Encyclopedia
of
SOUTHERN BAPTISTS

Encyclopedia of SOUTHERN BAPTISTS

I

Ab - Ken

BROADMAN PRESS
Nashville, Tennessee

© 1958 BROADMAN PRESS
Nashville, Tennessee

All rights reserved.

International copyright secured.

Library of Congress Catalog Card Number: 58-5417
Printed in the United States of America
7.5057K.S.P.

EDITORIAL COMMITTEE

Clifton Judson Allen, Ph.D. (Chairman), Editorial Secretary, Sunday School Board of the Southern Baptist Convention

Robert Andrew Baker, Th.D., Ph.D., Professor of Church History, Southwestern Baptist Theological Seminary

John Hall Buchanan, Th.M., D.D., Pastor, Southside Baptist Church, Birmingham, Alabama

Norman Wade Cox, Th.M., D.D., Executive Secretary, Historical Commission of the Southern Baptist Convention

Leo Taylor Crismon, M.S.L.S., Ph.D., Librarian, Southern Baptist Theological Seminary

Montraville Walker Egerton, BA., LL.B., Senior Partner, Egerton, McAfee, Armistead & Davis, Attorneys, Knoxville, Tennessee

Porter Wroe Routh, A.B., LL.D., Executive Secretary-Treasurer, Southern Baptist Convention Executive Committee

MANAGING EDITOR
Norman Wade Cox, Th.M., D.D.

ASSOCIATE EDITOR
Judson Boyce Allen, M.A.

THE GENERAL COMMITTEE

This committee was composed of the following who were delegated by their agency to represent it in the work of developing and creating ENCYCLOPEDIA OF SOUTHERN BAPTISTS:

I. SOUTHERN BAPTIST CONVENTION AGENCIES

AMERICAN BAPTIST THEOLOGICAL SEMINARY
Sedberry, Leland Stanford, Sr., Th.M.
Executive Secretary-Treasurer, Southern Baptist Commission on the American Baptist Theological Seminary

BROTHERHOOD COMMISSION
Schroeder, George William, M.S., LL.D.
Executive Secretary

CARVER SCHOOL OF MISSIONS AND SOCIAL WORK
Lansdell, Emily K., M.A., LL.D.
President

CHRISTIAN LIFE COMMISSION
Miller, Acker C, Th.M., D.D.
Executive Secretary

EDUCATION COMMISSION
Cornett, Richard Orin, M.S., Ph.D., D.Sc.
Executive Secretary-Treasurer

EXECUTIVE COMMITTEE
Routh, Porter Wroe, A.B., LL.D.
Executive Secretary-Treasurer

FOREIGN MISSION BOARD
Means, Frank Kester, Th.D.
Secretary for Latin America

GOLDEN GATE BAPTIST THEOLOGICAL SEMINARY
Carleton, William Augustus, Th.D.
Dean and Professor of Church History

HISTORICAL COMMISSION
Cox, Norman Wade, Th.M., D.D.
Executive Secretary

HOME MISSION BOARD
Caylor, John, Sr., A.M., D.D.
Editorial Secretary, Department of Editorial Service

NEW ORLEANS BAPTIST THEOLOGICAL SEMINARY
St. Amant, Clyde Penrose, M.A., Th.D., Ph.D., LL.D.
Professor of Church History

RADIO AND TELEVISION COMMISSION
Duncan, Clarence Edgar, Jr.
Associate Director

RELIEF AND ANNUITY BOARD
Reed, R. Alton, A.B., Th.B.
Executive Secretary

SOUTHEASTERN BAPTIST THEOLOGICAL SEMINARY
Duncan, Pope Alexander, M.S., Th.D.
Professor of Church History

SOUTHERN BAPTIST FOUNDATION
Holcomb, Thomas Luther, B.P., Th.G., D.D., LL.D.
Executive Secretary

SOUTHERN BAPTIST HOSPITALS
Tripp, Edgar Franklin, D.D., LL.D.
Executive Secretary-Superintendent

SOUTHERN BAPTIST THEOLOGICAL SEMINARY
Crismon, Leo Taylor, M.S.L.S., Ph.D.
Librarian

SOUTHWESTERN BAPTIST THEOLOGICAL SEMINARY
Baker, Robert Andrew, Th.D., Ph.D.
Professor of Church History

SUNDAY SCHOOL BOARD
Allen, Clifton Judson, Ph.D.
Editorial Secretary

II. WOMAN'S MISSIONARY UNION
Mather, Juliette Edla, B.M.T., M.A.
Editorial Secretary

III. STATE CONVENTION AGENCIES

ALABAMA
Macon, Leon Meertief, Th.M., D.D.
Editor, *The Alabama Baptist*

ARIZONA
Garrett, Wilkins Barry, Jr., M.A., Th.M.
Editor, *Baptist Beacon*

ARKANSAS
Bridges, Benjamin Lafayette, A.B., D.D.
Executive Secretary-Treasurer, Arkansas Baptist State Convention

CALIFORNIA
Looney, Floyd
Editor and Business Manager, *The California Southern Baptist*

DISTRICT OF COLUMBIA
Stith, Milton Chandler
Executive Secretary, District of Columbia Baptist Convention

FLORIDA
Stracener, William Guy, D.D.
Editor-Manager, *Florida Baptist Witness*

GEORGIA
King, Spencer Bidwell, Jr., Ph.D.
Chairman, Department of History and Government, Mercer University

ILLINOIS
Purdue, William Joseph, B.E., M.R.E.
Pastor, Winstanley Baptist Church, East St. Louis, Ill.

KANSAS
Gibson, Hoyt Sidney, A.B., M.Ed.
Editor, *Baptist Digest*

KENTUCKY
Crismon, Leo Taylor, M.S.L.S., Ph.D.
Librarian, Southern Baptist Theological Seminary

LOUISIANA
Gayer, Theodore Wilmot, Th.M., D.D.
Retired, former Superintendent, Louisiana Baptist Children's Home

MARYLAND
Thomas, Clifton Cromwell, D.D.
Executive Secretary, Maryland Baptist Union Association

MISSISSIPPI
Quarles, Chester Leland, A.M., Th.M., D.D.
Executive Secretary, Mississippi Baptist Convention Board

MISSOURI
Medearis, Thomas Whittier, B.D., D.D.
General Superintendent, Missouri Baptist General Association

NEW MEXICO
Stagg, Harry Perkins, B.A.
Executive Secretary, New Mexico Baptist Convention

NORTH CAROLINA
Carpenter, Levy Leonidas, Th.D., Ph.D.
Editor and Business Manager, *Biblical Recorder*

OHIO
Roberts, Raymond Everett, B.T.
General Secretary, State Convention of Baptists in Ohio Affiliated with Southern Baptist Convention

OKLAHOMA
Gaskin, Jesse Marvin, A.B.
Pastor, First Baptist Church, Heavener, Okla.

OREGON-WASHINGTON
Milam, Robert Edward, Th.M., D.D.
Executive Secretary-Treasurer, Baptist General Convention of Oregon-Washington

SOUTH CAROLINA
Sims, Charles Furman, Th.D., D.D.
General Secretary-Treasurer, General Board of the State Convention of the Baptist Denomination in South Carolina

TENNESSEE
Pope, Charles Wesley, M.A., D.D., LL.D.
Executive Secretary-Treasurer, Tennessee Baptist Convention

TEXAS
Elliott, Leslie Robinson, Th.D.
Director of Libraries, Southwestern Baptist Theological Seminary

VIRGINIA
Cousins, Solon Bolivar, B.A., D.D., LL.D.
Chairman, Department of Bible and Religion, University of Richmond

EXECUTIVE COMMITTEE

Pope, Charles Wesley, Chairman
Cornett, Richard Orin, Secretary
Holcomb, Thomas Luther
Macon, Leon Meertief
Schroeder, George William

INTRODUCTION

THIS ENCYCLOPEDIA was planned, supported, and produced by Southern Baptists themselves, working together through all their organized agencies. Those who led in the project had a conviction that Southern Baptists have become increasingly self-conscious, and that they need historical insight, objective evaluation, and adequate information for a consistent understanding of their basic premises if they are to continue to grow and prosper with soundness. In addition, those outside their fellowship are increasingly desirous of some means of understanding them. All these needs could be supplied only by a reliable encyclopedia. This is not an official encyclopedia of Southern Baptists; it could not be because of the way in which they define their polity. It is, however, the most competent work that those who produced it could create, and time will prove its validity.

These volumes present Southern Baptists in the context of their history, their present organization, and their maturing methodology. Eight hundred and ninety-nine writers contributed 4,349 articles, and a qualified editorial staff prepared the manuscript for publication. In it all a dedicated effort was made to provide Southern Baptists and all others who are interested with the facts that are necessary to a genuine understanding of Southern Baptists—their past, their present life, and their work.

History.—In 1927 the Southern Baptist Convention adopted a resolution expressing a need for an encyclopedia, but no agency felt able to undertake the project. An early historical committee made ambitious plans but accomplished little. Later the Convention set up the Historical Commission, and it was chartered to protect and promote the "history interests of the Southern Baptist Convention." From the beginning of his work, in February, 1951, as the Commission's first executive secretary, Norman Wade Cox felt that one of his major responsibilities was to communicate to Southern Baptists the knowledge and appreciation of their history which would give them a firm basis for self-understanding and sound growth. Several publications were conceived. The most important and most ambitious of these was this ENCYCLOPEDIA, which the Commission's secretary felt was urgently needed. Others agreed with him that there was a real need but did not see how the work could be done. Despite this widespread doubt, he felt that the co-operative method of work characteristic of Southern Baptists would make the book possible, and in August, 1952, he shared his beliefs and plans with the Historical Commission. The Commission approved the idea and voted for him to develop and promote the project. Gradually other leaders were convinced, and other agencies expressed interest.

During 1953 a general encyclopedia committee was formed, composed of representatives of the various Convention agencies and state bodies. Each representative was appointed to study the proposed encyclopedia and report to his respective board or agency. The committee was formally organized in December, 1953, and approved the encyclopedia project in principle. Thereafter, this committee was the group through which Southern Baptists were persuaded to undertake and carry through the work. At this December meeting the committee elected an executive committee and an editorial committee, and chose Norman W. Cox managing editor. At the next meeting, in June, 1954, the committee adopted a report from the editorial committee, outlining detailed plans and specifications and financial arrangements for the project. By December, 1954, nearly all the several bodies—the Executive Committee and the various boards, institutions, and commissions of the Southern Baptist Convention; the Woman's Missionary Union, auxiliary to the Southern Baptist Convention; and the twenty-four state conventions—had formally committed themselves to the project. Eventually approval came from all.

The general committee implemented the plan by which the work would be done. Each co-operating agency was to assume responsibility for providing a section of the content and a proportionate share of the overhead expense. The editorial committee, with the managing editor and his staff, was made responsible for all decisions regarding content, editorial revision, and arrangement. The managing editor was made business manager and treasurer of the encyclopedia funds.

Relatively more responsibility fell thereafter on the editorial committee, which consisted of Clifton J. Allen, chairman, Robert A. Baker, John H. Buchanan, Norman W. Cox, Leo T. Crismon, M. W. Egerton, and Porter W. Routh. William J. Fallis, editor of Broadman Press, and Judson B. Allen, ENCYCLOPEDIA associate editor, also participated in committee meetings. These men met formally four times each year and were always available, individually and collectively, for consultation and advice. They formulated all editorial policies, took an active part in planning the work, and made in every way a creative and indispensable contribution.

In planning for the content of the ENCYCLOPEDIA, various categories of necessary information were formulated. Finally it was decided that a complete and thorough coverage could be achieved by assembling material under fifty-seven different categories, such as, Bible, theology, church history, church music, religious education, evangelism, and material covering the history and work of each Baptist state convention and each Convention agency. Taken together, these areas give a comprehensive picture of Southern Baptists, past and present. Each category was assigned to a person with special competence in that area, and a committee was appointed to assist him. Then, with guidance and correlation from the central office at the Historical Commission, each committee formulated titles for enough monographs to give proper coverage to its particular area. The best writers available were enlisted to do the research and write the articles. Each committee, and especially each chairman, was made responsible for verification and preliminary editing. The central editorial office was responsible for correlating and editing all the material, and for preparing a complete and unified manuscript for the publisher.

Staff and writers.—Slightly more than nine hundred men and women produced this work. These people are the recognized leaders of the denomination, and are serving in positions of influence and large responsibility. They assumed the extra burden of this work, which in many cases was considerable, because they realized the importance of the project to the denomination. Out of the first hundred asked to assume major responsibility, only two declined. The rest accepted with alacrity, and their response was typical.

All writers and editors were enlisted to work in the area of their specialties. Articles on state history and work were assigned to those who had long experience in that area. Articles dealing with history or theology were written by men professionally trained in those fields. Articles on church methods were written by men who had formulated those methods or who had worked with them intensively in classroom and local church situations. Altogether 899 writers have contributed the 4,349 monographs that compose the contents of this ENCYCLOPEDIA. Of this number 289 have earned doctoral degrees, 301 have graduate degrees ranging from M.A. to to Th.M., 135 have either a B.A. or a B.S. degree. The remaining number are persons whose experience qualified them for their assignments. Approximately four-fifths of the copy was prepared by those holding a graduate degree. Most of the area editors were engaged in editing and publishing or were scholars experienced in research and writing. They bore a major responsibility in planning, writing, and carrying through to the end with a multitude of details.

Editorial procedure.—In accordance with the co-operative plan on which the project was based, the various area editors bore responsibility for a major part of the work. In co-operation with the central editorial office, they planned their work and enlisted writers of the monographs for which they were responsible. Twenty one-day training clinics were held across the country so that one was within reach of every writer. In these clinics the area editors planned their work with the managing editor of the ENCYCLOPEDIA and guided their writers in the preparation of the needed monographs. When the writing and revision were done, they checked and verified all of the material, edited and revised it further where needed, and forwarded it to the managing editor. A central editorial staff was assembled, and procedures were put in operation so that each monograph could be evaluated, checked, revised, styled, and copied for the printer with maximum efficiency. During this phase of the work some material was revised again. All of it was carefully studied and evaluated. Needless detail and subjective evaluation were eliminated. Terminology and expression were revised so as to make the whole work as consistent as possible throughout. Omissions and duplications were noted and corrected. Everything possible was done to produce a work which would be complete, consistent, accurate, and thoroughly objective.

Pictures.—In addition to the comprehensive information provided in monographs, the ENCYCLOPEDIA includes a collection of photographs to present what is typical of Southern Baptists in a wide range of subjects. Illustrated are church buildings, children's homes, hospitals, homes for the aged, colleges, student center buildings, state convention offices, and headquarters for Convention agencies and institutions and for Woman's Missionary Union. Each picture was chosen because it was representative and typical. In all, ninety-two pages, printed on special paper and inserted at intervals throughout both volumes, have been included.

Acknowledgments.—This work owes its existence to many institutions and a large number of persons. It would be impossible to mention them all, but it would be unthinkable to omit mention of some who have made vitally significant contributions. Gratitude should first be expressed to the sponsoring agencies: the Executive Committee and the several boards, commissions, and institutions of the Southern Baptist Convention; the Woman's Missionary Union, Auxiliary to the Southern Baptist Convention; and the twenty-four state conventions which co-operated in the work. These agencies not only contributed in time and material, but provided substantial financial support as well. Each agency bore the expenses of its representatives to various encyclopedia meetings, of its own editorial office, and its pro rata share of the costs for the work of the central editorial office. In addition, these agencies shared in the cost of producing the background material, one fifth of the whole, which contributes so much to the value of the work. Altogether the co-operating groups spent not less than $80,000 to produce the manuscript and prepare it for publication. This subsidy has made it possible for the ENCYCLOPEDIA to be sold at a reasonable price and thus to be within the reach of all who need it.

Acknowledgment should also be made of the contribution made by the writers themselves, and by the various area editors. They individually bore heavy loads and collectively made a contribution exceeded by none. They gave willingly and gladly of their time and talent, and by their co-operation made the project an experience of rewarding satisfaction for those who have worked with it most closely and continuously. To all whose names appear on the pages which follow, deep gratitude is acknowledged for their dedicated research, writing, and rewriting which brought this venture into being.

Gratitude is also due to the employed staff for their able and abundant labors: Judson Boyce Allen, associate editor, without whom this work could not have been accomplished, ably served in many editorial capacities since January, 1955. He shared in the development of the titles of the monographs, preparation of the writer's style guide, evaluation of manuscript, revision and rewriting, and rendered many other services. He added much to what literary quality the work possesses. Associated with him on a part-time basis were Lynn E. May, Jr., Homer L. Grice, Rosalind Allen, Mera Cannon, and Mrs. Frank P. Ganick. These workers constituted a capable and much appreciated team.

In all of the work, the resources and capable staff of the Dargan-Carver Library, a joint project of the Sunday School Board and the Historical Commission of the Southern Baptist Convention, contributed much. A major burden of verification and reference work was borne by these persons. Many of the ENCYCLOPEDIA writers depended on the resources of the Dargan-Carver Library in their research. They received help unstintedly from the librarian, Helen Conger, and her associates, Jean Gladdish, Mrs. William D. Dunn, and Beatrice Preston.

The services of Mary Elizabeth Griffith, style consultant, co-ordinator, and editor, and her associates—Velma Darbo, Mrs. C. Everett Floyd, and Mrs. Hilton M. Austin—who efficiently handled the complicated problems of styling the manuscript, are greatly appreciated.

Mrs. Richmond O. Brown and her associates—Mrs. Kenneth L. Hayes, Mrs. William A. O'Leary, Mrs. R. Eugene Partee, Jr., Mrs. James E. Griggs, Jr., Mrs. Nathaniel R. Davis, Mrs. L. Willard Parker, Mrs. Lee A. Coker, Mrs. J. Carl Billingsley, Mary Alice Pruett, and Rosemary Colson—deftly handled the complex stenographic work and control of manuscripts so that each item was properly and safely filed, transferred, returned, reassigned, etc. This involved handling each of the 4,349 articles about twelve times in such a way that each could always be located.

Throughout all the work, the co-operation of the editor and staff of Broadman Press was most helpful. It was understood from the beginning that Broadman Press would accept the responsibility for publishing the ENCYCLOPEDIA. The editor of the Press, William J. Fallis, shared in the editorial planning at all stages. The work of the central editorial office was often expedited by his counsel. The ENCYCLOPEDIA staff and the staff of Broadman Press maintained a close and mutually helpful relationship.

Arrangement of material.—The monographs are in strictly alphabetical arrangement, with the exception of those dealing with associations. The associational monographs are arranged in groups under the names of their respective states. Cross references are provided to make all the material in the two volumes easily accessible. A subject which might be sought under different titles is treated only once, but cross references under alternate titles refer to it. All monographs are as complete as possible in themselves; however, some cross references refer to supplementary information. Biographical treatments are referred to by means of the abbreviation " (*q.v.*) " following incidental references to the person treated.

Bibliographies appearing with many of the monographs refer to sources of additional detailed information, especially to those works which should prove genuinely helpful and which should be fairly generally available. Works which were exceedingly specialized or which could be found only in few libraries or carefully guarded archives were omitted. Documents and obscure periodicals were omitted. Always the purpose was to achieve maximum usefulness for the general reader.

Content and usefulness.—The ENCYCLOPEDIA includes many kinds of material, all of it especially relevant to Southern Baptists. This relevancy, however, was not construed narrowly; in addition to material dealing specifically with Southern Baptist work, history, personalities, and methods, other information was included which Southern Baptists need in order to understand themselves in their setting and relations. Thus general doctrinal material, information on other religious groups, and history of Baptist work prior to the organization of the Southern Baptist Convention in 1845 are included. About 20 per cent of the articles deal with general background, having to do with the history of Christianity, other denominations, other Baptist bodies, the Bible, theology, ecclesiology and polity, evangelism, missions, ethics, music, preaching, stewardship, education, etc. The remainder of the content is given to histories of Southern Baptist state conventions, associations, organizations, institutions, publications, agencies, and personalities. Also included are articles which describe and interpret special Southern Baptist distinctives, controversies, crises, and patterns of organization and work; other articles give essential factual information.

It is, of course, impossible to present in this work *the* Baptist position, for there is no such thing; and this work has no authority to give expression to it. However, the facts of Baptist history which are here presented are incontrovertible, regardless of the interpretations one may wish to place on them. The descriptions of Baptist procedure are equally factual. Doctrinal and theological articles were written by persons who are, of course, responsible for their own interpretations, but who have also gained such respect and confidence from Southern Baptists that their work can be fairly regarded as representative.

Most Southern Baptists will be pleased with what they find in this work; some will probably be displeased. This is to be expected. In spite of their varied backgrounds, Southern Baptists are firmly united on basic doctrine. At the same time some of them disagree with a fervency that occasionally amounts to acrimony about some matters of practice and thought. Even so, these matters are not usually made a test of fellowship among them. Writers were not chosen on the basis of their known loyalty to one or another of the coteries of belief with which many Southern Baptists align themselves. They were chosen on the basis of their known competence in the field in which they were asked to write. On the basis of this competence, they were encouraged to write what they believed to be the truth. The editors, of course, accepted responsibility for assistance in putting the material in proper form, but they left to the writers responsibility for the accuracy of their statements and for their interpretations.

Those who read this ENCYCLOPEDIA extensively will doubtless be surprised many times. In some instances they will find that the truth about a given subject is different from what is commonly believed. It will become increasingly evident that one cannot understand anything until he knows its history. If one reads all the state convention histories, he will find that each is similar in much but that each has distinctive differences that are the result of the special forces that affected the pattern of its developing life. One will clearly see that these Southern Baptists, in spite of their basic unity, have many differences that sometimes lead to misunderstandings. Their common faith, their history, and their guiding sense of mission tie them firmly together. At the same time they vehemently argue with one another about such things as alien immersion, various millennial and dispensational concepts, open and close communion, etc. But these disagreements are not allowed to become disruptive, because Baptist belief in liberty and in the competency of the individual gives each one the inalienable right to interpret such matters for himself. Hence, they are not allowed to become a bar to fellowship in co-operative denominational relationships.

The facts contained in these volumes, therefore, will prove that Southern Baptists have much that they can profitably learn from one another. A common awareness and understanding of their differences can help to strengthen their co-operative unity. But even more, Southern Baptists will profit from the knowledge that they will gain about their past. They should discover in these volumes that they have a rich heritage. They will find that they have made major achievements, that they have overcome hampering weaknesses, and that they have passed through severe trials. They will probably become convinced that their survival and prosperity are in many ways providential and that they have been preserved so that their distinctive message and mission can have a continuing witness.

This ENCYCLOPEDIA should serve a variety of persons and needs. Many pastors will need to refer to it repeatedly for information relevant to some situation in their ministry. Those who prepare programs, teach, or have to answer questions can find help in these source books. Those who are puzzled about many things in Baptist life can get the answers here. Students who write theses and dissertations on their denomination or some aspect of its life will find this work invaluable as a basic reference source. Editors, teachers, and denominational leaders of every degree and responsibility will find in it a compendium of information that will serve them well. For all who use it, Baptist or non-Baptist, it can be the gateway to genuine understanding of this major denomination.

CLIFTON J. ALLEN
NORMAN W. COX

ACKNOWLEDGMENT

In behalf of all who will benefit by the use of this work it is appropriate to record our indebtedness to the managing editor. The need for such a publication had long been felt. Men of vision dreamed about it. But Norman W. Cox conceived a way to translate the vision into reality. His propagation of the idea convinced the leadership of Southern Baptists that the encyclopedia must be published, and he enlisted the support to achieve it. His knowledge of Baptist life and thought and his judgment and zeal have a fruitage in these two volumes of immeasurable importance for the continuing mission of Southern Baptists and for the wider witness of the total Christian community.

CLIFTON J. ALLEN
Chairman, Editorial Committee

AREA EDITORIAL STAFF

I. BACKGROUNDS

BIBLE
Summers, Ray, Th.D., Chairman
Cousins, Solon Bolivar, B.A., D.D., LL.D.
Fisher, Fred Lewis, Th.D.
Francisco, Clyde Taylor, Th.D.
Hester, Hubert Inman, Th.D., D.D.
Watts, James Washington, Ph.D.

CHURCH ADMINISTRATION AND RELIGIOUS EDUCATION
Dobbins, Gaines Stanley, M.A., Th.D., LL.D., D.D., Chairman
Chapman, James Horton, A.M., Th.M., Vice-chairman
Grey, James David, Th.M., LL.D.
Heacock, Joe Davis, D.R.E.
Howse, William Lewis, Jr., M.A., D.R.E., L.H.D.
Pettigrew, William Robert, Th.M., D.D.
Scales, Robert Sylvesta, A.B., D.D.

CHURCH MUSIC
Sims, Walter Hines, B.Mus., M.A., D.Mus., Chairman
Angell, Warren Mathewson, M.Mus., Ed.D.
Bennett, Carlyle Dean, B.S., M.S.M., Mus.D.
Heeren, Forrest Henry, M.S., M.A., Ed.D.
Patterson, Edgar Allen
Patterson, Floyd, M.M., M.A., Ph.D.

ETHICS
Binkley, Olin Trivette, B.D., Ph.D., D.D., Chairman
Glass, Victor Thomas, Th.D.
Insko, Chester Arthur, M.A.E., B.D., Th.D.
Maston, Thomas Bufford, D.R.E., Ph.D.
Ransom, Guy Harvey, M.A., Th.D.
Waddell, Henry Clayton, Th.D.

EVANGELISM
Leavell, Roland Quinche, A.M., Th.D., D.D., LL.D.

HISTORY
St. Amant, Clyde Penrose, M.A., Th.D., Ph.D., LL.D., Chairman
Barnes, William Wright, A.M., Th.D., L.H.D., D.D.
Carleton, William Augustus, B.S., Th.D.
Stealey, Sydnor Lorenzo, Ph.D., D.D.

MISSIONS
Goerner, Henry Cornell, Ph.D., Chairman
Brown, Lawrence Avery, Th.D.
Guy, Robert Calvin, B.A., Th.D.
Hipps, John Burder, Th.M., S.T.M., M.A., D.D.
Lansdell, Emily Kilpatrick, M.A., LL.D.
Lawrence, John Benjamin, M.A., LL.D.
Sadler, George Washington, M.A., Th.M., D.D.

OTHER BAPTIST BODIES
McClellan, Albert Alfred, Th.M., D.D.

PASTORAL CARE
Oates, Wayne Edward, Th.D., Chairman
Bell, Arthur Donald, D.R.E.
Elder, James Lyn, Th.D.
Price, John Milburn, Jr., M.R.E., Th.D.
Segler, Franklin Morgan, Th.D.
Young, Richard Knox, Th.D.

PREACHING
Stanfield, Vernon Latrelle, Th.D., Chairman
Murphy, Joel C., Th.D.
Naylor, Robert Ernest, Th.M., D.D.
Nelson, Dotson McGinnis, Jr., Th.D.
Northcutt, Jesse James, Th.D.
Patterson, Eugene Nelson, Th.D.

STATISTICS
Edmunds, Jacob Pinckney

STEWARDSHIP
Moore, Merrill Dennis, Th.M., D.D.

THEOLOGY
Moody, Dale, Th.D., Chairman
Clark, Theodore Roscoe, Th.D.
Humphrey, George Caldwell, Th.D.
Hunt, William Boyd, Th.D.
Newman, Stewart Albert, Th.D., D.D.
Trentham, Charles Arthur, Th.D., Ph.D.

II. SOUTHERN BAPTIST CONVENTION

AMERICAN BAPTIST THEOLOGICAL SEMINARY
Sedberry, Leland Stanford, Sr., Th.M.

Area Editorial Staff

BROTHERHOOD COMMISSION
Schroeder, George William, B.A., M.S., LL.D.

CARVER SCHOOL OF MISSIONS AND SOCIAL WORK
Carver, George Alexander, M.A.

CHRISTIAN LIFE COMMISSION
Miller, Acker C, Th.M., D.D.

EDUCATION COMMISSION
Cornett, Richard Orin, M.S., Ph.D., D.Sc.

EXECUTIVE COMMITTEE
Routh, Porter Wroe, A.B., LL.D., Chairman
McClellan, Albert Alfred, Th.M., D.D.
Moore, Merrill Dennis, Th.M., D.D.

FOREIGN MISSION BOARD
Means, Frank Kester, Th.D., Chairman
Greer, Genevieve, B.A.
Hickerson, Amy Compere (Mrs. Clyde Vernon), B.L., B.M.T.
Sadler, George Washington, M.A., Th.M., D.D.

GOLDEN GATE BAPTIST THEOLOGICAL SEMINARY
Carleton, William Augustus, Th.D.

HISTORICAL COMMISSION
Cox, Norman Wade, Th.M., D.D.

HOME MISSION BOARD
Caylor, John, Sr., A.M., D.D., Chairman
Dowis, Solomon Franklin, Th.M., D.D.
Lawrence, John Benjamin, M.A., D.D., LL.D.
Seigler, O. M., Th.M., D.D.

NEW ORLEANS BAPTIST THEOLOGICAL SEMINARY
St. Amant, Clyde Penrose, M.A., Th.D., Ph.D., LL.D., Chairman
Davidson, Nelle Catherine, B.S. in L.S.
Leavell, Roland Quinche, A.M., Th.D., LL.D.
Watts, James Washington, Ph.D.

RADIO AND TELEVISION COMMISSION
Duncan, Clarence Edgar, Jr.

RELIEF AND ANNUITY BOARD
Reed, R. Alton, A.B., Th.B., Chairman
Chaffin, Floyd B., A.B., Th.B., M.R.E., D.D., LL.D.

SOUTHEASTERN BAPTIST THEOLOGICAL SEMINARY
Duncan, Pope Alexander, M.S., Th.D., Chairman
McDowell, Edward Allison, Jr., Ph.D., D.D.
Stealey, Sydnor Lorenzo, Ph.D., D.D.
Strickland, William Claudius, Th.D.

SOUTHERN BAPTIST FOUNDATION
Holcomb, Thomas Luther, B.P., Th.G., D.D., LL.D.

SOUTHERN BAPTIST HOSPITALS
Tripp, Edgar Franklin, D.D., LL.D.

SOUTHERN BAPTIST THEOLOGICAL SEMINARY
Crismon, Leo Taylor, M.S.L.S., Ph.D., Chairman
Dillard, Badgett, B.A., M.R.E.
Dobbins, Gaines Stanley, M.A., Th.D., LL.D., D.D.
Lumpkin, William Latane, Th.M., Ph.D.
McCall, Duke Kimbrough, Ph.D., LL.D., D.D., Litt.D.
Mueller, William Arthur, M.A., S.T.M., Ph.D.

SOUTHWESTERN BAPTIST THEOLOGICAL SEMINARY
Baker, Robert Andrew, Th.D., Ph.D., Chairman
Barnes, William Wright, A.M., Th.D., D.D., L.H.D.
Bell, Arthur Donald, D.R.E.
Johnson, Charles Price, A.B., M.R.E., Th.D.
Thompson, Sara Virginia, M.M.Ed., B.S. in L.S.
Williams, John Howard, Th.M., D.D.

SUNDAY SCHOOL BOARD
Allen, Clifton Judson, Ph.D., Chairman
Fallis, William Joseph, Th.D.
Grice, Homer Lamar, M.A., D.D.
Ingraham, Harold Edward, Th.G., D.C.E.
Waite, Florida

III. WOMAN'S MISSIONARY UNION
Mather, Juliette Edla, M.A., B.M.T.

IV. STATES

ALABAMA
Macon, Leon Meertief, Th.M., D.D., Chairman
Davis, Oscar Adams, Th.M., D.D.
Floyd, Mrs. Louise Platowsky
Sulzby, James Frederick, Jr., A.B., Litt.D.

ARIZONA
Garrett, Wilkins Barry, Jr., M.A., Th.M., Chairman
Maben, Jack Knox, B.A.
Stephens, Walter Colquitt, B.S.
Rock, Clifton Vaughan, B.S.

ARKANSAS
Bridges, Benjamin Lafayette, A.B., D.D., Chairman
James, Theo Thomas, Th.D.
Selph, Bernes K., Th.D.

CALIFORNIA
Looney, Floyd, Chairman
Carleton, William Augustus, B.S., Th.D.

Long, Haskell B., B.S.
Springer, James Verner, A.B., B.S.T.

DISTRICT OF COLUMBIA
Stith, Milton Chandler

FLORIDA
Stracener, William Guy, D.D., Chairman
Garwood, Harry Crawford, Th.M., Ph.D.
Mathis, Arthur William, Th.M.

GEORGIA
King, Spencer Bidwell, Jr., M.A., Ph.D., Chairman
Burch, John Burke, B.D.
Cleverdon, Leroy Geach, A.M., Th.D., Ph.D.
Jackson, Arthur, Th.M., D.D.
Merritt, James White, LL.D.
Newton, Louie DeVotie, A.M., D.D., LL.D., Litt.D.
Stephens, Leonard Abraham, M.A., Ph.D.

ILLINOIS
Purdue, William Joseph, B.E., M.R.E.

KANSAS
Gibson, Hoyt Sidney, A.B., M.Ed.

KENTUCKY
Crismon, Leo Taylor, M.S.L.S., Ph.D., Chairman
Boone, William Cooke, M.A., D.D.
Jewell, George Raleigh
Rone, Wendell Holmes, Th.M.

LOUISIANA
Gayer, Theodore Wilmot, Th.M., D.D., Chairman
St. Amant, Clyde Penrose, M.A., Th.D., Ph.D., LL.D.
Tinnin, Finley Watson, D.D.

MARYLAND
Clause, Harry Paul, Th.D., Chairman
Ruark, Elmer Francis
Woodward, Robert Franklin, B.D.

MISSISSIPPI
Abrams, Joseph Robert, Jr., Chairman
Boyd, Jesse Laney, Th.M.
Hamlet, Charles Buck, III, Th.M.

MISSOURI
McGinty, Hilary Herbert, Ph.D., Chairman
Carlin, Opal Rowena, A.B., B.L.S.
Hester, Hubert Inman, Th.D., D.D.

NEW MEXICO
Myers, Lewis Alexander, Th.M., Chairman
Baker, Mrs. Richard Thomas, Sr., B.A.
DuLaney, Arthur A., Th.D.
Inlow, Eva Richard, M.A.
Stumph, Calowa William, B.A.

NORTH CAROLINA
Carpenter, Levy Leonidas, Th.D., Ph.D., Chairman
Gaddy, Claude Fisher, M.A.
Gardner, Eugene Norfleet, M.A., Th.M., D.D.
Huggins, Malloy Alton, A.M., LL.D.
Williams, William Harrison, Th.M., D.D.

OHIO
Roberts, Raymond Everett, B.T.

OKLAHOMA
Gaskin, Jesse Marvin, A.B., Chairman
Ramay, Marion Edgar, LL.B., Th.M., D.D.

OREGON-WASHINGTON
Milam, Robert Edward, Th.M., D.D.

SOUTH CAROLINA
* Daniel, Robert Norman, M.A., Ph.M., Litt.D., LL.D., Chairman
Jones, Samuel Hovey, Th.D., D.D.
Tucker, Robert Cinnamond, B.S., in L.S., M.A.

TENNESSEE
Frey, Leibert Garland, Chairman
Taylor, Oury Wilburn, A.B., D.D.

TEXAS
Elliott, Leslie Robinson, Th.D., Chairman
Estep, William Roscoe, Jr., Th.D.
Johnson, Roy Lee, Th.D.

VIRGINIA
Cousins, Solon Bolivar, B.A., D.D., LL.D., Chairman
Brown, Raymond Bryan, S.T.M., Th.D., Editor
Hartz, Dennis Wilson, B.A.
Oliver, Ellen Douglas, B.A., M.R.E.
Peyton, Edward Voorhees, D.D.
* Deceased

CONTRIBUTORS

Abrams, Joseph Robert, Jr.
Ackland, Donald Frank
Adams, William Walter
Adkins, Luther Pryor
Airey, Mrs. Ethel
Aldredge, Henry Truman
Alexander, Elizabeth Quarles
Alexander, Mary Charlotte
Allen, Andrew Quincy
Allen, Clifton Judson
Allen, Judson Boyce
Allen, William Cox
Alley, Reuben Edward, Jr.
Alley, Reuben Edward, Sr.
Allison, Beverly Gray
Anderson, Park Harris, Jr.
Armstrong, Marjorie Moore
Ashcraft, Jesse Morris
Atchison, Ray Morris
Atkins, Willie Clyde
Atkinson, Paul
Autrey, Cassius Elijah
Averett, Clyde Wesley

Babb, Winston Chandler
Baekkelie, Egil A.
Bagby, Robert Harwood
Baggett, Hudson Doyle
Bagley, George Edwin
Baker, Ira Lee
Baker, Mrs. Richard Thomas, Sr.
Baker, Robert Andrew
Baldwin, Cecil Ainsworth
Barnard, Floy Merwyn
Barnes, Ernest Richard
Barnes, John Evan, Jr.
Barnes, Robert Bryant
Barnes, William Wright
Barnette, Henlee Hulix
Barnette, Jasper Newton
Barry, James Clinton
Bartlett, Eugene Monroe, Jr.
Barton, Vernon Wayne
Barton, William Henderson
Batts, Henry Lewis
Beggs, Hilda Harland
Bell, Arthur Donald
Bell, Robert Emmet
Belote, James Dalby
Belt, Loren James

Bennett, George Willis
Bennett, Thomas Miles
Bergstrom, Herbert Eugene
Berkstresser, John Emory, Sr.
Berry, William Hafford
Berry, Winford Jennings
Biggerstaff, William Palmer
Binkley, Olin Trivette
Binns, Walter Pope
Bishop, Julius Ivyloy
Black, Charles Herman
Black, John Robert
Blackburn, Geoffrey H.
Blackmon, George Truett
Bland, Thomas Albert
Bodie, Mrs. Patton
Bonner, Francis Wesley
Boone, William Cooke
Bowen, Claud Ballard
Bowling, Lura Lucille (Mrs. Leslie Monroe)
Boyce, William Arthur
Boyd, Jesse Laney
Bozeman, Albert Snead
Bradford, Wendell
Bradley, Sam Ed
Branch, Douglas McKinley
Brannock, Willis Herbert
Brannon, J. D.
Brewer, James Franklin
Briggs, Argye Mary McCanlies
Briggs, Shirley
Brimm, Hugh Alexander
Brooks, Mrs. Walter
Brothers, Lionel Raymon
Brough, Anne Wade Roark (Mrs. Charles Hillman)
Brown, Archie Earl
Brown, Joseph Everingham
Brown, Lawrence Avery
Brown, Rachel Fair
Brown, Raymond Bryan
Brown, Richmond Otto
Brown, Willis Alfred, Sr.
Browne, Philip Dale
Bruce, Daisy
Bryan, Charles Willis
Bryan, Gainer E., Sr.
Bryant, Cyril Eric, Jr.
Bryant, Eugene

Bryant, James Raleigh
Bullard, George Woodrow
Burke, Kenneth Edison
Burkhalter, Frank Elisha
Burney, Frank Swanson
Burney, John Harrison
Burns, Herman Franklin
Burns, Percy Pratt
Burton, Joe Wright
Burts, Charles Watson
Bush, Charles Edwin
Butler, Richard Pearl
Buzbee, Glenwood
Byrd, Annie Ward

Cagle, Albert Rayo
Callaway, James Emory
Callaway, Timothy Furlow
Cameron, Harry L.
Campbell, Leslie Hartwell
Canclini, Santiago
Cantrell, James Clifton
Carleton, Jacob Paul
Carleton, William Augustus
Carlin, Opal Rowena
Carlson, Carl Emanuel
Carlson, Ernest Leslie
Carpenter, Coy Cornelius
Carpenter, Kathryn Ellen
Carpenter, Levy Leonidas
Carpenter, Nollie Wilbur, Jr.
Carroll, James Elton
Carswell, William Jones
Carter, Harry Lee
Carter, John Franklin
Carter, Thomas Edwin
Cartlidge, Jared Irving
Carver, George Alexander
Cash, Amos Boyd
Cathey, Wheeler Clifton
Caudill, Robert Paul
Cauthen, Eloise Glass (Mrs. Baker James)
Caylor, John, Sr.
Chapman, James Horton
Cheatham, James Douglas
Cheney, Irvin, Jr.
Clark, Charles Barton
Clark, Edward Thomas
Clark, Franklin Gustavus
Clark, James Lewis

Clark, Theodore Roscoe
Clasen, Winifred
Clegg, Albert Lawrence
Clegg, James Lloyd
Cleverdon, Leroy Geach
Clinard, Harold Gordon
Clonts, Forrest William
Coates, Fletcher
Coggins, Aileen
Cole, James Franklin
Coleman, James Plemon
Collier, Earl Matthew
Collins, Lloyd W.
Colson, Howard Paul
Colton, Clarence Eugene
Compere, Ebenezer Lattimore
Conger, Helen
Conrad, Carl Everett
Conway, Florrie
Cook, Milliard Judson
Cooke, Lawson Hill
Cooper, Clifton Earl
Cooper, Davis Clay, Jr.
Cooper, Milburn Newton
Corder, Benjamin Loyd
Corley, Odus Marion
Cornett, Richard Orin
Corzine, Jesse Lynn
Costello, Mrs. Lela Beall
Cottrell, Nobel Thomas
Cousins, Paul Mercer
Cousins, Solon Bolivar
Cowsert, Jack Jimmerson
Cox, Carey Edward
Cox, Ernest Eugene
Cox, James William
Cox, Joseph Powhatan
Cox, Norman Wade
Cox, Truett
Crabtree, Asa Routh
Crane, James Dreher
Crawford, Robert Shaver
Crawley, James Winston
Creasman, William Clarence
Crismon, Leo Taylor
Crocker, Everett Gordon
Cross, Irvie Keil
Crouch, Austin
Crouch, William Henry
Crow, Hilton Jones (Mrs. G. D.)
Crowe, John Marvin
Culbertson, Ambrose Brazier
Cullom, Willis Richard
Culpepper, Charles Lee, Sr.
Culpepper, Hugo Hurlston
Culpepper, Ola Lane (Mrs. Charles Lee, Sr.)
Cunningham, Collis

Dale, William Pratt, II
Dalrymple, Guy Harold
Dalton, Jack Parker
Daniel, Larkin Taylor
*Daniel, Robert Norman

Davenport, Arthur Stuart
*Davidson, Blount Ferrell
Davidson, David Nathaniel
Davidson, James Edward
Davis, Edwin Summers
Davis, Francis Asbury
Davis, William Penn
Daw, Carl Pickens
Dawson, Joseph Martin
Deere, Derward William
Dempsey, Dancy Spurgeon
Deusner, Charles Ford
Deusner, Edwin Earl
Dickey, Grady Gaither
Di Domenica, Angelo
Dobbins, Gaines Stanley
Dobbs, Hubert Lee
Dobbs, William Claibourne
Dodd, Damon Clifford
Doke, W. H.
Dotson, Clyde Johnson
Dowell, Fred Mitchell, Jr.
Dowell, Spright
Dowis, Solomon Franklin
Dozier, Edwin Burke
Drake, Charles Leo
Driskell, Herman Lamar
Drumwright, Huber Lelland, Jr.
Duke, Guyle Nelson, Jr.
Dunaway, Edwin Eagle
Duncan, Benjamin Harrison
Duncan, Clarence Edgar, Jr.
Duncan, Pope Alexander
Durst, John Kemp
Dwyer, Eddie Lo Elmer

Eaglesfield, Carrol Frederick
Easley, John Allen
Eby, Frederick
Edge, Findley Bartow
Edmonson, Lousia Bennett (Mrs. T. E.)
Edmunds, Jacob Pinckney
Edwards, James Thomas
Egerton, Montraville Walker
Elder, James Lyn
Elliott, Leslie Robinson
Ellis, David Alvin
Estep, William Roscoe, Jr.
Estes, Joseph Richard
Ethridge, Waller Maurice
Evans, Joshua Levering

Fallis, William Joseph
Falwell, Reuben Hale, Jr.
Farmer, Foy Johnson (Mrs. James S.)
Ferguson, Odessa Lyons (Mrs. George R.)
Fields, Ermon Elmer
Fields, Marion Horace
Fishel, Lawrence Lavern
Fisher, Fred Lewis
Fite, Daniel Harley
Flanders, Henry Jackson, Jr.
Flynn, Jean Martin

Ford, Glynn Roland
Forderhase, Verlin Fred
Forrester, Clifton Arthur
Foshee, Howard Bryce
Fox, Baynard Francis
Francisco, Clyde Taylor
Franks, Jesse Dee
Fredmund, Immanuel
Free, Laurence Adam
Freeman, John D., Jr.
Frey, Leibert Garland
Fuller, James Woodrow
Fussell, William Rupert

Gabhart, Herbert Conway
Gaddy, Claude Fisher
Gallman, Rawdon Lee
Gardner, Eugene Norfleet
Garrett, James Leo
Garrett, Wilkins Barry, Jr.
Garrison, George Frank
Garrison, Searcy Slaton
Garrott, William Maxfield
Garwood, Harry Crawford
Gaskin, Jesse Marvin
Gayer, Theodore Wilmot
Gibbs, John Wesley
Gibson, Hoyt Sidney
Gibson, John Frank
Giddens, Earold Donovan
Giddens, Howard Peterson
Gideon, Virtus Evans
Gilbreath, John Albert
Gilewicz, John
*Gilliam, Norris
Glass, Victor Thomas
Glass, Wiley Blount
Glaze, Redus Edgar, Jr.
Goerner, Henry Cornell
Gooding, Marion William
Goodrich, Arthur Leon
Goodson, Carl Edward
Goodwin, Rex Dean
Graham, Finlay Morrison
Grant, James Marse
Grant, Mrs. James Richard
Graves, Allen Willis
Graves, Harold Keaster
Gray, Elmer L.
Gray, Ione
Green, Charles Sylvester
Green, James Milburn
Greene, Glen Lee
Greer, Genevieve
Greer, Isaac Garfield
Gregory, Ernest Jackson
Gregory, Harold Davis
Gresham, Felix Morris
Grey, James David
Grice, Homer Lamar
Griffin, Gladys Morris (Mrs. Charles M.)
Griffith, Benjamin Woodward, Jr.
Groner, Pat Neff
Gross, Arthur Lee

Contributors

Groves, Florence Belle
Gruver, Kate Ellen
Gulley, Julius Paul
Gunn, Jack Winton
Guy, Robert Calvin

Hackley, Woodford Broadus
Haight, Elmer Francis
Halbeck, Frank
Hall, Charles Bonner
Hall, David Clarence
Hall, Dick Houston, Jr.
Hall, William Franklin, Sr.
Hallock, Edgar Francis, Jr.
Hamlet, Charles Buck, III
Hamlett, Mayme Lucille
Hamric, Ethalee
Hamrick, John Asa
Harbuck, Donald Bradford
Hardie, George MacFarlane
Harrell, William Asa
Harris, Frank Carleton
Harris, Ransom Baine
Harris, Robert Lawson
Harris, Thomas Lafayette
Harrison, Guy Bryan, Jr.
Harvey, Paul Caspar
Harvey, Sam Allen
Harwell, Hoyt Horace
Harwell, Jack Dempsy
Haskins, Thomas Paul
Hastings, Carroll Brownlow
Hastings, Robert Jean
Havins, Thomas Robert
Hayes, James Madison
Heacock, Joe Davis
Head, Eldred Douglas
Hearn, Charles Aubrey
Heath, Daryl Ivan
Hebard, Roger Deaver
Heeren, Forrest Henry
Henderson, Carrie Wilhite (Mrs. W. C.)
Henderson, Eula Mae
Hendricks, Garland Alford
Henry, Auguie
Hensley, John Clark
Hester, Hubert Inman
Hickerson, Amy Compere (Mrs. Clyde Vernon)
Hiett, Dollie Eulalia
Higginbotham, Frederick Rhodes
Hill, Mrs. Arthur Byrd
Hill, Eugene Lowell
Hillyer, Herbert Sydney
Hinson, Arthur
Hipps, John Burder
Hobbs, Herschel Harold
Hodges, Jesse Wilson
Hoffa, Vergie May (Mrs. James M.)
Holcomb, Clifford Augustus
Holcomb, William Lamar
Holloway, Thomas Thornton

Holmes, Richard Lafayette
Hook, James Don
Hopkins, Charles Howard
Hough, Raymond Franklin, Sr.
Howard, Alva Roscoe, Jr.
Howse, William Lewis, Jr.
Hoyt, James Alfred, Jr.
Hudgins, Frances Eugenia
Hudgins, William Douglas
Hudson, Robert Lofton
Huey, Henry Jeremiah
Huggins, Malloy Alton
Hughey, John David, Jr.
Humphrey, George Caldwell
Hunt, William Boyd
Hurt, John Jeter, Jr.
Hutcherson, Curtis Alvin

Ingle, Clifford
Ingraham, Harold Edward
Ingram, Ben
Inlow, Eva Richard
Insko, Chester Arthur
Ivey, Robert Allison
Ivey, Willis Leon

Jackson, Arthur
Jackson, Herbert Cross
Jackson, Walter Andrew
James, Minnie Kennedy (Mrs. William Carey)
*James, Powhatan Wright
Janes, Horace Lee
Jenkins, Albert Ellison
Jenkins, George Miley
Jewell, George Raleigh
Johns, Thomas Maxwell
Johnson, Charles Price
Johnson, Hansford Duncan
Johnson, Kimball
Johnson, Lafayette Demetrius
Johnson, Mary Lynch
Johnson, William Buren
Johnston, Edwin Dargan
Joiner, Edward Earl
Jones, Billy Walker
Jones, Charles Walton
Jones, Edwin Holmes
Jones, Irene A.
Jones, John Estill
Jones, Samuel Hovey
Jones, Vasile William
Jones, Warren Francis

Keegan, Gilbert Kearnie
Keene, Frank Archie
Kendall, William Fred
Kennedy, James Hardee
Kilpatrick, William Heard
King, Bernard Dodson
King, Jessie Mae
King, Joe Madison
King, Spencer Bidwell, Jr.
Kirkley, Jesse Merle

Kmeta, Ivan A.
Knight, Walker Leigh
Kolb, Robert Francis
Koon, Victor
Kuhnle, Harold

Lackey, Thomas Bert
Laing, Wesley Newton
Lambdin, Jerry Elmer
Lane, William Thomas
Latch, Ollie
Lawrence, John Benjamin
Lea, Cecil Francis
Leavell, Roland Quinche
Lee, George Avery
Lee, Robert Lett
Leek, Charles Franklin
Leichliter, Gould A.
Leininger, Louis Lee
Leonard, Charles Alexander
Lester, Malcolm
Leuschner, Martin Luther
Levy, George Edward
Lewis, John Moore
Lewis, Walter Oliver
Lighthouse, Lucy Laurene
Link, William Calhoun, Jr.
Littell, Franklin Hamlin
Littleton, Homer Richerson
Lockard, Gertrude Inez
Long, Garis Thomas
Looney, Floyd
Lord, Fred Townley
Lott, Janie Mae
Lott, Theodore Franklin
Loving, Robert Edward
Loving, William Rush
Lower, Mark Antony
Luck, Joe Fred
Lumpkin, William Latane
Lynes, Benjamin Obadiah
Lyon, Louise Jackson (Mrs. Henry Louis)

Macon, Leon Meertief
Maguire, Clyde Merrill (Mrs. John)
Manley, Jack Hamilton
Manning, Jack Warren
Mantiply, Victor Edsel
Maples, Lewis Emerson
Martin, James Curtis
Martin, Lewis Waller, Sr.
Martin, Robert William, Jr.
Martin, William Plunkett
Massey, Dyar Edwin, Jr.
Maston, Thomas Bufford
Mather, Juliette Edla
Mathis, Arthur William
Matthews, Charles DeWitt, Jr.
Matthews, Ruby Hyatt (Mrs. Lucien)
Maxey, Henry Truman
May, Lynn Edward, Jr.
McCall, Duke Kimbrough

McCan, Robert Lee
McCartney, Mrs. Mable Holmes
McClellan, Albert Alfred
McClung, Robert Lee
McDanel, Ralph Clipman
McDonald, Erwin Lawrence
McDonald, Florence H.
McDormand, Thomas Bruce
McDowell, Edward Allison
McDowell, Emily Sawyer (Mrs. William Herbert)
McElrath, William Nold
McGee, William Kay
McGinty, Hilary Herbert
McGlothlen, Gaye Lilburn
*McGlothlin, William Joseph
MacGorman, John William
McIlroy, Minnie Douglas
McIntire, Russell Martin
McKay, Charles Lloyd
McLeod, John Angus
McLin, William Robert
McManus, Harold Lynn
McMillan, Mary Alberta
McMinn, Joe Billy
McMurray, Mary Jo Henry (Mrs. J. D.)
McNabb, Polly Anna
McRae, Jane Carroll (Mrs. J. D.)
Mein, Mildred Cox (Mrs. John)
Mercer, Moses Eli
Meredith, Helen
Merritt, James White
Middlebrook, John B.
Middleton, James Wallace
Middleton, Robert Lee
Milam, Robert Edward
Miller, Acker C
Miller, Joe Hardy, Sr.
Mitcham, Mrs. Thelma Mardis
Mitchell, John Henry
Mitchell, Merle Amon
*Mixon, Forest Orion
Moncrief, Adiel Jarrett, Jr.
Moody, Dale
Moore, David Otto
Moore, Edward Harmon
Moore, Eugene Tillman
*Moore, Hight C
Moore, John Allen
Moore, Lamire Holden
Moore, Merrill Dennis
Moore, Robert Cecil
Moore, Walter
Moore, William Dewey
Morgan, Leonard Lafayette
Morgan, Oscar Okla
Morgan, Samuel Lewis
Morrison, Thomas Henry, Jr.
Morton, Hugh Dudley
Morton, William Hardy

Moses, Colter Hamilton
Mueller, William Arthur
*Mullins, Edgar Young
Murch, James DeForest
Murdoch, John Cochran
Murphree, Bob
Murphy, Joel C.
Murphy, Mrs. Pat
Murrie, Benjamin Jackson
Muse, William Taylor
Myers, Lewis Alexander

Naylor, Robert Ernest
Neal, La Venia
Neiger, Fred Eugene
Nelson, David A.
Nelson, Dotson McGinnis, Jr.
Newman, Stewart Albert
Newport, John Paul
Newton, Louie DeVotie
Nichols, Buford Lee
Nielson, Richard Elmer
Noe, Fred W.
Noonkester, James Ralph
Nordenhaug, Josef
Norfleet, Frank Ford
Norgaard, Johannes
Norman, Kenneth Glen
Northcutt, Jesse James
Northington, Mary
Norwood, Josephine Carroll

Oates, Wayne Edward
O'Bannon, Retta
O'Dell, Mrs. Kathryn McGlothlin
Offutt, Garland
Ohrn, Arnold Theodore
Olive, Eugene Irving
Ousley, John Wiley
Owen, Richard Newton
Owens, John Joseph
Owens, Loulie Latimer (Mrs. Ollin J.)

Palmer, John Norris
Palmer, Robert Leland
Parker, James Benjamin
Parker, Raymond Austin
Paschal, George Washington
Pate, Billie Homer
Patterson, Floyd
Patterson, Frank Willard
Patterson, Joye
Patterson, William Morgan
Paulette, Richard Carrington
Pearson, Thomas Alton
Pennebaker, John Howard
Perry, Edwin Fleetwood
Perry, Marion Walter
Peterson, Hugh Raymond
Peterson, Monte Raymond
Petre, Adalbert M.
Pettus, Herschel Crockett
Pharr, Lamar Keener

Phelps, Ralph Arloe, Jr.
Pierce, Herbert Miner
Pile, Josephine
Pitt, William Davis
Pitts, Rubin Clayton
Polhill, Lucius McLendon
Ponder, James Lowell
Pope, Charles Wesley
Posey, Shelton Gambrell
*Poteat, Edwin McNeill, Jr.
Powell, Mary Patricia
Prather, Mrs. R. W., Jr.
Pratt, Eugene Talmadge
Preston, William Hall
Price, John Milburn, Jr.
Price, John Milburn, Sr.
Price, Theron Douglas
Prince, Aaron Erastus
Provence, Ruth
Pruden, Edward Hughes
Puckett, Garnett Eaton
Pugh, Roberta
Purdue, William Joseph
Purdy, Harold John
Puryear, Mrs. George Washington
Pylant, Agnes Durant (Mrs. Lake)

Raines, Luther Henry
Ramay, Marion Edgar
Ramm, Bernard Lawrence
Ransdell, John William
Ratliff, John Durwood
Ray, Lewis Clinton
Ray, Willis Jackson, Jr.
Reap, John William
Reavis, Henry Clay
Redden, Lawrence Drew
Redford, Samuel Courts
Reeves, Gordon Crawford
Reid, Avery Hamilton
Reid, Orvil Wilson
Reynolds, William Jensen
Rhodes, Lewis Elliot
Rhys, William Joseph
Richardson, Frank Craig
Richardson, Rupert Norval
Richardson, Vernon Britt
Riddle, John Roberts
Ridenour, Crea
Rigdon, Raymond May, Jr.
Ritchey, George Arch
Ritter, Lacy Milton
Roach, Dewey Revero
Roark, Harry McCullough
Robbins, Albert Wayne
Robbins, Ray Frank
Roberts, Frances Everett
Roberts, John Elgin
Robinson, Arabella Barton (Mrs. H. L.)
Robinson, Berneice Marie
Robinson, Maude Edwina
Robinson, Robert Lee
Rockett, Dewey Hobson

Contributors

Rogers, James Sterling, Sr.
Rone, Wendell Holmes
Rose, Thomas Andrew
Rosser, John Leonidas
Roth, Jewell Edward
Routh, Eugene Coke
Routh, Porter Wroe
Ruark, Elmer Francis
Rule, Walter Stuart
Russell, Joseph Jamison
Rust, Eric Charles
Rust, Ray Pearce
Rutledge, Arthur Bristow
Ryburn, Frank Marion
Ryland, Garnett

Sadler, George Washington
St. Amant, Clyde Penrose
St. John, Evalois
Salley, John Cecil
Sampson, Farris Athelstan
Sanderford, Matthew Anderson
Sanders, Albert Neely
Sanders, Harold Glen
Sandidge, John Pleasant, Jr.
Sauls, Henry Sylvester
Saunders, Marjorie
Sawyer, James Albert
Scales, James Ralph
Scales, Robert Sylvesta
Scantlan, Samuel William
Schlafer, Frederick George
Schroeder, George William
Scofield, Mary Ellen
Scudder, Cleo Wayne
Sedberry, Leland Stanford, Sr.
Seefeldt, Harold Christian
Segler, Franklin Morgan
Segler, John Coy
Seigler, O. M.
Sewell, Bailey Otis
Sewell, William Lamar
Shamburger, William Marsh
Shaw, Jack
Shields, Oliver Rebhan
Shinto, William Mamoru
Shipp, Vernon Edwin
Shrader, William Wesley
Sims, Walter Hines
Sinclair, Helen
Singleton, Janice Ruth
Skelton, Eugene Lamar
Skidmore, Clyde Beecher
Smiley, David Leslie
Smith, Budd Elmon
Smith, Buren Cortez
Smith, James Leslie
Smith, Lemuel Edward
Smith, Noel
Smith, Ralph Lee
Smith, Robert Houston
Smith, Sam Mayer
Smith, Taylor Clarence
Smith, William Cheney, Jr.

Soileau, Robert R.
Somerville, Wendell C.
Sommerkamp, Theo Enoch
Spell, Howard Edgar
Spencer, Harry Lee
Spencer, Lee Bowen
Spiro, Robert Harry, Jr.
Springer, Rudolph Arden
Stagg, Frank
Stagg, Harry Perkins
Stagg, Louis Anatole, Jr.
Stagg, Paul Leonard
Stainback, Arthur House
Stallings, Oscar Monroe
Stanfield, Max Carman
Stanfield, Vernon Latrelle
Starkey, James Wesley
Stealey, Sydnor Lorenzo
Stearns, Ada
Stenstrom, Julian Lovejoy
Stephens, Julius Harold
Stephens, Walter Colquitt
Stewart, Mack Patrick, Jr.
Stiansen, Peder
Stigler, Willie Leonard
Stith, Milton Chandler
Stockstill, Eugene Hunter
Stokes, Henry Jerome, Jr.
Stone, Eugenia Wootton
Storer, James Wilson
Stout, Elta Cooperood (Mrs. W. I.)
Stracener, William Guy
Strange, William Ernest
Strickland, William Claudius
Stroupe, Henry Smith
Strutz, Eric
Stumph, Calowa William
Stupka, Vincent Peter
Sullivan, Herman Taylor
Sullivan, James Lenox
Summers, Mrs. Luther Davis
Summers, Ray
Sutton, Frank Wesley
Swift, Roy Lee
Swilley, Monroe Franklin, Jr.

Tanner, Andrew Daniel
Taylor, Eldred Martin
Taylor, Noel Myron
Taylor, Raymond Hargus
Taylor, Sara Frances
Taylor, Walter Fuller
Taylor, Wilburn Stanley
Tedford, Leroy Carson
Terrell, Robert Francis
Theisz, George Elmer
Thomas, Ida Margaret Jackson (Mrs. G. W.)
Thomasson, Florence
Thompson, Sara Virginia
Tibbs, Albert Elias
Tidwell, Donavan Duncan
Timberlake, W. Burman
Tinnin, Finley Watson
Todd, Byron Franklin

Town, William Forrester, Jr.
Treadway, Charles Franklin
Trejbal, Helen Victoria
Trent, Robbie
Trentham, Charles Arthur
Tripp, Edgar Franklin
Trueblood, Elwyn Judson
Truex, Madge Nicholson (Mrs. C. M.)
Trutza, Earl Hester (Mrs. Petre)
Tucker, Charles Rolfe
Tucker, Robert Cinnamond
Tull, James Estol
Turlington, Henry Eugene
Tyner, Elbert Clement

Udvarnoki, Ruby Daniel (Mrs. Bela)
Underwood, Richard Vance
Ussery, Annie Wright (Mrs. Gordon)

Van Ness, Noble
Vaughan, William Curtis
Venting, Albert
Voda, Melba Beaird
Vollmer, Albert Martin
Von Hagen, Keith Croswell

Waddell, Henry Clayton
Waite, Florida
Waldrup, Rufus Earl
Walker, Elbert Henry
Walton, William Truett
Wamble, Gaston Hugh
Ward, Richard Hiram
Ward, Wayne Eugene
Warden, Francis Marion
Warr, John Carey
Washburn, Alphonso Victor, Jr.
Waterhouse, William Edward
Watkins, Esther Pearl (Mrs. R. H.)
Watts, James Merideth
Watts, James Washington
Waud, Gilbert Burton
Wayland, John Terrill
Weaver, Ellis Neely
Webb, Marion Buel
Webb, Perry Flynt, Jr.
Weber, Paul
Webster, James Aldean, Jr.
Weeks, Dorothy Louise
Welsh, James Elwood
Wenger, Margaret Noffsinger (Mrs. Milo E.)
Wesberry, James Pickett
West, George Allen, Jr.
Westmoreland, Mrs. Lillie Ballard
Westmoreland, N J
Wharton, James
Wheeler, Troy Val

White, Blanche Sydnor
White, David Lewis
White, Glenn Foster
White, William Richardson
Whitten, Charles William
Whittington, Richard Henry
Whittington, William Madison
Wilbanks, Charles Estes
Wilds, Ruth Lawton (Mrs. George J., Jr.)

* *Deceased*

Williams, Hubert Ethridge
Williams, James Toy
Williams, John Daniel
Williams, John Howard
Williams, Leslie Spencer
Williams, Loren Raymond
Williams, William Harrison
Williamson, Edgar
Williamson, Edgar Stanley
Winburn, Mrs. Hardy Lathan

Winchcole, Dorothy Clark
Winters, Doyle Newburn
Wood, Levi Davis
Wood, Nathan Rillstone
Woodson, Hortense Caroline
Woodward, Robert Franklin
Woolley, Davis Collier
Wright, Leslie Stephen

Yates, Kyle Monroe, Jr.
Young, Richard Knox

ILLUSTRATIONS

	Facing Page
Presidents of the Southern Baptist Convention.	36–37
Early Pioneer Baptist Churches.	68
Buildings Typical of 14,000 Southern Baptist Country Churches in 1956.	69
First Baptist Church, Leroy, Ala.	100
First Baptist Church, Salem, Ill.	100
Alabama Baptist Children's Home, Troy.	101
Connie Maxwell Children's Home, Greenwood, S. C.	132
Mississippi Baptist Children's Home, Jackson.	Between 132–133
Oklahoma Baptist Orphans' Home, Oklahoma City.	Between 132–133
Texas Baptist Children's Homes.	133
Virginia Baptist Children's Home, Salem.	164
Virginia Baptist Home, Inc., Culpeper.	165
Texas Tech Baptist Student Center, Lubbock.	196
University of Alabama Baptist Student Center, Tuscaloosa.	196
University of Miami Baptist Student Center, Miami, Fla.	197
University of Oklahoma Baptist Student Center, Norman.	197
Baylor University, Waco, Tex.	228
Carson-Newman College, Jefferson City, Tenn.	229
Furman University, Greenville, S. C.	260
Georgetown College, Georgetown, Ky.	261
Howard College, Birmingham, Ala.	292
Howard Payne College, Brownwood, Tex.	293
Louisiana College, Pineville.	324
Mercer University, Macon, Ga.	325
Mississippi College, Clinton.	356
Ouachita Baptist College, Arkadelphia, Ark.	357
Stetson University, DeLand, Fla.	388
Union University, Jackson, Tenn.	389
University of Richmond, Virginia.	420
Wake Forest College, Winston-Salem, N. C.	421
William Jewell College, Liberty, Mo.	460
First Baptist Church, Charleston, S. C.	461
First Baptist Church, Augusta, Ga.	492

	Illustrations
First Baptist Church, Greenville, S. C.	493
First Baptist Church, Columbia, S. C.	524
First Baptist Church, Mobile, Ala.	525
First Southern Baptist Church, Phoenix, Ariz.	556
Truett Memorial Baptist Church, Hayesville, N. C.	556
First Southern Baptist Church, San Diego, Calif.	Between 556–557
First Southern Baptist Church, Sanger, Calif.	Between 556–557
First Baptist Church, Nashville, Tenn.	Between 556–557
Walnut Street Baptist Church, Louisville, Ky.	557
First Baptist Church, Winston-Salem, N. C.	588
First Baptist Church, West Palm Beach, Fla.	589
First Baptist Church, El Dorado, Ark.	620
First Baptist Church, Jennings, La.	621
First Baptist Church, Decatur, Ga.	652
First Baptist Church, Jackson, Miss.	653
Family Night, First Baptist Church, Meridian, Miss.	684
First Baptist Church, Greensboro, N. C.	685
First Baptist Church, Jackson, Mo.	716
First Baptist Church, Clinton, Mo.	716
First Baptist Church, Clovis, N. Mex.	717
First Baptist Church, Roanoke, Va.	808
First Baptist Church, Oklahoma City, Okla.	809
First Baptist Church, Lancaster, S. C.	840
First Baptist Church, Smithville, Tenn.	841
First Baptist Church, Dallas, Tex.	872
First Baptist Church, Hattiesburg, Miss.	873
Dauphin Way Baptist Church, Mobile, Ala.	904
First Baptist Church, New Orleans, La.	905
First Baptist Church, Lubbock, Tex.	936
First Baptist Church, Richmond, Va.	937
First Baptist Church, Tulsa, Okla.	968
Southern Baptist Theological Seminary, Louisville, Ky.	969
Southwestern Baptist Theological Seminary, Fort Worth, Tex.	1000
New Orleans Baptist Theological Seminary, Louisiana.	1001
Golden Gate Baptist Theological Seminary, Berkeley, Calif.	1032
Southeastern Baptist Theological Seminary, Wake Forest, N. C.	1033
Carver School of Missions and Social Work, Louisville, Ky.	1064
American Baptist Theological Seminary, Nashville, Tenn.	1065
Sunday School Board, Nashville, Tenn.	Between 1096–1097
Woman's Missionary Union Headquarters Building, Birmingham, Ala.	1128
Foreign Mission Board Headquarters Building, Richmond, Va.	1129
New Mexico Buildings.	1160

Illustrations

Alabama Baptist Convention Building, Montgomery.	1161
Centreville Baptist Church, Alabama.	1161
Maryland State Convention Headquarters, Baltimore.	1192
Louisiana Baptist Building, Alexandria.	1192
Mississippi Baptist Convention Building, Jackson.	1193
Kentucky Baptist Building, Middletown.	1193
Baptist Building, Dallas, Tex.	1264
Oklahoma Baptist Building, Oklahoma City.	1264
South Carolina Baptist House, Columbia.	1265
Virginia State Convention Building, Richmond.	1265
Arizona Baptist Building, Phoenix.	1296
Florida Baptist Convention Building, Jacksonville.	1296
Illinois State Convention Building, Carbondale.	1297
Missouri Baptist Building, Jefferson City.	1297
Georgia Baptist Building, Atlanta.	1328
Tennessee Baptist Convention Headquarters, Nashville.	1328
Southern Baptist Hospital, New Orleans, La.	1329
Baptist Memorial Hospital, Jacksonville, Fla.	1360
Oklahoma Baptist Hospitals.	Between 1360–1361
Georgia Baptist Hospital, Atlanta.	1361
Missouri Baptist Hospital, St. Louis.	1392
Baptist Memorial Hospital, Houston, Tex.	1393
Baton Rouge General Hospital, Louisiana.	1424
North Carolina Baptist Hospital and Bowman Gray School of Medicine, Winston-Salem.	1425
Baptist Memorial Hospital, Memphis, Tenn.	1456
Baylor University Hospital, Dallas, Tex.	1457

ABBOT, HENRY (b. London, England, c. 1745; d. North Carolina, May, 1791). Son of John Abbot, canon of St. Paul's, London, he ran away to America in 1765 as a youth. With moderate education he became a schoolteacher. In 1758 he was baptized without an experience of conversion, by Joseph Parker (c. 1705–91), a General Baptist minister. Later he was converted, and accepting the doctrines of the Regular Baptists, he traveled widely as an itinerant preacher. About 1764 or 1765 he became pastor of Shiloh Church, Camden County, N. C., and was one of the ministers present at the constitution of the Kehukee Association in 1769. He became dissatisfied with his baptism and was immersed the second time. In 1775 he led in constituting the branch of Shiloh Church at Yeopim (formerly Yoppim) into a separate organization and became pastor there also. He was a member of the conventions which considered the North Carolina and federal constitutions, and proved himself an able advocate of religious liberty. J. A. EASLEY

ABBOTT'S CREEK CHURCH. Established as a station of the Sandy Creek Church, about 30 miles away, it was the second Separate Baptist church in North Carolina. Upon its constitution as an independent body, probably in 1756, Daniel Marshall became the ordained pastor of the church. While at Abbott's Creek, Marshall spread Separate doctrines even into Virginia and led his church in becoming a constituent of Sandy Creek Association in 1758. After Marshall and some members of the church migrated to South Carolina, in 1760, the church organization seems to have failed, although the members retained their religious interest under the ministry of visiting Separate Baptist preachers and Moravian missionaries who held services in neighborhood homes. In 1772 a Baptist minister, Stotsmann, was a resident in the area. A reorganization of the church, of which there is no written record, occurred in 1777, and another in 1783, with George Pope as pastor. Pope remained with the church for many years, representing it at the Sandy Creek Association as late as 1814. During the Great Revival he baptized about 500. In 1825 the church withdrew from Sandy Creek to join in the formation of Abbott's Creek Union Association, taken over by the antimissionary element in 1832. As a result the church split, one part becoming antimissionary, the other joining in the formation of the Liberty Baptist Association, a Separate body. G. W. PASCHAL

ABEOKUTA BAPTIST BOYS' HIGH SCHOOL. See NIGERIA, MISSION IN.

ABEOKUTA BAPTIST GIRLS' SCHOOL. See NIGERIA, MISSION IN.

ABERDEEN MALE ACADEMY. Established in 1874 at Aberdeen, Miss., with J. W. Bozeman as principal. The academy is now extinct.
J. L. BOYD

ABSTINENCE. Abstinence in general is the exercise of the disciplines of self-control. As such, its practice is essential to the growth of personal character and the well-being of human society. The term in its common usage among Southern Baptists means total abstinence from the use of intoxicating beverages.

The total abstinence position is religiously conditioned. Those who abstain from the use of alcoholic beverages because of their religious convictions believe that the Bible sustains their views. Varying attitudes toward biblical interpretation, however, lead to differences of opinion at this point. Many find proof tests in the Bible which they believe forbid any use of beverage alcohol. Others find texts which they claim support the practice of moderate drinking and which, they say, teach true temperance. Some point out that the great burden of the biblical attitude on the subject is directed against drunkenness.

Most Baptists believe that a thorough and comprehensive study of the Bible, supplemented by scientific knowledge of the nature and effect of alcohol, demands total abstinence from the use of intoxicating beverages as a Christian duty and a Christian responsibility. Three scriptural teachings support this view: (1) The purpose of God in the creation of man. Man is to glorify God and to finish His work. (2) The purpose of God in the redemption of man. God is to remake man in the image of His Son. (3) The purpose of God in the destiny of man. Man is to be seen as a light in the world holding forth the word of life.

Scientific studies show that alcohol used as a beverage in small or large amounts affects its user. It is a narcotic and acts as a depressant. It releases the inhibitions and lowers moral restraint. It weakens the judgment. It dulls the sense of co-ordination and timing essential to safety in this machine age. Its continued use even in moderation affects the health, the emotions, and the personality. These resultant characteristics are inconsistent with Christian character; they make one unfit for the "high calling of God in Christ Jesus."

The ethical case for abstinence grows out of a true sense of man's obligation to others. The source of this obligation is found in Christian love. Each man is his brother's keeper, and must bear the burdens of his fellows. He must not place a stumbling block in someone else's road. Paul's illustration of eating meat that had been offered to idols is appropriate here. Paul had no compunctions of conscience in eating this meat. But if a less mature Christian thought it was wrong, then he would abstain from eating it. Paul's genuine love for others enabled him to do this.

Another side of the ethical case for abstinence is the fact that the use of beverage alcohol often harms and hurts others. No person has the right to injure others in his home or community. Nor does the exercise of his personal liberty give him the right to threaten the public safety on streets and highways. Liquor-caused accidents on the public highways have killed in the same length of time more people than were killed in World War II. Moreover, alcoholism is 5.5 per cent more prevalent in America than cancer, 3.2 per cent more prevalent than tuberculosis, and more than 100 times more prevalent than polio.

Numerical statistics, of course, do not reveal the full results of the use of alcohol as a beverage. Its use affects all areas of human relations and is involved in many subtle ways in economic and governmental problems. The Southern Baptist Convention has through the years held the position that the only solution for this problem for the individual and for human society is total abstinence.   A. C. MILLER

ACADIA BAPTIST ACADEMY. A boarding, standard, state-approved high school owned and operated by the Louisiana Baptist Convention, established in 1917 primarily as a mission undertaking. The success of several smaller efforts together with the growth of French mission work caused Pastor W. J. Westberry of Pilgrim Rest Baptist Church, Eunice, to offer 20 acres of land and $2,000 for the first building; the Home Mission Board paid the salaries of two teachers. In 1919 the property was transferred to the Executive Board of the Louisiana Baptist Convention. The school was chartered as an educational institution in 1922. It offers grades 8 through 12, instruction in Bible, sacred music, and religious education, and remedial work to adults. It appeals especially to young people who have volunteered for special work but who have not finished high school.

Property consists of 71 acres of land with 20 buildings adequate for accommodating 125 students. By action of the Louisiana Baptist Convention in Nov., 1947, the academy was made an integral part of the 10-year program of expansion for Louisiana Baptists, and preliminary plans were laid for completely redesigning the school plant to accommodate at least 250 students. The state convention in 1954 placed the academy in the Cooperative Program for its support. Four hundred and twenty-five students have graduated from the school. In 1954 the enrolment was 111, the budget was $100,000. Net worth was $233,525.98 with no indebtedness.

BIBLIOGRAPHY: Acadia Baptist Academy, *Annual 1917–18 to 1954–55.* Louisiana Baptist Convention, *Annual 1917–54.* C. P. St. Amant, *A Short History of Louisiana Baptists* (1948).   MRS. T. E. EDMONSON

ADAM. The first man, into whom God creatively imparted the capacity to live in His image. The Hebrew word *Adam* means man; Adam is the representative man, in biblical thought. What happens to all men stems from what happened to Adam. All men are in the racial solidarity of Adam and have sinned like him. All men are outside the garden in the wilderness of sin and death, because in Adam men rejected God, and thought themselves, through pride, to be self-sufficient.

Christ, the last Adam, is representative of the new humanity. By faith in Christ the divine image is restored in man.

See also MAN and INFANTS, SALVATION OF.
        E. C. RUST

ADAMS, GEORGE F. (b. Dorchester, Mass., 1802; d. Baltimore, Md., Apr. 16, 1877). Clergyman, teacher, and a founder of the Maryland Baptist Union Association. He was baptized in Ohio in 1812, was licensed to preach in 1822, and entered Columbian College, Washington, D. C., in 1824 to prepare for the ministry. He was ordained in 1827. In 1829 he became principal of the college, and pastor of a group which formed the E Street Church in Washington. The D.D. degree was conferred upon him in 1859 by Columbian College. During 1830–35 he was principal of the Ladies' Academy in Falmouth, Va., and assistant pastor in a Baptist church in Fredericksburg, Va. He went to Baltimore, Md., in 1836, serving for seven years as pastor of Calvert Street Church, later known as High Street Church. When the Civil War started, he went back to Virginia, but returned to Baltimore to serve as a city missionary (1863–65). In 1865 he took charge of a school for girls in Onancock, Va. In 1867 he became pastor of the Baptist church at Hampton, Va., where he served until failing health caused him to retire and return to Baltimore in 1876.
        MRS. LESLIE M. BOWLING

ADAMS, JAMES McKEE (b. Raleigh, N. C., Oct. 17, 1886; d. Louisville, Ky., Sept. 17, 1945). Theological professor, biblical lecturer, author. Son of David Thomas and Anne Marie (Nowell) Adams, he received A.B. and M.A. degrees from Wake Forest College and attended Crozer Theological Seminary, Chester, Pa., 1910–11. Adams received his Th.M. degree in 1920 and his Ph.D. degree in 1929 from Southern Baptist Theological Seminary in Louisville, Ky. While a seminary student, he was appointed a fellow in systematic theology by Edgar Young Mullins (*q.v.*), seminary president. Adams became assistant professor in theology in 1921 and associate professor in 1925. The following year, he began his 20-year professorship of biblical introduction. On 11 trips to Europe and the Near East in archeological study and research, Adams' enthusiasm increased as he saw material remains from Bible times. His classes reflected this enthusiasm.

Author of the *Syllabus for Biblical Introduction Studies* (1926); *Biblical Backgrounds* (translated into several languages for use in schools and seminaries) (1934); *The Heart of the Levant: Palestine and Syria* (1937); *Our Bible* (1937); and *Ancient Records and the Bible* (1946), Adams also contributed numerous articles to magazines. William Owen Carver (*q.v.*), a colleague and former teacher of Adams, said: "Dr. Adams was a man of devout, persistent, unostentatious, sometimes I thought unconscious, piety. He was always religious without the slightest show of religiosity."

J. MORRIS ASHCRAFT

ADAMS, MALDON BROWNING (b. Clarksburg, W. Va., 1869; d. Maysville, Ky., Apr. 18, 1945). Minister and educator. Son of John Browning and Martha Columbia (Holden) Adams, he was educated at Broaddus Classical and Scientific Institution, Clarksburg, W. Va., 1888–90, and Southern Baptist Theological Seminary, where he received the Th.B. degree in 1893. After being ordained to the ministry by the New Castle Baptist Church, New Castle, Ky., in 1891, he served as pastor of the church until 1893, after which time he held pastorates at North Fork Baptist Church, Mason County, Ky., 1893–98, and First Baptist Church, Frankfort, Ky., 1898–1910.

Adams served as corresponding secretary (1910–13), vice-president (1918), and president (1918–22) of the Baptist Education Society of Kentucky; and as president of Georgetown College, Kentucky (1913–31). Under his administration the college eliminated the old Georgetown Academy which had been an adjunct of the school since its beginning; in 1919 Georgetown was placed on the list of approved colleges by the Association of Colleges and Secondary Schools of the Southern States and became a member of the American Association of Colleges.

Adams was president of the Kentucky State Baptist Young People's Union, 1889–1904; president of the Kentucky Anti-Saloon League, 1900–07; and assistant moderator of the General Association of Baptists in Kentucky in 1909. He was president of the Standardization Commission of the Southern Baptist Convention, 1923–27; chairman of the Kentucky Commission for the Selection of Rhodes Scholars, 1913–19; president of the Kentucky Association of Colleges and Universities; member of the Kentucky Education Association; and president of the Southern Baptist Education Association for the term 1926–28. An able scholar and a student of the Bible, Adams wrote the weekly Sunday school lesson treatments for the *Western Recorder* for many years.

GEORGE RALEIGH JEWELL

ADMINISTRATION, SOUTHERN BAPTIST PATTERNS OF. The Southern Baptist Convention has carried on its business since its organization in 1845 by the election of trustees, and by making the trustees responsible for the selection of administrative officers.

In the first Convention held in 1845, it was stated in Article 5 of the constitution:

The Convention shall elect at each triennial meeting as many boards of managers, as in its judgment will be necessary for carrying out the benevolent objects it may determine to promote, all of which boards shall continue in office until a new election. Each board shall consist of a president, vice-president, secretaries, treasurer, auditor and fifteen other members, seven of whom, including one or more of the officers, shall form a quorum for the transaction of business. To each board shall be committed, during the recess of the Convention, the entire management of all the affairs relating to the object with whose interest it shall be charged, all of which management shall be in strict accordance with the constitutional provisions adopted by this Convention, and such other instructions as may be given from time to time. Each board shall have power to make such compensation to its secretaries and treasurer, as it may think right; to fill the vacancies occurring in its own body; enact its own bylaws; have an annual meeting at any place it may appoint, and other meetings at such times and places as it may think best; keep a record of its proceedings, and present a report of them to the Convention at each triennial meeting.

In 1915 the Convention amended its constitution and bylaws to provide that the corresponding secretary or administrative officers should be elected by the Convention itself, rather than by the directors or trustees elected, but this provision was revoked by the Convention in 1924, when it again provided, as in the original constitution, that the trustees or directors elected by the Convention should select their own administrative officer.

The constitution now provides that each board may elect "executive, administrative, finance, and investment committees if desired." The boards are also authorized to elect "a president, a recording secretary, a treasurer, an executive secretary who may be named as treasurer, and such other officers as may be required." In describing the duties and officers of boards, it states: "All officers shall be subject to the control and direction of their board in matters pertaining to the board's work and obligations." It states further: "The executive secretary of each board and the president of each institution shall be its executive head and shall carry on the work as the board may direct."

The recording secretary is instructed by the constitution to "keep a record of all board meetings . . . in fireproof safes or vaults," and the treasurer of each board is instructed to "follow approved methods of accounting, keep the

Adoption

books, receipt for all monies and securities, deposit all funds with a depositary approved by the board, and render full statements as required to the board or to this Convention. The treasurer shall not pay out money except as the board may order and direct."

Each agency is authorized to prepare its own bylaws, and the detailed processes of administration in each agency are outlined in its bylaws and approved by the board.

Matters which are presented to the Convention dealing with areas which have been assigned to specific boards may be committed to those boards by the Convention, or the Convention may decide to commit the matter for study to a special committee for recommendation either to the board involved in the area or to report direct to the Convention.   PORTER ROUTH

ADOPTION. See SONSHIP.

ADVENT. The coming of Christ to Bethlehem; also the beginning of the Christian year. The observance of Advent began in Gaul, Spain, and Italy toward the end of the fifth century. In the West the Advent season begins on the nearest Sunday to St. Andrew's Day (Nov. 30), and extends through four Sundays, which in the Anglican service emphasize the second coming, the Holy Scriptures, the Christian ministry, and the first coming of Christ. Advent also contemplates the different ways of Christ's coming. Thus the second coming of Christ and the last judgment are emphasized in this season.

See also PAROUSIA.

BIBLIOGRAPHY: C. H. Dodd, *The Coming of Christ* (1951). A. Schweitzer, *The Quest of the Historical Jesus* (1950).   CHARLES A. TRENTHAM

ADVENTISTS. Religious sects which believe that the second coming of Christ and the beginning of the millennium are near at hand. The movement was founded by William Miller (1782-1849), who was of Baptist background, but beliefs similar to those held by Adventists were held in England as early as 1820. The Seventh-Day Adventists, largest of the Adventist bodies, was organized in 1845.

Other prominent Adventist bodies are Advent Christians, organized in 1861; the Evangelical Adventists; the Church of God; the Life and Advent Union, organized in 1848; the Church of God in Jesus Christ, or Age-to-Come Adventists, organized in 1913; and the Primitive Advent Christian Church. Outstanding doctrines of most Adventists are soul sleeping; annihilation of the wicked; Saturday held as the sabbath; millennium period finding world without inhabitants; the atonement merely beginning on the cross and continuing in Christ's priesthood; noncreedalism; the Ten Commandments used as a moral standard; the Bible as the basis of faith; membership by baptism (usually immersion); a usually negative morality—no smoking, drinking, dancing, theater; the world evil in nature; separation of church and state; tithing most important; gifts of prophecy; and salvation by grace.

See also MILLERITE MOVEMENT.

BIBLIOGRAPHY: H. K. Carroll, *The Religious Forces of the United States* (1895). E. T. Clark, *The Small Sects in America* (1949). *Encyclopaedia Britannica* (1949). L. E. Froom, "Seven-Day Adventists," *The American Church of the Protestant Heritage*, ed., V. Ferm (1953). P. E. Mayer, *The Religious Bodies in America* (1954). F. S. Mead, *Handbook of Denominations in the United States* (1951). M. Phelan, *Handbook of All Denominations* (1915). C. F. Potter, *The Faiths Men Live By* (1954). R. G. Torbet, "Baptist Churches in America," *The American Church of the Protestant Heritage*, ed., V. Ferm (1953). J. K. Van Baalen, *The Chaos of Cults* (1947).

C. EARL COOPER

ADVOCATE. A small antimission periodical edited and published in Illinois by Daniel Parker (q.v.) from 1829 to Sept., 1831, when he discontinued it for lack of funds.

LYNN E. MAY, JR.

AFRICA, MISSIONS IN. See GOLD COAST, MISSION IN; LIBERIA, MISSION IN; NIGERIA, MISSION IN; and SOUTHERN RHODESIA, MISSION IN.

AGE OF ACCOUNTABILITY. To be accountable means to be responsible for one's moral actions, to be answerable for one's conduct. This presumes in the person held accountable a measure of general intelligence which is lacking in infants and the mentally deficient but present in a normal adult. The age of accountability is that invisible boundary a person crosses when he has matured to the point at which he can justly be held answerable for his conduct. The Jews considered a boy a *son of the Law* at the age of twelve. Influenced by heredity and environment, individuals mature at different rates; some powers develop faster than others; thus no precise age of accountability may be specified.

See also RESPONSIBILITY.   BERNARD RAMM

AGE SECURITY PLAN. Inaugurated Jan. 1, 1936 (later revised), to provide old age or disability income for pastors and lay workers of churches affiliated with the Southern Baptist Convention. Member and employer each paid 3 per cent of member's salary, up to a maximum of $4,000 per year. The combined dues plus interest, at the time of retirement, determined the amount of annuity paid. This plan was revised on Nov. 1, 1940, as Age Security-B and operated for church employees who were not eligible to participate in the Ministers Retirement Plan or some other group plan. The revised plan provided an administrative expense deducted from the employer contributions. On Sept. 1, 1952, the plan was revised to the present plan, Age Security-C. Participation is accepted on the basis of 3 per cent or 5 per cent dues matched by the employer, with no maximum salary basis. A member may leave service, hold his certificate, and upon reaching retirement age receive the annuity provided by the total accumulations. If he elects to withdraw from the plan upon leaving service, for each year of membership he will receive 10 per cent of the employer accumulations in addition to his own.

MABLE MCCARTNEY

AGED, DENOMINATIONAL HOME FOR. An institution frequently supported by special contributions from interested individuals within a given religious group, together with the assistance of denominational appropriations and special offerings. Such a home furnishes support and care for aged persons who, because of previous service or for some other Christian considerations, are regarded as the responsibility of the denomination.

Institutional care for the aged, like the allied science of geriatrics, is a comparatively recent development, particularly among Baptists. Prior to the present century, care given to older people came usually from the family and relatives. But the modern trend away from large family establishments encompassing several generations, and the relative instability of the family as a modern institution, have made this arrangement less adequate. In addition, the marked increase in numbers of people living to advanced age has created a problem with which too few families can cope. Modern emphasis on sanitation and public health and on diet, together with the effectiveness of medical science, has lengthened the average life span in the United States by 27 years in a single generation. People often outlive their social groups, and sometimes even their immediate families. The older they grow, the more apt they are to find themselves without close or concerned kin, and therefore without a home.

Like other areas of benevolence, the care of the aged is coming to be regarded in some measure as the responsibility of religious groups. Often a real obligation binds a church or denomination to care for those who, whether lay or clergy, have devoted many years to the service of the church. Baptists in the South have only recently begun to face this need. As of 1955 the following states had homes in operation: District of Columbia, Kentucky, Maryland, Missouri, North Carolina, Texas, and Virginia. In Georgia, Florida, and Oklahoma homes were either under construction or definitely planned. The total value of all homes in operation as of Dec. 31, 1954, was $3,622,199. The homes were variously supported. Some were partially endowed; some received a percentage of Cooperative Program receipts; and all depended in some degree on special offerings and gifts. Significant sums have come from older people of means who have a special appreciation of the needs of their contemporaries.

J. T. EDWARDS

AGENCY OF THE SOUTHERN BAPTIST CONVENTION. The concept of the boards named by the Southern Baptist Convention serving as agents of the Convention was present at the time of its organization in 1845, but the term "agency" is not found in official documents until 1925 when a plan for new policies for the "boards and agencies" was adopted. In that same year authority was given to the committee on business efficiency to get any information desired from "Convention agencies." The 1926 Southern Baptist Convention *Annual* lists all the boards, institutions, commissions, and standing committees under the title "Agencies of the Convention" for the first time. An agency is considered as a permanent organization and different from a special committee.

The agencies of the Southern Baptist Convention are classified as follows: *General Boards.* —Foreign Mission Board, Home Mission Board, Relief and Annuity Board, The Sunday School Board. *Institutions.*—Golden Gate Baptist Theological Seminary, New Orleans Baptist Theological Seminary, Southern Baptist Theological Seminary, Southwestern Baptist Theological Seminary, Southern Baptist Foundation, Southern Baptist Hospital. *Institutions not owned but fostered by the Convention.*—The American Baptist Theological Seminary. *Commissions.*— The Education Commission, The Southern Baptist Commission on the American Baptist Theological Seminary, The Christian Life Commission, The Radio and Television Commission, The Historical Commission, and Brotherhood Commission.

The Executive Committee is not considered and is not listed as an agency of the Convention since it is the Convention *ad interim.* Although it is not listed as an agency, the Convention By-Laws state: "The Executive Committee shall be the fiduciary, the fiscal, and the executive agency of the Convention in all its affairs not specifically committed to some other board or agency." The agencies of the Convention are listed in By-Law 6.

PORTER ROUTH

AGES. See DISPENSATION and ETERNITY.

AGNOSTICISM. A term derived from the Greek *a*-privative (not) and the verb *gignōskein* (to know). Agnosticism is the theory that reason cannot penetrate beyond empirical judgment and that metaphysical or theological views cannot have definite proof. That is to say, agnosticism is a habit of mind (not a system) which recognizes an intrinsically Unknowable and thus despairs of a metaphysic or a theology. *Metaphysical* agnosticism, in contrast to skepticism, T. H. Huxley maintains, is not the denial of the possibility of all knowledge, but only a denial of the possibility of knowledge of ultimate reality. *Theological* agnosticism denies the possibility of acquiring knowledge about God or immortality either by the "natural light of reason" (Descartes), by empirical judgment (Schleiermacher, D. C. Macintosh), or by revelation (the church).

Ajloun Hospital

BIBLIOGRAPHY: E. A. Burtt, *Types of Religious Philosophy* (1939) Chapter VI. R. Flint, *Agnosticism* (1903). T. H. Huxley, H. Wace, et al., *Christianity and Agnosticism: A Controversy* (1899). J. Ward, *Naturalism and Agnosticism*. The Gifford Lectures delivered before the University of Aberdeen in the years 1896–1898 (1899).   J. B. MCMINN

AJLOUN HOSPITAL, AJLOUN. See JORDAN, MISSION IN.

ALABAMA ASSOCIATIONS.

I. Extant. ALABAMA-CRENSHAW. Formed in 1934 by the consolidation of Alabama Association with five remaining churches and the Crenshaw County Association, formerly New Providence, with 20 churches. The association adopted articles of faith. In 1954, 31 churches reported 193 baptisms, 4,514 members, $86,770 total gifts, $6,054 mission gifts, $207,890 property value, and $6,134 church debt.

AUTAUGA. Constituted at Autaugaville Baptist Church, Dec. 17, 1950, with eight churches, two out of Montgomery Association, five out of Unity Association, and one other church in Autauga County. It adopted articles of faith. In 1954, 13 churches reported 72 baptisms, 2,432 members, $122,525.56 total gifts, $9,680.94 mission gifts, $459,360.50 property value, and $101,427.90 church debt.

BALDWIN. Constituted at Bay Minette Baptist Church, Oct. 8, 1914, with 20 churches from Mobile and one church from Elim associations. In 1954, 33 churches reported 348 baptisms, 5,709 members, $241,747.16 total gifts, $33,297.15 mission gifts, $705,477.00 property value, and $26,318.00 church debt.

BARBOUR. Constituted as Eufaula Baptist Association, Nov. 13, 1854, of churches mainly in Barbour County. The name was changed to Barbour County Baptist Association, Oct. 8, 1935, at Old Mt. Zion Baptist Church. It adopted articles of faith. In 1954, 25 churches reported 215 baptisms, 4,023 members, $85,091.00 total gifts, $14,379.50 mission gifts, $519,100.00 property value, and $28,764.00 church debt.

BESSEMER. Constituted of seven churches at the First Baptist Church in Bessemer, Oct. 18, 1899. Disbanded in 1906, the association reorganized with 30 churches from Birmingham, Mud Creek, and Pleasant Grove associations at Seventh Street Baptist Church in Bessemer, May 29, 1949. It adopted articles of faith. In 1954, 37 churches reported 781 baptisms, 14,383 members, $550,511.85 total gifts, $85,931.48 mission gifts, $1,935,383.00 property value, and $133,286.00 church debt.

BETHEL. Constituted in 1820 of churches, principally from Bethlehem Association, one of which was Bassett's Creek Church in Clarke County. The following question and answer were recorded in the minutes of 1834: "Is the purchase of lottery tickets, a species of gambling! Answered in the affirmative." The association manifested a missionary spirit early in its life. In 1954, 30 churches reported 160 baptisms, 4,657 members, $130,351 total gifts, $17,840 mission gifts, $394,721 property value, and $11,385 church debt.

BETHLEHEM. Originally constituted in 1816 as Beckbe, which was changed to Bethlehem in 1827, with a few churches in Clarke and Washington counties. It was the second association formed in Alabama, and the first formed on Alabama soil. Under the leadership of Alexander Travis (*q.v.*), who arrived in 1817, Bethlehem was missionary from its founding. As new churches were organized its area increased, finally extending from the Mississippi border to the eastern boundary of Conecuh County, and from the southern boundary of Lowndes County to the Gulf. Messengers to its annual meetings often traveled 150 miles on horseback, requiring a week each way, stopping overnight at prearranged settlements to which throngs of people came to hear them preach. In 1954, 25 churches reported 283 baptisms, 5,113 members, $123,494 total gifts, $22,132 mission gifts, $429,500 property value, and $38,200 church debt.

BIBB. Constituted at Centerville Baptist Church, Nov. 12, 1902, with 19 churches in Bibb County. It adopted articles of faith. In 1954, 34 churches reported 116 baptisms, 4,318 members, $82,311.76 total gifts, $14,900.21 mission gifts, $217,650.00 property value, and $2,585.00 church debt.

BIGBEE. Constituted as Central Association in 1845 at Jones Creek Church, near the village of Epes in Sumter County. In 1852 the name was changed to Little Bigbee Association, and in 1853 it was changed to Bigbee Baptist Association. In 1954, 15 churches reported 48 baptisms, 2,099 members, $78,774.28 total gifts, $15,266.54 mission gifts, $259,500.00 property value, and $5,000.00 church debt.

BIRMINGHAM. Constituted as Canaan Association at Canaan Meeting House, Jefferson County, Sept. 16, 1833, of 10 churches, seven of which were dismissed from Mt. Zion Association, one from Cahaba Association, and two newly constituted in St. Clair County. The association organized in protest against a decision made by the Mt. Zion Association in the previous year, no longer to "hold correspondence with" the Baptist State Convention of Alabama and the Baptist Tract Society. The new association adopted a constitution containing two articles thought by some irregular, which provided for the promotion of "domestic missions, the education of pious and promising young men hopefully called of God to the ministry" and for the furtherance of "all the benevolent plans now cherished and supported by evangelical christians." The name was changed to Birmingham Baptist Association on Oct. 10, 1890. The Birmingham Baptist Hospital and the Highland Avenue Baptist Hospital, both located in Birmingham, belong to the association. Howard College and the headquarters of the Woman's Missionary Union are located in Birmingham. *The Alabama Baptist* is published here. In 1954, 113 churches reported 3,038 baptisms, 69,369 members, $3,407,414.73 total gifts, $642,793.08 mission gifts, $3,437,594.00 property value, and $1,538,366.00 church debt.

BLOUNT. Constituted as Warrior River Association in 1860 of churches chiefly from Blount County. Its name was changed to Blount County Baptist Association, Oct. 20, 1906. In 1954, 68 churches reported 495 baptisms, 9,975 members, $103,538.07 total gifts, $8,077.94 mission gifts, $369,288.00 property value, and $5,738.00 church debt.

BULLOCK-CENTENNIAL. Constituted in 1876 as Centennial Association of churches most of which were in Bullock County. It changed the name to Bullock-Centennial Baptist Association at Midway Baptist Church, Oct. 17, 1917. It adopted articles of faith. In 1954, 13 churches reported 60 baptisms, 1,638 members, $42,573 total gifts, $7,476 mission gifts, and $187,500 property value.

BUTLER. Constituted of 20 churches in Butler County at Brushey Creek Church on Nov. 20, 1903. It adopted articles of faith. In 1954, 31 churches reported 249 baptisms, 5,281 members, $127,668 total gifts, $19,837 mission gifts, $301,750 property value, and $3,200 church debt.

CAHABA. One of the most historic associations in the state, constituted at Cahawba Valley Church, Oct. 3, 1818, with 10 churches from Cahawba (now Bibb), Greene, Hale, Jefferson, Perry, and Tuscaloosa counties. The Alabama Baptist State Convention was organized at Salem Church, Oct. 28, 1823, and the Manual Labor Institute was established at the outskirts of Greensboro in 1833. About 1838 the *Family Visitor,* formerly published at Wetumpka by John D. Williams, was given to the denomination, moved to Marion, and issued under the name *Alabama Baptist.* Founded at Marion were Judson College in 1839 and Howard College in 1841. The Domestic Mission Board, now the Home Mission Board of the Southern Baptist Convention, was organized at Marion in 1845. "Greensboro was once Baptist headquarters in Alabama." In 1954, 31 churches reported 130 baptisms, 4,204 members, $87,890.53 total gifts, $18,534.76 mission gifts, $326,272.43 property value, and $5,005.00 church debt.

CALHOUN. Constituted with 29 churches, most of which came out of Tallasseehatchie and Coosa River associations, at Jacksonville Baptist Church on May 27, 1892. Articles of faith were adopted. In 1954, 77 churches reported 1,222 baptisms, 21,333 members, $726,907 total gifts, $93,150 mission gifts, $2,548,661 property value, and $234,202 church debt.

CAREY. Constituted in 1855 of churches in Clay, Tallapoosa, and Randolph counties. It adopted articles of faith. In 1954, 32 churches reported 97 baptisms, 5,006 members, $48,874.84 total gifts, $7,707.61 mission gifts, $336,069.00 property value, and $2,100.00 church debt.

CENTRAL. Constituted of four churches at Shiloh in Elmore (then Coosa) County, Oct., 1845. It adopted articles of faith. The influence of the antimissionary struggle going on throughout the state was strongly felt in this section. The Wetumpka, an antimission association, had been recently organized; but the missionary position of Central Association was positive and most emphatic. It began co-operation with both the state and the Southern Baptist conventions at its second session. In 1868 the Home Mission Society stated, Northern Baptist, "Let us unite heart and hand, as far as we can, and the providence of God shall direct . . . especially in aiding to lift up millions of freedmen to the exercise of all rights and duties of citizenship." Feeling that the statement had been made to humiliate the South, the association sent a delegate to the Southern Baptist Convention proposing to withdraw unless the Convention dissolve all connection with the Home Mission Society. The Convention refused to receive the delegate because the association had not contributed $100 to its work. The association did not withdraw from the Convention but did express its disapproval of its action. In 1954, 22 churches reported 132 baptisms, 3,182 members, $75,117 total gifts, $7,603 mission gifts, and $188,000 property value.

CHEROKEE. New name of Tallasseehatchie and Ten Islands Association formed in 1880 by consolidation of Tallasseehatchie Association constituted of six churches in the Creek country, principally in Calhoun (then Benton) County in 1834, and Ten Islands Association constituted at Mt. Zion Church, Calhoun (then Benton) County, in 1853. The name was changed to Cherokee County Missionary Baptist Association in 1892. The association should not be confused with Cherokee County Baptist Association, formerly Liberty Association, Etowah County, and now DeKalb County Baptist Association. It adopted an abstract of principles. The 1954 minutes state, "The Cherokee County Missionary Baptist Association has no convention meetings in which official action is taken." In 1954, 35 churches reported 204 baptisms, 4,286 members, $81,740 total gifts, $10,404 mission gifts, $348,850 property value, and $2,577 church debt.

CHILTON-UNITY. Constituted at the First Baptist Church in Clanton, Oct. 27, 1953, by the merger of Chilton County Association, constituted in the Baptist Academic School building in Thorsby, Dec. 4, 1901, of 12 churches in Chilton County formerly in Mulberry Association; and some of the churches which came out of Unity Association, constituted at Shady Grove Church in Autauga County in 1855 of the churches in Autauga Association and of seven churches in Mulberry Association. It adopted articles of faith. In 1954, 45 churches reported 273 baptisms, 9,158 members, $212,738.15 total gifts, $21,142.71 mission gifts, $680,807.00 property value, and $17,000.00 church debt.

CHOCTAW. Constituted as Antioch Association of 13 churches in Choctaw County in 1883. Articles of faith were adopted. The name was changed to Choctaw County Baptist Association in 1918. In 1954, 32 churches reported 77 baptisms, 2,826 members, $62,890 total gifts, $8,630 mission gifts, $168,707 property value, and $3,100 church debt.

CLARKE. Constituted as South Bethel Association at Grove Hill of 24 churches comprising the second district of Bethel Association, Nov. 7, 1883. Articles of faith were adopted. The name was changed to Clarke County Baptist Association in 1901. In 1954, 47 churches reported 176 baptisms, 7,352 members, $187,316 total gifts, $31,538 mission gifts, $613,017 property value, and $67,996 church debt.

CLAY. Constituted of 11 churches, formerly in Boiling Springs Association, at Ramah Church, Delta, Ala., Nov. 25, 1898. It adopted an abstract of principles. In 1954, 14 churches reported 35 baptisms, 1,371 members, $7,671.17 total gifts, $856.95 mission gifts, and $41,700.00 property value.

CLEAR CREEK. Constituted of 11 churches, mostly in Winston County, at Rock Creek Church, Oct. 9, 1874. Troubled at times by the Landmarkers, the association continued to maintain its missionary zeal. It adopted a declaration of faith. In 1954, 42 churches reported 178 baptisms, 5,805 members, $94,518.00 total gifts, $11,091.05 mission gifts, $333,700.00 property value, and $15,000.00 church debt.

CLEBURNE. Constituted of 20 churches, most of which had been granted letters by Harmony Baptist Association for that purpose, at Edwardsville Baptist Church, Oct. 27, 1899. It adopted articles of faith. In 1954, 35 churches reported 150 baptisms, 5,123 members, $67,209 total gifts, $3,857 mission gifts, $356,700 property value, and $18,138 church debt.

COFFEE. Constituted at Calvary Baptist Church, Enterprise, Oct. 20, 1908, by the consolidation of Haw Ridge Association, which changed its name to Coffee County Association at Rockey Head Church in Dale County, Oct. 11, 1905; and Pea River Association which also changed its name to Coffee County Association in 1905. It adopted an abstract of faith. In 1954, 37 churches reported 601 baptisms, 9,127 members, $235,610.00 total gifts, $33,765.99 mission gifts, and $57,626.00 church debt.

COLBERT-LAUDERDALE. Constituted by the consolidation of Colbert Association and Lauderdale Association, formerly Florence Association, at the First Baptist Church, Sheffield, Oct. 25, 1932. It adopted articles of faith. The state convention owns and operates a student center at the Florence State Teachers College, purchased in May, 1954. In 1954, 50 churches reported 622 baptisms, 12,535 members, $503,479 total gifts, $54,318 mission gifts, $1,811,365 property value, and $308,378 church debt.

COLUMBIA. Constituted of 12 churches, mostly in Henry and Houston counties, at Bluff Springs in 1885. It adopted articles of faith. In 1954, 45 churches reported 620 baptisms, 12,487 members, $404,299.53 total gifts, $68,175.39 mission gifts, $1,224,000.00 property value, and $99,156.00 church debt.

CONECUH. Constituted of 20 churches in Conecuh County, some of which came out of the division of Conecuh Baptist Association at Fairfield Baptist Church, Oct. 27, 1903. In 1954, 25 churches reported 98 baptisms, 3,951 members, $85,961 total gifts, $10,510 mission gifts, and $255,529 property value.

COOSA RIVER. Constituted of five churches in Talladega County in the region occupied by the Creek Indians at Talladega Meeting House, Nov. 8, 1833. It adopted articles of faith. In 1854 it organized the Baptist Male High School at Talladega, which closed in 1866. In 1885 the association set up an Indigent Ministers Fund. The state convention owns and operates an assembly at Shocco Springs near Talladega. In 1954, 62 churches reported 724 baptisms, 12,034 members, $333,576.21 total gifts, $69,991.87 mission gifts, $2,500,000.00 property value, and $82,059.47 church debt.

COVINGTON. Constituted as Zion Baptist Association in 1857. It adopted articles of faith. The name was changed to Covington County Baptist Association in 1903, and back to Zion Baptist Association in 1904. Again in 1932 it changed to Covington County Baptist Association. In 1954, 45 churches reported 446 baptisms, 7,398 members, $251,080.41 total gifts, $48,762.00 mission gifts, $759,577.00 property value, and $28,447.00 church debt.

DALE. Constituted in 1886 as Newton Association of churches, mostly in Dale County. It adopted articles of faith. The Southeast Alabama Collegiate Institute, now disbanded, was established by the Newton church and taken over by the association in 1903. The name was changed to Dale County Baptist Association in 1907. In 1954, 31 churches reported 243 baptisms, 5,611 members, $99,911 total gifts, $18,737 mission gifts, $395,800 property value, and $1,225 church debt.

DEKALB. Constituted in 1842 as Liberty Association, Etowah County, at Bethany Church in what is now Etowah County. The name was changed to Cherokee County Baptist Association in 1844, and again to DeKalb County Baptist Association at Corinth Church in 1905. A declaration of faith and practice was adopted. In 1954, 54 churches reported 379 baptisms, 10,760 members, $198,418.57 total gifts, $27,718.83 mission gifts, $690,760.00 property value, and $22,374.00 church debt.

EAST CULLMAN. Constituted as Cullman Association of a few churches lettered out of Sulphur Springs Association at Good Hope Church, 1883. It adopted articles of faith. Because of its large territory it divided into two bodies, East Cullman and West Cullman, in 1947. In 1954, 47 churches reported 222 baptisms, 7,860 members, $80,828 total gifts, $10,690 mission gifts, and $364,100 property value.

EAST LIBERTY. Constituted as Liberty Association, Chambers County, of 12 churches in the territory known as the Creek nation which came out of the dissolution of the Choctaw Association at Lafayette, Sept. 26, 1836. Article 7 of the constitution stated, "This association shall not engage in the missionary enterprises of the day, but leaves churches and members to exercise their judgment in all such cases." This was repealed in 1839. The name was changed to East Liberty Association in 1885. Philadelphia Confession of Faith was adopted. In 1954, 40 churches reported 382 baptisms, 10,115 members, $347,727.31 total gifts, $53,211.70 mission gifts, $1,662,500.00 property value, and $105,081.00 church debt.

ELMORE. Constituted on Nov. 3, 1914, of 23 churches, most of which came out of Montgomery and Central associations, at Good Hope Church. It adopted articles of faith. In 1954, 37 churches reported 360 baptisms, 7,532 members, $191,749 total gifts, $27,345 mission gifts, $491,450 property value, and $21,662 church debt.

ESCAMBIA. Constituted on Jan. 13, 1903, of seven churches, five of which came out of Conecuh Baptist Association, at Brewton Baptist Church. It adopted articles of faith. It declined to recognize women as messengers. In 1954, 30 churches reported 299 baptisms, 6,417 members, $191,646 total gifts, $27,930 mission gifts, $699,200 property value, and $24,609 church debt.

ETOWAH. Constituted on Nov. 7, 1884, of 19 churches at Mt. Carmel Church near Gadsden. It adopted articles of faith. The association owns the Gadsden Memorial Baptist Hospital. In 1954, 74 churches reported 1,131 baptisms, 22,467 members, $830,009 total gifts, $128,703 mission gifts, $2,480,635 property value, and $87,420 church debt.

FAYETTE. Constituted of 14 churches as New River Baptist Association in Oct., 1871. The name was changed to Fayette County Baptist Association in 1919. Articles of faith were adopted. In 1954, 35 churches reported 131 baptisms, 3,603 members, $45,926 total gifts, $8,595 mission gifts, $180,850 property value, and $2,400 church debt.

FRANKLIN. Constituted on Oct. 21, 1898, as Shady Grove Association of six churches in Franklin County at Shady Grove Church. Articles of faith were adopted. The name was changed to Franklin County Baptist Association in 1919. In 1954, 23 churches reported 197 baptisms, 4,594 members, $98,537 total gifts, $11,977 mission gifts, $405,000 property value, and $35,200 church debt.

FRIENDSHIP. Constituted at Cleveland Baptist Church, Nov. 29, 1955, of 15 churches which withdrew from Blount County Baptist Association in order to co-operate more fully and freely with the Alabama Baptist State Convention and the Southern Baptist Convention in their mission programs. Constituting churches were Second, Blountsville, Cleveland, Concord, Fairview, and Hayden, in Altoona; South, Mt. Pleasant, and Mt. Tabor, in Hopewell; and First, Pleasant Mount, Sunnyside, Union Chapel, Union Hill, and Village Springs, in Oneonta. The name chosen was Friendship Missionary Baptist Association of Blount County. In the 1954 minutes of the Blount County Association these 15 churches reported 143 baptisms, 2,919 members, $60,667.42 total gifts, and $6,761.54 mission gifts, $175,000.00 property value, and $4,000.00 church debt.

GENEVA. Constituted in 1876 as Sandy Creek Association of churches mostly in Geneva County. It adopted articles of faith. In 1954, 30 churches reported 301 baptisms, 6,181 members, $142,476 total gifts, $12,866 mission gifts, $364,000 property value, and $6,250 church debt.

JUDSON. Constituted of churches in southeast Alabama in 1851. It adopted articles of faith. In 1954, 21 churches reported 144 baptisms, 4,151 members, $91,696 total gifts, $13,597 mission gifts, $327,000 property value, and $5,217 church debt.

LAMAR. Constituted on Oct. 30, 1911, of eight churches which withdrew from Yellow Creek Association. It adopted articles of faith. In 1954, 26 churches reported 79 baptisms, 2,663 members, $55,447 total gifts, $5,577 mission gifts, $260,000 property value, and $9,500 church debt.

LIMESTONE. Constituted on Sept. 5, 1916, at Round Island Baptist Church, of 13 churches in Limestone County which came out of North Liberty Association. In 1954, 23 churches reported 281 baptisms, 5,290 members, $103,314.70 total gifts, $12,948.00 mission gifts, $345,280.00 property value, and $37,325.00 church debt.

LOOKOUT MOUNTAIN. Constituted in 1874 as Cedar Bluff Association of churches in northeast Alabama. It adopted articles of faith. Gaylesville Academy, one of the Home Mission Board's mountain schools established in 1906 and discontinued in 1923, was located in the bounds of the association. The name was changed to Lookout Mountain Missionary Baptist Association in 1928. In 1954, 22 churches reported 126 baptisms, 2,456 members, $35,035 total gifts, $3,389 mission gifts, $133,430 property value, and $7,673 church debt.

MADISON-LIBERTY. Constituted on Nov. 2, 1838, as Liberty Association, Madison County, of six churches forced out of Flint River Association in consequence of "inquisitorial decrees of that body." The name was changed to North Liberty in 1884 as there were several associations named Liberty. It changed again to Liberty in 1918, and to Madison-Liberty in 1920. In 1954, 38 churches reported 567 baptisms, 11,039 members, $347,128.86 total gifts, $38,584.00 mission gifts, $1,497,659.00 property value, and $75,849.00 church debt.

MARION. Constituted of churches in northwest Alabama in 1924. It adopted articles of faith. In 1954, 20 churches reported 82 baptisms, 3,284 members, $55,664 total gifts, $8,047 mission gifts, $361,500 property value, and $29,506 church debt.

MARSHALL. Constituted at Albertville Baptist Church, Dec. 3, 1887, of 13 churches formerly in Warrior River Association and one church formerly in Mt. Carmel Association. It adopted articles of faith. In 1954, 64 churches reported 639 baptisms, 14,046 members, $336,370 total gifts, $31,075 mission gifts, $1,157,517 property value, and $78,084 church debt.

MINERAL SPRINGS. Constituted of 11 churches formerly in Sulphur Springs Association, at Mineral Springs Baptist Church, Jefferson County, Dec. 15, 1893. It adopted an abstract of principles. In 1954, 30 churches reported 172 baptisms, 3,840 members, $85,680.65 total gifts, $7,358.19 mission gifts, $197,034.00 property value, and $10,484.00 church debt.

MOBILE. Constituted of the churches which withdrew from the Gulf Coast Association as the Mobile Baptist Union in 1880, and changed its name to Mobile Baptist Association in 1886. Providence Association was constituted of churches in Alabama and Mississippi at Providence Church in Jackson County, Miss., in 1855 and changed its name to Gulf Coast Association on May 24, 1878. The association dates its beginning from the organization of the Providence Association and celebrated its centennial Oct. 18–20, 1955. It adopted a declaration of faith. The association owns and operates Citronelle Baptist Assembly and Baptist Fellowship Center for Negroes. In 1954, 69 churches reported 2,197 baptisms, 36,581 members, $1,595,335 total gifts, $262,926 mission gifts, $5,497,585 property value, and $565,852 church debt.

MONTGOMERY. Constituted of 16 churches in Montgomery, Elmore, and Autauga counties at Wetumpka Baptist Church, Oct. 13, 1882. It adopted abstract of principles of the Alabama Association. At the organizational meeting it set up a financial goal for objects fostered by the state mission board and apportioned the amount among the churches. The Alabama Baptist state headquarters is located in Montgomery, the capital of the state. The association has a revolving expansion fund for the purchase of property for new work. A Negro center, with property valued at $15,000, is owned and operated jointly by the association and the Negro association, with the co-operation of the Home Mission Board, which pays the director's salary. The association provides $2 for each $1 that the Negro association provides. In 1954, 38 churches reported 790 baptisms, 20,850 members, $932,975 total gifts, $178,393 mission gifts, $3,287,912 property value, and $608,420 church debt.

MORGAN. Constituted in 1920 of 31 churches, mostly in Morgan County. It adopted a statement of belief. In 1954, 52 churches reported 500 baptisms, 12,090 members, $350,177 total gifts, $64,278 mission gifts, $1,286,594 property value, and $114,935 church debt.

MUD CREEK. Constituted in 1891 at Mud Creek Church of 16 churches in the western part of Jefferson County. It adopted an abstract of principles. In 1888 the association organized a literary school at Oak Grove and operated it until the county took it over. In 1954, 31 churches reported 159 baptisms, 3,544 members, $72,669 total gifts, $4,090 mission gifts, $188,150 property value, and $7,144 church debt.

MUSCLE SHOALS. Constituted as Big Bend of Tennessee River Association of nine churches in Franklin, Lawrence, and Lauderdale counties, at Russell Valley Church in Franklin County on July 15, 1820. It adopted an abstract of faith. The name was changed to the Muscle Shoals Association of Baptists in 1821. The antimissionary spirit was strong, and in 1829 a majority of the churches were opposed to any missionary effort. A resolution, condemning Campbellism, which was making some inroads upon the churches, was adopted in 1829. A ministers' meeting was organized in 1835. The missionary party had been increasing, and in 1844 the Muscle Shoals Home Mission Society was organized, meeting at the same time and place as the association. The society formulated a plan of missionary work to be carried on by the association, which was adopted, thus making the association, nominally at least, a missionary body. The antimission churches withdrew and formed another association called by the same name and claimed that they constituted the original association, though a majority of the churches remained with the missionary party; and the anti-association has dwindled so that if it is in existence, it is scarcely known. In 1954, 26 churches reported 184 baptisms, 4,748 members, $79,752 total gifts, $6,009 mission gifts, $327,900 property value, and $7,557 church debt.

PICKENS. Constituted in Sept., 1835, as Union Association of 19 churches which came out of Buttehatcha Association at Bethany in Pickens County. An effort to organize as an antimissionary association failed. Articles of faith were adopted. The name was changed to Pickens Baptist Association in 1924. In 1954, 33 churches reported 106 baptisms, 4,008 members, $85,783.60 total gifts, $15,131.26 mission gifts, $411,733.00 property value, and $10,071.00 church debt.

PINE BARREN. Constituted in May, 1950, of churches which embraced the northern half of Bethlehem Association at Friendship Church, Wilcox County. J. B. Hawthorne (q.v.), who began his career in Mobile as a lawyer, entered Howard College and became a theological beneficiary of the association in 1858. It adopted articles of faith. In 1954, 12 churches reported 54 baptisms, 1,472 members, $54,179 total gifts, $11,545 mission gifts, $212,350 property value, and $66,800 church debt.

PLEASANT GROVE. Constituted as Blue Creek Association of six churches in Jefferson County at Blue Creek Baptist Church, Oct. 31, 1902. It adopted the articles of faith of Harmony Association. The name was changed to Pleasant Grove Missionary Baptist Association in 1912. In 1954, 17 churches reported 73 baptisms, 1,838 members, $24,470 total gifts, $794 mission gifts, $61,142 property value, and $300 church debt.

RANDOLPH. Constituted of 19 churches from Rock Mills Association and some churches of Arbacoochee Association at Rocky Branch Church, Randolph County, Nov. 2, 1900. It adopted articles of faith. In 1954, 29 churches reported 124 baptisms, 5,060 members, $93,297 total gifts, $16,979 mission gifts, $398,920 property value, and $7,801 church debt.

RUSSELL. Constituted as Harris Baptist Association of six churches in Russell and Lee counties at Brownville Baptist Church, now the First Baptist Church in Phenix City, Oct. 26, 1886. Articles of faith were adopted. The name was changed to Russell Baptist Association at Oswichee Baptist Church in 1913. In 1954, 28 churches reported 438 baptisms, 7,274 members, $261,950 total gifts, $28,348 mission gifts, $1,050,000 property value, and $91,019 church debt.

ST. CLAIR. Constituted as Cahaba Valley Association in 1867. The name was changed to St. Clair County Baptist Association at New Prospect Church near Fairview, Sept. 10, 1898. An abstract of principles was adopted. It presumably consolidated with North St. Clair Baptist Association in 1918, retaining the name of St. Clair Association. In 1954, 62 churches reported 376 baptisms, 8,534 members, $183,410 total gifts, $19,140 mission gifts, $692,450 property value, and $21,435 church debt.

SALEM-TROY. Formed by the consolidation of Salem Baptist Association, constituted of eight churches which withdrew from Conecuh River Association because of its antimissionism at Salem Church, Pike County, in Nov., 1839; and Troy Baptist Association, constituted of 4 churches which withdrew from the Salem Association, Nov. 7, 1884. A joint conference of the two associations was held at the First Baptist Church at Troy, May 5, 1904; and the consolidation was completed at Henderson Baptist Church, Aug. 10, 1904. Articles of faith were adopted. In 1954, 34 churches reported 259 baptisms, 6,455 members, $102,943.58 total gifts, $17,454.67 mission gifts, $330,800.00 property value, and $16,271.60 church debt.

SAND MOUNTAIN. Constituted of churches in northeast Alabama at Pleasant View Church in 1917. It adopted articles of faith. In 1954, 27 churches reported 102 baptisms, 3,515 members, $41,449 total gifts, $3,039 mission gifts, $120,600 property value, and $428 church debt.

SARDIS. Constituted of churches in southern Alabama in 1895. It adopted articles of faith. In 1954, 24 churches reported 115 baptisms, 2,844 members, $27,766 total gifts, $504 mission gifts, $95,600 property value, and $6,771 church debt.

SELMA. Constituted of 11 churches from Alabama and Cahaba associations at Shiloh Church in Dallas County, Oct. 30, 1883. Articles of faith of Alabama Association were adopted. In 1920 the Alabama Baptist Hospital was located in Selma, with the Good Samaritan Annex for Negroes. Because of financial difficulties the hospital was leased to Physicians and Surgeons Hospital Society, Inc., Feb. 28, 1931, and finally sold to the bondholders in 1936. Selma University, begun about 1877, is located in Selma, and through the years has been influential in the development of Negro leadership in the South. Kathleen Mallory (*q.v.*), a leader of Southern W.M.U., came from this association. In 1954, 20 churches reported 245 baptisms, 5,617 members, $262,441.37 total gifts, $57,719.00 mission gifts, $697,212.00 property value, and $128,295.00 church debt.

SHELBY. Constituted at Bethel Church, Shelby County, in Oct., 1851. Articles of faith were adopted. The name of the association has been intermittently changed from Shelby Missionary Baptist Association to Shelby Baptist Association to Shelby County Baptist Association, and at present its constitutional name is Shelby Baptist Association, though it is called Shelby County Baptist Association in the 1954 proceedings. In 1954, 45 churches reported 290 baptisms, 6,664 members, $204,973 total gifts, $24,893 mission gifts, $664,321 property value, and $24,678 church debt.

SIPSEY. Constituted of 14 churches in the western part of the state at Moore's Bridge Church, Fayette County, Nov. 14, 1890. It adopted articles of faith. In 1954, 15 churches reported 75 baptisms, 1,341 members, $10,120 total gifts, $2,496 mission gifts, and $40,000 property value.

SULPHUR SPRINGS. Constituted of churches in Jefferson, Walker, and Blount counties at Sulphur Springs Baptist Church in 1872. It adopted articles of faith. In 1954, 23 churches reported 115 baptisms, 2,658 members, $34,549 total gifts, $3,619 mission gifts, $82,753 property value, and $1,865 church debt.

TALLAPOOSA COUNTY. Constituted of 20 churches in Tallapoosa County, formerly in East Liberty, Central, and Carey associations, at Dadeville, Oct. 31, 1915. It adopted articles of faith. In 1954, 36 churches reported 352 baptisms, 6,838 members, $203,012 total gifts, $25,054 mission gifts, $984,000 property value, and $64,496 church debt.

TENNESSEE RIVER. Constituted of six churches in Jackson County which came out of Duck River Association (Tenn.) at Friendship Baptist Church, Fackler, in Sept., 1853. The association omitted four annual sessions during the Civil War; and while it held its 97th annual session in 1954, the association was 101 years old in that year. It adopted articles of faith. Scottsboro Baptist Institute at Scottsboro and Tennessee River Institute at Bridgeport were located within the bounds of the association. In 1954, 40 churches reported 317 baptisms, 5,551 members, $107,202.45 total gifts, $14,756.16 mission gifts, $558,859.00 property value, and $14,533.00 church debt.

TUSCALOOSA. Constituted of 13 churches in Tuscaloosa and Bibb counties, most of which were dismissed from Cahaba Association, at Hopewell Meeting House 5 miles east of Tuscaloosa, Mar. 7, 1834. It adopted articles of faith. A strong antimission sentiment resulted in what was known as "The Big Split" and the beginning of Baptist growth. The Alabama Atheneum that paved the way for Central College was sold to the Methodists in 1836 and became Tuscaloosa Female College. The state convention owns and operates a student center near the state university. In 1954, 59 churches reported 875 baptisms, 16,531 members, $546,776.66 total gifts, $103,111.00 mission gifts, $992,647.00 property value, and $287,512.00 church debt.

TUSKEGEE. Constituted of 17 churches which withdrew from East Liberty Association because of its growing opposition to missions, at Tuskegee Baptist Church, Jan. 2, 1846. It adopted articles of faith. In 1850 the association established the East Alabama Female College at Tuskegee. In 1954, 22 churches reported 286 baptisms, 7,322 members, $398,777 total gifts, $52,155 mission gifts, $1,449,900 property value, and $232,062 church debt.

UNITY. Constituted of the churches in Autauga Association and seven churches in Mulberry Association at Shady Grove Church in Autauga County in 1855. It adopted articles of faith. In 1953 a joint committee from Chilton County Association and Unity Association recommended the merger of the two associations. A majority of those present voted for the merger, but a majority of the churches did not agree. The churches that did agree joined with Chilton County Association to form Chilton-Unity Baptist Association. The rest of the churches continued co-operation as Unity Missionary Baptist Association. In 1954, 11 churches reported 46 baptisms, 1,669 members, $24,427 total gifts, $3,818 mission gifts, $79,000 property value, and $2,000 church debt.

WALKER. Constituted as North River Association of churches, most of which were in Walker and Tuscaloosa counties, under the leadership of David Andrews who openly avowed his acceptance of Arminian principles, in 1835. The name was changed to Walker County Baptist Association in 1935. A declaration of faith was adopted. The Home Mission Board established Eldridge Academy in Walker County in 1906 and discontinued it in 1931. In 1954, 66 churches reported 480 baptisms, 10,204 members, $44,865 total gifts, $24,325 mission gifts, $496,250 property value, and $21,309 church debt.

WASHINGTON. Constituted of nine churches in Washington County at Rocky Ridge Church near Loper, Nov. 5, 1909. It adopted the articles of faith of Antioch Association. In 1954, 31 churches reported 156 baptisms, 3,500 members, $86,572.46 total gifts, $9,077.81 mission gifts, $354,567.00 property value, and $15,929.00 church debt.

WEST CULLMAN. Constituted as Cullman Association of a few churches lettered out of Sulphur Springs Association at Good Hope Church in 1883. It adopted articles of faith. Because of its large territory it divided into two bodies, East Cullman and West Cullman, in 1947. In 1954, 50 churches reported 319 baptisms, 9,451 members, $20,946 mission gifts, $155,275 total gifts, $982,410 property value, and $213,253 church debt.   BLOUNT F. DAVIDSON

II. Extinct. ALABAMA. Fourth association in the state, constituted Dec. 13, 1819, with four churches, all in Montgomery County. The scene of much dissension in early years, it later became the banner association in the state in missionary zeal. In 1828 the association purchased, upon the death of his master, a Negro slave named Caesar who had been converted and ordained to preach, and gave him his liberty to preach where God might direct; everywhere he went the whites listened to him with respect. Weakened numerically because a number of churches withdrew to form new associations, Alabama consolidated with Crenshaw County in 1931 to form Alabama-Crenshaw Association.

ANTIOCH. A "new test" association, organized in 1839 with six churches, most of which came out of and made the first breach in Bethlehem Association. The last available record was the minutes of the 103rd annual session of the Antioch Baptist Association of the Primitive Faith and Order.

ANTIOCH. Constituted in 1883 of 13 churches in Choctaw County. Its name was changed to Choctaw Baptist Association in 1918.

ARBACOOCHEE. Organized in 1851 of churches in the eastern part of the state, mostly in Lamar and Cleburne counties. The last reference to the association is in the state convention minutes of 1913.

BECKBE. Constituted in 1816 of a few churches in Clarke and Washington counties. It was the second association formed in Alabama and the first formed on Alabama soil. In 1827 it changed its name to Bethlehem Association.

BEULAH. A "new test" association, constituted Nov. 17, 1838, of 11 churches in Chambers, Russell, and Tallapoosa counties in Alabama and two churches in Troupe and Heard counties in Georgia at Enon Church, Chambers County. The last available reference was to a ministers' meeting on June 27, 1839.

BIG BEND OF TENNESSEE RIVER. Constituted of nine churches in Franklin, Lawrence, and Lauderdale counties at Russell Valley Church in Franklin County on July 15, 1820. The name was changed to the Muscle Shoals Association of Baptists in 1821.

BLUE CREEK. Constituted of six churches in Jefferson County at Blue Creek Baptist Church on Oct. 31, 1902. The name was changed to Pleasant Grove Missionary Baptist Association in 1912.

BOILING SPRINGS. Constituted in 1860 of churches in Clay, Cleburne, and Calhoun counties. At the 39th annual session in 1898, the executive committee made the following report: "No money at our command, no demand made upon us, consequently we have done nothing." At the same session the report of the committee on destitution stated: "Your committee after investigating are glad to report that we find no destitution within our border." At the last session in 1899 each church was granted a letter to one of the following associations: Clay County, Cleburne County, Calhoun County, and Coosa River. Following this action the association was dissolved.

BUTTEHATCHA. A "new test" association, constituted of eight churches, three of which were dismissed from Cahaba Association on Oct. 6, 1826. In 1834 about 16 churches were dismissed to form Union Association. In 1838 the following decree was passed: "We will not hereafter correspond with any Missionary Associations; . . . the painful sense that we experienced, being associated with persons favorable to the missionary scheme, or effort system; and in order to guard against a future innovation upon our peace and harmony, we enter our protest against all such institutions, as we think falsely so called benevolent." Some of its churches were incorporated in other bodies, and others have become extinct.

CAHABA VALLEY. Constituted in 1867. The name was changed to St. Clair Association at New Prospect Church near Fairview on Sept. 10, 1898.

CANAAN. Constituted of 10 churches, seven of which had been dismissed from Mt. Zion Association, one from Cahaba Association, and two newly constituted churches, at Canaan Meeting House, Jefferson County, on Sept. 16, 1833. The name was changed to Birmingham Baptist Association, Oct. 10, 1890.

CEDAR BLUFF. Constituted in 1874 of churches in northeast Alabama. The name was changed to Lookout Mountain Missionary Baptist Association in 1928.

CEDAR CREEK. Constituted of 11 churches at Heflin Baptist Church, Cleburne County, on Nov. 4, 1892. Articles of faith were adopted. It dissolved in 1903.

CENTENNIAL. Constituted of churches most of which were in Bullock County in 1876. The name was changed to Bullock-Centennial Baptist Association at Midway Baptist Church on Oct. 17, 1917.

CENTRAL. Constituted in 1845 at Jones Creek Church, near the village of Epes in Sumter County. In 1852 the name was changed to Little Bigbee, and in 1853 to Bigbee.

CENTRAL LIBERTY. Constituted of churches in Bibb and Hale counties in 1885. It adopted abstracts of principles; it disbanded in 1912.

CHATTAHOOCHA RIVER. Constituted prior to 1840. It was influenced by Jeremiah Kimbass and James Cattenhead, both violently opposed to missions, Bible societies, sabbath schools, etc. Several of its churches were missionary and went into other associations. It dissolved about 1840.

CHEROKEE COUNTY. Constituted as Liberty Association, Etowah County, at Bethany Church in what is now Etowah County in 1842. The name was changed to Cherokee County Baptist Association in 1844, but not to be confused with Cherokee County Missionary Baptist Association, an active association. The name was changed again to DeKalb County Baptist Association at Corinth Church in 1905.

CHILTON COUNTY. Constituted in the Baptist Academic School building in Thorsby of 12 churches in Chilton County formerly in Mulberry Association on Dec. 4, 1901. It merged with Unity Association at the First Baptist Church in Clanton on Oct. 27, 1953, to form Chilton-Unity Association.

CHOCTAW. Constituted in 1834 of 16 churches, nine in Mississippi and seven in Alabama. It dissolved in 1838, and from the ruins of the body four other associations were constituted: Liberty, Sumter County, the Louisville in Mississippi, the Friendship, and the new Choctaw. No further information about the last two is available.

COLBERT. Constituted at Liberty Church, Town Creek, in 1897. Consolidated with Lauderdale County Association at First Baptist Church, Sheffield, to form Colbert-Lauderdale Association.

CONECUH RIVER. Constituted in 1827. In Sept., 1839, delegates from 12 churches met and passed the nonfellowship decree, requesting the association to do so. As a result the missionary churches left the association. The association evidently divided, for in 1921 there were two Primitive associations, Conecuh River No. 1 and Conecuh River No. 2. There are no further records of either association.

CRENSHAW COUNTY. Constituted as New Providence Association of 17 churches in Covington, Coffee, and Crenshaw counties at Bethel Church in 1889. In 1903 the name was changed to Crenshaw County Association. In 1934 Crenshaw County Association and Alabama Association consolidated to form Alabama-Crenshaw Association.

CULLMAN. Constituted of a few churches lettered out of Sulphur Springs Association at Good Hope Church in 1883. It adopted declaration of faith. Because of its large territory it divided into two bodies in 1947, East Cullman and West Cullman.

EBENEZER. Constituted of 18 churches, 17 of which withdrew from Alabama Association because it refused to adopt the nonfellowship resolution, at Breast Work Church in Dec., 1838. In the last record available it was listed as a Primitive association in 1906.

EUFAULA. Constituted of churches mainly in Barbour County on Nov. 13, 1854. It adopted abstract of faith. The name was changed to Barbour County Baptist Association on Oct. 8, 1935, at Old Mt. Zion Baptist Church.

FLINT RIVER. The oldest association in Alabama, constituted of 17 churches in Alabama and Tennessee at Bradshaw's Meeting House, Lincoln County, Tenn., Sept. 26, 1814. In 1822 the association divided, the southern division retaining the original name. The northern division was called Richland Association. A fierce conflict between the missionary and antimissionary forces began early in the life of the association, with the antis finally getting control and passing the famous nonfellowship resolution that divided the association. In 1838 the missionary forces withdrew and formed Madison-Liberty Association. The last available record was of the 94th annual session, held with the Flint River Church on Oct. 2–4, 1908. The lengthy minutes of this session contained almost exclusively the discussion of the question, "Who are the Primitive Baptists?"

FLORENCE. Constituted of seven churches at Union Grove Church on Dec. 15, 1888. Articles of faith were adopted. The name was changed to Lauderdale Association in 1904. It consolidated with Colbert Association at First Baptist Church, Sheffield, Oct. 25, 1932, to form Colbert-Lauderdale Association.

GILLIAM SPRINGS. Constituted of churches in north Alabama in 1895. It disbanded in 1920.

HARRIS. Constituted of six churches in Russell and Lee counties at Brownville Baptist Church, now the First Baptist Church in Phenix City, Oct. 26, 1886. The name was changed to Russell Baptist Association at Oswichee Baptist Church in 1913.

HAW RIDGE. Constituted in 1889. The name was changed to Coffee County Association in 1905.

LAUDERDALE. Constituted as Florence Association of seven churches at Union Grove Church on Dec. 15, 1888. Articles of faith were adopted. The name was changed to Lauderdale County Baptist Association in 1904. It consolidated with Colbert Association at First Baptist Church, Sheffield, Oct. 25, 1932, to form Colbert-Lauderdale Baptist Association.

LEE COUNTY. Constituted of 18 churches at Concord Baptist Church near Blecker on Oct. 24, 1929. It disbanded in 1931, its churches going to East Liberty, Tuskegee, and Russell associations.

LIBERTY, CHAMBERS COUNTY. Constituted of 12 churches in the territory known as the Creek nation which came out of the dissolution of the Choctaw Association at Lafayette, Chambers County, Sept. 26, 1836. The name was changed to East Liberty Association about 1884 as there were several associations named Liberty.

LIBERTY, ETOWAH COUNTY. Constituted at Bethany Church in what is now Etowah County in 1842. The name was changed to Cherokee County Baptist Association in 1844, and again changed in 1905 to DeKalb County Baptist Association at Corinth Church.

LIBERTY, MADISON COUNTY. Constituted of six churches forced out of Flint River Association by the intolerance of that body on Nov. 2, 1838. The name was changed to North Liberty Association in 1884 as there were several associations named Liberty. It was changed again to Liberty in 1918, and to Madison-Liberty in 1920.

LITTLE BIGBEE. Constituted in 1845 at Jones Creek Church near the village of Epes in Sumter County under the name Central Association. In 1852 the name was changed to Little Bigbee, and in 1853 to Bigbee.

MACEDONIA. Constituted in 1880 of churches in Washington County. It adopted articles of faith. Most of its churches went into Washington Association, and the association disbanded about 1919.

MULBERRY. Constituted at Cahaba Valley Church in 1828 of churches in Autauga, Bibb, Dallas, Perry, Shelby, and Talladega counties, most of which were dismissed from Cahaba Association. In 1855 some of the churches merged with Autauga Association to form Unity Association. At Pleasant Grove Church a motion prevailed at the 74th annual session, Oct. 16, 1901, that the association give way to a county association; and at the Baptist Academic School building in Thorsby, the Chilton County Baptist Association was organized on Dec. 4, 1901, dissolving the Mulberry Association.

NEW PROVIDENCE. Constituted of 17 churches in Covington, Coffee, and Crenshaw counties at Bethel Church in 1889. In 1903 the name was changed to Crenshaw County Association. In 1934 Crenshaw County Association and Alabama Association consolidated to form Alabama-Crenshaw Association.

NEW RIVER. Constituted of 14 churches, most of which were in Fayette County, in Oct., 1871. The name was changed to Fayette County Baptist Association in 1919.

NEWTON. Constituted of churches, mostly in Dale County, in 1866. The name was changed to Dale County Baptist Association in 1907.

NORTH LIBERTY. Constituted on Nov. 2, 1838, as Liberty Association, Madison County, of six churches forced out of Flint River Association in consequence of inquisitorial decrees of that body. The name was changed to North Liberty in 1884 as there were several associations named Liberty. The name was changed again to Liberty in 1918, and to Madison-Liberty in 1920.

NORTH RIVER. Constituted in 1835 of churches, most of which were in Walker and Tuscaloosa counties, under the leadership of David Andrews who openly avowed his acceptance of Arminian principles. The name was changed to Walker County Baptist Association in 1935.

NORTH ST. CLAIR. Constituted of 15 churches in the northern judicial division of St. Clair County at Ashville Baptist Church, Oct. 6, 1909. Abstract of principles of St. Clair County Baptist Association was adopted. The name was changed to St. Clair County Baptist Association in 1918.

PEA RIVER. Constituted in 1877. The name was changed to Coffee County Association in 1905.

PILGRIM'S REST. Constituted on Nov. 11, 1837, of 12 churches which seceded from Union Association at Rehoboth Church, Greene County. A paragraph from a circular adopted at its first session stated, "Theological schools unwarranted in the word of God, and dangerous to religious liberty. Wherever they have been organized . . . they have been a source of persecution, and bloodshed on the church of Christ." The association evidently divided, since records reveal two Primitive associations by the same name, Pilgrim's Rest No. 1 and Pilgrim's Rest No. 2.

PROVIDENCE. Constituted in 1855 of churches in Alabama and Mississippi at Providence Church in Jackson County, Miss. The name was changed to Gulf Coast Association on May 24, 1878. In 1880 the Alabama churches withdrew and formed the Mobile Baptist Union which changed its name to Mobile Baptist Association in 1886.

RICHLAND. Constituted as the northern half of Flint River Association at the time of the division in 1822. It sent a corresponding letter to Muscle Shoals Association in 1827, which is the last reference to this association.

ROCK MILLS. Constituted in 1871. Articles of faith were adopted. It dissolved in 1900 to organize a county association.

SALEM. Constituted of eight churches formerly in Conecuh River Association, which refused to remain under the antimission yoke, at Salem Church, Pike County, in Nov., 1839. It adopted an abstract of faith. It consolidated with Troy Association at Henderson Baptist Church on Aug. 10, 1904, forming Salem-Troy Baptist Association.

SANDY CREEK. Constituted in 1877 of churches mostly in Geneva County. The name was changed to Geneva County Missionary Baptist Association in 1888.

SHADY GROVE. Constituted of six churches in Franklin County at Shady Grove Church on Oct. 21, 1898. Articles of faith were adopted. The name was changed to Franklin County Baptist Association in 1919. Evidently a few churches continued the Shady Grove Association, for it was disbanded in 1941, its churches going to Franklin, Marion, and Clear Creek associations.

SOUTH BETHEL. Constituted at Grove Hill of 24 churches comprising the second district of Bethel Association, Nov. 7, 1883. Articles of faith were adopted. The name was changed to Clarke County Baptist Association in 1901.

TALLASSEEHATCHIE. Constituted of six churches in the Creek country, principally in Calhoun (then Benton) County, in 1834. It consolidated with Ten Island Association in 1880 to form Tallasseehatchie and Ten Island Association. The name was changed to Cherokee County Missionary Baptist Association in 1892.

TALLASSEEHATCHIE AND TEN ISLANDS. Formed by the consolidation of Tallasseehatchie Association and Ten Islands Association in 1880. The name was changed to Cherokee County Missionary Baptist Association in 1892.

TEN ISLANDS. Constituted at Mt. Zion Church, Calhoun (then Benton) County, in 1853. It consolidated with Tallasseehatchie Association in 1880 to form Tallasseehatchie and Ten Islands Association. The name was changed to Cherokee County Missionary Baptist Association in 1892.

TROY. Constituted on Nov. 7, 1884, of four churches which withdrew from Salem Association. It adopted articles of faith. It consolidated with Salem Association at Henderson Baptist Church, Aug. 10, 1904, forming Salem-Troy Baptist Association.

UNION. Constituted of 19 churches which came out of the Buttehatcha Association at Bethany in Pickens County in Sept., 1835. An effort to organize as an antimissionary association failed. The name was changed to Pickens Baptist Association in 1924.

WARRIOR RIVER. Constituted in 1860 of churches chiefly from Blount County. The name was changed to Blount County Baptist Association on Oct. 20, 1906.

YELLOW CREEK. Constituted of churches which withdrew from Canaan Association in 1861. In 1911 eight churches from which the association withdrew formed Lamar Association; it disbanded about 1913.

ZION. Constituted in 1857. Articles of faith were adopted. The name was changed to Covington County Baptist Association in 1903; it changed back to Zion Baptist Association in 1904; and in 1932 the name again changed to Covington County Baptist Association.

BLOUNT F. DAVIDSON

ALABAMA BAPTIST. The first Baptist papers were private correspondence and the circular letter which was read at associations. Efforts to establish a denominational paper were made prior to 1835. The first of these efforts was made by William Wood in 1834 when he issued a small Baptist paper named the *Southwestern Baptist Pioneer* at Jacksonville in Calhoun County. It was short-lived. At the state convention in 1835, action was taken to enlist G. F. Heard, of Mobile, as editor of a paper, which, however, never materialized.

John D. Williams founded a Baptist paper at Wetumpka, Ala., in 1835, called *The Family Visitor.* In 1840 Edwin David King, a layman, purchased this paper and moved it to Marion, Ala., as a publicity outlet for Judson College. It was renamed *The Alabama Baptist,* and Milo Parker Jewett was the editor. In 1842 Howard College was founded at Marion and its president, S. S. Sherman, became editor. In 1849 A. W. Chambliss purchased the paper and changed its name to *The Alabama Baptist Advocate.* In the next three years it absorbed the subscription list of the *Western Recorder,* published in New Orleans, and of the *Mississippi Baptist.* It was renamed the *Southwestern Baptist.* In 1852 it was sold and was moved to Montgomery, Ala., where it was edited by Samuel Henderson and A. Williams. Two years later it was moved to Tuskegee, with Henderson as editor-in-chief. Shortly thereafter, it was purchased by the Alabama Baptist State Convention, with Henderson remaining as its editor. H. E. Talliaferro became editor in 1856 and remained until about 1861.

In 1865 Henderson, who had been editor during the Civil War, was arrested for making strong attacks on the Yankees and was forced to agree not to publish any longer in Alabama. The paper was then moved to Georgia, merged with the *Christian Index,* and renamed *Christian Index and Southwestern Baptist.* This arrangement lasted until 1872. In 1872 the Alabama Baptist State Convention, meeting in Talladega, voted to re-establish *The Alabama Baptist* at Marion, with E. T. Winkler as editor. Later the paper was given to the Alabama Baptist State Convention and was moved to Selma, with John L. West as editor. It was burned out in 1877, but was revived in 1881 by W. C. Cleveland, who was editor until 1884. In 1884 J. G. Harris bought the paper and moved it to Montgomery. Those serving as editors in Montgomery were C. W. Hare, James Pope, and W. B. Crumpton, who served for one year and purchased a half interest in the paper.

In 1902 Hare sold the paper to Frank Willis Barnett, who moved it to Birmingham. It was then renamed the *Southern Alabama Baptist* but shortly resumed its present title. In 1919 the state convention purchased the paper, and W. F. Yarborough acted as editor until Leslie Lee Gwaltney was elected in April to fill that position permanently. The paper was again moved to Montgomery but a few months later it was moved back to Birmingham because of inadequate printing equipment. On July 1, 1950, Leon Meertief Macon succeeded Gwaltney as editor and business manager. Three editors served a total of 65 years: Harris, 17 years; Barnett, 17 years; and Gwaltney, 31 years.

At the end of 1954 the *Alabama Baptist* was still owned by the Alabama Baptist State Convention and was edited by Macon. The circulation was 73,000. There were 1,442 churches which sent the paper to their families on the budget plan.

The paper operated under its own board of nine members elected by the convention, one-third each year. The board elected the editor. The convention subscribed $6,000 a year from the Cooperative Program. The equipment, valued at $6,998.28, was mostly office furniture, including Addressograph and Graphotype machines. The paper owned the editor's home. The paper was printed by contract with the Birmingham Printing Company. The editor wrote all checks, and the bookkeeping was done in the paper's office. The files of the paper were incomplete but had been microfilmed. The address was 614–16 Stallings Building, Birmingham 3, Ala. Besides the editor, there were four other employees.   LEON MACON

ALABAMA BAPTIST ADVOCATE. See ALABAMA BAPTIST.

ALABAMA BAPTIST CHILDREN'S HOME, THE. Founded July 8, 1891, by Mariah L. Becton Woodson of Selma, Ala., in memory of her mother and father, Mary C. and James Short, her brother, James Monroe Short, and her son, William Short DeLoach. Established as the Louise Short Baptist Widows and Orphans Home, it became the Alabama Baptist Children's Home on Nov. 15, 1938. The estate of Mrs. Woodson, valued at $30,000, was deeded to the Baptist state convention, which appointed David Ingram Purser (*q.v.*), G. S. Anderson, Hugh Shepherd Darby Mallory (*q.v.*), and others to serve on a board of trustees, to advertise for and receive bids on a location. The trustees selected Evergreen, Ala., as a temporary location, and appointed J. W. Stewart financial secretary and agent. Within a few weeks after the home opened on Mar. 8, 1893, 21 children had been received. From March to November of the first year, the home had cash receipts of $1,152.43, while operating expenses totaled $842.58, leaving a balance of $309.85.

Stewart became superintendent in 1893 and served until Jan. 1, 1910, and again from 1917 to 1923. The home was moved from Evergreen to Troy in 1923, at which time three two-story brick cottages had been completed. In 1955 buildings, which totaled 25, included eight cottages for children, a hospital, recreational building, seven residences, a laundry, and barns. The home has 231 acres of land with total property value of approximately $1,000,000. With adequate facilities for 190, the home serves approximately 300 children each year.

Its annual operating budget is $225,000, of which one month's expenses come from the Cooperative Program and the remainder from special gifts. Approximately three fourths of operating costs come through a Christmas cash offering. Children attend public schools and First Baptist Church, Troy. College training is offered to those who qualify. Children, accepted into the home on the basis of need, may be orphan, half-orphan, or from broken homes.

E. E. COX

ALABAMA BAPTIST ENCAMPMENTS. The first Alabama Baptist summer encampment was held at Shelby Springs, Ala., Aug. 22–29, 1910. The second assembly was held at Shocco Springs, near Talladega, Ala., Aug. 21–28, 1911. The third assembly was held at an assembly site purchased by a group of Baptist leaders appointed by the state convention, known as the Alabama Baptist Encampment Commission, Inc., located on a hilltop just west of Pelham, Ala., and called Pelham Heights. The property consisted of 55 acres of land. Buildings and facilities were constructed and lots sold to individuals and church groups at $100 each. Due to the lack of financial support from the convention, repairs were not made and the buildings deteriorated. It was felt the assemblies could not meet there again without spending a large sum of money, and in 1920 it was decided to dispose of the property and secure another site. Several offers were received, the Mentone, Ala., mountain site being the most attractive. The price was $60,000, and the company holding the property agreed to allow $20,000 for the Pelham Heights property. However, it was found that the convention could not make the purchase because of restrictions in its charter. A private corporation was formed, $15,000 paid down on the property, and a mortgage given for the balance, which was to be secured by sale of lots to churches, associations, and individuals. In 1921 Baptists held their first assembly at Mentone. The Mentone site was abandoned in 1932 due to inadequate water supply and sanitary facilities for such large crowds of people and lack of financial support from the convention. The assemblies were held at Judson College through 1935. In 1936 arrangements were made to have assemblies at Shocco Springs, near Talladega, continuing through 1940. Because the United States took Shocco Springs for housing for its workers, arrangements were made to meet at Cook Springs in 1941 and through 1943. In 1944 the assemblies were again held at Judson College and met there through 1947. Jewett Hall burned at Judson College on July 15, 1947, leaving no alternative but to secure another place of meeting for the assemblies. On Nov. 12, 1947, authorization was given for the purchase of Shocco Springs property. The property was secured for $62,500 cash, paid from state missions funds, and included 40 acres of land, 3 hotels, 14 cottages, an auditorium, dining room and kitchen, swimming pool, and a bunkhouse. It could accommodate about 400 people. The summer of 1948 all departments held assemblies at Shocco Springs. Since its purchase there have been constructed 10 classrooms, two hotels, a new dining room seating 600 people, a kitchen, a new office, an adequate water system, a new sewage system tied on to Talladega lines, and 12 cabins. Property totaling 181.3 acres was added to the original 40 acres in 1955.

Capital funds from the Cooperative Program receipts give $15,000 each year to Shocco Springs for construction of new buildings, the present funds being set aside for a new auditorium. Operations and maintenance are cared for out of receipts during the summer's operations. In the summer of 1955, 6,471 people attended the assembly for various weeks.   GEORGE BAGLEY

ALABAMA BAPTIST FOUNDATION, THE. The earliest efforts to establish a foundation in Alabama were made by W. B. Crumpton (q.v.) while president of the convention (1917–18). L. L. Gwaltney made a similar effort while he was president of the convention (1935–37). At the convention in 1937, A. Hamilton Reid offered a resolution to appoint a committee to look into the forming of a foundation. At the convention in 1939, Gwaltney offered a resolution that a committee be appointed to study the feasibility of a foundation for Alabama. Reid, who was chairman of the resolutions committee, made a report to the convention in 1940 recommending the founding of a foundation. It was adopted. The foundation received its first $1,000 in July, 1940, and reported its holdings to be $511,331.76 in 1954. From the inception of the foundation in 1940 through 1954, the total amount of $101,327.70 was disbursed by the foundation to Baptist institutions and agencies.

Pat Roberson, Pell City, has been president of the trustees from the beginning. He kept the books in his bank at Pell City, made certified audits, and wrote all checks until a secretary was employed. In Oct., 1954, Leslie Wright was employed as its first executive secretary. The foundation is located at Baptist headquarters, 403 S. Perry St., Montgomery. Its board has 15 members. It holds in trust monies for agencies of the state Baptist convention and Southern Baptist Convention. Reid, who is executive secretary of the state executive board, is also treasurer of the foundation board.
   LEON MACON

ALABAMA BAPTIST HISTORICAL SOCIETY. An agency for gathering historical materials. In 1834 the Alabama convention requested all concerned to collect church histories and designated a historian. Hosea Holcombe promoted this action, which resulted in 1840 in the publication of his *History of the Baptists of Alabama.* A society was organized in 1893, resulting in *The History of Alabama Baptists* by Benjamin Franklin Riley. In 1903 George E. Brewer revived new interest and John R. Tyson was elected first president of a new organization, which brought about the publication of Riley's *Memorial History of Alabama Baptists.*

The present society was organized Nov. 18, 1936. A constitution was approved in 1937, and a second constitution adopted Nov. 21, 1946. James H. Chapman headed the original committee (1933), and since then has continued as curator. Officers are a president, four regional vice-presidents, curator, secretary, and treasurer, nominated by the society and elected by the Alabama convention. The society meets annually as an executive committee. Archives are at Howard College.   JAMES H. CHAPMAN

ALABAMA BAPTIST STATE CONVENTION.
   I. Baptist Beginnings. *Pioneer times.*—The history of Alabama Baptists prior to the organization of the state convention in 1823 closely parallels the story of the settlement of the area. Alabama has a good system of navigable rivers, and immigrants moved into the territory either along or adjacent to these streams. The first settlements were along the Tennessee River in the north and the Tombigbee River in the south. After the War of 1812, the settlers swarmed into the area between the Black Warrior and the Cahaba rivers and into the valleys of the Coosa and the Alabama. Eastward toward the Georgia line in the east central and southeast sections, the presence of the Creek Indians until after the treaty of Mar. 24, 1832, by which they ceded their lands to the United States, held the settlers to "a few hardy pioneers." There were Baptists, laymen and preachers, among the immigrants, and whenever 10 or 12 of them settled in a community, they met together and organized a church. By 1825, two years after the founding of the convention, there were 6 associations, 128 churches, 70 ministers, and nearly 5,000 members.

Meetinghouses, preachers, and feuds.—In every section "Baptist preachers followed in the wake of all settlements, no matter how remote from the throbbing pulse of the great outside world"; and wherever one of them discovered the location of a group of immigrants holding the Baptist faith, he organized a church.

It was traditional in the older states for Baptists to give their churches the same name as that of the neighboring stream. The first two churches constituted in Alabama were Flint River and Bassett's Creek. Also, such names as Town Creek, Mill Creek, Pond Creek, and Fork of Butta Hatchie in the Muscle Shoals Association, and Pigeon Creek, Murder Creek, and Olive Branch in the Beckbe Association indicate that the practice was limited by neither time nor place.

The first churches were constituted in private homes, and worship was continued there until a church could be built. Building churches was no easy task. There was plenty of timber, but it was hard to convert into lumber. Consequently, like the homes of the settlers, the first churches were rude log cabins with no floors and only wooden shutters at the doors and windows. The seats were split logs with the flat surfaces turned up, supported by short forks driven into the ground. Only the pulpits distinguished these frontier churches. They were large square or circular enclosures, reached by a number of steps and having a door which could be easily fastened. They symbolized the apocalyptic figure of the lighted candlestick, with the pulpit as the candlestick, and the minister as the light in it. In view of the obviously uncomfortable conditions, it is little wonder that in good weather the people often either built a brush arbor or met in a near-by grove.

The Baptist preachers were, in most cases, as rough and ready as their places of worship. Undaunted by the fact that they normally served three or four churches, they farmed during the week, lest someone should accuse them of preaching for money, only "knocking off" soon enough to reach their church field in time for the Saturday business meeting and the Sunday preaching. During the week they "chewed and digested" their Bibles, even going so far as to tack to the plow a piece of paper with passages scrawled on it, so that they could commit whole chapters to memory. Unfortunately, however, their studies ended here. Their preaching was almost entirely exhorting, and they relied on physical exertion to compensate for mental deficiency. In fact many of them seemed to be exponents of the philosophy that "schoolin ain't necessary as long as I've got good wind." Truly, they needed "good wind" as well as leather lungs, for their two- and three-hour sermons were preached in a high sing-song monotone, ordinarily referred to as the "ministerial whine," which on a quiet night could be heard for from one to two miles.

"Called" rather than trained as they were, many of these farmer preachers faced problems that would have stumped a seminary doctor, for the membership of their churches was often divided in doctrine and torn by dissension. The people had come from different churches in different states, all with preconceived opinions of church life and order. "They were drawn together in a new region, in an incoherent mass, without regard to social congeniality or ideas in consonance respecting church life. This was a primal cause of the feuds and dissensions among the members of the earliest Baptist Churches, and this in time, led to much laxness of discipline among the first Baptists in Alabama." Equally as high as church discipline on the agenda of topics for dispute were foot washing and missions. In an attempt to combat dissension and establish some common bond of sentiment, the circular letter was instituted. This was a treatise, written by assignment, on some topic of general interest such as "church government, church discipline, baptism, communion, missions, etc." In spite of all efforts, the feuds became so bitter that "it was regarded as a bit of good fortune if a church could be represented in its letter to the Association by the language 'We are at peace and harmony among ourselves.'" But Alabama Baptists continued to grow.

The Tennessee River Valley.—In 1807 the general surveyor for the Mississippi Territory was authorized to contract for the survey of public lands in his jurisdiction to which the Indian title had been extinguished. The work started in North Alabama in Madison County. Surveyed lands were reported to the Land Office at Nashville, Tenn., in May, 1809, and the sales started in August of the same year. Already, some 5,000 settlers had moved into the country. Described as "the pioneer type, generally a poor and honest race, simple in their manners, living peacefully . . . ," they had come mostly from Virginia, North Carolina, and Georgia in search of good, cheap land.

In the vanguard were three Baptist ministers —John Nicholson, John Cantebury, and Zadock Baker. It is not strange, therefore, that the Baptists organized the first church in Madison County. On Oct. 2, 1808, about 11 or 12 members, under the guidance of Nicholson, gathered at the home of James Deaton, a few miles northeast of Huntsville, and constituted the Flint River Baptist Church. This was a beginning; and from that time forth, in spite of scattered settlements and lack of roads, "the ministerial trio," soon joined by eight other immigrant ministers, worked and traveled. They organized the Flint River Association, Sept. 26, 1814, composed of 17 churches, with 1,021 members, located in both Alabama and Tennessee.

This association never prospered in accordance with the population of the area because as late as 1823, the 16 member churches in Alabama had a membership of only 903. Many Baptists had squatted on lands in Madison County before they were surveyed and put on the market. At the time of the land sales, they failed to obtain the land they had selected and consequently moved. This broke up some churches and weakened others. In general, the movement was westward along the Tennessee River, and the work which these pioneer Baptists had started in one home, they continued in another. John Davis (q.v.), who styled himself "Flat-footed John Davis" because of his plain and forcible style of preaching, was the guiding light. Writing of him years later, his son said,

> He was a man of limited means, and though of a strong and vigorous intellect, had only the imperfect education of the pioneers of that day. His chief study was the Bible, and a few volumes of history, which formed his only library. Although a Baptist minister of high standing, he occupied himself during the week with ordinary farm labor, and could never be induced to accept any compensation for his services in the church. This would have been according to his belief, "serving the Lord for hire."

In 1817 he assembled 32 members and constituted the Russell Valley Church. He also helped it organize several other churches. By 1820 there were nine Baptist churches in the "Big Bend" of the Tennessee River, and three years later, at the time of the formation of the state convention, there were 22. In order to avoid the mistakes of the Madison County Baptists who had remained for "a number of years without making any apparent progress in religious work . . . ," due in large part to their hostility to missions, the "Big Bend" Baptists appointed two ministers as missionaries on each side of the river. They also adopted the circular letter device as a substitute for books and denominational publications.

The Tombigbee settlements.—White people began to settle along the Tombigbee, north of the west Florida boundary line, as early as 1800, and there was a steady but moderate increase until the War of 1812. This was temporarily checked by serious Indian troubles in 1813. After the cessation of hostilities with the Creeks, however, "the flood-gates of Virginia, the two Carolinas, Tennessee, Kentucky, and Georgia were hoisted, and mighty streams of emigration poured through them. . . . Log cabins sprang, as if by magic, into sight. Never before or since has a country been so rapidly peopled."

For 10 years this Tombigbee region was virtually without the benefits of organized religion. There had been a Roman Catholic church at St. Stephens under the Spanish, but the first Protestant minister heard in the area was the famous Methodist, Lorenzo Dow, who passed through St. Stephens in 1803 and stopped long enough to hold services. Tradition has it that a Baptist minister visited the area shortly afterward, only to find his offer to hold religious services rudely refused and himself threatened with physical violence. He was seized, placed in a canoe, taken across the river, and warned that "if he again set foot within the limits of the town, he would be promptly tarred and feathered."

It was not until 1810 that the Baptists secured a firm foothold in the region, at which time William Cochrane came from Georgia to begin his labors in Clarke County. Another Baptist named Gorham worked in neighboring Washington County for a short time until his death. It was still a third minister, James Courtney, who succeeded in organizing a church. This was the Bassett's Creek Church, constituted on Mar. 31, 1810, with 20 members—the first Baptist church in south Alabama and the second in the entire Alabama section of the Mississippi Territory. Almost simultaneously, Joseph McGee, "a man of more than ordinary pulpit ability," and Jacob Parker constituted the Oaktuppa Church northward in the Little Bigbee section of Sumter County. From this time forward the Baptists were active in the tier of counties west of the river to the Mississippi line, as well as in those stretching east from the river toward the Creek territory.

The physical difficulties were terrible. This was canebrake country, with the cane on each side of the trail "as high as a man on horseback could reach with an umbrella," and the trails so narrow that the saddlebags of the travelers rubbed the cane on either side. The physical obstacles encountered and overcome by Alexander Travis (q.v.), who came to Alabama from South Carolina and became the principal agent in laying the foundations of the Baptist churches in Conecuh and Monroe counties, furnishes a case in point. He frequently walked from his home in Conecuh County to Claiborne in Monroe County—a distance of 40 miles—to meet his appointments to preach. "When the bridgeless streams were swollen, the dauntless missionary would strip himself bare, secure his clothing from the waters by holding them aloft with one hand, while with the other he would swim to the opposite side, re-dress himself, and go on his way rejoicing."

Devotion and exertions of this nature could not fail to succeed. By 1816 there were enough churches in Clarke and Washington counties to organize the Beckbe Association. Eight years later, this association included 17 churches located in five counties—eight in Conecuh County, three in Washington, three in Monroe, two in Clarke, and one in Covington—with a total membership of 481.

The Coosa and the Alabama River valleys.—Settlers moved into this region in numbers a few years later than they did into north and south Alabama, but once started, they came with a rush. As always, there were Baptists and Baptist preachers among them. In June, 1818, James McLemore constituted Antioch Church, the first church of any denomination organized in Montgomery County. During the next year McLemore and another Baptist minister, Electius Thompson, constituted two more churches. A fourth church was added to these three through the work of Lee Compere (q.v.), an English Baptist missionary to Jamaica who came to Alabama after short sojourns in South Carolina and Georgia, and R. S. Daniel. These

Alabama Baptist Convention

four churches—Antioch, Bethel, Elim, and Rehoboth—all in Montgomery County joined together on Dec. 13, 1819, to form the Alabama Baptist Association. L. C. Davis, self-styled "The Club-Ax," was the first moderator. A Revolutionary soldier who had frozen and starved at Valley Forge, Davis was as filled with religious zeal in 1819 as he had been with patriotism in 1777. His preaching was a "strange conglomeration of ridicule, sarcasm, exhortation, denunciation, pathos, humor, and zeal." It was a fact known to all in his audience that he was "ready to sustain with physical force, if necessary, any utterances which fell from his lips while in the pulpit." Like many eccentrics, he always attracted a large audience. His utterances, especially the "merciless invectives" which he used so unhesitatingly, became household sayings. This ability to focus men's attention on religious affairs made "The Club-Ax" a useful minister and contributed much to the growth of the Alabama Association. Weak in the beginning, it had only 200 members in 1820, but it prospered as the country expanded, new churches were organized, and the older ones grew. In 1821 the association had 441 members; in 1824, 874 members; and 10 years later, 2,000 members.

The Black Warrior and Cahaba River valleys.—Settlers came into both ends of this area at approximately the same time. Men who passed through what was to become Jefferson County with Andrew Jackson, on their way south to fight the Indians, remembered the beautiful valleys and big springs. When the fighting was over, they came back to build homes. The first settlers came into Jones Valley from Huntsville in 1815, and by the next year there were enough Baptists to organize a church. On Mar. 27, 1819, Hosea Holcombe (*q.v.*), a pioneer Baptist minister and historian, gathered nine persons at the home of John and Sarah Jacks and constituted the Ruhama Baptist Church. One of these charter members was a female Negro slave. This occurrence was not unusual, as a great number of Negroes, particularly slaves, were members of Baptist churches in Alabama. Some belonged to churches like the African Huntsville Baptist Church, where the whole membership was colored, and others belonged to the white churches. In fact as the slave population increased with the growth of the plantation system, it was not uncommon to find churches composed of from one half to two thirds colored members. Ruhama grew, and only two months after its organization, it erected a log meetinghouse and increased its membership to 132.

A hundred miles to the south, at the other end of the Black Warrior and Cahaba River valleys, settlers poured into the Black Belt after the War of 1812 to found the "Cotton Kingdom of Alabama." The acquisition of Mobile Bay, and with it free access to the Gulf of Mexico for all of the hinterland along Alabama's great river system, gave impetus to the movement. White settlers first came to Greensboro (originally called Troy), one of the oldest towns in Greene County, in 1816. By this time there were scattered settlements stretching from Greene County northward to Blount County and many Baptist churches were organized. On Oct. 3, 1818, 10 churches united to form the Cahaba Association. It prospered and within two years the number of churches had increased to 23.

One of the leaders in the work was Joseph Ryan, who is said to have been the first Baptist minister in Greene County. He is also credited with organizing nearly all of the Baptist churches in the area now included in Greene, Hale, and Perry counties. After preaching for a few years in Georgia, Ryan came to Greene County in 1818. Shortly thereafter, he gathered eight people in a log schoolhouse just east of Greensboro on the Marion Road and constituted the Salem Church, an event of great importance for Alabama Baptists in the near future.

By 1823 the Baptists of Alabama had six associations, but there was no general state convention. Instead, they gave their support to the old nation-wide Triennial Convention, which had been organized by Luther Rice (*q.v.*) in 1814. There were leaders in Alabama who thought it was time to organize a state convention, but the discord in the individual churches and the associations was so great that the suggestion of any innovation was dangerous. After months of anxious discussion, J. A. Ranaldson, the initial supporter of the movement, sent out written invitations to a meeting to discuss the project. His daring was rewarded. In Oct., 1823, the delegates whom he had invited met at Salem Church near Greensboro and organized the Alabama Baptist State Convention.   WILLIAM PRATT DALE

II. History of Convention. The constitution on Oct. 28, 1823, of the Baptist State Convention of Alabama came as an outgrowth of missionary enthusiasm fired by the pioneer work of William Carey (*q.v.*), Adoniram Judson (*q.v.*), and Luther Rice (*q.v.*). By this date missionary societies had been organized in many Baptist churches, and often in the villages and counties as well.

Fifteen delegates from these missionary societies, "agreeable to the proposal and arrangement made" the year before, came together at Salem Church, near Greensboro, to constitute the convention. They elected as president Charles Crow (*q.v.*), pastor of the Siloam Church of Marion, and as secretary, J. A. Ranaldson (*q.v.*) of Claiborne, a missionary agent of the Mississippi Missionary Society and previously a missionary to Louisiana of the American Baptist Board of Foreign and Domestic Missions.

A missionary convention.—Though the name of the convention did not contain the word "missionary," it was clearly a missionary convention for the purpose of "promoting missions and religious instruction throughout the state, to aid . . . the General Convention of the Baptists in the United States, in extending the benefits of the gospel to the heathen, and in improving the education of the Gospel Ministry."

The convention began immediately to carry out the purpose for which it was organized. First there was an accounting of the funds received by Ranaldson, the agent, during the time he had worked in the state. For missions he received $193.42, for education, $51.25, for Bible distribution, $18.50, for subscription to the *Latter Day Luminary* and the *Columbian Star*, $99.50: a total of $362.67.

In addition, there had been given a gold watch and two pairs of socks, which were to be sold and the receipts given to missions. Also, for the Indian mission there had been given two boxes of clothes, stock, and provisions which had been turned over to Lee Compere (*q.v.*), the missionary to the Indians.

The convention was organized with a board of managers composed of 18 including the six officers. Before the convention adjourned, 15 domestic missionaries were elected as representatives in different parts of the state: for the northern district—Henry W. Hodges, Jeremiah Burns, Henry Petty, and Sion Blythe; to the middle district—William Moseley, James McLemore, Isaac Suttle, Moses Crawson, Charles Crow (*q.v.*), William Calloway, Joseph Ryan, John Henry, and Hosea Holcombe (*q.v.*); in the southern part of the state—Alexander Travis (*q.v.*) and Dempsey Winbourne. Only Winbourne, Holcombe, Crow, Calloway, and Ryan were listed as delegates.

In further seeking to accomplish the purposes of the convention, Ranaldson was unanimously elected as agent for the coming year. The constitution states that an "agent employed shall use his constant endeavors to promote the interests of the convention by forming societies, attending anniversaries; and by collecting and imparting general information." At the second annual meeting Ranaldson was re-elected agent.

Opposition to missions.—The agents did not find the work of the newly formed convention very well received. There were people scattered throughout the state in almost every church who feared that the formation of a convention was a step toward centralized power, to destroy the liberties won so recently by the Revolution. There was also marked opposition to the missionary purposes of the convention because the antimission forces at work at this time in Kentucky, Tennessee, and North Carolina were also reaching into Alabama. Evidence of this opposition is seen in the fact that only three agents reported to the next convention, meeting at Siloam Church in Marion. They were Sion Blythe, Alexander Travis, and Hosea Holcombe, one from each of the three districts. In addition a report was made by John Ellis, who was appointed to fill the vacancy caused by the death of Winbourne.

The officers and agents of the convention at first endeavored to hold the Baptists of the state together, regardless of whether they were in agreement with the missionary purposes of the convention. In 1843 the recording secretary listed the Baptist associations, indicating whether the association had made "effort at missions" or "anti-effort," "effort mixed," or was "missionary." Earlier, some associations were listed as "new test," which was a designation given to some of the "anti-mission" bodies which considered nonparticipation in missions activities a "test" of fellowship. Those who were opposed to missions, domestic and foreign, were opposed to all the "societies" which were promoting the various phases of denominational work and wanted to have no part in any of the so-called "institutions of the day."

As early as 1829, a resolution was adopted which sought to enlist the antisocieties group to support the objects of the convention, as follows:

Believing that it is the duty of all Christians to encourage and support every object that is calculated to advance the interests of the Redeemer's Kingdom Army men, and persuaded that Bible societies, tract societies, Sabbath schools and all such institutions are eminently suited to the purpose, resolved, that we earnestly recommend them as worthy of the most prayerful attention, and liberal support of our brethren.

The annual circular letter, which served as a forerunner of the denominational paper, was written on a timely topic at the direction of the convention and distributed in the printed minutes. In 1829 the circular letter recognized the "opposing medium of action" in matters of missions and warned the brethren against insidious agents who were at work in the state. It also urged the brethren to give to the support of the teaching and to the printing and distribution of the Bible and books. These were the closing words: "These things we leave with you hoping that the day is not far distant when we shall see eye to eye and be all of one heart and one mind, in the things which make for peace and salvation."

But co-operation did not come; finally, the opposers walked out of the churches, formed their own churches which did not affiliate with the state convention, and called themselves "primitive Baptists."

The missionary churches which were left became stronger and more mission-minded than ever. So did the state convention, which participated in and supported the work of the American Baptist Board of Foreign and Domestic Missions, sending representatives to the triennial meetings and funds in increasing amounts for the support of missions, both foreign and domestic.

However, in 1843 the convention, in revising the constitution, omitted the reference to the General (Triennial) Convention and delineated the "business of the convention" as: missions, ministerial education, Bible translations and distribution, Sunday schools, religious periodicals, tracts, and temperance. The trend was away from the Triennial Convention.

Missions and the slavery issue.—About the same time that the lines were forming separating the antimissionary churches from those mildly or positively missionary, there arose yet another problem. The American Baptist board had refused to send as foreign missionaries those who were slaveholders. This condition immediately caused Alabama Baptists to question the advisability of supporting the mission enterprises of the Triennial Convention. In 1844 this query was presented from the Tuscaloosa Church: "Is it proper for us at the South to send any more money to our brethren at the North, for missionary & other benevolent purposes, before the subject of Slavery be rightly understood by both parties?"

The convention approved this reply: "Slaveholders are eligible and entitled, equally with non-slaveholders, to all the privileges and immunities of their several unions; and especially, to receive any agency, mission or other appointment, which may fall within the scope of their operations or duties." The convention voted to send copies of this report to all the Northern societies and to withhold funds until a reply was received.

The board of directors of the convention declared the replies from the North unsatisfactory and agreed to follow the suggestion received from the Virginia Foreign Baptist Mission Society that a Southern convention be held. Delegates were appointed to meet in Augusta, Ga., May 8, 1845, and the Southern Baptist Convention was organized. The 1845 convention approved the action to dissolve all connection with the board of the Triennial Convention and the American Baptist Home Mission Society.

The Baptists had suddenly come to grips with the slavery issue. Their approach was not entirely negative. The positive approach resulted in showing themselves missionary in spirit and deed to the slaves. A resolution had been adopted the year before committing the convention to "solemnly recognize the duty of using all practicable and legal methods for communicating *religious instruction orally* to the people of color within our borders. And finding more than a quarter of a million of them within the limits of Alabama, we feel it our duty to provide for their moral and religious interests." The resolution further urged that services be held for the slaves, and that all masters be encouraged to impart religious instruction. The resolution was not heartily received by all, but the convention continued to consider the religious instruction of colored people a duty. As a result the convention voted to have a catechism published to be used in teaching slaves. "The Catechetical Instructor," which was designed to be used in teaching slaves and in "Sabbath schools," was approved and recommended to the use of the churches.

Thus the slavery issue advanced the cause of missions and education in the state, and this crisis forced the convention to face the need of bringing the gospel to the heathen at home as well as sending "bearers of the gospel" to other lands. In order to meet these needs, the people had to be taught to give more adequately to these causes. A report on "Systematic Benevolence" in 1848 called on the churches to "devise some plan by which the contributions of every individual may be directed into the proper channels." These suggestions were ordered printed and distributed to every pastor in the state.

Education.—From the first the convention supported education. For the first few years offerings were contributed to Columbian College. Each annual session heard a report on education, encouraging the young preachers to prepare themselves and restating the convention's purpose over against that of the antimission group.

In 1833 the convention meeting at Grants' Creek, Tuscaloosa County, voted to begin a school. Funds were raised, and in 1835 the Manual Labor Institute opened near Greensboro. The financial stress of 1837, along with certain internal discord, caused the convention in special session at Marion in Dec., 1837, to instruct the trustees to sell the property and pay the debts of the school.

This failure in establishing an educational institution did not change the purpose of the convention; it only changed the methods of educating the preachers. In 1839 the convention authorized the committee on education to buy $100 worth of books to be loaned to ministers. In certain instances books and financial aid were given to young preachers.

By 1841 the convention which met at Talladega was ready to consider the founding of a school for boys and young men at Marion. The school was chartered as Howard College and began its first semester in 1842 with S. S. Sherman as principal. The convention meeting in Montgomery in 1842 heard the reports of the opening of Howard College and accepted the generous offer of the board of trustees of Judson Female Institute, presenting this four-year-old school to the convention.

Another action of the 1842 convention was the decision to establish a religious periodical, *The Alabama Baptist*, which was commended to the special favor of the churches. Also, the convention voted to revise the constitution and take necessary steps to insure the incorporation of the body.

The convention in 1851 approved the use of a new hymnal, *The Baptist Psalmody*, arranged and edited by Basil Manly, Sr. (*q.v.*), and Basil Manly, Jr. (*q.v.*), and published by the Southern Baptist Publication Society.

Ministerial education.—One of the primary purposes of the convention was the education of preachers. This was the work of the "committee on education," which was succeeded in

1844 by the "Alabama Baptist State Education Society—auxiliary to the Baptist State Convention." This society was to raise funds to assist indigent young men of the Baptist denomination, studying for the ministry. This work continued as a regular function of one committee or another of the convention until 1883, when the Board of Ministerial Education was formed to administer the funds for financial assistance to ministerial students in the colleges and the seminary.

After the establishment of Howard and Judson colleges, the convention took under consideration the general education of Baptist children. In 1848 a special committee recommended that schools auxiliary to Howard and Judson colleges be begun in all counties and be supported by tuition fees. The convention was not long in recognizing the inability of the Baptists to do this task alone; the 1852 convention passed a resolution to the effect that a committee be appointed to awaken public legislative action on the establishment of free schools by the state legislature.

This aroused interest brought many denominational schools into being. Some were taken over by the convention; others were operated independently. In 1857 the Central Female College became an institution of the convention, and Newton Institute was accepted by the convention in 1907.

In order to "co-ordinate and correlate, equip and endow" the various Baptist schools, an education commission was formed with a secretary to work in the state. The work of the commission as to correlation was limited to a combined approach for the raising of funds to relieve financial pressure and to build up endowment of all the schools.

Bible society and Sunday schools.—The convention committed itself to the Sunday school work in 1829, since Sunday schools were "calculated to advance the Redeemer's Kingdom." The "Sabbath schools" were commended to the people each session thereafter, and the pastors were requested to preach a sermon on the Sabbath schools and "present a plan suited to the needs of the church." In 1853 the churches were urged to keep the schools going the whole year instead of closing during the winter months.

The Alabama Baptist Bible Society had been in operation since 1836 as an auxiliary to the convention. Its main purpose was to distribute Bibles and to encourage gifts for Bible publication and translation. The organization encouraged the reading of Bibles and good books. This society was reorganized as the "Bible Board of the Southern Baptist Convention" in 1851. In 1860 the Alabama Baptist Bible and Colporteur Society (the name had been changed in 1856) was absorbed by the convention, with the promise that a Bible board of the convention would be elected to promote the distribution of Bibles and books and to promote the work of the Sunday schools and the reading of tracts and good literature.

There was a division in the convention in the period just before the Civil War because of some unfavorable reaction to the use of books and literature in the Sunday schools which were published by the Southern Baptist Publication Society. Because of this situation and the outbreak of war, no reports on Sunday schools were given for several years, though there were some references in the minutes to the "Sabbath School Board" and a "Sunday School Convention."

In 1869 the convention voted to revise the constitution, incorporating in it "education of the youth" and "publication and distribution of religious tracts and periodicals."

At the 1879 session a committee was appointed on "statistics," to gather information in regard to Sunday schools and to promote the cause of Sunday schools in any way possible. The committee's work brought about the establishment by the convention of a State Sunday School Board, auxiliary to the Sunday School Board of the Southern Baptist Convention. The board was located in Talladega with T. C. Boykin as the secretary and evangelist. This early effort resulted in the formation in 1874 of the State Mission and Sunday School Board, which came to be the State Mission Board in 1875, with T. M. Bailey (*q.v.*) as secretary.

The president of the board said the work of the board was the main work of the convention. Therefore, one of the purposes for re-establishing *The Alabama Baptist* at this time was to have a medium for promoting the main work of the convention. The board authorized by the convention employed a secretary (or superintendent) of Sunday school work in 1906, who also promoted Baptist Young People's Union work until 1917, when a secretary was employed by the board.

The convention passed resolutions for several years recommending an encampment or summer assembly until 1910, when the first encampment was held at Shelby Springs, followed by one at Shocco Springs in 1911, and at Pelham Heights for several years thereafter. These encampments were at first operated by a special committee of the convention and were not a part of the work of the board.

The Executive Board.—In 1914 the State Board of Missions had grown so cumbersome that after special study a reorganization was effected, giving the board the new name Executive Board, composed of 36 members and being organized into departments of work. This board was to employ a secretary-treasurer, employ agents, and devise plans for the work of the convention. All funds contributed were to go through the treasurer of the board for distribution.

The board made advances forward in this new plan. W. B. Crumpton (*q.v.*), who had served 28 years as corresponding secretary of the State Board of Missions, was made secretary emeritus and placed in charge of the colportage work. Bunyan Davie (*q.v.*) worked as general colporteur, carrying on the distribution and sale of Bibles and books. The old Bible Society in 1856 began this work, which was taken over by the board in 1880.

Beginning in 1904, the board worked with a convention committee on co-operation which correlated the needs of all the agencies of the denomination and set an annual convention budget with goals for financial contributions to meet the need of each cause. This same committee made a suggested apportionment to each association and recommended that each church accept a quota on the basis of mission gifts the year before. This plan was enlarged on a five-year basis in co-operation with the Southern Baptist Convention in 1919, when the 75 Million Campaign was launched. In 1925 it became the Cooperative Program.

The Alabama Baptist.—This publication was purchased by the convention in 1919, and L. L. Gwaltney became the editor.

Baptist Foundation.—In 1921 Crumpton had proposed a Baptist foundation, and 19 years later (1940), the convention established the foundation for the purpose of receiving and investing gifts and bequests made to the convention and its interests. This foundation employed a full-time secretary in 1954.

Benevolent enterprises.—The attention of the convention had been repeatedly called to the obligation of caring for aged and infirm preachers and their families. In 1851 a special committee was set up to take this matter in hand and secure funds for this cause. The efforts were sporadic, and recommendations were passed requesting the association to handle the matter until a central committee was set up in 1880 with offices in Selma to secure and disburse funds for aged and infirm ministers. Later, this project was taken over by the board until in 1914 it was placed in the hands of a Board of Aged and Infirm Ministers Relief Fund, which operated independently with a secretary. In 1903 the Alabama Baptist Ministerial Benefit Society was instituted and was "heartily endorsed" by the convention. This society continues to function as a mutual benefit society for preachers and their wives.

In 1863 the convention approved the efforts to establish an Orphans' Asylum, especially for children of deceased soldiers. It was not until J. W. Stewart came to the convention in 1892 with a proposal to begin a home that the convention established an orphans' home at Evergreen.

The convention voted in 1920 to establish a hospital. Convention committees had been studying the possibilities of a hospital since 1905, but not until the spirit of enlargement took hold of the convention was the project realized. The hospital opened in Selma in 1922 and operated until it was leased to a private corporation and the debt liquidated.

Women's work.—In 1881 the "central committee on women's work" was appointed by the board. This committee corresponded with women over the state, urging the organization of women's missionary societies. The excellent response to this project, as reported to subsequent conventions, resulted in the convention's authorization of the appointment in 1885 of the Central Committee, which was located in Montgomery with a corresponding secretary. After opposition arose to the women's work, the committee was not re-elected. A few years thereafter, the state mission secretary stated that the "women were quietly working" and indicated it might be time for a central committee to be renamed by the convention. The next year, 1889, the Central Committee was elected by the convention, and offices were located in Birmingham. This was the beginning of the Alabama Woman's Missionary Union. In 1893 the first annual meeting of the "W.M.U. of Alabama, Auxiliary to State Convention" was held in Montgomery, and a record of it carried in the convention minutes.

Laymen's work.—Since 1888, when the first "Alabama Baptist Laymen's Association" was organized as an auxiliary to the convention, reports were made from time to time recommending the employment of a secretary, with the board supervising. The name of the movement was changed in 1926 to Baptist Brotherhood, and with the change of the name came new emphasis. That year, the convention authorized the Executive Board to arrange for promotion of the Brotherhood by the Sunday School Department. It was not until 1946 that the Brotherhood Department of the board was established.

Student work.—Work among students on the state college and university campuses came to the attention of the convention in 1922, when a representative of the Inter-Board Commission of the Southern Baptist Convention addressed the body. The next year, the convention appointed a commission on Baptist needs at educational institutions. The report of this commission resulted in assisting with the erection of church buildings in educational centers and the establishing of the student program, including Baptist Student Union work at the schools and colleges and the beginning of the Department of Student Work in 1926.

Negro work.—Beginning in the days of slavery, the convention has turned its attention from time to time to the missionary opportunities among the Negro people. However, little was done other than to offer assistance and to pass resolutions. After many years the Department of Negro Work was established by the board July 1, 1951, with a full-time secretary.

Church music.—The board brought into being in 1954 the Department of Church Music, and a full-time secretary began work May 20.

Evangelism.—Since the first Sunday school secretary was given the work of evangelism, the board has had special evangelists. However, with a greater emphasis upon organized evangelism, the board established a department with a director in charge of promotion in 1938.

Temperance.—When the constitution of the convention was revised in 1842, it included "temperance," a matter that had been claiming the attention of the convention with resolutions for several years. A few years before (1838), the convention had sent delegates to a state "Temperance Convention meeting in Tuskaloosa [*sic.*]." Baptist leaders in the state had been at the forefront in the cause of temperance. W. B. Crumpton and L. L. Gwaltney were recognized leaders in the forces opposing the use and sale of beverage alcohol. The convention has co-operated with other denominations in supporting the organized effort of temperance and abstinence. Churches and individuals are urged to contribute financially to the state organization for promoting temperance.

Historical committee.—In 1933 the convention created a committee to preserve Baptist historical materials. As a result of the work of that committee, the Alabama Baptist Historical Society was organized in 1936.

Growth.—From a small beginning in 1823, the convention has grown in 1954 to a host of Baptists numbering 597,913 members. Only three cities in the state can now adequately accommodate the annual meeting, Birmingham, Mobile, and Montgomery.   DAVIS C. WOOLLEY

III. Program of Work of Alabama Baptists. The Baptist State Convention of Alabama was originally incorporated by a special act of the legislature of Alabama, approved Feb. 17, 1860, which act was later amended by an act of the legislature approved Feb. 22, 1887. At present the convention operates under a charter granted by the legislature of Alabama, approved Feb. 14, 1923.

Purpose of the convention, as set forth in Article III of the constitution, is:

1. To offer an agency of cooperation for the churches.
2. To promote the preaching of the gospel in Alabama and throughout the world.
3. To support ministerial and Christian education.
4. To publish and distribute Christian literature, including the Bible, if desirable.
5. To organize and promote all phases of work fostered by this convention and the Southern Baptist Convention.
6. To aid any benevolent or moral movements it may deem promotive of God's kingdom.

The convention performs its functions through certain boards, commissions, and committees which it elects in its annual sessions, in conformity to its constitution and bylaws, in the following manner:

Meetings.—The convention meets annually at a time and place chosen the previous year, with any called meetings which may be found necessary to expedite and validate its actions. These meetings are made up of messengers from the churches and associations on the following bases:

1. From the churches: one messenger from each co-operating church and one additional messenger for each 100 members above the first 100; or one messenger for each additional $250 above the first $250 contributed to the work of the convention.

2. From the associations: one messenger for the first 1,000 members, or fraction thereof, and one additional messenger for each additional 1,000 members; provided, however, that no association may be entitled to more than five messengers.

These messengers assembled in convention hear reports of all their organized work, both on a statewide and a convention-wide level, and take whatever appropriate action they deem advisable. They adopt a budget and allocate anticipated Cooperative Program receipts to their several agencies and institutions.

Officers of the convention are a president, a first vice-president, a second vice-president, a recording secretary, a statistical secretary, and a treasurer. The president may not serve more than two successive terms; the two secretaries may serve indefinitely; the treasurer is usually the executive secretary of the executive board.

The actions of the convention are binding upon itself but not upon the churches. In 1956, 2,717 churches reported 619,274 members, $19,987,702.32 total gifts, of which $1,908,866.04 went to the Cooperative Program and $690,-357.06, to designated mission objects. The convention divides its receipts as follows: 47 per cent to Convention-wide causes and 53 per cent to state causes.

Executive board.—The convention elects its own executive board, consisting of its president and one member from each co-operating association (75 in 1956), with an additional member if $10,000 was contributed to the work of the convention the previous year and an additional member for each $30,000 contributed above the first $10,000; plus five women members elected from the state at large, though no two of these may be from the same association. One third of the entire number is elected each year for three-year terms, and no member may serve more than two successive three-year terms.

The board holds two meetings a year—one usually immediately prior to the annual state convention, to formulate its report and to approve a budget for recommendation to the convention; the other at a time chosen, ordinarily in December, to allocate funds to the several departments under its jurisdiction, namely, evangelism, city missions, rural and associational missions, missionary pastors, Sunday School Department, Training Union Department, Department of Student Work, Brotherhood Department, Department of Church Music, Department of Negro Work, and Shocco Springs Assembly.

The board is charged with the duty of electing an executive secretary, of employing all heads of departments of state mission work, and of administering and promoting all the work of state missions. It does not, however, have authority to lease or to sell property belonging to the convention valued at more than $50,000, or to mortgage property, issue bonds, contract obligations, or increase the indebtedness of the convention or any of its agencies or institutions without the specific instructions of the convention, either in a regular meeting or a special meeting called for that announced purpose.

Administration committee.—From the membership of the executive board, the convention elects annually an administration committee, composed of 15 members, one of whom is the convention president—who serves as chairman—and two of whom are women. This committee meets as often as necessary, upon call of the chairman and the executive secretary of the board. Its specific duty is to prepare annually a proposed budget for convention approval. The committee acts under authority of the convention or of the executive board on all matters committed to it by them and handles emergency administrative matters, although it is not permitted to involve the board or convention in financial obligations or project any new plans of work not authorized by the board or convention.

Education.—The convention owns and operates two senior colleges, Howard and Judson. The affairs of the colleges are handled by boards of trustees—36 for Howard and 27 for Judson—elected by the convention. The convention in 1955 appropriated $200,000 to Howard for its operating expenses and $95,000 to Judson. In addition it provided $392,592.20 to Howard and $78,518.45 to Judson for their building needs out of its capital needs fund.

In 1956 Howard was engaged in a building program on a new campus in the southern suburbs of Birmingham and expected to move from its old campus in the East Lake community of Birmingham in the fall of 1957. The college enrolled 1,688 students on its campus in 1955–56, plus an additional 1,900 students in its 50 extension centers. The extension center project among Southern Baptist state colleges is known as the Howard Plan. Howard was chartered in 1842.

Judson is situated in Marion, Ala., and is one of the few all-female schools left in the nation. It was founded in 1838 and claims to be the oldest Baptist woman's college in the world. In 1956 it reported a student body of 250, with its dormitory space crowded. New building programs were under way for several years, and the newest addition was scheduled for occupancy during the 1956–57 school term.

The convention provides a small subsidy for ministerial education, all of which now goes to students for the ministry at Howard College. The allocation produced $21,491.86 for this purpose in 1955. The fund is administered by a board of ministerial education of 15 members elected by the convention.

Orphanage ministry.—The convention owns and operates a children's home at Troy, Ala., which cared for 247 children in 1954–55. The home shares a small percentage ($21,000 for operating and $15,000 for buildings) of cooperative funds and, by agreement, makes an annual appeal at Christmas for funds from the churches. Its receipts in 1955 were $266,164.69 from all sources. It also participates in the capital fund for buildings. Its affairs are under the control of a board of trustees of 15 members elected by the convention.

Weekly paper.—The convention publishes a weekly newspaper, *The Alabama Baptist*, in Birmingham. Its affairs are in the hands of a board of directors of nine members elected by the convention. It receives an annual appropriation of $6,000 to supplement its income from subscriptions and advertising. Circulation now totals 75,000. Its pages are used for general religious news and to promote all phases of the work of the denomination.

Investment foundation.—The convention maintains a holding corporation, called the Baptist Foundation. This unit receives and invests various bequests, legacies, and other gifts for the several institutions. Its operations are controlled by a board of trustees of 15 persons elected by the convention, and employs the services of a full-time secretary.

Department of Evangelism.—A full-time secretary of evangelism gives himself to the work of evangelism and general promotion. Annual state-wide evangelistic conferences have been held since 1947, giving emphasis to this work. Baptisms have increased through the years, until a total of 28,726 were reported in 1955.

City missions.—Three full-time city mission programs are carried on under the state board—at Birmingham, Mobile, and Montgomery. With the exception of a small subsidy from the Home Mission Board, these programs are financed entirely out of associational and state mission funds. Regular reports are submitted by each city mission superintendent, and new churches are constantly being constituted under their direction. They also direct all phases of the organized life of the denomination in their areas.

Rural and associational missions.—In each of the remaining 72 associations, a missionary is provided, the associations bearing the major part of the cost. A full-time superintendent directs and correlates their activities. The missionaries on the field counsel pastors and other church leaders, assist in setting up calendars of activities, aid in securing pastors and pastoral supplies, and generally provide liaison services between the churches and the convention program, promoting in all areas of denominational life.

Aid to missionary pastors.—Perpetually, there are churches in strategic locations which need supplemental aid to pastors' salaries, in order to procure able men to lead them. The convention provides this aid over a period of two years. The number of pastors so aided in 1955 was 67.

Sunday schools.—A Sunday School Department is operated by the state board, with a secretary and three associates, besides office clerks. This department promotes Sunday school work throughout the year, with frequent clinics and study courses. Enrolment in the Sunday schools of the state reached 454,702 in 1955. Vacation Bible schools are an important phase of this work and have seen rapid growth in the convention. In 10 years, from 1945 to 1954, the number of Vacation Bible schools in the state increased from 1,004 to 2,462. Enrolment by then reached 214,194.

Training Union.—The Training Union Department sponsors a continuous program of training in the churches for the members themselves. Fully organized for all ages, this unit meets generally on Sunday evenings an hour before the evening worship. On a statewide level, the department is manned by a secretary and three associates, plus office personnel. Various types of enlargement campaigns and training courses are engineered by the state staff. Total members reported by the churches in their Training Unions in 1955 was 184,732.

Student work.—The Department of Baptist Student Union functions under the direction of a secretary, who is assisted by an office secretary and an employed director on each of nine college campuses in the state and at the Baptist Hospital in Birmingham. Baptist Student Union organizations are maintained at other institutions of higher learning in the state wherever permitted. The union seeks to enlist the Baptist students in active life of the churches near the college centers.

Brotherhood.—The Brotherhood Department undertakes to enlist the laymen of the churches in all the program of the denomination and of the churches where they are members. The department, with its secretaries, is taking over the Royal Ambassador program in the churches. Brotherhood figures for 1955 were 26,324 enrolled, not including Royal Ambassador membership.

Church music.—The board has established a Department of Church Music, with a full-time secretary. By means of frequent schools of music, hymn sings, advocacy of standards of excellence in music, emphasis on the use of higher quality hymns in the churches, etc., this department has contributed notably to the realm of better values in praise and worship in the churches and their organizations.

Negro work.—This department, with its secretary, has done much to alleviate the condition of Negroes with regard to their efficiency in church matters. Working primarily through their schools of higher learning, pastors' groups, and other selected leadership, in addition to Vacation Bible schools, the department has succeeded in elevating their standards of church functions and loyalties.

Summer assemblies.—For the past eight seasons, the board has operated a summer assembly program at Shocco Springs, a former resort which it now owns, near Talladega. For the summer season of 1955, a total of 6,471 campers attended the assembly. Programs of all departments of the board's work are promoted. A full-time manager, with some time given to advising churches about their building plans, is in charge of the assembly management. The programs themselves are planned by the particular department in charge of a given week. A similar operation is carried on by the Mobile Baptist Association at its camp at Citronelle, with the state fostering certain weeks, and at other sites by an increasing number of associations.

Aid to churches.—Several times each year, a small number of church buildings are destroyed by fire, tornado, or other calamity, and the board provides a modest sum to each to aid them in rebuilding their houses of worship.

Retirement and relief of ministers.—The board not only provides its part as a participant in the Southern Baptist retirement plan for its own employees but supplies the percentage required for the pastors in the state to participate in the several plans. It also promotes a Mother's Day offering for those on the relief rolls. In 1956, 547 pastors were in one or more of the Southern Baptist Convention retirement plans.

Administration and promotion.—The executive secretary bears the prime responsibility of administration and promotion. Members of his staff include: assistant to the executive secretary, financial and statistical secretary, secretary to the executive secretary, bookkeeper, two office secretaries, a minister's retirement fund secretary, and a financial clerk. The office handles all mission contributions from the churches, receipting them for the same, and disburses checks to proper recipients. It also supervises various properties and investments of the board and generally promotes all the work, including every convention-wide interest.

Social service.—A Christian Life Commission studies moral and social conditions throughout the year, such as liquor, gambling, divorce, church-state integration tendencies, racial relations, trends toward militarism, materialism, economic injustices, welfare state, corruption in government, and vice of all kinds. The commission reports its findings to the convention each year. Its personnel is elected annually by the convention.

Woman's missionary work.—Although the state Woman's Missionary Union acts as auxiliary to the convention, it works in full cooperation with the convention's program. It elects its own officers and administrative staff, but its funds are handled by the board's executive secretary-treasurer, and its schedule of activities is integrated with those of the convention. It holds its own separate state convention meeting each year, as well as regular district and associational meetings, in the promotion of its own work and the cause of missions. Its youth organizations are Young Woman's Auxiliary, Girl's Auxiliary, and Sunbeam Bands. Its offices are located in the same building as the state board offices, and a mutually helpful relationship exists between the two organizations.

IV. ALABAMA, STATISTICAL SUMMARY

Year	Associa-tions	Churches	Church Mem-bership	Baptisms	S. S. Enrol-ment	V.B.S. Enrol-ment	T. U. Enrol-ment	W.M.U. Enrol-ment	Brother-hood En-rolment	Mission Gifts	Total Gifts	Value Church Property	State Capital Worth
1823	6	128	5,000	....	....	....	....	....	....	....	....	....	....
1830	12	235	12,454	1,964	....	....	....	....	....	....	....	....	....
1840	31	507	25,026	3,751	....	....	....	....	....	....	....	....	....
1850	..	....	....	....	....	....	....	....	....	....	....	....	....
1860	..	....	....	....	....	....	....	....	....	....	....	....	....
1870	..	....	....	....	6,771	....	....	....	....	$ 5,705.35	....	....	....
1880	54	1,097	75,000	4,789	5,840	....	....	....	....	2,336.42	....	....	....
1890	71	1,457	96,888	4,392	24,475	....	....	....	....	1,043.07	$ 21,839.85	....	....
1900	80	1,769	129,545	6,682	44,577	....	....	....	....	10,649.48	155,951.77	$ 740,422.00	....
1905	79	1,891	150,945	7,690	62,554	....	....	....	....	40,534.39	206,046.64	1,255,354.00	....
1910	77	2,002	184,385	9,706	92,739	....	....	....	....	55,626.92	396,153.82	1,718,147.00	....
1915	76	2,133	213,086	15,966	124,460	....	4,000	....	....	56,256.08	676,306.26	2,877,233.00	....
1920	77	2,057	227,531	12,736	152,885	....	....	20,000	....	68,060.54	647,548.52	3,723,555.00	....
1925	76	2,120	274,732	16,394	167,396	....	23,686	31,800	....	108,039.32	1,931,125.84	5,464,852.00	....
1930	75	2,007	302,829	16,250	188,382	3,830	33,392	30,152	....	*781,564.54	2,072,551.23	9,073,751.00	....
1931	75	2,062	312,805	18,880	201,070	5,000	40,217	38,591	....	#322,476.48	1,944,528.06	13,431,428.00	....
1932	74	2,075	320,596	17,915	210,716	3,435	46,243	41,617	....	264,882.65	1,845,322.96	13,399,698.00	....
1933	73	2,107	328,409	14,708	203,166	4,324	48,177	47,308	....	232,926.02	1,393,734.68	12,831,183.00	....
1934	72	2,179	335,607	14,372	204,314	3,134	48,858	37,462	....	199,256.35	1,098,572.91	12,624,534.00	....
1935	72	2,131	345,667	16,643	208,843	6,000	44,431	39,618	....	138,439.49	1,250,320.95	12,608,431.00	$2,700,000.00
1936	72	2,196	352,855	13,926	205,768	8,139	45,184	39,457	....	170,420.60	1,387,395.15	12,482,314.00	....
1937	72	2,211	362,035	15,436	202,045	12,000	49,241	39,553	....	190,532.11	1,488,413.95	12,483,209.00	....
1938	72	2,232	375,009	20,555	218,119	15,918	52,651	47,463	....	216,991.95	1,287,371.38	12,520,928.00	....
1939	72	2,272	391,199	20,903	234,801	22,304	59,517	47,768	....	236,416.99	1,873,722.18	13,004,918.00	....
1940	72	2,302	397,915	17,406	227,802	24,427	57,842	47,078	....	249,641.83	2,045,184.39	13,019,251.00	....
1941	71	2,306	401,017	13,483	224,203	40,995	60,425	45,518	....	295,878.22	2,174,403.89	13,354,477.00	....
1942	71	2,314	409,039	15,106	214,277	37,935	51,017	42,560	611	301,894.43	2,508,042.10	13,883,682.00	....
1943	71	2,327	416,969	14,794	212,529	37,033	49,248	41,682	377	365,806.30	3,130,124.12	14,425,537.00	....
1944	71	2,331	426,347	16,552	217,514	46,990	51,657	41,080	303	490,466.00	3,628,789.04	14,820,707.00	....
1945	71	2,453	434,844	20,311	232,932	70,175	38,211	45,105	404	646,731.37	4,930,851.65	15,565,561.00	2,800,000.00
1946	71	2,455	456,131	18,247	250,954	94,320	58,944	50,094	1,511	1,068,762.31	5,426,703.92	17,182,527.00	....
1947	72	2,501	478,058	20,282	272,893	117,120	73,034	56,127	2,302	972,026.93	6,892,800.94	18,583,704.00	....
1948	72	2,551	489,172	22,787	293,006	139,031	88,414	64,097	3,436	1,176,772.23	7,533,548.12	21,692,433.00	....
1949	73	2,553	511,109	25,059	328,169	146,147	104,724	69,128	3,548	1,121,701.91	9,129,337.37	26,330,551.00	....
1950	73	2,587	530,423	26,358	350,048	160,304	121,959	78,440	6,253	1,307,311.81	11,198,110.59	32,362,617.00	....
1951	74	2,622	552,543	25,727	360,156	168,010	129,065	76,817	6,582	1,454,708.78	11,443,616.32	38,180,924.00	....
1952	74	2,663	565,573	23,205	377,381	144,123	140,637	86,708	8,615	1,401,524.85	13,519,577.73	44,778,912.00	....
1953	74	2,683	581,770	28,196	396,389	198,578	157,278	89,523	11,928	1,579,666.73	13,849,112.54	53,881,802.00	....
1954	74	2,697	597,913	29,636	437,457	214,194	173,801	99,055	15,296	1,832,885.50	16,012,545.19	60,748,711.00	....
										2,163,909.31	18,590,694.60	68,916,882.00	9,300,000.00
										3,220,799.12			

* This figure includes 75-Million and all Missions, Education, and Benevolences.   # This figure includes all Missions, Education, and Benevolences.

BLOUNT F. DAVIDSON

Hospitals.—Although the state convention owns no hospital of its own, it appropriates small amounts to two hospitals in Birmingham, operated by the churches of that area, and has made small gifts to a Baptist hospital in Gadsden. It once owned and operated a hospital in Selma but disposed of that facility.

Temperance.—No organization exclusively promoting temperance is sponsored by the convention, but it encourages support for the Alabama Temperance Alliance, setting a date each year for special offerings to that organization and receiving and forwarding funds to it.

Bible distribution.—Having no facility of its own for the worldwide distribution of the Scriptures, the convention invites contributions from the churches to the American Bible Society, setting aside a date in its calendar for such appeal and offerings and receiving funds for them to be forwarded to their office.

BIBLIOGRAPHY: W. W. Barnes, *The Southern Baptist Convention 1845–1953* (1954). E. Berry, *Labor of Love Through Alabama Baptist Woman's Missionary Union* (1940). E. C. Betts, *The Early History of Huntsville, Alabama 1804–1870* (1916). W. C. Bledsoe, *History of Liberty (East) Baptist Association of Alabama* (1886). J. T. Christian, *A History of the Baptists* (1926). W. B. Crumpton, *A Book of Memories* (1921). J. E. Dean, *Baptists in Greensboro, Alabama* (1938). D. Everett, *The Dixie Frontier* (1948). M. B. Garrett, *Sixty Years of Howard College* (1926). J. S. Graham, *A History of Clarke County* (1923). L. L. Gwaltney, *Forty of the Twentieth, or the First Forty Years of the Twentieth Century* (1940); *World's Greatest Decade* (1949). T. E. Huey, *Ruhama, The Story of a Church 1819–1945* (1946). H. Holcombe, *A History of the Rise and Progress of the Baptists in Alabama* (1840). H. Kephart, *Our Southern Highlanders* (1936). L. Manly, *History of Judson College* (c. 1915). B. F. Riley, *A Memorial History of the Baptists of Alabama* (1923); *The History of the Baptists of Alabama* (1895). J. Shackelford, *History of the Muscle Shoals Baptist Association* (1891). C. A. Stakeley, *History of the First Baptist Church of Montgomery, Alabama* (1930). W. W. Sweet, *The Story of Religion in America* (1939). T. J. Taylor, "Early History of Madison County," *Alabama Historical Quarterly*, I (1930). A. K. Walker and J. O. Colley, *The Story of the Alabama Baptist Children's Home* (1945). E. W. Yerby, *The History of Greensboro, Alabama* (1908). DAVIS C. WOOLLEY

ALABAMA CENTRAL FEMALE COLLEGE (1857–1923). A high school and junior college located at Tuscaloosa, Ala., founded by a local group of Baptists "to advance the interest of the denomination and to advance the cause of religion." The school, which was annually commended by the Alabama Baptist State Convention for its religious and cultural contributions to young women, was made an institution of the convention in 1922. The buildings, including the former state Capitol, which had been leased to the school, burned in 1923 and were never rebuilt. JAMES E. DAVIDSON

ALASKA, BAPTISTS IN. Baptist mission work has been conducted in Alaska since the middle of the 1880's. At the annual meeting of the American Baptist Home Mission Society in 1885, "the Corresponding Secretary announced that mission work was to be carried forward in Alaska partially by the aid of the Government." In 1887 the announcement was made that "Rev. W. F. Roscoe and wife, missionaries to Alaska, reached their destination at Kodiak Island . . . September 22, 1887." As well as missionaries appointed by the society, they were teachers under appointment of the Government. The society listed through several years one, two, or three missionaries, but no church was reported organized nor were any baptisms recorded. In 1900 the board of the society reported that work in Alaska was confined to Skagway. An organized church there received during the preceding year one by baptism and 13 by letter, with 31 members in all. J. C. Jordan was pastor. The town of Skagway did not develop as expected, and in 1903 the mission work was moved to Valdez, where G. S. Clevanger was pastor. In the report of the board to the annual meeting of the society, 1909, there is a survey of the preceding 25 years of work:

Far to the northward lies Alaska, where now we have no mission work. The Woman's American Baptist Home Mission Society has maintained for many years an orphanage at Wood Island. . . . In 1899 when Skagway seemed to be the commercial entrepot to the Alaskan gold fields, the society appointed a missionary and built a chapel and parsonage there; but the collapse of the place which has dwindled to the proportions of a village thwarted our endeavors. Subsequent work at Copper Centre yielded small returns. Attempts were made to occupy Valdez and Seward, but these places had been taken by two other denominations in contravention of a long-standing comity agreement that this region should be considered Baptist territory; other denominations have also their sections of Alaska.

In 1917 two officials of the society, C. A. Woody and Bruce Kinney, visited Alaska to study the situation with reference to the reopening of the mission. During these years the Woman's Home Mission Society continued to conduct the orphanage at Kodiak (Wood Island), caring for 60 or 70 orphan children each year. Apparently, the orphanage was doing excellent work with these children, who attended a government school near by. The missionary work seemed to be moving very slowly. In 1932 the board of the society reported that the only Baptist church building in all Alaska, at the orphanage on Wood Island, was falling down. However, the church made some progress, and in 1935 it was reported that "the church is affiliated with the West Washington State Convention and is making regular contributions. The Sunday-school has been graded and a Vacation Church School was conducted last summer. A number of the older boys and girls recently took a stand for Christ." In 1936 the report of the Woman's Home Mission Society says:

One of the outstanding events was the appointment of Rev. Clarence Riley for evangelistic work on Kodiak Island and other islands of the vicinity.

Alaska, Baptists in

... For more than forty years Baptists have been responsible for a certain territory on which the orphanage is located and it is a great joy that at last it is possible to begin this first piece of Protestant work on Kodiak Island.

The next year, 15 baptisms were reported. In 1939 the Woman's Home Mission Society reported: "Baptists are responsible for the evangelizing of a certain area in southeastern Alaska, and it has been a joy to extend the work to include the village of Ouzinkie and Spruce Island. ... All of the work at Kodiak and Ouzinkie is now known by the term, 'Kodiak Baptist Mission.'" At the beginning of the 1940's government activities on Kodiak Island began to increase, accompanied by rapid population growth. The American Baptist Home Mission Society sent W. A. Warner to make a survey and to inaugurate an active church program at Kodiak. A church building was constructed in 1940 but it soon became inadequate. In 1950 an educational building was added to the facilities; in that year 20 were baptized into the fellowship of the Kodiak church, and 16 were received by letter. It was reported to the annual meeting of the society that "on May 1, we began the operation of the Cordova Community Hospital. This is a twenty-bed hospital, the only service of its kind in a large area around Cordova. By arrangement with the Presbyterian denomination and upon the invitation of the local church, the Cordova Presbyterian Church has now become the Cordova Community Baptist Church." Apparently, at the beginning of the 1940's, the Kodiak Church was the only Baptist church in Alaska. The Cordova Church became Baptist in 1951.

The work of Southern Baptists in Alaska might be termed indigenous. The work was not begun by sending missionaries by some mission board; it was started by Baptists in the area.

Chaplain Aubrey C. Halsell said that if he ever lived in a community where there was no Baptist church he would organize one. That took place in 1943 when he was stationed in Anchorage, Alaska. Major Halsell and Chaplain Jewel D. Foster, another Baptist, with the marvelous co-operation of fifteen soldiers and two civilians as charter members, organized the First Baptist Church in Anchorage. After much prayer two well located lots (424-426 Sixth Avenue) with a burned out residence on one of them was found. They were priced at $5,000. Those loyal Baptists with God's help raised the $2,000 down payment—remodeled and rebuilt the structure into a temporary church building. The first worship services were held there Sunday, January 3, 1944.

"Competitive denominations" (as they put it) soon put pressure through army sources and had the leaders sent to the Aleutian Islands. The others carried on the work and Captain G. C. Demott was asked to supply until the first civilian pastor, William A. Petty, could arrive from the Southern Baptist Seminary. In the summer of 1940 after graduation from Ouachita College, Rev. Mr. Petty made a mission survey to Alaska with the intention of returning after his Seminary training. He arrived June 19. By this time, other Southern Baptist preachers had come to Alaska and started churches.

Rev. C. O. Dunkin and wife were having great success in Fairbanks. The first worship service was held September 17, 1944, the day the Anchorage church celebrated its first anniversary. Dr. J. T. Spurlin came to Juneau from a church in Detroit, Michigan, in August, 1945. In February, 1946, by the grace of God, he had organized a Baptist church there. One of the members sent all the way to Finland for her church letter. Reverend Felton H. Griffin arrived from Texas, and in June, 1945, was called as the second pastor of the Anchorage Church. Rev. Mr. Petty had resigned to do mission work and establish a Bible School (College of Alaska), and also to work toward the establishment of an orphanage.

On March 27-28, 1946, these three banded together in Anchorage to form the Alaska Baptist Convention.

The newly formed convention not only brought together representatives from the increasing number of Southern Baptist churches, thereby developing fellowship and strengthening morale; it also led to acquaintance and fellowship between the Southern group and the Northern Baptists who had been working in a portion of Alaska 60 years.

When the Alaska Baptist Convention met in Fairbanks we had with us a visitor Reverend Lincoln B. Wadsworth of the Department of Cities—Home Mission Society of the Northern Baptist Convention.

Though A.B.C. is not associated with the Northern Baptist Convention we understand each other better because of this visitor and we feel that better relationships will result from this visit.

We also had Brother Glenn Chandler from the Kodiak church visiting our convention. He was given a place on the program and gave us much information on the work in the Children's Home in Kodiak.

Brother Chandler returned with the Anchorage group and spent the following Sunday with the Anchorage church. We hope that the day may come when all Baptist work in Alaska will be an active part of the Alaska Baptist Convention. Before going to Fairbanks Brother Wadsworth visited with the churches in Juneau, Anchorage, and Kodiak.

The convention met with the Kodiak church in 1951.

They have been sending fraternal messengers to the Convention for the past three years now, and we are happy to have them. ... This year we have another Northern Baptist church in the territory. They took over the Presbyterian Hospital and church at Cordova.

In the Northern Baptist Year Book, 1952, reference is made to this event. The Kodiak church building was constructed in 1950.

The adequacy of this building was shown August 14-16, 1951, when Kodiak was host to the annual meeting of the Alaska Baptist Convention. Fifty-seven delegates came by chartered plane, and were housed on cots in the various rooms of the church. This still left room for the entire convention to be served three meals each day in the dining room of the church.

The annual meetings of the convention have shown year by year the progress of the work, at the same time being instrumental in stimulating the work. In the 1955 meeting there were reported 21 churches and 5 stations; 508 baptisms for the year; 3,618 members; church property valued at $1,486,525; contributions of $257,895.50, of which $38,717.63 were appropriated to missions. The work was being carried on among whites, Negroes, Indians, and Eskimos. When the first one or two churches were formed, Negroes and whites were in the same church. The Negroes desired a church of their own, and, with the help of their white brethren, two churches were soon organized. All of these racial groups are affiliated in the convention.

In 1948 the Southern Baptist Convention requested the Home Mission Board to look into the desirability and possibility of assisting the work in Alaska. In 1949 the board began such assistance in appropriation of money for the construction of church buildings and appointing missionaries. The Alaska convention quite early began to contribute to the Cooperative Program of the Southern Baptist Convention. In 1956 the Home Mission Board ceased to work in the area as a frontier mission field but began to co-operate with the Alaska Baptist Convention in the same way it co-operates with other state conventions. L. A. Watson was elected by the Home Mission Board and the Alaska Baptist Convention as superintendent of missions in the territory.

With the rapid increase of population (77 per cent increase from 1940 to 1950) the Baptist work has increased steadily and rapidly.

BIBLIOGRAPHY. F. A. McCaulley, *Survey* (1948). Alaska Baptist Convention, *Proceedings, 1950, 1955*. Southern Baptist Convention *Annuals, 1948, 1950, 1951*.   SOLOMON F. DOWIS

ALASKAN PETITION. Baptist churches were begun in Alaska by leadership of Southern Baptists doing military service in the territory. The churches were already co-operating in and financially supporting the work of Southern Baptists through its constituted boards. The Memphis Convention, 1948, authorized the Home Mission Board to assist the churches in developing their work. In 1950 the Southern Baptist Convention was petitioned by Alaskan Baptists for admission as a convention. In 1951 a special committee reported to the San Francisco meeting of the Convention clarifying the constitution of the Southern Baptist Convention by amendment concerning the receiving of constituencies into the Convention and clarifying the status of Southern Baptist churches in the territory of Alaska co-operating with the Convention. The Convention is composed of representatives from co-operating churches. Representation on the boards of the Convention is determined by the numerical strength of Baptists in a given territory or state.

JAMES W. MIDDLETON

ALBEMARLE BAPTIST HOME FOR THE AGING. Began operation Dec. 7, 1953, at Albemarle, N. C., with facilities for 35 residents. The property, formerly used for hospital purposes, was remodeled and equipped and was valued in 1955 at $250,000. The home is directed by a board of trustees elected by the state convention and a general superintendent chosen by the trustees. Applicants for admission to the home must be at least 65 years of age, able to dress and come to meals; they must be church members. If they have no funds, the cost of their keep is met by a special day offering and an allotment from the Cooperative Program.   JAMES M. HAYES

ALBIGENSES. The Albigenses (from Albi, a town in Southern France) were kin to Bogomiles, and root back in Manicheism. They are more or less identical with the Cathari. Appearing in various groups in the 12th century, they show no doctrinal uniformity. The following emphases are typical: rejection of the Trinity, belief that Moses was a tool of Lucifer, who was considered to be the God of the Old Testament; belief in the doctrine of transmigration of souls. They held that Christ was a creature, although a perfect heavenly creature, who taught truth on earth and returned to heaven after seeming to die. Salvation was attained by accepting the doctrine and by the laying on of hands by the *perfect*. Sexual intercourse even within marriage was the most heinous of sins. Their uprightness, moral earnestness, and steadfastness during persecution attracted the allegiance of thousands, but they were finally extirpated by the Roman Catholic inquisition and state repression.

BIBLIOGRAPHY: *New Schaff-Herzog Encyclopedia of Religious Knowledge* (1950). H. J. Warner, *The Albigensian Heresy* (1922).   T. D. PRICE

ALEXANDER, WALTER RICHARDSON (b. Philadelphia, Pa., Sept. 23, 1889: d. Dec. 13, 1954). Executive secretary of the Relief and Annuity Board. The son of William Booth and Martha Kay (Foreman) Alexander, he was educated in the Philadelphia public schools and attended Temple University at night. After receiving his call to the ministry, he attended Crozer Theological Seminary and graduated in 1916. He received the D.D. degree from Furman University in 1931.

Alexander married Eva Elizabeth Edge, June 29, 1911. They had one daughter, Ruth (Alexander) Cowell. His first pastorate was with First Baptist Church, Winchester, Va. (1916–18). There followed pastorates at First Church, Stamford, Tex. (1918–21); Mantua, Philadelphia (1921–22); First Church, Rock Hill, S. C. (1922–28); and First Church, Florence, S. C. (1928–42). After serving as a state board member of the Relief and Annuity Board from 1940–42, he joined that board as associate secretary, and served in that position until 1947. He became executive secretary in 1947, upon the retirement of Thomas J. Watts, and served until his death, Dec., 1954.

While serving as president of the Church Pensions Conference, Alexander was instrumental in the passage of a bill numbered HR-6000, which made Social Security for the pastor strictly voluntary. He traveled extensively in the British Isles, Egypt, and Palestine, and from these travels came the book *Holy Hours in the Holy Land*. He also wrote *All Out for God* and a study course book, *Doing Likewise*.

RETTA O'BANNON

ALEXANDRIA BAPTIST HOSPITAL. In 1916 a small 20-bed hospital was donated to the Louisiana Baptist Convention by a group of Alexandria physicians. The gift was made on condition that the convention take immediate steps to enlarge the facilities of the institution and operate it as a general hospital. A board of managers was appointed and the convention assumed charge on Feb. 1, 1917.

A statewide campaign for funds was launched, and in 1919 the name was changed to Alexandria Baptist Hospital. When the convention assumed control, the property consisted of a lot and three small buildings with a total value of $25,000. It had a debt of $9,700. Since its opening the hospital has treated 140,958 patients for which it has received $13,271,508.41.

In 1954 the value of land, buildings, and equipment was $2,009,083.09, with a debt of $435,574.22. The hospital treated 20,906 patients for which it received $1,463,172.11. It did charity work in the amount of $28,251.

It has 250 beds, serves patients of all races, and maintains a school of nursing, which had an enrolment of 49 in 1954. It is an accredited institution but has not been approved for internship. It received $2,400 from the Cooperative Program and $4,211.47 in designated gifts in 1954.

R. HOUSTON SMITH

ALIEN IMMERSION. A baptism, regularly performed in the name of the Trinity, on confession of faith in Jesus Christ as Saviour, by an administrator who belongs to a different ecclesiastical fellowship or church order; he is an alien. Some Baptist churches reject such immersion, holding that the administrator is an alien and is not authorized by the proper authority. Other Baptist churches accept the immersion on the principle that each church is the final authority. Those who reject alien immersion have never come to agreement among themselves as to how alien must alien immersion be in order to be alien. Some Baptists reject an immersion not performed by one of their own particular group of Baptists, authorized by one of their own churches. Others accept an immersion performed by anyone authorized by any Baptist church, whatever be the distinctively qualifying adjective.

Underlying the rejection of alien immersion is the theory that a qualified administrator of baptism must have a succession of authority back through the centuries to the 12 apostles and Jesus Christ.

Those who accept alien immersion do so on two grounds. Negatively, they reject the theory of succession of authority on the ground that, if it be made the test and cannot be proved, doubt is cast upon every baptism; it thereby ceases to be the answer of a good conscience to God (I Peter 3:21). On the positive side, they insist that a church is the highest authority under Jesus Christ in governmental and spiritual matters. Therefore, a church may ordain a man, thereby authorizing him to perform baptism. By the same token, the church may accept a baptism on confession of faith, by whomsoever performed, thereby regularizing for themselves the baptism so performed.

This disagreement on theory and practice stems from the very beginning of the English-speaking Baptist movement of the 17th century. The leaders of that day—Eaton, Spilsbury, Jessey, Kiffen, Tombs, Bunyan, Grantham, *et al.*—divided among other things on the question of "owning" parish churches to be churches of Jesus Christ, and the inferences therefrom. Congregations divided on the issue but continued to fellowship one with another. Consequently, no major confessional statement has raised the question. Each church has been left free to make its own decision.

Alien immersion is a subject on which Southern Baptists have widely differed throughout the years. They inherited from their Baptist forebears in England such disagreement. The churches in some areas have largely accepted into their membership without rebaptism persons who had been immersed upon the profession of their faith into the membership of non-Baptist churches, if and provided that at the time of their immersion they held the same concept of baptism and its purpose that Baptists consider necessary to receive the ordinance. In other areas the number who do or do not accept such persons is varied. In still other areas, all or nearly all require persons to be rebaptized who have previously been immersed into churches of another body, even in some instances churches of another Baptist general body. At times alien immersion appears to be a geographical question: pastors sometimes adapt their attitudes on the question to that of the area in which they labor at the time.

The only way the exact percentage that do or do not accept alien immersion could be determined would be by a poll of all of the churches. It is evidently true that a large majority of Southern Baptist churches do not accept without rebaptism those whose baptism they regard as alien. For generations this subject has been the source of thorny debate among Southern Baptists. During the last century only a few times has it been made a test of fellowship for the co-operation of Baptist churches in the membership and work of associations and conventions.

BIBLIOGRAPHY: T. Crosby, *History of English Baptists*, I (1738). *The Sumter Discussion on the Authority of the Administration of Baptism* (1903).

W. W. BARNES

ALIGNMENT, BAPTIST GENERAL CONVENTION OF OKLAHOMA. After the Civil War, the Home Mission Board was forced by financial circumstances virtually to abandon mission work in Indian Territory. This occasioned the entrance of the Home Mission Society (Northern Baptist) into this field and resulted in a series of divisive issues which led to the existence of four conventions for a brief period (1898–1900) in what is now the state of Oklahoma. Two of these were in Indian Territory (the eastern part of Oklahoma), and two were in Oklahoma Territory (western part). In each territory one convention co-operated with the Home Mission Society and one with the Home Mission Board. In 1900 both conventions in each territory consolidated, and a problem each newly organized body immediately faced was that of denominational alignment. The result was a plan to co-operate with both the Home Mission Board and the Home Mission Society which became known as "dual alignment."

First to adopt dual alignment was the Baptist General Convention of Indian Territory in its organizational meeting at Durant, Sept. 6, 1900. The plan adopted called for co-operation with both mission bodies. Each was to supply $4 for each $1 raised by the convention, up to a limit of $4,000. Each mission board also was to supply at least $1,000 for new church buildings. The two conventions in Oklahoma Territory met at Blackwell, Oct. 5, 1900, and consolidated to form the Oklahoma Baptist State Convention and adopted a similar plan of dual alignment.

The two territorial conventions met in Shawnee, Nov. 9, 1906, to consolidate and form the present Baptist General Convention of Oklahoma. The policy of dual alignment was continued on the basis of dividing equally between the Home Mission Board and the Home Mission Society all offerings for home missions, and between the Missionary Union of Boston and the Foreign Mission Board at Richmond all offerings for foreign missions.

The first annual report of the board of directors of the convention, made in 1907, shows that under the dual alignment policy the mission boards had given $8,000 each to mission work in Oklahoma and $3,000 each for new buildings.

Dual alignment continued until 1914. Steps leading to single alignment began two years before with a series of discussions and intermittent correspondence. Action taken in the 1913 state convention called for the appointment of a joint committee of 27 members, 9 each from the Oklahoma, Northern, and Southern Baptist conventions. Subcommittee chairmen named were Cortez Stubblefield (q.v.), Oklahoma; George E. Horr, Newton Centre, Mass., Northern Baptist; and Joshua Levering, Baltimore, Md., Southern Baptist. No general meeting of the joint committee was ever held because the Northern Baptist committee declined to act on the matter. They held the issue was one to be settled by Oklahoma. Consequently, July 28, 1914, the executive board passed a recommendation that Oklahoma form single alignment with the Southern Baptist Convention in work where all three co-operating conventions were concerned. This did not apply to any work fostered singularly by either the Home Mission Board or the Home Mission Society. The recommendation was given final convention approval at Shawnee, Nov. 18, 1914.

See also DUAL ALIGNMENT.   J. M. GASKIN

ALLDREDGE, EUGENE PERRY (b. Brooksville, Ala., May 30, 1875; d. Nashville, Tenn., Feb. 22, 1953). Clergyman and statistician. The son of P. G. and Emma Vicie (South) Alldredge, he received the following degrees: Baylor University, B.A., 1900, M.A., 1901, Th.B., 1903, and D.D., 1920; Southern Baptist Theological Seminary, Th.M., 1904; Ouachita College, Arkadelphia, Ark., D.D., 1917. He married Barbara M. Taliaferro, Oct. 4, 1904; children—Eugene Perry, Jr., and Mary. Following her death he married Mrs. Elkin Lightfoot Lockett, Nov. 27, 1940. He was ordained to the Baptist ministry in 1899 and served as pastor in Amarillo and Dallas, Tex., 1905–07, and as state secretary of missions for the Baptist Convention of New Mexico, 1911–12.

In the days when the struggle in New Mexico was intense between those supporting the Northern Baptist Convention and those who wished a single alignment with the Southern Baptist Convention, he was influential in securing alignment with the Southern Baptist Convention. He also served as pastor of Immanuel Baptist Church, Little Rock, Ark., 1913–19, and as executive secretary for the Arkansas Baptist State Convention, 1919–20. Keenly interested in moral issues affecting public life, and especially the cause of prohibition, he participated actively in public affairs and in movements affecting civic righteousness and public morality.

In 1920 he accepted the position as secretary of the Department of Survey, Statistics, and Information of the Sunday School Board of the Southern Baptist Convention and served in this capacity until his retirement in 1945. He gave himself to statistical work with a sense of mission and helped Southern Baptists become aware of the value of statistical information. The procedures and standards he established for district association minutes have been reflected in more accurate and complete Southern Baptist records.

He served as a member of the Constitutional Convention of Arkansas in 1916 (only minister in that body); and as a member of the Charities and Corrections Commission of Arkansas for four years. He was a member of the American Statistical Association, American Academy of Political and Social Science, and American Economic Association. He was a prolific writer, contributing many articles for religious journals, and was author of the following books: *Southern Baptist Handbook,* yearly (1921–45); *Southern Baptists Working Together* (1924); *The New Challenge of Home Missions* (1926); *One Hundred Successful Country Churches* (1922); *Southern Baptists in World Service* (1936); *101 Expository Sermons* (1941); *Forty Sermon Studies from the Book of Jonah* (1942); *Soul-*

winning Sermons (1943); *Sunshine and Shadows*, poems (1944); *Cowboys and Coyotes* (1945); *The New Racial Situation* (1946); *Unionizing Southern Baptists* (1948); *While Southern Baptists Sleep* (1949). He was editor of *The Quarterly Review,* 1941–46.

J. P. EDMUNDS

ALLIED CHURCH LEAGUE FOR ABOLITION OF BEVERAGE ALCOHOL.

The Allied Church League, Inc., was organized in Greensboro, N. C., Mar. 25, 1943, by the following religious bodies in the state: Associate Reformed Presbyterians, Baptists, Congregational Christian, Disciples of Christ, Episcopal, Evangelical and Reformed, Friends, Lutherans, Methodists, Moravians, Pentecostal Holiness, Pilgrim Holiness, and Presbyterians.

The objectives of the organization are: "To promote Christian citizenship and civic righteousness, including sobriety and total abstinence, . . . to work, organize and prosecute campaigns against alcoholic beverages, along educational, legislative and all other lines; to engage in all forms of activities to combat the manufacture and sale of alcoholic beverages."

The first organizations for temperance began in the state about 1820 in the form of temperance societies. The first no-license territory was created in 1838 when the legislature prohibited the granting of licenses within one mile of Wake Forest College. The first important step toward legal prohibition came in 1874 when townships were given the right to vote on the issue. The organization of the league was preceded by two statewide organizations. The Anti-Saloon League was organized in Raleigh on Feb. 6, 1902, with the aim of abolishing the saloon. In 1933 the United Dry Forces was organized in the same city to fight the repeal of the Eighteenth Amendment.

The work of the league is supported financially by designated amounts from the various co-operating denominations and is controlled by trustees nominated by these groups.

W. P. BIGGERSTAFF

ALL-SOVIET COUNCIL OF EVANGELICAL CHRISTIANS AND BAPTISTS.

Because there is no precise information available concerning the religious situation in Russia, it is not possible to give certified statements. Therefore, this article is merely a conservative statement compiled from trustworthy sources.

In his brochure *Baptists in the U.S.S.R.* (1943) James Henry Rushbrooke says of Baptist beginnings:

> In Tsarist days there existed in Russia two organized groups, known respectively as the "Union of Baptists" and the "Union of Evangelical Christians." The difference of name was due to independent origin, and to years of separated activity. Both Unions, however, were known abroad as Baptist; both became members of the Baptist World Alliance, and both have been represented in its Executive Committee. Shortly after the establishment of the Soviet Government they expressed their essential unity by accepting a common declaration of faith and order, and since the Nazi invasion they have in a joint appeal addressed the Baptists of all lands as "co-religionists." These two bodies include as far as is known, the whole of the Baptists of the U.S.S.R.

In an outline of early history, Rushbrooke sheds some light on the duality of Baptist organization:

> The beginnings of the Russian Baptist movement are traceable to religious awakenings during the latter half of the 1860's, in certain southern regions, Transcaucasian Tiflis and Ukrainia. In Transcaucasian Tiflis lived a merchant named Nikita Voronin, a leader of the Molokan community. The subject of baptism had come up for discussion among the Molokans, and Voronin gave himself to the study of New Testament teaching on the matter. The result was a profound spiritual experience . . . and a change of outlook which led him to desire baptism as a believer. He was ignorant of the existence of such people as Baptists; only after his convictions had taken form did he learn from a German artisan that they were shared by thousands even millions in other lands. Around Nikita Voronin, who was baptised on the 20th of August, 1867, there gathered a small group to form in 1868 the earliest Baptist church. . . . Meanwhile in Ukrainia the "Stundist" movement, originating among German colonists, had begun to gain Russian adherents; and among these "Stundism" . . . came during the "seventies" to assume a definitely Baptist form, largely owing to contact with the stronger movement spreading from the Caucasus. With the formation of the Russian Baptist Union in 1884, assimilation was complete.

Thus the main stream of Russian Baptist life, its source in Caucasia, receiving a strong tributary from the southwest, flowed onward as the Union of Baptists.

In the middle of the 1870's another movement started, which like the "Stundist" eventually became Baptist both in doctrine and polity. In certain respects it differed from that we have described [above]. It was northern instead of southern; at the outset it was largely aristocratic rather than popular; and it owed much to direct influence from abroad. An Englishman, Lord Radstock, a "pietist" of the "Plymouth Brother" type, had been invited by a Russian woman of high social standing to come to St. Petersburg, and the first of a series of visits took place in 1874. His preaching in the houses of members of the aristocracy proved effective. [Members of the nobility were converted and] began to evangelize working people and peasants on their estates, to print and distribute tracts, and to organize Christian philanthropic efforts.

In 1888 a man named Ivan S. Prokhanoff appeared in Baptist ranks and soon proved to be a great leader, able, educated, and dynamic. He traveled abroad, studied in the Baptist college of Bristol, England, and in the universities of Berlin and Paris, and returned to St. Petersburg as a professor. The Union of Evangelical Christians was organized under his influence in 1908.

The communist revolution, because of its atheistic emphasis, brought on an inevitable clash with religion, a clash first felt in the Orthodox Church, state church at that time.

The Baptist position with reference to the

revolution was generally one of aloofness. Baptists supported the laws enacted by the government against the Orthodox Church because they had suffered at the hands of the Orthodox hierarchy. The government welcomed this support, but when Baptists opposed the government's rigid censorship of all printed matter of the churches and the closing of Sunday schools, they, too, began to feel communist suppression.

The law of 1929 was directed mainly against evangelicals and Baptists. It granted freedom of worship, but not of propaganda; at the same time it granted freedom of propaganda to atheists and anti-religionists.

At about the time of the enactment of this law, the All-Soviet Council (or Union) of Evangelical Christians and Baptists was organized. This council is an agency of the government, designed to give the government control of evangelical churches. Corresponding in purpose, authority, and even in organizational form, to the Patriarchal Synod of the Orthodox Church, the council has 12 members, appointed by the government. The headquarters of the council are in Moscow, with some of the members residing in Kiev, Riga, and Tallina.

For the organization of the council Russia is divided into 70 regions, with a presbyter or supervisor over each of them. The presbyters are appointed by the 12-member Council; through them and local presbyters the organization reaches the local church level.

Under this form of state control, evangelical Christians and Baptists share alike with the Orthodox Church in the measure of religious freedom granted. They have freedom of worship only; all activities and open expressions of interest in the work of the churches must be confined within places of worship. It appears to be the government's theory that religion is concerned only with rites and ceremonies and, therefore, religious freedom can mean only the freedom required for the observance of these formalities.

This sort of restricted freedom does not agree with the Baptist conception of the purpose and function of the New Testament church. It rules out evangelism and world missions by denying the right of propaganda.

Under the Soviet system all religions are on an equal footing before the law. No church group receives preferential recognition or subsidies from the state or outside religious organizations. The government owns all church properties, and all are at the disposal of the government. Churches pay rental charges for the use of their buildings.

Baptist churches in Russia have a high moral standard for their members; thus it is not easy to become a church member. Of the reported 520,000 registered Baptist church members in Russia, however, about 20 per cent are young people over 17 years of age.

All religious instruction of children must be confined to the homes and directed by the parents, since Sunday schools are not allowed.

Every church has a choir, and observes choir-practice hours, with rehearsals attended by other members in addition to Baptists. In connection with the rehearsals Bible truths may be emphasized, thus affording a limited opportunity for evangelism.

Many converts are baptized into the churches every year, and Baptists, well organized for carrying on their work, are making steady progress. There are many churches in Siberia and in the Caucasus.

Baptists in Russia form the backbone of Protestantism at the present time because of their clear doctrinal teachings and their effective organization. As a Christian group they have a strong influence in Russia.

At present there is no frontal attack on religion in Russia. The government seems to be employing the milder policy of religious toleration, without overly offending the consciences of religious citizens, hoping by a slow process of educational and psychological attrition to suppress, intimidate, and finally destroy religion.

There is no economic discrimination against citizens because of their religion. The religionists seem more or less content with the present order of things. They follow the party line, supporting official ideas of the government on international affairs and keeping silent on internal political and social matters. Indication of this attitude is their universal approval of the so-called Russian peace plan. The All-Soviet Council publishes a monthly journal which provides material for use in services and private Bible reading and current news of happenings in the congregations. It has recently been promised permission to publish an edition of the Russian Bible and also a hymnbook.

Spiritual and physical vigor is displayed by leaders of the council, particularly by the 70 supervisors who travel long distances visiting the more than 5,000 congregations under their charge. Some of these journeys are undertaken by foot. Few congregations have full-time ministers; rather most of them are served by ministers who are in their positions because of their intensive study of the Bible or their eloquence. About 500 have received instruction in ministers' training institutes in Leningrad or Moscow. There are 5,400 Baptist churches in Russia, 3,000 ordained pastors, and 2,400 unordained pastors. The total Russian Baptist constituency is variously estimated at from two million to four million.   J. D. FRANKS

ALTO FRIO BAPTIST ENCAMPMENT. A Texas encampment organized in 1920 on the Frio River near Leaky, Tex., in District 6. A movement originated by Bruce Roberts, Billy Mitchell, and S. M. York resulted in the organization of this encampment.   J. E. ROTH

AMBASSADOR LIFE. A magazine with world outlook for Baptist boys, which began in June, 1946, as a 24-page monthly. Woman's Missionary Union's executive committee proposed that

World Comrades, the Girls' Auxiliary publication, "launch and sustain" a Royal Ambassador magazine until it could support itself. The name *Ambassador Life* was suggested by nine-year-old Bob Lutz of Biloxi, Miss., in a contest for Royal Ambassadors. Published by Woman's Missionary Union, the magazine contains programs for Junior and Intermediate Royal Ambassadors, stories, features, news from chapters and individual Royal Ambassadors, camping, handicraft, recreation, hobby suggestions, book reviews, and helps for counselors and embassies. The subscription rate, originally $1 a year, was increased to $1.50 in Oct., 1952. J. Ivyloy Bishop, first Southern Baptist Convention-wide Royal Ambassador secretary, served until Dec., 1953, when B. W. Jackson, Royal Ambassador secretary for North Carolina, became guest editor. Subscriptions to *Ambassador Life* have increased from 11,548 to 59,705 by 1955.

MARY PATRICIA POWELL

AMERICAN BAPTIST ASSOCIATION. A Landmark Baptist body, organized in Texarkana, Ark., Nov. 24, 1905. Known first as the Baptist General Association, the name was officially changed to American Baptist Association (A.B.A.) in Dec., 1924.

A long and bitter controversy among Southern Baptists over the primacy of the local church in preaching the gospel, administering the ordinances, and doing mission work gave birth to the American Baptist Association. Although the Big Hatchie Association in Tennessee had adopted certain Landmark tenets as early as 1851, it was not until 1854 that the term "Landmark" was attached to the dissenters. It became a distinguishing name after 1855.

The first state organization of Landmark Baptists was formed at Troup, Tex., in 1899 and was called the East Texas Baptist Convention. Later in the same year at Lindale, Tex., the name was changed to Missionary Baptist Association of Texas. In Arkansas, Landmarks slipped away from the convention in 1901, and organized a state association in Oct., 1902. Attempts for reconciliation between the convention and the association failed at both state and Southwide levels. Early in the 1920's, all major Landmark associations united to form the present American Baptist Association. It is composed of approximately 2,200 churches in the United States with a combined membership of 286,691.

The American Baptist Association is composed of churches as units, with each church represented equally at all business sessions of the association. All authority for preaching the gospel, administering the ordinances, and evangelizing the world is vested in the local church. The original Landmark ecclesiology which makes the first New Testament church and succeeding associations of churches co-terminous with the kingdom of God, as advocated by James Robinson Graves (*q.v.*), Amos Cooper Dayton (*q.v.*), James Madison Pendleton (*q.v.*), and others, is still held by most affiliates of the American Baptist Association.

The association promotes extensive local, district, and interstate missions, but is weak in foreign mission work, having work in only four fields in 1955.

A number of schools, including a seminary in Little Rock, Ark., are operated by affiliate churches of the American Baptist Association. A publishing house and headquarters are maintained in Texarkana, Ark., with J. Alvan Rester as business manager, and A. L. Patterson as secretary of missions. It owns and operates an orphanage at Texarkana, Ark., caring for from 15 to 25 children each year.

In 1950 the American Baptist Association split, and the minority group was organized into the North American Baptist Association.

See also BAPTIST MISSIONARY ASSOCIATION, TEXAS, and NORTH AMERICAN BAPTIST ASSOCIATION.

J. DON HOOK

AMERICAN BAPTIST CONVENTION. The organization of Baptists in the Northern states of the United States. It was formed in 1907 and was called the Northern Baptist Convention. In 1950 the name was changed to American Baptist Convention. Prior to 1907 Northern Baptist churches expressed themselves co-operatively through societies organized at various dates for specialized functions: the American Baptist Foreign Mission Society, Woman's American Baptist Foreign Mission Society, the American Baptist Home Mission Society, Woman's American Baptist Home Mission Society, American Baptist Publication Society, the American Baptist Education Society, and the American Baptist Historical Society. Each society was incorporated and was autonomous. Each performed the missionary, publication, educational, or historical function indicated by its name. Each was dependent upon essentially the same group of churches for its support. Members of these societies from the churches met annually on consecutive days in a series of "May anniversaries" to hear reports and transact business of the societies.

History of the early societies.—The early history of the American Baptist Convention is the history of societies that grew out of Baptist beginnings in America. The first Baptist organizations in America were the First Baptist churches of Providence and Newport, R. I., founded about 1638. Baptist churches increased their strength slowly after this beginning in colonial America. The first association of Baptist churches was the Philadelphia Baptist Association, organized in 1707 by two churches in Pennsylvania and three in New Jersey, later joined by other churches in Virginia, Maryland, Delaware, Pennsylvania, New Jersey, New York, and Connecticut.

Meanwhile, variations were developing among Baptists in America. The General Six-Principle Baptists were organized in Rhode Island in 1670, the Original Free Will Baptists were organ-

PRESIDENTS

of the

SOUTHERN BAPTIST CONVENTION

Ministers, educators, lawyers, and business men—these twenty-eight leaders were drawn from thirteen states for service and honor.

WILLIAM B. JOHNSON
1845–1849

R. B. C. HOWELL
1851–1857

RICHARD FULLER
1859–1861

P. H. MELL
1863–1871

JAMES P. BOYCE
1872–1879, 1888

JONATHAN HARALSON
1889–1898

W. J. NORTHEN
1899–1901

JAMES P. EAGLE
1902–1904

E. W. STEPHENS
1905–1907

JOSHUA LEVERING
1908–1910

EDWIN C. DARGAN
1911–1913

LANSING BURROWS
1914–1916

J. B. GAMBRELL 1917–1920	 E. Y. MULLINS 1921–1923	 GEORGE W. McDANIEL 1924–1926	 GEORGE W. TRUETT 1927–1929
 W. J. McGLOTHLIN 1930–1932	 FRED F. BROWN 1933	 M. E. DODD 1934–1935	 JOHN R. SAMPEY 1936–1938
 L. R. SCARBOROUGH 1939–1940	 W. W. HAMILTON 1941–1942	 PAT M. NEFF 1944–1946	 LOUIE D. NEWTON 1947–1948
 ROBERT G. LEE 1949–1951	 J. D. GREY 1952–1953	 J. W. STORER 1954–1955	 C. C. WARREN 1956–1957

ized in Virginia and North Carolina in 1727, and the first Seventh Day Baptist church was formed in Germantown, Pa., in 1728. The Great Awakening (c. 1739) divided many other Baptists in America into Regular and Separate Baptists but also stimulated evangelism and missionary activity and marked the beginning of rapid expansion of Baptist work. In 1767 the Warren Association, Warren, R. I., was formed. In 1802 the first statewide missionary organization of Baptists, the Massachusetts Baptist Missionary Society, came into being. This society initiated missionary work that reached far beyond the borders of the state.

The conversion of Adoniram Judson to the Baptist position in 1813 led to the formation of the General Missionary Convention of the Baptist Denomination in the United States for Foreign Missions (Triennial Convention) in Philadelphia in 1814. This body, now known as the American Baptist Foreign Mission Society, became the first of a group of societies that co-operated nearly a century later to organize the American Baptist Convention. The Baptist General Tract Society, now known as the American Baptist Publication Society, was formed in Washington, D. C., in 1824. Mission activities of Massachusetts Baptists led to the organization of the American Baptist Home Mission Society in 1832, to win "North America for Christ." The majority of Baptist churches in the United States co-operated in the work of these societies until tension over slavery caused the churches in the South to separate from them and form the Southern Baptist Convention in 1845.

Later, still other societies were formed. The American Baptist Historical Society was started in 1852; the Woman's American Baptist Foreign Mission Society, in 1871; the Woman's American Baptist Home Mission Society, in 1877; and the American Baptist Education Society, in 1888.

First steps toward organization of a denomination that would bring the societies closer together were taken in 1896, when delegates from the churches attending the May meetings called for appointment of a Commission on Systematic Beneficence. A commission on co-ordination was formed, and to the May meetings in 1901, it recommended: (1) that the same delegates be seated at meetings of all societies; (2) that a mid-year meeting of executive officers of the societies be called to co-ordinate their activities; (3) that the societies agree to make a joint appeal to the churches for support; (4) and that a committee of nine be appointed to make further study and report in 1902. This plan was adopted, and in 1902 a committee of 15 was chosen to make the further study. In 1903 the committee advised against any merger of the societies.

A call for a general meeting of all the societies was issued in 1906, to be held in connection with the May anniversaries in 1907 in Washington, D. C. The American Baptist Missionary Union (in 1910 the name was changed to American Baptist Foreign Mission Society), the American Baptist Home Mission Society, and the American Baptist Publication Society responded to the call and met in Calvary Baptist Church, Washington, D. C., May 16–17, 1907. Here a committee of 15 was appointed to draft a plan of organization that would preserve the independence of the local church and at the same time co-ordinate denominational work.

The societies at the 1907 meetings reported the following results of the previous year of work: The two foreign mission societies had 578 missionaries working in Burma, Assam, South India, Siam, China, Japan, Africa, and the Philippine Islands. They also had 4,551 native workers. There were 1,294 churches with 137,438 members. In addition, there were 1,917 schools of all grades on the mission fields. To support this work, they had received from the churches, individuals, annuities, legacies, and income from funds, a total of $928,153.77.

The home mission societies had 1,805 missionaries and teachers entirely or partly supported by them. These people worked among Negroes, Indian Americans, Spanish-speaking Americans, European immigrants, Japanese, and Chinese, and in Cuba, Mexico, Puerto Rico, and Alaska. Receipts from all sources totaled $750,717.54. In 1907 the American Baptist Home Mission Society celebrated its 75th anniversary. A summary report showed that the society in 75 years had commissioned a total of 34,049 workers, and that 6,113 churches had been organized all over the United States.

The American Baptist Publication Society in 1907 listed 33 publications with a total circulation of 2,144,214 copies. It was supporting 141 missionary colporteurs and Sunday school missionaries and had founded 44 new churches and 333 Sunday schools during the year. Its missionaries had distributed 12,000 Bibles among 12 nationality groups. Bible institutes were reported among Negro people, both North and South. A report of activities since 1824, when the society was founded, recorded the organization of 14,197 Sunday schools and 1,589 churches. With book stores in Philadelphia, Boston, Chicago, St. Louis, Atlanta, and Dallas, the society reported a publishing income of $719,775.64. Income from all other sources was $217,536.42.

A tentative organization was effected at the 1907 meeting in Washington, and Charles Evans Hughes, later chief justice of the United States Supreme Court, was elected president. W. C. Bitting, St. Louis, Mo., was elected corresponding secretary, an office which he held for 20 years. The Northern Baptist Convention was incorporated legally under the laws of the state of New York on June 6, 1910. Section 2 of "An Act to Incorporate the Northern Baptist Convention" states that "The objects of the corporation shall be to give expression to the opinions of its constituency upon moral, religious, and denominational matters, and to promote denomination unity and efficiency in efforts for the evangelization of the world."

American Baptist Convention

By-laws of the new corporation provided that "the constituency of the Northern Baptist Convention shall be all Baptist churches in the United States which co-operate in its work." They also provided: (1) that delegates be appointed by the churches and co-operating organizations with the voting privilege by each society extended to all delegates seated in the convention; (2) that there be an executive committee composed of officers, former presidents, and 30 other members, 15 of whom should be laymen, this committee to act for the convention between sessions; (3) that the legal independence of each co-operating society be guaranteed, but each society be required to agree "to regulate expenditures in accordance with the budget to be annually approved by the Convention" and "to solicit funds only on the approval of the Finance Committee given between the Annual meetings of the Convention"; (4) and that the relationship between a society and the convention could end on one year's notice from either party.

The new convention included "co-operating organizations" (the societies) and "affiliating organizations" (Baptist state conventions and standard Baptist city societies). Provision was made in 1939 for any "national Baptist body" in the territory of the American Baptist Convention, "which indicates its willingness to co-operate whole-heartedly in the purpose and objects" of the convention, to relate itself to the convention as an "associated organization" upon nomination by the general council, invitation by the convention, and a vote of acceptance of the invitation by the organization. Provision was also made for subsidiary boards and councils, some of which were formed at later dates. One such board was the General Board of Promotion, created in 1920 to review the work of the convention, its boards and societies, in the fall of each year, and to make plans and prepare a budget for the ensuing year. This was a widely representative board with members from all agencies of the convention besides members at large. Its responsibility included policy-making as well as fund-raising. In 1924 its name was changed to the Board of Missionary Co-operation. Because some saw in this agency a threat to the autonomy of the local churches and possibly an effort to gain control of the societies, the Board of Missionary Co-operation was abolished in 1934, and its promotional functions were given to a new Council on Finance and Promotion with a membership representing all agencies and the churches at large. The name of the Council on Finance and Promotion was changed to Council on Missionary Co-operation in 1950.

The executive committee of the convention was replaced by a general council, to which the standing committees of the convention became responsible. The general council was composed of members, none of whom could be a salaried officer of any agency of the convention, plus the officers of the convention. It was given "all the powers vested in the Northern Baptist Convention and which the Convention has not expressly reserved to itself."

The following agencies were also created by the convention or came into relationship with it in subsequent years:

The Board of Education was initiated by the convention in 1909, when a committee of college presidents and other leaders was appointed to study denominational education. At the annual meeting of the convention in 1912, a 21-member board was chosen. The interests of the American Baptist Education Society were merged with the new board. Its purpose was to increase interest in Christian higher education, to provide a ministry to Baptist students attending state universities, and to assist Baptist-related schools and colleges in securing financial aid. In 1944 this board was integrated with the board of managers of the American Baptist Publication Society, the resulting body becoming known thereafter as the Board of Education and Publication.

The Ministers and Missionaries Benefit Board was established by the convention in 1911 and was incorporated in 1913. Its purpose is "to administer its funds for benefit of worthy ministers and missionaries who have served the Baptist denomination, their wives, widows, and their dependent children; . . . to promote interest in the better maintenance of the ministry." A retiring pension fund was added to the program in 1920, and family protection benefits were offered in 1951 and 1954. In 1956 this board became the first church group to offer accident and health benefits to its members. In 1956 grants on account of need (not a part of the pension program) were being paid at the rate of about $200,000 a year, and emergency assistance at the rate of about $100,000. There were, on Dec. 31, 1955, 3,462 dues-paying members of the pension fund, with more than 85 per cent of the eligible ministers and missionaries included. On the same date the assets of the board were $55,109,063.

The National Council of American Baptist Men began in 1922 as the National Council of Northern Baptist Men. It was founded to develop Christian fellowship, spiritual growth, and united action among laymen.

The Ministers Council was organized in 1936. It works to lift educational standards for ordination to the ministry, to develop procedures in placement of ministers, to establish minimum salary plans, to recruit candidates for the ministry, and to encourage reading and in-service training of pastors.

The Council on Christian Social Progress was established in 1941. It has a directive from the convention to study the field of human relations and events in a broad perspective in order to find ways for the churches to apply the teaching of Jesus Christ in human affairs. Among the major features of the Council on Christian Social Progress are the United Nations and Washington Churchmen's Seminars to help the laity assume responsibility as Christians in national and international affairs. Recognizing that there can be no world peace until there is peace in one's own community, the Council also has a program of education and correction to help churches combat such social evils as liquor and narcotic traffic, gambling, obscene literature and movies, juvenile delinquency, economic exploitation, and unemployment.

The National Council of American Baptist Women was formed in 1951, including all the women members of the churches of the American Baptist Convention. Through this council the women are united in a program to develop deeper devotion to Jesus Christ, to participate in the program of the American Baptist Convention, and to support missions. Each year the council collects a Love Gift offering for the unified budget of the convention. The 1954-55 offering was $462,704.44.

American Baptist Assembly was formed in 1944 when the American Baptist Convention acquired an 1,100-acre lake-front estate at Green Lake, Wis., for summer conference uses. Each year, 20,000 young people and adults attend conferences here for fellowship and leadership training in missions, evangelism, Christian education, and stewardship.

The Baptist Youth Fellowship and the Baptist Student Movement are two youth organizations that grew out of a program formed before 1907.

Relations with other Baptist bodies.—Northern Baptists came into the Baptist World Alliance when it was organized in 1905 and thereby gave formal evidence of their desire to have fellowship with all Baptists. They co-operate with other Baptist groups in the Baptist Joint Committee on Public Affairs, an organization which they helped to create in 1938. Because of the missionary activity of the Home Mission Society among foreign language groups in America, some of the foreign language conferences of Baptist churches have had relationships with the convention. In 1956 the Norwegian Baptist Conference united with the American Baptist Convention. One other Baptist group has united with the American Baptist Convention: the Free Baptists, an Arminian group, which came into the convention in 1911. Their missionary and educational work was merged with similar work of American Baptists at that time.

In 1932 a group of churches withdrew to form the General Association of Regular Baptists. It now numbers 726 churches with 124,039 members. In 1947 a group of churches withdrew from the American Baptist Convention to form the Conservative Baptist Association. The group had formerly been organized as a Fundamentalist fellowship within the convention. This body reported 998 churches with 250,000 members in the *Yearbook of American Churches*, 1957. These two groups had failed to win majority support for a creedal test of membership in the convention, and so they separated to form their own organizations.

The American Baptist Convention voted in 1955 to join with several other Baptist groups in North America to emphasize evangelism in a "Baptist Jubilee Advance," beginning in 1959 and culminating in 1964 in a celebration of the 150th anniversary of the forming of the General Missionary Convention of the Baptist Denomination in the United States for Foreign Missions.

Co-operation with others.—American Baptists co-operate with other evangelical Christian bodies in various ways. They were among the founders of the Federal Council of Churches of Christ in America in 1908. The convention voted in 1939 to join the World Council of Churches which was then in process of formation. In 1948 the convention voted to approve formation of the National Council of Churches of Christ in the United States of America. This body was constituted in 1950. In the years following World War II, American Baptists co-operated with other Christians in a worldwide relief program.

Budget and organizational changes in progress in 1957.—The American Baptist Convention adopted for 1957 a budget (not including income from investments held by the various societies) of $8,764,527 for its world mission work. This budget provides:

For the foreign mission boards, $2,053,879 for use for missions in Burma, Assam, Bengal-Orissa, South India, Belgian Congo, Thailand, Hong Kong, Japan, the Philippines, and Europe. The boards have 415 missionaries in these areas. Their mission work included 2,872 schools and 81 hospitals and dispensaries. A major emphasis of the boards is on the training of indigenous leaders for the churches and institutions so that there is a high ratio of national workers and also baptized believers in the churches.

For the home mission boards, $1,050,126 for use in the United States, Alaska, Mexico, Nicaragua, El Salvador, Cuba, Haiti, and Puerto Rico. These boards have emphasized the training of Latin American leaders for churches on the mission fields, as well as the training of Negro, Indian, and foreign-language-speaking workers from their respective groups. The home mission boards have pioneered in a number of ministries, the latest of which is a program to combat juvenile delinquency.

For missionary work by Baptist state conventions and standard Baptist city societies, $2,554,865. Rural and city missions, evangelism, Christian teaching, and church extension are included in this work.

For the Board of Education and Publication, $902,527 for use in 75 student centers on college and university campuses; in aid to 56 Baptist-related schools, colleges, and seminaries; in evangelism work among boys and girls, recruitment and training for the ministry, lay leadership training; and in Christian teaching in home, church, and community.

For the Ministers and Missionaries Benefit Board, $348,649. Grants in aid and emergency assistance were being paid at the rate of $300,-

000 per year, while the pension fund had 3,462 dues-paying members, 85 per cent of those eligible. The board had assets of $55,109,063.

Other budget items include radio and television, world relief, the Council of Christian Social Progress, work with American Baptist men and women, co-operative work with other denominations, and promotion.

In 1955 the American Baptist Convention was in the process of changing its structure. In 1950 the general council and the convention chose the first full-time general secretary, Reuben E. Nelson. Since that time studies were made of the organizational structure with a view to increasing the efficiency of the work. The general director of the Council on Missionary Co-operation was made an associate secretary of the convention by action of the convention in annual session at Seattle, Wash., in 1956. Staff members of convention agencies were, at the same time, formed into a Staff Committee on Program Co-ordination under the chairmanship of the general secretary. Looking toward further structural changes, the convention chose a committee to study the present organization and determine what further changes should be recommended.

The American Baptist Convention, in 1955, had 1,513,697 members in 6,490 churches. Sunday schools enrolled 969,007 pupils. Baptisms in that year numbered 62,625. Contributions for all purposes were $66,294,515. Church property was valued at $356,026,570. In the same year the total number of ordained ministers was listed in the *Yearbook of American Churches* as 8,000, including 5,305 pastors having charges.   R. DEAN GOODWIN

AMERICAN BAPTIST FOREIGN MISSION SOCIETY. Grew out of the first national Baptist organization for support of overseas missions, the Triennial Convention, organized May 21, 1814, in Philadelphia, Pa., to provide support for missionaries Adoniram and Ann Hasseltine Judson (*q.v.*). Inspired by Luther Rice (*q.v.*) the organization's purpose was "diffusing the knowledge of the religion of Jesus Christ, by means of missions, throughout the world."

After separation of North and South in 1845, the convention was reorganized in the North as the American Baptist Missionary Union with headquarters in Boston, Mass. In 1910 it became the American Baptist Foreign Mission Society and a co-operating body of the Northern Baptist Convention. At the annual meeting of this Society and the Woman's American Baptist Foreign Society in Atlantic City, N. J., May 24, 1955, the administration of the two bodies was integrated, with the resulting organization called the American Baptist Foreign Mission Boards. The office of general secretary was created, and overseas public relations, missionary personnel, budget, and treasury departments were established.

MISSION FIELDS, 1954

Burma—established 1814.

India—Assam, Bengal-Orissa, South India, established 1836.

China—South China, established 1836; evacuated after communist occupation 1953. East China, established 1843; evacuated 1950. West China, established 1890; evacuated 1952.

Hong Kong—first work established 1843; current work, 1953.

Japan—established 1872.

Africa—Belgian Congo, transferred from Livingstone Inland Mission 1884.

Philippines—established 1900.

Thailand—established 1835 for Chinese and discontinued for work in China 1842; re-entered 1950 among Chinese and Karens.

Europe—co-operative relationship with autonomous Baptist organizations in France, Belgium, Denmark, Norway, Finland, and Germany; until 1949, also Poland and Czechoslovakia; previous relationship with Russia, Estonia, Latvia, and Lithuania. One representative of the society has headquarters in Zurich, Switzerland.   IRENE A. JONES

AMERICAN BAPTIST HOME MISSION SOCIETY. The agency through which Baptists in the Northern states of the United States carry on missionary work within their own territory and in certain other regions. The society was organized in New York City on Apr. 27, 1832, largely through the efforts of John Mason Peck (*q.v.*) and Jonathan Going. Peck, who had been one of the very few home missionaries appointed by the Baptist Triennial Convention, inspired the organization. Going promoted the idea among individuals and churches in the East and served for five years as the society's first corresponding secretary. Peck continued to serve in the West until his death in 1856. Although organized by Baptists in fellowship with the Triennial Convention, the society was not constituted as a denominational agency. Its cohesive force was the zeal of those committed to its purpose to win "North America for Christ." This creditable aim, to regard the whole continent as its mission field, brought many problems in later years, as it clashed with similar intentions of other missionary organizations, notably those of Southern Baptists.

DATA

	1934	1954
Financial assets	$10,122,411	$14,543,865
Annual budget	1,150,605	1,821,029
Missionaries	610	264
National workers	7,877	7,411
Society membership	1,475,540 *	1,512,265 **
Organized churches overseas	3,226	4,724
Church members overseas	352,413	521,404
Sunday schools	2,916	3,142
Sunday school enrolment	119,351	171,503
Baptisms	13,559	27,703

* Identical with membership of Northern Baptist Convention.
** Identical with membership of American Baptist Convention.

At first the society was supported by individuals and churches in both North and South. The slavery issue, as well as the complaint that Southern missions were being slighted by the society, led to the withdrawal of Southern supporters in 1845. The result was the founding of the Southern Baptist Convention and its Board of Domestic Missions.

The history of the society since 1845 is marked by two features: expansion and comity agreements. In 1832 there were 900 churches in the West; by 1896 there were 7,470. Membership rose from 32,000 to 581,000 during the same period. Work among national groups began with the Negro population and gradually expanded to include every major foreign language group in the United States. Missionary activities extended outside the borders of the United States to Mexico, Central America, the islands of the Caribbean, and Canada. Under the leadership of Secretary Henry L. Morehouse (1879–93, 1903–17), the society initiated a program for assisting churches in construction of edifices. This led eventually to the establishment of the Department of Architecture in 1920.

The rapidly expanding program of the society led naturally to a clash with the interests of other mission groups. Within the Northern Baptist fellowship, the work of the Publication Society was seen to parallel that of the Home Mission Society at many points. A series of conferences between the two societies, beginning in 1918, gradually produced an equitable solution: Supervision of all missionary activities was assumed by the Home Mission Society; expenses were shared between the two societies.

The missionary enterprises of the Home Mission Society clashed, also, with Baptist groups outside the Northern Baptist fellowship. In the case of Free Baptists, the problem was solved by union with that denomination in 1911. Similar proposals for union with Southern Baptists were consistently resisted by the latter. It was necessary, however, for the Home Mission Society to confer with the Home Mission Board of Southern Baptists from time to time as special problems arose in various localities. The Fortress Monroe Agreement of 1894 approved co-operative and combined efforts to assist Negro Baptists. Likewise, the Home Mission Society agreed to withdraw its work from New Mexico in 1912 and Oklahoma in 1914 to end competition with the Home Mission Board. This same disposition to reach comity agreements has been demonstrated in missionary activities outside the United States and even on an interdenominational level through co-operation with the Federal Council of Churches.

In 1955 the society had $25,492,712 in assets and an income for the fiscal year of $1,072,127, of which slightly over 50 per cent came from contributions. There were 950 missionaries, working on 423 fields. Baptisms were one for every 12 members in Latin America and one for every 25 members in the United States.

Specialized services included the juvenile protection program, which provided through junior citizens' camps for 350 delinquent children yearly and assisted churches in helping thousands of others. There was work with Spanish-speaking people in 18 states and pastor training provided through the Spanish American Seminary. The society's 11 educational centers for Negroes trained church leaders for Baptists of that race. The rural church center at the American Baptist Assembly at Green Lake, Wis., provided in-service training for rural ministers and their wives. Bacone College, Murrow Home for children, and missionaries in six states ministered to the Indians. A hospital ministry contributed to work in Alaska. In Central America and the West Indies, national pastors and missionaries served in 309 churches and 1,145 missions and outstations, which had 48,137 members in a Baptist constituency of 218,650. A recently established fund, called "Churches for New Frontiers," provided assistance for financing and planning church buildings. Sixty homes and hospitals, which not long before had become related to the home mission program, were serving 33,000 people from the American Baptist Convention constituency.

Undergirding the society's entire work, the Department of Evangelism, with a staff of four national leaders, seven area directors, and three regional missionaries, worked in co-operation with state conventions and 16 state directors.

Until 1955 the society, in co-operation with the Woman's American Baptist Home Mission Society, Baptist state conventions, city societies, and the Board of Education and Publication, composed the Associated Home Mission Agencies. Even before the various women's missionary societies were amalgamated in 1877 into Woman's American Baptist Home Mission Society, efforts were made to bring the women into an affiliation with the American Baptist Home Mission Society that would eliminate duplication and overlapping in home mission work among American Baptists. Official committees were at work from 1902 onward.

On May 19, 1955, integration was accomplished. This was not a merger; it was necessary for the two societies to maintain their legal identities for fiduciary relationships. Boards of managers, known as the American Baptist Home Mission Boards, are identical, with 52 voting members. Bylaws are practically identical. The integrated societies are closely unified with the American Baptist Convention but constitute a distinct entity, not a board or agency of the Convention. The annual meeting of the boards comes during the annual session of the American Baptist Convention. Other meetings may be called if necessary. The officers and board members of the societies are nominated by the committee on nominations of the American Baptist Convention and are elected by the societies. The membership of the societies is composed of all missionaries appointed by the societies, all accredited delegates to the annual meeting of the American Baptist Convention, and all annual members appointed by affiliated Baptist churches.

BIBLIOGRAPHY: R. A. Baker, *Relations Between Northern and Southern Baptists* (1948). W. W. Barnes, *The Southern Baptist Convention* (1954). W. Cathcart, ed., *The Baptist Encyclopedia*, I (1881). W. W. Sweet, *The Story of Religion in America* (1930). R. G. Torbet, *A History of the Baptists* (1950). H. C. Vedder, *A Short History of the Baptists* (1907). C. L. White, *A Century of Faith* (1932). V. WAYNE BARTON, MARGARET NOFFSINGER WENGER, and HERBERT C. JACKSON

AMERICAN BAPTIST MISSIONARY UNION. See AMERICAN BAPTIST FOREIGN MISSION SOCIETY.

AMERICAN BAPTIST PUBLICATION SOCIETY. Until 1944, when combined with another organization, the official publishing agency of Northern Baptists and the American Baptist Convention. The society was organized Feb. 25, 1824, as the Baptist General Tract Society, in the home of George Wood, Washington, D. C. It was chartered as an independent society and not as an agency of the General Missionary (Triennial) Convention. Noah Davis of Maryland and James Knowles of Washington, D. C., were instrumental in the organization. The first year receipts from contributions totaled $363.80 and 696,000 pages of tracts were issued. In 1826 the society moved to its permanent home in Philadelphia, Pa. At first publications were limited to tracts and Sunday school supplies. In 1840 the name of the society was changed to American Baptist Publication and Sunday School Society, anticipating a much broader scope of publication and education endeavor. In the year 1844 the first bound volumes were produced, with the issue of the writings of Andrew Fuller. Again the name of the society was changed, this time to American Baptist Publication Society. The broad purposes of the society were stated in its new constitution (1844): "to promote evangelical religion by means of the Bible, the printing press, colportage, and the Sunday school."

Colporteurs were first employed in 1840 and Sunday school missionaries in 1867. The latter concentrated their labor in the South and West. Periodical publications began in 1856, with the purchase of the *Young Reaper*, and expanded through the years to include scores of monthly and bimonthly issues. In 1862, colportage work came to be promoted by a subsidiary missionary department, having separate offices and accounts. Agents of this department carried society publications throughout home and foreign lands. Beginning in 1869, a growing number of branch offices were established in the principal cities of the United States. The profits of the society were regularly channeled through its missionary department.

So broad was the education and missionary work of the society that its program inevitably overlapped the program of other societies of the Northern Baptist fellowship. Efforts to correct such needless overlapping of work occupied Northern Baptists from 1918 to 1944. The problem of missions was solved when the publication society began in 1918 to surrender its mission work to the supervision of the Home Mission Society. An equitable plan was devised for the sharing of mission expenses whereby the publication society continued to channel much of its profits into mission work.

Prior to 1944, education work of Northern Baptists was promoted by both the publication society and the board of education. The former confined its work largely to the churches. The latter, established as a convention agency in 1912, promoted secondary and higher education as well as education on the church level. By official action of the Northern Baptist Convention in 1944, there was established the Board of Education and Publication combining work of the above groups under a single organization. Since Northern Baptists changed their name to American Baptists in 1950, this agency acquired the name of the Board of Education and Publication of the American Baptist Convention.

BIBLIOGRAPHY: *American Baptist Year-Book* (1920). W. Cathcart, ed., *The Baptist Encyclopedia*, II (1881). W. W. Sweet, *The Story of Religion in America* (1930). R. G. Torbet, *A History of the Baptists* (1950). H. C. Vedder, *A Short History of the Baptists* (1907). C. L. White, *A Century of Faith* (1932). "Your Board of Education and Publication" (1955).

V. WAYNE BARTON

AMERICAN BAPTIST REFLECTOR. Had a shorter history than *The Baptist*. O. C. Pope began the *Baptist Reflector* at Morristown, Tenn., in 1874. He sold it in 1878 to W. D. Mayfield, who moved it to Nashville. J. B. Chevis bought it in 1881. J. M. Robertson bought it and moved it to Chattanooga, where he combined it with *The American Baptist*, of that city. He also bought the *Baptist Sun*, of Rome, Ga., from G. A. Nunnally. Later, Robert J. Willingham, pastor of the First Baptist Church, Chattanooga, and A. W. McGaha were in possession of the paper until Edgar E. Folk bought it. He was its editor-owner until he combined it with *The Baptist* in Aug., 1889.

RICHARD N. OWEN

AMERICAN BAPTIST THEOLOGICAL SEMINARY. An institution of learning for the education and training of Negro ministers and religious workers, organized in 1924, jointly owned and controlled by the National Baptist Convention, Inc., and the Southern Baptist Convention, located at 1800 White's Creek Pike, Nashville, Tenn.

The first resolution toward the establishment of a Negro theological seminary was offered by Edgar Young Mullins (*q.v.*) at the Southern Baptist Convention, St. Louis, Mo., May 15, 1913. In the resolution the Convention pledged its sympathy and support to the National Baptist

Convention in this undertaking and authorized the appointment of a committee of nine to study the matter and bring back a report the following year. The committee was composed of Mullins, Orren Luico Hailey (*q.v.*), Arthur James Barton (*q.v.*), Benjamin Cox, William Elrie Atkinson (*q.v.*), James Marion Frost (*q.v.*), Benjamin Franklin Riley, George White McDaniel (*q.v.*), and Joseph Jefferson Bennett. The committee recommended that such a seminary be established, but that the institution be under the government and control of the National Baptist Convention.

Because of conditions resulting from World War I and a division in the National Baptist Convention, the founding and opening of the seminary was delayed until the year 1924. The National Baptist Convention was divided into two groups over the principle of denominational ownership and control of denominational institutions and agencies. The two groups were known as the Boyd group, rejecting this principle, and the National Baptist Convention, Inc., accepting it. Efforts were made to reconcile the two factions. Meetings were held in Alexandria, La., Little Rock, Ark., Galveston, Tex., and a final meeting in Nashville, Tenn., on Nov. 12, 1918; but they were without success. The Boyd faction purchased some property in East Nashville, Tenn., and chartered a National Baptist Theological Seminary, with a self-perpetuating board of trustees.

The other group, as it was recorded, "in the meanwhile . . . remained fixed in their purpose to cooperate with the Southern Baptist Convention in the building and promoting [of] the theological seminary which had been planned for since 1913."

In 1919 Hailey was elected as general secretary of the commission on the seminary.

Five principles of management were agreed upon by the joint commission of the two conventions:

First, there shall be two governing bodies, one to hold and control the property, the other to organize and conduct the affairs of the seminary.

Second, that the board holding the property shall consist of 12 members, 8 to be elected by the Southern Convention and 4 by the National Convention.

Third, that the number of the members of the board to direct the affairs of the seminary shall be determined by the National Convention, and shall be in proportion of two to one to be elected by the National and Southern Conventions respectively.

Fourth, each board shall elect its own officers. The president of the "governing body" shall be a member of the National Convention, U. S. A. and the secretary of that body shall be a member of the Southern Baptist Convention and a paid officer.

Fifth, the president of the seminary shall be a member of the National Baptist Convention, U. S. A.

The location of the proposed seminary was considered in the first meeting of the representatives of the two conventions, held at Nashville, Tenn., Sept. 18, 1913. The following quotation is from the first report of the committee:

Resolved that the question of the location of the seminary be for the present deferred, but that we express the conviction that it should be located in one of the following cities: Memphis, Tenn., Nashville, Tenn., Birmingham, Ala., Atlanta, Ga., or Louisville, Ky., provided proper inducements are offered for its location.

Resolved, further, that the matter of the location be brought to the notice of the proper authorities in these cities by the Cor. Sec. of the Educational Board of the National Baptist Convention, with a view to ascertaining what inducements, financial and otherwise, they may be ready to offer.

Resolved, further, that the Seminary be located where it will do the greatest good to the greatest number.

There were present at this meeting: Mullins, chairman, Riley, Hailey, Frost, and Cox, representing the Southern Baptist Convention; from the committee of the National Baptist Convention, E. C. Morris, chairman, T. J. Searcy, Sutton E. Griggs, William T. Amiger, J. H. Henderson, Josiah William Bailey (*q.v.*), and J. D. Crenshaw.

From Memphis came a letter dated Dec. 1, 1914, stating: "We have not been able to clear fifteen acres of ground as a site nor raise Fifteen Thousand Dollars in cash." This letter was signed by H. C. Shepherd, president, and T. O. Fuller, secretary, of the local committee. From Nashville a letter was received stating: "I have been informed that Memphis was given until December 16th to prepare a gilt-edge negotiable paper as a guarantee of the fulfilment of her proposition. Nashville is very much interested in this matter and I am advised to write and ask you to give us the true status of the matter as it now stands." This letter was signed by Arthur Melvin Townsend, president of Roger Williams University, and was dated Jan. 2, 1915.

The seminary was located at Nashville, Tenn., on land adjacent to Roger Williams University. The seminary was opened on Oct. 1, 1924. The enrolment consisted of 28 students for the ministry and two women studying missions. The first faculty consisted of Amiger, dean and acting president, J. H. Garnett, and Hailey. Griggs was elected the first president.

The buildings were provided by the Southern Baptist Convention according to agreement, and the furnishings were provided by the National Baptist Convention. The buildings are Griggs Hall Dormitory, with a capacity of 90 students, which houses the dining room, kitchen, and cafeteria; the J. B. Lawrence Administration Building, which provides offices for the faculty and staff, classrooms, and a temporary chapel; the T. L. Holcomb Library, with a capacity of 50,000 volumes and reading rooms to provide for an enrolment of 300 students; a central heating plant; eight duplex apartments and three dwellings, which provide housing for students and faculty.

There were 74 students enrolled in 1956. The highest enrolment recorded was 118 in 1946–47.

The school offers a B.D. degree for college graduates doing three years' work, a B.Th.

degree for high school graduates doing four years' work, and a B.R.E. degree for high school graduates doing four years' work. A certificate in Christian training is given for two years' work to students below the high school level. A diploma in theology and a certificate in Christian training are offered in extension training units and correspondence courses.

Publications include *The Seminarian,* published by the seminary. *The Helping Hand* and *The Call,* both now discontinued, were published by the Southern Baptist Commission on the Seminary.

Each convention is represented by a commission, which is the fiscal agency of the convention. The National Baptist Commission is composed of six members appointed by that convention. The Southern Baptist Commission is composed of 20 members—12 trustees and 8 members of the Holding Board—all elected by the Convention.

The functions of the Southern Baptist Commission are summarized by the actions of the Convention up to 1928, as follows:

The Commission is authorized and instructed by the Convention to receive and distribute such funds as the Southern Baptist Convention provides for the Seminary. It is authorized by the Convention to receive and handle all monies and valuables contributed for the current support, the permanent endowment, or for any other interest of the Seminary; and is also authorized to invest any funds that it may have in hand for the benefit of the Seminary, as it may think proper, and to apply the proceeds of all such funds for the best interests of the Seminary, according to its best judgment.

The commission also serves as the promotional agency for the seminary among Southern Baptists.

The years 1931–33 were the most critical in the history of the seminary. Roger Williams College had closed in 1927 to merge with Howe Institute, Memphis, Tenn. The trustees of the seminary proposed to sell the property, and the school rented quarters from Meharry Medical College, paying $50 per month rent. The school found itself in serious financial difficulties, and the board of directors voted not to open in the fall unless financial relief was found. Trevecca College, owned and operated by the Nazarenes, occupied the former seminary property during 1931–33 and proposed to buy it, but did not. The seminary returned to its original site in July, 1933. Its current obligations were met, and, through the heroic work of Garnett and James Clarence Miles (professors, 1931–56), the school was put back on its feet.

The presidents of the seminary and their terms of office are as follows: Griggs, 1925–26; Amiger, 1927–29; Garnett, 1930–32, dean and acting president; Roy A. Mayfield, 1932–34; James M. Nabritt, 1936–44; Ralph Waldo Riley, 1944–56; Victor Thomas Glass, 1956–   , acting president.

The general secretaries of the commission on the seminary and their terms of office are as follows: Hailey, 1919–34; Eugene Perry Alldredge (*q.v.*), 1934–49; Leland Stanford Sedberry, 1949–   .

During the first 20 years of the existence of the seminary, Southern Baptists gave an average of $10,000 per year to its support. Since 1944 gifts have increased and for both capital needs and current operations have averaged $100,000 per year. During the past 19 years, National Baptists have given an average of $12,718.31 per year to the support of the seminary. Because the National Baptist Convention has no systematic plan of raising funds, the institutions and agencies of the convention must depend largely on financial appeals for support.

The assets of the seminary as of Dec. 31, 1955, were listed as follows: total permanent fund assets, $15,425.00; total fixed assets, $679,350.61; total current assets, $50,763.15; total assets, $745,539.15.   L. S. SEDBERRY

AMERICAN BIBLE SOCIETY. A worldwide missionary organization, founded in 1816, which aids in Bible translation, publishes Scriptures without note or comment, and distributes without profit. As "Scripture specialist" for churches and mission agencies, it provides editions for varied needs, such as Gospels for widespread distribution; two-language editions for people learning new languages; large-type volumes for new literates and persons with poor vision. For the blind it provides raised-letter Scriptures and "talking book" records. It seeks to reach the overlooked, in prisons, orphans' homes, hospitals, migrant camps, remote rural areas, etc. It co-operates with Bible societies of other nations in meeting worldwide needs.

Distribution is normally by sale because people appreciate the Book more when they make a personal investment. In many fields Scriptures are priced below cost to place them within reach of the people. In cases of special need, they are given without charge. In 1955 the society distributed 908,000 Bibles, 1,612,739 Testaments, and 12,397,614 portions, making a total of 14,918,353 volumes in some 200 languages. Included were 1,397,101 volumes donated to chaplains for distribution to United States Armed Forces.

The work is supported by gifts from churches and individuals. Gifts in 1955 amounted to $2,770,490.04. Because Southern Baptists consider its work essential to their own world missions program, state conventions and the Southern Baptist Convention have adopted resolutions requesting churches to contribute to the society. In 1955 Southern Baptist gifts of $115,631 ranked second among gifts from all denominations, totaling $804,998.

With headquarters in New York, the society has offices in 16 cities of the United States, foreign agencies in 16 countries, and sub-agencies throughout the world. The work is directed by a board of managers and an advisory council representing over 50 denominations, which regularly includes Southern Baptists. The society publishes an annual report; its official magazine is the *Bible Society Record*.

THOMAS T. HOLLOWAY

AMERICAN INDIAN MISSION ASSOCIATION. Founded on Oct. 27, 1842, in Cincinnati, Ohio. The meeting had been called as an outgrowth of the anniversary of the Western Baptist Publication and Sunday School Society, observed in June at Louisville. Isaac McCoy (*q.v.*) led in the establishment of the new association for "promotion of the spiritual and temporal interests of the Aborigines," and served as its first corresponding secretary till his death in 1846. In 1844 the association established "fraternal correspondence" with the Triennial Convention and took over its western Indian mission stations. Extensive evangelism was carried on, but increasing financial difficulty caused the transfer of all work in 1855 to the Board of Domestic Missions of the Southern Baptist Convention.

WILLIAM N. MCELRATH

AMERICAN SUNDAY SCHOOL UNION. An agency located at Philadelphia, Pa., which began as the Sunday School and Adult Union in May, 1817, when there were not more than 100 Sunday schools in the United States. By 1824, when it became the American Sunday School Union, it had become almost national in scope, and had organized 723 schools that averaged 10 teachers and 70 pupils to the school. It was composed of individuals from evangelical denominations who believed in establishing and developing Sunday schools throughout the country, made gifts for its work, and applied for membership. It had no direct or indirect denominational relationships, but for its officers and board of managers, who had to be laymen, it chose men who belonged to churches of different denominations, and judiciously distributed them among its various committees. Its literature of all kinds was to be evangelical, but not in any way sectarian. For example, no book could be published unless every member of the publication committee gave his approval. From the beginning it aggressively and enthusiastically promoted the establishment of Sunday schools in every part of the country. Its schools were not church schools, and they used the union's literature. When churches developed in a community and became able to have their own schools, the union's school either ministered to those who did not attend a church school or ceased to operate.

The union had three basic purposes: (1) to publish suitable Sunday school literature; (2) to select scriptural passages and prepare lesson materials; and (3) to organize and maintain schools in needy places.

By 1832 the union's 78 missionaries had organized 2,867 Sunday schools in rude huts, log cabins, and sod houses. At the Richmond, Va., session of the Baptist Triennial Convention in 1835, it was reported that the union had established more than 16,000 schools with an average attendance of about 125,000 teachers and nearly 1,000,000 pupils.

In 1832 the union launched its Mississippi Valley enterprise to establish in two years throughout the Mississippi Valley (nine states, parts of Pennsylvania and Virginia, and the Northwestern Territory) a Sunday school in every destitute place where it was practicable to do so. It began this vast program with less than a thousand dollars, but the people gave generously of their money and enabled it within four years to organize nearly 10,000 schools in the valley and the South.

The six South Atlantic states (Virginia to Alabama) and Florida Territory, in 1833, asked for a campaign similar to that in the valley. The union responded with a five-year program to plant and sustain schools in every neighborhood where practicable and if wanted. This area of more than 300,000 square miles, with a population of about 4,000,000, of whom about 500,000 were white children, had only 213 known schools in 1826. In the valley states there were six known schools in Kentucky, three each in Mississippi and Tennessee, and one in Louisiana. The results of the Southern campaign were substantial, but not as phenomenal as those in the Mississippi Valley.

Henry Clay Trumbull said that in 1832 the union was the common pivot of nearly all organized Sunday school work in the country. James Barnett Taylor (*q.v.*) said at the Southern Baptist Convention, Richmond (1846), "Nearly all Sunday schools in Virginia were brought into existence mainly through the efforts of this institution." This was true, no doubt, in all the Southern states.

The union limited its activities mostly to sparsely and newly settled communities and unchurched areas. It did much of its work before the various denominations were able to do such work. As they became able, and as churches were established, the destitute places in which the union worked became more circumscribed. However, between 1890 and 1915 it found places to organize 43,500 schools, and reorganize or revive 9,000 other schools. During its first 86 years (1824–1900) it established 121,038 schools.

The work of the Sunday School Union constantly broadened. In 1826 it began its first system of uniform lessons; and in 1827 it instituted its long and successful program of teacher training, for which it issued lesson helps, manuals, and guides. Besides its lessons for pupils and guidance materials for teachers, it also began and continued the publication of many kinds of books that belonged to its larger field of ministry. It pioneered in the creation of juvenile literature and the establishment of Sunday school libraries. In 1846 it began production of a library of 100 bound volumes to sell for $10, but made available to new schools for $5. It led in the establishment of national Sunday school conventions, with delegates from 15 of the 24 states present at the first convention at Philadelphia in 1832. It established a newspaper-size weekly in Jan., 1831, *The Sunday-School Journal,* the first of its kind in the world. The paper became a semiweekly in 1843, and was succeeded by *The Sunday-School Times* in 1859. This paper was sold to private parties in 1861 because of financial difficulties. The union then began (Mar., 1861) a monthly, *The Sunday-School World,* 8 x 10 inches in size, which could be bound year by year.

The union gave up its own uniform lesson plan to co-operate in the establishment of the Uniform Lesson System in 1872, and issued the first lesson papers for the new lessons. It prepared the way for the organization of the International Sunday School Association. It was a pioneer in providing help for Sunday school and church building plans. It created a Sunday school consciousness among the people and thereby made it possible for the early denominational Sunday school organizations to do more and better work.

The union's policy was to keep out of the many and often bitter doctrinal controversies that prevailed throughout the country. Because ministers generally led these controversies, its constitution forbade their serving as officers or being on the 36-man board of managers. However, many of the field men and missionaries were ministers.

The union necessarily kept out of its literature the presentation of any biblical doctrine from a denominational viewpoint. This inevitably led the denominations, in time, to make their schools church schools, and get them to use the lesson materials they had prepared in keeping with their own doctrinal interpretations. A certain amount of friction between the union and the several denominations was inevitable, but the union's wise policies and judicious management through the years kept it within bounds. As sparsely settled areas and destitute communities throughout the country decreased, and the denominations became strong, the union's sphere of labor became steadily more restricted, but it continued to work in its own chosen field, and was still active and helpful in the 133rd year of its ministries (1956).

BIBLIOGRAPHY: M. C. Brown, *Sunday-School Movements in America* (1917). E. W. Rice, *The Sunday-School Movement and the American Sunday-School Union (1780–1927)* (1917, revised 1927).

HOMER L. GRICE

AMHERST ACADEMY. A school at North Catawba, N. C., under Baptist control in the 1880's and 1890's, under R. L. Moore (*q.v.*). It was endorsed by Catawba River and Caldwell associations.   D. L. SMILEY

AMITE FEMALE SEMINARY. Established in 1853 at Liberty, Miss., and tendered to the Mississippi Baptist Association in 1854. The school, chartered in 1856, flourished under its principal M. S. Shirk until Union troops destroyed it during the Civil War.   J. L. BOYD

AMMON, THOMAS (b. Louisa County, Va., 1740's [?]; d. Bourbon County, Ky., 1811). Preacher, Revolutionary patriot. Wicked in his youth, he had a remarkable conversion experience and became a member of the Crooked Run Baptist Church in Culpeper County, Va. Later, he was "raised up for the ministry" in that church. For preaching without permission from the state, he was imprisoned in Culpeper prison, about 1774. "It is a tradition in the family that he preached through the window of the prison to crowds, and that his voice was so strong that he could be heard for a mile in the open air, either preaching or singing."

On Sept. 8, 1767, Ammon married Elizabeth Anderson. He left Virginia and went to Kentucky around 1789. He was the first and only pastor of Hickman's Creek Separate Baptist Church in Fayette County, Ky., organized about 1790. In the minutes of Elkhorn Association, 1803, 1805–08, he is listed as an ordained minister in Brush (or Brushy) Fork Church and a messenger to the association.   LEO T. CRISMON

AMUSEMENTS AND RECREATION, SOUTHERN BAPTIST ACTIONS CONCERNING. Occasionally the Convention has approved resolutions by its Social Service or Christian Life Commission and by individuals, condemning such varied activities as "beauty contests" and "bathing revues," which were considered "evil and evil only"; "card-playing . . . and late joy-riding"; "flippant jazz entertainment"; and "all cheap vaudeville programs."

The dance hall has been condemned as "lascivious and deadly"; and the dance, as fleshly and sinful, a corrupt, corrupting, and gross evil, which, accompanied by immodest dress, close physical contact of the sexes, and lack of restraint, "undermines the morals of our young people." Pastors and parents should seek to check and abolish its "growing menace." The marathon dance was seen as merely the "nauseating excess to which this destroyer of" modesty and morals had gone.

While the Convention has recognized that the motion picture is attended by "the large majority of the total population," that it has tremendous power and "should be harnessed for harmless amusement, for education and for the Kingdom of God," nevertheless it has been considered "for the most part vicious and corrupting," a creator of depraved tastes, and a contributor to "the disintegration of the moral fibre of our people." It has done the latter by its display of indecency and lust, along with the "eternal triangle," and by depicting scenes of "gambling, drinking, organized vice, divorce and general immorality," the last of which it tends to glorify and glamorize.

The Convention has attempted at times to take more positive action with regard to the motion picture problem. Church members and parents have been advised to discriminate in the choice of pictures. The Convention once recommended that motion pictures should be reformed, controlled by the state, or abolished like the liquor traffic. The Convention has urged the motion picture industry to clean up, has condemned "blind selling" and "block booking," and has approved the work of the Legion of Decency, sponsored by Roman Catholics, and the Protestant Film Association.

T. B. MASTON

ANABAPTISTS. A polemical term applied to certain evangelical groups of the 16th century by their enemies. It derives from the Latin form of the Greek original, *anabaptismos* (to rebaptize; German noun, Wiedertäufer), and was used to make those to whom it was applied liable to the ancient penalties against the Donatists, death penalties reaffirmed by the Imperial Edicts of Charles V (Speyer, 1528, 1529). There was, however, little relation between the two—Anabaptists and Donatists, because the Anabaptists rebaptized as a recognition of the personal faith of the one being baptized, while the Donatists rebaptized because they doubted the efficacy of baptism administered by priests not of their persuasion. Anabaptists themselves protested against the term, preferring to be called Christians or brethren, and asserting that "the Scripture teaches nothing of infant baptism; and they who will be baptized according to God's word must first be believers." Anabaptists, in fact, believed in a gathered church, united in a covenant and disciplined according to the plain teaching of the New Testament. Believers' baptism was, in a period dominated by the post-Constantinian territorial establishments, an inevitable consequence of the Free Church view and was instituted near Zurich on Jan. 21, 1525.

As a polemical term, Anabaptist was applied with deliberate lack of precision to all who attacked the evils of state-church systems, Roman Catholic and Protestant. (The most noted opposition writers were Luther, Justus Menius, Zwingli, Heinrich Bullinger.) Anabaptists have been called "the Bolsheviki of the sixteenth century." The *Täuferakten,* a series of volumes now being published by the *Verein für Reformationsgeschichte* (with assistance from the American Mennonites), clearly indicate, however, that the theologians and lawyers of the territorial churches were aware of differences between the various protesting groups. Unfortunately, even to this day many reputable historians have depended upon the polemical propaganda against the Anabaptists, rather than upon the primary sources of the movement itself, in categorizing Anabaptists as *Schwärmer* (enthusiasts) and revolutionaries. In the 16th century defenders of coercive establishments (Roman Catholic, Lutheran, Calvinist) regarded religious voluntaryism as subversive doctrine and perverse practice: An intact Christendom, with confessional conformity enforced by law and sealed in the sufferings of exiles and the blood of martyrs, was assumed to be worth the price. Today, with another and more sensitive view of religious obligation and liberty coming into its own, Anabaptists are beginning to be accorded more respectful treatment. If Anabaptists, anti-Trinitarians, individual spiritualizers, and prophets properly are lumped together at all, it is under such a neutral term as "the left wing of the Reformation."

In former times, when church historians still depended upon secondary and polemical sources, it was customary to trace the origins of protest to the Zwickau prophets (Storch, Stübner, Zwilling), Karlstadt, and Thomas Müntzer. The essential characteristics of the protest were said to be apocalypticism, special revelations, and political revolution. The final results were seen in the Peasant Revolt (1525–26) and the Davidic Kingdom at Münster in Westphalia (1534–35), with the Dutch *Doopsgezinde* a tired, postrevolutionary fragment gathered together by Menno Simons. This view of the Anabaptists made it possible for later champions of the established order such as Karl Holl to continue to condemn all voluntaryism and Free Church views:

Müntzer represented already the thoughts which sound so modern: religious reform is impossible without a simultaneous social reform.... The thought of establishing the Kingdom of God on earth and carrying out in connection with it a comprehensive political and social reform appeared anew in the English revolution.... At this point our German conception is sharply different from that of the sect-influenced English-American. Holding together in the State, furthering and deepening the commonweal, is a value to us which stands higher than the freedom of movement of the individual.

In fact, however, Anabaptists proper repudiated chiliasm, were pessimistic about the world and its direction, and were almost exclusively concerned with the internal order and life of the true church *(die rechte Kirche).*

Anabaptism had its beginnings in the circle which gathered about Ulrich Zwingli, Zürich preacher and reformer. The key figure was Conrad Grebel (c. 1498–1526); associates were Felix Manz, Wilhelm Reublin, Georg Blaurock. (Balthasar Hübmaier, whom Henry C. Vedder chose for Putnam's *Heroes of the Reformation* series, is no longer regarded as a key figure in the movement itself, although his writings were important and his martyrdom impressive.) It slowly became clear, in the process of internal discussions and finally public debates, that Zwingli had decided to effect a conservative reformation of the church according to the decisions of the Town Council. At this point certain of his most vigorous supporters, demanding a restitution of New Testament teaching and order, pulled away to become what Walter Rauschenbusch later called "the root and branch party of the Reformation." (For the Anabaptists the key word is *restitutio* rather than *reformatio.*) Zwingli's view was that what was plainly antiscriptural should be eliminated from parish life and worship, but on other points his attitude was permissive. The Swiss

Anabaptists

Brethren, as they are now called, were convinced that the Bible gave a clear picture of what the Lord expected of his disciples.

The Anabaptists were savagely persecuted, and during the first decade some thousands died by burning, drowning, or beheading. Their property was subject to confiscation, and many wandered homeless and unemployed. Their books and tracts were destroyed, and it has only recently become possible to reconstruct the main outlines of their history and testimony. In spite of barbarously severe measures employed by both Roman Catholic and Protestant territorial churches, congregations were gathered and disciplined. From 1526 until the Jesuit Counter-Reformation, Bohemia and Moravia provided centers of refuge, and there the Christian communist colonies of the Hutterite Brethren took shape under Jakob Huter (?–1536), Peter Riedemann (c. 1490–1556), Peter Walpot (c. 1520–78). These colonies sent missioners throughout the known world, and at a time when the established churches were content to accept the principle of the Peace of Augsburg (1555) —*cuius regio eius religio*— (the religion of a ruler is the religion of his country) —were unique for implementing the mandate of the Great Commission (Matt. 28:16–20; Mark 16:15).

Protestantism apparently came first to the Lowlands as a type of Anabaptism, but in a form inclined toward apocalypticism, prophetism, and a Docetic teaching on the natures of Jesus Christ. Melchior Hofmann (c. 1495–1543) was a leading figure. After the tragic affair at Münster, however, in which thousands from the Lowlands were involved, Menno Simons (1492?–1561) came to the fore and gathered a people on main-line Anabaptist principles. His position on violence and special revelations was clear from the start. In his first book to John à Lasco (1544) he wrote:

> ... as before God who knows our hearts, we are clear of all their abominable doctrine, uproar, mutiny, bloodshed, plurality of wives and the like abominations. Yea we hate and from all our heart oppose them as acknowledged heresies, as snares to the conscience and deceit, as deception of souls and pestilential doctrine. ...

In the words of Cornelius Krahn,

> As Luther defined his position against the "enthusiasts" (*Schwärmer*), so Menno took his stand against a like aspect of "Anabaptism" (*Täufertum*). Indeed his very first writing waged this battle, in which he placed himself directly against the kingdom of Münster—which was a product of the allegorizing of Scripture and chiliastic prophetism. He comes forward boldly not for truth through a "revelation or heavenly inspiration" but rather through the "expressed, written word of the Lord." He wants to know nothing of "his own opinions, dreams, and visions." He angrily cried out in a defensive writing that he was neither an Elias nor an Enoch nor a "third David" nor yet a seer or prophet.

Although the Anabaptists in the Lowlands were first called Menist in an Act of 1544 aimed at the more radical groups of Batenburgers, the Dutch wing came to be known generally as Mennonites—although they themselves continued to use the term *Doopsgezinde* (*Taufgesinnten*). In the 17th century, as Holland became a center of toleration, the movement became an accepted part of the national culture. The American Mennonites are actually descended in the main from Swiss and South German families.

The leading figure of the South German Brethren was Pilgram Marpeck (?–1556), an engineer and lay leader whose Bible-centered leadership and writings played an important part in shaping the Anabaptist testimony. Only two copies of his *Vermahnung*, three copies of his *Verantwortung*, and two copies of the *Testamentserleütterung* are left, and the recent rediscovery of his role in the movement is revealing proof of the suppression endured in his generation and after. Of special significance was his work in holding off the spiritualizing influences of individual seers who agreed with the Anabaptists in criticizing the "fallen" post-Constantinian church but repudiated the practice of disciplined Christian community. Just as the integrity of Anabaptist testimony was threatened by the revolutionaries, so was it jeopardized from within by the men of the Inward Word (such as Johannes Bünderlin, Sebastian Franck, Caspar Schwenckfeld). Marpeck repudiated the mystical and individualistic note and succeeded in holding the Anabaptists proper fast to the Bible.

In all wings of the movement, certain main teachings stood out. The "fallen" church was marred by union of church and state power, a monopoly of church government by theologians and jurists (professionals), an excessively proud hierarchy, a decline in congregational life and lay initiative, lack of missionary passion and activity, accommodation to the world and the use of violence, a magical teaching on the sacraments, baptized unbelief, and promiscuity of church "membership." Against the territorial pattern of culture-religion (whether Roman Catholic or Protestant), they proclaimed a free church governed by the Holy Spirit and ruled by Jesus Christ, the head of the church. Against conformity enforced by the sword, they asserted, not the right of the individual to believe as he pleased, but the duty of every believer to participate in the attainment of a doctrinal and ethical consensus as to the meaning of discipleship. Reading and expounding the Bible, they concluded that true discipleship involved several points:

Believers' baptism.—The first of the Seven Schleitheim Articles (1527) denounced promiscuous baptism of all children in a given territory and affirmed the acceptance of baptism as a conscious decision in which the believer participates in the new birth in Christ Jesus. By so doing he submits to the discipline of the Christian covenant, coming under the Ban.

Spiritual government.—Separation from evil and participation in congregational discipline were necessary consequences of Christian decision. The individual was in no sense left alone nor regarded as sufficient to himself.

After the people have received the Word of God and through water baptism in the presence of the church have put themselves under obligation to God to live according to the Word, and if they are ready to walk in newness of life and henceforth not to let sin reign in the mortal body, they still have need of medicine, because men are by nature children of wrath, evil and incapable, whereby the foul and stinking flesh together with the poisoned members may be somehow cut off, in order that the whole body may not be dishonored and corrupted.

The ban was only the outer limit of control; within the congregational life a whole structure of admonition, exhortation, and fraternal care made the Christian testimony a collective manifestation.

Community.—The logic of Christian sharing led the Hutterites to a communism of consumption modeled on the Acts of the Apostles. The other wings of the movement, however, limited the control to a strenuous practice of refugee relief, mutual aid, fraternal assistance among the brethren.

Item: our Christian faith says, a holy Christian church and a communion (*Gemeinschaft*) of saints; whoever now recognizes the communion (*Gemeinschaft*) of saints with the mouth but does not maintain Community (*Gemeinschaft*), he is false.

The Lord's Supper.—The third of the Seven Articles (1527) and second of the Five Articles (1547) repudiated a magical view of the Mass, and the Supper was practiced as a symbol of fellowship existent in the body of Christ (the church). In this understanding of the supper, the Anabaptists were in the line of the Brethren of the Common Life and the Swiss Reformation. The faithful were not adoring spectators at a sacrifice but themselves partook of the commitment to be the living temple and be broken in suffering and sacrifice like the Lord himself.

Apostolic nonresistance.—Anabaptists were not "pacifists" in the modern sense but rather New Testament nonresistants. They were obedient to government and prayed for civil rulers but refused to take the oath required of all vassals and to serve as magistrates. This reserve toward civil government was in part due to the common practice of compulsion in religious matters, to the use of violence and revolution, and to their own sense of destiny as the church of the martyrs. The Bible, which tells of the Good Shepherd, frequently calls his flock "the sheep."

By sheep Christians alone were meant. A sheep is a meek, weaponless, submissive beast, that has no other defence for itself than to run as long as it can and may. And it resembles the governance of the sword not at all, as little as a sheep resembles a wolf or lion.

The most direct descendants of the Anabaptists, the Mennonites and Hutterites of North America, still maintain the peace testimony, not in a utopian and modern form, but as a mark of what they believe Christ expects of his disciples. This position, however, is now much studied and debated; for it is clear that a representative government, where each participates to some degree in the work of the magistrate (*Obrigkeit*), is far different from the tyranny of despotic or totalitarian regimes.

The relations between the Anabaptists and the British General Baptists have only recently been established. The significance of the classical testimony of the free church pioneers for the present day is just beginning to be appreciated. Theological seminaries and graduate schools, particularly in America, where the Anabaptist pattern of church-state relation is now accepted as normative, have just within the decade begun to study the Anabaptist movement for light on present theological and socio-ethical situations. There is evidence of the coming of a general renaissance of Anabaptist studies and a more articulate appreciation of the life, martyrdoms, and testimonies of them as the forerunners of the free church way.

See also MENNONITES.

BIBLIOGRAPHY: H. Barge, *Andreas Bodenstein von Karlstadt* (1905). H. S. Bender, *Conrad Grebel* (c. *1498–1526*) (1950); *The Mennonite Encyclopedia* (1955). H. Böhmer, *Studien zu Thomas Müntzer* (1922). G. Bossert, ed., *Quellen zur Geschichte der Wiedertäufer: Herzogtum Württemberg* (1930). A. Cornelius, *Geschichte des Münsterischen Aufruhrs* (1855). H. E. Dosker, *The Dutch Anabaptists* (1921). R. Friedmann, "Recent Interpretations of Anabaptism," *Church History*, XXIV (1955). F. Heyer, *Der Kirchenbegriff der Schwärmer* (1939). K. Holl, "Luther und die Schwärmer," *Gesammelte Aufsätze zur Kirchengeschichte*, I (1932). J. Horsch, *The Hutterian Brethren* (1931); "Menno Simons' Attitude toward the Anabaptists of Münster," *The Mennonite Quarterly Review* (1936); *Mennonites in Europe* (1942). C. Krahn, *Menno Simons* (1936). F. H. Littell, *The Anabaptist View of the Church* (1952). A. Lohmann, *Zur Geistigen Entwicklung Thomas Müntzers* (1931). L. Müller, ed., *Glaubenszeugnisse oberdeutscher Taufgesinnten* (1938). N. Müller, *Die Wittenberger Bewegung, 1521 und 1522* (1911). W. Rauschenbusch, "The Zürich Anabaptists and Thomas Müntzer," *The American Journal of Theology*, IX (1905). P. Ridemann, *Account of Our Religion, Doctrine and Faith* (1950). R. J. Smithson, *The Anabaptists* (1935). T. J. van Braght, *A Martyrology of the Churches of Christ commonly called Baptist* (1850–53). H. C. Vedder, *Balthasar Hübmaier: The Leader of the Anabaptists* (1905). F. O. zur Linden, *Melchior Hofmann, ein Prophet der Wiedertäufer* (1885). FRANKLIN HAMLIN LITTELL

ANALYTICAL REPOSITORY, THE. The first Baptist newspaper in Georgia and one of the first in the United States. Henry H. Holcombe, pastor of Savannah's First Baptist Church, published the bimonthly paper in Savannah, Ga., from May–June, 1802, to Mar.–Apr., 1803, when he suspended the publication for lack of popular support. JOHN J. HURT, JR.

ANDERSON, JAMES HUGHES (b. Point Pleasant, Ky., Nov. 6, 1862; d. Knoxville, Tenn.,

Anderson College

May 22, 1949). Son of Samuel W. and Martha Bentley Anderson, was a successful merchant and businessman in Knoxville, Tenn., for many years. He was one of the founders of the Miller Department Store, Inc., in Knoxville. His education was in public schools. He was an outstanding businessman and Christian layman, for many years a deacon and a Sunday school teacher in the First Baptist Church of Knoxville. He put great emphasis upon stewardship, and beginning with the tithe, he moved on to give nearly all his income through his church, with the exception of modest living expenses. For some years his weekly check through the church was $1,000. Over a period of years, he gave more than a million dollars, largely designated for missions. He made a lasting contribution toward the development of the Cooperative Program of Southern Baptists. He was eager to witness for Christ and demonstrated unfailing loyalty to his pastor and to his church.

His business ability made him a valuable leader of his denomination. He was a member of the Foreign Mission Board of the Southern Baptist Convention, a member of the Executive Committee of the Southern Baptist Convention, vice-president of the Southern Baptist Convention, and chairman of the Layman's Missionary Movement of the Southern Baptist Convention, now known as the Brotherhood. He also served as chairman of the board of trustees of the Southern Baptist Theological Seminary of Louisville, Ky., and as a member of the executive board of the Tennessee Baptist Convention. He served as a trustee of Carson-Newman College, Jefferson City, Tenn., and as president of the Tennessee Baptist Convention.

HAROLD STEPHENS

ANDERSON COLLEGE. Chartered Feb. 14, 1911, at Anderson, S. C., the college began as a result of community interest in the education of women under Christian auspices. An earlier expression of this interest in 1848 had produced Johnson Female Seminary, named for its first president, William Bullein Johnson (q.v.), whose leadership in the education of women left a deep impression on the community, but the college closed in 1863 due to the Civil War.

In 1910, under the leadership of the Anderson Chamber of Commerce, a group of citizens raised $100,000 in pledges and secured the gift of a site for a new college for women. Convinced that it should be affiliated with a religious denomination, and in view of the strength of Baptists, the leaders offered the money and site to the South Carolina Baptist state convention, meeting in Laurens in Nov., 1910. The convention formally accepted the offer and appointed 15 trustees to possess the property and carry out the project "for the benefit of the Baptists of South Carolina." H. H. Watkins, who had presented the Anderson memorial, became president of the board of trustees.

Anderson College opened Sept. 18, 1912, with an enrolment of 75 students and a faculty and staff of 15, under John A. Chambliss, president, and John K. Breeden, dean of the faculty. Primarily a liberal arts college for women, the college offered special courses in music, art, speech, and domestic science. At the beginning of the presidency of John Ellington White (q.v.) in 1916 additions were made to the dormitories, and another building was constructed to provide for an enlarged student body which reached 291. Financial support for operating the college was derived almost wholly from student fees, while money for buildings and equipment was made possible through gifts from the South Carolina Baptist convention and individual donors.

Following White's resignation in late 1927, Annie Dove Denmark, dean of women, became the fifth president. Early in her administration the college became a junior college and began its new career in the fall of 1930. Financial difficulties, along with an increasing need for a junior college in the state, led to the change. The music department continued intact under Grace Louise Cronkhite; a high school department was added; and men were admitted the next year as day students. Miss Denmark served as president until her retirement in May, 1953. Near the end of her administration the college was included in a 10-year program of the state convention which was to provide nearly $1,000,000 for capital needs. At the same time, the Baptist contribution for operation was stabilized at a higher level.

In June, 1953, Elmer Francis Haight, formerly professor of religion and chaplain at Furman University, became sixth president of the college. During the first two years of his administration, an almost complete change of faculty and staff personnel occurred, and thorough renovation of buildings, the addition of new equipment, and the authorization of a $100,000 library building have been effected.

The college, situated on a 32-acre campus in a residential section, has two dormitories, an administration building, and recreation building all under one roof, and includes an auditorium seating 650. The college has no debt, owns property valued at nearly $350,000, and has an endowment fund of over $40,000. During the 1954-55 session the college enrolled a total of 385 students, including 158 private pupils in special departments. The faculty and staff totaled 38 persons. Graduates in liberal arts, receiving the Associate of Arts diploma, are accepted by South Carolina senior colleges as juniors. The cost of operation for the 1954-55 session, approximately $166,000, was derived from student fees and the South Carolina Baptist convention. In the period of 1913-55 the college graduated a total of 1,697 students.

E. F. HAIGHT

ANDERSONVILLE INSTITUTE. An academy at Andersonville, Tenn., founded c. 1897, which served for several years as a "feeder" for Carson-Newman College. President C. T.

Carpenter in 1902 stated the following twofold purpose for the academy: "(1) To provide the elements of higher education; (2) To train young men and young women for positions as teachers, especially in public schools." Although Clinton and Midland associations owned and controlled the school, it was for several years prior to its dissolution under the supervision of the Southern Baptist Home Mission Board, from which it received support through 1917. LYNN EDWARD MAY, JR.

ANDREWS, GEORGE WASHINGTON (b. Raleigh, N. C., Nov. 10, 1861; d. Atlanta, Ga., Apr. 28, 1934). Of Scotch-English ancestry, he obtained a limited private education, then became an apprentice in the railway shops in Raleigh. He rose to master mechanic and then was an insurance salesman until 1904. In that year, because of his achievements as superintendent of the Woodward Avenue Sunday school in Atlanta, he was employed as Sunday school evangelist or field secretary (variously called) of the mission board of the Georgia Baptist Convention, and retained this position the rest of his life. He was a pioneer in Sunday school grading, teacher training, and planning and provision of adequate buildings and facilities for Sunday school teaching. In 1886 he married Lucy Jackson Day, of Manchester, Va.
H. LEWIS BATTS

ANGELS. Angels are spiritual created beings of a higher order than man and not subject to the limitations imposed by the physical order, within which man's historical existence must be worked out. Angels have no physical bodies but, like man, possess free will. They form an unseen host of guardian beings sent to minister to man (Heb. 1:16). The existence of angels cannot be demonstrated by sense experience; we know of them only by revelation. In biblical thought angels increase in prominence as the divine relation moves to its climax in Christ. To the seer of Daniel, they were the mediators of revelation. Christ taught their existence and spoke frequently of both good and evil angels. His understanding of his own redemptive mission was bound up intimately with the existence of angels, especially with the reality of the devil. New Testament writers were convinced that angels, and especially evil powers, were operative in the universe; they believed that Christ defeated the evil powers in the cross and resurrection. The good angels, described as great in number, "legions" (Matt. 26:53), are God's messengers (Luke 1:28; Heb. 1:14); they guard God's children (Matt. 18:10); they form the heavenly host which joins issue with the powers of darkness (Rev. 12:7); they execute divine judgment (Matt. 12:39, 49; 16:27; 26:31; II Thess. 1:7); they witness the conduct of men (I Cor. 4:9). Yet angels must learn the mysteries of God's grace through the church (Eph. 3:8–10; I Pet. 1:12), even though they see God face to face (Matt. 18:10). E. C. RUST

ANGLICAN CHURCH. That group of Christians embraced in the Church of England and its related bodies in the United Kingdom. Two views are widely held with regard to its origin. Anglican churchmen insist that it is the historic Christian church which was planted in England in the third century and was firmly established by Augustine after 597. Some, however, assert it to be a creation of the 16th-century Protestant Reformation. In any case, the divorce controversy between Henry VIII and the papacy culminated in a series of acts of Parliament (1529–36) separating the English Church from Rome and specifically (1534), in the Act of Supremacy, declaring the king to be "the only supreme head in earth of the Church of England." Henry VIII did not permit the church to adopt Protestant theology or polity. Archbishop Thomas Cranmer (1489–1556), however, under Edward VI (ruled 1547–53), led England toward Protestantism, which, despite Roman Catholic reaction in Mary's reign (1553–58), was largely confirmed under Elizabeth (1558–1603).

This church has been the established (state) church in England since 1559, except for a brief period (1643–60) during the Civil War and the Commonwealth. Of some 42 million Englishmen today, three million are members of the Anglican Church. In communion with it is the Episcopal Church in Scotland (disestablished 1689) with 106,000 members, the Episcopal Church in Ireland (disestablished 1871) with 400,000 members, and the Episcopal Church in Wales (disestablished 1920) with 200,000 members. Episcopal churches throughout the world are in fraternal association with the Anglican Church and each other by means of Lambeth Conferences which have met regularly since 1888.

The Anglican Church is episcopal in structure, formal in mode of worship, and evangelical in theology. The Elizabethan 39 Articles of Faith (1563), still considered the basic summary of theological beliefs, embody a moderate Calvinism. They appeal to the Scriptures as the sole authority in things spiritual and assert justification by faith. Also basic are the Catechism and the two Books of Homilies which date from Edward VI. Church liturgy is regulated by the Book of Common Prayer. Infant baptism and sprinkling are practiced. Transubstantiation, purgatory, and the celibacy of the clergy are rejected.

The clergy consists of deacons, priests, and bishops who are appointed by the sovereign on the advice of the prime minister. Of the two ecclesiastical provinces, Canterbury ranks first and is largest, having 29 dioceses; York embraces 14. Each is headed by an archbishop, Canterbury's being considered the primate of all England. Church law is framed by a church assembly composed of houses of bishops, clergy, and laity.

BIBLIOGRAPHY: C. Garbett, *The Claims of the Church of England* (1947). H. Gee and W. J. Hardy, comps., *Documents Illustrative of English Church*

History (1896). A. H. Hore, *History of the Church of England from William III to Victoria*, 2 vols. (1900). P. Hughes, *The Reformation in England*, Vol. 1 (1952). K. S. Latourette, *A History of Christianity* (1953). M. W. Patterson, *A History of the Church of England* (1909). Society for Promoting Christian Knowledge, *Doctrine of the Church of England* (1938). W. R. W. Stephens and W. Hunt, eds., *A History of the English Church*, 8 vols. (1901–10).

ROBERT H. SPIRO, JR.

ANN HASSELTINE YOUNG WOMAN'S AUXILIARY. Functioning on college, university, and seminary campuses in Southern Baptist Convention territory, Ann Hasseltine or college Young Woman's auxiliaries totaled 148 in 1955. Woman's Missionary Union interest in young women engaged in higher education began in 1889 by granting to Mrs. Adelia M. Hillman of Mississippi leaflets on missions "for distribution among the students of the college at Clinton." In 1910 Woman's Missionary Union recommended that a college correspondent be appointed to promote missions among young women in colleges, and named Susan B. Tyler (later Mrs. Curtis Lee Laws) to that position, an office which she held until 1921 when Juliette Mather succeeded her. Miss Mather served until 1948 when Margaret Bruce became young people's secretary, the title used since 1927.

Following a recommendation that a college correspondent be selected in each state to cooperate with the general college correspondent of the union, work was extended to Baptist and non-Baptist colleges through campus representatives. As early as 1839 or 1840, the Ann Hasseltine Missionary Society was organized at Judson College, Marion, Ala., and in 1914 the name Ann Hasseltine was adopted for all college Young Woman's auxiliaries. When the Baptist Student Missionary Movement of North America was developing in 1914, Kathleen Moore Mallory (*q.v.*), executive secretary of Woman's Missionary Union, was a member of its advisory board. Later the union co-operated with the Inter-Board Commission and then with the Baptist Student Union, through which it continues to promote Young Woman's Auxiliary.

From 1925 until 1933, Ann Hasseltine auxiliaries maintained a fund known as Our Sisterhood Special for scholarships and incidental expenses connected with the study in the United States of four young women from Romania and Hungary. However, this venture was discontinued to avoid the possibility of lessening Young Woman's Auxiliary loyalty to the Cooperative Program.

The Window of Y.W.A., the auxiliary's publication, followed the Ann Hasseltine Y.W.A. Bulletin, distributed from 1921 until 1929.

See also YOUNG WOMAN'S AUXILIARY.

JULIETTE MATHER

ANNE LUTHER BAGBY COLEGIO, SAO PAULO. See BRAZIL, MISSION IN.

ANNIE ARMSTRONG OFFERING. See WOMAN'S MISSIONARY UNION.

ANNUITIES, GIFT. First authorized by the Commission on Ministerial Relief and Annuities (later became Relief and Annuity Board) Sept. 25, 1917, initial contract issued Feb. 26, 1919. The plan is designed to leave a part of the principal sum as a gift to the board for charity. It also guarantees life income to annuitant (donor). The Southern Baptist Convention directed this board in 1933 to fund all gift annuity contracts for any of the Convention agencies. In funding gift annuity contracts, the board holds the annuity reserves; the contracting agency receives the gift portion. The rates are actuarially computed. The present rate basis is: 1937 Standard Annuity Mortality Table, female ages rated as one year younger, interest at 3 per cent, 50 per cent residuum, loading 5 per cent of total gift. L. T. DANIEL

ANNUITY FUND, (OLD). First plan operated by Relief and Annuity Board. The first certificate was issued July 1, 1919. This plan was closed to new members Sept. 30, 1930. Premiums paid by members, based on age at entry, provide one fifth of the cost of benefits, and denomination pays four fifths of the cost. Annuity begins at age 68, or earlier if total and permanent disability occurs. Amount of annuity is $500 per year, payable in monthly instalments of $41.67. This plan also provides for widow annuity in the amount of $300 annually, payable $25 monthly for remainder of the widow's life or until her remarriage. If member dies after annuity begins, annuity is payable to widow who was married to him when he became an annuitant. If no widow survives, minor children receive the $300 per year until last child reaches age 21. MABLE H. MCCARTNEY

ANNUITY PLAN, SAVINGS. A savings plan, inaugurated in 1930, operated by the Relief and Annuity Board as a service for ministers, missionaries, and full-time workers in churches, boards, and institutions affiliated with the Southern Baptist Convention. It provides for deposit of any sum of money with the board, to draw interest (current rate 3 per cent). The interest is payable semiannually, or it may be left with the board and added to the principal. At the request of the certificate holder, part or all of his credits may be applied toward a Life Annuity contract with provision for survivor benefits. All or part of deposits may be withdrawn upon request to the board.

MABLE H. MCCARTNEY

ANNUITY PLAN, SERVICE. The first contributory plan offered by the Relief and Annuity Board, approved by Southern Baptist Convention in May, 1930, and put into operation Jan. 1, 1932. The plan was not generally accepted; only 126 certificates were issued. It was closed to new members Jan. 1, 1938. The plan provided: a maximum retirement annuity of 50 per cent of average salary over 35 years of service; widow's benefits of 50 per cent of husband's benefit; annuity for total disability, and for orphans; and a death benefit in maximum amount of $500. Dues were 2½ per cent of salary by member, and 8 per cent by church.

MABLE H. MCCARTNEY

ANNUITY PLAN, SPECIAL DEFERRED. Offered to ministers and layworkers employed by the denomination. The member takes out units of $100 per year, payable semiannually, quarterly, or monthly. Purchases are limited to five units per member. Three options are available: monthly life annuity, based on age of member at entry; monthly refund life annuity which guarantees full cash value; or return of all payments plus interest in cash settlement. Loans not in excess of total cash value may be made at 5 per cent, without other collateral. Thirty-one-day grace period is allowed in payment of premiums.

MABLE MCCARTNEY

ANNUITY, SPECIAL (LIFE). Inaugurated by the Relief and Annuity Board in 1929. It is a single-premium annuity issued in units of one thousand dollars or multiples thereof. The annuitant receives a guaranteed amount beginning at an agreed specified date and continuing for the lifetime of the annuitant. A completely funded plan with no gift portion, it is issued on single life or on joint and survivor with husband and wife as annuitants.

L. T. DANIEL

ANTHROPOMORPHISM. Derived from the Greek compound *anthrōpos* (man) and *morphē* (form), this term implies the assumption that human characteristics are present in nonhuman beings (e.g., gods, angels, demons, ghosts), in the forces of nature (e.g., wind, rain, storm), and in certain abstract ideas (e.g., justice, hope, peace, law, love). The term, however, is applied primarily to the tendency to conceive of deity in the image of man. Physical or psychical characteristics may be posited upon God.

In Greek culture this religious application is seen in Homer and Hesiod, who described the gods as being born, wearing clothes, and having voice and body. Against this "crass" personification Xenophanes, Aristotle, Cicero, and other thinkers remonstrated, but with little success.

In Jewish culture, also, anthropomorphic details are noted in the corporeal descriptions of the deity and his entourage and in the description of man as created in God's image (*imago dei*). But anthropomorphism is pre-eminently evidenced in Christian culture, where historically God becomes man in Christ, after which man and God become inextricably related in the life process.

BIBLIOGRAPHY: Cicero, *De Natura Deorum* (*The Loeb Classical Library*, 1950). C. L. Drawbridge, *Common Objections to Christianity* (1931) Chapter XV. C. Hartshorne and W. L. Reese, eds., *Philosophers Speak of God* (1953).

J. B. MCMINN

ANTICHRIST. The term "antichrist" is found in the Bible only in I John and II John. In I John 2:18 "many antichrists" are mentioned. They deny that Jesus is the Christ (I John 2:22) or that he came in the flesh (II John 7). The "spirit of antichrist" (I John 4:3) is already in the world. I John 2:18 refers to an individual antichrist, they have "heard" that "antichrist shall come." While not using the term, Paul describes the man of lawlessness (II Thess. 2:3) who is a necessary prelude to the *parousia* of Christ and is to be destroyed at his coming (II Thess. 2:8). A dual concept involving a political world power is presented (Rev. 13:16; 17:10–11; 19:19–20), with a priesthood enforcing emperor worship (Rev. 13:15). The abomination of desolation (Dan. 11:31) probably influenced the development of the antichrist idea. The term is used to refer to the personage with unusual powers who at the end of the age will be an opponent of the Messiah or will attack the Messiah's people.

BIBLIOGRAPHY: G. Milligan, *St. Paul's Epistles to the Thessalonians* (1908). D. A. Nelson, "A Critical Study of Antichrist and Related Ideas in the New Testament."

DAVID A. NELSON

ANTIMISSION MOVEMENT. An extreme application of Calvinism, affecting largely the uncultured congregations of the frontier, which led them to oppose all evangelical effort and to depend instead on a rigid double predestination. The movement was begun about 1819 on the frontier by local preachers who were suspicious of the missionary movement being promoted by the Baptist Triennial Convention, which had been organized in 1814. These frontiersmen "were uneducated and prejudiced, but exceedingly capable in their understanding and manipulation of human nature as it existed around them." When Luther Rice and others made their first journeys through Kentucky and Tennessee, they were met with prejudice, suspicion, and hostility, and a movement soon arose in opposition to their cause.

The leaders of the movement had several reasons for their attitude. Their opposition to Arminian Methodism led them to be extreme in the opposite direction, hence into hyper-Calvinism. They could find no scriptural justification for missionary societies or any other man-made organizations and feared the power of the Baptist Board of Foreign Missions to become a locus for the centralization of authority. In addition, largely because of their own deficiencies, they were suspicious and jealous of ministers who were educated and paid for their labors, and therefore could not accept the visitors from the Eastern cities who came advocating the cause of missions.

John Taylor, Alexander Campbell, and Daniel Parker became the main leaders of antimissionism. In 1781 Taylor had come to Kentucky, where he established several churches. In 1819 he published a tract entitled "Thoughts on Missions," opposing the idea, which exhibited more passion and prejudice than reason and logic. He later charged that Rice's main object was to get money. Campbell was Presbyterian but changed his views on baptism in 1813 and was invited to join the Redstone Association in Virginia. He remained a Baptist until 1830, when he organized the Campbellite movement, the beginning of the Christian Church. He was editor of a periodical called the *Christian Baptist,* which circulated widely in the West. Campbell professed sympathy toward missions but objected to the mission board because he thought it unscriptural. Parker was a product of the frontier, and his work was confined to Kentucky, Tennessee, Illinois, and Texas. He would ask questions at association meetings in such a manner as to awaken opposition to missions. John Mason Peck, missionary to the West, met Parker twice in debate and won, but said of him: "I have never before met with so determined an opposer to missions in every respect."

The antimission movement was largely confined to the frontier, but its influence was felt throughout the Southern states. It began in Kentucky with Taylor's tract, "Thoughts on Missions," but spread rapidly. Many churches and whole associations followed these leaders. They still called themselves Baptists but used such adjectives as "Old," "Old School," "Primitive," "Predestination," "Original," and in one case "Antimissionary" to distinguish themselves from ordinary missionary Baptists. From 1820 to 1840, they wrecked the missionary cause on the frontier and created confusion in the older states, throughout the South and beyond. They reached their zenith about 1840. From that time they began to decline, but not before causing untold harm to the cause of missions in the South.

Baptists lost a large percentage of their total strength to the antimission movement. A large number left the denomination with Campbell, though the exact figure cannot be accurately estimated, as no sources on this point are available. Others refused to join the Baptists because of the controversy. Schools and colleges were not founded in the West during this time, further delaying the growth and progress of Baptists for lack of trained leadership. Those who remained with the denomination became more energetic in promoting missions and the Baptist program throughout the South. The separation was complete by the time the Southern Baptist Convention was organized in 1845.

BIBLIOGRAPHY: R. Babcock, *John Mason Peck* (1864). D. Benedict, *A General History of the Baptist Denomination in America, and Other Parts of the World* (1848). J. T. Christian, *A History of Baptists,* Vol. II (1926). C. T. Goodsell, *The Baptist Anti-Missionary Movement in America* (1924). A. H. Newman, *A History of the Baptist Churches in the United States* (1915). J. H. Spencer, *A History of Kentucky Baptists,* Vol. I (1886). W. W. Sweet, ed., *Religion on the American Frontier: The Baptists* (1931). J. Taylor, *History of Ten Churches* (1823).

A. W. ROBBINS

ANTINOMIANISM. The word is formed by the combination of *anti,* against; and *nomos,* law. The theory of antinomianism rests upon a misinterpretation of Romans 6:14: ". . . ye are not under the law, but under grace." It is a view of salvation stressing the freeness of salvation through faith and denying (more or less) the claims of the law (Mosaic, moral), and ranging from mild or *passive* forms to extreme or *active* forms. Paul, in his effort to relate grace to law, encountered both types: (1) the mystics who maintained a *passive indifference* to law (Mosaic law, good works, etc.), and (2) the libertines who, though "clean" in the "spirit" by "faith," actively engaged in immorality that the "grace of God might abound." This was a complete perversion of Paul's teaching and his reaction is seen in a number of places in the New Testament (e.g., Rom. 3:5-8; 5:15 to 6:34; II Tim. 3:1-13; Titus 1:10-16).

Antinomian teachings have continued to appear from time to time in Christian history. Among certain gnostics of the second and third centuries (Adamites, Cainites, Satanites) antinomianism was common. Some of the "spiritual ones" of the middle ages (e.g., Amalric of Bena, d. 1204) actually regarded harlotry as not sinful. Antinomianism became a serious issue in the 16th and 17th centuries, largely as a result of a misunderstanding of Luther's teachings. A bitter controversy raged between Luther and Melanchthon on the one hand and Agricola, Amsdorf, and Cordatus on the other. In England a hyper-Calvinistic theology with its supralapsarian interpretation of sin and its doctrine of irresistible grace produced antinomian tendencies (especially among Particular Baptists). One of the most chaotic antinomian sects to appear in England was the "Ranters" who reportedly engaged in degrading moral practices (some reports probably exaggerated). Andrew Fuller and John Ryland (Baptists) wrote vigorously against the antinomians, especially against the "Sandemanians" and "Johnsonians." In New England Anne Hutchinson (1590-1643) and her followers disturbed the orthodox with antinomian teachings. Antinomianism is not dead. Some groups today teach that a "spiritual" perfection is possible for the "elect," while the sins of the flesh remain a matter of indifference. Other antinomian tendencies can be seen in those who stress the spiritual and eschatological aspects of salvation and ignore the social and ethical demands of the gospel.

BIBLIOGRAPHY: T. Gataker, *Antinomianism Discovered and Confuted* (1652). S. Fisher, *Baby Baptism Mere Babism* (1653). J. Fletcher, *Works; Story of the Rise, Reign, and Ruine of the Antinomians, Familists and Libertines that Infected the Churches of New England* (1644). T. Crisp, *Works* (1690). D. Bogue, *History of Dissenters* (1808-12). J. Belcher, *The Complete Works of Andrew Fuller* (1845). D. Neal, *History of Puritans* (1848). C. F. Adams, *Three Episodes of Massachusetts . . .* (1892). W. Beyschlag, *New Testament Theology* (1894). A. Harnack, *History of Dogma* (1896). A. H. Newman, *A Manual of Church History* (1904). A. H. Strong,

Systematic Theology (1907). W. T. Whitley, *A History of British Baptists* (1923). A. C. McGiffert, *A History of Christian Thought* (1946). A. C. Underwood, *A History of British Baptists* (1923). *The New Schaff-Herzog Encyclopedia of Religious Knowledge* (1949). F. Hildebrandt, *From Luther to Wesley* (1951). TED R. CLARK

APOLOGETICS. This term refers to the setting forth of the grounds for the Christian claim to the true knowledge of God. It differs from the *apology* which is a reply to a specific objection, and from *Christian evidences* which is a subdivision of apologetics dealing with the supernatural and factual validation of revelation. Apologetics is the master plan which governs the form and strategy of apologies.

Although Roman Catholicism develops its apologetics within the framework of Thomism, Protestantism has never fixed upon a specific apologetic. However, the writings of Augustine, Calvin, and Luther have had a pervasive influence. Apologists are considered *rationalists* if they find the test for revelation in one or more of the laws of logic (e.g., Augustine) and *empiricists* if they find the test for revelation in an examination of nature or experience (e.g., Joseph Butler). The *autopistic* school believes that Christianity is validated within itself (e.g., John Calvin), while the *evidential* school believes that Christianity is verified through Christian evidences (usually considered apart from philosophical considerations; e.g., William Paley).

The outstanding Southern Baptist apologist of recent times, E. Y. Mullins (*q.v.*), was influenced by personalism in philosophy and followed the empirical school, as witnessed by his faith in the validity of theistic proofs.

The writings of Soren Kierkegaard and Karl Barth created a new era of apologetics in the 20th century by a radical challenge to traditional apologetics and philosophy through new conceptions of faith, revelation, and divine transcendence. BERNARD RAMM

APOSTASY. The word occurs twice in the New Testament (Acts 21:21; II Thess. 2:3; for the Greek, *apostasia*). In classical Greek it referred to a deserting of one's military post, the revolt of a soldier from his commander, or a revolt against an alliance. In the Old Testament (LXX) it meant rebellion against either the king or God himself. In the papyri "apostasy" has been used to signify "rebels," "deserters," and "rowdies." In the New Testament Paul is charged with deserting from Moses (Acts 21:21). The Thessalonians are told by Paul that before the return of Christ there shall be the manifestation of the man of sin (lawlessness) and rebellion (II Thess. 2:3). Most commentators interpret this as a desertion from the Christian religion. Apostasy thus means a rebellion against accepted religion, a desertion from one religion to another either by force or voluntarily.

There are other expressions equivalent to apostasy to be found in the Old Testament, in inter-biblical literature, and in the New Testament itself. In the history of the church appear numerous instances of apostasy, with much severe legislation against them. Apostasy was uniformly considered more serious than heresy.

See also BACKSLIDING. BERNARD RAMM

ARCHEOLOGY, BIBLICAL. The discipline which, by a systematic study of the remains of ancient Near Eastern cultures, seeks to recover the total historical and cultural setting of the lands and societies contemporary with the production of the Hebrew-Christian Scriptures. More directly, it seeks to view the Bible in the perspective of this total cultural background and to apply all relevant material from it to the interpretation and illumination of the scriptural message. Biblical archeology is distinguished from general archeology, therefore, by its concern with a special interest rather than by the employment of a special technique.

It is not within the purpose or province of archeology to attempt to prove or disprove the Bible, for the validity of Scripture involves matters of faith and subjective experience and is therefore not subject to scientific proof or disproof. However, historical and cultural confirmations of the Bible frequently occur as a result of archeological study. Such occurrences, however, are benefits accompanying the study rather than the goal of the research. It is more important to gain understanding and illumination of the Bible; for, though a particular passage may be valid for all ages, it was written against the historical and cultural background of the time of its writer and was intended, first of all, to be understood by the writer's contemporaries. By recovering this historical and cultural setting (which the original readers and hearers knew, but which, during the lapse of the centuries, present-day readers have often lost), archeology makes the reader, in a sense, the author's contemporary and thus helps him understand the writer's times and his modes of expression. Accordingly, the greatest over-all achievement of archeology has been the reconstruction, from innumerable literary references and from countless material remains, of the historical and cultural framework of life in the ancient Near East. Viewed from the perspective provided by this cultural pattern, the Bible has been rediscovered in some important aspects of its nature.

Historical and geographical reliability.—Confidence in the essential dependability of the narratives associated with the various periods of biblical history has resulted from the discoveries of recent years. Unknown and forgotten empires have been recovered and reconstructed, biblical cities and towns have been reliably identified and located, the history of biblical times is being rewritten and, on occasions, written for the first time—further supplementing the Bible. Especially is this true with respect to the patriarchal narratives. They have, in times past, been frequently regarded as unauthentic. Now, however, the result of archeological study has proved that they present a true picture of the prevailing social customs and legal practices of their day. Furthermore, these customs do not fit into the cultural patterns of later periods. Similar evidences relating to subsequent periods in biblical history have created more confidence among scholars in the essential validity of biblical narratives. Accompanying this confidence has come a renewal of appreciation for the reliability of the oral transmission of Israel's early traditions.

Literary relationships.—The recovery of a large amount of literature of the biblical world has made it abundantly clear that the languages in which the Old and New testaments were written were common means of communication in those times. The accumulation of materials written in biblical and related languages, as well as the discovery of actual biblical texts and versions, has resulted in tremendous forward strides in the sciences of textual criticism and lexicography. Consequently, many lexicons and grammars of the Greek and Hebrew languages have been outdated. The study of this mass of literary material has inspired confidence in the essential faithfulness of transmission represented by our best Greek texts of the New Testament and by the Massoretic text of the Old Testament. We may expect that most of the future progress along the line of literary research will come in a better understanding of the use of words, figures of speech, and idioms of the language.

Religious superiority.—Archeology has contributed significantly to the understanding of the religious concepts of Israel, as related to those of its contemporaries. When biblical literature is compared with the literature of Israel's neighbors, the similarity of expression, figures of speech, and poetic parallelisms is clearly evident. Of equal significance with this similarity of thought forms, however, is the content which they were made to carry and the use to which they were put by the biblical writers. The contrast between the polytheism of Israel's neighbors and Israel's own faith may be seen in this difference: The polytheistic systems personified the forces of nature as gods, whereas Israel's faith was in a personal God, who was himself in control of nature's phenomena. It is no longer possible to maintain seriously that the religion of Israel was close to that of Canaan. Against the total background of ancient Near Eastern life, Israel's culturally superior contemporaries appear decisively inferior in their religious concepts.

History of archeological studies.—This history may be divided into the following periods: The period of beginnings (1800–90) was characterized largely by the search for museum pieces but, nevertheless, witnessed the first scientific exploration of Palestine (1838) by Edward Robinson and the opening of excavations in the several countries of the Near East. The second period (1890–World War I) witnessed the beginning and early development of scientific techniques in archeology. This era was inaugurated by Flinders Petrie's observations in 1890, which led to the development of the science of pottery chronology; progress in field techniques was largely due to the improved methods introduced by G. A. Reisner and C. S. Fisher. The third period began with the establishment of the Palestine Department of Antiquities in 1920 and spanned the years between the two world wars. In activity, techniques, and interpretation it was a period of unparalleled progress. Several national archeological societies were at work in the field, techniques of excavation were further improved, pottery chronology was developed to a reliable procedure, and accumulated materials and information became sufficient to attempt objective historical and cultural reconstruction of Near Eastern society. Cessation of field activities during and subsequent to World War II afforded scholars an opportunity to interpret the mass of previously accumulated materials. The resulting effort of W. F. Albright to reconstruct and evaluate the religious concepts of ancient man in *From the Stone Age to Christianity* (1940) inaugurated a fourth period of archeological history, which might well be characterized as the period of early maturity, for it is at this level of interpretation that archeology achieves its chief goal. Albright's lead was followed (among others) by Frankfort, Wilson, Jacobsen, and Irwin in their *Intellectual Adventure of Ancient Man* (1946), by C. J. Gadd's *Ideas of Divine Rule in the Ancient East* (1948), and by Dentan's (editor) *The Idea of History in the Ancient Near East* (1955). Since 1950, in spite of tensions and divisions in the Near East, field work in archeology has entered a period of renewed activity.

BIBLIOGRAPHY: W. F. Albright, *Archaeology and the Religion of Israel* (1942); *From the Stone Age to Christianity* (1940). G. A. Barton, *Archaeology and the Bible* (1937). M. Burrows, *What Mean These Stones?* (1941). J. Finegan, *Light from the Ancient Past* (1946). G. E. Wright and F. V. Filson, *The Westminster Historical Atlas to the Bible* (1945).

WILLIAM H. MORTON

ARCHITECTURE, CHURCH. The science and technique of designing a building which can at once suitably house the activities of a given congregation and at the same time express the "sense of deity" of that congregation. A church building has two functions: It serves the needs of the people and is at the same time the house of God.

Architecture in relation to the worship of God is first seen in the history of Israel—in the detailed specifications given by Jehovah for his tabernacle (Ex. 25–27) and in the building of the Temple by Solomon (I Kings 5–6). References in the New Testament to the meeting places of the early Christians do not imply the existence of buildings built specifically for worship. At times believers assembled in private homes for services (Rom. 16:5; I Cor. 16:19). Public halls were doubtless used. As persecution arose, secret places were used for worship. When buildings began to be erected, the values of Christian faith and the needs arising from the nature of the church gave direction to the development of distinctive elements of architectural design suitable for churches. Basically, this development was an outgrowth of the attempt to provide houses that met the needs of Christian worship, which at first was the major activity of the assembled congregation. The tastes of ruling monarchs and the prevailing customs of the people were also influential. Various styles developed and succeeded each other: Romanesque, Byzantine, Gothic, Renaissance, Georgian, and Victorian. Currently, churches are still built in many of these styles, also in styles which may be loosely called "contemporary" or "modern." It is true, however, that the Romanesque, and more particularly the Gothic, styles—since these styles were the creation of the peculiarly church-centered culture of the Middle Ages—probably most

Increase in Southern Baptist Church Property, 1950–1955

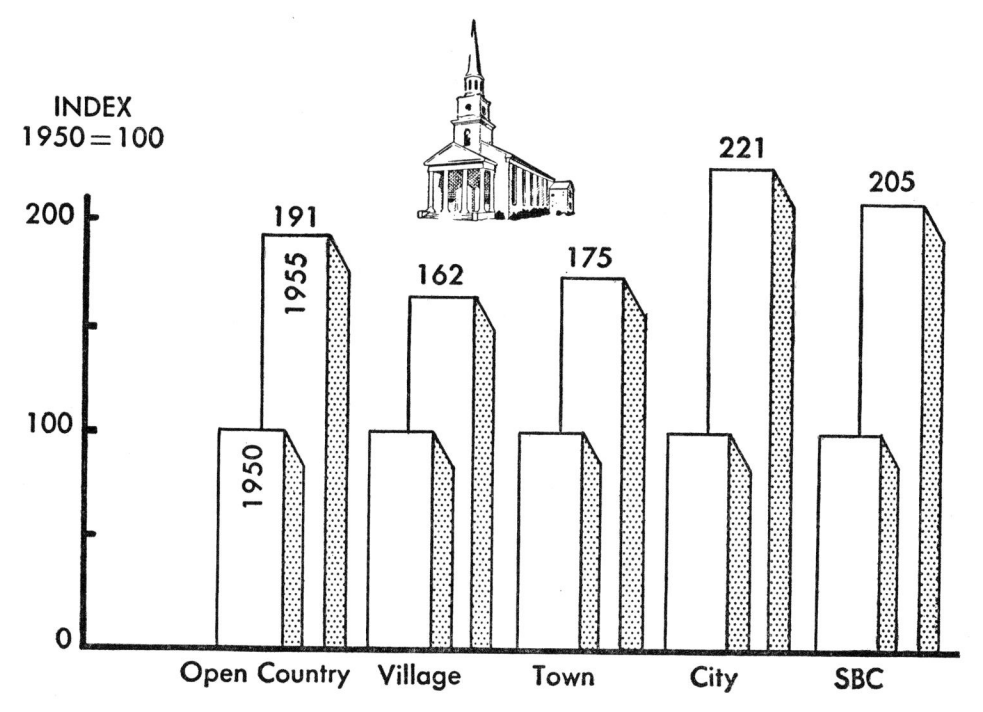

INDEX 1950 = 100

Open Country 1950=100, 1955=191
Village 162
Town 175
City 221
SBC 205

deserve to be called "Christian architecture."

From the beginning the use of a church building has had some influence on its design and arrangement. The needs of the worshiper are uniquely important. In fact, "the greatest and most fundamental change in church design of the Gothic period over the churches of Egypt, Periclean Greece and Maya is the relation of the building to the human being. . . . The church, by this time, had begun to recognize man as an integral part of the building scheme and to provide for him in the integration and planning of its parts." In modern architecture this trend toward functionalism has been especially marked. Conscious use has been made of the resources for expression inherent in various materials and types of structure. Always foremost are two considerations: the effect of the building on the worshiper and its convenience for his use.

Architecture in Southern Baptist churches has been greatly affected in its development both by prevailing styles and by the needs of Southern Baptist organizations and programs. These two influences have not always been combined happily, but over the years there has developed a growing architectural understanding of Southern Baptist organizational distinctives and needs. This in turn has resulted in the creation of buildings that have been a major factor in the growth of the denomination.

The first buildings were simple halls, in which the people could meet for worship. They were small, for congregations were small. All activities were conducted within this one room; and what Bible study classes there were, were conducted in a corner. As the Sunday school movement grew, it became an influential factor in the design of church buildings. Rooms were constructed at the side and rear of the one-room building. Many provided a place for the Sunday school beneath the auditorium.

The Akron Plan, a strictly utilitarian double-purpose arrangement developed in Akron, Ohio, came into existence in 1867 and soon affected all sections of the country. Gradually, the churches realized, however, that the same space could not be efficiently used for both educational and worship purposes. Therefore, churches, according to their ability, sought to provide for these needs separately. As long ago as 1926, Isaac Jacobus Van Ness (q.v.) interpreted this concept as follows:

> The purpose for which we are building will determine largely the character of structure. It has come about, therefore, that Southern Baptists have developed a distinct type of church architecture in which a great auditorium for preaching is built alongside an equally great structure for teaching purposes.

His statement had reference primarily to large churches, but the principle he formulated has guided the building plans of churches of all sizes. Most affected, of course, were plans for educational space, because the work of religious education had become a major distinctive of Southern Baptist churches. As programs enlarged to include not only teaching and training but also music, fellowship, banquets and dinners, recreation, and dramatics, the need for new arrangements of space and new building design contributed to the development of church architecture. The coming, also, of elaborate departmentalization, with closely graded age divisions for more specialized teaching and training, added to the complexity of the buildings which large churches needed for their educational work.

In the design of their sanctuaries for worship, Baptists have developed few distinctive patterns but have largely used traditional forms. Occasionally, an intense concern for the practical has led to the building of auditoriums designed purely for the accommodation of large groups of people, largely lacking in aesthetic values for worship. Generally, churches have sought for both efficiency and worshipfulness. Baptist emphasis on the importance of the preaching ministry has led to the centrally placed pulpit. The ordinance of baptism is regularly given large architectural emphasis; the ordinance of the Lord's Supper does not require similar provision. Choirs are provided for in numerous ways but are usually seated behind the pulpit, facing the congregation.

Within the first decade of this century, the Baptist Sunday School Board expressed concern for the promotion of better church buildings. A book on the subject by Prince Emmanuel Burroughs (q.v.) was published in 1917. Under Burroughs' aggressive leadership the board carried on a continuous ministry, emphasizing the importance of properly designed church buildings, all the while serving the churches with a program of guidance. In 1940 the Department of Church Architecture was established as an entirely separate unit, with William Asa Harrell as secretary. At that time the department was serving about 100 churches a month. In 1956 the department handled an average of over 730 requests for service per month, sending out to the churches literature, advice, sketches of suggested building layouts, etc. This department seeks to promote the functional, cultural, and spiritual values of church buildings among Southern Baptist churches. The current era is one of expansion and much building activity. During the decade from 1945 to 1955, the total evaluation of Southern Baptist church property increased from $276,089,711 to $1,323,453,534.

BIBLIOGRAPHY: American Institute of Architecture, *The Handbook of Architectural Practice* (1943). M. Anderson, *Planning and Financing the New Church* (1944). P. E. Burroughs, *Church and Sunday School Buildings* (1917); *How to Plan Church Buildings* (1926); *Let Us Build* (1938). H. F. Evans, *The Sunday School Building and Its Equipment* (1916). D. J. Fleming, *Christian Symbols* (1940). W. A. Harrell, *Planning Better Church Buildings* (1947). D. Holisher, *The House of God* (1946). W. H. Leach, *Protestant Church Building* (1948). J. R. Scotford, *The Church Beautiful* (1945). E. Short, *A History of Religious Architecture* (n.d.). P. Thiry, R. M. Bennett, and H. L. Kamphoefner, *Churches and Temples, Encyclopedia Americana* (1952). W. W. Watkins, *Planning and Building the Modern Church* (1951). F. R. Webber, *The Small Church* (1939); *The Small Church—How to Build and Furnish* (1939); *Church Symbolism* (1927).

W. A. HARRELL

ARENDALL, CHARLES BAKER (b. Nathalie, Halifax County, Va., Aug. 18, 1880; d. Mobile, Ala., Feb. 20, 1946). Active in denominational life and pastor of Dauphin Way Baptist Church, in Mobile, Ala. It was at this church where he did his greatest work. Under his ministry it became the largest church in the Mobile Association; he led in erection of several buildings, the latest of which were the auditorium and two educational units—all part of the present plant. Arendall was vice-president of the Alabama Baptist State Convention, a member of its executive board, a trustee of Southern Baptist Hospital in New Orleans and of the Southern Baptist Theological Seminary, Louisville, Ky., and a leader in religious and civic affairs in Mobile. Much in demand as a speaker, he was known for his evangelistic zeal, his shepherd heart, and his marked ability as an administrator. Greatly feared by the elements of lawlessness in his community, he became a powerful deterrent to crime and organized vice in the area. His other pastorates included the First Baptist Church of Madison, Ga., where he married Kate Peacock on July 2, 1913; Parkview Baptist Church, Portsmouth, Va.; and First Baptist Church, Troy, Ala. He was graduated from Lynchburg, Va., High School; from Richmond College (A.B.); and from Southern Baptist Seminary (Th.M.). Howard College later conferred upon him the D.D. degree. His parents were John J. and

Olivia (Lacy) Arendall. His children were Charles Baker, Jr., John Thomas, Edgar Mullins, and Robert Alexander. One son, Edgar M., became a minister and attained prominence in his own right.   H. H. HARWELL

ARGENTINA, MISSION IN. Organized in Buenos Aires, Dec. 1, 1904, with Sidney McFarland Sowell (*q.v.*), Joseph Lancaster Hart, Tennessee Hamilton Hart, Frank James Fowler, Daisy Cate Fowler, King Wolsey Cawthon, and Lillian McCall Cawthon as charter members. Rosario and Buenos Aires were the first mission centers. Public services in Spanish began Nov. 20, 1904, with a sermon preached by Sowell. The first "regular Baptist church" of Argentina was organized Apr. 2, 1905, at 1552 Lima Street, Buenos Aires, with eight charter members; the first converts Cosmo Misetti and Marcos Zambianco were baptized in La Plata River on May 2, 1905. The mission initiated the Argentine Baptist Convention with the motion "to request the churches of the Argentine Mission to send delegates to Rosario Tuesday after the first Sunday in December, 1908, to form a Baptist Union."

From Buenos Aires expansion was planned toward the south, but in 1912 the mission began looking northward and westward. Progress came in 1912 with the opening of work in Uruguay; in 1917, Chile and the Argentine cities of Cordoba and Mendoza; in 1918, Paraguay; later the Argentine cities of Bahia Blanca, Tucuman, and Cipolletti.

The women's work, from the beginning, has been indigenous in that the national women have taken the initiative without a missionary executive secretary of Woman's Missionary Union. The missionary women were authorized in 1931 to administer the organization's Cox Fund for helping young women do full-time work in the churches, especially among children and young people. In 1954 Clara Bell Hagler Freeman became the first full-time Woman's Missionary Union worker.

Publication work began in 1908 with a paper and Sunday school literature. Now this work is carried on by an agency of the national convention, though a missionary is administrator.

James M. Justice was the first president of the theological seminary organized in Buenos Aires, Aug. 1, 1911. The first faculty included Justice, Sowell, Robert M. Logan, and Thomas Spight. Succeeding presidents were Sowell, Santiago Canclini, and William Lowrey Cooper. A girls' training school was opened in Buenos Aires in 1937. In 1946 this school was combined with the older training school in Rosario. As early as 1936 Chile was invited to send students to Argentina for theological studies. Tentative plans for a new seminary were approved by the Foreign Mission Board in 1943, but the present International Baptist Seminary was not organized until 1950; on Feb. 2, Everett Gill, Jr., the Board's Latin American secretary at that time, was present when the old seminary and training school were merged and the new school was founded to serve Argentina, Chile, Paraguay, Uruguay, and Bolivia.

During the first generation of mission work, the individual missionaries had national helpers who were employed directly by the mission. Since 1927 the mission has worked with churches and not with individual nationals. A further step was taken in 1930, when the Argentine convention was invited to name a committee to study and consult with the mission regarding the allocation of subsidy money. In that same year, the handling of building and loan funds was delegated to the Argentine convention's Home Mission Board. This procedure was followed for a number of years, and then the administration fell back into the hands of the mission. The mission is conferring with the convention with a view to setting up mixed committees of nationals and missionaries having authority to administer fraternal aid through building and loan funds.

In 1955 the mission had 47 missionaries. Of the 158 churches, with more than 10,000 members, about two-thirds were self-supporting. The convention was making plans to adopt a financial plan based on the Cooperative Program, and the mission and convention were co-operating in projection of an extensive program of religious education in the churches.

HUGO H. CULPEPPER

ARGENTINE BAPTIST CONVENTION. Organized Dec. 31, 1908, with five churches and Thomas Spight, a missionary, as president. The churches had developed as a result of the work of Southern Baptist missionaries who entered the country in 1903. Sidney McFarland Sowell (*q.v.*), who arrived in Buenos Aires Nov. 30, 1903, was the first missionary and was followed a few months later by Joseph L. and Tennessee (Hamilton) Hart. The Foreign Mission Board now has 47 missionaries in Argentina.

Pablo Bessón (*q.v.*), "a herald of Christian liberty," was a Swiss pastor who began the Baptist work in 1881. Fighting for liberty of conscience, he opened the way for future work. At the beginning of Southern Baptist efforts, there were already three Baptist churches, as a result of the labors of Bessón, pastor of Central Church of Buenos Aires, the first of the three. These churches entered the convention immediately after its organization. Bessón baptized the first Argentine Baptist in the river called *Rio de la Plata*, Dec. 23, 1883.

With the extension of work into Uruguay, the convention was called the River Plata Baptist Convention. Later, Paraguayan Baptist churches were added. In 1948 the Uruguayan churches withdrew to form the Uruguayan Baptist Convention; in 1956 the churches of Paraguay withdrew. Thus the convention again includes only Argentina.

With 169 churches and 159 annexes, the convention represents more than 12,000 members. There are 246 Sunday schools with 1,476 teachers

Arizona, Baptist Convention of

and officers and an average attendance of 9,150. Eight regional associations co-operate with the convention, besides two "auxiliary" conventions —the Woman's Missionary Union and the Young People's conventions, both of which work within their respective fields.

The Mission Board of the Argentine convention supports seven couples who work in eight churches and several annexes located in areas to the south and north of the country. In the south the work in "Tierra del Fuego" (land of the fire) is more austral than Baptist work in any other place.

The International Baptist Theological Seminary, Buenos Aires, was organized in 1953 to serve Argentina, Uruguay, Paraguay, and Chile. Under supervision of the Southern Baptist Foreign Mission Board, it is administrated by a board of directors with representatives from all of these countries. It has ample and modern buildings and a growing number of professors and students. The seminary replaced an older one which served only the Argentine convention, existing almost from the beginning of the work.

Social work is represented by the Baptist Old Peoples' Home located in the city of Rosario, and the Children's Home in Esperanza, Province of Santa Fe. Both are supported entirely by churches of the Argentine convention. The Publications Board edits numerous books and publishes the Baptist monthly magazine, *El Expositor Bautista*, initiated by the Argentine convention, and other auxiliary magazines, including *Tribuna Evangelica* for young people.

S. CANCLINI

ARIZONA, BAPTIST GENERAL CONVENTION OF.

I. Baptist Beginnings. James C. Bristow, from Humansville, Mo., preached the first Baptist sermon in Arizona under a cottonwood tree at Middle Verde the second Sunday in Oct., 1875. The Lone Star Baptist Church, located near Prescott and later moved to that town, was the first Baptist church organized in the state. R. A. Windes was the pastor and the first ordained Baptist preacher in Arizona. The Arizona Baptist Central Association was organized in 1881, reorganized as the Arizona Baptist Association in 1893, and as the Arizona Baptist Convention in 1901. In 1894 there were seven churches and in 1904, 14 churches.

Calvary Baptist Church was organized in Phoenix in Apr., 1917, with 72 members who had withdrawn from the First Baptist Church over charges of "liberalism" in the mother church. C. M. Rock (*q.v.*) of Asheville, N. C., was called as pastor. Because of friction over the Interchurch World Movement, 72 members withdrew from this church to organize the First Southern Baptist Church of Phoenix on Mar. 27, 1921. In May, 1921, Rock was recognized as a messenger to the Southern Baptist Convention, meeting in Memphis, Tenn., and in August the church was received into the fellowship of the Southwestern Baptist Association of New Mexico, meeting in Las Cruces.

In 1925, a need being evident for a closer fellowship within the state, a meeting for the purpose of organizing an association was called in the First Southern Baptist Church, Phoenix, Sept. 20. Messengers came from the First Southern Baptist churches in Buckeye, Prescott, Glendale, and Phoenix, and the First Baptist churches of Chandler and Willcox. A later meeting was held on Nov. 26 with the First Southern Baptist Church in Buckeye. The constitution of Gambrell Memorial Association was effected here with the First Southern Baptist churches of Buckeye, Glendale, Phoenix, and Prescott; First Baptist churches of Chandler and Willcox; Grace Baptist Church, Phoenix; and First Pima Baptist Church, Sacaton.

W. C. STEPHENS

II. History of General Convention. On Sept. 21, 1928, at the fourth annual session of the Gambrell Memorial Association in Globe, Ariz., the Baptist General Convention of Arizona was constituted. The convention voted to continue its relation with the New Mexico convention until Dec. 31. The executive committee was empowered to complete plans for the fall organization. J. O. Willett (*q.v.*), pastor of the First Pima Baptist Church, Sacaton, was elected president.

On Dec. 6, 1928, the adjourned session of the Baptist General Convention of Arizona met with the First Southern Baptist Church of Phoenix to complete the organization. Messengers were seated from the First Southern Baptist churches of Phoenix, Prescott, and Buckeye; First Baptist churches of Chandler and Willcox; Grace Baptist Church, Phoenix; Calvary Baptist Church, Glendale; and First Pima Baptist Church, Sacaton. Later in the session, Calvary Baptist Church of Casa Grande was seated. Thus the convention was formed of these churches with the date of their organization:

Chandler	First Baptist	1915
Willcox	First Baptist	1917
Young	Young Baptist	1919
Phoenix	First Southern Baptist	1921
Sacaton	First Pima Baptist	1923
Buckeye	First Southern Baptist	1925
Phoenix	Grace Baptist	1925
Glendale	Calvary Baptist	1926
Globe	First Southern Baptist	1926
Prescott	First Southern Baptist	?
Casa Grande	Calvary Baptist	1928

Of the above-named churches, Grace, Phoenix, and First, Willcox, later withdrew to affiliate with the Northern Baptist Convention. First Southern, Globe, and First Southern, Prescott, disbanded. Since that time, another First Southern, Prescott, and Trinity, Globe, have been constituted. Also, First Southern, Glendale, earlier mentioned, merged with the group constituting Calvary Church.

In Sept., 1928, when the Baptist General Convention of Arizona was organized with 10 churches, there were 36 Northern Baptist churches in the state. In 1955 the general convention reported 219 churches, of which 119 were within Arizona, the others being in the states affiliated with the Arizona convention. In 1955 the Arizona Convention of American (Northern) Baptist Churches reported 33 churches. In 1955 the Arizona Baptist Convention (Conservative) reported 45 churches. Only seven churches have left the Northern Baptist Convention to become Southern Baptist. Two churches have changed from Southern to Northern (American).

Soon the new convention found itself beset with hardships. A transient population, lack of funds, religious prejudice of Catholics, Mormons, Northern Baptists, and even within Southern Baptist ranks, slowed the progress.

In Mar., 1928, a joint committee composed of Edgar Young Mullins (q.v.), Isaac Jacobus Van Ness (q.v.), Baron DeKalb Gray (q.v.), Arthur James Barton (q.v.) (Southern Baptist Convention), and F. W. Freeman, J. F. Herget, D. J. Evans (Northern Baptist Convention) met to discuss the Baptist situation in Arizona. Among their findings were these recommendations:

> . . . that none of the general agencies of the Southern Baptist Convention in the present disturbed condition of affairs in Arizona, send representatives into the State of Arizona . . . [and] that in harmony with the 1912 Statement of Principles they [Northern and Southern churches] strive to co-operate to the utmost of their ability toward the fulfillment of the general ideal set forth in said statement.

Of special significance and encouragement to Arizona Southern Baptists was the attendance (on basis of money contributed to Southern Baptist Convention work) of their messengers at the Southern Baptist Convention, Memphis, Tenn., May, 1929. Their presence was accorded formal recognition by George Washington Truett (q.v.). Later in the same meeting, they were given representation on the Home Mission Board, Sunday School Board, and the Executive Committee.

In Mar., 1929, Miss Floy Hawkins became the first foreign missionary (China) to go out from Arizona Southern Baptists.

New Mexico continued to help Arizona churches, which had formerly been an association of their convention, and in 1931 their Sunday school secretary, Sanford Stanton Bussell (q.v.), became Arizona's third corresponding secretary. Headquarters for the new convention were established in Bussell's home, where the first issue of *The New Testament Baptist News*, a four-page monthly, was mimeographed, June, 1932. The name was changed (second issue) to the *Arizona Baptist Beacon*. A state Brotherhood organization, John D. Davis, president, was completed at the 1932 state convention and reorganized in 1941.

W. A. Jenkins and George W. Graham were invited to visit Arizona in 1935 and make a thorough investigation of Baptist work. Conferences, to which Northern Baptist brethren were invited, were held at First Southern Baptist Church, Phoenix, and in Prescott. These fraternal conferences resulted in better spirit between conventions. There were 15 churches with 3,194 members in 1939 when Bussell retired.

H. A. Zimmerman, former missionary to Brazil, became executive secretary in Oct., 1939. Headquarters were established at 215 Home Builders Bldg., Phoenix. The *Baptist Beacon* doubled in size and was published semimonthly. Mar. 3–4, 1942, two associations were organized: Central and Gila Valley.

Willis J. Ray was elected executive secretary in June, 1944. Growth of the work made necessary a division of duties. Bussell was elected secretary of educational work, and after his death in 1947, he was succeeded by Joe E. Jones. The present secretary of religious education, Howard Halsell, was elected in 1952. Educational work was first divided in 1944, when Norman Fromm, fourth-time worker, became Baptist Student Union secretary. In 1946 Paul Davis became Training Union secretary. The work was combined from 1952 to 1955, when Sid Davis was elected associate for B.S.U. and church music. In Oct., 1956, Ernest B. Myers became Training Union secretary.

A general missionary evangelist, L. B. Wilkinson, was first elected in 1929 and served one year. Other attempts to finance evangelistic programs failed until Horace Lee Janes was elected, 1942–43. Milton E. Cunningham began his service as state evangelist in 1945, assisted by two fieldworkers. In Sept., 1944, the first home missionaries were appointed for Mexican work in Tucson. That year, the Home Mission Board employed the first superintendent of city missions in Phoenix. By 1956 there were 41 Home Mission Board missionaries. Frank Sutton became superintendent of missions under the Home Mission Board, 1952. Outside help from the Sunday School Board, Home Mission Board, the W.M.U. organizations of the Southern Baptist Convention, and of Texas and Virginia, was largely responsible for the significant mission growth in the state.

Plans for a Baptist college were inaugurated at the 1946 state convention, with $3,000 pledged. Grand Canyon College, Prescott, formally opened with 101 students in Sept., 1949. The college was moved to an 80-acre campus in Phoenix in 1951; it became fully accredited in 1952. Presidents of the college have been Willis J. Ray, Leroy Smith (acting), B. O. Herring, Glen Eason (acting), and Loyed R. Simmons.

The *Baptist Beacon* became a weekly newspaper in 1946. It was edited by executive secretaries until W. Barry Garrett was chosen editor in 1947. A circulation of 11,800 was reported in 1956.

The Baptist Building was replaced in 1949

Arizona, Baptist Convention of

after a fire with a modern two-story office building. Aug. 16, 1956, the convention announced purchase of property valued at $187,000, exclusive of land, on W. McDowell Road, for a new headquarters building.

By 1955 Arizona convention territory included churches in Utah, Colorado, Wyoming, Idaho, Nevada, Montana, North and South Dakota. Nov. 21, 1955, 80 churches withdrew to form the Colorado convention.

Gambrell Memorial Assembly first met in 1926 at Groom Creek. Thereafter, quarters were rented at Pine Lawn or Episcopal Assembly Grounds, Prescott. During the 1946 convention C. Vaughan Rock (son of C. M. Rock), chairman of the assembly committee, presented plans for purchasing assembly grounds and raised $3,000. In 1947 plans for purchasing the grounds were discontinued until the college could be established. In Aug., 1955, the 29th annual assembly was held at Paradise Valley Ranch, Prescott, property of state convention.

In Feb., 1956, Ray was elected executive secretary of the Colorado convention. Garrett served as interim secretary until Oct., 1956, when Charles L. McKay accepted the position.

Two histories of the convention have been published: *A Highway in the Desert*, Mrs. C. B. Maxwell (1941); *A Highway in the Desert*, Vol. II, Mrs. G. D. Crow (1952).

MRS. G. D. (HILTON) CROW

III. Program of Work of Arizona Baptists. The executive board, administrative body of the Baptist General Convention of Arizona, consists of a member from each association, with 10 other members at large; it has authority to supervise and control all business and work of the convention, including missions, stewardship, evangelism, education, literature, church organizations, beneficences, camp activities, and employment and the setting of salaries in the interim of the annual sessions.

Arizona's state mission program includes general missionaries and pastoral subsidy in co-operation with the Home Mission Board, city and pioneer missions, and administration of a church revolving loan fund. Accomplishments of the program in 1954 included constitution of 32 new churches, organization of two associations, provision of supplemental salaries for 70 pastors, and employment of seven general missionaries and a superintendent of missions. A limited church loan fund known as the Trust and Memorial Fund had loans totaling $205,135.66 to 70 churches in 1954. A city missions program is provided in Phoenix.

The department of religious education, established in 1944, reported 10 years later in 1954, enrolments of 28,210 in Sunday school; 10,615, Training Union; and 1,554, Brotherhood. Student unions had been established on five college campuses, and membership in 182 churches totaled 26,379. The Department of Evangelism, created in 1948 in co-operation with the Department of Evangelism of the Home Mission Board, has encouraged the holding of revivals in every church, which have resulted in 3,111 baptisms and net gains of 4,300. The department of Woman's Missionary Union reported 60 societies in 74 churches with 1,287 members in 1950; four years later, membership had increased to 2,683, with 246 auxiliaries, which had 2,782 members. The Department of Brotherhood and Foundation was created in 1952, when there were 40 Brotherhoods with 855 members. Two years later, the number of Brotherhoods had doubled and membership totaled 1,569. The Baptist Foundation of Arizona was incorporated in 1950 to receive, hold, and sell properties for Baptist institutions.

Historian of the Arizona convention, 1944-52, Mrs. Murray Parsons, collected historical data on the churches composing the convention during its first 25 years.

A fund has been accumulating through the years for the opening of a children's home or child placement agency, but at present no home has been opened. Grand Canyon College, with seven buildings, had an enrolment in 1954-55 totaling 352.

Arizona's Baptist Building houses the convention offices, Baptist Book Store, and rental space. At Gambrell Memorial Assembly six buildings accommodate 300 persons, and a program of development is under way.

The *Arizona Baptist Beacon* has been the organ of publicity of the state convention since 1928. Originally a mimeographed monthly sheet, it became a weekly publication in 1949. Since it served churches in eight northern states affiliated with the Arizona convention, its name was changed to *Baptist Beacon* in 1950. With a circulation of 10,150 in 1955, the paper is financed by advertisements, subscriptions, and the Cooperative Program. The Arizona Baptist convention operated on a budget of $443,220 in 1954-55.

State expenditures.—The following is a list of disbursements made by the Baptist General Convention of Arizona from Nov. 1, 1953, to Sept. 30, 1954.

Administration	$19,188.37	
Arizona Baptist Beacon	21,659.80	
Co-operative Missions	64,564.71	
Department of Evangelism	11,558.17	
Department of Religious Education	19,208.04	
Foundation and Brotherhood	7,361.78	
Southwide Appropriations	52,521.22	
State Missions	16,368.22	
Women's Missionary Union	10,612.90	
Colorado Christian Education	1,632.58	
Grand Canyon College	85,495.31	
Miscellaneous Disbursements	11,451.36	
Transfer Items	9,717.14	$331,339.60

WILLIS J. RAY

IV. ARIZONA STATISTICAL SUMMARY

Year	Associations	Churches	Church Membership	Baptisms	S. S. Enrolment	V.B.S. Enrolment	T. U. Enrolment	W.M.U. Enrolment	Brotherhood Enrolment	Mission Gifts	Total Gifts	Value Church Property	State Capital Worth
1830													(Explanation: This column includes total value of Schools, Children's Homes, Hospitals, Foundation, Buildings, etc.)
1840													
1850													
1860													
1870													
1880													
1890													
1900													
1905													
1910													
1915													
1920	1	10	1,641	133	835	176	335	354	....	$ 4,971.97	$ 29,604.73	$ 58,525.00	* Present Worth
1928	1	11	1,896	177	1,534	....	523	296	....	4,010.88	25,879.16	76,200.00	
1930	1	13	2,001	196	1,638	136	547	237	....	4,519.21	37,069.12	107,925.00	
1931	1	13	2,283	220	1,944	....	602	408	....	3,753.04	43,382.83	148,765.00	Children's Home Fund $35,000
1932	1	13	2,860	247	2,419	....	662	310	....	4,068.11	23,668.46	179,400.00	
1933	1	14	2,604	196	....	....	....	....	....	3,139.28	....	....	
1934	1	16	2,770	165	1,761	....	730	519	67	4,457.35	27,155.46	135,200.00	Assembly property $42,000
1935	1	16	2,786	234	1,848	....	607	530	....	4,614.84	29,896.90	133,125.00	
1936	1	16	2,991	130	1,949	....	640	743	32	6,033.23	38,691.55	147,250.00	
1937	1	16	2,957	248	2,250	635	787	927	5	6,065.10	47,767.76	178,950.00	Baptist Building $100,000
1938	1	16	3,193	361	2,856	751	812	....	32	6,031.67	40,060.60	185,175.00	
1939	1	16	3,448	368	3,448	1,055	1,166	....	125	4,768.49	48,601.38	162,550.00	Grand Canyon College (approx. net worth) $86,358
1940	1	17	3,647	184	3,300	1,110	1,028	687	123	8,410.52	41,412.53	166,025.33	
1941	1	19	4,080	397	3,355	1,131	943	707	92	12,041.37	46,099.81	182,450.00	
1942	1	25	4,541	252	3,500	1,551	955	798	110	14,767.30	149,667.07	256,750.00	Trust and Memorial Fund $150,000
1943	2	26	5,029	344	4,210	2,258	1,358	845	114	27,011.72	214,729.50	371,500.00	
1944	2	32	5,781	476	4,996	4,092	1,465	....	....	42,405.35	289,375.12	932,310.00	
1945	5	51	6,834	743	6,690	....	1,569	1,767	412	56,392.96	399,832.78	1,236,305.00	Baptist Beacon $25,000
1946	5	56	7,845	867	8,140	6,335	2,654	1,840	529	59,452.23	414,858.54	1,603,046.33	
1947	5	63	10,198	1,056	9,755	7,740	3,056	1,999	561	83,411.01	578,470.76	1,855,661.14	
1948	5	71	10,953	1,127	12,606	8,199	4,210	2,049	604	100,428.21	567,527.16	2,177,437.00	Total $438,358
1949	6	77	12,268	1,323	12,923	8,384	4,452	3,163	569	94,177.13	732,266.00	2,859,442.00	
1950	9	88	14,257	1,512	14,240	11,843	5,117	3,325	871	126,389.00	902,225.00	4,327,912.00	
1951	11	115	17,310	1,723	17,543	13,534	6,468	4,056	1,279	149,174.54	1,240,540.00	5,388,389.00	
1952	15	155	22,079	2,336	21,648	15,800	6,551	5,512	1,554	185,077.16	1,561,326.00	6,497,059.00	
1953	18	183	26,379	3,111	28,024	15,800	10,580	5,512	1,554	205,011.26	1,561,326.00		
1954	21	219	32,605	4,044	34,897	19,593	14,011	5,543	2,345	279,461.51	2,391,613.00		

BERNEICE ROBINSON

ARIZONA ASSOCIATIONS.

I. Extant. ARKANSAS VALLEY. Organized in Oct., 1954, by messengers from five churches which withdrew from the Southern Baptist Association of Colorado for convenience and fellowship. Articles of faith were adopted. In 1954 six churches reported 48 baptisms, 299 members, $15,099.00 total gifts, $1,539.85 mission gifts, $36,500.00 church property, and $15,800.00 church debt.

CATALINA. Organized Oct. 11, 1946, at Tucson, Ariz., by messengers from 6 churches in Pima County. Articles of faith were adopted. It is the first Arizona association to own a camp and the first to establish work among the Mexicans. The first B.S.U. building, purchased by the Baptist General Convention of Arizona, is just outside the campus of the University of Arizona at Tucson. In 1952 three churches left Catalina to form Cochise Association. In 1954, 12 churches and 2 missions (including Mexican mission) reported 433 baptisms, 2,924 members, $63,328 total gifts, $35,744 mission gifts, $593,500 property value, and $209,989 church debt. Catalina and Cochise share a district missionary.

CENTRAL. Organized Mar. 2, 1942. Messengers from 16 churches located in Maricopa, Yavapai, and Graham counties met in first annual session at Glendale, Ariz., Oct. 12, 1944. Articles of faith were adopted. It is the mother association of churches which later organized Grand Canyon, San Carlos, Mohave, and Estrella. A district missionary serves Central and Estrella. Phoenix, located in Central, is the state capital and headquarters for the Baptist General Convention of Arizona. It is the home of the first Southern Baptist church organized in Arizona, the first mission work among the Chinese in Arizona, and Grand Canyon College. In 1954, 31 churches and the Chinese mission, reported 750 baptisms, 8,268 members, $449,880 total gifts, $105,771 mission gifts, $1,563,332 property value, and $398,220 church debt.

COCHISE. Organized Oct. 12, 1953, at Douglas, Ariz., by messengers from three churches which withdrew from Catalina because of distance. The newly organized church at Willcox joined the association. Articles of faith were adopted. In 1954 six churches reported 91 baptisms, 555 members, $21,096 total gifts, $2,674 mission gifts, $45,425 property value, and $10,543 church debt.

DENVER. Organized in 1954 by messengers from the 12 churches remaining in the Southern Baptist Association of Colorado after 14 churches had withdrawn to form two new associations. Articles of faith were adopted. A district missionary serves Denver, Pike's Peak, and Arkansas Valley associations. In 1954, 21 churches reported 255 baptisms, 1,929 members, $215,990 total gifts, and $598,150 property value.

ESTRELLA. Organized Oct. 16, 1951, by 31 messengers from eight churches in Central Association. Articles of faith were adopted. A district missionary serves Estrella and Central. In 1954, 10 churches reported 237 baptisms, 1,833 members, $75,990 total gifts, $13,540 mission gifts, $273,500 property value, and $78,444 church debt.

GILA VALLEY. Organized at Casa Grande, Mar. 3, 1942. Messengers from 10 churches located in Pima, Maricopa, and Pinal counties attended the first annual meeting at Casa Grande. Articles of faith were adopted. It is the mother association of churches which helped organize Catalina and Yuma. Gila Valley shares a district missionary with Yuma, San Carlos, and Mt. Graham. In 1954, 17 churches reported 211 baptisms, 2,949 members, $136,896 total gifts, $21,827 mission gifts, $677,000 property value, and $113,651 church debt.

GRAND CANYON. Organized at Prescott in 1946 by messengers from six churches in Coconino and Yavapai counties. Articles of faith were adopted. Included in its work were churches from Utah and Colorado until they were strong enough to form the Utah Association. A district missionary serves Grand Canyon, Little Colorado, and Mohave. In 1954 five churches reported 91 baptisms, 647 members, $24,835 total gifts, $3,344 mission gifts, $119,000 property value, and $43,979 church debt.

LITTLE COLORADO. Located in Navajo and Apache counties, in northeastern Arizona, organized in 1950 by messengers from four churches. Articles of faith were adopted. A district missionary serves Little Colorado, Mohave, and Grand Canyon. In 1954 eight churches reported 97 baptisms, 1,057 members, $44,263 total gifts, $6,904 mission gifts, $191,000 property value, and $31,145 church debt.

MOHAVE. Organized in 1951 by messengers from four churches in northwestern Arizona and southern Nevada. Articles of faith were adopted. A district missionary serves Mohave, Grand Canyon, and Little Colorado associations. In 1954 four churches reported 32 baptisms, 294 members, $15,560 total gifts, $3,556 mission gifts, $29,000 property value, and $8,800 church debt.

MONTANA. Organized at Cheyenne, Wyo., Sept. 7, 1953, by messengers from six churches. Articles of faith were adopted. In 1954 six churches reported 52 baptisms, 372 members, $33,104 total gifts, $55,000 property value, and $3,300 church debt.

MOUNT GRAHAM. Organized Dec. 17, 1951, at Clifton, Ariz., by messengers from four churches. A district missionary serves this and three other associations. They also own a camp site. In 1954 six churches reported 60 baptisms, 612 members, $32,082 total gifts, $13,886 mission gifts, $64,000 property value, and $12,389 church debt.

NORTH DAKOTA. Organized Dec. 14, 1954, at Williston, N. Dak., by messengers from four churches. Articles of faith were adopted. In 1954 six churches reported 32 baptisms, 142 members, $8,273 total gifts, and $1,500 property value.

OLD FAITHFUL. Organized Sept. 7, 1953, at Cheyenne, Wyo., by messengers from six churches. Articles of faith were adopted. A district missionary serves the Wyoming, Montana, Dakota district. In 1954, 13 churches reported 133 baptisms, 749 members, $82,772 total gifts, $8,098 mission gifts, $251,900 property value, and $182,860 church debt.

PIKE'S PEAK. Organized in Sept., 1954, by nine churches which withdrew from Southern Baptist Association of Colorado for convenience and fellowship. Articles of faith were adopted. In 1954, 11 churches reported 309 baptisms, 1,262 members, $111,636 total gifts, and $308,600 property value.

SAN CARLOS. Organized at Globe, Ariz., Oct. 12, 1946, by messengers from six churches in Gila, Navajo, and Graham counties. Articles of faith were adopted. In 1954, having lost churches to other newly organized associations, four churches reported 32 baptisms, 479 members, $22,063 total gifts, $4,332 mission gifts, $37,410 property value, and $23,000 church debt.

TWIN BUTTES. Organized Oct. 3, 1953, at Pocatello, Idaho, by messengers from four churches. In 1954 five churches reported 40 baptisms, 250 members, $13,856 total gifts, $1,689 mission gifts, $43,500 property value, and $18,840 church debt.

UTAH. Organized at Flagstaff, Ariz., Oct. 3, 1950, by messengers from five churches in Utah and Colorado at the fifth annual session of Grand Canyon Association. Articles of faith were adopted. Three of the original churches, Denver, Casper, and Idaho Falls, have become a part of three new associations, Denver, Old Faithful, and Twin Buttes, respectively. A district missionary serves Utah and Twin Buttes associations. In 1954, 12 churches reported 91 baptisms, 783 members, $38,164 total gifts, $7,056 mission gifts, $155,832 property value, and $73,189 church debt.

YUMA. Organized July 8, 1952, at Wellton, Yuma County, Ariz., by messengers from four churches which withdrew from Gila Valley because of distance. Articles of faith were adopted. A district missionary serves Yuma, Gila Valley, Mt. Graham, and San Carlos. In 1954 five churches reported 91 baptisms, 734 members, $39,142.00 total gifts, $3,990.05 mission gifts, $210,500.00 property value, and $70,100.00 church debt. HILTON J. CROW

II. Extinct. GAMBRELL MEMORIAL. Organized Oct. 26, 1925, by messengers from nine churches located in Maricopa, Gila, and Yavapai counties. Articles of faith were adopted. It became a co-operating association of New Mexico Baptist Convention Nov. 26, 1926, but dissolved Sept. 21, 1928, when the association organized into the Baptist General Convention of Arizona.

SOUTHERN BAPTIST ASSOCIATION OF COLORADO (COLORADO-WYOMING). Organized at Denver, Colo., Oct. 14, 1952, by messengers from seven churches in Colorado and one in Wyoming. Each affiliating church indicated its acceptance of the New Hampshire Declaration of Faith. In 1953, 26 churches reported 345 baptisms, 2,115 members, $154,387 total gifts, and $375,944 church property. In 1954 this association was divided into three associations known as Denver, Pike's Peak, and Arkansas Valley.

WYOMING-MONTANA. Organized Feb. 17, 1953, at Casper, Wyo., by messengers from three Wyoming churches and one from Montana. The articles of faith were adopted. Sept. 7, 1953, this association and a portion of North Dakota became the Wyoming-Montana-Dakota district and was divided into two associations, Old Faithful and Montana. HILTON J. CROW

ARIZONA BAPTIST AFFILIATES. See WESTERN BAPTISTS AFFILIATED WITH ARIZONA.

ARKANSAS ASSOCIATIONS.
I. Extant. ARKANSAS VALLEY. Organized June 29, 1920, by 10 churches from Mt. Vernon Association, located in Phillips, Lee, and Monroe counties. The association owns a missionary's home and employs a superintendent of missions. In 1954, 26 churches reported 441 baptisms, 7,137 members, $259,114 total gifts, $51,576 mission gifts, $1,098,500 property value, and $102,306 church debt.

ASHLEY COUNTY. Organized by 18 churches Oct. 17, 1950, located in Ashley County, formerly affiliated with Bartholomew Association. It employs a superintendent of missions. In 1954, 20 churches reported 224 baptisms, 5,005 members, $164,089 total gifts, $25,731 mission gifts, $576,485 property value, and $47,024 church debt.

BARTHOLOMEW. Organized in 1846 by seven churches located in Drew, Ashley, and Bradley counties. It has articles of faith and employs a superintendent of missions. In 1954, 26 churches reported 297 baptisms, 5,936 members, $166,950 total gifts, $32,220 mission gifts, $685,050 property value, and $115,936 church debt.

BENTON COUNTY. Organized in 1885 by 19 churches located in Benton County by uniting Bentonville and Springtown associations. It employs a superintendent of missions. In 1954, 24 churches reported 365 baptisms, 5,893 members, $261,815 total gifts, $47,948 mission gifts, $730,310 property value, and $99,538 church debt.

BIG CREEK. Organized in 1874 by churches in Fulton County. It has articles of faith and employs a superintendent of missions. In 1954, 14 churches reported 50 baptisms, 1,159 members, $24,939 total gifts, $2,190 mission gifts, $80,600 property value, and $7,979 church debt.

BLACK RIVER. Organized in 1914 by six churches in Lawrence County. It has articles of faith and employs a superintendent of missions. In 1954, 28 churches reported 217 baptisms, 4,381 members, $120,117 total gifts, $14,109 mission gifts, $585,900 property value, and $46,703 church debt.

BOONE COUNTY. Organized Sept. 17, 1951, by 18 churches in Boone County. These churches came out of Boone-Carroll which divided in order to enlarge local missionary work. Boone has had a superintendent of missions most of the time. In 1954, 21 churches reported 166 baptisms, 2,631 members, $88,133 total gifts, $11,810 mission gifts, $506,500 property value, and $77,867 church debt.

BUCKNER. Organized as a part of Concord in 1870. About 1880 the churches in Scott County organized as Concord South; and in 1891 the name was changed to Buckner, in honor of J. H. Buckner, missionary to the Indians and first president of Buckner College. It has a superintendent of missions and articles of faith. In 1954, 30 churches reported 213 baptisms, 3,898 members, $83,096 total gifts, $19,190 mission gifts, $198,300 property value, and $32,901 church debt.

BUCKVILLE. Organized in 1890 by nine churches located in Garland and Montgomery counties, most of them from Saline Association. It has articles of faith and a part-time superintendent of missions. In 1954 seven churches reported 2 baptisms, 332 members, $2,782 total gifts, $547 mission gifts, $10,000 property value, and $50 church debt.

CADDO RIVER. Organized Oct. 8–10, 1853, by five churches at Mt. Gilead Church in Montgomery County. It has articles of faith and has usually had a superintendent of missions. In 1954, 17 churches located in Pike, Clark, and Montgomery counties reported 65 baptisms, 1,751 members, $34,417 total gifts, $4,896 mission gifts, $130,550 property value, and $7,778 church debt.

CAREY. Organized Mar. 11, 1916, by 14 churches in Dallas, Calhoun, and Clark counties, 11 of which had previously been in Judson Association. It adopted articles of faith; usually it has a superintendent of missions for whom it owns a home. In 1954, 15 churches reported 143 baptisms, 3,408 members, $135,762 total gifts, $27,500 mission gifts, $294,800 property value, and $13,801 church debt.

CAROLINE. Organized in 1853 near Austin by five churches located in Lonoke and Prairie counties. In 1900 it had 59 churches located in Lonoke, Prairie, Pulaski, White, and Woodruff counties. Parts of seven associations have come from it. It has adopted articles of faith, employs a superintendent of missions, and owns a home for him. In 1954, 25 churches located in Lonoke and Prairie counties reported 226 baptisms, 5,437 members, $181,911 total gifts, $30,674 mission gifts, $816,060 property value, and $113,993 church debt.

CARROLL COUNTY. Organized Nov. 2, 1950, by seven churches located in Carroll County. Boone-Carroll, of which it was formerly a part, dissolved, forming two associations so that local mission efforts might be increased. Carroll County has a superintendent of missions. In 1954 eight churches reported 114 baptisms, 1,147 members, $62,027 total gifts, $6,281 mission gifts, and $174,000 property value.

CENTENNIAL. Organized in 1945 by six churches in Arkansas County, formerly in Harmony Association. It usually has a superintendent of missions. In 1954, 10 churches reported 199 baptisms, 3,248 members, $139,839 total gifts, $28,118 mission gifts, $498,500 property value, and $38,748 church debt.

CENTRAL. Organized in 1919 by seven churches in Garland, Saline, and Hot Springs counties. Most of these came from Saline Association which was predominantly "Landmark." Central regularly employs a superintendent of missions and owns a home for him. It has articles of faith. In 1954, 35 churches reported 617 baptisms, 14,032 members, $493,178 total gifts, $75,267 mission gifts, $1,888,692 property value, and $234,038 church debt.

CLEAR CREEK. Organized in 1872 by five churches in Crawford and Franklin counties. It has articles of faith, owns assembly grounds, and has a superintendent of missions. In 1954, 27 churches in Johnson, Franklin (north of the Arkansas River), and Crawford counties reported 397 baptisms, 4,673 members, $173,316 total gifts, $23,940 mission gifts, $832,500 property value, and $153,950 church debt.

CONCORD. Organized in 1870 by 12 churches from Dardanelle Association, located in Sebastian, Scott, Franklin, and Logan counties. About 1878 it divided into Concord North, and Concord South, the southern part later forming Buckner Association. Concord has articles of faith and employs a superintendent of missions. In 1954, 37 churches reported 1,003 baptisms, 18,801 members, $703,695 total gifts, $133,259 mission gifts, $3,023,000 property value, and $304,345 church debt.

CONWAY-PERRY. Organized in 1948 when churches in Conway County united with Perry County Association. It has a superintendent of missions. In 1954, 15 churches reported 96 baptisms, 1,736 members, $55,221 total gifts, $12,209 mission gifts, $128,000 property value, and $25,000 church debt.

CURRENT RIVER. Organized Oct. 7, 1881, with six churches formerly in Cane Creek (in Missouri), located in Randolph and Clay counties. Articles of faith were adopted. It employs a superintendent of missions and, with adjacent associations, owns and operates Ravenden Springs Assembly. In 1954, 19 churches reported 156 baptisms, 3,061 members, $67,969 total gifts, $9,591 mission gifts, $334,500 property value, and $4,000 church debt.

DARDANELLE-RUSSELLVILLE. Organized at Morrilton in 1932 by the union of Dardanelle and Russellville associations, composed of 30 churches located in Yell, Pope, and Conway counties. It employs a superintendent of missions. In 1954, 23 churches located in Yell and Pope counties reported 271 baptisms, 4,092 members, $105,357 total gifts, $24,863 mission gifts, $227,700 property value, and $4,000 church debt.

DELTA. Organized Sept. 26, 1929, at Lake Village by 20 churches located in Desha and Chicot counties. It employs a superintendent of missions and owns a home for him. In 1954, 34 churches reported 372 baptisms, 7,838 members, $218,666 total gifts, $40,219 mission gifts,

$565,585 property value, and $14,694 church debt.

FAULKNER COUNTY. Organized as Greenbrier Association, changing its name to Faulkner County in 1928 because of a conflict with another association also called Greenbrier. It has a superintendent of missions and owns assembly grounds. In 1954, 25 churches reported 128 baptisms, 3,748 members, $92,595 total gifts, $12,668 mission gifts, and $345,100 property value.

GAINESVILLE. Organized as Bethlehem Association with the name changed in 1883, to enhance the founding of a Baptist school at Gainesville, which never materialized. It has articles of faith, a superintendent of missions, and owns interest in Ravenden Springs assembly grounds. In 1954, 17 churches, located in the eastern part of Clay County, reported 138 baptisms, 2,322 members, $74,103 total gifts, $12,023 mission gifts, $181,700 property value, and $2,581 church debt.

GREENE COUNTY. Organized Nov. 11, 1925, by eight churches formerly in Gainesville Association, located in Greene County. It has a superintendent of missions and owns a home for him. In 1954, 38 churches reported 400 baptisms, 7,269 members, $162,859 total gifts, $25,355 mission gifts, $609,400 property value, and $77,215 church debt.

HARMONY. Organized in 1918 by seven churches in Jefferson, Cleveland, and Lincoln counties. The churches came out of Friendship Association because it was a strong "Landmark" body. Harmony has a superintendent of missions and a home for him. In 1954, 32 churches reported 430 baptisms, 12,289 members, $482,885 total gifts, $80,896 mission gifts, $1,759,000 property value, and $162,751 church debt.

HOPE. Organized in 1907 by 13 churches in Hemstead and adjacent counties. It has a superintendent of missions and a home for him. In 1954, 39 churches, in Miller, Hemstead, Lafayette, and Columbia counties, reported 648 baptisms, 11,121 members, $514,020 total gifts, $83,441 mission gifts, $2,012,306 property value, and $226,078 church debt.

INDEPENDENCE. Organized in 1850 by nine churches located in and adjacent to what is now Independence County. It has a superintendent of missions and owns assembly grounds. In 1954, 17 churches reported 104 baptisms, 3,544 members, $75,037 total gifts, $19,659 mission gifts, $362,469 property value, and $5,182 church debt.

LIBERTY. Organized in 1845 by churches in Union County which belonged to Saline Regular Association, a body which aided and encouraged the organization. Prior to the Civil War Liberty sponsored a female college at Camden. In 1850 it had about 24 churches. It has articles of faith, owns an assembly ground, has a superintendent of missions, and owns a home for him. In 1954, 47 churches, located in Union and Ouachita counties, reported 699 baptisms, 16,-842 members, $856,378 total gifts, $205,052 mission gifts, $3,565,753 property value, and $409,254 church debt.

LITTLE RED RIVER. Organized in 1872 by churches in Cleburn County. It usually has a superintendent of missions and has articles of faith. In 1954, 17 churches reported 114 baptisms, 2,326 members, $33,458 total gifts, $7,015 mission gifts, $142,000 property value, and $4,714 church debt.

LITTLE RIVER. Organized in 1915 by 13 churches in Little River, Sevier, and Howard counties. It has a superintendent of missions. In 1954, 28 churches reported 242 baptisms, 4,772 members, $127,371 total gifts, $22,307 mission gifts, $436,990 property value, and $40,975 church debt.

MISSISSIPPI COUNTY. Organized Oct. 20, 1925, by 12 churches in Mississippi County previously in Mt. Zion Association. It has a superintendent of missions and owns a home for him. In 1954, 38 churches reported 858 baptisms, 13,191 members, $769,950 total gifts, $59,387 mission gifts, $1,582,100 property value, and $121,682 church debt.

MOUNT ZION. Organized at Mt. Zion Church in Greene County, Sept., 1852, by five churches, previously in New Salem Association, which had dissolved. In 1902 it established Woodland Baptist College at Jonesboro, maintained about 15 years. It has articles of faith. It has a superintendent of missions and owns a home for him. In 1954, 29 churches reported 622 baptisms, 8,956 members, $336,938 total gifts, $52,610 mission gifts, $1,231,600 property value, and $102,889 church debt.

NEWTON COUNTY. Organized Oct. 21, 1944, by four churches in Newton County, previously in Boone-Carroll Association. It usually has a superintendent of missions. In 1954, five churches reported 31 baptisms, 290 members, $8,090 total gifts, $1,030 mission gifts, $42,766 property value, and $1,657 church debt.

OUACHITA. Organized in 1867 by churches in Polk County. It published articles of faith in 1902 and now has a superintendent of missions. In 1954, 19 churches reported 207 baptisms, 2,969 members, $69,244 total gifts, $10,250 mission gifts, $192,950 property value, and $7,745 church debt.

PULASKI COUNTY. Organized Nov. 9, 1916, by 16 churches previously in Caroline Association. Caroline aided and approved the organization. Pulaski has a superintendent of missions. In 1954, as the largest association in the state, its 75 full-time churches reported 1,644 baptisms, 32,557 members, $1,571,592 total gifts, $312,385 mission gifts, $6,243,248 property value, and $1,097,987 church debt.

RED RIVER. Organized near Hope in 1848 by five churches in southwestern Arkansas. At one time it included churches in Clark, Nevada, Hemstead, Columbia, Howard, and Sevier counties, but at present includes only Clark and Nevada. It took action in 1884 which led to the founding of Ouachita College, located in the association. It has articles of faith (1899), employs a superintendent of missions, and owns a home for him. In 1954, 33 churches reported 212 baptisms, 5,985 members, $146,457 total gifts, $28,786 mission gifts, $751,800 property value, and $41,825 church debt.

ROCKY BAYOU. Organized in 1833 or 1840 (two accounts found) and in early years extended through the present Izard, Fulton, Randolph, Lawrence, Independence, Sharp, and Stone counties in Arkansas, and some territory in Missouri. In 1849 the Missouri churches withdrew and formed another association. Rocky Bayou now has churches only in Izard and Sharp counties. It has a superintendent of missions. In 1954, 15 churches reported 58 baptisms, 1,457 members, $18,767 total gifts, and $3,935 mission gifts.

STONE-VAN BUREN-SEARCY. Organized in 1932 by the union of Van Buren and Stone County associations, under the name Stone-Van Buren. "Searcy" was added to the name in 1944 since churches from Searcy County had joined the association. Annual sessions date from the organization of Stone County Association in 1917. The present association usually has a superintendent of missions, and has articles of faith. In 1954, 19 churches, in Stone, Van Buren, and Searcy counties, reported 180 baptisms, 2,440 members, $54,809 total gifts, $6,789 mission gifts, $115,450 property value, and $3,000 church debt.

TRI-COUNTY. Organized Oct. 20, 1925, by eight churches in Cross, Crittenden, and St. Francis counties. The churches came out of Mt. Zion and Mt. Vernon associations. At first named St. Francis County Association, the name was changed to Tri-County in 1926. It has a superintendent of missions. In 1954, 34 churches reported 666 baptisms, 6,360 members, $366,578 total gifts, $41,786 mission gifts, $1,162,674 property value, $203,854 church debt.

TRINITY. Organized in Nov., 1937, by seven churches in Poinsett County. It has a superintendent of missions. In 1954, 30 churches reported 498 baptisms, 6,237 members, $141,713 total gifts, $17,355 mission gifts, $595,512 property value, and $43,188 church debt.

WASHINGTON-MADISON. Organized Sept. 11, 1941, by merging Washington County and Madison County associations. It has a superintendent of missions. In 1954, 25 churches reported 343 baptisms, 6,232 members, $295,433 total gifts, $41,032 mission gifts, $890,100 property value, and $141,967 church debt.

WHITE COUNTY. Organized in 1926 by 15 churches in White County, previously in Caroline Association. It has a superintendent of missions. In 1954, 30 churches reported 267 baptisms, 4,582 members, $108,940 total gifts, $18,503 mission gifts, $589,000 property value, and $56,500 church debt.

WHITE RIVER. Organized in 1840 by five churches in north central Arkansas, formerly in Spring River Association which dissolved that year. White River led in establishing and maintaining Mountain Home College, 1893-1933. In early years it embraced a large part of north central Arkansas and the part of southern Missouri now in Baxter and Marion counties. It has a superintendent of missions and articles of faith. In 1954, 15 churches reported 84 baptisms, 2,223 members, $50,587 total gifts, $7,826 mission gifts, $185,200 property value, and $16,500 church debt.

WOODRUFF COUNTY. Organized Nov. 18, 1928, by eight churches in Woodruff County. It has a superintendent of missions and articles of faith. In 1954, 13 churches reported 79 baptisms, 2,032 members, $60,965 total gifts, $11,553 mission gifts, $178,500 property value, and $623 church debt.

II. Extinct. ARKANSAS. Organized about 1841, perhaps in north central part of Arkansas. It evidently lasted only a short time.

ARKANSAS COUNTY. Organized in 1920 by 15 churches in Arkansas County, previously in Grand Prairie Association. It was discontinued about 1930.

BENTONVILLE. Organized in 1860 by merging Old Mt. Zion and Fayetteville United Baptist associations. Located in Benton and Washington counties, it had 43 churches in 1870. In 1885 it united with Springtown Association to form Benton County Association.

BETHLEHEM UNITED BAPTIST. Organized in 1853 by four churches, three in northeast Arkansas and one in Missouri. They had formerly been in Black River Association, Missouri. In 1854 the name was changed to Bethlehem Association of United Effort Baptists. "Effort" was added to distinguish the association from the Hardshells who opposed evangelistic efforts, but in 1855 the word was dropped. In 1883 the name was changed to Gainesville to enhance the establishment of a Baptist institute at Gainesville which never materialized.

BLUE MOUNTAIN. Organized in 1874 by churches located in Searcy and Stone counties. It had 13 churches in 1917. In 1954, with 20 churches, it affiliated with the American Baptist Association. It has articles of faith.

BOONE-CARROLL. Organized Nov. 9, 1937, by 19 churches, in Boone and Carroll counties. It was a union of Carroll County and Crooked Creek associations. It dissolved Sept. 6, 1951, forming Carroll County and Boone County associations.

BUFFALO. Organized in 1838 by churches in and adjacent to Marion County. This association became Hardshell and existed as such in 1897.

CADDO RIVER, SOUTH. Organized Oct. 8, 1910, by nine churches in Montgomery County. It adopted articles of faith. By 1913 the name had been changed to Caddo River Valley, and no records later than 1919 have been found.

CARROLL COUNTY. Organized in 1870 in Carroll County. It merged with Crooked Creek Nov. 9, 1937, forming Boone-Carroll Association. It adopted articles of faith.

EARLY PIONEER BAPTIST CHURCHES

SATERS CHURCH, Lutherville, Md. Exterior and interior. Organized Nov. 17, 1742, when Henry Sater deeded "one acre of land for a meeting house, burying place and all other conveniences, for the church and congregation, forever and to the end of the world." Structure was built early thereafter and is still used. Contains original brick brought from England.

WOODVILLE CHURCH, Miss. Original building, front columned section, erected by slave labor in 1809 and still in use. Membership 1956 was 400 with property valued at $150,000. Educational unit serves 400.

KIOKEE CHURCH, Appling, Ga., near Augusta. Oldest Baptist church in state, constituted 1772 by Daniel Marshall who served as pastor until his death in 1784. This building erected in 1808, photo by Hugh Cross.

SANDY CREEK CHURCH, N.C. Organized by Shubal Stearns, Daniel Marshall, and others in 1755. This artist's conception of original building shows the structure typical of the majority of the first country church buildings prior to 1825.

HALF MOON BLUFF CHURCH. Organized 1812, was the first non-Catholic church in Louisiana outside of New Orleans. Picture is artist's conception of the original building, which had a dirt floor, one door, two windows, and a mud chimney.

BUILDINGS TYPICAL OF 14,000 SOUTHERN BAPTIST COUNTRY CHURCHES IN 1956

ZION CHURCH, Clinton, Tenn. Typical of approximately 3,500 Southern Baptist churches.

FALLING CREEK CHURCH, Goldsboro, N. C. Like about 3,000 other churches, it has been remodeled by addition of Sunday school rooms at the rear.

BEFORE AND AFTER, Wallerville, Miss., church. Where Dr. J. B. Gambrell was baptized, showing the building erected in 1854 and the one which replaced it in 1937. It is typical of about 3,000 churches.

COLUMBIA. Organized in 1852 by churches in Columbia and Lafayette counties. It has articles of faith and continues as a "Landmark" association.

CONCORD, SOUTH. Organized about 1878 by churches from Concord Association located in Scott County and adjacent territory. The name was changed to Buckner Association in 1891.

CROOKED CREEK. Organized in 1867 in Boone County. It merged with Carroll County to form Boone-Carroll in 1937. It adopted articles of faith.

DARDANELLE. Organized in 1854, in west central Arkansas, from Dardanelle to Fort Smith, including churches on both sides of Arkansas River. Churches in the western part formed Concord in 1870; and churches north of the river formed Russellville in 1880. In 1932 Dardanelle merged with Russellville, forming Dardanelle-Russellville.

FAYETTEVILLE. Organized in 1871 by four churches in Washington County. It has articles of faith and, with 13 churches, affiliates with American Baptist Association. Convention churches withdrew and organized Washington County Association in 1918.

FOURCHE VALLEY. Organized in 1887 in Perry County. In 1896 it had seven churches and nine preachers, with total salaries of $1,250. In 1942 the name was changed to Perry County.

FRIENDSHIP. Organized about 1872, located in Jefferson, Lincoln, Drew, and Cleveland counties. Convention churches withdrew and organized Harmony in 1918.

GRAND PRAIRIE. Organized in 1874, located in Prairie, Arkansas, and Monroe counties. It published articles of faith in 1914. In 1954, with 19 churches, it was classified "Landmark."

GREENBRIER. Organized Oct. 10, 1884, with 19 churches in Faulkner County, from United Association. The name was changed to Faulkner County in 1928. Articles of faith were adopted.

HOWARD COUNTY. Organized in 1893 by 20 churches in Hemstead and Howard counties, which came out of Southwestern Association. Convention churches withdrew in 1915. Extant as "Landmark," 1954, it had seven churches located in Howard County. It has articles of faith.

HOWARD COUNTY No. 2. Organized Oct. 23, 1925, by five churches in Howard and Hemstead counties. The churches soon returned to adjacent associations.

JONESBORO. Organized in 1898 by a few rural churches in Craighead County; it had 13 churches in 1902. Soon after, it became and has remained "Landmark."

JUDSON. Organized in 1854 by seven churches in Bradley, Dallas, and Ouachita counties. Convention churches withdrew from it and formed other associations. It affiliated with American Baptist Association in 1954. It has articles of faith.

LITTLE ROCK. Organized Nov., 1824, by three churches in Pulaski and Saline counties. It was the first association in the state. Although in 1828 it had eight churches in Pulaski, Saline, Clark, Perry, Faulkner, and Crawford counties, it dissolved before 1832.

MACEDONIA. Organized in 1885 by churches in Scott and Yell counties. It had articles of faith and in 1892 reported nine churches with a total of 388 members.

MADISON COUNTY. Organized in 1887 by some churches in Madison County. In 1914, with 13 churches, it published articles of faith. It merged with Washington County Association in 1941 as Washington-Madison Association.

MILLER COUNTY. Organized in 1903 by seven churches which withdrew from Texarkana Association. It adopted articles of faith and bought a home for its superintendent of missions. No records are available after those of 1906.

MOUNTAIN. Organized in 1868 in Scott County. It had 10 churches in 1872. It became extinct about 1878, for causes unknown. It had articles of faith.

MOUNT VERNON. Organized about 1856 by churches in St. Francis and Phillips counties. Convention churches withdrew and formed other associations, leaving it "Landmark." Mt. Vernon established Forrest City Baptist College in 1876. In 1954 it reported 12 churches affiliated with the American Baptist Association.

NEW SALEM. Organized in 1848 by two churches in Craighead County. After only four years, Mt. Zion Association was organized in its place.

NORTHWESTERN ARKANSAS MISSIONARY. Organized in 1869 by the merging of Fayetteville United and Old Mt. Zion. It was located in Crawford, Washington, and Benton counties. In 1877 it became Bentonville Association.

OLD MT. ZION. Organized in 1840 in northwest Arkansas. It had 11 churches in 1851 and merged with Fayetteville United Baptist Association in 1860.

OSCEOLA. Organized in 1872 by seven churches in Mississippi County. In 1899 it had seven churches and 233 members. It disbanded in 1900, and the churches went into Mt. Zion Association.

PEE DEE. Organized in 1883 by churches in Stone and Van Buren counties. Named after the church where it was organized, it had six churches in 1893 and had adopted articles of faith. Its last meeting was held about 1918, and most of the churches went into the organization of Van Buren County Association in 1923.

PERRY COUNTY. Organized in 1887 as Fourche Valley Association. The name was changed to Perry County in 1942 and to Conway-Perry in 1948.

PIKE COUNTY. Organized in 1905. In 1906 it had 11 churches in Pike and Clark counties. Convention churches withdrew about 1927 and joined Caddo River Association leaving Pike County "Landmark." It adopted articles of faith.

PINE BLUFF. Organized in 1863 by churches in and adjacent to Grant County. In 1902 it had

Arkansas Associations

42 churches in Grant, Jefferson, Saline, and Pulaski counties. Convention churches withdrew shortly after 1902 leaving it wholly "Landmark." In 1954 it had 64 churches. It has articles of faith.

POINT REMOVE. Organized in 1843 eight miles northeast of Adkins by 12 churches in Pope and Conway counties. It has articles of faith and exists as a Primitive association with four churches in Logan, Franklin, and Pope counties.

RUSSELLVILLE. Organized in 1880 by churches in Pope and Johnson counties, which withdrew from Dardanelle Association due to difficulty in crossing the Arkansas River. It had 30 churches in 1896. In 1932 it united with Dardanelle to form Dardanelle-Russellville Association.

ST. FRANCIS. Organized in 1831 at Franklin in St. Francis County. It dissolved or became Hardshell about 1850.

SALEM. Organized in 1840 in and near Washington County. It was probably Hardshell from its beginning but definitely so in 1846.

SALEM. Organized by four churches in the Batesville area in 1847. Due to internal strife it lasted only one year.

SALINE. Organized in 1836 by six churches in Saline, Hot Springs, Clark, and Hemstead counties. In 1847 it requested the organization of a state convention. Due to anticonvention attitudes prevailing in it, the convention churches later withdrew and joined or formed other associations. Saline, affiliated with the American Baptist Association, has 45 churches.

SEBASTIAN COUNTY. Organized at Mansfield Oct. 27, 1920, by eight churches in the southern part of Sebastian County. It disbanded soon after this, and the churches went back into Buckner Association.

SOUTHEAST ARKANSAS, GENERAL ASSOCIATION OF. Held its seventh session at Warren, June 16–18, 1882; 18 churches were represented. W. E. Paxton was moderator, and James Bryant Searcy (*q.v.*), secretary.

SOUTHWESTERN. Organized in 1880 in southwestern Arkansas. In 1915 it adopted articles of faith. In 1954, with 16 churches located in Miller, Little River, and Sevier counties, it affiliated with the American Baptist Association.

SPRINGFIELD. Organized in 1871 in northwest Arkansas.

SPRING RIVER. Organized in Nov., 1829, the second association in the state, by five churches in Lawrence, Independence, and Izard counties. Due to personal conflicts Spring River disbanded in 1840, having 14 churches and 284 members. It adopted articles of faith.

SPRING RIVER. Organized in 1868 by a few churches which came out of Rocky Bayou Association, in Sharp, Randolph, Lawrence, and Izard counties. It had 19 churches in 1875 and is "Landmark."

SPRINGTOWN. See STATE CORNER.

STATE CORNER. Organized in 1872, by churches in northwest Benton County and southwest Missouri. The name was changed to Springtown in 1873. It merged with Bentonville to form Benton County Association in 1885.

STATE LINE. Organized in 1873 by five churches in Missouri. Churches in Randolph County, Ark., united with it, so that, by 1888, 10 member churches were in Missouri, 11 in Arkansas. The Missouri churches were lettered out to form another association. State Line helped to establish and maintain Maynard Baptist Academy at Maynard, 1899–1926. When the association disbanded in 1923, the eight churches joined Current River Association. It adopted articles of faith.

STEVEN'S CREEK. Organized in 1880, in White and Jackson counties. It adopted articles of faith and reported 21 churches in 1909. Convention churches withdrew, leaving it "Landmark." Steven's Creek is affiliated with the American Baptist Association.

STONE COUNTY. Organized Sept. 26, 1919, by 10 churches in Stone County. It adopted articles of faith. In 1932 it merged with Van Buren County Association to form Stone-Van Buren Association.

STONE-VAN BUREN. Organized in 1932 by the union of Stone County and Van Buren County associations. Annual sessions date from the organization of Stone County Association in 1919. In 1944 the name was changed to Stone-Van Buren-Searcy.

TRACE RIDGE. Organized in 1888, in Searcy and Van Buren counties. It became "Landmark."

UNION. Organized in 1841 in southwestern Arkansas. It became extinct during the Civil War.

UNION. Existed in 1850's, in Conway, Searcy, and Van Buren counties.

UNION. Organized in 1871, in southwestern Arkansas. It became and has remained "Landmark."

UNION. Organized in 1879 in Searcy, Marion, and Stone counties.

UNITED. Organized in 1874, located in Faulkner and Conway counties. In 1884 several churches withdrew to help form Greenbrier Association. It is "Landmark."

VAN BUREN COUNTY. Organized at Pee Dee Church Oct. 19, 1923, by eight churches in Van Buren County. It adopted the rules of decorum and the articles of faith of Pee Dee Association, and the constitution of Stone County Association. In 1932 it united with Stone County forming Stone-Van Buren Association.

WASHINGTON COUNTY. Organized in 1837 by 12 churches in Northwest Arkansas. It became Hardshell and extinct.

WASHINGTON COUNTY. Organized Nov. 26, 1918, by four churches in Washington County. In 1941 it merged with Madison County as Washington-Madison Association.

WHITE RIVER VALLEY. Organized in 1870 in Jackson County. In 1905 it reported 10 churches and 479 members. It disbanded about 1910, and churches joined Black River Association.

L. C. TEDFORD

ARKANSAS BAPTIST. Established as the Arkansas state paper by vote of the Arkansas Baptist Convention in 1858. The first issue was printed in Little Rock, Jan., 1859, and the subscription price was $2 a year. In four months the circulation reached 1,600 subscribers, and by the second year it had increased to 2,200. Privately owned and published in Little Rock, the paper had a continuous publication for two years and five months when the Civil War forced its discontinuance.   B. H. DUNCAN

ARKANSAS BAPTIST. Founded in 1868 at Little Rock by N. P. Moore. The paper existed only 10 weeks, and its subscription list was transferred to the *Central Baptist* of St. Louis, Mo.   B. H. DUNCAN

ARKANSAS BAPTIST. Founded at Beebe in 1879 by Joshua Hill who sold it a few months later to J. H. Ruberson. Ruberson moved the paper to Judsonia, changing its name to *Arkansas Baptist Banner*. He sold it to James P. Green who was publishing it in 1881. The paper no longer exists.   B. H. DUNCAN

ARKANSAS BAPTIST. Established in 1887 when the state convention changed the name of *The Evangel* to *Arkansas Baptist*. In 1896 W. A. Clark, acting mission secretary, became editor. During his editorship the paper gave less and less support to the state convention and its institutions, and when the convention met in Hope in 1900, "the editor was severely reprimanded for not supporting the Convention program and workers." Clark promised to change his policies during 1901 but did not keep his promise. He and other anti-convention individuals owned controlling stock in the paper. Therefore, in 1901 the convention renounced the *Arkansas Baptist* as the state paper and took action for its replacement, establishing another paper in 1902 called the *Baptist Advance*.   B. H. DUNCAN

ARKANSAS BAPTIST. Established in 1933 when the state convention changed the name of the *Baptist Advance* to *Arkansas Baptist*. From 1933 to 1940 J. I. Cossey edited and published the paper under lease. Under L. A. Myers of New Orleans, elected editor and business manager in 1940, the list of subscribers to the paper increased from 6,000 to 14,000. C. E. Bryant, assistant editor beginning in Feb., 1943, became editor when Myers resigned in June of that year. Under Bryant, who resigned May 1, 1947, to accept a position with the executive committee of the Southern Baptist Convention, the circulation rose to 28,308. B. H. Duncan was chosen as Bryant's successor.

In 1955 circulation of the *Arkansas Baptist* was 47,334, with 431 churches sending the paper to their families, on the budget plan. The paper has equipment valued at $12,000 which includes office furniture, Addressograph machines, and a Graphotype machine. It receives an allocation of $15,000 a year from the Cooperative Program.   B. H. DUNCAN

ARKANSAS BAPTIST ASSEMBLY. An encampment site owned and developed by Arkansas Baptists to accommodate various summer meetings held to promote phases of the program of the state convention. The first such meeting was recommended as early as 1904 and was held at Brown's Springs near Arkadelphia in July, 1905. The next assembly was held at Arkadelphia in July, 1906. For 10 or 12 years the assemblies were held at Arkadelphia where Ouachita College facilities were available. In 1913, in addition to the assembly at Arkadelphia, one was held at Cushman and one at Monte Ne.

Since 1923 the state assembly has been held near Siloam Springs. At first it was under the direction of the state B.Y.P.U. organization. Later it was transferred to the Arkansas Baptist executive board, then later to the Arkansas convention itself.

Three men have served as directors: Herbert Hamilton, secretary of Sunday school and training union department, 1923-27; Jacob Pinckney Edmunds, 1928-36; and Edgar Williamson, 1937-56.

The assembly property, owned by Arkansas Baptists, consists of 170 acres of land and more than 125 buildings, including dormitories, cabins, tabernacle, dining hall, faculty building, bath house, rest rooms, etc. Property, buildings, and equipment are valued at $108,800.

Kitchen facilities are of modern design. The water filter system and the water are approved by the State Health Department. For recreation there are two modern tennis courts and a swimming pool, 40 by 75 feet, which was built in 1955 at a cost of $24,000.

In 1954 the registration reached 1,300 and in 1955, 1,559. Two jubilee anniversary sessions of the assembly were observed during 1956: the first, June 28-July 3; the second, July 5-10.

In addition to serving as a means of promoting the program of Arkansas Baptists, the assembly sessions have proved effective in the enlistment of leadership. Many who first made decisions at the assembly are preaching and serving as missionaries and in other full-time Christian activities.   EDGAR WILLIAMSON

ARKANSAS BAPTIST FOUNDATION. An agency of the Arkansas Baptist State Convention, created "to serve any benevolent, charitable, educational or missionary undertaking, institution or agency fostered by, or having the official sanction of, the Arkansas Baptist State Convention." Its function is "to receive, by bequest, devise, gift, purchase or lease, either absolutely or in trust, any property, real, personal or mixed, and to administer such property, to convey such property, to invest and reinvest the same, or the proceeds thereof," as the directors may deem advisable. The foundation was created by the Arkansas Baptist State Convention on recommendation of its executive

Arkansas Baptist Hospital

board. The principal promoters of the idea were B. L. Bridges, J. G. Cothran, and B. H. Duncan. A proposed charter was presented to the convention and approved in 1948. The charter was issued under the laws of Arkansas Apr. 25, 1949.

When gifts are designated, the instructions of the donor must be carried out. Undesignated funds are administered by the board on instructions from the convention. The foundation is managed by a board of nine directors elected by the convention for terms of three years each, "each of whom shall be a regular member of a Missionary Baptist church which is in active co-operation with the Arkansas Baptist State Convention." This board is responsible directly to the convention for the management of foundation affairs. The first executive secretary of the foundation was John D. Freeman, who served from July 1, 1950, to Feb. 1, 1951, after which there was no secretary till Sept. 15, 1952, when W. A. Jackson, the present secretary, assumed the office. The operating budget of the foundation is supplied by the convention from Cooperative Program receipts. The budget for 1954 was $6,000. The total assets of the foundation as of Dec. 31, 1954, were $17,512.32, of which $5,961.08 were institutional funds. Investment income of $399.68 and capital funds of $9,047.53 were received during 1954.

W. A. JACKSON

ARKANSAS BAPTIST HOSPITAL. An institution at Little Rock, Ark., founded Nov. 1, 1920, by the Arkansas Baptist State Convention. The present building, which cost $500,000, was opened Jan. 1, 1935. A $1,500,000 addition providing 125 more patient beds opened in Jan., 1956.

From its beginning through Dec. 31, 1955, the hospital served 213,314 patients. Income from patients for the period from June 30, 1941, through Dec. 31, 1955, was $16,042,278.43; denominational income for period from June 30, 1948, through Dec. 31, 1955, was $226,846.36; designated gift income for the same period was $930,687.69.

The hospital consists of three wings, six stories high; a five-floor school of nursing and dormitory building; and a six-floor medical arts building. Value of the buildings and equipment as of Dec. 31, 1955, was $3,319,435.53; of the land, $121,126.83. Total assets as of Dec. 31, 1955, were $4,402,377.16; total indebtedness was $1,174,812.50.

In 1955 the capacity was 300 beds; in 1956, 425 beds. There were 15,760 patients admitted in 1955. Income from patients in 1955 was $1,975,684.43; denominational income, $45,000; and designated gift income, $148,083.17. Value of charity and free service in 1955 was $168,232.53.

The hospital operates a three-year diploma school of nursing for women and men; the faculty consists of 14 members. Enrolment in the school was 215 on Dec. 31, 1955.

The hospital is approved for internship by the Joint Commission on Accreditation of Hospitals. It is a member of the American Hospital Association and the Arkansas Hospital Association. It serves all races and denominations. J. A. Gilbreath has been the administrator since 1947.

J. A. GILBREATH

ARKANSAS BAPTIST STATE CONVENTION.

I. Baptist Beginnings. The history of Arkansas Baptists prior to the organization of the state convention in 1848 is the story of the gradual development of a pioneer mission field. From the beginning of Baptist work in the state among the early settlers in 1814 to the organization of the convention, numerous obstacles, such as physical barriers of the wild country, danger from Indians, shortage of preachers, Campbellism, and antimissionism, hampered the growth of Baptists in the state. Nevertheless, Arkansas Baptists overcame these hindrances and, with the assistance of the American Baptist Home Mission Society, made remarkable progress during the first 34 years of their history. The gradual organization of associations slowly led to more centralized thinking on the part of the Baptists. With practically no denominational development beyond the associations and almost no previous institutional development, Arkansas Baptists came together in 1848 and formed the Arkansas Baptist Convention.

EARLY RELIGIOUS BEGINNINGS. In the first half of the 19th century, thousands of settlers migrated into the Mississippi Valley, of which the territory of Arkansas was an integral part. Many of the people who migrated through Missouri into northeastern Arkansas were Baptists. George Gill, a Baptist preacher, entered the territory in 1814 and settled on White River at a place called Mount Olive, where he preached his first sermon on Christmas Day, 1814. Many credit him as being the first Baptist to preach in Arkansas, although John Mason Peck (*q.v.*) indirectly suggested John Clark, who traveled through the territory in 1810, as a claimant for the honor. Gill, formerly of South Carolina and Virginia, labored for the rest of his life in the northeastern part of Arkansas as an effective preacher, organizer of churches, and writer.

The Bethel Association of southeastern Missouri appointed James Phillip Edwards as a missionary to the Arkansas territory in 1817. He made an extensive preaching tour of the territory during that same year, traveling over 1,000 miles. Together with Benjamin Clark and Jesse James, Edwards organized in 1818 a church (later called Salem) with 12 members in the Fourche a Thomas settlement (later known as Columbia). The members of this first Baptist church in Arkansas were largely pioneers from Kentucky who had settled on the Fourche a Thomas River in northeastern Arkansas around 1815, when the white population of the entire territory was less than 400. John Young Lindsey, one of these Baptist pioneers, became a prominent leader among Arkansas Baptists for almost half a century.

Poor transportation, the wildness of the country, danger from Indians, and a shortage of preachers accounted in part for the slow growth of Baptists in the state. Edwards, while on a missionary tour in 1819, organized a second church in the territory, but the available records do not mention its name. The Pecannerie Church, located on the Arkansas River south of the present site of Morrilton, was, according to the best available sources, constituted the same year. Edwards, Clark, and William Street, under appointment of the Bethel (Missouri) Association, made a 250-mile tour in the state in 1832 and organized the Little Flock and Union churches in what is now Lawrence County. The Kentucky Church, organized around 1832 and served by Lindsey as pastor for many years, is probably the oldest church in the state with a continuous existence.

EARLY ORGANIZATIONAL BEGINNINGS. The year 1824 marked the beginning of an organizational movement which culminated in the formation of the state convention. Silas Toncray, a silversmith-preacher, came in 1824 to the village of Little Rock from Kentucky, where he had served as clerk of the Long Run Association. Toncray and his brother-in-law, Isaac Watkins, organized a Regular Baptist church in Little Rock in July, 1824. The following November, these two men organized the Little Rock Church, Salem Church in Clark County, and the Arkansas Church at Pecannerie Settlement into the short-lived Little Rock Association of Regular Baptists, the first Baptist Association in Arkansas.

Missionary activities flourished in 1825, resulting in the organization of several churches: Little Flock on Terre Noire Creek in what was then Clark County, Little Flock in Crawford County, Mount Pleasant (located at the present site of Pittman), and possibly others. The Little Rock Church in 1825 constructed a meetinghouse, the first known church building of any faith in the state. Both the territorial legislature and the state constitutional convention later convened in this small log building.

Upon the invitation of several Baptists in Arkansas, David Orr came into the state in 1827 from Missouri to do mission work. Through his itinerant ministry in northeastern Arkansas, he established numerous churches and at least two associations. Apparently, John Mason Peck was his only rival as to distance covered. By 1829 Orr had established several churches and organized them into the Spring River Association. Orr, who also served as a missionary for the American Baptist Home Mission Society for many years, reported in 1833 the organization of eight churches and one association since he had begun his work. He also pointed out the spiritual destitution that he found in some areas. "I have visited places where grown-up people had never heard a sermon from a Baptist preacher." Orr, Lindsey, and others constituted at least 13 churches between 1828 and 1831. The organization of the American Baptist Home Mission Society in 1832 marked the beginning of a new era of expansion and growth in Arkansas Baptist history.

THE WORK OF THE AMERICAN BAPTIST HOME MISSION SOCIETY. From the time of its organization in 1832 to the early 1900's, the American Baptist Home Mission Society worked to evangelize the state of Arkansas. During the period 1832–48, the society gave support to a number of missionaries in Arkansas. Between 1833 and 1841, the body commissioned 27 men to labor in the state. These missionaries reported 813 weeks of work and 105 baptisms. Though they collected no money for the society, the body expended $2,725 for mission work in the state during this period. From 1842 to 1848, the society commissioned 13 men, who reported 503 weeks of labor and 180 baptisms. The missionaries collected only 69 cents for the society, even though the body appropriated $1,400 for their work.

Those who labored as appointees of the society included such capable men as David Orr, W. B. Karr, Benjamin Clark, and Thomas Mercer. The society paid or supplemented the salaries of the missionaries, many of whom had previously come into the state with no financial backing whatever. The missionaries organized numerous churches in the state, at times five or more in a single year (1836).

THREATS TO BAPTIST PROGRESS. The "Reformers," who preached the heretical doctrines of Alexander Campbell, invaded Arkansas in the late 1820's. The First Baptist Church of Little Rock unwittingly granted some Reformers permission to conduct revival services in their building. Thus, with their "foot in the door," the Campbellites quickly gained complete control of the church. Other Baptist churches also became victims of the Reformers. Many of them, however, such as the Kentucky Church of Saline County, successfully withstood the Campbellite attacks.

The antimission movement, which entered Arkansas in force in the 1830's, engaged the Baptists of the state in a struggle of over 35 years and greatly hampered their progress. Numerous churches joined the movement in its opposition to missions. Other churches suffered discord and regression at the hands of the antimissionary members who remained within their fellowship. At least three associations joined the movement. The St. Francis Association, organized in eastern Arkansas in 1831, became an antimission body and by 1850 had ceased to exist. The Washington County and Salem associations (1840) in the northwestern part of the state also joined the movement. Both from within and without, the attacks of the antimissioners plagued Arkansas Baptists and slowed their progress even up to 1870. In the period 1840–60, antimissionary Baptists made

Arkansas Baptist State Convention

up almost one fourth of the total Baptist population in the state.

BUILDING TOWARD A STATE CONVENTION. Prior to 1830 not a single Baptist church existed in southern Arkansas. Only five were located in the central part of the state. Of the 17 active churches in 1832, only three were located in the south. In that year Baptists in Union County, including immigrants from Louisiana, organized Liberty Church (near Lawson), the first one in the extreme south. The period 1833-48 was an era of growth and expansion, during which the organization of churches and associations laid the groundwork for the organization of the Arkansas Baptist Convention. This growth was augmented by immigration, removal of the Indians to the Indian Territory (Oklahoma), and assistance from the American Baptist Home Mission Society. The renewal of organizational activity in 1833 resulted in the organization of at least five new churches in various parts of the territory. These included two churches in the south, Hillsboro in Union County and Mount Olive in Hempstead County. In 1834 at least three churches were constituted.

The period following 1835 marked a growing corporate consciousness in Arkansas, both politically and religiously. A growing population, advancing civilization, and developing culture inspired the people of this pioneer territory to unite in an effort to promote their common welfare. They attained statehood on June 13, 1836. The state held its Constitutional Convention in the Baptist church building in Little Rock. More centralized thinking on the part of Baptists led to additional organization beyond the level of the local church. In Oct., 1836, six Baptist churches of southwestern Arkansas in Saline, Clark, Hot Springs, and Hempstead counties, with a total membership of 78, met at Spring Creek (now Benton) Church and organized Saline Association. This association, the first in the southern part of the state, proposed to invite into its membership all churches in the area south of the Arkansas River and running west to Indian Territory. Saline Association began the movement that culminated in the formation of the state Baptist convention. In 1837, 12 churches located west of White River and north of Arkansas River organized Washington County Association. When this body became antimissionary in 1840, some of its churches withdrew and formed the Salem Association. By 1846, however, it also became antimissionary. The Spring River Association of northwestern Arkansas disbanded in 1840, but its churches organized Rocky Bayou Association under the leadership of David Orr and White River Association under the guidance of George Gill. These are the two earliest Arkansas associations with a continuous history.

The missionary activities of such men as Gill, William Nutt, Sherrod Winningham, P. S. G. Watson, and others effected the organization of numerous churches and several associations in the 1840's. Under their leadership Arkansas Baptists organized in 1843 more churches than in any previous year in the state's history. From 1843 to 1848, over 20 churches were organized in the southern part of the state and more in other areas. The Baptist membership during these years increased from 800 to over 2,700. During this period also, the Saline Association "lettered out" some of its churches in 1845 to form Liberty Association in the southernmost part of Arkansas and others in 1848 to constitute the Red River Association in the southwest.

In only 30 years the Baptists of Arkansas grew from one small church with 12 members in 1818 to at least 84 active churches, 9 associations, and 2,749 members by 1848. The population of Arkansas during approximately the same period grew from 400 whites (1815) to a total population of 209,897 (1850). There was little denominational and almost no institutional development during this period. The Baptists secured a charter from the state in 1845 for an educational institution, but it was operated for only a brief time. They established no denominational paper. There were few unifying factors to bring the Baptists of the state together.

J. S. ROGERS, SR., and LYNN E. MAY, JR.

II. History of Convention. While Arkansas was yet a pioneer mission field, the Baptists who sensed the need for more extensive cooperation between the churches and associations of the state organized the Arkansas Baptist State Convention. The history of this convention is the story of Baptist people who, in spite of numerous obstacles and lengthy delay, ultimately secured unity, established permanent institutions, and organized an effective denominational program.

ORIGIN. The Saline Association in 1847 passed a resolution which suggested that the "time was ripe" for the organization of a state convention to unite Arkansas Baptists. This body invited the other associations in the state to unite with it in effecting such a coalition. On Sept. 21, 1848, 71 men and one woman, Mrs. D. Spakes from Harmony Church, representing 23 churches from Saline and Liberty associations, gathered at Brownsville Church in Tulip, Ark., and organized the Arkansas Baptist State Convention. The new body chose Isaac C. Perkins, president, and S. Steveson, recording secretary. In 1848 Arkansas Baptists comprised nine associations: the St. Francis, organized in 1831; Saline, 1836; Washington, 1837; White River, 1840; Rocky Bayou, 1840; Liberty, 1845; Salem, 1847; New Salem, 1848; and Red River, 1848.

Purpose.—The convention's original constitution, which has since remained substantially the same, stated that the primary object of the convention

shall be to supply the destitute regions within its bounds with the unadulterated word of life and a living ministry, and to aid, by appropriate and scriptural means, all destitute and feeble churches, and also supply the community with such books as may be approved by this body, and as may be thought best calculated to communicate information as to the distinctive doctrines and ordinances of the gospel of Christ as received by our denomination. The Convention may whenever consistent with the conditions of the treasury adopt means for the advancement of education and also the cause of Foreign Missions.

The constitution further stated: "The Convention shall be composed of delegates from Baptist Associations, Churches, and individual contributors who are members of Baptist Churches in good standing. Associations shall be entitled to five and churches to three delegates to the Convention."

In no way was the convention to infringe on the liberty of the churches. The constitution guaranteed this through the following provision: ". . . this Convention shall have no ecclesiastical jurisdiction, nor even act as an advisory council, nor in any way interfere with the constitution of any church or association."

The new convention acknowledged the need for an educational institution in the state to train its ministry. The committee on ministerial education recommended as early as 1850 that definite steps be taken toward providing such an institution. Although Arkansas Baptists established no permanent work in the early years of the convention, they showed a vital interest in foreign missions, Sunday schools, colportage, etc.

ORGANIZATION. At its earliest meeting the convention recognized its need for a body to control and carry out its work ad interim. The convention thus created an executive committee, which consisted of the elected officers of the convention and 10 or more managers, and which was to transact the business of the convention between its annual sessions. A president, two vice-presidents, recording secretary, corresponding secretary, and treasurer were to be elected at each annual meeting.

OTHER CONVENTIONS. When Arkansas Baptists organized their convention, the state was still frontier territory. Efforts to construct a centralized organization and program of work for the denomination encountered such obstacles as poor transportation and communication. The state convention consisted of churches and associations located in the southern part of the state and held its meetings in that area. Baptists in the north who felt the need of a larger co-operative organization found it impractical to unite with the Baptists of the state convention because of the above obstacles. Accordingly, about 20 churches met in Batesville, Sept. 14, 1850, and organized the White River Baptist Convention. This body engaged in an active mission program in the northern part of the state for several years. Baptists in eastern Arkansas organized the General Association of Eastern Arkansas sometime after 1850. These general bodies, each seemingly trying to outdo the other, assumed full responsibility for their own section of the state. No conflict of jealousy appeared between them since each seemed to consider its organization as being auxiliary to and not in competition with the others.

UNREALIZED ENTHUSIASM. The Baptists who organized the Arkansas convention in 1848 had high aspirations for the denomination's work in the state. The constitution of the body provided for a program of work with a wide scope. During the first 18 years of its history, however, the convention made few permanent accomplishments. Though the body expressed its vital interest in foreign missions, the convention in its "infancy" could do little "to advance this . . . cause." Arkansas Baptists contributed a total of $50.55 for home missions in 1848. Their gifts to missions gradually increased during the following years. Even though the convention voted to establish an educational institution and succeeded in appropriating some funds toward that end, the Civil War disrupted its plans, and the body failed to accomplish the desired end. The convention in 1858 voted to establish a denominational newspaper which would have the support of the convention. This enterprise, which seemed on the way to prosperity, suspended its operations in 1861 at the outbreak of the Civil War.

A marked enthusiasm characterized the proceedings of the 1859 session of the convention. The body secured a charter that year from the state for its incorporation. The future of organized Baptist work in the state looked bright indeed, but the upheaval of the Civil War disrupted and destroyed the initiative of the Baptists and practically destroyed their organization. The 1859 convention was the last really constructive convention until 1867.

GROWING A DENOMINATIONAL LIFE. The population of the state increased from 209,897 in 1850 to 435,450 in 1860. In spite of the aftermath of the Civil War, Arkansas Baptists multiplied rapidly between 1868 and 1899. During this period they grew from 18 associations, 331 churches, which reported 578 baptisms and 12,637 members, to 48 associations, 1,279 churches, which reported 3,793 baptisms and a total of 68,476 members. As they grew in number, the Baptists of Arkansas also grew in the spirit of co-operation as they organized their program of work. Whereas there had been several general bodies prior to the war, now they largely united in the effort to propagate their faith through a more closely knit organization than had been previously employed.

From its beginning, the Arkansas Baptist Convention took measures to safeguard the autonomy of the local church. While still maintaining their autonomy in the last three decades of the century, the local churches tended to "centralize power in the Convention proper, or in the various committees and boards of the Convention." The tone of the report of the convention's state mission board in 1872 reflected this growing tendency. The board reported to the conven-

Arkansas Baptist State Convention

tion that during the past year the *board* had employed six part-time missionaries to whom the *board* had paid $885.45. The convention in the 1870's delegated authority to its corresponding secretary whereby he could act in behalf of the convention, in harmony with its wishes, between the sessions of the executive board. This office ultimately developed into that of state executive secretary. The matter of "delegated authority" and centralization became the source of much controversy among Baptists in the state, particularly around the turn of the century.

Unlike previous years, Arkansas Baptists from 1869 to 1900 made their greatest strides toward achieving permanent institutions through the convention. This pertained especially to the establishment of educational institutions and the state departments of the convention. Most of the contemporary institutions and departments originated during this period.

Though Arkansas Baptists had organized Sunday schools in their churches for many years, the state convention made the first step toward formal recognition of the Sunday school enterprise in 1871. At that time the body appointed a five-man advisory committee to "gather statistics, and to advise in reference to the Sunday-school work in the State." Out of this developed the statewide but short-lived Sunday School Convention. The state convention resumed control of the state Sunday school work in 1874. After experimenting with a variety of promotional methods, the convention established in 1895 the Department of Sunday School and B.Y.P.U. Work. The convention later organized the Training Union Department out of the above combined department.

As they have sensed the need for further organization, Arkansas Baptists have organized other departments of state work, including the departments of Church Music, Brotherhood, Student Union, and Evangelism. The present effective state program is the result of a gradual growth in co-operative work on one hand, while the churches maintained their autonomy on the other.

The work of the women in the state, which was recognized by the convention as early as 1883, culminated in the organization of the Woman's Missionary Union, Auxiliary to the Arkansas Baptist State Convention. The forerunner of this organization, the Central Committee, functioned in the state for several years to stimulate the women of the churches in missionary efforts and giving. The Arkansas Woman's Missionary Union elected Mrs. J. P. Eagle as the first president of the organization. The women's work has contributed much to the missionary endeavor of Arkansas Baptists.

In 1938 the convention adopted the retirement plan of the Relief and Annuity Board of the Southern Baptist Convention, which is presently known as the Ministers' Security Plan. It went into effect in 1941.

GROWING CO-OPERATION. During the years following the Civil War, the Baptists of Arkansas learned well the lesson of co-operation among their churches, with bodies outside of the convention, and with those auxiliary to it. The American Baptist Home Mission Society, which had maintained missionaries in the state since 1832, continued its work in Arkansas after the Civil War, even though it was a Northern organization. This relationship existed between the society and the individual churches, rather than with the convention as such. The Domestic (Home) Mission Board of the Southern Baptist Convention began operations in Arkansas in 1851. These two agencies worked within the state for many years without conflict. When differences did arise in the 1880's, the state convention in 1882 voted that any church could co-operate with either of the above agencies; and, should the society or board refuse aid to a church, the convention would decline to co-operate with that agency. On that basis the convention continued to maintain harmonious relations with both the society and the board for several years, but the state body ultimately gave its full support to the Home Mission Board. During this period the American Baptist Publication Society maintained a missionary in the state who devoted most of his time to the promotion of Sunday school work. The convention welcomed this assistance.

CONTROVERSY AND SCHISM. In the latter 19th century a controversy over methods of mission work developed that created discord and ultimately resulted in a division in the ranks of Arkansas Baptists. At the meeting of the 1872 convention, James Robinson Graves (*q.v.*) of the Southern Baptist Publication Society of Memphis, Tenn., appeared on the scene. On Sunday he preached at the Baptist church from the text, "The veil of the temple was rent in twain. . . ." He spoke three hours and held his audience spellbound. The beginning of a unified program and the appearance of Graves, the exponent of local church autonomy, was destined to play a large role in the Landmark schism that was soon to plague Arkansas Baptists. The "first open note of opposition to a paid Corresponding Secretary of State Missions" arose at the 1888 session of the convention. Opposition leaders objected to the executive board's helping weak churches; insisted that boards and conventions were heretical, whereas associations and committees were scriptural; objected to co-operation with the Southern Baptist Convention; and opposed the employment of state secretaries. Those who thus opposed the convention were largely followers of Graves.

The resulting Landmark crisis severely tested the convention. The state convention's effort to restore harmony within its ranks led to smaller programs and less results. Men who came to Arkansas from other states provided most of the leadership for the Landmark element. Ben M. Bogard, who came to the state in 1899 to become pastor of the church at Searcy, entered the fight against a corresponding secretary and became the main leader of the Landmark movement in Arkansas for the next 50 years. The Landmark element and the convention supporters both refused to yield ground in the conflict. As a result, the Landmark churches withdrew from the convention and organized the General Association of Baptists, Apr. 10–11, 1902, at Antioch Baptist Church in Little Rock. By 1920 the Landmark Baptists in the state had a membership of approximately 38,000. After the withdrawal of the Landmarks, the weakened but united convention progressed in all areas of its work.

The body met in Conway in 1902 and drafted a new constitution, whereby the convention consisted of church messengers only. The convention in 1921 changed the constitution to provide for an executive board of 15 members and a general secretary. A constitutional amendment in 1955 gave each association one member on the board for each 5,000 members or major fraction thereof, provided that no association be entitled to more than five members.

PUBLICATIONS. The convention operated 10 years without an official publication. In 1858 the body voted to establish and support a state denominational newspaper, and the *Arkansas Baptist* began publication late that year or early in 1859, with P. S. G. Watson as editor. The outbreak of the Civil War forced the suspension of the promising but short-lived paper. N. P. Moore published in 1868 several issues of a paper, which the convention recommended, called the *Arkansas Baptist*. The convention for many years recommended to its constituents The *Baptist*, edited in Tennessee by J. R. Graves, and endorsed it as "the organ for the State." T. B. Espy and T. P. Boone secured the convention's endorsement for their paper, the *Western Baptist*, 1874–76. Two papers, *Arkansas Baptist Banner* and *Arkansas Baptist Index*, published in the 1880's, do not seem to have obtained the recognition of the convention. The convention endorsed the *Arkansas Evangel*, which began publication in 1880, as its "own state paper." The publishers changed the name of the paper to the *Arkansas Baptist* in 1887. The convention withdrew its recommendation of this publication in 1901, when it became a Landmark organ. Arkansas Baptists then endorsed the publication of the *Baptist Advance* in 1902. The name of the paper was changed to *Arkansas Baptist* in 1933 and is now owned by the convention.

INSTITUTIONS. Arkansas Baptists have developed several institutions to help carry out their missionary and educational enterprises. They incorporated in their original constitution provision for educational work. As early as 1856, the body appointed a board of managers to investigate the possibility of establishing a college for the education of its youth. The convention in 1858 employed an agent to collect funds to be used as endowment for the proposed institution and appointed seven men as trustees. By 1860 the Baptists had secured $75,000 endowment for a college, but in the Civil War all funds were lost. Soon after the war, the convention reasserted its desire for a state Baptist college but did not realize this objective until 1886. For several years in the 1870's, the convention endorsed Mississippi College at Clinton, Miss., and assisted some of its young people who were studying there. Several Baptist associations established schools which received the commendation of the convention, but most of them were short-lived. Arkansas Baptists took definite steps toward the establishment of a state Baptist college in 1883, when they appointed an Educational Commission for that purpose. In 1886, after 30 years' delay, Arkansas Baptists established Ouachita College at Arkadelphia, with J. W. Conger (*q.v.*) as president, as its first permanent institution and its only permanent educational institution.

In 1897 the convention accepted the offer of property in Monticello for a Baptist home for orphans and organized and chartered what is now known as Bottoms Baptist Orphanage. Arkansas Baptists established a second benevolent institution in 1920, the Arkansas Baptist Hospital. The convention also owned and operated a hospital in Pine Bluff for several years.

THE GENERAL SECRETARY. At first the occupant of this position was known as "General Agent." This officer has been variantly called corresponding secretary, mission secretary, general secretary, and is presently known as executive secretary. Though an employee of the executive board, he is recognized by the convention as its representative. The first one to occupy this position was Isaac C. Perkins, who was also the first president of the convention. His successors were:

A. J. Smith, 1853
T. J. Smith, 1854
T. H. Compere, 1855
W. E. Trawick, 1856–61
J. B. Searcy, 1867
M. D. Early, 1886–89
J. F. Love, 1903–06 (*q.v.*)
R. C. Bowers, 1907–08
J. S. Rogers, 1908–10
J. T. Christian, 1910–12 (*q.v.*)
R. M. Inlow, 1914
J. S. Rogers, 1915–18
B. L. Bridges (acting secretary), 1929
T. D. Brown, 1930

B. L. Bridges assumed the position in 1931 and has continued in it.

TWENTIETH-CENTURY PROGRESS. Although the convention lost numerous churches and some associations through the Landmark schism, the co-operating churches rallied to the convention and enabled it to make marked progress. The institutions of the state body continued to grow in usefulness and in value. The 75 Million Campaign stimulated Baptist growth in the 1920's. Arkansas' quota for the five years was

Arkansas Baptist State Convention

$3,200,000. The Baptists of the state contributed a total of $2,228,413.97, but at the same time accumulated an indebtedness of $249,000 through spending "anticipated" funds on the capital needs of its institutions. This debt continued to assume larger proportions until 1927, when it amounted to approximately $1,259,000, which included a bond issue of $900,000. The executive board found it impossible to pay even the interest on the debt and keep a semblance of activities in missions and education operating. In 1930 the convention made no provision in its budget for Southwide causes. That year, Arkansas Baptists contributed only $39,000 to state work. After all plans failed, the convention reluctantly made an arrangement with its creditors to settle the debt at 35 per cent. Beginning with the election of B. L. Bridges as secretary and following his capable and dedicated leadership and the sacrificial service of Otto Whitington (*q.v.*), Arkansas Baptists gave themselves to paying their debts in the dark depression years. By 1938, through a campaign for $329,000 and placing a mortgage on their hospital, they raised sufficient funds and paid off their creditors according to the terms of settlement. In 1943 they voted to press on to redeem their honor by paying the 65 per cent of the principal of their debts that had been legally forgiven. They achieved their goal in 1952.

Throughout its history Arkansas has been a fertile mission field. The work of state missions, through strengthening weak churches, organizing new churches, promoting the work of evangelism, etc., has greatly stimulated Baptist growth. This work has been largely under the direction of the executive board, except for an interim between 1921 and 1926, when this work was under the direction of a state mission board created in 1921. The convention organized in 1944 a department of rural missions, now known as the Department of Evangelism, to assist in state mission work. In 1955 the Arkansas convention reported 1,139 churches, 277,860 members, a budget of $1,205,375, and property valued at $4,097,147.73.

T. L. HARRIS and LYNN E. MAY, JR.

BIBLIOGRAPHY: G. H. Allen, "A History of the Arkansas Baptist State Convention" (1952). Arkansas Baptist State Convention, *Annuals*, 1848–1956. A. A. DuLaney, "History of Baptist Education in Arkansas" (1933). A. McPherson, "Some Facts About the Early Baptists of Arkansas," *Baptist Advance* (Aug. 28, 1924). D. O. Moore, "The Landmark Baptists and Their Attack upon the Southern Baptist Convention Historically Analyzed" (1949). F. F. Norfleet, "A History of Arkansas Baptists to 1900" (1950). J. S. Rogers, *History of Arkansas Baptists* (1948). J. B. Searcy, "Baptists in Arkansas," *Publications of Arkansas Historical Association*, I.

III. Program of Work of Arkansas Baptists.
ORGANIZATION. The general convention of Arkansas Baptists is composed of messengers from regular Baptist churches who meet annually in November or on a special call of the executive board. The convention is composed of three messengers from each church with one additional messenger for each 100 members of a church or major fraction thereof, but with no church entitled to more than 10 messengers. The state convention constitution provides complete independence for each church within the convention.

The officers of the convention are a president, two vice-presidents, a treasurer, and a recording secretary. These are the only permanent officers. The president appoints the standing committees. There were 17 such committees appointed in 1954, which were created to consider such subjects as home missions, hospitals, orphanage, radio ministry, social service, Christian education, the Cooperative Program, the Arkansas Baptist Foundation, and the executive board. The president of the convention also appoints a nominating committee, and this committee nominates persons for membership on boards, agencies, and commissions.

THE CONVENTION EXECUTIVE BOARD. The annual convention elects an executive board made up of members from the bounds of each association on a membership basis, but with no more than five members from any association. These members are elected for a three-year term and may succeed themselves only once. This board is the convention's legal and business agent administering the convention's business in the interim between the annual meetings. The executive board meets regularly three times a year but is subject to the call of the president at any time. For the forwarding of its work, the board organizes itself into a number of standing committees representing the activities it will carry on. The committees have advisory power only, and their chairmen make up the executive committee of the board. "These committees shall function in an advisory capacity only. . . . Each advisory committee shall be composed of from three to seven members and no one shall be a member of more than one committee, except in the case of the Executive Committee." These advisory committees serve as a liaison between the departmental heads and the executive board as well as the constituents of the state convention.

The executive committee of the board is its most important committee, being empowered to act for the board between sessions, provided that it shall never exercise any authority contrary to the expressed will of the board. This committee meets quarterly or on the call of the chairman, and a majority of its members constitute a quorum. The executive committee makes final recommendations on employing all department heads and associates. Such recommendations are made with the consent of and in co-operation with the executive secretary and must be submitted to the board for approval or rejection. Further, the executive committee makes recommendations to the board touching finances, budgets, and general policies and programs. It passes upon salaries of the administrative office as well as the various departments, and acts in all emergencies between meetings of the board. In all the activities the executive committee serves to assist the executive secretary in formulating general objectives of the Co-operative Program for each year. The executive board and the executive secretary serve as promotional agents in each of the associations within the convention's territory.

The executive officers of the board are the executive secretary, his associate, and such other persons as the work requires. The executive secretary is held responsible by the executive board for the promotion, general supervision, co-ordination, bookkeeping, and general management of all work undertaken. He also directs all persons employed by the board through the department organizations.

PROGRAM OF MISSIONS AND BENEVOLENCES. The Arkansas Baptist State Convention undertakes to promote a full program as recommended by the Southern Baptist Convention and as the needs of the state require. It has 14 departments and agencies through which this program is forwarded.

Arkansas is predominantly an agricultural and rural state. An aggressive state missions program is therefore maintained. Negro work is promoted through a director for that purpose within the State Missions Department. A Negro fieldworker is employed, and aid to the Negro Baptist college of the state is given. Direct missions are promoted through two state evangelists, and these men cover the entire convention strengthening weak churches, organizing new ones, making surveys, and holding revivals. In co-operation with the Southern Baptist Home Mission Board, city mission work is directed by a full-time superintendent of city missions. Institutional work is carried on at some tax-supported institutions through chaplains maintained by Arkansas Baptists, and associational missions are promoted through aid given on salaries to local missionaries within the associations. It is the aim of the convention to have a local missionary in each of the associations in the state; in every case, however, employed and directed by the local association. The budget for state missions in 1954 was $139,334 of which $90,000 came from the Cooperative Program, $23,602 from the offering for state missions, and $11,249 from Southern Baptist Convention agencies.

Hospitals.—Arkansas Baptists also own and operate the Baptist Hospital at Little Rock, valued at $2,461,201, with a 425-bed capacity. Baptists in this state also have one-third interest in ownership and operation of the Baptist Memorial Hospital in Memphis, Tenn., sharing with Tennessee and Mississippi.

Children's Home.—In the area of benevolences, Arkansas Baptists own and support Bottoms Baptist Orphanage at Monticello. This home is operated by a board of 18 persons elected by the convention.

Gifts to world causes.—For these purposes Arkansas Baptists have set aside 45 per cent of their distributable budget receipts. In 1954 these gifts amounted to $428,482.90.

Christian education.—Knowing that Christian education is the lifeblood of the denomination, Arkansas Baptists own and operate Ouachita Baptist College, a fully accredited senior co-educational institution. Ouachita was organized in 1886 in Arkadelphia. Its total enrolment in the 1955–56 school year was 803 students. In 1955 the convention gave to the school $150,000 for operating expenses and $35,300 for capital improvements. Arkansas Baptists give $30,000 a year on operational expense of Southern Baptist College at Walnut Ridge, although the school is not owned by the convention.

Baptist Student Union.—This organization is rapidly expanding in this state. Plans have been made for Student Union buildings with full-time secretaries to be operated adjacent to each of the state tax-supported educational institutions. It was decided that costs of constructing these buildings would be shared equally by the local churches in the college area and the state convention. In 1956 four such buildings were built, and another was under construction. Chairs of Bible instruction were not maintained.

Sunday school and Training Union.—A secretary and an associate in both the Sunday School and Training Union departments promote a steadily enlarging work in these areas. At the end of the 1953 associational year, Sunday schools of Arkansas Baptists had enrolled 201,005 pupils. The Training Union had enrolled 90,458. These departments are aggressively operated because of the conviction of Arkansas Baptists that religious education is the real heart of the denominational program.

PUBLICATIONS AND PROMOTION. The convention publishes its own denominational paper, the *Arkansas Baptist,* a weekly that goes out to more than 47,000 subscribers. Through this medium information regarding each department of state work is kept before the people. The executive secretary is given a full page each week to promote the Cooperative Program and other phases of Baptist life. Matters that are controversial and divisive are generally screened from publication by the editor. It is felt that this paper should mold public sentiment in favor of the denominational program as organized and promoted by the executive board acting for the convention. The editor, through editorials, keeps before the people various ideas concerning specific problems and programs.

Evangelism.—A Department of Evangelism is one of the newest co-operative activities. Organized to promote evangelism in the local church and in the convention at large, this department is proving helpful in planning associational simultaneous revivals and state evangelistic conferences, and in general promotion throughout all Arkansas. The departmental secretary reported 15,052 baptisms in Arkansas Baptist churches for the year 1955.

Brotherhood.—Another agency for the prop-

IV. ARKANSAS STATISTICAL SUMMARY

Year	Associations	Churches	Church Membership	Baptisms	S.S. Enrolment	V.B.S. Enrolment	T.U. Enrolment	W.M.U. Enrolment	Brotherhood Enrolment	Mission Gifts	Total Gifts	Value Church Property	State Capital Worth
1828	1	16	124	11									
1831	2	27	189										
1840	4	37	810										
1851	9	129	4,483	23									
1860	16	321	11,341	310									
1870	28	547	30,297	1,272									
1880	38	870	35,997	1,030	5,000								
1890	42	1,125	55,497	1,662	5,500					$ 6,612.32			
1900	47	1,321	71,419	4,725	9,154			21		59,936.73		$ 246,625.00	$ 92,500.00
1905	50	1,372	84,808	4,241	18,943			47		101,001.64		488,708.00	60,000.00
1910	51	1,534	106,528	5,809	24,213			40		157,086.45		720,857.00	49,450.00
1915	52	1,483	114,713	7,243	41,047		3,200	74		34,642.47		1,496,835.00	39,450.00
1920	49	1,234	102,914	7,278	57,865		6,916	3,972		90,749.64	359,534.64	1,957,951.00	270,950.00
1925	41	953	106,374	6,213	50,415		7,250	7,302		95,469.87	371,751.83	1,810,101.23	404,158.34
1930	45	827	108,860	7,988	87,206	1,928	13,729	701		330,649.92	1,003,159.04	4,223,025.00	857,203.89
1931	45	820	110,962	6,848	84,339	3,830	15,747	961	30	324,647.87	1,212,374.80	6,317,430.00	2,547,295.86
1932	43	803	112,815	7,691	86,247	10 sch	18,780	14,675		248,085.20	1,218,693.82	6,170,833.00	3,998,764.93
1933	43	824	119,876	8,668	87,995	965	20,474	15,010		146,884.86	943,673.17	5,597,929.10	2,886,480.96
1934	42	822	125,827	9,432	89,993	1,640	22,054	16,937		116,132.12	778,897.49	5,248,740.00	3,323,570.99
1935	42	853	129,903	8,414	90,985	2,330	23,087	10,860		87,295.99	685,017.10	5,384,798.00	2,927,164.80
1936	40	872	132,870	7,458	96,566	4,020	25,130	18,800		112,177.31	746,220.28	5,374,264.00	3,098,090.69
1937	40	864	135,854	7,462	99,182	5,129	29,450	21,815		122,062.25	783,863.23	5,413,316.00	2,438,608.06
1938	40	892	145,386	6,965	99,831	9,047	33,337	21,815		129,049.33	878,647.57	5,484,690.00	2,245,268.41
1939	40	892	152,773	10,501	108,089	13,648	35,013	22,000		291,741.47	1,059,688.11	5,578,990.00	2,780,025.54
1940	40	929	154,635	11,854	118,055	12,496	45,100	25,312		166,608.79	1,032,898.35	5,714,722.00	2,865,830.08
1941	40	903	158,443	11,636	122,864	151	41,464	26,490		174,976.23	1,143,720.85	5,657,782.00	3,081,023.46
1942	40	904	170,017	8,923	117,126	18,372	39,953	27,775		194,869.85	1,283,944.83	5,870,712.00	3,222,509.23
1943	40	973	169,171	8,046	118,526	160	36,090	28,154		279,816.00	1,641,111.34	6,453,803.91	3,293,996.67
1944	40	920	176,292	7,577	106,680	161	26,712	26,396	667	290,186.61	1,709,571.54	6,837,585.00	3,291,681.13
1945	40	887	181,060	8,183	105,501	170	28,024	15,574	503	391,702.76	2,233,040.77	7,410,421.00	3,551,680.93
1946	42	892	189,930	9,539	113,356	185	28,278	16,619	390	471,637.51	2,712,729.62	8,307,796.00	3,408,842.67
1947	42	920	200,572	9,930	123,974	296	33,278	28,248	677	601,070.00	3,314,104.00	9,603,314.00	2,781,784.77
1948	42	1,034	211,728	11,476	135,543	31,254	39,507	22,702	2,327	823,417.00	4,058,590.00	11,372,893.00	3,237,357.72
1949	42	961	218,514	13,947	148,400	36,375	43,296	23,021	2,240	922,470.00	5,629,260.00	14,858,787.00	2,639,857.71
1950	43	992	35,306	14,560	160,305	39,285	51,015	25,896	4,427	976,480.00	5,663,111.00	16,617,943.00	3,819,755.02
1951	44	1,033	242,156	16,367	172,254	43,706	61,462	28,502	4,910	1,192,800.41	6,955,931.20	20,351,274.27	3,985,994.84
1952	45	1,003	252,930	14,023	81,406	47,850	67,546	31,315	6,433	2,069,697.77	8,617,799.81	23,429,692.00	4,000,700.03
1953	45	1,043	261,277	14,948	169,187	56,660	73,319	31,843	6,441	1,154,840.00	7,463,317.00	28,874,978.00	5,201,567.60
1954	45	1,093	273,323	13,418	186,520	64,724	75,555	30,242	8,322	1,505,495.00	8,389,662.00	33,641,717.00	5,134,848.51
	45	1,137		14,693	201,005	49,480	81,416	35,492	8,347	1,638,267.00	8,997,833.00		5,937,738.46
							90,458	39,380	8,850	1,721,929.00	10,001,492.00	36,731,384.00	7,811,045.23

GEORGE TRUETT BLACKMON

agation of denominational principles and the development of the male constituency is the Brotherhood Department. It has taken over the responsibility for the Royal Ambassadors and now pursues vigorously a man-boy program for the teaching of missions and the development of the spiritual life.

SPECIAL PROGRAMS AND SERVICES. Other departments operated by Arkansas Baptists are a Church Music Department, promoting and developing a fully graded, worshipful music program for all churches; a foundation controlled by a separate board seeking bequests and gifts to be invested in kingdom endeavor; and assemblies and camps for summer activities, pointing up denominational work generally and missions in particular.

OTHER GENERAL ACTIVITIES. Special committees and commissions are appointed from time to time to study the program of work being undertaken and bring recommendations as to how this may be improved. A recent survey committee studying capital needs of our convention agencies and institutions for the years 1956–60 has reported needs which will be met over that period in the amount of $1,086,000.

The Arkansas Baptist Historical Society is an organization set up by the convention for the purpose of collecting and preserving historic materials of the convention. A board of control is elected to direct this work. Historical data of worth is kept in the library room of Baptist headquarters building.

Besides furthering ministerial education through its support of Ouachita College, the convention provides annually a sum of money for grants in aid to needy ministerial students. A ministerial board of education passes on the applications.

Budget.—In 1955 the Arkansas Convention adopted the following budget for its local state program:

Department of Evangelism	$ 10,000.00
State Missions Department	85,000.00
Southern Baptist College	30,000.00
Arkansas Baptist	15,000.00
Orphanage	45,000.00
Hospital School of Nursing	30,000.00
Hospital Charity Fund	15,000.00
Sunday School Department	19,000.00
Training Union Department	18,000.00
Church Music Department	7,500.00
B. S. U. Department	30,000.00
Ouachita College	175,000.00
Brotherhood Department	18,000.00
Foundation Department	7,000.00
State Assembly	5,000.00
Promotion and Convention Fund	11,000.00
Emergency Reserve Fund	7,200.00
Ministerial Education	8,400.00
Memphis Hospital	10,000.00 $546,100.00

DAVID O. MOORE

ARKANSAS EVANGEL, THE. Founded in 1880 as a result of the inauguration by T. B. Espy of the Arkansas Baptist Printing and Publishing Company for the purpose of publishing a Baptist paper in Arkansas. Espy and James Bryant Searcy (*q.v.*) were the original editors. Espy died before the first issue of the paper, which carried his obituary, was published. Originally published at Dardanelle, *The Evangel* was moved to Little Rock in 1885. In 1887 the state convention changed the name to *Arkansas Baptist*.

B. H. DUNCAN

ARLINGTON ACADEMY. Associational school of Mecklenburg and Cabarrus associations, established at Arlington, N. C., in 1903, on a lot adjoining Arlington Baptist Church. Two years later the trustees were authorized to dispose of the property, for lack of support.

D. L. SMILEY

ARMED FORCES, RELIGIOUS WORK IN. The United States now has a continuous program of training for military service, which intends that in the course of 20 or more years each able-bodied man in this country will have had two or more years of training in some branch of military service.

In July, 1946, the Home Mission Board requested the Chaplains Commission of the Southern Baptist Convention to promote a ministry through the churches to the men returning from military service. Special emphasis was given to those who had accepted Christ while in the service of their country and had not been baptized. J. D. McCready and Troy B. Yopp were appointed by the commission to promote the work. Most commendable results were realized.

The Chaplains Commission, together with the Co-operative Missions Committee of the Home Mission Board, in 1952, enlarged this movement with a threefold purpose: (1) to encourage churches and pastors to plan a program to prepare young men for the experiences which will come to them while they are away from their homes and churches, (2) to encourage churches to sustain communication with men while they are in service, (3) to enlist returned servicemen in the life of the churches on their release from military duty. E. L. Ackiss, a retired navy chaplain, is promoting this work for the board in co-operation with other Southern Baptist agencies.

The present military setup in our country calls for a continuous spiritual ministry to those in military service; therefore, the work of the

Arminianism

chaplain is in constant demand and requires its share of the total Southern Baptist ministry.

O. M. SEIGLER

ARMINIANISM. The view of James (Jacobus) Arminius (1560-1609), professor in the University of Leyden and preacher in the Reformed Church of the Netherlands. Arminius protested strongly against the Calvinistic doctrines of irresistible grace and unconditional election. He magnified man's freedom of choice, teaching that although God knows in advance a man will sin of his own free choice, God does not predestine him to do so. Arminius insisted that freedom exists only where there is ultimate choice. Arminian Baptists began in 1609, with John Smyth who was converted to the Baptist position. They are opposed to Calvinists or Particular Baptists.

BIBLIOGRAPHY: W. Walker, *A History of the Christian Church* (1949). K. S. Latourette, *A History of Christianity* (1953).

CHARLES A. TRENTHAM

ARMSTRONG, ANNIE WALKER (b. Baltimore, Md., July 11, 1850; d. Baltimore, Md., Dec. 20, 1938). Woman's Missionary Union leader. Daughter of James D. and Mary (Walker) Armstrong, she did not become a Christian until she was 19, after which she was baptized by Richard Fuller (*q.v.*) into the Seventh Baptist Church of Baltimore, Md. She left Seventh Church with 117 others, joined Eutaw Place Baptist Church at its organization, Feb. 20, 1871, and taught the infant class there for at least 30 years.

She led in framing the constitution of Woman's Missionary Union which made the organization auxiliary to the Southern Baptist Convention instead of an independent body with power to collect and administer its own money and send out its own missionaries. Never discouraged, "Miss Annie" wrote, spoke, planned indefatigably. In 1899, while corresponding secretary of Woman's Missionary Union, she was absent from the Mission Rooms, which served as the Woman's Missionary Union office, for nearly two weeks due to sickness, and it was the first time this had occurred in 11 years. "The clerk made daily visits to the home—and the work was continued." She refused to accept a salary from 1900 until her resignation in 1906, when the union voted that the corresponding secretary must be paid. The fact that she did not approve of establishing the W.M.U. Training School in Louisville added to her reasons for resigning.

Caring for her own travel expenses until 1901, Miss Armstrong traveled great distances—3,300 miles in 21 days, visiting 19 places, and making 26 addresses. Besides writing leaflets for Woman's Missionary Union, Miss Armstrong, at the request of the editors, started a young people's Scripture department in *Kind Words*, a "Folks and Facts" column, and two departments in *The Teacher*. She was a frequent contributor to the two mission publications, *Foreign Mission Journal* and *Our Home Field*. In 1888, after conference with Henry Allen Tupper (*q.v.*), secretary of the Foreign Mission Board, Miss Armstrong wrote by hand letters to all the societies, asking them to contribute to the first Christmas offering, which resulted in $2,833.49 for Lottie Moon in China. She led Woman's Missionary Union to enlarge its efforts in providing organizations for Negro Baptist women and children and in publishing literature for them.

As memorials to Miss Armstrong, Woman's Missionary Union voted in 1907 to give $5,000 to a Home Mission Board mountain school and $5,000 to a hospital in China. The Annie Walker Armstrong building, erected at Burnsville, N. C., was dedicated in 1908 in appreciation of her service. More permanent memorials are the Annie Armstrong Offering for Home Missions and the structure of Woman's Missionary Union, which she led in establishing.

JULIETTE MATHER

ARMSTRONG, JAMES (b. Hempstead, Rockland County, N. Y., Mar. 20, 1776; d. Wilkes County, Ga., Aug. 28, 1835). Minister, denominational officer, and agent for Mercer University at its beginning. While quite young he was left an orphan when his father, with 22 others, was massacred by Indians while assembled for worship. He was reared by Joseph Barker, a Presbyterian, and prepared for the Presbyterian ministry.

In early manhood he moved to Savannah, Ga., and taught in the male academy there, later becoming cashier of a bank. Though elected a Presbyterian elder, he was not satisfied with infant baptism, and in 1810 joined the Baptist church. During the War of 1812 he moved to Wilkes County, settling near Fishing Creek meeting house, and was ordained to the ministry by Fishing Creek Baptist Church on Oct. 11, 1821. He served this church with great success for 14 years, and was also pastor of Greenwood, Goshen, and Lincolnton churches for almost nine years. He was closely associated with Jesse Mercer and others in the first efforts to establish a seat of learning at Penfield and was a member of the committee which selected Penfield as a site for Mercer Institute. Not long afterward he resigned his pastoral charges and gave full time to the collection of funds for buildings and for the support of the faculty. He was one of the eight regularly appointed messengers entering into the organization of the Georgia Baptist Convention in 1822, and he served as treasurer of the convention from 1833 to 1835. During the severe cold winter of 1834-35, ever loyal to duty in seeking endowment for Mercer, he was stricken with a painful disease which caused his death.

JAMES P. WESBERRY

ARMSTRONG, JAMES CLAYTON (b. Franklin County, Mo., 1848; d. Liberty, Mo., 1937). Pastor, editor, and college librarian. Converted in 1867, he united with New Hope Church in

Franklin County and decided that same year to enter the ministry and go to college. He worked his way through William Jewell College, Liberty, Mo., by teaching Greek and Latin. This institution awarded him the A.B. degree, 1874, the A.M. degree, 1875, and later conferred on him the D.D. degree. After his marriage to Emma Pendleton in 1877, they moved to St. Louis, Mo., where he joined the staff of the *Central Baptist*. He edited this paper from 1893 until its consolidation with *The Word and Way*. Armstrong served as pastor of the following Missouri churches: Garrison Avenue (now Delmar Avenue), St. Louis; First Baptist, Mexico; Westport, Kansas City. The Missouri convention had him on its State Board of Missions, 1918–22. His college alma mater utilized his services first as a trustee, 1893–1922, then as librarian, 1922–37. His scholarship, sincere piety, and winsome Christian spirit won for him the confidence and affection of all who knew him.   OPAL R. CARLIN

ARMSTRONG, LAURA DELL 'MALOTTE' (b. Graham, Nordaway County, Mo., Feb. 3, 1886; d. Plattsburg, Mo., May 13, 1945). Missouri and Convention-wide Woman's Missionary Union leader. Daughter of James Wesley and Mary (Eddy) Malotte, she had a distinguished Huguenot and Pilgrim ancestry with her father and grandfather, both prominent Baptist ministers in northwest Missouri, of French Huguenot descent. Her mother was a lineal descendant of William Eddy, vicar of St. Dunstan's Church, England, during the early 17th century. His four children settled in Plymouth Colony 10 years after the landing of the Mayflower. In order to provide educational advantages for their daughter and three sons, her parents moved to Maryville, Mo., where Laura Dell later graduated from Northwest Missouri State Teachers College and then taught in the public schools in Bolckow and Clearmont, Mo. On Sept. 4, 1907, she married Frank Wade Armstrong, a Maryville attorney and active Baptist layman.

Elected member of the executive board of the Missouri Baptist General Association in 1919, Mrs. Armstrong served continuously until 1936. From 1923 to 1934, she was president of the Woman's Missionary Union of Missouri, and from 1933 to 1945, of the Convention-wide Woman's Missionary Union. A member of the Executive Committee of the Southern Baptist Convention, 1927–45, she was also member-at-large of the Baptist World Alliance, 1934–45.

In 1920 she was named state Woman's Missionary Union college correspondent in Missouri; later, as president, she appointed a committee to make plans with the state board and Inter-Board Commission of the Southern Baptist Convention for the first Missouri Baptist Student Union conference, which met in Jan., 1925, at Hardin College, Mexico, Mo. The first mission study institute in Missouri was held under her administration in 1932. As president of the Convention-wide W.M.U., she served for 12 years on the editorial staff of Woman's Missionary Union magazines—*Royal Service, The Window of Y.W.A.,* and *World Comrades*. Her Convention-wide position also made her chairman of the board of trustees of Woman's Missionary Union Training School (now Carver School of Missions and Social Work), and she was largely responsible for erection of the school's present building adjacent to the Southern Baptist Theological Seminary in Louisville, Ky. Another significant achievement of her administration was the designation of $10,000 of the Golden Jubilee Offering to the National Baptist Negro women's work for the publication of necessary literature and for financing cooperative institutes where white and Negro women could meet together to discuss better methods of promoting the missionary program.

Memorials established to Mrs. Armstrong include the Armstrong Terrace at Carver School; the maternity ward of the first Southern Baptist hospital erected in South America, located in Asuncion, Paraguay, gift of the Missouri Woman's Missionary Union; the Armstrong Memorial Training School, Rome, Italy; and the Baptist Seminary, Havana, Cuba, both established by Woman's Missionary Union.   MRS. C. M. TRUEX

ARMSTRONG MEMORIAL TRAINING SCHOOL, ROME. See ITALY, MISSION IN.

ARMY OF NORTHERN VIRGINIA, REVIVAL IN. One of the most spectacular and influential revivals of religion in American history occurred in the Confederate Army of Northern Virginia beginning in the fall of 1862 and continuing until Apr., 1865. In the revival, which reached its climax in the period Aug., 1863, to May, 1864, there were not less than 15,000 professions of conversion, perhaps many more.

The revival appeared first in camps and hospitals around Richmond and in isolated army units in western Virginia. It followed a period of inactivity and demoralization in the Confederate Army. Strong religious influences prevailed in the army at the time of its organization when "scarcely a company moved without some public religious service, and it was considered a most important part of each man's equipment that he should carry in his knapsack a copy of God's word." A large proportion of officers in the Army of Northern Virginia were Christians, and during the first months of the war the Confederate Army was amply provided with religious tracts and books, and nearly every regiment had its prayer meeting.

Following the first battle of Manassas, however, the army suffered serious demoralization, when vice and drunkenness became common. The months of inactivity following Manassas led many people to believe that the one great victory had virtually ended the war and that England and France would soon recognize the independence of the South. Confederate disasters in early 1862 restored Southerners to their senses, and the religious tone of the army improved decidedly. A number of competent chaplains joined the army in this period.

When Jackson's corps returned to the lower Valley of Virginia following the Sharpsburg campaign, a revival spirit was manifested in its midst, and when the army moved to the Rappahannock and faced Burnside, the revival greatly accelerated. Between the battles of Fredericksburg and Chancellorsville there was a mounting wave of religious interest, with generals and their staffs often attending the open air services. Barksdale's Mississippi brigade alone reported 500 professions at Fredericksburg. After the preaching services, conducted by missionaries, pastors, and colporteurs, as well as chaplains, groups of soldiers gathered around the firestands, where religious conversation continued for an hour or two. Often 15 or 20 conversions occurred in these groups.

The disastrous campaigns of Gettysburg and Vicksburg did not dampen the army revival. Instead, the revival reached its greatest proportions when the army returned from Gettysburg and rested along the Rapidan. The Second and Third Army Corps under Lee's command were particularly affected. Without chaplains, brigades of 2,000 men met for prayer. Jones estimates that there were at least 5,000 conversions between Aug., 1863, and Jan., 1864. Presbyterians, Methodists, and Baptists provided the most prominent preachers; the Domestic Mission Board of the Southern Baptist Convention led in colportage work and in providing army missionaries. In the desperate struggle around Petersburg early in 1865 Pickett's division experienced the revival, and a week before the evacuation of Richmond chaplains reported revivals in four brigades, with large additions to churches from other brigades.

Prayer, letters from home, tracts, godly officers, chaplains, and missionaries were instrumental in continuing the revival. As a result of it, many southern churches experienced revival during the summer and fall of 1865; the number of ministerial students increased sharply after the war; and the South was sustained and rehabilitated in large measure during the dark days of reconstruction by those who had experienced the army revival.   W. L. LUMPKIN

ARNOLDISTS. A sect begun *c.* 1130 through the reformatory preaching of a young priest, Arnold of Brescia, in northern Italy. Zealous for a reformation of the Church in its life, rather than in its organization and doctrine, he attacked the riches and temporal power of the Church, advocating the separation of church and state and a return to apostolic poverty on the part of the clergy. Arnold and his followers seem to have followed Catholic doctrine and accepted the hierarchy of the Church. He gained a large following, especially in Rome, but the pope had him burned as a heretic in 1155. Arnold's followers propagated his ideas until *c.* 1200.   LYNN E. MAY, JR.

ART, RELIGIOUS. Religion has always inspired the artist to give his best to honor and to glorify his God in architecture, painting, and sculpture. Almost all the great religions, pagan and Christian, have produced great art. By far the greater number of works of art existent today have a religious purpose or subject matter.

From Sumeria, later Babylonia, religious statuettes survive, dating to about 3,000 B.C. Religion embodying belief in after-life determined the nature of Egyptian art and produced colossal pyramids, cliff tombs, and temples. Assyrian, Indian, Chinese, and other Eastern civilizations left monumental religious architecture and sculpture.

Epitomizing classic architecture and sculpture, the Parthenon of Pericles, a temple to Athena, has stood almost 2,400 years as probably the finest tribute to deity yet devised by man.

Christian art was cradled in Roman times—at first escaping the historical state influence—and was much given to symbols such as the cross, fish, and vine as subjects of high significance to inspire spiritual worship, superseding the ancient idolatry.

Roman catacombs preserve remarkable Christian mural paintings and sarcophagi dating from the late first to the fifth centuries. In A.D. 323 Constantine made Christianity the state religion, which determined that religious art should be thus dominated for 1,200 years. The architecturally important basilica type churches created in this period preserved Christian art in the form of stiff, formal mosaics, until Constantinople fell in 1453. The fall of Rome in 476 submerged the fine arts in the collapse of the Western world. In 726 Byzantine Emperor Leo forbade the worship of images; and many artists fled to Italy and northern Europe, then dominated by the conquering Gothic races. Late in the 11th century the enduring Roman church developed the Romanesque architecture which by the 13th century had evolved into the artistically significant Gothic type churches, ideal vehicles for symbolical and decorative sculpture, stained-glass windows, and great tapestries.

Thirteenth-century Francis of Assisi helped change the psychology of religion from authoritarian formalism to that of love, joy, and kindness, freeing religious painters to depict the dramatic human life instead of the eternal repose of the divine.

Giotto (1267?–1337), the first great Florentine painter, made way for progress culminating in the High Renaissance, the zenith of Christian art, a period like no other, when the grand patrons, the Roman Church and great nobles, extravagantly employed extraordinary talents to produce the most famous works of religious art, such as Leonardo's (1452–1519) *Last Supper*, Raphael's (1483–1520) exquisite madonnas, Michelangelo's (1475–1564) Sistine Chapel murals and great sculptures. Titian (1477–1576) led Venetian painters in contributing much to the supremacy of the Italians as religious artists.

Concurrently art awakening was progressing

in northern Europe where the Van Eycks (1366?–1441), great Flemish religious painters, developed oil painting, which provided freer expression for all subsequent painters. Lutheran Albrecht Durer (1471–1528), in distinctive German style, produced the expressive *Praying Hands* and the *Four Apostles,* possibly the greatest Protestant painting.

El Greco (1542–1614), although circumscribed by the weird mysticisms and symbolisms of Catholic Spain, attained high spiritual expression in a painting style called "modern."

Flemish Peter Paul Rubens (1577–1640) and the immortal portrayer of the highest and deepest in personal spiritual emotions, Dutch Rembrandt van Rijn (1606–1669), made enormous contributions in the 17th century. Since Rembrandt, greatest artist of the Reformed faith, no great religious painter has emerged; and religion has inspired few important artists, especially in Protestant countries. Important 20th-century art has been little devoted to religion, and the great flame of religious art, millenniums old, burns low past mid-century. American museums afford excellent examples from almost all the great European painters except Leonardo and Michelangelo.

BIBLIOGRAPHY: T. Craven, *A Treasury of Art Masterpieces* (1939). A. B. Loucheim, *5000 Years of Art* (1946). W. Lowrie, *Art in the Early Church* (1947). S. W. Orpen, *The Outline of Art* (1923).

HERMAN F. BURNS

ASCENSION. See CHRISTOLOGY; JESUS CHRIST

ASHEVILLE BAPTIST. Paper first known as the *Blue Ridge Baptist.* It was established in 1890 by J. A. Speight who became the editor. When the paper was moved to Asheville, N. C., its name was changed to *Asheville Baptist.* Its failure was due to lack of financial support.

L. L. CARPENTER

ASHPOLE INSTITUTE. The associational school of Cape Fear Association, located at Leesville, Robeson County, N. C. Officially known as Cape Fear Baptist Associational High School, the school was founded at the 1877 session of the association and opened Feb. 11, 1878. Stinceon Ivey, pastor at Leesville, was the principal of the school.

Although the school was in a healthy condition in 1882, and was endorsed by Robeson Association the following year, it died for lack of support in 1900.

D. L. SMILEY

ASSAM AND MANIPUR, COUNCIL OF BAPTIST CHURCHES OF. Organized in 1950 in co-operation with the American Baptist Foreign Mission Societies, with the plan to meet quadrennially for fellowship to attain a sense of Baptist unity. The All-Assam Baptist Convention, forerunner of the council, was formed in 1914 with 1,000 representatives of over 20 languages and tribes. Several large associations follow tribal and language groupings, and Christian periodicals are published in the vernaculars. The Assam Christian Council, organized in 1937, sponsored the founding of a Union Christian College opened on Aug. 16, 1952, on a 1,000-acre campus in the mountains at Barapani, the site given by the chief of a large hill tribe. International youth camps, to which students come from as far as Burma and Japan, aided with campus and buildings.

In 1943 Assam became the terminus for thousands of refugees pouring out of Burma before the invading Japanese, and mission stations nearest Burma suffered considerable war damage. It was there that the forces of the United Nations turned the tide which contributed to the Allied victory in 1945. During 1945–49 an evangelistic spirit increased the church membership from 79,000 to 95,000.

Assam was opened as a mission by missionaries in Burma who sought a way into China and a route into Burma from the north. Nathan Brown (b. 1807; d. 1886) in Moulmein set out with Oliver T. Cutter (b. 1811; d. 1881) and a printing press, arriving Mar. 23, 1836, in Sadiya, Assam, northeastern India. Brown translated the New Testament and other Christian literature into Assamese.

The British Commissioner encouraged establishment of stations on the plains among the Hindu Assamese and immigrants coming to work on the vast tea gardens. Penetration of the mountainous areas, accomplished in 1867, opened the way to primitive animistic and head-hunting tribes—the Garos to the west and several tribes of warlike Nagas near the Burma and China borders, where six million people speak 80 languages and dialects. The province came within British India in 1838.

The largest growth has come among the hill tribes, who early adopted self-support and evangelism as their responsibilities. Missionary Edward Payson Scott (b. 1832; d. 1869), armed only with his Bible and violin, won his way past the spears of the Nagas, reduced their language to writing, and translated the Scriptures. The Garos have 500 churches, every one self-supporting, and since 1900 have been sending missionaries to other tribes.

DATA

	1934	1954
Churches	923	1,632
Baptisms	2,165	6,303
Church members	53,534	119,577
Missionaries	64	46
Council workers	854	1,279
Students	12,052	16,037
Schools	443	525
Patients	29,694	28,671
Hospitals & Dispensaries	10	14
Field contributions	$20,779	$118,651

Jorhat, accessible to both the plains and the hills, is the location of the Baptist theological seminary. The Assamese Bible Training School is located at Golaghat. The largest of the four interrelated medical centers, located at Jorhat, cares for the local community and workers in the tea gardens and provides treatment for tuberculosis and leprosy. Youth in Baptist areas are reached through hostels for men and women students in the large government schools at Gauhati, and also through the field program directed by a full-time missionary and his associates appointed by the council.   ADA STEARNS

ASSEMBLIES, GEORGIA. The summer assembly program in Georgia functions largely in terms of organizations, and is not based upon any one central and highly developed assembly site. Although some attempts have been made to develop a central assembly, the various programs, organizations, and emphases have largely been promoted in independent meetings held at varying locations.

Plans for development of the state's first Baptist assembly at Blue Ridge were presented by William Warren Landrum to the Georgia Baptist Convention, 1908, during its meeting at Madison. The following summer, 1909, the first state assembly was held. The new auditorium, erected under the supervision of Edward George Willingham, was dedicated. This service occurred during the meeting of the Baptist Young People's Union of Georgia at Blue Ridge. The Mary P. Willingham School for girls at Blue Ridge, 1916–31, was requested by the convention to assume full direction of the summer assembly program, a function it performed, 1918–23. The school was closed in 1931.

The Training Union assembly of Georgia, then called the B.Y.P.U., began in June, 1929, at the Riverside Academy, Gainesville; Edwin Smith Preston, state secretary, was director. It continued to meet at Riverside each summer through 1933; at Shorter College, Rome, 1934–41; at Tift College, Forsyth, 1942–46; and at Mercer University, Macon, 1947–56. Gainer E. Bryan, Sr., has been state secretary and director since 1938.

The school of religious education, a part of the Baptist Sunday school program of Georgia, was begun at Tift College, Forsyth, 1935. It has continued to meet there. The Lake Louise Assembly, which meets later in the summer, was also founded by Tiny Walter Tippett, state Sunday school secretary, 1949.

The 1954 convention, meeting in Augusta, authorized the appointment of a special committee to "study the feasibility of establishing an assembly in Georgia." This committee was to report "through the executive committee to the convention." The committee met in 1955. David James Evans, Atlanta, chairman, appointed a survey committee, but no recommendations were made.   GAINER E. BRYAN, SR.

ASSEMBLIES, LOUISIANA. Beginning in 1924 the encampment idea sprang up all over the state. Interested groups organized regional camps as "supplementary to, and not substitutes for, the state encampment, [to] serve . . . their respective territories." Some of these regional encampments are still in existence:

Southwest, at Dry Creek, began in 1924, "built around a revival."

Central, organized in 1928, first two meetings at Camp Grant Walker near Pollock, moved to Olla in 1930, now known as *Northeast.*

Northwest, organized in 1926 at Mansfield, last reported in 1931.

Lake Arthur, first session in 1929 on grounds rented from Methodists, had last session in 1944.

Southeast, began in 1947, met at Mandeville, originally known as the Strawberry Encampment, grew into District XI.

Clara Springs was organized in 1953 by District VIII.

Woman's Missionary Union, 50 acres 14 miles south of Alexandria, was purchased in 1954.

See also LOUISIANA BAPTIST ENCAMPMENT.

G. AVERY LEE

ASSEMBLIES, VIRGINIA. In 1908 the Baptists of Virginia held their first encampment at Buckroe Beach, Va., with an emphasis on the work of Sunday schools. Training Union conventions were begun at Virginia Beach and were held there annually from 1910 until 1936. Assemblies promoting Sunday school work continued there until 1930. Important to the churches of western Virginia was the Intermont Assembly held at Virginia Intermont College, Bristol, Va., 1913–32. One of the signal factors in the strengthening of Baptist Sunday school and Training Union work during past years was the annual encampment at Virginia Beach, where classes, conferences, and lectures were a significant part of the program. Distinguished speakers from all over America came to address the assemblies. The Sunday School Department moved its assembly to Massanetta Springs, near Harrisonburg, Va., in 1933, after encampments at Virginia Intermont College in 1931–32. In 1937 the Training Union Department began its summer program at Massanetta Springs also. However, the facilities of this Presbyterian Assembly are no longer adequate to meet the needs of the highly successful assemblies directed by the Sunday School and Training Union departments. The full development of "Eagle Eyrie," Lynchburg, Va., will allow the expansion of the present significant program of assemblies.   RAYMOND BRYAN BROWN

ASSEMBLY, SUMMER. A summer gathering of people from the churches, usually for a week or 10 days, on property owned by the denomination or leased for the purpose, on a district, state, or Convention-wide basis, for inspiration, fellowship, instruction, and recreation. Most district and state assemblies offer periods for Bible study; classes in Sunday school, Training Union, Woman's Missionary Union, and Brotherhood work; personal or group interest conferences; and preaching. However, a few states operate assemblies for the entire summer with a different emphasis each week. Convention-wide assemblies are operated at Ridgecrest, N. C., and Glorieta, N. Mex. The variety of the

program is indicated by the fact that at these two assemblies week-long conferences are conducted related to Sunday school, Training Union, Woman's Missionary Union, Young Woman's Auxiliary, Brotherhood, church music, student work, audio-visual aids, church library, church recreation, public relations, home missions, foreign missions, Bible study, and Christian writers; also, related to the work sponsored by the Christian Life Commission, Historical Commission, Radio and Television Commission, and Relief and Annuity Board. Many of the conferences meet simultaneously. Mornings and evenings are given to classes, conferences, demonstrations, addresses, and sermons, while the afternoons are reserved chiefly for rest and recreation.
J. M. CROWE

ASSOCIATION, THE DISTRICT. The genesis of Baptist general co-operative bodies is found in the conference at Jerusalem (Acts 15; Gal. 2), and in the co-operative benevolence of New Testament churches (Acts 11:27–30; II Cor. 8–9; Rom. 15:15–32; I Cor. 16:2–6).

These churches were independent of one another; but, in their sympathetic understanding and co-operative effort, were interdependent. The church at Jerusalem had no control over the church at Antioch, but it was interested in the welfare of the saints of the young church in that great city (Acts 11:22). This spirit was mutual (Acts 11:29–30).

Doctrinal differences growing out of the conversion of the Gentiles led to the Jerusalem council. The brethren, in sharp disagreement at first, talked things through and came to a clear understanding. They agreed on a statement to send to the churches, a decree which began: "It seemed good unto us, having come to one accord, to choose out men and send them unto you . . . who themselves also shall tell you the same things by word of mouth" (Acts 15:25–27 ASV).

Baptist associations had a similar beginning. They preceded Baptist conventions by 180 years. As early as 1642–43 Baptist "associations" were convening among English Baptists for counsel and correspondence. By 1655, several groups had been formed and the title "association" was well recognized. Then followed, under Charles II, a long struggle for existence. Baptists who crossed the Atlantic to the New World were persecuted, particularly in Massachusetts and Virginia.

In 1707 the Philadelphia Association was organized. Prior to that date general meetings, without any formal organization, had been held for discussion of matters of faith, polity, discipline, and evangelism. In 1707 five small churches in the Philadelphia area, typical of which were the Pennepack (founded in 1688) and the Philadelphia (organized in 1698), formed "an association of messengers authorized by their respective churches to meditate and execute designs of public good." Its plan was similar to that of Baptist associations in England and Wales, and, in defining its relation to the churches, it set the pattern for Baptist associations for years to come. Next after the Philadelphia Association were organized the Charleston (1751), Sandy Creek (1758), Kehukee (1760), Ketocton (1766), Warren (1767), Stonington (1772), Redstone (1776), and Shaftsbury (1780).

Churches were autonomous, and the association had no authority over the churches except as fellowship might be withdrawn from churches for defections in doctrine or practice.

> Various churches relied upon the Association for advice and even for the settlement of disputes. At times it acted in the capacity of a council for ordination. . . . The Association was careful to examine the credentials of itinerant preachers and to warn the churches of such as were imposters . . . queries concerning communion, baptism, church membership, ordination, the place of women in the church and the propriety of using musical instruments in the service. . . . The decision was left to the local church.

"Associations tended to take on an advisory capacity, declining the power of discipline, and in every way possible leaving the church to make decisions for itself." In 1766 the Philadelphia Association admonished messengers not to hasten away from the association before adjournment. An outstanding feature of early associations was the writing of circular letters, partly because there were so few papers. These letters touched various phases of doctrine, polity, church and home life, and missions. The pattern of such a letter was set by the Jerusalem council.

As a basis of doctrinal agreement, the Philadelphia Association adopted in 1742 as a statement of faith the London Confession of Particular (Calvinistic) Baptists of 1689, the controlling influence of which was the Westminster Confession, altered to suit Baptist views. The Philadelphia Confession was adopted by many churches and associations and was a great influence in stabilizing and strengthening the doctrinal position of American Baptists. Almost a century after the Philadelphia Confession of Faith was adopted by the Philadelphia Association, the New Hampshire Confession, moderately Calvinistic, was approved by the board (5 members) of the New Hampshire convention. Later, in 1867, with some revision, it was incorporated by James Madison Pendleton (*q.v.*) in his *Church Manual*, and came to be adopted by many of the associations. An interesting story is told of the effort to agree on a doctrinal statement when a group of brethren met to organize the first missionary Baptist association in the Republic of Texas. One half of the preachers in the group were missionaries; the other half, antimissionaries. Several days were spent in a fruitless effort to agree on a constitution and articles of faith. About four months later, the missionary group met, Oct. 8, 1840, and organized the Union Association.

Associational Missions

For many years the early associations followed the custom of sending messengers as visitors to adjoining associations. To be appointed a visitor or correspondent to another association was considered an honor.

The annual association meeting was the most significant Baptist gathering of the year, continuing three or four days, with an attendance frequently of several hundred messengers and visitors.

At present, the average Southern Baptist church conceives the association of Baptist churches with which it is affiliated to be an organization through which it voluntarily co-operates with the other member churches for special mission ministries within the associational area, and from which it gains the values such an organization can contribute to the churches in the manifold areas of their interest and co-operation. Therefore, a Baptist association in the matter of polity is free to determine what churches it will admit to its fellowship and whether it will continue to receive the messengers of those who have already been admitted, just as the churches are free to decide whether they will or will not be in co-operative relationship with the association.   E. C. ROUTH

ASSOCIATIONAL MISSIONS. The mission program of the Baptist district association is the means by which the efforts of all the Baptist churches in a local geographical area are concentrated and directed so as to provide a strong and balanced church ministry to all the people living in that area. The association exists to promote programs and establish churches which can provide in the best possible way for the religious needs of its actual and potential constituency.

The association is the agency through which churches collectively engage in activities beyond their capabilities as individuals. This has been true from the beginning of the associational plan of organization, and was clearly pointed out when Samuel Jones, moderator of the Philadelphia Association, wrote to James Manning of Warren, R. I., on the occasion of the formation of Warren Association:

For, as particular members are collected together and united in one body, which we call a particular church, to answer those ends and purposes which could not be accomplished by any single member, so a collection and union of churches into one associational body may easily be conceived capable of answering those still great purposes which any particular church could not be equal to.

These early associations had many purposes and uses, but one of the first and most important was the promotion of missions. In 1755, four years after its organization, the Charleston Association, first in the South, "observed with concern the unevangelized condition of many places in the back-country in neighboring provinces. Oliver Hart, pastor of the First Baptist Church [Charleston] and moderator of the Association, was authorized to procure the services of a missionary to take the gospel to these places. He secured Rev. John Gano."

All programs of associational missions are built on a thorough knowledge of the area and the people which the program is intended to serve. This knowledge is usually secured by means of a complete survey of the population of the area concerned and a thorough analysis of the area's churches, businesses, schools, industries, and all other factors which might affect its growth and character. On the basis of this information it can be determined which areas can support new churches and which areas are in need of a temporarily or permanently subsidized mission program. The varied activities which the association promotes are then tailored specifically to meet the varied and specific needs of all the different classes of people living within the bounds of the association's ministry. By means of a well-planned and correlated calendar of activities, which includes all these activities, a balanced and continuous program can be planned and promoted.

As it adapts its program to meet the needs of the people, the association becomes involved in many different kinds of activity. For its established and developed churches, the association provides leadership in the development of a full educational and evangelistic program. It provides, or promotes, training schools for church leaders, teachers, music leaders, and workers of all sorts. It integrates evangelistic effort, and helps in the promotion of simultaneous crusades. It provides leadership and organizational help in enlargement campaigns. For the inspiration and development of all its constituency, it plans and provides a summer assembly program. It helps the churches fulfil their social responsibilities by conducting informative institutes on problems concerning the family, juvenile delinquency, temperance, etc., and helps to make the churches concerned with the improvement of their own communities.

Because the association acts more often as a co-ordinator than as an executive, it can only carry on a ministry to unchurched areas by encouraging and guiding the work of the churches within its area. These churches do much of the work that is done. They sponsor missions and good will centers with leadership and financial aid. They sometimes furnish from their membership enough leadership to make the beginnings of new churches, and help financially to get them established.

The associational mission responsibility is as large and as varied as the need which the association faces. In some areas there are numbers of military personnel who need to be integrated into the life and work of the local church. In others there are minorities who can be helped by Christian influence and special training. In all areas there are social problems—such as juvenile delinquency, broken homes, liquor, gambling, and crime—which need to be dealt with, either by the association and the churches themselves or by church members as informed and interested citizens. In either case the association provides leadership and encouragement to the actions of its constituency.

In addition to its program of local and internal mission work, the association also provides a means of communication between local churches and the denomination as a whole. It is through the association that the churches report on the progress of their work to the denomination, thus giving Southern Baptists their only reliable basis of denominational statistics. In addition, the association serves to inform the churches of the needs and plans of the whole denomination. The association is the most immediate channel through which the churches extend their effort and influence, through voluntary co-operation, not only to the territories in their own neighborhood, but also into the area of the whole denomination, and through foreign missions into the rest of the world.

H. S. SAULS

ASSOCIATIONS, EXTINCT. The large number of associations which, at one time or another, existed as a part of the Southern Baptist constituency and which no longer appear in Southern Baptist reports have been classified as extinct associations. These organizations disappeared, dissolved, or were dropped for a number of reasons.

Some of the extinct associations were dissolved because of failure to achieve uniformity of doctrine in member churches. This was true of Mero Association in Tennessee, which was constituted in 1796 and which seven years later was disbanded because of internal dissension. The suspicion with which these early groups regarded doctrinal irregularity is shown in what I. M. Allen says of Red River Association:

The Red River Association is a faithful daughter of old Kehukee in North Carolina, whence she emigrated about forty years ago. In doctrine she is hyper-calvinistic, and treats with neglect, not to say contempt all who dare to differ from her views. Revivals out of her own precincts she affects to regard as spurious and entirely enthusiastic, although she would gladly receive into her own bosom the most doubtful characters that present themselves on such occasions. To all the benevolent operations of the day she is violently opposed. In 1812 this Association contained 2,387 members. In 1805, it had 2,000. We learn that it is now reduced to less than 1,000.

Although most associational constitutions specifically prohibit interference with local church activities, actually in practice associations did attempt to control the doctrine of the churches. Associations invented and enforced with rigor various tests of fellowship. A group, for instance, called by their opponents "new test" associations,

. . . introduced a *new test* of fellowship, by which, friendship to any of the benevolent operations of the day, or contribution to them, is made an offense punishable with exclusion from church communion. All these are rapidly diminishing, and will soon become extinct.

Some associations, instead of being destroyed by controversy, were captured by some emergent heresy and left the denomination, becoming, at least as far as co-operative relatedness was concerned, extinct. In addition to the major defections brought on by antimissionism, Campbellism, Landmarkism, and Gospel Missionism, there were many small vagaries of doctrine or method which carried off an occasional association or group of associations. Since 1875 there have been only minor defections.

The cause of extinction often was less drastic. Many associations merely changed their names or divided and took new names. They were divided for many reasons, usually in the interest of efficiency. Constituencies that were too large or too scattered for efficient work would divide into smaller, more workable units.

Other associations became extinct because of a willingness to follow the change to a county unit system. Still others were dissolved because of lack of support, or died with the institutions they were organized to support.

The general trend, of course, is toward stability of organization. Changes in associational organizations which do occur are made for reasons of expediency or efficiency rather than because of controversy.

See also presentations of extinct associations, under names of various states.

CARL P. DAW

ASSOCIATIONS BEFORE 1845. The first association formed in America, the Philadelphia (Pa.), 1707, played a vital role in the formation of four of the next five—Charleston (S. C.), 1751; Kehukee (N. C.), 1765; Ketocton (Va.), 1766; and Warren (R. I.), 1767. These, with the Sandy Creek (N. C.), 1756, had an important part in the formation and pattern followed by many of the associations formed before 1845. The theory was generally accepted that such an organization "would have a tendency to impart stability, regularity, and uniformity" to the Baptist movement as a whole.

In a day before state or national denominational papers, the various associations adopted the custom of exchanging minutes and circular letters. These were read to the messengers and visitors which assembled at the annual meetings. The highlights of these minutes and letters were often included in the local minutes in order that all might profit from them. Much care was given to the preparation of the circular letters to the corresponding associations. These bodies also exchanged messengers, who were allowed to preach and to give oral or written reports on their own activities and those of neighboring bodies. These reports and messages "fired" the preachers and others present with a joy and enthusiasm that enabled them to return to their work with renewed energy and zeal.

Another benefit which grew out of the annual meeting of the association was the preaching done by the ministers on their way to and from the meetings, since some often traveled

Associations Before 1845

150–200 miles. Also, throngs sometimes attended these sessions who listened to the deliberations and preaching, and presented pleas for ministers to be sent into their neglected areas. The answer to these requests was a regular order of business in the annual sessions of many of the associations. The messengers recommended that ministers "be requested to consider the situation" of the needy churches and districts and that they "visit them as often as possible," that the "churches liberate their ministers by placing enough means in their hands" so they "could give themselves to full time domestic missions" in the destitute regions. Various associations responded to the challenge by establishing a fund to pay expenses and by appointing preachers to serve in these areas for a few months or a year. Preachers and churches readily complied with this plan.

Another way in which the associations assisted in imparting stability to the Baptist movement was their effort to bring about doctrinal uniformity. This was done in several ways; first, by the adoption of what came to be known as the Philadelphia Confession of Faith. This, with some modifications, was adopted by many of the associations before 1845. In addition, these bodies sent their more capable ministers to confer with churches and preachers who were considered irregular in their doctrinal views with the purpose of restoring them to the accepted tenets. Perhaps the most positive plan was the institution by the Philadelphia, in 1759, of the custom of designating annually one of its strong ministers to preach upon a specific doctrine at the next session. This practice was quickly followed by most of the other bodies with the result that the doctrinal sermon came to hold a very high place on the program in the annual associational meetings.

Another effective method was the use of the circular letter to treat one of the doctrines. These "papers were very helpful to the churches." At other times doctrinal questions were discussed in session, and the conclusions were printed in the minutes in order that those who had attended might be benefited.

From the time William Carey went to India, many of the associations became concerned over the matter of foreign missions. This interest was increased upon the receipt of news that the Adoniram Judsons and Luther Rice had become Baptists soon after reaching India. When Rice returned to this country he found that the associational organization offered an excellent basis for his campaigns of information, inspiration, and fund-raising for the Judsons and for missions in general. At first he was welcomed at all of these meetings. In a few years, however, a number of associations, following the lead of the Kehukee, Red River (Tenn.), and Little River (Tenn.), became "violently opposed" to missions as well as to those who sponsored the preaching of the gospel to all men. This antimission movement threatened to split asunder the work in all regions and brought about a spirit of antagonism and division that has been a hindrance to the cause of missions ever since.

Many associations throughout the South became interested in the evangelization of the Indians and adopted measures to promote the effort. The Negroes throughout the period of slavery generally attended and became members of the white churches. However, there were all-Negro churches in several Southern states. When any movement was set under foot by the owners or the state to abridge the freedom of the Negro to attend worship, white church members and the associations were quick to protest.

The associations, following the example set by the Philadelphia, Charleston, and Warren, took the lead in sponsoring institutions of learning in order that there might be a better-trained ministry. This task was taken over by the state conventions as they were organized, but the associations continued to raise money to pay tuition and other expenses of needy ministerial students in various states. These bodies also sponsored Bible societies, Sunday schools, and other benevolent causes. Here again they were challenged by the hyper-Calvinistic element in their midst.

From the foregoing it can be seen that the associations before 1845 played a vital role in the growth and pattern followed by the Baptists in the United States before the organization of a permanent convention.

BIBLIOGRAPHY. T. Armitage, *A History of the Baptists* (1871). I. Backus, *A History of New England with Particular Reference to the Denomination of Christians Called Baptists* (1871). D. Benedict, *A General History of the Baptist Denomination in America, and Other Parts of the World* (1813). J. L. Boyd, *A Popular History of the Baptists in Mississippi* (1930). L. Burkitt and J. Read, *A Concise History of the Kehukee Association from Its Original Rise to the Present Time*, ed. J. Biggs (1834). J. T. Christian, *A History of the Baptists of the United States* (1945). W. Fristoe, *A Concise History of the Ketocton Baptist Association* (1808). W. Furman, *A History of the Charleston Association of Baptist Churches in the State of South Carolina* (1811). Z. T. Leavell and T. J. Bailey, *A Complete History of Mississippi Baptists from the Earliest Times* (1904). J. Mercer, *History of the Georgia Baptist Association* (1838). A. H. Newman, *A History of the Baptist Churches in the United States* (1915). G. W. Purefoy, *A History of the Sandy Creek Baptist Association from Its Organization in A.D. 1758 to 1858* (1859). B. F. Riley, *A Memorial History of the Baptists of Alabama* (1923); *A History of the Baptists in the Southern States East of the Mississippi* (1898). T. O. Schilling, *Abstract History of the Mississippi Baptist Association for One Hundred Years 1806–1906* (1906). R. B. Semple, *A History of the Rise and Progress of the Baptists in Virginia* (1894). W. W. Sweet, *Religion on the Frontier: The Baptists* (1931). C. B. Williams, *A History of the Baptists in North Carolina* (1901). S. Wright, *History of the Shaftsbury Baptist Association from 1781 to 1853* (1853). H. C. Vedder, *A History of the Baptists in the Middle States* (1898).

JAMES CLARK

ASSURANCE. In the New Testament the joyous certainty of salvation is the normal Christian experience, the Holy Spirit bearing inner witness with the believer that he has become a son of God (Rom. 8:15–16; Gal. 4:6), and also assuring him of final and complete deliverance (Eph. 1:13–14; 4:30). "Full assurance" is a rich phrase (Col. 2:2; I Thess. 1:5; Heb. 6:11; 10:22). Yet the New Testament refers to an incomplete faith which needs to grow (John 2:23–25; 7:31; 8:30–31; 10:42) and suggests the possibility of a saving faith without assurance (I John 5:13). Since assurance is grounded in a person, not on a proposition (II Tim. 1:12), it is expressed more consistently by a life of Christlike devotion (I John 3:10–24) than by the selfish enjoyment of salvation as a status.

BIBLIOGRAPHY: A. S. Yates, *The Doctrine of Assurance* (1952).   W. BOYD HUNT

ASUNCION BAPTIST HOSPITAL. See PARAGUAY, MISSION IN.

ATHEISM. This word is derived from the Greek *a*—not and *theos*—God; hence it is the denial of the validity of the idea of God. Philosophically opposed to theism and pantheism, atheism attempts to account for the universe in purely naturalistic terms. As a system of thought, it is as old as the history of thought itself. Vast atheistic systems arose early in India and China as well as among the Greek atomists. Eighteenth century unbelief is embodied in the *Systeme de la Nature,* which Voltaire called the Bible of atheism.

BIBLIOGRAPHY: C. C. J. Webb, *Religion and Theism* (1934). N. K. Smith, *Hume's Dialogues Concerning Natural Religion* (1947).   CHARLES A. TRENTHAM

ATHENS BAPTIST FEMALE COLLEGE. Founded in 1901 at Athens, Tenn. The property was purchased from the Methodist Episcopal Church, South, and the school opened in 1901 as the only Baptist female school in East Tennessee. It is now extinct.   LYNN EDWARD MAY, JR.

ATKINSON, WILLIAM ELRIE (b. Alabama, July 24, 1852; d. Arkansas, Nov. 8, 1935). He graduated from Washington and Lee University and practiced law at Prescott, Ark., until Jan., 1889; then was attorney general of the state of Arkansas from 1889 to 1893, and was chancellor of the 9th District Chancery Court from 1921 until his death. He was one of the founders of Ouachita Baptist College, Arkadelphia, Ark., in 1885 and served continuously as chairman of the board until his death. For three years, 1906–08, he was president of the Arkansas Baptist State Convention. In 1893 he married Eliza M. Powers of Augusta, Ky. Three children survived this union. He was buried at Conway, Ark.   PAUL ATKINSON

ATLANTIC INSTITUTE. Baptist academy at Morehead City, N. C. Organized in 1900 under the guidance of Atlantic Association, the school was incorporated by the state legislature and opened in 1901. A. W. Setzer was the first principal, succeeded in 1904 by W. L. Beach. The school closed in 1907.   D. L. SMILEY

ATLAS NEWS SERVICE, RIO DE JANEIRO. See BRAZIL, MISSION IN.

ATONEMENT. This term is used to interpret the death of Christ for man's sins. When Paul wrote to the Corinthians, "For I delivered unto you first of all that which I also received, how that Christ died for our sins according to the scriptures" (I Cor. 15:3), he not only laid bare the heart of the New Testament message; he also expressed the essential idea of the Christian doctrine of atonement. The term originated from the old English expression, *at one,* signifying agreement or reconciliation between parties. As early as the Geneva Bible (1557), "at one" was used in the religious sense of reconciliation between God and man: "We pray you that ye be at one with God" (II Cor. 5:20). The term "atonement," however, was used to express ideas beyond the meaning of reconciliation. In the Old Testament "atonement" is used frequently, with a meaning involving the idea of propitiation (atonement as covering the sin or offense). The King James Version uses "atonement" only once in the New Testament (Rom. 5:11), and then for the idea of reconciliation. Due in part to its predominant Old Testament background, the term "atonement" dropped into disuse during the early part of the 20th century, when the abiding worth of the Old Testament was little appreciated. In recent years it has come into general usage again, but its meaning in current discussions is quite controversial. The problem arises over whether Christ's death as atonement involves the fuller meaning of propitiation and expiation or only the simpler meaning of expiation and reconciliation. To discern whether the latter interpretation is adequate is of primary importance for understanding the New Testament witness.

The Old Testament preparation.—Especially with reference to the atonement, the Old Testament is the key to the New. Such terms as "sacrifice," "death," "blood," "redemption," "atonement," "covenant," "sin," "forgiveness," "righteousness," and the like, were already of special significance to the Jews of Jesus' day. Centuries of special revelation and religious heritage had conditioned the Jews to the vocabulary of atonement. Three principles govern the Old Testament interpretation of these terms.

1. The initiative in atonement in the Old Testament is always God's. Man, who is sinful, cannot himself provide a way of approach to God, who is holy. Leviticus 17:11, after indicating that the life of the flesh is in the blood, adds: "And I have given it to you upon the altar to make an atonement for your souls." Peter Taylor Forsyth comments: "Given! Did you ever see the force of it? 'I have given you the

blood to make atonement. This is an institution which I set up for you to comply with, set it up for purposes of My own, on principles of My own, but it is My gift.'" Atonement, in the Old Testament context, is God's gift before it is man's response.

2. Although God provides the atonement, he also requires it. It is God who has been sinned against; it is God's wrath which is propitiated. George Buchanan Gray recognizes this element of propitiation as primary in the Old Testament meaning of atonement. God abhors evil. He cannot simply overlook it.

3. The Old Testament nowhere suggests that atoning efficacy is inherent in the sacrifice itself. If the psalmists and prophets stress that God requires obedience and not sacrifice, it is not because they consider these antithetical. Rather, what they condemn is insincere and hypocritical offering of sacrifice.

Beyond these principles which guide in the interpretation of atonement in the Old Testament is the remarkable anticipation of Christ's sacrificial work in the concept of the Suffering Servant in Isaiah 40-66. In 53:10 particularly, the redemptive action of the Servant is pictured not only as originating with Jehovah himself but also as a guilt offering of the Servant himself in death. This prophecy, however, along with other Old Testament anticipations, did not prepare the Jews of Jesus' day for the idea of a Messiah who would fulfil his mission by dying a violent and sacrificial death. It remained for Jesus himself to link together these two ideas of messiahship and sacrificial suffering.

The New Testament witness.—"But when the fulness of the time was come, God sent forth his Son, made of a woman, made under the law, to redeem them that were under the law, that we might receive the adoption of sons" (Gal. 4:4-5). The final revelation of God was made at the cross; everything else in the New Testament record is subordinate to this central event.

1. The primacy of the cross is emphasized in Jesus' own understanding and interpretation of his mission. Mark's Gospel shows that Jesus interpreted his mission in terms of his death: Jesus' baptism was a self-identification with sinners (1:9-11); the voice from heaven at the baptism and at the transfiguration, by reflecting the language of Isaiah 42:1, associated Jesus with the Suffering Servant prophecies of Isaiah 40-66 (1:11; 9:7); Jesus' temptations reflected his refusal to resort to any short cuts in the fulfilment of his mission (1:12-13); he knew the bridegroom must be removed (2:19-20); he plainly announced that he would suffer and die (8:31-32; 9:31; 10:32-34); he said he was giving his life a ransom for many (10:45); he spoke of having a cup to drink and a baptism with which to be baptized (10:38-40; 14:36); in the parable of the wicked tenants, he showed his awareness that he would be rejected violently (12:1-12); he announced his betrayal (14:17-21, 41); he said his blood was the blood of the new testament, to be shed for many (14:22-25); he agonized in Gethsemane (14:34-42); he cried in dereliction from the cross (15:34). These references show conclusively not only that Jesus assigned the central place in his mission to his death but also that he interpreted it in terms of the prophecy of the Suffering Servant, of sacrifice, and of ransom.

2. The cross is also central in the New Testament writings of Jesus' interpreters. Their universal emphasis on the supremacy of Jesus' death is the crowning evidence of the unity of the New Testament.

(1) In Acts 1-12 we have the record of the earliest Christian preaching, clearly establishing one thing from the very beginning. The salvation these early disciples preached was proclaimed in the name of Jesus (Acts 2:21, 38-40, 47; 3:6, 19; 4:13; 5:31; 8:35; 10:43). Although they did not make explicit the connection between Jesus' death and the forgiveness of sins, such a connection is implicit in all they claimed. They were vividly aware that human wickedness destroyed Jesus (Acts 2:21; 3:14-15; 5:30; 7:52), but they also saw his death as a fulfilment of the Scriptures in line with the purpose of God (Acts 2:23; 3:18, 24; 4:11; 7:52; 8:30-35; 9:22; 10:43). The background of their thinking, in Isaiah 53, is indicated by references to Jesus as Servant (Acts 3:13, 26; 4:27, 30).

(2) First Peter, written many years after Pentecost, provides a point of comparison with Peter's preaching in Acts. As would be expected, there is evidence of doctrinal development. First Peter was written for the practical purpose of encouraging Christians undergoing persecution. Jesus' passion is therefore presented as the supreme example of innocent suffering patiently endured. But the meaning of Christ's death is by no means limited to the idea of an example. Three important passages are basic to the message of I Peter: "Forasmuch as ye know that ye were not redeemed with corruptible things . . . but with the precious blood of Christ, as of a lamb without blemish and without spot" (1:18-19); "Who his own self bare our sins in his own body on the tree, that we, being dead to sins, should live unto righteousness: by whose stripes ye were healed" (2:24); "For Christ also hath once suffered for sins, the just for the unjust, that he might bring us to God" (3:18). These references clearly indicate the sacrificial and substitutionary nature of Christ's death.

(3) Paul gives the atonement its fullest biblical treatment. One cry is heard in all he writes, "God forbid that I should glory, save in the cross of our Lord Jesus Christ" (Gal. 6:14). Paul's glorying in the cross beggars language. He borrows images from varied and widely separated areas of life: from the slave market, redemption; from the law court, justification; from war, reconciliation; from death, making alive; from the family and the law court, adoption; from commercial debt, forgiveness; from horticulture, engrafting; from ritual, washing. He employs legal terms, but the context is always ethical and vital: The believer's supreme

possession is the Spirit of Christ. The sweep of Paul's thought is universal. There is no blessing the cross has not secured, no enemy it has not destroyed. The accusations of the law are silenced, the slavery of the flesh is broken, the curse of sin is borne, and the fear of death is cast out (cf. Rom. 8:33–39). The riches of the cross are unspeakable (II Cor. 9:15) and unsearchable (Eph. 3:8). Such fulness and complexity of thought warn against any attempt to reduce Paul's interpretations to a single principle or theory. In any effort to systematize his teaching, primary ideas should be taken into account: God and Christ are one in the work of the cross (II Cor. 5:19); Jesus' death reveals both the love of God (Rom. 5:8) and the love of Christ (Gal. 2:20); the cross demonstrates the righteousness of God (Rom. 3:25); by the cross we are saved from his wrath (Rom. 5:9); Jesus took the sinner's place (II Cor. 5:21) and bore the sinner's curse (Gal. 3:13); yet the believer also dies and rises—he dies to sin and rises to righteousness (Rom. 6:5–11); Jesus' death was an open triumph over cosmic principalities and powers (Col. 2:15); by the cross God reconciled all things to himself (Col. 1:20). These ideas, along with other essential elements, clearly involve a substitutionary and propitiatory interpretation of the atonement.

(4) The sacrificial significance of Jesus' death is the entire message of the book of Hebrews. Christ, the perfect High Priest, provides full and unhindered access to God; he is the final sacrifice for sin, by which the new covenant is established (Heb. 9:11 to 10:18). Unique in this teaching is the stress it places on the dual aspects of the sacrifice as final and the priestly ministry as continuing. Thus, in one aspect, Christ is seated at the right hand of God in token of a task completed (1:3, 13; 8:1; 10:12; 12:2); his sacrifice was made once for all (2:27; 9:12, 26–28; 10:10, 12); he provided eternal salvation (5:9) and eternal redemption (9:12), offered himself through the eternal Spirit (9:14), and shed the blood of an eternal covenant (13:20). In the other aspect Jesus' high priestly ministry continues in heaven (4:14–16; 6:19–20; 7:25–26; 8:1–2; 9:24; 10:20–21). This dual presentation enriches the New Testament witness.

(5) Two distinctive emphases in the Johannine writings (the Fourth Gospel; I, II, and III John; and Revelation) should be noted. John's referring to Jesus' lifting up and glorification in the Fourth Gospel instead of to his exaltation, as elsewhere in the New Testament, is interpreted as a reference to Jesus' death (3:14; 8:28; 12:23–28, 32; 13:31–33; 17:1–5). John is teaching that the cross is the climax of the whole process of the incarnation. The Fourth Gospel, along with I John, stresses that Jesus' lifting up in death is the cosmic defeat of Satan and the overcoming of the world (John 12:31–33; 14:30; 16:11, 33; I John 3:8; 5:4; Revelation).

It is evident that the fuller meaning of atonement, involving propitiation and expiation, is required for adequate interpretation of biblical materials. Jesus' death was far more than the reconciling work of one who acted as man's representative. God himself, in the person of his Son, took the sinner's place, both as substitute for the individual and as representative of the race, and propitiated the righteous wrath of God by expiating sin. Concerning this conclusion several observations should be noted: (1) In Christ's redemptive work there is never the slightest hint of personal warfare between Father and Son; (2) Christ's death is both the commending of God's love and the bearing of God's wrath; (3) there is a tension between the work of the earthly Jesus on the cross as finished, and the work of the risen Christ through the Spirit as continuing; (4) Christ's work has both an individual and a cosmic reference; (5) what Christ does for man in redemption leaves man utterly and unspeakably in his debt.

The doctrinal interpretation.—Many theories have developed regarding the central meaning of the doctrine of the atonement. Although not one of these interpretations is wholly adequate in itself, each conserves some aspect of New Testament truth.

1. The closest thing to a theory of the atonement in the first centuries of Christian history was the *ransom* or *patristic* theory, which interpreted Jesus' death as a ransom to Satan for man's release. Scriptural in its view of Christ's death as a ransom and in viewing the cross as a victory over Satan, this theory goes beyond Scripture in holding that the ransom was paid to Satan. Until recent times the patristic theory was considered too crude to express the essential ideas of the cross. Gustaf Aulén, however, has revived it in his *classical* theory, in which the emphasis shifts from the idea of Jesus' death as a ransom to Satan to the idea of Jesus' whole life and resurrection as a defeat of the powers of cosmic darkness and evil. The influence of Aulén's thought is evident in the writings of Sydney Cave, W. T. Conner (*q.v.*), James S. Stewart, and William Hordern. This tendency represents one of the chief trends in contemporary interpretation. Writers who stress the cosmic aspect of Christ's work often speak of "eternal atonement."

2. In orthodox circles the *satisfaction* or *substitutionary* theory is the most prominent. The satisfaction theory first found definite expression in Anselm (1033–1109) and was modified by the Reformers into the substitutionary (sometimes *penal*) theory. For Anselm the alternative was either penalty or satisfaction, with God choosing the latter; while for the Reformers, God chose penalty as satisfaction. In the post-Reformation period the views of the Reformers were often interpreted with extreme legalism. Hyper-Calvinism, with its view of a literal substitution and limited atonement (i.e., that Christ died for the elect only), developed in this period. According to hyper-Calvinism, if Christ had died for the nonelect, their suffering eternally in hell would mean the exacting of the

penalty twice, once from Christ on the cross and once from the sinner in hell. This, it was charged, would be unjust. The most virile group of English Baptists in the 18th century were infected with this hyper-Calvinism. Holding to a limited atonement, they were called Particular Baptists, as opposed to General Baptists, who viewed the atonement as unlimited (i.e., that Christ died for all men). Hyper-Calvinism persisted among Baptists in America longer than in England. It was dominant in the theology of James P. Boyce (*q.v.*). The main stream of orthodox thought, however, has followed a modified Calvinism, which interprets Christ's substitutionary death in ethical and non-legalistic terms. This view claims the support of evangelical scholars such as Dale, Denney, Forsyth, H. R. Mackintosh, and Mozley. It was the view of Edgar Y. Mullins (*q.v.*) and W. T. Conner. Today it is challenged principally by C. H. Dodd and Vincent Taylor, who reject the elements of propitiation and substitution. Dodd prefers to speak of an impersonal wrath of God and of the expiation of sin; Taylor stresses the categories of sacrifice and representation. This tendency to eliminate propitiation and substitution, while stressing sacrifice or expiation, is a second chief trend in contemporary interpretation.

3. The moral influence theory, originating with Abelard (1079–1142), omits any reference to the elements of propitiation and substitution, finding the only barrier to reconciliation in man alone. It views the cross as such a demonstration of Jesus' love and loyalty to the Father as to move man to repentance and faith. Although this theory's advantage is its stress upon the cross as a demonstration of love, its inadequacy as a complete rationale of the atonement is quite generally recognized at the present.

Theories and interpretations of the atonement are essential, although the cross is infinitely more than any theological formulations about it. Mackintosh, saying that we fail to understand the cross, not because we lack intelligence, but because we are not good enough, evidenced real insight into man's dilemma with regard to the atonement.

See also CROSS, EXPIATION, and PROPITIATION.

BIBLIOGRAPHY: G. Aulén, *Christus Victor* (1931). E. Brunner, *The Mediator* (1947). W. T. Conner, *The Cross in the New Testament* (1954). J. Denney, *The Death of Christ* (1911). P. T. Forsyth, *The Cruciality of the Cross* (1948). L. W. Grensted, *A Short History of the Doctrine of the Atonement* (1951). L. Hodgson, *The Doctrine of the Atonement* (1951). T. H. Hughes, *The Atonement* (1949). L. Morris, *The Apostolic Preaching of the Cross* (1956). J. K. Mozley, *The Doctrine of the Atonement* (1915). O. C. Quick, *The Gospel of the New World* (1944). V. Taylor, *Jesus and His Sacrifice* (1943); *The Atonement in New Testament Teaching* (1945); *Forgiveness and Reconciliation* (1948).
W. BOYD HUNT

ATTRIBUTES OF GOD. Those characteristics and modes of God's being (power, life, truth, holiness, love, etc.) which express his essential nature and existence, usually classified as (1) those that express what God is in himself, independent of the universe, and (2) those that express God's relations to the universe. Some (Sydney Cave, A. C. Knudson, Emil Brunner, *et al.*) have rejected the traditionally rigid schematization of the attributes as too abstract, insisting that the personal nature of God prohibits such clear-cut distinctions in attributes as internal and external, quiescent and operative, metaphysical and ethical, etc. Emil Brunner, especially, has attacked those theologians who obscure the biblical teaching of God's attributes with speculative ideas derived from Greek thought. A well-known listing of the attributes may be found in A. H. Strong, *Systematic Theology* (1907).

See also GOD.

BIBLIOGRAPHY: E. Brunner, *The Christian Doctrine of God* (1950). L. R. Farnell, *The Attributes of God* (1925). A. C. Knudson, *The Doctrine of God* (1930).
TED R. CLARK

AUDIO-VISUAL AIDS. A term to identify the many teaching materials which are predominantly visual and/or audio-visual in nature. These include films, filmstrips, charts, graphs, posters, objects, observation trips, flat pictures, stereographs, and other visual media.

Though mechanical aids combining sound and sight are recent developments, various forms of visuals have been used for centuries in religious education. The reading of Exodus and Leviticus impresses one with the visual element in Levitical system. Note other Old Testament examples in I Kings 11:29; Isaiah 6:1–13; Jeremiah 18:1–10; 19:1–13; Ezekiel 4:1 to 5:17; and Jonah 4:1–11. The visual element in Jesus' teaching is pronounced. The two ordinances, baptism and the Lord's Supper, are pictures of basic spiritual truths.

Drama and religious art have always been used extensively in religious instruction. In periods of history when few people could read, some kind of visual help was essential. The development of the camera and modern photographic and sound recording processes gave a new emphasis to visual media. As early as 1898 a film on the Oberammergau Passion Play was produced and circulated to church audiences. The present emphasis on audio-visual aids in religious education is of ancient origin, but the plan for producing, distributing, and using them is of recent development.

The first significant recognition of audio-visual aids by a Southern Baptist agency came in 1938 when Southwestern Baptist Theological Seminary introduced a course on the use of these materials in a church program. In 1942, after exploratory conferences, the Sunday School Board of the Southern Baptist Convention joined a co-operative effort of several Protestant denominations and formed the Religious Film Association to select and distribute religious films to churches. The Visual Education Service, a department of the Sunday School Board, was started in 1943.

Both the Home and Foreign Mission boards of the Southern Baptist Convention developed active programs of audio-visual production and promotion in the 1940's. In 1948 the Southern Baptist Convention assigned to the Sunday School Board the responsibility of producing and distributing Southern Baptist audio-visual aids. The next year the board discontinued its distribution arrangement with the Religious Film Association and set up its own audio-visual libraries in connection with its Baptist Book Stores. The question of film production came before the Convention again in 1949 and the Radio Commission of the Southern Baptist Convention was asked to become the production agency with the Sunday School Board acting as distributor. Another recommendation was approved by the Convention in 1950 reassigning to the Sunday School Board responsibility for the production of these materials.

EARL WALDRUP

AULICK, AMOS LINDSEY (b. Falmoth, Ky., Oct. 9, 1882; d. Santa Cruz, Calif., Aug. 5, 1953). Pastor and educator. The youngest of 10 children, he spent his early years on his father's farm. At the age of 16 he was converted in a revival conducted by Jesse Warren Beagle (*q.v.*). He was graduated from a business college at Lebanne, Ohio, and then attended Georgetown College until poor health forced him to go to the West. After some time on a ranch in Colorado, he entered Baylor University. Later he earned the B.A. degree from the University of New Mexico, the Th.B. degree from Southwestern Baptist Theological Seminary, the M.A. degree from Colgate University, the B.D. degree from Colgate Seminary, and the Th.D. degree from the University and Seminary of Dubuque.

He was married to Marie Walters Cook in Waco, Tex., Aug. 26, 1908. They had one child who died in infancy.

Aulick served as Sunday school and Training Union secretary of Arkansas and as educational secretary of the Baptist Student Missionary Movement of America. In this work he visited college campuses, organizing mission bands and enlisting students in mission service.

Among his pastorates were Pulaski Heights Baptist Church, Little Rock, Ark.; University Baptist Church, Austin, Tex.; Trinity Baptist Church, Oklahoma City, Okla.; and Central Baptist Church, Clovis, N. Mex.

He was always intensely interested in Christian education, and while a pastor he served as a trustee of Southern Baptist Theological Seminary and Oklahoma Baptist University. From 1935 until 1942 he was head of the Bible department of Oklahoma Baptist University. From 1944 until 1948, he served as Bible teacher in connection with Eastern New Mexico University. While filling this position he led in a successful campaign for funds to erect the Baptist Student Center and Bible Chair Building adjoining the campus.

In 1948 he became head of the New Testament department in Golden Gate Baptist Theological Seminary. He performed valuable service in greatly strengthening the teaching staff and in attracting students to the new seminary. In addition to his seminary duties he was active in the general program of California Baptists, and at the time of his death he was serving as president of the Southern Baptist General Convention of California. WILLIAM A. CARLETON

AURORA, THE. A Baptist monthly newspaper, now extinct, published at Murfreesboro, Tenn., from 1859 to *c.* 1862, and edited by Mrs. E. M. Eaton. LYNN E. MAY, JR.

AUSTRALIA, BAPTIST UNION OF. The beginnings of Baptist work in Australia go back to the early days of the colonization of this country. In 1778 the first shipload of unhappy convicts arrived in Australia from England to start the new colony of South Wales. When these convicts were leaving England, the English Baptists had asked the government to allow a Baptist minister to go with them. But they had been told that they "could not send a Baptist minister, as there were no Baptists among the convicts." Forty-three years later, in Apr., 1831, the first Baptist church service to be held in Australia was conducted in the "long room" of the Rose and Crown Inn, Castlereagh Street, Sydney. The preacher was John McKaeg. Governor Bourke granted the infant church a block of land in Bathurst Street and the first Baptist church was built there. It continued in use as the Central Baptist Church in New South Wales until 1937 when a new and larger church was erected in George Street.

In 1832 John McKaeg resigned as minister, and the infant church wrote to the Baptist Missionary Society in England asking that a missionary be sent to take charge of the Sydney Baptist Church. On Monday Dec. 1, 1834, John Saunders landed in Sydney. He was minister of the church for many years. By July, 1858, there were four Baptist churches in New South Wales, and in that year they banded together into the New South Wales Baptist Association. The association was not able to keep going with so few churches, but in 1868 it was reorganized, this time with 11 churches and 360 members. In 1870 it changed its name to the Baptist Union of New South Wales.

The day after John Saunders arrived in Sydney, another Baptist minister from England, Henry Dowling, landed in Hobart, Tasmania. A Baptist church was formed there in June, 1835, with Dowling as the minister.

In 1838, three years after the founding of Melbourne, Baptist church services were conducted in a tent in Collins Street, Melbourne. In 1842 the first Baptist church in Melbourne was constituted. In 1843 John Ham became the first minister of the Collins Street Baptist

Australia, Baptist Union of

Church which has been the Central Baptist Church in Melbourne ever since. The discovery of gold in Victoria in 1851 meant a great influx of people, and by 1858 there were 10 Victorian Baptist churches which formed into the Victorian Baptist Association. In 1862 this became the Baptist Union of Victoria.

In 1843 Baptist work began in Adelaide, South Australia. In 1855 Queensland Baptists, who for six years had been combining with the Congregationalists and Presbyterians in the United Evangelical Church, formed into the first Baptist church in Queensland. In 1859 the Baptist church building was opened, and 20 people were baptized on the same day. In 1894 the first Baptist church in Western Australia was formed under the leadership of J. H. Cole of Melbourne.

In 1901 the federation of the six states of the Commonwealth took place; and seven years later, on Sept. 22, 1908, the first meeting of the Australasian Baptist Congress was held in the Bathurst Street Baptist Church, Sydney, when delegates from the six states of Australia and New Zealand were present. On the closing day of the congress, the following motion was passed: "In the opinion of this Congress the time has arrived for the formation of an Australasian Baptist Alliance." The organization envisaged was to embrace the Baptists of the six states of Australia and New Zealand. This was not realized; but it was the germ of the idea that led to the formation of the Baptist Union of Australia in 1926. The Baptist Union of New Zealand remained a separate entity, having no organic connection with the Baptist Union of Australia.

Among the leaders of those early days who did much to bring the Baptist Union of Australia into being were F. W. Norwood, J. C. Martin, A. J. Waldock, J. A. Packer, Q. Stow Smith, J. H. Goble, and C. J. Tinsley.

The constitution of the Baptist Union of Australia was adopted at the inaugural assembly of the union held in the Burton Street Tabernacle, Sydney, Aug. 25—Sept. 1, 1926. The union's functions are clearly defined in the constitution which states:

1. *Objectives.* (a) To foster the spirit of fellowship and co-operation among the Baptist Unions of the Commonwealth of Australia, and to exhibit their substantial unity in doctrine, polity and work.

(b) To confer upon matters vitally concerning the Baptist churches of the Commonwealth, and the progress of the Kingdom of God, in India and elsewhere.

(c) To initiate and carry out in conjunction with any State Union or Unions, such work as it may consider desirable and to do such work remitted to it by any such Union or Unions as shall be undertaken by it.

2. *Proviso.* Except in regard to matters referred to it by any State Union or Unions, the Union shall exercise no authority whatever over its constituents.

3. *Constituency.* The Union shall consist of the existing State Baptist Unions of the Australian Commonwealth and of such other Baptist Unions as may hereafter be formed in the Commonwealth and admitted as constituents by the assembly of such Union.

The headquarters of the union are located in Melbourne, Victoria. Baptists are found in all six states of the Commonwealth of Australia and are most numerous in areas of greatest population, i.e., along the eastern, southern, and southwestern coast lines. In these areas the respective state capitals of the mainland of Australia—Brisbane, Sydney, Melbourne, Adelaide, and Perth—contain 4,721,763 of the total population (9,313,291) of Australia, and the Baptist churches in these five cities number about 300 compared with a total of 546 Baptist churches for Australia.

Baptist work in Australia is organized on a state basis. There are six states of the Commonwealth—New South Wales, Victoria, Queensland, South Australia, West Australia, and Tasmania. Within each state the traditional pattern of Baptist life has been followed by churches binding together into associations on a geographical basis. There are approximately 35 district associations functioning in Australia at present.

Statistics for Baptist churches in Australia are as follows:

NUMBER OF BAPTIST CHURCHES IN AUSTRALIA

	N.S.W.	Vic.	Q'land.	S.A.	W.A.	Tas.	Total
1934	117	119	63	88	25	18	430
1954	169	143	92	90	31	21	546

CHURCH MEMBERSHIP

	N.S.W.	Vic.	Q'land.	S.A.	W.A.	Tas.	Total
1934	10,552	8,330	4,201	5,052	1,560*	1,400*	31,095
1954	12,040	8,355	5,024	4,151	1,647	1,497	32,714

SUNDAY SCHOOL MEMBERSHIP

	N.S.W.	Vic.	Q'land.	S.A.	W.A.	Tas.	Total
1934	13,501	12,450	4,800	7,367	2,055*	2,000*	42,173
1954	13,500	11,820	8,014	5,754	2,523	2,118	43,729

BAPTISMS

	N.S.W.	Vic.	Q'land.	S.A.	W.A.	Tas.	Total
1954	639	288	163	118	109	72	1,389

*Approximate figures, no statistics available.

Though divided geographically by state boundaries, Australian Baptists are united doctrinally. There is frequent interchange of ministers and members between different states and churches.

The official organ of the Baptist Union of Australia is *The Australian Baptist*, which is published weekly at the Australian Baptist Publishing House, Sydney. It has a circulation of approximately 4,600. It serves all the states but particularly New South Wales, South Australia, West Australia, and Tasmania. The other two states, Queensland and Victoria, publish their own monthly papers, *The Queensland Baptist* and *The Victorian Baptist Witness*, respectively. A monthly missionary magazine, *Vision*, is published by the Australian Baptist Foreign Mission. It has a circulation of over 10,000.

There are four theological colleges training young men for the ministry—the Queensland Baptist Theological College located in Brisbane, the New South Wales Baptist Theological College located in Sydney, the Victorian Baptist Theological College located in Melbourne, and the South Australian Baptist Theological College located in Adelaide. The total enrolment of the four colleges is approximately 80 students.

There is also the Missionary and Deaconess Training Institute located in Melbourne where female students are trained as missionaries and as deaconesses. The present enrolment is five for overseas work and four for work in Australia.

In New South Wales the Bedford Business College, commenced in 1943, provides a commercial education for 24 girls. In Victoria there are three associated grammar schools—Carey, Strathcona and Kilvington. Carey was founded in 1923; its property is valued at $750,000; the enrolment is 800 boys. Strathcona was founded in 1944; its property is valued at $80,000; the enrolment is 227 girls. Kilvington was founded in 1947; its property is valued at $85,000; the enrolment is 266 girls. In South Australia, King's College, owned jointly by the Congregationalists and Baptists, has an enrolment of 250 boys. All four grammar schools provide education up to matriculation standard.

While so much of Baptist work in Australia is organized on a state basis—e.g., theological education, home mission work, youth work, evangelism, etc.—the Baptist Union of Australia is playing an increasingly important role in the over-all development of work in this land. Much of its work is delegated to the following boards of the union:

Home Mission Board.—This board, with headquarters in Sydney, initiated work in the Australian Capital Territory and brought into being in 1929 the first Baptist church of Canberra, Australia's capital city. It opened a second Baptist church in North Canberra in 1952. It is also responsible for missionary work among the Australian aborigines. In 1947 work was begun among the Waibris at Yuendumu. In 1956 there was a staff of four missionaries. This board also assists the Marribank Aborigine Mission Station commenced by the West Australian Union in 1952. Substantial help is given to the Queensland and West Australian home mission committees for pioneer work in the sparsely populated areas of central and northern Australia.

Educational Board.—The Educational Board co-ordinates the theological training of the state unions. It has an extramural course of ministerial training and is at present training eight men. It encourages postgraduate work among ministers and grants certificates for same.

Young People's Board.—This board, whose headquarters is in Melbourne, commenced publishing Sunday school literature in 1939. In that year there were four publications, and 17,500 individual books or booklets were produced. There are now 10 periodical publications, and in 1955, 270,000 individual pieces of literature were produced. This board also produces textbooks for Christian education. Its Sunday school publications have been adopted by the New Zealand Union. A few South African schools also use them. There is co-operation with the Federal Board of Christian Education of Churches of Christ at kindergarten, primary, and Bible class levels. In each state there is a well-organized youth department and either a full-time youth director or a part-time youth secretary. Annually, Sunday school Scripture examinations are held for more than 8,000 entrants. In the local churches there is a variety of youth organizations—Christian Endeavour, Boys' Brigade, Girls' Brigade, Fellowship Group, Pathfinder Club, Scout and Guide troops, Missionary bands, etc. The Young People's Board seeks to co-ordinate all these organizations in the Baptist Youth Fellowship of Australia.

Board of Evangelism.—This board, with headquarters in Sydney, encourages evangelistic efforts and often brings to Australia outstanding evangelists from overseas. A recent development has been the production of Baptist radio programs.

Women's Board.—The Women's Board, which is located in Sydney, seeks to co-ordinate the women's work in the churches. It also provides a course of leadership study for women.

Men's Board.—Likewise, the Men's Board, which is located at Melbourne, seeks to co-ordinate the men's work in the churches. There are now approximately 300 men's societies functioning in Australian Baptist churches.

Board of Literature.—This board, with headquarters in Melbourne and trading under the name Clifford Press, has been functioning for nine years. It has produced half a million booklets during that period.

Advisory Board.—This board seeks to facilitate the transfer of ministers from one state to another.

Annuity Board.— With assets of over £30,000, this board is responsible for the administration of the Ministerial Annuity Scheme which enables participating ministers to receive annuity payments on retirement.

In 1950 the Australian Baptist Historical Society was formed. Its objects, as set out in the constitution, are "to encourage the preservation of historical records of Baptist life and witness; to collect into libraries materials of Baptist history; to encourage research into this field; to facilitate the dissemination of this knowledge; to establish a liaison with other similar societies." Many documents and objects pertaining to the early days of Baptist work in Australia are now in its possession.

The Australian Baptist Publishing House, Ltd., located in Sydney, was formed in 1912 with individual shareholders. In 1952 it passed into the control of the Baptist Unions of Australia. It publishes *The Australian Baptist, Vision,* and other denominational literature.

The Australian Baptist Foreign Mission is an incorporated society consisting of six state missionary societies which federated in the year 1913. Prior to 1864 the Baptist churches of Australia supported the work of the Baptist Missionary Society, sending their contributions direct to London. In that year a Baptist missionary society was formed in Adelaide and accepted responsibility for support of Indian workers of the Baptist Missionary Society in the Faridpur district of Bengal, India. A similar society was started in Melbourne in 1865 and supported Indian workers at Mymensingh in Bengal.

In 1882 the first Australian Baptist missionaries, Ellen Arnold and Marie Gilbert, were sent to Faridpur by the society in Adelaide. In 1885 missionaries were similarly sent from Melbourne to Mymensingh.

In due course Baptists of the other states of Australia followed the example of those in South Australia and Victoria, forming societies, sending out missionaries, and taking over territory in the field of the Baptist Missionary Society in East Bengal. Overlapping and duplication of operations and fraternity of spirit and purpose eventually resulted in the federal organization with headquarters, first in Adelaide and then in Melbourne.

When India was divided into the two self-governing states of India and Pakistan in 1947, the original field of the Australian Baptist Foreign Mission was included in East Pakistan. As new work, however, had been opened in Assam only three months earlier, the mission had a field in India also. There are now 120 churches, having a total membership of 7,000 in Pakistan, and 30 churches in India, having a total membership of 1,800, connected with the mission.

In 1949 the society began work in the Western Highlands of the territory of New Guinea among a completely primitive people. In 1956 two churches were constituted there with a total membership of 100. Plans are being developed for extension into the Central Highlands of Dutch New Guinea.

The Australian Baptist Foreign Mission supports 33 missionaries in Pakistan, 12 in India, and 37 in New Guinea. The total income by contributions and legacies in 1934 was £14,250 (approximately $32,000) and in 1954 £72,500 (approximately $163,000). G. H. BLACKBURN

AUSTRALIAN BAPTIST FOREIGN MISSION SOCIETY, THE. Officially constituted Aug. 27, 1912, a natural outgrowth of the federation of the states of Australia into a commonwealth in 1900. Formerly, the states had established foreign mission societies to undertake missionary work chiefly in Bengal. The Australian Baptist Foreign Mission now operates in the eastern Bengal section of East Pakistan; in the Goalpara and Kamrup districts of Assam, India; and in the highlands of New Guinea. In Assam the districts occupied are populated by Muslims, Hindus, Buddhists, and a large number of tribal people among whom most of the mission's work is done. Work in the eastern Bengal area, with a population of almost 13 million, is divided into two classes, work among the Bengalis and more fruitful work among the Garos, who are primitives and therefore less bound by traditionalism than the Bengalis. The highlands of New Guinea, inhabited by animistic stone-age people, became a mission field in 1949. Medical, educational, linguistic, and evangelistic work has been developed. However, due to the primitive character of the people, progress toward establishment of churches is slow.

Since the first state mission was founded in 1864, approximately 260 missionaries have been sent out by Australian Baptists. In Dec., 1955, 82 missionaries were under appointment. The mission's annual budget in 1955 was approximately $170,000. H. R. PETERSON

AUTHORITY. The search for authority in Christianity has developed three major types of thought. The first type appeals to the authority of the church and becomes, after a long history of development, the distinctive view of Roman Catholicism. In the early church the letters of Cyprian (c. A.D. 200–258), Bishop of Carthage, emphasized the authority of the church, which in the Middle Ages became centralized in general councils. In modern Roman Catholic history the struggle over authority in the Church was finally resolved in the Dogma of Papal Infallibility in 1870. This Vatican Decree declares that the "definitions of the Roman Pontiff are irreformable of their own nature (*ex sese*) and not by reason of the Church's consent."

The second type of thought related to authority, the characteristic view of conservative Protestantism, appeals to the authority of the Scriptures. The Westminster Confession, drawn up in 1646, says: "The authority of the Holy Scripture, for which it ought to be believed and obeyed, dependeth not upon the testimony of any man or church, but wholly upon God (who is truth itself), the Author thereof; and therefore it is to be received, because it is the Word of God." All historic Baptist confessions express this view of biblical authority. Southern Baptists have produced no original confessions of faith, but the views expressed by Edgar Young Mullins (*q.v.*) on the Bible as the final authority in faith and practice agree with the revised edition of the New Hampshire Confession of Faith approved by the Southern Baptist Convention in 1925. Authority of the Spirit has been advocated in the third type of thought as a source of authority superior to the Scriptures. Robert Barclay, who in 1678 formulated the fifteen propositions of the Quakers, expresses this third type as follows:

From these revelations of the Spirit of God to the saints have proceeded the Scriptures of truth.... Nevertheless, because they are only a declaration of the fountain, and not the fountain itself, therefore they are not to be esteemed the principal ground of all truth and knowledge, nor yet the adequate primary rule of faith and manners. Nevertheless, as that which giveth a true and faithful testimony of the first foundation, they are and may be esteemed a secondary rule, subordinate to the Spirit from which they have all their excellency and certainty. . . .

The seat of authority in Christian faith is Christ. In his earthly life he spoke not as a scribe but as one who had authority (Mark 1:22), and after his resurrection he declared that all authority in heaven and on earth had been given to him (Matt. 28:18). The authority of the church, the Scriptures, and the Spirit is rightly understood in relation to him. The authority of the church comes, not from the insights of flesh and blood (Matt. 16:13-20), but from the presence of Christ (Matt. 18:15-20) and the power of the Holy Spirit (John 20:22-23). Any claim to ecclesiastical authority apart from the Christ of the Scriptures and the Holy Spirit degenerates into religious despotism. The true authority of the church is exercised in making disciples of all nations (Matt. 28:19-20) and in making known through her mission the manifold wisdom of God (Eph. 3:10). The authority of the Scriptures is derived from the fact that they are fulfilled in Christ (Luke 4:21; 24:44-48) and bear witness of him (John 5:39). Searching the Scriptures is insufficient if those who search refuse to accept Christ. The Holy Spirit bears witness of Christ (Acts 5:31), and his authority comes not from himself but from Christ (John 16:13). Failure to relate the experience of the Holy Spirit to the historical revelation of God in Christ as recorded in the Scriptures produces a false subjectivism and substitutes vague mysticism for vital faith. Recognition of the supreme authority or lordship of Christ increases rather than decreases reverence for the church of which he is the head (Eph. 1:22; 4:15; 5:23; Col. 1:18; 2:10), the Scriptures in which he is found (Acts 3:24; 8:35), and the Holy Spirit whom he gives (John 3:34; 7:37-39; 14:14, 17, 25-26; 15:26-27; 16:7-15).

BIBLIOGRAPHY: C. Bergendorff, *Christ as Authority* (1947). R. E. Davies, *The Problem of Authority in the Continental Reformers* (1946). J. N. Geldenhuys, *Supreme Authority* (1953). E. Y. Mullins, *Freedom and Authority in Religion* (1913).   DALE MOODY

AUTHORITY OF THE SOUTHERN BAPTIST CONVENTION. The charter of the Southern Baptist Convention authorizes the "eliciting, combining, and directing the energies of the BAPTIST DENOMINATION OF CHRISTIANS, for the propagation of the gospel. . . ." Questions raised as to the adequacy of this authorization to cover all of the functions of the Convention issued in the adoption of an Enabling Act by the General Assembly of the State of Georgia, whereby the general statement of authority of the charter would be specifically enlarged. Specifically affirmed was the right of the Convention

to conduct schools for the training of the youth; to own and operate for itself or for others printing plants, publishing houses, and any desired methods or means for the dissemination of news and information; to own and operate hospitals, nurses' homes and any and all kinds of institutions for the alleviation of pain and suffering; to own and operate for itself or others orphan asylums, old people's homes and any and all institutions for the care of the needy and dependent; to conduct and carry into effect any plan for the care, maintenance and support of its workers and employees who may have become disabled, been retired, or otherwise made eligible for the benefits of said plan, and in connection therewith to conduct a plan for the establishment and payment of annuities in connection therewith. . . .

This legal authority of the Convention is limited by its constitution, *Article IV, Authority:* "While independent and sovereign in its own sphere, the Convention does not claim and will never attempt to exercise any authority over any other Baptist body, whether church, auxiliary organizations, association, or convention." This limitation is prompted by the theological proposition that each church is independent and autonomous. No other body may usurp the authority of any church.

Churches may voluntarily associate themselves in larger bodies to accomplish specific objectives and may delegate to such bodies certain functions, but the primary responsibility for these functions continues to rest with the churches. The delegation of these functions by any church may be rescinded by that church, and the church may withdraw its voluntary co-operation from the body, e.g., the Southern Baptist Convention. The authority, therefore, of the Convention is derived from the churches whose messengers make up the corporate body in its annual sessions. This authority flows in only one direction—from the churches to the Convention. It may not be used by the Convention to control any church or even to bind a church to the decision of its messengers expressed in vote on the Convention floor. Since the churches create other Baptist bodies, associations, or conventions, these, whether larger or smaller than the Southern Baptist Convention, are not within its jurisdiction, nor is it within theirs.

The church, however, is not sovereign but is under the lordship of Christ, its head. The Convention, when its resolutions and activities represent the mind of Christ, acquires a kind of spiritual authority, though never in an exclusive sense. For example, when it provides a channel for world missions, the Convention has a spiritual claim upon the co-operation of the churches. The churches must either use the channels of the Convention or find for themselves some other means of carrying out the commission of Christ. The actions of the Convention, therefore, have weight for individuals, churches, and other organizations. This is not authority in any legal sense, though it is the means whereby the Convention secures co-operation and compliance with its decisions.

Under specific legal authority as an independent corporation, the Convention may act and may project these actions beyond the range of its limited legal authority. It does this through the voluntary acceptance by others of a given action as having spiritual authority because it represents a proper interpretation of the mind of Christ. Thus, a Convention program on stewardship with an emphasis on tithing is enabled to reach into the life of most of the churches without impairing the independence of any church. Convention resolutions on ethical issues carry weight, not because the Convention has authority to enforce them or assess penalties upon those who ignore them, but simply because the weight of the opinion of a large percentage of the messengers automatically commends the statement to the conscience of church members and claims at least a careful examination by the individual church member to ascertain whether it rests upon proper biblical authority and is an interpretation of the mind of Christ. DUKE K. MCCALL

AUTRY, ALLEN HILL (b. Denton County, Tex., Mar. 16, 1865; d. Little Rock, Ark., Feb. 1, 1932). Minister. His father was a doctor, minister, and farmer, who moved with his family from Texas to Greenwood, Ark., in 1868. Autry was converted at age 16 and began a ministry which lasted 50 years. He was educated at Buckner College in Arkansas and William Jewel College in Missouri. He married Mary E. Nifong, Booneville, Ark., Apr. 29, 1891. To them were born seven children: Ruth, Harvey, Esther, Mary, John, Paul (M.D.), and Daniel (M.D.). He led in building six church structures at Booneville, Magazine, Dardanelle, Springdale, Hope, and Nashville, Ark. He was financial secretary of Ouachita College; missionary for Arkansas Baptists and for the Southern Baptist Home Mission Board; three times president of the Arkansas Baptist Convention. He was the author of three books and many pamphlets. An enthusiastic advocate of fundamental Baptist doctrines, he debated his views with Campbellites and Methodists. Friends credited him with having committed to memory large portions of the Bible. MRS. WALTER BROOKS

AVEN, MRS. MARY BAILEY (b. Black Hawk, Miss., Apr. 8, 1868; d. Greenwood, Miss., Oct. 14, 1945). Woman's Missionary Union leader. As an infant, she moved with her parents to Winona, Miss., where she was educated by private governesses and at Winona Female Institute. On Feb. 24, 1887, she married Algernon Jasper Aven, who conducted a private school for boys in Winona. After her husband became a member of the faculty of Mississippi College in 1889, she moved with him to Clinton. About 1895 Mrs. Aven organized the first glee club at Mississippi College and was its director for many years. From 1894 to 1896, she served as president of the Mississippi Woman's Missionary Union and zealously urged the missionary societies to provide for young women. Secretary of the state organization in 1897–98, she also served on the Central Committee between 1898 and 1916 as corresponding secretary, vice-president, and first state "leader of tithing" in 1914. During her second term as state president from 1916 to 1934, Mrs. Aven led the Woman's Missionary Union convention to meet separately from the Mississippi Baptist Convention.

BIBLIOGRAPHY: Mississippi W.M.U., *Hearts the Lord Opened, The History of Mississippi W.M.U.* (1954). C. B. HAMLET III

AVERETT COLLEGE. In 1859 a group of citizens of Danville, Va., secured a charter from the legislature for the Union Female College. The college made modest progress until the Civil War. In 1864, due apparently to the unpopularity of the word "union," the charter was amended to make the name Roanoke Female College. Subsequent changes of name were Roanoke College and Roanoke Institute. Finally, in 1917, the present name was adopted to honor two Danville citizens, Samuel W. and John T. Averett, who had given loyal support to the school for 20 years.

In 1914 the school was organized as a junior college and was accredited as such by the Virginia State Board of Education. It is now on the accredited list of the Southern Association of Colleges and Secondary Schools and belongs to Southern and national associations of junior colleges. The high school division was discontinued in 1936.

As is true of many private schools, there were serious financial troubles in the early years. In 1910 the property had to be sold to pay debts, but friends rallied to the support of the college; the present campus in the western part of Danville was purchased and a central building erected. The most recent addition to the physical plant is a building containing a gymnasium and music rooms. When funds are available, an auditorium will be added.

The president, Curtis V. Bishop, has served since 1936. The college is governed by a self-perpetuating board of trustees nominated by the Virginia general association. Income from Cooperative Program receipts for 1955–56 amounted to $66,200, and total assets were $725,585. There is an endowment of $49,000. Enrolment for 1955–56 was 258. Since its founding the school has graduated 2,284 young women.

RALPH MCDANEL

AXIOMS OF RELIGION. In 1908 Edgar Young Mullins (*q.v.*), president of Southern Baptist Theological Seminary, Louisville, Ky., published *The Axioms of Religion,* a new interpretation of Baptist faith that has been generally accepted as standard. The six axioms are (1) theological: the holy and loving God has a right to be sovereign; (2) religious: all men have an equal right of access to God; (3) ecclesiastical: all believers have a right to equal privilege in the church; (4) moral: to be responsible, the soul must be free; (5) religio-civic: a free church in a free state; and (6) social: love your neighbor as yourself. In 1935 Harold W.

LEROY, ALA., CHURCH. (Before and after), 1904 and 1953. There are about 2,500 country churches of this type.

FIRST BAPTIST CHURCH, Salem, Ill. Constituted 1837, present auditorium of modified Gothic erected 1950 to accommodate approximately 1,000. Membership 1956 over 1,200, capacity of educational unit 1,340, property worth $750,000.

ALABAMA BAPTIST CHILDREN'S HOME (q.v.), Troy. Founded 1891, serves an average of 300 children annually in eight cottages, seven residences, hospital, and recreation building on a 200-acre campus and farm, which have a value of $1,000,000.

Tribble, Mullins' successor in the chair of theology in the seminary, issued a widely used revision and adaptation of the book under the title *The Baptist Faith*. DALE MOODY

AYCOCK, CHARLES BRANTLEY (b. Wayne County, N. C., Nov. 1, 1859; d. Birmingham, Ala., Apr. 4, 1912. Governor. Son of Benjamin and Serena (Hooks) Aycock, he was converted under the ministry of A. C. Dixon while a student at the University of North Carolina, from which he was graduated in 1880. On May 20, 1881, he married Varina D. Woodard, to whom three children were born: Ernest, Charles B., Jr., and Alice (Mrs. Clarence Poe). After her death Aycock married Cora L. Woodard, to whom were born William W., Mary (Mrs. L. P. McLendon), Connor W., John Lee, Louise, Frank, and Brantley. Aycock practiced law in Goldsboro; served as superintendent of Wayne County schools; and was United States district attorney for eastern North Carolina, 1892–98. As governor of North Carolina, 1901–05, Aycock proved to be a progressive and forward-thinking leader by introducing a new era of material expansion and economic progress in the state. He was recognized as an advocate of improved public education, insisting on equal opportunities for Negro and white children; of improved labor laws; of pensions for Confederate soldiers; of the care of the mentally ill. Without any increase in taxes, he ended his term as governor with money in the treasury. He died while speaking in Birmingham, Ala., in behalf of universal education.

BIBLIOGRAPHY: R. D. W. Connor, *North Carolina, Rebuilding an Ancient Commonwealth*, Vol. II (1929). R. D. W. Connor and C. Poe, *The Life and Speeches of C. B. Aycock* (1912).

C. SYLVESTER GREEN

AYERS, THOMAS WILLBURN (b. Ayersville, Ga., Dec. 22, 1858; d. Atlanta, Ga., Jan. 5, 1954). Medical missionary to China. Ayers, who united with the Carnesville (Ga.) Baptist Church when he was 15 years old, graduated in 1886 from the College of Physicians and Surgeons in Baltimore, Md. In 1878 he married Minnie Skelton, and on Oct. 30, 1900, was appointed by the Foreign Mission Board for medical work in Hwanghsien, Shantung, China. Ayers built the Warren Memorial Hospital in Hwanghsien, the first hospital built by Southern Baptists on a foreign field. He left China in 1926 because of the ill health of his wife.

OLA L. CULPEPPER

B

BACKSLIDING. This term refers to a temporary condition of turning back or away from the zeal of one's profession of faith in God and an interruption of fellowship with God. Backsliding manifests itself in failure to participate in worship with fellow Christians, in the development of ingratitude, in a stubborn and rebellious will, and in a reversion to wrong and sinful habits and practices. When this condition persists, it raises a question as to the validity of one's profession of faith.

See also APOSTASY. GEORGE C. HUMPHREY

BACKUS, ISAAC (b. Norwich, Conn., Jan. 9, 1724; d. Nov. 20, 1806). Evangelist, historian, apostle of religious liberty. He came from a pure Congregational background which rejected the Saybrook Platform of 1708. The evangelism of the Great Awakening at first offended him, but in 1741 he was converted. He refused to join the Norwich, Conn., church, for it contained unregenerate and undisciplined persons, and discountenanced "experimental religion." A Separate or New-Light church was formed by converts of the revival, and Backus joined it. In 1746 he felt a call to preach; thereafter, he insisted that educational qualifications and ecclesiastical ordination are invalid without an internal call. After some experience as a lay preacher, he was called in 1748 as pastor of a Separate church in Middleboro, Conn., where he lived for 58 years. In 1749 he married Susannah Mason of Rehoboth; they had nine children. In 1749 two members of his church adopted believer's baptism, and Backus inclined to the same position until several factors forced him to recant. In Apr., 1751, he vowed to God to restore discipline, but by July, 1751, he came to see that a disciplined church is inconsistent with infant baptism; he remained with his church, but refused to baptize infants. In 1756 he became a Baptist; several of his members formed a Baptist church and called him as pastor. For the next 50 years he served conspicuously as evangelist, historian, and advocate of religious freedom. He is especially distinguished as an apologist for liberty and as an historian. In 1772 Backus became the agent of the Warren Association, formed in 1767, in promoting religious liberty. In 1774 he presented Baptist grievances to the Continental Congress in Philadelphia, which were denied by the Massachusetts delegates. For the next dozen years Backus engaged in a controversy over religious liberty, advocating his position in pamphlets, newspapers, sermons, and petitions. The point of chief difference was the power of the state to tax for the support of religion. Interestingly enough, Backus employed principles which American colonists used against England: (1) "it is essential to liberty that representation and taxation go together"; (2) causes must be tried by unbiased judges; and (3) "it is not the PENCE but the POWER" to impose the pence to which objection is made. Some Baptists were willing to conciliate the state by securing certificates, paying taxes, and then suing for their recovery, but Backus objected on two counts: (1) the concession implies that the state has power over religion; and (2) it weakens the purity of Baptist churches by encouraging "covetous men" to enlist as Baptists for partial tax exemption. His celebrated *History of New England,* designed to validate his plea for religious liberty, was begun around 1770 and published in parts after 1777. He continued his work on the history until after 1800, making extensive journeys, checking original sources, and engaging in a wide correspondence to insure accuracy. He also wrote on the nature of the church and on doctrinal matters. Religious freedom is the legacy of Backus and his Baptist conferers to all Americans. Fortunately, Backus lived to see the First Amendment to the Constitution adopted; but, unfortunately, he did not live to see the complete fall of the standing order in New England, even though he had laid his lethal ax to the root of that tree.

HUGH WAMBLE

BACONE, ALMON CLEMATUS (b. Scott, Courtland County, N. Y., Apr. 25, 1830; d. Muskogee, Indian Territory, Apr. 22, 1896). Educator, leader in organizing the Baptist Missionary and Educational Convention of Oklahoma and Indian Territories. He was a graduate of the University of Rochester. In 1886 he introduced a resolution to encourage and finance deserving youth, "that we may be able to raise up trained Christian workers for this Territory." He organized Indian University at Tahlequah in 1880, which moved to Muskogee in 1885 and was renamed Bacone College after Bacone's death in 1896. Baptist academies and other missions interests at Tahlequah, Atoka, and among the Plains Indians claimed an interest in his labors. Bacone served with singular fidelity and purity of purpose, possessing "an honest, great and patient soul, leaving behind him a record of industrious, unselfish and honorable life." He is buried in a small cemetery adjoining the campus of the school he founded.

GLENWOOD BUZBEE

BACONE COLLEGE. Founded in 1880 at Tahlequah, Cherokee Nation, as Indian University; was the first institution for higher learning to be established in what is now Oklahoma and is the only Christian school of college rank exclusively for Indians. The name was changed to Bacone College in 1896 in honor of Almon Clematus Bacone (*q.v.*).

Bacone came to Tahlequah in 1878 to teach in the Cherokee Male Seminary, a school established by the Cherokee government. He soon came to believe that more could be accomplished in a Christian school than in a tribal institution. On Feb. 9, 1880, with three students, in a tiny room in the Baptist mission house in Tahlequah, he began the operation of a school based upon what he considered sound Christian and educational principles. On Dec. 18, 1880, the Board of the American Baptist Home Mission Society voted to appoint him principal of the Indian Normal and Theological School at Tahlequah, his salary to be retroactive to Sept. 1, 1880.

It was apparent that a more central location for the school would be very helpful and in 1881 Bacone visited the Creek Council, the legislative body of the nation, in session at Okmulgee, and requested a grant of 160 acres upon which to build a school. The request was rejected at first but due to the earnest labors of William McCombs, a Baptist minister and a member of the Council, the matter was brought up for reconsideration, and the grant was approved.

Bacone, Joseph Samuel Murrow (*q.v.*), and Daniel Rogers (*q.v.*) selected the new site a few miles northeast of Muskogee. A marker on the present campus indicates the spot where the three knelt and dedicated the grounds to Christian education for the American Indians. John D. Rockefeller was one of the first donors to the work, and the first building was called Rockefeller Hall. The school opened in its new location in May, 1885, with 70 students.

For several years whites as well as Indians were admitted. Among some of the well-known graduates are Patrick Hurley, Secretary of War under President Herbert Hoover, and William Oziah Leach, former president of the Baptist General Convention of Oklahoma.

In 1920 a campaign sponsored by the General Education Board of the Northern Baptist Convention and the Home Mission Society of the same convention resulted in gifts of more than $810,000 for operating expenses, endowment, and buildings.

Francis W. Thompson, who served as president for seven years, resigned in 1954 and in 1956 no successor had yet been named.

In 1955 enrolment was 185; total enrolment since school's establishment, 16,500; the present college property was valued at $786,679.46; and the endowment amounted to $387,150.48.

BIBLIOGRAPHY: E. C. Routh, *The Story of Oklahoma Baptists* (1932). W. A. Carleton, *Not Yours but You* (1954). C. C. Rister, *Baptist Missions Among the American Indians* (1944). *The Watchman Examiner,* Jan. 13, 1955.

WILLIAM A. CARLETON

BACONIAN, THE. Published at Bacone College, was founded in May, 1898, by Almon Clematus Bacone (*q.v.*). It was published quarterly by a board of managers elected by the students. Subscriptions were 50 cents a year. Patrick J. Hurley, United States Secretary of War, 1929–32, was editor while a student at Bacone. Latest extant files at Bacone date to Vol. XI, No. 4, May, 1908.
J. M. GASKIN

BAGBY, ANNE LUTHER (b. Kansas City, Mo., Mar. 20, 1859; d. Recife, Brazil, Dec. 23, 1942). Missionary to Brazil. Daughter of John Hill Luther who moved from Missouri to Texas in 1877 and served 13 years as president of Baylor College, Anne's thoughts were first turned to foreign missions by a missionary from Africa. Her support as missionary to her chosen field, Brazil, was guaranteed in 1880 at a meeting of the Texas Baptist Convention. The Texas General Association took similar action concerning the support of William Buck Bagby (*q.v.*), whom Anne Luther married Oct. 21, 1880. They were appointed as missionaries Christmas week and sailed for Brazil in Jan., 1881. Anne Bagby spent 61 years in Brazil before her death, Christmas week, 1942. Of the nine Bagby children, two died in infancy, two in young manhood, and the remaining five, all Brazilian-born, became missionaries, Ermine (Mrs. S. W. Sowell, d. 1939) to Argentina, the others to Brazil: Taylor, Albert Ian, Helen (Mrs. W. C. Harrison), and Alice (Mrs. Harley Smith). The name of the mother was perpetuated in the Anne Bagby School for Girls (*Colegio Batista Brasileiro Ana Bagby*), founded at São Paulo in 1902.

BIBLIOGRAPHY: J. M. Carroll, *History of Texas Baptists* (1923). A. R. Crabtree, *Baptists in Brazil* (1953). H. B. Harrison, *The Bagbys of Brazil* (1954). B. Oliver, *Baptists Building in Brazil* (1942).
E. C. ROUTH

BAGBY, WILLIAM BUCK (b. Coryell County, Tex., Nov. 5, 1855; d. Porto Alegre, Brazil, Aug. 5, 1939). Missionary to Brazil. Converted under the preaching of Rufus C. Burleson (*q.v.*), then president of Waco University and pastor of the First Baptist Church, Waco, Bagby was one of the first pupils of Benajah Harvey Carroll (*q.v.*), who succeeded Burleson as pastor of the Waco church and taught theology to the preachers in the Waco school. Bagby graduated from the university in 1875 and was teaching school at Plantersville when he was ordained to preach, Mar. 16, 1879. He and Anne Ellen Luther married on Oct. 21, 1880, were appointed missionaries to Brazil in December of that year, and sailed the following month. The Bagbys were two of five members of the first Brazilian Baptist church, organized Oct. 15, 1882; Zachary Clay Taylor (*q.v.*), Mrs. Taylor, and Antonio Teixeira (the only one Brazilian) were the other members. The second church was constituted at Rio de Janeiro, July 24, 1884. The Bagbys lived in Rio until Oct., 1901, when they moved to São Paulo. Among early converts under the preaching of Bagby was F. F. Soren who became pastor of the First Baptist Church, Rio de Janeiro, and served there 33 years. Five of the nine Bagby children became missionaries to South America.

BIBLIOGRAPHY: L. M. Bratcher, *Soren* (1938). A. R. Crabtree, *Baptists in Brazil* (1953). E. Gill, Jr., *Pilgrimage to Brazil* (1954). H. B. Harrison, *The Bagbys of Brazil* (1954).
E. C. ROUTH

BAHAMAS, MISSION IN. Organized June 23, 1953, by four missionaries of the Southern Baptist Foreign Mission Board, Mr. and Mrs. H. H. McMillan, sent to the Bahamas in 1951, and Mr. and Mrs. John Mein, sent in 1953. In 1953 Mr. and Mrs. E. O. Ray replaced the McMillans, who had returned to the United States.

The first Baptist church in the islands was organized in 1790, a result of the labors of a freed slave from South Carolina. The Baptist Missionary Society of England sent its first missionary to the Bahamas in 1839 and maintained representatives there until 1929.

The Southern Baptist mission founded the Bahamas Baptist Bible Institute on Sept. 15, 1953, and enrolled 33 students for night classes the first year. A monthly paper, *The Baptist Messenger*, begun in 1954, is distributed to Baptist churches without cost. The mission produces a regular radio program over the local station.
MILDRED COX MEIN

BAHAMAS BIBLE INSTITUTE. See BAHAMAS, MISSION IN.

BAILEY, CHRISTOPHER THOMAS (b. Williamsburg, Va., Oct. 24, 1835; d. June 5, 1895). Editor. Son of William Bailey, he studied at William and Mary College and Richmond College. Later, Wake Forest College conferred upon him the D.D. degree. Bailey was ordained to the ministry in 1858. During the Civil War he served for a short while as a private. After the war he came to North Carolina (1865) and became master of the Reynoldson Academy in Gates County. Bailey was pastor of Baptist churches in Edenton, Hertford, and Warrenton, N. C., and in the Sandy Creek Association. In 1875 he became proprietor of the *Biblical Recorder* and continued until 1895. Bailey served as trustee of Wake Forest College and Shaw University and was president of the North Carolina Baptist State Convention, 1885–86. In 1865 he married Annie Sarah Bailey, daughter of Josiah Clanton Bailey, a Baptist minister of Greenville County. To them were born five children: Sallie (Mrs. Wesley N. Jones) (*q.v.*), C. T., Jr., Josiah W., Edmunds Lamar, and Bayard Yates.

BIBLIOGRAPHY: J. Bailey, "Dr. C. T. Bailey," *Biblical Recorder* (Jan. 2, 1935). W. Cathcart, ed., *The Baptist Encyclopedia*, Vol. I (1881).
W. H. WILLIAMS

BAILEY, JOSIAH WILLIAM (b. Warrenton, N. C., Sept. 14, 1873; d. Raleigh, N. C., Dec. 15, 1946). United States Senator. Bailey, the son of Christopher Thomas (*q.v.*) and Annie Sarah Bailey, was a Christian politician whom the press nicknamed "Holy Joe." His father and grandfather were both preachers. After he received the B.A. degree from Wake Forest College in 1893, he assisted his father in editing the *Biblical Recorder* and then succeeded him as editor, 1895-1907. After studying law for several years at Trinity College (now Duke University) and Wake Forest Law School, he secured admittance to the state bar in 1908 and began to practice law at Raleigh. From 1913 to 1921, he held the position of United States collector of internal revenue.

Although he practiced law, Bailey had a decided flair for politics. He lost his first campaign in the middle twenties but won the race for senator in 1930, with the largest majority ever given a North Carolina senatorial candidate, and served with distinction for 16 years. In the Senate he held many important posts: Commerce Committee chairman, chairman of Committee on Air Commerce, high-ranking member of Finance Committee, Post Office and Post Road Committee, and Senate Claims Committee. He also initiated significant wartime legislation. An eloquent speaker and a man of deep convictions, the Senator was known as a "man who speaks his own mind clearly and freely votes his convictions straight down the line." Bailey held LL.D. degrees from Wake Forest College (1931), Colby College (1938), and Duke University (1941). Elon College, North Carolina, conferred on him the Litt.D. degree in 1939. From his marriage to Edith Pou, Aug. 16, 1916, five children were born: James Hinton Pou, Annie Elizabeth, Josiah William, Jr., Edith Pou, and Sallie.

W. H. WILLIAMS

BAILEY, THOMAS M. (b. Graceville, County Antrim, Ireland, Dec. 27, 1829; d. Greenville, S. C., 1923). Businessman, preacher, missionary, and denominational leader. He attended Moravian school; then conducted business in Dublin. Called to preach at age 16, he was appointed at the age of 21 by the Foreign Mission Board of Moravian Church to St. Thomas Island, Danish West Indies, and then to St. Croix for four years. Bailey came to the United States in 1855. He was baptized into the fellowship of Gilgal Baptist Church, South Carolina, in 1856. He moved to Alabama in 1858, as pastor of Cahaba Church; he was pastor of various country and village churches in Alabama until 1874, when he was chosen general evangelist of the state Sunday school board. The board's report to the state convention in 1875 stated, "Work full of blessings . . . could not find a brother more richly endowed with gifts for its performance." In Aug., 1875, Bailey was appointed by the state mission board as evangelist and financial secretary of the State Mission and Sunday School Board of the Alabama Baptist State Convention. He served continuously for 10 years with "distinction, ability, and efficiency." The work progressed in all areas. Bailey was called the founder of state missions in Alabama; his work gave stability and permanence to the state mission board.

He was elected a corresponding editor of *The Alabama Baptist,* 1877; completed the unification of Baptist groups in Alabama, 1878; and greatly extended Sunday school work and raised it to a plane on which it was destined to expand to unlimited dimensions. His "comprehensive and successful" administration "wrought prodigies in Alabama." His 10 years of tranquillity and progress was known as the "golden era" of Alabama Baptist history. Bailey resigned Dec., 15, 1885, to assume a similar position in South Carolina. He served 25 years as active secretary of the state mission board in South Carolina and 12 years as secretary emeritus; he was known for his contributions in helping weak churches and in colportage work. He died at age 94 in Greenville, S. C., and was buried in Springwood Cemetery.

BIBLIOGRAPHY: W. Cathcart, *The Baptist Encyclopedia* (1883). J. S. Dill, *Lest We Forget* (1938). B. F. Riley, *History of the Baptists of Alabama, 1808-1894* (1895); *A Memorial History of the Baptists of Alabama* (1923).

LESLIE S. WRIGHT

BAINES, GEORGE WASHINGTON, SR. (b. near Raleigh, N. C., Dec. 29, 1809; d. Belton, Tex., Dec. 28, 1882). Pastor, educator, editor. His early years were spent in North Carolina, Georgia, and Alabama. He graduated from the University of Alabama; he was converted at 23 years of age near Tuscaloosa, Ala.; and he was ordained at 27 years in 1836. Baines moved to northern Arkansas in 1837, where he spent seven years, organized three churches, baptized 150 people in a sparsely settled area, served one term in the state legislature, and married Melissa Ann Butler, Oct. 20, 1840. Yielding to call of duty, he settled in Mt. Lebanon, La., in 1844 and served churches in that area. He also served as superintendent of schools of Bienville Parish. Six years later he moved to Texas and became an eminent figure in that state. For all of his 32 years in Texas his name appears in every convention annual and in many association minutes. He was pastor at Huntsville, Independence, Anderson, Fairfield, Springfield, Butler, Florence, and Salado. He was the editor of the first paper, *The Texas Baptist,* 1855-61. He was president of Baylor University for two years. Later he served as field agent for the state convention and the education commission. He served with unremitting toil for 48 years in spite of frail health. Such men as Zacharius N. Morrell (*q.v.*), Robert Emmett Bledsoe Baylor (*q.v.*), Sam Houston (*q.v.*), and M. V. Smith, who preached his funeral, testify as to his piety, wisdom, ability, and stainless character. He was the third in the line of four generations of Baines who were Baptist preachers.

BIBLIOGRAPHY: J. B. Link, ed., *Texas Historical and Biographical Magazine,* Vol. 1 (1891).

L. R. ELLIOTT

BAKER, ELIJAH (b. Lunenburg County, Va., 1742; d. Salisbury, Md., Nov. 6, 1798). Minister. He was of humble parentage, and there is no record of his boyhood. In 1769 he was converted and baptized by Samuel Harris and promptly began to exhort. He became a constituting member of Meherrin Baptist Church in 1771. Success in his native county prompted him to become an itinerant preacher, and from 1773 to 1775 between Richmond and Hampton several churches were planted by his ministry. In 1776 he moved to the eastern shore where he continued a similar ministry until his death, having found no less than 10 churches. In 1782 he led in the formation of Salisbury Association. As the first Baptist preacher in that section of Virginia, Baker suffered much opposition and frequent persecution. His imprisonment at Accomac for 56 days in 1778 on complaint of Episcopal churchwardens is the last recorded instance of suffering of this sort by Baptist preachers in the state. Among other indignities he suffered abduction and was committed to the keeping of the captain of a sailing vessel, who had been instructed to carry him to another country as a disturber of the peace. The conduct of the prisoner soon gave the captain reason to believe otherwise, and he ordered him put ashore. Baker was married to Sarah Copeland, but no lineal descendants are known. His burial place is unknown, but a monument to his memory stands in the churchyard of the Drummondtown Baptist Church in Accomac, Va. His life was best summarized by two who knew him well; John Leland said that Baker was "a man of low parentage, small learning and confined abilities. But with one talent, he did more than many do with five." Lemmon wrote, "In Mr. Baker, I found the Israelite indeed, the humble christian; the preacher of the gospel in the simplicity of it; and the triumphant saint, in his last moments."

CARRINGTON PAULETTE

BAKER, HARRIET A. (b. Powhatan County, Va.). Missionary educator. She was appointed by the Foreign Mission Board of the Southern Baptist Convention, Mar. 5, 1849. Sailing the following March, she arrived in Canton in July, 1850. The board reported: "Sister Harriet Baker has gone . . . attempting the establishment of a school for female children. This is an experiment, the beneficial influence of which remains to be tested." Apparently to meet this question John Lewis Shuck (*q.v.*) wrote to the board: "Soon after the arrival of Miss Baker here (Shanghai, Feb. 2, 1851) our mission passed a formal resolution, authorizing her to commence a *female* boarding school. . . . The general opinion among missionaries seems to be that when a mission has a boarding school for one sex, there should . . . be a similar school for the other sex . . . for one young person carefully brought up in a mission school to be compelled to marry another brought up under . . . heathenism . . . would be . . . throwing away . . . toil." Ill health forced Miss Baker to resign Dec. 5, 1853. Returning to this country, she made her home with her brother in the West. For some time afterward the board was opposed to the appointment of single ladies as missionaries. Harriet Baker's missionary career was brief, but she pioneered in education for girls.

J. LEVERING EVANS

BAKER, JOSEPH S. (b. Liberty County, Ga., Aug. 17, 1798; d. Quitman, Ga., July 23, 1877). Inheriting considerable property from his mother, Baker studied at Yale and Hampden Sidney in Virginia before taking up the practice of medicine there. Poor management cost him the estate by early manhood.

Study of the Bible influenced him as a young man to leave the Presbyterian church of his family and be immersed as a Baptist. He soon forsook the medical profession to serve as a missionary, evangelist, and pastor in Virginia. He moved to Georgia in 1840 as pastor of the Columbus Church. Baker served as coeditor of *The Christian Index* from Oct. 7, 1842, until the end of the year. He then went to Penfield, became editor, and served until Dec. 14, 1848. In 1849 he moved to Atlanta and started a newspaper, the *Atlanta Luminary* (afterward the *Atlanta Intelligencer*) which was the town's first newspaper. He served churches in Florida and Georgia from 1850 to 1865 when he retired to Quitman.

Baker never bothered about personal possessions and gave himself fully to the ministry. He was courageous as an editor, but some thought him "too fond of controversy" and too caustic in his writing. His stubbornness thwarted conciliation with the result that his resignation was probably more of necessity than of choice.

JOHN J. HURT

BALL, CHARLES THOMAS (b. Oxford, N. C., Feb. 3, 1866; d. Fort Worth, Tex., Jan. 26, 1943; buried Crowley, Tex.). Pastor, teacher, youth leader, seminary president. Reared in North Carolina, he secured his A.B. degree from Wake Forest College in 1898. He graduated with the Th.M. degree from Southern Baptist Theological Seminary, Louisville, Ky., in 1903. From 1904 to 1911, he was dean of the Bible department at Simmons College (now Hardin-Simmons University); from 1911 to 1919, he was professor of comparative religion and missions in Southwestern Baptist Theological Seminary. In connection with his professorship of missions, he assisted in organizing the seminary extension department. He was the founder of the Baptist Student Missionary Movement in 1912, providing vigorous leadership until 1920. This organization is generally regarded as the forerunner of the Baptist Student Union. From 1920 to 1925, he was executive secretary of the

Ball, Fleetwood James

American Baptist Student Union. In 1925 Ball became pastor of the Winsinoming Baptist Church of Philadelphia, Pa. In that same year he led in the establishment of the Eastern Baptist Theological Seminary and became its first president. He married Mary Agnes Peterson of Winston-Salem, N. C., on Nov. 30, 1897. To them were born Marie Elizabeth and Charles E. Ball. CHARLES P. JOHNSON

BALL, FLEETWOOD JAMES (b. Cherry Creek, Pontotoc County, Miss., Mar. 16, 1876; d. Lexington, Tenn., May 1, 1941). Pastor, evangelist, recording secretary of the Tennessee Baptist Convention, and denominational leader. Son of Martin and Lizzie (McKay) Ball, he was fifth and last in a line of Baptist ministers. He graduated with the B.S. degree from Union University, 1896, and took the English course at Southern Baptist Theological Seminary. Later Union awarded him the D.D. degree. He married Flossie Lee Melton, May 14, 1907, who died Dec. 8, 1918. Four daughters, Mary Elizabeth, Flossie Melton, Lily McKay, and Martha Joe, all graduated from Union University. Ball served the following churches as pastor: Friendship (Henry County) 1894–1903, Henry, Denmark, Malesus, Cottage Grove (12 years), Erin, Union Academy, Mount Nebo, Wildersville, Huntingdon, Parsons, Perryville, and Decaturville. He was pastor, First Baptist Church, Lexington, Tenn., 34 years (Dec., 1902–Dec., 1936). During this time he served the following rural churches which met in the afternoon: Rock Hill, Sand Ridge, Piney Creek, Chapel Hill, and Union. When roads were bad, he walked. He led Cottage Grove, Perryville, and Lexington in building houses of worship. Ball served as moderator of Western District Association for several years and of Beech River Association for 31 years; was recording secretary of the state convention 25 years; contributed the column entitled "Among the Brethren" in the *Baptist and Reflector* for 40 years; was actively connected with operating Baptist Memorial Hospital and Union University; was a member of the Tennessee Baptist mission board 10 years, a correspondent of the *Commercial Appeal*, an editorial assistant for the *Lexington Republican*. A score of young men in Henderson County at one time bore the unusual name Fleetwood. ROBERT L. PALMER

BALM INSTITUTE. A school at Balm, N. C., organized in 1904 by Mt. Calvary Baptist Church of the Three Forks Association. The school closed after one year. D. L. SMILEY

BANNER AND GLEANER. The short-lived result of a merger of the *Baptist Banner*, published from Benton, Ill., and the *Baptist Gleaner*, published from Fulton, Ky., which was accomplished on Sept. 14, 1881, by the editors of the two papers, William Pinckney Throgmorton (*q.v.*) and John Newton Hall (*q.v.*). High water contributed to the financial failure of the joint editorship, which ended when Throgmorton returned the paper to Benton in the spring of 1882. The paper was continued under the name *Baptist Banner*. B. J. MURRIE

BAPTISM. The two symbols of primary significance in the Christian faith are baptism and the Lord's Supper. It is difficult to set forth a term that will properly categorize these symbols because any word selected can be defined in various ways. To avoid the term "sacrament," we have used "ordinance" to specify baptism and the Lord's Supper. The word "ordinances" in the King James Version is a translation of the Greek word meaning "traditions" (I Cor. 11:2). However, Paul, in the use of the word "traditions" in this verse, had reference to all that Jesus said and taught, and the synonym for "ordinance" in the dictionary is "sacrament." We have avoided "sacrament" because of the magical implications of the word. However, the word, when originally used by the Romans, meant a pledge of allegiance of a Roman soldier to the ideals of the Roman army. If "sacrament" were used in the way it was originally used, it would be a good word to specify both baptism and the Lord's Supper. But to avoid being misunderstood as to our meaning of these symbols, it might be more appropriate to call baptism and the Lord's Supper "symbols of our Christian faith."

The meaning of the word baptizō.—The verb *baptizō* is an intensive or iterative form of the verb *baptō*, and both words have the meaning "to dip" or "to plunge." The verb *baptō* occurs 16 times in the Septuagint (the Greek translation of the Old Testament). All these examples have the meaning "to dip" or "to plunge," and most of them are a translation of the Hebrew word *tabal*, which means "to dip." In classical and postclassical Greek the intensive form *baptizō* is used in both the literal and metaphorical senses. In Plato we find the metaphorical usage in such expressions as "soaked in wine" or "getting into deep water" (i.e., an argument). In the Septuagint the word *baptizō* is found four times. Three of these examples (II Kings 5:14; Judith 12:7; Sirach 24:25) are used in the literal sense of dipping, while the fourth (Isa. 21:4) seems to have the metaphorical meaning as found in Plato.

In the New Testament the word *baptizō* occurs 75 times, and *baptō* is found three times. About one half of the occurrences of *baptizō* are in relation to the ministry of John the Baptist. In all these examples the meaning of the word is in complete accord with the meaning "to dip" discovered in classical Greek literature and the Septuagint. Therefore, the original meaning and usage of the Greek word which is transliterated into English by the word "baptize" is beyond question.

The origin of Christian baptism.—Since the ceremonial use of water is common to all religions, attempts have been made at various times to show that New Testament baptism has been affected by pagan influences and particularly by the Greek mystery cults. Such attempts have met with no success. Since Christianity had its rootage in Judaism, it is only logical to turn to Judaism to seek the source of Christian baptism.

The baptism which Jesus commanded in Matthew 28:19-20 must of necessity be interpreted in the light of the baptism proclaimed by John, and John's baptism in turn must be viewed against the backdrop of the Judaism of that day. John's baptism most assuredly finds its earliest historical connection in the Levitical washings of the Old Testament; nevertheless, this is by no means a full explanation of his rite. A closer connection is seen in the use of water by the prophets (Isa. 1:16; Jer. 4:14; Psalm 51:2; Isa. 4:4; Ezek. 36:25). The prophets not infrequently employed the metaphor of washing to represent ethical purification. The closest prototype of John's meaning of baptism among the prophetic utterances is found in Ezekiel 36:25-26.

In addition to the ethical implications of water which he inherited from the prophets, John was also acquainted with the bath required of Gentiles before they were admitted to Judaism. (It is now believed by the majority of New Testament scholars that there is sufficient evidence for the existence of the proselyte bath for entrance into Judaism in the first century A.D.) There were similarities between John's baptism and the proselyte bath. Both were complete immersions and were performed once for all. Both symbolized a change of thought and a self-dedication to a new way of life. However, there are also differences with respect to the two rites. The baptism of John was a public affair, while the proselyte bath could be administered in the presence of two or three witnesses. John's rite symbolized a change of life, not merely a change of creed. Because of this difference, John could call upon Jew and Gentile alike to submit to his baptism.

The two distinctive elements in the preaching of John were a demand for repentance in view of approaching judgment and a prediction of the immediate arrival of the "Coming One," and both these elements were related to John's baptism. His mission of repentance and baptism was based upon the prophetic anticipation of national washing or purification before the coming of the messianic era, which would issue in judgment. Those who repented and were baptized would escape this terrible day of judgment, which was the wrath of God.

John's baptism and Christian baptism.—Some Baptists contend that John's baptism and Christian baptism were essentially the same. Other Baptists maintain that there was a decided difference between the two. The majority of Baptists are undecided on the issue. The New Testament evidence indicates that the two baptisms were distinct. John called upon the people to repent and be baptized because the Coming One was about to make his appearance, but he did not call upon them to believe that Jesus of Nazareth was Lord. The disciples of John could confess belief in one who was to come without becoming the disciples of Christ. As a matter of fact, some of the disciples of John were jealous of the popularity of Jesus (John 3:25 ff.). When John was in prison, there was doubt in his mind, since Jesus did not execute judgment, as to whether Jesus was the person he had proclaimed as coming (Matt. 11:2 ff.; Luke 7:18 ff.). Many Jews were full of expectation that the Messiah was coming, but they were unable to acknowledge Jesus as Messiah because he was not the kind of Messiah they expected. So it was quite possible for a Jew to profess the preaching of John and receive his baptism, yet reject the claims of Jesus.

In the book of Acts, we learn of a group of disciples who had not received the Holy Spirit. Paul asked the men, "Into what then were you baptized?" Their reply was, "Into John's baptism." Immediately, Paul explained John's baptism as one of repentance and belief in the one coming after John. This one Paul interpreted as Jesus. After this explanation the men were baptized into the name of the Lord Jesus (Acts 19:1 ff. RSV). In following Paul's interpretation, the essential difference between John's baptism and Christian baptism is a difference of belief. John's disciples were baptized after repentance and belief in the Messiah who was to come, while Christian baptism is repentance and belief in Jesus as Messiah and Lord who has come, been crucified, and been raised from the dead. This same idea was set forth by Peter on the day of Pentecost (Acts 2:32-41). One cannot be baptized into the name of Jesus Christ until after a recognition that he is Christ and Lord through the resurrection. Finally, it is also to be noted that John looked upon his rite as something preparatory, provisional, and to be superseded by a greater baptism (Mark 1:8).

Jesus and John's baptism.—Why did Jesus submit to John's baptism? This has been a problem for Christians since the second century A.D. A large number of interpretations have been advanced to escape what appears to be a difficult situation and to relieve Christianity of a certain embarrassment. But if it is borne in mind that the repentance which John preached held not simply the negative aspect but the positive aspect as well, there is no recognizable difficulty. The positive side of repentance is usually ignored. The positive meaning of repentance is a bent of spirit toward conformity to the divine will with the endeavor for righteousness and submission to the rule of God. Jesus, being baptized by John, began his ministry with a declaration to Israel of his dedication to the purposes and intentions of God.

Both the heavenly voice and the descent of the Spirit authenticated the action of Jesus. The baptism of Jesus was a confirmation of his own consciousness of his messiahship and served as a definition of the nature of that messiahship, which was along the lines of suffering, trial, and death.

The authority for Christian baptism.—The practice of baptism in the early church was not an innovation of the disciples nor a mere continuance of the rite of John the Baptist; its origin was based on a command of Jesus. After his resurrection Jesus appeared to the 11 disciples on a mountain in Galilee and said, "Go ye therefore, and teach all nations, baptizing them in the name of the Father, and of the Son, and of the Holy Ghost; teaching them to observe all things whatsoever I have commanded you: and, lo, I am with you alway, even unto the end of the world" (Matt. 28:19–20).

The mode and subjects of Christian baptism.—Occasionally, a member of another Christian group will refer to Baptists as those Christians who believe in baptism. While the designation is correct, this does not mean that other Christian groups do not believe in baptism. The distinction that should be made is with respect to the mode and subjects of baptism. Baptists, in following the New Testament teaching on baptism, believe that the proper manner of baptizing is immersion, and that the person to be baptized is one who believes in Jesus Christ.

That immersion was the correct form of baptism in New Testament times is supported by the Greek word *baptizō*, which means "to dip" or "to plunge." For the apostle Paul nothing but immersion could express an identification with Christ in his death, burial, and resurrection (Rom. 6:3 ff.). Furthermore, the descriptive words of baptism of the Ethiopian eunuch by Philip, "they both went down into the water, . . . they came up out of the water" (Acts 8:38–39 RSV) can only mean immersion. It is admitted that, at the beginning of the second century A.D., pouring was allowed if circumstances arose where immersion was found to be impossible, but the author of Didache, our source for this information, nowhere suggested that this mode could prevail as normative for Christians.

Reliable New Testament scholars of both Protestant and Catholic communions readily admit that the New Testament evidence unquestionably sets forth immersion as the proper mode for Christian baptism. When they employ the modes of sprinkling or pouring, they do so, not on the basis of New Testament authority, but for the sake of convenience or in consideration of the health of the individual to be baptized.

From the New Testament there is no basis for the view that the character of baptism was so completely altered that it became a rite to which unconscious infants as well as responsible people could be admitted. All the references to individuals who were baptized include only those who believed that Jesus was Lord and confessed that belief. Believer's baptism is the only kind of baptism known in New Testament times. Baptists do not believe that baptism is restricted to adults. Children as well as adults are capable of making a personal profession of faith in Christ. Since infants are not in the position of having a personal faith in Christ, any baptism which is performed in their case cannot express the meaning of Christian baptism.

In recent years theologians of other denominations have denounced the established views of their denominations relative to the practice of infant baptism by stating that such a practice is not in accordance with the teaching of the New Testament. Some of these, while setting forth believer's baptism as the New Testament teaching, still contend that it is legitimate to continue the practice of infant baptism on other than a scriptural basis.

The meaning of Christian baptism.—For our knowledge of the meaning of baptism in the New Testament, we are indebted to Paul and Peter. The prevailing meaning of Christian baptism for Paul is a symbol of union with Christ and unity of believers in Christ.

1. Union with Christ. The most characteristic expression used by Paul to describe the nature of the Christian life was the formula "in Christ" and cognate expressions (used no less than 164 times in his epistles). The expressions were shortened forms of "in the name of Jesus Christ" and "in the name of the Lord Jesus." From three passages in Paul's epistles, the "in Christ" relationship is set forth as a relationship which is properly symbolized by baptism (Rom. 6:1–14; Gal. 3:27–28; Col. 2:10–12).

The main argument of Paul throughout the epistle to the Romans is that every individual comes into a right relationship with God by faith and by faith alone. To remove any thought that the gospel of faith which he proclaimed would lead people to continue in sin, the apostle replied, "God forbid. We who died to sin, how shall we any longer live therein?" (Rom. 6:2 ASV). For him faith in Christ carried with it death to sin. At this place in his argument, the symbolism of baptism offered Paul the best illustration of the precise point he desired to make, namely, the intimacy of the union which faith achieves between the believer and Christ. In the baptismal act—the disappearance of the believer under the water and his emergence—Paul saw a striking symbol of the union with Christ in death and in life which comes through faith. In baptism the believer identifies himself with the will and purpose of Christ. There is a dramatic reenactment of the death, burial, and resurrection of Jesus. The convert is immersed into the water. This means a dying with Christ. He remains there for a moment under the surface. This means being buried with Christ. He emerges from the water. This means being raised with Christ. Baptism marks a break with the old life and all its associations and a pledge to a new life of attachment to Christ. Paul used the great events of the passion to explain the transformation of his own life and the lives of others which had been accomplished through union with Christ by faith and had been demonstrated in the act of baptism.

In Galatians 3:27, Paul used the metaphor of clothing in connection with baptism. The verb "to put on" or "to clothe," which is used in this verse, means in this instance "to take on the character or standing of the person designated." The person here designated is Christ. Paul looked upon baptism as depicting a union with Christ to such an extent that in the experience it is as though the believer is casting aside his old garments and putting on new garments, i.e., Christ. In Colossians 3:5–17, Paul enlarged upon the metaphor of clothing in its relation to baptism. He pointed out that certain things were to be put off, and others were to be put on. We are to put off the old clothes of the old life and put on the new clothes of the new life, which correspond to the character of Christ.

2. A symbol of unity of believers. While the predominant significance of baptism for Paul was union with Christ, he also reminded his readers that it was a symbol of the unity of believers in Christ. On three occasions in the context of baptism (I Cor. 12:13; Gal. 3:28; Col. 3:11), he ruled out all racial and class distinctions, thus showing that baptism was a visible bond of union among all believers. It matters not whether a person is Jew or Greek, freeman or slave, because it is one Spirit who is operative in them all. Baptism is a symbol and pledge of the unity of those who through faith have received the one Spirit, a unity of which they are made fully conscious by the joyful experiences which enter their hearts when they are baptized into Christ.

It has been maintained by some New Testament scholars that the apostle Paul injected a magic effect into baptism, but there is no basis for this statement. Baptism of itself could effect nothing, according to Paul's theology. Paul's contention for faith in Christ as the sole means for a right relationship with God rules out any such notion. If Paul had thought of baptism in sacramental terms, he would not have made the statement about baptism which we find in I Corinthians 1:16–17. But he did emphasize that, in full submission to baptism, a person deepens his response to Christ. The power of baptism to enrich the life of an individual depends entirely on the faith of his changed will. Christian baptism, then, has decided ethical commands. To make baptism effective, we are to live a new life dedicated to God.

If a person is baptized and does not follow what is suggested in the symbol of baptism, his baptism becomes ineffective. We could compare this situation to that of a Jew who was circumcised but did not submit to the law. In substance Paul said that a good pagan was better off than a bad Jew (Rom. 2:1 ff.). It is possible for baptism to mean nothing more than the external rite of circumcision meant to some of the Jews in Paul's day.

3. Peter's concept of baptism. In I Peter 3:21, the negative and positive distinctives of Christian baptism are set forth. Negatively stated, baptism is "not the putting away of the filth of the flesh." The removal of dirt or ceremonial uncleanness is not the meaning of Christian baptism. Positively stated, Christian baptism is "the dedication of a right attitude toward God."

From Paul and Peter we conclude that Christian baptism means a union with Christ and a union with believers in Christ with the full intention of following God's will in identification with Christ.

See also JESUS CHRIST.

BIBLIOGRAPHY: K. Barth, *The Teaching of the Church Regarding Baptism* (1948). F. C. Bryan, *Concerning Believer's Baptism* (1943). H. Cook, *What Baptists Stand For* (1947). D. G. Dix, *The Theology of Confirmation in Relation to Baptism* (1946). W. F. Flemington, *The New Testament Doctrine of Baptism* (1948). J. C. Lambert, *The Sacraments in the New Testament* (1903). H. G. Marsh, *The Origin and Significance of the New Testament Baptism* (1941). H. H. Rowley, "Jewish Proselyte Baptism," *Hebrew Union College Annual*, XV (1940).

T. C. SMITH

BAPTISM, ADMINISTRATION OF. Baptists accept as good administration of the ordinance of baptism that practice, however varying, which takes knowledge of and does credit to three major considerations: (1) The administration should reflect faithful obedience to New Testament teachings and to the example of Jesus. Such obedience is shown in baptizing only believers, and baptizing only by immersion in the name of the Trinity. (2) The administration should inspire the maximum religious experience in the one being baptized, but in no way suggesting any saving efficacy in the ordinance. (3) The administration should afford effective Christian witness to others.

Proper administration of baptism, and effective use of such Scripture passages as Romans 6:4; Matthew 3:5–6; Mark 1:4–5; Matthew 28:19–20; Luke 3:12–21; and Colossians 2:12 will clearly and dramatically show the identification of the candidate with the buried and resurrected Lord.

As soon as practicable after the profession of faith by the candidate, and acting under authority of the local church, the administrator will arrange for the baptismal service. The candidate should be given adequate counsel concerning the religious meaning of baptism and its method of observance.

A committee from the church should be carefully chosen to aid in preparation for baptism. All possible needs should be anticipated. The place, whether indoors or outdoors, should be made ready. Adequate dressing space should be provided, water temperature checked for comfort, and every consideration extended toward making the service effective.

The actual administration of baptism should be done in a worshipful manner. The pastor helps the candidate into the baptistry, and repeats a formula similar to the following: "_____ _____, upon your profession of faith in Jesus Christ as Saviour and Lord, and in obedience to his command, I baptize you in the name of the Father, the Son, and the Holy Spirit. Amen."

The candidate is then lowered gently beneath the water, raised with unhurried motion, and assisted from the baptistry. This procedure will enable the ordinance to be observed in simple and chaste beauty.

Regardless of the place, baptism can be administered with meaning and dignity whenever the administrator plans wisely. Ultimately, the attitude and planning ability of the administrator are the decisive factors in the meaningful observation of the New Testament ordinance of baptism.

BIBLIOGRAPHY: G. S. Dobbins, *The Churchbook* (1951). E. T. Hiscox, *The Star Book for Ministers* (1878); *The Baptist Directory* (1859). J. R. Hobbs, *The Pastor's Manual* (1925). J. D. Morrison, *Minister's Service Book* (1937). A. W. Palmer, *The Art of Conducting Public Worship* (1939). J. M. Pendleton, *The Baptist Manual* (1912). EDWIN F. PERRY

BAPTISM, MODES OF. The word "baptize" is derived from the Greek word *baptizō*, which means to dip or to immerse. The overwhelming weight of scholarship is agreed upon this primary meaning and acknowledges also that New Testament baptism was immersion. Thus, philologically and etymologically speaking, there is only one mode of baptism, and that is immersion.

There has been much disagreement, however, upon the necessity of adhering to the New Testament mode. Historically baptism has been used to refer to a variety of modes, with sprinkling (aspersion) and pouring (affusion), as well as immersion, the chief ones.

The first-century Christians practiced immersion as a symbol of the death to sin and resurrection to new life previously accomplished in conversion (*cf.* Rom. 6:1-5), and it continued to be the preferred mode until the Middle Ages. From the time of Tertullian (*c.* 150–225), single immersion was supplanted by trine immersion, with the candidate being dipped three times, once each in the name of the Father, the Son, and the Holy Spirit. However, during this period affusion was recognized as valid where difficulties prevented immersion.

From the 13th-century onward, aspersion was practiced along with immersion and affusion in the Roman Catholic Church, although affusion is the accepted mode today. But the Eastern Church retained trine immersion and does until the present.

Immersion was practiced in the West in the 16th century by certain Anabaptist groups, especially in Poland, and in the 17th century in Holland by the Rhynsburgers, from whom it spread to the English Baptists. Since then Baptists have been consistent exponents of the practice.

The rise of modes other than immersion was inextricably bound up with the growth of the sacramental interpretation of baptism, i.e., it is a channel of saving grace (*ex opere operato*) without which one *cannot* be saved. Such an interpretation led to affusion and aspersion where circumstances of health or climate prevented immersion and also led to infant baptism.

Another factor in the rise and continuation of modes other than the one in the New Testament is the belief that the mode is unimportant. John Calvin (1509-64) wrote, "Whether the person who is baptized be wholly immersed, or whether thrice or once, or whether water be poured or sprinkled upon him, is of no importance." Attaching no importance to the mode accounts for the prevalence of modes other than immersion in those churches standing in the Reformed tradition as well as those in the Lutheran and Anglican traditions.

Baptists and certain other denominations and sects feel, however, that the mode *is* important and point to three lines of investigation which support their practice of immersion: (1) the philology of the Greek word transliterated *baptize*, (2) the history of the ordinances as practiced from the first to the 13th century, (3) the symbolism (Rom. 6:1-5) intrinsic to the ordinance.

BIBLIOGRAPHY: K. Barth, *The Teaching of the Church Regarding Baptism* (1948). A. Carson, *Baptism in Its Mode and Subjects* (1860). W. Cathcart, *The Baptism of the Ages* (1878). J. C. Chrystal, *A History of the Modes of Christian Baptism* (1861). J. Conant, *Meaning and Use of Baptizein* (1864). A. H. Newman, *A Manual of Church History* (1902). W. H. Whitsitt, *A Question in Baptist History* (1896). RAYMOND A. PARKER

BAPTISM IN THE SPIRIT. See HOLY SPIRIT.

BAPTIST, EDWARD (b. Mecklenberg County, Va., May 12, 1790; d. Marengo County, Ala., Mar. 31, 1863). Pioneer denominational leader in Virginia. The ninth child of William Glanville Baptist, a wealthy merchant and planter, and Margaret (Langston) Baptist, he was educated at Hampden-Sydney College and ordained in 1815. He married Eliza J. C. Eggleston on May 17, 1817, and was the father of seven children.

The first college graduate to enter the Baptist ministry in Virginia, he was the originator of the movement which resulted in the formation of the Baptist General Association of Virginia and was the drafter of its constitution. He served as the first vice-president of the Virginia Baptist Education Society. As the first teacher engaged by that society, he opened his home to young men desiring to prepare for the ministry and, in Aug., 1830, founded Dunlora Academy in Powhatan County, Va., with an enrolment of nine students. The University of Richmond grew from this institution. For many years he served as a member of the Baptist Board of Foreign Missions for the United States. In 1835, after a notable ministry in his native state, he moved to Marengo County, Ala., and served as pastor of Spring Hill, Uniontown, Demopolis, and Dayton Baptist churches. He was a trustee of the University of Alabama and was instrumental in organizing several churches in that state.

Widely known as a man of judgment, integrity, and piety and as an able and eloquent preacher, he wrote extensively for Baptist periodicals and exerted an influence among Baptists which was second to no man of his day. Having independent wealth, he never accepted a salary from a church during his entire ministry. A monument marking his grave in Oakland Cemetery, Faunsdale, Ala., was erected by the trustees of the University of Richmond in Aug., 1955, and is inscribed as follows: "Edward Baptist, A.M. 1790–1863/ Eminent Baptist Minister of Alabama and Virginia/ A Founder of the Baptist General Association of Virginia/ Trustee of the University of Alabama/ Founded at Dunlora Plantation in Powhatan County, Virginia/ the Academy which later became the University of Richmond/ Erected by the Trustees of the University of Richmond, August, 1955." JACK MANLEY

BAPTIST, THE. The first paper published by Baptists south of the Ohio River and west of the Appalachian Mountains to achieve continuity of publication. It was issued in Jan., 1835, by Robert Boyté Crawford Howell (q.v.) at Nashville, Tenn. By 1860 this religious weekly was reputed to have attained the widest readership of any Baptist paper. J. R. Graves (q.v.) made this paper a powerful factor in shaping the thinking of Baptists in the mid-South and Southwest. Consolidated with the *American Baptist Reflector*, Aug. 22, 1889, it became the *Baptist and Reflector*. In 1921 this was bought by the Tennessee Baptist Convention, and has since been its official journal.

Howell issued a prospectus for *The Baptist* in Sept., 1834, before leaving Norfolk, Va., and after receiving a call to Nashville to become pastor of the First Baptist Church. Sixteen hundred subscribers were reported at the end of the first year (1835). Howell edited the paper for 13 years. He made it a strong advocate of co-operative work and of the newly formed Baptist state convention of Tennessee organized at Mill Creek in Davidson County, Oct. 24, 1833. Howell gave the paper to the Baptist General Association of Tennessee in 1846. Through its education board the association named James Robinson Graves (q.v.) associate editor, Nov. 21, 1846. Graves changed the name to *The Tennessee Baptist* in May, 1847. He became the editor in July, 1848. James Madison Pendleton (q.v.) and Amos Cooper Dayton (q.v.) became his associate editors in 1858 but later resigned because of the Civil War. Publication was suspended in 1862 at Nashville, because of the capture of the city by the Union army, and resumed at Memphis, Feb. 1, 1867, with its original name *The Baptist*.

Graves made *The Baptist* the champion of Landmarkism in 1851. He contended for no ministerial or ecclesiastical affiliation by Baptists who would recognize a church of other denominations as a church. He held to the doctrine of historical succession for Baptist churches, and believed that the observance of the Lord's Supper should be restricted by a church to its own members. Graves suffered a stroke in Aug., 1884, but continued as a special editor till his death in 1893. RICHARD N. OWEN

BAPTIST ACADEMY, LAGOS. See NIGERIA, MISSION IN.

BAPTIST ADVANCE. Founded in 1902 to replace the *Arkansas Baptist*, which the convention renounced as state paper in 1901. N. R. Pittman, pastor at Fort Smith, M. L. Thomas, pastor of Second Church, Little Rock, and Arthur James Barton (q.v.), secretary of missions in Arkansas, helped to found the paper. The Advance Publishing Company had been formed to promote it. Serving with Barton as editor were Edmund James Archibald McKinney (q.v.) and Sam Eaton, assistant editors. When Barton resigned the editorship in 1904, J. J. Hurt, Sr., replaced him. James Franklin Love (q.v.) served as editor for a few months in 1905, with McKinney as his assistant. From 1906 to 1918, under McKinney as editor and business manager, the paper gained rapidly in circulation and prestige. Hardy Latham Winburn (q.v.) was interim editor from Jan. 1, 1919, to July 1, 1919, when J. S. Compere accepted the editorship. In 1931 L. M. Sipes became editor and served for two years, publishing the paper under a lease from the Arkansas Baptist State Convention. The paper, called the *Baptist Advance* from 1902 until 1933, became the *Arkansas Baptist* in 1933 by action of the convention. B. H. DUNCAN

BAPTIST AND REFLECTOR. Volume I, Number 1, appeared in Nashville, Tenn., Aug. 29, 1889, and was the continuation of *The Baptist*, Memphis, Tenn., and the *American Baptist Reflector*, Chattanooga, Tenn. The Tennessee Baptist Convention purchased it in 1921 and established the Tennessee Baptist Press, with a nine-man board of directors to operate it. This board was to elect the editor after his nomination by the executive committee of the state convention, and to select the treasurer, whose accounts would be handled as a special account in the state mission funds. The paper was not to have any allocation from the convention's Cooperative Program funds. The

Baptist Argus, The

circulation of the paper was 60,438 in 1954, with 453 churches having the paper in their budgets for family distribution. In 1956 the Tennessee Baptist Press had equipment valued at about $50,000 and printed the paper by contract, the contractor using the equipment.

The editors under convention ownership have been: J. D. Moore for about four years; O. E. Bryan, executive secretary of the state convention, *ad interim* editor; John D. Freeman (1925–33); O. W. Taylor (1933–1950); and Richard N. Owen (1950–   ).

Through its antecedents the paper goes back to the first issue of *The Baptist*, Jan., 1835, and the *American Baptist Reflector*, 1874.

The Baptist was begun as a small monthly, by R. B. C. Howell (*q.v.*), who became pastor of the First Baptist Church, Nashville, Jan., 1835. He changed it to a semimonthly in 1837. He merged it into *The Banner and Western Pioneer*, Louisville, Ky., after its February issue of 1839. There was a section in this paper under "The Baptist," which Howell edited through Nov. 3, 1842. *The Baptist* reappeared in Nashville, June 29, 1844, as Volume I, Number 1, with Howell as editor. He gave the paper to the Baptist General Association of Tennessee and North Alabama in the fall of 1846. Through its education board it at once contracted with J. R. Graves (*q.v.*) (then 26) and Alex B. Shankland to publish the paper and establish a depository, and made Graves assistant editor. The name was changed to the *Tennessee Baptist* May 8, 1847. Graves became editor in July, 1848, and soon increased the circulation to about 12,000. The paper suspended publication in Feb., 1862, when the Union army captured Nashville, and began again in Memphis, Feb. 1, 1867, as *The Baptist*, Volume I, Number 1, with Graves as editor. The paper again became the *Tennessee Baptist* with the issue of Sept. 9, 1882; and again *The Baptist* July 9, 1887, with the first issue following the combination of the *Tennessee Baptist* and the *Baptist Gleaner* of Fulton, Ky. (established 1879), J. B. Moody, owner and editor. Graves and Moody were the owner-editors of the combined paper. *The Baptist* combined with the *American Baptist Reflector*, Chattanooga, Tenn., E. E. Folk (*q.v.*), editor-owner, Aug., 1889, and became the *Baptist and Reflector*, at Nashville. Two months later, O. L. Hailey, Graves' son-in-law, bought Moody's interest, and a little later was given Graves's interest. Graves had a stroke in Aug., 1884, and a serious injury from a fall a few years later, but continued as an associate or contributing editor after Hailey succeeded him as editor.

Albert R. Bond bought Folk's interest in 1917. Later, M. R. Cooper bought the paper and edited it until the Tennessee Baptist Convention bought it. Hight C Moore served briefly as editor after Cooper.   RICHARD N. OWEN

BAPTIST ARGUS, THE. A weekly begun at Louisville, Ky., on Oct. 28, 1897, by the Southern Baptist Theological Seminary to promote the cause of the Baptist Young People's Union. J. N. Prestridge, pastor of the First Baptist Church, Williamsburg, Ky., was prevailed upon to become its editor, and Marion Palmer Hunt (*q.v.*), then pastor of the Twenty-second and Walnut Street Baptist Church, Louisville, Ky., was the assistant editor. Shortly thereafter, Thomas D. Osborne, an experienced newspaperman, became identified with the paper as news editor. Members of the Southern Seminary faculty also were involved in the work. In 1908 Editor Prestridge, having become interested in promoting the idea of a Baptist World Alliance, changed the name of the paper to *The Baptist World*, May 7, 1908. It retained this name until it was merged with *The Western Recorder* and the *Kentucky Mission Monthly* in 1919.   GEORGE RALEIGH JEWELL

BAPTIST BANNER. A Baptist newspaper started in 1876 at Cumming, Ga., by J. M. Wood and J. J. Morris. When fire destroyed the paper in 1881, Wood moved it to Gainsville where it continued publication until its suspension in 1883. Other editors associated with the paper were James C. Blackstone and D. M. Breaker. The *Banner* had a large circulation in northeast Georgia for several years.

JOHN J. HURT, JR.

BAPTIST BANNER, THE. Published at Shelbyville, Ky., and Louisville, Ky., from 1834 to 1851. In 1851 its name was changed to the *Western Recorder*. During nine of its years—1839–48—it was called *The Baptist Banner and Western Pioneer*.

See also WESTERN RECORDER.

GEORGE RALEIGH JEWELL

BAPTIST BANNER AND WESTERN PIONEER, THE. See WESTERN RECORDER.

BAPTIST BATTLE FLAG. A Missouri paper first published in La Grange, June 1, 1875, with David B. Ray, editor. Its purpose was to "prove that the Baptist church is 'the only Christian community which has stood since the days of the apostles.'" It was "not designed to be a state paper, but to occupy a field in polemic and historical theology unoccupied by any periodical in the world." In June, 1877, the *Battle Flag* was consolidated with the *Baptist Herald* although it retained its original name until July 23, 1879, when it became the *American Baptist Flag*.   J. R. BLACK

BAPTIST BEACON. The official publication of the Baptist General Convention of Arizona. Founded in June, 1932, by S. S. Bussell as a monthly mimeographed four-page paper under the name *The New Testament Baptist News*, it was changed to *Arizona Baptist Beacon* with the second issue. On Nov. 27, 1952, it became *Baptist Beacon* because it was serving Southern Baptist churches in a nine-state area (Arizona,

Nevada, Utah, Idaho, Colorado, Wyoming, Montana, North Dakota, and South Dakota). In Oct., 1939, the *Arizona Baptist Beacon* was increased to eight pages and was published semimonthly. It became a weekly in Jan., 1946. At first the executive secretaries of the Arizona convention also served as editors. These were S. S. Bussell, H. A. Zimmerman, and Willis J. Ray. W. Barry Garrett, the present editor, became the first full-time editor June 1, 1947. Circulation reached 11,800 in 1955. For several years every church in the Arizona convention has sent the *Baptist Beacon* to every family through the church budget plan. The *Baptist Beacon* has no separate committee or board, but is under the direct supervision of the executive board of the Baptist General Convention of Arizona. Offices are maintained in the Doctor's Building (convention headquarters), 312–316 W. McDowell Road, Phoenix, Ariz.   W. BARRY GARRETT

BAPTIST BEACON. Established Nov. 15, 1895, at Muskogee, Indian Territory (Okla.). Its motto was "Holding Forth the Word of Life" (Phil. 2:16). Consisting of 8 pages, size 11 × 14 inches, the paper sold for $1.50 the year. B. F. Stamps was editor and publisher. The paper is now extinct.   J. M. GASKIN

BAPTIST BEACON. Established Oct. 9, 1896, at Ardmore, Indian Territory (Okla.). A bi-weekly, 15 × 22 inches in size, consisting of four six-column pages, the paper sold for $1 the year. J. F. Young was editor and business manager; J. W. Tinnin, publisher. In 1898 the paper was 13 × 20 inches in size and issued at $1.50 per year; and in 1899, size 11½ × 13 inches, it consisted of 16 four-column pages, with Lucius Robertson and James Malcolm Newman, associate editors. The paper no longer exists.   J. M. GASKIN

BAPTIST BEACON, THE. A newspaper published at Knoxville, Tenn., c. 1880. It flourished for a brief duration.   LYNN E. MAY, JR.

BAPTIST BIBLE FELLOWSHIP. Organized in a Fort Worth, Tex., hotel May 24, 1950, by a group of ministers who the previous day had severed their relationship with the World Fundamental Missionary Baptist Fellowship and the Bible Baptist Seminary of Fort Worth. The break was due to "the dictatorial methods" of J. Frank Norris. At Denton, Tex., on May 24 a statement of the aims of the organization was signed by 14 ministers. Springfield, Mo., was chosen as the organization's headquarters, where it was chartered under the laws of Missouri; it established the three-year Baptist Bible College and the weekly publication *Baptist Bible Tribune*. In 1955, 471 churches contributed a monthly average of $33,634.08 to the organization; 426 students were enrolled in the college and 72 missionaries were serving 14 fields. The organization adheres to the basic historic doctrines of Baptists, with emphasis on the premillennial return of Christ to the earth.
   NOEL SMITH

BAPTIST BULLETIN. A New Mexico paper published by Northern Baptists at Roswell in 1910–11. It was edited by Perry Wilson Longfellow (*q.v.*) and was published simultaneously with the Southern Baptist paper *New Mexico Baptist* at Portales.
   MRS. RICHARD THOMAS BAKER, SR.

BAPTIST CHAMPION. A semimonthly, published at Macon, Ga., from July 15, 1859, to Apr. 26, 1860. Joseph Walker was editor and proprietor, until Samuel Boykin (*q.v.*) bought the subscription list and transferred it to the *Christian Index*.   SPENCER B. KING, JR.

BAPTIST CHRONICLE (Extinct). See BAPTIST MESSAGE.

BAPTIST CHRONICLE AND GEORGETOWN LITERARY REGISTER, THE. Published at Georgetown, Ky., edited by Uriel B. Chambers during 1830–32. The initial issue of this periodical had been called *The Baptist Herald and Georgetown Literary Register*. A monthly, it succeeded *The Baptist Recorder* of Bloomfield, Ky., and was succeeded by *The Baptist Banner*, Shelbyville, Ky., which later moved to Louisville, Ky. Complete files and microfilm of this magazine are in the library of Southern Baptist Theological Seminary.
   BIBLIOGRAPHY: J. H. Spencer, *History of Kentucky Baptists* (1886).   GEORGE RALEIGH JEWELL

BAPTIST CHRONICLE AND MONTHLY MONITOR. A monthly edited by Joseph S. Baker at Columbus, Ga., from May, 1840, to June, 1841.   SPENCER B. KING, JR.

BAPTIST CIRCULAR. Started in Aug., 1858, by John Lewis Shuck (*q.v.*), pastor of First Baptist Church, Sacramento, Calif., and edited by him until early 1860 when he resigned his pastorate due principally to the slavery controversy which had arisen in the church. Upon his resignation the paper was moved to San Francisco where it became known as *The Evangel* with D. B. Cheney, editor. Shuck served as associate editor for a few months before returning to his South Carolina home in 1860. *The Evangel* soon lost its Southern Baptist characteristics although it continued as a general religious publication for 20 years. During the Civil War California's position as a "free" state closed all work of the Southern Baptist Convention, changing the status of the various churches and missions started by Southern Baptist missionaries and pastors.
   W. BURMAN TIMBERLAKE

BAPTIST COLLEGE SEARCHLIGHT. A Negro publication (now extinct) started at Muskogee, Creek Nation (Okla.), in 1899. The four-page paper, 13 × 20 inches in size, was published by J. F. Gordon in the interest of the Negro college and Baptist church at Muskogee. The price was $1 per year.   J. M. GASKIN

BAPTIST COLLEGIATE INSTITUTE (1898–1930). An elementary and high school for boys and girls located at Newton, Ala. It was founded and operated by Newton Baptist Church until 1907, at which time its ownership and control was assumed by the Alabama Baptist State Convention. A. M. Tate, first principal, served for many years. The school was primarily noted as a feeder for Howard and Judson colleges. An attempt to operate the school as a junior college failed in 1930.
JAMES E. DAVIDSON

BAPTIST CORRESPONDENT (1859–61). Before settling in Alabama in 1857, William Calmes Buck (q.v.), a Virginian, had served as pastor in Louisville, Ky., and Columbus, Miss. While in Louisville, he had edited the *Baptist Banner and Western Pioneer*. In May, 1857, he accepted a call to the Baptist church at Greensboro, Ala.; and later at Marion he commenced publication of the *Baptist Correspondent*, a weekly. Late in 1861 Buck suspended publication of his paper and joined the Confederate army as a missionary.
RAY M. ATCHISON

BAPTIST COURIER, THE. The official organ of the Baptist state convention in South Carolina, published weekly in Greenville. It began publication under the name *Working Christian* in Yorkville (York), July 1, 1869, with Tilman R. Gaines (1834–99) as editor. Previously, April–August, 1866, Gaines had edited a paper called *Baptist Church and Sunday School Messenger*.

In a meeting of the state convention in York, July 22–25, 1869, A. K. Durham presented a resolution commending the *Working Christian* to the support of Baptists. *Working Christian* was moved to Charleston and began publication there May 19, 1870, with Gaines as editor. Later it was moved to Columbia, where it was first published Oct. 19, 1871. The paper continued publication as the *Working Christian* until Sept. 20, 1877, when it appeared under its new name, *The Baptist Courier*.

James Alfred Hoyt (q.v.) purchased *The Baptist Courier* from Charles M. McJunkin, an associate of Gaines, and Abner Whateley Lamar became editor with the issue published Sept. 26, 1878. Hoyt moved the paper to Greenville Mar. 20, 1879. The issue of Jan. 15, 1880, lists Hoyt and J. A. Chambliss as editors, with Lamar, James Clement Furman (q.v.), and William Strickland as associate and corresponding editors. Andrew Jackson Spears Thomas (q.v.) became one of the editors and proprietors of the paper June 1, 1891. After the death of Thomas in 1911, Zechariah Thornton Cody (q.v.) and J. C. Keys assumed control.

The state convention, meeting in Columbia in Dec., 1920, voted to purchase *The Baptist Courier* from Cody and Keys for $24,000. A board of trustees composed of 15 men was elected to manage the paper, with Cody continuing as editor; and Jacob Smiser Dill, circulation manager. Robert Francis Terrell succeeded Dill as circulation manager in 1926, a position he now holds (1956).

Cody died Mar. 7, 1935, and was succeeded by William Cox Allen who served until his resignation, Mar. 28, 1940. Jesse McGarity Burnett, who succeeded Allen in 1940, died Oct. 30, 1947. After an interim editorship until May 15, 1948, Samuel Harry Jones, the present editor (1956), assumed his duties. *The Baptist Courier* is now published weekly, except the first week in January and one week in August, in Greenville. With a news magazine format, the paper is printed on newsprint, 10-inch, three-column pages; it uses 24 pages with an occasional 16-page issue. Controlled by a 15-man board of trustees elected by the state convention, *The Baptist Courier* is chartered by the state of South Carolina. Its circulation Dec. 1, 1955, was 91,034, with 760 churches subscribing for every family. The convention contributes $35,000 annually to its support. Hiott Press prints the paper on contract, and since the paper owns no real estate, it rents its offices from Hiott Press. A complete file of *The Baptist Courier* is in the Furman University Library; it has been microfilmed.

BIBLIOGRAPHY: G. W. Gardner, "A Historical Sketch of *The Baptist Courier*," *The Baptist Courier* (1921). R. W. Sanders, "Baptist Journalism in South Carolina," *The Baptist Courier* (1921).   S. H. JONES

BAPTIST DIGEST. First issued Dec. 3, 1945, in two-page mimeographed form, as *Southern Baptist Beams*, temporarily edited by N J Westmoreland as the publication of the Kansas Southern Baptist fellowship. Orbie Russell Clem was named editor at the organization of the fellowship Nov., 1945. In Mar., 1946, the paper was named the official publication of the newly organized Kansas Convention of Southern Baptist Churches. Clem was confirmed in his editorship Apr. 24, 1946. The paper appeared as *Kansas Southern Baptist Beams* May 1, 1946, and as a four-page monthly July 5, 1946. In annual session Nov. 11, 1953, the state convention voted to establish a seven-member board of directors to direct the state Baptist paper. In quarterly session Mar. 22, 1954, the board of directors changed the name to *Baptist Digest*, named Hoyt Sidney Gibson editor, and adopted statement of policy regulating operation of the paper. Circulation at that time was 2,758; in Dec., 1954, it was 4,283. Weekly publication was begun Oct., 1954.   HOYT S. GIBSON

BAPTIST FEMALE COLLEGE. Established at Pontotoc, Miss., in 1858, almost immediately after the suspension of Mary Washington Female College. The school was directed by William L. Slack and his wife, and one of their students expressed her opinion of them in the algebraic equation, "Two Slacks equal one Tight." Mrs. Modena Lowrey Berry (q.v.) was one of the students in the school before it closed in 1878. J. L. BOYD

BAPTIST FLAG, THE. Weekly paper first published Jan. 1, 1875, at La Grange, Mo., as *The Baptist Battle Flag and Church Historian*, edited by David Burcham Ray (1830–1922). On June 27, 1877, the place of publication was changed to St. Louis. On July 23, 1879, the name was changed to *American Baptist Flag* with "and Church Historian" added on editorial page; however, this was dropped at the end of the year.

On Apr. 21, 1898, John Newton Hall (q.v.) (1849–1905) was made editor, and publication offices were maintained in St. Louis, Mo., and Fulton, Ky. After Feb. 18, 1904, the St. Louis office was no longer maintained. On May 4, 1905, the name became *The Baptist Flag*. On July 17, 1924, the paper was merged with the *Diagram of Truth* and published at Nashville, Tenn., as *The Diagram of Truth and American Baptist Flag*. On Jan. 22, 1925, the paper was again published at Fulton, Ky. as *The Baptist Flag*. In Oct., 1925, it was sold to the *American Baptist* of Memphis, Tenn. LEO T. CRISMON

BAPTIST FORUM. A newspaper edited and published by Silas L. Morris in Atlanta, Ga., 1910–12. This paper succeeded *The Bible Studio* in 1910. JOHN J. HURT, JR.

BAPTIST GENERAL ASSOCIATION OF MIDDLE TENNESSEE AND NORTH ALABAMA. See TENNESSEE, BAPTIST GENERAL ASSOCIATION OF.

BAPTIST GLEANER, THE. A weekly publication printed at Fulton, Ky., from 1879 until June 29, 1887, when it was consolidated with *The Baptist* of Memphis, Tenn. The editors were John Newton Hall (q.v.) (1849–1905) and Joseph Burnley Moody (q.v.) (1838–1931).
 LEO T. CRISMON

BAPTIST HELMET, THE. A newspaper, now extinct, published at Vandalia, Ill., 1839–45.
 LYNN E. MAY, JR.

BAPTIST HERALD, THE. First published at Lebanon, Mo., its office was moved to St. Louis in June, 1877, when it became consolidated with the *Baptist Battle Flag* under that name. J. R. BLACK

BAPTIST HERALD AND GEORGETOWN LITERARY REGISTER, THE. Published at Georgetown, Ky. It was the successor to *The Baptist Recorder*, Bloomfield, Ky. It was issued under this title only once dated Jan., 1830. Thereafter it appeared during 1830–32 as *The Baptist Chronicle and Georgetown Literary Register*. GEORGE RALEIGH JEWELL

BAPTIST HISTORICAL RECORD. A monthly first published in Cochran, Ga., under the name *Our Church History*. Walter M. Lee, editor, changed the name to *Baptist Historical Record* after moving to South Carolina to become pastor of the Immanuel Baptist Church of Westminster, and the first issue of this 12-page paper under its new name appeared in Oct., 1926, listed as Volume I, Number 6. The purpose of the periodical was to aid in preserving the early history of Baptists in the South. The last known issue of *Baptist Historical Record* appeared in Oct., 1927.
 ROBERT A. IVEY

BAPTIST HOSPITAL, BARRANQUILLA. See COLOMBIA, MISSION IN.

BAPTIST HOSPITAL, CHENGCHOW. See CHINA, MISSION IN.

BAPTIST HOSPITAL, EKU. See NIGERIA, MISSION IN.

BAPTIST HOSPITAL, GAZA. See GAZA, MISSION IN.

BAPTIST HOSPITAL, GUADALAJARA. See MEXICO, MISSION IN.

BAPTIST HOSPITAL, INC. (Mid-State). An institution at Nashville, Tenn., owned and operated by the Tennessee Baptist Convention since Apr. 21, 1948. Formerly known as the Protestant Hospital, it was given to the Tennessee convention with the understanding that the convention would expand and improve its facilities, make it a standard hospital, and place it on a par with other hospitals owned by the Baptist denomination in Tennessee. After the transfer, an expansion program was projected and successfully completed.

From the beginning of Tennessee Baptist administration until 1955, the hospital's total patient income was $7,240,000; $319,000 was received from the denomination; and $10,652 from designated gifts. In 1955 the 18 buildings, with land and equipment, were worth $3,500,000, and there was an indebtedness amounting to $280,000. In 1955 the hospital had 242 beds, and served 16,895 patients. Income was $2,274,973, and $69,248 was received from the denomination. The hospital is approved for intern and resident training; it is approved and accredited by the joint commission on accreditation, the American Medical Association, the American Hospital Association, and the Tennessee Hospital Association. The hospital admits only white patients. D. A. ELLIS

BAPTIST HOSPITAL, JOINKRAMA. See NIGERIA, MISSION IN.

BAPTIST HOSPITAL, KWEILIN. See CHINA, MISSION IN.

BAPTIST HOUR, THE. The history of the *Baptist Hour* dates back to 1938, when Samuel

Franklin Lowe (q.v.) urged the Southern Baptist Convention, meeting in Richmond, Va., to explore the possibilities of religious broadcasting. At that meeting Lowe was appointed chairman of a seven-member committee charged with making the survey.

In 1939 at Oklahoma City the survey group recommended to the Convention that a committee be continued to make a study of the best methods of religious broadcasting, and that that committee be empowered to raise money through private donations to promote Baptist broadcasts. With an operating fund of $1,200 from the Sunday School Board, the committee set in motion plans for a *Baptist Hour* program. These plans were approved at the 1940 Convention in Baltimore, Md.

The first 13-week *Baptist Hour* series began in Jan., 1941. Monroe Elmon Dodd (q.v.) delivered the first message on the half-hour evangelistic program; and was followed by George Washington Truett (q.v.); Adiel Jarrett Moncrief, Jr.; Theodore Floyd Adams; Ellis Adams Fuller (q.v.); John Clyde Turner; John Richard Sampey (q.v.); Clyde Calhoun Morris; Charles Oscar Johnson; John Hall Buchanan; Thomas Luther Holcomb; John Leonard Hill; and William Wistar Hamilton. The series was carried by 17 stations in 11 states.

At the 1942 Convention in San Antonio the *Baptist Hour* network was reported at 32 stations. Lowe was made director of the committee at this meeting.

World War II forced cancellation of the scheduled Convention in Memphis in 1943. Lowe's report, which was filed with the Executive Committee of the Convention, showed a gain in network to 37 stations, eight of which had a power of 50,000 watts.

In 1945 the first quarter series was followed by 13 additional programs in April, May, and June; and the program was heard each Sunday during the first six months of 1946. During both years the broadcast was presented on a 37-station network. The *Baptist Hour* came of age in the Convention at the 1946 meeting in Miami, Fla. The name "Radio Committee" was replaced by the name "Radio Commission," and the commission was recognized as an agency of the Convention, receiving a direct and proportionate share of Cooperative Program receipts.

In 1947 the *Baptist Hour* was heard over 52 stations. By 1948 the number had increased to 63. At the 1949 Convention in Oklahoma City, Okla., the commission announced a full-time *Baptist Hour* beginning in October of that year. On Oct. 2, 1949, the full-time *Baptist Hour* began over 120 stations of the American Broadcasting Company. The network schedule was terminated in June, 1950, for lack of funds.

The programs were offered transcribed to independent radio stations, and 180 stations scheduled the broadcasts. The *Baptist Hour* was not heard during the fourth quarter of 1950. On the first Sunday in Jan., 1951, the transcribed programs were resumed on the 180-station network. Time was purchased on 50 other stations. By the end of 1951 the *Baptist Hour* had been logged by 273 stations in 24 states and 3 foreign territories. By Apr. 1, 1952, the number of stations had grown to 300 in 26 states and 4 foreign territories.

Associate Director Dupree Jordan was made acting director following the death of S. F. Lowe Oct. 4, 1952. The commission elected Paul Morris Stevens director in Aug., 1953. By the end of that year 330 stations in 28 states and 7 foreign territories had scheduled the *Baptist Hour*. Beginning with the last quarter of 1955, 376 stations had accepted the broadcast, including a seven-station Far East network originating in Manila. The *Baptist Hour* is produced transcribed each week by the Radio and Television Commission of the Southern Baptist Convention. The commission was moved from Atlanta, Ga., to Fort Worth, Tex., June 1, 1955.

THEODORE LOTT

BAPTIST LEADER (Negro). In Aug., 1900, J. H. Eason was editor of this Anniston religious weekly. The paper gave some attention to civic and political affairs. W. S. Stratman was associate editor, and the Alabama Colored Baptist State Convention was proprietor.

RAY M. ATCHISON

BAPTIST LEADER. A newspaper published and edited at Cumming, Ga., by A. J. Kelly and Jesse Williams, 1891–92, and by Williams alone, 1893–96. Williams in 1897 sold the paper to A. E. Booth who named his publication *North Georgia Baptist* and continued it until 1901. Both publications seem to have been simply local town papers which carried secular news while bearing a Baptist label with limited denominational news items.

JOHN J. HURT, JR.

BAPTIST MEMORIAL HOSPITAL. Located in Jacksonville, Fla., established by the hospital commission of the Southern Baptist Convention under its Louisiana charter and a permit granted by the state of Florida, July 18, 1953.

A committee from Jacksonville, Fla., submitted a proposal to the hospital commission of the Convention offering to contribute $1,000,000 and an adequate site if the board would construct and operate a hospital in the city of Jacksonville. The board studied the situation carefully, approved it, and submitted it to the Executive Committee of the Convention for its consideration. The committee in turn approved the request and brought it before the Convention meeting in St. Louis, Mo., in May, 1947. The proposal was adopted, provided the transfer of money and site could be made within the business and financial plan of the Convention. The site consisted of 15 acres on the bank of the St. Johns River, and the transfer of site and money to the board was made on June 25, 1953.

The Wolfson Foundation contributed $250,-

000 to erect the Wolfson Memorial Children's Hospital in connection with the Baptist Memorial Hospital. The amount was later increased to $315,000, and still later to $565,000.

The contract for the building was signed in July, 1953, and construction was begun. The original contract called for a bed capacity of 182 with other sections to be roughed in for completion after the hospital opened and money was available. However, since there was such a need for more hospital beds in Jacksonville, the hospital commission asked permission of the Executive Committee of the Convention to borrow more money in order to finish the entire building bringing the capacity to 310 beds. The first unit of 182 beds was completed and was opened to receive patients Sept. 13, 1955.   FRANK TRIPP

BAPTIST MESSAGE. The official newspaper of the Louisiana Baptist Convention. The publication, which eventually became the *Message*, was founded in 1886, on recommendation of a special committee of the state convention. It was supported by 331 pledged two-dollar subscriptions, and it was to be called the *Baptist Chronicle*. The editorial office was located in Shreveport. W. C. Friley was appointed editor, with the understanding that he would make the paper "his own private enterprise," supported by the promised backing of the convention. The paper functioned so ably in support of the convention program that the next year it was reported that "whatever success has crowned the efforts of the Executive Board can be, to a very large extent, attributed to this" newspaper.

Friley, an able preacher but an inexperienced editor and administrator, soon gave up the *Chronicle*, and William Sidnor Penick (q.v.), pastor of the First Baptist Church in Shreveport, became editor for the interim. In 1887 the *Chronicle* was adopted by the convention as its official organ. In 1888 it was bought by R. M. Boone, who edited it until 1903. Then the paper was purchased by a stock company and edited by various men, including Bruce Benton, John Benjamin Lawrence, and David Lawrence, until 1912, when Edwin Oswald Ware (q.v.) purchased it and published it until 1919. Ware then sold his paper to the convention. It was renamed the *Baptist Message*, and W. H. Barton became editor. He served until Sept., 1920.

On Oct. 1, 1920, the present editor, Finley W. Tinnin, at the request of the executive board, became editor and manager of the paper. At that time there were less than 6,000 subscribers, and increasing circulation was the major problem. In 1923 the budget plan was adopted, and the churches were asked to subscribe to the paper for every resident family in their memberships. By 1928 the circulation had reached 23,000, a total exceeded only by the 27,000 circulation reported by the Georgia *Christian Index*.

During the depression of 1929–36, the circulation dropped to 6,000. A campaign sponsored by the state Woman's Missionary Union in 1938 resulted in about 7,000 new subscribers. Since then circulation has increased every year until the paper reported on Sept. 1, 1955, a circulation of 54,489. There were 476 churches that included the paper in their budgets and 442 churches that used a club plan.

The business affairs of the *Message* are supervised by an operating committee elected by the executive board of the Louisiana convention. The convention appropriates $12,550 annually for the paper, and a financial reserve of $43,973.27 has been accumulated. The *Message* has mailing equipment which cost $5,613. Due to a fire, the paper does not have a file of its issues prior to 1919, but most of the issues from the beginning have been located and microfilmed by the Southern Baptist Historical Commission.   F. W. TINNIN, SR.

BAPTIST MESSENGER. A newspaper published at Pensacola, Fla., near the beginning of the 20th century. The Florida Baptist State Convention purchased the paper with 460 subscribers in 1904 for $60. This gave the *Florida Baptist Witness* the co-operation of Baptists in west Florida.   W. G. STRACENER

BAPTIST MESSENGER. Official organ of the Baptist General Convention of Oklahoma, founded in Oklahoma City, Okla., by Clarence Perry Stealey (q.v.), owner and editor, May 15, 1912. It continued as a private publication until it was purchased by the Baptist General Convention of Oklahoma in 1919 for the sum of $5,000. Stealey continued as editor until 1928. Circulation at the time of convention purchase was 5,000; one year later it had reached 8,500.

The Stealey Controversy growing out of the issues involving fundamentalism and evolution, resulted in Stealey's removal as editor of the *Messenger* as of Dec. 31, 1927. A committee composed of Andrew Potter (q.v.), J. W. Gillon, R. C. Miller, and J. B. Rounds edited the paper until Eugene Coke Routh assumed the editorship Feb. 15, 1928. Routh was born at La Grange, Tex., Nov. 26, 1874. An A.B. graduate of the University of Texas in 1897, he was ordained to the ministry May 12, 1901. He was an evangelist during 1901–03; pastor at Lockhart, Tex., 1903–07; editor, *South Texas Baptist*, San Antonio, 1907–12; associate editor, *Baptist Standard*, Dallas, Tex., 1912–14; and editor-in-chief of the *Standard*, 1914–28. Editor of the *Baptist Messenger*, Feb. 15, 1928, to May 15, 1943, he went to Richmond, Va., as editor of *The Commission*, 1943–48, when he retired to Lockhart, Tex. He is author of *Life Story of Dr. J. B. Gambrell* (1929), *Story of Oklahoma Baptists* (1932), *Reading the Bible* (1934), *Are All Roads the Same?* (1941), *The Word Overcoming the World* (1941), *Evening and Morning in China* (1950), *Adventures in Christian*

Journalism (1950), *Who Are They?* (1951), *Scattered Abroad* (1952), *Baptists on the March* (1952), *According to the Scriptures* (1956), and editor, *The Southern Baptist Convention—1845–1953*, by W. W. Barnes.

Prior to Routh's editorship the *Messenger* was printed by various commercial printers in Oklahoma City, and from Apr., 1928, to Oct. 29, 1953, it was printed by the Oklahoma Baptist University Press, Shawnee, Okla. It was printed by the Leader Press, Oklahoma City, Nov. 5, 1953, to Oct. 28, 1954. Beginning with the issue of Nov. 4, 1954, it has been printed by its own press in the Baptist Building, 1141 N. Robinson, Oklahoma City, Okla.

E. C. Routh was succeeded by his son, Porter, in the editorship of the *Messenger* July 15, 1943. During E. C. Routh's time circulation grew to 25,000, and during Porter Routh's term as editor it increased to 36,000. Albert McClellan was editor Oct. 1, 1945, to Aug. 1, 1949, and during this time circulation reached 47,000. Jack Linton Gritz, the present editor, succeeded McClellan Aug. 1, 1949.

In 1956 the *Messenger* had 18 employees, seven full-time and four part-time in the press room; five full-time and two part-time in the editorial office. Value of the press and equipment was $84,792; and the operating budget was $150,000, with $22,000 from the Cooperative Program, $96,000 from subscriptions, $20,000 from special church editions, and $12,000 from advertising and other sources. In 1955–56 the Messenger Press printed ten books. Circulation of the paper in 1956 reached 76,000. Published weekly except the first issue in August and the last in December, the *Messenger* costs $2 per year for individuals, $1.75 per year by the club plan, and $1.60 in the church budget plan. Accounts are handled through the state convention's bookkeeping department, but the *Messenger* office keeps its own set of books showing receipts and disbursements. The editor is elected by the board of directors of the convention, makes semiannual reports to the board and annual reports to the convention. Two advisory committees serve the *Messenger* annually, one from the convention's board of directors, appointed when it organized following the convention's annual session in November, and the other elected by the convention itself. A complete file of the paper is in the *Messenger* office.   J. M. GASKIN

BAPTIST MESSENGER, THE. A monthly newspaper, now extinct, published at Woodbury and Readyville, Tenn., 1882–86, with J. M. D. Cates as editor.   LYNN E. MAY, JR.

BAPTIST MESSENGER, THE. A paper published in 1874 in Jasper, Tex., with W. M. Reece as editor.   E. C. ROUTH

BAPTIST MIRROR. A newspaper published at Cuthbert and Macon, Ga., and edited by E. Z. F. Golden from 1898 to Jan., 1900, when it was discontinued.   JOHN J. HURT, JR.

BAPTIST MISSIONARY ASSOCIATION. The official title for a general body of Texas Baptists first organized at Troupe, July 6, 1900, under the name of East Texas Baptist Convention, the name being changed the same year at a subsequent meeting (Dec. 6–8) at Lindale to Baptist Missionary Association of Texas. The organization of this new body was the culmination of several years of bitter controversy within the Baptist General Convention of Texas. The controversy first flared in 1894 when S. A. Hayden, owner and editor of the *Texas Baptist Herald*, proposed to the convention certain reforms which stirred up a divided reaction. The conflict thus inaugurated was intensified by many exchanges of accusation and criticism between Hayden and James Britton Cranfill (*q.v.*), owner and editor of the *Texas Baptist Standard*. It involved newspaper competition and personal jealousy, and ultimately it found its way into the courts of the state. When in 1897, 1898, 1899, and 1900 Hayden was denied a seat in the annual convention, the issue of church sovereignty was brought into the limelight of the controversy. Hayden contended that the local church was the sovereign authority in matters pertaining to the composition of the convention, and that the convention had no right to refuse eligibility to membership without denying the church a right to send its messengers. James Bruton Gambrell (*q.v.*), then executive secretary of the general convention, expressed the opposing view in this statement: "A church cannot delegate its powers to merge its sovereignty through delegates into a general body. It may send messengers to represent its views and wishes, but not delegates invested with its sovereignty of authority." The issue revolved around this question: Was the convention constituted of churches represented by their messengers or of individuals as messengers from the churches without authority from the churches sending them?

There were several precursory, informal, and unofficial meetings of interested parties to consider the possibility and feasibility of organizing a new convention. The first meeting was held in San Antonio in 1897 after Hayden's first denial of a seat, and another was held in Waco in 1898. A "consultation meeting" was held in Dallas, July 4, 1899, and the final meeting followed the convention in Dallas, Nov., 1899. In all of these preliminary meetings, Hayden vigorously opposed the establishing of another general body of Baptists; however, when the new body was organized, he identified himself with it.

Messengers from 30 churches in east Texas constituted the new body of Baptists. When it was learned that other Baptists from over the state wished to become identified with this new group, the name was changed to include all Baptists of the state who wished to co-operate with the new organization. At the second annual meeting, held at Jack Creek near Mexia in 1901, 244 churches were represented. The largest number of churches represented at the annual meeting was in 1904, when 563 churches were enrolled. The 1954 meeting in Houston was represented by 248 churches.

Owned and operated by the Baptist Missionary Association are the following: Jacksonville College at Jacksonville, the Texas Baptist Orphanage at Waxahachie, a state paper called the *Baptist Progress,* and the Baptist Progress Book Store at Dallas. Another institution, the Texas Baptist University at Dallas, organized in 1905, became extinct in 1912. The mission program of the association is carried on through a Board of Missions, the members of which are elected at the annual meeting. An executive secretary is employed by the board to direct the mission program, which in 1954 included six full-time and two part-time state mission workers, and 54 foreign missionaries, including 34 native workers.

In 1933 a committee was appointed by both general Baptist bodies in Texas for the purpose of studying the possibility of a unification of the two groups. This committee of 25 from each body, headed by Morris A. Roberts of the Baptist Missionary Association and Franz Marshall McConnell (*q.v.*) of the general convention, worked out a statement of principles which involved a few changes in the constitutions of both bodies. The general convention in session (1934) in San Antonio adopted unanimously the proposed changes in the constitution. The Baptist Missionary Association, meeting a week later in Dallas, rejected the proposed changes. Thus was thwarted a movement which appeared to be well on its way toward bringing unification of the two bodies.

See also AMERICAN BAPTIST ASSOCIATION.

BIBLIOGRAPHY: J. M. Carroll, *A History of Texas Baptists* (1923). J. B. Cranfill, *Cranfill's Chronicle* (1916); *Hayden-Cranfill Trial* (1900). B. F. Fuller, *A History of Texas Baptists* (1900). J. B. Gambrell, *Baptists and Their Business* (1919). T. C. Kuykendall, *An Answer to "Circular Letter to the Baptists"* (1909). J. B. Link, *Historical and Biographical Magazine,* vol. II (1892). F. M. McConnell, *The Agreement and Differences Between the Two Baptist General Bodies in Texas* (1913); *Mission Plans and the Baptist General Convention Compared with the Baptist Missionary Association* (1911). W. H. Parks, *History of the Baptist Missionary Association of Texas* (1912). B. F. Riley, *A History of Texas Baptists* (1907). M. A. Roberts, *Eye Opener or Compendium of Facts Regarding Texas Baptists* (1921); *Our Baptist Missionary Association* (n.d.). R. C. Vance, *The Baptist Missionary Association from 1900 to 1953* (1955).   C. E. COLTON

BAPTIST MISSIONARY SOCIETY (of Great Britain). Founded Oct. 2, 1792, at Kettering, England, by William Carey (*q.v.*) and 13 other young men, this was the first modern missionary society. Based upon the principle of voluntary membership of those sufficiently interested to make financial contributions to the spread of the gospel, it set the pattern which was quickly followed by other denominations, both in Europe and in America, and earned for Carey the title "Father of Modern Missions." It has continued for more than a century and a half to be the principal agency through which Baptists of Great Britain have carried on foreign mission work.

The original name, "The Particular Baptist Society for Propagating the Gospel among the Heathen," was soon shortened to "Baptist Missionary Society," which became more appropriate when in 1891 the mission work of General Baptists was merged with that of Particular Baptists. Two other organizations, the Women's Missionary Association (previously known as the Baptist Zenana Mission) and the Medical Mission Auxiliary, were merged with the Baptist Missionary Society in 1925.

India, the first field entered in 1793, has continued to be of primary interest. Unsuccessful missions were attempted in Sierra Leone in 1795 and in Burma in 1807. Ceylon was entered in 1812 and became a permanent field. Work was done in the East Indies from 1813 to 1826. The West Indies were entered in 1814, to become one of the most successful enterprises. Missions were inaugurated in Brittany in 1834. In 1844 a successful African mission was planted in the Cameroon region, but this was turned over to the Basle Society after Germany annexed the territory. China was entered in 1845 and continued to be an important field until 1950. The Congo mission was launched in 1878, to develop into an extensive undertaking, extending into Angola. Other temporary fields were Norway (1863–85); Italy (1870–1921); Japan (1878–83); and Palestine (1886–1905). Limited new projects in Hong Kong, Malaya, and Brazil were begun in 1953.

In 1955 the Baptist Missionary Society had 343 active missionaries assigned to 7 major fields, with 2,326 organized congregations, 100,886 church members, and a total Christian community of 313,214. They maintained 1,266 day schools, 2 colleges, 14 theological and training schools, 11 hospitals, and 2 orphanages. The income for the year 1954–55 was £300,726 ($842,032).

The following is a summary of work in the several fields in 1955:

Field	Missionaries	Churches	Church Members
India	138	455	32,470
Pakistan	36	130	5,728
Ceylon	10	31	1,609
Congo	109	1,225	27,072
Angola	28	253	9,898
Jamaica	11	235	23,621
Trinidad	5	17	488

Six missionaries are employed on special projects: in Hong Kong, Malaya, Brazil.

The Baptist Missionary Society is located at 93 Gloucester Place, London W.1, England.

H. C. GOERNER

BAPTIST MONITOR AND POLITICAL COMPILER. Published at Bloomfield, Ky., from

Apr. 22, 1823, to Jan. 27, 1824. Edited by Stephen Ray, the paper called itself "religious, political, literary, agricultural and miscellaneous." The final two issues, Feb. 3 and 19, 1824, were issued and dated at Bardstown, Ky., in the same county. The issue for Feb. 19, 1824, says that, owing to the sectarian nature of the name of the paper, it would henceforth be known as *The Telescope.* No such name has ever been found. Relatively little actual Kentucky news was printed in the paper. Most of the articles were from other states and countries, and many were copied from other publications. Most of its issues are on microfilm in the library of Southern Baptist Theological Seminary.

GEORGE RALEIGH JEWELL

BAPTIST MOVEMENTS, RECENT MINOR. Small groups whose original churches withdrew from either the Northern and Southern Baptist conventions or some other body, usually in special advocacy of some tenet of orthodoxy which they felt was being neglected or attacked. These groups have been the most outspoken advocates of that extreme supernaturalism, which until the 20th century was characteristic of traditional American evangelical Christianity. They have resisted with tenacity any group or teaching which they alleged had minimized or rationalized the importance of miracles, divine revelation, literal biblicism, dispensationalism, or the letter of their concept of New Testament ecclesiology. These groups came into prominence as their position of traditional supernaturalism was challenged by a complex combination of factors during the first half of the 20th century.

The total impact of each component and the varied actions and reactions of ideological and historical forces defy description. Radical criticism of the Bible; the projection of evolutionary and materialistic theories; the enlarging grip of rationalism; the open challenge of theological liberalism; the rapid development of ecumenical organization; the loss of immediate democratic control in some denominations because of the great increase in size and benevolent activities; and the almost frantic effort to diagnose the political, social, and economic ills of a world constantly in crisis—these trends brought deep cleavages in doctrines and methods of operation that brought schism in the ranks of several denominations.

Baptists in particular were affected because their emphasis on the Bible as their basis for doctrinal and organizational life made them quite vulnerable to schism under attack from Fundamentalist thinking. Long before the opening of the 20th century, American Baptists had disagreed and separated on matters of doctrine as well as on methods of organizing and doing benevolent work. The surrounding conditions of the first half of the 20th century, however, brought additional strife.

Three of the more important of the Baptist schisms involve the Conservative (Fundamentalist) movements, the General Association of Regular Baptist Churches, and the Southern division of the Fundamentalist movement, Norrisism—all of these movements stemming basically from the same general background. Other localized organizational and institutional protests against theological liberalism also appeared during this period.

The Conservative movements.—It became evident by 1920 that there were two opposing factions in the Northern Baptist Convention—the Fundamentalists (so called because of their championship of the "Christian fundamentals") and the Liberals (ranging from moderates, who desired to maintain denominational unity, to rationalists, who denied all the beliefs of traditional supernaturalism). The two views clashed when the Fundamentalists (later called Conservatives) questioned the orthodoxy of Baptist foreign missionaries. An unsuccessful effort was made to secure the adoption by the Northern Baptist Convention of the New Hampshire Confession of Faith. From 1923 until 1943, the Conservatives fought with the Liberal leaders for control of the convention, accusing them of departing from the old-time Baptist faith, particularly with reference to the trustworthiness of the Scriptures. In reply the Liberals charged the Conservatives with trying to make an adjudicating presbytery out of a Baptist convention by demanding the adoption of rigid doctrinal standards of orthodoxy.

As a result, the latter group, on Dec. 15, 1943, met in Chicago and organized the Conservative Baptist Foreign Mission Society for the purpose of insuring the doctrinal soundness of Baptist foreign missionaries. By 1954 the society had 300 missionaries on foreign fields. Five years later, this group formed the Conservative Baptist Home Mission Society. These bodies were organized under the old society method; viz., one organization for each benevolent activity on a completely voluntary basis. On May 17, 1947, at Atlantic City, N. J., the Conservative Baptist Association of America was organized for fellowship by churches sympathetic with their views. This association in 1956 reported 998 churches with 250,000 affiliated members.

The General Association of Regular Baptist Churches.—The same protest against theological liberalism, but with greater Landmark antipathy against organizational forms, accounts for the rise of the General Association of Regular Baptist Churches, which was organized in May, 1932, with headquarters at Chicago, Ill. This body differed from the Conservative movements in that it sought to avoid organization of "elaborate machinery" for benevolent work. It determined not to create "another Baptist mission board." The association, formed as a fellowship only, carries on missionary and other benevolent activity through independent Baptist agencies organized by others. An approved list of such independent agencies is maintained and regularly scrutinized to insure doctrinal regularity. The same policy is followed in the support of Baptist schools. The permanent organization of the association is a council of 14 members, half of whom are elected annually to a two-year term. Two delegates from each church, irrespective of its size, are permitted to vote for these officers. In 1956 the association reported 726 churches with 124,039 members in affiliation.

Southern Fundamentalism.—One of the early Southern leaders of the Fundamentalist movement was John Franklyn Norris (q.v.), of Fort Worth, Tex. On May 10, 1923, along with T. T. Shields of Toronto, Canada, and William B. Riley of Minneapolis, Minn., Norris helped organize the Bible Baptist Union, the purpose of which was to combat modernism among Baptists. These leaders united in making acrimonious attacks upon alleged modernism in Baptist bodies and institutions throughout the land. Norris was refused a seat in the Tarrant County Baptist Association in 1922 and in the Baptist General Convention of Texas in 1924. However, his movement was pared away from the national body after 1926, when he killed a Fort Worth businessman, for which he was later acquitted. He continued independently, organized a seminary and a world Fundamentalist fellowship, and secured a large following. On May 25, 1950, a serious schism in his movement resulted in the organization of a separate section, named Baptist Bible Fellowship, which is strongly premillennial, in Springfield, Mo. Since the death of Norris on Aug. 20, 1952, the movement has declined.

BIBLIOGRAPHY: *Baptist Bible Tribune* (1950–56). W. W. Barnes, *The Southern Baptist Convention* (1954). S. G. Cole, *The History of Fundamentalism* (1931). B. Y. Landis, ed., *Yearbook of American Churches (for 1957)* (1956). *The Baptist Bulletin* (1935–56). *The Fundamentalist* (1927–56). *The Searchlight* (1917–27). R. G. Torbet, *A History of the Baptists* (1950). C. E. Tulga, *The Foreign Missions Controversy in the Northern Baptist Convention* (1950).

ROBERT A. BAKER

BAPTIST NEW MEXICAN. The official spokesman of the Baptist Convention of New Mexico which owns and prints it, the *Baptist New Mexican* has been in continuous publication since 1912. It has been served by 11 editors, and from the beginning has had for its slogan, "A Paper in Every Baptist Home." Published with 16 pages, it has a circulation of 16,000 weekly, through 203 church budgets.

The paper came into existence with the consolidation of smaller publications, organs of the New Mexico Baptist Convention (Northern) and the Baptist General Convention (Southern). Divided in polity, each felt the need of union and the presence of the paper to bring it about. Papers which merged were *The Baptist Bulletin* (Northern), published at Roswell and edited by Perry Wilson Longfellow (q.v.), 1910–11; and the *New Mexico Baptist* (Southern), published at Portales and edited by Eugene Perry Alldredge (q.v.), 1910–11. As a result of the union of the two conventions at Clovis in 1912, the *Baptist New Mexican* came into existence, with headquarters moved to Albuquerque.

The first editor, S. B. Calloway, served only three months. In 1913, the convention's executive secretary, Elmer B. Atwood, became editor, serving through 1918. Editors following Atwood have included Coleman Craig, James Weston Bruner, William Park, Calowa William Stumph, Henry Clay Reavis, Horace Burns, Harold E. Dye, George Ward Fenley, and Lewis Alexander Myers.

Editors are elected by the New Mexico State Mission Board and approved by the Convention. A committee of the board, known as the *Baptist New Mexican* Committee, counsels and brings quarterly reports. The convention-owned building provides offices for five staff members. All receipts are turned over to the convention, which pays the bills. Aside from circulation and advertising income, the board supplements the subscription price of $1 by 50 cents for each church budget subscriber, thus encouraging the top record in Baptist family coverage, 16,000 in 1955. This is 98 per cent of total family possibility.

The publication varied from 4 to 16 pages until 1941, since which time the 16-page size has been consistently maintained. The paper varied from a monthly to a bimonthly to a weekly, maintaining a weekly basis since 1920. Advertising is restricted to Baptist agencies and to noncommercial, educational items. The annual budget was $30,000 in 1954, subscriptions and advertising amounting to $20,000 annually. Statistical reports indicate that this paper is a Southern leader in circulation coverage.

MRS. RICHARD THOMAS BAKER, SR.

BAPTIST NEWS. A privately owned weekly, established and edited at Du Quoin, Ill., by W. P. Throgmorton (q.v.) from Nov. 16, 1895, to June 14, 1902. Featured serially was an unpublished book of 55 chapters on Illinois Baptist history through 1900 by E. W. Hicks (1841–1919). The paper was consolidated with the *Central Baptist*, St. Louis, Mo. The largest circulation of the *News* was 3,200.

B. J. MURRIE

BAPTIST NEWS, THE. First published in Dec., 1888, at Honey Grove, Tex., by Lewis Holland and John H. Boyet. In Aug., 1889, Boyet sold his interest to Holland. The paper was moved to Dallas; Robert Taylor Hanks bought half interest from Holland in 1890, and the name of the paper was changed to *Western Baptist*.

E. C. ROUTH

BAPTIST OKLAHOMAN. Published in Oklahoma City, Okla., and edited by Adoniram Judson Holt (q.v.). It consisted of 12 or more pages, 8½ x 11 inches, and was adopted as the official organ of the Baptist General Convention of Oklahoma sometime prior to 1911. It no longer exists.

J. M. GASKIN

BAPTIST PIONEER (Negro). A weekly, probably established in the late 1870's. In 1882 the *Baptist Pioneer* was edited at Selma by W. H. McAlpine, president of the Alabama Baptist Normal and Theological School. Associate editors were J. Dozier, Uniontown; Charles O. Boothe, Selma; and Albert Franklyn Owens, Mobile. The *Pioneer* was not only published under the auspices of the theological school but was also intended to be an organ for the Missionary Baptist Convention of Alabama (Negro). Owens was editor in 1884–85.

RAY M. ATCHISON

BAPTIST PRESS. A news gathering and distribution service sponsored by the Executive Committee of the Southern Baptist Convention. It began in 1946 as the Southern Baptist Press Association (SBPA) issued by the Sunday School Board's Department of Survey, Statistics, and Information, Porter Routh, secretary. In 1946, under the leadership of Duke Kimbrough McCall, the Executive Committee assumed responsibility for the Baptist Press and in 1947 elected C. E. Bryant as director of publicity. The Baptist Press has been enlarged to include: a foreign edition, mailed monthly, for Baptist papers outside of the United States; a features section, including articles of general interest for state Baptist papers; and a children's page, which is offered to subscribing state papers for a small fee each week. The director is Albert McClellan, and the editorial assistant is Theo Sommerkamp. The mailing address is 127 Ninth Avenue, North, Nashville, Tenn.

See also PUBLICITY, CHURCH.

ALBERT MCCLELLAN

BAPTIST PRESS, HONG KONG. See HONG KONG-MACAO, MISSION IN.

BAPTIST PROGRAM, THE. A magazine first published by the Commission on 1925 Program of Southern Baptists. The earliest copy now known to be in existence is dated Jan. 22, 1925. It is believed that this is the first printed. Ownership was transferred to the Executive Committee of the Southern Baptist Convention in 1927. In 1931 the name was changed to the *Every Member Canvass* when ownership of the paper was assumed by the Promotion Committee of the Southern Baptist Convention. The name was changed back to *The Baptist Program* with the issue of Apr. 15, 1932, ownership having been reassumed by the Executive Committee with the dissolution of the Promotion Committee and the assumption of its work by the Executive Committee. The following men have served as editors: Frank E. Burkhalter, 1925–30; Walter M. Gilmore, 1930–47; C. E. Bryant, 1947–49; Albert McClellan, 1949– . *The Baptist Program* is exclusively for pastors, state workers, educational workers, and others who are employed by the churches or the denomination. It publishes only that which is in harmony with the adopted program of Southern Baptists. Monthly circulation is 30,000. The mailing address is 127 Ninth Avenue, North, Nashville, Tenn.

ALBERT MCCLELLAN

BAPTIST RECORD. The official journal of the Mississippi Baptist convention since Jan. 1, 1919, when the convention purchased the paper for $8,800. The paper then became the sole convention-sponsored successor of a series of Baptist papers that had existed, beginning in 1836, some of convention sponsorship. Plautus Iberus Lipsey (*q.v.*) was editor upon its purchase in 1919 and served until his retirement in 1941. He was succeeded by A. L. Goodrich, who served until his death in 1956. W. C. Fields was elected to succeed him.

The *Baptist Record* had its origin in Clinton in Feb., 1877, when it began publication under convention sponsorship with James Bruton Gambrell (*q.v.*) as editor and M. Thomas Martin (*q.v.*) as business manager. In 1879 it was moved to Jackson, and by 1887 it was in private hands. It was consolidated with the *Southern Baptist* at Meridian in 1887 as *Southern Baptist Record*. In Jan., 1888, J. A. Hackett became managing editor, and he became sole editor when Gambrell resigned. In 1890 the *Mississippi Baptist*, official journal of the General Association of Southeast Mississippi with Nathan Lytle Clarke as editor, entered the field with headquarters at Newton. It was published until 1927.

In 1890 the *Baptist Layman,* a monthly publication consisting mostly of clippings from other papers, made its appearance in Winona with W. O. Hurt as editor. In 1894 T. J. Bailey, Winona pastor, became editor. By 1898 it had become a weekly with J. L. Johnson, Sr., as editor.

As a result of the demand for one state Baptist paper, the Mississippi Baptist Publishing Company, a stock company with a capital of $10,000, was formed with the endorsement of the 1898 convention. This company purchased the *Southern Baptist Record* and the *Layman* and consolidated them into a paper called *The Baptist,* which was in reality a continuation of the original *Baptist Record*. James Bryant Searcy (*q.v.*) was editor, and T. J. Bailey, business manager. Searcy was editor only a short time, succeeded by Bailey, who served until 1912. In 1906 the original name of *Baptist Record* was restored.

By Oct., 1956, the circulation was 89,282, having increased from 4,001 in 1941. This large increase was due to emphasis on the every-family plan, a budget plan in which the *Record* is sent to every family of the local church, and the church pays monthly. More than 1,100 churches use this plan. In 1956 the paper was converted from the conventional tabloid form to an eight-page, seven-column newspaper.

The *Baptist Record* is operated by the Mississippi Baptist convention board. The board elects all personnel annually, including the editor. The convention annually elects a *Bap-*

tist *Record* advisory committee, which advises on editorial matters with the editor upon his request.

The paper is supported by subscription fees and advertising. Any and all earnings are turned back into the work of the denomination. It receives no subsidy or allocations from the convention board. All monies received by the *Baptist Record* bookkeeper are turned over to the convention board bookkeeper, who pays all bills on requisition by proper *Baptist Record* authorities. The paper is printed on contract by a Jackson publishing company and mailed from the Baptist Building in Jackson, where the paper has its headquarters. The paper owns mailing, addressographing, and office equipment valued at $18,927.58.   A. L. GOODRICH

BAPTIST RECORD, THE. A paper published in Luling, Tex., in 1890, with J. B. Hardwicke, editor.   E. C. ROUTH

BAPTIST RECORDER, THE. Published 1825–26 at Bloomfield, Ky. It succeeded *The Baptist Register* of the same city, and in 1830 became *The Baptist Chronicle* and *Georgetown Literary Register,* edited in Georgetown, Ky. George Waller and Spencer Clack were joint editors of *The Baptist Recorder.* Only one copy of this paper is known to be in existence, and that is a photostat.

BIBLIOGRAPHY: G. R. Jewell, "Tabular History of the Western Recorder," *Western Recorder* (Dec. 19, 1935). F. M. Masters, *A History of Baptists in Kentucky* (1953). V. I. Masters, "Facing the Past and the Future at the End of a Century," *Western Recorder* (Dec. 24, 1925). W. D. Nowlin, "The History of the *Western Recorder,*" *Western Recorder* (Dec. 24, 1925). J. H. Spencer, *History of Kentucky Baptists* (1886).   GEORGE RALEIGH JEWELL

BAPTIST REFLECTOR, THE. See AMERICAN BAPTIST REFLECTOR.

BAPTIST REGISTER, THE. Begun at Bloomfield, Ky., by George Waller and Spencer Clack, presumably on Dec. 15, 1825. It probably was the successor to *The Baptist Monitor and Political Compiler,* also of Bloomfield, and was succeeded by *The Baptist Recorder* of Bloomfield. No copies of this paper are known to be in existence.   GEORGE RALEIGH JEWELL

BAPTIST REPORTER. An extinct Georgia Baptist newspaper published at Excelsior, 1886–87, and at Guyton in 1888. J. A. Scarboro was editor of the paper; W. L. Geiger, associate.   JOHN J. HURT, JR.

BAPTIST RIVAL. A weekly newspaper for Negroes, established in 1902, Republican in politics, printed each Friday at $1 per year. Peter Rozena Neil was editor, and Ezell Willie Perry, associate editor during 1908–09. The paper, which had four pages (15 × 22 inches), was finally suspended about 1916.   J. M. GASKIN

BAPTIST SENTINEL, THE. A monthly probably started in Nov., 1869, and edited at Lexington, Ky., by Adolphus Spalding Worrell, editor; D. B. Ray, assistant editor. B. W. Whilden, Marshallville, Ga., and C. E. W. Dobbs, Lexington, Ky., were corresponding editors. Beginning with the Jan., 1871, issue, W. H. Felix, Covington, Ky., was added as a corresponding editor. Some issues are at the Divinity School of the University of Chicago.
   GEORGE RALEIGH JEWELL

BAPTIST SIGNAL. Originated in Ardmore, Indian Territory (Okla.), in 1898. Consisting of eight pages (13 × 20 inches), the paper sold for $1.50 per year. Jesse Mercer Green (*q.v.*) and W. H. Kuykendall were editors and publishers. Later J. M. B. Gresham was editor and manager, and Luman Lucius Smith (*q.v.*) an associate editor. The paper is now extinct.
   J. M. GASKIN

BAPTIST STANDARD. A weekly paper, established by members of the First Baptist Church, Nashville, Tenn., published from Nov. 10, 1858, till Nov. 17, 1860. Its primary purpose was to present the evidence in the trial of James Robinson Graves which resulted in his exclusion Oct. 18, 1858, to reply to his varied and continued attacks upon the church, and to make clear to the public the differences between the church and Graves about church government and the limitations of associations, general associations, and state conventions with reference to the internal affairs of a church. Pastor Howell said: "The church was dumb. It had no medium through which to speak to the public. It was soon perceived that a weekly paper . . . was an imperative necessity." The paper having successfully accomplished its purpose, and Graves's effort to disrupt the Southern Baptist Convention having failed, it ceased publication.

See also GRAVES-HOWELL CONTROVERSY.
   HOMER L. GRICE

BAPTIST STANDARD. Established as a weekly in 1889 by R. T. Hanks, pastor of the First Baptist Church, Dallas. Hanks, who had purchased the subscription list of the extinct *Baptist News,* a publication of the previous year, and used it to gain his first subscribers, called his publication the *Western Baptist.* In 1892 M. V. Smith and James Britton Cranfill (*q.v.*) bought the *Western Baptist,* moved it to Waco, and changed the name to the *Texas Baptist Standard.* With a circulation of 6,000 when Smith and Cranfill bought it, the *Standard* had been created to counteract the influence of S. A. Hayden, editor and publisher of the *Texas Baptist and Herald.* After Smith's death in 1893 and a fire which destroyed offices and printing material in 1894, debts forced Cranfill to seek help. Finally, in 1898 Christopher C. Slaughter (*q.v.*) of Dallas bought half interest in the *Standard* with the provision that the paper move back to Dallas. That same year the publication was incorporated as the Baptist Standard Publishing Company. George W. Carroll purchased a third interest in the paper in 1900, and three years later Slaughter sold out to Cranfill who divided with Carroll, giving both equal shares. In 1904 Carroll became sole owner and named J. H. Gambrell as editor.

After five years in which the paper changed hands several times, stability came in 1909 when George Washington Truett (q.v.), H. Z. Duke, James Bruton Gambrell (q.v.), Charles D. Fine, and Robert Cooke Buckner (q.v.) bought the publication. Robert Henry Coleman (q.v.) was named business manager, and J. B. Gambrell (brother of J. H.) became editor. Under this ownership the paper was freed of a $30,000 debt and given to the convention in Mar., 1914. Eugene Coke Routh, who had been associate editor for three years, became editor. When the *Standard* assumed management of the Baptist Book Store in Dallas in 1919, however, it began a period of indebtedness which grew worse until 1925 when the book store was transferred to the Sunday School Board in Nashville, Tenn., and the Texas executive board. Circulation of the paper at that time was about 20,000, and the debt was more than $30,000.

With Routh's resignation in 1927 F. M. McConnell (q.v.) was named editor, and although circulation slowly increased, the paper operated with almost a yearly deficit until 1934 when denominational agencies began to share in the expense of publicizing the work. In 1937 the Texas convention gave the publication $79,249.75, which erased all debt, and the corporation has operated debt free ever since. Circulation in 1942 increased from 51,000 to 72,056. Seventeen district pages, each edited by a district missionary and circulated only within the missionary's district, were started in 1942, and 37 new local church pages more than doubled the former number. The year before, Southern Baptists had established a committee to increase circulation of state papers.

Following McConnell's retirement in 1944 when circulation of the *Standard* had grown to 110,000, David M. Gardner was elected editor. In every year of his editorship circulation increased and finances improved.

Circulation at the close of 1954 was 286,854, and more than 2,300 of the state's churches were subscribing for every family. A board of directors, appointed by the Texas General Convention, which owns the paper, elects the editor annually. The convention allotted $11,000 to the paper in 1954 through the Cooperative Program, approximately 4 per cent of its operating costs. The paper operates independently of other agencies, committees, or institutions, even in financial matters, and is housed in its own building, a large two-story brick structure in the heart of Dallas. The *Standard* has a complete microfilm file of all back issues, including much of the *Texas Baptist and Herald* but not the *Western Baptist*.

BIBLIOGRAPHY: J. M. Carroll, *A History of Texas Baptists* (1923). J. B. Link, *Texas Historical and Biographical Magazine*, Vol. II (1892). B. F. Riley, *History of the Baptists of Texas* (1907).

WALKER L. KNIGHT

BAPTIST STUDENT, THE. A magazine issued monthly, except July-September, by the Sunday School Board of the Southern Baptist Convention to promote the spiritual growth of Baptist students and the work of the Baptist Student Union on campuses served by Southern Baptists. It was first issued Sept., 1922. The magazine contains news articles on student life and treatments of live issues and current student problems. In 1956 the circulation was 19,300.

G. KEARNIE KEEGAN

BAPTIST STUDENT UNION. A name adopted at Palacios, Tex., in 1920 and applied to the movement which since has become the college or university student organization of Southern Baptists. The movement had beginnings in small sporadic organizations on Southern campuses. As early as 1905, a group of Baylor University students were "praying definitely" that Texas Baptists might assume responsibility for a religious program for their students. Later, in 1914, the Home Mission Board launched the Baptist Student Missionary Movement in Fort Worth, Tex., which was to promote the study of missions among students. By 1919 Texas Baptists had become interested enough to authorize the employment of a state student secretary; Joseph P. Boone was elected. In 1921 the movement became Convention-wide in scope and acquired official status through the authorization by the Southern Baptist Convention of an Inter-Board Commission to direct the work. After laying the foundations for the movement, the Inter-Board Commission at the suggestion of the Southern Baptist Convention transferred its responsibilities to the Sunday School Board.

Under the leadership of Frank Hartwell Leavell (q.v.) and his successor Gilbert Kearnie Keegan, the Student Department of the Sunday School Board developed a complex program of activities. Leavell has defined the Baptist Student Union as "the connecting link between the college and the local church in the college center. . . . It keeps before the student the objectives and activities of the church . . . [and] is a recruiting and training activity for local churches" and the denomination.

The B.S.U. program includes many emphases and activities. Students are encouraged to join the local church while at college and participate in its program, reaping the values which can come only through a normal church life. Campus devotional emphases, including the prayermate movement and individual and group Bible study and worship, offer opportunities for spiritual development. Personal evangelism is stressed and training offered. Focus weeks are designed to help students understand their religion in the context of contemporary world thought and action and relate their faith to the whole of life. Mission programs provide knowledge of world need, give opportunity to share in special student mission projects, and inspire students to life commitment. Periodic conventions and retreats offer information, inspiration, and fellowship which challenge to maximum Christian living. These and many other emphases seek to lead the Baptist student in a maturing Christian experience to the end that he becomes an increasingly effective witness for Christ in his church and in every area of his life. G. KEARNIE KEEGAN

BAPTIST SUN. A mediocre newspaper of north Georgia, published at Gainesville in 1877-78, edited by J. A. Scarboro.
JOHN J. HURT, JR.

BAPTIST TELEGRAPH AND FLORIDA EMIGRANT. A newspaper founded by James McDonald in 1848 and published in Jacksonville, Fla. Insufficient finances forced its suspension after a few years. W. G. STRACENER

BAPTIST TELESCOPE. A paper founded by W. A. G. Brown, edited by N. Bowen, 1859-60 and 1881-83. After Bowen's death in 1884, Joseph E. Carter became editor and changed the name of the paper to *Western North Carolina Baptist*. L. L. CARPENTER

BAPTIST TRAINING UNION. The term used to designate the training organization in Southern Baptist churches. It is the part of the educational program conducted by a church on Sunday evening in the period before the preaching service. It is organized, controlled, operated, and co-ordinated with the total educational program by the church.

Membership.—All of the members of a Baptist church, and members of their families who are not Christians, are invited to be members of the Training Union. Baptist church members are classified as active members, and all others are classified as associate members.

Aim and objectives.—The aim of the Training Union is training in church membership. Its objectives are: (1) to increase spirituality; (2) to stimulate growth in Christian character, attitudes, and skills; (3) to give a working knowledge of the Bible; (4) to educate in Baptist life, including distinctive doctrines; (5) to cultivate the Baptist spirit; (6) to encourage participation in the Baptist program in church and denomination; (7) to increase understanding of and Christian behavior in the world situation in all areas of human endeavor.

Grading.—The Training Union is graded on the same lines as the Sunday school from Nursery children through Adults, ranging from single units for each age group in small churches to multiple departments in large churches.

Organization.—The general and department officers, leaders, associate leaders, sponsors, and counselors are elected by the church, and some union officers are approved by the church. The guide for organization, meetings, and activities is the Standard of Excellence.

Method.—The method of training in this organization is individual participation in all of the studies and activities. In the Nursery, Beginner, and Primary departments, learning situations based on life experiences of the children are created so that the children may participate normally in the informal teaching procedure. In all other departments the members take part in the studies, discussions in the meetings, daily Bible reading and prayer, group worship, giving to the church, the work of officers and committees, visitation, social life, and missionary activity, because these are the things in which church members participate in normal church life.

Curriculum materials.—The curriculum materials of the Training Union are published by the Sunday School Board of the Southern Baptist Convention. They consist of graded lesson courses; a Daily Bible Reader's Course with suggestions for daily prayer and a prayer calendar of home and foreign missionaries; and a graded textbook study course. There are more than 75 (1956) books in the textbook study course. These are arranged under 10 subjects in each department as follows: principles and methods, the church, the Christian life, the Bible, doctrine, the home, missions, stewardship, soul-winning, and the denomination. These courses are taught in special five-night training schools, usually Monday through Friday.

The periodical publications (fourth quarter, 1956) used by the Baptist Training Union are as follows: *The Baptist Training Union Magazine; The Nursery-Beginner Leader; Every Day with Nursery Children;* Teaching Pictures for Nursery Children; *Every Day with Beginners;* Teaching Pictures for Beginners; *The Primary Leader; Every Day with Primaries;* Teaching Pictures for Primaries; *The Junior Leader; Baptist Junior Union Quarterly I; Baptist Junior Union Quarterly II; The Intermediate Leader; Baptist Intermediate Union Quarterly I; Baptist Intermediate Union Quarterly II; Baptist Young People; Baptist Married Young People; Baptist Young Adults; Baptist Adults; The Bible Reader's Guide and Missionary Prayer Calendar.*

Supplementary materials for the curriculum are published in *The Baptist Training Union Magazine.* These include assembly programs, materials for the recreational program, helps for the associational organization, and helps for all officers of the Training Union.

Special projects.—Youth Week is sponsored annually in Baptist churches by the Training Union. This comes usually in the first week of April. It is a project in which all of the places of leadership in the church are assigned by the church for one full week to the older Intermediates and Young People. For several weeks

Baptist Training Union Magazine

in advance they are given special training for this project. Baptist Youth Night on the associational level is sponsored on Saturday evening at the close of Youth Week. Christian Home Week is sponsored by the Training Union, in co-operation with the Sunday school. It begins on the first Sunday in May and closes on Mother's Day. The Training Union Department of the Sunday School Board originated the idea for this week in 1939. An orientation course for new church members, *Your Life and Your Church,* is sponsored. "M" Night, on the first Monday in December, is a special project on the associational level for launching the Training Union program for the ensuing year.

Associational and state organizations.—The associational Training Union is the district associational organization for helping the churches to establish and maintain Training Unions. State Training Union conventions and assemblies have the same purpose on the state level.

Convention-wide assemblies.—The Training Union Department of the Sunday School Board conducts two Convention-wide leadership assemblies, one at Glorieta, N. M., and the other at Ridgecrest, N. C. Three weeks are devoted to each of these assemblies. Each week has a complete program. The work of the Training Union and of the whole denomination is sponsored in these assemblies.

Origin and development of the Baptist Training Union.—It developed from Baptist Young People's Union which was for young people 17 years of age and above. Its first paper was the *Young People's Leader,* published from 1894–1900. *The B.Y.P.U. Quarterly* appeared in 1900. In the fourth quarter of 1908 the Sunday School Board published the first issue of *The Junior B.Y.P.U. Quarterly* for ages 13 through 16. This indicated that the Baptist Young People's Union had been graded into two units, the Senior B.Y.P.U. and the Junior B.Y.P.U. With this arrangement the work expanded rapidly, but usually there were only two organizations in a church. Then in 1914 the group plan of organization was put into the *B.Y.P.U. Manual.* This led to multiple unions in a church. During the period from 1914 to 1920, some large churches employed Baptist Young People's Union directors to supervise the work. From 1918 to 1921, a further step in grading took place. A union was set up for the real Juniors, ages 9 through 12, so that the old Junior union was reclassified as the Intermediate Baptist Young People's Union. The Sunday School Board responded by publishing graded literature for these three departments. During the period from 1920 to 1925, it became obvious that the churches needed general officers to develop, expand, direct, and supervise this work of training in church membership. This led to the organization of all the unions in a church into the general B.Y.P.U. organization. The Baptist Sunday School Board published *A General B.Y.P.U. Organization* by Jerry Elmer Lambdin in 1925. This was a manual or handbook for general B.Y.P.U. officers.

The Baptist Adult union and the Children's Story Hour for children below the Junior department emerged in the decade 1920–30. The Sunday School Board studied this movement carefully and issued a lesson course for adults in 1929. This course was published during that year in *The Monthly B.Y.P.U. Magazine. The Baptist Adult Union Quarterly* was issued in the first quarter of 1930. The first materials for the weekly meeting of the Children's Story Hour, under the title, "The Bible Story Hour," were published in the graded Sunday school periodicals; *Graded Bible Lessons, Teacher's Textbook,* and *Graded Bible Lessons for Primary Pupils.* This was not found to be satisfactory, so it was discontinued in 1935. From 1935 to 1937, materials for the Children's Story Hour were published in *The Baptist Training Union Magazine. The Story Hour Leader* was issued in 1937. It was succeeded in 1950 by *The Primary Leader* and *The Nursery-Beginner Leader.* Complete sets of materials for the Nursery, Beginner, and Primary departments are now available for the children and for the leaders.

Upon the recommendation of Lambdin, secretary of the B.Y.P.U. Department, the name Baptist Training Union was adopted by the Sunday School Board, June, 1934, and was recommended to all of the states, associations, and churches. It was universally adopted before the end of that year.

As of 1955, 21,217 churches in the Southern Baptist Convention had a Training Union, with a combined enrolment of 2,223,502.

J. E. LAMBDIN

BAPTIST TRAINING UNION MAGAZINE, THE. A monthly magazine published by the Sunday School Board of the Southern Baptist Convention. First published as *The B.Y.P.U. Magazine* in July, 1926, the name was changed to *The Baptist Training Union Magazine* in 1935. Its chief purpose is to provide resource and guidance materials for Training Union workers. Its contents include general articles and helps on all phases of Training Union work. These helps take the form of equipment suggestions, educational procedures, assembly programs for departments, Bible drills, suggestions for building and presenting programs, socials, how-to-do-it suggestions for officers and committees, and associational programs. The circulation in 1956 was 291,011.

J. E. LAMBDIN

BAPTIST TRIBUNE. Published in Dallas, Tex., owned by James Britton Cranfill (*q.v.*). The *West Texas Baptist* and the *Southern Baptist,* purchased by the *Baptist Tribune* in 1905 and 1906 respectively, were both merged with it. In Apr., 1907, the *Baptist Tribune* was sold to the *Baptist Standard.*

E. C. ROUTH

BAPTIST UNION INSTITUTE. Established at Glennville, Ga., in 1890, fostered by

Baptist Union Association. It existed until about 1910.
ARTHUR JACKSON

BAPTIST WATCHMAN. Founded at South McAlester, Indian Territory (Okla.), in 1893. With eight pages, 13 × 22 inches, it sold for $1.50 per year and was issued each Thursday. In 1893 it merged with *The Indian Missionary* and continued as the official organ of the Baptist Missionary and Educational Convention of Indian Territory, a relationship formerly sustained by the *Missionary*. The convention reported final suspension of the paper in 1894.
J. M. GASKIN

BAPTIST WATCHMAN, THE. A weekly newspaper, now extinct, published at Knoxville, Tenn., 1855–59, and edited by Matthew Hillsman.
LYNN E. MAY, JR.

BAPTIST WORKER. Founded and edited by Alonzo Nunnery, it was issued bimonthly at Mangum, Okla., beginning in 1909. On July 13, 1910, it was changed to a weekly, and in 1911 it was moved to Granite, Okla. From Jan. 26, 1921, until publication was suspended in Nov., 1939, it was published at Chickasha, Okla. The only surviving institution of the A. Nunnery Movement in Oklahoma, The *Worker* was no longer issued after the passing of its editor Sept. 24, 1939.

BIBLIOGRAPHY: R. D. Hebard, "The A. Nunnery Movement in Oklahoma" (Thesis, Southwestern Baptist Seminary, 1944).
J. M. GASKIN

BAPTIST WORKMAN. A New Mexico paper published at Roswell in the period 1905–06. Edited by Henry F. Vermillion, it became extinct in 1906.
MRS. RICHARD THOMAS BAKER, SR.

BAPTIST WORLD, THE. Published from 1908 to 1919 at Louisville, Ky. It was a continuation of *The Baptist Argus* and was merged with *The Western Recorder* and *The Kentucky Mission Monthly* in 1919. It is now being continued under the name of *The Western Recorder*. A complete file is in the library of Southern Baptist Theological Seminary.
GEORGE RALEIGH JEWELL

BAPTIST WORLD ALLIANCE. A fellowship comprehending all national or regional organizations of Baptists who desire to co-operate with it, established to disseminate information, provide the basis for worldwide communion, and function when necessary as a means for the expression of concerted opinion. The Alliance will be treated under seven heads: definition, preparation, organization, history, work, results, and status.

Definition.—This world organization of Baptists is only in a very limited sense an alliance. A more accurate title would be "The Baptist World Fellowship." What it always has been and is has been too generally misunderstood, because the average person has thought of it in terms that its official name connotes. Its founders had no thought of setting up an administrative or legislative Baptist body. The Alliance has always regarded such matters as the exclusive and rightful responsibility of the several Baptist bodies of the national and/or regional conventions throughout the world. The missionary, benevolent, and educational work of these respective Baptist bodies is exclusively their responsibility, and the Alliance in no respect is concerned with it.

The basic organizational foundation of every Baptist body is that it is composed of members whom it has chosen to constitute its membership. From the beginning the Baptist World Alliance has been an organized *fellowship,* dedicated to the emphasis of the essential oneness in Jesus Christ as the Saviour and Lord of the Baptist peoples of the earth. As such it has recognized all organized Baptist bodies that have in their fellowship churches, associations, societies, unions, conventions, etc., and that desire association with other such Baptists in a world fellowship.

Throughout the years, without variation, the sessions of the Alliance have been called congresses. These congresses have been composed of Baptists of all nations. They rely upon the executive committee of the Alliance to provide a fitting program of inspiration and information. No individual or group is bound by any pronouncement of the Alliance. Keeping in mind the original purpose of the Alliance, that of fellowship and a common witness to the saviourhood and lordship of Jesus Christ, the addresses, resolutions, and suggestions are, therefore, the responsibility of the speaker or commission offering such proposal. There are many Baptists who would like to see more democracy in the Alliance, by which they mean more opportunity for expression from the floor in all the procedures of the Alliance. However, from the beginning its constitution and bylaws have provided for practically every action to be taken within the executive committee, including the naming of all committees, the making of programs, the setting up of the executive staff, the making of budgets, etc. All such matters are delegated by the constitution and bylaws to the executive committee. It should be said that the membership of the executive committee is excellently representative of the Baptists of the various conventions, etc., and that the first 50 years of the life of the Baptist World Alliance have shown it to be purely a fellowship conference of the Baptist peoples of the earth. As such it has proved to be of satisfying value and especially rewarding to the Baptists whose life and work are spent in areas where they are overshadowed by a state church or non-Christian religions.

Preparation.—About 1678, a 17th century General Baptist in England, Thomas Grantham, is quoted as saying: "I could wish that all congregations of Christians of the world that are baptized according to the appointment of Christ would make one consistory at least sometimes to consider matters of difference among them." In 1790 John Rippon, a well-known British Baptist preacher and hymn writer and editor of *The Baptist Annual Register,* wrote an editorial in which he said:

To all the baptized ministers and people in America, England, Ireland, Scotland, Wales, the United Netherlands, France, Switzerland, Poland, Russia, and elsewhere, with a desire of promoting a universal interchange of kind offices among them, and in serious expectation that before many years elapse (in imitation of other wise men) a deputation from all these climes will meet probably in London to consult the ecclesiastical good of the whole, which is now submitted to their superior wisdom.

Two years after Rippon published that editorial suggesting a world organization of Baptists, William Carey sailed for India. Twenty-three years later, the conversion of Adoniram Judson and Luther Rice to Baptist beliefs and practices vitally extended the orbit of Baptist interest. The dream first manifest in Grantham, repeated in Rippon, had its stirrings in other hearts, but never came to effective focus until 1904, when John Newton Prestridge (*q.v.*), editor of *The Baptist Argus,* Louisville, Ky., later named *The Baptist World,* blew the trumpet call for its creation. He was quickly joined by Archibald Thomas Robertson (*q.v.*), of the Southern Baptist Theological Seminary; Robert H. Pitt (*q.v.*), editor of *The Religious Herald,* Richmond, Va.; and William Warren Landrum, pastor of the First Baptist Church, Atlanta, Ga. John Howard Shakespeare, editor of *The Baptist Times and Freeman,* London, quickly caught the significance of the proposal made by his American brethren and gave it his hearty endorsement. He, with John Clifford, Alexander Maclaren (*q.v.*), and other British leaders, in Oct., 1904, extended to the Baptists of the world the invitation to meet in London in July, 1905, in co-operation with the Baptist Union of Great Britain and Ireland. Baptists in 23 nations responded to the invitation. Among them were 50 Negroes from the United States. The first world gathering of Baptists became an accomplished fact in Exeter Hall, London, July 11-18, 1905.

Organization.—The Baptist World Alliance was wellborn under happy auspices. British Baptists, with world approval, designated the greatest Baptist expository preacher of the last three centuries, Alexander Maclaren of Manchester, to serve as a provisional president to preside over the first session. While the program was in progress they appointed a representative committee to recommend a plan of organization, a procedure for future congresses, and to develop a constitution and bylaws. Their report was adopted on Monday, July 17. It contained the following:

Whereas, in the providence of God, the time has come when it seems fitting more fully to manifest the essential oneness in the Lord Jesus Christ as their God and Saviour of the Churches of the Baptist order and faith throughout the service and co-operation among them, while recognizing the independence of each particular church and not assuming the functions of any existing organization, it is agreed to form a Baptist World Alliance, extending over every part of the world.

ARTICLES

1. Designation. This Alliance shall be known as "The Baptist World Alliance."
2. Membership. Any general Union, Convention or Association of Baptist churches shall be eligible for membership in the Alliance.
3. Officers. The Officers of the Alliance shall be: a President, a Vice-President from each country represented in the Alliance, a Treasurer, a British Secretary and an American Secretary.
4. The Executive Committee. The Executive Committee shall consist of the President, Treasurer, Secretaries and twenty-one other members, all of whom, together with the officers, shall be elected at each General Meeting of the Alliance and enter upon office at the close of each meeting.
5. Powers of Executive. The Executive Committee shall have the power of filling up vacancies which may occur among the officers and the Executive when the Assembly is not in session. It shall be the first business of the Executive Committee, after its appointment, and the forming of this Alliance, to frame the by-laws for the administration of business.
6. General Meeting. The Alliance shall meet in general assembly ordinarily once in five years, unless otherwise determined by the Executive Committee, the specific date and place to be determined by the Executive Committee, which shall have power to make all necessary arrangements therefor.

This basic original preamble and constitution in a half century has experienced no radical changes but shows some growth. After the changes of 1955 it reads:

The Baptist World Alliance, extending over every part of the world, exists in order more fully to show the essential oneness of Baptist people in the Lord Jesus Christ, to impart inspiration to the brotherhood, and to promote the spirit of fellowship, service and co-operation among its members; but this Alliance may in no way interfere with the independence of the churches or assume the administrative functions of existing organizations.

I. NAME

This organization shall be known as the Baptist World Alliance.

II. NATURE AND FUNCTIONS

Serving as the nerve center and corporate will of Baptists throughout the world the Alliance shall:
(1) Have as one of its primary purposes the safeguarding and maintenance of full religious liberty everywhere, not only for our own constituent churches, but also for all other religious faiths.
(2) Serve as an agency for propagating Baptist principles and tenets of faith, objectives and distinctive principles throughout the world.
(3) Serve as an agency to make surveys throughout the world with a view to furnishing facts to the various Baptist groups and counselling with them in establishing work in new fields when such service is requested.

(4) Serve as a world-wide agency in making such use of the radio and press as may be practicable in preaching the Gospel, propagating Baptist principles, and promoting common tasks of Baptists throughout the world.

(5) Arrange and conduct preaching missions throughout the world.

(6) Co-operate with Baptist groups in instituting and administering relief funds as occasion may require.

(7) Gather news by means of correspondents in the various Baptist groups, and disseminate it by use of bulletins, Baptist and other papers, and radio; and, when feasible, by a Baptist world publication.

In ministering in any one or all of these fields of service, the Baptist World Alliance shall limit its activities strictly within its annual budget.

III. Membership

Any general Union, Convention, or Association of Baptist churches, or general Foreign Baptist Missionary Society, or Conference of Baptist churches on a mission field, which is not already an integral part of a Convention, shall be eligible for membership in the Alliance subject to the approval of the Executive Committee.

IV. Officers

The officers of the Alliance shall be the President, nine Vice-Presidents, a General Secretary, with such other Secretaries as the Executive Committee may deem desirable, and two Treasurers (Eastern and Western Hemispheres).

The Baptist World Alliance in General Meeting shall elect the above-mentioned officers upon the nomination of the Nominating Committee. Nominations from the floor of the General Meeting for any of the foregoing officers may also be in order. If found desirable the General Meeting may refer the election of the Secretaries and Treasurers to the Executive Committee.

In the event of the death of any Secretary or Treasurer, or their failure to act, the Administrative Committee shall nominate name or names to the Executive Committee as successors. The election is to be made at the next meeting of the Executive Committee, but in cases of extreme emergency may be held by mail.

V. Executive Committee

The Executive Committee shall consist of the Officers of the Alliance, Past Presidents, Past General Secretaries, and thirty-nine other members who shall be elected at the General Meeting of the Alliance, and shall enter on office at the close of such meeting. These thirty-nine shall represent all six continents as provided in the By-laws, due consideration being given to the geographical distribution of Vice-Presidents and Treasurers. The Executive Committee shall also have power to co-opt not more than nine additional members. The Women's Department and the Youth Department shall each nominate two members to the executive.

VI. Functions of the Executive Committee

It shall be the function of the Executive Committee:

(1) To transact the business of the Alliance between General Meetings, and to supervise the administration of any undertaking projected by the Alliance.

(2) To appoint an Administrative Sub-Committee as indicated in VII below, and to appoint such standing or special committees as it may deem necessary, and to determine their duties.

(3) To arrange local, regional, continental or other conferences as may be considered desirable.

(4) To fill vacancies in the offices and in the committees of the Alliance.

(5) To fix the time and place of the General Meeting of the Alliance, unless these have been determined by the Alliance in General Meeting, and to make all necessary arrangements therefor, including the preparation of the program.

(6) To nominate for appointment by the Alliance in General Meeting, a Nominating Committee, a Business Committee, a Resolutions Committee, and other committees to serve during the sessions of the General Meeting.

VII. Administrative Sub-Committee

The Executive Committee shall appoint from its members an Administrative Sub-Committee of seven including at least one woman. The members of this committee shall reside within reasonable distance of the headquarters city of the Alliance, and serve as an Advisory Committee to the General Secretary, and shall have power to act for the Executive Committee *ad interim* with the understanding that all its actions shall be reported promptly to the members of the Executive Committee.

The President of the Alliance, the General Secretary, the Western Hemisphere Treasurer, and such ex-Presidents and Vice-Presidents as live within reasonable distance from the headquarters of the Alliance shall be *ex-officio* members of the Administrative Sub-Committee.

The Administrative Sub-Committee, in co-operation with the General Secretary and Treasurers, shall be charged with the responsibility of soliciting funds for the support of the Alliance. The sources of income shall be an appropriation by each constituent Convention, Union, or Association within the Alliance, free-will offerings by local churches on Baptist World Alliance Sunday, and voluntary gifts.

The Administrative Sub-Committee, with the General Secretary and Treasurers, shall be charged with the responsibility of submitting each year a proposed budget to the Executive Committee, which committee shall have full authority to act on the budget.

VIII. Meetings

The Alliance shall assemble in General Meeting ordinarily not less than once in five years.

IX. Representation in General Meeting

Each body represented in the Alliance may appoint messengers to the General Meeting on a basis to be determined by the Executive Committee.

X. Amendments

No change shall be made in this Constitution except by a two-thirds majority of those present and voting at a General Meeting after at least two days' notice of the proposed action.

The over-all authority is invested in the executive committee. It meets annually. In 1955 it consisted of 66 members representing 27 countries. The administrative committee composed of 12 members conducts the work of the Alliance under the general plan of operation approved by the executive. Minutes of all the meetings of the administrative committee are

Baptist World Alliance

sent to the executive committee. Sessions of the Alliance are customarily scheduled at five-year intervals, but have several times been canceled or postponed because of war or political unrest.

The Alliance has been fortunate in its leadership, foremost of which always is the president and general secretary. During the interim between meetings, usually they visit all the countries that are related to the Alliance. Many visits are made to deal with particular situations as they develop.

The nine presidents have been: John Clifford, elected 1905; Robert Stuart MacArthur, 1911; Edgar Young Mullins (q.v.), 1923; John MacNeill, 1928; George Washington Truett (q.v.), 1934; James Henry Rushbrooke, 1939; Charles Oscar Johnson, 1947; Fred Townley Lord, 1950; Theodore Floyd Adams, 1955. Until 1928 it was customary to have two secretaries. One, who might be called the senior secretary, lived in London; the other lived in the United States. The secretaries throughout the 50 years have in reality functioned as the executive officers of the Alliance. John Howard Shakespeare served from 1905 until 1925. He was the secretary of the British Baptist Union. With him it was a part-time job, but his service was abundant. His American counterpart was John Newton Prestridge, then Robert H. Pitt, Clifton D. Gray, and Louie DeVotie Newton. In 1924 James Henry Rushbrooke became eastern secretary and served until 1928, when he became the first general secretary. His services to the Alliance were extraordinary. Upon his election to the presidency in 1939, he retired in favor of Walter Oliver Lewis, who served until 1948. Upon his retirement he was succeeded by Arnold Theodore Ohrn, of Norway.

Until 1940 the headquarters were in the Baptist House in London. Due to the constant threat of the destruction of the British Baptist headquarters from the German blitz, early in 1940 Rushbrooke came to the United States with the request of the London committee that the headquarters be temporarily moved to Washington. This transfer was made in 1941. Upon the recommendation of the executive committee, the Copenhagen conference voted in 1947 for permanent transfer. It is now located in the Baptist Building, 1628 Sixteenth St., N. W., Washington, D. C. The Alliance jointly owns this excellent property with the Baptist Convention of the District of Columbia.

History.—The eight volumes of the record of the proceedings of the Baptist World Congress are rich with information concerning Baptist life all over the world for the 50 years from 1905 through 1955. Although the Alliance is a fellowship and not a functioning organization with institutions and programs to promote and large sums of money to be raised and an adequate leadership personnel to train and enlist, it is, nevertheless, an effective organization that has created a striking history. Its history exploits intangible values of rich meaning. One never-to-be-forgotten high light of every program has been the roll call of the nations, when not infrequently high levels of dramatic force are attained by the nationals of that area as they present themselves and their situation in some fashion that conveys to their audience their story while their speaker in a brief response interprets it.

These meetings have furnished a rostrum from which the more able leaders of Baptist people among the nations, in an atmosphere frequently charged with emotion, have delivered sermons, addresses, and pronouncements that have lighted lamps that do not go out in the souls of those who hear them.

The first congress was in London in 1905, when Clifford, Mullins, and Maclaren added new dimensions to the thinking and experience of the Baptists of 23 nations.

The second congress, in Philadelphia in 1911, heard a sermon from Thomas Phillips, of Bloomsbury Baptist Church, London, on "Grace and Glory" that some of his auditors 40 years later described as the most moving message they had ever heard. Notable at that congress was the presence of a large Russian delegation and the spontaneous raising of more than $30,000 to establish a Baptist seminary in Russia.

The Philadelphia congress chose Berlin and 1916 as the next place and time of meeting, but the world was enveloped in World War I, and there could be no meeting until 1923 in Stockholm.

In the 12 years between Philadelphia, in 1911, and Stockholm, in 1923, the world had been convulsed by the catastrophe of World War I. The leadership had grown older. MacArthur had died. Truett was the congress preacher. Mullins' address on "Religious Liberty" stirred the body, in which many were present who had suffered the pains of persecution because this liberty had been denied them. A notable feature of the Stockholm congress was the report of Rushbrooke as Baptist Commissioner for Europe. He had been elected on July 23, 1920, at the postwar London conference of the Baptist World Alliance executive committee and mission board secretaries. The time needed a man like Rushbrooke to be their traveling ambassador to small Baptist groups of the many European countries, and to be willing to press the plea of their world fellowship with the diplomats and state authorities who, because of their disposition or because of pressure from others, laid restrictions upon their freedom to do their work. He was remarkably effective in many countries. His representations and intercession brought helpful relaxation of persecution and pressures. The aged Shakespeare, long the Alliance's influential general secretary, who had largely directed the work of the organization since 1905, of necessity was slowing down. Mullins was elected president.

The fourth congress convened in Toronto, Canada, June 23–29, 1928. President Mullins had suffered a stroke a few days before. By his request Truett read his presidential address and presided at most of the session. The largest attendance of "delegates" and visitors ever recorded until then was present, of whom 4,856 registered as delegates. John MacNeill of Canada was elected president. After the Stockholm meeting Mullins and Rushbrooke had made a world tour, during which they conferred with Baptist leaders and spoke to large audiences in many countries. Among other things, they found a lack of understanding of the functions of the Alliance. This situation prompted Rushbrooke to present a statement to the Toronto congress, setting forth a detailed definition of the Alliance. In answer to those who doubted its permanency or feared its potential power, Rushbrooke said:

> It is as a purely fraternal association, whose members are bound to one another by the silken cords of love, that it holds its place in Baptist life. It stands to refute the idea that only by iron bands of ecclesiastical machinery, by papacy or episcopacy or synod, can Christian men be held together; and by its very existence it demonstrates that with liberty in Christ there can also be full and joyous oneness in Him. Our Alliance is indeed unique in the earth. No formal contract binds us each to each—any one of the constituent groups could secede at any moment; their adhesion is in the strictest sense voluntary. . . . Individualists we are, standing for the supreme value and the solemn and separate responsibility of every human soul; isolated we are not, for in Him we are indissolubly united. The Baptist World Alliance demonstrates that our polity has room for the unforced expression of an inward and spiritual unity which no human scheme can either create or destroy.

Since 1923 Rushbrooke had given his full time to the Alliance. His contributions were of remarkable value. He proved himself to have been a man specially prepared of God for the mission to which his Baptist brethren called him.

The Baptists of Germany first sought, in Philadelphia, to have the Alliance meet in Berlin. The invitation had been accepted for 1916. The date fell in the middle of World War I. This invitation was renewed in Toronto and accepted for 1933. Conditions in Germany under Hitler caused it to be delayed a year, until Aug. 4–10, 1934. President MacNeill's health prevented his attending. His death followed about two years later. Again Truett presided and at its close was elected president. The acute tensions in the country made the situation difficult. In his address of welcome F. W. Simoleit said: "Today, through the grace of God, with joy and gratitude, in the jubilee year of Oncken, Carey and Spurgeon, we greet this glorious assembly in Berlin." German President Hindenburg died the day before the congress opened, and three days later, Adolf Hitler declared himself Führer. In such an atmosphere, Baptists from every part of the world gave their witness to a free church in a free state, and a remarkable local press treatment of the meetings was appreciated by the visitors. Hitler, who had just come into power, asked that a delegation from the congress meet with the Reichsbishop to receive official welcome. Rushbrooke, Truett, Lee Rutland Scarborough (q.v.), Louie DeVotie Newton, Arnold Theodore Ohrn, and several others received that assignment. Rushbrooke, who spoke German fluently, made a notable response to the Reichsbishop, stating frankly and clearly the Baptist position on separation of church and state, the priesthood of the believer, the equality of believers, and the autonomy of the local church.

The sixth congress was held in Atlanta, July 22–29, 1939, with 12,445 registered delegates, and an average attendance at all the sessions of 40,350. At the pageant session 60,100 persons attended by actual count of the automatic gate machines. More than 100,000 persons registered as guests during the sessions. A feature of the Atlanta congress was Truett's presidential address on the Baptist mission and message. Rushbrooke was elected president, succeeding Truett. Walter Oliver Lewis was elected general secretary, succeeding Rushbrooke. Ohrn delivered the congress sermon. President Franklin Delano Roosevelt sent an official welcome from the United States. Broadcasts of the sessions were carried on all American networks, and three broadcasts went to foreign lands. It was the largest and most colorful congress in the history of the Alliance. Fear had been expressed that there might be difficulty with the racial situation, but no major incident occurred, and large numbers of both races attended every session. An invitation to meet in Burma in 1944 was accepted, but World War II intervened.

The seventh congress met in Copenhagen, Denmark, July 29—Aug. 3, 1947. Rushbrooke had died on Feb. 1 that year, and C. J. Tinsley, vice-president, Australia, presided at Copenhagen. The first world gathering of Baptists after World War II, the Copenhagen congress, sought to restore the fellowship of Baptist people. The session proved to be one of the turning points in Baptist world fellowship. Harold C. Phillips of Cleveland delivered the congress sermon on the text: "Other Foundation Can No Man Lay."

C. O. Johnson of St. Louis was elected president. A manifesto on "Religious Freedom" was read by Stanley Stuber, which was unanimously adopted and widely published.

Three years after the Copenhagen congress the Alliance met in Cleveland, Ohio, July 22–27, 1950. Fred Townley Lord, London, was elected president, succeeding Johnson; and Ohrn, who had been made general secretary in 1948, directed the details of the Cleveland congress. Melbourne Evans Aubrey, London, delivered the congress sermon.

So many Baptists wanted to attend the Jubilee (Ninth) Congress in London, July 16–22, 1955, that the attendance had to be limited. It met in Royal Albert Hall with President Lord presiding. Its program was dedicated to a review of the blessings of God upon its ministry, and to a search for understanding of the challenges which the present and the future brought to it. Despite the disasters that two world wars and the communistic revolution had brought, plus the terrible reign of persecution that had beset Baptist people in many lands, the London meeting brought to those who were there, and has been communicated by them to millions, the fact that hitherto the Lord had led them and that their God could be depended upon as they faced a new 50 years. Theodore Floyd Adams was elected president. Joel Sorenson of Sweden, who had served as youth secretary since 1948, resigned. Robert Stanley Denny was elected associate secretary for youth work, his office to be in the Alliance headquarters in Washington. Ohrn continued as general secretary. The Women's Committee and the Youth Committee were changed to departments at the London congress, with Mrs. George Martin as the head of the women's work and Sorenson, head of youth activities.

Work.—From the beginning the work of the Baptist World Alliance has been financed by a budget provided by the conventions, unions, and associations of the co-operating Baptist groups. At the first the Baptist Union of Great Britain and Ireland contributed the largest single amount to the budget of the Alliance. With the coming of World War I, the source of financial support steadily shifted to the United States, with the Southern Baptist Convention and the Northern Baptist Convention assuming the major share of the Alliance budget which for 1956 was $57,000. Of this amount, the Southern Baptist Convention gave $30,000; the American Baptist Convention, $15,000; other conventions, $6,000; Baptist World Alliance Sunday and other gifts, $5,000; and miscellaneous, $1,000.

In addition to the staff and headquarters in Washington, a London office is maintained in the Baptist Church House, 4 Southampton Row, WC1. An associate secretary is in charge of this office. Henry Cook has served as interim active secretary there since the London congress in 1955. The London office is maintained by the Alliance budget. Contributions from British Baptists and the continental groups are received and administered in the London office.

A vital part of the work of the Alliance organization is to keep various Baptist groups in the world informed about each other. The extent to which this can be done is limited, but what is done is highly valuable. Since Jan., 1954, the monthly news bulletin, *The Baptist World*, has been published to provide the constituency of the Alliance with needed information.

In the interim between the meetings of the congress, the tours of the president and the general secretary are scheduled to enable them to attend some of the meetings of nearly all of its co-operating bodies. Their messages and personal contacts serve to stimulate the desired sense of world Baptist fellowship. Special crises develop that call for special activity on the part of the officers and sometimes of the executive. When the area to be covered, the number of people to be served, the small budget, and few workers are considered, a large amount is accomplished.

In 1940, under the pressure of circumstances created for the British Baptist Missionary Society because of World War II, Rushbrooke presented the Southern Baptist Convention a request for a loan of $150,000 with which to sustain them in that emergency crisis. Southern Baptists considered the request and decided with hearty unanimity to grant the request as a gift and not as a loan.

Results.—The results of the ministry of the Baptist World Alliance are principally intangible but richly valuable. It has brought to small minority groups, giving their testimony in the face of overwhelming odds, the consciousness that 300 years ago all Baptists were worse off than they are; that in these centuries in some nations Baptists have become strong, free, respected, and numerous, with great institutions and facilities for services; and that they, by being faithful to the same Christ, are opening the door for their children to attain the realizations that others have reached whose forebears began earlier. To Baptists more privileged, the Alliance furnishes the knowledge of needs and opportunities. This awakens them to greater effort.

While Baptists all have many areas of unity of faith and practice particularly in the essential distinctives, their fellowship in the Baptist World Alliance has brought them a consciousness of differences that are secondary and are not a test of fellowship. These differences largely are the result of the cultural backgrounds from which the various national groups have come, or they are the variations in human interpretation of the same sources.

In 1905, when the Alliance was founded, there were approximately 6,000,000 Baptists in the world. In 1955, when the Jubilee Congress met in London, there were 20,693,358 Baptists in the world, as follows: Europe, 1,106,154; Asia, 642,157; Australia and Oceania, 45,345; Central America and West Indies, 98,437; South America, 132,345; North America, 18,447,012.

Status.—Fifty years of history have brought to the Baptist World Alliance its cordial acceptance as an institution for effective world fellowship for Baptists. Thousands of national leaders have attended one or more meetings. Its representatives have been heard by audiences in whatever countries Baptists are to be found. The ability and wisdom of its presidents, secretaries, and executive committee members through 50 years have earned a good report and created such reservoirs of good will, confidence, and appreciation in the hearts of the Baptists of the world that the ministry of the Alliance should continually accelerate in fruitfulness through the years ahead.

CONNIE MAXWELL CHILDREN'S HOME (q.v.), Greenwood, S. C.
Top: Two of the 19 children's cottages. Center: Bailey Administration Building, built in 1955 for $84,000.
Bottom: Jeanette Murdoch Cottage, named for staff member who served for more than 50 years. The campus has 100 acres.

MISSISSIPPI BAPTIST CHILDREN'S HOME (q.v.). Established in 1864, now located at Jackson. It annually serves 175 children on a 100 acre campus with 17 buildings valued at $1,017,215.

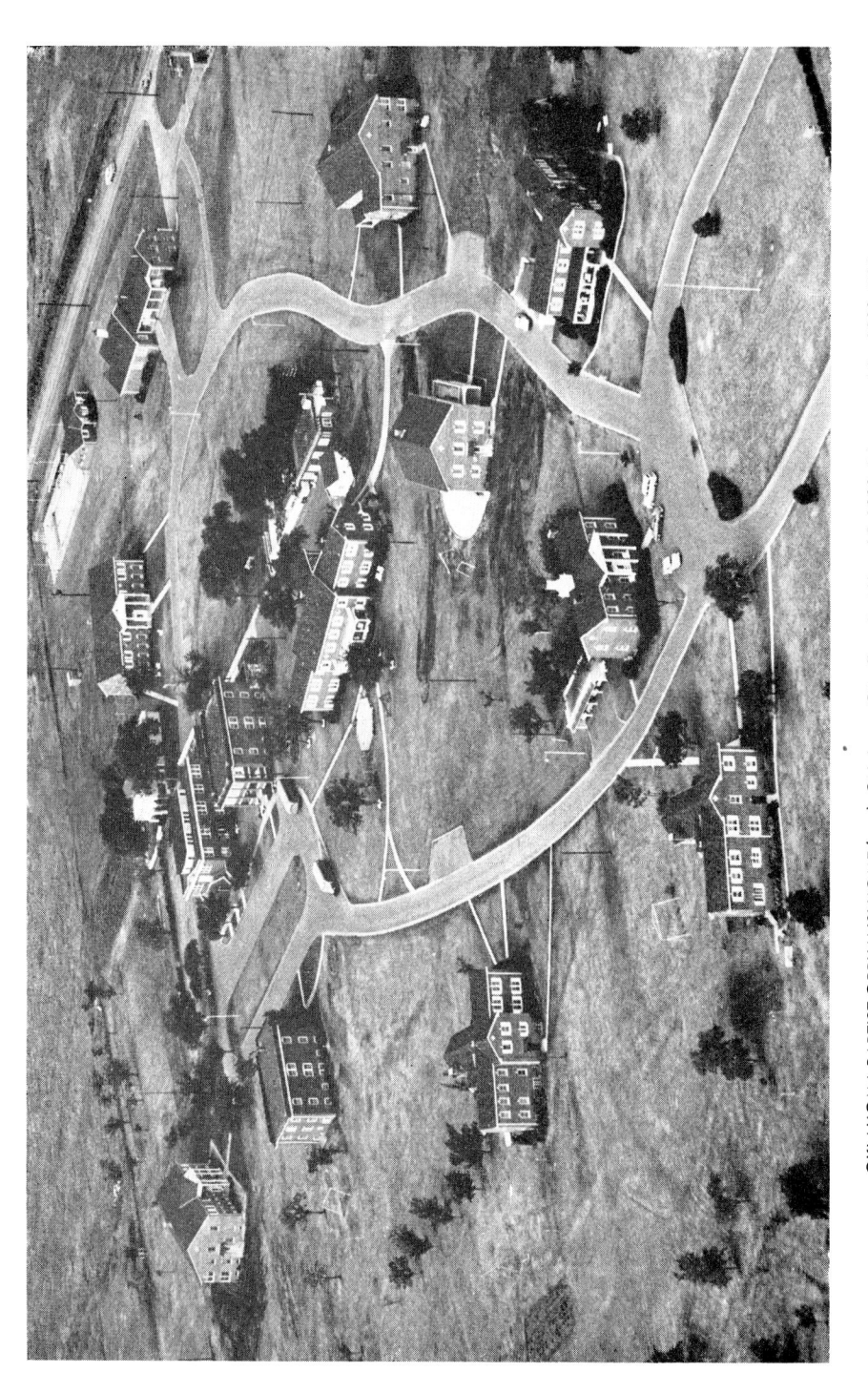

OKLAHOMA BAPTIST ORPHANS' HOME (q.v.), Oklahoma City. Founded Mar. 15, 1903. It has cared for 1800 children in 53 years and serves 215 children annually on a 40-acre campus and an 800-acre farm valued at $1,500,000.

TEXAS CHILDREN'S HOMES. Top: Administration building, Mexican Baptist Home, San Antonio, has a capacity of 96. Second: Chapel, Texas Baptist Children's Home, Round Rock, has a capacity of 180. Third: Maris Welcome Center, Buckner Orphans' Home, Dallas, organized in 1879, facilities for 700. Bottom: Cottage on campus of South Texas Home, Beeville, accommodations for 48. Total investment exceeds $10,000,000.

Baptist World Alliance

Figures of Baptist church membership as at Feb., 1955, unless otherwise indicated. Statistics for some areas are incomplete.

EUROPE

Austria	850
Belgium	494
Bulgaria	676
Channel Isles	492
Czechoslovakia	5,000
Denmark	7,300
England	200,967
Estonia [1]	—
Finland	3,139
France	3,184
Germany	98,875
Holland	6,763
Hungary	14,003
Ireland	4,961
Isle of Man	46
Italy	4,169
Latvia [1]	—
Lithuania [1]	—
Norway	7,393
Poland	7,015
Portugal	1,429
Rumania	65,880
Scotland	19,235
Spain	2,300
Sweden	34,915
Switzerland	1,871
U.S.S.R.	512,000
Wales	100,195
Yugoslavia	3,002
Total for Europe	**1,106,154**

[1] *Estimate for Estonia, Latvia, and Lithuania not included in total—12,000.*

ASIA

Burma	142,499	
Ceylon	1,605	
China—proper	90,000	*1941 Estimate)*
Hong Kong and Macao	6,067	
Formosa (Taiwan)	2,704	
India	349,489	
Indonesia	84	
Israel	44	
Japan	12,040	
Jordan	22	
Korea	4,844	
Lebanon	102	
Malaya	421	
New Guinea	—	
Pakistan	11,168	
Philippines	19,805	
Thailand	1,263	
Total for Asia	**642,157**	

AUSTRALASIA AND OCEANIA

Australia	31,588
New Zealand	11,052
Hawaii	2,705
Total for Australasia and Oceania	**45,345**

AFRICA

Algiers	—
Angola	8,786
Belgian Congo	94,998
Cameroons, British	10,896
Cameroons, French	10,931
Egypt	20
Ethiopia	—
French Equatorial Africa	3,000
Gold Coast	2,079
Kenya	—
Liberia	12,000
Mozambique	—
Nigeria	44,355
Nyasaland	1,010
Rhodesia, Northern	686
Rhodesia, Southern	629
St. Helena	96
Sierra Leone	429
South Africa	30,420
Spanish Morocco	50
Total for Africa	**222,385**

CENTRAL AMERICA AND WEST INDIES

Bahamas	16,000
Costa Rica	385
Cuba	14,412
El Salvador	2,685
Guatemala	—
Haiti	28,457
Honduras	1,147
Jamaica	23,617
Nicaragua	3,464
Panama	1,200
Puerto Rico	6,320
Trinidad and Tobago	750
Total for Central America and West Indies	**98,437**

SOUTH AMERICA

Argentina	11,545
Bolivia	1,000
Brazil	109,241
Chile	5,812
Colombia	2,007
Ecuador	29
Guiana, British	245
Guiana, Dutch	100
Paraguay	679
Peru	493
Uruguay	716
Venezuela	478
Total for South America	**132,345**

NORTH AMERICA

Alaska	275	
Canada	144,353	
Mexico	15,482	
United States		
American Baptist Convention	1,564,210	
Baptist General Conference of America	49,981	
National Baptist Convention, Inc.	4,557,416	
National Baptist Convention of America	2,645,789	
North American Baptist General Conference	45,121	
Seventh Day Baptist General Conference	6,259	
Southern Baptist Convention	8,182,305	*(1954)*
15 Other Baptist Bodies	1,235,821	
		18,286,902
Total for North America		**18,447,012**

Baptist Young People's Union

Europe	1,106,154
Asia	642,157
Australasia and Oceania	45,345
Africa	222,385
Central America and West Indies	98,437
South America	132,345
North America	18,447,012
Grand Total	20,693,358

(Excerpt from *Baptist World Fellowship* by F. Townley Lord, Broadman Press, 1955)

BIBLIOGRAPHY: Alliance Congress Volumes: London (1905), Philadelphia (1911), Stockholm (1923), Toronto (1928), Berlin (1934), Atlanta (1939), Copenhagen (1947), Cleveland (1950), London (1955). *The Baptist World Alliance Handbook* (1939). W. W. Barnes, *The Southern Baptist Convention* (1954). J. C. Carlile, *The Story of English Baptists* (1905). E. R. Fitch, *The Baptists of Canada* (1911). J. D. Franks, *European Baptists Today* (1952). L. G. Jordan, *Negro Baptist History* (1930). F. T. Lord, *Baptist World Fellowship* (1955). A. H. Newman, *A History of the Baptist Churches in the United States* (1915). Fannie Clardy Prestridge, *The Baptist World Alliance: Its Beginning* (1939). H. C. Vedder, *A Short History of the Baptists* (1907).

LOUIE DEVOTIE NEWTON

BAPTIST YOUNG PEOPLE'S UNION, SOUTHERN BAPTIST CONVENTION. Organizations for Baptist young people appeared in a few Baptist churches between 1881 and 1891. The Baptist Young People's Union started in Southern Baptist territory as a "Department of the Green" of the B.Y.P.U. of America, 1891–95. The question of sponsorship by the Convention was debated in annual meetings 1893–95. The B.Y.P.U., Auxiliary to the Southern Baptist Convention, was organized in Atlanta, Ga., Nov., 1895, with headquarters located in Birmingham, Ala. This organization was recognized by the Convention in May, 1896. It continued to function through 1909, when its work was assigned to a committee appointed annually by the Convention. This committee co-operated with the Sunday School Board in the development of materials and the promotion of the B.Y.P.U. until 1918, when the full responsibility was entrusted to the board, which had published B.Y.P.U. literature since 1894. The first publications were: *Young People's Leader* (1894), changed from a monthly to a weekly in 1896 and succeeded by the *B.Y.P.U. Quarterly* in 1900; *B.Y.P.U. Manual* (1907) by Landrum Pinson Leavell (q.v.), revised edition in 1914; *Junior B.Y.P.U. Quarterly* (1908); and *Junior B.Y.P.U. Manual* (1916) by Ernest Eugene Lee.

The B.Y.P.U., in the early years, was vigorously set forward by Isaac Jacobus Van Ness (q.v.), both as pastor and later as editorial secretary of the board. The B.Y.P.U. Department of the board was established in 1918 with Leavell as secretary. He became the moving force in the development and promotion of B.Y.P.U. activity in Southern Baptist churches. Following his death in 1929, Jerry Elmer Lambdin became the secretary of this department of work.

The growth of B.Y.P.U. work led by 1921 to grading into age groups—Junior (9–12), Intermediate (13–16), and Senior (17 and above). The Adult union and the Children's Story Hour emerged in the period 1920–30. The concept of a general B.Y.P.U. organization including all the units arose, and the Sunday School Board published a book in 1925 describing the plan for church supervision and leadership. Adult programs, first published in the *B.Y.P.U. Magazine* in 1929, became the *Baptist Adult Union Quarterly* in 1930. Thus the movement developed into a fully graded church training program for all age groups; and in 1934 the name was changed to the Baptist Training Union.

J. E. LAMBDIN

BAPTIST YOUNG PEOPLE'S UNION OF AMERICA. The term applied to the national organization of B.Y.P.U.'s, which in turn designated organizations of young people in Baptist churches designed to promote Christian growth and loyalty. The forerunner of this organization was the Loyalist Movement (1887) started by O. W. Van Osdel, pastor at Ottawa, Kans. The motto was "Loyalty to Christ, in All Things, at All Times." At Chicago in 1890, in a conference of Northern Baptist leaders, plans were made to organize Baptist young people for more active service in the churches and denomination. Fourteen states had held meetings of Baptist young people. *The Loyalist* (Chicago, 1890) was the official publication of the Loyalist Movement. A general convention, with 1,621 people enrolled, representing Canada, District of Columbia, and 29 states, was held in the Second Baptist Church, Chicago, Ill. W. H. Geistweit, of Minneapolis, Minn., suggested that, since the projected organization was to take in hosts of young people in the North, and the South, and Canada, the name be Baptist Young People's Union of America. The name was adopted, and headquarters were established in Chicago. The movement was promoted by big conventions, held annually with few exceptions. The object of the B.Y.P.U.A., as the organization came to be called, was: (1) unification of Baptist young people; (2) increased spirituality; (3) stimulation in Christian service; (4) edification in Scripture knowledge; (5) instruction in Baptist doctrine and history; (6) enlistment in missionary activity through existing denominational organizations. The national organization sponsored weekly meetings in churches, daily Bible reading, and study courses called Christian Culture Courses. The B.Y.P.U.A. and the American Baptist Publication Society alternated through the years in publishing the literature, as follows: *The Loyalist* (1890); *Young People's Work* (1890); *Young People's Union* (1891); *The Baptist Union* (1893); *Service* (1904); *The Junior Baptist Union* (1898); *Our Juniors* (1904). By 1909 B.Y.P.U.A. activity was confined largely to the territory of the Northern Baptist Convention, since Canadian Baptists and the Southern Baptist Convention were already promoting their own B.Y.P.U. work. The B.Y.P.U.A. went out of existence in 1941. The Board of Education and Publication of the American Baptist Convention has continued to sponsor Sunday evening young people's work in the churches of the convention. J. E. LAMBDIN

BAPTISTS. Because of their distinct doctrines, polity, and practice, Baptists of the 20th century believe that they are in a line of spiritual succession from Jesus and the churches and Christians of New Testament days. One cannot find Baptist churches, as they are known today, in every century since Pentecost. Competent scholars have located some Christian groups prior to the 17th century who believed and cherished various doctrines and practices now held by Baptists. In most instances these groups, however, held to doctrines and practices that would disqualify them for membership in the average 20th-century Baptist church or association. Established historical evidence testifies that in the 16th century Hubmaier, Grebel, and others developed, in the midst of the Reformation, a radical wing of dissent which produced small "gathered churches" throughout central Europe. These insisted upon baptism of believers only. They frequently practiced sprinkling or pouring. Hubmaier "baptized" 300 out of a milk pail. Not only as to the act of baptism, but also in several other particulars, there were doctrinal differences between these Continental Anabaptists and English Baptists: The former were, generally speaking, Pelagian; the latter, Arminian or Calvinistic; as to the person of Christ, the Anabaptists were Socinian, if not Unitarian; English Baptists, in the beginning at least, were Trinitarian. Later there developed a Unitarian element among General (Arminian) Baptists. Anabaptists had a connectional ecclesiology; English Baptists began with an insistence upon the independence of each congregation. After three fourths of a century, General Baptists had developed a semiconnectionalism. Particular Baptists held tenaciously to independency. In relation to the state (civil government), Anabaptists forbade their members to take part in civil and military activity. English Baptists recognized the right and the duty of Christians to participate as citizens in the affairs of this world as well as in the affairs of the kingdom of God. In regard to property, there was a tinge of communism in the life of Anabaptists. English-speaking Baptists have always recognized the right of private property but have recognized also the duty of Christian stewardship.

The Mennonites (Anabaptists) in Europe and America have never recognized Baptists as historically related to them. In 1790 John Rippon, in the dedication of his *Baptist Annual Register,* included them in his plan for "all the Baptized Ministers and People (to meet) probably in London," in a world alliance. The Mennonites, sensing a difference, did not respond. They were not included in the invitation to organize the Baptist World Alliance in 1905.

In the last year of the reign of Elizabeth I (1558–1603) and throughout the whole reign of James I (1603–25), persecution raged in England against all who left the state church. James said: "I will make them conform, or I will harry them out of the land." Dissenters fled from England to Holland, the freest country in Europe. John Smyth and his congregation, refugees in Holland, began baptism anew at the beginning of the 17th century. He baptized himself (*se-baptist*) and then baptized all the others, by sprinkling or pouring. Smyth decided that they should have received succession of baptism from their neighbors, the Mennonites (Anabaptists). Thomas Helwys and a minority (three men and four or five women) of the congregation disagreed with Smyth and the majority as to the necessity of baptismal succession. Each group excommunicated the other. After Smyth's death (1612) his group was absorbed into the Mennonite fellowship.

Origin.—Helwys and his followers, believing that spiritual succession is the only type of succession taught in the New Testament, conducted their worship as a separate, distinct congregation. Believing that they should give their witness "where Satan's throne is," they returned to London (1612) and set up the first English Baptist church. Other churches arose on English soil after the same pattern and manner. From that period (first quarter of the 17th century) to modern times, recognizable Baptist churches may be seen in many lands.

In the discussion of the source of authority and the forms of government thereunder, which came to a head in England in the 17th century, three types of government emerged in the discussion: monarchy, representative democracy, and pure democracy. The New Testament in English (Tyndale, 1525, onward) brought forth comparable studies and conclusions in the ecclesiastical sphere. Three types of church polity appeared in the closing decades of the 16th century—episcopacy, presbyterianism, and independency. James I vowed he would enforce episcopacy to the extent of suppression or exile for Presbyterian or Independent dissenters. Thousands fled to Holland. After the return of Helwys and his church, other Independent groups began to appear. Their beginnings in many localities are uncertain—it was best for their health not to be too well known to the state-church authorities.

Three stages in the development of independency led to the full New Testament position: (1) At the point of government, studies in the origins and development of the civil law (the law from the early Roman Republic onward) and in the New Testament as to church law led to the position that under God the people are the source of authority. "Governments derive their just powers from the consent of the governed." Individuals left the Church of England, rejecting episcopacy and the half-way stage (Presbyterianism), and formed Independent congregations.

(2) The second stage would normally arise after they were separate, apart, governing themselves under democratic processes. Who could become members, citizens, of this little democracy? If all the citizens thereof are voting members, then one desiring to be a member must come of his own free choice—a believer. Hence, these groups rejected infants as fit subjects for membership. Those of the Independents who balked at this second stage of development ultimately were called Congregationalists.

(3) The third stage completed the development into the full New Testament position. When a believer chooses to ask for membership in this little Christian democracy to become a voting citizen thereof, upon the basis of what prerequisite shall the present citizens vote to receive him? Upon the symbol of the death and resurrection of the Lord Christ and of the death of the believer to his old life and the rising to walk in newness of life—baptism, immersion (Rom. 6:1-4).

Helwys' church was Arminian in theology. The definite rise of a Calvinistic church is given in an old manuscript. Out of Jacob's Independent Church (London, 1616) arose two or more Baptist churches according to the sequence of the three stages enumerated above. In 1633 a group seceded on the question of baptism; another, in 1638. The original group divided again in 1640 into almost equal parts. The group approving immersion sent Richard Blunt to Holland to secure immersion from a congregation of immersing Mennonites. The greater number of Independents who favored immersion rejected the thought of such succession. The congregation that secured it dropped the thought of the necessity of baptismal succession about four years later. John Spilsbury, the leader of the group of 1638, said: "Where there is a beginning somebody must be first; baptizednesse [sic] is not a necessary qualification in the baptizer." The compiler of this document wrote within the circle of London Baptist life. This is just an example of how at least one Independent Congregation came to the full New Testament position. By 1644 there were at least seven Calvinistic Baptist congregations in the London area. Representatives of these churches published a confession of faith in that year. Would that some country editor had gathered and preserved information concerning the beginnings in the counties! Without recourse to any other basis and authority than the New Testament, those Independent New Testament assemblies came into being.

The Arminian Baptists had, a generation before, made their pronouncement on the question. About 1613, after Smyth's death, the remnant of his followers put forth a confession. Article 81 reads: "That there is no succession in the outward church, and that all succession is from Heaven, and that the new creature only hath the thing signified, and substance, whereof, the outward church and ordinances are shadows."

One of the members in Jacob's Independent Church who moved on to the third step (immersion) was Mark Luker. The son of Benjamin Luker, a Greek merchant in London, he was born in 1605. He could have been a nephew of the Patriarch at Constantinople. He emigrated to America and assisted in the beginnings there. He was a charter member of the First Baptist Church, Newport, R. I. (1644).

Name.—There has been a wrong conception of the name Baptist and its significance. It has been associated in history and in significance with John the forerunner of Christ who baptized. The true origin of the name is found otherwise.

Independent congregations, as indicated above, took the third stage in development and accepted immersion of believers as New Testament baptism. They disagreed concerning the status of state-church parishes from which they had separated. Some Independents recognized parish churches as true churches unbaptized; others denied their Christian status. In the records of the Independent church bearing the name of Henry Jacob, there is this statement in the year 1633: "Sundry of ye church whereof Mr. Jacob and Mr. John Lathrop had been Pastors, being dissatisfied with ye Churches owning of English Parishes to be true churches desired dismission."

Those who were immersed on confession of faith were branded Anabaptists (rebaptizers). They insisted that they baptized and vigorously rejected the name Anabaptist. For example, in 1644 the seven churches in and around London put forth a confession of faith "of those Churches which are commonly (Though falsly [sic]) called Anabaptists"; and likewise in 1660 the Arminian Baptists published a confession of faith, "set forth by many of us, who are (falsely) called Anabaptists." To shun the name Anabaptists and at the same time to differentiate themselves from parish churches and unimmersed Independents, they called themselves Baptized Churches.

Thomas Grantham, the great leader of the General (Arminian) Baptists, in his book *Christianismus Primitivus* (1678), never uses the title "Baptist" church or churches. He uses the term "Baptist" (or the plural) many times to refer to individuals, but when he refers to them in corporate capacity, he always says, *Baptized* church (or the plural). He uses the term at least 76 times. It is to be noted that John Rippon, as late as 1790, dedicated the first number of his *Baptist Annual Register* to "all the Baptized Ministers and People, etc."

In America these believers did not call themselves Baptists or Baptist churches until well after the middle of the 18th century. There were several varieties of names: Baptized Congregations; Congregations Holding Believers' Baptism; Congregations of the People Owning Believers' Baptism; Churches of Christ; and Baptized Churches of Christ. (See Philadelphia

Association, 1729–87.) When, in Virginia in 1787, the Regular and the Separate Baptists united, they named themselves United Baptist Churches of Christ. These are not, strictly speaking, names but are descriptive adjectives to distinguish these churches from others. The two shorter forms, Baptist Church of Christ and Baptist Churches, came to be generally used.

In the final development of the name, the descriptive adjective "baptized" came to be modified and shortened in popular usage to "Baptist," so that by the time the 18th century closed and the 19th century was opening, the term Baptist had come to be the accepted title.

A distinction must be made between the commonly used adjective or noun "Baptist" and the name given to John, the forerunner of Jesus. This adjective, Baptist, that is used as a proper name is the modified perfect participle of the verb "to baptize." It indicated not only the rite but also the teaching illustrated in the rite. The name given to John is found in two forms: the most common form in the Greek—*ho baptistes*—is an adjectival form meaning agent. The less used form—*ho baptizon*—is a present participle form which means the same thing, one who does something. The distinction to be drawn is that, in the case of John the Baptist, he was so designated because he was doing something, or was the agent in the revelation of God, doing the same thing. The translation should be John the Baptizer. In the case of the English Baptists of the 17th and 18th centuries, they were so called because something was done to them (perfect participle) to illustrate their firm belief and teaching, distinguishing them from others.

In the first half of the 19th century, there arose a movement in America that made a deep inroad into Baptist ranks. It claimed to reject all human and man-made nomenclature and to hold to the divine name only. In so doing, this group reverted to the error against which Paul protested in I Corinthians and Philippians and again made the name of Christ a sectarian appellation. The evangelical content in the name *Baptized Church of Christ* was lost, and the new denomination became semi-sacramental. The Baptists, holding tenaciously to the original evangelical content in their developing name, dropped the phrase "of Christ" to avoid any appearance of association with the new lapse into sacramentalism. Since the name *Baptist* connotes both the rite of immersion and the evangelical significance thereof, they were content with the evangelical teaching and avoided the semi-sacramentalism associated with the phrase "of Christ."

Groups.—There have been, from the theological point of view, two distinct types of Baptists: those who accept the teaching of John Calvin and those who accept the teaching of James Arminius. The statement is usually made by Baptist and non-Baptist writers that English Baptists divided into two groups. Just the opposite was the case. Their churches were not united in a denominational group. They appeared as independent, self-governing congregations, disagreeing in theology. It was the era of the rise of the controversy associated with the names of Calvin and Arminius, beginning in Holland. Those developing Baptist congregations gathered into two groups distinguished by the names *Particular* (Calvinistic) and *General* (Arminian) Baptists. These were the two general groups. There were other qualifying adjectives in each of these major groups, according as certain phases of doctrine or practice were insisted on.

They did not develop into distinctly separate groups until later, and then chiefly in America. There were those who insisted upon the Jewish sabbath as being the day of worship for all Christians. Perhaps here is some influence of John Calvin. He taught the continuity between the Jewish religious system and the Christian church, substituting baptism for circumcision in the case of infants and applying the name "Sabbath" to the first day of the week. Some of the English-speaking Baptists held to the seventh day as the sabbath day. These were called Seventh Day Baptists. Some held to the six principles enumerated in Hebrews 6:1–2. The last, the laying on of hands on believers after the baptism, is the only item in the list differentiating them from other Baptists; hence, they are called Six Principle Baptists. In the formative period in England, the several views and practices were intermingled.

In America the churches that retained the sixth principle (mainly New England, Pennsylvania, and New Jersey) have formed a separate body. In America, again, geographical and other influences have produced other distinct groups. The United States Census Bureau (1936) lists 20 groups. There are, in addition, a few others.

Relations with the state.—1. Attitude of Christians toward the state. Here is evidence wherein English Baptists are differentiated from Continental Anabaptists. The Declaration put forth by Thomas Helwys and his group (1611), the first English Baptist confession of faith, Article 24, states:

> That Magistracie is a Holie Ordinace off God, that every soule ought to bee subject to it not for feare onelie, but for conscience sake . . . that wee are to pray for them, for God would have them saved and come to the knowledge off his truth. And, therefore, they may bee members off the Church off Christ, reteining their Magistracie.

The Particular Baptists (1646) set forth a similar attitude of the Christian toward the state. Article 50 in the confession of that date says: "It is lawfull for a Christian to be a Magistrate or Civill Officer; and also it is lawfull to take an oath, so it be in truth, and in judgement, and in righteousnesse."

Judging from the conduct of both General and Particular Baptists during the political turmoil of the middle of the 17th century, they held to such opinions concerning the attitude of the Christian toward the state even before they embodied them in formal declarations. Such have been the belief and conduct of Baptists in England and America ever since. In some countries in modern times, due to special political conditions, Baptists have held aloof from participation in political life.

2. Attitude of the state toward Christianity. Helwys and his group say in the confession already stated, Article 9:

Off his (Jesus Christ) church, he also being the onely Law-giver, hath in his Testament set downe an absolute and perfect rule off direction, and all persons, at all times, to bee observed; Which no Prince, nor anie whosoever, may add to, or diminish from, as they will avoid the fearefull judgments denounced against them that shal so do (Revelation 22:18–19).

A generation later the General Baptists, as a denomination, approved a confession of faith (1660) to present to King Charles II. In Article 24 they say:

That it is the will, and mind of God (in these Gospel times) that all men should have the free liberty of their own conscience in matters of Religion, or Worship, without the least oppression and persecution, as simply upon that account; and that for any in Authority otherwise to act, we confidently believe is expressly contrary to the mind of Christ.

In Article 25 they say: "But in case the Civil Powers do, or shall at any time impose things about matters of Religion, which we through conscience to God cannot actually obey, then we with Peter also do say, that we ought in such cases to obey God rather than man."

The Particular Baptists were just as clear in their attitude of freedom of conscience and worship as were the General Baptists. In their confession published in 1677 (reissued 1689), Article 21, section 2: "God alone is Lord of the Conscience, and hath left it free from the Doctrines and Commandments of men which are in anything contrary to his Word, or not contained in it. So that to believe such Doctrines, or obey such Commands out of Conscience is to betray true liberty of Conscience."

During these troublous times Baptists of all shades of opinion thought and wrote a great deal on the question of liberty. Benjamin Evans in his book *The Early English Baptist,* Vol. I, sums up:

The pen was wielded, and from the press various works issued in defence of Baptist principles. Against the ignorance, the intolerance, the cruelty of the ruling faction, they appealed. Sentiments were uttered then which have exerted the most benignant influence on society. [These were] Sentiments which surpliced hypocrites, wanton courtiers, and a sensual monarch, could not appreciate, but which Williams, Taylor, Milton, Locke, in after years, heard with rapture and propagated with success. Scarcely were they heard at first. The rigid Presbyterians, as well as the Right Divine Episcopalians, repudiated them. But they were not powerless. In the senate and in the church they worked, and on them rests the mighty structure of England's liberties.

It was in America, however, that the superstructure envisioned by Evans was brought into reality.

In the history of the founding and development of the 13 American colonies, Massachusetts and Virginia stand out as the centers of religious intolerance. In Massachusetts the Congregational church leaders drove Roger Williams and others to Rhode Island (1636); a short time thereafter John Clarke likewise was driven to Rhode Island by state-church authorities in Massachusetts. These two great leaders in both the religious and political spheres laid the foundations of the first state government granting absolute religious liberty in the history of the world. Four or five years before they initiated their government, Lord Baltimore secured a charter from the government of Charles I (1632). Under this charter an act was passed by the colonial legislature of Maryland (1649), tolerating the worship of all who confessed the deity of Jesus Christ. Williams went far beyond that, both in theory and fact. He and Clarke contended that any man, whether Christian, Jew, Mohammedan, or pagan, had full religious liberty (much more than legal toleration). Clarke was a more sedate, political philosopher. Williams was the extremist who forced others to know that he was present. Clarke had much to do with getting a charter from the government of Charles II (1663) that was so well written and so comprehensive in its fundamental principles that it served the colony and state for 180 years of struggle and development.

In Virginia the Church of England was the established church. Within the first half-century after the founding of Jamestown, the colonial legislature passed an act (1661) imposing a fine of 2,000 pounds of tobacco upon parents who refused to have their babies christened. Not until near the middle of the 18th century did the Baptists in Virginia make much progress and impression. In 1768 five Baptist preachers were imprisoned in Fredericksburg, Va. The severest charge that the prosecuting attorney could make against them before the court was: "May it please your worships these men are great disturbers of the peace, they cannot meet a man upon the road, but they must ram a text of scripture down his throat."

The troubles leading to the American Revolution were becoming serious by this time. Baptists of Virginia formed a general body in order to bring their influence to bear. The two groups, Regulars and Separates, appointed committees that worked together as the General Committee and for 12 years fought the union of church and state, which had been in operation for more than a century and a half. They enlisted the sympathy and support of several leaders in Virginia political life whose names are stars in American history—Jefferson, Madison, Mason, Pendleton, Wythe, and others of less fame. They succeeded first through the political leading of these men in disestablishing the Church of England, and after the Revolution in securing title of the landed endowments of the Church of England to the state of Virginia.

When a new federal constitution was prepared, "in order to form a more perfect union," and submitted to the 13 independent states, there was a question as to whether Virginia would adopt it. The Baptists were afraid of the proposed constitution because it contained no assurance of religious liberty. Patrick Henry was the leader of the party opposed to adoption, and the Baptists followed him. James Madison, "Father of the Constitution," was the leader for adoption. If he were not elected to the state convention which would consider adoption, Henry would carry the day. In a half-day conference with John Leland (q.v.), Madison convinced him that the best way would be to adopt the Constitution and then amend it as might be seen necessary. Leland accepted Madison's argument and assurance; through his leadership and support Madison was elected to the convention. The new Constitution was adopted, and a Virginian was elected the first President under it. President Washington requested Madison to prepare such amendments as seemed to be necessary. The first one that Madison prepared fulfilled the promise to John Leland and the Baptists: "Article I. Congress shall make no law respecting an establishment of religion, or prohibiting the free exercise thereof . . ." (the second half of Article I deals with the freedom of speech and the press).

The example of the United States of America has carried the influence of Rhode Island and Virginia to the ends of the earth. The principle and practice of religious liberty now so widely proclaimed are the contribution of English-speaking Baptists to the life of the world of the 20th century.

Missions.—At the close of the 17th century and throughout the 18th century, evangelical Christianity was at a low ebb. English deism, German rationalism, and French infidelity were all the rage. In England and America there was little evidence of genuine Christianity. The Wesleyan revival in England and the Great Awakening in the American colonies began to turn the tide. Under the influence of the Wesleyan revival, Christianity in England was revitalized.

The expansion of the British Empire brought the people of England into contact with non-Christian peoples. An insignificant mender of shoes named William Carey (q.v.) became, under God, the voice to call English Christians to worldwide activity. His work in the realm of Protestant missions marks the beginning of a new era. Students of missions, regardless of denomination, recognize his work. C. H. Robinson, quoting Bishop Mylne of Bombay, says: "I should hardly be saying too much did I lay down that subsequent missions have proved to be successful, or the opposite, in a proportion fairly exact to their adoption of Carey's methods."

The Carey movement influenced American Baptist life to a great extent. William Staughton (q.v.), a theological student, was one of the subscribers to the first contribution to Carey's work (in the list of subscribers, his name is not given; the contribution of one-half guinea is designated *Anon.*). Staughton came to Georgetown, S. C., as pastor; from there he went to New Jersey; his great pastorate was in Philadelphia. Carey and his colleagues wrote letters to American Baptist pastors. These letters were read, either the original or copies, to Baptist congregations. The *Periodical Reports*, later enlarged into the *Baptist Missionary Magazine*, were sent from England to leading American pastors. Due to the refusal of the British East India Company to allow missionaries to travel in their ships, English Baptist missionaries to and from India traveled by way of New York. While waiting in New York for a ship going to India or England, they were guests of Baptists in New York, Philadelphia, and other near-by centers. Letters constantly passed between Carey and his fellow workers and John Williams of New York City and other pastors in the middle states. By the time of the famous Haystack Prayer Meeting (1806), American Baptists in the middle states, and especially in South Carolina, were awake to the work of British missions in India. Thousands of dollars were sent by ship captains and other means to assist in the work.

The conversion of Luther Rice (q.v.) and Adoniram Judson (q.v.), Congregationalist missionaries in the Far East, to Baptist views was the clarion call to arouse this mission interest in American Baptist life to enlarged endeavors. American Baptists had been doing mission work among the Indians, among the Negro slaves in the South, and among the emigrants to what was then the Far West. The missionary interest and activity aroused interest in other phases of Christian activity. Home missions, literary and theological education, benevolence, Sunday school work—all these and more were expanded in the life and activity of American Baptists due to the fervor of missionary zeal. The whole effort of expanding organizational life throughout the 19th century may be interpreted in terms of missionary motivation.

Education.—The minister among Baptists, as the word indicates, is a servant of his brethren. There is no distinction between clergy and laity. He is not, in the sight of God, on a level above his brethren. As a consequence the educational level of the ministry has been related to the educational level of the people generally. As the standard of education among the people has been raised, the level of ministerial education has been raised accordingly. In the beginning of the English-speaking Baptist movement, there were several men educated as Church of England clergy; others were educated, if at all, in private study. The contention of Baptists then, which has been held down to the present, was that a minister is divinely called, and that college and seminary training is not a necessary prerequisite.

As the great worldwide mission movement arose among American Baptists, it was recognized that a more widely trained leadership, both at home and abroad, was necessary. Before the Rice-Judson era there was in America one Baptist college, Brown University. In the generation following the beginning of that era, dozens of Baptist colleges were established, primarily for the training of ministers but not limited to that purpose. Ten or twelve of the oldest Baptist colleges in the South date from these years. In the early years in England, educated Baptist pastors conducted private schools. The same practice prevailed in the early years in America. Even down to the era following the Civil War, Baptist pastors of excellent training conducted private schools, several of their students being ministers. The young ministers read the books in the library of the pastor and preached under his general direction. With the increase of Baptist church members in the South and the rise of their economic level, the colleges accepted more and more nonministerial students. That fact itself increased, along with the state education, the level of education in the church membership. This growth in learning in turn called for an enlarged program of ministerial education. The increasing number of schools, collegiate and theological, has been determined by the need.

Polity and methods of work.—Baptist churches began in England as independent, self-governing bodies. On the basis of theology (Calvinism and Arminianism), the congregations gathered into two distinct fellowships. As the number of churches and church members increased, the General (Arminian) Baptists formed a national body, the General Assembly of General Baptists. This national assembly had jurisdiction over the constituent congregations. The church was defined as the sum total of all the churches. The first Baptists in America south of the Potomac were from this English group. Something of this vigorous corporate consciousness may be seen in Southern Baptist life as an inheritance from England.

The Particular (Calvinistic) Baptists were slower in forming a national body. Their insistence upon the independence of the church kept them from forming such a national body as the general assembly. The churches were grouped in associations, the meetings of which were occasions of fellowship and preaching. The Particular Baptists emigrating to America established their main center, to begin with, in the Delaware Valley. Out of that settlement came the Philadelphia Association. Immigration from that area into the South strengthened the Calvinism and Independency that had already entered this region. In New England a mild Calvinism prevailed among Particular Baptists, but the influence of other types from England and the Great Awakening in the first half of the 18th century combined to stress the local congregation. The political atmosphere in New England with an emphasis upon the "town meeting" had its influence on the New England emphasis on the local church.

The three distinct elements—Particular, Calvinistic, and Separate (product of the Great Awakening)—combined in the South to form the type of denominationalism found among Southern Baptists. A Baptist church is an independent, self-governing entity. So is every other Baptist organization. There is no ecclesiastical sequence. An association may not dictate to a Baptist church; conversely, a church may not dictate to an association. But in the South, especially, and certainly in a few instances outside the South, associations, that is to say, groups of churches associating together, may decide with which faction in a divided Baptist church the associated churches will hold fellowship. Many instances are on record to show that, both in principle and in practice, associations have recognized the minority in a divided church as the true church and have received it into fellowship.

The time-honored emphasis upon Baptist church independence has determined the methods of work in missions, education, and benevolence. When the Carey movement began, his association as such did not send him as a missionary to India, but a society of interested individuals supported him. Since the society was formed to raise money to support Carey, membership in the society was based on financial contributions. Other comparable societies were formed in British Baptist life. In America the same custom began. Societies carried on foreign missions, home missions, publication, education, benevolence, etc. These societies were not in the strictest sense denominational. This explains the fact in American Baptist history that the trustees or regents of supposedly Baptist schools have separated them from any connection with the denomination.

In the South the denominational or convention method has been preferred. When the Southern Baptist Convention was formed (1845–46), the constitution provided for two boards, for foreign and home missions, and for as many other boards as the Convention might see fit to set up. The members of these boards are named by the Convention in annual meeting, and the boards are responsible to the Convention. This method finds its explanation in the very definite corporate consciousness early existent in the thinking of Baptists in the South.

From very early days Baptist leaders felt the need of a national or even international fellowship with their brethren. Grantham said in his *Christianismus Primitivus:* "And when it shall please God to put it into the Hearts of the Rulers of the Nations, to permit a Free and General Assembly of the differing Professors of Christianity, for the finding out of Truth, we trust that some of the Baptized Churches will (if permitted) readily make their appearance with others to help on that needful work." This is more of a call for all evangelical Christians to gather together.

In 1790 John Rippon, pastor in London, began publication of the *Baptist Annual Register.* He dedicated the first number "To All Baptized Ministers and People . . . in Expectation that before many years elapse . . . a deputation from all these climes will meet probably in London to consult the ecclesiastical good of the Whole." Rippon included in his invitation the Mennonites (Anabaptists) in all the countries of the continent. They gave no recognition of the invitation.

The next suggestions of a world association of Baptists are found in American periodicals. In the *American Baptist Magazine*, May, 1824, a correspondent (Francis Wayland), under the pen name "Backus," proposed a national Baptist convention of the United States to be composed of the serveral state conventions. Among the objects of this national convention, one was "to correspond by delegation with our brethren in England, who would themselves see the benefit of such an association; and thus the Baptists on both sides of the Atlantic would be united in a solid phalanx."

The next suggestion of a world order is found in the *Religious Herald*, Mar. 16, 1843—a quotation signed by "Hanno" from the *American Star of the West*. The writer gave a record of the Proceedings of the World Association, held at Constantinople, Apr. 27 through May 15, 2042. In this fictional account of a meeting in the future, the word Baptist does not occur, but all the leaders, about eight or ten, bear names famous in Baptist history. After this manner, by way of fantasy, the writer showed that he conceived Baptists of the world some day meeting in a world association.

The next suggestion of a world meeting is found in the same paper, Apr. 11, 1895. A correspondent from New York City, not a Baptist, suggested a Pan-Baptist conference. A little later, the editor himself called for such a meeting. Archibald Thomas Robertson (*q.v.*) wrote: "Dr. R. H. Pitt, about ten years before 1905, had suggested a Pan-Baptist Conference. The time was not ripe for such and nothing came of it." However, it is barely possible that Robertson held to the suggestion in editor Pitt's editorial, and after nearly 10 years it came to light again. At any rate, Robertson wrote in the form of an editorial in the *Baptist Argus* (Louisville, Ky.) a call for a Baptist world alliance. J. N. Prestridge, editor of the *Argus*, became the spokesman, the prophet, of the new movement. He sent copies of his paper to Baptist leaders in every country of the globe. The response came with enthusiastic unanimity. Editor Prestridge is recognized around the world as the spiritual father of the Baptist World Alliance.

The Baptists of Great Britain issued an official invitation to their brethren throughout the world to meet in London, July 11, 1905. The World Alliance meets every five years. In July, 1955, the Alliance met again in London for the 50th anniversary celebration.

As the title indicates, this world organization is an alliance of the national conventions, unions, or conferences of the Baptists of the world. Churches as such do not hold membership. Individual Baptists or Baptist churches hold relationship with the Alliance only through the national body in which or with which they are affiliated. The purpose of the Alliance is fellowship. It has proved of great value for the mass of the Baptist church members of the world to be able in a measure to bring their united voice to speak at one point, on one subject. It has been worth much to the smaller and to the larger national Baptist bodies to come to know one another better.

Southern Baptists of the United States have taken a leading part in the life and work of the Alliance from the beginning. Southern Baptists have furnished four presidents of the Alliance. Small groups of Baptists in some of the nations of the world have been assisted in the midst of their own national surroundings by the friendship and fellowship of the Baptists of the world expressed through the executive committee of the Alliance. The headquarters of the Baptist World Alliance, first located in London, were moved to Washington, D. C., as a consequence of World War II.

BIBLIOGRAPHY: *Baptist Historical Society Transactions* I, (1908–09). H. S. Commager, *Documents of American History* (1949). W. Fristo, *History of the Ketocton Association* (1806). T. Grantham, *Christianismus Primitivus* (1678). C. F. James, *Struggle for Religious Liberty in Virginia* (1900). W. J. McGlothlin, *Baptist Confessions of Faith* (1911). A. H. Newman, *History of Baptist Churches in the United States* (1915). Mrs. J. N. Prestridge, *The Baptist World Alliance—Its Beginning* (1939). C. H. Robinson, *History of Christian Missions* (1915). R. B. Semple, *History of the Rise and Progress of the Baptists in Virginia* (1810). H. C. Vedder, *Balthasar Hubmaier* (1905). W. T. Whitley, *A History of the British Baptists* (1923). L. and M. Williams, *Serampore Letters* (*c.* 1892).

W. W. BARNES

BAPTISTS AND THE BIBLE. For Baptists there is one authoritative source of religious truth and knowledge. To that source they look in all matters relating to doctrine, polity, the ordinances, worship, and Christian living. That source is the Bible. Baptists hold that there are at least three assertions which must be made about the Bible in order to state its position in belief and life: The Bible is sufficient for man's religious needs. It is certain in its deliverance. It is authoritative for belief and conduct.

Sufficiency.—Belief in the sufficiency of the Bible is not meant to disparage other sources of religious knowledge. God has spoken to mankind in many ways throughout human history. Paul clearly shows that nature reveals some of the attributes of God, his "eternal power and Godhead" (Rom. 1:19–21). But he shows also that men do not follow the light of nature. Sin blinds them to much of the truth in nature. Conscience also teaches much concerning God. Its action is based on the distinction between right and wrong. No other explanation really explains conscience. God is the source of the ideal of right; yet, a bare knowledge of right is not enough. Again, the religious struggles and beliefs of men, even where they are defective or false, witness to God. Men have a belief in God which nothing can uproot. It is practically universal in extent. Even belief in many gods shows that man cannot escape from the idea of divinity.

However, it is true that none of these other sources of religious knowledge, nor all of them combined, are sufficient for our needs. The Bible gives the additional truth about God. In it we find not so much man seeking God as God seeking man. In and through the Bible God reveals himself to man. God's power for redemption is pledged to us in the Scriptures. In Jesus Christ, God spoke finally to mankind. The Bible is God's record of his gradual revelation leading up to the final revelation in Christ. No element of truth is wanting for our religious needs when we have really obtained the message of the Bible.

Certainty.—The Bible is a certain source of religious knowledge. Certainty is a relative term, but, as applied to the Bible as a source of religious truth, it means permanent dependability. Science sometimes speaks with great certainty. There are certain physical laws which men frame as a result of their scientific studies and which are in a measure final. Yet they are always subject to revision. Philosophy builds up world views and general theories, but none of these are absolutely certain in their appeal to the human reason, for other theories are easily conceived to set them aside. But in the case of the revelation of God in Christ, the matter is different. Christ's appeal to men does not leave them wavering and uncertain. When he comes into the heart and life, he satisfies. Men at once recognize the certainty and finality of his word, and his person as the revelation of God to man.

Authority.—The Bible is authoritative. This characteristic follows very obviously from its certainty and sufficiency, but a few words are needed as to the grounds for the assertion of the authoritativeness of the Scriptures. The Bible is not authoritative on account of human decrees about it. Church councils in the early centuries did not create the authority of the Bible. Early Christians did make certain declarations about the canon of Scripture, but the books of the Bible do not derive their authority from these decisions. The early councils simply recognized the books which bore in themselves the marks of their authoritativeness. The biblical writers of both the Old and the New Testaments claimed to speak for God. They declared that they were moved by the Holy Spirit. Jesus gave his own statement endorsing the Old Testament revelation. He also promised the presence and guidance of the Holy Spirit to his disciples. The New Testament writers recorded and interpreted the facts of the life and teaching of Jesus under the guidance of the Holy Spirit.

Finally, however, personal Christian experience is the most convincing witness to the truth of the Scriptures. They affect man more deeply than any other writing. They go into the innermost recesses of man's soul. They satisfy. They bring redeeming truth and reveal the redeeming power.

The whole Bible.—It is clear, then, that the Bible is an inspired book. There have been numerous theories of inspiration, but men never have been able to fathom fully the process by which God moves through his Spirit upon the hearts and minds of men. The great fact, however, is clear: God has given us a revelation of himself which is clear and authoritative. The Bible is not inspired in the sense in which a poet is "inspired." There are clear marks of special divine guidance in the revelation God gave us in the Scriptures.

One point needs elucidation here. Is the Old Testament authoritative equally with the New? The answer is not difficult. The Old Testament is authoritative for its purposes equally with the New. The Old Testament is authoritative as God's preparatory revelation. The New Testament is authoritative as God's completed revelation. All that is permanent in the Old Testament is carried over into the New. The moral and the ceremonial laws are fulfilled in Christ. The Ten Commandments all remain in force in the New Testament, but they are enforced in new ways: They are written on the heart; new motives are behind their observance. Practically all of them are repeated in one form or another in Paul's epistles, but now they are a part of the larger life in Christ. The Old Testament, then, is as authoritative as the New for its own end and purpose. It was a preparatory revelation. As such it is authoritative.

The Bible and science.—The Bible, then, is sufficient, certain, and authoritative for us in all matters of religion. It must be kept clearly in mind that the Bible is the book of religion. It is a mistake to think of it as a textbook on science or any other subject except religion. In conveying religious truth the writers of the Bible could gain a hearing for their inspired religious message only by employing the means of conveying ideas in common use. It is astonishing, indeed, how the Bible statements conform broadly and generally to the teachings of science. But the biblical writers had to use the language of appearances, of things as they looked to the ordinary eye, not the language of exact science.

Man has no right to declare that the Bible teaches science and a hundred other things, when it professes only to be God's revelation for religious need. It is equally foolish to find so-called "contradictions." We do not demand of a watch that it point directions, nor of a compass that it tell us the time of day. For its own ends the Bible is our only sufficient, certain, and authoritative guide. Those ends are religious.

Every man's creed.—Baptists hold that the Bible is for all. The right of private and individual interpretation is inalienable. Baptists have no creeds which they put in the place of the Bible. For them the Bible is final. Hence, Baptists should seek to produce the best scholarship and the greatest possible intelligence among the people in order that they may understand the Bible. The Bible requires interpretation. Many contradictory views have been drawn from it without warrant. Its real message is obtained only by careful, wise, sympathetic, and patient toil under the guidance of God's Spirit.

The final word.—Jesus Christ is the crown of the revelation recorded in the Scriptures. In him all is unified. The lordship of Christ is a fundamental Baptist teaching. In all our doctrine of the Bible we seek to express the meaning of Christ as disclosed therein.

It follows from all the preceding that the Bible is final in all questions of doctrine, polity, and Christian living. The doctrines of salvation, of the church, of the ordinances, of polity, and of the Christian life are derived from the Bible. In its teachings alone we find our sufficient, certain, and authoritative source of knowledge concerning all these matters.

The only basis of unity.—The one sure and certain road to agreement among all Christians is obedience to the New Testament teachings in all matters of doctrine, polity, worship, and life. To seek unity of view on any other basis is in effect an effort to uproot the fundamental principle of evangelical Christianity—the finality and authority of the Bible. Loyalty to the Bible would very soon destroy any form of unity otherwise established. For Baptists, then, it seems a hopeless undertaking to seek unity of view on any other principle. If the Bible is final and authoritative, why set forth plans of unity based on expediency or mutual concession of vital teachings? They can be only roundabout paths to new issues so long as the Bible remains authoritative and final. Baptists long and pray for complete agreement among Christians of all names. They are second to none in their desires in this direction. They especially desire that it be accomplished on a stable and lasting basis. They firmly believe that the Bible alone is such a basis.

For all Christians there should be one authoritative source of religious truth and knowledge. To that source they should look in all matters relating to doctrine, polity, the ordinances, worship, and Christian living—that source is the Bible. E. Y. MULLINS

(NOTE: This monograph was published as a tract by the Sunday School Board of the Southern Baptist Convention based on material previously prepared by E. Y. Mullins, and is used by permission.)

BAPTISTS IN THE FOUNDING OF THE NATION. While religious considerations entered into the founding and development of every American colony from New Hampshire to Georgia, it can be shown conclusively that only independents originally stood for full religious liberty and separation of church and state, which are the distinguishing principles of the American Republic established after the Revolution.

Practically every one of the settlers was a member of some church—nearly all Protestants, for Roman Catholics were not supposed to exist under the English Crown. Though all were looking for larger religious freedom, the extent to which each desired this freedom varied no little. The Anglican Cavaliers, who came to Virginia in 1607 and afterward on a company charter basis, wished an exclusive state church. Puritan Anglicans, who chose Massachusetts Bay in 1630 on a company charter basis, thought less of obtaining what the prior arrivals, the Pilgrims, sought—real religious liberty. Those of the Bay looked for a clime in which Protestantism might have a better chance to succeed than appeared possible in Europe. The Scotch-Irish Presbyterians, who later liked New Jersey, Penn's Woods, and the Valley of Virginia, bore deep resentment toward British rule, concentrated on political freedom, barely hoped for full religious freedom, and so did not fight for it.

Cecil Calvert, operating on an individual proprietary basis in Maryland, felt quite as much concern for the material prosperity of his colony as he did for the security for his fellow believers, the Roman Catholics; hence, he extended toleration—not religious liberty. Most certainly, that liberty was not extended to Jews, Deists, and Unitarians, who remained subject to the death penalty for their faith. William Penn, proprietor of a grant of land, while solicitous for his persecuted Quaker brethren, opened the door rather widely to those of contrary belief, to insure business success. But he still did not grant full religious liberty, for he restricted office-holding to those of a prescribed faith.

The common remark, "All the early settlers came in search of religious liberty," is far from true. Facts reveal that among them all, only the Pilgrim Fathers, Independents, landing at Plymouth in 1620, who had separated from the English Established Church and suffered continued persecution, desired full religious liberty. Even the Dutch, with a tradition of toleration in Holland, set up the Reformed church in New Amsterdam on a policy of excluding all outside their own faith. They maintained that policy until 1664, when the English took over and substituted in New York the Episcopal Church as the official church, which practiced limited toleration.

Up to the time of the Revolution, nine of the colonies supported an established church—Massachusetts, Connecticut, and New Hampshire preferring the Puritan Congregational Church; and Virginia, New York, Maryland, North Carolina, South Carolina, and Georgia clinging to the Anglican (Episcopal) Church. In all nine the state church imposed a strict conformity and inflicted penalties on dissenters. Rhode Island alone—which originated here, not in Europe—guaranteed full religious liberty for everybody. While Baptists bore much of the persecution, suffering banishment, fines, whippings, and imprisonment; only Quakers were actually put to death for their faith.

Among the American founders of religious freedom, all authorities are agreed that Roger

Williams heads the list. Focusing upon the last third of the 18th century, Anson Phelps Stokes, the former canon of the Washington Cathedral (Episcopal) and secretary of Yale University, in his monumental work, *Church and State in the United States,* puts statesmen who were laymen in the front rank. But Jefferson, Madison, Henry, and other statesmen stoutly opposed the position of their own church and worked heartily with Baptist ministers. Among the ministers whom Stokes selected were Isaac Backus (q.v.), a Baptist; John Witherspoon, a Presbyterian; John Carroll, a Roman Catholic; and John Leland (q.v.), a Baptist. Only Backus and Leland, however, worked primarily for full religious liberty and church-state separation. Stokes continues:

> The Baptists were the most active in view of their limited numbers. . . . The Baptist influence was due mainly to religious conviction. It was this that led members of this group to advocate and practice adult baptism—feeling that union with the Church should represent the free decision of the individual. . . . The more one goes into the story, the more one appreciates the outstanding contribution of their great leader, Roger Williams, in this field; but this has been more generally recognized than that of some of his more humble associates who had equally strong convictions on the subject and worked equally earnestly for the cause.

Roger Williams, in the colony of Rhode Island, set the pattern for the new republic. No scholar disputes this fact. This honor Williams shared to a degree with John Clarke, pastor of the Newport, R. I., First Baptist Church.

Oscar S. Straus, a Jew, after prolonged research into the origins of the nation, said: "Perhaps much more than we have realized Roger Williams became the real founder of the new Republic, which remains as lively an experiment today as when the young believer in separate church and state began the policy at Providence."

Concerning the charter of Rhode Island, former Chief Justice Charles Evans Hughes said: "This was the ancestor of the provisions for our Federal Constitution adopted one hundred and twenty-four years later and of the familiar provisions of similar import of the respective State Constitutions."

Perry Miller writes:

> Now, as all the world knows, this Separatist figures in history as the pioneer of religious freedom, even of democracy. . . . For the subsequent history of what became of the United States, Roger Williams possesses one indubitable importance, that he stands at the beginning of it. . . . As a figure and a reputation he was always there to remind Americans that no conclusion than absolute religious freedom was feasible to this society.

When the marble statue of Roger Williams was unveiled in the Hall of Fame in the nation's Capitol, Senator Anthony spoke words which may fitly signify our own estimate of him:

> In the history of all the world there is no more striking example of a man grasping a grand idea, at once, in its full proportions, in all its completeness. . . . Those who have followed him have not been able to add anything to the simple words in which he enunciated the principle, nor to surpass him in the exact fidelity with which he reduced it to the practical business of government.

The influence of succeeding Baptists on the thinking and action of Thomas Jefferson, often called "the Architect of the Republic," was pronounced. The fact is accounted for: first, by Jefferson's study of Sir Edward Coke, the early patron of Roger Williams; next, by his familiarity with the Rhode Island experiment; again, by his having many Baptist books in his library; and most of all, by his personal contact with Baptist churches and leaders such as John Leland. He wrote more letters of commendation of Baptists and their principles than of any other single religious group. In his published papers may be seen his acknowledgment of indebtedness to the Baptist church at Buck Mountain, near Charlottesville, which he often attended and applauded for its pure democracy; his message to the Goochland Baptist Association in response to their resolution passed in 1777; to the General Assembly of Rhode Island and Providence Plantations, 1801; to the Danbury Baptist Association, Connecticut, 1802; to the New Hope Baptist Church, Virginia, 1807; to the Appomattox Baptist Association, 1807; to the Baltimore Baptist Association, 1808; to the Ketocton Baptist Association, 1808; to six Baptist associations at Chesterfield, 1808; and to numerous individuals, particularly Leland.

Comparison of official utterances of Roger Williams and Thomas Jefferson reveal how nearly the two expressed themselves alike. Indeed, Williams, faithfully followed by oncoming Baptists, anticipated the framers of the United States governmental system. Ernest says: "In the Rhode Island Constitution adopted we have prefigured the Constitution of the United States and several states, by its principles, its preamble, bill of rights and body of civil and criminal laws."

Upon the foundation laid by Williams years prior, Isaac Backus built enduringly. In 1769 the Warren Baptist Association, next to Rhode Island, constituted a committee on grievances to protest violations of religious liberty and to work for separation of church and state. Backus became its agent and until his death pursued the work at his own expense, long after the committee had regarded its task completed. He wrote about 40 books and pamphlets, preached and lectured, riding on horseback some 60,000 miles up and down the Atlantic seacoast. With him were associated illustrious leaders like James Manning, first president of Brown University, and John Gano, pastor of the First Baptist Church of New York City. These men presented a memorial in respect to the Baptist contentions to the first Continental Congress and later to the Constitutional Convention of 1789, beseeching incorporation of their principles.

Doubtless, the most essential contribution of

Backus was the winning of pre-eminent statesmen like the Adamses, Franklin, Washington, and Hancock to ultimate support of these principles. For a generation Backus besieged the general court of Massachusetts for relief from abuses and took proper action with reference to religious persecutions and injustices. He had most to do with converting the major established churches to what is now called the American system.

A disciple of Backus, John Leland, also of the Massachusetts Warren Baptist Association, went to Virginia in 1775 to plead the principles of the Separatist Baptists, also to combat the severe religious persecution of Baptist preachers by the established Episcopal Church. Almost immediately, he was accepted as the most influential Baptist preacher in the commonwealth and aided powerfully in making the Baptists the majority group there. Settling near Orange, close by the home of James Madison, he speedily won the confidence of that rising young statesman. In fact Madison could never have been elected to public office but for the approval of Leland. Near Orange stands a monument in the Leland-Madison State Park, erected to commemorate a meeting between the two men at which it was agreed that Madison would work for a national bill of rights, and the essentials of the First Amendment guaranteeing full religious liberty were assented to, which was to become a part of the federal Constitution.

Subsequently, the Baptists of Virginia chose Leland to represent them before the state's general assembly, in order to procure complete church-state separation. Feeling his work had been finished in the South, in 1791 Leland returned to New England, where he became the instrument to bring tardy Connecticut in 1818 and halting Massachusetts in 1833 to disestablish the Standing Order (Congregational Church). He wrote many books and pamphlets, which were compiled by Miss L. F. Greene and published in one large volume.   J. M. DAWSON

BARACA-PHILATHEA MOVEMENT. A movement fostering the organization of Sunday school classes of men and women and promoting a popular program of study, fellowship, and service activities. A small Bible class of 18 men was organized by Marshall A. Hudson in the First Baptist Church, Syracuse, N. Y., Oct. 20, 1890. The name given to the class was "baraca." This name was derived from the word "berachah" found in II Chronicles 20:26, meaning "blessing." In 1893 Hudson organized the Philathea Class to enlist women for Bible study in the First Baptist Church. Emma W. Thursfield, the first teacher, taught the class for 17 years. The class name "Philathea" is a Greek word meaning "lovers of truth."

From these two classes the worldwide Baraca-Philathea movement resulted, with headquarters in Syracuse. The motto of the movement was "We Do Things." Nine thousand classes were registered by 1915, with a membership of nearly 1,000,000. Every state in the United States, many foreign countries, and 32 denominations were represented by the classes registered. In addition to Bible study, social life was stressed. Classrooms were used frequently each week for business meetings, Bible clubs, lecture courses, and entertainments of a social and intellectual nature. A strong class spirit was stimulated.

Generally speaking, the classes sustained a loose relation to the churches; though considered a part of the Sunday school, they were independent of church control. In many cases a program of independent activity developed which became detrimental to the church's fellowship and service. Loyalties became intense and tended to focus on the movement and the individual class instead of the church. Thus, denominations and local church leaders began (1915–20) to redirect the interest of men and women to a program of Bible study through classes integrally related to church control and work. In Southern Baptist churches the names Baraca and Philathea continued to be used, but connections with the national movement largely disappeared in 1920–25.   W. L. HOWSE

BARBOURVILLE BAPTIST INSTITUTE. A school at Barbourville, Ky., founded and maintained in part by the First Baptist Church of Barbourville (at that time called the Cumberland River Church) from 1900 to 1935. At the beginning its classes were held in the church building. The institute's first building was erected in 1902. It was also called the Southern Kentucky Baptist Institute. The Home Mission Board assisted the school for some years, as did the General Association of Baptists in Kentucky through its Baptist Education Society. However, the school's income was not sufficient to maintain high standards; and in 1935, during the depression, its property was purchased by the Knox County Board of Education.

GEORGE RALEIGH JEWELL

BARDSTOWN BAPTIST FEMALE COLLEGE. Established at Bardstown, Nelson County, Ky., in 1845, and served as a boarding school for young ladies until 1876. At that time it was incorporated into Bardstown Male and Female College, with H. J. Greenwell as principal. In later years the school was known as Bardstown Coeducational College. A total enrolment of 135 was reported for the session 1897–98. It was reported in the Nelson County Association Minutes for 1908: "The Bardstown Baptist Institute (Co-educational College), which for a number of years was the pride of this associational district, is both dead and abandoned."

HARGUS TAYLOR

BARROWISTS. English Separatists who propagated the views of Henry Barrowe in the late 16th and early 17th centuries. Barrowe was imprisoned c. 1586 and later hanged because his views were considered as heretical. He denied the authority of the queen in ecclesiastical matters, taught that the established church was a false church, and asserted that each congregation should govern itself. While in prison, he wrote several treatises which influenced large numbers to accept his teachings. Many were banished from England and were compelled to seek refuge in Holland.   LYNN E. MAY, JR.

BARTLETT, EUGENE MONROE, SR. (b. Waynesville, Mo., Dec. 24, 1885; d. Siloam Springs, Ark., Jan. 25, 1941). Gospel singer, composer, singing school teacher, editor, and publisher. The son of Hiram Bartlett, he married Joan Tatum in 1916. He was educated at Hall-Moody Institute, Martin, Tenn. He was head of Hartford Music Company, Hartford, Ark., a publishing company, 1918–35, and editor of a music magazine, *Herald of Song*. Bartlett was a member of the First Baptist Church, Hartford, Ark. He conducted three-week singing normals throughout Arkansas, Oklahoma, Texas, Alabama, and Tennessee.   WILLIAM J. REYNOLDS

BARTON, ARTHUR JAMES (b. near Jonesboro, Ark., Feb. 2, 1867; d. Nashville, Tenn., July 19, 1942). Minister, publicist. The son of William H. and Eliza (Morgan) Barton, he was ordained to the Baptist ministry in 1888. He was educated at Southwestern Baptist University (now Union University), Jackson, Tenn., (A.B., 1891) and was given honorary doctorates by Union and Baylor. He held pastorates in Tennessee, Arkansas, Texas, Louisiana, and North Carolina, and led five of these churches in the completion of a building program. He held executive positions with the Home and Foreign Mission boards, and with the state conventions in Arkansas, Texas, and Missouri. He was general director of the Cooperative Program Commission, Southern Baptist Convention, 1926–27; attended all but two or three of the annual sessions of the Southern Baptist Convention from 1891 to 1941; and was elected vice-president in 1932.

His most significant work was in the field of temperance and social service. He served as chairman of the Social Service Commission of the Southern Baptist Convention (and of the Standing Committee on Temperance that preceded it) from 1910 until 1942. The commission's annual reports to the Convention are classic statements of the Christian position on temperance, race relations, industrial problems, world peace, divorce, and related matters. These reports were written by the chairman (with the single exception of the 1942 report) and were approved by the commission and the Convention with only occasional slight changes.

He was an outstanding leader in the national temperance movement and had much to do with shaping national legislation that culminated in the adoption of the Eighteenth Amendment to the Constitution. He served as chairman of the committee which in 1911 framed the Sheppard-Kenyon Bill as to interstate shipments of liquor (same in substance as Webb Bill) and was president of the second national conference to promote this legislation, also chairman of the national conference, Washington, July, 1915, on wording of Sheppard-Hobson Resolution for Prohibition Amendment to the Federal Constitution, and chairman of the National Prohibition Constitution Committee. He served as superintendent of the Anti-Saloon League of Texas from 1915 to Oct., 1918, during which time Texas voted dry by a decisive majority. He represented the United States Government at the International Conference Against Alcoholism in Milan, Italy, 1913, and in Lausanne, Switzerland, 1921. He served as chairman of the National Executive Committee, Anti-Saloon League of America, 1924–34 (member from 1913), and president of National Conference of Organizations Supporting the Eighteenth Amendment, 1929–32, and also as a member of the executive committee of the National Temperance Council.
     HENDERSON BARTON

BARTON, PULASKI CLINGMAN (b. Greenville District, S. C., Oct. 13, 1856; d. Jonesboro, Ark., July 20, 1940). Denominational leader and deacon. He grew up on a farm, taught school, and was a successful businessman dealing in lumber and bricks. He was "exact and exacting on fundamental matters." He served his local church in almost every office and was treasurer, mission board chairman, and moderator of his association. He was three times president of the Arkansas Baptist Convention and for 25 years a member of its executive board. He was elected vice-president of Southern Baptist Convention in 1910, and presided at the Baltimore meeting in 1940. He was buried in the city cemetery in Jonesboro, Ark.

     MRS. H. L. ROBINSON

BASIC BAPTIST PRINCIPLES. Many efforts have been made to express the fundamental Baptist position in one sentence. William Owen Carver (*q.v.*) has expressed the Baptist principle in the phrase, "redeemed personality under the Lordship of Jesus Christ." There can be no true conception of Christianity without Christ and his authority over redeemed personality. From this central concept emerge the distinctive and vital doctrines of the Baptists.

This basic Baptist principle implies a number of essential parts:

1. The Bible is the inspired record of divine redemption. It is through the Bible that one learns about Christ and his teachings. The center of authority is not located in an institution, tradition, or well-formulated dogmas. Jesus Christ is the supreme authority, and his will and purpose are made known through the Bible, particularly in the New Testament. Any idea or institution is always evaluated by the conscientious Baptist in the light of the clear teaching of the Scriptures. It is this tenacious loyalty to the Scriptures that explains many of the attitudes of Baptists in relation to other Baptists and to the Christians of other denomi-

nations. "There is no substitute for the criterion found in the Holy Scriptures, or one that even approaches it in quality or certainty."

2. Another fundamental principle of the Baptists is that of salvation by divine grace through faith. This immediately eliminates salvation by works, or any merit on the part of man. Personal faith in Christ is the prerequisite for baptism, for church membership, and for fellowship in the Lord's Supper. Salvation by grace means that it is a gift, and that one does not pay for it, work for it, or give anything in exchange for it (Eph. 2:8–9). Though redemption is a gift which is not deserved, it is bestowed upon a person without money and without price. Salvation, offered as the free gift of God, is made possible for man on the basis of his personal repentance and faith (Luke 13:3; Acts 16:31; Titus 3:5–6). Thus the object of faith is a person, namely, the Lord Jesus Christ, who enters into the heart, not only as Saviour but as the reigning Lord.

3. Another Baptist principle closely allied to the preceding one is that the church should be composed only of regenerated persons. References to churches throughout the New Testament imply that they were companies of believers. It was after Peter's great confession of faith that Jesus said, "I will build my church" (Matt. 16:18). Baptists have always insisted that only those who have experienced the redeeming grace of God in their hearts should be admitted into the church. This insistence upon a regenerated church membership makes it impossible for Baptists to practice infant baptism. No parent, person, or institution has the authority to deprive the individual of the right to come to God for himself. "Every one of us shall account of himself to God" (Rom. 14:12).

4. The ordinances of a New Testament church, according to the Baptist interpretation, are two; namely, baptism and the Lord's Supper. These ordinances have no saving power. The term "sacrament" is avoided by Baptists because of the association of this idea with various forms of sacramentarianism. Baptists observe the ordinances, not because they have saving power, but because they have been commanded by the Lord Jesus Christ (Matt. 28:19–20; I Cor. 11:24–25).

Baptists have not accepted the doctrine of transubstantiation which implies that the bread and wine are literally transformed into the actual body and blood of our Lord, a view commonly held by Roman Catholics; or the theory of consubstantiation, the view held by Lutherans and some other groups, which implies that in and under, in some mystical way, there is the actual presence of the Lord in the symbols. Baptists insist on the symbolical meaning of both baptism and the Lord's Supper. These ordinances symbolize facts which constitute the heart of the gospel. The Lord's Supper signifies the shedding of the blood and the broken body of the Saviour.

The mode of baptism universally practiced by Baptists is the immersion of a believer in water "in the name of the Father, the Son, and the Holy Spirit" (Matt. 3:5–6, 16; Mark 1:9–10; John 3:23; Acts 8:38–39; Rom. 6:4; Col. 2:12). Only immersion can picture the death, burial, and resurrection of Jesus.

5. Still another basic Baptist principle is that of the competency of the individual soul before God and the priesthood of every believer. This principle is simple and arises out of acceptance of the dignity and worth of man as taught in the Bible. Man stands as a counterpart "over against" God, with the power of choice. "We ought to obey God rather than men" (Acts 5:29). Man is a dependent-independent being, but his dependence is always within the framework of freedom. "God places himself face to face with a free being. Every form of determinism, any thinking whatsoever which questions or completely denies human freedom, is wholly foreign to the Old and New Testaments." Such a conception endows human personality with great value and responsibility and vastly enlarges the horizons of the soul. Through the centuries this principle of individualism has been rendered ineffective by the intervention of the church, the priesthood, and the sacraments between the soul and God. This position is well expressed by Edgar Young Mullins (*q.v.*) in his *Axioms of Religion:* "All men have an equal right to access to God. Direct access to God through Christ is the law of the Christian life." According to Baptists there is no place in New Testament Christianity for a priestly and sacramental system.

6. Baptists have always contended for liberty of conscience and for freedom of worship and speech. John Locke, in his essay on toleration, says, "The Baptists were, from the first, the friends of liberty, just and true liberty, equal and impartial liberty." Bancroft, the American historian, says, "Freedom of conscience, unlimited freedom of mind, was from the first the trophy of the Baptists." Perry Miller, of Harvard, writes, "This Separatist, [Roger Williams] figures in history as the pioneer of religious freedom . . . of the splendid doctrine that a man's right to worship as he pleases is inalienably given him by nature and nature's God."

Roger Williams first espoused the cause of religious liberty in colonial America. The colony of Rhode Island was established on this principle, and the first Baptist church on the North American continent was established in Providence, R. I., in 1639. John Clarke, in 1644, established a Baptist church in Newport, R. I. Both of these leaders were determined that the concept of religious liberty, with the complete separation of church and state, would be the basic principle in the growing life of these colonies. Baptists patiently bore persecution for their beliefs; and finally, through the influence of George Washington, Thomas Jefferson, James Madison, and other leaders of the American colonies, they were able to see the principle of religious freedom adopted as the First Amendment to the Constitution of the United States.

A corollary to this principle of liberty of conscience is that of a free church in a free state. This involves the assumption of the burden of self-support and the foregoing of all participation in public funds collected by taxes. Baptists feel that any religious group anywhere in the world has the right to free and unhindered propagation of its message, within the framework of the commonly accepted requirements of public welfare. This prohibits the establishment or the support of any religious group by the state and affords the same civil status and opportunity to all. Furthermore, the rights of the atheist and the nonbeliever are secured in that he cannot be coerced in matters of conscience by the state.

7. Baptists hold a unique doctrine of church government. The local church is a sovereign body of baptized believers, covenanted together to carry out the will of God under the law of Christ, its head and lawgiver.

Each local Baptist church is a self-governing unit. No outside authority, board, conference, association, convention, or individual can exercise coercive control over the affairs of a Baptist church (Matt. 23:8–10). Baptist churches are related to other Baptist churches in associations, conventions, and alliances; but this relation is purely voluntary and advisory. Within the membership of a church, all are equal. The pastor of a Baptist church is the shepherd of the flock and the overseer of the work of the church, but his authority resides in his capacity for ministering according to the Scriptures rather than any mandatory power which he might assume.

Operating as a simple democracy, the church decides matters by the vote of the congregation after full, free, and open discussion. Under Baptist procedure the majority rules. When the vote of the congregation is taken, even on controversial issues, most of the members of a Baptist church feel the responsibility of abiding by the will of the majority. It is a part of the Baptist genius, not only to be independent in thought and action, but also to submerge minor considerations in the light of the larger loyalty to Christ and his kingdom. For this reason Baptist churches co-operate with churches of like faith and order to carry out the commission of their Lord Jesus Christ. Their co-operative service is a proof of their desire to do the will of God under the law of Christ. Therein is perceived the basic source of their unity which is derived from their fellowship under the lordship of Christ.

There is also a willingness among Baptists to work with Christians of other denominations in achieving some of the broad objectives of the kingdom of God. Facing such tasks as dealing with the serious moral issues of our times, and making a Christian impact on national and international problems, they join hands with all believers in Christ in such common efforts.

8. The acceptance of the lordship of Jesus places the obligation on each redeemed soul to give his witness to the gospel of salvation in Christ. Redeemed individuals brought into close, personal relation with Christ are constantly called to use their time, talents, faith, and material resources for the achievement of the objectives of the kingdom of God. The co-operation among the Baptist bodies of the world through the Baptist World Alliance is a visible sign of this sense of community. It is on the basis of the voluntary response in the heart of each individual that Baptists have endeavored to join together in a total program for witnessing to the world.

BIBLIOGRAPHY: W. W. Barnes, *The Southern Baptist Convention, 1845–1953* (1954). W. B. Boggs, *The Baptists, Who Are They and What Do They Believe?* (1898). W. C. Boone, *What We Believe* (1936). P. E. Burroughs, *The Baptist People* (1934). H. Cook, *What Baptists Stand For* (1947). E. C. Dargan, *The Doctrines of Our Faith* (1905). J. M. Dawson, *Baptists and the American Republic* (1956). D. P. Gaines, *Beliefs of Baptists* (1952). F. S. Mead, *See These Banners Go* (1936). P. Miller, *Roger Williams* (1952). L. R. Morgan, *The Lordship of Jesus* (1931). E. Y. Mullins and H. W. Tribble, *The Baptist Faith* (1935). R. G. Torbet, *A History of the Baptists* (1950). H. W. Tribble, *Our Doctrines* (1936). H. C. Vedder, *A Short History of the Baptists* (1907). W. R. White, *Baptist Distinctives* (1946). O. C. S. Wallace, *What Baptists Believe* (1934). I. J. Van Ness, *Training in the Baptist Spirit* (1914).

MONROE F. SWILLEY, JR.

BASIC CONCEPT, SOUTHERN BAPTIST CONVENTION. The Southern Baptist Convention, as it has developed, represents the middle concept of three popular alternatives at the time of its organization. The first concept was the society form of organization, composed of individuals, churches, and other organizations who wished to participate in the specific objectives of the society. While from the beginning the Southern Baptist Convention was organized to engage in other activities, its initial program was home and foreign missions. It was sometimes referred to as the Southern Missionary Convention. In other words, it was considered by some to be a missionary society. The second concept was that of a denomination of co-operating churches (not individuals and other organizations) and organized to carry on all types of religious activities, including missions, schools, publishing houses, etc. Third, there was a more highly developed denominational concept in which district associations would be made up of churches, state convention would be made up of district associations, and the Southern Baptist Convention would be composed of state conventions. Ultimately, perhaps, a worldwide Baptist organization would be made up of the larger (national) conventions.

In the course of development, the first and third concepts have found limited expression, but provision was made in the original constitution for the second concept, which has come to have general acceptance.

It should be noted that the denomination is

the creation of the churches. Its continued existence is determined by the desire of the churches to maintain it. Participation in the affairs of the denomination by any church is voluntary. The church may identify itself with the denomination or withdraw such identification. The church may co-operate with any program of the denomination or refuse to co-operate. On the other hand, the denomination is not required to recognize any specific church as a part of its constituency and may indeed withdraw its fellowship from a church previously so recognized.

Thus the Southern Baptist Convention, while made up of voluntarily co-operating churches, has a life of its own which is the result of that measure of the Christian witness delegated to it by the churches and the resources for Christian witnessing committed to it. The Southern Baptist Convention, therefore, is not the least common denominator of agreement among all the co-operating churches but a majority opinion arrived at by democratic processes. Consequently, the churches whose messengers vote against a proposal may continue to support that proposal in their support of the Southern Baptist Convention as such. For example, a new institution may be created by the Convention against the judgment of the messengers of a relatively small number of churches. Yet, these churches, by their continued giving through the Cooperative Program, may actually support the new institution. Should, however, all the churches withdraw their co-operation in the Convention, it and its independent life would cease to exist.

The advantages of the concept of a denomination made up of churches to carry on all types of religious activities include the following: The denomination is a flexible instrument which can be adapted to changing circumstances and needs. Not only can more agencies of a given type, such as seminaries, be created, but also new types of agencies, such as the Public Affairs Committee, can be developed. These agencies can be enlarged in proper ratio to one another according to the judgment of the Convention. For example, larger resources may be put to the service of foreign missions than any other single agency. The agencies are under the direct control of the Convention. This control is implemented both by the selection of trustees or directors of the agencies and also by the allocation of funds. Also, the Convention has direct access to the churches. The denomination has in the churches the New Testament unit for eliciting, combining, and directing the activities of individual Christians. DUKE K. MCCALL

BASIC DYNAMICS OF SOUTHERN BAPTISTS. Any large organization finds its basic dynamics in many forms. The Southern Baptist Convention includes the following:

1. The concept of the competence of the individual in matters of religion focuses the concern of both the churches and the denomination upon all kinds of men and women. Social, cultural, class, sectional, and geographical distinctions are submerged in concern for people as such. Ordinary people are expected to share in the witness of the gospel in all types of positions or responsibility. The methods and language for the communication of the gospel are controlled by the abilities of individuals to understand, without reference to any artificial cultural standards.

2. A simple faith in the Bible as the authoritative revelation of God provides the basis for dogmatic assertions about the claims of God. It is assumed that the Bible is able to communicate an understanding of the message of God to all who read it sincerely, seeking to know and willing to be led of the Holy Spirit. The Bible is central in private devotions and in all public worship. All theological statements and actions and programs designed to carry out the commands of God are tested by the Bible. The Bible is therefore the norm of Baptist life and provides both a sense of unity and also an actual degree of uniformity. Whereas the church must face each new historical crisis and therein determine what is expedient, the understanding of the Bible as authoritative provides the record of events from which guidance may be secured when the church confronts any new situation.

3. The emphasis upon freedom is a basic dynamic of Southern Baptists. Freedom for the individual conscience and for the church has provided room in which each can grow unfettered by governmental or ecclesiastical controls. Freedom is a natural expression of the dignity of the individual and is therefore very appealing. In the face of the emphasis on the competence of individuals in matters of religion and the right of men to seek the will of God for themselves in the Bible, there is an element of diversity within the Southern Baptist Convention which can only be encompassed by this emphasis on freedom.

4. The sense of mission under the divine authority of Jesus Christ provides a tremendous dynamic. The denominational program is measured by its relation to this mission to make known to all men everywhere the redemption which God through his love has provided in his Son. While welcoming the witness of other Christians, Southern Baptists believe themselves to be responsible under God for the proclamation of the gospel so long as there is one person in the world who has not heard the "good news."

DUKE K. MCCALL

BATON ROUGE GENERAL HOSPITAL. In 1944 the Louisiana Baptist Convention accepted from the Charity Ward Association of Baton Rouge a gift of a 52-bed hospital operating under the name Baton Rouge General Hospital. The gift was accepted on the condition that the convention add to the facilities or construct a new hospital with a 250–300 bed capacity. A campaign for $600,000 was successfully conducted in Baton Rouge. The convention added $200,000 to this amount, and a 250-bed hospital was constructed on a new site. The name was retained. The hospital began operation Jan. 30, 1950, under the direction of a board of trustees elected by the convention.

In 1954 the hospital owned eight buildings and land with a total value of $3,495,321.33. It owed $1,488,470.85. It had treated a total of 164,137 patients for which it received $7,391,-742.67. Its patient income in 1954 was $1,924,-015. It received $2,400 from the Cooperative Program, and $22,510.43 in designated gifts. The hospital did $19,942.75 worth of charity work. A school of nursing is maintained and had 48 enrolled in 1954. The hospital serves all races and is accredited and approved for internship.

R. HOUSTON SMITH

BATTLE, ARCHIBALD JOHN (b. Powelton, Hancock County, Ga., Sept. 10, 1826; d. Sept. 29, 1907). At the age of 10 he moved to Alabama, graduated from University of Alabama in 1846, and in 1847 was appointed tutor of ancient languages. The same year he married Mary E. Guild, of Tuscaloosa, Ala. A professorship at East Alabama Female College followed in 1852, and in 1853 he was ordained to the ministry by the Tuskegee Baptist Church. In 1855 he became pastor of the Tuscaloosa Baptist Church; in July, 1856, was elected professor of Greek at University of Alabama; in July, 1860, accepted the presidency of Alabama Central Female College, an institution which he had founded; in 1865 was elected president of Judson Female Institute at Marion, Ala. In July, 1872, he was inaugurated president of Mercer University, Macon, Ga., which position he held until 1879. He then served as interim pastor of First Baptist Church in the city for one year.

Battle was a cultivated scholar, and belonged to a family of social prominence. As a minister, he prepared full manuscripts before preaching, and was acclaimed for his book, *A Treatise, Psychological and Theological, on the Human Will* (1876). The D.D. degree was conferred on him by three institutions: Howard College, Columbian College, and the University of Georgia.

HENRY J. STOKES, JR.

BAYLOR, ROBERT EMMETT BLEDSOE (b. Lincoln County, Ky., May 10, 1793; d. Gay Hill, Washington County, Tex., Dec. 30, 1873). Lawyer, Texas Baptist leader. Son of Walker and Jane (Bledsoe) Baylor, he was born in 1793, the same year in which two other careers of importance to Texas began, those of Stephen F. Austin and Samuel Houston (q.v.). Baylor's education in a country school and academy was ended by service in the War of 1812, but was resumed when he began the study of law in the office of his uncle. After serving in the Kentucky Legislature, Baylor entered law practice in Alabama, where he also served in the Legislature in 1824, and was sent to the 21st Congress of the United States in 1828. Commander of Alabama Volunteers during the Creek Wars of 1836, Baylor was converted and ordained a Baptist minister in 1839. That same year, at the age of 48, Baylor went to Texas. A bachelor, he gave his life to his state and church, and took as his motto one which later became the motto of the university named for him, *Pro Ecclesia–Pro Texana*. Baylor organized a missionary school in Fayette County in 1839, assisted in the organization of Union Baptist Association in 1840, and, with William Milton Tryon (q.v.) and others, organized the Texas Baptist Education Society in 1841. Baylor served as judge of the Third Judicial District of the Republic of Texas and on the Republic's Supreme Court. With Tryon and James Huckins (q.v.), he prepared and secured passage of the act which established Baylor University. A member of the Constitutional Convention after the annexation of Texas, Baylor gave the first $1,000 to Baylor University and served as its first law professor, as trustee, and as acting president on occasion. He gave these services to the university and to his denomination without charge.

While traveling his districts in the enforcement of the law, Baylor organized both churches and courts, holding court by day and preaching the gospel by night.

BIBLIOGRAPHY: O. W. and H. B. Baylor, *Baylor's History of the Baylors* (1914). Baylor University Papers (Baylor University, Texas Collection). R. E. B. Baylor Papers (Baylor University, Texas Collection). Mrs. G. J. Burleson, *Life and Writings of Rufus C. Burleson* (1901). J. M. Carroll, *History of Texas Baptists* (1923). J. W. Hale, "Judge Baylor in Perspective" (1950). E. L. Jennett, ed., *Biographical Directory of Texas Conventions and Congresses* (1941). J. B. Link, *Texas Historical and Biographical Magazine* (1891). Z. N. Morrell, *Flowers and Fruits in the Wilderness* (1872).

GUY B. HARRISON, JR.

BAYLOR UNIVERSITY. An institution of higher learning owned and operated by the Baptist General Convention of Texas. Founded in 1845 while Texas was a republic, the university has grown until enrolment on the main campus at Waco, Tex., and professional branches at Dallas and Houston was 6,818 for the 1954-55 session (ending Aug., 1955).

Baylor University owes her founding chiefly to Judge Robert Emmett Bledsoe Baylor (q.v.), an attorney who combined preaching with law, and two pioneer missionaries, James Huckins (q.v.) and William Milton Tryon (q.v.) appointees of the American Baptist Home Mission Society, who in 1841 initiated an Education Society in Union Baptist Association, a group of churches in the Houston area. When the society met in 1844, "it was resolved to found a Baptist university in Texas upon a plan so broad that the requirements of existing conditions would be fully met, and that would be susceptible of enlargement and development to meet the demands of all ages to come."

The university was chartered by an act of the Ninth Congress of the Republic of Texas, Feb. 1, 1845. In his *A History of Texas Baptists*, James Milton Carroll (q.v.) says that Tryon and Baylor, making application for the charter, realized that no name had been selected for the new school. Baylor urged the name Tryon because the idea of a Baptist university in Texas had originated with Tryon, also its strongest promoter. Tryon insisted on the name Baylor; and over Baylor's protest Tryon, who held the pen, wrote "Baylor University" into the charter.

The town of Independence, Washington County, made the highest of four bids for the school's location, including a two-story frame building. First classes in the preparatory department met May 18, 1846, with one teacher, Henry F. Gillette, and 24 students, male and female. The school was thus one of the first coeducational institutions in America.

Among the first contributors were Judge Baylor, who gave $1,000 before making application for the school's charter, and General Sam Houston, who gave $330 for the education of young ministers, and the use of his law library.

Gillette directed the school until the arrival from Georgia of its first president, Henry Lea Graves (*q.v.*). In 1847 Graves organized a collegiate department, and in 1849 he added lectures in law. He resigned in 1851, and was succeeded by Rufus C. Burleson (*q.v.*), who announced a course of study leading to graduation. The university granted its first degree in 1854 to Stephen Decatur Rowe, who was professor of ancient languages and resident graduate at Baylor in 1856. A woman, Mary Gentry Kavanaugh, graduated in 1855.

The university was divided into male and female departments in 1851, with Burleson serving as president of the university and principal of the male department, and Horace Clark (*q.v.*), principal of the female department. Disagreement over spheres of authority between the two leaders resulted in Burleson's resignation in 1861, at which time he took the entire faculty and the senior class of the male department to Waco where he took over Waco Classical School, fostered by Waco Baptist Association, and had the school rechartered as Waco University.

Miraculously the university at Independence survived this blow at the very time other young schools of the South and Southwest had to suspend operations due to the Civil War. Actually Texas Baptists were successful in keeping both Baylor and Waco universities open during the war and reconstruction period.

George Washington Baines, Sr. (*q.v.*), succeeded Burleson at Baylor University (Independence) and in 1863 was followed by William Carey Crane (*q.v.*) during whose presidency the female department became Baylor Female College (1866), a separate institution. From 1866 to 1886 Baylor University was a male school. By 1885 new courses, which later developed into departments and schools, had broadened the curriculum. After 22 years of heroic struggle to keep the university going, Crane died in 1885, and Reddin Andrews, an alumnus, became president.

In 1886, when the Baptist General Association and the Baptist State Convention were combined to form the Baptist General Convention of Texas, Baylor University was consolidated with Waco University, of which Burleson had been head since his resignation as president of Baylor at Independence, and the resulting institution was rechartered as Baylor University at Waco. By the end of 1887, Baylor was established on the present campus in Waco, with Burleson as president of the combined schools.

When Burleson retired in June, 1897, J. C. Lattimore served as chairman of the faculty and administrative offices until Oscar Henry Cooper (*q.v.*) became president in 1899. Cooper's chief contributions to Baylor were the securing of F. L. Carroll Library and George W. Carroll Science Hall, and the raising of academic standards which brought academic recognition to the university.

Samuel Palmer Brooks (*q.v.*), an educator and statesman, succeeded Cooper in 1902, serving as president until his death in 1931. Brooks added new departments and organized the schools of education, law, business, and music. In addition, Baylor acquired three professional schools in Dallas: the college of medicine (1903); the school of nursing (1917); and the college of dentistry (1918). The school of pharmacy, established in 1904, was discontinued in 1931. The Texas Baptist Memorial Hospital at Dallas, renamed Baylor University Hospital in 1920, was a part of the college of medicine until 1943 when the college of medicine was transferred to Houston. The Baylor Theological Seminary, established in 1905, became Southwestern Baptist Theological Seminary, a separate institution, in 1908, and was moved to Fort Worth in 1910.

Pat Morris Neff (*q.v.*), former governor of Texas, alumnus and president of the board of trustees for many years, became president in June, 1932. Under his direction the endowment was increased and teachers' salaries raised. Library and laboratory facilities were improved and extended, old buildings were redecorated and refurnished, and five new buildings were erected. In 1945, in spite of difficulties incident to World War II, Baylor celebrated her centennial anniversary.

William Richardson White, a minister, was elected president following Neff's resignation in 1947. White took office Feb. 1, 1948. Under his administration, the university has made unprecedented growth both in capital assets and academic standards. The Ph.D. degree has been inaugurated. Seven new buildings have been erected. The university holds steadfastly to its basic educational philosophy of blending Christian understanding into classroom and laboratory study.

On the university's main campus in Waco are the college of arts and sciences, the schools of business, education, law, music, and nursing, and the graduate school. The Baylor college of dentistry, graduate research institute, and Bay-

Baylor University

lor Hospital are located at Dallas, and the Baylor college of medicine at Houston. The Baylor Graduate School is affiliated with Baylor University Hospital in Dallas and Brooke Army Hospital of the Brooke Army Medical Center in San Antonio through which it extends credit for approved residency training programs and original research. In San Antonio graduate study programs (for military personnel) are operated on a co-operative basis between Brooke Army and Baptist Memorial hospitals.

The university is a member of the Association of Texas Colleges, the Southern Association of Colleges and Secondary Schools, the Association of American Colleges, the American Council on Education, the Conference of Deans of Southern Graduate Schools, and the American Association of University Women. The college of medicine is rated Class A by the Council on Medical Education and Hospitals and by the Association of American Medical Colleges. The college of dentistry is provisionally approved by the Council of Dental Education of the American Dental Association. The school of law is a member of the Association of American Law Schools and is on the approved list of the American Bar Association. The school of music is a member of the National Association of Schools of Music. The department of journalism is accredited by the American Society of Journalism School Administrators. The radio department is approved by the University Association for Professional Radio Education. The school of business is an associate member of the American Association of Collegiate Schools of Business.

Baylor general library contains 227,000 volumes covering every phase of the college curriculum. The library also subscribes to 1,100 journals and magazines and is a selective depository for documents of the United States Government. There are varied specialized libraries, including the J. B. Tidwell (q.v.) Bible Library with 12,000 volumes, the Armstrong-Browning Library, which contains the world's largest collection of materials related to Robert and Elizabeth Browning (13,000 items), the Texas collection of historical and contemporary materials on the Southwest, and the Law Library whose 25,000 volumes include trial and appellate decisions as far back as English courts of 1263. There also is at Baylor the John K. Strecker Natural History Museum containing approximately 100,000 specimens of Southwestern life. The Baylor Theater, directed by Paul Baker, with Eugene Calvin McKinney as professor of religious drama and playwriting, trains young people for creative writing, church drama, television, and film production projects of Southern Baptists. The theater, operating in a modern and highly flexible plant, has been especially noted for its dramatic experimentations.

A busy campus program is arranged for training students for Christian citizenship. The student body at Baylor operates its own student government under a constitution adopted in an unusual constitutional convention and approved by the school administration and faculty. The students publish a newspaper, *The Daily Lariat*, and a yearbook, *The Round-Up*, and operate their own campus radio station, KYBS. A complete intercollegiate athletic program, with Baylor a member of the Southwest Athletic Conference, proves a strong adhesive force for school spirit. Social clubs for both men and women students are organized under provisions of the Student Body Constitution and supervised by faculty sponsors.

Christian principles dominate the Baylor campus, in the classroom and out. Faculty members are employed after careful consideration of religious belief and practice. All freshman and sophomore students meet three times weekly for religious services in the university chapel. Students conduct the Baylor Religious Hour to which hundreds come voluntarily for worship each Wednesday evening. Devotional services are held on the campus each morning and at noon on school days.

The university's net worth in Waco, Dallas, and Houston in 1955 was $30,000,000, which has built up steadily during White's administration at an average increase of $2,000,000 a year in buildings and endowment. A $50,000,000 fund drive is in progress for the 10-year period 1953–63. The university's endowment is $7,500,000.

A budget of $10,000,000 annually serves the three campuses, half of which is for operation of the main campus at Waco. Income for educational expense is derived from endowment earning (8 per cent); Baptist convention allocations (8 per cent); gifts (21 per cent); tuition (55 per cent); and miscellaneous earnings (8 per cent).

Twenty per cent of the students enrolled in the fall of 1955 came from outside of Texas, listing home addresses in 44 states and 24 foreign countries. There were 600 ministerial students and 100 volunteers for mission service.

Between 80,000 and 90,000 students have attended Baylor in its more than 100 years, of whom 23,621 have graduated (through 1955). Baylor has furnished more missionaries for the Southern Baptist Foreign Mission Board than any other college or university. William Buck Bagby (q.v.), Southern Baptists' first missionary to Brazil, was a Baylor graduate, as is Baker James Cauthen, executive secretary of the Foreign Mission Board, and James Winston Crawley, the board's secretary for the Orient.

Among other former students are Benajah Harvey Carroll (q.v.), founder of Southwestern Baptist Theological Seminary; Albert Sidney Burleson, United States Postmaster General; William Sidney Graves, Major General, United States Army; Lee Rutland Scarborough (q.v.), president of Southwestern Baptist Theological Seminary; George Washington Truett (q.v.), pastor; George White McDaniel (q.v.), pastor; Pat Morris Neff (q.v.), governor of Texas; Samuel P. Brooks, Baylor president and statesman; Dixon Wecter, educator and historian;

United States Senator Thomas Terry Connally; United States Senator Price Daniel. Four of these, Truett, Scarborough, Neff, and McDaniel, were presidents of the Southern Baptist Convention, and Truett was president of the Baptist World Alliance, 1934–39.

Baylor's strengthening emphasis on church leadership, Christian citizenship, and world missions has caused the university motto *Pro Ecclesia, Pro Texana* (For the Church, for Texas), as originated by President Burleson in 1851, now to be interpreted by Baylor administrators as *Pro Deo, Pro Patria, Pro Mundo* (For God, for Country, for the World).

BIBLIOGRAPHY: J. M. Carroll, *A History of Texas Baptists* (1923). J. M. Dawson, *A Century with Texas Baptists* (1947). J. M. Price, *Ten Men from Baylor* (1945). L. M. Russell, "A History of Baylor University" (in preparation 1956).   C. E. BRYANT

BAYLOR UNIVERSITY HOSPITAL. A unit of Baylor University, located at Dallas, Tex., owned and operated by the Baptists of Texas and governed by the Dallas executive committee of the Baylor University board of trustees.

Baylor, the largest Baptist hospital in the world and one of the largest non-tax-supported hospitals in the country, began in 1903, partly as a result of a banquet given at the Oriental Hotel on May 23, 1903, to honor Adolph Lorenz of Vienna, Austria, internationally known as "the bloodless surgeon of Vienna." George Washington Truett (*q.v.*), then pastor of the First Baptist Church in Dallas, was the principal speaker. With the subject "Hospitals, the Result of Christian Influence," Truett concluded his message with the challenge, "I raise the question at this time—a notable period in the history of our city—is it not now time to begin the erection of a great humanitarian hospital, one to which men of all creeds and those of none may come with equal confidence?" On the following Oct. 16 the state of Texas granted a charter to the Texas Baptist Memorial Sanitarium which opened in the Good Samaritan Hospital, formerly owned by Charles M. Rosser. On Nov. 4, 1904, Christopher C. Slaughter (*q.v.*) turned the first spade of dirt for the erection of the sanitarium, and five years later, Oct. 14, 1909, its doors were opened to receive patients. By amendment of its charter authorized Dec. 11, 1920, the Texas Baptist Memorial Sanitarium became Baylor Hospital, and on July 16, 1936, by a new charter the legal name of the institution became Baylor University Hospital.

One after another, additional buildings were added to the Baylor-in-Dallas campus. In Mar., 1918, through the generosity of Slaughter and others, a Nurses' Home and Training School building was completed and occupied. Soon afterward the Women's and Children's Building was constructed at a cost of $750,000. E. R. Brown and his wife gave funds with which Florence Nightingale Maternity Hospital was erected in 1937. Due to the need for enlargement to meet increasing demands, actual construction was begun in Feb., 1948, on the $5,550,000, seven-floor George W. Truett Memorial Unit, dedicated Thanksgiving Day, 1950. Net value of the hospital's properties amounts to over $10,000,000. From 1909 to 1955, 654,538 patients were admitted to Baylor. Treatment and free hospitalization had been provided to thousands of charity patients at an annual cost of more than $325,000.

Baylor was the birthplace of the first group hospitalization plan, now known as the Blue Cross. Through experimental work in Baylor's blood bank the Adtevac method of drying plasma was developed. Baylor scientists received international acclaim for perfecting a method of producing a serum to indicate types of the Rh blood factor.

Accredited by the Joint Commission on Accreditation, the American Medical Association, and the approval agencies of various training programs offered, the hospital is one of the teaching units of the Southwestern Medical School of the University of Texas, and is recognized as both a teaching and research center.
   MARJORIE SAUNDERS

BAYS, JOSEPH L. (b. Pendleton District, N. C., Dec. 28, 1786; d. Matagorda County, Tex., June, 1854). Pioneer Baptist preacher. The youngest of seven sons, Bays moved with his family to Kentucky in 1794 where his father soon died. He never went to school but had for his only teacher, his mother, and his only textbook, the Bible. Conducting prayer meetings and beginning to preach at 16, Bays soon moved to Missouri, where at 18 he married Roseina Wicher. With 32 other families he followed Moses Austin to Texas in 1820.

Bays, who was more than six feet tall and weighed about 250 pounds, could at times be heard singing or preaching two or three miles. "He never read his Bible in public, always quoting the lesson from memory. The hymn, also, he lined from memory, and led the singing himself. . . . His sermons were never more than 35 or 40 minutes long." While emigrants tarried at a camp on the Sabine River, Bays preached to them, and among his converts was a Universalist preacher, "Billy" Cook, whom Bays immersed. He also preached the first Baptist sermon on Texas soil, across the river from the camp. After giving medical aid to Moses Austin, ill at the home of Hugh McGuffin near the Sabine camp, Bays followed Austin's son, Stephen F., to San Felipe, Tex., in 1821 while preaching there, again contrary to Catholic law, he was arrested, but escaped and returned to Louisiana.

Although according to tradition, Bays fought under General Sam Houston at the Battle of San Jacinto and was commissioned by Houston afterward to pacify the Indians in east Texas, the extant state archives cannot verify either statement. His latter years were saddened when his wife and one of his sons became Mormons and left him to move to Utah. Bays lived during his last years with his daughter, Susan, wife of Peter DeMoss, in Matagorda County.

L. R. ELLIOTT

BEAGLE, JESSE WARREN (b. Campbell County, Ky., 1868; d. Cynthiana, Ky., Nov. 16, 1945). Home Mission Board worker. Beagle was a farmer in New Richmond, Ohio, until he was licensed to preach, at the age of 29, by the First Baptist Church of New Richmond. Later, Beagle, with his wife and two children, moved to Georgetown, Ky., where he entered Georgetown College, also serving rural pastorates and a church in Covington.

From 1915 to 1925, Beagle was field secretary of the Home Mission Board in Kentucky and Missouri. In Nov., 1925, the Home Mission Board transferred Beagle to the department of Independent and Direct Missions "comprehending the work among foreigners, Indians, Negroes, the deaf mutes, Jews, and soldiers and seamen." After 27 years, he retired from the Home Mission Board, on Nov. 14, 1942, due to ill health. Beagle was the author of two books: *People of the Jesus Way* and *His Precious Promises* (1943).

JOHN CAYLOR

BEALE, GEORGE WILLIAM (b. Cabinford, Westmoreland County, Va., Aug. 21, 1842; d. Hague, Va., July 15, 1921). Confederate soldier, minister, historian. Oldest of seven children of General R. L. T. and Lucy Marie (Brown) Beale, he was educated at Fleetwood Academy, Culpeper Military Institute, Piedmont Academy, and, following his military service, at Southern Baptist Theological Seminary. Beale spent four years in the Confederate Army and was wounded. He was a favorite among the men he led in battle. Beale was baptized in 1861 at Nomini Ferry, Westmoreland County, Va., where he baptized his father 12 years later. Machodoc Church ordained him Oct. 18, 1868.

On Dec. 3, 1879, he married Mary A. Bouic, daughter of a Rockville, Md., judge.

Beale's six pastorates were Machodoc and Pope's Creek (1868–74); Gay Street, Georgetown (1874–79); Beth Car and Walnut (1879–83); Buchanan and Enon (Hollins) (1883–94); Coan and Fairfield (1894–1905); Menokin and Nomini (1905–19). He was president for two years of the Baptist General Association of Virginia.

Beale prepared a revised and extended edition of *Semple's History of the Rise and Progress of the Baptists in Virginia*, published in 1894, and edited and published *History of the Ninth Virginia Cavalry*, left in manuscript by his father. Chairman of the committee which prepared the historical statement which now appears in the front of the *Virginia Baptist Annual*, Beale also wrote *A Lieutenant in Lee's Army*, his own story of the war years, and *The Moral Dignity of the Sunday School Work*.

CLAYTON PITTS

BEAUCHAMP, HARVEY (b. Crawfordsville, Ind., May 17, 1866; d. Dallas, Tex., Oct. 21, 1938). Pioneer fieldworker of the Sunday School Board of the Southern Baptist Convention. He was the son of S. A. and Jennie (Bland) Beauchamp. His youth was spent in Texas, where his parents moved when he was 10 years of age. At the age of 17, he entered William Jewell College. In 1889 he went to Eureka Springs, Ark., to do mission work, and very shortly thereafter was called as pastor of the First Baptist Church. There he married Laura W. English. Later he served the church at Springdale.

From this pastorate he was called to the secretaryship of the state mission board of the Arkansas Baptist State Convention. In 1905 he was elected as field secretary of the Sunday School Board. In this position he became a vigorous proponent of standards and of full age grading. In 1908 he outlined the Standard of Excellence, which became the accepted standard of direction and objectives for Southern Baptist Sunday schools. Later, Beauchamp designed the Advanced Standard of Excellence. He also developed Standards of Excellence for Sunday school classes and departments. In 1911 he wrote the book *The Graded Sunday School*. His leadership in this area led to his being called the "father of the graded Sunday school." Graded Sunday schools required graded buildings. This led him to advocate graded buildings for Sunday school work. To Beauchamp must be given much credit for initiating the movement for improved church buildings as a means to an improved teaching program. As a pioneer in Baptist Sunday school work, he helped to lay foundations and establish directions that account for modern Sunday school growth.

J. N. BARNETTE

BEAUREGARD MEMORIAL BAPTIST HOSPITAL. The construction of a Baptist hospital in De Ridder was authorized by the Louisiana Baptist Convention in 1947. The 30-bed hospital opened Feb. 20, 1950. Since that date 9,002 patients have been treated. The hospital is conditionally accredited and serves patients of all races. It is not approved for internship and has no school of nursing.

Land, buildings, and equipment were valued at $215,557.51 in 1954 and the hospital had no debt. The patient income in 1954 was $129,476.40; it received $569.48 from the denomination and did charity work in the amount of $527.10. The total income 1950–55 was $478,927.58.

BIBLIOGRAPHY: Louisiana Baptist Convention *Annual* (1947, 1954). C. P. St. Amant, *A Short History of Louisiana Baptists* (1948).

R. HOUSTON SMITH

BEESON ACADEMY (1907–22). A school on the elementary and high school level founded and operated by the Home Mission Board of the Southern Baptist Convention at Pisgah, in Jackson County, Ala. In the appropriations to mountain schools by the board in 1922, Beeson was not included. It was combined with another school.

JAMES E. DAVIDSON

BELGIAN CONGO MISSION. Transferred to the American Baptist Missionary Union by the Livingstone Inland Mission in 1884. Belgian Congo is thickly populated by Bantu tribes speaking many dialects, chiefly Kikongo and Lingala in Baptist areas. Early death rate of missionaries was staggering. The Belgian government, Roman Catholic, adopted a mission school-aid policy in 1920 in lieu of establishing public schools, but only in later years has this been implemented for Protestant schools. Illiteracy and poverty of the people have further retarded education. Training for pastors and teachers was opened on a union basis at Kimpese in 1909, with the Baptist Missionary Society, Swedish Covenant Mission, and American Baptists co-operating; and in 1952 five missions opened the Institut Medical Evangelique, offering a five-year course for doctors and shorter courses for midwives and nurses. Co-operating missions include Baptist Missionary Society, Christian and Missionary Alliance, Disciples of Christ Congo Mission, Swedish Covenant Mission, and American Baptists. A Protestant university is envisaged on the site of the medical school. The first Baptist Congolese to do graduate study outside of the colony graduated in Belgium with honors in 1955 and returned to the mission. Medical work includes a hospital on each station except Leopoldville, baby clinics and dispensaries in the villages, and treatment of leprosy. Uplift of womanhood has been a major effort since pioneer days, and today each station is building a woman's center. In spite of deficiency in higher training, Christians have evidenced native ability and dedication; a Congolese administrative body is being organized.

Mass movements have occurred in some areas, the most historic being the Pentecost of 1886–96. Two world wars brought an alarming trend toward secularism as tribal life in villages was disrupted for work in urban industry at substantial salaries.

Protestant co-operation strengthens the work through the Congo Protestant Council, established 1925; the International Committee on Christian Literature for Africa sponsored by the International Missionary Council, 1929; La Librairie Evangelique au Congo (LECO), publishing house providing Christian literature and texts and equipment for schools. The official organ of the council is *Congo Mission News;* of the mission, *Congo News Letter.*

DATA

	1934	1954
Baptisms	1,556	5,691
Churches and chapels	235	328
Church members	25,125	51,051
Missionaries	61	81
Congolese workers	2,041	1,698
Students	57,282	35,794
Schools	1,346	1,032
Patients	57,241	129,346
Hospitals, dispensaries	14	29
Field contributions	$ 4,214	$139,431*

* Incomplete.

ADA STEARNS

BELGRADE BAPTIST SEMINARY. See YUGOSLAVIA, MISSION IN.

BELL, THEODORE PERCY (b. Beaufort, S. C., Feb. 2, 1852; d. Asheville, N. C., Oct. 2, 1916; buried at Society Hill, S. C.). Pastor, denominational leader, and editor. He was educated at the University of South Carolina and the Southern Baptist Theological Seminary, attending the seminary at Greenville, S. C., 1874–76, and graduating from it at Louisville in 1880. He was ordained in 1875 and was pastor of rural churches while a student at Greenville. He served the First Baptist Church, Anderson, S. C., as pastor from July, 1880, through July, 1886. From Aug., 1886, through Apr., 1893, he was assistant corresponding secretary of the Foreign Mission Board and editor of the *Foreign Mission Journal.* He spoke effectively for the board at the annual state Baptist conventions and similar meetings and won the friendship and praise of the people. In his young manhood he had wanted to be a missionary to China. Strong missionary convictions and zeal for missions marked his entire life.

Bell became corresponding secretary of the Southern Baptist Sunday School Board, May 1, 1893, succeeding James Marion Frost (*q.v.*), who had been his pastor in Richmond. A month after Bell moved to Nashville, the Foreign Mission Board elected him corresponding secretary to succeed Henry Allen Tupper (*q.v.*), but he declined its call. While at the Sunday School Board he introduced Missionary Day and Children's Day, and led the board to make its first contribution to a Bible fund. During his three years of service, he did much to strengthen and enlarge the work of the board. He was succeeded by Frost, who again became secretary Mar. 1, 1896. He purchased *The Christian Index,* Atlanta, Ga., in Jan., 1896, with Isaac Jacobus Van Ness (*q.v.*), and was its senior editor until Jan., 1915, when ill health compelled his retirement. His editorial support of missions and of the Sunday School Board was vigorous and effective. He, with his associates, made *The Christian Index* an unusually strong denominational paper.

He was twice married: first to Ada Claybaugh, Talladega, Ala., in 1880, who bore him a son and two daughters, the younger of whom, Ada, served a term in China as a missionary; and later to Martha E. McIntosh, Society Hill, S. C., who was the president of the Woman's Missionary Union during its first four years (1888–91).

HOMER L. GRICE

BELLVIEW ACADEMY. A Baptist school in Cherokee County, N. C., located 10 miles south of Murphy, N. C. It was supported by the Western North Carolina, Liberty and Ducktown, and Haywood associations. Organized in 1892 with J. W. Lawing as principal, the school failed after a few years' operation. In Nov., 1899, representatives of Liberty and Ducktown Association met in Bellview with Baptists from Western North Carolina Association to discuss

Belmont College

a joint associational school. The site of the original Bellview school was offered and accepted, R. A. Sentell was elected principal, and the school opened Jan. 1, 1900, with an enrolment of 143 pupils. The school received grants of $125 and $250 from the state mission board during its first two years. In 1904 the school received $400 from the Home Mission Board. In 1906 the Western North Carolina Association ceded its share of Bellview to Liberty and Ducktown Association, after which the school declined. In 1909 an effort was made to move the school to a 25-acre campus at Friendship Baptist Church, 15 miles west of Murphy, but the move was not made. In 1910 the school closed in favor of Murphy Institute. D. L. SMILEY

BELMONT COLLEGE. A coeducational liberal arts college operated at Nashville, Tenn., by the Tennessee Baptist Convention since 1951. Prior to that time the institution had been a private preparatory school and junior college for girls, last known as Ward-Belmont College. In Jan., 1951, the board of trustees of Ward-Belmont, Inc., offered that institution to Tennessee Baptists for the price of the indebtedness, which was approximately $650,000.

A school for women named Ward Seminary was established in Nashville in 1865. Another school of the same general type, Belmont College, was established in the same city in 1890. In 1913 these two privately owned schools combined and became Ward-Belmont College, remaining a school for women. This school had a most prosperous growth and before closing enjoyed an international reputation as an outstanding school for women.

The executive board of the Tennessee Baptist Convention voted to purchase the Ward-Belmont property on Feb. 27, 1951. Part of the property was to be used as Baptist state headquarters. On Mar. 13, 1951, the executive board voted to offer to Cumberland University as much of the Ward-Belmont property as was needed for school purposes provided the trustees would agree to move the college of arts and sciences to the Ward-Belmont campus. The law school was to be left in Lebanon.

The board of trustees of Cumberland University met Mar. 18, 1951, and voted to keep both the law school and the college of arts and sciences at Lebanon. The Tennessee state board then announced that a coeducational college would be operated on the Ward-Belmont campus and that no funds would be available for the operation of Cumberland University after June 8, 1951. Cumberland University was then transferred back to its former trustees on May 21, 1951.

The executive board had selected a board of trustees for Ward-Belmont Feb. 27, 1951. These trustees selected Belmont College as the name of the school to be operated on the newly acquired campus. They asked Warren F. Jones, president of Union University, to secure a faculty and make the arrangements necessary for the opening of a junior college in September following. Jones served as acting president through the 1951–52 session.

The establishment of a coeducational Baptist college in the geographical center of Tennessee, in the home city of the Sunday School Board, and in one of the chief centers of Southern Baptist denominational work seemed most auspicious. The Southern Association of Colleges gave approval to the continued membership of Belmont College, and it therefore has been operated from the beginning as an accredited school on the junior college level.

The board of trustees elected R. Kelly White on Aug. 8, 1952, as the first president of Belmont College. Plans for a strong Baptist college in this great Baptist center were carefully made. Belmont soon began to fulfil fond expectations of friends. In 1953–54, 308 students, under a capable faculty and living on a campus with adequate room for growth, testified to Belmont's rapidly recognized worth. The 1955–56 enrolment passed the 500 mark, and the college seemed destined to become a large one. A liberal arts college offering both general and specialized education, Belmont granted degrees of Bachelor of Arts and Bachelor of Science first in 1954–55. A fully accredited junior college, in 1956 it was in the process of becoming accredited also in its senior division.

The property of Belmont College in 1955 was valued at $2,042,302. Between the years 1952 and 1954 part-time faculty increased from 6 to 13 and full-time faculty from 12 to 25. The operating budget for 1954–55 was $354,747.64.

HARLEY FITE

BELO HORIZONTE COLEGIO. See BRAZIL, MISSION IN.

BENGAL-ORISSA: THE CHRISTIAN SERVICE SOCIETY. The administrative body in charge of the work in three provinces, West Bengal, Orissa, and Bihar, among people speaking five different languages. Roma Kanto Sahu, an Oriya, is executive secretary. The general pattern of organization, including quarterly meetings, follows that established by the General Conference of Free Baptists, which opened work in Orissa in 1836. Amos Sutton, a British Baptist, was the first missionary. Work was transferred to the American Baptist Foreign Mission Society in 1911; work for women was transferred in 1916. Eli Noyes (b. 1814; d. 1854) and Jeremiah Phillips (b. 1812; d. 1879) and their wives were the first American missionaries.

Progress has been difficult in these strongly Hindu and densely populated provinces where poverty is prevalent. Two animistic rural tribal groups, the Santals and Koras, slightly exceed the Oriyas in number of Christians. The Santals in Bengal and neighboring provinces have an interdenominational Christian council of their own, as do the provinces of West Bengal and Bihar, providing co-operation in production of Christian literature, promotion of Christian home, family life, and other programs. The Santals co-operate with the National Christian Council, which is also the representative of overseas mission boards in such governmental matters as securing of visas. Only restrictions in issuing visas for missionaries delay the opening of medical and agricultural work. Vocational training is available in schools at Bhimpore, Hatigarh, and Balasore, where the Boys' High and Technical School is recognized as one of the best of its kind in India. Churches in Khargpur, a railroad center for the railway running between Calcutta and Bombay, and in Jamshedpur, the largest steel center in Asia, include in their membership workmen and others from all parts of India. A Christian center in Khargpur provides Christian social services for the industrial community. Present legislation prohibiting observance of caste will contribute to major changes in the basic and industrial life of India. The English publication of the mission is *Tidings*.

DATA

	1934	1954
Organized churches	39	49
Baptisms	149	203
Church members	2,762	3,592
Indian workers	279	208
Missionaries	30	29
Students	3,766	3,138
Schools	114	39
Dispensary patients	9,500	8,450
Field contributions	$5,747	$11,152

ADA STEARNS

BERNARD, HUGH ROBERTSON (b. Robertson County, Tenn., Jan. 25, 1843; d. Athens, Ga., Aug. 8, 1916). An early leader in development of organized work among Baptists in Georgia. He served as convention treasurer, 1896–1902; as field secretary, Mercer University, 1896–1901; as auditor of the state mission board and secretary of the committee on co-operation, 1906–16; and as acting secretary of the state mission board, 1914. He is best known among Baptists for the Bernard Schedule, a plan for regular support of Convention causes through designating groups of associations to give emphasis to specific causes on certain months and to other causes other months. In this manner each association stressed each cause on a regular schedule. He was editor and publisher of *The Southern Advance* (1902–05) and tracts and pamphlets of interest to Baptists in Georgia. He served as pastor of country churches in and around Oconee County for more than 25 years. On Aug. 22, 1867, he married Mary E. Weatherly of Athens, Ga. They had six children.

BERNARD D. KING

BERRY, MRS. MODENA LOWREY (b. Farmington, Alcorn County, Miss., Nov. 16, 1850; d. Blue Mountain, Miss., Jan. 31, 1942). College founder. The oldest child of Mark Perrin Lowrey (*q.v.*), she with her father and her sister, Maggie, founded Blue Mountain College in the autumn of 1873. William Edwin Berry purchased half interest in the school at the suggestion of M. P. Lowrey, and then married Modena, June 20, 1876. Mother Berry, as Mrs. Berry was called, was actively connected with the college until her 84th birthday in 1934 when she retired, accepting the title vice-president, emerita, but she remained college mother until her death. On Nov. 16, 1942, a portrait of Mother Berry was placed in the Mississippi Hall of Fame.

BIBLIOGRAPHY: D. E. Guyton, *Mother Berry of Blue Mountain* (1942). R. N. Sumrall, *A Light on a Hill, a History of Blue Mountain College* (1947).

C. B. HAMLET III

BESSON, PABLO (b. Noda, Switzerland, Apr. 4, 1848; d. Buenos Aires, Argentina, Dec. 30, 1932). One of the founders of the Free Presbyterian Church of Switzerland and France, Besson was converted later to the Baptist position and worked in Belgium and France as a Baptist missionary. He joined French Baptists in Argentina in 1881 and won a large measure of religious liberty, civil registration, civil legal marriage, and civil burial from the Catholic-dominated government. He assisted the first Southern Baptist missionaries sent to Argentina in 1903 and later became pastor of the Central Baptist Church, Buenos Aires. In 1905 he married Margaret Meally Graham (d. 1931), widow of an English Baptist missionary.

BIBLIOGRAPHY: J. N. Prestridge, *Modern Baptist Heroes and Martyrs* (1911). J. C. Quarles, *Christ in the Silver Lands* (1937). Ione Gray "Don Pablo Besson—The Opportunity and the Man Met," *The Commission* (Sept., 1951).

E. C. ROUTH

BESTOR, DANIEL PERRIN, SR. (b. Suffield, Conn., Feb., 1797; d. Mobile, Ala., Apr. 9, 1869). Baptist minister of wide influence as a pulpiteer, educator, and legislator. He was trained in the advanced schools of New England and studied law at Lexington, Ky. At 22 he was converted and began preaching immediately. Around 1819 he moved to Athens, Ala., thence to La Grange in the Tennessee Valley where he later founded a school, the La Fayette Academy (a school of high grade for young women). As one of a presbytery, he helped constitute the Courtland Church, May 5, 1827, and was its pastor for six years. He moved to Greensboro in 1833 and there, too, established a female school which immediately gained statewide popularity. In 1834 he helped organize a Manual Labor School although he doubted the wisdom of such a school. He became first theology lecturer, and later he was elected to the chair of theology; the school closed in 1837. He was elected to be secretary of the Home Mission Board in 1845. In 1846 Bestor settled in Sumter County where he farmed and preached. He bought a plantation in Mississippi in 1856, but made his residence in Mobile. Other pastorates he served included Spring Hill, Gainesville, Sumterville, Livingston, Mobile, and Columbus, Miss., which he served until his death. All of his services were nonremunerative. He served in the Alabama and Mississippi legislatures, and he was a member of the board of trustees of the University of Alabama during the administration of Basil Manly, Sr. (*q.v.*). Frequently he was asked to serve as president of colleges and high schools and to serve as pastor of churches in the North, but he felt that his adopted section was God's place for him. He was "the forerunner of higher education in Alabama, not alone of the Baptist denomination, but of the state," and he had a particular interest in the education of the ministry. It was said that he was "without a superior in the state, intellectually or oratorically," and that he was a possessor of much wit. In 1826 he married Elizabeth J. Townes, daughter of John L. Townes and Mrs. Bledsoe Townes, daughter of Thomas G. Blewett, Columbus, Miss.

BIBLIOGRAPHY: T. M. Owen, *History of Alabama and Dictionary of Alabama Biography* (1921). B. F. Riley, *A Memorial History of Baptists of Alabama* (1923); *History of the Baptists of Alabama* (1895).

R. H. FALWELL

BETHANY CAMP. Started about 1940 at Beechwood (Owen County), Ky., operated and supported by the Woman's Missionary Union of Owen County Baptist Association. Facilities are owned by the county school board. The purpose of the camp, operated two weeks annually, is a spiritual ministry to boys and girls with emphasis on Royal Ambassadors and Girls' Auxiliary.

ELDRED M. TAYLOR

BETHEA BAPTIST HOME. At the meeting of the South Carolina Baptist state convention in 1949 J. Elwood Welsh, chairman of a committee from Fairfield Association, recommended that the convention establish a Baptist home for the aged. The committee was appointed "to make further study of this matter and report at the next regular session of the Convention." The committee reported in 1950, and the following year a second committee indicated that Percy A. Bethea and his wife of Darlington, S. C., had made an offer of $100,000 in cash plus a building site for a home. In 1952 the convention approved a recommendation made by a committee of the general board that the Betheas' offer be accepted. The convention adopted a constitution for the home, elected a board of trustees in 1953, and secured a charter Jan. 29, 1954. Arthur Lee Gross, then director of South Carolina retirement plans, was elected superintendent-treasurer to begin work Jan. 1, 1955. Needs of the home are provided through one week's Sunday school offerings, inclusion in church budgets, the Cooperative Program, and individual gifts.

ARTHUR L. GROSS

BETHEL ACADEMY. Associational school at Bethel, N. C., operated during the Civil War period by Flat River Association under the direction of T. J. Horner.

D. L. SMILEY

BETHEL BAPTIST CHURCH, MISSOURI. Organized July 19, 1806, in Cape Girardeau County, two miles southeast of Jackson, Mo., Bethel Church was the first non-Catholic religious organization and the first permanent Baptist church west of the Mississippi River. The well-preserved minutes housed in the archives of the Missouri Historical Society at William Jewell College, Liberty, Mo., show that this church was constituted by David Green, a minister, and George Lawrence and Henry Cockerham, deacons, at the home of Thomas Bull, with 14 charter members present. The log building erected in 1812 was the first non-Catholic house of worship west of the Mississippi River. Nothing remains of the building, but the site is the property of the Missouri Baptist General Association.

The records show that during the early years Bethel was a vigorous and missionary-spirited organization which was the mother of nine churches and which helped numerous others. Unfortunately, in later years the remaining members became antimissionary, and finally in 1867 the organization ceased to exist. The First Baptist Church of Jackson is virtually a continuation of Bethel Church, being constituted largely by those from Bethel who favored missions.

CURTIS A. HUTCHERSON

BETHEL BAPTIST ENCAMPMENT. Purchased in 1945 and put into operation in 1946 at Visalia, Ky. Owned and supported by the North Bend and Campbell County Baptist associations, the camp is operated seven weeks per year and is used for all church organizations proposing to provide a Christian atmosphere for all campers.

ELDRED M. TAYLOR

BETHEL COLLEGE. A Baptist liberal arts, coeducational junior college, located in Hopkinsville, Ky. The college began as Bethel High School in 1854, the culmination of a desire of the Baptists of Hopkinsville and the surrounding territory to provide a school in which young people could receive an education beyond the ordinary public or private schools. The movement for the school began to take shape in 1853, when public-spirited citizens of Christian and adjacent counties raised funds by private contribution to buy six acres of land in a residential section of Hopkinsville. The cornerstone for the first building was laid in 1855, and this four-story structure, which today houses the administrative offices, the dining hall, chapel, and classrooms, was completed in 1857. With its massive columns it continues to be one of the most beautiful examples of Greek architecture in Kentucky.

In 1859 the school was given a new charter as Bethel Female College. In 1890 a charter was secured legalizing this name and granting the institution the power to confer the usual bachelor degrees. In 1916 it was decided to cease offering degrees and make the college a junior college under the name of Bethel Woman's College.

A further change of charter, in 1951, under the leadership of William Edwin Richardson changed the name to Bethel College and made it coeducational.

While Bethel has been a Baptist school from its beginning, many faiths are represented in the student body. Each student is encouraged to attend the church of his choice. Since its founding a total of 1,497 have been graduated.

The operating budget for the school year 1955–56 was $88,489, of which $42,881 was received from the General Association of Baptists in Kentucky, $9,386 from private donations, $35,515 from student tuition and fees, and $707 from endowment. The endowment in 1956 was $14,566, and buildings and grounds were valued at $432,176. The library in 1955–56 contained 10,576 volumes.

Bethel College is accredited by the Southern Association of Colleges and Secondary Schools and is a member of the American Association of Junior Colleges. Enrolment for the year 1955–56 totaled 151 full-time and 67 part-time or special students. ERWIN L. MCDONALD

BETHEL COLLEGE. Operated at Russellville, Ky., from 1854 to 1933, and in its day, a school of notable accomplishments. Founded originally as Bethel High School, or Academy, by Bethel Baptist Association, the institution opened Jan. 3, 1854, with a faculty of Benjamin Turner Blewitt, principal, and George L. Hayes, assistant; and a student body of 25 young men. The school was chartered on Mar. 9, 1854. The next year, Fred B. Downs, H. H. Skinner, Augustus Maasberg, and Colby A. Smith were added to the faculty. As the school succeeded, its friends became more ambitious for it, and sought to make it a college. The Kentucky legislature issued a charter Mar. 6, 1856, giving the school the power to operate as a college, and even as a university if it so desired. The Green River Baptist Educational Society assumed control and operated the school for years. It opened as a college in the fall of 1856, and the student body was increased to 150. The college received a needed stimulus when H. Q. Ewing, at the time president of its board of trustees, gave an unconditional gift of $10,000 and a conditional gift of $10,000 worth of real estate, provided $30,000 could be raised from other people. Judge E. M. Ewing, the first president of the Bethel High School trustees and the father of H. Q. Ewing, made a similar proposition, offering a cash gift of $3,000 and 80 acres of land in Chicago, provided the full amount was reached. President Blewitt raised another $3,000, and by the middle of 1859, the goal was attained.

During the Civil War the school was interrupted. Many of the students enlisted, and the buildings were used as a hospital for soldiers. Blewitt resigned as president in the summer of 1861, later becoming head of other educational institutions in Kentucky and St. Louis, Mo. Bethel reopened in Sept., 1863, with George Hunt as its head. A year later, he was succeeded by J. W. Rust, who anchored the college on a firm footing. The fourth president was Noah K. Davis, a scholar and author in the field of mental and moral philosophy and the son of the founder of the American Baptist Tract Society. He remained five years, later going to the University of Virginia.

Upon his resignation in 1873, the trustees placed an 1860 alumnus—Leslie Waggener, who had been on the faculty since 1866—in charge of affairs, calling him chairman of the faculty, presumably so that they could look around for a new president. He managed the school under that title for three years, until the trustees decided to make him president. Under that title he served five years, from 1877 to 1883, then resigned to go to the University of Texas. There he became professor of English, history, and literature, chairman of the faculty, and later the school's first president, 1895–96. Waggener Hall, on the University of Texas campus at Austin, is named for him.

Again the trustees turned to an alumnus for leadership of the school in 1883 when they asked James H. Fuqua, of the second graduating class (1858), to become chairman of the faculty. He remained in that work until 1887, when he asked to be relieved of the administrative duties, though he remained on the faculty. For some years he was superintendent of education in Kentucky. The sixth president was W. S. Ryland, who remained 11 years (1889–98), having the longest administration of any of the men who presided over the institution. He had been on the faculty since 1880 and had served as chairman of the faculty for two years prior to his election to the presidency in 1889. Subsequent presidents have been E. S. Alderman, 1898–1902; W. H. Harrison, 1903–07; James D. Garner, 1907–09; F. D. Perkins, 1909–13; H. G. Brownell, 1913–17; Robert Hill Tandy, 1917–18; George Franklin Dasher, 1918–24; William C. James, 1924–28; O. W. Yates, 1930–31; Frank M. Masters, 1931–33.

In its early years, prior to the removal of Southern Baptist Theological Seminary to Kentucky in 1877, Bethel maintained a professorship of biblical and pastoral theology for the benefit of the large proportion of its students studying for the ministry. For most of its years, Bethel was strictly a small liberal arts college, but with a level of achievement significantly above what should have been expected of a school so small and so lacking in resources. Large numbers of its graduates continued in postgraduate study, and many of them achieved real prominence in many fields. Eventually, its limited income, insufficient patronage, evaporated denominational support, and competition from state-supported institutions led into bankruptcy in Feb., 1933. GEORGE RALEIGH JEWELL

BETHEL FEMALE COLLEGE. Established by Bethel Association, Georgia, as one of two Baptist schools for young women which it planned to establish in the rapidly filling region between the Flint and Chattahoochee rivers. The one at Villa Nova failed, but Bethel was successfully opened at Cuthbert, Ga., Feb. 16, 1852. Fifteen trustees had been elected and the charter approved Dec. 22, 1851, in which the school was named Baptist Female College of Southwestern Georgia. Jesse H. Campbell (*q.v.*) had first promoted the idea of the college, and the trustees elected Adam T. Holmes president and Thomas Muse (*q.v.*) agent of the school. In 1863, with metal stripped from the roof for war purposes, the building was used as a military hospital, and since the trustees were unable to continue the school, they turned the property over to the state in 1877 to be used for an agricultural college.   ARTHUR JACKSON

BETHEL HILL INSTITUTE. A Baptist school at Bethel Hill, Person County, N. C., founded in 1888 by J. A. Beam. In 1899 B. D. Thames became principal. In 1904 the school's main building was destroyed by fire. The state built on the spot a high school which continued for many years under the direction of Mrs. J. A. Beam.   D. L. SMILEY

BETHEL MALE COLLEGE. Established in 1893 at Cuthbert, Ga., sponsored by Bethel Association. The association sold the property to the town of Cuthbert in 1903 and invested the money derived from its sale, using it for a scholarship fund for students from Bethel Association going to Mercer University or other schools.   ARTHUR JACKSON

BETHEL TRAINING SCHOOL. Located at Guthrie, Ky., a feeder school for Bethel College, Russellville, Ky., operated during 1892-97. Its building is still standing. When Bethel College ceased to operate the extension school, the building was occupied by Walton College for a few years, and is now used by the Guthrie Graded School.   GEORGE RALEIGH JEWELL

BETHEL WOMAN'S COLLEGE. See BETHEL COLLEGE (Hopkinsville).

BEULAH BAPTIST MALE INSTITUTE. A Baptist school at Madison, N. C., formed by moving Milton Baptist Male Academy to Madison and merging it with another school there. It was opened in July, 1857, and was closed during the Civil War.   D. L. SMILEY

BIBLE, THE. *Definition.*—The word "Bible" is the term universally used to designate the aggregate of the books which compose the Holy Scriptures of the Christian faith. In the English usage the word is singular in number, though it came to this form from the Greek plural (*ta biblia*). The earliest use of the designation "the books" is apparently that given in Daniel 9:2, a reference to prophetic writings. In I Maccabees 12:9 the title "the holy books" is found. The designation appears to have been commonly used as a Christian reference to the Old Testament. Later, perhaps in the fourth and fifth centuries, it was extended to embrace the New Testament. Thus through popular usage and under the guidance of the Holy Spirit, "the books" came to be regarded as "the Book"—the Bible.

There is a total of 66 books included in the Bible—39 in the Old Testament and 27 in the New Testament. They were written by an undetermined number of authors over a period ranging from approximately 1400 B.C. to approximately A.D. 100. These books reflect remarkable variety—history, law, prophecy, poetry, biography, letters. Yet, along with this widely ranging variety, there is amazing basic unity.

These books have been gathered into groups according to the specific emphasis given and the type of literature to which they belong. One of the first groupings, disclosed in the Scriptures themselves (Luke 24:44), is that of the Jewish canon of the Old Testament, in three parts: the law (five books: Gen., Exod., Lev., Num., Deut.); the prophets (eight books: Josh., Judg., Sam., Kings, Isa., Jer., Ezek., and the Minor Prophets, called also "The Twelve"); the writings (11 books: Psalms, Prov., Job, Song of Sol., Ruth, Lam., Eccl., Esther, Chron., Dan., Ezra-Neh. as one book). Another arrangement embraces both the Old Testament and the New Testament collections: the Pentateuch (the first five books), the historical books (the next 12), the poetical books (six), the Major Prophets (four), the Minor Prophets (12). Likewise, five divisions of the New Testament: Gospels (four), history (one), Pauline epistles (13), general epistles (eight), prophecy (one).

The New Testament authors used the following titles in referring to the Old Testament: "the scriptures" (Matt. 21:42; Mark 14:49; Luke 24:32; John 5:39; Acts 18:24; Rom. 15:4), "the holy scriptures" (Rom. 1:2), "the sacred writings" (II Tim. 3:15 ASV), "the law and the prophets" (Matt. 5:17; Acts 13:15), "the law" (John 10:34; 12:34; I Cor. 14:21), "the oracles of God" (Rom. 3:2).

The Bible was written in three original languages: the Old Testament, in Hebrew with a few brief passages in Aramaic; the New Testament, in Koine Greek, which was commonly spoken at that time.

The word "testament" means will or covenant. In its two broad divisions, the Bible treats of two covenants. The old covenant (Old Testament) records the covenant of the law written on tables of stone. The new covenant (New Testament) is the covenant of grace written in the heart. It was foreseen by Jeremiah (Jer. 31:31-34) and discussed in Hebrews 8:8-13 as having its fulfilment in the redemptive work of Christ. Because of the weakness of his flesh, man failed to attain righteousness on the terms of the old covenant of the law (Rom. 8:3; Gal. 3:11). But under the new covenant of grace, man appropriates the benefits of the redemptive work of Christ and is clothed in God's righteousness (Gal. 2:20; Eph. 2:5, 8; Heb. 8:12-13).

In reality the Bible is the history of an

idea—the idea of redemption. It was written to record God's redemptive purpose for mankind. All other phases of its contents are incidental to the realization of this supreme objective—whether history or prophecy, poetry or law, type or antitype—all move toward the peak of revelation, Christ as Redeemer, coming to focus on Calvary. This accounts for the underlying unity of the Bible. Its 66 books are actually one book, disclosing one theme—man's salvation from sin through the atoning death of Christ. For the Christian the Bible is the inspired Word of God. This is its claim throughout its pages—a claim not only attested by thorough research but also fully substantiated in personal experience. E. D. HEAD

Unity of the Bible.—The Bible is distinguished by unity in diversity. The diversity is external and manifold; the unity, organic and profound. The Bible's diversity can be briefly summarized. Its 66 books, treating of Jews and Gentiles of three continents and covering more than 12 centuries, represent numerous authors with widely differing cultures and literary abilities. Using Hebrew, Aramaic, or Greek, and written in prose or poetry, these books contain history, law, prophecy, poetry, proverbs, Gospels, letters, and epistles. This content, concerned with God, man, and the universe, attracts archeologists, anthropologists, geographers, historians, philosophers, psychologists, scientists, and theologians.

The Bible's unity is manifest in many ways. (1) It is manifest in the Bible's central purpose. From Genesis to Revelation, the Bible wrestles with a religious problem: sin marring man's home, life, and relationships. The Bible ends with that problem fully solved. This religious purpose makes the Bible one Book. (2) It is manifest in the Bible's central person. From Genesis to Revelation, the Bible tells the story of persons, divine and human. By his incarnation Jesus unites in himself deity and humanity, thus becoming the Bible's central person. (3) It is manifest in the Bible's central message. The Bible's messages, varied and comprehensive, result in one message: the revelation of God—his being, his attributes, and his will for man. (4) It is manifest in the Bible's central mind. The Bible is the product of many minds: Jews, Gentiles, angels, prophets, saints, and sinners. But always there is one overruling mind—the mind of God. (5) It is manifest in the Bible's central action. The Bible is a book of action. But always God is the chief actor, working to accomplish one end—to get men to act with God, in obedience to his laws and will, in establishing and perfecting his reign in all the earth. (6) It is manifest in the Bible's central function. That function is not to answer all of man's questions and desires but to provide for his need for redemption in order that, through the Bible's adequate resources, man may come to salvation and spiritual maturity. (7) It is manifest in the Bible's continuity. Biblical history unfolds through successive ages, but with never a complete break. Prophets use the past to illuminate the present in the interest of a growing revelation and a richer future realization. (8) It is manifest in the Bible's steady progress toward completion. The Bible moves from plan and promise to performance and fulfilment; from types and shadows to antitypes and realities; from the outward and imperfect to the inward and perfect; from the temporal and changing to the eternal and enduring; from a covenant written on stone to a covenant written in the heart; from sin exposed and a promised Redeemer to sin mastered through the redeeming Christ. (9) It is manifest in the Bible's enduring vitality. Critics, unbelievers, governments, civilizations, and literatures come and go, but the Bible's vitality endures: man's one book, not of theories and speculation, but of redemption and life. W. W. ADAMS

Authority of the Bible.—The authority of the Bible rests in the fact that it is the divinely inspired record and interpretation of God's self-revelation to man, and that it is the instrument of the Holy Spirit in leading men to Christ and the Christian way.

God's revelation in and through the life and history of the people of the old covenant was most important for his redemptive purposes. This preparatory revelation is recorded and interpreted in the Old Testament. The climax of God's revelation was reached in the coming of Christ and the bringing into existence of the people of the new covenant. The authority of Christ and his power, therefore, are primary. In fact, the life of Christ and the early church preceded the New Testament chronologically; nevertheless, the books of the Bible are indispensable to the Christian movement. Only a divinely inspired literature coming from the apostolic circle could present the original form of the revelation of God to man in its purity and distinctness. The recorded faith and witness of the apostolic circle are an integral part of the original act of divine revelation "into" and "in" and "through" history.

During the Patristic and Medieval periods there evolved the doctrine that the authority of tradition and the dominant church stood side by side and on an equality with the Bible. The Bible used by the Roman Church included the Old Testament Apocrypha. The Roman position was fixed at the Council of Trent (1545–63).

Reacting against this view, the Protestant Reformers taught that the Bible (excluding the Old Testament Apocrypha) not only was divinely inspired and authoritative but was the completely sufficient literature for matters of faith and conduct. In fact, Calvin and certain Anabaptists contended that nothing was to be believed and taught in the churches unless it had the sanction of the Bible or of clear inferences from it. The plain and literal sense of the Bible was held to be primary. It was contended that all parts of the Bible were inspired and authoritative, although not all parts were equal in importance. The illumination of the Holy Spirit was held to be necessary for a genuine understanding of the Bible. Baptists have carried the Calvinistic doctrine of authority to its logical conclusion and have thus made the Bible the sole rule of faith and practice.

Since the Reformation liberal Protestantism has tended to minimize the absoluteness of the Bible's authority. The theology of crisis or neo-orthodoxy emphasizes that the Bible does not convey truth to the human mind apart from the divine act of revealing which takes place in the subjective encounter. Conservatives criticize the fact that the neo-orthodox writers fail to emphasize properly the integrity and authority of the written Word of God.

That it has divine origin, status, and authority is claimed by the Bible itself. It traces its authorship through the human writing to the Holy Spirit. This claim has been vindicated through the centuries by the external and internal power of the Bible. Externally, the Bible has exhibited its power and authority by its circulation and use, translation, survival through criticism, and influence. Internally, its power and authority are seen in its realism, historical core, doctrines, unparalleled treatment of certain themes, and in its power as an agent of the Holy Spirit to lead men to Christ and the Christian way in life and doctrine.

The authority of the Bible is both objective and subjective. It is a divinely inspired and authoritative historical record and interpretation of God's revelation in history and thus constitutes an objective authority in religion. Yet, it exerts its authority in an internal and subjective manner. The authority of the Bible is not rigid and mechanical. It is a living and pulsating Book which is used by the Holy Spirit to constrain without compelling and to lead without forcing. It is a Book through which the Holy Spirit works to lead men to the living Christ and guide in the Christian way. JOHN P. NEWPORT

Finality of the New Testament message.— The finality of the New Testament message rests upon two facts: (1) that Christianity is the final religion, and (2) that the New Testament is a true and adequate presentation of Christianity. These facts have important implications for Christian belief and practice.

Nothing is more real, when one reads the New Testament, than the sense of having reached finality in God's redemptive work. In the Old Testament is the atmosphere of preparation, not finality. Moses foretold the coming of another prophet (Deut. 18:15); Abraham was the beginning of God's movement to bless men (Gen. 17:1–7); Malachi prophesied the coming Son of Righteousness (Mal. 4:1–2). The whole tone is one of incompleteness and expectancy of what God is going to do. This atmosphere is changed in the New Testament; men speak of what God has done in Christ. God has spoken in Christ (Heb. 1:1–3), reconciled the world to himself in Christ (II Cor. 5:19), and brought grace and truth into existence through Christ (John 1:17). Walter Thomas Conner (*q.v.*) states the theme of Hebrews as "the supremacy of Christ and the finality of his religion." This is the theme of all the New Testament; for the sense of finality, of completeness, of having reached something which cannot be superseded or improved is the basic foundation of all its teaching.

The New Testament message, then, is final if it is a true and adequate presentation of the gospel of Christ with its demands on faith and life. That it is believed to be true and adequate is shown by the formation of the New Testament canon. The inclusion of the books we have is evidence of the conviction of Christians through the ages that what is contained in the New Testament is true; the refusal to add to the collection of New Testament books is evidence of the conviction that it is adequate. While the New Testament must be interpreted and applied by each generation, it has proved in all ages to be reliable and adequate, bringing men to God and pointing the way to proper Christian behavior.

This does not mean that Christianity is static; it seeks to understand and apply the New Testament to life in a changing world. Progress and advance toward the perfect ideal of Christ is the aim of all Christian thought and struggle. This advance, however, must be within the framework of the New Testament. To seek to improve upon its message is to depart from it; to depart from it is to depart from truth.

This is the basis for the belief that the New Testament is the sole and sufficient guide for Christian belief and conduct for churches and individuals. Since the Old Testament finds its completion in the New, the New Testament alone has the quality of finality. All Christian belief and practice must be derived from an interpretation of the New Testament and the application of its principles.

This is also the basis for believing that Christianity is a universal religion, that it alone will meet the needs of men of all ages and lands. Finality cannot be shared; all other religions must be either false or inadequate. Christians, therefore, feel it their duty to evangelize the world. FRED L. FISHER

*Human experience and the Bible.—*The Bible was directed to basic human problems and situations. Man has undergone no fundamental change as to his essential nature during recorded history. The Bible was written to meet situations developing in the experiences of men or in anticipation of experiences that would develop. The approach in the Old Testament was more direct and specific. In the New Testament we find a more indirect and general application. In both Old and New testaments, teaching and doctrine are indissolubly connected with duty and practice.

The Bible deals with living situations which are usually obvious, immediate, and local. Sometimes we have proverbs and philosophical meditation, but even they are reflections from observations either objective or subjective. The Old Testament situations usually relate to the Chosen People or those with whom they had contact. The New Testament deals largely with needs and problems arising in the churches. Even the Gospels were written to meet developing situations among early Christians as to the historical facts and spiritual truth about the person of Christ. Prophecy had both an immediate and remote application to living experiences.

The approaches in the Old Testament and the New Testament differ considerably. Much of the Old Testament is directed to Israel or its leaders. The approach is usually political and social. There are frequent individual applications, but usually it is the nation or the group that is addressed. In the New Testament the churches are approached, but individual, personal life problems are given the main emphasis. In the Old Testament social sins are specified and condemned. In the New Testament personal sins are condemned and exposed. In the Old Testament God deals with the sins of Israel and those of surrounding nations. In the New Testament the Lord and inspired writers expose hypocrisy, insincerity, and immorality of religious leaders and professing disciples.

The New Testament writers did not seem concerned about reforming the world. They were concerned about keeping the fountain of the faith and life of the disciples pure. They were thinking of the integrity of the salt and the clarity of the light. They felt that corruption and darkness would be arrested and pushed back by these as they multiplied and maintained their genuineness. There were no frontal attacks on the national and social ills of the day, but principles and concepts were proclaimed that would uproot these ills with the process of history. Freedom of the spirit must ever be primary; otherwise, external freedoms will be arbitrary, artificial, and temporary because devoid of a creative, nurturing root.

A God who is holy, just, righteous, and merciful would naturally expect these qualities in his followers. That is the conclusion reached by the prophets and teachers of Israel. Their conception of God was so high and so relevant to life that they stood out in bold contrast to surrounding nations. In the New Testament the great doctrines were always related to great deeds. In fact, right living grows out of right believing. It is a dynamic relationship between root and fruit. Anything else is either abnormal or spurious. W. R. WHITE

BIBLIOGRAPHY: S. A. Cartledge, *A Conservative Introduction to the New Testament* (1938). J. D. Davis (revised by H. S. Gehman), *The Westminster Dictionary of the Bible* (1944). M. Dods, *The Bible, Its Origin and Nature* (1908). C. T. Francisco, *Introduction to the Old Testament* (1951). C. R. Gregory, *Canon and Text of the New Testament* (1920). B. F. Westcott, *A General Survey of the History of the Canon of the New Testament* (1889).

BIBLE BAPTIST. A newspaper published at Waycross, Ga., and edited by E. R. Carswell, Jr., in 1898. Carswell was sharp in his attacks on *The Christian Index* (Ga.). The *Bible Baptist* is now extinct. JOHN J. HURT, JR.

BIBLE BOARD, SOUTHERN BAPTIST CONVENTION. This board, created by the Convention and located in Nashville, Tenn., 1851–63, had four secretaries, all ministers: William Calmes Buck (*q.v.*), until the spring of 1854; Amos Cooper Dayton (*q.v.*), Sept., 1854, to Apr., 1858; Edward Payson Walton, June, 1858, to May, 1859; Matthew Hillsman (*q.v.*), June, 1859, to Jan., 1860; and Littlebury W. Allen, 1860–61. The board suffered constantly from a lack of funds, since many churches supported the American and Foreign Bible Society. From the fall of 1857 until 1861, it was the victim of a bitter controversy between Landmarkers and anti-Landmarkers for its control. The Convention made it responsible for colportage and Sunday school work in addition to its Bible work. When the Civil War began, secretary Allen left Nashville, without resigning, to work with the Confederate soldiers in Virginia. The board suspended work when the Union army captured Nashville in Feb., 1862. The Convention took steps at its 1861 session toward the combination of the Bible Board with the Southern Baptist Publication Society, Charleston, S. C., but this effort failed. The Convention then abolished the board at the 1863 session, not being able to communicate with it, but did not get its last report until 1866, a year after the war ended. The Bible Board worked closely with local and state colportage and Bible societies during its 10 years. What it experienced was a part of the painful and often costly efforts Southern Baptists had to make through many years in order to develop a cohesive and effective denomination. HOMER L. GRICE

BIBLE DISTRIBUTION. The Bible as every man's book, meant for all men of every race in every age, was the concept of primitive Christianity. During the first centuries of the Christian era, when propagation of the Word, whether spoken or written, was the chief concern of the church, the expansion of Christianity was prodigious. The concept of the Bible as the Book of the clergy came with the Dark Ages; later, the invention of the printing press and the coming of the Reformation gave the Bible back to the laity. Bible reading and prayer circles gave rise to the revivals of the 18th century on both sides of the Atlantic; out of these came Bible societies (British and Foreign Bible Society, 1804; American Bible Society, 1816) whose activities have paralleled the modern missionary movement.

Correlation between Bible distribution, evangelism, and church expansion is unmistakable. This is the conclusion of A. M. Chirgwin after a three-year worldwide survey sponsored by the United Bible Societies, the clearinghouse since

Bible Distribution

1946 for 24 national Bible societies. Bible distribution is promoted not only through these but also by denominational agencies such as the (Baptist) Bible Press of Brazil, the Chinese Baptist Publication Society, and by other missionary and church-related organizations.

Methods used for the distribution of the Bible include Bible society agencies, book stores, book deposits in churches, radio ministries, airplane ministries which drop Gospels on remote villages, colporteurs, and volunteer workers. While full-time colporteurs and Bible women are decreasing in number, the number of volunteer workers and total distribution of the Scriptures are increasing. Workers visit bazaars and markets, board public conveyances, visit homes, and in effect go wherever the people are. The effective Bible agent attempts to bring those interested in the Bible into contact with a church or mission.

Persons who purchase a Bible usually have more interest in reading it than those who receive it as a gift. There is a place, however, for planned free distribution. Baptists on mission fields often use this plan: first week, prayer and preparation; second week, systematic visitation from house to house, leaving a Gospel in each home; third week, revival services; fourth week, a second visit to homes of those who show interest in the gospel. Of Brazilian Baptists, who use almost a third of a million Gospels annually in their campaign, Chirgwin says, "No church in Brazil uses Scriptures more consistently, and none grows more rapidly."

A United Bible Society summary gives the total circulation by all Bible societies in 1950 as 2,497,208 Bibles; 3,424,748 Testaments; 15,878,271 Gospels and other portions; a total of 21,800,227. With a billion people able to read and another 50 million learning to read each year, the importance of Bible distribution looms large.   F. W. PATTERSON

BIBLE DISTRIBUTION. In the South Bible distribution was quite limited until the organization of the American Bible Society (1816), the American Sunday School Union (1824), and the Baptist General Tract Society (1824), which became the American Baptist Publication Society in 1840. Near the middle of the 19th century, most of the Southern states had in various combinations Bible, tract, Sunday school, and colportage societies with depositories and book stores. Before 1847 they were usually auxiliary to the American Baptist Publication Society. Then they became auxiliary to the Southern Baptist Publications Society, Charleston, S. C., and to the Southern Baptist Bible Board after 1851. The Tennessee Baptist Publication Society, chartered Feb. 2, 1848, had for its objects "the purchase and publication of Bibles, Testaments, religious and sabbath school books, tracts and other publications of moral tendency, and the same to sell and distribute gratuitously in the destitute portions of our country, through colporteurs and otherwise." This indicates the general nature of all these agencies who employed missionaries and colporteurs for full- and part-time work.

After the Civil War Southern Baptists again depended largely on the American Baptist Publication Society for many years for Bible distribution. With the creation of the Southern Baptist Sunday School Board (1891), a new era dawned for Bible, book, and tract distribution. It made available free Bibles to missionaries and other Christian workers for distribution among needy people; also, it co-operated with the missionaries of the Home Mission Board and the various state boards in getting Bibles, religious tracts, and books to the people. With the establishment and expansion of its book stores into every state of the Southern Baptist Convention, its close relations with the state staffs of Sunday school and Training Union workers, and its supply of free biblical, doctrinal, and evangelistic tracts to all ministers and churches requesting them, the Sunday School Board has largely obviated the need during recent decades for colporteurs. However, the work done in earlier years by a host of humble colporteurs and missionaries, who carried and sold religious books and Bibles, was a major contribution to the development of Southern Baptist life.   HOMER L. GRICE

BIBLE INSTITUTE, FLORIDA BAPTIST. Established to train for the ministry men who had not taken advantage of earlier educational opportunities, sponsored by South Florida Association, the Institute opened in the First Baptist Church, Lakeland, on Sept. 7, 1943. Three years later it opened on its first campus with 72 students, and the following year, on Nov. 19, 1947, the Florida Baptist State Convention recognized it as a worthy Baptist school and included it in the state mission offering. Leon M. Gambrell served as president from Nov., 1946, until May, 1952, after which Arthur H. Stainback assumed the executive post. In Sept., 1954, the institute opened on its new 160-acre campus in Graceville, Fla. It owns 12 buildings, a poultry research farm, and a hatchery, both used for student employment. Endowment is valued at $250,000. With an enrolment of 136 in 1955, the school held membership in the Association of Southern Baptist Bible Institutes and the American Association of Bible Institutes. The annual budget, exclusive of the dining room, totals approximately $84,000, given by Southern Baptist churches in designated gifts, by individuals, and the Florida Baptist State Convention's state mission offering.   A. H. STAINBACK

BIBLE INSTITUTE, THE. An educational institution designed for those ministers who, because of age or for some other reason, lack needed training which they cannot get elsewhere. The call to preach is sacred to Baptists. When this call comes to young men, the problem of training is not too difficult. For nearly 100 years Southern Baptists have been able to

VIRGINIA BAPTIST CHILDREN'S HOME (q.v.), Salem. Established in 1892, it serves annually more than 350 children with full- or part-time care. It includes 12 cottages, gymnasium, infirmary, printing shop, dairy barn, and other property valued at $1,500,000.

VIRGINIA BAPTIST HOME, INC. (q.v.), Culpeper. Completed in 1950, this eight unit building serves 200 aging people. Its cost was $1,500,000.

offer college and seminary training to the young preacher. Many have not accepted the offer, but it has been available. The call has not always come to men in their youth. Sometimes it has been heard and heeded by mature men, who more often than not have inadequate literary training and only a fair acquaintance with the Scriptures.

To solve this problem, some colleges maintained a high school or an academy adjacent to the campus. These offered an opportunity for the untrained to get ready for college work.

For years Southern Baptists maintained mountain schools, scattered about in various areas of the South, which offered high school training to the local youth but maintained dormitories for out-of-town students, many of whom were mature. Kentucky, Virginia, Louisiana, Texas, and Tennessee still have at least one such academy each. These schools offered limited Bible studies, but were still quite helpful to individuals who could not otherwise have had any education at all.

In addition, the seminaries have made a place for the noncollege student. Some seminary leaders believed that such provision should always be made. They encouraged young men to go to college, but took care to offer the noncollege student the same opportunities as the college graduate. Later the two educational areas were separated by the accrediting agencies in all the seminaries.

After World War I, Southern Baptists set up the Baptist Bible Institute in New Orleans under the co-operative efforts of the Home Mission Board, the Sunday School Board, and the Mississippi and Louisiana state conventions, in order to provide training for noncollege men and to serve as a center of Baptist work in its Catholic area. However, the enrolment of an increasingly larger percentage of college graduates caused the school to be changed to a theological seminary.

Meanwhile Bible institutes were begun in several areas. Among them were the West Kentucky Institute at Clinton, Clear Creek, at Pineville, Ky., the Baptist Bible Institute, Lakeland, Fla., and Fruitland Bible Institute in North Carolina. These Bible Institutes offer training for those who are inadequately equipped for college and seminary study, or who prefer institute training to college training. The curriculum consists of courses in English Bible, church history, church work, sermon preparation and delivery, pastoral service, and related subjects. In addition, basic studies are offered in regular academic fields and particularly in corrective English. Actually this work combines literary training of several levels with theological studies. The present tendency is for the state conventions to support these schools, since they are at college and subcollege levels.

Property valuation of these institutions in 1956 was $1,064,000. Endowments totaled $50,000. Where the institutes have had strong leadership, their services have made a lasting impression. In 1956 the total spring term enrolment of the group was 486, not including the enrolment at the Southern Foundation of Illinois.

See also EDUCATION, SOUTHERN BAPTIST.

LEE GALLMAN

BIBLE READERS' COURSE, THE. The Bible Readers' Course is a systematic plan for individual, daily Bible reading. Developed and promoted by the Training Union, the course provides a five-year cycle of references. Each daily reference is accompanied by a key verse, a devotional comment, a prayer thought, and the names of Southern Baptist missionaries having birthdays on that date. The daily lists of names of missionaries are taken from the missionary prayer calendar, which is promoted jointly by the Training Union and the Women's Missionary Union.

During the first two years of the five-year cycle the references provide a plan for reading through the books of the Bible. References for the first two months of each quarter are in Old Testament; New Testament books are read during the third month of each quarter. During the second two years of the five-year cycle the references are organized around great themes of the Christian faith. The references for the final year of the cycle guide in a reading through of the New Testament.

The first step in the development of the course came when the Education Committee of the B.Y.P.U. of the South provided, in 1911–12, a two-year plan for covering the entire Bible through daily Bible readings. This plan replaced in the Baptist Young People's Union Quarterly the B.Y.P.U. of America references for daily Bible reading which formerly had been carried in that quarterly. This course was repeated four times before the two-year topical course was added in 1918. The one-year course of reading through the New Testament was added in 1924. The prayer thought and missionary prayer calendar were added in 1935. Bible reading helps or devotional comments have been a part of the course from the beginning.

All of the elements in the course are carried each quarter in the Training Union quarterlies for Young People and Adults. The references also are carried in the Training Union quarterlies for Juniors and Intermediates, and they provide the basis for the devotional comments in the devotional magazine *Open Windows*.

RAYMOND M. RIGDON

BIBLE SOCIETY, AMERICAN AND FOREIGN. Organization formed in New York on May 12, 1836, in protest against the refusal of the American Bible Society to appropriate funds for the printing and circulation of the translations made by Baptist missionaries in India and Burma, in which the words relating to baptism were rendered by those equivalent to immersion. Delegates from 23 states in 1837 met in Philadelphia and completed the organization of the society, which proposed "to promote a wider circulation of the Holy Scriptures in the most faithful versions that can be procured." When chartered in 1848, the society had already gained, with few exceptions, the united support of the Baptists of America. In the beginning the society largely confined itself to aiding missionaries in publishing their translations. When the organization began to publish English versions, a conflict arose between those who desired a new version in English and those who favored the standard English version. The former group withdrew in 1850 and formed the American Bible Union. The sharp controversy between the union and the society, which soon divided the denomination on the question of Bible circulation, eventually led Baptists to withdraw their support from the rival organizations and in 1883 to turn over Bible work at home to the American Baptist Publication Society and foreign distribution to the American Baptist Missionary Union. After an ineffective struggle against overwhelming denominational sentiment, the two rival Bible societies quietly passed out of existence.

LYNN E. MAY, JR.

BIBLE STUDIO, THE. A Baptist newspaper of Georgia established in 1906 as the successor of *The Guardian. The Bible Studio* was replaced by the *Baptist Forum* in 1910.

JOHN J. HURT, JR.

BIBLE TRANSLATION AND DISTRIBUTION. As of May, 1956, the Bible had been published, as a whole or in part, in 1,092 different languages and dialects. No other book can approach this record. This remarkable achievement was largely accomplished in the 19th and 20th centuries, much of it in relation to the modern missionary movement. As late as A.D. 1800, only 71 languages and dialects had seen some part of the Bible in print—50 in Europe, 13 in Asia, 4 in Africa, 3 in America, and 1 in Oceania. In the next 30 years 86 new languages received some part of the Bible, 66 of them outside of Europe. The process has continued unabated.

Baptists have played a worthy part in the translation of the Scriptures. William Carey (*q.v.*), pioneer Baptist missionary to India, left a record which has never been equaled. With the aid of native scholars, he translated the entire Bible into six different languages (Bengali, Oriya, Hindi, Marathi, Sanskrit, and Assamese), the New Testament and part of the Old into five languages, the entire New Testament into 18 additional languages, and at least one gospel into five more tongues: a total of 34 languages in which some part of the Bible was rendered.

Adoniram Judson (*q.v.*), pioneer Baptist missionary from America, translated the Bible into Burmese in 1835. Among other Baptists who translated some part of the Bible into a new language were Sarah Hall Boardman (Talaing); Nathan Brown (Assamese and Japanese); W. G. Crocker and Ivory Clark (Bassa); W. F. Thomas (South Chin); Joshua Marshman, Josiah Goddard, and William Dean (High Wenli Chinese); Horace Jenkins (Kinhwa Chinese); S. B. Partridge (Swatow Chinese); T. J. Keith, E. G. Phillips, and M. C. Mason (Garo); Ola Hanson (Southern Kachin); J. H. Vinton, Francis Mason, and D. L. Brayton (Pwo Karen); Jonathan Wade and F. Mason (Sgaw Karen); C. H. Harvey and H. Richards (Kongo); W. Pettigrew (Manipuri and Tangkhul Naga); C. B. Banks (Mongo); S. W. Rivenburg (Naga); E. W. Clark (Ao Naga); Eric Lund and Braulio Manikan (Panayan); A. C. Bowers (Rabha); J. N. Cushing (Shan); J. T. Jones (Tai); A. Sims (Teke); J. M. Carvell (Mikir); H. Cope (Chin); W. H. Leslie (Hungana); H. D. Brown (Bolia); J. H. Telford (Lahu); B. J. Anderson (Lhota Naga); J. E. Tanquist (Rengma Naga and Sema Naga); M. Vincent Young (Wa); Johnston Lykins and James H. Chute (Shawnee); John Davis (*q.v.*) and J. Lykins (Muskogee); Henry Frieland Buckner (*q.v.*) (Muskogee); Moses Merrill (Oto).

The printing and distribution of Bibles has largely been the work of nondenominational Bible societies. The British and Foreign Bible Society was founded in London in 1804, with Joseph Hughes, a Baptist, as its first secretary. In 1816 the American Bible Society was organized. Baptists gave strong support to this organization until 1836, when the society refused to aid in the printing of a Bengali Bible in which the Greek work *baptizō* was translated "immerse." Partly as a result of this, Baptists founded the American and Foreign Bible Society in 1837. When this organization failed to issue an English version in which the word *baptizō* was rendered "immerse," another society was founded in 1850, called the American Bible Union. These two separate Baptist Bible societies continued until 1883, when "it was decided that Bible work at home was to be carried on by the American Baptist Publication Society, while that for foreign distribution was to be carried on by the American Baptist Missionary Union."

Southern Baptists founded a separate Bible board, with headquarters in Nashville, Tenn., in 1851. It failed to gain solid support, and was abolished in 1861. Gradually, Southern Baptists turned their support to the American Bible Society. This increased rapidly after 1945. In the five-year period from 1949 to 1954, Southern Baptist contributions to the American Bible Society increased from $76,384 to $112,064. In 1954 the Southern Baptist contribution was second only to that of the Methodist church. The American Bible Society was allowed each year to present its work on the program of the annual meeting of the Southern Baptist Convention. Through their Foreign Mission Board, Southern Baptists also supported publishing houses in El Paso, Tex., Rio de Janeiro, Brazil,

Buenos Aires, Argentina, and Ibadan, Nigeria. Bibles were printed only at the Rio center.

H. C. GOERNER

BIBLICAL BACKGROUNDS.
I. Old Testament Times. Old Testament times were the restless seas that produced the great kingdoms of old. There flowed through them, however, a stream as separate from them as the Gulf Stream is from the oceans, a benevolent and saving influence, the worship of Yahweh. The kingdoms of the ancient world were built on culture, commerce, and conquest for gain. Israel drew many benefits from the endeavors of civilized men but, in spite of lapses, was intended to be a religious community, different from her neighbors.

ANCIENT BABYLONIA. *Prehistoric Era.*—Semites were in the north, Sumerians in the south. Sumerian culture was well advanced in architecture, art, and literature; its mythological epics, including those of creation and the flood, were probably familiar to the patriarchs of the Bible; its polytheism, however, its religious sanction of immorality, and its practice of human sacrifice were spurned by all worshipers of Yahweh. The early chapters of Genesis make the development of Yahweh worship their theme, and they credit the Yahweh worshipers with convictions about religion and moral conduct that contradict the idolaters. The poetic passages, Genesis 2:23; 3:14-19; 4:23-24; 9:25-27, are presented as quotations from early sources and reflect a culture as high as the Sumerian but also a theology and an ethic markedly different from pagan religion.

City-kingdoms. (*c.* 4000-2360 B.C.).—Kish, Lagash, Nippur, Akkad, Umma, Erech, Ur, and Opis were the most prominent ones. The culture included great libraries, temples, art, and commerce, all reflecting the seductive influence of idolatry.

Empires.—The Akkadian Empire, *c.* 2360-1960 B.C., took its name from the Akkad mentioned in Genesis 10:10. It was founded by Semites who absorbed Sumerian culture. Nineveh became a focal point in the north. About 2070 the empire reorganized with Ur as the capital. Terah, Abram, and Lot probably left Ur in this period and settled at Haran, a city of the Arameans in Syria. Hammurabi, who lived 1748-1675, was a great leader in this culture. His legal code and others were used extensively in the Pentateuch but were purified and made more humane.

ASSYRIA. *Early Period.*—Assyria was founded by Semites from Babylonia, *c.* 2500 B.C., with a Semitic language, a Babylonian culture, and an idolatrous religion. Ashur and Mari rose to power, *c.* 1960-1700; other peoples were gradually subjugated by a military state and an absolute monarchy motivated by desire to control trade. Abraham moved out of Babylonia over its trade routes, seeking to escape idolatry and led by divine call.

Empires.—At this time, *c.* 1400-745 B.C., came domination of Babylonia, Syria, and other countries established by Tiglath Pileser I, *c.* 1150. Asshurnasirpal II, 884-860, temporarily restored the empire. Shalmaneser III, 860-824, made Israel pay tribute. During the Second Empire, 745-612, established by Tiglath Pileser III, Babylonia was annexed; and Samaria was carried captive by Sargon II in 722. Amos and Hosea had predicted this catastrophe as a result of the corruption of Israel by idolatry. Judah was invaded by Sennacherib in 701. Nineveh was destroyed in 612 by Medes, Babylonians, and others, as had been predicted by the prophets Nahum and Habakkuk as a result of Nineveh's bloody rule.

NEO-BABYLONIAN EMPIRE. This period lasted from 612 to 539 B.C. World supremacy was attained under Nebuchadnezzar II, 604-562. The captivity for Judah, which had been predicted by Isaiah and Micah, came to pass. Daniel was taken away in 604, Ezekiel in 598. By the time of restoration, as predicted by the same prophets, Jewish reaction against idolatry had eliminated it from Jewish life.

EGYPT. During the predynastic era Egypt was a mixture of Hamites, Semites, and others. The calendar was invented 2421 B.C.; agriculture, trade, art, and government advanced; religion was mythological, and Pharaoh was a god. At the time of the early dynasties and after (*c.* 2850-1720), the priesthood was predominant, and there was a pantheon of gods. Worship was characteristically licentious and included the practice of human sacrifice. During this period the pyramids were built. The Middle Kingdom (*c.* 2150-1720) brought a great civic order based on law and expansion into Canaan. During the Hyksos Period (*c.* 1720-1550) and the New Kingdom (*c.* 1570-1065), nomadic culture introduced by the Hyksos invaders made possible Abraham's sojourn and Joseph's career. Under the New Kingdom, Canaan and Syria were dominated, and the Israelites were oppressed. Moses was trained as a prince; the Israelites were forced to learn many skills and given opportunity by Egypt's later decline to use them in establishing themselves as a nation. During the Late Period (*c.* 1065-332) there was constant interplay of political, commercial, and idolatrous influences between Egypt and Israel, from Solomon's time onward. Yahweh worship in Israel was undermined by these and similar influences in Canaan.

PERSIA. Racial and linguistic features link the Medes and Persians with the Japhite peoples of Genesis 10. Zoroastrian dualism supplanted the old polytheism, *c.* 900 B.C. The empire was established by conquests of Cyrus the Great over Media in 549, Lydia in 546, and Babylonia in 538; Aramaic was adopted by the Jews for popular use and many contributions to civilization made through it; normative Judaism made great strides toward the universal outlook which Christianity brought to fulfilment later. In 536 a Jewish remnant was granted permission by Cyrus to return to Palestine and rebuild the Temple; Artaxerxes I permitted the second group to return in 458 under Ezra. Jerusalem was rebuilt in 445 under Nehemiah. The Persian empire was absorbed into the Greek Empire of Alexander the Great, c. 332.

J. WASH WATTS

II. Intertestamental Times. The intertestamental period includes the time between the writing of the latest book of the Old Testament and the beginning of the New Testament records. Thus, for some it dates well back into the Persian period (538–331 B.C.), and for others it begins in the Maccabean period (167–63), depending upon one's critical views regarding certain books of the Old Testament. In either instance the period covered is one of considerable importance.

Following the death of Alexander the Great in 323 B.C. and the consequent division of his empire, the Jews were dominated by the Ptolemaic rulers of Egypt. This political alignment prevailed until 198, when Antiochus the Great defeated the Egyptians at Panium, and the Jews came under the control of the Seleucid rulers of Syria.

One of these Seleucid rulers, Antiochus IV (Epiphanes), was of particular importance to this period. His accession to the throne in 175 B.C., his efforts to enforce Greek culture upon the Jews, and his ruthless determination to destroy the Jewish religion led to the outbreak of the Maccabean rebellion in 167. At this time Mattathias, a priest who was outraged by the pagan oppressions, and his five sons—Judas, Jonathan, Eleazar, John, and Simon—challenged all who were zealous for the law to revolt against the Syrians and to punish the apostate Jews who collaborated with them. During the conflicts of the next several years, the Jews achieved religious liberty under Judas in 165 and political liberty under Simon in 142. Following the victory of Judas, the Temple was cleansed and rededicated, an event which was celebrated annually in the Feast of Dedication (John 10:22); and a few months after the victory of Simon, the Jewish nation conferred upon him and his descendants permanent authority as ruling high priests; thus, the Hasmonean dynasty was established.

Simon (143–135 B.C.) ruled until his assassination at the hands of his son-in-law. He was succeeded by his son, John Hyrcanus (135–104), who took advantage of the dynastic dissensions among the Syrian rulers to enlarge the borders of his rule, so that, at the time of his death, the Jewish state was at the height of its power. He was succeeded by his son Aristobulus I (104–103), who became the first of the Hasmonean rulers to adopt the royal title "king of the Jews." His short and violent reign was succeeded by the long and violent reign of Alexander Janneus (103–76), a brother whom he had imprisoned and who later married his widow Salome Alexandra. He was succeeded by Salome Alexandra (76–67), widowed a second time, during whose reign the Pharisees were permitted for the first time to have an important place in the government. Following her death there was a period of intermittent civil strife as her two sons, Hyrcanus II and Aristobulus II, fought over the throne. Their quarreling and the period of Jewish political independence were both ended by the Roman conquest of Jerusalem under Pompey in 63, thus initiating the Roman period in the history of the Jews which provided the political background of the world into which Jesus Christ came.

The intertestamental period was important for several reasons: During this period the Jews were dispersed over wide areas of the Mediterranean world; Greek culture left its impress upon Jewish thought; the biblical message was made available to Greek-speaking people through the translation of the Hebrew Scriptures in the Septuagint; the Jewish sects were fully developed; and important developments took place in the doctrines of God, sin, the law, angelology, and demonology, and particularly eschatology, as is evidenced in the study of the Old Testament Apocrypha and Pseudepigrapha.

J. W. MACGORMAN

III. New Testament Times. JEWISH WORLD. At the beginning of the New Testament era, Jewish people were to be found in practically all of the Mediterranean world and as far east as ancient Shushan. In Palestine itself the Jews had been under control of the Romans since 63 B.C; although a large measure of home rule was allowed, they were never able to lose consciousness of the fact that they were a subject people. The hand of the tax collector and of the Roman legionnaires was always in evidence. The destruction of Jerusalem by the Romans in A.D. 70 marked the end of the Jewish nation as a political entity and, according to Josephus, put an end to the perpetual sacrifice in the Temple.

Religious attitudes of the Jewish world found expression in a number of religious parties or sects. Of these groups the Pharisees, the Sadducees, and the Essenes were the most influential. The Pharisees thought of themselves as the guardians of the law and went to fantastic ends to keep out any liberal interpretations. That they were popular with the common people cannot be doubted. The Sadducees, though less numerous than the Pharisees, were more powerful, since they represented the aristocratic and more liberal element who were slowly coming to the position that the law needed supplementary revelation for its interpretation and application. Their control of the Temple and its worship gave them an enviable position and one which they were careful to guard and exploit. The Essenes represented the extreme pietistic attitude of the day and were severe ascetics. These and other sects made their contributions and also supplied their share of hindrances to progress.

The synagogue as a place of religious instruction and worship, the Temple as a place of sacrifice and worship, and the Sanhedrin as an ecclesiastical court constituted the three major institutions of Jewish life in the first century. H. E. SPELL

IV. New Testament Times. GRECO-ROMAN WORLD. The conditions which Christianity found in the Greco-Roman world determined the character of its history for several centuries and have profoundly affected that history to the present time. The human race was already old and numerous, differentiated by color, language, culture, religion, mental and moral characteristics. The civilized peoples lived on a strip of land some twenty degrees in width, lying southeast by northwest in S. Europe, N. Africa, and S. Asia, most of it in N. Temperate zone. In E. half lay India, China, Japan, in W. half the Semites, Greeks, and Romans. The two portions knew and influenced each other very little. Outside this strip all mankind was barbarous or savage, destitute of all elements of civilized life, such as settled life, written language, literature, art, architecture, music, the sciences. No means exist for knowing the population of the world at that time even approximately.

Christianity was born near the center of the W. half of civilized mankind. Here it worked for five centuries and this Greco-Roman world we must now study.

1. *Politically* most of it was subject to the Romans; lay around Mediterranean with c. 100,000,000 population. Its government consisted of (a) central authority—Emperor and Senate; (b) provincial governors appointed by emperor and senate; (c) local municipal governments. It was firm and in the main just, with much local freedom; brought all races under law, preserved order, prevented petty internecine strifes, suppressed robbery, built good roads, kept open communications by sea and land between all parts of the Empire; its judges, in the main, just, its law faithfully administered; it was regarded by early Christians as a providential preparation for the coming of Christ. Its law and legal procedure have profoundly influenced the subsequent history of Europe.

2. *Races and Their Distribution.* Many peoples intermingled and greatly mixed. (1) *Latins* in Italy, N. Africa, Spain and Gaul, which were largely Latinized. (Compare their languages.) The military and governing classes everywhere were Romans; Latin the official language. (2) *Greeks* in Greece and its islands, Asia Minor, Syria, N. and E. Palestine, Egypt, the coasts of Italy, Sicily, Rome, S. E. Gaul, and elsewhere. (3) *Jews* (a) Palestinian (b) the Dispersion, mostly commercial people in the cities of Egypt, Cyprus, Syria, Asia Minor, Greece, Macedonia, Italy, Spain, Mesopotamia, Persia and farther East. (4) *Other Semites* (a) Syrians in Syria and Mesopotamia; (b) Arabs in Arabia; (c) Phoenicians in Phoenicia and North Africa; (5) *Other native populations* (a) Celts in Gaul, British Islands and Galatia; (b) Copts in Egypt; (c) Berbers in North Africa; (d) various native peoples in Asia Minor and Southeast Europe.

Surrounding the Empire were the Germans on the north, still barbarous; on the east the Persians, Parthians, Scythians; on the south various desert tribes in Asia and Africa.

3. *Social and Economic Conditions.* (1) Many *slaves*, white, captives in war, without legal rights, and often cruelly treated; (2) *woman* was debased, with few rights often immoral; children were poorly educated and little regarded; (3) there were extremes of wealth and poverty (200,000 mendicants in Rome alone). Agriculture, manufacture and commerce still primitive.

4. *Culture.* The masses even of civilized peoples were everywhere illiterate; no system of public schools; education was in private schools and by tutors; books few and costly, made by copying with the hand; education was literary, rhetorical, artificial. Sources of culture were various: (1) That of ancient Egypt, Babylonia, Assyria and Persia had largely perished. Only the ruins of their architecture and sculpture remained. (2) The primitive native populations had never possessed much culture. (3) The culture of Persia had affected the Empire little, that of India and of China perhaps not at all. (4) The golden age of *Grecian* culture was past, but the language had been widely diffused by commerce, colonization and war (Alexander), and was the chief vehicle of culture for that world. The elements of Greek culture were: (a) A beautiful, flexible and expressive language, widely distributed; (b) an extensive literature, which still serves as models in dramatic, lyric and epic poetry, in oratory and in history; (c) art and architecture (Doric, Ionic and Corinthian); (d) philosophy, which has deeply affected philosophy and theology to the present time. The most influential philosophers were Pythagoras (c. 582–510 B.C.), Socrates (469–399), Plato (427–347), Aristotle (384–322); Zeno, founder of the Stoic school (340–260); Epicurus (342–270), and Pyrrho, founder of the Skeptics (360–270). Philosophy was the religion and the moral support of the more intelligent—"a schoolmaster to bring the Greek to Christ." (5) *Romans*, contributed law, stable government, internal order, good roads, open seas. Their literature and philosophy were dependent upon Greek models, but Latin ultimately became the language of theology and learning for the Western world, and held that position till recently. (6) *Jews* cannot be said to have contributed anything of importance to culture. Their contribution was in the realm of religion and morals.

5. *Religion.* All peoples were religious; their religions were national; i. e., not personal or universal. They related almost exclusively to the ordinary affairs of the present life—propitiating the gods to appease their anger and enlist their aid in personal and national matters—for health,

happiness, good crops, victory, safety; there was belief in future life, but it was shadowy, uncertain and uninviting. The greater gods were national, but there were local and household gods or spirits, e. g., nymphs and sprites of Greeks, lares and penates of Romans. All, except Judaism, were polytheistic, with male and female divinities often immoral; only in Judaism was there union of morals and religion. All had sacrifices, priesthoods, temples, sacred seasons, more or less ritual, but little or no religious instruction. Roman conquests and commercial intercourse were breaking down religious prejudices by bringing all religions into contact with one another. (1) In Greek religion the gods were personifications of the powers of nature resting on a semi-pantheistic basis; aesthetic, intellectual, but morally feeble; inadequate conception of sin, uncertain belief in immortality; rich in mythology, creative of beautiful and impressive temple architecture but no Bible, distinctly religious literature or religious instruction. (2) In Roman religion the gods were personifications of the functions of society, the reproduction of a roman household; public worship was ceremonial and legal, conducted by the State; emperor worship was later required of all subjects; Roman religion much more serious but less stimulating than the Greek; no Bible, religious literature or instruction. (3) In Jewish religion: (a) One living God, holy, the creator and upholder of all things; monotheism; (b) high moral precepts with religious sanction; (c) hope of a Messiah; golden age in the future; one temple, a priesthood, ritual; synagogues for non-sacrificial worship and instruction; Bible and instruction. (4) Syrian, Egyptian, and other religions were widely distributed, often grossly immoral, rarely elevating. Worship of Cybele, Isis, Mithra, etc., was spreading over the Empire. Last century B.C. was an age of skepticism, but through efforts of Augustus and others, faith in the fundamentals of religion was reviving during the first Christian century.

6. *Morals.* Political life was debased. Provincial governors often became rich by graft and oppression. The Emperor, often made by the army and controlled by favorites, slaves and concubines, was supreme and growing more despotic with the centuries; the *Senate* and subordinate officials subservient, venal, cringing. *Amusements* among Greeks and Romans were mostly outdoor sports—gladiatorial shows, races, the theater—were idolatrous and morally degrading. The *army* was efficient, but cruel, war almost constant. *Slavery* was extensive and corrupting. *Literature* was often debased; morals had little religious sanction. There was boundless sexual immorality of most revolting character, divorce, low regard for children; abortion frequent, exposure and murder of children allowed; theft, graft, oppression, gambling, and drunkenness were common.

Into this world came Christianity to redeem and transform the whole life of the whole race. It grappled with men and conditions as it found them, with what result Christian history has to relate.

(NOTE: This section is from *A Guide to the Study of Church History* by W. J. MCGLOTHLIN. Used by permission.)

BIBLIOGRAPHY: J. M. Adams, *Ancient Records and The Bible* (1946). W. F. Albright, *From the Stone Age to Christianity* (1946); "Old Testament World," *The Interpreter's Bible*, Vol. I (1952). G. A. Barton, *Archaeology and the Bible* (1937). J. H. Breasted, *A History of Egypt from the Earliest Times to the Persian Conquest* (1912). R. H. Charles, ed., *The Apocrypha and Pseudepigrapha of the Old Testament in English* (1913); *Religious Development Between the Old and the New Testaments* (1914). W. H. Davis and E. A. McDowell, *A Source Book of Interbiblical History* (1948). H. and H. A. Frankfort, J. A. Wilson, T. Jacobsen, and W. A. Irwin, *Intellectual Adventure of Ancient Man* (1946). E. J. Goodspeed, *The Apocrypha: An American Translation* (1938). F. Kenyon, *The Bible and Archaeology* (1940). S. N. Kramer, *Sumerian Mythology* (1944). W. E. Oesterley, *The Books of the Apocrypha* (1914); *An Introduction to the Books of the Apocrypha* (1935). R. H. Pfeiffer, *History of New Testament Times: with an Introduction to the Apocrypha* (1949). J. B. Pritchard, ed., *Ancient Near Eastern Texts Relating to the Old Testament* (1950). H. H. Rowley, *The Relevance of Apocalyptic* (1947). E. Schurer, *A History of the Jewish People in the Time of Jesus Christ*, 5 vols. (n.d.). C. C. Torrey, *The Apocryphal Literature* (1945). J. E. M. White, *Ancient Egypt* (1952).

BIBLICAL LANGUAGES. The major languages in which the Scriptures were originally written were Hebrew and Greek. The Old Testament was written, over a period of some 1500 years, in Hebrew, but it included a few short passages in Aramaic. These are found particularly in Daniel and Ezra. The New Testament was written in Greek, during a period conservatively estimated at 60 years.

The Hebrew of the Old Testament was primarily the language of the Jewish people and never achieved international use. It is one of the Canaanite dialects of northwest Semitic and is thus closely related to Aramaic, Ugaritic, and Moabite. Etymologically, Old Testament Hebrew is well developed. Even in the earliest writings can be found a varied and expressive vocabulary. Words were well defined. The language was concrete, not lending itself to the expression of abstract thought; and, therefore, it helped to shape the personal and vivid character of the Hebrew religion. In this picturesque, graphically concrete language, the creation is described as the personified breath of God brooding upon the face of an unknown void symbolized by deep waters, and the care and providence of God are affirmed in the expression, "The Lord is my shepherd." This is language rich in meaning, but it is meaning closely connected to and symbolized by material existence. It is meaning which is metaphorical rather than philosophical, evocative rather than scientific.

Hebrew syntax, on the other hand, is quite undeveloped and limited. Exactness of expression is impossible, especially with regard to tenses. Strictly speaking, Hebrew can express only two kinds of action—that which is completed, and that which is incomplete. The perfect tense denotes action which is finished; but it may refer to completed action in the present, in the past, or in the future. The imperfect denotes incomplete action, but again with no connection to a particular point in time. In fact the true meaning of any Hebrew verb is determined primarily by the context. Thus the Hebrew language is, because of its very structure, unsuited to exact explanation and analysis —the exploration of precise relationships between ideas, between events, or between man and God. It is a language most suited to simple affirmation; therefore, an ideal language for a religion founded on belief, on faith, on the affirmation of God and the truth of his laws.

The Greek of the New Testament is generally quite different from Hebrew, but in some ways it is quite similar. Like the Hebrew, the Greek of the New Testament is a vernacular language. Called Koine (common) Greek, it was the universal language of the Mediterranean world. It was a language of commerce and trade, of law, of everyday affairs—the most concrete kind of Greek. But this Koine Greek had quite different roots from Old Testament Hebrew. Greek had been the language of Homer and later was the language of the greatest of ancient philosophies. In developing from the classical to the Koine, the language, of course, changed; but the changes affected vocabulary and style more than grammar and syntax, and the expressive resources of the language were not lost.

This Koine Greek is a language of exactness. Vocabulary is highly developed. It includes not only a wealth of concrete expressions and a rich metaphorical and poetic tradition, but also the abstract terminologies of philosophy and logic. Words are highly inflected, revealing with precision fine shades of meaning and relationship. A well-developed system of prepositions carries this analysis of relationships still further. Most elaborate of all is the system of tenses; unlike modern English, it is not so much temporal as descriptive. Although it can refer to particular points in time—past, present, future—it is more concerned with the *character* of a given action. The tense system deals with fine distinctions between linear action (action which is continued over a period of time), point action (action which is specific, precise, and discrete), and completed action.

Thus the New Testament writers, provided with a language rich in resources for exact analysis as well as rich description, had a medium well suited for the explanation and description, in great detail, of those completed historical events—the life, death, and resurrection of Christ—on which the Christian faith is based. The Old Testament writers had a language suited to the revelation of a God who must be trusted to perform some unknown future redemptive act; the New Testament writers had a language suited to the revelation of the good news of a Saviour who had performed that redemptive act and who must in some measure be understood as well as trusted. Both languages, in their concreteness, in their vernacular quality, were closely related to life and to the problems and condition of human beings. They thus were suited for the revelation of a religion with its good news of redemption and righteousness for all men.   JUDSON BOYCE ALLEN

BIBLICAL RECORDER. One of the earliest publications established by North Carolina Baptists, founded in 1833 by Thomas Meredith (*q.v.*). The first issue of the paper was published Saturday, Jan. 4, 1834, in Edenton, when its full title was *Biblical Recorder and Journal of Passing Events*. Meredith served as editor, and at the same time was pastor of the Edenton Baptist Church. Immediate forerunner of the *Biblical Recorder* was the *North Carolina Baptist Interpreter*, a monthly publication, which first appeared Jan. 17, 1833, edited by Meredith in Edenton. After the first issue of the *Biblical Recorder*, however, no other issue appeared until Jan. 7, 1835. In the meantime, Meredith had become pastor of the First Baptist Church, New Bern, where he published the second issue of the paper and continued publication until Jan. 18, 1838, when the paper was moved to Raleigh, a more central part of the state. Since that date the *Biblical Recorder* has been published regularly except in 1842 when no issues appeared for lack of financial support and about six months in 1865 at the close of the Civil War.

Since Meredith's principal aim was the promotion of objects of the Baptist state convention, the *Biblical Recorder* contained articles on missions, education, and Sunday schools, as well as theological discussions and church news. In setting forth the proposal for establishment of the *Biblical Recorder* in the Sept., 1834, issue of the *Interpreter*, Meredith wrote:

> The periodical now proposed will be strictly a Baptist publication, and will be primarily devoted to interests of our denomination, in the region of country through which it is destined to circulate. It shall, however, be conducted on principles of Christian liberality, and shall so far contain information touching the interests and operations of other evangelical societies as shall give it some claim at least to the notice of friends of religion in general.

The paper, characteristically a family religious paper at its establishment, has continued as such throughout its history.

Early in 1838 Meredith received the subscription list and good will of the *Southern Watchman*, the South Carolina Baptist paper, and merged the two papers under the title, *Biblical Recorder and Southern Watchman*. The connection with South Carolina Baptists continued for only a short time, however.

Editors since Meredith, who served until his death Nov. 13, 1850, have included James Dunn Hufham (*q.v.*), 1861–67; John Haymes Mills (*q.v.*), 1868–73; Christopher Thomas Bailey (*q.v.*), 1875–95; Josiah William Bailey (*q.v.*),

1895–1907; Hight C Moore, 1908–17; Livingston Johnson (*q.v.*), 1917–31, James Sadberray Farmer (*q.v.*), 1931–38; George Washington Paschal (*q.v.*), acting editor, 1938–39; John Calvin Slemp, 1939–41; and Levy L. Carpenter, since 1942.

Although the *Biblical Recorder* was privately owned until 1938, it has always been described as the organ of the Baptist State Convention of North Carolina and in more recent years as the journal of the Baptist State Convention of North Carolina. In 1938 the state convention bought the paper and the Recorder Building following action taken at the annual meeting of the convention in Raleigh, Nov. 15–17, of that year. At that time the *Recorder* committee of five was enlarged to 15, with instructions to complete business transactions, select an editor, and present a certificate of incorporation to the next convention. By the following year these instructions were carried out with the transfer of the paper and all its properties, including the building, to Biblical Recorder, Inc., the selection of John Calvin Slemp, as editor, and the signing of a certificate of incorporation dated Dec. 15, 1939.

Circulation of the paper in 1954 was 58,457, with 1,087 churches having a *Recorder* club and 387 having the every-family plan. The paper's own board of directors, consisting of 16 men from various sections of the state, elects the editor and other members of the staff, and makes an annual report to the convention. Each year the *Recorder* receives from the convention through the Cooperative Program $28,800, which provides a supplement of 50 cents each on every-family subscriptions and pays for sending complimentary subscriptions of the *Recorder* to active Baptist pastors in the state, North Carolina students in Southern Baptist seminaries, North Carolina missionaries on foreign fields, and libraries and hospitals in the state. Property owned by the paper, including the furniture, a Speedaumat Addressograph, and other fixtures and equipment, is valued at $5,812. The paper is printed by contract on a flatbed press by the Bynum Printing Company of Raleigh. Practically complete files of the *Biblical Recorder* from the beginning of the *North Carolina Baptist Interpreter* in 1833 are kept in fireproof vaults of Wake Forest College, and 100 years (1833–1932) of these files have been microfilmed.

BIBLIOGRAPHY: L. Johnson, "Baptist Newspapers in the State," *The Growth of 100 Years of North Carolina Baptists, 1830–1930* (1930). G. W. Paschal, *History of North Carolina Baptists* (1930). H. S. Stroupe, "History of the *Biblical Recorder*, 1835–1907, as Recorded in Its Files" (1937).

LEVY L. CARPENTER

BIBLICAL STUDIES, SOUTHERN BAPTIST. The contribution of Southern Baptists to the study of the Scriptures may be summarized under four headings: (1) translation, (2) interpretation, (3) emphases, (4) writings.

Translation.—In the field of translation, two main productions should be noted: the Bible Union Version (New Testament, 1891; Old Testament, 1912; published together, 1912), and the translation of the New Testament by Charles B. Williams, 1937. To a lesser extent Southern Baptist scholars had a part in producing the Revised Standard Version (New Testament, 1946; Old Testament, 1951).

The Bible Union Version was a joint work of a group of Baptist scholars from both the North and the South. The Southern Baptist members were John A. Broadus (*q.v.*) and John R. Sampey (*q.v.*), both professors in the Southern Baptist Theological Seminary. This "Baptist Bible," as it has been called, has the unique distinction of using the words "immerse" and "immersion" instead of "baptize" and "baptism." Although it is a remarkably accurate version, it never came into widespread use even among Baptists.

The New Testament translation by Charles B. Williams is distinguished by its preservation of the Greek tenses, its accurate rendering of Greek idioms, and its choice of modern everyday English, which suggests well the flavor of the original Koine. This version may be said to be a significant contribution to New Testament study, and it has had a fairly wide reception, though not at all as wide as such versions as Weymouth, Moffatt, and Goodspeed.

The Revised Standard Version, a product of the joint labors of scholars representing many denominations, had on its original committee Sampey and Archibald Thomas Robertson (*q.v.*), both professors in the Southern Baptist Theological Seminary. Robertson died in 1934 and was not replaced by a Southern Baptist. Sampey retired from the committee in 1938, and his place was taken by his colleague, Kyle M. Yates.

Since both Robertson and Sampey were members of the committee a relatively short time, and since Yates, though a member 13 years, was not as active as some of the other members, the Southern Baptist contribution to the Revised Standard Version cannot be considered outstanding.

Interpretation.—Two words—"conservative" and "evangelical"—suitably sum up the nature of the best of Southern Baptists' contribution to the interpretation of the Bible.

John A. Broadus, professor of New Testament, may be thought of as outstanding among the earlier Southern Baptist Bible interpreters. His *Commentary on Matthew* is still widely used, and his *Harmony of the Gospels* had great influence in its day.

Another interpreter of great influence was Benajah Harvey Carroll (*q.v.*), whose long years of teaching the English Bible at Baylor University and later at Southwestern Seminary helped to mold the attitude of a host of ministerial students toward the Bible. His 17-volume *Interpretation of the English Bible*, which has had widespread use by Southern Baptist preachers, has doubtless done its share to help keep the pattern of their Bible teaching conservative.

Progressive in approach, yet at the same time conservative, were such teachers as Sampey, Robertson, William Owen Carver (*q.v.*), H. E. Dana (*q.v.*), and William Hersey Davis (*q.v.*). All these were masters of the grammatico-historical method and completely abreast of critical Bible knowledge, but at the same time thoroughly evangelical in their attitudes and positions. Of these, Robertson deserves special mention. His monumental work, *A Grammar of the Greek New Testament in the Light of Historical Research* (1914), marked him in his day as one of the half-dozen leading New Testament Greek scholars of the world. He was also the most prolific writer of all Southern Baptist Bible scholars, having to his credit more than 40 volumes on New Testament subjects, as well as numerous articles in theological journals, Bible dictionaries, and encyclopedias.

Emphases.—The rank and file of Southern Baptist people have throughout their history maintained a conservative attitude toward the Bible. They have accepted it as the Word of God and therefore authoritative in religious faith and practice.

The biblical emphasis is central in each of the theological seminaries which Southern Baptists have established. Much importance is thus attached to Bible knowledge in the training of preachers, and this, naturally, is both a reflection of the popular attitude within the denomination and an influence upon that attitude. Similarly, the Sunday school lesson courses produced and promoted by the Sunday School Board have not been only Bible-based but Bible-centered. This is true of both the widely used Uniform Lesson Series and the more restricted Graded Series. Indeed, the leadership in Southern Baptist Sunday school work conceives of the Sunday school primarily as a Bible-teaching agency. Popular Bible study for all age groups on Sunday morning has become one of the most outstanding features of Southern Baptist church life.

Writings. It is impossible in this limited space to list more than a few of the significant writings of Southern Baptist Bible scholars. The following deserve special mention: J. McKee Adams, *Biblical Backgrounds* (1934), *Ancient Records and the Bible* (1946); John A. Broadus, *Commentary on Matthew* (1886), *Harmony of the Gospels* (1893; revised by A. T. Robertson, 1922); B. H. Carroll, *An Interpretation of the English Bible*, 17 Vols. (1913); W. O. Carver, *Missions in the Plan of the Ages* (1909); H. E. Dana, *The New Testament World* (1937), *The Epistles and Apocalypse of John* (1937); William Hersey Davis, *Beginner's Grammar of the Greek New Testament* (1923); Clyde T. Francisco, *Introducing the Old Testament* (1950); H. I. Hester, *The Heart of Hebrew History* (1949), *The Heart of the New Testament* (1950); Edward A. McDowell, *The Meaning and Message of the Book of Revelation* (1951); A. T. Robertson, *Syllabus for New Testament Study* (1902; fifth edition enlarged, 1923), *Epochs in the Life of Paul* (1909), *A Grammar of the Greek New Testament in the Light of Historical Research* (1914; five editions), *World Pictures in the New Testament*, 6 Vols. (1930–33); John R. Sampey, *Syllabus for Old Testament Studies* (1903; fifth edition revised 1924); Frank Stagg, *The Book of Acts* (1955); Ray Summers, *Worthy Is The Lamb* (an interpretation of the book of Revelation, 1951); J. B. Tidwell, *The Bible, Period by Period* (1923); J. Wash Watts, *A Survey of Old Testament Teaching*, 2 Vols. (1947); Kyle M. Yates, *The Essentials of Biblical Hebrew* (1938), *Preaching from the Prophets* (1942), *Preaching from the Psalms* (1948).

HOWARD P. COLSON

BIBLICAL THEOLOGY. A branch of doctrinal studies which attempts to set forth the basic teachings of Scripture in their own historical and literary context. The scope may include the entire Bible or each Testament separately or other natural divisions of Scripture, such as the epistles of Paul, the Synoptic Gospels, or the writings of John.

All theology claims to be biblical, but the distinguishing characteristic of biblical theology is its principle of organization. It does not attempt to erect a systematic structure of doctrine into which the Bible may be fitted verse by verse in the old "proof text" way; rather, it attempts to discover in each book the unifying theme which integrates and interprets the entire work, relating all other teachings to this central theme. The subdivisions of the theme are determined then, not by some logical or systematic order, but by the nature of the biblical material itself. This usually means that the divisions will be historical (e.g., Mosaic period, post-Exilic, etc.) because the basic nature of the Bible is its interpretation of specific events, such as the redemptive acts of God in the life of Israel, the ministry of Jesus, and the early church. Sometimes the particular events become the main divisions of the doctrinal teaching, and at other times the type of literature is a determining factor (e.g., legislative codes, wisdom literature, etc.).

Such a method of organization is most easily applied to a single book; but the problem increases as the scope is widened to include all of the writings of a single author, an entire Testament, or the entire Bible. Some scholars have pronounced it an impossible task; but Christians must continue in this task because they are convinced of the essential unity of the Bible in its divine authorship, in its central theme of the redemptive acts of God in history culminating in the life, death, and resurrection of Jesus Christ, and in its authoritative place in the life and faith of Christians.

The formal beginning of this discipline may be located in the inaugural address of Johann Philipp Gabler as professor of theology at the University of Altdorf, Germany, on Mar. 30, 1787, when he gave an "Oration on the Proper Distinction between Biblical and Dogmatic Theology." The practice of this discipline is apparent whenever Christians seek to bring forth from the Scriptures their essential teaching and relate it to the whole body of Christian truth and to all aspects of Christian living.

BIBLIOGRAPHY: M. Burrows, *Outlines of Biblical Theology* (1946). A. B. Davidson, *Theology of the Old Testament* (1904). R. C. Dentan, *Preface to Old Testament Theology* (1950). W. Eichrodt, *Theologie des Alten Testaments* (1933). G. B. Stevens, *Theology of the New Testament* (c. 1899).   WAYNE E. WARD

BIBLIOGRAPHY, BAPTIST. An essential step in the study of any subject is the preparation of a list of manuscripts and printed works relating to the subject. Much has been written by and about Baptists, but no satisfactory list of these writings has been available to guide the student of Baptist life.

The earliest of several efforts which have been made to compile Baptist bibliographies was completed in 1864 by William Crowell, author of an article in *The Missionary Jubilee* (1865) entitled "Literature of American Baptists, from 1814 to 1864." Crowell was prejudiced against the Confederate states, but did include some references to Southern writings. A. H. Newman's *A Century of Baptist Achievement* (1901) contained Kerr Boyce Tupper's article entitled "Baptist Contributions to Literature During the Nineteenth Century," which helped to fill in the last half of the century.

The next effort, a British project, produced the only comprehensive and full Baptist bibliography which has yet been published in its entirety. This was William Thomas Whitley's *A Baptist Bibliography: Being a register of the chief material for Baptist history, whether in manuscript or in print, preserved in England, Wales, and Ireland*, Vol. I, 1526–1776 (1916); Vol. II, 1777–1837 (1922). Whitley included among his thousands of titles Baptist works listed in Charles Evans' massive *Bibliography of American Books* down to 1776 and those in W. E. McIntyre's *Baptist Authors: A Manual of Bibliography*. The latter was a Canadian publication and covered only the alphabetical section A–Day.

By far the most extensive list of Baptist materials ever attempted is Edward C. Starr's project entitled *A Baptist Bibliography: Being a register of printed material by and about Baptists; including works written against the Baptists*, Section A (1947). Three additional volumes, which carry the work from B through Colby, have now (1956) been published in mimeographed form. The author expects to produce one volume a year until all his findings have been published. His file includes a total of approximately 85,000 cards, and he estimates that the project will run to 15 volumes.

Starr, currently curator of The American Baptist Historical Society, Rochester, N. Y., is the outstanding bibliographer among Baptists in the United States. His comprehensive publication includes works relating to all Baptists everywhere from 1609 to date and is based on a thorough study of all important sources of information. For example, it includes Baptist works listed in the publications of Whitley, McIntyre, and Evans named above and also those in William Cathcart's *Baptist Encyclopedia* and Joseph Sabin's exhaustive *Dictionary of Books Relating to America*. The author checked his findings against the holdings of the principal college and seminary libraries and the ten million cards in the Union Catalog of the Library of Congress. Starr's work not only names Baptist publications but tells where copies are located. When completed, it will be the guide to the study of Baptist history and practices that research scholars have needed.

Although not a full bibliography, Leo T. Crismon's recent article entitled "The Literature of the Baptists," *Religion in Life*, XXV (winter, 1955–56), is a useful guide to materials about the Baptists. Often quite helpful are the bibliographies in the many articles and books on specific phases of Baptist history now in print. These lists are not designed to be exhaustive but they do contain references to source material for those who want additional information.

HENRY SMITH STROUPE

BIGGS, FRANCIS SEXTON (b. Norfolk, Va., Nov. 1, 1857; d. Baltimore, Md., Nov. 16, 1939). Prominent Baptist layman of Baltimore. His father, Major Joseph John Biggs, was a North Carolinian, and his mother, Isabelle Anderson (James) Biggs was a Philadelphian. Her mother, Elizabeth Sexton James, was a Friend. Biggs moved to Baltimore in 1869. He was a member, successively, of the Franklin Square, Fulton Avenue, North Avenue (McCormick Memorial) and University churches. He was president of the Church Extension Society for 13 years (1920–32), and for more than 50 years he was a member of the Maryland Baptist State Mission Board. He was also one of the incorporators of the Baptist Children's Aid Society, and was very active in that organization for many years. A man of splendid balance, Biggs was quick to see the possible humor in any given situation. He had a genuine humility—the inevitable expression of a deeply reverent nature. His upright posture and carriage were indicative of his mind and spirit. In his active maturity he was a striking figure, and in his later years he possessed a distinguished dignity. As an indication of his interest in things of the spirit, he took up the study of Greek grammar at 75, in order to understand his New Testament better.

FRANCIS A. DAVIS

BIRMINGHAM BAPTIST HOSPITALS. Nonprofit voluntary general institutions, owned by the Birmingham Baptist Association and operated by a board of 15 trustees. The Birmingham Baptist Hospital was purchased from W. C. Gewin, in Jan., 1922, and began accepting patients as a Baptist institution. Highland Avenue Baptist Hospital was leased in 1930 and purchased in 1934. Hospitals are accredited by the Joint Commission on Accreditation of Hospitals. Ownership of the hospitals changed hands in 1949. The hospital corporation was deeded to the Alabama Baptist State Convention as a gift from the Birmingham Baptist Association. Property was given back to the Birmingham Baptist Association within the year.

Development of modern scientific methods of diagnosis and treatment has necessitated many changes since beginning. After studying several plans for enlarging and modernizing facilities, the Birmingham Baptist Association authorized an expansion program in 1950. A campaign to raise funds was launched, and hospital trustees negotiated a loan for construction of east and north wings to add 90 patient beds and new modern facilities for surgery, radiology, and laboratories. These wings were ready for occupancy in early 1953. In late 1955 plans were readied for addition of a fourth floor to these wings, to house the obstetrical department. A reallocation of space at Highland Avenue was planned to add 10 beds, thereby increasing total bed capacity from 300 to 350. The School of Nursing, in existence at time of purchase, is fully accredited nationally and has graduated 755 students. Other components of the teaching program include intern training program, pathology residency, School of Medical Technology, and School of X-ray Technology.   JANIE LOTT

BISHOP. The title *bishop* (*episkopos*), originating and used extensively in Greek politics and found frequently in the Septuagint (II Kings 11:19; Neh. 11:9 ff.; Isa. 60:17, etc.), appears only four times in the New Testament (Acts 20:28; Phil. 1:1; I Tim. 3:1–2; Titus 1:7; possibly, I Peter 2:25), signifying *overseer*, the chief official of the local congregation. Being conjoined with the titles and functions of *elder* and *pastor* (cf. Acts 20:17, 28; Titus 1:5, 7; I Peter 5:1–2; probably, Eph. 4:11), the New Testament office of bishop shows much variation but little individual character. As it later developed, the office was probably an elevation out of the presbytery, rather than a localization out of the apostolic order. Although the qualifications are explicit (I Tim. 3:1–7; Titus 1:7–9), the duties (I Tim. 3:2; 5:17; Eph. 4:11–12), ordination (cf. Acts 14:23; Titus 1:5), tenure, and remuneration (I Tim. 5:17–18; I Peter 5: 2–3) of the office remain obscure and inconclusive.

The history of the office of bishop indicates an early tendency to become rigid and individualized, beginning with Ignatius (Bishop of Syrian Antioch, *c.* 110–117), who presents the hierarchical structure of bishop, elder, and deacon. Its contemporary connotations, grounded upon a subapostolic basis, deviate widely from the New Testament office. Perhaps for this reason Southern Baptists have disallowed the title to describe the leader in the church, preferring *pastor*.

BIBLIOGRAPHY: E. C. Dargan, *Ecclesiology* (1905). C. Gore, *The Ministry of the Christian Church* (1889). K. E. Kirk, ed., *The Apostolic Ministry* (1946). J. B. Lightfoot, *Dissertations on the Apostolic Age* (1892). T. W. Manson, *The Church's Ministry* (1948).   J. B. MCMINN

BLACK, JOHN WILLIAM (b. Rowan County, Ky., Dec. 13, 1875; d. Covington, Ky., May 15, 1950). Attorney, pastor, Kentucky Baptist leader. After attending Newfoundland Normal, a private school, Black taught school in the mountains of Kentucky, became an attorney, and was elected county attorney for Rowan County. On Jan. 3, 1896, he married Jennie L. Adkins, by whom he had one daughter and five sons. In 1916, while county attorney, Black decided to enter the ministry and began preaching at Howard's Mill, near Morehead and Mt. Sterling, Ky., about May 1 of that year. He was ordained June 1, 1916.

Although Black attended Southern Baptist Theological Seminary only a few months, he remained throughout life an avid reader and a student of the Bible. A logical thinker and a pleasing pulpit speaker, he held pastorates in Levee, Jackson, Wheatley, and Dry Ridge, Ky. During his 13-year pastorate at Latonia Baptist Church, Covington, Ky., which began May 1, 1926, he became recognized as one of the leading pastors of the state.

Black was clerk of Three Forks Association and moderator of Concord Association, member of the executive board of the General Association of Baptists in Kentucky and of its appropriations committee for seven-year periods, moderator of the general association, and its general secretary-treasurer from 1939 to 1946.

GEORGE RALEIGH JEWELL

BLACK HAWK SEMINARY. Established in Carroll County, Miss., in 1839 with E. W. Tripp as principal. The school was commended by the Baptist state convention as a female seminary of high order, but there is no record of the length of its duration.   J. L. BOYD

BLAIRSVILLE COLLEGIATE INSTITUTE. Founded by Notla River Association, Georgia, in 1905. After 1909 the school, a member of the Mercer system, was supported by the Home Mission Board, which assumed complete control in 1925 and transferred the property to the local board of education for use as a public school in 1929.   ARTHUR JACKSON

BLAKE, WILLIAM PACKER (b. Martinsburg, Pa., Nov. 14, 1857; d. Hyattsville, Md., Apr. 11, 1946). Baptist minister, editor, educator, missionary, and denominational statesman. In Mar., 1875, Blake entered printer's trade in Ohio and moved the same year to Singer's Glen, Va., to pursue that trade until 1878. That year he was licensed to preach, then entered Southern Baptist Theological Seminary, 1878–80. He was ordained at Weldon, N. C., Dec. 12, 1880, and was pastor there, 1880–83, when he moved to Indian Territory to succeed Henry Freeland Buckner (*q.v.*) as missionary to the Creek Indians. On Dec. 1, 1887, he became superintendent of the Seminary Academy for Seminole Indian girls at Sasakwa, Indian Territory. From 1894 to 1906, he served at Emahaka Academy near Wewoka, Okla., when he resigned to enter general mission work.

He was cofounder of the *Indian Missionary* in 1884 and coeditor until the next year; later he was associate editor of the *Western Baptist*. He gained denominational prominence by leadership in the Baptist Missionary and Educational Convention of Indian Territory, the Baptist General Convention of Indian Territory, and the Baptist General Convention of Oklahoma as recording secretary of these bodies consecutively, 1892–1918. Active service in educational circles included various Indian mission schools and the founding of Oklahoma Baptist University. He is buried in Fort Lincoln Cemetery, Washington, D. C. J. M. GASKIN

BLANC, HENRY DANIEL (b. Third Creek Community, Knox County, Tenn., Jan. 31, 1872; d. Knoxville, Tenn., Sept. 3, 1952). Lumberman and financier. He was the son of a Swiss immigrant who settled in Knox County soon after the Civil War. Despite limited opportunities for an education, he rose swiftly from sawmill hand to owner of a lumber business and became one of East Tennessee's most outstanding and beloved philanthropists. A mayor of Knoxville spoke of him as "the expert stairway builder whose skill was known as far west as the United States extends" and "who took the Lord as a senior partner to whom he paid 10 per cent of the profits of his business for over 50 years." Blanc believed his success in business was due to this partnership with God in returning to him the tenth of his income. He once said that as a young man he wanted more than anything in the world to be a preacher, but God had other plans; he wanted him to be his businessman.

He operated a successful lumber business in Knoxville, was a director of the Home Building and Loan Association and the Home Federal Savings and Loan Association there. Through his influence some of the surplus of the company was invested in a total of $1,000,000 in loans to 57 churches in the Knoxville area. He also lent his personal funds to churches, and at the time of his death at least 15 churches in the Appalachian region annually observed Henry D. Blanc Day in appreciation of his gifts to their building funds.

He was converted at about 13 years of age and joined the Third Creek Baptist Church. He held numerous offices of trust and responsibility—Sunday school superintendent, teacher, and deacon in the First Baptist Church, Knoxville.

Aware of his lack of education, he desired it for others. He gave large gifts to Carson-Newman College on whose board of trustees he served for 34 years. He financed the building of Blanc Hall for men students, and his leadership and gifts helped to pave the way for the entrance of the college into the Southern Association of Colleges. He was chairman of the building committee and a large contributor to the building of the East Tennessee Baptist Hospital in Knoxville, Tenn. In his many philanthropic church and civic activities, he was wise, alert, and progressive.

He was married on May 18, 1896, to Bergie Adelia Hinton. To this union were born nine children. WILLIAM F. HALL

BLAYLOCK, ARDEN PLEASANT (b. Greenwood, Ark., Dec. 1, 1897; d. Little Rock, Ark., Mar. 18, 1937). Pastor and evangelist. His parents were natives of Greenwood. He was educated in elementary schools conducted by his father in Magazine (Ouachita) Academy, Arkadelphia, Ark., and in the Southern Baptist Theological Seminary. In May, 1934, he received the D.D. degree from Ouachita College.

Blaylock married Irene Mitchell, Youngville, N. C., Oct. 25, 1922; they had three children—Betty, Billie, and Joseph. He was ordained May 16, 1917, and became noted as an able New Testament evangelist. Through several years there was an unusually large number of conversions in his revivals. A powerful pulpiteer, he held two successful pastorates: one was at Field Street Baptist Church, Cleburne, Tex., 1929–31; the other was at First Baptist Church, Little Rock, Ark., 1931–37. He was a denominational leader, a strong contender for civic righteousness, and a useful and influential citizen.

O. M. STALLINGS

BLECKLEY MEMORIAL INSTITUTE. Established in 1913 in Clayton County, Ga., as a result of a gift of property by the widow of Chief Justice Logan E. Bleckley to the Georgia Baptist convention. A member of the Mercer system in 1920, the school was controlled by the Home Mission Board until 1924 when it merged with Hiawassee Institute.

ARTHUR JACKSON

BLIND, MINISTRY TO THE. See BRAILLE BAPTIST, THE, and BRAILLE EVANGEL, THE.

BLUE MOUNTAIN COLLEGE. A senior college for women, located at Blue Mountain in the hill country of northern Mississippi, 75 miles southeast of Memphis, Tenn. The college was founded as an institute for women in 1873 by Mark Perrin Lowrey (*q.v.*), with the assistance of his daughters Modena (Mrs. Modena Lowrey Berry [*q.v.*]) and Margaret. It was chartered as a college in 1877. Operated as a private institution from 1873 to 1919, the college had Lowrey for its first president, who served until his death in 1885, and then Lowrey's two sons, William Tyndale Lowrey (*q.v.*) and Bill Green Lowrey, who served in alternate terms until 1925. Miss Modena Lowrey, who married William Edwin Berry in 1876, served successively as "Lady Principal" and vice-president of Blue Mountain until her retirement in 1934, and during that time became widely known as Mother Berry of Blue Mountain. Her husband, who had purchased half interest in the school in 1876, served as professor and part owner until his death in 1919.

Blue Mountain's enrolment increased from 51 during its first year to 141 in 1884–85. The total number of college graduates since its founding was 2,341 in 1955. In its various divisions, including the former grammar and high school divisions, Blue Mountain has served approximately 7,100 students. The grammar school and high school divisions, which had been maintained since the beginning of the college, were abolished respectively in 1922 and 1925.

Always Baptist in sympathies, Blue Mountain College was donated by its owners in 1919 to the Mississippi Baptist convention, which has been in charge of its operation since that time. President Lowrey stated in his report in 1919 that Blue Mountain College was donated to the convention free of debt through "generosity of the Jennings family" amounting to $100,000. He concluded by saying that "Blue Mountain College, therefore, is the gift to the Convention of the Lowrey and Berry families, the Jennings family and the Hearn family." Since 1925 Lawrence T. Lowrey, a grandson of the founder, has served as president of the college. Blue Mountain has been continuously accredited by the Southern Association of Colleges since 1927. It has been a member of the Association of American Colleges since 1928.

Distinguished alumnae of the college include Mary Raleigh Anderson, long-time missionary to China, and Susan B. Riley, professor of English at George Peabody College for Teachers and since 1951 president of the American Association of University Women. Although a college for women, Blue Mountain has under special circumstances admitted a few men as students. Its eight men graduates include David E. Guyton, professor emeritus of history and Rotary district governor during 1951–52, and George Duke Humphrey, president of the University of Wyoming since 1945.

The present replacement value of the college plant is estimated at $1,460,000; endowment totals $529,400. The current budget of $238,280 comes from endowment, $16,780; student fees, $152,000; and the co-operative program of the Mississippi Baptist convention, $69,500. Enrolment, Sept., 1954, through Aug., 1955, was 341.

The distinctive policy and atmosphere of Blue Mountain are attributable to a blending of several factors: the college's sense of its mission as a Christian institution; traditions created by the founding family; a carefully studied balancing of "liberal" with "vocational" learning; the student activity and student life made possible in a small college for women; vigorously administered system of student government and student honor; and a mingling within the college of certain cosmopolitan influences with the nativist and regional culture of the mid-South.

WALTER F. TAYLOR

BLUE MOUNTAIN MALE ACADEMY. A Mississippi Baptist school chartered in 1882 with T. B. Winston principal. Seventy-five students were enrolled in 1885, and four years later Blue Mountain Female College purchased the academy, appointing J. N. McMillin principal and B. G. Lowrey manager. The school closed in 1902.

J. L. BOYD

BLUE RIDGE BAPTIST. Founded by D. B. Nelson and published at Hendersonville, N. C., with Joseph E. Carter as principal editor, 1883–86. In 1890 it was turned over to J. A. Speight, who continued the publication, but moved it to Asheville, changing its name to *Asheville Baptist*. The paper failed due to lack of financial support.

L. L. CARPENTER

BLUE RIDGE INSTITUTE. A school at North Wilkesboro, N. C., under Baptist control in 1900. Three Forks Association endorsed it as a denominational school.

D. L. SMILEY

BLUEFIELD COLLEGE. The movement to establish a Baptist college in southwest Virginia began in 1915, when the Baptist General Association of Virginia appointed a committee to consider the establishment of a school for boys somewhere in the area. The committee reported favorably at the association meeting in 1916, but lack of money, the war, and other factors caused a postponement of action.

In 1919 a new committee of the general association was appointed to revive the idea of a college, and in August of that year a delegation from Bluefield offered a gift of land and $75,000 on condition that the new college be located in that city. The committee and the general association accepted the offer, and R. A. Lansdell, elected as the first president of Bluefield College, began a campaign to raise funds. Fund raising, selection of faculty, and building were difficult tasks, and the first session did not begin until Sept., 1922. Four years of high school and the first year of college were offered in the first session. The second year of college work was added in the second session, and the high school work was ultimately dropped.

While the school was projected as a junior college for men, women day students were admitted from the beginning, and since 1951 they have been admitted to residence.

Lansdell served as president until 1926. Presidents who have succeeded him are: J. Taylor Stinson, 1926–27, 1930–34; Oscar E. Sams, 1927–30; Edwin C. Wade, 1934–46; Charles L. Harman, 1946– . The college is accredited by the state of Virginia and the Southern Association of Colleges and Secondary Schools and holds membership in the American Association of Junior Colleges.

In addition to more than $700,000 contributed by Virginia Baptists for capital and operating expenses, the Home Mission Board of the Southern Baptist Convention has contributed $60,000. From the Virginia capital funds budget the college was able to complete a modern library building in 1955. Total assets are $719,707. There is an endowment of $117,187, and denominational contributions for the past session were $105,903. The total enrolment for 1955–56 was 285.

RALPH MCDANEL

BOATWRIGHT, FREDERIC WILLIAM (b. White Sulphur Springs, W. Va., Jan. 28, 1868; d. Richmond, Va., Oct. 31, 1951). For 51 years president of the University of Richmond, formerly Richmond College. The son of Reuben Baker and Elizabeth (Woodruff) Boatwright, he was married on Dec. 23, 1890, to Nellie Moore Thomas, daughter of John V. and Virginia (Moore) Thomas, of Taylorsville, Ky. They had two children, Frederic and Evelyn Moore.

He entered Richmond College at the age of 15 and graduated in 1887 with the A.B. degree. He earned the A.M. degree the following year. Graduate study in French and German was continued abroad at Halle and Paris, and later in Leipzig. During 64 years of service to the University of Richmond as teacher, president, and chancellor, his pioneering leadership in liberal education was nationally recognized. Outstanding offices in the educational field included membership on the executive committee of the Association of American Colleges and president of the Virginia–North Carolina Intercollegiate Athletic Conference. Honorary degrees were awarded by Mercer, Georgetown, and Baylor universities, and the Medical College of Virginia.

Upon his election to the presidency of Richmond College in 1895 at the age of 27, a storm of controversy arose centering chiefly around his youth and lack of proven administrative ability. He made time his friend, and every passing year wrote a new chapter of progress in the history of the growing college. In 1895, with its meager endowment sunk in Confederate bonds, Richmond College had a good name but little else. Its total resources amounted to $500,000; it had a faculty of nine, a student body of 186, and a campus of 13 acres located at Grace and Lombardy streets in the heart of Richmond. When Boatwright gave the trustees his final report after 51 years as president, Richmond College had become the University of Richmond, had foresightedly moved to a new campus of 300 acres on the western edge of the city, and had assets listed at more than $7,000,000, including $3,000,000 in endowment. The annual income was $650,000. The faculty numbered more than 100, and the student enrolment was 2,300.

Boatwright, while conservative in temperament, was a courageous exponent of academic freedom. "We must encourage our teachers and students to think," he said, "and we should not be surprised when they do not think alike." That position he steadfastly defended against all encroachments.

His personal integrity and strong Christian faith were recognized by his denomination, and he was elected to its most responsible positions, including that of president of the General Association of Virginia Baptists.

Boatwright's tall, arrow-straight bearing and friendly, but never familiar, manner commanded respect in all circles. As he completed a half century as president of his alma mater, Douglas Freeman wrote of him: "Willing to trust time but not to wait on it . . . a humanist who sensed the new science . . . an educator who always had the spirit of evangelism . . . architect of great academic designs on foundations of sure finance . . . adding day by day, he multiplied everything by ten."

His funeral service was held in the Cannon Memorial Chapel of the university that is his enduring monument.

BIBLIOGRAPHY: *Directory of American Scholars* (1942). *National Cyclopaedia of American Biography*, XI (1901). *Who's Who in America*, VI (1910–11). *Who's Who in America* (1950–51).

VERNON B. RICHARDSON

BODY OF CHRIST. Used in reference to the church, the term "body" is distinctively Pauline. Generally *to soma tou Christou* or *hen soma* is acknowledged to be used ecclesiologically in I Corinthians 10:16 f.; Romans 12:4 f.; Ephesians 1:23; 2:16; 3:6; 4:4, 12, 16; Colossians 1:18, 24; 2:19; 3:15, although some would add I Corinthians 11:29 and Romans 7:4. "Body of Christ" in meaning is intimately related to Christ's headship, to the concept "in Christ," to *koinonia* or "fellowship," and to the figures of "building" and "bride." Contemporary theologians disagree as to whether the phrase is only a metaphor or to be taken literally as a mystical organism. A similar division exists concerning the church as the continuing incarnation of Christ, an idea advocated by William Owen Carver (*q.v.*). Most Baptists have not accepted this view.

See also CHURCH.

BIBLIOGRAPHY: E. Best, *One Body in Christ* (1955). W. O. Carver, *The Glory of God in the Christian Calling* (1949). J. R. Nelson, *The Realm of Redemption* (1951). L. S. Thornton, *The Common Life in the Body of Christ* (1942).

J. LEO GARRETT

BOGOMILES. A sect which appeared in Bulgaria shortly after A.D. 1100, as a fusion of earlier groups (Paulicians and Messalians). They belong, broadly, to the Manichean tradition. The Bogomiles ("friends of God") considered matter, especially the flesh, to be sinful, hence opposed marriage, despised the body, and practiced rigorous asceticism. They rejected the Mosaic writings while accepting the Psalter, the Prophets, four Gospels, writings of the apostles, and various apocryphal books. Both dualistic and Docetic, they taught that Christ (the *Logos*, or redeeming principle) descended from heaven, entered the virgin Mary through her right ear, and seemed to have a human body, but in reality did not. The passion, death, and resurrection of Jesus are all thus Docetic. Their doctrine of the Trinity is Sabellian. They reverenced demons to avoid harm from them; rejected baptism, the Lord's Supper, and the use of images; and forbade eating of meat and enjoined fasting. They were active in Byzantine Empire until they were extirpated in the 15th century.

BIBLIOGRAPHY: *New Schaff-Herzog Encyclopedia of Religious Knowledge,* VIII (1950). D. Obolensky, *The Bogomils* (1948). T. D. PRICE

BOLIVIAN BAPTIST CONVENTION. Organized in 1935 as the Bolivian Baptist Union with six member churches. All delegates were laymen, and neither pastors nor missionaries could vote or hold office. The union accepted the responsibility of supporting one home mission church, with more new churches organized as a result. In 1949 the union agreed to give voting privileges to pastors and missionaries making them eligible to hold office. At present 32 churches comprise this steadily growing union. Churches reported 130 baptisms in 1954. A Board of Home Missions, composed of Bolivians and Canadians, has power to take executive action in starting new causes, arranging pastoral changes, studying areas of need, and fostering special evangelistic witness.

Canadian Baptists began missionary work in Bolivia in 1898; however, in 1939 only 10 Canadian missionaries were at work. H. S. HILLYER

BOND ISSUES OF THE SOUTHERN BAPTIST CONVENTION. The Southern Baptist Convention as a corporate entity has floated only two bond issues. The first one was known as the bond issue on behalf of the Baptist Convention of New Mexico, issued in 1929. The other was a bond issue, in 1938, to consolidate some of the debts of the Convention and its agencies.

In 1929 the executive committee of the Baptist Convention of New Mexico appealed to the Executive Committee of the Southern Baptist Convention to recommend to the Convention that it "procure a loan for the purpose of consolidating the indebtedness of the New Mexico Convention to be supported by a first mortgage on the property, or properties, of the New Mexico Convention."

In response to this appeal the Executive Committee recommended "that the Convention procure and provide a minimum sum of $35,000.00 per year and a maximum not to exceed $40,000.00 per year for work in New Mexico." The Convention adopted an enabling act, to do all things necessary to carry out the will of the Convention as expressed in its act providing for the New Mexico program,

to borrow in the name and behalf of this Convention the sum of not more than $250,000 for the purpose of refinancing the present indebtedness of the New Mexico Convention and to procure and provide in cash an annual irrevocable sum of not less than $25,000.00 out of the total sum provided for the whole New Mexico program, and that such annual sum shall be hypothecated to the service of the principal and interest of such loan.

That the Executive Committee cause said loan to be secured by a first mortgage on college property of the New Mexico Convention . . . the loan to be secured by said mortgage to extend over a period of not more than fourteen years.

That the Executive Committee through its proper officers be and is hereby instructed and empowered to execute, in the name and as the obligation of the Southern Baptist Convention, any and all bonds, contracts and agreements necessary to give this action effect in the solution of the New Mexico problem.

In 1930 a report was made to the Convention stating:

Pursuant to the instructions of the Convention, the Executive Committee negotiated a bond issue amounting to $250,000.00. The bond issue was floated through Bitting & Company, of St. Louis, Mo., with the St. Louis Union Trust Company as trustee. The bonds are "First Mortgage Six Per Cent, Serial Gold Bonds," and are the obligation of the Southern Baptist Convention.

In 1937 the Executive Committee in its report to the Convention recommended

that the Executive Committee of the Southern Baptist Convention be . . . authorized and directed to issue bonds of the Southern Baptist Convention not to exceed the sum of Six Hundred Thousand ($600,000) Dollars. . . .

That a service charge of not more than Sixty Thousand ($60,000) Dollars per year . . . shall be a first charge against the distributable funds of the Cooperative Program coming to the Southern Baptist Convention. . . .

Said bonds . . . shall bear a rate of interest not to exceed five (5%) per cent.

In 1938 the Executive Committee recommended:

That the Executive Committee be authorized to sell to the Relief and Annuity Board, and that the Relief and Annuity Board be authorized to purchase $274,000.00 of the proposed $565,000.00 of the Southern Baptist Convention bond issue which was authorized by the Convention last year.

In 1939 the Executive Committee reported that in 1938 it had issued the bonds in the amount of $565,000, with the American National Bank, Nashville, Tenn., as trustee.

"This bond issue in 1938 constitutes the only direct obligation of the Southern Baptist Convention and of the Executive Committee on behalf of the Convention." AUSTIN CROUCH

BOOK CONCERN, BAPTIST. Retail book store located at Louisville, Ky. It was incorporated on May 8, 1890. William Patrick Harvey (*q.v.*), long the auditor of the Southern Baptist Convention, was the first president. The other officers were: T. T. Eaton, vice-president; Theodore Harris, treasurer; and Thomas D. Osborne, secretary. Its board of directors was made up of these officers together with Basil Manly, Jr. (*q.v.*), George W. Norton I, John B. McFerran, Joseph Burnley Moody (*q.v.*), and James G. Caldwell.

After its organization the Baptist Book Concern purchased *The Western Recorder* from Harvey, McFerran and Co. and the religious books from the Charles T. Dearing Book Store.

After some years J. Henry Burnett became manager and bookkeeper for the firm and remained there for some time. He later managed Liberty Female College, Glasgow, Ky., and was for 26 years a secretary of the Southern Baptist Convention. Others connected with the store through the years were Calvin M. Thompson, Sr., Jonathan G. Bow, John William Porter (q.v.), Henry C. McGill, and Wiley J. Smith.

During much of its existence the Baptist Book Concern, in addition to its retail bookselling and its publishing of *The Western Recorder,* was also a publisher of Baptist books.

The Baptist Book Concern disposed of *The Western Recorder* in 1919. The Sunday School Board of the Southern Baptist Convention secured the Baptist Book Concern in 1925 and changed its name to the Baptist Book Store. It was the first unit in the series of chain book stores the board now operates throughout the country.

The person having the longest connection with this organization was Miss Christina Stokmann. She began as a stenographer, 1916–23, but left Baptist employment in 1923 to accept a position in the city buyer's office. In 1927 the Sunday School Board asked her to return to the Baptist Book Concern as its manager. In that capacity she remained for 27 years (1927–54). She retired in December of 1954.

The present manager is Davis C. Hill.

BIBLIOGRAPHY: J. S. Johnston, *Memorial History of Louisville,* Vol. II (1896). B. T. Kimbrough, *Jubilee in '53, The Sesquicentennial History of the Long Run Association of Baptists* (1953).

GEORGE RALEIGH JEWELL

BOOK STORES, BAPTIST. A group of 50 stores owned and operated by the Sunday School Board of the Southern Baptist Convention as a service to the denomination. Exclusively retail, the stores major in selling religious books, Bibles, and supplies for all church organizations. Audio-visual equipment is also sold, and many of the stores operate religious film libraries. A special service for church libraries is offered. Church music, songbooks, and hymnals are also emphasized. Open to the public, the book stores observe generally the same store hours as other retail establishments in the community but are maintained primarily to serve Southern Baptist churches and their members. Each store has an assigned trade territory, promotes sales over the counter and by mail order, and invites charge accounts with churches and individuals. Policies are set by the Sunday School Board, but each manager has considerable freedom to manage the store under set policies and procedures. Central financial accounting done at the Sunday School Board includes all matters except accounts receivable (charge accounts with customers). Each store is a separate operation, yet part of the whole. Co-operative purchasing of goods for resale, combined advertising, and other standard procedures are maintained, resulting in more efficient operations and ultimate benefit to the denomination. Income from store operations becomes a part of the board's earnings budgeted for religious educational purposes and other denominational activities supported by the board.

As of Sept., 1956, the Baptist book stores in the following cities are the ones operated by the Sunday School Board: *Alabama:* Birmingham and Mobile. *Arizona:* Phoenix. *Arkansas:* Little Rock. *California:* Fresno, Huntington Park, and Oakland. *Colorado:* Denver. *Florida:* Jacksonville, Miami, and Tampa. *Georgia:* Atlanta and Savannah. *Illinois:* Carbondale. *Kansas:* Wichita. *Kentucky:* Louisville and Owensboro. *Louisiana:* Alexandria, New Orleans, and Shreveport. *Maryland:* Baltimore. *Mississippi:* Jackson. *Missouri:* Kansas City and St. Louis. *New Mexico:* Albuquerque. *North Carolina:* Charlotte and Raleigh. *Ohio:* Columbus. *Oklahoma:* Oklahoma City and Tulsa. *Oregon:* Portland. *South Carolina:* Columbia and Greenville. *Tennessee:* Chattanooga, Knoxville, Memphis, and Nashville. *Texas:* Austin, Dallas, Fort Worth, Houston, Lubbock, and San Antonio. *Virginia:* Richmond and Roanoke. Each school year, stores are operated on Southern Baptist seminary campuses, and during the summer season stores are also operated at the Ridgecrest and Glorieta assemblies. KEITH C. VON HAGEN

BOONE, ARTHUR UPSHAW (b. Elkton, Ky., Sept. 7, 1860; d. Memphis, Tenn., Jan. 29, 1956). Pastor, denominational leader, author. He was the son of Higgason Grubbs and Martha Maria (Edwards) Boone, and a descendant of Samuel (brother of Daniel) Boone. He worked on the farm and attended country schools. Boone attended Southern Baptist Theological Seminary, 1885–87. He was ordained to the ministry in 1887 and served as pastor at Elkton, Smith's Grove, and Leitchfield, Ky., 1887–91. He was awarded the D.D. degree by Union University, Jackson, Tenn., in 1900. On Apr. 30, 1891, he married Eddie Belle Cooke of Bowling Green, Ky. (d. 1925). They had two children: William Cooke and Martha Maria (Mrs. Frank H. Leavell). His second marriage was to Ida McIntosh in 1927.

Boone served as pastor at Clarksville, Tenn., 1891–98, and at First Baptist Church, Memphis, Tenn., 1898–1930. Retiring as pastor in 1930, he served as interim pastor for several years at First Baptist Church, Tulsa, Okla.; First, Shawnee, Okla.; Shelbyville and Springfield, Tenn.; Immanuel, Nashville, Tenn.; First, Tampa, Fla.; First, Montgomery, Ala. He then served as pastor-chaplain of Baptist Memorial Hospital, Memphis, Tenn., of which he was one of the founders, for nine years, finally retiring in 1944. Boone served on various boards and committees, including the Tennessee Baptist State Board; trustee, Baptist Memorial Hospital of Memphis; trustee, Union University; trustee, Southern Baptist Theological Seminary; and the Sunday School Board of the Southern Baptist Convention. He served as president of the Tennessee Baptist Convention for six years, 1903 through 1908. He wrote numerous articles which were published in the denominational papers and as tracts. In his late years he published a small book, *Four Score Years and Nine*. A biography of Dr. Boone, by Mrs. Leslie S. Howell, was published by the Oklahoma Baptist University Press in 1932. He was listed for many years in *Who's Who in America*.   WILLIAM COOKE BOONE

BOONE, JESSE BYNUM (b. Northampton County, N. C., Oct. 1, 1836; d. Hendersonville, N. C., June 17, 1908). Educator. Son of Benjamin and Nancey Boone, he was educated at Buckhorn Academy, Wake Forest College, and Southern Baptist Theological Seminary, Greenville, S. C. He married Sadie Maddrey Jan. 31, 1877. Boone served as state missionary in Charlotte, Salisbury, and Statesville, N. C., and was elected superintendent of the first graded school in Charlotte. Boone held pastorates in Southampton County, Va., Northampton County, Windsor, and Union, N. C., and Moberley, Mo. He was president of Judson College, Hendersonville, N. C., 1883–89, serving as pastor of the Baptist church there 1885–88. During his presidency, arrangements were made by the United States Government for a group of girls from the Cherokee Indian reservation to become students at the college. Boone served as general manager of the Thomasville Baptist Orphanage, Sept. 2, 1895, to Sept. 1, 1905, succeeding its founder, John Haymes Mills (*q.v.*). His wife served as superintendent of the orphanage. With outstanding ability as a practical schoolman, Boone erected a central building at the orphanage, taking the school work out of the dormitories and starting a graded school. Several other new buildings and a waterworks system were constructed during his administration.   I. G. GREER

BOONE'S CREEK BAPTIST ASSOCIATION CAMP. Started in 1954 at Trapp (Clark County), Ky., operated and supported by the Boone's Creek Baptist Association. Facilities and property of the Corinth Baptist Church are used for the camp, with four weeks of Royal Ambassador and Girls' Auxiliary camps held annually. The purpose is to give a spiritual ministry to boys and girls.   ELDRED M. TAYLOR

BORDEN, GAIL, JR. (b. Norwich, N. Y., Nov. 9, 1801; d. Borden, Tex., Jan. 11, 1874). Inventor, surveyor, school founder, newspaperman, factory owner, and benefactor to many. Supposedly the first Anglo-American baptized in the Gulf of Mexico west of the Mississippi, Borden became a Baptist Sunday school missionary to the poor and to travelers; a trustee of the Texas Baptist Education Society, which founded Baylor University; an officer in the local temperance society at Galveston; and a deacon and clerk in the Baptist church there.

Borden had less than two years of formal schooling but became captain of a local militia in Indiana at 20. He arrived at Galveston in 1829, later became a surveyor for Stephen F. Austin's colony, and assumed many of the duties of Austin's private secretary. He founded the *Telegraph and Texas Register* at San Felipe in 1835, prepared the first topographical map of Texas, and in 1836 helped lay out the site for Houston. A Galveston alderman, Borden helped rid the island temporarily of gamblers, and in 1842 directed insular defenses against an expected Mexican invasion.

Borden began inventing in the mid-1840's, experimenting with large-scale refrigeration to prevent yellow fever, using a terraqueous machine which would travel on land or water, and a meat biscuit of dehydrated meat and compounded flour. After securing a patent for condensed milk in 1856, Borden established factories for its production in Connecticut, New York, Illinois, Maine, and Pennsylvania. His other inventions included processes for condensing fruit juices, beef extract, and coffee. After the Civil War he established a meat packing plant at Borden, Tex., and a sawmill and coopery at Bastrop. In 1873 Borden built a freedmen's school and a white children's school, organized a Negro day school and a Negro Sunday school, aided in erecting five churches, maintained two missionaries, and partially supported numerous poorly-paid teachers, ministers, and students.   JACK D. HARWELL

BORUM, JOSEPH HENRY (b. Prince Edward County, Va., July 20, 1816; d. ?). Pastor and author. Though limited in formal schooling, he studied privately and achieved a good education. He moved with his family to Wilson County, Tenn., in 1828. Converted in a Methodist camp meeting Sept. 20, 1836, he joined a Methodist church pending his immersion. After delaying his baptism for almost a year, the church invited a presiding elder to preach on the subject. He declared that although immersion was valid baptism, he considered it to be "indecent, vulgar and dangerous to health, and that no decent person would submit to it." Borum thereupon united with the Beaver Creek Baptist Church, Fayette County, which immersed him on Aug. 17, 1837. About a month later he began to preach. The Covington church ordained him Sept. 21, 1845.

He served as pastor of many churches in West Tennessee. In conjunction with George Whitfield Young, he helped to organize the following churches: Elam, Hermon, Salem, Grace, Pleasant Plains, Ripley, and Dyersburg. His contemporaries described him as "an excellent preacher, . . . very successful in establishing churches and building up the cause of Christ in destitute regions. Perhaps no man in West Tennessee has been so universally successful."

Borum acted as an agent for the Brownsville College in West Tennessee, the West Tennessee Baptist Convention, and the Southern Baptist Publication Society, Memphis. He published in 1880 *Biographical Sketches of Tennessee Baptist*

Ministers. By his marriage to Ann Christy Brooks on Feb. 9, 1841, he had nine children.

W. LEONARD STIGLER

BOSCOBEL COLLEGE. A female school at Nashville, Tenn., founded in 1889. The institution opened with J. P. Hamilton as president, 11 teachers, and 100 pupils. The property was valued at $75,000 in 1892. Literature, music, art, and elocution were the major subjects of instruction. J. G. Paty, H. G. Lamar, and C. A. Folk also served the institution as president during its brief career of about 14 years. Inadequate financial support forced the college to close *c*. 1904.

LYNN EDWARD MAY, JR.

BOTTOMS, GEORGE WASHINGTON (b. Henrico County, Va., June 16, 1848; d. Texarkana, Ark., Sept. 3, 1924) and **IDA M. (BLANKENSHIP) BOTTOMS** (b. Cass County, Tex., Dec. 8, 1860; d. Texarkana, Ark., Dec. 21, 1944). Texarkana philanthropists who made a fortune in the lumber business and gave liberally to Southern Baptist work. They were married Nov. 18, 1882. Charter members of Beech Street Baptist Church, Texarkana, Ark., and active in its work, they made their largest gifts to home missions. A trust fund for the Home Mission Board produced approximately $1,000,000 in income between 1919 and 1956 for work in Cuba and among foreign language groups in the United States.

Other substantial gifts went to the Foreign Mission Board; Southern, Southwestern, and New Orleans Baptist seminaries; Ouachita (Arkadelphia, Ark.), Central (Conway, Ark.), and Mary Hardin-Baylor (Belton, Tex.) colleges; Buckner (Dallas, Tex.) and Bottoms (Monticello, Ark.) orphanages; Baptist State Mission Board of Arkansas; sanitorium work in Arkansas; to build churches in Palestine and Brazil; as well as to their home church.

Their name is attached to the trust fund; to a church in Nazareth, Palestine; to an orphanage and a dormitory in Arkansas; and to a chair of missions. Mrs. Bottoms' will after her death in 1944 provided for a trust fund in excess of $600,000, the proceeds of which were designated: one fourth to Southern Baptist Theological Seminary, and one eighth to each of the following: Buckner Orphanage, Bottoms Orphanage, Home Mission Board, Foreign Mission Board, Arkansas Baptist State Hospital, and Southwestern Baptist Theological Seminary. Their known gifts approximate $2,000,000, not including income from the two trust funds.

BIBLIOGRAPHY: B. H. Price, "Baptist Benefactor Passes to Heavenly Home," *Arkansas Baptist*, XLIV (Jan. 3, 1945). L. M. Stegall, *History of Beech Street Baptist Church* (1934). *Texarkana Gazette* (Jan. 11, 1945).

A. B. RUTLEDGE

BOTTOMS BAPTIST ORPHANAGE. An institution owned and supported by Arkansas Baptists, located at Monticello, Ark. It was established in 1894 as the result of a "gift of love" on the part of Hannah Hyatt, who, after she had gathered 25 homeless children in her childhood home, offered it and 80 acres of land to the Arkansas Baptist state convention. One hundred sixty acres were added in 1902, making the present total 240 acres. It was incorporated in 1895. In 1924 the name was changed to Bottoms Baptist Orphanage in honor of Mr. and Mrs. G. W. Bottoms of Texarkana. The governing board consists of 18 trustees elected by the convention.

The plant consists of 15 buildings: two two-story dormitories, an administration building, a farm manager's home, and various farm buildings. Three cottages were built in 1954–55. A milk pasteurizing building and a combination recreation and assembly building were planned for construction in 1956.

At the end of 1955 the audit showed the net worth of the home as $700,550.19. The expense for 1955 was $108,997.69, which provided for 138 children; $45,000 came from the Cooperative Program; and $87,999.31 through the Thanksgiving Offering. The Capital Need Budget provided $25,000 in 1954 and $10,000 in 1955.

The children attend the public schools and the First Baptist Church in Monticello. Children who show capacity for further education are assisted either by scholarships, interested friends, or the Home Helper Fund. Provision is always made for every child who leaves the home.

H. C. SEEFELDT

BOTTOMS TRUST FUND. On July 31, 1929, Mrs. George Washington Bottoms (*q.v.*), of Texarkana, Ark., executed a trust indenture in which she named the Texarkana National Bank of Texarkana, Tex., as trustee and the Home Mission Board of the Southern Baptist Convention as beneficiary. The trust indenture, among other things, directed the board to transfer to the trustee named therein the 1,000 shares of capital stock of Crowell and Spencer Lumber Company of Long Leaf, La., which were given to the board by Mrs. Bottoms and her husband, George Washington Bottoms (*q.v.*), in 1918.

The trust indenture, as originally drawn, contemplated the erection of a school in Havana, Cuba. When it became evident that the income from the trust would be inadequate to erect and maintain the proposed school, the trust was adjusted by mutual agreement between Mrs. Bottoms and the board on Apr. 14, 1933, to provide that the assets of the trust be held by the trustee "in trust for the following uses, benefits, and purposes, to-wit: to use the future income from the cash and securities in the trust for the use and benefit of the board, and at and under its direction, for religious, educational and/or benevolent work in Cuba, the Canal Zone, and/or among foreigners in this country."

During the intervening years up to Feb. 1, 1956, the board has received from this trust $790,337.23, to which can be added approximately $110,000 income received by the board on the gift of Crowell and Spencer Lumber Company capital stock made by the Bottomses in 1918, prior to the establishment of the Bottoms Trust Fund, making the total income received from the two sources $900,337.23 for administration in accordance with the provisions of the gift and/or trust. The trustee's statement as of Feb. 1, 1956, shows that it still holds in trust United States Government bonds of the approximate value of $600,000, 100 shares of the capital stock of Crowell Land and Mineral Corporation, 200 shares of the capital stock of Meridian Land and Mineral Corporation, and cash in the amount of $1,022.92.

During Mrs. Bottoms' latter years she set up a living trust under which she disposed of her personal estate; and in addition to the income heretofore referred to, the board has thus far received from her estate additional distributions totaling $90,000.   G. FRANK GARRISON

BOWEN, THOMAS JEFFERSON (b. Jackson County, Ga., Jan. 2, 1814; d. Ga., Nov. 24, 1875). Missionary to Africa and Brazil. After fighting in the Creek Indian War, spring of 1836, and doing military service in Texas, Dec., 1836, to Nov., 1839, Bowen was converted in Oct., 1840, began preaching in 1841, and was appointed missionary to central Africa, Feb. 22, 1849. He visited Monrovia, Badagry, and Abeokuta, where he labored many months. When Bowen returned to America for a brief visit, he married Lurenna Henrietta Davis, May 31, 1853. In July they sailed for Africa, built a mission house at Ijaye, and in June, 1854, Bowen baptized his first convert. The Bowens moved to Ogbomosho in autumn, 1855, but various factors caused their return to America in the spring of 1856. In 1859 Bowen was commissioned by the Foreign Mission Board to open a mission in Brazil, but ill health compelled him to leave there early in 1861, and the Brazil mission was abandoned. From 1868 to 1874 he traveled in Texas and Florida, and on Nov. 24, 1875, he died while in Georgia away from his family. He was the author of *Central Africa* and *Grammar and Vocabulary of the Yoruban Tongue*.

BIBLIOGRAPHY: C. E. Maddry, *Day Dawn in Yoruba Land* (1939). H. A. Tupper, *Foreign Missions of the Southern Baptist Convention* (1880). M. E. Wright, *Missionary Work of Southern Baptist Convention* (1902).   E. C. ROUTH

BOWMAN ACADEMY. A school of Mitchell Association, and later of Roan-Grandfather Mountain Association located at Bakersville, Mitchell County, N. C. First efforts to establish a school in Mitchell Association in 1888–89 were unsuccessful, but in 1899 the association established Bowman Baptist Seminary to serve the people in that area. The trustees secured a building at Bakersville, formerly used as a school by J. C. Bowman, for whom the academy was named. In 1901 the school was opened with W. W. Baker as principal. Beginning in 1905, the school received financial assistance from the Home Mission Board's program of aid to mountain schools and by 1922 had received more than $15,000 for maintenance and improvements. In 1909 the name of the school was changed to Mitchell Collegiate Institute, and in 1911 it was taken over by the Roan-Grandfather Mountain Association. World War I cut short the rapid growth of the school, and in 1921 only 55 pupils were enrolled. Two years later the school closed for "lack of loyalty."

D. L. SMILEY

BOWMAN GRAY SCHOOL OF MEDICINE OF WAKE FOREST COLLEGE, THE. An expansion of the two-year school of medicine founded at Wake Forest College in the fall of 1902. When it was moved to Winston-Salem, Sept. 10, 1941, and became a fully accredited four-year school, the name of Bowman Gray was given the school in honor of its principal benefactor up to that time. The first dean of the two-year school was Fred K. Cooke. Coy C. Carpenter succeeded Cooke as dean and was the principal organizer of the four-year school in Winston-Salem. As the medical school of Wake Forest College, it is an institution of the Baptist State Convention of North Carolina.

Thirteen students enrolled in the first class in 1902. The third class, 1905, included Thurman Delna Kitchin, president of Wake Forest College from 1930 to 1950, and Wingate M. Johnson, who served 20 years on the board of trustees—the last three as its president—and later became professor of clinical medicine in the school.

In 1941, the first year of the four-year school, the student body numbered 73. Since 1941 the entering class has been limited to 54 students selected from 600 to 1,200 applicants. Through June, 1955, there had been 594 graduates.

The buildings are all connected and under the same roof with the North Carolina Baptist Hospital. The total value of buildings and equipment in 1955 was $1,880,108.80. The total budget in 1938 was $20,000.00; in 1941 it was $184,590.73; and in 1955, $1,084,000.00. The income consists of student fees and other earnings plus $50,000 a year from the undesignated endowment income of Wake Forest College, income from a $2,000,000 designated endowment fund and gifts and grants.

The school is on the approved list of all medical school accrediting agencies in the United States, including the Council on Medical Education of the American Medical Association and the Association of American Medical Colleges.

COY C. CARPENTER

BOYCE, JAMES PETIGRU (b. Charleston, S. C., Jan. 11, 1827; d. Pau, France, Dec. 27, 1888). Seminary founder, administrator, Convention president. Boyce was the first child of Ker Boyce and his second wife, Amanda Jane Caroline Johnston, both of whom were Scotch-Irish with Presbyterian background. Boyce's father never affiliated with any church, but his mother became a Baptist at an uncertain date. Since his father was one of the wealthiest men in South Carolina, Boyce received excellent opportunities for cultural and social development. Educated at Charleston College (1843–45), Brown University (1845–47), and Princeton (1849–51), Boyce became enamored of systematic theology under the teaching of Princeton's Charles Hodge. Francis Wayland of Brown was influential in the development of Boyce's teaching method and his concept of theological education.

When he went to Brown to prepare for a legal profession, Boyce was not a Christian; but during his first year, he was stimulated by Wayland's evangelical chapel talks. When Boyce returned to Charleston in the spring of 1846, he was converted under the preaching of Richard Fuller (q.v.), and when he returned to Brown he became interested in religious activities. During the year 1846–47 he decided, against his father's desire, to become a minister. Boyce married Elizabeth Llewellyn Ficklen of Washington, Ga., in Dec., 1848, and they had three daughters.

Editor of *The Southern Baptist*, a weekly paper, from Nov., 1848, to Apr., 1849, Boyce accepted the pastorate of First Baptist Church, Columbia, S. C., after two years at Princeton. Examiners at his ordination in Nov., 1851, asked Boyce if he planned to give his life to preaching. "Yes," he replied, "provided I do not become a professor of theology," and in 1855 he resigned the pastorate to become professor of theology at Furman University. Two years later he became agent of South Carolina Baptists in raising $70,000 for the newly proposed seminary.

Regarded as the founding father of Southern Baptist Theological Seminary although the idea of a central seminary did not originate with him, Boyce was the strongest advocate of theological education from 1856 on. When the seminary was established in Greenville, S. C., in 1859, he became the first chairman of the faculty, which included John Albert Broadus (q.v.), Basil Manly, Jr. (q.v.), and William Williams (q.v.).

Although Boyce taught various subjects including theology, homiletics, New Testament, and church history, he is primarily noted for his administrative ability and concept of theological education. He raised the money to establish the seminary, and after the school was suspended during the Civil War, Boyce led in its reopening in 1865, believing its suspension would set theological education back a generation or more. At the first meeting of the seminary's professors after the war, Broadus proposed: "Suppose we quietly agree that the Seminary may die, but we'll die first." Resources in the seaboard states were very limited after the war and Boyce had lost most of his estate, but he gave liberally to the school. In 1870 when the seminary seemed doomed, Boyce said, "I'll spend every cent I have rather than suspend."

Due to adverse economic conditions, the trustees in 1871 reluctantly decided to relocate the seminary. Boyce spent five years in residence in Louisville, Ky., before relocation, trying to raise needed funds. A financial depression in 1874 and opposition of some Kentuckians who thought the seminary would impair their two colleges made his task more difficult. After the seminary's relocation, Boyce initiated several campaigns to raise money for operation and capital needs and received generous gifts from Louisville, Georgia, and New York donors. When Boyce's administrative skills were sought by others, he turned down the presidency of Mercer and Brown colleges and of railroad, bank, and manufacturing businesses to remain with the seminary.

Boyce's concept of theological education is defined in his inaugural address at Furman in 1856. Entitled "Three Changes in Theological Institutions," it embodied the foundation principles of the seminary: (1) Each minister, regardless of his educational background, should have access to theological instruction, for otherwise the mass of the ministry cannot be adequately trained. (2) Able students should be given special courses to develop their abilities, for Baptists need their own thinkers and writers. (3) Each professor should subscribe a doctrinal statement, or "abstract of principles," agreeing to teach nothing contradictory to the statement, thereby insuring doctrinal soundness.

The most important principle was the first, for although it was commonly held that classical training is prerequisite to theological training, Boyce called this a "false principle" which God has rejected in calling unlettered men to preach. The task of a seminary is to provide for the churches an adequate ministry from those who are divinely called; "the opportunity should be given to those who cannot or will not make thorough scholastic preparation to obtain that adequate knowledge of the truths of the Scriptures, systematically arranged, and of the laws which govern the interpretation of the text in the English version, which constitutes all that is actually necessary to enable them to preach the Gospel, to build up the churches on their most holy faith, and to instruct them in the practice of the duties incumbent on them."

Boyce served as president of the Southern Baptist Convention from 1872 to 1879 and again in 1888.

During his last 17 years occasional attacks of gout made Boyce irritable. In 1888 he went to Europe for a rest and died in southern France on Dec. 27. His epitaph fittingly reads, "First President of the Southern Baptist Theological Seminary; to him, under God, the Seminary owes its existence." HUGH WAMBLE

BOYKIN, SAMUEL (b. Milledgeville, Ga., Nov. 24, 1829; d. Nashville, Tenn., Nov. 3, 1899). First editor of the Sunday School Board of the Southern Baptist Convention. His father, Samuel Boykin, was a distinguished, wealthy, and highly cultured physician; his mother, Narcissa Cooper, was the daughter of Thomas Cooper, a wealthy tither and deacon and the leading Georgia Baptist layman of his day. After graduation from the University of Georgia in 1851, he traveled in Europe for six months. He received an M.A. degree from the University of Georgia in 1854. In July, 1859, he became editor of the *Christian Index*, Macon, Ga., and he purchased it from the Georgia Baptist convention in May, 1861. He was ordained as a Baptist minister in Sept., 1861. The Civil War compelled him to suspend the *Christian Index* in early 1865, but he resumed publication in 1866 and during that year sold it. Boykin began publication of the *Child's Index* in Oct., 1862, but he had to suspend its publication along with the *Christian Index* in early 1865. He reissued it in early 1866 as the *Child's Delight*, when a reviewer wrote, "It comes nearer filling our idea of what a child's paper should be than any we have ever seen." In 1870 he sold it to the first Sunday School Board of the Southern Baptist Convention, Memphis, Tenn., when it was combined with *Kind Words* under the name *Kind Words and Child's Delight*. From Feb., 1870, until his death in Nov., 1899, he was its editor—under the first Sunday School Board until its abolishment in June, 1873; under the Domestic [Home] Mission Board until July, 1891; and then under the second Sunday School Board until his death. When the Home Mission Board established a series of Sunday school quarterlies, Jan., 1887, he served as their editor and continued in this capacity when they were transferred to the Sunday School Board.

The Sunday School Board in 1916 made a gift of $10,000 to the Home Mission Board, one half of it to be the Samuel Boykin Memorial Fund for church buildings in memory of Boykin as "the first editor of the Sunday School Board, previously editor for the Home Mission Board, and for many years before that almost the chief pioneer and genius in making Sunday school literature for the Baptists of the South."

Boykin served only one church as pastor—the Second Baptist of Macon, Ga. Because of partial deafness, he gave his life to religious writing and editing. He served as the agent of the Georgia Baptist Bible and Colporteur Society from its organization in 1858 through 1859. He was the author of two books, *Memoirs of Howell Cobb* and the *History of the Baptist Denomination in Georgia*. The latter, published by the *Christian Index* in 1881, does not bear his name, but he wrote on the flyleaf of one copy (in the Dargan-Carver Library, Nashville, Tenn.): "This book was written entirely by me, during eight months of hard labor, one half my time being given to it exclusively. . . . Two thirds of the sketches [in the back of the book] were written by me, founded on facts furnished by others, I being familiar with most of the persons."

As an editor, Boykin dealt with issues clearly and forcefully but without personal vituperation or sarcasm. He wisely refrained, as the editor of *Kind Words*, from participating in the controversy about the creation of the Sunday School Board but gave himself to preparing the literature needed by the churches.

He married Laura Nisbett, Macon, Ga., in 1853, who survived him along with one of his two daughters, Mrs. Eugenia (Boykin) Dashiell. She bore testimony to her father's "liberality in the support of his denomination and of the needy that were near him." He was buried in Macon, Ga. HOMER L. GRICE

BOYS' RANCH TOWN, OKLAHOMA. A home for delinquent or underprivileged boys, founded in 1953 on a 160-acre tract of land 13 miles northeast of Oklahoma City, by the Baptist General Convention with funds provided from a $500,000 gift by Mr. and Mrs. James Morton Johnson. The gift, made in memory of the Johnsons' son Jimmy, who died of polio at the age of 14 years, was to be divided, $100,000 to be used for immediate buildings and the balance to be held in a trust endowment for the institution. On June 1, 1953, Jesse Anderson Russell became resident manager of the ranch, and later that month the first boy was admitted. Millard Judson Cook became superintendent on Nov. 1, 1953. On Oct. 12, 1953, a ground-breaking ceremony was held for the initial $100,000 building, a one-story, four-wing structure, which was dedicated Nov. 9, 1954. M. JUDSON COOK

BRAILLE BAPTIST, THE. A monthly magazine for the blind, in grade 1½ Braille, published by the Sunday School Board of the Southern Baptist Convention since Oct., 1946. It is designed chiefly to enable sightless persons to participate in their church activities. Hence, it reproduces lessons from *Sunday School Adults* and programs from *Baptist Adult Union Quarterly*, together with other features and articles. The magazine is supplied on request and without cost to blind people. The circulation in 1956 was 1,450. DONALD F. ACKLAND

BRAILLE EVANGEL, THE. A religious magazine for the blind, published in Fort Worth, Tex. It was inaugurated in 1946 by Edwin Wilson, who has served as its editor. He enlisted a group of Christian leaders from various states of the South to serve as a board of directors. It was designed to provide reading material, drawn chiefly from various religious publications, for visually handicapped persons, featuring articles of inspirational, evangelistic, and educational value. It has depended on voluntary contributions as a source of income. CLIFTON J. ALLEN

BRANTLY, JOHN JOYNER (b. Augusta, Ga., Dec. 29, 1821; d. Macon, Ga., June 8, 1902). From 1826–38, Brantly lived in Philadelphia, where his father William Theophilus Brantly, Sr. (*q.v.*), was a well-known preacher. When his father assumed presidency of Charleston College in 1838, young Brantly entered there as a sophomore. While visiting in Georgia he was converted at the church of Pastor Shaler Granby Hillyer (*q.v.*) in Milledgeville. Graduating in 1841, he taught for four years in Georgia and North Carolina academies; but being called to the ministry, he was ordained by the Fayetteville, N. C., church, his first pastorate. In 1850 he became pastor of the Newberry, S. C., church, serving there until appointed professor of English at Mercer in Jan., 1867. He was also pastor of the Penfield Church. A teacher of national reputation, he was awarded an LL.D. degree by Mercer in 1891 and in 1893 retired.   BENJAMIN W. GRIFFITH, JR.

BRANTLY, WILLIAM THEOPHILUS, JR. (b. Beaufort, S. C., May 18, 1816; d. Baltimore, Md., Mar. 6, 1882). Minister and educator. The son of William T. Brantly, Sr. (*q.v.*), and Anna (McDonald) Brantly, he was taken to Philadelphia in 1824, when his father accepted a pastorate there. He was reared and educated in the North, and graduated from Brown University with high honors in 1840. After his ordination on Dec. 27, 1840, he became pastor of the First Baptist Church, Augusta, Ga., where he remained until 1848. Then, after eight years at the University of Georgia as professor of belles lettres, history, oratory, and evidences of Christianity, he went in 1856 to Philadelphia as pastor of Tabernacle Baptist Church. At the beginning of the Civil War, he moved to Atlanta, and was pastor of the Second Baptist Church, 1861–1871. Moving then to Baltimore, he held the pastorate of the Seventh Baptist Church there until 1882.

Called "one of the best classical scholars and most charming preachers of his denomination," Brantly was a recognized leader. He edited the Georgia *Christian Index* during the latter half of 1866. He was a trustee of Mercer University, 1842–1851, 1863–1871, and was offered the presidency of the school in 1865 but found it necessary to decline, thus repeating the experience of his father, who had declined the same offer in 1839.   BENJAMIN W. GRIFFITH, JR.

BRANTLY, WILLIAM THEOPHILUS, SR. (b. Chatham County, N. C., Jan. 23, 1787; d. Augusta, Ga., Mar. 28, 1845). One of the most powerful preachers of his age, who helped establish First Baptist Church, Augusta, Ga., and was the first editor of the *Christian Index* (which name he gave to the Baptist paper *The Columbian Star*). He removed the denominational weekly from Philadelphia to Washington, Ga., and passed it on to the editorship of Jesse Mercer in 1833.

During the wave of revivalism in 1802, young Brantly was converted under the preaching of George Pope. So zealous was the lad of 15 that he would regularly ask permission to preach to the congregation after the regular service was over. Graduating from South Carolina College with distinction, he was called at the age of 22 to become rector of Richmond Academy in Augusta, Ga. There being no Baptist church in Augusta, Brantly began preaching on Sunday in the academy meetinghouse. Anxious to devote full time to the ministry, he accepted a call in 1811 to the church at Beaufort, S. C., where he remained for eight years until recalled to Augusta to serve in his former position and as pastor for the Baptist Praying Society of Augusta. After three years of preaching at the academy he was able to lead the congregation to erect a church building, which was dedicated on May 6, 1821.

In 1826 when Henry Holcombe, pastor of the First Baptist Church of Philadelphia, was dying, he was asked to name a successor; Brantly was named. He accepted and moved in April to Philadelphia, where he became ranked immediately as one of the most powerful preachers of that city. In 1837 Brantly accepted the call to First Baptist Church, Charleston, S. C. Shortly afterward he was named president of the College of Charleston. Smitten by a paralytic stroke on July 18, 1844, Brantly died on Mar. 28, 1845.

Brantly was twice married: in 1809 to Mrs. Annie McDonald Martin, who died in 1818; and in 1819 to Mrs. Margaret Joyner. He was a capable classical scholar and a preacher of widely recognized abilities. A Boston reviewer, speaking of the first sermon Brantly published, said: "This sermon is evidently the production of a man of genius." Brantly wrote *Themes for Meditation* (1837).   BENJAMIN W. GRIFFITH, JR.

BRAZIL, MISSION IN. As early as 1850 Southern Baptists considered opening mission work in Central and South America. A band of Southerners emigrated to Brazil after the Civil War and founded a colony at Santa Barbara, São Paulo, where a group of Baptists organized a church in 1871. The next year the church presented the first of a series of requests to the Foreign Mission Board to send missionaries to the Brazilians. At the meeting of the Southern Baptist Convention in 1880, A. T. Hawthorne, having visited Brazil, pleaded with the convention to take advantage of favorable conditions and send missionaries to that friendly country. The convention authorized the board to open the mission. William Buck Bagby (*q.v.*) and Anne Luther Bagby (*q.v.*) were appointed in Dec., 1880, and landed at Rio de Janeiro, Mar. 2, 1881. After a year's study of the language and the people, and the arrival of Zachary Clay Taylor (*q.v.*) and Kate Crawford Taylor, the two men made a survey of the fields and decided to open work in Salvador, Bahia. A Brazilian ex-priest, Antonio Teixeira de Albuquerque, had moved to São Paulo and united with the Baptist church in Santa Barbara. He joined with the four missionaries in organizing the first national Baptist church of Brazil in the capital city of Bahia, Oct. 15, 1882.

In spite of opposition and persecution, in which Bagby was hit on the forehead with a stone and knocked unconscious while preaching, the membership grew to 25 within the next year. The first male convert, John Baptist, became an evangelist and pastor.

Bagby opened work in Rio de Janeiro and organized the First Baptist Church with only four members, Aug. 24, 1884. A Presbyterian preacher, C. I. Mesquita, came to the Baptists and served as an evangelistic worker. E. H. Soper, an English missionary to sailors in Rio, joined the church, adding strength and encouragement to the working force.

The pioneer missionaries adopted the plan of opening work in the larger cities, with the purpose of carrying the gospel to every province of the empire. Rio de Janeiro became the center of activities for South Brazil, and Salvador (later transferred to Recife) for the North.

Invited by his former enemies, Teixeira began preaching in his home town, Maceió, Alagoas, and led his father, mother, and others who had opposed him to become Christians. On May 17, 1885, Teixeira and Taylor organized the Maceió Church with 10 members.

When the empire fell with the proclamation of the Brazilian republic, Nov. 15, 1889, Baptists had gained a costly foothold. Bagby and others had suffered from yellow fever, which took the life of one, Maggie Rice. Three men and five women were not able to withstand the climate, and returned to the States. The Bagbys, Z. C. Taylors, and Emma Morton (later Mrs. Solomon L. Ginsburg) were the missionaries on the field when the empire fell. Four churches, 312 members, four ordained ministers, and eight unordained workers represented the Baptists.

The new government disestablished the Catholic Church and proclaimed religious freedom, a great encouragement to all evangelical Christians; the board appointed a growing number of able young people who presented themselves and asked to be sent to Brazil; new centers were entered, and by 1900 churches were multiplying at an increasing rate. Capable young Brazilians such as Thomaz da Costa, F. F. Soren, Theodoro Teixeira, Francisco de Miranda Pinto, Benjamin and Joaquim Paranagua joined Baptist ranks, adding their strength and prestige to the new religion.

Evangelism was carried on by the distribution of literature, the opening of new fields with Sunday schools and Bible study, and the preparation of evangelical groups to be organized as churches. The definite establishment of work in a new center usually represented the service of preachers and teachers who in some cases suffered persecution and failure until their Christian testimony broke down opposition.

In 1891 Bagby organized a church in the city of Campos, a center from which work spread throughout the state of Rio, and to the north into the states of Espírito Santo and Minas Gerais. The church in Belo Horizonte, organized in 1898, and the First Baptist Church of São Paulo in 1899, became centers of activity in the states of Minas and São Paulo. The First Baptist Church of Vitoria, Espírito Santo, organized in 1903 by Z. C. Taylor and Albert Lafayette Dunstan, became a strong center from which Baptist work, under the leadership of Loren Marion Reno, spread to the most important centers throughout the state and into the borders of Minas.

Solomon L. Ginsburg and Erik Alfred Nelson (q.v.) organized the first church in the Amazon Valley in the city of Belem in 1897, and Nelson organized the First Baptist Church of Manaos in 1900. From Manaos Nelson carried the gospel to numerous towns and cities in the valley for nearly half a century.

During the first 25 years the pioneers had blazed the trails into the far interior, they had sowed the seed of Truth and had organized churches as outposts of the Kingdom of Christ. The churches were few and widely separated, without adequate houses of worship and with insufficient leadership, yet there was in the Baptist brotherhood a number of choice spirits who had passed through fiery trials in accepting the Gospel, and were taking their stand by the side of the foreigners to give the Gospel to the Brazilian people. Local associations, missionary societies and a few primary schools had been organized, and in some sections Baptists were winning favor because of the transforming power of the Gospel, and because of their interest in education and social development.

The organization of the Brazilian Baptist Convention in 1907 marked the beginning of a period of expansion, with the development of national and foreign missions, the production and publication of literature, and the establishment of institutions for Christian and theological education.

The organization of the North and South Brazil Missions in 1910, at the suggestion of T. Bronson Ray (q.v.), has contributed to progress and efficiency. In 1947 the missionaries of the Amazon Valley organized the Equatorial Mission. With a population of 64,000,000, Brazil's three missions represent Southern Baptists in 47 per cent of the territory of South America. Their constitutions define their mthods of work and their responsibilities to Southern and Brazilian Baptists.

As the work has progressed, with a growing number of theologically trained pastors and the development of national institutions, the service of the missionary has become more specialized. Brazilian pastors have developed strong missionary churches and are taking on larger responsibilities of leadership. The missions ask for missionaries prepared for special types of service. Everett Gill, Jr. (q.v.), Latin American secretary, 1941-54, counseled with the missions and sought appointees prepared to meet their numerous requests. Missionaries of the Southern Baptist Foreign Mission Board, elected by the Brazilian Baptist Convention, serve as presidents and teachers of the seminaries, director of the publishing house, and heads of departments of the Brazilian Sunday School Board. Field missionaries co-operate with Brazilian state boards. And the missions, as organizations and representatives of the Foreign Mission Board, continue opening work in unoccupied

Brazil, Mission in

centers, either in co-operation with state boards or in some cases on their own initiative. All stages of missionary progress are represented, with numerous cities and populous regions open to the gospel and still unoccupied.

In 1894 a group of missionaries and Brazilian pastors organized a nonprofit, property-holding board, incorporated under Brazilian law. This board still exists, independent of the national convention, and holds the titles to many valuable properties. Some of the institutions are now incorporated and hold the title to their property, valued at millions of dollars.

In 1900 Bagby, Z. C. Taylor, Ginsburg, and J. J. Taylor merged their local papers and their assets, and organized the Publication Committee for the purpose of founding and publishing a national paper, *The Baptist Journal*. The first number was published Jan. 10, 1901. As a denominational organ *The Baptist Journal* came under the supervision of the national convention in 1907, and has maintained, for more than 50 years, a high standard of religious journalism.

The two building and loan boards, organized by the North and South Brazil Missions and supported by the Foreign Mission Board, are helping, through rotating loans, to build churches, schools, and orphanages. These boards have helped many churches to construct adequate buildings, thus contributing to their prestige, growth, and efficiency.

The Bible Press, organized in 1940 under the leadership of Thomas Bertram Stover and Jack Jimmerson Cowsert, has published and distributed 750,000 Bibles and New Testaments. Stephen Lawton Watson and William Edison Allen, with the help of Crabtree, A. Ben Oliver, and Brazilian scholars, revised the Almeida version of the New Testament published in 1955. Work is well advanced on the Old Testament.

The Woman's Missionary Union of Brazil, auxiliary to the national convention, organized in 1908, grew in strength and missionary service, and in 1925 took on new vigor under the leadership of Minnie Levatta Landrum. Since 1935 its national president, Ester Dias, has represented the organization in Brazil and abroad. In 1954 there were 872 women's societies, 297 young women's auxiliaries, and 502 children's societies, with a total membership of 25,868. The women provide fieldworkers, literature and training for their organizations, contribute to home and foreign missions, and with the help of Southern Baptist women support two training schools for Christian workers, which in 1954 enrolled 96 girls.

The Atlas News Service, led by William Hafford Berry, maintains a department of journalism, a daily radio program, and records hymns and Bible readings for use in open-air services and in private homes.

The missions have led in the founding of schools, which give courses from kindergarten through junior college. Anne Bagby, John Watson Shepard, Otis Pendleton Maddox, Harvey Harold Muirhead, Alonzo Bee Christie, Adolph John Terry, John Mein, Paul Clay Porter, Helen Bagby Harrison, Joseph Arnol Harrington, Robert Elton Johnson, Bernice Ruth Neel, and many others have led in the founding and development of schools in Rio de Janeiro, São Paulo, Belo Horizonte, Campos, Porto Alegre, Recife, Maceió, Natal, Fortaleza, Jaguaquara, Corrente, and other centers.

The two theological seminaries were departments of the American Baptist College of Recife and the John W. Shepard College of Rio de Janeiro until 1936, when they were separated and their administrative boards elected by the convention. With appropriations from the Southern Baptist Foreign Mission Board, the seminaries have constructed administration buildings, which are adding to their efficiency in the training of a growing national ministry.

The seminary of North Brazil, organized in 1902 and developed under the direction and leadership of Muirhead, William Carey Taylor (q.v.), Leslie Leonidas Johnson, Arnold Edmund Hayes, John Mein, W. C. Harrison, and other missionaries, in co-operation with Brazilian colleagues, offers standard courses, and in 1953 matriculated 55 students. David Mein is the present president, with a strong faculty of missionaries and Brazilian teachers.

The South Brazil Seminary of Rio was organized in 1908 by Shepard. Alva Bee Langston, Allen, Crabtree and other missionaries and Brazilian colleagues have contributed to the development of the institution, which enrolled 85 students in 1954 and graduated 23 in 1955. A four-year course, with Hebrew and Greek, is offered to college graduates. The seminary publishes a theological review. Oliver is the present president, and the faculty includes five missionaries and six Brazilians.

Taylor (W. C.), Langston, Muirhead, and Crabtree have written theological textbooks for students and pastors, some of which are used in other evangelical seminaries and by Catholics and Jews. A vast amount of evangelical literature for Sunday schools, Training Unions, pastors, and workers, by missionaries and Brazilians, is flowing constantly from the press.

Baptists, though relatively few in number, are making an impact on the religious and social life of Brazil. Catholics are pleading to Europe and the United States for missionary help and seeking to improve their ministry to the underprivileged classes, but they are handicapped by their feudalistic background, loss of prestige, and the influence of communism. Thousands of Brazilians are without any religious leadership and training. Political corruption, illegitimacy, social injustice, religious ignorance, and superstition are still widespread.

With 179 missionaries and more than 650 Brazilian pastors and workers, Baptists are growing in numbers, culture, virility, and influence because of their emphasis on the authority of the Scriptures, a regenerated church membership, a high standard of Christian ethics, missionary zeal, the training and education of children, and emphasis on the dignity and worth of the individual in his social and religious rights and responsibilities.

A. R. CRABTREE

BRAZILIAN BAPTIST CONVENTION. When William Buck Bagby (*q.v.*) organized the church in Salvador, Bahia, Oct. 15, 1882, Antonio Teixeira de Albuquerque, the only Brazilian Baptist at that time, was one of the five charter members. Converted by reading the Bible while studying for the priesthood, he continued his study of the Greek New Testament, and wrote his apologetic, *Why I Left the Church of Rome*, which has been used effectively for 75 years in the evangelization of Brazilians. As preacher, evangelist, pastor, and writer, his brief period of service until his death in 1887 helped to lay the foundations for the progress of Brazilian Baptists.

With churches established in strategic centers and missionary societies and local associations spread from Manaos to São Paulo, with 26 ordained Brazilian pastors and as many unordained preachers and colporteurs and more than 1,000 baptisms in 1906, missionaries recognized that the time had come to organize these potential forces for the promotion of unity, co-operation, and nation-wide planning.

Celebrating the 25th anniversary of the establishment of the mission, messengers from 39 of the 83 churches, representing more than 5,000 Baptists, met in Salvador and on June 22, 1907, organized the Brazilian Baptist Convention, electing F. F. Soren, president; Joaquim Lessa and João Borges da Rocha, vice-presidents; Theodoro Teixeira and M. I. Sampaio, secretaries; and Zachary Clay Taylor (*q.v.*), treasurer.

At its organization the convention sent the following telegram to the President of the Republic, Afonso Pena:

> The First Brazilian Baptist Convention, commemorating the 25th anniversary of the entrance of their first evangelists in the national territory, greets the Nation in the Person of your Excellency, praying and working for the prosperity and advancement of Brazil. Signed, Bagby and Taylor.

The convention organized the Home and Foreign Mission boards, the College and Seminary Board of Rio de Janeiro, the Education Board, and three other boards which were merged in 1922 in the Sunday School and Young People's Board, which also included the publishing house. Later the American Baptist College and Seminary of Recife came under the convention; it voted in 1936 to separate the theological seminaries from the colleges, electing their first administrative boards.

The National Convention stimulated the organization and cooperation of denominational forces throughout the Baptist ranks, and led to the development of a comprehensive program, including home and foreign missions, publications, education and benevolences. Brazilian Baptists, under the leadership of their missionaries, follow the general plans of the Southern Baptist Convention, but they bring to these plans their own national and personal characteristics in their methods of work.

The Baptist Journal, founded by the publication committee of the mission in 1901, came under control of the national convention. With William E. Entzminger, Theodoro Teixeira, Moysés Silveira, and Almir Goncalves as successive editors, the *Journal* has contributed to Christian culture, denominational unity, Baptist prestige and progress.

With limited resources, the Brazilian Home Mission Board led the way in opening work in the states of Rio Grande do Sul, Goyaz, and Mato Grosso. Unable to man these fields, the board received missionaries and financial help from the mission. Under the leadership of Lewis Malen Bratcher for 28 years, an expanding work developed in the interior. In 1953, 49 missionaries, 23 colporteurs, 28 teachers, and five nurses represented work in a Bible institute, an orphanage, 21 schools with an enrolment of 1,525, and three medical dispensaries. The Brazilian Foreign Mission Board maintains work in Portugal and Bolivia.

In 1928 the Brazilian Relief and Annuity Board was organized under the leadership of Stephen Lawton Watson. His successor, A. N. Mesquita, has continued to enlist the co-operation of pastors and churches in the development of a growing capital to care for retired pastors and widows of pastors.

The convention meets annually for the transaction of business, and functions *ad interim* through its executive committee. In 1953, 1,123 churches, with 674 Brazilian pastors, reported 9,172 baptisms, 114,324 members, and 1,179 Sunday schools with an enrolment of 121,357.

The convention co-operates with the missions in the direction of the American Baptist College of Recife, the John W. Shepard College of Rio de Janeiro, the North Brazil Seminary, the South Brazil Seminary, and the Carroll Publishing House of Rio. The convention also co-operates with state boards and other denominational organizations.

Brazilian Baptists, through their convention, are taking part in the activities of the Baptist World Alliance. They promoted a Latin American Baptist convention and sponsored the meeting of the Baptist World Youth Congress in Rio de Janeiro with 32 nations represented in 1953. They have contributed to relief programs in Latin America and Europe.

A. R. CRABTREE

BRAZILIAN BAPTIST FOREIGN MISSION BOARD. In 1907, 25 years after Southern Baptist missionaries had organized their first church in Salvador, Bahia, 43 messengers, representing 83 churches with approximately 5,000 members, met in the same city and organized the Brazilian Baptist Convention, with its boards, including the Brazilian Baptist Foreign Mission

Board, "to help preach Christ beyond the national frontiers, in all America and all the world." At the first meeting the board elected William Buck Bagby (q.v.) as corresponding secretary and asked him to accept an invitation to visit a group of churches in Chile. After visiting the 11 churches in 1908, in company with W. T. D. McDonald, a Baptist worker of the Missionary Alliance, Bagby led them in the organization of the Chilean Baptist Union, representing 500 members. The Brazilian Baptist Foreign Mission Board contributed to the support of their work until 1918 when it was taken over by the Foreign Mission Board of the Southern Baptist Convention. In 1908 the Brazilian Baptist Foreign Mission Board sent Zachary Clay Taylor (q.v.) to Portugal, where he organized the church of Pôrto with 10 members. They sent their first missionary to Portugal in 1911. In 1955 they supported two missionaries, co-operating with 17 pastors and 22 churches with 1,520 members.

The Brazilian Baptist Foreign Mission Board opened work in Bolivia in 1947, and in 1955 they had seven missionaries, co-operating with six Bolivian workers and eight churches with 360 members. — A. R. CRABTREE

BRAZOS INSTITUTE. A coeducational school promoted by Noah T. Byars (q.v.) and established at Palo Pinto, Tex., in 1860 by Brazos River Association. It was maintained until the spring of 1861. — RUPERT N. RICHARDSON

BREWER, CHARLES EDWARD (b. Wake Forest, N. C., July 12, 1866; d. Raleigh, N. C., May 1, 1941). Educator. Son of John Marchant and Ann Eliza (Wait) Brewer and grandson of Samuel and Sarah Merriam Wait. He was educated in Wake Forest elementary schools, Vine Hill Male Academy of Scotland Neck, Wake Forest College (M.A., 1886), Johns Hopkins and Cornell universities (Ph.D., 1900), with LL.D. degrees from Baylor University and Wake Forest College. He served as professor of chemistry at Wake Forest, 1889–1915, and was the first dean of the college, 1912–15. In 1915 he became president of Meredith College, which moved to a new site and enjoyed notable progress during his administration (1915–39). He served as president emeritus, 1939–41. Brewer participated in denominational, educational, and civic affairs. He was clerk of Central Association for 26 years, recording secretary of the Baptist State Convention of North Carolina, 1908–15, first chairman of the Laymen's Movement Committee of the state convention, organizer of the Glenn Royall Sunday School near Wake Forest and its superintendent for 14 years, organizer of Berean Class in First Baptist Church, Raleigh, and its teacher for many years. He was elected president of the North Carolina Teachers' Association for one year, and held a similar position in the North Carolina College Conference for one year. He was a member of the board of town commissioners of Wake Forest, 1901–15; life member of the Raleigh Rotary Club, member of its board of directors, and president for one year. He married Love Estell Bell, Shawboro, N. C., Oct. 28, 1891, and they had two children, Ellen and Ann Eliza. — W. R. CULLOM

BREWTON-PARKER JUNIOR COLLEGE. A coeducational institution located near Mount Vernon and Ailey in Georgia. It was chartered Apr. 28, 1904, under the name of Union Baptist Institute. Classes began Sept. 12, 1905. The name was changed to Brewton-Parker Institute in 1914, honoring the founders J. C. Brewton and W. C. Parker; and to Brewton-Parker Junior College in 1948. The school was first owned by the Daniell, Tatnall County, and Telfair associations. The number of co-operating associations was finally increased to 20. At the beginning all pupils in the community were admitted, but since 1948 only junior college students have been enrolled.

The original board of trustees had as its officers J. C. Brewton, chairman; W. T. Burkhalter, vice-chairman; J. D. Rabun, clerk; and A. B. Hutcheson, treasurer. The first building was erected in 1905 on 15 acres of land lying about midway between the towns of Mount Vernon and Ailey. The land was donated by Mrs. Eliza Fountain and a Negro man, W. C. Crawley.

J. C. Brewton served as president from 1905 to 1913, and again in 1919. He was closely identified with the institution until his death in 1939. J. W. Palmer has served as clerk of the board of trustees since 1907. Presidents since Brewton have been: R. E. Robertson, 1914–16; B. B. Smith, 1917–18; L. S. Barrett, 1919–22; A. M. Gates, 1922–41; R. L. Robinson, 1942–46; C. T. Ricks, 1947–49; M. P. Campbell, 1950–53; and M. A. Murray, since 1953.

Expansion and development has brought added acreage and several buildings. The school was raised to junior college level in 1927.

The fidelity of the college to its original purpose to educate young people under Christian influence has sent graduates to pastorates and other areas of Christian service and has equipped many others for useful Christian citizenship and for leadership in business and the professions. Eight former students are foreign missionaries: Tom Gullatt, Rev. and Mrs. Charles Whaley, Rev. Heyward Adams (retired), Rev. and Mrs. J. B. Durham, Miss Vera Campbell, a former science teacher, and Miss Blanche Bradley. Bible is required for graduation.

The school ranks high in junior college athletic circles. In basketball the Southeastern regional championship was won in 1948; and in 1953 and 1954 Brewton-Parker placed 10th and 8th, respectively, in the national tournament.

The college is accredited by the Georgia State Department of Education. A diploma entitles the holder to a teacher's certificate. The chief financial benefactors of the college since 1940 have been Columbus Roberts, W. A. Wilcox, and J. E. Parker. In 1955 there were eight college buildings and a president's home on the 132 acres which make up the campus. The estimated financial value of its property was $500,000. The cash endowment was $202,886.75. There were 6,000 volumes in the library.

R. L. ROBINSON

BRIDGEPORT ACADEMY. A school known also as the Tennessee River Institute, founded by the Home Mission Board of the Southern Baptist Convention at Bridgeport, Ala., in 1909. The Chamber of Commerce deeded the properties formerly occupied by Alatennga College, valued at $25,000, to the board. The school was combined with Eldridge Academy in 1927.

JAMES E. DAVIDSON

BRISTOL FEMALE COLLEGE. A school at Bristol, Tenn., founded *c.* 1868 as Bristol Female Institute, with J. F. Kincanon as principal. The school was chartered as a college in 1871 and had D. C. Wester as president in 1881. The institution operated 36 years but did not open its doors in 1904.

LYNN EDWARD MAY, JR.

BRISTOW MEMORIAL HOSPITAL. In 1954 the Bristow Memorial Hospital Foundation asked the Oklahoma convention to lease this newly constructed 30-bed hospital at Bristow, Okla., on a 25-year agreement. The lease, at $25 per year, was signed Oct. 1, 1954, and the hospital was dedicated Dec. 5, 1954. Building and equipment are valued at more than $350,000.

TOM E. CARTER

BRITAIN AND DOMINIONS, BAPTISTS OF. *England.*—English Baptists, as a self-conscious, self-perpetuating denomination, can be traced back to the year 1641. Baptist principles, doctrine, and polity may be found earlier but cannot be demonstrated to have existed together in entirety or without deviation until the 17th century.

Baptist beginnings in England were twofold, originating in what are now called General Baptists and Particular Baptists. British Baptists, especially Particular Baptists, experienced their greatest period of development and expansion in the 17th century, about 1645–90. With the Act of Toleration (1689), Baptists experienced a decline in Britain which has never fully been overcome. Baptists flourished during the Commonwealth and Protectorate; some held high office in the government, and many filled important roles in Cromwell's army. Baptists were, without exception, congregational in polity. The only connection above the local organization among Particular Baptists, until the formation of the Baptist Union (1813), came as a result of Baptist participation in the army. The "associations" that had been organized for purposes of recruitment and defense in the 1640's were continued after the hostilities as the government began to settle the army in occupied territories. Baptists, who were numerous in the army, quite naturally carried over the organizational plan and the name "association" into their churches as they established them in these territories. Many Baptists in the army were "preachers," and all were evangelists. It is not, therefore, surprising that great expansion, both in churches and in numbers, characterized this period.

In the latter part of the 17th century and in the 18th century, General Baptists came under a cloud, and the Calvinistic Baptists dominated the scene until the conversion of Dan Taylor (1738–1816) and the formation of the New-Connextion General Baptists (1770). The old General Assembly of General Baptists (1654) had become infested with various Socinian doctrines, including both universal restoration and unitarian views of God. Particular Baptists were able, with a few exceptions, to avoid these errors, but they came very heavily under the influence of a nonevangelical hyper-Calvinism. John Gill (*q.v.*) of London was a leader in this defection. His ultraconservatism at last led him to forsake the general application and invitation of the gospel. The history of Particular Baptists in the 18th century consisted chiefly in their transition from this type of lifeless Calvinism to a broader, more evangelical, yet still strongly Calvinistic and conservative, viewpoint. Andrew Fuller (*q.v.*) (1754–1815) and John Ryland (1753–1825) were in the vanguard of the new evangelicalism. With this new perspective, it is not difficult to explain the revival of interest among the Particular Baptists, both for the work at home and for the experiment by William Carey (*q.v.*) (1761–1834) and the Mission Society (1792) in Serampore.

After conversion to Baptist principles, Dan Taylor sought company among the Particular Baptists of the Yorkshire area, but he was turned away, principally because of his Arminian sentiments, a carry-over from his connection with the new Methodism. He was finally immersed at the hands of a General Baptist minister in Nottinghamshire. Taylor soon was linked with the General churches in Lincolnshire and with the general assembly in London. Very quickly, Taylor wearied of the threadbare theology and dated social customs of the assembly. After several unsuccessful attempts to get Baptists into the Leicestershire evangelical movement, he finally hit upon the plan of a "new connection" of Arminian Baptists, particularly in the Leicestershire area. On June 6, 1770, the New Connexion of General Baptists was constituted in London for the purpose of reviving "experimental religion or primitive Christianity in faith and practice." The organizing was done over the loud protests of the assembly, in session at the same time. Gradually the old assembly and the New Connexion lost all touch with each other, and eventually the assembly almost completely frittered away into a thoroughgoing Unitarianism.

The 19th century was marked by the ministries of three able yet diverse preachers: Robert Hall, Jr. (*q.v.*) (1764–1831), Charles Haddon Spurgeon (*q.v.*) (1834–92), and Alexander Maclaren (*q.v.*) (1825–1910). Hall showed signs of future greatness even as a precocious child. He was one of the truly great orator-preachers of modern times. His influence was on a rather high level, and his sermons have little appeal today because of their involved style and an ornate eloquence long since gone from the pulpit. Spurgeon was quite different; his greatest influence and appeal have been to the rank and file of people. Not so well educated, he was an untiring and prolific student of the Bible, as his sermons testify. His most notable contribution was his long ministry in London at the Metropolitan Tabernacle. Maclaren, of Manchester, was alike a prodigious Bible scholar and a preacher of some popularity and of great power among his following. He was not so conservative as Hall and Spurgeon but was much more so than John Clifford (1836–1923).

British Baptist life in recent years has been marked by the organization of two important general bodies: the Baptist Union of Great Britain and Ireland and the Baptist World Alliance. In 1891 final union of the great majority of General and Particular Baptists was effected through the Lancashire and Cheshire Association and the Baptist Union, originally chartered in 1813 in the Old Southwark Church. John Clifford, a General Baptist, was instrumental in this accomplishment. A number of Baptist churches in England and Scotland are not affiliated with the Union. The Baptist World Alliance came into existence in 1905 by action of the First World Baptist Congress, then meeting in London. It was chartered as "a voluntary association of Unions, Conventions and Associations of Baptist churches," which extends "over every part of the world." The Baptist World Alliance

exists in order more fully to show the essential oneness of Baptist people in the Lord Jesus Christ, to impart inspiration to the brotherhood, and to promote the spirit of fellowship, service and co-operation among its members; but this Alliance may in no way interfere with the independence of the churches or assume the administrative functions of existing organizations.

Interfaith groups with which British Baptists have aligned themselves are the National Council of the Evangelical Free Churches and the British Council of Churches, an arm of the World Council of Churches. They have steadfastly resisted both national and world appeals for organic union with non-Baptist groups. English Baptists at present number around 207,101.

Scotland.—Baptists have never been strong in Scotland. Their beginnings can be traced back to the days when Cromwell's army occupied the land, but a more substantial foundation was laid by the work of Archibald McLean (1733–1812) and Robert Haldane (1764–1842). The McLeanite movement was of a distinctive type, very clannish, imbibing of the Sandemanian doctrine of faith as intellectual assent, and bearing striking similarities to the American movement of Alexander Campbell (1786–1866). Haldane and his brother breathed the breath of evangelism and missions into the Scottish Baptists. Baptists in Scotland today number 19,704.

Ireland.—The Baptists of Ireland have a history begun and closed by the army of Cromwell. Fewer than a dozen churches were established by the soldiers, of which half have not survived. There are approximately 4,476 Baptists in Ireland today.

Wales.—Welsh Baptists have been characterized by their rather low cultural level, by the indigenousness of their churches where the old Welsh dialect is still widely used, and by recurrent waves of emotionalism and revivals. Christmas Evans (*q.v.*) (1766–1838) was a preacher of some stature, and he exerted a stabilizing influence on the work. In the churches of Wales today there are 105,922 Baptists.

Canada.—The Baptist witness in the Maritime Provinces of Canada dates from the establishment of the first church at Horton in 1778. In 1906 various groups united to form the United Baptist Convention. The first Baptist church in Ontario claims 1776 as the founding date, and the first in Quebec, 1794. The first Baptist work to be done in the three western provinces of Canada was by John Morton in 1862. In 1875 the first church was officially organized as a result of the mission efforts of the Ontario Baptists. The Baptist Convention of British Columbia was organized in 1897, at which time Baptists in the United States withdrew the financial aid they had been giving. In 1909 Baptists in western Canada formed the Baptist Union of Western Canada; and in 1944, the general body, the Baptist Federation of Canada. There are 141,239 Baptists associated with the federation today.

South Africa.—The first Baptist group to organize a church in South Africa was at Crahamstown in 1820. The Baptist Union of South Africa was organized in 1877, and today it has 24,360 members.

Australia.—The Bathurst Street Baptist Church in Sydney, New South Wales, was officially constituted a church in 1836. The last province in Australia to receive the Baptist witness was in Western Australia, where a Baptist church was organized in Perth in 1894. The Baptist Union of Australia was formed in 1926, and today it has approximately 31,460 members. In New Zealand the first Baptist church was organized in Nelson in the year 1851 as a result of the mission work of the Baptists of Sydney. In 1882 the Baptist Union of New Zealand was organized; it has a membership close to 10,000 today.

BIBLIOGRAPHY: T. Crosby, *The History of English Baptists* (1738–40). J. Ivimey, *A History of English Baptists* (1811–30). R. G. Torbet, *A History of* the *Baptists* (1930). A. C. Underwood, *A History of the English Baptists* (1947). W. T. Whitley, *A History of British Baptists* (1923).

EUGENE H. STOCKSTILL

BRITTAIN, CHARLES MERCER (b. Coyners, Ga., Dec. 16, 1873; d. Jan. 12, 1943). Minister, denominational leader. Son of Jabez Marshall and Ida (Callaway) Brittain, he received his education in the grade schools of Covington, Ga., Emory College, and Mercer University, graduating from the latter in 1898. During the Spanish-American War he served as Army Christian Commissioner for the Y.M.C.A. In Dec., 1899, he was ordained to the ministry; and June 27, 1900, he married Susie Marie Moore of Macon, Ga. To them were born five sons.

After eight years as pastor and high school teacher in Georgia, he went to Florida, being pastor at Kissimmee two years and at Lake City one year. While in the latter city, he was elected trustee of the newly founded Columbia College. After two years as pastor in Alabama, he returned to Florida to teach in Columbia College and serve as business manager of the institution, which conferred on him the D.D. degree. During his years at Columbia College, Brittain served two years as editor of the *Florida Baptist Witness* and continued contributing to the paper afterward. When the college closed in 1918, he served a year as pastor at Ocala and then was elected associate secretary of the Florida Baptist State Board of Missions. After the death of S. B. Rogers, the executive secretary-treasurer, Brittain was elected to succeed him. In 1941, due to failing health, Brittain resigned his position and was elected executive secretary-treasurer emeritus.

H. C. GARWOOD

BROADDUS, ANDREW, I (b. Caroline County, Va., Nov. 4, 1770; d. Dec. 1, 1848). Minister, teacher, hymn writer. Son of John Broaddus, a schoolteacher and farmer, Andrew was the youngest of 12 children. Educational facilities were few, and Broaddus had only a few months in school, but his father may have taught him for a time. He had a thirst for knowledge and a retentive memory, and read every book he could find. According to Jeremiah Bell Jeter (*q.v.*), when candles were scarce the "aspiring boy" would lie on his breast on the floor, poring over his book by the dim light of the pine knot on the hearth.

Since Broaddus' father was a member of the Episcopal Church, Andrew was forbidden to attend religious worship conducted by the Baptists. However, young Broaddus, under the influence of Theodoric Noel, an effective Baptist minister of his day, was baptized May 28, 1789, and became a member of Upper King and Queen Baptist Church.

Broaddus and his close friend, Robert Baylor Semple (*q.v.*), preached their first sermons at the home of Mrs. Lowrie in Caroline County, Dec. 24, 1789; and Broaddus was ordained at Upper King and Queen Church, Oct. 16, 1791. He held pastorates in Caroline County churches, Burrus's and Bethel, and at Fredericksburg, and was largely responsible for organization of the Bethel and Fredericksburg churches.

Supported primarily by a school he taught in Caroline County, Broaddus was very proficient in English literature, Latin, and Greek. After teaching he served as pastor of Upper Zion, Beulah, Mangohic, Salem, and Upper King and Queen churches. Although recognized by city churches, Broaddus confined his ministry to the country. He was invited to preach as a supply minister with either a view to a call, or was actually called, to large churches in Boston, New York, Philadelphia, Baltimore, Norfolk, and the First Baptist Church in Richmond, all of which he declined except Richmond, where he served as pastor for a few months. Jeter thought Broaddus declined the work of the larger churches "because of an unfortunate nervous sensitiveness which rendered him timid among strangers."

Gifted as a writer, Broaddus frequently contributed articles for the *Religious Herald* and other papers. He wrote several books, including a reply to Thomas Paine's attack on Christianity, which he entitled *The Age of Reason and Revelation*. A writer of hymns and a compiler of hymnals which found widespread use among Baptist churches of the South, his three hymnal compilations are *Collection of Sacred Ballads* (1790), *The Dover Selection of Spiritual Songs* (1828), which contains one of his original hymns, and *The Virginia Selection of Psalms, Hymns, and Spiritual Songs* (1836), containing three of his original hymns.

Moderator of Dover Association for eight years, Broaddus declined the D.D. degree offered him by Columbian College, Washington, D. C., because he doubted the wisdom of ministers' accepting such exterior decorations. Broaddus married four times, and his third wife was Jane C. Broaddus, sister of his second wife and widow of his nephew, by whom he had seven children, one of whom, Andrew Broaddus, Jr., succeeded his father as pastor of Salem Church. When Andrew Broaddus became pastor at Salem in 1820, he began a famous triumvirate of Andrews—father, son, and grandson—who served the Salem pastorate consecutively for 106 years.

BIBLIOGRAPHY: A. Broaddus, *Bible History Particularly adapted to the use of Schools and Families* (1816); ed., *The Dover Selection of Spiritual Songs* (1828); *The Extra Examined*, a reply to A. Campbell's *Millennial Harbinger Extra* (1831); *Virginia Selection of Psalms, Hymns, and Spiritual Songs* (1836). J. B. Jeter, *The Sermons and Other Writings of the Rev. Andrew Broaddus with a Memoir of His Life* (1852).

L. M. RITTER

BROADDUS, WILLIAM F. (b. near Woodville, Va., Apr. 30, 1801; d. Fredericksburg, Va., Sept. 8, 1876). Minister. Son of William F. and Susannah (Ferguson) Broaddus, he was educated in private schools and became a teacher when he was 16. At 18 he married Mary Ann Farrar. Given careful religious training by his mother, Broaddus was converted under the preaching of Ambrose C. Booten of Luray, Va., and was baptized by him in the Hawksbill Creek. In 1823 he was ordained at "F. T." church and became its pastor. He held other pastorates at Mt. Salem, Bethel in Frederick County (now Clarke County), and Long Branch in Fauquier County, Va.

Because of his public advocacy of missions, Sunday schools, Bible tracts, and temperance societies, Broaddus was denied a seat in Ketocton Association although he was pastor of Bethel Church, a member of the association. On that occasion James Sowers and William Kerfoot, delegates from Bethel, withdrew, stating that they could not continue as members of a body from which their pastor had been excluded. For several years Broaddus encountered, and spoke against, the antimission spirit which dominated many northern Virginia churches.

From 1840 to 1850 Broaddus was pastor of four churches in Kentucky, while living at Lexington, Shelbyville, and Versailles, after which he returned to Virginia and became pastor of the Fredericksburg church in 1853. Taken as a hostage by Union officers in the Civil War, Broaddus was taken to prison in Washington, but returned two months later. In Jan., 1863, he became pastor of the church in Charlottesville, Va. Broaddus declined a call to return to the Fredericksburg pastorate in 1865, although he moved back to Fredericksburg and remained there until his death, raising money for the education of orphans of Confederate soldiers.

L. M. RITTER

BROADMAN PRESS. Trade name of the general book publishing enterprise of the Sunday School Board of the Southern Baptist Convention. "Broadman" was coined by John Leonard Hill, book editor, 1922–49, from the last names of John Albert Broadus (q.v.) and Basil Manly, Jr. (q.v.), secretary and president, respectively, of the first Sunday School Board. The first books to bear this imprint appeared in 1934. In 1956 the Sunday School Board was also producing church supplies, visual aids, records, and anthems under this imprint.

General book publishing by the board began in 1898 with the release of *The Story of Yates the Missionary* by Charles E. Taylor (q.v.). Although such publishing had been prohibited in the establishment of the board, the Convention reacted favorably to this venture. Without official authorization for book publishing, however, James Marion Frost (q.v.), executive secretary of the board, could not use its funds for that purpose. A special fund had been set up to underwrite the Yates book; two other endowments of the same amount were given by Banjamin E. Garvey and Pinckney Daniel Pollock (q.v.), and 12 books were financed through 1913 by these funds with a total sale of 73,000 copies. When the American Baptist Publication Society closed its last branch in the South, the Convention in 1910 "authorized and urged [the board] to enter . . . on the work of supplying the brethren of our churches with books, tracts, hymn and song books, and indeed all supplies . . . such as are suitable and desirable." Despite Convention endorsement, the development of a book program was slow; from 1911 to 1921, only 59 books were published, and 24 of these were study books for the growing Sunday schools and other church groups.

In 1922 John L. Hill, dean of Georgetown College, Ky., was elected book editorial secretary, and the board made a joint publishing arrangement with the George H. Doran Co., New York, to promote some of its general books on a national basis. Isaac Jacobus Van Ness (q.v.), executive secretary of the board, had already (1919) pointed out the need for a neutral imprint for general books and for wider distribution of such books through a system of book stores. Until the depression of the 1930's, the annual list of general books ranged from 17 to 28; in 1931–35 that list was reduced to an average of 10 books. Since then, except for the period of wartime paper shortage, the annual list has ranged from 15 to 31 (in 1956). The first salesman for Broadman books was employed in 1946, when Broadman's trade advertising began.

When Hill retired in 1949, William J. Fallis succeeded him as book editor. A study of book interests and needs initiated an aggressive program during the next several years in book design, production, and promotion, and manuscript solicitation. The joint publishing arrangement which began with the Doran house was inherited by Harper and Brothers, but in 1954 this relationship was severed so that Broadman books might be promoted independently on a national scale. In 1956 the staff of Broadman Press had been increased in proportion to the growth of the press during the preceding five years; it included: Joseph F. Green, Jr., general book editor, Kate Ellen Gruver, children's book editor, and Mary Christian, missions book editor. Design and production plans were projected through the Art and Operations departments of the board; promotion and sales were carried on by the Advertising and Merchandise Sales departments to reach both the Southern Baptist constituency and readers across the country. G. R. Welch Co. was the Canadian representative. Broadman books were manufactured by several printers of national reputation. In 1956 the catalogue listed 220 books in print for children, young people, and adults; for preachers and other church leaders; and in these categories: Bible study, missions, sermons, fiction, inspiration, personal Christian living, biography, doctrine, religious education, ethics, recreation, and music.

See also SUNDAY SCHOOL BOARD and CONVENTION PRESS.

BIBLIOGRAPHY: P. E. Burroughs, *Fifty Fruitful Years* (1951). J. M. Frost, *The Sunday School Board: Its History and Work* (1914). WILLIAM J. FALLIS

BROADUS, JOHN ALBERT (b. Culpeper County, Va., Jan. 24, 1827; d. Louisville, Ky., Mar. 16, 1895). Scholar, teacher, preacher, and denominational leader. The fourth child of Major Edmund and Nancy (Sims) Broadus, he came into a home which, though not wealthy, was distinguished by intelligence, culture, and piety. When he was about 16, he was converted. His early education had been at home and in a private school. From 1844 to 1846 he taught in a small school and engaged in disciplined independent study. In the fall of 1846 Broadus entered the University of Virginia to prepare for the ministry, receiving the M.A. degree in 1850. During the next year he taught in a private school in Fluvanna County, Va., preached in small country churches, and diligently studied church history, theology, sermons, and the Bible. During this year two notable events occurred—his ordination, Aug. 12, 1850, and on Nov. 13, 1850, his marriage to Maria Harrison, a daughter of Gessner Harrison (1807–62), professor of ancient languages at the University of Virginia.

Calls of various kinds came to the young teacher, and he finally accepted the post as tutor in Latin and Greek at his alma mater and pastor of the Baptist church at Charlottesville. After one year he resigned his teaching position in order to devote full time to his pastorate. This he did with the exception of two years when he was given a leave of absence to serve as chaplain at the University of Virginia.

In 1858 Broadus was asked to become a member of the faculty of the new Southern Baptist Theological Seminary. Though he had a part in planning the institution, he declined the offer because of his attachment to preaching and pastoral work. After months of struggling with the decision, he agreed to become a member of the first faculty when the seminary opened in Greenville, S. C., in 1859. For the next 36 years he was professor of New Testament interpretation and homiletics, and his life was inextricably bound to the school.

While the seminary was closed during the Civil War, Broadus preached in small churches and spent some time as chaplain in Lee's army in northern Virginia. When the seminary reopened in 1865, it struggled for existence and remained open largely because of the heroic efforts of Broadus and James Petigru Boyce (1827–88). However, during this period of stress and strain, Broadus did some of his best work. In 1870 he published *On the Preparation and Delivery of Sermons*, a book which has become a classic in its field. Broadus received nationwide recognition as a preacher and teacher and was offered many influential pastorates, professorships, and other positions.

The last years of Broadus' life brought increasing recognition. He published the following works: *Lectures on the History of Preaching* (1876, revised, 1896); *Commentary on the Gospel of Matthew* (1886); *Sermons and Addresses* (1886); *Jesus of Nazareth* (1890); *Memoir of James Petigru Boyce* (1893); *Harmony of the Gospels* (1893); twenty or more pamphlets, tracts, etc.; and many periodical articles. In 1889 he gave the Yale Lectures on Preaching and is the only Southern Baptist ever to be accorded this honor. He died Mar. 16, 1895, almost at the zenith of his fame, and was buried in Cave Hill Cemetery in Louisville, Ky.

There were three children from Broadus' first marriage: Eliza S., Annie Harrison, who married W. Y. Abraham, and Maria Louisa. His first wife died on Oct. 21, 1857, and on Jan. 4, 1859, he married Charlotte E. Sinclair, who bore him five children: Samuel S., Caroline, Alice V., who married S. C. Mitchell, Ella Thomas, who married A. T. Robertson, and Boyce.

Throughout his life Broadus engaged in a dual work—teaching and preaching. As he stood before classes and congregations, he soon won their confidence. He was a well-proportioned man of medium stature, with unusually expressive brown eyes and a countenance which expressed kindliness and sincerity. However, it was not his person but rather his manner of speaking which attracted attention. He had accurate knowledge, a clarity of expression which made the difficult simple, and an enthusiasm which was transmitted to his listeners.

V. L. STANFIELD

BROADWAY PLAN OF CHURCH FINANCE, THE. What has come to be known as the Broadway Plan of Church Finance in California began in Broadway Baptist Church in Houston, Tex., in 1936, when an attorney, J. S. Bracewell, who at that time served the church as Sunday school superintendent, saw the need for more buildings, yet realized that no money was available with which to build them. Bracewell conceived and developed a plan whereby the church would issue bonds (bonds are called notes in California legal terminology) bearing 5 per cent interest maturing over a period of 13½ years. The bonds would be sold to members and friends of the church. His plan provided that the church would deposit in a trust account $2 per week for each $1,000 in securities issued in order to meet principal and interest payments as they came due. So successful was the venture that Bracewell was soon asked to help other churches project the same plan. In local parlance it became known as the Broadway Plan, and in order to meet the demand Bracewell began processing applications for it through his law firm. As of Jan. 1, 1956, 1,200 churches of 18 major denominations in 35 states, Alaska, and Canada had issued $55,000,-000 in securities on which every payment on interest and principal had been made on time.

In July, 1951, a contractual agreement was established between Bracewell and the executive committee of the board of directors of the Southern Baptist General Convention of California which provided that a branch office known as the Broadway Plan of Church Finance in California would be opened in the convention office in Fresno with S. G. Posey as executive director and Miss Edna Bowling as secretary. On June 30, 1956, at which time the contract had been in force five years, 256 California churches had issued a total of $8,044,100 in bonds.

BIBLIOGRAPHY: F. Looney, *History of California Southern Baptists* (1954).   S. G. POSEY

BROOKE, WILLIAM SELDON (b. Cumnor, King and Queen County, Va., June 24, 1878; d. Columbia, S. C., Sept. 8, 1949). Pastor, South Carolina Baptist leader. Son of Elizabeth Garrett and Philip Edward Brooke, he joined historic Mattaponi Baptist Church at nine years of age, the church which later licensed him to preach. Brooke attended Fork Union Military Academy, Virginia, received the B.A. degree from the University of Richmond in 1907 and the Th.G. degree from Southern Baptist Theological Seminary in 1911.

After serving as pastor at Branch's Baptist Church during his student days, Brooke held other pastorates at Second Baptist Church, Danville, Va., where he was ordained in June, 1907, and at churches in Greenville, Va. (1912-16), Johnston, S. C. (1916-22), and Lake City, S. C. (1922-29). His going to South Carolina in 1916 opened the way for special denominational service when he was elected the first field man and enlistment secretary of the state convention's general board. While serving in that position, Brooke promoted the every-member canvass, "God's acre," and other project plans for church financing. Upon the death of General Secretary-Treasurer Charles Alfred Jones (q.v.), Brooke was appointed to act in that position until his election as general secretary-treasurer in Nov., 1942. He served in that capacity until his death. Brooke married Janie Louise Fulton of Danville, Va., in 1913.

BIBLIOGRAPHY: R. N. Daniel, *Furman University, a History* (1951). J. S. Ramond, *Among Southern Baptists* (1936).   W. C. ALLEN

BROOKS, SAMUEL PALMER (b. Milledgeville, Ga., Dec. 4, 1863; d. Waco, Tex., May 14, 1931). College administrator, educator. After moving to Texas when he was five, Brooks worked on farms and railroads, beginning when he was 14 until he was 22. At 23 he was teaching country schools; seven years later he received an A.B. degree from Baylor University and an A.M. degree from Yale in 1902. President of Baylor University in 1902-31, Brooks led Baylor in its growth from a small college to full university status. During his administration he organized the Baylor Medical and Dental colleges, the schools of Law, Nursing, and Pharmacy, the Theological Department, the Texas Association of Colleges, and the Texas Peace Society. Brooks was president of the Baptist General Convention of Texas, the college section of Texas State Teachers Association, Southern Sociological Congress, Southern Baptist Education Society; vice-president of the Southern Baptist Convention and of the American Peace Society; and corresponding secretary of the Texas Baptist Educational Commission. In addition Brooks was a member of the International Peace Commission and a candidate for the United States Senate.

BIBLIOGRAPHY: Baylor University, *Diamond Jubilee* (1921). Brooks Papers, Texas Collection, Baylor University, Waco, Tex. J. M. Dawson, *Brooks Takes the Long Look* (1931). Texas State Historical Association, *The Handbook of Texas* (1952).
   GUY B. HARRISON, JR.

BROTHERHOOD, BAPTIST. An organization of Baptist men, originally founded for the promotion of missions, but later a general-purpose organization emphasizing the total denominational program and seeking to enlist men who are church members in a more active participation of stewardship. One incentive to the development of the organization was an appreciation on the part of some Southern Baptist leaders of the effectiveness of the Woman's Missionary Union in promoting its program. At the 1907 meeting of the Southern Baptist Convention, in Richmond, Va., the organization which was to be later known as the Brotherhood was founded on recommendation brought by Joshua Levering (q.v.) of Maryland and William Jonathan Northen (q.v.) of Georgia. The organization was called the Laymen's Missionary Movement of the Southern Baptist Convention. It operated under this title from 1907 to 1926. From 1927 to 1950 it was known as the Baptist Brotherhood of the South. Since 1950 it has operated under the title of Brotherhood Commission of the Southern Baptist Convention.

The year after its founding, the new organization elected an executive secretary, John Thompson Henderson (q.v.), who promoted the work with vigorous effectiveness. A definite policy and program was soon formulated. The Laymen's Movement, it was said, existed for pastors as well as laymen; was not a society or separate organization; did not send out missionaries; but had as its purpose the enlistment of men for inspiration and instruction of the world mission task of the Convention. Henderson led in setting up a functioning organization. In every state there was to be an over-all committee elected at the annual state meeting. This committee was to see that the work was presented to every district and association and was to try to get a local committee of three appointed in each association to promote the work there. Rallies were to be held at intervals, with laymen in charge and speaking. Every church was to have two or three men to promote the work, distribute literature, and (prior to the establishing of the Cooperative Program) take pledges for missions.

Henderson led in the setting up of organizations in every state but two. Almost immediately after the Convention action which established the organization, the various states

TEXAS TECH BAPTIST STUDENT CENTER, Lubbock. Air conditioned and includes recreational facilities, library, and Bible student classrooms, cost $70,000 in 1952.

UNIVERSITY OF ALABAMA BAPTIST STUDENT CENTER, Tuscaloosa. Completed in 1954, it houses the manifold activities of a large student constituency. Cost $220,000.

UNIVERSITY OF MIAMI BAPTIST STUDENT CENTER, Miami, Fla. Erected in 1950 at a cost of $57,000, emphasis is given to Bible study, mission activities, fellowship, intramural sports, and vocational guidance.

UNIVERSITY OF OKLAHOMA BAPTIST STUDENT CENTER, Norman. Serves the varied interests of Baptist students. It was completed in 1953 at a cost of $165,000.

began to act. In July, 1907, in Mississippi, a committee was appointed to get the Laymen's Movement started there. This committee reported to the state convention in 1908, and the work was adopted.

In 1908 two men were appointed in Texas to investigate the movement. They reported to the Texas state convention, but no organization on a statewide basis was set up until 1915. However, an executive committee on Laymen's Movement was elected, which each year reported to the state convention praising the work of the Laymen's Movement in the Southern Baptist Convention.

In 1910 a committee was appointed in North Carolina to study the movement. The following year the convention heard addresses on the subject, but no organization was established. As late as 1924, there was still no state organization for Laymen's Movement in North Carolina.

The Laymen's Movement was first presented in Illinois at the state ministers' conference in Harrisburg in 1912. Each year from 1914 to 1928, statewide laymen's meetings were held. W. E. Williams of Eldorado, Ill., served as chairman of the movement in Illinois from 1912 to 1926.

In Alabama the Laymen's Movement was slow in taking hold. In the period 1916–25 the reports to the state convention were primarily concerned with what was going on in the Southern Baptist Convention.

In Arkansas during 1916–25, no state organization was established to promote the Laymen's Movement. There were, however, ministers' and laymen's conferences held in the years 1916, 1923, 1924, and 1925. These meetings, held two days before the opening of the Arkansas state convention, seemed to have little to do with the Laymen's Movement.

In Florida in 1916 at the state convention at Live Oak, Henderson spoke about the Laymen's Movement. An executive committee for the state was appointed which reported progress to the next three state conventions.

In Georgia the Laymen's Movement was well organized by 1916. The state was divided into 25 districts with workers in each one, and by 1920 it was reported that "men in much larger numbers are attending the associational and conventional meetings; thousands of capable men were active in the 75 Million Campaign."

Baptists in Kentucky were quick to adopt the Laymen's Movement. By 1916 they had their state, district, and association officers elected and working.

In Louisiana the Laymen's Movement was slow in getting started. The state's 1917 report reveals a "suspension of the ardor and enthusiasm for this movement." Each year, however, state conventions were held for Baptist laymen. The reports reveal that Henderson was present every year in these meetings trying to promote the Laymen's Movement. The 1925 report states: "The convention meeting in Shreveport last year adopted the report on laymen's work which contained this suggestion: the appointment of a state committee composed of nine zealous laymen, but this action seems to have been overlooked."

Henderson was again present at this meeting and suggested that a mass meeting be called at Alexandria, La. This was done, and an organization was established which started the Laymen's Movement on the road to success in Louisiana.

In Mississippi the Brotherhood work was not organized on a statewide basis until 1944. It was customary to have a pastors' and laymen's convention each year in connection with the state convention of Mississippi Baptists.

In South Carolina the laymen met for state conventions, but no Brotherhood organization was established until 1931. That year Henderson spoke to a special statewide convention held in Columbia. About 500 were present.

In Tennessee the laymen's work was confined largely to state conventions and mass meetings until about 1925. In the years prior to this, Henderson and William David Powell (*q.v.*) kept up the mission interest among the men.

From its beginning, and into the early twenties, the Laymen's Missionary Movement was almost purely a spontaneous organization, promoted and carried on somewhat independent of the regular state conventions but, of course, in sympathy with their work. After 1920 the state conventions began to express a more concrete interest in the work of their laymen, and the promotion of the Laymen's Movement came to be more and more a regular part of the work of the denomination.

In Kentucky in 1920, the autonomous state committee which had been leading in the Laymen's Movement recommended to the state convention that a state secretary be elected to head the movement and to work in close harmony with the Home and Foreign Mission boards. A man was secured, and by 1925, 50,-000 tithers had been enlisted among the laymen. In Virginia a state laymen's secretary was secured in 1921. In Tennessee the laymen's work was made the responsibility of the Sunday school and B.Y.P.U. department, and a full-time secretary was not secured until 1940. In Missouri the work was combined with the stewardship department and was for a time promoted largely through the men's Sunday school classes. A full-time secretary was elected in 1934. In Mississippi the movement was not organized on a statewide basis until 1944, when a state secretary was elected and a separate department established for this work. In New Mexico the state convention and the Laymen's Movement grew up together, and in 1926 the state secretary for Sunday school and enlistment was asked to spend part of his time in the laymen's work. South Carolina depended on a state Brotherhood chairman from 1931 until the election in 1947 of a state Brotherhood secretary.

Brotherhood, Baptist

By 1956 the movement was largely integrated into the organized life of the denomination. In all, 23 states in the Southern Baptist Convention had state Brotherhood secretaries. These states and secretaries are as follows: Alabama, William Jesse Isbell, Jr.; Arizona, William Daniel Lawes; Arkansas, Nelson Tull; California, Walter F. Bisbee; Florida, Gary A. Ratterree; Georgia, Bernard Dodson King; Illinois, George Edward Wheeler; Kansas, Shaw Belew; Kentucky, Lucien Edwin Coleman; Louisiana, Fred Forester; Maryland, Allen Jack Beck; Mississippi, Wilburn Roberts; Missouri, Walter P. Arnold; New Mexico, Howard Carroll Sivells; North Carolina, Horace Bernard Easom; Ohio, John Henry Ashcraft; Oregon-Washington, Paul Alexander McCasland; Oklahoma, John Allen Pennington; South Carolina, John Alexander Farmer; Tennessee, Paul Robert Cates; Texas, Leldon Hunter Tapscott; Virginia, George Lee Euting.

As state organizations and programs came gradually into being, the Convention-wide organization provided leadership, inspiration, and guidance. In 1910 the secretary, Henderson, reported to the Southern Baptist Convention that he had "delivered one hundred and fifty addresses in the interest of the Movement that year, had visited every one of the fifteen states of the Convention, and had attended conferences in Huntington, West Virginia, and New York."

In 1912 the executive committee of the Laymen's Movement suggested that a "great convention of men" be held sometime during the next year. The report was adopted, and the executive committee projected and held a "General Convention of Baptist Laymen" in Chattanooga, Tenn., Feb. 4-6, 1913. More than 1,200 men attended. In 1913 another convention of Baptist men was held in Dallas, Tex., with more than 1,100 men in attendance. At the Southern Baptist Convention in 1914, the headquarters for the Laymen's Movement were moved from Baltimore, Md., to Chattanooga, Tenn.

Until 1926 Henderson, as executive secretary, was largely responsible for the work. In that year L. A. Ellison, a banker from Oklahoma, was elected associate secretary of the Baptist Brotherhood of the South. George J. Burnett succeeded Ellison in 1927. T. J. York succeeded Burnett in 1931 and established his headquarters in Little Rock, Arkansas. He died suddenly in 1933, and Lawson H. Cooke, a banker from Richmond, Va., came to the office in 1936, establishing headquarters in Memphis, Tenn. Henderson resigned as secretary of the Baptist Brotherhood of the South, July 1, 1938, after having served 30 years. At the Convention in Richmond, Va., in 1938, he was elected secretary emeritus for life. Because of his outstanding work as associate secretary, Cooke was elected Henderson's successor. Cooke served as executive secretary of the Baptist Brotherhood for 15 years, 1936-51. George W. Schroeder, who was serving as associate secretary of the Brotherhood Commission at the time, was elected his successor. James M. Sapp became associate secretary in June, 1952. David T. Mashburn was elected as a second associate secretary in August, 1953. A third associate, Edward Hurt, Jr., was added in 1955.

In 1926 a new name for the Laymen's Movement, which had been first applied to the movement in Alabama in 1921, was adopted by the Southern Baptist Convention. The executive committee of the Laymen's Missionary Movement recommended to the Southern Baptist Convention at that time that the name be changed from Laymen's Missionary Movement of the Southern Baptist Convention to the Baptist Brotherhood of the South. It was felt that this new name would "include the entire denominational program, rather than having it restricted to just one phase of it." The Convention concurred and voted the change.

In Apr., 1936, an extension office for the Brotherhood work was established in Memphis, Tenn., which, in turn, became the location of the main and permanent headquarters in 1938. Since that time the facilities have been gradually expanded. In 1936 one room about 15 feet square was rented in the Commerce Title Building on Main Street in downtown Memphis. The rental lease of $25 a month was signed. Ten years later the Brotherhood Commission was occupying a suite of five rooms in the same building. In 1951 the commission purchased property at 1548 Poplar Avenue in Memphis. It now owns its own headquarters building.

In 1956 Schroeder, executive secretary of the Brotherhood Commission, reported that there were 10,246 church Brotherhoods in existence, with an enrolment of 289,387 men. The *Brotherhood Journal*, a quarterly magazine for the men, had a circulation of 390,000 in 1955. During that same year more than 2,000,000 pieces of literature were produced and distributed by the Brotherhood Commission offices.

Until 1950 the work of the Brotherhood was under the direction of a standing committee of the Convention. In that year a commission was created, and Brotherhood work was thus constituted as a regular agency of the Southern Baptist Convention. With this change also came the shortening of the name of the organization from Baptist Brotherhood of the South to Brotherhood Commission. In churches the organization is known simply as the Baptist Brotherhood.

Throughout its history the Brotherhood has sponsored and promoted a varied program. Now based on the local church group, which was foreshadowed in the Men's Unions which first began to spring up over the Convention in 1917, beginning in churches in Hopkinsville, Ky., Albuquerque, N. Mex., Macon, Ga., and Knoxville, Tenn., the Brotherhood has consistently tried to enlist the men of the church in increasingly active support of the church program.

In the beginning, a primary interest was missions and missionary stewardship. During the

Convention meeting in Houston, Tex., in 1915, Henderson proposed that the laymen undertake to erase the debts of the Home and Foreign Mission boards, which amounted to $120,000. The states responded in different ways. In Florida in 1916 a committee was appointed to enlist laymen and "in a quiet way" to secure the $2,500 which was Florida's apportionment of the debt. In Kentucky by 1916 officers of the movement were working, and they reported that "our laymen, before the meeting of the Southern Baptist Convention, raised $2,614.95 with little or no cost to the Boards to apply on the deficits of the two Boards." In Tennessee in 1916 the laymen gave $4,432.27 toward the debts of the mission boards. The other states responded more or less, and the total sum secured was $13,254.28. Again in 1917 the appeal was made. The Brotherhood executive committee asked for "emergency men" to sign pledges, and letters were sent out to laymen in every state. Arkansas received honorable mention for the response of their men to this call.

In an effort to promote interest in the work, the Southern Baptist Convention in 1932 recommended that a special "Layman's Day" be set aside each year for special emphasis. The first such day of emphasis was Apr. 9, 1933.

Evangelism has also been a part of the work of the Brotherhood. As early as 1939, Cooke was urging the men to promote evangelism through their local churches; and as the simultaneous revival plan of evangelism came into use in the Convention, the Brotherhood was used actively in its promotion.

Church advertising has been promoted by the Brotherhood since 1948. That year began the campaign to use the men to get the church program advertised through newspapers, billboards, radio, magazines, and other such secular media.

The Man and Boy Movement came into existence about 1949. Schroeder that year wrote a pamphlet called "Introducing, Adopting, Promoting, the Man and Boy Movement." In it he said that the main objective of the movement was to "encourage men to invite and take unchurched boys to Sunday school."

In 1954, by action of the Southern Baptist Convention, responsibility for the Royal Ambassador organization, which had been founded and until then sponsored by the Woman's Missionary Union, Auxiliary to the Southern Baptist Convention, was transferred to the Brotherhood Commission. A plan was arranged for transfer over a period of three years. Edward Hurt, Jr., was elected associate secretary of the Brotherhood Commission in charge of the Royal Ambassador work.

All of this work is promoted by the staff of the Brotherhood in co-operation with the secretaries employed by the various states of the Convention. In addition to promoting missions, the Brotherhood now interests itself to some extent in every phase of the church and denominational program: stewardship and benevolence, devotions and daily prayer, Christian education, pastoral support, every-member canvass, mass meetings for men, evangelism, and missionary education of boys through the sponsoring of Royal Ambassadors. A program of educational promotion through the use of a wide variety of promotional and informational literature is carried on.   ARCHIE E. BROWN

BROTHERHOOD JOURNAL. A quarterly publication containing information concerning the Brotherhood work as it is progressing throughout the Convention, suitable program materials which the Brotherhoods may use, and many other additional helps aimed to assist Brotherhood leadership. It is the major Brotherhood publication, and every Brotherhood member is encouraged to receive and read it. Circulation was 120,000 per quarter at the beginning of 1957.   GEORGE W. SCHROEDER

BROTHERHOOD NEWS. A news sheet covering the progress of the Brotherhood endeavor throughout the Southern Baptist Convention. It is published quarterly. The publication contains four pages, two of which are printed in the offices of the commission and deal with various features of the Brotherhood endeavor that are Convention-wide in their aspects. Two pages are left blank. It is made available to the various state Brotherhood departments in bulk. These departments, in turn, print state Brotherhood news on the two blank pages and then mail direct to their Brotherhood leadership. Quarterly circulation was 52,000 at the beginning of 1957.   GEORGE W. SCHROEDER

BROUGH, CHARLES HILLMAN (b. Clinton, Miss., July 9, 1876; d. Washington, D. C., Dec. 26, 1935). Educator and statesman. Son of Charles Milton Brough, banker and mining executive in Ogden, Utah, and mayor of Ogden two terms, and Flora M. (Thompson) Brough, teacher, Central Female Institute, now Hillman College, Clinton, Miss. C. H. Brough's degrees include these: B.A. from Mississippi College, Clinton, 1893; Ph.D. from Johns Hopkins, 1898; LL.B. from University of Mississippi, 1902; LL.D. from University of Arkansas, 1917; he also attended Baylor University in 1917 and Mississippi College in 1920. He was professor of history and economics, Mississippi College, 1899–1901; professor of history, economics, and philosophy, Hillman College, 1903–04; professor of economics and sociology, University of Arkansas, 1904–16. He married Anne Wade Roark, Franklin, Ky., June 17, 1908. He was Governor of Arkansas two terms, 1917–21; president of Southern Sociological Congress, 1915. He belonged to numerous clubs and orders. He was a Baptist deacon in Fayetteville and Little Rock, president of Central College, Conway, Ark., 1928–29, and vice-president of the Southern Baptist Convention, 1918. Brough was highly regarded as a leader and as a campaign speaker for his denomination and his country.   MRS. C. H. BROUGH

BROUGHTON, JOSEPH MELVILLE (b. Raleigh, N. C., Nov. 7, 1888; d. Washington, D. C., Mar. 6, 1949). North Carolina governor. The son of Joseph Melville and Sallie (Harris) Broughton, he received his early education in the public schools of Raleigh and in 1910 earned his A.B. degree from Wake Forest College. Later this institution, Davidson College, and the University of North Carolina all conferred on him the LL.D. degree. Upon the completion of a year's study at Harvard University Law School in 1914, he opened a law practice in Raleigh, which he continued until 1940. The offices to which he was elected and the ministries that he performed indicate something of his diversified interests and the public demand for his services. The city of Raleigh chose him as city attorney, president of the Chamber of Commerce, and member of the school board. The state of North Carolina selected him as president of its bar association, elected him to its senate, and ultimately made him governor. Wake Forest College, Shaw University, and the University of North Carolina appointed him to their boards of trustees. A popular speaker, he keynoted the state Democratic convention and twice addressed the National Governors' Conference. He served Tabernacle Baptist Church of Raleigh as Sunday school superintendent continuously, 1913–41, and taught a Bible class for 25 years.

The people of North Carolina in 1940 elected Broughton, who never lost a political contest, as governor. His administration led to the enactment of the teachers' and state employee's retirement law and a nine-month school law, and to the reorganization of the state hospitals and correctional institutions. He brought about legislation adding the 12th grade to the public school system, and launched the movement for a broader hospital and medical care program in the state. He won his final political victory with election to the United States Senate Nov. 2, 1948, to fill the unexpired term of the late Josiah W. Bailey (q.v.), and to a full term, beginning Jan. 3, 1949, but died Mar. 5, 1949. Broughton and Alice H. Wilson, whom he married Dec. 14, 1916, had four children: Alice Wilson, Joseph Melville, Jr., Robert Bain, and Woodson Harris.
W. H. WILLIAMS

BROUGHTON, NEEDHAM BRYANT (b. Raleigh, N. C., Feb. 14, 1848; d. Raleigh, N. C., May 26, 1914). Publisher, Baptist layman. The eldest son of Joseph and Mary (Bagwell) Broughton, he had only a meager education. In his early teens Broughton was apprenticed in the office of the *Raleigh Register*. At 16 he went to Washington and later to New York to work as a typesetter. At 23 he returned to Raleigh as an employee of C. B. Edwards (later Edwards and Broughton Printing Company). He united with the First Baptist Church, Raleigh, in 1864; 10 years later he was a leader in organizing the Tabernacle Baptist Church there. He distinguished himself as a Christian layman. He was a Sunday school teacher in the early years; in 1876 he was elected Sunday school superintendent, serving in this capacity 37 years; he became secretary of the Baptist state convention; and he was at one time part owner of *Biblical Recorder* and a trustee of Meredith and Wake Forest colleges. At the same time he was active in state, political, and cultural movements. Broughton married Caroline R. Lougee, Raleigh, May 20, 1869, and to them were born six children: Edgar E., Effie (Mrs. Charles B. Park), Mary Nelson (Mrs. S. O. Garrison), Rosa C., Carrie L., and N. B., Jr.
C. SYLVESTER GREEN

BROWN, ALBERT ERSKINE (b. Jefferson City, Tenn., Aug. 6, 1863; d. May 30, 1924). Educator. Son of William Albert Gallatin Brown, first president of Mars Hill College, and Margaret (Pattison) Brown, he was one of five children, all teachers, three of whom were ordained ministers. Brown studied at Carson-Newman (from which he received the D.D. degree) and Judson colleges. He was converted at age of 16 at Carson-Newman and ordained to the ministry in 1889. He taught at Fairview Institute, near Asheville, for eight years and served as pastor of churches at Beaverdam, Berea, Mt. Carmel, and West End. Brown was secretary of the mission board of the Western North Carolina Convention and later became president of that convention. He served as moderator of the Buncombe Association and as assistant corresponding secretary of the North Carolina Baptist State Convention.

Brown was intensely interested in the education of mountain youth. In his early ministry he devoted himself to evangelism, but later, distressed by the ignorance of mountain preachers, he set himself to the task of founding and developing mountain schools. In 1899 he resigned the pastorate in order to organize and superintend the work in the Southern mountain regions, which was supported by the Baptist state convention and the Home Mission Board of the Southern Baptist Convention. At one time these schools totaled 40, with an enrolment of more than 6,000. A collection of Brown's sermons and addresses may be found in Mars Hill College library. In Mar., 1885, he married Lamanda Whitaker, to whom were born five children: William H., Jessie (Mrs. D. A. Greene), Beatrice (Mrs. Carl Gossett), Mack, and Mary (Mrs. Ray C. Hamrick).
W. H. WILLIAMS

BROWN, CLINTON CAPERS (b. Barnwell County, S. C., Feb. 2, 1852; d. Richmond, Va., June 14, 1921). Pastor, professor, writer. Son of Clementine and Barry H. Brown, he grew up on his father's large plantation in Barnwell, S. C. Brown was baptized at Greenville, S. C., Apr. 9, 1871, and ordained at Barnwell, July 26, 1874. Educated at Washington and Lee University, Furman University, and Southern Baptist Theological Seminary, 1872–74, Brown became professor of Latin and mathematics at Sumter Eclectic Female College, 1886–89. For 39 years he served as pastor of the First Baptist Church, Sumter, S. C., from Jan. 1, 1875, until July 1, 1914. A prolific writer, Brown contributed articles to state papers of the Southern Baptist Convention, and for a number of years he wrote an article each week for the *Baptist Courier*. He was the author of *Thoughts Toward Sunset*, *Uncle Dan'l and His Friends*, and *History of the First Baptist Church, Sumter, S. C.* In 1903 he participated in a notable debate with J. J. Porter, Joplin, Mo., on the subject, "The Practice of Alien Immersion Subverts Baptist Principles as Taught in the New Testament." He was prominent in the beginning of the South Carolina Baptist Board for the Relief of Aged and Indigent Ministers. Genial in spirit, sympathetic in heart, and fertile in brain, he found relaxation from toil in writing for the Baptist press.

BIBLIOGRAPHY: C. C. Brown, *History of the First Baptist Church, Sumter, S. C.* (1938); *Thoughts Toward Sunset* (1920); *Uncle Dan'l and His Friends* (n.d.). J. W. Porter, *The Sumter Discussion* (1903). J. R. Sampey, ed., *Southern Baptist Theological Seminary 1859–89* (1890). *Religious Herald* (Oct. 8, 1908).

WILLIAM R. MCLIN

BROWN, HENRY ALFRED (b. Rockingham County, N. C., Sept. 28, 1846; d. Winston-Salem, N. C., Apr. 25, 1929). Minister. Son of Robert Brown, schoolteacher and farmer, and Sarah (Troth) Brown, he attended district and preparatory schools in Guilford County, N. C., and was graduated from Wake Forest College in 1871. He served in the Junior Reserves during the War Between the States. Converted in 1865, Brown soon felt an unmistakable call to the ministry and was ordained in 1871. He entered active work as a missionary of the state mission board. He served as pastor of First Baptist Church, Fayetteville, 1874–77, and First Baptist Church, Winston-Salem, 1877–1917. Brown and Bishop Edward Rondthaler, of Southern Moravian Church, came to Winston-Salem about the same time, when the village had about 1,000 inhabitants. They worked together in influencing its moral and religious growth. No man ever had a stronger grip on a community than Brown. He was known as "The Pastor Beloved." When he retired at 71, he was elected pastor emeritus of all the Baptist churches in Winston-Salem. To him and his wife, Julia Cain, of Fayetteville, were born three children: Henry Wingate, Addie (Mrs. W. O. McCorkle), and Eloise (Mrs. H. S. Stokes).

BIBLIOGRAPHY: G. T. Stephenson, *The Pastor Beloved* (1925).

W. H. WILLIAMS

BROWN, JOSEPH EMERSON (b. Pickens District, S. C., Apr. 15, 1821; d. Atlanta, Ga., Nov. 31, 1894). Statesman and benefactor of the Southern Baptist Theological Seminary. Brown grew up in the remote interior mountains of Union County in north Georgia, worked as a farm laborer, and acquired a basic education in local schools. At 19 he began studies at Calhoun Academy, Anderson District, S. C. After several years he returned to Canton in north Georgia, where he read law and served as principal of Canton Academy. Admitted to the bar in 1845, he was graduated from the Yale Law School in 1846.

In 1847 he married Elizabeth Grisham, the daughter of a Baptist minister, and two years later, as a Democrat, was elected to the Georgia senate. He served as a presidential elector in 1852, and became judge of the Blue Ridge Superior Court Circuit in 1855. Two years later he was nominated for governor as a compromise candidate after five strong politicians had canceled each other out. His election was a complete denial of the tradition of aristocratic leadership which had held sway in Georgia for many years, but in spite of inexperience, he served until 1865 and proved to be a strong executive who aggressively promoted his opinions over all opposition. As governor he supported sound money, advocated state support of education, and reformed his militia in anticipation of war. His strong belief in state sovereignty led him, during the Civil War, to sharp disagreement with President Davis, particularly over the claims of the central government to a share in the control of Georgia state troops.

Although imprisoned briefly by the Federal Government in 1865, he soon adjusted himself to the new state of affairs and supported the congressional policies of reconstruction in Georgia, thereby bringing on himself the odium of former associates. He became a Republican and served as chief justice of the Georgia supreme court from 1868 to 1870. In that year he resigned to lease from the state its Western and Atlantic Railroad, of which he became president, and in whose administration he had effected profitable reforms while governor. In 1871, when the governor who had appointed him to the bench of the Supreme Court became involved in charges of corruption, Brown returned to the Democratic party. As a Democrat, he became a United States Senator in 1880 and served until his retirement in 1891.

Brown was converted in 1842 and remained throughout his life an active church member, after 1866, of the Second Baptist Church in Atlanta. He served as a trustee of the Southern Baptist Theological Seminary from 1872 to 1877, and again from 1880 to 1894, and was president of the board from 1883 to 1894.

In addition to the Western and Atlantic Railroad, he was also president of the Southern Railway and Steamship Company, the Walker Coal and Iron Company, and the Dade Coal Company, and achieved wealth quite rapidly. In his business practices, Brown was like many others who achieved success during the 19th century. He used convict labor leased from the state on favorable terms and took advantage of various opportunities permitted by the government which are not legal today. But his generously large gifts to many causes helped to temper the "hostility aroused by his political apostasy." He gave $50,000 to the University of Georgia for a loan fund, a like amount (in 1880) to the Southern Baptist Theological Seminary for desperately needed endowment, and smaller sums to his church, Mercer University, and other causes.

BIBLIOGRAPHY: [Samuel Boykin], *History of the Baptist Denomination in Georgia, with Biographical Compendium* (1881). "Joseph Emerson Brown," *Dictionary of American Biography*, III (1929). H. Fielder, *A Sketch of the Life and Times and Speeches of Joseph E. Brown* (1883). A. B. Moore, *Conscription and Conflict in the Confederacy* (1924). F. L. Owsley, *States Rights in the Confederacy* (1931). C. M. Thompson, *Reconstruction in Georgia* (1915). C. V. Woodward, *Origins of the New South* (1951).

MALCOLM LESTER

BROWN, JOSEPH EMERSON, CHAIR OF THEOLOGY. On Feb. 11, 1880, Joseph Emerson Brown (*q.v.*), former governor of Georgia and United States senator, contributed $50,000 to Southern Baptist Theological Seminary, Louisville, Ky., for the purpose of establishing a Chair of Theology. The endowment was given on the basis that it would be used only for that purpose and not for other expenses. In a letter to the seminary, Brown wrote that he had for some time been considering the propriety of making a large gift to some institution of higher education. He had wished that one of his sons might feel called into the ministry, and since apparently that had not happened, Brown decided to help educate the sons of others for that work. This donation came at a most needful time, for James Petigru Boyce (*q.v.*), president of the seminary, had asked the entire faculty and student body to join in special prayer that someone would give $50,000 for the endowment of a chair.

Securing other gifts which, with the funds already invested, would yield the necessary income then became the problem. At this point, George Washington Norton (1814–89), of Louisville, suggested an amendment to the charter, requiring that the principal of all contributions for endowment made since Feb. 1, 1880, be held forever sacred and inviolate, only the income to be expended —and if any part of the principal were used for expenses, then the whole should revert to the donors— and that a Financial Board of five business men in Louisville should be elected every year to invest the principal, hold the securities, and pay over the income to the Treasurer of the Seminary.

After this amendment was approved on Mar. 31, 1880, Norton and his brother, William Frederick Norton (1820–86), each offered to give a generous sum toward the proposed $200,000 for the endowment of the chair. Within two years the total amount was received and invested, and the seminary's existence was no longer in danger. Incumbents of the Joseph Emerson Brown Chair of Theology have included Boyce (1880–89), Franklin Howard Kerfoot (*q.v.*) (1889–99), Edgar Young Mullins (*q.v.*) (1899–1928), Harold Wayland Tribble (1929–47), and Dale Moody (1954–   ).

LEO T. CRISMON

BROWN, OBADIAH BRUEN (b. Newark, N. J., July 20, 1779; d. Washington, D. C., May 2, 1852). Civic leader and first regular pastor to serve the Baptist denomination in the capital city. He married Elizabeth Reilly Jackson, a widow. In May, 1807, he left Newark, N. J., which had been founded by his great grandfather Obadiah Bruen in 1667, and went to Washington to be pastor of the First Baptist Church. The church had been organized in Mar., 1802, but it had had only voluntary or itinerant ministers until Obadiah Brown was called. He was not only a pioneer preacher for the denomination in that area but also an important leader in the civic and educational growth of the new federal city as well as the nation itself, which was in its infancy. His pastorate lasted for 43 years, at which time he retired from the ministry. It was with great regret that the members of the church received his resignation as pastor, and he remained as a member until his death. For nearly half a century he was an active worker. He was affectionately known throughout the city as "Pastor Brown" or "Father Brown." Many famous people worshiped in his congregation—notably Luther Rice (*q.v.*), who organized the first Sunday school in this country in his church in 1819. It was also in 1819 that Obadiah Brown, Luther Rice, Spencer Cone, and Enoch Reynolds raised the sum of $6,000 toward the purchase of land for Columbian College. Obadiah Brown was the first president of the board of that college, which later became George Washington University.

DOROTHY CLARK WINCHCOLE

BROWN, SANFORD MILLER (b. Yadkin County, N. C., July 12, 1855; d. Kansas City, Mo., Sept. 21, 1938). Pastor, editor, and denominational leader. Educated in public and private schools of North Carolina, he was ordained to the ministry in 1876. The following year he moved to Missouri, where he served as pastor of several churches until he became editor of the *Central Baptist* in 1884. Two years later the Missouri convention elected him secretary of its state mission board. He resigned in 1892 and for four years labored in Kansas City as a pastor and as superintendent of missions. In 1896 he founded the official publication of Missouri Baptists, *The Word and Way*, which he edited until his death. Brown promoted the Baptist cause through his paper, helped to place scores of churches on a sound financial basis through his skilful guidance, and assisted numerous churches in erecting new buildings. He organized five churches in Kansas City and dedicated hundreds of others throughout the state. In addition to his contributions as a religious journalist, he wrote several books and many songs. He was married to Lulu Everingham in 1887.

MRS. R. W. PRATHER, JR.

BROWN MEMORIAL THEOLOGICAL SEMINARY, BUDAPEST. See HUNGARY, MISSION IN.

BROWN UNIVERSITY. The first Baptist college in America. It was founded in Warren, R. I., in 1764 as Rhode Island College, through the efforts of the Philadelphia Association, primarily to educate young men for the ministry. This state was chosen because many of its legislators were Baptists who were more favorable to the chartering of the institution.

James Manning, a graduate of the College of New Jersey (now Princeton) became president, and the school opened in Sept., 1765. Four years later the first class of seven graduated.

Philadelphia, Charleston, and Warren associations, the most important during the latter 18th century, staunchly supported the college. Morgan Edwards toured England to solicit funds for the new institution; Hezekiah Smith toured the South, South Carolina and Georgia in particular. All sections continued to give their support until other Baptist colleges were organized nearer home.

In compliance with an offer by the trustees to move the college to the Rhode Island city which raised the most money, it was moved to Providence in 1770, where it has remained. The financial condition of the institution continued acute for many years.

The name was changed to Brown University in 1804 when Nicholas Brown, in response to another offer by the trustees, gave $5,000 "for the establishment of a professorship" in oratory. Mr. Brown continued his gifts to the university for many years—until the amount became approximately $160,000.

Throughout the first 150 years the university had only nine presidents, an indication of the stability of the institution and its leaders.

Brown has furnished many capable religious leaders not only to Baptists but to other denominations as well. Probably the most outstanding to Southern Baptists was John Albert Broadus (q.v.). It has also trained many political, medical, military, and judicial leaders, as well as college presidents and teachers.

BIBLIOGRAPHY: I. Backus, *A History of New England with Particular Reference to the Denomination of Christians Called Baptists* (1811). D. Benedict, *A General History of the Baptist Denomination in America, and Other Parts of the World* (1813). W. C. Bronson, *The History of Brown University 1764-1914* (1914). R. A. Guild, *Chaplain Smith and the Baptists, or Life, Journals, Letters, and Addresses of the Rev. Hezekiah Smith, D.D. of Haverhill, Massachusetts* (1885); *History of Brown University with Illustrative Documents* (1867); *Life, Times, and Correspondence of James Manning and the Early History of Brown University* (1864).　JAMES L. CLARK

BROWNING COLLECTION, BAYLOR UNIVERSITY. Acquired under the inspirational drive of A. Joseph Armstrong (1873–1953), and reputedly the world's largest collection of materials related to Robert Browning, English poet (1812–89), and his wife, Elizabeth Barrett Browning (1806–61). Known as the Armstrong-Browning Library, the collection contains 13,000 items, including all first editions of Browning's works, personal articles, and other books dealing with the poet. Armstrong, who considered Browning's poetry high in Christian optimism, sought out the Browning memorabilia in 37 transoceanic trips during his 40 years as chairman of Baylor's English department (1912–52). The collection is housed in a magnificent white marble building erected on Baylor's Waco campus in 1950 at a cost of $1,500,-000, mostly raised by Armstrong.　C. E. BRYANT

BROWNSVILLE FEMALE COLLEGE. A school founded in 1851 at Brownsville, Tenn., by the West Tennessee Baptist Convention. The first class (four students) was graduated in 1851. The school grew steadily in numbers, strength, and influence. Later the school admitted young men, possibly as day students only. The catalogue for the school year 1890–91 listed the names of 187 students, 48 of which were men. The school was merged with Jackson University in 1893.　HARLEY FITE

BROWNWOOD INSTITUTE. A private finishing school for girls opened at La Grange, Ga., early in the 1840's. Although not owned or controlled by the Western Association in which it was located, the institute was headed by Baptist men and recognized by the association. The *Christian Index* pronounced the school "among the best literary institutions in the South" in 1854, but it ceased to exist before the Civil War.　ARTHUR JACKSON

BRYAN, OSCAR EUGENE (b. Mississippi, Aug. 4, 1873; d. Tennessee, Jan. 24, 1933). Pastor; denominational leader; author; editor. Son of Jacob Allen and Mutelle (Armour) Bryan, he was a student at Baylor University, 1900–06, and a graduate in theology from Southwestern Baptist Theological Seminary, 1916. He received D.D. degrees from Baylor and from Georgetown (Ky.) College in 1921 and the LL.D. degree from Union University in 1931. He was engaged in general evangelistic work before becoming evangelist of Southwestern Seminary. From 1913 to 1916, he served as pastor of Tabernacle Baptist Church, Waco, Tex., and from 1916 to 1921, as secretary of the Kentucky Baptist state board. He headed the department of evangelism and enlistment, Home Mission Board, 1921–23, and was budget director for the 75 Million Campaign of the Southern Baptist Convention, 1923–24. Bryan served as executive secretary (previously termed corresponding secretary) of the Tennessee Baptist State Convention, 1924–33.

On Sept. 2, 1903, he married Fannie Elizabeth Davidson of Glen Flora, Tex. She helped originate the Sunbeam Band, edited the *Sunbeam Magazine*, wrote Baptist literature, and worked to evangelize the Jews. Bryan bequeathed much in character to his children: Dr. William Ray Bryan, National Cancer Research Institute, inventor of the rotary blood shaker, who taught at Vanderbilt University, New York University, and Duke University medical schools, and married Lulu Lawton Leavell, daughter of J. B. Leavell; Annie Frances, who married W. B. Dowell, Jr., nephew of Spright Dowell, former president Mercer University; Oscar Eugene, Jr., chaplain, United States Air Force, Alaska; Mary Elizabeth, who married Harold Hollis, sports writer, Duluth *News Tribune;* Harriet Newell, who married John R. Olson, research radiologist, University of Indiana.

Notably successful in denominational work, Bryan was able to win the co-operation of Baptist leaders in the trying period which followed the 75 Million Campaign. His sound judgment and capable business management enabled him to lead Tennessee Baptists to reduce the indebtedness on their institutions by $750,000. Called "the father of the Cooperative Program" because he introduced it in Tennessee before it became a Southern Baptist policy, he spent his later years trying to convince the churches of its merit. "Pay as you go if you possibly can," was one of his principles.

Bryan wrote numerous tracts, edited *Mission Monthly* while secretary in Kentucky, and published *The Great Commission* in 1932. Acquaintances said that in him courtesy and courage were blended and that he possessed doctrinal soundness, missionary passion, and scholarly gentleness.   ROBERT PALMER

BRYAN, ROBERT THOMAS (b. Duplin County, N. C., Oct. 14, 1855; d. San Antonio, Tex., Apr. 3, 1946). Missionary to China. Son of John Alexander and Mary (Oliver) Bryan, he graduated from the University of North Carolina and the Southern Baptist Theological Seminary. Appointed by the Foreign Mission Board in 1885, Bryan sailed for China in November and served in Chinkiang, Yangchow, and Shanghai. He founded Ming Jang Boys' School and a Bible class which became the theological department of Shanghai Baptist College and Seminary. A preacher and teacher, he was also a translator and an able student of the Chinese language, for which he prepared books for study.   J. T. WILLIAMS

BRYAN BAPTIST ACADEMY. A coeducational school at Bryan, Tex., transferred to the state convention about 1910. Enrolment reached 154 in 1916 but declined thereafter, and the school was closed about 1917.

RUPERT N. RICHARDSON

BUCHAREST BAPTIST SEMINARY. See ROMANIA, MISSION IN.

BUCK, WILLIAM CALMES (b. Shenandoah County—now Warren, Va., Aug. 23, 1790; d. Waco, Tex., 1872). Preacher, editor, author. Youngest son of Charles and Mary (Richardson) Buck, he was self-educated, knew Latin and philosophy, and learned Greek and Hebrew after 50 years old. Converted in 1807 at the age of 17, he was baptized in Apr., 1808, and immediately began to exhort in public meetings. Licensed to preach at 22, he began a two-year period of itinerant preaching. He served his home church as pastor for about five years before moving to Kentucky in 1820, where he spent 13 years in Union County as frontier preacher and missionary. He married Maria Lewright in 1815. After her death in 1822, he married Miriam Field in 1829.

Buck went to Louisville in 1836 to be pastor of First Baptist Church. Here, between 1839 and 1850, he had an editorial career with the *Baptist Banner and Western Pioneer.* During this period he founded East Baptist Church in Louisville and a church in Jeffersonville, Ind. Losing the paper and almost bankrupt, he moved to Georgetown, Ky., in 1851; but shortly afterward, he was offered the position of corresponding secretary of the Bible Board with headquarters in Nashville, Tenn. When he was left with five small children by the death of his second wife, traveling became all but impossible; he served in pastorates in Columbus, Miss., 1854, and Greensboro, Ala., 1857. In 1858 he went to Selma, Ala., where he took up editorial work, publishing *The Baptist Correspondent* for two years.

The Civil War period was spent as missionary evangelist to churches, camps, and hospitals. In 1866 he bought a farm near Waco, Tex. There he lectured at Waco University on theology and preached in churches around Waco until his death. In 1856 he wrote *Philosophy of Religion* (really a systematic theology), and in 1858, *Science and Life.* He also edited a hymnal.

BIBLIOGRAPHY: A. Yager, *Sketch of the Life of Wm. Calmes Buck* (n.d.).   VICTOR MANTIPLY

BUCKNER, HENRY FRIELAND (b. Newport, Tenn., Dec. 18, 1818; d. Eufaula, Okla., Dec. 3, 1882). Missionary to the Creek Indians of Indian Territory. He came to Eufaula, Creek Nation, under appointment by the American Indian Mission Association, arriving Mar. 7, 1849. According to Joseph Samuel Murrow (*q.v.*) "he made a stronger impression on the Creek Nation than any other man."

His father, Daniel Buckner, was a Baptist minister who was excluded from a church in Tennessee because of his mission activities. H. F. Buckner was licensed to preach in 1839 and the same year entered Alabama University, where Basil Manly, Sr. (*q.v.*), was president. He was married Nov. 22, 1842, to Lucy Ann Dogan, daughter of Samuel Dogan, M.D., a Baptist minister of Pulaski County, Ky. In 1846 he was appointed a missionary to the mountain people of eastern Kentucky, Virginia, and Ohio by the Baptist General Association of Kentucky. Two years later the Indian Mission Association of Louisville gave him his commission to the Creeks. He made a close study of the Creek language, wrote a Creek grammar with an illustrative alphabet, and translated a hymnbook and much of the New Testament into Creek. During the Civil War he moved to Texas, where he was pastor first at Linden and then at

Independence. In 1870 he returned to his work among the Creeks. He was successful in keeping Southern Baptists interested in Indian missions, and it was largely through his influence that the Levering Mission School was established near Wetumka. He was buried near Eufaula, Okla., in the garden back of the home built for him by Baptist friends.

BIBLIOGRAPHY: E. C. Routh, *The Story of Oklahoma Baptists* (1932). WILLIAM A. CARLETON

BUCKNER, HENRY FRIELAND (HAL) (b. Dallas, Tex., Oct. 13, 1878; d. Dallas, Tex., Jan. 16, 1951). Preacher, missionary, denominational leader, and administrator and builder of Buckner Orphans Home. The youngest of six children of Robert Cooke and Viena Buckner, he was educated in Dallas public schools; Old North Texas Baptist College, Jacksboro, Tex.; Baylor University; and Southern Baptist Theological Seminary. Honorary D.D. and LL.D. degrees were given him by Howard Payne College and Hardin-Simmons University.

Buckner was ordained to the ministry Dec. 23, 1900, and he spent 10 years in evangelistic and pastoral ministries, serving churches in Texas and Oklahoma. From 1909 to 1919, he was in China as a missionary, during which time he was professor of New Testament interpretation and acting president of Graves Theological Seminary, where he helped to train 500 Chinese Baptist ministers.

He served the orphans' home from 1919 to 1951, during which time it achieved the distinction of being the first eleemosynary institution in Texas to be fireproof in all its principal buildings. He established and accredited a school system of 12 grades and broadened the benevolent program. Among his slogans were the following: "Care for more children and do more for the children cared for"; "that which is good for my child is good for an orphan child"; "that which is not good enough for my child is not good enough for an orphan child"; and "that which I hope to supply for my child, by the grace of God I will endeavor to supply for an orphan child."

Buckner married Bertha Aston in Jacksboro, Tex., on Sept. 4, 1901; they had four children.
G. G. DICKEY

BUCKNER, ROBERT COOKE (b. Madisonville, Tenn., Jan. 3, 1833; d. Dallas, Tex., Apr. 9, 1919). Editor, Texas Baptist leader, and founder of Buckner Orphans Home. The fifth of six children of Daniel and Mary Buckner, he was born in a log cabin, and when he was five years old, his father moved the family to Somerset, Ky. Converted and baptized at the age of 11, Buckner was ordained to the ministry six years later in his father's church in Somerset, Nov. 13, 1852. He became pastor at Albany, Ky., where he married Viena Long June 7, 1854.

Buckner attended Georgetown College in Georgetown, Ky., where he distinguished himself in Latin, Greek, and theology.

In 1859, after serving several pastorates in Kentucky, the young minister moved with his family by wagon to Paris, Tex., where he became pastor of First Baptist Church in 1861, serving until 1873. At the close of his pastorate in Paris, Buckner began publication of *The Religious Messenger*, a paper dedicated to the cause of Christian living and the spread of the Baptist enterprise in Texas. This venture in the newspaper field gave him the opportunity to launch the movement for the establishment of Buckner Orphans Home in 1879, of which he served as president and general manager until 1919. Buckner was editor and founder of another newspaper, *The Texas Baptist*, 1876–83; general agent of the Baptist General Association, 1868–69; and president of the Sunday school convention of the general association, 1875–80. Buckner served also as the association's superintendent of missions, 1877–82, and president, 1880–85. For 20 years he served as president of the Baptist General Convention of Texas, 1894–1914.

BIBLIOGRAPHY: J. B. Cranfill and J. L. Walker, *R. C. Buckner's Life of Faith and Works* (1914). L. R. Elliott, ed., *Centennial Story of Texas Baptists* (1936). G. G. DICKEY

BUCKNER BAPTIST BENEVOLENCES. Buckner Orphans Home at Dallas, Tex., a corporation and parent institution of Buckner Baptist Benevolences, was founded and chartered under the laws of Texas in 1879 by Robert Cooke Buckner (*q.v.*) (1833–1919) upon authority given him by a deacons' convention in 1877. The first children admitted to the home for care were placed in a rented frame structure in Dallas, Dec. 2, 1880, but in the spring of 1881, the children were moved into a new building erected on the home's original 44-acre site chosen by the founder; the site comprises part of the present campus eight miles east of downtown Dallas.

Buckner Orphans Home has from its beginning been Baptist owned and Baptist controlled. The founder was responsible to a board of directors elected by the deacons' convention until fusion of the Baptist State Convention of Texas and the Baptist General Association of Texas into the Baptist General Convention of Texas in 1886. From that date until 1914, he was responsible to a self-perpetuating board of directors. At the Abilene convention of 1914, Buckner, on behalf of the deacons' convention, offered the property of Buckner Orphans Home to the Baptist General Convention of Texas, with the proviso that certain stipulations of its charter be observed. The convention accepted the institution on recommendation of a committee appointed to study the proposal. The governing body of the institution is a board of 27 deacons elected annually by the convention as trustees, who in turn elect nine directors from their own number to operate the home through an administrator.

Buckner Baptist Benevolences now comprise

six units and properties: Buckner Orphans Home at Dallas, Tex., for neglected and dependent children, consisting of 2,500 acres of land and 24 principal buildings, founded in 1879; Bethesda Home at San Antonio, Tex., for unwed mothers, consisting of 12 acres of land and two buildings, added in 1949; Buckner Boys Ranch at Burnet, Tex., for delinquent boys, consisting of 3,600 acres of land and 14 buildings, added in 1951; Mary E. Trew Home at Dallas, for the aged, consisting of four acres of land and one building, added in 1954; Texas Baptist Haven at Houston, Tex., for the aged, consisting of 45½ acres of land and two buildings, added in 1955; and Girls Ranch at Breckenridge, Tex., for delinquent girls, consisting of 640 acres and two buildings, acquired in 1955. The total property value of all units as shown in the annual audit of Aug. 31, 1955, was $9,681,880.30. The total budget for all units in 1954–55 was $753,017.55.

Buckner Baptist Benevolences are not included in the Cooperative Program of Texas Baptists, but are supported by income from endowment held by the Baptist Foundation of Texas, which provides about one third of the annual cost of operation; income from farms, rents, interest, dividends, etc.; income from church and individual contributions; and income from bequests. The total income from church and individual contributions for the past 30 years has amounted to $8,863,322.96 or an average of $295,444.10 per year.

The boys of Buckner Boys Ranch attend public schools of Burnet, Tex., but the boys and girls of Buckner Orphans Home attend Buckner Home Academy, their own private school, operated on the home's campus. Even preschool-age children attend their own play school, nursery school, and kindergarten. The high school offers a general academic curriculum and courses in business training, home economics, and Bible, all accredited; its vocational division is designed to offer courses in photography, offset printing, drafting, cabinetmaking, carpentry, upholstery, cosmetology, radio, barbering, baking, plumbing, electricity, auto mechanics, agriculture, dairying, and poultry husbandry.

The institution operates on a plan known as the academy plan. The children live in dormitories, three to six in a room with a bath connecting every two rooms. There is a central dining room for children of school age; cooking and serving, sewing, and laundry services are performed outside the residence buildings, so that group mothers may have more time to give the children personal attention. In addition to school and home services, the academy plan provides a church ministry. Buckner Home Baptist Church has its own Sunday school, Training Union, Brotherhood, Woman's Missionary Union, Royal Ambassador, and Girls' Auxiliary organizations. The plan furnishes opportunity for educational training of a cultural, academic, spiritual, and vocational nature.

Graduates of the academy may go to college by means of scholarship aid granted them by Baptist colleges and universities in Texas, loans from the home's student loan fund, and income from certain marketable, vocational skills utilized in part-time jobs after class hours. Those who do not attend college are assisted in securing satisfactory employment upon departure from the home.

All children born in Bethesda Home are placed for adoption, and all child-adoption services for the entire organization are transacted by that unit. Case workers as such are not employed by the institution, but their function is performed by other members of the staff.

The numbers of individuals cared for in 1954–55 were 685 in Buckner Orphans Home, 47 in Boys Ranch, 35 in Bethesda Home, and 24 each in Trew Home and The Haven. The per capita cost for the year was $988.

BIBLIOGRAPHY: J. B. Cranfill and J. L. Walker, *R. C. Buckner's Life of Faith and Works* (1914). L. R. Elliott, *Centennial Story of Texas Baptists* (1936). *The Baptist Standard* (1951). G. G. DICKEY

BUDAPEST WOMEN'S TRAINING SCHOOL. See HUNGARY, MISSION IN.

BUDGET OF THE CONVENTION. The bylaws of the Convention, Article 9 (5) (g), states that the Executive Committee shall have the responsibility

... to recommend to the Convention a comprehensive budget for the Convention and for all its agencies, which budget shall include the budgets of all the agencies of the Convention as approved by the Executive Committee, together with the percentage of Convention funds which may be allocated to each cause. The Executive Committee shall not recommend any percentage allocation of funds for any agency or institution for which the Convention does not elect trustees or directors.

In setting up the budget, each agency is instructed by the Convention to submit to the Executive Committee for its approval (1) an itemized estimate of its receipts for the next fiscal year, and (2) an itemized estimate of its expenditures for the next fiscal year.

The bylaws of the Executive Committee state that the finance committee of the Executive Committee

... shall study and make recommendations concerning the budgets and audit reports of the Convention and its agencies. Recommendations concerning the allocation of Cooperative Program funds shall be initiated in the Finance Committee and brought to the Executive Committee after consultation with the Administrative Committee.

The budget for the agencies of the Convention is determined by the cash receipts, distributable and designated, for the regular work of the previous year, not including wills, bequests, and special gifts for specific purposes, and any debt incurred within the current year must become a preferred item in the budget of the Convention year immediately following.

The finance committee and the Executive Committee also take into consideration the estimate of the receipts for the next fiscal year presented at the time of the budget, in accord with Section I of the Business and Financial Plan.

To meet emergencies which might arise during the year, the agencies are authorized to borrow for seasonable needs with the understanding that the borrowing shall not exceed the amount of its budget allowance for the year remaining at the time of borrowing.

In regard to capital investments, an agency or institution is not allowed to create any liability or indebtedness except that which can and will be repaid out of its anticipated receipts for current operations within a period of three years, without the consent of the Convention or the Executive Committee. In order to obtain such approval, the agency must file a statement showing the source of such anticipated receipts.

PORTER ROUTH

BUENOS AIRES INTERNATIONAL SEMINARY. See ARGENTINA, MISSION IN.

BULLETIN SERVICE, BAPTIST. A service for the editing and distributing of pre-printed bulletins or worship service folders to churches for use either on Sunday or as mail-out papers during the week. The service was established in 1926 by the Commission on Cooperative Program and edited by Frank E. Burkhalter, publicity director for the commission. Earliest known issue of the service is for May 21, 1926. The Bulletin Service was transferred to the newly created Executive Committee in 1927. The Baptist Bulletin Service has remained the property of the Executive Committee except for a brief period in 1931-32 when the Promotion Committee of the Executive Committee had separate status. Editors of the Bulletin Service have been Frank E. Burkhalter, 1926-30; Walter F. Gilmore, 1930-47; C. E. Bryant, 1947-49; Albert McClellan, 1949- . In 1955 churches used a total of 12,139,109 copies of the Bulletin Service, averaging more than 1,000,000 monthly. The mailing address is 127 Ninth Avenue, North, Nashville, Tenn.   ALBERT MC CLELLAN

BUNYAN, JOHN (b. Elstow, near Bedford, England, Nov. 28, 1628; d. London, England, Aug. 31, 1688). English pastor and author. He was the son of a tinker. When John was 16, his mother and sister died, and his father remarried almost immediately. The shock and painful readjustment created a prolonged religious struggle which ended in his conversion.

Bunyan served briefly in the Parliamentary army, where ideas of democracy and sectarianism were strong. With a bride he returned home to ply the tinker's trade. While working in Bedford one day in 1653, he saw three women "sitting at the door in the sun, and talking about the things of God." He drew near to listen and found "their talk was about a new birth." These "poor godly women" were members of a small Bedford congregation, organized by John Gifford in 1650, which later became Baptist. The overheard conversation was the turning point of his life. He became a member of the congregation, then a deacon, and finally the pastor.

Bunyan was imprisoned in 1660 after five years of lay preaching. His prosecutors promised freedom if he would pledge to stop preaching his Baptist doctrines. He would make no such promise, despite the fact that his second wife needed help with his four small children, the oldest of whom was "my poor blind daughter, who lay nearer my heart than all I had besides." Bunyan was in prison until 1672, and he was imprisoned again in 1676.

Bunyan's formal education was meager; yet, he became a serious student because of his desire to serve his Lord. His continuing popularity rests on three masterpieces: *Grace Abounding* (1666), the remarkable story of his own religious struggle; *The Pilgrim's Progress* (1676), written in prison, the most popular book ever written in English; and *The Holy War* (1682). In *The Pilgrim's Progress,* Bunyan included several original hymns. A few of these have been included in compilations of hymns, but only one is in common usage today. It is the "war song" of Valiant, "Who would true valor see." It has been amended to "He who would valiant be." He wrote 57 other books and pamphlets, most of them expanded sermons. Bunyan's was "an awakening ministry" centered on salvation by grace through faith. In later years he assumed the duty of spokesman for those of his persuasion and increasingly emphasized doctrines related to the church.

Bunyan was an open-membership Baptist, and was also in fellowship with the Congregational churches of the Bedford area. Believer's baptism was observed in his church during his ministry. He accepted those who had been baptized as infants, provided they were godly, professing Christians. Bunyan pleaded for baptism by immersion, but he asked for "a bearing with our brother that cannot do it for want of light." He saw the unity of all Christians as a major New Testament teaching.

Bunyan was buried in Bunhill Fields, London's nonconformist burial ground.

ROBERT L. MC CAN

BURKITT, LEMUEL (b. Chowan County, N. C., Apr. 26, 1750; d. Nov. 5, 1807). Minister. Son of Thomas and Mary Burkitt, he was baptized in July, 1771, by Henry Abbot (*q.v.*) into the Yeopim branch of the Shiloh Church. In Nov., 1773, he was ordained by Jonathan Thomas (d. 1774) and John Meglamre (1730-99) to become pastor of Sandy Run Church (Bertie County), which he served for 34 years. He was a leader in the Kehukee Association, serving as its clerk for over 30 years and giving direction to Baptist life in the eastern half of the state for as long. He was a strong advocate of a converted church membership, a preacher of unusual power, introducing into North Carolina in 1801 the revival from Tennessee and Kentucky. He and Jesse Read wrote the history of the Kehukee Association up to 1803. He edited two or three collections of religious songs. He was one of the representatives chosen to consider the question of the state's acceptance of the federal Constitution.

J. A. EASLEY

BURLESON, RUFUS COLUMBUS (b. Flint River, south of Decatur, Ala., Aug. 7, 1823; d. Waco, Tex., May 14, 1901). Pioneer Texas minister and educator. He was the seventh child of Jonathan and Elizabeth (Byrd) Burleson and was through his mother descended from the Byrd family of Virginia. He was taught at home until the age of seven, after which he attended the limited short-term frontier schools of the day. In 1837 he entered Summerville Academy, where he studied for two years; then he entered Nashville University, only to be forced to leave after one year because of bad health brought on by too much study. He recuperated quickly, however, and after a period of teaching began to preach. He was ordained at Starkville, Miss., in 1845, and in Jan., 1846, continued his education in the Western Baptist Theological Seminary at Covington, Ky., from which he graduated in June, 1847.

Appointed to mission work in Texas, he went to Gonzales, then in 1848 accepted the pastorate of the Baptist church in Houston, where he stayed about three years. In June, 1851, he succeeded Henry Lea Graves as president of Baylor University, then a small, struggling school at Independence, Tex., with two small buildings and 51 students, which had been founded only six years before by the Baptist Education Society in Texas. Burleson, with the help of agents, brought the school to a position of relative strength. Buildings were erected, salaries were paid with greater regularity, and instruction in law was added to the curriculum. However, friction developed between Burleson and Horace Clark, the head of the nearly independent girls' department of the school, involving personal differences and a conflict over authority, which by 1861 led to Burleson's resignation.

He went to Waco and became president of a Baptist school there, accompanied by his faculty and by the entire senior class of the male department, who refused to receive their diplomas from any other person. The school, renamed Waco University, managed to remain open throughout the Civil War and in 1865 was made coeducational. By 1868 it was receiving support from the Baptist General Association of Texas, which included most of the northern part of the state. The school grew in strength, helped, no doubt, by the growing prosperity of its region, while Baylor University at Independence gradually declined. There was some sentiment for consolidation, but disagreement between factions delayed the event until 1886. That year the two schools were consolidated at Waco under the name Baylor, with Burleson as president. Under his leadership Baylor achieved a permanent position of prominence in Texas education. He continued to serve, in spite of disagreements with his trustees, until 1897, when he was retired, made president emeritus, and given full salary. He died three years later.

In addition to his work as a college administrator, Burleson also figured prominently in the leadership of his denomination and in the development of education in Texas generally. At various times he served as president of several of the general associations and conventions of Texas Baptists. He served various pastorates in addition to his regular duties. During the Civil War he was a chaplain of a Texas regiment.

For about five years, after 1874, Burleson was Texas agent for the Peabody Education Fund and in this position made a major contribution to his state. He worked to persuade the people of Texas of the importance of a free public school system. Paralleling this effort was his part in influencing Governor O. M. Roberts and the Texas legislature of the need for a normal institute to prepare the teachers who would be demanded when the public school system was established. One of the agencies Burleson used in his work as a Peabody agent was the Texas State Teachers' Association, which he helped to organize in 1878–80. The teachers had three objectives: a public schools system, a normal institute, and a state university. As a cofounder of the association Burleson figured in all three of the objectives, even the establishment of the University of Texas.

Altogether he made a distinct and significant contribution to his state and his denomination. In person he was "a man of high ideals, devoted to the promotion of education and of his church. He was of a kindly disposition and a playful humor; but he was noted also for a naive egotism and great tenacity of opinion, traits which sometimes involved him in unprofitable controversy."

BIBLIOGRAPHY: Baylor University Records, Texas Collection, Baylor University. G. J. Burleson, *The Life and Writings of Rufus C. Burleson* (1901). R. C. Burleson, "My Life Work and Sixty-third Birthday," Texas Collection, Baylor University; R. C. Burleson Papers, Texas Collection, Baylor University. J. M. Carroll, *A History of Texas Baptists* (1907). W. C. Crane Papers, Texas Collection, Baylor University. J. W. Gunn, "The Life of Rufus C. Burleson" (1951). J. B. Link, *Texas Historical and Biographical Magazine* (c. 1891). Imogene Burleson Radney, "A History of the Peabody Education Fund in Texas" (n.d.). B. F. Riley, *A History of Texas Baptists* (1907). Texas State Historical Association, *Handbook of Texas* (1952). Waco University Records, MS, Texas Collection, Baylor University.

GUY B. HARRISON, JR.

BURLESON COLLEGE. A coeducational school opened at Greenville, Tex., in 1895 under the direction of the Hunt County Baptist Association. It became a junior college under control of the Baptist General Convention in 1899 and was continued until mounting annual deficits necessitated its being closed in 1930. In 1924 it had 471 students.

RUPERT N. RICHARDSON

BURMA BAPTIST CONVENTION. Opened in 1813 as the first mission field of American Baptists through their first missionary, Adoniram Judson (b. 1788; d. 1850) (q.v.). The convention, administrative body for some 200,000 Baptists in Burma, has representatives from 16 tribal groups, each of them speaking a different dialect or language, which promote their work through their own associations. The Burmese are mainly Buddhists and are the dominant race. From them came Judson's first converts, with resulting churches organized in the Burma Baptist Churches Union. The largest subdivision of the convention is the Karen (Sgaw-speaking), numbering 88,000, with 12 associations united in the Karen Baptist Convention. There are 15,000 Pwo Karens in three associations. The three principal animistic tribal groups in the hills are subdivided into associations which guide the co-operation of some 30,000 Shans, 28,000 Northern Chins, 20,000 Kachins. In 1953 Thra Tun Shein, a Karen, was elected general secretary for all Burma. The conventions and associations have 2,700 workers. Mission property is being transferred to the convention or to local certified holding bodies. The women's organizations make strong and varied contribution to the work.

The Karens, with over 1,000 churches throughout the district, for many years have administered their own self-supporting educational and medical work centered in Bassein in the south, probably the largest mission center in the world before World War II. To meet the demands for higher education the American Baptist Foreign Mission Society established Rangoon Baptist College, later called Judson College, in Rangoon. This college, by Government action, was not reopened after World War II. However, compensation funds from the government made possible a comprehensive program for higher education and student Christian centers. Related to the Burma Baptist Convention are over 400 association secondary schools; 13 seminaries and Bible schools; 19 union schools; agricultural demonstration centers; and four hospitals in strategic areas, two of which provide treatment for leprosy.

Missionary Judson translated the Bible into Burmese and compiled a dictionary, both of them still in general use. A large body of Christian literature, in the several languages of the country, has been translated or written by missionaries and printed and distributed by the Baptist Mission Press of Rangoon. The press was discontinued after World War II as a printing establishment, but the publication and distribution services continue on a wide scale, making use of bookmobiles for the printed page and for audiovisual aids. There is full co-operation with the National Christian Council of Burma.

The Japanese invasion from the south in 1942 led to the martyrdom of many pastors, church workers, and village Christians; missionaries had to flee; there was extensive destruction of property. The Japanese, turned back in Assam by allied forces, retreated down the length of the country, causing further destruction and loss of property. In 1948 more than a century of British occupation came to an end in the bloodless establishment of the Union of Burma, outside the Commonwealth. Following independence the country was torn by civil strife in which a segment of the Karens was involved, resulting in loss of life and property and displacement of people. By 1953 an agreement was reached whereby a Karen state was set up within the Union of Burma in the Tenasserim area. From the days of the Judsons there has been a close bond of fellowship and co-operation between the American missionaries and the churches. The official organ of the American Baptist Mission of Burma is *Burma News*. Convention groups have periodicals in their own vernaculars.

DATA

	1934	1954 *
Churches	1,518	1,714
	(1,053 self-supporting)	(1,454 self-supporting)
Baptisms	3,963	8,106
Church members	131,940	c. 200,000
Missionaries	155	60
National workers	2,991	2,703
Students	39,796	32,319
Schools	825	463
Patients	45,494	54,311
Hospitals and dispensaries	14	19
Field contributions	$131,646	$242,586

* Incomplete.

ADA STEARNS

BURNETT, J. HENRY (b. Auburn, Ky., May 6, 1872; d. Hendersonville, N. C., Nov. 3, 1956). Recording secretary of the Southern Baptist Convention from 1918 to 1946. The son of Joseph H. and Laura (Huff) Burnett, he attended Auburn College. He married Marietta Abbot of Louisville, Ky., in 1899. They had four sons, George Lee, Oscar Weaver, J. Henry, Jr., and Robert Sibley, and one daughter, Catherine. Burnett was active in church work during his adult life. He was a deacon in several churches, as well as a Sunday school teacher and superintendent at various places in Virginia, Tennessee, and Kentucky. Burnett is the author of the *Hand Book on Institution Management*.

MARY ELLEN SCOFIELD

BURNETT, JOHN J. (b. Big Creek, now Del Rio, Cocke County, Tenn., Jan. 22, 1854; d. Jefferson City, Tenn., July 3, 1937). Minister and biographer. His parents were J. J. and

Mary Louise (Huff) Burnett. His early education was at Mossy Creek school in East Tennessee, which he entered in his 20th year after his conversion the preceding year. He graduated from what is now known as Carson-Newman College, Jefferson City, Tenn., in 1877. He was also a graduate of the Southern Baptist Theological Seminary, Louisville, Ky. His first pastorate was in Winchester, Tenn. Other pastorates were in Tokyio, Mo.; Harriman, Del Rio, and Jefferson City, Tenn. After his retirement from the pastorate, he wrote *Sketches of Tennessee's Pioneer Baptist Preachers* (1919).

HAROLD STEPHENS

BURNEY, THOMAS JEFFERSON (b. Greene County, Ga., Apr. 29, 1801; d. Madison, Ga., 1876). Lawyer, merchant, and planter. His family moved to Morgan County when he was quite young. He was entered in an "old field school" to a Scotch-Irishman, attended grammar school at Monticello, Ga., at 13, and did farm labor for two years. He learned bookkeeping as clerk in the United States land office in Cahaba, Ala., and was in the commission business in Mobile in 1822. He attended a course of law lectures at Judge Tucker's school in Winchester, Va. He was twice married, first to Cornelia M. Walker, Jan. 15, 1829, who bore him four children; and then to Mrs. Julia Shields Bryan, Sept. 13, 1837, who bore him six children. From early boyhood, he had deep religious convictions, was baptized by Adiel Sherwood, and joined the church Nov., 1834. He was among the organizers and first trustees of Georgia Female College, Madison, in 1850. He was a trustee of Mercer University for 34 years (1842–76), treasurer of the Georgia Baptist Convention from 1844 to 1876, and treasurer of Mercer University from 1844 to 1874. To him was due much credit for having so well safeguarded Mercer's financial interest through strenuous and trying times. FRANK S. BURNEY

BURNT CHIMNEY ACADEMY. A school at Burnt Chimney, N. C., supervised by trustees selected "from Baptist ranks." King's Mountain Association endorsed it. D. L. SMILEY

BURROUGHS, PRINCE EMMANUEL (b. Caldwell County, Tex., Dec. 31, 1871; d. Gainesville, Ga., May 22, 1948). Pastor, author, and long-time educational secretary of the Sunday School Board of the Southern Baptist Convention. His conversion occurred when he was 10 years old. He spent two years in Centenary College, and he graduated from Baylor University at 19. He was ordained to the Baptist ministry, and following a short pastorate at Wichita Falls, Tex., he enrolled in the Southern Baptist Theological Seminary and earned the Th.M. degree in 1896. He was awarded the D.D. degree by Hardin-Simmons University (1906) and by Baylor University (1907). After serving churches in Kentucky, he returned to Texas as pastor of First Baptist Church, Temple, and later he went to Broadway Baptist Church, Fort Worth. As a member and secretary of the board of trustees of Southwestern Baptist Theological Seminary, he was influential in moving it to Fort Worth. On Oct. 1, 1910, he was called to the Sunday School Board to direct the work of teacher training, serving at first as office secretary and later (1913) as educational secretary. On the foundation laid by Bernard Washington Spilman (*q.v.*), Landrum Pinson Leavell (*q.v.*), and others, Burroughs set up a system of records and built a training course from 8 to 57 books by 1943.

One of his major contributions to Southern Baptist life came through interpreting the need for adequate building facilities for the church program of worship and education. From 1914 to 1940 he directed the board's ministry in this area, at which time an entirely separate department of architecture was created. From 1927 to 1936 Burroughs was head of the Department of Church Administration and editor of the *Church Administration* magazine as long as it was published (1927–30). In 1940, still serving as secretary of the Educational Department, he was elected secretary of the Division of Education and Promotion, which position he occupied until retirement in 1943.

He was the author of the following books: *Outlines of Bible History* (1913); *Winning to Christ* (1914); *Old Testament Studies* (1915); *The Present-Day Sunday School* (1917); *Church and Sunday School Buildings* (1917); *Building a Successful Sunday School* (1921); *A Complete Guide to Church Building* (1923); *How to Plan Church Buildings* (1925); *Growing a Church* (1927); *The Functioning Church* (1928); *Our Lord and Ours* (1928); *Our Church and Ours* (1928); *Honoring the Deaconship* (1929); *The Baptist People* (1934); *The Grace of Giving* (1934); *Let Us Build* (1938); *Fifty Fruitful Years* (a history of the Sunday School Board, 1941); *The Spiritual Conquest of the Second Frontier* (a history of the First Baptist Church of Nashville, Tenn., 1942).

He was married twice—first to Corinne Gayle Alexander, 1898; and then to Corinne Gayle Riley, 1937. A. V. WASHBURN

BURROWS, JOHN LANSING (b. Albany, N. Y., Feb. 14, 1814; d. near Augusta, Ga., Jan. 2, 1893). Minister. His father, Samuel Burrows, who died when the son was six years old, was captain of an American privateer in the War of 1812; his mother, a Miss Lansing, was of old New York Knickerbocker stock. Young Burrows attended Union College, Schenectady, N. Y., and graduated also from Andover Theological Seminary. In 1835 he was ordained in Poughkeepsie, N. Y., and in the same year married Adeline Benthuysen. After about a year as a co-pastor with Archibald McClay in New York City, Burrows engaged in educational work in Elizabethtown and Shelbyville, Ky. In 1840 he became pastor of the Sansom Street Baptist Church, Philadelphia, Pa.; four years later he organized the Broad Street Church there. In 1854 he accepted a call to the First Baptist Church, Richmond, Va., and remained there for 20 years. While serving there and in other pastorates in the South, he was appointed to many important committees in Virginia and in the Southern Baptist Convention. He was a trustee of Richmond College, president of the Education Board, and in 1873 organized and directed a $300,000 campaign for the school. He was for six years president of the Foreign Mission Board and three times vice-president of the Southern Baptist Convention. In 1874 he accepted a call to the Broadway Baptist Church, Louisville, Ky., remaining there until 1882 when he became pastor of the Freemason Street Baptist Church, Norfolk, Va. Soon after arriving on his new field, he conducted in his church a revival that lasted five weeks. Though 68 years old, he became a leading force in the general life of the city. In 1891, because of declining health, Burrows resigned his pastorate, and went to live with his son Lansing Burrows (q.v.), then pastor in Augusta, Ga. He died on a Monday morning after preaching on Sunday at a country church called Wares, 30 miles from Augusta. Memorial services were held in Augusta, Louisville, and Richmond. Burial was in Hollywood Cemetery, Richmond, Va. His children were Lansing, Mason Mitchell, and a daughter, who married W. Winston Fontaine.

J. L. ROSSER

BURROWS, LANSING (b. Philadelphia, Pa., Apr. 10, 1843; d. Americus, Ga., Oct. 17, 1919). Pastor, statistician, secretary of the Southern Baptist Convention. His parents were John Lansing Burrows (q.v.) and Adelaide (Van Benthuysen) Burrows, both of Knickerbocker descent. The senior Burrows was pastor of the First Baptist Church, Richmond, Va., where his son Lansing was reared and converted in May, 1858, at the age of 15. He entered Richmond College but subsequently, 1859, transferred to Wake Forest College, which suspended operation during the Civil War. At the war's end the college reopened, and a diploma was issued to him as a senior of the class of 1861. Burrows earned and received the A.M. degree at Princeton, 1871. The D.D. degree was twice conferred upon him: first by Madison (now Colgate University), 1871; second by Bethel College, Russellville, Ky., 1882. He received the LL.D. degree at Union University, Tennessee, 1896.

During the Civil War, Burrows endured more vicissitudes than combats. He enlisted on Apr. 25, 1861, at Richmond, and was assigned to the Fayette Artillery as sergeant. He was captured at Winchester, Va., Sept. 19, 1864, and imprisoned at Ft. Delaware until near the close of the war; then he was exchanged as an incurable prisoner and returned to Richmond.

In the summer of 1867 he married Lulie Rochester, daughter of Charles H. Rochester of Kentucky. She died, after several years' illness, in Nashville in 1901 during her husband's pastorate there.

Burrows was ordained a Baptist minister in July, 1867, at Stanford, Ky., where he was teaching in a seminary. During his 50-year ministry he served eight churches as pastor: Stanford, Ky., 1867; Lexington, Mo., 1867–69; Bordentown, N. J., 1870–76; Newark, N. J., 1876–79; Lexington, Ky., 1879–83; Augusta, Ga., First Baptist, 1883–99; Nashville, Tenn., First Baptist, 1899–1909; Americus, Ga., 1909–16, in which latter year he retired from the pastorate.

For 33 years, 1881–1913, Burrows was recording secretary of the Southern Baptist Convention, and was denominational statistician, 1881–1919. He was elected president of the Convention three times: 1914, 1915, 1916. For a decade, 1899–1909, while residing in Nashville, he was a member of the Sunday School Board; then, after moving to Americus (1909), he was for another 10 years, until his death, its state member for Georgia. For a score of years he contributed to the Baptist *Teacher* and *Adult Bible Class Quarterly*. He was the editor of *The Baptist Hymn and Praise Book* (1904), to which he contributed six original hymns.

He was twice a citizen of Georgia, and during each period of residence in that state he was a member of the Mercer University board of trustees (1890–99 and 1912–19). He was survived by a son and a daughter and was buried in Mt. Olivet Cemetery in Nashville, Tenn.

EDWIN S. DAVIS

BURT, ROBERT EUGENE (b. Drew County, Ark., 1882; d. Houston, Tex., 1943). A Houston and Dallas oil operator, Burt was chairman of the executive board of the Baptist General Convention of Texas from 1918 to 1928. For 26 years he was a trustee of Mary Hardin–Baylor College, 1916–42, and president of its board, 1926–34. Burt, also a trustee of Baptist Memorial Hospital from 1913 to 1921, headed its board the last three years of this trusteeship. During the depression of the 1930's, Burt endorsed Texas Baptist notes for millions of dollars at Houston banks after Dallas institutions had extended the denomination all the credit they felt was justified. Along with Manson Horatio Wolfe (q.v.), Burt provided funds which enabled James Milton Carroll (q.v.) to write *A History of Texas Baptists*, published in 1923. Burt Hall, a dormitory at Mary Hardin–Baylor College, was a gift of Burt and his wife in 1919.

BIBLIOGRAPHY: *Baptist Standard* (Jan. 30, 1919; Nov. 3, 1938; Aug. 26, 1943). F. E. Burkhalter, *A World-Visioned Church* (1946). J. M. Carroll, *A History of Texas Baptists* (1923). L. R. Elliott, ed., *Centennial Story of Texas Baptists* (1936). *Who's Who in America* (1938–39).

FRANK BURKHALTER

BURTS, CHARLES ELFORD (b. near Honea Path, Abbeville County, S. C., Dec. 5, 1867; d. Columbia, S. C., Nov. 18, 1939). Pastor, South Carolina Baptist leader. Son of Richard Ward

Bush, John Curtis

and Amanda (Latimer) Burts, he received the A.B. degree from Furman University in 1893 and the Th.M. degree from Southern Baptist Theological Seminary in 1898. Burts held pastorates at Gallatin, Tenn. (1890–1900), First Baptist, Macon, Ga. (1927–1933); and South Carolina churches in Blackville (1900–04), Edgefield (1904–10), Columbia (1910–19), Newberry (1926–27), and St. Matthews (1933–39). Secretary-treasurer of the general board of the South Carolina convention (1919–24) and director of Cooperative Program Commission of the Southern Baptist Convention (1924–26), Burts was director (1933–38) and president (1938–39) of the South Carolina Federated Forces for Temperance. Elected president of the South Carolina convention (1936–39), his presidential address, "The Layman," was published at request of the 1938 convention. An acquaintance of Burts's of long standing said, "If I were called upon to name the chief quality of this man, I would say it was leadership. All of his faculties conspired to make his leadership a success."

BIBLIOGRAPHY: R. W. Burts, "Autobiography" (n.d.). J. C. Hemphill, *Men of Mark in South Carolina* (1908). *The Baptist Courier*, Vol. 71 (Nov. 23 and Nov. 30, 1939). W. S. Utsey, ed., *Who's Who in South Carolina* (1935). CHARLES W. BURTS

BUSH, JOHN CURTIS (b. Pickettsville, Pickens County, Ala., June 17, 1845; d. Mobile, Ala., June 19, 1910). Cotton factor and twice mayor of Mobile, Ala. Bush was first elected in 1897, during which time "he gave Mobile a very honest, economical and efficient government." He was widely known for his many charities, among which were frequent gifts to the poor of his city; he also made frequent large donations to his church and denomination, included among which were initial major gifts toward building programs in his own church (First Baptist, Mobile) and more than half of the money required to purchase a headquarters building for the Baptist state executive board in Montgomery. He attended Howard College and the University of Alabama. He enlisted in the Confederate army, taking part in the Battle of Murfreesboro and rising to the rank of quartermaster-sergeant. After the close of the Civil War, he entered the University of Mississippi where he was graduated (class valedictorian) in 1867. One unit of the educational building at First Baptist, Mobile, was named in his honor. His parents were Albert Peyton Bush and Sarah Ann Williams. He married Ruth Sarah Tarrant, Nov. 30, 1869, in Marion, Ala. His children were: T. G., Felix, Sarah (Mrs. A. W. Brooks), J. C., Jr., Ruth (Mrs. Sexton), Marie (Mrs. Arthur Glover Gage). He served as treasurer, deacon, and Sunday school superintendent of his church. One son, J. C., Jr., was also well known for his philanthropies.

H. H. HARWELL

BUSH THEOLOGICAL SEMINARY. See CHINA, MISSION IN.

BUSHYHEAD, JESSE (b. Amohee, Ga., Sept., 1804; d. Westville, Okla., July 17, 1844). Pioneer Indian Baptist preacher and Christian statesman, a prominent spiritual and civic leader of the Cherokee nation at the time of the Indians' removal to the Indian Territory over "The Trail of Tears" in 1838–39. He was converted in 1830 and ordained to the ministry in 1833. He organized a Baptist church soon after his detachment of nearly 1,000 Indians arrived in the Indian Territory Feb. 13, 1839. Bushyhead helped write the Cherokee nation's constitution, and from 1840 until his death he served as the second chief justice of the Cherokee Supreme Court. He was the first president of the Cherokee Temperance Society, and interested himself in a variety of civic, religious, and educational projects. Shortly before his death he helped to found the *Cherokee Messenger,* the first newspaper in what is now Oklahoma. Hostile conditions prevailed in the Cherokee nation in Bushyhead's time, and he was the only man of any standing who traveled freely over the nation unarmed except for his Bible. He is buried near Westville, Okla.

BIBLIOGRAPHY: J. M. Gaskin, *Trail Blazers of Sooner Baptists* (1953). E. C. Routh, *The Story of Oklahoma Baptists* (1932). J. W. Thoburn, *History of Oklahoma* (1916). J. M. GASKIN

BUSINESS AND BUSINESS MEETINGS, CHURCH. The usual democratic procedures of Baptist churches are based on the same scriptural grounds which Baptists claim for their doctrine and ordinances. Believing that the New Testament form of church government was democratic, Baptists have consistently followed the same congregational pattern of self-determination on the basis of majority vote. The requirements of true democracy demand that church business meetings be held in order that congregational decisions may be reached on matters that require such action. Each church makes its own rules, but most of them follow similar procedure.

Baptists generally agree that all questions affecting the organization or operation of the church must be decided in open business session. Routine matters, however, can be disposed of under some established policy or pattern, adopted by the church as a convenient standing rule. Through the years the average church, by resolution or special motion, creates a significant body of such operational policies, which do not have to be renewed but continue indefinitely until, in the judgment of the church, a change is needed. In this way the church in business session is relieved of unnecessarily detailed considerations, and many duties can be assigned to designated individuals, committees, or groups, with authority to act.

Congregational determination of the business affairs of a church began at Jerusalem, where there was apparently a very simple organization made up of believers meeting together. Under leadership of the apostles and the Holy Spirit, there was gradual development. Earliest congregational action is indicated in the choosing of Matthias to succeed Judas (Acts 1:26) and the election of the first deacons (Acts 6:3-5). Record of the Conference at Jerusalem (Acts 15) indicates that the apostles expressed the opinions that prevailed and the elders and brethren agreed, but it would seem that all alike were free to express themselves, each opinion advanced by a member of the group being given proper consideration. Definite church action was taken here in the selection of representatives to be sent to Antioch.

At the time when a church is organized, or as soon thereafter as possible, three important actions are necessary to initiate an effective organization: (1) a parliamentary authority should be adopted containing rules governing procedure in business meetings; (2) the number of members required to be present for the transaction of business should be established; (3) a fixed monthly or quarterly date for the holding of regular business meetings should be agreed upon and an understanding reached relative to the manner in which special meetings may be called. It is obvious that unless some quorum requirements and regular meeting dates are observed, a small group might undertake to determine a matter at a time and place unfairly chosen, and in such a manner as not to fully represent the wishes of the congregation as a whole.

In the typical Baptist church the pastor serves as moderator, although another individual may be chosen for the position. While pastor and deacons are recognized as church officers, they do not have any preferred right in a business meeting. Care should be exercised to keep every meeting on a democratic basis and to follow parliamentary practice.

The moderator is responsible for presiding, directing the course of the meeting, seeing that each member is protected in the right to be heard, requiring that discussion be addressed to the chair and be kept both pertinent and well ordered, and seeing that no proper item is omitted from consideration. He should apply parliamentary rules as needed and rule against personal attacks or abusive remarks. An adequate and proper order of business should be followed. Accurate records of all business meetings should be kept by the church clerk, and a duplicate copy should be filed in the church office or elsewhere for safekeeping. Following the reading of minutes, reports of committees and/or organizations and recommendations of deacons or other officers should be heard, after which old and new business may be dealt with. All procedure should be in keeping with the usual routine followed by democratic bodies. Each business session should be closed with prayer and may include other devotional elements in accord with local custom and as time permits.

Numerical growth of modern churches, along with complicated living and working conditions, has led to the disposition to leave business decisions to comparatively small groups. For this reason especially it is important that full advance publicity be given to each meeting and that all members be given an opportunity to be present. The challenging of any decision on the grounds of insufficient notice of meeting should be made unnecessary.

Many matters of routine nature, such as building care and alterations, certain financing procedures, the selection of certain personnel for church employment, and the carrying out of detailed procedure relative to purchase of property or supplies, may be entrusted by congregational action to deacons, committees, staff members, or other individuals. Thus the necessity of too frequent business meetings can be eliminated. Baptists hold that democracy is not violated by the delegation of authority to individuals or groups, provided this is done by specific action of the body.   NORRIS PALMER

BUSINESS AND FINANCIAL PLAN OF THE CONVENTION. The Business and Financial Plan of the Southern Baptist Convention is actually a part of the Convention's constitution and bylaws. It regulates and directs all financial matters involving the Convention as a body and determines courses of procedure where new or additional agency or Convention projects are proposed. In general, it is the Convention's "law" regarding all business procedures.

The first recorded mention of a Business and Financial Plan is found in the minutes of the Southern Baptist Convention for 1937, where, on page 43, the Convention received from the Executive Committee the following recommendation: "That the Executive Committee of this Convention be instructed to formulate plans and policies looking toward the prevention in the future of the incurring of debts either by this Convention or its agencies."

This recommendation was adopted by the body, and in its session the following year, 1938, the report of the Executive Committee, in recommendation No. 13, set forth the Business and Financial Plan in its original form. This recommendation was adopted by the Convention, and in the Convention *Annual* for 1939, the Business and Financial Plan of the Convention appeared for the first time as a part of the body's constitution.

Initially, the Business and Financial Plan was a child of the great depression. Several years had been spent in trying to pay off huge debts on the Convention. Convention leadership realized the necessity of preventing, if possible, such a recurrence of debt. The wisdom of bringing all financial and business matters under control of the Convention was seen, and the section of the Convention's constitution under which it now operates its business and financial affairs was the outcome.

During the years since its adoption a few minor changes have been made, but the plan

Business Efficiency Committee

is largely in its original form. Covered in this section of the constitution are principles governing the budget of the Convention; budgets of the agencies; responsibility for arriving at budgets to be recommended to the Convention for adoption; limitations as to the authority of any agency to borrow money; distribution of Cooperative Program receipts; limitations upon special financial campaigns by any agency; regulations concerning trust funds, special gifts and annuities, capital investments, contingent reserve funds for individual agencies, methods of making audits and financial reports; regulations concerning the initiating of new enterprises; etc.

The Business and Financial Plan of the Convention may be altered by two-thirds of the messengers present and voting at any time except on the last day of the Convention. The Business and Financial Plan of the Southern Baptist Convention is printed in the annuals of the Convention on the pages immediately following the bylaws.   W. DOUGLAS HUDGINS

BUSINESS EFFICIENCY COMMITTEE. A committee appointed by the Southern Baptist Convention in 1925 to study the business methods of the denominational agencies of the Convention. The agencies were heavily in debt at this time. Following the close of World War I, various religious bodies put on special campaigns to raise funds to take advantage of the new missionary opportunities throughout the world. The Southern Baptist Convention in 1919 launched the 75 Million Campaign to raise $75,000,000 for religious work at home and abroad, with $15,000,000 annually for five years. A committee was appointed to work out the details and to promote the campaign, with Lee Rutland Scarborough (*q.v.*) director. After a vigorous campaign, the members of the churches enthusiastically pledged $92,000,000; but because of the financial depression, the final collections amounted to approximately $58,500,000, which was about $34,000,000 less than the pledges, and nearly $17,000,000 less than the $75,000,000 goal.

It was under these conditions of financial difficulties in the denomination that Austin Crouch, of Tennessee, with George White McDaniel (*q.v.*) presiding, made the following motion at the Convention in Memphis, Tenn., May 14, 1925, which was adopted:

> That a committee be appointed to study the business methods of the Convention and make recommendations to the Convention next year; the committee to be composed of one from each State and the District of Columbia, one-half at least to be laymen, and no one of the committee shall be an employee of the Convention or any of its agencies. Authority shall be given the committee to secure any facts or information desired from any and all Convention agencies.

The committee secured the necessary information concerning the various agencies, and a sub-committee consisting of W. M. Whittington, Mississippi, chairman, E. Hilton Jackson, District of Columbia, and Austin Crouch, Tennessee, was appointed to put the report in final form for presentation to the Convention. The committee made its report to the Convention meeting in Houston, Tex., May 12, 1926, with the following recommendations:

> . . . that the convention at this time commit itself to budget control, and that the Executive Committee of the convention be instructed to present a suggested, detailed, combined budget to the convention next year.
>
> . . . that the convention go on record as favoring a single agency to function along the lines presented in this report, and that the committee on business efficiency be instructed to work out the details of such agency and present it to the convention next year.
>
> . . . that your committee on business efficiency be continued; that it make a full, complete, and analyzed survey of the work, policies, activities, and other matters of the convention and all of its agencies.

The committee made its report to the Convention meeting in Louisville, Ky., on May 4, 1927, and recommended, among other things, that (1) the Convention commit itself to the policy of having an operating budget as a financial working basis for itself and its agencies, (2) that the Executive Committee be organized with permanent headquarters and office force, and that all the work then being done by the Cooperative Program Commission be taken over by this Executive Committee, (3) that each agency prepare an operating budget for presentation to the Convention the next year, which should not exceed the agency's cash receipts for the past year, and (4) that a committee be appointed to make a further survey of all the work done by the Convention through all its organized agencies except the Foreign Mission Board, the Sunday School Board, and the Relief and Annuity Board, and to make a report to the Convention the next year.

This committee was appointed with L. L. Gwaltney (*q.v.*), chairman, and it made its report to the Convention in Chattanooga, May 16–20, 1928. Recommendations were made concerning Inter-Board Commission, Hospital Commission, Home Mission Board, and the Education Board. It was recommended that the Education Board be discontinued, and "that the Executive Committee of this Convention be recognized as the successor in law to the Board of Education, and that all of the interests and obligations of the Education Board, financial, legal and otherwise, be and are hereby committed to the Executive Committee of this Convention."   AUSTIN CROUCH

BUSSELL, SANFORD STANTON (b. Waxahachie, Tex., Sept. 26, 1879; d. Phoenix, Ariz., Oct. 3, 1947). Minister, Arizona Baptist leader. Ordained to the ministry in 1906 by a Baptist church in Italy, Tex., Bussell graduated from Southern Baptist Theological Seminary in 1910. For the next 10 years he served as pastor in

Oklahoma and Texas. He left Oak Cliff Baptist Church in Dallas to serve as chaplain in Europe during World War I. Called to New Mexico as state Sunday school and Baptist Young People's Union secretary in 1921, Bussell resigned four years later to enter Baptist Student Union and Brotherhood work. In 1931 he became executive secretary of the Baptist General Convention of Arizona and began promotional work of all convention departments. A guiding spirit in denominational progress in Arizona, Bussell was president of the Baptist General Convention of Arizona from 1940 to 1942 and education secretary of the convention from 1944 until his death.

CARRIE W. (MRS. W. C.) HENDERSON

BUTLER, CHARLES (b. Camilla, Ga., Dec. 29, 1879; d. in Florida, Oct. 12, 1929). Gospel singer and evangelist. He attended Mercer University and studied music in Boston, Mass. He married Edith Anderson of Springfield, Ill., in 1910. A baritone soloist of unusual ability, Butler joined the evangelistic party of R. A. Torrey and Charles M. Alexander and for several years toured America and England with this group. He toured with the Billy Sunday evangelistic party as soloist, returning to serve as song leader for R. A. Torrey, replacing Alexander. He made a most significant contribution during World War I, singing and leading singing in the army camps. He was ordained to the Baptist ministry in Spartanburg, S. C. For a number of years his singing of "On Jordan's Stormy Banks" became a tradition by popular demand at the annual sessions of the Southern Baptist Convention. He is the author-composer of one published gospel song, "No Other Name" (1926).

WILLIAM J. REYNOLDS

BUTLER, DARIUS LEONARD (b. Sevier County, Tenn., Oct. 17, 1876; d. Mar. 9, 1952). Merchant and financier. He contributed over half a million dollars to Baptist causes, led in the financial affairs of Baptist institutions in East Tennessee, and helped them to make significant increases in endowments and physical assets.

As a boy, Butler moved from Sevier County to the Byington community, Knox County, Tenn. He graduated from Carson-Newman College in 1901, married Bertie Maples, whom he had met on the campus, and entered partnership with her father in the mercantile business. Later he was involved in real estate and banking. A typical businessman of the era of individualism, Butler held denominational offices for many years. He was for 41 years a member of the executive committee of the trustees of Carson-Newman College, for 40 years a deacon, and for 30 years treasurer of the First Baptist Church, Jefferson City, Tenn. He served as a director of the East Tennessee Baptist Hospital and was a member of the building committee and chairman of the enlargement campaign for Carson-Newman College. He gave and worked to replace the college's burned administration building, together with Henry David Blanc built its Butler-Blanc Gymnasium, and gave largely to build the old boys' dormitory. With Mrs. Butler, he gave the Maples Memorial Library. In his will he left a substantial sum for the college's endowment, and $20,000 for a new boys' dormitory. He and his wife also gave a trust fund of $200,000 to the Tennessee Baptist Foundation, and designated the income for the Cooperative Program.

Butler's only son Thales L. Butler died in 1937 at the age of 26, and the inheritance which he would have received was used toward the erection of the educational building of the First Baptist Church, Jefferson City. The Butlers placed their son's personal organ there, and later gave a pipe organ for the church.

ROBERT PALMER

BUTLER, DAVID EDWARD (b. Wilkes County, Ga., Mar. 9, 1818; d. Madison, Ga., Aug. 29, 1886). Orphaned at nine years of age, Butler lived with relatives in Washington, Ga., until 1834, when he entered Mercer Institute. Following further study at Washington in 1837 and two sessions in law at the University of Virginia, he was admitted to the Georgia bar in 1840 and practiced law in Washington until 1850. During the next 10 years he engaged in mercantile and agricultural pursuits in Augusta, Morgan, and Lowndes counties.

In 1861, at the age of 43, Butler was ordained to the ministry by the Baptist church at Madison. Thereafter, as pastor in Madison, Milledgeville, Monroe, Conyers, and Jackson, he was active in supporting whatever promoted the interests and welfare of Georgia Baptists. From 1854 to 1880 he was a member of the executive committee of the Georgia Baptist convention and was its president from 1872 to 1877. From 1874 to 1878 he was editor of *The Christian Index*. A strong advocate of Christian education, he served Mercer University as a trustee from 1854 until his death, 20 years of that time as president of the board, and was active in the founding (1878) and promotion of the Georgia Baptist Female Seminary (now Brenau College) at Gainesville.

Butler married Virginia Walton of Madison, Ga., in 1850. They had six children.

HAROLD L. MCMANUS

BYARS, NOAH TURNER (b. Spartanburg, S. C., May 17, 1808; d. Brownwood, Tex., Aug. 18, 1888). Texas patriot and frontier missionary. Although little is known of Byars' life before his arrival in Texas in 1835, once there he opened a blacksmith shop at Washington-on-the-Brazos, and in his shop both the Texas Declaration of Independence and the Constitution of the Republic of Texas were formulated. Displaying true revolutionary spirit, Byars enlisted as armorer for the Texan forces and engaged in the San Jacinto campaign. Between

1837 and 1841 he lived at Houston and Bastrop, serving as justice of the peace and sergeant-at-arms of the senate during meetings of the Texas congress.

Converted in 1824, Byars resisted what he termed a persistent call to the ministry until 1841. However, while residing at Webberville, Tex., he requested ministerial license of the Macedonia Baptist Church, and the church ordained him Oct., 1841. Following ordination, Byars served a church in Burleson County, but he was soon unhappy. Beckoned by the frontier, he was designated by the Domestic Mission Board as missionary in Navarro County in 1845, and the Baptist state convention employed him in 1848. From that date on, Byars was closely affiliated with the convention or with associations on the extreme frontier until 1884. Traveling on horseback and covering more than 100,000 miles, he helped constitute more than 60 churches and also organized five associations.

BIBLIOGRAPHY: *Texas Historical and Biographical Magazine*, I–II. T. R. Havins, "N. T. Byars—A Study in Baptist Missions on the Frontier" (1941).

T. R. HAVINS

BYERS, JOHN HENRY (b. Near Enterprise, Ark., Sept. 27, 1872; d. Fort Smith, Ark., Feb. 25, 1953). Indian Territory preacher. He was baptized by Pilgrim's Rest Baptist Church, near Mansfield, Ark., at the age of 16. He studied in two Arkansas colleges, Buckner at Witcherville and Ouachita at Arkadelphia. On Jan. 13, 1892, he married Mona Ann Cacy. After his second sermon, June, 1893, his church licensed him to preach. He was pastor or missionary in eastern Oklahoma and in Arkansas for 57 years and moderator of Buckner Association (Ark.) for 20 years. One of the Folsoms (Choctaw), whose family established Folsom's Chapel, gave Byers' father land near what is now Cowlington, Okla. The elder Byers was burned out by hostile Indians in 1874, and though he had valid leases, he refused to fight. He gave the property to A. F. Cowling, for whom the present town of Cowlington, Okla., was named. Cowling participated in the organization of the Short Mountain Association. Byers suffered many physical and mental hardships while preaching in Indian Territory. He was buried at Mansfield, Ark.

BIBLIOGRAPHY: H. M. Pierce, "John Henry Byers," *Chronicles of Oklahoma* (1954); "Great Heart of Indian Territory and Western Arkansas," *Quarterly Review* (July, 1955).

HERBERT M. PIERCE

BYRD, JAMES EDWARD (b. Covington County, Miss., May 10, 1872; d. Knoxville, Tenn., Oct. 21, 1937). Mississippi Baptist leader. Mississippi's second state Sunday school secretary, Byrd succeeded Landrum Pinson Leavell (*q.v.*) in 1903 and served 34 years. From humble beginnings as a country schoolteacher and later a merchant in Mount Olive, Byrd became a leader of Mississippi Baptists, who twice elected him president of the state convention. He is among the few laymen awarded a D.D. degree by Mississippi College. A world traveler, Byrd went to Rome in 1907 for the World Sunday School Convention; in 1910 he attended the International Sunday School Convention in San Francisco, and in 1923, the Baptist World Alliance in Stockholm, when he also toured the British Isles, Europe, Egypt, and the Holy Land. Byrd served in the Mississippi legislature from 1900 to 1904. He was a trustee of Mississippi Woman's College from its beginning in 1912 until the time of his death in 1937. He served for nine years as trustee of Mount Olive public schools, and was appointed by Governor M. J. Connor as a member of the Central Board of Trustees of the University and Colleges of Mississippi.

C. B. HAMLET III

C

CALEDONIA ACADEMY. Founded at Caledonia, Ark., by Liberty Baptist Association in 1920. The academy operated on income from tuition and appropriations from the Arkansas Baptist State Mission Board; it had three buildings financed locally. Enrolment was 31 in 1924–25 and 44 in 1925–26, the year in which it closed.

H. D. MORTON

CALENDAR OF ACTIVITIES. A comprehensive schedule, arranged by a committee each year, of activities, promotional emphases, programs, and causes promoted by Southern Baptists. It provides a maximum of efficiency through the elimination of conflicts and duplications in the promotional work of various agencies of Southern Baptists. The schedule does not determine policy with regard to dates and programs but provides a working basis for general co-operation. The earliest mention of the idea of such a schedule or calendar for the whole denomination was in 1933 when the

Executive Committee recommended that all Cooperative Program causes be given "calendar time . . . as a means of keeping our people informed." A year later the Executive Committee reported adoption of a calendar of denominational activities to emphasize home and foreign missions the first quarter; hospitals and education in the states the second quarter; seminaries and Relief and Annuity Board in the third quarter; and state missions, orphanages, and state papers the fourth quarter. The committee was composed exclusively of representatives of Southern Baptist Convention and state agencies. The Executive Committee, in 1937, recommended that the Convention committee on committees name the calendar committee. In 1938 the new committee made its first report. In 1941 the report of the calendar committee contained this statement, "The meeting this year was held in advance of the regular June meeting of the Executive Committee so that the calendar, as approved by the committee, could be submitted . . . to the Executive Committee . . . for adoption." This procedure made it available sooner than usual. Prior to 1948 the calendar had been reported to the Convention in the year which it covered. In that year the committee submitted its regular report covering the 1948 calendar. In addition a second calendar was submitted for 1949, setting a pattern for the ensuing years. The Committee on Denominational Calendar does not make a policy concerning dates and programs. It only calls attention to conflicts and duplications and co-ordinates principal dates into a calendar.   ALBERT MC CLELLAN

CALI INTERNATIONAL SEMINARY. See COLOMBIA, MISSION IN.

CALIFORNIA, SOUTHERN BAPTIST FOUNDATION OF. Established in 1952 by the Southern Baptist General Convention of California upon recommendation of the convention's board of directors to serve as an investment agency for the convention and its auxiliary corporations. The convention elected a board of directors at the 1952 session in San Jose, Calif. Julian L. Stenstrom was elected executive director of the foundation. The foundation became a California nonprofit corporation June 5, 1953. It makes no investments except in securities offered by Southern Baptist churches or by institutions owned and controlled by the Southern Baptist General Convention of California. Assets in 1955 totaled $400,000.
    JULIAN L. STENSTROM

CALIFORNIA, SOUTHERN BAPTIST GENERAL CONVENTION OF.
I. Baptist Beginnings. When California was admitted to statehood Sept. 9, 1850, Baptist work in the area had already begun. Osgood Church Wheeler, with a commission from the American Baptist Home Mission Society, arrived in San Francisco Feb. 28, 1849. On July 6 of the same year, he organized the First Baptist Church of that city, the first Baptist church in California. Many Baptist preachers came with the gold seekers in the next two years. They were not connected with any mission agency, but some of them were active in establishing churches. Among the first churches constituted were the First Baptist Church of Santa Clara, organized Mar. 1, 1851, by Joseph Morris of Alabama; Santa Rosa Baptist Church, organized by Stephen Riley of Missouri in 1852; and El Monte Baptist Church, organized by Robert Fryer of Arkansas in 1853. The first baptism to be administered in California took place on Oct. 21, 1849, in San Francisco Bay. The candidate was Thomas Kellam of Virginia.

Thousands from the Southern states moved to California before 1855, and many of these were members of Baptist churches. Southern Baptists considered California as their mission responsibility from the very beginning. At the second annual session of the Southern Baptist Convention in Richmond, Va., June, 1846, a committee consisting of I. T. Henton, D. B. Shepherd, J. Huckens, C. Tyree, and G. M. Thompson was appointed on "New Fields of Labor for Domestic Missions." When the committee made its report to the Convention in 1849, attention was called to the migration of many Southerners into California and the need for missionaries in that distant territory. The Convention approved the report and the recommendations of the committee, but the Domestic Mission Board contended that its work should be confined to the 14 slaveholding states. The board also contended that the expense of sending missionaries to California would not be justified because the people were so bent on getting gold that they would not pay any attention to the preaching of the gospel.

The Convention continued to override the Domestic Mission Board's contention that its activity should be confined to the 14 slaveholding states and in 1853 declared that its field embraced all portions of the country. John Lewis Shuck (*q.v.*), a former foreign missionary of the Triennial Convention, was appointed a missionary to California by the Domestic Mission Board in 1854. He did outstanding work among the Chinese. He also served for six years as pastor of the First Baptist Church of Sacramento, during which time a new house of worship was erected and the church became "the largest and most efficient Baptist church in the state." In 1858 Shuck began publishing the *Baptist Circular,* which was taken over by D. B. Chaney two years later. He was very active in associational and convention activities and assisted in the organization of churches and in the general missionary program of Baptists all over the state. In 1859 he was given the title of general missionary to California, and on Jan. 1, 1860, he moved to San Francisco in order to be nearer the center of his work. On Jan. 1, 1861, he resigned his position with the mission board and accepted a pastorate in South Carolina.

One of Shuck's greatest contributions was his success in enlisting others in mission interests. It was he who encouraged E. J. Willis to surrender to the call of the ministry. Willis, an attorney from Charlottesville, Va., went to California in 1849 and was elected the first county judge of Sacramento County. The First Baptist Church of Sacramento was organized in his home. In July, 1854, he began the editorship of a Baptist paper called *The Pacific Recorder*, sponsored by the California Baptist State Convention, founded in 1853. In Aug., 1854, he resigned his judgeship and was ordained to the ministry. Upon the recommendation of the California convention, he was appointed a missionary by the Domestic Mission Board of the Southern Baptist Convention. In Nov., 1854, he opened a mission in Oakland which, on Dec. 7 of that same year, he organized into the First Baptist Church of Oakland. This became one of the great Baptist churches of California. In 1856, at the request of the San Francisco Association, Willis went to Virginia to attempt to raise funds for Baptist mission work in California. Prolonged illness in his family prevented his return to Oakland, and he became pastor of the Leigh Street Baptist Church in Richmond, Va.

Harvey Gilbert, another missionary of the Southern board, served for a time as pastor at Oakland and then in 1858 settled in Marin County, where he organized a church at San Rafael and established the San Rafael Baptist Institute.

The Domestic Mission Board employed at least 15 missionaries to California during the years 1854–61. Among the places where these missionaries organized churches are Santa Cruz, Benicia, San Ramon, Morago Valley, Centerville, Sonora, and Texas Springs. These early churches were missionary-minded and loyal to the Southern Baptist Convention. In the Convention minutes for 1855, California is listed as one of the 15 Southern states and is commended for exceeding in gifts to home missions Tennessee, Arkansas, Texas, Kentucky, Louisiana, North Carolina, and Florida.

In these years all of the California churches, whether they were organized by missionaries from the American Baptist Home Mission Society or the Southern Baptist Home Mission Board, were in the same associations and state convention. Very little friction existed between the Northern and Southern elements in the Baptist ranks.

In 1861 the Southern Baptist Home Mission Board decided to curtail mission work in California because of the necessity for "retrenchment." This withdrawal of support did not mean the complete abolishment of Southern Baptist work in California. However, the Civil War and the trying years which followed weakened the work. References to California occur in the Southern Baptist Convention minutes for 1860, 1870, 1872, and 1873. In 1881 the Home Mission Board reopened a mission among the Chinese in San Francisco. This work was closed in 1884, although a church organized during this period still continues to exist. The early churches organized by the Southern Baptist missionaries became affiliated with the American Baptist Home Mission Society.

Southern Baptist work began anew in California with the organization of the First Southern Baptist Church in Shafter with 16 members on May 10, 1936. Every charter member had belonged to a Southern Baptist church elsewhere before moving to California. At the organization meeting Joe Hardcastle was called as supply pastor; he was succeeded Aug. 15, 1936, by Tom H. Rains, who had been pastor of many of the members where they lived in Oklahoma.

Sam Wilcoxon, from Eastside Baptist Church, Paragould, Ark., accepted the pastorate at Shafter Nov. 10, 1937. Wilcoxon set about to promote a full-scale Southern Baptist program. Mrs. Wilcoxon organized a Woman's Missionary Society Apr. 6, 1938. In Feb., 1938, the church turned down a proposal from a Landmark missionary, Silas Hill, that the church affiliate with that group.

By early 1939 there were Southern Baptist churches in Shafter, Oildale, and Lamont. In the meantime a church organized at Taft in 1928 came over from the Landmarks and joined with Southern forces. Messengers from the four churches organized San Joaquin Valley Missionary Baptist Association at Shafter Apr. 13, 1939. Thurman D. Ellis was elected moderator and Corbin Ogilvie, clerk. Thirteen men were elected to the executive board. Woman's Missionary Union officers elected were Mrs. Edith Billingsley, president; Mrs. Averil Mouser, vice-president; and Mrs. Ora Ware, secretary-treasurer. Training Union officers elected were Tilman Hull, president, and Corbin Ogilvie, director. Donald Graves was elected Sunday school superintendent. No Brotherhood officers were elected. No records were kept of the activities of the board or the association's officers, but reports read to the first annual meeting, which convened the following September, included one by Dud Poyner of his activities as missionary. The association proceeded with an aggressive missionary program, and when it convened for its second annual session in Shafter, it had grown so that messengers were present from 13 churches with a total membership of 1,038.

Robert W. Lackey, who was serving half time as associational missionary and half time as pastor of the First Southern Baptist Church in Bakersfield, came to the second annual meeting of the association with a proposed constitution for a state convention. During a brief adjournment of the association on the afternoon of Sept. 13, 1940, messengers from 13 churches organized the Southern Baptist General Convention of California and elected Sam Wilcoxon, president; Vester E. Wolber, recording secretary; and Robert W. Lackey, corresponding secretary-treasurer. A board of directors consisting of nine men was elected.

WILLIAM A. CARLETON

II. History and Program of General Convention. *Constitution and bylaw structure.*—The constitution designated the body as the Southern Baptist General Convention of California and provided that it consist of messengers appointed by Southern Baptist churches in California co-operating with and contributing to the work of the convention. Each church was entitled to three messengers for the first 50 members or fractional part thereof and one additional messenger for each 50 members there above or major part thereof, but no church was allowed more than 10 messengers. It declared that the object of the convention was to furnish a means by which the Southern Baptist churches in California in their sovereign capacity could work together in promoting all denominational enterprises, but it disclaimed any ecclesiastical authority or power whatever and avowed that it would never assume to write creeds or to exercise judicial or legislative control over the churches. The officers included a president, two vice-presidents, a recording secretary, an assistant recording secretary, an executive secretary-treasurer, and a historical secretary, all of whom were to be elected annually.

In order to handle the necessary affairs of the convention, provision was made for the appointment of boards, trustees, and standing committees, who were required to make reports of all matters committed to them.

Provision was made for a board of directors, consisting of the president and recording secretary of the convention and nine other members, one-third of whom would retire each year and not be eligible for re-election for a year. The board would appoint all missionaries and other workers, fix their salaries, and determine their fields of work. In case of a vacancy, the board would elect an executive secretary-treasurer whose initial duty it would be to superintend the work of the board and make a full report of the work committed to it. Meetings would be held annually and more often if deemed wise; designated funds would be applied according to the designation of the donors, and all undesignated funds would be divided and sent to the agencies of the Southern Baptist Convention according to the percentage agreement. The constitution could not be amended without a year's notice unless a proposed amendment was recommended by the board of directors three months in advance and all churches notified. The section dealing with the sovereignty and independence of churches could not be amended.

Bylaws adopted declared that the business and property of the convention would be managed and controlled by the board of directors; that an executive committee be elected to handle matters committed to it by the board; that the executive secretary-treasurer of the convention be designated as the custodian of all funds; and that the recording secretary and the president of the board be responsible for signing all contracts authorized by the board. The board of directors was given authority to provide auxiliary corporations in harmony with the convention and subject to the general control of the board of directors. No agency of the convention was permitted to launch any enterprise calling for the expenditure of money beyond regular operating expenses without the approval of the board of directors.

From the beginning the corresponding secretary was known as the executive secretary, and in 1944 the constitution appeared in the annual with executive secretary substituted for corresponding secretary. The records do not indicate that the change was ever made officially. In 1943 the convention refused to adopt an amendment recommended by the board of directors to limit representation to churches which neither received alien immersion nor practiced open communion. Instead, the messengers approved a resolution which declared that the convention was opposed to the practice of open communion and the reception of members with alien immersion. The reason advanced for rejecting the amendment was that it would conflict with an article in the constitution which forbade the convention to write creeds and exercise control over the churches.

In 1944 the constitution was amended to increase the number of board members from 9 to 15. In 1947 the board was increased to 21 members; and in 1951, to 27 members. In 1946 the constitution was amended to permit messengers from churches in border states to be seated. In 1951 after a long debate, the constitution was amended to state "that messengers shall not be seated in this convention from any church that receives persons with alien immersion or practices what is commonly called open communion."

Denominational affiliation.—At the second meeting of the board of directors after the convention was organized, it was agreed that 10 per cent of all undesignated funds be channeled through the Southern Baptist Convention's Cooperative Program and that R. W. Lackey would be sent to the 1941 meeting of the Southern Baptist Convention with a petition for recognition as a co-operating constituency. The petition was presented to the Southern Baptist Convention meeting in Birmingham, Ala., and the following were appointed a committee to study the question: Arthur James Barton (*q.v.*), John Jeter Hurt, James Burley Rounds (*q.v.*), and Walter Pope Binns.

When the Convention met in San Antonio, Tex., a year later, Binns, in the absence of the committee chairman, Barton, who was ill, moved that the committee be continued for another year and that three new members be added. Rounds brought a minority report calling for immediate recognition of California. His motion drew opposition from Dodd and other Southern Baptist leaders as well as Louis J. Julianel, pastor of the First Baptist Church, San Francisco, Calif., who was present to object to what was commonly called "the invasion of Southern Baptists into Northern Baptist territory." After a long debate the Rounds motion prevailed, and California was admitted.

Expansion and activity.—For two years after the convention was organized, the executive secretary also served as head of the Sunday school and Training Union work, but in Mar., 1941, Mrs. J. O. Crow was elected corresponding secretary of Woman's Missionary Union and B. G. Good was elected Brotherhood secretary, both serving without pay. In 1941 *Southern Baptist Stamina*, edited by G. Dallas Faulkner, was adopted as the official state Baptist paper. May 8, 1942, Faulkner was relieved as editor but did not turn over the masthead of the paper. In June, 1942, the first issue of *The California Southern Baptist* appeared as the official organ of the convention, with Lackey as editor. On Dec. 29, 1942, John A. Farmer was elected Sunday school and Training Union secretary after the board had requested financial assistance from the Baptist Sunday School Board. Others who have held the position are Ellis B. Evans, Fred J. Porter, and W. Alvis Strickland. B. N. Lummus at the same time became the convention's first general missionary. In Oct., 1943, Naomi Readdy of Texas became the first Woman's Missionary Union executive secretary to be employed and paid a salary. On Apr. 7, 1944, the board agreed to join with the Home Mission Board in a city missions program in the cities of San Diego, Los Angeles, and Oakland–San Francisco and to employ two additional missionaries to work in the 1,000-mile-long state, with the understanding that the Home Mission Board would pay all the salaries of the city superintendents and half the salaries of the missionaries.

Widespread opposition to Lackey, who had served as editor of *The California Southern Baptist* in connection with his duties as executive secretary, resulted in his not being reelected by the convention in 1944. Floyd Looney was elected editor of *The California Southern Baptist*, an eight-page monthly, and was paid a part-time salary until Dec. 18, 1946, when the paper was enlarged and he was employed full time. Atha Floyd Crittendon succeeded Lackey as executive secretary May 3, 1945, and held the position until Nov., 1950.

In Feb., 1946, the Sunday school and Training Union department had been divided and the Brotherhood work assigned to the Sunday school department. A new department of Training Union and Baptist student work was set up and headed by Russell Ware. Provision was made in the 1955 budget for an associate in the Training Union–Student Department with an understanding that he divide his time with the promotion of church music. The Brotherhood work was separated from the Sunday school department, and Julian L. Stenstrom became the first full-time Brotherhood secretary Aug. 15, 1951. A year later he took the initiative in establishing the California Southern Baptist Foundation and became its executive secretary while still serving as Brotherhood secretary. The Brotherhood began cosponsorship of the Royal Ambassadors with Woman's Missionary Union in 1952. In Sept., 1954, the Brotherhood Department and the foundation were separated, with Julian L. Stenstrom heading the foundation and Walter F. Bisbee, who had been serving as Royal Ambassador secretary, heading the Brotherhood Department. C. E. Wilbanks was elected to head a new department of evangelism Aug. 24, 1948.

Shelton G. Posey succeeded Crittendon as executive secretary Jan. 1, 1951; at the first meeting of the board after he took office, the Department of Co-operative Missions and Stewardship was set up, and A. C. Turner was elected to direct it.

A summer assembly, started by San Joaquin Valley Association in the summer of 1940, was taken over by the convention as soon as it was organized. A committee of the board of directors serves as assembly board. The chairman of the committee is also chairman of the annual program committee. A president, vice-president, and secretary of the assembly are elected annually by those who attend. Rented quarters were used each year until 1956, when the assembly was held for the first time on the convention's own grounds, known as Jenness Park.

Since July, 1951, the convention has held a contractual relationship with J. S. Bracewell, Houston, Tex., attorney, founder and owner of the Broadway Plan of Church Finance. Through this arrangement the convention assists churches in issuing bonds to finance building programs. The executive secretary of the convention serves as executive director of the Broadway Plan of Church Finance and is paid an additional salary for his services. In 1956 the convention through its board of directors was operating departments of administration, co-operative missions and stewardship, Sunday school, Training Union-Student Union-church music, Brotherhood, evangelism, and Woman's Missionary Union with a total of 21 full-time employees and several part-time workers. There were 14 general missionaries assigned to specific areas, and 44 mission pastors whose salaries were paid in part by the convention board and the Home Mission Board. The convention owned and operated *The California Southern Baptist*, a weekly publication staffed with an editor and two other full-time employees.

The total budget was $704,500, which was received through the Cooperative Program, special offerings, income of *The California Southern Baptist*, and contributions made by the Home Mission Board and the Sunday School Board of the Southern Baptist Convention.

The board of directors, by constitutional provision, manages and controls all the business and property of the convention. The board, consisting of 27 members, plus the convention's president and recording secretary, is divided into eight committees. To do the work committed to it, the board holds three regularly scheduled meetings each year and as many additional meetings as deemed wise in carrying out the work committed to it.

Auxiliary corporations.—Auxiliary corporations of the convention include Sunny Crest Children's Home, California Baptist College, and the California Southern Baptist Foundation. Golden Gate Baptist Theological Seminary, located at Berkeley, previously owned and operated by the convention, passed to the control of the Southern Baptist Convention in 1950.

Statistical summary.—In 1955, 32 associations with 542 churches reported 10,351 baptisms, 89,177 members, $5,082,702 total gifts, and $245,241.74 gifts through the Cooperative Program. The state convention budget, 1955–56, was $704,500.

FLOYD LOONEY

CALIFORNIA ASSOCIATIONS.

I. **Extant.** CALVARY. Organized Sept. 8, 1941, with five churches at First Baptist Church, Bell Gardens. In 1954, 28 churches reported 541 baptisms, 4,786 members, $260,170 total gifts, $34,991 mission gifts, $780,300 property value, and $300,034 church debt. E. RICHARD BARNES

CENTRAL VALLEY. Organized as Central Valley Association of Southern Missionary Baptists Oct. 4, 1945, in Modesto, Calif., by messengers from eight churches. Total membership of the participating churches was 790. In 1954, 23 churches reported 456 baptisms, 3,503 members, $164,954 total gifts, $18,402 mission gifts, $577,540 property value, and $227,384 church debt.

DELTA VALLEY. Organized in 1953 by eight churches from Central Valley Association. Articles of faith by J. M. Pendleton were adopted. In 1954, 10 churches reported 138 baptisms, 1,163 members, $83,876 total gifts, $6,109 mission gifts, $170,500 property value, and $74,726 church debt. BILLIE H. PATE

EAST CONTRA COSTA. Organized following the annual meeting of the Contra Costa Association in 1953 with 14 churches, which were previously affiliated with the Contra Costa Association. In 1954, 14 churches reported 158 baptisms, 1,833 members, and $117,532 total gifts of which $6,613 was given through the Cooperative Program. In 1955, 15 churches reported 326 baptisms, 2,379 members, $122,490 total gifts, and $6,262.15 Cooperative Program contributions.

FLOYD LOONEY

FEATHER RIVER. Organized in 1954 by messengers from 10 churches located in northeastern California and western Nevada, five of which had been affiliated with Sierra-Butte, one with Sacramento-Sierra. In 1954, 10 churches reported 129 baptisms, 911 members, $47,815 total gifts, $4,011 mission gifts, $91,500 property value, and $29,200 church debt. SAM A. HARVEY

FRESNO. Organized with five churches from the Fresno-Madera Association Nov. 13, 1950. A sixth church was added before the first annual meeting in 1951. Total church membership in 1950 was 1,374. In 1954, nine churches reported 223 baptisms, 2,484 members, $107,880 total gifts, $16,877 mission gifts, $425,000 property value, and $118,302 church debt.

FRESNO-MADERA. Originally called Fresno, organized at Oildale during the 1944 session of the San Joaquin Association. Messengers from 13 churches asked for letters of dismissal, and a 14th church sent messengers with a petitionary letter to the new association's first executive board meeting. Total church membership at the first annual session was 1,529. In 1954, 20 churches reported 361 baptisms, 3,020 members, $108,128 total gifts, $9,523 mission gifts, $322,350 property value, and $46,194 church debt.

J. LESLIE SMITH

GOLDEN GATE. Organized in 1949 when the New Golden Gate Baptist and the Golden Gate Southern Baptist associations merged with 15 churches in the San Francisco Bay area participating. In 1954, 27 churches reported 352 baptisms, 3,303 members, $187,000 total gifts, $22,742 mission gifts, $645,375 property value, and $232,559 church debt. CHARLES E. BUSH

HARMONY. Organized in 1951 by eight churches located along the coast north of Los Angeles to Ventura. The parent organization, Pacific Association, was meeting with the First Southern Baptist Church, Grover City, when there was a peaceable division of the territory. In 1954, 13 churches reported 183 baptisms, 1,991 members, $115,688 total gifts, $18,130 mission gifts, $338,542 property value, and $119,914 church debt. DARYL I. HEATH

LOS ANGELES. Organized by messengers from five churches Sept. 5, 1943, at Prairie Avenue Baptist Church, Hawthorne. The association began operation of California Baptist College in the First Southern Baptist Church of El Monte Sept. 18, 1950. A camp site in Orange County (since sold) was purchased Nov. 8, 1950. The association contributed member churches to Orange County, San Gabriel Valley, and San Fernando Valley associations. In 1954, 59 churches reported 1,778 baptisms, 14,622 members, $743,399 total gifts, $90,236 mission gifts, $9,332,589 property value, and $1,053,157 church debt. BOB MURPHREE

MID-WAY. Organized Sept. 26, 1950, in Turlock, Calif., with six churches from Central Valley Association. In 1954, 15 churches reported 315 baptisms, 1,836 members, $66,467 total gifts, $8,062 mission gifts, $246,750 property value, and $55,045 church debt. BILLIE H. PATE

MOJAVE DESERT. Organized in 1948 by five churches, two from Calvary and three from San Joaquin Valley associations. Churches are scattered over a 25,000 square mile area mostly in the Mohave Desert in towns and communities where American Baptists (for the most part) by a comity agreement have refrained from building churches. In 1954, 10 churches reported 248 baptisms, 1,616 members, $91,132 total gifts, $12,154 mission gifts, $296,500 property value, and $12,900 church debt.

E. RICHARD BARNES

MONTEREY. Organized following the adjournment and dissolution of Salinas–Santa Clara Association in the fall of 1947 by messengers from seven churches. In 1954, 21 churches reported 237 baptisms, 2,568 members, $120,011 total gifts, $13,501 mission gifts, $311,850 property value, and $119,448 church debt. FLOYD LOONEY

NEVADA. Organized July 20, 1955, at Tahoe Village, Lake Tahoe, Calif., by seven churches affiliated with Feather River Association in California. Churches in Nevada continue to work with the Southern Baptist General Convention of California. Nevada's first meeting was held in connection with the annual meeting of Feather River Association. Organization of the Nevada Association completed a link of Southern Baptist fellowship from Miami Beach to Puget Sound. WENDELL BRADFORD

NORTH BAY. Organized Oct. 10, 1952, at Vacaville by messengers from nine churches located in Napa and Solano counties. All the churches were previously affiliated with Redwood Empire Association. In 1954, 12 churches reported 183 baptisms, 1,696 members, $83,475 total gifts, $7,612 mission gifts, $320,616 property value, and $148,450 church debt.

NORTH COAST. Organized in 1951 along the California coast from Garberville to Crescent City by six new churches which reported 347 members at the association's first annual meeting in 1952. Most of the churches were organized by Golden Gate Seminary students and by Southern Baptist Tentmakers, a movement initiated by the Home Mission Board. In 1954, 11 churches reported 168 baptisms, 980 members, $53,234 total gifts, $5,107 mission gifts, $164,300 property value, and $71,406 church debt.

CLYDE B. SKIDMORE

ORANGE COUNTY. Organized Oct. 10 and Nov. 20, 1952, at Palm Street Baptist Church (now First Southern) of Anaheim. Nine churches participated in the organization. In 1954, 13 churches reported 308 baptisms, 1,955 members, $138,837 total gifts, $14,442 mission gifts, $399,750 property value, and $124,979 church debt.

PACIFIC. Organized in 1946 with six churches from Calvary and Fresno associations. Distances were so great that these churches found it difficult to attend meetings of the associations with which they were affiliated. Pacific had increased to 13 churches by 1951, at which time eight withdrew to form Harmony Association. In 1954, six churches reported 77 baptisms, 788 members, $35,863 total gifts, $3,857 mission gifts, $130,500 property value, and $36,048 church debt. THOMAS A. ROSE

REDWOOD EMPIRE. Organized in 1949 by nine churches located west and north of San Francisco Bay which had previously affiliated with Contra Costa Association. Since 1949 North Bay, North Coast, and Yokayo associations have been organized by churches in the area originally covered by Redwood Empire. In 1954, 11 churches reported 145 baptisms, 1,097 members, $61,525 total gifts, $6,353 mission gifts, $292,817 property value, and $99,502 church debt.

CLYDE B. SKIDMORE

SACRAMENTO-SIERRA. Organized in 1948 with seven churches located near Sacramento and in western Nevada. In 1954, 20 churches reported 335 baptisms, 2,668 members, $130,621 total gifts, $14,772 mission gifts, $508,000 property value, and $154,318 church debt. SAM A. HARVEY

SAN DIEGO. Organized and given the name Southern Baptist Association at a meeting of messengers from six churches in the First Southern Baptist Church, San Diego, Apr. 11, 1943. In 1954, 19 churches reported 717 baptisms, 5,622 members, $378,629 total gifts, $37,681 mission gifts, $1,414,488 property value, and $479,828 church debt. FLOYD LOONEY

SAN FERNANDO VALLEY. Organized Apr. 7, 1953, at the First Southern Baptist Church of North Hollywood with eight churches from Los Angeles Association and one mission. In 1954, 14 churches reported 338 baptisms, 2,536 members, $171,276 total gifts, $21,012 mission gifts, $563,950 property value, and $295,467 church debt.

BOB MURPHREE

SAN FRANCISCO–PENINSULA. Organized as San Francisco Association by eight churches, four of them from Golden Gate Association, with its first annual meeting Oct. 18, 1951, at First Southern Baptist Church, San Francisco. By 1954 the name had been changed to San Francisco–Peninsula Southern Baptist Association. In 1954, nine churches reported 192 baptisms, 1,430 members, $76,053 total gifts, $9,478 mission gifts, $314,000 property value, and $125,749 church debt. RICHARD V. UNDERWOOD

SAN GABRIEL VALLEY. Organized Oct. 14, 1954, with nine churches from Los Angeles Association. In 1955, 20 churches reported 356 baptisms, 2,726 members, $179,099 total gifts, $21,003 mission gifts, and $710,042 property value.

BOB MURPHREE

SAN JOAQUIN VALLEY SOUTHERN MISSIONARY. Organized Apr. 13, 1939, by messengers from four churches in Shafter, Oildale, Taft, and Lamont. At the second annual meeting held in Shafter in 1940 there were messengers from 13 churches located from Ontario north to Port Chicago. On the afternoon of the second day of the meeting the association adjourned to organize the Southern Baptist General Convention of California. In 1954, 19 churches reported 544 baptisms, 4,240 members, $260,909 total gifts, $28,981 mission gifts, $780,382 property value, and $164,554 church debt.

WINIFRED CLASEN

SAN JOSE SOUTHERN BAPTIST. Organized in Oct., 1947, following the dissolution of Salinas–Santa Clara Association for the purpose of forming San Jose and Monterey associations. Eight churches reported 50 baptisms, and a total membership of 415 and church property valued at $12,100 in 1948; $24,131 was given for local expenses, and $3,135 was contributed to missions. In 1955, 17 churches reported 314 baptisms, 2,089 members, and $140,050.00 total gifts, of which $9,403.71 was given through the Co-operative Program. FLOYD LOONEY

SEQUOIA. Organized late in 1949 after messengers from First Southern Baptist churches in Tulare, Visalia, Porterville, and Woodlake were refused seats at the annual meeting of the Tulare-Kings Association in Tipton because they had received members into their fellowship who were baptized upon authority of Northern Baptist churches. Total church membership in 1949 was 563. In 1954, seven churches reported 212 baptisms, 1,286 members, $42,617 total gifts, $5,610 mission gifts, $130,175 property value, and $25,585 church debt.
DARYL I. HEATH

SIERRA-BUTTE. Organized in 1948 with six cooperating churches, resulting from the decision to disband Sacramento Valley Missionary Baptist Association in order to form two associations. In 1954, 17 churches reported 304 baptisms, 2,053 members, $100,923 total gifts, $13,-948 mission gifts, $196,866 property value, and $66,453 church debt. WINIFRED CLASEN

SIERRA FOOTHILLS. Organized Oct. 25, 1954, by messengers from five churches in Placer and Nevada counties. The churches had been members of Sacramento-Sierra Association until their friendly withdrawal "because of the geographic situation." The five churches had 650 members at organization. In 1955, seven churches reported 170 baptisms, 896 members, $39,938 total gifts, $4,881 mission gifts, and $157,800 property value. SAM A. HARVEY

WEST CONTRA COSTA. Organized following the annual meeting of the Contra Costa Baptist Association of California in 1953 with 13 churches which previously affiliated with the Contra Costa Association. In 1954, 13 churches reported 351 baptisms, 3,148 members, and $138,811 total gifts, of which $11,732 was given through the Cooperative Program.
FLOYD LOONEY

YOKAYO. Organized in Oct., 1953, by nine churches from Redwood Empire Association. In 1954, 11 churches reported 131 baptisms, 710 members, $38,588 total gifts, $4,409 mission gifts, $70,500 property value, and $24,050 church debt. CLYDE B. SKIDMORE

II. Extinct. FEATHER RIVER. Organized in 1944 in northern California by two Baptist churches, Linda (which later changed its affiliation from the Southern to the Northern Baptist Convention) and Oroville (which later became Landmark). It was disbanded upon the formation of Sacramento Valley Missionary Baptist Association Oct. 2, 1945. SAM A. HARVEY

GOLDEN GATE SOUTHERN BAPTIST. Organized in 1941 by Port Chicago and Oroville churches, although 17 churches were represented by the time of the associational meeting. Most of them were near San Francisco, but a few were so far away that letters, rather than messengers, were sent to the annual meeting. In 1944 the association elected trustees and assumed financial support of Golden Gate Seminary. It dissolved in 1949 when Golden Gate Southern and New Golden Gate merged to form Golden Gate Baptist Association.

NEW GOLDEN GATE. Organized in 1948 with nine churches, all located in the San Francisco Bay area. It operated for little more than one year when it merged with Golden Gate Southern to form the Golden Gate Baptist Association. CHARLES E. BUSH

NORTHWEST. Organized Apr. 25, 1947, at Springfield, Ore., with messengers from two Washington and five Oregon churches. Former organizations in which churches in these areas worked were known as the Coastal Area Mission and later the Inter-State Baptist Mission.

Messengers from churches in Washington and Oregon were received into the fellowship of the Southern Baptist General Convention of California, Nov. 7, 1947. On Apr. 13, 1948, at Portland, Ore., messengers from 15 churches organized the Baptist General Convention of Oregon, later known as the Baptist General Convention of Oregon-Washington. Churches in Oregon and Washington continued to send 25 per cent of Cooperative Program gifts to the California convention until the Oregon-Washington body was recognized by the Southern Baptist Convention. California Southern Baptists in turn paid the salary of a missionary assigned to Washington and Oregon, and departmental workers continued to give assistance. WENDELL BRADFORD

SACRAMENTO VALLEY. Organized Oct. 2, 1945, with eight churches from a wide area of northern California. Before the second annual session the name was changed from Sacramento Valley to Sacramento Valley Missionary Association. It was dissolved at the adjournment of the fourth annual session in Oct., 1948, in order to organize Sacramento-Sierra and Sierra Butte associations. At that time it had 14 member churches with 1,306 members. SAM A. HARVEY

SALINAS–SANTA CLARA. Organized in the fall of 1946 by messengers from 11 churches which had previously cooperated with Central Valley Association. The only annual meeting of the organization was held with the First Baptist Church, Gilroy, Oct. 2–3, 1947, at which time 11 churches reported 125 baptisms and 871 members. The association disbanded to form two associations in the same territory.
FLOYD LOONEY

SAN FRANCISCO–MARIN. Organized Feb. 1, 1947, at First Baptist Church, San Rafael, with four churches from Golden Gate Association. After the first annual meeting, Oct. 16–17, 1947, two newly organized churches sought fellowship with the association. By 1949 the association had disbanded, and churches were affiliated with other associations in the San Francisco Bay area.

SAN FRANCISCO–PENINSULA. With the exact date of organization unknown, it held its first annual meeting, Oct. 13, 1950, with two churches represented, Central Baptist (now First Southern) of San Mateo and Immanuel Baptist of San

Francisco. The next year San Mateo affiliated with San Francisco Association, which has since become known as San Francisco–Peninsula Association. The original San Francisco–Peninsula Association was left with only one church, Immanuel, which has never affiliated with any other association. In 1951 the two churches reported 12 baptisms, 112 members, and $7,403 total gifts.   RICHARD V. UNDERWOOD

TULARE-KINGS. Organized June 10, 1948, with 11 churches from Fresno Association. A 12th church was added at the first annual meeting Oct. 25–26, 1948, when the churches, all located in Tulare and Kings counties, had 830 members. In 1949 the association disbanded, and most of the churches affiliated with Fresno-Madera Association.   J. LESLIE SMITH

CALIFORNIA BAPTIST COLLEGE. A four-year liberal arts college located on a 70-acre campus in Riverside, Calif., established as a result of the 1947 meeting of Los Angeles Association when a resolution was adopted which committed the association to the establishment of a college. Subsequent to the meeting the association's executive board elected five men to serve as trustees of what the board called California Baptist University and made the provision to appropriate 10 per cent of the association's income for establishment of the college.

An effort to open the school in Pasadena in 1949 with Clyde J. Garrett as president ended in confusion when a controversy arose between the association and leaders of the Southern Baptist General Convention of California. Garrett resigned in the interest of harmony, and P. Boyd Smith succeeded him as president. The school opened under the name California Baptist College in the building of the First Southern Baptist Church in El Monte, Sept. 18, 1950, with 10 faculty members and 74 students. At the request of the association, ownership and control of the institution passed to the Southern Baptist General Convention of California June 1, 1954. Early in 1955 the school was moved from El Monte to its present 70-acre campus located in Riverside. In 1955 the school had 270 students and was operating on an annual budget of $264,700.   BYRON F. TODD

CALIFORNIA SOUTHERN BAPTIST, THE. First published in June, 1942, as Volume I, Number 8, after the board of directors of the Southern Baptist General Convention of California had failed to secure the masthead of *Southern Baptist Stamina* from G. Dallas Faulkner, recently dismissed as editor.

The volume and issue numbers of *The Stamina* were incorporated in the first issue of *The California Southern Baptist*. The paper, a four-page monthly, was edited by R. W. Lackey, executive secretary of the state convention, until 1944 when Floyd Looney became part-time editor while serving as pastor of First Southern Baptist Church in Tulare. Previous to that several efforts had been made to employ a full-time editor and to increase frequency of publication.

In 1944 circulation was less than 1,000, but by early 1946 circulation had doubled, and the paper was issued bimonthly. In the meantime Looney resigned his pastorate, devoting half time to the paper and serving as vice-president and field representative of Golden Gate Seminary which the state convention adopted in 1945. On Jan. 1, 1947, Looney was asked to serve on a full-time basis as editor of the paper, which was increased to 16 pages and issued bimonthly. The paper, which has a present circulation of 21,000, has been published weekly since Jan., 1954.   W. B. TIMBERLAKE

CALIFORNIA SOUTHERN BAPTIST STATE ASSEMBLY. Southern Baptists in California held their first summer assembly at Greenhorn Mountain, 55 miles northeast of Bakersfield, in 1940, a few weeks before the state convention was organized. That year it was sponsored by the San Joaquin Valley Association, but the next year it was taken over by the state convention. The attendance the first year was 65; the following year it was 256. Each year through 1944, the assembly met at Greenhorn, using facilities owned by Kern County. In 1945 Camp Sierra, owned by the Methodists and located in the high Sierras 65 miles east of Fresno, was rented for the assembly, which had an attendance of 500. The same year an effort to purchase a half-million dollar Y.W.C.A. camp known as Asilomar located near Monterey failed because of a controversy with some Northern Baptists from New York who were members of the Y.W.C.A. board. The assembly in 1946 was held in the Y.W.C.A. property where, due to a reduced attendance, it operated at a loss to the convention.

From 1947 to 1954, the assembly was held each year at Beulah Park near Santa Cruz, in property which was rented from the Nazarenes. In 1955 the assembly was held on the campus of California Baptist College at Riverside. An effort in 1947 to purchase an abandoned army camp at Watsonville from the War Assets Administration for one dollar failed.

In 1953 Central Valley Association gave the convention 160 acres of land located in the high Sierras near Sonora, with the understanding that it be developed as a permanent assembly site. In 1954 development plans were projected for the site, officially named Jenness Park Baptist State Assembly.   ELMER L. GRAY

CALL TO FOREIGN MISSION SERVICE. Southern Baptists have believed consistently in a special divine call to foreign mission service. Biblical support for this belief is found in such passages as Acts 13:2 and Galatians 1:15–16. Emphasis is commonly given to the effective call, the individual's subjective assurance concerning God's will for him, such an assurance being held as prerequisite to fruitful missionary service. There has been comparatively little attention to the method or process used by God to induce a sense of call. Southern Baptists would generally agree, however, that many different agencies and influences may contribute to awareness of a personal call. Fluctuations in the number of persons professing a call to foreign mission service reflect the changing circumstances of Southern Baptist history and the measure of effectiveness of those agencies and means which should evoke the sense of call.

Historically there has been considerable latitude of interpretation among Southern Baptists concerning the relationship of the call to foreign mission service to the call to special Christian service other than foreign missions. One extreme view is that all ministers are under obligation to serve abroad unless there is some evident objective hindrance. The opposite extreme view is that no one should become a foreign missionary unless he feels such strong compulsion as to make him unable to serve in the homeland. The call to foreign missions usually is felt as a distinctive call, often growing out of an earlier general call to Christian service.

BIBLIOGRAPHY: J. W. Crawley, "The Call to Foreign Missions among Southern Baptists, 1845–1945" (1947).

JAMES WINSTON CRAWLEY

CALLAWAY, ENOCH (b. Wilkes County, Ga., Sept. 14, 1792; d. Sept. 12, 1859). Minister. He came from a family which has furnished Georgia and the South with 40 Baptist preachers in many generations. Most of them were descended from Thomas Callaway, an Episcopal vestryman in Virginia. Enoch Callaway and his preacher cousins, Joshua and Francis, were born in Wilkes County during George Washington's first presidential term. Enoch was the son of John and the grandson of Thomas Callaway. He was baptized into the Sardis Baptist Church at 16 years of age, ordained by the same church on Nov. 7, 1823, and served it for 32 years as pastor. His other churches were Rehoboth, County Line, and Beaverdam in Wilkes County, and Baird's and Milltown in Oglethorpe County. He had little formal education other than what he learned in the "old field schools" of his childhood. He and all the other Callaways were taught by their fathers to believe not only that salvation is by grace through faith in Jesus Christ, but also that God is "holy and just," that there is "a hell to be saved from and a heaven to be saved to."

Enoch married Martha Reeves on Dec. 5, 1811. Of their 14 children, four died in childhood. Two sons became Georgia Baptist preachers: Abner Reeves Callaway, who was the father of Fuller E. Callaway, the La Grange industrialist; and Brantly Mercer Callaway, who was for 35 years successor to his father as pastor of the church at Sardis, and for 20 years a trustee of Mercer University, serving for six years as chairman of the board. Five grandsons of Enoch became Georgia Baptist preachers: John Sanders Callaway, John F. Cheney, William Binns, Pat Rhodes, and L. S. Barrett. A great-grandson is Walter Pope Binns, president of William Jewell College in Liberty, Mo., since 1943. Though he was tedious and unattractive as a speaker, Enoch was a faithful pastor who "excelled in exhortation." His sermons "combined the doctrinal, practical, and experimental." Of rugged character, he was a man of strong moral convictions, thoroughly missionary in outlook.

T. F. CALLAWAY

CALLING. See VOCATION.

CALVINISM. Calvinism is the system of theology of John Calvin (1509–64), whose basic doctrine is the sovereignty of God. Man's first duty is to do God's will. This will is supremely presented in the Scriptures which are interpreted through the Holy Spirit. God in Christ redeems the elect who live by faith in union with Christ and are thus enabled to do God's will. Calvinist Baptists, or Particular Baptists, came out of the Jacob-Lathrop congregation in London in 1633. In 1644 they drew up in 52 articles a confession of faith accepting Calvinistic teachings and embracing the immersion of believers as the only valid baptism.

See also PREDESTINATION.

BIBLIOGRAPHY: J. Calvin, *The Institutes of the Christian Religion* (1895).

CHARLES A. TRENTHAM

CAMEROONS, BAPTISTS IN. About 1845 an English Baptist missionary, Alfred Saker, started work in the area of Africa called the Cameroons with the Baptist Missionary Society (Great Britain), and he had considerable success. Since World War I, Baptist work has been carried on in French territory by Baptist missionaries from France, working in close conjunction with the interdenominational Paris Missionary Society. In British territory the sponsoring missionary body is the North American Baptist General Conference (the former German-American group). The Baptist convention in French Cameroun is called the Union of Baptist Churches in Cameroun (*Union des Eglises Baptistes du Cameroun*). The membership figure in 1953 was 10,930. (This union should not be confused with a dissident group calling itself *Eglise Baptiste Camerounaise*, which claims nearly as many members.) The Baptist churches in British Cameroons are organized separately as the Cameroons Baptist Convention. The membership in 1955 was reported as approximately 15,000. The latest development is the organization of the European Baptist Missionary Society and the start of completely new work among primitive people in an unevangelized area of French Cameroun. This work is being pioneered by Maurice Farelly and his wife, who is a medical doctor.

ARNOLD T. OHRN

CAMP CARSON. Since 1949 an assembly of Tennessee Baptists. It was established after the adoption, at the 1946 session of the Tennessee Baptist Convention, of a directive authorizing its executive board to purchase two camp sites, one in the eastern and one in the western sections of the state. Camp Carson is located at Carson Springs, Cocke County, six miles from Newport, Tenn., and serves the eastern section of the state. The camp is comprised of 150 acres, 30 acres of which were given by Ben Hooper and 120 acres given by Charles T. Rhyne. In 1955 there were two large dormitories adequately caring for 235 campers, a dining hall, caretaker's home, staff house, and the stone Stokley Chapel with seating capacity of 1,000. The summer program is sponsored by the various departments of the convention: W.M.U. and Auxiliary organizations, Sunday school, Training Union, Brotherhood, and Baptist Student Union. The camps were first suggested by the Tennessee W.M.U. and their existence is due largely to the hard work and gifts of that organization. The camp program of the convention, which program includes Camp Linden in the western section, receives $20,000 annually from the W.M.U. and $4,640 from the state mission board.

Since the inception of the camp program in 1949 at Camp Carson and in 1950 at Camp Linden and through the summer program of 1954, the aggregate attendance has been estimated at over 20,000 with 200 professions of faith and 600 dedications. It has been estimated by the business manager's office of the convention that Tennessee Baptists have assets in the amount of $400,000 in these two camps.

HERBERT C. GABHART

CAMP COPASS. One of two Texas encampments organized in 1948. It is located near Denton, Tex., in District 12. J. E. ROTH

CAMP GARAYWA, MISSISSIPPI. Located south of Clinton, Miss., this camp, which is owned and operated by Mississippi Woman's Missionary Union, opened in 1947. It consists of 26 well-constructed frame buildings—an auditorium, activities building, 18 cabins, 3 bath houses, a canteen, and custodian's house. Recreational facilities include a large swimming pool. The name Garaywa (pronounced Gay-ray-way) is a combination of the initial letters of the three auxiliary groups sponsored by Woman's Missionary Union, and it typifies the purpose of the camp. The camp program begun in 1935 by the women's organization in Mississippi grew to the point that it became necessary to provide adequate, permanent facilities or discontinue the camping program, which by 1940 was reaching annually more than 2,500 young people. Thus plans were made in 1942 to provide a permanent camp site, for which Mississippi College gave a 40-acre tract of wooded land. Over a period of five years the Mississippi Woman's Missionary Union contributed $60,295.07 in a "beyond the goal" drive of the State Mission Week of Prayer offering. A campaign in 1946–47 resulted in gifts totaling $109,279.19. Construction began in 1946 for the first camping season the following year.

In a 14-week camping period weekly attendance averages 200, and in addition to this summer program for young people's organizations, the camp has become the meeting place for adult leadership groups—state, district, associational, and local officers. It has also been used by other denominational groups, including Baptist Student Union, Training Union, Sunday school, Brotherhood, pastors, and associational missionaries. Heated buildings make possible year-round use of the camp, which is valued at $225,919.79. EDWINA ROBINSON

CAMP JOY. Opened in 1952 at Brownsville, Ky., owned and supported by the Baptists of the southern region. Camps are conducted five weeks annually promoting missionary education and denominational activities, emphasizing Royal Ambassador and Girls' Auxiliary work. Facilities are available to co-operating churches in the southern region. ELDRED M. TAYLOR

CAMP KAVANAUGH. A Methodist camp at Crestwood, Ky., rented for one week each year from 1946 until 1950 by the central region Woman's Missionary Union for Royal Ambassador and Girls' Auxiliary camps. The 1950 camp was held at Cedarmore in conjunction with Long Run Association's camp. Since 1951 central region Woman's Missionary Union has again been renting the facilities of Camp Kavanaugh.

ELDRED M. TAYLOR

CAMP LINDEN. Since 1950 an assembly of Tennessee Baptists. It was established after the adoption, at the 1946 session of the Tennessee Baptist Convention, of a directive authorizing its executive board to purchase two camp sites, one in the eastern and one in the western sections of the state. The camp is located on Buffalo River in Perry County, eight miles from Linden, Tenn., and serves the western area of the state. It is composed of 100 acres of land, a large dormitory to accommodate 200, small dormitory, staff house, dining hall, open-air auditorium, caretaker's house, conference house, and many recreational facilities.

The summer program is sponsored by the various departments of the convention: W.M.U. and Auxiliary organizations, Sunday school, Training Union, Brotherhood, and Baptist Student Union. The camps were first suggested by the Tennessee W.M.U., and their existence is due largely to the hard work of that organization. The camp program of the convention, which program also includes Camp Carson in the eastern part of the state, receives $20,000 annually from the W.M.U. and $4,640 from the state mission board.

Since the inception of the Camp program in 1949 at Camp Carson and in 1950 at Camp Linden and through the summer program of 1954, the aggregate attendance has been estimated at over 20,000 with 200 professions of faith and 600 dedications. It has been estimated by the business manager's office of the convention that Tennessee Baptists have assets in the amount of $400,000 in these two camps.

HERBERT C. GABHART

CAMPAIGN TALKING POINTS. A magazine published by the Conservation Commission of the Southern Baptist Convention for the purpose of publicizing the 75 Million Campaign. There are 10 issues on file in the offices of the Executive Committee of the Southern Baptist Convention. The first is dated Sept. 15, 1923, and the last Nov. 7, 1924. The masthead carries the explanation, "Sent to preachers only." Frank E. Burkhalter, publicity director of the Southern Baptist 75 Million Campaign, served as editor.   ALBERT MCCLELLAN

CAMPBELL, JAMES ARCHIBALD (b. Harnett County, N. C., Jan. 13, 1862; d. Fayetteville, N. C., Mar. 8, 1934). Educator, son of Archibald Neill and Humy (Betts) Campbell. He was educated at local short-term schools, Oak Dale Academy, and Wake Forest College, returning after years of teaching to graduate at Wake Forest with his two sons (A.B., 1911; D.D., 1926). His life was given to the education of poor boys and girls. With that in mind, on Jan. 5, 1877, he started a one-room school, about 12 miles from his home, with 16 students. This became Buie's Creek Academy, later Buie's Creek Junior College, later Campbell College. He was ordained to the Baptist ministry in 1886, and served as pastor of Hector's Creek, Friendship, Buie's Creek (for nearly 40 years), Spring Branch (for about 44 years), Dunn, Benson, Holly Springs, Mt. Tabor, Erwin, Coats, and Green Level churches. A versatile individual, for years he edited *The Little River Record;* was clerk of the Little River Association for 52 years; served as president of the Bank of Buie's Creek; filled the presidency of the board of trustees of Wake Forest College; led in the movement that prohibited the sale of liquor in Harnett County and then in all of North Carolina; farmed as a hobby, and used his profits for the support of needy students. He married Cornelia Pearson in 1890. His children were Leslie Hartwell, Arthur Carlyle, and Elizabeth Pearson (Mrs. A. E. Lynch). In frequent demand as a speaker, he had an irrepressible wit and stock of common sense, combined with sympathy and understanding, that touched the minds and hearts of his hearers. He remained president of Campbell College until his death and was buried in Buie's Creek cemetery.

See also CAMPBELL COLLEGE.

LESLIE HARTWELL CAMPBELL

CAMPBELL, JESSE HARRISON (b. McIntosh County, Ga., Feb. 10, 1807; d. Columbus, Ga., Apr. 16, 1888). Pastor and author. Converted in 1822 at the age of 16, Campbell began immediately to preach and for nearly half a century was pastor of Baptist churches, chiefly in middle Georgia. An interested and active participant in the organized life of Georgia Baptists, he was a trustee of Mercer University for more than 30 years beginning in 1838, and was instrumental in founding Cuthbert Female College and Marshall College. Primarily an evangelist, he was a zealous advocate of missions, serving for five years as agent for the Southern Baptist Foreign Mission Board in Georgia. At the state convention of 1877 he introduced the resolution that led to the establishment of the state mission board in Atlanta.

He was a frequent contributor to religious periodicals, and his *Georgia Baptists: Historical and Biographical* (1874) was the first published history of the Baptist denomination in Georgia. In 1877 Mercer University conferred on him the D.D. degree upon his retirement from the active pastorate. Campbell was for four years (1843-47) state agent for the deaf and dumb and was influential in persuading the legislature to provide a school for mutes at Cave Springs in 1848. During his years of retirement in Columbus, Ga., he was popularly known as "the servant of God's poor" because of his benevolent activities among the underprivileged of the city. He was buried at Columbus.

BIBLIOGRAPHY: [S. Boykin], *History of the Baptist Denomination in Georgia with Biographical Compendium* (1881). *Christian Index* (Apr. 19, 1888). S. G. Hillyer, *Reminiscences of Georgia Baptists* (1902). B. D. Ragsdale, *Story of Georgia Baptists* (1932-38).   HAROLD L. MCMANUS

CAMPBELL, ROBERT CLIFFORD (b. Cleveland County, N. C., July 2, 1888; d. Galax, Va., Mar. 25, 1954). Denominational leader, pastor, writer. Son of R. P. and Lettie (Melton) Campbell, he finished Boiling Springs (N. C.) High School in 1911, attended Wake Forest College, 1911-12, and graduated from Carson-Newman College in 1915. In 1921 Campbell attended Southwestern Seminary. Ordained in 1910, he married Ella Myra McCurry on May 24, 1911.

Campbell served 10 different churches as pastor: Clifton, S. C.; Second Baptist Church, Shelby, N. C.; First Baptist churches in Canton, Scotland Neck, and Hickory, N. C.; in Belton and Lubbock, Tex.; in Columbia, S. C.; and in Little Rock, Ark.; and Popular Springs Church, N. C. His published works include numerous religious booklets and pamphlets and 14 books: *Heaven or Hell, Which?* (1931); *Modern Evils* (1933); *Universal Message* (1936); *Youth and Yokes* (1938); *The Coming Revival* (1939); *Militant Christianity* (1940); *A Quest for God* (1941); *Around the Cross* (1942); *Rocks of the Ages* (1944); *Keeping the Foundations* (1945); *The Christ of the Centuries* (1947); *The Right Way* (1949); *God's Plan* and *How Firm a Foundation* (1954).

Campbell, elected vice-president of the Southern Baptist Convention in 1953, served as executive secretary of the Baptist General Convention of Texas from 1936 to 1941. He had a major role in starting two of Southern Baptists' greatest movements, one of which was stewardship and tithing. His booklet on stewardship entitled *God's Plan*, widely read and adopted by many churches, sold approximately 500,000 copies. Campbell was also originator of the annual statewide evangelistic conference which spread to other states in the Southern Baptist Convention. W. M. SHAMBURGER

CAMPBELL COLLEGE. A four-year junior college located 30 miles south of Raleigh, N. C., founded with 16 students on Jan. 5, 1887, as Buie's Creek Academy by James Archibald Campbell (q.v.). The school was owned, operated, and financed by its founder until 1925. The academy grew rapidly from its beginning in a one-room building until 1900, when 310 students from 27 North Carolina counties and three other states assembled in a large three-story structure. On Dec. 20, however, fire destroyed the entire plant except for a large, open tabernacle used solely for commencement exercises. "To the Stars Through Difficulties," the school motto, characterized efforts of friends who by 1903 had erected a three-story brick administration building on the original site, now known as Kivett Building. Other buildings were added by 1926 on the 32-acre campus: Treat Dormitory for girls, Pearson Building for the lower grades, Layton Dormitory for boys, Old Gymnasium, Carrie Rich Memorial Library, and D. Rich Administration Building. In 1925 the state convention purchased from the founder the entire plant at approximately $28,000, with the understanding that Campbell would pay off a debt of $20,000 still due on Layton Dormitory.

After North Carolina's statewide public high school system was established in the 1920's, Campbell secured permission from North Carolina Baptists to convert the institution into a junior college. Buie's Creek Junior College, as it was called, began in 1926, and its name was changed by the convention to Campbell College in 1927.

After Campbell died in 1934, his son, Leslie Hartwell Campbell, succeeded him as president. His first major achievement was obtaining accreditation for Campbell College by the Southern Association of Colleges and Secondary Schools in 1941. World War II seriously curtailed enrolments, and postwar years brought on problems of overcrowding. In the meantime internal structural changes included the separation of the public school from the junior college and dropping the first two years of high school, leaving a standard four-year junior college.

The entire plant was valued at $1,500,000 in 1954, and endowment, listed at cost price in the 1954 audit, amounted to $178,514.01. Operating on a budget of $431,246.44 in 1954–55, Campbell College had an enrolment of 641 for the regular session, or 782 including summer school.

LESLIE H. CAMPBELL

CAMPBELLISM. A movement which stems from an early 19th-century group of preachers in Kentucky, Ohio, and Pennsylvania who began a "reform" movement to "return to the simplicity and authority of the Scriptures." They rejected "man-made creeds" and institutions, which produce religious multiplicity, and urged all Christians to unite in strict adherence to the simple teachings of the Bible. An outstanding leader was Alexander Campbell, whose Irish-born father, Thomas Campbell, seceded from Presbyterianism to found "the Christian Association of Washington" (Pennsylvania) on Aug. 17, 1809, a group which professed to speak or keep silence in strict accord with the Scriptures. The association constituted itself, on May 4, 1811, at the Brush Run Church, which later ordained Alexander Campbell to the ministry. Alexander, Thomas, their wives, and three church members were immersed and became Baptists. For 17 years thereafter Brush Run Church belonged to the Redstone Baptist Association, though with mounting tension. Separation came in 1830.

The powerful preaching of Alexander Campbell, Barton W. Stone, and others, spread the doctrines in several states. Some Baptist ministers embraced Campbellism; occasionally whole congregations joined, or large majorities, as in the case of the First Baptist Church in Nashville. The most influential Campbellite doctrine was baptism for the remission of sins, following "a good confession" (i.e., of the divinity of Jesus) and the promise to obey the Gospels. By mid-19th century, the Christian church was the fourth largest in Tennessee, preceded only by Baptists, Methodists, and Presbyterians. Many Baptist bodies that followed Campbell felt that they were joining a reformation, not changing their denomination. Campbell's followers were not much affected by the issue of slavery.

The Reformation split into two wings, the progressives favoring missionary societies and instrumental music in church, and the conservatives opposing these additions. By 1936 the progressive Campbellites had in Tennessee alone 116 churches with 23,899 members, and property worth $1,731,236.

Campbellism was largely Arminian in doctrine, holding that "a saved person could be lost if he did not endure to the end." Two of their basic Scripture passages, often quoted in defense of their doctrine, were Acts 2:38 and John 3:5.

See also CHURCHES OF CHRIST and DISCIPLES OF CHRIST.

BIBLIOGRAPHY: W. E. Garrison and A. T. DeGroot, *The Disciples of Christ* (1948). E. C. Routh, "Campbellism and the Church of Christ," *Baptist and Reflector* (Jan. 26, 1956). R. PAUL CAUDILL

CAMPBELLSVILLE COLLEGE. Baptist junior college located in Campbellsville, Ky. Its forerunner was Russell Creek Academy, which opened in Sept., 1907, as an institution of the Russell Creek Baptist Association. Organized by those who wanted a school where the Bible would be taught daily, the school has kept the Bible at the center of its curriculum.

First head of the school was W. G. Welbourn, who had the title of principal. By 1956 the college had a faculty and administrative staff of 25 and an enrolment of 373 full-time students. Graduates to that date totaled 2,172.

BAYLOR

UNIVERSITY,

TEXAS

. . . Waco

. . . Dallas

. . . Houston

BAYLOR UNIVERSITY (q.v.), Texas. Founded in 1845. Top: Pat Neff Hall, main campus, Waco. Center: College of Dentistry, Dallas. Bottom: College of Medicine, Houston. Total enrolment approximately 7,000, property valued at almost $27,000,000.

CARSON-NEWMAN COLLEGE (q.v.), Jefferson City, Tenn. Founded 1851, enrolment 2,184 for 1955–56 session. Administration building pictured is one of 27 structures on campus valued at approximately $2,600,000.

The elevation of the Russell Creek Academy to the rank of a junior college was authorized at the annual meeting of the General Association of Baptists in Kentucky, in Covington, in Nov., 1923. As a result of this action, legal requirements were met for changing the name of the school to Campbellsville College, in 1924, and it has since been operated by Kentucky Baptists.

In 1933 the college was admitted to membership in the Kentucky Association of Colleges and Secondary Schools organized that year. It has been accredited by the Southern Association of Colleges and Secondary Schools since 1949, and it is a member of the American Association of Junior Colleges.

Campbellsville College is coeducational, and it offers the liberal arts courses which prepare its graduates to go on to senior colleges, with no loss of credit, to work toward A.B. and B.S. degrees. Pre-professional courses are also offered in several fields, along with terminal courses for those who do not plan to continue their education beyond junior college.

In 1956 the college, led by John Maurice Carter (1911–   ), who has headed the school since 1950, established the Campbellsville College Student Industries. Through the industrial program the college can now provide employment for scores of students who find it necessary to earn part or all of their expenses while attending college.

In recent years the college has had a close working relationship with the Kentucky State Education Department and has developed a strong teacher-training program. A high percentage of its graduates teach in the public schools of the state.

In 1955–56 the college buildings and grounds were valued at $1,000,000, including the administration building, a men's dormitory, two dormitories for women, a chapel, a gymnasium, and a student inn. The endowment at this time was $74,076.

For the school year of 1955–56, Campbellsville had an operating budget of $139,949. Of this, $42,879 was received from Kentucky Baptists; $18,004 from donations; $76,745 from student tuition and fees; and $2,321 from endowment.

ERWIN L. MCDONALD

CAMPOS COLEGIO. See BRAZIL, MISSION IN.

CANADIAN ACADEMY. A coeducational school at Canadian, Tex. It came under the control of the convention in 1905. Lack of patronage necessitated its being closed in 1913.

RUPERT N. RICHARDSON

CANADIAN BAPTIST FOREIGN MISSION BOARD. Organized May 10, 1912, a year after royal assent to legislation necessary for the act of incorporation had been given. Thus Canadian Baptists from coast to coast united in their overseas missionary enterprise. Canadian Baptist missionary interest went back 97 years, however, when in 1814 at Chester, Nova Scotia, an offering was received for the "poor heathen" amounting to $24.22. In 1845 the first Canadian Baptist missionary volunteers R. E. Burpee and his wife went to Burma under the Triennial Convention. Missionaries served abroad under American boards until 1873 when John McLaurin saw an opportunity for a Canadian Baptist effort in unoccupied Telugu territory in India and wrote home describing it. The convention replied favorably and established the Telugu mission, which now has 160 churches, 45,000 members, 428 schools, a theological seminary, a Bible school for women, 7 hospitals, and 3 dispensaries. In 1898 the Canadian Baptist Board opened a Bolivian mission which includes at present 32 churches, 22 schools, a prosperous rural project, a theological seminary, and a powerful radio station. On Jan. 1, 1954, the board took over the Angola Evangelical Mission in Portuguese West Africa. Canadian Baptists, numbering 143,000, support 124 active and 47 retired missionaries, with an annual budget of approximately $550,000.

H. S. HILLYER

CANON, HISTORY OF. OLD TESTAMENT. *Meaning of the term.*—The English word "canon" is related to the Hebrew word *qaneh*, "reed," and the Greek word *kanon*, "rod." The concept of a reed or straight rod led to the meaning of anything standardized or normative. It was not until the fourth century A.D., however, that the term was used by Athanasius as indicative of the collection of written material which was the standard of faith and doctrine. Even though the word itself was not used in regard to the books of the Old Testament, the concept of writings which were normative for faith and teaching is ancient. This concept is conveyed by the use of terms such as "Scripture," "Holy Scripture," and "Scriptures" in referring to the books of the Old Testament.

Books contained in the Old Testament canon. —The 39 books of the Old Testament canon are divided into three distinct divisions, recognized as varying in their authority for Hebrew worship. They are known as Torah, Prophets, and Writings.

The Law (Torah) was revered more highly than any other literature. The five books of Law are known under the titles of Genesis, Exodus, Leviticus, Numbers, and Deuteronomy. The Prophets are divided into three sections. The earlier Prophets are Joshua, Judges, I and II Samuel, I and II Kings. The later Prophets are Isaiah, Jeremiah, and Ezekiel. The Twelve Prophets are Hosea, Joel, Amos, Obadiah, Jonah, Micah, Nahum, Habakkuk, Zephaniah, Haggai, Zechariah, and Malachi. The Writings contain the writings of the wise men who, being led by God, brought wisdom to bear upon the problems and thoughts of mankind. These books are Psalms, Proverbs, Job, Song of Songs, Ruth, Lamentations, Ecclesiastes, Esther, Daniel, Ezra, Nehemiah, I and II Chronicles.

Tradition of writing and canon.—Josephus

preserves a tradition that the scriptures of the canon were written between the time of Moses and Ezra. According to this tradition the era for the Old Testament canonical literature was between Moses and King Artaxerxes. Furthermore, the authors of the books were Moses, Joshua, Samuel, David, Jeremiah, Ezra, the men of Hezekiah, and the Great Synagogue.

In 4 Esdras, Ezra is given a more important part in the canonization than Josephus gives him. After the Scriptures were destroyed at the destruction of Jerusalem in 587 B.C., it was necessary for them to be rewritten. It is stated that Ezra dictated 94 books to his assistants in 457 B.C. Of the 94 books, he published the first 24, which coincide with the 22 books of the Jewish canon. Such traditions held sway in many circles until the 18th century, but facts have not been produced to support this tradition.

Time of canonization.—The fixation of the three groups of Scripture indicate three separate periods of canonization. Thus, canonization was a process reached by consent rather than by a council-inspired edict.

The fact that the Samaritans recognized only the Pentateuch and rejected the other writings of the Jews indicates clearly that the Law was canonized prior to the break between the two groups. This schism is dated in and after the time of Nehemiah (444–432 B.C.). Such acceptance shows the date at which the first section of canonization was finished. How much earlier it was recognized is a subject for debate.

The second division of the Old Testament canon received recognition by *c.* 200 B.C. Jesus ben Sirach wrote Ecclesiasticus *c.* 190 B.C., in which he took notice of the "Law and the Prophets." This notice indicates a growing process, in that the body of Prophets was added to the previously recognized Torah. Such process may have been finished much earlier but definitely not later than *c.* 200 B.C.

The identification of the third division as authoritative writing is not so positive as that of the others. In the prologue to the book of Ecclesiasticus, the grandson of ben Sirach mentioned in 132 B.C. "the Law and the Prophets and the rest of the books." This statement certainly implies a type of collection which was regarded as authoritative, even though the terminology does not define accurately the contents. However, I and II Maccabees (*c.* 125–70 B.C.) and Philo (*c.* 20 B.C. to A.D. 50) show a definitely formed canon which was divided into three sections as "law, prophets, and writings." The repeated references in the New Testament to such a body of writings support the evidence furnished by noncanonical writings in establishing the conviction that the canon was a definite body of literature prior to *c.* A.D. 100.

The closing of the canon.—The Old Testament canon was not officially declared closed by any synod or council. However, the council of Jamnia, *c.* A.D. 100, was important as one of the last official bodies to work on the problem of canonization. This council did not seek to determine the exact and comprehensive list of books in their proper order. On the other hand, it discussed the books of Ezekiel, Proverbs, Song of Songs, Ecclesiastes, and Esther as to their right to remain there. The books of Chronicles also came into the discussion and were given approval.

The writings were not formulated as a standard in faith and doctrine in one year or in one generation. The process through which this was accomplished has not been clearly ascertained, but there are some definite principles upon which canonization was determined.

Principles of canonization.—The place which an account of history or prophetic utterance gained in the worship life of the people insured its perpetuation. Some unusual and effective purpose was necessary to bring about the actual writing of an account in the time of scarcity of scribes and scribal materials. Much material was preserved in the repeated retelling of stories and events which highlighted the closeness of the families, tribes, and clans. Each new crisis presented an occasion for recounting the purpose of God for the people as revealed in their history. As the people met disaster and catastrophe, their spiritual leaders authenticated their messages by historical records. The effective use of important events, such as the Exodus and the Exile, enhanced the value of the account in the eyes of kin and community. Thus, adding to the recognized fact of God's inspiration, the account gained a hallowed function in worship.

Much material was preserved, as times progressed, in actual written documents. Only those documents which were authoritative and valuable could be carried throughout their history. These documents were priceless for reasons other than material content. They were valuable by virtue of the individual through whom God sent the messages. This is more emphatically seen in the prophets. Men of God were inspired to proclaim a message which was recognized as authoritative because it was "thus saith the Lord." This message, brought through a man who knew he was a messenger of God and who was recognized by the people as such, was immediately accorded a place of respect, reverence, and use in their worship.

It can be easily recognized that the worship patterns of the Hebrew people match the periods of history through which the canon developed. There is a definite relationship between the national history and the national worship. The acts of the person, the tribe, or the nation, the words of the leaders in war and worship, and the specific manifestations of God's power and grace toward the Hebrews were honored, respected, revered in use, and eventually canonized.

BIBLIOGRAPHY: H. C. Alleman and E. E. Flack, *Old Testament Commentary* (1948). A. Bentzen, *Introduction to the Old Testament* (1948). F. Buhl, *Canon and Text of the Old Testament* (1892). E. E.

Flack, "Canon of Scripture," *The Text, Canon, and Principal Versions of the Bible* (1956). A. S. Geden, *Introduction to the Hebrew Bible* (1909). A. Jeffery, "The Canon of the Old Testament," *The Interpreter's Bible*, Vol. I (1952). G. Ostborn, *Cult and Canon* (1951). H. H. Rowley, *The Growth of the Old Testament* (1950). H. E. Ryle, *The Canon of the Old Testament* (1925).   JOHN JOSEPH OWENS

CAPERTON, ALEXANDER COTTON (b. Jackson County, Ala., Jan. 4, 1831; d. Leitchfield, Ky., Jan. 18, 1901). Educator, preacher, editor. He received his education in the public schools, at Mississippi College, graduating in 1856, and at Rochester Theological Seminary, graduating in 1858. He was ordained in 1858 by the church at Clinton, Miss. During the Civil War he turned to the farm to support his family; after the war he held pastorates in Memphis, Tenn., Mayfield, Ky., and Evansville, Ind. In 1871 he became coeditor, then editor and proprietor, of *The Western Recorder*. He was also editor and proprietor of the *American Baptist*, a paper published in Louisville, Ky., for Negroes. He established a book and publishing house in Louisville and was an active member of the missionary and Sunday school boards of his denomination in Kentucky. He spent the later years of his life on his farm near Leitchfield, Ky., where he combined farming with preaching at destitute places near by. Caperton was married and had seven children, one of whom, Mary Ellen Caperton, with her husband Thomas Brown Craighead, was a missionary for many years in southeastern Europe. Their son, Walter Eugene Craighead, and his wife became missionaries, serving in Russia and South America.   LEO T. CRISMON

CAREY, WILLIAM (b. Paulerspury, Northampton, England, Aug. 17, 1761; d. Serampore, India, June 9, 1834). Father of modern missions. He was the author of *An Enquiry into the Obligations of Christians to Use Means for the Conversion of the Heathens* (1792); preacher of the sermon at the Baptist associational meeting in Nottingham, May 31, 1792, on text of Isaiah 54:2–3 and the theme, "Expect great things from God; attempt great things for God"; and leader in founding The Particular Baptist Society for Propagating the Gospel among the Heathen (later named the Baptist Missionary Society) at Kettering on Oct. 2, 1792, which in turn launched the "society method" of missionary support and direction, and the whole modern evangelical missionary endeavor. With physician John Thomas he went to India under the appointment of the Baptist Missionary Society, devoting 41 of his 73 years to India without a return to his homeland. He was an able linguist and translator; a botanist of considerable reputation; and a missionary statesman par excellence.

Carey, who was born into a devout Anglican home, had an avid appetite for books. He was influenced most by the *Voyages of Captain Cook*, Guthrie's *Geographical Grammar*, the biographies of John Eliot and David Brainerd, and the Bible. Debates with fellow apprentice shoemaker John Warr, a Nonconformist, and a guilty conscience over a petty dishonesty led to a conversion experience in 1778. Three years later he became a charter member of the Congregational church at Hackleton. His contact with John Sutcliff of the Particular (Calvinist) Baptists and study of the Greek New Testament led to the conviction that baptism must be by immersion following a confessional experience. John Ryland baptized him in the River Nene on Oct. 5, 1783, and he later joined a Baptist church (Olney). He pastored successively at Moulton and Leicester, supplementing his meager income by teaching school and making shoes. During these years he acquired a profound linguistic skill through the study of Hebrew, Latin, Greek, French, and Dutch. Burdened with the "vastness of heathenism" and the "urgent duty which rested upon the Christian church to supply that need," he prepared the *Enquiry*, "one of the greatest achievements of Carey's career." After stimulating the organization of the missionary society in Kettering, he became its first missionary. Reaching India on Nov. 11, 1793, he endured six years of extreme trials before establishing the noted missionary colony at Serampore. He soon mastered numerous Indian languages, preached in the vernacular, labored constantly for the conversion of individuals, and led in establishing 20 churches and mission stations in India by 1814. His linguistic ability gained for him a 30-year professorship of Bengali and Sanskrit languages in the crown college, Fort William, of Calcutta. The leading figure in the "Serampore Trio," with William Ward assisting him as printer and Joshua Marshman as educator, Carey sought to give the Indian people literary tools and resources that would enable them to evangelize their own country. Therefore, he led in building a paper mill, setting up a printing press, publishing the first Indian newspaper, and publishing the Bible in the language of the people. From his life's earnings he contributed over £40,000 to mission work in India. This noted linguist superintended the translation of the Bible into 42 Oriental tongues and thus made the Word of God accessible to a third of the world. In spite of a fire in 1812 that destroyed the press and valuable manuscripts, the Serampore press issued during Carey's lifetime 212,000 copies of the Scriptures. Carey also wrote grammars and dictionaries for six major Indian languages, translated many Sanskrit classics into English, and functioned as government censor for literary productions.

Serampore College, which Carey and his colleagues established in 1810 to train Christian leadership, remains today one of the outstanding educational institutions of Asia and stands as a tribute to its founder's original vision and careful planning. His prolonged efforts for social reform led to the passage of laws prohibiting the heathen practice of infanticide, disposing of children for religious or economic motives; and abolishing the suttee rite of burning widows on the funeral pyres of their husbands. Carey, who was a century ahead of his day in insights into co-operative Christianity, is beyond doubt "the greatest and most versatile Christian missionary sent out in modern times."

HERBERT C. JACKSON and LYNN E. MAY, JR.

CARNES'S DEFALCATION. The defalcation of the treasurer of the Home Mission Board was the greatest financial calamity ever to strike the work of the Southern Baptist Convention. The stealing of the funds of the board, which was carried out over a period of years, came to light in Aug., 1928. Clinton S. Carnes became treasurer of the Home Mission Board during the Convention year 1919–20 and was given authority to handle the papers and the funds of the board over his own signature. He had a penitentiary record in the city of Atlanta, but it was not discovered until after the defalcation. He was an expert bookkeeper and accountant, and seemingly had no difficulty in securing a position in a firm of accountants during the period of World War I when men who had ability were difficult to secure. With the best recommendations from business sources and church sources the board engaged his services. By authority from the board, he was empowered to borrow money from banks in different states to carry on the work of the board. He so manipulated his financial dealings that his criminal acts were committed legally in different states. When his conduct came to light, it seemed to the lawyers employed by the board that it would be next to impossible to assemble all of the various threads of evidence necessary to convict him on his different acts of thievery. Since his crimes were committed legally in different states, he could not be tried in Georgia upon the indictments for every individual act.

Carnes returned to Atlanta and confessed his defalcation. He pleaded guilty to one of the indictments committed in Georgia and was sentenced to the limit the law allowed upon that conviction. He had taken $226,126.86 from the church building fund and $683,334.14 from the general fund of the board, making a total of $909,461. He assigned to the board all his known assets, estimated at a minimum value of $225,000. Upon conviction his bond of $50,000 was paid to the board. On his person when he was arrested were found $3,000 in traveler's checks. The sum of these amounts repaid nearly one third of the amount of the defalcation.

The fact of defalcation and the amount of money involved, coming on the very eve of the depression that hit the fall of 1929, left the board and its work in a fearful situation. But churches of the South came forward with special offerings, on Baptist Honor Day, to relieve the immediate situation in the amount of $389,164.35. Other special gifts amounted to $28,518.79. These gifts, together with Carnes's bond and his assets assigned to the board, amounted to $629,683.14, or more than two thirds of the total defalcation. Under wise and efficient management the board carried on a greatly limited work, and succeeded in clearing all debts by 1943. Much credit is due to Archibald Cunningham Cree (q.v.), who served briefly during the crisis as interim secretary, and later to Secretary J. B. Lawrence and his co-workers and the members of the board in meeting the situation so successfully.
W. W. BARNES

CAROLINA BAPTIST. Founded as a medium of communication to carry on convention work after the Western North Carolina Baptist Convention became an independent body in 1847. James Blythe published the paper at Hendersonville, N. C., 1853–55. When publication was suspended, the list of subscribers was taken over by *Biblical Recorder*.
L. L. CARPENTER

CAROLINA BAPTIST. A monthly publication which originated in Greenville, S. C., in Sept., 1845, with T. W. Haynes editor. The subscription rate was $1.25 per year for the 24-page periodical. In Mar., 1846, the paper was moved to Charleston because of the editor's health. Haynes had been able to work on only two issues of the monthly while the paper was published in Greenville. A friend assisted with the others. After 12 issues of the *Carolina Baptist* had been distributed, publication of the paper was terminated in Aug., 1846.
ROBERT A. IVEY

CARROLL, ALLIE MURPHEE (b. Troy, Ala., Sept. 8, 1861; d. Troy, Ala., Nov. 5, 1938). A member of the Children's Home Board; superintendent of the Salem-Troy Association of Woman's Missionary Union; District W.M.U. vice-president; a state W.M.U. trustee. In 1913 she gave to the Foreign Mission Board $30,000 to establish the Carroll Publishing House in Rio, Brazil, as a memorial to her deceased husband, U. S. Carroll. Mrs. Carroll was educated in the public and private schools of Alabama. She was most active in civic affairs in her town, being president of the Nineteenth Century Club, Music Club, and Civic Improvement Club.
MRS. HENRY LYON

CARROLL, BENAJAH HARVEY (b. near Carrolton, Carrol County, Miss., Dec. 27, 1843; d. Fort Worth, Tex., Nov. 11, 1914). Pastor, teacher, denominational leader, author. He led in the founding of Southwestern Baptist Theological Seminary, and served as president of the seminary until his death. He was one of 12 children born to Benajah and Mary Eliza (Mallard) Carroll. His father was a Baptist minister who supported his family by farming. He moved with his parents to Arkansas in 1848 and to Burleson County, Tex., in 1858.

At 16 he entered Baylor University, then located at Independence, Tex. When the Civil War began, he enlisted in the Texas Ranger service to guard the Texas frontier. In 1862 he enlisted in the regular army. First assigned to the Seventeenth Regiment of Texas Infantry, he served to the end of the war.

Although his college career was interrupted by the war, Baylor University granted him the B.A. degree. In later years he received honorary M.A. and D.D. degrees from the University of Tennessee and the LL.D. degree from Keatchie College, La.

He was converted in 1865, following a period of bitter struggle with skepticism, as he later recorded in his famous sermon, "My Infidelity and What Became of It." The same year he united with the Baptist church at Caldwell, Tex. He was ordained to the gospel ministry the following year.

In 1866 he was married to Ellen Virginia Bell. To them were born nine children: Hassie, Ellen, Hallie, Jimmy, Guy Sears, B. H., Jr., Charles, Katherine, and Annie Louise. After the death of his first wife, he married Hallie Harrison in 1899. To them was born one son, Francis Harrison.

Following the war years, he preached to small churches in Burleson County and found it necessary to teach school for three years in order to pay debts incurred during the war. He served as pastor of Providence Church, Burleson County, and New Hope Church, McLennan County. In 1870 he was called to the pastorate of First Baptist Church, Waco, where he served until 1899 when he was elected corresponding secretary for the Texas Baptist Education Commission.

Always intensely interested in higher education, he taught theology and Bible in Baylor University from 1872 to 1905. He organized the Baylor Theological Seminary in 1905, and led in the founding of Southwestern Baptist Theological Seminary, whose charter was granted Mar. 14, 1908. At this time he became president of the seminary where he served until his death. The seminary was moved to Fort Worth in 1910.

He was known as an influential denominational leader. He served on several state and Southern Baptist Convention committees, making notable addresses in the interest of various areas of denominational work. He gave particular emphasis to evangelism, prohibition, Christian education, and the work of home missions.

The published works of Carroll total 33 volumes, comprising special addresses, doctrinal discussions, sermons, and expositions. His best-known work is *An Interpretation of the English Bible*, a commentary of 13 volumes. Outstanding books of sermons are *Jesus the Christ*, *Baptists and Their Doctrines*, and *Christ and His Church*. There are yet 15 volumes of unpublished materials.

He possessed an outstanding personality. Towering several inches over six feet, he made a commanding appearance. In later years he wore a flowing white beard. Endowed with a powerful and pleasing voice, he was widely known for his oratorical ability. Many stories are told concerning his unusual intellectual ability and especially with regard to his gift of memory. Certain spiritual experiences which he related indicate the depth and fervor of his piety and devotion to Jesus Christ. Shortly before his death he summoned Lee R. Scarborough, whom he had suggested to become his successor as president of Southwestern Seminary, and said to him, "Lee, lash the Seminary to the heart of the Saviour." He died Nov. 11, 1914, and was buried in Oakwood Cemetery, Waco, Tex.　　　　　　　FRANKLIN M. SEGLER

CARROLL, JAMES MILTON (b. Monticello, Ark., Jan. 8, 1852; d. Fort Worth, Tex., Jan. 11, 1931). Pastor, college administrator, Texas Baptist historian. One of 12 children born to Benajah and Mary (Mallard) Carroll, he was six years of age when the family moved to Texas. Due to the turbulent times in which Carroll grew up, his elementary education was seriously impaired. His father died when he was 10 and his mother by the time he was 16. At 19, he married Sudie Wamble, and a short time later, was licensed to preach by the old Liberty Baptist Church in Burleson County. In Jan., 1873, Carroll entered Baylor University at Independence and graduated five years later with the M.A. degree.

Overshadowed by his more famous brother, Benajah Harvey Carroll (q.v.), J. M. Carroll's contributions to the Baptist denomination have all but been in eclipse. Of the large number of pastorates which he held, among the most outstanding were First Church, Lampasas; First Church, Waco; and Riverside Park Church of San Antonio. He served as secretary of the Texas Baptist Education Commission; statistician of the Baptist General Convention of Texas; corresponding secretary of the Sunday School Convention of Texas; and agent of the Foreign Mission Board. Founder and first president of San Marcos Baptist Academy, Carroll was also president of Oklahoma Baptist University and Howard Payne College. He led in the organization of the short-lived Carroll College of McAllen, Tex.

Carroll's love of nature made of him an enthusiastic hunter and a collector of hunting stories. With one of the largest collections of birds' eggs in Texas, he had a national reputation as an ornithologist. An ardent prohibitionist, he left a pastorate to lead in the prohibition movement. Carroll's published works include his most outstanding literary achievement, *A History of Texas Baptists*; a biography of his older brother, *B. H. Carroll, the Colossus of Baptist History*; and a work published posthumously, *The Trail of Blood*. He also prepared *Texas Baptist Statistics* (1895), which was used in the preparation of *A History of Texas Baptists*.

BIBLIOGRAPHY: J. M. Carroll, *A History of Texas Baptists* (1923); B. H. Carroll, *the Colossus of Baptist History* (1946); *The Trail of Blood* (1931). J. B. Cranfill, "The Last of the Carrolls," *The Baptist Standard* (Jan. 22, 1931). J. M. Dawson, *Century* with *Texas Baptists* (1947). I. E. Gates, "J. M. Carroll," *The Baptist Standard* (Jan. 29, 1931). B. J. W. Graham, ed., *Baptist Biography*, Vol. II (1920).

W. R. ESTEP, JR.

CARROLL COLLEGE. A school at Denmark, Tenn., founded in 1850. "In 1850 the West Tennessee Baptist Convention was organized primarily for the purpose of supporting Carroll College." The college later passed from under Baptist control.   LYNN EDWARD MAY, JR.

CARROLL COUNTY INSTITUTE. Founded as a mission school in 1918 and operated by the Home Mission Board and the Arkansas Baptist State Mission Board. Later called No-Ark Academy, it had three buildings and an average enrolment of 84; it closed in 1930.   H. D. MORTON

CARROLLTON FEMALE COLLEGE. A school in Carrollton, Miss., which came under Baptist control in 1889 with Z. T. Leavell as president. Rated as a school of high order, the college had an enrolment of 120 in 1891, but was sold to the city for a high school in 1896.

J. L. BOYD

CARSON, WILLIAM HENRY (b. Sheffield, Ala., Dec. 27, 1887; d. Nigeria, West Africa, May 20, 1954). Missionary to Nigeria. Educated at Howard College and Southern Baptist Theological Seminary, Carson was pastor of Grace Baptist Church, Baltimore, Md., at the time of his appointment to Nigeria in 1918. He served as vice-principal and later as principal of the Baptist College and Seminary, Ogbomosho; superintendent of missions in Benin and Warri provinces and Niger Delta; editor of the *Nigerian Baptist;* and pioneer in radio evangelism. He carried on work in the delta with a motor launch provided by friends in America. On Sept. 16, 1914, Carson married Grace Schimmel (1891–   ).

BIBLIOGRAPHY: *The Commission* (July, 1954). *Missionary Album* (1954). C. E. Maddry, *Day Dawn in Yoruba Land* (1939).   E. C. ROUTH

CARSON-NEWMAN COLLEGE. A coeducational institution at Jefferson City, Tenn., founded in 1851 by the Baptist Education society of East Tennessee as Mossy Creek Missionary Baptist Seminary. The name was successively changed to Mossy Creek Baptist College in 1855, to Carson College in 1880, and, as a result of being merged with Newman College for girls in 1889, to Carson-Newman College, the name it bears today. Except for a short interruption during the Civil War, the institution has been in operation every year since its organization.

Two years after initial steps for the establishment of what is now Carson-Newman College had been taken, the school opened for the reception of students in Sept., 1851, with William Rogers as president. The following Dec. 5th, the institution obtained a charter as The Mossy Creek Missionary Baptist Seminary, but four years later changed its name to Mossy Creek Baptist College. Its first graduate was Richard Scruggs of Sweetwater, Tenn., in 1855. Two brick dormitories were completed in 1857. During the difficult period following the Civil War, Jesse Baker in 1869 succeeded in raising the necessary funds to satisfy all outstanding debts and is thus credited with saving the college. When the institution became more prosperous in 1876, it purchased an adjacent estate from Andrew Jackson Mountcastle. The building was used for the college offices and classes until 1892, after which it served for many years as a dormitory. In 1880 James Henderson Carson, of Dandridge, made a bequest of $17,000 to the institution as an endowment fund for ministerial students. In appreciation the school changed its name to Carson College.

This institution became Carson-Newman College in 1889, when it merged with Newman Baptist Female College, and entered a new period of expansion. The latter school had begun as a seminary for young ladies, occupying the building known as Old College on the original Carson College campus, and which was under the direction of Professor William Thomas Russell. Later, the board of trustees of Carson College ceded the property to the trustees of the girls' school. The latter then secured a charter for the new institution, which they named after William Cate Newman and other members of the Newman family, who had contributed $10,840 to the school. The newly merged college constructed a classroom administration building, which was started by a gift of $1,500 from the American Baptist Publication Society. This building and many valuable records were completely destroyed by fire on Dec. 13, 1916. The college completed the present administration building in 1918, which it named in honor of John Thompson Henderson (*q.v.*), president from 1893 to 1903, for his outstanding leadership. The American Baptist Education Society made an important contribution to the college when it offered in 1899 and then contributed $15,000 after the college had met the terms of its conditional gift: to raise $60,000 by July 1, 1901. Encouraged by its new funds and benefactors, the school erected three buildings within a short period—a "first class Young Ladies' Home" named Henderson Hall for C. W. Henderson of Knoxville, completed in 1899; Sarah Swann Home, built by Alfred Reuben Swann in honor of his mother, in 1905; and Davis Hall for men, raised to the memory of L. Wallace Davis, the following year. All three structures are still in active use and stand in good repair. Two major additions to the institution's capital followed some years later. In 1918 the churches of East Tennessee rallied to raise $200,000 so that the college became eligible for an additional gift of $100,000 from Swann and James Hughes Anderson. Not only substantial physical expansion and deepened financial resources but also considerable academic development and transition to convention control characterized the first decades of the new Carson-Newman College.

Three presidents have served the college since 1920, Oscar Ernest Sams (1920–27), James Thomas Warren (1927–48), and Daniel Harley Fite (1948–   ). During Sams's administration the institution expanded its physical plant, increased its endowment, and raised its academic standing. The college started a summer school program in 1921 and constructed the Butler-Blanc Gymnasium in the same year. With the help of a $20,000 gift from Henry Daniel Blanc (q.v.), a trustee of the college, Blanc Hall for men was completed in 1924. After the constituency of the college had raised $125,000, the General Education Board in 1822 gave $75,000 toward endowment which had now grown to almost $500,000. This gift and another of $70,200 from the Tennessee Baptist Convention cleared the college of all debts, assisting greatly in meeting the conditions necessary for membership in the Southern Association of Colleges and Secondary Schools. This association admitted Carson-Newman in Dec., 1927.

Similar gains characterized the administration of Warren. The institution gained membership in the Association of American Colleges in 1928, during his first year as president. The college added a long-needed science building to its facilities in 1939 and acquired an infirmary in 1940. The erection of two other structures just after World War II initiated a period of expansion unequaled in the history of the institution. In 1946 the school bought the residence of Jesse McGarity Burnett, president of the college from 1912 to 1917, for use as a dormitory. Later additions to this building have brought its capacity to 96 students. Money donated by the Holston Baptist Association made possible the purchase in 1947 of Holston Home to serve as residence for the president of the college. A new and modern heating plant was added the same year.

Under the administration of Fite, the college continued the expansion of its physical plant begun in 1946 and made marked academic progress. Within a few months of his inauguration in Oct., 1948, the institution launched the 1949 enlargement campaign. Income from this effort, supplemented by unused income from a fund-raising effort in 1941 and by substantial gifts from personal donors, made possible the erection of the Maples Library, Chambliss Fine Arts Building, and the Cecil Hurst Baker Memorial Building. The institution constructed the library building in 1949, which it named in honor of the wife and family of Darius Leonard Butler. The Fine Arts Building, completed in 1950, carries the name of Judge Alexander W. Chambliss and pays tribute also to Ocoee Baptists, who contributed generously to its erection. The Elbert Lane Willson cafeteria in the Baker Memorial Building was put into service at the beginning of the fall term of 1951; the student center officially opened at homecoming that October; and during the spring term of 1952, the Home Economics Department moved into its extensive new facilities in this building. In Sept., 1954, the college completed an 82-girl unit of a suite-type residence for women, named Bertie Maples Butler Hall. In August of the next year the school began construction on a four-story residence hall to house 196 men. Other improvements include the reconditioning of all the former structures, the laying of over a mile of sidewalks, extensive landscaping of the campus, and the addition of four new tennis courts.

According to Charles D. Johnson, "Physical and financial improvement has been matched, if not exceeded at Carson-Newman by academic progress." Of a faculty numbering 65, only three have less than the Master of Arts degree; over 40 per cent hold the Doctor's degree or have completed all the resident work required as active candidates for this degree. Since World War II, both the college curriculum and enrolment have more than doubled, with 1,184 full-time students attending the college during the 1955–56 school year. In Jan., 1955, the curriculum provided 15 departments with majors in 19 fields, minors in 7 others, and 10 special programs of study including pre-engineering, pre-forestry, medical technology, prelaw, premedical, and elementary education. The college also offered an off-campus program for Christian education with 97 preachers and 624 laymen enrolled in 20 off-campus centers throughout East Tennessee during the fall term of 1955. The college therefore served a total of 1,905 students during that same term. Estimated value of the property (1955) is $2,106,700. With an endowment of $741,580.59, the institution operates on a current budget of $851,064.07.

Carson-Newman College is among the top 15 per cent of all the colleges and universities that have the largest number of graduates listed in *Who's Who in America*. Over 10,000 students have attended the college since its founding, with 3,697 of these receiving degrees. At least 2,350 have entered the ministry, 1,072 have become missionaries or have devoted their lives to other areas of religious service, and 2,160 have chosen the teaching profession, many of these becoming college educators. Ten have been selected to serve as college presidents; two have been United States senators, and two have become governors of their states. Four have been elected to Congress; one has been a United States Supreme Court justice, with many others becoming state and federal judges. Another graduate attained the highest office among Baptists, president of the Baptist World Alliance, and the contributions of two others have been enshrined in football's hall of fame. Thousands have taken useful places in society as Christian businessmen or as Christian wives and mothers. They have also, through their Christian training, assumed positions of leadership in their churches and greatly enriched the life of their communities, their nation, and their world.

DANIEL HARLEY FITE

CARVER, WILLIAM OWEN (b. Wilson County, Tenn., Apr. 10, 1868; d. Louisville, Ky., May 24, 1954). Minister, educator, author, and missionary statesman. Son of Alexander Jefferson and Almeda Adaline (Binkley) Carver, he was the second of 11 children. When Carver was 19 his mother died, after which his father remarried and had nine children by his second wife. Carver's father, a farmer and mill operator, was a Baptist deacon; and his mother, a devout Christian, had a profound influence upon her son's life. Before going away to college Carver told his mother that he felt called to the ministry, after which he secured the sanction of his church, New Hope, at Hermitage, Tenn., in his call.

During his final years as a student at Richmond College, Richmond, Va., Carver held his first pastorate at Concord Church, Caroline County, from 1889 to 1891. He also served at the same time as supply pastor for Mount Horeb Church in a near-by community. After receiving the M.A. degree from Richmond College in 1891, Carver returned to his Tennessee home expecting to spend the next year paying off college debts. He became pastor of his home church where he was ordained Dec. 25, 1891, and also began his studies in Southern Baptist Theological Seminary. After leaving the seminary in 1893 Carver became professor of philosophy and ancient languages in Boscobel College, Nashville, Tenn., and pastor of South Union Church, Church Hill, Ky. In Jan., 1895, he resumed his studies in Southern Seminary, receiving the Th.M. degree that year and the Th.D. in 1896.

Carver became instructor in New Testament at Southern Seminary in 1896 and also taught some courses in homiletics and theology. In 1899 he introduced a course in comparative religion and missions, and the following year became head of the missions department, the position in which he served until his retirement in 1943. In 1900 and again in 1907–08 Carver visited and studied missions in Europe. In 1922–23 he toured mission fields in South America and the Orient. Carver's advice on missionary problems was sought by both missionaries and board secretaries. From 1936 to 1944, he represented the seminary as a member of the executive committee of the American Association of Theological Schools. From its organization in 1939, he was a member of the American Theological Committee, a subsidiary of the World Conference on Faith and Order, and in this connection wrote the paper on Baptist churches which appeared in *The Nature of the Church*, published in 1952.

Instrumental in founding the Woman's Missionary Union Training School at Southern Seminary in 1907, Carver taught there for many years while also teaching in the seminary. The name of the school was changed to The Carver School of Missions and Social Work in 1953. Charter member and for a long time president of the Southern Baptist Historical Society, Carver was largely responsible for the founding of the Historical Commission of the Southern Baptist Convention. In recognition of his contribution to the preservation of Baptist history, the library of the Historical Commission in Nashville, Tenn., when merged with the Dargan Memorial Library of the Sunday School Board in 1953, was named The Dargan-Carver Library. He was also a member of the Kentucky Baptist Historical Society and the Baptist Historical Society of Great Britain and Ireland.

Carver was managing editor of the *Review and Expositor* from 1920 to 1942, contributing editor of the *Commission* for 12 years, and frequent contributor to other journals. Carver's 19 published books include *History of the New Salem Baptist Church, Nelson County, Ky.* (1901); *Baptist Opportunity* (1907); *Missions in the Plan of the Ages* (1909); *Missions and Modern Thought* (1910); *The Acts of the Apostles* (1916); *All the World in All the Word* (1918); *The Bible a Missionary Message* (1921); *The Self Interpretation of Jesus* (1926); *Thou When Thou Prayest* (1928); *The Course of Christian Missions* (1932); *How the New Testament Came to Be Written* (1933); *The Rediscovery of the Spirit* (1934); *The Furtherance of the Gospel* (1935); *Sabbath Observance* (1940); *Christian Missions in Today's World* (1942); *God and Man in Missions* (1944); *Why They Wrote the New Testament* (1946); *The Glory of God in the Christian Calling* (1949); *Out of His Treasure* (unfinished memoirs, published posthumously in 1956).

He married Alice Hughes Shepard in 1897, and they had six children, two of whom became foreign missionaries.

GEORGE A. CARVER and H. C. GOERNER

CARVER SCHOOL OF MISSIONS AND SOCIAL WORK. Located at 2801 Lexington Road, Louisville, Ky., operated from 1907 to 1953 as Woman's Missionary Union Training School for Christian Workers, under the auspices of Woman's Missionary Union, Auxiliary to the Southern Baptist Convention; in 1953 the trustees adopted and the Woman's Missionary Union approved the present name, better describing the enlarged program of the school and honoring William Owen Carver (*q.v.*), who had been largely instrumental in the establishment of the W.M.U. Training School, had been its first professor, and had continued as faculty member and counselor throughout the school's history. In May, 1956, at the annual sessions of Woman's Missionary Union and the Convention, actions were taken by which the Convention would assume responsibility for and control of the school.

The W.M.U. Training School was formally inaugurated on Wednesday, Oct. 2, 1907, at exercises in the Broadway Baptist Church, Louisville, Ky., as the culmination of developments reaching back into the 19th century. Ezekias Z. Simmons (*q.v.*), missionary to China since 1870, while in America on furlough in 1899 proposed to Foreign Mission Board Secretary Robert Josiah Willingham (q.v.) the establishment of a school for training women missionaries, to be located near and conducted in close relationship with the Southern Baptist Theological Seminary. With the encouragement of Willingham and the approval of the seminary faculty, Simmons presented his plan to the Woman's Missionary Societies of Walnut Street and Broadway Baptist churches in Louisville. Though enthusiasm was aroused, full development of the project was delayed several years.

It is recorded that one young woman attended classes in the seminary in 1884–85. By 1891 married women had been attending seminary classes along with their husbands, and "occasionally, also, some unmarried women had quietly listened to lectures." In the fall of 1904 four young women came to Louisville for the specific purpose of attending seminary classes. They were Clemmie Ford of Tennessee, Rena Groover of Georgia, Alice Huey of Alabama, and Ella Jeter of Oklahoma. Three of these subsequently served as foreign missionaries, Rena Groover Shepard in Brazil, Alice Huey and Ella Jeter Comerford in China.

Though they received no formal credit for their work, the seminary faculty did "record their names, grade their papers, and certify them to the committee of women in Louisville organized to provide a home" for them. This committee was formed following a meeting called for the purpose in 1904 by Eliza Somerville Broadus, daughter of John Albert Broadus (q.v.). Soon, with Edgar Young Mullins (q.v.) and William Owen Carver (q.v.) as advisory members representing the seminary, it became a board of managers for the Training School Home.

On Thanksgiving Day, 1904, the four original students moved into a house at 125 Fourth Street (later renumbered 923 South Fourth) which the board had rented. Others joined them, and before the end of that academic year a number of unmarried women were taking advantage of seminary classes. A special lecture course in Practical Work for ladies alone, conducted by Carver, enrolled 14 married women and 11 single women during the 1904–05 session.

During the summer of 1905, the board rented a larger house at 720 (later renumbered 728) West Broadway and appealed to the women of the South for support. This support was finally gained after patient, prayerful labor by those who saw the need for the school.

In 1907 the seminary trustees voted to surrender "to the Woman's Missionary Union . . . the entire management and control of the Woman's Training School, in connection with our Seminary, and that we offer to the Training School all the advantages of our classrooms." The Louisville group in charge of the training school also offered to Woman's Missionary Union "the furnishings collected during the three years of its existence, valued at $900, also to subscribe $500 towards a Building Fund for the Woman's Missionary Union Training School."

At Richmond, Va., in May, 1907, under the leadership of its president, Fannie E. S. Heck (q.v.), the Woman's Missionary Union voted unanimously to adopt the school. Full ownership and control was vested in Woman's Missionary Union, the school to be conducted on its behalf by

(a) A Board of Managers consisting of one member from each State, Territory or District connected with the W.M.U. together with the Pres., Cor. Sec., and Treas. of said Union. (b) A Local Board of Managers composed of twenty-one Baptist women of Louisville. (c) An Advisory Board of seven members, two of whom shall be Baptist laymen residents of Louisville or its vicinity, and three of whom shall be the Cor. Secretaries of the For. Miss. Board, the Home Miss. Board and Sunday School Board of the Southern Baptist Convention.

A building at 320 (later renumbered 334) East Broadway was purchased for $20,500 and by Oct., 1907, $17,000 had been raised toward the cost of the building and its furnishing. At the opening exercises James Marion Frost (q.v.), on behalf of the Sunday School Board, presented a check for $20,500 on condition that the Woman's Missionary Union use the remainder of their $17,000, after paying for alterations and equipment, as nucleus for a $20,000 endowment fund.

Maud Reynolds McLure (q.v.) was chosen first principal and she gave distinguished leadership in the development and growth of the school for 16 years. From an enrolment of 32 boarding students and 5 day students the first year there were 131 boarders and 43 day students the last year of her principalship. She is honored in Woman's Missionary Union memory as one of the "Five Founders" of the school along with Fannie E. S. Heck, who as president of Woman's Missionary Union led enthusiastically in the movement to establish the school; Eliza Broadus, who was largely instrumental in the formation of the original group of Louisville women to establish the Training School Home and who served as a member of the local board of managers of the school from its beginning until 1926; Mrs. George B. Eager, who "more than any other one person was responsible for the adoption of the Home and the authorization of the W.M.U. Training School," and who was vice-chairman of the local board, 1907–08, and chairman, 1908–26; and Mrs. Samuel E. Woody, who was chairman of the local board in 1907–08 and again in 1926–31, and vice-chairman, 1908–26.

The early success and growth of the school made it apparent that larger quarters would soon be needed, and in 1910 an enlargement fund was started. In 1914 Woman's Missionary Union purchased the house on the corner lot adjoining the school for $20,142, thereby providing immediate additional space and assuring room for the eventual erection of a larger building. At that time the Sunday School Board made a gift of $10,000 to the school's enlargement fund.

An enrolment for the 1915–16 session of 64 boarding and 22 day students made immediate the need for new quarters, and Woman's Missionary Union voted in May, 1916, to raise "$98,000.00 from 98,000 Baptists" to add to $52,000 already in the building fund. The school's needs were placed before the 1916 meeting of the Convention, and "Dollar Clubs" were formed throughout the Convention territory. Louisville friends alone contributed more than $30,000.

During the 1916–17 session three rented buildings on the north side of Broadway housed the school while the way was cleared for the new home. On Apr. 5, 1917, the cornerstone was laid for the new "House Beautiful" on the southwest corner of Preston and Broadway. Isaac Jacobus Van Ness (q.v.) was present for the occasion to give an additional $10,000 from the Sunday School Board for the enlargement fund. The still uncompleted building was occupied Sept. 15, 1917, and on May 22, 1918, the completed "house and all within its walls" were dedicated to "Him whose we are and whom we serve."

The continued growth of the school made necessary the purchase in Apr., 1921, of the residence adjoining the school on the west for $18,000.

From its establishment in 1912, the Good Will Center has been a notable feature of the school's life and ministry. In 1921 Carrie U. Littlejohn of South Carolina, a 1915 graduate of the school, joined the staff as teacher of practical missions and director of the center. She was elected in 1923 to serve as acting principal. She served as associate principal, 1925–30; as principal, 1930–48; and as president, 1948–51. In 1925 Janie Cree Bose, for the previous 12 years leader for Woman's Missionary Union of Kentucky, was elected principal, and gave significant leadership to the school for the next five years.

The initial curriculum of the school offered a three-year course with classes in Old Testament and New Testament, Sunday school pedagogy, personal work, domestic science, music and public speaking, and lectures on medicine and principles of nursing for the entering students. The following years offered further work in Bible and courses in systematic theology, church history, comparative religion, and missions, ecclesiology, and electives in the seminary curriculum.

Some of the classes were given in the W.M.U. Training School, but until 1926 the students went to the near-by seminary for a large part of their work. Following the removal of the seminary in 1926 to its Lexington Road campus, all Woman's Missionary Union Training School classes were taught at the school. A full-time professor of Bible was added to the staff, seminary professors came to the school to offer other courses which the students had previously taken at the seminary, and with funds provided by the Sunday School Board a new department of Christian education was added to the curriculum.

Until 1937 the local board of managers had the principal responsibility for the operation of the school. On May 10, 1937, the general board of Woman's Missionary Union authorized a revision in the school's charter so as to provide for a board of trustees elected annually by W.M.U., to consist of the president, executive secretary, and treasurer of Woman's Missionary Union, a representative from each state Woman's Missionary Union represented in the Convention, three members at large, and seven resident members. In this board was vested the responsibility to elect faculty and staff, adopt the operating budget, and determine the policies of the school.

Also in 1937, in a move toward re-establishing the original close relationship with the seminary and provide more adequately for the growth of the school, Woman's Missionary Union authorized the inauguration of a building project. In Aug., 1937, a seven-and-one-quarter-acre tract at 2801 Lexington Road, immediately adjoining the seminary, was purchased for $27,500. In 1939, $50,000 was set aside from the Woman's Missionary Union special Golden Jubilee gift, to be used in the new building for the unit containing the chapel to be known as the Fannie E. S. Heck Memorial Chapel. At the same time a building committee was appointed and a campaign was authorized to raise $100,000 toward the central unit of the building, "to be regarded as the Maud Reynolds McLure Memorial."

To perpetuate in the building the names of the three other founders the three distinct parts of the dormitory, an east hall, a west hall, and a central hall, were named, by vote of the trustees in Feb., 1941, Broadus, Eager, and Woody. Subsequently, to honor Mrs. Frank W. Armstrong (q.v.) the terrace on the north side of the building was named the Armstrong Terrace.

A ground breaking ceremony on the new site was held Mar. 20, 1940, and the cornerstone was laid Oct. 2, 1940, with the first four students who lived in the original training school home present for the occasion. The beautiful Georgian building was completed during the summer of 1941, at a cost of $353,016.85, and the school opened its first session in its new home on Sept. 16, 1941, with 91 boarding students and 83 day students.

There were four exercises of dedication for the new building. The first occurred when about 175 of the alumnae and other former students gathered the second week of Sept., 1941, for a homecoming and "to symbolize the transfer of their loyal devotion from the old to the new site." The next week the faculty and student body received the new property "as the excellently appointed place for their mutual activities." On Founders' Day, Oct. 2, 1941, the formal dedication took place, the address being given by Mrs. Armstrong, president of the school's board of trustees as well as of Woman's Missionary Union, and one whose vision and leadership had been so important in the successful completion of the project. The final dedication was made in the Heck Memorial Chapel on Feb. 25, 1942, in connection with the annual meeting of the board of trustees, by which time the project had been fully paid for.

The academic year 1942–43 saw the return to the school's original plan of coeducational arrangements with the seminary, whereby the entire seminary curriculum was available to W.M.U. Training School students. At the same time the distinctive classes taught at the school by its own faculty were strengthened in the fields of missionary, education, community missions and social work, personal evangelism, church music, religious journalism, public speaking and religious drama, and stenography and office practice.

An integral part of the school's program from the beginning has been training in practical missions. As a regular part of their program, students are assigned to specific placements in the churches, missions, hospitals, settlements, and institutions of the community for their development in missionary interest, race relations, personal evangelism, and better methods in group work. Thus they receive guided experience through which they learn to apply in their later Christian service the teachings of the classroom.

The value of this type of experience was early recognized and led to the establishment of a Good Will Center (known until 1915 as the Baptist Training School Settlement), owned and operated by the school, which was first opened on Oct. 25, 1912, in a rented building at 512 East Madison Street, in a needy neighborhood of the city. In Oct., 1913, a near-by residence at 524 East Madison was purchased by Woman's Missionary Union at a cost of $5,000 to house the center.

The practical experience in social service in the center has helped train students as future directors and workers in numerous settlements, institutional churches, and other institutional situations in the homeland and on the mission field. As early as 1914, former students of the school were directing settlements in Meridian, Miss.; Norfolk, Va.; Atlanta, Ga.; and Richmond, Va.

In its practical ministry through a varied program of religious education and wholesome recreation for the people of the community, the center was soon reaching hundreds of lives a year, so that, even with the acquisition of an adjoining building in 1922, the quarters were still too small. The report for the year May 1, 1923, to May 1, 1924, showed "Total Attendance in All Organizations at the Center of 10,524."

In Jan., 1925, the executive committee of Woman's Missionary Union authorized the construction of a "model and adequate Good Will Center to replace the two old buildings." By Oct. 10, 1925, the new center had been constructed on the site of the old buildings.

In 1940 the character of the neighborhood in which the center was located was rapidly changing. The Negro population was increasing, a government housing project was being completed in a near-by slum clearance, and the Presbyterian Colored Mission was developing a large community center. The Good Will Center was admirably situated for extension of that work, and on Aug. 17, 1940, the executive committee of Woman's Missionary Union approved the sale of the center to the Presbyterian mission for $16,000.

Plans and surveys were begun to determine the location of a new Good Will Center in an underprivileged section of the city not already adequately served by any other evangelical group. Ultimately the survey committee recommended to the school's trustees, in Mar., 1950, that property at 1818 Portland Avenue, Louisville, be purchased. This house, in a crowded section of the city, was bought and remodeled at a total cost of $19,547.46. The gratifying response in attendance and interest made it immediately evident that enlarged quarters would be required in the near future.

Adequate previous preparation of its students and strengthening of its academic standards have been continuing interests of Carver School. In 1945 the board of trustees adopted the following rules for admission of students:

Applicants for admission as graduate students must have a bachelor's degree from some institution of recognized standing; college graduates who have had at least one full year of experience in some sort of work between high school and college, during or since college years are given first consideration. *Applicants for admission to the course leading to the Bachelor of Religious Education* degree must have completed at least two years of college work; no applicant with less than two years of college work will be admitted.

In 1951 Carrie U. Littlejohn submitted her resignation as president of the school, to take effect June 30, 1951. The trustees officially stated, "The Board collectively and individually reluctantly accepts the termination of her leadership and desires to record sincere and abiding appreciation of the worthy service of Dr. Littlejohn." For 30 years she was identified with the school, 23 of which she served as principal and president. A student of Converse College, Spartanburg, S. C., and a graduate of Woman's Missionary Union Training School, she also received the B.R.E. degree from the Hartford School of Religious Education and an M.S. degree in education from Northwestern University. During the period of her service to the school, she attended summer sessions of the University of Chicago and George Washington University. In 1944 Georgetown College conferred upon her the LL.D. degree. Through her years of leadership she steadily strove for an expanding curriculum, higher educational standards, and increased library facilities. In paying tribute to her upon her retirement, the board recorded these words:

> With judicious skill she has selected her faculties and staffs and maintained a high level of efficiency on a most economical basis. Through the years she has taken an increased interest in the training of day students in addition to boarding students, and was especially interested in the wives of the Seminary students. Year after year she has fitted her student body into the life of a great seminary with consummate skill and the least possible disruption. Throughout the years she has been able to meet every problem with open vision, clear thinking, hard work, Christian consideration and determined purpose in the interest of a more perfect service of the School in its Christian mission. Dr. Littlejohn's executive ability was further manifested in the building program which gave to us our present commodious building which is the epitome of beauty and utility. Upon her shoulders fell the major burden of overseeing this project. Countless decisions were forced upon her in addition to her usual duties. Her works praise her through this monument in brick and stone known as the Woman's Missionary Union Training School for Christian Workers.

At its annual meeting in Louisville, Feb. 28–Mar. 1, 1951, the trustees elected Emily K. Lansdell of Hephzibah, Ga., as president, to assume office July 1, 1951. She came to the position with a rich background. After appointment under the Foreign Mission Board in 1946 she taught for three years in the University of Shanghai. During the next two years she assisted the Personnel Department of the Foreign Mission Board in visiting colleges, presenting world missions, and counseling with students interested in the field. She had previously taught in the high school in her home town and a year at Campbell College in North Carolina. She received an A.B. degree from Coker College in South Carolina, an M.A. in English from Duke University, and an M.S. in oriental culture from Yale, and did graduate study in the University of Georgia, Columbia University, Woman's Missionary Union Training School, and the College of Chinese Studies in Berkeley, Calif. In 1952 Mercer University conferred upon her the LL.D. degree. She, in close co-operation with Mrs. George R. Martin, president, 1945–56, of Woman's Missionary Union and of the school's trustees, led in the development of the school's expanded program.

On May 12, 1952, Woman's Missionary Union in annual session at Miami, Fla., approved recommendations of the trustees of the school that the faculty, curriculum, and building be enlarged in order to meet more adequately some challenging needs along the lines of missions and church social work. It was further voted that the name of the school be changed, that classes be opened to men who might need the specialized curriculum which the school would offer, and that no person be denied admission because of cultural or racial differences.

A gradual enlarging of the curriculum is in process with no sudden departure from the patterns of the past. The school continues to offer the degrees of Bachelor of Religious Education and Master of Religious Education, with general preparation for Christian workers. The program of study differs from the formal and classical curriculum of religious education in its stress on understanding people and the social situation. Those who have already completed the requirements for the M.R.E. degree at the Carver School or have had similar work in another institution are offered an additional year of specialized study in social work, Christian education, or missions, for which the M.S. is given.

The social work course is planned because of the conviction that many missionaries at home and overseas, particularly women, and other denominational workers such as Good Will Center workers, church social workers, workers in Baptist children's homes and other institutions need a specialized training different from that of the pastor and the educational director of a local Baptist church. The training emphasizes an awareness and understanding of social situations and problems and the knowledge and techniques of meeting individual and group needs in the spirit and power of the Christian gospel. Courses offered include social group work, social casework, cultural anthropology, community organization, child welfare, intercultural relations, law and social work, selected areas of study in social pathology such as divorce, alcoholism, gambling, and criminal behavior. At the same time there is included enough basic preparation in the study of Bible, religious education, and related subjects to equip general Christian workers.

A program of advanced missionary training is being developed for furloughed missionaries and overseas missionary candidates. Students who have already completed the requirements for the M.R.E. degree in Carver School or similar work elsewhere may be candidates for an M.S. degree on the basis of an additional year of intensive work designed to equip the missionary for the task of working with people of other cultures and races. Courses have been established in phonetics and linguistics, literacy education, basic medical information, cultural anthropology, world revolutionary forces, the philosophy of missions, and area studies in the lands where the Foreign Mission Board operates.

The library has an important place in the expanding program of the school. Located in the east wing of the building, it was given by Woman's Missionary Union of North Carolina as a memorial to Mrs. Sallie Bailey Jones (q.v.). It now contains 12,000 volumes and 100 current periodicals. Also available to the students of the school are the resources of the seminary library of some 76,000 volumes, and the excellent facilities of the Louisville Free Public Library.

The enlargement program of the school does not undertake to duplicate unnecessarily courses already offered at the neighboring seminary, but provides that its students will continue to take some classes at the seminary. Classes at Carver School are likewise available to seminary students. Representatives of the seminary faculty serve on the faculty council of Carver School.

In addition to the president, the teaching staff of Carver School for 1955–56 included six full-time and 10 part-time faculty members.

From its organization through the academic year 1955–56, the school enrolled approximately 4,000 students, of whom 2,519 were boarding students. The day student group, for the most part, consisted of wives of seminary students. Through May, 1956, the school had awarded 1,883 degrees or certificates. The first man to receive a degree from Carver School was Louis G. Stone of Oklahoma, who received the M.R.E. degree in social work in 1955 and then joined the staff of the Missouri Baptist Children's Home, Pattonville, Mo. The continuing basic missionary purpose of the school is reflected in the 402 of its former students who have gone, or as of May, 1956, were under appointment to go, as foreign missionaries to 29 countries. In the home field at least 100 have done mission work under home, state, and city mission boards. More than 100 have served through Woman's Missionary Union as executive, young people's and office secretaries, treasurers, and fieldworkers; nearly 200 have worked as church secretaries, pastors' assistants, youth workers, and educational directors; more than 50 have done Good Will Center work. Many others have found their fields of service with Sunday school and Training Union departments; as student secretaries and faculty and staff members in colleges and special schools; as teachers in mission schools, Bible schools, and public schools; and as workers in orphanages and other social work situations. Most of the day students and a large number of the boarding students who subsequently married ministers have put their training to service through local churches.

Through the years Woman's Missionary Union has assumed responsibility for the full maintenance and support of the school. The Sunday School Board has had a continuing interest in the school, and since 1919 financial support from the Convention has been given to the school through the Education Board, the Executive Committee, and the Cooperative Program. For the year ending Dec. 31, 1955, income for the operation of the school was from the following sources: Cooperative Program allotment, $61,000.00; Sunday School Board, $500.00; Woman's Missionary Union, $45,500.00; board, room, and fees, $33,999.83; interest on endowment, $7,573.04.

On Dec. 31, 1955, the assets of the school included eight and one-quarter acres of land fronting on Lexington Road with the building erected in 1941 and a large colonial residence on the corner of Lexington and Upland roads purchased in 1954; the total value of land, improvements, buildings, equipment, and furnishings was listed at $799,500; and the Good Will Center at 1818 Portland Avenue, listed at $23,750. In addition the school had on hand $320,000 received from the Cooperative Program for the erection of a new academic hall. Plans soon were under way for the construction of this new building.

Other funds held on the same date for the use of the school included endowment funds, $300,087.58; scholarship fund, $29,700.00; Margaret M. Norton Fund, $11,100.00; and Good Will Center reserve fund, $18,870.00. The cash held in all funds brought the total assets to $1,565,914.19.

At Kansas City, Mo., on May 26, 1956, the executive board of Woman's Missionary Union approved, and on May 28, 1956, the Woman's Missionary Union in annual session adopted the following recommendations:

We reaffirm our conviction of the need for the program offered by the Carver School of Missions and Social Work.

We are gratified that the Theological Committee of the Southern Baptist Convention has recognized that there is a definite place for the school in the areas of church social work and missionary training.

We further believe that if the Southern Baptist Convention likewise recognizes these needs in the training of Christian workers and is ready to undertake the support and control of the school, it is wise for Woman's Missionary Union to transfer the school to this larger body of which we are members.

We appreciate the generosity of the Theological Committee in proposing that one-half of the trustees shall be nominated by Woman's Missionary Union to the Committee on Boards of the Convention and we shall continue to show our interest in the school, particularly through these trustees.

We therefore recommend in the event that the Southern Baptist Convention accepts the proposals of the Theological Committee:

1. That a committee from Woman's Missionary Union be appointed to formulate necessary changes in the by-laws of Woman's Missionary Union in regard to the Carver School of Missions and Social Work and submit these for consideration by the Executive Board of Woman's Missionary Union at its January 1957 session and thereafter for publication in *Royal Service* and for adoption by Woman's Missionary Union at the 1957 annual session.

2. That the same or another committee be appointed to work with the Southern Baptist Convention's Theological Committee in the details of the transfer to the Convention of the school.

3. That this committee explore ways in which Woman's Missionary Union can fulfill its trust in certain funds and properties now held by Woman's Missionary Union for Carver School of Missions and Social Work, safeguarding the purpose for which these funds and properties were given and also allowing flexibility within the framework of this purpose as the school continues to grow and adjust to changing needs and situations. The committee will report to the January 1957 session of the Executive Board of Woman's Missionary Union and the matter will be submitted for consideration by Woman's Missionary Union at the 1957 annual session.

On May 31, 1956, the Convention adopted the following recommendations of its subcommittee to study the financial relation of the Carver School to the Convention:

Recommendation No. 3

...*The Executive Committee shall not recommend any percentage allocation of funds for any agency or institution for which the Convention does not elect trustees or directors.* (Note: Not to take effect until 1957 Convention)

Recommendation No. 4

Believing that there is a definite place for the Carver School of Missions and Social Work in the areas of church social work and missionary training, we recommend with regard to the Carver School:

(1) That if the Southern Baptist Convention is to allocate funds on a percentage basis to the Carver School it do so only upon provision that the Woman's Missionary Union amend its charter and bylaws.

(2) That when the charter and bylaws of the Woman's Missionary Union be changed to permit it, the trustees of the Carver School shall be elected by the Southern Baptist Convention, one-half of whom shall be nominated by Woman's Missionary Union to the Committee on Boards of the Convention and elected by the Convention, and that the Carver School shall then operate as an institution of the Southern Baptist Convention within the Business and Financial Plan of the Southern Baptist Convention.

(3) That in the event Woman's Missionary Union shall be agreeable to the above recommendations, the Committee on Theological, Religious, and Missionary Education of the Convention be authorized to work with Woman's Missionary Union in matters pertaining to details to be presented to the Southern Baptist Convention for consideration as soon as possible.
GEORGE A. CARVER

CARY, LOTT (b. Charles County, Va., 1780; d. Liberia, Nov. 10, 1828). Leader of the first group of Baptist missionaries to go from Virginia to a foreign land. He was born a Negro slave, learned the alphabet from the New Testament, led in the organization of the Richmond African Baptist Missionary Society, became a missionary to Africa, and served as governmental agent for the colony of Liberia. He was reared on a farm about 30 miles east of Richmond, Va., the only child of pious parents. After he became a worker in a Richmond warehouse, he learned to read by studying the third chapter of the Gospel of John. Further education was received in an evening school for young Negro men, conducted by William Crane, father of William Carey Crane (*q.v.*), of the First Baptist Church of Richmond, Va. Encouraged by his church, First Baptist, he preached among the Negroes of Richmond and vicinity with great success, earning their confidence and respect. In 1813, with aid of white friends, he purchased freedom from slavery for himself and his family.

The missionary propaganda of Luther Rice which spread rapidly in Virginia found a ready response in Lott Cary. He aroused among his Negro brethren a lively interest in the spiritual condition of Africa. The Richmond African Baptist Missionary Society, whose contributions were to go to a Baptist mission in Africa, was organized in Apr., 1815, with Cary as secretary. This was the first Baptist mission society in the country whose support came largely from Negroes. Cary was joined by Collin Teague, a fellow preacher of his own race, in a growing determination to go to Africa to preach the gospel. With William Crane's help, they were accepted as colonists to Liberia and appointed missionaries by the board of the Baptist General Convention in Apr., 1819. Following a year of study these two were ordained by the First Baptist Church and with five companions organized themselves into a church. They sailed for Africa in Jan., 1821.

Cary's integrity and ability were so apparent in his missionary endeavor that he was asked to conduct the affairs of the colony of Liberia. His work ended abruptly in 1828, when he was killed in an accidental explosion of gunpowder, while fortifying the colony against a threatened attack by natives.
CLAYTON PITTS

CASWELL BAPTIST ASSEMBLY. Following action of the North Carolina Baptist Convention in its 1945 and 1946 sessions, the general board presented a recommendation which the convention adopted to lease some property and open an assembly in June, 1948, at historic Fort Fisher, located about 12 miles southeast of Wilmington. The assembly was named Seaside. Then early in 1949 opportunity came to purchase old Fort Caswell, located on the ocean at the mouth of Cape Fear River, from the United States Government. The price finally agreed upon was $86,000, although the government appraiser had placed a replacement value of $1,480,000 upon the 250 acres of land, the paved roads, water system, and about 70 buildings. In 1949 the state convention approved the purchase, although by a divided vote. Seaside Assembly, after operating two years at Fort Fisher, ceased to exist when the assembly was transferred to Fort Caswell in the spring of 1950 and became Caswell Baptist Assembly. With R. K. Redwine as director of the assembly at both locations, attendance through the summer of 1955 totaled 35,856.
M. A. HUGGINS

CATAWBA RIVER BAPTIST ACADEMY. A Baptist School which opened in Jan., 1859, near Morganton, N. C.
D. L. SMILEY

CATHARI. See NOVATIANS.

CATHCART, WILLIAM (b. Londonderry, Ireland, Nov. 8, 1826; d. Guynedd, Pa., July 8, 1908). American Baptist pastor, historian, editor, author, and cyclopedist. The son of James and Elizabeth (Cously) Cathcart, he was reared in the Presbyterian church, but became a Baptist in Jan., 1846, at the age of 19. He was educated at the University of Glasgow, Scotland, and at Horton Baptist Theological School, Yorkshire, England. In 1850 he was married to Eliza Caldwell. Early in the same year he was ordained pastor of the Baptist church of Barnsley, England, where he served for three years.

Cathcart's political ideas and his strong anti-state church sentiments caused him to be attracted to the United States. He came to New York on Nov. 18, 1853. In December of the same year he accepted the call of the Third Baptist

Church of Groton, Mystic River, Conn., where he remained as pastor until Apr., 1857. He then became pastor of the Second Baptist Church of Philadelphia where he remained 27 years.

Cathcart was an ardent exponent of the distinctive doctrines of his denomination. He was a staunch supporter of the Bible Union in the dispute concerning the translation of the terms having to do with baptism. His attacks on the strong Sabbatarian views which prevailed among many of his fellow ministers often involved him in controversy.

In 1873 the University of Lewisburg recognized Cathcart's scholarship by conferring on him the D.D. degree. In 1876 he succeeded Howard Malcom as president of the American Baptist Historical Society. His deep interest in history compelled him to devote much energy and time to the promotion of the activities of this organization. He continued as president of the society until 1884. He left the pastorate this same year because of failing health, but remained active in Baptist affairs for many years, devoting much of his time to editorial work and original writing on historical subjects.

In 1885, at the request of the Baptist Ministerial Union of Pennsylvania, he prepared a paper on "The Baptists in the Revolution." This paper was later enlarged to become a work entitled *The Baptists and the American Revolution*.

He is best remembered as the editor of *The Baptist Encyclopedia*, published in 1881. Other works in addition to the two mentioned are *Christian Union, Mock and Real; The Claims of Large Cities upon the Friends of Jesus; The Lord's Day Not the Sabbath of the Jews; The Lord's Supper and Unbaptized Participants; The Papal System; The Progressive Changes of the Infallible Church; The Remarkable Preservation of the Hebrew and Greek Scriptures;* and *Roots of the Tree of Liberty*.

BIBLIOGRAPHY: W. Cathcart, *The Baptist Encyclopedia* (1881). *Dictionary of American Biography* (1929). J. B. Filson, *History of the Second Baptist Church, Philadelphia* (1886). *The New Schaff-Herzog Encyclopedia of Religious Knowledge* (1908). E. C. Starr, *A Baptist Bibliography* (1954).

WILLIAM A. CARLETON

CAVE SPRINGS FEMALE SEMINARY. A Georgia school founded in 1849 with W. D. Cowdry as the first principal. During the Civil War, with Shaler Granby Hillyer (*q.v.*), principal, it operated in conjunction with the boys' school, Hearn Academy. After the war it operated separately, but was consolidated again with Hearn in 1883.

ARTHUR JACKSON

CEDAR RUN ACADEMY. A North Carolina school under Baptist control in 1886. It was endorsed by Brier Creek and Caldwell County associations.

D. L. SMILEY

CEDARMORE KENTUCKY BAPTIST ASSEMBLY. Purchased by the Long Run Baptist Association in 1949, located at Bagdad, Ky. It was used as an associational and regional camp during 1950, operated by Long Run Association. The general association of Baptists in Kentucky purchased Cedarmore in 1951, and the Kentucky Baptist State Assembly was moved from Clear Creek Springs, Pineville, Ky., to Cedarmore at Bagdad. Providing inspiration, dedication, information, and Christian fellowship, camps and assemblies are held by various departments of the state for 12 weeks annually. Camps include Royal Ambassadors, Girls' Auxiliary, and Young Woman's Auxiliary. Assemblies and rallies include Sunday school, Training Union, Woman's Missionary Union, Business Woman's Circle, Brotherhood, and Baptist Student Union. The camp's assets in 1955 were valued at $190,972.61.

ELDRED M. TAYLOR

CENSORSHIP BY RELIGIOUS GROUPS OF SECULAR PUBLICATIONS. Many Christian citizens have become greatly alarmed at the flamboyant display of salacious material freely accessible to youth today. The Roman Catholics with their National Organization of Decent Literature have long been working most effectively toward a solution to this serious problem. Others, such as Methodists and Episcopalians, have spoken out against the evils and dangers of obscene literature. Southern Baptists have also become alerted and active in opposing this kind of publication. On May 16, 1920, George Washington Truett (*q.v.*), addressing a meeting of the Southern Baptist Convention from the east steps of the national Capital, said: "We will take free speech and a free press, with all their excrescences and perils, because of the high meaning of freedom, but we are to set ourselves with all diligence not to use these great privileges in the shaming of liberty." A strong resolution concerning obscenity was adopted both at the 1949 and 1953 Convention meetings. Since then the editorial department of the Sunday School Board has given much thought through its various publications to this problem. Many of the editors of Baptist state papers have written boldly on its evils, and the Christian Life Commission has also made some study and pronouncements. Many individual members of churches have been quite active.

JAMES P. WESBERRY

CENTENNIAL, SOUTHERN BAPTIST CONVENTION. The celebration of the 100th anniversary of the Convention which had been organized on May 8, 1845. Definite preparations to make the occasion an historic event began as early as 1939, when the Executive Committee appointed a Centennial Session Program Committee. The latter completed all program arrangements for the centennial session that was to be held in Atlanta, Ga., May 8–13, 1945, with a pilgrimage on the 14th to Augusta, where a century before the Convention had been organized. But conditions incident to World War II prevented the Baptists from convening for their annual session in 1945. Although prohibited from consummating plans made for the historic observance, the denomination conducted a "Baptist Hour" centennial broadcast on May 6, 1945, part of which originated from the First Baptist Church of Augusta, the birthplace of the Convention. War conditions frustrated original plans, but Southern Baptists formally observed their centennial at the evening session, May 15, 1946, of the Miami Convention. Addresses by Louie D. Newton on "The Work We Sought to Do, and Did Begin," and by W. R. White on "Carrying on with 'Widening Reach and Heightened Power,'" and the showing of the film, *The Romance of a Century*, prepared by the Sunday School Board, highlighted the program conducted before an estimated audience of 8,000.

R. PAUL CAUDILL

CENTRAL AFRICA. See NIGERIA, MISSION IN.

CENTRAL BAPTIST. A Missouri state Baptist paper resulting from the consolidation of the *Missouri Baptist Journal* and *The Record* in Aug., 1868, effected to remove friction which had developed between the two Baptist elements in the state during the Civil War. John Hill Luther was editor, with Adin A. Kendrick and Norman Fox his associates in 1870. Luther and William Pope Yeaman (*q.v.*) edited the paper from 1875 until Oct., 1877, when William Ferguson became editor. The paper was sold to William Harrison Williams in 1882. On Nov. 20, 1912, a committee representing both papers recommended the purchase of the subscription list of the *Central Baptist* by *The Word and Way*, published by the Western Baptist Publishing Company. The purchase was transacted for $7,000.

J. R. BLACK

CENTRAL BAPTIST HOSPITAL. Located at Lexington, Ky., a general short-term hospital, fully accredited by the Joint Commission on Accreditation, with a capacity of 173 beds and 25 bassinets. It was dedicated on May 9, 1954, and it received its first patient on May 12, 1954. However, the organization was started in 1945 when a group of interested physicians and laymen organized the Central Baptist Hospital, Incorporated, which led in the plans for development. Ground was broken on May 9, 1948, and the foundation, basement, and footing were finished. As additional funds were obtained, the steel structure was erected.

However, progress was slow, and in 1950 the hospital board of trustees appealed to the General Association of Baptists in Kentucky for financial help. In 1951 the Hospital Commission of Kentucky Baptists was organized, and the Lexington project became a statewide effort. Almost $2,000,000 was borrowed against a mortgage of Kentucky Baptist Hospital in Louisville for the completion of Central Baptist Hospital.

Patients are ministered to regularly from Kentucky, Tennessee, West Virginia, Virginia, and Ohio, as well as other states throughout the nation. Medicine, surgery, and obstetrics are the three major services with qualified doctors in attendance in each department. Homer D. Coggins is administrator.

H. L. DOBBS

CENTRAL COLLEGE. A school for women, located at Conway, Ark.; owned and operated by the Arkansas Baptist State Convention from 1892 to 1950. Encouraged by G. W. Bruce, who had had to send his daughters out of the state for their education and so saw the need for a college for women in Arkansas, the Arkansas convention in 1890 authorized the establishment of such an institution. A plot of ground was donated by A. P. Robinson, who was not a Baptist. One building served as dormitory, classrooms, dining room, and kitchen. Furniture except for pianos and china was given by G. W. Bruce, who also stood as guarantor for the payment of other pledges to provide money for buildings and equipment. Many of these pledges were never paid, and in fulfilment of his guarantee Bruce gave his own money, his three-story brick home on an 80-acre plot in the west part of Conway, and valuable river bottom farms.

The school opened with a small enrolment in 1892, under the presidency of C. M. Williams. It began as a four-year college, but was made a junior college in 1922 and was accredited as such in 1925 by the North Central Association of Colleges and Secondary Schools.

The college was moved to Camp Robinson in North Little Rock in 1947, but due to lack of patronage and financial support was closed in 1950. The property at Conway, consisting of the original building, a three-story brick dormitory which when erected was considered the finest dormitory in Arkansas, an indoor swimming pool, and several smaller buildings, was sold in 1951 to the North American Baptist Association (Landmark). Its value was about $150,000.

DAISY BRUCE

CENTRAL FEMALE INSTITUTE. See HILLMAN COLLEGE.

CENTRAL GEORGIA BAPTIST. A newspaper edited by J. A. Scarboro and published in Macon, Ga., for a few months in 1889.

JOHN J. HURT, JR.

CENTRAL INSTITUTE (1854–59). A high school for boys and girls founded by the Central Baptist Association, near Wetumpka, Ala. It collapsed under heavy debt in 1859.

JAMES E. DAVIDSON

CENTRAL MESSENGER. A paper published in Brownwood, Tex., with W. T. Curtis and W. R. Earp as editors. It merged with the *Baptist Standard* in 1921.

E. C. ROUTH

CENTRAL MISSISSIPPI FEMALE COLLEGE. Established by Yazoo Baptist Association at Lexington, Miss., in 1853 to replace Lexington Male and Female Academy. With A. W. Chambliss principal, the school flourished after it was chartered and had 116 students enrolled in 1855. It closed during the 1860's.

J. L. BOYD

CENTRAL MISSOURI STATE COLLEGE CHAIR OF BIBLE, WARRENSBURG. Established Sept., 1949, on property acquired through Irving L. Bush, Clinton, Mo., as a memorial to his mother. An approved curriculum was adopted by the Central Missouri State College curriculum committee Dec. 11, 1950. All courses are fully accredited by the college, and the Bible professor must meet the certification requirements of the college. Earl Harding, pastor of First Baptist Church, Warrensburg, served as the first professor of Bible. Curtis A. Hutcherson assumed this position Sept. 1, 1952. CLIFFORD INGLE

CENTRAL TEXAS BAPTIST CONVENTION. A Texas general body organized at Dublin, Tex., Nov. 12, 1880. Always a weak body, it began with high hopes of enlisting all the churches between the Brazos and the Rio Grande. Its collections proved negligible. In the meeting at Abilene in 1884 the unwisdom of its struggle had become evident, and it therefore disbanded in 1885 at Hico in confession of its conviction that Baptists of the state should unite. Perhaps its experience, along with that of the brethren in north and east Texas, actually assisted in bringing about in 1886 the consolidation which was desired by all Texas Baptists, who finally realized that fragmentary effort, however fervent, was inadequate.

J. M. DAWSON

CHAMA VALLEY MEDICAL CENTER. Established as a mission clinic with a medical emphasis in Parkview, N. Mex. An earlier effort to provide such a center was Clovis Hospital, which became extinct in 1938. The center's establishment followed action of the New Mexico Baptist Convention in 1952, led by Harry P. Stagg, executive secretary. E. Kay Bryan and his wife, former medical missionaries to China, were called in 1952 to the superintendency of the institution.

The center stands alone, in an area of a 70-mile radius, in the type of service it renders. Near by the Parkview Baptist Church serves both personnel and constituency in a spiritual way. Parkview, a rural village in the thickly populated Spanish area of the Chama Valley country, provides many mission opportunities. In 1954 medical service receipts totaled $19,915; investments amounted to $70,000, included the clinic building, the doctors' and nurses' home, clinical supplies, and an ambulance Jeep.

DOYLE WINTERS

CHANEY, BAILEY E. (flourished 1790–1823). Pioneer preacher in Louisiana and Mississippi. Coming from South Carolina to the Natchez Country c. 1793, he joined the Cole's Creek (Salem) church of which his father (William Chaney) was the first known deacon. He removed to Louisiana c. 1798 and preached the first Baptist sermon in that state c. 1799, for which he suffered a jail sentence. Upon his release he returned to Mississippi where he served three terms in the house of representatives, Mississippi Territory, 1809, 1813, and 1814. The Salem church engaged him as clerk for nearly two years. However, the membership repeatedly brought against him charges of drunkenness and disorderly conduct, and the church finally excluded him. But in Jan., 1823, it restored him to fellowship and granted him a letter of dismission to join the Bethlehem Baptist Church, Jefferson County. In April of the following year the church "Resolved, That Brother Chaney be required to give up the Church Book." J. L. BOYD

CHAPLAIN. A clergyman attached to military and quasi-military units who serves such personnel in the realm of religion and morality. The United States Government commissions chaplains for the army, navy, air force, and national guard. Veterans Administration hospitals and the Civil Air Patrol also have chaplains. A chaplain must be ordained, endorsed by his denomination, and have adequate educational, mental, moral, and spiritual qualifications. His principal functions are providing for public worship and instruction, administering rites and ordinances, visiting and counseling, instructing in character guidance, and encouraging participation in personal devotions and public religious fellowship. While not required to conduct religious services contrary to the forms of his denomination, the chaplain is morally obligated to serve the religious needs of his entire command through co-operation with other chaplains, civilian clergymen, and other qualified personnel.

The military chaplaincy is an institution of long standing. In ancient times Hebrew priests led the Israelites marching around the crumbling walls of Jericho. In Europe chaplains represented one of the state religions; but in America the Continental army and Congress made a revolutionary policy of choosing a chaplain holding the belief of a majority of each regiment.

The chaplains, at first, also served as teachers in the army and secretaries to the captains in the navy. Each colony had its own plan of religious ministry to the military until the Revolutionary War. Legal provision for a chaplains corps was made July 29, 1775. The Revolution began with a disorganized system of volunteer preachers but closed with an excellent corps of brigade chaplains. Since that time the field of service for chaplains has continued to enlarge so that today this program of ministry has become as wide and varied as that of a vocational worker in any other field of Christian work.

Southern Baptists began a planned ministry to the army and navy through chaplains and other media in 1853, the state Baptist conventions beginning their co-operation in 1860.

The Civil War was accompanied by a great wave of religious revivals. Since each side claimed its cause a holy one, religious fervor prevailed in all the camps. Southern Baptists played an important part in the religious work done for Southern soldiers, through the efforts of boards, colporteurs, the Board of Domestic Missions (Home Mission Board), denominational leaders, printing companies, and chaplains.

The government of the new Southern Confederacy depended upon religious leaders of the South to give moral and spiritual guidance to the people in general and to the soldiers in particular during the war days. Baptist soldiers by far outnumbered any other Christian group; therefore Baptists were also in the lead in their spiritual ministries to these men. Religious work in the army was diversified. At times the religious worker accompanied the regiment on its march and preached as he found opportunity. At other times he moved from camp to camp, preached, counseled, and distributed tracts to soldiers in different camps.

Colporteurs were provided and supported by state mission boards. Some of the greatest services made to soldiers in this war were provided by pastors of the stronger Baptist churches in the South and by denominational leaders. Prominently mentioned in this type of service were: Sylvester Landrum, Lansing Burrows (q.v.), Isaac Taylor Tichenor (q.v.), John Albert Broadus (q.v.), Jeremiah Bell Jeter (q.v.), and James Barnett Taylor (q.v.). They preached on week ends, held revivals in the camps, and as a result, when the war closed a sweeping revival was experienced throughout churches over the South.

Congress provided in 1901 that prospective chaplains should be endorsed by their respective religious denominations. Southern Baptists along with some other groups were slow to assume the responsibility for the endorsement of men for the chaplaincy until 1914.

Growing out of the lack of organization and co-ordination of the spiritual ministries to the men in World War I, the National Defense Act in 1920 provided that chiefs of chaplains be appointed to serve for terms of four years, who would supervise the work of all chaplains in the army. Later, a similar provision was made for the other branches of the military. Since this provision was made, the following Baptists have served as chief of army chaplains: Alva Brasted, 1933-37; Roy Parker, 1949-52; Ivan L. Bennett, 1952-54.

When World War II brought enormous problems in procurement of sufficient numbers of chaplains to meet suddenly expanded needs, it was decided to apportion to each denomination the responsibility for supplying sufficient numbers of chaplains to meet assigned quotas. The response was gratifying—within less than three years, 8,171 chaplains were on active duty in the army. Southern Baptists bore their part of this responsibility.

To expedite Southern Baptist work through the chaplaincy, the Southern Baptist Convention in Birmingham, Ala., in 1941, authorized the Home Mission Board: (1) to have charge of Southern Baptist work in the military, (2) to give denominational endorsement to Baptist preachers who qualify for the chaplaincy, and (3) to co-operate with the state mission boards in religious work contiguous to the military camps. The Home Mission Board immediately organized the Chaplains Committee. By May, 1944, Southern Baptist chaplains in all branches of the military numbered approximately 1,000.

In 1944 the Chaplains Committee became the Chaplains Commission of the Southern Baptist Convention. The commission has had three chairmen since its beginning as a committee in 1941: Ellis A. Fuller, Dick H. Hall, Jr., and O. M. Seigler. Alfred Carpenter was appointed director in 1941. He was sent on missions by the Department of Defense in connection with religious work to be done overseas in military establishments in 1945, 1947, and 1949, and was sent by the Chaplains Commission to Alaska, Korea, and Japan in 1954. The director aids in procurement of chaplains, counseling with them on posts of duty, and helps in launching camp services and evangelistic campaigns, and in promoting denominational conferences and assemblies for the chaplains.

Since the close of World War II, the sphere of service for the chaplains has been greatly enlarged in scope. During this period, the United States Government has stationed troops, more or less permanently, at bases all over the world. The families of military men in the States and in some overseas assignments are permitted to be with them, making the populace on military instalments similar to that in an average community. The chaplains, therefore, must give a spiritual ministry to the families of the military personnel. Added to this duty is the responsibility of building good will among the nations where these armies are located. To meet increased demands, the Chaplains Commission appointed George W. Cummins, a former navy chaplain, as associate director in Oct., 1955.

The expansion of the religious work in the navy has kept pace with the general development of the United States Navy. Burgess Allison, commissioned in 1823, was the first Baptist chaplain to be commissioned for the navy. Three other Baptist chaplains were commissioned for the navy during the period 1825-41. Five others were commissioned from 1842 to 1860. During this period only 24 chaplains were on duty. Two Baptist chaplains were outstanding in their services during the period 1850-80. They were Joseph Stockbridge, made a commodore in 1873, and John Benglass.

Baptist naval chaplains increased from five to 17 during 1917-18. These men, along with the chaplains from other Christian groups, gave significant service to the more than 50,000 men in the United States Navy. Special mention of Southern Baptist chaplains is made of E. L. Ackiss and John W. Decker. During World War II, Baptist naval chaplains increased to 254. Chapels were constructed at most of the navy bases in operation on United States soil and on many islands of the seas.

Since Mar. 3, 1865, chaplains have been provided by the government for military hospitals on a part-time basis. On Nov. 28, 1945, a provision was made for full-time service for the men in veterans' hospitals. In 1955 it was reported that 42 Southern Baptist chaplains were serving in veterans' hospitals.

The most recent branch to be formed in the military is the air force. Until 1948 it served in conjunction with the army, but in 1949 a chief of the air force chaplains was appointed, and since that time all air force chaplains have been under the chief of chaplains for that branch.

O. M. SEIGLER and HAROLD G. SANDERS

CHARITY AND CHILDREN. Publication of the Baptist Orphanage of North Carolina, Inc., first issued on July 14, 1887, approximately 20 months after the orphanage was founded. Mailed to several hundred friends of the orphanage, the paper had for its first editor John Haymes Mills (q.v.), the institution's founder. Although difficulties and uncertainties plagued the paper in its early years, it became more firmly established in 1895 when Archibald Johnson (q.v.) of Red Springs became editor. Thirty-five years later Martin Luther Kesler (q.v.), general superintendent of the orphanage from 1905 to 1932, wrote: "Every issue of the paper, from that day to this has been a page of our history. It is the right arm of the institution and one of the most widely read papers among Southern child welfare publications." Johnson served as editor until his death in 1935, succeeded by John Arch McMillan until 1949, when J. Marse Grant assumed the editorship. Printed in a modern plant on the campus, which was given to the orphanage by the late Robert M. Idol of Winston-Salem, the paper is mailed in bundles to Sunday schools of Baptist churches in North Carolina and also to individual subscribers. Circulation was 48,000 on Dec. 31, 1954. The *Charity and Children* print shop trains men for the printing industry. MARSE GRANT

CHARLESTON, S. C., FIRST BAPTIST CHURCH. The oldest Baptist church in the South, organized Sept. 25, 1682, in Kittery, Me., William Screven (q.v.), pastor. Compelled by persecution to move south, the church migrated to South Carolina, traditionally before June, 1684, where the congregation established the settlement of Somerton near Charleston on the Cooper River. Though the time of Screven's arrival in South Carolina is uncertain, the earliest known record of his presence in the state is dated Dec. 7, 1696. A group of immigrants, "pious and respectable Dissenters from Somersetshire in England," led by Humphrey Blake, and another group from north of England, led by Lord Cardross, united with the church and strengthened it. Both of these groups traditionally arrived in the 1680's. About 1693 the church moved its seat of public worship from Somerton to Charleston (then called Charles Town), where it met "in a temporary building or in the home of William Chapman." On July 18, 1699, William Elliott gave to the church by deed the lot on which it now stands. The congregation soon erected a building which they later enlarged. The body completed the present building in 1822. Of the last building Robert Mills (noted architect, 1781-1855), who designed it, said, "It is purely Greek in its style, simply grand in its proportions and beautiful in its detail."

This church has exercised a formative influence upon Southern Baptists. It led in setting forth much of the pattern later adopted by the denomination in the following areas: theology, organization, education, civil and patriotic endeavors, home missions, and foreign missions. The modified Calvinistic theology of Baptists in the South today is essentially the same as that embraced by the Charleston church over two and one-half centuries ago. Under Screven's leadership in 1700, the church adopted with slight modifications the Second London Confession of Faith of 1689, which was later adopted by the Philadelphia Association. This Calvinistic confession became the pattern for most American Baptists.

The Charleston church and its leaders took initial steps in formulating much of the organized life of the denomination. According to Baptist principles, the church was organized as an autonomous body. Through one of its pastors, Oliver Hart (q.v.), the church led in the organization of the Charleston Association Oct. 21, 1751, the first association in the South. The association conducted most of its meetings in the building of Charleston church until 1778. This church in conjunction with another congregation in 1819 confronted the Charleston Association with the need for a more efficient and extensive union among the Baptists of South Carolina. This action led to the organization of the State Convention of the Baptist Denomination in South Carolina on Dec. 4, 1821, the first state convention planned in the United States and the first organized in the South. Here, too, it is generally accepted, the first organized women's work in the South originated in the Wadmalaw and Edisto Female Mite Society. As early as 1812 the Charleston Association received a contribution from this society. Richard Furman (q.v.), while pastor at Charleston, in 1814 helped to draft the constitution of the Triennial Convention, the first general organization of Baptists in America. Initial steps in the development of the work of Christian education resulted from the work of the church's leadership and membership. In 1755 the church took the lead in forming the Religious Society, one of the early organizations for the education of Baptist ministers in America. William Mason in 1757 opened a day school in the church, where reading, writing, arithmetic, etc., were taught. This was apparently a private enterprise, but the church was co-operative in allowing the use of its facilities. Furman University, the oldest Baptist college in the South, grew out of the work of the church and its pastor, Richard Furman. Two of the four founders of the Southern Baptist Theological Seminary, Basil Manly, Jr.

($q.v.$), and James Petigru Boyce ($q.v.$) (the latter, the first president of the seminary), were from this church, trained in its Sunday school.

The church also made contributions to civil and patriotic affairs. During the Revolution the church lent about 300 pounds sterling to the American Government. The body stood so firmly in behalf of American independence that its property was confiscated when Charleston fell into the hands of the British. In 1788, when the convention meeting to ratify the United States Constitution needed a "more commodious place," Richard Furman offered the use of the First Baptist Church building; evidence has not been found that the offer was accepted.

The missionary interest of the church expressed itself in the beginning of associational and home missions in the South. Records of the Society for the Propagation of the Gospel in Foreign Parts declare that where their missionaries went in this area they found themselves preceded by the Baptists. Largely through its pastor, Oliver Hart, the church in 1755 led the association to send out John Gano ($q.v.$), rightly designated as the first associational missionary in the South. In the 1720's and 1730's the church established missions which later became autonomous churches. This principle of Baptist growth is clearly stated in the minutes of the church by James Tupper (1819–68), who said that people can be reached effectively only by "occupying every accesible [sic] point with sanctuaries." He further stated, "When a church has more members than it can actively employ, the withdrawal of a portion to constitute a new interest is advantageous."

The church also manifested a very early interest in foreign missions. It supported William Carey ($q.v.$) to the extent of contributing a sizable portion of the money raised for him in America. In May, 1814, at the insistence of the congregation, the pastor, Richard Furman, attended the Triennial Convention in Philadelphia. Furman served as president of this convention, the first organized effort of Baptists in America for the support of foreign missions, from 1814 to 1820.

The period from Richard Furman to the Civil War was characterized by learned pastors, great revivals, numerous volunteers for the ministry, deep spirituality, a large increase in membership, large offerings for missions, and new churches. Of the five pastors of the period, three were college presidents and one an editor. The membership reached 1,926 by 1860.

The war scattered and depleted the membership and seriously damaged the building. During the pastorate of Andrew Jackson Spears Thomas ($q.v.$), the congregation with great sacrifice renovated the building for the bicentennial in 1883. A cyclone in 1885 and an earthquake in 1886 made it necessary for the struggling congregation to repair its building extensively for the third time in four years.

In 1891, having no pastor, "due to financial conditions and extreme misfortune, the church closed." However, a group of the faithful climbed in a window to hold regular prayer meetings. In 1893 Lucius Cuthbert led in reopening the church and served as pastor until 1900. From that time until 1940, the church, with fluctuating progress, nobly struggled for existence. The congregation expanded the church lecture room into an educational building in 1940, greatly enlarged it in 1947, and further enlarged it in 1956. The church has operated a kindergarten and day school since Sept. 12, 1949.

BIBLIOGRAPHY: W. Furman, *A History of the Charleston Association* (1811). R. G. Torbet, *A History of the Baptists* (1950). L. Townsend, *South Carolina Baptists, 1670–1805* (1935). H. A. Tupper, ed., *Two Centuries of the First Baptist Church of South Carolina, 1683–1883* (1889).

JOHN A. HAMRICK

CHARLESTON ASSOCIATION, GENERAL COMMITTEE OF. A committee established in 1791 by the Charleston, S. C., Association to assume the work of the older religious society. Named the General Committee for the Charleston Baptist Education Fund, the chartered body was subject to churches of the association. The idea of such a committee originated in 1789 when "a proposition was also brought forward, to recommend a mode for forming funds in the several churches, in order to assist pious young men in their studies for the ministry, and other things of a pub[l]ic nature. . . ." The association unanimously approved the proposition; and in 1790 a plan for the committee was presented which embodied (1) a "charity sermon" to be preached once a year in each church, at which time a collection would be taken to aid in the education of "pious young men," and (2) the forming of a committee consisting of one member from each church to "receive the collections" and "examine candidates for the churches' bounty." From its first meeting in 1791 the committee functioned regularly until 1875. Gradually evolving into an associational missionary body, the committee merged its efforts with the association under a new constitution in 1875.

BIBLIOGRAPHY: R. N. Daniel, *Furman University, a History* (1951). W. J. McGlothlin, *Baptist Beginnings in Education; A History of Furman University* (1926). L. Townsend, *South Carolina Baptists, 1670–1805* (1935).

JOE MADISON KING

CHASTAIN, JAMES GARVIN (b. Itawamba County, Miss., Dec. 18, 1853; d. Richton, Miss., Feb. 20, 1954). Missionary to Mexico. Baptized Dec. 21, 1873, Chastain was ordained June 17, 1875. He graduated from Mississippi College and received a Th.M. degree from Southern Baptist Theological Seminary. Appointed to Mexico in June, 1888, Chastain was an evangelistic worker there for 30 years. After leaving Mexico in 1913 because of revolution, he served under the Home Mission Board for 10 years, in Cuba and Florida. Chastain married Lillian Wright (1860–1927) Nov. 20, 1888, by whom he had two sons and two daughters. Chastain attended foreign mission conference at Ridgecrest

Baptist Assembly when he was nearly 100 years old.

BIBLIOGRAPHY: B. J. W. Graham, *Baptist Biography*, Vol. III (1923). *The Commission* (April, 1954). J. G. Chastain, *Thirty Years in Mexico* (1927).

E. C. ROUTH

CHASTITY. See VIRTUE, CHRISTIAN.

CHATTAHOOCHEE HIGH SCHOOL. A coeducational school opened in 1902 at Clermont, Ga., sponsored by Chattahoochee Association. A member of the Mercer system in the 1920's, the school existed until 1925.

ARTHUR JACKSON

CHAUDOIN, WILLIAM N. (b. Robertson County, Tenn., Aug. 20, 1829; d. LaGrange, Fla., Jan. 22, 1904). Pastor, denominational worker. Son of John Mims and Sarah (Calthorp) Chaudoin, he received little formal education but improved his learning throughout his life by wide reading and study. Converted and baptized at the age of 16, he preached his first sermon two years later in the same church. May 16, 1850, he married Caroline Frensley. In 1851 he was ordained pastor of Charity Church near Nashville, Tenn. Two years later he was called to the Second Church, Nashville. During a revival there he developed the pulmonary infection which handicapped him for the remainder of his life. After a year as agent of the Bible Board of the Southern Baptist Convention, he moved to Macon, Ga., where he was elected principal of Georgia School for the Blind. During the Civil War he preached to soldiers in camps in Virginia. From 1865 to 1870, he served as pastor of churches in southwest Georgia. Beginning in 1870, he was commissioned as agent of the Domestic and Indian Mission Board of the Southern Baptist Convention and later made district secretary of the board for Georgia and Florida. In 1879 he was commissioned by the Georgia Baptist Convention as its general missionary. During the 1870's he contributed to the *Christian Index*, of Georgia, editing the Florida department of that paper.

Having been forced for several years to spend the winters in Florida because of his health, he moved to the state in 1880; that same year the Florida Baptist convention elected him its president and the corresponding secretary and treasurer of its newly created State Board of Missions. Mar. 24, 1886, he was elected to the board of trustees of DeLand College, afterward John B. Stetson University. Feb. 13, 1893, the college voted to confer on him the honorary D.D. degree. Chaudoin Hall of the university was named in his honor.

BIBLIOGRAPHY: [S. Boykin], *A History of the Baptist Denomination in Georgia, with Biographical Compendium and Portrait Gallery of Baptist Ministers and other Georgia Baptists* (1881). L. D. Geiger, *Florida Baptist Witness* (1899). E. H. Reynolds, Sr., *Florida Baptist Witness* (1904).

H. C. GARWOOD

CHEKIANG-SHANGHAI BAPTIST CONVENTION, EAST CHINA. As early as 1873 Baptists in Chekiang and Kiangsu (Shanghai) provinces organized the Chekiang Baptist Association, later the Chekiang-Shanghai Baptist Convention. The China Baptist Council, organized in 1922, co-ordinated the Chekiang-Shanghai Baptist Convention, the Ling Tong Baptist Convention of the South China Mission, and the Szechuan Baptist Convention of the West China Mission; the council was composed of five Chinese and three missionaries from each field. East China was in the forefront of missions in transferring administrative responsibility to national leaders. In 1930 the China Baptist Alliance was organized to bring together all Chinese Baptist churches regardless of the mission society which fostered them.

Baptist work in East China began in 1843 with the establishment of a mission at Ningpo by D. J. Macgowan, M.D. (b. 1815; d. 1893), American Baptist missionary. The first convert was baptized Nov. 21, 1847, and the first church organized. The New Testament, translated by Josiah Goddard (b. 1813; d. 1854), was printed in 1853. Baptist work suffered reverses during the Taiping Rebellion (1845–1865) and the Boxer Rebellion of 1900, but Baptists south and north founded in 1908 Shanghai Baptist College (University in 1911) with a plant valued in 1926 at $1,000,000. When the Chinese Republic was proclaimed Feb. 12, 1912, the old-style educational system was abolished, and Christians promptly developed educational and medical work, with most of the institutions under Chinese administrators by 1927.

The Chekiang-Shanghai Baptist Convention largely administered work during the undeclared war by Japan, which began in 1931 with seizure of Manchuria and culminated in 1937 with a full-scale invasion. General internment of missionaries during World War II began early in 1943. Missionaries returned after furlough and undertook rehabilitation of the work and reconstruction of property. As a result of the Communist invasion from the north in 1948, with the People's Republic of China formed Oct. 1, 1949, all missionaries had to be evacuated. The evacuation was completed by 1950 with most of the missionaries transferring to other fields. Christian work continues with Chinese leaders, but suffers all the disabilities imposed by Communist control.

DATA

	1934	1949 *
Churches	36	35
Baptisms	404	—
Church members	3,431	5,826
Missionaries	56	1
Chinese workers	490	641
Students	7,389	7,616
(Univ. of Shanghai 2,681)		
Schools	43	26
Patients	45,889	134,329
Hospitals and dispensaries	5	7
Field contributions	$23,801	—

* Latest figures.

ADA STEARNS

CHEROKEE BAPTIST COLLEGE. Founded in 1853 at Cassville, Ga., in Bartow County. Citizens of Cassville projected the school in Nov., 1853, and the charter was approved in January of the following year. Thomas Rambaut was the first president, or "Chairman of the Faculty." Neither the school nor the Cherokee Baptist Convention which sponsored it survived the Civil War. ARTHUR JACKSON

CHEROKEE BAPTIST CONVENTION. A body organized by representatives of Middle Cherokee, Coosa, and Tallapoosa associations meeting at Cassville, Ga., Nov. 23, 1854, for the furtherance of education and the fostering of missions. Its primary basis seems to have been a desire to support the Cherokee Baptist College, which was founded the same year at Cassville.

One of the instrumentalities of the new convention was a paper called *The Landmark Banner and Cherokee Baptist,* published first at Rome, Ga., in Oct., 1859, under the editorship of Jesse M. Wood. In June, 1860, the paper was moved to Atlanta. The exigencies of the Civil War brought financial embarrassment, and the paper passed into other hands and subsequently went out of existence.

The Cherokee Baptist Convention gained support from the Tallapoosa, Ellijay, Arbacoochee, State Line, and Noonday Baptist associations. The war, however, appears to have crushed the convention and its enterprises. The minutes of the Middle Cherokee Association for 1866 show that a motion to appoint delegates to the Cherokee Baptist Convention was indefinitely postponed. EDWIN D. JOHNSTON

CHEROKEE BAPTIST HIGH SCHOOL. Opened at Adairsville, Ga., in 1901, partially supported by Middle Cherokee Association. In 1917 the property was sold, and proceeds in Liberty Bonds were donated to Bessie Tift College for a student fund. ARTHUR JACKSON

CHEROKEE INDIAN BAPTIST ASSEMBLY. Founded in 1950 by Roe Beard and wife, missionaries of the Home Mission Board to the Cherokees, it occupies 21 acres of land six miles east of Tahlequah, Okla. Grounds and buildings are valued at about $25,000. The first year's registration was 445, and in 1956 it was 230. Sponsored by the Cherokee Baptist Association, it is financed by registration fees of $1 per person and by special gifts from the churches of the association and the Home Mission Board.
J. M. GASKIN

CHEROKEE MESSENGER. A newspaper published at Rome, Ga., which was approved by the Floyd County Association in 1897. A. B. S. Moseley was the first to publish the paper for the association. The paper became extinct by 1911. JOHN J. HURT, JR.

CHEROKEE MESSENGER. A monthly paper published by Evan Jones and Jesse Bushyhead (*q.v.*) and the first newspaper of any kind published in what is now Oklahoma. It was issued by the second printing press in the Cherokee Nation, located at Breadtown. Later called *Cherokee,* the paper was originally called *Baptist,* with Volume I, Number 1 being issued in Aug., 1844. The Baptist Mission Press was furnished by the Baptist Mission Board of Boston, Mass., and was accompanied to the Cherokee Nation by Hervey Upham, a practical printer, who executed the press work on the early editions. The periodical, a 16-page, two-column paper issued irregularly, was primarily devoted to religious and temperance topics. It was printed mostly in Cherokee characters using the alphabet invented by Sequoyah. The first edition, comprising 1,600 copies, contained less than four columns of English. The paper, with its first 12-number series running from Aug., 1844, to May, 1846, was issued at 50 cents a year, payable in advance. Volume I, Number 1 (Aug., 1844) consisted of a portion of Genesis, Psalm 1, Bunyan's *Pilgrim's Progress,* Peter Parley's *Universal History,* the Cherokee alphabet, sounds, vowels and consonants, brief specimens in Cherokee grammatical forms, and an account of the Going Snake Temperance Society. Although publication was suspended in 1846, John Buttrick Jones (*q.v.*) revived the paper in Sept., 1858, and issued it every alternate month at 40 cents a year. It consisted of 16 pages in pamphlet form and again was printed principally in the Cherokee language. On Sept. 5, 1859, it reported a circulation of 2,000 copies for each of the five numbers issued in its new series. The paper was permanently suspended, probably not later than 1860, due primarily to general strife in the Cherokee Nation apparently engendered over the slavery issue in the face of impending conditions which led to the Civil War. J. M. GASKIN

CHILDREN'S AID SOCIETY, MARYLAND BAPTIST. A Baptist children's home providing for unfortunate and needy Baptist children, established in 1920. The home was duly incorporated under the laws of Maryland, and the first meeting of the trustees was held on Oct. 22, 1920. The first trustees were W. M. McCormick (*q.v.*), Francis S. Biggs (*q.v.*), A. William Field, W. A. Gunton, and J. Edward Tyler, Jr. The original officers were: president, McCormick; vice-president, E. M. Sturtevant; secretary, Field; and treasurer, Francis A. Davis.

The purpose for which the corporation was formed was thus stated: "The care of orphan children, and other children needing attention because of neglect or dependence; to throw around them the atmosphere of a private Christian home, with the influence and safeguards there found." To best accomplish this work, the Placing Out System (now known as foster home service) was adopted.

In the beginning the work was conducted with great difficulty, resulting in a temporary arrangement with the Henry Watson Children's Aid Society to help in establishing the enterprise.

Soon thereafter, Grace Tyler became the executive secretary and continued in office until 1926 when Margaret Brooke became the fieldworker, with Mrs. J. W. C. Brittingham as assistant executive secretary.

In 1921 the society was able to care for only nine children. The allocation from the 75 Million Campaign was 4 per cent of the distributable funds. In 1922 there were 35 children under the care of the society.

In 1923 Miss Tyler said in her annual report: "We want every one to understand that our aim is to befriend every needy Baptist child in Maryland. We are contemplating changing our corporate name to The Baptist Children's Aid Society." Twenty-seven of the 39 children under the care of the organization were in their own homes.

In 1924 the name of the organization was changed as recommended by Miss Tyler. In President McCormick's report of 1925, he stated that a woman's advisory board of 10 members had been appointed. At that time the cost of caring for the children was $225 per year. During the same year the Maryland Baptist Cooperative Program was inaugurated, and the society continued to receive the same percentage of the contributions as during the 75 Million Campaign. Mrs. Brittingham was elected executive secretary and served until 1936 when she resigned. Carolyn G. Henderson was elected as executive secretary and served until 1949 when, upon her retirement, Mrs. J. M. Hoffa was elected to serve in this capacity.

In 1928 the total assets of the society were only $12,718.09, and it was necessary for the trustees to borrow $3,000 for current expenses.

Willoughby M. McCormick (q.v.) and many other Maryland Baptists have contributed to the Children's Aid. In 1954 total assets were over $193,000. An annual budget of $23,000 was provided. Ninety-three children, representing 29 families, received service. Twenty-four went out of care, including one adoption. Presently, service is given to 66 children of whom six are orphaned or part-orphaned and 29 deserted by one or both parents. The society pays board, costing from $10 to $16 weekly. It supplements food budgets, provides clothing, and secures required medication. Its aim is to provide love and security, with special emphasis placed upon Christian training.

The present officers of the corporation are: president, Rowland McD. Ness; vice-president, William D. Pitt; secretary, Laurence A. Free; treasurer, Francis A. Davis; executive secretary, Virgie M. Hoffa.

BIBLIOGRAPHY: J. T. Watts, *Rise and Progress of Maryland Baptists* (n.d.). VIRGIE M. HOFFA

CHILDREN'S HOME, THE DENOMINATIONAL. An institution for neglected, dependent, and destitute children, owned and operated by Southern Baptists through one of their state associations and conventions. Presently there are 27 Baptist children's homes. Homes that were originally established some 50 to 75 years ago to minister to orphan children only now find that only 5 per cent or less of their children are full orphans. Almost all of their children are from broken homes, and more than 50 per cent of them have both parents living. Baptists are operating children's homes because there is a tremendous need to provide Christian care for those children who, through no fault of their own, find themselves without a home.

Baptist children's homes, in general, have three distinct fields of service. The first service is institutional care. This is by far the largest area of service offered by Baptist homes. Children's needs are provided for in group living. This was the original purpose of orphanages and remains so in present children's homes. Here the child receives Christian training and educational and cultural advantages, which are the heritage of every American boy and girl. Without exception, Christ and his teachings are emphasized above everything else in Baptist children's homes.

The second phase of service, foster home placement by the institution under the auspices and supervision of the institution, fulfils the need of some children for a more normal, homelike atmosphere for growth and development. Some children simply cannot accept group living. They are not equipped emotionally to cope with the competition and stresses that come from the closeness of so many other children. Many Baptist children's homes now offer this service to children entrusted to their care.

The third phase of service is mother's aid. In this type service the child or children remain in their own homes with a mother who has proven that she can manage well, that she loves her children, and that she can give them far more than any institution or foster home, but she needs financial help. After proper study and planning by the institution, money is provided on a monthly basis to supplement whatever income is in the home in order to keep the family together and prevent a break-up of the home.

In these three fields of service carried on by 27 Southern Baptist children's homes, administered independently by the different state institutions, some 6,395 children were cared for in 1955.

The investment through the years by Baptist people in real estate, endowment, equipment, etc., to carry on this work runs over 29 million dollars. In 1955 the income for the operation and maintenance of all Baptist children's homes amounted to approximately $5,278,000. Every dollar came from Baptist sources, given freely for the cause of dependent childhood.

The scope of the child care services rendered by Baptist people on the Southern Baptist Convention level is tremendous. Since the founding of the first Baptist orphanage in the South in the late 1860's, it is conservatively estimated that more than 56,000 children have been served by Southern Baptist children's homes.

The strong thread of emphasis from the beginning remains: Christian living in a Christian atmosphere administered and supported by Baptist Christian people.   R. F. HOUGH

CHILD'S INDEX. A monthly, edited and published by Samuel Boykin (q.v.) at Macon, Ga., from Sept., 1862, to Apr., 1865. It was superseded by the *Child's Delight,* which was later (Jan., 1866) merged with *Kind Words,* founded by the first Sunday School Board of the Southern Baptist Convention.   SPENCER B. KING, JR.

CHILE, MISSION IN. Impressed by the heroic work of William David Thompson MacDonald (q.v.) and his Chilean associates, and by the great evangelistic opportunity Chile offered, T. Bronson Ray (q.v.), following a visit to South America in 1914, secured aid for Chilean Baptists from the Foreign Mission Board. In 1917 Joseph Lancaster Hart, a missionary on furlough from Argentina, stirred the Baptist church at Murray, Ky., to guarantee the salary of a missionary couple for Chile. As a result William Earl and Mary (Skidmore) Davidson began work in Santiago, Chile, that year. They organized the first Baptist church there in 1920 with seven members and a second church in 1921.

Robert Cecil and Mary (Pimm) Moore began a new station at Concepción, third city of Chile, in 1919, organizing seven churches between 1920 and 1933. Hart was transferred from Argentina in 1921 and located at Temuco, the center of work established by MacDonald. Following a vigorous evangelism and training schedule in that whole area until 1933, he served briefly in Concepción, and in 1936 opened a new field in Antofagasta, where he organized the first Baptist church and maintained outstations in saltpeter and copper mining centers.

Each missionary had student helpers; and MacDonald, Moore, and Davidson held winter institutes for preachers. Hart and James William McGavock, who reached Chile in 1922, began a Bible institute in Temuco, which was moved to Santiago and enlarged as a seminary under McGavock in 1939. A women's training school, begun in 1942 by Georgia Mae Ogburn, soon merged with the seminary.

Nora Agnes Graham (q.v.) went to Chile in 1920 to found a Baptist school in Temuco, which she opened with 10 students in Apr., 1922. Assisting her were Cornelia Brower, Tennessee Hamilton Hart, and later Anne Nora Laseter and Marjorie Spence. The school added prestige to Baptist work throughout south Chile.

A Baptist paper, *La Voz Bautista,* was started by MacDonald in 1908, with Hart as editor, 1922–23, followed by Moore who served for 12 years, after which the paper was turned over to the Chilean Baptist Convention. Moore opened a book store and began publishing tracts and books in 1920; publication work is now under the convention.

Mrs. Hart and Mrs. Moore organized a national Woman's Missionary Union in 1923; Mrs. Moore was executive secretary until 1949 and has been editor of the women's publications since 1922. Catherine Johnson McGavock and Susan Roberta Ryan developed Sunbeam work, and Mary Elizabeth Buch McConnell started Vacation Bible schools.

Chief problems of early missionaries were self-support for churches and working relations with nationals. There were few paid pastors, but about 100 lay preachers were trained. Creation of the Co-operative Board of Mission and Convention in 1936 threw responsibility on nationals, with excellent results. The mission proposed and the convention accepted in 1953 a goal for self-support for each church. Excellent church buildings have been provided by the Jarman Foundation and Lottie Moon offerings. A good will center, founded by Lois Hart in 1940, is located at Antofagasta. A children's clinic and day school are connected with it. The mission was legally incorporated in 1922 as Sociedad Evangélica Bautista. The five mission stations, maintained by 37 missionaries, are Antofagasta, Valparaíso, Santiago, Concepción, and Temuco.

                                    R. CECIL MOORE

CHILEAN BAPTIST CONVENTION. German colonists organized the first Baptist church in Chile in 1892, and a Christian and Missionary Alliance representative, H. L. Weiss, a Mennonite who arrived in Chile in Apr., 1897, extended German Baptist work among the Chileans. William David Thompson MacDonald (q.v.) worked with the alliance from 1899 to 1907. Encouraged by a visit from William Buck Bagby (q.v.) from Brazil, he led in organizing the Chilean Baptist Convention in June, 1908, with five churches and 300 members. In 1914 the Southern Baptist Foreign Mission Board began giving the convention financial aid.

In 1926 a joint administrative board of the convention and the Baptist Mission was named and in 1936 was reorganized as the Co-operative (executive) Board. A building and loan board was launched in 1942, and a national Woman's Missionary Union was organized in 1923.

Colegio Bautista, a Baptist academy and high school begun by missionaries in 1922, has 450 students and a Chilean principal, Timoteo Gatica, elected in 1947. A theological seminary, begun as a Bible institute by missionaries in Temuco in 1923 and later moved to Santiago and expanded to include a training school for women, also has a Chilean president, Honorio Espinoza, and has 22 students.

Espinoza is editor of a Baptist paper, *La Voz Bautista,* begun in 1908 by MacDonald. Four other magazines, one for women and three for children, are published. The Co-operative Board publishes tracts and books and maintains four book stores, the first begun in 1920 by Robert Cecil Moore. After some sporadic attempts at radio preaching, regular radio work began in 1950. A Sunday school board was named in 1925, with emphasis on teacher training.

The Chilean Baptist Convention was legally

incorporated in Oct., 1947. In 1955 it included 59 churches with 6,406 members. Self-supporting churches increased from 5 per cent in 1920 to 65 per cent in 1955.   R. C. MOORE

CHILEAN SEMINARY, SANTIAGO. See CHILE, MISSION IN.

CHILIASTIC BODIES. Sectarian groups holding a common view centered in the millennium, a position held by many of the early Christian fathers until Origen. In fact, these views were most universal until the time of the Gnostics. Dionysius of Alexandria and Augustine delivered a temporary deathblow to millennialism until just prior to A.D. 1,000.

Psychology, perhaps more than theology, played a great part in the ascendency of chiliasm, for wherever the view was held with greatest tenacity, it was preceded with some great moral, mental, economical, physical, social, or political stress. Chiliastic views revived during the Reformation, the Peasants' Revolt, the English, French, and American Revolutions, the American Civil War, and the two world wars.

Usually chiliastic bodies have set a date for the bodily return of Christ to the earth. Some of the dates that have been set are: 500, 1000, 1365, 1367, 1525, 1689, 1694, 1730, 1826, 1835, 1836, 1838, 1844, 1864, 1868, 1870, 1873, 1889, 1891, 1902, 1914, and 1923.

Chiliasm holds that Christ shall come from heaven as a warrior and shall vanquish the anti-Christian world. Those who died for the faith shall rise first and reign with Christ 1,000 years on earth, at which time Satan is loosed for a season. God then destroys Satan, resurrects the remaining dead, and performs the last judgment. Although the Greek church and the German and Swiss reformers threw out the old view of chiliasm, the Western church retained it.

Religious bodies that have adopted chiliastic views are Anabaptists, Mennonites, Holiness sects, fundamentalists within non-millennial churches, Jehovah's Witnesses, and forty or more sects, including the "Prophets of Zwickau," a group headed by Thomas Münster.

BIBLIOGRAPHY: "Anabaptists," *The Universal Standard Encyclopaedia* (1955). H. K. Carroll, *The Religious Forces of the United States* (1895). E. T. Clark, *The Small Sects in America* (1949). *Encyclopaedia Britannica*, XX, XV (1949). L. C. Froom, "Seventh-Day Adventists," *The American Church of the Protestant Heritage*, ed., V. Ferm (1953). P. E. Mayer, *The Religious Bodies in America* (1954). F. S. Mead, *Handbook of Denominations in the United States* (1951). M. Phelan, comp., *Handbook of All Denominations* (1915). C. F. Potter, *The Faiths Men Live By* (1954). *The Western Recorder* (Sept. 21, 1916). R. G. Torbet, "Baptist Churches in America," *The American Church of the Protestant Heritage*, ed., V. Ferm (1953). J. K. Van Baalen, *The Chaos of Cults* (1947).   C. EARL COOPER

CHILTON UNITY HIGH SCHOOL. A coeducational school located at Thorsby, Ala., founded *c.* 1905 by the Unity and Chilton County associations. An effort on the part of the trustees to pass control of the school to the state convention failed, and the school closed shortly after 1912.   JAMES E. DAVIDSON

CHINA, MISSION IN. The first missionary appointed by the Foreign Mission Board after its organization in 1845 was appointed to China. Thus, China is Southern Baptists' oldest mission field and was, for a century, their largest. Southern Baptists usually date their work in China from 1836, when John Lewis Shuck (*q.v.*) and Henrietta Hall Shuck (*q.v.*) arrived there. The Shucks, although Southerners, went out under the Triennial Convention. After the Southern Baptist Foreign Mission Board was organized, Shuck became affiliated with it, and the work begun in Canton was continued by Southern Baptists.

During the century following Southern Baptist beginnings in China four missions were organized and developed. The missions, organizations of missionaries located in general areas, planned the work to be done in the various stations, through preaching places, schools, hospitals, etc. The four missions established in China were South, Central, North, and Interior.

The South China Mission dates from 1836 (1845). Canton was the first and central station, but other stations were opened and manned by missionaries at Kweilin, Kong Moon, Macao, San Ooi, Shiuchow, Shiu Hing, Waichow, Wuchow, and Yingtak.

The Central China Mission was opened in 1847, when Matthew Tyson Yates (*q.v.*), Shuck, and T. W. Tobey began work in Shanghai, with other stations established at Soochow, Chinkiang, Yangchow, Wusih, and Kunshan.

North China Mission had its beginning in 1859, when Jessie B. Hartwell and James Landrum Holmes (*q.v.*) arrived in Chefoo, with Holmes settling in Chefoo, and Hartwell in Tengchow. In later years Hwanghsien was recognized as the central station of the mission. Other stations were Dairen (in Manchuria), Laichow, Laiyang, Tsingtao, Pingtu, Tsinan, and Tsining. Harbin, Manchuria, opened as a station of the North China Mission, was recognized as Manchuria Mission a few years before World War II.

The Interior China Mission was opened in 1904, when Wesley Willingham Lawton (*q.v.*) and William Eugene Sallee (*q.v.*) located at Chengchow, Honan. In 1908 Sallee opened a station at Kaifeng, which became the school center of the mission. Later, Kweiteh in Honan and Pochow in Anhwei became stations of the Interior Mission.

Each mission had its own organization, including a separate treasurer. There was little communication and correlation among them at first. Many North China and all Interior missionaries had their bank accounts in Shanghai. They agreed that one treasurer could serve the three missions, and began to operate under this plan in 1924 with the treasurer in Shanghai.

The South China Mission came in with them in 1938.

As mission work expanded a need was felt for closer relations among the missions, and between them and the board in Richmond. To meet this need and to assist the board's executive secretary, Milledge Theron Rankin (q.v.) was elected first secretary for the Orient, holding that office until he was elected executive secretary of the board Jan. 1, 1945. Baker James Cauthen became secretary for the Orient Jan. 1, 1946, serving during the evacuation of missionaries from China under Communist pressure.

Outstations were opened in areas surrounding the stations. As converts were won, churches were established; as churches increased in number, associations were organized for fellowship and inspiration; as more local associations were organized, the original associations became conventions. In each of the four mission areas, conventions were established: Leung Kwong, Kiangsu, North China, and Honan-Anhwei. The next step, a national convention, was organized in 1948 as the China Baptist Convention and was functioning when missionaries were forced to leave China due to Communist oppression.

Of necessity, missionaries had to be pastors of the early churches, although the trend led toward Chinese pastors. As soon as devout Chinese could be found and trained, they were called to serve as pastors, thus relieving the missionaries to encourage and help in the organization of other churches.

Missionaries established schools in most of the stations and encouraged churches to establish primary schools as part of their work. The schools varied from primary to college and theological seminaries. Although the schools provided general education, the Bible occupied the central place in the curriculum. Through schools, thousands of young people became Christians.

Old China provided education for some of its boys but made no provision for educating girls. Thus Rosewell Hobart Graves (q.v.), believing the Chinese Christians would take care of the boys, advocated establishing a school in Canton for girls. Pooi Ching Boys Academy was established in Canton. With a small beginning, it was still struggling along with about 40 boys in 1913, but it belonged to the Chinese and they were proud of it. About 1915 the school began to grow and needed more buildings. Local people did what they could and sent a representative to collect money from Chinese abroad. At the beginning of the Chinese-Japanese war in 1937 the academy had a student body of 3,500, ranging from primary through high school. Pooi Ching established a branch in Hong Kong which was expanded after the war, thus when Communists took over, the Chinese continued a strong Christian school in Hong Kong, which had an enrolment of more than 3,000 in 1955.

Southern and Northern Baptists worked together in establishing Shanghai Baptist College and Seminary in 1905. After about 25 years the seminary department was discontinued, but the college maintained a strong department of religious instruction. In the early days the president and heads of departments were missionaries. J. T. Proctor was president of the college; Robert Thomas Bryan (q.v.), of the seminary. After a short term Proctor resigned and F. J. White became president, serving for about 25 years. Then, Herman Chan-En Liu (q.v.), T. K. Van, and Henry Lin, in order, held the position. By popular request of Chinese Baptists the name of the school was changed to University of Shanghai, and it became one of the great Christian schools in China.

Bible training was provided in each of the four missions, at Graves Theological Seminary in South China, through Bible classes and seminary department of the university in Central China, at Baptist Theological Seminary, Hwanghsien in North China, at Honan Baptist Bible School in Interior China, and at All-China Baptist Theological Seminary, which began at Kaifeng and was moved to Shanghai.

Graves Seminary, the oldest of the Bible schools, began as a Bible class in the home of Rosewell Hobart Graves (q.v.). The students followed three months of school work with three months of itinerant preaching. To serve with Graves, other teachers, both Chinese and missionary, were added to the faculty. For 75 years this school trained hundreds of men.

In the beginning all the seminaries received Christian Chinese men who could read their own language. Christian witnessing and good standing in a Baptist church were requirements for admission. Most of the men became effective in Baptist advancement.

As the educational standard of Chinese Christians became higher, there appeared a need for a seminary where college men could be given instruction in keeping with their ability. A committee, appointed from each of the four missions to study the need and possibilities, selected Kaifeng as a central location, leading to the opening of the China Baptist Theological Seminary there in 1938 in borrowed buildings. In the autumn of 1940, when missionaries were being evacuated, classes were suspended, but in 1941-42 some members of the faculty and student body continued seminary work in Shanghai. The first class was graduated Feb. 13, 1943, the day before the missionary faculty was called up for Japanese concentration camp.

After World War II, due to disturbed conditions in the Interior, the trustees chose Shanghai as the permanent home of the seminary. Permanent buildings were erected on the Baptist Compound there, and a promising beginning was made until atheistic communism closed in and put a stop to the work.

In addition to the seminaries for men, emphasis was given to the training of women. Pooi In Women's Bible School was established to give rudimentary education to wives of theological students, but it developed into an efficient training school for women preparing for special Christian service. Bible schools and informal training classes for women were provided in several other mission stations. A few years before the war a woman's training school was established in Shanghai on the Baptist Compound. It was not reopened after the war, but women students were admitted to the China Baptist Seminary.

The first Southern Baptist hospital in any foreign land was Warren Memorial at Hwanghsien. Thomas Willburn Ayers (*q.v.*) was its first doctor. Other hospitals in China were Mayfield-Tizzner in Laichow, Baptist hospitals in Pingtu, Yangchow, Chengchow, and Kweilin, Stout Memorial in Wuchow, and a hospital-clinic at Pochow in the Interior Mission. The Leung Kwông Hospital in Canton is not a mission hospital, but is a vital part of Baptist work, owned and operated by the Baptists of Leung Kwông Convention. At times a missionary doctor has assisted in it.

The value of the printed page in spreading the gospel was recognized by the early missionaries, resulting in a growing conviction that Baptists should do their own printing so as to have the literature needed to teach doctrines adequately. Thus the China Baptist Publication Society was organized in Canton in 1899. The organization body consisted of representatives of the South China Mission of Southern Baptists and the similar Northern Baptist mission at Swatow. The society's purpose was to serve all Baptists in China, with representatives of the two American boards participating in it. Although co-operation of the two South China missions was excellent, personnel and funds came largely from Southern Baptists, and the partnership was dissolved in 1937. The Foreign Mission Board refunded to the American Baptist Foreign Mission Society without interest its investment in the publication society.

Robert Edward Chambers was recognized as founder of the society and was elected its corresponding secretary, a position he held until his death. The work began with one foot-powered press, with other presses and machinery added according to demand. Land was secured and suitable buildings erected on the river bank near Tungshan, Canton.

It became apparent that Shanghai would be a better center from which to reach quickly all Baptists in China, and the publication headquarters were moved there in 1926. The buildings and equipment in Canton were sold and printing was done by contract in Shanghai. In 1929 a lot in the heart of Shanghai was purchased, and in 1930–31 an eight-story office building was erected, into which the society moved Jan. 1, 1932. This building became headquarters for Baptists in China, with offices provided for the China Mission treasurer, secretary for the Orient, secretary of the Kiangsu convention, and finally for the executive secretary of the China Baptist Convention.

The society published tracts, theological textbooks, and study course books for Sunday school, Training Union, and missionary societies. A full line of literature for the Sunday school and Training Union was prepared and published. A prime objective at the beginning, to publish Bibles with the correct word for baptism, resulted in the publication of many editions of Bibles, New Testaments, and Gospel portions, which were widely used. Hymnbooks for the churches and *True Light Monthly Magazine* were also published.

In Oct., 1940, political disturbance in the Far East was such that the Foreign Mission Board advised evacuation from China of all women and children, especially women who had children, and all missionaries whose furloughs were due in 1941. During late 1940 and early 1941 more than 100 missionaries were evacuated. At the outbreak of the war, Dec. 7, 1941, 89 missionaries were in China and 10 in the Philippines, eight of them at the Peking Language School which had been moved to the Philippines and two in transit home in Manila.

At the outbreak of the war all missionaries in occupied territory were either placed under house arrest or otherwise limited in their movements. Those in Hong Kong and the Philippines were interned as soon as the Japanese captured them. Missionaries in Macao were severely restricted. Those in Wuchow and Kweilin moved on west ahead of the Japanese advance in China. Some were repatriated on the first trip of the *Gripsholm* in the summer of 1942, others on the ship's second trip in 1943. Those in the Philippines were interned until liberated by American forces.

As soon as Japanese surrender was in sight, missionaries became eager to re-enter China. Three men were sent by the first available passage, and a few others were sent later to study the situation and make provision for missionaries to return as soon as possible. They found residences, school buildings, and churches devastated by Japanese occupation and vandalism. As arrangements were made for housing, the flow of missionaries grew until most members of the prewar staff were back on the field, along with new missionaries just appointed. Communist domination prevented the reopening of stations at Hwanghsien, Laichow, Laiyang, Pingtu, and Kweiteh, but all other stations were opened.

Toward the end of 1947, it became apparent that the antiforeign hatred of the Communists would prevent missionaries from continuing their work. Thus another evacuation began, with some missionaries leaving just ahead of Communist occupation, while some remained to try to work under the new regime. Chengchow and Kaifeng had to be evacuated by air lift over Communist lines. The Chengchow Hospital staff and vital equipment were taken by air lift to Hankow and then sent by train to Kweilin. As conditions became worse, station after station was evacuated, until all Southern Baptist missionaries were out of China proper.

During the years of war and two evacuations only two Southern Baptist missionaries were lost by violence. Rufus Gray (*q.v.*) died at the hands of the Japanese in Baguio, Philippines, while William Wallace (*q.v.*) was killed by Communists in Wuchow.

Former China missionaries are now serving in Korea, Japan, Formosa, Hong Kong, Macao, Philippines, Thailand, Malaya, Indonesia, and Hawaii. They work entirely with Chinese in Formosa, Hong Kong, and Macao. In other countries, except Japan and Korea, although first contacts were with Chinese, missionaries are reaching other races as well. Strong seminaries are operating in Formosa and Hong Kong.

J. T. WILLIAMS

CHINA BAPTIST PUBLICATION SOCIETY, SHANGHAI. See CHINA, MISSION IN.

CHINA MISSION ADVOCATE. A monthly journal of 32 pages published for only one year, 1839, by the Roberts Fund and China Mission Society of Kentucky. It was begun by action at the annual meeting of the society in Louisville, Ky., on Nov. 2, 1838. The editor was John L. Waller.

WILLIAM M. SHINTO

CHINESE, HOME MISSIONS TO. The Home Mission Board began work with the Chinese of California by appointing John Lewis Shuck (*q.v.*), who served 1854–60 in Sacramento, and J. B. Hartwell, who served in San Francisco from 1879 until the work was abandoned in 1884. Beginning in 1870, B. W. Whilden served for a while among the Chinese working on plantations and railroads in the South.

The board took up the Chinese work it is now doing by the appointment of Ollie Lewellyn, San Antonio, Tex., 1924; Margaret Jung, Phoenix, Ariz., 1940; Mary Etheridge, El Paso, Tex., 1941; and Mary Nelle Lyne, Berkeley, Calif., 1946. Thomas Lowe, missionary in Berkeley, began the work in San Francisco, Calif., in 1949. M. W. Rankin was loaned by the Foreign Mission Board to begin work in Los Angeles, Calif., in 1951, and Mary Etheridge and Nina Gillespie were transferred to Tucson, Ariz., in 1955.

Other Chinese mission work is being done by local forces, sometimes with the help of summer mission workers and part-time missionaries of the Home Mission Board in Norfolk, Va.; Charleston, S. C.; Augusta, Ga.; Miami, Fla.; and Houston, Tex.

The following have worked under the Home Mission Board with the Chinese after having served as foreign missionaries in China: J. Lewis Shuck, George Pearcy, J. B. Hartwell, Mary Nelle Lyne, and M. W. Rankin. Many Home Mission Board workers of Chinese extraction are products of missions in China.

In 1956 the Home Mission Board employed 13 missionaries with the Chinese. The budget for salaries and operational expense was $21,000. The board owns properties with a total evaluation of $255,000 in San Antonio, Tex.; El Paso, Tex.; Phoenix, Ariz.; Los Angeles, Calif.; and San Francisco, Calif. Local Baptist forces own properties for Chinese work in Norfolk, Va., and Houston, Tex. There are Chinese Baptist churches at San Antonio, Tex.; Houston, Tex.; Los Angeles, Calif.; and San Francisco, Calif. The other work is in the form of missions, mission centers, or an effort to integrate the Chinese into the Anglo-American Baptist churches. The estimated Chinese population of the Southern Baptist Convention territory is 80,000.

LOYD CORDER

CHINESE BAPTIST CONVENTION. An all-Chinese convention of Baptists, organized in 1948, which grew out of the work of Southern Baptist missionaries. Several factors prevented organization of a national Baptist convention in China prior to 1948. Mission work was begun in widely separated areas of China, where people spoke different dialects, and travel between them was difficult, dangerous, and expensive. Baptist organization beyond the church level consisted in local associations and provincial conventions. One convention, Kwong Siu, was organized 51 years ago.

Missionaries of various Baptist boards first sensed the desirability of nation-wide fellowship and organized the China Baptist Alliance in the early 1900's. The alliance, which met several times at irregular intervals, was attended by missionaries, and at its last meeting welcomed several English-speaking Chinese Baptists. Following the China Baptist Alliance era the idea of a national convention of Chinese Baptists was considered. It failed to materialize, partly because of political disturbances, but largely because of a difference in working policy.

The national situation changed after about 1920 when the national language (Mandarin) began to be taught in most of the schools throughout China. As a result, educated people from the various provinces could converse intelligibly. A few rail and motor roads, better coastal steamers, and airplanes made travel easier, and these improved conditions opened the way for renewed thought of a national Baptist convention. Messengers from the four areas in which Southern Baptist missionaries were stationed met in Shanghai in 1948 and organized the China Baptist Convention, a small but important beginning in national organization. They felt the need of a general secretary through whom they could correlate and promote Baptist work in the provinces represented, and elected T. K. Van to that position soon after the convention was organized. Because of the extreme poverty of the Chinese following the devastation of World War II, the Foreign Mission Board provided financial assistance to help the convention become well established.

Communist control forced most of the missionaries to leave China soon after organization of the convention, and a Communist order to cut off all relations with Americans was discussed at an early meeting of the group. Messengers made an earnest plea to be allowed to receive aid from America for one more year, but the request was denied. In the face of this denial, the Chinese representatives voted to assume full responsibility for the convention and their churches.   J. T. WILLIAMS

CHOCTAW ACADEMY. An interracial boys' school—primarily Indian—at Great Crossings, Scott County, Ky. It was apparently founded in 1818 (although not by that name) by the Kentucky Baptist Missionary Society through the leadership of Richard M. Johnson. The latter continued to guide the school when it received sanction from the Triennial Convention and support from the government in 1825. At one time at least 100 were enrolled, but the school declined after the first decade and was closed c. 1845.   WILLIAM N. MCELRATH

CHOCTAW INDIANS, MISSISSIPPI. Work with these Indians, who had escaped deportation by the United States Government to reservations in the West, was begun in 1849, when the Mississippi Baptist Convention voted "to sustain at least one teacher of the true religion of Christ among the Choctaws," then resident in Jasper, Kemper, Leake, Neshoba, and Winston counties. In 1879 the General Association of Regular Baptists in southeast Mississippi began evangelistic work among the Choctaws through a superintendent who had oversight over four of their native preachers. By request the state convention and the Home Mission Board agreed to cooperate, the Home Mission Board assuming the responsibility of a missionary, beginning in 1920. The state convention board began in 1924 to supplement the work and in 1931 assumed full responsibility as the Home Mission Board made curtailments. In 1945 the Home Mission Board resumed supporting a missionary, and the convention board increased its annual supplementary appropriations to assist the work. In 1945, $1,000 was appropriated; in 1947, $8,000; in 1948, $4,000, and similar amounts in later years. Through the New Choctaw Association, Sunday schools, W.M.U. work, training courses, music schools, and camps for boys and girls are featured.   MARION W. PERRY

CHOCTAW MALE COLLEGIATE INSTITUTE. Established by Choctaw Baptist Association at Macon, Miss., and chartered in 1852. The final outcome of the school is uncertain.
                               J. L. BOYD

CHOWAN COLLEGE. "A female school of high order," authorized by the Chowan Baptist Association meeting at Ramoth Gilead Church on May 19, 1848. At that time a report was made that about $1,000 in cash and pledges was in hand, most of which had been given on condition that the school be located in Murfreesboro, N. C. The offer for its location there was accepted. Later, churches of Portsmouth Association in southeastern Virginia were invited to share in building the school. The old academy lot and brick building known as Banks School, on the north side of Murfreesboro, were purchased for $1,225, and Chowan Baptist Female Institute opened on Oct. 11, 1848. A stock company was soon organized to provide more room and assure continuation of the new Baptist school, and the next year 28 acres of land were purchased on the south side of Murfreesboro, where a four-story building, known as The Columns, was erected.

In July, 1859, the stockholders returned the school to the two associations, but debts were incurred during Civil War operation which led to organization of another stock company in 1868 to save the institute by assuming the debts. On June 25, 1878, the stockholders turned the school over to the Baptist denomination rather than to the associations. With its name changed to Chowan College in 1911, the school became one of the colleges of the state convention and shared in the funds of the 75 Million Campaign of 1919. It became coeducational in 1925 and a junior college in 1937.

Due to struggles caused by World War II, the college closed in 1943 for six years. It was reopened in 1949 after $250,000 had been spent in remodeling the plant, building four cottages for boys and a home for the president. Between 1951 and 1956 the college again became well established. The campus was enlarged by the purchase of 56 acres of land adjoining the original 54-acre site. A graphic arts department was inaugurated with a building erected for it, and the department grew beyond anticipation. The college graduated by 1955 a total of 938 students. In 1954 endowment totaled $5,760, and property value, $153,598.57. Enrolment was 301 in 1954–55, when the school operated on a budget of $193,500. Presidents of Chowan College include Archibald McDowell (*q.v.*), John B. Brewer, John Catre Scarbrough (*q.v.*), Charles P. Weaver, H. Hadden Dudley, and F. Orion Mixon, who has served since 1951.
                               F. ORION MIXON

CHRIST. See JESUS CHRIST.

CHRISTIAN, JOHN TYLER (b. Lexington, Ky., Dec. 14, 1854; d. New Orleans, La., Dec. 18, 1925). Pastor, professor, historian. Son of Marion Washington and Amada Martinie Christian, he was educated at Bethel College, Russellville, Ky., receiving B.A. and M.A. degrees; and he made seven trips to Europe for postgraduate work. Ordained in 1876, Christian held pastorates at First Baptist Church, Chattanooga, Tenn., 1883–86; East Baptist Church, Louisville, Ky., 1893–1900; Second Baptist Church, Little Rock, Ark., 1904–11; First Baptist Church, Hattiesburg, Miss., 1913–19; and others. For several years secretary of missions for both Mississippi and Arkansas, Christian served as chairman of an informal conference of friends in Houston, Tex., 1915, who met to consider the founding of a theological seminary at New Orleans, La., and later he was a member of the special committee appointed to bring the enterprise before the Southern Baptist Convention in 1917. Professor of Christian history and librarian at Baptist Bible Institute, New Orleans, from 1919–25, Christian traveled repeatedly in Europe and the Near East for study and the collection of books. He donated his personal library consisting of over 15,000 volumes to Baptist Bible Institute. A member of the Society of Christian Archaeology of Greece, the Academy of History of France, the Academy of Science, Arts and Belles Lettres of the Mediterranean, and the American Society of History, Christian was author of *Close Communion* (1892); *Americanism, or Romanism, Which?* (1895); *Did They Dip? an Examination of the English Baptists* (1897); *Baptist History Vindicated* (1899); *Baptism in Sculpture and Art* (1907); *A History of the Baptists* (1923); and *History of the Baptists of Louisiana* (1923).

BIBLIOGRAPHY: "Historical Sketch," *Bulletin of the Baptist Bible Institute* (1924–25). J. M. King, "John Tyler Christian, A Study of His Life and Works" (1953) A. N. Marquis, ed., *Who's Who In America* (1926–27).   J. WASH WATTS

CHRISTIAN BAPTIST, THE. Edited and printed by Alexander Campbell at Buffalo, Va. (now Bethany, W. Va.), between July 4, 1823, and July 5, 1830. *The Christian Baptist*, a monthly, was Campbell's propaganda journal, widely read in the West. Purporting to evince truth and expose error, it sponsored his peculiar ecclesiological views and attacked others. It was discontinued after the split between Baptists and Reformers in 1830, but Campbell had already begun to publish the *Millennial Harbinger* (1830–70), dedicated to the "destruction of sectarianism" and "the development and introduction" of the millennium.   HUGH WAMBLE

CHRISTIAN EDUCATION, NORTH CAROLINA COUNCIL ON. Organized by the Baptist State Convention of North Carolina, meeting in Winston-Salem in 1943, with a total of 25 members. This council succeeded an education commission established by the convention's general board in 1942. It was the council's duty

... to meet at the call of the General Secretary at least quarterly to consider ways and means of further correlating the work of the various institutions and make recommendations upon the same to the Board of Trustees of the institutions involved, to the end that each may be of the greatest possible service in the cause of Christian education; to study and give consideration to the needs of the institutions and make recommendations to the General Board of the Convention concerning the disposition of funds which may be available for current operating support; to formulate plans for increasing the interest and support of Baptist people everywhere in their educational program; and ... make an annual report to the Convention upon such plans.

The council was first embodied in the convention's constitution in 1946, which added to it "the members of the Education Committee of the General Board and eight members at large," and provided that "the Chairman of the Committee on Education of the General Board shall be Chairman of the Council, and the President of the Woman's Missionary Union shall be Vice Chairman." In the same year the powers and duties of the council were specified in Article IV of the bylaws. Membership of the council was changed again by convention action in 1951 with the omission of the executive committee chairman of the board of trustees of each college, the general secretary of the convention, and the eight members at large. Required to hold at least three sessions annually, the council, with offices in Raleigh, has had for its first and only executive secretary Claude F. Gaddy since July 1, 1946.   CLAUDE F. GADDY

CHRISTIAN EDUCATION, THE COMMITTEE OF TWELVE ON, KENTUCKY. Because of the failure of the Baptist Education Society of Kentucky (1906–42) to develop an educational policy, its dissolution in 1942 was brought about by action of the General Association of Baptists in Kentucky in 1941, and a committee of 12 on Christian education was appointed (1) to study the whole subject of Christian education, (2) to inform the people and stimulate interest, (3) to recommend allocation of funds, and (4) to report to the general association. It was stipulated that after June 30, 1942, only the schools which presented "annually to the nominating committee of the general association two names for each vacancy on its Board of Trustees" should "share in the proceeds of the Co-operative Program of Kentucky Baptists." This committee was composed of 12 members, four members being appointed each year for three-year terms. No employee of any of the educational institutions was eligible for membership on the committee. The committee was authorized in 1941 to raise $750,000 for Baptist education in Kentucky, and the amount was increased to $1,500,000 in 1942. J. G. Cothran was elected director of the committee. Up to Nov., 1945, the schools had received over $307,000 through this movement, which was superseded by the Department of Christian Education.   LEWIS C. RAY

CHRISTIAN HERALD (1865–72). A weekly, first published on July 21, 1865, at Moulton, Ala., by D. C. White and Josephus Shackelford and edited by Shackelford. According to the paper's self-stated aim, it was "Devoted to the Dissemination of Religious Truth and Bible Doctrines, Education, Temperance, Agriculture, &c." The *Herald* was transferred first in 1867 to Tuscumbia and, again, sometime between Aug. 20, 1869, and July 27, 1871, to Nashville, Tenn. In 1872 it was purchased by J. J. Toon, of Atlanta, and merged with the *Christian Index*. At various times Shackelford was assisted by J. M. D. Cates, T. T. Eaton, J. M. Phillips, and A. B. Cates. While it survived, the *Herald* "proved an important agency for the rehabilitation of Baptist churches and Baptist benevolent, educational and missionary enterprises in its immediate field." RAY M. ATCHISON

CHRISTIAN INDEX, THE. The publication of the Georgia Baptist convention, the third oldest religious weekly in the United States, and the second oldest Baptist paper. First published as *The Columbian Star*, it began with the issue of Feb. 2, 1822. *The Christian Secretary* (Presbyterian) was the first religious weekly; *The Christian Watchman*, founded in 1819, was the first for Baptists.

The Columbian Star, taking its name from Columbian College in Washington, D. C., was founded to provide "missionary and other religious intelligence, as well as a medium for inculcating sound theological doctrines and pure moral precepts." Luther Rice (*q.v.*) was one of the founders, and James Davis Knowles was editor.

Moved to Philadelphia, Pa., in 1827, it was edited by William Theophilus Brantly, Sr. (*q.v.*), pastor of the First Baptist Church there. The name was enlarged in 1829 to *The Columbian Star and Christian Index* to "indicate its religious character." The name was reduced to *The Christian Index* with the issue of Jan. 1, 1831.

Brantly, formerly a pastor in Augusta, wrote to Jesse Mercer (*q.v.*) in May, 1831, suggesting removal of the *Index* to some "central point" where it would serve "Carolina, Georgia, and Alabama." Financial details are lacking, but Mercer apparently acquired the paper for the cost of a printing plant in Washington, Ga., where he was identified as editor and proprietor beginning with the issue of Sept. 14, 1833. He wrote in that issue: "One of the chief excellencies of a religious publication is in its presenting, in one view, the sentiments of the denomination; by which an opportunity is afforded for . . . a full investigation; whereby in the exercise of Christian candor and mutual forbearance, through divine influence, it may be hoped a successful effort may be made to bring all into the unity of the spirit and the bond of peace."

Mercer gave the *Index* to the Georgia Baptist convention at its meeting in May, 1840. It had property valued at $2,000 and $3,000 due in accounts which Mercer also donated along with a new font of type worth $500. Mercer was well convinced of the value of a denominational paper. ". . . let me exhort and admonish, nay, let me beseech you *to hold fast to the Index*," he wrote in a later issue. He apparently had in mind the paper's historic financial difficulties when he added: "That such a publication is needed in the south is acknowledged by many, but too few feel the right sort of zeal in the cause."

The paper was moved to Penfield in December. Financial troubles plagued it most of the time until sold in 1861 by the convention to Samuel Boykin (*q.v.*) and C. M. Irwin of Albany for $2,200. They continued publication in Macon, where the *Index* had moved in 1857. At the time of sale $5,500 was due from subscriptions and circulation was around 2,000.

Civil War years multiplied difficulties. Subscription prices went from $2 to $20 in 1864 when eggs were selling for $6 a dozen in Macon. The *Index* missed some issues, probably all of those for the first part of 1865. With the issue of Nov. 9, 1865, J. J. Toon was listed as proprietor, and Atlanta as the place of publication.

Other papers were absorbed by the *Index*, including the *Christian Herald* from Tennessee. In 1878, the paper was a combination of the *Florida Baptist*, the *Southwestern Baptist*, the *Christian Herald*, and the *Index* with a ministry in Florida, Tennessee, Alabama, and Georgia. The paper remained strong in its missionary zeal and for temperance but, as from the beginning, printed general news. It had "The Farmer's Index" section.

The Georgia Baptist convention regained the *Index* in 1920, paying $40,000 to The Index Printing Company. B. J. W. Graham was the editor and principal stockholder in the company.

Louie DeVotie Newton, Georgia director of publicity for the Baptist 75 Million Campaign and formerly a professor at Mercer, was elected editor and took charge in mid-January. He started the boost in circulation, gave the paper a more general appeal, and attracted Southern Baptist Convention recognition by engaging its leaders as authors. He served through 1929, resigning to become pastor of the Druid Hills Baptist Church in Atlanta where he was a deacon when called to the pulpit. O. P. Gilbert, pastor at Brunswick, succeeded Newton in Jan., 1930, and was editor until he died Apr. 8, 1947. He was succeeded July 6 by John Jeter Hurt, Jr., who was with the Associated Press as writer and editor.

The affiliation of the *Index* with the Georgia Baptist convention remained in 1956 much as in 1920 when it was acquired. The paper's own board of directors, having immediate supervision, nominates the editor for election by the executive committee, the corporate executive body of the Georgia convention.

Circulation in June, 1956, was 90,469 and had doubled in the previous six years. The greater part of this circulation was provided by a church budget plan through which 670 churches sent the paper to their members. Circulation and advertising revenue, plus $17,500 from the convention for advertising and promotion, provided a budget of $150,000 for 1956. Contract printing in Atlanta with Western-Perry involved two thirds of the budget. The *Index* had its own bank account, and this with other physical assets gave a 1955 audit value of $35,379.

Several libraries joined with the *Index* in 1950 for microfilming all known issues. The microfilm starts with the first (Feb. 2, 1822) issue of *The Columbian Star*. The *Index* has some bound volumes starting in 1825 and most of them after 1876. JOHN JETER HURT, JR.

CHRISTIAN LIFE COMMISSION, THE. An agency of the Southern Baptist Convention. Its purpose is to emphasize the Christian's responsibility in social relations with special reference to marriage and the family, crime and juvenile delinquency, industrial relations, race relations, beverage alcohol, Christian citizenship, and such other problems relating to social morality that may confront the Christian conscience.

This commission was established by the Convention in 1913 under the name of the Social Service Commission. The next year its work was combined with the standing committee on temperance, created in 1908, and was called the Temperance and Social Service Commission. In 1920 the temperance work was incorporated in that of the Social Service Commission. This name was retained until May, 1953, when it was given its present name.

During the first 11 years of service of this commission (1908-19), the chief emphasis in its work was temperance as it related to the growing traffic in beverage alcohol. Under the leadership of Arthur James Barton (q.v.) as its chairman, the commission led Southern Baptists in a sustained and aggressive opposition to the manufacture, sale, and use of alcohol as a beverage. The annual reports of the commission to the Convention during this period and the energetic leadership of its chairman contributed much to the creation of a public opinion that resulted in the adoption of the Eighteenth Amendment to the national Constitution outlawing the manufacture and sale of beverage alcohol within the territorial limits of the United States.

The commission then turned its attention to other social problems, such as the continuing activity of the liquor traffic, the need for law enforcement, the growing crime wave, the divorce evil, the demoralizing effect of the motion picture, growing unrest among minority groups, injustices in industrial relations, disregard for the sabbath, obscene literature, race-track gambling, and other vital issues.

The commission foresaw the development of these conditions. In 1921 they proposed a constructive program which would be positive in its emphasis. "Southern Baptists have scarcely begun to enter the great and ever widening field of social service," they wrote; then added the recommendation that serious attention be given to the advisability of establishing a permanent headquarters office and to the employment of a qualified man to have charge of the social service ministry of Southern Baptists. This proposal was urged in each annual report of the commission except two (1927, 1928) from 1921 through 1932.

When the commission did not offer this recommendation in 1933, Edwin McNeill Poteat (q.v.) offered an amendment to its report calling for the appointment of a committee to consider the advisability of creating an agency of social research in connection with the Social Service Commission. This committee was appointed with Poteat as chairman. It was continued without a report being given in 1934 and brought its first report in 1935. Action on this report was deferred for one year and the committee was enlarged by the appointment of one additional member from each state. In 1936 the enlarged committee made its final report, recommending that the agency be established. After an extended debate from the floor, the matter was finally disposed of by a motion to lay the question on the table.

After the death of Barton in 1942, Jesse Burton Weatherspoon (1886-) professor of preaching at the Southern Baptist Theological Seminary, Louisville, Ky., became the chairman of the commission. He had been a member of the commission since 1930. His insight into movements of mounting tensions in the civic and religious life of our nation enabled him to evaluate and interpret these movements in terms of Christian truth and responsibility.

In its report of 1946, the commission submitted to the Convention two significant recommendations. One asked for the appointment of a committee of nine to consider the responsibility of Southern Baptists in the growing problems of racial understanding and adjustment. The report of this committee to the 1947 Convention was reaffirmed in 1948 and distributed widely in brochure form. It was the basis for further progress in racial understanding, which resulted in the acceptance by the Convention of the recommendation offered by the Commission in 1954 on desegregation in the public schools.

The second recommendation in the 1946 report requested that the executive committee restudy the proper functions of the commission and set out more clearly the scope of its work. In its report to the Convention in 1947, the executive committee defined the field and work of this commission and suggested the need for the employment of qualified personnel in the promotion of its program and, in support of this, proposed an operating budget of $10,000 for 1948, which was approved.

The commission in its annual session at Ridgecrest the following August voted to elect Hugh Alexander Brimm now head of the department of sociology and human relations, Carver School of Missions and Social Work, Louisville, Ky., as its executive secretary-treasurer under full-time employment and to establish the headquarters office at Louisville, Ky. Brimm served until Dec. 31, 1952. He was succeeded by Acker C Miller on Jan. 1, 1953, who is the present secretary.

Since its office was established in 1947, under its executive leadership the commission has developed its program under the following objectives:

1. To co-ordinate and seek to unify the work of other agencies in areas of Christian morality and social responsibility

FURMAN UNIVERSITY (q.v.), Greenville, S. C. Founded 1826, enrolment 1,413 in 1955–56 session. Classroom building pictured is located on new campus where 20 major buildings are to be erected for an estimated $15,000,000.

GEORGETOWN COLLEGE (q.v.), Georgetown, Ky. Founded in 1798, enrolment 1,380 in 1955–56 session. Its 25 buildings are worth $2,350,000.

2. To emphasize the nature and extent of our Christian responsibilities

3. To provide factual and authentic information that will help our people to understand the issues of our day in terms of Christian faith and practice

4. To develop and distribute an informational and interpretive literature on the Christian's responsibility in social areas

5. To suggest and formulate plans of Christian action in the areas of moral and social evil

6. To conduct Christian Life conferences at Southern Baptist assemblies and in co-operation with churches and associations

7. To co-operate with state and associational committees on social service, temperance, or civic righteousness in promoting this work throughout the Convention.

BIBLIOGRAPHY: W. W. Barnes, *The Southern Baptist Convention* (1954). Christian Life Commission, *Minutes* (Aug., 1952). A. C Miller, "Christian Life Commission—Principles, Purposes, Procedures" (n.d.). Social Service Commission, *Minutes* (Aug., 1947).

A. C MILLER

CHRISTIAN LIFE COMMISSION AND SOCIAL SERVICE, VIRGINIA. Originated in 1911 by action of the Virginia Baptist General Association, at the request of Edwin Charles Dargan (*q.v.*), president of the Southern Baptist Convention. Reflecting the rise of the social gospel movement and acknowledging indebtedness to figures such as Walter Rauschenbusch (*q.v.*) and Charles Spurgeon Gardner (*q.v.*), the committee concerned itself from the beginning with the whole gamut of social issues. Robert Frazer was chairman of the first committee.

The work of the committee, under the state mission board, at first consisted of lectures at the encampment at Virginia Beach, Sunday school institutes, Baptist Young People's Union meetings, and encouragement to churches to instruct their congregations in the social message of the Bible.

The committee has had far-reaching educational influence in arousing social consciousness. In its annual report it treats not only such conventional themes as gambling and alcoholism, but more venturesome issues, industrial problems, and social justice. In 1954 it commended the Supreme Court of the United States for declaring segregation unconstitutional in public schools.

The name of the commission has been changed several times. For a while it was called the Social Service-Temperance Committee. In 1943 its work was taken over by the Committee for the Promotion of Moral Education and Legislation, but in 1944 the Social Service Committee was restored in name and function. The most recent change was in 1953 when the name was changed to the Christian Life Committee to correspond with the Christian Life Commission of the Southern Baptist Convention.

PAUL L. STAGG

CHRISTIAN MAGAZINE, THE. A Baptist newspaper begun in Knoxville, Tenn., in 1846 and edited by a local pastor, H. Sears. The paper had a very brief existence. LYNN E. MAY, JR.

CHRISTIAN REPOSITORY. See FORD'S CHRISTIAN REPOSITORY.

CHRISTIAN SCIENCE. A religious order founded by Mrs. Mary Baker Eddy (1821-1910), who published the first edition of her *Science and Health* in 1875. By 1879 her disciples banded themselves into the Church of Christ, Scientist, proposing to constitute a "church designed to commemorate the word and works of our Master, which should reinstate primitive Christianity and its lost element of healing." Today the mother church in Boston, Mass., with more than 3,000 branches throughout the world, seeks to perpetuate a theology and discipline derived partially from biblical prooftexts and partially from purely philosophic presuppositions. A basic tenet of this faith is "that the mortal sense of life, with all its sin and sickness, derives from the carnal mind which is enmity against God and is to be corrected by a right understanding of the perfect man revealed through Christ Jesus." Christian Scientists, therefore, declare as the "natural and indispensable phenomenon of religion" the healing of the sick by means of refusing to accept the reality of evil in any form and constantly reasserting "the real man's freedom from what seems to be a life of mingled good and evil."

BIBLIOGRAPHY: G. G. Atkins, "Christian Science," *An Encyclopedia of Religion* (1945). E. F. Dakin, *Mrs. Eddy: The Biography of a Virginal Mind* (1930). M. B. Eddy, *Science and Health with Key to the Scriptures* (1909). V. Ferm, ed., *Religion in the Twentieth Century* (1948). E. A. Kimball, "Answers to Questions Concerning Christian Science" (1909). L. Rosten, ed., *A Guide to the Religions of America* (1955). C. P. Clifford, "The A B C of the Christian Science Religion," *The Christian Science Sentinel* (Nov. 24, 1928).

GEORGE M. JENKINS

CHRISTIAN TIMES. A Baptist newspaper, now extinct, started in Chicago, Ill., Aug. 31, 1853, by a committee of the Chicago Baptist Association, and edited for three months by an "association of clergymen." The following November, the association transferred the paper to a private firm. *The Witness* of Indianapolis, Ind., in 1867 merged with the Chicago paper, which thus became *The Christian Times and Witness*. The same year, on the consolidation of the *Michigan Christian Herald* with the Chicago paper, the proprietors renamed their journal, *The Standard*. Leroy Smith edited this publication from 1853 to 1896. The paper was suspended in 1926. LYNN E. MAY, JR.

CHRISTIAN WATCHMAN. A newspaper that began publication in 1866 with J. B. Hamberlin as editor. This Mississippi paper, which is now extinct, also had as editors H. M. Atkins, Joseph Sorsby, and Theodore Whitfield.

A. L. GOODRICH

CHRISTIANITY, HISTORY OF. Christianity is the religion to which followers of Christ adhere and the doctrines and life which flow from their faith. The two major traditions within the movement are the Catholic and Protestant, with considerable variety of belief and practice within each. Catholicism emerged in the second century A.D. and exhibited a structured church at the end of that century. From this basic Catholic movement several types of Catholicism have developed—Roman, Greek, Anglo-, and a multitude of smaller groups, such as the Coptic, the Jansenist, and Old Catholic churches. Protestantism appeared in the 16th century, representing a break with the Roman Catholic tradition and also expressing a movement of protest against Catholicism which may be seen across the centuries in the ancient and medieval periods. Protestantism quickly divided into four basic types—Lutheran, Reformed, Sectarian, and Anglican. These types in turn were further divided by external pressures and internal disputes as Protestantism was established in Europe and spread to America.

Primitive Christianity.—The Christian faith, rooted in the Hebrew heritage, finds its focus in the figure of Jesus Christ. The "Lordship of Christ inaugurated by His resurrection and exaltation to the right hand of God," says Oscar Cullmann, ". . . is the center of the faith of primitive Christianity." He was Lord of life and the spearhead of a new community of grace called the church, "the body of Christ." The massive figure of Jesus Christ, dominating and unifying the New Testament records, was the bearer of the kingdom of God which invaded human history in him. The kingdom came with Christ, and the demonic powers were defeated. C. H. Dodd says, "Something has happened which has not happened before, and which means that the sovereign power of God has come into effective operation." The kingdom of God, long prophesied, was proclaimed as a present reality. History thus became the interim between Christ's initial coming, when the "powers of the age to come" were decisively set against the powers of evil, and his final coming, when the conquest will be brought to completion.

Since Christ is Lord, he is master of life, sin, death, and history; therefore, he was remembered and interpreted by his followers, for whom he was still alive through his resurrection from the dead. The new age had come, and a divine radiance gripped the group for whom he was Lord. As a consequence of the new life which came with Christ, communities called churches were formed.

Organization was simple, though the exact form of the primitive Christian communities is problematical. People who performed functions of leadership became officers of these churches —bishops, elders, and pastors. (These three terms probably refer to the same office.) The deacons functioned first as distributors of alms and eventually served as aids to the bishops. The rites of the churches were baptism and the Lord's Supper, which symbolized, respectively, Christian conversion and Christ's self-sacrifice for sin. Baptism points to the very heart of the gospel because it portrays the participation of the believer in Christ's death and resurrection. The Lord's Supper is a memorial of the mighty drama of redemption and a reminder of Christ's constant presence with his people.

The worship of the churches was patterned after the ritual of the Jewish synagogues—prayer, praise, hymns, preaching, and the "breaking of bread." The first Christians were Jews who continued to worship in the synagogues but for whom Jesus was the long-expected Messiah. They held informal services in private houses in addition to the ritualistic services in the synagogue. This Jewish Christianity was challenged by Paul, who detached Christianity from the shell of Judaism in which it first appeared and stressed its universal genius. Paul believed that divine grace and human faith were the only conditions of salvation. One's race had nothing to do with it. The gospel, as he conceived it, challenged all barriers which bring enmity among men and envisaged a new humanity in Jesus Christ.

This mighty faith left the literary deposit known as the New Testament. The four Gospels, the Acts of the Apostles, the letters of Paul, the General Epistles, Hebrews, and Revelation make up the New Testament. These classical criteria of the Christian faith were not established by the Catholic or Protestant churches, which, of course, had not yet appeared, but grew out of the life of the primitive Christian communities.

Catholicism.—The burst of enthusiasm which centered in Jesus Christ the Lord, victor over sin and death, showed signs of waning in the latest New Testament writings. E. F. Scott believes the Epistle to the Hebrews, for example, indicates that "the earlier glow of conviction had given place to a mood of lassitude. . . ." The internal bonds which held the early Christians together began to weaken with the passing of the first generation, and external bonds began to appear. By the turn of the century, knotty theological questions were developing, and the dynamic faith of the first Christians was beginning to manifest doctrinal rigidity.

The term "catholic," meaning universal, was first applied to the church in the second century in a letter of Ignatius. By A.D. 200 this embryonic Catholicism issued in a definite Catholic Church with a constitution (centered in the bishop), a creed (the emerging Apostles' Creed), and a canon (the developing New Testament writings). The "fixing of tradition," in Adolf Harnack's words, was a consequence of the assaults of the heresies known as Gnosticism and Montanism upon the Christian movement. These assaults forced the Church Fathers to define Christianity doctrinally. Internal confusions also made theological formulas necessary. The authority of the episcopate was more firmly established than before.

Bishops in the New Testament were "overseers" of local congregations. In the second century these collegiate bishops were displaced by the ruling bishop, who allegedly stood in apostolic succession. The appearance of a single bishop with authority over his congregation and with the prestige of an alleged connection with the apostles is the first major development in the history of the Catholic hierarchy. In the third century the bishop had extended his authority from a single church to a group of churches known as a diocese, and he became a diocesan bishop. The diocesan bishops in the cities were called metropolitans, of whom the most powerful were in large cities like Alexandria, Antioch, Constantinople, and Rome. The relationship among them was that each was *primus inter pares*—first among equals. The bishop of Rome finally achieved ascendancy over his colleagues as a consequence of the Mohammedan conquests, which placed Constantinople (Rome's only important rival) under constant threat of capture. Another factor which accounts for the priority of the Roman bishop was the growing importance of the city and church of Rome. The Eternal City had been the residence of the emperors, and the church there quickly became the largest in Christendom. The collapse of the Roman Empire in the fourth and fifth centuries produced growing political chaos, upon which the church capitalized by providing a center of social order. This increased the prestige of the Roman bishop.

The Old Catholic Church became the Roman Catholic Church when the bishop of Rome became the primary bishop in the west. *Primus inter pares* became *primus*—and Romanism was born. Various dates have been suggested by historians to mark this momentous event. Innocent I, who became Bishop of Rome in A.D. 401, is regarded by some as the first Roman bishop who was looked upon as the primary bishop, not only of Rome, but of the church as a whole. Others suggest Gregory the Great, who was consecrated Bishop of Rome in 590. Perhaps the position of priority of the Roman bishop was not completely achieved until the Mohammedans swept in a two-pronged fashion from Medina, on the one hand, along the North African coast and then northward to Tours in France, where Charles Martel turned them back in 732, and, on the other hand, across Syria and into Asia Minor, posing a threat to Constantinople. The Eastern bishoprics were overrun, leaving Rome unscathed, powerful, and largely alone in its supremacy.

The pre-Roman Catholic period also saw significant theological developments. The earliest statement of the Apostles' Creed, an explanation of the baptismal confession in opposition to Gnosticism, appeared first in Rome between A.D. 150 and 175. The trinitarian form of this historic creed strongly influenced subsequent theological thought. The Nicean (325) and Chalcedonian (451) creeds, dealing respectively with the relation of the Father to the Son and the person of Christ, were final definitions for Catholic orthodoxy, except for minor refinements.

The formative features of the sacramental system were established, though the elaboration of the details of the seven sacraments was carried on through the Middle Ages. For example, belief in the "real presence" of Christ in the Mass was clearly held by A.D. 250, but the doctrine of transubstantiation, which purports to tell *how* Christ is present, was not defined until 1215. The church, which in primitive Christianity was a community of the redeemed, became an agency of redemption. In the mid-third century, Cyprian said, "There is no salvation outside the church." Baptism, which in early Christianity was a symbol of conversion, became both an instrument of salvation and a rite of initiation. Infant baptism became increasingly widespread after Christianity became a state church in the fourth century, and the doctrine of original sin was structured. The doctrine of infant baptism and the idea of a state church go hand in hand. The doctrine was strengthened by the belief that salvation lay in the church, into which infants should be baptized, and the belief that infants were infected with original sin from which baptism freed them, permitting entrance into heaven in case of death.

It should be noted that there was in this period a constant protest by a variety of sects, such as the Montanists, Novatians, and Donatists, against the claim that the Catholic Church was the sole custodian of the divine revelation.

Roman Catholic Church.—The Roman Catholic Church was the dominant institution in the Middle Ages. It allied itself with feudalism and Greek thought and forged a social and theological unity which persisted to the Reformation. The theological achievement of the medieval church was expressed by scholastic thinkers, supremely by Thomas Aquinas in his *Summa Theologica*. This is a theology of continuity between God and man, revelation and reason, the kingdom of God and the Catholic Church. The seven sacraments, in the sole custody of the Catholic Church, are the channels of divine grace. Baptism cleanses the soul of all previous sin, original and/or actual, and restores the supernatural virtues lost in the fall. Penance furnishes absolution for mortal sins committed after baptism and assigns satisfactions for the possible removal of remaining penalty. Holy Eucharist offers the substance of Christ's body and blood to the believer and re-enacts his sacrifice for sin. Confirmation of the young by the bishop serves as a source of spiritual strength and provides the final prerequisite for the first communion. Extreme unction prepares the soul for the next life through the application of holy oil to the dying. Marriage, sacramentally conceived, supplies divine aid which enables the contracting parties to fulfil the Christian purpose of their relationship. Ordination, by the imposition of the bishop's hands, transmits apostolic authority to the ordainee, enabling him to dispense the sacraments.

The Middle Ages, the period from the collapse of the ancient Roman Empire to the Reformation, saw the appearance of an ecclesiastical society in which church and state were closely related. The Holy Roman Empire and the church often found it to their mutual advantage to support each other, though conflicts developed from time to time. This meant that the leaders of the church—the pope, the archbishops, and the bishops—and the leaders in the state—the kings and the feudal lords—worked out a relationship which resulted in the interaction of the two institutions. Roman Catholic theology shows the influence of feudalism, for example, in the satisfaction theory of the atonement worked out by Anselm, and feudalistic life was heavily influenced by Catholic beliefs. Many bishops were also feudal lords. The pope, as the "vicar of Christ," came to wield vast political power. No wonder Edwyn Bevan writes that "the new position which Christianity had acquired in the world made a greater difference to the character of Christianity than it did to the character of the world."

Monasticism absorbed those sensitive souls who rebelled against the compromise between the church and the world. This movement, which began in Egypt in the third century, was introduced into the West by Athanasius. The Benedictine order, which appeared in the sixth century, is the best example of early Western monasticism. The Cluniacs, Cistercians, Dominicans, and Franciscans, who sought to reform the church in the later Middle Ages, were not able to stem the rising tide of administrative and moral abuses which led to the Protestant Reformation.

The growth of nationalism in England, France and Spain weakened the authority of the pope in Europe. The Gallican Church in France is only one of several examples of a national church which refused to be subservient to the papacy.

The Babylonian Captivity of the papacy (1309–77), when the pope lived at Avignon, a French city, and the great schism (1378–1416), when the church was embarrassed by the spectacle of two and, for a brief period, three popes, greatly diminished the prestige of the Roman Catholic Church in Europe.

The humanism of the Renaissance turned men's minds away from the church to the past in a concern for the Greek and Roman classics and to a scientific interest in nature and human nature. The man-centered direction of humanistic thought, opposed to the claim of the church to dominate the intellectual life, played an important part in shattering the medieval pattern and prepared the way for the Protestant Reformation.

Economic difficulties, brought on by a time of inflation as result of the stimulation of trade which came out of the Renaissance and the discovery of the New World in the west, posed grave problems for the church. The need to raise revenue lured the church into the imposition of more and more taxes which made the people increasingly restive. The sale of indulgences precipitated the Reformation.

It should be noted that in 1054 Eastern tendencies within the Roman Church burst the bonds which had contained them, and the Greek Catholic Church, sometimes called the Orthodox Church, was born. A dispute in the ninth century involving matters of belief and practice between Photius, Patriarch of Constantinople, and Pope Nicholas I intensified growing ill feeling between East and West which finally led to a division two centuries later and the rise of the Greek Catholic Church under the Patriarch Michael Cerularius.

Protestantism.—The term "Protestant," first used at the second Diet of Speyer in 1529, designated a minority of the German Reichstag who protested against proposed legislation which would have ended the Lutheran territorial churches in Germany. It was quickly applied to the rising movement of protest against the Roman Catholic Church in the 16th century. Protestants were soon those, led by the Reformers, who wished to cleanse the Catholic Church of the accretions, ecclesiastical and theological, accumulated across the centuries and to restore primitive Christianity.

The development of Protestantism into a variety of types was the outgrowth of the freedom of interpretation which followed the overthrow of Catholic authority, resulting in national Protestant churches, and the growing religious freedom which permitted divisions within these churches.

The Lutheran Church appeared in Germany as a consequence of the reformatory activities of Martin Luther and his circle. Luther's attack upon Roman Catholic theology was centered first upon the theory of indulgences in his *Ninety-five Theses* and was extended to include the entire sacramental system in *The Babylonian Captivity of the Church*. Against the Catholic view that man can live above mortal sin, Luther insisted that sin persists in the life of the Christian upon every level of moral and spiritual growth. The Christian is righteous and unrighteous at the same time—*justus et peccator simul*. Against the claim that a priestly class holds the sacraments in custody and possesses the sole power to administer them, Luther held that man's constant need of God's pardoning and empowering grace is met by the steady availability of that grace in Jesus Christ to the believer without benefit of clergy. Since all Christians are priests, no priestly class is required, and priestly absolution is without effect. The peace of the Christian is not the peace of goodness but the peace of being completely known and all forgiven.

The Lutheran church was regulated by Protestant princes, who, in some measure, used it to maintain their positions in German society. Luther attached undue veneration to political order and was extremely suspicious of revolutionary tendencies, which, because of human depravity, he believed would lead to anarchy.

The Peasant's Revolt, which Luther opposed with all his might, threw the peasants into the rising Anabaptist movement, which stressed religious liberty and the separation of church and state, and which favored emerging democratic tendencies. Divisions appeared among the Anabaptists, producing a bewildering variety of belief and practice. The Mennonites are a contemporary sect derived from the Anabaptists. Emphasis upon the visible church made up of baptized believers is a common denominator of the movement. The Anabaptists and other Protestant sects contributed heavily to the idea of democracy.

The Reformed type of Protestantism was established in Geneva by John Calvin and his followers. It spread into France (Huguenots), Holland (Dutch Reformed), Scotland (Church of Scotland), England (Presbyterian church), and America (Presbyterian church). Reformed churches are commonly governed by presbyters, or elders, distinguishing them from episcopal and congregational organizations. Unlike Lutheranism, which was attached deeply to one land, Calvinism was projected into many lands and a variety of cultures. The activism of the Reformed faith is rooted in theological belief. "The drive of Calvinism," says Roland Bainton, "stems from optimism as to God despite pessimism as to man." Perry Miller describes this faith similarly as "cosmic optimism in the midst of anguish" and, writing about the Puritans in New England, says, "they were too busy waging war against sin, too intoxicated with the exultation of the conflict to find occasional reversals, however costly, any cause for deep discouragement." A Calvinist on the Continent, in England, or in the New World could say in times of despair, "The blight is upon the earth, but it will not end that way."

Calvin's monumental theological treatise, *The Institutes of the Christian Religion*, has exerted an influence upon Protestantism far beyond the specifically Reformed tradition. Calvinism has been transmitted in various degrees to sectarian Protestantism, often through Puritanism. God's sovereignty and human depravity are the focal points of this theology with consequent emphasis upon divine grace as the only means of salvation. *The Westminster Confession of Faith*, adopted in England in 1646, is the most important creedal statement of Calvinism.

The Zwinglian movement was quickly absorbed into Reformed Protestantism, though Zwingli's nonsacramental view of the Lord's Supper was largely adopted by sectarianism. The Reformed faith, somewhat more optimistic about human possibilities than the Lutheran view permitted, was more hopeful than Lutheranism concerning the transformation of society toward Christian ends and much more active in seeking to establish the kingdom of God on earth.

The sectarian type of Protestantism was expressed at first by the Anabaptists, whose descendants today are the Mennonites and Hutterites, and among whose spiritual children may be numbered the Quakers and to a degree, also, the Baptists and some Congregationalists. A church composed exclusively of baptized believers is basic to the sectarian view. The community as a whole could never comprise the church, which should be completely separated from the state. The sects generally opposed the use of creeds and insisted upon the Bible alone as the rule of faith and practice. Sectarianism was particularly fruitful in its contributions to the development of democratic doctrines. The Levellers in England especially emphasized the principle of equality. Franklin H. Littell has shown conclusively in his *Anabaptist View of the Church* that historians of the Reformation have commonly misunderstood the character of Anabaptism and underestimated its significance. His criticism of Reformation historiography may be extended to the sectarian movement in general. It also should be noted that certain creative consequences of sectarianism in both Christian and political thought have been overlooked by both secular and church historians.

English Baptists emerged out of the sectarian movement in the Reformation and exhibited an affinity with principles expressed in numerous earlier sects. Three Separatist leaders guided a group to Holland early in the 17th century to escape disabilities imposed by the English Crown. John Smith, Thomas Helwys, John Merton, and their followers came into contact with the Mennonites in Holland. Smith became increasingly sympathetic with them. Helwys and Merton, who remained radical Separatists, led a large group back to England in 1611 and established a church which was the progenitor of the General Baptist churches. The term "general" was adopted by these Baptists because they believed that the atonement was available generally to all who would believe. In the 1630's a defection in an Independent church resulted in the appearance of a group who soon called themselves Particular Baptists because they held that the benefits of Christ's death were extended only to the "particular" ones who constituted the elect. By the early 1640's immersion had been adopted by both General and Particular Baptists as the proper mode of baptism. In the 18th century the General Baptists were weakened by defections to Unitarianism, and the Particular Baptists failed to grow because of preoccupation with a hyper-Calvinistic theology which largely neutralized their evangelistic and missionary concern. The two groups of English Baptists grew gradually in the last century and finally came together, after several splits and mergers, in 1891 to form the Baptist Union of Great Britain and Ireland. In 1952 there were approximately 350,000 Baptists in Great Britain and Ireland.

The Anglican type of Protestantism appeared in the 16th century when the Church of England emerged as a distinctive historical entity. The Reformation in England was actuated initially by a growing nationalism. After the break with the Roman Catholic Church during the reign of Henry VIII, the Church of England remained largely Catholic with a new head, the king, who displaced the pope. Because of the youth and frailty of Henry's son and successor, Edward VI, the country was ruled by a council which was strongly Protestant in its sympathies. England, therefore, became thoroughly Protestant, though there followed immediately an equally thorough Catholic period during the reign of "Bloody" Mary. Elizabeth I was determined to preserve the peace of her realm in the religious settlement, and the Church of England embodied her desire for comprehensiveness. *The Thirty-nine Articles*, a modification of Thomas Crammer's *Forty-two Articles*, and the 1552 *Prayer Book* were adopted. Richard Hooker's treatise entitled *The Laws of Ecclesiastical Polity* states the ecclesiology of the emerging church.

The religious settlement was not satisfactory to the Puritans, who, though remaining in the Church of England, sought to purify it of "Romish" elements; to the Separatists, who separated from the church precisely because these elements were not eliminated; and to the Roman Catholics, who hoped their church would be re-established. English Baptists, who appeared as a distinctive historical movement in the early 17th century, were derived from the Separatist movement, though their principles were exhibited, more or less, by earlier sectarian groups. Baptists in England and America made noteworthy contributions to the doctrine of religious liberty.

From the beginning the Church of England, of which the Episcopal Church in America is a branch, occupied a mediating position between the Catholic and Protestant traditions. Consequently, there are tendencies in the Church of England in both directions. The high church stresses the Catholic heritage and the low church, the Protestant point of view. There is now a strong movement within the clergy of the Anglican communion to minimize the Protestant element in its history and to stress the Catholic tradition. This viewpoint portrays Anglicanism as the expression of the authentic Catholic faith from which the Roman Church deviated centuries before the Reformation. It should be noted, however, that the laity tends to stress the Protestant element, and that in America the church is known as "Protestant Episcopal." The Church of England has spread throughout the British Commonwealth and to America.

The history of Protestantism is marked by rather distinctive periods. Following the Reformation there was a tendency toward creedal orthodoxy, which identified the Christian faith with theological expressions of it. This Protestant scholasticism pervaded particularly the Lutheran and Reformed churches and resulted in preoccupation with theological niceties which weakened the missionary outreach of these churches. In the meantime the Roman Catholic Church was reinvigorated by the Council of Trent (1545–63) and the rise of the Society of Jesus (Jesuits), and Catholic missionaries were sent into hitherto untouched areas.

Pietism in Germany was a reaction to the excessive intellectualism of the scholastic theology. Centered in Halle University and led by Jacob Spener, pietism emphasized the personal side of the Christian faith. The same emphasis may be seen in England in the Wesleyan movement and in the Great Awakening in America in the 18th century. A period of rationalism in Germany and England was followed by the theological romanticism of the 19th century. The German theologians, F. D. E. Schleiermacher, whose major work is *The Christian Faith*, and Albrecht Ritschl, whose basic treatise is *The Christian Doctrine of Reconciliation and Justification*, were the chief figures in this movement. Schleiermacher's theological subjectivism and Ritschl's historical and ethical emphasis blended, especially in America, to produce the outstanding features of theological liberalism. Adolph Harnack and Wilhelm Herrmann were advocates of Ritschlianism, but Karl Barth, Herrmann's student, broke away from this theology, which he felt was inadequate amid the realities of contemporary history. His biblical realism, with a variety of modifications, now dominates the Protestant theological scene. Barth's massive and monumental *Kirchliche Dogmatik* combines the comprehensiveness of Aquinas, the objectivity of Calvin, and the scientific concern of Schleiermacher.

American Protestantism is an importation from Europe, modified by the situation in America to which it was adapted. It is marked by great denominational diversity, due to the fact that America was a haven for the persecuted religious groups of Europe, and because liberty of interpretation was available first in Rhode Island and the middle colonies and eventually throughout the new country. The frontier experience of American Christianity produced further development and doctrinal diversity. Methodists and Baptists were particularly successful in dealing with the dynamics of frontier life and reaped heavy numerical rewards.

The Calvinism which the Puritans brought to America was modified, though theology has played a minor role in American Christianity. The only distinctive American theology was developed by Jonathan Edwards, who combined an imaginative Calvinism and American revivalism. The New England theology which Edwards founded persisted until the end of the 19th century, when it succumbed to the rising power of theological liberalism. The scholarly and scholastic Calvinism of the Princeton school of theology, forged by Charles Hodge in the last century, partially persists today in conservative Protestant thought. Fundamentalism, which appeared as a distinctive movement early in the century, reached its height in the 1920's and 1930's and then declined. By 1940 liberalism in theology was on the defensive, and neo-orthodoxy, inspired by the biblical realism of Barth and others, was on the upsurge.

However, Christianity in this country is not deeply concerned with theological foundations and is basically activistic. The plight of the contemporary world has chastened somewhat the optimism of American Christianity, and there is now at least the beginning of theological searching, symbolized by Reinhold Niebuhr. "Theology is one of the conduits of faith," Niebuhr says, "without which the water which rises in the springs of Evangelicalism runs into the sand." Perhaps Christian theology, which degenerated into a "thin diagram of possibility" in the liberal movement, will again become "the full round of a dominant view of the world."

American Christianity, which presents a bewildering complex of belief and practice, exhibits the individualistic, experimental, and optimistic temper of the American character. In 1954 there were more than 400 religious groups in this country. Two of these are native to America: The Church of Jesus Christ of Latter Day Saints, called Mormons, started by Joseph Smith in 1830; and the Church of Christ Scientist, called Christian Science, begun by Mary Baker Eddy in 1875. In spite of widespread diversity and religious eccentricity, the ecumenical movement dominates the American Protestant scene; all large denominations except the Missouri Synod Lutherans and Southern Baptists belong to the World Council of Churches. The deepening concern for a more adequate liturgy in some denominations, hitherto committed to a high degree of spontaneity in worship, tends to bring Christian groups together in a common pursuit of historic liturgical forms.

Baptists appeared in the American colonies in Rhode Island in the 1630's. Churches were organized in Providence and Newport. Baptist principles, dominant in these churches from the beginning, were sufficiently pervasive by the late 1640's to set them apart as full-fledged Baptist churches. These Baptists and their English counterparts insisted upon immersion as the proper mode of baptism, administered only to believers, a nonsacramental concept of baptism and the Lord's Supper, congregationalism in church government, and the separation of church and state. These were subversive and dangerous doctrines in those days!

Baptist growth in America was the result, in some measure, of the coincidence between the belief in religious freedom and the democratic political philosophy which, sweeping over America in the 18th century, became a basic element in the Constitution of the new nation. The noncreedal and nonsacramental position of the Baptists appealed to the American frontiersman, who knew the Bible stories but was unfamiliar with the Christian creeds and for whom sacramentalism seemed rather remote and unreal in the midst of the intensely practical demands of his life in the wilderness. The Baptist farmer-preacher or schoolteacher-preacher who established many academies could communicate with the American pioneer, because they spoke the everyday language of the people rather than the jargon of the learned. The Presbyterian church contributed greatly to civilizing the frontier through a highly educated ministry and the founding of numerous schools and thus quietly projected itself into the substance of the American heritage, but the Baptists and the Methodists with their itinerant preachers won converts at a much higher rate and thus became the strongest denominations in this country. In 1954 there were at least 18 million Baptists and more than 10 million Methodists in the United States.

American Catholicism was relatively weak until the mid-19th century, when migration from Europe, especially Ireland, brought several million Catholics to these shores. This projected the Church into a position of prominence in the nation and brought forth some anti-Roman Catholic sentiment. The Roman Catholic Church has been largely an urban movement in America, though in recent years efforts to extend the faith into rural areas have increased. The authoritarian character of Catholicism has created serious problems for the Church in the American democratic scene and has produced a certain restiveness in some Catholic circles. Perhaps an "American Catholicism" is emerging.

Modern Roman Catholicism.—The Roman Catholic Church reasserted itself in the Counter-Reformation, involving the Council of Trent (1545–63), where the scholastic theology was reaffirmed and the medieval outlook in general was confirmed, and in the organization of the Society of Jesus by Ignatius Loyola, authorized in 1540 by Paul III, who also reorganized the Spanish Inquisition in 1542. Within a century the Counter-Reformation had largely spent its force, due to the decline of Spain as a world power and the loss of prestige by the Jesuits, who, despite prohibition in their own constitutions, engaged in colonial trade and, in general, incurred the hostility of the Catholic clergy. Pope Clement XIV finally abolished the order in 1773. The Popes of the 17th and 18th centuries were not men of commanding force. The growth of European nationalism with the companion tendency for the church in each country to regard itself as a national church was symbolized by the Gallican movement in France. Furthermore, Protestantism had triumphed in northern Europe.

The Edict of Nantes (1598), which guaranteed freedom for French Protestantism, was revoked in 1685 and resulted in the expulsion of the Huguenots. The virtual removal of the Protestant witness from France and the power of the Jesuits in this period resulted in the imposition of a "Jesuit type" of Catholicism upon the country and the consequent narrowing of the choice of the people to either a constricted Romanism or the rationalism of Voltaire and his associates. It is not surprising that the French Revolution swept away the church, the crown, the nobility, and kindred institutions and dealt a blow to the Roman Catholic Church from which it has never really recovered. In

1793 the Jacobin Clubs succeeded in abolishing Christianity itself. Napoleon realized that the people were at least nominally Catholic and, with restrictions, permitted the Church to function again. Protestants were also granted religious rights. Anticlericalism became part and parcel of the French mentality, particularly for intellectuals, due to the tendency of the Church in revolutionary France to align itself with privilege.

The opposition of the Church in France to liberty stands in sharp contrast to the American experience in this matter. Here Christianity has largely stood on the side of freedom. More than a century ago Alexius de Tocqueville saw this and said, "In France I had almost always seen the spirit of religion and the spirit of freedom marching in opposite directions. But in America I found they were intimately united and that they reigned in common over the same country."

From the time of the Great Schism, a debate raged within the Roman communion concerning the question of the seat of supreme authority in the Church. Was it in a Church council or in the pope? In the 19th century the question was given an uncompromising answer in the ultramontanist movement, which asserted the ultimate authority of the papacy. Ultramontanism, strengthened by the restoration of the Jesuits by Pius VII in 1814, reached its climax in 1870 in the decree of papal infallibility, which declared that the *ex cathedra* utterances of the pope concerning "a doctrine of faith or morals" are free from error. Thus the absolute papal monarchy, implied across the centuries, became an explicit institution. Other papal triumphs in the 19th century were the proclamation of the immaculate conception of the Virgin Mary in 1854 and, 10 years later, the *Syllabus of Errors*, which, while condemning some things most Christians oppose, repudiated the doctrine of the separation of church and state and asserted the superiority of parochial to public schools.

Though the Papal States were removed from the pope's jurisdiction by Victor Emmanuel in 1870, the power of the pope in both the Church and the world did not greatly suffer. A secular task which the pope was ill equipped to discharge was thus assumed by the state. The prestige of the papacy in the early 20th century was high, due largely, perhaps, to the stature of the men who occupied the Roman throne. Following World War II the Catholic Church assumed a major role in the struggle against communism, though it is worth noting that in Europe communism is strongest in the southern part where the Church is dominant.

The authoritarian character of the Roman Church makes it inflexible and ties it too much to its past. The medieval theological outlook was reaffirmed and Catholic "modernism" condemned by Pius X in 1907. It is too Roman to be truly Catholic, in the sense of "universal," which is what the word means. Kenneth Scott Latourette has said that "the Roman Catholic Church is handicapped, probably permanently and increasingly, by being too closely bound to a particular cultural tradition and by being based primarily upon a small section of the globe." The growth of Romanism is, therefore, problematical, particularly in view of the fact that the Catholic Church is a minority movement in both the Soviet Union and the United States.

BIBLIOGRAPHY: R. Bainton, *The Reformation of the Sixteenth Century* (1952). A. G. Baker, *A Short History of Christianity* (1940). I. A. Dorner, *History of Protestant Theology*, 2 vols., translated by G. Robson and S. Taylor (1871). A. Harnack, *History of Dogma*, 7 vols., translated by N. Buchanan (1894); *The Constitution and Law of the Church in the First Two Centuries*, translated by F. L. Pogson (1910). K. S. Latourette, *A History of Christianity* (1953); *Anno Domini* (1940); *The Christian Outlook* (1948). R. Niebuhr, *The Nature and Destiny of Man*, 2 vols. (1941, 1943). W. O. E. Oesterley, *The Jewish Background of the Christian Liturgy* (1925). W. W. Sweet, *The Story of American Religion* (1940). W. Walker, *A History of the Christian Church* (1919). C. PENROSE ST. AMANT

CHRISTOLOGY. The systematic interpretation of the person and work of Jesus Christ. The materials for Christology, found in abundance in the Synoptic Gospels, are developed in the christological passages in Paul, John, and Hebrews. Although Hebrews has never dominated a period of Christian history, it may be said in general that the metaphysical concern with the person of Christ in the ancient period was guided by the Logos Christology of John, while the speculations on the saving work of Christ in medieval Christianity were rooted more in Paul. Mystical interest in the imitation of Christ in his passion provided background for the recovery of the "historical Jesus" in the 19th century. Recent emphasis on "the Christ of faith" in reaction against "the Jesus of history" movement requires a restatement that maintains a balance not only between "the historical Jesus" and "the Christ of faith" but also between the biblical foundations and the historical formulations. This may be summarized by a consideration of Christ as the Messiah of Israel, as the mystery of godliness, and as the mediator between God and man.

The Messiah of Israel.—Eusebius of Caesarea (?260–?340), the famous church historian, spoke of our Lord as "the divine and heavenly Word, who is the only High Priest of the universe, the only King of all creation, and the only Prophet among His Father's prophets." Protestant theology, following this clue, has described the threefold office of Christ as prophet, priest, and king. Older Protestant thought gave most emphasis to the priestly work of Christ, and the tendency during the last century has been to speak much of the prophetic work of Christ, but the present turn of events has stimulated strong affirmations of the kingship of Christ. In the light of this historical background, the messianic work of Christ may be summarized under three biblical words describing his nature and work: prophet, priest, and potentate.

1. The prophetic work of Christ pertains to both his *mission* and his *message*. True prophets were sent from God and produced signs to indicate the approval of God on their mission. When Nicodemus came to Jesus, these two facts were recognized when he said: "Rabbi, we know that you are a teacher come from God; for no one can do these signs that you do, unless God is with him" (John 3:2 RSV). Both of these facts were fully evident in the mission of Jesus, for he was conscious of the fact that he was sent from God and came on a unique mission. At one place Jesus is actually called "the apostle and high priest of our confession" (Heb. 3:1 RSV), and the Gospels give abundant evidence of the messianic mission of Jesus. There are both passive and active aspects of this consciousness (John 12:44-47). Jesus is clearly in the role of a prophet, but he is far more than a prophet.

The signs of his mission were also abundant while God "bore witness by signs and wonders and various miracles and by gifts of the Holy Spirit" (Heb. 2:4 RSV). He had all the signs, wonders, and powers of Moses, and this had not happened before in Israel (Deut. 34:9-12). His mighty works were powers in relation to nature, wonders in relation to man, and signs in relation to God. The course of nature was altered, the awe of man was stimulated, and a medium of revelation was provided. The Gospel of John has seven great signs, beginning with the turning of water into wine and coming to a great climax with the raising of Lazarus from the dead. All of the miracles of Jesus are to be understood in the light of this messianic mission.

The message of Jesus was also cast in the role of a prophet. The poetic and parabolic form of his teachings were after the form of the inspired prophetism of the Old Testament. When one reads such poetic passages as the Lord's Prayer in Matthew 6:9-13 or the parable of Mark 12:1-12, the kinship with Hebrew prophecy becomes obvious. The content of his message as well as the form recalls the prophets of the Old Testament. As Amos had the theme of righteousness; Hosea, that of steadfast love; and Isaiah, the holiness of God, Jesus came preaching on one theme with many variations: the kingdom of God. It is very clear, especially in reading the Gospel of Matthew, that Jesus is the prophet like Moses raised up by God (Deut. 18:15-19; Acts 3:22-23; 7:37).

2. The work of Christ was also priestly. Through the offering of *sacrifices* and the promise of the *servant* of the Lord, the way was prepared for the sufferings and perfect obedience of the Son of God. The sacrifice of Christ has both historical and eternal significance. The historical is summed up in the words of Paul, who said: "Him who knew no sin he made a sin offering for our sake, so that in him we might become the righteousness of God" (II Cor. 5:21, author's translation). This historical sacrifice was both *sinless* and *substitutionary*. It was sinless because Christ "knew no sin." The suggestion that Christ possessed a sinful nature or that he did acts of sin not only rejects the testimony of the Scriptures but also removes the standard by which all sin is recognized and rebuked (Heb. 4:16). This historical sacrifice was also substitutionary. Christ was "made a sin offering for our sake." To this fact the Scriptures give repeated testimony, but Galatians 3:13 goes so far as to say that "Christ redeemed us from the curse of the law, having become a curse for us" (RSV).

The eternal sacrifice relates the death of Jesus to both *finality* and *faith*. The sacrificial death of Jesus is final because it happened once, never to be repeated. Hebrews is distinctive in teaching that Christ "appeared once for all at the end of the age to put away sin by the sacrifice of himself" (9:26 RSV). It was "by a single offering" that he "perfected for all time those who are sanctified" (10:14 RSV). And this points to the importance of faith, a second theme given major attention in Hebrews. The eternal sacrifice brings eternal salvation only to those who have saving faith.

Jesus was also the Servant of the Lord promised in Isaiah 53. As the Servant of the Lord, the sufferings of Christ were *voluntary* and *vicarious*. They were voluntary because the will of neither the Father nor the Son was forced in the sublime submission of the cross. Freely God willed to give his Son, and freely the Son became submissive to the Father's will. Jesus could say: "I seek not my own will but the will of him who sent me" (John 5:30 RSV); yet it was just as true when, speaking of his life, he said: "I have power to lay it down, and I have power to take it again" (John 10:18 RSV). The vicarious element in the sufferings of the Servant were central in Isaiah 53, and the fulfilment of these promised benefits came to us through the One who gave himself up for us (Gal. 2:20). Jesus was the good shepherd who gave his life for the sheep (John 10:11), and he now appears "in the presence of God on our behalf" (Heb. 9:24 RSV). This is the supreme revelation of the love of God (I John 4:10), and this leads to the role of Christ as potentate.

3. First Timothy 6:15 speaks of "the blessed and only Potentate, the King of kings, and Lord of lords." Jesus is indeed the King of kings. In the Old Testament the Lord was the true King (Psalm 24:7-10), and the kings of Israel were his representatives. The dark despair that followed their failure was relieved by the promise of the Messiah as king (Isa. 9:6-7). This promise was fulfilled when Mary conceived by the Holy Spirit One who would rule on the throne of David forever (Luke 1:31-35). The vivid portrait of Jesus as King in humiliation in John 18:33 to 19:22 is balanced by the vision of the King coming in glory in Revelation 19:9-16. Jesus Christ is "the faithful witness, the firstborn of the dead, and the ruler of kings on earth" (Rev. 1:5 RSV).

Christology

Christ is also Lord of lords. In the Old Testament no essential of faith is more important than the cry at Mount Carmel: "The Lord, he is the God; the Lord, he is the God" (I Kings 18:39). The burning question was not whether there was a God, but who was God. Israel knew that the true and living God was the Lord, who brought them "out of the land of Egypt, out of the house of bondage" (Ex. 20:2). That was the reason behind the first of all commandments: "Hear, O Israel: The Lord our God is one Lord; and you shall love the Lord your God with all your heart, and with all your soul, and with all your might" (Deut. 6:4 RSV). When the New Testament writers added to the statement that the Lord is God the confession that Jesus is Lord, they intended to proclaim nothing less than belief in the deity of Christ. The confession that Jesus is Lord was filled with such meaning that Paul declared that no person could say it "except by the Holy Spirit" (I Cor. 12:3 RSV). By the humiliation and exaltation of our Lord Jesus Christ, God has revealed that every tongue should "confess that Jesus Christ is Lord, to the glory of God the Father" (Phil. 2:11). When the consummation of the ages comes, one called the Word of God will be revealed as "King of kings, and Lord of lords" (Rev. 19:16).

The mystery of godliness.—Jesus is more than the Messiah of Israel. He is also the mystery of godliness (I Tim. 3:16), who as the eternal Son of God appeared in history and was exalted to the right hand of God with all authority in heaven and on earth.

The *eternity* of Christ, commonly called preexistence, rejects all efforts to establish a point in time or eternity at which the Son of God was not. Resurrection (Rom. 1:3), baptism (Mark 1:11), and birth (Luke 1:35) are all inadequate points of departure to express the high Christology of Christian faith. Only one who is God's eternal Son is worthy of worship. In the New Testament Paul presents Christ primarily as the eternal wisdom of God. Against the background of the Old Testament teaching, the letters of Paul abound in implications of this eternal relation (Phil. 2:5; Col. 1:15–18; I Cor. 2:6–9; 8:6; 10:4; 15:44–49; II Cor. 8:9; Gal. 4:4; Rom. 8:3; I Tim. 1:15). John builds this eternal relation more on the idea of the word of God, which is also deeply rooted in Old Testament teaching. As the "Son of man" (John 3:13), the "I am" (John 8:38, 42, 48), and the "Son of God" (John 17:1, 5, 24), this eternal relation is proclaimed. Revelation adds the idea of Christ as the Alpha and the Omega to this conception (Rev. 1:8, 11; 21:6; 22:13). Hebrews, although less influential than Paul and John in historical theology, unites both the wisdom and the word in proclaiming Christ as the radiance of God's glory and the stamp of God's substance (Heb. 1:1–4).

The *epiphany* (appearance, II Tim. 1:10) of Christ in history also presents both a Pauline and a Johannine emphasis. Protestant theology, following the lead of Philippians 2:5–11, has given more attention to the humiliation of the Servant, while Anglican theology follows more John's teaching on the incarnation of the Word (John 1:1–18). Both are valid New Testament teachings, and the word "epiphany" is here used to embrace both ideas.

The *humiliation* of our Lord, outlined in Philippians 2:6–8, makes reference to two forms of Christ. The first is the form of God and contrasts the first and last Adam along the lines of I Corinthians 15:45; Romans 5:14. In Genesis 3:5–6 the first Adam attempts to become equal with God by eating of fruit snatched from the tree, but in Philippians 2:6 the last Adam "counted not the being on an equality with God a thing to be grasped" (author's translation). The second form is that of the Servant, and the contrast between the two Adams continues. In Genesis 2:7 the first Adam comes into existence by the special act of God, while Philippians 2:7 indicates that Christ became man by God's miraculous act. Paul uses the same Greek word (*ginomai*) in Romans 1:3; Galatians 4:4; Philippians 2:7 that is used in Genesis 2:7. It is not the common word (*gennao*) for natural generation, found in Galatians 4:23. This seems to indicate that Paul believed that the first Adam and the last Adam came into existence by a special act of God. The main difference between the two was that one was temporal and "of the earth," while the other was eternal and "from heaven" (I Cor. 15:47).

The *incarnation* of the Word in the union of deity and humanity is described in the magnificent hymn in John 1:1–18. Christ is declared to be the eternal Word of God shining forth as the Light of the world even before his entrance into humanity in the flesh of Jesus (John 1:6–13). The eternity of the Word is rooted in such Old Testament passages as Genesis 1 and Psalm 33:6, where God created by his word. The Word of God existed before all created things and is the agent by which God created whatever has a beginning. The entrance of the Word into humanity is related to this universal presence in the world as focused light is related to diffused light. The universal Light which came out of eternity and floods the world with his presence was focused in all his fulness in the flesh of Jesus. According to John 1:14–18, this focused Light was both unique and concrete. The concreteness of the Word is the union of the eternal and the historical, of deity and humanity, while the uniqueness of the Word means that the revelation and redemption in Christ are never repeated.

The *exaltation* of Christ creates considerable conflict in current discussions. Conservatives differ, liberals devaluate it, and radicals seek to eliminate the "myths" from the New Testament picture. The stages of Christ's exaltation include the descent into Hades, the resurrection, the ascension, and the enthronement at the right hand of God. The descent doctrine, once pushed into the background, has received new attention in such works as Bo Reicke, *The Disobedient Spirits and Christian Baptism*. Many New Testament passages suggest the teaching (Matt. 12:29, 40; 16:18; 27:52-53; Acts 2:27-31; Rom. 10:6-8; Col. 2:15; Eph. 4:8-10; I Tim. 3:16; I Peter 3:18 to 4:6; Rev. 1:18). The resurrection of Christ is commonly recognized as the central teaching of New Testament faith, but much heated debate centers on the idea of the empty tomb. The ascension, mentioned less in the New Testament (Luke 24:49-51; Acts 1:1-12; Mark 16:19; John 3:13; 6:62; 20:17; I Tim. 3:16), has difficulties in adjusting to the modern scientific view of the world; but it is still maintained with considerable success. The enthronement at the right hand of the Father is almost as central to New Testament faith as the resurrection, and it is basic for the teaching of the lordship of Christ. In the New Testament John puts emphasis on crucifixion, Paul on resurrection, and Hebrews on the enthronement, but all of these stages in the exaltation may be harmonized with the total teaching of each. The bias of the thinker has much to do with the conclusions on this phase of Christology.

The mediator between God and man.—This is the climax of Christology. Christ is not a mediator in the sense of an intermediary such as Moses, who received the law through the angels (Gal. 3:19-20), but he is the mediator of a covenant that is better (Heb. 8:6) and new (Heb. 9:15; 12:24). This statement does not deny the true humanity of the Lord, who was himself man (I Tim. 2:5), but it does declare that it is God himself who is confronted in the humanity of Jesus. It is at this point that the virgin birth of Christ became so important in the opposition of the early church to those who denied the humanity of Christ. In modern times when many argue for the deity of Christ on the basis of the virgin birth, it becomes important to call attention to the defense of the humanity of Christ in the struggle of early Christianity. The growth of Christ, along with his birth, is important for understanding the humanity of our Lord, and it is important to notice how closely it is related to the virgin birth in Luke 2:52. The messianic temptations of Christ (Luke 4:1-13; Matt. 4:1-11) are also abundant evidence of the humanity of Jesus (Heb. 2:5-18; 4:15). The emphasis of Hebrews, along with the passion narratives of the Gospels, rules out every denial that Jesus was truly man. The author of Hebrews found no difficulty in moving from the deity of Christ in Chapter 1 to the profound statement of the humanity of Christ in 5:7-10.

The humanity of Christ apart from deity is not sufficient for a true and perfect mediator. Only one who is truly God as well as truly man can save men from their sins. If he is not God, he has no power to save; and if he is not man, he has no right to save. Through humanity the deity of Christ is revealed in word and deed. The prophets proclaimed the word of God, but Jesus was the Word (John 1:1-18). This was with authority (*exousia*, Mark 1:22) and fulfilled the law of Moses (Matt. 5:21, 27, 33, 38, 43). The absoluteness of his teaching is seen in his proclamation of the nearness of the kingdom of God in his preaching and in his person. His works as well as his words were evidence that God had visited his people and made himself known in the flesh of Jesus. The unique life of Christ, who worked miracles in nature and men (Matt. 21:11; 4:6; Luke 7:16; 24:19; Acts 2:22-23; John 3:2; 4:19; 6:14; 7:40; 9:17; 20:31) and who lived a sinless life among men (Luke 5:8; Heb. 4:15; II Cor. 5:21), was sufficient evidence for faith. The unique life was sealed by a unique death that revealed that Jesus was no ordinary man among men (Mark 15:39).

Historical development of Christology.—In the dynamic drama of historical revelation, belief in both the humanity and the deity of the Lord are found side by side in the assurance of faith. It was not until efforts were made to explain the incarnation in the terms of the metaphysical speculations of Greek philosophy that the travail of thought and the threat of heresy haunted man's faith.

At least four major crises arose regarding man and salvation before the definition of Chalcedon brought comparative agreement among the faithful. The first crisis came when Arius (A.D. 256-336) championed a creature Christology that thought of Christ as an intermediate being between the uncreated and all other created beings. This denial of the eternal sonship of Christ was condemned as heresy at Nicea in A.D. 325. A second crisis came when Apollinarius (?331-?392), bishop of Laodicea, attempted to explain the humanity and deity of Christ as a combination in which the body and soul of Jesus were declared human, and the mind or spirit of Christ was declared divine. This rejection of the human mind of Jesus was repudiated at Constantinople in A.D. 381; thus the first two tests of orthodoxy had defended the deity of Christ, in opposition to Arius, and the humanity of Christ, in condemning Apollinarius. The next crisis came when Nestorius refused to speak of Mary as the mother of God (*theotokos*). He was willing to call her the mother of Jesus the Son of God, but the idea that Mary bore God was repugnant to interest in the humanity of Christ. In a decision still hotly debated, Nestorius was condemned first at Ephesus in A.D. 431 and then at Chalcedon in A.D. 451. The fourth major crisis centers around Eutyches (A.D. 378-454), who taught that the divine and human natures of Christ became one divine-human nature in the incarnation. He claimed Christ was *of* two natures, but he was not *in* two natures after he became flesh. At the Council of Chalcedon in A.D. 451, this doctrine was declared heresy, along with the teachings of Apollinarius and Nestorius. The famous definition, based on the so-called Tome of Leo and generally regarded as orthodox unto this day, reads as follows:

We, then, following the holy Fathers, all with one consent, teach men to confess one and the same Son, our Lord Jesus Christ, the same perfect in Godhead and also perfect in manhood; truly God and truly man, of a reasonable soul and body; consubstantial with the Father according to the Godhead, and consubstantial with us according to the Manhood; in all things like unto us, without sin; begotten before all ages of the Father according to the Godhead, and in these latter days, for us and for our salvation, born of the Virgin Mary, the Mother of God, according to the Manhood; one and the same Christ, Son, Lord, Only-begotten, to be acknowledged in two natures, *inconfusedly, unchangeably, indivisibly, inseparably;* the distinction of natures being by no means taken away by the union, but rather the property of each nature being preserved, and concurring in one Person and one Subsistence, not parted or divided into two persons, but one and the same Son, and only begotten, God the Word, the Lord Jesus Christ; as the prophets from the beginning concerning him, and the Lord Jesus Christ himself has taught us, and the Creed of the holy Fathers has handed down to us.

The definition has, of course, been vigorously challenged at times, but no other definition has been able to gain enough support to supplant it.

Reaction to Chalcedonian Christology has been varied. In the Middle Ages the chief concern centered in the death of Christ. Anselm (1033–1109) of Canterbury interpreted the death of Christ as a satisfactory reparation paid to God for human sin; Peter Abelard (1079–1142) saw in it the revelation of God's love, which turned man to God; and Bernard of Clairvaux (1091–1153) prepared the way for the recovery of the historical Jesus by making the sufferings of Christ the object of mystical contemplation. All of these elements are found in the Christology of Thomas Aquinas (1224–74), but *The Life of Christ* by Ludolf of Saxony (d. 1377) and *The Imitation of Christ* issued by Thomas à Kempis (1380–1471) illustrate a growing concern for the Jesus of history.

In the Renaissance, Erasmus (?1446–1536) placed the teachings of Jesus at the center of his humanistic interest in Jesus, while the Reformation continued the effort to understand the death of Christ. Luther (1483–1546) was primarily interested in the penal sufferings of Christ for man's salvation and the universal presence of Christ's person, especially as related to the Lord's Supper. Although Calvinism was in basic agreement with Luther on the penal and substitutionary death of Christ, the idea of universal presence was rejected. Orthodox Protestantism remained loyal to Chalcedonian Christology even during the times when the rationalist would permit no higher view of Jesus than a supreme moral teacher.

Several currents in modern thought have modified Chalcedonian Christology. A psychological interest reaches back to Schleiermacher (1768–1834), who, under the influence of Romanticism, interpreted Christ as Redeemer of men and founder of the Christian church, insofar as there is participation in the perfection of Christ's own God-consciousness. The efforts of William Sanday, *Christologies Ancient and Modern* (1910), to locate the divinity of Christ in the subliminal consciousness and the suggestions of W. R. Matthews, *The Problem of Christ in the Twentieth Century* (1950), that Jung's theory of the racial unconscious may help to understand the temptations of Jesus and his relation to the human race continue this concern with the mind of Jesus. An ethical movement that grew out of Ritschl's (1822–89) revolt against metaphysical speculations makes the vocation of the historical Jesus as the revealer of the kingdom of God the focus of attention. This new appreciation for the historical Jesus flowered in such works as Sir John Seeley's *Ecce Homo* (1865), published anonymously, but the reaction of this movement against metaphysical reflection led to a radical distinction between the gospel *of,* and the gospel *about,* Jesus. A third trend that turned with Thomasius (1802–75) to the old Protestant doctrine of the *kenosis* (emptying, Phil. 2:7) of Christ to meet the challenge of the critical study of the gospels has created a stir among the orthodox. The critical theories of *Formgeschichte,* especially in the writings of Rudolf Bultmann, deepened the dissatisfaction with the static concepts of Chalcedonian Christology. Some of these trends are found in the earlier writings of Karl Barth and Emil Brunner, but those who accept the general results of the radical reduction of historical facts in extreme form criticism give emphasis to revelation as an event in history. This is a special concern for Paul Tillich, *The Interpretation of History* (1936), Otto Piper, *God in History* (1939), and John Knox, *On the Meaning of Christ* (1947). The historical reinterpretation of Jesus as Leader, Saviour, and Victor in the thought of Karl Heim has found a strong advocate in W. M. Horton, *Our Eternal Contemporary* (1942). A philosophical movement led by William Temple, *Christus Veritas* (1924), and Lionel S. Thornton, *The Incarnate Lord* (1928), undertakes to relate the cosmic Christ to A. N. Whitehead's philosophy of process. Most of the modern theories have value when interpreted in a more inclusive context that does not reject other valid teachings on the person of our Lord. Christology today has turned in the direction of balance that offers hope that contemporary discussions may arrive at an agreement different in terminology and deeper in understanding but not far from the distinctive patterns of the definition of Chalcedon.

See also INTERCESSION OF CHRIST and SINLESSNESS OF JESUS. DALE MOODY

BIBLIOGRAPHY: D. M. Baillie, *God Was in Christ* (1955). G. C. Berkouwer, *The Person of Christ* (1954). P. T. Forsythe, *The Person and Place of Jesus Christ* (1909). J. S. Lawton, *Conflict in Christology* (1947). H. R. Mackintosh, *The Person of Jesus Christ* (1913).

CHURCH. *Meaning of the word.*—In nonbiblical Greek the word *ecclesia* ordinarily connotes an assembly of citizens, summoned (for example) from their homes by a herald to gather for specific business at an appointed time and place. The word stresses not what they are called out from, but rather the *purpose* for which they come together. Occasionally, ecclesia is used of a general meeting of a *koinon* or brotherhood. It is never used as the title of a religious group *per se*.

In the Septuagint, the Old Testament in Greek translation, two words are used which relate directly to this study: *ecclesia* and *synagoge*. These terms are roughly synonymous and refer to the people met for religious purposes, especially for worship. But there are also notable differences in the words. *Synagoge* ordinarily translates the Hebrew word *'edhah* and is especially frequent in Exodus, Leviticus, Numbers, and Joshua. *Ecclesia*, ordinarily translating *qahal*, is used with great frequency especially in such later books as Chronicles, Ezra, and Nehemiah. *Synagogue-'edhah* as referring to the society of Israel, assembled or unassembled, seems originally to have been a more comprehensive and abstract word than *ecclesia-qahal*. It appears, however, that *ecclesia*, originally the more definite and formal word, came to combine (after the Exile) the shades of meaning belonging both to itself and to *synagoge*. For the Jews, therefore, who spoke Greek, *ecclesia* meant the whole society or congregation of Israel as well as any assembly of that congregation. In other words, *ecclesia*, originally more specific and tangible, had taken on broader and more abstract connotations.

This interpretation of the growth of the meaning of this word is indirectly substantiated by a notice of what was happening to the other word, *synagoge*, in the Apocrypha. There *synagoge* seemed to be coming to mean (perhaps in distinction from *ecclesia*) the local congregation more specifically than the unassembled congregation. By the middle of the first century of the Christian era, both words had ceased to be current in Judaism and had been displaced by one word which did service for both: *k'neseth*.

In the New Testament the church (*ecclesia*) appears as the result of God's redemptive action, as the object of his continuing interest, and as the organ of his saving purpose for the world. It is constituted through Christ as the "New People of God," i.e., as the new and true Israel. This gathering and constituting of a messianic people is implicit in the idea of messiahship itself. The Shepherd is no shepherd without a flock.

The church as it appears in the New Testament is both one and many, both holy and sinful. It is led by, but is greater than, its ministry. It is thought of functionally as fulfilling in history the cosmic intention of Christ, through immediate and total fellowship with him. This fellowship, being much more than a human spirit of camaraderie, involves radical participation in Christ's victory over sin and death, in his spirit of sacrifice and absolute obedience to the Father's will, and in his sonship and final exaltation.

Because the great fact of Jesus Christ thus pours such new content and meaning into the word *ecclesia*, it is necessary in the New Testament to interpret the word from the reality, more than the reality from the word.

We now must consider more fully and in turn: first, the nature of the church; second, the function of the church; and third, the relation of the church to churches.

The nature of the church.—Perhaps the nature of the church can best be indicated in its relation to the triune God, as this relationship appears in characteristic figures of speech: (1) a royal priesthood to God; (2) the body of Christ; and (3) the community of the Holy Spirit.

The biblical doctrine of the church has its clearest point of departure in the narrative of Exodus 19. This passage discloses the nature and purpose of the mighty, saving act of God in the deliverance from Egypt. A virtually anonymous mass of men was here being welded into a kingdom-unit in history on the basis of vocation and mission. They were to be to God "a kingdom of priests and a holy people." This means that they were to manifest God's character in their own common life and were to lead others to do the same. They had been laid hold on by God and delivered by his mighty hand. Since this is the end for which men were made, this royal-priestly society apprehends ultimate reality and therefore becomes, in one sense, an end. But since this same redeeming encounter is the desire of God for all men, this royal-priestly society becomes a means through which God reaches to others, to "all the families of the earth."

The significance of this passage for our subject lies in its being the presupposition of the New Testament conception of the church as the reconstituted people of God; and in one epistle (I Peter 2:9–10) it is even taken over bodily and applied to the Christian church. The Old Testament narrative in many respects gathers around the measure and manner in which the holy Israel of the calling became too much an Israel of the flesh. In turn, the revelation through a holy people was mediated through a holy remnant and at last through the Holy One: the Suffering Servant and Son of Man.

In Jesus Christ the Holy One was in our midst to redeem us from our sin and to fulfil the destiny which we had forfeited through wilful self-assertion. In him the revelation given to patriarchs and prophets in varying portions and manners (Heb. 1) was incarnate in clarity and fulness. For in him, who was both perfectly sinless and perfectly obedient to the Father's will, the very being and purpose of God were revealed. Those who by faith saw that this was so, who by grace were incorporated into his divine life, and upon whom the Spirit came in regenerating power, were made to be the church. To them passed the vocation and mission of

Israel. Here is God's household (Gal. 6:10) and God's temple (II Cor. 6:14 ff.; Eph. 2:11–22), in which society the believing confess their faith in an utter dependence upon the Father God, who has made himself known in the Son by the Spirit; and the believing then turn to the world in the discharge of their priestly-prophetic ministry, with a will to bring all men to the same confession.

The church is also the body of Christ (I Cor. 12; Rom. 12; and Eph.). This figure of speech is used to stress the common life which we share in Christ. Believers are said to be incorporated into Christ, to have put on Christ, to have been baptized into Christ. Those who are thus assimilated to him, who live under him as head, have union with him and with one another in him. Having become members of Christ, they become members, also, of one another.

There is one Christ, one Head. "There is one body, and one Spirit, even as ye are called in one hope of your calling" (Eph. 4:4). The church is this body of Christ, through one Spirit and one calling. As there is one Christ, so there is one church, one body. For members to be divided from one another is for Christ himself to be divided (I Cor.).

Men become members of Christ's body through his own gracious act of incorporation. We do not ourselves create this church; we may only be added to it and then represent and manifest it. For the question of whether or not Christ has, or is to have, his own spiritual body, is a matter over which local congregations have no control.

The church as "body" sees the "members" incorporated into Christ, God's Son, by a faith expressed in baptism and sealed by the Holy Spirit. These members grow up in all things into him who is their Head (Eph. 4:15), and who will present them faultless and blameless to the Father, who will take up habitation among them by the Spirit (Eph. 2:22).

The church is the community of the Holy Spirit. The church as the "fellowship of the Spirit" is the characteristic emphasis of the book of Acts (cf. also II Cor. 13:14; Phil. 2:1). A group of men who would otherwise have only a sociological significance and be related together as by voluntary social contract, being subject only to the laws which pertain to all other social groups, are transformed by the Holy Spirit into a fellowship and rendered fit for service.

This view sees the church wherever the Holy Spirit is present with regenerating power and finds the distinctiveness of the faith in the change which is produced in the believer. This profound change in the very being of the believer, which is the distinctive work of the Holy Spirit, is stressed in Acts much more than regularity in either doctrine or polity. Without this life-changing experience the church fails to be the church, for it is constituted, not of the dead or profane, but of those whom the Spirit has quickened and sanctified to God. Neither sound theology nor right polity can substitute for the presence and work of the Holy Spirit in the making of the church.

It should not need to be said, however, that theology and experience are not mutually exclusive. Indeed, no doctrine of the church is adequate which neglects either. It is important that the Baptist tradition, expressed in the historic English and American Baptist confessions of faith, gives representation to this many-sided biblical witness on the doctrine of the church.

Every known Baptist confession of faith before 1833 (including the First and Second London Confessions of the Particular Baptists, and the Standard Confession and the Orthodox Creed of the General Baptists in England; and the confessions of the Philadelphia, Charleston, and Warren associations in America) has a strong and unmistakably plain article on the church. For in the historic Baptist faith, as in the New Testament, the church is God's Israel, his royal priesthood, his household and temple. It is the pillar and ground of truth, in which is confessed a living faith in God, in which is shared a common life in the body of Christ, and in which is wrought the transformation of life by the power of the Holy Spirit.

The function of the church.—The function of the church answers to the nature of the church. Just as the church is a royal priesthood to God, so does it function in a ministry of worship. As the church is the body of Christ, so does it function in a ministry of the Word of God, of which Christ was the very incarnation. As the church is the fellowship of the Spirit, so does its fellowship always overflow into service. Obviously, however, as the New Testament pattern clearly shows, the church functions naturally through churches.

1. The worship of God. The church as a royal priesthood exists to serve the altar of God the King. The Christian priesthood offers no sacrifice on the church's altar. Our High Priest has himself entered once and for all into the holy of holies to put away sin by the sacrifice of himself (Heb. 2:9; 7:27; 9). Because that sacrifice entailed the death of him who offered it, it cannot be repeated. Because it was absolutely and finally efficacious for all the requirements of God's purpose and man's need, it need not be repeated. The Roman Catholic intention to repeat Christ's sacrifice in the celebration of the Mass in effect denies the absolute and final character of Christ's work on the cross. The Christian priesthood finds its distinctive function, therefore, not in acting from God's side in the offering of sacrifices on man's behalf; it rather acts from man's side, as it leads men in faith to present their bodies a living sacrifice to God (Rom. 12:1).

A church's worship hours are prostituted when they are consistently used for promotional or other ends. The meeting of men with the living God is an end in itself. The only proper reference beyond this is that all men should have the same encounter and live out its implications. A church, thus, has a great responsibility to make available, to all who will share it, a profound experience of corporate worship. This is, one may well suppose, the most significant and challenging of all human endeavors. God, who is Spirit, can be only spiritually discerned. Revealed omnipotence is to sinners a horrible sight. Even all-sufficient grace may be surgical in its operation. True worship, thus, requires insight, awe, and courage. The worship of the living God is not an occasion where philanthropically minded men promote a human institution deemed worthy of their support. Nor is it a flight from reality for purposes of mystical contemplation. Neither is it a series of stimuli contrived to produce certain emotional responses.

The worship of God, rather, takes thought, planning, preparation, dedication, and, usually, patient waiting. It aims, here on earth, at recognizing the awful holiness of God's being ("Hallowed be thy name"), at discovering the majesty of God's ruling power ("Thy kingdom come"), and at co-operating with the imperious purposes to which we are subject ("Thy will be done"). Apart from the fear (awe, reverence) of God, men are not persuaded; apart from the love of Christ, men are not constrained; apart from the new creation of grace, old things do not pass away (II Cor. 5:11–17). It is the aim of a church at worship to make these things vivid and persuasive.

2. The Word of God. The church as the body of Christ exists to proclaim the Word of God, which was incarnate in Jesus; and to this Word inspired witness has been borne in Holy Scripture.

The "word of God" means just what it says. It is God's living intention voiced for our redemption, through media of his own choosing. The prophets, law, and writings; the Gospels and Epistles, are God's written Word for us just because they do translate this living Word of God into human speech and formulate it for our instruction and nurture. The Bible, so conceived, becomes our chief textbook and religious authority. It remains timelessly relevant because God is unchanging. It cannot be supplemented or revised, not because prophets of God are not still translating his living Word into speech through preaching, but because our faith, which is grounded and fulfilled in God's final Word, his Son and Christ, finds all its foundations resting upon and all its hopes consummated in the saving event which has already happened. To what happened, inspired witness has already been given. It is this event, and its meaning, which must ever remain the burden of all Christian preaching. The voiced gospel of today is powerful and relevant, therefore, just in the measure that it encounters, interprets, and applies the truth already revealed.

Our faith is thus always set within the dialectic of backward and forward. We turn backward to the Bible, but also forward through the Bible to the living Word of God to which the Bible bears authoritative witness. By the Holy Spirit we worship the living God in the living Word. For, in a splendid phrase of Hendrik Kraemer, "the Word was made, not book, but flesh, and dwelt among us." In the measure that the church receives, understands, and obeys the Word of God—in that measure it functions in keeping with its nature as the body of Christ.

3. The service of God. The church as a fellowship of the Spirit exists to discharge a spiritual *diakonia*, a service or ministry (cf. Eph. 4:11–12; Acts 2; Eph. 5–6). The church must receive the gift and filling of the Holy Spirit in order to carry out its spiritual mission. Those who stand outside the covenant are not moved to the kingdom of God by a church which fails to embody and manifest the grace about which it preaches. Those who stand without the covenant do not accept a criticism of life which reaches them from a church which does not stand under the judgment of its own gospel. The world, the flesh, and the devil do not bow the neck before a church which in its own life has not rejected the world, the flesh, and the devil.

But the church which humbles itself at the altar of its Lord, which accepts the judgment of its own gospel, and which puts to death the mind of the "flesh"—that church will know the abiding Presence, it will speak the Word with authority, and it will lay imperative claims on the forms and institutions of the world's life. For it is through the church's witness as means, and through its common life as end, that the spiritual-ethical demands of the kingdom of God are brought redemptively to bear on the lives and relationships of men.

A figure of speech from Paul (Phil. 3:20 Moffatt), catches up all three of these elements of worship, word, and service: "We are a *colony* of heaven." Wedel gives a stirring interpretation of this. The Roman colony, in Paul's day, existed on the frontiers of the empire in an alien land. There Roman citizenship (*politeuma*) would be a treasured possession. There Roman culture, speech, and manners would be zealously fostered. The individual by himself could not keep alive the traditions of the homeland. Corporate life alone would suffice. "For the colony was both memory and foretaste of home. Roman citizen and barbarian neighbor might be outwardly scarcely distinguishable. Yet what a difference in ultimate loyalties, in heart's longing or in memories."

This is a true parallel to the life of God's people in the world. On the frontiers of the world's life, which blaze in the conflagrations of human passions and pride, the church sets up its altar, proclaims its word, and performs its service in the spirit of lowliness. This church, set in society as its servant and yet over against society as its conscience, will prove to be the world's guiding light and saving salt.

Thus the church worships God through the

Church Administration

Word by the Spirit. In worship and witness it proclaims the very Word which it has received from the God it worships. And it carries the overflow of both word and worship into mission and service.

The church and churches.—What has been said of the church to this point makes urgent the question: What is the relationship of *the* church to *a* church? For it is in churches that the church lives between God and the world. Further, what has been said of the church refers neither to a merely lovely ideal nor to a reality which is only invisible. *The* church is truly known only to faith, because it is constituted in and by the Holy Spirit. For this reason it may in one sense be described as invisible. But the church becomes visible in churches—in actual, visible, local companies. What this involves may (in part) be dealt with under the topics of: (1) the one and the many; and (2) the principle of the gathered church.

The church is manifested and embodied in churches. God alone determines the membership of the church. A church must seek to reflect God's action of election and redemption. The church derives its ultimate character not from its membership but from its Head. Its proper members are chosen by him, not by us. But the membership of local churches, which believers do control, must be determined by a sense of true churchmanship; i.e., churches must—so far as it is possible for us to make them so—be reflections and embodiments of God's church.

The distinctive Baptist witness to the dignity and importance of the local church is set squarely within the framework of the Baptist witness to the primacy of the church universal. Early Baptists had a high doctrine of the local congregation precisely because they took with radical seriousness the reality of the church of God. A local church was important just because it was meant to be, in its own time and place, the embodiment of the whole church. In every congregation was the fulness of churchmanship, because in every congregation were present faith in God, fellowship in Christ, and the transformed life of the Spirit. Every congregation was thus in intercourse with Ultimate Reality, God himself. No one congregation had larger right of access to the divine presence than another. Therefore, no one congregation could coerce the will of another; and for the same reason no group of congregations could act in matters touching any one congregation, except as that congregation had freely willed it so.

Each church was independent. But all churches were interdependent. They were congregations expressing a common faith, walking together in a common calling, and sharing a common experience. Their interdependence was expressed in the principles of association and co-operation. The independence appeared in each church's freedom to determine its own ministry and discipline. But it was always the participation of each church in the life of the whole church which gave to it importance, authority, and relevance. If this historic Baptist truth today sounds strange in any Baptist ears, its valid place in the Baptist doctrine of the church may be studied, in its uniform consistency, in every Baptist confession of faith, British and American, which appeared before 1833.

A local church becomes a manifestation and embodiment of the church by the principle of gathering and the process of disciplining its members. The church is visible because it is a voluntarily cohering group of regenerated believers already embodying and manifesting what older Baptist confessions of faith called the "Catholick Church." Its members are "gathered" to God out of the "world."

Further, in our Baptist tradition churches are not clubs to which individuals with similar preferences and prejudices belong. A church must stand under the Word of God and not under subjectivistic whim. The churches betray themselves when they permit their own constituency to imagine that church membership is simply a phase of "the respectable way of life," or that it is the custodian of "values" from which members may pick at will. Rather, a church must aim at nothing less than the full nurture of its members in the knowledge and admonition of the Lord. To achieve this, each member must understand that he enters by faith into a community of mutual instruction, rebuke, and aid. If necessary, the integrity of the community must be preserved by the use of the ban of censure or excommunication. The church of God, embodied in churches, is no society of self-assertion, nor does it exist for the cultivation of individual opinions—even individual opinions about God. It is rather the community of faith, hope, and love, within which individuals' opinions and assertions are significant only as they are brought into obedience to the mind of Christ and minister to the interests of his gospel. Such a church has the freedom of grace and the responsibility of truth. It bows to no authority lower than Christ but finds its glory in ministry to the least, the lowly, and the lost.

See also BODY OF CHRIST.

BIBLIOGRAPHY: W. O. Carver, *The Glory of God in the Christian Calling* (1949). R. N. Flew, *Jesus and His Church* (1938). F. J. A. Hort, *The Christian Ecclesia* (1898). G. Johnston, *The Doctrine of the Church in the New Testament* (1943). F. H. Littell, *The Anabaptist View of the Church* (1952). J. R. Nelson, *The Realm of Redemption* (1951). L. Newbigin, *The Household of God* (1954). E. A. Payne, *The Fellowship of Believers* (1952). H. W. Robinson, *Baptist Principles* (1945).   THERON D. PRICE

CHURCH ADMINISTRATION. A church after the New Testament pattern has been described as "an organized body of baptized believers, equal in rank and privileges, administering its affairs under the headship of Christ, united in the belief of what he has taught, covenanting to do what he has commanded, and co-operating with other like bodies in kingdom movements." Since a Baptist church is committed to the principle of "administering its affairs," the problems and responsibilities of effective church administration increase with the variety and complexity of church organization. By administration is meant the effective application of principles of polity and details of practice to the affairs of the institution by qualified persons.

The word "administration" has as its root the word "minister." To minister is to serve; to administer is to serve for given purposes with appropriate means. "Leadership" is not a New Testament word; its nearest equivalent is "servantship." Jesus said: "Whosoever will be great among you, let him be your minister; and whosoever will be chief among you, let him be your servant: even as the Son of man came not to be ministered unto, but to minister, and to give his life a ransom for many" (Matt. 20:26–28). This revolutionary concept of greatness is basic in the practice of church administration.

The objectives of church administration are both similar to and different from objectives in the administration of other institutions. In business and industry, administration has been described as "the necessary activities of those individuals (executives) in an organization who are charged with ordering, forwarding, and facilitating the associated efforts of a group of individuals brought together to realize certain defined purposes." Yet there are observed differences between business administration and church administration. Church administration is concerned primarily with persons, with property only as it ministers to persons. Church administration focuses attention on eternal values, on temporal values only as they relate to eternal. Church administration acknowledges the sole sovereignty of God in Christ through the Holy Spirit as revealed in the Scriptures, the rulership of men only as they submit to divine authority. The ultimate objectives of church administration are those of Christ, that the kingdom of God may come and his will be done on earth as in heaven.

Congregational basis of administration.—The immediate purpose of church administration is twofold: (1) to manage efficiently the affairs of a congregation; (2) in and through the process, to develop to the fullest extent possible the Christian personality of every member of the congregation. Baptists hold that the New Testament ideal has been missed if there is failure at either of these points. A papal or episcopal form of church government, which locates final authority in the clergy, might conceivably be more efficient in the management of the church's affairs than a democratic form. Admittedly, there is calculated risk in placing the management of the affairs of the church in the hands of all the members. There is no claim that democracy is a perfect form of management. The underlying assumption, however, that the development of Christlike personality through freedom and responsibility is of more worth than managerial efficiency, is a New Testament fundamental. If the rulers are the ruled, and if, in this process of self-government, each individual is developed both in freedom and in responsibility, the ultimate outcome will be greater efficiency in the conduct of the affairs of the church than if its management were in the hands of a select few.

As numbers increase, both in the local congregation and in the denomination, the necessity for delegation of responsibility and authority likewise increases; however, the principle of democracy is maintained through the election by the people of their representatives. Yet it is an essential of Baptist polity and practice that proposals made by their elected representatives be referred to the congregation for consideration and approval or disapproval.

Baptists insist on the implementation of this principle at every important point of the life of the church. (1) The congregation votes to receive all new members. (2) The congregation elects its ministers, deacons, superintendents, teachers, and all other responsible lay officers. (3) Each member of the congregation, irrespective of age or financial or social status, has the right of discussion and of vote on an equality with every other member. (4) Relationships with other bodies are voluntary and involve or imply no authority of one body over another, except that of influence.

Congregational autonomy obviously places heavy responsibility on a church for the education of its constituency. While there can be no external coercion, a Baptist church has the right to expect of its members such attendance on and participation in its services of study and worship as will equip each member for competency in the discharge of his duties as a voting member. The exercise of discipline is therefore a prerogative of a Baptist church. By "discipline" is not meant punitive measures connoted by the papal concept of "excommunication," but teaching and training to prevent lapses, admonition and counseling with a view to reclaiming those who have lapsed, and ultimate withdrawal from those who resist all efforts at their reclamation. Since membership is always voluntary, withdrawal from membership is likewise a voluntary privilege. Transfer of membership to another church is the privilege of any member. As a rule, such letters are exchanged only with churches of like faith and order.

In all of these matters, the congregation governs. It is local, autonomous, independent yet interdependent, free to make its decisions uncoerced by any superior body or by the state. Baptists believe that in this practice of congregationalism, there is stronger cohesion than in a polity that is more authoritarian and less democratic.

Responsibility of pastor and deacons.—The principle of delegation of responsibility and authority is essential to democracy. Jesus Christ,

Church Administration

himself the sole head of the church, gathered about him a group of men whom he "ordained" or "appointed," thus distinguishing them from other of the disciples. (See Matt. 10:1–8; Mark 3:13–15; Luke 6:12–16; John 10:15–17.) The New Testament abounds in references to this concept of the man of God divinely called to the service of Christ through a church as its pastor.

The pastor has many administrative duties, concerned with all areas of the church's activity, including: (1) the planning and supervision of worship services; (2) the program of teaching and training; (3) the work of evangelism and missions; (4) the supervision and enforcement of discipline; (5) the administration of the church organizations; (6) stewardship and church finance; (7) work with the sick or bereaved and aid to the indigent; (8) the social program of the church and its fellowship activities; (9) community service; and (10) the church's contribution to the work of the whole denomination.

The listing of these areas of pastoral administration at once points to the fundamental function of the administrator: to delegate and supervise, rather than to perform all duties himself. Baptists hold that there is nothing which the pastor does (unless it be of a civil or contractual nature) which could not be delegated by him or the church to an unordained member. Thus a layman, authorized by his church, can preach, teach, pray, administer the ordinances, supervise the organizations, visit the sick, bury the dead, serve on councils and committees, or render any other service whatever. In line with traditional Baptist practice, certain of these functions will ordinarily and properly be fulfilled by the ordained pastor; others will be delegated to lay members.

Early in the life of the churches, "servants of the church" were known as *deacons*. The Greek word *diakonos* is the exact equivalent of the Latin word *minister*. The administrative functions of deacons were not significantly different from those of pastors. There is little New Testament justification for a sharp distinction between the responsibility of the pastor as being "spiritual" and that of the deacon as being "material." Yet in order that pastors may give themselves more fully "to prayer, and to the ministry of the word," deacons may well be expected to perform many of the administrative functions of the church. Deacons are more likely to be specialists in the field of finance, and therefore particularly qualified to care for the church business.

It is customary in Southern Baptist churches for deacons to serve as trustees or legal representatives of the church, especially in matters pertaining to church property. Deacons may well serve on the committee on church property which is responsible for maintenance and repair. Deacons will almost always be represented on the finance committee. Deacons often serve as general church officers, such as treasurer, financial secretary, clerk. Deacons and their wives often constitute the committee on the ordinances, preparing for and assisting in the administration of baptism and the Lord's Supper. As a rule, deacons are given responsibility as ushers, although not exclusively; in this capacity they serve as collectors of the offerings. Deacons ordinarily constitute important members of the building committee, giving guidance to building projects at the request of the church. Deacons are expected to take active interest in the several organizations of the church and can render effective service in oversight of these organizations in accordance with assignments made and accepted for such unofficial supervision. Deacons can do much to promote evangelism and missions, giving intelligent and prayerful leadership to these basic enterprises. The entire body of deacons, under guidance of pastor and chairman, may be so subdivided that each deacon will have specific as well as general responsibilities.

Executive organization of the church.—Correlation and integration of the several church organizations is usually effected through the *church council*. This "council for counsel" consists of pastor, staff members, and representatives from the several organizations, who meet to make reports to one another, to share problems and needs, to approve a calendar of activities, to set up objectives and secure cooperation in their attainment, to discuss proposals and clarify them for presentation to the church for action, to develop and deepen the spirit of teamwork, and in many other ways to unify the work of the church. Churches seeking correlation according to this plan are usually careful to indicate that the church council has no legislative authority, does not supersede the deacons, has no control over the organizations, but is representative and advisory.

For actually doing its work, the typical Baptist church is organized functionally. The function of worship is under the guidance of the pastor and shared by the leader of music, the choirs, and the ushers. There is no prescribed order of worship services, each church being free to devise its own order. The functions of music leadership, ushering, teaching, training, study and promotion of missions, enlistment and utilization of men, Christian action and social service are responsibilities of officers, teachers, leaders, committees, nominated to and elected by the church.

Church staff.—A significant trend in modern Baptist churches is an increasing use of professional leadership. The unpaid, part-time pastor who was able to satisfy the needs of pioneer churches has given way to the settled minister, assisted in most churches by one or many other paid employees, all necessary to lead the complex organizational programs which increasingly prevail. According to size and needs, a church may employ, in addition to the pastor, (1) a church secretary or secretaries; (2) minister of education; (3) minister of music; (4)

age-group specialists—workers with children, young people, adults; (5) assistant to the pastor; (6) business administrator; (7) hostess; (8) supervisor of visitation; (9) student director; (10) counselor. Rarely will a church have all of these staff members, and their titles vary widely, but a staff whose responsibilities are specialized somewhat as indicated above has become fairly common among many of the larger Baptist churches. Procedures in calling the staff member to a position in a church vary, but in the main, employment follows recommendation to the church by the pastor and a church-appointed personnel committee.

Staff relationships cannot be authoritatively prescribed, since each church is free to make its own arrangements. However, in general practice the pastor is recognized as the chief of staff. While of necessity there is a specialization of function, the ideal is teamwork in the achievement of common goals. Staff members are not employed primarily to relieve members of responsibilities, but rather to enlist the total membership in the total work of the church, providing guidance for an ever-increasing number of fellow workers rather than substituting professional for lay service.

Educational administration.—Departmentalization on an age basis has been found by experience to be a simple, practical, functional method of organizing and administering the church educational program. Regular promotion from department to department provides for progression and makes possible specialization on the part of those who deal with the same age group from year to year. Departmentalization carries over into other aspects of the church's life, providing congenial groups for purposes of service, fellowship, worship, evangelism.

Records.—For many reasons Baptist churches need accurate and adequate records. The high value placed on the individual calls for full information regarding each person from his entrance into church membership until his dismissal or death. Not always have Baptist church clerks been diligent to secure and revise such information. It is expected, however, that when a member is received, there shall be entered on an appropriate record book or file vital statistics which provide information from reception to dismissal or death. In addition, various church organizations keep separate records on their particular membership. These records not only serve the purpose of obtaining the facts, but constitute a program of work and an effective plan for character building. The ideal of person-mindedness held by Baptists emphasizes the necessity and the value of records in all the organizations and in all the activities of the church.

Enlistment.—The voluntary principle, basic in Baptist church polity, involves an especially difficult problem as to the enlistment of members. Baptists hold to "believers' baptism," that is, to the belief that only those are baptized into the fellowship of a church who are competent to decide for themselves and who of their own volition apply for baptism and consequent church membership. From that point onward, the relationship, together with all activities and duties, is on a voluntary basis. No compulsion other than that of moral suasion is allowed. Consequently, a member may attend the services of his church or not, he may enter into the activities of its organizations or not, he may support the church financially or not, according to his uncoerced choice. The member voluntarily subscribes to a covenant which is binding on his conscience but which cannot be enforced in the event of neglect of duty, immorality, heresy, violation of the covenant, and similar dereliction, except by withdrawal of fellowship.

Since members themselves take the initiative in applying for transfer of membership when they move from one community to another, the problem of nonresidency assumes large proportions. Realization of the seriousness of this problem has led to concerted efforts on the part of churches to encourage their members to transfer membership to the churches where they live.

The problem of inactivity and "backsliding" is not peculiar to Baptists, but again the principle of voluntariness accentuates the difficulty of the problem. Historically Baptists have rejected the "confirmation class." In the main, Baptists have depended on family instruction and teaching in the Sunday school and in the Training Union to prepare members for fruitful church membership. Many churches utilize the "new members' class," by means of which the newly received member is enrolled for a period of intensive study of the essentials of churchmanship. The operation of this plan has tended to reduce inactivity and unenlistment.

BIBLIOGRAPHY: C. J. Allen, *For You and Your Church* (1950). A. W. Blackwood, *Pastoral Leadership* (1949). P. E. Burroughs, *The Functioning Church* (1928). G. S. Dobbins, *Building Better Churches* (1921); *The Churchbook* (1951). A. Flake, *Building a Standard Sunday School* (revised 1950). E. T. Hiscox, *The New Directory for Baptist Churches* (1894). J. E. Lambdin, *The Baptist Training Union Manual* (revised 1952). K. Mallory and M. Christian, *Manual of Woman's Missionary Union* (1949). B. B. McKinney and A. W. Graves, *Let Us Sing* (1942). R. E. Naylor, *The Baptist Deacon* (1955). E. Noland, *The Six Point Record System* (1941). J. M. Pendleton, *Church Manual* (1912). G. W. Schroeder, *Brotherhood Guidebook* (1950). J. L. Sullivan, *Your Life and Your Church* (revised 1955). R. C. Walton, *The Gathered Community* (1946).

GAINES S. DOBBINS

CHURCH AND COMMUNITY. A church is a community of believers who are redeemed by the grace of God, seeking to understand the mind of Christ, bound together in the love of Christ, under compulsion of the Holy Spirit to minister to human needs, and commissioned by Christ to engage in a world task. As a contemporary fellowship of the redeemed, the church is commissioned to be the heart of life for the human community. Through its minister and its ministry a church brings the gospel to bear upon every basic human impulse and need. It works within the world, yet it is not of the world.

Life in world society begins with the individual human being. Each person is a sinner and is in need of redemption. The church bears witness to the redemptive grace of God, which any person may accept for himself through faith in Jesus Christ.

An individual lives in a world along with other individuals. In home, school, work, and play it is necessary for one person to share with and communicate to others. Human beings are interdependent. The church, through its preaching, pastoral, personal, and service ministries, brings the mind of Christ to bear upon every relationship of man with man. In so doing, the church affords to people who inhabit the earth a source of divine wisdom, a guiding light, a way of life, and eternal truth for contemporary living.

Each person is a free moral agent, forced to choose between the distortion of the flesh and the leading of the Spirit. There are differences of opinion about the mind of Christ and degrees of obedience to the will of Christ. Tensions result where persons come together, and the peace and well-being of the human community are threatened by such evils as listed in Galatians 5:19–21. The love of Christ, revealed in his earthly life and triumphant at the cross and in the resurrection, is proclaimed by the church as the divine impulse and power for human endeavor.

Man, a free moral agent living with other men, finds himself in need of help and hope from outside himself, powers which other men cannot give him. The church bears witness to the power of the Holy Spirit, which is operative in the life of a consecrated Christian, compelling him to consider the needs of others and to assume responsibility for helping to fulfil those needs.

The whole world, embracing people of every race and color and creed, is the field of endeavor for the church. A local church is a fellowship or a community with a mission to fulfil in the larger world community. A local church is independent, yet all churches are interdependent. And the whole world is dependent upon the witness and work of the churches for a true sense of spiritual values and for a proper sense of moral direction.

The spiritual and moral destiny of man on earth is affected by the devotion and enthusiasm with which the churches seek to guide the life of their respective human communities. Though the origin of the church is not of this world, the people who constitute the church live in this world. While a church is giving its message to its community, it is at the same time receiving something from its community—ideas, customs, habits, economic capacity. A church holds property and has income and, therefore, cannot escape economic responsibility. It engages in a program of education, indoctrination, and service; therefore, it cannot escape social responsibility. The church seeks to change the world to its ways, knowing that if it fails to do so, it will be conformed to the ways of the world. The church undertakes to achieve a regenerate society by means of the work and influence of regenerate individuals working together as a community within a community.

There must be someone to lead the way in a church, keeping the community of the redeemed always conscious of God's purpose and work for men. The pastor, called of God and ordained by a local church, assumes this role.

A pastor speaks to individuals, interpreting the Bible in terms of its application within contemporary life. He calls attention to the evils of the world and helps Christians understand their responsibilities within the world. He upholds the divine ideal and challenges men to strive to reach it. He is God's spokesman to the community of the redeemed, and he speaks for the redeemed to the rest of the world.

BIBLIOGRAPHY: J. Baillie, *What Is Christian Civilization?* (1945). A. A. Beaven, *The Local Church* (1937). G. A. Beaver, *Christ and Community* (1950); *Church and Community* (1938). O. T. Binkley, *The Churches and the Social Conscience* (1948). P. R. Clifford, *The Mission of the Local Church* (1953). J. M. Dawson, *Christ and Social Change* (1937). C. A. Ellwood, *The Reconstruction of Religion* (1922). C. S. Gardner, *The Ethics of Jesus and Social Progress* (1914). H. Harvey, *The Church: Its Polity and Ordinances* (1879). K. S. Latourette, *Missions Tomorrow* (1936). S. Mathews, *The Church and the Changing Order* (1913). A. J. W. Myers, *Christian Life in the Community* (1919). H. Seifert, *The Church in Community Action* (1952). G. Stewart, *The Church* (1938). W. H. Wilson, *The Evolution of a Country Community* (1913).

GARLAND HENDRICKS

CHURCH AND SCHOOL. A newspaper published at Rome, Ga., which in 1880 was commended by the Georgia Baptist convention. This body also appealed to the paper's editor, G. A. Nunnally, to expand the paper into a missionary journal for the South. The publication is now extinct.

JOHN J. HURT, JR.

CHURCH AND STATE. *Baptists and the church.*—The earliest English Baptists—Smyth, Helwys, Spilsbury, Keach—held that a true New Testament church is a body of regenerated and baptized believers. Such believers become members of the visible church through confession of their personal faith in Jesus Christ as Lord and Saviour. In the dramatic ordinance of baptism, the symbol of Christ's death and resurrection, the believer declares his faith before many witnesses in a conscious act of obedience and life commitment. By this act of believer's baptism, a pledge is given to forsake all known sin and to acknowledge Christ's rule over man's total life.

In his presidential address at the sixth Baptist World Alliance Congress at Atlanta, Ga., in the summer of 1939, George W. Truett expressed the Baptist doctrine of the church thus:

> Concerning the church, Baptists hold that it is a Divine institution, not evolved from the changing conditions of society, but expressing the mind of Christ; that it is an enduring institution, adapted to all times and climes; that it is the custodian of the truth, to hold and teach it to the end of time, and to all peoples. They hold that a church of Jesus Christ is a spiritual institution, and that it is a pure democracy, without disbarment of franchise to any member, on the ground of nationality, race, class or sex. There are two ordinances of the church—Baptism and the Lord's Supper, neither as a means of salvation, but both figurative and commemorative. It is a vital Baptist principle that spiritual birth must precede church membership and these two ordinances.

While Baptists insist on this view of the church, derived from the New Testament, they also have a sense of fellowship and spiritual union with all other genuine Christians of every church.

Early Baptists and their successors have also consistently defended the doctrine of the autonomy of the local church. Each local congregation within the Baptist fellowship is competent to order its own affairs under the leadership of the Holy Spirit. The exclusive lordship of Jesus Christ, the head of the church, is the norm and basis for the faith and practice of each local church.

Baptists also acknowledge the "universal priesthood of all believers." While they recognize the different gifts which Christ has bestowed upon the members of the church, they do not acknowledge an essential difference between clergy and laity. Every Christian is to be a witness to Christ, and any group of regenerated and baptized believers may constitute a church, ordain ministers, administer the ordinances, exercise church discipline, and engage in preaching and evangelism. Needless to say, this emphasis upon the dignity and rights of the local congregation has not prevented Baptists from organizing associations, state conventions, national conventions, and, since 1905, the Baptist World Alliance.

Baptists and the state.—Throughout their history Baptists have held that the state is ordained of God. It is established to restrain and punish evildoers and to protect human rights. The state is obligated to safeguard the personal, economic, civic, and religious rights of all of its citizens. But Baptists likewise insist that the state has no right or competency to interfere with the religious persuasions of men. Baptists believe in a free church within a free state, each competent within its own sphere and each bound to respect the other. However, man's supreme loyalty belongs to God alone. Baptists, therefore, deny to the state the right or duty to protect the doctrines of the Christian church or to prefer one church to another.

In most of the churches stemming from the Reformation, the principle of coercion in religious and ecclesiastical matters was accepted. Baptists gratefully recognize that most of these churches have by now given up this principle. Baptists, however, have from the very beginning of their history insisted on separation of church and state and its implication, complete religious liberty or soul freedom as man's inalienable right given to him by God. Thomas Helwys wrote in a book which he addressed to the king of England, James I: "The king is a mortall man, & not God, therefore hath no power over ye immortall soules of his subiects, to make lawes & ordinances for them, and to set spirituall Lords over them."

Coercion, whether by secular or ecclesiastical powers, Baptists hold to be hostile to the deepest interests of the Christian faith. They consider coercion of religious convictions to be utterly contrary to the example and teachings of Jesus Christ, the sovereign Lord of conscience and the only head of the church. Baptists have defended the principle of religious liberty, that is, the individual's right to worship God or not to worship him at all, throughout their history. John Bunyan, the tinker of Bedford, endured twelve years of imprisonment because he advocated soul freedom and the principle of a free church in a free state. This freedom, of course, does not imply moral or doctrinal license. The local church is free to purge itself by means of spiritual discipline of unworthy or heretical members. But that discipline, according to the New Testament, is strictly spiritual, never physically or legally coercive, and secular governments have no share in it whatever.

The 1646 edition of the London (Particular Baptist) Confession of Faith of 1644 declares:

> And concerning the worship of God, there is but one Law giver, which is . . . Jesus Christ. . . . So it is the magistrate's duty to tender [allow] the liberty of men's consciences . . . (which is the tenderest thing unto all conscientious men, and most dear to them, and without which all other liberties will not be worth the naming, much less enjoying) and to protect all under them from all wrong, injury, oppression, and molestation. . . . And as we cannot do anything contrary to our understandings and consciences, so neither can we forbear the doing of that which our understandings and consciences bind us to do; and if the magistrate should require us to do otherwise, we are to yield our persons in a passive way to their power, as the saints of old have done.

Maurice A. Levy rightly said at the Berlin Congress of 1934: "The idea of voluntariness and independency renders intolerable both a church-controlled state and a state-controlled church. However, separation of church and state need not be of such a type as to imperil the permeation of the common life by the spirit of Jesus."

In view of these principles, Baptists defend the right of Christian or pagan to follow the dictates of conscience in the matter of religious worship. Any state or ecclesiastical system that tries to coerce the conscience is therefore resisted in the name of man's supreme loyalty to God.

Open problems.—The advocacy of sound principles is one thing; the realization of those principles is quite another matter. Although Baptists agree in principle regarding the separation of church and state, they differ in their interpretations and practices. Baptists are not fully agreed with regard to the scope and range of a Christian's political responsibility. They make no consistent stand on the problem of pacifism or nonparticipation in war, nor with regard to several specific issues which have not been legally defined. These issues include: the use of public funds for parochial schools and private Christian hospitals, social security benefits for ministers, Bible reading and the teaching of religion in public schools, and the institution of the chaplaincy.   WILLIAM A. MUELLER

CHURCH BUILDING LOAN FUND. Begun in 1883 to assist Southern Baptist churches in their building programs. Almost from the beginning the leadership of the Southern Baptist Convention, and more especially those associated with the work of its Home Mission Board, recognized the need for a church loan fund; however, it was not until Isaac Taylor Tichenor (*q.v.*) came to the executive secretaryship of the board in 1883 that any effort was made to raise such a fund. During that year a contribution of $500 was received to begin the fund.

Pursuant to the Convention's adoption of a recommendation made by a special committee appointed to consider the matter, G. A. Nunnally was put in the field to raise money for the loan fund. Everywhere he went, he met with gratifying success. His success, however, gave rise to the fear on the part of some of the leaders of the Convention that the raising of money for the loan fund would overshadow other mission undertakings. The board in its report in 1885 said:

Leading brethren, several of whom are in charge of our state boards, have expressed the desire that money for church building should not be raised by appeals to the churches, as is usually done for missions, but that it should be done by the methods adopted in raising endowments for our colleges.

The board recommended that this procedure be followed; Nunnally resigned, and the department was discontinued. Some money was raised for the fund and a few churches were helped, but it was not until 1903, when the board "requested the W.M.U. to inaugurate a Tichenor Memorial . . . Loan Fund," that a real effort was made to raise a building and loan fund. By 1910 this effort on the part of the Woman's Missionary Union had resulted in the raising of only $20,000. The Convention in annual session that year had its attention called to the fact that there were not less than 4,500 homeless churches in the Convention territory and was challenged "to do something worthy of a great denomination of Christian people in assembling the proposed Church Building Loan Fund of $500,000."

Year after year the Convention's attention was called to the growing need for an adequate church loan fund; and although the fund had only grown to $76,000 by 1912, a committee appointed to study the matter made the following recommendation: "Your committee would therefore recommend that the Board be instructed again to enter with expedition upon an aggressive campaign to raise a Church Building Loan Fund of $1,000,000."

In 1913 L. B. Warren was employed as superintendent of the Church Building Loan Fund in the hope of reaching the $1,000,000 goal in a relatively short time; however, due to the fact that the Judson Centennial fund-raising campaign was claiming large attention, no intensive campaign was begun until 1915. Two principal methods were adopted—the soliciting of memorials to be recorded in what was known as the Hall of Fame, and the selling of gift annuity bonds—both of which proved quite fruitful. Warren kept the matter continuously before the people, and in 1922 the board reported that the Church Building Loan Fund had passed the million-dollar mark, the goal set as the first unit in the great undertaking. The report attributed the signal success of this feature of work largely to the persistent and efficient efforts of the superintendent, L. B. Warren, who had been with the board nine years.

Notwithstanding the fact that no intensive campaign for funds has been put on since 1922, the fund has continued to grow, its growth coming largely from payment on unpaid pledges totaling $575,216.17 as of May 1, 1922, sale of annuity bonds, and earned income. As of Dec. 31, 1955, the Church Building Loan Fund had a corpus of $2,110,692.32, with 212 outstanding loans totaling $2,098,230.37, and with about $800,000 worth of loans approved to be made when funds were available.   G. FRANK GARRISON

CHURCH COUNCIL, THE. A group, sometimes called the pastor's cabinet or executive committee, which meets to consider all the plans, emphases, and meetings of each organization of the church to correlate these with associational, state, and Convention-wide Baptist work, and to set up a co-ordinated church calendar of emphases, events, and activities. The council, an advisory body authorized by the church, meets regularly or at the pastor's call. It is composed of the pastor, church officers, staff members, and the heads of all existing church organizations. The recommendations made are referred to the church for approval. A typical meeting consists of prayer, the reading of the minutes, and a discussion of each organization's activities and meetings for the coming month (or quarter). At the pastor's direction, the church educational program is integrated with all other activities, and a calendar of events is adopted. This organization is a means of keeping the main purpose of the church paramount and of bringing the organizations to function as parts of a total program of evangelism, training, stewardship, and missions. It delegates leadership and responsibility while promoting harmony among leaders. The entire church program is presented to each organization, thus preventing conflicts, friction, or duplications of effort. It may secure co-operation from what might be independently operated groups within the church. CLAUD B. BOWEN

CHURCH COVENANT, BAPTIST. The church covenant came to Baptists as part of their English Separatist heritage. It was the custom of the Separatists to establish their churches on the basis of a covenant, agreeing upon certain doctrines and promising to forsake others and walk together. The pre-Baptists such as the congregation of John Smyth covenanted together, but with the acceptance of immersion practiced upon believers (c. 1641), Baptist churches began to be constituted on that basis instead, thus displacing the covenant.

However, the covenant was still considered essential to the well-being of the congregation, since "one of the basic ideas underlying the 'gathered church' was mutual committal to one another linked with mutual care of one another."

Perhaps the single most important contribution to the church covenant among the Baptists of America was made by J. Newton Brown, who, in 1833, presented to the Baptist Convention of New Hampshire a confession of faith with attached covenant, which that body adopted. Brown subsequently published both confession and covenant in 1853; and they were again published in 1867 and 1890, all under the title of the New Hampshire Confession of Faith. This covenant was widely used, and is still the accepted covenant of most Baptist churches. In the form published among Southern Baptists, it is as follows:

Having been led, as we believe, by the Spirit of God, to receive the Lord Jesus Christ as our Saviour, and on the profession of our faith, having been baptized in the name of the Father, and of the Son, and of the Holy Spirit, we do now, in the presence of God and this assembly, most solemnly and joyfully enter into covenant with one another, as one body in Christ.

We engage, therefore, by the aid of the Holy Spirit, to walk together in Christian love; to strive for the advancement of this church, in knowledge, holiness, and comfort; to promote its prosperity and spirituality; to sustain its worship, ordinances, discipline, and doctrines; to contribute cheerfully and regularly to the support of the ministry, the expenses of the church, the relief of the poor, and the spread of the gospel through all nations.

We also engage to maintain family and secret devotions; to religiously educate our children; to seek the salvation of our kindred and acquaintances; to walk circumspectly in the world; to be just in our dealings, faithful in our engagements, and exemplary in our deportment; to avoid all tattling, backbiting, and excessive anger; to abstain from the sale and use of intoxicating drinks as a beverage, and to be zealous in our efforts to advance the kingdom of our Saviour.

We further engage to watch over one another in brotherly love; to remember each other in prayer; to aid each other in sickness and distress; to cultivate Christian sympathy in feeling and courtesy in speech; to be slow to take offense, but always ready for reconciliation, and mindful of the rules of our Saviour to secure it without delay.

We moreover engage that when we remove from this place we will, as soon as possible, unite with some other church, where we can carry out the spirit of this covenant and the principles of God's Word.

BIBLIOGRAPHY: C. Burrage, *The Early English Dissenters in the Light of Recent Research* (1912). W. Cathcart, ed., *The Baptist Encyclopedia* (1881). E. T. Hiscox, *The New Directory for Baptist Churches* (1894). W. J. McGlothlin, *Baptist Confessions of Faith* (1911). E. A. Payne, *The Fellowship of Believers* (1952). A. Peel and L. Carlson, eds., *The Writings of Robert Harrison and Robert Browne* (1953). D. Sheppard, *Baptist Confessions of Faith and a Summary of Church Discipline* (1831). R. Walton, *The Gathered Community* (1946).

RAYMOND A. PARKER

CHURCH EXTENSION LOAN FUND. Set up by the Home Mission Board from general funds of the board and from March Week of Prayer funds, which it has been permitted to use for such purposes, to assist churches affiliated with the Southern Baptist Convention in acquiring or erecting houses of worship, educational plants, and pastoriums. Under present rules assistance may not be given to churches which have been constituted for more than seven years.

The establishment of this fund, which was originally designated as the Church Extension Fund, was authorized by the board in annual session Nov. 28-29, 1944, in the initial amount of $100,000. An appropriation in that amount was made Dec. 28, 1944. Other appropriations were made from time to time, both from general funds of the board and from March Week of Prayer funds, until as of Dec. 31, 1955, the corpus of the fund amounted to $1,484,222.88.

While this fund has enabled many young churches to erect a first or second unit, which they could not otherwise have had, the corpus of the fund is inadequate to meet the demands on the part of young churches, and the board has secured Convention permission to borrow a total of $3,500,000 for the account of this fund. On Dec. 31, 1955, the fund had loans outstanding to 360 churches in the total amount of $3,416,380.49 with sufficient loans approved to completely use up the remaining credit available to it. G. FRANK GARRISON

CHURCH EXTENSION SOCIETY, BALTIMORE BAPTIST. Organized in 1854 to confer with groups to raise funds for the establishment of Baptist churches in Baltimore, Md. In 1905 activities of the society were extended to include the entire state. Originally, individuals were solicited by members of the society for funds to meet the need as churches were established, but since 1929 the state association has made yearly appropriations to the society. Today, work of the society is supported through the Cooperative Program. Gifts from the society have made possible the building programs of most of the churches in the state.

HARWOOD BAGBY

CHURCH FINANCE. Baptists in common with other denominations have used many plans and methods for the support of the financial programs of the churches. These methods through the years have undergone significant change. Stewardship and the tithe as taught in the Bible have had small part in such programs in most eras in church history. In certain of these periods, the dominant churches were supported by the state funds provided by a compulsory state tax. In other periods the effort was made to meet the comparatively small needs of a church by gifts from a few people and other methods. Recent years have seen a significant change from these concepts.

Baptists generally have refused such methods of church finance as: (1) State support, used by most churches in Europe through the centuries. Baptists have consistently believed in and practiced separation of church and state. (2) Gambling and games of chance. (3) Petty merchandising including bazaars, rummage sales, cake sales, oyster suppers, carnivals, etc. To Baptists each of these methods degrades the church and her Lord. (4) Apportionments made to church members by officials in the church, and to churches by a "higher" authority such as conference or bishop. (5) Pew rental. This method was nevertheless used for some time by a few churches in the South, e.g., First, Richmond, Va., and First, Savannah, Ga.

Several methods followed by Baptists at varying times, include pastoral self-support, loose offerings, subscription lists, subscription in public services, budget programs, individual offering envelopes, every-member canvass, the Sunday school, the unified budget, "fund raising," and the new church finance program of Southern Baptists.

Self-support by the pastor was one of the first methods used in America. This method resulted from the people's strong and positive reaction against the state church tax. David Benedict in *Fifty Years Among the Baptists* (published 1860) spoke of the self-supporting character of the ministers, frequently as farmers, teachers, and skilled artisans, and their success in sometimes becoming wealthy, for the times, while planting churches in the wilderness. This was in consequence of a natural and easily understandable but violent reaction away from the oppression, greed, dishonesty, and simony which was practiced by certain state churches in Europe, notably Catholic, and in some states in America in Colonial days. It has required generations to get away from this reaction and back to the scriptural principles and methods.

Loose offerings, received in the worship services, have long been the major basis of many church finance programs. Alone, they have proved totally inadequate.

Subscription lists raised by one or two key men in a congregation when there arose some special need marked an advance. These were sporadic and the persons solicited were usually a small circle of the faithful leaders, with no effort made to reach the larger portion of the congregation.

Subscriptions in public services were frequently taken where there was some special need in the program. The sporadic nature of such efforts, ostentation, the embarrassment to givers of small ability, and lack of any plan for reaching the entire membership proved weaknesses of this plan.

Budget programs began to be more popular after World War I. In 1924 the Conservation Commission of the Convention employed Oscar Eugene Bryan (q.v.) as budget director to encourage the churches to adopt annual financial budgets. A budget is a record of anticipated receipts and expenditures usually for one year; it is an authorization to expend certain funds, and it is a method of controlling expenditures and preventing over-expenditure. In making a budget, the church names a budget planning committee representative of the entire congregation which anticipates the financial needs of the church program for the forthcoming year. It sets these figures down, together with all anticipated income. After necessary adjustments are made and the budget is adopted by the church, it becomes the financial program for the year, subject to modification only by subsequent action of the church. The budget plan put system into church finances and laid the necessary groundwork for reaching the entire membership in the financial program of the church, thus spreading the load, and raising the increasingly large amounts needed in the local and missionary programs. The budget has proved indispensable for a successful church finance program.

The individual offering envelope plan magnifies the importance of the individual in the program of the church, reminds him of his responsibility to the church program, stimulates giving as an act of worship, makes possible a record of the individual's gifts for his and the church's information, stimulates increased giving and Christian development. The envelopes are packaged and dated; the package bears the member's name, and each envelope contains a date and the number assigned to the member on the church records. Duplex envelopes have been used, with one side for gifts to local expenses and the other for missions. Unified budgets are considered the superior plan by Baptists. With the unified budget a single envelope is used.

The every-member canvass developed after 1918. Visitors or canvassers go into the home of each member, explain to him the program of the church, and seek his pledge to the budget for the coming year. This magnifies the individual, seeks to realize the New Testament injunction in I Corinthians 16:2, "let every one of you lay by him in store," undertakes to reach the last member of the congregation, and secures greatly increased amounts of money for local, benevolent, and missionary programs.

Using the Sunday school in the church's financial program began in some churches not long afterward. This plan was pioneered by Southern Baptists. Its early application was described by Arthur Flake (*q.v.*). In this plan, as it is now generally applied, the Sunday school and church members pledge to a unified budget, seeking to reach agreed class and department goals relating to number of pledges, number of tithers, and amount of weekly pledges. The offering to the unified budget which includes expenses of the Sunday school as a part of the total church program is received in the Sunday school and in the worship service. This plan is not one of financing the church through the Sunday school, but one in which the church uses the Sunday school in its finance program. The budget and the entire finance program are the responsibility of the church. The Sunday school performs certain functions as indicated and as requested by the church.

Southern Baptists are almost unique in their use of this plan, which is successful among them because in many Sunday schools 50 to 60 per cent of the enrolment is composed of young people and adults. But pledges to the budget and pledges to tithe are received from small children as well, with approval of their parents. Thus they are trained in stewardship while young.

The unified budget is another advance pioneered by Southern Baptists. It is a comprehensive program of church finance providing one budget for everything the church does. This includes (1) the world mission and local mission programs of the church; (2) the local program with its salaries and utilities, literature, and expenses of the Sunday school including each class and department, Brotherhood, Training Union, choir program, etc.; and (3) the building program of the church.

One budget means one church program, supporting the whole kingdom program as one. It means one appeal—the members are asked to support the total program with one pledge. Each person brings, in one envelope, his entire weekly contribution to all causes, and the amount is divided by the church treasurer as the church voted in adopting its budget. It means one treasury receiving and handling all money and paying all bills. One budget means one loyalty, first to the church, and then to an organization as a part of the church.

The unified budget plan simplifies the church's financial program, eliminates the confusion of many appeals, magnifies the responsibility for the entire program, puts church finances under church control where they properly belong, encourages the use of offering envelopes, facilitates the use of the Sunday school in the church finance program, reaches those who do not remain for the worship service, makes it easy to give to missions through the Cooperative Program on the percentage basis, increases the offerings, and provides a superior educational opportunity to train young people to give to spread the gospel throughout the whole world.

The "fund raising" concept is a more recent development. Promoted by commercial organizations in recent years, this combines and uses principles which have been proved in the experience of many churches, e.g., seeing every member to secure his pledge. A trained director is on the field for the length of the campaign, usually from 4 to 13 weeks. Canvassers are trained, and a detailed program of publicity, promotion, and preparation is followed, using prepared materials.

The forward program of church finance of Southern Baptists, developed in consequence of action of the Southern Baptist Convention meeting in Miami, Fla., in 1955, and presented for the Convention's adoption in Chicago, Ill., in 1957, offers to Southern Baptists a complete and integrated program embodying the successful experience of churches, denominations, and fund-raising organizations. It is based upon the convictions that church finance is a spiritual task, that system is needed as well as dedication, that scriptural stewardship including the tithe is the basis for a Christian program of church finance, that each church has the responsibility for reaching every member in its finance program, that love is the motive for all Christian giving, and that missions is an essential stimulus to larger giving.

This church finance program has a complete and detailed calendar for a four-week campaign, plus a period of preparation and a period of follow-through; it is an organization including pastor, general chairman, steering committee, committees on budget planning, budget promotion, budget pledging, loyalty dinner, etc. It offers a plan for an objective study of the giving record of the church and its members, a workbook for developing a more complete program of work and budget program for the church, and a plan for determining the approximate giving potential of the church. It uses the unified budget plan and the Sunday school organization for teaching a special stewardship lesson, setting and reaching class and department goals for pledgers, tithers, and weekly amounts pledged to the budget, receiving pledges in a pledge service, and receiving offerings to the unified budget in weekly offering envelopes. It also provides a planned program of publicity and promotion including four issues of a church campaign newspaper and a budget folder for local imprinting. It offers forms to be used in letters, the campaign newspaper, and printed and mimeographed materials used in the campaign. It proposes a loyalty dinner for the congregation, a pledge day, visits by canvassers, and a victory day. There is also included a follow-through program, with the provision of individual offering envelopes to every member of the church and Sunday school (in most churches at least through the primary department), an individual stewardship record and report of gifts sent quarterly to each individual, procedures to assist in adhering to the budget as adopted by the church and for better handling of church and mission funds.

The church finance program was produced to meet the purposes and needs and to use the facilities and programs of a Baptist church. It has been refined and simplified so that it may be used in the average Baptist church with local leadership, after study of the basic *Guidebook of Fund Raising and Church Finance* (1956) in, for example, a state or associational church finance clinic.   MERRILL D. MOORE

CHURCH GROWTH, PRINCIPLES OF. More than a hundred years of Southern Baptist history have made clear the principles underlying church growth. Some of these principles for successful church work are as follows: being divinely located, scripturally organized (Acts 11:9–30), and soundly and scripturally financed (Acts 11:24 and I Cor. 16:2); having a good minister (Acts 11:24); using good laymen (Acts 13:1); having a distinct membership (Acts 11:26) who are Spirit-guided (Acts 13:2), evangelistic (Acts 11:24), missionary (Acts 13:3), spiritual (II Peter 3:18 and Heb. 10:25), praying (Acts 13:3), and co-operative (I Cor. 3:9). The following items may well summarize the factors within a church that affect its growth: (1) positive doctrinal conviction, (2) evangelistic zeal, (3) co-operative spirit, (4) effective organization. In all this the pastor's leadership is basic. When these characteristics prevail, churches grow numerically as long as there are people to reach, but a church in a growing and homogeneous community grows more rapidly.

Certain Southern Baptist distinctives have appeared in utilizing religious education for church development. These distinctives have largely grown out of Baptist doctrines and reflect their democratic philosophy. They are as follows:

A major emphasis upon the use of laymen and lay women.—Churches that have operated on this principle of using to the fullest extent the ability of the members, through the Sunday school, the Training Union, the Brotherhood, the W.M.U., and special committees have had great numerical and spiritual growth.

A sound program of stewardship and church finance based on enlisting members first in the educational work of the church.—Surveys have indicated that from 80 to 90 per cent of the financial support of a church comes from its members who are enrolled in the Sunday school and the other church agencies.

A denominationally projected program of co-operative educational activities that does not interfere with church autonomy.—Southern Baptists have, through the years, developed a program suited to their own genius and have, therefore, looked less and less to sources outside the denomination for guidance. This attitude has given the churches a program strengthened by continuity rather than one handicapped by the frequent and sudden changes that would have inevitably occurred under interdenominational influence, or because of the fluctuation of leadership in the individual church. This program has also given the churches simplicity of organization, continuity of emphases, definiteness in goals, adaptable methods, and steady progress. Since an informed membership has been the basis for co-operation in all this, an intensive training program has been essential.

In the Sunday schools the principal factors in church growth have been best illustrated. The five essential steps in enlargement were first enumerated by Arthur Flake (*q.v.*) in 1922. These were: (1) The constituency must be known. A complete census is necessary for finding those who are available for membership and where they live. (2) The organization must be enlarged. Since Sunday school enrolment approximates 10 pupils for each worker, reaching more people directly depends upon more workers. (3) Suitable space must be provided. The amount and arrangement of the space limits or facilitates the organization. When space is saturated, growth is curtailed. (4) Workers must be trained and set to work. The best workers, thoroughly prepared, are necessary for numerical and spiritual growth of members. (5) Visitation must be maintained. Personal visitation is basic, not only to good salesmanship, but in reaching people for the full ministry of the churches. Enrolment and attendance increase in proportion to the number of personal visits. This principle has a strong New Testament basis (Acts 4:42).   A. V. WASHBURN

CHURCH MUSIC. See MUSIC, CHURCH.

CHURCH MUSICIAN, THE. A monthly magazine published by the Sunday School Board of the Southern Baptist Convention. The first issue appeared Oct., 1950. It is prepared for all church music leaders, instrumentalists, and choir singers. The contents include articles on graded church music education, administration, methods, materials, techniques, and hymnology; also various helps such as programs, units of work, and miscellaneous information. A graded music section, removable from the magazine and containing music for all choirs, is included in each issue. The circulation in 1956 was 56,002.   W. HINES SIMS

CHURCH NIGHT. See FAMILY NIGHT.

CHURCH OFFICERS AND ORGANIZATION. Baptist churches have traditionally elected officers in addition to the two—pastor and deacon—specifically mentioned in the Scriptures. These additional officers increase the efficiency of the church. In the beginning these officers were responsible primarily for church records and finances, but in recent years, as church organizations have grown more complex, many varied positions have been created to meet needs as they have arisen.

The officers most commonly found in contemporary Baptist churches include the church clerk, the treasurer and financial secretary (sometimes assisted by paid personnel), trustees, music director, ushers, the principal officers of the educational organizations, and their subordinates. These latter include the Sunday school superintendent, the Training Union director, the president of the Woman's Missionary Union, the Brotherhood president, and others.

Though sometimes nominated from the floor before election by the church, these officers are usually presented to the church by a nominating committee. Such a committee studies the needs of the church to be met by these officers and then after prayer seeks out the best-qualified members of the church to fill the positions. At the time of their report to the church other nominations may be received, but usually the work of the committee will be accepted. This committee will normally take the person chosen by the W.M.U. or Brotherhood as their nominee for the principal officer in each of those organizations.

In most instances, these church officers begin their period of service at the beginning of the church year, either October 1 or January 1, without formal recognition service. There is a growing practice, however, to hold a service of dedication in which all church officers, including those serving in the various auxiliary organizations, are committed to their tasks. This service helps to give dignity and importance to the various officers and clearer understanding of their duties to those elected. There is increasing concern in the churches that their officers know their tasks and how to perform them.

The primary consideration in the selection of any church officer is the Christian character and experience of the person being considered for the office. These officers are expected to be convinced Baptists in their doctrinal belief and faithful in worship, in private devotion, and in service. There are also distinctive qualifications and duties for each officer.

Church clerk.—The church clerk must have not only the ability to write, but also the ability to keep accurate records and to present them attractively. Interested in all that the church does, the clerk develops church records which are the basic materials of church history. He should be faithful in attendance and active in the full life of the church and thus able to know what is essential to the record. The clerk should keep accurate records of all church meetings and make them available for approval and filing. The clerk is responsible for the church roll, recording additions and losses. He reports requests for letters to the church and upon its approval issues letters. Likewise, he writes to other churches for the letters of those who present themselves for membership.

Treasurer and financial secretary.—In smaller churches there is usually one man chosen to perform the task of caring for the church's money. In larger churches both a treasurer and a financial secretary are used. The treasurer is responsible to the church to count, deposit, and report to the church all monies received. (Many churches, large and small, have a committee that counts the offerings following each service and certifies the total.) He makes all payments by check upon the authority of the church, either by an adopted budget or by specific action. Checks are usually countersigned by the financial secretary or some other individual designated by the church. The treasurer is usually a member of the budget committee. For his protection and for the protection of the church, he is often bonded.

The financial secretary sometimes assists the treasurer in counting the money and recording each individual gift. He records all receipts and expenditures and seeks to keep the items of the adopted budget in balance. He makes a periodic report to each contributor regarding his record of giving.

Trustees.—Most states require specific persons in each church to be the legal holders of the property. They are usually chosen for their business judgment and integrity. Having no authority except as delegated by the church in business session, trustees act for the church in the purchase and sale of property and its improvement.

Ushers.—Usually Baptist churches have ushers to assist in the worship services. They are a group of men who are chosen to seat the people, attend to their comfort, and keep the general atmosphere of the service worshipful.

Music director.—The music director should have not only musical talent but also consecration to the task of leading worship through the use of music. Frequently such a person assists the pastor in the selection of the hymns, leads the music in the service, and directs the choir in its special musical numbers. In larger churches, there may be a number of choirs graded by age. The number of such choirs is being increased yearly.

Sunday school superintendent and Training Union director.—These officers are chosen by the church because of their interest in, and demonstrated ability to direct, the activities in their respective fields. Their duties are rather definitely described in the literature provided by the Southern Baptist Sunday School Board. These officers head an organization of many people chosen to assist them.

Presidents of Woman's Missionary Union and Brotherhood.—These officers are chosen by their respective groups according to the procedures of their particular organization. Their duties are well defined in the literature provided by each organization. Each of these organizations enlists a large group of officers to work with its president to accomplish the purposes of the group.

BIBLIOGRAPHY: G. S. Dobbins, *Building Better Churches* (1947); *The Churchbook* (1951).

HAROLD K. GRAVES

CHURCH PENSIONS CONFERENCE. Originally organized in 1915 as the Interdenominational Secretaries Conference. The name was changed to Church Pensions Conference in 1931, and the conference was expanded to include actuaries, treasurers, and other financial officials. The purpose of the conference is to study development and problems related to administration and finance of ministerial pension systems. Its organization and promotion was largely the work of Actuary George A. Huggins of Philadelphia. Membership consists of 25 pension boards of various religious groups and holds annual meetings in New York City. Membership embraces 148,000 congregational units, 134,000 ministers, and more than 35,000,000 church members with actuarial reserves in 1953 exceeding $312,500,000 and total funds approximating $440,000,000.

FRED W. NOE

CHURCH PROPERTY AND THE LAW OF TRUSTS. It is a fundamental principle of law declared in the First Amendment to the Consitution of the United States, and by constitution or statute in the individual states, that civil government may not enact laws or regulations concerning the establishment or exercise of religion.

Accordingly:

So far as the purely ecclesiastical or spiritual features of a church or religious society are concerned the Civil Courts have steadily asserted their want of jurisdiction to hear and determine any controversy relating thereto (45 Am. Jur. p. 768).

But religious associations do have civil relationships which lie within the jurisdiction of the courts. Contracts (45 Am. Jur. p. 783), torts (45 Am. Jur. p. 784), taxation (51 Am. Jur. p. 589 *et seq.*), and ownership and use of property (45 Am. Jur. p. 757 *et seq.*), among others, are matters which are independent of and are not controlled by ecclesiastical beliefs and practices; and laws affecting them do not come within prohibitions of constitutions and statutes affecting the establishment or exercise of religion.

. . . whenever rights of property are involved, the law must interpose equally in those instances where the dispute is as to church property and in those where it is not (45 Am. Jur. p. 769).

Baptist churches are never defined in terms of property, so no ecclesiastical question is involved in the ownership of property. When a church acquires property, it is generally acquired in trust for the purposes of the church. If this trust is specifically declared, then the courts enforce the trust and require the property to be used for the purpose of the trust, regardless of any church action (45 Am. Jur. p. 771). If the property is acquired by conveyance without specific declaration of trust, the courts determine whether or not a trust is implied (45 Am. Jur. p. 775) and enforce implied trusts as fully as declared ones. Where division or schisms occur in a church, that part of the church which fulfils the purpose of the trust maintains the right to the use of the property (45 Am. Jur. p. 775 *et seq.*). Where property is acquired by a church and no limitation is imposed upon the uses to which the property is to be devoted by the conveyance, the weight of authority is to the effect that the property is held under an implied trust coextensive with the fundamental and characteristic doctrines of the church as held at the time the property is acquired, and the civil courts will exercise their jurisdiction at the instance of a faction of the church, however small, which remains loyal to those doctrines, to prevent the diversion of the property to another use (46 Am. Jur. pp. 775–777).

Thus it may be stated that practically all donations to a church of property, money, and other valuables are held by the church in trust and cannot be diverted by any kind of congregational majority to the use of an organization differing in fundamental and characteristic doctrines from those held at the time the property, money, and valuables were acquired.

MONT W. EGERTON

CHURCH STAFF. The paid professional or clerical employees of a local church, who are responsible for leading the church to achieve its purposes and carry on its program. Although the concept of a multiple ministry has basis in the New Testament, the traditional pattern of Southern Baptist practice until the present century was that the church have only one minister, the pastor. Due to scarcity of pastors and smallness of congregations, the pastor often served more than one church. However, at the turn of the 20th century this pattern began to change. First, more and more churches were able to support full-time pastors. Then, as the churches grew in size and promoted a more and more complex program of activities, increasing demands being made upon the pastor made it necessary to secure additional workers. Clerical workers were the first to be added to the church staff. Later, educational workers were employed. The first such worker was Robert H. Coleman, who became assistant to the pastor and Sunday school superintendent at the First Baptist Church in Dallas, Tex., in Dec., 1904. In the next 11 years Louis Entzminger, William P. Phillips, and Clarence S. Leavell assumed similar positions with other churches. Since that time more and more churches have found a need for workers in addition to the pastor, and the church staff has become more or less typical of modern Southern Baptist churches.

Due to the growing comprehensiveness and complexity of the church program, the need for specialized assistance has increased. To meet this need several specialized vocations have developed, in many cases, so rapidly that often there is confusion between the titles these vocational workers are given by the churches and the functions they are expected to perform. In spite of this confusion in practice, the main positions which may be included on a church staff have been more or less defined. Following is a partial list of the positions on the church staff with a brief statement concerning the primary function of each. Most churches do not have nearly all these staff members, but have only two or three staff members in addition to a secretary or secretaries. Often one worker fills several of the positions described below.

Pastor.—He is responsible for preaching and performing the pastoral ministry, and for the supervision of the total church program, including the staff. In his relationship with staff members, he is to be accepted as the chief. Difficulties arise here when this principle is not observed.

Associate (or assistant) pastor.—He assists in the pastoral ministry, and in visitation. Some churches are employing a minister who has had specialized training in counseling to serve as associate pastor with counseling as his primary responsibility.

Minister of education.—This worker is to promote, direct, co-ordinate, and improve the total educational work of the church.

Minister of music.—This worker organizes and directs the church choirs. He seeks to lift the level of music appreciation in the various areas of church life, and, in conjunction with the pastor, to deepen the experience of worship for the total church membership.

Church (or business) administrator.—He supervises the financial aspects of the life of the church. All purchases for the church are made through him.

Adult director, youth director, elementary director.—These age-group specialists supervise, promote, and correlate the work of their respective age groups in all agencies of the church. The few very large churches have a paid worker for each departmental division, i.e., Nursery, Beginner, Primary, Junior, Intermediate, Young People, and Adult.

Church kindergarten teacher.—This worker directs the weekday church kindergarten.

Recreation director.—This worker promotes, correlates, and supervises the total recreational program of the church.

Secretary.—There are various types of secretaries that may be on a church staff: the church secretary, the promotional secretary, the financial secretary, the educational secretary, the personal secretary, etc. These, of course, have different responsibilities.

Church visitor.—This worker visits the sick, the shut-in, the prospects, and the unsaved.

Church hostess.—This worker is responsible for the planning and preparation of meals that are served at the church.

The pastor is called by the church upon recommendation of the pulpit committee. The other staff members are usually called by the church upon recommendation of the personnel committee, of which the pastor is a member.

FINDLEY B. EDGE

CHURCH TEMPERANCE COUNCIL, INC., VIRGINIA. Organized in Richmond, its present location, in May, 1946. It was the result of three years of promotion by representatives of the Baptist General Association of Virginia "to unite various Church forces in Virginia in one agency or organization, to promote by educational and other means civic righteousness, and abstinence from the use of alcoholic beverages and other narcotics."

The council is directed by 21 trustees, elected or re-elected annually by the eight church groups (denominations) which contribute to its financial support. Annually a president, vice-president, secretary, and treasurer are elected by the trustees from among their number. The council employs a full-time executive secretary and other secretarial assistants. W. RUSH LOVING

CHURCHES OF CHRIST. An American restorationist denomination, existing originally as the conservative wing within the Disciples of Christ, reported separately for the first time in the religious census of 1906. They had actually achieved complete separation from the Disciples several years earlier, but their lack of centralized organization delayed acquisition of this information.

Two main issues—the use of instrumental music and the utilization of mission societies—provoked the controversy leading to the conservative group's withdrawal. Placing a melodeon in the church at Midway, Ky. (1860), inaugurated this dispute, but it was not until 1864 that any serious note of alarm was sounded. J. W. McGarvey (1829–1911), conservative leader within the Disciples, writing in the *Millennial Harbinger*, struck out against the use of musical instruments in the church, insisting that no element in public worship was legitimate unless the New Testament specifically authorized it. With the death of Alexander Campbell (1788–1866), the powerful leader of the movement and one of its founders, the "most serious" of all controversies arose concerning missionary societies. In attacking the American Christian Missionary Society of the Disciples, the conservatives employed some antisociety declarations written by Campbell at an earlier period. They opposed not only mission societies but "all forms of representative gatherings" as well. About this time Benjamin Franklin (1812–78), editor of the *American Christian Review*, cast his influence with the conservative cause. The *Gospel Advocate* had earlier taken the same position. Leading the liberal group arrayed against Franklin and his followers was Isaac Errett (1820–88), progressive editor of the *Christian Standard*. Although unresolved, these controversies slowly died out around 1875, and the strict restorationists, constituting about one fourth of the Disciples, began withdrawing into a separate, non-co-operating group called the "Churches of Christ."

The Churches of Christ regard themselves as a restoration of Christianity to its original pattern and purity, not merely as a new sect. They hold that all other groups have perverted God's plan, and own no creed but the New Testament. "Where the Scriptures speak, we speak; where the Scriptures are silent, we are silent" is their self-acknowledged canon of orthodoxy. Even the Holy Spirit cannot direct, inspire, or empower except through the words of the Bible. Salvation is obtained through a process of obedience to the commands of the gospel: faith, repentance, confession, baptism by immersion, and perpetual obedience. Faith, strictly speaking, consists of intellectual assent to the testimony of the New Testament, which any man may exercise without divine assistance. Their worship each Lord's Day includes singing (without instruments), teaching, contributing of money, prayer, and the Lord's Supper.

Although void of all interchurch organizations, the Churches of Christ are not congregational. Each local body is ruled by elders (bishops, pastors) and served by deacons, chosen by and from the congregation. Not even the minister (preacher, evangelist) has a vote in determining church policy. Only the ruling elders exercise such authority.

These churches are intensely evangelistic and have missionaries in foreign countries sent out from the local congregations. What they have consistently opposed is not missions, but cooperative mission efforts which necessitate superchurch organizations. Accordingly, they have no publishing houses, editorial boards, official doctrinal statements, or authorized statistical reports. All of their literature is published and distributed privately. Social, benevolent, and educational institutions (including colleges) are maintained by members of the Churches of Christ and in some instances by individual churches, but they do not officially represent the churches as a group or have any organic connection with them.

Churches of Christ are largely concentrated in Texas, Tennessee, Kentucky, Alabama, Arkansas, and Oklahoma. In 1953 they numbered 1,500,000 in 15,000 churches. The number of preachers (none of whom ever receive formal ordination) was reported to be 15,500 in 1952.

See also CAMPBELLISM.

BIBLIOGRAPHY: G. C. Brewer, *Foundation Facts and Primary Principles* (1949). E. T. Clark, *The Small Sects of America* (1949). J. H. Cobb, "Churches of Christ," *Encyclopaedia Britannica*, V (1956). M. M. Davis, *How the Disciples Began and Grew* (1949). W. E. Garrison, *An American Religious Movement: A Brief History of the Disciples of Christ* (1945); *Religion Follows the Frontier: A History of the Disciples of Christ* (1931). B. C. Goodpasture, "Churches of Christ," *Twentieth Century Encyclopedia of Religious Knowledge*, I (1955). T. W. Grafton, "The Transition Period," *The Reformation of the Nineteenth Century*, J. H. Garrison ed. (1901). T. W. Phillips, *The Church of Christ* (1943). Z. T. Sweeney, ed., *New Testament Christianity*, II, III (1930). E. West, *The Search for the Ancient Order*, 2 vols. (1947). B. Y. Landis, ed., *Yearbook of American Churches for 1955* (1954).
DON B. HARBUCK

CITIZENSHIP, BAPTIST CHRISTIAN. Christian citizenship is a distinctive quality that pervades the human relations of the child of God. It is the participation of the loyal subject of God in the affairs of group life here on earth. In this participation he seeks to represent Christ as his master and to bring credit to God as his ultimate sovereign. This means that he takes his stand thoughtfully in terms of principles, that he is careful not to push his own selfish interests, that he treats present issues as part of a larger conflict, and that he gives his fellow men all the respect and consideration which he desires for himself.

The essence of right living, according to New Testament teaching, lies in the enjoyment of a right relationship to God through full acceptance and response to Christ. By divine act new forces are released in human experience. The spiritual results which are described as "fruits of the Spirit" become personality or character traits in the lives in which God prevails. These are not limited to church-related activities; rather, as Paul stated, Christians are to "do all to the glory of God" (I Cor. 10:31).

Although the above dynamic view of the Christian life seems clear enough at present, the history of Christendom has many long chapters in which the term "Christian" is applied to regimentation of minds, to coercion of convictions, or to persecution of saints. Usually these movements have been in defense of established political, economic, or ecclesiastical interests. At other times the dynamic quality of Christian citizenship has failed for lack of specific attention or lack of group effort to give a clear witness to the divine love, will, and power as revealed in Christ.

Although loosely called Anabaptists by some in Colonial beginnings, Baptists in America have differed sharply at one point from the Anabaptist concept of the believer's relationship to the state. They emphatically received the European sect's teachings concerning separation of church and state and full religious liberty for all; but in searching the Scriptures to recover the pattern of the early church, they, unlike the Anabaptists, found nothing which demanded withdrawal from political life. On the contrary, they construed Jesus' words, "Render . . . unto Caesar the things which are Caesar's" (Matt. 22:21), not only as an injunction for obedience to civil law but as warrant for participation in the government.

With Martin Luther, Baptists have regarded citizenship duties as generally defined by the apostle Paul in Romans 13. However, they have never accorded to the state any such powers as did Luther, whom they believe substituted an authoritarianism of the state similar to that previously exercised by the Roman Catholic Church, thus veering toward totalitarianism in the state and encouraging reliance of the church upon the state.

Baptists hold strictly to the belief that the church is a gathered company of regenerated members, never coterminous with the population and hence functioning differently from the state. From the days of Roger Williams, founder of their first church in America (1639), Baptists have stood for democracy in political government, no matter to which party they belonged. They stress the obligation of each to vote.

The Baptist movement has been marked by a strong effort to release the dynamic forces engendered by freedom of conscience, of worship, and of religious expression. No particular social or political patterns have been adopted as integral parts of the movement. Many have objected to war, to oaths, or to other civil procedures, but the churches as corporate groups have not prescribed set patterns of civic behavior.

The Baptist emphasis on the priesthood of all believers and on the independence of the churches from the state has called upon the membership, under the guidance of the Spirit, to play an active and constructive role in the community. Although the resulting quality of citizenship has been uneven, varying with personal devotion and with adequacy of instruction, Baptists have made significant contributions to the cultivation of a free way of life and to that idea of personal competency which is basic to true democracy.

The friendly, understanding attitude of Roger Williams toward the American Indians and to their culture foreshadowed the Baptist insight that religion consists not in national culture patterns but in full responsiveness to God. Baptist leadership in the foreign missionary movement has sprung out of those same basic presuppositions. Hence Baptists have sought to be loyal and constructive citizens but never chauvinistic or uninterested in the well-being of all mankind.

Since Baptist churches have been viewed and advanced as fellowships of believers, they have sought to avoid aligning themselves with any particular economic interest or class but rather to enhance the understanding of God's concern for righteousness and love on the part of all. Similarly, the churches have avoided "politics" in the sense of partisan interests, but have expected the church members to use their commitment to God in their political affairs.

In the United States, as in other countries, individual Baptists, never as official representatives of their churches, have frequently been elected to public office, have been appointed to various stations in government, or have led in political movements, notably in reform measures. Baptists have been foremost in support of their country's most distinguished constitutional principles of religious liberty and church-state separation, which, as universally recognized, they helped most to establish. Baptists have furnished two presidents of the United States, Warren G. Harding and Harry S. Truman. They have had at least one head of the United States Supreme Court, Charles Evans Hughes. Every Congress has included Baptists in the Senate and House of Representatives. Many Baptists have served as governors in the states.

Expressive of the Baptist conception of the Christian's responsibilities to civil government is the following statement from Pat M. Neff, twice governor of Texas, later president of Baylor University, and president of the Southern Baptist Convention:

> The government is just as good and just as bad as the people make it. At all times it reflects the people's desires. . . . While the state should not oppress religion and religion should not coerce the state, it is unquestionably true that every Christian should be a politician to the extent of taking an active interest in every public question that touches the moral and material welfare of the people.

Neff based his statement on the examples of Moses, John the Baptist, Paul, and Jesus.

Southern Baptists, like other Baptist bodies, have long fostered an agency, now called the Christian Life Commission, which conducts researches into social questions and attempts to recommend attitudes and action. They also strongly support the Joint Committee on Public Affairs, maintained jointly by six national Baptist bodies in Washington, D. C.

Baptists are more pleased with the aim toward which they have worked than with their own level of civic achievement. The many points at which Christian participation in group and national life has fallen prey to the rationalizations of economic, social, or political aspirations are well known to students of history. These failures, however, next to divine revelation itself, are the most conclusive evidence of the importance of a church fellowship that is committed to God rather than to a prevailing social order or to an authoritarian clergy.

As choices involved in Christian citizenship become more complex and involved, as forces of evil and self-interest become more powerfully entrenched, and as organs of public communications bear in more forcibly on public opinion, Baptists will undoubtedly need to draw closer together in order to have a clear Christian witness. The numerous very difficult issues will call for extended study and discussion in the local, as well as in the larger, fellowships in order to apply the principles of the Scriptures under the guidance of the Spirit with Christian consensus.

J. M. DAWSON and C. EMANUEL CARLSON

CITY MISSIONS. A co-operative work involving the Home Mission Board, a state mission board, and a local association, designed to promote the total denominational program within a given metropolitan area, and emphasizing missions, ministry to minority groups, aid to mission areas, and the development of new or unchurched sections. The program has as its goal "to meet all the needs of all the people through the enlistment of all the churches."

The modern Home Mission Board program of city missions was authorized by the board on Nov. 7, 1940, in the following words: "Resolved that the Executive Secretary be instructed to project a city mission program, looking to the establishment of city missions in the South as funds shall be provided this next year." Prior to this time the Convention had been for long years interested in New Orleans, and before the Civil War had had work in other Southern cities. The very first city mission work of Southern Baptists was authorized by the Convention at the time of its organization in 1845. The work was to begin in New Orleans, under the direction of the Board of Domestic Missions. The board planned to work by establishing and aiding new churches. This policy was followed for the first 15 years of the board's history. Churches were aided in more than 30 cities. City mission programs consisting of aid by the board to church-sponsored activity and work were set up in Montgomery, Ala.; Richmond, Va.; Augusta, Ga.; and San Francisco, Sacramento, Oakland, Santa Cruz, and San Ramon Valley, Calif., by 1860. With the coming of the Civil War, the work came to an end. Nothing of interest is recorded about city missions until the inauguration of the present program. The work began with two programs set up and operated by the Home Mission Board in 1941 in Houston, Tex., and Atlanta, Ga., with Loyd Corder and S. F. Dowis, respectively, superintendents. In 1941 two other cities were added: Washington, D. C., and Birmingham, Ala. By the end of 1943 there were 21 city mission programs in operation under the Home Mission Board. As of Jan. 1, 1956, there were 52 city mission programs in operation in the Southern Baptist Convention.

The city mission program was begun as a co-operative program between the Home Mission Board and the local city association. On Jan. 1, 1951, it was made a co-operative work with the state mission boards and the associations.

The first pamphlet written to guide the church in its local mission work, which was entitled "A Local Church Mission Program," was by C. C. Warren, pastor of the First Baptist Church, Charlotte, N. C., who pioneered in this work. This pamphlet was printed by the Home Mission Board in 1948.

The first Convention-wide superintendent of city missions was S. F. Dowis, Atlanta, Ga., who assumed this work on Jan. 1, 1943, under the direction of the Home Mission Board. Because of enlarged duties as secretary of Co-operative Missions, J. P. Carter of Louisville, Ky., was chosen to assist in the direction of city mission work on Feb. 1, 1943. Later Carter went to a pastorate at Flagler Street Church, Miami, Fla., and Leland Waters of Richmond, Va., was chosen to supervise the work.   S. F. DOWIS

CLARK, HORACE (b. Charlestown, Mass., July 7, 1819; d. Feb. 23, 1909). Educator and ordained Baptist minister, later an Episcopalian rector. At the age of 14, he moved with his mother to Illinois and attended Shurtleff College at Alton. He moved to Kentucky in 1841 and married in 1844. For four years he was principal of Henry Academy, Newcastle. Moving to Texas in 1850, Clark became principal of the Female Department of Baylor University the following year, a position he held until 1871. During his tenure a controversy with Rufus C. Burleson (q.v.) resulted in Burleson's removal to Waco to head the school which, after a later merger, continued as Baylor University. Later, without public explanation or comment, Clark changed his church affiliation and was ordained to the Episcopal priesthood in 1879. He served as rector of the Church of the Good Shepherd, Corpus Christi, Tex., from 1880 to 1898.

BIBLIOGRAPHY: *Journal of the Sixtieth Annual Council of the Protestant Episcopal Church in the Diocese of Texas Held in All Saints Church* (1909). C. B. Wilson, "Baptist Educational Efforts in Texas, 1829–1900" (1934).   R. N. RICHARDSON

CLARKE, JOHN (b. Suffolk, England, Oct. 8, 1609; d. Newport, R. I., Apr. 28, 1676). Minister, statesman, and advocate of religious liberty. Born of well-to-do parents, he was the sixth of eight children and the third of "five sons, four of whom ultimately settled in Newport, R. I." The obscurity of his early life prohibits certain knowledge of any connection with an educational institution "unless a John Clarke of the University of Leyden is to be identified with him, but his intellectual outlook reveals a breadth of view not entirely ascribable to self-training, while various evidences point to some erudition." At the age of 28, having been educated in some manner to a high degree of proficiency in medicine, law, and theology, Clarke emigrated to New England, where he hoped to find freedom of conscience. When he arrived in Boston in Nov., 1637, the general court had just taken rigorous action against the Antinomians. He identified himself with this defeated group, which immediately recognized him as a leader, and joined with them in a determined effort to establish a new colony on the basis of civil and religious liberty. Clarke and 18 others formed a company and through the assistance of Roger Williams (q.v.) on Mar. 24, 1638, consummated the purchase of the island of Aquidneck in Narragansett Bay (now Rhode Island) from the Indians. Though William Coddington became governor, Clarke, as a physician and preacher, was "equally a leader" and helped establish the principle of religious liberty in the colony. By 1640 he had gathered a church at the new settlement of Newport which he served as pastor until his death. Its early history is obscure, but this body became Baptist both in doctrine and practice no later than 1648. While conducting religious services at Lynn, Mass., in 1651 in the home of William Witter, a nonresident member of his church, Clarke and his colleagues, John Crandall and Obadiah Holmes (q.v.), were arrested and then put in prison, charged with unauthorized preaching, denying the lawfulness of infant baptism, and other offences. Sentenced to be fined or whipped, Clarke escaped punishment only after a friend without

HOWARD COLLEGE (q.v.), Birmingham, Ala. Model of the new $11,000,000 campus.

HOWARD
PAYNE
COLLEGE

The new 50,000-volume Walker Memorial Library at Howard Payne College, Brownwood, Texas, was opened in 1952. It provides modern library facilities for a student body of more than a thousand students.

The new million-dollar girls' dormitory was opened September 1, 1955. It provides modern dormitory facilities for 254 women students.

his knowledge paid his fine of 20 pounds. Later that same year the people of Rhode Island sent Clarke and "Williams to England to protect the interests of the colony." They soon accomplished their immediate objective and Williams returned, but Clarke remained in England for 12 years before obtaining his ultimate objective, a more suitable and liberal royal charter for Rhode Island. During these years he supported himself by practicing as a physician, by preaching, and by mortgaging his property in Newport. He published in London in 1652 *Ill Newes from New England or a Narrative of New England Persecution,* which recounted the Lynn, Mass., episode and advocated liberty of conscience.

In spite of much discouragement, difficulty, and delay, Clarke secured from Charles II on July 8, 1663, a charter for Rhode Island that not only enlarged the boundaries of the colony but also provided for full civil and religious liberty, stating "that noe person within the colonie, at any time hereafter shall be in anywise molested, punished, disquieted or called in question for any differences in opinions in matters of religion. . . ." Upon his return to Newport in 1664, the colonists elected him to the general assembly for several years, and three times elected him deputy governor, while at the same time he continued to serve as minister and physician. The colony also appointed him to codify and revise its laws in 1666. He retired from public life in 1672 and spent his last years in study and religious work.

Besides his 1652 publication, he wrote a strongly Calvinistic confession of faith, a concordance, and a lexicon. Thrice married, Clarke had one child, a daughter who died in infancy. By his will he left the bulk of his property in trust for religious and educational purposes.

LYNN E. MAY, JR.

CLARKE, NATHAN LYTLE (b. Burke County, N. C., Feb. 7, 1812; d. Decatur, Miss., Sept. 11, 1906). Pastor, church organizer, editor. After moving to Mississippi in 1840, Clarke was ordained in 1841, and served as pastor of the Decatur church from 1848 until his death. He was also missionary for Mount Pisgah Baptist Association in 1849, and held office in the association continuously from 1850. Leader in the organization of the General Association of Southeast Mississippi in 1855, Clarke was its only president until his death. He founded the *Mississippi Baptist* in 1891, which he edited for 15 years as the organ of the general association. Clarke organized about 100 Mississippi churches and made Kemper, Leake, Scott, Smith, Neshoba, Simpson, Covington, Jones, Jasper, Lauderdale, and Newton counties a Baptist stronghold. Clarke Memorial College, named for him, was established at Newton, Miss., in 1907. Clarke always preferred the more conservative atmosphere of the general association to the more aggressive and progressive state convention.

BIBLIOGRAPHY: J. L. Boyd, *A Popular History of the Baptists in Mississippi* (1930). L. S. Foster, *Mississippi Baptist Preachers* (1895). R. A. Venable, "Rev. N. L. Clarke, An Appreciation," *The Baptist Record* (1906).

C. B. HAMLET III

CLARKE MEMORIAL COLLEGE. A junior college at Newton, Miss., owned and operated by the Mississippi Baptist Convention. Founded in 1907 by the General Association of Regular Baptists in Mississippi, it was named in memory of Nathan Lytle Clarke (q.v.), a preacher who died in 1906. A former effort to establish this school as East Mississippi College had failed. Newton was chosen for the school's location because of its centrality and the attractive offer made to the locating committee. The first session opened Sept. 22, 1908, with six teachers, S. B. Culpepper as president, and an enrolment of 104. By the next session enrolment had increased to 214.

In 1913 the Mississippi Baptist Convention, responding to an appeal from the board of trustees, named conditions under which it would accept and operate the college. When these conditions were met, the college property was conveyed in Apr., 1914, to a convention-elected board of trustees who assumed responsibility for operation. However, in 1930 when the convention discontinued support, Clarke College was operated privately under lease from 1931 to 1946 with trustees functioning as custodians of the property. The convention reassumed responsibility for the college in 1945 and has operated it as a convention institution since June 1, 1946.

The original college plant included two dormitories and a school building, all of wood, erected on a 40-acre plot given by the people of Newton. The first boys' dormitory, burned in 1909, was replaced that year by the present brick building, and the original school building, which burned in 1924, was replaced by the present academic building the following year. In Nov., 1955, college holdings consisted of 230 acres of land, including 60 acres of campus and housing area and 170 acres of farm and woodland. The operating plant included the academic building, housing classrooms, laboratories, and auditorium; two dormitories (the girls' dormitory built in 1952 and 1954); the dining hall and library (1949); the office building (1953); the gymnasium (1954); and the music building (1946). On the site where the original girls' dormitory burned in 1954 a library building is being erected. The college owns 54 faculty and student homes; and the Board of Ministerial Education owns 30 homes for ministerial students on property adjoining the campus, which the college donated to the board in 1945. With a building fund of $85,000 and endowment of $129,000 Clarke College had a total income in 1954–55 of $126,000, of which $58,351.62 came from Cooperative Program receipts. The college had its largest enrolment of 565 in 1950–51. Enrolment in 1954–55 was 454.

The first class of nine graduated in 1911,

and since then the total number of graduates has been approximately 1,200. The college conferred B.A. or B.S. degrees until 1919 when it definitely took its place as a junior college. It was accredited by the Mississippi Junior College Commission in 1926, one of the first two schools thus recognized; and it has held membership in the Southern Association of Colleges and Secondary Schools since 1952. JOHN F. CARTER

CLEAR CREEK BAPTIST SCHOOL. Located in a mountain region at Pineville, Ky., it seeks to improve the Christian leadership by providing training for men and women who feel called to special Christian service and who do not have the educational background to qualify them to attend college or seminary. It had its beginning in 1926 when Lloyd Caswell Kelly, who was to be its first president, and R. P. Mahon conducted a two-week school for preachers, at Clear Creek. From this developed the Clear Creek Mountain Preachers Bible School.

For several years the session was for one month. Later the length of term was extended to four months. In 1946 the school was chartered by the Kentucky legislature and has since been in session two full semesters each year. A new charter adopted in 1956 changed the name of the institution to Clear Creek Baptist School.

The school has buildings and grounds valued at $453,495 and endowment, as of 1955–56, of $2,032, for a total of $455,527. Kelly Hall, the large, native-stone administration building, includes classrooms, library, dining hall, administrative offices, and living quarters for single students. Other buildings include a church-furniture factory, an auditorium, and more than 50 apartment houses and cottages, all of native-stone construction.

In 1955–56 the enrolment was 102 as compared with an enrolment of 12 the first year the school was open. In 1956 expenses totaled $74,280, of which $48,824 was received from the General Association of Baptists in Kentucky, $18,135 from gifts, and $12,110 from student fees.

Clear Creek had graduated (as of 1955–56) a total of 156. Operating in the adult education field, it offers three-year, noncredit courses mainly in Bible and church administration.

Dennis Merrill Aldridge, the second president, has headed the school since 1954. The school is owned and operated by, and its trustees are elected by, the General Association of Baptists in Kentucky. ERWIN L. MC DONALD

CLEAR CREEK MOUNTAIN SPRINGS ASSEMBLY. Founded in 1924 at Pineville (Bell County), Ky., when interested Baptists in southeastern Kentucky purchased 450 acres of ground for the site. The encampment's purpose was to give inspiration and information emphasizing all phases of church and denominational life. Vacation Bible schools, boys' camps, and mountain preachers' schools were also held there annually. Clear Creek, the only state Baptist assembly in Kentucky after 1931, was operated as the state Baptist assembly until 1951 when Kentucky Baptists purchased Cedarmore and moved the state assembly from Clear Creek. Boys' and girls' camps are still held each summer at Clear Creek, promoted and conducted by the Clear Creek Mountain Preachers' Bible School. ELDRED M. TAYLOR

CLEBURNE MALE AND FEMALE INSTITUTE. A school which opened in the Cleburne Baptist Church, Cleburne, Tex., in 1866 and passed to the control of Alvarado Association in 1870. Enrolment, preparatory and college, exceeded 200 at times, but the school closed in 1878 for lack of patronage.

RUPERT N. RICHARDSON

CLERICALISM. Primitive Christianity exhibited neither uniformity in local church organization nor a central administrative authority. The most complex order common toward the close of the first century involved a dual ministry of collegiate or presbyter-bishops and deacons, with groups of bishops or presbyters (these were then synonymous terms) heading a single congregation. The concept of a monarchical bishop in apostolic succession, the superintendent of the Christian life of a single city, was a part of the second-century development of a triple clerical differentiation (bishop, presbyter, and deacon), the rigid ancient Catholic Church organization, and sharp cleavage between clergy and laity. In the third century, while the Roman bishops maneuvered for superiority of jurisdiction, a growing sacerdotalism gave recognition to major and minor orders of the clergy, accentuated the combination of city and adjacent rural areas into a diocese supervised by a diocesan bishop and facilitating local rural worship, and reflected the superior dignity of the great city bishops. Upgrading of clerical rank in the fourth century, accompanied by additional power through clerical exemption from taxation and recognition of the clergy as a privileged class, produced the metropolitans and patriarchs, bishops respectively of the capital centers of province and empire. Subsequently, vested with greater power and advantage in a declining empire, the Roman bishops, the popes, took upon themselves the function of Christ's vicegerent and claimed, more successfully in the West than in the East, hegemony over all Christendom, subject to the judgment of God alone.

BIBLIOGRAPHY: J. C. Ayer, Jr., *A Source Book for Ancient Church History from the Apostolic Age to the Close of the Conciliar Period* (1952). G. P. Fisher, *History of Christian Doctrine* (1908). A. Harnack, *The Constitution and Law of the Church in the First Two Centuries* (1910). K. S. Latourette, *A History of Christianity* (1953). T. M. Lindsay, *The Church and the Ministry in the Early Centuries* (1902). J. T. Shotwell and L. R. Loomis, *The See of Peter* (1927). B. H. Streeter, *The Primitive Church, Studied with Special Reference to the Origins of the Christian Ministry* (1929). W. Walker, *A History of the Christian Church* (1945). GLEN LEE GREENE

CLEVELAND MILLS SCHOOL. A Baptist school at Cleveland Mills, N. C., under direction of W. B. Dove in 1896 and W. D. Burns in 1898.

D. L. SMILEY

CLINTON COLLEGE. An academy and college operated in Clinton, Hickman County, Ky., from 1874 to 1914. Founded as a school for girls, it became coeducational in 1883 as the result of a merger with a school for boys in the same area. The school was sponsored by the West Union Baptist Association, which in the 1870's occupied the territory in Kentucky west of the Tennessee River and east of the Mississippi River, and was known as "The Purchase." The first president was T. N. Wells; the first building, erected on land given by Robert Moore, was built in 1875. In 1883 enrolment was 200.

GEORGE RALEIGH JEWELL

CLINTON SEMINARY. A school for girls operated in Clinton, Ky., for a while, beginning in 1830.

GEORGE RALEIGH JEWELL

CLOPTON, ABNER W. (b. Pittsylvania County, Va., Mar. 24, 1784; d. probably Charlotte Court House, Va., Mar. 20, 1833). Pastor, organizer of the first temperance society in Virginia, promoter of tract societies. Son of Christian parents "in comfortable circumstances," Clopton, at 19, had an unhappy marriage which ended in divorce in 1809 and left its imprint of gloom on his life. He was educated at the University of North Carolina and studied medicine in Philadelphia. Personal reflection during a severe illness resulted in Clopton's conversion, and he was baptized into the membership of Shockoe Church in Aug., 1812. He taught in a private school in South Carolina, tutored at the University of North Carolina, and served on the faculty of a Female Seminary in Melton, N. C., after which he returned to Virginia as pastor of Ash Camp and Mossingford churches in Charlotte County.

Agent for several years for the Baptist General Tract Society, Clopton organized more than 100 auxiliaries in Virginia. He helped fellow preachers who had little education by furnishing them good books, and was agent for Columbian College, Washington, D. C., for about two years before his death. Clopton wrote several strong articles for the *Christian Index* of Philadelphia, confuting the followers of Alexander Campbell, and urged associations to adopt resolutions rejecting Campbell's tenets. The extremes to which he went in controversy, however, often became a handicap. Clerk of the Virginia general association and a member of its board, Clopton did his most outstanding work in temperance reform. Largely as a result of his efforts, the Virginia Society for the Promotion of Temperance was organized Oct. 27, 1826, the first temperance organization in the state.

CLAYTON PITTS

CLOPTON, SAMUEL CORNELIUS (b. New Kent, Va., Feb. 7, 1816; d. Canton, China, July 7, 1847). Missionary to China. The first missionary appointed by the Foreign Mission Board after its organization, Clopton attended Richmond College, Columbian College, and Newton Theological Seminary. On Apr. 14, 1846, he married Keziah Turpin; the following June 22 he and his wife, with George and Frances (Miller) Pearcy, sailed for Canton. Clopton died after a brief illness when he had been in China only nine months.

GENEVIEVE GREER

CODY, ZECHARIAH THORNTON (b. near Franklin, Henry County, Ala., May 21, 1858; d. Greenville, S. C., Mar. 7, 1935). Editor. He was the son of Edmund, a Baptist minister and planter, and Sarah (Henderson) Cody, and a descendant of James Cody, Irish emigrant to Virginia about 1740. Z. T. Cody attended country and village schools, Mercer University, Carson-Newman College, and Southern Baptist Theological Seminary, receiving the Th.M. degree in 1887. He received the D.D. degree from Bowden College, Ga., and La Grange College, Mo., and LL.D. degrees from Georgetown College and Furman University. He was ordained at the Second Baptist Church, Atlanta, Ga., July, 1885, and was pastor at Portland Avenue Church, Louisville, Ky., 1885–87; Buck Run, Ky., Jan. to June, 1887; Mays Lick, Ky., 1887–90; Georgetown, Ky., 1890–1901; First, Greenville, S. C., 1901–11; Wellford, S. C., and Roebuck, S. C., 1914–15; and Wellford, 1915–35. He served on numerous boards, committees, and commissions of the South Carolina and Southern Baptist conventions, including a mission to Europe, and preached the annual sermons for the South Carolina convention in 1907 and the Southern Baptist Convention in 1912. Cody was joint owner and editor of the *Baptist Courier* from 1911 until it was sold to the South Carolina Convention in 1920 and edited the paper until his death. As editor, he rendered an outstanding service to the Baptist denomination in South Carolina and in the South, and was active in the work of the Baptist World Alliance. He made for the *Courier* a foremost position among Southern Baptist papers. He was a theologian of the first rank; and his theological, doctrinal, and literary temperament was reflected in his editorials. His theology comprehended the cosmic Christ. Though conspicuously able as an editor, he never felt that he had left the ministry or pastorate.

On Nov. 9, 1887, he married Susan Isabella Anderson of Kentucky. Two children were born to them, Lois and Edmund. In a memorial issue of the *Baptist Courier,* Mar. 21, 1935, tributes were paid him by numerous individuals, institutions, and organizations in the state, the South, the North, and England. He was acclaimed a great editor, Christian statesman, eminent theologian, denominational leader, faithful pastor, friend to all denominational causes, and pre-eminently a preacher.

BIBLIOGRAPHY: J. C. Hemphill, *Men of Mark in South Carolina* (1908). G. W. Lasher, *BaptistMiniste-*

rial Directory (1899). R. N. Daniel, *Furman University, a History* (1951). Southern Baptist Convention, *Annual* (1955). S. C. Baptist Convention, *Annual* (1955). S. C. Baptist Convention, *Annual* (1954). *Baptist Courier*, Mar. 14, 1935; Mar. 21, 1935; Jan. 30, 1936.

W. C. ALLEN

COKER COLLEGE. A woman's college in Hartsville, S. C., founded in 1908 by James Lide Coker in co-operation with a number of missionary Baptist associations in South Carolina. Its forerunner was the Welsh Neck Baptist High School, founded by Coker and the Welsh Neck Association in 1894, because of the absence at that time of state high school education in the area. The college took over all properties of the high school and was organized under its charter with minor changes as to name and amount of property the college could own. Directed by a board of trustees elected from eastern and southern South Carolina Baptist associations, the college, although Baptist, was not sectarian in policy and was neither owned nor controlled by the Baptist state convention. For some years the state convention made annual contributions to the support of the college, but in 1944 all direct relations with and responsibilities to Baptist associations and the convention were terminated, and a self-perpetuating board of trustees took over direction of the school. Coker was no longer to be affiliated with a Christian denomination but was to remain a distinctly Christian college. The board of trustees is composed of 25 members, 15 elected at large, five elected by alumnae, and five chosen by the Coker College Foundation.

Student self-government was instituted in 1915–16 and has continued since that time, with students assuming responsibility for most of the regulations governing conduct. Various associations and clubs exist on the campus, and religious life is fostered through the Christian Association and denominational groups which serve to relate the student to the local church. Scholastic interest is manifested in such clubs as Sophiades, the drama club, glee club, and departmental clubs. The students publish a semimonthly newspaper, a literary magazine, and a college annual. Scholarships, undergraduate and graduate, are offered for students of recognized ability.

The college holds membership in the Association of American Colleges, the Southern Association of Colleges and Secondary Schools, and the National Association of Schools of Music, and is on the approved list of the American Association of University Women. The first Baptist college in South Carolina admitted to the Southern Association of Colleges and Secondary Schools, Coker confers both B.A. and B.S. degrees. The college library, occupying the second floor of the administration building, contains 30,000 volumes, well balanced in various fields of study. Plans have been drawn for a library building. The campus totals 25 acres in three divisions, the campus proper consisting of 14 acres and 10 buildings; the athletic field for tennis, hockey, and other field sports; and Prestwood Lake property for boating and other water sports. Two new buildings, the William Chambers Coker Science Building and the Margaret Coker Lawton Music Building, erected at an approximate cost of $400,000, provide quarters for science, music, and other departments. The college has real property valued at $1,500,000 and an endowment of $1,500,000, consisting primarily of gifts from the Coker and Joseph James Lawton (*q.v.*) families.

BEN INGRAM

COLDWATER BAPTIST FEMALE SEMINARY. Established by Coldwater Baptist Association at Chulahoma, Marshall County, Miss., in 1851. Chartered in 1852 with J. R. Hamilton as president, the school had eight teachers and an enrolment of 104 in 1856. Destruction caused by a tornado and increasing debts threatened the school's closing, but it continued to exist until Civil War damages forced it to close in 1866.

J. L. BOYD

COLEMAN, JAMES SMITH (b. near Beaver Dam, Ky., Feb. 23, 1827; d. Mar. 29, 1904). Pastor. The only child of Elisha and Susanna (Maddox) Coleman, he was well educated.

He was converted at the age of 11 and was baptized on Mar. 10, 1838. At the age of 15, he first felt a call to preach but turned aside from it. The call was renewed, however, and he was licensed to preach May 27, 1854, and ordained in October. He accepted the care of Sandy Creek Church in Butler County one Sunday per month, spending the remainder of his time as missionary of the Gasper River Association. In this capacity and as pastor, he baptized over 1,000 persons in four years. From first to last, he served the following churches in Kentucky as pastor: Sandy Creek, Salem, Beaver Dam, Buck Creek, Green Brier, West Point, Sugar Grove, Mt. Carmel, Greenville, First and Walnut Street churches in Owensboro, Bell's Run, Whitesville, Hartford, Madisonville, Morgantown, Grand River, Livermore, and Pleasant Ridge. He was a Landmark successionist, denying the validity of all other denominations.

Coleman edited the *Green River Baptist* at Hartford, Ky., during the Civil War and helped to save the *Western Recorder* from going out of existence after the war. He was a colporteur and book agent. Invited to the Walnut Street Baptist Church in Louisville, Ky., and to a church in Sacramento, Calif., he declined both offers, because he preferred to remain in the Green River country and work with the small churches. In the years 1867–70, he was appointed as an evangelist by the General Association of Baptists in Kentucky. He organized the Baptist church at Madisonville in 1870.

On May 6, 1846, he married Rachel Chapman; to this union 11 children were born. After the death of his first wife, he married Mrs. Josephine Field on Dec. 24, 1877.

During his lifetime, Dr. Coleman was moderator of the association 29 times. He was moderator of the Kentucky general association 16 times. After 50 years in the ministry, he collapsed from nervous exhaustion brought about by his strenuous labor, and he died after two years of illness.   LEO T. CRISMON

COLEMAN, ROBERT HENRY (b. Bardstown, Ky., Nov. 1, 1869; d. Dallas, Tex., Feb. 13, 1946). Songbook publisher, church musician, denominational worker. After attending public schools and Georgetown College in Kentucky, Coleman moved to Plano, Tex., in early manhood, where he operated a drugstore and was editor of the *Plano Courier* for three years. He was later assistant secretary of Young Men's Christian Association in Dallas. In Dec., 1903, Coleman became assistant to George Washington Truett (*q.v.*) at First Baptist Church, Dallas, and became superintendent of the Sunday school in 1910, continuing in that position until his death, except from 1909 to 1915, when he was business manager of the *Baptist Standard*. Coleman, director of music for the Baptist World Alliance in Stockholm, Sweden, in 1923, was president of the state Baptist Young People's Union, 1899–1902 and 1914–22, and was its corresponding secretary, 1903–06. The R. H. Coleman Publishing Company, which he operated, published at various times 32 different hymnals and collections of religious songs. The company pioneered in the publishing of hymnals and religious songs for many years, during which time it was the principal source of church music for Southern Baptist churches. Coleman sold the publishing business to the Southern Baptist Sunday School Board in 1944.

BIBLIOGRAPHY: *Encyclopedia of American Biography* (First Series) Vol. 50.   F. M. RYBURN

COLLEGE, THE DENOMINATIONAL. "The church and the four-year college have been the chief agencies responsible for the rapid rise of the United States to its prominence as a world power," writes Guy E. Snavely in the opening sentence of his book recording the contribution of the church to higher education in the United States.

In 120 years no one has improved on Lyman Beecher's declaration of the value of the colleges and schools of that day, predominantly church-related:

> Colleges and schools are truly the intellectual manufactories and workshops of the nation, and in their design and results are pre-eminently republican institutions. They break up and diffuse among the people that monopoly of knowledge and mental power which despotic governments accumulate for purposes of arbitrary rule, and bring to the children of the humblest families of the nation a full and fair opportunity of holding competition for learning, and honor, and wealth, with the children of the oldest and most affluent families . . . giving thus to the nation the select talents and powers of her entire population.

(The above quotation is used by permission from *The Church and the Four-Year College* by Guy E. Snavely [New York: Harper & Brothers, 1955]).

Of the first 120 colleges founded in the United States, about 100 were established under church auspices, and there were only 17 state institutions among the 246 colleges founded by the year 1860. The primary purpose of most of these colleges was identical with that of the Colonial colleges founded a century or more earlier: to educate men for the ministry. More than half the graduates of Harvard during its first 60 years became ministers, as did nearly three fourths of the graduates of Yale during its first 12 years.

The developing democratic concept of educational opportunity for all that was responsible for the free public school movement in the 19th century served to broaden the role of the denominational colleges to include the higher education of lay persons as well as clergy. As greater and greater numbers were enrolled in college, and as state-supported colleges and universities came into being, the concern of church groups over the trend toward "education without religion" led to the founding of large numbers of denominational colleges during the last seven decades of the 19th century.

The swift rise of the public school systems, virtually complete in the North by about 1860, also gave rise to an unprecedented demand for teachers. In the South, where the public schools developed more slowly in the beginning and were further delayed by the War Between the States, a similar need was created by the numerous elementary schools and academies initiated under church and private auspices. Thus, the education of teachers became, and still remains, one of the basic purposes of the denominational college, resulting from the conviction that teachers educated in a Christian college are needed in the public schools. The founding of colleges for women and the change to coeducational status of many denominational colleges further broadened the objectives of denominational higher education.

As higher education became more extensive and more complex, the denominational colleges grew in numbers, in size, and in curriculum. Some, controlled by self-perpetuating boards of trustees, found substantial sources of income outside denominational sources and became large, independent universities like the University of Chicago and the University of Southern California. Others, such as Brown, Emory, and Duke, retained denominational ties while achieving virtual financial and operational independence. Still others, such as Baylor University and Southern Methodist University, became moderately large while retaining strong denominational relationships and relying to a large degree on denominational sources of income. The same trends were seen among the denominational colleges that remained small. Some drifted away from denominational relationships, some retained denominational ties out of choice, others remained under close denominational control.

By 1950 there were in the United States 1,857 institutions of higher education, of which 710 were church controlled, 507 privately controlled, and 640 publicly (state, county, or municipally) controlled. Many of the 507 listed as privately controlled in 1950 were to some degree church-related, the relationship varying from a completely nominal one to a co-operative and fraternal relationship closer than many of those listed as church-controlled.

In 1955 the following distribution of four-year denominational colleges and universities in the United States was listed: American Baptist, 24; National Baptist Convention of America, 4; Southern Baptist, 29; Seventh Day Baptist, 2; Congregational, 23; Disciples of Christ, 15; Lutheran, 12; other Lutheran bodies, 18 (1 to 5 each); Methodist, 77; other Methodist bodies, 15; Presbyterian, U.S.A., 40; Presbyterian Church in the United States, 17; other Presbyterian bodies, 9; Roman Catholic, 95; Church of the Brethren, 6; Church of Christ, 4; Church of the Nazarene, 6; Evangelical and Reformed, 8; Evangelical United Brethren, 7; Five-Year Meeting of Friends, 5; Society of Friends, 4; Mennonite, 5; Protestant Episcopal, 7; Seventh Day Adventist, 9; other denominations, 18.

As the denominations have built their colleges, so have the colleges built their denominations. In many cases the formation of an educational society for the purpose of starting a college was the first step toward denominational organization at the state or district level. In other cases fledgling denominational organizations which founded colleges achieved thereby an immediate centrality of purpose and response to leadership that resulted in vigorous denominational growth even before the colleges had time to produce the "seed corn" of denominational advance—educated, consecrated Christian leaders.

Basically the denominational college is the expression of a conviction that secular education at the college level lacks a vital part of what Christian youth must have in order to attain its full potential in service to God and man. It is easy to give lip service to the idea of Christian higher education without grasping its full import. "Education plus," *complete* education, education of heart and soul along with hand and mind—these are some of the well-worn phrases used to express the idea that Christian education goes beyond secular education in its scope and purpose. But those who examine only the slogans of Christian education miss its very reason for existing—the difference it makes in how Christian young men and women invest their lives.

Psychologists tell us that the most formative and impressionable years are those of early childhood. The college years, though, are the decisive ones, those when directions are set and destinies determined. The normal ages at which one chooses a life companion, a lifework, a social pattern—all are within the normal span of the college years.

It is during the college years that the elements of leadership must emerge or be sidetracked. The determination to succeed must breed willingness to pay the price in effort. The ideals of worthy life and worthy service must take control, if they are ever to do so. Minds that are crossing horizons in science, history, and psychology must relate these to Christian faith and Christian experience if the latter are to remain at the center of life's purpose.

For the young person who has had the advantages of a Christian home and a good upbringing, the early college years bring the most severe test of personal convictions, standards of conduct, and sense of values. Away from the immediate influence of parents, the home church, and friends of long standing, one's attitudes, convictions, and motives must stand on their own during the crucial period when they are crystallizing into a relatively permanent, adult pattern.

College brings increased pressures. The student who has had a rather easy time in high school finds it difficult to do satisfactory work in college. Fear of failure, fear of not being liked, fear of responsibility—these and other disturbing elements make life difficult for the average college freshman. He needs answers to the most vital questions of life, answers that give him faith, courage, determination, motivation. He needs the Christian college.

It is not primarily the trustees who make a college Christian, though they can do much to help. Neither is it the administration, though much of the responsibility rests here. No one will deny the importance of the faculty as a basic factor in making a college Christian. The identity of the Christian college, though, is vested just as intimately in its majority of high-principled Christian students who participate enthusiastically in a Christ-centered educational program. No other single factor is so essential to the Christian college as the predisposition toward worthy activities, worthy living, and worthy objectives that results inevitably when consecrated Christians are in the majority among the students.

The idea that the Christian college functions primarily through a sheltered environment is a misconception. There is evil in every college. In a Christian college there are the same temptations and the same problems, though perhaps in lesser degree. The students vary from best to worst—academically, morally, socially. But the solid majority who set the pace in the Christian college are those who hold to Christian standards of leadership, conduct, and even of popularity. The ne'er-do-wells, the frivolous ones, and the incorrigibles are on the outer fringe, and the steady current of Christian purpose moves past them, through them, and beyond them. Indeed, the very genius of the Christian college is this momentum of purposeful Christian youth that catches up and carries forward with it all who will join.

The denominational colleges of today face

probably two decades of mushrooming enrolments, of mounting costs of operation, and of shortages of qualified teachers. Their basic problem, however, remains that of leading their respective constituencies to recognize the essential worth and basic task of the denominational college.

In this the widespread tendency to identify the denominational college as an institution for recruitment and training of personnel for church vocations is both principal asset and greatest handicap. It is an asset in that it causes the constituency to recognize the necessity of the denominational college. It is a handicap in that it hinders recognition of the larger task, that of preparing Christian youth to meet the demands of Christian citizenship and leadership in secular vocations offering great opportunity for Christian influence, such as teaching, journalism, social work, the healing arts, government, and others. Only as Christian leaders, parents, and youth come to recognize the unique ministry of the Christian college in blending Christian purpose with maturing mentality, and Christian convictions with the pattern of youthful aspiration, can the Christian college realize more than a small fraction of its full potential.

Of late the picture has brightened considerably. The worth of the church and private colleges is being proclaimed by corporations and foundations, and support from these sources is growing rapidly. The precedent-shattering gift of the Ford Foundation, announced in Dec., 1955, dramatized the importance of college faculties, and of church and private colleges, to a degree never before approached. Too, there are signs of progress among the denominations themselves, increasing financial support, attention to the need for denominational colleges in the large cities, surveys of need, potentialities and problems of the institutions, and formulation of long-range plans. One probability is most apparent: the rising tide of interest in and support for private colleges, combined with swelling enrolments, will cause many denominational colleges to sever or weaken denominational ties. The denominations that propose to keep their colleges must face up to the needs and make full use of their services. More denominational colleges are lost through neglect than are killed by design.

BIBLIOGRAPHY: E. P. Cubberley, *A Brief History of Education* (1922). J. D. Russell, *Number and Accredited Status of Institutions of Higher Learning in the United States.* G. E. Snavely, *The Church and the Four-Year College* (1955). D. G. Tewksbury, *The Founding of American Colleges and Universities Before the Civil War* (1932).   R. ORIN CORNETT

COLLEGE ASSOCIATION OF BAPTIST TEACHERS OF RELIGION. See RELIGIOUS EDUCATION, PROFESSIONAL ASSOCIATIONS.

COLOMBIA, MISSION IN. Baptist work in Colombia began in 1844 on the English-speaking islands of San Andres and Providence, Colombian possessions off the coast of Nicaragua, through Philip Livingston, sea captain, United States consul, and Baptist minister. Spanish-speaking Cuban missionaries began Baptist work in continental Colombia. Henry William Schweinsberg and Joseph Lancaster Hart made a preliminary survey of the field for Southern Baptists in Nov., 1941.

Southern Baptist mission strategy provided a missionary staff sufficient for rapid development of strong churches in key centers from which evangelistic efforts would branch out in surrounding regions. Foreign Mission Board and Jarman Foundation funds made possible the purchase of suitable properties for the churches. Evangelism, indoctrination of converts, stewardship, Christian education, promotion of religious education in the churches, and training of national leadership have been primary emphases.

Missionaries are located in five cities. Schweinsberg began work in Barranquilla in 1942, with the first church organized that year. In 1943 Thomas Lawton Neely opened work in Cartagena; the following year a church was organized there. James Ulman Moss and John Nathaniel Thomas went to Cali in 1946; a church was organized in 1948. Gerald Riddell entered Bogota, the capital city, in 1947; in 1949 a church was organized. Thomas began work in Medellin in 1955.

Following the division of the Colombian-Venezuelan Convention because of travel difficulties, the Colombian Baptist Convention was organized in 1952. It includes home and foreign missions, a national Baptist paper (*El Heraldo Bautista*), promotion of religious education, stewardship, and evangelism, and partial support of an orphanage. A national Woman's Missionary Union organized in 1950 sponsors young people's work, camps and institutes, and weeks of prayer for home and foreign missions.

The International Baptist Theological Seminary, graduate school for the training of pastors and Christian workers of Central America and northwestern South America, opened in Mar., 1952. Ben Harold Welmaker became the first president of the school. Julius Raht Hickerson, who laid plans for the institution, was killed in a 1951 plane disaster. Property has been bought near Cali for future buildings.

The Baptist Hospital at Barranquilla serves Baptists and other evangelical Christians. Roy Cloud McGlamery, medical missionary (resigned 1953), opened the first clinic in 1948. The hospital building, in use since Oct., 1950, was dedicated Feb., 1956. George Hiram Kollmar is director of the institution.   CREA RIDENOUR

COLOMBIAN BAPTIST CONVENTION. Baptist churches in Colombia and Venezuela were organized in a joint convention in Feb., 1949, but the 10 Colombian Baptist churches (not including three churches on San Andres Island) formed a separate convention Jan. 16, 1952. Fifteen churches now compose the Colombian Baptist Convention, contributing a minimum of 10 per cent of their incomes to the convention through a Cooperative Program. The convention, directed by an executive committee, publishes a monthly periodical, *El Heraldo Bautista*.

In 1954 home and foreign mission boards were organized. The foreign mission board is accumulating funds and holding them in reserve until a missionary can be sent out. The home mission board helps support four churches and contributes toward the support of a large mission congregation. The resources of the boards are increased by two special offerings annually.

HELEN MEREDITH

COLORADO BAPTIST GENERAL CONVENTION, HISTORY OF. Looking forward to organization of the Colorado convention, a regional convention was organized in Temple Church, Denver, May 5, 1954. Fifty-seven churches from Colorado, Wyoming, Montana, and North and South Dakota formed the convention. Ten of the churches were affiliated with the New Mexico Baptist Convention, but all the others co-operated with the General Convention of Arizona. Formed without administrative or executive function, the regional convention had a threefold objective: fellowship, promotion, and co-operation. A total of 348 registered for the meeting, probably the first regional convention of its nature ever held in the history of Southern Baptists.

A second such meeting was held at Denver Temple Church, Nov. 22–23, 1954, when registration reached 370. The third convention was held at First Southern Baptist Church, Casper, Wyo., Apr. 25–26, 1955. At this meeting the group voted to dissolve the regional body in order to organize the Colorado Baptist General Convention.

Thus, on Nov. 21, 1955, 690 persons, 331 of them authorized messengers from 90 churches, met at First Southern Baptist Church, Colorado Springs, and organized the Colorado Baptist General Convention. Churches from five Western states were represented in the new convention: Colorado, Wyoming, Montana, North Dakota, South Dakota, and Nebraska. Thirteen of the 90 churches were formerly affiliated with the New Mexico Baptist Convention, and the others, with the Baptist General Convention of Arizona. The group adopted a budget for 1956 totaling $108,850, of which $70,000 was anticipated through the Cooperative Program from churches, the remainder from Home Mission Board, Sunday School Board, and designated gifts. Twenty per cent of the budget was allocated to the Southern Baptist Convention, 80 per cent to state missions. The meeting was presided over by Paul W. Davis, president of the Baptist General Convention of Arizona, the sponsoring organization. A provisional constitution was approved, and William Caswell Bryant was elected convention president.

FRANK W. SUTTON

COLPORTAGE. See Bible Distribution.

COLUMBIA COLLEGE. At a special meeting in Lake City on July 24–25, 1907, the Florida Baptist State Convention unanimously approved a recommendation of its education committee for establishment of a Baptist college in Lake City to be owned and controlled by the convention. The new school formally opened Oct. 1, 1907, with 133 students enrolled. Its affairs were to be administered by a board of 20 trustees, all of whom were to be members of Florida Baptist churches and elected by the convention. The college property, consisting of 355 acres, eight buildings, and $15,000 in cash, was a gift to the convention from the city council of Lake City. Enrolment of the school grew steadily during its first year, from 133 to more than 200 in later years. Beset with financial difficulties, however, almost from the beginning, the school had increasing problems when Florida experienced a disastrous drouth in 1908. Convention support did not meet operating expenses, and debt piled up year after year. Finally, with a debt of approximately $50,000, the institution was forced to close in Aug., 1918. Two years later, the convention deeded the property of Columbia College to Lake City and discharged the board of trustees.

E. EARL JOINER

COLUMBIAN COLLEGE. Later (1874) Columbian University and since 1903 George Washington University. The school opened with a theological department in 1821 under the auspices of the Triennial Convention (the General Missionary Convention of the Baptist Denomination in the United States) and by authority of a charter granted by Congress. Statesmen like Washington and Monroe had advocated a great national university at the capital, but the Baptists, under the stimulus of Luther Rice's grand concept of a great national Baptist missions-education program, were the only non-Catholics to attempt the project. Rice had raised $6,000 in 1819 and purchased a site. The charter provided for trustees and students of any religious conviction and for teaching of regular classical subjects: law, medicine, and divinity. The board of trustees was practically self-perpetuating. The college opened humbly with the removal by the Convention of its little Theological Institution in Philadelphia with eight students to the new site. William Staughton became president and Ira Chase and Alva Woods theological teachers. Expansion was rapid at first, but by 1824 financial difficulties, under Rice's management, beset the college. In 1825 Chase and the theological department left to establish the Newton Theological Institution in Massachusetts. In 1826 the Convention abandoned the project except to nominate trustees (which they did until 1847). And thereafter Baptist support was by individuals and local groups and was never adequate. In 1832 Congress voted about $25,000 aid. In 1852 the Maryland Baptist Union Association assumed partial control. In 1861 the government took over the buildings, but repaired and returned them in 1865. In 1889 young women were admitted. In 1903, because of poor financial support, control was lost by Baptists and the name changed, leaving no Protestant educational program in the capital to oppose Catholic strength. In 1920–22 some Baptists tried to restore Baptist control, but lost the opportunity due to lack of funds.

BIBLIOGRAPHY: A. H. Newman, *The History of Baptist Churches in the United States* (1915). B. F. Riley, *A History of Baptist Churches in the Southern States East of the Mississippi* (1898). R. G. Torbet, *A Social History of the Philadelphia Baptist Association, 1707–1940* (c. 1945). S. L. STEALEY

COMITY AGREEMENTS. Comity agreements between Northern and Southern Baptists have never been so specific and territorial as the term signifies when related to different faiths. They have usually applied to some particular tensions between the two groups.

Before 1907 Northern Baptists functioned through their societies, having no general convention in the sense known among Southern Baptists. The American Baptist Home Mission Society and the American Publication Society operated rather vigorously in the South for more than half a century after the organization of the Southern Baptist Convention.

The first and perhaps the most historic comity agreement was the Fortress Monroe Comity Agreement of 1894. It derived its name from the place where the committees held their deliberations—Fortress Monroe, Va. The Southern Baptist Convention requested the American Baptist Home Mission Society to function in co-operation with the Home Mission Board of the Southern Baptist Convention in its operations in the South. The Home Mission Society resisted the idea but in time agreed to a joint conference on the idea. In the Fortress Monroe Agreement three things were considered: educational work among Negroes, evangelistic work among Negroes, and the territorial limits to the operation of the American Baptist Home Mission Society and the Southern Baptist Convention.

It was agreed, first, that it was inexpedient for two different organizations of Baptists to solicit funds or to establish missions in the same territory. In the second place it was recommended that when each group had work already established in adjoining or in the same territory, there should be no strife but good will and co-operation wherever practical. It was recommended, in the third place, that each body in establishing new work avoid entering a field where the other had work already initiated or established.

The specific agreements for implementation of these principles provided a co-operative program for work among the Negroes of the South. The Home Mission Society, Home Mission Board, state conventions in the South, and the Negro conventions were to move together in the support of educational and evangelistic operations. The Home Mission Society and the Home Mission Board worked together consistently. The part to be carried out by the state conventions and Negro conventions met only partial success.

The territorial limits were not clearly defined, nor has any subsequent comity conference agreed on specific description of territory. There has been the general idea of an imaginary line running south of Delaware, Pennsylvania, West Virginia, Ohio, Indiana, and Kansas, bisecting Illinois and Missouri. Each group has laid some claim to the southern territory west of Texas. Emigration from the South into the West, adjoining states, and great industrial centers of the central part of the nation has been going on with increasing momentum since the turn of the century. Many Southern Baptists are in that number. For various reasons they have organized churches, associations, and conventions. Sooner or later they seek affiliation with the Southern Baptist Convention.

The situation in New Mexico became rather acute in the first decade of this century. The American Baptist Home Mission Society grew very unhappy about what it considered the violation of the Fortress Monroe Agreement. The Home Mission Board had been receiving insistent requests for assistance for a number of years from Baptist churches in New Mexico. The matter was brought to the attention of the Southern Baptist Convention. When the Home Mission Society reacted very critically to such an idea, the Home Mission Board asked for another comity conference.

The committee from the Home Mission Society, composed of A. S. Hobart, H. L. Morehouse, L. C. Barnes, T. J. Villers, and D. G. Garabrant, and the committee of the Home Mission Board, composed of J. E. Briggs, Sam D. Jones, Governor J. M. Terrell, Baron DeKalb Gray (*q.v.*), and James Franklin Love (*q.v.*), met in Washington, D. C., Apr. 15, 1909. They unanimously agreed that the Home Mission Board of the Southern Baptist Convention should relieve the Home Mission Society of the Northern Baptist Convention of all mission work in New Mexico, expending an amount "next year" equal to that expended by the Home Mission Society "this year" and taking over the Navaho missions property at its cost to the Home Mission Society. This was contingent upon the consent of New Mexico Baptist Convention. They agreed, also, that the question of territorial adjustment be considered settled for at least five years. They further agreed that in case both the Home Mission Society and the Home Mission Board ratified the recommendations of the conference, a joint communication should be addressed to the churches of New Mexico expressing the hope that they would regard this arrangement with favor.

This agreement was ratified by the Home Mission Board and presented to the Southern Baptist Convention with the understanding that nothing in the statement would be so construed as to limit any church, association, or any other

Baptist body in the free exercise of the inalienable right to make such alignment for co-operation as would, in its judgment, be for its own good and for the furtherance of its work. The agreement was adopted by the Southern Baptist Convention but rejected by the Home Mission Society, due to the clarifying clause on free self-determination of churches and other Baptist bodies.

Due to the absence of any joint agreement among Northern and Southern Baptists on the New Mexico operations, the situation deteriorated as to united action. The New Mexico Baptist Convention split over the problem. The Southern Baptist Convention appointed a committee headed by Arthur James Barton (q.v.), seeking to resolve the situation, but to no avail. However, the tragic situation in New Mexico caused both groups to see that another conference was imperative.

The committees met in Old Point Comfort, Va., Sept. 27–28, 1911, and again at Hot Springs, Jan. 24–25, 1912. The principles adopted in these conferences replaced the statements adopted at Fortress Monroe and in subsequent meetings prior to this conference. Whatever guiding principles now applicable to present relations between Southern and American Baptists stem from the final statement agreed upon at Hot Springs in 1912. The subsequent committees headed by Charles William Daniel (q.v.), W. R. White, and T. C. Gardner of the Southern Baptist Convention, in conference with committees from the American Baptist Convention, reiterated these principles and statements adopted in 1912.

R. A. Baker succinctly sums up the three fundamental principles as follows: (1) the independence of the local Baptist church; (2) the moral interdependence and co-operation of Baptist churches; and (3) the advisory nature of all denominational organizations. Three practical applications of the idea of comity were enunciated: (1) The giving of financial aid by a denominational organization should not impair the free autonomy of any church. (2) Denominational organizations should sacredly regard the rights of sister organizations and churches to the end of promoting unity, harmony, and free self-determination. (3) Baptist bodies should never hinder or injure the work of any other Baptist group.

There were other definite, specific recommendations for resolving the distressing friction in New Mexico. These laid the foundation of a day of unity and progress after a period of bitter struggle. The accelerated emigration from the South, and the financial limitations of the Home Mission Society accentuated a complete change-over to a single affiliation with the Southern Baptist Convention and one state convention.

The Southern Baptist Convention made one admitted blunder in its comity practices, in its session in San Antonio, Tex., when it received a group of churches in California as a unit instead of recognizing them as individual churches. This was rectified in its 1944 session.

Several facts and principles emerge in the study of comity agreements between Northern and Southern Baptists:

1. The independence and autonomy of local churches and voluntary and advisory nature of denominational bodies among us make rigid disciplines incongruous and impossible.

2. The immigration of thousands of Southern Baptists into the North and West has produced a new situation.

3. The tremendous switch in the relative strength of the American Baptist and Southern Baptist conventions calls for adjustment.

4. Most of our problems have arisen from our not being sufficiently realistic in a changing situation.

5. There is a great reservoir of good will at the heart of, and in the leadership of, each group sufficient for Christian fellowship and Christian orientation. W. R. WHITE

COMMISSION. See GREAT COMMISSION.

COMMISSION, THE. A monthly periodical, first published by the Foreign Mission Board from Jan. 15, 1849, to Jan. 15, 1851. Its editor was the board's corresponding secretary, James Barnett Taylor (q.v.). A second periodical by the same name was published from June, 1857, to June, 1861, with Alvam Maer Poindexter (q.v.) as editor. Poindexter's statement of the magazine's purpose was: "To impart information, to enforce duty, to keep the subject of missions constantly before the minds of pastors and brethren, to induce self-devotion to missionary work, to excite and guide the spirit of prayer with reference to missions."

The present magazine bearing the name *The Commission* began in Jan., 1938. Charles Edward Maddry, executive secretary of the board, served as its editor for five years, until the board was free of debt and able to add an editor to its staff.

Eugene Coke Routh, with 36 years of experience with Baptist periodicals in Texas and Oklahoma and a vital interest in world missions, became editor May 15, 1943. Two of his books, *The Word Overcoming the World* (1941) and *Scattered Abroad* (1952), cover the history of Southern Baptist foreign missions from the beginning. Following the retirement of Routh in May, 1948, Josef Nordenhaug became editor of the magazine. After serving for two years, he became president of the Baptist Theological Seminary in Switzerland. Since 1950 the board's secretary of education and promotion has served as editor of *The Commission*.

The Commission includes articles by Foreign Mission Board personnel, reports on mission work by area secretaries and by missionaries serving on the fields, features devoted to new types and areas of work, letters from missionaries, photographs and factual briefs of missionary appointees, and reviews of mission books and films. In 1955 circulation of the magazine was 113,880, with the individual subscription rate at $1.00 per year and church subscription rates for every family in the church, 55 cents per year.

Associate and managing editors serving *The Commission* from 1938 to 1956 have been Inabelle G. Coleman, Nan F. Weeks, Archibald M. McMillan, Marjorie Moore (Mrs. O. K.) Armstrong, and Ione Gray. GENEVIEVE GREER

COMMUNION. See LORD'S SUPPER.

COMMUNISM. In the contemporary Soviet sense, a social system which is based upon a materialistic interpretation of reality, and which seeks to establish a classless society by the elimination of private property through revolutionary methods. The theoretical foundations of this type of communism lie in the teachings of Karl Marx. The word signifies different things in different contexts. Originally, the term meant "common ownership." In this sense communism goes back to Plato's *Republic*, in which he advocated a type of utopian society based on a limited community of ownership of private property. The early Christian church practiced a form of common ownership (Acts 2:43-45; 4:32-35), and throughout the Middle Ages monastic orders and certain religious sects (Waldenses and Albigenses) practiced communism to some degree. Secular communistic groups were established by Robert Owen in England and America in the 18th century. Fruitlands and Brook Farm were famous secular communistic societies in America in the 19th century.

Marx's philosophical theories appear most clearly in the *Communist Manifesto* (called the creed of the Communists and written in collaboration with Friedrich Engels) and *Capital* (called the bible of communism). From philosophers G. W. F. Hegel and Ludwig Feuerbach, Marx derived his theory of dialectical materialism. He conceived of history as a dialectic, developing from one form of organization through conflict to the next higher stage by an inevitable, self-determining, progressive movement. This dialectic of history comes to its end in a classless society. From this theory Marx derived his view of historical materialism, which is the notion that the causes of all social change are changes in the modes of production and exchange. He distinguished five stages in economic history: primitive communism, slavery, feudalism, capitalism, and the socialism which has not yet arrived.

The force behind the dialectic of history, claimed Marx, is the struggle between the owning class (the bourgeoisie) and the working class (the proletariat). By appropriating the difference between what the worker produces and what he is paid in wages, the owning class exploits the working class. Thus Marx conceived of labor-time as the measure of value, but he noted that the laborer gets barely enough to live on. The profit which goes to the employer Marx called "surplus value," which he believed rightly belonged to the worker.

Marx reasoned that the class struggle between the owners and the workers would become so intense that eventually the workers would rise up and take over the means of production and exchange. Then the social utopia would be a reality. During the period of reconstruction, a dictatorship of the proletariat would have to be established to inaugurate the program and to put down counterrevolutions.

Since the state, in Marx's opinion, is the instrument of the bourgeoisie to protect their own interests, the first task of the revolution was to capture and to use it. But the state will eventually "wither away" as the proletarian revolution establishes the classless society.

Religion is "the opiate of the people." Thus Marx summed up the communistic attitude toward religion. He said that religion is false, a "reflex of the real world." It is a tool of reaction to calm the desires of the exploited for justice and to ease the consciences of the exploiters. But religion will wither away when its capitalistic ground is removed and religious ideas are educated out of the new generation. Morality in Marxism is relative to time, place, and class. The moral code is the product of particular social needs. It is entirely subordinated to and derived from "the interests of the class struggle of the proletariat." Thus right conduct is that which assists the revolution, the overthrow of capitalism, and the establishment of communism.

From Marxism are derived two major social movements: modern socialism and communism. The former differs from the latter in that it minimizes class warfare, replaces revolutionary action with gradualism, rejects confiscation of property without reimbursement, converts the political state to democratic purposes, and rejects the transitional dictatorship. In communism, socialism is but an intermediate phase which must be consolidated under the dictatorship of the proletariat. The end result is the Communist society, in which class divisions are ended, the state abolished, and men live by the principle: "From each according to his ability; to each according to his need." This is the type of social movement which took root in Russia.

In Russia Marx's followers divided into the Bolsheviki (majority) and Mensheviki (minority) parties. The former advocated revolutionary and the latter evolutionary methods for the advancement of communism. The Bolshevists seized power after the October Revolution of 1917 under the leadership of V. I. Lenin (1870-1924). Lenin's most important contribution to communism was in the field of party organization and tactics. He held that the Party, well disciplined and trained, was necessary to guide and indoctrinate the masses before and after the revolution.

Joseph Stalin (1879-1953), Lenin's successor, also gave new direction to Marxism. The Party was converted into a centralized and all-powerful bureaucracy; the Marxian theory of the state was abandoned; an agrarian policy was adopted, contrary to Lenin's teaching; equalitarianism was condemned; and a new theory of revolution, "socialism in one country," was formulated.

Georgi M. Malenkov succeeded Stalin as head of the Russian state in 1953 and in 1954 resigned, confessing incompetence. He was succeeded by Nikolai Bulganin.

Russian victories in war and diplomatic triumphs at Teheran, Yalta, and Potsdam greatly extended the sway of communism. Communist governments were imposed upon every nation in eastern Europe except Greece. With the beginning of the "cold war" in 1947 between Russia and the free nations, Russia set up an international organization called the Communist Information Bureau (Cominform), whose aims were to direct propaganda against the United States and to cripple the European Recovery Plan.

Communist domination also increased in Asia. Under the leadership of Chou En-lai and Mao Tse-tung, China became Communist. Chiang Kai-shek's nationalist army was defeated in 1949 but still held the island of Formosa. Large areas of French Indo-China had come under Communist control by 1950.

The United States has been a special target of the Communists. Stalin thought that the "Communist Party of the United States is one of the Communist parties to which history has given decisive tasks from the point of view of the world revolutionary movement." The Communist Party of the United States was founded in Chicago in 1919. William Z. Foster, national chairman of the United States Communist Party, clearly stated the aims of the Party when he said: "The American Soviet government will be organized along the lines of the Russian Soviets, . . . will join with the other Soviet governments in a world Soviet Union, . . . will be the dictatorship of the proletariat."

While the Communist Party has never had more than 100,000 members in the United States, its members have been able to penetrate to some degree into government, education, labor unions, the motion picture industry, and other important areas of American life. In 1949 the United States began a campaign to curtail the activities of American Communists, with the result that 11 party members were convicted in court. In 1953 President Eisenhower tightened security measures for federal employees.

In spite of its inevitable involvement in Russian nationalism, communism is a world movement, which has as its goal to effect revolution in every nation. The *Manifesto* closes with a vigorous appeal to win the world for communism:

The Communists disdain to conceal their views and aims. They openly declare that their ends can be attained only by the forcible overthrow of all existing social conditions. Let the ruling classes tremble at a Communist revolution. The proletarians have nothing to lose but their chains. They have a world to win.

Working men of all countries, unite!

BIBLIOGRAPHY: J. C. Bennett, *Christianity and Communism* (1949). R. N. C. Hunt, *The Theory and Practice of Communism* (1951). D. M. Mackinnon, *Christian Faith and Communist Faith* (1953). K. Marx, *Communist Manifesto* (1950); *Capital* (1906). E. E. Palmer, ed., *The Communist Problem in America: A Book of Readings* (1951). E. Rogers, *A Christian Commentary on Communism* (1952). H. G. Wood, *Christianity and Communism* (1933).

HENLEE BARNETTE

COMPERE, EBENEZER LEE (b. near Montgomery, Ala., Feb. 6, 1833; d. Old Dallas, Ark., Nov. 26, 1896). Ninth child of Lee and Susannah Voysey Compere, he was converted and baptized in Montaches Creek Church, Mississippi, in 1849, and preached his first sermon in Mooresville Church in 1851. Compere was educated at Mercer University and Mississippi College, where he received the B.A. and M.A. degrees in 1857 and 1860. He began work as a pastor in Fort Smith, Ark., in 1860, devoting half of his time to work among the Cherokees in Indian Territory. After serving during the Civil War as a chaplain under Stand Watie, Compere returned in Mar., 1866, to his work in Fort Smith, which extended from Little Rock west into Indian Territory. He continued this missionary service until his death in 1896, part of the time employed by the Board of Domestic and Indian Missions, part of the time working independently, organizing churches and sometimes serving as pastor. In 1876 Compere assisted in organization of the General Association of Western Arkansas and the Indian Territory at Charleston, Ark., recognized in 1878 as one of the 21 organizations entitled to representation in the Southern Baptist Convention. Compere was its first moderator and presided over every session except two until 1897. He assisted in the establishment of Buckner College at Witcherville, Ark., chartered in 1879, and helped to begin *The Indian Missionary* at South Canadian, Indian Territory, organ of the general association, for which he wrote many articles. Compere's *Indian Missions for the Five Great Southern Tribes* was published just a few weeks before his death. Seized with a nervous chill during the last session of the general association in 1896, Compere died shortly after this at his home in Old Dallas, Ark.

BIBLIOGRAPHY: A. C. Hickerson, *The Westward Way* (1945).

MRS. AMY COMPERE HICKERSON

COMPERE, LEE (b. Market Harborough, Leicestershire, England, Nov. 3, 1790; d. Navarro County, Tex., June 15, 1871). Pastor, denominational leader, superintendent of Creek Indian Mission in Alabama where he prepared vocabulary and translated Scriptures in their language. He married Susannah Voysey in Nov., 1815. His second marriage was to Sarah Jane Beck, 1836. Converted at the age of 15, he studied under Sutcliff at Olney. He was appointed to Jamaica and sailed Nov. 21, 1815, together with two members of Ryland's church at Broadmead. He began work at Old Harbor, then settled in Kingston. "Much enfeebled by the inclemency of the weather," he resolved to go on to America in 1817.

Compere sailed for Charleston, S. C., became associated with Richard Furman (q.v.), and received help from a ministerial aid fund that had been established for training young ministers. He attended the organization of the state convention of South Carolina as a delegate from Charleston Association, Dec. 1, 1821. He also participated in the organization of the Georgia Baptist Convention, June 27, 1822, and the Alabama convention in 1823, and in 1829 he was its president. He attended the first permanent organization of the Mississippi Baptists, Dec. 4, 1836, and was elected to what we would call today the state mission board; his son-in-law, S. S. Lattimore, was elected first general agent, or as we would say today, executive secretary.

In 1823 he became superintendent of Withington Station, a mission for Creek Indians located in Alabama and "under the patronage of the Baptist Board of Missions of the United States, directed by the joint counsel of the Ocmulgee, Georgia, Ebenezer, and such other associations as may hereafter co-operate with them. . . . According to the regulations prescribed by the general government for Indian improvement." Outstanding features of his ministry to the Creeks was the preparation of a complete vocabulary of their language and translations of portions of the Scriptures. The work was heartily supported until feelings between Indians and white citizens became tense over the dealings of the government, which culminated in the McIntosh affair. Support was withdrawn by Georgia Baptists in 1825; the mission was not concluded until the removal of the Creeks west of the Mississippi in 1829, and Compere continued as superintendent until that time.

He organized the First Baptist Church of Montgomery, Ala., and became its first pastor in Nov., 1829. He founded and was president of the Montgomery Bible Society.

He moved to Mississippi in 1833, settled in Yazoo County, and organized and was president of the Mississippi Education Society. He was deeply involved in the missionary-antimissionary controversy, and was excluded from a Baptist church "because he was a missionary. But another church . . . received him into fellowship immediately."

After brief periods in Tennessee and Arkansas, he moved to Texas, where he lived the last years of his life with his son Thomas Hichichee. *The Freeman* of England and *The Queen's Newsman* of Jamaica carried accounts of his life's service and of his death, as did the American Baptist papers.

"In sentiment and in practice he was a wholesouled *Missionary* . . . without seeming effort commanding the respect of the highest and most distinguished."

His youngest son, Ebenezer, wrote of him, "He ever held to regular baptism, restricted communion, and a strictly Baptist pulpit. But the steady, Christian life, the meek, prayerful, forgiving spirit, he regarded as far more important than mere regularity."

MRS. AMY COMPERE HICKERSON

CONCRETE COLLEGE. A school founded in 1865 by J. V. E. Covey at Concrete, DeWitt County, Tex., not far from Cuero. Although the institution was owned by Covey and was not in a legal sense a denominational school, the relation of Covey to the Baptists of the area was so close and the Baptists' confidence in the school was such that it was practically a Baptist institution. The close fraternal relationship is evidenced by the fact that Covey was pastor at Concrete; also he was elected vice-president of the state convention in 1867. The state convention annual of 1867–68 carried full-page advertisements of Concrete College. Colorado Association went on record as recommending the institution. In 1866 Covey secured Woodlief Thomas as associate director of the school. Under the leadership of these two men, the school served its section of the state well and enjoyed an unusual patronage. In 1873 it had a faculty of 12 and student enrolment of 250. The school was closed in 1880.

RUPERT N. RICHARDSON

CONFEDERATE BAPTIST. Published in Columbia, S. C., from Oct. 1, 1862 to Jan. 25, 1865. Presumably Sherman's burning of Columbia, Feb. 25, 1865, brought about discontinuance of the paper. The four-page *Confederate Baptist*, which had for its motto "Render unto Caesar, the Things That Are Caesar's and unto God the Things That Are God's," was published on Wednesdays and sold for $2 per year. The paper was read not only by people at home but by soldiers in the Confederate army. A prospectus of *The Confederate Baptist Review*, a monthly, appeared constantly in the *Confederate Baptist* during 1864, but there is no evidence that this paper was ever published.

ROBERT A. IVEY

CONFESSION. The acknowledgment of sin to a representative of a church, such as a priest, for the purpose of absolution or counsel. In the Roman Catholic Church the act of confession involves for the confessor the fulfilment of assigned penance; the priest has the right to decree requirements for proper fulfilment of penance and give or refuse absolution. The Greek Orthodox Church expects confession annually, while the Anglican Church provides opportunity as often as the penitent seek it. Baptists hold that confession of sin is indispensable for proper relationship with God; they insist, however, that confession is a personal matter between the individual and God.

BOB SOILEAU

CONFESSIONS OF FAITH, BAPTIST. Few Christian groups have confessed their faith so freely as the Baptists, but no group has been more reluctant than they to elevate these confessions into authoritative symbols or creeds. Baptists have thought of their confessions of faith as manifestos of prevailing doctrine, with each manifesto purporting to stand only for the particular group in whose name it was put forth. Critical periods in Baptist history have generally been productive of new confessions, which have been published in the name of assemblies, conventions, associations, local churches, or even individuals. With changing conditions the confessions have usually been revised or discarded.

Outstanding uses for which Baptist confessions have been designed are the following: (1) as instruments for securing toleration for Baptists, through silencing false accusers; (2) as bases for the association of churches; (3) as educative instruments to strengthen and clarify convictions; (4) as missionary documents; and (5) as means of combating heretical or proselyting movements. Unique features of Baptist confessions have especially concerned the position and worth of the believer, the nature of the church, freedom of conscience and separation of church and state, and the missionary obligation of individuals and churches. Evangelical fervor and tenderness of tone have characterized the confessions, which, also, have almost invariably made room for the concept of the universal or invisible church.

The background of Baptist confessions.—The earliest Baptist confessions were produced against the background of the Protestant Reformation, a movement productive of numerous creeds and confessions. The several Protestant groups sought by means of confessional documents to distinguish their points of view from those of one another. Taking for granted prior evangelical creeds, they did not purport in every case to set forth comprehensive summaries of Christian doctrine.

The pioneer Baptist confessions have a direct line of descent from certain 16th-century documents which might be considered their immediate forerunners. These earlier documents were particularly products of two movements, the radical wing of the Continental Reformation known as Anabaptism, and English Separatism.

A majority of the group of English Separatists of Lincolnshire who became exiles in Amsterdam about 1608, under the leadership of John Smyth, sought to join the Dutch Anabaptists (Mennonites) in 1610. Several confessional statements were exchanged by the two groups. A minority party of the English, led by Thomas Helwys, rejected the idea of union with the Mennonites. In 1611 this group of about 10 published a confession of 27 articles justifying its separate stand. It went beyond the confessions of Smyth and his followers in urging local church autonomy, in denying a succession in church life, and in rejecting Mennonite prohibitions against oaths, bearing arms, and participating in government. This first English Baptist confession was taken to England when the small church returned to bear its witness in the homeland in 1612 and to become the mother church of the General Baptist denomination.

English Baptist associational confessions.—The Particular (or Calvinistic) Baptists appeared in England in the 1630's, coming directly out of the Separatist movement. They held that Christ died for the elect (a particular atonement), while the General Baptists insisted that he died for all men. During the unsettled period of the Civil War and the Commonwealth (1640-60), attacks on the part of opponents, plus the missionary demands of the time, caused Baptists to give attention to the association of churches and induced them to make specific formulations of their faith. The period was more productive of confessions, mostly associational, than any similar period of Baptist history. Noteworthy confessions of the time include the following:

1. The London Confession, 1644. The rapid growth of Baptist sentiments in the London area by 1644 called forth serious opposition to them. Several scurrilous works appeared in the years 1642–44, each seeking to arouse popular suspicion against the Baptists and to confuse people concerning their identity.

To distinguish themselves from both the maligned Anabaptists and the General Baptists, the seven Particular Baptist churches of London determined to prepare a confession of their faith. The confession of 1596 of the London Separatist church of Francis Johnson was used as a model for a larger and more comprehensive document, one of the noblest Baptist confessions of all time. It largely anticipated the Westminster Confession of the Presbyterians (1646), though it was marked by a warmer spirit. It was the first modern confession of Western Europe to require immersion as the only mode of baptism. The confession, though received with skepticism in non-Baptist circles, helped acquaint the English with Baptist views. A second edition (1646) was instrumental in securing legal toleration for the Baptists. Several other editions appeared in the 17th century.

2. The Faith and Practice of Thirty Congregations, 1651. This General Baptist document appears to have been used as an instrument of formal association by churches of the Midlands. It is significant as the first General Baptist confession to represent more than one church.

3. The True Gospel Faith, 1654. The first attempt of the young, aggressive Quaker movement to "occupy" London called forth this confession from some General Baptist churches, since bands of itinerant Quaker preachers, aiming their proselyting efforts especially toward Baptist groups, found their greatest success among the General Baptists. John Griffith led fellow churchmen in preparing a polemic against the Quakers, to which they attached a private confession of one Thomas Lover as a declaration of their faith. The confession used "dipped" for "baptized" and is the first Baptist confession to prescribe laying of hands upon all baptized believers. It appears to have made London Gen-

eral Baptists aware of the Quaker threat and to have steadied the churches in a time of crisis.

4. The Midland Confession, 1655. Seven articles of faith served the Midland Particular Baptists as a doctrinal basis for their association. The confession was intended primarily for instructional and disciplinary uses.

5. The Somerset (or Western) Association Confession, 1656. The Somerset Association, one of the oldest of Particular Baptists, at its seventh meeting, in 1656, published a confession. The Epistle Dedicatory of the document indicates that Quaker inroads were chiefly responsible for its publication, though the confession may have been drawn up earlier.

6. An Antidote Against the Infection of the Times, 1656. Five congregations of "close" Particular Baptists in Wales organized by John Myles, in order to confute the Quakers, published a unique confession in 1656.

To the same period belong also private confessions of John Spilsbery, John Bunyan, Vavasor Powell, and others. New associational confessions occasionally appeared in 18th-century England, but they were seldom published.

English Baptist general confessions.—1. The Standard Confession, 1660. The confession of the General Baptist General Assembly (organized 1654) was called forth in 1660 by the uneasy state of politics immediately before the Restoration. Because Baptists had been prominent in the army and in politics under the Commonwealth, they were now regarded in some quarters as dangerous plotters. To answer the false charges of adversaries, the assembly issued a confession of 25 articles which was presented to King Charles II in July, 1660.

London General Baptists were preponderantly represented in the confession of 1660, but not all London General Baptists approved it. Before 1659 a group of churches there, led by John Griffith, urged the adoption of the "six principles" of Hebrews 6:1-2 as the sole creedal standard. The new symbol became a divisive issue in the general assembly by 1660. The assembly approved an article on laying on of hands, but even this action did not keep the Griffith churches in the group. In 1665 the assembly appeased the dissidents by adopting both the 1660 confession and the six principles. In 1690 there was another division, and the Six-Principle Baptists set up their own assembly.

A general assembly of 1663 revised and reaffirmed the confession of 1660. From that time it was called the Standard Confession. Serving the churches as a basis of union for well over 40 years, the confession was especially valuable as a specific, stabilizing body of doctrine during the dark years of repression, 1664–72, when little intercourse and organization were possible.

2. The Assembly Confession, 1677 and 1689. The Restoration brought upon dissenters a period of severe testing. The renewal of persecution drew dissenting groups nearer to one another. Fear of a return of popery to England furnished further stimulus to interdenominational co-operation. Baptists and Congregationalists wished to form a united front with the strong Presbyterian body. Particular Baptists of the London area took the lead in 1677, putting out their revision of the Westminster Confession. William Collins of London did most of the work of editing the new confession. Major alterations of the Westminster creed were made on the doctrines of the church and the ordinances, but the purpose of the new confession was to show "hearty agreement" with Presbyterians and Congregationalists.

At the first general meeting of Particular Baptists, Sept., 1689, following the ascension of William and Mary to the English throne, a general assembly of this group was formed, and the confession of 1677 was approved. Known as the Assembly or Second London Confession, this became one of the most influential of all Baptist confessions. Benjamin Keach of London worked over and condensed the document in 1697, and it was then published in the name of the churches of Keach and his son, Elias. In this form it found its way to America.

3. The Orthodox Creed, 1678. General Baptists quickly followed the example of their Particular brethren when a large segment of them from several Midland counties prepared a new confession to "unite and confirm all true Protestants." Their Orthodox Creed was also designed to refute certain current heretical views regarding Christ. The Westminster Confession again served as a model, but it was followed less closely than in the confession of 1677. The general assembly never adopted the confession of 1678.

4. The Somerset Confession, 1691. A protest against the heightened Calvinism of the Second London Confession came from the west of England in 1691. Churches of the area issued a 27-article confession, which reflected the changing theology of Thomas Collier (cf. the Somerset Confession of 1656) and his wish to include General as well as Particular churches within his circle.

5. The Unity of the Churches, 1704. This document was designed to reunite two General Baptist bodies whose doctrinal differences dated from a 1696 schism.

6. Articles of Faith of the New Connexion, 1770. The Evangelical Awakening of the second half of the 18th century gave the General Baptists a new start with the movement of Daniel Taylor known as the New Connexion of General Baptists. At its formation in 1770, this New Connexion drew up a confession to which, for a few years, new ministers had to subscribe. The articles continued in use for most of the next century.

7. Doctrinal Statement of the Baptist Union, 1888. The Baptist Union of Great Britain and Ireland, formed in 1888 and including Particular and General Baptists after 1891, adopted a brief doctrinal statement in the former year. It has not known wide use.

Confessions of Faith, Baptist

American Baptist confessions.—No confessions are known to have been used among the early Baptists of New England. In the South some of the earliest Baptists held Arminian views, and these seem generally to have acknowledged the Standard Confession of 1660. Their movement was overwhelmed, however, in the second half of the 18th century by Calvinistic Baptists who looked to Philadelphia as their center. It was in the Philadelphia area that the most prominent early confession was circulated in America.

1. The Philadelphia Confession, 1742. Elias Keach of London was converted and became pastor in this area in 1688. Returning to London in 1692, he became pastor of a church there. The articles of faith which he and his father published in 1697 in the name of their churches were almost exactly the Assembly Confession, with the addition of articles on hymn singing and laying on of hands. This so-called "Keach's Confession" became the confession of the Philadelphia Association (organized 1707). This confession came either directly from Elias Keach to Philadelphia or by way of Welsh Baptists, whom Benjamin Keach had influenced before their coming to America. Welsh Baptists were prominent in the early history of the Philadelphia Association, and they insisted upon hymn singing and laying on of hands. For many years before its formal adoption by the association in 1742, the confession was the accepted doctrinal standard among churches of the area. It was first printed for the association by Benjamin Franklin in 1743, having the two articles added to the Assembly Confession by the Keaches. A treatise on discipline was appended to it.

Many early associations adopted the Philadelphia Confession, among them the Kehukee of North Carolina (1765), the Ketocton of Virginia (1766), the Warren of Rhode Island (1767), and the Charleston of South Carolina (1767). This last association rejected the article on laying on of hands. It was in the area of the Carolinas that the confession exerted extraordinary influence, especially among Baptists who had once held Arminian views. Throughout the South it shaped Baptist thought generally and has perhaps been the most influential of all confessions. Local church covenants still reflect its outlook.

The Separate Baptist movement, coming out of the Great Awakening of New England, at first rejected all confessions of faith. However, the Separate General Association of Virginia cautiously adopted the Philadelphia Confession in 1783. This confession also served as the basis of union of Separate and Regular Baptists in Virginia in 1787. It passed into the background of Baptist affairs in the 19th century, though it continued to be referred to in America as "the Baptist Confession."

2. Articles of Faith of the Kehukee Association, 1777. What was perhaps the first purely American Baptist confession was adopted by the Kehukee Association in 1777. A document of 17 articles, it was designed to meet objections of Separate Baptist churches to the Philadelphia Confession and to declare against Arminianism and lax disciplinary standards. The articles are still in use by the Kehukee Primitive Association.

3. Terms of Union of United Baptists of Kentucky, 1801. Regular and Separate Baptists in Kentucky united in 1801 on the basis of a brief original doctrinal statement of 10 articles.

4. Principles of Faith of the Sandy Creek Association, 1816. The famous Sandy Creek Separate Baptist Association of North Carolina adopted, with the help of Luther Rice (*q.v.*), 10 principles of faith in 1816.

5. The New Hampshire Confession, 1833. The rise of Free Will Baptists in New England after 1780, under the pioneer leadership of Benjamin Randall, resulted in some theological accommodation on the part of Calvinistic Baptists of that area. In 1830 the convention of New Hampshire authorized the preparation of a new confession, asserting that known declarations of faith were not "in precisely the same language as it is desirable they should be." The Calvinism of the group was restated in very moderate tones in a confession which was published in 1833.

This document might not have become known outside of New Hampshire except for the work of one of its authors, J. Newton Brown, who, 20 years later, was editorial secretary of the American Baptist Publication Society. In 1853 Brown revised the confession on his own authority and published it in *The Baptist Church Manual*. Articles on "Repentance and Faith" and "Sanctification" were added by him. In Brown's and other manuals the confession became the most widely distributed creedal declaration of American Baptists. Its silence on the doctrine of the universal church made it particularly adaptable to the emphasis of the "Landmark" Baptists of the South, following its introduction by J. M. Pendleton (*q.v.*). Landmark Baptists of the Southwest (now the American and the North American Baptist associations) adopted the confession in 1902, along with a supplementary doctrinal statement. Also, in 1933 the General Association of Regular Baptists, a movement of protest against theological liberalism and denominational policies in the Northern Convention, adopted the New Hampshire Confession, with a premillenial interpretation of its last article.

6. Treatise of the Free Will Baptists, 1834 and 1935. The Free Will Baptist movement of New England resisted the use of confessions until 1832. The general conference of the body adopted a treatise or confession in 1834 which was revised in 1869. The merging of this large group of Baptists with the Northern Convention in 1911 did not mean entire disuse of the treatise. In the South the "Original Free Will Baptists" continued their separate existence, and their general conference formulated a treatise in 1935, based on that of the New England group. A revision of this treatise, adopted in

1948, continues in use by churches of the National Association of Free Will Baptists.

7. *Fundamentalist Confessions, 1921 and 1923.* The fundamentalist-modernist controversy of the 1920's produced several new Baptist confessions. The Fundamental Fellowship of the Northern Convention adopted a short confession of Frank M. Goodchild in 1921. This group sought unsuccessfully the approval of such a declaration by the Northern Convention. Even a resolution that the New Hampshire Confession be recommended to the churches was rejected by that body. The Goodchild Confession was adopted by the Conservative Baptist Foreign Mission Society in 1943 and later became the doctrinal platform of the Conservative Baptist Association of America. Another Fundamentalist organization among Northern Baptists, the Baptist Bible Union, produced a confession in 1923.

8. *Statement of Faith of the Southern Baptist Convention, 1925.* In the Southern Baptist Convention the controversy over evolutionary theory led, in 1925, to the adoption of a statement of faith by that body. This statement was an enlargement of a statement of principles of 1919 (based upon the New Hampshire Confession) which had been prepared as a worldwide greeting to Baptists following World War I. The Sunday School Board has continued to publish the document under the title *Baptist Faith and Message.*

The Sunday School Board of the National Baptist Convention, U.S.A., Inc., published in *The Baptist Standard Church Directory* (1929) articles of faith taken from the New Hampshire and the Southern Baptist Convention confessions. These articles are the only confession known to represent American Negro Baptists.

Confessions of other nationalities.—Baptist confessions among groups other than English and American Baptists include the following: Confession of the German Baptist Union (1849, revised in 1944); Confession of the Swedish Baptist Union (1861); Confession of the French Baptist Union (1879); Confession of the Convention of Ontario and Quebec, Canada (1925). Some other Baptist unions employ doctrinal bases or basic statements of belief.

BIBLIOGRAPHY: J. M. Cramp, *Baptist History* (1869). T. Crosby, *History of English Baptists* (1738). W. J. McGlothlin, *Baptist Confessions of Faith* (1911). G. W. Purefoy, *A History of the Sandy Creek Baptist Association* (1859). R. B. Semple, *History of the Rise and Progress of the Baptists of Virginia* (1894). J. H. Spencer, *A History of Kentucky Baptists* (1886). W. T. Whitley, *A Baptist Bibliography* (1916).

WILLIAM L. LUMPKIN

CONGER, JOHN WALTER (b. Jackson, Tenn., Feb. 20, 1857; d. Fort Smith, Ark., Apr. 7, 1924). Organizer and first president of Ouachita College. He was graduated from Southwestern Baptist University (later Union University), Jackson, Tenn., with the A.B. degree in 1878, received the A.M. degree in 1883, and the LL.D. in 1896. He spent most of his time after graduation in organizing or administering several schools, and in June, 1886, was elected president of Ouachita College, Arkadelphia, Ark., which he organized, and which opened on Sept. 6, 1886, with six teachers and 100 students. Under his leadership an administration building was completed by June, 1889, at a cost of about $40,000. A girls' dormitory, a conservatory, and a president's home were also built during his presidency. He served until 1908, when he resigned to become president of Union University for two years. He then became president of Central College, Conway, Ark., and served from 1911 to 1919.

Conger is credited with being Arkansas Baptists' most important leader in the field of education. The success of Ouachita College was in large measure his personal achievement; although agents were hired at various times to raise money for buildings, Conger was responsible for administration, enlistment of students, and securing whatever money was necessary for the school's support beyond tuition and fees.

Conger was married twice; in 1882 to Carrie McKinney, who died the next year; and in 1884 to Tenny Hamilton, who bore him four children, and who died in 1923. Conger was buried with his second wife on the campus of Ouachita College.

J. S. ROGERS, SR.

CONGREGATION, THE LOCAL. Except for first-century Christianity and the Bible, no one seems to know the antecedents for congregationalism among Baptists. It is known that early English Baptists practiced great freedom in the local church, it being free and independent. The emphasis was so strong, in fact, upon self-government of the local church that not even an association of churches was founded by Baptists until 1653. The General Assembly of the General Baptists, formed in 1671, attempted an overlordship which some believe contributed to its partial failure. It was partially this fear by the churches of an overlordship which made organization into associations and conventions so difficult in the early years of Baptist life.

The tenacious desire for complete self-government in the local church has kept Baptists wary of creed-makers. W. J. McGlothlin (*q.v.*) says:

Being congregational and democratic in church government, Baptists have naturally been very free in making, changing, and using Confessions. There has never been among them any ecclesiastical authority which could impose a Confession upon their churches or other bodies. Their Confessions are, strictly speaking, statements of what a certain group of Baptists, large or small, did believe at a given time.

As early as 1612, the election of officers for the church was a congregational procedure. As late as 1928, an Executive Committee report to the Southern Baptist Convention, growing out of a dispute over an "evolution clause" Oklahoma Baptists had demanded, brought into clear focus again, not only that local congregations among Baptists were autonomous, but that all

Baptist groups were so considered. South Carolina, like other Southern Baptist states, so recognized this independence that it wrote into its first constitution that the convention "shall recognize the independence and liberty of the churches." Eventually, the word "delegate" was changed to "messenger," implying no overlordship, and messengers came to be sent from churches only rather than from other Baptist bodies to the meetings of general bodies.

BIBLIOGRAPHY: W. W. Barnes, *The Southern Baptist Convention, 1845–1953* (1953). J. C. Carlile, *The Story of English Baptists* (1905). *The Carolina Baptist* (Sept., 1845). H. K. Carroll, *The Religious Forces of the United States* (1893). J. T. Christian, *A History of the Baptists* (1922). V. Ferm, ed., *The American Church of Protestant Heritage* (1953). J. C. Furman, "Historical Discourse" (1852). C. M. Griffin, *The Story of South Carolina Baptists* (1934). W. B. Johnson, an address, *The Edgefield Advertiser* (May 7, 1845). M. M. Lappin, *Baptists in the Protestant Tradition* (1947). W. J. McGlothlin, *Baptist Confessions of Faith* (1911). "The Philadelphia Confession," *The Baptist Encyclopaedia* (1881). L. Townsend, *South Carolina Baptists, 1670–1805* (1935). H. C. Vedder, *A Short History of Baptists* (1907). H. Woodson, *Giant in the Land* (1950).

C. EARL COOPER

CONNER, WALTER THOMAS (b. Cleveland County, Ark., Jan. 19, 1877; d. Fort Worth, Tex., May 26, 1952). Theologian, educator. The son of Philip Orlando and Frances (Monk) Conner, he moved with his parents from Arkansas to a Taylor County, Tex., farm at the age of five. Converted during a Methodist revival and baptized into the Baptist church at Caps, Tex., Conner was ordained a Baptist minister in Oct., 1899. Educated in ungraded country schools, at Simmons College, Baylor University (A.B., 1906; M.A., 1908), and Baylor Theological Seminary (Th.B., 1908), he was pastor of rural and village churches at Tuscola, Caps, Eagle Lake, Rock Island, East Bernard, Blum, and Rio Vista, Tex. A student in Rochester, N. Y., Theological Seminary during 1908–10, Conner was also supply pastor of the Congregational Church, Wheatville, N. Y. He received the B.D. degree in 1910. He joined the faculty of the Southwestern Baptist Theological Seminary at the time of its removal to Fort Worth in 1910, succeeding Calvin Goodspeed (q.v.), and served for 39 years as professor of systematic theology. During 1914 he studied in the Southern Baptist Theological Seminary, from which he received the Th.D. degree in 1916 and the Ph.D. degree in 1931. Additional study was done at the University of Chicago in 1910 and 1920. His books were written as follows: *A System of Christian Doctrine* (1924), *Gospel Doctrines* (1925), *The Resurrection of Jesus* (1926), *The Teachings of Mrs. Eddy* (1926), *The Teachings of "Pastor" Russell* (1926), *The Epistles of John* (1929), *Revelation and God* (1936), *Personal Christianity* (1937), *Christian Doctrine* (1937), *The Christ We Need* (1938), *The Faith of the New Testament* (1940), *The Gospel of Redemption* (1945), *What Is a Saint?* (1948), *The Work of the Holy Spirit* (1949), and *The Cross in the New Testament* (1954). A frequent contributor to theological journals and to denominational publications, Conner lectured to Bible conferences and summer assemblies and held supply pastorates and evangelistic meetings. He was the first pastor of the Seminary Hill Baptist Church, now the Gambrell Street Baptist Church, Fort Worth, Tex. In 1907 he married Blanche Ethel Horne, and they were the parents of six children: Mary, John Davis, Arnette, Blanche Ray, Neppie Lee, and Sarah. Mrs. Conner, together with her husband, has pioneered in a Christian ministry to the Chinese in Fort Worth.

Conner combined in his own teaching certain aspects of the theological systems of three of his teachers, Benajah Harvey Carroll (q.v.) of Baylor, Augustus Hopkins Strong (q.v.) of Rochester, and Edgar Young Mullins (q.v.) of Louisville. Influenced in early years by personalism, Conner gave stress to the self-consistency of the divine attributes, tended toward kenoticism in Christology, leaned toward Calvinism on election, moved from a modified penal theory to an interpretation of the cross approximating Aulen's *Christus victor* idea, insisted that justification was "vital" and not "declarative," and changed from postmillennialism to amillennialism in eschatology. Although giving much emphasis to Christian experience and the work of the Holy Spirit, the Conner theology was not purely mystical. While critical of Barth's paradoxism and denial of general revelation, Conner was somewhat influenced on revelation by contemporary movements and did not attempt to set forth a theory of inspiration. Conner's doctrinal position, classroom method, missionary zeal, and characteristic wit were woven into the fabric of Southwestern Baptist Theological Seminary and its alumni.

BIBLIOGRAPHY: *Who's Who in America*, Vol. 26 (1950–51). J. M. Price, ed., *Southwestern Men and Messages* (1948). L. R. Scarborough, *A Modern School of the Prophets* (1939).

J. L. GARRETT

CONNIE MAXWELL CHILDREN'S HOME. Established by the South Carolina Baptist convention in 1891, with the first child admitted May 22, 1892. Governed by a board of 15 trustees elected by the convention, the home is located in Greenwood, S. C., on an 800-acre tract of land, 470 acres of which was a gift of the late John Chappell Maxwell and his wife with the proviso that the institution be located in Greenwood and bear the name of their daughter, Connie Maxwell, who died at eight years of age. The name was changed in 1946 from Orphanage to Children's Home, to embrace the program of care for children from homes broken by divorce and separation. The home has served about 3,000 children since its establishment.

Consisting of 35 buildings, the plant includes 20 cottages in which children live, church, infirmary, library, print and wood shops, school, administration building, five staff cottages, and auxiliary buildings. Livestock, poultry and truck farms, print and general maintenance shops are operated in connection with the home.

In 1954 total assets were over $2,000,000, including land, buildings, equipment, and permanent endowment funds of $500,000. An annual budget of $325,000 provided care for 450 children, with 65 per cent of the budget coming from monthly offerings of Sunday schools, 20 per cent from the Cooperative Program, and 15 per cent from endowment funds, personal gifts, and relatives of children.

The purpose of the children's home is to provide Christian training and development for children in South Carolina who are not given adequate care and protection by their own parents and relatives. A carefully selected staff of 55, including seven trained social workers, Christian home life emphasis, an organized church on the grounds, public school education, recreational activities, a preventive emphasis on medical care, and training in manual skills have advanced this purpose.

Extra-institutional services, such as mother's aid, foster family care, and adoption, instituted in 1925 had become by 1948 an integral part of the total program, providing flexibility in meeting the changing needs of children. Special attention is now being given to follow-up work for graduates, who, through loan funds and a plan of self help, have opportunities for college education and other special training. Social services, provided for children who can be returned to their own families, require intensive work with the families of the children under care. Assistance of pastors, laymen, and social agencies in planning and counseling has produced many resources in broken families for the future welfare and development of children.

SAM M. SMITH

CONSCIENTIOUS OBJECTORS. Those who refuse combatant training and service in the armed forces of the United States because of religious convictions. The National Service Board for Religious Objectors reported to the House Armed Service Committee on Apr. 19, 1948, that 11,997 men were classified as conscientious objectors during World War II. The Social Service Commission reported to the 1944 Southern Baptist Convention that 23 members of their churches were enrolled as conscientious objectors. Southern Baptists have made no provisions to care for conscientious objectors in camps. The Convention has, however, made several recommendations and pronouncements relative to the over-all matter. The 1940 Convention recognized the right of a conscientious objector to his convictions and instructed its Executive Committee to provide facilities for his registration with the denomination. In 1944 the Convention approved the commission's report in which it was stated:

. . . The preservation of freedom of conscience which is basic to every freedom of our cherished democracy is the first charge upon the Christian churches of America in the midst of this global war. . . . That the secretary of the Executive Committee be authorized to receive and transmit to the National Service Board any funds that persons or churches may desire to contribute to this cause.

In 1946 the Convention requested the Executive Committee to study the matter of reimbursing the agencies who lent assistance to its members while in camps. The Convention also urged the President of the United States to grant amnesty at the earliest possible moment to those objectors still held in camps or prisons. The commission also recommended opposition to peacetime military conscription.   H. C. GABHART

CONSECRATION. See SANCTIFICATION.

CONSERVATIVE BAPTIST ASSOCIATION OF AMERICA. Organized May 17, 1947, at Atlantic City, N. J., a wholly independent and separate Baptist group. It is a successor to the Fundamentalist Fellowship (founded 1920) that operated within the Northern Baptist Convention in protest against the "inclusive" policy of Northern (American) Baptists under which missionaries of both liberal and conservative views were sent out to foreign fields. Complete separation from American Baptists was slow and did not come until 1951. In Aug., 1954, Conservative Baptists reported 596 churches as completely affiliated and 203 others as affiliated only with a local conservative association. In 1955 it had 998 churches with 970 ministers and 250,000 members. However, in 1954, 1,634 churches contributed to its $1,500,000 foreign mission program that supported or helped support 331 missionaries. The association maintains a paper called the *Highlights*.   ALBERT MCCLELLAN

CONSERVATIVE BAPTIST FOREIGN MISSION SOCIETY, THE. A 20th-century fundamentalist movement, founded in the Tabernacle Baptist Church in Chicago, Ill., Dec. 15, 1943. It was initiated by the Fundamentalist Fellowship in protest over the alleged "modernism" of the American Baptist Foreign Mission Society. The Conservative Foreign Mission Society was an outgrowth of the Back to the Bible Movement which was launched in 1920. The function of the society is to carry the gospel to all parts of the world exclusive of the North American continent which is served by the Conservative Baptist Home Mission Society. The society's first mission endeavors were in India and China. Sixty-six missionaries were under appointment by Dec., 1945; and by Sept., 1949, this number had increased to 132 active missionaries in 11 countries. In 1954 there were 320 missionaries and appointees of the society. These were at work in more than a dozen mission fields of the world. The total income for the year ending Apr. 30, 1954, was $1,330,557.70.   L. A. BROWN

CONSTITUTION, SOUTHERN BAPTIST CONVENTION. The fundamental definitions which the Southern Baptist Convention has developed and adopted to guide it in its work. In spite of numerous amendments, the constitution of the Southern Baptist Convention has undergone surprisingly little real change since its adoption by "the delegates from Missionary Societies, Churches, and other religious bodies of the Baptist Denomination, in various parts of the United States, met in Convention, in the city of Augusta, Georgia," in May, 1845. The Southern Baptist Convention was established "for the purpose of carrying into effect the benevolent intentions of our constituents, by organizing a plan for eliciting, combining and directing the energies of the whole denomination in one sacred effort, for the propagation of the Gospel." Its constitution still contains this purpose, almost entirely in these same words. Throughout the years the basic organization has been the same. The Convention has consistently done its work through boards, institutions, and commissions following the denominational pattern in which it began. It has been the one agency through which Southern Baptists have done all their co-operative work, of whatever character, outside the areas of associations and state conventions.

Aside from amendments which have proved temporary and amendments which were designed to add emphasis rather than change meaning, the changes which have been made in the constitution have grown out of the needs of the Convention's growing organization, work, and program. These changes were made in pragmatic fashion through the years, and in 1946 a comprehensive revision was adopted, which eliminated conflicts and inconsistencies and increased explicitness and precision of statement. In addition several changes were made. The president of the Convention was made a member of each of the several boards and of the Convention's Executive Committee. A system of rotation was set up which made board members ineligible for more than two successive three-year terms. Exceptions were made in the case of those whose special services in medical, legal, or financial matters made it advisable that they be continued as board members.

The article which has been most often changed is number 3, dealing with representation. From the beginning, the Convention has based representation on contributions, reasoning that the giving of money is the most obvious proof of co-operation, and that the constituency of the Convention should be from those churches and church members which support it. This money basis of representation has come under repeated attack, usually because of Landmarkism or Gospel Missionism, but it is still in force, presently as an alternative to representation based on membership.

Other limitations have also been placed on membership. In 1859, as a result of Landmark opposition to visiting fraternal messengers from other denominations, there was added to the original article the words, "provided that no person shall be a member of the convention who is not a member in good standing of a regular Baptist church." The same prohibition is implicit in the present definition of messengers as persons "who are members of missionary Baptist churches co-operating with the Convention." In 1885 messengers were defined as "brethren" instead of simply as "members" in order to prohibit the admission of women. This limitation was removed in 1918.

Another article which has been often changed is the present number 11, dealing with meetings of the Convention. In the beginning the Convention met triennially, then biennially, later annually. Registration at Convention sessions has increased from 236 in 1845 to 12,254 in 1956. Changes in this article were made as problems arose, and reflect the increasing complexity of arrangements for meetings brought on by increasing attendance.

Most other changes, which have affected the Convention's bylaws and its business and financial plan more than the constitution itself, have been a reflection of the Convention's growth from its simple beginnings suited to its then present situation to the essentially more complex structure made necessary by its enlargement. The development of the Executive Committee of the Convention and the founding of new boards, institutions, and commissions have been reflected in the constitution. The coming of new methods, such as the Cooperative Program, have necessitated certain amendments. But in spite of all these changes, the basic essence of the constitution has remained unchanged. The convention plan of organization, which provides for a single denominational organization through which all co-operating churches carry on all their denomination-wide work, was defined by the constitution adopted in 1845, and has remained the basis of Southern Baptist denominationalism. FRANK NORFLEET

CONSTITUTION AND BY-LAWS OF A BAPTIST CHURCH, NORTH CAROLINA. Prior to 1954 very few Baptist churches in North Carolina operated their affairs according to a printed constitution and by-laws, but following the North Rocky Mount Baptist Church case, the value of such a document became more apparent. During the 1953 annual session of the state convention, a motion was passed authorizing the appointment of a committee of five to work with the general secretary in preparing a suggested constitution and by-laws for a Baptist church. This committee was to report to the general board and distribute copies of the suggested constitution and by-laws to the churches. Since Nov., 1954, several thousand copies have been distributed to churches throughout the state and beyond.

The suggested constitution deals with the purpose and membership of the church; meetings; church officers; and general items, such as, license and ordination of ministers, affiliation with associations and conventions, and property holding. The by-laws deal with specific meetings for worship, observance of the ordinances, and the transaction of business. Listing other church officers and heads of the organizations with their duties and responsibilities, the by-laws also suggest several standing committees with a detail of their duties. Election and function of the nominating committee receive special consideration. The three addenda included with the printed document are (1) the church covenant; (2) the Articles of Faith adopted by the Southern Baptist Convention in 1925; and (3) some suggested rules of order for use in regular business sessions of the church. G. W. BULLARD

CONVENTION, THE STATE BAPTIST. The concept of a Baptist state convention in 1955 was that it is an organization created out of Baptist experience to enable Baptist churches and other Baptist bodies to serve the missionary, educational, benevolent, stewardship, civic, and other needs through the state area and, by co-operation with larger bodies, to extend their ministry around the world. Like all other Baptist bodies, the state convention chooses its own membership and is sovereign within the bounds set by its constitution. The Baptist principle of voluntary co-operation enables the state convention to render vital ministries to its own constituency and to be the vehicle through which its constituency can efficiently minister to many interests which they feel called to serve within their own state, and through which they can participate in the larger ministries of the Southern Baptist Convention and the Baptist World Alliance. The co-operative organization next larger than the district association, the state convention is the body through which Baptists provide for themselves institutions and programs of promotion and missions, which are related to a local area but which cannot succeed without the support of a constituency larger than that of the district association.

The first co-operative organizations of Baptists, associations, began to be organized more than a century before the beginning of the state conventions. These associations were organized for fellowship and counsel. There were few newspapers in the early days, and information was gained from circular letters and correspondence. The annual meetings of Baptists strengthened the bonds of faith and, through profitable discussions, found answers to perplexing problems involving Baptist doctrines and polity.

Associational meetings revealed the need for something else. The foreign mission awakening, first in the sending out of William Carey (q.v.), then in the conversion of Adoniram Judson (q.v.) to the Baptist position, followed by the vigorous promotion of missions by Luther Rice (q.v.), gave many associations clearer visions of world needs and obligations and pointed the way toward new forms of organization. Kentucky Baptists, for example, made attempts "to organize a state body to provide for a more extended field of co-operation in missionary endeavor than that of the district association." The first such state convention in the South was formed in South Carolina, Dec., 1821; the second, in Georgia, June, 1822. In several of the states, such as Virginia, Kentucky, and Missouri, these state bodies were called general associations, in order to avoid the opposition engendered by the name "convention."

Early efforts at organization were often unwisely defined or were too much opposed to be able to accomplish a great deal. Antimissionism, Campbellism, Landmarkism, and various disagreements over methods of carrying on the work delayed or frustrated many efforts at organization. In Kentucky the first state organization, called the Kentucky Baptist Convention, lasted only from 1832 to 1837, when it was succeeded by an organization which survived. In Virginia the first state organization, after the initial General Association of the Separate Baptists of the state, was the General Committee (1784–99), then the General Meeting of Correspondence of the United Baptist Associations in Virginia. This body was largely ineffectual, because although it "continued its annual sessions, its constitution gave it almost nothing to do." This misfortune, according to Garnett Ryland, was due to the "great jealousy in the district associations and among Baptists generally of any body that was supposed to be able to encroach on the liberties and prerogatives of the churches."

Rival conventions within a single state also delayed progress. In Texas the first association, Union, was organized in 1840. The Baptist State Convention was formed in 1848; the Baptist General Association, in 1868; and three others, later. There were two schools, Baylor University and Waco University, and two rival papers, the *Texas Baptist Herald* and *The Texas Baptist*. In 1886 a program of consolidation was effected which resulted in one general state body, the Baptist General Convention of Texas; one university, Baylor, removed from Independence to Waco; and one Baptist paper, the *Texas Baptist and Herald*. In what is now the state of Oklahoma, there were at one time four general bodies, two in Indian Territory and two in Oklahoma territory, which grew out of conflict between the Home Mission Society (Northern Baptist) and the Home Mission Board (Southern Baptist). In New Mexico, Oklahoma, Missouri, and Illinois, controversies were precipitated by similar issues involving divided loyalties to North and South.

The state bodies, from the beginning, stressed foreign missions, the enlargement of district associations to reach destitution in the state, Sunday schools, the publication of Baptist papers, pastoral support, and ministerial education. These interests led naturally to the founding of institutions and the eventual development of promotional programs, which together occupy most of the energies and resources of state conventions. In 1955 most Southern Baptist state conventions owned and supported schools, hospitals, assemblies, orphanages, and other benevolent institutions. They shared in the planning and promotion of activities related to every phase of Baptist life and work. They co-operated with other groups in work on various social problems. In addition, they were involved in the administration of endowments and trust funds and in helping to provide for the relief and retirement of their ministers. E. C. ROUTH

CONVENTION PRESS. Publishing medium of the Sunday School Board of the Southern Baptist Convention for books and booklets of strictly denominational character, designed to be sold exclusively through the Baptist Book Stores and publishing houses owned by other denominations. Until 1934 when Broadman Press was introduced, the Sunday School Board published all its books under its own name. As "Broadman" gained recognition during the next two decades, some of the Sunday school and Training Union study books were published under that imprint, as were also some books published for Woman's Missionary Union and the Foreign Mission Board. On Feb. 10, 1955, however, the Sunday School Board adopted "Convention Press" as the imprint for all such books, plus other general books which would be designed primarily for Southern Baptist readers. Thus, the Broadman imprint was reserved for general trade books, while Convention Press secured a larger and better controlled distribution for curricular and denominational books.
See also SUNDAY SCHOOL BOARD and BROADMAN PRESS. WILLIAM J. FALLIS

CONVENTION TEACHER. See TEACHER, THE.

CONVERSION. The term as it is used popularly among Southern Baptists refers to the experience of repentance (what man does) and regeneration (what God does). It is used to describe that unique experience in which an individual is united with God in Christ and is made into a "new creature." It is the experience of which Jesus spoke when he said to Nicodemus, "Ye must be born again." This unique experience happens only once and is needed only once.

Used in this way, the term "conversion" is not an entirely accurate designation for the experience described above. The word comes from the Latin, *conversio,* a turning round, revolving, revolution (Greek, *epistrepho,* to turn to, to turn oneself about).

There are different types of conversion experience, varying from the highly emotional, cataclysmic experience to the quiet acceptance of Christ as Saviour and commitment to him. The outward expression of the experience is often greatly influenced by the kind of life the person has lived previously.

One's view of the conversion experience is closely related to his doctrine of man and his doctrine of the church. On the basis of the universality of sin, Baptists have held that all stand in need of regeneration. The child, even the child of Christian parents, is not a member of the kingdom of God. However, before the period of accountability the child is "safe" in God's prevenient grace.

Regeneration is a highly individualistic and personal matter. For this reason Baptists have rejected infant baptism since in this sacrament the family and the church are acting in behalf of the child without the conscious, free, personal choice of the child. The nurture given by the church and the Christian family is not minimized, but after the church, the family, and all other influences have done all they can for the individual, the individual's relationship with God in Christ is sealed—and must be—by his own free, conscious, voluntary choice.
See also SALVATION, REPENTANCE, REGENERATION. FINDLEY B. EDGE

CONVICTION OF SIN. The experience of the sinner in which he recognizes that his life is not in harmony with the will of God. Conviction is the work of the Holy Spirit, who brings home to the sinner what sin is, in the light of the righteousness and holy love of God, as these are revealed in Christ. Conviction is related at every point directly to Christ. The remorse and despair of himself which the sinner experiences before Christ, is preparatory to repentance and the acceptance of the salvation which Christ bestows. J. E. TULL

COOPER, DAVIS CLAY, SR. (b. Anniston, Ala., May 22, 1866; d. Oxford [suburb of Anniston], Ala., Nov. 15, 1943). Prominent Baptist layman and businessman in central Alabama for half a century. The son of Charles J. and Harriet (Johnson) Cooper, he married Annie Constantine in June, 1888. To that union were born five children: Davis Clay, Jr., Annie A., Roberta (Mrs. W. K. Weaver), Dominique F., Bessie Mae, and Eugene C. He was educated in common schools and at Oxford College, Oxford, Ala.

Cooper's business ability is evident from the following positions he held and activities in which he participated: He was president of Bank of Oxford at age 22; he established Oxford Oil Mill, a cotton mill, and a street railway; he was mayor of Oxford for 25 years; he was a Mason, and chairman of the Oxford board of education.

Most active in church and denominational life, he was often selected for important denominational positions. He served as president of Calhoun Sunday School Convention for 15 years (1901–16); as moderator of Calhoun Baptist Association for 44 years; as vice-president of the Alabama Baptist State Convention (1906, 1915, 1919, 1925); as president of the Alabama Baptist State Convention (1927); as member of the state board of missions and its successor, the executive committee of the state convention for 39 years (1904–43), serving 12 years as president or chairman; as a trustee of Howard College for 20 years; as a member of Howard College Endowment Commission for 28 years; and as vice-president of the state Anti-Saloon League.

GARNETT E. PUCKETT

COOPER, OSCAR HENRY (b. Carthage, Tex., Nov. 22, 1852; d. Abilene, Tex., Aug. 22, 1932). Educator, university president. Son of William Henry and Catherine Hunter (Rosser) Cooper, he graduated from Yale University in 1872 and did further study at Yale and the University of Berlin. He married Mary Bryan Stewart in 1886. Superintendent of Public Instruction in Texas from 1886 to 1890, and superintendent of Galveston schools from 1890 to 1896, Cooper served as president of Baylor University, 1899–1902, and Simmons College, 1902–07. For six years, 1909–15, he maintained Cooper Training School for boys at Abilene, after which he returned to Simmons College as chairman of the faculty and professor of philosophy and education, continuing in that position until his death. He was president of the Association of Texas Colleges in 1923.

BIBLIOGRAPHY: M. Baggett, "The Life and Work of Oscar Henry Cooper, Texas Educator" (1945). *Who Was Who in America, 1897–1942* (1942).

RUPERT N. RICHARDSON

CO-OPERATION, EUROPEAN BAPTISTS. The first Baptist witness in Europe was related to the Pietistic movement of laymen in the late 18th century. In 1832 the Triennial Convention of Baptists in America appointed a general director and a missionary, both sailing to France. After 1882 the American Baptist Missionary Union established the policy of engaging Europeans rather than missionaries and sending financial aid and a "representative." Their work came to be largely concentrated in the northern countries of Europe, and Southern Baptists took responsibility in the South. There was close co-operation between them and with British Baptists. Publications have been a major means of evangelism. The greatest success has been in Germany. In Scandinavia, Baptist churches are not only almost entirely self-supporting but maintain foreign mission work, principally in the Belgian Congo. The seminary at Hamburg attracts theological students from a wide area. Opposition from both Roman Catholics and state churches has been severe, but the attitude of the state churches has become more permissive in recent years. In Russia in 1940 Baptist sympathizers were estimated at five million, but in 1945 when the Council of the United Baptists, Evangelical and Pentecostal Churches and Groups in the U.S.S.R. was organized, Baptist membership was 350,000, with an estimate of three million sympathizers. Refugee and relief work and the reclamation of youth indoctrinated with Nazi and communistic doctrines were major postwar efforts. Fellowship between Baptists of East and West Germany is restricted. The European Baptist Federation organized in 1952 was fostered by the seventh congress of the Baptist World Alliance, which met in Copenhagen in 1951. Figures for church membership in 1934 and 1953 (latest) reflect radical changes brought about after World War II by displacement of peoples, closing of the Iron Curtain, division of Germany into East and West, and general disruption of normal life and economic and political stability.

CHURCH MEMBERS

1934		1954	
Austria	300	Austria	850
Belgium	255	Belgium	494
Bulgaria	690	Bulgaria	676 (1941)
Czechoslovakia	2,914	Czechoslovakia	3,155 (1941)
Denmark	3,030	Denmark	7,301
Estonia	7,183	Estonia	10,000
Finland	3,162	Finland	3,139
France	1,594	France	3,184
Germany	67,977	Germany	99,812
Great Britain and Ireland	402,959	Great Britain and Ireland	325,896
Holland	4,372	Holland	6,763
Hungary	12,936	Hungary	20,000
Italy	4,025	Italy	17,372
Latvia	10,804	Latvia	12,000
Lithuania	1,091	Lithuania	1,000
Norway	6,881	Norway	7,393
Poland	13,532	Poland	7,015 (1941)
Portugal	423	Portugal	1,429 (1952)
Romania	58,277	Romania	65,880 (1952)
Spain	1,401	Spain	2,300
Sweden	67,388	Sweden	34,915
Switzerland	1,651	Switzerland	1,871
U. S. S. R.	—	U. S. S. R.	512,000
Yugoslavia	1,877	Yugoslavia	3,002
Total	674,722	Total	1,147,447

ADA STEARNS

CO-OPERATION, FORMULA OF BAPTIST. Baptist churches in Great Britain, both General and Particular, were indigenous to that nation. The two branches, independent of each other, advanced by logical steps from the Established Church to Puritanism, to Separatism, and finally into a Baptist church. The first English Baptist church as such began in Amsterdam, Holland, among a company of English Separatists led by John Smyth. Having accepted the theology of Arminius, they believed in a general atonement, and that belief gave ground for their name as General Baptists. This doctrine also supported their contention "that the magistrate is not by virtue of his office to meddle with religion, or matters of conscience . . . but to leave Christian religion free, to every man's conscience." Soon after organization a part of the congregation returned to England, where, in 1611 or 1612 at Spitalfields, London, they founded the first Baptist church in England. By 1660 there were more than 100 General Baptist churches in England, and the movement had spread to America, exerting a strong influence in New England, New York, Virginia, and North Carolina.

A Particular Baptist church appeared in London as early, possibly, as 1633. The congregation adopted Calvinistic theology with its strict interpretation of the atonement, and so they were called Particular Baptists. In 1689 representatives of 107 Particular Baptist churches met in London to adopt a confession of faith written in 1677. English Particular Baptists exerted great influence upon Baptists in the New World through their historic confession. In 1742 the Philadelphia Association adopted the confession of faith of 1689 in a slightly amended form. The Philadelphia Confession played a determining role in the subsequent history of American Baptists.

Among Particular Baptists who signed the confession in 1689 some said "that we cannot hold Church-communion, with any other than Baptized-believers, and Churches constituted of such; yet some others of us have a greater liberty and freedom in our spirits that way. . . ." These differences were mentioned in an appendix "as having a direct reference unto the controversie between our brethren and us" but in a way "that the distance between us and our brethren may not be by us made more wide. . . ."

> [Since] those who do consult the Word of God, cannot yet arrive at a full and mutual satisfaction among themselves . . . yet inasmuch as these things are not of the essence of Christianity, but that we agree in the fundamental doctrines thereof, we do apprehend, there is sufficient ground to lay aside all bitterness and prejudice, and in the spirit of love and meekness to imbrace and own each other therein; leaving each other at liberty to perform such other services, wherein we cannot concur apart unto God, according to the best of our understanding.

Baptists first appeared in Virginia in Prince George County. The congregation corresponded with General Baptists in England and subsequently received Robert Norden as a "messenger" and pastor. The small congregation appears to have flourished for a while; then it withered away, but not before members of the group had moved to eastern North Carolina, where they organized a General Baptist church. The movement took root there, resulting in the formation of about 15 churches within a decade. The Arminian theology of these General Baptists attracted visitors from the Philadelphia Association who showed the churches the error of their way and persuaded them to adopt the London Confession of 1689. In 1765 these reformed congregations organized the Kehukee Association of Regular Baptist churches. The term "Regular" applied to Particular Baptists in America.

In 1743 a group of Baptists moved into northwest Virginia and organized a church which received corrective treatment by the Philadelphia Association in 1751, becoming a Regular Baptist Church "in connexion with" that association. Dormant at first, the Regular Baptist movement in that area began to take hold after 1760. Within a few years it had taken over the whole Northern Neck above and below Fredericksburg.

In 1754 Shubal Stearns (*q.v.*), a product of the New Light movement in New England, arrived in northern Virginia, where he stayed with the Regular Baptists for a season. Becoming dissatisfied, he moved to a settlement on Sandy Creek in North Carolina, where he founded Sandy Creek Baptist Church in 1755. Under the leadership of Stearns, the New Lights soon spread through eastern North Carolina and into Virginia. A few years later, these Separates, as they were called in Virginia, moved northward until they occupied much of the territory south of the Rappahannock River. In 1773 the Separates had churches in 28 of the 60 counties of the state.

By 1785 Baptists had established themselves in all sections of Virginia, but they were seriously divided. Regular Baptists, in direct line from the Particular Baptists of England, had strength through the northern part of the state. They held to the theology of Calvin and placed emphasis upon the confession of faith. As a rule their ministers were well trained and their churches orderly in worship.

Separate Baptists were in the line from English General Baptists—with modifications. Many of their pastors and churches accepted Arminianism with its doctrine of general atonement. Separates were slow to adopt formal statements of doctrine or confessions of faith. They vigorously contended for individual freedom and religious liberty under the law. It is likely that they lacked orderliness in worship and that their ministers often displayed great emotionalism in preaching.

Following the Revolutionary War, Baptist leaders in Virginia saw that, while the division was real, time had tempered the differences between the two groups. They believed that unity might be won under the guidance of the Holy Spirit. In 1783 the General Association of Separate Baptists had adopted the Philadelphia Confession with apparent timidity and stated provisions. In 1777 the Kehukee Association had admitted four Separate churches and adopted a modified form of the confession. In 1786 the Ketocton Association of Regular Baptists took the initiative by sending a delegation to the General Committee of Separates, "and they were received upon equal footing with those from other associations." This gave rise to formal action: "It is recommended to the different associations [Separates] to appoint delegates, to attend the next General Committee, for the purpose of forming an union with Regular Baptists."

In 1787 "agreeable to appointment the subject of union of Regular and Separate Baptists was taken up" by the two groups in joint session at Dover meetinghouse. The Separates enumerated their objections to union, which were "chiefly matters of trivial importance." The Regulars complained that "the Separates were not sufficiently explicit in their principles, having never published or sanctioned any confession of faith; and they kept within their communion many who were professed Arminians. . . ." Each side had stated its case and argued its defense. Everyone seemed thoroughly justified in himself "so that all minds were much mollified before the final and successful attempt for union."

Under these auspicious circumstances the Baptists of Virginia jointly accepted the terms of union in the following words: "The committee appointed to consider the terms of union with our Regular Brethren, Reported: that they conceived the manner in which the Regular Baptist confession of faith has been received by a former association, is the ground-work for such union." After debate the general committee received the report of the committee on union with an explanation which excels as an example of sympathetic forbearance and righteous compromise for the sake of Christian fellowship. The explanation:

To prevent the confession of faith from usurping a tyrannical power over the conscience of any, we do not mean, that every person is bound to the strict observance of every thing therein contained; yet that it holds forth the essential truths of the gospel, and that the doctrine of salvation by Christ and free unmerited grace alone, ought to be believed by every christian, and maintained by every minister of the gospel. Upon these terms we are united; and desire hereafter that the names Regular and Separate, be buried in oblivion; and that, from henceforth, we shall be known by the name of the *United Baptist Churches of Christ, in Virginia.*

So Virginia Baptists made common cause 100 years before their prototypes in Great Britain achieved that happy Christian state.

BIBLIOGRAPHY: Burkitt and Read, *A Concise History of the Kehukee Baptist Association* (1805). W. J. McGlothlin, *Baptist Confessions of Faith* (1911). G. Ryland, *The Baptists of Virginia* (1955). R. B. Semple, *A History of the Rise and Progress of the Baptists in Virginia* (1810). A. C. Underwood, *A History of the English Baptists* (1947). H. C. Vedder, *A Short History of the Baptists* (1907).

REUBEN ALLEY

CO-OPERATION: TERMS OF GENERAL UNION IN KENTUCKY, 1801. Until their union in 1801, early Kentucky Baptists were known as either Separates or Regulars. Separates, noted for their evangelism, radical independence, and aversion to confessions of faith, during the period of emigration far outnumbered Regulars, who subscribed to the Philadelphia Confession and practiced interdependence. Their independence and doctrinal ambiguity, however, prevented Separates from meeting frontier problems, and they tended to become Regulars. Of the first 25 Baptist preachers to go to Kentucky before 1785 only one was unmistakably a Regular in the East, whereas 20 were Separates; at the end of 1785, however, 18 were Regulars, and only seven were Separates. Four attempts at union were made. The effort following the revival of 1785 failed because Separates withdrew when the Philadelphia Confession was approved. In 1789 Separates bitterly rejected any creed but the Bible. They became so susceptible to heresy, however, that several Separates withdrew in 1793 and formed the Tates Creek Association of United Baptists, endorsing Regular doctrine but neither adopting the confession nor uniting with the Regulars.

It was the Great Frontier Revival, begun in 1800, which led to a union. Regulars became more zealous in evangelism, and Separates became more concerned about doctrinal soundness and interdependence. At the request of the Elkhorn Association (Regular), delegates of the Elkhorn and South Kentucky associations (Separate) met at Howards Creek Church, Clark County, in Oct., 1801, and united on "The Terms of General Union":

We, the committees of Elkhorn and South Kentucky Associations, do agree to unite on the following plan:

1st. That the Scriptures of the Old and New Testament are the infallible word of God, and the only rule of faith and practice.

2nd. That there is one only true God, and in the Godhead or divine essence, there are Father, Son and Holy Ghost.

3rd. That by nature we are fallen and depraved creatures.

4th. That salvation, regeneration, sanctification and justification are by the life, death, resurrection, and ascension of Jesus Christ.

5th. That the saints will finally persevere through grace to glory.

6th. That believers' baptism by immersion is necessary to receiving the Lord's supper.

7th. That the salvation of the righteous and punishment of the wicked will be eternal.

8th. That it is our duty to be tender and affectionate to each other, and study the happiness of the children of God in general; to be engaged singly to promote the honor of God.

9th. And that the preaching Christ tasted death for every man [universal atonement], shall be no bar to communion.

10th. And that each may keep up their associational and church government as to them may seem best.

11th. That a free correspondence and communion be kept up between the churches thus united.

Unanimously agreed to by joint committee: [*nine signatures*].

Other Baptists endorsed this statement, so the union became more extensive than the Elkhorn and South Kentucky associations. They gave up their former names and began to call themselves United Baptists.   HUGH WAMBLE

CO-OPERATION, THEORY OF. The basis of co-operation is provided in the body of Christ. Unity is required to spread the gospel throughout the world. The basis of this unity is revealed in the prayer of Jesus which included his disciples in all ages: "Neither pray I for these alone, but for them also which shall believe on me through their word; that they all may be one; as thou, Father, art in me, and I in thee, that they also may be one in us: that the world may believe that thou hast sent me" (John 17:20-21). This is a prayer for unity with a purpose—world evangelism.

Co-operation by Southern Baptists is first within and then through the church. Individual co-operation in religious enterprises through nonchurch organizations should not be condemned, but the normal channel is for individuals within the fellowship of a church to determine by church action the direction and degree of co-operation with other Christians in various organizations and enterprises. The interrelatedness of Christians through Christ involves them in each other's needs, as is demonstrated in the collection taken by Paul among the Christians in Corinth for the saints in Jerusalem. This same sense of unity has produced, for example, the Relief and Annuity Board of the Southern Baptist Convention, through which co-operating Southern Baptists provide for the needs of retired or incapacitated ministers. As Jesus was concerned for the welfare of men, so Baptists co-operate to provide hospitals, children's homes, and homes for the aged to provide for human need, in addition to organizations such as the Christian Life Commission to study the moral and social situation. Again, Baptists co-operate to provide schools after the example of Jesus the Great Teacher, in which all students can receive an education based on Christian truth, and in which many receive teaching which is designed to prepare them for leadership in the churches. In all of these, the ultimate objective is evangelism, which requires Baptist co-operation especially at the point of missions.

Baptists' co-operation is made necessary by tasks too large for a small number of Christians to accomplish or tasks in which the co-operation of a large number of Christians is more efficient and more effective. From another point of view, channels of co-operation must be provided if any one Christian is to carry out in any measure all of the requirements of the New Testament. What is involved may be illustrated in the Cooperative Program. Each contributor has a proportionate part in many types of benevolence, healing, teaching, and witnessing throughout his own state, his nation, and the world. No one Christian could begin to do so many diverse things in so large an area if he worked alone.

Co-operation, however, is not confined to the giving of money to support joint enterprises. There is co-operation in counseling, in planning programs, and in the execution of programs. This fact may be illustrated particularly in the realm of Bible study. The churches co-operate through the Southern Baptist Convention to maintain the Sunday School Board. Here is developed, by denominational counseling and planning, a program which can be executed only through the co-operative participation of the individual members of churches.

Thus co-operation in the Southern Baptist Convention is rooted in Christian fellowship, and is designed to provide mutual aid and encouragement in Christian growth and to bear witness to the gospel throughout the world. Co-operation is implemented through the churches by the participation of members in the giving of time, talent, and counsel, as well as money. It is at all points voluntary since neither the individual nor any group of Christians may be coerced.

The relation of the Southern Baptist Convention and the various state Baptist conventions is important. By agreement much of the promotion of the interest of the Southern Baptist Convention is carried on through the offices of the state conventions. Also by agreement the financial support of the Southern Baptist Convention and its agencies passes through the offices of the state conventions, with the state conventions determining the proportion of Cooperative Program funds which is ultimately forwarded to the Southern Baptist Convention. Designated funds are forwarded intact. This relationship between the Southern Baptist Convention and the state Baptist conventions is entirely voluntary and subject to cancellation by either. Both conventions have the authority to approach the churches directly, but convenience and efficiency have prompted the arrangement whereby state Baptist conventions operate in specific areas between the Southern Baptist Convention and the churches. The authority of the Convention can operate on the basis of interdependence as well as independence and is not impaired by the delegation of a function or functions so long as the Convention continues to be responsible for those functions in a final sense.

See also INDEPENDENCY AND CO-OPERATION, BAPTIST.

DUKE K. MCCALL

CO-OPERATION IN MISSION WORK. Southern Baptists, although not affiliated with interdenominational organizations which might require compromise of basic convictions, believe that certain values may be gained through voluntary co-operation with other denominations in advancing the kingdom of God. Although strong in their desire for co-operation with other Christians, Southern Baptists have firmly held that co-operation must not be contrary to scriptural teaching concerning the lordship of Christ, the way of salvation, the voluntary principle in religion, soul liberty, a regenerated church membership, believer's Baptism, and separation of church and state.

During the closing years of the 19th century, when much was said on the question of Christian union, Southern Baptists gave consideration to invitations from the Protestant Episcopal church, Presbyterians, Methodists, Disciples of Christ, and other evangelical groups. The attitude of Southern Baptists was clearly expressed in 1919 by James Bruton Gambrell (*q.v.*), then president of the Southern Baptist Convention, when, in response to the invitation to join the Inter-Church World Movement, he said:

We would not discount the good done by our brethren of other denominations, not excepting Roman Catholics; but facing the present world situation, we are bound in faithfulness to preach the full truth covering the whole field of divine revelation and make Christ's program, given in the Great Commission, effective wherever men live and need the Truth. In so doing we will serve Christ and all the world in the fullest measure.

In 1908 the Home Missions Council, in which a number of evangelical denominations co-operated for the promotion of missions in the United States, was formed. In later years the American Baptist Home Mission Society of New York joined representatives of other missionary societies in a survey of a few states in which certain allotments of territory were accepted by Baptists representing the society with the approval of state conventions. According to this plan the American Baptist Home Mission Society agreed not to enter territory which had been allotted to other co-operating denominations. Northern Baptists approved this plan, but Southern Baptists felt that it was too restrictive. The Foreign Mission Board of the Southern Baptist Convention faced conditions quite different. With the exception of a period from 1919 to 1938, the Foreign Mission Board co-operated with the Foreign Missions Conference of North America from the time of its organization in 1893 until 1950. This conference never imposed any limitations of territory, personnel, or policies on co-operating missionary agencies; it was an entirely voluntary association. That relationship was helpful, especially during World War II, because of complex international problems. In 1950, however, when the National Council of Churches was formed, the Foreign Missions Conference of North America expressed its desire to enter the merger, which included the Home Missions Council, the Federal Council of the Churches of Christ in America, and related organizations. The Foreign Mission Board of the Southern Baptist Convention then voted unanimously to withdraw from the conference.   E. C. ROUTH

CO-OPERATION WITH OTHER DENOMINATIONS. It was nearly 50 years after the organization of the Southern Baptist Convention before Southern Baptists gave an official expression of interest in their relationship to other denominations, although the denominational press had written about it and various agencies had voiced concern.

Evidently, the young denomination, struggling for its existence in the difficult years immediately before and following the Civil War, had all it could do to keep its own work going. Official convention effort to determine the extent of co-operation that should exist between Southern Baptists and other denominations did not appear until the annual meeting in Fort Worth, Tex., in 1890. It was then that the Convention's Committee on Christian Union made its report.

The Convention recognized the desirability of all Christians' agreeing "in all important points of doctrine and polity," and that "there is a standard recognized as authoritative by all Christians—namely, the Bible." The report pointed out—in those early days when membership in the denomination's churches numbered only 1,200,000—"the gravity of the problem of bringing different denominations to see alike on important subjects concerning which they now differ." It was careful to say, however, that Southern Baptists recognized "in the teaching of Scripture the only basis on which such agreement is either possible or desirable." The report proposed that representative scholars from other denominations join with Baptist scholars in determining "just what is the teaching of the Bible on the leading points of difference of doctrine and polity between the denominations, in the hope that they can, at least, help to a better understanding of the issues involved." It ended by urging that results of the study "be widely published in all denominational papers . . . that progress may be made toward true Christian union."

Fraternal relations have always prevailed between Southern Baptists and other denominations. Friendly greetings were early exchanged annually between the Convention and other religious bodies. However, as early as 1855, the Convention turned down a resolution authorizing that "clergymen and brethren of other denominations be affectionately invited to seats in this body," and welcomed only "ministers of our denomination." In the 1859 Convention a similar resolution calling on the president to "tender to the preachers of other denominations of Christians the regard and respect of this Convention, and invite them to seats upon this floor," was, after some discussion, withdrawn.

The 1891 Convention recognized the necessity of interdenominational co-operation in at least one area. It authorized its president to act with representatives from other denominations in formulating a common statement favoring "the universal substitution of arbitration in the place of war as a means of settling difficulties among the nations of the world." This action was in response to a communication from the Assembly of the Presbyterian Church in the United States.

The 1912 Convention adopted a report approving Southern Baptist participation in the World Conference on Faith and Order. The report pointed out that the plan for the conference "does not involve any compromise of principles on the part of those who participate. It merely looks to a fraternal and general conference on doctrine and polity with a view to a better understanding and closer union among all Christians." The committee's reply to the invitation to the conference incorporated Southern Baptists' historic position of avoiding "entanglements" in any organic union, but it expressed happy willingness "to confer with our brethren of other communions on the great matters which have been referred to us by our various Christian bodies." The report continued to explain the Baptist position in detail:

We are thankful to recognize that there is increasing spiritual unity among all the true followers of our Lord, and we heartily engage to promote by all suitable means the furtherance and strengthening of this real, impressive and growing union among all Christians. We recognize further the feasibility, and in many cases the desirability, of a larger degree of cooperative union among the various bodies of Christians. But we cannot as yet see the way clear to the formation of any federal directive body which will manifest this union in an organic way. We think, however, that this matter should be fully discussed and frankly considered from every point of view, that all the difficulties in the way may be duly considered and such cooperation as is possible may be secured and perpetuated. We are sure that the discussion of church order and a closer fellowship cannot fail, if conducted in the spirit of our Lord, to result in a better understanding and a larger degree of combined action in many useful directions.

With regard to questions of doctrine and polity, we are sure that under present conditions, uniformity, or any organic union based upon that, cannot be expected. . . . We shall rejoice therefore, to meet in a World Conference with our brethren of other faiths, praying with them that we may all be led to see the truth and work together for the bringing in of the kingdom of our Lord Jesus Christ.

In 1913 the Convention noted the time lag necessary in arranging for such a comprehensive meeting of denominations and proposed that

the various Commissions employ the interval of waiting in seeking to arouse within their own denominations a deeper interest in Christian unity, in enlisting other Christian bodies near to themselves in practice, and in considering and studying both the differences and agreements between the various Christian communions with a view to better understanding.

An informal conference on world faith and order, which Southern Baptist representatives were unable to attend, met in New York on May 8, 1913. It suggested, among other things, the appointment of a committee of scholars from all the communions that were planning to participate in the conference, "who shall spend, if need be, years in formulating the questions on which we are now at difference. It is hoped that such a committee of scholars and earnest Christians would succeed in finding a greater measure of agreement than we now, in our isolation, suppose exists."

By the 1914 Convention at least 35 of the leading bodies of Christians throughout the world had appointed commissions to engage in the study, among which was the Southern Baptist Convention. At this same Convention a long "Pronouncement on Christian Union and Denominational Efficiency" was adopted. It rejoiced in "the many evidences of increasing interest in the subject of Christian union among Christian people everywhere." However, it carefully set out the Southern Baptist insistence on keeping clear of interfaith agreements that might influence doctrinal compromises. The report said specifically:

We believe that the highest efficiency of the Southern Baptist Convention in the propagation and confirmation of the Gospel can be attained:

1. By the observance of strict loyalty to Christ as the head of the church . . .
2. By preserving a complete autonomy at home and abroad, unembarrassed by entangling alliances with other bodies holding to different standards of doctrine . . . church life and church order.

The 1915 Convention converted the commission to study world faith and order, previously appointed annually, into a standing commission, with the Convention president and secretaries representing Southern Baptists in this capacity. The years 1914–17 saw efforts to reach agreements for a study conference on world faith and order among the various communions give way before the turmoil brought on by World War I. At the 1918 Convention, however, the Southern Baptist commission said:

It is our judgment that such a conference as is proposed, held in the spirit of love and mutual respect, would result in large blessings to our common Christianity. It would certainly promote a better understanding among the different and differing denominations—a thing very desirable.

Reaction had set in, however, as a result of the encroachments that were made by the military on the freedom with which the denominations thought they should be allowed to function in wartime. James Bruton Gambrell's (q.v.) address to the 1919 Convention severely criticized the government's wartime policy of reducing the effectiveness of denominational services to the men in arms. He quoted a secretary of the War Department as saying: "The whole desire of the department is in the interest of breaking down, rather than emphasizing, denominational distinctions."

A committee report supplementing the president's address concluded:

Your Committee would . . . say that Baptists favor Christian union on the basis of the Holy Scriptures, but insist that union on any other basis is not desirable, nor with Baptists possible. We will both labor and pray for a Scriptural union, but deplore all efforts to promote union on any other basis. We cherish for our fellow-believers in all communions a deep and abiding love, but we believe that all attempts to bring incongruous elements into one mass-movement will inevitably promote discords, strifes, and spiritual deterioration—results we would deeply deplore.

By 1932 reaction against the union movement had become so strong that the Convention reversed its position on having a commission to study, along with scholars of other communions, points of doctrinal differences and agreements among denominations, by declining to appoint delegates to the proposed World Conference of Faith and Order.

In 1937 the Convention merely cited its 1932 decision and refused again to appoint representatives to the World Conference on Faith and Order, scheduled to meet in Edinburgh, Scotland. However, this same Convention authorized George Washington Truett (q.v.), who would be traveling in Europe as president of the Baptist World Alliance, to attend the Conference on Church, State and Community at Oxford, England, "as spokesman of this Convention." The 1938 Convention, because of Truett's inability to fulfil his intention of attending the Oxford conference, elected John Richard Sampey (q.v.), the current president, to represent Southern Baptists at both the Conference on Church, State and Community at Oxford and the Conference on Faith and Order at Edinburgh.

The 1938 Convention unanimously adopted a conciliatory but firm report on interdenominational relations which indicated that Southern Baptists would not budge in their refusal to compromise themselves doctrinally in any form of organic union. Summarized, the report said:

We would issue a fraternal warning to our brethren of every communion of the danger of a man-made union. It would constitute a powerful monopoly fraught with many possible perils for the world. . . . Such . . . power would be too much for human nature. We can conceive of it as a great temptation to some would-be world dictator. . . . Only a union dominated by spiritual believers, perfected by spiritual motives . . . would be safe for the world. This is our profound conviction.

Our message to our brethren of other communions is that since the present divided condition of Christendom is unquestionably the result of departures from the simple teaching of the Scriptures, the only possible road to organic union is back to the Scriptures, fairly interpreted. . . .

Pending the working out of the problem of union we are glad to say that we stand ready at all times to co-operate with all our fellow Christians and our fellow citizens . . . in every worthy effort for the moral and social uplift of humanity.

The appointment by Franklin D. Roosevelt, on Dec. 24, 1939, of a government representative to the Vatican with the rank of ambassador, was given a stinging rebuke at the 1940 Convention. The Convention also declined an invitation for Southern Baptists to become a member of the proposed World Council of Churches. Although the tone of the Convention's reply was cordial, it left no doubt about why it rejected the invitation:

Directly replying to your invitation, permit us to advise that the Southern Baptist Convention is a voluntary association of Baptists for the purpose of eliciting, combining and directing the energies of our denomination in missionary activity at home and abroad, and in educational and benevolent work throughout the world. Our Convention has no ecclesiological authority . . . The thousands of churches to which our Convention looks for support . . . would disapprove of any attempted exercise of ecclesiastical authority over them.

In a world which more and more seeks centralization of power . . . we are sensible of the dangers of totalitarian trends. . . . We wish to do nothing that will imperil the growing spirit of co-operation on the part of our churches in . . . giving the gospel of Christ, as we understand it, to all men everywhere. In the light of these considerations, we feel impelled to decline the invitation to membership in the World Council of Churches.

In successive years the Convention adopted resolutions of protest against the United States Government for continuing diplomatic relations with the Vatican.

The 1947 Convention endorsed a proposed amendment to the federal Constitution that would have clearly prohibited "sectarian appropriations to non-public educational institutions . . . of any kind."

Seeking a countermove to offset growing Roman Catholic influence in American life, the 1948 Convention endorsed the newly formed organization, "Protestants and Other Americans United for the Separation of Church and State," popularly known as POAU. The Convention also declined to send even an "observer" to the World Council of Churches meeting that summer in Amsterdam, Holland.

In 1949 the Convention refused to "place Southern Baptists in a compromising position . . . toward organic union with religious bodies that do not believe or practice the New Testament Baptist principles. . . ." In 1950 it reaffirmed "our convictions that Southern Baptists cannot enter into organic connections with the Federal Council of Churches of Christ in America, or in any other organization that would compromise Baptist principles. . . ." In the years 1951–53 each annual Convention declined to affiliate the denomination with any interfaith movement and urged a more strict indoctrination of Baptists in the tenets of their own faith.

The traditional Southern Baptist position on relations with other religious communions is, perhaps, best summarized in a report written for presentation to the 1919 Convention by J. B. Gambrell:

Baptists have, as we profoundly believe, a distinct witness to bear and our message must in no way be . . . enfeebled. It is our inescapable duty to bear this message . . . to the uttermost part of the world. To syndicate our denomination with other denominations would impair, if not destroy, this message. . . . Let us, then, while heartily bidding godspeed to all who love our Lord in sincerity and truth, . . . be busy about our own tasks, the tasks which, if neglected by us, will never be accomplished.

C. DE WITT MATTHEWS

CO-OPERATIVE MISSIONS. The Co-operative Missions Department of the Home Mission Board was set up by action of the board at the annual meeting on Dec. 4, 1946, and S. F. Dowis was elected secretary of the department. On Jan. 1, 1947, the department began to function. Co-operative missions consists of certain phases of work carried on by the Home Mission Board in co-operation with the state mission boards. The state mission boards employ and direct the missionary personnel; the Home Mission Board provides program, counsel, and literature for promotion of the work and conducts conferences on the state and Convention levels in the interest of a uniform mission program for the entire Convention. The Home Mission Board makes allocations of funds for this work so far as they are available.

Co-operative Missions

Various programs of work are included in the Co-operative Missions Department.

City missions was a co-operative work with associations until 1950, when the board turned to state mission boards for selection of superintendents and direction of activities.

The rural church program began as a cooperative work with the state boards and was placed under the direction of the Co-operative Missions Department on Jan. 1, 1947. Included in the rural church program is the plan for a superintendent of missions in each state, a staff of associational or general missionaries, and such special missionaries as needed in certain areas.

The rural church survey program was first outlined by John D. Freeman as an Eight-Day Rural Church Revival and was later revised and promoted by John W. Wells of the Home Mission Board.

The Co-operative Missions Department published through the Home Mission Board a book as a guide for associational mission work, entitled *A Mission Program for the Baptist Association*, by Dowis. A pamphlet by Eldred Taylor of Louisville, Ky., was published in Feb., 1955, entitled "The Missionary." Another pamphlet provided by the department is "The What-Why-How of the Association" by Sam Scantlan of Oklahoma City, published Dec., 1955.

The western mission work was begun with city mission programs in Albuquerque, N. Mex., on Jan. 1, 1944; Phoenix, Ariz., on Sept. 1, 1944; Tucson, Ariz., on Nov. 1, 1945; San Diego, Calif., on Sept. 1, 1944; Los Angeles, Calif., on Aug. 1, 1944; San Francisco, Calif., on Dec. 1, 1944; and Fresno, Calif., on July 1, 1946. These programs were all transferred to a general mission program for the western states, Jan 1, 1947. On this same date the work in all the states west of Texas and Oklahoma became a part of co-operative missions. In 1942 there were only 254 churches in this total area. At the close of 1955, the work covered all the 15 states west of Texas and Oklahoma, with 6 state conventions: New Mexico, Arizona, California, Oregon-Washington, Kansas, and Colorado. In these are 78 associations and 1,192 churches.

The mountain mission program was authorized by the Home Mission Board in its annual meeting, Nov., 1946, and the first allocation for this work was made by Woman's Missionary Union from the Annie Armstrong Offering. On Feb. 1, 1948, A. B. Cash, superintendent of city missions, Columbus, Ga., began to work out the county unity mission program for the mountain areas in co-operation with the Kentucky state board. A pamphlet outlining the program was written by Cash under the title "Plan Enlarged Mountain Mission Program" and published in Feb., 1952. This work has spread to other states and is still under the direction of Cash.

The pioneer mission work includes all the work in states east of the Mississippi from its headwaters, consisting of Iowa, Minnesota, Wisconsin, Michigan, Illinois, Indiana, Ohio, West Virginia, Pennsylvania, Delaware, and New York. The work is sponsored by the state conventions of Missouri, Arkansas, Illinois, Kentucky, Virginia, Maryland, and Ohio, with which the Home Mission Board co-operates, and is under the direction of Cash.

The military personnel program is a phase of co-operative missions carried on in co-operation with the Sunday school, Training Union, B.S.U., and Brotherhood, in the interest of moral training and character-building of the youth in military service. The program was authorized by the Home Mission Board at the annual meeting on Dec. 3, 1952. E. L. Ackiss, a retired Navy chaplain, was elected by the board on Jan. 1, 1953, to direct the work. His pamphlet, "Southern Baptist Ministry to Pre-Inductees and Service Youth," sets forth the program and commends the material of the other agencies in this field. This is a five-point program: (1) a program of orientation before entering the service; (2) a contact program to keep the church in touch with the person while in service; (3) a contact and service program for his family while he is away; (4) vital contact with the chaplain while in service; (5) adjustment counsel and assistance upon coming out of service.

The broken home and juvenile delinquent program for reclamation of juvenile delinquents had several demonstrations of interest through city mission programs and the Brotherhood Commission. The Brotherhood initiated the Man and Boy Movement, by which a man would assume responsibility for a boy who was not in Sunday school and church. The work continues and has helped many boys. The city mission program in Louisville, Ky., initiated a home for boys known as "Boys Estate," and the Knoxville, Tenn., program set up a sponsorship movement which has proved effective. The broken home program calls for an experienced man to serve as a volunteer counselor and helper at the court level. Court officials will refer to him those seeking divorce, if they are willing to go for free counsel and help.

The trailer camp ministry was initiated by the Home Mission Board in co-operation with South Carolina in Feb., 1953, when the Savannah River Project was under construction. Chester R. Murphy was sent there by the Home Mission Board to minister to the thousands living in trailers. When the project was finished, homes were built, and five new churches were left on the field. Murphy was moved to Portsmouth, Ohio, where another project was under construction. He remained there until Sept. 1, 1955, when the project was finished there and this phase of the work discontinued.

In 1946 J. B. Lawrence, executive secretary-treasurer of the Home Mission Board, became concerned about many Southern Baptists' taking correspondence Bible courses from sources which were not in agreement with Southern Baptist interpretation of the Bible. Therefore, the Home Mission Board authorized a free correspondence Bible course, and Dowis, secretary of co-operative missions, was asked to write the lessons and promote the course. In the last quarter of 1946, the first lesson was written on "The Life and Ministry of Christ." There were 10 lessons written on this theme from the Four Gospels during 1950–52, comprising Book I. Book II, consisting of 10 lessons, was prepared between 1952 and 1955 on the rest of the New Testament. More than 10,000 people had enrolled in the course during the five years, and above 500 had completed all 20 lessons. The requirements for enrolment are that the person must be 16 years of age, take the lessons for home study, and agree not to substitute them for any literature provided for the departments of the church work; that every person must enrol for and complete each lesson before securing the next one. No credit is given for the work, but a small certificate is given after each lesson to show completion of it. Beginning with 1956, the lessons started with the Old Testament and were to follow through book by book until it was completed. s. f. dowis

COOPERATIVE PROGRAM. A unified appeal for all denominational causes, state and Convention-wide, a program of co-operation, not among state conventions nor among churches, but between the Southern Baptist Convention as an organization and each separate state convention as an organization. This co-operation involves three things, all related to the question of money: the soliciting, the securing, and the dividing of funds.

After the 75 Million Campaign a Conservation Commission was set up to conserve the results accomplished by the co-operative work done in the campaign. This was succeeded by the Future Program Commission, which in 1925 recommended to the Southern Baptist Convention that "from the adoption of this report by the Convention our co-operative work be known as the 'Cooperative Program of Southern Baptists.'" The Cooperative Program Commission was discontinued in 1927, on the following recommendation: "We recommend that all the work now done by the Cooperative Program Commission be taken over by the Executive Committee." In 1929 the Convention recommended "that all sums collected in the various states for Southwide objects shall be forwarded monthly by each state secretary to the Executive Committee which shall become the disbursing or distributing agent of the Convention."

The state convention sets a goal of the amount of money it will try to raise for the Cooperative Program for the next year's work and decides upon the division by percentages between the state convention work and the Southern Baptist Convention work, of the distributable funds that may be secured. The percentages going to the state and to the Southern Baptist Convention differ among the states. Some states divide on a 50–50 basis; other states, on a 60–40 basis; and some, in work in new states, on a 75–25 basis—75 per cent for the state work and 25 per cent for the Convention.

The Cooperative Program includes all distributable funds, all designated funds, and all special offerings, such as the Woman's Missionary Union Lottie Moon Offering for foreign missions, the Annie Armstrong Offering for home missions, offering for state missions, etc. In reality, all funds received for any cause included in the Cooperative Program, whether they be distributable, designated, or special funds, belong to the Cooperative Program. Designated funds and special offerings for a cause cannot be divided. They must go according to the wish of the donor.

The churches in a state send their contributions for the Cooperative Program to the state headquarters, where the distributable funds are divided, so much for Convention-wide and so much for statewide causes, according to the percentages fixed by the convention of that state for the distribution of the total funds—that is, for all the denominational causes fostered by the state convention and those fostered by the Southern Baptist Convention. The state headquarters retains all the funds going to the state and distributes these funds to the state agencies according to the percentages fixed by the state convention.

All of the money—distributable, designated, and special funds—belonging to Southern Baptist Convention causes is sent by the state convention headquarters to the treasurer of the Executive Committee, who is the executive secretary of the Southern Baptist Convention, Nashville, Tenn. The Executive Committee divides all of the distributable funds thus received among the Convention agencies according to percentages fixed by the Southern Baptist Convention, and to each agency the designated and special funds, if there be any.

There are distinct advantages in the Cooperative Program. The individual can make an offering, week by week or month by month, to all the causes fostered by the Southern Baptist Convention and by his own state convention. The church can and should put on an every-member canvass and secure pledges to be paid month by month or week by week to all the causes. A great advantage to the agencies is that they receive funds regularly. The Executive Committee distributes funds weekly to Southern Baptist agencies. The agencies of the states also receive their funds regularly.

The work of promoting the Cooperative Program is carried on mainly by the spoken message—such as sermons, addresses, and teaching—and by the written word—such as by articles and tracts on the causes included in the Cooperative Program. These give the individual information concerning all the work the denomination is doing. The best method that has yet been devised for securing necessary funds for all the denominational causes is the plan known as the every-member canvass. The object of the annual every-member canvass by a church

Copass, Benjamin Andrew

is to secure, so far as possible, from every member a pledge to contribute regularly to the church budget, which includes the Cooperative Program.

The Cooperative Program is scriptural. The work supported by the Cooperative Program may be classified under three heads: missions, teaching, and benevolence. Missions is preaching the gospel at home and abroad. According to the command of Christ (Acts 1:8), this gospel is preached in all the world. The teaching of the doctrines and principles of Christianity and the will of Christ expressed in his commandments is enjoined in the New Testament. The benevolent work of the denomination refers to the work done in order to secure the happiness and well-being of the needy. This includes children's homes, hospitals, and ministerial relief.

The Cooperative Program is scriptural in its objectives and methods. The plan is, of course, through co-operation of individuals and churches. Paul gave a fine example of co-operative effort. He had urged the churches in different sections to make contributions for the poor at Jerusalem, and the method for raising this money was according to his instruction to the church in Corinth: "Upon the first day of the week let every one of you lay by him in store, as God hath prospered him, that there be no gatherings when I come" (I Cor. 16:2). The appeal of Paul and the Cooperative Program is to individuals.   AUSTIN CROUCH

COPASS, BENJAMIN ANDREW (b. Jackson County, Tenn., May 29, 1865; d. Fort Worth, Tex., Jan. 2, 1950; buried Waxahachie, Tex.). Pastor, professor at Southwestern Seminary, author. His parents were Charles Wesley and Lucinda (Bowman) Copass. After irregular attendance in country schools he enrolled in Willette Academy, Willette, Tenn. His parents moved to Kentucky where he was converted at Rock Bridge in 1879. He attended Bethel College, Russellville, Ky., where he received the A.B. degree in 1890 and the A.M. degree in 1893. The college conferred the D.D. degree upon him in 1898. He attended the Southern Baptist Theological Seminary from 1891 to 1894, completing the regular course of study. The seminary did not confer degrees at that time. He studied at the University of Chicago during the summer of 1919.

Copass was ordained to the ministry in 1889. His first pastorate was in Clinton, Ky., 1894–96, where Clinton College was located. Other pastorates were in Los Angeles, Calif., 1896–98; Marksbury, Ky., 1898–1901; Waxahachie, Tex., 1901–06; San Marcos, Tex., 1906–12; and Denton, Tex., 1912–13.

From 1914 to 1918, he served as associate secretary of the executive board of the Baptist General Convention of Texas under James Bruton Gambrell (q.v.). In 1918 he was elected professor of Old Testament Interpretation in Southwestern Baptist Theological Seminary, a position he held until his retirement in 1942.

Copass published a number of books and articles. Among them were: *The Message of Hosea* (1906); *Amos* (1939); *Isaiah, Prince of Old Testament Prophets* (1944); and *A Study of the Prophet Micah* (1950). He was aided in this last work by his colleague, E. Leslie Carlson. Other works in mimeograph form were used as textbooks for his classes.

On May 29, 1894, he married Cloantha Williams, daughter of the vice-president of Bethel College. She died in Waxahachie, Tex., in 1902. They had four children. In 1904 he married Crickett Keys. To this union three children were born. Copass was a Mason, a Democrat, and a member of the Phi Gamma Delta fraternity.

BIBLIOGRAPHY: J. M. Price, *Southwestern Men and Messages* (1948). J. S. Ramond, *Among Southern Baptists* (1936). L. R. Scarborough, *A Modern School of the Prophets* (1939).

E. L. CARLSON and RALPH L. SMITH

COPASS, MRS. BENJAMIN ANDREW (b. Danville, Ala., July 4, 1873; d. Seattle, Wash., Aug. 20, 1952). Woman's Missionary Union leader. Known as Crickett Keys Copass—after her marriage—she moved with her family to Cleburne, Tex., in 1877 when she was only four. Mrs. Copass began her career as a teacher at the age of 17 and continued to attend Baylor University, Waco, Tex., during the summer. She married Benjamin Andrew Copass, pastor in Waxahachie, Tex., in 1904, and he later became professor of Old Testament at Southwestern Seminary in Fort Worth. President of the Woman's Missionary Union of Texas from 1931 to 1946, Mrs. Copass was one of the first women elected to the executive board of the Baptist General Convention of Texas. She served 15 years as chairman of the advisory board of the Southwestern Seminary Training School. Her published works include *That They May See; Give Ye Them to Eat; Women of Destiny in the Old Testament; Women of Destiny in the New Testament;* and the chapter "The Women and Their Work" in the *Centennial Story of Texas Baptists*.

BIBLIOGRAPHY: Baptist General Convention of Texas, *Centennial Story of Texas Baptists 1836–1936* (1936). R. T. Patterson, *Candle by Night* (1955). Woman's Missionary Union, *Minutes* (1931–46).

EULA MAE HENDERSON

CORRELATION, COMMITTEE ON. One of the most persistent problems in Southern Baptist life has been the overlapping of organizations and duplication of activities which have added unnecessarily to the burden of church workers. This has been in part due to the creation of new committees, commissions, and departments of the boards, each wanting a special week in the local church. Stimulated by public sentiment, the Southern Baptist Convention has appointed committees to study the matter.

LOUISIANA COLLEGE (q.v.), Pineville. Founded in 1906, enrolment 1,284 in 1955—56 session. Alexandria Hall, pictured, built in 1923, is one of 10 buildings valued at over $2,000,000.

MERCER UNIVERSITY (q.v.), Macon, Ga. Founded in 1833, enrolment 1,571 in 1955–56 session. Administration building, pictured, completed in 1874. Its 53 buildings valued at $3,000,000.

The first was in 1937 when on motion of George W. Sadler the Convention appointed a committee to study the matter. The committee made its final report to the Convention in San Antonio in 1942. Probably its greatest achievement was in moving the Convention to vote that a church would not be out of order if it varied from the regular organizations in an effort to find a better way of doing things.

The second committee was appointed by the Southern Baptist Convention at its meeting in Miami, Fla., in 1946, on motion by P. E. Burroughs. In a personal letter he stated that if the committee were large enough, representative enough, and continued its studies long enough, something definite could be done. With Gaines S. Dobbins as chairman, one of the distinctive things this committee did was to send out an extensive questionnaire to 11,500 pastors throughout the South, answers to which revealed a strong sentiment for, and valuable suggestions on, correlation. An outcome of this committee's work was the Inter-Agency Council from the Home Mission, Foreign Mission, Sunday School, and Woman's Missionary Union boards to consider matters of common interest to all of them.

At the meeting of the Southern Baptist Convention in Kansas City, May 31–June 2, 1956, a recommendation was brought by the Executive Committee and adopted by the Convention that another committee be appointed by the Convention "to study the functions of the agencies and boards and their relationship with the churches, the state conventions, and other boards and agencies."

The final outcome from this study on correlation is not evident now (June, 1956).

J. M. PRICE

CORYELL COUNTY BAPTIST ASSOCIATION ENCAMPMENT. A Texas encampment organized for the Young Woman's Auxiliary members of the First Baptist Church, Gatesville, Tex., in Aug., 1933. During the years following the camp's organization members of the Young Woman's and Girl's auxiliaries from churches in adjacent towns took part in the camp programs, which had a special emphasis on missions. Boys from neighboring churches attended the camp in 1942, at which time the five churches represented in the coeducational attendance asked Coryell County Association to assume management of the camp as an annual affair for all associational churches. In 1947, 255 young people were registered at the camp, the largest number on record. District and associational missionaries, pastors, and Woman's Missionary Union officers have assumed much of the responsibility for the camp's program.

J. E. ROTH

COSBY ACADEMY. A school in East Tennessee. "In 1912 Mr. A. E. Brown, of the Home Mission Board of the Southern Baptist Convention, made a proposition to the East Tennessee Baptist Association, if the people of the community would furnish a part of the money, the Home Mission Board would match the money and establish a high school on Cosby Creek." Nearly everyone in the locality made a contribution, often of materials or labor. The school began with two buildings. Later two others were built. In 1936 the Baptists sold the school to the county board of education. For some 24 years Cosby Academy was the principal educational and religious influence among the young people on Cosby Creek and for miles around.

HARLEY FITE

COSTA RICA, MISSION IN. Baptist work started in Costa Rica in 1943 with a Bible study group meeting in private homes. On Dec. 6, 1943, the First Baptist Church of San Jose was organized with 49 members. When an appeal for aid was made to Paul Carlyle Bell, Sr., Southern Baptist Home Mission Board representative in Panama, Bell examined the work and recommended support, which was granted by the board on Mar. 2, 1944. In 1947 a national Baptist convention was formed with four churches. Van Earl and Waurayne (Duree) Hughes became resident missionaries in 1948. The work was transferred to the Foreign Mission Board the following year, and the Hugheses remained as missionaries of the Foreign Board. In 1950 Mr. and Mrs. Charles Willis Bryan were also appointed for Costa Rica, the same year in which a Bible Institute was organized. By 1955 the institute included 18 students, seven ordained pastors, eight Baptist churches, and a membership of 395.

CHARLES W. BRYAN

COSTA RICAN BIBLE INSTITUTE, SAN JOSÉ. See COSTA RICA, MISSION IN.

COTTAGE VISITOR. A paper edited by N. Bowen, 1867–71. Publication was resumed in 1880 as *Baptist Telescope*.

L. L. CARPENTER

COTTINGHAM, CLAYBROOK (b. Ottoman, Va., May 4, 1881; d. Mexico City, Mexico, Aug. 17, 1949). Baptist educator and denominational statesman. Converted in 1894, Cottingham was educated at Richmond College (B.A., 1899; M.A., 1900) and was awarded the LL.D. degree by Baylor University (1920). Cottingham's long career as a Christian educator in Louisiana began in 1902 when Mt. Lebanon Baptist College selected him professor of Greek and philosophy. In 1905 he became president of that college. When Louisiana College was founded in 1906, he was chosen as its first professor of Greek and philosophy; four years later he became president. Challenging Louisiana Baptists to recognize the claims of Louisiana College and Christian education, Cottingham gained their co-operation in building a strong Baptist college for the state. His life was dedicated to teaching and training men and women to serve Christ more efficiently. During his administration (1910–41), Louisiana College developed from a struggling, unknown institution with assets of $46,814 into a strong, standard, and widely recognized college with assets of over $1,000,000. Assuming the presidency of Louisiana Polytechnic Institute in 1941, Cottingham led that institution to progress numerically and economically and to acquire national academic standing. Upon his resignation in 1949, Cottingham contemplated a career of public speaking. He served as an executive in numerous posts in his profession and denomination, e.g., Southern Baptist Education Association, Louisiana Teachers' Association, Rotary International, etc. He was the only two-time president of the Alexandria Rotary Club, serving 1924-25 and 1927-28; he was governor of District 17 in 1928-29 and director of Rotary International, 1930-31; he was an active deacon in his church from 1912 until his death; he was president of Louisiana Baptist Convention for three years. He was buried in Greenwood Memorial Park, Pineville, La.

BIBLIOGRAPHY: C. Cottingham, "Reports of the President to the Board of Trustees of Louisiana College," (1910-41); "Report of My Administration as President of Louisiana Tech" (1949). J. P. Durham and J. S. Ramond, eds., *Baptist Builders in Louisiana* (1937). "Official Program for 25th Anniversary Celebration," *Old Grads Exchange* (May, 1935). C. P. St. Amant, *A Short History of Louisiana Baptists* (1948). S. F. Tillman, comp., *Tilghman-Tillman Family 1225-1945* (1946).

LYNN EDWARD MAY, JR.

COUNTRY LINE CHURCH. Organized in 1772, according to Asplund, and 1783, according to Benedict. The church is located in Caswell County, southwest of Yanceyville, N. C., a section where Shubal Stearns, Daniel Marshall, and other Separate Baptists labored; it was for a half century faithful to the Separate Baptist tenets. It co-operated with Virginia churches which affiliated with the Roanoke District Association until Roanoke was divided in 1794, Country Line joining other North Carolina churches in the formation of Flat River Association. In 1806 Flat River divided, and the western division, to which Country Line belonged, became known as the Country Line Association. In the early years both church and association, under the leadership of such men as Thomas Miller and Barzillai Graves, were progressive, supported missions, benevolences, Sunday schools, and corresponded with other missionary Baptist associations. In 1832, influenced by James Osbourn of Baltimore and John Stadler, pastor of the church, both church and association became antimissionary. Since that time the Country Line Church has remained antimissionary and, with scarcely a dozen members, belongs to the Primitive Upper Country Line Association. G. W. PASCHAL

COVENANT. In biblical thought, a mutual agreement between two parties which carries with it certain mutual obligations and promises, morally binding upon both. At the human level, where the two parties are equal, for example, David and Jonathan, the covenant carries equal promise and obligation. However, when one party is God, he takes the initiative and the covenant is an act of grace. Man cannot dictate the conditions of the covenant; God determines them. God promises certain things to the "covenant man" and demands certain things of him. The covenant is a gracious command which man is set free to accept. Once man has accepted the covenant, it is binding upon him as it is binding upon God because of his nature. Man must fulfil the moral obligations laid upon him by the covenant, and God graciously fulfils his promise, abiding faithful to his Word.

In God's covenant with Israel, the obligations were expressed through the successive strata of the Mosaic law and made clear to Israel by prophets through the divine Word. God's initiative and grace were evidenced by his free choice and election of Israel and his promise that through her all nations of the earth would be blessed. Israel's failure to fulfil her obligations reveals a sinful perversity from which man cannot deliver himself. Hence the Old Testament promised a new covenant in which God would again take the initiative and recreate man from within, making it possible for man to respond to God's demands to live in the obedience of faith. This new covenant was established in Christ.

The church, like Israel, is a covenant community. It is the fellowship of those who are bound to God and to one another by the outpoured life of Christ. God's grace in Christ's atoning death has established a new covenant with sinful man. The divine gift of faith has made it possible for man to respond in faith and to live in the covenant relationship. Such a life of reconciliation to God means a life of fellowship and love with others, so that the church is a community of those who are covenanted to God and so covenanted to one another.

Covenant is grounded in God's grace and faithfulness; it finds its expression in man's own faith, in loyalty to God, and in loving service of and loyalty to fellow men.

BIBLIOGRAPHY: H. H. Rowley, *The Bible Doctrine of Election* (1950). N. Snaith, *Distinctive Ideas of the Old Testament* (1946). E. C. RUST

COX COLLEGE. A private school for girls started by John Edmonds Dawson (*q.v.*) in Jan., 1843, at La Grange, Ga., soon taken over by Milton E. Bacon. Chartered under the name La Grange Female Seminary, it became La Grange Collegiate Seminary for Young Ladies two years later, and Southern and Western Female College by another charter in 1852. Ichabod F. Cox, who took over the school in 1857, continued control until his death in 1887. During the period of his leadership the college was named for him and for the Cox family, several members of which were teachers in the school. In spite of opposition from the La Grange populace, Cox College was moved to

Manchester (now College Park), a more accessible and desirable location, in 1895. In its new location it became Southern Female College and began declining steadily two years after its move. The school retained strong Baptist connections throughout its existence, especially at La Grange, where faculty and trustees were predominantly Baptist.   ARTHUR JACKSON

CRAB ORCHARD ACADEMY. A secondary school in Cumberland County, Tenn., founded in 1901 and "fostered by the Big Emory Association." The school was under the direction of a Professor Bailey. It closed about 1906.

LYNN EDWARD MAY, JR.

CRAIG, ELIJAH (b. Orange County, Va., c. 1743; d. Georgetown, Ky., 1808). Farmer, minister, educator. The son of Toliver and Polly (Hawkins) Craig and the brother of Lewis and Joseph Craig, Elijah Craig received but a limited education. He was converted in 1764 through the ministry of David Thomas (q.v.). The following year, encouraged by Samuel Harris (q.v.), Craig began to hold meetings on Sundays on his tobacco farm in Orange County. In 1766 he and two others traveled to North Carolina to get James Read (1722-98) to baptize new converts. After being baptized in May, 1771, Craig became pastor of the Blue Run Church. "Some time after this the sheriff came to where he was plowing, arrested him, and carried him before a magistrate" in Culpeper County on the charge of his having preached the gospel contrary to law. During his imprisonment, which caused injury to his health, Craig preached through the prison's gates to the people. After a month he was released by giving bond. At another time, for similar reasons, he was imprisoned in Orange County. The date is uncertain. These experiences and a study of the Scriptures soon developed "the tobacco-barn exhorter into one of the most popular and influential preachers in Virginia." In the fall of 1744, he was elected by the Virginia Baptist General Association as one of three "apostles," in an effort to revive the office referred to in Ephesians 4:11.

In 1786 Craig removed to Kentucky, bought 1,000 acres of land in what is now Scott County, and laid off a town which was at first called Lebanon but later called Georgetown. Entering into speculation, he erected the first saw and grist mill, then the first fulling mill, the first rope works, and the first paper mill in Kentucky. While serving as pastor of the Great Crossings Church in Scott County, he got into difficulty with Joseph Reding (1750?-1815), whom some members desired as their pastor, and was excluded from the church in Jan., 1791. Apparently restored to membership, he attended Elkhorn Association as a messenger from the church in 1792, 1793, and 1794. He left the church to enter into the constitution of McConnell's Run Church in Sept., 1795.

A pioneer in education, Elijah Craig established his classical school at Georgetown in 1788. According to John H. Spencer, the historian of Kentucky Baptists, "he wrote two pamphlets, one to prove that a settled pastor of a church is not entitled to any compensation for his services in that capacity. The other was titled 'A Portrait of Jacob Creath.' They were both written in a bad spirit." Considered to be the greatest preacher of the three Craig brothers, he continued to preach until near the end of his life.

LEO T. CRISMON

CRAIG, JOSEPH (b. Orange County, Va., c. 1747; d. Fayette County, Ky., c. 1827). Preacher and farmer. The son of Toliver and Polly (Hawkins) Craig and the brother of Elijah and Lewis Craig, Joseph Craig was converted to Christianity during his early years and was baptized under the ministry of Samuel Harris (q.v.) and Dutton Lane (1732-1801). Soon after his conversion he began exhorting sinners, and although persecuted by the authorities in Spotsylvania County, Va., he in each instance managed to elude them, even when hunted by dogs. Many stories are told of his eccentricity, in Virginia and after coming to Kentucky, probably with his brother Lewis and the "Travelling Church," in 1781. He is thought to have been the first and only pastor of the Head of Boone's Creek Church, which was constituted in Fayette County, Ky., in 1785 and was dissolved soon after 1790. Unsuited to the pastoral office, he probably never had another pastorate but continued as a zealous and diligent exhorter. Chiefly by farming, Joseph Craig became the richest of the three brothers. He maintained an unblemished reputation in his personal life. He reared six sons and four daughters, all of whom became respectable citizens, most of them being prominent in church life.   LEO T. CRISMON

CRAIG, LEWIS (b. Orange County, Va., 1741; d. Mason County, Ky., 1824). Minister who was imprisoned for his preaching. The son of Toliver and Polly (Hawkins) Craig and the brother of Elijah and Joseph Craig, Lewis Craig grew up on a farm and received little education. At an early age he married Betsy Landers. Under deep religious conviction for a long time and loudly exclaiming his own condemnation to others, he began his ministry before he himself was assured of salvation. After conversion he continued his preaching for some time before he was baptized. Many were converted under his ministry. During this period he was indicted by a grand jury for "preaching the gospel contrary to law," but perhaps there was no conviction. On June 4, 1768, Craig, with two others, was seized by the sheriff while engaged in public worship and after trial was imprisoned for a month. In Nov., 1770, Craig was ordained and became minister of the Upper Spotsylvania Church, which he had been instrumental in gathering. In the summer of 1771, he was imprisoned for three months in Caroline County for preaching "contrary to license." During his ministry in Virginia, he was instrumental in gathering three other churches in Dover Association—Tuckahoe, Upper King and Queen, and Essex.

In the fall of 1781, Craig left Virginia for Kentucky, accompanied by most of the members of the Upper Spotsylvania Church. In Dec., 1781, the group, called the "Travelling Church," arrived in what is now Garrard County, Ky., south of the Kentucky River. There they met for worship and took the name of Gilberts Creek. In 1783 Craig and most of the members moved North of the Kentucky River into Fayette County and joined the South Elkhorn Church. He was active in the organization of Elkhorn Association in 1785. During his stay in Fayette County, Craig speculated in land and suffered heavy loss. About 1792 he moved to Bracken County (Mason County), where he was called "the father of Bracken Association." His death in 1824 was sudden and in accordance with a previous premonition.   LEO T. CRISMON

CRAIG-MAYES BAPTIST ASSEMBLY. Located at the east edge of Disney, Okla., on a 20-acre tract of land, owned and operated by the Craig-Mayes Association. Its first session was at Northeast Baptist Assembly grounds Aug. 10–15, 1953, when 262 registered, and there were 16 conversions. First session on the present grounds was July 12–16, 1954. A $10,000 loan negotiated for original development is being liquidated in $2,000 annual payments. In 1955, 200 registered, there were six conversions, and six surrendered for special service. It received $2,250 from the associational budget in 1955–56, $2,000 designated for debt retirement.
                                            J. M. GASKIN

CRAIN, JOHN DEAN (b. Greenville County, S. C., Oct. 25, 1881; d. Greenville, S. C., Jan. 10, 1955). Pastor, leader in Christian education. Son of David Hoke and Jane (Suddeth) Crain, farm people of the isolated, mountainous "Dark Corner," Crain, whose early schooling was meager, entered North Greenville Academy at 17 and began a 12-year struggle for an education. In 1910 he received the A.B. degree from Furman University. Converted at 19, Crain was ordained in Oct., 1907, and held chief pastorates at City View and Pendleton Street, Greenville; and Park Street, Columbia. A trustee of Furman University, 1923–24, he was one of its chief money raisers and policy makers. He also served on the Sunday School Board, 1932–49; was first vice-president of the Southern Baptist Convention in 1942; president of the South Carolina Convention in 1927, 1928, and 1929.

Known for his dynamic faith, deep convictions, and formidable adherence to New Testament doctrines, Crain was called the Noble Commoner. His imagination and incisive humor made him a distinct individual. In 1914 he published *A Mountain Boy's Life Story;* later, "My Position as a Baptist on Baptism" and "Bible Lessons." On June 10, 1908, Crain married Ellen Douglas Wilson.

BIBLIOGRAPHY: J. D. Crain, *A Mountain Boy's Life Story* (1914). *Furman University Magazine* (Dec., 1954). Furman University, *The Bonhomie* (1910). *Piedmont* (Jan. 10, 17, 1955). L. B. Westmoreland, "A Biography of J. Dean Crain" (1955).
                                            LILLIE B. WESTMORELAND

CRANE, WILLIAM CAREY (b. Richmond, Va., Mar. 17, 1816; d. Independence, Tex., Feb. 27, 1885). Pastor, editor, educator. Son of William and Lydia Crane, he was educated under private teachers, and attended "Gravel Hill" Academy in 1826, Mount Pleasant Classical Institute in 1831, Richmond Academy in 1832, Virginia Baptist Seminary (Richmond College) in 1832, Hamilton Literary and Theological Institute in 1833, and Madison (Colgate). In 1834 Crane entered Columbian College (George Washington University) and received his A.B. and A.M. degrees in 1836 and 1839. Ordained to the ministry in 1838, Crane became pastor at Montgomery, Ala., on Mar. 17, 1839. After holding other pastorates, he served as president of Mississippi Female College, 1851–57, of Semple Broaddus College in Mississippi, 1859–60, and Mount Lebanon College in Louisiana. While at Mount Lebanon he was also coeditor of the *Mississippi Baptist.* Cofounder and vice-president of the Mississippi State Historical Society, Crane was for two years general agent of the American Tract Society. Crane moved to Texas in Sept., 1863, to become president of Baylor University at Independence where he served for 22 years. Under his leadership and through the expenditure of his own funds, the university was able to survive the trying years of the Civil War and Reconstruction. Crane was one of the South's greatest scholars and educators, a prolific author, and the biographer of Sam Houston. He led in the establishment of Sam Houston Normal Institute, the reorganization of the public school system following Reconstruction, and the establishment of the University of Texas.

BIBLIOGRAPHY: G. J. Burleson, *Life and Writings of Rufus C. Burleson* (1901). J. M. Carroll, *The History of Texas Baptists* (1923). W. C. Crane Papers, Texas Collection, Baylor University, Waco, Tex. F. Eby, *History of Education in Texas* (1925). H. Ford, "The Life and Work of Dr. W. C. Crane" (1926). E. Hyden, "The Relation of William Carey Crane to the Bible Revision Movement in the Antebellum South (1949). J. B. Link, *Texas Historical and Biographical Magazine* (1891). D. L. Smiley, "The Antebellum Professor as Seen in the William Carey Crane Collection" (1948). D. L. Smiley, "William Carey Crane, Professor of Old Mississippi," *Journal of Mississippi History* (Apr., 1950). H. Snapp, "The Mississippi Career of William Carey Crane" (1953). E. B. Thompson, "William Carey Crane and Texas Education," *Southwestern Historical Quarterly* (Jan., 1955). C. G. Wolfskill, "The Educational Philosophy of William Carey Crane" (1947).
                                            GUY B. HARRISON, JR.

CRANFILL, JAMES BRITTON (b. Parker County, Tex., Sept. 12, 1858; d. Dallas, Tex., Dec. 28, 1942). Editor, author and compiler of various religious books, Texas Baptist leader.

After practicing medicine for several years from 1879 to 1882, Cranfill was ordained a Baptist minister in 1890. He served as editor of *Gatesville Advance, Waco Advance, Texas Baptist Standard,* and *Baptist Tribune,* and was financial secretary of Baylor University and superintendent of Baptist mission work in Texas. Candidate for vice-president of the United States for the National Prohibition Party in 1892, Cranfill was a trustee of Southwestern Baptist Theological Seminary, 1909–42, and of the Relief and Annuity Board, 1920–42. He was vice-president of the Baptist General Convention of Texas in 1928. Author of *Cranfill's Chronicles, Courage and Comfort, From Nature to Grace, Cranfill's Heart Talks, From Memory,* and *Fifty Golden Years* (a biography of Mrs. W. L. Williams), Cranfill was joint author of *R. C. Buckner's Life and Works,* compiler and editor of treatises and sermons by Benajah Harvey Carroll (q.v.) and James Milton Carroll (q.v.) and of various books of sermons by George Washington Truett (q.v.), including *We Would See Jesus, A Quest for Souls,* and *God's Call to America.*

F. M. RYBURN

CRAWFORD, NATHANIEL MACON (b. Oglethorpe County, Ga., Mar. 22, 1811; d. Tunnel Hill, Ga., Oct. 27, 1871). Minister, theologian, and college president. As the son of William H. Crawford, a United States senator from Georgia, secretary of the treasury under James Monroe, American minister to France, and one-time candidate for the presidency, Nathaniel Macon Crawford enjoyed unique cultural and educational advantages in boyhood. He was educated in the schools of Washington, D. C., and at the University of Georgia where he graduated with highest honor in 1829 in a distinguished class which included George F. Pierce, a future Methodist bishop and college president; Thomas G. Scott, a future Episcopal bishop; and Shaler Granby Hillyer (q.v.), a distinguished Baptist minister and educator.

Crawford studied law and was admitted to the bar. However, he soon turned to teaching and served as professor of mathematics at Oglethorpe University, a Presbyterian institution, from 1837 to 1841. Although he was brought up a Presbyterian, he became a Baptist after his Baptist wife, the former Anne Katherine Lazer, influenced him to study the New Testament teaching on the meaning of baptism. Ordained a Baptist minister in 1844, he served as pastor such important churches as that at Washington, Ga., in 1844–45 and the historic First Baptist Church of Charleston, S. C., in 1846–47.

Returning to teaching, Crawford was appointed to the faculty of Mercer University in 1847 as professor of biblical literature. In 1854 he was elected president of Mercer, but he resigned in 1856 because of dissension in the faculty. He returned to Mercer as president in 1858, after serving in 1856–57 as professor of mental and moral philosophy at the University of Mississippi and in 1857–58 as professor of systematic theology at Georgetown College. In 1865 Crawford became president of Georgetown College and served in that capacity until his retirement early in 1871.

Noted as a life-long student, Crawford was an accomplished linguist, mathematician, and philosopher as well as a theologian. He was described by his colleague, John Leadley Dagg (q.v.), as a man of learning, talent, and popularity. Although he published one book, *Christian Paradoxes,* he wrote little, and his contributions to Southern Baptists were largely made as a classroom teacher, a counselor of men with ability and promise, and a college executive.

BIBLIOGRAPHY: S. Boykin, ed., *History of the Baptist Denomination in Georgia* (1881). J. H. Campbell, *Georgia Baptists: Historical and Biographical* (1874). B. D. Ragsdale, *Story of Georgia Baptists,* Vol. I (1932).

MALCOLM LESTER

CRAWFORD, TARLETON PERRY (b. Warren County, Ky., May 8, 1821; d. Dawson, Ga., Apr. 7, 1902). Missionary to China. Crawford graduated from Union University, Murfreesboro, Tenn., in 1851, and received a D.D. degree from Richmond College in 1879. Appointed missionary to China in Jan., 1851, he married Martha Foster on the following Mar. 12. In Mar., 1852, Crawford and his wife arrived in Shanghai, where they established a boys' school and engaged in evangelistic work. In 1863 they moved to Tengchow, Shantung Province, for reasons of health. Due to his peculiar views of missions and methods of conducting mission work, Crawford, with others, withdrew from the board and in 1894 established the Gospel Mission in Taianfu.

W. B. GLASS

CRAWFORD HIGH SCHOOL. Opened in Dalton, Ga., in the fall, 1873, with William Clay Wilkes principal. Authorized by the Georgia Baptist convention, the school was operated by the trustees of Mercer University. It became the Joseph E. Brown Institute in 1883.

ARTHUR JACKSON

CREAL SPRINGS COLLEGE AND CONSERVATORY OF MUSIC. Opened Sept. 22, 1884, as Creal Springs Seminary. In Aug., 1888, a charter was granted by the state of Illinois and the name became Creal Springs Seminary Company. In Jan., 1894, the name was changed, by charter, to Creal Springs College and Conservatory of Music. It was located in Creal Springs, Williamson County.

Henry Clay Murrah and Gertrude Brown Murrah erected a building in 1884 that was used for both living quarters and school work. Four years of academic courses and two years of college work were offered. It began as a school for women only but soon became coeducational. On opening day only six were admitted but by the end of the year 12 were taking college work, 31 preparatory work, 7 primary work, and 9 music.

The charter provided that management of

CREATH, JOSEPH WARNER DOSSEY (b. in Virginia, Feb. 3, 1803; d. Cameron, Tex., July 28, 1881). Pioneer minister, missionary, and denominational leader of Texas. Creath, whose father, William Creath (1768–1823), and four brothers were ministers, was converted at 21 and began preaching a year later. After graduating from Virginia Baptist Seminary (now University of Richmond) in 1837, he served pastorates in Virginia until 1846, when he went to Texas as a missionary of the Southern Baptist Domestic Mission Board. Creath spent the remainder of his life as general missionary of the Baptist state convention of Texas preaching throughout the state, organizing churches, counseling, writing letters and articles, and raising money for missions and church buildings. He raised funds for a church building and parsonage at San Antonio, constituted churches at Beaumont and Corpus Christi, and died on a mission tour while projecting plans for churches at Abilene, San Angelo, Laredo, and El Paso. Creath served as president of the Baptist state convention, vice-president of the Southern Baptist Convention, and president of the trustees of Baylor University.   D. D. TIDWELL

CREATION. Biblical revelation affirms that God is absolute Creator. The universe is wholly dependent upon his creative will.

God the Creator.—Of itself the world can offer God nothing. God, sufficient in himself and in the communion of his own trinitarian nature, enjoys the fulness of love. Therefore, if God creates, it is an act of grace. He wills to create a world to be a home for created spirits to share in and reflect back his love. In creation it is God as Holy Trinity who acts. Genesis 1 affirms that God created by his word; Proverbs argues that wisdom was by God's side as a master workman in the moment of creation; the New Testament brings these thoughts to fulfilment by holding that Christ is the Word of God and the Wisdom of God through whom all things were created. The eternally preexistent Son is the agent of creation, as he is also the mediator of redemption. Further, the Holy Spirit, who recreates man after the divine image and works the miracle of regeneration, brooded over the deep in the moment of creation, bringing order out of chaos; thus the Spirit is God's immanent activity in the created as well as the redeemed order.

Absolute creation and sustenance.—Biblical revelation makes it clear that God created out of nothing. He did not work with pre-existent material but brought into being the material which he created into his world. The divine word in creation emphasizes that the world came into being by a free act of the divine will. God commanded, and the world became. Thus, everywhere the created order is directly dependent upon God's will. The laws which the scientist studies in his laboratory are expressions of the habitual divine activity. The regularity of nature is a revelation of God's faithfulness. Miracle is no alien intrusion but God's heightened, creative intervention into the natural order for his particular purpose of redemption. A special activity of God within his created order supersedes, for the time being, his normal creative and sustaining activity. Hence, God did not start the world going and leave it to run according to fixed laws which he had ordained. Creation implies providential government. At every point of the process, God is present, guiding and sustaining the creative movement which he originated. The sustaining of the world is the continuation of creation.

Knowledge of God the Creator.—This knowledge has not come by intellectual speculation. However reasonable it may appear to some that the existence of the universe implies an uncaused Cause and that the design of the universe implies a great Designer, counterarguments can easily be given by the materialists and naturalists. Belief in creation is the result of an experience of redemption. Both the Old and New Testaments present this order of derivation. The God who can use the forces of nature to work the salvation of his chosen people must be the God who created and sustains those forces. God, who can remake the human heart and reconcile man to himself, must be the one through whom all things came into being. Christ, the saving mediator, must also be the divine mediator in creation. The world was made through him.

BIBLIOGRAPHY: E. C. Rust, *Nature and Man in Biblical Thought* (1953).   E. C. RUST

CREE, ARCHIBALD CUNNINGHAM (b. Innerleithen, Peebleshire, Scotland, Mar. 9, 1872; d. Spartanburg, S. C., Dec. 15, 1944). Pastor and denominational executive. He was educated at Wake Forest College (M.A., 1898) and the Southern Baptist Theological Seminary (Th.M., 1900; Ph.D., 1905), and was given the LL.D. degree by Mercer University (1920). Ordained in 1894, he served various churches in South Carolina, Kentucky, Tennessee, and Georgia from 1900 to 1912, and was enlistment secretary of the Southern Baptist Home Mission Board, 1912–15. In Mar., 1915, he became executive secretary of the executive committee of the Baptist Convention of the State of Georgia. In 1919, as director of the 75 Million Campaign for Georgia, he led his state in subscribing more than $10,000,000. Later he succeeded in leading the Georgia convention in a program of debt retirement, and in enlarged enlistment efforts. He left

Georgia in Mar., 1930, to become pastor of the First Baptist Church, Salisbury, N. C., and served there until 1941. After the emergency created in the affairs of the Home Mission Board by the Carnes defalcation, Cree, as temporary acting executive secretary-treasurer, took charge of the board's affairs and succeeded in helping the board to attain a position of relative financial safety.   SEARCY S. GARRISON

CREEDS. Christianity since the apostolic era has sought to express the essence of its gospel in confessions, creeds, or symbols. The New Testament writings themselves contain numerous confessional statements (Matt. 16:16; Rom. 10:9-10; I Cor. 8:6; 12:3; 15:3-7; Eph. 4:4-6; Phil. 2:6-11; I Tim. 6:12-16; I Peter 3:18-22; I John 4:2, 15, *et al.*). Probably the most basic of all confessions was "Jesus is Lord." Persecution, polemics, baptism, and worship occasioned such early confessions, most of which were basically christological.

The Apostles' Creed in its present form seems to have originated in the sixth, seventh, or eighth century. However, its core, called the Old Roman Symbol (R), dates from the second century and is discernible in the writings of Ireneus, Tertullian, Marcellus of Ancyra, and Rufinus. The tradition of a fragmentary authorship by the 12 apostles has been discredited since the 15th century. The symbol R, patterned after the threefold structure of the baptismal formula, stresses historical events concerning Jesus and is thus strongly christological. Some contend that R originated as a polemical weapon against Marcion and Gnosticism; others favor a catechetical and missionary purpose.

The Nicene or Niceno-Constantinopolitan Creed consists of its Nicene form (325) and of the additions following the term "the Holy Spirit," made, if not at the Council of Constantinople (381), by the time of the Council of Chalcedon (451), together with the Western addition of the *filioque* clause. Anti-Arian and anti-Macedonian in phraseology, it declares the deity of Christ and of the Holy Spirit. It was the first creed to obtain authority in both East and West. The Creed of Chalcedon with its doctrine of the two natures in the one person of Christ the God-Man was not only anti-Arian and anti-Apollinarian but mediated between Eutychianism and Nestorianism. The Athanasian Creed, erroneously attributed to Athanasius from the 9th to the 17th centuries, seemingly originated in the Latin West. Written as a "dogmatic psalm" and containing damnatory clauses, it reflects Augustine's doctrine of the Trinity as well as Chalcedonian Christology.

Eastern Orthodoxy, despite its relative doctrinal fixity, has produced several confessional documents, the most significant of which have been the Protestantizing Confession of Cyril Lucar (1631), the anti-Protestant Confession of Dositheus (1672), and the Russian Catechism of Philaret (1839).

Of the distinctly Roman Catholic creeds, the most determinative, the canons and decrees of the Council of Trent (1564), were produced in reaction to Protestantism and gave precise formulation to certain doctrines which had been developing under Scholasticism, viz., tradition, the Apocrypha, original sin, justification, the sacraments, purgatory, indulgences, relics, and images. Tridentine theology was popularly expressed in the Profession of the Tridentine Faith (1564) and taught in the Roman Catechism (1566). Pius IX's decree *Ineffabilis Deus* (1854) defined the immaculate conception of Mary, the Vatican Council (1870) decreed the dogma of papal infallibility, and Pius XII's *Munificentissimus Deus* (1950) defined the assumption of Mary.

Protestant confessions, unlike the ancient Greek creeds, were written in Latin or a modern language, were detailed in scope, and were polemical in purpose. Earliest of the Anabaptist confessions were probably the Seven Articles from Schlatten am Randen (1527) and Hübmaier's Twelve Articles (1527), but the most elaborate Anabaptist confession was the *Rechenschaft* (*c.* 1540) of Peter Rideman, the Hutterite. Oldest of the major Protestant confessions is the Augsburg Confession (1530), prepared by Melancthon. It, its Apology (1531), Luther's two catechisms (1529), the Schmalkald Articles (1537), and the controversy-terminating Formula of Concord (1577) constitute the authoritative symbols of Lutheranism. The Reformed Confessions, more numerous than the Lutheran, were produced in the various nations where Calvinism was planted. Among the more important were the Thirty-nine Articles (1553, 1563), the Gallican (1559), the Scotch (1560), the Belgic (1561), the Heidelberg (1563) by Ursinus and Olevianus, and Bullinger's Second Helvetic (1566) confessions. Later Reformed confessions, such as the Remonstrance (1610), the Canons of Dort (1619), and the Helvetic Consensus Formula (1675), dealt with issues within Protestantism. The Westminster Confession (1648), with its rootage in the Lambeth Articles (1595) and the Irish Articles (1615) and its emphasis on the Scriptures and the sabbath, has been widely influential in Britain and America. The Savoy Declaration (1658) of English Congregationalism and the Second London Confession (1677) of Particular Baptists were adaptations of the Westminster Confession. The Mennonites produced the Waterlander Confession by Ries and Gerrits (*c.* 1580) and the Dort Confession (1632). Barclay's Apology (1675) represented the Quaker view, while the Racovian Catechism (1605) was the standard for Socinianism. From the Thirty-nine Articles, John Wesley produced the Twenty-five Articles (1784) for American Methodism.

American confessions include the moderately Calvinistic New Hampshire Confession of Baptists (1833), the Free Will Baptist Confession (1834), the unofficial yet influential "Declaration and Address" by Thomas Campbell (1809), the Cumberland Presbyterian Confession (1813), the Boston Declaration of Congregationalists (1865), and the Statement of Fundamental Truths of the Assemblies of God (1916).

BIBLIOGRAPHY: O. Cullmann, *The Earliest Christian Confessions* (1949). J. N. D. Kelly, *Early Christian Creeds* (1950). A. C. McGiffert, *The Apostles' Creed* (1902). W. J. McGlothlin, *Baptist Confessions of Faith* (1911). P. Schaff, *The Creeds of Christendom* (1877).

J. LEO GARRETT

CRIME. Any act, or failure to act, which is forbidden or proscribed by law, the failure to abide by such law being punishable by fine, imprisonment, banishment, death, or other punitive treatment, as the particular state may prescribe. Crime is one of the most costly and one of the most universal social problems of mankind. It has been estimated that the annual cost of crime in America is between $13,000,000,000 and $16,000,000,000.

Types of crime.—Crimes may be divided into several categories. When classified as to their degree of reprehensibility, they are either felonies or misdemeanors. Although there is some variation as to classification by the several states, usually such crimes as murder, burglary, rape, grand larceny, arson, and treason are considered to be felonies. As such, they are usually punishable by imprisonment in a state prison or by death. In some instances a felony may be punishable by fine or by both fine and imprisonment.

Other crimes, such as drunkenness, disturbing the peace, petit larceny, and traffic violations which do not cause serious injury are classified as misdemeanors. These are punishable by a fine or a short jail sentence.

Crimes may be committed by individuals, by groups, or by gangs. Thus, organized crime is the control of an illegal business in a specific geographical area by a crime syndicate, whose operations may include such crimes as gambling, prostitution, bootlegging, commercial rackets, and political graft. In recent years attention has been directed by Congressional investigations and the reports of crime commissions to "white collar" crime. This includes violations of the law by businessmen, executives of large corporations, and persons in positions of private or public trust. "White collar" crime is committed by misrepresentation, fraudulent advertising, illegal use of money, unfair labor practices, embezzlement, and other violations of private and public trust.

Extent of crime.—In 1954 the Federal Bureau of Investigation estimated that 2,267,250 major crimes were committed in the United States. This was an average of one crime committed every 13.9 seconds throughout the year. For seven consecutive years including 1954, there was an increase in the crime rate for the nation. Between 1950 and 1954 the population of the country increased 7 per cent; during the same period the nation's criminality increased 18.4 per cent.

The major crimes listed by the FBI for the year 1954 were as follows:

Murder and non-negligent manslaughter	6,850
Manslaughter by negligence	5,410
Rape	18,030
Robbery	67,420
Aggravated assault	93,540
Burglary—breaking or entering	519,190
Larceny—theft	1,340,870
Auto theft	215,940

Crime in the South.—According to information from the Federal Bureau of Investigation in 1954, the urban crime rate in states of the South in several categories exceeded the rate for the rest of the nation. (See table below.) This was true of a majority of the Southern states in the categories of murder, assault, burglary, and auto theft.

URBAN CRIME RATES, 1954, BY GEOGRAPHIC DIVISIONS AND STATES
(Offenses known per 100,000 inhabitants. Population based on 1950 decennial census.)

Division and State	Murder and non-negligent manslaughter	Robbery	Aggravated assault	Burglary—breaking entering	Larceny—theft	Auto theft
TOTAL (all states)	4.8	71.2	85.0	444.9	1,037.8	187.0
South Atlantic	10.0	59.1	229.9	518.5	1,139.3	236.4
Delaware	5.7	53.4	21.4	509.2	1,519.4	233.2
Florida	10.1	76.4	100.9	869.1	1,473.5	233.3
Georgia	16.6	46.5	198.7	488.2	965.3	250.3
Maryland	7.7	67.3	155.3	462.2	1,037.9	444.2
North Carolina	11.0	29.7	367.0	396.9	929.9	142.8
South Carolina	7.2	31.1	105.1	489.7	1,226.4	151.0
Virginia	10.0	66.2	245.0	473.0	1,385.1	239.0
West Virginia	3.5	23.2	60.6	274.0	661.2	109.2
East South Central	12.9	50.3	117.4	482.2	779.4	194.4
Alabama	14.8	36.0	119.7	524.4	770.6	127.4
Kentucky	9.8	89.7	156.2	530.9	1,086.8	303.8
Mississippi	9.4	17.3	48.4	371.2	592.7	99.7
Tennessee	14.7	45.0	111.3	449.7	623.8	204.0
West South Central	8.9	49.3	95.2	527.7	1,225.0	259.5
Arkansas	6.4	56.7	92.2	407.8	836.5	102.5
Louisiana	10.7	75.6	93.4	275.5	727.6	444.4
Oklahoma	5.4	37.4	38.2	505.0	1,221.1	162.4
Texas	9.7	45.7	109.9	600.9	1,375.0	259.1

Crime and Christian responsibility.—Reports and recommendations of the Christian Life Commission to the Southern Baptist Convention contain the following practical steps for individual Christians and church groups to follow in meeting the challenge of crime: (1) study of crime and the conditions that produce it; (2) investigation of the treatment of criminals; (3) promotion of Christian teachings in the home to prevent crime; (4) co-operation with law enforcement agencies in the community to reduce crime; (5) assistance in the rehabilitation of those who have been released from jail or prison. HUGH A. BRIMM

CRISES, SOUTHERN BAPTIST. From the days of their beginnings until 1944, in all the areas of their life, Southern Baptists enjoyed seasons of prosperous harmony and progress, alternating with longer periods of critical adversity sufficiently serious to be called crises. The forces which precipitated these trials inflicted severe damage and were painful to those who had to endure them. In retrospect Baptists feel that divine providence used each grave crisis to develop within Southern Baptists as a people, and in the organizations that express their co-operative life, blessings which they could never have otherwise obtained.

These crises affected in one way or another much of Baptist life. The doctrine, polity, organization, and institutions of modern Southern Baptists have been tested by controversy. In every case the pattern of events has been the same. First there would be proposed a theory which was either an extreme conclusion drawn from a valid doctrine or a distorted position close enough to Baptist ideas to be attractive and far enough away to be corrupting. Many people would adopt this new theory, and there would be a division, often accompanied by heated controversy. Southern Baptists would then be forced to clarify or redefine the aspect of doctrine or polity in question. Dissident elements would withdraw, and Southern Baptists would be left reduced in numbers but committed more strongly than ever to their distinctive and newly understood position. Always their gain in understanding and in commitment has more than compensated for their loss in numbers and has led to greater accomplishments than could have been achieved by the denomination as it existed before the crisis occurred.

There have been seven of these crises. In one way or another, they have all been dealt with in other articles in this work. In this monograph an effort is made to pinpoint them in a way that will reveal the underlying trends which are the meaning of the historical facts elsewhere treated. The seven crises are as follows:

Antimissionism.—When Baptists in America launched their missionary enterprise with the organization of the Triennial Convention in 1814, they obtained immediate and gratifying response from individuals, churches, and associations, which looked with favor upon the venture, organized mission societies, and contributed to the cause of missions. But within a decade many of them had joined a violent antimission movement that endangered the whole forward trend of the denomination. Baptists lost to it approximately 45 per cent of their membership, including many entire churches and associations, between 1820 and 1845.

Numerous factors account for the rise, spread, and devastating effects of this movement, which was largely a Baptist phenomenon and had little effect on other denominations. The average Baptist of that day had little education, possessed little knowledge of distinctive Baptist doctrine or principles, but was quite committed to the authority of the Scriptures, and had a firm but naïve concept of the sovereignty of God. Thus he was highly susceptible to any propaganda which was persuasively proclaimed as biblical. Powerful leaders such as John Taylor (*q.v.*) in Kentucky; Daniel Parker (*q.v.*), an extreme hyper-Calvinist, in Tennessee, Kentucky, Illinois, and Texas; and James Osburn in Virginia and North Carolina, who all claimed biblical support for their written and hortatory attack upon mission principles, methods, and leaders, etc., convinced thousands to join the anti-movement. Hyper-Calvinism (an extreme form of Calvinism maintaining that if a man was destined by God to be lost, he would be lost and no amount of preaching would do any good) gave the movement a quasi-theological basis and was often employed to bolster and justify other arguments against exerting any effort to evangelize the lost. The work of missions, according to Parker, involved in addition "acts of such gross and supreme folly that no Christian should engage in them." Widespread illiteracy, which in turn bred suspicion and fear of new methods and educated leaders, contributed strongly to the success of anti-evangelistic propaganda, which was often quite vicious. John Taylor, speaking of missions, said, "Money and power is the watchword of the whole scheme," and accused the missionary agents of "aiming at Lordship over God's heritage." The scarcity of denominational papers and mission agents to counteract these false views in many areas allowed the movement to inflict severe damage to the cause of missions. However, in spite of tremendous loss of membership, churches, and associations, and serious delay in their progress caused by these "hardshells," Baptists came forth from this trial more committed to the causes of missions and education than ever before. The crisis forced Baptist members, churches, and associations to take a stand on the question under attack. When the denomination was rid of antimission elements, it grew all the faster in numbers and missionary giving for having lost them. Thus the struggle with antimissionism helped to make Southern Baptists a stronger missionary denomination.

Campbellism.—During the same period in which the denomination wrestled with antimissionism, another rival, Campbellism, arose, which by the 1820's posed a serious threat to Baptist beliefs, unity, and progress. Inflamed controversies afflicted Baptist churches and associations. Sometimes entire churches joined the interlopers, while others divided. The Campbellites secured control of original churches in several important Southern cities. Churches in Pennsylvania, Ohio, Tennessee, Virginia, Indiana, Illinois, Kentucky, and Missouri suffered heavy loss. Within a decade Baptists lost approximately 20 per cent of their membership.

The large defection of Baptists to this movement was caused by a combination of factors. Because Alexander Campbell and his followers, who posed as reformers endeavoring to restore the New Testament church, were affiliated with Baptist associations from 1813 to 1830, churches generally received them into their pulpits without any suspicion of their menace to Baptist doctrine, polity, and fellowship. The idea of reform appealed to many because of their background of radical dissent. Their uncritical nature plus the persuasiveness of the Campbellites caused many to embrace Campbell's whole doctrinal system, in spite of its rejection of vital Baptist doctrines and principles. The average church member of the early 19th century knew little about Baptist doctrine. He did maintain a strict view toward local church autonomy, baptism by immersion, and authority of the Scriptures. Apparently Campbell, who professed to uphold these views, took this "container of Baptist attitude" and filled it with counterfeit knowledge. He eventually rejected as unscriptural all organization beyond the level of the local church, which attitude endangered the vital Baptist principle of co-operation. He substituted a merely intellectual concept for genuine faith and required no experience of regeneration prior to baptism. Vitriolic controversies developed in churches and associations between Campbellite and anti-Campbellite elements. Open division frequently resulted. Had it not been for men with informed convictions concerning the fundamental doctrines of Christianity, those who claimed to offer a New Testament restoration would have wrecked Southern Baptist life.

Baptists, however, successfully opposed their opponents through several means. Associations adopted anti-Campbellite resolutions. Newspapers wrote against their views. Churches barred them from their pulpits and withdrew fellowship from those who accepted their teachings. Gradually Baptists shut out the discordant elements, surviving greatly reduced in numbers but more thoroughly committed to the distinctive doctrines which opposition had brought them more clearly to understand: the necessity of spiritual regeneration, the symbolic character of baptism, and the necessity for a definition of the New Testament church would be the basis of fruitful co-operation. This definition they worked out in their later struggle with Landmarkism.

Method.—The centralized convention plan of organization, which William Bullein Johnson (*q.v.*), heir to the denominational concept of Richard Furman (*q.v.*), led Southern Baptists to adopt in 1845, had been desired by many Southerners from 1814, but was not finally accepted for 60 years. In the beginning the society plan as used by Baptists in the North competed for favor, but for most of the period, Landmarkism was the chief and almost overpowering rival.

Unlike the two previous crises, which split the denomination, this trial divided the minds of the people and remained a source of contention and confusion for an extended period. The Convention labored for many years under both internal and external pressure to revert to the society plan of organization. Landmarkism at home and Gospel Missionism abroad, by their vigorous opposition to the board system of mission work, created controversy that threatened to destroy the program of work of Southern Baptists. In the end, however, through facing and overcoming this opposition, they became more committed to their own distinctive methods than ever before.

Robert Boyté Crawford Howell (*q.v.*), pastor of the First Baptist Church of Nashville, Tenn., who saw firsthand the devastating effects of hyper-Calvinism, antimissionism, Campbellism, and anticipated the far-reaching effects of Landmarkism, wrote in 1863, while a prisoner of war of the Union army:

Now for the third time within forty years, the desolation of the Baptist churches in Tennessee was complete. They were first rent, overthrown and destroyed by the violence of the controversy on the doctrine of *Predestination;* they were secondly crushed and scattered by the Reformation of Mr. Campbell; they were thirdly severed and prostrated by the Mission controversy. Scarcely did they begin fairly to recover from one calamitous division when they fell into another. Would to God this had been the last! But alas, yet another awaited us, still more destructive! Will the Baptists of Tennessee ever be united, and labor together continuously in the cause of Christ?

Landmarkism.—Southern Baptists had far from fully recovered from the ravages of Antimissionism and Campbellism when they had to confront internal opposition in the form of Landmarkism. This movement created dissension, threatened division, sought control of the Convention, and in many ways jeopardized Southern Baptist life and work for 50 years.

Because Landmark doctrines were extreme or distorted versions of normal Baptist beliefs, they were quite dangerous to orthodoxy, particularly when promoted by so skilled an advocate as James Robinson Graves (*q.v.*). Frequently it was difficult to oppose the positions without being made to appear to attack some fundamental tenet of Baptist faith. Through proclaiming himself as the champion of local church autonomy and the restorer of vital practices of the New Testament church, Graves won thousands of adherents, especially among those who feared the growth of centralization within the Convention. He appealed to the denominational pride of Baptists, who had been a despised and scorned sect for so many years, by asserting that they were the only true church, and he advanced what appeared to many to be convincing historical proof of his claims. The powerful leadership of Graves, J. M. Pendleton (*q.v.*), and Amos Cooper Dayton (*q.v.*), who were all skilled with tongue and pen, provided the movement with a formidable momentum.

Perhaps its chief threat was the contention that the local church, not conventions and boards, should administer mission activities. If Southern Baptists had accepted this view with its implications, it would have destroyed their convention and prevented the development of the work of state conventions. The growing power and uncompromising spirit of the Landmarkers caused them to threaten to split churches, associations, and conventions if these bodies rejected their doctrines and demands. Their agitation and appeal to prejudice resulted in divided opinion and bitter, prolonged controversies that had devastating effects on Southern Baptist life and work. Had the Civil War not intervened, Landmarkers would likely have caused a major split in the denomination. Though they failed to destroy or divide the Convention, they did create Landmark and anti-Landmark factions in many churches, associations, and state conventions, which hindered the development of a stronger denominational program for many years. But the denomination had no recourse except to endure them until in large degree they defeated themselves.

The withdrawal of the Landmarkers in 1905 to form their own organization greatly aided Southern Baptists. This separation augmented the growth of denominational consciousness and strengthened the Convention for its larger tasks of the 20th century. On the other hand, the movement bred a congregational exclusiveness still influential in the denomination's life. Paradoxically, Landmark emphases and methods encouraged the growth of denominationalism and resulted in Southern Baptists' becoming more committed to their own distinctive principles and methods than ever before.

1865–92.—The three decades following the Civil War were critical years for Southern Baptists. In the beginning economic prostration prevented them from engaging in an aggressive mission program at home and abroad and caused many to advocate that the Convention be dissolved. The question of reunion with Northern Baptists, as favored by some Southern leaders and stimulated by the Northern Home Mission Society, created controversy in Convention sessions for some years. The Convention in 1882 almost decided to abolish the Home Mission Board. If this had been done, it would have been a major step toward the total disintegration of the Convention and its program of work.

The dire financial distress of Southern Baptists resulted from the loss of their wealth during the war and the economic privations of Reconstruction days. Although the economic factor may have been an underlying motive behind the move toward reunion with Northern Baptists, the principal factor appears to have been the sentiment of some who wished to dissolve the Convention and return to the society plan of organization. In the light of this, some leaders, in both North and South, insisted that the reason for the 1845 separation of Baptists had been slavery, and that since slavery no longer existed, Baptists should unite and thus facilitate the work of the denomination. The most dangerous peril to the Convention, however, evolved from the work of the Home Mission Society in the South. Its aggressive program and its alliance with many of the state conventions cut off the Home Mission Board from much of its territory and support. Some of these conventions apparently excluded the board from their territory because they had their own problems and saw no real need for the board's work. Because of the weakened and destitute condition of the board, the Convention in 1882 seriously considered abolishing it. Had this been done, there is little doubt that the Foreign Mission Board would soon have lost its strength, and the Convention would have disintegrated. But the Convention voted to continue the board, relocated it, and elected as corresponding secretary, Isaac Taylor Tichenor (*q.v.*). He promoted a policy of single alignment, based on a platform of aggressive sectional loyalty, which eventually forced the Home Mission Society out. By 1892 the Southern Baptist Convention had reclaimed its territory, and state conventions joined in hearty sympathy and co-operation with the Home Mission Board.

Baptists of the South came from this period of testing determined to maintain their identity and separate program of work, to which they have since remained loyal. They also had gained an appreciation of the vital place of the Home Mission Board and were committed to its support.

Religious publications.—Southern Baptists for 46 years had no permanent program of religious publication. Thus they were unable to supply their churches with literature distinctively Southern in origin and emphasis and therefore could not retain the undivided allegiance of their constituency. As they sought to develop such a program, they encountered numerous obstacles and vigorous opposition from within and without. The effort of Landmarkers to gain control of the denomination's publication business resulted in extended delay in the development of a permanent institution. This, combined with the effects of the Civil War, financial depression, etc., ultimately caused the termination of early publication efforts in the South. As a result a majority of the churches turned to the American Baptist Publication Society for their literature needs, especially in the 1870's and 1880's.

The expansion of Sunday school literature by Tichenor in 1887 was a direct attack upon the Southern business of the Publication Society and thus forced Baptists in the South to decide once and for all the question of publications.

Since many believed that the literature of the society, which was in part produced by Southern writers, was doctrinally sound and adequate to meet their needs, they failed to see the need for a new institution. But others sensed the importance of distinctively and purely Southern publications and pressed for an independent program of publication. The conflict between these two factions, which the society fostered because of its determination to retain its lucrative business in the South, resulted in spirited contests in churches, associations, and conventions. In spite of this internal opposition, and in the face of the aggressive program of the society through its agents and newly established branch houses in the South, and the relentless attacks from both sources upon Southern publications, the Convention in 1891 established the Sunday School Board. Although the task seemed impossible, this institution, by producing suitable literature of excellent quality, by appealing to the sectional loyalty of the people, and by refusing to indulge in bitter retaliation, eventually triumphed over its opposition, gained as friends most of its former critics, and secured the patronage of its constituency. The Sunday School Board has, since created, promoted, and obtained acceptance for large programs of religious education based on its materials. In addition the board has almost from the beginning provided, in addition to printed materials, a full program of instruction in methods serving the church. This program, added to publications, has been responsible for much of the denomination's growth.

Finances.—Southern Baptists, from their beginning until 1940, found themselves handicapped in their work by recurring financial crises. For most of this period, the denomination depended upon special campaigns for funds ordinarily conducted independently by its various boards and agencies, which often competed with each other. Since the funds were usually paid in at the end of the year, these bodies generally operated on anticipated income, which at times failed to materialize, often resulting in debts and retrenchment. Financial depressions intensified the problem. Most churches, associations, and conventions had no systematic plan for collecting or spending their monies and thus were forced to gear their program to a fluctuating income. But no previous economic trials compared with the one that followed the 75 Million Campaign and continued until the early 1940's.

The failure of the campaign, caused largely by economic depression in the 1920's, in addition to overexpansion by Convention agencies on the basis of anticipated income, resulted in a mounting debt for both state and Southern Baptist Convention causes. The latter by 1926 had accumulated a debt of over $6,500,000. That of the states was proportionately even larger. Because of the disaster of recurring depression, the plight of the average church member by 1933 was the same as that of the denomination —large debts and little or no income. As a result the total gifts of Baptists decreased that year almost 63 per cent below the all-time high of 1928, although they were still over any pre-75 Million Campaign total. While membership increased a million between 1920 and 1933, mission gifts fell from a peak of over $14,000,000 to less than $4,000,000 in the same period and did not reach $14,000,000 again until 1945. Drastic reduction in income frequently forced the Convention to renew its loans without any payment on principal. At times even the interest could not be paid. The desperate condition of their organized work, which could not expand and in most cases had to be curtailed, produced deep despondency among the people. Their morale was at the breaking point. Discouragement overcame denominational workers. Creditors clamored for payment of loans, while some even threatened legal proceedings to collect or throw the Convention's agencies into bankruptcy.

In spite of what seemed like an almost hopeless situation, Baptists weathered the financial storm, paid their debts, and profited greatly by their experience. Though the 75 Million Campaign left them deeply in debt, it gave Southern Baptists the methods which were the foundation of success—co-ordinated planning and enlistment, systematic giving to a co-operative program, and percentage distribution of receipts. Through the application of these methods and an unprecedented emphasis on stewardship, the denomination not only released itself from debt by 1944 but also gathered momentum for the years of accelerating expansion which followed.

See also AMERICAN BAPTIST HOME MISSION SOCIETY; ANTIMISSIONISM; CAMPBELLISM; CHURCHES OF CHRIST; DIRECT MISSIONISM; GRAVES-HOWELL CONTROVERSY; HOME MISSION BOARD; LANDMARKISM; PRIMITIVE BAPTISTS; SOCIETY, THE BAPTIST; and SUNDAY SCHOOL BOARD.

LYNN E. MAY, JR.

CROSBY, THOMAS (Lived c. 1740 at Southwark, London). The author of English Baptists' first self-conscious attempt at a complete history. Crosby was not a historian by training or natural interest. The historical materials of Benjamin Stinton (1676–1718), Crosby's pastor at Goat Street, were given to Crosby upon the former's early and untimely death. These papers apparently had been successively in the possession of Henry Jessey (1601–63), pastor of the Jacob's Church, 1637–63; William Kiffin (1616–1701), long-time pastor of the Devonshire Square Church in London; and Richard Adams (d. 1716), copastor and pastor of the Devonshire Square Church, 1690–1716. Crosby, feeling his inadequacy and hoping to find a more "able hand" to complete the work of Stinton, meanwhile began to "digest the materials in their proper order, and supply the vacancies." Failing to find anyone, he besought Daniel Neal (1678–1743), Puritan historian, who was preparing his *History of the Puritans,* to include Stinton's material on the Baptists in the work. Crosby says,

"I was surprized to see the ill use Mr. Neal made of these materials; and that the rise and progress of the English Baptists . . . were contained in less than five pages of his third volume; and that too with very great partiality."

Crosby, incensed by this treatment and desiring to vindicate the Baptists from the disgrace of Neal's misrepresentations, forthwith commenced his own history, which he published as *The History of the English Baptists, from the Reformation to the Beginning of the Reign of King George I* in four volumes. The first volume appeared in 1738 and the third and fourth in 1740.

Crosby is chiefly valuable for his biographical particulars of the earlier "Baptist" ministers. His work is trustworthy as a mere compendium of isolated facts and events but is completely uncritical in the finer points of historical method. The absence of cohesion, a very apparent apologetic and appalling style, and poor arrangement of material make it almost completely useless as an authority. Crosby also published *A Brief Reply to Mr. John Lewis* (1738) and *The Book-keeper's Guide* (1749).

BIBLIOGRAPHY: C. Burrage, *The Early English Dissenters* (1912). T. Crosby, *The History of English Baptists* (1738–40). J. Ivimey, *A History of English Baptists* (1811–30). EUGENE STOCKSTILL

CROSBY ACADEMY. A secondary school at Crosby, Tenn., founded c. 1922. It reported in 1924 an enrolment of 110 and property valued at $25,000. It operated under the supervision of the Southern Baptist Home Mission Board until 1930, and was closed for lack of support in 1932. LYNN EDWARD MAY, JR.

CROSS. The term in New Testament usage came soon to stand for more than the outward form of Christ's death, being used as a brief term for the saving work of Christ (I Cor. 1:18). Paul first used the expression "the cross of Christ" (I Cor. 1:17). Death on the cross was a shame and a curse (I Cor. 1:23; Gal. 3:13; Heb. 12:2; 13:3), yet the cross became the revelation of God's wisdom and power (I Cor. 1:18, 24). By the cross God reconciled all things to himself (Col. 1:20; 2:14; Eph. 2:16); by it the believer is crucified to self (Gal. 2:20), to the flesh (Gal. 5:24), and to the world (Gal. 6:14).

See also ATONEMENT. W. BOYD HUNT

CROSS AND BAPTIST BANNER, THE. A four-page weekly paper begun at Frankfort, Ky., Oct. 13, 1832. The earliest presently available issue bears the date of Jan. 2, 1834, and it is Volume II, Number 6. Only it and the issues for Feb. 6, 13, 20, 1834, are now extant. Early references to the title are always *The Cross and Baptist Banner*, but the four extant issues bear only the title *The Cross*. The editor was Uriel B. Chambers and the publisher was W. B. Holeman. On Mar. 28, 1834, it was merged with *The Baptist Journal of the Mississippi Valley* to form *The Cross and Baptist Journal of the Mississippi Valley* and was published at Cincinnati. LEO T. CRISMON

CROW, CHARLES (b. Newberry District, S. C., 1770; d. June 12, 1845). A pioneer Baptist minister and denominational leader. He was received for baptism by the Bush River Baptist Church, Newberry District, S. C., Sept. 4, 1802, was ordained by this church Aug. 29, 1807, and served as pastor from Oct. 9, 1816, until he migrated to Alabama in 1819. In 1822 he founded the Hopewell Baptist Church in Perry County and became its pastor. Together with William Callaway he was cofounder of the Siloam Baptist Church in Marion in June, 1822, and served as its first pastor until 1830. He helped institute Fellowship Church in Perry County, and he served Shiloh Church for three years. In 1829 he became pastor of the Oculmulgee Baptist Church, which he served until his death. When the Alabama Baptist State Convention was organized at Salem Baptist Church near Greensboro in 1823, he became the first president. He was one of the first missionaries to be appointed when the state was divided into three districts, northern, middle, and southern. In 1835 he was one of the vice-presidents of the Convention. He was moderator of the Cahaba Association almost all of his life in Alabama. He was married twice; his first wife was named Sarah, and his second, Sarah McCraw (1832). He had four children by his first wife: Elijah, Silas, Joshua, and Elizabeth. He is buried at Oculmulgee churchyard near Marion, Ala.

BIBLIOGRAPHY: H. Holcombe, *A History of the Rise and Progress of the Baptists in Alabama* (1840). J. B. O'Neall and J. A. Chapman, *The Annals of Newberry in Two Parts* (1892). T. M. Owen, *History of Alabama and Dictionary of Alabama Biography* (1921). B. F. Riley, *The History of the Baptists of Alabama* (1895); *A Memorial History of Baptists in Alabama* (1923). R. H. FALWELL, JR.

CROWDER, JOSEPH WADE (b. Macon County, Tenn., Mar. 27, 1873; d. Fort Worth, Tex., July 20, 1954; buried "Greenwood," Fort Worth). Pastor, teacher, director of Southwestern Seminary Extension Department. He attended the public schools in Macon County, Tenn., 1879–92. He was converted in Allen County, Ky., in 1886. In 1897 he moved to Texas and was licensed to preach in 1899. After serving as a pastor for five years, he entered the Southwestern Baptist Theological Seminary and earned the E.B. degree in 1908. In 1911 he earned the B.A. degree from Baylor University, and in 1934 he was awarded the D.D. degree by Webster University. Additional study was completed at Temple University in 1902 and at the University of Chicago in 1916. From 1910 to 1919 he taught English Bible in Southwestern Seminary, and from 1920 to 1943 he served as director of the Seminary Extension Department. His main literary contribution was the collecting and editing of the works of Benajah Harvey

Carroll (*q.v.*). He furnished the manuscripts for all but four of the 35 volumes of Carroll's published works. He married Allie Mae Marrow June 1, 1897. They had two children: Carroll M. and Noma (Mrs. W. J. Hodson). His first wife died Apr. 1, 1934, and on May 11, 1935, he married Mrs. May Fair. His life may be characterized by two words expressed by a friend at his retirement from the seminary, "faithful" and "efficient."

BIBLIOGRAPHY: J. M. Price, *Southwestern Men and Messages* (1948). J. S. Ramond, *Among Southern Baptists* (1936). L. R. Scarborough, *A Modern School of the Prophets* (1939).   RALPH L. SMITH

CRUCIBLE OFFERING. A supplementary method employed during the Southern Baptist debt-paying campaign for 1933. Also known as the Crucible Service Campaign and as the Old Gold Campaign, it was planned to be not in lieu of but supplemental to the self-denial cash offering, which was being promoted each year. Altogether, these efforts were planned to reduce the 18-million-dollar indebtedness of Southern Baptists, nearly six million of which was on Convention-wide institutions and the remainder on state institutions.

Baptists were urged to give through their churches old gold, silver, and precious stones. "Watches, chains, rings, lockets, brooches, medallions, pendants, cuff links, bracelets, spectacle frames, cameos, pins, dental scraps, sterling pieces and old jewelry of every kind" were suggested. These were to be purchased by the Crucible Service Company of Philadelphia. The company agreed to advertise the campaign, furnish promotional literature, pay transportation charges to Philadelphia, and to do the smelting and refining for 20 per cent of the proceeds. Eighty per cent would be returned to the state executive secretaries who agreed to divide the same on a fifty-fifty basis between Convention-wide and state debts. It was estimated that each of the 950,000 Baptist homes had at least $4 worth of jewelry, suggesting a potential of nearly four million dollars. The promotion committee of the Convention was charged with its promotion. Based on initial estimates of the potential, the results were disappointing. An incomplete report through mid-May, 1933, showed a gross of $16,297.75.   ROBERT J. HASTINGS

CRUCIFIXION. See JESUS CHRIST.

CRUMP, FRANK T. (b. Richmond, Va., Jan. 6, 1867; d. Richmond, Va., Sept. 26, 1951). Educated in the public schools of Richmond, he entered business in that city and owned and operated a box company until elected treasurer of the Baptist General Association of Virginia in 1919. This post he held for 30 years and also served as executive secretary of the same group from 1937 to 1944. For some years he was superintendent of the Sunday school of the Second Baptist Church of Richmond. In 1930 when the whole denomination was deeply in debt, he proposed a plan of liquidation of debt which would prevent the crippling of the current work of the denomination. An ardent supporter of the Cooperative Program, he prepared several sketches for its promotion which have continued in use ever since, among them the familiar lighthouse, the balances, and the encircled world. He was married to Nannie Ellyson, daughter of James Taylor Ellyson. They had one son, James Taylor Ellyson Crump.   CARRINGTON PAULETTE

CRUMPTON, WASHINGTON BRYAN (b. Camden, Wilcox County, Ala., Feb. 24, 1842; d. Montgomery, Ala., Mar. 9, 1926). Pastor, author, and denominational leader. He was the son of Henry T. and Matilda (Bryan) Crumpton. At the age of 13, Crumpton joined the church. He attended Georgetown College but was not graduated. After serving as a sergeant in the Confederate army, Crumpton was discharged as a lieutenant. He was licensed as a minister in 1866 and was ordained in 1870. As pastor, he served in six Alabama churches and in the First Baptist Church, Meridian, Miss. Returning to Alabama, he served as state evangelist in eight associations. In 1883 he was elected a member of the state mission board and two years later was chosen corresponding secretary of the board. Crumpton was among the first to promote a unified plan of contributions for the churches and the enlistment of children and young people in denominational enterprises. His other promotional plans included the organization of the Alabama Baptist Bible and Colportage Board, and the founding of the State Mission Quarterly. After 10 years of service, he resigned from the board to become financial secretary of Georgetown College (Kentucky). In 1899 he was again chosen secretary of the mission board in Alabama and promoted the work effectively through his oral and written messages. During this time he organized the Alabama Anti-Saloon League and served as its first president. Resigning as secretary of the mission board in 1913, Crumpton remained in office until the election of his successor, finally retiring from this post in 1916 as secretary emeritus. He continued to serve as state director of colportage, and as president of the state convention (1917–19). Crumpton's writings included his "Trip Notes," printed in *The Alabama Baptist,* and the following books: *A Book of Memories 1842–1920, Our Baptist Centennials, Daily Devotionals,* and, as co-author, *The Adventures of Two Alabama Boys.*

BIBLIOGRAPHY: W. B. Crumpton, *A Book of Memories 1842–1920* (1921). B. F. Riley, *A Memorial History of the Baptists of Alabama* (1923). W. P. Wilks, *Biographical Dictionary of Alabama Baptists 1920–1947* (1947).   GARNETT PUCKETT

CRUTCHER, GEORGE HARVEY (b. Lewisburg, Tenn., July 12, 1870; d. Tampa, Fla., Feb. 27, 1944). Pastor, missionary, evangelist, professor. Son of Charles J. and Elizabeth (Welch) Crutcher, he was educated in the Lewisburg public schools, after which he attended Union University, Jackson, Tenn., receiving the B.S. degree in 1896, and Southern Baptist Theological Seminary. Crutcher's early spiritual experiences occurred in the Baptist church in his community, and he was ordained to the ministry in 1891. After serving as pastor at Shelbyville, Tenn., from 1897 to 1899, he went as a missionary of the Foreign Mission Board to Mexico in 1899 and remained at Torreon, Coahuila, until a severe attack of smallpox and consequent ill health forced his return home. He held other pastorates, served as evangelist of the Home Mission Board, 1909–12, secretary of missions for Louisiana, 1912–20, and professor of evangelism and applied Christianity, Baptist Bible Institute, New Orleans, 1920–27. After two years in retirement in Florida due to illness, Crutcher remained there until his death, serving as pastor of Fifth Avenue Church, St. Petersburg, 1927–28, and Riverside, Tampa, 1929–44. Crutcher was a leader in the movement for the establishment of Baptist Bible Institute. He met informally with John Tyler Christian (q.v.), Monroe Elmon Dodd (q.v.), Adoniram Judson Holt (q.v.), Plautus Iberus Lipsey (q.v.), and John Benjamin Lawrence to discuss the matter at Houston, Tex., in 1915, and served on the committee of three which presented the proposal to the Southern Baptist Convention at New Orleans in 1917.

BIBLIOGRAPHY: J. G. Chastain, *Thirty Years in Mexico* (1922). J. T. Christian, *History of Baptists of Louisiana* (1923). J. WASH WATTS

CUBA, BAPTISTS IN. The Baptist work in Cuba had its beginnings in the island's two struggles for independence from Spain. The first effort for independence occurred in the decade, 1868–78. The Foreign Mission Board reported to the Southern Baptist Convention in 1879 as follows:

In reference to Cuba as an inviting field, Rev. J. B. Hamberlin, of Mississippi, addresses the Board thus: "There are now three Baptist ladies who have just returned to that island from this vicinity. They were refugees here during the long civil war in Cuba. They were Catholics before, but while here they learned of Jesus by a sweet personal experience, were received into one of our Gulf Coast churches, are now full of love to the Saviour, and are anxious to work for His Cause. They begged me to call the attention of our American brethren to the Island of Cuba, and to assist in sending them a Missionary at the earliest day possible. They have wealth, intelligence, and through their aid I believe the Lord is opening a special door for the pure Gospel in that benighted, priest-ridden land."

In 1881 the board again made reference to Cuba:

At the last meeting of the Baptist State Convention, of Mississippi, the following resolution was adopted:
"*Resolved*, That a committee of three be appointed to look after the establishment of a Christian mission on the Island of Cuba, and report at the next meeting of this Convention."

The Chairman of the appointed committee, Rev. J. B. Hamberlain, wrote to the Board: "The three Baptist sisters I wrote you of a year or two ago, are still in Cuba, and longing for a pastor or missionary, and are able to help support one. . . . The names, etc., of these ladies should be kept private as a protection to them. They believe that they would be severely persecuted if known to the Catholics. Your Board should send the missionary or missionaries. We believe that, if sought for, one or more could be found, and would be sustained. We suggest that you make of the Secretary of State at Washington, inquiries as to the toleration or protection of Baptist missionaries in Cuba." . . . the Board . . . did not feel at liberty to do more than to make the inquiries of the Secretary of State, requested by the committee of the Mississippi Convention. The reply of Mr. Blaine is as follows:

"SIR—I have received your letter of the 8th instant, wherein, representing the Southern Baptist Convention, you inquire, 'Whether the Spanish or Cuban Government would protect or tolerate Baptist missionaries in Cuba: and, if not, whether our Government would do anything, by treaty or otherwise, to secure protection for any of our citizens, whom the above-named Convention might appoint as missionaries to that Island?'

"In reply, I have to observe that, while the existing treaty relations between the United States and Spain protect the rights of our citizens, as such, no assurance can be given in advance as to the action of foreign authorities toward the missionaries themselves or in respect to their work. This Government, however, is always ready to give all due protection to Americans, if their rights as citizens are infringed. I may add that it is not thought likely that your agents in Cuba will meet other or greater obstacles than in the countries named by you, where the Convention already has missions. I am, sir, your obedient servant. [Signed] JAMES G. BLAINE."

At the meeting of the Convention in 1886, the Foreign Mission Board reported:

In 1879 and in 1881 the Board reported this subject [Missions to Cuba] to the Convention. In the latter year the Convention decided that the time had not come for our Board to enter that field. Recently new religious interest has sprung up in the Island. Through the courtesy of the Home Board the attention of our Board was called to the subject; and by the invitation of prominent brethren of Florida, deeply interested in a Cuban mission, our Corresponding Secretary visited the Baptist Convention of that State, last November, in order to obtain further information which might aid the Board to decide wisely whether it should undertake this new mission. From the action of the Florida Convention we extract the following:

"We conceive that this Convention is able to undertake this work at once, *i.e.*, the preliminary or provisional work—to go and prepare the way, to lay foundations, to throw up breast-works, and hold the fort till the Foreign Mission Board of the Southern Baptist Convention can come to the rescue, which we hope will be not later than the next meeting of the Southern Baptist Convention."

The means of doing all that the Providence of God indicates should be done, are in the hands of God's people, and the question of duty in the premises is respectfully submitted to the wisdom of the Convention.

At the same session of the Southern Baptist Convention (1886), the Home Mission Board

Cuba, Baptists in

reported the correspondence that had passed between the board and W. F. Wood, missionary of the Home Mission Board in Key West, concerning the development of Cuba through contact with Cuban converts in Key West.

The Foreign Mission Board was promptly advised of these remarkable events, and requested to enter this door which God's providence had opened to the Baptists of the South. Learning from its Corresponding Secretary that the Board could not at that time improve so promising an opportunity, the Home Mission Board asked the consent of the Foreign Board to enter that field, and hold it until such a time as they might be ready to take it, or until the Convention should instruct us to transfer it to their hands. The consent thus sought was not obtained.

The Florida convention . . . resolved themselves to assume the burden and bear it until the denomination should come to their relief. As that convention does all its work in co-operation with the Home Mission Board, it has voluntarily reported this work to us, and placed the names of its missionaries in Cuba upon our roll.

At this session of the Convention, the work in Cuba was put under the Home Mission Board.

Between Cuba's first rebellion and the second (in the 1890's), Baptists secured a foothold on the island through contact with Cubans who had immigrated to American cities on the Gulf Coast—Mobile, Biloxi, Tampa, Key West. Some converts in these cities, returning to Cuba, increased the number of believers on the island.

Adela Fales came in contact with the truth of the gospel in Biloxi. She read devotedly *Kind Words*, the magazine for children begun by the first Sunday School Board of the Southern Baptist Convention and continued by the Home Mission Board upon the consolidation of the two boards (1873). The Fales family left Biloxi, returned to Cuba, and then went to Key West; there Adela again found her beloved *Kind Words*. In Key West there were about 5,000 Cubans. Pastor Wood of the Baptist church opened a mission among the Cubans, aided by Miss Fales, whose knowledge of English and Spanish was a great assistance. In 1885 the Home Mission Board reported to the Convention that promising beginnings were being made. "Already the seed that has been sown has brought forth fruit. A young man of Cuban parentage, and of marked ability and consecration to the work of the Lord, has been licensed to preach the gospel."

Some preparation for the spread of the gospel in Cuba came from Bibles, distributed by unknown hands, that lay hidden for years, even for a generation. In two or three port cities, a Christian ship captain, taking sugar to American and other ports, would give a Bible to a sugar planter as an act of friendship. The planter would courteously receive the Bible but hide it in his home. His own son or perhaps his grandson might find the Bible as a child, read a portion, and later in manhood accept the gospel as preached by a national or by an American missionary.

Between the meetings of the Southern Baptist Convention in 1885 and 1886, Wood wrote to the Home Mission Board

. . . that there was an urgent request for him to visit Havana; that members of his church, natives of Cuba, had gone back to their homes, and meeting others there, had began a work for the Master [,] that scores of people under their teachings had abandoned the Catholic faith, and were seeking for the pure light of the Gospel.

After the Convention placed the work in Cuba under the Home Mission Board, the work continued to expand. Its greatest need was met when the board bought the Jané (Hah-náy) Theater. The building, dedicated Feb. 15, 1891, is located at the corner of Zulueta and Dragones streets, at almost the very center of the city at that time. The building, called the Baptist Temple (*Templo Bautista*), has been the headquarters of the Southern Baptist work on the island—the Calvary Baptist Church (Spanish), the English-speaking church, the seminary (in the beginning), the preparatory school, the printery, and apartments for some of the mission workers.

The work on the island continued to prosper until the outbreak of the second war for independence (1895). All the national pastors were forced to leave. They went to various cities in Florida and continued there to work among Cuban refugees, some of whom were members of churches in Cuba.

When our preachers were constrained to leave the Island of Cuba in consequence of the war, the work was left in the hands of pastorless churches.

With commendable fidelity and zeal they have kept up the weekly prayer meetings, the Sunday services, their Sunday schools and their day schools. Letters advising us of persons converted in these meetings and who desired to be baptized, have been received from time to time. While many of the members of the churches have left Havana, some going into the army and others becoming refugees in this country, there yet remained quite a number in that city who are earnestly engaged in promoting the cause of Christ among the masses about them.

At the close of the Spanish-American War and after the independence of Cuba was recognized by Spain, the Home Mission Board began to re-establish its work on the island. The board entered into an agreement with the American Baptist Home Mission Society (Nov. 23, 1898) under which the eastern half of the island was transferred to the society, the Home Mission Board retaining the four western provinces, about half of the area.

The war had demoralized the mission work, almost wiping it out. The property in Havana remained and some individual believers were left but were scattered far and wide. National pastors returned from Florida to rebuild almost from the bottom. The seemingly prosperous prewar progress proved to be unstable. The first leader and general missionary under the board,

Alberto J. Diaz, was found to be lacking in an adequate understanding of Baptist fundamentals, and ultimately, the board was forced to dismiss him. But under his regime national pastors of genuine worth and leadership were discovered.

C. D. Daniel went to Cuba under the board in Jan., 1901. His family were among the emigrants from the South to Brazil after the Civil War, while he was a small child. Later, the family returned to the States, and after graduation from Baylor University, Daniel was sent to Brazil as a missionary. When his health gave way, he returned to Texas to work among the Mexicans. His facility in Portuguese, acquired as a child, enabled him to learn to speak Spanish like a native. He came to know the Mexican and the Cuban peoples as well as their language. After Diaz resigned from service under the Home Mission Board (Aug. 2, 1901), Daniel carried on in English and in Spanish. The church at Havana was reorganized and the work extended into the other three provinces: Santa Clara, Matanzas, and Pinar del Rio. Upon the few remains of the prewar work, Daniel began to develop the work in the four western provinces and gave direction that came to fruitage under the long superintendency of Moses Nathaniel McCall.

This missionary came to Havana, Feb. 15, 1905, as pastor of the English-speaking congregation, looking forward to learning Spanish and entering into that phase of the work, also. Soon after he arrived the health of Daniel, already delicate, became worse, and he had to lead the work under the Home Mission Board without knowledge of the language. He learned the Spanish language and the Cuban people in the hard school of experience. For 42 years he led Cuban Baptists. His deep piety, practical wisdom, and genuinely understanding love for the Cubans as a nation and as individuals gave direction and character to the Baptist movement. Three fundamental principles underlay all his work:

[1.] . . . no country can be evangelized by forces from without. . . . It would seem reasonable then that we major on the native born preacher.

[2.] . . . forces from without are auxiliary, and the burden must be principally on the native born preacher and the [native] Christians. . . .

[3.] . . . fraternal relations should be just as frank and sincere between the missionary and the Cuban brethren as they would be if we were of the same nation and tongue.

In keeping with the first principle, a seminary was opened in 1906 with six students, three more coming later in the year. The facilities were inadequate, but a start was made in the right direction. The six students proved themselves in their leadership of the churches in the years ahead. One of them is now (1956), and has been for a score of years, president of the convention. Livingston I. Mays joined McCall on the faculty the first year but retired at the end of the year. McCall was the faculty the second year. In the middle of the third year, Feb., 1909, W. W. Barnes joined McCall as director of the Colegio Cubano-Americano and teacher of the national ministerial students. Barnes left May 31, 1922.

In 1906 a step was taken to implement the second fundamental principle enumerated by McCall. The few churches and mission stations were widely separated. Travel was expensive. The national preachers and church members had little realization of denominational fellowship and no opportunity to develop any. A West Cuban Baptist Convention was begun Feb. 6, 1905, with the organization being completed the next year. It was small in members, to be sure, and inexperienced in co-operative endeavor, but it was a beginning. The subsequent development in numbers, in co-operative fellowship, in achievement has long since justified the venture of 1905. As a part of the convention effort and as a medium of communication, a paper, *La Voz Bautista*, was begun.

McCall himself was the embodiment of the third fundamental principle. He entered into understanding of Cubans. He lived, labored, traveled, and thought as they did. He loved them with the fervor and sincerity of a New Testament apostle, and they returned the sentiment in kind.

McCall began with eight churches having 300 members. He led in the establishment of many day schools, the organization of a Sunday school association, the Woman's Missionary Union, the Federation of Baptist Training Unions, and the men's Brotherhood. During his ministry, due principally to the generosity of Mrs. George W. Bottoms and the Bottoms Trust Fund, many church buildings and pastors' homes were built or acquired. The seminary, closed for some years, was reopened in a new building in one of the suburbs of the city. At the death of McCall, Mar. 8, 1947, he left a strong, well-organized work with more than 60 churches, approximately 6,000 members, and more than 50 trained pastors.

After having served with McCall for 18 years, Herbert Caudill became superintendent of Cuban missions, May, 1947. Under his leadership the work has grown (1956) to 84 churches with 8,244 members and more than 150 preaching stations. The Home Mission Board has 144 workers on the island, including nationals and American missionaries. An assembly has been established in the beautiful Valley of Yumurí, Metanzas Province. The seminary has grown to an enrolment of 24 students. It was reopened in 1936 with 11 resident and two nonresident students. Its purpose is to continue to fulfil the first fundamental principle laid down by McCall in the program for the evangelization of Cuba—the training of a national leadership. This reopening was made possible by funds from the Bottoms Trust. Religious work among the students in the University of Havana has been started. There are about 100 Baptist students enrolled and a half dozen Baptists on the faculty. Miss Ondina Maristany, native of eastern Cuba, graduate of Los Colegios Internacionales near Santiago, University of Havana, and Southwestern Baptist Theological Seminary, is the Baptist Student Union secretary, beginning Feb. 1, 1954. A Student Center building has been recently completed (1956). Many new church buildings and pastors' homes have been built. The total value of Baptist mission property in western Cuba is $1,576,381.40.

Cuban Baptists have an old folks' home and a hospital and clinic. The Baptist Convention of Western Cuba promotes a strong program of evangelism and stewardship. For the year 1955, 508 baptisms were reported, and the churches contributed $129,758.49. The Sunday school association reported 389 Sunday schools with 16,004 enrolled. The Federation of Baptist Training Unions reported 163 unions with 2,533 enrolled. The Woman's Missionary Union had 75 societies and 181 auxiliaries, with a total enrolment of 3,286. The Baptist Brotherhood had 54 church Brotherhoods with an enrolment of 863.

BIBLIOGRAPHY: H. Caudill, *Our Cuban Field* (1954). M. N. McCall, *A Baptist Generation in Cuba* (1942). A. S. Rodriguez, *La Obra Bautista en Cuba Occidental* (1930).   LOYD CORDER

CULTURE AND EDUCATION OF SOUTHERN BAPTIST MINISTER. See EDUCATION, SOUTHERN BAPTIST; MINISTER, THE SOUTHERN BAPTIST; and THEOLOGICAL EDUCATION.

CUMBERLAND COLLEGE. Baptist junior college located in Williamsburg, Ky. The first suggestion for establishing this college came in 1887 from the Mount Zion Baptist Association, meeting at Bethlehem. R. C. Medaris was appointed financial agent to receive funds for the school. Late in the same year, a special session of the association was held in Williamsburg. Green Clay Smith spoke for the movement, and a total of $4,000 was subscribed. At the same session articles of incorporation were drafted. The Kentucky legislature granted a charter on Apr. 6, 1888. The first building was erected and the school opened as Williamsburg Institute on Jan. 7, 1889.

Principal founders included Green Clay Smith, John Newton Prestridge (1853–1913), James P. Mahan, John W. Siler, A. Gatliff, and T. B. Mahan.

W. J. Johnson moved to Williamsburg as principal of the new school and pastor of the Williamsburg Baptist Church, in 1889. In tribute to him and his success in raising money for the school, one of the dormitories bears his name. Becoming absorbed in fund-raising, Johnson yielded the presidency to E. E. Wood, who was virtually president until the spring of 1919, although John Newton Prestridge was actually president for a brief time. Under Wood's administration the school acquired an enviable record for thorough work and scholarly attainments.

The struggle for endowment of the school has been long and difficult, but also fruitful. In 1892 the trustees obtained a conditional pledge of $10,000 from the American Baptist Education Society, provided an additional $25,000 be raised. To secure the American Baptist gift, A. Gatliff personally contributed $10,000, his first large gift to the school. By the close of 1892, the endowment had reached $40,000 and the building fund for Johnson Hall was nearing completion. The new building was occupied on Jan. 1, 1894.

Through his will, J. W. Siler, long-time treasurer of the school, left his entire estate of $50,000 to the school, in 1912. Other large gifts included a gymnasium and $16,000, by Ancil Gatliff and $10,000 by Mrs. J. P. Mahan. Recently the people of Williamsburg have provided the new and spacious A. Gatliff Memorial building which includes a chapel, classrooms, and administration offices.

Under the presidency of James M. Boswell, who has headed the college since June 1, 1947, the enrolment has grown rapidly, reaching a total of 572 full-time students in 1955–56, plus 80 special and part-time students. Cost of operation (1955–56) was $203,456, of which $42,631 was from Kentucky Baptists; $27,864, from donations; $94,451, from student tuition and fees; and $38,510, from endowment. Endowment as of 1955–56 totaled $708,390, and property value, $1,377,304, for a total of $2,085,694. The college library contains 12,000 volumes.

From the opening of the school to 1956, a total of 2,265 had been graduated.

Cumberland College is a member of the Association of Kentucky Colleges and Secondary Schools, the American Association of Junior Colleges, and the Southern Association of Colleges and Secondary Schools. It is operated by Kentucky Baptists and its trustees are elected by the General Association of Baptists in Kentucky. The college is liberal arts and coeducational.   ERWIN L. MCDONALD

CUMBERLAND INSTITUTE. A school in Cumberland Gap Association, Tenn., founded c. 1902 as the property of the association and valued at $5,000. H. B. Clapp served as president. The school is now extinct.
   LYNN EDWARD MAY, JR.

CUMBERLAND UNIVERSITY. A college and law school, founded in 1842, owned and controlled by Tennessee Baptists 1946–51, and still in partial operation. In 1945 the trustees proposed to transfer to the Tennessee Baptist Convention "the entire holdings of the university, real estate, buildings and equipment, endowment of around $150,000, and all bequests." The school had formerly operated under the auspices of the U.S.A. Presbyterian Church and then independently for a period. The law school, offering a one-year course, had educated many successful lawyers, and had enjoyed for many years an international reputation.

The conditions of the transfer of Cumberland University to the Tennessee Baptist Convention were these: (1) that the school be maintained as a four-year coeducational college with university rating; (2) that the name Cumberland University be retained; (3) that within a reasonable time the endowment be increased to not less than $500,000, to enable the institution to qualify for membership in the Southern Association of Colleges. The Tennessee executive board voted unanimously to accept the offer of the Cumberland University trustees. In Jan., 1946, the property was formally transferred to the Tennessee Baptist Convention. The following November, Cumberland University reported to the Tennessee Baptist Convention as a school under Baptist control and patronage, with a student body of 517 and endowment of $371,000.

In spite of efforts made to meet the conditions under which Cumberland had been accepted, the school declined. A campaign for funds did not pay expenses, but resulted only in increased indebtedness. Lack of accreditation brought a steady decline in enrolment. In 1951 the offer of the trustees of Ward-Belmont College in Nashville to sell their holdings to the Tennessee convention was seen as an opportunity to get a needed headquarters building for the convention and at the same time provide for Cumberland University a much more promising location, all for less expense than the $750,000 which was the estimated cost of a new convention headquarters building. After the Tennessee executive board had voted, on Feb. 27, 1951, to purchase the Ward-Belmont property, the Cumberland trustees were asked to agree to remove their college of arts and sciences to the Ward-Belmont campus. This the trustees refused to do, and the Cumberland University property was returned to the group from whom the Baptists had received it in 1946.

HARLEY FITE

CURRICULUM OF RELIGIOUS EDUCATION. The planned content of religious teaching, or the course of study through which churches lead their members in order to help achieve for their minds, souls, and characters certain predetermined goals. The necessity for planning is obvious, for only through planning can results be predicted or controlled. Curriculum may include many elements. One theory holds that it consists of all of life's experiences, since all experiences influence what people become. Thus all that a pupil might do at school, at home, at the office, or in play becomes a part of curriculum. In spite of the experiential basis of learning, this theory is impractical as a basis for church work, because of the impossibility of planning and control comprehensive enough to organize all of life. For the church, curriculum includes only those activities planned and directed by the church itself to achieve its aims. In a more restricted sense, curriculum is conceived as a planned and prepared course of study, which includes both information to be learned and guidance in desirable attitudes and skills.

Religious education has been described as an effort to lead people toward Christlikeness and to make good citizens in the kingdom of God. It, therefore, attempts to provide a curriculum which employs every legitimate procedure designed to accomplish its task. In the planning of curriculum, recognition is made of basic social realities. A person's needs are influenced by his culture, which varies greatly with environment. Needs are also influenced by the times in which a pupil lives, whether in war or peace or in economic prosperity or depression. There are also spiritual and moral realities. Pupils are lost in their sins. There is the sense of need for security. There is spiritual illiteracy, confusion in matters of right and wrong, and a lack of neighborliness.

In the light of such needs, curriculum seeks to nurture the growing religious and moral life of the pupil. Objectives have been determined to furnish a pattern by which curriculum should be built. These objectives help to determine the methods, materials, and measurements to be employed by the leadership, and are as follows: (1) To develop a consciousness of God in human experience and to recognize him as creator and ruler of the universe. (2) To develop an understanding and appreciation of the personal life and teaching of Jesus that will lead to complete surrender of heart and life to him as Saviour and Lord. (3) To develop a Christian character in keeping with the teaching and spirit of Jesus. (4) To develop an interest in service to others as a contribution to the building of a Christian social order. (5) To develop an understanding of the meaning and mission of a New Testament church and a complete and dedicated loyalty to its purpose. (6) To understand God's purpose for the home and the importance of the Christian family. (7) To know and accept the Bible as the divinely inspired Word of God and to make it the rule and guide of one's personal life. (8) To build a Christian philosophy of life in harmony with the teachings of the Bible.

Although activities and experiences of life are a vital part of curriculum, all experiences are not properly educative. If such activities are to be beneficial, they must be wisely selected and directed toward worthy goals. This means the teacher or leader of the unit is of major importance. Learning comes by the steps taken to do something about a purpose upon which both teacher and pupil have agreed. In order to provide guidance for the process, printed lesson materials are prepared. These are supplemented by many types of audio-visual aids. As the knowledge, attitudes, and conduct of those pupils who constitute the unit group improve, the church is improved and with it the community, and even the faraway areas of the world.

Printed lesson materials are provided in several forms for Southern Baptists. These materials are intended to meet the needs of all the educational organizations of the church: the Sunday school, the Training Union, the music groups, the missionary organizations and their auxiliaries, and all their respective classes for leadership training. The materials are varied in content, dealing with such subjects as Bible study, evangelism, missions, personal and social problems, ethics, doctrine, theology, church polity, educational methodology, recreation, drama, and music. They are planned to appeal to given age groups, or occasionally to special interest groups, thus supporting the age-graded departmental organization characteristic in Southern Baptist churches. In addition, care is taken to see that the materials are thoroughly usable by workers at all levels of training and experience and are adaptable to the needs of local church situations.   JOE DAVIS HEACOCK

CURRY, JABEZ LAMAR (at first Lafayette) **MONROE** (b. Lincoln County, Ga., June 5, 1825; d. Richmond, Va., Feb. 12, 1903). "Farmer, lawyer, legislator, soldier, teacher, diplomat, writer, author, manager of Peabody and Slater Funds, Special Ambassador," Curry was United States Minister to Spain, 1885-88; Ambassador Extraordinary, 1902; an ordained Baptist minister; trustee, Southern Baptist Theological Seminary; president, Virginia General Association; and president, Foreign Mission Board. A member of the Alabama legislature, and a Representative in the United States and Confederate congresses, he was "a staunch Southerner, but . . . above all a great American." He was president, Howard College, 1865-68; professor, Richmond College, 1868-81, later president of the trustees. A pioneer and promoter of education for white and Negro, Curry addressed superbly every legislature in the South, where he had "a greater personal influence than any other man." He had "a broad love of humanity, unwavering faith in God and country." Curry attended private schools; he graduated from Franklin College (University of Georgia) and Harvard, Dane Law School. Mercer University and University of Georgia gave him the LL.D. degree, and University of Rochester, the D.D. degree. In 1837 the family moved to Alabama, the state that placed his figure in Statuary Hall, Washington. In 1847 Curry married Ann Alexander Bowie (d. 1865); their children were Susan Lamar and Manly Bowie. He married Mary Worthan Thomas in 1867.

BIBLIOGRAPHY: E. A. Alderman and A. C. Gordon, *J. L. M. Curry, A Biography* (1911). J. L. M. Curry, *Civil History of the Government of The Confederate States with some personal reminiscences* (n.d.); *Constitutional Government in Spain* (1889); *The Southern States of the American Union considered in their Relations to the Constitution of the United States and to the Resulting Union* (1895); *Establishment and Disestablishment or Progress of Soul Liberty in the United States* (1889); *Protestantism: How far a failure?* (n.d.); *The present Condition of Religious Liberty throughout the world* (n.d.); *An appeal to the Southern Representatives in Congress and to the friends of free schools in the south* (n.d.)

J. P. Rice, *J. L. M. Curry, Southerner, Statesman and Educator* (1949). G. Ryland, *The Baptists of Virginia, 1699-1926* (1955). G. B. Taylor, *Virginia Ministers* (1915).   J. LEVERING EVANS

CURTIS, RICHARD, JR. (b. Dinwiddie County, Va., May 28, 1756; d. Amite County, Miss., Oct. 28, 1811). Pioneer minister. Mississippi's first Baptist preacher, Curtis came with a group of settlers from the Great PeeDee, S. C., and settled on Cole's Creek, north of Natchez, in 1780. Under his leadership the first Baptist church in Salem was constituted in Oct., 1791, although Curtis was only a licentiate. Forced back to South Carolina by Roman Catholic persecution in 1795, he was ordained while there and returned to Mississippi in 1798, when the Natchez country came under the United States. Curtis helped in the organization of the first association, the Mississippi, in 1806, and attended the association for the last time Oct. 19, 1811, a few days before his death. He was buried in the yard of a friend in whose home he died on Beaver Creek, and a marble shaft in his memory stands near by in the cemetery of Ebenezer Church.

BIBLIOGRAPHY: J. L. Boyd, *A Popular History of Baptists in Mississippi* (1930). J. T. Christian, "Sketch of Early Mississippi Baptist History," *Goodspeed's Biographical and Historical Memoirs of Mississippi* (1891). L. S. Foster, "Baptist Pioneers," in Z. T. Leavell and J. J. Bailey, *History of Mississippi Baptists* (1904); *Mississippi Baptist Preachers* (1895). Z. T. Leavell, "Early Beginnings of Baptists in Mississippi," *Publications of the Mississippi Historical Society* (1901). C. H. Otken, "Richard Curtis in the Country of the Natchez," *Publications of the Mississippi Historical Society* (1901).   C. B. HAMLET III

CUSETTA SEMINARY. A high school for girls located at Cusetta, in Chambers County, Ala., founded *c.* 1849 with J. W. Williams as president.   JAMES E. DAVIDSON

CYRENE INSTITUTE. Opened in Decatur (Seminole) County, Ga., in 1910, sponsored by Bowen Association. It existed until 1914.
   ARTHUR JACKSON

CZECHOSLOVAK BAPTIST CONVENTION OF NORTH AMERICA. Organized in Chicago in June, 1912, after the Union of the Slavic Baptist People in America, of which it previously had been a member, was dissolved. The convention, largely in the Chicago and Cleveland areas, had as its principal founders Vaclav Kralicek, Matthew Steucek, Jan Kana, August Meereis, Vaclav Hlad, and Jan Valastiak.

A missionary organization since its inception, the convention supported numerous missionaries in Czechoslovakia until the present Communist regime took over, at which time the government assumed the financial support of local pastors; leaders of Baptist work in Czechoslovakia were imprisoned. In addition to missionary work in the United States, Canada, and Czechoslovakia, the convention has supported seven native missionaries in Haiti, West Indies, since 1949.

The convention's monthly publication, *Pravda A Slavna Nadeje (The Truth and Glorious Hope)*, is in its 37th year, with Jan P. Piroch and Karel Marek, editors.

The Women's Mission Union, organized in 1923, supports a missionary in Haiti and sends annually hundreds of packages of clothes to relieve Czechoslovak refugees in Germany, Austria, and Italy.

Present mission emphasis is in Canada, with thousands of new Canadians of Czechoslovak background in Toronto, London, Ontario, Montreal, and Winnipeg, Manitoba. Membership on the foreign fields is more than three times as large as the convention's constituency.

Member churches support the work of the Czechoslovak Baptist Convention in addition to contributions to other conventions, such as the American Baptist Convention to which churches in its territory belong. In 1954, 17 member churches reported 89 baptisms, 2,050 members, and $7,642.31 total income.

Present officers include: Daniel Evan, president; Paul Struharik, vice-president; Vincent P. Stupka, secretary; and John A. Jeren, treasurer.

VINCENT P. STUPKA

D

DAGG, JOHN LEADLEY (b. Middleburg, Loudoun County, Va., Feb. 13, 1794; d. Hayneville, Ala., June 11, 1884). Baptist pastor, theologian, and college president, and one of the most learned of Southern Baptist theologians. Although he never received a formal college education, he mastered Latin, Greek, Hebrew, and higher mathematics. While pursuing his studies by candlelight, he permanently impaired his eyesight and, in later life, had to do most of his writing and reading with the assistance of others.

Before his ordination to the ministry in 1817, Dagg worked at his father's trade, as a saddler, taught school, studied medicine, and fought as a soldier in the War of 1812, during which he witnessed the bombardment of Fort McHenry at Baltimore.

Baptized into the fellowship of Ebenezer Church in Loudoun County, Va., in 1812, Dagg began preaching in 1816 and was ordained in 1817. After his ordination he served several churches in Loudoun, Fairfax, and Fauquier counties. In spite of his conviction that the dignity of the ministry required the undivided attention of a minister maintained by his parishioners, he was compelled by financial necessity to resume teaching. During the early 1820's he conducted a school for girls at Middleburg and was later principal of the Upperville Academy.

Despite the handicaps of defective eyesight and lameness, Dagg accepted the pastorate of Fifth Baptist Church of Philadelphia in 1825. An outstanding advocate of temperance, missions, and benevolences, he was a founder of the Pennsylvania Missionary Association which later became the Pennsylvania Baptist Convention. During his Philadelphia pastorate he was prominent in the proceedings of the Triennial Convention and served that body as a vice-president and as a member of the board of managers. He was also a trustee of Columbian College and a leader in the work of the American Baptist Home Mission Society, the American and Foreign Bible Society, and the Baptist General Tract Society which became the American Baptist Publication Society. Owing to the partial loss of his voice in 1834, he was forced to give up the work of the pastoral ministry. He then accepted the presidency of Haddington College, a manual labor school near Philadelphia for the education of Baptist ministers, and there began his career as a professor of theology.

After leaving Haddington he became president of the Alabama Female Athenaeum at Tuscaloosa, Ala., in 1836. While in Tuscaloosa he was associated with the elder Basil Manly (*q.v.*), who as president of the University of Alabama conferred the D.D. degree upon Dagg in 1843.

On the recommendation of President Manly, Dagg was appointed professor of theology and president of Mercer University in 1844. He served as president until 1854 but continued as professor of theology until 1856. Patrick Hues Mell (*q.v.*), who was Dagg's colleague during his Mercer presidency, testified that he never knew a better or more successful college president than Dagg. According to Mell, President Dagg found the university in a state of depression but left it in a high state of prosperity. Dagg was particularly successful in building up a theological seminary at Mercer which had no equal in the South before the Civil War.

Retiring from the Mercer faculty in 1856, Dagg lived with relatives at Madison, Cuthbert, and Forsyth, Ga., until 1870 when he removed to Hayneville, Ala., where he died in 1884. During his years of retirement Dagg wrote the books on theology which established his fame as a theologian. In 1857 he published the first volume of his *Manual of Theology* which was on *Christian Doctrine*. The second volume, which was on *Church Order*, appeared in 1858. His book on *Elements of Moral Science* was published in 1860 and his *Evidences of Christianity* followed in 1869. Dagg's theology was biblical rather than philosophical; he adhered to a position of moderate Calvinistic Augustinianism. Although Dagg wrote many other tracts and essays, the aforementioned works were the ones which were most influential in Southern Baptist schools, where they displaced texts by Northerners such as Francis Wayland. Dagg's writings were described by Jeremiah Bell Jeter (q.v.) as being "distinguished by the clearness of his intellect, the purity of his taste, the extent of his knowledge, the value of his theological works, and his shrinking modesty."

Dagg was first married to Fannie H. Thornton of Virginia, the mother of his son, John Francis Dagg, who was also a minister and college president and editor of the *Christian Index*. His second wife was Mrs. Mary Young Davis, the mother of Noah K. Davis, the philosopher.

BIBLIOGRAPHY: J. L. Dagg, "Autobiography of John L. Dagg" (Mercer University, MS). [Samuel Boykin], *History of the Baptist Denomination in Georgia and Biographical Compendium* (1881). F. G. Lewis, "John Leadley Dagg," *Dictionary of American Biography* (1930). H. H. Straton, "John Leadley Dagg" (1926). MALCOLM LESTER

DAINGERFIELD BAPTIST ENCAMPMENT. One of four Texas encampments organized in 1946. It is located near Lone Star, Tex., in District 1. J. E. ROTH

DALLAS COLLEGE. A school which opened in temporary quarters in Dallas, Tex., in 1875 under control of Elm Fork Association. There was a more auspicious opening in a new plant in 1878. The school was closed in 1881 for lack of patronage. RUPERT N. RICHARDSON

DANA, HARVEY EUGENE (b. Warren County near Vicksburg, Miss., June 21, 1888; d. May 17, 1945). Pastor, educator, professor, seminary president, author. He was the third of four children born to Charles Martin and Eva (Smith) Dana. He was converted at the age of 12 in the Antioch Baptist Church where his father, a farmer, was a deacon. He dedicated his life to the ministry in response to God's call and preached his first sermon at 18 years of age.

Entering Mississippi College at 18 he earned the Ph.B. and A.B. degrees in 1911. He was granted the Th.D. degree by Southwestern Baptist Theological Seminary in 1921. He studied at the University of Chicago and at the University of Dubuque, and he received an honorary LL.D. degree from Ottawa University in 1939.

He was married to Tommy Elizabeth Petty on July 13, 1909. Two daughters, Eugenia Elizabeth and Elsie Marie, were born to them.

Pre-eminently an educator, he was professor of New Testament at Southwestern Seminary from 1919 to 1938. He excelled in the classroom. Students made it a practice to return repeatedly to hear again special lectures which were full of human interest and dramatic imagination. He was elected president of Central Baptist Seminary, Kansas City, Kans., in 1938, where he served until his death in 1945. He was widely recognized for his scholarship in New Testament background, criticism, and exegetical interpretation of the Greek New Testament. He was a member of the Society of Biblical Literature and Exegesis and of the American Research Society.

A noted author, he began a series of scholarly books early in his teaching career. The following books comprise his published materials: *Authenticity of the Holy Scriptures; Manual for the Study of the Greek New Testament; Introduction to the Critical Interpretation of the New Testament; The Epistles and Apocalypse of John; An Expositor's Harmony of the Synoptic Gospels; Jewish Christianity; New Testament Times; Manual of Ecclesiology; Searching the Scriptures; The Holy Spirit in Acts; The Heavenly Guest; The Ephesian Tradition; The Life and Literature of Paul; The New Testament World;* and *Lee Rutland Scarborough, A Life of Service*. His writing includes numerous articles and essays and a volume of unpublished materials on the life and literature of Paul.

Ordained in 1908, Dana was a popular preacher, and he was in constant demand for conventions, encampments, and revival meetings. He loved the pastorate and served many churches as supply and interim pastor throughout his teaching career. His pastorates included Fort Gibson, Utica, and Hermanville in Mississippi; Allen Avenue in Fort Worth, Alvord, and Graford in Texas; and the First Baptist Church, Ardmore, Okla. In all his work his ministry with young people was particularly effective, and he gave both material and spiritual aid to the multitudes of them who were attracted by his personal charm and genuine friendship. He made many personal financial sacrifices to assist struggling seminary students with their obligations.

While serving as president of Central Seminary, he died of a heart attack May 17, 1945, and was buried in Highland Park Cemetery, Kansas City, Kans. FRANKLIN M. SEGLER

DANBURY, GEORGE WASHINGTON (b. Warren, Ohio, Apr. 3, 1848; d. DuQuoin, Ill., Jan. 22, 1931). Minister, home and foreign missions secretary, children's home superintendent. Left an orphan at an early age, Danbury enlisted during the Civil War in Company I, 4th Ohio Volunteer Cavalry, Jan. 4, 1864. He was mustered out July 5, 1865. After attending school in Lebanon, Ohio, Danbury made a trip around the world which included a visit to the

Holy Land. When he returned he settled in southern Indiana and married Lydia Perry, Oct. 27, 1869. Converted and baptized in Little Pigeon Baptist Church in Spencer County, about 1874, Danbury served his first pastorate there after the church ordained him on June 10, 1877. He moved with his family to Olney, Ill., in 1884, served as missionary of Olney Association, and later became pastor of the Baptist church in Olney until 1886.

He held several other pastorates in Illinois until Nov., 1889, when he moved to DuQuoin, Ill., which was his home until his death.

Superintendent of Sunday school work in Illinois for 12 years under the Illinois Baptist State Association, Danbury was connected with the anti-saloon league from 1904 to 1912. He was later financial secretary of Ewing College. Under direction of the state association, he established Carmi Baptist Orphanage in 1917 and was its superintendent for four years. Danbury served Nine Mile Association as clerk and treasurer for 38 years. He was instrumental in organization of the Illinois Baptist State Association and later served as its clerk and moderator.

ARCHIE E. BROWN

DANIEL, CHARLES WILLIAM (b. Monticello, Ark., May 6, 1874; d. Atlanta, Ga., Feb. 4, 1951). Pastor. The son of William Dudley and Effie (Clayton) Daniel, he was converted at the age of 11 and received his higher education at Union University, Jackson, Tenn., and at Southern Baptist Theological Seminary. He was ordained in 1893 by First Baptist Church, Jackson, Tenn. He married Alice Calhoun in Nashville, Tenn., Feb. 11, 1897. Four children were born to them. He held the following pastorates: Texarkana, Tex., 1896–98; Pine Bluff, Ark., 1898–1903; Covington, Ky., 1903–05; Fort Worth, Tex., 1905–09; Atlanta, Ga., 1909–28; Richmond, Va., 1928–34; El Dorado, Ark., 1934–43. He retired from active work in 1943.

Many of his friends termed him an expository preacher without a peer in his time. Commonplace among Baptists became this statement about Daniel: "He not only believes the Word but preaches it with peculiar insight, understanding, and power." He was fearlessly true to his convictions. He served the Baptist denomination in many capacities, but was most esteemed for his expository preaching.

MRS. LUCIEN MATTHEWS

DANIEL, ROBERT NORMAN (b. Gravel Hill, Va., Nov. 30, 1888; d. Greenville, S. C., Sept. 20, 1956). Educator. The son of John Robert and Florence Lillian (Hall) Daniel, he was educated in the grade school, Scottsville, Va., Fork Union (Va.) Military Academy, the University of Richmond (A.B., 1907; A.M., 1908), and the University of Chicago (Ph.M., 1911). On June 24, 1914, Daniel married Frances Evelyn Pack of Greenville, S. C. Their children are Frances Evelyn, Robert Norman, Elizabeth Sanderson, and Charles Pack. Daniel was associate professor of English, Furman University, 1911–14, and head of the English department, Georgetown College (Ky.), 1914–20. In 1920 he returned to Furman University and held the following positions: head of the English department, 1920–56; dean, 1922–48; dean emeritus, 1948–56; acting president, 1938.

Daniel was awarded the Litt.D. degree (Georgetown College, 1942) and the LL.D. degree (Furman University, 1948). He was author of *Furman University, a History* (1951), a history of the First Baptist Church, Greenville, S. C., which is in process of publication, and was chairman of the editorial committee for the South Carolina section of the *Encyclopedia of Southern Baptists*. Recognized as an authority on Robert Browning's works, Daniel was an active Baptist layman, serving on occasion as pastor, deacon, and Sunday school teacher.

FRANCIS W. BONNER

DANIELL HIGH SCHOOL. Established in 1891 at Vidalia, Ga., in the Daniell Association from which it received its name. It existed until about 1896.

ARTHUR JACKSON

DANISH BAPTIST FOREIGN MISSION SOCIETY. From 1877 to 1919, Danish Baptists sent financial support and personnel to the American Baptist Foreign Mission Society. Several Danish missionaries served in the Lower Congo during this period under this society. In 1921–22 Danish Baptists supported Godtfred Pedersen who worked among Muslims in Bulgaria. From 1923 to 1927, they co-operated with the Mission Board of the Swedish Baptist Union, sending one evangelist and two nurses to Basakata in the Congo. In 1928 the Danish Baptist Foreign Mission Society launched its own mission in Ruanda-Urundi, a region in the Belgian Congo which was formerly part of German East Africa. A ripe field in a thickly populated district was taken over from the Neukirchener-Mission, a German society which had been forced to evacuate during World War I. In 1931 a Baptist church was formed in Musema. A second church was founded in 1942 in Rubura. During World War II Denmark was cut off from the mission field, and Danish Baptists in the United States assumed support of the work in Ruanda-Urundi. This support continued on a co-operative basis after the end of the war. The united budget of Danish and Danish-American Baptists in 1955 amounted to Kroner 163,796 ($30,000). In 1956 a staff of 17 missionaries and five national ministers served two churches in Ruanda-Urundi with 2,262 members. There was a hospital at Musema, 136 schools with 2,743 pupils, and a teacher-training school with about 80 enrolled.

JOHANNES NORGAARD

DANISH BAPTIST GENERAL CONFERENCE OF AMERICA, THE. Danish Baptist missionary work in America dates back to 1856, when the first Danish Baptist church was organized at Raymond, Wis. At the 50th anniversary in Albert Lea, Minn., there were approximately 50 member churches, located in Michigan, Illinois, Wisconsin, Iowa, Minnesota, Nebraska, and South Dakota, with state conventions and state missionaries. In 1910 the general conference was organized at Harlan, Iowa. A 300-page book, *Seventy-Five Years of Danish Baptist Mission Work in America*, was published as a part of the 75th anniversary observance. During the next years the conference began contributing financial assistance to the mission field, opened by Baptists of Denmark with four missionaries in Belgian Congo, where they also supported three missionaries of the American Baptist Foreign Mission Society. A Danish Baptist Memorial Home for the aged, valued at $300,000, has been built at Harlan, Iowa, and the conference archive is housed in this building. The theological seminary, originated in Morgan Park, Ill., in 1884, moved to Des Moines, Iowa, in 1913 and became affiliated with Northern Baptist Theological Seminary, Chicago, Ill., in 1925. Since the work has become entirely American, no students have enrolled for several years, and churches have consolidated with American Baptists and other groups. The conference publishes a monthly paper, *The Watchman*. A special "Centennial Edition," published in 1956, marks the observance of the 100th anniversary, which included a centennial conference at Albert Lea, Minn.   I. FREDMUND

DARGAN, EDWIN CHARLES (b. Darlington Co., S. C., Nov. 17, 1852; d. Chicago, Ill., Oct. 26, 1930). Minister, teacher, editor, and author. He was the son of John Orr Beasley and Jane Francis (Lide) Dargan. His father was a minister at Darlington, S. C., and a friend of James A. Furman; his grandfather, Timothy Dargan, was also an eminent Baptist minister. During his youth contact with his father's wide circle of acquaintance gave Dargan knowledge of many people, some of them of considerable importance. At the age of 21 he received the M.A. degree from Furman University, Greenville, S. C., and in 1877 was graduated from the Southern Baptist Theological Seminary, which at that time was also located at Greenville. He received honorary degrees from Washington and Lee University (1888 and 1920) and from Baylor University (1904).

After serving as supply pastor of First Baptist Church, Wilmington, N. C., he was ordained in 1876, then served as pastor at Bottetourt (Hollins), Big Lick (Roanoke), and Bonsack, Va., 1877–81; of First Baptist Church, Petersburg, Va., 1881–87; in Dixon, Calif., 1887–88; and of Citadel Square Baptist Church, Charleston, S. C., 1888–92. Then from 1892 to 1907, he was professor of homiletics at Southern Baptist Theological Seminary, where he made a major contribution first as a teacher and then, with the appearance in 1905 of the first volume of his *History of Preaching*, as a definitive historian. Leaving the seminary, he was pastor of First Baptist Church, Macon, Ga., 1907–17. In that year he became editorial secretary of the Southern Baptist Sunday School Board, where he remained until 1927, devoting his time largely to the production of expositions for use in the Sunday school and bringing to his position the dignity of his significant reputation as a scholar and writer. He was a member of the International Sunday School Lessons Committee from 1918 to 1928, serving as its chairman in 1920–21. In addition to his *History of Preaching*, two volumes of which have been published (1905, 1912), he wrote *Notes on Colossians* (American Commentary, 1890), *Ecclesiology* (1897, 1905), *Doctrines of Our Faith* (1905), *Harmony Hall, Recollections of an Old Southern Home* (1912), *Exposition of the Epistle to the Romans* (1914), *The Changeless Christ and Other Sermons* (1919), *The Art of Preaching in the Light of History* (1922), and *The Bible, Our Heritage* (1924).   JOHN D. FREEMAN

DARGAN-CARVER LIBRARY. A joint historical and research library operated by the Sunday School Board and the Historical Commission of the Southern Baptist Convention. The last work of Edwin Charles Dargan (q.v.) was in the position of editorial secretary of the Sunday School Board. At his death, his personal library, bequeathed to the board, became the nucleus of a reference library to serve the need of editors and other employees in connection with the board's publication work. William Owen Carver (q.v.), in addition to his career as a seminary professor, served for years as chairman of the Southern Baptist Convention Historical Society which he organized in 1938, and he led in the accumulation of a substantial collection of basic historical material. After May, 1947, when the Southern Baptist Convention authorized the Historical Society to have the status of a Commission, it was given authority to employ a staff and establish itself as a chartered body. In 1949 the Sunday School Board approved a recommendation of its executive secretary, Thomas Luther Holcomb, that it offer to provide offices for the Historical Commission and the facilities to house its historical collection. Thus, the collections of the commission and the board were integrated under an agreement adopted Mar. 8, 1951, between representatives of the society (later, the commission) and the board. The new joint library, appropriately renamed the Dargan-Carver Library, was formally dedicated on June 16, 1953. In 1956 approximately 45,000 books had been accessioned and 59,000 items of archival material processed.

With the unusual co-operation of the Sunday School Board in providing the space and staff for the integrated library, the commission under the direction of its executive secretary, Norman Wade Cox, has gathered the largest collection on microfilm of Baptist source material in the world. It includes rare church histories, diaries, registers, church records, associational minutes, and denominational periodical files.

The Dargan-Carver Library, in its operation, functions as a department in the Service Division of the Sunday School Board. The director of this division and the executive secretary of the Historical Commission are the joint directors of the library, which is being used extensively by Southern Baptists.

The work of the library is threefold: (1) It serves the board staff, particularly those with editorial responsibility, and writers preparing curricular materials by providing source materials and research and verification assistance. (2) It offers materials for intensive and exhaustive research in the field of Baptist history. (3) With the Historical Commission, it is acquiring and conserving the valuable historical materials which are in danger of being destroyed by fire, war, time, and simple carelessness. The microfilm service of the commission exists to guarantee the vital records of Baptist past and present against further loss. The Dargan-Carver Library serves as a depository of these materials.

See also HISTORICAL COMMISSION, SOUTHERN BAPTIST.   HELEN CONGER

DAVID, WILLIAM JOSHUA (b. near Meridian, Miss., Sept. 28, 1850; d. Bellville, Tex., June 25, 1919). Missionary to Africa. David, whose father died when he was very young, felt called as a missionary to Africa at the age of 16. Although his wealthy grandfather objected, young David sold his horse and saddle and entered Mississippi College in 1869. He graduated from Crozier Theological Seminary in 1874, also taking a short medical course in New York. On Jan. 5, 1874, the Foreign Mission Board requested David to raise funds for African missions, and 10 months later, Nov. 3, 1874, the board appointed him as a missionary to Africa. David, the first representative of the board to go to Africa after the Civil War, sailed with a Negro appointee, W. W. Colley, on Jan. 5, 1875. Forced to return to Richmond in 1878 due to ill health, he married Nannie Bland and induced the board to allow his wife to sail to Africa with him on Dec. 18, 1879. Illness again forced David home in 1883; but while in the States he collected $5,000, lumber, and other materials for construction of the First Baptist Church in Lagos, the capital city of Nigeria. In the church which he erected in 1887, standing today as a landmark, a memorial tablet was unveiled in 1921 by David's missionary daughter, Nannie B. David. After losing his first wife, who was buried at sea May 20, 1885, David married Mrs. J. E. Greer, a widow, and they sailed for Lagos Jan. 10, 1886. Three years later, ill health caused him to leave Africa, never to return. George W. Sadler called David "an intrepid traveler," "a powerful preacher," "an able builder." David organized Fifteenth Avenue Church, Meridian, Miss., in Jan., 1891; Ohio Street (now Second Baptist), Pine Bluff, Ark., 1903; Bellville, Tex., 1906; and Woodland, Houston, Tex., Mar. 4, 1916.

BIBLIOGRAPHY: L. S. Foster, *Mississippi Baptist Preachers* (1895). G. W. Sadler, *A Century in Nigeria* (1950). N. F. Weeks, comp., *Builders of a New Africa* (1944).   C. B. HAMLET III

DAVIDSON, BLOUNT FERRELL (b. Montgomery, Ala., Dec. 16, 1886; d. Montgomery, Ala., Sept. 23, 1956). Pastor, associational missionary, chaplain, active in denominational and civic affairs. After attending school at Starke University in Oklahoma and William Jewell in Missouri, he began his career in real estate and insurance. He entered the ministry in 1911 and served churches in Arkansas and Missouri. He did associational missionary work in Missouri, Louisiana, and Montgomery, Ala. He served as chaplain, in the armed services with rank of lieutenant colonel. While serving with the Montgomery Association, he led in the organization of 13 new churches, directed the organization of Alabama Baptist Negro Center, negotiated and directed the purchase of property on which the Normandale Baptist Church is now being built, initiated a move to build a $3,000,000 hospital, and initiated a move to buy a large tract of land which was sold in lots in order to get a plot of ground for Ridgecrest Baptist Church.

Davidson served as secretary-treasurer of the Montgomery Ministerial Association and was very active in church and civic affairs. He will be remembered for his vigorous efforts to preserve the principle of separation of church and state and for his opposition to alcoholic beverages. He was married to Magdalene (Margaret) Higgins; they had one daughter, Mrs. Harold Lee of Danville, Va. At the time of Davidson's death he was working on all the monographs for the ENCYCLOPEDIA OF SOUTHERN BAPTISTS which pertained directly to the executive board of the Alabama Baptist State Convention.

LEON MACON

DAVIE, BUNYAN (b. Old Spring Hill, Barbour County, Ala., Dec. 10, 1852; d. Nov. 18, 1939). Merchant, educator, and lay religious worker, serving as superintendent of education in Barbour County, and as colporteur for the Alabama Baptist State Convention. The son of Marshal C. and Jane E. (Bass) Davie, he married Harriett Jones, Troy, Ala., and they had five children: Eunice, Louise, Lois, Bunyan, and Paul. Excerpts from an annual report as colporteur show that Davie traveled 5,038 miles in 333 days, delivered 227 addresses, held 120 stereopticon services, sold 2,680 books, and visited 171 homes. He was a member of the committee in 1907 that recommended the buying of property for Baptist state headquarters. His annual reports on Sunday school work, written more than 50 years ago, reveal deep insight concerning adequate buildings, teacher training, grading, evangelization, and enlistment. He was esteemed for his character and consecration.

BIBLIOGRAPHY: Anonymous, *Memorial Record of Alabama* (1893). W. B. Crumpton, *A Book of*

Memories 1842–1920 (1921). W. P. Wilks, *Biographical Dictionary of Alabama Baptists 1920–1947* (1947).

CARLOS CUNNINGHAM

DAVIESS COUNTY INDIAN MISSION ASSOCIATION. Founded in 1845 at the second meeting of Daviess County (now Daviess-McLean) Baptist Association of Kentucky. It is credited with having awakened missionary zeal in the parent body and received support from it for several years.

WILLIAM N. MCELRATH

DAVILLA INSTITUTE. A coeducational school, at Davilla, Milam County, Tex., maintained by the Leon River and Little River associations from about 1873 until about 1878.

RUPERT N. RICHARDSON

DAVIS, JONES EDGAR (b. Lone Jack, Mo., Mar. 22, 1873; d. Independence, Mo., June 4, 1944). Editor, missionary to Mexico. After graduating from William Jewell College in 1899, Davis pastored churches in Missouri before his appointment to Mexico by the Foreign Mission Board, July 5, 1904. He established a printery in Toluca, Mexico, in 1905 and founded the Baptist Spanish Publishing House at Leon in 1906. When revolution led to removal of the publishing house to El Paso, Tex., Davis continued as manager until his retirement in 1943. Editor of *El Expositor Biblico*, 1907–44, Davis wrote several published works including *El Evangelismo, Manual del Evangelismo Personal,* and *El Camino de la Vida.*

FRANK W. PATTERSON

DAVIS, MARY HILL (b. Greenville, Ga., c. 1860; d. Dallas, Tex., Nov. 28, 1934). Woman's Missionary Union leader. As a young child, she moved with her family to Texas in 1870 and later married F. S. Davis, a Dallas, Tex., physician. She served as recording secretary of the Texas Woman's Missionary Union from 1898 to 1906 and as president, 1906–31. During the period of her service, she attended every meeting of the executive board and convention and paid her own expenses until 1922. Her president's addresses at the annual meetings, compiled in *Living Messages*, indicated her knowledge of literature and world conditions and her devotion to Baptist causes. During Mrs. Davis' presidency the circle plan for Woman's Missionary Societies was inaugurated; the week of prayer for state missions was begun; and the name of the state organization was changed from Baptist Women Mission Workers to Woman's Missionary Union. The offering taken in Texas during the Week of Prayer for state missions bears her name.

BIBLIOGRAPHY: O. B. Davis, *Mary Hill Davis* (1949). R. T. Patterson, *Candle by Night* (1955). Mrs. W. J. J. Smith, *Baptist Women 1830–1930* (1933). Woman's Missionary Union, *Living Messages* (1935). Mrs. W. L. Williams, *Golden Years* (1921).

EULA MAE HENDERSON

DAVIS, WILLIAM HERSEY (b. Norfolk County, Va., Jan. 20, 1887; d. Elizabeth City, N. C., Sept. 10, 1950). Theological professor, pastor. Son of Quinton Clarence and Sarah Elizabeth Davis, received B.A. and M.A. degrees from the University of Richmond in 1912 and 1913. Davis attended Southern Baptist Theological Seminary, earning Th.M. and Th.D. degrees, and spent one year in study at Berlin, Leipzig, and Oxford. After marrying Mabel Lee Sewell in 1912, he was ordained six years later, after which he served pastorates at North Vernon, Ind., Deer Park, Louisville, and Finchville, Ky. Professor of New Testament interpretation at Southern Baptist Theological Seminary beginning in 1920, Davis was made head of the department in 1934, four years after he had become director of the seminary library. He was a member of the American Philological Association, the Society of Biblical Literature and Exegesis, Phi Beta Kappa, and Sigma Phi Epsilon. Author of *A Beginner's Grammar of the Greek New Testament* (1923) and *Greek Papyri of the First Century* (1933), Davis served as co-author with Archibald Thomas Robertson (*q.v.*) of *A New Short Grammar of the Greek Testament* (1931) and with Edward Allison McDowell of *A Source Book of Interbiblical History* (1948).

McDowell, long associated with Davis, has written:

> But above all his virtues as a teacher was Dr. Davis' love for his students. . . . He possessed the faculty of making the individual student, whether in the seminary or in a North Carolina summer preachers' school, feel that his teacher was his friend and was interested in him personally.

Davis possessed the quality of interpretative imagination to the degree that all his knowledge—in various fields—was brought to its focal point in a given passage of Scripture. Rejecting allegory and typology consistently, he insisted upon historico-grammatical principles as the valid tools of interpretation. During his last several years of teaching, mimeographed copies of his lectures were prepared from stenographic notes, and these copies are available in the seminary library.

J. ESTILL JONES

DAVIS HOSPITAL. An institution at Pine Bluff, Ark., instituted by a benevolent society in 1909 and operated by the Arkansas Baptist state convention from 1920 to 1942. During this time it was under the management of a board of local citizens of all denominations and was self-sustaining with the exception of some income from gifts.

The hospital was at all times open to all races and religions, and a large amount of charity work was done. It became an accredited institution while under Baptist control and was increased from a 50- to a 65-bed unit.

In order to render more adequate service to its area during the strenuous war years, the convention deeded the hospital to the city of Pine Bluff, Ark., in 1942, and government aid was then obtained which paid for enlargement and improved equipment, and which made possible an enlarged service to the community.

While operated by the Baptists the institution served 24,947 patients. Patient income was $846,496; denominational income was $25,800; other gifts amounted to $33,092; and $59,105 was expended on charity patients. The value of the property when deeded to the city was estimated at $75,000, and the institution was free from debt.

JOHN W. REAP

DAWSON, JOHN EDMONDS (b. Washington County, Ga., Mar. 7, 1805; d. Tuskegee, Ala., Nov. 18, 1860). Minister. The second son of Major John E. Dawson, former Virginian, he attended school in Madison and at Mount Zion. In 1824 he married Eliza Walker, daughter of John Walker of Morgan County. He was converted by the preaching of Adiel Sherwood (q.v.) during the session of the Ocmulgee Association in 1827. Though active in church, he did not begin to preach until 1834, following the death of his wife. Ordained by the Indian Creek Church, Morgan County, in Jan., 1835, he moved immediately to Eatonton, where he became pastor. During this year he married Mary Sandford of Eatonton. In 1836 he accepted the church in Columbus and settled on a plantation in what was known as Indian Nation, across the Chattahoochee River. Due to crop losses, Indian warfare, and constant danger, he returned to middle Georgia in 1837 to preach again in Eatonton. Later, moving to Madison, he conducted a female academy. In 1842 he accepted a pastorate at La Grange. In order to avoid too heavy a strain on the resources of the church and provide a needed supplement to his income, he became principal of the female academy there. After a successful five-year stay in La Grange, Dawson returned to Columbus in 1847, remaining there as pastor until his retirement in 1856. During this time he went to New Orleans to survey the religious needs of that city for the Home Mission Board.

In addition, he was for a period in 1858 agent of Mercer University, working to encourage support for Christian education. He became editor of the *Southwestern Baptist* in Tuskegee in 1859 and continued until his death. Although without college training, John Edmonds Dawson through his own efforts became a possessor of considerable knowledge. A tablet has been erected to his memory in his church at Columbus, and he was buried in that city.

HENRY J. STOKES, JR.

DAWSON, LEMUEL ORAH (b. Chambers [now Lee] County, near Waverly, Ala., Apr. 24, 1865; d. Birmingham, Ala., Jan. 14, 1938). Pastor, denominational leader, teacher, author. He attended the regular schools of Chambers County; he graduated (B.A. degree) from Howard College, then at Marion, in 1886 having held the offices of quartermaster and post adjutant of the college, and ranking as senior captain which was the highest office in the college; he graduated from the Southern Baptist Theological Seminary in 1889 and did postgraduate work under John Albert Broadus (q.v.) at the same institution. His education also included studies in Germany and a postgraduate course in Columbian University, Washington, D. C. At the age of 18 he became a Baptist minister. He became pastor in Tuscaloosa in Dec., 1892, where he served for 32 years. During this long pastorate he refused calls to leading churches in the Southern states at much larger salaries because of his conviction of God's ministry for him in Tuscaloosa; also he declined the presidencies of several colleges (including Howard, 1902), secretaryships of mission boards, and the editorships of church periodicals. He was a member of the board of trustees of Howard College, a trustee of the Alabama Central Female College (19 years), a trustee of the Southern Baptist Theological Seminary, a member of the Alabama state board of missions, a member of the Baptist education commission; one of the founders and for 10 years president of the Baptist Young People's Union; a national guard chaplain in 1913; chairman of the building committee of Druid Hills City Hospital, Tuscaloosa; president of the Alabama Baptist State Convention in 1921; and at one time professor of Bible and church history, Howard College. He was honored by the Edgewood Baptist Church in Birmingham when it changed its name to L. O. Dawson Memorial Baptist Church. Dawson wrote for the religious and secular press. He served as associate editor of the *Alabama Baptist*, was founder and editor of the *Franklin Advocate* of Howard College, and was one of the founders and editor-in-chief of the seminary magazine, now the *Review and Expositor*, Louisville, Ky. He wrote *After Fifty Years*, and many pamphlets and tracts. He was married on Oct. 30, 1890, to Margaret Samuel Logan. They had two children: Andrew Lewis and Eugene Reese.

BIBLIOGRAPHY: T. M. Owen, *History of Alabama and Dictionary of Alabama Biography* (1921). B. F. Riley, *A Memorial History of Baptists of Alabama* (1923). W. P. Wilks, compiler, *Biographical Dictionary of Alabama Baptists 1920–47*.

R. H. FALWELL, JR.

DAWSON SPRINGS ASSEMBLY. See WEST KENTUCKY BAPTIST ASSEMBLY.

DAY OF THE LORD. See ESCHATOLOGY AND JUDGMENT.

DAYTON, AMOS COOPER (b. Plainfield, N. J., Apr. 4, 1813; d. Perry, Ga., June 11, 1865). Author, editor, controversialist. Dayton quit school at 16 because of bad eyesight and became a schoolteacher at 17. He employed a reader at the medical college he attended, from which he was graduated in 1834. Frail health caused him to go South, where he at first lectured on phrenology and kindred subjects. He married Lucile Harrison at Shelbyville, Tenn., and then went with his bride to Florida, where he lived three years. From about 1839 until 1852, he resided in Columbus and Vicksburg, Miss., where he was a dentist.

Dayton was originally a Presbyterian, but he joined the Baptist church in 1852. Shortly afterward Dayton met James Robinson Graves (*q.v.*), who asked him to write something for the *Tennessee Baptist*. What he wrote impressed Graves, who said, in substance, "I do not know what else you can do, but you can write." Thereafter the two men were close friends and coworkers. Dayton became corresponding secretary of the Southern Baptist Bible Board, Nashville, Tenn. (organized 1851), Sept. 4, 1854, and served until Apr. 5, 1858, when he resigned because of serious opposition from some of the board members. They objected to some of his operational procedures and to the amount of time he was giving to the affairs of the Sunday School Union, both as its president and as a writer for it. He, a Landmarker, was supported by Landmarkers on the board and opposed by those who were not Landmarkers.

Dayton and Graves planned for and led in the temporary organization of the Southern Baptist Sunday School Union at Nashville, Tenn., Oct. 23, 1857, and its permanent organization at Memphis, Tenn., Dec., 1858. He was president of the union through 1858 and its corresponding secretary until he moved to Atlanta, Ga., just before the Union army captured Nashville in Feb., 1862. He also served in 1859 as the moderator of the Baptist General Association of Tennessee and North Alabama.

As a supporter of Graves in the Graves-Howell controversy, he was one of the minority excluded by the Nashville First Baptist Church Feb. 15, 1859, following Graves's expulsion Oct. 18, 1858. The charge against him was that he was a schismatic.

Dayton was editor of the *Baptist Banner* (a Landmark paper), Atlanta, Ga., 1863–64. In it he printed 16 letters addressed to Samuel Boykin (*q.v.*), editor of the *Christian Index*, Atlanta, on the question, "Can Baptists without violating the Scriptures conduct missionary operations by boards and conventions?" (His answer was no.) Boykin reprinted the letters and replied to them. This correspondence contained perhaps the most complete and the ablest discussion of the subject that appeared.

Dayton moved to Perry, Ga., in the summer of 1863, to become president of Houston Female Institute, and served until his death in Apr., 1865, from tuberculosis. He had four daughters and two sons.

Dayton was a frequent contributor to the *Tennessee Baptist* before, during, and after the period when, with James Madison Pendleton (*q.v.*), he was an associate editor (May, 1858, to Oct., 1959). He had a weekly column, either as president or corresponding secretary of the Sunday School Union, on Sunday schools and the work of the union. His fictional story, *Theodosia Ernest*, or *Heroine of Faith*, began in the paper Dec. 1, 1855, and appeared in book form in 1856. It went into several editions, 14,000 copies selling in the first six months and 18,000 in the first year. Volume II, *Theodosia Ernest*, or *Ten Days in Search of the Church*, reached its 28th edition in 1858. (These two books reflected much of the struggle through which Dayton himself went before becoming a Baptist.) He kept a journal, 1853–63. Other books written by Dayton during 1857–59 were *The Infidel's Daughter, Pedobaptist and Campbellite Immersions, Baptist Fact and Methodist Fiction, The Baptist Sunday School Question Book*, Vols. I and II, and the booklet (a sermon preached at the first annual session of the Sunday School Union in 1859 at Canton, Miss.), *How Children May Be Brought to Christ*. All his books, mostly controversial, were published by Graves, Marks & Co. (South-Western Publishing House), Nashville, Tenn.

BIBLIOGRAPHY: J. H. Borum, *Biographical Sketches of Tennessee Baptist Ministers* (1880). J. J. Burnett, *Sketches of Tennessee Pioneer Baptist Preachers* (1919). W. Cathcart, *The Baptist Encyclopedia* (1880). L. D. Phillips, "Sketch of A. C. Dayton," *Tennessee Baptist* (Jan. 29, 1870).

J. CLARK HENSLEY and HOMER L. GRICE

DEACON. A transliteration of the Greek word *diakonos*, signifying in spoken usage a servant or minister (e.g., Rom. 13:4; 15:8; I Cor. 3:5; Eph. 6:21; I Tim. 4:6), but technically designating an officer in the church (*ekklesia*). In the latter sense, *diakonos* occurs only three times: Philippians 1:1, in connection with *episkopos* (bishop); I Timothy 3:8–13, in the context of qualifications for the diaconate; Romans 16:1, in the feminine sense, *deaconess* (*Phoiben . . . diakonon tes ekklesias tes en Kenchreais*). The obscurity of the office raises the question of its origin, nature, and duties. Some scholars resolve this difficulty by inferring from the appointment of the seven (Acts 6:1–6) the implicit beginnings of the later diaconate; their inferences, however, shade into equivocation. Whatever the case, the office was a new institution, not borrowed from Jewish economy, but evolved from an emerging need within the *ekklesia*.

Scarcity of data on the diaconate has led to widespread differences among denominations. In the Catholic Church deacons are inferiors in the ecclesiastical *cursus honorum;* in the Episcopal Church, clergymen of lowest grade; in the German Protestant Church, assistant ministers; in the Reformed Church, part of the local consistory; in the Methodist Church, junior ministers; in the Presbyterian, Congregational, Christian, and Baptist churches, administrators of benevolences and financial affairs. Ultimate scriptural justification is claimed for all of these classifications.

The diaconate in Southern Baptist churches consists of a board of counselors elected by the local congregation (usually in keeping with qualifications listed in I Tim. 3:8–13) and ordained by a council (presbytery) to assist the pastor in serving the *ekklesia*. Although Baptist polity permits a wide latitude of form and practice, the deacon usually renders an administrative and officiating ministry.

See also ORDINATION.

BIBLIOGRAPHY: H. E. Dana and L. M. Sipes, *A Manual of Ecclesiology* (1944). C. Gore, *The Ministry of the Christian Church* (1889). "The Historic Diaconate," *Theology*, LVIII (Nov., 1955), 405–436. J. B. Lightfoot, *Dissertations on the Apostolic Age* (1892). W. R. McNutt, *Polity and Practice in Baptist Churches* (1935). B. H. Streeter, *The Primitive Church*, The Hewett Lectures, 1928 (1929).

J. B. MCMINN

DEAF, MISSIONS TO. Work with the deaf was begun by the Home Mission Board of the Southern Baptist Convention with the appointment of J. W. Michaels (1852–1942) (*q.v.*) in 1906 as evangelist to the deaf. Subsequent leaders of missions to the deaf were A. O. Wilson (1867–1939) (*q.v.*), J. W. Gardner (1884–   ) and Carter E. Bearden (1928–   ). As of 1956 the deaf population of the territory served by the Southern Baptist Convention was estimated at 100,000. The board had 10 missionaries, and 75 churches were providing a ministry to the deaf.

The principal feature of the board's program of work for the deaf is to employ general missionaries to serve areas of one to four states, leading and helping the churches to take interest in the deaf of their respective communities, and to provide leadership, materials, and space for their participation in regular church services. The Home Mission Board also publishes Sunday school literature and provides black-and-white silent movie films of sign-language sermons for the deaf.

The Southern Baptist Conference of the Deaf and several statewide conferences promote the unity and cohesion of mission efforts among these people. New Orleans Baptist Theological Seminary offers a course in dactylology (the universal sign language for the deaf) for those who wish to work in this area.   LOYD CORDER

DEATH. The condition following the escape of the soul from the body. Hebrew Scriptures emphasize a place of silent forgetfulness in the depths of the earth called *Sheol* (Psalms 86:13; 88:12; Prov. 15:24). To the Hebrew, death was not annihilation but a transition to a shadowy existence. Death was regarded as being "gathered unto their fathers" Judg. 2:10; II Kings 22:20), or to "Abraham's bosom" (Luke 16:22). Death was associated with sin (Gen. 3:19, 22). The resurrection of the dead to a reward or punishment did not find expression in the Hebrew Scriptures until very late in the Old Testament period (Dan. 12:2 f.). The grave is man's "long home" (Eccl. 12:5), a concept closely akin to Egyptian thought. Like the Egyptians and Babylonians, the Hebrews placed in tombs objects which they thought would be useful to the dead.

In the New Testament death is frequently associated with sin. It is difficult, however, to determine whether physical or spiritual death (banishment from God) is meant. The relationship of death to evil is clearly set forth (I Cor. 15:56), "The sting of death is sin." Christ's clearest statement concerning death and its sequel is, "I am the resurrection, and the life" (John 11:25). He regarded death for the believer as an entrance into a fuller fellowship with God (John 14:2 f.).

See also IMMORTALITY and INTERMEDIATE STATE.

BIBLIOGRAPHY: J. Baillie, *And the Life Everlasting* (1951). A. E. Taylor, *The Christian Hope of Immortality* (1946).   CHARLES A. TRENTHAM

DEBATE AND CONTROVERSY, BAPTIST WRITINGS IN. Historically, Baptist polemical and apologetic writings began with 17th-century England, assumed great variety and scope in America throughout the 19th century, and, by their general replacement in the 20th century with intradenominational discussions of specific problems in polity, indicate a maturing of the Baptist denomination and imply a recognition throughout Christendom of the status and significance of the Southern Baptist Convention. The known continuity of the modern Baptist movement began with the debate and controversy sparked in 17th-century England over soul liberty and the rejection of sprinkling and infant baptism. Prominent in this development were such men as: Thomas Helwys, a man of power and influence, who was detested both for the liberty of conscience for which he pleaded and for the immersion which he practiced; Henry Jessey, a man of great learning, who came to reject sprinkling and infant baptism and so changed from Episcopal to Baptist affiliation; William Kiffin, a wealthy merchant and Baptist pastor, who, through his position of political influence, was able to shield and protect his persecuted brethren; John Smyth, of whom it is said in Whitley's treatise, "He announced that he would be, as Bacon put it, a 'true pioner [sic] in the mine of truth'; he was persevering in following every clue, in declining to bow to mere custom or tradition, in recurring to first principles, in acting on what he discovered"; John Spilsbury, pastor of a dissenting Baptist church with a Calvinistic bent; and Roger Williams, the founder of Rhode Island, whom A. B. Strickland has described as a man of "unyielding tenacity of purpose, a man who could grasp a principle in all its bearings and who could incorporate it in a social compact."

Neve and Heick point out that, although the Anabaptists represented essentially a practical and moral rather than a doctrinal movement, the spiritualistic trait in their churches gave much stimulation to theological thought. Such thinking provided the basis for *Individualism*, some of the leaders of which have been mentioned in the preceding paragraph. However, the formal development of nonconformist theology began with the Congregationalists of the 19th century. Baptist theology of the 19th century was represented by such men as John Foster, John Hinton, and John Clifford. Neve and Heick quote Selbie as saying that typically, theologians of this period were not "cloistered academics, but, generally speaking, men with pastoral experience, and a wide knowledge of human nature." Their zeal, unsupported by a foundation of comprehensive and thorough Bible study, undoubtedly contributed to the disputatiousness of the times.

Concerning the *Liberalism* controversy, which began in the latter part of the 19th century, Neve and Heick state, "Though the Baptists were at first rather slow in accepting the new learning, an extreme type of radicalism made great headway among them." Two of their first liberal thinkers were E. G. Robinson and Crawford Howell Toy (*q.v.*). The most eminent Baptist scholar was H. W. Robinson, who, in *The Christian Doctrine of Man* (1911), laid stress on the religious and moral concept of man as opposed to the rational and esthetic view of man inherent in Greek thought. John Albert Broadus (*q.v.*), H. B. Hackett, and Edgar Young Mullins (*q.v.*) are among Baptist theologians who have exerted a conservative force in American Calvinism and have made a real contribution to Biblical study.

Ritschlianism, under which theology became a historical and practical discipline, aroused interest in America at the beginning of the 20th century, along with William James' *pragmatism*. The Baptist scholar, W. N. Clarke, who wrote an *Outline of Christian Theology* (1898), based religious authority plainly on Christian experience. Fortunately, "the gospel of the New Testament has never lacked men who have combined faith in the Gospel with scholarly attainment," and such a man was Archibald Thomas Robertson (*q.v.*), a prolific writer and profound linguist, whose *A Grammar of the New Testament Greek in the Light of Historical Research* is a monumental achievement in American theological scholarship.

Doctrinally, Baptist polemical and apologetic writings may be considered under the three classifications of J. F. Curtis: "Those which have been by degrees conceded in theory by many of the most enlightened of other denominations; those which form the remaining points still controverted; and those which, though always held in common by evangelical Christians, require the acknowledgment of Baptist principles to be advocated with due force and consistency." Or, as W. T. Whitley has expressed it, such debate and controversy may be viewed as the protests against the following perversions: pouring and sprinkling as baptism; infant baptism; sacerdotalism and sacramentalism; churches composed of others than believers, such as their relations, neighbors, and moral friends; rules of faith and practice being laid down by priests; and accepting sources of authority other than the New Testament.

As has been implied, some of these controversies inherent in Baptist history have, at one time or another, been prominent in the public eyes, while others are of such a nature as to have remained largely within private groups of professional theologians. By far the most spectacular and prolific of the doctrinal controversies have been concerned with the conditions and mode of water baptism.

Ecclesiastically, Baptist polemical and apologetic writings may be loosely classified as expressing differences between Baptist and non-Baptist denominational groups, as being intradenominational, as contrasting the positions of the American and Southern Baptist conventions, and as providing instruction for Baptist peoples.

Baptists have probably been engaged in more debate with the Disciples of Christ than with any other Christian denomination. This group was organized by Alexander Campbell in Pennsylvania in 1810 and is an offshoot of the Sandemanian sect of Scotland, which dates back to 1719. Campbell was essentially Arminian, holding that the Holy Spirit had unchecked access to the hearts of believers, but that he could not influence the hearts of unbelievers. Of such sects Whitsitt has written, "The literalism which is an abuse of Protestantism was pretty well displayed in each of them, and in several instances it became absurd and injurious." Some of the public debates between Baptists and Campbellites have been faithfully transcribed and make interesting reading. In 1857 Franklin (Disciples) and Fisher (Baptist) debated three propositions: "Do the Scriptures teach that baptism, administered as the Lord intended, to a proper subject, is for the remission of past, or alien sins? Do the Scriptures teach the doctrine of total, hereditary depravity? Do the Scriptures teach that the saints can apostatize, fall from grace, and be lost?" In 1872 Ray (Baptist) and Lucas (Disciples) debated which of their church organizations possesses the Bible characteristics which entitle it to be regarded as the visible church, or kingdom, of Jesus Christ. In 1874 Crawford (Baptist) and Sweeney (Disciple) debated their points of difference in faith and practice as touching upon Calvinism and the design of baptism.

Around 1800 two forms of heresy, Unitarianism and Universalism, were plaguing Baptists. The pseudo-intellectualism of the former fell on stony ground with respect to most Baptist congregations, and their moderately Calvinistic theology curbed the latter. In 1844 Pingree (Universalist) and Waller (Baptist) debated, "Do the Scriptures teach the ultimate holiness and salvation of all men?" In 1908 Strain (Universalist) and Porter (Baptist) debated, "The Bible and reason teach that all men will finally be made holy and happy"; and "The Bible and reason teach that a part of mankind will suffer endless misery."

In 1876 Graves (Baptist) and Ditzler (Methodist) in "The Great Carrollton Debate" argued six propositions:

I. Immersion in water is the act which Christ commanded His apostles to perform for Christian baptism.

II. Infant baptism, as practiced by the Methodist

Church South, is authorized by the Word of God.

III. Christian baptism is prerequisite to the Lord's Supper.

IV. The M.E. Church at Carrollton, Missouri, possesses the Scriptural characteristics of a church of Christ, or a branch of the same.

V. Believers in Christ are the only subjects Christ commanded His apostles to baptize.

VI. It is possible for a truly regenerate and adopted child of God to apostatize so as to be finally lost.

John William Porter (*q.v.*) has sounded the warning, "While Baptists have been engaged in an age-long conflict, their warfare is not yet ended. The last great battle is yet to be fought and won. This battle is destined to be between the Roman Catholics and the Baptists."

Regarding intradenominational controversy J. F. Love has written, "The indomitable Baptist spirit of today was forged in persecution," but, "having won our battle for religious liberty and the right of conscience, some Baptists forgot themselves, and disputes arose among them over missions, Sunday Schools, and Conventions, with the disastrous results of strife first and then division." The development of an educated ministry and of an effective missionary enterprise was hindered during the first quarter of the 19th century by the "antimission controversy," whose forces claimed that Sunday schools, missionary societies, and theological seminaries were without scriptural justification, and that centralization of authority threatened Baptist democracy.

A source of considerable controversy has been "Old Landmarkism," which James Robinson Graves (*q.v.*), the leading proponent, defined as "the characteristic principles and policy of true Baptists in all times since the ascension of Christ." He set forth seven "marks." Graves campaigned vigorously against the Pedobaptists, alien immersion, and pulpit affiliation. The Landmarkists established their own mission work under the direction of the local churches, in opposition to Convention board missions, and thus furthered the "antimission controversy."

The "antislavery controversy" was, of course, settled by the Civil War. Foss and Mathews have edited a collection of documents revealing the practice and sanctioning of slavery by Baptists, with the objective of "exposing spiritual wickedness in high places" so as to further the "amelioration of the condition of out-cast humanity." Torbet wrote of the slavery issue, "The majority of Baptists were cautious about the issue because of their preference for unity, their hesitancy to have the church interfering in civil affairs, and the presence of slave-holding members in their churches." Nevertheless, the controversy resulted in a schism between Northern and Southern mission activity in 1845.

Individual Southern Baptists, when moving into a community where American Baptist churches already exist, often do not align themselves with such churches, claiming that they find liberal doctrinal views prevailing, to which they cannot accede. The fact that such individuals have repeatedly organized their own churches and associations and then applied for and received recognition by the Southern Baptist Convention has been a source of friction. According to Baker, the aforementioned doctrinal objections include "open communion, alien immersion, affiliation of the Northern convention with the Federal Council of Churches, interdenominational comity agreements, and the inclusive policy in missionary appointments."

Baptist church libraries are filled with didactic and promotional writings for instruction in Baptist heritage, doctrinal beliefs, and distinctive polity. G. E. Horr summarizes the matter:

In the last three centuries the Baptists have stood for many different things. Their positions have necessarily been influenced by the issues of the times, by the current interpretations of the Scriptures, and by the spiritual vision of their leaders. . . . It is amazing, when we come to think of it, from how many vagaries and fanaticisms we have been delivered.

W. R. White sounds the challenge, "I am convinced that Baptist distinctives are absolutely indispensable to the basic needs of the developing world order before us. I am deeply concerned that we have spiritual fellowship and unity with other Christians but without betraying a most sacred trust."

The status of Baptists today, gained through debate, controversy, persecution, and schism, is a living testimony to the vigorous plain-spokenness of both leaders and people since the post-Reformation period.

BIBLIOGRAPHY: R. A. Baker, *Relations Between Northern and Southern Baptists* (1948). W. Cathcart, *The Baptist Encyclopedia* (1881). J. T. Christian, *Baptist History Vindicated* (1899). J. Crawford and J. S. Sweeney, *Debate on the Points of Difference in Faith and Practice between the Two Religious Bodies Known as the Disciples of Christ and the Regular Baptists Embracing the Subject of Calvinism and the Design of Baptism* (1875). T. F. Curtis, *The Progress of Baptist Principles in the Last Hundred Years* (1856). H. M. Dexter, *The True Story of John Smyth* (1881). A. T. Foss and E. Mathews, *Facts for Baptist Churches* (1850). B. Franklin and T. J. Fisher, *Debate on Some of the Distinctive Differences between the Reformers and Baptists* (1858). R. Fuller and F. Wayland, *Domestic Slavery Considered as a Scriptural Institution* (1845). J. R. Graves, *Old Landmarkism: What Is It?* (1881). J. R. Graves and J. Ditzler, *The Great Carrollton Debate* (1876). G. E. Horr, *The Baptist Heritage* (1923). J. F. Love, *What Is the Matter with the Baptists?* (1926). R. Mason, *The Church That Jesus Built* (n.d.). J. L. Neve and O. W. Heick, *A History of Christian Thought* (1946). E. M. Pingree and J. L. Waller, *A Debate on Universalism* (1845). J. W. Porter, *The World's Debt to the Baptists* (1914). D. B. Ray and J. R. Lucas, *Church Discussion: Baptists and Disciples* (1873). J. S. Seiss, *The Baptist System Examined, the Church Vindicated, and Sectarianism Rebuked* (1859). W. B. Selbie, *Congregationalism* (1927). A. J. Strain and J. J. Porter, *Religious Debate* (1908). A. B. Strickland, *Roger Williams* (1919). R. G. Torbet, "Dissension and

Strife," *A History of the Baptists* (1950). W. R. White, *Baptist Distinctives* (1946). W. T. Whitley, *The Works of John Smyth* (1915); *The Witness of History to Baptist Principles* (1897). W. H. Whitsitt, *Origin of the Disciples of Christ* (1888); *A Question in Baptist History: Whether the Anabaptists in England Practised Immersion Before the Year 1641* (1896). J. D. GREY

DEBT AND SOUTHERN BAPTISTS. This mention of debt refers to the obligations of denominational organizations financed by contributions of the individual Baptists, organizations like churches, district associations, state conventions, Southern Baptist Convention, and institutions like schools, colleges, hospitals, orphans homes, etc. Beginning with the early days of our Baptist work in the United States some denominational enterprises either collapsed or became seriously embarrassed because their promoters entered into contracts, depending upon pledges which for some reason were not paid, and on expected contributions which failed to materialize.

There are many reasons why Baptists go in debt. Debts are sometimes made in order to take advantage of opportunities for the advancement of the work, to provide facilities for increasing possibilities for usefulness. This, done within the bounds of reason, is ordinarily a good thing to do. Debts, on the other hand, are sometimes made because of an emergency over which the denomination has no control. To illustrate, a church building may be destroyed by fire, and to rebuild would evidently necessitate some debt; and as to denominational work as a whole, a financial depression affects all denominational work just as it affects all business. All financing propositions through borrowing money should be conservative, with the payments small enough to be met promptly.

In order to carry on their work the Baptists, like business concerns and governments, frequently go in debt. The attitude of Baptists is, by and large, like the attitude of every honest person. When they make debts, they expect and intend to pay them, they do everything in their power to pay them, and usually do pay them promptly, though sometimes it takes more time than was expected. In making debts, small or large, the denominational body should consider, first, the absolute need for making a financial obligation, with a careful study of the minimum need, at the time, of the proposed project, with plans for expansion later. Payments should be planned that can be reasonably met. It should be remembered that borrowing money is not raising money, but is making a contractual obligation to be paid in a certain way and at a certain time. Sometimes the obligations or denominational enterprises may be self-liquidating, as in the case of hospitals, college dormitories, etc., which produce income.

The 75 Million Campaign was launched to take advantage of the worldwide opportunity for service. Doors to mission fields were opening, everywhere opportunities for expansion were present. On the surface, the financial condition of the country seemed excellent, and the people had money. The campaign was launched for 75 million dollars, to be paid over a period of five years, with an annual payment of 15 million dollars. Conditions were favorable. Members of the churches were enthusiastic and pledged $92,000,000. On the basis of the amount pledged, institutions were enlarged, new missionaries were appointed by state and Convention-wide boards, and every phase of the denominational work was expanded commensurate with the pledges made. Then the depression struck hard. The members were able to pay on their pledges during the five-year period only $58,000,000, which left debts of something like $17,000,000 or $18,000,000, on state and Convention causes. This left the Southern Baptist Convention and its agencies with a debt of $6,500,000.

It should be realized there is great difficulty in paying burdensome debts. Debts usually have to be paid when the source of income has been reduced. The voluntary gifts which support the denomination come from people whose income has been reduced, people who themselves have financial burdens. In addition the current work must be carried on, and there is a minimum beyond which expenses cannot be reduced without destroying the work entirely. Then a certain amount must be paid each year on interest and retirement of the loan. In paying debts the first thing that has to be done is to stop increasing indebtedness by running deficits. To stop making debts one of two things—or, better, both—should be done: expenses should be reduced to the minimum, and income should be increased as much as possible. When the debts of the Convention became burdensome, the Executive Committee studied the income and the expenditures of the agencies over several years and found that the receipts were being reduced practically 12 per cent a year. Therefore, the Convention adopted the committee's recommendation that the agencies make their next year's budget 12 per cent less than their cash receipts of the year before. In the face of burdensome debts throughout the country, the Convention in 1933 adopted the Baptist Hundred Thousand Club, to increase the income of the denomination. It seemed to many that it was a simple plan and could easily be carried out—namely, get one hundred thousand people to pledge to pay $1 per month over and above their regular subscriptions through the churches, until the debts of all Southwide agencies were paid, or the pledge was canceled by the subscriber. All of the income was to be applied on debts. If successful, that meant $1,200,000 annually to be applied on debts. It was a simple and easy plan but, for various reasons, the membership of the churches did not at first respond wholeheartedly. Because of this, it took a little over seven years to raise the first year's goal. The total raised by the Hundred Thousand Club, on the $6,500,000

MISSISSIPPI COLLEGE (q.v.), Clinton. Founded in 1826, acquired by Baptists 1850. Top: Old chapel used by Union troops as hospital and stable in their march on Vicksburg. Neo-Grecian architecture is typical of antebellum South. Bottom: Administration building named in honor of D. M. Nelson, long-time president. Thirty-three buildings house more than 2,000 students.

OUACHITA BAPTIST COLLEGE (q.v.), Arkadelphia, Ark. Classes began in 1886, present enrolment exceeds 800. Forty buildings are valued at over $2,000,000.

debt was $2,627,822.36 in the 10-year period 1933-43. The rest of the $6,500,000 debt was paid by funds from other sources. These outstanding debts were paid in 1943, with a balance of nearly $50,000, from the Hundred Thousand Club, which in 1944 was given to the Relief and Annuity Board, to the reserve fund of the Old Annuity Plan.

Growing out of the experience in dealing with past debts, the Executive Committee recommended that each agency of the Convention create a reserve fund. This recommendation was adopted by the Convention, as follows:

Each agency of this Convention shall set up as soon as possible a reserve for contingencies to provide for deficits that may occur either through decreased receipts or through emergencies or both. The maximum amount of contingent reserve of any agency shall be determined by the agency, subject to the approval of the Convention.

This reserve fund of an agency can be used to meet temporary emergencies, or a prolonged period of unfavorable business conditions, to enable the agency to retrench its expenditures gradually rather than abruptly.   AUSTIN CROUCH

DECATUR COLLEGE. The only junior college operated by Texas Baptists, successor to Northwest Texas Baptist College which opened in Sept., 1892, in a temporary building on the Decatur town square. The first commencement was held in the new, native stone, three-story building May 28, 1893. Despite valiant struggles to overcome customary difficulties in building, Northwest College was sold at an auction in 1896 for $13,000.

In 1897 Jesse Lawrence Ward (q.v.), pastor of First Baptist Church, Decatur, spurred on by Benajah Harvey Carroll (q.v.), and after an all-night conference with James Milton Carroll (q.v.), decided to present to the Baptist General Convention of Texas, meeting in San Antonio, an offer to purchase the property of Northwest College for $7,000. The convention bought the college, changing the name to Decatur Baptist College in 1897 and establishing it as a junior college to be a feeder for Baylor University. The world's oldest junior college opened its doors under its new name with 75 students in Sept., 1898. B. F. Giles, president, was succeeded by Ward, 1900-07. Following the presidencies of Josiah Blake Tidwell (q.v.), 1907-09, and W. C. Carver, 1909-14, Ward returned as president to fight for the school's existence until 1950. Otis Strickland, former student and pastor of First Baptist Church, Cisco, was his successor.

Properties of the college, which had an enrolment of 268 in 1955 and endowment of $289,515, include brick dormitories, an administration building, gymnasium, well-lighted football field, heating plant, dairy barn, 20 housing units for married students, and the president's home. Income from tuition, interest from endowment, and appropriation from the Texas Baptist Convention, totaled $312,151 in 1956.

Offering regular junior college work and terminal and vocational training, Decatur College is the only Baptist school in Texas which provides basic education for adults past public school age. The school is a member of the Texas Junior College Association, American Association of Junior Colleges, Association of Texas Colleges, and is approved by the Texas Educational Agency.   MRS. R. H. WATKINS

DECREES. A decree is a decision, a plan, a purpose of God formed in eternity and realized in time. The important decrees refer to creation, preservation, and salvation. All evangelical theologians concede that God has made decrees, but they differ over the extent (Calvinism versus Arminianism) and the order (supra-, sub-, and infralapsarianism) of the decrees. The entire subject is treated authoritatively with an exposition of all major positions held with reference to the decrees in Benjamin Warfield's *The Plan of Salvation*.   BERNARD RAMM

DEISM. A rationalistic and naturalistic view of the relation of God to the universe, expressed in terms of radical transcendence, resulting in a denial of divine revelation and providence (miracles, incarnation, etc.) and of faith as essential to man's experience of God, and regarding human reason as alone capable of discovering religious truth in the laws of nature. Deism appeared in England in the 17th and 18th centuries under the leadership of Lord Herbert of Cherbury, John Toland, Matthew Tindal, *et al.* English Baptists (John Gill, John Ryland, Andrew Fuller, *et al.*) were strong opponents of this movement, which struck at the very foundations of the Christian gospel.

BIBLIOGRAPHY: J. Butler, *The Analogy of Religion* (n.d.). J. Orr, *English Deism: Its Roots and Fruits* (1934).   TED R. CLARK

DELL SCHOOL. A Baptist academy at Delway, Sampson County, N. C. After two years of preparation, the school opened on Sept. 2, 1902, with C. M. Beach as principal and W. N. Johnson, business manager. In 1903 and again in 1907 the school was chartered by the state legislature, and in 1909 was admitted to the system of secondary Baptist schools established by the state convention. In 1907 the Cape Fear–Columbus Association pledged $600 toward the support of the school, but Dell, with a debt of over $8,000, was forced to close.   D. L. SMILEY

DEMENT, BYRON HOOVER (b. Silver Springs, Wilson Co., Tenn., May 17, 1863; d. New Orleans, La., Mar. 17, 1933). Pastor, professor, seminary president. Son of John Henry and Nancy Jane (Morrow) DeMent, he was educated as a boy in country schools, Sunday school, and church. At the age of 17, according to notes made by DeMent himself in a small copy of the New Testament, he memorized the whole of it. DeMent graduated from Peabody College, Nashville, Tenn., (then University of Nashville) and received the scholarship medal in 1885. After teaching school at Bell Buckle, Tenn., in 1886–87, he attended the University of Virginia and won the debator's medal but was forced by ill health to drop out. DeMent received the Th.D. degree from Southern Baptist Theological Seminary in 1900. Converted in 1881 and ordained in 1886, he held pastorates at Bell Buckle; Mt. Shiloh, Mt. Ed, Hebron, Buena Vista, and Lexington, Va.; 22nd and Walnut Street Church, Louisville, Ky.; First Church, Waco, Tex.; and First Church, Greenwood, S. C. He served as professor of practical theology and Hebrew at Baylor University, 1903–04, and professor of Sunday school pedagogy and assistant in theology and Hebrew, Southern Seminary, 1906–14. First president of Baptist Bible Institute, New Orleans, La., 1917–28, DeMent served as professor of New Testament exposition and Bible doctrines, 1928–33. He was a member of the Sunday School Lesson Committee of the Southern Baptist Convention and director of the assembly at Ridgecrest, N. C. DeMent wrote Sunday school lesson notes for *Baptist World* for six years; also *Bible Readers Life of Christ* (1928) and *The Inspiration of the Bible* (1931).

BIBLIOGRAPHY: B. H. DeMent, "Notes" (Recorded on the flyleaf of a New Testament used by him and still in possession of David C. DeMent, New Orleans, La.). J. T. Gwatkin, "Founder's Day Address" (1939). A. N. Marquis, ed., *Who's Who in America*, (1932–33).   J. WASH WATTS

DEMOCRACY. The word "democracy" may be used in three ways. (1) Democracy is a form of social organization which is characterized by popular sovereignty by means of representative constitutional government. (2) Democracy is an ethical ideal in which the essential equality, liberty, and intrinsic worth of every individual become the norm for the establishment of freedom and order in society. (3) Democracy is an affirmation of belief in the potentialities of the common man and in the power of truth and right to be both apprehended and applied in society. The foundation of this affirmation is the belief that God the Creator has given a moral law by which man is to be governed. Although the religious foundation of democracy has been challenged by naturalistic thought in the 20th century, the religious roots of democracy have been evident. These roots may be found in the Bible and in Christian history.

As an ideal and a faith, democracy is very old. As a form of social organization, democracy in modern society dates from the 16th century. Its growth closely paralleled the rise and expansion of Protestantism, especially Puritanism, from the European continent and England to the United States of America. Specific religious roots of democracy which are found in the Puritan-Protestant tradition include the doctrines of the sovereignty of God, man, the church, the state, and Christian vocation.

The English word "democracy" is derived from the Greek word *demokratia,* which means rule of the people. The Greeks supplied more than the word, however. The Athenian democracy of the fifth century was an early example of representative government. The Greeks also instituted a democratic constitution under Cleisthenes. Although the Greeks supplied some of the political theory upon which democracy is based, their own attempts to maintain a democratic government failed, largely because of the thoroughgoing secularism and lack of national unity which marked their culture.

The Judaic-Christian revelation in the Bible furnished religious ideals for the rise of democracy as a system of government. The social organization of the Hebrew nation was, ideally, theocratic. Actually, the nation moved from the time of Moses' leadership to a period of rule by priestly judges and, finally, to a limited monarchy. The covenant relation with God, the divine law in the form of an ethical decalogue, and the humanitarian provisions for slaves, laborers, widows, orphans, the poor, and the foreign traveler, served to guarantee a basic respect for the rights of individuals. In this way, therefore, the Old Testament record of Hebrew history contributed to democratic ideas.

A study of the New Testament indicates that Jesus did not place approval on any particular governmental system. However, Georgia Harkness notes four emphases in the teaching of Jesus which are fundamental requisites for true democracy: (1) the primacy of respect for personality; (2) an emphasis upon love of God and neighbor which places obligations above rights; (3) Jesus' realistic view of both the limitations and possibilities of human nature; (4) the inseparableness of personal piety and social responsibility as indicated in the continuity between faith in God and love for neighbor.

The historical courses of democracy and Christianity have not always run parallel. "For most of its history the Christian Church never dreamed that political democracy was a natural or even possible consequence of its faith and ethic. And even in the last few generations only a minority of Christians, only one tradition within the Church, has been consistently affiliated with political democracy." Puritanism has consistently been instrumental in the establishment of democracy, principally in the English-speaking world. In England the zenith was reached in the Puritan revolution in the middle of the 17th century. Simultaneously, in New England Roger Williams and other left-wing Protestants were declaring the separation of civil and ecclesiastical authority. By the time of the American Revolution, every right asserted in the Declaration of Independence had been discussed in sermons by the New England clergy.

The Christian roots of democracy in America have followed Calvinist and sectarian emphases. The emphases upon the sovereignty of God in both Calvinism and sectarianism served originally to undermine political and ecclesiastical absolutism. The doctrine of the church as the society of the redeemed in which decisions relating to church life were to be made by the membership or their representatives contributed to an appreciation of freedom of discussion as an essential of democratic procedure. Furthermore, the sectarian concept of the church as a gathered community based upon voluntary association of members in a covenant relationship gave to political thinkers of a Puritan background, such as John Locke, an idea of the state as a social contract calling for the consent of the governed. Left-wing sects, in insisting upon a structural and functional separation of church and state, fostered and consistently reaffirmed this arrangement as both Christian and democratic. The doctrine of the Christian calling has special importance for the Christian in politics. The Christian magistrate is to fulfil God's purpose in the sphere in which he works, just as is the Christian pastor. In recent Protestant political ethics the need has been cited for a renewed emphasis upon politics as a Christian vocation.

Christian political theory maintains that a realistic appraisal of man is essential for the survival of democracy. Both man's potentialities and his sinfulness are recognized in Christian political theory. Man's potentialities, as one created in the image of God, emphasize his essential equality and his personal liberty. Both Christian and democratic thought accentuates man's intrinsic personal worth and the necessity of equality of opportunity for all men because of their relation to God. The emphasis upon liberty includes freedom of thought, action, and individual expression within the limits of conscience and general welfare. Because of man's sinful nature, however, it is necessary to restrain his egoistic attempts to express liberty and equality. Therefore, democracy exists to restrain sin through its emphasis upon fundamentally just law. Reinhold Niebuhr states the case succinctly: "Man's capacity for justice makes democracy possible; but man's inclination to injustice makes democracy necessary."

BIBLIOGRAPHY: A. M. Baldwin, *The New England Clergy and the American Revolution* (1928). L. Dewar, *An Outline of New Testament Ethics* (1949). R. H. Gabriel, *The Course of American Democratic Thought: An Intellectual History Since 1815* (1940). G. Harkness, *The Modern Rival of Christian Faith: An Analysis of Secularism* (1952); *The Sources of Western Morality: From Primitive Society Through the Beginnings of Christianity* (1954). A. E. Holt, *Christian Roots of Democracy in America* (1941); *This Nation Under God* (1939). J. H. Nichols, *Democracy and the Churches* (1951). R. Niebuhr, *The Children of Light and the Children of Darkness* (1944). P. Ramsey, *Basic Christian Ethics* (1951). E. F. Scott, *The Ethical Teaching of Jesus* (1949). A. P. Stokes, *Church and State in the United States*, three volumes (1950). E. Troeltasch, *The Social Teaching of the Christian Churches*, trans. Olive Wyon, two volumes (1949).

THOMAS A. BLAND

DEMONS. The word "demon" does not occur in the King James Version. The Greek words *daimōn* and *daimonion* are usually translated "devil." "Devilish" (*daimoniōdēs*) and "possessed with a devil" (*daimonizomai*) also occur. Among the Greeks "demon" denoted a god or divinity, then a messenger from the gods, and finally (and vaguely) some sort of personal guardian as in the remarkable case of Socrates. In biblical references (LXX and N.T.) the devil or demon is always evil. Literature on the subject of demons is enormous, and a number of theories exist attempting to explain how ethnic demonism was absorbed into the scriptural record.

Certain remarkable features stand out in the Gospel passages concerning demons. Christ treated demons as realities, and if he held any other opinion of them (such as accommodating himself to contemporary beliefs about illness), he said nothing to indicate it. Demons are considered one of the terrible manifestations of sin, a part of the satanic kingdom. Possessed people are regarded as sick and treated with tenderness and care (not with the brutality so uniformly and unfortunately connected with the treatment of the abnormal). The demons are aware that Christ is the Son of God. There is remarkable restraint in the biblical record which is free from speculation, fantasy, and mythology.

BERNARD RAMM

DENMARK, BAPTIST UNION OF. The first Baptist church in Denmark was organized by Julius Köbner and J. G. Oncken in Copenhagen, Oct., 1839, with 11 members. Köbner, a Danish Jew, was a co-worker of Oncken in Germany, and a pioneer in Baptist work in Denmark. From 1865 to 1879 he was pastor of the First Baptist Church in Copenhagen (Kristuskirken); he wrote many of the hymns still used by Baptists in Denmark and Germany.

Severe persecution was directed against the Baptists until 1849 when the Danish Constitution granted religious freedom to dissenters. Full civil recognition of the Baptist churches came more than 100 years later (1952). In 1956 the Baptist Union formed the largest free church group in Denmark with a membership of 7,500 in 40 churches.

Danish Baptists have had active interest in foreign missions since the middle of the last century. In 1928 they organized their own mission in Urundu, Belgian Congo, where national membership now exceeds 2,000. About 12 Danish missionaries work with a number of national pastors, maintaining a hospital, seminary, and over 100 grade schools.

The Danish Women's Society has 2,400 members in 56 societies. Since 1946 Danish Baptists have co-operated with Norway and Sweden in the Scandinavian Seamen's Mission in San Francisco, and since 1928 pastors and missionaries have been trained at the seminary in Tollose, a village about 30 miles west of Copenhagen. An academy and folk high school, also located in Tollose, provide Christian education for young people. A Scout movement, started in 1931, enrols approximately 2,000 boys and girls. The Baptist Publication Society produces devotional

Denominational Calendar

and Baptist literature as well as the weekly paper, *Baptisternes Ugeblad*, with a circulation of 3,000. Other periodicals are *Dag over Danmark* and *Fredsbudet*. Baptist headquarters are located in Tollose.

BIBLIOGRAPHY: J. D. Franks, ed., *European Baptists Today* (1952). I. Barnes, *Truth is Immortal* (1955).

JOSEF NORDENHAUG

DENOMINATIONAL CALENDAR. See CALENDAR OF ACTIVITIES.

DENOMINATIONALISM. A spirit of oneness and loyalty among the people of a particular denomination, i.e., those who are bound together by a large measure of agreement with regard to doctrines and polity and by a desire for co-operation among the various churches holding these tenets. Growing out of a need for unity in wider kingdom work, denominationalism took shape among Particular Baptists in the formation of the first association in England in 1653; among General Baptists in the formation of the General Assembly, 1671; the Six Principle Baptists in 1690; and the Assembly of the Free Grace General Baptists organized in London, 1770.

Baptists in America originated mainly from England. Thus, when the Philadelphia Association was formed in 1707, American Baptists found themselves attempting to grow a single stalk of denominationalism out of two English Baptist roots: Calvinism and Arminianism. Calvinism triumphed in Philadelphia and remained to color the life of Baptists, particularly as they spread southward.

The growing denominational spirit took on several phases. In 1814, in order to support Luther Rice (*q.v.*) and Adoniram Judson (*q.v.*), Baptists formed a general convention; in 1817 the constitution was changed to include home missions; but in 1820 denominationalism suffered a setback as home missions was eliminated, and separate societies were formed to care for different aspects of the work. In spite of the fact that the denominational method had split, the purpose had become pretty well formed: to do together what could not be done singly.

The denominational spirit continued to grow. In 1824 the General Tract Society was organized. In 1832 the American Baptist Home Mission Society was formed. But it was not until the formation of the Southern Baptist Convention in 1845 that the society method was changed to boards. Although Calvinism, concern for freedom of the local church, and Landmarkism hindered, by 1859 the denominational spirit had fairly well cemented Baptists of the South; by 1916 the seeds for the Executive Committee had been planted; and by 1924 the Cooperative Program took root, later to grow into full-grown denominational co-operation.

BIBLIOGRAPHY: W. W. Barnes, *The Southern Baptist Convention, 1845-1953* (1953). J. F. Brownlou, "On Consolidating the Boards," *Baptist Standard* (Jan. 25, 1917). W. C. Buck, *Baptist Banner and Western Pioneer* (Feb. 15, 1844). J. C. Carlile, *The Story of English Baptists* (1905). W. Cathcart, "Philadelphia Confession of Faith," *The Baptist Encyclopedia* (1881). V. Ferm, ed., *The American Church of the Protestant Heritage* (1953). M. M. Lappin, *Baptists in the Protestant Tradition* (1947). W. J. McGlothlin, *Baptist Confessions of Faith* (1911). J. Rippon, ed., *The Baptist Annual Register* (1790-1802). J. B. Taylor, *Memoir of Luther Rice* (1841). A. L. Vail, *Baptists Mobilized for Missions* (1911). H. C. Vedder, *A Short History of Baptists* (1907). F. Wayland, *The American Magazine* (Nov., 1823; Jan., 1824; May, 1824).

C. EARL COOPER

DEPRAVITY. Man's tendency toward evil, inherited from Adam. Total depravity indicates that every area of man's personality has been affected by sin which was introduced by the fall of Adam. However, total depravity does not mean that every man is as bad as he can be or that every man is as bad as every other man, but that he is totally incapable of saving himself. Some theologians who believe in total depravity also recognize that there is much natural good in man, although his controlling disposition is toward evil; if he is saved, God by his grace must take the initiative.

See also SIN.

BIBLIOGRAPHY: R. Niebuhr, *The Nature and Destiny of Man* (1944). W. T. Conner, *The Gospel of Redemption* (1945).

CHARLES A. TRENTHAM

DERIEUX, WILLIAM THOMAS (b. Essex County, Va., May 6, 1853; d. Columbia, S. C., Mar. 4, 1938). Pastor, state mission leader. Son of Arthur Plumard and Virginia Gatewood (Clarkson) Derieux, he was educated at Council's School, the University of Richmond, and Southern Baptist Theological Seminary. Following his ordination by the Grace Street Baptist Church, Richmond, Va., Derieux held pastorates at Bainbridge Street Baptist Church, Richmond; First Baptist Church, Spartanburg, S. C.; Venable Street Baptist Church, Richmond; and First Baptist Church, Suffolk, Va.

Assistant missionary secretary of the South Carolina Baptist convention from 1906 to 1910, and state mission secretary from 1910 to 1926, Derieux held that position as secretary emeritus from 1926 until his death. His lifelong ambition, that every textile community in South Carolina should have at least one Baptist church, was realized before his death.

J. ELWOOD WELSH

DESIGNATED GIFTS. Gifts set apart or given for a certain purpose. A designation may be, first, a general designation, as for the Cooperative Program. Such funds would be distributed according to the percentages of distribution adopted for the Cooperative Program. Second, there is a selective designation from objects in the Cooperative Program, as foreign missions. Such funds could be used by the Foreign Mission Board for any purpose. Third, there is a special designation, for instance, the work of the Foreign Mission Board in Africa. Then the specific designation may be very specific, such as for a certain missionary working in Nigeria, under the Foreign Mission Board.

The attitude of the Southern Baptist Convention toward designated gifts is set forth in its business and financial plan, as follows:

Designated Gifts.—The Convention binds itself and its agencies faithfully to apply and use all such gifts as designated by the donor.

Trust Funds.—Each agency of the Convention is hereby instructed and ordered to keep all trust funds and designated gifts (for they are trust funds) sacred to the trust and designation; that they be kept separate from all other funds of such agency; that they are not to be used even temporarily for any other purposes than the purpose specified; and that such funds shall not hereafter be invested in the securities of any denominational body or agency.

AUSTIN CROUCH

DETERMINISM. Derived from the Latin compound *de* (from, concerning) and *terminus* (limit, end), *determinism* denotes the theory that every fact or event in the physical universe and human history is an instance of a definite causal pattern. There are at least two types of determinism: mechanistic (physical) and teleological (psychical). The former implies that every single event in the universe is fixed and limited by a certain number of laws and principles, and that, with the knowledge of these laws, it is theoretically possible to deduce and to predict every event of the future. The latter asserts that each event is determined by antecedent conditions, but that it also illustrates an unfolding cosmic design.

Only in its teleological sense does this term have any remote bearing upon Baptist thought. In this sense it is roughly the correlative of the religious term "predestinarianism" (Augustine and Calvin).

See also PREDESTINATION.

BIBLIOGRAPHY: J. E. Skinner, "Predestination and Determinism," *Anglican Theological Review* (1955). Spinoza, "The Ethics," *Philosophy of Benedict de Spinoza*, trans., R. H. M. Elwes (n.d.). J. Ward, *Realm of Ends.* The Gifford Lectures delivered at the University of St. Andrews in the years 1907–10 (1911). Paul Weiss, *Man's Freedom* (1950). J. B. MCMINN

DEVIL. Word applied in Scripture to Satan, to demons, and to man (John 6:70; cf. Matt. 16:23). The word derives from a Greek word meaning slanderer, accuser. "Satan" is a transliteration of the Hebrew word meaning adversary, resister. Since the Scriptures do not present abstractions, good and evil are never represented as abstract ideas or concepts. Good issues from the God of all goodness, and evil stems from a spirit of complete iniquity, i.e., the devil or Satan. His origin is a mystery. Appeals to Ezekiel 28 and Isaiah 14 are considered inconclusive by most expositors. The devil is presented as having superhuman power but remains a created and limited being operating only within the permissive will and sovereignty of God. He is the enemy of God and man and the lord over a host of fallen angels. The devil is variously called a liar, the tempter, the evil one, the old serpent, the murderer, and the dragon, each title emphasizing some particular characteristic of his person or activity. Historic Christianity has accepted the existence of a personal devil as a matter of divine revelation. Although religious liberalism rejected this doctrine, there has been serious reconsideration of it in recent theology.

BERNARD RAMM

DeVOTIE, JAMES HARVEY (b. Oneida County, N. Y., Sept. 24, 1813; d. Griffin, Ga., Feb. 16, 1891). First corresponding secretary of the Georgia Baptist State Mission Board. The son of pious Presbyterian parents, DeVotie was converted at the age of 16. At 17 he went to Savannah, Ga., to join an uncle in business. He attended First Baptist Church and began serious study of the New Testament. He was baptized on Dec. 2, 1831, and immediately felt called to preach. He attended Furman Theological Seminary and was ordained in Mar., 1833, to serve the Baptist church at Camden, S. C.

From 1835 to 1856 DeVotie served pastorates at Montgomery, Tuscaloosa, and Marion, Ala. He was active in the establishment of Howard College and of the *Alabama Baptist*.

DeVotie became pastor of the First Baptist Church, Columbus, Ga., in 1856. He led in the organization of the public school system of Columbus and served as the first president of the board of trustees. After a brief service as chaplain of the Second Regiment of Georgia Volunteers in the Confederate Army, he returned to his pastorate and throughout the war collected and administered relief funds. New church buildings were erected in Columbus and in Griffin, where he became pastor in 1870.

The newly organized Georgia Baptist State Mission Board elected DeVotie as its first corresponding secretary in 1877. As secretary DeVotie's talents and experience were employed successfully in organizing and developing support of missions. Increased gifts were collected at decreased cost, and under DeVotie's leadership the state mission board was established as the collecting agency for the Southern Baptist Home and Foreign Mission boards.

DeVotie was married to Miss Christian Margaret Noble in 1835, and to this union five children were born. In 1873 he married Mrs. Georgiana Lucia Pyron, and to this union four children were born.

SEARCY S. GARRISON

DICKINSON, ALFRED ELIJAH (b. Orange County, Va., Dec. 3, 1830; d. Richmond, Va., Nov. 20, 1906). Minister and denominational leader. He was the son of Ralph and Frances A. S. (Quisenberry) Dickinson. His family moved to Louisa County during Dickinson's infancy. He was baptized at the age of 17. He received his B.A. degree from Richmond College and his M.A. from the University of Virginia. He was married three times, first to Fannie Taylor who bore him four children, James Taylor, Fannie (Mrs. Samuel M. Torian), Nellie, and Janie; then to Lou Craddock, who bore him a daughter, Hallie; and lastly to Bessie Bagby. Pastorates held include Forest Hill which ordained him, First Baptist of Charlottesville, and Leigh Street in Richmond. He was superintendent of Baptist colportage and Sunday school work in Virginia. In 1865 he became partner of Jeremiah Bell Jeter (q.v.) in ownership and publication of the *Religious Herald*, Richmond College, and destitute churches. Trustee of Richmond College 36 years, he raised large sums for the school in numerous campaigns. Dickinson was general agent of the Army Colportage Society during the Civil War. A popular speaker to Northern audiences, he was a principal promoter of good feeling between Baptists of the South and North after the war. Always a promoter of peace which sacrificed no principle, his poise in heated debate contributed largely to the tradition of sanity in Virginia Baptist deliberative bodies.

CARRINGTON PAULETTE

DILLAHUNTY, JOHN (b. Kent County, Md., Dec. 8, 1728; d. Nashville, Tenn., Feb. 8, 1816). His family name was French, *De LaHunte,* and his ancestors were French noblemen. His parents were Catholics. He married a Quakeress, Hannah Neal, of Talbot County, Md., after which both he and his wife were excommunicated from their respective churches. Four years after their marriage, he and his wife came to Neuse, N. C., near New Bern, where he became sheriff of Craven County.

The first gospel sermon he ever heard was by George Whitefield, by which he was strangely moved. He was later converted under the ministry of Shubal Stearns (q.v.) and Daniel Marshall (q.v.) and was baptized by Philip Mulkey. When a Baptist church was organized, he became a deacon and shortly thereafter was licensed to preach. This congregation was dispersed by the Revolution. He reorganized the scattered flock in 1781 in Jones County, N. C., after which he was chosen the pastor and was ordained to the gospel ministry. He served this church fruitfully for 15 years. During his pastorate in Jones County, N. C., the Episcopalians, whose Tory minister had fled the country, came under the influence of his preaching and gave to his church their good building. Many of the members of this Church of England were converted and were received into the Baptist church by immersion.

He came to Tennessee in Mar., 1796, where he organized the Richland Creek Baptist Church near the present Belle Meade section of Davidson County, of which Nashville is the county seat. The Richland Creek church was the first Baptist church on the south side of the Cumberland River. The pastor, Elder Dillahunty, as he was known, was regarded as an eminent and successful minister for more than 55 years. He served as pastor of this church until his death.

He and his wife died suddenly on the same day and were buried in the same grave in Davidson County, Tenn., in the heart of Belle Meade. The chapel in the Baptist Hospital, Nashville, Tenn., is called the Dillahunty Memorial Chapel, being furnished in his memory by churches of Nashville Baptist Association.

HAROLD STEPHENS

DILLARD, JAMES EDGAR (b. Danville, Va., June 3, 1879; d. Nashville, Tenn., July 9, 1953). Minister, college president, author, first Convention director of promotion. The son of Edward Banks and Annie (Robertson) Dillard, he graduated from William Jewell College (A.B.) 1900, (D.D.) 1913; Clarksburg (Mo.) College (A.M.) 1901; Howard College (LL.D.) 1927. He was ordained in 1898 at Centralia, Mo. He married Lillian Cotton Madison, St. Louis, Mo., Jan. 15, 1903, and they had two children, James Edgar, Jr., pastor in Florida and Georgia; and Lilyan (Mrs. Wheeler Tracy) of Evanston, Ill.

Dillard began preaching at 16. He held pastorates at Sturgeon, Mo.; Macon, Mo.; Delmar, St. Louis, Mo.; First, St. Joseph, Mo.; and Southside, Birmingham, Ala., 1918–36. He was president of Clarksburg College, 1901–07; president of the Alabama convention, 1933–34; second vice-president of the Southern Baptist Convention, 1932–33; a trustee of Howard College, and book editor of *Alabama Baptist*, 1918–36.

He was a member of the Convention's Future Program Commission in 1925, created when the Cooperative Program was created, and chairman of the Cooperative Program Commission, 1925–27. He was president of the Executive Committee, 1927–36. He was the first director of promotion, for the Cooperative Program and Hundred Thousand Club from Aug. 2, 1936, until his retirement in July, 1947. He then served as director of promotion, emeritus. He led in payment of all Convention debts and was praised for realizing the aim "Debt Free in '43."

A wide reader and facile writer, he had a photographic memory. He reviewed several books weekly for 18 years in the *Alabama Baptist*. He wrote *We Southern Baptists* (1937); *What Next?* (1940); *Bible Stewardship* (1941); many tracts; and hundreds of brief articles on debt payment and mission support.

BIBLIOGRAPHY: J. S. Ramond, comp., *Among Southern Baptists* (1936). *Who's Who in America* (1953).

MERRILL D. MOORE

DILLARD, RYLAND THOMPSON (b. Caroline County, Va., Nov. 17, 1797; d. 1878). Pastor. Dillard was well educated, studied law, and began practicing it in Winchester, Ky., where he had moved in 1818.

Though a member of the Episcopal church, Dillard did not enter a "living experience" as a Christian until 1823, after a period of struggle. He related his experience and was baptized by Ambrose Dudley (q.v.)—whose granddaughter was Dillard's wife—into Bryants Baptist Church. He soon felt called to preach and was licensed by Bryants Church, 1824; he was ordained in the same year when called to the East Hickman Church. He preached at East Hickman about 46 years, also being pastor of David's Fork Church for 26 years. To these two churches Dillard devoted the majority of his ministry. For a short time he was pastor of Providence, Ephesus, Paris, and Clear Creek churches.

In 1843 he was appointed superintendent of public instruction for the state; he proved an able administrator. W. THOMAS LANE

DIRECT MISSIONISM (GOSPEL MISSIONISM). First threatened the existence of the Southern Baptist Convention in 1858–61. James Robinson Graves (q.v.) was its foremost advocate and ardent champion. With reference to the work of its Foreign Mission Board he said editorially in the *Tennessee Baptist*, Sept. 4, 1858, that he did not believe "our missionary machinery is scriptural or expedient. The scriptural plan is clearly exemplified in the New Testament, and is simple and effective. The sooner we return to it, the better for us and the world." He contended that only a church, or sometimes a group of churches, had the right to select, send, and support a missionary, and should send his salary through a commercial agency. In other words, missions should be conducted directly rather than through a convention or its board.

Graves was not alone in his views. Among other able men who agreed with him was Nathaniel Macon Crawford (q.v.), the president of Mercer University, Georgia, who, in an article published in the *Tennessee Baptist* Sept. 4, 1858, said that the missionary Baptists were right in supporting missions, and that the antimissionary Baptists were right in declaring the Southern Baptist missionary machinery to be unknown to the gospel. He then added: "The churches in the apostles' time sent out and sustained missionaries. Let our wealthy churches, and Associations of churches, now appoint their own missionaries."

Graves agitated this subject for months and made it dominant at the 1859 session of the Convention at Richmond, where it was discussed for more than a day. Graves himself spoke several hours. Although only the Foreign Mission Board was directly involved, his contentions applied also to the other boards of the Convention and to state conventions. The boards would have been useless and the Convention would have had but little to do had he won, but he lost. After all that was involved had been made clear, and misunderstandings had been clarified, the Convention voted almost unanimously to continue its methods for selecting, appointing, directing, and supporting missionaries. However, it voted for the board to transmit at cost any funds which a church or an association might give to support its missionary. Graves expressed satisfaction with the decision but soon renewed his opposition with even more vigor and determination. He charged that the Convention was episcopal and hierarchical in nature and dominated by city pastors.

At this time Graves was the undisputed leader of the aggressive and divisive Landmark movement, very demanding, and supported by many able men and a large following in some areas and some following in many areas. Since direct missions was an integral part of Landmarkism, it could not be separated from either Graves's efforts to make Landmarkism dominant in Southern Baptist life or his aggressive controversy with Robert Boyté Crawford Howell (q.v.) and many other prominent Southern Baptists. For a year or more there was a widespread fear that he would split the Convention and establish a Landmark convention for his followers. For example, he delivered an editorial ultimatum that one half the Convention boards and their secretaries must be Landmarkers, and closed by saying, "Let one or two other changes be made, and the denomination would again be united in missionary work—otherwise never."

Several state conventions wrestled desperately with the problems Landmarkism and direct missions created. However, many of his followers, when they became familiar with the implications of a split, declined to follow him. Samuel Boykin (q.v.), editor of the *Christian Index*, Georgia, wrote editorially, Oct., 1860, that he had traveled considerably and talked with many, and that he had found all against anything like a further division of the denomination (such as those caused by Alexander Campbell and the antimissionary Baptists), that disputes were gradually dying down, and that a decision had been reached not to let the Landmark or the board question become a test of fellowship.

Thus the crisis passed. The Civil War and the Reconstruction period followed. The South was prostrate. Both the churches and the denomination struggled desperately to re-establish themselves. Then the agitation for direct missions again appeared, but under the new name of "gospel missionism."

The leader in this movement was Tarleton Perry Crawford (q.v.), who went as a missionary to the Orient in 1851 and served many years in North China. He went under the auspices of the Foreign Mission Board, but under the patronage of the Big Hatchie Association, Tennessee, which underwrote his salary, but which salary the board often had to pay. (It was at Cotton Grove in this association that Landmarkism began in 1851. The Big Hatchie was one of the strongest Landmark associations.)

In May, 1885, Crawford returned to the United States on his own responsibility and at his own expense to acquaint the board with views he and some of his associates had come to hold. From 1885 until 1893, gospel missionism plagued the board. Its champions were bold, aggressive, and frequently insubordinate. They had the support of many who had imbibed the views of Graves on direct missions. The board acted with restraint, much patience, and good judgment until gospel missionism ceased to be an issue.

The gospel mission contentions were substantially as follows:

1. A local church, or group of churches, should select, send, and sustain its own missionary (direct missions), and to it only should the missionary be responsible and make reports. He should major on evangelism rather than preaching and teaching, and have liberty to do his work in his own way and at places of his choosing.

2. No money should be used for the support of schools.

3. No native should be paid for religious work, and no financial help should be given to native churches.

4. A missionary should suffer hardship, even unto death, if and when he fails to receive support from his supporting church in America. (This contention of D. W. Herring may not have been shared by others.)

5. A missionary should wear native dress, live in a native house, and eat native food, thereby completely identifying himself with the natives.

Finally Crawford wrote a tract, "Churches to the Front," which led the board to remove his name from the list of missionaries. The president of the board said: "If the Convention should accept the ideas advanced in Dr. Crawford's tract entitled 'Churches to the Front,' it would simply commit suicide, and in its fall would crush other organizations of Baptists."

Missionary Roswell Hobart Graves (q.v.), Canton, wrote "Board or No Board" to answer the contentions of the gospel missioners. It appeared in the *Christian Herald,* Virginia, Oct. 12, 1893. It was "so plain in statement, fine in spirit, and exhaustive in argument" the board printed it as a tract for free distribution. The controversy ended when the board "separated" T. P. Crawford and T. J. League because they would not resign, and the others resigned: Mrs. Crawford, Mrs. League, G. P. Bostick, D. W. and Mrs. Herring, and later, W. D. King and Miss Fannie Knight.

Thereafter, gospel missionism ceased to be an issue in the Convention. The churches and associations that believed in Landmarkism, including direct or gospel missions, did but little for missions. In 1905 they organized the Baptist General Association and made Texarkana, Ark.-Tex., headquarters and had no further connection with the Southern Baptist Convention. In 1924 they changed the name to American Baptist Association. In 1950 a minority withdrew and organized the North American Baptist Association, with headquarters at Little Rock, Ark. Both groups, however, adhered to gospel missionism or direct missions, and other Landmark doctrines.

See also GOSPEL MISSIONISM.

BIBLIOGRAPHY: J. S. Rogers, "The Landmark Baptist Division Over Mission Methods [in Arkansas], 1901," *History of Arkansas Baptists* (1948). R. G. Torbet, *A History of the Baptists* (1950). H. A. Tupper, "Theory and Conduct of our Missions," *A Decade of Foreign Missions, 1880–1890* (1891).

HOMER L. GRICE

DISCIPLES OF CHRIST. Also called Christians, an American religious body founded by Thomas Campbell (1763–1854), his son Alexander (1788–1866), and Barton Warren Stone (1772–1844). Thomas Campbell was a minister of the Secession (independent Presbyterian) Church in Ireland. In 1807 he emigrated to western Pennsylvania, accepting a charge in the Presbytery of Chartiers. Campbell's independent spirit and belief in Christian unity led to controversy with the Presbyterians and, in 1809, to the formation of the Christian Association of Washington (Pa.). That same year he issued the "Declaration and Address," a 30,000-word statement of Christian belief, to which his youthful son Alexander subscribed. Chief among its principles are these: (1) the essential unity of the church of Christ (proclaimed in John 17); (2) church co-operation in diversity; (3) the return to simple, primitive Christianity; (4) "no creed but Christ"; (5) supremacy of the New Testament; (6) congregational government.

At Brush Run, Pa., was established (1811) the first congregation of the Reformers, as Campbell's group styled themselves. From 1813 until 1827, they were affiliated with various Baptist associations. Despite agreement on immersion of adult believers only, congregational polity, strong biblical emphasis, and a mutual antipathy for creeds and confessions of faith, Reformers and Baptists drifted apart after 1826.

Alexander Campbell emerged by 1820 as the leading thinker, organizer, and expositor of the Reformers, now preferring the name Disciples of Christ. He established the *Christian Baptist* (1823), which he replaced (1830) with the *Millennial Harbinger,* strongly emphasizing the second coming. Advocating New Testament Christianity without human innovations, he waged war on missions, Sunday schools, and sectarian societies. In 1840 he founded Bethany College in western Virginia. Until his death in 1866, Alexander Campbell traveled incessantly, preaching and debating before large audiences throughout the eastern United States and abroad.

The denomination—an outgrowth of a movement created to unify all disciples of Christ—grew rapidly. Especially significant was the early union of the Disciples with a similar group called "Christians," led by Barton W. Stone. In 1906 schism developed among the Disciples over the use of instrumental music in public worship, and a number of churches withdrew to form the "Churches of Christ." By 1954 this latter group had grown to 1,600,000, organized into 16,500 churches. In 1955 the Disciples reported 8,419 churches, 2,029,963 members, 7,404 ordained ministers, and 8,601 Sunday schools enrolling 1,288,238. The denomination is the eighth largest American evangelical communion.

Disciples co-operate in an International Convention with headquarters in Indianapolis, Ind., and work closely together through the United Christian Missionary Society and other agencies. Riley B. Montgomery is president (1956) of the International Convention.

See also CHURCHES OF CHRIST.

BIBLIOGRAPHY: B. A. Abbott, *The Disciples—An Interpretation* (1924). P. Ainslie, "Disciples of Christ, or Christians," *Encyclopaedia Britannica*, VII (1956). A. Campbell, *The Memoir of Elder Thomas Campbell* (1861). M. M. Davis, *How the Disciples Began and Grew* (1915). W. E. Garrison, *Alexander Campbell's Theology* (1900); *Religion Follows the Frontier—A History of the Disciples of Christ* (1931). E. Gate, *History of the Disciples of Christ* (1905); *Early Relation and Separation of Baptists and Disciples* (1904). T. W. Grafton, *Alexander Campbell* (1897). F. D. Kershner, "Disciples of Christ," *Encyclopedia Americana*, IX (1956). R. Richardson, *Memoirs of Alexander Campbell* (1888). H. K. Rowe, "Alexander Campbell" and "Thomas Campbell" in A. Johnson, *Dictionary of American Biography*, III (1929). W. W. Sweet, *Our American Churches* (1924); *The Story of Religion in America* (1930). B. B. Tyler, *A History of the Disciples of Christ* (1894). P. H. Welsheimer, *Concerning the Disciples* (1935). R. F. West, *Alexander Campbell and Natural Religion* (1948). H. L. Willett, "Disciples of Christ," *Hastings Encyclopaedia of Religion and Ethics*, IV (1909). ROBERT H. SPIRO, JR.

DISCIPLINE. An activity of Christian churches, under the direct control of the congregation, to preserve conformity in doctrine and practice and to foster the spiritual well-being of members individually and corporately. Authority is based upon the express words of Jesus, the accepted Lord of the individual church (Matt. 16:18; 18:17); and upon New Testament principles and practices reflecting churches as autonomous bodies, members of which voluntarily submit to the jurisdiction of the whole body (Acts 6:3; I Cor. 5:4 ff.; II Cor. 2:5-7; I Thess. 5:12 ff.; II Thess. 3:6; I Tim. 5:20).

A church is called to share in and to show forth the holiness of its Lord. In the Bible this call "involves the consecration and actual sanctification of its individual members." The members of a church are confronted by the ideal of moral and spiritual growth. But they are promised forgiveness when they come short of this ideal. There is always some measure of tension and conflict between the true nature of Christians as saints and their realization of saintlike character.

Three principal concerns of a church, growing out of this situation and touching on the integrity of its own life, are the maintenance of the purity of its doctrine, the unity of its fellowship, and the holiness of its members. It follows that, with respect to its inner life, a church must look on nothing with greater apprehension than impure teaching (heresy), disruption of fellowship (schism), and moral and spiritual lapse (sin).

To all these dangers a church addresses its discipline. In the widest sense discipline includes, positively, the cultivation of sound doctrine, sound unity, and sound character. Negatively, discipline has to do with censures of whatever sort which put the heresy, factiousness, or sinfulness of a member under appropriate penalties. In the narrower sense discipline usually refers to a church's action against sin and moral lapse, looking toward the offender's reclamation. This is the responsibility, in the final analysis, of the whole congregation.

The nature of a church's life, being spiritual, requires spiritual means, insights, and objectives for the exercise of church discipline. Discipline must therefore not be separated from a biblical understanding of sin and grace; it must express love rather than spite; it must aim at the protection of the church and the reclamation of the offender.

The books of discipline, which once were in wide use among Baptists in America, ordinarily have opening chapters on church doctrine, church officers, conditions of reception into membership, and the duties of members. These are followed by chapters on how to deal directly with members who, after right instruction and credible profession, have fallen into sin. These measures are "commonly called Church-Censures, which differ in their nature according to the Nature and Degree of Offence." There were three such degrees:

Rebuke.—This is the lowest censure, aiming at pointing out an offense, admonishing the offender, and reclaiming him from sin. Rebuke was administered for such things as: revealing the weakness of a brother to others; contentiousness over worship practices which do not have explicit scriptural warrant or rejection; neglect in attending business meetings of the church, etc.

Suspension.—This penalty followed the conviction of an offending member and set him aside "from Office, from the Lord's Table, and from the Liberty of judging or voting" on a church issue. More grave than rebuke, suspension was administered for such causes as: gossip and backbiting, refusal of one's domestic or civic responsibilities through sloth, or refusing to receive the church's rebuke for some offense. On credible repentance the offending member was to be restored.

Excommunication.—This is a censure of the highest degree, "is a judicial Act of the Church, in which by the authority of Christ, she cuts off and entirely excludes an unworthy Member, from Union and Communion with the Church, and from all Rights and Privileges thereof." This exclusion affected the spiritual activities of man and never involved temporal or civil penalties. Neither did it forbid attendance on the ministry of the Word.

Excommunication was exercised against all sins which violated the letter of the Ten Commandments, all civil crimes which called for severe corporal punishments (provided the human laws are not contrary to divine law), and all scandalous actions which exposed the church to contempt.

The exercise of discipline was indispensable, in churches of believers only, for maintaining their character as "gathered" communities, i.e., as communities which had been "separated from the world and unto God."   THERON D. PRICE

HISTORY OF DISCIPLINE. With the passing of the apostolic age, discipline in the old Catholic church came under the jurisdiction of the rising episcopate. However, small antichurchly groups through the centuries resisted episcopal discipline in favor of a congregational or presbyterial form. This was most often done in an effort to preserve the pattern of primitive Christianity.

The Reformation emphasis upon biblical authority brought the New Testament pattern into clearer relief. Continental Protestantism of the 16th century saw the episcopal discipline being challenged seriously by a presbyterial form. In the time of Edward VI in England (1547–53), according to the practice of at least one Reformed church, discipline was meted out by elders, subject to approval of the congregation. In the 17th century Baptists and Congregationalists emerged as the two strongest advocates of congregational discipline.

A 16th-century Anabaptist statement of belief, from Bern, Switzerland, records: "If a brother sees his brother going astray he should, in accordance with the command of Christ, warn and chastise him in a Christian and fraternal way, as everyone is obligated by love to do." An early Mennonite confession of faith (c. 1580) says: "Ecclesiastical discipline or extreme punishment is ... an external action among believers. ... Wherefore special care must be taken that no one be condemned in the church who has not beforehand been condemned by the Word of God." The Orthodox Creed of 1678 (Baptist) states: "Christ hath given to his church a subordinate power [for discipline and government]."

In America the practical implications of congregational discipline came to an early flowering among Congregationalists and Baptists. The Separatists at Plymouth were of this polity before it spread to neighboring New England colonies. Though the local church exercised final authority, Congregational churches often delegated certain matters of discipline, for advice only, to committees of unions or associations. The records of an Illinois church, 1834, record "the whole duty of prosecuting the case further [after following Matt. 18] devolves on the church."

Baptists have traditionally practiced congregational discipline. Its frequency of implementation and effectiveness have depended on the local congregation. W. W. Sweet lists over a hundred offenses dealt with by local Baptist churches on the American frontier. At present, congregational discipline is still a stoutly defended ideal among Baptists. At regular and called business sessions of the church, all members in good standing have equal voting rights on matters that confront the body. With increasing delegation of tasks to committees, many churches follow in practice a presbyterial form. More discerning churches make a distinction between delegation of work and delegation of authority. To the extent that authority is delegated, the church has ceased to exercise congregational discipline.   JOE KING

DENOMINATIONAL SELF-DISCIPLINE. More than they themselves realize, Southern Baptists have inherent resources for self-discipline. These resources are operative in the fields of doctrine and polity and in the co-operative features of their denominational life. They exercise themselves as disciplinary forces and follow a pattern which Baptists in the South have been evolving from the early 18th century to the present.

It is important that there has been a period of several generations in which to evolve Baptist resources of self-discipline, as these resources were not born with full growth. They were developed as the individual Baptist, equally a member of his church and his general bodies, sought to fulfil his Christian obligations. As no Baptist body has the authority to bind any other Baptist body, and as no Baptist body has the authority to bind even its own future action (except regarding property and other relationships governed by civil law), its denominational discipline cannot be established by legislative action. Bodies may act but not legislate—except through long-sustained unanimity of action which establishes binding or near-binding rules through the gradual building of a tradition, through what in effect becomes the principle of common law. This gradualism and the dependence upon Scripture as the final authority result in a large measure of conservative stability. In addition, because of the lack of legislative and binding enactments, Baptist bodies possess a large measure of real freedom of action which, within the space of a generation, can effect marked changes.

Discipline with respect to doctrine.—Although the churches had their own confessions of faith, they repeatedly sent "queries" to their associations for guidance in doctrinal interpretation. Although the association's judgments in these matters could be either accepted or rejected, they resulted in the establishment of norms for the association which made it difficult for any constituent churches effectively to promulgate any extreme or tangential doctrinal errors. Messengers from one church could report questionable doctrinal interpretations of another church to the association. In such instances the association would usually appoint a committee to consider the matter with the church in question.

The entrance of Separate Baptists into the stream of Southern Baptist life in 1755 introduced opposition to both church and associational confessions of faith. This difference was resolved in 1787 in Virginia and shortly thereafter in other states, resulting in co-operation between the two groups, each respecting the views of the other. Those associations formed before *c.* 1900 usually adopted confessions of faith, many following the example of the Charleston Association (1767) in adapting the Philadelphia Confession. Associational confessions were identical with or similar to the confessions which had been adopted by the co-operating churches. Then, when a church applied for affiliation with an association, the association appointed a committee to examine the church's confession of faith. That practice still prevails. In this way the association admits to co-operative relationship only churches whose confessions of faith, or articles of faith as they now often are called, are consistent with the confessions of faith that other churches in its fellowship have adopted. Thus, there is established doctrinal uniformity among the churches of the association. This step is an essential condition to obtaining the associational relationship. The relationship is voluntary on the part of both the church and the association and may be dissolved by either, should doctrinal positions become sufficiently divergent, or for any other reason.

Gradually, there developed the belief that it was not at all essential that an association have articles of faith, inasmuch as the churches initiated the adoption of articles of faith, and no churches were received into associational fellowship whose articles of faith were not in harmony with the articles of faith of affiliated churches. By 1956 about one third of the associations in the Southern Baptist Convention had no articles of faith. In spite of any accepted theory to the contrary, in a practical way the relationships between the churches and the association to which they are affiliated are the most immediate and intimate of the various relationships which exist between separate Baptist bodies. Each, therefore, has a strong corrective power of doctrinal discipline at its command. Though seldom used because the necessity infrequently arises, it positively exists and is available when needed. Therefore, state conventions and the Southern Baptist Convention have but rarely given consideration to doctrines in their deliberations, as that subject is felt to be amply safeguarded in the associations, which are in closer contact with the churches and which traditionally have accepted this responsibility.

The Southern Baptist method of ordaining ministers (and deacons) is one which tends to produce uniformity of doctrine among these leaders. A presbytery, usually composed of ministers from the association, questions the ministerial candidate and recommends his ordination to the church. Although the ordination is done in the name of the church, it is the presbytery which performs the laying on of hands which generally has been considered a necessary part of the ceremony.

Discipline with respect to polity.—Baptist polity developed and became established in much the same way as did the statements of Baptist doctrine. Many of the "queries" from the churches to the association were regarding this matter. The very principle of association became defined within the early associations.

While books have been written concerning Baptist polity, their contents cannot be thought of as definitive. The general concepts are in what may be thought of as the realm of unwritten law. They are traditions established by time and general usage.

Because there is considerable latitude for the practice of methods and processes within clearly established and widely accepted bounds, deviations from the established principles and practices of Baptist polity are infrequent. Such deviations as do occur are often considered of less importance than the continuance of co-operative enterprise and are quietly tolerated in a spirit of mutual forbearance.

In their early history Southern Baptists looked for specific scriptural directives for their actions and for a significant period hesitated or even refused to act in matters on which the Scriptures were silent. This dependence upon Scripture gives a measure of stability to Southern Baptist action but allows change in harmony with changing patterns of interpretation. Of late, Southern Baptists have tried to pattern their purposes and actions after what they conceive to be the spirit of the New Testament, as in the case of Woman's Missionary Union, Baptist Training Union, etc., without being so insistent as formerly on specific scriptural directive.

As it was during the process of its establishment, so now Baptist polity continues to find resources for the practical discipline of deviations. New developments have called for the creation of new patterns. Their shapes have been developed in relation to established principles in a way that is held consistent with Scripture and with the central missionary message and purpose of Christianity as understood by Baptists. Dedicated people imbued with such concepts do realize the need for correction when errors arise. The guidance of the Holy Spirit, therefore, becomes a significant resource in the discipline of polity deviations.

Discipline with respect to co-operative features.—Every Southern Baptist belongs to a Baptist church in affiliation with a general body. Through this affiliation these churches together accomplish joint ventures in Christian service. Some ventures are continuing, and others are temporary, but all are voluntary. The major emphases at early Colonial associational meetings were evangelistic and devotional. The venture that sought to bring all American Baptists into co-operative effort resulted from the desire to evangelize, both at home and abroad. This national effort eventually resulted in the American and the Southern Baptist Conventions. Other general bodies have developed whose affiliated churches usually come from within the

Discipline

geographical bounds of individual states. Thus, the Southern Baptist denomination has developed, from a geographical and a quasi-organizational point of view, a pyramidal structure with churches forming the base and with associations and then state conventions leading to the apex, the Southern Baptist Convention. Theoretically and organically, such a pyramid does not exist; practically and functionally, it does, at least to the extent of being used as a working mechanism.

Devotional and evangelistic emphases and the great desire to encourage home and foreign missions still are vital to all general bodies. However, as co-operative ventures became more numerous, more varied, and more complex, the general bodies, through experience or by mutual agreement, or simply in practice, limit themselves to certain areas of endeavor. For example, colleges and universities are primarily the responsibility of the state conventions, theological seminaries are primarily the responsibility of the Southern Baptist Convention, and hospitals have become the direct concern of associations, state conventions, and the Southern Baptist Convention.

Although each general body has its own responsibility, the program of the Southern Baptist Convention, with its boards, commissions, institutions, and committees, sums up most of the co-operative desires of Southern Baptists and thus this Convention has become the agency which initiates specific plans for accomplishing these desires. These plans often suggest patterns of action for all the co-operating general bodies and churches which support the Convention's program. The roles of all are implied in a single, unified program for voluntary co-operation.

Just as associations have become the denomination's guardian for doctrinal discipline, the Southern Baptist Convention has given co-operative goals and unity of purpose, plans, and action to other denominational units. Loyalty to this program has become a major criterion by which Southern Baptists are known and recognized. Significant deviation from this program labels itself as the beginning of defection.

Yet all the while, each unit of the denomination has disciplinary resources by which it may correct the mistakes of the other units. This, of course, includes the power to cause the modification of the co-operative program of the Southern Baptist Convention. If the action of boards, institutions, commissions, and committees of the general bodies is consistent with the faith and convictions of their constituencies, the warmth of their fellowship and their joint sharing together enrich the life of each. Should there be deviation, each unit, each individual, in the utilization of his liberty and in the operation of the voluntary principle, has the opportunity to influence correctively the deviate. This discipline of deviation is effective because each is conscious of the practical interdependency of one on the other, and all general bodies are conscious that their existence depends on the co-operation of the churches.

Discipline with respect to Baptist history.—An understanding of the facts of Baptist history studied in context would seem to be a legitimate source of self-discipline. However, as Southern Baptists have never given much emphasis to even the events of Baptist history, denominational history is largely a latent source for self-discipline. Southern Baptists do not know their past well enough for its disciplinary influence to be greatly felt throughout the denomination. Conversely, there exist popular misconceptions held by Baptists concerning their own history which point to the need for drawing on this potential source and developing a strong self-discipline in this field.

Although Southern Baptist traditions, growing out of their heritage from the radical wing of the 16th- and 17th-century reformations, have created invisible forces which have affected their reactions and directions, Southern Baptists have little historical understanding as to how many of these traditions became established or how they developed into their presently recognizable forms. They know little of traditions which have been outgrown, and they seldom think in terms of developing new traditions. In the continuing development of denominational self-discipline, it is now being felt by many leaders throughout the Southern Baptist Convention that knowledge and understanding of the facts of Baptist history are a necessity. Efforts are being made to write Baptist history and to promote its study by all Southern Baptists. An outstanding example of the vitality of this movement is the rise of various historical societies and commissions among Southern Baptists.

Finally, the principle of denominational self-discipline is rooted in the tradition of church members who are free and, at the same time, responsible. All churches and general bodies are composed, not of each other in any hierarchical, corporate, or legal relationship, but of individuals. Each individual Christian, related equally as he is to his church, to his association, to his state convention, and to the Southern Baptist Convention, must of necessity maintain consistency and harmony among these bodies in order to maintain consistency and equilibrium within his own being. Baptist denominational unity, progress, and purpose are ultimately based on and derived by individuals who share a similar context of doctrine, polity, and co-operation. The combination of these, plus the force and effect of tradition, serves to create adequate organization and motivation to achieve the providentially appointed mission of Southern Baptists.

See also POLITY, BAPTIST CHURCH.

BIBLIOGRAPHY: *A Confession of Faith, Put Forth by the Elders and Brethren of Many Congregations of Christians (Baptized upon Profession of their Faith) in London and in the Country. Adopted by the Baptist Association in Charlestown, South Carolina. To Which is Annexed a Summary of Church-*

Discipline (1774). S. L. Greenslade, *Schism in the Early Church* (1953). A. Harnack, *The Mission and Expansion of Christianity in the First Three Centuries* (1908). M. M. Knappen, *Tudor Puritanism* (1939). W. J. McGlothlin, *Baptist Confessions of Faith* (1911). E. Payne, *The Fellowship of Believers* (1952). W. W. Sweet, *Religion on the American Frontier: The Baptists* (1931); *Religion on the American Frontier: The Congregationalists* (1939). W. Walker, *A History of the Congregational Churches in the United States* (1899). R. G. Torbet, *A History of the Baptists* (1950).

FLOYD PATTERSON

DISESTABLISHMENT OF STATE CHURCH, VIRGINIA. For 169 years, from the settlement of Jamestown in May, 1607, to the adoption of the state constitution in June, 1776, the Church of England was established, supported, and governed in Virginia under the laws of England and the colony. For another 10 years after 1776 the Church of England held this role in a modified fashion.

As early as 1623 laws required the establishment of houses for worship in the Virginia Colony, such worship to be only in accordance with the canons of the Church of England. Citizens were fined for absenting themselves from worship, disparaging a minister, or failing to have their children baptized. There were efforts to enforce conformity by "whippings and brandings" in the mid-1600's.

The Act of Toleration (1689) was first applied in Virginia in 1699 when a Presbyterian minister, Francis Makemie, received from the constituted authorities a license to preach as a dissenter. Records indicate that at least some Regular Baptists conformed to the requirement to apply for a license and to take the prescribed oath, but Separate Baptists refused to recognize the right of any civil power to regulate preaching or places of worship. The Separates grew rapidly from about 1755 on and soon became an important factor in the struggle to abolish the Established Church.

On June 4, 1768, five Baptist ministers were arrested while preaching in Spottsylvania County, and three of them served 43 days in jail. Although they had been attacked repeatedly by unruly mobs, this was the first of many instances when Baptist preachers in Virginia were imprisoned for their refusal to abide by the Toleration Act.

Baptists began to petition the House of Burgesses for relief in 1770. Their first petition concerned the requirement that their ministers bear arms under militia law and attend musters, "by which they are unable to perform the duties of their function," but this petition was rejected. Baptists ignored a restriction prohibiting dissenting ministers from preaching in meetinghouses not particularly mentioned in their licenses. Petitions multiplied, not only from Baptists, but from other dissenters as well, as sentiment against the Establishment grew. The American Revolution speeded up the progress of disestablishment, since the war period called for union and harmony among all classes. Persecution of all dissenters ended, though inequalities of status remained.

In 1775 Baptists asked for and obtained from the Colonial Convention permission for dissenting clergymen to conduct worship and preach to the soldiers who preferred their own ministers to the chaplains. The following year, June 12, 1776, the convention adopted the historic Declaration of Rights, the 16th Article of which, as reported to the convention, stated that "all men should enjoy the fullest toleration in the exercise of religion." On motion of James Madison, however, the article was amended to read, "all men are equally entitled to the free exercise of religion." A radical difference existed between these two concepts, which Madison distinguished, ably defending the cause of religious freedom. The adoption of his amended 16th Article marked an important step in the disestablishment.

When the first general assembly met at Williamsburg, Oct. 7, 1776, it was flooded with petitions, some asking that the Establishment be abolished, others predicting dire consequences to the moral and religious life of Virginia unless it were maintained. After lengthy debate, a compromise was reached; laws prohibiting the exercise of any mode of worship were repealed; dissenters were exempted from supporting the state church; and even the requirement for support of the Protestant Episcopal Church (the Anglican Church was cut off from Virginia by the Revolution) by its own members was suspended until the next session of the general assembly. However, the principle of state regulation of churches was reaffirmed, and the question of a general assessment to support all churches was reserved for later decision.

Between 1776 and 1779 the struggle continued in the general assembly. From one session to the next the tax for support of the Established Church was suspended, until at the end of 1779 it was abolished. But the Episcopal clergy still hoped for a general taxation for support of all churches, enjoyed a near monopoly on marriage fees, and possessed the rich glebes (plantations bought with tax money in colonial days and given to the church for support of its clergy).

Many religious groups which opposed a state church hoped for the support of all churches by general taxation, with each individual's taxes going to the church of his choice. Baptists were said to offer the chief opposition to such a general assessment. In 1784 the general assembly submitted the proposed taxation to the people, but opposition was apparently overwhelming, and the proposal died in committee the following year, never to be resurrected.

By 1784 proponents of religious equality had secured a satisfactory marriage law, placing the ministers of all denominations on equal footing regarding the solemnization of marriages. With little of the Establishment remaining, the Protestant Episcopal Church was incorporated in 1785, empowering the vestries and clergymen with the supervision of the church and doing away with all state control. The Act of Incorporation, however, was objectionable to Baptists and others, in that it implied a state-church relationship which ought not to exist and confirmed to the Episcopal church possession of the glebes. After the Act of Incorporation was repealed in 1787, and the glebes were sold by act of the assembly in 1802 with proceeds devoted to public use, a preferred church no longer existed in Virginia. In the meantime, James Madison had again presented the "Bill for Establishing Religious Freedom," first offered by Jefferson in 1779, and on Jan. 19, 1786, it became law.

See also EPISCOPAL ESTABLISHMENT IN VIRGINIA.

L. D. JOHNSON

DISPENSATION. The Greek word (oikonomia) occurs seven times in the New Testament, is translated "dispensation" four times and "stewardship" three times. Its root meaning is that of a stewardship, a management, a disposition of goods or affairs.

Dispensation is used frequently in theological literature to indicate the modes of God's administration of his kingdom. The Old Testament is thus referred to as the old, the legal, the Jewish, or the material dispensation, and the New Testament is accordingly called the new or the Christian dispensation.

However, the word has acquired special meaning with a school of interpretation (dispensationalism) which divides sacred history into seven periods, during each of which a special administration (dispensation) prevails. According to C. I. Scofield, "these periods are marked off in Scripture by some change in God's method of dealing with mankind or a portion of mankind, in respect to the questions of sin and of man's responsibility. Each of the dispensations may be regarded as a new test of the natural man, and each ends in judgment—marking utter failure." Dispensationalism follows a very strict literalism in biblical interpretation and has never been affirmed by any outstanding Baptist theologian.

See also ETERNITY.

BERNARD RAMM

DISTRICT OF COLUMBIA BAPTIST CONVENTION. Baptist work began in Washington shortly after the new national city was occupied. The first recorded meeting of Baptists was on July 5, 1801, four months after the inauguration of President Thomas Jefferson and eight months after the first meeting of Congress in the city.

The first worship service of Baptists was held in the newly built Treasury Building. Lewis Richards, pastor of the First Baptist Church of Baltimore, Md., officiated. Eight months later, on Mar. 7, 1802, the First Baptist Church of Washington, D. C., was organized in a private home with six charter members. Four visiting ministers were present at this meeting: Elders Lewis Richards, Adam Freeman, Jeremiah Moore, and William Parkinson, the recently elected chaplain of the House of Representatives. Jeremiah Moore, who had earlier been imprisoned in Virginia for the preaching of Baptist doctrine, preached the sermon. At the second meeting, held a week later in the Fountain Inn, plans were made for the purchase of property and the erection of a building, a project speedily undertaken and completed by fall of the same year. The building was located on the southwest corner of Nineteenth and I streets on a lot purchased for $225. Parkinson and various visiting clergymen supplied the pulpit until May 31, 1807, when Obadiah B. Brown of Newark, N. J., was elected pastor and began a ministry that lasted for the next 43 years.

Discipline was unusually strong in Baptist churches of this period. Of the six founding members of the Washington church, three were later excommunicated, and two withdrew in dissent to form another church. The statement of doctrine was similar to most evangelical churches of the day, except that baptism was specified as immersion. The church had at least three rules of discipline that were fairly rigidly enforced: (1) Attendance was required of all members at all meetings of the church, good and sufficient reasons for absence to be given at the next meeting after absence therefrom. (2) Each member was to pay his share of the expenses according to his ability. (3) The members were not to remove to distant parts without informing and consulting with the brethren. Pews were rented to the public and were advertised in the newspapers. Forty-four pews brought in an annual revenue of $309 in 1809.

During its first five years the little church depended entirely upon visiting and supply preachers for its ministerial services. The most regular supply was Parkinson, who had been present at the founding of the church.

The most stabilizing influence upon the tiny congregation (27 members) was that of Obadiah B. Brown. His ministry was one of the most notable to be found in the religious history of the capital city. During the early period of his ministry with the church, he also found time to fill a clerkship in the post office, at a salary of $1700, in order to be of less expense to the struggling church. He was a leader in the city's civic and educational progress. He was chaplain of the House, one of the founders and president of the board of trustees of Columbian College, president of the Baptist General Tract Society (later the American Baptist Publication Society), and one of the original trustees of the Washington City Orphan Asylum.

The Second Baptist Church of Washington, D. C., was organized as the Navy Yard Baptist Church on June 3, 1810, under the leadership of Joseph and Sarah Borrows and three other members of First Church—Bartleson Fox, Clement Boswell, and Harvey Bestor—all of whom held letters of dismission from First Church. The organizational meeting was held in McLeod's schoolhouse with three ministers present: William Grinstead; Robert Latham; and Jeremiah Moore, who had preached the dedicatory sermon of First Church. The group continued to meet in the schoolhouse until September of that year, when a small frame building was erected near the corner of Fourth and G streets, S. E. Moore preached the first sermon, and he continued to serve the church until his death in 1814.

Moore was succeeded at Navy Yard (Second) by an equally colorful clergyman, Spencer Cone, a former legitimate actor of some note who had retired from the stage in 1812 decrying the lack of advancement in the theater and the want of public appreciation. He had been a member of the Philadelphia and Baltimore Company, considered the most talented company in the country, which appeared in Washington for a short theatrical season in 1808 and 1809. In 1814, while a clerk in the Treasury Department, he preached his first sermon before the Navy Yard Church. On June 25, 1815, upon presenting a letter from the First Baptist Church of Baltimore and preaching a sermon to the great satisfaction of the members, he was received into the membership of First Church and licensed as a clergyman. As pastor of Second Church, his eloquence attracted such large crowds that a new brick church was built on the corner of Virginia Avenue and Fourth Street in 1823. A Sunday school was formed the same year. Under the influence of Henry Clay, Cone was appointed chaplain of Congress. After 1821 the church was officially known as the Second Regular Baptist Church of Washington, D. C. The ministry of Cone continued until about 1827, after which he had a long and distinguished ministry in New York City. By Mar., 1827, the membership had grown to 100.

Significant in the life of early Baptists in Washington was the arrival in 1813 of Luther Rice (q.v.), termed by William Heth Whitsett (q.v.) "the magician of American Baptist Life." From then until his death in 1836, he made Washington his headquarters, contributing directly to the establishment of a number of local and national Baptist institutions, among them the first nation-wide Baptist journal, *The Columbian Star*, a religious weekly begun in 1818; the first Baptist missions magazine, *The Latter Day Luminary;* the first Sunday school in the city, begun in First Church in 1819; the establishment of the first Baptist college in the South, Columbian College, now George Washington University, chartered in 1821; and the organizing of the first Baptist publication society, the General Tract Society, later the American Baptist Publication Society.

Sent out as a Congregationalist missionary to Burma after his graduation from Andover Theological Seminary in 1810, Rice, like Adoniram and Ann Judson (q.v.), became a Baptist, following study of his Greek New Testament and after his arrival in Burma. While the Judsons remained on the field, Rice returned to America to lay the missions cause before Baptists. When the General Missionary Convention of the Baptist Denomination was formed in Philadelphia, Pa., May 18, 1814, Judson was appointed as its missionary to India and Rice as its missionary to America to interest Baptists in the cause of missions. His biographers describe him as being of the crusader type, thin, tall, nervous, and possessing great religious zeal. He literally traveled all over the South and the North preaching the causes of missions and education and raising funds for the support of Baptist causes. His great passion was the establishment of a major Baptist university that would provide educated evangelical leadership.

The Sunday school started by Rice in First Church in 1819 was the first in the city. It was a union school, with teachers of different denominations participating; Negro children were taught in a separate part of the room.

Early in the year 1817, Rice conceived the idea of establishing a Baptist college in Washington. In 1819 Rice, Brown, Cone, and Enoch Reynolds formed a Literary Association for the purpose of buying land for such a college. That same year 46½ acres on the outskirts of Washington, now the area of Meridian Hill Park, from about Fourteenth and Florida, N. W., to about Euclid Street, were purchased for five or six thousand dollars. The money for the college was raised by the Literary Association, and John Quincy Adams, William H. Crawford, and John C. Calhoun were among the contributors. The institution was named Columbian College. A charter was obtained from Congress, the first ever granted, on Feb. 9, 1821, and the inauguration of the faculty took place on Jan. 9, 1822. Brown was elected president of the board of trustees; Reynolds, secretary; and Rice, treasurer. Four buildings were constructed. The first commencement was held on Dec. 15, 1824, and was attended by the president of the United States, James Monroe, the secretaries of State, War, and Navy, leading members of both houses of Congress, and Lafayette, who happened to be on his famous visit to the United States at this time. Afterward, all the distinguished guests dined with the board of trustees and the faculty.

The first president of the college was William Stoughton, of Philadelphia, who was also professor of general history, belles-lettres, rhetoric and moral philosophy, divinity, and pulpit eloquence. The college had a preparatory division and schools of medicine, law, and theology, along with the regular collegiate division. One of the requisites for admission to the freshman class was the correct reading and writing of Greek and Latin. The college was essentially financed through the funds raised directly by Rice in his journeys over the country. In 1826 the General (Triennial) Convention, the parent mission society sponsoring Luther Rice, severed its connections with the institution and Rice in order that it might devote its interest fully to foreign missions. In 1827 the entire faculty, including the president, resigned in a body; however, the college reopened in 1828. Never financially secure and never adequately supported by Baptists in general, the college had many closings and reopenings during its history as a Baptist institution. In 1904 the charter was changed so that the college might no longer be considered a Baptist institution. Negotiations by Southern Baptists in 1923-24 to regain control of the university through the promise of two million dollars of forthcoming support to be paid $300,000 annually proved to be unsuccessful, since the trustees preferred that the university remain undenominational.

Rice spent the last years of his life working feverishly to keep the college alive. He died in Edgefield District, S. C., while on a money-raising tour for the college.

Another Baptist project that originated in Washington and in which Rice shared was the founding of the first Baptist publishing house at 923-25 E Street in the center of Washington. It was here, at the Mission Press as it was called, that the two Baptist periodicals, *The Columbian Star* and the *Latter Day Luminary*, were published. It was here, also, that a book by Ann Hasseltine Judson (*q.v.*), *A Particular Relation of the American Baptist Mission to the Burman Empire*, was published in 1823. Early in 1824, Noah Davis, a pastor of Virginia, wrote to the editor of *The Columbian Star*, his former classmate at Columbian College, concerning a plan for forming a tract society in Washington comparable to the American Tract Society among the Congregationalists. The idea was highly approved by the editor, Rice, Brown, and others, and the Baptist General Tract Society was formed on Mar. 25, 1824. Brown was elected president, and Davis was elected general agent. In 1826 this society was moved to Philadelphia and eventually became the American Baptist Publication Society.

The third Baptist church in Washington was organized as Central Baptist Church in 1827 under the leadership of George F. Adams (*q.v.*), a student at Columbian College. The church met in the city hall for a number of years and then moved to the center of town on Ninth Street. In June, 1834, the white members of First Church moved from the Nineteenth and I Street address to a new structure at Tenth and E streets, N. W., not far from Central. The old building was turned over to the Negro membership. In 1835 Central Church was disbanded, and its property went to First Church.

The third permanent Regular Baptist church in the city was established as the Third Baptist Church on Oct. 6, 1842, with 21 members. The new church was directly encouraged and sponsored by Second (Navy Yard) Church. The first sermon was preached by George F. Adams, former pastor of Central Church. All the departments—Sunday school, regular prayer meetings, female prayer meetings, and a monthly concert of prayer for missions—began to function. In 1843 George Whitefield Samson, a graduate of Brown University of the class of 1839 and a student at Newton Theological Seminary, was called as pastor. His ministry continued, with the exception of three years, until 1859, when he became president of Columbian College. For three years the church met in a hired assembly room and in various locations in the general locality of *The Columbian Star* office on E Street. It finally settled on a location on the south side of E Street between Sixth and Seventh and took as its official name E Street Baptist Church. Much later the name was changed to Temple, which is the present name.

E Street Church (Temple) appears to have been the first Baptist church in the city to be formed without Negro membership. The records of First Church show that Negroes were received by baptism and letter as early as 1803, and it is likely that the Negro membership in both First and Second equalled or exceeded the white membership. The records show that white and Negro were baptized together in the Potomac River or Rock Creek and received the right hand of fellowship simultaneously. Many of the Negroes in First Church were slaves of prominent families. Although Negroes were segregated inside the church, they received the same spiritual instruction.

The Nineteenth and I Street building of First Church was turned over to the increasing colored membership in 1833, when the white members built a new building at Tenth and E streets, N. W., but the two were still considered one church unit until years later. Negro members were received into the fellowship at Tenth Street as late as 1845, and there were Negro members in the congregations of nearly all white Baptist churches until and after 1865. The present Negro First Baptist Church, with a membership of over 2,500, still meets at the Nineteenth and I Street location, part of the old building still being used in the present structure. In 1848 Negro members from Second Church formed the Second Baptist Church, Colored, a church which was later received into the Columbia Association. The trend toward independent Negro church congregations increased, likely, as an assertion of a new-found democracy. After the war there were no less than seven Negro churches with a total membership of over 3,000.

Of the three early churches, First, Second, and Temple (E Street), the last, itself a product of local missions, proved to be the most prolific during this period. It was responsible for the establishment of five new churches between 1853 and 1862. In 1853 a number of Baptists from various local churches, but principally from Temple Church, formed the Fourth Baptist Church, sometimes called the Thirteenth Street Baptist Church. Thomas C. Teasdale was called as pastor. In 1857 an impressive building, located on the east side of Thirteenth Street between G and H, was dedicated before an audience including President Pierce and various government officials.

In 1857 Temple Church started a mission, on what was then known as the "Island," which was later constituted as the Island Baptist Church. It is now known as Fifth Baptist

Church. The church flourished rapidly. It had a strong Sunday school, and it prospered spiritually under the 40-year ministry of its first pastor, Chastain C. Meador. Fifth Church has been a strong church during its entire history.

In 1850 Obadiah Brown retired from the pastorate of First Church due to ill health and was succeeded by Stephen P. Hill, a member of the church. Late in the 1850's Fourth and First churches merged, taking the name of First and both assuming the debt on the Thirteenth Street property. Thus, First Church moved into the Thirteenth Street church building, and the two pastors continued to serve the one congregation as copastors, preaching on alternate Sundays, until 1860, when George W. Samson, pastor of Temple Church, became simultaneously president of Columbian College and pastor of First Church.

In Dec., 1861, the old First Church building at Tenth and E streets was sold, and a year later it was completely destroyed by fire.

The war period was a time of disturbance and confusion in all the local Baptist churches, with Northern and Southern sentiments running high. Some Southern members withdrew and left the city, often upsetting the budgets of the churches. Most of the Baptist pastors found secular employment during the war years. Joseph Spencer Kennard, who succeeded Samson at E Street (Temple), applied for a position in the Treasury Department and was immediately employed. After a meeting in which a majority refused to receive Northerners as members of the church, he sorrowfully resigned. Meador became a storekeeper but remained pastor of Fifth. Temple (E Street) essentially split. One faction, about one third of the membership, formed the element that eventually became Sixth or Calvary Baptist, and the other element moved into the academy of one of the members, Zalmon Richards (former principal of the Preparatory School of Columbian College, former superintendent of schools in the District of Columbia, and the first president of the National Education Association), when the Government took over the building for a hospital. Samuel M. Shute, professor of English in Columbian College, served as acting pastor until 1876. During the war First Church managed to remain on an even keel under the leadership of Samson, who served without salary. Abram D. Gillett of New York City, a former minister in the American Chapel in Paris, served as pastor of First from 1863 to 1869. He was succeeded by J. H. Cuthbert.

Calvary Church was organized on Sept. 24, 1862, in the F Street Presbyterian Church with 31 members of E Street Church under the leadership of Joseph Kennard, the former pastor of E Street. In June, 1862, Amos Kendall, Andrew Jackson's postmaster general, a close friend of Kennard's, and one of Washington's most distinguished citizens, but not a member of any church at this time, made the proposition that if the new group would build a $100,000 church, name it Calvary, and call his family's pastor, T. R. Howlett, in New Jersey, he would give $60,000 of the amount. The church was duly organized, Howlett agreed to come, the additional $40,000 was raised, and the church was speedily built. Thus came into being a church that has been one of the strongest Baptist influences in the city. After a rather dramatic conversion Kendall joined Calvary Church and was baptized in E Street Church by Kennard on Apr. 2, 1865. During his few remaining years he provided a strong Christian influence.

On Dec. 15, 1867, Calvary Church was completely destroyed by fire. The total loss was estimated at $134,000. With $50,000 provided by insurance and an additional $15,000 donated by Kendall, a new building was immediately constructed. Meanwhile, the congregation, which by this time numbered 600, accepted the invitation of a Presbyterian Church to meet in their sanctuary.

In 1873 E Street Church sent out a colony to organize North Church, near Columbian College. This church existed for 14 years, then merged with First Church, which planned to move to the same area. It was one of the original charter churches of the Columbian Association. In 1878 members from E Street organized the Metropolitan Baptist Church, which grew rapidly. J. W. Parker, pastor of E Street Church, became its minister. In Feb., 1879, the pastor of Calvary Church accepted the call to become pastor of E Street Church, bringing 125 members with him. In 1881 E Street organized Brookland Baptist Church.

In 1889 J. J. Muir, a Scotchman, became pastor of E Street (Temple) Church and began a long and distinguished pastorate which lasted until 1924. The same year, First Church sold its Thirteenth Street building to the Concordia Lutheran Church and constructed a new building in suburban Washington, at Sixteenth and O streets.

Washington Baptist churches have been members of four district associations. First Church, in the year of its organization, was admitted into the Baltimore Association. Second (Navy Yard) Church was received into the same fellowship on Oct. 17, 1811. The Baltimore Association met with the First Church of Alexandria, Va., which was a member of the same association, in 1819. In 1820 First Church of Washington and First Church of Alexandria were granted letters of dismission by the Baltimore Association to organize a new association, the Potomac, in Virginia.

In 1832 some opposition to Sunday schools and missionary, Bible, and tract societies as being "worldly" societies resulted in dropping from the Baltimore Association all churches "uniting with and encouraging others to unite in worldly societies." This doctrine, which was adopted in 1836 when the association met at Black Rock, Baltimore County, and which has since been labeled "Black Rockism," effected a schism in the Baltimore Association, and a new association, the Maryland Baptist Union, was formed Oct.

District of Columbia Baptist Convention

27, 1836, with Washington Second (Navy Yard) being one of the charter members. All the other Washington Baptist churches, except First, finally joined this association and remained as members until a Washington association was formed. Washington Baptists shared in the General Missionary Convention of the Baptist Denomination, formed in Philadelphia, May 18, 1814, better known as the Baptist Triennial Convention. From 1822 to 1826, the headquarters offices of this convention were in Washington.

The first efforts to establish a Washington city Baptist association occurred in 1877 in the formation of the Columbia Association of Baptist Churches, now the District of Columbia Baptist Convention. On Nov. 14 of that year, letters of dismissal were granted by the Maryland Baptist Union to Second, E Street (Temple), Calvary, Fifth, North, and Gay Street (Georgetown, First) churches to form this city association. It was formally constituted on Nov. 26, 1877. The first moderator was James C. Welling, president of Columbian College. First Church was admitted to this association in 1882.

During this period the Sunday school movement was at a high peak of interest. In 1880 the total membership of the seven churches was 1,641, and the total membership of their Sunday schools was 2,613. A central figure in the development of the Sunday school movement at this time was William Stickney, superintendent of the Calvary Sunday school for 18 years, president of the Maryland and District of Columbia Baptist Sunday School Association from 1871 to 1874, and one of the organizers of the Columbia Association of Baptist Churches. Most of the new churches established thereafter began as Sunday schools.

In Jan., 1882, co-operating with the American Baptist Home Mission Society, the executive board of the association employed O. Ellyson, pastor of Berryville Church, Clark County, Va., as general missionary for the association. This office proved to be an effective instrument of church extension for years to come. From 1877 to 1900, eight churches were organized: Metropolitan, 1878; Wisconsin Avenue, 1880; Brookland, 1881; Anacostia, 1884; Grace, 1884; Maryland Avenue, 1891; East Washington Heights, 1894; and Hyattsville, 1898. In 1884 the association took definite steps for the support of the Woman's Baptist Home, established in 1880. Mission work among the Chinese dates back to 1900. The Southern Baptist Convention met in Washington with the First Baptist Church in 1895. In 1899 the Association's charter of incorporation was renewed. The first tenure of 22 years had expired; the second tenure was more optimistically set at 1,000 years. At this time the constitution was also revised to indicate the right of the association to receive and disburse funds, a point not clear from the rather loose powers granted by the original constitution. In 1902 a centennial celebration of Baptist work in the city was held.

After considerable planning the Northern Baptist Convention was organized in Calvary Church in May, 1907. In addition to its organizational meeting in 1907, the Northern Baptist Convention met in Washington in 1926 and in 1933. In 1933 both the Southern and Northern conventions met in Washington in a joint one-day session.

From 1900 to 1925, Baptists in the city devoted their energies mainly toward the relief of the indebtedness of Baptist institutions, the strengthening of mission churches, and a general co-operative effort toward denominational establishment. Since 1925 local Baptists have sought to define more clearly their relation to the two major national conventions and through them to a broader national and world mission outlook. The efficiency of the operation of local work has been increased tremendously in recent times.

Between 1900 and 1925, 13 churches were organized: Kendall, 1901; Centennial, 1902; Bethany, 1904; National Memorial, 1906; Fountain Memorial, 1907; Capitol Heights, 1910; Congress Heights, 1910; Petworth, 1912; Church of the Redeemer—Italian language—1915; Takoma Park, 1919; Central, 1923; Chevy Chase, 1923; and Silver Spring, 1924. In 1914 a Baptist home for children was founded. In recent years it has been relocated on Cedar Lane in Bethesda, Md.

In 1919 a unified budget to include all the work of the association and the objects of the Northern and Southern conventions was adopted —the division to be one third to the Northern Convention, one third to the Southern Convention, and one third for local causes.

Immanuel Church, founded in 1906 as a mission of First Church, was in 1919 designated as a national Baptist memorial church to the memory of Roger Williams. Five hundred dollars was contributed by the Northern and Southern conventions toward the construction of a new sanctuary. The name is still legally Immanuel, although the church is known as National Memorial. Ground for the new building was broken by Warren G. Harding, President of the United States, in 1921. The structure was occupied in 1926, and it was formally dedicated in 1933 during the joint meeting of the two conventions.

In 1922 Henry W. O. Millington, pastor of Brookland Church, became local Baptist executive secretary. Downtown offices, known as Baptist headquarters, were established in the Munsey Building. In 1924 the headquarters were moved to the Woodward Building, where they remained until 1929, when they were transferred to 715 Eighth Street, N. W., near Calvary Church. In 1947 they were moved to the present address, 1828 Sixteenth, N. W., to a building owned jointly with the Baptist World Alliance. Millington served until his retirement May 1, 1936, when he was succeeded by Rufus Washington Weaver (q.v.), pastor of First Church.

In 1937 the local organization was completely reconstituted as the District of Columbia Baptist Convention. A completely new and modern constitution was written and adopted the same year, the essential feature being the broadening of the powers and function of the executive committee. Since Weaver's retirement in 1943, M. Chandler Stith, former pastor of Brookland Church, has served as executive secretary.

Since 1925, 24 local Baptist churches have been established: Riverdale, 1934; Bethesda, 1934; Brookmont, 1934; Luther Rice Memorial, 1941; Christ, 1943; Covenant, 1945; Avondale, 1946; Suitland, 1950; Trinity, 1950; Briggs, 1952; Hillandale, 1952; Wheaton, 1952; Carmody Hills, 1953; Clifton Park, 1953; Forest Heights, 1953; Temple Hill, 1953; Temple Hills, 1954; Bethel, 1954; Morningside, 1954; Parkway, 1954; Pennsylvania Avenue, 1954; Gaithersburg, 1955; Hillcrest, 1955; and Forestville, 1955.

In addition to the recent success in establishing new churches in the suburban area and the general improvement of all phases of local Baptist work, of recent historical note is the completion and dedication on Christmas Day, 1955, of a new million-dollar building by First Baptist Church. Most of the other older churches have constructed new buildings or enlarged their original ones.

In 1954-55, 51 churches and 7 chapels reported 34,203 church members, 28,107 Sunday school members, 2,089 baptisms, $461,125.35 mission gifts, $3,881,952.40 total expenditures, and $12,589,339.53 total property value.

R. BAINE HARRIS

Program of Work of District of Columbia Baptists. *Executive Board.*—The administrative board of the District of Columbia Baptist Convention is composed of the elected officers of the convention; all past presidents of the convention who are members of churches within the convention; chairmen of all standing committees, the active president and treasurer of, and two members elected by, the Sunday school, Training, women's and men's organizations, in each of which at least one third of the churches of the convention participate; the board of managers of the Baptist Home for Children and the Baptist Home of the District of Columbia; the executive secretary; the secretary of the executive committee; the pastors, assistant pastors, and treasurers of the several churches and not less than two or more than ten additional members from each church, to be named by the church in its report to the convention, the number to be determined as follows: two for the first 250 members and one for each additional 250 members or major fraction thereof. The D. C. convention grants to this board authority to supervise and control all business and work of the convention in the interim of the annual sessions. Five meetings of the board are held annually, a simple majority of church representatives constituting a quorum. The board has as its president and secretary those persons so elected by the annual convention.

The executive board elects members of its executive committee at the close of the last session of the annual convention. Nine members so elected—three pastors, three laymen, and three women—together with the elected officers of the convention and the chairmen of convention committees, compose the full executive committee. This committee has the authority to act for the executive board in all matters in interim of board meetings. The executive committee is named as the budget committee and instructed to prepare a suggested budget yearly for the consideration of the board. The vice-president of the convention is named chairman of the executive committee.

The executive board elects the executive secretary, whose duties are enumerated in the constitution. He is to promote interest in the denominational program and administer funds set aside for the evangelistic, missionary, educational, and benevolent work of the convention. He is to give guidance and leadership to all of the administrative and promotional plans of the convention as specified by it in its constitution. M. Chandler Stith, in 1956 the executive secretary, came to this office in 1943.

In 1943 the Convention created four departments to promote and maintain the divisions of work assumed by the convention—Education, Institutions, Missions and Evangelism, and Promotion.

Missions and evangelism.—The D. C. mission program includes pastoral and building subsidy, a city mission program, the Woman's Baptist Missionary Association, and the Men's Brotherhood Council. In 1954, 18 chapels and missions were aided with subsidies from this department. William J. Crowder is director of the department.

Education.—This department is responsible for the promotion and administration of Sunday school, training organization, Baptist Student Union, student aid, and literature. Howard D. Rees is secretary of B.S.U.; Winston H. Ambrose, secretary of Department of Education.

Institutions.—District of Columbia Baptists have two institutions. Baptist Home for Children is located on a 31-acre tract of land in Bethesda, Md. It is fully approved by the Board of Welfare of the state of Maryland. The home is supported jointly by budget appropriation of the convention and offerings from the churches. Capacity of the home is 52 children, housed in two large English-manor type buildings. Jack Shorrow is superintendent.

Baptist Home of District of Columbia is a home for aged. Care can be provided for 28 guests. Plans have been drawn for a new home of triple the present capacity. The home is supported by convention budget appropriation and by direct offerings of the churches.

In 1947 the Baptist building was purchased jointly by the convention and the Baptist World Alliance. This four-story building houses the offices of the convention on the first and second floors and those of the Baptist World Alliance, with the Joint Conference Committee on Public Affairs, on the third and fourth floors.

Promotion.—The *Capital Baptist* is the organ of publicity of the convention. J. O. Duncan, director of promotion, reports a circulation of 5,000. The paper is supported by budget appropriation and subscriptions. The department is charged with the responsibility of promoting all work fostered by Baptists in the District of Columbia convention.

Membership and giving.—In 1954 there were 50 churches co-operating with the District of Columbia convention, with a total membership of 34,203. There were 2,060 baptisms. Total contributions amounted to $2,426,569.62; gifts to the Cooperative Program amounted to $68,493.24. The convention budget for the year 1954–55 was $290,828.   M. CHANDLER STITH

BIBLIOGRAPHY: J. R. Garrett, "Historical Notes on the Second Baptist Church" (1947). R. W. Weaver, "The Story of Washington Baptists" (c. 1941). W. A. Wilber, *The History of the Columbia Association of Baptist Churches, Fifty Years, 1877–1927* (1928); *Temple Baptist Church, Washington, D. C., Through Ninety Years* (1932). L. W. Wilkinson, *Early Baptists in Washington, D. C.* (1925). D. Winchcole, *The First Baptists in Washington, D. C.* (1952).

DISTRICT OF COLUMBIA BAPTIST HOME (FOR AGED). A home for the aged, organized in 1880 at the suggestion of Mrs. Amelia Powell and Sara Wood. They interested Mrs. Carter Gray, who gave property at 55 H Street, N. W., for the home. The home was opened with two guests. Shortly after this the board of managers was formed.

The records of the District of Columbia Circuit Court show that the articles of incorporation were taken out Mar. 25, 1880. In 1888 a special effort was made for contributions to purchase a new home, and the property at 3248 N Street, N. W., was acquired. In 1898 a three-story dormitory of 20 rooms was erected behind this property, giving each of the 19 guests a private room. The home in 1956 housed 31 ladies. During a period of 65 years 207 ladies entered the home. In 1956 there were 36 names on the waiting list.

In 1952 the charter was changed permitting the admission of men into the home; however, in 1956, due to crowded conditions, no men had been admitted.

The financial resources of the home are from (1) interest on the endowment, (2) an allotment from the budget of the District of Columbia Baptist Convention, (3) funds or property of guests which is turned over to the home for investment, (4) direct contributions from the churches, individuals, and the annual tea, (5) entrance fees and new guests. That fee was $750, of which $200 was reserved for burial funds. The endowment funds are administered by the board of trustees, a self-perpetuating board which, by agreement with the District of Columbia convention, elects trustees previously nominated by the executive board of the convention. The board of trustees directs the financial policy of the home and handles the investment of its funds while co-operating with the board of managers in working out the general policy under which the home is operated.

In recognition of the need for more space, the trustees have purchased a little more than two acres of land at Nebraska Avenue and Ward Circle, directly across the street from American University, providing a place for a new home.
     R. BAINE HARRIS

DISTRICT OF COLUMBIA BAPTIST HOME FOR CHILDREN. Established by the District of Columbia convention in 1914, located in Bethesda, Md., on a 37-acre tract of land purchased by the trustees with funds derived from the sale of a tract of land given by John B. Lord as the original site.

The plant consists of two spacious buildings housing 52 children and 12 staff members. The governing boards consist of a board of lady managers elected by member churches of the convention on a membership rate basis, and a board of 10 trustees elected by the convention.

In 1954 total assets were in excess of $700,000, including land, buildings, equipment, and endowment funds of $175,000. An annual budget of $45,000 provided care for an average of 34 children. Support is shared about equally by convention budget appropriations and by direct gifts.

The purpose of the home for children is to provide care, Christian training, love, and a home atmosphere for children of member churches of the convention who are not provided with adequate care and protection by their own parents or relatives. A dedicated staff, Christian home life emphasis, educational facilities, recreational activities, and good medical care advance this purpose.

Every effort is made to provide social services for children who can be returned to their own families. Educational provision for those leaving the home without family assistance after graduating from high school is offered, and fellowship supervision is normal procedure.
     M. CHANDLER STITH

DISTRICT OF COLUMBIA HEADQUARTERS BUILDING. The District of Columbia Baptist Convention and the Baptist World Alliance in 1947 jointly purchased the "Edie Mansion," 1628 Sixteenth Street, Northwest, Washington, D. C., as headquarters building for both organizations. The price paid for the Baptist Building was $105,000. Offices of the staff of the District of Columbia convention are located on the first and second floors. An auditorium seating 100, a dining room seating 85, a library, and quarters for the custodian are also located on these floors. The Baptist World Alliance offices, located on the third floor, house the staff of this organization. The fourth floor contains the offices for the staff of the Joint Conference Committee on Public Affairs, and two guest rooms. Adequate space is available for conferences and committees—local, national, and international.
     M. CHANDLER STITH

DIXON, AMZI CLARENCE (b. Shelby, N. C., July 6, 1854; d. Baltimore, Md., June 14, 1925). Pastor and evangelist for more than 50 years. The son of Thomas and Amanda Dixon, he was baptized at the age of 12 along with 97 others in a revival led by his father. He was educated at Shelby Academy and at Wake Forest College from which he graduated in 1874 with a determination to invest his life in the service of God. He was ordained in 1874, and in 1875 he enrolled as a student at the Baptist Theological Seminary, Greenville, S. C. He became pastor of the Baptist church at Chapel Hill, N. C., a university town, where his evangelistic gifts resulted in many conversions of students and townspeople alike.

Early in 1880 Dixon became pastor of the Baptist church in Asheville, N. C., and in July of that year he was married to Susan Mary Faison of Warsaw, N. C. In 1882 he was invited to become president of Wake Forest College, but he declined this offer to accept the pastorate of the Immanuel Baptist Church, Baltimore, Md. After a highly successful ministry of eight years at the Baltimore church, he accepted the pastorate of the Hanson Place Baptist Church, Brooklyn, N. Y., serving from 1890 to 1901.

His work in Brooklyn was marked by evangelistic zeal, support of the temperance cause, and frequent controversy over liberal teachings, especially evolution. In 1893 he was associated for one month with D. L. Moody preaching to the throngs that were in attendance at the World's Fair. Leaving Brooklyn in 1901, Dixon began a ministry at Ruggles Street Baptist Church, Boston, Mass., which continued until Oct., 1906, when he became pastor of the Moody Church, Chicago, Ill. From Chicago Dixon left America to accept the pastorate of Spurgeon's Tabernacle, London, England, where he served from 1911 to 1919, a period which covered the trying days of World War I.

For several months following his London ministry, he was engaged in Bible conferences, in evangelistic meetings, and in writing and preaching in support of the Fundamentalist movement. While attending a missionary conference in China in 1922, his wife died following a brief illness. Returning to America, he accepted the pastorate of the University Baptist Church of Baltimore which had recently been organized. To this new but very promising work he gave the closing years of his ministry from 1921 to 1925. In 1924 he married Helen C. Alexander, widow of Charles M. Alexander, widely known evangelistic singer. He died in 1925 and was buried in Druid Ridge Cemetery, Baltimore, Md.

BIBLIOGRAPHY: J. W. Chapman, *The Life and Work of Dwight L. Moody* (1900). Helen C. A. Dixon, *A. C. Dixon—A Romance of Preaching* (1931).

W. H. BRANNOCK

DOCTRINAL CONTROVERSY, ALABAMA. Doctrinal controversies among Alabama Baptists were primarily on the church and associational level. The issue of missions, which affected Bible societies and benevolent activities, formed a continuing dispute throughout the state during Baptist formative years. The opponents of missions were termed "new testers" and their movement was dubbed "anti-ism." In 1822 the Alabama Baptist Association appointed a committee to poll their churches to "ascertain their minds relative to missions." In 1837 churches and associations began to "split" over the question, with antimissionary adherents forming their own groups. By 1839 five associations had divided over the issue. Attempts at reconciliation with their opponents were made by the missionary bodies, but these failed, and such efforts were abandoned by 1850.

Circular letters prepared on subjects of church unity, discipline, and doctrinal issues were adopted by the associations for distribution to the churches as a means of instructing them on Baptist practices and beliefs. These were discontinued after 1846 when religious papers began to be more widely available.

Resolutions were adopted by the associations from time to time dealing with the tenets of the Baptist faith. The Alabama Baptist Association in 1832 issued a warning of certain Baptist ministers who were propagating the Sabellian heresy. In 1834 the Tuscaloosa Baptist Association took note of schisms being caused by certain preachers who were advocating Arminian views in their Calvinistic churches. The Muscle Shoals Baptist Association expressed its position on valid baptism in 1848 and in 1870, the former action on the performance of the ordinance by "regularly authorized Baptist ministers" and the latter "against recognizing . . . the immersion of Pedo-Baptists and Campbellite societies." In 1888 this association adopted resolutions clarifying the issue of church independence and associational authority. The Liberty (East) Baptist Association protested, in 1853, the revision of the Scriptures by the American Bible Union.

Many of the early churches and associations practiced foot washing as an ordinance of the New Testament. In 1853 Landmarkism was injected as a divisive issue in the state. Religious liberty has been a recurring theme in the history of the Baptists of the state. In 1824 a memorial was addressed to the national congress "in favor of religious liberty." The centennial of the nation in 1876 was used as an occasion to provide information on "the sufferings and persecutions of the fathers" for religious freedom. The separation of church and state was an issue in 1949 on the question of accepting government funds to build hospitals.

W. E. WATERHOUSE

DOCTRINAL STATEMENTS, OKLAHOMA. Official actions of the Baptist General Convention of Oklahoma concerning doctrine have largely been related to two major problems: ecumenism and evolution.

On the problem of evolution an action was taken in 1919, refusing to retain any faculty member of Oklahoma Baptist University "who denies that God is the Creator of the universe and substitutes any materialistic doctrine of evolution for the Bible account of creation." After the McDaniel statement denying the validity of evolutionary theories was adopted by the Southern Baptist Convention in Houston in 1926, the Oklahoma convention acted to require the members of the O.B.U. faculty to endorse that statement, and voted to withhold from Southwide institutions their pro rata amount of Oklahoma contributions until the seminary faculty members had also endorsed that statement.

With regard to ecumenism, the Oklahoma convention decided in 1919 that the Inter-Church World Movement was "inimical to denominational solidarity" and that no money should be contributed from Oklahoma toward the construction of the Roger Williams Memorial Church in Washington, D. C., because if that church at any time should approve alien immersion or federation comity, it would "grossly misrepresent the profound convictions of the Baptists of Oklahoma." In 1949 it was decided that all "churches which accept alien immersion, practice open communion or affiliate with the Federal Council, World Council or any other similar unionizing organization, shall be considered unsound in faith and practice."

In addition, the Oklahoma convention in 1919, stimulated by controversy over the rising Nunnery movement, and on the occasion of Nunnery's unseating, claimed as "inherent in all organizations, and essential to organization, the right of a Baptist convention to prescribe and enforce the conditions of admission into its membership and continuance therein."

M. E. RAMAY

DODD, MONROE ELMON (b. Brazil, Tenn., Sept. 8, 1878; d. Long Beach, Calif., Aug. 6, 1952). Pastor of the First Baptist Church of Shreveport, La., from 1912 until his retirement in 1950, except for seven months with Temple Church of Los Angeles in 1927. He founded Dodd College, a Shreveport junior college for women (which later closed), in 1927; was president of both the Louisiana Baptist Convention and the Southern Baptist Convention; and was a member of the executive committee of the Baptist World Alliance. A graduate of Union University, he was awarded several honorary degrees. He was a member of the 75 Million Campaign commission, was influential in the founding of Baptist Bible Institute (New Orleans Baptist Theological Seminary) and in the launching of the Cooperative Program of Southern Baptists. He wrote extensively, led in raising some $6,000,000 for Baptist causes, traveled around the world on missionary tours, and preached through interpreters in 47 languages and dialects. Dodd, whose ministry was largely pulpit-centered, preached 18,000 sermons, baptized 7,000 converts, performed 2,118 marriages, traveled 500,000 miles, and received some 15,000 new members into the Shreveport church.

G. L. GREENE

DODD COLLEGE. A junior college for girls in Shreveport, La., established by the M. E. Dodd Foundation, opened in 1927 and closed in 1942. The foundation offered the school to Louisiana Baptists if the state convention would raise $200,000 in five years to build dormitories. The amount was not realized, and after the time had expired, the convention asked the foundation to release it from further financial obligations. In 1941 the foundation gave the property to the Louisiana Baptist Convention on condition that it would assume all debts. The convention then sold the property to Centenary College.

BIBLIOGRAPHY: C. P. St. Amant, *A Short History of Louisiana Baptists* (1948).

T. W. GAYER

DODSON, OBADIAH (b. Halifax County, Va., 1792; d. De Soto Parish, La., 1854). Pastor, missionary, author. He was converted in 1812 and was baptized by his father, Elias Dodson, into Mill Baptist Church, Pittsylvania County, Va. He served in the armed forces during the War of 1812. Dodson began preaching in 1819. He moved to Tennessee in 1822, where he was ordained to the ministry and helped establish many churches. In 1850 he moved to Rusk County, Tex., where he remained only one year. He moved to De Soto Parish, La., in 1851 and served as a missionary of the Louisiana Baptist Convention until his death in 1854. He kept a record of his baptisms and before his death had baptized over 4,000 converts. He was author of a widely read booklet, *Fifteen Reasons for the Proper Training of Children.*

R. H. WARD

DOGMA. Greek *dokein*, "to seem," denotes an established opinion, hence a doctrine or body of doctrine, especially of religion. The term occurs in the New Testament, but only in the sense of a decree or statute (Luke 2:1; Acts 17:7). In its broader meaning it came into use by the fourth century as official, definitive statements were made by Christian leaders and groups.

BIBLIOGRAPHY: A. Harnack, *History of Dogma*, I, N. Buchanan, tr. (1895). A. Neander, *Lectures on the History of Dogmas*, I, J. E. Ryland, tr. (1866). A. H. Newman, "Dogma, Dogmatics," *New Schaff-Herzog Encyclopedia of Religious Knowledge*, III (1909). J. H. Thayer, *A Greek-English Lexicon of the New Testament* (1886).

E. F. HAIGHT

DONATISTS. A schismatic movement, originating in North Africa in the early fourth century as one of the results of the Diocletian persecution. Certain bishops had surrendered the sacred writings of the Church to Roman officers for burning. This was thought of as a form of apostasy by stricter Christians. The stricter group gathered (after A.D. 316) around Donatus the Great, forming their own churches in opposition to the Great Church. The basic issue was the nature of the Church's holiness: was it that the Church could be the mediator of holy things, specifically the sacraments (so

Catholics); or must the priests who mediate the sacramental grace also be holy (so Donatists)? This issue was also complicated and aggravated by other very real elements in North Africa, so that in one sense the struggle was one of urban (Catholics) against rural (Donatists), as well as Roman colonists (Catholics) against Numidian natives (Donatists).

The most interesting point for church history lies in the problem posed for the Catholics as how to deal with the Donatists, since the Donatists professed the same faith and celebrated the same sacraments as the Catholics. Augustine (d. 430) granted that Donatists were orthodox in the Catholic sense but schismatic in that they had forsaken love and broken ecclesiastical unity. The movement was wiped out by the advance of Islam across North Africa in the late seventh century.

BIBLIOGRAPHY: W. H. C. Frend, *The Donatist Church* (1952). *New Schaff-Herzog Encyclopedia of Religious Knowledge*, III (1950). G. G. Willis, *St. Augustine and the Donatist Controversy* (1950).

T. D. PRICE

DOYLE INSTITUTE. A school at Doyle, Tenn., chartered in 1884 as Doyle College. Nine acres of land on which the school was located were purchased from G. W. Doyle for $5, and the school opened in 1884 with 142 students and a two-story brick building. The first president was William Huff.

The school was first operated by the Union Association of Baptists. From 1904 through 1927 the Home Mission Board assisted in its support, and during 1924-36 it was partly financed by White County. In 1924 the school had an enrolment of 200 and property valued at $100,000. The school building and part of the grounds were sold to the White County Board of Education on July 27, 1936, for $4,000. The dormitory and some of the land were given to the Doyle Baptist Church for a pastor's home. The Home Mission Board was refunded about $1,500, and the remainder of the assets were given to the Baptist church for repairs.

Among the school's graduates was William Owen Carver (*q.v.*) of the Southern Baptist Theological Seminary.

HARLEY FITE

DOZIER, CHARLES KELSEY (b. La Grange, Ga., Jan. 1, 1879; d. Kokura, Japan, May 31, 1933). Missionary to Japan. Dozier graduated from Mercer University in 1903 and from Southern Baptist Theological Seminary in 1906, the year in which he married Maude Burke. Founder of Seinan Gakuin, Southern Baptist school in Fukuoka, Dozier's last words, "Seinan, be true to Christ," are written in its chapel. Appointed to Japan in 1906, Dozier served as professor in the theological seminary, principal of the night school, dean and later president of Seinan Gakuin, and pastor of the Seinan Gakuin Church. The Doziers' two children Edwin and Helen (Mrs. Timothy Pietsch) are missionaries to Japan.

MRS. FOY FARMER

DRAKETOWN BAPTIST INSTITUTE. Established by Concord, Harmony, Tallapoosa, Carrolton, and Bethlehem associations in 1905 in Haralson County, Ga. It existed until about 1918.

ARTHUR JACKSON

DRAMA, CHURCH. A religious drama is that dramatic production which helps an audience and participants to experience a sense of God's presence, a consciousness of fellowship with him as well as a vital relationship and responsibility to their neighbors throughout the world. It seeks to make religious truths real by dramatizing them in everyday life situations. It can minister to individuals of all age levels because interest in dramatic productions is universal. Subject matter of religious drama is varied. It may come from the Bible itself or from the stories of men's struggles to follow Jesus Christ.

During the early history of America, drama in the churches was not tolerated. The Puritans of England, who had closed all theaters as the "Devil's Churches," influenced the attitude in the colonies. In the 18th and 19th centuries a few courageous individuals began to use drama, and in the 20th century a more universal attempt to use it was made. At first drama was used as a teaching aid in Sunday school with children, dramatizing Christmas and Easter stories and later giving pageants with a variety of themes. Enthusiastic audiences received them even though most material was poorly written and lacking in good direction and equipment. Later, plays with interesting plots and good character portrayal were written. Young people were the participants. Evening services were used for the production. Churches have begun to plan adequate space and equipment for drama. Organizing drama groups in churches is another definite trend.

Southern Baptist churches have been some slower than other denominations in using religious drama; but since they began they have made singular progress, especially in providing space and equipment. In 1923 a course in storytelling and dramatization was offered in the school of religious education at Southwestern Baptist Theological Seminary. At first some of the professors opposed it. Now three drama courses are offered in this seminary, and two religious dramas are presented each year. Other seminaries and denominational colleges now offer such courses.

Frank Hartwell Leavell (*q.v.*), former Baptist Student Union secretary, provided a course in religious drama at the Ridgecrest BSU Retreat beginning in 1939. Other assemblies since then have done this. The Ridgecrest Baptist Assembly now employs a drama director for the staff.

The latest development in this field (1956) is the appointment of a drama consultant in the Church Recreation Service of the Sunday School Board of the Southern Baptist Convention. This department promotes religious drama festivals throughout the Convention. They seek to lift the standards of church drama, both in writing and production. FLOY BARNARD

DRUMMOND, NORVELL ROBERTSON (b. Pinola, Miss., Aug. 25, 1878; d. Dec. 10, 1942; buried near Columbia, Miss.). Teacher, denominational leader, author. The son of Richard and Matilda (Beasley) Drummond, he was reared near Columbia, Miss., and graduated from the state university, B.A. degree, in 1901. He served as teacher and superintendent of schools in Columbia, Miss. In his mature years, deeply impressed by a tragic accident claiming the life of his small son, he surrendered to full-time Christian service and was ordained on Jan. 16, 1917. He enrolled at Southwestern Baptist Theological Seminary, Fort Worth, Tex., in 1917 and earned the Th.M. degree in 1920 and the Th.D. degree with distinction in Jan., 1923. Additional study was completed at the University of Dubuque in Iowa and Northwestern University in Illinois.

From 1920 through 1930, he taught education administration at Southwestern Seminary, Fort Worth, Tex. From 1930 to 1936, he was educational director, First Baptist Church, Oklahoma City, Okla. From 1936 until his death, he was editorial associate at the Baptist Sunday School Board, Nashville, Tenn. He was author of *The Education Function of the Church* (1924), and from 1933 to 1935, he was president of Southwestern Baptist Religious Education Association.

On Mar. 16, 1905, he married Pearl Magee; their children are Robert and Margaret. A man of quiet and solid personality, Drummond lived through others. He was known for his dry sense of humor and served effectively as teacher, leader, and writer.

BIBLIOGRAPHY: J. C. Schwarz, ed., *Who's Who in the Clergy*, Vol. I (1935-36). A. DONALD BELL

DUAL ALIGNMENT. The purpose, policy, and program of a local Baptist church, a Baptist association of churches of like faith and order, or of a Baptist state convention which co-operates with more than one national convention at the same time. In Baptist life a church is said to be doubly aligned when it is aligned at the same time with both the American (formerly Northern) Baptist Convention and the Southern Baptist Convention. A doubly aligned church uses the program of organization and work of both conventions as it may choose, and also financially supports the missionary and institutional life of both conventions.

In the United States dual alignment has been practiced by churches in the state of Missouri and the city of Washington, D. C. Within the last few years some churches in California have considered such alignment but have not officially declared it.

The only area other than the District of Columbia where dual alignment has been definitely undertaken and practiced is in Missouri. Following is a brief account of the convention affiliation of the Missouri Baptist General Association from its inception in 1834 until it came to be made up of churches which were affiliated with both conventions.

During the first decade the Missouri Association was declared to be "auxiliary to the American Baptist Home Mission Society." In 1846 the Missouri Association voted in its convention meeting to become "auxiliary to the Southern Baptist Convention." In 1869, by vote of the convention, the words "auxiliary to the Southern Baptist Convention" were dropped. This action left the Missouri Association without any organic auxiliary relation to any missionary organization. In 1888 the Missouri Association adopted a resolution which provided for the Board of General Home and Foreign Missions consisting of 19 members. This board was charged with the responsibility of raising funds in the state of Missouri and forwarding such funds to the different mission agencies. These funds were distributed according to the following rule:

We further instruct this board in all its operations carefully to respect the known preferences of brethren, churches and associations, and to divide all funds not otherwise designated on a basis derived from a comparison of the receipts in Missouri of the several boards for the past five years.

This unification program of operation came to be known as the Missouri Plan, and the Missouri Association followed this manner of operation until its annual meeting in 1919, held in St. Louis, when it voted to align itself with the Southern Baptist Convention. Some few churches in the state are still doubly aligned and co-operate with both American and Southern Baptist conventions, but the Missouri Baptist General Association follows the program of the Southern Baptist Convention in its promotion and missionary ministry.

See also ALIGNMENT, BAPTIST GENERAL CONVENTION OF OKLAHOMA. O. R. SHIELDS

DUCK RIVER (AND KINDRED) ASSOCIATION OF BAPTISTS. Composed of a group of independent and mildly Calvinistic churches that are loosely organized together for fellowship only. They are located principally in the mountains of East Tennessee and in Alabama, Georgia and Mississippi. Sometimes called Separatist Baptists, these churches are historically related to the Old Elk River Association; they were separated from that group in 1825. Later, in 1843 the Old Duck River Association divided over the question of missions and publications. The Duck River (and kindred) Association churches took the position that Christ died for all and that all should be invited on gospel terms. Ministers are ordained by two or more ministers, and the churches teach a milder form of Calvinism than that taught both by the Elk River and Old Duck River associations. The Duck River (and kindred) churches added foot washing to the ordinances. In 1952 there were 326 churches and 9,720 members. ALBERT MCCLELLAN

DUCK RIVER MALE ACADEMY. A school at Fairfield, Tenn., established in 1858. Its charter placed it under the control of Duck River Association.   LYNN EDWARD MAY, JR.

DUDLEY, AMBROSE (b. Spotsylvania County, Va., 1750; d. near Lexington, Ky., Jan. 27, 1825). Pastor. His father was perhaps named Robert Dudley. Ambrose Dudley was converted while serving in the colonial army during the Revolutionary War. He felt called to preach about the same time. After preaching in Virginia for several years, he came to Lexington, Ky., and soon was pastor of the Bryant's Station Church, which had been organized in Apr., 1786. On Aug. 26, 1801, David's Ford Church of 267 members was dismissed from the Bryant's Station Church, and Dudley soon became pastor of it also.

He was often moderator of Elkhorn Association, and in 1801 he was a member of the committee which arranged the Terms of General Union between the Regular and Separate Baptists in Kentucky. Dudley was also active in the Licking Association, serving as moderator for several years.   LEO T. CRISMON

DUNCAN, ROBERT SAMUEL (b. Lincoln County, Mo., Apr. 27, 1832; d. Montgomery, Mo., Apr. 21, 1909). Pastor, denominational statesman, and author. The son of a Baptist minister, he received his education in the public schools of Missouri. The Bethlehem Church of Lincoln County in Aug., 1855, ordained him to the ministry. After he had served several churches as pastor, the Southern Baptist Foreign Mission Board appointed Duncan as its agent for Missouri. For many years he did much to stimulate missionary interest and to systematize mission work in the state. One of his most valuable contributions to his denomination was in the field of historical writing. His interest in learning about Baptist beginnings in Missouri led him to begin collecting material as early as 1858. After almost a quarter of a century of gathering materials, research, and writing, Duncan published in 1882 *The History of Missouri Baptists*. In addition to this, he made frequent contributions to the denominational press.

BIBLIOGRAPHY: W. P. Yeaman, *History of Missouri Baptist General Association* (1899).

MRS. R. W. PRATHER, JR.

DURHAM, ALLEN PINCKNEY (b. Cuthbert, Ga., Sept. 29, 1853; d. Mansfield, La., Nov. 18, 1939). Pastor, associational missionary, evangelist. He traveled with his family from Georgia to Louisiana where they settled in a community just south of Winnfield. At the age of 19, "he was converted and baptized into the fellowship of Sardis Church near Winnfield." In June, 1886, he was ordained to the ministry by the Baptist church of Atlanta, La. During his lifetime "Apple Pie" Durham, as he was affectionately known, served as pastor of about 40 churches, most of them fourth-time churches. He is credited with more than 5,000 conversions, 2,720 baptisms, and several hundred funerals. His ministry, in addition to successful pastorates, included that of associational missionary and state evangelist. In 1922 he returned to the pastorate where he remained until his death.

J. C. MURPHY

DURHAM, COLUMBUS (b. Rutherford County, N. C., Apr. 28, 1844; d. Nov. 14, 1895). Minister. Durham was the son of Micajah and Esther (Baxter) Durham. He was baptized in Sept., 1860. At the age of 17, he entered the Confederate army, and during the war he conducted prayer meetings among the soldiers. Durham entered Wake Forest College, 1867, and was graduated in 1871. While he was pastor of Goldsboro First Baptist Church (1871–76), the membership of the church more than doubled, and a pastor's study and parsonage were built. From the pastorate of the Durham First Baptist Church (1876–87), he was called to be corresponding secretary of the Baptist state convention and served in that capacity until his death in 1895. Durham was an outstanding leader of North Carolina Baptists for more than a quarter of a century. He married Lila Waters, to whom were born three children.

BIBLIOGRAPHY: W. Cathcart, *The Baptist Encyclopedia* (1881). R. C. Lawrence, "Dr. Columbus Durham: Missionary Baptist," *Biblical Recorder* (Oct. 25, 1939).   E. NORFLEET GARDNER

DURHAM FEMALE INSTITUTE. A school in Montgomery County, N. C., under Baptist control in the 1890's with E. L. Middleton as principal. Montgomery County Association endorsed the school.   D. L. SMILEY

DYKE, LODIRE JUDSON (b. Warren, N. J., July 16, 1840; d. Oklahoma City, Okla., Feb. 22, 1927). Baptist pastor and pioneer missionary. A graduate of Colgate University (1871) and Hamilton Theological Seminary (1873), he married Lucinda Stetson in 1863. She died in 1877, and he married Georgia F. Frazer, Aug. 6, 1889. He served two years in the Union army, was ordained in 1873, and after serving pastorates in Pennsylvania, Ohio, and Kansas, he came to Indian Territory where he served under the American Baptist Home Mission Society, 1890–1901. From 1901 to 1904, he was missionary to Wichita and Caddo Indians, and from 1905 to 1907, he was financial secretary for Murrow Indian Orphanage. He is buried at North East, Pa.   LEE B. SPENCER

E

EAGER, GEORGE BOARDMAN (b. Jefferson County, near Rodney, Miss., Feb. 22, 1847; d. Jacksonville, Fla., Mar. 21, 1929). Seminary professor, minister, editor. A courier at 16 in the Confederate Army, Eager was serving as sergeant major in Griffith's Brigade when the Civil War ended. After graduating from Mississippi College in 1872 and Southern Baptist Theological Seminary in 1876, he served as pastor of Baptist churches in Lexington, Va. (1876–78), Knoxville, Tenn. (1878–80), Mobile, Ala. (1880–87), Danville, Va. (1887–90), Anniston, Ala. (1890–92), and Montgomery, Ala. (1892–1900). Professor of biblical introduction and pastoral duties in Southern Seminary from 1900 to 1920 Eager retired at 73 to become the seminary's first professor emeritus. Eager served as editor of the *Review and Expositor* and contributed to publications of the Baptist Sunday School Board. He married Anna Banks Coor-Pender of Jackson, Miss., Feb. 21, 1879.   GAINES S. DOBBINS

EAGLE, JAMES PHILLIP (b. Maury County, Tenn., Aug. 10, 1837; d. Little Rock, Ark., Dec. 20, 1904). Governor of Arkansas, and president of the Arkansas Baptist Convention. In 1839 the family moved to a farm in Lonoke County, Ark., where he was reared. After serving in the Confederate Army till the end of the war, he returned to Lonoke and, although over 30 years old, continued his education there and at Mississippi College, Clinton, Miss. He married Mary Kavanaugh Oldham of Kentucky. He joined the church in 1867 and was ordained a minister two years later. He served several terms in the state legislature, was speaker of the house in 1885, and was a delegate to the state constitutional convention in 1874. In 1888 he was elected governor of Arkansas, serving two terms. Elected president of the Arkansas Baptist Convention in 1880, he served 25 years in this office. In 1902 he was elected president of the Southern Baptist Convention and was twice re-elected. After retiring from the governor's office in 1893, he returned to farming and to preaching to Baptist congregations that were without financial means to have a regular preacher. On his death he left a bequest of $13,160 to Ouachita College.
   EDWIN E. DUNAWAY

EAGLE EYRIE ASSEMBLY. "Eagle's Nest," an estate of approximately 200 acres, purchased in Nov., 1950, for $31,500, located near Lynchburg, Va. It is being developed by the Baptists of Virginia as a place of assembly. The Board of Missions and Education employed Herbert R. Carlton as its first secretary of the Department of Summer Assembly in 1952. He was succeeded by William O. Beasley in 1956.

Plans call for an auditorium, classrooms, departmental buildings, a dining hall, four or five hotel units, 48 cottages, and recreational facilities to care for 1,500 persons per week. English Hall, named for the English family of Altavista, Va., was completed in the summer of 1956, at a cost of approximately $280,000 with furnishings. Roads have been completed, and water tanks, water and sewer lines, disposal plant, and pumping station have been installed.
   RAYMOND BRYAN BROWN

EAGLEVILLE SCHOOL. A secondary school at Eagleville, Tenn., founded *c.* 1887. S. M. Savage was principal in 1888 and had 170 pupils. In 1890 the school had J. N. Huff as principal, 6 teachers, 169 students, and was affiliated with Southwestern Baptist University, Jackson, Tenn. It is now extinct.   LYNN EDWARD MAY, JR.

EAST ALABAMA FEMALE COLLEGE (1850–71). A school for girls known also as Tuskegee Female College, located at Tuskegee, Macon County, Ala. It was reported in 1859 to be one of the three big sisters of female education in Alabama, the others being Judson College and the Alabama Central Female College. A devastating fire closed the school in 1871.
   JAMES E. DAVIDSON

EAST MISSISSIPPI COLLEGE. Established under the leadership of William Thigpen at Garlandsville, Jasper County, in 1881, by the General Baptist Association of Southeast Mississippi. The school was chartered and moved to Sylvarena, Smith County, in 1886, but it reverted to a high school the following year. It is now extinct.   J. L. BOYD

EAST MISSISSIPPI FEMALE COLLEGE. Established about 1865 by Baptists of Aberdeen, Miss., with W. E. Chambliss president. It was backed by Aberdeen Baptist Association, but no further records of its operation exist unless Aberdeen Female College, presided over by W. E. Bacon in 1877, was the same school.
   J. L. BOYD

EAST TENNESSEE, GENERAL ASSOCIATION OF BAPTISTS OF (1844–75). Organized at Mossy Creek in Aug., 1844, as the successor of and by the East Tennessee Baptist Convention. The latter organization was auxiliary to the Tennessee Baptist Convention (organized Oct. 25, 1833) but declined to be auxiliary to the Baptist General Association of Tennessee, organized in May, 1842, to succeed the Tennessee Baptist Convention. It included four associations, to which more were later added. Its constitution restricted representation to churches and associations that contributed funds. It limited itself to one purpose, the support of the gospel in destitute places within its bounds. It restricted its board of managers to 10 men and its treasurer to a deacon. Its territory was all Tennessee east of the summit of the Cumberland Mountains.

The general association had 10 missionaries and 2 missionary agents in 1846. At its session in 1850, it heard its first sermon on Sunday schools and learned from the missionary sermon that in 1816 Luther Rice had established the United Missionary Society of the Tennessee and Holston associations.

The East Tennessee Baptist Education Society, organized in Oct., 1842, became related to the general association, which organized Carson College at Mossy Creek in 1850.

At its 1852 session the general association heard its first committee report on Sunday schools. Its 1859 session was probably its stormiest, for the friends of James Robinson Graves (q.v.) provoked several hours of controversy with reference to the seating of Robert Boyté Crawford Howell (q.v.), a visiting minister, as a messenger. A small minority group, they withdrew from the general association after their defeat.

It appears that the general association ceased operation at some period during the Civil War, for the East Tennessee Missionary Union was organized in 1867. The next year it organized itself into the Baptist General Association of East Tennessee and adopted a constitution.

In 1872 seven associations reported that they had each had a Sunday school convention, and one association reported a Sunday school in every church. The association appointed a missionary to do Sunday school work and to cooperate with the Southern Baptist Sunday School Board at Memphis.

The general association voted (1873) in favor of unification with the general associations of Middle and West Tennessee; but in 1875, a year after the organization of the Tennessee Baptist Convention, it voted to postpone the merger indefinitely. However, as time passed, co-operation by churches and associations with the state convention led the general association at its 1885 (and last) session by a rising vote to dissolve and adjourn *sine die*. This completed the efforts begun in 1833 to bring all Baptist churches and associations of the state together in one harmonious and continuing organization, the Tennessee Baptist Convention.

BIBLIOGRAPHY: W. Cathcart, *Baptist Encyclopedia* (1881). R. B. C. Howell, *A Memorial of the First Baptist Church, Nashville, Tennessee*, Vol. 1 (1867).

HOMER L. GRICE

EAST TENNESSEE BAPTIST HOSPITAL. An institution established in 1943, and owned and operated by the Tennessee Baptist Convention since 1949. The hospital was the result of a resolution presented by a pastors' conference to the Knox County Baptist Association in Oct., 1943, requesting the association to appoint a commission responsible for the establishment of a Baptist hospital in Knox County. Many civic and business institutions joined the association in raising funds for buildings and equipment, and the hospital was chartered in Apr., 1944. The school of nursing was opened Mar. 15, 1948, and the first patient was received Nov. 26 of the same year. On Nov. 16, 1949, the Tennessee Baptist Convention assumed control. Since the hospital was opened, until 1954, a total of 56,865 patients were served, and 9,798 babies were delivered. Total income from patients was $8,739,-285.57; $385,211.60 was received from the denomination, and $1,959,817.25 came from designated gifts. In 1954 the hospital had 254 beds and 36 bassinets. The three buildings, with land and equipment, were valued at $4,349,935, and debt totaled $782,460.14. That year 12,956 patients were admitted, and the total income was $1,760,489.08, of which $91,277.60 came from the Cooperative Program and $42,590.85 from designated gifts. Free medical care worth $74,321.79 was given. The school of nursing had 150 students. The hospital is approved for internship and is fully accredited. It serves only white patients.

D. A. ELLIS

EAST TENNESSEE MISSIONARY UNION. See EAST TENNESSEE, GENERAL ASSOCIATION OF BAPTISTS OF.

EAST TEXAS BAPTIST. Published for a brief period in Jacksonville, Tex., with W. F. Dorris, editor. Its subscription list was transferred to the *Baptist Standard* in 1912.

E. C. ROUTH

EAST TEXAS BAPTIST COLLEGE. Chartered as the College of Marshall in 1912, continued as a junior college with an academy until 1937, and as a junior college alone until 1944, when as a senior college its name was changed to East Texas Baptist College.

The original movement for its founding grew out of a Methodist dinner in First Methodist Church, Marshall, to celebrate a fund-raising victory for Southern Methodist University and in response to congratulations extended by W. T. Tardy, local Baptist minister. Tardy urged the Methodists to establish a school in Marshall, and a Methodist layman, Marvin Turney, replied, "If you will build a Baptist college here, I will give you the first thousand dollars." Another Methodist layman made a similar offer. Thus with Tardy as chairman, a multidenominational council was formed to select and purchase a site and effect the organization of a school.

The school opened in June, 1917, with 33 enrolled; the total fall enrolment in 1917 was 374 with 40 in the college department.

Thurman C. Gardner, first president, served from 1913 until 1916. The Baptist General Convention of Texas assumed ownership of and responsibility for operating the institution as a junior college in 1914. The denomination now operates the institution through a board of trustees, administrative staff, and faculty. Five buildings were completed by Sept., 1917, with a total value of $275,000.

J. Wesley Smith, professor and dean of the college for 35 years, was three times acting president, and is at present chairman, division of religion. Arthur K. Tyson, chairman of the history department from 1944 to 1954 became president of the Mary Hardin–Baylor College in 1954.

Under the administration of H. D. Bruce, president since 1942, enrolment has increased from 99 to 688; two new dormitories, a chapel-music hall, dining-recreation hall, science building, and library-administration building have been built, and all old buildings remodeled at a cost of $2,000,000.

The college, with an endowment of $319,611.62, has admitted 12,850 students. Enrolment in Sept., 1955, was 688. Accredited by the Association of Texas Colleges and the Texas Education Agency, the school operated in 1955–56 on a budget of $471,000, which came from tuition, fees, convention appropriation, interest from endowment, churches, and special gifts. Total property value of the 168-acre campus and 11 buildings is estimated at $2,603,538.97.

BIBLIOGRAPHY: J. H. Boyd, *History of College of Marshall* (1944). W. T. Tardy, *Trials and Triumphs* (1919). WALLER M. ETHRIDGE

EAST TEXAS BAPTIST CONVENTION. A Texas general body organized at Overton, Tex., Dec. 12, 1877, by 37 messengers from 19 churches. The meeting came about after Cherokee Association, seat of eastern disaffection in the 1850's, issued a call to the churches of its section "to consider the propriety of a permanent organization for missionary work in Eastern Texas." Before its last session at Center in 1885, the East Texas Convention met eight times. The attitude of the East Texas Convention is best understood from the following resolutions:

Whereas, there is a large amount of destitution in the section of our State known as Eastern Texas, and the strength and resources of our churches are mostly undeveloped and unemployed, and

Whereas, the strength and power of the other two great missionary bodies in the State are directed to the supply and cultivation of other territory and there exists the same necessity for organization of a third body as there ever did for the second: therefore be it

Resolved, that, as the result of painful experience in the past, we now regard it as inevitable necessity for us to do our own work in the best way we can, if we are ever to meet our obligations to Christ and our fellow men.

Resolved, that we do now in the fear of God and depending upon Him for help, proceed to organize a general missionary Convention for Eastern Texas.

J. M. DAWSON

EAST TEXAS BAPTIST ENCAMPMENT. Organized in 1943 near Newton, Tex., in District 3. Oscar Perkins, one of the leaders in its organization, is president of the encampment.

J. E. ROTH

EAST TEXAS BAPTIST INSTITUTE. A school established at Rusk, Tex., called Academy of Industrial Arts, in 1907, better known as Rusk Academy and as Rusk Junior College. It had its beginning under the Cherokee Baptist Association in 1895, was transferred to the Baptist General Convention in 1897, was made a junior college in 1918, and was closed because of financial difficulties in 1928. In 1920 it had 351 students.

RUPERT N. RICHARDSON

EASTERN CUBA BAPTIST CONVENTION. The first missionaries of the American Baptist Home Mission Society and the Woman's American Baptist Home Mission Society entered eastern Cuba in 1889, and five years later the Eastern Cuba Baptist Convention was organized. The convention includes 125 churches, 140 missions and outstations, and nine associations. Total church membership is 6,753 in a Baptist constituency of 35,000. The Board of Missions, the oldest promotional structure in the convention, supports a staff of missionaries largely engaged in rural areas. The Board of Evangelism and Stewardship promotes a church program for all ages; recently, the Baptist Youth Federation in co-operation with the board, organized preaching missions. The Board of Christian Education and Publication assisted in 1955 in six young people's assemblies, two boys' and girls' camps, two women's spiritual retreats, and two inspirational gatherings for laymen.

The Federation of Baptist Laymen was organized in 1955, with progress in individual stewardship a result. Pastors are being requested to organize classes for the preparation of lay preachers and Sunday school teachers. The women have long been organized as the Association of Woman's Societies of the Baptist Churches of Eastern Cuba. As a part of their stewardship the women give an extra gift each year called the Gift of Talents.

The seminary, in its seventh year in 1956, has students in charge of missions and preaching stations while in training, under supervision of faculty members and near-by pastors. Seminary graduates are engaged in missionary work or are exerting leadership in churches already established. Some are in the United States for graduate work. For the first time a worker among students, a seminary graduate, is serving the University of Oriente. Twenty-two day schools with a staff of 155 teachers reach 2,613 students, serving as significant missionary agencies.

MRS. MILO E. WENGER

EASTERN TEXAS, BAPTIST CONVENTION OF. A Texas general body which existed under this name from 1855 to 1867. It was a continuation of the first Baptist General Association of Texas which was organized at Larissa in 1853. Among its stated objects were the "revival of experimental and practical religion," raising a fund for the education of young ministers, and promotion of education in general. This convention assumed sponsorship of Tyler University, begun by Cherokee Association, which suspended in 1857 on account of a disastrous fire and thereafter, until the Civil War, confined its efforts to the education of young women. This convention abrogated the money basis for representation, which was to come from associations only, but allowed auxiliaries to send representation in proportion to money contributed. The next session amended "to admit one delegate from each church without money basis and one additional for every $10 contributed . . . and any Baptist in good standing upon his paying $5 to the funds of the Convention." At Bonham a further amendment allowed one delegate to each church of 30 members, one more for each additional 30, and three delegates to each association of 500 members and one additional for a second 500, and so on. At its first session a subcommittee, after investigation of complaints concerning the methods and policies of the Baptist State Convention of Texas, reported, "We regard the difficulty between brethren East and West, to be amicably settled." On Oct. 12, 1867, the name was changed to the Baptist General Association of Texas.

J. M. DAWSON

EATON, THOMAS TREADWELL (b. Murfreesboro, Tenn., Nov. 16, 1845; d. Grand Junction, Tenn., June 28, 1907). Son of Joseph H. Eaton, pastor of the Baptist church of Murfreesboro and president of Union University at Murfreesboro. Thomas Eaton was educated at Union University and at Madison (Colgate) University (1860–61). During the Civil War he served in the Seventh Tennessee Cavalry of the Confederate army. After the war he attended Washington and Lee University, where he received the A.B. degree in 1867 and the D.D. degree in 1878. He became professor at Union University (1867–72). He was ordained in Murfreesboro in Feb., 1870, and served as pastor in Lebanon, Tenn., 1870–72. He was pastor in Chattanooga, 1872–75; and in Petersburg, Va., 1875–81. He was pastor of Walnut Street Baptist Church, Louisville, Ky., from 1881 until his death.

In 1887 Eaton became editor of the *Western Recorder*, serving until his death. A forceful advocate of his views, he used the columns of this paper to support those opposed to William Heth Whitsitt (q.v.), and was instrumental in bringing about his resignation from the presidency of Southern Baptist Theological Seminary. He was for many years a trustee of Georgetown College, Southwestern University, and of the Southern Baptist Theological Seminary. He was an active and influential member of the American Society for Religious Education, the American Sunday School Association, and the Southern Baptist Missionary Association. He served four years as moderator of the General Association of Baptists in Kentucky.

"Dr. Eaton, at the time of his death, was doubtless the most potent and influential personality among the Baptists of the South."

LEO T. CRISMON

EBENEEZER HIGH SCHOOL. Opened at Dudley, Ga., in 1901. By 1914 the property had reverted to its donor I. J. Duggan.

ARTHUR JACKSON

ECCLESIOLOGY. See CHURCH.

ECUADOR, MISSION IN. Organized in Sept., 1950, after the arrival in Quito of William Milton and Lois (Nichols) Haverfield and Everett Gordon and Bettye Ruth (Williams) Crocker. Garreth Elbert and Elaine (Giltner) Joiner began service a year later; at the same time the Haverfields transferred to Mexico.

The congregation in Quito was organized into the Central Baptist Church, Mar. 12, 1952; church property was purchased in 1954. A second Baptist center was opened in Quito in Nov., 1955.

Baptist work began in Guayaquil in July, 1953, with the arrival of Howard Lee and Dorothy Dell (Moore) Shoemake. The first church service was held Jan. 3, 1954. At the beginning of 1956, Guayaquil had three Baptist centers, all with regular church services.

In addition to Baptist work in the two principal cities of Ecuador, there are two small churches in the province of Guayas which for many years have been independent churches holding Baptist beliefs and using Baptist literature. They officially became Baptist churches in 1954.

E. GORDON CROCKER

ECUMENICAL MOVEMENT, THE. A movement which seeks a larger degree of unity among the Christian communions of the world. The term "ecumenical" is derived from a Greek word meaning "the whole inhabited earth." In its adjectival form the term has been used to designate certain authoritative councils of the Catholic Church from the fourth through the eighth centuries, as well as various worldwide denominational conferences. The modern use of the term is applied to the union movement which dates from the 1910 meeting of the International Missionary Conference at Edinburgh. The impetus from this meeting set in motion the movement embodied in the World Council of Churches, which is the international organizational expression of the ecumenical movement. There are three periods discernible in this movement: ecumenical antecedents, 1529–1910; the ecumenical movement, 1910–38; and the World Council of Churches, 1938–present.

Ecumenical Movement, The

Ecumenical antecedents, 1529–1910.—The historical antecedents of the ecumenical movement are to be found as far back as the 16th century Reformation. In 1795 the London Missionary Society became the first of a number of interdenominational bodies which eventually led to the Edinburgh conference of 1910. The most influential of all 19th-century interdenominational bodies was the World's Evangelical Alliance, which was formed at London in 1846. However, the Edinburgh conference of 1910 crystallized the interdenominational co-operation of the preceding century and gave birth to the modern ecumenical movement.

By far the most important action taken at Edinburgh and that which gives Edinburgh its unique place in ecumenical history was the adoption of a report of the commission on "Cooperation and the Promotion of Unity." This report emphasized the necessity of unity and suggested that federation and increasing co-operation were necessary steps to eventual organic union. It was during the course of the discussion of this report that the motion was made that a continuation committee of the Edinburgh conference be set up as the agency through which increased co-operation could be made possible. Andrew Fraser made the motion with the understanding that it was only a small step in the direction of organic union.

The ecumenical movement, 1910–38.—From 1910 to 1938, the ecumenical movement developed along three distinct lines embodied in the Life and Work, Faith and Order, and International Missionary movements. The first Life and Work conference was held, largely under the guidance of the Federal Council of Churches of the United States, at Stockholm in 1925. Two years later, the first conference on Faith and Order met at Lausanne, largely as a result of Anglican leadership. Both conferences followed the Edinburgh pattern in the setting up of continuation committees to carry on the work between conferences and to make plans for future meetings.

Even though the ecumenical movement developed along three apparently independent lines of interest, these were mutually interdependent movements. The leaders and the delegates involved in the various conferences were often the same. Each movement was primarily concerned with what was termed "the reunion of Christendom" and was worldwide in influence and interest.

The World Council of Churches, 1938–present.—The idea of a world council of churches did not originate with the 1937 meetings of the Life and Work and the Faith and Order movements. Since 1933 the most able leaders of the two movements had been in almost constant contact, seeking to prepare the way for the action that took place at the Oxford and Edinburgh conferences of 1937. It was just before these meetings were to convene that a subcommittee of 35, gathered at Westfield College in London, put the finishing touches on the plans for setting up a joint committee from representatives of the Life and Work and the Faith and Order movements.

In May, 1938, the full committee met at Utrecht to write a constitution for the proposed World Council of Churches. In addition to the writing of the constitution, the conference proposed that a provisional committee should be formed in order that the essential natures of the Life and Work and the Faith and Order movements might be preserved in the new council.

Ten years later, the first assembly of the World Council of Churches was called to order on Aug. 22, 1948. There were present for this meeting 351 delegates representing 150 denominations from 44 countries. The last official action of this first assembly of the World Council of Churches was the drafting of the "Message" to be sent to fellow Christians who were not at Amsterdam and to "all who are willing to hear." In substance, the "Message" stated that, although not of one faith or of one baptism, those meeting at Amsterdam did confess one Lord, who is the basic principle of unity. Upon that basis they told the world, "We have met together and *intend to stay together.*" In addition, the "Message" condemned war and divisions among Christians. It emphasized the fact that the task of reconstruction had just begun, and it called upon the Christians of the world to join in this task by implementing those decisions reached at Amsterdam.

The second assembly of the World Council of Churches, held in Aug., 1954, at Evanston, Ill., in many ways may prove to be the most significant of all conferences of the modern ecumenical movement. Certainly, it attracted more attention than any preceding ecumenical conference. In typical American fashion the opening of the second assembly was ushered in by the gigantic Festival of Faith witnessed by 125,000 persons in Soldiers' Field, Chicago, Ill. Fully twice as many delegates as in any previous ecumenical conference attended the daily sessions of the second assembly. The *Christian Century* reported: "Through 17 days of August, 1,242 men and women representing 132 of the 163 Protestant and Orthodox communions in the World Council of Churches met on the Northwestern campus in Evanston, Illinois."

Although many Baptist groups participate in the activities of the ecumenical movement, to date (1957) the Southern Baptist Convention has not affiliated with the National Council of Churches or the World Council of Churches. Three reasons account for this attitude of aloofness on the part of Southern Baptists: (1) a distinctive doctrinal position, (2) a strong congregational ecclesiology, and (3) practical considerations. Some ministers and churches throughout the Convention co-operate with local church councils and with various agencies of the National and World councils. However, the vast majority of Southern Paptists either ignore or reject outright the challenge of ecumenical

Christianity, choosing instead the denominational pattern of connectionalism as superior to that which they feel to be embodied in the leadership, methods, and goal of the ecumenical movement.

BIBLIOGRAPHY: M. J. Bradshaw, *Free Churches and Christian Unity* (1954). W. R. Estep, Jr., *Church Union and Southern Baptists* (1955). W. R. Hogg, *Ecumenical Foundations* (1952). J. Marsh, *The Significance of Evanston* (1954). C. McIntire, *Twentieth Century Reformation* (1945). C. C. Morrison, *The Unfinished Reformation* (1953). S. Neill, *Towards Church Union* (1952). J. H. Nichols, *Evanston* (1954). G. B. Oxnam, *On This Rock* (1951). R. Pache, *The Ecumenical Movement* (1950). Rouse, Ruth, and Neill, Stephen Charles, ed., *A History of the Ecumenical Movement 1517–1948* (1954). C. E. Tulga, *The Case Against the World Council of Churches* (n.d.). W. A. Visser 'T Hooft, ed., *The First Assembly of the World Council of Churches* (1949); *The Evanston Report* (1955).

W. R. ESTEP, JR.

ECUMENICALISM. The word "ecumenical" is derived from the Greek *oikoumene*, which means the whole inhabited earth, thus worldwide or universal. In the history of the church, the term was first used in reference to the general synods of Nicaea (325), Constantinople (381), Ephesus (431), and Chalcedon (451). In later usage the term was enlarged to include three other general synods, the decisions of which are accepted by both the Roman and Greek Catholic churches. These include the second Council of Constantinople (553), the third Council of Constantinople (680), and the second Council of Nicaea (787). In the strict sense the term "ecumenicalism" is applied to the theology of the seven ecumenical councils.

However, the term in current usage is applied to the 20th-century movement which seeks a greater degree of understanding and unity among the Christian communions of the world. Ecumenical leadership is divided over the ultimate goal of the movement. Some leaders in the World Council of Churches hold that nothing is desired beyond the rather loose federation which now characterizes the movement; others insist that the movement must not be satisfied with anything less than the union of all Christendom in one worldwide, visible church organization.

Historically, the modern ecumenical movement dates from the World Missionary Conference held at Edinburgh in 1910, although the beginnings of the movement antedate the 20th century by several hundred years. To date, the movement in its organizational aspects embraces one third of organized Christianity. Southern Baptists, Missouri Synod of Lutherans, some fundamentalist bodies, and Roman Catholics are not represented in the World Council of Churches.

W. R. ESTEP, JR.

EDINBURGH MISSIONARY CONFERENCE. An interdenominational, international missionary conference held at New College, Edinburgh, Scotland, June 14–23, 1910. Over 1,200 delegates attended, representing 159 missionary societies of Great Britain, the continent of Europe, and America. Technically termed The World Missionary Conference, it is popularly known as The Edinburgh Conference.

Similar conferences date back to 1854, but "Edinburgh, 1910" is recognized as a landmark in the development of Christian co-operation. It was a deliberative and consultative conference, rather than a series of inspirational mass meetings, as some previous gatherings had been. It sought co-operative action in essential Christian tasks, rather than agreement in theology or polity. It brought into being a Continuation Committee, which in turn instituted the International Missionary Council as a permanent agency of interdenominational co-operation.

The program at Edinburgh centered around the reports of eight commissions, as follows: (1) carrying the gospel to all the non-Christian world; (2) the church in the mission field; (3) education; (4) the missionary message; (5) the preparation of missionaries; (6) the home base of missions; (7) relation of missions to governments; (8) co-operation and the promotion of unity. The discussion and findings were published in nine volumes, one for each commission and one general volume.

The Foreign Mission Board of the Southern Baptist Convention appointed eight delegates to the Edinburgh Conference, including S. J. Porter, field secretary, William H. Smith, educational secretary of the Board, and Edith C. Crane, corresponding secretary of Woman's Missionary Union.

H. C. GOERNER

EDISTO ACADEMY. A Baptist coeducational school at Seivern, Aiken County, S. C., founded in 1915. The school closed in 1934 because of conditions resulting largely from the economic depression. While primarily a high school, Edisto offered training on the elementary level and, for a while, one year's work at the college level.

William Henry Cannada, previously a missionary to Brazil, was the school's first president, although preliminary promotional work was done by Thomas H. Posey, a near-by pastor. Marion Buel Webb, principal for three years, became president in 1930. The plant consisted of three buildings and 331 acres of land. Student enrolment at the peak was 112.

Trustees elected by Aiken, Edgefield, Edisto, Lexington, Ridge, and Fairfield associations operated the academy until 1922, when ownership was transferred to the South Carolina Baptist state convention. The school was discontinued by the convention in 1932 "with profound regret" but continued under associational control until 1934.

MARION BUEL WEBB

EDUCATION, MINISTER OF. The title given to the person who, under the leadership of a pastor and in co-operation with the members of a church, guides and promotes the edu-

Education, Southern Baptist

cational and training activities of that church. He is concerned with developing, organizing, administering, and promoting an adequate program of education and training to enable the church to reach its constituency and provide it with adequate curricula and instruction. In the last 40 years an increasing number of churches have felt a need for the services of such a person, and the ministry of education has finally come to be considered a vocation, professional in nature and based upon formal vocational training. The work itself, however, is not new. Churches carried on educational activities long before they felt any need for professional administrators. Scarcity of pastors and typically small church groups made the "one man" church necessary in early American life. However, many changes in church life—increasingly large congregations, a developing idea of the church's educational responsibility, an increase in the number and complexity of organizations, the development of new and more detailed educational methods—have created a special need for ministers of education.

This consideration of education as a part of the work of the church is based upon biblical teaching. J. M. Price in *A Survey of Religious Education* (1940) gives a detailed account of the "ministry of teaching" in Bible times. Specific New Testament references usually cited on this point are I Corinthians 12:27-28; Ephesians 4:11; Acts 20:17, 28; Philippians 1:1.

Opinions vary on the propriety of ordination for ministers of education. Some, such as Clark Hensley in *The Pastor as Educational Director* (1946), feel that full-time ministers of education should be ordained, but also allow a place for nonordained lay workers. This is a new development in a limited area in Baptist life. No "orders of the ministry" are described in the New Testament, but the teaching ministry of Baptist churches has produced need for several types of workers, including (1) the minister of education (often also responsible for music); (2) the age-group specialist, working with child, youth (including students), and adult groups; (3) the organizational specialists usually found in state and Convention-wide headquarters; and (4) full-time recreational, visual education, journalism, and editorial workers, as well as teachers at home and on mission fields. To these are added hospital chaplains, Good Will Center and emergency-home workers, and others. All these require definite calling and specialized preparation.

Some of the requisite personal qualities include (1) genuine conversion; (2) sense of divine vocation; (3) love for people; (4) wholesome personality; (5) true ideals and vision; (6) specific emotional qualities such as initiative, courage, faithfulness, and creativeness; (7) a mixture of educational skill and evangelistic zeal.

The duties of a minister of education in a local church are summed up by Findley B. Edge in *Does God Want You as a Minister of Education?* (1951). Edge emphasizes the need for coordination, supervision, and promotion. Specific responsibilities include outlining the program, training the leadership, directing the activity, personal counseling, and visitation. Gaines S. Dobbins says that the minister of education should "harness the powers of all organizations to the denominational program of world service."

Preparation usually includes a bachelor's degree from an accredited college or university and the degree of Master of Religious Education from a seminary. These six years of study include the arts, biblical subjects, educational theory, and church administration.

The minister or director of education is generally called by the church, is accepted as colaborer by the pastor, accepts his leadership, and relates himself to the members as advisor and friend. He does not assume or eliminate their work but helps them to do it better.

BIBLIOGRAPHY: G. S. Dobbins, *The Church Book* (1951). F. B. Edge, *Does God Want You as a Minister of Education?* (1951). G. L. Guffin, *Pastor and Church* (1955). J. C. Hensley, *The Pastor as Educational Director* (1946). J. M. Price, et al., *A Survey of Religious Education* (1940). J. D. Smart, *The Teaching Ministry of the Church* (1954).

J. M. PRICE, JR.

EDUCATION, SOUTHERN BAPTIST. "The early Baptist ministers (in the South) were men of spiritual fervor, native ability, but possessing little education. In 1791 there was not a single college man in all the Baptist ministry of the South." So wrote Rufus Washington Weaver in 1931, explaining that an educated ministry was not encouraged until college-trained Baptist ministers from the North led forward-looking Southern Baptists in the establishment of schools for the training of young ministers. "Southern Baptists owe a great debt," Weaver said, "to Northern men like Wait, Meredith, Furman, Sherwood, Jewett, Sherman, Graves, Eaton, Tryon, Huckins and others who initiated the founding of our older Baptist institutions."

What is believed to be the first organized effort for education among Baptists in the South was the action of the Charleston (S. C.) Baptist Association in establishing in 1755 a fund for aiding young ministers to secure an education, by defraying part or all of their living expenses while each studied under an older minister. Interrupted by the War for Independence, this pattern of support of ministerial education was revived in 1790 under the leadership of Richard Furman, when the General Committee for the Charleston Baptist Educational Fund was established. In addition to aiding young men who were educated in the homes of ministers, the general committee, during the period 1790-1825, assisted others to attend Rhode Island College (now Brown University) established under Baptist auspices in 1765, the South Carolina College (now the University of South Carolina), and Columbian Col-

STETSON UNIVERSITY (q.v.), Florida. Top: Administration building, DeLand. Bottom: College of Law, St. Petersburg. Campus and buildings, including Student Union center and new law library, valued at more than $6,000,000

UNION UNIVERSITY (q.v.), Jackson, Tenn. Three of the nine major buildings valued at $1,612,229. Top: Student Union building and chapel. Left: Barton Hall, principal administration building. Right: Gymnasium, which includes accommodations for 2,500 spectators.

lege, founded in 1821 in Washington, D. C., under the leadership of Luther Rice and with the support of Baptists from both North and South.

The early interest of Baptists of the South in Columbian College faded rapidly in the first decade after its founding, as the education societies and state conventions in South Carolina, Kentucky, Georgia, North Carolina, and other states set about establishing academies, seminaries, and colleges of their own.

The earliest educational institutions operated by Baptists in the South were academies, such as that established by John M. Roberts, pastor of the High Hills Baptist Church in South Carolina, prior to Nov. 1, 1800; and that operated by Silas Mercer from 1793 to 1796 in Georgia, at Salem.

By the end of the first half of the 19th century, Baptist and other academies were numerous in the South, though most were privately owned. It was common for an educated minister to earn a substantial share of his livelihood by operating a tuition grammar school or private academy. In some areas opposition to a salaried ministry made it virtually necessary for a minister to support himself by some activity outside the ministry, and the operation of a school was thus often advantageous to both the minister and the community.

During the period 1845–60 hundreds of Baptist schools were organized. Most were small schools which existed for only a few years. Many were schools and academies for women, numbering nearly a hundred during this period.

Virtually wiped out by the Civil War, Baptist academies sprang up again throughout the South following Reconstruction and at the turn of the century, when interest in Christian education was spurred by the rapid growth of tax-supported education and the fear of its consequences. By 1920 the number of academies controlled by organized Baptist groups much exceeded 50. Of these, 36 were mountain academies, receiving substantial support from the Home Mission Board, and enrolling more than 6,000 students. The number of privately controlled academies operated by Baptists during this period cannot be accurately estimated. It is probably safe to say that at least 600 different institutions of this type came into existence under Baptist auspices during the period 1800–1920, most of them during either the decade preceding the Civil War or the early part of the 20th century.

The culmination of the public high school movement, later in the South than in the North, eliminated most of the private and denominational tuition academies. The mountain academies operated by the Home Mission Board dropped from 36 in 1922 to 19 in 1930, and the board ceased altogether its support of these schools in 1931. The total number of academies under distinctly Baptist auspices was listed at 31 in 1930 and 12 in 1940. Some entered the field of higher education as the public high schools took over the secondary education field.

The number of Baptist academies has since decreased to eight, all of which receive support from their respective state Baptist general bodies. Though the Baptist elementary and secondary schools have given way to public education, they served a vital purpose and rendered a great service in their day. Hundreds of the great leaders of Southern Baptists were given their start toward education and leadership by these schools, and tens of thousands benefited from their ministry.

Earliest of the educational institutions established under the auspices of a state Baptist organization in the South was Furman University, founded Dec. 20, 1825, and opened Jan. 18, 1827, as the Furman Academy and Theological Institution at Edgefield, S. C. It was moved to the High Hills of Santee in 1829, to near Winnsboro in 1837, and to Greenville in 1851.

The Baptists of Kentucky were also among the first in the South to establish a denominational school. A charter for the Georgetown Literary and Theological Institution, later Georgetown College, was secured in 1829 by the Kentucky Baptist Education Society.

The Virginia Baptist Seminary, later Richmond College (1840) and the University of Richmond (1914), was founded by the Virginia Baptist Education Society in Richmond in 1832, after two years of experimentation in the instruction of ministerial candidates in the homes of ministers.

Mercer Institute, which later became Mercer University, opened Jan. 14, 1833, at Penfield, Ga. The early contributions of this institution can be witnessed in the fact that of 192 Baptists listed in Cathcart's *Baptist Encyclopedia* (1881) who attended a Southern Baptist college, 43 had attended Mercer University.

Wake Forest Institute, later Wake Forest College, was chartered Dec. 18, 1833, following several years of planning and discussion among North Carolina Baptists, led by Samuel Wait.

Judson College (1838) and Howard College (1842) in Alabama, Baylor University (1845) and Mary Hardin–Baylor College (1866) in Texas, Chowan College (1848) and Mars Hill College (1856) in North Carolina, Tift College (1847) in Georgia, William Jewell College (1849) in Missouri, Mississippi College (given to Baptists in 1850), Carson-Newman College (1851) in Tennessee, Bethel College (1854) in Kentucky, and Averett College (1859) in Virginia, complete the list of extant colleges and universities operated under distinctly Baptist auspices before the Civil War.

Between the close of the war and the end of the 19th century, several Southern Baptist colleges now extant were established, chiefly in the border states. Among these are Hannibal-LaGrange College (former LaGrange College), Hannibal, Mo. (1866); Blue Mountain College, Blue Mountain, Miss. (1873); Union University, Jackson, Tenn. (1874); Shorter College, Rome, Ga. (1877); Southwest Baptist College, Bolivar, Mo. (1878); Stetson University (formerly De-

Land Academy), DeLand, Fla. (1883); Virginia Intermont College, Bristol, Va. (1884); Ouachita Baptist College, Arkadelphia, Ark. (1886); Campbell College, Buie's Creek, N. C. (1887); Cumberland College, Williamsburg, Ky. (1888); Howard Payne College, Brownwood, Tex. (1890); Meredith College, Raleigh, N. C. (1891); Decatur Baptist College, Decatur, Tex. (1891); Hardin-Simmons University (originally Simmons College), Abilene, Tex. (1891); North Greenville Junior College, Tigerville, S. C. (1892); and Wingate College, Wingate, N. C. (1897).

Eight senior colleges and nine junior colleges have been founded or taken over by Southern Baptists since 1900. The senior colleges include Louisiana College, Pineville, La. (1906); Oklahoma Baptist University, Shawnee, Okla. (1910); Wayland College, Plainview, Tex. (1910); William Carey College, Hattiesburg, Miss. (given to Mississippi Baptists in 1911); East Texas Baptist College, Marshall, Tex. (1914); University of Corpus Christi, Corpus Christi, Tex. (1947); Grand Canyon College, Phoenix, Ariz. (1949); California Baptist College, Riverside, Calif. (1950); and Belmont College, Nashville, Tenn. (1951).

The junior colleges founded since 1900 are Norman College, Norman Park, Ga. (1900); Brewton-Parker Junior College, Mount Vernon, Ga. (1904); Campbellsville College, Campbellsville, Ky. (1907); Gardner-Webb College, Boiling Springs, N. C. (1907); Clarke Memorial College, Newton, Miss. (1908); Anderson College, Anderson, S. C. (1911); Bluefield College, Bluefield, Va. (1920); Southern Baptist College, Walnut Ridge, Ark. (1941); and Truett-McConnell Junior College, Cleveland, Ga. (1946). Many of the colleges listed were founded as academies, institutes, or seminaries, reaching college status as opportunity permitted or as the need dictated.

Of the many academies, institutes, and colleges for women, established under Southern Baptist auspices, one missionary training school, six senior colleges, and three junior colleges remain. Some have ceased to exist; others have severed their connections with Baptist groups. Most, of course, were tuition schools established during the era preceding the growth of the public high school movement, and discontinued along with the other academies and institutes as public high schools became widespread. Senior colleges for women now include: Blue Mountain College, Judson College, Mary Hardin–Baylor College, Meredith College, Shorter College, and Tift College. Junior colleges for women are Anderson College, Averett College, and Virginia Intermont College. Several of these admit male day students.

Among Southern Baptist colleges are all kinds: excellent, good, fair, and poor. More of them (73 per cent), percentagewise, are fully accredited than of tax-supported colleges as a group, church colleges, private colleges, or all colleges of the United States, as a group.

Numbering 30 senior colleges and 21 junior colleges, they are distributed throughout 16 states, from Virginia to California, with the greatest concentrations in Texas (8), North Carolina (7), and Georgia (6). Their enrolments are predominantly (75 per cent) Southern Baptist, although they currently enrol only about 19 per cent of Southern Baptists who are now in college.

During the 1955–56 school year, the 51 colleges enrolled 45,429 regular and 7,146 special, extension, and correspondence students—an all-time high. Of these, 6,448 were ministerial students and 1,637 were mission volunteers. Enrolments in the seven seminaries during the same period totaled 5,428 regular and 457 special students, and in the eight academies and four Bible schools were 2,944 students. Of seminary students, 3,894 were ministerial students and 844 were mission volunteers. Of the students in the academies and Bible schools, 440 were ministerial and 63 were mission volunteers.

Although the curricula of the 30 senior colleges and universities are centered largely in the liberal arts, specialized and professional training in a wide variety of fields is available. The Bachelor's degree is available with a major in any of 45 academic subjects, from art to zoology, and curricula leading to professional degrees are available also in dentistry, hospital administration, law, medical technology, medicine, music, pharmacy, and other fields. Combination degree programs are also available in engineering and several other fields.

Of many problems facing the colleges at this time, probably the most serious at present are those of (1) maintaining faculties that are well-qualified, both professionally and in Christian witness, in the face of a growing general shortage of college teachers; (2) expansion of facilities and operating budgets in keeping with rising enrolments; and (3) the perennial problem of increasing the degree to which the Baptist population understands the vital role of the Christian college.

The major problems of the state conventions, in connection with the colleges they support, are (1) equitable division of Christian education funds among the colleges, according to both need and service opportunity, (2) accurate evaluation and equitable meeting of the needs of both the existing institutions and the populous areas not adequately served at present by Baptist colleges, and (3) the need for continued progress toward closer co-ordination of the objectives, methods, public relations programs and curricula of colleges supported by the same state convention. In connection with point 2, it is pertinent that not one of the five largest (local) associations of Southern Baptists, together listing a total of more than 550,000 members, is served by a local Baptist college.

The Southern Baptist Convention itself faces difficult problems in the area of theological education. The rate of growth of the denomination requires an ever-increasing rate of production of seminary-trained ministers, education

Growth of Southern Baptist Schools and Colleges
1940–1954 *

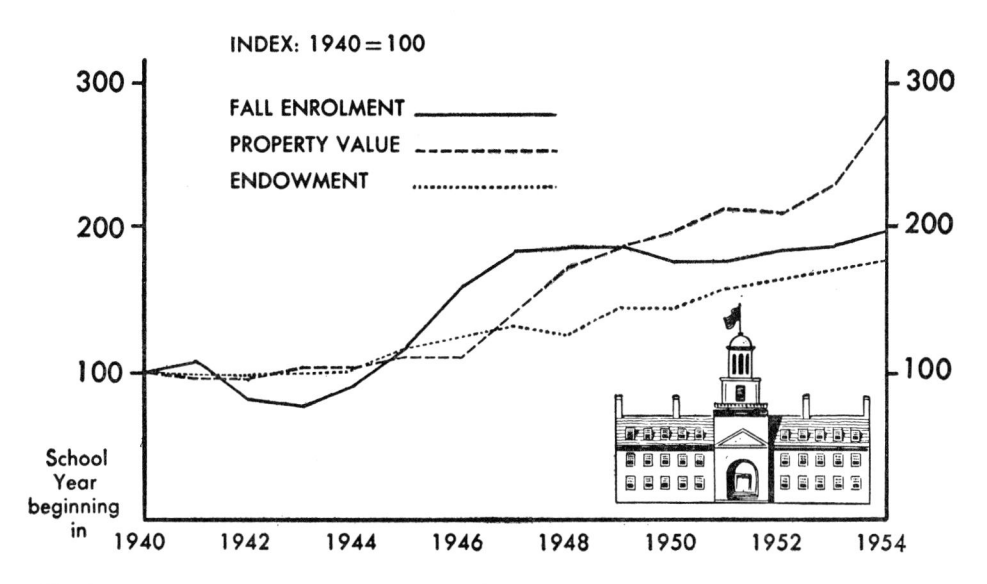

*Theological institutions, Senior and Junior Colleges.

directors, and church music directors. Also, the geographical growth of the Convention has resulted in areas of great potential which cannot be served adequately by the existing seminaries. The difficult problem of the Convention is that of developing a plan for meeting the needs of these areas without impairing the service of the existing institutions.

The last 35 years have witnessed at least five significant changes in the pattern of education among Southern Baptists. First, the denomination has largely gotten out of the field of secondary education, the eight remaining secondary schools being either military institutes or mission schools in areas of special need.

Second, the support and control of theological education have been assigned to the Southern Baptist Convention itself, and the support of the colleges to the state conventions. The original purpose of most of the early colleges (except those for women) was the education of candidates for the ministry, and this is still one of their major objectives. As the opportunity developed for theological education in seminaries supported by the Southern Baptist Convention itself, however, and as the standardization movement among the colleges of the South made it increasingly difficult for an accredited college to offer theological degrees, the older colleges with theological departments replaced these by departments of religion offering only basic courses, terminal undergraduate and preseminary work. The colleges have ceased to grant theological degrees, and do not offer work in this field beyond the level of the pre-seminary curriculum. Two offer the Master of Arts degree with a major in religion. All the senior colleges offer the Bachelor of Arts degree with a major in religion.

Third, along with other denominations and the state educational systems as well, Southern Baptists have largely given up the idea of separate colleges for men and women. The colleges for women which remain are those in which a strong tradition has been coupled with a superior program capable of sustaining interest and support in the face of a national trend in the opposite direction.

Fourth, the self-perpetuating board of trustees has become the exception instead of the rule. The state conventions, in a majority of cases, select the trustees of the colleges they support, and insure a further degree of control through rotating terms of office. Many schools are still in a transition stage in which the convention nominates and the trustees elect, or vice versa, and a few still have outright self-perpetuating boards, but the trend is definitely in the direction of control of selection of trustees by the state convention.

Fifth, financial support of Southern Baptist colleges through widespread solicitation of funds in the churches has been replaced largely by provision of annual appropriations through the state convention budgets. Primarily the result of the rapid growth of giving through the Cooperative Program and the attendant growth and stabilization of the financial programs of the state conventions, this marked shift in the pattern of financial support is probably the most significant development of all time in the life of these colleges. In 1955 the 63 colleges, academies, and Bible schools received $9,269,678 through state Baptist convention offices, compared with $5,309,875 in 1951. Until the last five years the appropriations were almost exclusively for operations, but as of Dec., 1956, only two of the state conventions failed to include funds for capital purposes in the appropriations.

See also BIBLE INSTITUTE, THE; THEOLOGICAL EDUCATION; and WEEKDAY RELIGIOUS EDUCATION.

BIBLIOGRAPHY: C. D. Johnson, *Higher Education of Southen Baptists* (1955). W. J. McGlothlin, *Baptist Beginnings in Education* (1926). G. W. Paschall, *History of Wake Forest College* (1935). B. D. Ragsdale, *Story of Georgia Baptists* (1932).

R. ORIN CORNETT

EDUCATION BOARD. An agency of the denomination intended to co-ordinate and promote the work and support of the educational institutions and interests of Southern Baptists. Pursuant to authorization May 16, 1919, of the creation of an education board, the agency was incorporated Mar. 23, 1920, under the laws of Alabama, with headquarters in Birmingham. The first executive officer was James Edgar Dillard (q.v.), who served as acting corresponding secretary until William Carey James took office as corresponding secretary on July 1, 1920. Successors were John Walter Cammack, who served from Oct. 1, 1924, until May 19, 1927, and Rufus Washington Weaver (q.v.), who served from Oct. 7, 1927, until the discontinuation of the board in 1928. Albert Richmond Bond was editorial secretary from Aug. 1, 1920, to Jan., 1927.

In the first report of the Education Board, May 12, 1920, its mission was described as threefold:

First, to enable the denomination as a whole to function in the realm of education. Second, to enable our educational institutions, individually and collectively, to function in the work of the denomination. Third, to enable the denomination and its schools unitedly to function more largely in the life of the world today.

The initial report also described as necessary the organization of the board into at least three departments: the Department of Publicity and Propaganda, the College Department, and the Student Department. By 1924 the board was organized into seven departments: Surveys, Publicity, Institutions, Student Life, Teacher Bureau, Legal and Legislative, and Standardization and Promotion. Throughout the reports of the board, references to its primary responsibilities consistently emphasize (1) the creation and maintenance, among Southern Baptists, of an educational conscience conducive to rightful appreciation of Christian education and adequate support of Southern Baptist schools; and (2) co-ordination and co-operation of Southern Baptist schools in the interests of academic quality and Christian influence.

The Education Board made its most significant contributions through the production and distribution of materials on Christian education, the initiation and promotion of fund-raising efforts for the schools, the compilation of reports on Baptist education, and the setting up and publicizing of standards for Christian schools. Its principal difficulties included financial problems and the perpetual struggle to define and establish its proper area of service within the pattern of activities of the Convention agencies.

On May 18, 1928, the Convention voted to discontinue the Education Board and replaced it with an Education Commission, directing that the properties and obligations of the board be transferred to the Executive Committee. The board ceased its actual operations on Oct. 1, 1928; but considerations affecting the transfer of property and obligations necessitated continuation of the board as a legal entity until 1932, and an account in its name was carried on the books of the Executive Committee until June 15, 1938.

Early in its existence the board acquired a principal interest in the Ridgecrest Assembly, and as majority stockholder controlled its operation until Oct. 1, 1928.

During its nine years as a functioning organization, the board received from all denominational sources $2,214,756.67, and disbursed to denominational causes and institutions $2,588,417.41. Its receipts for its own work totaled $228,183.49. Indebtedness at the time it ceased operation was $387,442.40, including $106,787.79 (in excess of receipts for this purpose) advanced to colleges and seminaries, plus $27,142.62 accumulated interest on same, and $216,743.95 spent on improvements to the Ridgecrest Assembly property, plus $42,768.14 accumulated interest and bond issue expense. Property value totaled $799,929.34, including: Ridgecrest Assembly, $605,416.84, Nuyaka Indian School, $80,000.00, Umatilla (Florida) Assembly, $114,512.50.

R. ORIN CORNETT

EDUCATION COMMISSION OF THE SOUTHERN BAPTIST CONVENTION. An agency established on a temporary basis in 1915, changed to permanent status in 1917, replaced by the Education Board in 1919, and re-established in 1928 following the decision of the Convention to discontinue the Education Board.

From 1931 to 1951, the work of the Education Commission was conducted on a voluntary basis, and at the personal sacrifice of much time and effort by its chairman during that period, Charles D. Johnson, and the secretary-treasurer, Spright Dowell. There was no employed staff until Feb. 1, 1951, when a central office was established in Nashville, Tenn., and the first executive secretary, Richard Orin Cornett, took office. The staff has since increased to five persons.

The Education Commission was incorporated Dec. 10, 1951, under the laws of Tennessee.

According to its charter, which was approved by the Southern Baptist Convention in 1952, the commission was established: ". . . to serve the educational interests of the Southern Baptist Convention and any and all agencies now or any time hereafter created by, controlled by, fostered by, or officially sanctioned by the Southern Baptist Convention." It "may serve at its discretion any and all agencies created by, controlled by, fostered by, or officially sanctioned by any church, association, convention or Baptist group co-operating with the Southern Baptist Convention."

During the period of its existence prior to the creation of the Education Board, the commission devoted most of its efforts to study of the need for and scope of service of such an agency. When it was re-established in 1928, its purpose was clearly stated by the Convention, as follows:

The duties of this Commission shall be to stimulate and to nurture interest in Christian education, to create educational convictions, and to strive for the development of an educational conscience among our people. . . . In short, this Commission shall be both eyes and mouth for Southern Baptists in all matters pertaining to education.

As early as 1930, the commission was operating by means of committees active in five areas: survey and statistics, publicity, reports and programs, standards, and interrelationships. Despite the handicap of a very limited budget covering only the expenses of meetings and the cost of correspondence, the commission contributed, during the period of Johnson's chairmanship, guidance and encouragement at many vital points. Its consistent emphasis upon standardization and upon the need for qualified, consecrated faculty, and its never-ceasing campaign to stir the educational conscience of Southern Baptists were invaluable in a period in which the fortunes of Southern Baptist educational institutions were repeatedly at stake. Its role as an official voice for Christian higher education was particularly valuable during the stressful years of the depression, when school after school encountered financial problems without precedent. By focusing attention upon specific needs and problems as they became acute, the commission accomplished during this period results which were far out of proportion to the meager financial outlay provided.

A significant step was taken in 1937 when publication of *Southern Baptist College News and Views* was initiated. Renamed *The Southern Baptist Educator* in 1947, this periodical continues to be a vital factor in co-ordinating and furthering the work of Southern Baptist educational institutions. Other publications of the commission are the *Southern Baptist Campus Directory*, published at four-year intervals beginning in 1954; *Southern Baptist Career News*, a monthly vocational guidance periodical for teen-age young people; and various tracts, pamphlets, and leaflets.

The commission has encouraged and subsidized in part the production of several college textbooks and reference volumes. Three of the most significant of these are *The Heart of Hebrew History* and *The Heart of the New Testament*, both by Hubert Inman Hester, and *Higher Education of Southern Baptists*, by Charles D. Johnson. The first two are textbooks used widely for college courses in the Bible, and the third is an institutional history of higher education among Southern Baptists.

The work of the Education Commission embraces a sixfold program of services, as follows:

1. Stimulation and encouragement of interest in Christian education is accomplished through (1) maintenance of a central source of information; (2) production of articles and features for denominational publications; (3) publication of *The Southern Baptist Educator, Southern Baptist Career News, The Southern Baptist Campus Directory,* tracts, and other materials; (4) organization and correlation of promotional efforts in behalf of Christian higher education; and (5) annual reports to the Southern Baptist Convention.

2. Specific institutions are served through (1) operation of a faculty placement service free to Baptists, supplying candidates for faculty positions in Southern Baptist institutions; (2) surveys and consultation on specific problems; (3) circulation of useful ideas and techniques; and (4) provision of special services requested by individual institutions.

3. Organized Baptist groups are served through (1) conducting of surveys at the request of state conventions and state convention boards and committees, and (2) counsel and survey services to groups interested in starting Baptist educational institutions.

4. Co-operative effort among Southern Baptist educational institutions and agencies is promoted.

5. Educational conferences and projects are sponsored.

6. A church-and-college co-ordinated program of vocational and educational guidance for Southern Baptist youth is promoted and maintained.

Central feature of the promotional efforts of the commission is the annual Convention-wide emphasis on Christian education in April, which was begun in 1954. In each of the three years, 1954 through 1956, the annual April emphasis resulted in features, articles, lessons, and programs in more than a score of Convention-wide periodicals with combined circulations in excess of four million, and wide coverage in the state Baptist papers reaching more than a million Baptist homes. In addition, more than two million tracts and leaflets on Christian higher education and on the Christian approach to vocational choice were distributed.

One of the most important phases of the commission's work includes surveys conducted at the request of state Baptist conventions, executive boards and committees, and local associations. Among these have been the surveys of

Kentucky Baptist colleges and schools (1951), of those in Texas (1952), of those in Mississippi and Georgia (1953), of the potentialities for a Baptist college in Atlanta (1954) and in Houston (1954), of the Louisiana Baptist educational institutions (1955), of the potentialities for a Baptist college in Louisville (1956), and of the capital needs of the Baptist schools of Georgia (1954) and Missouri (1955). Special assistance has been provided also in the working out of formulas for division of Christian education funds among the Baptist schools in Texas and Georgia (1953), and in Kentucky (1956).

A vital ministry was begun in 1954 in the production of materials for the vocational and educational guidance of teen-age Baptist youth. This program aims at co-ordination of the efforts of colleges, churches and denominational agencies working for an improved stewardship of the vocational and intellectual potential of Baptist young people.

Closely co-ordinated with the work of the Education Commission are the activities of the Southern Association of Baptist Colleges and Schools. Composed of the administrative officers of all Southern Baptist educational institutions, this organization makes available to the commission a supply of highly competent personnel for dealing with problems of Christian higher education.   R. ORIN CORNETT

EDUCATION IN MISSIONS. Impelled by the desire to reinforce evangelism by every possible technique, Southern Baptists logically have used general education. In 1910 William Owen Carver (*q.v.*) wrote: "Church buildings, hospitals, printing plants, school buildings, missionaries' homes, . . . constitute in many ways an impressive advantage for the work of Christianizing the life of the nations. They give assurance to the workers, provide facilities for the work, and proclaim to the people the benevolence of its purpose."

The ministry of education has a biblical basis: "And the things that thou hast heard from me among many witnesses, the same commit thou to faithful men, who shall be able to teach others also" (II Tim. 2:2). To this Southern Baptists have endeavored to be faithful. In addition, the law of reproductive spiritual life, which guarantees continuity of leaders, calls for education. Schools are the places that best disseminate it. Christian schools and colleges produce leaders as well as converts. Southern Baptist schools, for primary and secondary as well as higher education, are fundamentally essential for the training of denominational leaders.

Just as Baptists have been concerned to have trained leaders, they have been zealous for an intelligent laity. They recognize the need for churches that are consciously independent and autonomous, characteristics which are fostered by knowledge gained in Christian mission schools. Constitutions of national conventions on many mission fields evidence an understanding of this educational responsibility and a concern for encouraging the same principles in the establishment of national mission boards.

Baptists have not only effectively used schools in combating superstition and idolatry, but also have used them in helping to avoid the conceit of gnosticism. General education has helped students develop their abilities constructively and has increased the influence and prestige of the missionary. "The influence of the missionaries was increased after the founding of mission schools." Even though some secondary schools have been developed with less religious emphasis than others, all have offered sound general education with a strong spiritual basis. "The mission schools conducted by the Baptists and other denominations in the West largely laid the foundations for an educational system in Indian Territory and were the best schools of which we can find trace during this period in the early history of education in what is now Oklahoma." Likewise, on many foreign fields for decades the mission-established schools were the sole educational institutions, e.g., in Nigeria: "For a long while the Government depended upon mission schools alone for education."

Schools and colleges have been fields as well as instruments for a program of evangelism, through students who have demonstrated in daily living the Christian principles gained in the schools. Regarding the Near East, W. O. Carver wrote, "Educational missions have constituted the most effective means of service and instrument of progress." Reporting on mission work in Chile for the year 1954, Hubert and Jean Middleton recorded:

The thirty-second anniversary of the founding of the Baptist school in Temuco was celebrated on October 18 with the dedication of the Agnes Graham memorial auditorium. On this occasion, R. Cecil Moore began a series of revival services in the school. Through such services, Bible classes, daily chapel programs, and constant testimony within the school, a large number of the students have been won to the Lord, and six boys have made known their desire to follow the Lord's call to preach the gospel. In its spiritual and cultural ministry the school has reached out into many areas of life in Chile.

Nearly every field has given a similar testimony, but only one other is quoted here:

The Bible is a textbook throughout the twelve grades of the Hawaiian Baptist Academy. Its teachings make amends, in part, for the lack of Christian influence in the homes of many of the students. Without undue pressure, almost every pupil enrolled in the fifth through the twelfth grades makes decisions for Christ during a yearly revival. This year the school will graduate its first twelfth grade and begin to turn back into the churches and colleges a stream of young people from a Christian school.

In summary, as stated by Henry C. Vedder, "Baptists felt the necessity of a better education for their children," so they felt the necessity of it for converts or inquirers on mission fields. Schools and colleges have contributed to civil governments, produced graduates with higher ideals, trained a steady stream of teachers for schools of every grade, and taught church doctrines and methods of personal evangelism.

L. RAYMON BROTHERS

EDUCATION SOCIETY, THE. Organized in Washington, D. C., May 16, 1888, "to assist in formulating wiser plans in the founding of new schools and in the erection of buildings for new institutions of learning." The society arose largely through the influence of Henry L. Morehouse, corresponding secretary of the Home Mission Society. The first corresponding secretary of The Education Society was F. T. Gates of Minnesota. Before a year had passed, John D. Rockefeller, Sr., had provided the society with $100,000.

The outstanding achievement of the society came under the leadership of Gates (1888-93) in establishing the University of Chicago. Rockefeller gave $600,000 for the project. Gates and T. W. Goodspeed led in securing another $400,000. From 1888 to 1902, 46 institutions, including the University of Chicago, received $1,354,002.53 from the society by raising $3,106,484.17 according to the terms of the grants. Thus, a total of $4,460,486.70 was added to the funds of approved institutions.

In spite of such apparent success, The Education Society was terminated in 1902. This may be attributed to several factors. First, most of the money handled by the society was designated for institutional grants. Relatively little was received for operating expenses. Within five years after its inception, the society had insufficient funds to maintain a secretary. In the declining years (1893-1902), Morehouse served without salary while at the same time employed as field secretary of the Home Mission Society. Then, notably, except for a few hundred dollars, most of the gifts to the society were from one man: Rockefeller.

The Northern Baptist Convention established a Board of Education in 1912 to resume the functions of the society, then dead 10 years. In 1944 the board was merged with the Publication Society. This new agency became known after 1950 as The Board of Education and Publication of the American Baptist Convention.

BIBLIOGRAPHY: L. A. Crandall, *Henry Lyman Morehouse, A Biography* (1919). R. G. Torbet, *A History of the Baptists* (1950). H. C. Vedder, *A Short History of the Baptists* (1907). C. L. White, *A Century of Faith* (1932). "Your Board of Education and Publication" (brochure, 1955).

V. WAYNE BARTON

EDUCATION SOCIETY OF KENTUCKY, BAPTISTS. Organized on June 26, 1906, at Richmond, Ky., by the Baptist Educational Committee of Kentucky "to co-ordinate our schools and bring them closer to the denomination." The society represented all parts of the state. From 1908 it reported regularly to the General Association of Baptists in Kentucky, and its reports were printed in the minutes of the general association. The former committee had been an agency appointed by and reporting to the general association. The latter society was a body chartered under the laws of Kentucky with a membership made up of persons who contributed as much as $100 through it to any one of the Baptist schools in Kentucky. The schools, to participate in the funds raised by the society, had to change their charters to coincide with the charter of the society. Edgar Young Mullins (*q.v.*) (1860-1928) was the first president. The schools were under the direction of the society (not the general association) since they submitted two names for each vacancy on their boards of trustees, and the society elected one of them at its annual meeting held in conjunction with the General Association of Baptists in Kentucky.

Originally, the society attempted to raise $500,000 for educational work in Kentucky, but the effort was not successful. The society promoted various other financial campaigns for the support of the schools and distributed the funds to the schools. Also, funds which were allocated by the general association for education were distributed by the society.

There was little further development in the general association's purpose to control the schools during the life of this organization. In 1941 a committee on Christian education, appointed in 1940, recommended, "that the General Association of Baptists in Kentucky request the Baptist Education Society of Kentucky to take such steps immediately as to bring about the dissolution of the said society as a chartered body. . . ." In consequence of the adoption of this recommendation, the society was dissolved on Nov. 11, 1942.

LEWIS C. RAY

EDUCATIONAL BUILDINGS, CHURCH. See ARCHITECTURE, CHURCH.

EDUCATIONAL COMMITTEE OF KENTUCKY, BAPTIST. Prior to 1897, a committee on schools and colleges reported annually to the General Association of Baptists in Kentucky. In this year the committee, with Thomas Treadwell Eaton (*q.v.*) as chairman, recommended that the schools should be brought under denominational control by allowing the general association to elect their trustees. In 1898 this committee pointed out that Baptist schools in other states were under control of the Baptist bodies in their respective states, and it recommended that "a standing committee be appointed to be known as the Baptist Educational Committee of Kentucky," to take the place of the older committee. The new committee was to consist of nine members, three of whom should go out of office each year, and it was to "consider how far it may be practicable and wise to go toward bringing these institutions under the control" of the general association, as well as "to guide these institutions in the successful prosecution of their work."

The personnel of the committee changed somewhat from year to year; however, most of the men whose terms expired immediately succeeded themselves, and T. T. Eaton remained chairman from 1897 until his death in 1907. In 1904 in the committee's report it expressed concern about making the schools permanently secure for the denomination and it stated that "some brethren favor having the trustees chosen by the General Association," but that others thought that "the Boards of Trustees should be self-perpetuating." After the death of T. T. Eaton, William Joseph McGlothlin (1867–1933) became chairman for two years (1908–09), then the committee was succeeded by the Baptist Education Society of Kentucky. The committee failed in its primary purpose of bringing the schools and colleges under the control of the general association.

LEWIS C. RAY

EDWARDS, JOHN RODDEN (b. Hinds County, Miss., Sept. 10, 1851; d. Ruston, La., Apr. 25, 1938). Pastor and denominational leader. At the age of 24, he surrendered to the call to preach and was licensed by Antioch Church of Warren County, Miss. He came to Shiloh in Union Parrish, La., in Dec., 1876, and entered Concord Institute, where he remained for the rest of the session and part of the following year. He was ordained by Shiloh Church, July 14, 1878, during the session of the Louisiana Baptist Convention. In 1883 he enrolled in Mississippi College. After spending part of two years there, he took up his second pastorate at Downsville, La. From there he moved to Ruston, where he served eight years before moving to Mt. Lebanon, where he was pastor of the church and president of Mt. Lebanon College. He was for three years president of the Louisiana Baptist Convention, and he served for many years as member of the state mission board and of the education commission.

J. C. MURPHY

EDWARDS, SAMUEL (b. Putnam County, Tenn., Aug. 29, 1880; d. Salisbury, N. C., Feb. 15, 1955). Pastor and advocate of denominational affiliation. Edwards earned two academic degrees, LL.B. from Cumberland University Law School (1906) and A.B. from Carson-Newman College (1910). He was converted at 24 while a student at Cumberland and was baptized by Samuel Howell into the Boiling Springs Church near by.

Edwards was elected county judge of Putnam County in Tennessee in 1910, soon after he began practicing law at Cookeville. In 1913 he succeeded in reviving a defunct church in Cookeville; it was reorganized with nine members and later became the First Baptist Church there. After futile efforts to secure a pastor, the church in 1917 asked Edwards, though a layman, to "carry on and conduct services as usual." This he "tried to do in approved ministerial style minus salary." The following year he was ordained by the church and during his 20-year pastorate had over 1,000 conversions. His doctrinal sermons were effective in stemming the tide of Campbellism in that section. Edwards was instrumental in bringing the independent Stone Association into the Tennessee convention in 1919. He also influenced other nonaffiliating churches in the surrounding area to unite with associations co-operating with the convention.

In 1938 he became pastor of the Baptist church at Mountain City, Tenn., and several surrounding rural churches. Ten years later, he retired and moved to Salisbury, N. C.

In addition to religious tracts and doctrinal articles, Edwards wrote "History of Stone Association" (1944) and *History of Cookeville Baptist Church* (1933).

BIBLIOGRAPHY: S. Edwards, *History of Cookeville Baptist Church* (1933); "History of Stone Association," *The Baptist and Reflector* (Nov. 30, 1944).

F. M. DOWELL, JR.

EGAN, BARTHOLOMEW (b. Killarney, Ireland, Dec. 10, 1795; d. Shreveport, La., 1879). Educator, physician, statesman. Son of James Constantine Egan, he attended Killarney College and graduated from Dublin University. Following his marriage to Eliza Cormick, he emigrated to the United States, settling in Dinwiddie County, Va. In his adopted state he soon became a leading educator. While teaching at Charlottesville, he studied medicine and began to practice. At Danville, Va., he united with the Baptist church.

In 1847 Egan moved to Mt. Lebanon, La., and led in establishing Mt. Lebanon University, being the first president of the board of trustees. On Aug. 2, 1855, he was appointed president *pro tem* of the university and professor of language and mental and moral hygiene, in which position he served for more than two years without pay. In 1848 he and 12 other men organized the Louisiana Baptist Convention. During his residence in Louisiana, Egan filled the following positions: presidential elector, surgeon general of Louisiana, superintendent of the state laboratory at Mt. Lebanon, and member of the board of supervisors of the state seminary at Pineville.

T. W. GAYER

ELDER. From *presbuteros* in its technical sense, adopted from the synagogue and found only in the Acts and the Pastoral Letters, and translated elder (presbyter). An elder is an administrative and pedagogical official (I Tim. 5:17) in the local congregation (*ekklesia*). Frequently, the term appears as a synonym for bishop or pastor but never for deacon. As early as Ignatius (Bishop of Syrian Antioch, c. 110–117), however, elder became the second grade of a threefold hierarchy: deacon, elder, bishop.

Contemporary uses of the term vary widely. Southern Baptists employ generally the functional term "presbytery" as the official title of an ordination council (cf. I Tim. 4:14).

BIBLIOGRAPHY: C. Gore, *The Ministry of the Christian Church* (1889). K. E. Kirk, ed., *The Apostolic*

Ministry (1946). J. B. Lightfoot, *Dissertations on the Apostolic Age* (1892). B. H. Streeter, *The Primitive Church* (1929).

J. B. MCMINN

ELDRIDGE ACADEMY (1906–31). An elementary and high school for boys and girls located at Eldridge, in Walker County, Ala. The successor to the West Alabama Male and Female College, it was founded jointly by the Alabama Baptist Convention and the Home Mission Board of the Southern Baptist Convention. It was operated by the Home Mission Board until 1931 and was noted as a feeder for Howard and Judson colleges.

JAMES E. DAVIDSON

ELECTION. The purposeful, sovereign choice of God in calling or choosing nations and individuals in whom and through whom he accomplishes his will. Abraham and his descendants were graciously chosen to be servants of God (Gen. 12:1–3). Through the work of the Suffering Servant, God calls people of all cultures and races to be his servants (Isa. 49:6; 65:13–16; Eph. 2:4 f.; I Peter 2:9). As a miracle of divine grace, election is independent of merit (Deut. 7:6–8; Deut. 9:4 f.), although it entails responsibility commensurate with privilege (Amos 3:2). Fruitfulness is characteristic of the elect (John 15:16). God's choices may be deemed arbitrary in the sense that they depend solely upon his sovereign will, but his choices are not irrational or capricious. They are manifestations of his gracious redemptive nature (Isa. 55:8 f.; Rom. 11:33). Through his redemptive activity in behalf of Israel, God has a claim on Israel's service (Exod. 19:4 f.). Through his redemptive activity in Christ, he has a claim on all men; to be in Christ means to be a debtor to all men (Rom. 1:14). In electing men to redemption and service, God initiates the action in response to man's need (John 6:44) and in accordance with God's eternal purpose (Eph. 1:4; 2:8–9).

GEORGE C. HUMPHREY

ELLIS, RICHARD (b. in Virginia, Feb. 14, 1781; d. Bowie County, Tex., Dec. 20, 1846). Lawyer, judge, Texas state senator. A delegate to the convention which met in 1836 at Washington-on-the-Brazos, Tex., Ellis was unanimously chosen president of the convention and was presiding on Mar. 2 and Mar. 17 when the Texas declaration of independence was signed and the state's first constitution adopted. His name was affixed to the famous document with those of others present. Ellis was elected to the Texas congress four times between 1836 and 1840 and served as president *pro tem* of the senate until Mirabeau B. Lamar was inaugurated vice-president.

Although he had only common school education, Ellis studied law and was admitted to the bar and elected a Franklin County, Ala., delegate to the state's 1819 constitutional convention. In 1820 he was elected judge of the fourth Alabama circuit and served there until moving to Pecan Point, Bowie County, Tex., Feb. 22, 1834. He was a member of the first Texas Baptist Education Society board of managers. After his death in 1846, Ellis was buried in a family cemetery three miles from New Boston. His body, with that of his wife, was removed to the state cemetery in Austin, Tex., in 1929, and a bronze statue of Judge Ellis was erected at Waxahachie, county seat of Ellis County, in 1936.

BIBLIOGRAPHY: J. M. Carroll, *A History of Texas Baptists* (1923). L. R. Elliott, ed., *Centennial Story of Texas Baptists* (1936). W. P. Webb and H. B. Carroll, eds., *The Handbook of Texas* (1952).

JACK D. HARWELL

ELLYSON, HENRY KEELING (b. Richmond, Va., July 31, 1823; d. Richmond, Va., Nov. 27, 1890). Baptist layman, Virginia Baptist leader, civic official. Although he had no classical or collegiate education, Ellyson spent several years in private schools, became a printer's apprentice at the age of 14, and opened his own printing business in 1841. While Ellyson was learning the printing trade, his father died; and his mother and sisters were dependent upon him. Based on sound business practices and absolute integrity, he established a thriving business, and won the confidence of the people of the city. In 1854 Ellyson was elected to the Virginia House of Representatives and served two terms; in 1857 he was elected sheriff of Richmond, a position which he held until 1865. In 1870 he became mayor of Richmond.

Following the Civil War, Ellyson and James A. Cowardin revived the *Daily Dispatch*, the most influential journal in the state, and Ellyson devoted the rest of his business life to the paper. He was active also as a director in banking, railroad, insurance, and steamboat companies.

Leading Baptist layman of his time in Virginia, Ellyson became the first secretary of the State Mission Board of the Baptist General Association of Virginia in 1847 and served in this capacity until his death, never missing a meeting and refusing every offer of remuneration. His tenure was during one of the periods of largest and soundest growth experienced by Baptists in the state. He served for seven years as secretary of the general association. Secretary of the Southern Baptist Convention in 1853 and vice-president in 1882, Ellyson was director of the American Baptist Publication Society and trustee of the Southern Baptist Theological Seminary. He was a member of the Foreign Mission Board for 20 years and published at his personal expense *The Southern Baptist Missionary Journal*. He was a trustee of Richmond College for 22 years and president of the board during the last four years of his life.

Baptized at the age of 20, Ellyson was a member of the Second Baptist Church, Richmond, where he was superintendent of the Sunday school for most of the rest of his life. Ellyson served on the board of trustees of Richmond Theological Seminary and was loved and honored by the Negro brethren. For a year (1847) he published *The Baptist Guardian*, edited by his pastor, J. L. Reynolds (1812–77). In June, 1843, he married Elizabeth P. Barnes.

CARRINGTON PAULETTE

EMINENCE MALE AND FEMALE SEMINARY. Established in 1861 at Eminence, Ky., as a private secondary school for girls under the patronage of the Sulphur Forks Baptist Association. In 1863 boys were admitted, and it continued operation under various appellations until 1882.

GLYNN R. FORD

ENID GENERAL HOSPITAL (Enid, Okla.). In 1953 officials of the Enid General Hospital Foundation approached convention leaders with a proposal to deed this hospital, equipment, and other assets to the Oklahoma convention. Complete agreement was reached Oct. 12, 1953, and the hospital was accepted two days later. This 135-bed hospital is valued at $1,191,084. Total assets in 1954 were $1,283,430, with indebtedness of $61,363.75. The hospital has a school of nursing which has been in operation since 1917. It accepts an average of 21 students each year.

TOM E. CARTER

ENLARGEMENT CAMPAIGN. A method of Sunday school and Training Union field work, first popularized by Arthur Flake (*q.v.*) soon after he became secretary of the Southern Baptist Sunday School Board's Department of Sunday School Administration in 1920. It was first developed in Sunday school work; later, it was adapted to Training Union promotion. The term is used to describe a one-week or eight-day intensive campaign in a church to enlarge and improve the Sunday school or Training Union organization. Essentially the campaign is an exhaustive listing and visiting of prospects, followed by the creation of new classes (or unions) and departments to take care of the consequent increased enrolment. The fundamental principle on which this work is based is a belief in the formation of additional organizational units followed by thorough visitation on the part of enlisted leaders as the best means of growth and expansion.

For success the enlargement campaign must be carried out by a large group of carefully trained workers, whose enlistment and instruction in methods is the crucial part of the whole effort. On the basis of past experience, a detailed and rather elaborate procedure has been formulated, which includes the following steps and activities:

Preparation.—When a given church has been thoroughly committed to the program, and a suitable time has been chosen, this procedure is followed: (1) A faculty, adequate to instruct all necessary workers, is engaged and a master schedule formulated. (2) Preparation is made for a religious census. The territory is defined and properly divided. Adequate workers are enlisted to discover the religious preference and affiliation of everyone who lives in a given area. Also, the church roll is checked with the rolls of the various organizations to list as prospects all church members who do not belong to the educational organizations.

The work of the campaign.—This work includes these operations: (1) The taking of the religious census on the opening Sunday. The information is classified, tabulated, arranged in lists by age groups, and made ready for use. This census provides the church with names and addresses of prospects and leads to better understanding of the religious needs of the community. (2) The planning of new organizational units. On the basis of the information obtained through the census and prospects discovered from other sources, classes and departments are formed, involving the adjustment of former units and the creation of completely new units composed of prospects. One of the major objectives of the enlargement campaign is this creation of new classes and departments. (3) The enlistment and training of workers who will be the teachers and workers in existing units and in new units. Generally the church provides classes in the evening for a week. Books on departmental administration, on the various age levels, or some other suitable books are taught. (4) The provision of space for the newly organized units. Usually, by means of more efficient planning and utilization, churches can provide space for many new organizational units within existing buildings. Sometimes an enlargement campaign is carried on as a church enters a new educational building. Sometimes supplementary space has to be obtained on a temporary basis. (5) The adoption of an efficient system of records. Southern Baptist churches generally use the record system prepared and recommended by the Sunday School Board. (6) The visitation of prospects. In a systematic way all the prospects discovered in the census are visited, and a definite effort is made to enlist them in the unit to which they have been assigned. The newly created organizations will have been planned to provide for every age group. (7) The installation of the new organization. No enlargement campaign is complete until the new departments and classes (or unions) are actually put into operation.

Follow-up and conservation.—After an enlargement campaign, the primary work of the church is to maintain and fill its enlarged organization. This is done in many ways. In the Sunday school, for example, a weekly officers and teachers' meeting is held, which provides regularly and systematically for further training. Visitation is continued and intensified. Standards of Excellence—the patterns of organizational efficiency promoted by the Sunday School Board—are adopted as the goal of each class and department. The work which is done is directed toward the attainment of these standard requirements. Finally, evangelism is emphasized, and an effort is made to bring new members of the educational organizations to Christian conversion and to active church membership.

Variations.—There are two major variations of the enlargement campaign as practiced by Southern Baptist churches. One, called the "inside" enlargement campaign, is generally used by Training Union organizations. The census is eliminated, and prospects are found on the church roll, the Sunday school roll, and from other lists of prospects. This type of campaign has been widely used. In recent years, in larger churches, it has become more a matter of continuous visitation in an effort to enlist all the members in all church activities. In addition enlargement campaigns have been expanded to include larger areas than the local church. Association-wide simultaneous campaigns are often conducted. These provide for more efficient coverage of the community and, by means of general meetings and centralized planning, intensify effort and promote efficiency. The first such effort was a simultaneous Sunday school enlargement campaign conducted in San Antonio, Tex., Sept. 23-30, 1923. The first record of a simultaneous association-wide campaign involving rural churches is of that conducted in Marion County Association, South Carolina, Nov. 7-14, 1926.   HAROLD E. INGRAHAM

ENLISTMENT. In Southern Baptist usage the securing of support from church members for their church and denominational program, and the encouragement of co-operation. The Southern Baptist concept of enlistment has grown in two ways: in relation to a constantly expanding program, and because of increasingly efficient enlistment methods. In general, this growth may be described as a progress from the specific to the general. In the beginning, specific causes were promoted in an effort to create a supporting group of specially interested people. Currently, Southern Baptists promote a complex and integrated program of activities and interests in an effort to gain the support of all the people for the whole range of denominational activities. Over the whole period of their history, enlistment has been a major concern of Southern Baptists.

In the field of missions this interest was manifested in 1845 when the new Southern Baptist Convention created two mission boards in order to enlist, encourage, and direct its constituents in missionary endeavor. Perhaps the greatest single stride taken in the early days in informing and enlisting the churches in the support of missions came through the organization of the women's work. This movement existed at first as isolated local societies. The first Convention-wide meeting of Baptist women took place in Baltimore, Md., in 1868, under the leadership of Mrs. Ann J. Graves. For many years the work continued as local societies functioning under the direction of state committees. In 1875 the Southern Baptist Convention took official recognition of their work. After many years of opposition to its desire to be included in the Convention itself, in 1888 in Richmond, Va., the ladies organized for Convention-wide work as the Executive Committee of the Woman's Missionary Societies (auxiliary to the Southern Baptist Convention). In 1890 in Fort Worth, Tex., the present name was adopted—Woman's Missionary Union, auxiliary to the Southern Baptist Convention. Its first executive secretary was Annie Walker Armstrong (*q.v.*).

From the beginning the Convention realized the need for Christian publication and education, and so founded the Bible Board in 1851 for the specific purpose of circulating Scriptures. Its scope was enlarged in 1855 to include Sunday school and colportage work. In 1863 this agency gave way to a Sunday School Board, located in Greenville, S. C., with Basil Manly, Jr. (*q.v.*), as its first president, and John Albert Broadus (*q.v.*) as its first salaried director. From 1873 to 1891, this work was committed to the Home Mission Board. At that time the present Sunday School Board was organized with James Marion Frost (*q.v.*) as its first corresponding secretary. From meager beginnings as the publisher of Sunday school literature and the promoter of Sunday school work, this board has expanded to almost unbelievable proportions in literature and book publication; built a field force; developed a study course series; promoted Training Union work, Baptist student work, and church music; and in many other ways provided assistance in the religious education program of the local church.

During the last quarter of the 19th century, the training of children through the women's societies led responsible people to be concerned about the enlistment of the men to support the entire program of the churches. The Laymen's Missionary Movement, an interdenominational organization, began and soon covered the United States and Canada. In 1907 the Southern Baptist Convention founded its own men's organization, with J. Harry Tyler as chairman. In 1908 John Thompson Henderson (*q.v.*) was elected as its first general secretary. The Laymen's Movement took as its three emphases organization, education, and inspiration. In its first report to the Convention, it stated its purpose to be missionary. In 1926 its name was changed to the Baptist Brotherhood of the South, with its headquarters located in Memphis, Tenn., since 1938.

The problem of unaffiliated church members has been of perennial interest to Southern Baptists. This is evidenced by the action of the 1916 Convention which adopted a resolution offered by K. A. Handy urging the pastors to notify other churches within the Convention area of the removal of Baptists to their church fields. In recent years work on this problem has become an integral feature of the program of the Department of Evangelism of the Home Mission Board.

Permeating all the foregoing efforts has been Southern Baptists' interest in the enlistment of its people in stewardship. As early as 1895,

Georgia Baptists recognized the need of a program of enlistment to "unify and systematize" the work of their churches, and adopted a Regulation Schedule, a plan for systematic giving to the causes of their convention. Definite steps were taken in 1897 when a standing committee on co-operation was appointed to enlist non-co-operating churches to promote a plan of systematic and proportionate giving, and to present an annual budget of convention needs, with suggestions as to the improvement of denominational methods. This emphasis developed through the years until in 1916 the State Mission Board organized a department of enlistment with J. Fred Eden, Jr., as its enlistment fieldworker.

At the Southern Baptist Convention level this matter was brought into focus by the 75 Million Campaign which was projected in 1919 for the purpose of raising $75,000,000 for all of the Convention causes over a period of five years. In 1925 a committee on business efficiency was appointed to make a study of the Convention and of all its agencies. As the result of their study, this committee in 1927 was enlarged and continued as the Executive Committee of the Southern Baptist Convention with Austin Crouch as its first executive secretary. Its duties, among other things, are to act for the Convention ad interim in matters not otherwise provided for; to act for the Convention in matters of property; to receive, receipt, and disburse all funds; and to conduct the general work of promotion.

Consequent with the development of the Executive Committee, the budget plan of financing the work of the Convention was adopted. This plan came to be known as the Cooperative Program, of which the Executive Committee said in its 1939 report to the Convention: "The Cooperative Program is the greatest step forward in Kingdom finance Southern Baptists have ever taken." Since that time denominational growth has been founded on the co-operative principle, and enlistment of Southern Baptists is for the support of the whole program. HERSCHEL H. HOBBS

ENLOW MINISTERIAL AID FUND. Established in 1872 at Bethel College, Russellville, Ky., by bequests from two Kentuckians, James Enlow and William Price, to aid ministerial students. On closing of this college in 1933, the fund was transferred to Georgetown College in Kentucky where it maintains its identity and purpose. Valuation as of Nov. 1, 1956, was $21,079.22, and the yield was about 4 per cent. BAYNARD F. FOX

EPISCOPAL ESTABLISHMENT IN VIRGINIA. From 1776 until 1785 the Church of England was officially the state church of Virginia, although not supported by taxation. The Church of England Establishment ended with the Revolution, but many persons were not prepared to follow Jefferson, Madison, and the Baptists into full separation of church and state. They hoped, with Patrick Henry and others, to provide tax support for all churches, each paying his tax to the church of his choice. The general assessment proposal was abandoned in 1786 after long debate, and Jefferson's "Bill for Establishing Religious Freedom" was adopted.

In 1784 the Episcopal Church was incorporated, removing it one step further from state relationship. Other denominations, however, notably Baptists, opposed the Incorporating Act on the grounds that it implied a relationship between church and state which ought not to exist and confirmed to the Episcopal Church the possession of public property in the form of glebes (lands paid for by tax money in colonial days and assigned to the churches for support of the clergy). After the Incorporating Act was repealed in 1787, and the glebe lands were sold by act of the legislature in 1802, with proceeds going to public use, disestablishment was complete.

See also DISESTABLISHMENT OF STATE CHURCH, VIRGINIA. L. D. JOHNSON

EQUATORIAL BRAZIL, MISSION IN. See BRAZIL, MISSION IN.

ESCHATOLOGY. In theology the term refers to those events by which God will bring human history to a close and usher in the eternal state. A study of the term necessarily involves the relationship of eschatological events to each other and to the historical order as well as the nature of events.

New Testament references to eschatology present an apparent paradox. At times eschatological events are referred to as future events, while at other times they are explicitly described as present realities. Consequently, some persons view eschatological events as altogether future, in terms of "the day of the Lord," judgment, destiny, and even the heavenly kingdom and the reign of Christ, which they hold are yet to come. Others, such as C. H. Dodd (*Apostolic Preaching*), believe that the Gospels are primitive apostolic preaching presenting a "realized eschatology." According to this view the incarnation with the established kingdom of Christ, the death, resurrection, and ascension of Christ, and the manifestation of Christ at Pentecost, all constituted "The Day of the Lord"; judgment and destiny have already entered human experience.

A balanced account of New Testament sources indicates that biblical eschatology involves both present and future aspects. That is, some eschatological entities are now in a state of realization, but this does not exhaust their fulfilment. With the first coming of Christ, the redemptive order broke into the present world in a fuller sense and is being realized, but there are future aspects which coincide with the second coming.

One of the prominent factors in the Old Testament was the living expectancy of a better day for Israel, an idea often expressed by the terms "the day of Jehovah" and "the last days." W. J. Beecher points out that while "the day of the Lord" had a number of meanings in the Old Testament, it never indicated a specific time. The day, believed to be near and impending, was to be a time of divine retribution and spiritual deliverance. The coming of Christ with the inauguration of his spiritual kingdom in the first century was the arrival of the "day of the Lord," although the fuller realization was in the future (II Tim. 3:1; Heb. 1:2).

According to the first epistle of John, a major aspect of eschatology, realized through forgiveness, is eternal life, or the quality of life known as enduring relationship with God. Just as spiritual death or separation from God was a reality among men in biblical times, so eternal life, entering into their human experience, became a like reality. Eternal life was not broken by physical death, which became the glorious entrance into a fuller life with Christ, transcending man's earthly experience.

The nature of life immediately beyond death is indicated in a few Scriptures but is not given major emphasis. The account of Lazarus and Dives teaches that Hades, the term indicating the general abode of the dead, is a state of conscious being. Paul (Phil. 1:23) indicates that life beyond death for the redeemed is a state of fellowship with God. While righteous souls are free from suffering, they still await bodily resurrection, judgment, and ultimate destiny in an intermediate state which transcends earthly experience; for in it, Paul anticipated, the soul realizes more fully the spiritual world which has broken into human existence.

Along with the New Testament certainty that the messianic age had arrived is the expectation of future consummation. Both Christ and the New Testament writers looked forward to ultimate triumph through the coming of the kingdom of God in its fullness (I Cor. 15:24), a consummation to be realized by the Parousia, the second coming of Christ. While the writers presented basic principles for Christian progress, they lived in expectancy of Christ's return. Although some interpreters insist on a millennial reign of a temporal king as an essential phase of Christ's triumph in the consummation of his redemptive work, the fact that is certain and of major significance is that Christ is to triumph with the redeemed in the final culmination of his work on earth. All his enemies, including death, the greatest enemy, are to be overcome, and the ultimate goal of an eternal kingdom is to be realized (I Cor. 15:23-28; Phil. 2:10-11).

Christ is to return not only to consummate his redemptive work, but to bring the redeemed to appropriate ends or to the eternal kingdom of God (I Cor. 15:24). New Testament writers also thought of the Parousia as the time of a general resurrection and final judgment. In fact, one of the primary purposes of Christ's return is judgment and not salvation. All men of all time are to stand before Christ and be judged according to works (Rev. 20). Destiny will already have been determined. Final judgment will be for the manifestation of character, the rendering of rewards, and the final vindication of God.

The biblical concept of the resurrection is one general resurrection preceding final judgment. It will be universal in scope, including both righteous and unrighteous (John 5:20-21; Acts 24:15; Rev. 20:11-13).

The resurrection body of Christ and Paul's writing in I Corinthians 15 are evidences of bodily resurrection. Although the nature of Christ's body after he left the tomb is not known, the fact remains that he possessed a body and that it was visible, although not limited to temporal locations. Paul describes the resurrection body as a spiritual body (I Cor. 15:44), pointing out that it will be glorified in form. While it is to come forth from the old body of flesh and bones, and in some way be a continuation of it, the new body will not be composed of the particles of flesh and blood that constituted the old carnal body. Paul indicates that the new body will be composed of immortal and incorruptible essence. The New Testament makes no explicit statements about the nature of the body of the wicked.

The last phase of eschatology is the nature of final destiny. The New Testament record, limited in this aspect, does suggest several characteristics of heaven and hell as ultimate destiny for the redeemed and the wicked.

The New Testament speaks of heaven as both a state and a place. When the writers consider heaven's transcendent glory, they naturally think of a state of being, a state of character and eternal fellowship with Christ and the redeemed. Heaven is thus primarily a state of sinless perfection, of freedom from the limitations of all that is sensual and material. The symbols of Revelation suggest that heaven will be a state of highest moral values, of perfect fellowship and protection, and of unending service and sustenance. Not only will heaven be a state of perfect peace and happiness, but a state of realized rewards (Matt. 25:21; Luke 19:12-27).

In another sense heaven is described as a place. Jesus said, "I go to prepare a place for you" (John 14:2). The fact that heaven was thought of as the realization of God's eternal kingdom naturally suggested the term place, as did the idea of glorified resurrected bodies. There is a hint of a renovated world or universe (II Pet. 3:13). Obviously, however, the character of heaven transcends in importance the idea of locality. Hell, like heaven, is also described as both a state and a place. Because hell is thought of as the realm eternally separated from heaven, it is referred to as a place. As the fulfilment of selfishness and the negation of heaven, hell is a state. Strong language is used to describe hell as a state of unending suffering and punishment. But, as language limited New Testament writers in describing the splendent glory of heaven, so language limited them in describing the awful anguish and torture of souls in hell.

See also MILLERITE MOVEMENT.

BIBLIOGRAPHY: L. Berkhof, *The Kingdom of God* (1951). E. Brunner, *Eternal Hope* (1954). R. H. Charles, *A Critical Study of the Doctrine of the Last Things* (1949). O. Cullmann, *Christ and Time* (1951). H. A. Guy, *The New Testament Doctrine of the Last Things* (1949). T. A. Kantonen, *The Christian Hope* (1954). S. Salmond, *The Christian Doctrine of Immortality* (1901). W. G. T. Shedd, *The Doctrine of Endless Punishment* (1887).

E. L. DWYER

ESTONIA, BAPTISTS IN. The Estonians, who speak a language similar to Finnish, are nearly all Lutherans. The Baptists in Estonia grew out of a revival movement of 1877, which in some instances degenerated into fanatical excesses, but which did have saner elements who organized groups of believers. These Baptists were influenced by those in Latvia. The leaders were often imprisoned, but behaved with great courage, preaching to the criminals imprisoned with them, and excited some popular sympathy. The worst persecution occurred during the later years of Czar Alexander III (reigned 1881–94). Soon after World War I a seminary was opened just outside Tallinn (Reval) under the leadership of Adam Podin, who had preached in many prisons all over the Russian Empire and done much to alleviate the lot of a colony of lepers in Estonia, and who had once been condemned to death but had escaped execution. The seminary was badly damaged during World War II.

W. O. LEWIS

ETERNAL LIFE. Sometimes spoken of as everlasting life or simply as life and especially prominent in the writings of John. The Johannine emphasis upon eternal life is closely related to the Synoptic emphasis upon the kingdom of God or the kingdom of heaven. Paul in his writings refers to a similar relationship when he speaks of the redeemed as having "died to sin" and having been made "alive unto God in Christ Jesus" (Rom. 6:11).

Specifically, eternal life is not mere continuation of existence; it is a life of personal knowledge of and fellowship with God (John 17:3), made possible only through Christ, showing itself in one's present experience, possession, and relationship (John 3:36; 5:24; 6:47). Christ assures man that eternal life is a future reality. In the resurrection, the saved will enter into fuller life with God, while the unsaved will enter into a state of greater condemnation (John 5:24–29).

J. W. OUSLEY

See also IMMORTALITY.

ETERNITY. Eternity is God's being. In philosophical thought it is pictured either as timeless being or as the comprehension of all time in God's eternal NOW. Both views are alien to biblical revelation. God's eternity is not the negation of time. The biblical revelation is historical, and God's redemptive purpose is fulfilled in time. God saves men by becoming flesh, entering into and working redemptively within time. Equally, however, God's eternity is no static *now* in which past, present, and future are alike present to God. God knows the end from the beginning. God, the living God, acts, and his eternity must imply movement. Hence the Bible talks of God's eternity in terms of unending time, everlastingness—not implying that God is limited by time, for he creates and sustains it, but implying that the succession of time has reality for him. His eternity is the whole which embraces all times and from which all times spring. His past and future are always within his *now*, but that *now* is a movement in which he wills to live through "his time" while at the same time ordering and sustaining it.

Man's time is not something he can so order and control; rather his time is controlled by God. Man's time is divided because of his sin and creatureliness. His past is beyond reclaim and lives on in his memory, with the corresponding sense of guilt. Man's future is "not yet" and is generally beyond his control. Only the living present has reality. Christ, however, reclaims man's past, forgives his guilt, and assures his future. Thus man may enter into eternal life. His fear of the future, and of past guilt, is met by reconciliation in which God integrates his life, giving him a share in His eternity.

Hence the Bible can speak of life on earth as in this present evil "age," and of the future with God as the "coming age," which lies beyond the present, yet in which man may already live by His grace. God is Lord of the "ages." All ages are embraced within his eternity and take their content from it.

See also DISPENSATION.

BIBLIOGRAPHY: O. Cullmann, *Christ and Time* (1951). J. Marsh, *The Fulness of Time* (1952).

E. C. RUST

ETHICS, CHRISTIAN. The term applies to (1) the ethical principles enunciated by Jesus, (2) the character and conduct of Christians, and (3) the systematic study of the presuppositions and norms of Christian behavior. The qualities of Christian character are analyzed in a separate monograph. This article deals with definitions of ethics; purpose and methods of Christian ethical inquiry; distinctive features of Christian morality; and fundamental issues, theoretical and practical, confronting the Christian conscience today.

Definitions.—In modern English usage there is a broad distinction between ethics and morals. *Ethics* is the science of morals, and *morals* is the practice of ethics. Earlier, however, the two words were fully synonymous, and they are so used in this monograph. Ethics is defined as "the systematic study of reflective choice, the standards of right and wrong by which it may be guided and the attainable goods towards which it may be directed." Christian ethics may be defined as the theory and practice of the Christian moral life in history and in contemporary society. It is that part of Christian theology which deals with the moral criteria of conduct in the light of what God has done for men in Jesus Christ.

Purpose and methods.—The critical and constructive study of Christian ethics is carried on within the Christian community. Its purpose is to articulate the norms of Christian behavior and to achieve precision and consistency in Christian conduct.

Christian ethical inquiry is bifocal. It looks to the Bible and the moral reflection of Christian teachers for clarification of its norms and motives and to the social sciences for knowledge of the social contexts within which its imperatives operate and for tested methods of implementing moral decisions. Competent interpreters of the Christian life manifest lofty standards of intellectual integrity, respect for the dignity and worth of the individual, concern for justice in human relations, and reverence for Christ. They wrestle with the problems of their age and culture, examine issues in the perspective of the mind of Christ, and mark out the direction of Christian action in personal and group relations.

The historic types of Christian ethics are delineated in the writings of Henry Sidgwick, Ernst Troeltsch, Anders Nygren, Kenneth E. Kirk, and H. Richard Niebuhr. Two methods are prominent in the history of moral reflection. The teleological method attempts to define the goal (e.g., happiness, wisdom, self-realization, the vision of God) for which man strives. The deontological method begins with the moral requirements by which decisions may be guided and tested and asks what the law requires. Christian ethical inquiry begins with God as the source of moral obligation and asks what he requires of his children. It may anticipate and evaluate the consequences of a proposed course of action, but it disavows success as the sole criterion and raises the crucial question: What is the right action in this concrete ethical situation in the sight of God, whose will is manifested in Jesus Christ as holy love?

The vitality of contemporary Christian ethical thinking appears in two systematic treatises, one by Emil Brunner, the other by George Thomas, both notable for scope and depth. Brunner defines Christian ethics as "the science of human conduct as it is determined by Divine conduct," relates ethics to theology, and works out a comprehensive theory of Christian behavior based upon the presuppositions of the Reformers, chiefly Luther and Calvin, who rediscovered the basis of evangelical ethics in the saving activity of God in Jesus Christ. Thomas explicates the biblical foundations and social implications of the Christian moral ideal and presents an illuminating analysis of the relation of Christian ethics to moral philosophy.

Distinctive features.—1. The Christian ethic of justice and love has a religious basis. It issues out of, and is interlocked with, the Christian gospel. It is grounded in the reality of God as revealed in Jesus Christ and deals with the principles of human response to God's action in creation and redemption. It teaches every person saved by grace through faith to seek first God's kingdom and righteousness.

The central ethical principle underlying the diversity of values and injunctions in the Old Testament is that of obedience to God's will. This unifying principle appears in the imperatives of the Decalogue, and in the profound insights of the prophets, who saw clearly that God is the source of man's freedom and worth and that the primary requirements of the moral law are justice and mercy. "These two words, *justice and covenantal faithfulness,* with all their varied connotations and associations, are the key words of Israel's ethics."

In the New Testament moral principles are stated and concrete ethical situations are examined in the light of God's saving acts in Christ. This dynamic interrelation of gospel and ethics is reflected in the structure of Paul's thinking. In the epistle to the Romans, a penetrating exposition of the gospel (chaps. 1–11) is specifically and inextricably linked with an explication of the ethics of the new life (chaps. 12–15). Moreover, C. H. Dodd has demonstrated that four of the main themes of moral teaching in the New Testament involve distinctively Christian motives or sanctions: Christian eschatology, imitation of Christ, membership in the body of Christ, and the primacy of love.

This linkage of gospel and ethics is in harmony with the mind of Christ as it is disclosed in the Gospels. The moral imperatives of Jesus are grounded in his knowledge of God and of the personal relationship between God and man, and they can be understood only in the light of what he said about the kingdom of God and the cross. His ethical teaching, summarized in the Sermon on the Mount, calls for obedience to God's righteous rule, marks out with perfect clearness the moral principles of action, and presents concrete examples of right behavior. After an exegesis of the Sermon, A. M. Hunter writes:

As we call ourselves followers of Christ, we must acknowledge that Christ does set before us a real design for living which challenges every thoughtful disciple. He does tell us: (1) the kind of people we ought to be; (2) the influence we ought to exert in the world; (3) the way in which, as Christians, we ought to behave socially; (4) the kind of worship we ought to render; (5) the attitude we ought to have towards earthly and heavenly treasures; and (6) the manner in which we should treat our fellow-men.

2. The Christian ethic is a social ethic. Human beings live in a network of personal and social relations, and the Bible teaches that the love of God and the love of neighbor are in-

separably related. The sociological characteristics of the Christian ethic are identified by Troeltsch as individualism and universalism. The disciple of Jesus Christ is a responsible member of the Christian community. He belongs to the household of faith. He participates in the Christian fellowship (*koinonia*). He has a sense of personal responsibility and of social solidarity, and he orders his life by the principles of freedom, fellowship, and service.

The Christian community, whose members acknowledge Jesus Christ as Lord and treat each other as brothers, lives alongside other communities in human society. The Christian, therefore, faces the question: What am I, as a disciple of Jesus, to do in relations with my neighbors, Christian and non-Christian? This ethical question is at the center of Paul's exposition of Christian morality. Saved by the grace of God through faith and undergirded by the sustaining fellowship of believers, the disciple of Jesus grows in maturity, loves his neighbor, speaks the truth, is mindful of the needs of others, manifests a forgiving spirit, and performs the duties of citizenship in a manner that is worthy of the gospel of Christ.

3. The Christian ethic is an ethic of the Holy Spirit. The Christian moral life is guided and sustained by the Holy Spirit and therefore transcends legalism and moralism. The Holy Spirit is at work in the Christian fellowship. He produces a moral transformation in the believer, draws believers together in the community of faith and love in which Jesus is acknowledged as the Lord of life, interprets the mind of Christ, gives disciples of Jesus wisdom and power for the adventure of Christian living, and makes an impact upon human society through the minds of Christian citizens. He may be resisted (Acts 7:51), grieved (Eph. 4:30), and quenched (I Thess. 5:19) by proud and cruel men and women, but he is the source of love, joy, and peace in the Christian life.

Fundamental issues.—1. Is the Christian pattern of life theoretically valid? Today interpreters and advocates of Christian ethics have to deal, not only with disparity between the ethical teaching of Jesus and the daily behavior of his followers, but also with the view that the Christian moral standards have lost their authority. At the beginning of an exposition of the faith of a moralist, A. E. Taylor affirms that the soundness of "the Christian ideal of human character and the Christian rule of life" is the "infinitely serious issue"; and Hastings Rashdall devotes 61 pages of his interpretation of Christian ethics to an analysis of objections to the moral teaching of Christ. After a rigorous study of New Testament ethics, E. F. Scott concludes that the principles which Jesus laid down are valid and that the ethic of Jesus "can lose its authority only on the one condition that love, truth, goodness should some day cease to be regarded as the highest ideals."

2. Is the Christian ethic relevant to the personal choices and social issues confronting men here and now? An affirmative answer to this question is indicated by the fact that Jesus did not formulate and enforce a code but marked out the principles of action and left his disciples free to apply them in changing social contexts under the guidance of the Holy Spirit. The ethical insights of the New Testament are most clearly and directly applicable to the face-to-face relation of one person with one neighbor, but they also illuminate the search for a Christian course of action amid the social structures and human problems of a technical civilization; and the relevance of Christian morality is manifested in the dynamic relation of Christian love to justice and in the responsibility of Christian witnesses, who take the moral teaching of the Sermon on the Mount seriously, "to claim the whole range of human living under the sovereignty of the living Christ."

3. A few thinkers are exploring the relation of Christian ethics to eschatology, economics, and politics, but much remains to be done. A major task confronting the churches in the second half of the 20th century is the development of a Christian social ethic based upon biblical truth and sound social theory, which will provide guidance and stimulus for effective Christian conduct in marriage and the family, in economic and political responsibilities, and in interracial and international relations. This task will require an attitude of moral earnestness toward the human problems of an industrial society, intellectual integrity, and the co-operation of Christian theologians, Christian social scientists, and other "fellow workmen for God," whose thinking is directed, not primarily by personal preferences and social customs, but by a sense of Christian vocation and the principles of Christian ethics upon which the moral structure of the universe rests.

BIBLIOGRAPHY: R. Anshen, ed., *Moral Principles of Action* (1952). F. R. Barry, *The Relevance of Christianity* (reprinted 1947). J. Bennett, *Christian Values and Economic Life* (1954). E. Brunner, *The Divine Imperative* (1947). M. C. D'Arcy, *The Mind and Heart of Love* (1947). L. Dewar, *An Outline of New Testament Ethics* (1949). C. H. Dodd, *Gospel and Law* (1951). A. M. Hunter, *Design for Life* (1953). J. A. Hutchison, ed., *Christian Faith and Social Action* (1953). K. E. Kirk, *The Vision of God* (1931). H. R. Niebuhr, *Christ and Culture* (1951). R. Niebuhr, *The Children of Light and the Children of Darkness* (1944). A. Nygren, *Agape and Eros* (1953). R. C. Petry, *Christian Eschatology and Social Thought* (1956). P. Ramsey, *Basic Christian Ethics* (1950). H. Rashdall, *Conscience and Christ* (1916). A. T. Rasmussen, *Christian Social Ethics* (1956). E. F. Scott, *The Ethical Teaching of Jesus* (1933). Henry Sidgwick, *Outlines of the History of Ethics* (reprinted 1939). A. E. Taylor, *The Faith of a Moralist* (reprinted 1951). W. Temple, *Christianity and Social Order* (1942). G. Thomas, *Christian Ethics and Moral Philosophy* (1955). E. Troeltsch, *The Social Teaching of the Christian Churches* (reprinted 1949). P. Wheelwright, *A Critical Introduction to Ethics* (revised 1949). A. Wilder, *Eschatology and Ethics in the Teaching of Jesus* (1950).

OLIN T. BINKLEY

EUROPE, MISSIONS IN. See EUROPEAN BAPTIST THEOLOGICAL SEMINARY, SWITZERLAND; HUNGARY, MISSION IN; ITALY, MISSION IN; ROMANIA, MISSION IN; SPAIN, MISSION IN; and YUGOSLAVIA, MISSION IN.

EUROPEAN BAPTIST THEOLOGICAL SEMINARY, SWITZERLAND. Established in Ruschlikon, Switzerland, by the Southern Baptist Foreign Mission Board in 1949 to offer theological training to pastors, teachers, and missionaries, combining high scholastic standards with evangelistic zeal; and to promote international fellowship and co-operation among the Baptists of Europe. The seminary property, a country estate five miles from Zurich, was purchased in 1948. On the seven-acre campus three more buildings and a library wing have been constructed since that time. Students are recommended by their own churches and endorsed by the Baptist union and the seminary trustee in their own country. The regular four-year course leading to the Bachelor of Divinity degree requires completion of 128 semester hours of study, a 10,000-word dissertation, and a final oral examination. Only students with certificates of complete pre-university schooling in their own countries (*Abitur, Artium, Bacchalaureate, Matura*) are admitted to B.D. study, but students may take a shorter course suited to their future work. The *Matura* is not required of such term students. Scholarships covering room and board are available for European students. The faculty consists of a professor in each of the following fields: Old Testament, New Testament, biblical backgrounds, theology, church history, and practical theology. The library contains major reference works, standard books, current literature, and periodicals in each field. Emphasis is placed on the collection of Baptist historical material for Europe. The language of instruction is English, but much of the reference literature is in German and French. Liaison with the various European Baptist unions is maintained through trustees from each nation, who meet annually. During the summer, between the school semesters, Ruschlikon serves as a Baptist center for conferences in which pastors, young people, laymen, chaplains, teachers, students, missionaries, and women's groups come together for fellowship, study, and inspiration.

JOSEF NORDENHAUG

EUROPEAN BAPTISTS. Baptist denominational groups in the countries of Europe are essentially modern groups. European Baptists claim no direct historical connection between themselves and the Anabaptists or other sects. They rather trace their beginnings to various national movements spearheaded by leaders like Johann Gerhard Oncken, Julius Kobner, John Elias Feisser, Fredrick L. Rymker, Frederick Olaus Nilsson, Henri Pyt, and others. The oldest of these national movements appeared in the early part of the 19th century. In all of them, the essential and most noteworthy characteristic was spontaneity. Baptist groups in all these countries grew out of the Bible study and prayer of individual Christians as they sought fellowship with each other and as they organized their churches and eventually became a movement.

These national Baptist movements were for the most part indigenous in character, in that they were not the product of efforts sponsored under foreign leadership. It is true that the influence of Oncken, through the movement begun by him in Germany, was either directly or indirectly connected with the beginnings of similar movements in many countries, but this connection was based more on the German support and encouragement of other groups as they arose rather than on any active mission work. Therefore, because of its indigenous origin, Baptist life and work in Europe developed along national lines, taking character and direction from the homeland setting of national traditions, culture, and outlook. As national movements they continued to develop in the traditionally nationalistic European pattern. There were no organic connections between these bodies. It is true that there were loose organizational fellowship ties which transcended national boundaries. The Union of Associated Churches of Baptist Christians in Germany and Denmark is one example of this kind of organization. But there was never organic union with administrative powers.

In their organizational life, these nationalistically minded Baptist groups were naturally influenced by the concepts of life and organization traditionally accepted in their countries. There never developed in Europe any consistent and distinctive Baptist pattern of activity, organizational form, or terminology. In addition, the national orientation of European Baptists tended to increase their consciousness of their minority status. Lacking the strength which firm international fellowship would have given them, they have had a tendency to feel inadequate in the face of constant reminders of the power, prestige, and sometimes hostility of the great state churches.

Their relative weakness has also deprived European Baptists of the ability to develop institutions, particularly educational institutions, which are a primary basis of denominational strength. Facilities for the training of church leaders have never been adequate, and the lack of trained leadership has greatly hampered growth. State-controlled educational systems offering only that religious education approved by the state church have never been able to supply European Baptists with the kind of leadership necessary.

In spite of these limitations, however, Baptists in Europe have made significant progress. Refusing to be overdiscouraged by their minority position, they have grown in numbers and prestige. In all of the countries of Europe Baptists have greater influence and prestige than their numbers would ordinarily justify. They have consistently demanded of their members a high

European Baptists

level of personal conduct in civic and social affairs, have been uncompromisingly biblical in their doctrines, and have thus won a good measure of respect in most European countries.

As a rule, Baptists in Europe have achieved an efficient working organization. The denominational enterprises supported by their national organizations include such institutions and agencies as Sunday schools, other youth organizations, evangelistic programs, missionary enterprises in their own countries and in foreign lands, schools (particularly Bible schools for the training of their ministers), and various social service institutions. Women's societies and laymen's organizations, where found, are usually carried on independently of the national Baptist unions, but work in close co-operation with them.

European Baptists have not as yet experienced the strength and stimulus which the united witness of their combined resources would make possible. National prejudices and antipathies, born out of centuries of international strife and conflict, have at times been reflected even in their religious attitudes and programs. If these limitations, and the isolation born of such strictly national origins, could be overcome in some sort of organic association, many of the most besetting problems of European Baptists would be largely solved.

In recent years European Baptists have made definite progress in the direction of international unity. Four genuinely European organizations have been established: (1) The European Baptist Federation, an international organization which brings together all of the national Baptist groups in Europe in co-operative fellowship. This organization officially came into being at a meeting in Paris in Oct., 1950. (2) The European Baptist Women's Union, first proposed at the meeting of the Baptist World Alliance in Copenhagen in 1947, and definitely organized the year following at the meeting of the Executive Committee of the Baptist World Alliance in London. (3) The European Baptist summer conference, held in the Baptist Theological Seminary in Ruschlikon-Zurich, with a program organized on an international basis and sponsored by the Seminary. The first conference season opened in the summer of 1950. (4) The European Baptist Foreign Missionary Society, officially founded in 1954, with headquarters in Zurich, Switzerland. Its missionary field is the Camaroons in North Africa. The society has two missionaries in the field, and others are in training preparing to go. Six European National Baptist unions have officially united for the support and administration of the work of the society. This is the first time in their history that European Baptist national bodies have entered into organic union for the support of a common, continuing Baptist enterprise.

Perhaps one of the most far-visioned enterprises of Baptists in Europe, pointing toward the dissolution of age-old barriers that have so long separated European Baptist peoples, is the Baptist Theological Seminary at Ruschlikon-Zurich, Switzerland. This international institution was founded in 1949 by the Foreign Mission Board of the Southern Baptist Convention, U.S.A., with the approval of the Baptist World Alliance. Sponsored by the Southern Baptist Foreign Mission Board, it is a school whose primary purpose is to serve the needs of Baptists in all the nations of Europe. It is international in its design and its personnel. Many nations are represented on its board of counselors, its faculty, and in its student body. Its constituency is international. The influence of this institution, through its training of church leaders and its summer conference program, has contributed constructively toward the unity and co-operation in service of European Baptists.

The following statistical information, as supplied by responsible European Baptist leaders, will give a fair picture of the resources, as of 1955, which may be drawn upon as European Baptists face the future. The figures given represent the totals in each category for all Baptist groups in western Europe, exclusive of Russia, Poland, Czechoslovakia, Hungary, Rumania, and Bulgaria.

There are in Europe today 4,915 Baptist churches; 522,991 church members; 2,969 pastors; 153 non-clergy full-time workers; 6,479 Sunday schools; 459,697 Sunday school pupils; 55,301 Sunday school teachers; 201 youth organizations; 221 theological students now in training; 41 full-time home missionaries (mainly evangelists); 16 gospel tents being used for evangelistic services; 48 social service institutions, such as orphanages, homes for the aged, hospitals (in Germany), deaconess homes, etc.; 506 foreign missionaries; 49 periodicals, general and missionary; and 9 publishing houses.

It is significant to note that the Sunday school enrolment includes only small children and young people up to 15 years of age, since there are no classes provided in European Sunday schools, as a rule, for adults. This means that there is at present, already under the direct influence of the churches, a great evangelistic opportunity with the possibility of a correspondingly great increase in church membership.

The outlook for the future reveals difficult problems which must be faced and inspiring opportunities which may be seized. In the opinion of their leaders, the problems and the needs are summarized as follows: (1) extensive war damages to church properties not yet repaired, due in some cases to governmental regulations restricting the building of churches; (2) the shifting of populations to new townships, cities, and housing areas, making urgent the need for new churches; (3) provision of chapels for Baptist refugee congregations, particularly in western Germany where thousands of Baptists have come from the communist East to make their homes, settling in cities and communities where there are no Baptist churches; (4) a divided Germany, making a unified Baptist program impossible; (5) the great need among the youth of East Germany; (6) secularism and materialism felt everywhere, deadening to spiritual Christianity; (7) the great need for trained ministers and workers; (8) decline in Christian family life; (9) overwhelming traditions of the state churches; (10) need for men and means for starting new work in strategic places; (11) the loss of missionary activity and power.

These opportunities are listed: (1) the potentialities of work among the young people; (2) the possibility of establishing strong Baptist centers and churches in new housing areas; (3) evangelism especially among children and young people; (4) the existence of free churches as a living demonstration and proof of the New Testament pattern; (5) the willingness of Roman Catholics to listen to the gospel proclaimed in open air meetings (Ireland).

European Baptist leaders face the future with problems, but with optimism and hope, seeing their greatest opportunities growing out of their greatest difficulties.   J. D. FRANKS

EUROPEAN RELIEF, SOUTHERN BAPTIST PROGRAM OF. After World War I the Foreign Mission Board asked the Southern Baptist Convention for European reconstruction funds. Some relief was sent to France, 1919–20. The conference in London, July 19–23, 1920, attended by James Bruton Gambrell (q.v.), James Franklin Love (q.v.), Edgar Young Mullins (q.v.), and George Washington Truett (q.v.), gave new impetus to European relief when Southern Baptists accepted mission responsibility in Hungary, Italy, Romania, Russia, Spain, and Yugoslavia. Reconstruction and relief responsibility also included Austria, Germany, Latvia, and Poland. By 1921 Southern Baptists had sent $140,000 and $100,000 worth of clothing. The 75 Million Campaign limited the appeals by the Foreign Mission Board to the churches for relief funds, while outside agencies, under no such restraint, collected large untabulated amounts. British, Canadian, Northern (American), Swedish, and Baptists in 14 other nations participated in European relief. During the severe famine in Russia in 1921–22, Everett Gill, Sr. (q.v.), Hoyt E. Porter, and W. O. Lewis served to relieve distress there. In 1923 the Convention was $70,000 short of the annual goal for European relief. By 1924 this relief program was practically finished, but in 1925 Hoyt E. Porter was still in Russia distributing money and clothing.

Up to 1945 the World Emergency Committee of the Foreign Mission Board had received $1,127,000 for relief, most of it for China, but some for Europe. The Miami Convention in 1946 adopted a goal of $3,500,000 for world relief. By September the same year $4,000,000 had been raised. After the World Congress in Copenhagen, 1947, the Baptist World Alliance adopted a relief program with R. Paul Caudill as chairman. The executive committee of the Baptist World Alliance in London, Aug. 15–17, 1948, worked out details. The clothing center in New Orleans, La., was put at the disposal of the Baptist World Alliance relief committee. W. O. Lewis was appointed to co-ordinate work among refugees and displaced persons. Between the congress in Copenhagen, 1947, and in London, 1955, 8,780 persons had been resettled outside Europe. The center in New Orleans up to Feb., 1950, processed five million pounds of clothing valued at $4,250,000, most of which went to Germany. From Aug. 1, 1947, to Mar. 31, 1950, Southern Baptists gave $1,279,776.16 for European relief. The Southern Baptist Convention along with other Baptist conventions continued their own direct relief work in addition to that which they channeled through the Baptist World Alliance program. The refugee program in Paris directed by Edwin A. Bell (American Baptist Convention) and Roy F. Starmer (Southern Baptist Convention) aided 2,500 refugees (half of them Romanians), Dec., 1948 through Apr., 1950. J. D. Franks was Southern Baptist relief representative, 1948–54, during which time $250,000 was spent for relief and rehabilitation in Austria, Belgium, Germany, France, Holland, Norway, Poland, and Yugoslavia. The relief and rehabilitation work consisted in providing food, shelter, clothing, medical aid, resettlement of refugees and displaced persons, and rehabilitation of damaged church property.

JOSEF NORDENHAUG

EVANGELICAL BAPTIST CHURCH, INC., GENERAL CONFERENCE OF THE. A free will Baptist group organized in 1935 and formerly known as the Church of the Full Gospel, Inc. Located mostly in North Carolina, these people are in close fellowship with the Free Will Baptists and exchange ministers with the Wilmington Conference of the Free Will Baptist Church. Their doctrinal position is almost identical to the Free Will Baptists. In 1952 they reported 31 churches, 2,200 members, 3,100 in Sunday school, and 22 ministers. A paper, *Quiet Hour News*, is published in Goldsboro, where headquarters are maintained at 1601 Rose Street.   ALBERT MCCLELLAN

EVANGELISM (from Greek *eu*, well; *aggelos*, messenger). The activity of a messenger of God taking the good news of the truth in Christ to unbelievers, announcing the gospel, publishing good tidings, going "every where preaching the word" (Acts 8:4). The word "evangelist" (*euaggelistes*) occurs three times in the New Testament (Acts 21:8; Eph. 4:11; II Tim. 4:5). In Ephesians 4:11 evangelists are listed third among apostles, prophets, pastors, and teachers. The evangelist was not a separate ecclesiastical order, for apostles (Acts 8:25), deacons (Acts 21:8), and indeed all early disciples exercised the function (Acts 8:4). Evangelists functioned both as traveling missionaries and as settled preachers.

Since apostolic times all Christian sects have developed various methods and programs of evangelism, both personal and mass. Evangelists have used preaching, teaching, writing, and later, printing, radio, and other means of communication. They have utilized church, home, school, and often the state as propagation agencies. Worldwide missionary enterprises have established churches, schools, hospitals, and charitable institutions for evangelistic purposes.

EVANGELISM IN THE BIBLE. The type of evangelism which has borne fruit through the Christian era is that which was rooted by the Old Testament prophets and which flourished fruitfully with Jesus and the apostles.

Old Testament prophets.—The Old Testament is saturated with vital evangelism. Moses preached mighty evangelistic sermons (Deut.). Joshua read the blessings and curses of God (Josh. 8:35) and called for a decision (24:14–15). Zerubbabel resumed worship of Jehovah (Ezra 3:1–6). Ezra prayed, and a revival followed (Ezra 9–10); he read the law, and the people obeyed it (Neh. 8:1–8). The burden of Isaiah's mighty book is evangelistic (cf. chaps. 1; 2; 5; 40–66). Jeremiah lamented over Judah. Ezekiel, like a watchman, warned the wicked to turn and live (33:1–20). Daniel commended soul-winning (12:3). Hosea's prophetic writing described sin, appealed for repentance, and exhorted men to respond to the love of God. Joel called to fasting and prayer, promised the outpouring of God's Spirit, and described multitudes who were in the valley of decision. Amos preached both the personal ("Prepare to meet thy God," 4:12) and the social application ("But let justice roll down as waters, and righteousness as a mighty stream" 5:24 ASV) of the evangelistic message. Jonah led in a mighty city-wide evangelistic preaching mission in Nineveh. Micah voiced the Lord's appeal to his people, foretold Christ's coming, and showed the way to return to God (6:1–8). Nahum exalted God's goodness, warned of his severity, and extolled the evangelist who would bring good tidings of peace (1:15). Habakkuk surveyed world problems and prayed for revival (3:2). Zephaniah predicted the day of wrath and warned people to seek the Lord. Zechariah proclaimed apocalyptic revelations, reproved disobedience, besought men to hearken, return, see, and obey. Malachi declared God's love, rebuked priests and people, promised the Coming One, and exhorted to return to the law of Moses.

John the Baptist.—John the Baptist ushered in New Testament evangelism (Luke 3:18). Preaching and baptizing by immersion were his two principal methods. His essential message was, "The kingdom of heaven is at hand," for which men should repent of sin and believe on the Lamb of God (Matt. 3:1–12; John 1:29–36). His violent language startled men from their self-complacency, and multitudes came from widespread areas (Matt. 3:5) to be baptized by him. Jesus approved the evangelism of John by being baptized by him (Matt. 3:13; Mark 1:9; Luke 3:21).

Jesus.—Jesus is the norm for evangelists. He came to seek and to save those who were lost (Luke 19:10). His dedication to this ministry was incessant (John 9:4). His efforts at soul-winning touched Pharisees, Sadducees, Herodians, Zealots, rulers, Samaritans, Galileans, Greeks, and Romans. He dealt with common people, publicans, lechers, harlots, little children, wise men, soldiers, beggars, fishermen, lovely women, and taxgatherers. He won souls while they were fishing, collecting taxes, sitting on a well curb, in homes, on the highway, at meals, in private conferences, and at social engagements. He used praying, preaching, teaching, and healing for evangelistic purposes. He denounced hypocrites, wept over the erring, exhorted the unrepentant, encouraged the outcast, humbled the haughty, prayed for his murderers, and saved a sinner on a cross beside him. He established the New Testament church and committed to it the keys of the kingdom of heaven (Matt. 16:18–19), which include soul-winning, evangelism, and missions. Just prior to his ascension, he gave the imperative, evangelistic, Great Commission (Matt. 28:18–20).

The twelve apostles.—The apostles took the commission of Jesus seriously (Matt. 28:18–20; Acts 1:8). The revival at Pentecost fixed their standards for evangelistic endeavor. Peter and John were intensely active in Jerusalem, preaching, witnessing, and working miracles amid opposition and persecution. They extended their work to the Samaritans (Acts 8:14). Peter went to the Gentiles in Caesarea (Acts 10:24 ff.) and Antioch (Gal. 2:11). His writing ministry was addressed to the "elect who are the sojourners of the Dispersion in Pontus, Galatia, Cappadocia, Asia, and Bithynia" (I Peter 1:1 ASV). He made good use of the keys of the kingdom (Matt. 16:19). John was exiled on Patmos for his testimony concerning Jesus Christ (Rev. 1:9). Tradition says he spent his latter years at Ephesus, where he won many disciples and wrote books. No book of Scripture is more evangelistic than John's Gospel (John 20:31).

Andrew, called by Jesus to become "a fisher of men" (Mark 1:17), first led his brother Simon to the Lord (John 1:41). He brought the inquiring Greeks to Jesus (John 12:20 ff.). Traditional writings of later centuries say he evangelized in Bithynia, Scythia, and Achaia, where he was crucified. James the son of Zebedee was called to apostleship when Jesus addressed Peter and others, saying, "Fear not; from henceforth thou shalt catch men" (Luke 5:10). Martyrdom cut short his evangelistic career. Traditions about Matthew speak of his preaching 15 years in Palestine, then in foreign countries such as Syria, Macedonia, Media, Parthia, Persia, and Ethiopia. Similar traditions tell of Philip in Phrygia, Bartholomew in Parthia, Thomas in India, James the son of Alpheus in Jerusalem, Judas (called Thaddeus) in Syria and Edessa, and Simon Zelotes in Jerusalem, where he is said to have succeeded James the brother of Jesus as bishop or pastor of the Jerusalem church. Most of these suffered martyrdom for their witnessing for Christ.

The Jerusalem church.—Evangelism in the church at Jerusalem reached its peak at Pentecost (Acts 2). The disciples followed the divine order; namely, prayer (Acts 1:14), personal witnessing to others under the Spirit's power (Acts 2:6-8), and preaching the gospel of Christ (vv. 14 ff.). Three thousand were baptized (v. 41). The program of evangelism was continued thereafter by teaching new converts, fellowship, observance of the Lord's Supper, and prayer (v. 42). The believers soon numbered 5,000 men (Acts 4:4) and continued to multiply greatly (Acts 6:7). Other methods of evangelism were miracles, stewardship of possessions, steadfastness amid vigorous persecution, and sending out missionaries. Peter and John went as evangelists to Samaria. Deacon Philip went to Samaria, Gaza, and Caesarea. Peter went to Lydia, Joppa, and Caesarea, preaching to both Jews and Gentiles. The evangelistic zeal of the church was gradually chilled and eventually killed by the antiracial and antimissionary spirit of the Judaizers, who opposed evangelizing Gentiles unless they would become Jewish proselytes as well as Christians (Acts 15:1, 5).

The deacons.—The term "deacon" (Greek *diakonos*, a table server) in the New Testament indicated filial service to God and fraternal service to men. The seven men appointed in Jerusalem to serve the tables of the poor (Acts 6:2-3) were later called deacons. The deaconship had become an ecclesiastical office when Paul wrote Philippians 1:1 and I Timothy 3:8-13. Although the primary function of deacons was to dispense alms, Stephen and Philip, "full of the Holy Ghost and wisdom" (Acts 6:3), became witnesses of the Word. Stephen was martyred for preaching and debating in favor of the cause of Christ. Philip was known as "the evangelist." His work extended to Samaria (Acts 8:5), Gaza (v. 26), Azotus, and Caesarea (v. 40). He was a settled evangelist in Caesarea more than 20 years later, when Paul and Luke visited in his home (Acts 21:8-10). He fulfilled Paul's requirement of "ruling their children and their own houses well," for his four daughters had the gift of prophecy. Philip, as a deacon-evangelist, exercised such functions as preaching, working miracles, driving out evil spirits, and baptizing. He used both personal soul-winning and mass evangelism.

The apostle Paul.—Evangelism reached its widest geographical results under the apostle Paul. The dynamic basis of his life of evangelism is found in his conversion and call (Acts 9:1-22; 22:6-21; 26:12-18). His experience near Damascus immediately inspired him to evangelize, for "straightway he preached Christ in the synagogues, that he is the Son of God" (Acts 9:20). The story of his evangelistic tours is told by Luke in Acts 13-28. Paul's vision and methods grew with experience. His work on Cyprus was personal soul-winning, dealing with the sorcerer Bar-Jesus and the Roman deputy Sergius Paulus. Seeing the gospel's power, he took the Roman name of Paul and turned toward great Roman city centers in Asia Minor. He did extensive evangelistic work in Pisidian Antioch, Iconium, Lystra, and Derbe. During his second evangelistic tour he saw a vision of a man of Macedonia, which set his mind on winning Roman provinces (Acts 16:9). By the end of the third missionary tour, his expanding vision encompassed the Roman Empire as his evangelistic opportunity, and he planned to visit faraway Spain. During his imprisonment in Rome, he began planning for world conquest.

His zeal to evangelize transcended all racial, political, national, and territorial boundaries. Two great doctrinal tenets which permeated his evangelism were the deity of Christ, as opposed to the Gnostic heresy, and the universality of the gospel, as opposed to the narrow exclusiveness of the Judaizers. The gospel he preached was applied both personally and socially. He exalted the church as the divinely ordained institution for propagating the gospel. Paul's methodology is described in I Corinthians 9:22: "I am made all things to all men, that I might by all means save some." He used every worthy method to win souls. He was perennially a man-to-man, personal soul-winner. He dealt personally with all types of people, such as a Roman proconsul, a sorcerer, a demon-possessed girl, a businesswoman and her household, a jailer, a runaway slave, a Greek physician, a Greek philosopher, a ruler of a synagogue, a professor, sailors and soldiers of the Roman Empire.

His preaching was virile and dynamic. He preached in synagogues, on the streets, before kings, in school buildings; on shipboard, in the face of a howling mob, in prison, in the Athenian marketplace, and on Mars Hill. His evangelistic sermons were varied in style. Beyond preaching he used teaching, miracles, letter-writing, disputation, collecting money, and visitation in his work of evangelism. He was a man of fervent, incessant prayer.

The apostle conserved and perpetuated the results of his soul-winning. He organized churches, ordained ministers and deacons, trained converts by instruction and direction of their Christian activities. His evangelism was geographically inclusive, doctrinally scriptural, personally all-embracing, socially Christlike, and organizationally permanent in its structure. His ideals, his message, and his methods were those of Christ.

HISTORY OF EVANGELISM. The westward march of early Christianity can be traced approximately by the evangelistic emphasis in great cities. These city centers were universally cosmopolitan, prosperous, and influential.

Jerusalem.—This city was the center of evangelism at Pentecost and during the subsequent persecution (Acts 8:1, 4, 14, 25). Evangelism in Antioch and elsewhere had to be approved by the Jerusalem leaders (Acts 15:1-35). Evangelistic zeal in Jerusalem eventually was dissipated by the withering antimissionary spirit of those exclusionists who demanded that Gentile Christians become obedient to the Mosaic law.

Antioch in Syria.—Capital of the Roman province Syria, Antioch was the cradle of Gentile evangelism and missionary aggression during the second half of the first century A.D. Antioch was "Queen of the East," next in importance to Alexandria and Rome. Paul began his three missionary journeys from Antioch (Acts 13:1 ff.; 15:36 ff.; 18:22-23). The disciples were first called Christians there (Acts 11:26). The groves and baths of Daphne, licentious pleasure resorts dedicated to Apollo and Artemis, were five miles from Antioch. Worldliness and wickedness eventually infiltrated the Christian community and chilled its evangelistic fervor. Postapostolic writers attributed the hated doctrines and deeds of the Nicolaitans (Rev. 2:6, 15) to Nicholas, a proselyte from Antioch who was one of the seven (Acts 6:5), but who brought licentiousness into the churches. However, evangelism lasted until John Chrysostom (345-407), a mighty evangelistic preacher and writer who was born and reared in Antioch.

Ephesus and Alexandria.—Strong centers of evangelism and missionary expansion developed in these cities during the second and third centuries, and from them Christianity spread throughout the Roman Empire. Ephesus was visited by Paul during his second and third missionary journeys, at which times the church grew, and rapid progress against the worship of Diana was made. The location, wealth, and political prominence of Ephesus gave it great advantage in spreading the gospel. Across the Mediterranean, Alexandria was strategically located. Tradition strongly states that Mark the writing evangelist carried the gospel there. Christianity spread throughout Egypt, Nubia, Ethiopia, and Abyssinia. One of the first Christian theological schools was founded in Alexandria. Pantenus (A.D. 180), its first head, was followed by Clement (A.D. 202) and Origen (A.D. 232). Origen is credited with temporarily defeating paganism and Gnosticism through his philosophical learning. From Alexandria emerged such Christian writers as Julius Africanus, Dionysius, Gregory, and Eusebius. The Gnostic heresy, denying the essential deity of Jesus, took its toll both in Ephesus and Alexandria.

Constantinople.—This was the city inaugurated as the new seat of the Roman Empire in A.D. 330 by Constantine. For three centuries it was characterized by a strong theological and ecclesiastical spirit. Its evangelistic zeal radiated Christianity as far as Ireland, Scotland, and Germany. Important ecumenical councils were held here, shaping doctrinal thought for centuries. Evangelism was gradually subdued and finally destroyed by the union of church and state, by formalism in worship, by liturgy supplanting spirituality, and by the spread of Mohammedanism.

Rome.—This was the center of evangelistic aggression from about 600 to 1050, and beyond. Evangelism has intermittently flourished and faded there until this day. Gibbon in his *Decline and Fall of the Roman Empire* accounts for the evangelistic victories of Christianity by (a) the zeal of the early Christians; (b) their doctrinal emphasis on the resurrection, immortality, future rewards for righteousness, and the promise of the return of the Lord Jesus Christ; (c) the preaching and character of the Christians; (d) the perfect life of Jesus as an incentive for noble living; and (e) strong ecclesiastical organization.

Evangelism spread from Rome to the Irish, Scotch, Anglo-Saxons, Germans, and Scandinavians. In 597 a monk named Augustine was sent to preach to the Anglo-Saxons. They in turn evangelized the Germans across the Rhine, the Franks, and the Frisians. The Anglo-Saxon Boniface became the apostle to Germany. In the ninth century the Germans evangelized Denmark, Norway, and Sweden. Greenland, Iceland, and other islands were turned to Christianity.

Unfortunately, the dying Latin language was retained in the liturgy and the Latin Vulgate. Eventually, Bible instruction died with the language, and biblical theology decayed. Infant baptism became practically universal. Preaching and personal soul-winning sadly declined. Monasteries at first fostered Bible scholarship, scriptural teaching, evangelistic preaching, and Christian service; but eventually, they deteriorated in zeal and power. Indulgences, pardons for sin purchased with money to the church, supplanted repentance; confession to priests replaced confession to God; faith in the saving power of the church and its ordinances supplanted faith in Jesus Christ. Some anti-Catholic evangelism flourished during this period under dissenting believers, such as the Nestorians, Paulicans, Bogomiles, and others. In spite of persecution, they believed and practiced many biblical teachings. Sporadic efforts, such as those under Francis of Assisi (1182-1226) and Savonarola (1452-98) in Florence, continued for centuries within the Roman Church.

France.—Some aggressive evangelism flourished in France during the 12th, 13th, and 14th centuries, especially when the papacy was located at Avignon (1309-77). This was manifested by the growing power of the pope and was expressed in the aggressive spirit of the Crusades. However, the struggle for power between the pope and the state rulers, schism in the church, and the unholy results of the Crusades prevented any very significant, permanent contribution being made to evangelism. An important revival occurred in the Rhine Valley under John Tauler (1300-61), the greatest of the mystics. His followers emphasized prayer and union with God, and his influence lasted more than 100 years.

Protestant evangelism flourished in France under John Calvin (1509-64). This highly educated priest, converted from Roman Catholicism, was driven to Geneva by persecution. He became the chief preacher, teacher of theology, and writer of Protestantism following Luther. Writing was his most effective method of propagating his beliefs. His *Institutes of the Christian Religion* shook Protestantism. His theological tenets became directives for multitudes in Italy, Poland, Germany, Netherlands, England, Scotland, and the American colonies. The French Huguenots, Scottish Covenanters, English Puritans, and American Pilgrim Fathers were all profoundly influenced by his evangelistic writings on doctrine. Religious wars largely ended aggressive evangelism in France after Calvin.

Germany.—During the 16th century study of the Bible kindled such evangelistic fires in Germany and beyond in Western Europe that the ecclesiastical walls of Roman Catholicism were burned down sufficiently for the spirit of New Testament Christianity to be freed. The influence of John Wycliffe of England (1320–84) reached John Huss of Bohemia (d. 1415), encouraging him and his followers to read and teach the Bible. Martin Luther (1483–1546), an Augustinian monk of Germany, came under the influence of the Hussites. The monastery gave him ample time for Bible study. The text, "The just shall live by faith," became the rallying point of his thinking, leading him to break with the Roman Catholic Church. In 1517 he nailed 95 theses, or religious propositions, to the cathedral door at Wittenberg, Germany. This action set in motion the Protestant Reformation, the mightiest evangelistic movement since Pentecost. The remaining 30 years of Luther's life were spent in vigorous evangelism. Luther, one of the most versatile evangelists of Christian history, was preacher, teacher, scholar, debater, translator and expositor of the Bible, author, hymn writer, organizer, and personal soul-winner.

Luther's evangelism transformed the religious life of most of Western Europe. Contemporary with Luther and followed by him came Zwingli of Switzerland, Calvin of France, Knox of Scotland, and the Anabaptists. Luther's influence also spread into Scandinavia, Poland, Bavaria, Bohemia, Moravia, etc. The Lutheran denomination is one of the strongest in America, attesting the strength of his evangelism. After Luther vital Christianity was preserved in Germany largely through a movement called Pietism, which flourished in spite of the ravages of religious wars, dogmatic orthodox controversy, and heterodox rationalism. Some leading German Pietists who kept evangelism alive were John Arndt (1555–1621), Paul Gerhardt (1607–76), Philip Jakob Spener (1663–1729), the New Testament interpreter Albrecht Bengel (1687–1752), and Count Nicolaus Ludwig Zinzendorf (1700–60). Their methods were devotional hymn singing, incessant preaching of the doctrines of grace, distribution of the Scriptures, and educational institutions for training ministers and missionaries.

Evangelism during the Protestant Reformation reached a high standard with the Anabaptists, so called for demanding believer's baptism of those who had been sprinkled in infancy. Conrad Grebel broke with Zwingli. Feliz Manz, George Blaurock, and Wilhelm Reublin were vigorous evangelists. The latter, driven to Germany by persecution, won Balthasar Hubmaier to his belief. Hubmaier, a learned doctor of theology, baptized no less than 6,000 in one year. He, Manz, and others suffered martyrdom, but their preaching and writing spread their doctrines as far as England. "With respect to the relationship between Anabaptists and Baptists, it is safe to say that the latter are the spiritual descendants of *some* of the former." Convictions about scriptural doctrines have kept alive the evangelistic zeal of early Anabaptists and modern Baptists.

Spain and Portugal.—The Iberian Peninsula has never produced vital, New Testament evangelism. Spain's chief methods of preservation of the Catholic faith have been a state church, the Inquisition, and persecution of dissenters. Spanish and Portuguese settlements in America experienced forceful imposition of Catholicism upon the natives, with occasional exceptions of benevolence. It is "a story of attempted cooperation in the common service of God and Mammon and Moloch."

Great Britain.—Evangelism in the British Isles has run the scale of all types and degrees, including missionary conquest of the native Angles, persecution, compulsory state church membership, zealous preaching during the Protestant Reformation, Wesleyan revivalism, foreign missions, and fervent pastoral evangelism. The forerunners of modern evangelism in Britain were John Wycliffe and others who translated the Scriptures. The humble Lollards interpreted the Bible and were led to oppose the Romanists in theology and social applications of the gospel. John Knox (1505–72) of Scotland was Britain's outstanding evangelist of the Protestant Reformation. He was forceful, earnest, courageous, and a dynamic doctrinal preacher, setting the pattern for evangelism in his time. Scotland followed him in forsaking Catholicism. Anabaptists appeared in England early in the 16th century. By 1573 there were at least 50,000, evangelistically preaching the doctrines of the Bible as the rule of faith and practice, separation of church and state, and baptism for believers only. The 17th century witnessed revival under the Puritans, encouraged by writings of John Bunyan (*q.v.*) and John Milton.

British evangelism reached its peak in the Wesleyan revivals of the 18th century, against a background of moral and spiritual degeneration. John and Charles Wesley, George Whitefield, and others were the leaders. These men were of the "Holy Club" of Oxford students, nicknamed the Methodists. Their emphasis was on the necessity for regeneration rather than mere state church membership. Whitefield (1714–70) was the spell-binding preacher; Charles Wesley (1707–88), the sweet-spirited hymn writer; and John Wesley (1703–91), the central figure, an indefatigable worker, incessant personal soul-winner, scholarly thinker, and genius in organization. He studied, preached, taught, wrote, collected money, erected chapels, and led moral movements for social welfare. Before his death he was directing 511 preachers on definite preaching circuits. He organized 120,000 followers into "societies" which emerged into Methodist churches. His influence spread throughout England, Scotland, Wales, Ireland, and the American colonies. The Wesleyan revivals produced philanthropy, abolished slavery, relieved penal laws, reformed prisons, and gave rise to popular education. England was saved from the counterpart of the French Revolution, which began in 1789.

Modern foreign missions was begun by the Baptist cobbler, William Carey (q.v.) (1761-1834) of Northamptonshire, who went to India in 1793. Pastoral evangelism in Britain reached its peak with Charles Haddon Spurgeon (1834-92) in the Baptist Metropolitan Tabernacle in London. His evangelistic influence circled the globe through his personal soul-winning, expository preaching, publication of 50 volumes of sermons, editorial and expository writing, organization of Spurgeon's College for training ministers, and many charitable programs.

Occasional revival fires have burned during preaching missions led by American evangelists such as Dwight L. Moody and Billy Graham. The Moody revivals were strengthened by the co-operation of Henry Drummond of Scotland, who continued the revival efforts among students after he became professor in the University of Glasgow. A revival swept Wales in 1904-06. Under the leadership of a young ministerial student, Evan John Roberts, the intensely religious spirit of the Welsh was inflamed like spontaneous combustion. There was a minimum of preaching and no organization. Youth were the leaders in singing, prayer, and testimony during long night sessions. Over 100,000 professed conversion in a population of 2,000,000. There were amazing results in elimination of feuding, drunkenness, profanity, and dishonesty. The revival greatly promoted good literature, charity, better education, and happier home life.

HISTORY OF EVANGELISM IN AMERICA. Evangelism early became vital in the religious life of North America. Like a mountain stream, it has been alternately swift and stagnant, now a torrent and now smooth, usually refreshing but occasionally too turbulent. The net results have been amazingly beneficial.

Colonial America and the United States.—Aggressive evangelism had its birth in New England in 1734 under the preaching of Jonathan Edwards (1703-58), after some embryonic movements previously. Edwards' preaching at Northampton, Mass., emphasizing justification by faith, initiated the Great Awakening, which spread throughout the American colonies. The revival was strengthened by the work of George Whitefield of England, Gilbert Tennett of Pennsylvania, Theodore Frelinghuysen of New Jersey, and many others. Whitefield's influence upon religious life in the South appears to have been indirect. Although he preached from Georgia northward, he was received more warmly in the Northern colonies than in the Southern. The evangelistic tide ebbed during the wars of the middle of the century but flooded again after the American Revolution. Revivals became prominent in colleges such as Dartmouth in 1781, Yale and Princeton in 1783. The Revival of 1800 (approximately 1785-1812) produced mighty results in fixing the pattern of denominational life in the United States. The preaching of Charles Grandison Finney (1790-1875) sustained evangelism in the northeastern states during the middle of the 19th century. A mighty wave of evangelism by laymen swept the Northern states in 1857-58 but was dissipated by the Civil War. A spontaneous torrent of fervent evangelism moved through the Southern armies during this period. Following the war, evangelistic standards were set by Dwight L. Moody on the highly organized, city-wide, union plan. Moody's style has been followed by such evangelists as B. Fay Mills, Reuben A. Torrey, J. Wilbur Chapman, Major W. E. Penn (q.v.), William A. (Billy) Sunday, and others.

Southern Baptist Convention.—The Southern Baptist Convention was organized in 1845 with evangelism at home and abroad as its primary purpose. During the preceding century intrepid pioneer Baptist evangelists, such as Jeremiah Walker and Benjamin Watkins of Virginia, Shubal Stearns (q.v.) and Thomas Ethridge of North Carolina, Daniel Marshall (q.v.) of Georgia, Richard Curtis, Jr. (q.v.), of Mississippi, had laid the foundations. The Southern Baptist Convention immediately organized a "Board of Domestic Missions" (Marion, Ala., 1845) to evangelize Negroes, Indians, and the Catholics around New Orleans. (The name was changed in 1882 to Home Mission Board.) Its evangelism has been extended to many bilingual groups, the deaf, mountaineers, Jews, soldiers, migrants, and city slum dwellers. Its missions extend to Cuba, the Canal Zone, the far West, and Alaska. The Home Mission Board's Department of Evangelism has been the pace-setter for Southern Baptists, specializing in city-wide and association-wide simultaneous campaigns. State mission boards have followed with secretaries of evangelism vigorously promoting urban and rural programs, creating evangelistic literature, holding statewide and associational conferences, establishing new preaching stations, publicizing methods and results of soul-winning. Pastoral evangelism and perennial church programs have been increasingly emphasized. Personal soul-winning, preaching in meetings of one to three weeks' duration, Sunday school evangelism, distribution of tracts, youth revivals, establishment of branch churches, organized visitation evangelism by laymen, and many other methods have been used extensively and successfully. During the two decades 1936-56 the evangelistic advances of Southern Baptists are revealed in the following statistics of baptisms:

Year	Baptisms
1936	191,993
1937	204,567
1938	256,814
1939	269,155
1940	245,500
1941	209,593
1942	209,127
1943	202,301
1944	216,820
1945	256,699
1946	253,361
1947	285,152
1948	310,226
1949	334,892
1950	376,085
1951	375,525
1952	354,384
1953	361,835
1954	396,857
1955	416,867

American (formerly Northern) Baptist Convention.—The Northern Baptist Convention was organized in Washington, D. C., May 17, 1907, co-ordinating the work of the existing American Baptist Publication Society, American Baptist Missionary Union, and American Baptist Home Mission Society, the last of which has been the convention's chief agency for promotion of evangelism. The name was changed to American Baptist Convention on May 24, 1950. In 1908 the convention supported two evangelists-at-large, Cornelius Woelfkin and James Allan Francis, and co-operated with 14 state Baptist conventions in supporting evangelists. The evangelists-at-large were discontinued in 1911, and co-operation with the states was extended. By 1919 the territory had been divided into Eastern, Central, and Western districts or divisions, with a director or general evangelist for each.

The superintendents (sometimes called secretaries) of evangelism for the Home Mission Society have been as follows: Herbert F. Stilwell (1919–26), Benjamin T. Livingstone (1926–30), Charles S. Detweiler (1930–36), Walter E. Woodbury (1936–56). Stilwell's work was devoted to holding evangelistic conferences with preachers, promoting simultaneous campaigns, and aiding in the development of state evangelistic programs. Livingstone introduced throughout the Northern Baptist area a program called Friendly Visitation Evangelism for Laymen. Detweiler administered the growing funds of the Home Mission Society appropriated for co-operation with state evangelistic groups and promoted use of an "Aid to Devotional Reading of the Bible," which he wrote for evangelistic purposes. Woodbury's 20 years of fruitful work were given to versatile methods of promotion, such as intensive organization of perennial programs in seven regional areas, annual evangelistic conferences at Green Lake, Wis., and director of a movement called Printed Page Evangelism. Because of the declining popularity of the protracted meeting or preaching mission method in the Northern states, Woodbury majored on promoting and directing five-day home visitation crusades, both in individual churches and in simultaneous city-wide campaigns, in which he trained hundreds of picked lay workers to go in teams of two into homes for personal soul-winning. He directed a program of "Winning the Children for Christ" through a team of seven women evangelists. His department employed a full-time director of evangelism for American Baptist youth. Woodbury co-operated with the Evangelistic Department of the National Council of Churches. During his last year in office (1955), the convention reported 62,625 baptisms, one to every 24.1 members, the best ratio reported in the 20 years that records have been kept.

The American Baptist Convention fosters missionary evangelism among Negroes, Indians, Mexicans, Cubans, and Porto Ricans, through methods such as preaching, educational institutions, literature, social work, and colportage.

Negro Baptists.—Negro Baptists, who number over 7,000,000, have two conventions: the National Baptist Convention of America, organized in 1895, and the National Baptist Convention of the United States of America, Incorporated, which separated from the original body in 1915. Their evangelism has been intensively promoted within the churches rather than through extensive organized campaigns, due largely to economic reasons. The two Baptist conventions comprise practically half the Negro population in America. Eloquent, imaginative, and emotional preaching has been the chief method of evangelism. Fervent, spiritual congregational singing has been characteristic.

REVIVALS IN AMERICA. American evangelism has moved forward through four mighty revival periods and has been retarded by wars and depression.

The Great Awakening.—The Great Awakening (1734–70, approximately) was contemporary with the Wesleyan Revival in England. It had as a background the transplanting of various European groups in colonial America, usually resulting in disastrous spiritual degeneration, but also in introducing Puritanism, Pietism, and other spiritual influences from Europe. Rationalism from Germany, atheism from France, and deism from England fostered godlessness and immorality. State church control bred coldness in worship and persecution of dissenters. The "Half-way Covenant" adopted in 1662 in Massachusetts, admitting children of faithful parents into full church membership without personal Christian experience, had filled churches with the unregenerate. Fidelity to the marriage vow often was sneered at. Dissenters like Quakers and Baptists were being imprisoned, flogged, fined, and banished. Against this dark background evangelistic fires were kindled by great preaching. The flames first burst out in Northampton, Mass., under Jonathan Edwards

(Congregationalist). They were fanned by the mighty sermons of Gilbert Tennett (Presbyterian) and his colleagues of the Log College evangelists in Pennsylvania, by Theodore J. Frelinghuysen (Dutch Reformed) in New Jersey, and by scores of others of lesser fame but similar passion.

The southern phase of the revival (1754–90, approximately) resulted in a tremendous increase in the number of Baptists. Shubal Stearns (q.v.) and Daniel Marshall (q.v.), products of the New England awakening, came to North Carolina in 1755 and established the Sandy Creek Church, out of which grew 42 churches in 17 years. The itinerant ministry of these men and their converts, which extended throughout the south and west, brought about a general awakening in those regions. The preaching of Marshall, Samuel Harris, and other evangelists, for example, effected a revival in Virginia by which Baptists increased in 36 years from six small churches in 1754 to 204 churches with 20,443 members in 1790. During this period many migrated to Kentucky, where Baptists, largely through revivals, grew in eight years from three small churches to 42 churches with a membership of 3,105. Baptists multiplied proportionately in North Carolina, South Carolina, Georgia, and Tennessee.

The Great Awakening firmly fixed aggressive evangelism in the religious life of America. Christianity was restored to favor, dead churches were quickened into new life, and home life was purified. Missions and education became a fixed part of the Christian responsibility. For the first time in the history of government, absolute religious liberty was granted by Roger Williams to citizens of Providence Plantations in Rhode Island (1636). Within a generation about one seventh of the population of New England was converted, and corresponding numbers in other colonies.

The revival of 1800.—This revival had scattered beginnings in churches and colleges for nearly 20 years following the Revolutionary War. The revival reached its peak about 1800 but continued until the War of 1812. King George's War, the French and Indian War, and the Revolution wrought spiritual havoc to the results of the Great Awakening. Godless immorality, atheism in colleges, drunkenness in society, and infidelity in marriage prevailed. There were few trained ministers, most of whom were formalistic and spiritually powerless. But toward the dawn of the new century, isolated spontaneous revivals began to appear. Religious awakenings came in colleges such as Dartmouth, Yale, Princeton, Hampden-Sydney, Williams, and others. Timothy Dwight, grandson of Jonathan Edwards, became president of Yale in 1795. He and a student named Lyman Beecher led the college in a mighty revival beginning in 1802.

Regional revivals in churches first began about 1785 along the James River in Virginia among some praying Baptists now free from persecution by state church officials. These revivals soon spread south into Georgia. A notable revival appeared in Lee, Mass., in 1792 and spread through New England. Western Pennsylvania had a strong manifestation of power in 1795 and again from 1802 to 1804. The most spectacular manifestations came among the Scotch-Irish settlers in the mountains of eastern Kentucky and Tennessee. Camp meetings began to draw people from great distances to stay long periods, hearing continuous preaching from groups of preachers. These revivals began to produce "the jerks," violent physical demonstrations of nervous excitement, moaning, fainting, people lying on the ground like dead, some shrieking to God for mercy. The sermons centered on fear of damnation and punishment in hell fire.

In spite of these emotional excesses in some areas, vast permanent influences for good were set in motion at home and abroad. Atheism in colleges received a body blow from which it did not recover for a century. The Presbyterians were multiplied by three; the Baptists, by four; the Methodists, by five. Denominational life was fixed by the issuance of the first denominational papers, by organization for sending out home missionaries, by vast multiplication of denominational colleges, by establishment of orphanages, and by the beginning of the Sunday school movement. The famous "Haystack Prayer Meeting" at Williams College in 1806 and the subsequent influence of its leader, Samuel J. Mills, while in Andover Seminary led in 1812 to sending Adoniram Judson (q.v.), Luther Rice (q.v.), Gordon Hall, Samuel Nott, and Samuel Newell to India as America's first foreign missionaries. The hundreds of volunteers for the ministry coming from the college revivals demanded theological seminaries such as Andover, Princeton, Union in Virginia, and Yale Divinity School.

Revival of 1857–58.—This revival resembled a nation-wide laymen's prayer meeting. The years 1848–57 had been prosperous. The gold rush to California, expanding railroads and industries, growing cities and dying churches, worldly pleasure and low morals characterized the times. Wall Street broke, and depression began in Oct., 1857. A laymen's noonday prayer meeting was started on Fulton Street, New York, and the laymen's weekday prayer meeting movement spread over the Northern states. Amazing spiritual results came in 1858, when at least a million people united with churches. The Revival of 1857–58 was confined almost wholly to Northern states, its strength being abated by the Civil War.

Revivals in the Confederate army.—Revivals swept the Confederate armies in unusual power during the latter part of the Civil War, following the drunkenness, gambling, vice, degeneration of morals, and decline of church life earlier in the conflict. Great Christian leaders like Robert E. Lee, Stonewall Jackson, and Jefferson Davis exerted their influence for God.

Chaplains and many high-ranking officers were aggressive spiritual leaders and soul-winners, such as Kirby Smith, J. E. B. Stuart, John B. Gordon, J. William Jones (q.v.), D. H. Hill, W. N. Pendleton, M. P. Lowrey (q.v.), J. B. Gambrell (q.v.), William W. Bennett, Lansing Burroughs, Sr. (q.v.), William E. Hatcher, Sr. (q.v.), John A. Broadus (q.v.), and hundreds of others. A tidal wave of revival increased as the war moved on. Soul-winning, prayer meetings in camp, impassioned evangelistic preaching, and distribution of hundreds of thousands of Bibles and tracts were some of the methods used. It is said that at least 150,000 soldiers were converted, among them many generals and high officers. Thousands left the army to enter the ministry or missionary service. The Christian spirit in the revival was taken home to enable the Southern people to go spiritually victorious through military defeat and harsh reconstruction.

EVANGELISTIC PERSONALITIES INFLUENCING BAPTISTS. Baptists in the colonies had been persecuted too persistently to prosper and produce great leaders before the Great Awakening. Out of that revival Baptists began to emerge. They have been influenced strongly by great evangelists of other denominations.

1. Jonathan Edwards (1703–58), a Congregationalist, combined the powers of a scholarly mind and a fervent heart in preaching doctrinal sermons. Pulpiteering was his mightiest force, Calvinism his doctrinal pattern, and Bible exposition his method. He stirred both intellect and emotions. It is not difficult to trace some broad characteristics of Baptist evangelistic preaching back to the influence of Edwards.

2. George Whitefield (1714–70), a Church of England preacher turned Methodist, was at 25 England's most popular preacher, drawing audiences by the thousands, swaying them with emotional, musical voice and sensational preaching. He preached grace, regeneration, and perseverance of the saints. He traveled to America 13 times, preaching from Georgia to New England. He preached 18,000 times in 34 years. Whitefield is the prototype of hosts of Baptist itinerant evangelists who never serve as pastors but go everywhere preaching to win souls, leaving matters of church membership, Bible teaching, indoctrination, and enlistment of the converts to settled pastors.

3. Isaac Backus who was born in Connecticut in 1724, Shubal Stearns who was born in Boston in 1706, and Daniel Marshall who was born in Connecticut in 1706, were converted in the Great Awakening, and later became Baptists through Bible study concerning controversy about infant baptism, religious liberty, and the Established Church. Backus helped organize a Baptist church at Middleborough, Mass., in 1756, of which he was pastor 50 years. The rapid growth of Baptists in New England was in a large measure due to his influence. He became the vigorous advocate of freedom of religion and separation of church and state, doctrines always so dear to Baptists. Stearns, who was like Whitefield in magnetic, powerful preaching, went South in 1754 to Virginia and later to North Carolina. He organized the Sandy Creek Church, Guilford County, N. C., and later the Sandy Creek Association. It later was divided into three associations, in Virginia, North Carolina, and South Carolina, each of which multiplied in membership rapidly. Daniel Marshall, brother-in-law to Stearns, organized churches in North Carolina and Virginia. Having already made a truly apostolic record, Marshall at 64 moved into Georgia in 1771, establishing the first Baptist church in Georgia at "Old Kiokee." When arrested for preaching, he converted both the constable and the magistrate. He lived to see six Baptist churches in Georgia and the Georgia Association formed (1784). His son Abraham Marshall (q.v.) continued his pioneer, itinerant evangelizing and organization of churches.

4. Charles Grandison Finney (1792–1875), Presbyterian revivalist, pastor, and educator, went far to crystallize methods of the "protracted meeting" conducted by itinerant evangelists and has tremendously influenced Baptists as well as other evangelicals. His life span bridged the gap between John Wesley and Dwight L. Moody. A lawyer in Adams, N. Y., converted at 29, he said he had a retainer from the Lord Jesus Christ to plead his cause. He conducted protracted meetings in many great cities of the Northeast, during which tens of thousands were converted. With legal logic and Scripture texts, he refuted the extreme Calvinism which denied use of one's will in repentance or use of one's efforts to win others to Christ. He preached without notes, standing in the aisle level with people rather than from a high "pill-box" pulpit. He demanded the use of one's will according to his knowledge, emphasized prayer and baptism of the Holy Spirit, and adopted the Methodists' plan of the "anxious seat" and "inquiry room." During his latter years he was president of Oberlin College, where he lectured, trained young evangelists, and wrote his *Revival Lectures*, still widely read. His discussions on prayer, the Holy Spirit, preparation for a revival, wisdom in soul-winning, instruction to sinners and converts, evangelistic sermonizing, and conservation of results are widely influential today.

5. Dwight L. Moody (1837–99), Congregationalist, set the standard for mass evangelism for all denominations during two generations following the Civil War. Utilizing the successful methods of Finney and others, he multiplied and perfected methods of preparation and publicity in a city before the start of the preaching mission, use of theaters and tents, organization of district prayer meetings, house-to-house solicitation for attendance, strong finance committee work, use of large groups of other preachers for extension services in shops and schools, daily conferences with the workers for prayer and discussion of promotion methods, and em-

phasis on the ministry of music through the leadership of a professional song leader. As never before, he perfected methods of uniting all denominations into co-operative campaigns. His evangelism exerted nation-wide and worldwide influence on moral and spiritual affairs. His methods have been followed by all subsequent union evangelists, such as Mills, Chapman, Reuben A. Torrey, "Gipsy" Smith, Billy Sunday, George Stuart, Sam Jones, and Billy Graham.

ORGANIZED MASS EVANGELISM. This is the name given to all types of approach to people in groups. Its methods have gradually evolved from the revival times of Jonathan Edwards to the present. Mass evangelism has always been criticized by some, usually the highly intellectual. Certainly, misuses of mass evangelism have merited criticism. Mass psychology has been used at times to sway groups into excessive emotions, with disastrous reactions. Superficial results come when people join a church under mere impulse and excitement. Mass evangelism occasionally has received some hard body blows from its advocates because of their greediness for a stupendous "love offering," their unworthy desire to report large numbers of converts, their crude antics and slangy jokes to attract crowds, their loose criticism of churches and preachers, their unsound theology and lack of reverence toward God, or their cheap sensationalism. In spite of occasional defects of evangelists, however, mass evangelism itself has brought infinitely great spiritual values. It has capitalized on the inspiration of the crowds to attract multiplied millions to hear the gospel and to accept Christ. Higher social and civic ideals have been advanced, vice and the liquor traffic have often been curtailed, home life has been purified, and church life has been strengthened. Better relations between denominations have been formed, multitudes of youth have been inspired to enter the ministry or missionary careers, and denominations have advanced in mighty programs of education and missions, through the results of organized mass evangelism. It has been generally true that Baptists have co-operated in union mass meetings, and they have been consistent in using mass evangelism themselves. Even so, Baptists produced no world-famous mass evangelist until Billy Graham.

CHURCH-CENTERED EVANGELISM. Baptists have generally concentrated efforts on church-centered evangelism rather than the out-of-the-church, tabernacle type. The "keys of the kingdom" (Matt. 16:18-19), given by Christ specifically to the church, are interpreted by Baptists to mean soul-winning, evangelism, and missions. Baptists find ingatherings of members better in church-centered evangelism and employ it because they do not make use of infant baptism, immigration, or a state church to build membership. In church-centered programs Southern Baptists have used all methods, such as individual church revival meetings, educational evangelism, visitation evangelism, extension services, radio, new missions, and distribution of literature, becoming all things to all men that they might win some. The church organizations have been mighty forces for church-centered evangelism. The mission boards have promoted evangelism in mission stations with the hope that they will eventually become churches. Traditionally, simultaneous crusades have been held in church buildings rather than tabernacles or theaters. Associational and state evangelistic conferences have majored on promoting church-centered perennial programs of evangelism.

DENOMINATIONAL EVANGELISTS. Although famous union evangelists have been scarce among Baptists, the ranks of dynamic denominational evangelists among Southern Baptists have been full and illustrious.

1. Major W. E. Penn (1832-95) was an outstanding pioneer among Southern Baptist full-time evangelists. Born in Tennessee, he became a major in the Confederate army. Like Finney, he turned from the practice of law to evangelism at 43. He conducted meetings, organized like Moody's, in Texas, California, many Southern states, England, and Scotland; but, unlike Moody, his meetings were sponsored by Baptist churches only. He preached doctrines of grace with special emphasis on Baptist distinctives. He had a companion song leader, used a portable organ, called sinners to the "anxious seat," prevailed in prayer, studiously avoided clap-trap sensationalism while using a lawyer's skill in denouncing hypocrisy and appealing for a decision for Christ. It is estimated that converts in his revivals numbered about 150,000, nine tenths of whom joined Baptist churches. A vast number of youth volunteered for the ministry under his preaching.

2. Thomas Theodore Martin (q.v.) was born in Mississippi in 1862, first a teacher, then a pastor. He became one of Southern Baptists' most unusual, yet typical professional evangelists. His major emphasis was on teaching the plan of salvation. He also diligently expounded the Bible on the doctrines of the church, heaven and hell, the second coming of Christ, etc. He cared little for publicity, avoided emotional appeals, directed his appeals to the intellect with fiery logic, and proved his points by Bible exposition. Avoiding self-publicity, he never revealed the numbers of the converts in his meetings. He attracted intense admirers and also bitter critics, especially among other denominations when he expounded Baptist beliefs. During his latter years he devoted much time to an organization of young preachers called Blue Mountain Evangelists, which was not perpetuated after his death. In his latter days he became consumed with fighting the theory of evolution and lost some of his evangelistic leadership. He was the author of about 15 volumes on doctrinal subjects and against evolution. He was the most influential evangelist in the mid-South in the zenith of his power.

3. George W. Truett (q.v.) (1867-1944),

more than any other American, shaped the life of Baptists through pastoral evangelism. His Christlike character, his clear-voiced, silver-tongued oratory, his power to stir the deeper emotions, his pastor heart, and his impassioned zeal for souls made him undisputed leader of the growing forces of Southern Baptists. During his pastorate (1897–1944) the First Baptist Church, Dallas, Tex., became the largest white Baptist church in the world. His extensive evangelistic efforts reached out in great church- and city-wide Baptist revivals, in evangelistic conferences, in keeping evangelism in the forefront while he was president of the Southern Baptist Convention and of the Baptist World Alliance. The Commission on Evangelism of the Baptist World Alliance was instituted in 1939 while he was president. He preached to cowboy groups in Texas, filled extensive engagements in colleges, held camp meetings in his native North Carolina hills, and preached frequently on the mission fields of Europe and South America. He drew capacity crowds as no other Southern Baptist ever did. He avoided excessive emotional demonstrations, sensationalism, and compromise, as well as alliances with other denominations which might have weakened his doctrinal message. He urged Southern Baptists to remain true to the Bible and to preach the doctrines of grace; yet he avoided offense to others while preaching his Baptist convictions. Only the records of heaven can tell how much his influence helped Southern Baptists to become the most evangelistic and most rapidly growing denomination in the 20th century.

4. Educational evangelists compose another category. Most of the outstanding evangelists, such as Spurgeon, Edwards, Tennett, Finney, Moody, and others, in their latter years have promoted education for young evangelists. This has been true among Southern Baptists with Lee Rutland Scarborough (*q.v.*), Edgar Young Mullins (*q.v.*), John R. Sampey (*q.v.*), William Wistar Hamilton, Sr., Ellis Adams Fuller (*q.v.*), and others. Scarborough (1870–1945) is typical. He was a personal soul-winner, an impassioned evangelistic preacher in church revivals, founder of the chair of evangelism and its professor while a faculty member and later while president of Southwestern Baptist Theological Seminary, author of a number of books on evangelism, and leader of a two-year program of evangelism (1938–40) while president of the Southern Baptist Convention. The three oldest Convention-owned seminaries, Southern Baptist Theological Seminary at Louisville, Southwestern Baptist Theological Seminary at Fort Worth, and New Orleans Baptist Theological Seminary at New Orleans, through the years have been strongly evangelistic and missionary under the influence of the above-mentioned and other leaders and authors. The younger seminaries are following the same pattern.

5. William Wistar Hamilton, Sr. (1868–   ), is typical of Southern Baptist mission board leaders of evangelism. Holding the Th.D. degree from Southern Seminary, successful as a pastor and later as president of the Baptist Bible Institute (now New Orleans Baptist Theological Seminary), author of many books on evangelism, he served two periods, 1906–09 and 1918–21, as superintendent of evangelism for the Home Mission Board. He maintained a large staff of evangelists and specialized in city-wide simultaneous meetings. He kept evangelism vibrant and on a high plane, concentrated in church buildings rather than union meetings in tabernacles or tents, even during the heyday of popularity of the Billy Sunday type of sensational union meetings. His influence upon Southern Baptist evangelism was far-reaching, typical of the methods used by Home Mission Board evangelists. Other Home Mission Board superintendents have been Weston Bruner, 1910–17; O. E. Bryan, 1922–23; Ellis A. Fuller, 1925–27; Roland Q. Leavell, 1937–42; Fred Eastham, 1942–46; C. E. Matthews, 1947–55; Leonard Sanderson, 1955–   .

TRENDS IN CURRENT EVANGELISM. Revivalists, methods, and manifestations differ, but the fire of evangelism is the same. All revivals have had the background of low moral and spiritual conditions, war, or chaotic financial situations. Revivals have started usually with church people and have been accompanied by prayer, concern for souls, and manifestations of divine power. Following World War I, new sects appeared with aggressive evangelism and rapid growth, working usually on the outskirts of cities among the less educated people, preaching holiness, calling themselves various names, such as Adventists, Pentecostals, Church of God, Nazarenes, and Jehovah's Witnesses. Some of these are growing into sizable denominations. In college and wealthy circles the Oxford Group Movement gained some headway by inviting prominent people to their "houseparties" to witness to them, but the movement has waned. During and after World War II, the Youth for Christ movement—in which union Saturday night youth meetings were held, with evangelistic singing, witnessing, and youth sermons—flourished all over the nation and in some foreign countries, but its popularity is on the wane. National hook-up radio programs have been used, such as the *Lutheran Hour* with Walter Maier as preacher, the *Old Fashioned Revival Hour* with Charles Fuller as preacher, and *The Hour of Decision* with Billy Graham as preacher. The *Baptist Hour* by the Radio and Television Commission of the Southern Baptist Convention has combined evangelism with devotion, Bible exposition, and doctrine. Television is slowly moving into the evangelistic field. The upsurge of evangelism since World War II in other countries has brought extensive results in the two defeated nations, Germany and Japan. The crusades of Billy Graham in England, Scotland, continental Europe, and India have brought results placing him as the peer of Edwards, Finney, and Sunday.

Personal soul-winning.—Emphasis on personal soul-winning has been growing steadily since

Moody's campaigns. His initial interest in evangelism began with soul-winning in the Chicago Y.M.C.A. and among soldiers in the Civil War. He held training classes for soul-winners during his campaigns and initiated similar courses in Moody Bible Institute. Such organized personal work has been utilized by Chapman, Torrey, Sunday, Hamilton, Graham, and virtually all evangelists. Volumes of books and tracts have been written on methods of personal work. Guy Black of the Methodist church has promoted visitation evangelism by teams of two, based on Luke 10:1-17, sometimes eliminating preaching. Visitation evangelism has been publicized by A. Earl Kernahan, Dawson C. Bryan, and others, and has been used widely by Walter E. Woodbury and associates in the Department of Evangelism of the American Baptist Home Mission Society. This type of evangelism has increased in popularity with the increasing difficulty of drawing unbelievers into preaching services. Its weakness is in the tendency to enrol people in the churches without deep convictions aroused by burdened prayer and impassioned gospel preaching.

Perennial pastoral evangelism.—This type of evangelism has been growing in recent years. A half-century ago, many churches depended almost wholly on the annual revival meeting for their ingathering. Today, almost all larger evangelical churches have additions on profession of faith regularly on Sundays. Pastors plan annual programs with at least one week in each month dedicated to something evangelistic, such as a religious census, visitation, a revival meeting, establishment of a mission, vacation Bible school, Sunday school decision days, youth revival, study course in soul-winning, family program, radio evangelism, and the like. Some churches without special campaigns are having more baptisms perennially than Spurgeon had in London.

Evangelism through church organizations.—The notable 20th-century growth of Sunday school, Baptist Training Union, Woman's Missionary Union, and Brotherhood organizations has fostered evangelism. The Sunday school has proved to be the most potential church organization for evangelism, reaching more unbelieving and unaffiliated people than any other. The closeness of teachers to pupils, Bible lessons, visitation to the unsaved, training soul-winners through study courses, and emphasis upon preaching attendance are all used by pastors for evangelism. While missions is the chief evangelistic objective of the Woman's Missionary Union, the young people's organizations and personal service department are effective evangelistic agencies in local churches. Evangelism is being emphasized increasingly in the Brotherhood through boys' work and deputation service in unchurched areas. Enlistment of new converts and conservation of evangelistic results are rapidly developing in technique and extent through the Training Union, as it takes new converts, assigns them to church activities, promotes daily prayer and Bible reading, teaches classes in personal soul-winning, and sends young Christians on evangelistic missions to jails, unchurched sections, new missions, and areas for social service.

Simultaneous evangelistic campaigns.—The union simultaneous evangelistic campaign plan was developed fully by Moody in Chicago during the World's Columbian Exposition in 1893, when he used approximately 80 assistant evangelists. They preached on the streets, under tents, in vacant stores, and in churches. City-wide simultaneous campaigns by Southern Baptists were promoted by Hamilton and Fuller, early superintendents of evangelism of the Home Mission Board, with a staff of full-time evangelists on a salary basis. They held revival services in all the churches of a city each night for two weeks, with a joint meeting in some centrally located Baptist church each weekday morning.

The Department of Evangelism, abandoned during the depression of 1929-33, was reactivated in 1937 with Leavell as superintendent, but with no staff of evangelists. He specialized in city-wide and association-wide simultaneous crusades, each church having a visiting pastor for evangelist. His emphasis was on pastoral church evangelism and associational programs. The superintendent visited each city or association months before the campaign and set up an organization with (1) director general, (2) director of publicity, (3) director of preparation, (4) director of conservation, (5) director of extension services, and (6) treasurer. An over-all budget was apportioned to the churches, and a six-weeks' program of preparation was set up for all churches to follow simultaneously. During the campaign all pastors, visiting evangelists, and singers met for breakfast five days each week, during which time they gave reports. The superintendent conducted a school of methods of pastoral evangelism and led in seasons of prayer. Later, these simultaneous crusades, under superintendent Matthews, were expanded to include entire states, sections of the South, and even the entire Southern Baptist Convention area. Widespread interest in evangelism was created, and far-reaching results came, but churches found it difficult to secure visiting evangelists for the broader areas.

Evangelistic programs by mission boards.—Evangelistic superintendents under various state mission boards began to appear about 1937, although previously many states had employed full-time evangelists only for holding revival meetings. These superintendents worked in co-operation with and often under the leadership of the Home Mission Board superintendents, organizing city-wide and association-wide campaigns, planning perennial programs for the states, holding annual state and associational conferences, creating literature, directing publicity, and conducting revival meetings. They located unchurched areas and co-operated in organizing preaching mission stations and churches. Tremendous evangelistic results have come through the Home Mission Board's Department of Direct Missions, with hundreds of missionaries working with bilingual groups, mountaineers, Negroes, Indians, Jews, seamen, and the deaf. The Department of City Missions has promoted expansion of mission stations in cities under sponsorship of the stronger local churches in the cities, a method which has been signally successful in promoting soul-winning and enlistment. The Foreign Mission Board has kept evangelism to the forefront, with educational and medical missions as means to the evangelistic end. Gradually, the revival meeting plan and simultaneous campaign method have grown on foreign fields.

Evangelism and denominational educational institutions.—Evangelism has been promoted in virtually all Southern Baptist educational institutions but has flourished particularly in seminaries. Departments of evangelism are maintained in most American and all Southern Baptist seminaries, with survey courses required for graduation. Programs of field mission work are directed through students, with street preaching, visitation to jails and social work institutions, maintenance of preaching missions, operation of rescue missions, and radio evangelism. Some seminaries require weekly reports on evangelistic activities and results, with no credit given for any classroom work unless all mission assignments have been fulfilled. Many volumes on evangelism have been written by seminary faculty members. One seminary's statistics show that sufficient people are won to Christ and church membership by students and faculty every school week to form at least two good-sized Baptist churches, if the people were in the same localities.

Evangelistic literature.—Finney's *Revival Lectures,* published in 1835 and revised in 1868, was the most widely read book on evangelism in the 19th century. The majority of the 19th-century literature on evangelism consisted of histories of the revivals of that and the previous century. Books on the psychology of revivals began to appear toward the end of the 19th century, culminating with *Varieties of Religious Experience* by William James in 1905, the most influential. Books on revival methods and the technique of personal soul-winning rapidly increased during the first three decades of the 20th century. Volumes of evangelistic sermons from almost all great evangelists, both contemporary and of the past, have been popular during the past two decades. Likewise, a number of books on methods of two-and-two visitation evangelism have been recently published. Southern Baptist authors of evangelistic literature have been chiefly from the seminaries, the Department of Evangelism of the Home Mission Board, and other denominational agencies. A partial bibliography of Southern Baptist writings is given below: J. N. Barnette, *One to Eight* (1954); *The Place of the Sunday School in Evangelism* (1945). L. E. Barton, *Helps for Soul-Winners* (1945). P. E. Burroughs, *How to Win to Christ* (1934). A. Crouch, *The Plan of Salvation* (1924). G. S. Dobbins, *A Winning Witness* (1938); *Evangelism According to Christ* (1949); *Winning the Children* (1953). H. W. Ellis, *Fishing for Men* (1941). O. O. Green, *Normal Evangelism* (1910). W. W. Hamilton, Sr., *Bible Evangelism* (1921); *Wisdom in Soul-Winning* (1929); *A Bible Revival* (1940). P. W. James, *George W. Truett: A Biography* (1939). F. H. Leavell, *Christian Witnessing* (1942). R. Q. Leavell, *Winning Others to Christ* (1936); *Helping Others to Become Christians* (1939); *Saving America to Save the World* (1940); *The Romance of Evangelism* (1942); *Evangelism: Christ's Imperative Commission* (1951). C. E. Matthews, *The Southern Baptist Program of Evangelism* (1949); *Every Christian's Job* (1951); *A Church Revival* (1955). C. L. McKay, *The Call of the Harvest* (1956). E. Y. Mullins, *Talks on Soul Winning* (1920). W. L. Muncy, Jr., *New Testament Evangelism for Today* (1941); *Evangelism in the United States* (1945). J. C. Owen, *The Romance of Soul Winning* (1936). L. R. Scarborough, *With Christ After the Lost* (1919; revised by E. D. Head, 1952); *A Search for Souls* (1925); *How Jesus Won Men* (1926). E. O. Sellers, *Personal Evangelism* (1923); *Evangelism in Sermon and Song* (1946).   ROLAND A. LEAVELL.

EVANGELISM, HOME MISSION BOARD PROGRAM OF. The work of the missionaries of the Home Mission Board from the very beginning was mainly evangelistic in character. During the War Between the States the work of army missions, begun by the board in Jan., 1862, was altogether evangelistic. After the war men specifically called "evangelists" were employed by the board. In 1866 there were 12 men employed by the board designated "evangelists" who were located in Virginia, North Carolina, Alabama, Mississippi, Kentucky, and Missouri. In 1867 Florida and Texas were added to the list of states in which evangelists of the Domestic Board (Home Mission Board) labored. For several years thereafter the board continued to do the work of evangelism. The men were employed individually and the fields of labor designated. Those employees of the board who were designed missionaries combined the work of evangelism with pastoral ministration.

At the meeting of the Convention in 1904, Len G. Broughton of Georgia presented for consideration the proposition "that the Convention appoint a committee of twelve pastors, not members of any Convention Board, to be known as the Committee on Evangelism for the Needy Sections in Convention Territory." The paper suggested somewhat the method that the committee of 12 would follow in carrying out the work of evangelism. The Convention referred the question to a committee of five to report the following year. In 1905 the committee of five made a long report on the subject of evan-

Evangelism, Board Program of

gelism during the year. The committee made extensive inquiry among the leaders in the several states:

> It is manifest to all that there has come about an awakened interest in the subject of evangelistic work. There is an atmosphere of evangelism. By evangelism we mean no new thing. It has been recognized and felt through all these years. . . . It has for its end the salvation of the lost and edification of the saved—that edification which has as its aim the better, fuller, more complete equipment of the individual member of the church. . . . There must, of course, be made the distinction between the evangelism which is needed, and that which has gained a reputation. There is a great difference between the real God-sent evangelist, and the peripatetic, non-responsible traveler whose sound is heard, but whose affiliation and connections are as uncertain as the doctrines he preaches. The pure and true New Testament Evangelist greatly needs a larger place in our lives and work today because of the widely prevalent, vague, and superficial views on the subject.

The committee recommended that a committee of five be appointed to take the whole matter under consideration to study it a year and report to the Convention on the "Work of Evangelism in the Several States of the Convention." The Convention adopted the report and appointed Len G. Broughton, Georgia; George Washington Truett (*q.v.*), Texas; W. W. Hamilton, Kentucky; W. M. Vines, Virginia; and Andrew Jackson Spears Thomas (*q.v.*), South Carolina.

At the next meeting of the Convention in 1906 the committee of five made a long report covering the status of evangelism and evangelistic efforts in the Southern territory.

> But with all our opportunity as Southern Baptists there is a serious weakness. We have the evangelistic soil; we have the evangelistic spirit; but we need a better evangelistic organization. To be sure, this work is, and ought to be, under the direction of the churches, just as every other agency of the denomination is. It is our profound conviction that the supreme centers of evangelism are the churches . . . but why should Southern Baptists not be better organized? . . . We have a larger number of people scattered over a larger territory, and they are of such a temperament as that organization would be more helpful. It is true that our Home Mission Board has been doing a great deal of evangelistic work through its missionaries. They have done more during the last few years than ever before. . . . The states that have tried a plan of employing special evangelists are enthusiastic over the results obtained, but this kind of organization is not fully meeting the needs. What we need is organization that will more vigorously push evangelism throughout all this Southern country.

The committee recommended that the Convention instruct the Home Mission Board to create a Department of Evangelism. After a speech by Benajah Harvey Carroll (*q.v.*) of Texas the report was adopted.

Home Mission Board evangelism had its origin in an enthusiastic atmosphere and was promoted by the most capable men in the Convention. Its beginning was not without opposition, however; some esteemed and cautious brethren were afraid that such a movement would infringe upon the rights of the local churches. After Carroll proved by the Word of God that the evangelist is an appointee of God to do the work of the most permanent character in the kingdom; that he, like the apostles and pastors, was to be set in the church; that the New Testament church stated clearly the peculiar functions and qualifications; that the office of the evangelist was higher in importance than that of the pastor; and that the Word of God offered many illustrations of the work of the evangelist in the first century, the Convention voted enthusiastically to authorize the Home Mission Board to proceed with the work of organized evangelism.

William Wister Hamilton, Sr., was elected in 1906 as the first general evangelist of the Home Mission Board. Under the leadership of Secretary Baron DeKalb Gray (*q.v.*), the board initiated the department. It was expected to be self-sustaining. Each church in which an evangelistic meeting was held was asked to take care of the salaries of the workers who came as helpers, and to give even more in order that the Home Mission Board workers might preach in meetings to be held in mission churches.

The salaries and expenses of the men in the department were paid by the board; the offerings, small and great, were sent to the board as contributions to its evangelistic program. The workers would be relieved of criticism because of offerings taken in the meetings. Hamilton was designated general evangelist, and five other evangelists were associated with him during the first two years. The number was increased to 11 the third year.

The department under Hamilton pioneered in several fields of evangelism. First, he led in city campaigns, the first of which was planned for Wilmington, N. C., with only two workers employed at that time. They were the general evangelist and W. D. Wakefield; Fred Hale, pastor of the First Baptist Church, was the leader. These meetings were so blessed in the number led to accept Christ, and in the healing of church troubles, that from this time the Home Mission Board evangelism took on new meaning for Southern Baptists. Evangelistic pastors and consecrated singers were in increasing numbers ready and willing to become members of the staff. In 1907 Hamilton conducted a citywide revival in St. Joseph, Mo., and later in Atlanta, Ga., and other larger Southern cities. Ordinarily one half of the churches in a given city conducted revivals, each with its own evangelist, the first two weeks, and the other half of the churches the following two weeks. Each day a union service was conducted in a different one of the co-operating churches. Directors of the campaign spoke in these union services. This was not always the procedure. In one such city campaign there were 2,611 additions to the Baptist churches. One of the results in

UNIVERSITY OF RICHMOND (q.v.), Va. Boatwright Memorial Library, above, dedicated 1955, cost $1,000,000, houses 100,000 books, a priceless Baptist historical collection; university administration offices occupy the ground floor.

WAKE FOREST COLLEGE (q.v.), Winston-Salem, N. C. One hundred twenty-two years old. Moved from Wake Forest to its new $20,000,000 campus in 1956.

these simultaneous crusades was that the converts were received into the congregation where the decision was made, and the membership had the added privilege of being locally active and useful.

City campaigns of the above nature and with variations were used by the Home Mission Board evangelist to help solve the complex problem of city evangelism. John William Porter (*q.v.*) said: "The problem of making converts of our city population has been one of the most difficult questions with which Baptists have had to deal"; but it appears from the record that from this time onward, Southern Baptists began to make positive evangelistic progress in cities. The evangelists of the board not only went as a body to conduct city-wide campaigns under the leadership of the general evangelist, but also went individually through the Convention territory holding revivals in local churches.

In the summer of 1908, some conferences on evangelism were conducted to stimulate the preachers and laymen to a more concerted effort in soul-winning. One of these conferences was held at Hot Springs, Ark., in the summer of 1908. The speakers were Edwin Charles Dargan (*q.v.*) of Macon, Ga., Lee Rutland Scarborough (*q.v.*) of Abilene, Tex., and H. A. Porter of Louisville, Ky. Conferences on evangelism were held on Friday, Saturday, and Monday before the meeting of the Southern Baptist Convention in 1908. Such subjects as "How to Get Ready for Revival," "Drawing the Net," and "Caring for the Young Converts" were discussed.

The Home Mission Board asked the general evangelist to prepare a mission study book which could be used in classes in the churches. The subject chosen was Bible Evangelism. The book discussed the meaning, the messenger, the message, the motives, the methods, the mistakes, the membership, the mission, the money, the music, the measure, and the Master in evangelism. Illustrations and suggestions for review were given at the close of each chapter. In the last pages there were added helps for those who would be winners of souls. Scripture passages were cited that presented "God's Word to the Lost," and "God's Word to the Saved."

Under the leadership of Hamilton, the Home Mission Board encouraged a sane evangelism. This placed evangelism among Southern Baptists on a much higher plane than it had been previously. There were elements in much of the evangelism of that day that deserved censure. It needed the lift which the Home Mission Board evangelistic staff offered. A description of a typical evangelist employed by the board is quoted in a state Baptist paper. *The Home Field,* Mar., 1908, is quoted as saying, "He is pre-eminently what is termed a safe evangelist. He has neither pulpit juggling nor high pressured methods. He uses the Word of God as a basis of everything he says and the personal equation is out of sight."

Evangelists of the Home Mission Board during this period were characterized by a spirit of denominational loyalty. In spite of sentimental unionism, which seemed to dominate the times, these evangelists presented a gospel that was consistent with our faith, and with love to all they pursued the even tenor of their God-appointed way.

Hamilton resigned in the fall of 1909 to return to the pastorate. He was succeeded by Weston Bruner who was elected general evangelist, effective Feb. 1, 1910. For seven years Bruner was head of the department. The peak year under his leadership was 1916. There were 20 evangelists of the Home Mission Board who won 20,709 for baptism. The board under the vigorous leadership of Bruner addressed itself with enthusiasm and skill to the task of evangelizing the South. It was felt that the time had come to launch a major offensive in the homeland in the field of evangelism. Porter in supporting the vigorous drive of the department said, "Unless we meet the problem here, sooner or later, we shall withdraw our forces beyond the seas."

One of the major contributions made to evangelism during Bruner's tenure was the associational campaign. The first such effort tried by the department was in 1915, in North Greenville Association in Northwestern South Carolina. The plan worked admirably. Each church had an excellent meeting. The associational meeting that followed was regarded as the best they had ever had. Immediately following this initial effort eight to ten other associational campaigns were conducted with success.

In 1912 the Department of Evangelism had a special evangelist to the colleges, one to the mountain areas, and another to the Negroes.

The Home Mission Board reported to the Southern Baptist Convention that through the evangelistic staff there were added to the churches by baptism 60,276, by letter and otherwise 23,893, making a total of 84,169. These were only a part of the tabulated results. By this year the department had begun to organize several associations for evangelistic efforts and had discovered that the principle of co-operation could be effectively applied in the rural sections as well as in the cities. In *The Home Field,* Apr., 1916, much publicity was given to revivals among the Negroes. The good effect was far beyond what had been anticipated by the Home Mission Board.

Bruner resigned in 1917. Hamilton returned in 1918 for another period of four years as general evangelist. It was during this period that the board decided that its evangelistic work should attain not only soul-winning results, but also the strengthening of churches in other respects. The evangelists undertook to assist the local churches in many of their problems, such as increasing pastors' salaries and raising money for church debts and church buildings. Hamilton resigned in 1922 and was succeeded by Oscar Eugene Bryan (*q.v.*) as general evangelist. In June of that year the board approved the recom-

Evangelism, Board Program of

mendation of Secretary Gray to combine the departments of Evangelism and Enlistment. This was done because of financial difficulties and the need for retrenchment.

The report to the Southern Baptist Convention in May, 1923, states that

notwithstanding the unprecedented retrenchment, made imperative by financial conditions, results per worker during the year will compare well with the results of any previous year. Last year the department reported 46 workers with 22,089 additions to the churches. This was 480 additions per worker. This year we had twenty-eight workers. These workers reported 17,452 additions to the churches. This is an average of 626 additions per worker. The department is making progress along the lines of efficiency.

At the time of this report only 24 workers were on the staff, including singers and preachers. During 1922 the amount of money appropriated was $85,000. The department spent $72,842.05 of the amount.

O. E. Bryan resigned from the Department of Evangelism in June, 1922, to accept the position of budget director of the 75 Million Campaign. For six months the department had no superintendent; then Bryan was pressed to return to the department. He accepted and resumed his duties June 1, 1924. There were fewer city-wide and simultaneous campaigns as the result of having no superintendent. The Home Mission Board report to the Convention May, 1924, included from the department a total of 8,128 additions to the churches. Bryan remained only a brief time. He resigned to become secretary of missions for the state convention of Tennessee.

Ellis Adams Fuller (q.v.) became superintendent of the department Oct. 1, 1925. He made several definite contributions to the methods of evangelism while serving as superintendent of the department. He began evangelistic efforts on a statewide basis. The first was held in Florida, Feb., 1927. Oklahoma, South Carolina, North Carolina, and other state conventions voted to launch similar efforts under Fuller's leadership. Charles Alfred Jones (q.v.), general secretary-treasurer of the general board of the South Carolina convention, in presenting the matter to the Convention, called for a great statewide simultaneous campaign on soul-winning.

These statewide campaigns were similar in character to the city-wide campaigns conducted by Hamilton. Each pastor filled out a questionnaire asking for detailed information concerning evangelistic possibilities in his field. He indicated five evangelists or pastors and five singers, any one of whom would be acceptable to the church. It was necessary for him to secure the approval of his church. This information was sent to the office of the superintendent of evangelism in Atlanta. All of the churches, making such approval and expressing the desire to be included in the campaign, were supplied with evangelists or singers or both. The pastors were urged to do their own preaching if possible. All the members of the evangelistic staff of the Home Mission Board were concentrated in that part of the state.

Out-of-state pastors and evangelists also were invited to assist in the campaigns. An evangelistic committee functioned in each association, and all were co-ordinated with the statewide effort as well as it was possible to co-ordinate such an effort. Every co-operating church displayed a large streamer to announce the special service, and it was planned that each church advertise as much as it thought wise and was capable of doing. These meetings were not held in temporary tabernacles, but in local churches under pastoral leadership. Thousands of church members all over the state united in prayer for an effective simultaneous soul-winning drive. Fuller resigned Oct. 1, 1928, to accept the pastorate of the First Baptist Church, Atlanta, Ga. The department was discontinued for eight years and three months, due to the financial crisis following the depression and the defalcation of C. S. Carnes of the Home Mission Board. Roland Quinche Leavell became secretary of evangelism Jan. 1, 1937. At the meeting of the Southern Baptist Convention in St. Louis in 1936, Secretary Lawrence of the Home Mission Board announced that the Department of Evangelism was being re-established. The members of the Convention cheered. Monroe Elmon Dodd (q.v.), pastor of the First Baptist Church of Shreveport, interrupted the announcement to make a motion that the Convention approve these plans. The messengers present voted an enthusiastic approval.

Mrs. George Washington Bottoms (q.v.) of Texarkana had agreed to give $5,000 per year for two years to help re-establish the department. Leavell brought in sufficient offerings from the meetings which he held and from the royalties on his books to take care of the expenses of the department in those days of financial struggle.

When Leavell became secretary of evangelism many pastors throughout the Convention territory had individual programs of evangelism for the churches; but they did not have a concerted and co-ordinated plan of aggressive evangelistic strategy. Leavell planned to give them one. The approach had to be different from that of former years. There was no staff of evangelists to conduct meetings. Leavell was the sole member of the staff. It was planned to train the rank and file of church members to do evangelism. On June 4, 1936, Secretary Lawrence, in preparation for this sort of program, sent the following message for the consideration of the Sunday School Board:

Our Board proposes to launch as soon as possible, an evangelistic program which is suitable for the age in which we live. We propose to elect a superintendent and then work with him in developing an adequate program of evangelism. We realize that evangelism in this day must have thorough preparation through teaching and be followed by thorough teaching and training. The Sunday School Board does have this means and organization for doing this work. We would like, therefore, to have the endorsement and closest co-operation of the Sunday School Board in the full use of the Sunday school organization for teaching the Word and its Training Union organization for training young converts to the kingdom through the churches.

The reply from the Sunday School Board was: "Our Board agrees to co-operate in every possible way with the Home Board through our Sunday School and Baptist Training Union Departments. It is, of course, understood that we are not assuming any financial obligation." The Sunday School Board voted to co-operate with the Home Mission Board in a Convention-wide evangelistic program. Thus major emphasis was placed on personal evangelism for laymen as well as for ministers. In 1938 Leavell laid strong emphasis on "person to person evangelism." Along with an emphasis on training and using personal soul-winners came the emphasis on home evangelism. An effort was made to establish family altars.

The emphasis in those days was not on personal evangelism alone. Leavell led the forces of the Southern Baptist Convention into the field of mass evangelism. He was the pioneer in simultaneous crusades. The first effort under his leadership was held in Tampa, Fla., in 1937. He directed many similar city-wide campaigns. In a report given by him in Aug., 1938, he said: "Southern Baptists will practice mass evangelism by seeking to have a protracted meeting in every one of our 24,844 churches. An effort will be made to have preaching in every destitute place and in every unchurched community."

Leavell gave a vital lift to Southern Baptists' evangelism by producing some fresh and helpful literature on evangelism and by leading out in personal evangelism augmented by the teaching and training ministry of the Sunday School Board. He made a definite contribution to mass evangelism by pioneering in simultaneous city-wide crusades, and by an appeal to all the churches to hold revival meetings in their local fields as well as in out-of-the-way places. He resigned, effective as of Apr. 1, 1942, to return to the pastorate.

Fred Eastham, pastor of the First Baptist Church of Wichita Falls, Tex., was elected Dec. 15, 1944, to take the place left vacant by the resignation of Leavell more than two years before. He began by jointly conducting with M. E. Dodd a city-wide simultaneous campaign in Nashville and then one in Shreveport. He inaugurated a Sunday evening evangelistic broadcast over KWBU, 50,000-watt station in Corpus Christi, Tex.

Southern Baptists put on a special effort in 1945 to win a million souls to Christ during the year. Dodd headed the campaign. Eastham reported to the Southern Baptist Convention in 1946 that a total of 256,144 were baptized in 1945. He continued: "We are well into 1946. Crusades, revivals, and brush-arbor meetings are being held all over our Convention. Our State Boards are electing secretaries of evangelism and they are giving to these departments a substantial budget."

Eastham resigned Oct. 1, 1946, to accept the pastorate of the First Baptist Church of Springfield, Mo. C. E. Matthews, secretary of evangelism of the Baptist General Convention of Texas (Dallas), was elected to succeed Eastham Nov. 7, 1946.

The Southern Baptist Convention voted at St. Louis in 1947 to recommend: first, a unified program of evangelism for all the state conventions and churches; second, that each state convention create a Department of Evangelism; third, that all associations be organized with two officers of evangelism, an organizer and a general chairman; fourth, that stress be placed in mass evangelism, chiefly the associational simultaneous method. This was the first time the Convention had ever voted on a definite program of simultaneous evangelism.

In June, 1937, the first statewide evangelistic conference ever conducted was held at Seminary Hill, Fort Worth, Tex. It proved such a blessing that other states began to hold similar meetings. Matthews and other leaders began to promote these meetings for all the states. At the Convention in 1948, he reported that there would be held in every state and the District of Columbia an evangelistic conference in the winter of 1949. He further announced that the Home Mission Board Week at Ridgecrest would give major emphasis to evangelism.

The superintendent recognized the importance of working in close conjunction with the Convention-wide and statewide leaders. He cleared every major change and move in evangelism through the denominational leadership. He worked through the Executive Committee of the Southern Baptist Convention and in close co-operation with the heads of the Sunday school, Training Union, Brotherhood, and Woman's Missionary Union, as well as the promotional officers of the Convention. Without the hearty endorsement and the support of all the agencies of the Convention, the evangelism of the Home Mission Board could not succeed. The Department of Evangelism at its annual meetings in Nashville often had present the executive secretaries of the state conventions and the editors in order to keep its program properly co-ordinated with the interests and activities of the various states.

Matthews called a meeting, Dec., 1948, of all the secretaries of evangelism and all the executive secretaries of the states who could attend to work out and correct the script to be used in "Southern Baptist Program of Evangelism." This meeting was held in the First Baptist Church of Dallas. Every secretary of evangelism of the various states was present. The tasks of the secretaries of evangelism were clearly defined:

1. Find and promote the best methods of evangelism known.

2. Hold annual statewide evangelistic confer-

ences for the purpose of inspiration and promotion. Major emphasis was put on the unified program. The leaders thought that without the unified program it would be impossible to mobilize nearly 30,000 churches and seven million Baptists in soul-winning. Wholly dissatisfied with the evangelistic accomplishments of the past, the group who met in Dallas decided to do something different.

3. Agree to give proper effort to the promotion and conduct of simultaneous crusades.

4. Emphasize the use of the association as the basis of operation for the simultaneous crusades.

As early as 1948, therefore, major emphasis was being given by Matthews to mass and personal evangelism. This is the first time such an emphasis had been given to associational simultaneous crusades. The method had been used before, but not so extensively. A definite church program of visitation evangelism, functioning through church agencies from week to week the year around, was promoted. In May, 1949, the department began to promote big-scale simultaneous evangelism for the first time. It was to do it on the basis of a section of the Convention territory at the same time. During Apr. 8–23, 1950, all the 8,441 churches and the missions west of the Mississippi River conducted a simultaneous effort. Then the following year, Mar. 25–Apr. 8, 1951, all the 18,158 churches east of the Mississippi River engaged in a simultaneous crusade. The Home Mission Board reported to the Convention in 1950, through the Department of Evangelism, that the crusade in the 8,441 churches resulted in a total of 376,085 baptisms, which was an all-time high for one convention year. The comparable report for the crusade in the 18,158 churches east of the river gave as the result of the crusade 120,000 for baptism during the two weeks' effort. This was the largest single evangelistic effort ever undertaken in the history of the Convention. In 1951 the churches of the Convention reported 375,525. Many of the churches east of the river had experienced revival and an increasing number of additions in 1950 while they were preparing for the crusade of 1951.

In 1951 the Department of Evangelism sent C. Y. Dossey to South America in conjunction with the Foreign Mission Board to conduct simultaneous crusades in Argentina, Paraguay, and Uruguay. These meetings were successful. Simultaneous evangelism had worked everywhere it had been tried at home and abroad. In 1952 the department conducted three successful simultaneous crusades in Kansas, Alaska, and Cuba. Seventy Southern Baptist pastors and evangelists left Miami, Fla., Jan. 2, 1953, for a week's simultaneous revival in Jamaica. Guy Bellamy, secretary of Negro work of the Home Mission Board, directed the effort.

During 1953 Southern Baptists began planning for a nation-wide simultaneous revival. These plans were discussed and approved by the Executive Committee and later were approved by the Convention. During this year 361,835 baptisms were reported.

Three important events happened for the advancement of evangelism in 1954. The National Baptist Convention, Inc., U.S.A., approved the setting up of a Department of Evangelism with a full-time secretary to supervise the work throughout the United States jointly with the Department of Evangelism of the Home Mission Board of the Southern Baptist Convention. Immediately thereafter Matthews assisted the newly elected secretary to prepare a book for the Negroes similar to *The Southern Program of Evangelism*. The Sunday School Board launched a drive to enrol a million new members in the Sunday schools of the Convention. The Department of Evangelism assisted the Sunday school forces in every way possible, because for several years the number of baptisms had been almost a direct ratio to the number of new folk enrolled in the Sunday schools of the Convention. For the year 1954, 396,857 were baptized. In June, 1954, the Department of Evangelism in co-operation with the Department of Direct Missions of the Home Mission Board conducted a simultaneous crusade among the American Indians.

At the meeting in Dec., 1954, at Nashville, of all the state secretaries of evangelism, special study and concern was given to the crusade to be held in the spring of 1955. At previous meetings of these secretaries, all the plans and details had been thoroughly worked out for the crusade. The territory was divided into three zones running across the nation from east to west. The tropical zone included Cuba and all or parts of the Gulf states from the Atlantic to the Pacific, including southern New Mexico, Arizona, and California. The dates were Mar. 6–20. The central zone included some 12,000 churches and missions in the central part of the Convention territory. The crusade in this area was conducted Mar. 27–Apr. 10. The northern zone embraced the northern part of the Convention territory and the pioneer states. Part of the Alaskan effort was included in this period. The revival in the northern zone began Easter Sunday and ran for two weeks. All the states reported that some 300,000 united with the churches during the crusade. This was the largest organized effort ever to be reported in the history of evangelism. Never before had so many churches and preachers been enrolled in an effort to seek a revival at one time.

Due to failing health Secretary Matthews asked to be relieved of the responsibility of heading the Department of Evangelism of the Home Mission Board at the end of 1955. Leonard Sanderson, secretary of evangelism for Tennessee, was named to succeed Matthews. He began his services Jan. 1, 1956. Matthews was asked to serve during 1956, as much as his health would permit, in an advisory capacity to assist Sanderson and his associates in the promotion of the world crusade in evangelism for 1959.
　　　　　　　　　　　　　　　　C. E. AUTREY

EVANGELISM, RELIGIOUS EDUCATION AND. The educational basis of church work and growth, which has been increasingly the distinctive emphasis of Southern Baptist activity since the founding of the Southern Baptist Sunday School Board in 1891 and even before, makes necessary the closest possible relationship between religious education and evangelism. Southern Baptists, who have always been thoroughly and emphatically evangelical in all their activities, have come to consider their programs of religious education as the basic means through which to achieve their enlistment and evangelistic purposes.

Enlistment of new church members can be based upon many methods, some of which Baptists would consider erroneous, others merely inexpedient or insufficient. Some groups have depended upon infant baptism, geographical parishes, and legal constraints to provide prospective members. With these methods Baptists cannot agree. Others have depended almost solely upon revivals or upon the ministry of preaching. A few are not at all evangelistic but rely upon their moral or religious prestige (which may be very real) to influence persons to present themselves for membership. Southern Baptists also emphasize preaching and revivals and try to cultivate in their churches and members exemplary character, but they depend fundamentally on results achieved through teaching.

The educational approach involves all the organizations of the church, with particular emphasis upon two: Sunday school and the Baptist Training Union. Woman's Missionary Union and the Brotherhood also have evangelistic programs. All of the work of these organizations is planned to include evangelistic emphases, and many features are primarily directed toward the enlistment of the unchurched. The Sunday school curriculum is thoroughly biblical in doctrine, interpretation, and subject matter. Specific themes of study vary widely, but all of them are directly related to that fundamental character change which is regeneration. The curriculum does deal with problems of Christian growth and maturity, but never in such a way as to lose sight of or minimize the meaning and importance of the point of beginning, which is the acceptance of Christ as Saviour. Whatever its subject, the curriculum is designed to have a constant appeal to the lost.

Sunday school methods are important. The Sunday school is organized into small, face-to-face groups, in which teachers can cultivate the sound knowledge and the intimacy and openness of personality which are the basis of spiritual decisions of genuine and lasting character. The teacher can know the needs and problems of his pupils and is thus in a position to lead them more effectively than any other person in the church. In addition, the Sunday school works systematically at enlistment. Sunday school organization and methods make it possible to reach every possible prospect within a given community with a maximum of efficiency. New people are brought into the Sunday school as members. Then, in an atmosphere of Bible study, they are given the information and encouragement which should lead them to decide to become members of the church.

The church schedule which brings together the ministries of teaching and preaching is also important. In Southern Baptist churches Sunday school is regularly held before the morning worship service on Sunday, and Sunday school members are regularly encouraged to attend the worship service. There, under the ministry of preaching, they can be led to profess decisions made, or cultivated, in the Sunday school.

The Baptist Training Union and the other educational organizations of the church are designed primarily for church members, but they, too, have distinct evangelistic emphases. Most fundamentally of all, the members of these organizations are encouraged to work individually with their friends and associates to bring them to Christ and the church. The curricula of these organizations contain specific guidance in this work of personal evangelism, and in addition, there are provided for all age levels, beginning at the age of nine, graded study courses dealing in detail with the methods of personal work and emphasizing its importance. Thus every church member, of whatever age, is led to help in the church's evangelistic program, and this division of responsibility leads to a large multiplication of achievement.

Any non-Christian who may join one of these church organizations which are primarily designed for church members is led toward a decision for Christ in several ways. The curricula of these organizations are also biblically based and thus contain evangelistic content. In addition, the new member is thrown into immediate and intimate contact with the church's most active and consecrated members and is necessarily influenced by their lives, characters, and testimonies. An effort is also made, as a general rule, to enlist this kind of member in the Sunday school, where a more direct evangelistic appeal will be made.

Southern Baptists feel that this educational approach to evangelism has several distinct advantages. First, it gives new church members a sounder basis for their decision than the too often temporary emotional experience produced in overly enthusiastic revivals. In fact the educational approach leads to the idea that the decision for salvation, the decision to become a church member, is more a culmination than a crisis. Second, it is an approach suited to the peculiar needs of Southern Baptist churches. The educational method provides for the elaborate division of responsibility and work so necessary to the large organizations which many churches have become. Through the educational approach trained staff members can most efficiently help their churches minister effectively to large and increasingly urbanized constituencies by capitalizing on the relatively trained efforts of many of their church members. Third, the educational approach, because of its effectiveness as a method of enlistment and evangelism, benefits the church members themselves and the denomination as a whole. By engaging church members in personal work, it helps them toward Christian maturity. By its emphasis on evangelism, it implies and demands support for missions, both at home and abroad. By its emphasis on salvation as the door to church membership, it helps to preserve the purity of the body of Christ, the church.

JUDSON BOYCE ALLEN

EVANGELISTIC METHODS IN FOREIGN MISSIONS. These vary with geography, cultural and economic conditions, longevity of the mission, and personnel. All methods, however, are geared to taking the gospel, through word and example, to as many individuals as possible, pressing for commitment and then encouraging fellowship and growth in a New Testament church so that mature Christian witness completes the cycle. So-called educational, medical, agricultural, and social service missions all have the same ultimate purpose.

For the "go" in the Great Commission, the wheelbarrow, ricksha, pack animal, canoe, and sailing craft have been superceded in most of the world by the bicycle, automobile, launch, steamer, and airplane. Radio, recordings (disc, wire, tape), and public address systems may proclaim the gospel when personnel is scarce or entrance into an area is forbidden. To the literate, tracts, papers, pamphlets, magazines, books, and Scripture portions multiply avenues of evangelism. Moving pictures, slides and filmstrips, flannelgraph, puppets, and flat pictures tell a simple story to the less literate. Music, vocal and instrumental, is also effective.

In Japan, evangelism in strategic centers has the definite objective of developing strong parent-churches in accessible cities. Procuring strategic property (indicative of permanency) for services and for housing personnel precedes a widely advertised, well-timed, intensive, and extended evangelistic campaign by a team of preachers, personal workers, and musicians, added to the locally assigned national and missionary personnel. Intensive instruction prepares inquirers for baptism, after which, as a group, they become ready relatively early for church organization and self-support. Later, a series of meetings by another team spurs growth and solidifies the program, which, well established, becomes the center for a similar program in contiguous areas.

Seasonal or periodic evangelism is dependent more on persistent, aggressive, advance planning, local and area-wide, than on weather, agricultural or industrial lay-by seasons, vacations (holidays), or other sociological conditions. The employment of tents, open-air forums, street preaching, auditoriums, chapels, and churches varies with circumstances. Preaching missions, manned from abroad or locally, spearhead new work and strengthen what is already established. Systematic visitation by Christians heads the list for advertising meetings, although placards, posters, invitation handbills, newspaper, radio, and public address announcements, or other means must not be minimized for total effect. Simultaneous (Convention-wide) activities among churches aid in interest generated, prayer and personnel exchange, and co-operation. Where two yearly campaigns occur, experience proves that one locally planned (autonomous) and the other co-operatively conceived are most beneficial.

Perennial evangelism (in local churches) depends on prayerful planning, careful organization, and persistent work. Utilization of regular worship for evangelistic preaching and the creation of an atmosphere of expectancy for decisions is essential. Training and organization of church membership (especially Sunday school teachers) in personal soul-winning and insistence on implementation during the week bring results. Consecutive, monthly, week-end evangelistic services with visiting preachers, and organized systematic visitation evangelism by Bible women, laymen, and particularly by lay officials of the church are effective.

Personal evangelism has always found women missionaries and national Bible women leading the way, with national evangelists and seminary and training school students contributing materially. Women's and young people's community mission projects enlist less-trained personnel; in Japan, a Volunteer Movement sends out personal workers in pairs. Colporteurs have made personal work a part of their job while selling Christian literature.

Class evangelism for language-student missionaries consists in English Bible classes with or without interpretation, developing into national language classes in missionaries' homes, where women missionaries frequently make their major contribution. A secretary of the Foreign Mission Board (Charles Edward Maddry) once said, "The missionary home is exhibit 'A' on the mission field." Demonstration classes in homemaking (cooking, child-care, sewing, etc.), always accompanied with a Bible lesson, tie in with parent-teacher (chiefly mothers) meetings of church-directed kindergarten and primary schools, offering contacts for visitation and personal work. Youth and young couples' classes are other sources for evangelism. Before the literacy movement launched by Frank C. Laubach, missionary women conducted reading classes, which were exciting experiences for both pupils and teachers.

Specialized evangelism includes newspaper and radio media, where space or time is bought and messages are disseminated, with fan mail coming in for answer by letter and various types of literature (tracts, papers, Scripture portions, lending library, etc.) or with recorded messages (disc, wire, tape) for the blind and other groups. These media are related to the nearest church and workers. Workshop and office evangelism utilizes relatively free times before work, noon and other recesses, and after-work periods for classes and preaching. Evangelistic methods are directed through hospitals and sanatoriums, prisons and reformatories. Student evangelism, through Bible classes, discussion groups, and a student-center program, differs materially from the American Baptist Student Union program because of the small number of Christians. Missionary evangelism endeavors to enlist actively in a program of evangelism and intelligent support American overseas personnel who are employed in business, professional, government, and military occupations.

Half the battle of evangelism is in the area of conservation and follow-up of persons who have made a commitment. Careful planning is necessary to absorb transfers or utilize them as nuclei for new work. Only Convention-wide or association-wide planning and close co-operation can consummate the ultimate goals of evangelism, the continuation of evangelism by the converts.

EDWIN DOZIER

EVANS, CHRISTMAS (b. in Wales, Dec. 25, 1766; d. Swansea, Glamorganshire, South Wales, July 19, 1838). Preacher and evangelist. Born of poor parents who derived his name from his birthday, Evans was reared by a disreputable uncle after his father's death. At the age of 18, he joined the Arminian Presbyterians. In spite of his lack of learning and his self-abnegation, his fellow Christians asked him to preach. His first sermon and prayer were memorized, but his delivery and the effect of the sermon were prophetic of his future. A Calvinistic Baptist challenged Evans on baptism; in preparing to defend infant baptism, he became privately persuaded that true baptism is believer's baptism; thus he became a Baptist by conviction. However, he was primarily an evangelist whose interest transcended denominational lines, minimized church order, and led him into extensive itineration.

Evans never received a formal education, but he became skilled in Hebrew, Greek, Latin, and English. His desire for learning is seen in the fact that, in order to be able to use the Scriptures, he learned to read in a month's time. His chief sources were the Bible, *Pilgrim's Progress*, and the theological works of John Owen, an Independent.

In an age noted for its theological preaching, Evans became famous as an evangelist. His localized ministry was discharged in five places: Lleyn in Caernarvon, Angelsea, Caerphilly in Glamorgan, Cardiff, and Caernarvon. His longest pastorate was in Angelsea (1791–1826), where he served 10 preaching stations and received an annual salary of £17. His evangelistic zeal was temporarily arrested by the rigid legalism of Sandemanianism (a source of American Campbellism); this brought on a struggle of soul from which he emerged stronger in zeal. His 10 preaching stations doubled in two years, and 600 converts were made. As a preacher he was in great demand, not only in all of Wales but also in England. He preached his first associational sermon about 1792 as a last-minute substitute, but the sermon made him famous; he preached a total of 173 associational sermons.

Evans was a great preacher because his understanding of sin made his preaching urgent, his personal experience of salvation made it convincing, and his exaltation of the Saviour made it magnetic.

HUGH WAMBLE

EVANS, KATHERINE (KATE) **F.** (b. Painesville, Amelia County, Va., Dec. 1, 1842; d. Thonzé, Burma, Mar. 3, 1918). For five years Miss Evans sought appointment as a missionary to Burma. She became the first appointee of the Woman's American Baptist Foreign Mission Society, sailing from New York Dec. 16, 1871, and reaching Rangoon the following Feb. 25. Her spirit is shown in this excerpt, her first letter: "In Burma at last! All the weary years of waiting, and of heart-sickening disappointment seem like a dream now. To be here is ample compensation for all."

Co-operating with the desire of the missionaries, Katherine Evans went to Thonzé, a single station without railroad or post office. She was given charge of education for girls, which meant pioneering against prejudice. In 1906 she returned from furlough for literary work in Rangoon. At a woman's prayer meeting in Kemendine she was stricken with paralysis from which she never fully recovered; she died seven years later and was buried at Thonzé.

Her associates summarized "the brilliant career" of "our gifted sister" in these words: "As an educator of Burman youth . . . and as a translator of religious literature into colloquial Burmese . . . she had few equals, if any."

J. LEVERING EVANS

EVERETT, WILLIAM WADE (b. Chelsea, Mass., Aug. 23, 1871; d. Washington, D. C., Mar. 14, 1949). Layman and denominational leader. Educated in public schools of Washington, he studied business law at Columbian College. In 1888 he was employed by Woodward and Lothrop as messenger; he became general manager in 1913 and president of the firm in 1942. He was long recognized as one of Washington's leading businessmen. For 60 years he was a member of Calvary Baptist Church, where he rendered outstanding service as superintendent of the Sunday school, trustee, and generous financial supporter. As president of the District of Columbia convention, he led in all progressive moves, such as the establishment of Baptist headquarters and the expansion of the homes for children and the aged. He served on every important conference committee of the District of Columbia convention, dealing with such matters as the return of George Washington University to the denomination, and others where the American and Southern Baptist conventions were involved. He was a wise and

EVERGREEN ACADEMY. Located at Evergreen, in Conecuh County, Ala., founded by Alexander Travis c. 1840, with Horatio Smith as first principal. In 1881 the school was reported to be "an excellent literary institution."

JAMES E. DAVIDSON

EVOLUTION. A fundamental assumption in biology which asserts that, by a mechanism not yet determinately known, biological forms change into other biological forms. Species are not fixed but are changeable, and over a period of time, new species derive from previous ones. The theory was given a testable formulation by Darwin (1859); since then a number of mechanisms have been proposed to account for the process, none of which has yet made its way to a full acceptance among the biologists. The argument for the validity of the theory is based upon a composite picture made up of elements from paleontology, comparative morphology, and genetics.

BERNARD RAMM

EWING COLLEGE. Began as a high school on Dec. 25, 1867, in Ewing, Ill. On May 29, 1874, a collegiate department was added and thereafter the institution was known as Ewing College. At the outset the college was undenominational, but in 1877 it became a Baptist school and in the year 1908 aligned itself with the Illinois State Association, which was affiliated with the Southern Baptist Convention. In Oct., 1919, the Illinois State Association assumed full responsibility of the college.

John Washburn was the first principal of the high school and was also elected as first president after the collegiate department was added. During the first year as a college there were 84 students enrolled in the spring session and 83 in the fall session, and 5 were graduated with the Bachelor of Arts degree. Departments of music, theology, and commerce were later added to the curriculum.

During its 51 years of operation, Ewing College had 10 presidents, the first of which served at three different intervals: 1874–75, John Washburn; 1875–76, J. W. Patterson; 1876–77, John Washburn; 1877–80, William Shelton; 1880–90, John Washburn; 1890–1911, J. A. Leavitt; 1911–12, W. A. Matthews; 1912–15, E. L. Carr; 1915–17, Arthur E. Summers; 1917–20, H. M. Tipsword; 1920–21, H. A. Smart; 1921–25, August Griesel, dean and acting president. Financial difficulties arose during the years of World War I, and in 1925 Ewing College was forced to cease operations after accumulating an indebtedness of $60,000.

Because of incomplete records, it is not possible to learn how many students were served by the school, but 335 were graduated during the years 1879–1914.

J. C. MARTIN

EXALTATION (OF CHRIST). See CHRISTOLOGY.

EXCELSIOR ACADEMY. Established in Bulloch County, Ga., in 1875, a private school with all teachers Baptist. The community which grew up around the school took its name, but the school was short-lived. J. C. Brewton, one of its students, became one of its best-known teachers.

ARTHUR JACKSON

EXCELSIOR HIGH SCHOOL. A Baptist school at Atkinson, N. C., conducted in the early 1900's by J. J. Payseur and his wife. Payseur was pastor of the Atkinson Church and vice-moderator of Wilmington Association. In 1903 a committee was appointed to bring the school into a more "vital" relationship with the association, but nothing came of the effort.

D. L. SMILEY

EXECUTIVE COMMITTEE OF THE SOUTHERN BAPTIST CONVENTION. The "fiduciary, the fiscal, and the executive agency of the Convention in all its affairs not specifically committed to some other board or agency." It is instructed "to act for the Convention ad interim in all matters not otherwise provided for." It is "to be named in transfers of real and personal property for the use and benefit of the Convention either by deed, conveyance, will, or otherwise and to affix the seal of the Convention to all approved transactions."

The first half century of Southern Baptist history was marked by its organization, its disruption and disturbance by the Civil War, by the emergence of new agencies, by the development of state conventions with a state consciousness, and finally by a sense of direction which produced conscious study of the type of organization needed to achieve the desired goals.

The state convention of Georgia in 1898 presented to the Southern Baptist Convention through the Home Mission Board a resolution asking for "the observance of the year 1900 as a year of thanksgiving by our Baptist churches in which special efforts be made to more fully inform them of the gracious fullness of the Divine blessings received during this century, and to better organize and equip them for the mighty work which lies before them in the century to come."

A committee was appointed known as the "Committee on Co-operation," and its report at the Southern Baptist Convention in New Orleans in 1901, brought by Franklin Howard Kerfoot (q.v.), of Georgia, its chairman, was referred to a committee headed by James Bruton Gambrell (q.v.), of Texas.

This committee brought in the following recommendations:

1. That this Convention renew its declaration formerly made that we will give special attention to the primary object of the Convention, the eliciting, combining, and directing of the energies of the de-

nomination in one sacred effort for the propagation of the gospel throughout the world.

2. That a special agency be employed, to be known as the Committee on Co-operation of the Southern Baptist Convention, . . . and located in Baltimore. . . . We recommend further that this committee be authorized to employ a secretary, fix his remuneration, and also provide such other agencies as in their judgment may be necessary.

3. We recommend the acceptance of the offer of the Baltimore brethren to give $4,000 a year for three years, or so much thereof as may be necessary, toward the expenses of the work; provided the Sunday School Board of the Convention be authorized to appropriate for the same object $3,000 a year for the same time.

4. That the committee work in the closest co-operation with all the existing boards, and in the interest of all the boards of this Convention.

5. We especially recommend that the Committee on Co-operation be instructed to seek to work with and through the state boards, and in the interest of the state organization co-operating with this Convention.

6. We recommend the adoption of the Appeal of the Committee of Nine in these words: "We earnestly invite every state association or convention, and every state board, to co-operate with us in a vigorous, specific movement of this kind along such lines of co-operation as can be mutually agreed upon in each state."

7. We recommend that the details of the work be left to the wisdom of the Committee on Co-operation.

After considerable discussion the Convention turned down the concept of a "committee on co-operation," and although there was considerable discussion in Southern Baptist papers, the matter was not presented to the Southern Baptist Convention again until 1913, when John Ellington White (q.v.), Georgia, introduced the following resolution:

That a commission of seven judicious men among us be appointed by the president of the Convention, of which he shall be chairman, which shall, during the coming year, make a careful study and a thorough examination of the organization, plans and methods of this body, with a view to determining whether or not they are best adapted for eliciting, combining and directing the energies of Southern Baptists and for securing the highest efficiency of our forces and the fullest possible enlistment of our people for the work of the Kingdom.

One proposal, that all of the boards should be combined into a single board as had been done in a number of the states, was turned down by the Convention. In 1916, M. H. Wolfe, Texas, proposed, "That Articles V to X of the Constitution of this Convention be amended and revised so as to create one strong executive board which shall direct all of the work and enterprises fostered and promoted by this Convention." The report of the committee dealing with the matter, which was presented in 1917, stated:

That the boards of the Convention remain separate, . . . and believing that some improvement in the method of conducting the work would be obtained by the creation of a standing committee of the Convention to act for the body between its sessions in ways hereafter set forth, we recommend that an executive committee of seven, representing the different parts of the territory of the Convention, be selected annually by the Convention. . . . The duties of the committee shall be to have oversight of the arrangements for the meetings of the Convention, with power to change both the time and place of meeting in case an emergency arises making such change necessary; that this committee shall act for the Convention ad interim on such matters as may arise pertaining to the general business of the Convention and not otherwise provided for in its plan of work; that this committee shall also be empowered to act in an advisory way on all questions submitted to it on matters arising between the boards of this Convention, but only on request of one or more of the boards concerned; that this committee shall have no further duties except as other things may be specifically committed to it by the Convention itself at its annual meeting.

Members of the first Executive Committee of seven were: Manson Horatio Wolfe (q.v.), Texas; Livingston Johnson (q.v.), North Carolina; George E. Hays, Kentucky; Joseph Cole Stalcup (q.v.), Oklahoma; Zechariah Thornton Cody (q.v.), South Carolina; Edwin Charles Dargan (q.v.), Georgia; and S. M. Brown (q.v.), Missouri.

In 1919 the Executive Committee was enlarged in membership by the following bylaw change:

That there shall be chosen an Executive Committee composed of the president and secretary of the Convention, one member from each of the boards of the Convention, and one additional member from each state represented in the Convention. The president and secretary of the Convention shall be ex officio chairman and secretary of the committee; the members from the boards shall be elected by the boards, and the members from the states shall be selected by the Convention, and have no official connection with the Convention or any of its agencies.

The committee was given further responsibility in 1926 by the adoption of the preliminary report of the Committee on Business Efficiency: "In order to preserve the autonomy of the Southern Baptist Convention, its Executive Committee shall have the authority of the Convention for fixing total objectives, for allocating funds to its various agencies and recommending same to the Southern Baptist Convention for adoption." The boards and agencies of the Convention were also instructed to submit their proposed budgets for review by the Executive Committee, and approval by the Convention.

In 1927 the full report of the Committee on Business Efficiency was made to the Louisville Convention. It stated: "One of the greatest needs of the Convention at this time is to have a thorough, detailed, and analytical survey made of all the affairs and activities of the Convention and its agencies."

Problems called attention to included (1) making a workable budget, (2) raising sufficient money to care for the consolidated operating budget, (3) allocation of funds, (4) providing for the needs of the institutions of the Convention, (5) paying off the indebtedness of the agencies of the Convention, (6) increasing the work of the agencies of the Convention. The report continued as follows:

> After the most earnest consideration, we are convinced that the Convention should have some agency keep in close touch with all the work of the Convention and its agencies. The affairs of the Convention and its agencies are too varied and too great to be handled effectively without it. It is evident to us that the affairs of the Convention have suffered greatly in the past from lack of such agency. The logical agency to do this is the Executive Committee of the Convention. . . . We make specific recommendation for the enlargement of the functions of the Executive Committee.

The recommendations that were adopted and incorporated in the Convention By-laws are essentially the same as found in By-law 9, setting forth the duties of the Executive Committee.

In addition to the enlarged function of the Committee adopted in 1927, the report recommended that the work of the Cooperative Program Commission be taken over by the Executive Committee. It also gave certain instructions regarding financial matters and business procedure to the agencies of the Convention.

The "task" for the Executive Committee for 1927–28 included the following:

> (1) That it make a complete survey of the work of the Convention and its agencies; (2) That it make a full and complete statement of the basis of co-operation of the Southern Baptist Convention with co-operating state conventions and state boards; (3) That it work out with the agencies of the Convention the form for making financial statements; (4) That it work out with each agency a form for the auditor's report suitable to the agency's type of work; (5) That it investigate certain matters regarding annuities issued.

After the Executive Committee had handled the responsibility for promotion for several years, the Convention in 1931 recommended:

> That a Promotion Committee, to be composed of one member from each co-operating state and the District of Columbia, and the executive heads of the Foreign Mission Board, the Home Mission Board, Sunday School Board, Relief and Annuity Board, Southern Baptist Theological Seminary, Southwestern Baptist Theological Seminary, Baptist Bible Institute, Woman's Missionary Union, and Baptist Brotherhood, together with 11 pastors and 10 laymen representing the Convention at large, be established and that the 21 members elected by the Convention shall be elected for one, two, and three years, and that no member shall be eligible to succeed himself immediately.

It was further stated:

> While the administrative functions of the Convention ad interim shall be performed by the Executive Committee, we recommend that the Promotion Committee be charged with establishing the goal of the Co-operative Fund, and the ratio of distribution of undesignated Southwide funds, of suggesting standards of co-operation, of recommending the objects among Southwide causes to be included in the program, of recommending the ratio of division of the co-operative funds as between Statewide and Southwide causes in each state; and of promoting the Co-operative Program. This committee shall be charged with all negotiations with state conventions and state boards, and with other co-operating agencies in matters that pertain to the Cooperative Program; and it shall be the authorized agency to conclude all agreements with state agencies for the conduct of the Program in the several states and for the method of handling the Southwide funds raised in the states, and for other related matters.

This separation of functions did not work satisfactorily, and in 1933 the Southern Baptist Convention recommended:

> 1. That the work of promoting the program of the Southern Baptist Convention, which has been in the hands of the Promotional Agency of Southern Baptists, be consolidated with that part of the work of this Convention which is in the hands of the Executive Committee, and be done under the leadership of that Committee through the heads of Southern Baptist Convention boards and institutions, as named by By-Law 5, and the W.M.U. secretary and the secretary of the Baptist Brotherhood, in the interest of unity, economy, simplicity, and efficiency.
>
> 2. That the Convention instruct its Executive Committee to take over leadership of this work of promotion at the earliest practicable date; organize itself fittingly and adequately for the new task; and plan the details of all such promotional programs as may be committed to it by the Convention, or may be found necessary, in conference with the heads of the Southwide boards and institutions, who are, under this policy, to be the principal contact parties with the field for such work of promotion. The very heart of this matter is in the mobilizing, co-ordinating and using the splendid promotional possibilities dormant in the great operating agencies of the Convention.

In setting up the new Church Finance Program in 1955, the Convention further stated:

> It is our understanding that the primary responsibility for the origination, development, and promotion of the financial program of the Southern Baptist Convention among the churches is given to the Executive Committee and to the Promotion Committee of the Executive Committee, working in co-operation with the several agencies of the Southern Baptist Convention for the implementation of this program.

The Executive Committee as constituted by the Convention in Louisville in 1927 had its first full meeting in Nashville in 1927, and voted to establish its headquarters in that city. Austin Crouch was elected the first executive secretary, a position he held until retirement in 1946. Duke K. McCall served as executive secretary-treasurer from 1946 until he was elected president of the Southern Baptist Theological Seminary in 1951. Porter Routh was elected executive secretary-treasurer in 1951.

The work of the Executive Committee is divided into three parts, dealing with administrative, promotional, and publication matters. The executive secretary is "the executive officer of the entire work of the Executive Committee including general responsibility for the promotional work of the Committee." He has the "administrative responsibility in connection with all of the affairs of the Executive Committee of the Southern Baptist Convention, and the affairs of the Convention as outlined in Bylaw 9. He shall render such services as the churches and other denominational organizations may require to the limit of his ability."

The Executive Committee is composed of four standing committees: (1) Administrative, (2) Promotion, (3) Finance, (4) Convention Arrangements.

The duties of the Administrative Committee are "to consider all matters related to the administrative work of the Executive Committee, including agreements with co-operating state organizations or agencies as to the basis of cooperation, such other matters as may be referred to it, and to employ such help as may seem wise for the conduct of the office of the Executive Committee."

The Committee on Promotion has as its duty "the promotion among all our constituency of the Cooperative Program and any special efforts authorized by the Southern Baptist Convention; such promotion to be in harmony with the agreements with the several state agencies."

The Finance Committee is charged with the responsibility to "study and make recommendations concerning the budgets and audit reports of the Convention and its agencies. Recommendations concerning the allocation of Cooperative Program funds shall be initiated in the Finance Committee and brought to the Executive Committee after consultation with the Administrative Committee."

The Committee on Convention Arrangements has the responsibility of making arrangements for the meetings of the Southern Baptist Convention in accordance with the bylaws of the Convention, and recommending through the Executive Committee to the Committee on Time, Place, and Preacher the place or places for future Conventions.

The Executive Committee handles all Convention funds. It receives and receipts for all current funds of the Convention, including Cooperative Program and designated funds. Such funds are received from the states and distributed. Cooperative Program funds are distributed according to the percentages adopted by the Convention, and designated funds according to the stipulation of the donors. A monthly report of all receipts and disbursements is compiled and sent to all of the agencies, to the state secretaries, to the state Baptist papers, and to others who might be interested. Annual reports of all receipts and disbursements are presented in the *Book of Reports*, made to the Convention, and published in the Convention *Annual*. Receipts from all of the states and individuals and disbursements to all of the agencies or other designated causes are checked each year by a certified public accountant. All checks must be signed by two bonded employees.

The agencies of the Convention present their needs to the Finance Committee of the Executive Committee in its December meeting. The allocation of Cooperative Program funds agreed on by the Finance Committee must be approved by the Administrative Committee, and then by the entire Executive Committee. The recommendations then go to the Southern Baptist Convention, and of course they are subject to change by the Southern Baptist Convention. Generally, however, the Southern Baptist Convention has accepted the recommendations of the Executive Committee in the matter of the allocation of Cooperative Program funds.

The Executive Committee is also instructed to present to the Convention each year a consolidated and comprehensive financial statement of all agencies of the Convention, showing the assets and the liabilities of all the agencies, and the cash receipts of the year. This statement is presented to the Executive Committee and then to the Convention, and is printed in the Convention *Annual*.

The committee is instructed by the bylaws to recommend a comprehensive budget for the Convention and its agencies, which budget shall include the budgets of all the agencies of the Convention as approved by the Executive Committee, together with the percentage of Convention funds which may be allocated to each cause. A new provision included in 1956 states that the Executive Committee shall not recommend any percentage allocation of funds for any agency or institution for which the Convention does not elect trustees or directors. The agencies present their budgets to the December meeting of the Executive Committee, and they are then presented to the Convention as a part of the annual report of the Executive Committee. In the case of organizations, like the Baptist World Alliance, where financial assistance is given by the Convention, the sum is included in the Convention Operating Budget, but no percentage allocation is made.

As the administrative agency of the Convention, the Executive Committee looks after those affairs not specifically committed to some other board or agency. This provision assures that all matters that come up which might involve the Convention will receive attention. The Committee is also empowered to act for the Convention ad interim in all matters not otherwise provided for. It must notify all boards, agencies, and institutions of the actions of the Convention, and advise with them as to the best way of promoting all the interests of the Convention. It does not have authority to control or direct the several boards, agencies, and institutions of the Convention. But it is instructed and commissioned to study the affairs of those boards, agencies, and institutions of the Convention, and to make recommendations to them concerning needed adjustments and also to make whatever recommendations concerning them to the Convention it deems advisable.

For example, the Executive Committee has surveyed the needs of the various agencies from time to time in regard to the capital needs program. At times of threatening debt, defalcation of trusted employees, unanticipated reverses, and in the failure of the Convention itself to act on some matters which involved an agency, the Executive Committee has taken action. For example, no agency can make an appropriation to any cause or for any purpose other than the promotion of its own work except by the approval, or upon the instruction, of the Convention or of the Executive Committee. An agency cannot undertake a special financial campaign for budget needs, endowment, building, equipment, or other purpose until it first receives the endorsement and approval of the Convention or its Executive Committee. An agency cannot create any indebtedness except such as can and will be repaid out of current operating receipts within a period of three years, without the consent of the Convention or the Executive Committee. In order to obtain this approval, the agency must file a statement showing the source of such anticipated receipts. The amount of bond on persons who handle funds or securities for the Convention must be approved by the Convention or its Executive Committee.

The Executive Committee is responsible for promotion and publicity, in co-operation with the other agencies and institutions of the Convention. When the work of the Co-operative Program Commission (originally known as the Commission on the 75 Million Campaign) was committed to the Executive Committee, Frank Burkhalter came from that Commission to the Executive Committee as director of publicity. He was succeeded by Walter Murchison Gilmore (q.v.), who served from 1930 until his death in 1946. C. E. Bryant served as director of publicity from 1947 through 1948. He was succeeded by Albert McClellan, who came as director of publications in 1949.

The following services to Southern Baptists are furnished through the Executive Committee's Division of Publications:

The Baptist Bulletin Service.—Owned and edited by the Executive Committee for the purpose of informing Southern Baptists about all phases of work. The bulletins, which are used by hundreds of churches for their Sunday announcements, are printed and distributed by the Baptist Sunday School Board under provisions of a contract signed Jan. 1, 1945.

Stewardship Tract Service.—A service which provides to Southern Baptists through the state offices a large array of tracts on various phases of stewardship and the denomination's Cooperative Program.

The Baptist Program.—A magazine which is mailed free of charge to all pastors, state workers, and other denominational agents. Published monthly, it strives to inform pastors of the over-all Convention program, and to aid them in their promotion of kingdom work.

Baptist Mat Service.—Another medium through which the Executive Committee seeks to aid the pastor in the promotion of denominational activities.

Baptist Press.—A service to the denominational and secular press. In co-operation with the editors of the state Baptist papers and publicity departments of Southern Baptist Convention agencies, this service gathers news of wide interest and makes it available in regular releases for publication.

James Edgar Dillard (q.v.) served 13 years as director of promotion until his retirement in July, 1947. He was succeeded by Merrill D. Moore, who assumed his duties Jan. 12, 1948. The director of promotion has the responsibility of promoting the Cooperative Program, the Every-Member Canvass, the Church Finance Program of Southern Baptists, and the various emphases which are set by the Convention in the field of promotion from year to year.

In keeping with the Convention provision, the Promotion Division does its work through the various state conventions and through the agencies of the Southern Baptist Convention. In connection with the meeting of the Executive Committee in December and June, there is held a Joint Promotion Conference to consider all promotion recommendations and plans to be presented to the Southern Baptist Convention. This conference group is made up of the editors, state secretaries, and promotion secretaries in all of the states, the secretaries and presidents of the various Southern Baptist Convention agencies, and other pastors and individuals who are brought in for assistance from time to time. Recommendations go from the Joint Promotion Conference to the Promotion Committee, a subcommittee of the Executive Committee, then to the Executive Committee for approval, and finally to the Convention itself, which is the ultimate authority.

The Committee on Convention Arrangements of the Executive Committee is charged under the Convention Procedure to investigate possible invitations for the Convention's annual meeting and to bring a summary of findings with a recommendation or recommendations to the Committee on Time, Place, and Preacher.

The Executive Committee is charged with having oversight of the arrangements for the meetings of the Convention, with authority to change both the time and place of the meetings in accordance with the provisions of Article XI, Section 3, of the Constitution.

The director of publications for the Executive Committee has served as press representative for the Southern Baptist Convention, and the agencies are instructed to have information which will be of interest in the hands of the press representative in advance of the Convention. Through the Committee on Convention Arrangements, contacts are made with the local committee, hotel reservations are worked out, contracts for the auditorium, etc., are prepared, exhibit space is allocated, and other general plans are made for the meeting of the Southern Baptist Convention.

In dealing with other Baptist groups, the Executive Committee is authorized to "act in an advisory capacity in all questions of co-operation between the different agencies of the Convention, and between the agencies of the Convention and those of other conventions, whether state or national."

A subcommittee of the Administrative Committee has charge of the Van Deusen Opdyke Scholarships, which are awarded annually to candidates chosen from the mountain boys and girls within the territory of the Southern Baptist Convention.

The Executive Committee also has the responsibility for the printing and distribution of the Southern Baptist Convention *Annual*.

The expenses for the Executive Committee are provided through the Convention Operating Budget, which is made possible through an allocation of the Cooperative Program, and by an additional $60,000 from the Sunday School Board each year.

The Executive Committee is made up of the president of the Convention, the senior secretary of the Convention, the president of the Woman's Missionary Union, and one member from each co-operating state of the Convention having 25,000 members or more. When a state convention has 250,000 members, it is entitled to an additional representative, and one additional representative for each 250,000, with no state having more than five. When a state has more than one representative, at least one shall be a lay person. No salaried official of the Convention or any of its agencies, or any member of any board or board of trustees or commission of the Convention or any salaried official of any state convention or of any agency of a state convention may be a member of the Executive Committee. These restrictions do not apply in case of the president and senior secretary of the Convention. PORTER ROUTH

EXPERIENCE. A designation for both the sensory phenomena of an event and the resultant values. Religious experience ranges from "an uneasiness and a solution" to the mystic's consciousness of identity with divinity.

By Christian experience is meant the totality of the experience which the believer shares through his fellowship with God in Christ. It is the process by which the great body of objective data of the Christian revelation becomes subjectively meaningful to the individual. Experience is the personal appropriation of the common intellectual and historical heritage of Christianity as a vital constituent of life.

BIBLIOGRAPHY: W. R. Matthews, *God in Christian Thought and Experience* (1947). H. N. Wieman, *Religious Experience and Scientific Method* (1926).
A. ELLISON JENKINS

EXPIATION. This term does not appear in the Authorized Version. Older theologians used the term very little and then in a sense synonymous with propitiation. However, in current theological discussion a sharp distinction is often drawn between expiation, as atoning action directed toward the removal of sin or guilt, and propitiation, as atoning action directed toward satisfying the wrath of God. Many writers follow C. H. Dodd in rejecting the idea of propitiation altogether in favor of the simpler idea of expiation. A better viewpoint comes from an interpretation of the biblical idea of atonement which includes the ideas of both expiation and propitiation.

See also ATONEMENT and PROPITIATION.

BIBLIOGRAPHY: L. Morris, *The Apostolic Preaching of the Cross* (1956). V. Taylor, *The Atonement in New Testament Teaching* (1945). W. BOYD HUNT

EXTENSION CENTERS, BAPTIST COLLEGE. Two types of educational programs are: (1) the off-campus extension of the regular program offered on the college campus, with identical courses and credits; (2) a missionary type of adult education in which courses do not exactly correspond nor are credits interchangeable with the regular college program, but where the needs of pastors and other religious workers are met through specially designed courses. Some extension centers combine features of these two types.

The extension program among Southern Baptist colleges had its beginning in Sept., 1942, in Jasper, Ala., when Gilbert L. Guffin, pastor of the First Baptist Church, organized the first center, which was destined to become the pattern for many to follow. This center was related to Walker Junior College, a private institution, which gave credit for the studies taught by Guffin. The Jasper center originated in a request from ministers for an adult education program which would meet their needs and better prepare them for service to the churches while they were making their living in secular jobs. From a beginning of 19, this center's enrolment increased to more than 100, with some students driving as far as 200 miles round trip per night through all kinds of weather to sit three hours in classes, after working all day.

A group of Alabama Baptist leaders in 1946, recognizing the possibilities of the work in Jasper, decided to project such a program from Howard College in Birmingham, with a view to making it a statewide program. Guffin was asked to head the program, thus beginning what has come to be known as the Howard Plan. Guffin began in Jan., 1947, with the program as an integral part of the college's curriculum and the support of the Alabama Baptist State Convention.

Georgia Baptist leaders considered the program in 1948 and recommended it to the Georgia Baptist convention, which approved the recommendation and asked Mercer University, Macon, to administer the program, beginning in Jan., 1949. Leaders of the Tennessee Baptist Convention and the presidents of the Baptist colleges of that state considered the plan in 1949. Carson-Newman College, Jefferson City, projected the program in Sept., 1950.

Meanwhile, in 1944 Gardner-Webb Junior

College, Boiling Springs, N. C., began organizing night classes on the campus for adults, both ministers and laymen. After two years the program lapsed. In the fall of 1950, a department of church-community development was organized, carrying a program into the surrounding associations. This was a modified form of the Howard Plan and the beginning of a permanent extension work. Other state bodies and Baptist colleges became interested and began some type of extension work. Campbellsville Junior College, Campbellsville, Ky.; Oklahoma Baptist University, Shawnee, Okla.; and the University of Richmond, Va., projected their programs in the fall of 1951. Louisiana Baptist College, Pineville, La., began a center at Lake Charles; and Ouachita College, Arkadelphia, Ark.; Union University, Jackson, Tenn.; and Clarke Memorial Junior College, Newton, Miss., all began work in 1952, but the last named continued its work for only a brief time. Belmont College, Nashville, Tenn., began work in 1953, and Baylor University, Waco, Tex., began work in Dallas in 1955. Georgetown College, Georgetown, Ky., has carried on some type of extension work spasmodically since 1946, and Hardin-Simmons University, Abilene, Tex., has conducted correspondence courses and some off-campus instruction. Furman University, Greenville, S. C., has conducted regional schools for ministers during the summers.

The extension centers are planned in strategic localities, meeting usually in some church, with classes one or more nights a week. The curriculum is planned to meet the needs of ministers and religious lay leaders; to strengthen their work and the work of the whole denomination. Special certificates of achievement for completing specified work are awarded at appropriate "graduation" exercises on the college campuses, often in connection with regular commencement activities.

The 1954–55 enrolment in the 168 centers operated by 11 colleges totaled 7,035, of whom 1,851 were ministers. The faculties are made up largely of active pastors and college teachers, all of whom have the academic training and spiritual development necessary for teaching. Many of the teachers hold doctorates in their respective fields. During 1954–55, 694 teachers were used in the program, with a total of 856 different teachers having taught a total of 28,857 different students during the history of the program.

PARK HARRIS ANDERSON, JR.

F

FACTOR, JAMES (b. *c.* 1798; d. Sasakwa, Okla., Nov. 6, 1896). Seminole Indian, language interpreter, Baptist preacher, reported to be the first Baptist convert among the Seminoles. Persecuted by Seminoles hostile to Christianity, he was imprisoned, but his intimate friendship with Chief John Jumper (*q.v.*) led the latter to befriend him with continual postponements of trial until he was released. Instrumental as interpreter for Joseph Samuel Murrow (*q.v.*), he helped persuade Jumper to abandon Presbyterianism to unite with the Baptists. Factor and Jumper became members of the Ash Creek Baptist Church the year it was organized (1860) and went with the church when it aligned with the Confederacy in the Civil War. Factor was ordained in 1865. He is buried 11 miles southwest of Wewoka, Okla.

J. M. GASKIN

FAIRVIEW COLLEGIATE INSTITUTE. A Baptist school at Fairview, Buncombe County, N. C., founded in 1888 by W. A. G. Brown. In 1892 the school was adopted as the associational school of Buncombe Association, and trustees were appointed to govern it. In 1893, with A. B. Justice as principal, the school was chartered by the state legislature and its title legally transferred to the association. The school's debt was described as "desperate," and Fairview was closed shortly after 1900.

D. L. SMILEY

FAITH. The trustful, believing response to God, in which God makes himself known to man (Eph. 2:8; John 17:3) and man entrusts himself into the keeping and direction of God (John 3:36; Acts 16:31). Faith is God's work (John 6:44) and man's privilege and responsibility (John 5:39). Right relationship with God is, at all times and in all periods of history, faith and trust (Rom. 4:1–8).

Distinction should be made, however, between an intellectual assent to a creed, sometimes called a confession of faith, and an experience of grace in which one commits himself to God. "Faith" is sometimes used to designate various denominations, such as "the Catholic faith," "the Presbyterian faith." In the New Testament the substance and truth of revelation is called "the faith" (Acts 6:7; 13:8; 14:22).

GEORGE C. HUMPHREY

FALL BRANCH SEMINARY. A male school at Fall Branch, Tenn., founded *c.* 1851 with L.

Bennett as principal. This secondary school was "under the patronage" of Holston Association until *c.* 1870 when it was reorganized as Masonic Normal College.   LYNN EDWARD MAY, JR.

FALL OF MAN. Traditionally, the original commission of sin by the first human beings, together with man's resulting change of nature and status. Man's fall from the created state, described in the Adam-Eve narrative (Gen. 3) and alluded to in the New Testament (Rom. 5:12; I Cor. 15:21 f.; II Cor. 11:3; I Tim. 2:14), was classically formulated as a doctrine by Augustine. Twentieth-century liberalism under the impact of evolution has denied both the historicity and actuality of a human fall and taught instead man's ascent. Neo-orthodoxy, also denying the historicity, teaches either a suprahistorical fall or the individual "fall" of every man. Some conservative Protestant and all Roman Catholic theologians teach the historicity. Roman Catholic theology, however, relates the historical fall to its doctrine of Adam's superadded gift. The fall resulted in such consequences as alienation from God, disruption among men, depravity, and death.

See also MAN and SIN.

BIBLIOGRAPHY: E. Brunner, *Man in Revolt* (1947); *The Doctrine of Creation and Redemption* (1952). J. Orr, *God's Image in Man* (1905). F. R. Tennant, *The Origin and Propagation of Sin* (1906).

   JAMES LEO GARRETT

FALLS CREEK ASSEMBLY. The only assembly owned and operated by the Baptist General Convention of Oklahoma, located on 195 acres of land in the Arbuckle Mountains six miles southeast of Davis, Okla. The original site consisted of 160 acres which James Burley Rounds (1876–   ) and William Durant Moorer (*q.v.*) located from a picture they saw in a barber shop in Davis in 1917. Purchase price of the site was $1,200, and Rounds took a personal option on it by securing $200 to hold it temporarily. He and Moorer "had been appointed a committee to look out and locate a Baptist Assembly grounds that our B.Y.P.U. State Convention might further such an enterprise." The first assembly on the grounds was held Aug. 16–26, 1917, with total registration 273.

By the second session there were four buildings on the grounds; two pavilions, one given by Frank Tripp and another by the Salt Fork Valley Association in honor of their missionary H. E. Hogan; Howell Hall, provided by the state Woman's Missionary Union, and the Pollyanna Club House erected by the young women of the state. That year the state Baptist Young People's Union deeded the assembly to the convention debt free.

In 1920, with 1,200 attending sessions, there were 40 classes covering all phases of Baptist work from the pastorate to Sunbeams. Ground was broken for a tabernacle type auditorium, to be constructed out of steel and concrete. In 1926–27, a large dam was built on a creek passing through the assembly grounds, at a cost of $7,800, financed by the sale of shares at $50 each, which entitled the holder to fishing, boating, and duck hunting privileges for 13 years. In 1927 property value was $32,500, with only $812 debt.

In 1928 the assembly outgrew its facilities. The tabernacle was large enough to accommodate only half the attendance. It was replaced by the Moorer-Rounds Tabernacle, a 60 × 90 foot structure, dedicated by Isaac Jacobus Van Ness (*q.v.*) on Sunday morning of the assembly's next annual session.

Beginning in 1922, Rounds was requested by the convention's board of directors to act as business manager of the assembly in an attempt to balance its business affairs; on Nov. 2, 1922, the assembly showed an overdraft of $6,199. Rounds was succeeded in Dec. 1924, by Thaddeus H. Farmer.

During Farmer's administration, continuing until 1936, the number of buildings on the grounds increased from 36 to 100. Following his resignation, the assembly's affairs were placed under the Convention's board of directors, with a Falls Creek committee selected from the board's membership annually, an arrangement still in force. The committee directs all affairs of the assembly except the program, which through the years has remained the responsibility of the Sunday school and Training Union (now religious education) secretary.

In 1938 registration totaled 7,865, and at the convention's annual board meeting Dec. 6, 1938, action was taken to enlarge the Moorer-Rounds Tabernacle to seat 5,000 instead of 1,500. This was completed for the 1939 assembly. At the assembly's 25th anniversary, Aug. 4–14, 1941, registration reached a high mark of 9,009 with 4,869 average daily class attendance. War conditions caused a decrease in attendance in 1942 and cancellation of the 1943–45 sessions. Because its growth had overtaxed its physical facilities, in 1952 the assembly was divided into two seven-day sessions in which it had the cumulative total of 18,419 full-time registrations, the highest in its history up to that time.

A series of one-week Royal Ambassador and Girl's Auxiliary camps, running alternately, precedes the annual assembly several weeks each summer. In 1954, the Woman's Missionary Union broke ground for a new camp site, Nunny-Cha-ha, atop the highest point in the Arbuckle Mountains. The cumulative registration in 1955 for the split assembly was 21,561, a new record high. In 1956 convention-owned property value totaled $193,297; church and privately owned properties were valued at approximately $350,000. The 1955 assembly budget was $88,704, with $13,000 of this amount from the Cooperative Program. In 1956 Thomas Edwin Carter succeeded Millard Judson Cook as business manager.

BIBLIOGRAPHY: W. L. Stigler, "A History of the Institutions of the Baptist General Convention of Oklahoma" (1945).

   TOM E. CARTER and J. M. GASKIN

FALLS CREEK INDIAN BAPTIST ASSEMBLY. Organized 1947, meets annually on the Falls Creek Assembly grounds. Registration reports showed a total of 333 in 1947, and 509 in 1956, representing 23 tribes. Financed by registration fees and annual grants from the Oklahoma Woman's Missionary Union and the Southern Baptist Home Mission Board, it is governed by its own constitution and elects officers annually. J. M. GASKIN

FAMILY NIGHT. Designated by a variety of names, the Wednesday evening fellowship meeting of the church, involving a common meal and a variety of other activities. To some degree a development of the last 15 years, Family Night is observed in a large and growing number of Southern Baptist churches. Specific schedules and arrangements vary. The "Church Night" plan provides 30 to 45 minutes for supper, followed by an hour for meetings of organizations. Some churches have Brotherhoods and W.M.S. circles and auxiliaries; some, Sunday school teachers' meetings and W.M.U. auxiliaries, while others vary the programs to include Baptist Training Union planning meetings, study classes, choir rehearsals, or other activities. All assemble afterward for the prayer service. Special groups may meet before supper or after prayer meeting.

Other churches have Family Night primarily for fellowship and prayer. At the meal, time is taken to sing, introduce visitors, thank those serving the food, report news about the church family, and enjoy special musical or dramatic features. Prayer service follows immediately in the sanctuary, with hymns, periods of prayer, special music, and a Bible study or devotional talk by the pastor. When the Sunday school workers' council is held, the superintendents meet before supper, and departmental meetings are after prayer service. Other special meetings may be arranged at either of these times. When all of a family comes for several meetings on one night, time is saved and the transportation problem simplified. Meals provided at the church at nominal cost encourage many to attend who otherwise would not do so.

Since the time of the early disciples, who, "breaking bread from house to house, did eat their meat with gladness" (Acts 2:46), fellowship at meals has drawn Christians together. The churches that have consistently followed this plan have experienced an increasing sense of vital fellowship within their membership. Aside from practical values, the custom of having many families of a church to have a meal together each week helpfully serves to develop the elements of spiritual solidarity that characterize a congregation as a family in Christ.
WALTER MOORE

FAMILY VISITOR. A weekly, and the first newspaper planned and sanctioned by the Alabama Baptist State Convention. Edited by John D. Williams, the initial issue appeared in Wetumpka on Nov. 12, 1836. About 1839 ownership was transferred to Edwin D. King and Milo P. Jewett, who moved the paper to Marion, where it later became, under Jewett's editorship, the original *Alabama Baptist*.
RAY M. ATCHISON

FARMER, JAMES SADBERRAY (b. near Norwood, N. C., Feb. 6, 1875; d. near Raleigh, N. C., Feb. 27, 1938). Editor. The oldest son of Thomas Croson and Martha Keziah (Thompson) Farmer, he attended Norwood High School, Bethel Hill Institute, and was graduated from Scottsburg Normal College, Scottsburg, Va., 1899. Ordained in 1899, he spent one year as missionary in the Roanoke Association. He served as pastor in Rocky Mount two years; was field representative for the *Biblical Recorder*, 1902–08; was secretary-treasurer of the Biblical Recorder Publishing Co., 1909–38; and was editor of the *Biblical Recorder*, 1931–38. During his long association with the *Biblical Recorder*, he held pastorates in country churches: Midway, New Hope, Chalybeate Springs, Fuquay Springs, and Millbrook. He married Myrtle Hart Farmer, who died in 1920. In 1922 he married Foy Johnson Willingham and to this marriage were born two children.

BIBLIOGRAPHY: B. J. W. Graham, *Baptist Biography* (1923).
FOY J. FARMER

FATHERHOOD OF GOD. Generally the authority and concern of God over all that is dependent on his care. In a more special way God is Father according to the pattern of the prayer in John 17 where Jesus prays for himself, his disciples, and all people who will ever believe.

In the inner circle God is the Father of Christ. Many passages in the New Testament evidence this; the Gospel of John designates God as "Father" 119 times. The *love* of the Father is in the Son. In the obedient life of Jesus, the Father loves the Son so much that he "hath given all things into his hand" (John 3:35) and "sheweth him all things that himself doeth" (John 5:20); but in the sacrificial death the love of the Father for his obedient Son comes to full focus (John 10:17). The final hour pulls back the veil, disclosing the Father's love for the eternal Son in glory (John 17:24).

In the middle circle God is the Father of those who believe. The Heavenly Father's love is mediated through the Son to the disciples; and the Father's love is bestowed on believers because they love the Son, keep the word of the Son, and believe that the Son came from the Father. John always reserves the term "Son" for Jesus, but he stresses the fact that all who have been born from above are children of God, who are taught to worship the Father in spirit and truth.

In the outer circle God is the Father of all men (Eph. 3:14; 4:6; I Cor. 8:6), not in the same sense in which he is the Father of Christ or of those who believe; but he is over all and cares for all. In creation he made all men his offspring (Acts 17:29), fulfilling one function of fatherhood. In redemption the Father's love reaches out for all who are lost in sin and thus deprived of the joys of salvation in the Father's presence (Luke 15:11–32). In providence God provides for both the just and the unjust (Matt. 5:43–48), an idea of fatherhood which some Baptists reject, although representative Baptist theologians teach it.　　　　　　DALE MOODY

FELIX, WILLIAM H. (b. Woodford County, Ky., Oct. 6, 1838; d. Clearwater, Fla., Jan. 6, 1912). Minister. He attended schools in Woodford and later enrolled in Georgetown College, Kentucky, graduating in 1860. In 1859 he was licensed by Hillsboro Church, where he later preached his first sermon. His first pastorate was at New Castle, Ky., in 1860. After a brief ministry in Pilgrim Church, New York City, he returned to Kentucky in 1870 to become pastor of First Church, Covington, where he served 14 years. After several brief pastorates he was called to First Church, Lexington, in 1887 and served till Jan. 1, 1898, when he took charge of David's Fork Church. Because of illness he resigned this pastorate in 1908. Felix was for a long time a trustee of the Southern Baptist Theological Seminary. He helped organize the Baptist Education Society of Kentucky.

In 1861 Felix married Mattie Hayden and four daughters were born to them. After his wife's death in June, 1870, he married Camilla Hemingray in 1874. They had two children.

LEO T. CRISMON

FELLOWSHIP. The doctrine of the fundamental unity and interdependence of believers in Christ; the touchstone of the church.

Three New Testament terms, with cognates, convey the idea of fellowship: *koinonia* (fellowship, communion), *hen* or *henotes* (one, unity), and *soma* (body).

Koinonia and its cognates provide not only the content of fellowship but also the root of the term "communion." The root means "common," as distinguished from "individual"; it implies commonality or mutuality. The primary meaning is participation in the same thing; association is a derived and secondary meaning. The New Testament terms convey three basic ideas: (1) the relation of a believer with God the Father, Son, and Spirit; (2) the relation of believer with believer; and (3) the demonstration of interdependence between believer and believer. The third idea is closely connected with the second, as the practical expression of interdependence.

The fundamental unity of Christians is derived from the fact that each believer is related to God the Father, through Christ, and in the Spirit. It was on this basis that John appealed for a fellowship of believers (I John 1:3–10). Each believer is a member of a Christ-centered community, a heavenly community, over which Christ is Lord (I Cor. 1:9). This community is either created by the Spirit or constitutes the sphere in which the believer participates in the Spirit (II Cor. 13:13). In this community there can be no dual religious loyalty. In worship one establishes fellowship with the object of his worship. Therefore, idolatry is to be abhorred; Christianity has nothing in common with heathenism (I Cor. 10:14–20). By participating in the Lord's Supper, one affirms Christ's lordship over his life.

The relation of a believer with God requires a similar relation of believer with believer. The lack of such a relationship between believers belies one's alleged relationship with God (I John 1:6–7). Mutual care is required of believers. The maintenance of harmonious relationships among Christians is of such prime importance that compromise with idolatry (either actual or apparent) must be rejected lest tender consciences be offended and the relationship between believers be broken (I Cor. 10:23 ff.). The Supper, therefore, is a social meal, as well as a personal communion with Christ. Inasmuch as Christians have the Spirit in common (Phil. 2:1), they are to resolve their differences and cultivate love. A believer resolves differences when he confirms his fellowship with God by holy living; by so doing he also strengthens fellowship among believers (I John 1:6 ff.). Love controls all activity and becomes virtually synonymous with fellowship (cf. I John 1:3 ff.; 2:9 ff.), for love is the essential element of the common life.

The fellowship of believers is not an abstract theory of interdependence and interrelatedness, but a relationship which is demonstrated in practice. In the New Testament believers shared in evangelism to the Gentiles and sealed their partnership by giving the right hand of fellowship to each other (Gal. 2:9). In the fellowship of faith, slavery was relieved by spiritual, if not legal, equity and equality (Philem. 6). Social, racial, and economic barriers to fellowship were overcome by a common religion. Fellowship might assume the outward character of a "collection" or "contribution" by Gentiles for needy Christians in Jerusalem (Rom. 15:26; II Cor. 8:14; 9:13; Heb. 13:16). This collection was the Gentiles' expression of gratitude for the evangelical blessing which Jewish Christians had shared with them; it was a pledge of equality in the scattered Christian community and an instrument whereby fellowship was strengthened. Fellowship was a common life in which all things, both material and spiritual, were shared (Acts 2:42 ff.; 4:32). The common life of the Jerusalem church was not an economic communism nor a socialization of goods, but the spontaneous solution of the economic problem created by the social disabilities of early Christianity.

The terms for "one" or "unity" refer primarily to the relationship between God and believer, a similar relationship to that sustained between Father and Son (John 17:22). The secondary meaning of the terms is the life of man in the light of God. Believers are gathered

Fellowship, Right Hand of

up in a unity which is preserved by divine aid; this preservation demonstrates the validity of Christian faith and becomes the basis of evangelical appeal to the world (John 17). One cooperates with God in the preservation of unity with God by assuming a threefold responsibility. First, mutual care protects a person from sin and preserves the integrity and purity of the community. Second, if one sins, he must assume full responsibility for his guilt. Third, if one sins, those who are not guilty are to bear with compassion the sins of the offender lest they themselves succumb to pride. Mutual care means that one responsibly shares the burdens of others while assuming complete responsibility for his own (Gal. 6:1–6).

The most descriptive term of the corporate nature of the church is "body." Both the supremacy of the Head and the interrelation of members are emphasized in this corporate nature. The church is the body of Christ, who is the Head (Eph. 1:23–24; 4:12 ff.). The Head was made supreme by divine action (Col. 1:18). The Head is the source of unity and the fountain of nourishment (Eph. 4:16; Col. 2:19). The church must submit to its Head. The body is a complex organism of interrelated members, with each necessary to the body, and with the condition of each member affecting all other members. A member cannot separate from others without repudiating its own character and crippling the body (I Cor. 12:12–27). Each member has a specific function; the various functions, or "gifts," are complementary, not competitive. Operating together, they achieve the objective of the church (Rom. 12:4–8). If there is any exaltation, it is the exaltation of the most insignificant member (I Cor. 12:22–24). All members have one gift in common—love; without it the exercise of other gifts is meaningless and irrelevant (I Cor. 13).

Baptists have held a view of the disciplined or gathered church in which fellowship is central. Fellowship is maintained by requiring personal faith in Christ of each person who seeks membership, by requiring holy living of each member, by exercising congregational government in which none (including the minister) is pre-eminent, by associating with fellow Christians in missions, benevolence, and worship, and by strengthening the awareness of Christ's lordship by means of identification with him in baptism and communion with him and his followers in the Lord's Supper.

BIBLIOGRAPHY: E. A. Payne, *The Fellowship of Believers* (1952). L. S. Thornton, *The Common Life in the Body of Christ* (1942). R. C. Walton, *The Gathered Community* (1946). H. Wamble, "The Concept and Practice of Christian Fellowship" (1956).

HUGH WAMBLE

FELLOWSHIP, RIGHT HAND OF. The custom of the hand shake, practiced by the Romans, Greeks, Hebrews, and most other peoples of antiquity, is an expression of sympathy by means of contact, a method of clinching a bargain or expressing a covenant. The "right hand of fellowship" was extended in ordination services in Puritan New England. Increase Mather (1639–1723), a Congregational minister, said that he was surprised when asked by the Baptists to "give the right hand of fellowship" when he assisted in the ordination of a Baptist. By 1801 the practice of extending the right hand of fellowship to new members was common among Baptists. This practice, which continues to the present, involves a distinction between Christian fellowship and church fellowship. The first is given by all Christians and the latter by the local church or by the pastor. Fellowship is extended in some churches upon the admission of the individual to the church, but in others, after baptism or the receipt of a church letter.

BIBLIOGRAPHY: I. Backus, *Church History of New England from 1620 to 1804* (1853). J. Hastings, ed., *Encyclopaedia of Religion and Ethics* (1913). J. M. Pendleton, *Church Manual* (1950). W. W. Sweet, *Religion on the American Frontier; The Baptists* (1931). "Terms of Communion," *Baptist Manual* (1835).

LAWRENCE CLEGG

FELLOWSHIP SUPPER. See FAMILY NIGHT.

FERGUSON, BARBOUR VAUGHN (b. Floyd County, Va., July 12, 1883; d. Fort Smith, Ark., Sept. 14, 1953). Pastor. His parents were William and Signora (Ramsey) Ferguson. He was ordained by Sandy Creek Church near Ringold, Va., Apr. 24, 1909. He attended private schools and Reidsville Seminary, and graduated from Leaksville Spray Institute and from Wake Forest College (N. C.) in 1912. He studied two years at Southern Baptist Theological Seminary, Louisville, Ky. During his career Ferguson was pastor of only two churches: First Baptist, West Durham, N. C., 1914–16; and First Baptist, Fort Smith, Ark., 1916–50. He was president of the Arkansas Baptist State Convention two terms and served as a trustee of the Relief and Annuity Board and the Southern Baptist Theological Seminary. In 1913 he married Mae Reynolds of N. C., who died in 1938. He married Margaret Jones Fowler of Prescott, Ark., in 1939.

MRS. PAT MURPHY

FINANCIAL PLANS, DENOMINATIONAL. Plans for raising and administering money for the support of missionary and educational work by Baptist churches have included early missionary societies, conventions, financial agents, special offerings in the churches, the 75 Million Campaign, the Co-operative Program, the work of state mission offices and Southern Baptist Convention Executive Committee, and the Business and Financial Plan of the Southern Baptist Convention.

Missionary societies.—Baptist missionaries to the Indians were supported by churches and associations as early as 1778. The influence of the missionary movement in England under William Carey (*q.v.*) spread to America. The

Massachusetts Missionary Society was formed in 1802 and others followed.

Luther Rice (q.v.) was employed as agent of another such society. Throughout the nation missionary societies, which were composed of both men and women, sprang up where Rice visited. Female "mite" societies were also organized. Because of opposition to missions in many of the churches, these missionary societies were composed only of interested individuals within a church or association.

Educational societies were established for the support of academies or colleges. Even Sunday school societies operated Sunday schools in or near the buildings of the churches where there was opposition to the church's operating such an organization itself.

The missionary and educational societies sought to band the members together for prayer, disseminate information concerning the work, raise monies for its support, and safeguard the autonomy of the churches by helping to keep them from involvement in an ecclesiastical organization. They did make beginnings in promotion and support of the work, and laid groundwork for more successful programs of support to come later. Societies in churches sent delegates to societies in states, and to the General Missionary Convention in the United States of America for Foreign Missions (Triennial Convention), which was organized in 1814. This organization was in reality a foreign mission society, composed of individuals interested in missions or sent by bodies interested in missions, whether churches, associations, or state conventions.

Enlargement of the work in other fields than foreign missions was made by organizing other societies for home missions, education, and publication, a separate and independent body for the prosecution of each object. After the division of the Triennial Convention in 1845, these several independent societies were the channels of missionary co-operation in the North. In 1907 the Northern (now American) Baptist Convention was formed to integrate these several societies in a denominational entity. The societies remain autonomous to this day.

Conventions.—The Southern Baptist Convention formed in 1845 followed a different principle of denominational organization. William Bullein Johnson (q.v.) described it as "a single Convention embodying the whole denomination together, with separate and distinct boards for each object of benevolent enterprise, located at different places, and all amenable to the Convention." At the organizational meeting in 1845 two boards were established: Foreign Mission Board, Richmond, Va., and Board of Domestic and Indian Missions, Marion, Ala. Success of the new Convention's work is seen in the report that in the 30 years prior to 1846 Baptists in the South contributed $250,656 to home and foreign missions. In the 13 years after 1846 they contributed to the same causes $650,698 or an average annual contribution seven times greater than before the organization of the Southern Baptist Convention.

State conventions had been organized prior to 1845 in many states, and others have been organized until in 1956 there were 23 related to the work of the Southern Baptist Convention.

Financial agents.—Each mission board, college, or other missionary agency or institution had full responsibility for raising its own funds until later plans were developed. Financial agents were employed to solicit funds from individuals and to take special offerings in the churches. Furman Institute, later Furman University, employed such agents in 1845. Typical agents sought to secure "bonds" or pledges from individuals of means. These pledges were payable over a period of from three to five, or even 10 years. The needs of these causes were so great in the early years, in the distressed economy following the Civil War, and in the 20th century that the collections made by the financial agents kept the work alive in many cases. Weaknesses in the plan were obvious, however. The bonds, or pledges, were payable over too long a period, so that collections were low, averaging from 20 to 60 per cent of pledges. The results of this plan were often tragic. Colleges, orphanages, mission boards, and later hospitals went afield, secured pledges, borrowed money against them, built or expanded with the borrowed money, failed to collect, and found themselves all but hopelessly in debt. In many cases it had to be decided whether an institution would sue its contributors for collection of pledges. Such experience has indicated the wisdom of securing pledges for 12 months rather than for longer periods.

The agent plan was expensive, and after high costs were paid, the amount available for the cause was correspondingly small. Expenses came out of first receipts. One of the basic faults of the plan was that it was of necessity built on the idea of dependence on a few persons of significant means. No plan for broad-based support had been developed.

Special offerings in the churches.—Field agents preached in the churches and took special collections for their causes. Pastors led in taking special offerings and forwarding them direct to the institution or agency. Certain special offerings in more recent years have become fixed annual offerings and continue to be a part of the support of these causes to the present.

The 75 Million Campaign.—This campaign introduced several new and strengthening factors. All missionary, educational, and benevolent causes supported by the denomination in the states and in the Convention were grouped together, and support from the constituency was sought jointly for all. For the first time plans were set in motion to reach the masses of the Baptist people for the support of all the missionary causes. For the first time all the people, whether they were persons of small or large means, were led to think in terms of significant and worthy amounts for missionary support.

Even the plan of five-year pledges, dropped immediately after the campaign, had value in helping to lift the sights of the people to more worthy levels and larger amounts. Best of all, probably, was the plan of making payments on pledges with regularity: annually, monthly, and weekly, with emphasis given to weekly payments. Rather than a few field agents, organizers were named in every state, association, and church. A corps of volunteer canvassers was set up in each church. A competently planned and thoroughly organized program of promotion and information was undertaken. Each church became an organization for securing missionary support, and "each pastor a personal representative of each missionary cause." Funds were sent from the churches through the state mission board offices.

Cooperative Program.—This plan, begun in 1925, conserved all the advantages of the 75 Million Campaign. To this it added the value of an annual campaign for pledges, which reaches more people and secures more collectible pledges. It ties the campaign for missionary support to the annual campaign for the support of the local program. Increasingly it is seen that the task of every member is to support the local and the world mission programs of his church.

State and convention promotion.—Assistance in promotion of stewardship and the Cooperative Program has increasingly been provided by the office of the state mission secretary. Collections have gone through his office. Since 1932 offerings for all Convention causes have been received and transmitted by the office of the Executive Committee of the Convention. Leadership of the promotion work of the Convention is the responsibility of the Committee.

Business and financial plan.—To strengthen its procedures for securing, handling, and expending of missionary funds, the Convention has developed since 1927 a Business and Financial Plan. This plan provides controls in promotion matters; in the collection of funds; in handling, accounting, reporting, and expending funds; and in the assuming of indebtedness. This plan makes for greater efficiency, assures the largest return for mission funds, develops confidence in the work of the Convention, and assists in securing increasing support for the causes. MERRILL D. MOORE

FINLAND, BAPTISTS IN. Finnish Baptists are divided into two groups. A few over 1,000 speak Finnish; over 2,000 speak Swedish. Most Finns are Lutherans. The history of the Swedish-speaking Baptists began during the Crimean War in 1855, when the British fleet occupied the Oland Islands. While the British were there, Swedish ministers preached to the Swedish-speaking inhabitants on these islands, which belong to Finland. When the English battleships left, the Swedish preachers had to leave to escape arrest at the hands of the Russian authorities.

In 1856 some copies of Andreas Wiberg's book on baptism reached the islands from Sweden. The reading of this book led three men to go to Stockholm to be baptized. One of them was a customs inspector named Fagerström. He and five others who were baptized formed a church.

About this time a few Baptists were brought before the Archbishop of Turku (Abo) in the mainland. The unexpected result was the conversion of the archbishop's son and daughter, who crossed to Stockholm and were baptized by the Baptists. They returned to Finland and became active members of the Swedish-speaking church in Jacobstad near Vaasa. A church had been organized there in 1869.

In the early years there was no organized Baptist work among the Finnish-speaking people. A separate convention was started among the national Finns in 1903. Both groups have headquarters at Vaasa. There is active evangelistic work among the young people of Finland, but a shortage of trained preachers in both groups. W. O. LEWIS

FISHER, THOMAS JEFFERSON (b. Mt. Sterling, Ky., Apr. 9, 1812; d. Louisville, Ky., Jan. 11, 1866). Evangelist. He had little formal education. In 1828 he was converted, joined the Presbyterian church at Paris, Ky., and began to study the Bible diligently. Feeling that he was not scripturally baptized, he left the Presbyterian fellowship and was baptized into the fellowship of David's Fork Baptist Church by Jeremiah Vardeman (*q.v.*). Feeling a call to preach, he left home and went to Middletown, Pa., to study; later he studied in Pittsburgh under Elder S. Williams, pastor of the Baptist church there. In 1832 he was licensed to preach in Pittsburgh. In 1834 he was ordained and became pastor of the Baptist church at Lawrenceburg, Ky. He moved to Mill Creek Church near Bardstown in 1835. In Oct., 1836, he married Elizabeth Naylor.

His greatest work was as an evangelist, begun around 1836, in a turbulent time in Kentucky when many were forsaking Baptist churches to follow Alexander Campbell. He held protracted meetings from Missouri to Maryland but mostly in Kentucky. During a period of more than 30 years, he held more than 500 meetings, during which an estimated 10,000 persons professed faith in Jesus Christ. VICTOR MANTIPLY

FLAKE, ARTHUR (b. La Grange, Fayette County, Tex., Nov. 17, 1862; d. Memphis, Tenn., July 3, 1952). Sunday school and Training Union pioneer. He married Lena Nelson of Mississippi in 1895. He was educated in the schools of Bell County, Tex., and in South Belton Institute. He was converted in 1893, at the age of 31. He then became a traveling salesman and a department store manager. In 1895 he organized in his church at Winona, Miss., the first B.Y.P.U. in the state. In 1899 he helped organize the Mississippi State B.Y.P.U. Convention and served as the president until 1903. He also served as a volunteer Sunday school superintendent and was so successful that he was elected in

1909 as field worker by the Sunday School Board of the Southern Baptist Convention.

Flake's main work at first was in the area of Sunday school promotion, but later he gave his time chiefly to B.Y.P.U. promotion. However, in 1920 he was placed in charge of the board's new department of Sunday School Administration. In this position he did his major lifework. He developed, standardized, and popularized a philosophy and methodology of Sunday school organization and administration on which most future work was based. Among other things, he initiated (1) the enlargement campaign; (2) the five-step formula in building a Sunday school (discover the possibilities, enlarge the organization, provide a place, train the workers, and visit the prospects); (3) *The Sunday School Builder*, a monthly magazine which he edited from 1920 to 1936; (4) books and leaflets on Sunday school work; and (5) the Sunday school clinic idea. He improved and projected (1) Training Union administration; (2) the Sunday school Standards of Excellence; (3) the Six Point Record System; (4) the church library movement; (5) the weekly officers and teachers' meeting; (6) grading and the principle and method of multiplying units—classes and departments; (7) the associational Sunday school organization.

He was the author of the following books: *Building a Standard Sunday School* (1922), *Sunday School Officers and Their Work* (1923), *Young People's and Adult Departments* (1925), *Senior B.Y.P.U. Administration* (1926), *The True Functions of the Sunday School* (1930), *The Sunday School and the Church Budget* (1931), *Life at Eighty As I See It* (1944). He was the co-author with Carribel R. Blankenship of *The Department Sunday School* (1924), with Emma Noland of *The Sunday School Secretary and the Six Point Record System* (1924), and with Leona Lavender of *Rural and Village Sunday Schools* (1927).

The most widely distributed of his books was *Building a Standard Sunday School*. More than any other volume, it has given guidance and motivation for the expansion of Southern Baptist Sunday school work. Flake's methodology was practical but creative. His philosophy of Sunday school work was based on experience. The impact of his leadership made an immeasurable contribution to Sunday school growth and improvement. H. E. INGRAHAM

FLORIDA ASSOCIATIONS.
I. Extant. ALACHUA. Organized in 1847 by eight churches in North Florida east of the Suwannee River, all of them granted letters by the Florida Association to form a new association. It adopted articles of faith at the time of organization, and in 1848 had 13 churches and 479 members. It co-operated with the Florida and West Florida associations in forming the Florida Baptist Convention in 1854. In 1954, 22 churches reported 202 baptisms, 4,084 members, $132,803 total gifts, $17,279 mission gifts, $407,-163 property value, and $9,232 church debt.

BEULAH. Organized in 1879 by a group of churches from Santa Fe and Alachua associations in north central Florida. In 1881 the association had 11 churches and 548 members. Articles of faith based on the New Hampshire Confession were adopted. In 1954, 27 churches reported 149 baptisms, 4,462 members, $113,284 total gifts, $11,729 mission gifts, and $328,300 property value.

BLACK CREEK. Organized in 1913 with six rural churches in Clay County, adopting articles of faith in 1915. In 1954, 21 churches in Clay, Bradford, and Duval counties reported 305 baptisms, 3,056 members, $73,892 total gifts, $5,017 mission gifts, $217,300 property value, and $9,608 church debt.

BREVARD. Organized in 1953 with seven churches in Broward and Volusia counties, adopting articles of faith in 1954. In 1954, 10 churches reported 174 baptisms, 3,094 members, $157,079 total gifts, $19,965 mission gifts, $520,053 property value, and $49,046 church debt.

CHIPOLA. Organized in 1925 as the Jackson County Baptist Association with 30 churches reporting at the first annual meeting in 1926, most of them from the West Florida Association. Articles of faith were adopted in 1936, and the present name, Chipola, in 1945. In 1954, 36 churches reported 279 baptisms, 6,076 members, $154,247 total gifts, $12,190 mission gifts, $739,236 property value, and $35,109 church debt.

FLORIDA. Organized in 1842 by churches which withdrew from the Ochlochnee Association after it adopted an anti-missions article in its decorum. In 1843 Florida Association had 10 churches in Jefferson, Leon, Madison, Gadsden, Duval, and Jackson counties. Originally it included all missionary Baptist churches in Florida and some in Georgia, but the last Georgia church withdrew in 1877. In 1846 it lettered out all member churches east of the Suwannee River and those west of the Chattahoochee, the former group organizing Alachua Association and the latter West Florida Association. With articles of faith adopted early in its existence, it initiated moves which resulted in the establishment of Madison Baptist Female College in 1849 and the Florida Baptist Convention in 1854. In 1954, 36 churches reported 511 baptisms, 12,459 members, $505,758 total gifts, $53,391 mission gifts, $1,852,242 property value, and $133,723 church debt.

GADSDEN. Organized in 1951 with six churches in Gadsden County, adopting articles of faith. In 1954, eight churches reported 70 baptisms, 917 members, $39,213 total gifts, $3,474 mission gifts, and $127,950 property value.

GRAVES. Organized in 1890 with seven churches east of the Choctawatchee and west of the Yellow rivers in northwest Florida. It adopted articles of faith. In 1954, 18 churches reported 194 baptisms, 2,679 members, $43,847 total gifts, $5,511 mission gifts, and $158,100 property value.

Florida Associations

GULF STREAM. Organized in 1948 by nine churches on the lower east coast of Florida, which withdrew from Palm Lake and Miami associations to form a new association. In 1954, 17 churches reported 512 baptisms, 6,900 members, $424,010 total gifts, $60,947 mission gifts, $1,619,384 property value, and $329,562 church debt.

HARMONY. Organized in 1879 by seven churches in north central Florida which withdrew from Santa Fe River Association. Articles of faith were adopted in 1886. In 1954, 18 churches reported 129 baptisms, 3,092 members, $81,086 total gifts, $9,193 mission gifts, and $317,859 property value.

HOLMES COUNTY. Organized in 1924 with 18 churches in Holmes County, most of them from Bethel Association which became extinct. It adopted articles of faith in 1927. In 1954, 25 churches reported 168 baptisms, 3,205 members, $60,873 total gifts, $3,954 mission gifts, and $209,158 property value.

INDIAN RIVER. Organized in 1889 with six churches from Wekiwa and St. John's River associations in Brevard and Volusia counties. The New Hampshire Confession of Faith was adopted at the time of organization. In 1890 eight churches reported 298 members. In 1954, 14 churches reported 349 baptisms, 5,253 members, $232,426 total gifts, $33,854 mission gifts, and $708,343 property value.

JACKSONVILLE. Organized in 1879 as St. Mary's River Baptist Association; name changed to Jacksonville Association in 1901. It originally had four churches in northeast Florida and southeast Georgia adjacent to St. Mary's River; some of its Georgia churches remained until after 1900. Articles of faith were adopted in 1893. In 1954, 68 churches reported 2,686 baptisms, 41,875 members, $1,624,994 total gifts, $204,261 mission gifts, $6,627,744 property value, and $817,023 church debt.

LAFAYETTE. Organized in 1891 with nine churches in Lafayette County. Articles of faith, adopted in 1891, made footwashing an ordinance of the churches, continued until 1927. In 1954, 16 churches reported 36 baptisms, 1,828 members, $42,113 total gifts, $3,268 mission gifts, and $118,500 property value.

LAKE COUNTY. Organized in 1924 with 12 churches in Lake County, from Alachua, Wekiwa, and other associations. It did not adopt articles of faith. In 1954, 18 churches reported 355 baptisms, 4,578 members, $237,496 total gifts, $46,671 mission gifts, and $884,500 property value.

MARION. Organized in 1885 by 13 churches in Marion County which withdrew from Alachua to form a new association. It adopted Alachua's constitution which included articles of faith. In 1954, 29 churches reported 295 baptisms, 7,230 members, $256,903 total gifts, $39,379 mission gifts, $856,385 property value, and $57,887 church debt.

MIAMI. Organized in 1909 with seven churches, 369 members in Dade, Broward, and Palm Beach counties. It organized four Seminole Indian churches and in 1927, promoted the East Coast Assembly. In 1954, 48 churches reported 2,631 baptisms, 36,539 members, $1,980,731 total gifts, $398,288 mission gifts, $7,255,869 property value, and $1,241,897 church debt.

MIDDLE FLORIDA. Organized in 1900, 11 churches, 629 members from Madison, Lafayette, and Taylor counties. It adopted articles of faith at the time of organization. In 1954, 38 churches reported 268 baptisms, 6,757 members, $207,168 total gifts, $25,987 mission gifts, $648,025 property value, and $10,556 church debt.

NEW RIVER. Organized in 1872. Its oldest records are lost, but at its ninth annual session, 1880, it reported 13 churches, some of them previously members of Santa Fe River Association. In 1880 most of its churches were in Bradford County, with a few in Columbia and Alachua counties. Articles of faith appear in the 1881 minutes. In 1954, 19 churches reported 110 baptisms, 2,986 members, $95,778 total gifts, $12,551 mission gifts, and $359,800 property value.

NORTHEAST FLORIDA. Organized in 1938 by nine churches, mostly in Nassau County, which withdrew from Jacksonville Association. Articles of faith appear for the first time in the 1948 minutes. In 1954, 20 churches reported 238 baptisms, 4,074 members, $126,701 total gifts, $18,109 mission gifts, $390,054 property value, and $13,088 church debt.

NORTHWEST COAST. Organized in 1934 by 10 churches which withdrew from West Florida Association. Articles of faith were adopted in 1943. In 1954, 21 churches reported 609 baptisms, 8,538 members, $358,047 total gifts, $38,150 mission gifts, and $1,110,900 total property value.

OKALOOSA. Organized in 1922 as Okaloosa County Baptist Association, with 18 churches from New Santa Rosa and Graves associations. It adopted the present name in 1926. According to article I of the Okaloosa constitution, articles of faith "adopted by the Southern Baptist Convention" are the basis of fellowship and cooperation. In 1954, 22 churches reported 361 baptisms, 4,019 members, $152,202 total gifts, $16,788 mission gifts, and $557,750 property value.

ORANGE BLOSSOM. Organized in 1932 with 19 churches, most of them from Peace River Association. Articles of faith were published in the 1934 minutes. In 1954, 30 churches reported 266 baptisms, 7,580 members, $254,135 total gifts, $27,887 mission gifts, $850,040 property value, and $43,951 church debt.

PALM LAKE. Organized in 1938 by seven churches which withdrew from Miami Association in order to organize in the territory north and west of Miami. Although Palm Lake did not adopt articles of faith, its constitution gives it the right to drop any church from its connection "which it shall deem corrupt in faith or practice." In 1954, 17 churches reported 460 baptisms, 8,128 members, $93,744 total gifts,

$11,749 mission gifts, $1,381,942 property value, and $73,227 church debt.

PASCO. Organized in 1885 as Hernando Association by nine churches which withdrew from South Florida Association to form a new organization. Ten new churches joined at the first annual meeting, and articles of faith published in the church manual of the American Baptist Publication Society were adopted. In 1888 the association adopted the name Pasco. In 1954, 12 churches reported 180 baptisms, 2,902 members, $111,889 total gifts, $16,605 mission gifts, and $289,200 property value.

PEACE RIVER. Organized in 1876 as Manatee Missionary Baptist Association by six churches which withdrew from South Florida to form a new association. It adopted articles of faith at its organization and adopted its present name in 1897 to avoid confusion with Manatee River Baptist Association, organized in 1892. In 1954, 24 churches reported 214 baptisms, 5,182 members, $255,583 total gifts, $34,499 mission gifts, $1,040,500 property value, and $35,827 church debt.

PENSACOLA BAY. Organized in 1887 after the Pensacola and Milton churches "called an advisory convention" to discuss organization of a new association of Florida churches which were members of Elim Association in Alabama. All the Baptist churches in Escambia, Santa Rosa, and Walton counties were invited to co-operate in the organization, but Florida churches of the Elim Association did not respond at this time, and efforts failed to persuade Graves Association to join. Pensacola Bay Association grew slowly but steadily. In 1954, 38 churches reported 1,086 baptisms, 18,928 members, $886,427 total gifts, $106,744 mission gifts, $2,668,445 property value, and $311,908 church debt.

PINELLAS. Organized in 1932 as the Pinellas County Baptist Association by eight churches which withdrew from Tampa Bay Association to form a "more cohesive" association "of immediate accessibility." Minutes of 1933 include "An Appeal For Unity in Doctrine And Practice Among Our Churches" emphasizing requirements for the ordinance of baptism. The association adopted the present name in 1950. In 1954, 22 churches reported 639 baptisms, 11,360 members, $697,114 total gifts, $87,713 mission gifts, $2,318,529 property value, and $225,925 church debt.

ST. JOHN'S RIVER. Organized in 1877 as North St. John's River Baptist Association by seven churches in Clay and Putnam counties which withdrew from Santa Fe River to form a new association of greater contiguity. Articles of faith appear in the minutes of 1879. Churches in St. John's and Volusia counties were added later; the present name was adopted in 1881. In 1954, 31 churches reported 425 baptisms, 7,188 members, $269,239 total gifts, $39,721 mission gifts, $816,677 property value, and $20,720 church debt.

SANTA FE RIVER. Organized in 1857 as the Santa Fe River Missionary Baptist Association, with churches of the Alachua Association and from the original Suwannee Association which by majority vote became anti-missionary in 1845. In 1862 the association had 32 churches in the northeast Florida counties of Nassau, Duval, Clay, Putnam, Columbia, Hamilton, Alachua, Baker, Bradford, and Lafayette. It adopted articles of faith in 1868. Footwashing was not included; however, in 1869 the association voted to table a statement in a committee report that footwashing as an ordinance of the gospel was contrary to Baptist principles and practice. In 1954, 28 churches reported 359 baptisms, 8,217 members, $298,104 total gifts, $40,995 mission gifts, $1,057,700 property value, and $206,520 church debt.

SANTA ROSA. Organized in 1907 with six churches from Elim and Pensacola Bay associations. With 11 churches by 1909, eight of them united with Smyrna to form New Santa Rosa Missionary Baptist Association in 1913. It adopted the present name and articles of faith in 1921. In 1954, 15 churches reported 135 baptisms, 3,199 members, $86,233 total gifts, $7,417 mission gifts, and $320,500 property value.

SEMINOLE. Organized in 1914 by 17 churches in northeastern Wekiwa Association, in Lake, Seminole, and Brevard counties. Seminole adopted articles of faith of the Wekiwa Association from which 13 of its churches had withdrawn to form a more accessible association. In 1954, 30 churches reported 625 baptisms, 12,536 members, $507,650 total gifts, $58,953 mission gifts, $2,033,735 property value, and $81,046 church debt.

SHILOH. Organized, adopting articles of faith, in 1950, with 12 churches, 11 of them from South Florida Association. In 1954, 19 churches reported 261 baptisms, 5,286 members, $44,011 total gifts, $14,544 mission gifts, $529,600 property value, and $60,599 church debt.

SOUTH FLORIDA. Organized in 1867 by 12 churches from Alachua Association which granted letters to its churches south of the Withlacoochee River to form a new association. It adopted a constitution and articles of faith at its organization. In 1954, 60 churches reported 1,555 baptisms, 25,089 members, $116,365 total gifts, $139,209 mission gifts, $254,050 property value, and $168,898 church debt.

SOUTHWEST FLORIDA. Organized in 1924 with 15 churches in Manatee and Sarasota counties, most of them lettered out by Tampa Bay Association. Articles of faith were adopted in 1926. In 1954, 23 churches reported 571 baptisms, 8,051 members, $345,848 total gifts, $48,612 mission gifts, $1,264,800 property value, and $168,-898 church debt.

SUWANNEE. Organized in 1873. Its early history is obscure, due to loss of records, but it is not to be confused with the original Suwannee Association, organized in 1835, which became anti-missionary in 1845. In 1885 this second Suwannee Association reported 20 churches with 581 members in Suwannee, Alachua, and Hamilton counties (most of them in Suwannee). The minutes of 1885 record articles of faith, including footwashing, which "should be observed immediately after the Lord's Supper." In 1891 the provision for footwashing was appended to the effect that "in no case, shall this article be so construed as to make it a test of fellowship." After 1911 this article was dropped. In 1954, 33 churches reported 188 baptisms, 5,543 members, $150,074 total gifts, $14,606 mission gifts, and $369,399 property value.

TAMPA BAY. Organized in 1911 by 18 churches which withdrew from South Florida Association, believing "two associations can do more work than one; that greater convenience in attending our gatherings and other influences, will tend to develop interest in associational work." Articles of faith based on the New Hampshire Confession of Faith, were adopted in 1935. In 1954, 63 churches reported 1,598 baptisms, 26,142 members, $1,091,914 total gifts, $162,577 mission gifts, $3,865,000 property value, and $263,204 church debt.

WEKIWA. Organized in 1870. Its early history is unknown, but in 1882 it adopted articles of faith and had 21 churches in central Florida counties. In 1954, 31 churches reported 976 baptisms, 15,199 members, $661,120 total gifts, $108,711 mission gifts, $2,284,100 property value, and $1,562 church debt.

WEST FLORIDA. Organized in 1847 after Florida Association granted letters in 1846 to churches west of the Chattahoochee River. The new association included 15 churches in Florida and several in Alabama. In 1849 West Florida adopted articles of faith. In 1854 it approved a motion to co-operate with Florida Association in the organization of the Florida Baptist Convention. Joshua Mercer, missionary agent to the association, was moderator for several of its early years. In 1954, 19 churches reported 79 baptisms, 2,617 members, $44,957 total gifts, $6,618 mission gifts and $199,500 property value.   H. C. GARWOOD

II. Extinct. BETHEL. Organized in 1905 with 13 churches in Holmes and Jackson counties in West Florida. Its churches joined the Holmes County Association, organized in 1924, and the Jackson County Association, organized in 1925.

CALOOSA. Organized in 1916 by six Lee County churches which withdrew from Peace River Association. It ceased to exist in 1918 when its churches were invited to reunite with Peace River Association.

CENTRAL. Organized in 1903 as the New Santa Fe Association. The name was changed to Central in 1906. It dissolved in 1925 after losing some of its stronger churches.

ELIM. Organized in 1886 with churches in Alabama and in Santa Rosa and Escambia counties in Florida. "In 1902 the Alabama churches pulled out and left the churches of the two Florida counties in the Elim Association." In 1910 the Florida churches of the old Elim Association in Santa Rosa County organized as Pensacola Bay Association.

GENEVA. Organized in 1876 with churches in Alabama and Florida. Only two Florida churches were members in 1891. It became a member of the Alabama Baptist Convention.

HAMILTON. Organized in 1882, with eight churches, three of them in Georgia. Suwannee Association approved its organization. Hamilton dissolved in 1905 after losing churches to other associations.

HERNANDO. Organized in 1885 by nine churches from the South Florida Association. In 1888 the name was changed to Pasco Baptist Association.

JACKSON COUNTY. Organized in 1925 with about 30 churches, most of them from West Florida Association. In 1945 the name was changed to Chipola.

LITTLE RIVER. Organized in 1914 by four churches which withdrew from Beulah Association because of "Biblical principles." It accepted an invitation to rejoin Beulah Association in 1916 and ceased to exist independently.

MANATEE MISSIONARY. Organized in 1876 by six churches from South Florida Association. In 1897 the name was changed to Peace River.

MANATEE RIVER. Organized in 1892 by six churches from Manatee Missionary Baptist Association. In 1902 it disbanded and its churches returned to South Florida Association.

MIDWAY. Organized before 1879. It is mentioned in 1879 and 1881 minutes of South Florida Association.

MOUNT OLIVET. Organized in 1900, the minutes of its organization being the only record of its existence. It was never reported to the Florida Baptist Convention.

NEW SANTA FE. Organized in 1903 with six churches, four from New River Association in Alachua County. In 1906 the name was changed to Central. In 1925 the association dissolved, after losing several of its stronger churches.

NEW SANTA ROSA. Organized in 1912 with churches from Santa Rosa and other associations. It ceased to exist when most of its churches joined the Santa Rosa Association in 1924.

NEW WEST FLORIDA. Organized in 1905 as Bethel. The name was changed to New West Florida in 1909, and back to Bethel in 1911.

ROCKY CREEK. Organized in 1888 by eight churches, the majority from West Florida and Jackson County associations. It dissolved in 1925, making no report to Florida Baptist Convention after that date.

ST. MARY'S RIVER. Organized in 1879 with four churches, two in Georgia and two in Nassau County, Fla. In 1902 the name was changed to Jacksonville Association.

SANDY CREEK. Organized in 1876. The only minutes known to exist are dated 1882.

SMYRNA. Organized in 1912 by nine churches from Pensacola Bay Association. In 1913 it joined the churches from Santa Rosa Association to form the New Santa Rosa Association.

SUWANNEE. Organized in 1835 on a missionary basis in Columbia County. By majority vote in 1845 it became anti-missionary, and in 1847 adopted the name Suwannee River Primitive Baptist Association.   H. C. GARWOOD

FLORIDA BAPTIST. A newspaper inaugurated by the Santa Fe River Association in 1872 and approved by the Florida Baptist State Convention the same year. Its first editor was Hugh Bowen McCallum, native of Tennessee, former chaplain in the Confederate army, organizer and first pastor of a Baptist church in Lake City. T. E. Langley and John Henry Tomkies became associate editors. The paper published its first issue in Feb., 1873, in Lake City. The lack of financial support forced the paper to suspend publication in 1875; convention efforts to revive its publication failed. McCallum moved to Jacksonville, Fla., and briefly renewed the publication of the denominational paper, but the stringency of the times forced him to suspend his publication. He transferred his subscription list to the *Christian Index* of Georgia and became editor of its Florida department page. Editor L. A. Fish for a brief time renewed the publication of the *Florida Baptist* in the 1880's at Live Oak, Fla.

W. G. STRACENER

FLORIDA BAPTIST CHILDREN'S HOME, JACKSONVILLE. Incorporated Dec. 16, 1926, as the Baptist Children's Home of the Jacksonville Association, it formally opened Jan. 1, 1927. Its name was changed on Oct. 7, 1932, to Baptist Home for Children. The home is owned and operated by the Jacksonville and Northeast Florida associations, and one third of its 27 trustees are elected each year for a three-year period. Although several superintendents have served for short periods only, Brinson MacGowan served from 1931–44. Silas M. Bishop has been superintendent since 1948.

Operating expenses are provided largely by regular monthly budget gifts from churches in the two associations and a percentage of the annual state missions offering, but the home receives no Cooperative Program support. There is a small foundation fund and an educational fund for children eligible for college study. Property includes 57.5 acres and six buildings. The home, which follows the "cottage plan" with central dining hall, kitchen, and storage room, operates its own farm and dairy. In 1955 there were 77 children in the home.

JOHN H. MITCHELL

FLORIDA BAPTIST CHILDREN'S HOME, LAKELAND. The need for a children's home in Florida was brought to the attention of the Florida Baptist State Convention meeting in DeLand in 1899. As a result the convention adopted a resolution, asking "that a committee of seven members be appointed to take into consideration the questions of establishing a Baptist Orphanage, and . . . that said committee report on the matter at the next meeting of this Convention." Reporting to the next convention, the committee requested "that said committee be incorporated into a Board of Trustees of said Orphans' Home."

The trustees of Florida Baptist Orphanage, which had its name changed to Florida Baptist Children's Home in 1925, made their first report to the Florida Baptist Convention in Dec., 1901. They reported that the home had been located at Arcadia, and "the sum of $5,450 had been subscribed toward equipping and maintaining this institution." A charter was granted the board of trustees on Apr. 14, 1902, and two years later on Feb. 1, 1904, the first child was admitted to the home.

Florida Baptist Children's Home offers institutional and boarding home care to children who must be relocated and gives aid to worthy mothers who are left without sufficient funds to rear their children. Through 1954 the home served 1,533 children, 235 of them in 1954 alone, when the home operated on a budget of $127,705.68.

Supported by churches and church organizations, the Cooperative Program, individuals, and Woman's Missionary Union, Florida Baptist Children's Home has its present property at Lakeland, Fla., where it moved in 1948; the property consists of 182 acres of land, nine cottages for children, a chapel, administration building, a superintendent's home, Gaines Vocational Building, two houses for employees, and four utility buildings. A four-acre orange grove on the campus adds to the property value, which was estimated at $732,451.45 in 1954.

The children attend public schools and church services in Lakeland. Studied care is given to each child admitted, and opportunity is provided for vocational training through the public schools and on the campus. Children are encouraged to finish high school, and those who are capable and wish to attend college are assisted through the Student Loan Fund. Assistance is given those seeking employment.

T. M. JOHNS

FLORIDA BAPTIST FOUNDATION, THE. Since 1947 the official agency of the Florida Baptist State Convention, charged with responsibility for the custody and investment of various permanent funds owned by Florida Baptists. A proposed form of charter had been submitted to the convention meeting in Tampa in its 1946 session, and that body authorized the brethren presenting the matter to "proceed with the legal incorporation of the body." This was done on Apr. 1, 1947, and the trustees elected at the Tampa convention served as the incorporators.

The foundation is empowered to own and hold real estate to the value of $1,000,000. Its objects, as set forth in its charter, are:

To encourage, motivate, and facilitate the making of gifts, donations, and benefactions by deed, will, gift annuity contracts or otherwise, for the advancement, promotion, extension, and maintenance of the Florida Baptist State Convention and the various causes and objects now or at any time hereafter fostered, approved, endorsed, or officially sanctioned by the Florida Baptist State Convention or the Southern Baptist Convention or for any other purpose embraced within the scope of the objects of this corporation as set forth in this Charter.

Gould A. Leichliter, first full-time executive secretary of the foundation, began his service on Jan. 1, 1953. The operating budget of the foundation office is provided by the Florida Baptist Convention. In 1954 the operating budget amounted to $13,500. As of Sept. 30, 1955, the foundation held on behalf of various objects and agencies invested funds totaling $418,191.43.   GOULD A. LEICHLITER

FLORIDA BAPTIST HISTORICAL SOCIETY. Organized Nov. 15, 1951, at Winter Haven, Fla., under the leadership of Pope A. Duncan, Thomas Hansen, and others to collect and preserve material and information concerning the history of Florida Baptists as reflected by the activities of the Florida Baptist State Convention, associations, agencies, institutions, churches, and individuals. Its officers and executive committee are elected by the Florida state convention, and collected material of the society is deposited in the archives of Samson Library at Stetson University. Harry C. Garwood, curator since 1954, has gathered and processed a substantial collection of materials, many of which are reproduced on microfilm. All materials have been indexed and printed.
JAMES A. SAWYER

FLORIDA BAPTIST STATE CONVENTION.
I. Baptist Beginnings. Baptist beginnings in Florida date from about the turn of the 19th century. Many of the settlers in Georgia and Alabama, living near the Florida border, began to farm strips of Florida land within short distances of their homes. Slowly a brave-hearted few dared to cross over into Florida to reside, although Spanish authorities and Seminole Indians constantly threatened life and property. Among these new settlers were a number of Baptists who opened their homes to missionary-minded preachers with regular pastorates in Alabama and Georgia. Neighbors were invited, and services were conducted despite a Spanish law ordering such worshipers imprisoned. The first Baptist preacher to devote his full time to preaching in Florida was Fleming Bates, who assembled enough Baptists in the Pigeon Creek Community (Nassau County) to organize a church. On Jan. 7, 1821, a presbytery, consisting of Bates and Elder Isom Peacock, met with the Baptists who had in hand their church letters from Sardis Baptist Church of Georgia, and Pigeon Creek Baptist Church was organized. This was the first Baptist church organized in Florida. Messengers were sent from this church to the Piedmont Baptist Association in Georgia, and membership was secured in that association. Inasmuch as the United States had purchased Florida, although not yet having taken formal possession, Bates and the church felt that the Spanish authorities would not oppose their organizing a Baptist church. Nevertheless, they breathed a sigh of relief when the United States took formal possession on July 16, 1821. Immediately after the Spanish flag was lowered and the Stars and Stripes of the United States was raised, Bates conducted a religious service and preached a sermon. Men could now worship God according to the dictates of their conscience.

Meanwhile, in west Florida E. H. Calloway, of Alabama, was at work to establish a church in Jackson County. On Mar. 12, 1825, a presbytery, composed of Calloway and Jeremiah Kembril, met with a group of 19 Baptists at Bethlehem, three miles south of the Alabama line, and organized the Bethlehem Baptist Church (now called Campbellton Baptist Church). An edifice was constructed of logs. Since the only other Florida Baptist church was across the state, it appeared wise for this group to join the Chattahoochee Association of Alabama. It was the dream of Bethlehem that soon other churches could be organized and that an association could be formed in west Florida. Encouraged by the Bethlehem church, the Sardis Baptist Church was organized within the year in Jackson County.

In 1828 a Baptist church with five male and seven female members was constituted at the Casa Bianca plantation, two miles south of Monticello; Benjamin Manning, Sr., was called to be pastor. In Leon County in July, 1829, 10 Baptists met with Henry Miller and Theophilus Hardee and were regularly constituted into Indian Springs Baptist Church; Hardee was called to be pastor. The fertile land in Bradford County was settled with people from Georgia, South Carolina, and Virginia; and Baptists of this group organized the Providence Baptist Church on Oct. 6, 1832. The Baptist cause prospered in this county, and the following year the New River Baptist Church was founded. In Washington County, of west Florida, a group of pioneers determined to have a Baptist church, and as the result of their efforts the Orange Hill (Hickory Hill) Church was established in 1834. In its first report to the West Florida Association in 1851, a Sunday school and a prayer meeting were included. Several members of the well-known Mercer family of Georgia moved into this section, including Joshua Mercer, brother of Jesse Mercer (q.v.) of Georgia. In Jefferson County, near Aucilla, the Kinsey and Walker families formed the Elizabeth Baptist Church in 1834; Jesse Goodman was called as pastor.

Each new church dreamed of the day when an association could be formed in Florida. By 1835 there were eight Baptist churches in Florida, and in several other communities regular religious services were held; it was only a matter of time before a church would be organized in each place. Many of the preachers and church members believed that the day had come for a Florida Baptist association. On Sept. 26, 1835, the churches sent messengers to convene at the Providence Baptist Church in Columbia County to organize the first association of Florida Baptists. This association was named the Suwannee Association. So great was the need for having an association within the borders of the state to unify the work and to aid in developing the cause, and so eager were messengers to perfect an organization, that no questions were asked concerning doctrine. All who called themselves Baptists were readily accepted. It soon became evident that within this new body there were two groups: one advocated special missionary activity, Sunday schools, revival meetings, and ministerial education; the other was antimissionary. These two groups were at cross purposes for 10 years. The strongest churches and the majority of church members of the Suwannee Association were overwhelmingly missionary. Some of the missionary churches withdrew in 1842 to take part in the creation of the Florida Association. The antimissionary churches, finding themselves beaten in scriptural debate at the hands of the missionary-minded Baptists, decided upon a "coup." In the 1845 annual session they arrived early; and, as the known messengers from missionary churches arrived, they were refused seats. The Suwannee Association then voted to become an antimissionary body.

The American Baptist Home Missionary Society of New York saw the needs of the scattered Baptists of Florida and in 1837 sent one missionary to the territory. However, this missionary served for only 13 weeks. In the decade from 1832 to 1841, the society spent $400 in Florida and was represented by three missionaries. In this same period the society had 96 missionaries in Missouri. The problem was not one of finances but rather that of securing brave and able men to come to Florida, where lurking Indians were often upon the warpath and where scattered people lived in places accessible only by boat or dim trail. In 1836 James McDonald, a Baptist convert from Catholicism, came to east Florida as a missionary of the society. There he found three churches with 60 members (including some colored adherents). During the Seminole Indian War, McDonald had opportunity to preach the gospel at the many funerals he was called upon to conduct.

In the early days lurking Indians made churchgoing dangerous. From 1836 to 1840, people usually carried guns with them to church. Worship services were at times broken up by raiding Indians. In the Indian wars nearly every hearthstone had been stained with blood. Homes were burned and stock was stolen. Even in such times new churches were established. Under the leadership of McDonald, the Bethel Baptist Church (First Baptist Church) of Jacksonville was organized in July, 1838, with four white members and two Negro slaves. The meeting place was the government blockhouse. Within two years a church building was erected which is reputed to have been the first church edifice in Jacksonville. With true missionary zeal, McDonald in 1841 constituted the Baptists of Nassau County into the Sharon Baptist Church, later called Callahan Baptist Church.

Near Madison on June 20, 1841, a small group of seven Baptists formed the Concord Baptist Church. Richard Johnson Mays donated to the church 20 acres of land. He was ordained by Concord as a deacon and in the same year was ordained as a minister. This church later acted as host church when the Florida Baptist Convention was organized. Under the guiding hand of Mays, the Baptist church of Monticello was organized in the fall of 1841 with six members, four of whom were women. The new church immediately called Mays as pastor.

In 1836 William B. Cooper came from South Carolina to this area of middle Florida. A former student at Furman Institute and a graduate of Columbian College of Washington, D. C., Cooper was disturbed by the attitude of the antimissionary members of the Suwannee Association. He believed that a line should be drawn and that an entirely missionary body should be organized. The course of action that led to the formation of the Florida Association was largely the work of Cooper. A call went out to the churches to convene at the Salem Church, Leon County, on Oct. 22, 1842, to create a new association to be called the Florida Association. A temporary organization was formed, and the first regular meeting of the new body was set for Oct. 16, 1843, with Ebenezer Church. Messengers from Ebenezer, Indian Springs, Elizabeth, Concord, Monticello, Aenon, Providence, Bethel, and Sardis churches attended. The constitution stated that "the Association thus organized shall have no power to lord it over God's heritage, nor infringe upon the internal rights of the churches." The body was to provide general union, to advise churches, to appropriate monies, and to look into orthodoxy. Each church sent messengers to the annual meetings. The actions of the association in no way bound the local church; the local church could accept or reject any action of the association. In 1846 the Florida Association placed a missionary in the field. Plans were made to establish a college. A church was organized in Tallahassee, the capital of Florida, and the Florida Association contributed mission funds to aid in the erection of a church building.

When Florida became a state in 1845 there were 644 Baptists living in the geographical area between the Chattahoochee River and the Escambia Bay. Representatives from 11 Florida churches and three Alabama churches assembled on the Saturday before the second Sunday in Nov., 1847, at Bethlehem Church for the purpose of organizing the West Florida Baptist Association. Since the Florida Baptist

Convention did not exist, the assembly agreed to affiliate with the Alabama Baptist Convention. A missionary was placed at work in the field to promote the gospel and to aid in building a church edifice in Marianna.

As the Florida population spread southward and eastward, Baptist churches were quickly organized. In 1847 messengers from 13 churches located in Alachua, Benton, Columbia, Duval, Marion, and Nassau counties convened and established the Alachua Missionary Baptist Association. One of the first items of business was to try to devise means of securing a missionary.

South Florida, with its fresh-water lakes, fertile soil, and beneficial climate, offered an ideal home for the white settler. The Indians and wild beasts that roamed the forests, however, constituted a menace. The federal government erected forts to hold the Indians in check, and hunters soon took care of the beasts. Among the earliest settlers were some Baptist preachers. Preaching services were carried on in the scattered homes of the pioneers. The Hurrah Baptist Church (Alafia) was organized in Hillsborough County in 1850. James M. Hayman had been converted in a meeting conducted by missionary John Tucker at Lake Lindsey, Fla. He began missions in Bartow, Tampa, and Socrum. The work at Bartow progressed rapidly, and a church was constituted Sept. 3, 1854. This church was named Peas Creek (later changed to Peace Creek and then to First Baptist Church).

On Nov. 22, 1853, while the Florida Baptist Association was in session with Olive Church, Thomas County, Ga., a farsighted messenger suggested that the time had come for Florida to have its own state Baptist convention. Discussion revealed that it was the "unanimously expressed opinion" of the association that it was "proper, expedient, and practicable" to establish a convention in Florida to unite the strength of Florida Baptists in the "promotion of the Kingdom of God." Committees were appointed to contact the pastors of the Alachua and Florida associations to enlist their co-operation in this proposed venture. These committees met with a favorable response, and definite plans were made to create a state convention at the next annual meeting of the Florida Association.   JACK P. DALTON

II. History of Convention. Oct. 21–24, 1854, West Florida Association, meeting with Union Academy Church in Jackson County, Fla., adopted the following resolution: *"Resolved,* That we adopt the resolution in the Florida Baptist Association regarding a State Convention to be styled THE FLORIDA BAPTIST STATE CONVENTION, and that Messengers from this Association co-operate. . ." Messengers were appointed to attend the 1854 Florida Association and assist in organization of the convention. The Alachua Association also appointed representatives to meet with those of the other two associations.

The Florida Association met with Concord Baptist Church, Madison County, Fla., Nov. 18–21, 1854. A special committee recommended to the association: "That, after a free interchange of opinion on the subject, they deem the measure advisable, find the brethren from said associations fully authorized to go into an organization, and recommend that such organization be consummated immediately." The report was adopted. On Monday evening, Nov. 20, the delegates from the three associations met in the "parlor" of the local pastor, R. J. Mays, and proceeded with the organization. After considerable discussion a constitution for the new state convention was drawn up and adopted. Officers elected for the first year were R. J. Mays, president; D. G. Daniel, secretary; S. C. Craft, assistant secretary; and John Cason, treasurer. An executive committee, composed of H. Z. Ardis, Craft, W. B. Cooper, B. S. Fuller, W. H. Goldwire, and W. J. Blewett, was elected and instructed to apply to the Florida legislature for the incorporation of the Florida Baptist State Convention. Correspondents were appointed to Salem Association, Alabama; Eufaula Association, Georgia; Judson Association, Alabama; Bethel Association, Georgia; and the Baptist Convention of Georgia.

The group voted to hold the next session in Union Academy Church in Jackson County, Fla., "on Friday before the first Sabbath in December 1855." The Florida convention minutes were printed at the office of the *Tennessee Baptist,* Nashville, Tenn., in conjunction with the minutes of Florida Association for 1854.

During the early years the great distances to travel and the financial condition of the people hindered the work of the convention. In 1868 West Florida Association took the following action: "On motion agreed to dispense with appointing delegates to the Florida Baptist Convention for the present."

The size of some of the early conventions was small, with only 15 delegates and two visitors attending the meeting in Madison in 1871. That year five men received aid as missionaries from the American Baptist Home Missionary Society. The need of a general evangelist or agent to travel over the state, visiting churches and associations to bring them into closer union and co-operation with the convention, was reported as the convention's greatest need. A proposal, inaugurated by Santa Fe River Association, for establishment of a state denominational paper was heartily approved. The convention voted to appoint two assistant editors from different sections of the state.

On July 1, 1873, Kinsey Chambers began work as part-time state evangelist. His report to the 1873 convention stated that he had traveled 1,688 miles, spoken 105 times, made 54 family visits, aided in constituting one church, baptized seven, and collected $68.95. His expenses amounted to only $10.75 for the period of five months. The convention inaugurated an effort to have every member in each church contribute at least one cent per week for state missions.

In 1876 a February meeting of the convention was held in Gainesville to try to prevent suspension of *The Florida Baptist*, the state denominational paper. H. B. McCallum, founder and editor, was given cash and pledges and asked to revive the paper if he could do so without expense to himself. The struggle to maintain a state evangelist also continued.

In 1880 W. N. Chaudoin became president of the convention. Under his leadership the State Board of Missions was inaugurated.

STATE BOARD OF MISSIONS. The State Board of Missions was organized in 1880, with W. N. Chaudoin serving as corresponding secretary and treasurer.

The first years of its organization it employed two missionaries and raised for all purposes $150, and there were added to all the church (which the missionaries helped) that year through pastors and State missionaries, thirty-one men and women.

In Dec., 1882, Chaudoin reported to the state convention a close co-operation with the Home Mission Board of the Southern Baptist Convention. That board appropriated $2,000 for the work of the Florida board for the year 1883 and asked Floridians to duplicate the amount. By the following year the number of missionaries, including both full-time and part-time workers, had increased from nine to 23. These missionaries supplied 54 churches and 44 mission stations.

The State Board of Missions not only sponsored state missions but also created greater interest in foreign missions, which resulted in larger contributions. Florida exceeded the quota of $500 for foreign missions requested by the Southern Baptist Convention in Waco, Tex., in 1883. The following year, the state again raised more than the quota, sending in $606.09. Much of the credit for these increases in mission funds was due to the efforts of the women of the state.

INSTITUTIONS. *Stetson University.*—The idea of a Baptist school was presented in 1875 and again in 1881, but not until 1883 was action taken on the proposal. That year $560 was pledged and a committee was appointed to lay plans for beginning a Florida Baptist school. In 1883 H. A. DeLand, a Baptist, founded an academy in DeLand, Fla. The school first met in the lecture room of the Baptist church, but the following year DeLand erected a two-story academy building, now known as DeLand Hall, on a four-acre site at the northeast corner of Minnesota Avenue and Woodland Boulevard. When the committee on location for a Baptist college visited DeLand, he offered them this land and building with its fixtures and $10,000 if the denomination would raise an additional $10,000. This offer was accepted by the convention at Jacksonville in Dec., 1885.

The school name was changed to DeLand College, and in 1887 the legislature of Florida granted it a charter under the name of DeLand University. The development of the school was unusually rapid because of the gifts of John B. Stetson of Philadelphia, C. T. Sampsom, and others. Stetson's first contribution was a large amount toward the construction of a dormitory building, now known as Stetson Hall. Because of Stetson's continued interest, the trustees, at DeLand's request, changed the name of the institution to John B. Stetson University. The Stetson family has contributed more than a million dollars to the university.

From a small denominational academy begun more than 70 years ago, Stetson has become a modern Christian university. In addition to occupying its original campus in DeLand, its college of law was moved in 1955 to a million-dollar campus in St. Petersburg. Since its incorporation, Stetson has had four presidents: John Franklin Forbes (1885–1903), Lincoln Hulley (1904–34), William Sims Allen (1934–47), and J. Ollie Edmunds (1948–   ).

Columbia College.—When the University of Florida was moved from Lake City to Gainesville, the former campus, together with $15,000 in cash, was offered to any denomination to establish a school there. Florida Baptists, at a special session of the convention held at Lake City in July, 1907, voted to establish Columbia College. The school opened Oct. 2, 1907, with a faculty of nine and 133 pupils. G. A. Nunnally served as president until June, 1909, when he was succeeded by H. W. Tribble. After Tribble's death early in 1912, A. P. Montague became president. Because of debts due to inadequate endowment, and with the United States' entry into World War I, the college was closed for the duration. In 1920 the convention decided to return the property to the city of Lake City and to concentrate its educational efforts in Stetson University.

The orphanage.—In 1899 C. S. Farriss offered a resolution that the convention consider the establishment of a Baptist orphanage or children's home. The resolution was adopted and a committee was appointed to confer and report at the next meeting of the convention. The first contribution to the orphanage was made in 1900 by Mrs. W. D. Chipley, of Pensacola, who pledged $100 a year to the enterprise. A gift of land and negotiable notes, to the amount of $5,400, by the people of Arcadia led the trustees to decide to locate the home there. By 1904 W. L. Mahon, acting as financial agent, was able to secure sufficient donations to build and equip a two-story ($10,000) brick building. After the completion of the structure, the total indebtedness was but $1,500, which was more than covered by pledges. Bartlett Bean and his wife were elected as the first superintendents. On Feb. 1, 1904, Florida Baptists opened the first denominational orphanage in the state, and by the end of the first year there were 23 boys and girls in the home. Three years later there were 43 children in the home and a cash balance of $3,465.47

after the payment of all bills. After seven years as superintendent, Bean's health failed and he was succeeded on Apr. 1, 1911, by J. E. Trice. Trice served until T. M. Johns, the present superintendent, succeeded him in 1932. The Florida Baptist Children's Home (the legal name of the orphanage since 1921) having outgrown its original location in Arcadia, was moved in 1948 to a modern campus in Lakeland.

CONSTITUTIONAL STRUCTURE AND ADMINISTRATION. The constitution, adopted in 1854, provided that the body should be known as the Baptist Convention of the State of Florida. Its objects were: (1) To unite the influence and pious intelligence of the Baptists within its bounds, and thereby facilitate their union and co-operation. (2) To form and encourage plans for the revival of experimental and practical religion in the state and elsewhere. (3) To aid in giving effect to useful plans of the several associations. (4) To afford an opportunity to those who may conscientiously think it their duty to form a fund for the education of pious young men who may be called, by the Spirit and their churches, to the Christian ministry. (5) To promote pious and useful education in the Baptist denomination.

Each association was entitled to send 10 delegates to the convention, and provisions allowing for additional delegates from associations having more than a thousand members were stated. Auxiliary societies contributing $50 to the funds of the convention were allowed a delegate for each $50 so contributed. Each individual contributing $10 annually was a member of the convention.

A president, secretary, assistant secretary, and treasurer were to be chosen annually by ballot. The constitution also provided that an executive committee consisting of at least seven members, chosen by ballot, would attend to the business of the convention during its recess. In true Baptist style the constitution provided that none of the decisions of the convention "shall be binding on the associations or auxiliaries." Affiliation with the Southern Baptist Convention was provided for in the 13th article, which reads: "When its funds will justify, this body may send delegates to the Southern Baptist Convention."

For a time the affairs of the convention were conducted in open meeting with the executive committee acting for the convention during the recess, but after the organization of the State Board of Missions in 1880 the latter body assumed the duties of the convention in recess. In 1902, however, L. D. Geiger, then serving as corresponding secretary and treasurer, asked the legislature of Florida for an act of incorporation for the mission board. The act was passed, and the State Board of Missions legally and officially became the Florida Baptist Convention.

During World War I, religious and educational work suffered. However, in 1919 Southern Baptists launched the 75 Million Campaign. Florida was asked to raise one million dollars for all purposes during the five years of the campaign, and the members of 462 of Florida's 682 churches promised $1,373,057.06. The responsibility of collecting and enlisting the unenlisted occupied the energies of Secretary S. B. Rogers and the convention for five years. In the final report of the campaign, Florida is credited with raising $1,009,416.89, oversubscribing its quota by a larger percentage than any other state.

After 17 years as chief executive officer of Florida Baptists, Rogers died in office Aug. 16, 1926. He was succeeded by C. M. Brittain, who served until his retirement in 1941. Charles H. Bolton followed him, giving vigorous leadership to Florida Baptist work until 1944. The present executive secretary, John Maguire, assumed his office Jan. 15, 1945.

DEPARTMENTS OF WORK. The first department to be organized was the women's work. In 1881 Mrs. N. A. Bailey was selected corresponding secretary for the state. In her first report Mrs. Bailey reported two Ladies' Associational Missionary Unions and 26 missionary societies, half of which were new. After Mrs. Bailey's death in 1886, Mrs. L. B. Telford succeeded to the office. In 1893 she reported 63 women's societies and 29 children's organizations. Mrs. Telford died in July, 1893, and was succeeded by Jennie Spalding, who served as secretary for 18 years. During her first year the Woman's Missionary Union of Florida was formed during the meeting of the convention at Plant City. Miss Spalding was succeeded by Mrs. H. C. Peelman. Following Mrs. Peelman's retirement after 25 years of service, Miss Louise Smith became secretary. The growth of women's work is shown by the increase of receipts from 16 per cent of the total contributions in 1882 to 27 per cent in 1937.

A Sunday school was organized as early as 1844 according to records of the First Baptist Church, Key West. The work was not organized on a statewide basis until 1909, when Louis Entzminger became secretary of Sunday school and B.Y.P.U. work. He was followed in 1911 by George Hyman, who served until 1914. W. W. Willian became secretary in Apr., 1916; at that time there were 497 Sunday schools with an enrolment of 40,976. Since Willian's retirement (after 30 years of leadership) Thomas M. Collins, Glenn M. Bridges, and C. F. Barry have served as Sunday school secretary.

The first state convention of the Baptist Young People's Union was held Apr. 6–7, 1897. The following year, according to the first known report, there were 41 unions in the state. Except for a brief eight months in 1920 when O. K. Armstrong served as B.Y.P.U. secretary, the work was led by a combination Sunday school–Training Union worker until 1938. The present secretary, O. K. Radford, began his work in 1926, as assistant to W. W. Willian, in the fields of both Sunday school and Training Union. Radford is the only secretary the separate Training Union Department has had. Under his guidance this department has grown until in 1954 there were approximately 90,000 enrolled in the work.

While the laymen's movement was first considered by the convention in 1909, it was not until 1928 that W. G. Upchurch was selected as the first Brotherhood secretary. After being discontinued during the depression, state work was again resumed in 1936 with election of Hugh F. Latimer, who served as secretary until 1939. Secretaries since then have been J. Harrison Griffin, 1939–45; C. A. Holcomb (combination Music-Brotherhood secretary), 1945–50; and G. A. Ratterree, since 1950.

Organized in 1945, the Church Music Department (for six years in combination with the Brotherhood Department) was headed by Clifford A. Holcomb until Dec., 1952. On Jan. 15, 1953, W. G. Stroup became secretary of a separate Church Music Department. He was also business manager of camps and assemblies.

The DeLand Assembly was started in 1919 in the buildings of Stetson University. It continued almost without interruption (except for war years) under the direction of W. W. Willian. After the retirement of Willian, O. K. Radford has served as director. Approximately 800 young people and adults attend annually. The second oldest assembly is the West Florida, begun in 1928 at DeFuniak Springs and moved later to Panama City. This assembly, serving churches in the western part of the state, now operates on the West Florida Assembly grounds owned by the convention. In 1952–53, in addition to the assemblies mentioned, Florida Baptists operated an East Coast Assembly at Stuart which was moved to Ft. Pierce in 1954. Combined attendance at assemblies and camps runs above 2,800 annually.

GORDON C. REEVES

III. Program of Work of Florida Baptists. The State Board of Missions of the Florida Baptist Convention is incorporated as the Florida Baptist Convention. The corporation is subject to the convention of messengers which meets annually.

Members of the board are elected by the convention for three-year terms, one for each 10,000 members (but not more than three in all) from each of 39 associations. The convention president and board membership must include at least three women. Only the convention president or a Stetson University trustee may serve currently on the board and on any other Florida Baptist Convention agency. Board membership is terminated by death, by removal, by non-co-operation with the association or convention, or after three unexcused absences from board meetings.

The convention president serves as president of the board; and there is a recording-statistical secretary, without vote. The board, quorum 20, meets quarterly and on call of the president and executive secretary-treasurer, at convention expense except for the annual meeting at the convention.

An executive secretary-treasurer is employed by the board to have general supervision of all departments, to recommend all secretaries, evangelists, or special agents; to handle all funds, subject to the order of the Florida Baptist Convention; to make and publish estimates, fix objectives, and recommend a budget not to exceed Cooperative Program receipts for the previous year; to provide financial support for convention work and aid institutions in the area by funds provided through the special annual state mission offering. In return for such aid, local institutions are expected to agree not to canvass for funds outside the territory agreed upon by the board and the institutions.

Six departments participate in state mission work—Brotherhood, co-operative missions, music, camps and assemblies, Baptist student, Sunday school, and Training Union. The Woman's Missionary Union is an auxiliary to rather than a department of the work. In return for 24 per cent of the Cooperative Program dollar Stetson University provides full tuition scholarships for approved ministerial students. New enterprises involving expenditures must be voted by two consecutive annual conventions. This restriction does not apply to the regular work of an agency.

Duties of the associate to the executive secretary and director of promotion include the preparation and distribution of literature, tracts, and posters on stewardship, tithing, and the Cooperative Program. Teams representing the whole mission program visit annual associational meetings; 12 leadership conferences are held in the state. This department also handles news service and public relations.

The department of camps and assemblies under the direction of the associate to the executive secretary operates three summer assemblies, offering eight-day classes in Sunday school, Training Union, W.M.U., and music; and provides a week of conferences for ministers in September.

All departments of state work follow a general plan of working through associations. However, the grouping of associations varies with departments. The promotion department provides 12 leadership conferences and also sends teams supplementing the state workers to visit each association. The co-operative missions department divides the state for city or rural missionaries into 14 districts. The Sunday school department works with an organization in each association and holds four district conferences for the training of associational leaders. The W.M.U. holds methods conferences in 11 strategic places. The Training Union works with every association, dividing the state into eight districts. The music department groups the state into six districts for music festivals. Each association is organized for work with each department, which arrangement affords flexibility and does not require the same person to be an officer in many departments.

Associational mission work is mainly integrated with the activities of co-operative missions department workers. Each associational executive committee has a missions committee to encourage the sponsorship of new work and to give local guidance to the work of the missionaries. Applications for mission money allotments are approved by the executive committee of the association before they are presented to the state board.

Each department does work that might be called associational missions through the encouragement of the associational organizations to enlist and train the churches in all departments of the work. Only one association, Miami, is served by a full-time associational missionary.

Mission work among minorities or language groups is primarily directed by the Home Mission Board. The W.M.U. set aside a part of the special state mission offering to build a home for the missionary to the Spanish at Immokalee.

Church building funds have been provided as direct, non-repayable grants, subject to retain title or reverter clause in favor of the state board of missions in event the properties pass to some other group. Because this reverter clause was not satisfactory to missions or sponsoring churches, changes were made, and for 1953–54 approximately 95 per cent of funds were issued on a repayable basis, without interest for five years, then at 3 per cent interest until paid off. This plan is known as the new work revolving fund. Any church or mission hampered by a reverter clause may be released by refunding the actual amount the board has put into the work.

A building loan fund of $24,500 has been available at 5 per cent with personal endorsement for each $250. The Hargrave Loan Fund of $5,300 for rural churches requires 5 per cent interest paid to the donor.

The co-operative missions department operates through a secretary and associates in 14 districts. Four of these who work in cities of 150,000 or more are known as city missionaries and the other 10 are known as rural missionaries. Both rural and city missionaries survey areas for new work, secure church sponsorships for work in new locations, and aid in securing suitable strategic properties. In 1954, $65,000 was allocated for new work.

There are two general methods of granting aid. The board may make a direct grant, and then hold the title to the property or protect itself by a reverter clause in case affiliation with the convention should cease. Or, the board may allocate funds without interest for five years, secured by a lien at 6 per cent in the event the church ceases to co-operate with the convention. As the church refunds this amount, it is credited (1) with a contribution to the new work revolving fund and (2) with the satisfaction of the lien.

Rural or district missionaries work with associational officers and with pastors, offering plans in building and remodeling, giving information on mission programs and methods, encouraging stewardship and evangelism. Encouraging stewardship involves stewardship meetings in churches and assistance in making church and missionary budgets. The co-operative missions department also promotes the Southern Baptist program of evangelism, encouraging association-wide, city-wide, or state-wide evangelistic campaigns. A three-day state evangelistic conference is an annual event in January.

The Sunday school department employs a secretary, three associates, and two office secretaries. The first line of work is through 39 associational organizations meeting monthly as service organizations for the churches. The secretary of the department or one of the associates attends three of these meetings a year in each association. A group of age-group specialists for all departments of Sunday school work are available to go for small honorariums to church or association-wide schools. Each age-group specialist sends a quarterly bulletin. Special dates and emphasis for 1954–55 included five district leadership conferences, which prepared associational workers for promoting the work among the churches. Vacation Bible school clinics are held in each association before the time for the summer Vacation Bible schools. A statewide Sunday school convention is held each February, and a one-week statewide leadership clinic majoring on better Bible teaching is held in the fall.

The department promotes and secures faculties for from 6 to 10 association-wide enlargement campaigns each year, in which a team of workers stays with each church for five days and guides in plans for enlargement. Occasionally the department sends workers to individual churches for either departmental study courses or enlargement, but it concentrates on the association as a working unit. One period per day in each of three eight-day assemblies is conducted in Sunday school work and Bible study. A state record of training is sent monthly to pastors and superintendents, and an associational spotlight bulletin is sent to all associational leaders and educational directors in the churches.

The Training Union department employs a secretary with three associates. The 39 associations are organized with voluntary workers serving the churches. Nine approved workers specializing in the work of the different departments go on call and for small honorariums. The department majors on association-wide enlargement campaigns, seeking to enlarge Training Union organization and membership in every church simultaneously. The department fosters associational leadership schools in methods for workers in churches.

The state is divided into eight districts of about five associations each, and a Training

Union convention is held in each district before the summer months. The programs are held in the afternoon and evening, and one feature is the selection of district winners of sword drill and better speakers' tournaments. The winners go to the state assembly at DeLand to compete for state representative. Two state representatives are sent at Training Union expense to the annual Southwide tournament at Ridgecrest Assembly.

The department provides classes in Training Union work one hour per day in the three eight-day assemblies held each summer. The secretary writes the associational directors every month and sends quarterly bulletin reports to associational leaders and educational directors. Some help, particularly in the area of enlargement, is given in individual church schools.

The executive board of the Woman's Missionary Union, auxiliary to Florida Baptist Convention, consists of a state president and all state officers; state chairmen of committees on missions, stewardship, mission study, and prayer; the recording secretary; and up to 10 local resident members. Its staff consists of the executive secretary, assistant to the executive secretary, and a youth secretary, an R.A. secretary, and an office worker. Its purpose is to promote the study of missions, to stimulate gifts to missions, and to lead members to be missionaries.

The program of the W.M.U. includes work through associational organizations; a two-day state leaders' conference for associational leaders; 11 methods conferences in strategic places; a daily period of classes in each of three assemblies; three special seasons of prayer: foreign missions in November and December; home missions in March; and state missions in September. The W.M.U. also holds eight five-day camps for girls and five for boys. One boys' camp lasts two weeks. The W.M.U. organizes a week-end Y.W.A. conference in the spring and a G.A. conference in the fall; an R.A. Congress and a Young Men's Missionary Conference; it carries on correspondence and provides promotional material and leadership for all these. The W.M.U. reported 847 societies in 1,006 churches (81 per cent), 773 R.A. chapters, and a grand total of 3,854 organizations. The budget for 1954 was $37,573.95.

The Brotherhood department is led by a secretary, and reported 561 churches with active Brotherhoods and functioning organizations. The Brotherhood participated in the three assemblies at DeLand, Fort Pierce, and Panama City.

The Baptist Student Union works in co-operation with Baptist churches in college communities, seeking to enlist students in Christian comradeship, Bible study, prayer, church membership, denominational loyalty, and kingdom advancement. The state B.S.U. organization, affiliated with the Southwide B.S.U. department, operates through a state secretary located at the University of Florida. With one associate, he serves also as secretary of the local B.S.U. Other secretaries serve Florida State University at Tallahassee, Stetson University at DeLand, University of Miami at Miami; one secretary serves Southern (M.E.) College at Lakeland, Tampa University at Tampa, and Stetson Law School at St. Petersburg, Fla. The B.S.U. operates through councils of student workers and local church members and through a state council. Over 5,500 Baptist students were enrolled in colleges and universities in Florida in 1953. Some students work in service projects during summer months.

Although little money is spent for purchase of time, some churches are using radio. In Jacksonville church programs are on the air about 376 hours a year. There are but two 30-minute TV programs each Sunday in the state, one by the B.S.U. of Miami University and one by Northwood Baptist Church of West Palm Beach.

Florida Baptist Historical Society, H. C. Garwood, curator-treasurer, is located at Stetson University, DeLand. The collection, known as the Stetson Baptist Archives, has been indexed and printed lists are available. Approximately a thousand items of early Baptist history in the Southern Baptist territory have been microfilmed. Only a few Baptists pay the annual dues of $1 for membership in the society.

The music department of two workers and three summer fieldworkers arranged for music directors in 39 associations; held four music planning conferences, 52 music schools with lessons in directing, hymn playing, and song leading; several associational music festivals and four state festivals in different areas. The department conducted music classes at each period during the three assemblies and a 10-day music camp at Harmony Bay Assembly.

Stetson University has an investment in buildings and endowment of $3,113,830; an enrolment of 1,653 students, with 127 teachers and officers; and a library of 146,800 volumes. One hundred and twenty-seven ministerial students and many more full-time volunteers to mission fields or Christian vocations are receiving preparation. Stetson, in co-operation with churches and associations, provides tuition scholarships for outstanding students or lay leadership. With less than one-twentieth of the college enrolment in Florida, Stetson has about one third of the names listed in current *Who's Who* and more individual names than all other private colleges in the state combined. A total of $160,652.12 was received for current operations and ministerial education.

The Baptist Bible Institute, with buildings at Lakeland and a new location at Graceville, Fla., is operated by a board of independent trustees. It provides training in Bible, music, and secretarial work for students not prepared for regular college or seminary training. It received $4,908 from the special state mission offering.

The convention assists the work of the Florida Normal and Industrial College for

Negroes at St. Augustine by 8 per cent of the annual state mission offering. The W.M.U. undertakes to raise an additional $15,000 for the college.

The Florida Baptist Children's Home, Lakeland, Fla., is owned by the convention and operated by a board of trustees elected by the convention. It has 145 children in residence and has served 192 on the campus in the year 1955, having assisted a total of 235 in all branches. It assisted 42 through its mother's aid program. Through the convention it received $148,313.99.

The Jacksonville Baptist Home for Children is sponsored by the Jacksonville and the Northeast Florida associations. It received 12 per cent of the special annual state mission offering, or $4,908.64.

The Baptist Memorial Hospital, 800 Miami Road, Jacksonville, is a Southern Baptist institution with a 310-bed capacity and 70 bassinets. It is fully air-conditioned, and has a strategic location for serving city, county, and southeastern territory.

South Florida Baptist Hospital, Plant City, is Baptist in name but operated by an independent board of trustees. The same is true of the Baptist Hospital at Pensacola.

The convention co-operates in the plans of the Relief and Annuity Board of the Southern Baptist Convention. The executive secretary-treasurer of the convention assists in processing applications for entrance and for benefits. According to records in the state office, there were on Jan. 1, 1955, 321 people participating in the various plans.

The Florida Baptist Foundation was chartered in 1947 to serve any cause or agency fostered or sanctioned by the convention. It has received $434,949.78 and 17 wills conveying assets to the foundation.

The convention is friendly to the work of the American Bible Society, making mailing addresses available for certain appeals and providing a place on the state convention program.

The United Florida Drys, supported mainly by the Florida Baptist Convention and the Methodist denomination, with offices in Lakeland, Fla., employs a full-time secretary to promote a program of education and legislation seeking to curtail the sale and use of alcoholic beverages. This organization received 16 per cent of the special state mission offering, or a total of $3,272.42.   ARTHUR W. MATHIS

BIBLIOGRAPHY: S. Boykin, *History of the Baptist Denomination in Georgia with Biographical Compendium Compiled for the Christian Index* (1881). *Christian Index* (May 20, 1880). T. F. Davis, "History of Jacksonville and Vicinity, 1513–1924" (1925). *Florida Baptist Witness* (Jan. 2, 1901). O. J. Frier, "A Memorial Sketch of the Life and Ministerial Labors of Rev. J. H. Newman. One of the Pioneer Baptist Preachers of South Florida. Who Passed to His Reward Above, July 9, 1902" (n.d.). A. H. Newman, *A Manual of Church History* (1903). P. Mays, "Richard Johnson Mays, Pioneer Preacher Patriot," Madison County Historical Society, *Second Annual* (1941). R. W. Weaver, "Centennial Address 1825–1925" (1925).

FLORIDA BAPTIST WITNESS. Authorized by the Florida Baptist State Convention in session in Lake City in 1883, the first issue of the *Florida Baptist Witness* appeared Jan. 17, 1884. After one year's publication in Lake City, the paper was moved to DeLand where fire destroyed the publishing house. L. B. Plumer, who became editor in 1887, changed the name of the paper to the *Florida Witness*, but heavy debt soon forced the paper to be sold. First purchased by William D. Turnley, the paper was sold to Milton F. Hood in 1888, and then to J. C. Porter, under whose guidance the circulation reached 4,000 by 1892. Porter, who erected a three-story brick building to house the *Witness* offices, continued to edit the paper until he sold its subscription list, shortly before his death in 1904, to W. L. C. Mahon of Arcadia. Mahon moved to Jacksonville and secured as partners in purchasing and publish- the paper W. A. Hobson and D. H. McMillan. Hobson was successful in getting the agreement of John B. Stetson to merge the *Southern Baptist*, established in Apr., 1903, with the *Witness;* the consolidated paper, which first appeared on June 1, 1904, was called *Southern Baptist Witness*. Stetson contributed $7,000 to establish the paper on a sound basis. When Hobson requested to be relieved of editorial responsibilities, negotiations were entered into which resulted in acquisition of the paper by the convention. On Dec. 26, 1904, the trustees purchased for $60 the list of the 460 subscribers and the good will of the *Baptist Messenger* of Pensacola. The *Witness*, which had no presses of its own, contracted its printing and moved in rapid succession from Jacksonville to Orlando to DeLand to Ocala, during which time its name was shortened to *Southern Witness*. The name of the paper was changed back to *Florida Baptist Witness* in 1908.

Faced with financial difficulties and debt, the paper returned to private ownership when the convention sold it on Mar. 13, 1912, to W. D. Nowlin of Lakeland. Nowlin sold the paper in 1914 to a group in Arcadia who employed as editor A. J. Holt, who served until Feb., 1918, when the *Witness* returned to convention ownership. J. W. Mitchell, editor and owner of the *Baptist Banner* of Parkersburg, W. Va., was secured as editor on Apr. 15, 1918; and during his 10-year tenure of the post, he built circulation from less than 3,000 to 7,500.

Financial difficulties and deficits increased with the coming of the depression in the 1930's, and the *Witness* committee offered Edward Davis Solomon of Louisiana editorship of the paper on a lease arrangement under which its only financial obligation was a stated small subsidy. Solomon served as editor from June 1, 1931, until Aug. 15, 1949, and built circulation of the paper from fewer than 2,000 paid-up subscriptions to more than 23,000. Solomon's

IV. FLORIDA STATISTICAL SUMMARY

Year	Associations	Churches	Church Membership	Baptisms	S. S. Enrolment	V.B.S. Enrolment	T. U. Enrolment	W.M.U. Enrolment	Brotherhood Enrolment	Mission Gifts	Total Gifts	Value Church Property	State Capital Worth
1830													(Explanation: This column includes total value of Schools, Children's Homes, Hospitals, Foundation, Buildings, etc.)
1840													
1850													
1860													
1870													
1882	12	222	8,059	593									
1890	10	173	7,384	587	3,686								
1899	23	459	22,620	1,302	10,474					$ 6,149	$ 44,404		
1906	24	519	27,969	2,064	12,600					44,548	252,130	$ 286,945	
1910	25	598	39,017	3,130	19,577					58,114	315,232	1,923,006	
1915	29	730	54,951	4,191	38,566		4,654	10,739		131,127	654,744	2,944,202	
1920	29	751	65,094	3,813	38,114		15,841	14,373		328,711	1,586,952	12,962,180	
1925	31	838	99,075	6,449	80,240			21,187		106,524	1,356,212	10,914,440	
1930	31	751	115,705	6,617				21,187		106,524	1,356,212	10,914,440	
1931	31	748	116,118	6,712	84,843		18,312	19,948		111,071	1,259,399	10,760,616	
1932	32	760	121,522	7,284	92,373		21,802	21,541		201,505	1,061,800	9,236,037	
1933	32	761	122,189	7,103	111,432		22,603	25,476		120,417	859,793	9,052,897	
1934	33	787	129,323	7,117	90,594		19,628	22,448		143,189	966,087	8,875,182	
1935	33	835	132,544	6,049	94,678		18,315	23,296	776	155,643	1,049,083	8,105,386	
1936	33	788	133,201	6,343	96,474		17,071	27,679	1,095	162,937	1,207,639	7,317,336	
1937													
1938	33	789	145,209	9,357	106,669	10,965	32,049	30,872	2,097	177,950	1,407,151	8,242,456	
1939	36	817	155,965	11,307	116,457	13,196	33,872	29,170	2,052	201,953	1,495,390	8,604,244	
1940	36	808	162,396	8,875	117,343	16,585	37,978	32,958		231,615	1,572,260	8,900,565	
1941	35	773	165,247	7,715	120,544		39,086	36,175		272,046	1,909,259	8,912,642	
1942	35	806	167,122	8,239	110,723		41,622	31,633		328,721	2,081,284	9,275,728	
1943	35	829	176,688	8,336	110,826		31,460			532,833	2,866,171	9,650,262	
1944	36	826	184,140	8,883	116,765		36,258	29,132		653,509	3,361,988	10,308,031	
1945	36	833	199,483	13,173	130,271		36,382	28,956		843,176	4,629,407	9,865,169	$ 469,131 (Children's Home & Convention assets only)
1946	36	813	201,480	11,297	133,841	32,551				909,024	5,497,539	12,283,822	
1947	36	813	201,480	11,297	133,841	32,551				909,024	5,497,539	12,283,822	
1948	36	897	242,804	15,286	180,016	53,393	52,062	37,247	5,504	1,068,059	6,967,706	20,717,750	
1949	36	914	261,527	17,467	193,499	62,189	58,561	40,477	7,361	1,225,361	8,062,219	26,920,041	
1950	36	911	278,668	18,460	214,402	74,802	68,889	42,127	8,157	1,350,204	9,423,025	29,214,329	
1951	38	952	296,704	18,877	224,927	79,177	76,298	43,303	9,380	1,348,871	9,978,676	33,788,394	
1952	38	976	311,955	18,163	241,574	88,567	76,851	47,436	10,282	1,536,275	9,674,071	38,481,655	
1953	38	1,006	330,220	19,430	259,903	94,764	86,449	47,488	11,373	1,766,150	13,282,230	44,101,646	
1954	39	1,038	369,294	20,196	298,064	94,764	99,750	53,693	12,597	1,947,094	14,819,219	50,903,129	5,202,952

FRANK C. RICHARDSON

introduction of the budget subscription plan, his persistent good will, and his loyalty to the denominational program contributed to the circulation increase. During the last year of his editorship he served as a salaried employee of the newly created Florida Baptist Witness Commission. On Aug. 15, 1949, William Guy Stracener became editor of the *Witness*, and under his administration the paper's circulation rose to 40,172 by 1956.   W. G. STRACENER

FLOWERS, FRANK CHEATHAM (b. Rutherford, Tenn., June 7, 1871; d. Jan. 1, 1928). Leader in children's home work in Louisiana. Flowers, a poor farm boy, was converted in 1886 at the age of 15. He was graduated from Union University, Jackson, Tenn., in 1901. Thereafter he held pastorates in Oregon, Idaho, Tennessee, Louisiana, and Mississippi. In 1917 he returned to Louisiana, settling in Amite. On Jan. 1, 1918, he became superintendent of the orphanage at Lake Charles. In 1925 it was moved to a 430-acre tract at Monroe, La., and its name was changed to Louisiana Baptist Children's Home. The number of children cared for increased from 43 to 175, the facilities from one to five buildings, the property value from $40,000 to $250,000. Flowers was first married to Louise Dance, to whom were born three children; after her death he married Benna Goar. He is also known as the writer of a column entitled "Billie and His Pa" in the *Baptist Message*.   CARL CONRAD

FOLK, EDGAR ESTES (b. Haywood County, Tenn., Sept. 6, 1856; d. Nashville, Tenn., Feb. 12, 1917). Minister, editor of the *Baptist and Reflector*, the official newspaper of Tennessee Baptists. A son of Baptists, Folk was converted at the age of 13. He joined the Brownsville Baptist Church and immediately began preaching. After attending Haywood County schools and Wake Forest College, he was graduated from the Southern Baptist Theological Seminary in 1882. The First Baptist Church, Murfreesboro, Tenn., ordained him the same year, and he became its pastor. In 1886 he was pastor at Millersburg and Falmouth, Ky., and in 1887–88 at Albany, Ga.

In 1888 he married Elizabeth Handly of Nashville, Tenn. That same year he became editor of the *Baptist and Reflector*, serving until his death in 1917. He was a member of the Southern Baptist Sunday School Board and was for some time its president. He was one of the 10 men present at the first meeting on May 26, 1891. During its early years, when the Sunday School Board was struggling to establish itself, Folk provided space in his office for James Marion Frost, the Board's first secretary. Folk was also president of the Tennessee Anti-Saloon League, and is said to have done more than any other man for the cause of temperance in Tennessee. He was the author of five books—*Mormon Monster, Plan of Salvation, Baptist Principles, A Southern Baptist in Eastern Lands, The Folk-McQuiddy Discussions*—and of one tract, "Why a Baptist and Not a Campbellite."   WILLIAM F. HALL

FOLSOM, PETER (b. 1809; d. Feb. 9, 1885). Converted at Johnson's Choctaw Academy in Kentucky, 1829, he was the first of his tribe to become a Baptist. He came to Indian Territory soon after 1830 and helped to organize the first Baptist church among the Choctaws in 1836. He was the first Choctaw to be ordained to the ministry in the Choctaw Nation. Intense in his zeal for Christ, he probably organized more churches, preached more sermons, and helped to ordain more preachers than any other man among the Choctaws. He was instrumental in getting the American Indian Mission Association transferred to the Southern Baptist Convention in 1855.   L. E. MAPLES

FORBES, LILIAN STEVENSON (b. Eminence, Ky., Sept. 5, 1869; d. Jackson, Miss., May 30, 1945). Pioneer in elementary Sunday school work for Southern Baptists. She was educated in Louisville, Ky., in the elementary schools, the Female High School, and the old Normal School, an institution for training public school teachers.

At the age of 12 or 13, she was converted under the preaching of Dwight Lyman Moody and baptized by Henry Allen Tupper (q.v.) into the membership of East Baptist Church, Louisville. There she taught her first Sunday school class, a group of Junior boys.

For a short time Miss Forbes taught school; later she filled a responsible business position. Then she went into religious work, serving as pastor's assistant and as church secretary. She wrote the first closely graded lessons for Juniors published by Southern Baptists, collaborating in that work with Annie Laurie Williams (q.v.). For five years she served as secretary of elementary Sunday school work in Alabama and for an interim period carried the responsibility of the Alabama Sunday school secretaryship.

When Lilian Forbes became secretary of the Elementary Department of the Sunday School Board in 1918, that work existed only in name. She organized and trained elementary workers in various states of the Southern Baptist Convention and promoted the work of Cradle Roll, Beginner, Primary, and Junior groups, developing standards and eventually providing a worker for each age group. During her 17 years of service, the Sunday School Board began publication of the *Elementary Messenger* (at first a free publication), a Primary superintendent's manual, and a Junior superintendent's manual. In 1927 the board began the observance of Home Co-operation Week, an outgrowth of Children's Day. Miss Forbes wrote *The Home Department of the Sunday School* (1916), the first book on extension work published by Southern Baptists. She also wrote *Program Material for Beginner and Primary Workers* (1922). In addition, she carried a heavy schedule of field work, teaching and making addresses throughout the South.

Miss Forbes retired Apr. 1, 1935, to make her home with relatives in Mississippi. Of her work Isaac Jacobus Van Ness (*q.v.*), then executive secretary of the Sunday School Board, said:

At a time when the work in Elementary departments needed to be systematized and made more and more effective, she began a pioneer work. With wonderful faithfulness and in the finest spirit, she has labored for these years, not only carrying to the churches and to our conventions her own message, but gathering about herself in the office and in the various states, co-workers who shared her spirit and her enthusiasm.

. . . Others will . . . build upon the foundations which she made and profit by the spirit which she had.

ROBBIE TRENT

FORD, REUBEN (b. probably Goochland County, Va., *c.* 1742; d. 1823). Pastor and associational clerk. He was converted at the age of 20 in a meeting led by Whitefield and Davis and was baptized seven years later, in 1769. In 1771, while a member of Lower Spottsylvania Church, Ford participated in the formation of the first Separate Baptist Association. Having led in the formation of the Goochland Church in 1771, he became its pastor. Out of the Goochland Church, with Ford's help, came Dover, Chickahominy, Licking Hole, Hungry, and Hopeful churches. His entire pastoral services were given to Goochland and the churches growing out of Goochland Church.

While a strong and beloved pastor, Ford also served denominational causes. Elected clerk of the Dover Association in 1786, he held that post for more than 30 years. During much of that period he was also serving as clerk of the general committee, or the general meeting of correspondence. Through these offices, as well as by choice, he was at the heart of the struggle in Virginia for the separation of church and state. "To him, more than to any other . . . was the duty committed of waiting on the General Assembly with petitions and memorials respecting religious rights."

BEN LYNES

FORD'S CHRISTIAN REPOSITORY, THE. Published at Louisville, Ky., from 1852. It succeeded *The Western Baptist Review*, of Frankfort and later Louisville, Ky. Its earliest editors were John Lightfoot Waller (*q.v.*) and Charles D. Kirk. In 1866 it was moved to Memphis, Tenn.; and in 1871 it was transferred to St. Louis, Mo., where it became known as *Ford's Christian Repository*, for its editor, S. H. Ford. Much of the credit for the success of the periodical should be given to Ford's brilliant, precocious wife, Mrs. Sally Rochester Ford—a woman of rare intellectual and literary gifts.

GEORGE RALEIGH JEWELL

FOREIGN MISSION BOARD.

I. History of the Board. At the 1844 session of the Triennial Convention in Philadelphia, the year preceding the organization of the Southern Baptist Convention, Francis Wayland of Brown University was elected president. He represented the conservative group opposed to slavery. The Philadelphia convention declared neutrality, but the Acting Board of Boston declared later, in response to an inquiry from Alabama Baptists the following November, that it would not appoint a slaveholder a missionary. In the light of that decision, Baptist leaders, North and South, were agreed that further co-operation was impossible. Wayland wrote Jeremiah Bell Jeter (*q.v.*), Richmond, Va., "You will separate of course. I could not ask otherwise. Your rights have been infringed." Secular and ecclesiastical publications expressed similar views.

Early in Mar., 1845, the Virginia Baptist Foreign Mission Society issued a call for a consultative convention to meet in Augusta, Ga., May 8 of that year, to consider, among other things, the organization of a foreign mission society to do any sort of denominational work that seemed wise, particularly missions and possibly theological education, and distribution of Bibles and other religious publications.

Three hundred and twenty-seven messengers from 11 states met at Augusta (34 represented two or more constituencies, leaving a net enrolment of 293). One of the vital questions was whether the society or the denomination plan would be adopted—separate and independent bodies for the prosecution of each object, as had been followed in the Triennial Convention, or the unification of the whole denomination with separate and distinct boards for each object of benevolent enterprise. Substantially, the latter plan was finally adopted. "It was truly a denominational convention comprehending within its scope any phase of work, missions, education, benevolence, etc., that the Convention would desire to perform." The charter was secured under the laws of Georgia, Dec. 27, 1845, and was revised in 1943 to be continued in perpetuity and to provide basis in law for the authority granted the Executive Committee. Only two boards were formed in 1845: Foreign Mission Board at Richmond, Va., and Domestic Mission Board at Marion, Ala.

Organization of Foreign Mission Board.—The constitution of the newly organized Southern Baptist Convention provided that at each meeting (first triennial, then biennial, finally annual) "the Convention shall elect . . . as many Boards of Managers as in its judgment will be necessary for carrying out the benevolent objects it may determine to promote, all which boards shall continue in office until a new election."

After the adoption of the constitution on May 10, 1845, the Convention adopted the following resolutions:

Resolved, That the Convention appoint a Board of Managers for Foreign Missions, and also one for Domestic Missions, and that a committee be appointed to nominate the members of such boards. . . .

Resolved, that the Board for Foreign Missions be located at Richmond, Va. . . .

Foreign Mission Board

The following brethren nominated as members of the Board of Managers for Foreign Missions were elected:

President, Jeremiah B. Jeter, (q.v.), Va.

Vice-presidents: E. Bell, Virginia; W. Crane, Maryland; R. Fuller (q.v.), South Carolina; B. M. Sanders, (q.v.), Georgia; I. T. Hinton, Louisiana; T. Meredith (q.v.), North Carolina; H. Malcom, Kentucky; C. K. Winston, North Carolina; T. G. Blewett, Mississippi; W. H. Bayless, Arkansas; B. Manly (q.v.), Alabama; J. McDonald, Florida; E. Kingsford, District of Columbia; R. Hughes, Missouri.

C. D. Mallary (q.v.), corresponding secretary; M. T. Sumner, recording secretary; Archibald Thomas, treasurer; Charles T. Wortham, auditor.

Managers: A. B. Smith, R. Ryland (q.v.), A. Snead, A. G. Wortham, W. H. Jordan, H. Keeling, J. Thomas, Jr., J. Snead, A. Fleet, Th. Hume, E. L. Magoon, Wm. H. Gwathmey, W. A. Baynham, J. Tallman, Sr., T. W. Sydnor.

At the first triennial meeting of the Southern Baptist Convention at Richmond, June 10-15, 1846, there were no changes except on the personnel of the Foreign Mission Board nominated by a committee of one from each state. C. D. Mallary declined the office of corresponding secretary for health reasons and prior engagements with the Georgia convention. Four other men elected to that office declined. At the 1846 convention James Barnett Taylor (q.v.) was unanimously elected.

Some of the factors that doubtless influenced the Augusta Convention to designate Richmond, Va., as the location of the Foreign Mission Board were:

(1) Richmond was the approximate center of the Baptist constituency along the Atlantic Seaboard.

(2) It was near the seaports through which would be handled most of the passenger and freight traffic to foreign fields.

(3) Banking centers in that area would enable the board to handle, expeditiously, remittances to other countries.

(4) Richmond was close to the heart of Southern Baptists. Virginia Baptist preachers had been imprisoned for daring to preach the gospel without permission of the Established Church.

(5) The Virginia Baptist Foreign Mission Society had issued the call for Southern Baptists to meet in Augusta, Ga., in 1845. The first Baptist missionaries from the South to China were sent from Virginia and the first missionaries appointed by the Foreign Mission Board were Virginia Baptists.

(6) Among the spiritual giants in the Augusta Convention were James B. Taylor, the first permanent corresponding secretary of the board; Jeremiah B. Jeter, first president; and Archibald Thomas, first treasurer, all of whom were residents of Richmond.

(7) Virginia was the home of one of the three established Baptist papers in the South, the *Religious Herald,* faithfully supporting the work of the Foreign Mission Board.

First missionaries.—Among the first missionaries appointed by the new Southern Baptist board were two men who had labored in China under the Triennial Convention, J. Lewis Shuck (q.v.) and Issachar Jacox Roberts. Shuck and his wife, Henrietta (Hall) Shuck, were the first American Baptist missionaries to China, having sailed in 1835. Henrietta Hall made a confession of faith in Christ in a camp meeting in which the pastor, J. B. Jeter, was assisted by James B. Taylor. She was baptized by Jeter. The Shucks lived first at Macao, a Portuguese colony, and then at Hong Kong, British Territory, both near Canton; they went to Canton after five Chinese ports were opened to trade, and Shuck organized the first Baptist church at Canton, Nov. 27, 1844. Shuck preferred to continue his labors in China under the auspices of the Foreign Mission Board of the Southern Baptist Convention and was appointed by the board and assigned to Shanghai. He was in the United States at the time of his appointment in 1846, having brought his children home following the death of his wife in 1844.

Roberts, who had served as missionary in Canton under the Kentucky China Mission Society, auxiliary to the Triennial Convention, was invited to accept appointment with the Southern Baptist Board.

Preceding the appointment in 1846 of Roberts and Shuck, the Southern Baptist Foreign Mission Board had commissioned its first two missionaries to China, Samuel C. Clopton (q.v.), Aug. 4, 1845, and George Pearcy, Nov. 3, 1845.

Financial negotiations with the Triennial board.—One of the resolutions of the Augusta Convention in 1845 pertained to adjustment of financial claims:

Resolved, That the Foreign Mission Board of this Convention be instructed to communicate with the acting Board of the Baptist Triennial Convention, in reference to any claim we may have upon that Convention, or any claim which that body may have, or think they have upon us, and that the said Board report fully at the next meeting of this Convention.

At the first meeting of the Foreign Mission Board in Richmond, May 20, 1845, two committees were approved, one to advise what fields should be occupied, the other to correspond with the Boston (Triennial) board concerning the matter of assuming a portion of the field formerly supported by the united body and to express readiness to pay a part of the outstanding obligations against the Boston board. The response by the Boston board, through a committee headed by Francis Wayland, was to the effect that the general board did not think it should make any claim on the Southern board for any portion of the obligations made by the general board prior to the organization of the Southern Baptist Convention.

At the 1846 Convention in Richmond, the Foreign Mission Board reported an agreement with the general (Triennial) convention on a resolution adopted by the general board:

Resolved, That it is inexpedient, either for the General Convention or for those who may have retired from it, to make any claim, the one upon the other respecting the property of the said General Convention on the one hand, or the payment of its present debts on the other.

Choice of mission fields.—William Carey (*q.v.*) and John Thomas, the first missionaries sent out by English Baptists in 1793, chose India as their first mission field, although Carey had been inclined toward a mission in some of the islands in the Pacific. Carey was influenced by Thomas, who, in the employ of the East India Company as surgeon, had made two voyages to India and had learned enough Bengali to encourage Carey to begin the translation of the New Testament into that language.

Because of the opposition of the British East India Company, Carey and his associates, including William Ward, who set up a press, were compelled in Jan., 1800, to establish their mission at Danish Serampore instead of British Calcutta.

Adoniram Judson (*q.v.*), who had been given temporary residence at Serampore by English Baptists after he had been converted to Baptist views, went to Rangoon, where English Baptists had formed and then discontinued a mission, and formally constituted a Burmese mission. Under the leadership of Luther Rice (*q.v.*), whose conversion to Baptist views had been similar to that of Judson, American Baptists mobilized their forces in May, 1814, and assumed support of the Judsons.

When the Foreign Mission Board of the Southern Baptist Convention was constituted in 1845, English Baptists had been in North India half a century and in Ceylon since 1812. American Baptist (Triennial Convention) missionaries had been in Burma since 1813, among the Telugu in southeast India since 1836, and in Siam (now Thailand), Portuguese Macao, British Hong Kong, and mainland Canton since about the same time. When the Southern Baptist Convention was organized, J. Lewis Shuck, American Baptist missionary since 1836, and Issachar Jacox Roberts, who had started a mission in Canton in 1844, chose to work with Southern Baptists.

Of the fields in Asia, China made a greater appeal to the Southern Baptist Foreign Mission Board than any other. It was the oldest nation in the world, with the largest population and with more widely distributed adherents of major non-Christian religions (Confucianists, Moslems, Buddhists, and Taoists). China was considered the land of greatest need and opportunity; and on June 30, 1845, Jeter, the president of the board, offered the following preamble and resolution, which was adopted at its next meeting, July 7, 1845:

The empire of China presents the widest and most important field for Christian missions in the world. For centuries it has been carefully closed against the ministers of Christ. Recently God has opened the way for the introduction of the gospel into that dark land of heathenism. Five ports of the empire have been declared free for the labors of Christian missionaries, under solemn treaty stipulations. The efforts of the Baptist missionaries in China during the last year have been crowned with encouraging success. Just at this crisis events wholly unanticipated have hastened the formation of the Southern Baptist Convention. To the vast and inviting fields of China all eyes were anxiously turned. In view of this consideration, relying on the sympathy and co-operation of the churches, and above all confiding in the God of missions, and earnestly praying for his guidance and blessing—therefore,

Resolved, That with as little delay as possible, we will proceed to establish missions in the free ports of China, or such of them as may be selected for the purpose. . . .

In the first annual report of the Board of Foreign Missions is the following reference to prospective mission fields: "China is open. Africa is accessible. God has gone before us and prepared the way, inviting us to follow."

American Baptists had already become interested in Africa through the settlement in Monrovia, Liberia, of a church of seven members, with Lott Cary (*q.v.*), as pastor, which had been organized in Richmond, Va., and sent to Liberia in Jan., 1821, for the purpose of beginning work in Africa. Several missionaries were supported in that field by the Triennial Convention before 1845, and by the Southern Baptist Convention before the Civil War. After the war Nigeria, where a mission was begun in 1850, became Southern Baptists' one African mission. The Negro National Baptist Convention continues to direct foreign mission work in Liberia.

At the 1846 Convention a committee reported on "New Fields of Labor for Foreign Missions":

Resolved, That whilst for the present it would be unwise for the energies of our Foreign Mission Board to be diverted from China, and our contemplated mission in Africa; yet it is proper that they should direct their preliminary enquiries to other fields, and especially to Mexico, South America and Palestine, with a view to the future establishment of missions in those regions, if their means should justify it, and the providence of God should open an effectual door.

It was two decades before missionaries of the board entered areas other than China and Africa.

Agents.—Two vital problems facing the young Foreign Mission Board of the Southern Baptist Convention were (1) the securing of capable, consecrated missionaries; and (2) the expense of sending them to the foreign fields and supporting them afterward. Through all the years missionaries have received meager salaries, but their living must be provided.

For the reason that they had been far removed from the offices of the Triennial Convention and were provided with very little literature acquainting them with missionary needs and opportunities in foreign fields, pastors and people in the South were at a great disadvantage in developing interest in world missions. Moreover, many of them had been affected by antimissionary propaganda.

Consequently, the Foreign Mission Board found in the very beginning that some means must be devised to acquaint the churches, most of them in isolated communities, with the foreign mission enterprise. The board's secretary could not reach all of them. It was necessary to secure "agents" especially equipped and appointed for the purpose of acquainting and enlisting the Southern Baptist constituency through visitation of churches, associations, conventions, and other public meetings, as well as by personal solicitation. The first man selected for this purpose was William B. Johnson, president of the Convention. He agreed (May 12, 1845) to "make a tour among the churches in behalf of the Foreign Mission enterprise." He gave several months to that work, and met a hearty response wherever he went.

Consequently, the board began to plan for agents in every state. The plan was used for several years, although it was difficult to secure suitable men.

Antimissionary spirit.—With the growth of the missionary spirit and the expansion of missionary activities among American Baptists, resistance to the missionary message and methods increased. It found expression in ridicule of education, charges that mission boards were seeking to dominate churches, alleged misuse of mission funds, and attacks on missionary leaders. John Taylor, Daniel Parker, Alexander Campbell, and their followers criticized Luther Rice and other friends of missions. One correspondent wrote, "In my opinion every individual who contributes to the missionary operations is ignorantly contributing to the downfall of the American Republic."

Concerning the antimissionary spirit A. H. Newman wrote:

The Antimissionary movement constitutes the saddest and most discreditable feature of modern Baptist history. . . . From 1820 onward the Anti-effort Baptist became aggressive and, in many cases, malignant. . . . Anti-effort Associations in many instances passed resolutions disfellowshiping any church that should take any part in missionary or educational enterprises.

In one form or another, the antimissionary spirit has found expression from the days of Luther Rice and Judson to our own time, wherever Baptists have sought to obey Christ's teachings to go into all the world and preach the gospel to every creature. Frequently, it has been rooted in personal frustrations or prejudices.

Graves-Howell controversy.—In Jan., 1835, Robert Boyté Crawford Howell (*q.v.*) preached his first sermon as pastor of the First Baptist Church in Nashville, Tenn. With the consent and support of the Nashville church, he started *The Baptist.* In 1846 James Robinson Graves (*q.v.*) became associated with him in editing *The Baptist* and in 1848 became sole editor.

For seven years Howell was pastor of the Second Baptist Church, Richmond; he returned to First Baptist Church, Nashville, in 1857.

In that interval James Madison Pendleton (*q.v.*), then pastor of the First Baptist Church, Bowling Green, Ky., published in the *Tennessee Baptist* a series of articles in which he raised the question whether Baptists ought to recognize pedobaptist preachers as gospel ministers. This was the beginning of the Landmark controversy, led by Graves and others. The controversy involved more, however, than the pedobaptist issue. Concerning the Foreign Mission Board, Graves said in an editorial comment in the *Tennessee Baptist:*

We do not believe that the Foreign Mission Board has any right to call upon the missionaries that the churches send to China or Africa, to take a journey to Richmond to be examined touching their experience, call to the ministry, and soundness in the faith. It is a high-handed act, and degrades both the judgment and authority of the Church and Presbytery that ordained him, thus practically declaring itself above both.

In the Southern Baptist Convention, Richmond, that year the issues were fully debated, and Graves declared himself satisfied by the explanations of the Foreign Mission Board. But for several years efforts were made to eliminate the financial basis of co-operation and change the Convention into an ecclesiastical body composed of churches.

Howell and First Baptist Church of Nashville steadfastly opposed the Landmark program and its objectives. The Nashville church withdrew fellowship from some of the leaders of the movement, including Graves. Graves opposed the re-election of Howell as president of the Southern Baptist Convention. Howell was re-elected but immediately resigned, thus removing the personal element from the contest and leaving the Convention free to debate the fundamental issue of the method or methods of mission work.

Crisis of 1859.—The Southern Baptist Convention meeting in Richmond in 1859 debated the question of methods in missions. In the *Tennessee Baptist* Graves had discussed the relation of the Foreign Mission Board to the churches. Graves in the South and Francis Wayland in the North represented the sentiment of Baptists who claimed that churches and associations, rather than boards, should select, appoint, and support foreign missionaries. Every phase of the question was discussed in the Richmond Convention. Such leaders of missions as Matthew T. Yates (*q.v.*), James Petigru Boyce (*q.v.*), Alvam Maer Poindexter (*q.v.*), and W. P. Chilton pointed out that under the proposed plans a church or association might, after a brief season, withdraw its support, and the mission would suffer or be discontinued. A board representing the entire denomination would be enabled, to a much greater degree, to sustain the work of any given missionary or in any chosen field. There is as much scrip-

WILLIAM JEWELL COLLEGE (q.v.), Liberty, Mo. Founded 1849. Jewell Hall, above, built 1851. Seventeen buildings serve more than 700 students annually.

FIRST BAPTIST CHURCH (q.v.), Charleston, S. C. Formed 1682, Greek structure seating 1,000 built 1822. Membership 1956 over 1,300.

tural precedent for a board as for an association. Furthermore, a board or committee with a knowledge of the entire area and of mission stations could more intelligently and more effectually direct the missionary enterprise. Duplication would be avoided and the resident missionaries would be strengthened and encouraged by the spirit of co-operation. A full day was given to debate, with Graves leading. The Foreign Mission Board explained in detail all of its plans and policies. All questions were answered and criticisms were apparently allayed, especially after Graves had stated that he intended to vote for the report of the board. However, in 1869 Graves proposed an amendment to eliminate the financial basis of co-operative work and to change the Convention to an ecclesiastical body composed of churches rather than individual messengers. Thirty years later, the Foreign Mission Board faced a similar situation in the gospel missions controversy.

Civil War.—At the beginning of the Civil War, Southern Baptists had sent missionaries to two foreign countries, China and Africa. The Foreign Mission Board was cut off from communication with the missionaries by the federal blockade. Richard Fuller of Baltimore, president of the Southern Baptist Convention, secured permission from the Secretary of State in Washington for funds of the board in Richmond to be sent by flag of truce to Baltimore. More than $2,000 was sent in this way to William Crane of Baltimore, who in turn arranged with Isaac T. Smith of New York for it to go to missionaries of the Foreign Mission Board. During the rest of the war, Baptists in Maryland, District of Columbia, Kentucky, and Missouri (border territory) assisted greatly in supporting Southern Baptist foreign missions.

Missionaries in China in 1860 were Matthew T. Yates, who landed in Shanghai Mar. 10 of that year after a visit to the United States; Rosewell H. Graves (*q.v.*), who arrived in Canton Aug. 14, 1856; Charles W. Gaillard, who reached Canton late in the summer, 1854 (killed in typhoon July 27, 1862); James Landrum Holmes (*q.v.*), who was appointed in 1858 (martyred 1862, Chefoo, Shantung); J. B. Hartwell, who was appointed in 1858; John G. Schilling, who reached Canton, Aug., 1860 (retired to America, 1864); George W. Burton, who arrived in Shanghai, Mar., 1852 (retired to America, 1861, and in dark days of war made available to China missionaries some funds he had in Shanghai); and Tarlton Perry Crawford (*q.v.*), who returned to China in 1860 after a visit to America.

Some of the missionaries, particularly Yates, secured secular work which enabled them to carry on. The London Missionary Society contributed to the work of Graves. Some funds were provided for missionaries in China and Africa through sale of cotton on the English market by blockade-running. Missionaries in China expressed the sentiment, "War or no war, the mission must go on." From July, 1863, to Jan., 1866, Yates did not receive one cent of salary. He supported himself and his family by working four hours a day as interpreter for the Shanghai Municipal Council.

The Taiping Rebellion in China coincided with the Civil War in America. These wars interfered seriously with everything but preaching. Through a period of 10 years, 1860–70, Southern Baptists sent to China only two missionary couples.

A situation similar to that in China developed in Africa. The Yoruba (Nigeria) Mission was opened in 1850 by Thomas J. Bowen (*q.v.*), but from 1858 to 1874, no missionaries to Nigeria were appointed by the Foreign Mission Board. T. A. Reid, R. H. Stone and his wife, and A. D. Phillips labored in Nigeria under the most difficult conditions. Phillips remained at his post during the entire period of the war. During the years from 1868 until William Joshua David (*q.v.*) went out from America in 1874 under appointment of the Foreign Mission Board, the Wesleyan Methodists looked after the little Baptist congregation and the chapel at Lagos.

The work in Nigeria was retarded by tribal conflicts. Ijaiye, where the first Baptist church in Nigeria was founded in 1852, was destroyed in 1862. The little group of Baptists found refuge in Abeokuta, and the Baptist church in what became known as the Ijaiye section of Abeokuta has been regarded as the mother church in Nigeria. Moses L. Stone, a refugee boy from Ijaiye who later was called the Spurgeon of the Yoruba country, and Sarah Harden, widow of J. M. Harden, helped to hold Baptists together during the dark years. J. M. Harden, a Negro missionary in Liberia who was transferred to Lagos, Nigeria, in 1854, the founder of the first Baptist church in Lagos, died in May, 1864. Charles E. Maddry writes of the Hardens: "Mrs. Harden was truly a mother in Israel to our early missionaries. After her husband's death, she became the chief stay and support of our little Baptist church in Lagos. It was all that was left in an organized way, of eighteen years of labor by the missionaries of our Board in Nigeria."

After twenty-five years.—As early as 1850, the attention of the Foreign Mission Board was directed to Roman Catholic Europe, but nothing was done then because of lack of funds. A little more than a year before the close of James B. Taylor's administration as secretary, the board decided to open work either in France or Italy. Other denominations were at work in that area, but there was an urgent conviction that the Baptist message should be given to southern Europe. The occupation of Italy by King Victor Emmanuel in Sept., 1870, and the consequent opening of doors that had been kept closed by temporal powers of the papacy seemed a providential opportunity for Baptists.

The first missionary appointed for Italy was William N. Cote. Toward the end of 1873, George Boardman Taylor (*q.v.*), a son of Secre-

Foreign Mission Board

tary Taylor, began his ministry and spent most of the remaining years of his life in Italy, until his death 34 years later. The next year after his arrival in Italy, he baptized into the fellowship of the Milan Baptist Church a man named Enrico Paschetto, whose two sons Lodovico and Paolo became outstanding Baptist leaders in Italy.

During the administration of Henry Allen Tupper (q.v.) as secretary (1872-93), the board extended its work into three new areas—Mexico, Brazil, and Japan. William David Powell (q.v.) went from Texas to find out, if possible, how John Westrup (q.v.), first missionary of Texas Baptists to Mexico, was killed. He found the diary of the young missionary, in which the last entry was: "Four baptisms today. Go back and teach them next week." Powell kept asking himself, "Who will teach them now?" He wrote the Foreign Mission Board, offering to take up the work begun by Westrup in 1880. Powell was appointed in 1882 and spent 16 years in Mexico.

Following the Civil War, General A. T. Hawthorne left the South to become a voluntary exile in Brazil. When he returned to Texas, he was converted in a meeting held by William Evander Penn (q.v.), an evangelist, and immediately started making appeals to Baptists to send missionaries to Brazil. The first appointees for Brazil, William Buck Bagby (q.v.) and Anne Luther Bagby (q.v.), sailed in Jan., 1881.

Probably the most significant phase of the closing years of Secretary Tupper's administration was the entrance into Japan. Southern Baptists had appointed missionaries to Japan in 1860, but they never reached that land. Two of them, John Quincy Adams Rohrer and Sarah Robinson Rohrer, sailed but were lost at sea. No other attempts were made to open missionary work in Japan until 1889 when, in response to the urgent plea of Southern Baptists in convention, John William McCollum (q.v.) and his wife were appointed and finally located at Fukuoka, where a Baptist high school, college, university, and woman's training school are now in operation. In one of his first letters to McCollum, Tupper wrote: "Remember, my brother, that you are to lay the foundations of an eternal work. Look a hundred years ahead." The McCollums were joined by Ernest Nathan Walne and his wife in 1892.

Decision concerning reunion, 1879.—During the Reconstruction era after the Civil War, there were occasional suggestions, North and South, that Southern Baptists reunite with Northern Baptists. Such discussions and the consequent uncertainties concerning the future course of the Southern Baptist Convention tended to affect interest in both domestic and foreign missions. The issue came to a head in the 1879 Convention, which met at Atlanta.

After the question had been debated for half a day, John Albert Broadus (q.v.) introduced the following proposal, which, when adopted, pledged Southern Baptists in convention to an aggressive and constructive missionary program:

Resolved, That five brethren be appointed by this Convention to bear to our Baptist brethren of the Northern States, at their approaching anniversaries, expressions of our fraternal regard, and assurances that, while firmly holding to the wisdom and policy of preserving our separate organizations, we are ready, as in the past, to co-operate cordially with them in promoting the cause of Christ in our own and foreign lands.

Following that decision both mission boards, home and foreign, affirmed their purpose to go on, and adopted plans to that end. The next year the Foreign Mission Board appointed missionaries to enter new fields, Mexico and Brazil. The Home Mission Board, the name of which had been changed in 1874 from Domestic and Indian Mission Board, moved to Atlanta, Ga., in 1882, elected as secretary Isaac Taylor Tichenor (q.v.), and enlarged its missionary program.

Gospel missions.—In the late 1880's and early 1890's, a movement led by T. P. Crawford, for years an honored missionary in North China, advocated the view that missionaries should be supported by churches and not through boards (a revival of the Landmark controversy), that no schools should be conducted by the missions, and that the foreign missionaries should live like the people among whom they served, in housing, dress, and food. A number of missionaries followed Crawford and engaged in independent work because the board would not adopt their plans. The work of the North China Mission was crippled for a time but revived with the coming of new missionaries and the return of J. B. Hartwell. For several years the mission work of Baptists, both South and North, felt the effects of the Gospel Mission propaganda. Finally, the more vocal Landmark element withdrew from the Convention and in Mar., 1905, organized at Texarkana, Ark., a Landmark association.

Beginning the 20th century.—The administration of Robert Josiah Willingham (q.v.) as secretary (1893-1914) was characterized by an awakening of Southern Baptists to ever-enlarging world mission opportunities, expressed in the Judson Centennial Movement launched at the 1912 Southern Baptist Convention; the wider enlistment of Baptist laymen, which had its beginning at a laymen's conference preceding the 1907 Convention and the subsequent service rendered by John Thompson Henderson (q.v.), secretary from 1908 until 1938 (with the name changed in 1926 to Baptist Brotherhood of the South); the Baptist World Alliance, the first session of which was held in London in 1905 (Willingham was on the program of the second meeting at Philadelphia in 1911); the Foreign Missions Conference of North America (interdenominational), attended in the early years by Willingham and Ray; and the World Mission Conference at Edinburgh in 1910 (attended by W. R. Smith and S. J. Porter, then on the secretarial staff of the Foreign Mission Board). Two new mission fields were entered during

Willingham's period as secretary—Argentina (1903) and Uruguay (1911).

Pablo Besson (*q.v.*), called the Baptist Apostle of the River Plate, opened the way for the first missionary appointees to Argentina in 1903: Sidney McFarland Sowell (*q.v.*), Joseph Lancaster and Tennessee (Hamilton) Hart, and King Wolsey and Lillian (McCall) Cawthon. They were followed a few months later by Frank James and Daisy (Cate) Fowler. When Sowell and Hart applied to the board for appointment, Willingham asked, "Don't you know that our board has no work in Argentina?" They insisted that God was calling them to Argentina, and the board agreed to send them to the new field—a wise decision, as the years revealed.

The first Southern Baptist missionaries to Uruguay were James C. and Helen (Taylor) Quarles, who transferred from Argentina in 1911. They were followed a year later by a brother and sister-in-law, Lemuel Cleveland and Jennie (Saunders) Quarles.

Judson Memorial Campaign.—A significant advance step taken by the Convention in the interest of foreign missions was the launching, in 1912, of the Judson Memorial Campaign. After reviewing the development of world missions since Adoniram and Ann Hasseltine Judson went to the Orient in 1812, and then forecasting future possibilities and progress, the Southern Baptist Convention adopted the recommendation "that the Baptists of the South undertake the raising of a million dollar educational fund for the adequate equipment and enlargement of our educational institutions in foreign fields, . . ." T. Bronson Ray (*q.v.*) was asked to lead in the campaign to raise the special funds. Despite the interruption of World War I, the goal was oversubscribed, reaching the high mark of $1,250,000. Every phase of the foreign mission program was blessed by this offering given by Southern Baptists.

Coincident with the administration of James Franklin Love (*q.v.*), executive secretary of the Foreign Mission Board, 1915–28 were a number of significant steps in the development of the Southern Baptist Convention: creation of the Relief and Annuity Board (1918), incorporation of the Baptist Young People's Union into the work of the Sunday School Board (1918), admission of women as messengers to the Convention (1918), opening of the Baptist Bible Institute (1917), authorization of the Tuberculosis Sanatorium (1918), opening of the Southern Baptist Hospital (1926), projection of the Cooperative Program (1925), and enlargement of the Executive Committee (1927).

Chile was entered as a new mission field in 1917. The Baptist pioneer in Chile was a Scotsman, William David Thompson MacDonald (*q.v.*), who, to quote T. Bronson Ray, wrote "a new chapter in the Acts of the Apostles." With the aid of Bagby, he led in organizing the Baptist Union in Chile in 1908. The first Southern Baptist missionaries, William Earl and Mary (Skidmore) Davidson, were not appointed until 1917.

Several countries in the Near East and in Europe, where Baptist work was already established, became Southern Baptist mission areas in 1920, although missionaries were not located immediately in all of them. Missionaries were stationed in Spain in 1921, in Romania and Palestine in 1923. Baptist work in Hungary and Yugoslavia received financial support from Southern Baptists, although no missionaries were stationed in Hungary until 1935 and none in Yugoslavia until 1938.

The 75 Million Campaign.—When the 1919 session of the Southern Baptist Convention met in Atlanta following the close of World War I, there were appeals from several sources for an enlarged financial program. At the preceding Convention the Education Commission had proposed a five-year program to raise $15,000,000 for the Baptist schools of the South. Early in the proceedings of the 1919 Convention, the Relief and Annuity Board had requested the Convention to authorize an appeal for $75,000,000 for reserve and endowment of that board. All such suggestions and requests were referred to a Committee on Financial Aspects of Our Denominational Program. The Convention adopted the recommendation of that committee: "In view of the needs of the world at this hour, in view of the numbers and ability of Southern Baptists, we suggest that in the organized work of this Convention we undertake to raise not less than $75,000,000 in five years."

Plans were made for an organization to carry out the program, with Lee Rutland Scarborough (*q.v.*) as general director of the campaign. The total subscription amounted to $92,630,923, but, because of the financial depression and other factors, at the end of the five-year period, the collection amounted to $58,591,713.69. During the five years, boards and institutions had projected their plans on the basis of anticipated receipts of at least $75,000,000. This policy resulted in heavy indebtedness on most of the interests and institutions. The Foreign Mission Board had sought to meet urgent needs and had appointed new missionaries and enlarged necessary facilities, buildings, and equipment in foreign fields. Missionaries on life contracts could not be recalled great distances overnight. But one of the most tragic results of the outcome of the campaign was the inability of the Foreign Mission Board to send out a large number of missionary volunteers who were qualified and approved for foreign service. Before the end of the decade, the Foreign Mission Board was under a crushing indebtedness of more than a million dollars.

T. B. Ray, who had been connected with the Foreign Mission Board from 1906 and had taken an active part in the advance of the mission enterprise, served as executive secretary from 1929 to 1932. During those years no new fields were opened. The board was trying desperately to hold steady through the depression years.

Hundred Thousand Club.—At the 1933 session of the Southern Baptist Convention, total liabilities of nearly $6,000,000 were reported. The Foreign Mission Board reported notes payable totaling $1,127,417.17. At that Convention the Baptist Hundred Thousand Club was adopted with recommendations:

> That the object of the Club be the liquidation of the present debts of all of the agencies of the Southern Baptist Convention.
>
> That the membership of the Hundred Thousand Club consist of persons paying one dollar (1.00) per month over and above their regular subscriptions through the churches.

There was a gratifying response to the plan, and complete deliverance from debt for the Convention and all of its agencies was achieved in 1944. At the Apr. 13, 1943, meeting in Richmond, the Foreign Mission Board celebrated the payment of the last note due the banks and was able to report in 1944 no indebtedness and no interest paid—for the first time since its creation in 1845.

After this experience with debt, the board adopted a plan to create a reserve, in line with the policy of the best business institutions, as a safeguard against possible contingencies that might develop in the future.

The administration of Charles E. Maddry covered this period of financial difficulty, and the world war which followed. Secretary Maddry visited all of the Southern Baptist foreign mission fields during his administration and was in Honolulu Dec. 8, 1941, when that city was attacked by Japanese war planes. As a way station between America and the Orient, the Hawaiian Islands were formally aligned with the Southern Baptist Convention in 1941.

When Maddry retired, the board expressed in fitting words the appreciation of Southern Baptists and their evaluation of his missionary leadership:

> His twelve years as secretary was a period of expanding horizons for us and for him . . . and in every department of our growing work administrative wisdom has been shown in meeting each new situation, in establishing new fields, and increasing the number of missionaries wherever doors have been open.
>
> Noteworthy among the many achievements of this administration has been more than a million dollars given for the relief of the hungry in the famine-stricken areas of other lands.
>
> . . . Our Foreign Mission Board has been blessed of God in the men who have been our secretaries. Each faced problems springing out of the period in which he served. Each did his day's work, and faithfully. . . . In that noble succession Dr. Maddry walked. . . .

Advance Program.—During the administration of M. Theron Rankin (*q.v.*), 1945–53, a score of new fields were entered by missionaries of the Foreign Mission Board. In the Near East a mission station was opened in Lebanon in 1945, and a station in Jordan in 1952. In Latin America, Paraguay was entered in 1945; Venezuela, Costa Rica, and Guatemala in 1949; and Ecuador and Peru in 1950. In Africa, missionaries entered the Gold Coast in 1947 and Southern Rhodesia in 1950. Because of the Communist domination of China, missionaries gradually left their missions there, primarily to protect Chinese Baptist nationalists, and following apostolic precedent "they that were scattered abroad went every where preaching the word" (Acts 8:4). Missionaries who had served in China entered Korea, Formosa, the Philippines, and Thailand in 1950, and Malaya and Indonesia in 1951. The first international seminary of Southern Baptists was opened in Zurich, Switzerland, in 1948.

Early in 1948 Rankin proposed an Advance Program with a goal, specified the following year, of 1,750 missionaries and an over-all annual budget of $10,000,000. He cited the following objectives for the Advance Program:

(1) To multiply and strengthen every useful channel for preaching the good news of God in Christ Jesus

(2) To increase the facilities for training national Baptist leaders

(3) To provide and maintain hospitals to strengthen medical missions in our Baptist foreign mission fields

(4) To maintain Baptist publication organizations in all areas for providing Bibles, Sunday school literature, Woman's Missionary Union materials, magazines, books, and other forms of Christian literature in the language of each country

(5) To project definite missions to Moslems, featuring direct evangelism, medical work, and schools—including the Near East and North Africa

(6) To enlarge plans for training leaders for Italy, Spain, Balkan countries, and the Near East

(7) To provide facilities for mission work recently started or projected in new areas in Latin America

(8) To enlarge program for Japan, Hawaii, and other fields in the Orient

(9) To study mission possibilities in unoccupied areas in Africa.

From 1948 until his death, Rankin continued to stress the specific objective of the Foreign Mission Board—1,750 overseas missionaries and an annual over-all budget of $10,000,000. In his last report to the Southern Baptist Convention in May, 1953, he stressed the objective of missionaries of the Foreign Mission Board who, wherever they go—whether to Nigeria, where our missionaries have served for over 100 years, or to Indonesia, where they have served only one year—seek to lead people to a personal faith in Christ Jesus as Lord and Saviour, to bring them together in churches for worship of God and service in his kingdom, to teach them and train them in stewardship and in co-operative service, and to aid them in developing their own schools and institutions for training their pastors and other church workers.

The title of Rankin's last written message before his death in the July, 1953, *Commission* was "Do Southern Baptists Dare Follow God?" In it he said:

These forces of advance have been stirring among Southern Baptists. Already they have carried us farther than many of us dared to hope when the Foreign Mission Board announced its program of advance in 1948. But it is becoming evident that we have advanced only to the door, where we are seeing the world in a new way. We are becoming conscious of new dimensions. . . .

. . . I am much more afraid of standing at the door of the new day of advance in the coming of God's kingdom and of having God pass me by as he moves on, seeking those who will dare to follow him out into the world of this day. I wouldn't *dare* be left standing there!

When Baker James Cauthen became executive secretary in Jan., 1954, the board had 900 missionaries in active service, a little more than half the Advance Program goal. In 1955 there were more than 1,000 missionaries in foreign service for the first time in the history of the Southern Baptist Convention. In 1956 the missionary recruitment program of the board was strengthened, and a goal of 125 appointments per year was set. Missionaries entered Honduras in 1954, and the board named missionaries to Pakistan, Tanganyika, and Kenya in 1956.

II. Missionary Finance and Sources of Income. *Support of missionaries.*—The Foreign Mission Board of the Southern Baptist Convention provides modest support for its missionaries. For years the annual salary was $800; then the amount was increased to $1,000 each. The wife is paid the same amount as the husband, with an allowance of $250 (minimum) or $300 for each child. Where the country in which they work is suffering from inflation, a reasonable increase in salary is paid. Traveling expenses and homes for the missionaries are provided, as well as sick benefits. There is probably no missionary in our service who could not earn more money in the homeland. For example, a young medical missionary, before she went to her chosen field on a salary of $1,000 a year, was assured of an income of $10,000 a year in her practice as a skilled physician and surgeon in one of the largest cities in the South. Yet she is happier as a missionary because she has the conviction that she is where God wants her to be.

There are at least five ways in which support of missionaries may be provided:

1. Working one's way. Matthew T. Yates did that when shut off from the South by the blockade during the Civil War. In China he was given a government job as interpreter, but that limited his service as a full-time missionary. The apostle Paul is sometimes quoted as authority for this plan on the basis of such Scripture references as I Thessalonians 2:9; II Thessalonians 3:8; Acts 18:3; 20:34. But by the side of those statements should be put other statements of Paul, as I Corinthians 9:14; II Corinthians 12:13 (in which he asks the church at Corinth to forgive him the wrong of not permitting them to share with him the missionary burden). Other churches did share the burden with him: II Corinthians 11:9 (ASV), "the brethren, when they came from Macedonia, supplied the measure of my want"; Philippians 4:15-17; Romans 15:27.

2. Going as an "independent" missionary, with other individuals or churches (not co-operating with organized groups) supporting him. A number of missionaries who began as "independents" came to see the wisdom of co-operative service and sought appointment by the Foreign Mission Board of the Southern Baptist Convention in a relationship in which they rendered very effective service.

3. Faith missions. A notable example was the China Inland Mission founded by Hudson Taylor. His dominating motto was to "move men through God by prayer alone." He thought men should not be asked for money, and no debts should be incurred. There have been other faith movements, but none reached the mark set by the China Inland Mission as it stressed the power of prevailing prayer. While "faith" missions were evangelical in certain fundamentals, they failed as a rule to magnify churches built after the definite scriptural pattern and did not stress the training of the Christian ministry. To that extent they lacked compliance with the full teaching of the New Testament and failed to lay enduring foundations as indicated by Jesus when he said, "I will build my church; and the gates of hell shall not prevail against it."

4. Gospel missions. That plan which insists that churches, not missionary organizations, appoint and support missionaries has been tried out by Southern Baptists. When for any reason a church withdrew its support, the missionary was disabled. Some of the best missionaries in the ranks of Southern Baptists came to us after the gospel mission policy had failed.

5. Co-operative missions. The scriptural pattern provides that in carrying out Christ's program of teaching, preaching, and healing, churches co-operate with one another. If one church fails, the work will go on. Paul enlisted the churches in the areas which he visited, in ministering to the suffering saints in Judea. The churches, in not just one province but in others, had a share in that task. The persons chosen to transmit and direct the offerings, whether called "committees" or "boards" or by some other designation, made sure that the proper distribution was made. The Cooperative Program of Southern Baptists assures the unity, continuity, and expansion of our world mission assignment, with fellow Christians in thousands of churches having a part in the ministry of more than 1,000 men and women, under appointment of our Foreign Mission Board, working in lands in every continent.

According to the 1956 budget adopted by the 1955 Southern Baptist Convention, $3,800,000 of the Cooperative Program fund was allotted to the Foreign Mission Board, with 75 per cent of all receipts over $10,000,000 going to that board. In addition to the Cooperative Program funds, the Lottie Moon Christmas Offering and other designated items are sent to the Foreign Mission Board. In 1954, according to the report of the treasurer of the Foreign Mission Board, $4,772,-123.14 was received through the Cooperative Program; $1,539,230.62, designations; $3,600,-765.44, Lottie Moon Offering.

Lottie Moon Christmas Offering.—In the closing months of 1887, Charlotte (Lottie) Diggs Moon (*q.v.*), who had gone from Virginia to North China in 1873, wrote an article for the *Foreign Mission Journal*, suggesting that Southern Baptist women set apart the week before Christmas as the week of prayer and offering for world missions.

The following May, Southern Baptist women met in Richmond, at the time of the Southern Baptist Convention, and were organized into what was known later as Woman's Missionary Union, Auxiliary to the Southern Baptist Convention. They accepted Miss Moon's challenge, passed on to them by Henry A. Tupper of the Foreign Mission Board. Plans were made for the first offering to be taken in Dec., 1888. She had asked that two new missionaries be sent to reinforce her in Shantung Province. The offering was sufficient for three. The annual December offering (named in 1918 the Lottie Moon Christmas Offering) increased from year to year, until in 1954 it totaled $3,600,765.44 (for the W.M.U. year ending the following April, $3,957,821.00).

Through the Lottie Moon Offering, Southern Baptists provide salaries of 125 missionaries, funds for evangelistic work, and current expenses of hospitals, seminaries, training schools, pastors and church workers, publication houses, and homes for missionaries. A vast amount of work is done which, without the Lottie Moon Offering, would be impossible.

George W. Bottoms Endowment Fund.—In 1918 Mr. and Mrs. George W. Bottoms of Texarkana, Ark., gave to the Foreign Mission Board $100,000 to provide an office building as headquarters for the board. In 1922 the board reported the purchase of property in Richmond which was occupied until 1943. The full amount of the gift was not expended in the purchase of the first two buildings. Subsequent gifts were made to the work of the board in Palestine (Nazareth), Brazil (Rio de Janeiro), and other mission fields around the world.

Henry A. Brown Memorial Fund.—In 1944 the Foreign Mission Board received more than $42,000 worth of securities given by a member of the First Baptist Church, Winston-Salem, N. C., to be known as the Henry A. Brown Memorial Fund. The friend who started the fund wished to remain anonymous; but the fund, which honors the memory of the man who was for many years the beloved pastor of the Winston-Salem church, appealed to this church, and sums of money have been added to it and paid out as decisions are made concerning its use. For some time the church has been interested in missionary projects in Latin America. In 1956 the Brown Memorial provided funds for the basic unit in the first Southern Baptist hospital in Mexico.

Estate of W. R. Spight.—During the pastorate at Decatur, Ala., of W. Y. Quisenberry, one of the most zealous advocates of foreign missions that Southern Baptists have ever known, a young businessman and wholesale grocer, W. R. Spight, became interested in foreign missions. At the time of his death in Sept., 1936, he left an estate valued at more than a million dollars. After making appropriate gifts to relatives and ample provision for his sister, Mrs. Seneca R. Burr, he left the remainder of his estate to the W. R. Spight Religious and Charitable Trust, appointing his sister as executrix. Provision was made for distribution of his estate as follows: Foreign Mission Board, 50 per cent; Home Mission Board, 3 per cent; state mission board, 2 per cent; Southern Baptist Theological Seminary, 15 per cent; Baptist Bible Institute (now New Orleans Baptist Theological Seminary), 10 per cent; Howard College, 10 per cent; Judson College, 2 per cent; Union University, 8 per cent.

Mr. Spight's will specified that this gift to the Foreign Mission Board was to be used "exclusively in the furtherance and expansion of foreign mission work by the employment of new and additional qualified missionaries for foreign mission work and their reasonable expense and charges."

The estate has been in process of liquidation since the death of Mrs. Burr, Nov. 27, 1950. According to the treasurer of the Foreign Mission Board, the board received between 1938 and 1950 a total of $300,000, and between 1950 and 1955 a total of $610,000 from liquidation of the estate—all to be used toward the appointment of new missionaries. The money is being gradually used each year in the appointment of new missionaries, as provided in the budget. It is contemplated that in a few years this fund will be closed out completely.

Jarman Foundation.—W. Maxey Jarman, a Baptist layman of Nashville, Tenn., became interested several years ago in the Foreign Mission Board's program in South America. Through the Jarman Foundation, projected by his father, J. F. Jarman, he has given through the Foreign Mission Board over a period of years more than $1,500,000, most of it designated for Baptist church buildings in South America, due to his conviction that substantial buildings on the principal streets are more attractive than shabby houses on side streets. Gifts from this foundation have provided buildings in Buenos Aires and Rosario, Argentina; Santiago, Temuco, and Valparaiso, Chile; Barranquilla, Cali, Cartagena, and Bogota, Colombia; San Jose, Costa Rica; Quito, Ecuador; Lima, Peru; Caracas, Venezuela; and Montevideo, Uruguay.

III. Types of Mission Work. In the beginning Southern Baptist mission work in the two fields,

China and Africa (until 1870 when Italy was entered), was restricted largely to evangelism. At the end of the first half-century, only four more countries had been entered: Italy, Mexico, Brazil, and Japan. There were no hospitals, no publication societies, few schools. At the turn of the century, the work began to expand. Southern Baptists were seeing more clearly that the new fields must ultimately be evangelized by the nationals rather than by the relatively few missionaries that could be sent. In Nigeria, for example, the 1955 report indicates that only one missionary was serving as a pastor, while 272 Nigerians were pastors. The missionaries were engaged in evangelistic work and in training national personnel.

The Shantung revival.—During the 1930's a revival swept Shantung Province in North China. In the Foreign Mission Board report for 1933, we find the following paragraph concerning the revival:

> The revival in Pingtu aroused all Shangtung [sic] and has attracted visitors from fields afar, . . . to study the work of the Holy Spirit . . . business men have put aside remunerative positions and are now giving all their time to the spread of the glad news. . . . Others stay by their business but put soul-winning first.

Similar stories came from Hwanghsien, Tsinan, Laiyang City, Tsingtao, Chefoo. The widespread revival was characterized in every community by confession of sin, intercession, filling of the Holy Spirit, heart-searching by the church members, Bible study, soul-winning, affirmative answers to the question—"Have you been born again?" Southern Baptist missionaries reported great blessing in their work from this revival.

Missionary teachers.—The first missionaries to China began by teaching the children and giving the Scriptures to the people. Mission schools have justified their existence by reaching adults in the homes through children in the schools, by winning students to Christ through contacts with Christian teachers, and by training Christian nationals for leadership among their own people. As various mission bodies entered China, they opened schools of elementary grade. Mission schools preceded government schools in Hong Kong. The oldest Southern Baptist school in China with continuous existence (except for brief interruptions because of war), is a boarding school for girls, Pooi To, begun in 1888. Janie L. Sanford Graves was principal for 35 years. Growing out of Pooi To was Pooi In, training school for women founded in 1909 by Valleria Page Greene. The Pooi Ching school for boys was opened in 1889. Other schools were established later in other centers in China. Shanghai College began its first term in 1909.

One of the first references to schools in Nigeria, West Africa, was in 1876 to a "day school" with 40 pupils, sponsored by the young church at Lagos. To William Joshua David goes the credit for erecting the first Baptist school building of what is now Nigeria, during the school year 1883-84, the beginning of Lagos Academy. Struggling pioneer missionaries in Nigeria realized the increasing need for schools. The Nigerian Baptist Seminary had its beginning in 1897 with a small group of young Nigerian pastors who were taught the Bible by Charles Edwin Smith (*q.v.*). Baptist schools have been the most effective agencies in winning Nigerian Moslems to Christ.

Similar stories may be told of the successful work done through Christian schools in every mission field entered by Southern Baptist missionaries. A heavy responsibility rested on the missionaries to look after the training of the Christian forces in these new areas. As the various missions began to enlarge their educational facilities, to build academies and colleges, theological seminaries, and training schools for women, these Christian schools proved to be great evangelizing agencies. In 1955 the board had theological seminaries in 22 foreign mission areas with a total enrolment of 896.

Orphanages in four countries and Good Will Centers in seven link Christian teaching with social service.

Medical missionaries.—We are told in the Gospels that Jesus went about teaching, preaching, and healing. After evangelism and Christian education came Baptist hospitals, clinics, and dispensaries. Baptists began to send medical missionaries—doctors and nurses—calling for hospitals and clinics. This expansion meant more doctors, more nurses.

Except for brief, intermittent hospital ministries, the first Baptist hospital in China was established at Hwanghsien (Warren Memorial) in 1900 by Thomas Willburn Ayers (*q.v.*). The first trained nurse sent to any foreign mission field was Jessie L. Pettigrew, who entered Warren Memorial in 1902 (married to W. B. Glass in Mar., 1916).

The first Southern Baptist hospital in Africa was begun by George Green at Ogbomosho, Nigeria, in 1907. The first leper colony was founded by Basil Lee Lockett (*q.v.*) in 1932, near Ogbomosho.

The 1955 report of the Foreign Mission Board listed 11 hospitals in 8 countries (4 in Nigeria), and 29 clinics in 11 countries. There were 27 missionary physicians in 10 countries, 24 national physicians, 38 missionary nurses, and 119 national nurses.

Printing presses in mission fields.—The people of other lands were provided with Christian literature—tracts, periodicals, books. Along with the production of wholesome literature, literacy programs were promoted.

The first words of an East African chief, when taught to read, were, "Give me a book!" Baptist missionaries and nationals have been encouraged to project and promote the printed page. William Carey in India was reinforced by the printer, William Ward; Adoniram Judson in Burma, by George Hough; John Taylor Jones in Siam, by Robert Davenport. An indispensable factor in every mission field has been the printed page.

The China Baptist Publication Society was organized Feb. 28, 1899, in Canton. Robert Edward Chambers was the leader in this significant enterprise. Co-operating with the missionaries were four Chinese men on the board of directors. In 1926 the general offices were removed from Canton to Shanghai.

The Brazilian Publication Society, located at Rio de Janeiro, had its beginning Jan. 1, 1901. It sends out periodicals, books, and tracts in the Portuguese language. The Brazilian Bible Press, organized in 1940 in connection with the publication society, has published more than 250,000 Bibles and New Testaments and was the first agency in Brazil to publish the entire Bible in Portuguese.

Toward the close of 1904, J. Edgar Davis set up a small printing press at Toluca, Mexico, then at Leon. In 1916, because of antireligious legislation in Mexico, the plant was moved to El Paso, Tex., where the Baptist Publishing House published Baptist literature for distribution in 35 Spanish-speaking countries.

Other Baptist publishing centers are found in Buenos Aires, Argentina; Santiago, Chile; Ibadan, Nigeria; Tokyo, Japan (Jordon Press). One of the most unusual publishing institutions is the Baptist Press, Hong Kong, which supplies Christian literature in the Chinese language to the Philippines, Malaya, Indonesia, Thailand, and Formosa. Missionaries engaged in publication work number 44 in 16 nations, serving in co-operation with 278 nationals.

Thus Southern Baptists are carrying out Christ's program of preaching, teaching, and healing.

IV. Organization and Program of the Board.
New Departments.—In the closing months of 1845, the first missionaries, Clopton and Pearcy, had been appointed. In 1846 Shuck and Roberts, who had already labored in Macao, Hong Kong, and Canton, were appointed; also Yates, the same year. Less than a dozen missionaries were serving in 1846. In Jan., 1956, 1,020 Southern Baptist missionaries were serving in 35 countries.

The expansion of the foreign mission activities of Southern Baptists, in areas and in number of missionaries, calls for administrative patterns that provide adequate organization, resources, and personnel. There was a time when, with less than a half-dozen mission fields and relatively few missionaries, one man, who served as corresponding secretary with one or two assistants, could look after the work of the board. That is no longer possible. With nearly 40 mission fields and more than 1,000 missionaries in active service, the administrative staff must have an efficient organization and enlarged personnel.

The present elected staff of the Foreign Mission Board consists of executive secretary, assistant to the executive secretary, secretary for the Orient, secretary for Latin America, and secretary for Africa, Europe, and the Near East; president of the international theological seminary in Switzerland; treasurer, assistant treasurer, and business manager; the secretary for missionary education and promotion, associate secretary for audio-visual education, associate secretary for promotion, associate editor of *The Commission*, and book editor; secretary for missionary personnel, assistant secretary for missionary personnel, and assistant secretary for missionary personnel—student representative. All are reinforced by capable assistants.

Regional secretaries.—In *Charles E. Maddry, an Autobiography*, the author describes the origin of the regional plan adopted by the Foreign Mission Board while he was executive secretary:

I realized early in my service with the Board that the work was worldwide in its ramifications and that one man alone could never meet the responsibilities and direct the operations of five hundred missionaries widely separated in sixteen different countries on three continents. In addition to the supervision of the work abroad, there was the conduct of the work in the homeland. . . .

On my visit to Japan and China in 1935, . . . I had already made up my mind to recommend to the Board on my return the election of a regional secretary for the Orient. . . . Dr. [J. B.] Weatherspoon [who accompanied Dr. Maddry to the Orient] advised me to wait until we reached Canton and see Missionary M. T. Rankin before making a decision. He had been a missionary in South China for twenty years, was widely known in mission circles throughout China, and was greatly beloved by missionaries and national Christians alike. For some years he had been president of the Graves Theological Seminary in Canton. He had married Valleria Greene, a daughter of Dr. George Greene, a North Carolinian and a missionary beloved in China. . . .

Dr. Weatherspoon and I . . . laid before Dr. Rankin our plans for the reorganization of our foreign mission work in the Orient and offered him the position. He was greatly surprised and could not give his answer at once. Some three weeks later . . . he notified us that he would accept the call of the Board as the call of God. We had cabled our recommendation to the Board in Richmond and in a few days received a cable in reply, saying that Dr. Rankin had been elected regional secretary for the Orient. . . .

As I visited the other mission fields in Europe, Africa, the Near East, and Latin America, I recommended the election of regional secretaries for these areas. My recommendations were accepted by the Board, and Dr. George W. Sadler who had served many years as a missionary in Nigeria was elected [1939] for Europe, Africa, and the Near East, and W. C. Taylor was elected [1936] for Latin America. Dr. Taylor was succeeded [1941] by Dr. Everett Gill, Jr. [*q.v.*].

Maddry, who became executive secretary emeritus in 1945, was serving as secretary of the North Carolina Baptist convention when he became executive secretary of the Foreign Mission Board in 1933. It was during his 12 years of service that the board emerged from the era of debt into a continuing era of expansion. He was succeeded by Rankin, who initiated the Advance Program, designed to accelerate the expansion.

When Rankin became executive secretary in

1945, Baker James Cauthen, who had been missionary to China since 1939, was elected secretary for the Orient. Cauthen was acting professor of missions at Southwestern Theological Seminary and a pastor in Fort Worth when he was appointed to China.

After Rankin's death in 1953, Cauthen became executive secretary, and in 1954 James Winston Crawley, appointed missionary to China in 1917 and transferred to the Philippines in the evacuation of missionaries from North China in 1948, became secretary for the Orient. Crawley was a pastor in Kentucky at the time of his missionary appointment.

Sadler, who continues as the board's regional secretary for Africa, Europe, and the Near East, had served in Nigeria as principal of the college and seminary in Ogbomosho. In 1949, while the international theological seminary in Zurich was in its first session, he served as president. In 1953 he served as acting executive secretary of the Foreign Mission Board. He was an army chaplain during World War I.

After the death of Everett Gill, Jr., Frank Kester Means, who had been head of the board's Department of Education and Promotion since the department's beginning, became secretary for Latin America. Before joining the Foreign Mission Board staff, he was professor of missions at Southwestern Theological Seminary.

An ex officio member of the Foreign Mission Board staff, L. Howard Jenkins, after service as a member of the board since 1915, became its president in the same year that Maddry became executive secretary (1933). He was of invaluable service to the cause of missions during the days when debt threatened the board. A Richmond businessman, he has given his time freely to foreign missions through 40 years of continuous connection with the Foreign Mission Board.

Department of Missionary Personnel.—Not only are many more missionaries appointed yearly, but the procedure in appointing missionaries is much more complex than it was in the early years. Because the few fields that had been entered then were composed, for the most part, of people who had not the degree of culture now attained by many groups, the requirements for new appointees were not so rigid. But with world progress in inventions, modern methods of communication and transportation, and a greatly increased proportion of nationals who have college and university training, present-day volunteers must measure up to higher standards of preparation before they are qualified for appointment. Around the world nationals are earning graduate degrees. They keep in touch with world problems. Their great-grandfathers, like ours, had no telephones, no radios, no TV's, no automobiles, no airplanes, no movies. Today these descendants are shuttling back and forth across oceans and continents.

To aid in bringing young people to missionary appointment, a Department of Missionary Personnel was added to the organization of the Foreign Mission Board in July, 1943. The function of the department is to interview and correspond with young people interested in foreign mission service, to advise them of opportunities on the foreign mission field and of the preparation required, and to help the board select candidates best qualified for missionary service.

J. W. (Bill) Marshall, secretary of the Department of Student Work in Texas since 1938, was the new department's first secretary. He was succeeded in 1948 by Samuel E. Maddox, born in Rio de Janeiro, appointed missionary to Brazil in 1946. When Maddox entered the pastorate, Elmer S. West, Jr., a Virginia pastor, became secretary of the Department of Missionary Personnel (1953).

Members of the personnel department make and maintain contacts with young people, not only in Southern colleges, universities, seminaries, and training schools, but in conventions, summer assemblies, and special missionary meetings. Through personal visits and correspondence, they counsel with volunteers and seek to strengthen their purpose to be world missionaries.

Candidates for appointment have conferences with one of the board's administrative secretaries before going to Richmond. Each candidate has a thorough physical examination at an approved hospital, which may reveal any unsuspected physical trouble. In recent years, in these times of tense personal and social relationships, the board has found it wise to have sympathetic Christian psychiatrists determine the volunteers' emotional stability, their reactions in possible contingencies, and their ability to get along with people, especially their associates in service. In Richmond candidates for missionary service are examined regarding their Christian experience in conversion, their definite call to missionary service, and their soundness in scriptural teachings.

Missionary education and promotion.—The gratifying growth in missions has been made possible by a strong home base, by missionary-minded churches with a far-reaching program of missionary education and promotion; 3,524 Southern Baptist churches shared in schools of missions in 1954. This activity is a part of the Department of Missionary Education and Promotion, which includes *The Commission,* an annual graded series of mission study textbooks, the publication of pamphlets, and various forms of visual education.

In Nov., 1906, the Foreign Mission Board elected T. Bronson Ray to the newly created position of educational secretary. By the following May he had organized 84 mission study classes. In 1907 he edited *Highway of Mission Thought,* a collection of historical missionary addresses, the second volume published by the Baptist Sunday School Board (the first being *The Story of Yates the Missionary*). The program of mission study classes has grown steadily. Mission study literature is prepared for various age groups—Adult, Young People, Intermediate,

Review of Foreign Missions, 1940-1955

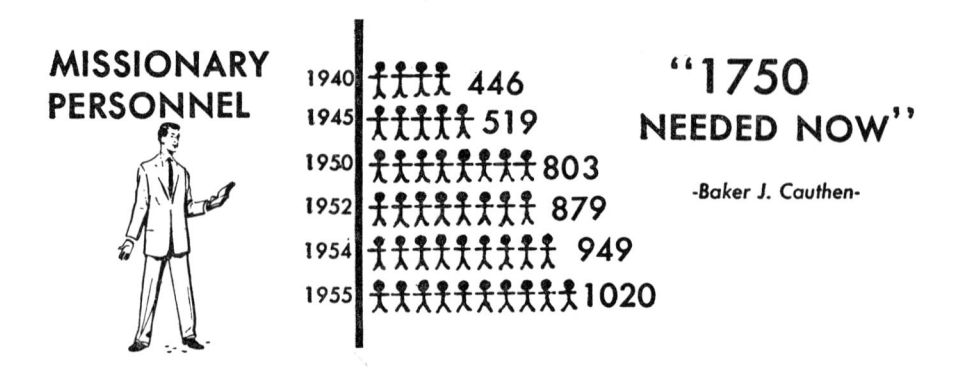

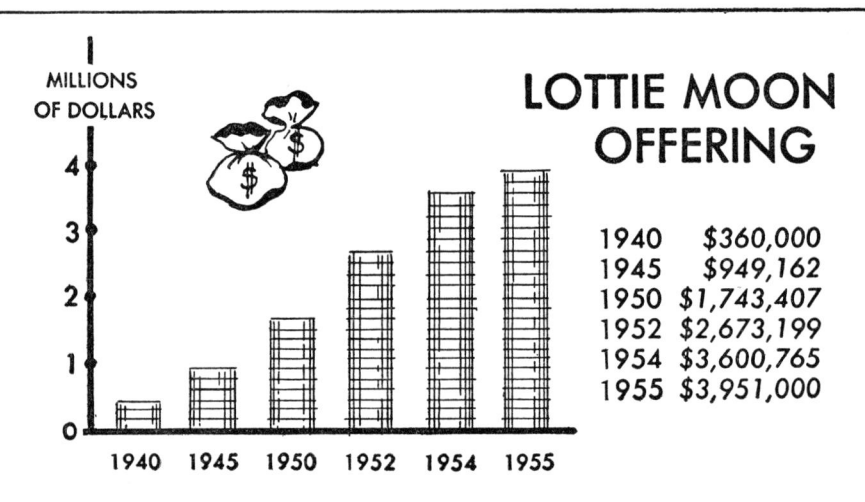

MISSIONARY PERSONNEL

Year	Count
1940	446
1945	519
1950	803
1952	879
1954	949
1955	1020

"1750 NEEDED NOW"
-Baker J. Cauthen-

LOTTIE MOON OFFERING

1940	$360,000
1945	$949,162
1950	$1,743,407
1952	$2,673,199
1954	$3,600,765
1955	$3,951,000

MISSIONS and GIVING

- ■ Foreign Mission Board Receipts from SBC States
- .... All Mission Gifts through churches
- ——— Total Gifts through churches

INDEX 1940=100

F.M.B. RECEIPTS

1940	$1,345,918
1945	$3,486,564
1950	$5,884,661
1955	$10,896,500 (Est.)

Junior, and Primary—covering in a cycle of years every country served by Southern Baptist foreign missionaries. The publication and distribution of these books is carried on in a cooperative relationship with the Sunday School Board of the Southern Baptist Convention.

Initiated in July, 1947, the Department of Missionary Education and Promotion was directed by Means until his election as secretary for Latin America. Eugene Lowell Hill, missionary to China, where he served with Graves Theological Seminary in Canton (1936–49), and Malaya (from 1951), became secretary in 1956.

Missions.—Not all of the administrative work connected with missions is in Richmond. With the goal of ultimate responsibility located in mission fields and the growth of the spirit of nationalism, increasing importance is attached to missions in the various areas.

A Mission consists of all regularly appointed missionaries who are in active service within specified territorial limits defined and agreed upon by the Mission and the Foreign Mission Board. . . . The Mission is the agency through which the Foreign Mission Board functions on the field, and through which the members of the Mission conduct a cooperative program of work. . . . It must have powers of self-government and freedom of action on the field in harmony with the Board's responsibility to the Southern Baptist Convention. . . . Provision should be made, just as rapidly as possible, for the national Baptist constituency to assume full financial and administrative responsibility in the work.

Periodicals of Foreign Mission Board.—Early in its service the Foreign Mission Board arranged for the publication of missionary periodicals. In its report to the 1846 Convention, the board prefaced its report on "Publication" with the statement:

In the early part of their official year, the Board made arrangements to publish appeals and missionary intelligence, for the purpose of increasing the interest of the churches in this cause, through the columns of various southern papers of our denomination, the Religious Herald being considered, on account of its convenience, the organ of direct communication. A gratifying attention to this subject has been shewn by our editorial brethren. . . .

. . . the Board have made arrangements to issue a monthly, to be entitled, the "Southern Baptist Missionary Journal" [beginning June, 1846, with eight pages given to the Domestic Mission Board beginning Oct., 1846].

At the Nashville Convention in 1849, announcement was made that an additional small and inexpensive periodical, *The Commission,* was being published for the board. In 1851 both publications were discontinued and superseded by a monthly paper called the *Home and Foreign Journal.* In 1857 the Foreign Mission Board reported that a magazine, *The Commission* (second by that title), had been initiated.

During the Civil War both the *Journal* and *The Commission* were suspended. Publication of the *Home and Foreign Journal* was resumed in 1868. This publication was discontinued in 1875 but reappeared in Apr., 1876, as *The Foreign Mission Journal.* With the exception of a brief period (1895–96) when the publications of the two mission boards were consolidated under the title *The Mission Journal,* the Foreign Mission Board continued *The Foreign Mission Journal* until 1916, when, by instruction of the Convention, *The Foreign Mission Journal* and *The Home Field* were consolidated as *The Home and Foreign Fields.* This arrangement continued until Jan., 1938, when, on account of declining circulation, the two boards again resumed publication of their own magazines, *The Commission* (title for the third time) and *Southern Baptist Home Missions.*

Headquarter's buildings.—Although the Foreign Mission Board's headquarters staff has occupied several different buildings, it has been located in Richmond, Va., since its beginning in 1845. The first meeting of the board was held in the library of the Second Baptist Church, Richmond. Subsequent meetings in 1845 and 1846 were held in the parlors of the First, Second, and Grace Street churches.

In 1846 Taylor, first secretary of the Foreign Mission Board, had his office in his home in Richmond. On Jan. 4, 1847, he moved the home of the board to the basement of the old First Baptist Church building on East Broad Street, which was occupied, rent free, for a quarter of a century.

Soon after Tupper became secretary in 1872, the office of the board was moved to the upstairs rooms over Ellyson's Store, adjoining the present Travellers Building on Main Street. In 1888 the headquarters of the board was transferred to the Merchants National Bank Building, where it remained until 1918. The next move was to the Presbyterian Building on South Sixth Street, where one floor was occupied except for the small chapel, which was shared with the Presbyterian officials.

In 1935 the board decided to occupy the fifth floor of the building at Sixth and Franklin streets, purchased several years before. In the late summer of 1943, because of the need for more room and the necessity of getting away from the noise of the downtown district, the board purchased a building at 2037 Monument Avenue. As world activities expanded, the adjacent building, on the corner, was purchased. In 1956 property on which a new headquarters building would be erected was purchased in the 3800 block on Monument Avenue.

The first home the board owned, at Sixth and Franklin, was purchased through a gift of $100,000 to the Foreign Mission Board in 1919 by Mr. and Mrs. George W. Bottoms, Texarkana, Ark. The board invested this sum in the Sixth and Franklin streets building and other income-producing real estate in Richmond. The two buildings on Monument Avenue cost only $71,500.

Missionary qualifications and procedures.—Candidates for service in a foreign field must possess certain qualifications before appointment by the Foreign Mission Board:

Foreign Mission Board

1. A genuine experience of the regenerating grace of God and a clear understanding and acceptance of the Holy Scriptures as the Word of God

2. A deep sense of the call of God to be a foreign missionary and a clear committal to the will of God for his life

3. Physical, educational, and emotional resources which measure up to standards which the Foreign Mission Board has learned through experience are necessary qualifications for successful missionary service

4. A degree from an accredited senior college and a bachelor's degree from a Southern Baptist seminary. For a missionary wife, a minimum of two years' training beyond a senior high school, either in a college or seminary. In addition, for a man, two years of continuous service in a pastorate or in related practical experience

5. Usually an age between 24 and 32 years. Under certain conditions, the Foreign Mission Board will consider appointment of candidates up to 35 years of age.

Candidates for appointment who meet qualifications (the board decides from information furnished by applicant, commendation by personal references, personal interviews with secretaries of the board, and by satisfactory examination in approved hospitals) are brought to Richmond for consideration by the board, with special reference to physical condition, Christian experience, definite call to missionary service, and doctrinal beliefs. Full information concerning qualifications for missionary service may be secured by writing the Personnel Department, Foreign Mission Board, Southern Baptist Convention, P.O. Box 5148, Richmond 20, Va.

Special appointees.—This term refers to a person who is appointed for only one term as a foreign missionary, with the possibility of permanent appointment at the successful completion of the first term, upon the recommendation of the mission of that particular field, the area secretary, and approval by the Foreign Mission Board. Special appointees, like permanent appointees, must have had a background of definite conviction concerning a call to foreign mission service. Usually, the initial appointment for only one term is due to some lack, to a small degree, in the matter of physical condition, education, or practical experience, with the possibility that such deficiency may be remedied during the one term of service. About one half of the special appointees are recommended for appointment at the end of first term and do excellent work.

Policies and regulations.—Policies and regulations relating to missionaries are clearly defined by the Foreign Mission Board with reference to qualifications, terms of service, furloughs, salaries, expenses, allowances, pensions, language study, reports, deputation work, retirement, etc. Terms of service vary from three to five years, first term; from three (in tropical areas) to six years, subsequent terms. In practically all fields the term of furlough is one year. The age of retirement is 65, voluntary; 70, mandatory.

The basic annual salary for each missionary is $1,000 ($2,000 for missionary couple). The pension is $900 a year, based upon 20 years of completed service, or fewer years in case of total and permanent disability while in the service of the Foreign Mission Board. The board holds a general policy for group life insurance providing $1,000 term insurance coverage for each missionary, premium being paid by the board. One-half certified medical bill is paid for each member of a missionary family. A basic allowance of $250 per year is granted for children up to 10 years of age, and $300 from 10 to 21 years, or until children under 21 marry or become self-supporting.

No work is opened and supported by special gifts without approval of the mission in any given area. Individual missionaries are not to make direct appeals for special gifts to support individual projects. These regulations do not refer to personal gifts, over which the board, of course, has no control.

Financial fluctuations.—This term has much more significance to world missionary enterprises than it had a generation ago. No longer does any country live to itself. Argentina is affected financially by what happens in Arkansas, and Colorado is affected by what is done in Colombia, South America. The whole world is sensitive to the fluctuations of the American dollar. At one time two Mexican pesos were equal in value to one American dollar. According to a recent quotation, it takes eight pesos to equal an American dollar in value. World missionary organizations such as the Foreign Mission Board must take all of these financial factors into account to determine the amount needed for modest living requirements for missionaries—much less, as a rule, than their service would command in this country. For example, during the days of terrific inflation in China, $3,000 would not purchase nearly as much as $900 would under normal conditions. Because of financial fluctuations the Foreign Mission Board must keep its finger on the financial pulse of the world.

V. Personalities and Institutions. *Presidents of Foreign Mission Board.*—Presidents of the board have been Jeremiah Bell Jeter, 1845–49, 1853–66, 1867; R. B. C. Howell (*q.v.*), 1850–53; J. L. Burrows (*q.v.*), 1866, 1868–70, 1872–74; J. L. M. Curry (*q.v.*), 1871, 1872, 1874–86; H. H. Harris (*q.v.*), 1886–95; C. H. Winston, 1896–1901; J. B. Hutson, 1902–16; William Ellyson, 1916–19; R. E. Gaines, 1920–32; and L. Howard Jenkins, 1932– .

Corresponding (executive) secretaries, Foreign Mission Board.—These have been James Barnett Taylor (*q.v.*), June, 1846, to Dec., 1871; Henry Allen Tupper (*q.v.*), Feb., 1872, to June, 1893; Robert Josiah Willingham (*q.v.*), Sept., 1893, to Dec., 1914; James Franklin Love (*q.v.*), June, 1915, to May, 1928 (home secretary, May,

1914, to June, 1915); T. Bronson Ray (*q.v.*), Oct., 1929, to Dec., 1932 (had served as secretary of education, assistant secretary, foreign secretary); Charles Edward Maddry, Jan. 1, 1933, to Dec., 1944; Milledge Theron Rankin (*q.v.*), Jan. 1, 1945, to June 27, 1953; and Baker James Cauthen, Oct., 1953– .

Treasurers of the Foreign Mission Board.—Treasurers have been Archibald Thomas, 1845–58; Edwin Wortham, 1859–74; John C. Williams, 1875–1909; R. R. Gwathmey, 1910–19; George N. Sanders, 1920–26; E. P. Buxton, 1926–49; and Everett L. Deane, 1950– .

Pioneer and outstanding missionaries.—Representatives of the missionaries who laid foundations in evangelism, education, literature, or medicine are mentioned here. Many more deserve to be in this list. Most of them served many years. Some were martyrs to the faith (Westrup, Holmes, Gray, Wallace): T. W. Ayers (*q.v.*), China; W. B. Bagby (*q.v.*) and Mrs. Bagby (*q.v.*), Brazil; R. E. Beddoe, China; T. J. Bowen (*q.v.*), Nigeria; L. M. Bratcher, Brazil; R. T. Bryan, China; J. G. Chastain (*q.v.*), Mexico; J. S. Cheavens and Mrs. Cheavens, Mexico; W. J. David (*q.v.*), Nigeria; J. E. Davis (*q.v.*), Mexico; C. K. Dozier and Mrs. Dozier (*q.v.*), Japan; Everett Gill, Sr., and Mrs. Gill (*q.v.*), Europe; Solomon Ginsburg, Brazil; Agnes Graham (*q.v.*), Chile; R. H. Graves (*q.v.*) and Mrs. (Janie Sanford) Graves, China; Rufus Gray (*q.v.*), China (Philippines); George Green and Mrs. Green (*q.v.*), Nigeria; George Greene and Mrs. Greene, China; J. B. Hartwell, China; J. L. Holmes (*q.v.*), China; Willie Kelly, China; George H. Lacy, Mexico; W. W. Lawton (*q.v.*), China; B. L. Lockett (*q.v.*), Nigeria; John W. Lowe, China; Carie Green Lumbley (*q.v.*), Nigeria; J. W. McCollum (*q.v.*), Japan; W. D. T. MacDonald (*q.v.*), Chile; Charlotte (Lottie) Moon (*q.v.*), China; E. A. Nelson (*q.v.*), Brazil; L. W. Pierce and Mrs. Pierce, China; W. D. Powell (*q.v.*), Mexico; Lucile Reagan, Nigeria; J. H. Rowe and Mrs. Rowe, Japan; Eugene Sallee (*q.v.*), China; Naomi Schell, Japan; John W. Shepard (*q.v.*), Brazil; J. L. Shuck (*q.v.*), China; S. M. Sowell (*q.v.*) and Mrs. Sowell, Argentina; T. B. Stover, Brazil; George B. Taylor (*q.v.*), Italy; Z. C. Taylor (*q.v.*), Brazil; William Wallace (*q.v.*), China; E. N. Walne, Japan; J. O. Westrup (*q.v.*), Mexico; Mary D. Willeford, China; Calder Willingham, Japan; Matthew T. Yates (*q.v.*), China.

Outstanding nationals.—This list of national leaders is brief but representative. The objective of the Foreign Mission Board, in each field served by our missionaries, is to co-operate with Baptist churches and general bodies in developing a national leadership, qualified to direct God's work in their countries if and when missionaries are withdrawn. Most of the leaders in this list are no longer living: Majola Agbebi, Nigerian Baptist pastor and leader; John Agboola, Nigerian Baptist teacher and pastor; Juan Domingo Alvarez, organizer of first women's society in Chile; Chang Wen-kai, editor, *True Light Magazine*, Shanghai; Thomaz da Costa, corresponding secretary, Brazilian Baptist Foreign Mission Board; Carlos de la Torre, gifted Baptist preacher and physician, Buenos Aires, Argentina; Matsuta Hara, president, Seinan Jo Gakuin, Kokura, Japan; Joseph M. and Sarah Marsh Harden, Baptist leaders in Nigeria in days of war; John Y. Lee, secretary, China Baptist Publication Society; Mrs. F. Y. O. Ling, president, All-China Woman's Missionary Union, Shanghai; Herman Chan-En Liu (*q.v.*), president, University of Shanghai; Nathaniel D. Oyerinde, educator and pastor, First Baptist Church, Lagos, Nigeria; Mrs. Yoneko Ozaki, president, Woman's Missionary Union of Japan; Joaquim Noqueira Paranagua, Baptist physician and leader, Corrente, Brazil; Enrico Paschetto, Baptist scholar, editor, teacher, and author, of Rome, Italy (father of two distinguished sons, Lodovico and Paul Paschetto); K. Shimose, president, West Japan Baptist Convention, Fukuoka; Francisco Fulgencio Soren, pastor, First Baptist Church, Rio de Janeiro, Brazil (succeeded by his son, John F. Soren); Moses Ladejo Stone, pastor, First Baptist Church, Lagos ("Spurgeon of Nigeria"); Theodoro Rodrigues Teixeira, editor *O Jornal Baptista*, Rio de Janeiro, Brazil (Teixeira and Soren were the first men won to Christ by Bagby); Alejandro Trevino, pastor and president of Mexican Baptist Convention, Monterey.

Leading institutions and organizations.—With the expansion of Southern Baptist foreign mission interests and activities, institutions and organizations have increased; secondary schools and colleges, hospitals, theological seminaries, and training schools have been established in most areas. Some, because of age or distinctive service, need to be mentioned:

1. Schools and colleges. (1) China. Pooi To Girls' School and Pooi Ching Boys' School are among the oldest schools on Southern Baptist mission fields. Established in Canton with branches in other cities, the Hong Kong branches have become the main schools since missionaries were forced to leave mainland China. The girls' school reported in 1955 more than 1,400 students and the boys' school, more than 4,000. In two revivals (1955 report) over 1,300 students signified their decision to accept Christ. The Baptist theological seminary had 54 students enrolled.

Other leading schools, maintained for many years before the Communist regime in China, were Graves Theological Seminary in Canton, the North China Seminary in Hwanghsien, the Pooi In Woman's Bible School in Canton, and the University of Shanghai.

(2) Japan. In Fukuoka, Seinan Gakuin school enrolled (1955 report) 4,000 students, junior high school through the university and theological seminary. With its enrolment of 1,500, Seinan University is Southern Baptists' largest university overseas. Seinan Jo Gakuin, Kokura, a girls' school offering work through junior college, had 1,619 students. Over 500 of the

students and teachers are baptized Christians.

(3) Brazil. There are two older theological seminaries, in Rio de Janeiro and in Recife, Pernambuco. More than 300 pastors have studied in the Rio seminary. Colleges and training schools are located in both Rio and Recife. The Kate White Domestic School is located in Salvador, capital city of Bahia.

(4) Argentina. Two international theological seminaries are located in Spanish-speaking South America: Buenos Aires, Argentina; and Cali, Colombia (a new school).

(5) Chile. One of the best-known schools in Latin America is the *Colegio Bautista*, Temuco, directed for its first years by Agnes Graham. The seminary at Santiago is training badly needed national preachers.

(6) Mexico. The theological seminary at Torreon had 51 students in 1954. Since its beginning at Torreon in 1901, it has "traveled an eventful and extremely difficult road," to quote Everett Gill, Jr., but the days ahead are full of promise.

(7) Nigeria. One of the oldest and most distinctive theological seminaries in the foreign fields is located at Ogbomosho. It began in 1897. Now affiliated with the Southern Baptist Theological Seminary in Louisville, its graduates are awarded degrees by that institution.

(8) Europe. Two well-known international institutions in Europe are the seminary at Ruschlikon, Zurich, Switzerland, and the Armstrong Memorial Training School for women at Rome.

2. Hospitals. (1) China. Among the leading Baptist hospitals in China before the days of Communist control were Warren Memorial in Hwanghsien, Stout Memorial in Wuchow, Mayfield-Tyzzner in Laichowfu, Oxner-Alexander Memorial in Pingtu, and the Chengchow and Kweilin hospitals.

(2) Nigeria. There are four Baptist hospitals in Nigeria, the largest being at Ogbomosho, reporting 1,518 in-patients in 1954. Many patients, some Moslems, have been led to Christ in this institution, founded in 1907. Several hundred lepers are patients in the leper hospital near Ogbomosho. In 1953, 1,353 patients were undergoing treatment for leprosy. In an evangelistic meeting in that colony, 75 professed faith in Chirst. A considerable percentage of lepers are members of the Baptist church in the leper colony.

(3) Near East. A distinctive medical and surgical service is given in the two hospitals, Ajloun (Jordan) and Gaza (Palestine).

(4) Latin America. The three Baptist hospitals in Spanish-speaking America are in Asuncion, Paraguay; Barranquilla, Colombia; and Guadalajara, Mexico.

(5) Orient. Hospitals were opened in 1955 in Korea and Japan.

3. Publications. Institutions that are making far-reaching contributions to Christian training are the Casa Bautista de Publicaciones (Baptist Publishing House) in El Paso, Tex.; the Baptist Publishing House in Rio de Janeiro, Brazil; the publishing house in Buenos Aires, Argentina; the Jordan Press, Tokyo, Japan; and the new publishing house at Ibadan, Nigeria. The value of their literature is illustrated in a letter received by the Spanish Publishing House at El Paso from a former Roman Catholic priest: "I was baptized last night into a Baptist church. Thank you for having printed the books that helped me to understand the full truth of the gospel."

The Baptist Press at Hong Kong—supplying Christian literature in the Chinese language to the Philippines, Thailand, Malaya, Indonesia, and Formosa—carries on the work begun by the China Baptist Publication Society, first in Canton and later in Shanghai.

See also GRAVES-HOWELL CONTROVERSY and DIRECT MISSIONS.   E. C. ROUTH

FOREIGN MISSION BOARD OF THE NATIONAL BAPTIST CONVENTION, U. S. A., INCORPORATED. Organized in 1895 for the purpose of "planning and executing the foreign mission work of the National Baptist Convention." Its headquarters are in Philadelphia, Pa.

The board is composed of nine members chosen from the state in which the board is located and one member recommended by each state delegation and approved by the National Baptist Convention. Work is established on the continent of Africa in Liberia, Sierra Leone, Ghana, Nyasaland, Union of South Africa, and Basutoland, and also in the Bahama Islands, Nicaragua, Okinawa, and Japan. The board operates two hospitals, Carrie V. Dyer Memorial Hospital, Monrovia, Liberia, West Africa, and the James E. East Hospital, Nyasaland, East Africa.

More than 1,200 churches have been established by the board in Africa alone with a collective membership of 375,000. Mission schools and colleges have 18,500 students enrolled; the total value of the board's property holdings exceeds $1,000,000. The board has 30 principal stations with numerous tributaries; Pilgrim Baptist Mission, Issele Uku, Nigeria, West Africa, has 35 substations for work in adjacent villages and accessible communities and areas. A staff of 700 American and native workers serve on the foreign fields.

This agency is not to be confused with the National Foreign Mission Board of America.

GARLAND OFFUTT

FOREIGN MISSIONARIES, SOUTHERN BAPTIST CONVENTION, 1845–1955. Since the organization of the Foreign Mission Board in 1845, a total of 2,087 missionaries have been appointed. These may be divided approximately as follows: men, 805; women, 1,282. About 140 of the missionaries were born in 28 foreign countries; some 60 of them were children of missionaries.

Early records indicate that the first married women went to the mission field only as "wives of missionaries." They were not officially appointed, as were their husbands, and in some instances were not considered as missionaries.

Apparently, the first single woman was appointed by the Southern board in 1849. Harriet A. Baker was appointed for missionary service in China "for the purpose of attempting the establishment of a school for female children, and as an experiment, the beneficial influence of which remains to be tested." Miss Baker returned to the States in 1853, and for some years afterward "the Board was opposed to single women becoming missionaries." It was not until in the early 1870's that unmarried women were appointed "to work among the women and children."

The missionaries are listed alphabetically. Included also are place of birth, country or countries in which the missionary served or is serving, and years served in each country. Where information is incomplete, it is because it was not available.

Abell, John Curthbert, Jr., M.D.; Tex.; Nigeria, 1951- .
Abell, Betty C. (Roorbach) (Mrs. J. C., Jr.); Tex.; Nigeria, 1951- .
Abernathy, Gertrude Inez; N. C.; China, 1908-13.
Abernathy, John Arch; N. C.; China, 1925-49; Korea, 1950, 1951- ; Philippines, 1950-51.
Abernathy, Jewell (Leonard) (Mrs. J. A.); Ark.; China, 1925-49; Korea, 1950, 1952- ; Phillippines, 1950-52.
Adair, J. B.; Tex.; Nigeria, 1941-50.
Adair, Desser Jewell (Whisenant) (Mrs. J. B.); Tex.; Nigeria, 1941-50.
Adams, Wayne Womack; Va.; China, 1908-43.
Adams, Floy (White) (Mrs. W. W.); Ala.; China, 1908-43.
Adams, Heyward Lander; S. C.; Nigeria, 1948-53.
Adams, Dorothy (Anderson) (Mrs. H. L.); Ark.; Nigeria, 1948-53.
Aden, Joseph; Sweden; Brazil, 1893-97.
Alderman, Jennie; S. C.; China, 1936- .
Alexander, Mary Charlotte; Tex.; China, 1920-52; Hong Kong, 1952- .
Alexander, Minnie; Tex.; China, 1921-34.
Allen, James Ross; S. C.; Brazil, 1919-52.
Allen, Margie (Hammond) (Mrs. J. R.); Ga.; Brazil, 1919-52.
Allen, Olive; Tenn.; Hawaii, 1948- .
Allen, William Edison; Miss.; Brazil, 1921- .
Allen, Edith Caroline (Ayers) (Mrs. W. E.); Ark.; Brazil, 1921- .
Anders, James Clarence; Va.; Nigeria, 1927-35.
Anders, Carolyn (Loring) (Mrs. J. C.); Calif.; Nigeria, 1927-35.
Anderson, Charles James Fox; Va.; Italy, 1900-04.
Anderson, Mary (Jordan) (Mrs. C. J. F.); N. C.; Italy, 1900-04.
Anderson, John Todd, M.D.; S. C.; China, 1915-18.
Anderson, Minnie (Middleton) (Mrs. J. T.); N. C.; China, 1915-19.

Anderson, Mary Raleigh; Miss.; China, 1910-23.
Anderson, Maurice John; Minn.; Hawaii, 1943-47; China, 1947-53; Hong Kong, 1953- .
Anderson, Kitty Thordis (Thomstad) (Mrs. M. J.); Norway; Hawaii, 1942-47; China, 1947-53; Hong Kong, 1953- .
Anderson, Park Harris; Ky.; China, 1907-26, 1930-38.
Anderson, Pansy (Green) (Mrs. P. H.); N. C.; China, 1910-17.
Anderson, Paneuma (Barton) (Mrs. P. H.); S. C.; China, 1915-26, 1930-36, 1937-38.
Anderson, Susan; Ga.; Nigeria, 1918- .
Anderson, Theresa King; China; China, 1948-49; Philippines, 1949- .
Andrews, Hazel; Tenn.; China, 1916-29.
Andrews, William Parker; N. C.; Chile, 1950- .
Andrews, Constance (Wildes) (Mrs. W. P.); Mass.; Chile, 1950- .
Appleby, David Perry; Mo.; Brazil, 1924-25.
Appleby, Rosalee (Mills) (Mrs. D. P.); Miss.; Brazil, 1924- .
Applewhite, Calvin Winfield, M.D.; Ga.; Indonesia, 1955- .
Applewhite, LaVerne (Viverette) (Mrs. C. W.); Miss.; Indonesia, 1955- .
Askew, David Curtis; Miss.; Japan, 1947- .
Askew, Mary Lee (Trenor) (Mrs. D. C.); Miss.; Japan, 1947- .
Askew, Dolphus Fay; Ala.; Argentina, 1940- .
Askew, Julia (Reaves) (Mrs. D. F.); Ala.; Argentina, 1940- .
Austin, Stella Asalee; N. C.; Nigeria, 1949- .
Ayers, Sanford Emmett; China; China, 1921-25, 1934-41, 1947-55.
Ayers, Winnie Davis (Bennett) (Mrs. S. E.); Miss.; China, 1921-25, 1934-39, 1947-55.
Ayers, Thomas Willburn; Ga.; China, 1900-34.
Ayers, Minnie (Skelton) (Mrs. T. W.); Ala.; China, 1900-34.

Bach, Jean; Ky.; Nigeria, 1948- .
Badger, Ted Orris; Tex.; Philippines, 1953- .
Badger, Mary Ellen (Byerly) (Mrs. T. O.); Iowa; Philippines, 1953- .
Bagby, Albert Ian; Brazil; Brazil, 1939- .
Bagby, Thelma (Frith) (Mrs. A. I.); Ark.; Brazil, 1938- .
Bagby, Olive Elliott; Va.; China, 1914-23.
Bagby, Samuel Adams; Va.; Brazil, 1941-46.
Bagby, Sara (Lavender) (Mrs. S. A.); Va.; Brazil, 1941-46.
Bagby, Taylor C.; Brazil; Brazil, 1918-55.
Bagby, Frances (Adams) (Mrs. T. C.); Va.; Brazil, 1918-55.
Bagby, William Buck; Tex.; Brazil, 1880-1937.
Bagby, Anne (Luther) (Mrs. W. B.); Mo.; Brazil, 1880-1937.
Bailey, Gracia Imogene; Tex.; Brazil, 1947- .
Bailey, James Mansfield; Tenn.; China, 1924-38.
Bailey, Ethel Ray (Stoermer) (Mrs. J. M.); Ky.; China, 1924-38.
Baker, Clifton Ayers; S. C.; Brazil, 1917-39.

Foreign Missionaries, 1845–1955

Baker, Mary (Hammond) (Mrs. C. A.); Ga.; Brazil, 1917–45.
Baker, Dwight L.; Mo.; Israel, 1950– .
Baker, Emma E. (Weatherly) (Mrs. D. L.); Va.; Israel, 1950– .
Baker, Effie Evelene; Tex.; Japan, 1921–32.
Baker, Harriet A.; Va.; China, 1849–53.
Baker, Mattie Alida; S. C.; Brazil, 1923– .
Baldwin, Willie Kate; S. C.; Nigeria, 1939–48.
Barker, John A.; Va.; Brazil, 1888–89.
Barker, Lillie (Easterby) (Mrs. J. A.); S. C.; Brazil, 1888–89.
Barlow, Hannah Lee; Va.; Japan, 1951– .
Barratt, Clifford Irene; S. C.; China, 1921–50; Formosa, 1950– .
Barrick, Charles Ransom; Mo.; Nigeria, 1922–25.
Barrick, Elva June (Sawyer) (Mrs. C. R.); Okla.; Nigeria, 1922–25.
Bartley, James Willard, Jr.; Ga.; Uruguay, 1952– .
Bartley, Peggy Jean (Place) (Mrs. J. W., Jr.); Tex.; Uruguay, 1952– .
Barton, Addie; Tex.; Mexico, 1884–1921.
Bausum, Robert Lord; S. D.; China, 1920–51; Formosa, 1951– .
Bausum, Euva (Majors) (Mrs. R. L.); Tex.; China, 1924–51; Formosa, 1951– .
Beall, Jeanette Ellen, M.D.; Kans.; China, 1919–53.
Beaumont, John F.; Va.; Nigeria, 1856–57.
Beck, Emily Virginia; Ind.; Argentina, 1921–29.
Beddoe, Robert Edward, M.D.; Tex.; China, 1909–27, 1933–48.
Beddoe, Louella (Houston) (Mrs. R. E.); Ky.; China, 1909–27, 1933–48.
Bedford, Allen Benjamin; N. Mex.; Argentina, 1951– .
Bedford, LaNell (Watson) (Mrs. A. B.); Tex.; Argentina, 1951– .
Bell, Ada C.; Va.; China, 1914–22.
Bell, Frances; Ala.; Nigeria, 1949–52.
Bell, Lester Carl; Tex.; Brazil, 1950– .
Bell, Bessie Wayne (Giddens) (Mrs. L. C.); Okla.; Brazil, 1950– .
Bell, Paul Carlyle, Jr.; Tex.; Guatemala, 1953– .
Bell, Carolyn (Crunk) (Mrs. P. C.); Tenn.; Guatemala, 1953– .
Belote, James Dalby; D. C.; Hawaii, 1940–47; China, 1947–50; Hong Kong, 1950– .
Belote, Martha F. (Bigham) (Mrs. J. D.); Miss.; Hawaii, 1940–47; China, 1947–50; Hong Kong, 1950– .
Bender, William Dean; Kans.; Nigeria, 1955– .
Bender, Novella B. (Chism) (Mrs. W. D.); Ky.; Nigeria, 1955– .
Bengtson, Nils John; Sweden; Spain, 1928–40.
Bengtson, Elin (Jerngren) (Mrs. N. J.); Sweden; Spain, 1928–48.
Benson, James Horatio; Tex.; Mexico, 1906–18, 1921–42.
Benson, Daisy (Fitzmaurice) (Mrs. J. H.); Tex.; Mexico, 1906–18, 1921–42.
Berry, Edward Grady; Brazil; Brazil, 1953– .
Berry, Lois J. (Roberts) (Mrs. E. G.); Tenn.; Brazil, 1948– .

Berry, William Hafford; Ark.; Brazil, 1922– .
Berry, Olga (Oliver) (Mrs. W. H.); Ark.; Brazil, 1922– .
Bice, John Lankford; Miss.; Brazil, 1923– .
Bice, Blanche (Hamm) (Mrs. J. L.); Tenn.; Brazil, 1923– .
Bigham, Sarah Kathryn; S. C.; China, 1946–55.
Bitner, James Henry; Tex.; Chile, 1953– .
Bitner, Fern (Weaver) (Mrs. J. H.); Tex.; Chile, 1953– .
Blackman, Lonnie Elwood; N. C.; China, 1922–38; Hawaii, 1938– .
Blackman, Gladys (Yates) (Mrs. L. E.); N. C.; China, 1922–38; Hawaii, 1938– .
Blair, Martin Stone; Tex.; Argentina, 1919–54.
Blair, Cora (Hancock) (Mrs. M. S.); Fla.; Argentina, 1919–54.
Blair, William Judson; Argentina; Argentina, 1949– .
Blair, Dorothy (Sullivan) (Mrs. W. J.); Ark.; Argentina, 1949– .
Blankenship, Adrian Emory; Ark.; Brazil, 1945–48, 1950– .
Blankenship, Mary (Hall) (Mrs. A. E.); Tenn.; Brazil, 1945–48, 1950– .
Bledsoe, Hilda Rebecca; Ga.; Hawaii, 1949–55.
Bond, Alfred Luther; Ohio; China, 1860–60.
Bond, Helena (Dameron) (Mrs. A. L.); Md.; China, 1860–60.
Boone, Clarence Dixon; N. C.; Mexico, 1921–25.
Boone, Esther (Stacy) (Mrs. C. D.); Ark.; Mexico 1921–25.
Bostick, Attie (Mrs. T. J. League); N. C.; China, 1916–45.
Bostick, Edward May, Jr.; S. C.; China, 1923–37.
Bostick, Nell Darden (Lawrence) (Mrs. E. M., Jr.); N. C.; China, 1923–37.
Bostick, George P.; N. C.; China, 1889–92, 1912–26.
Bostick, Bertha (Bryan) (Mrs. G. P.); Ky.; China, 1889–90.
Bostick, Mary J. (Thornton) (Mrs. G. P.); Ala.; China, 1889–92.
Bostick, Lena (Stover) (Mrs. G. P.); Va.; China, 1912–28.
Bostick, Wade D.; N. C.; China, 1910–36.
Bostick, Flora (Holloway) (Mrs. W. D.); N. C.; China, 1910–34.
Bouldin, George Washington; Ala.; Japan, 1906–33.
Bouldin, Maggie (Lee) (Mrs. G. W.); Tenn.; Japan, 1906–33.
Bowden, Beulah Beatrice; N. C.; Mexico, 1908–12.
Bowdler, George Albert, Sr.; Chile; Argentina, 1919–55.
Bowdler, Ruth (Nicholson) (Mrs. G. A., Sr.); Iowa; Argentina, 1919–55.
Bowdler, George Albert, Jr.; Argentina; Guatemala, 1951–54.
Bowdler, Caroline (Rhyne) (Mrs. G. A., Jr.); S. C.; Guatemala, 1951–54.
Bowen, Thomas J.; Ga.; Nigeria, 1849–59; Brazil, 1859–61.
Bowen, Lurenna Henrietta (Davis) (Mrs. T. J.); Ga.; Nigeria, 1853–59; Brazil, 1859–61.

Bowlin, Ralph Treece; Ala.; Southern Rhodesia, 1950- .
Bowlin, Betty J. (Thedford) (Mrs. R. T.); Tex.; Southern Rhodesia, 1950- .
Bradley, Blanche; S. C.; China, 1918-51.
Bradshaw, Melvin Joel; Va.; Japan, 1950- .
Bradshaw, Edith (Claytor) (Mrs. M. J.); W. Va.; Japan, 1950- .
Branch, Chester Wilder; Fla.; Mexico, 1922-37.
Branch, Rebecca (Rogers) (Mrs. C. W.); S. C.; Mexico, 1922-37.
Brantley, Maurice Eugene; Fla.; Nigeria, 1940-53.
Brantley, Louise (Doyle) (Mrs. M. E.); Okla.; Nigeria, 1940-53.
Branum, Irene Thelma; Ark.; China, 1946-51; Korea, 1951- .
Brasington, James Bryan; S. C.; Peru, 1955- .
Brasington, Victoria (Young) (Mrs. J. B.); Fla.; Peru, 1955- .
Bratcher, Lewis Malen; Ky.; Brazil, 1918-53.
Bratcher, Artie (Porter) (Mrs. L. M.); Ky.; Brazil, 1918- .
Bratcher, Robert Galveston; Brazil; Brazil, 1949- .
Bratcher, Lois J. (Heaton) (Mrs. R. G.); Tenn.; Brazil, 1949- .
Braun, Milton L.; N. Y.; China, 1918-29.
Braun, Mary (Young) (Mrs. M. L.); Pa.; China, 1918-29.
Brewer, Nadyne; Tex.; Brazil, 1952- .
Bridges, Glenn McLeen; Okla.; Brazil, 1948- .
Bridges, Mary Ruth (Pennington) (Mrs. G. M.); Tex.; Brazil, 1948- .
Brittain, Milner Callaway; Ga.; China, 1935-43.
Brittain, Mary (Brown) (Mrs. M. C.); Ark.; China, 1935-43.
Britton, Thomas C.; N. C.; China, 1888-1934.
Britton, Nannie (Sessoms) (Mrs. T. C.); N. C.; China, 1888-1934.
Brock, Lonnie Ross, Jr.; N. C.; Brazil, 1953- .
Brock, Barbara (Howard) (Mrs. L. R., Jr.); Tenn.; Brazil, 1953- .
Brooks, Lucy Ernelle; N. C.; Nigeria, 1947- .
Brooner, Mary Aileen; Kans.; Southern Rhodesia, 1952- .
Brothers, Lionel Raymon; Ky.; Nigeria, 1936- .
Brothers, Leola (Smith) (Mrs. L. R.); Ga.; Nigeria, 1936-51.
Brothers, Mary C. (Adams) (Mrs. L. R.); Fla.; Nigeria, 1948- .
Brower, Cornelia; N. J.; Chile, 1921- .
Brown, Cordelia Edna; Vt.; China, 1910-16.
Brown, Homer Arbon, Jr.; Ill.; Nigeria, 1948- .
Brown, Mildred (Steckler) (Mrs. H. A.); Ill.; Nigeria, 1948- .
Brown, Lorne Eckhardt, M.D.; Canada; Persian Gulf, 1949-51; Jordan, 1951- .
Brown, Martha V. (Allen) (Mrs. L. E.); Tenn.; Persian Gulf, 1949-51; Jordan, 1951- .
Brunson, John Alexander; S. C.; Japan, 1888-92.
Brunson, Sophia (Boatwright) (Mrs. J. A.); S. C.; Japan, 1888-92.
Bryan, Charles Willis; Tex.; Costa Rica, 1950- .

Bryan, Martha Anna (Christian) (Mrs. C. W.); Ga.; Costa Rica, 1950- .
Bryan, David; Ala.; China, 1914-26.
Bryan, Mildred (Thorne) (Mrs. David); Ala.; China, 1914-26.
Bryan, Eugene Kay; Tex.; China, 1943-52.
Bryan, Ruth (Howell) (Mrs. E. K.); Tex.; China, 1943-52.
Bryan, F. Catharine; China; China, 1908-51.
Bryan, John Nelson, M.D.; Tenn.; China, 1946-52.
Bryan, Leta Rue (Riddle) (Mrs. J. N.); Tex.; China, 1946-52.
Bryan, Nelson Augustus, M.D.; Tenn.; China, 1920-51; Korea, 1951- .
Bryan, Frances (Allison) (Mrs. N. A.); Tenn.; China, 1920-51; Korea, 1951- .
Bryan, Robert Thomas; N. C.; China, 1885-1937.
Bryan, Lula (Freeland) (Mrs. R. T.); N. C.; China, 1885-1908.
Bryan, Mamie (Sallee) (Mrs. R. T.); Ky.; China, 1909-37.
Bryant, William Howard; Ala.; Chile, 1939- .
Bryant, Sarah (Allred) (Mrs. W. H.); Ala.; Chile, 1939- .
Buckner, Hal F.; Tex.; China, 1909-19.
Buckner, Bertha (Aston) (Mrs. H. F.); Tex.; China, 1909-19.
Buddin, Horace Everett; S. C.; Brazil, 1948- .
Buddin, Virginia (Morgan) (Mrs. H. E.); Brazil; Brazil, 1948- .
Bumpus, Claud Ramey; Ark.; Brazil, 1953- .
Bumpus, Frances M. (Beindorff) (Mrs. C. R.); Ark.; Brazil, 1953- .
Burch, Vella Jane; N. C.; Switzerland, 1952- .
Burks, Edgar Harold, Jr.; Mo.; Nigeria, 1955- .
Burks, Linnie J. (Joslin) (Mrs. E. H., Jr.); Mo.; Nigeria, 1955- .
Burton, George Washington, M.D.; Tenn.; China, 1851-61.
Burton, Anna M. (Bennett) (Mrs. G. W.); Ga.; China, 1853-61.
Buster, Waller Ray; Tex.; Brazil, 1923- .
Byrd, Juanita Carolyn; Miss.; China, 1929-46.

Cabaniss, Asa Bruce; Va.; China, 1850-59.
Cabaniss, Elvira (Adkisson) (Mrs. A. B.); Va.; China, 1850-59.
Cabiniss, Lucy Carter; Va.; Mexico, 1888-95.
Cader, Burley Edward; La.; Brazil, 1951- .
Cader, Ulene (DeWeese) (Mrs. B. E.); N. C.; Brazil, 1951- .
Cadwallader, Chester Samuel, Jr.; Tex.; Guatemala, 1952- .
Cadwallader, Dorothy Irene (Bell) (Mrs. C. S., Jr.); Tex.; Guatemala, 1952- .
Cain, Dora Lee; Ga.; China, 1904-06.
Calcote, Ralph Victor; Miss.; Japan, 1951- .
Calcote, Gena Myrle (Wall) (Mrs. R. V.); La.; Japan, 1951- .
Caldwell, Pearl; Miss.; China, 1910-47.
Callaway, Merrel Price; Ga.; Lebanon, 1942-45; Palestine, 1945-46; Persian Gulf, 1947-51; Jordan, 1951-52.
Callaway, Elizabeth (Fountain) (Mrs. M. P.);

N. J.; Lebanon, 1942–45; Palestine, 1945–46; Persian Gulf, 1947–51; Jordan, 1951–52.
Callaway, Tucker Noyes; Ga.; Hawaii, 1945–47; Japan, 1947– .
Callaway, Elizabeth (Clark) (Mrs. T. N.); Tenn.; Hawaii, 1945–47; Japan, 1947– .
Campbell, Charles Wallace; Tex.; Argentina, 1953– .
Campbell, Bernadene (Kimmey) (Mrs. C. W.); Tex.; Argentina, 1953– .
Campbell, Vera Leona; Ga.; Japan, 1950– .
Campbell, Viola Dee; N. C.; Mexico, 1942– .
Cannada, William Henry; S. C.; Brazil, 1902–12.
Cannada, Norma Clara (Jenkins) (Mrs. W. H.); Ky.; Brazil, 1902–12.
Canning, Harold Braselton, M.D.; Ga.; Nigeria, 1946–53.
Canning, Cornelia Lena (Barker) (Mrs. H. B.); S. C.; Nigeria, 1947–53.
Canzoneri, Mabel Antonina; Tex.; Nigeria, 1947– .
Capshaw, Martha Jean; Ky.; Colombia, 1954– .
Carlisle, Jean Evelyn; Tenn.; Mexico, 1955– .
Carlisle, Robert Lee, Jr.; Miss.; Uruguay, 1940– .
Carlisle, Ruth (Newport) (Mrs. R. L., Jr.); Okla.; Uruguay, 1940– .
Carney, Mary Ruth; Tex.; Brazil, 1951–55.
Carr, Jo; Ala.; China, 1915–19.
Carroll, Daniel Marion, Jr.; W. Va.; Argentina, 1953– .
Carroll, Betty Alice (Cowan) (Mrs. D. M., Jr.); N. C.; Argentina, 1953– .
Carroll, Kate; Tex.; Brazil, 1910–12.
Carson, William H.; Ala.; Nigeria, 1918–54.
Carson, Grace (Schimmel) (Mrs. W. H.); Ala.; Nigeria, 1918– .
Carter, William Percy, Jr.; S. C.; Chile, 1954– .
Carter, Kate (Callaway) (Mrs. W. P., Jr.); Tenn.; Chile, 1954– .
Carver, George Alexander; Ky.; China, 1933–46.
Carver, Emma Saxon (Rowe) (Mrs. G. A.); Ky.; China, 1933–46.
Cason, J. H.; Tenn.; Nigeria, 1856–57.
Cason, Mrs. J. H.; ( ); Nigeria, 1856–57.
Cate, Carolyn Louise; Tenn.; Lebanon, 1954–55; Egypt, 1955– .
Cather, Douglas Cookman; Va.; Gold Coast, 1953– .
Cather, Sarah Ellen (Bragg) (Mrs. D. C.); Tenn.; Gold Coast, 1953– .
Caudle, Cora; N. C.; Nigeria, 1918–24.
Cauthen, Baker James; Tex.; China, 1939–45.
Cauthen, Eloise (Glass) (Mrs. B. J.); China; China, 1939–45.
Caver, Mary Ellen; Ala.; Nigeria, 1925–29.
Cawthon, King Woolsey; Ga.; Argentina, 1903–07.
Cawthon, Lillian (McCall) (Mrs. K. W.); Ga.; Argentina, 1903–07.
Chambers, Robert Edward; Va.; China, 1894–1932.
Chambers, Mattie (Hall) (Mrs. R. E.); Va.; China, 1895–1905.
Chambers, Julia (Trainham) (Mrs. R. E.); Va.; China, 1901–17.
Chambers, Christine (Coffee) (Mrs. R. E.); Tex.; China, 1913–47.
Chamlee, Roy Zebulon, Jr.; Ga.; Peru, 1955– .
Chamlee, Martha Jo (Brooks) (Mrs. R. Z., Jr.); Ill.; Peru, 1955– .
Chaney, Edith Arlene; Ark.; Nigeria, 1945– .
Chapman, J. Griffin; Ky.; Japan, 1921–26.
Chapman, Vecie (King) (Mrs. J. G.); Tex.; Japan, 1921–26.
Chappell, Catherine Flo; Ga.; Brazil, 1952– .
Chappell, LeRoy Norcross; N. C.; China, 1888–95.
Chappell, Mary Ella (Moore) (Mrs. L. N.); N. C.; China, 1888–95.
Chastain, James Garvin; Miss.; Mexico, 1888–1921.
Chastain, Lillian (Wright) (Mrs. J. G.); Va.; Mexico, 1888–1921.
Cheavens, John S.; Mo.; Mexico, 1898–1921.
Cheavens, Katherine (Herndon) (Mrs. J. S.); Mo.; Mexico, 1898–1929.
Cheek, Major Oswald; Ky.; China, 1923–31.
Cheek, Lilla Katherine (Thomas) (Mrs. M. O.); Tex.; China, 1923–31.
Cheesman, John H.; ( ); Liberia, 1849–71.
Cheyne, John Richard; Ill.; Southern Rhodesia, 1954– .
Cheyne, Marie (Golson) (Mrs. J. R.); Ala.; Southern Rhodesia, 1954– .
Christie, Alonzo Bee; Ky.; Brazil, 1907–46.
Christie, Anna (Cloud) (Mrs. A. B.); Mo.; Brazil, 1907–46.
Clark, Charles Barton; La.; Venezuela, 1951– .
Clark, Shirley (Risk) (Mrs. C. B.); Mo.; Venezuela, 1951– .
Clark, Clarence Ford, Jr., M.D.; Tenn.; Japan, 1953– .
Clark, Sadie Pauline (Watts) (Mrs. C. F., Jr.); N. C.; Japan, 1953– .
Clark, Clyde Eugene; Iowa; Venezuela, 1952– .
Clark, Betty Lou (Young) (Mrs. C. E.); Mo.; Venezuela, 1952– .
Clark, George Harold; Ill.; Malaya, 1954– .
Clark, Anna (Evanos) (Mrs. G. H.); Ill.; Malaya, 1954– .
Clark, Van Brun; Tex.; Mexico, 1909–14.
Clarke, Coleman Daniel; Japan; Hawaii, 1945–48; Japan, 1948– .
Clarke, Jennie (Sheffield) (Mrs. C. D.); Ga.; Hawaii, 1945–48; Japan, 1948– .
Clarke, James Avery; Miss.; Nigeria, 1949–53.
Clarke, Joyee (Van Osdol) (Mrs. J. A.); Miss.; Nigeria, 1949–53.
Clarke, William H.; Ga.; Nigeria, 1854–59.
Clarke, W. Harvey; Ga.; Japan, 1898–1936.
Clarke, Lucille (Daniel) (Mrs. W. H.); Ga.; Japan, 1899–1933.
Clawson, William Marion; La.; Mexico, 1953– .
Clawson, Kathryn J. (Odum) (Mrs. W. M.); La.; Mexico, 1953– .
Claxon, W. Neville; Ky.; Gold Coast, 1948–49; Nigeria, 1949– .
Claxon, Emma (Osborne) (Mrs. W. N.); Ky.; Gold Coast, 1948–49; Nigeria, 1949– .

Clement, Lora Amelia; S. C.; China, 1915-50; Malaya, 1950- .
Clifton, R. Aldine; Tex.; Brazil, 1920-25.
Clifton, Leslie Truett (Davis) (Mrs. R. A.); Tex.; Brazil, 1920-25.
Cline, Pervy Augustus, Jr.; N. C.; Thailand, 1955- .
Cline, Georgia Frances (Smith) (Mrs. P. A., Jr.) Ala.; Thailand, 1955- .
Clinkscales, Thomas Newton; Ala.; Brazil, 1941- .
Clinkscales, Rosalie E. (Duggan) (Mrs. T. N.); La.; Brazil, 1941- .
Clinton, William Lee; Ga.; Brazil, 1951- .
Clinton, Marion F. (Hulme) (Mrs. W. L.); Ga.; Brazil, 1951- .
Clopton, Samuel Cornelius; Va.; China, 1845-47.
Clopton, Keziah (Turpin) (Mrs. S. C.); Va.; China, 1846-48.
Clor, Elsie B.; Russia; Palestine, 1927-42.
Cobb, Daniel Robert; S. C.; Thailand, 1954- .
Cobb, Fannie (Morris) (Mrs. D. R.); Ky.; Thailand, 1954- .
Cobb, Jane Maude; Ga.; Hungary, 1935-38.
Cobb, Mary Virginia; Ga.; Lebanon, 1952- .
Cockburn, Samuel Herbert; Canada; Argentina, 1950- .
Cockburn, Violet Stewart (Hay) (Mrs. S. H.); Canada; Argentina, 1950- .
Cockrum, Buford Edgar, Jr.; Tenn.; Nigeria, 1947- .
Cockrum, Virginia Mae (Irwin) (Mrs. B. E., Jr.); Tenn.; Nigeria, 1947- .
Coggins, Ross Calvin; Tex.; Indonesia, 1955- .
Coggins, Doryce Annette (Lengefeld) (Mrs. R. C.); Tex.; Indonesia, 1955- .
Cole, Edward Lamar, M.D.; Ark.; Mexico, 1946- .
Cole, Oneita (Henley) (Mrs. E. L.); Tex.; Mexico, 1946- .
Cole, George McDaniel; Tex.; Peru, 1952-53.
Cole, Norma Ray (Ives) (Mrs. G. McD.); Tex.; Peru, 1952-53.
Coleman, Inabelle Graves; N. C.; China, 1943-52; Formosa, 1952- .
Colley, W. W.; Va.; Nigeria, 1874-79.
Collins, Margaret Saye; Ga.; China, 1946-52; Philippines, 1952- .
Combs, Edgar Jackson, Jr.; Mo.; Colombia, 1943-45.
Combs, Dorothy (Carpenter) (Mrs. E. J., Jr.); Tex.; Colombia, 1943-45.
Compere, James Seth; Ark.; Nigeria, 1905-10.
Compere, Pen (Lile) (Mrs. J. S.); Ark.; Nigeria, 1905-10.
Compton, Charles Earl, Jr.; Tex.; Brazil, 1950- .
Compton, Betsy (Dunning) (Mrs. C. E., Jr.); N. C.; Brazil, 1950- .
Congdon, Wilfred H.; Colo.; Nigeria, 1937- .
Congdon, Esther Etta (Bassett) (Mrs. W. H.); Colo.; Nigeria, 1938- .
Connely, Frank Hutchins; Mo.; China, 1916-52; Japan, 1952- .
Connely, Mary (Sears) (Mrs. F. H.); China; China, 1916-52; Japan, 1952- .

Conner, Lola Marie; Fla.; China, 1944-50; Formosa, 1950- .
Conrad, Florence; Tex.; Japan, 1921-29.
Cook, Strother Moses; Ky.; Nigeria, 1884-86.
Cooke, Sallie Burnam; ( ); Mexico, 1891-92.
Cooper, William Lowrey; Miss.; Argentina, 1939- .
Cooper, Tommie Katherine (Tomlinson) (Mrs. W. L.); Miss.; Argentina, 1939- .
Copeland, Edwin Luther; W. Va.; Japan, 1948- .
Copeland, Louise (Tadlock) (Mrs. E. L.); N. Mex.; Japan, 1948- .
Corder, Leota Blanche; Tex.; China, 1925-46.
Cote, William N.; Canada; Italy, 1870-73.
Couch, Lawanda Faye; La.; Nigeria, 1954- .
Councilman, Bessie Estelle; N. C.; Argentina, 1943-49.
Coupland, Laura Helen; Tex.; China, 1920-29.
Cowan, Anna Lucille; Mo.; Israel, 1948-51; Lebanon, 1954-55; Jordan, 1955- .
Cowherd, Charles Philip; Va.; China, 1946-51; Indonesia, 1951- .
Cowherd, Marian Peeler (Gray) (Mrs. C. P.); S. C.; China, 1940-51; Philippines, 1951-52; Indonesia, 1952- .
Cowley, William Austin; Ky.; Nigeria, 1955- .
Cowley, Audrey Carr (Evans) (Mrs. W. A.); Fla.; Nigeria, 1955- .
Cowsert, George Bagby; Brazil; Brazil, 1952- .
Cowsert, Hilda Kathryn (Bean) (Mrs. G. B.); N. C.; Brazil, 1952- .
Cowsert, Jack Jimmerson; Miss.; Brazil, 1920- .
Cowsert, Grace (Bagby) (Mrs. J. J.); Tex.; Brazil, 1920- .
Cox, Addie Estelle; Ala.; China, 1918-51; Formosa, 1951-55.
Cox, Laura; N. C.; Mexico, 1910-27.
Cox, Ona Belle; Mo.; Brazil, 1948- .
Cozzens, Katherine; Tex.; Brazil, 1941- .
Crabtree, Asa Routh; Va.; Brazil, 1921- .
Crabtree, Mabel (Henderson) (Mrs. A. R.); Va.; Brazil, 1921- .
Crabtree, Mildred Irene; Tex.; Nigeria, 1946- .
Craighead, Albert Brown; Romania; Italy, 1951- .
Craighead, Rhoda Mae (Miller) (Mrs. A. B.); Ga.; Italy, 1951- .
Craighead, Walter Eugene; Ala.; Romania, 1938-48; Paraguay, 1948- .
Craighead, Hazel (Thomson) (Mrs. W. E.); Mich.; Romania, 1938-48; Paraguay, 1948- .
Crane, James Dreher; Tex.; Mexico, 1945- .
Crane, Edith Eleanor (Carden) (Mrs. J. D.); Iowa; Mexico, 1945- .
Crawford, Frances Nadine; Tex.; Colombia, 1954- .
Crawford, Mary Katherine; Ga.; China, 1922-51; Hawaii, 1951- .
Crawford, Tarleton Perry; Ky.; China, 1851-92.
Crawford, Martha (Foster) (Mrs. T. P.); Ala.; China, 1851-92.
Crawley, James Winston; Tenn.; Philippines, 1947-54.
Crawley, Margaret (Lawrence) (Mrs. J. W.); Tex.; Philippines, 1947-54.

Foreign Missionaries, 1845–1955

Crocker, Everett Gordon; Tenn.; Ecuador, 1949– .
Crocker, Bettye Ruth (Williams) (Mrs. E. G.); Tenn.; Ecuador, 1949– .
Crocker, William Elwyn; N. C.; China, 1899–1919.
Crocker, Bessie (Thackston) (Mrs. W. E.); S. C.; China, 1899–1900.
Crocker, Jessie (Swann) (Mrs. W. E.); Scotland; China, 1903–28.
Crosland, Daniel Frank; S. C.; Brazil, 1904–24.
Crosland, Maude (Carter) (Mrs. D. F.); S. C.; Brazil, 1904–24.
Cross, Eugene Mosley; Miss.; Hawaii, 1947–54; Philippines, 1954– .
Cross, Ardis Ethel (Ward) (Mrs. E. M.); Tex.; Hawaii, 1947–54; Philippines, 1954– .
Crotwell, Mary Elaine; Ala.; Philippines, 1948– .
Crouch, Edward Hansford; Okla.; Brazil, 1923–47.
Crouch, Ura Georgia (Hallmark) (Mrs. E. H.); Tex.; Brazil, 1923–47.
Crouse, Jessie; Tex.; Argentina, 1922–25.
Crowder, Calvin Ray; Ala.; Nigeria, 1954– .
Crowder, Imogene (Thomason) (Mrs. C. R.); Ala.; Nigeria, 1954– .
Crutcher, George H.; Tenn.; Mexico, 1899–1900.
Crutcher, Lamira Eugenia (Kimbrough) (Mrs. G. H.); Tenn.; Mexico, 1899–1900.
Cullen, Paul Shelby, M.D.; Tex.; Nigeria, 1950– .
Cullen, Ida (Wright) (Mrs. P. S.); Tex.; Nigeria, 1950– .
Culpepper, Charles Lee, Sr.; Tex.; China, 1923–52; Formosa, 1952– .
Culpepper, Ola (Lane) (Mrs. C. L., Sr.); Tex.; China, 1923–52; Formosa, 1952– .
Culpepper, Charles Lee, Jr.; Tex.; China, 1944–52; Formosa, 1952– .
Culpepper, Donal (Jones) (Mrs. C. L., Jr.); Wis.; China, 1944–52; Formosa, 1952– .
Culpepper, Hugo Hurlston; Ark.; China, 1940–41; Philippines, 1941–47; Chile, 1947–53; Argentina, 1953– .
Culpepper, Ruth (Cochrane) (Mrs. H. H.); Ark.; China, 1940–41; Philippines, 1941–47; Chile, 1947–53; Argentina, 1953– .
Culpepper, Robert Harrell; Ga.; Japan, 1950– .
Culpepper, Kathleen (Sanderson) (Mrs. R. H.); Va.; Japan, 1950– .
Cunningham, Collis; Ga.; Japan, 1922–26.
Cunningham, Hester (Faulkner) (Mrs. Collis); Ala.; Japan, 1922–26.

Dailey, Arthur Renich; Ky.; Colombia, 1942–53.
Dailey, Clotilde Dorothy (Elam) (Mrs. A. R.); Ohio; Colombia, 1942–53.
Daniel, Charles D.; Ala.; Brazil, 1885–92.
Daniel, Lena (Kirk) (Mrs. C. D.); Tex.; Brazil, 1885–92.
Daniel, J. Carey; Tex.; China, 1910–14.
Daniel, Jewell (Leggett) (Mrs. J. C.); Tex.; China, 1909–27.
Daniel, Ruby Inez; N. C.; Hungary, 1935–45; Nigeria, 1945–46.
DaVault, Elijah E.; Tenn.; China, 1884–87.
DaVault, Laura A. (Murrah) (Mrs. E. E.); Ky.; China, 1884–92.
David, Nannie Bland; Nigeria; Nigeria, 1919–29.
David, Vernon Leroy; Miss.; Spain, 1924–35; Argentina, 1935–51.
David, Ava Burton (Manning) (Mrs. V. L.); Mexico; Spain, 1924–35; Argentina, 1935–48.
David, William Joshua; Miss.; Nigeria, 1874–94.
David, Nannie (Bland) (Mrs. W. J.); Va.; Nigeria, 1879–85.
David, Justa (Greer) (Mrs. W. J.); Miss.; Nigeria, 1885–94.
Davidson, Minor; Okla.; Malaya, 1955– .
Davidson, Mary Elizabeth (Boydstun) (Mrs. Minor); Okla.; Malaya, 1955– .
Davidson, William Earl; Mo.; Chile, 1917–26.
Davidson, Mary (Skidmore) (Mrs. W. E.); Ohio; Chile, 1917–26.
Davis, Alberta Lee; Fla.; Argentina, 1922–28.
Davis, Burton de Wolfe; Pa.; Brazil, 1945– .
Davis, Sarah Blanche (Nesbitt) (Mrs. B. de W.); S. C.; Brazil, 1945– .
Davis, J. Edgar; Mo.; Mexico, 1904–43.
Davis, Mary E. (Gamble) (Mrs. J. E.); Va.; Mexico, 1904–43.
Davis, Horace Victor; Ca.; Brazil, 1953– .
Davis, Ruby Dare (Fletcher) (Mrs. H. V.); N. C.; Brazil, 1953– .
Davis, Margie Estelle; La.; Nigeria, 1951–54.
Davis, Martha Mae; Tex.; Mexico, 1953–54.
Davis, Robert Carr, Jr.; Tex.; Hawaii, 1951– .
Davis, Ida Pearl (Anderson) (Mrs. R. C., Jr.); Tex.; Hawaii, 1951– .
Davis, William Ralph; Miss.; Nigeria, 1950– .
Davis, Cora Joyce (Merritt) (Mrs. W. R.); Miss.; Nigeria, 1950– .
Dawes, Joseph Vedale; Wis.; China, 1910–36.
Dawes, Laura (Moore) (Mrs. J. V.); Mo.; China, 1910–32.
Day, John; Va.; Liberia, 1846–59.
Deal, Zach Jeremiah, Jr.; Va.; Colombia, 1947– .
Deal, Barbara (Williams) (Mrs. Z. J., Jr.); N. C.; Colombia, 1947– .
Demarest, Mary Celia; N. Y.; China, 1919–51; Formosa, 1951– .
Dennard, J. S.; Ga.; Nigeria, 1853–54.
Dennard, Fannie (Smith) (Mrs. J. S.); Ga.; Nigeria, 1853–54.
Deter, Arthur Beriah; Mo.; Brazil, 1901–40.
Deter, May (Scrymgeour) (Mrs. A. B.); Canada; Brazil, 1901–40.
Dickson, Charles William; Tex.; Brazil, 1947– .
Dickson, Juanita Jo (Wilcox) (Mrs. C. W.); Tex.; Brazil, 1947– .
Dodd, Monroe Elmon; Tenn.; Mexico, 1904–05.
Dodd, Emma (Savage) (Mrs. M. E.); Tenn.; Mexico, 1904–05.
Dodson, Flora; Ky.; China, 1917–52; Hong Kong, 1952– .
Donath, A. C.; Tex.; Nigeria, 1935–43.
Donath, Christena (Breazeale) (Mrs. A. C.); Tex.; Nigeria, 1935–43.
Donnelly, Dorothy Evelyn; S. C.; Brazil, 1948–51.

Dorrough, Robert L., M.D.; Ala.; Philippines, 1955- .
Dorrough, Mary Blanche (Gilliland), M.D. (Mrs. R. L.); Ala.; Philippines, 1955- .
Dotson, Clyde J.; Ala.; Southern Rhodesia, 1950- .
Dotson, Hattie (Thigpen) (Mrs. C. J.); Ala.; Southern Rhodesia, 1950-55.
Dowell, Theodore Hulet; Okla.; Korea, 1953- .
Dowell, Oma Lee (Russell) (Mrs. T. H.); Okla.; Korea, 1953- .
Downing, James L.; Mo.; Brazil, 1891-93, 1899-1902, 1914-24.
Downing, Addie (Martin) (Mrs. J. L.); ( ); Brazil, 1891-93, 1899-1913.
Downing, Ruth (Mitchell) (Mrs. J. L.); Mo.; Brazil, 1916-24.
Doyle, Lonnie Adolphus, Jr.; Miss.; Brazil, 1949- .
Doyle, Janelle (Hartwick) (Mrs. L. A., Jr.); Tex.; Brazil, 1949- .
Dozier, Charles Kelsey; Ga.; Japan, 1906-33.
Dozier, Maude Adelia (Burke) (Mrs. C. K.); N. C.; Japan, 1906-44; Hawaii, 1944-51.
Dozier, Edwin Burke; Japan; Japan, 1933-41, 1946- ; Hawaii, 1941-46.
Dozier, Mary Ellen (Wiley) (Mrs. E. B.); N. C.; Japan, 1933-41, 1946- ; Hawaii, 1941-46.
Dozier, Helen Adelia; Japan; Japan, 1935-38.
Drayton, Boston J.; S. C.; Liberia, 1848-66.
Dunn, Mary Lou; Tex.; Spanish Publishing House, 1938-42.
Duffer, Hiram F., Jr.; Tex.; Spanish Publishing House, 1947-52; Mexico, 1952- .
Duffer, Charlotte Catherine (Martinez) (Mrs. H. F., Jr.); Calif.; Spanish Publishing House, 1947-52; Mexico, 1952- .
Duggan, Janie (Pritchard) (Mrs. J. R.); N. C.; Mexico, 1889-94.
Duggar, Ambrose Camp; Ala.; Brazil, 1923-29.
Duggar, Elsie Louise (Sampey) (Mrs. A. C.); Ky.; Brazil, 1923-29.
Dunaway, Archie Grover, Jr.; Miss.; Nigeria, 1947- .
Dunaway, Margaret (Lanier) (Mrs. A. G., Jr.); Tenn.; Nigeria, 1947- .
Dunstan, Albert Lafayette; Ga.; Brazil, 1900-37.
Dunstan, Sallie (Silvey) (Mrs. A. L.); Ga.; Brazil, 1900-47.
Durham, Jonathan Bryant; Ga.; Nigeria, 1950- .
Durham, Ina (Martin) (Mrs. J. B.); Ga.; Nigeria, 1950- .
Dutton, Mattie; Mo.; China, 1899-1906.
Duval, Louis M.; Canada; Nigeria, 1901-30.
Duval, Alice M. (Spragg) (Mrs. L. M.); Canada; Nigeria, 1902-35.
Dwyer, Anne Lucille; Va.; Lebanon, 1954-55; Egypt, 1955- .
Dyal, William M., Jr.; Tex.; Guatemala, 1953- .
Dyal, Edith (Colvin) (Mrs. W. M., Jr.); Ark.; Guatemala, 1953- .
Dyer, Robert Allen; La.; Japan, 1940-48.
Dyer, Mary Lawrence (Mills) (Mrs. R. A.); N. C.; Japan, 1940-48.
Dyson, Albert Hampy; Tex.; Nigeria, 1955- .

Dyson, Ethel Ruth (Widick) (Mrs. A. H.); Tenn.; Nigeria, 1955- .

Eager, John Howard; Miss.; Italy, 1879-98.
Eager, Olive M. (Board) (Mrs. J. H.); Va.; Italy, 1879-98.
Eaglesfield, Carrol Frederick; Kans.; Nigeria, 1944- .
Eaglesfield, Ida Pauline (Gadberry) (Mrs. C. F.); Tex.; Nigeria, 1944- .
Eavenson, Ira Dennis; Miss.; China, 1920-29.
Eavenson, Nancy (Miller) (Mrs. I. D.); Miss.; China, 1920-29.
Echols, Lilla Elizabeth; Ga.; China, 1923-30.
Eddinger, Sarah Rebecca; N. C.; Chile, 1945-51.
Eddleman, Henry Leo; Miss.; Palestine, 1935-42.
Eddleman, Sarah (Fox) (Mrs. H. L.); Ark.; Palestine, 1937-42.
Edens, Olive Theodosia; Tenn.; Nigeria, 1916-30.
Edwards, Francis Marion; Miss.; Brazil, 1907-24.
Edwards, Helen Frances (Eustis) (Mrs. F. M.); N. Y.; Brazil, 1915-30.
Edwards, Frank Khal; Ala.; Nigeria, 1950- .
Edwards, Roberta J. (Cox), M.D. (Mrs. F. K.); Tex.; Nigeria, 1945- .
Eidson, Ada Christine; Ga.; Argentina, 1952- .
Elam, Elma; Mo.; Nigeria, 1923-41.
Elder, Robert F.; New Zealand; Argentina, 1920-40.
Elder, Effie (Hay) (Mrs. R. F.); New Zealand; Argentina, 1920-40.
Eldridge, Eva May; Tenn.; Nigeria, 1955- .
Ellis, Martha Thomas; Ala.; Argentina, 1937-43.
Elliott, Darline; Tex.; Colombia, 1943- .
Emanuel, Beverly Paul; Okla.; Japan, 1950- .
Emanuel, Rebekah Sue (Jackson) (Mrs. B. P.); Okla.; Japan, 1950- .
Enete, William Walters; La.; Brazil, 1924- .
Enete, Crystal (Armstrong) (Mrs. W. W.); Mo.; Brazil, 1924- .
Engleman, Loren Otho Paul; Mich.; Mexico, 1925-37.
Engleman, Maggie Amanda (Whaley) (Mrs. L. O. P.); Tenn.; Mexico, 1925-37.
Entzminger, William Edwin; S. C.; Brazil, 1891-1930.
Entzminger, Maggie (Griffith) (Mrs. W. E.); N. C.; Brazil, 1891-1921.
Entzminger, Amelia Charlotte (Joyce) (Mrs. W. E.); England; Brazil, 1923-31.
Epperson, Barbara; Mo.; Nigeria, 1953- .
Ernest, Mary Lee; Ala.; Hawaii, 1947- .
Etter, Roscoe; Tenn.; China, 1921-25.
Etter, Frances (Duggin) (Mrs. Roscoe); Tenn.; China, 1921-25.
Eubank, Peyton A.; Ky.; Nigeria, 1881-92.
Eubank, Laura Boardman (Houchens) (Mrs. P. A.); Mo.; Nigeria, 1881-92.
Eudaly, Nathan Hoyt; Tex.; Mexico, 1948-52; Spanish Publishing House, 1952- .
Eudaly, Marie (Saddler) (Mrs. N. H.); Mo.; Mexico, 1948-52; Spanish Publishing House, 1952- .
Evans, Philip S., M.D.; Conn.; China, 1901-38.

Evans, Mary (Levering) (Mrs. P. S.); Md.; China, 1901–38.
Everett, Mina; Mo.; Brazil, 1885–87.
Ewen, Betty Jane; Tex.; Nigeria, 1951– .

Faile, George Marion, Jr., M.D.; S. C.; Nigeria, 1953– .
Faile, Alice K. (Johnston) (Mrs. G. M., Jr.); S. C.; Nigeria, 1953– .
Fairchild, James H.; Miss.; Brazil, 1948–49.
Fairchild, Frances (Felder) (Mrs. J. H.); Miss.; Brazil, 1948–49.
Falwell, Reuben H.; Ky.; China, 1947–48.
Falwell, Rowena (Gunter) (Mrs. R. H.); Miss.; China, 1947–48.
Farmer, Gladys Elizabeth; Ga.; Hawaii, 1948–51.
Fenderson, Eunice Marian; Minn.; Palestine, 1936– .
Fergeson, William Joel; Tex.; Nigeria, 1948– .
Fergeson, Elizabeth (Hale) (Mrs. W. J.); Tex.; Nigeria, 1948– .
Ferrell, William Hasel; Miss.; Argentina, 1952– .
Ferrell, Opal Miriam (Young) (Mrs. W. H.); Miss.; Argentina, 1952– .
Fielden, Robert Luther; Tenn.; Brazil, 1950– .
Fielden, Myra Jane (Rankin) (Mrs. R. L.); Tenn.; Brazil, 1950– .
Fielder, Joseph Thomas; Tex.; China, 1920–25.
Fielder, Lula Addie (Taylor) (Mrs. J. T.); Tex.; China, 1920–25.
Fielder, Lennox Gerald; China; Japan, 1954– .
Fielder, Jo Beth (McKneely) (Mrs. L. G.); Tex.; Japan, 1954– .
Fielder, Wilson; Tex.; China, 1912–49.
Fielder, Maudie (Albritton) (Mrs. Wilson); Tex.; China, 1914–49.
Fine, Earl Martin; Kans.; Nigeria, 1952– .
Fine, Roberta Marie (Robson) (Mrs. E. M.); Kans.; Nigeria, 1952– .
Fite, Horace Wilson, Jr.; Ark.; Brazil, 1950– .
Fite, Salle Ann (Taylor) (Mrs. H. W., Jr.); Tex.; Brazil, 1950– .
Fitzgerald, Ara Dell; Tenn.; Brazil, 1919–25.
Flournoy, William M.; Ala.; Mexico, 1882–85.
Flournoy, Victoriana (Muller) (Mrs. W. M.); Mexico; Mexico, 1882–85.
Fontnote, Audrey Viola, M.D.; Neb.; Japan, 1952– .
Ford, Charles Shelby; Fla.; Nigeria, 1952– .
Ford, Dorothy Lucille (Taylor) (Mrs. C. S.); Mo.; Nigeria, 1952– .
Ford, Ruth Lucille; Ill.; China, 1935–53; Indonesia, 1953– .
Foreman, Blonnye Holmes; Ark.; Brazil, 1934–55.
Fort, Milton Giles, Jr., M.D.; Tex.; Southern Rhodesia, 1952– .
Fort, Wana Ann (Gibson), M.D. (Mrs. M. G., Jr.); La.; Southern Rhodesia, 1952– .
Foster, James Alcorn; Miss.; China, 1947–49; Philippines, 1949– .
Foster, Zelma Rosa (Van Osdol) (Mrs. J. A.); Miss.; China, 1947–49; Philippines, 1949– .
Fowler, Frank James; Fla.; Argentina, 1904–33.

Fowler, Daisy (Cate) (Mrs. F. J.); Tenn.; Argentina, 1904–36.
Fowler, Franklin Thomas, M.D.; Argentina; Paraguay, 1947– .
Fowler, Dorcas Ann (Hauk) (Mrs. F. T.); Okla.; Paraguay, 1947– .
Francis, Thomas Houston; Ky.; Israel, 1950–53.
Francis, Mary Helen (Alvey) (Mrs. T. H.); Ky.; Israel, 1950–53.
Frank, Victor LeRoy; Ill.; China, 1947–49; Hong Kong, 1949– .
Frank, Irma (Mangels) (Mrs. V. L.); Ill.; China, 1947–49; Hong Kong, 1949– .
Franks, Martha Linda; S. C.; China, 1925–52; Formosa, 1952– .
Franks, Ruben I.; Tenn.; Chile, 1950– .
Franks, Edna Mae (Pugsley) (Mrs. R. I.); Ark.; Chile, 1950– .
Fredenburg, Mary Evelyn; Mich.; Nigeria, 1947– .
Freeman, Zachary Paul; Tenn.; Argentina, 1921–34, 1941–53; Uruguay, 1934–40.
Freeman, Clara B. (Hagler) (Mrs. Z. P.); Ill.; Argentina, 1921–34, 1941– ; Uruguay, 1934–40.
Freeland, Margaret Estelle; Tex.; Nigeria, 1954– .
Fryer, Ross Bruce, Jr.; Tex.; Indonesia, 1955– .
Fryer, Mary Lynn (Baker) (Mrs. R. B., Jr.); Ark.; Indonesia, 1955– .
Fulghum, Sarah Frances; Ga.; Japan, 1918–28.
Fuller, Aletha Blanche; Tex.; Nigeria, 1951– .
Fuller, Essie Mae; Ala.; Brazil, 1920–41.
Fuller, Ronald W.; Minn.; China, 1948–49; Macao, 1949– .
Fuller, Margaret (Royston) (Mrs. R. W.); Mo.; China, 1948–49; Macao, 1949– .
Funderburke, Sarah; S. C.; China, 1918–36.

Gaillard, Charles W.; S. C.; China, 1853–62.
Gallimore, Arthur R.; N. C.; China, 1918–47.
Gallimore, Gladys (Stephenson) (Mrs. A. R.); Tenn.; China, 1918–47.
Galloway, Edward D.; Ga.; China, 1945–49; Thailand, 1949–52.
Galloway, Sara Betty (Ellis) (Mrs. E. D.); Ky.; China, 1946–49; Thailand, 1949–52.
Galloway, John L.; Scotland; China, 1910–48.
Galloway, Lillian (Todd) (Mrs. J. L.); Calif.; China, 1910–48.
Gardner, Hattie Mae; S. C.; Nigeria, 1935– .
Garner, Alex Franklin; Ark.; Argentina, 1952– .
Garner, Charleta Alma (Beindorf) (Mrs. A. F.); Ark.; Argentina, 1952– .
Garrett, Doris Orene; Tex.; Nigeria, 1954– .
Garrett, James Lee; Ga.; Brazil, 1949– .
Garrett, Mary Joe (McCollum) (Mrs. J. L.); Ga.; Brazil, 1949– .
Garrett, Marvin Lucius; Tenn.; Nigeria, 1951–55; Southern Rhodesia, 1955– .
Garrett, Mary Ellen (Wooten) (Mrs. M. L.); Ohio; Nigeria, 1946–55; Southern Rhodesia, 1955– .
Garrott, William Maxfield; Ark.; Japan, 1934–46, 1947– ; Hawaii, 1946–47.

Garrott, Dorothy Shepard (Carver) (Mrs. W. M.); Ky.; Japan, 1935– .
Gassaway, Marion; S. C.; Mexico, 1893–95.
Gaston, James McFadden; Brazil; China, 1908–35.
Gaston, Annie (Gay) (Mrs. J. McF.); Va.; China, 1908–35.
Gaultney, Jerry Bradford; Ala.; Nigeria, 1953– .
Gaultney, Virginia (Skipper) (Mrs. J. B.); Ala.; Nigeria, 1953– .
Gaventa, William Carter, M.D.; Ga.; Nigeria, 1949– .
Gaventa, Alice (Price) (Mrs. W. C.); Tenn.; Nigeria, 1949– .
Gill, Everett, Sr.; Mo.; Europe, 1904–08, 1910–20, 1921–39.
Gill, Emma Geraldine (Williams) (Mrs. Everett, Sr.); Va.; Europe, 1904–08, 1910–20, 1921–39.
Gillespie, Alfred Leigh; Tenn.; Japan, 1946– .
Gillespie, Viola Rose (Boyd) (Mrs. A. L.); Ind.; Japan, 1946– .
Gillespie, Arthur S.; N. C.; China, 1931–52.
Gillespie, Pauline (Pittard) (Mrs. A. S.); N. C.; China, 1931– .
Gilliam, Elsie; Va.; China, 1910–12.
Gilliland, William McKinley; Ala.; Nigeria, 1942– .
Gilliland, Martha Christine (Jordan), M.D. (Mrs. W. McK.); Ala.; Nigeria, 1942– .
Gillis, Carroll Owens; Mo.; Argentina, 1937–48; Spanish Publishing House, 1948– .
Gillis, Mary Lou (Appleman) (Mrs. C. O.); Mo.; Argentina, 1937–48; Spanish Publishing House, 1948– .
Ginsburg, Solomon L.; Poland; Brazil, 1892–1927.
Ginsburg, Amelia Caroline (Bishop) (Mrs. S. L.); England, Brazil, 1892–1893.
Ginsburg, Emma (Morton) (Mrs. S. L.); Ky.; Brazil, 1889–1934.
Glass, Lois Corneille; China; China, 1935–50; Japan, 1950– .
Glass, Margaret Beatrice; Miss.; Argentina, 1941–49.
Glass, Wiley Blount; Tex.; China, 1903–45.
Glass, Eunice (Taylor) (Mrs. W. B.); Tex.; China, 1902–14.
Glass, Jessie Ligen (Pettigrew) (Mrs. W. B.); Va.; China, 1901–45.
Glaze, Andrew Jackson, Jr.; Miss.; Argentina, 1953– .
Glaze, Sue Eugenia (Johnson) (Mrs. A. J., Jr.); S. C.; Argentina, 1953– .
Golden, Rosa; Ala.; Mexico, 1905–09.
Goldfinch, Sydney Langston; S. C.; Uruguay, 1939–45; Paraguay, 1945– .
Goldfinch, Sarah Frances (McCaw) (Mrs. S. L.); S. C.; Uruguay, 1939–45; Paraguay, 1915– .
Goldie, Robert Frederick, M.D.; N. Y.; Nigeria, 1947– .
Goldie, Edna Mae (Muhlbacker) (Mrs. R. F.); N. Y.; Nigeria, 1947– .
Goldsmith, Peter Hair; S. C.; Mexico, 1891–94.
Goldsmith, Mamie (Furman) (Mrs. P. H.); S. C.; Mexico, 1891–94.
Goodale, Hervey; Mass.; Nigeria, 1849–50.

Goodman, George Edwin; Tenn.; Brazil, 1921–22.
Goodman, Dora (Nelson) (Mrs. G. E.); Ky.; Brazil, 1921–22.
Goodroe, Helen; Ga.; Colombia, 1952–53.
Goolsby, Alyne; Miss.; Brazil, 1899–1908.
Gordon, Richard Edward; Va.; Philippines, 1952– .
Gordon, Audrey Gertrude (Jolly) (Mrs. R. E.); N. C.; Philippines, 1952– .
Gould, Mary Frances; Ohio; China, 1948–50; Thailand, 1950– .
Graham, Finlay Morrison; Scotland; Palestine, 1947–48; Jordan, 1948; Lebanon, 1948– .
Graham, Julia Saccar (Hagood) (Mrs. F. M.); Tex.; Palestine, 1946–48; Jordan, 1948; Lebanon, 1948– .
Graham, Nora Agnes; Tex.; Chile, 1920–47.
Grant, Worth Collins; N. C.; Japan, 1950– .
Grant, Kathryn (Stephens) (Mrs. W. C.); S. C.; Japan, 1950– .
Graves, Alma Norean; La.; Japan, 1936–41, 1947– ; Nigeria, 1941–46; Hawaii, 1946–47.
Graves, Myra E. (Mrs. H. L.); Tex.; Mexico, 1885–86.
Graves, Rosewell Hobart, M.D.; Md.; China, 1855–1912.
Graves, Eva Mills (Gaillard) (Mrs. R. H.); N. Y.; China, 1853–64.
Graves, Jane (Norris) (Mrs. R. H.); Md.; China, 1872–88.
Graves, Janie Lowrey (Sanford) (Mrs. R. H.); Miss.; China, 1887–1936.
Graves, William Walthall; Tex.; Argentina, 1953– .
Graves, Ada (Gillett) (Mrs. W. W.); Ariz.; Argentina, 1953– .
Gray, Ora Elizabeth; S. C.; China, 1936–53; Malaya, 1953– .
Gray, Rufus Franklin; Fla.; China, 1940–42.
Grayson, Alda; N. C.; China, 1921–50; Hawaii, 1950– .
Green, George, M. D.; England; Nigeria, 1906–45.
Green, Lydia B. (Williams) (Mrs. George); Va.; Nigeria, 1907–45.
Green, Jessie L.; Ga.; China, 1936–51; Malaya, 1951– .
Greene, Anna M.; N. C.; China, 1898–1903.
Greene, George Washington; N. C.; China, 1891–1911.
Greene, Valeria (Page) (Mrs. G. W.); N. C.; China, 1891–1934.
Greene, George William; China; China, 1920–32.
Greene, Louise (Bomar) (Mrs. G. W.); Ky.; China, 1920–32.
Greene, Lydia Earle; S. C.; China, 1925–50; Hawaii, 1950–53; Malaya, 1953– .
Greer, Dorothy Jenell; Tenn.; Hawaii, 1942–47; China, 1947–51; Thailand, 1951– .
Gregory, Ernest Jackson; Tex.; Mexico, 1923–34.
Gregory, Ina M. (Johnson) (Mrs. E. J.); Tex.; Mexico, 1923–34.
Griffin, Bennie Theodore; Tex.; Nigeria, 1939– .

Griffin, Alice Maude (Latham) (Mrs. B. T.); Tex.; Nigeria, 1939– .
Grober, Glendon Donald; Miss.; Brazil, 1955– .
Grober, Marjorie Ann (Steele) (Mrs. G. D.); Ky.; Brazil, 1955– .
Groves, Blanche; Tex.; China, 1920–53; Hawaii, 1953–54; Hong Kong, 1954– .
Gruver, Kate Ellen; Canal Zone; Israel, 1938–48; Palestine, 1948–51.
Guest, Lena Ethel; S. C.; Nigeria, 1947– .
Gullatt, Tom Dean; Ga.; Japan, 1950– .
Gullatt, Mary (Studdard) (Mrs. T. D.); Ga.; Japan, 1950– .
Gunn, Alvada; Ga.; China, 1920–26.

Hagood, James Henry; Tex.; Palestine, 1943–46.
Hagood, Martha, M.D.; Ala.; Japan, 1953– .
Hagood, Ruth Virginia; Tex.; Nigeria, 1946–49.
Hairston, Martha Elizabeth; Ark.; Brazil, 1951– .
Halbrooks, Fred Eubern, Jr.; Ala.; Brazil, 1955– .
Halbrooks, Hazel Lillian (Crow) (Mrs. F. E., Jr.); Ala.; Brazil, 1955– .
Halcomb, N. W.; Ky.; China, 1881–86.
Halcomb, Mattie M. (Roberts) (Mrs. N. W.); Ky.; China, 1883–85.
Hale, Elizabeth Neal; N. C.; China, 1934–52; Malaya, 1952– .
Hale, Sarah; Tenn.; Mexico, 1888–1900.
Hall, Harold Edward; Okla.; China, 1933–52.
Hall, Alice Mellichamp (Wells) (Mrs. H. E.); S. C.; China, 1929–52.
Hall, Nell; Tex.; China, 1922–25.
Hallock, Edgar Francis, Jr.; N. Y.; Brazil, 1941– .
Hallock, Zelma (Curnutt) (Mrs. E. F.); Okla.; Brazil, 1941– .
Halsell, Thomas Erle; Ark.; Brazil, 1955– .
Halsell, Mary Elizabeth (Tolson) (Mrs. T. E.); Ark.; Brazil, 1955– .
Haltom, William Earl; Ark.; Hawaii, 1947– .
Haltom, Ruth (Miller) (Mrs. W. E.); Okla.; Hawaii, 1947– .
Halvarson, Carl Maurice; Colo.; Japan, 1952– .
Halvarson, Ruth (Ayres) (Mrs. C. M.); Kans.; Japan, 1952– .
Hambleton, George Forrest; Ohio; Japan, 1900–06.
Hambleton, Elizabeth (Spaulding) (Mrs. G. F.); Ky.; Japan, 1901–06.
Hamilton, David Luke; La.; Brazil, 1905–24.
Hamilton, Jennie (Albertson) (Mrs. D. L.); Tex.; Brazil, 1905–24.
Hamilton, Jephthah Erastus; La.; Brazil, 1899–1904.
Hamilton, Lora (Black) (Mrs. J. E.); Tex.; Brazil, 1899–1904.
Hamlett, Peter Wilkerson; Va.; China, 1907–47.
Hamlett, Lettie (Spainhour) (Mrs. P. W.); Va.; China, 1909–53.
Hamlett, W. A.; Tex.; Palestine, 1921–21.
Hamlett, Mrs. W. A.; Palestine, 1921–21.
Hammett, Mary Frances; S. C.; Nigeria, 1944– .
Hampton, Roberta Elizabeth; Okla.; Mexico, 1954– .

Hannah, Lolita Irene; Tenn.; Japan, 1925–35.
Harden, Joseph M.; Md.; Liberia, 1850–62.
Hardy, Clemmie Dupree; Tex.; Brazil, 1936– .
Hardy, Ethel Lee (Cooper) (Mrs. C. D.); Tex.; Brazil, 1936– .
Hardy, Cora Ney; Ky.; Nigeria, 1947– .
Hardy, Hubert L., Jr.; Ky.; Chile, 1950– .
Hardy, Ruby Nell (Brown) (Mrs. H. L.); Ky.; Chile, 1950– .
Hare, Zemma; Tex.; China, 1920–41.
Hargrove, Henry Lee; Tex.; China, 1919–22.
Hargrove, Viola (Frizzell) (Mrs. H. L.); Wis.; China, 1919–22.
Harmon, Ethel Rebecca; Ky.; Nigeria, 1938– .
Harper, Leland James; Mo.; Paraguay, 1950– .
Harper, Helen Elizabeth (Wicks) (Mrs. L. J.); Mo.; Paraguay, 1950– .
Harper, Winfred Ozell; Tex.; Nigeria, 1950– .
Harper, Juanita (Taylor) (Mrs. W. O.); Tex.; Nigeria, 1950– .
Harrington, Fern; Mo.; China, 1940–48; Philippines, 1948– .
Harrington, Joseph Arnol; Mo.; Brazil, 1938– .
Harrington, Edna Earle (Looper) (Mrs. J. A.); Ark.; Brazil, 1938– .
Harris, Clifton E.; Ark.; China, 1946–54.
Harris, Ann (Kilman) (Mrs. C. E.); Tex.; China, 1946–54.
Harris, Hendon Mason; Miss.; China, 1910–29, 1935–51.
Harris, Florence (Powell) (Mrs. H. M.); Mexico; China, 1910–29, 1935–51.
Harris, Josephine; Ark.; Hawaii, 1946– .
Harris, Lindell Otis; Mo.; Hawaii, 1945–53.
Harris, Connie Mae (McElyea) (Mrs. L. O.); Mo.; Hawaii, 1945–53.
Harris, Robert Lawson; N. C.; Peru, 1950– .
Harris, Mary Lillian (Culpepper) (Mrs. R. L.); Ga.; Peru, 1950– .
Harrison, William Coleman; Ky.; Brazil, 1924–29; 1936– .
Harrison, Helen (Bagby) (Mrs. W. C.); Brazil; Brazil, 1923–29, 1936– .
Hart, Joseph Lancaster; Va.; Argentina, 1903–21; Chile, 1921–47.
Hart, Tennessee (Hamilton) (Mrs. J. L.); Ky.; Argentina, 1904–21; Chile, 1921–47.
Hart, Lois Emily; Argentina; Chile, 1941– .
Hartwell, Anna B.; China; China, 1892–1940.
Hartwell, Charles Norris; Calif.; China, 1909–27.
Hartwell, Jesse B.; S. C.; China, 1858–1912.
Hartwell, Elizabeth H. (Jewett) (Mrs. J. B.); Ga.; China, 1858–70.
Hartwell, Julia (Jewett) (Mrs. J. B.); Ga.; China, 1872–79.
Hartwell, Charlotte (Norris) (Mrs. J. B.); Md.; China, 1881–1903.
Hartwell, Nellie; Calif.; China, 1887–91.
Harvey, Gerald Scott; Mo.; Southern Rhodesia, 1954– .
Harvey, Eunice (Listrom) (Mrs. G. S.); Mo.; Southern Rhodesia, 1954– .
Harvey, Wiley W.; Ind.; Nigeria, 1884–91.
Harvey, Cora F. (Caspar) (Mrs. W. W.); Ind.; Nigeria, 1884–91.
Hastey, Ervin Elmer; Okla.; Mexico, 1952– .

Hastey, Ethel Ruth (Tyson) (Mrs. E. E.); Okla.; Mexico, 1952- .
Hatchell, William Felix; La.; Mexico, 1900-38.
Hatchell, Jessie (Ennis) (Mrs. W. F.); Ala.; Mexico, 1900-31.
Hatcher, Minnie Frances; Ga.; Hawaii, 1952-55.
Hatton, William Alvin; Tex.; Brazil, 1947- .
Hatton, Catherine (Jordan) (Mrs. W. A.); Ark.; Brazil, 1947- .
Haverfield, William Milton; Ga.; Ecuador, 1918-52; Mexico, 1952- .
Haverfield, Lois (Nichols) (Mrs. W. M.); Tex.; Ecuador, 1948-52; Mexico, 1952- .
Hawkins, Dorine; Okla.; Brazil, 1944- .
Hawkins, Flora Floy; Tex.; China, 1935-48.
Hawkins, Fred Lee, Jr.; N. C.; Brazil, 1955- .
Hawkins, Mariruth (Barker) (Mrs. F. L., Jr.); Tenn.; Brazil, 1955- .
Hawkins, Nora E.; Tex.; Brazil, 1921-27.
Hawkins, Thomas Benton; Va.; Argentina, 1921- .
Hawkins, Lou Ellen (Combs) (Mrs. T. B.); Ala.; Argentina, 1921- .
Hayes, Arnold Edmund; Ala.; Brazil, 1919-54.
Hayes, Helen (Ford) (Mrs. A. E.); Ky.; Brazil, 1919-54.
Hayes, Charles A., M.D.; Ill.; China, 1901-43.
Hayes, Alice (Johnson) (Mrs. C. A.); M. D.; Iceland; China, 1901-43.
Hayes, Ida B.; Minn.; Mexico, 1893-1920.
Hayes, Ruth Everley; Ill.; China, 1947-53; Indonesia, 1953- .
Hays, George Howard; Mo.; Japan, 1948- .
Hays, Helen (Mathis) (Mrs. G. H.); Ky.; Japan, 1948- .
Hayward, John Charles, M.D.; Mich.; Korea, 1953-54.
Hayward, Josephine (Myre) (Mrs. J. C.); Wash.; Korea, 1953-54.
Head, Emily Virginia; Tex.; Colombia, 1950-53.
Headrick, Harvey Otis; La.; Brazil, 1950- .
Headrick, Betty Lucille (Colvin) (Mrs. H. O.); La.; Brazil, 1950- .
Hearn, Thomas Oscar, M.D.; Ala.; China, 1907-25.
Hearn, Lizzie (Penn) (Mrs. T. O.); Md.; China, 1907-25.
Henley, Sarah Lou; Tex.; Nigeria, 1955- .
Hensley, Eula; Ky.; China, 1908-09.
Hern, William Orval; Mo.; Lebanon, 1954- .
Hern, Nancy (Hunter) (Mrs. W. O.); N. C.; Lebanon, 1954- .
Herring, David Wells; N. C.; China, 1885-92; 1907-29.
Herring, Maggie (Nutt) (Mrs. D. W.); N. C.; China, 1885-92.
Herring, Alice (Rea) (Mrs. D. W.); Australia; China, 1907-29.
Herring, George N., M.D.; China; China, 1920-27.
Herring, Marion Clayton (Poulson) (Mrs. G. N.); N. Y.; China, 1920-27.
Herring, James Alexander; China; China, 1935-53.
Herring, Nan (Trammell) (Mrs. J. A.); S. C.; China, 1935-53.
Herring, Mary Lee; China; China, 1938-42.
Hester, Earl; Okla.; Romania, 1929-37.
Hickerson, Julius Raht; Tenn.; Colombia, 1949-51.
Hickerson, Vivian (Dunn) (Mrs. J. R.); Tex.; Colombia, 1949-54; Ecuador, 1954-55.
Hickman, William Aubrey, Jr.; Fla.; Paraguay, 1950- .
Hickman, Jane (Graham) (Mrs. W. A., Jr.); Fla.; Paraguay, 1950- .
Hicks, Marlin Russell; Ark.; Chile, 1950- .
Hicks, Dorothy (Gilbert) (Mrs. M. R.); Miss.; Chile, 1950- .
Hicks, Wade Bryant; S. C.; Philippines, 1955- .
Hicks, Peggy Lenora (Greene) (Mrs. W. B.); Ga.; Philippines, 1955- .
Hickson, Frederick C.; S. C.; China, 1884-86.
Hickson, Mrs. F. C.; China, 1884-86.
High, Thomas O'Conner; S. C.; Nigeria, 1955- .
High, Katharine Frances (Younts) (Mrs. T. O.); N. C.; Nigeria, 1955- .
Highfill, Virginia Barnes; N. C.; Japan, 1950- .
Hill, Eugene Lowell; Tex.; China, 1935-51; Malaya, 1951-55.
Hill, Louise (Heirich) (Mrs. E. L.); Minn.; China, 1935-51; Malaya, 1951-55.
Hill, John Baker; S. C.; Nigeria, 1955- .
Hill, Louise (Lewis) (Mrs. J. B.); Ala.; Nigeria, 1955- .
Hill, Leita; Ga.; Japan, 1921-22.
Hill, Mary Virginia; W. Va.; Nigeria, 1950-51.
Hill, Patrick Henry; Fla.; Nigeria, 1949- .
Hill, Jane (Knight) (Mrs. P. H.); Ga.; Nigeria, 1949- .
Hill, Ronald Callahan; N. C.; Thailand, 1952- .
Hill, Evelyn (Pittman) (Mrs. R. C.); N. C.; Thailand, 1952- .
Hine, Emma May; Md.; China, 1915-24.
Hines, William Earle; N. C.; China, 1922-25.
Hines, Ruby Burton; Tex.; Brazil, 1944- .
Hipps, John Burder; N. C.; China, 1913-51.
Hipps, Lydia Belle (Brown) (Mrs. J. B.); Iowa; China, 1921-24.
Hipps, Margaret F. (Stroh) (Mrs. J. B.); Colo.; China, 1926-51.
Hites, Laird Thomas; Mo.; Brazil, 1918-25.
Hites, Emma (Massey) (Mrs. L. T.); Mo.; Brazil, 1918-25.
Hollaway, Ernest Lee, Jr.; Ark.; Japan, 1949- .
Hollaway, Ida Nelle (Daily) (Mrs. E. L., Jr.); Ill.; Japan, 1949- .
Hollingsworth, Tom Connally; Tex.; Argentina, 1950- .
Hollingsworth, Minnie Marcelle (Sullivan) (Mrs. T. C.); Ark.; Argentina, 1950- .
Hollis, James Dewey; Ala.; China, 1948-49; Macao, 1949- .
Hollis, Emma Corinne (Dickson) (Mrs. J. D.); Ala.; China, 1948-49; Macao, 1949- .
Holmes, Evan Festus; Ala.; Chile, 1947- .
Holmes, Josephine M. (Haney) (Mrs. E. F.); Tex.; Chile, 1947- .
Holmes, J. Landrum; Va.; China, 1858-61.
Holmes, Sallie J. (Little) (Mrs. J. L.); Va.; China, 1858-91.

Foreign Missionaries, 1845–1955

Hooker, Rufus Walker; Miss.; Mexico, 1899–1921.
Hooker, Lila (Nelson) (Mrs. R. W.); Miss.; Mexico, 1900–21.
Hoover, Annie A.; Ark.; Japan, 1949– .
Hopewell, Gladys Geneve; Ky.; China, 1946–51; Thailand, 1951–54; Formosa, 1954– .
Hopkins, Linnie; Tenn.; Mexico, 1908–10.
Horton, Frederick Mast; Pa.; Japan, 1950– .
Horton, Elvee (Wasson) (Mrs. F. M.); La.; Japan, 1950–.
Horton, Marilyn Frances; Fla.; Japan, 1952– .
Hoshizaki, Reiji; Calif.; Japan, 1955– .
Hoshizaki, Alice Asano (Masaki) (Mrs. Reiji); Hawaii; Japan, 1955– .
Howard, Stanley Proctor, Jr.; Mo.; Japan, 1949– .
Howard, Patsy Ruth (McGee) (Mrs. S. P., Jr.); Tex.; Japan, 1949– .
Howell, E. Milford; Tex.; Nigeria, 1943– .
Howell, Eleanor Katherine (O'Haver) (Mrs. E. M.); Ind.; Nigeria, 1943– .
Howse, Ruby Jackson; Okla.; Chile, 1940– .
Huckaby, E. M., M.D.; Miss.; China, 1904–08.
Huckaby, Fannie (Ray) (Mrs. E. M.); Tex.; China, 1905–08.
Hudgins, Frances Eugenia; Va.; China, 1948–50; Thailand, 1950– .
Hudson, Lenora Carlton; Tex.; Japan, 1949– .
Huey, Mary Alice; Ala.; China, 1907–41; Hawaii, 1941–46.
Hughes, Van Earl; Tex.; Costa Rica, 1949– .
Hughes, Waurayne (Duree) (Mrs. V. E.); Tex.; Costa Rica, 1949– .
Hughey, John David, Jr.; S. C.; Spain, 1947–52; Switzerland, 1952– .
Hughey, Theodosia Evelyn (Wells) (Mrs. J. D., Jr.); S. C.; Spain, 1947–52; Switzerland, 1952– .
Humphrey, J. Hugh, M.D.; Okla.; China, 1936–51.
Humphrey, Edith (Felkel) (Mrs. J. H.); Okla.; China, 1936–51; Hawaii, 1955– .
Humphrey, Viola; Tex.; China, 1921–39.
Humphrey, James Edward; N. C.; Nigeria, 1948– .
Humphrey, Rachel (Thompson) (Mrs. J. E.); N. C.; Nigeria, 1948– .
Humphries, Carol Leigh; N. C.; Nigeria, 1951– .
Hundley, Lillie Mae; Tex.; China, 1923–52; Hawaii, 1952– .
Hunker, William Carl; Ore.; China, 1946–49; Philippines, 1949–52; Formosa, 1952– .
Hunker, Jeanette (Roebuck) (Mrs. W. C.); Tex.; China, 1946–49; Philippines, 1949–52; Formosa, 1952– .
Hunnex, William J.; England; China, 1882–95.
Hunnex, Mrs. W. J.; Switzerland; China, 1882–95.
Hunt, Bertha Lee; Tex.; Brazil, 1920–44.
Hunt, Walter Taylor; Tex.; Philippines, 1953– .
Hunt, Aliene Emma (Brasher) (Mrs. W. T.); Tex.; Philippines, 1953– .
Hunter, Clifforde Elizabeth; Ga.; China, 1913–28.
Hurley, Dan T.; N. C.; Romania, 1923–31.
Hurley, Ida Rachel (Flake) (Mrs. D. T.); N. C.; Romania, 1923–36.
Hurst, Harold Edward; Ill.; Honduras, 1952– .
Hurst, Alice J. (Leavitt) (Mrs. H. E.); Fla.; Honduras, 1952– .
Hurtt, Fannie George; Ala.; Nigeria, 1945–48.

Ingram, Edgar Allen; Tex.; Brazil, 1918–30.
Ingram, Lola (Cook) (Mrs. E. A.); Tex.; Brazil, 1918–30.
Ingram, Ray Porter; N. C.; Nigeria, 1944–51.
Ingram, Ada Alexander (Armstrong) (Mrs. R. P.); Okla.; Nigeria, 1944–51.
Isdell, Clarabel; Ala.; China, 1935–45.

Jackson, Ada; Ky.; Nigeria, 1943–50.
Jackson, Alma Mae; Tex.; Brazil, 1936– .
Jackson, Ernest A.; Va.; Brazil, 1903–28.
Jackson, Janette (Beasley) (Mrs. E. A.); Va.; Brazil, 1903–28.
Jackson, John Edward; S. C.; China, 1919–27, 1928–51; Japan, 1927–28; Philippines, 1951– .
Jackson, Mina (Garrett) (Mrs. J. E.); Tex.; China, 1921–27, 1928–51; Japan, 1927–28; Philippines, 1951– .
Jackson, Pauline; Ala.; Southern Rhodesia, 1955– .
Jackson, Stephen Pomeroy; Brazil; Brazil, 1941– .
Jackson, Pauline (Sheriff) (Mrs. S. P.); Okla.; Brazil, 1941– .
Jackson, William H., Jr.; Tex.; Japan, 1951– .
Jackson, Doris (Shirley) (Mrs. W. H.); Tex.; Japan, 1951– .
Jacob, Robert Augustus; Ky.; China, 1917–18, 1920–53.
Jacob, Floy Christine (Wright) (Mrs. R. A.); Ky.; China, 1922– .
James, Carmen Easley, M.D.; Tenn.; China, 1923–29.
James, Eulah Corinne (Pearson) (Mrs. C. E.); Tenn.; China, 1923–27.
James, Frederick S.; N. C.; Liberia, 1847–48.
James, J. Sexton; Pa.; China, 1846–48.
James, Annie Price (Safford) (Mrs. J. S.); Mass.; China, 1847–48.
James, Sallie Moss; Va.; China, 1934–48.
Jeffers, Irene; Ala.; China, 1923–51; Formosa, 1951– .
Jennings, George Edward; Tenn.; Spain, 1947–52.
Jennings, Frances Louise (Sharp) (Mrs. G. E.); Tenn.; Spain, 1947–52.
Jester, William Linville; Mo.; Nigeria, 1946– .
Jester, Daisy (Hicks) (Mrs. W. L.); Ky.; Nigeria, 1946– .
Jeter, Ella; Tex.; China, 1905–14.
Johnson, Cecil Warren; Okla.; Mexico, 1949–53.
Johnson, Lillian (Taylor) (Mrs. C. W.); Ga.; Mexico, 1949–53.
Johnson, Francis C.; S. C.; China, 1846–50.
Johnson, Joe Carl; Tex.; Brazil, 1949–55.
Johnson, Colene (Richards) (Mrs. J. C.); Tex.; Brazil, 1949–55.
Johnson, Johnni (Betty Jane); W. Va.; Japan, 1951–54.

Johnson, Leslie Leonidas; Tex.; Brazil, 1915-53.
Johnson, Sammie (Guynes) (Mrs. L. L.); Tex.; Brazil, 1915-53.
Johnson, Pearl; S. C.; China, 1924-53; Formosa, 1953- .
Johnson, Robert Elton; Ala.; Brazil, 1934- .
Johnson, Elizabeth Byars (Jackson) (Mrs. R. E.); Brazil; Brazil, 1934- .
Johnson, Roberta Pearle; N. C.; China, 1915-52.
Johnson, Sallie E.; Tex.; Brazil, 1892-94.
Johnson, Thomas Neil; Mo.; China, 1923-36.
Johnson, Belle (Tyner) (Mrs. T. N.); N. C.; China, 1923-36.
Johnson, Walter Leighton; Ky.; Mexico, 1938-42.
Johnson, Bessie (Kemper) (Mrs. W. L.); Ky.; Mexico, 1938-42.
Johnson, William Buren; N. C.; China, 1925-51; Indonesia, 1951- .
Johnson, Kate (Carper) (Mrs. W. B.); Va.; China, 1925-51; Indonesia, 1951- .
Joiner, Garreth Elbert; Tex.; Ecuador, 1950- .
Joiner, Elaine (Giltner) (Mrs. G. E.); Tex.; Ecuador, 1950- .
Joiner, James M.; Ga.; China, 1884-88.
Joiner, Mary (Eager) (Mrs. J. M.); Miss.; China, 1884-88.
Jones, Alexander L.; Va.; Liberia, 1846-47.
Jones, Dorothy Charlene; Tex.; Brazil, 1952- .
Jones, Florence; Mo.; China, 1907-43.
Jones, Frances Carter; Ky.; Nigeria, 1936-37.
Jones, J. Willie; Va.; China, 1860-61.
Jones, Kathleen Carmen, M.D.; Brazil; Indonesia, 1953- .
Jones, Marjorie Irma; La.; Nigeria, 1955- .
Jones, Robert Stanley; Ky.; Brazil, 1920-32.
Jones, Mary Ruth (Bowden) (Mrs. R. S.); Tenn.; Brazil, 1920-32.
Jones, Samuel Lee; Tex.; Southern Rhodesia, 1955- .
Jones, Dessa Ona (Knight) (Mrs. S. L.); Tex.; Southern Rhodesia, 1955- .
Jones, Susanna Emma; Ill.; Mexico, 1905-11.
Jones, William Walter; Tenn.; Brazil, 1924-29.
Jones, Lucia May (Rodwell) (Mrs. W. W.); Ga.; Brazil, 1923-29.
Jordan, Carl Fred, M.D.; Iowa; China, 1919-27.
Jordan, Eva (Sullivan) (Mrs. C. F.); Tex.; China, 1920-27.
Jowers, Sherman Clyde; La.; China, 1946-49; Philippines, 1949- .
Jowers, Alcie May (Pettigrew) (Mrs. S. C.); La.; China, 1946-49; Philippines, 1949- .
Joyce, Thomas Collins; England; Brazil, 1898-99.
Justice, James M.; N. C.; Argentina, 1908-18.
Justice, Mattie (Cox) (Mrs. J. M.); Ala.; Argentina, 1908-18.

Keith, Clara Upton; Ky.; Nigeria, 1915-25.
Kelley, Page Hutto; Ala.; Brazil, 1952- .
Kelley, Vernice (McIntosh) (Mrs. P. H.); Ala.; Brazil, 1952- .
Kelly, Willie; Ala.; China, 1893-1937.
Kendall, Douglas Edward; Mass.; Indonesia, 1955- .
Kendall, Emma Katherine (Kerr) (Mrs. D. E.); Ark.; Indonesia, 1955- .
Kendrick, Bertie Lee; N. C.; Hawaii, 1945- .
Kennedy, Colquitt Alexander; Okla.; Nigeria, 1946-49.
Kennedy, Lorene (Pfeiffer) (Mrs. C. A.); Okla.; Nigeria, 1946-49.
Kennedy, Thomas Jefferson; Tex.; Nigeria, 1954- .
Kennedy, Willie Mae (Rankin) (Mrs. T. J.); Tex.; Nigeria, 1954- .
Kennon, Annie Jennie; Ga.; China, 1899-1904.
Kerschner, G. W.; Pa.; Brazil, 1912-14.
Kerschner, Margaret (Miller) (Mrs. G. W.); Pa.; Brazil, 1913-14.
Kersey, Ruth May; Va.; Nigeria, 1920-55.
Kethley, Elizabeth; Miss.; China, 1918-29.
Kilgore, William Jackson; Tex.; Argentina, 1943-49.
Kilgore, Clara Barbara (Schmickle) (Mrs. W. J.); Mo.; Argentina, 1943-49.
King, Eunice Belle; Miss.; Brazil, 1928-34.
King, Harriette Law; China; China, 1935-53; Malaya, 1953- .
King, William Dawson; La.; China, 1914-35.
King, Ruth (Pye) (Mrs. W. D.); Ark.; China, 1914-35.
King, William Duncan; Ga.; China, 1891-93, 1908-09.
King, Mary L. (Barrow) (Mrs. W. D.); N. C.; China, 1908-11.
Kirk, James Palmer; N. C.; Brazil, 1947- .
Kirk, Maxie (Crawford) (Mrs. J. P.); Ky.; Brazil, 1947- .
Kirkpatrick, Mary Frank; Miss.; Nigeria, 1955- .
Knight, Charles William; Tenn.; Nigeria, 1940-52.
Knight, Elsie (Renfroe) (Mrs. C. W.); Ga.; Nigeria, 1947-52.
Knight, Doris Lynn; Ga.; China, 1920-52; Nigeria, 1952- .
Knight, Fannie E.; N. C.; China, 1889-94.
Knox, Martha Elizabeth; Mo.; Japan, 1950- .
Kolb, Raymond Lowrey; Miss.; Brazil, 1944- .
Kolb, Martha Ann (Cochran) (Mrs. R. L.); Ga.; Brazil, 1944- .
Kollmar, George Hiram, M.D.; N. J.; Colombia, 1950- .
Kollmar, Rosemary (Boston) (Mrs. G. H.); Tex.; Colombia, 1950- .
Koon, Victor; Tex.; China, 1925-35; Manchuria, 1935-40; Hawaii, 1940- .
Koon, Aurora Lee (Hargrove) (Mrs. Victor); Conn.; China, 1925-35; Manchuria, 1935-40; Hawaii, 1940- .
Kratz, Clarence Eugene; Ala.; Southern Rhodesia, 1952- .
Kratz, Dorothy (Gray) (Mrs. C. E.); Ala.; Southern Rhodesia, 1952- .

Lacy, George Holcombe; Ark.; Mexico, 1903-35.
Lacy, Minnie (Meek) (Mrs. G. H.); Ark.; Mexico, 1903-33.
Lacy, John H.; Va.; Nigeria, 1853-54.
Lacy, Olivia (Barkley) (Mrs. J. H.); N. C.; Nigeria, 1853-54.
Lair, Lena Valinda; Tex.; Nigeria, 1935- .

Lake, John; S. C.; China, 1903-39.
Lake, Pearl Clare Hall (Williams) (Mrs. John); Ind.; China, 1902-08.
Lake, Carrie (Bostick) (Mrs. John); S. C.; China, 1900-28.
Lake, Virginia (Lake) (Mrs. John); N. C.; China, 1933-39.
Lamberth, Margaret Elizabeth; Va.; Nigeria, 1952- .
Lancaster, Cecile; Tex.; Japan, 1920-45, 1947- ; Hawaii, 1945-47.
Landrum, Minnie Levatta; Miss.; Brazil, 1922- .
Lane, Dorothea Katherine; Ky.; Japan, 1951- .
Lane, Leonard Guy; N. Mex.; Nigeria, 1951- .
Lane, Daisy Marie (Brannan) (Mrs. L. G.); Tex.; Nigeria, 1951- .
Langley, Josephine Vivian; Ala.; Nigeria, 1946-53.
Langston, Alva Bee; S. C.; Brazil, 1909-36.
Langston, Louise (Diuguid) (Mrs. A. B.); Ky.; Brazil, 1909-36.
Langston, LaRue W.; S. C.; Brazil, 1914-17.
Langston, Marjory (Quattlebaum) (Mrs. L. W.); S. C.; Brazil, 1914-17.
Lanier, Minnie Lou; Ga.; Brazil, 1945- .
Lanneau, Sophie Stephens; Mo.; China, 1907-51.
Lansdell, Emily Kilpatrick; Ga.; China, 1943-51.
Larson, Ivan V.; Mo.; China, 1919-52; Philippines, 1952-54; Formosa, 1954- .
Larson, Edith (Drotts) (Mrs. I. V.); Mo.; China, 1919-52; Philippines, 1952-54; Formosa, 1954- .
Laseter, Anne Nora; Tex.; Chile, 1923- .
Lawton, Benjamin Ray; N. C.; Italy, 1947- .
Lawton, Mary (Patterson) (Mrs. B. R.); Nigeria; Italy, 1947- .
Lawton, Deaver Monroe; China; China, 1935-50; Thailand, 1950- .
Lawton, Dorothy (Dodd) (Mrs. D. M.); China; China, 1936-50; Thailand, 1950- .
Lawton, Mary Elizabeth; China; China, 1922-27.
Lawton, Olive Allene; China; China, 1924-50; Formosa, 1950- .
Lawton, Phebe Elizabeth; S. C.; Japan, 1923-26.
Lawton, Wesley Willingham, Sr.; S. C.; China, 1894-1936.
Lawton, Ida (Deaver) (Mrs. W. W., Sr.); Pa.; China, 1898-1936.
Lawton, Wesley Willingham, Jr.; China; China, 1934-53; Philippines, 1953- .
Lawton, Muriel (Ramsey) (Mrs. W. W., Jr.); China; China, 1936-39.
Lawton, Geraldine (Riddell) (Mrs. W. W., Jr.); Tex.; China, 1942-53; Philippines, 1953- .
Lea, Ola Vaden; Va.; China, 1925-50; Formosa, 1950- .
League, Thomas J.; S. C.; China, 1888-93.
League, Florence (Nightingale) (Mrs. T. J.); S. C.; China, 1888-93.
Leavell, Cornelia Frances; China; Hawaii, 1942-47, 1950- ; China, 1947-50.
Leavell, George W., M.D.; Miss.; China, 1912-35.
Leavell, Frances (Peay) (Mrs. G. W.); Ky.; China, 1912-35.
Leavell, Ullin W.; Miss.; China, 1920-29.
Leavell, Charlotte (Henry) (Mrs. U. W.); Ky.; China, 1921-29.
Ledford, Lowell Eugene; Ark.; Peru, 1955- .
Ledford, Shirley Ann (Stephan) (Mrs. L. E.); Ark.; Peru, 1955- .
Lee, Elizabeth Holt; Conn.; Palestine, 1947-51.
Lee, Joseph; S. C.; China, 1921-29.
Lee, Frances Elizabeth (King) (Mrs. Joseph); Tenn.; China, 1923-29.
Lee, Wyatt Wain; La.; Mexico, 1951- .
Lee, Edrie Elizabeth (Morris) (Mrs. W. W.); Tex.; Mexico, 1951- .
Lennon, Samuel Judson; N. C.; Thailand, 1955- .
Lennon, Harriett (Orr) (Mrs. S. J.); N. C.; Thailand, 1955- .
Leonard, Charles A.; N. C.; China, 1910-24, 1942-44; Manchuria, 1924-40; Hawaii, 1940-41, 1944-49.
Leonard, Evelyn (Corbitt) (Mrs. C. A.); La.; China, 1910-24, 1942-44; Manchuria, 1924-40; Hawaii, 1940-41, 1944-49.
Leonard, Marie Ruth; Kans.; Uruguay, 1922-27.
LeSueur, David Hardeman; Tex.; Mexico, 1903-35.
LeSueur, Allie (Roberts) (Mrs. D. H.); Tex.; Mexico, 1903-35.
Lide, Florence Coker; S. C.; China, 1913-50; Nigeria, 1950-54.
Lide, Francis Pugh; S. C.; China, 1920-51; Philippines, 1951- .
Lide, Bettie (Stephens) (Mrs. F. P.); Mo.; China, 1920-51; Philippines, 1951- .
Lide, Jane Wilson; S. C.; China, 1909-53.
Limbert, Rosemary; Ark.; Japan, 1950- .
Lind, Mary Elizabeth; Minn.; Paraguay, 1954- .
Lindsey, Robert Lisle; Okla.; Israel, 1944- .
Lindsey, Margaret (Lutz) (Mrs. R. L.); Ohio; Israel, 1944- .
Lingerfelt, James Elmer; Tenn.; Brazil, 1938- .
Lingerfelt, Nelle Jane (Self) (Mrs. J. E.); Tenn.; Brazil, 1938- .
Littlejohn, John Thomas, Jr.; S. C.; China, 1922-27.
Littlejohn, Marguerite (Pierce) (Mrs. J. T.); La.; China, 1922-27.
Littleton, Homer Richerson; Ga.; Nigeria, 1940-47; Gold Coast, 1947- .
Littleton, Ossie Ouida (Price) (Mrs. H. R.); Ga.; Nigeria, 1940-47; Gold Coast, 1947- .
Lockard, William David; Tex.; Southern Rhodesia, 1952- .
Lockard, Mary Sue (Sheffield) (Mrs. W. D.); Tex.; Southern Rhodesia, 1952- .
Locke, Russell Lloyd; Calif.; Nigeria, 1955- .
Locke, Veda Levina (Williams) (Mrs. R. L.); Ark.; Nigeria, 1955- .
Lockett, Basil Lee, M.D.; Tenn.; Nigeria, 1909-21, 1925-33.
Lockett, Josie (Still) (Mrs. B. L.); Tex.; Nigeria, 1909-11.
Lockett, Elkin Mozelle (Lightfoot) (Mrs. B. L.); Tex.; Nigeria, 1915-21, 1925-40.
Lockhart, Maxine; Tex.; Nigeria, 1955- .
Logan, Robert Mathers; Ireland; Argentina, 1909-35.

Logan, Rebecca (Adams) (Mrs. R. M.); Ireland; Argentina, 1909-36.
Logan, William Wayne, D.D.S.; Miss.; Nigeria, 1952- .
Logan, Dorothy (Cook) (Mrs. W. W.); Miss.; Nigeria, 1952- .
Long, Annie; Tex.; Mexico, 1915-27.
Long, Leonard; Okla.; Nigeria, 1934-38.
Long, Florence Candis (Major) (Mrs. Leonard); Mich.; Nigeria, 1934-38.
Long, Rebecca Violet; S. C.; Palestine, 1945-51.
Longbottom, Samuel Fletcher, Jr.; Fla.; Hawaii, 1954- .
Longbottom, Marian Laverne (Cross) (Mrs. S. F., Jr.); Tex.; Hawaii, 1954- .
Louthan, Alexander Doliphan, M.D.; Va.; China, 1905-20.
Louthan, Pauline (Lide) (Mrs. A. D.); S. C.; China, 1913-20.
Louthan, Elijah McIntyre; Va.; China, 1915-17.
Louthan, Gertrude (Richards) (Mrs. E. McI.); Canada; China, 1915-17.
Lovegren, Lloyd August, M.D.; China; Jordan, 1951- .
Lovegren, Alta Lee (Grimes) (Mrs. L. A.); Ga.; Jordan, 1951- .
Lovegren, Mildred Effie; China; China, 1944-50; Macao, 1950-53; Hong Kong, 1953- .
Low, Joe Edwin; Tex.; Nigeria, 1947- .
Low, Anita (Summerlin) (Mrs. J. E.); Tex.; Nigeria, 1947- .
Lowe, Clifford J.; Ga.; China, 1910-48.
Lowe, Julia (Martin) (Mrs. C. J.); N. Y.; China, 1910-48.
Lowe, John W.; Mo.; China, 1898-1941.
Lowe, Margaret (Savage) (Mrs. J. W.); Mo.; China, 1898-1941.
Lumbley, W. T.; Miss.; Nigeria, 1888-1906.
Lumbley, Mrs. W. T.; Ark.; Nigeria, 1888-95.
Lumbley, Carie (Green) (Mrs. W. T.); England; Nigeria, 1899-1906, 1907-28.
Lunsford, James Acree; Ky.; Brazil, 1940- .
Lunsford, Lena (Conway) (Mrs. J. A.); Okla.; Brazil, 1940- .
Luper, James Daniel; Brazil; Brazil, 1948- .
Luper, Julia Frances (Porter) (Mrs. J. D.); Neb.; Brazil, 1948- .
Lyne, Mary N.; Ky.; China, 1917-31.
Lyon, Roy Lenere; Tex.; Mexico, 1952- .
Lyon, Alma Ruth (Madden) (Mrs. R. L.); Tex.; Mexico, 1952- .

MacDonald, William D. T.; Scotland; Chile, 1919-34.
MacDonald, Mrs. W. D. T.; Chile, 1919-23.
MacKenzie, Julia K.; Ky.; China, 1894-1916.
MacLean, Ewart Gladstone; Canada; Nigeria, 1907-40.
MacLean, Addie Louise (Briggs) (Mrs. E. G.); Canada; Nigeria, 1907-40.
Macormic, Nova Marie (Leach) (Mrs. E. R.); Mo.; Mexico, 1946-49.
Maddox, Otis Pendleton; Ky.; Brazil, 1905-45.
Maddox, Effie (Roe) (Mrs. O. P.); Tenn.; Brazil, 1905-45.
Maddox, Samuel E.; Brazil; Brazil, 1946-48.
Maddox, Nadine (Sanders) (Mrs. S. E.); Mo.; Brazil, 1946-48.
Maberry, Annie J.; Miss.; Mexico, 1882-92.
Maer, Wynne Quilon; Miss.; Chile, 1925-48.
Maer, Berta Lou (Tooms) (Mrs. W. Q.); Tenn.; Chile, 1925-48.
Mahan, Doris Ruth; Tex.; Hungary, 1937-38.
Mahon, Robert Perry; Tenn.; Mexico, 1898-1920.
Mahon, Kate (Savage) (Mrs. R. P.); Tenn.; Mexico, 1898-1920.
Major, Alfred Roy; N. D.; Brazil, 1952- .
Major, Sarah Elizabeth (Myatt) (Mrs. A. R.); Ark.; Brazil, 1952- .
Manley, Kathleen Senter; Tenn.; Nigeria, 1934- .
Marchman, Margaret Randall; Ga.; Nigeria, 1941- .
Margrett, Anne (Sowell) (Mrs. H. G.); Argentina; Argentina, 1941- .
Marlar, Monda Vesta; Okla.; Southern Rhodesia, 1952- .
Marler, Lovelace Parkes; Miss.; Korea, 1955- .
Marler, Martha Ellen (Townsend) (Mrs. L. P.); Miss.; Korea, 1955- .
Marlowe, Elizabeth Rose; Ky.; China, 1921-49; Japan, 1949- .
Marriott, Cread C.; Mo.; China, 1910-40.
Marriott, Cora (Burns) (Mrs. C. C.); Mo.; China, 1910-40.
Marrs, Frank; Tex.; Mexico, 1900-35.
Marrs, Effie (Kincaid) (Mrs. Frank); Ohio; Mexico, 1900-35.
Martin, E. Pauline; Tenn.; Nigeria, 1955- .
Martin, Henry Dearman; Va.; Nigeria, 1954- .
Martin, Margaret Anne (McMullen) (Mrs. H. D.); Miss.; Nigeria, 1954- .
Mashburn, James Robert; Tenn.; China, 1922-35.
Mashburn, Annie Lois (Howard) (Mrs. J. R.); Tex.; China, 1922-29.
Mason, Roy; Ky; Brazil, 1924-26.
Mason, Nelle Gladys (Cooper) (Mrs. Roy); Mo.; Brazil, 1924-26.
Massengill, Mary Lou; Ky.; Japan, 1954- .
Masters, Helen Ruth; Fla.; Nigeria, 1950- .
Mathis, Virginia Bennett; La.; Hawaii, 1942-47; China, 1947-52; Philippines, 1952- .
Matthews, Jack Beacham; Ala.; Argentina, 1949- .
Matthews, Lois (Ware) (Mrs. J. B.); Fla.; Argentina, 1949- .
Matthews, Louis Brown; Ga.; Argentina, 1925-29.
Matthews, Reka Cornelia (Blanc) (Mrs. L. B.); Netherlands; Argentina, 1925-29.
Mayhall, David Norris; Miss.; Nigeria, 1950- .
Mayhall, Ollie Mae (Ware) (Mrs. D. N.); Miss.; Nigeria, 1950- .
Maynard, Nathan; Md.; Japan, 1894-1910.
Maynard, Bessie H. (Harlowe) (Mrs. Nathan); Va.; Japan, 1894-1910.
McBride, Nettie Grace; Ohio; China, 1915-18.
McCall, Louis Edmund; N. C.; Thailand, 1955- .

Foreign Missionaries, 1845–1955

McCall, Julia Marie (Seay) (Mrs. L. E.); S. C.; Thailand, 1955- .
McCamey, Howard Douglas, D.D.S.; Tex.; Nigeria, 1940- .
McCamey, Georgia (Cantrell) (Mrs. H. D.); Tenn.; Nigeria, 1940- .
McCarthy, Charles D.; Ireland; Brazil, 1898–99.
McCarthy, (Mrs. Charles D.); ( ); Brazil, 1898–99.
McClellan, Helen Iola; Mo.; Lebanon, 1948–50;
McCloy, Thomas; Scotland; China, 1889–1905.
McCloy, Mary (McWherrie) (Mrs. Thomas); Scotland; China, 1889–1905.
McCollum, J. W.; Ala.; Japan, 1889–1909.
McCollum, Dru (Collins) (Mrs. J. W.); Ala.; Japan, 1889–1909.
McConnell, Harry Cecil; Ohio; Chile, 1937- .
McConnell, Elizabeth (Buch) (Mrs. H. C.); Pa.; Chile, 1937- .
McConnell, Velma Frances; Ark.; China, 1940–41.
McCormick, Hugh Pendleton; Va.; Mexico, 1885–98.
McCormick, Anne P. (Perry) (Mrs. H. P.); Ala.; Mexico, 1885–98.
McCormick, Hugh Pendleton; Tex.; Nigeria, 1920–47; Hawaii, 1947- .
McCormick, Mary Katherine (Reeks) (Mrs. H. P.); La.; Nigeria, 1925–47; Hawaii, 1947- .
McCowen, Ruth, M.D.; Va.; China, 1881–86.
McCoy, Donald Burchard; Tenn.; Brazil, 1954- .
McCoy, Sterline (White) (Mrs. D. B.); Okla.; Brazil, 1954- .
McCoy, Grace; Mo.; Chile, 1923–27.
McCrea, Tully Foster; Miss.; China, 1904–34.
McCrea, Jessie (Read) (Mrs. T. F.); Pa.; China, 1904–34.
McCullough, Charles Wilson; Tex.; Colombia, 1943–53; Jamaica, 1953- .
McCullough, Avis (Chaffin) (Mrs. C. W.); Tex.; Colombia, 1943–53; Jamaica, 1953- .
McCullough, Helen Louise; Mo.; China, 1935–40, 1943- ; Hawaii, 1941–43.
McCullough, Nita Ruth; Fla.; Nigeria, 1953- .
McCullough, Ruby Miriam; Ala.; Mexico, 1948- .
McDaniel, Charles G.; Va.; China, 1902–43.
McDaniel, Nannie (Bartlett) (Mrs. C. G.); Va.; China, 1902–43.
McDavid, Lillian A.; S. C.; Mexico, 1891–95.
McDowell, Donald England; Md.; Paraguay, 1954- .
McDowell, May Christine (Vanderpoel) (Mrs. D. E.); N. J.; Paraguay, 1954- .
McGavock, James William; Ark.; Chile, 1922–44; Spanish Publishing House, 1944–53.
McGavock, Catherine Elizabeth (Johnson) (Mrs. J. W.); Tenn.; Chile, 1922–44; Spanish Publishing House, 1944–53.
McGavock, Margaret Page; Ky.; Spanish Publishing House, 1949–50.
McGee, John Sidney; N. C.; Nigeria, 1945- .
McGee, Doris (Thompson) (Mrs. J. S.); N. C.; Nigeria, 1945- .

McGinnis, William Harlem; Tenn.; Nigeria, 1950–52; Gold Coast, 1952- .
McGinnis, Josephine (Toomer) (Mrs. W. H.); Ky.; Nigeria, 1950–52; Gold Coast, 1952- .
McGlamery, Roy Cloud, M.D.; Okla.; Colombia, 1947–53.
McGlamery, Orlene (Ellis) (Mrs. R. C.); Miss.; Colombia, 1947–53.
McGuire, Victor V.; N. C.; China, 1919–25.
McIlroy, Minnie Douglas; Ore.; Argentina, 1923- .
McIntyre, Lila; N. C.; China, 1908–19.
McMillan, Archibald Memory; China; China, 1948–48.
McMillan, Margaret (King) (Mrs. A. M.); Ga.; China, 1948–48.
McMillan, Henry Hudson; N. C.; China, 1913–51; Bahamas, 1951–55.
McMillan, Lelia Memory (McNeill) (Mrs. H. H.); N. C.; China, 1913–51; Bahamas, 1951–55.
McMillan, Virgil Oliver, Jr.; Ala.; Japan, 1952- .
McMillan, Donabel (Pitts) (Mrs. V. O., Jr.); Ala.; Japan, 1952- .
McMinn, Mary Jane (Mollie); Mo.; China, 1889–98, 1921–40.
McMurray, Jesse Daniel; Okla.; Uruguay, 1945- .
McMurray, Mary Jo (Henry) (Mrs. J. D.); Okla.; Uruguay, 1945- .
McNealy, Walter Bayless; Ky.; Brazil, 1937- .
McNealy, Ymogene Martel (Alexander) (Mrs. W. B.); Va.; Brazil, 1937- .
McRae, James Thomas, M.D.; Miss.; Lebanon, 1950–52; Jordan, 1952–54; Egypt, 1954- .
McRae, Jane (Carroll) (Mrs. J. T.); La.; Lebanon, 1950–52; Jordan, 1952–54; Egypt, 1954- .
Meador, Deuflot Albertine; Tex.; Brazil, 1945–47.
Meadows, Joseph Guy, M.D.; Ala.; China, 1904–11.
Meadows, Dorcas Fidelia (Merriman), M.D. (Mrs. J. G.); Pa.; China, 1902–12.
Meadows, Julia; Ga.; China, 1904–19.
Medling, P. Paul; Tenn.; Japan, 1907–19.
Medling, Lena (Rushing) (Mrs. P. P.); Tenn.; Japan, 1907–20.
Medling, William Robert; Japan; Japan, 1946- .
Medling, Mary Louise (Gulley) (Mrs. W. R.); Tenn.; Japan, 1946- .
Mefford, Joseph Wilson, Jr.; Colo.; Spain, 1953- .
Mefford, Lila (Pritchard) (Mrs. J. W., Jr.); Colo.; Spain, 1953- .
Mein, David; Mich.; Brazil, 1944- .
Mein, Lou Demie (Segers) (Mrs. David); Ga.; Brazil, 1944- .
Mein, John; England; Brazil, 1914–53; Bahamas, 1953- .
Mein, Elizabeth (Felisenfield) (Mrs. John); Mich.; Brazil, 1914–46.
Mein, Mildred (Cox) (Mrs. John); Tex.; Brazil, 1934–53; Bahamas, 1953- .

Mercer, Dewey Edward; Ky.; Japan, 1955– .
Mercer, Margaret Ramona (Hall) (Mrs. D. E.); Tenn.; Japan, 1955– .
Meredith, Helen; Ga.; Colombia, 1942– .
Meredith, William Page, M.D.; Tex.; Nigeria, 1922–26.
Meredith, Dalkeith (Watson) (Mrs. W. P.); Tex.; Nigeria, 1922–26.
Meuth, Mary Sue; Ky.; Indonesia, 1955– .
Mewshaw, Robert E. Lee, M.D.; Tex.; China, 1916–26, 1934–48.
Mewshaw, Dell (Spencer) (Mrs. R. E. L.); Tex.; China, 1916–26, 1934–48.
Meyers, Francis M.; Ky.; Mexico, 1884–85.
Meyers, Mary Susan (Thompson) (Mrs. F. M.); Ky.; Mexico, 1884–85.
Middleton, Gordon K.; N. C.; China, 1920–29.
Middleton, Celia (Herring) (Mrs. G. K.); China; China, 1920–29.
Middleton, Hubert Kinson; N. C.; Chile, 1950– .
Middleton, Imo Jean (Anthony) (Mrs. H. K.); N. C.; Chile, 1950– .
Miles, Julia Virginia; N. C.; Philippines, 1948– .
Miller, Cynthia A.; Ala.; China, 1905–36.
Miller, Floryne Tipton; Tenn.; Japan, 1939–41, 1947– ; China, 1941–46; Hawaii, 1946–47.
Miller, Georgia Alice; Ga.; Nigeria, 1950– .
Miller, John Henry, M.D.; Ark.; China, 1941–47.
Miller, Jones Ivey; Tex.; Chile, 1946–55.
Miller, Winnie (Marshall) (Mrs. J. I.); Tex.; Chile, 1946–55.
Mills, Ernest Oscar; Wis.; Japan, 1910–42.
Mills, Grace Anne (Hughes) (Mrs. E. O.); Mo.; Japan, 1912–32.
Mills, John Edwin; Tex.; Nigeria, 1947– .
Mills, Virginia (Miller) (Mrs. J. E.); Tex.; Nigeria, 1947– .
Mitchell, Howard Barry; S. C.; Brazil, 1955– .
Mitchell, Laura (Tollison) (Mrs. H. B.); S. C.; Brazil, 1955– .
Mitchell, James Franklin; S. C.; Chile, 1943– .
Mitchell, Margaret (Pattillo) (Mrs. J. F.); Ala.; Chile, 1943– .
Moncure, John; Va.; Japan, 1909–13.
Montroy, Edyth Inez; Miss.; Nigeria, 1946– .
Moon, Charlotte Diggs (Lottie); Va.; China, 1873–1912.
Moon, Edmonia Harris; Va.; China, 1872–76.
Moon, Hazel Frances; Va.; Nigeria, 1947– .
Moon, James Loyd; Ala.; Brazil, 1951– .
Moon, Mary Hazel (Ford) (Mrs. J. L.); Ala.; Brazil, 1951– .
Moore, Bonnie Mae; Okla.; Nigeria, 1948– .
Moore, Elton; Miss.; Indonesia, 1954– .
Moore, Jean (Cooper) (Mrs. Elton); Miss.; Indonesia, 1954– .
Moore, Isabella; Ky.; Nigeria, 1937–46.
Moore, James Walton; N. C.; China, 1920–38.
Moore, Minnie (Foster) (Mrs. J. W.); Tex.; China, 1920–52.
Moore, John Allen; Miss.; Yugoslavia, 1939–41, 1955– ; Hungary, 1941–48; Switzerland, 1948–55.
Moore, Pauline Brooks (Willingham) (Mrs. J. A.); Ga.; Yugoslavia, 1940–41, 1955– ; Hungary, 1941–48; Switzerland, 1948–55.
Moore, Robert Cecil; Fla.; Chile, 1919– .
Moore, Mary Matilda (Pimm) (Mrs. R. C.); Fla.; Chile, 1919– .
Moore, Virginia Dale; Ariz.; Nigeria, 1952– .
Moore, Walter Mason, M.D.; Okla.; Nigeria, 1952– .
Moore, Charlean (DeBerry) (Mrs. W. M.); Okla.; Nigeria, 1952– .
Moore, William Dewey; N. C.; Italy, 1937– .
Moore, Alice (Speiden) (Mrs. W. Dewey); N. C.; Italy, 1937– .
Moore, William Donald, M.D.; N. C.; China, 1947–53.
Moore, Anne Byrd (Tucker) (Mrs. W. Donald); Ark.; China, 1947–53.
Moorhead, Marion Francis; S. C.; Japan, 1946– .
Moorhead, Thelma (Chandler) (Mrs. M. F.); Va.; Japan, 1946– .
Moorman, Mary E.; Ky.; China, 1904–36.
Morgan, Edgar Carter; China; Hawaii, 1948–54; Hong Kong, 1954– .
Morgan, Agnes (McMahan) (Mrs. E. C.); S. C.; Hawaii, 1948–54; Hong Kong, 1954– .
Morgan, Edgar L.; Mo.; China, 1905–32.
Morgan, Lelah May (Carter) (Mrs. E. L.); Ga.; China, 1905–32.
Morgan, Finis Alma Rhine; Ky.; Brazil, 1919–52.
Morgan, Gertrude (Weatherby) (Mrs. F. A. R.); Tex.; Brazil, 1919–52.
Morgan, Mary Neal; Ky.; Japan, 1950– .
Morgan, Quinn Pett; N. C.; Gold Coast, 1948–53.
Morgan, Lily Mae (Wingate) (Mrs. Q. P.); S. C.; Gold Coast, 1948–53.
Morris, Clinton Pope; Tex.; China, 1914–15.
Morris, Zollie (Dickinson) (Mrs. C. P.); Tex.; China, 1914–15.
Morris, John Glenn; Ga.; China, 1946–52; Thailand, 1952– .
Morris, Polly (Love) (Mrs. J. G.); Miss.; China, 1946–52; Thailand, 1952– .
Morrison, Cleo Bessie; Tex.; China, 1940–55; Philippines, 1955– .
Morrison, Martha; Ga.; Hawaii, 1946– .
Morton, Melissa May; Tenn.; China, 1920–24.
Mosely, Hartwell R.; S. C.; Mexico, 1888–94.
Mosely, Etna (Olliphant) (Mrs. H. R.); Miss.; Mexico, 1888–94.
Moss, James Ulman; Ala.; Colombia, 1945–50; Venezuela, 1950– .
Moss, Ruth May (Jordan) (Mrs. J. U.); Tex.; Colombia, 1945–50; Venezuela, 1950– .
Moxon, Winnifred Parker; Mass.; China, 1923–31.
Moye, John Luther; Ala.; Chile, 1922–29.
Moye, Esther Selina (Billingsley) (Mrs. J. L.); Ala.; Chile, 1922–29.
Muirhead, Harvey Harold; Tex.; Brazil, 1907–41; Spanish Publishing House, 1941–47.
Muirhead, Alyne (Guynes) (Mrs. H. H.); Tex.; Brazil, 1907–41; Spanish Publishing House, 1941–47.
Muller, Alfred Celso; Mexico; Mexico, 1946– .

Muller, Damaris Elisabeth (Jaccard) (Mrs. A. C.); Switzerland; Mexico, 1946– .
Mullins, Charles David; Ala.; Hawaii, 1955– .
Mullins, Sara Ruth (Young) (Mrs. C. D.); Ala.; Hawaii, 1955– .
Murphey, Milton; Ohio; Israel, 1952– .
Murphey, Martha Mae (Ladd) (Mrs. Milton); Ind.; Israel, 1952– .
Murray, Katie; N. C.; China, 1922–54; Formosa, 1954– .
Musgrave, James Everett; Mo.; Brazil, 1948– .
Musgrave, Jane (Everett) (Mrs. J. E.); Tex.; Brazil, 1948– .
Myers, Karl Johnson, Jr., M.D.; W. Va.; Nigeria, 1955– .
Myers, Mary Elizabeth (Lawton), M.D. (Mrs. K. J., Jr.); S. C.; Nigeria, 1955– .

Napier, Augustus Young; Ga.; China, 1904–32.
Napier, Lois (Davie) (Mrs. A. Y.); Ala.; China, 1905–32.
Neal, Charley Lee; Tenn.; Mexico, 1907–45.
Neal, Hallie (Garrett) (Mrs. C. L.); Tenn.; Mexico, 1907–45.
Neel, Bernice Ruth; Tex.; Brazil, 1921– .
Neely, Thomas Lawton; S. C.; Colombia, 1942–49; Venezuela, 1949–55.
Neely, Carolyn (Switzer) (Mrs. T. L.); S. C.; Colombia, 1942–49; Venezuela, 1949–55.
Neighbour, R. E.; Tex.; Brazil, 1893–95.
Neil, Lloyd H.; Tenn.; Colombia, 1952–53; Nigeria, 1953– .
Neil, Annie Lee (Thomas) (Mrs. L. H.); Tenn.; Colombia, 1952–53; Nigeria, 1953– .
Nelson, Enrico A.; Sweden; Brazil, 1898–1938.
Nelson, Ida (Lundburg) (Mrs. E. A.); Kans.; Brazil, 1898–1938.
Nelson, Loyce Neil; Ark.; Japan, 1950– .
Nelson, Gladys (Mosley) (Mrs. L. N.); Ark.; Japan, 1950– .
Newbrough, John W.; Tex.; Mexico, 1902–20.
Newbrough, Emma (Robertson) (Mrs. J. W.); Miss.; Mexico, 1902–04.
Newbrough, Eloise (Shimmins) (Mrs. J. W.); Kans.; Mexico, 1905–20.
Newman, Ada Lois; Tex.; Nigeria, 1945–48.
Newton, Alberta; N. C.; Nigeria, 1889–95.
Newton, Christopher Columbus; N. C.; Nigeria, 1889–94.
Newton, Cornelia (Herring) (Mrs. C. C.); N. C.; Nigeria, 1889–94.
Newton, Rachel Steeves; N. C.; China, 1922–30.
Newton, William Carey; N. C.; China, 1902–39.
Newton, Mary Louise (Woodcock) (Mrs. W. C.); N. Y.; China, 1902–39.
Nichols, Buford L.; Tex.; China, 1936–52; Indonesia, 1952– .
Nichols, Mary Frances (Hodges) (Mrs. B. L.); Tex.; China, 1936–52; Indonesia, 1952– .
Nichols, Sophia; S. C.; Brazil, 1947– .
Nix, Willard Voniver; N. C.; Japan, 1921–24.
Nix, Minta A. (Oxford) (Mrs. W. V.); La.; Japan, 1921–24.
Nixon, Helen; Tex.; Argentina, 1949– .
Norman, William Raymond, Jr., M.D.; Ala.; Nigeria, 1954– .

Norman, Lois (Williams) (Mrs. W. R., Jr.); Ala.; Nigeria, 1954– .
North, Henrietta F.; Conn.; China, 1887–1922.
Northrip, Ray Ulman; Okla.; Nigeria, 1939–46.
Northrip, Ruby Irene (Spencer) (Mrs. R. U.); Okla.; Nigeria, 1939–46.
Norwood, Evan Wilkins; S. C.; China, 1923–28.
Norwood, Emma (Wilson) (Mrs. E. W.); N. C.; China, 1923–28.
Nowell, Vivian Estelle; N. C.; Nigeria, 1938– .

Oates, Marion Davis; Ark.; Peru, 1949– .
Oates, Clifford Belle (Kingery) (Mrs. M. D.); Va.; Peru, 1949– .
Ogburn, Georgia Mae; Ala.; Chile, 1940– .
Olive, Howard Dudley; Tenn.; Philippines, 1955– .
Olive, Marjorie (Douglas) (Mrs. H. D.); Mo.; Philippines, 1955– .
Olive, Lucius Bunyan; N. C.; China, 1920–32, 1935–45.
Olive, Nell (Fowler) (Mrs. L. B.); N. C.; China, 1920–32, 1935–49.
Oliver, Albert Benjamin; Tex.; Brazil, 1935– .
Oliver, Edith (Deter) (Mrs. A. B.); Brazil; Brazil, 1935– .
Oliver, Edward Lee; Fla.; Japan, 1950– .
Oliver, Susan (Pyles) (Mrs. E. L.); Ky.; Japan, 1950– .
Oliver, John Samuel; N. C.; Brazil, 1950– .
Oliver, Virginia (Winters) (Mrs. J. S.); Ark.; Brazil, 1950– .
Olsen, Esther Amanda; Colo.; Nigeria, 1936–41.
O'Neal, Boyd Allen; Tex.; Brazil, 1949– .
O'Neal, Irma Edna (Schneider) (Mrs. B. A.); Tex.; Brazil, 1949– .
O'Neal, J. Paul; Ala.; Nigeria, 1940–46.
O'Neal, Meta (La Tuille) (Mrs. J. P.); Ala.; Nigeria, 1940–46.
Orr, Donald LeRoy; Ark.; Colombia, 1951– .
Orr, Violet (Rogers) (Mrs. D. L.); Okla.; Colombia, 1951– .
Orrick, Bailes William; Ark.; Uruguay, 1920– .
Orrick, Vera (Humphries) (Mrs. B. W.); S. C.; Uruguay, 1920– .
Owen, Carrie E.; Va.; China, 1921–23.
Owen, Frank Brooks, M.D.; Tex.; Indonesia, 1954– .
Owen, Virginia (Humberson) (Mrs. F. B.); Tex.; Indonesia, 1954– .
Owen, Jesse Colman; N. C.; China, 1899–1911.
Owen, Rebecca (Miller) (Mrs. J. C.); Pa.; China, 1900–1911.
Owens, Roswell Edward; Ga.; Palestine, 1928–48.
Owens, Doreen (Hosford) (Mrs. R. E.); Argentina; Palestine, 1928–48.
Owings, D. H.; S. C.; China, 1910–12.
Oxner, James M., M.D.; Miss.; China, 1903–07.
Oxner, Cora (Huckaby) (Mrs. J. M.); Miss.; China, 1903–11.

Page, Mary Frances; N. C.; Nigeria, 1950–54.
Parham, Robert Mereman, Jr.; Ga.; Nigeria, 1953– .
Parham, Jo Ann (Walton) (Mrs. R. M., Jr.); Fla.; Nigeria, 1953– .

FIRST BAPTIST CHURCH, Augusta, Ga. The Southern Baptist Convention was organized in it May 8, 1845. Church was organized 1817 as Baptist Praying Society with help of Daniel and Abraham Marshall. Membership 1956, 3,000; property evaluation, $675,000.

FIRST BAPTIST CHURCH, Greenville, S. C. Greek Revival auditorium built 1857, total property now worth $1,800,000. Entire building is air conditioned. The Southern Baptist Theological Seminary's first home was the building vacated in 1859 by this church when it completed this auditorium.

Parker, Alice; Va.; China, 1899-1939.
Parker, Earl; Ala.; China, 1922-54; Korea, 1954- .
Parker, Sarah (Gayle) (Mrs. Earl); Ky.; China, 1922-54; Korea, 1954- .
Parker, Franklin Calvin; Fla.; Japan, 1951- .
Parker, Harriett (Hale) (Mrs. F. C.); Tenn.; Japan, 1951- .
Parker, James B.; ( ); Brazil, 1920-24.
Parker, Annie (Thomas) (Mrs. J. B.); Brazil; Brazil, 1907-17, 1920-23.
Parker, John Alexander; Miss.; Chile, 1942- .
Parker, Ruby (Hayden) (Mrs. J. A.); Tex.; Chile, 1942- .
Parks, Robert Keith; Tenn.; Indonesia, 1954- .
Parks, Helen Jean (Bond) (Mrs. R. K.); Tex.; Indonesia, 1954- .
Parrack, Ira L.; Tex.; Brazil, 1906-06.
Parsons, Carrie Victoria; Va.; Philippines, 1948- .
Paterson, Ida; Ireland; China, 1921-28.
Patterson, Alonzo Scott; Fla.; Nigeria, 1910-26; 1937-50.
Patterson, Ione (Geiger) (Mrs. A. S.); Fla.; Nigeria, 1914-26, 1937-50.
Patterson, Frank Willard; Okla.; Spanish Publishing House, 1939- .
Patterson, Pauline (Gilliland) (Mrs. F. W.); Tex.; Spanish Publishing House, 1939- .
Patterson, Ira Newberne; Ala.; Nigeria, 1924- .
Patterson, Sara Lou (Bobo) (Mrs. I. N.); S. C.; Nigeria, 1924- .
Paulk, Erline; Ala.; Hawaii, 1948-51.
Peacock, Heber Fletcher, Jr.; Ariz.; Switzerland, 1950-55.
Peacock, Edith Tyner (Baucom) (Mrs. H. F., Jr.); N. C.; Switzerland, 1950-55.
Pearcy, George; Va.; China, 1845-55.
Pearcy, Frances (Miller) (Mrs. George); Va.; China, 1846-55.
Pearson, Fred Bunyan; Ala.; Palestine, 1922-24.
Pearson, Ruth (Casey) (Mrs. F. B.); Ala.; Palestine, 1922-24.
Pemble, Marguerite Joyce; Fla.; Brazil, 1952- .
Pender, Sallie Auris; Miss.; China, 1935-53; Hawaii, 1953-54; Malaya, 1954- .
Perry, Bernice Buel; Tex.; China, 1925-27.
Perry, May Edgel; Ga.; Nigeria, 1920- .
Perry, William Montgomery; Va.; Nigeria, 1902-03.
Perry, Virginia H. (Davis) (Mrs. W. M.); Pa.; Nigeria, 1902-03.
Pettigrew, Robert Edward; Tenn.; Brazil, 1904-34.
Pettigrew, Bertha (Mills) (Mrs. R. E.); Brazil; Brazil, 1907-31.
Pettigrew, Ruth; S. C.; China, 1920-52; Hong Kong, 1952- .
Pettit, Max Edward; Okla.; China, 1947-49; Philippines, 1949-52; Formosa, 1952-54.
Pettit, Ann (Snyder) (Mrs. M. E.); Va.; China, 1947-49; Philippines, 1949-52; Formosa, 1952-54.
Petty, Herman Leo; Idaho; Israel, 1953- .
Petty, June (Goodwin) (Mrs. H. L.); Tex.; Israel, 1953- .

Phillips, A. D.; N. C.; Nigeria, 1855-71.
Phillips, Fannie C. (Williams) (Mrs. A. D.); Ga.; Nigeria, 1855-56.
Phillips, Albert Rufus; N. C.; Argentina, 1921-26.
Phillips, Ruth (Cook) (Mrs. A. R.); Va.; Argentina, 1921-26.
Phillips, Mary Helen; Ill.; China, 1923-30.
Pierce, Ethel Margaret, M.D.; China; China, 1920-42.
Pierce, L. W.; Tex.; China, 1891-1922.
Pierce, Nellie (Miner) (Mrs. L. W.); N. Y.; China, 1891-1936.
Pierson, Abel Perly; Mexico; Mexico, 1944- .
Pierson, Coy Lee (Childress) (Mrs. A. P.); Tex.; Mexico, 1944- .
Pinnock, Samuel George; England; Nigeria, 1891-1925.
Pinnock, Mrs. S. G.; England; Nigeria, 1892-1925.
Plowden, Hannah Jane; S. C.; China, 1921-40; Hawaii, 1940- .
Poe, William Allen; Ala.; Nigeria, 1951-55; Gold Coast, 1955- .
Poe, Beth (Kelley) (Mrs. W. A.); Ala.; Nigeria, 1951-55; Gold Coast, 1955- .
Ponder, Wanda Lyvonne; Okla.; Paraguay, 1950- .
Pool, James Christopher; Tex.; Nigeria, 1934- .
Pool, Elizabeth (Routh) (Mrs. J. C.); Tex.; Nigeria, 1934- .
Popp, Violet Elizabeth; Md.; Jordan, 1953-54, 1955- ; Lebanon, 1954-55.
Porter, Asa Newton; Ky.; Mexico, 1908-21.
Porter, Laura (Boyd) (Mrs. A. N.); Tex.; Mexico, 1908-21.
Porter, Hoyt Echols; Miss.; Europe, 1921-25.
Porter, Paul Clay; Tex.; Brazil, 1922- .
Porter, Margaret (Johnson) (Mrs. P. C.); Tex.; Brazil, 1922- .
Porter, Ruth; Tex.; Paraguay, 1952- .
Porter, S. J.; N. C.; Brazil, 1893-94.
Porter, Mrs. S. J.; N. C.; Brazil, 1893-94.
Poteat, Edwin McNeil, Jr.; Conn.; China, 1917-29.
Poteat, Wilda (Hardman) (Mrs. E. McN., Jr.); Ga.; China, 1917-29.
Poteat, Gordon; Conn.; China, 1915-27.
Poteat, Helen (Carruthers) (Mrs. Gordon); Kans.; China, 1915-27.
Powell, Julius Carlyle; N. C.; Nigeria, 1919- .
Powell, Rosa (Hocutt) (Mrs. J. C.); N. C.; Nigeria, 1919- .
Powell, Mary Hester; Nigeria; Nigeria, 1949- .
Powell, William David; Miss.; Mexico, 1882-98.
Powell, Mary Florence (Mayberry) (Mrs. W. D.); Miss.; Mexico, 1882-98.
Price, Lottie W.; Pa.; China, 1893-1917.
Priest, R. W.; Miss.; Nigeria, 1856-57.
Priest, Mrs. R. W.; Miss.; Nigeria, 1856-57.
Priest, Sallie; Ky.; China, 1906-31.
Provence, Herbert Winston; S. C.; China, 1904-12.
Provence, Mary (Hall) (Mrs. H. W.); Va.; China, 1904-12.

Pruitt, Cicero Washington; Ga.; China, 1881–1936.
Pruitt, Ida R. (Tiffany) (Mrs. C. W.); Wis.; China, 1882–84.
Pruitt, Anna (Seward) (Mrs. C. W.); Ohio; China, 1888–1936.
Pruitt, Ida; China; China, 1912–20.
Pruitt, Samuel O.; S. C.; China, 1920–25.
Pruitt, Mary (Cullom) (Mrs. S. O.); S. C.; China, 1920–25.
Purser, Frank Moody; Ala.; Brazil, 1922–23.
Purser, Maude Elizabeth (Palmer) (Mrs. F. M.); Miss.; Brazil, 1922–23.
Puthuff, E. A.; Ky.; Brazil, 1885–88.
Puthuff, Emma (Fox) (Mrs. E. A.); Ala.; Brazil, 1885–88.
Putney, Nellie Lee; Va.; China, 1923–37.

Qualls, Samuel Alvis; Tenn.; Brazil, 1951– .
Qualls, Emmanetta Belle (Harbour) (Mrs. S. A.); Kans.; Brazil, 1951– .
Quarles, James C.; Va.; Argentina, 1908–11, 1918–52; Uruguay, 1911–18.
Quarles, Helen (Taylor) (Mrs. J. C.); Ky.; Argentina, 1908–11, 1918–52; Uruguay, 1911–18.
Quarles, Lemuel Cleveland; Va.; Argentina, 1910–13, 1929–50; Uruguay, 1913–29.
Quarles, Jennie (Saunders) (Mrs. L. C.); Va.; Argentina, 1910–13, 1929–50; Uruguay, 1913–29.
Quick, Oswald Jackson; Mo.; Japan, 1940–41; China, 1941–49; Philippines, 1949–51; Formosa, 1951– .
Quick, Mary Evelyn (Jones) (Mrs. O. J.); Mo.; China, 1946–49; Philippines, 1949–51; Formosa, 1951– .
Quillen, E. H.; Tenn.; Brazil, 1879–82.

Ragland, James Keith; Okla.; Lebanon, 1953– .
Ragland, Leola Lee (Kelley) (Mrs. J. K.); Okla.; Lebanon, 1953– .
Raley, Harry Llewellyn; S. C.; Formosa, 1954– .
Raley, Helen Frances (Bibb) (Mrs. H. L.); Miss.; Formosa, 1954– .
Ramsbottom, Minnie Ethel; Neb.; China, 1919–30.
Ramsour, Hilario B., Jr.; Tex.; Japan, 1939–40; Hawaii, 1940–41, 1946– ; Argentina, 1941–46.
Ramsour, Vera Mabel (Howard) (Mrs. H. B., Jr.); Tex.; Japan, 1939–40; Hawaii, 1940–41, 1946– ; Argentina, 1941–46.
Randall, Ruth; Mich.; Brazil, 1914–52.
Randle, Horace A., M.D.; England; China, 1894–98.
Randle, Mrs. H. A.; England; China, 1894–98.
Rankin, Manly Whitfield; S. C.; China, 1923–54; Malaya, 1954– .
Rankin, Grace Tennessee (Elliott) (Mrs. M. W.); Tex,; China, 1919–54; Malaya, 1954– .
Rankin, Milledge Theron; S. C.; China, 1921–35.
Rankin, Valleria (Greene) (Mrs. M. T.); China; China, 1920–35.
Rankin, Samuel Gardner, M.D.; Miss.; China, 1947–55; Hong Kong, 1955– .
Rankin, Miriam Elizabeth (Thomas) (Mrs. S. G.); S. C.; Hawaii, 1942–47; China, 1947–55; Hong Kong, 1955– .
Ratliff, John Durwood; N. Mex.; Honduras, 1952– .
Ratliff, Wynona Maxine (Haragan) (Mrs. J. D.); N. Mex.; Honduras, 1952– .
Rawlinson, Frank Joseph; England; China, 1902–21.
Rawlinson, Carrie (Dietz) (Mrs. F. J.); Md.; China, 1902–17.
Rawlinson, Florence (Lang) (Mrs. F. J.); Ohio; China, 1917–21.
Ray, Bonnie Jean; Ga.; China, 1918–50; Hawaii, 1950–54.
Ray, Daniel Brooks; China; Korea, 1953– .
Ray, Frances Jean (Deal) (Mrs. D. B.); Tex.; Korea, 1953– .
Ray, Emit Ozene; Tex.; Bahama Islands; 1954– .
Ray, Kathryn (McCluney) (Mrs. E. O.); Ariz.; Bahama Islands, 1954– .
Ray, Hermon S.; Conn.; Japan, 1934–37.
Ray, Rayberta Nell (Reed) (Mrs. H. S.); Ore.; Japan, 1934–37.
Ray, Jefferson Franklin; Miss.; Japan, 1904–42.
Ray, Daisy Winston (Pettus) (Mrs. J. F.); Ala.; Japan, 1904–42.
Ray, Rex; Tex.; China, 1919–51; Korea, 1951–55.
Ray, Janet (Gilman) (Mrs. Rex); China; China, 1921–51; Korea, 1951–55.
Ray, Stanley E.; Okla.; Nigeria, 1953– .
Ray, Ernestine Jane (Wilson) (Mrs. S. E.); Okla.; Nigeria, 1953– .
Rea, Elizabeth E.; Ill.; China, 1910–34.
Reagan, Lucille; Tex.; Nigeria, 1921–37.
Reeves, Harold Philmon; La.; Thailand, 1951– .
Reeves, Rose (Lengefeld) (Mrs. H. P.); Tex.; Thailand, 1951– .
Reid, Orvil Wilson; Okla.; Mexico, 1938– .
Reid, Jewell (Starr) (Mrs. O. W.); Okla.; Mexico, 1938–40.
Reid, Alma (Ervin) (Mrs. O. W.); Tenn.; Mexico, 1943– .
Reid, T. A.; Ga.; Nigeria, 1857–64.
Reid, Mary (Canfield) (Mrs. T. A.); S. C.; Nigeria, 1857–58.
Renfrow, Harold Edward; Mo.; Brazil, 1955– .
Renfrow, Nona Mae (Baumgartner) (Mrs. H. E.); Mo.; Brazil, 1955– .
Reno, Loren M.; Pa.; Brazil, 1904–35.
Reno, Alice (Wymer) (Mrs. L. M.); Pa.; Brazil, 1904–38.
Rice, Maggie; Mo.; Brazil, 1887–88.
Richardson, Frank Raymond; Tex.; Brazil, 1953–55.
Richardson, Doris Anatole (Morrison) (Mrs. F. R.); Tex.; Brazil, 1953–55.
Richardson, Jarrett Wood Henry, Jr.; Ala.; Nigeria, 1944– .
Richardson, Margaret L. (Sampson), M.D. (Mrs. J. W. H., Jr.); S. C.; Nigeria, 1944– .
Richardson, John S.; Ark.; Nigeria, 1924–33.
Richardson, Della (Black) (Mrs. J. S.); Okla.; Nigeria, 1924–33.
Ricketson, Robert Fleming; Ga.; China, 1936–52; Philippines, 1952– .

Ricketson, Bettie (Abernathy) (Mrs. R. F.); Okla.; China, 1936-52; Philippines, 1952- .
Riddell, Gerald Fred; Tex.; Colombia, 1944- .
Riddell, Virgie (Marion) (Mrs. G. F.); Miss.; Colombia, 1944- .
Riddell, Olive Pauline; Va.; China, 1919-53.
Ridenour, Emily Crea; Tenn.; Colombia, 1945- .
Riffey, John Leslie; Ark.; Brazil, 1935- .
Riffey, Prudence (Amos) (Mrs. J. L.); Ark.; Brazil, 1935- .
Rines, Annie Josephine; Tenn.; Nigeria, 1944- .
Roach, Benjamin Pleasant; Tenn.; China, 1904-18.
Roach, Laureola (Lloyd) (Mrs. B. P.); Va.; China, 1904-18.
Roberson, Cecil F.; Miss.; Nigeria, 1949- .
Roberson, Edith (Coats) (Mrs. C. F.); Miss.; Nigeria, 1949- .
Roberts, Frances Everett; S. C.; Paraguay, 1946- .
Roberts, Issachar J.; Tenn.; China, 1845-52.
Roberts, Virginia (Young) (Mrs. I. J.); Ky.; China, 1850-52.
Robertson, Naomi Brooks; Ky.; Nigeria, 1929-37.
Robertson, Reuben Boyd; Okla.; Argentina, 1950- .
Robertson, Jane (Meskimen) (Mrs. R. B.); Tex.; Argentina, 1950- .
Robinson, Gordon Eugene; Ore.; Nigeria, 1955- .
Robinson, Maxine (Williams) (Mrs. G. E.); Tex.; Nigeria, 1955- .
Robison, Oren Charles, Jr.; Okla.; Nigeria, 1952- .
Robison, Martha (Boaz) (Mrs. O. C., Jr.); Ky.; Nigeria, 1952- .
Rogers, Jesse M.; Tex.; China, 1916-31.
Rogers, Laura Judson (Learned) (Mrs. J. M.); Ohio; China, 1917-31.
Rogers, Lillie Otera; Tex.; Malaya, 1953- .
Rohm, Alma Hazel; Tex.; Nigeria, 1950- .
Rohrer, John Quincy Adams; Md.; Japan, 1859-60.
Rohrer, Sarah (Robinson) (Mrs. J. Q. A.); Pa.; Japan, 1859-60.
Roper, John Anderson, Jr., M.D.; S. C.; Lebanon, 1954- .
Roper, Ruth (Atkinson), M.D. (Mrs. J. A., Jr.); N. J.; Lebanon, 1954- .
Roper, Cleo Anita; Ga.; Nigeria, 1954- .
Ross, J. Wilson; Tex.; Mexico, 1950-53; Spanish Publishing House, 1953- .
Ross, Jimmie Ruth (Meek) (Mrs. J. W.); Tex.; Mexico, 1950-53; Spanish Publishing House, 1953- .
Rouse, William Thomas; Ala.; Brazil, 1904-05.
Rouse, Sallie (Milford) (Mrs. W. T.); Tex.; Brazil, 1904-05.
Rowden, Paul Dennis, Jr.; Ga.; Israel, 1951- .
Rowden, Marjorie Ann (Cole) (Mrs. P. D., Jr.); Ga.; Israel, 1951- .
Rowe, John Hansford; Va.; Japan, 1906-29.
Rowe, Margaret (Cobb) (Mrs. J. H.); Tex.; Japan, 1906-19.
Rowe, Carrie Hooker (Chiles) (Mrs. J. H.); Miss.; Japan, 1915-35.

Rowland, Ben; Tex.; China, 1913-26.
Rowland, Perle (Harrison) (Mrs. Ben); Miss.; China, 1907-26.
Rudd, Augustus Bartow; Va.; Mexico, 1888-98.
Rudd, Mae (Bagby) (Mrs. A. B.); Ky.; Mexico, 1889-98.
Rumphol, Ruth Myrtle; Wis.; Nigeria, 1951- .
Runyan, Farrell Edward; S. C.; Nigeria, 1946- .
Runyan, Elizabeth (Barnett) (Mrs. F. E.); S. C.; Nigeria, 1946- .
Russell, D. Rudalph; Tex.; China, 1948-49; Thailand, 1949- .
Russell, Joy (Day) (Mrs. D. R.); Tex.; China, 1948-49; Thailand, 1949- .
Russell, Francis Emily; Va.; Mexico, 1888-89.
Ryan, Susan Roberta; Ala.; Chile, 1945- .

Sadler, George Washington; Va.; Nigeria, 1914-32.
Sadler, Annie Laurie (Maynard) (Mrs. G. W.); Ala.; Nigeria, 1919-32.
Sale, Edmonia Bell; Va.; China, 1895-99.
Sallee, Hannah Fair; Ky.; China, 1913-53.
Sallee, W. Eugene; Ky.; China, 1903-31.
Sallee, Annie (Jenkins) (Mrs. W. E.); Tex.; China, 1905-47.
Sampson, Mary Hastings; Ky.; China, 1945-50; Philippines, 1950-51; Formosa, 1951- .
Sams, Audrey Marshall; Tex.; Argentina, 1946-50.
Sams, Helen Gertrude (McCubbin) (Mrs. A. M.); Mo.; Argentina, 1946-50.
Sanderford, Matthew Anderson; Tex.; Uruguay, 1952- .
Sanderford, Dora Jean (McDonald) (Mrs. M. A.); Tex.; Uruguay, 1952- .
Sanders, Florence Newton; Ga.; Mexico, 1907-12.
Sanders, Adria (London) (Mrs. F. N.); Tenn.; Mexico, 1907-12.
Sanders, Frances Marian; S. C.; Mexico, 1955- .
Sanders, Eva Mildred; Va.; Nigeria, 1931- .
Sanderson, Paul Edwin; Ala.; Brazil, 1950- .
Sanderson, Martha (Masden) (Mrs. P. E.); Ky.; Brazil, 1950- .
Sandford, Herman; Tex.; Nigeria, 1949-50.
Sandford, Juanita (Dadisman) (Mrs. Herman); Kans.; Nigeria, 1949-50.
Sandlin, Annie; Ga.; China, 1909-47.
Satterwhite, James Pumphrey, M.D.; N. C.; Japan, 1952- .
Satterwhite, Altha Loretta (Smith) (Mrs. J. P.); N. C.; Japan, 1952- .
Saunders, Davis Lee; S. C.; Nigeria, 1951- .
Saunders, Mary (Hogg) (Mrs. D. L.); S. C.; Nigeria, 1951- .
Saunders, Joel Roscoe; Tenn.; China, 1901-44.
Saunders, Mable (Earp) (Mrs. J. R.); Ark.; China, 1901-43.
Saunders, Letha Myrtle; Tex.; Brazil, 1938- .
Saunders, Mary Lucile; Mich.; China, 1939-52; Philippines, 1952- .
Savage, Loy Jesmine; Tex.; China, 1912-25.
Scaggs, Josephine Anna; Okla.; Nigeria, 1939- .
Scanlon, Alton Clark; Tex.; Guatemala, 1953- .
Scanlon, Sarah (Martin) (Mrs. A. C.); Ky.; Guatemala, 1953- .

Foreign Missionaries, 1845–1955

Scarlett, Lenora; Canada; China, 1910–48.
Schell, Naomi Elizabeth; N. C.; Japan, 1921–46.
Schilling, John G.; Germany; China, 1859–64.
Schilling, Kate (Lowther) (Mrs. J. G.) ; W. Va.; China, 1860–64.
Schmidt, Kermit Johnson; Ill.; Brazil, 1943–48.
Schmidt, Margaret Caroline (Foltz) (Mrs. K. J.) ; Okla.; Brazil, 1943–48.
Schweinsberg, Henry William; Australia; Colombia, 1941– .
Schweinsberg, Dorothy (Brickell) (Mrs. H. W.) ; Mo.; Colombia, 1941– .
Scott, Marcus J.; Tex.; China, 1921–22.
Scott, Leta Elizabeth (Denham) (Mrs. M. J.) ; Tex.; China, 1921–22.
Schwartz, Evelyn; Tenn.; Hawaii, 1949–52; Indonesia, 1952– .
Scoggin, Blainard Elmo; N. C.; Israel, 1949– .
Scoggin, Hannah Belle (Pearlman) (Mrs. B. E.) ; S. C.; Israel, 1949– .
Scull, Ancil Beach; Ind.; Indonesia, 1955– .
Scull, Rubye Lois (Northcutt) (Mrs. A. B.) ; Okla.; Indonesia, 1955– .
Sears, Stockwell Bettes; China; China, 1943–51; Indonesia, 1951– .
Sears, Darlyne (Horner) (Mrs. S. B.) ; Mo.; China, 1943–51; Indonesia, 1951– .
Sears, William H.; Mo.; China, 1891–1922.
Sears, Effie (Johnson) (Mrs. W. H.) ; Mo.; China, 1891–1904.
Sears, Grace (Boyd) (Mrs. W. H.) ; Australia; China, 1906–42.
Seats, V. Lavell; Ark.; Nigeria, 1941– .
Seats, Helen Elizabeth (Franklin) (Mrs. V. L.) ; Mich.; Nigeria, 1941– .
Seright, Gerald Ben; Okla.; Brazil, 1951– .
Seright, Kezzia Mae (Studebaker) (Mrs. G. B.) ; Okla.; Brazil, 1951– .
Sharpley, Dan Neal; Tex.; Brazil, 1948– .
Sharpley, Doris (Allred) (Mrs. D. N.) ; Tex.; Brazil, 1948– .
Shelton, Ray Ellis; Tenn.; Uruguay, 1949– .
Shelton, Mary Steele (McKee) (Mrs. R. E.) ; Ga.; Uruguay, 1949– .
Shepard, John W.; Tenn.; Brazil, 1906–31.
Shepard, Rena (Groover) (Mrs. J. W.) ; Ga.; Brazil, 1906–31.
Shepard, John Watson, Jr.; Brazil; Japan, 1948– .
Shepard, Jean (Prince) (Mrs. J. W., Jr.) ; Ill.; Japan, 1948– .
Shepherd, Charles R.; England; China, 1913–18.
Shepherd, Ellen (Hildebrand) (Mrs. C. R.) ; Ill.; China, 1913–17.
Sherer, Robert Charles; Ala.; Japan, 1948– .
Sherer, Helen (Mitchell) (Mrs. R. C.) ; Ill.; Japan, 1948– .
Sherwood, Wattie Bethea; S. C.; Brazil, 1918–52.
Sherwood, Eunice (Allen) (Mrs. W. B.) ; S. C.; Brazil, 1921–52.
Shiver, Mavis Gladys; Ala.; Japan, 1953– .
Shoemake, Howard Lee; Tex.; Colombia, 1947–53; Ecuador, 1953– .
Shoemake, Dorothy Dell (Moore) (Mrs. H. L.) ; Tex.; Colombia, 1947–53; Ecuador, 1953– .

Short, Lois Jaxie; Tex.; China, 1946–50; Hong Kong, 1950– .
Shuck, Jehu Lewis; Va.; China, 1846–53.
Shuck, Eliza G. (Sexton) (Mrs. J. L.) ; Ala.; China, 1847–51.
Shumate, Margie; Va.; China, 1914–50; Hong Kong, 1950–52; Thailand, 1952– .
Simmons, E. Z.; Miss.; China, 1870–1912.
Simmons, Maggie D. (McClamrock) (Mrs. E. Z.) ; Tenn.; China, 1870–1913.
Simpson, Blanche Virginia; Ill.; Brazil, 1936– .
Singleton, Ethel; La.; Chile, 1941–49.
Skinner, Katherine Ruth; Tex.; Mexico, 1947– .
Skinner, William, M.D.; Tenn.; Paraguay, 1950– .
Skinner, Frances (Lawrence) (Mrs. William) ; S. C.; Paraguay, 1950– .
Sledge, Randall Dothan; La.: Peru, 1954– .
Sledge, Dorothy (Sewall) (Mrs. R. D.) ; Minn.; Peru, 1954– .
Small, Tom Grisham; Tex.; Southern Rhodesia, 1955– .
Small, Mary Enid (Burnett) (Mrs. T. G.) ; Va.; Southern Rhodesia, 1955– .
Smelser, Alta; Iowa; Mexico, 1891–93.
Smith, Cathryn Lucile; Ga.; Brazil, 1946– .
Smith, Charles Edwin; Ark.; Nigeria, 1884–1909.
Smith, Florence (Blandford) (Mrs. C. E.) ; Ky.; Nigeria, 1884–84.
Smith, Cynthia (Morris) (Mrs. C. E.) ; Mo.; Nigeria, 1885–89.
Smith, Lucy (Shentson) (Mrs. C. E.) ; Wis.; Nigeria, 1891–1909.
Smith, Edwin Dargan, M.D.; S. C.; China, 1921–28.
Smith, Elizabeth (Mudd) (Mrs. E. D.) ; Ky.; China, 1921–28.
Smith, Essie Elizabeth; Ga.; China, 1923–30.
Smith, Harley; Tex.; Brazil, 1923–45.
Smith, Alice Anne (Bagby) (Mrs. Harley) ; Brazil; Brazil, 1920–45.
Smith, Hazel Irene; Okla.; Argentina, 1945–54.
Smith, Hoke, Jr.; Fla.; Colombia, 1952– .
Smith, Wanda Arleigh (Karnes) (Mrs. Hoke, Jr.) ; Tex.; Colombia, 1952– .
Smith, James Willis; Ga.; Israel, 1955– .
Smith, Mary Elizabeth (Flanders) (Mrs. J. W.) ; Ga.; Israel, 1955– .
Smith, Lucy Elizabeth; Mo.; China, 1936–49; Hong Kong, 1949–51; Japan, 1951– .
Smith, Mildred A.; Tex.; Nigeria, 1941–45.
Smith, Olive Bertha; S. C.; China, 1917–48; Formosa, 1948– .
Smith, Roscoe C.; Tenn.; Japan, 1921–26.
Smith, Sadie Gaines (Wilson) (Mrs. R. C.) ; Tenn.; Japan, 1921–26.
Smyth, Jerry Paul; Tex.; Brazil, 1953– .
Smyth, Frances Evelyn (Hennessee) (Mrs. J. P.) ; Ala.; Brazil, 1953– .
Snell, Oleta Elizabeth; Tex.; Chile, 1943– .
Snelling, Amy Ann; S. C.; Paraguay, 1955– .
Snow, Laura Frances; N. C.; Chile, 1955– .
Snuggs, Edward Thomas; England; China, 1904–12, 1914–35.
Snuggs, Josephine (Hebinger) (Mrs. E. T.) ; Hungary; China, 1904–12, 1914–32.

Snuggs, Faith Mary; China; China, 1922-35.
Snuggs, Harold Hebinger; China; China, 1922- .
Snuggs, Grace (Mason) (Mrs. H. H.); Va.; China, 1923- .
Solesbee, Willie Alsberry; Ark.; China, 1947-49; Philippines, 1949- .
Solesbee, Ella Ruth (Enloe) (Mrs. W. A.); Tex.; China, 1947-49; Philippines, 1949- .
Soper, Edwin Herbert; England; Brazil, 1885-93.
Soper, Grace (Mallaleer) (Mrs. E. H.); England; Brazil, 1886-93.
Sowell, Sidney McFarland; Va.; Argentina, 1903-42.
Sowell, Ermine (Bagby) (Mrs. S. McF.); Brazil; Argentina, 1903-39.
Spear, Bobby Lee; Okla.; Thailand, 1954- .
Spear, Norma Jean (Butler) (Mrs. B. L.); Okla.; Thailand, 1954- .
Speares, Carree; S. C.; Colombia, 1945-49; Chile, 1949-52.
Spence, Marjorie; N. C.; Chile, 1925- .
Spence, Raymond Morris; Tex.; Japan, 1948-55.
Spence, Inez (Gilliland) (Mrs. R. M.); Tex.; Japan, 1948-55.
Spencer, Alvin Elbert, Jr.; Ill.; Japan, 1952- .
Spencer, Doris Louise (Scalf) (Mrs. A. E., Jr.); N. C.; Japan, 1952- .
Spight, Thomas; Miss.; Argentina, 1905-20.
Spight, Ella (Fallas) (Mrs. Thomas); Mich.; Argentina, 1905-21.
Sprinkle, S. Dan., Jr.; Tex.; Argentina, 1955- .
Sprinkle, LaVora (Murfin) (Mrs. S. D., Jr.); Ind.; Argentina, 1955- .
Stallings, Hattie; Tex.; China, 1916-47.
Stamps, Drure Fletcher; Ga.; China, 1920-52; Hawaii, 1952-55.
Stamps, Elizabeth (Belk) (Mrs. D. F.); Va.; China, 1920-52; Hawaii, 1952-55.
Standley, Robert Ralph, Jr.; Ohio; Brazil, 1949- .
Standley, Bertha (Ewing) (Mrs. R. R., Jr.); N. Y.; Brazil, 1949- .
Stanton, Rufus Burleson; Tex.; Brazil, 1919-28.
Stanton, Marjorie (Taylor) (Mrs. R. B.); Brazil; Brazil, 1921-28.
Stapp, Charles F.; Tex.; Brazil, 1909-51.
Stapp, Mary (Shannon) (Mrs. C. F.); Tex.; Brazil, 1909-41.
Stapp, Willie Pearl (Dunston) (Mrs. C. F.); Ga.; Brazil, 1921-51.
Starmer, Roy Franklin; Okla.; Romania, 1938-49; Italy, 1949- .
Starmer, Lillie Mae (Hylton) (Mrs. R. F.); Tenn.; Romania, 1938-49; Italy, 1949- .
Starns, Fanny Louise; Miss.; Thailand, 1955- .
Steele, Eugene Earle; Ga.; China, 1920-29.
Steele, Leila Kathryn (Burnett) (Mrs. E. L.); Ga.; China, 1920-29.
Steelman, Isaac Newton; N. Y.; Mexico, 1892-96.
Steelman, Mrs. I. N.; N. Y.; Mexico, 1892-96.
Stein, Sallie; Va.; China, 1880-88.
Stenger, Bertha; N. Y.; Brazil, 1898-1900.
Stephens, Marjorie Lorraine; N. Mex.; Nigeria, 1952- .
Stephens, Peyton; Mo.; China, 1893-1924.

Stephens, Mary (Thompson) (Mrs. Peyton); Ky.; China, 1893-1942.
Stephens, Silas Emmett; Ga.; China, 1904-26.
Stephens, Irene Mouring (Carter) (Mrs. S. E.); Ga.; China, 1904-42.
Steward, Alberta Louise; Mo.; Brazil, 1935- .
Stewart, Reba Cloud; Ga.; China, 1919-36; Manchuria, 1936-42.
Stokes, Lucy Belle; Okla.; Japan, 1949- .
Stone, Richard H.; Va.; Nigeria, 1858-69.
Stone, Susan J. (Broaddus) (Mrs. R. H.); Va.; Nigeria, 1858-69.
Stout, William W.; Ky.; China, 1914-29.
Stout, Harriet (Campbell) (Mrs. W. W.); Ala.; China, 1914-29.
Stover, Sherrod Sylvester; Tex.; Brazil, 1940- .
Stover, Alice (Armstrong) (Mrs. S. S.); Tex.; Brazil, 1940- .
Stover, Thomas Bertram; S. C.; Brazil, 1922-54.
Stover, Ione (Buster) (Mrs. T. B.); Tex.; Brazil, 1923-48.
Stover, Etta Josephine (Withauer) (Mrs. T. B.); D. C.; Brazil, 1947- .
Stribling, Grace; S. C.; China, 1921-29, 1936-45.
Strother, Greene Wallace; La.; China, 1925-53; Malaya, 1953- .
Strother, Martha Lucile (Krause) (Mrs. G. W.); Neb.; China, 1925-53; Malaya, 1953- .
Strouse, George Henry; N. J.; Nigeria, 1903-04.
Strouse, Kate (Chidsey) (Mrs. G. H.); N. Y.; Nigeria, 1904-04.
Stuart, James Percy; Va.; Italy, 1908-17.
Stuart, Lillian (Lewis) (Mrs. J. P.); Kans.; Italy, 1908-18.
Stuart, Malcolm W.; Ala.; Hawaii, 1941-48, 1949- ; China, 1948-49.
Stuart, Edyth (Boyd) (Mrs. M. W.); Tex.; China, 1935-41; Hawaii, 1941- .
Sullivan, Patrick Donal; Tenn.; Brazil, 1940-50.
Sullivan, Janie (Nooner) (Mrs. P. D.); Tenn.; Brazil, 1940-50.
Summer, Mattie Vie; Ga.; China, 1920-37.
Summers, Mabel Miller; Ky.; Lebanon, 1948- .
Sundstrom, John; Sweden; China, 1910-31.
Sundstrom, Maude (Hubbard) (Mrs. John); N. Y.; China, 1910-31.
Sutherland, Daniel Francis; Ky.; Mexico, 1900-1900.
Sutherland, Louise (Eades) (Mrs. D. F.); Ky.; Mexico, 1900-1900.
Swann, Ada Ruth; N. C.; Lebanon, 1950-52.
Swann, Nancy; Tex.; China, 1912-20.
Swearinger, Jennie Lu; Tex.; Brazil, 1922-34.
Swenson, Erhardt Sven; Sweden; Argentina, 1923- .
Swenson, Anna M. (Granberg) (Mrs. E. S.); N. Y.; Argentina, 1923- .

Talley, Frances; N. C.; Japan, 1946- .
Tanner, Martha Julia; Ga.; Nigeria, 1946- .
Tatum, Ezra Frank; N. C.; China, 1888-1934.
Tatum, Alice (Flagg) (Mrs. E. F.); Me.; China, 1889-1914.
Tatum, Mona (Hall) (Mrs. E. F.); Canada; China, 1921-34.
Tatum, Hubert Rogers; Ga.; Hawaii, 1949- .

Tatum, Margaret (Gasteiger) (Mrs. H. R.); Tenn.; Hawaii, 1949- .
Taylor, Adrian S., M.D.; Ala.; China, 1906-16.
Taylor, Annie May (Cox) (Mrs. A. S.); Ky.; China, 1906-16.
Taylor, Ethel Fay; Fla.; China, 1943-50; Hong Kong, 1950-52; Indonesia, 1952- .
Taylor, Francis Willard; Tex.; Brazil, 1921-36.
Taylor, Caroline Elizabeth (Smith) (Mrs. F. W.); Tex.; Brazil, 1921-37.
Taylor, George Boardman; Va.; Italy, 1873-1907.
Taylor, Susan Spottswood (Braxton) (Mrs. G. B.); Va.; Italy, 1873-1884.
Taylor, Ida; Miss.; China, 1905-24.
Taylor, James Jackson; Ala.; Brazil, 1891-1924.
Taylor, Ada L. (Mrs. J. J.); Tenn.; Brazil, 1891-1926.
Taylor, Maye Bell; Tex.; Brazil, 1938- .
Taylor, Orville Walters; Ark.; Nigeria, 1955- .
Taylor, Evelyn Adella (Bonham) (Mrs. O. W.); Tenn; Nigeria, 1955- .
Taylor, Richard Vipon, Jr.; Ala.; China, 1912-27.
Taylor, Anne Russell (Sampson) (Mrs. R. V., Jr.); Va.; China, 1912-27.
Taylor, Sara Frances; S. C.; Argentina, 1945- .
Taylor, William Carey; Ky.; Brazil, 1915- .
Taylor, Grace (Cisco) (Mrs. W. C.); Ky.; Brazil, 1915- .
Taylor, Zachary Clay; Miss.; Brazil, 1882-1919.
Taylor, Kate Stevens (Crawford) (Mrs. Z. C.); Tex.; Brazil, 1882-94.
Taylor, Laura (Barton) (Mrs. Z. C.); Tex.; China, 1889-94; Brazil, 1894-1919.
Teal, Edna Earl; Ga.; China, 1910-43.
Tennison, Grayson C.; Tex.; Brazil, 1949- .
Tennison, Betty Jean (Waters) (Mrs. G. C.); Tex.; Brazil, 1949- .
Terry, Adolph John; La.; Brazil, 1912-45.
Terry, Lulie (Sparkman) (Mrs. A. J.); Fla.; Brazil, 1912- .
Terry, Virginia Katherine; Tenn.; Brazil, 1951- .
Tharpe, Edgar Jefferson; Ga.; Hawaii, 1947- .
Tharpe, Gertrude (Addis) (Mrs. E. J.); S. C.; Hawaii, 1947- .
Thomas, Isaac T.; Ala.; China, 1920-22.
Thomas, Annie Laura (Gary) (Mrs. I. T.); Ala.; China, 1920-22.
Thomas, John Nathaniel; England; Colombia, 1951- .
Thomas, Evelyn Vera (Arnold) (Mrs. J. N.); Canada; Colombia, 1951- .
Thomas, Thomas Moses; Ala.; China, 1904-08.
Thomas, Annie May (Griffith) (Mrs. T. M.); La.; China, 1904-08.
Thomason, Lillian; Tex.; China, 1923-39.
Thompson, Emma Belle; Ky.; China, 1900-17.
Thompson, Leslie Albert; Mo.; China, 1935-40.
Thompson, Pauline (Prosser) (Mrs. L. A.); Mo.; China, 1935-40.
Tilford, Frances Lorene; Tenn.; China, 1936-51; Formosa, 1951- .
Tinkle, Amanda Arvilla; Ark.; Nigeria, 1938- .
Tipton, William Henry; Tenn.; China, 1904-46.
Tipton, Nellie (Roberts) (Mrs. W. H.); Tenn.; China, 1904-07.
Tipton, Mary Greenlee (Bryson) (Mrs. W. H.); N. C.; China, 1909-46.
Tisdale, Billy Bob; Ark.; Philippines, 1955- .
Tisdale, Helen (McWilliams) (Mrs. B. B.); Tex.; Philippines, 1955- .
Tobey, Thomas W.; R. I.; China, 1846-49.
Tobey, Isabella (Hall) (Mrs. T. W.); Va.; China, 1846-49.
Todd, Anna Frances; Ky.; Colombia, 1945- .
Todd, Pearl; Ga.; China, 1921-50; Japan, 1950- .
Tolbert, Malcolm Oliver; Ill.; Brazil, 1952- .
Tolbert, Nell (Sills) (Mrs. M. O.); La.; Brazil, 1952- .
Tompkins, Allen Lloyd; Tenn.; China, 1920-22.
Tompkins, Lenor Irene (Thompson) (Mrs. A. L.); Ohio; China, 1920-22.
Torstrick, Melvin Eugene; Ky.; Chile, 1954- .
Torstrick, Shirley Mae (Lee) (Mrs. M. E.); Ky.; Chile, 1954- .
Townsend, Joseph Reed; Tex.; China, 1943-48.
Townsend, Oleta (Wilmoth) (Mrs. J. R.); Okla.; China, 1943-48.
Townshend, Sidney Joseph; England; China, 1917-38.
Townshend, Sarah Elizabeth (Crook) (Mrs. S. J.); England; China, 1917-38.
Trainham, Annie Genevieve; Va.; China, 1935-39.
Treadwell, Elmer Maurice; Tex.; Brazil, 1948- .
Treadwell, Winona (Purvis) (Mrs. E. M.); Tex.; Brazil, 1948- .
Treadwell, M. A.; Ala.; Japan, 1921-22.
Treadwell, Ruth (Espy) (Mrs. M. A.); Ga.; Japan, 1921-22.
Trimble, Selden Y.; Ky.; Nigeria, 1856-59.
Trimble, Mary E. (Moorhead) (Mrs. S. Y.); Ky.; Nigeria, 1856-59.
Truly, Mary Elizabeth; Tex.; Nigeria, 1938- .
Tucker, Louise; Ky.; China, 1910-21.
Tumblin, John Addison; S. C.; Brazil, 1921- .
Tumblin, Frances (Marrow) (Mrs. J. A.); Va.; Brazil, 1922- .
Tupper, Mary Caldwell; Ga.; Mexico, 1884-86.
Turlington, Henry Eugene; Fla.; China, 1946-50.
Turlington, Helen (Nobles) (Mrs. H. E.); Va.; China, 1946-50.
Turner, Jesse Valmore; Ark.; China, 1909-13.
Turner, Bonnie Belle (Tatum) (Mrs. J. V.); Ark.; China, 1909-13.
Turner, John William; Tex.; Lebanon, 1954- .
Turner, Mozelle (Hodge) (Mrs. J. W.); Tex.; Lebanon, 1954- .
Tyler, Grace; S. C.; Italy, 1952- .
Underwood, Joseph Buie; Tex.; Brazil, 1943-55.
Underwood, Mary Lea (Oxford) (Mrs. J. B.); La.; Brazil, 1943-55.
Van Lear, Valenza Marie; Va.; Nigeria, 1954- .
Vance, Shelby William, M.D.; N. C.; China, 1934-51.
Vance, Frances E. (Hudson) (Mrs. S. W.); Va.; China, 1934-51.
Vaughn, Mary Edith; Va.; Brazil, 1952- .

Vernon, Vance Ora; Ala.; Brazil, 1946– .
Vernon, Sue (Patrick) (Mrs. V. O.); Ala.; Brazil, 1946– .
Vineyard, Onis; Tex.; Brazil, 1940– .
Vingren, Carl; Sweden; China, 1905–08.
Vingren, Sigrid (Hjelm) (Mrs. Carl); Sweden, 1905–08.
Voorheis, Genevieve; Tenn.; Brazil, 1906–18.

Wagner, Lucy Elizabeth; Mo.; Korea, 1955– .
Wakem, John Bedrum; Syria; Nigeria, 1904–05.
Wakem, Linnie (Whipple) (Mrs. J. B.); Ohio; Nigeria, 1905–05.
Walden, Ruth Hannah; Va.; Nigeria, 1934– .
Waldron, Vada Mace; Tex.; Argentina, 1937– .
Walker, Blanche Rose; Tex.; China, 1910–38.
Walker, Catherine Berryhill; Ga.; China, 1946–52; Indonesia, 1952– .
Walker, Horace Glenn, M.D.; Okla.; Nigeria, 1936–47.
Walker, Mary Olive (Baldock) (Mrs. H. G.); Tex.; Nigeria, 1936–47.
Walker, Jack Earl, M.D.; Mo.; Nigeria, 1951– .
Walker, Sarah Ella (Cook) (Mrs. J. E.); Tex.; Nigeria, 1951– .
Walker, William Levi; Ky.; Japan, 1949– .
Walker, Mary Frances (Culpepper) (Mrs. W. L.); China; Japan, 1949– .
Walker, W. S.; Ga.; China, 1881–84.
Walker, Lillian Ellen (Mateer) (Mrs. W. S.); Pa.; China, 1883–84.
Wallace, William Lindsey, M.D.; Tenn.; China, 1935–51.
Walne, Ernest Nathan; Miss.; Japan, 1892–1935.
Walne, Claudia (McCann) (Mrs. E. N.); Ky.; Japan, 1892–1935.
Walne, Florence; Japan; Japan, 1919–34.
Walters, Mary Olivia; Fla.; Japan, 1923–29.
Walworth, Earl Harvey; Ill.; Mexico, 1955– .
Walworth, Martha Louise (Thomas) (Mrs. E. H.); Ala.; Mexico, 1955– .
Ward, Cecil Sylvester; Ala.; China, 1940–44.
Ward, Gertrude (Craig) (Mrs. C. S.); Ala.; China, 1940–44.
Ward, Josephine; Mo.; China, 1922–51; Formosa, 1951– .
Ward, Thomas Everett; Ill.; Nigeria, 1908–09.
Ward, Effie Levona (Ewing) (Mrs. T. E.); Ill.; Nigeria, 1908–10.
Ware, James Hamilton; Ga.; China, 1921–51; Hawaii, 1951– .
Ware, Mary Bibb (Long) (Mrs. J. H.); China, 1921–51; Hawaii, 1951– .
Wasson, Melvin Kenneth; Mo.; Nigeria, 1954– .
Wasson, Lillian (Strickland) (Mrs. M. K.); Ark.; Nigeria, 1954– .
Watkins, Elizabeth T.; S. C.; Japan, 1948– .
Watkins, Loretta Rees; Ala.; Nigeria, 1944–48.
Watkins, Asa Carrell; Ala.; Mexico, 1888–1908.
Watkins, Ava (Burton) (Mrs. A. C.); Ind.; Mexico, 1888–1904.
Watkins, Rosa (Schantz) (Mrs. A. C.); Neb.; Mexico, 1904–08.
Watson, James Ollin; Ga.; Argentina, 1950– .
Watson, Frances E. (Scott) (Mrs. J. O.); S. C.; Argentina, 1950– .
Watson, Leslie; Tex.; Japan, 1950– .
Watson, Hazel (Tunstead) (Mrs. Leslie); N. J.; Japan, 1950– .
Watson, Lila Florence; S. C.; China, 1919–50; Hong Kong, 1950– .
Watson, Stephen Lawton; S. C.; Brazil, 1914–50.
Watson, Annie L. (Miller) (Mrs. S. L.); S. C.; Brazil, 1914–50.
Watts, Emma Mildred; Ky.; Nigeria, 1952– .
Watts, James Washington; S. C.; Palestine, 1922–29.
Watts, Mattie Lelia (Reid) (Mrs. J. W.); S. C.; Palestine, 1922–29.
Watts, John Drayton Williams; S. C.; Switzerland, 1948– .
Watts, Winifred (Williams) (Mrs. J. D. W.); Ga.; Switzerland, 1948– .
Webb, William Jackson; Tex.; Mexico, 1941–48; Guatemala, 1948– .
Webb, Carra Inez (Tatum) (Mrs. W. J.); La.; Mexico, 1941–48; Guatemala, 1948– .
Webster, James B.; Vt.; China, 1908–26.
Webster, Alta (Newby) (Mrs. J. B.); Iowa; China, 1912–26.
Weeks, Wilma Jesseline; Neb.; China, 1936–49; Hawaii, 1949–53; Indonesia, 1953– .
Weller, Edith Rose; Ky.; Brazil, 1945– .
Wells, Grace; S. C.; China, 1923–43, 1947–52; Hawaii, 1943–47; Indonesia, 1952– .
Welmaker, Ben Harold; Tex.; Colombia, 1950– .
Welmaker, Janis (Loper) (Mrs. B. H.); Tex.; Colombia, 1950– .
West, Edith O.; Pa.; Brazil, 1920– .
West, Ralph Lee; S. C.; Nigeria, 1945– .
West, Frances (Murphy) (Mrs. R. L.); S. C.; Nigeria, 1945– .
Westbrook, Charles Hart; Ga.; China, 1912–53.
Westbrook, Annie May (Arnold) (Mrs. C. H.); Ga.; China, 1912–20.
Westbrook, Louise (Ellyson) (Mrs. C. H.); Va.; China, 1925–53.
Wester, William Smith; Ga.; Southern Rhodesia, 1955– .
Wester, Blanche Niada (Clement) (Mrs. W. S.); La.; Southern Rhodesia, 1955– .
Westrup, John O.; England; Mexico, 1880–1880.
Westrup, Thomas M.; England; Mexico, 1881–1881.
Whaley, Charles Lloyd, Jr.; Ga.; Japan, 1949– .
Whaley, Lois Eleanor (Linnenkohl) (Mrs. C. L.); Ga.; Japan, 1948– .
Wheat, Ruby Lemira; Okla.; China, 1944–51; Philippines, 1951–53; Korea, 1953– .
Whilden, Bayfield W.; S. C.; China, 1848–55.
Whilden, Eliza Jane (Martin) (Mrs. B. W.); S. C.; China, 1848–50.
Whilden, Mrs. B. W.; ( ); China, 1852–55.
Whilden, Lula; S. C.; China, 1872–1916.
Whirley, Carlton F.; Fla.; Nigeria, 1947– .
Whirley, Enid (Pate) (Mrs. C. F.); Ala.; Nigeria, 1947– .
Whisenhunt, Eph; Ga.; China, 1921–24.
Whisenhunt, Edith (Adair) (Mrs. Eph); Ga.; China, 1921–24.
White, Claudia J.; Md.; China, 1891–1901.

White, Philip Ernest; N. C.; China, 1924–27, 1935–41.
White, Mattie Macon (Norman) (Mrs. P. E.); N. C.; China, 1924–31, 1935–44.
White, Maxcy G.; S. C.; Brazil, 1914– .
White, Kate M. (Cox) (Mrs. M. G.); Iowa; Brazil, 1914– .
White, Georgia Pauline; S. C.; Brazil, 1918– .
Whitten, Charles William; Miss.; Argentina, 1947–53; Spain, 1953– .
Whitten, Nella Dean (Mitchell) (Mrs. C. W.); Miss.; Argentina, 1947–53; Spain, 1953– .
Whittinghill, Dexter Gooch; Ky.; Italy, 1900–39.
Whittinghill, Susy (Taylor) (Mrs. D. G.); Va.; Italy, 1905–39.
Whorton, Mary Jane; Ala.; Nigeria, 1953– .
Wiggins, Edith Ellene; Ga.; Nigeria, 1940–41.
Wilcox, Mary B.; N. Y.; Brazil, 1898–1900.
Wilcox, Everett G.; Mo.; Brazil, 1920–40.
Wilcox, Callie (Perrin) (Mrs. E. G.); Tex.; Brazil, 1920–41.
Wiley, James Hundley; Va.; China, 1921–47.
Wiley, Elizabeth (Ellyson) (Mrs. J. H.); Va.; China, 1921–47.
Wilkerson, Lonnie Otto; Tenn.; China, 1920–25.
Wilkerson, Edna (Wickes) (Mrs. L. O.); Tex.; China, 1920–25.
Willeford, Mary Davis; Tex.; China, 1901–36.
Williams, Lillian Rae; Ky.; Colombia, 1946– .
Williams, James Toy; Ala.; China, 1913–52.
Williams, Laurie M. (Smith) (Mrs. J. T.); Ga.; China, 1913–52.
Williams, Nicholas Butt; Ala.; China, 1871–76.
Williams, Jumille (Whilden) (Mrs. N. B.); S. C.; China, 1872–76.
Williams, Samuel Taswell; Va.; China, 1900–03.
Williams, Thelma Edna; Colo.; China, 1936–50; Formosa, 1950–54; Philippines, 1954– .
Williams, William Jackson, M.D.; Ga.; Nigeria, 1944– .
Williams, Leslie (Sands) (Mrs. W. J.); Okla.; Nigeria, 1944– .
Williamson, Norman F.; Ga.; Japan, 1918–37.
Williamson, Fannie L. (McCall) (Mrs. N. F.); Ga.; Japan, 1919–37.
Willingham, Calder Trueheart; Ga.; Japan, 1902–07, 1911–18.
Willingham, Bessie (Hardy) (Mrs. C. T.); Japan, 1902–10.
Willingham, Foy (Johnson) (Mrs. C. T.); N. C.; Japan, 1911–21.
Willis, Louise Edrington; Md.; China, 1922–29.
Willis, Sadie Miriam; Ark.; Argentina, 1943–47; Paraguay, 1947– .
Wills, James Edward; Miss.; China, 1908–16.
Wills, Sophie (Stark) (Mrs. J. E.); Ky.; China, 1914–16.
Wilson, David Alexander; La.; Mexico, 1886–97.
Wilson, Lizzie (Gooch) (Mrs. D. A.); Miss.; Mexico, 1886–97.
Wilson, Grace Elon; Tex.; China, 1940–42.
Wingo, Virginia; Ala.; Italy, 1949– .
Winn, W. P.; Ill.; Nigeria, 1896–97.
Winn, Alice (Shentson) (Mrs. W. P.); Wis.; Nigeria, 1896–97.
Wise, Gene Hale; N. Mex.; Brazil, 1950– .

Wise, Allene Ruth (Greenlaw) (Mrs. G. H.); Ariz.; Brazil, 1950– .
Withers, Mattie; Tenn.; Mexico, 1886–87.
Wofford, Azile May; S. C.; Argentina, 1923–27.
Wolfard, Rodney Bishop; Colo.; Brazil, 1953– .
Wolfard, Sue (White) (Mrs. R. B.); W. Va.; Brazil, 1953– .
Wollerman, Anna Mae Louise; Ark.; Brazil, 1950– .
Womack, Mary Ruth; Ala.; Nigeria, 1947– .
Wood, James Edward, Jr.; Va.; Japan, 1948– .
Wood, Alma Leacy (McKenzie) (Mrs. J. E., Jr.); Va.; Japan, 1948– .
Wood, Levi Davis; Miss.; Chile, 1939–48.
Wood, Ora (Smith) (Mrs. L. D.); Miss.; Chile, 1939–48.
Woodward, Frank Tennyson Neely; N. C.; China, 1924–48; Hawaii, 1948– .
Woodward, Mabel Elsie (Williams) (Mrs. F. T. N.); Ala.; China, 1924–37; Hong Kong, 1937–48; Hawaii, 1948– .
Wright, Lucy B.; Ga.; China, 1922–53; Korea, 1953– .
Wright, Morris Jesse, Jr.; Tex.; Japan, 1950– .
Wright, Joyce (Hickman) (Mrs. M. J., Jr.); Tex.; Japan, 1950– .
Wright, Robert Max, M.D.; Tex.; Korea, 1955– .
Wright, Paula (Perkins) (Mrs. R. M.); Tex.; Korea, 1955– .
Wyatt, Roy Blanton, Jr.; Va.; Spain, 1953– .
Wyatt, Mildred Joyce (Cope) (Mrs. R. B., Jr.); Tenn.; Spain, 1953– .

Yancey, Mary Ellen; Ala.; Nigeria, 1947– .
Yarnell, Carl Frederick, Jr.; Tenn.; Malaya, 1955– .
Yarnell, Mary Elizabeth (Pate) (Mrs. C. F., Jr.); Tenn.; Malaya, 1955– .
Yates, Helen Bernice; Va.; China, 1934–38.
Yates, Matthew Tyson; N. C.; China, 1846–88.
Yates, Eliza E. (Moring) (Mrs. M. T.); N. C.; China, 1846–94.
Yocum, Alfred Wolfe, M.D.; Va.; China, 1914–53; Korea, 1953.
Yocum, Daisy (Disney) (Mrs. A. W.); Md.; China, 1914–48.
Yong, Ch'in Sam; China; China, 1846–82.
Young, Emma; Ill.; China, 1883–89.
Young, Chester Raymond; Ky.; Hawaii, 1949– .
Young, Florence Alice (Baird) (Mrs. C. R.); Tenn.; Hawaii, 1949– .
Young, James Madderson, Jr., M.D.; La.; Lebanon, 1954–55; Egypt, 1955– .
Young, June (Buckner) (Mrs. J. M., Jr.); La.; Lebanon, 1954–55; Egypt, 1955– .
Young, Neale C.; S. C.; Nigeria, 1920– .

Zimmerman, Henry Albert; Ark.; Brazil, 1924–33.
Zimmerman, Jessie Mae (Earle) (Mrs. H. A.); Ark.; Brazil, 1924–33.

ROBERTA PUGH

FOREIGN MISSIONS AND THE COOPERATIVE PROGRAM. The Cooperative Program offers advantages in raising funds for foreign missions. It is far less expensive and more effective than field agents. It has greatly strengthened individual interest in the total program, which includes foreign missions, rather than fragmentary interest in one or more single aspects of the kingdom program. It has developed among Southern Baptists a unity which was born and nurtured in joint missionary endeavor. This spirit of unity has produced more funds for foreign missions and for every other cause. With the Cooperative Program every pastor and denominational worker is in effect a "field agent" for foreign missions.

The Cooperative Program provides other facilities and services essential to the foreign mission program. Luther Rice (q.v.) led Baptists in America to see that a foreign mission program alone is seriously deficient and led in the establishment of other work essential to foreign missions, notably a college and certain periodical publications. In addition to providing funds for the direct work of the Foreign Mission Board, the Cooperative Program has maintained colleges and seminaries for the training of missionary candidates to serve under the board. It has helped to maintain channels of communication for the board through state papers. It has built a stronger home base by maintaining a home mission program to help win the homeland to Christ. It has developed more fertile sources of mission volunteers by developing stronger churches through the church development programs of state and associational missions. The Cooperative Program has provided additional denominational support for retirement plans for missionary personnel. It has maintained hospitals which serve most of the missionaries on furlough. It has shown that foreign missions can be strong only as the home base is strong, and that foreign missions advances effectively only as all missions advance.

The Cooperative Program provides a sure long-range foundation for underwriting the enlarging financial program for foreign mission advance. It also provides a method for achieving a right balance between foreign missions and other causes. A perennial study is made of the comparative needs of the several causes, and the percentage of division of funds is made in Convention action every year, after annual examination of these comparative needs. This right balance is more nearly achieved as the Cooperative Program advances.

Foreign missions, on the other hand, helps raise more funds for all other missionary, educational, and benevolent causes. For many Christians it provides the largest motivation to Christian liberality, the effective central core for building mission programs, and a spearhead for advance in all mission work. Every church and every phase of missionary work becomes a base for world operations as it is related to the foreign mission enterprise. Foreign missions raises money for and contributes strength to each cause and institution every time an offering is made for it through the Cooperative Program. Some causes which lack the popular appeal of foreign missions, in spite of their importance to the kingdom, are not neglected in the ministration when offerings are made, as they might be without the Cooperative Program.

Foreign missions has been the major beneficiary of the Cooperative Program. Of all undesignated Convention Cooperative Program receipts from 1932 (when they were first handled through the office of the Convention's Executive Committee) through 1955, amounting to $87,072,705.84, foreign missions received $37,630,246.86, or 43.2 per cent, a larger percentage than any other cause. In the year 1954, for example, when 38.19 per cent of Convention Cooperative Program receipts went to the Foreign Mission Board, the next highest allocation was 12.64 per cent, to the Home Mission Board.

Foreign missions received much more funds through the Cooperative Program in 30 years than from all sources in the preceding 80 years. In 75 years, 1845–1919, the board received from all sources approximately $12,500,000. Including receipts from the five-year 75 Million Campaign, the total for 80 years amounted to $24,115,327.91. In 30 years of the Cooperative Program (1926-55), foreign missions received through the Cooperative Program alone a total of $42,664,159.30. This is $18,500,000 or 76.7 per cent more in the 30 years than was received by the board from all sources in the preceding 80 years of its history.

The Cooperative Program has provided the larger part of all funds received for foreign missions since 1925. In the period 1925–55, the board received from all sources, including Cooperative Program, designated gifts, Lottie Moon Christmas Offering, legacies, income from securities, subscriptions, and advertising for *The Commission,* and receipts of all other kinds, $119,751,146.68. The $42,664,159.30 from the Cooperative Program was 35.7 per cent of the total. When current contributions from living donors through Cooperative Program, designated gifts, and the Lottie Moon Christmas Offering only are considered, the percentage would be as much or more than it was in 1954, 48.2 per cent.

MERRILL D. MOORE

FOREIGN MISSIONS DURING THE CIVIL WAR. Soon after the beginning of the Civil War the federal authorities blockaded the South and, with the naval strength available, eventually made the blockade effective. The Foreign Mission Board was cut off from communication with the missionaries in China and Africa. Richard Fuller (q.v.) of Baltimore, president of the Southern Baptist Convention, secured permission from the secretary of state in Washington for the transmission to Baltimore, under the flag of truce, such funds as the board might have available.

At the meeting of the Maryland Association in 1861 the following motion, made by Fuller, was adopted:

That any churches having funds for foreign missions, be requested to pay the same to William Crane, and that brother Crane be requested to forward said funds to brother Isaac T. Smith of New York, and that we tender our acknowledgments to brother Smith for his Christian conduct and labor of love in behalf of our missionaries at all times, especially in their hour of trouble, when they have been cut off from the Board at Richmond. And that brother Crane be requested to act as our agent in reference to future communications with the missionaries.

In Dec., 1862, the Foreign Mission Board requested the following "judicious brethren"—Richard Fuller, J. M. W. Williams, Franklin Wilson (*q.v.*), Hiram Woods, Jr., Henry Taylor, A. F. Crane, and A. J. Lowndes—to act as a provisional board in Baltimore. Through the efforts of members of this committee, especially Fuller and Williams, who was elected corresponding secretary, and through the gifts, especially those of Hiram Woods, Jr., the work was carried on. The Baltimore provisional board raised, during 1862–65, $12,990.60 and expended $12,937.60, leaving a balance of $53 at the close of the war.

The Southern Baptist Convention at its meeting in 1866 expressed appreciation to the provisional board in Baltimore and to the Baptists in Maryland, the District of Columbia, and Kentucky for their generous aid during the period of the Civil War.

BIBLIOGRAPHY: W. W. Barnes, *The Southern Baptist Convention, 1845–1953* (1954). Southern Baptist Convention, *Annual* (1863, 1866, 1867).

W. CLYDE ATKINS

FOREKNOWLEDGE. A logical consequence of the doctrine of divine omniscience is the belief that God knows of future events. The three major positions concerning this foreknowing by God are: (1) Calvinistic—maintaining that since God has willed what is to happen in the future, he knows what will occur; (2) Arminian—holding that God, though he has not destroyed the free choice of man, may yet know what the choice will be; (3) Socinian—maintaining that God knows all that is knowable, but that future events dependent upon human free will are per se unknowable.

See also GOD.

BIBLIOGRAPHY: E. Brunner, *The Divine-Human Encounter* (1943). N. F. S. Ferre, *Faith and Reason* (1946). A. E. Garvie, *The Christian Belief in God* (1935).

A. ELLISON JENKINS

FORGIVENESS. The removal of sin which restores broken fellowship, by an act of God. God's forgiveness of man's sin is both a gift to man and a responsibility for man. God forgives according to his grace (Col. 1:14; Eph. 1:7), but he requires of man repentance (Mark 1:4; Luke 24:47; Acts 2:38; 5:31; 13:38; 26:18), confession (Jas. 5:15 f.; I John 1:9), and the forgiveness of others (Matt. 6:12, 14 f.; Luke 11:4). Only the blasphemy of the Holy Spirit is beyond forgiveness (Mark 3:28 f.). Man's forgiveness of others is related both to his devotion to God (Luke 17:3 f.; Matt. 18:15–35; Eph. 4:32) and to the discipline of the fellowship of the Spirit (John 20:22 f.).

BIBLIOGRAPHY: V. Taylor, *Forgiveness and Reconciliation* (1948).

DALE MOODY

FORK UNION MILITARY ACADEMY. In Dec., 1864, Wm. E. Hatcher, a Baptist pastor of Richmond, Va., married Virginia Snead of Fork Union, Va. Subsequently, the Hatchers acquired a summer home at Fork Union. As the years went by, Hatcher became more and more convinced of the need for a secondary school to serve the children of the village and the outlying areas. Ten citizens of the community were willing to guarantee the operation of the school for one year, and it opened in Oct., 1898, with 1 teacher and 19 boys and girls. Growth of faculty and students was consistent for the first few years.

Military regulations were adopted in 1902, and for the session 1904–05 an army officer was detailed to the school. Since that time the institution has maintained the highest standards of military instruction.

Hatcher was president of the school until his death in 1912. By that time debts had accumulated to such an extent that the future of the school was uncertain. In 1913 the trustees agreed to turn the school over to the denomination, which accepted it the following year.

From 1917 to 1930, the head of the school was N. J. Perkins. There was substantial growth in buildings and enrolment during his administration. The depression brought hard times, and the trustees selected the able and dynamic John J. Wicker as president in 1930. He succeeded in reducing the debt, erecting a number of buildings, and greatly increasing the enrolment during his 15 years of service. In 1945 Wicker's son, J. Caldwell Wicker, succeeded his father. The most important innovation of his administration was the "one subject plan," in which the student devotes all his time to one subject for a six-week period.

In 1955–56 the enrolment in the lower and upper schools combined was at capacity with 614 students. The total assets of the school are $2,199,347, and endowment is $596,064. Most of the income is from tuition and fees. The denomination contributed $16,296 in 1955. The school is fully accredited and is governed by a self-perpetuating board of trustees nominated by the Baptist General Association of Virginia.

RALPH MCDANEL

FORMOSA, MISSION IN. Christianity was first taken to the island of Taiwan, or Formosa as it is more generally known, by Spanish missionaries in the seventeenth century. Canadian and British Presbyterian missionaries have worked in the island for the past 80 years. Missionaries from other boards have gone to Taiwan only since 1945, when three million mainland Chinese fled to the island, 13,500 square miles in area, swelling its population to nine million.

Southern Baptists began mission work in Taiwan in Oct., 1948, when Olive Bertha Smith and Yang Mei Tsai were sent, the former by the Foreign Mission Board and the other by the frontier mission committee of the China Baptist Convention, to begin work among Mandarin-speaking people. Services began in Miss Smith's home in Taipeh. A church was organized Apr. 10, 1949, on Ren Ai Road with 30 Baptists from mainland China and 17 new members received for baptism.

Five missionaries arrived in Taiwan in 1950, seven in 1951, 10 in 1952, and six during the next three years. In 1951 churches were organized at Kaohsiung, Panchiao, Keelung, and Hsinchu, and in Taipeh, Amoy Street Church; in 1952, at Taichung and Chaiyi; in 1953, at Tainan and Chungli, and in Taipeh, Grace Church; in 1955, at Hsulintou, and in Taipeh, True Light Church and Chunghohsiang Church.

Church membership rose from 619 in 1951 to 3,835 in 1955. Sunday school attendance in 1955 was 7,123. Property with a total value of $521,-919.32, obtained jointly by the Foreign Mission Board and the local congregations, includes 13 church buildings and 14 chapels, a seminary, assembly grounds, and missionary residences.

The Taiwan Baptist Theological Seminary was organized in 1952. Sixty-five students are enrolled. Seven missionaries and eight Chinese are on the faculty.

The Taiwan Baptist Convention was organized in 1954.   C. L. CULPEPPER, SR.

FORMOSA (TAIWAN) BAPTIST CONVENTION. Organized July 12, 1954, with 35 messengers from 11 Baptist churches. Three national pastors and 20 missionaries took part in the meetings, held in the auditorium of the Baptist summer assembly grounds. The purpose of the convention was to promote fellowship and mutual aid among the Baptist churches in Taiwan. The organization consisted of the general officers of the convention and a number of committees, such as educational, training, missionary, summer assemblies, and evangelism, to promote the work of the convention. During its first year the convention sought to promote a theological seminary for the training of workers, electing trustees and sponsoring a Seminary Day throughout the convention territory. It assisted in the organization of three new churches, helped in the evangelization program through the churches and chapels, and fostered summer conferences for Intermediates and Juniors, Young People, and Adults. In 1955, 14 churches reported 1,199 baptisms, 3,835 members, 25 chapels, and 7,123 attending Sunday school.

C. L. CULPEPPER

FORMOSAN SEMINARY, TAIPEI. See FORMOSA, MISSION IN.

FORRESTER, ELDRED JOHN (b. Beaufort District, S. C., Nov. 14, 1853; d. Sparta, Ga., Nov. 11, 1932). Bible teacher and denominational official. He graduated from Furman University at the age of 22. His alma mater gave him the D.D. degree in 1893. He was also a graduate of the Princeton Theological Seminary and the Southern Baptist Theological Seminary. As a pastor, he served the Selma church in Alabama, the Hartsville and Greenwood churches in South Carolina, and the church at Washington, Ga. He was professor of Bible at Mercer University, 1905–18; treasurer of Mercer University, 1910–14; treasurer of the Georgia Baptist convention, 1905–32; and was on the executive committee of the convention at the time of his death. He wrote his own textbooks for his Bible courses at Mercer, was the author of *The Baptist Position* (Baltimore, 1893) and *A Righteousness of God for Unrighteous Men* (Nashville, c. 1926); and was one of the founders of the *Review and Expositor*, published by the Southern Baptist Theological Seminary at Louisville, Ky. Forrester was first married in May, 1887, to Elizabeth Dargan, daughter of J. O. B. Dargan, distinguished minister of South Carolina. She died after six years, leaving him with two small daughters. Later he married Margaret Dargan, sister to his former wife. His third wife was Mary Rebecca Duggan, daughter of John C. Duggan.   CLIFTON A. FORRESTER

FORT, ALLEN (b. Americus, Ga., June 7, 1882; d. Nashville, Tenn., Feb. 25, 1921). Pastor and denominational leader. The son of Allen and Floyd (Hollis) Fort, Allen Fort finished high school in Americus, Ga., and attended the University of Georgia for three years. During his junior year he returned home because of the failing health of his father, who was a lawyer. After studying law under an able jurist, he was admitted to the bar in 1901. In 1904 he was appointed solicitor by Governor Terrell of Georgia.

Converted at 14, Fort, at the age of 24, was ordained to the ministry at Americus. His first pastorate was at Dublin, Ga., and from there he went to Tabernacle Baptist Church in Chattanooga. Accepting a call to the First Baptist Church, Nashville, Tenn., Jan. 4, 1914, Fort served there until his death at the age of 39. During this ministry he asked Arthur Flake (q.v.) to lead a three-month enlargement campaign, which was one of the first in the Southern Baptist Convention.

Attractive in personality and physical appearance and an excellent speaker, Fort became one of Nashville's leading preachers. He received honorary degrees from Mercer University, University of Georgia, and Union University. He served his denomination as president of the local pastor's conference, president of the Sunday School Board, member of the Southern Baptist Commission on Negro Theological Education, member of the Executive Committee of the Southern Baptist Convention, and member of the executive board of the Tennessee Baptist Convention.   G. ALLEN WEST

FOSTER, L. S. (b. Tuscaloosa County, Ala., Dec. 18, 1847; d. ?). Pastor, editor, denominational leader, historian. In 1864 Foster entered the University of Alabama, but his college course was terminated when his father moved to Starkville, Miss. Baptized into the Starkville Baptist Church in 1865, Foster entered the Southern Baptist Theological Seminary at Greenville, S. C., in 1868. In 1871 he was ordained by the Starkville Baptist Church. Returning to the seminary in 1873, he completed the full course of study in 1875 with honors. Following his graduation, Foster served in Mississippi as a pastor and as a field-editor for the *Western Recorder* of Louisville, Ky. In 1879 he became pastor of the church in Louisville, Miss.; and in 1884 he became pastor of Fellowship Baptist Church in the "Natchez country," which stirred his interest in Baptist historical material. He was the animating spirit in the organization of the Mississippi Baptist Historical Society in 1888, and for years he served as corresponding secretary for the society. In Nov., 1893, he became associated with J. A. Hackett in the editorial work of the *Baptist Record*, and he was for several years the Mississippi correspondent of *The Examiner*, New York. His book, *Mississippi Baptist Preachers*, was published in 1895. On May 12, 1897, he and his wife founded the Mississippi Baptist Orphanage, and he became the first superintendent, serving until Sept. 1, 1903. When his health failed, he resigned as superintendent of the orphanage, and it was suggested in the Aug. 6, 1903, issue of *The Baptist Record* that he was going to Washington, D. C., to his son's for rest.

BIBLIOGRAPHY: J. L. Boyd, *A Popular History of the Baptists in Mississippi* (1930). L. S. Foster, *Mississippi Baptist Preachers* (1895).

C. B. HAMLET III

FOUNDATION, THE BAPTIST. A corporation established by a Baptist convention to receive, administer, invest, and reinvest endowments given to or placed in trust with the foundation, in order to produce income for a Baptist institution, agency, or cause fostered by the convention. The business of Baptist foundations is administered by trustees elected by the parent convention. Although the number of trustees varies with different states, in most instances trustees are elected for a term of years and may succeed themselves indefinitely. Some states require that trustees be successful Baptist businessmen. In some instances trustees are not permitted to serve on other convention boards or committees in order that impartial administration of foundation funds may be insured.

Baptist foundations serve the following specific purposes: (1) To provide a comprehensive, aggressive, and sustained promotional program for securing endowment funds, and to furnish a positive approach toward relieving financial needs of Baptist schools and other institutions. (2) To provide the wisest possible management of endowment funds in order to assure would-be contributors that funds will serve the purpose for which they are given in perpetuity, and to provide, by charter restrictions, conservative investment policies with all possible safeguards to protect such funds in perpetuity. (3) To remove endowment funds from exposure to emergencies that arise in institutions. (4) To place greater responsibility for securing endowment funds on the denomination, rather than leaving it wholly with the individual institution, and to make Christian education and other causes the responsibility of the entire Convention.

Philanthropists have long used the foundation idea in contributing to charitable and educational causes. Baptists began to adopt this plan at a time when Baptist institutions suffered severely for a lack of financial support. In the early 1920's North Carolina Baptists established a foundation, which, however, was nonaggressive. In 1931 Texas Baptists established their foundation to meet a serious emergency in Baptist institutions of that state. Within a few years this foundation had not only saved their institutions, but had also given impetus to the foundation movement. About 10 years later Georgia Baptists, without any knowledge of what Texas had done, were developing the same idea. Learning of the success of the Texas Baptist Foundation, they used it as an example to help put over the idea in Georgia. Within the next decade nearly every Southern Baptist state had a foundation. In addition, the Southern Baptist Foundation was established on Feb. 26, 1947.

Foundations are administered in various ways. In a few of the states the administration of funds is separate from the program of securing funds. In Texas, for instance, the foundation is concerned only with administration of funds. However, it co-operates with promotional workers, institutions, and individuals when called upon. The program for securing funds is under convention direction through the Department of Endowment, with an executive secretary and staff. In Georgia, administration of funds is entirely under foundation management. The promotional program is directed by the endowment committee, composed of the president and executive secretary of the convention, the institutional heads, five persons elected by the convention, and trustees of the foundation. The endowment committee employs and pays the endowment secretary out of a convention appropriation. In the past the foundation has elected the endowment secretary to serve the foundation as its executive officer, but this arrangement has come to be less than satisfactory. In some of the states the foundation is responsible both for securing and administering funds. Perhaps no two states have an identical plan. Foundation and endowment executives from all the states share their experiences and generally agree on certain fundamentals. Methods and policies of administering funds, however, vary with the several states. In some the convention directs institutions to place all endowments with the state foundation. This plan gets more immediate results. In other states more option is given. Generally state leadership encourages institutions to place their endowment funds with the foundation. There is increasing co-operation between institutions and foundations in securing funds, and there is some transfer of funds to foundations.

Through the denominational press and specially prepared printed matter, foundation and endowment executives have conducted a continuous publicity program. Opportunities to present the work of the foundation to denominational and church meetings are magnified. Mailing lists of prospects have been developed, and person-to-person programs of publicity go on continually. Through various programs of promotion, interest has been created and awareness of endowment needs has been awakened. Sources of endowment heretofore unknown are being uncovered, and techniques for tapping these resources are being developed. Some of the foundations are finding the trust annuity to be especially successful. According to this plan, an individual retains a portion or all of the income from property for himself or loved ones for life and at the same time makes sure that after death the income will go to some kingdom cause. Thus an assured income for life is provided, and the donor while living can give direction to the income from the residue of his estate for kingdom objectives after his death. Bequests in wills remain probably the greatest potential for the future security of Baptist institutions.

The Baptist foundation movement has constantly gained momentum. In the beginning there was uncertainty and opposition, with no pattern to guide those pioneering in this work. Now there is assurance, opposition is no more, and the work of the foundations is directed by men who are specialists in the field. At first results came slowly, but now there are often inquiries and gifts where no direct approach has been made. Co-operation between foundation executives and institutional heads is common. Appropriation for promotional work is generous, where there was formerly reluctance. Foundations have taken on an importance comparable with other major convention agencies. Funds for endowment purposes are being allocated to foundations by conventions. Total endowment assets held by both the Southern Baptist Foundation and state foundations are between 35 and 40 million dollars. But more significant is the enlarging field of interest out of which far more is expected to come in future years. ARTHUR JACKSON

FRANCE, FEDERATION OF EVANGELICAL BAPTIST CHURCHES OF. The first Baptist church of France was probably organized at Nomain by a group of persons who had been baptized by Henri Pyt, a Swiss evangelist. The first ordained pastors of France were Joseph Thieffry and Jean-Baptiste Cretin. In 1831 Howard Malcolm, while visiting France, heard of these two men. On his return to the United States, the story of their struggles was told to important persons of the Triennial Convention. The following year plans for undertaking work in France were envisioned. Erasmus Willard, who spent 21 years in France, led in the establishment of a Baptist church at Douai in 1835. One of the pioneers of the Baptist movement in France was François Vincent, grandfather of Henri Vincent, a president of the French Baptist Union.

Between 1871 and 1895 the Baptists progressed very rapidly. Many noted pastors and laymen from other Protestant churches joined their ranks with gladness; among them were Reuben Saillens, a forceful evangelist, poet, and hymn writer; Paul Besson, a learned pastor from Switzerland who later went to Argentina and became a widely famous Baptist pioneer there; Paul Passy, a well-known French economist. Baptist papers and literature were widely read throughout the land.

At the end of the 19th and the beginning of the 20th century, Baptist life in France was trying. Without a school for the training of pastors, it was difficult to maintain unity. Partly because of this lack and partly as a result of the two world wars, Baptist efforts became fragmented. In 1952 there were 17 churches in the federation. Connected with these organizations there were 1,000 baptized members and 3,000 sympathizers. Recently encouraging results were achieved in Lyon, Niort, and Metz. Plans have been considered for the establishment of summer assembly facilities, which are dependent on the co-operation of American, Southern, and French Baptists. GEORGE W. SADLER

FRASER, GEORGE BROADRUP (b. Washington, D. C., Oct. 4, 1890; d. Washington, D. C., Oct. 3, 1953). Lawyer, businessman, philanthropist. Fraser received the LL.B. and LL.M. degrees from National University, Washington, D. C., and was admitted to the bar when he was only 20 years old. He was a charter member of the Baptist Foundation; a president of the District of Columbia Baptist Convention; a recipient of an Outstanding Baptist Layman's Award in his area; treasurer of the Baptist Home of the District of Columbia convention for many years, and was president of its board at the time of his death. He was a member of the Executive Committee of the Southern Baptist Convention from 1944 to 1952, and from 1946 to 1952 served as president, being the first layman to hold this office. He also served as treasurer of the Western Hemisphere of the Baptist World Alliance. At the time of his death, Fraser was a member of the Calvary Baptist Church, Washington, D. C., and was teacher of the Florence M. Brown Class. Previously he had been a member of the Chevy Chase Baptist Church, where he was superintendent of the Sunday school for 24 years. An outstanding monument to his Christian generosity is the G. B. Fraser Building for Girls in the Taylor Orphanage in Rome (Centocelle), Italy. This is the only Baptist institution for the aged and orphans in Italy.

DOROTHY CLARK WINCHCOLE

FRATERNAL MESSENGERS. Persons sent by the Southern Baptist Convention to the annual sessions of other Baptist conventions or other religious bodies to further fraternal relations with these groups. The Convention in its formally adopted "Convention Procedure" authorizes appointment annually of fraternal messengers to specific Baptist bodies and provides for the election of such messengers to other groups as the occasion may require.

Torbet's *History of the Baptists* records the following events which appear to forecast the later action of the Southern Baptist Convention providing for fraternal messengers to other Baptist bodies: In 1870 the Southern Baptist Convention adopted a resolution which provided for maintaining cordial and co-operative relations with Northern Baptists. Again in 1879 the Convention voted to continue fraternal relations with Northern Baptists but "preserve our separate organizations."

Page 24 of the 1877 *Annual* includes the following statement: "J. P. Boyce of Kentucky . . . introduced to the Convention C. R. Blackall of Chicago, who addressed the body on the subject of Fraternal Relations."

The first reference concerning the appointment of fraternal messengers to other conventions is found on page 34 of the 1931 *Annual* in the form of a resolution, providing for the expenses of such messengers in certain instances.

Upon recommendation of the Convention's Executive Committee, the provision regarding fraternal messengers became a part of the Convention Procedure in 1936. The record of this action sets forth the fact that from time to time, confusion had arisen concerning the appointment of fraternal messengers to other Baptist bodies.

Each year there is published in the *Annual* the Convention charter, enabling act, constitution, bylaws, business and financial plan, and procedure. The procedure includes the following provision concerning fraternal messengers:

(1) The Convention shall send a fraternal messenger to the annual sessions of the American Baptist Convention, the National Baptist Convention of U.S.A., Inc., and the National Baptist Convention of America. The expenses of the fraternal messengers incurred while in attendance upon the conventions herein named, shall be included in the items of Convention expenses.

(2) The fraternal messenger to the American Baptist Convention shall be the president of the Southern Baptist Convention at the time of the meeting of the American Baptist Convention, and the fraternal messenger to the other named Conventions shall be the executive secretary of the Commission on the American Baptist Theological Seminary; provided, however, that if either of these brethren is unable to attend the respective conventions, he shall have authority to appoint a substitute.

(3) The fraternal messengers to other Baptist bodies or other religious bodies may be elected by the Convention as occasion may require. The expenses of such messengers shall be borne by the messengers themselves unless specifically provided for by the Convention.

Annually, provision is made in the Convention's order of business for recognition of and greetings from fraternal messengers from other bodies.

JAMES W. MERRITT

FREDDIE SHIPP COLLEGE. Established in 1893 at Cordele, Ga., and survived only one year.

ARTHUR JACKSON

FREE BAPTIST BANNER. An Oklahoma publication established in 1897. With four pages, 13 x 20 inches, the paper sold for $1 per year. Charles Stetson was editor; R. Y. Mangum, publisher. The paper is now extinct.

J. M. GASKIN

FREE BAPTIST VISITOR. A monthly publication (now extinct) issued at Coalgate, Okla., in 1906.

J. M. GASKIN

FREE WILL BAPTISTS, NATIONAL ASSOCIATION OF. The Free Will Baptist movement was begun in Perquimans County, N. C., in 1727, by Paul Palmer (1692–1763), whose threefold doctrine consisted of free grace, free will, free salvation. By 1750 other churches were organized in eastern North Carolina and northeastern South Carolina, and by 1800 total membership was reported at 25,000.

In 1780 Benjamin Randall (1741–1808) began the Free Will Baptist movement in New Hampshire, and the first quarterly meeting was organized in 1783. In 1827 the General Conference of Free Will Baptists was born, after which many churches were organized in Maine, Massachusetts, Rhode Island, Ohio, New York, Pennsylvania, and Canada. The Free Will Baptist movement split into Northern and Southern groups over the slavery issue in 1856. Consequently, the Northern movement retained the general conference organization, while the Southern group established its own General Conference of Free Will Baptists. The Northern conference was dissolved by merger with Northern Baptists in 1910, and the Southern group continued its conference until 1912.

In 1916 representatives from Free Will Baptist churches in Nebraska, Missouri, Oklahoma, and Texas met at Plattsburg, Mo., and organized a General Cooperative Association under the leadership of John H. Wolfe. The Eastern group reorganized at Nashville, Tenn., in 1921. Operating as independent groups until 1935, the two bodies then came together in Nashville, Tenn., and organized the National Association of Free Will Baptists. John L. Welch was elected moderator. Composed of 23 state organizations, the association comprises 4,200 churches with 450,000 members. There are independent Free Will Baptist churches in 19 other states with a combined membership of 50,000. One college is supported by the association, the Free Will Baptist Bible College, located at Nashville, Tenn. *The Free Will Baptist,* a weekly, *Contact* and the *Free Will Baptist Gem,* monthlies, are the denominational publications. The Woman's National Auxiliary Convention, Free Will Baptist Leagues, and the National Sunday School Convention are all auxiliaries of the association. Sunday school enrolment in 1955 was 375,000. Home mission fields are maintained in Tampa, Fla. (Cuban), Nebraska, Washington-Oregon, and Mexico, while foreign mission areas are North and South India, Cuba, Africa, and Japan. There are nine home and 14 foreign missionaries. Denominational headquarters are in Nashville, Tenn. The national association meetings are held annually in July. Free Will Baptists, Arminian in doctrine, hold three church ordinances: baptism by immersion, the Lord's Supper, and the washing of feet.

D. C. DODD

FREEDOM. Release, liberty, deliverance. In the Christian sense "freedom" means soul deliverance, new birth, God's gift vouchsafed through man's faith in God's redemption. It is the fruitage of the knowledge of truth (John 8:32) in Jesus Christ (John 14:6). It is a standing "in the liberty wherewith Christ hath made us free" (Gal. 5:1). Freedom is a fact in consciousness but is always relative in mortals, being limited by ignorance and disobedience. Freedom is accompanied by manifestations of release from fears and egoism—release from the law of sin and death (Rom. 8:2). Freedom implies release into a fellowship of obedience to God's known will.

See also RELIGIOUS LIBERTY.   P. D. BROWNE

FREEMAN, JOHN DOLLIVER (b. Milton, Nova Scotia, Aug. 12, 1864; d. Macon, Ga., Feb. 17, 1943). Pastor, theologian, teacher, and author. After attending the Liverpool Academy in Nova Scotia from 1876 to 1882, Freeman taught in the provincial public schools until he accepted a call to the ministry. He graduated from McMaster University in 1890 and later received the A.M. degree from Arcadia University, and the D.D. degree in 1914 from McMaster. From 1890 to 1902, Freeman served as a pastor of churches in Ontario and New Brunswick, and then until 1907 was pastor of the Bloor Street Church of Toronto. While pastor at Bloor Street, he attended the first meeting of the Baptist World Alliance at London in 1905 and delivered the inspiring keynote address on "The Place of Baptists in the Christian Church."

The Belvoir Street Church in Leicester, England, called Freeman as pastor in 1907. After 15 years in this pastorate, he went to the Hinton Baptist Church of Chesham, England, in 1922. During his Canadian and English pastorates, Freeman published eight volumes of fiction, poetry, and biblical studies. *Life on the Uplands* (1907), an interpretation and exposition of the 23rd Psalm, was perhaps his best and most widely known book. Returning to America in 1926, Freeman served interim pastorates at Euclid Avenue Church in Cleveland, Ohio, and at the First Church of Winnipeg, Manitoba. While Freeman was in Winnipeg, President Rufus Weaver of Mercer University (Ga.) offered him a professorship of Christianity at that institution. From 1927 to 1939, probably the most fruitful years of his ministry, Freeman taught a wide range of courses at Mercer in philosophy, biblical literature, and homiletics.

Greatly loved by many of his students and colleagues, he retired from the Mercer faculty in 1939, and spent final years as pastor of the Mt. Zion Baptist Church near Macon, Ga., and as a contributor to various religious periodicals. He was buried in the Mt. Zion churchyard.

BIBLIOGRAPHY: *Christian Index* (Mar. 4, 1943). *Proceedings of the Baptist World Congress* (1905). *Who Was Who in America* (1950).

MALCOLM LESTER

FREEMAN, WILLIAM AUGUSTUS (b. Little River County, Ark., Sept. 7, 1858; d. Shreveport, La., July 14, 1936), Pastor, evangelist, and missionary. Son of William M. and Mary Ann Freeman, William A. Freeman entered the Methodist ministry in 1883. He became a Baptist in Lewisville, Ark., in 1895 and was ordained as a Baptist minister that same year. Following his ordination, Freeman was engaged in evangelistic work (1895–98, 1901–03, 1911–12); from 1903 to 1906, he served as a missionary in Arkansas. During his ministry he served as pastor of the following Baptist churches: First Church, Texarkana, Tex. (1899–1901); First Church, Hope, Ark. (1903–05); Stamps, Ark. (1906); Magnolia, Ark. (1907); Chickasha, Okla. (1908–09); Cuero, Tex. (1911–12); Parkview, Shreveport, La. (1913–15); Vivian, La. (1916–19); Prescott, Ark. (1922–24); Vivian, La. (1925). Throat trouble prevented his preaching during the years 1919–22. Freeman retired in 1925 and lived in Shreveport until his death. He was the author of *The Devil Between the White Man and the Negro* (1907).

JOHN D. FREEMAN

FRENCH, HOME MISSIONS TO. The Home Mission Board is working among French-speaking people or people of French background in two areas. In Illinois, G. O. Foulon is the only worker. The larger number of French-speaking people are found in Louisiana where the area of activity of Home Mission Board missions is in a triangle from Alexandria southward to the Gulf of Mexico. In this area live 700,000 descendants of exiles from Acadia (Nova Scotia) who came to this area after the British conquered Canada (1763).

After Louisiana came under American con-

French Missions, Louisiana

trol (1803), three distinct groups developed in Louisiana—Creoles (descendants of original French and Spanish immigrants, mainly in New Orleans and surrounding areas), Acadians, and Anglo-Americans. The French-speaking people were Roman Catholic in religion. Because of language difficulty, there was very little evangelical work among them. Occasionally, a colporteur would venture into the French country. He did not receive much welcome because his books were in English, and the people's religion forbade them to read literature not approved by the Church authorities. The program of evangelical missions among the French depended largely upon the few French evangelicals. At the turn of the century, Ozeme Derouen, a Frenchman, was converted through contact with the colporteurs, and he became an evangelist among his own people.

One of the earliest foundation-builders was Thomas Rand, Jr., a native of Massachusetts. After graduation from Hamilton Theological Institution (Colgate) in 1838, he came South because of poor health. A well-educated man, he established a school in the French country and left an indelible imprint. Adolphe Stagg, famous in Louisiana Baptist history, has left on record: "I was never able to get away from the indelible impression made upon me by this man of God in the classroom." Stagg laid the foundations of evangelical work among the French. He was converted in 1870, and, although he was never employed directly by the Home Mission Board, he worked among the French.

The Louisiana Association, and later the Louisiana convention, carried on work among the French-speaking population within reach of Anglo-American churches. Toward the end of the 19th century, the Home Mission Board, under the leadership of Secretary Isaac Taylor Tichenor, began to enter into co-operative work with the boards of state conventions. In this co-operative program the Home Board and the state board of Louisiana began to employ missionaries among the English-speaking and the French-speaking populations. One of the outstanding missionaries in this co-operative work was Lucien C. Smith, employed first by the state mission board and then by the Home Mission Board. Smith established churches among the French; many French-speaking pastors came into service through his ministry; and numbers of mission stations were established. Other notable missionaries among the French include: J. H. Strother, J. I. Kendrick, S. O. Olivier, Berkman DeVille, Truman Granger, Eddie Savoie, Lawrence Thibodeaux, L. O. F. Cotey, Theo Cromier, Dolzey McGee, Amadie Janice, M. W. Salassi, P. B. Pettipas, H. H. Stagg, Herbert Hebert, Pershing Petrie, Alfred Schwab, Maurice Thibodeaux, Carl Conrad, Maurice Aguillard; also, many laymen with French names have made contributions to the Home Mission Board's ministry among the French.

Another important type of work is in the field of education. Quite early in the 19th century, Bible institutes were held for one or two weeks in various centers for training and evangelism. In the fall of 1910, a school was opened in Faquetaique, in the heart of the French-speaking area. The school survived for only two years, due to lack of financial support. Following the closing of the school, Mrs. Dora Jenkins carried on for two years. After the building in which this school was conducted was destroyed by fire in 1917, no further effort was made in the area. A work was carried on in the Baptist church building in Nunez, 1915–17, but it was closed for lack of funds. In 1915 Cotey began preaching among the Creoles in New Orleans. When the Baptist Bible Institute opened in 1918, Cotey closed his school to teach French in the institute for nine or ten years.

In 1916 the state board, under the leadership of corresponding secretary G. H. Crutcher, began a school near Houma. Grace MacFarland, a graduate of Southwestern Seminary, opened the school, but due to poor health she was able to carry on only for a year and a half. Students ranged from the ages of 5 to 27 years. This effort called attention to the great need, and Acadia Academy, which has had a long and profitable career, was established by the state mission board and Home Mission Board working together.

The founding of the Baptist Bible Institute (New Orleans Baptist Theological Seminary) in 1918 greatly advanced evangelical work among the French-speaking population. The work of students during their seminary years and the work of alumni who have gone into the work among the French-speaking people has had a large part in the development of this work during the past four decades.

Co-operative mission work among the French-speaking population is being carried on and supported by the state board and Home Mission Board. Improved economic conditions, the building of better roads, improved boat services, the development of industrial centers in Louisiana and southeast Texas, and the use of French programs over the radio have enlarged the work and brought greater success to Baptist missions.

BIBLIOGRAPHY. C. P. Sansom, "Baptist Work Among French-Speaking People of Louisiana" (1928).

JOHN CAYLOR

FRENCH MISSIONS, LOUISIANA. A joint work of the Home Mission Board and the Louisiana Baptist Convention involving "planning, counselling and working with French preachers, English speaking pastors of French groups, mission pastors of the Home Mission Board and mission pastors in French regions of the Louisiana Baptist Convention, and district and other missionaries in French areas."

"The first Baptist preacher in the bounds of the present state of Louisiana was probably

Bailey E. Chaney [*q.v.*] . . . in 1798 or 1799." Half Moon Bluff Church in Washington Parish, organized Oct. 12, 1812, was the first Baptist church in Louisiana. South Louisiana was settled by French colonists, most of whom were nominal Roman Catholics; and Baptist work was slow in beginning. The masses of the people were illiterate, and the language was an almost insurmountable barrier. Joseph Willis (*q.v.*) led in organizing the first Baptist church in Louisiana west of the Mississippi River, Calvary Church in St. Landry Parish, in Nov., 1812.

The first missionary officially employed by Louisiana Baptists to work with the French people was Adolphe Stagg (*q.v.*) (1834–1914). He was converted from Roman Catholicism and united with Mt. Olivet Baptist Church, Whiteville, in 1870. Thomas Muse (*q.v.*), Evergreen, said of Stagg in 1872: "In Adolphe Stagg we have an opening wedge. A Creole himself, more fluent in the French than in the English language, of high repute and extensive influence among his own people, it would be hard to find one more fitted to the work." Stagg assisted in constituting many churches, among them Opelousas, Eden, Mt. Nebo, Faquetique, and Memon (*sic*).

Baptist leaders in Louisiana were encouraged by the progress of French missions in 1888. The corresponding secretary reported: "In this mission since the last convention quite a number have been baptized, two churches organized and several other will be constituted in the near future. . . . The Executive Board . . . engaged Brother Aurelie Dauzart . . . to labor in conjunction with Brethren Stagg and Shaw."

Louisiana Baptists felt the need of developing the work begun by Stagg, but they had no French preacher. English-speaking men did what they could, but failed to accomplish much. Ozine Derouen (born *c.* 1870), a convert to Methodism in 1906, worked among the French people for the American Sunday School Union. Six of his converts asked to be "baptised like Jesus was baptised." This led Derouen to make an intensive study of New Testament teaching concerning baptism, and he became a Baptist. Louisiana Baptists in Jan., 1911, and the Woman's Missionary Union of Louisiana paid his salary. He baptized 35 converts in May, 1911.

When Derouen resigned because of ill health, C. B. Melancon was employed to replace him. Melancon had been converted through the witness of a Baptist neighbor and through reading his Bible.

The most notable convert of Derouen was L. C. Smith (1883–   ), who was baptized in 1910. During his years of training in Louisiana College and the Baptist Bible Institute he served as pastor of French churches and as missionary to the French. In 1924 he was elected superintendent of French missions for the **Louisiana Baptist Convention.** From 1936 to **1950,** he served the Home Mission Board of the Southern Baptist Convention as field missionary to the French.

L. O. F. Cotey, a native of France, did mission work among the French in Louisiana and also served for some years in the faculty of the Baptist Bible Institute.

Mrs. Mary Lou Jenkins, at one time president of the Louisiana Baptist Woman's Missionary Union, was very helpful in promoting mission work among the French. She supplemented salaries, provided scholarships, and was largely responsible for the beginning of the mission work in the Atchafalaya Basin. Mr. and Mrs. Ira Marks made a lasting contribution there.

The work of state missionaries in the French area has been supplemented by the mission work of the New Orleans Baptist Theological Seminary. Many of the churches have been organized by students and teachers. The French Baptist Radio Hour provides preaching in French, which reaches all French-speaking areas in the state. Carl Conrad is the present director of French missions.

BIBLIOGRAPHY: F. Brown, "Conversion and Early Work of O. Derouen," *The Baptist Message* (Sept. 22, 1932). J. Caylor, *In Evangeline's Country* (1954). J. T. Christian, *A History of the Baptists of Louisiana* (1923). K. O. Clawson, "The Influence of Mrs. Mary Lou (Johnson) Jenkins on Mission Work in Louisiana" (MS, 1950). J. P. Durham and J. S. Ramond, *Baptist Builders in Louisiana* (1934). M. L. Jenkins, *Around the World in Louisiana* (1937). Louisiana Baptist Convention *Annual* (1873–1955). *The Magnet* (1925–42). C. P. St. Amant, *A Short History of Louisiana Baptists* (1948). W. L. Stagg, Sr., *Adolphe Stagg, Life and Work* (1954). *Vision* (1946–56). M. S. Wagnon, "A Decade of Baptist Missions in the Atchafalaya Basin in Louisiana" (MS, 1949).

GRAY ALLISON

FRIENDSHIP ACADEMY. Founded in 1899 at Star City, Ark., by Friendship Association. It enrolled 150 the first year and had two buildings financed locally. The association operated the academy on income from tuition and voluntary contributions for 10 years.   H. D. MORTON

FRISTOE, WILLIAM (b. Stafford County, Va., 1748; d. Shenandoah County, Va., Aug. 14, 1828). Minister and itinerant. A son of middle-class parents, given so little education that he could scarcely read and write when grown, Fristoe educated himself. Converted at the age of 15, he was ordained at 21 to become pastor of his mother church Chappawamsic in 1769. After being pursued by a gunman intent on killing him, and after his arrest for preaching without a license, he fled to Philadelphia to seek advice from Baptists there. Following their advice, he qualified under the terms of the Toleration Act and procured a license.

Fristoe's labors covered many counties. He traveled long distances to serve churches established through his missionary efforts. The many churches he served included these: Chappawamsic, Hartwood (formerly Potomac), Broad Run, Thumb Run, Ebenezer, Buck Marsh, Grove,

Rockhill, Bethel, Zion, Salem, and Brentown. About 1801, while living in Stafford County, Fristoe despaired of God's blessing the people in that vicinity again, and he moved to Shenandoah County. In 1776 Fristoe participated in the formation of the first Baptist association in Virginia, the Ketocton; later he served it many times as moderator. In 1808 Fristoe published his one book, *A Concise History of the Ketocton Baptist Association.*   BEN LYNES

FRONTIER, BAPTISTS AND THE AMERICAN. The Baptists who migrated westward after the American Revolution settled on the continually receding free land, organized churches, associations, and schools, and prosecuted a vigorous missionary campaign. These pioneers contributed to the gradual civilizing of the frontier and in the process adapted themselves to the demands of what they discovered. One result was the rapid numerical growth of the Baptists. Another consequence was a certain modification of the Baptist outlook itself in the dynamic interplay of the Baptist witness and the frontier situation.

The frontier.—The frontier was both a *region* and a *process.* It was that region west of the settled area along the Atlantic seaboard. It was a process of change from the moment the wilderness was attacked with a view to making it habitable for civilized life to the time a settled community was established. Thus "the new west became the old west," as Frederic L. Paxson put it, "and the old west often ceased to be west at all."

It is important to distinguish between the frontier and theories about its bearing upon American life and thought. Frederick Jackson Turner, whose thesis about the frontier in *The Significance of the Frontier in American History* has greatly influenced the interpretation of American history, both defined the frontier and offered his view of its significance when he wrote that "the existence of an area of free land, its continuous recession, and the advance of American settlement westward *explain* American development." Thus the frontier may be defined as "the hitheredge of free land—the meeting point between savagery and civilization." This definition of the frontier, or one akin to it, is tenable. The difficulty with Turner's thesis arises when he says that the frontier can "explain American development." What the frontier was, is a fact. What its significance, if any, was and is in the "American development" is an interpretation of this fact.

It is also a fact that the Baptists were deeply involved in the dynamics of the frontier. Precisely how this fact should be interpreted—i.e., what consequences, if any, came out of this involvement and how these consequences are related to factors other than the frontier—is a matter on which there are widely differing views.

Organization.—Though several Baptist preachers, such as Squire Boone, the brother of Daniel Boone, entered the region across the mountains before the American Revolution, they left no permanent impressions and organized no churches. Spurred westward by economic difficulties on the Atlantic seaboard following the war and lured by free land on the frontier, the Baptists joined other Americans in the trek into the wilderness. Here they sought an "ampler ether, a diviner air," where they would be free from the "supercilious airs and opprobrium, with which the 'first families' of the tide water were accustomed to treat them."

Three Baptist preachers, Joseph Barnett, John Whitaker, and John Gerrard, were chiefly responsible for the formation of the first Baptist church west of the mountains, at Severns Valley, Ky., on June 18, 1781. In December of the same year, the Gilbert's Creek Church, called the "travelling church" because its members came in a body from Upper Spotsylvania, Va., to Kentucky, settled at Craig's Station and gathered for worship "around the same old Bible they had used in Spotsylvania." Several other Baptist churches came westward in the same curious manner.

The rude cabins of the settlers served for the first several years as meeting places for the Baptists on the frontier. This was possible in the beginning because the churches were usually quite small. Some time after the organization of the Forks of Elkhorn Church, an entry in the *Minutes* indicates that certain members were "appointed to seek out the most convenient place for a meeting house [and] also to fix what size would be most suitable." The father of Abraham Lincoln assisted in the construction of the Baptist church building on Pigeon Creek in Indiana in 1819. This meetinghouse was 26 × 30 feet, made of hewn logs, with a fireplace and chimney built of brick. More commodious and comfortable church buildings were commonly constructed 15 to 20 years after the organization of the average church.

The Elkhorn Baptist Association, the first west of the mountains, was formed on Sept. 30, 1785, by six churches which adopted the Philadelphia Confession of Faith in the home of John Craig on Clear Creek in Woodford County in central Kentucky. A month later, Oct. 29, the Salem Association, the second in the new west, was organized in western Kentucky. The Severns Valley Church joined this association. In 1787 seven Separate Baptist churches formed the South Kentucky Association. On Oct. 1, 14 years later, the Regular and Separate Baptists resolved their differences by agreeing upon a "plan" involving a theological adjustment which weakened the Calvinism of the Regular Baptists.

Doctrine.—The mild Calvinism reflected in the compromise of 1801 between the Separate and Regular Baptists, rather typical of doctrinal statements by Baptists on the frontier, is partly attributable to the influence of the frontier upon Baptist thought. Thoroughgoing Calvinism, preoccupied with God's sovereignty, human depravity, and predestination of the elect to salvation and the remainder to perdition, was ill equipped to deal with the dynamics of frontier life with its emphases upon man's ingenuity and a historical destiny determined in some measure by human virtue and effort. John Taylor, a frontier Baptist farmer-preacher, symbolized a widely shared distaste of the Baptists for what they considered excessive theological pre-occupation when he spoke disparagingly of "high toned predestinarians." The rugged demands of life in the western wilderness required a certain practical adjustment which left its mark upon American theology. The Baptists strengthened the pragmatic strain in their thought by vigorous participation in the frontier revivals and by embracing a pietism typified by Taylor, who recalled "a tide of heavenly joy" that flowed into his soul when he was converted.

The modified Calvinism of the Baptists brought forth by the frontier was of only secondary concern to the Baptist preacher, who was frequently also a farmer, with little or no formal education. Baptist confessions of faith, church covenants, and the doctrinal part of associational minutes are somewhat deceptive, in the sense that doctrinal matters were less important in the actual life of the churches than these documents would lead one to believe. For example, existing sermons by frontier Baptist preachers disclose a practical interest which the formal doctrinal statements of the churches and associations do not suggest. These preachers were steeped in the King James Version of the Bible, which they expounded in the context of their understanding of the mild Calvinism of Baptist doctrine.

Antimissionism.—From about 1820 for several decades, the antimission movement among frontier Baptists agitated and split the churches. In 1846 there were 68,068 Baptists in the United States who had embraced antimissionism. At least 50,000 of these lived on the frontier. Antimissionism appeared first among Baptists on the frontier and then moved eastward to the area along the Atlantic seaboard. Antimissionism was set off in Virginia and North Carolina through publications of John Taylor (*q.v.*) and Daniel Parker (*q.v.*). It was, therefore, initially a frontier phenomenon and found its greatest strength there. Those who embraced antimissionism were usually denoted "Primitive Baptists" and the movement called "Hardshellism." This tendency was largely confined to the Baptists, for there is no evidence of systematic opposition to missions among the Methodists and Presbyterians.

Taylor and Parker were severe critics of the missionaries. "To hear or read their reports," wrote Taylor in *Thoughts on Missions*, "it would seem as if the whole country was blank as to religion." His jealousy of the missionaries, especially those with formal education, was strengthened by his belief that missionary societies were too concerned about money, and that mission boards had no scriptural justification and violated Baptist polity. J. H. Spencer, the Kentucky Baptist historian, believed that Taylor eventually abandoned his antimission views.

Parker was the archenemy of missions on the frontier. He shared Taylor's suspicions concerning missions and grounded his objections on an ultra-Calvinism, involving a double-edged doctrine of predestination called Two-Seed-in-the-Spirit Predestinarian.

The divisions precipitated by antimissionism somewhat weakened the Baptist witness on the frontier; nevertheless, Baptist growth continued at a rapid rate. By the mid-19th century, the antimission movement had become a minor eddy in the main stream of the Baptist missionary enterprise.

Growth.—Baptists grew rapidly in America, not as a consequence of the migration of Baptists westward, but, as William Warren Sweet says, because of their "genius for making Baptists out of the raw material which the frontier afforded." For example, by 1810 there were in Kentucky 15 Baptist associations, 286 churches, and 16,650 members. A primary reason for Baptist expansion was the work of the farmer-preachers who, as Theodore Roosevelt in his *The Winning of the West* has observed, "lived and worked exactly as their flocks. . . . They cleared the ground, split rails, planted corn, and raised hogs on equal terms with their parishioners." John Taylor in his *History of Ten Baptist Churches* suggests several reasons for Baptist growth, which may be summarized as (a) simplicity of doctrine, (b) democracy of church and denominational organization, (c) closeness to the people, and (d) relevance to the frontier, which, as Sweet says, provided "a soil suited" to the "peculiar genius" of the Baptists.

Baptist growth was both conserved and accelerated by schools established on the frontier. Some frontier preachers were teachers in these schools. Many of these institutions were established by associations under the leadership of preachers. Though the farmer-preacher was the spearhead of Baptist expansion on the frontier, the significant role of the teacher-preacher must not be overlooked. Baptist teachers and schools gave stability and solidity to the Baptist movement in the west.

Thus the Baptists, a minority group of 10,000 at the time of the American Revolution, grew on the frontier into a strong denomination which by 1838 showed a membership in the United States of 490,636, with 6,945 ordained ministers and 401 associations. In 1846 the number of Baptists had increased to 655,536. In the early frontier period, Baptist churches were formed throughout the new west in the southern region and the area north of the Ohio River. The names of Baptist missionaries, preachers, teachers, and schools on the frontier are legion—and there are many more whose names are lost to history—and thus cannot be given; but this study could not claim adequacy even as a summary without reference to John Mason Peck (*q.v.*) (1789–1838). He cultivated a farm to pay expenses, traversed Missouri, Indiana, and Illinois, organizing Sunday schools and Bible societies, founded what became Shurtleff College in Illinois, and edited a religious paper. He and Jonathan Going were largely responsible for the formation of the American Baptist Home Mission Society in 1832. No wonder Kenneth Scott Latourette speaks of Peck as "the chief creator of nationally organized Baptist effort for the frontier."

See also WESTWARD EXPANSION, SOUTHERN BAPTIST.

BIBLIOGRAPHY: D. Benedict, *A General History of the Baptist Denomination in America and Other Parts of the World* (1813). B. H. Carroll, *Genesis of American Anti-Missionism* (1902). F. L. Paxson, *History of the American Frontier* (1924). G. W. Ranck, *The Travelling Church* (1891). T. Roosevelt, *The Winning of the West* (1900). J. H. Spencer, *A History of Kentucky Baptists* (1885). W. W. Sweet, *Religion in the Development of American Culture* (1952); *Religion on the American Frontier: The Baptists, 1783–1830* (1931). G. R. Taylor, ed., *The Turner Thesis* (1949). J. Taylor, *A History of Ten Baptist Churches* (1823); *Thoughts on Missions* (1819). F. J. Turner, *The Significance of the Frontier in American History* (1920).   PENROSE ST. AMANT

FROST, JAMES MARION (b. Georgetown, Ky., Feb. 10, 1848; d. Nashville, Tenn., Oct. 30, 1916). Pastor, denominational leader, founder and first secretary of the Sunday School Board of the Southern Baptist Convention. Being reared in Georgetown, Ky., he graduated from Georgetown College and there married Nanney Riley. He served as pastor of the following churches: First, Maysville, Ky.; Upper Street (now Calvary Baptist), Lexington, Ky.; First, Staunton, Va.; First, Selma, Ala.; Leigh Street, Richmond, Va.; First, Nashville, Tenn. His children were: Howard, Margaret, Marian, Marcellus, and Virginius.

While pastor in Richmond, Frost framed resolutions which led to the establishment of the Sunday School Board. He first advocated that the denomination produce its own printed literature through a board of publication under the direct control of the Convention and co-ordinate with the Foreign Mission Board and Home Mission Board. This was proposed in resolutions released through the *Religious Herald* on Feb. 27, 1890. The Baptist papers in the various states, except the *Baptist and Reflector* (Tenn.) and the *Western Recorder* (Ky.), opposed Frost's resolutions editorially. Frost's proposal was considered at the Fort Worth Convention (1890), and a Sunday school committee was set up, which served for one year with headquarters in Louisville. At the Convention in Birmingham the following year (1891), Frost made a motion that the matter be referred to yet another committee, consisting of one member from each state, and that their report be made a special order before that session of the Convention. Frost and James Bruton Gambrell, who were made a subcommittee to frame the report for the larger committee, held an all-day conference harmonizing their own views concerning the best approach to the perplexing problem. Compromises were reached whereby Gambrell would write the last paragraph of the report and Frost would pen the last sentence. Gambrell stressed complete freedom of the local church in purchasing its literature, while Frost pleaded that a fair chance be given the new board to live and prosper.

With President Jonathan Haralson presiding, the Convention dealt with the final resolutions which were read by Frost recommending a Sunday School Board. With the timely assistance of John Albert Broadus, the report was adopted without debate and with only 13 opposing votes. After much insistence Frost agreed to serve as first secretary of the board. On July 1, 1891, he came to Nashville, where the board was to be located. He was to experience considerable loneliness because many people, misunderstanding his mission, received him reluctantly. In borrowed quarters and handicapped by limited resources, Frost began his new duties. After having served only 18 months and still yearning for the pastorate, he felt that he could not decline the call to become pastor of the First Baptist Church in Nashville. In 1896, however, he returned to the secretaryship of the board and served in that capacity until his death in 1916.

Frost's decisions as first secretary largely determined the pattern of the board's future growth. He led it to be a publishing house instead of a printing enterprise. He worked for a strong and acceptable curriculum and further developed the graded series of lessons. He projected the Sunday school educational program as well as the teacher-training program. Also he worked out reliable standards for the measurement of efficiency in Sunday school progress. While he was interested in the development of Sunday school work even through interdenominational and nondenominational movements, he strove constantly to keep Southern Baptist Sunday schools closely related to the churches and denomination. This latter emphasis proved to be one of the major contributions of his ministry. He helped develop the Baptist Young People's Union. The board became the supplier of general materials for the churches and the denomination and entered into the book-publishing ministry during his tenure. In addition, Frost found time to write such outstanding books as *Moral Dignity of Baptism* (1905), *The Memorial Supper* (1908), *The School and the Church* (1911), *Our Church Life* (1909), *An Experience of Grace* (1908), and *Sunday School Board History and Work* (1914). At the time of his death, the board had prospered sufficiently to erect its own building of five floors at

161 Eighth Avenue, North, and dedicate it free of debt in 1914.

Frost's success is attributed to his pastoral heart, business ability, and unwavering devotion to an assignment which he felt was God-given. While never physically strong, he was able to endure 22 years of intense administrative pressure in the high office which he held. His health finally gave way, however, while he was en route to a field engagement in 1916. After much suffering he passed away at his home. Funeral services were held in Nashville and Louisville. Interment was at Cave Hill cemetery, Louisville, Ky.   JAMES L. SULLIVAN

FRUITLAND BAPTIST ASSEMBLY. In 1945 the North Carolina Baptist convention authorized the general board to secure a site and building in the eastern and western parts of the state for summer assembly grounds. For a site in Western North Carolina, the convention approved the Fruitland Baptist Bible Institute property but "authorized the Board" to develop the property for assembly purposes and provide a program during the summer of 1947, when the assembly opened for the first time. Since the Fruitland property was used for the Bible institute only during the winter, it seemed wise to use it for an assembly during the summer. B. G. Henry has directed the program since 1947, a period in which attendance has totaled 17,339. The present trend is toward providing camps for young people and planning special meetings for various groups on week ends.   M. A. HUGGINS

FRUITLAND BAPTIST BIBLE INSTITUTE. Located six miles from Hendersonville, N. C., it was originally one of the mountain schools operated jointly by the Home Mission Board and the Carolina Association. The establishment of public high schools made it difficult for the mountain schools to continue, and while a few became junior colleges, Fruitland was forced to close. Some indebtedness remained after closure, but the Baptist state convention assumed the debt for one-half interest in the property. While the convention made a study of possible uses for the property, it became apparent that the three schools for ministers conducted one week each summer were inadequate for ministers who could not "possibly go to college and seminary." The need for better training for them appealed to J. C. Canipe, pastor of the Boone Baptist Church, more strongly than to any other. In 1945 the general secretary of the state convention called attention in his convention report to the opening of "a school for the pastors in service" in Boone about Jan., 1946, and the general board of the convention requested the Home Mission Board "to surrender its share in the [Fruitland] property to the Convention in the event the committee found it could be used for some denominational purpose." In the meantime an effort was made to interest the Southern Baptist Convention in making the Ridgecrest Assembly property available for the use of pastors, not only in North Carolina, but those in South Carolina, Georgia, Tennessee, and Virginia "who are hungry for a chance for further study."

Early in 1946 the general board bought the interest of the Home Mission Board in the Fruitland property for $9,000, and reported to the convention that year that the experience gained from the experiment at Boone justified the expenditure of funds to put the Fruitland buildings in usable condition so that two or three six-weeks terms could be held during the winter months. Since Fruitland's beginning as a Bible institute, under Canipe's direction, about 1,000 men have enrolled, and an increasing number of the men continue for three years of eighteen weeks each. Except for meals, the cost of operating the school has been a part of the budget of the general board.   M. A. HUGGINS

FRUITLAND INSTITUTE. A Baptist school at Fruitland, Henderson County, N. C., the result of a desire on the part of Carolina Baptist Association to provide better educational facilities for its people. In 1896 plans were made for the establishment of a school in the associational area, and in 1898 a committee of the Carolina Association decided upon Fruitland as the location. On Jan. 2, 1899, the school was opened for a term of five months under its founder, Amos Isaac Justice (*q.v.*); there were 150 pupils.

In Dec., 1899, the board of missions of the state convention endorsed the school and incorporated it for educational mission work in the mountain district. Beginning in 1905 Fruitland Institute received annual assistance from the Home Mission Board of the Southern Baptist Convention. By 1931, when the board discontinued aid to mountain schools, Fruitland had received nearly $80,000, including over $40,000 for capital improvements. Fruitland made educational opportunities available to people who otherwise might not have had them in the mountain region of the state. In 1934 the school was supported by Carolina, Transylvania, and Buncombe County associations. It was a coeducational, fully accredited high school. Although closed in 1936, the school was later reopened as a Bible institute.   D. L. SMILEY

FUKUOKA WOMEN'S TRAINING SCHOOL. See JAPAN, MISSION IN.

FULLER, ANDREW (b. Wicken, Cambridgeshire, England, Feb. 6, 1754; d. Kettering, England, May 7, 1815). Preacher, pastor, missionary advocate, denominational leader, theologian, and writer. He joined with William Carey (*q.v.*) to bring the modern missionary movement and revival among British Baptists. Fuller became a Baptist at Soham when 16 years old. Though without special training, he was called as the church's pastor in 1775. In 1782 he accepted a call from the church at Kettering, Northamptonshire, where he remained until his death at the age of 61 in 1815. Though not a great

Fuller, Ellis Adams

preacher on a comparative scale, his sermons were effective.

Fuller, whose *The Gospel Worthy of All Acceptation* (1784) greatly influenced William Carey (1761–1834), was a firm supporter of the missionary enterprise. Not only did he serve tirelessly as secretary of the Baptist Missionary Society, but his theological work modified the spirit of the existing Calvinism in a way favorable to missions. His evangelical Calvinism was effectively stated in *The Calvinist and Socinian Systems Examined and Compared as to their Moral Tendency* (1894). An effective controversialist, Fuller was especially vigorous in his attacks upon the Deists, Socinians, and Scotch Sandemanians. Like Carey he was strongly opposed by hyper-Calvinist followers of John Gill (q.v.) and John Brine.

In addition to his many theological works— books, pamphlets, and articles—Fuller carried on a voluminous correspondence especially with the missionaries.

He has been compared with John Knox both as to his excellence and defects. Sincere, forceful, energetic, and self-denying, he was often harsh in administering reproof. In addition to the incalculable influence which Fuller has had upon British Baptists, he has greatly influenced American Baptists through his writings and example. He also served as an effective agent through which Adoniram Judson (q.v.) received news and monies from American Baptists during the War of 1812.

BIBLIOGRAPHY: W. G. Black, "Andrew Fuller," *Dictionary of National Biography* (1949–50). A. G. Fuller, "Memoirs of Mr. Fuller," *Works* (1833). A. H. Kirkby, "Andrew Fuller—Evangelical Calvinist," *The Baptist Quarterly* (Jan., 1954). J. Ryland, *Life and Death of Reverend Andrew Fuller* (1816).

POPE A. DUNCAN

FULLER, ELLIS ADAMS (b. Cross Hill, S. C., Apr. 1, 1891; d. San Diego, Calif., Oct. 28, 1950). Seminary president, pastor. Son of John Rhett and Ida Lee (Adams) Fuller. His father was a merchant and farmer. He attended Presbyterian College, Clinton, S. C., and received the A.B. degree in 1912. After serving as principal and teacher in public schools at Mountville and Union, S. C., from 1912 to 1917, Fuller enrolled in Southern Baptist Theological Seminary in 1917 and followed his graduation with the Th.M. degree by spending a year in postgraduate study. While at the seminary Fuller served as pastor of Hazelwood Baptist Church, Louisville, and the Campellsburg (Ky.) Baptist Church. Later pastorates were at South Main Street Church, Greenwood, S. C., 1922–24, and Earle Street Church, Greenville, S. C., 1924–25.

Fuller left the pastorate in 1925 to become superintendent of the Home Mission Board's department of evangelism and served until 1928. He then accepted a call to the pastorate of First Baptist Church, Atlanta, Ga., and during his 14 years in that capacity he led the church in moving from its downtown location to a more favorable semi-suburban site and in erecting an outstanding building. While in this pastorate, Fuller served as president of the Home Mission Board, 1928–42; chairman of the Georgia Baptist Hospital Commission, 1938–42; president of the Georgia Baptist convention, 1939–42, and of the Atlanta Christian Council; and trustee of Shorter College, Rome, Ga.

In May, 1942, Fuller was elected to the presidency of Southern Baptist Theological Seminary at the retirement of John Richard Sampey (q.v.), and Fuller took office just as the seminary was emerging from heavy indebtedness. During his eight-year tenure, enrolment increased from 520 to 951, the School of Church Music was established, 13 professors and 18 new buildings were added to the seminary. The buildings included an apartment for missionaries, the alumni memorial chapel, and a 96-family apartment building named Fuller Hall in his honor. Capital increases included the addition of 37 acres, $250,903 increase in endowment, and $2,575,995 in total property value.

Widely known as an evangelistic preacher, Fuller was in great demand for revival meetings; and a volume of his messages entitled *Evangelistic Sermons* was published posthumously (Broadman Press, 1953). Fuller died Oct. 28, 1950, following a heart attack which he suffered while preaching at the First Southern Baptist Church in San Diego, Calif. He married Elizabeth West Bates in 1925, and they had three children, Ellis Adams, Jr., Sara Elizabeth, and Ida Lee.

GAINES S. DOBBINS

FULLER, RICHARD (b. Beaufort, S. C., Apr. 22, 1804; d. Baltimore, Md., Oct. 20, 1876). Lawyer and clergyman. The ninth child in a family of 10, Fuller went to school in Beaufort and entered Harvard University in 1820. During his junior year, in Dec., 1822, he developed symptoms of what was thought to be tuberculosis and spent about a year in Northampton recuperating. When his class was graduated from Harvard in 1824, however, he was awarded a diploma in recognition of his past good record. Fuller's parents, Thomas and Elizabeth (Middleton) Fuller, became Baptists about the time of Richard's birth, but he was brought up more an Episcopalian than anything else. He married Charlotte Bull in 1831 and shortly afterward was converted, became a Baptist, and gave up the law practice, only recently begun, to enter the Baptist ministry as pastor of the Beaufort Baptist Church where he remained for 15 years.

In 1844 Fuller became involved in a public controversy, when at the request of the *Christian Reflector*, Philadelphia, he wrote an article which the paper published, explaining his belief in the biblical sanction for slavery. Answered by a fellow Baptist minister, Francis Wayland, Fuller began with him a long argument, which was published in 1845 in the book *Domestic Slavery Considered as a Scriptural Institution*. In 1847 Fuller became pastor of the

Seventh Baptist Church of Baltimore, accepting that pastorate primarily because of the unique position of Baltimore between the North and South, and remained there throughout the Civil War until 1871. Understanding the views of the North as well as the South, Fuller was able to hold his congregation together, even though sons of some members were fighting for the North and others for the South.

A denominational leader as well as a popular preacher, Fuller served as president of the Maryland Baptist Union Association in 1850 and preached the annual sermon in 1847, 1855, and 1859. He was president of the Southern Baptist Convention in 1859 and 1861 and preached the Convention's first annual sermon in 1846. At the Convention's meeting in 1869, Fuller spoke in behalf of the Southern Baptist Theological Seminary, emphasizing the need for an educated ministry. "The Bible is written in other languages," he said, "and we Baptists should see to it that we have men able to interpret them, and to state and defend our peculiar views." In an address on "domestic missions" in 1872, Fuller urged work among Negroes and pointed out the economical advantages of mission work close at home. He was leader of the Provisional Board in Baltimore, which carried on foreign mission work during the Civil War when the Foreign Mission Board in Richmond was cut off from communication with missionaries in China and Africa, and funds from the South were not available.

Under Fuller's leadership the Seventh Baptist Church increased in membership from 87 in 1847 to about 1,200 in 1867, at which time Fuller began to urge his members to erect a building for another Baptist church in Baltimore at Eutaw Place and Dolphin Street. With the building completed in 1871, Fuller and 132 of his Seventh Church members constituted the Eutaw Place Baptist Church, with Fuller serving as pastor until his death in 1871. Published writings of Fuller are *Baptism and the Terms of Communion: an Argument* (1854); *Sermons* (1860); *A City or House Divided Against Itself. A Discourse Delivered . . . on the First Day of June, 1865, Being the Day of National Fasting and Humiliation* (1865); *Sermons Delivered . . . During His Ministry with the Seventh and Eutaw Churches, Baltimore, 1847-76* (1877).

With the assistance of J. B. Jeter, Fuller published an edition of *The Psalmist* (1843), adding a supplement to make it more acceptable to Baptist churches in the South.

BIBLIOGRAPHY: J. H. Cuthbert, *Life of Richard Fuller* (1879). *Dictionary of American Biography*, VII (1931). W. CLYDE ATKINS

FUNDAMENTAL BAPTIST FELLOWSHIP, THE. A body of premillennial Baptists first organized in 1934 as the Premillennial Baptist Missionary Fellowship. This fellowship existed in an incipient form long before its actual formation in 1934 under the leadership of John Franklyn Norris (q.v.) and Clarence Perry Stealey (q.v.). They contended that less than three cents of every Cooperative Program dollar found its way to the mission field, but that the fellowship would send the entire amount directly to the missionary. This served the purpose of bringing together the Fundamental Baptist churches, that is, those which claimed to be the guardians of certain great truths of Christianity, in the Southwest, while offering a channel of missionary endeavor.

Norris, who in 1909 became pastor of the First Baptist Church of Fort Worth, very early in his career identified himself with Fundamentalism. As a result of the tremendous growth of denominational work in Texas after the turn of the century, Texas Baptists in 1914 consolidated their education commission with the state mission board and charged the executive board with the administration of all the affairs of the general convention. Norris opposed the new mission program. Definite signs of friction appeared between Norris' congregation and other churches of the local Tarrant County Association by 1917. That same year, his church sponsored an interdenominational Bible conference led by leading Fundamentalist preachers. By 1919 Norris was closely associated with the newly organized World's Christian Fundamentals Conference, and in 1923 he helped to form the ultrafundamentalist Baptist Bible Union of America. Tarrant County Association denied Norris and his church seats in 1922, and in 1924 the Texas general convention excluded them. He succeeded in alienating some ministers and churches from the denomination, enlisting them in his cause, and organizing a movement for "fundamental" Baptist churches. Norris gave the inspirational leadership for vicious attacks upon leaders, institutions, and agencies of the Southern Baptist Convention with the popular rallying cry of "modernism." The Fundamental Baptist Fellowship became nation-wide when Norris accepted the pastorate of Temple Baptist Church of Detroit in 1935. His church in Fort Worth in 1939 opened the Fundamental Baptist Bible Institute to teach "the whole English Bible." The World Baptist Fellowship, the enlarged organization of Norris' Fundamental Baptist Fellowship, adopted the institution and changed its name to the Bible Baptist Seminary. This school supplied the leaders that carried on the movement begun by Norris. Since his death in 1952, which deprived the fellowship of his dynamic drive, the movement has tended to slide into a mediating position. Some of its churches have sought co-operation with the Southern Baptist Convention. The characteristic difference of the fellowship lies in its shades of emphasis rather than divergent points of theology. As of 1956, the membership of this body consisted of several hundred churches and a few mission stations. WILBURN S. TAYLOR

FUNDAMENTALISM. An ultraconservative theological movement, and sometimes a reactionary religious attitude, which has cut across many denominations and affected all parts of Christendom. Its influence has been most acutely felt in American Protestantism since World War I. During the early years of the century, an increasing number of ministers and theological seminaries were accepting the critical approach to the Scriptures, together with a liberal theology which minimized or rejected the doctrine of the deity of Christ, weakened the orthodox teaching of depravity and sin, deplored the view of the atonement as divine satisfaction or vicarious substitution for the sinner, and particularly rejected belief in the visible return of Christ to establish his kingdom. Cries of consternation and warning were raised by conservative Christians, who, after many attempts to rally support from among various denominations, finally united in a 1909 meeting at Los Angeles, with plans to establish a Bible institute and enter the field of religious publication. Two wealthy laymen, Lyman and Molton Stewart, established the Stewart Evangelistic Fund and financed the publication of a series of 12 small volumes (1910–12), entitled *The Fundamentals: A Testimony of the Truth*. This work gave the name to the movement and included within it such an outstanding man as Edgar Young Mullins, (q.v.), president of Southern Baptist Theological Seminary, the leading theologian among Southern Baptists at that time.

This multivolume work has been called the "Bible of Fundamentalism." It sets forth the five unshakable "fundamental doctrines": (1) the virgin birth of Christ, presented always as a defense and proof of his deity; (2) the bodily resurrection of Christ (and Christians as well), set forth in refutation of theories of spiritual survival or natural immortality; (3) the inerrancy (infallibility) of the Scriptures, denying all scientific approaches to the Bible and asserting the absolute infallibility of all its historical, cultural, and geographical pronouncements because of its literal "verbal inspiration"; (4) the substitutionary theory of the atonement, denying all the liberal attempts to emphasize the "moral influence" theories of the work of Christ; (5) the imminent, physical second coming of Christ to usher in the millennial reign, interpreted as a refutation of all the evolutionary theories of inevitable progress toward a better and brighter world. Many of the contributors would have interpreted these fundamentals in differing fashion, but upon the bare statement of them, they were agreed.

In this outline of fundamentalist teaching can be seen a strange mixture of orthodox theology, on the one hand, and frantic efforts to rationalize and reinforce faith, on the other. With these efforts to defend and promulgate strict orthodoxy, many conservative Christians have had some sympathy; but most Christian theologians have expressed sharp disagreement with the basic misunderstanding of the nature of the Christian life and the character of biblical literature. They insist that, for the vital experience of personal faith in Jesus Christ, fundamentalism has often substituted intellectual acceptance of the doctrine of his deity, undergirded by a series of rational proofs. For a body of Holy Scripture which is interwoven with the saving acts of God in history, fundamentalists substituted a static book of doctrines and precepts, which is liable to all kinds of arrangements according to dispensational schemes, eschatological charts, and creedal "tests of fellowship."

The aggressive and militant attitude of fundamentalists has resulted in a long period of controversy in four major denominations: Presbyterians, Methodists, Disciples, and Baptists. With membership drawn from all of these, the World's Christian Fundamentals Association was founded in 1918, the Baptist weekly, *The Watchman Examiner*, becoming one of its voices. A schism was led in the Presbyterian church by J. Gresham Machen of Princeton Theological Seminary, resulting in the founding of the new Westminster Theological Seminary in Philadelphia and the emergence of the Bible Presbyterian Church, a fundamentalist denomination. The Methodists were involved in a group of splinter parties within the church and a rash of new periodicals to counteract the influence of the *Christian Century*. In 1923 a group of Baptist fundamentalists, led by J. Frank Norris, (q.v.), William B. Riley, and T. T. Shields, organized the Baptist Bible Union of North America.

Fundamental organizations were kept alive by Bible conferences and premillennial fellowships and promoted their teaching through such Bible schools as Moody Bible Institute, Wheaton College, Dallas Theological Seminary, and Fuller Theological Seminary. Many seminaries were founded to offset the liberal influence: Northern Baptist Theological Seminary to counteract the University of Chicago Divinity School; Eastern Baptist Seminary as a corrective to Crozer Theological Seminary, etc. Although fundamentalism was intended to be a nondenominational movement, it has often taken on the characteristics of a new denomination. The most authoritative work on fundamentalism is by Stewart G. Cole, *The History of Fundamentalism* (1931). As a specific theological movement, fundamentalism has already spent itself, but as an ultraconservative attitude, it will long be a considerable factor in the American church scene.

BIBLIOGRAPHY: S. G. Cole, *The History of Fundamentalism* (1931). The Bible Institute of Los Angeles, *The Fundamentals: A Testimony to the Truth* (1910–15).

WAYNE E. WARD

FUNDAMENTALISM, OKLAHOMA. Stemming mainly from alleged modernism and the evolution question, the beginnings of fundamentalism in Oklahoma may be attributed to the influence of C. P. Stealey. Outcomes of Stealey's activities were the Stealey Controversy and the ultimate removal of Stealey from leadership in the Oklahoma convention. On Nov. 10, 1926, the convention approved a resolution originated and introduced by Clyde Calhoun Morris. According to this resolution, undesignated funds were to be withheld from Southern Baptist institutions whose faculties refused to sign the McDaniel statement, a summary of doctrine which had been previously adopted by the Southern Baptist Convention. A year later the convention again approved the resolution. The issue was settled in Mar., 1928, when faculties of Southern and Southwestern seminaries signed the statement and all funds were forwarded in order.

Fundamentalism continued in Oklahoma under the leadership of W. Lee Rector, former professor at Oklahoma Baptist University and outspoken critic of Baptist life and institutions. Resigning as pastor of the First Baptist Church, Ardmore, Okla., Sept. 27, 1931, Rector led 300 members of the church to withdraw and form the First Orthodox Baptist Church of Ardmore. This church, with Rector as pastor, nominally supported convention work until 1935. Branding convention literature as modernistic, it then severed all convention connections and assumed the role of "mother church" to the so-called Orthodox Baptist Movement. In 1944 the church founded the Orthodox Bible Institute, which 10 years later claimed 25 students enrolled and 52 graduates. *The Orthodox Baptist*, a monthly publication, was founded in 1931.

On Nov. 11, 1948, a proposed constitutional amendment, fundamental in nature, was offered to the Oklahoma convention by Marion Edgar Ramey. The Ramey amendment, with the aim to stem the tide of liberalism in doctrine, proposed to restrict messengers from churches practicing open communion or alien immersion and from churches affiliating with the Federal or World council of churches or like organizations. A subject of year-long discussion, the amendment was changed to a resolution, offered by Ramey in substitute. According to the resolution, the words "Baptist churches" in the constitution were interpreted to mean "churches that are sound in faith and practice"; churches which violated principles in the proposed amendment were considered to be unsound in faith and practice. The resolution was adopted.

A survey in 1956 showed 38 churches in Oklahoma having definite fundamentalist persuasion and not co-operating with the Baptist General Convention of Oklahoma. Fifteen of these churches bear the name "Bible Baptist." A questionnaire sent to these 38 churches brought returns from only nine, which reported 3,038 members and property valued at $719,000.

J. M. GASKIN

FUNERAL PROCEDURES AMONG BAPTISTS. Funerals vary with the personality of the individual minister and the customs of the community. There is no church manual or book of procedure authoritatively published by the denomination. Various authors have written a pastor's manual including suggestive sermon outlines for funerals, and varying patterns of a burial service, but Baptists, unlike many ritualistic bodies, have no prescribed funeral service.

Some ministers have a pattern service from which they will not deviate, but the majority of funerals are conducted in accord with the wishes of the family and in co-operation with a funeral director. The length of the funeral has dwindled; today it is seldom over thirty minutes. In larger communities and in cities, most funerals are held in the chapel of the funeral home. In the rural areas and in communities without modern chapel facilities, funerals are more often held in the church than in the home.

Music has long had a place in the funeral. In many communities the congregation joins in the singing of two or three appropriate hymns; in still others hymns are sung by a choir or a small ensemble; in many larger towns and in the cities there seems to be a trend to instrumental music.

Occasionally, several ministers participate in a funeral service, but this arrangement is not so often used as formerly. Participation is often an imposition on the assisting ministers, who may have pressing obligations but who feel they cannot refuse. Except on rare occasions it is the feeling of ministers in general that funerals can best be conducted by the pastor or selected minister alone. At the cemetery few Baptist ministers use a ritualized committal service. A few verses of comforting Scripture and a closing prayer usually suffice.

The actual funeral service varies widely. Three things, however, almost always are characteristic: the reading of pertinent Scripture; a prayer or prayers; and a message of comfort and consolation to the family and friends. In most instances the message brought includes a word of personal appraisal of or tribute to the deceased, couched in language that will not tend unduly to arouse the emotions of the relatives present. In many sections the funeral sermon is still customary and is expected by the family and friends. The trend, however, is away from such procedure and toward a simple, comforting, devotional service. The majority of Baptists do not like an impersonal, formal, ritualistic funeral. Nor do they want the long "sermonic" type. In their hour of sorrow and bereavement, they feel the need of assurance, comfort, strength, hope, sympathy, and, above everything else, a sense of the presence of God.

When the deceased is a Christian—many times a very active and consecrated church member—the main objective of the funeral service is, through quiet worship, to give assurance and comfort to the family and to magnify in the hearts of those present the virtues and values of the Christian life. Often such an occasion affords the opportunity to present the worth of the Christian faith when hearts are tender and impressionable. Many times ministers are called upon to conduct services for those who are not church members and have no personal faith. In this situation the passages of Scripture, the prayers, and the message of the occasion are selected for the strengthening of the ones who remain. In cases of tragic death, or in unusual circumstances, the burden is on the minister to keep foremost in mind the needs of relatives and friends.

It is the custom of the Baptist minister to visit the home as quickly as possible after death has occurred. Often he is present when life ebbs away. At this time a prayer with the family may bring needed spiritual strength. Usually at a later period he returns to the family to confer about the service. All details, except those of the actual memorial service itself, are left in the hands of a funeral director.

The definite trend in funerals among Baptists is toward simplicity. Many customs, such as elaborate and expensive funerals, "viewing the remains," lengthy funeral sermons, two or more assisting ministers, and Sunday burials, are falling into disuse.

Some ministers prepare a copy of the Scripture passages used and a résumé of the message given and present them in an individually designed folder to the family at the close of the service. Some funeral homes now record or transcribe the service as a part of their professional services.

BIBLIOGRAPHY: A. W. Blackwood, *The Funeral* (1942). N. B. Harmon, *Ministerial Ethics and Etiquette* (1950); *The Pastor's Ideal Funeral Manual* (1942). J. R. Hobbs, *The Pastor's Manual* (1934). P. E. Irion, *The Funeral and the Mourners* (1954).

W. DOUGLAS HUDGINS

FURMAN, JAMES CLEMENT (b. Charleston, S. C., Dec. 5, 1809; d. near Greenville, S. C., Mar. 3, 1891). Minister, educator, editor. Son of Richard (*q.v.*) and Dorothea Maria (Burn) Furman, he was educated at the College of Charleston and Furman Theological Institution and preached from 1828 to 1844 in churches in the lower part of South Carolina. Licensed to preach in 1828 and ordained in 1832, Furman married Harriet Eloise Davis in 1833; and after her death in 1849, he married her sister, Mary Glenn Davis, in 1855.

He was active in moving Furman Theological Institution to Greenville, S. C., and changing it to a university, where he served as senior professor, 1844–52, chairman of the faculty, 1852–59 and 1879–81, and president, 1859–79. During the Civil War when Furman University was not operating, Furman taught in Greenville Baptist Female College. Active in the establishment of Southern Baptist Theological Seminary, he was an outspoken advocate of secession and a member of the South Carolina Secession Convention in 1860. From 1882 until his death, he was associate editor of the *Baptist Courier*. Furman was pastor of the First Baptist Church of Greenville from 1871 to 1875, served other churches, and played an active role in denominational affairs. His publications included *An Historical Discourse Delivered Before the Charleston Baptist Association*, "Memorial Sermon" (for John G. Landrum), and an address in *Minutes of Welch Neck Temperance Convention Held at Darlington Courthouse*. Furman displayed a remarkable ability to raise money for any cause in which he was interested and served as "an official of various Baptist boards, five times, for instance, vice-president of the Southern Association [Southern Baptist Convention], and seven times President of the State Association [S. C. Baptist State Convention]."

BIBLIOGRAPHY: W. Cathcart, ed., *The Baptist Encyclopaedia* (1883). H. T. Cook, *The Life Work of James Clement Furman* (1926). M. Furman, "A Family of Educators," *Education* (Mar., 1897). J. D. Wade, "James Clement Furman," *Dictionary of American Biography* (1928–36).

WINSTON C. BABB

FURMAN, RICHARD (b. Esopus, N. Y., Oct. 9, 1755; d. South Carolina, Aug. 25, 1825). Clergyman, patriot, educator, and pioneer denominational statesman. More than any other man, he created the basic organizational concepts that are unique in Southern Baptist denominational life. He was the son of Wood and Rachel (Brodhead) Furman, who moved to Charleston, S. C., shortly after his birth and to the High Hills of Santee in 1770. Furman's mind matured at an early age. When only a small child, he learned to read from the family Bible. He had less than a year of conventional schooling, but his father instructed him in mathematics and other sciences. By persistent, personal study he learned Latin, Greek, Hebrew, French, German, metaphysics, logic, history, and theology. He had a remarkable memory and mastered selections of poetry merely by reading them. In middle life he could recite correctly much of Homer's *Iliad* and portions of other classics that he had learned when only 11 years old. He acquired a knowledge of medicine and frequently ministered to the sick when no physician was available. Rhode Island College (now Brown University) recognized his attainments and granted him the honorary master's degree; both that institution and South Carolina College (now the University of South Carolina) gave him D.D. degrees.

Furman's spiritual heritage of evangelistic Calvinism determined his doctrine and tempered his preaching. He was converted in 1771 under the ministry of Joseph Reese at High Hills. Reese was a convert of Phillip Mulkey, who was in turn a convert of Shubal Stearns (*q.v.*); all were zealous, evangelical Calvinists. The union of the enduring qualities of the Regular and Separate Baptists in Furman made him the arch-prototype of the prevailing norm of the Southern Baptists of the 20th century. Furman began to preach at the age of 16 and became popularly known as the "boy-evangelist." Reese and Evan Pugh ordained him two years later, on May 10, 1774, as pastor of High Hills. After a fruitful ministry there of 13 years, he became pastor of the Charleston Baptist Church, which he served for the rest of his life. "In the community no minister ever enjoyed so large a share of general confidence and reverence." For 38 years he made "annual excursions" into various parts of the state, preaching the gospel and promoting the interests of the denomination. This itinerant ministry resulted in numerous revivals and the formation of many churches. His eloquence and fame as a preacher once opened for him an opportunity to preach in the United States Congressional Hall.

As an ardent patriot, Furman won many to the Colonial cause when the Revolutionary War began. He volunteered to fight, but Gov. John Rutledge persuaded him to continue as a propagandist among the Tories in western South Carolina, which he did with remarkable success. By his prayers and eloquent appeals, Furman so reassured the patriots that Cornwallis was said to have remarked that he "feared the prayers of the Godly youth more than the armies of Sumter and Marion." When Charleston surrendered, Cornwallis determined to make an example of this notorious rebel. He placed a price of £1000 on his head and forced Furman to flee from the state, not to return until after the war, in 1782.

A group of dissenters in 1776 called a meeting at High Hills to discuss religious liberty, of which Furman was a zealous advocate. His work contributed strongly to the constitutional change two years later which ended the established church in South Carolina. While serving as a delegate to the South Carolina constitutional convention in 1790, he obtained the passage of measures that discontinued the special privileges of the Episcopal church and granted the right of incorporation to all denominations.

Furman had a profound sense of the necessity and value of education. While a pastor in Charleston, in conjunction with Gen. Sumter and other leaders in the city, he helped to establish a literary society, and later a literary institution, Claremont Academy, near Statesburg. His interest in educating the masses in the Scriptures led him to assist in forming and directing the affairs of both the Charleston Bible Society and Religious Tract Society.

Stressing the importance of an educated ministry, Furman encouraged his fellow ministers, often unlearned men, suspicious of education, to overcome their prejudices and apply themselves to study. Such a one was Silas Mercer, who considered learning to be detrimental to true religion and was deeply prejudiced against it. After visiting Furman, Mercer came away convinced of the value of education and, for the rest of his life, was a diligent student and zealous promoter of learning. His son, Jesse Mercer (q.v.), helped to create an educational consciousness among Georgia Baptists, which led to the establishment of Mercer University.

Furman also recognized the need of young ministers for assistance in securing an education and devised means of providing it. For many years he gathered funds to send young men to Rhode Island College (later Brown University). In the annual meetings of the Charleston Association, he repeatedly stressed the importance of an educated ministry. He devised a plan for the systematic collection of money and led the association in 1790 to set up a permanent education fund. The association appointed Furman chairman of the committee (later called the General Committee) to direct the fund. The body elected him president of the general committee for 34 consecutive years. Under Furman's administration this fund provided assistance for training large numbers of young men, such as Jesse Mercer, who became prominent leaders of the denomination.

When the Triennial Convention was organized in 1814, Furman urged that provision be made for the education of ministers. His impelling address to the convention in 1817 aroused the delegates to include education in the denomination's program of work. Furman's plan, which was approved by the body, called for a central theological institution at Washington, with institutions preparatory to it in the separate states. A class of young men was gathered at Philadelphia under the instruction of William Staughton (q.v.), whom Furman had influenced to come to America in 1793, in anticipation of removal to Washington when funds permitted. The movement which Furman began resulted in the founding of Columbian College (now George Washington University); Furman University; Southern Baptist Theological Seminary, which grew out of the theological department of Furman; Mercer University; and others.

Furman was also a pioneer in the work of organizing his denomination on the district, state, and national bases. A Southern aristocrat and a Federalist in religion as well as politics, he advocated a more centralized ecclesiastical polity than many Baptists were willing to accept. Nevertheless, he conceived, initiated, and promoted much that is a vital part of Southern Baptist life and work today.

Through the influence he exerted upon its life and work, Furman led the Charleston Association to develop several ventures that marked the beginning of the basic distinctive forms from which came later Southern Baptist development. This body, under his leadership, set up an education fund for young ministers and organized the general committee, which not only directed this program but also came to serve in an executive capacity for the association. This committee foreshadowed the executive boards of associations and conventions. When his attempts to incorporate the Charleston Association failed, Furman secured in 1792 a charter for its general committee so that it could hold and distribute funds. He promoted a program of associational missions in 1802 and a more extensive program of itinerant preaching in 1817, in many respects similar to present-day associational and state mission programs, with a board to superintend the work. The Charleston Association chose Furman as its moderator for over 25 years.

Furman helped to organize and mold the character of the first state Baptist convention. As early as 1809, he expressed the hope that a plan might eventually be adopted to unite all associations in South Carolina to promote missions, education, and other important objects. His address to the Charleston Association in 1819 influenced the body to approve his plan for organizing a state convention and to print and distribute the address among the churches and associations of the state. The constitution of the new convention, which Furman helped to draft, embodied his ideas of a centralized denominational organization that comprehended within its scope the work of missions, education, Sunday schools, and other objects deemed useful by the body. He served for four years as president of the South Carolina convention, which became a model for the organization of conventions in other states.

Furman's far-reaching influence as a denominational statesman was even more extensive on the national level. He pointed out to the Charleston Association, as early as 1800, the need for an organization to unite the Baptists of America. The body voted with certain reservations to support such a coalition, if it were organized, and appointed Furman to secure the reaction of other associations to the idea. He also corresponded for several years with John Gano and Thomas Baldwin about uniting the denomination to promote missions and education. When the 33 delegates met at Philadelphia in 1814 to organize the Triennial Convention, they unanimously chose Furman president. As a member of the constitutional committee, he sought to construct a comprehensive denominational organization. The committee's first draft was rejected, probably because of its strong denominational emphasis. The delegates accepted the second draft after they had made several amendments. The convention re-elected Furman president in 1817. Through the impact of an address in which he advocated a "plan of education," he influenced the body to include ministerial education as one of its objects. This was a step toward the truly denominational organization that he had originally recommended. His denominational concept, however, waited many years to be realized on a national scale. Southern Baptists adopted in 1845 a plan of organization which comprehended within its scope any phase of work that the Convention should desire to perform. This was essentially the same plan that Furman had advocated at Philadelphia in 1814 and 1817 and had secured on the state level in 1821. It is significant that Furman's protégé and spiritual heir, William Bullein Johnson (q.v.), who wrote the original draft of the first constitution of the denomination, led Southern Baptists to adopt the centralized convention type of organization. Through Johnson, Furman's dreams were ultimately realized.

Twice married, Furman was survived by 15 children, among whom were Rachel, Wood, Richard, Samuel, Josiah, Charles Manning, James Clement, Anne Eliza, and William D. Several of Furman's sermons were published during his lifetime, and his eulogy of Alexander Hamilton may be found in H. T. Cook's *A Biography of Richard Furman*. He wrote several hymns, some of which were published.

For almost 50 years the outstanding pastor in the South, Furman was by reason of character and ability a leader in religious, educational, political, and humanitarian affairs. His influence as an educator and denominational statesman in particular has exerted a profound, determinative influence upon Southern Baptist life and work since his time.

BIBLIOGRAPHY: W. H. Allison, "Richard Furman," *Dictionary of American Biography*, VII (1928–36). H. T. Cook, *A Biography of Richard Furman* (1913). E. C. Dargan, "Richard Furman and His Place in American History," *Bulletin of Furman University* (July, 1914). H. C. Haynsworth, *Haynsworth-Furman and Allied Families* (1942). "Memoir of Rev. Richard Furman," *American Baptist Magazine* (Mar., 1826). H. A. Tupper, ed., *Two Centuries of the First Baptist Church of South Carolina* (1889). R. Furman, "Address to the Convention," *American Baptist Magazine* (Sept., 1817; 1818).

WINSTON C. BABB and LYNN E. MAY, JR.

FURMAN FITTING SCHOOL. Operated by Furman University in Greenville, S. C., providing college preparatory work from Sept., 1900, through May, 1916. The three-year program of study, an outgrowth of the university's preparatory department, was instituted to meet the problem of an increasing number of students not prepared for college and was expanded to four years for the 1915–16 term. Ninety-two students enrolled the first year, and enrolment averaged 88 for the school's 16-year existence with 82 enrolled during the final year. In May, 1916, Furman trustees discontinued the school because of the necessity for using fitting school facilities for college students. The provision of a new Greenville high school adequately provided for city patrons and was another factor in the school's closing. Headmasters of the Fitting School were Hugh Charles Haynsworth, Columbus Benjamin Martin, Allison William Honeycutt, George Smith Bryan, Richard Clyde Burts, and Luther Weeks Courtney.

DYAR EDWIN MASSEY, JR.

FURMAN UNIVERSITY. Originated in the Furman Academy and Theological Institution, authorized by the South Carolina Baptist state convention in Dec., 1825, and opened at Edgefield, S. C., Jan. 15, 1827, with Joseph Andrews Warne (1795–1881) as its first principal. The primary purpose of the founders was to educate candidates for the ministry, but provision was made for the admission of other students.

The first funds of the institution were $5,000 received from the estate of Thomas Gillison "to be applied to education [sic] purposes" and $400 from Basil Manly, Sr. (q.v.), which represented a part of the value of Manly's house and lot in Edgefield, acquired by the board of agents of the convention for $1,400. Only $1,000 of this sum was to be paid in cash, the balance to be a donation to the library.

Richard Furman (q.v.), for whom the school was named, had long promoted the idea of religious education in South Carolina as had Oliver Hart (q.v.) before him. Furman died in Aug., 1825, only a few months before the convention authorized establishment of a school. William Bullein Johnson (q.v.), president of the convention and chairman of the board of agents which acted for the convention, building on the ideas of Furman, led in the establishment of Furman Academy and Theological Institution, and later was a leading spirit in the establishment of Furman University.

Edgefield, S. C., was selected as the location for the new school in the hope that Georgia Baptists would join South Carolina Baptists in supporting it. Disappointed in this hope and faced by discouraging financial difficulties, the convention gave up the plant at Edgefield and early in 1829 placed the students in the home of Jesse Hartwell (1795-1859), pastor of High Hills Baptist Church in Sumter County. Under Hartwell the school became a theological institution, although there was instruction in academic subjects. Simple buildings were erected at the new location, principally at Hartwell's expense, and when the convention later purchased the main building, Hartwell apparently donated the lot on which it stood. A second teacher, Samuel Furman, a son of Richard Furman, was added in 1831, but mounting debts harassed the school, and both teachers resigned in 1834. As a result the institution was suspended and did not reopen until 1837 when it opened as a classical and English school on the manual labor principle.

In 1835 the convention elected a board of trustees for the Furman Theological Institution, and in 1836 placed the "superintendence and government" of both the projected manual labor school and the theological school in the hands of the board. The new start in 1837 was made on a farm of 557 acres near Winnsboro, S. C., purchased at a cost of $7,400. The next year the theological school was reopened under William Hooper (1792-1876), and for a short time the two departments of what was known as Furman Institution operated side by side. However, when the manual labor experiment proved unsuccessful, the convention took action in Dec., 1840, to abandon the classical and English school. Hooper resigned in 1839 and was succeeded by James L. Reynolds (1812-77), who headed the school until 1844. James Clement Furman (q.v.) then became senior professor, the title borne by all three of these men, and he reorganized the curriculum after the pattern of Newton Theological Institution. Associated with Furman were James S. Mims (1817-55), who had joined the faculty in 1842, and Peter C. Edwards (1819-67), who came in 1846.

Furman, Mims, and Edwards moved with the theological school to Greenville, S. C., where the convention had determined to establish a college and had even planned to raise $70,000 for that purpose. W. B. Johnson headed the committee recommending establishment of a college in Greenville, and Furman was chairman of the agents to raise the $70,000. In 1850 the state legislature chartered The Furman University. The article "the" was dropped when the charter of 1866 was issued.

On the first Monday in Feb., 1851, Furman Theological Institution began operation in Greenville, and a preparatory school known as The Furman University High School also began work. Mims taught theology; Edwards devoted his efforts principally to the preparatory subjects; and Furman raised the money. In June, 1851, a tract of land of approximately 25 acres was purchased from Vardy McBee for $3,750, and in Jan., 1852, a second tract of similar size was purchased from the same man for $3,765. On this campus a two-room cottage, used for classrooms, was the first building erected. Still in existence, it is used as the headquarters of an undergraduate club. The president's home was completed in 1852, and the main building, now known as Richard Furman Hall, was probably completed in 1854.

The collegiate department began operation in the autumn of 1852. Charles Hallette Judson (q.v.) had been elected to the faculty, and the three men who had come from Winnsboro, after resigning from the theological school, had become members of the university faculty. Furman became faculty chairman in Sept., 1852, and Judson, secretary. In 1859 Furman was elected president.

The university consisted of three departments, academic, collegiate, and theological. The academic offered preparatory work, while the collegiate department, organized on the basis of plans of the University of Virginia and Brown University, was to include six schools. In order to graduate, a student had to win the degree of Proficient (be placed in the first division) in prescribed studies in all the regular schools. A master's degree required the highest honor in each school plus mastery of Hebrew or one modern language. The theological department, which consisted of three schools, exegetical and systematic theology, ecclesiastical history, and sacred rhetoric, in 1859 was separated from the university to become Southern Baptist Theological Seminary.

Closed by the Civil War, the university did not reopen until 1866, at which time it began a long period of struggle for survival. In 1868 the situation became so desperate that President Furman was urged to abandon the "wreck." His reply was that he had nailed his colors to the mast and that if the vessel went down he would go down with it. In the 1880's the situation improved, largely through the efforts of Charles Manly (q.v.), president of that period (1881-97), and the financial agent, Richard H. Griffith

Furman University

(1825-94). During the 1897-1902 administration of Philip Andrew Montague (1854-1928), Furman's first lay president, financial improvements made possible the erection of a dormitory, chapel, and fitting school building. During the acting presidency (1902-03) of Judson a successful campaign for $100,000 endowment, led by Joel I. Allen (1850-1925), laid the financial foundation for the future of the university.

During the administration of Edwin McNeill Poteat (q.v.) from 1903 to 1918 the university advanced through the construction of a library building and science hall, considerable addition to the endowment, and strengthening of the curriculum, especially in the sciences. Sidney Ernest Bradshaw (1869-1938), professor of modern languages, served as acting president during the 1918-19 session, and William Joseph McGlothlin (q.v.), the next president (1919-33), led the 75 Million Campaign in South Carolina, from which $750,000 was allocated to Furman University. A successful alumni campaign, led by Bennette Eugene Geer, raised $325,000 to match $175,000 offered by the general education board, and soon after this the university, primarily due to Geer's influence, became a beneficiary of the Duke Endowment. A building program including a dormitory, central heating plant, refectory, gymnasium, and an infirmary incorporating an old student cottage was completed. Departments of education, physical education, economics, biology, and sociology were added and other departments strengthened.

In 1933, shortly before the death of McGlothlin, Greenville Woman's College and Furman University began a process of co-ordination which was legally consummated in 1938. During this period, under the leadership of Geer, who succeeded McGlothlin as president, the university sponsored an important community development project, largely financed by the general education board. Careful study and reorganization of the curriculum resulted in a major effort to improve instruction and the establishment of departments of speech, arts, political science, and home economics. The teaching of vocal music to men was emphasized, and courses in art and geology were added. Robert Norman Daniel (dean, 1922-48) served as acting president during the fall months of 1938.

Under John Laney Plyler, who has been president since Jan. 1, 1939, the university has steadily moved forward. It contributed to the World War II effort by conducting various training programs for military personnel, at the same time maintaining its liberal arts work. In the 1940's its indebtedness was paid off and its endowment materially increased. In 1951 the centennial of the university's location in Greenville and the 125th year of its history were celebrated.

With the launching of a movement for a new plant, buildings have been erected on a campus of 1,200 acres to the north of Greenville near Paris Mountain and in sight of the Blue Ridge Mountains. Plans call for a plant of about 20 major buildings to serve at least 2,000 students.

Enrolment for the 1955-56 session was 1,413 of whom 850 were men and 563 women. The summer session of 1955 enrolled 575. The university, whose administration, faculty, and library staff for 1955-56 numbered 99, offers B.A., B.S., B.A. in Music, M.A., and M.Ed. degrees. With the total value of the plants estimated at $6,008,945.41, $2,618,881.36 of this amount is represented by the old campuses and $3,390,064.05 by the new. The $4,974,094.88 endowment includes participation in the Duke Endowment. For current operations the Baptist state convention annually allots over $136,000 to the total annual budget of $1,022,017.79.

Furman University is a member of the Southern Association of Colleges, the Southern University Conference, the Association of American Colleges, and the South Carolina Association of Colleges. In 1929 it was placed on the approved list of the Association of American Universities and in 1945 on the approved list of the American Association of University Women. It is a liberal arts college member of the National Association of Schools of Music.

In its more than 100 years in Greenville, S. C., Furman University enrolled about 20,000 students and graduated 8,331. Graduates have gone into the ministry, teaching, medicine, the law, journalism, social work, politics, business, and other fields. Ministers among the alumni serve in churches or educational work in every county in South Carolina, in 24 other states, and in the District of Columbia. Since 1925, 10 out of 21 presidents of the South Carolina Baptist state convention have been Furman men. Alumni serve on the teaching or administrative staffs of more than 100 colleges, and 10 are college presidents. Sixty-nine alumni are listed in Volume 29 of *Who's Who in America*.

BIBLIOGRAPHY: H. T. Cook, *Education in South Carolina Under Baptist Control* (1912). R. N. Daniel, *Furman University, a History* (1951). W. J. McGlothlin, *Baptist Beginnings in Education; Furman University, A History of* (1926.)

ROBERT NORMAN DANIEL

G

GAMBLING. The deliberate wagering or staking of important or valuable considerations upon events which, so far as the parties to the wager can know, lie in the realm of pure chance or luck. Gambling involves the turnover of approximately 20 billion dollars a year in the United States. After an investigation into the activities of professional gamblers in this country, a special committee of the United States Senate concluded that gambling is controlled and promoted by some of the worst elements of the nation, who use tremendous sums of money for the corruption of public officials in local and state government.

Gambling is promoted by a variety of activities, both legal and illegal, but mostly illegal. The following outline is a brief summary of the more common gambling practices in the nation today: (1) *Horse racing* is legal in 26 states at present. It is estimated that 25 million persons attend the races every year and that they place $1,600,000 in bets at the pari-mutuel machines. Also associated with horse racing is the illegal business of bookmaking which amounts to about eight billion dollars per year. In addition to horse racing, gambling has become a big business in connection with many, if not all, professional sports. It has also invaded college athletics, creating serious scandals in recent years. (2) *Slot machines* are illegal in most states today; yet, they are played by some 14 million people and have a tremendous turnover of revenue. One reliable estimate for the country as a whole is that they gross more than four billion dollars a year for their operators. (3) *The numbers racket* is patronized annually by 15 million people who spend an estimated one billion dollars to play the numbers. This form of gambling has become a serious problem to American industry, creating a large economic drain on earnings in the industrial plants of the country.

Any discussion of the morality of gambling should begin with the fact that most forms of gambling are illegal in practically every part of the country. It is then apparent immediately that the Christian must hold gambling as wrong because it is a violation of the law. The Christian must also condemn gambling because of its effects. Gambling corrupts government and public officials. One Chicago gambler boasted that the handbook operators of that city could "deliver 200,000 votes" and unlimited financial support toward the election of a candidate favorable to them. In Miami a city councilman was offered $200,000 a year if he would let punchboards be brought into the city. In addition, gambling is inevitably associated with many social evils including organized crime and prostitution. It has always been dependent upon dishonesty and fraud for its existence. According to an eminent authority on mathematics who made a scientific study of gambling, it "has always been and always will be a crooked business." Finally, in addition to the above-mentioned reasons, the Christian must condemn gambling because it violates the image of God in human personality. Gambling leads one to cheat, steal, and lie in his dealings with his fellow man. It creates a craving to get something for nothing, at the price of suffering for others.   HUGH A. BRIMM

GAMBLING AND LOTTERIES, LOUISIANA. Louisiana Baptists on all organized levels warred against the rechartering of the Louisiana State Lottery, relic of a carpetbag legislature, and in the mid-1890's earned partial credit for its defeat. Thereafter the state enjoyed relative freedom from widespread organized gambling until, in the early 1930's, a dominant political machine apparently became allied with underworld gamblers. Subsequent impetus to the alignment of local and interstate operators in slot machines, bookmaking, etc., continued practically unabated for two decades, despite sporadic local reforms, and in defiance of the state's constitutional law and specific legislation prohibiting all forms of gambling. Intermittently Baptist voices attempted to define the pathological genius of the gambling problem and its amenability to the therapeutic values of the gospel as related particularly to the context of the contemporary social milieu. Throughout the period of 1952-55 a reform administration pursued a policy of rigid law enforcement, succeeded in breaking the hold of organized gambling upon the state, and suppressed slot machines, pinball payoffs, and previously unmolested church raffles and bingo, conducted chiefly by Roman Catholic churches. Louisiana Baptists consistently encouraged these late measures and continued agitation for the abolition of legalized race track gambling.

BIBLIOGRAPHY: J. T. Christian, *A History of the Baptists of Louisiana* (1923). B. Davidson and C. Hinch, "This Is A Raid!" *Collier's* (Apr. 1, 1955). E. Kefauver, *Committee Report on Organized Crime* (1951). G. W. McGinty, *A History of Louisiana* (1951). V. W. Peterson, *Gambling, Should It Be Legalized?* (1951). *West's Louisiana Statutes Annotated* (1951).   GLEN LEE GREENE

GAMBRELL, JAMES BRUTON (b. Anderson County, S. C., Aug. 21, 1841; d. Dallas, Tex.,

Gano, John

June 10, 1921). Editor, seminary professor, Texas Baptist leader. Son of Joel Bruton and Jane (Williams) Gambrell, he moved with his parents to northeast Mississippi when he was four years old. A scout for General Robert E. Lee in the Confederate Army, Gambrell fought at Gettysburg, was commissioned a captain, and was ordered to the Memphis territory. Before the close of the war he married Mary T. Corbell of Nansemond County, Va., on Jan. 13, 1864. After the war Gambrell enrolled in the University of Mississippi and served five years as pastor of Oxford Baptist Church. In 1877 he became editor of the *Baptist Record*, and in 1893 was elected president of Mercer University, Macon, Ga., where he served three years.

Gambrell became superintendent of missions in Texas in Dec., 1896, where he served until Feb. 10, 1910, when he resigned to become editor of the *Baptist Standard*, then owned by a group of representative Baptists. In 1912 Gambrell was elected a member of the faculty of Southwestern Baptist Theological Seminary but continued his duties as editor-in-chief of the *Baptist Standard* until Dec., 1914, when he was elected executive secretary of the Consolidated Board (missions and education) of the Baptist General Convention of Texas, at which time he resigned his positions with both the *Standard* and Southwestern Seminary. Gambrell served six years as secretary of the convention. In 1917 he was elected president of the Southern Baptist Convention and served in that position four terms. His death occurred only six months after he returned with Edgar Young Mullins (q.v.) from a visit to European Baptists.

BIBLIOGRAPHY: J. M. Carroll, *History of Texas Baptists* (1923). E. C. Routh, *Life Story of Dr. J. B. Gambrell* (1929).

E. C. ROUTH

GANO, JOHN (b. Hopewell, N. J., July 22, 1727; d. Frankfort, Ky., Aug. 10, 1804). Missionary and leading minister. He was a descendant of Francis Gerneaux, a French Huguenot of the 17th century who fled to America. Born of a Presbyterian father, Daniel Gano, and a Baptist mother, Sarah (Britton) Gano, he decided after a study of baptism to join the Baptist church at Hopewell, N. J. His early years were spent on a farm. Neighboring pastors tutored him in the classics and he attended classes at Princeton University although not matriculated there.

After his baptism he was called to the ministry. With others, sent by the Philadelphia Association, he made a missionary tour to Opekon Creek Church in Virginia in 1752. Returning to New Jersey, he was licensed and in May, 1754, was ordained. It was about this time that he was pastor of the church at Morristown, N. J. In the fall of 1754, on another tour to the South for the Philadelphia Association, he went as far south as Charleston, S. C., where he preached in the presence of George Whitefield (1714–70); he returned to New Jersey in the spring of 1755. Later in 1755, Gano was married to Sarah Stites, whose sister later married James Manning (1738–91), founder and first president of Rhode Island College, now Brown University, Providence.

When the Jersey Settlement on the Yadkin River in western North Carolina became a matter of concern to the Charleston Association in 1755, Oliver Hart (q.v.) was authorized to visit the Philadelphia Association later that year and obtain a missionary for the Yadkin area. John Gano was influenced to attend the Charleston Association in 1756, and at that time was sent by Charleston Association to the Yadkin. After his return to Morristown, N. Y., he yielded to the invitation to remove with his family to the Yadkin. He made the 800-mile trip in five weeks. The church was revived and strengthened. He remained there about two and a half years, leaving only after war with the Cherokee Indians broke out. During this stay on the Yadkin a son, Daniel, was born on Nov. 11, 1758.

Returning to New Jersey, he was called as pastor of the church in Philadelphia. This pastorate can be dated from his record of his daughter, Peggy, born Dec. 23, 1760. At the close of that brief pastorate he made another visit to North Carolina.

In 1762 Gano became pastor of the First Baptist Church of New York City, where he served for about 25 years, with the exception of 1776–83, when he served as a chaplain in the Revolutionary War. After the war the church grew to a flourishing condition, and he was recognized as a religious and civic leader. He was active in the affairs of Philadelphia Association, and he is reckoned as one of the founders of Brown University. He was elected a regent of the University of the State of New York (1784) and a trustee of King's College, now Columbia University.

His pioneering spirit persisted even after he became older; and, urged to visit Kentucky, he gave up his work in New York City, sold his property, and moved to Kentucky, arriving with his family at Limestone in Mason County on June 17, 1787. Later he moved to Lexington where he became pastor of the Town Fork Church. While still pastor of Town Fork Church he moved to Frankfort. In going to visit this latter place, Mrs. Gano fell from her horse and received injuries which made her a cripple the rest of her life. Soon after moving to the new location she died.

Having been called back to North Carolina to attend to property once owned there, in 1793, he met and married the widow of Captain Thomas Bryant, a daughter of Colonel Jonathan Hunt. He again visited South Carolina. Then after traveling to Kentucky and later to New York and Rhode Island, he left North Carolina with his wife on Sept. 30, 1794, and returned to Frankfort, Ky.

For two years he lived on land near Town Fork Church, but then moved back to Frankfort

FIRST BAPTIST CHURCH, Columbia, S. C. Begun 1809; where South Carolina secession convention met in 1860; later escaped torch of Union troops who sought to destroy it. Greek Revival architecture houses 1,500-seat auditorium, serves 1,600 in Sunday school.

FIRST BAPTIST CHURCH, Mobile, Ala. Founded 1835, membership 1956 approximately 1,700. Auditorium in classical Greek style erected 1845, seats 700, educational unit accommodates 960. Property valued at $900,000.

in the spring of 1798. In Sept., 1798, Gano fell from a horse and broke his shoulder. He recovered sufficiently to be able to preach. Later he suffered a paralytic stroke, which deprived him of the power of speech for a while, but he again "preached several times supported in his bed." He died at his home in Frankfort on Aug. 10, 1804. He is buried about four or five miles from Frankfort.

His manner of preaching is of great interest. Returning from his second tour of the South, "he visited an island where he was informed there never had been but two sermons preached." When the people collected, he preached to them from these words, "Behold, the third time I am ready to come to you, and I will not be burdensome to you." While a chaplain in the Revolutionary War, he was informed by his general that orders had been received to move on the next Monday, but that Gano was not to mention the matter until after the service on Sunday. At that service he preached from the words, "Being ready to depart on the morrow." On the trip to Kentucky in 1787 down the Ohio River, one of the boats was overturned and much of his property was lost, but all the men and the horses were saved. At his arrival at Washington, in Mason County, he preached from the text, "So we got all safe to land." When visited later by his son, Stephen, then pastor of the First Baptist Church of Providence, R. I., Gano preached from the words, "I am glad at the coming of Stephanus." In "an advanced age" he wrote his *Biographical Memoirs*, which were edited and published by his son, Stephen, at Providence, R. I., in 1806.

LEO T. CRISMON

GARDNER, CHARLES SPURGEON (b. Gibson County, Tenn., Feb. 28, 1859; d. Apr. 1, 1948, Richmond, Va.). Pastor, professor, author. Son of Stephen E. and Evelyn E. (Wood) Gardner, he was educated at the University of Richmond, Union University, and Southern Baptist Theological Seminary. He was ordained in 1883 and served as pastor in Trenton, Tenn., 1884–85; Brownsville, Tenn., 1885–86; Edgefield Church, Nashville, Tenn., 1886–94; First Church, Greenville, S. C., 1884–1901; and Grace Street Church, Richmond, Va., 1901–07. Gardner was married to Ariadne Turner of Brownsville, Tenn., Apr. 17, 1884. She died in 1914. They had three children—a daughter, Mrs. George T. Waite, who died in childbirth; a son, Charles, who was killed in France in World War I; and Claudia. Gardner's second marriage was to Mary Carter Anderson of Richmond, on Sept. 20, 1920.

Gardner was professor of homiletics and Christian sociology at Southern Baptist Theological Seminary, 1907–29, and then was professor emeritus for 19 years. He addressed the Baptist World Congress in London in 1905; preached the annual sermon before the Southern Baptist Convention in 1911; delivered an address before the World's Social Progress Congress, San Francisco, in 1915. He is the author of *The Ethics of Jesus and Social Progress* (1914); *Psychology and Preaching* (1918). After Gardner retired from the seminary, he moved to Richmond and remained there until his death. He was buried in the seminary lot at Cave Hill cemetery, Louisville, Ky.

William Owen Carver has said of him,

In character, culture, ideals and courageous insight and independence, Dr. Gardner was from the beginning marked for distinguished service. His consecration to Jesus Christ and devotion to the ministry of His gospel were as uncorrupted by any personal ambition or glory seeking as in any man whom I have ever known. . . . He was a man of deep and wide sympathies, of quiet gentleness, of thoughtful and conservative leadership, of unaggressive but unflinching courage. . . . His sermons were prepared with diligent, scholarly care and delivered with a quiet, deliberate and thoughtful eloquence which stimulated the attention of his hearers and challenged their response, while leaving them time to integrate their own emotions and thinking as they followed him in his delivery. . . .

LEO T. CRISMON

GARDNER, OLIVER MAX (b. Shelby, N. C., Mar. 22, 1882; d. New York, N. Y., Feb. 6, 1947). Governor, businessman, and Christian statesman. Gardner was the son of Oliver Perry Gardner, physician, farmer, and Confederate soldier, and Margaret (Blanton) Gardner. During his youth he made his home with his sister, Mrs. Clyde Hoey. Gardner was educated in the city schools of Shelby and at North Carolina State College of Agriculture and Engineering. From 1905 to 1907 he studied law at the University of North Carolina, where he received the LL.D. degree in 1931. He became a leader in both the business affairs and politics of his native state.

Gardner's interests were many. While in the university he was the only man ever to be elected captain of both the baseball and the football team. He was president of the Cleveland Cloth Mills, a director of the Sperry Corporation, and served on the board of directors of many other large business concerns. His first political office was in the state senate, where he served from 1911 to 1915. He was lieutenant governor, 1916–21, and governor, 1929–33. Although Gardner was governor in a period of depression, he did much for good roads and education in North Carolina. At the expiration of his term as governor, he established the law firm of Gardner, Morrison, and Rogers in Washington, D. C., where he was frequently called on for government service. President Franklin D. Roosevelt chose him as chairman of the Board of War Mobilization and Reconversion, and later President Harry S. Truman appointed him to succeed W. Averill Harriman as ambassador to Great Britain. A prominent Democratic official said of him, "He is too good to be true." Arthur Krock in the *New York Times* called him "a political philosopher of wide reading and deep thinking." Always interested in the affairs of his church, he taught for many years a Sunday school class in the First Baptist

Gardner, William W.

Church of Shelby, N. C., and was a founder of Gardner-Webb College.

BIBLIOGRAPHY: "Gardner, Oliver Max," *Current Biography* (1947).   W. H. WILLIAMS

GARDNER, WILLIAM W. (b. Barren County, Ky., Oct. 1, 1818; d. near Elk Creek, Ky., Dec. 1, 1894). Pastor, teacher, author. He was the eldest son of Richard and Jane Gardner. At the age of 20 he was converted and united with the Mt. Gilead Baptist Church, Todd County. In 1839 he was licensed to preach. Early in the spring of 1839 he entered Georgetown College. In 1844 he was ordained to preach and was called as pastor of Shelbyville Church. In 1847 he became pastor at Mays Lick Church in Mason County and served for 10 years. From 1857 to 1869 he was pastor of the church at Russellville. He also became professor of theology at Bethel College. He wrote *Bible Inspiration* (1886); *Church Communion, as practiced by the Baptists Explained and Defended* (1869); *Historical Sketch of Elk Creek Baptist Church for 100 Years, 1794–1894; Missiles of Truth* (1874); *Modern Dancing: in the Light of Scripture and Facts* (1893). His writings and preaching were marked by a simple, earnest style.   LEO T. CRISMON

GARDNER-WEBB COLLEGE. Located in Boiling Springs, N. C., the school was founded in 1905 by Kings Mountain and Sandy Run Baptist associations and began operation in 1907 as Boiling Springs High School. It became Boiling Springs Junior College in 1928 but continued to offer secondary school work as well as college subjects until 1948. Enrolment increased from 135 the first year to 472 for the 1955–56 session.

The school was renamed Gardner-Webb College on June 6, 1942, a name chosen by the trustees in honor of Oliver Max Gardner (*q.v.*) and his wife, the former Faye Webb, and their families. Gardner, former governor of North Carolina and ambassador to Great Britain, had given generously to the support of the school and was at that time active in a drive for its expansion.

Gardner-Webb College was accredited by the Southern Association of Colleges and Secondary Schools in 1948 for two years of college work. A member of the American Association of Junior Colleges and the Carolina College Conference, it is also accredited by the North Carolina Board of Education and the Federal Immigration Service for training of foreign students and is approved by the American Medical Association for two years of premedical training.

Unique in the operation of the college is its threefold program of community service. Through the Department of Public Relations, the college teaches adult education courses in Baptist churches throughout the piedmont Carolinas. The courses, taught at cost without college credit and organized through co-operation of the various Baptist associations, have an average annual enrolment of about 1,200. The Department of Guidance offers individual counseling service to the public and teaches courses in human relations, at cost, to overseers in local industrial plants. The college owns and operates Gardner-Webb College Community Health Center and Clinic, a modern 20-bed hospital, for use of the college and the community. The hospital averages 1,500 hospitalized patients and 18,000 outpatients annually. Administrators of the school include James Dwyre Huggins, first principal from 1907 to 1909; James Blaine Davis, first president of the junior college from 1928 to 1930; James Lineberry Jenkins, 1932–35; George Jackson Burnett, 1936–39; John Roland Cantrell, 1939–43; and Philip Lovin Elliott, since 1943.   JOHN ROBERTS

GAVELS, SOUTHERN BAPTIST CONVENTION. Eleven gavels, either possessing historical significance or expressing personal interest, have been presented to presiding officers of the Convention. (1) The Broadus Gavel stands out as the one continuously used. John Albert Broadus (*q.v.*), just back from a tour of the Holy Land, presented it (1872) to President James Petigru Boyce (*q.v.*) with these words:

Its handle is of balsam wood which grows by the River Jordan a beautiful fringe beneath whose shade the multitudes looked on as the Saviour was baptized; the head is of olive wood from the Mount of Olives from which he ascended to heaven. This simple mallet thus suggests to us the beginning and the end of our Lord's public work on earth.

(2) The Judson Gavel, made from a teakwood bedpost of Adoniram Judson (*q.v.*), was brought from Burma by President Monroe Elmon Dodd (*q.v.*) and presented to the Convention in 1935. (3) The Birmingham Gavel, a gift from R. H. Wharton to the Convention, was presented to W. W. Hamilton in 1941. (4) and (5) The Florida Gavels, one of ironwood and another of orange wood, were presented by Waldo E. Wood and F. G. "Pat" Railey, respectively, to President Pat Morris Neff (*q.v.*) in 1946. (6) The Charleston Gavel, made of mahogany wood from the old pulpit stand of the First Baptist Church, Charleston, S. C.—"the mother church of Southern Baptists"—was presented by J. A. Hamrick to President Louie DeVotie Newton in 1948. (7) The Oregon-Washington Gavel, symbolic of the Convention's expanding ministry in the Northwest, was presented by Roland P. Hood to President Robert Greene Lee in 1949. (8) The Rice Gavel, made from pine timber in the house where Luther Rice (*q.v.*) died, was presented by J. Aubrey Estes to President Lee in 1950. (9) The Bunyan Gavel, made from an oak piling in the foundation of the prison where John Bunyan was imprisoned and where he wrote *Pilgrim's Progress*, was presented by Milledge Theron Rankin (*q.v.*) to President Lee in 1950. (10) The Sandy Creek Gavel, made from a dogwood hitching post at the Sandy Creek Baptist Church, of which Shubal Stearns (*q.v.*)

was pastor in 1755, was presented by Barron E. Hunnicutt to President Lee in 1951. (11) The Texas Gavel, taken from wood in the church where the Baptist General Convention of Texas was organized in 1848, was presented by Stanley Wilkes to President James David Grey for his personal possession in 1953.   HIGHT C MOORE

GAY LECTURES. In 1893 and 1894 William David Gay (b. Oct. 8, 1867, Montgomery, Ala.; d. Aug. 11, 1949, Montgomery, Ala.) of Furman, Ala., previously a student at Southern Baptist Theological Seminary, from 1887 to 1889, gave to the seminary $5,000 for the endowment of a lectureship in honor of his businessman father, Julius Brown Gay (b. Sept. 9, 1830, North Carolina; d. Dec. 31, 1887, Montgomery, Ala.), to be called the Julius Brown Gay Lectureship. The subjects and the lecturers were to be chosen by the seminary faculty, and the initial course of lectures was delivered in Mar., 1895, by Henry Herbert Harris (*q.v.*), a professor in the seminary. Harris published the lectures as *Three Lectures on Missions* with the American Baptist Publishers' Society in 1895. The Gay Lectures, delivered 48 times, in 1954 were entitled "Great Epochs in Baptist History," delivered by C. Howard Hopkins, professor in Stetson University.   LEO T. CRISMON

GAYLE, PETER SMITH (b. Charlotte County, Va., May 20, 1802; d. Clinton, Miss., June 8, 1853). Converted and baptized in Charlotte County, Va., and ordained to the ministry in 1827 in Giles County, Tenn. With no formal schooling he became a Bible scholar, a preacher of superior abilities, and a devoted pastor with sound doctrinal principles. Migrating from his native Virginia to Tennessee at the time of great conflict between missionary and antimissionary parties (1826), he became a powerful "effort man" with widespread influence in favor of missions at home and abroad. He was called to the pastorate of First Baptist Church of Nashville, Tenn., 1831, just a year after it had been nearly destroyed by controversy over the Campbellism brought in through the preceding pastor, Philip Slater Fall. He began services in the Nashville Masonic Hall with only eight members but within two years had increased the membership to 40. He served a number of other churches in Tennessee, including one at Brownsville, one at Denmark, and First Baptist and Beale Street Baptist churches in Memphis. His last pastorate was at Clinton, Miss., where he served from 1850 until his death. He was one of the organizers of the Tennessee Baptist Convention and was the first president of the West Tennessee Baptist Convention. He was one of the leaders in the founding of the first Baptist education society, and before the organization of the Southern Baptist Convention he proposed a Tennessee Baptist Foreign Missionary Society to be auxiliary to the Triennial Convention. In the conflict over missions, Gayle was a zealous advocate of missions and education and of the work of the mission boards. During a time of intense conflict among Baptists, he developed skill in polemics with which he added strength to the cause of organized missionary advance. "Medium in size, somewhat stooped in shoulders, of pleasing address," he was a popular preacher and a formidable adversary in debate. In 1823 he was married to Mary M. Petters. To this marriage were born eight children.

WILLIAM F. HALL

GAYLESVILLE ACADEMY. An elementary and high school founded and operated (1907–22) by the Home Mission Board of the Southern Baptist Convention at Gaylesville, in Cherokee County, Ala. The school was reported to have enrolled 146 pupils the first year. It was discontinued in 1922.   JAMES E. DAVIDSON

GAZA, MISSION IN. Organized officially Feb. 8, 1954, when the Southern Baptist Foreign Mission Board adopted work which the Church Missionary Society of England had begun a hundred years before but could no longer support. James Thomas McRae represented Baptists in the transaction and began the work with the help, later, of another medical missionary, James Madderson Young, Jr. The mission includes a 92-bed hospital, a school of nursing for 30 students, an elementary school and kindergarten with an enrolment of 238 pupils, and a program of evangelism through Sunday schools, Bible classes, prayer meetings, ward services, and women's meetings. The area, 99 per cent Moslem, has a population of more than 300,000, of which approximately 200,000 are Arab refugees from the Palestine conflict of 1948. The mission property is on the main street in the heart of Gaza.   JANE CARROLL MCRAE

GEIGER, LORENZO DOW (b. Old Town, Marion County, Fla., Oct. 18, 1854; d. Apr. 21, 1909). Minister, editor. His parents were Abraham Elias and Sarah Ann Geiger. Converted at about the age of 17, Geiger joined the Stafford's Pond, or "Button Wood," Baptist Church in Levy County. About a year later he was licensed to preach and soon was ordained by the same church. His early education was interrupted by the Civil War. Later, working his way, he attended both private and public schools and afterward taught public school for several years. On Nov. 17, 1875, he married his cousin, Mattie Geiger. Four sons and two daughters were born to them. He combined farming with teaching and preaching until about 1884, when he gave himself wholly to the ministry. He became one of the most prominent and successful pastors and evangelists in the state of Florida, serving such churches as Micanopy, Leesburg, Ocala, Apopka, Brooksville, and Lakeland.

For several years he was associate editor of the *Florida Baptist Witness* and was also editor and proprietor of the *Orange County Citizen*.

In 1898 he was elected secretary of the Florida Baptist convention, serving until 1901, when he was elected corresponding secretary and treasurer of the Florida Baptist State Board of Missions. In 1902 Stetson University conferred on him the D.D. degree.   H. C. GARWOOD

GENERAL BAPTISTS. The distinguishing title of the oldest type of English Baptists and of several groups of American Baptists, including one or more contemporary denominations. Taking their name from their characteristic insistence upon the doctrine of a general atonement, these Baptists have held a fairly consistent Arminian theology.

The earliest English Baptist church of which there is knowledge was formed by a portion of the company of English Separatists which went in 1608 as exiles to Holland under the leadership of John Smyth of Lincolnshire. A short time later, Thomas Helwys, a member of Smyth's group, led a few of these exiles to separate from the Smyth party and to form a new church. Helwys' group returned to England two years later and settled outside the walls of London. Their church existed in spite of persecution and was later reckoned the first General Baptist church. By 1626 there were four or five like churches in various parts of England having fellowship with the Helwys church.

The Commonwealth period gave the General Baptists the opportunity to propagate their doctrines with new freedom. By 1660 their churches numbered 200 with at least 20,000 members. In 1653 a general organization of the Baptist churches in England was effected and was later called the General Assembly. The assembly met annually. In 1660 it adopted a confession of faith, for apologetic purposes, in the name of all the churches, which came to be called the Standard Confession and was widely used. As the century advanced, the theology of the General Baptists became more consistently Arminian.

General Baptists weathered the return of persecution after 1661 and were at the apex of prosperity at the Revolution in 1688, with 30,000 members. The period of toleration, 1689–1700, brought surprising decline, however, which continued into the next century. Doctrinal differences were perhaps the primary cause of this decline. A new beginning in General Baptist life was made in 1770 under the leadership of Daniel Taylor. As a by-product of the Wesleyan Revival, the New Connexion of General Baptists was organized. In 1891 the New Connexion body joined with the Particular Baptists in England, forming the Baptist Union of Great Britain and Ireland.

Early in the history of Baptists in America, General Baptists appeared. At first they joined with Calvinistic Baptists as members of the first churches of Providence and Newport, R. I., but they organized separate churches in 1652 and 1656. They erected the six principles of Hebrews 6:1–2 into a creed. Several Six-Principle churches were also planted in New Jersey, where today at least three congregations exist.

A church of General Baptists was formed in Virginia in 1714 and perhaps a few others later. Economic conditions encouraged the removal of most of these people into eastern North Carolina. There they experienced considerable growth, though many of their churches became Calvinistic after 1750. For a long time the North Carolina General Baptists called themselves the Original Free Will Baptist Church, but their official name today is the National Association of Free Will Baptists. Membership of this denomination, spread over several states, exceeds 120,000.

An Arminian Baptist movement began in 1779 in New Hampshire under the preaching of Benjamin Randall. By 1910 its churches had 90,000 members, but in 1911 it merged with the Northern Baptist Convention. Today the principal group in America claiming the General Baptist name is that which stems from the labors of Benoni Stinson in Indiana and neighboring states after 1822. The group was organized into a General Association of General Baptists in 1870, with a presbyterial type of organization. The group operates Oakland City College in Indiana and has approximately 58,000 members.

BIBLIOGRAPHY: W. H. Burgess, *John Smyth the Se-Baptist* (1911). D. C. Dodd, *The Free Will Baptist Story* (1956). T. Helwys, *Mistery of Iniquity* (1612). F. S. Mead, *Handbook of Denominations in the United States* (1956). A. Taylor, *The History of the English General Baptists* (1818). R. G. Torbet, *A History of the Baptists* (1950). W. T. Whitley, ed., *Minutes of the General Assembly* (1909).

W. L. LUMPKIN

GENERAL BAPTISTS, GENERAL ASSOCIATION OF. Organized Nov. 2, 1870, at Harmony church, Gallatin County, Ill. Denominational headquarters are in Poplar Bluff, Mo. The principal membership of General Baptists is in Missouri, Kentucky, Illinois, Indiana, Michigan, Tennessee, and Arkansas. The denomination has scattered membership in Ohio, Iowa, Kansas, Oklahoma, Arizona, Nebraska, and California. Benoni Stinson was largely responsible for the formation of the General Association, although he died prior to the actual organization.

General Baptists in the United States claim John Smyth and the English General Baptists as their historical founders. The transplanting of their doctrine to the colonies came through the immigration of English General Baptists. Due to the controversy over the doctrine of the laying on of hands, General Baptists died out along the seaboard, but the churches were renewed in the Middle West under the leadership of Stinson, who organized the oldest existing American General Baptist church in what is now the city of Evansville, Ind., in the fall of 1823. From this church the present denomination in the United States has developed.

In 1954 the General Association reported 40 associations, 677 churches, and 51,368 members as compared with 34 associations, 552 churches, and 34,884 members in 1934. A total of 4,704 additions were reported in 1954.

General Baptists publish a weekly paper, *The General Baptist Messenger,* a monthly, *The General Baptist Minister,* and a complete line of Sunday school literature in their own printing establishment in Poplar Bluff, Mo. They maintain a liberal arts college at Oakland City, Ind., which has a Bible department. They own and operate numerous camps for youth training in various states, maintain a home for the aged at Campbell, Mo., and Indian missions among the Cherokees in Oklahoma. Eleven foreign missionaries serve in the islands of Guam, Saipan, and Chi Chi Jima in the Pacific area.

General Baptists are Arminian in theology; foot washing is recognized as an ordinance among some of the associations, although its practice is disappearing. General Baptists practice open communion. Like other Baptists they are congregational in government and recognize the local church as the highest authority. A distinct feature of the denomination is its use of the presbytery both for ordination and control over the standing of ordained persons serving the churches. This organization, however, exercises no control over the membership of the ordained in his church.

The General Association maintains boards on home and foreign missions, minister's aid, publications, college, religious education, and women's work. These boards are under the absolute control of the General Association, which is made up of delegates from the local associations rather than from the local churches. In 1954 gifts totaled $1,452,881. Per capita giving in 1955 was slightly in excess of $30.

OLLIE LATCH

GENERAL CONFERENCE OF AMERICA, BAPTIST. Developed as a result of missionary work by American Baptists among the Swedish immigrants, it has operated as a general conference since 1879. Now fully Americanized, the fellowship endeavors to render a Christian witness to the whole community as well as to foreign lands. A pietistic emphasis has carried over from the Bible-reading prayer fellowships of the 19th-century Swedish countryside. This, in addition to missionary solidarity, provides the cohesion of the fellowship.

The general conference consists of over 400 churches with a membership above 50,000. The churches, extending from coast to coast, are concentrated in Minnesota and Illinois. During recent years there has been rapid growth.

The conference owns and operates Bethel College and Seminary, St. Paul, Minn.; the *Standard* (5750 North Ashland Avenue, Chicago 26, Ill.) is the official organ. The foreign mission program includes work in India (especially in the North Bank area of Assam), Ethiopia, Japan, the Phillipines, and South America. The Home Mission Board has missionaries as far north as Alaska and as far south as Mexico.

C. EMANUEL CARLSON

GENERAL CONFERENCE OF AMERICA, BAPTIST, FOREIGN MISSION BOARD. Organized as a separate and permanent board in 1944, the Board of Foreign Missions of the Baptist General Conference of America continued and expanded foreign mission work done by Swedish-American Baptists. Prior to 1944 missionaries of Baptist General Conference had been sent out under other boards, primarily the American Baptist Foreign Mission Society. A total of 122 conference missionaries had been provided for various fields between 1888 and 1945. Within six years under the advance program launched in 1944, 52 new missionaries were appointed. By June, 1955, the number had reached 75.

Up to 1955 seven fields had been entered by the board. China was entered in 1945, with a field in the North and one in the West. Withdrawal of China missionaries was necessary in 1950. Assam became the second field occupied, in 1946. Work was carried out on the north bank of the Brahmaputra River. A hospital was opened at Tezpur in 1954. Japan was entered in 1948, and work was developed in the Tokyo area and in Wakayama-Mie prefecture. A Philippine mission was inaugurated in 1949, first in Manila, then on the island of Cebu. Ethiopia was entered in 1950, Argentina and Brazil in 1955.

Income of the board for the year ending Mar. 31, 1955, was $257,268.86; and for the year ending Mar. 31, 1956, $325,455.74. The secretary of the board is John A. Wilcox, 5750 North Ashland Avenue, Chicago 26, Ill.

H. C. GOERNER

GENERAL MISSIONARY CONVENTION OF THE BAPTIST DENOMINATION IN THE UNITED STATES OF AMERICA FOR FOREIGN MISSIONS. See TRIENNIAL CONVENTION.

GEORGE BOARDMAN TAYLOR ORPHANAGE, ROME. See ITALY, MISSION IN.

GEORGE W. TRUETT ORPHANAGE, NAZARETH. See ISRAEL, MISSION IN.

GEORGETOWN COLLEGE. The first Baptist school west of the Alleghenies, established as Rittenhouse Academy in 1798. At a time in the nation's history when men were likely to overlook spiritual and intellectual values, the founders of Georgetown College envisioned the great need for Christian education in a wilderness community.

Building on the foundation of Rittenhouse Academy, Baptists of Kentucky opened Georgetown College under an incorporation act of the Kentucky legislature of Jan. 15, 1829. Impetus came from the missionary preaching of Luther Rice (*q.v.*) at Mount Pleasant, near Nicholasville, the previous summer, and from concern of Baptists for more enlightening of their people against the antimissions onslaughts of Alexander Campbell (1788–1866).

Issachar Pawling, a native of New Jersey who had for many years been a resident of Kentucky, donated his estate in trust to a board of trustees to be composed of Baptists, for the education of Baptist preachers. The trustees of Rittenhouse Academy transferred all of the property of the academy to the new college. An additional $20,000 was contributed by the citizens of Scott County. Shelbyville, Harrodsburg, and Georgetown all put in bids for the location of the college. In June, 1829, it was decided to locate it in Georgetown.

At the first meeting of the college trustees, Sept. 2, 1829, William Staughton (q.v.), Philadelphia, was unanimously elected president. But he died while on his way to Kentucky. Joel Smith Bacon, Newton Center, Mass., was the first president to be installed. In the second year, beginning in the fall of 1830, the Disciples of Christ seceded from Baptists of Kentucky and theological battle lines were drawn. There were various suits and injunctions against the college by rival groups seeking control of funds and property. Weary of strife, President Bacon resigned in the summer of 1832. The Campbellite controversy raged in 1833. In 1834 Thornton Fitzhugh Johnson, a Campbellite, began as president of the faculty and was responsible for operation of the school. Of the 11 students enrolled, seven were Campbellites. Baptists withheld support. In Oct., 1834, at a meeting of the Western Baptist Convention in Cincinnati, Baptists lamented the college as lost to the Baptist denomination.

Baptist interest in the school revived, however, and in June, 1836, the trustees and representative Baptists, with Johnson agreeing, appointed a Baptist president—Benjamin Franklin Farnsworth of New Hampton Institution, Massachusetts.

In November, Johnson left the Georgetown faculty to form his Collegiate Institute for Civil Engineers, taking 100 of the 120 students with him. Scott Countians were indignant about this new school, later designated Bacon College, but Farnsworth welcomed the break as clearing the air and leaving Baptists supreme in Georgetown College. Bacon College continued to flourish, however. The Georgetown College enrolment remained low, and President Farnsworth resigned in 1838.

Rockwood Giddings (1812–39), a young man who had been born and reared in New England and who had received his education at Colby College, Waterville, Me., where he had been a student of Farnsworth, was chosen president on Oct. 13, 1838. The eager young president died of overwork on the first permanent building, a structure which was erected by student and faculty labor. Bearing his name, Giddings Hall was completed under the presidency of Howard Malcom (1799–1879), whose eight years of administration witnessed the beginning of the college catalogue publication, an enlargement of the curriculum to include courses in music, and the founding of a college museum. Contemporary with such progress was the appearance of a boys' dormitory still known as Pawling Hall, named for Issachar Pawling, one of the founders of the college.

During the early life of the college a preparatory school was established in the college program to compensate for the lack of provision by the state of Kentucky for public high school education. Similarly, the establishment of a female seminary in 1845 by Jonathan Everett Farnam, a Georgetown College professor, provided education for young women. It was discontinued after a disastrous fire, but it was reorganized in 1869 by James Jefferson Rucker, who served as its leader during the remainder of its existence as a separate institution.

When war came in 1861, the college was progressing materially and spiritually under the leadership of Duncan Robertson Campbell (1814–65), who had become president in 1853. He had succeeded in securing pledges of more than $100,000, half of which were not collected. Notwithstanding this severe loss, the institution weathered the Civil War much better than many others. A $50,000 investment survived and proved an anchor during the critical and stormy period that followed.

The inauguration of Richard Moberley Dudley (1838–93) as president in 1879 ushered in 14 years of notable progress in the college. About $150,000 was added to the endowment, including $90,000 in new property values. His improvements in the curriculum, the addition of new departments and facilities, and, of primary importance, the adoption of a system of coeducation in 1892 placed the college in a prominent place as an educational force in the state.

With new buildings and increased endowment, Georgetown College accepted the challenge offered by the 20th century. Baron DeKalb Gray (q.v.), Joseph Judson Taylor (1855–1930), and Arthur Yager (1858–1941) gave distinguished leadership to the college until 1913 when Maldon Browning Adams (q.v.), was inaugurated as president. He served until 1930, and in that time the student body tripled, the faculty was greatly enlarged, and new buildings were added. By the close of the Adams administration, what had opened with daring in a small frame building with 30 students and four officers and professors now emerged as a standard college with seven brick buildings, a student body of 400, a faculty of 31 instructors, and endowed funds and real property valued at approximately $1,000,000.

In the 1930's Georgetown College suffered hard times. The college was frequently unable to meet its payroll. Notes given in the payment of salaries were discounted heavily by firms and persons cashing them.

Storms that rocked the college to its foundation broke upon the administration of Henry Noble Sherwood (1882–1956), head of the college from 1934 to 1942. The controversy began on the issue of alien immersion, but before it was settled, it involved the relationship of the college to Kentucky Baptists and the basic organization of the institution.

At the time of his election, Sherwood was a member of the Highland Baptist Church in Louisville. It was brought to the attention of the annual meeting of the General Association of Baptists in Kentucky in Henderson, in Nov., 1934, that he had been a member of a Christian church before he became a Baptist and that he had been received into a Baptist church in Indiana, and, subsequently, into the Louisville Baptist church without being baptized.

The Sherwood controversy focused attention anew upon the fact that Kentucky Baptists were supporting the college without having control of its operation. Older than the state Baptist general association, the college had never come under the direct control of the general association. The governing body of Georgetown College was the Kentucky Baptist Education Society, which was incorporated on Jan. 15, 1829, of 24 members. Until Nov., 1851, every member of this body was a "trustee," that is, the "board of trustees" of the society and the Kentucky Baptist Education Society were one and the same. This body controlled the college which began its first session on Jan. 11, 1830. These trustees were a self-perpetuating body, "empowered . . . to fill all vacancies in their own number caused by death, resignation, neglect, or otherwise." But in Nov., 1851, the membership of the Kentucky Baptist Education Society was enlarged so that it was composed of all "individuals who, since Jan. 1, 1840, had donated to the Kentucky Baptist Education Society $100 or shall do so in the future." Twenty-five members of the society were to compose a quorum. This society then was given the power to elect the board of trustees, consisting of 24 members, from its membership. This board of trustees controlled Georgetown College. This situation prevailed until 1906 when the Baptist Education Society of Kentucky was formed which promoted general Baptist education in Kentucky and to which all the Baptist colleges in Kentucky were related.

The charter of the Baptist Education Society of Kentucky was adopted as part of the charter of the Kentucky Baptist Education Society and all provisions of the charter of the Kentucky Baptist Education Society relating to its former power to elect trustees to operate Georgetown College were repealed. This change in the charter gave the Baptist Education Society of Kentucky the power to elect trustees on suitable nominations made by the Kentucky Baptist Education Society. The older of the two societies continued to meet at Georgetown at the time of spring commencement, and at this time it nominated two persons for each place to be filled on the board of trustees of the older society. The Baptist Education Society of Kentucky, meeting each fall in connection with the annual session of the General Association of Baptists in Kentucky, chose from these. So the college itself under this arrangement actually had no trustees. The Kentucky Baptist Education Society continued to be the actual governing group.

For the most of the Sherwood tenure, the General Association of Baptists in Kentucky withheld financial support. The enrolment dwindled. Under mounting pressure Sherwood resigned on June 1, 1942. He moved to Lexington where he soon united with Central Christian Church. He became chancellor and later president of Transylvania College, an institution of the Disciples of Christ.

Samuel Smythe Hill (1890–   ) was inaugurated as president in Sept., 1942. The General Association of Baptists in Kentucky resumed their financial support of the college, and a change in charter was made giving the general association the power to elect the trustees.

Under the administration of Henry Leo Eddleman (1911–   ), who became head of the college the spring of 1954, Georgetown reached new heights of achievement. For the school year of 1955–56 the college had a faculty staff of 56, a full-time enrolment of 886 and a total enrolment of 1,236. By this time there had been 3,768 graduates since the beginning of the college.

In 1955–56 the college received from Kentucky Baptists, $112,672 for operation; $14,896 from the same source for capital needs; $10,881 from gifts; $327,630 from student tuition and fees; and $27,242 from endowment. Its buildings and grounds were valued at $1,950,000 and endowment at $700,000 for a total of $2,650,000. The library, in 1955–56, contained 35,500 volumes.

Georgetown College is a member of the Association of Kentucky Colleges and Universities, Southern Baptist Education Association, Southern Association of Colleges and Secondary Schools, Association of American Colleges, and the National Conference of Church-Related Boards.

ERWIN L. MCDONALD

GEORGETOWN FEMALE SEMINARY. Established in Georgetown, Ky., by J. E. Farnham in 1846. From 1865 to 1869, the school was without a building but met in the home of its principal, J. J. Rucker. By 1886 the curriculum was such as to make it possible to obtain a degree equivalent to that granted by Georgetown College. By 1893 Female Seminary was fully merged with the college.

HARGIS TAYLOR

GEORGIA, BAPTIST CONVENTION OF THE STATE OF.

I. Baptist Beginnings. Early Baptist life in Georgia developed in three more or less successive stages: the first unorganized activities; the initiation of churches and associations; and the beginnings of denominational and missionary life. Baptists entered Georgia in two general

Georgia, Baptist Convention of

streams. The first, composed of Regular Baptists, came into the southern part of the colony, largely by way of Savannah. The second, made up of Separate Baptists, arrived mostly through Augusta and, in the main, settled northwest of that point.

The very first Baptists to settle in the colony came at its founding under James Edward Oglethorpe, English philanthropist, in 1733 or soon afterward. Among them were William Calvert of Lincolnshire, William Slack of Ireland, and Thomas Walker of Northampton. Later another early group, composed of Seventh Day Baptists from South Carolina, settled near Tuckaseeking about 1759 in present-day Effingham County. After about five years they returned to South Carolina. They were the first Baptists to observe the Lord's Supper in Georgia.

The first colonial antecedents of present-day Baptists known to assemble for worship in Georgia were gathered by Nicholas Bedgegood (c. 1730–74), pastor, Welsh Neck Church, S. C., and agent for George Whitefield at the orphan house, Bethesda, near Savannah. Having come to America in 1751, an Episcopalian, Bedgegood embraced the Baptist belief in 1757 and was baptized by Oliver Hart (q.v.) at Charleston. In May, 1763, in the creek in front of the orphan house, he baptized Benjamin Stirk (d. 1766), Georgia Baptist preacher, and his wife Mary (d. 1766), Thomas Dixon, agent for Whitefield at Bethesda, a man named Dupree, and (then, or later) Mrs. Hannah Barksdale Polhill (1732–80), forebear of the Georgia Polhills. To these Bedgegood also administered the Lord's Supper. However, the group dissolved without being constituted as a church.

Stirk moved to Saint Matthews Parish (Effingham County) in 1767 and started preaching at his own house, 18 miles above Savannah, and at "the widow Bell's" at Tuckaseeking, some 20 miles higher up the country. Following Stirk's death Edmund Botsford succeeded him at Tuckaseeking in June, 1771. About a year later he moved up the country and in 1773 established a church at New Savannah, which is now called Botsford Church.

The Separate Baptists from South Carolina began settling near Augusta about 1762. Over a period of several years, Daniel Marshall (q.v.), one of their strongest preachers, visited the colony from South Carolina, setting up preaching places at Quakers Settlement and Kioka (now Kiokee) a short distance above Augusta. On Jan. 1, 1771, Marshall moved to Georgia, and by the spring of 1772 he had led in the formation at Kioka of the first Baptist church in the province, which he served as pastor until his death in 1784. A true and lasting friendship between Marshall and young Botsford seems to have contributed largely to the subsequent gradual union of the Separate and Regular Baptists in Georgia. At Kioka, Marshall's encouragement helped produce a healthy group of ministers, among them being Abraham Marshall, son of Daniel Marshall, Alexander Scott (d. 1810), pastor, Black Swamp, S. C., Silas Mercer (1745–96), father of Jesse Mercer, (q.v.), Samuel Newton (d. 1771), minister, Loveless Savage (c. 1726–1815), minister, and Samuel Cartlidge (1750-c. 1843), minister.

After Kioka and Botsford the formation of churches continued until by 1789 there were 42 of them, 22 being in Wilkes County. There were also 33 ordained ministers, 39 licensed ministers, and 3,211 church members.

The first district association, Georgia, was established in 1784 or 1785. Hephzibah (1794), Sarepta (1799), and Ocmulgee (1810) associations were all formed from Georgia Association. Hephzibah Association lay to the south, Sarepta Association to the north, and Ocmulgee Association to the west of the parent body. Savannah Association (1802), later called Savannah River Association, was on the coast. Other associations formed before 1822 were Ebenezer (1814), Tugalo (1817), and Piedmont (1817). Ebenezer Association lay "in the forks of the Oconee and Ocmulgee rivers." Tugalo Association came mostly from Sarepta, with some churches from South Carolina. Piedmont Association was located on the upper side of the Altamaha River. In 1818, since Savannah River Association had a majority of its churches in South Carolina, its Georgia churches formed the Sunbury Association.

A series of conferences introduced the first efforts to secure a medium of co-operation among all the Baptists of the state. The Georgia Association arranged for a meeting at Powel's Creek (Powelton) in Hancock County on May 1, 1801, to plan for itinerant preaching. That meeting in turn called the attention of the association to the need for a missionary society in the state, and urged the "ministering brethren" to engage in itinerant labors. To a second conference at Powelton, Apr. 29, 1802, the various associations of the state sent 16 representatives. They reported encouraging results from the itinerant preaching of the year before. They discussed union among Christians of different denominations, and the conference proposed a General Committee of Georgia Baptists composed of three members from each association, with freedom to consider the strengthening of a "general union."

The third conference, also at Powelton, Apr. 29, 1803, with 24 ministers present, set up a permanent committee of 12, called "The General Committee of Georgia Baptists," and charged it to encourage and practice itinerant preaching, and to establish at the proper time an "English school" among the Creek Indians, as the "germ of a mission." Abraham Marshall of Kioka was chairman and Henry Holcombe (q.v.), secretary of the committee. The committee did nothing effective about Indian missions, but devoted its efforts to the establishment of a school for Baptists in Georgia. Known as Mount Enon Academy and located near Augusta, this school was the first venture of

Georgia Baptists as a group into the educational field. The committee was dissolved about 1810, having never been "cordially adopted by the denomination," but it had definitely prepared the way for the convention formed in 1822.

During this early period Baptists contributed to the public welfare of the state, principally as regards religious freedom. About 1768, while on a visit to the colony from his home in South Carolina, Daniel Marshall was arrested, was made to give security, and stood trial at Augusta for preaching in the Parish of St. Paul. He was threatened with severities if he preached any more in the neighborhood. This violation of conscience he successfully withstood, continuing to preach in that section and later baptizing the very constable who had arrested him. Also, at Savannah about 1789 Andrew Bryan (c. 1716-1812, first Negro Baptist pastor in Georgia), and his brother Sampson Bryan (c. 1746-1799, early Negro deacon), were imprisoned, and with others of their fellow Negro believers were publicly whipped, because as slaves they were holding religious services. These also resisted the oppression and, by perseverance and goodness of life, won public approval of their worship.

The first two constitutions of the state of Georgia had a provision that "no Clergyman, of any denomination, shall be a member of the General Assembly." In the constitutional convention of 1798, James Simms, a Baptist from the Kiokee church, successfully introduced a motion that this provision should apply to practicing attorneys also. The reaction that followed resulted in the omission of the whole provision. On Feb. 21, 1785, the General Assembly of the state passed an act for "the Establishment of and Support of the Public Duties of Religion," which provided for the use of tax money in support of public worship. The Georgia Baptist Association on May 16 of that year drew up and adopted a remonstrance against the act. This the state assembly considered but tabled in Jan., 1796. However, the act apparently never went into effect, as it was rendered void by the provision for freedom of worship in the constitution of 1798, which Jesse Mercer introduced in the constitutional convention.

The first missionaries in Georgia were the itinerant preachers. Early among them were Abraham Marshall and Edmund Botsford. The latter became known as the "flying preacher," because of his much travel with the gospel. Responsibility was felt early for the winning of the Negroes of the state. Those of them converted usually united with the same churches as did the white people. The first all-Negro church was formed at Savannah in 1788 as the result of the work of George Leile (b. c. 1751, preacher in Jamaica, also called George Sharpe) and Andrew Bryan, Negro preachers, and that of Thomas Burton, minister in South Carolina. Abraham Marshall was in charge of the service of constitution, as was he also in the case of the first African church in Augusta in 1793.

Early missionary vision resulted in the establishment in 1802 of *The Analytical Repository* by Henry Holcombe, pastor at Savannah. That publication is said to have been the earliest religious magazine in the South and the first Baptist missionary magazine in the nation. It had only six issues, four in 1802 and two in 1803, but it was a landmark in Baptist missionary development.

The missionary spirit that had showed itself from the beginning was greatly strengthened by news of the conversion of Adoniram Judson (q.v.) and Luther Rice (q.v.) to Baptist sentiments and by the visit of Rice to the state. Several associations organized for missionary activity. Savannah River was the first, in 1813, with Thomas Trowell and Allen Sweat (1783-1830), ministers, as its first employed itinerant preachers. On Dec. 17, 1813, a Baptist Foreign Missionary Society was formed at Savannah. A circular address from that body and its constitution were used by Jesse Mercer to stir Georgia Association to similar action. In 1815 that group resolved itself into a body for missionary purposes, and in 1816 adopted its first constitution, which called for "seven trustees to be denominated The Mission Board of the Georgia Association." In July, 1815, the Ocmulgee Missionary Society was formed in the association of that name. Another was begun by Sarepta in June, 1816, at the Moriah meetinghouse in Madison County, and Hephzibah formed one at Bark Camp Baptist Church, Feb., 1816.

The societies supported foreign as well as domestic missions. Georgia Association set up its mission board as a "component member" of the General Missionary Convention of the Baptist Denomination, which had headquarters at Philadelphia. Other associational societies also maintained correspondence with the mission board of that convention.

Mission societies among the women had their birth in this period, often being known as "Female Cent or Mite societies." The first known evidence of one is the remittance of $101 to the Baptist Board of Foreign Missions, June 23, 1817, by the "Female Mite Society" at Sunbury on the coast. A like society for the Athens area was formed at the Trail Creek Meetinghouse, July 13, 1819.

Sunday schools also had their beginning in this period. The first one seems to have been the one formed at Trail Creek in 1819 about two weeks ahead of the Female Mite Society there.

After the first surge of organized missionary zeal, an antimissionary spirit arose in some of the associations. Piedmont apparently followed that line from the beginning and continued so for about 30 years. Even Hephzibah, "with a Domestic Mission Society at Bark Camp, and a Foreign Mission Society at Louisville," became antimissionary by 1818 and continued so for 20 years.

Georgia, Baptist Convention of

Several associations in this period were trying to launch work among the Indians. The idea of the improvement and evangelization of these people had been in the thought of the Baptists of Georgia since about 1800. One of the original objectives of the general committee of Georgia Baptists set forth in 1803 was the establishment of a school among the Creek Indians. However, the time seemed not to be ripe, and the matter lay idle for some years.

In 1818 Georgia Association expressed definitely its belief that the Indians could be taught the things of God, and the chiefs of the Creek Nation stated that there was a desire among the Indians for instruction. In 1819 Ocmulgee Association sent Francis Flournoy (c. 1774–c. 1829), Georgia minister, as its agent to visit the Creek Nation to find a site for a school there, and in 1820 it adopted "A Plan of a School to Be the Germ of a Religious Establishment among the Creek Indians." The school was to be in the section between "the Euchee creek and the Tallapoosy river," and was to be directed jointly by Ocmulgee, Georgia, and Ebenezer associations. The latter two concurred in the plan, and the three together formed a board of managers. However, by 1823 the Ebenezer association withdrew from the plan, but the other two continued. Flournoy was offered the place of superintendent of the school but declined it. By the latter part of 1822 Lee Compere (q.v.) of South Carolina accepted the appointment. The mission and school were established by Ocmulgee and Georgia Associations with the co-operation of the board of managers of the Baptist General [Triennial] Convention of the United States. They were located at Withington Station about 30 miles south of the present site of Montgomery, Ala. Baptists also established a mission among the Cherokees, in 1821, at Coosawattee near the mouth of the Coosawattee River in the northwestern part of the state. This may have been the one maintained by Sarepta Association.

Co-operation by Georgia Baptists with work outside the state began as early as the visit of Hezekiah Smith (1737–1805), pastor, Haverhill, Mass., to Georgia about 1770 in the interest of Rhode Island College (Brown University). More extensive co-operation was evoked by the visit of Luther Rice to the area in 1813, and the subsequent formation of the Triennial Convention. A conversation between Rice and William Bullein Johnson (q.v.), pastor of the Savannah church, so encouraged Rice that he issued a call to the various local missionary societies in the country to send delegates to a central meeting at Philadelphia in May, 1814, where the convention was formed. Georgia also contributed financial support to the work of the convention. In his visit to Georgia, Rice also contributed greatly to the later establishment of Baptist schools in the state, as his activities revived the educational interest that had lain dormant after the unsuccessful efforts at Mount Enon.

In its 1820 session the Sarepta Association adopted a resolution offered by Adiel Sherwood (q.v.), calling for consideration by all the associations in the state of the propriety of organizing "a general meeting of correspondence." In 1821 Ocmulgee and Georgia associations concurred in the idea, the latter body proposing June 27, 1822, as the time and Powelton as the place of the first meeting of the proposed body. Representatives from Georgia and Ocmulgee associations met accordingly. Other associations delayed participation. A constitution was adopted, and the body was named The General Baptist Association of the State of Georgia. Jesse Mercer was elected president, Jabez P. Marshall (c. 1793–1832), pastor, Kiokee, secretary, and William Theophilus Brantly, Sr., (q.v.) assistant secretary. Thus Georgia Baptists launched their state convention.

W. J. CARSWELL

II. History of Convention. *Organization.*—In the years following the Powelton Conferences, Baptist life in Georgia was marked by many discouraging incidents, but a small band of leaders kept in touch with one another, cherishing the purpose to bring the churches closer together in the furtherance of the kingdom of God. Adiel Sherwood (q.v.) had offered a resolution in the Sarepta Association, meeting at Van's Creek, Oct., 1820, as follows: "Resolved, that we suggest, respectfully, to the consideration of sister Associations in the state, the propriety of organizing a general meeting of correspondence." The resolution was sent to the Georgia, Ocmulgee, Hephzibah, and Savannah River associations. The Georgia Association set June 27, 1822, as the day and Powelton as the place for the organization of one general association. Meanwhile, the Sarepta Association, at its session in 1821, reconsidered its action of 1820 and declined to send messengers to Powelton. Sherwood was at Powelton but not as a seated messenger, since his association had rescinded its action.

Answering the call of the Georgia Association for the meeting at Powelton on June 27, 1822, were the following messengers from that association: Jesse Mercer (q.v.), William Theophilus Brantly (q.v.), Winder Hilman, James Armstrong (q.v.), and Jabez P. Marshall. The Ocmulgee Association sent one messenger, Cyrus White. The messengers and visitors met in the Powelton meetinghouse and organized by electing Mercer as president and Marshall as secretary. Brantly was elected assistant secretary. It was then resolved that all members from distant churches and associations, lay members and ministers, together with the members of the Powelton Church, be invited to take part in the deliberations. Among those who accepted were Adiel Sherwood, Humphrey Posey (q.v.), Lee Compere (q.v.), and Elisha Perryman.

Mercer, Brantly, White, and Armstrong were appointed to draft a constitution, to be reported on the following day, and Posey was appointed to preach at the close of the second day's session. Sherwood's sermon on June 28, at the opening session, was based on Luke 3:4: "Prepare ye the way of the Lord." It is described as one of his greatest sermons, and it served to help prepare minds and hearts of delegates for the pending task of organizing the convention. Brantly then read the report of the committee on the constitution, explaining each section with earnest and cogent argument for adoption. He did not conclude his report until the following morning, June 29, when after extended deliberation the original constitution was adopted, as follows:

WHEREAS, it is highly expedient that a more close and extensive union among the churches of the Baptist denomination in the state of Georgia should exist, and that a more perfect consent and harmony and good understanding cannot be established without stated meetings of delegates from the several Associations, to confer together on subjects of general interest and plans of public utility; and to devise and recommend schemes for the revival of experimental and practical religion; for the promotion of uniformity in sentiment, practice and discipline; for the extension of the gospel by missions and missionaries, by Bibles and tracts, and for the fulfilment of that scriptural injunction, "provoke one another to love and to good works;" and since it hath seemed good to the Georgia and Ocmulgee Associations to make the first attempt to accomplish these important objects in the State of Georgia, and delegates being appointed from these bodies to meet in convention at such time and place as might be agreed upon, and these delegates, namely: Jesse Mercer, William T. Brantly, Winder Hilman, J. P. Marshall and James Armstrong, on the part of the Georgia, and Robert McGinty, J. M. Gray and Cyrus White, on the part of the Ocmulgee, having been appointed to convene at Powelton, June 27th, 1882, did accordingly assemble and adopted the following plan of operation:

1. This body is constituted upon those principles of Christian faith generally acknowledged and received in the Baptist denomination.
2. The constituents of this body are the Baptist Associations in the State of Georgia, or as many of them as may think proper to accede to the terms of this convention.
3. It shall be known and distinguished by the name of "The General Baptist Association of the State of Georgia," and shall form the organ of general communication for the denomination throughout the State.
4. Each Association may send not less than three and not more than five delegates to represent them in this body, and all delegates shall hold their appointments until others are elected to succeed them.
5. The officers of this union shall be a Moderator, and clerk and assistant clerk, who shall be appointed by ballot at each annual meeting, and shall form a committee of the body during the recess of the meeting; but this committee may be increased as occasion may require.
6. The Moderator shall perform the same duties that devolve on Moderators in the several Associations, and in addition to this, shall be authorized to call meetings of the committee in the interval of annual meetings should it be deemed expedient.
7. The clerk, who shall likewise be treasurer, shall enter in a book all the transactions of this body. The assistant clerk shall take charge of all distant communications to or from this body, and shall write all the letters which it may require.
8. Questions of difficulty may be referred from any of the Associations to the deliberation and advice of this body.
9. Acts and proceedings of this body shall be submitted, from time to time, to its constituents for inspection, and no decision shall be further binding upon any Association than the decisions of the Associations are upon the churches which compose them.
10. The following are the specific objects of this body: 1. To unite the influence and pious intelligence of Georgia Baptists, and thereby to facilitate their union and cooperation. 2. To form and encourage plans for the revival of experimental and practical religion in the State and elsewhere. 3. To promote uniformity of sentiment and discipline. 4. To aid in giving effect to the useful plans of the Association. 5. To afford an opportunity to those who may conscientiously think it their duty to form a fund for the education of pious young men who may be called by the Spirit and their churches to the Christian ministry. 6. To correspond with bodies of other religious denominations on topics of general interest to the Redeemer's Kingdom, and to promote pious and useful education in the Baptist denomination.
11. It shall have power to form rules, make arrangements and appoint committees for the accomplishment of any or all the above objects, provided none of these rules and arrangements shall be inconsistent with the Scriptures and the known principles of the Association.
12. Two-thirds of the whole number of delegates shall form a quorum, and a majority shall decide a question.
13. The above Constitution shall be liable to amendment or alteration by two-thirds of the delegates present, provided the change may have been proposed by a member of the General Association at the preceding meeting.

Jesse Mercer, Moderator.
J. P. Marshall, Clerk

The name was changed in 1827 to The Baptist Convention for the State of Georgia. It was deemed wise to appoint a committee to study the constitution in 1845 and recommend any changes needed, which the convention adopted in 1846. The constitution was amended slightly from time to time in the 19th century; in 1919 the present constitution was adopted, providing for membership "from regular Baptist Churches and Associations." A later amendment provides an executive committee composed of the officers of the convention and the presidents of the Sunday School Convention, the Baptist Training Union, the Woman's Missionary Union, The Baptist Brotherhood, the Baptist Student Union, and the Georgia Baptist Music Conference, ex officio, and "one member to be chosen from the territory of each cooperating District Association, and twenty additional members from the State at large." It will be noted that the name of the convention, as provided by the constitution adopted in 1919, is "The Baptist Convention of the State of Georgia."

Charters.—Charters of all institutions and agencies of the Georgia Baptist convention may be seen in brochure published by the convention in 1921, entitled "Charter and Constitu-

Georgia, Baptist Convention of

tion of the Baptist Convention of the State of Georgia and of Co-ordinate and Constituent Bodies." The original charter of the convention, granted by the General Assembly of Georgia, Dec. 22, 1830 (amended in 1837, 1838, and 1842), follows:

> Section 1. Be it enacted by the Senate and House of Representatives of the State of Georgia, in General Assembly met, and it is hereby enacted by the authority of the same, That from and after the passing of this Act, that Jesse Mercer, Moderator, Adiel Sherwood, Clerk, J. P. Marshall, Assistant Clerk, James Armstrong, B. M. Sanders, Jonathan Davis, and Thomas Stocks, who compose the present Executive Committee of the said Convention, and their successors in office, shall be, and they are hereby declared to be, a body corporate, by the name and style of the Executive Committee of the Baptist Convention of the State of Georgia, and by the said name and style shall have perpetual succession and power to use a common seal, to alter and amend the by-laws of the same; Provided, such by-laws be not repugnant to the laws and constitution of this State, or the United States.
>
> Section 2. And be it further enacted by the authority aforesaid, That the Executive Committee aforesaid, and their successors in office, elected agreeable to the Constitution of said Convention, shall have full power and authority, under the name and style of the Executive Committee of the Baptist Convention of the State of Georgia, by which name they shall sue, and be sued, in any court of law or equity in this State, and to take, hold and enjoy any real or personal property, to sue for, and recover all sum, or sums of money now due, or that may hereafter become due to said Convention, at any court of law or equity in this State, or at any tribunal having jurisdiction thereof, and the rights and privileges of said Convention to defend in any tribunal whatever; also to receive any bequests, or donations whatever, made to said Convention; and they shall be vested with all powers, privileges and advantages of a society incorporated; any law, usage or custom to the contrary notwithstanding.
>
> Assented to, Dec. 22, 1830.

Conflicting trends.—The first decade of the Georgia Baptist Convention was marked by deep differences of opinion regarding missions. These differences dated back to the earliest efforts at co-operation when the question of preaching to the Indians was suggested. With the developing years the conflict manifested itself in all forms of missions, at home and to the ends of the earth. A review of the minutes of the Convention reveals a constant conflict within the local churches and the district associations on the question of what the Bible teaches regarding the spread of the gospel.

Another conflict was created by the movement to establish schools and colleges for the training of the ministry. There was stout opposition to higher learning on the ground that God would call and prepare his preachers.

Still another conflict arose over doctrinal questions—baptism being one such issue. Personal conduct was another of the divisive issues in many of the churches. The question of stewardship was involved in the conflict over missions as well as pastoral support. The writings of Sherwood are particularly revealing in this early period of conflict.

Institutions.—Mercer Institute, later Mercer University, was opened at Penfield on the second Monday in 1833, with 39 students. The resolution authorizing the institution was offered by Adiel Sherwood at Buckhead Church, Burke County, when the convention met there in 1831. This important resolution follows: "Resolved, that as soon as the funds will justify it, this Convention will establish in some central part of the state a classical and theological school, which shall unite agricultural labor with study, and be opened for those only preparing for the ministry." The action of the convention was amended in 1832 as follows "admitting others besides students in divinity, under the direction of the Executive Committee." Billington McCarty Sanders (*q.v.*) was the first president of the institute. By amendment of the charter in 1837, the name was changed to Mercer University. The university was moved from Penfield to Macon in 1871.

The Forsyth Female Collegiate Institute, later Tift College, was granted a charter by the General Assembly of Georgia in 1849. Shorter College, located at Rome, began under the name of Cherokee Baptist Female College in 1873. Other charters of educational institutions having some relationship with the Georgia Baptist convention appear in the brochure above referred to and are as follows: Cox College, Hearn Academy, Brewton-Parker Institute, Norman Institute, Gibson-Mercer Academy, Blairsville Collegiate Institute, North Georgia Baptist College, Bleckley Memorial Institute, Mary P. Willingham School, and Piedmont Institute—Bunn-Belle Institute. Charters of the Georgia Baptist Children's Home and the Georgia Baptist Hospital appear in this brochure, as does the charter of the Holding Commission, an agency which served for some time and was then discontinued. The Truett-McConnell Junior College, established in 1947, is not included in the list of charters in the brochure above cited.

A number of Baptist schools and colleges, not included in the above list, appeared from time to time in the 19th century in Georgia. Notable among these were Locust Grove Institute, Cherokee Baptist College, and others, located at Madison, LaGrange, Perry, Cuthbert, Columbus, Cedartown, Griffin, and Gainesville. In 1957 there were six Baptist educational institutions in Georgia: Mercer University, Tift College, Shorter College, Norman College, Brewton-Parker Junior College, and Truett-McConnell Junior College. Other institutions owned and controlled by the convention were the Georgia Baptist Children's Home, Hapeville and Baxley, and the Georgia Baptist Hospital, Atlanta. The Georgia Baptist Home for the Aged was authorized by the convention in 1954, and plans were made to build it at Waycross.

Administration.—Administration of the con-

Georgia, Baptist Convention of

vention's activities began with the general committee in 1822, and under varying names committees carried on the administrative work until 1877, when James Harvey DeVotie (*q.v.*) became the first mission secretary. John G. Gibson succeeded DeVotie in 1891, serving until 1900, when Samuel Young Jameson (*q.v.*) was elected, serving until 1906. Joseph J. Bennett served from 1906 to 1914, when Archibald Cunningham Cree (*q.v.*) was elected to the post, with the expanded title of executive secretary-treasurer, serving until 1930. James W. Merritt served from 1930 to 1955 and was succeeded by Searcy S. Garrison, the incumbent.

The men who directed the work of the denomination devoted much of their time to voluntary administration—writing letters, visiting the churches and associations, compiling reports for the annual meeting of the convention, and issuing the minutes of the convention. The record would indicate that there were no salaried workers for most of this service to the denomination. With the establishing of the office of mission secretary in 1877, the pattern gradually developed into an efficient administrative system, serving as a clearinghouse for the growing work of Georgia Baptists and their co-operation with Southern Baptists in denominational work.

From the earliest days of the convention, dating from 1824, when Adiel Sherwood was named the first treasurer of the convention, there was a missionary pattern slowly but surely forming. Funds were received for foreign, domestic, and state missions, though there were no mission boards in the South until 1845. As early as 1829, James Reeves was recorded as a full-time "state mission worker." His salary in 1829 was $12 per month. John Wood is another state worker identified in 1829, who traveled 1,800 miles, constituted six churches, and baptized about 50 persons.

The unfolding story of state mission work in Georgia culminates in the Gainesville convention, 1877, when, upon motion of Jesse H. Campbell (*q.v.*), the Board of Missions was established in Atlanta and was composed of A. T. Spalding, D. W. Gwin, John H. James, J. M. Wood, J. H. Campbell, W. L. Goldsmith, and S. T. Jenkins. It was instructed to "take charge of missionary and Sunday School work in Georgia," and was authorized "to employ missionary and Sunday School workers, raise funds and expend them, using such agent or agents as they may deem necessary." Ragsdale, in his *Story of Georgia Baptists*, volume 3, comments:

> The establishment of the Board of Missions was followed by many pleasing results. The displacement of salaried agents for the Home and Foreign Boards worked for economy and better cooperation. The associations, instead of regarding simply their own destitution, developed State-wide outlook and interest. Work along many needed lines was strongly set forward in a spirit of fine harmony and joint effort. The good results everywhere manifest were due largely to the wise and fortunate choice of a man for Corresponding Secretary. J. H. DeVotie, with his varied experience and high reputation as pastor, his superior judgment and counsel, his genuine and genial piety, appeared to have come to the Kingdom for a time like that.

The work of state missions expanded rapidly, accounting for the steady growth of Georgia Baptists in new churches, effective evangelism, stewardship, and fellowship.

The work which has since grown into the convention's denominational program began, probably, with Sunday school work. The story appears to begin in Trail Creek Church, now First Church, Athens, in 1819. Adiel Sherwood, who had been in Georgia only about eight months, visited this church in June, 1819, and heard a man named Malone suggest that something be done to foster and promote the teaching ministry of the church. Isham Goss, pastor at Trail Creek, met with Malone and Sherwood at Trail Creek the first Sunday in July, 1819, and organized the first Sunday school in Georgia. When the convention met in Milledgeville in 1829—the year that marked the receipt of Josiah Penfield's (*q.v.*) initial gift for establishing what turned out to be Mercer University—the convention gave official approval to "the establishment of Sunday Schools in Georgia." In 1840 the convention appointed Sherwood, Adam Holmes, and Jonathan Davis to report on the "best method of promoting Sabbath school instruction in the churches." The Georgia Association reported 28 Sunday schools in 1829, with more than 1,000 pupils. The Georgia Association organized a Sunday school union in 1842. In 1853 the convention included in its minutes the "Address" from a recently organized state Sunday school association. Reference is made to a state Sunday school convention at Augusta in 1868.

Thomas Cooper Boykin came to Georgia from Alabama, Sept. 1, 1874, as the first superintendent of Sunday school work. He was to become famous as the editor of *Kind Words* and as one of the leaders who administered Sunday school work in Georgia and the South in the years leading up to 1891, when the Sunday School Board of the Southern Baptist Convention was established. It will be observed that Georgia Baptists had a department of Sunday school work three years before the State Mission Board was formed. Thus Sunday school work was the first organized administrative work of the convention.

George Washington Andrews (*q.v.*) became Sunday school secretary in 1904, upon the recommendation of Samuel Young Jameson (*q.v.*), then secretary of missions. He led Georgia Baptists in a great program of Sunday school development, aided by James W. Merritt and other capable and consecrated workers. One of the distinct features of Sunday school work in that period was the beginning of Vacation Bible schools, with Homer L. Grice, pastor at Washington, Ga., resigning his pastorate to go to Nashville as the first Vacation Bible school secretary for Southern Baptists.

Tiny W. Tippett succeeded Andrews as secretary of the department of Sunday school work in Georgia. He retired in 1956 after leading in major growth in the largest and most important phase of Georgia Baptist life.

Woman's Missionary Union is the second phase of the developing work of Georgia Baptists. Features of its early history are Martha Marshall and Kiokee, Charlotte Sherwood and Eatonton, Eliza Allen's letter to *The Christian Index* in 1837, Jesse Mercer's constant encouragement of the women, and the later days of the Woman's Missionary Society of the Second Baptist Church, Atlanta, which applied for membership in the convention when it met at Americus in 1874. The application was rejected, but in 1884, 10 years later, the Baptist Woman's Missionary Union of Georgia was organized in the Second Baptist Church, Atlanta. Emma Lenora Amos was the first state secretary and was succeeded by Evie Campbell, Susan Anderson, Mrs. Kate C. Wakefield, Maud Powell, Laura Lee Patrick, Mrs. A. F. McMahan, Mary Christian, and the incumbent, Janice Singleton (since 1940).

The Baptist Young People's Union of Georgia was approved by the convention, Apr., 1895. The state organization was formed in September of that year. The convention-wide B.Y.P.U. organization was formed in Atlanta in November of that year. Thirty-one churches were represented in the meeting at Macon when the Georgia body was organized. Jacob L. White, pastor of the First Baptist Church, Macon, was elected the first president of the organization; Frederick J. Paxon, secretary; and Ben H. Hardy, treasurer. There were years of struggle, but in 1913 the convention assumed responsibility for the salary of a full-time leader, and Frank H. Leavell (*q.v.*) was chosen as the first state secretary. Leavell was succeeded by H. Lewis Batts, Robert E. Connelly, Channing P. Hayes, Edwin S. Preston, and the incumbent, Gainer E. Bryan. When Leavell began his work in 1913, there were 40 local church unions. When he retired at the end of 1925, there were 1,670 unions. With that beginning Baptist Training Union work became one of the major factors in the total life of Georgia Baptists, reporting 177,577 members in 1955.

The Georgia Baptist Orphans' Home, now called the Georgia Baptist Children's Home, was organized by the Baptist women of Atlanta in the Second Baptist Church, July 13, 1888. Mrs. Belle K. Abbott was elected president of the board, and the home was opened Mar. 3, 1890, at 38 Formwalt Street. It was moved in September to 50 Capitol Avenue, and in 1892 it was again moved to Washington Street. In 1893 it was moved to 293 Courtland Street, and on Oct. 8, 1895, it was moved to its present site in Hapeville. The home was adopted by the convention in 1899, and James B. Taylor of Virginia was employed as superintendent, serving until 1903. He was succeeded by A. J. Beck, Lawson E. Brown, R. D. Hawkins, W. A. Johnson, Peter V. Rice, Thomas S. Scoggins, W. Patrick Anderson, Edwin Jesse White, Jesse L. Fortney, Oscar E. Rutland, and John Warr, the present manager, who began his work in Jan., 1950. Major expansion of the home included the purchase of valuable properties near Hapeville and at Baxley. Warr reported to the convention in 1955 that during the 83 years of the ministry of the home, 3,500 boys and girls had received Christian care, and that the home was caring annually for approximately 500 children. The property consists of 118 buildings and 1,700 acres of land. Only 25 per cent of the children applying to the home can be received because of lack of funds and space to care for them.

The Georgia Baptist Hospital dates from Thanksgiving Day, 1901, when Len G. Broughton led a group of friends in Atlanta Baptist Tabernacle Church to establish the Tabernacle Infirmary. In 1913 the Georgia Baptist convention bought the infirmary. It continued operation on Luckie Street until 1921, when it was moved to its present location, 300 Boulevard, N.E., in Atlanta. James M. Long served as superintendent from 1913 to 1922; he was succeeded by Eugene B. Elder, James B. Franklin, W. Daniel Barker, and the incumbent, Edwin B. Peel, who became administrator in June, 1946. The hospital is owned and controlled by the convention and is operated by the executive committee through a commission of five members, including the executive secretary-treasurer, who is treasurer of the hospital. Peel's report to the 1955 Convention revealed 23,959 patients for the first nine months of the year, with a plant capital of $5,777,562.03.

Other agencies represented in the administrative program of the Georgia Baptist convention include the Brotherhood Department, established in 1946, Bernard D. King, secretary; the Baptist Foundation, established in 1941, with Arthur Jackson serving as executive secretary until 1956, succeeded by Harry V. Smith; the Department of Music, established in 1950, Paul McCommon, secretary; the Department of Evangelism, established in 1936, with William H. Faust serving as secretary until his death, 1945. He was succeeded by Horace Cleveland Whitener, who served until his retirement in 1955, when he was succeeded by the incumbent, Reginald T. Russell. The Department of Student Work was established in 1925, with David B. Nicholson serving as secretary until his retirement in 1951, when the incumbent, Aubrey Hawkins, was elected secretary.

An important phase of the administrative work of the convention has been carried on by the office secretaries. Hugh Robertson Bernard (*q.v.*) filled this post until 1914, when he was succeeded by Spencer B. King, Sr. (*q.v.*). King served until 1919 and was succeeded by the incumbent, Buren C. Smith.

Office space for the convention's administrative program was rented until 1943, when the property at Peachtree and Baker streets, Atlanta, was purchased. This building houses the Baptist Book Store, now owned and operated by the Sunday School Board, and all the departments of the convention's work, including *The Christian Index*, purchased by the convention, Jan. 1, 1920.

The Christian Index, like Columbian College, was born in the fertile soil of Luther Rice's vision of a world missionary enterprise. Returning from Burma, with the pledge to Adoniram Judson that he would build the fires back home, Rice saw the need of a medium of propaganda for his great task, just as he saw the need of a school in which more ministers and missionaries would be trained. With this conviction and this vision, he established *The Columbian Star* in 1821 and Columbian College in 1822, at Washington, D. C.

Jesse Mercer saw the need of a medium of propaganda for Georgia Baptists and bought *The Columbian Star*, whose name had been changed to *The Christian Index*. He moved the paper to Washington, Ga., in 1833 and served for some time as editor of the paper. The final transfer of the paper to the convention occurred in 1840. In 1857 the paper was moved to Macon.

After brief editorships the convention sold the paper in 1861 to Samuel Boykin (*q.v.*) for $2,200. During the difficult days of the war, Boykin managed to keep the paper alive, and in 1866 he sold it to J. J. Toon for $2,000. Toon moved it that year to Atlanta and induced Henry Holcombe Tucker (*q.v.*) to accept the editorship. From that day the paper began to grow in favor with its increasing readers. There is an interesting interlude in this period of transition in which William Theophilus Brantly, Jr. (*q.v.*), pastor of the Second Baptist Church, Atlanta, served for some months as editor, thus linking his name with that of his father, who served as editor of the paper after it was moved from Washington to Philadelphia in the 1820's. Tucker was succeeded by David Shaver, but in 1878 Tucker returned to the editorship, succeeding David E. Butler, who had served as editor since 1874. Tucker's vigorous pen brought nation-wide attention to *The Christian Index* as a journal of real influence. In 1896 T. P. Bell (*q.v.*) bought the paper, and Isaac Jacobus Van Ness (*q.v.*) became associate editor and general manager. Van Ness left the paper in 1900 to become editorial secretary of the Sunday School Board. B. J. W. Graham joined Bell in 1900, and Graham became publisher of the paper in 1913 and editor from 1916 until Jan. 1, 1920, when his company sold the paper to the Georgia Baptist convention for the sum of $40,000. Louie DeVotie Newton served as editor of the paper from Jan., 1920, until Nov., 1929, when he accepted the pastorate of Druid Hills Baptist Church, Atlanta. Osceola Pinckney Gilbert served as editor from Nov., 1929, until his death, Apr., 1947. John Jeter Hurt, Jr., has served as editor since July, 1947.

The Christian Index has been the channel of information, enlistment, indoctrination, and inspiration for every cause and interest of the Georgia Baptist convention, the Southern Baptist Convention, and all the interests of co-operating Baptists from the day Jesse Mercer brought it to Georgia.

The 75 Million Campaign, launched by the Southern Baptist Convention in 1919, brought to the Georgia Baptist convention, as to every state in the territory of the Southern Baptist Convention, an unprecedented summons to undergird every missionary, educational, and benevolent agency and institution within the denomination. Never before had Southern Baptists been challenged by an appeal so comprehensive and convincing.

Archibald Cunningham Cree (*q.v.*) led the movement in Georgia, and he had the hearty and enthusiastic support of every denominational leader in the state, backed by every pastor and lay leader, from the most remote rural church to the largest city churches. A program of promotion was launched in the summer of 1919 which included every media of communication available—the daily and weekly newspapers, radio, billboards, *The Christian Index*, letters and cards, regional and associational mass meetings, with final emphasis within the local churches, seeking to reach every member of every church with this gigantic undertaking to raise the largest sum of money Baptists had ever given for the furtherance of the gospel.

Georgia was asked to raise seven and one-half million dollars, and when the final reports were tabulated in Dec., 1919, Cree was able to announce that over $10,000,000 had been subscribed. Southern Baptists, with a goal of $75,000,000, had subscribed $92,000,000. Not all of the pledges were paid, but the net result of the campaign remains one of the marvels of Baptist history. Every agency and institution was strengthened, and much progress was made. The Cooperative Program was one of the most notable by-products of the 75 Million Campaign.

Any estimate of the purpose and achievement of the Georgia Baptist convention, dating from 1822, and notably true in this generation, must take into account the fellowship of the people. There have been damaging schisms now and then, but through them all the people have maintained their commitment to their uniting fellowship. Strong men have differed on the basis of convictions regarding policies and, in rare instances, regarding doctrines; but they have never broken their fellowship. In one session of the Georgia Baptist convention in the 1930's, when the depression had thrust severe financial stress upon religious work, as upon all the economy, two prominent Georgia Baptist pastors were locked in bitter debate for several hours, but maintained through it all, not only respect for each other, but personal friendship. This is the sort of fellowship which is the basis of fruitful unity and co-operation.

LOUIE D. NEWTON

III. Program of Work of Georgia Baptists. THE EXECUTIVE COMMITTEE. On Dec. 22, 1830, eight years after the organization of the Georgia Baptist convention, the senate and house of representatives of the state of Georgia, in general assembly in Milledgeville, passed an act granting a perpetual charter to the executive committee of the Baptist Convention in the State of Georgia. The convention's present constitution, adopted in 1919 and amended in 1948 to enlarge executive committee membership, provides that the convention shall choose an executive committee consisting of 113 elected and 14 ex officio members. Members of the executive committee are divided into five groups, each with a different expiration date, and these groups are elected for terms of five years with the provision that the vacancies as terms expire shall be filled for terms of five years. Vacancies by reason of resignation or for other causes are filled for the period of the unexpired terms. No one connected in any way with an institution fostered by the convention is eligible for membership on the executive committee. No member, either elected or ex officio, shall be eligible for re-election after the expiration of his term of service until at least a year has elapsed. One member of the committee is to be chosen from each co-operating district association, 93 in number, and 20 additional members from the state at large. The ex officio members of the committee include the nine convention officers and the presidents of the departmental and auxiliary conventions. The associations from which members are to be chosen have the privilege of offering suggestions to the committee on nominations, but such suggestions are not binding upon this committee or the convention. Included in the committee's membership are pastors, laymen, and women, but there is no requirement governing representation of these groups on the committee.

Work of executive committee.—The executive committee has charge and control, except where otherwise directed by the convention, of all the work of the convention, including missions, education, and benevolences, in the interim between sessions of the convention.

When an unforeseen emergency occurs in any of the affairs of the convention, or in any of the interests it controls, that, in the judgment of the executive committee, requires action before the next session of the convention, the executive committee has full authority to take such action as it thinks will be best in the interim, and all parties are bound by its action, provided (1) that it must report to the next session of the convention all the facts in each case and what action it took; (2) that whatever action it takes in such cases will be binding only until the next session of the convention; and (3) that nothing in this article of the constitution shall be construed as giving the executive committee authority over any matters already committed by the convention to any of its boards of trustees, unless such boards decline to act.

Constitutional amendments.—The convention's constitution may be amended at any regular session by the vote of two-thirds of the messengers present and voting at the time; provided that no amendment shall be made later than the second day of the convention, and, further, that notice of the proposed change has been given in writing to the convention or in the state paper 90 days before its meeting.

Administration and other committees.—Four sessions of the executive committee are held during the year. The bylaws of the executive committee provide for the election of an administration committee of seven members, this committee to meet monthly and to have charge of the business of the executive committee between its sessions.

Provision is also made for the appointment of the following three standing committees: missions, education, and benevolence, with the entire membership of the executive committee equally divided among these groups. In broad outline the work of these committees is as follows: The committee on missions considers all applications and other communications touching the matter of missions and prepares and submits these to the executive committee as a whole. The committee on education reviews and presents to the executive committee matters concerning the entire field of education. The committee on benevolence prepares and presents matters concerning ministerial relief. (The work of the Georgia Baptist Hospital is directed by the Hospital Commission. The boards of trustees of the Georgia Baptist Children's Home and the Georgia Baptist Home for the Aged direct the work of these two institutions.)

The work of these standing committees is supplemented by the following special groups appointed by the executive committee: promotion committee, committee on aid to ministerial students and mission volunteers, committee on associational missions and city missions, Georgia Baptist Hospital Commission, and *The Christian Index* directors.

The education commission, elected by the convention, reports first to the executive committee.

The executive committee is charged with the responsibility of presenting a proposed budget to the convention each year and of making such other recommendations affecting the work and program of the denomination as it may deem wise and expedient.

The executive secretary-treasurer.—In addition to electing a president, vice-president, and recording secretary in its December meeting each year, following the session of the convention in November, the executive committee elects an executive secretary-treasurer, who serves as the chief executive officer of the convention. The executive secretary-treasurer has the responsibility of directing the work of the executive committee and is authorized to act for the committee in the areas of administration and promotion and in the supervision of the various phases and departments of state missions. The executive secretary-treasurer is authorized to sign papers and legal documents for the executive committee, either alone or with some other officer of the committee or convention as may be required.

The following condensed statement of some of the responsibilities of the executive committee, all of which constitute a part of the work of its executive secretary-treasurer, serves to reveal the scope of the committee's activities and its secretary's responsibilities:

Activities of the executive committee in the *field of promotion,* include promotion of the whole Cooperative Program; the every-member canvass, stewardship, and the enlistment of tithers; the special days in the Sunday schools and co-operation in the promotion of the special seasons of prayer and offering; the retirement and security plans for pastors; regional and state conferences; co-operation with all departments of state mission work and all agencies of the denomination in the promotion of the specific work committed to them. The executive committee directs the work of state missions; co-operates in efforts to increase the circulation of *The Christian Index;* co-operates with the churches and district associations in the promotion of the various phases of work, including associational work; and co-operates in all special efforts authorized by the convention.

The executive committee's work in the *area of administration* includes general supervision of all the work and interests of the convention committed to the executive committee; maintenance of offices, located in the Baptist Building, 291 Peachtree Street, Atlanta, referred to as Georgia Baptist state offices; receipt and disbursement, as instructed, of all funds contributed by churches and individuals and sent to the executive committee for the support of denominational causes; keeping and publication of accurate records of all funds received and disbursed and properly acknowledging all gifts from churches and individuals; administration of certain trust funds entrusted to the executive committee for specific purposes; keeping the records of the executive committee and the promotion of its work and plans; administration of certain phases of the retirement plans, such as handling applications from members for retirement; receiving from the Relief and Annuity Board, and, after making proper record, transmitting to the beneficiaries annuity checks for pastors who retire under the provisions of the retirement plans and widows who become beneficiaries; approving applications for ministerial relief; receiving and handling applications for pastoral aid. When such applications are approved by the executive committee, reports from the missionary pastors are received and recorded at the state office and checks issued to these pastors. Through a special committee, the executive committee receives and handles applications for associational missionary appropriations and, when such applications are approved, reports from the missionaries are received and recorded at the state office. The executive committee has direction of city mission work in co-operation with the Home Mission Board and direction of associational missionary work in co-operation with the district associations. It prepares all statistical tables and information for the minutes of the Georgia Baptist Convention each year. Blanks are supplied to association clerks for their use in furnishing material for the associational tables which appear in the convention minutes, and these tables are completed in the state office as to record of gifts of the churches to denominational causes.

The executive secretary-treasurer is treasurer and keeps the financial records of the executive committee and *The Christian Index;* he is also treasurer of the Georgia Baptist Hospital for all except current operating funds. All employees, including the executive secretary-treasurer, who handle funds are adequately bonded, and all records are regularly audited by a certified public accountant.

The executive secretary-treasurer arranges for, and notifies the members of, the meetings of regular and special committees appointed by the convention and the executive committee during the year and discharges other special instructions and responsibilities from the convention.

STATE MISSIONS. The convention has placed state missions under the direction of its executive committee. The following departments and phases of work are included in Georgia's state mission program: Evangelism, Sunday School, Training Union, Brotherhood, Church Music, Student Work, City Missions, Rural Work, Associational Missions, Missionary Pastors, Emergency Church Building Aid, State and Regional Conferences on Evangelism, Missions and Stewardship, Schools of Missions, Evangelistic Clinics, a full-time ministry to tubercular patients at Battey State Hospital at Rome, a part-time ministry to students in the School for the Deaf at Cave Spring, and a co-operative ministry with Negro Baptists. Woman's Missionary Union, auxiliary to the Georgia Baptist convention, renders effective service in the field of state missions.

Associational missions.—In 35 district associations missionaries are employed to promote programs of mission work and church development. The departments of state missions co-operate with the associations in the promotion, direction, and financial support of this work.

Missionary pastors.—Annually, approximately 100 missionary pastors receive salary supplements from state mission funds. These pastors serve churches in rural areas, mountain sections, industrial communities, cities, newly developed areas, and military centers, where financial assistance is required to maintain a regular church ministry. Pastoral aid applications require endorsement by the associations of which the churches making application are members.

Migrant workers.—Where migrant workers have been brought into agricultural sections of Georgia from Mexico to assist in harvesting operations, a ministry has been provided for these groups through the co-operation of the Home Mission Board.

Church building.—As a rule, church building appropriations are limited in amount and made only in emergency situations, such as the loss or damage of a building by fire or storm. All applications require approval of the local associations.

City missions.—Mission work is maintained in the five Georgia cities which meet the population requirement for this type of program. A superintendent directs the work in each place, and the Home Mission Board and the cities involved co-operate with state missions in support of city missions.

Rural work.—Development work among rural churches is a part of the general state mission program. Emphasis is given to rural work by associational missionaries and other departments of state missions. A statewide rural church conference has been inaugurated.

Evangelism.—A department of evangelism, with full-time secretary and staff, is maintained as one of the six regular departments of state missions. This department promotes evangelism through associational organizations, regional and statewide conferences, associational clinics, simultaneous crusades, revival meetings at mission points and in churches, and through a full-time ministry by one member of the staff to those in penal institutions. Organized effort is made to solve the problem of the absentee member by encouraging the transfer of church membership.

EDUCATIONAL MINISTRY. *Sunday School Department.*—This department maintains 14 full-time workers, including superintendents of teacher training, associational work, and Vacation Bible schools, and a worker for each department in the Sunday school. These staff members work with churches and associations in teacher training, enlargement, and promotion. During the summer months about 50 additional workers are employed to assist churches and associations in Sunday school and Vacation Bible school work, which is also the responsibility of the Sunday School Department. The activities of this department include a school of religious education; Sunday school conventions, state and regional; leadership conferences; planning conferences; special Vacation Bible school conferences; promotion of Sunday school organizations in each of the 93 associations; emphasis upon evangelism; and promotion of Bible Study Week in January of each year.

Training Union Department.—This department promotes Training Union work on a graded basis in the churches and associations through the efforts of seven full-time and a number of part-time workers. Activities of the department include study courses, central training schools, and association-wide campaigns and conferences. The annual Training Union Department program includes regional conventions, a state assembly, planning conferences, Bible or Sword Drill contests, and better speakers' contests. Promotion of "M" Night in every district association the first Monday night in December is also featured. An important objective of the Training Union Department is the organization of each association for the promotion of this phase of work among the churches.

Woman's Missionary Union.—This organization, which is auxiliary to the Georgia Baptist convention, is engaged in promoting state, home, and foreign mission work. A staff of eight, with offices in the Baptist Building, Atlanta, is maintained. Summer encampments are held at Camp Pinnacle, Clayton, and at Camp Glynn, Brunswick, owned by the W.M.U. This organization majors on mission education, seasons of prayer and offerings for missions, and stewardship of possessions. Its annual program includes a state convention, regional and associational meetings, and special conferences.

Off-campus centers for the education of ministers.—These centers, which were authorized and are supported by the convention, are directed by Mercer University under the leadership of a director and two assistants.

State encampments and assemblies.—Work of this type is promoted by various state mission departments at colleges and other places where facilities are available, and by the Woman's Missionary Union.

Regional conferences.—Ten one-day conferences on stewardship, missions, and evangelism, are held annually throughout the state, at which times emphasis is given to the entire denominational program and plans outlined for effective promotion of both regular and special features. Pastors, laymen, women, and associational officers are invited to attend these meetings.

Associational officers' conferences.—Each year a one-day conference of associational moderators, clerks, chairmen and members of executive committees, and other officers is held. Progress toward uniformity of plans and improvement in procedures result from discussions and exchange of ideas in these gatherings. Plans and future programs affecting the work of the churches, associations, and denomination are outlined for presentation to the churches through associational channels.

Schools of missions.—These schools are promoted on an associational basis in co-operation with leaders of the associations and of the Home and Foreign Mission boards.

Ministry at Battey State Hospital.—A full-time chaplain is provided in the state mission program to minister to the 2,000 patients and 500 employees of Battey State Hospital, Rome, an institution for the care and treatment of tubercular patients.

Ministry to the deaf.—A worker is employed to render service to those enrolled at the State School for the Deaf, Cave Spring, and to those who attend the Baptist church there. This worker regularly interprets the services in sign language for the benefit of those who are unable to hear.

Vacation Bible school.—This phase of work is promoted and directed by the Sunday School Department on an extensive statewide basis.

Department of Student Work.—This department ministers to Baptist students in 30 colleges through Baptist Student Unions in each of these institutions. The work is carried on in private institutions, in colleges of other denominations, in state schools, and in Baptist colleges. This department has a staff of 10 workers, and seven of these are campus directors of student work. At three locations student centers have been provided. Churches in college centers cooperate in providing and maintaining these centers. Programs of student guidance, counseling, and enlistment are part of the work of this department. Spring and fall retreats, a state student convention, and promotion and support of summer missions programs are activities of the Department of Student Work.

Brotherhood Department.—This department co-operates with the churches and associations in the organization, promotion, and development of Brotherhood work, the objective of which is to enlist men in support of the activities and programs of their churches and denomination. Evangelism, stewardship, Cooperative Program, and Royal Ambassador work are emphasized. Organization of associational Brotherhoods and committees is encouraged. This department promotes and gives direction to associational schools of missions. By agreement Royal Ambassador work has been transferred to the Brotherhood Department by the Woman's Missionary Union, and an assistant has been added to the department to aid in this new responsibility. During 12 weeks of each summer, camps are operated for Royal Ambassadors at Camp Pinnacle, Clayton, and Camp Glynn, Brunswick. Other activities of this department are regional conferences for Brotherhood officers, a statewide layman's meeting prior to the Georgia Baptist convention, and an annual Royal Ambassador Congress.

Radio committee.—A radio committee of five members, appointed annually by the convention, seeks to magnify the place and use of radio in the proclamation of the gospel and the teaching of the Bible. This committee co-operates with the Radio and Television Commission of the Southern Baptist Convention and responds to calls from other convention agencies for special service.

Church Music Department.—This, the youngest state mission department, ministers through training schools, festivals, and institutes conducted in the churches and associations, and in statewide events. The objective of this department is to aid the churches in their efforts to enlarge and improve the quality of chruch music programs. With a staff of four full-time workers, the Music Department emphasizes the associational approach, by means of which numbers of churches are reached and served in a single institute or training school. Summer workers are made available to a limited number of churches to supplement the work of the department in introducing graded choir programs and in training workers. Leaders in this department serve as music directors at state conventions and other general meetings.

Committee on Baptist history.—The convention elects and receives reports directly from the committee on Baptist history. This group is composed of eight members, and its work is supported by the convention. The committee has placed markers at a number of historical points and has arranged appropriate services to mark the unveiling of these markers. The committee has been authorized to recommend plans for production of a history of Georgia Baptists and for the preservation of the house of worship formerly used by Kiokee Church, Columbia County, the oldest Baptist church in the state, constituted in 1772.

INSTITUTIONS. *Colleges.*—The Georgia Baptist program of education includes three colleges of senior grade: Mercer University, Macon; Tift College, Forsyth; Shorter College, Rome; and three of junior grade: Norman College, Norman Park; Brewton-Parker College, Mount Vernon-Ailey; Truett-McConnell College, Cleveland. The convention elects trustees for the six colleges, provides financial support in its annual budget for these institutions, and receives yearly reports, including audits and financial statements, from each.

The convention's education commission has the responsibility of studying its educational program and making recommendations through the executive committee. A basic formula for the distribution of current operating funds, approved by the colleges and recommended to the convention by the commission, has been adopted. The commission also recommended a five-year program for providing minimum capital and repair needs of the six colleges through increased Cooperative Program contributions amounting to $5,562,969. This was adopted with the provision that the colleges secure funds from other sources to match the convention's appropriation for capital and repair needs.

The three senior colleges and the Georgia Baptist Hospital received grants from the Ford Foundation in 1956.

Children's Home.—The Georgia Baptist Children's Home, operating at Hapeville and

Baxley, provides for 500 children. By convention authority the home is given the privilege of seeking its support in designated gifts from churches, individuals, and foundations. Trustees are convention-elected on a rotating basis.

Georgia Baptist Hospital.—This institution, with a bed capacity of 550, including 75 bassinets, is owned and operated by the convention through its executive committee, which names a committee of five to supervise the hospital work. A school of nursing, training for doctors who serve as interns and residents, and training for technicians, all on approved bases, are included in the hospital's program. Its facilities include a professional building and a parking pavilion.

Ministerial relief and retirement.—The convention's retirement plans, administered by the relief and Annuity Board of the Southern Baptist Convention, include protection for pastors and their wives and for convention employees. Both plans have been liberalized since their inauguration, and both are classed as contributory plans. Relief appropriations are still provided in limited amounts to veteran pastors and their widows who did not secure membership in the retirement or security plans. Social Security is also made available for unordained convention employees.

Georgia Baptist Foundation and endowment committee.—The foundation, a chartered convention agency, is directed by nine trustees, who elect an executive secretary. This agency receives and administers trust funds for convention agencies; and its trustees, together with the presidents of the six Baptist colleges, the president and executive secretary-treasurer of the convention, and five other convention-elected members, constitute the endowment committee. This committee seeks to create endowment for the colleges and other institutions of the convention.

Home for the Aged.—The convention authorized establishment of its first Home for the Aged at Waycross, and construction is progressing under the direction of convention-elected trustees and an administrator employed by this group. The home is included in the convention's annual budget and is expected ultimately to care for a total of 300 persons.

PROMOTIONAL WORK. *The Christian Index.* The official organ of the convention, established in 1822, has a circulation of approximately 100,000. The paper is owned and operated by the convention through its executive committee, which annually appoints a board of directors of seven to co-operate with the editor in directing this work. *The Christian Index* is the chief source of information for Georgia Baptists regarding all phases of denominational work in this state and beyond. It serves as an agency of promotion and as a medium of information and of broad Christian culture.

Promotion.—While the executive secretary-treasurer gives general direction to promotion, working with him is a secretary of promotion and missions. The office was created Jan. 1, 1953. The administration committee is the committee on promotion. Promotion, carried on throughout the year, includes the following: creation and distribution of literature, educational and enlistment campaigns, constant publicity, and thorough organization of the state by associations. The objectives of the program of promotion are accomplished through correspondence, conferences, visits to churches, groups, district associations, and other gatherings, plus careful, long-range planning. The Cooperative Program is central in promotion. Special events are also emphasized, and all promotion is carried on in co-operation with churches and associations.

The teaching of stewardship through state-wide efforts has been featured in recent years, with definite results in enlarged support of church and denominational causes. Through associational organizations and otherwise, simultaneous stewardship study courses and revivals have been promoted on an every-church basis and special material provided for these efforts.

CO-OPERATIVE WORK. *American Bible Society.*—This group reports annually to the convention, which endorses the work of this organization and authorizes a financial appeal to the churches for support of its ministry on a designated Sunday in each year.

Temperance and social service.—A convention-elected commission of five members on social service reports annually. This commission's report deals with the evils resulting from the use of alcoholic beverages and with other social problems. The convention also makes provision in its annual budget for support of the Georgia Temperance League.

Work with other bodies.—Co-operative work is carried on with the Home Mission Board of the Southern Baptist Convention in programs of city missions, rural church development, evangelism, and a ministry to Negroes.

Negro Baptists.—Work with Negro Baptists, a part of the program of state missions, is carried on through the following channels: financial assistance in the support of a trained pastor for Trinity Baptist Church, Fort Valley, to make possible an effective ministry to students enrolled in the state college for Negroes located there; financial assistance in the maintenance of the headquarters of one convention in Atlanta; financial support of two institutes for pastors and other church leaders each year; and employment of a worker to expand the Georgia Baptist convention's ministry to the Negroes and to their churches of both conventions. This work is directed by the executive secretary-treasurer and the administration committee. This ministry follows in general the Home Mission Board's program of Negro work, which agency co-operates in its support.

Since changes occur from year to year, reference is made to the *Georgia Baptist Convention Minutes,* published annually, for detailed

IV. GEORGIA STATISTICAL SUMMARY

Year	Associations	Churches	Church Membership	Baptisms	S.S. Enrolment	V.B.S. Enrolment	T.U. Enrolment	W.M.U. Enrolment	Brotherhood Enrolment	Mission Gifts	Total Gifts	Value Church Property	State Capital Worth
1830													
1840													
1850	57	1,132	69,869	4,887									
1860	65	1,422	95,727	5,481									
1870	...	706	37,560	4,657									
1880	...	1,066	84,196	3,915						$ 10,181.86			
1890	...	1,288	...	5,514						20,329.97			
1900	...	...	...	...									
1905	82	2,120	213,325	12,427	78,137					15,607.41		$ 2,284,196.00	
1910	85	2,293	256,515	14,503	120,842					85,706.11		4,357,484.00	
1915	92	2,426	293,244	15,306	152,385					104,607.35		6,344,669.00	
1920	94	2,469	330,307	16,716						206,941.21			
1925	97	2,553	399,640	19,611		6,422				211,622.33			
1930	88	2,407	418,565	19,119	230,762	3,553	1,716	1,954		1,774,399.74	$ 1,017,880.00	17,533,344.00	
1931	88	2,410	427,874	20,400	251,183	4,420	1,912	2,179		568,170.79	2,722,397.45	17,137,043.00	
1932	89	2,430	441,756	21,553	264,459	3,524	1,982	2,265		411,414.95	2,358,278.95	17,164,856.00	
1933	85	2,376	450,610	18,424	265,766	5,855	2,015	2,373		367,525.79	1,975,135.01	16,989,643.00	
1934	84	2,408	457,941	18,988	260,670	4,927	2,037	2,391		311,067.50	1,751,064.74	16,774,494.00	$ 8,113,903.43
1935	84	2,392	462,849	16,669	250,741	7,224	1,992	2,455		299,866.71	2,002,323.88	16,831,953.00	
1936	84	2,407	470,362	16,510	250,418	9,336	1,869	2,483		350,243.08	2,148,880.33	17,128,081.00	
1937	85	2,414	481,206	18,307	252,870	12,500	1,894	2,396		392,111.60	2,419,987.43	17,495,552.00	
1938	86	2,434	499,404	24,111	263,456	15,091	2,181	2,699		449,674.83	2,568,017.72	17,888,203.00	
1939	86	2,421	505,839	22,276	268,987	16,188	2,542	2,977		457,806.29	2,891,544.92	18,350,966.00	
1940	86	2,428	520,546	22,427	278,525	24,951	2,957	3,064		442,113.33	3,039,423.82	19,127,585.00	
1941	86	2,459	530,952	17,268	269,010	33,888	3,095	3,132		583,596.72	3,468,583.40	19,628,645.00	
1942	86	2,476	539,617	17,562	259,231	35,215	3,055	3,088		667,161.37	3,495,355.58	20,457,113.00	
1943	87	2,491	552,360	16,451	254,556	34,348	2,942	2,932		650,510.83	4,112,505.52	21,040,256.00	
1944	87	2,511	566,231	18,664	259,731	31,383	3,052	2,814		910,228.08	5,140,282.72	21,986,243.00	$ 7,887,914.21
1945	88	2,531	581,599	21,057	286,311	52,194	3,319	3,069		1,436,443.49	6,339,825.03	23,220,437.00	
1946	88	2,559	598,728	20,798	293,845	70,025	3,818	3,266		1,772,688.79	8,651,563.54	26,020,776.00	
1947	88	2,588	615,854	23,781	318,771	97,404	4,213	3,502		2,265,245.06	9,428,703.52	30,298,936.00	
1948	87	2,567	629,491	26,192	350,114	115,393	5,123	3,738		2,170,319.13	10,736,469.23	36,200,299.00	
1949	88	2,584	651,265	28,571	387,309	133,257	5,995	4,093		1,998,298.23	12,331,026.61	42,550,117.00	
1950	90	2,614	675,305	31,280	426,175	145,351	111,463	97,159	17,229	2,751,621.86	13,608,751.98	48,530,631.00	
1951	90	2,654	701,821	32,670	446,461	156,463	122,542	98,487	19,696	2,232,752.54	15,821,214.80	60,318,179.00	
1952	90	2,684	718,808	27,027	467,165	158,916	132,222	101,845	21,981	2,803,566.14	19,104,568.28	70,912,971.84	
1953	90	2,720	738,250	29,956	486,536	183,221	146,898	110,389	24,754	2,970,237.55	17,983,637.87	80,956,542.20	
1954	92	2,748	760,024	33,379	549,962	220,167	165,801	120,170	29,404	2,950,883.29	21,214,046.65	90,480,688.73	$21,520,755.60
										3,272,790.73	24,429,877.70		
										3,546,120.99			

B. C. SMITH

records of the work, plans, and achievements, as well as the names of personnel, of the various departments and agencies through which the convention's work is carried on. Copies of the minutes are distributed each year to pastors and others, to college and seminary libraries, and to the Baptist offices of other states.

Additional current information is also available in the *Georgia Baptist Digest,* published and distributed annually to all Georgia Baptist churches by the executive committee of the Georgia Baptist convention.

The following table of distribution shows total credits to all causes made by the Georgia Baptist convention for the 12 months, Jan. 1, 1955, through Dec. 31, 1955.

BIBLIOGRAPHY: T. Armitage, *A History of the Baptists* (1889). D. Benedict, *General History of the Baptist Denomination in America, and Other Parts of the World* (1813). J. H. Campbell, *Georgia Baptists: Historical and Biographical* (1847 and 1874). W. Cathcart, *The Baptist Encyclopedia* (1881). *History of the Baptist Denomination in Georgia,* compiled for *The Christian Index* (1881). J. Mercer, *A History of the Georgia Baptist Association* (1838). A. H. Newman, *A History of the Baptist Churches in the United States* (1915).

GEORGIA ASSOCIATIONS.

I. Extant Associations. ALTAMAHA. Organized at Liberty Church, Jan. 7, 1945, by 14 churches located principally in Wayne County. Most of the churches came from the Piedmont and Con-

Causes	Undesignated	Designated Miscellaneous	Total for Year 1955	Total for Year 1954
Southern Baptist Convention Causes	$ 920,749.46	$ 515,251.79	$1,436,001.25	$1,269,926.75
State Missions	225,000.00	88,407.52	313,407.52	298,199.02
Executive Committee Loan (Ga. Baptist Hospital)	100,000.00		100,000.00	95,000.00
Georgia Baptist Hospital		182,642.17 (B)	182,642.17	190,042.64
Ministerial Education	3,500.00	14,105.08	17,605.08	16,530.67
Mercer University	90,000.00	153,042.22	243,042.22	140,899.06
Mercer University—Extension Department	24,000.00		24,000.00	24,000.00
Mercer University—Capital Funds	135,233.53 (A)		135,233.53	
Tift College	40,000.00	45,890.30	85,890.30	109,214.10
Tift College—Capital Funds	58,148.25 (A)		58,148.25	
Shorter College	40,000.00	71,903.18	111,903.18	65,685.92
Shorter College—Capital Funds	61,726.05 (A)		61,726.05	
Brewton-Parker Junior College	19,000.00	5,649.40	24,649.40	39,454.77
Brewton-Parker Junior College—Capital Funds	15,359.23 (A)		15,359.23	
Norman College	19,000.00	16,886.20	35,886.20	46,981.75
Norman College—Capital Funds	31,947.20 (A)		31,947.20	
Truett-McConnell Junior College	27,000.00	12,752.03	39,752.03	65,245.13
Truett-McConnell Junior College—Capital Funds	58,979.45 (A)		58,979.45	
Endowment Committee Expense	27,000.00		27,000.00	19,400.00
Education Commission—Expense	5,000.00		5,000.00	5,000.00
Georgia Baptist Foundation		32,399.21	32,399.21	59,164.91
Georgia Baptist Home for the Aged	25,000.00	11,795.63	36,795.63	
Committee on Georgia Baptist History	1,000.00		1,000.00	1,000.00
Georgia Baptist History	5,000.00		5,000.00	
Southern Baptist Encyclopedia	1,200.00		1,200.00	
Georgia Temperance League	4,600.00		4,600.00	3,600.00
The Christian Index	15,000.00		15,000.00	10,526.34
Baptist Woman's Missionary Union of Georgia	49,032.63		49,032.63	46,397.79
General Program Expense	100,909.88		100,909.88	101,202.39
Denominational Retirement Plans	107,919.87		107,919.87	77,842.00
Georgia Baptist Children's Home		582,394.99	582,394.99	541,019.39
B. W. M. U. Specials		3,783.64	3,783.64	4,778.51
Sundry Miscellaneous		104,996.86 (C)	104,996.86	254,521.00
1955 Totals	$2,211,305.55	$1,841,900.22	$4,053,205.77	$3,485,632.14 (D)
1954 Totals	1,846,535.07	1,755,080.91	3,601,615.98	

(A) *Total funds available for the six education institutions for capital needs and repairs was $361,393.71, of which $115,983.84 was brought over from previous year. These figures are included in the total of this column.*
(B) *This total includes $128,929.18 for charity offerings and $53,712.99 for the hospital building fund.*
(C) *This includes the following special gifts: special gifts to church buildings, $8,915.33; gifts to W.M.U. camps fund, $2,278.28; special funds for Southern Baptist seminaries, $3,150.00; special Atlanta Association gifts, $8,837.59; American Bible Society gifts, $4,371.58; Tift College specials, $17,927.74; Mercer University specials, $10,508.56; Shorter College specials, $18,365.50; and various sundry contributions, $30,642.28.*
(D) *This total does not include $115,983.84 shown as undistributed collections in 1954.*

JAMES W. MERRITT

solation associations. In 1954, 17 churches reported 131 baptisms, 2,847 members, $71,009.56 total gifts, $4,855.88 mission gifts, $393,373.00 property value, and $42,875.00 church debt.

APPALACHEE. Organized Oct. 31, 1835, at Freeman's Creek Church, Clark County, by three churches located in Clark, Oglethorpe, and Morgan counties. It adopted the Philadelphia Articles of Faith. Although the Monroe church is not listed as being in the organization of the association, the second annual session met at this church. Messengers were elected to the state convention in 1839. In 1954, 22 churches reported 261 baptisms, 5,256 members, $125,-388.35 total gifts, $16,884.55 mission gifts, and $600,500.00 property value.

ATLANTA. Organized Nov. 9, 1909, at the First Baptist Church, Atlanta, Ga., by 38 churches. Two of the churches in the organization had been members of the Roswell Association and the other 36 had been members of the Stone Mountain Association. All of these churches were located in and near Atlanta. Articles of faith were adopted conforming to Seminary Creed. This association is the largest one in the number of churches, membership, and contributions in the state. Located within its boundaries are: the headquarters of the Baptist Convention of the State of Georgia; the Georgia Baptist Hospital; one branch of the Georgia Baptist Children's Home; and the headquarters of the Home Mission Board of the Southern Baptist Convention. The association co-operates with the Baptist Convention of the State of Georgia and with the Southern Baptist Home Mission Board in a program of city missions. A superintendent of city missions is employed. The association also employs a full-time promotional director and a full-time office secretary. In 1954, 132 churches reported 4,830 baptisms, 105,379 members, $5,320,132.15 total gifts, $865,728.32 mission gifts, $20,299,336.04 property value, and $3,822,482.00 church debt.

AUGUSTA. Organized Nov. 28, 1949, at Curtls Church, Augusta, Ga., by 26 churches located in Richmond and Columbia counties and along the county line in Burke County. These churches withdrew from the Hephzibah Association when it decided to divide in 1949. The churches that remained in the Hephzibah kept the name of the old association. In 1925 articles of faith were adopted. The association co-operates with the state convention and the Southern Baptist Convention's Home Mission Board in a program of city missions. A superintendent of city missions is employed. In 1954, 32 churches reported 996 baptisms, 19,347 members, $1,033,527.26 total gifts, $103,952.26 mission gifts, $3,459,490.00 property value, and $412,202.00 church debt.

BEN HILL-IRWIN. Organized Oct. 22, 1924, at Irwinville Church, Irwinville, Irwin County, Ga., by 22 churches located in Irwin and Ben Hill counties. These churches came from the Mell and Little River associations. Articles of faith were adopted. In 1954, 22 churches reported 199 baptisms, 4,916 members, $143,667.98 total gifts, $23,977.51 mission gifts, $532,860.00 property value, and $7,081.00 church debt.

BETHEL. Organized in 1832 at Richland Baptist Church, Stewart County. Reports for its second year showed 21 churches located in Lee, Sumpter, Stewart, Baker, and Randolph counties in Georgia and Henry County, Ala. In 1839 this association made definite plans to engage in domestic mission work. Later it supported foreign mission work. It established and supported Cuthbert Female College of southwest Georgia and sometime later established a school for boys in the same community. The churches are located in Quitman, Randolph, Clay, Calhoun, Early, and Baker counties. The association employs an associational missionary and owns a home for the missionary. In 1954, 39 churches reported 210 baptisms, 7,104 members, $166,562.82 total gifts, $30,140.80 mission gifts, $692,600.00 property value, and $8,839.00 church debt.

BOWEN. Organized in 1856 by 18 churches located in Baker, Calhoun, Colquitt, Decatur, Early, and Miller counties in southwest Georgia. The place of organization is not known. This association employs an associational missionary. In 1954, 37 churches reported 256 baptisms, 7,308 members, $195,147.63 total gifts, $33,959.98 mission gifts, $785,397.00 property value, and $18,875.00 church debt.

CARROLLTON. Organized Oct. 24, 1874, in Carrollton County, by 17 churches located in Carroll and ajoining counties. An abstract of faith was adopted. The association employs an associational missionary. In 1954, 34 churches reported 368 baptisms, 9,603 members, $294,-843.97 total gifts, $26,034.03 mission gifts, $1,309,517.00 property value, and $5,167.00 church debt.

CATOOSA COUNTY. Organized in 1914 at Ringgold by churches coming from the Coosa and North Georgia associations. In 1915 there were nine churches located in Catoosa County. In 1954, 23 churches reported 257 baptisms, 5,310 members, $170,339.83 total gifts, $13,674.89 mission gifts, $482,333.21 property value, and $18,-345.00 church debt.

CENTENNIAL. Organized in 1883. The first annual session was at Barnesville Church, Lamar County. In 1889 at the sixth annual session it reported 14 churches located in Upson, Pike, Monroe, Crawford, Jasper, Butts, and Lamar counties. In 1954 the 36 churches composing this association were located in Upson, Monroe, Pike, and Lamar counties. The association employs an associational missionary. Tift College, a senior Baptist girls' college is located at Forsyth, Ga., in the area of this association. In 1954, 36 churches reported 408 baptisms, 9,395 members, $340,694.95 total gifts, $61,261.15 mission gifts, $1,575,578.00 property value, and $33,-710.00 church debt.

CENTRAL. Organized at Indian Creek Church, Morgan County, Feb. 1, 1834, by seven churches which had seceded from the Ocmulgee and Flint River associations. The churches were located in Morgan, Henry, and Monroe counties. The churches forming this new association recognized and approved sabbath schools, missions, education of ministers, and Bible, temperance, and tract societies. It became a member of the Baptist Convention of the State of Georgia. It adopted articles of faith of the Georgia Association. The churches are located in Putnam, Jones, Jasper, and Newton counties. In 1954, 26 churches reported 112 baptisms, 3,365 members, $73,547.97 total gifts, $14,098.42 mission gifts, $335,500.00 property value, and $323.00 church debt.

CHATTAHOOCHEE. Organized Mar. 1, 1926, at Hopewell Church, Hall County, by eight churches located in Hall, Habersham, Jackson, Gwinnett counties and one from the Cherokee nation. It employs an associational missionary. In 1954, 48 churches reported 489 baptisms, 17,040 members, $399,338.65 total gifts, $76,452.65 mission gifts, $1,742,334.00 property value, and $107,521.00 church debt.

CHATTOOGA. Organized Oct. 14, 1892, at the Summerville Baptist Church by 13 churches located principally in Chattooga County in northwest Georgia. Most of the churches seem to have come from the Coosa and the Cave Spring associations. In 1954, 32 churches reported 199 baptisms, 5,871 members, $87,330.14 total gifts, $12,487.14 mission gifts, and $401,900.00 property value.

COLQUITT COUNTY. Organized in 1912 by 22 churches located in Colquitt County. Article 2 of the constitution stated, "The Association shall be composed of white male members chosen by the respective churches." This association employs an associational missionary and owns a home for the missionary. In 1954, 39 churches reported 668 baptisms, 11,178 members, $256,848.29 total gifts, $27,384.55 mission gifts, $1,086,850.00 property value, and $130,200.00 church debt.

COLUMBUS. Organized in Nov., 1829, at New Hope Church, Harris County, by a small number of churches. At the 9th annual session in 1837, 26 churches reported 2,291 members. The churches were located in Talbot, Harris, Muscogee, and Meriwether counties. It has had a city mission program for many years and owns a home for its superintendent of city missions. This association is one of the largest in number of church members and in contributions in Georgia. In 1954, 43 churches reported 1,213 baptisms, 20,101 members, $889,121.74 total gifts, $135,663.74 mission gifts, $3,452,467.00 property value, and $444,279.00 church debt.

CONCORD. Organized Oct. 13, 1877, at Concord Baptist Church, Cobb County, by 11 churches coming from the Tallapoosa, Fairburn, and Noonday associations. These churches were located in Douglas, Cobb, and Paulding counties. This association employs an associational missionary. In 1954, 27 churches reported 412 baptisms, 8,761 members, $205,546.42 total gifts, $19,395.42 mission gifts, $900,000.00 property value, and $40,305.00 church debt.

CONSOLATION. Organized in 1894 at Consolation Church, Wayne County. There were 11 churches represented at the second annual session. Most of these churches came from the Piedmont and New Ebenezer associations. In 1954, 31 churches reported 293 baptisms, 6,882 members, $108,076.65 total gifts, $17,705.65 mission gifts, $487,660.00 property value, and $10,884.00 church debt.

COOSA. Organized in 1836 by several churches located in northwest Georgia. In 1842 there were 29 churches located in Cass, Cherokee, Floyd, Chattooga, Murray, and Walker counties. It became a member of the Baptist state convention of Georgia in 1842. It was the first association in Georgia to adopt the "Independent Plan" of conducting missions, employing David Foreman, a native Indian, as missionary to the Cherokees. This association employs an associational missionary and owns a home for the missionary. The churches are located mostly in Walker County, and all of the churches have full-time services. In 1954, 55 churches reported 689 baptisms, 11,738 members, $465,873.44 total gifts, $36,140.52 mission gifts, $1,521,000.00 property value, and $184,697.00 church debt.

DANIELL. Organized Nov. 8, 1890, at Vidalia Baptist Church, Montgomery County, by 13 churches located in Montgomery, Emanuel, Dodge, Laurens, and Tattnall counties. The association employs an associational missionary. In 1954, 38 churches reported 250 baptisms, 6,988 members, $125,251.66 total gifts, $25,398.66 mission gifts, $534,095.00 property value, and $6,170.00 church debt.

DODGE COUNTY. Organized in 1872 at Salem Church in Pulaski County as New Ebenezer Association. In 1874, 20 churches reported a total membership of 947 and 118 baptisms. The churches were located in Dodge, Pulaski, Laurens, and Montgomery counties. A considerable number of its churches withdrew and formed the Pulaski and Laurens County associations. It employs an associational missionary. In 1954, 32 churches reported 286 baptisms, 6,001 members, $130,427.02 total gifts, $16,494.29 mission gifts, $410,754.00 property value, and $9,151.00 church debt.

EBENEZER. Constituted Mar., 1814, at Cool Spring Church, Wilkinson County, by churches dismissed from the Hephzibah and Ocmulgee associations. The churches were located in Wilkinson and Twiggs counties. In 1954, 28 churches reported 171 baptisms, 4,321 members, $103,368.04 total gifts, $11,855.54 mission gifts, and $388,000.00 property value.

EMANUEL COUNTY. Organized Feb. 3, 1909, at Summit Baptist Church by 10 churches located in Emanuel County. The churches most probably came from Bulloch County and Miller associations. This association is located in one of the strongest antimission areas of the state. In 1954, 17 churches reported 243 baptisms, 3,164 members, $120,508.23 total gifts, $6,249.23 mission gifts, $332,500.00 property value, and $11,786.00 church debt.

ENON. Organized in Oct., 1900, at Enon Church, Hall County, by seven churches. In 1954, 13 churches reported 70 baptisms, 2,087 members, $11,138.01 total gifts, $1,127.66 mission gifts, $36,000.00 property value, and $308.00 church debt.

FAIRBURN. Organized in 1867. In 1871 it was composed of 19 churches located in Campbell, Douglas, Fayette, Cobb, Fulton, and Coweta counties. This association employs an associational missionary. In 1954, 36 churches reported 660 baptisms, 10,803 members, $320,882.89 total gifts, $28,172.20 mission gifts, $974,000.00 property value, and $25,259.00 church debt.

FLINT RIVER. Organized Oct. 16, 1824, at Rocky Creek Meetinghouse, Monroe County, by 14 churches dismissed from the Ocmulgee Association and six new churches. It declined to co-operate with the Baptist Convention of the State of Georgia for almost 20 years, but came into full accord after that time. Articles of faith are reported in earliest minutes preserved (1831). The association employs an associational missionary. In 1954, 57 churches reported 779 baptisms, 14,958 members, $551,994.32 total gifts, $85,912.25 mission gifts, $2,107,038.00 property value, and $234,913.08 church debt.

FLOYD COUNTY. Organized Oct. 4, 1893, at the First Baptist Church, Rome, Ga., by 25 churches coming from the Cave Spring and Oostanaula associations and located in Floyd County. Articles of faith were adopted. Shorter College, a Baptist college, is located at Rome. The association employs an associational missionary and owns a home for the missionary. In 1954, 57 churches reported 777 baptisms, 18,515 members, $622,313.52 total gifts, $59,519.50 mission gifts, $2,214,414.00 property value, and $87,295.00 church debt.

FRIENDSHIP. Organized at Friendship Church, Sumpter County, Nov. 24, 1859, by 24 churches located in Taylor, Marion, Macon, Lee, Webster, and Schley counties. It adopted the New Hampshire Confession of Faith. The association employs an associational missionary. The churches in 1954 were located in Sumpter, Macon, Schley, Marion, and Lee counties. In 1954, 33 churches reported 243 baptisms, 7,324 members, $240,447.14 total gifts, $34,825.82 mission gifts, $784,800.00 property value, and $28,280.00 church debt.

GEORGIA. Organized in 1784 by five churches located in what is now Columbia County. This was the first Baptist association formed in Georgia. Articles of faith seem to have been adopted (though the early records of the association have been lost). The Baptist Convention of the State of Georgia was organized within the bounds of this association (1822) at Powelton. In 1833, at Penfield, Ga., Mercer University had its beginnings within the bounds of this association. The churches are located in Greene, Wilkes, Oglethorpe, Taliaferro, Lincoln, and Columbia counties. It employs an associational missionary and owns a home for the missionary. In 1954, 51 churches reported 264 baptisms, 9,544 members, $280,881.77 total gifts, $43,077.97 mission gifts, $997,800.00 property value, and $12,117.50 church debt.

GILMER-FANNIN. Organized in 1915 by six churches located in Gilmer and Fannin counties in north Georgia. In 1954, 16 churches reported 106 baptisms, 2,424 members, $4,929.91 total gifts, $558.16 mission gifts, and $32,300.00 property value.

GOOD SAMARITAN. Organized at Friendship Church, Oct. 30, 1897. Most of the churches came from the Carrollton Association and were located in Carroll and Douglas counties. In 1954, 9 churches reported 22 baptisms, 861 members, $14,009.83 total gifts, $85.50 mission gifts, $35,500.00 property value, and $1,625.00 church debt.

GORDON COUNTY. Organized Oct. 30, 1896, at Bethesda Church, Red Bud, Ga., by nine churches located in Gordon County. These churches probably came from the Middle Cherokee Association. In 1954, 23 churches reported 145 baptisms, 5,170 members, $100,232.10 total gifts, $7,310.48 mission gifts, $305,700.00 property value, and $16,868.00 church debt.

GRADY COUNTY. Organized Nov. 22, 1911, at Long Branch Church in Grady County by 12 churches and known in the beginning as Taylor Association. This association employs an associational missionary. In 1954, 20 churches reported 174 baptisms, 4,886 members, $136,435.75 total gifts, $15,098.91 mission gifts, $364,950.00 property value, and $14,733.00 church debt.

HABERSHAM COUNTY. Organized at Cornelia Baptist Church, Habersham County, Nov. 28, 1921. In 1922 there were 16 churches located in Habersham County. Most of them had come from the Clarksville Association (now extinct). In 1954, 29 churches reported 250 baptisms, 7,085 members, $76,375.74 total gifts, $14,439.14 mission gifts, $584,500.00 property value, and $17,038.00 church debt.

HARALSON COUNTY. Organized Oct., 1917, by 13 churches located in Haralson County. The churches came from Harmony Association (now extinct). The association employs an associational missionary. In 1954, 21 churches reported 162 baptisms, 4,346 members, $107,487.77 total gifts, $10,550.77 mission gifts, $483,000.00 property value, and $7,800.00 church debt.

HEBRON. Organized in 1883 by 22 churches located principally in Elbert and Hart counties. The first session was held at Hendrys. It joined the Baptist Convention of the State of Georgia in 1884. In 1954, 48 churches reported 313 baptisms, 13,155 members, $178,250.90 total gifts, $32,745.90 mission gifts, $1,145,150.00 property value, and $352.00 church debt.

HEPHZIBAH. Organized in 1794 at Big Buckhead Church in Burke County by 19 churches located in Burke, Richmond, Jefferson, Warren, and Washington counties. The churches were dismissed from the Georgia Association in order to form a new association. This was the second Baptist association organized in Georgia. The Southern Baptist Convention was organized within the bounds of this association in 1845 at the First Baptist Church, Augusta, Ga. In 1925 the association adopted articles of faith. In 1949 the churches of this association, located within Richmond and Columbia counties, together with a few churches along the Richmond and Burke County line, withdrew and formed the Augusta Baptist Association. The churches located in Burke and Jefferson counties remained in the Hephzibah and kept that name. This association employs an associational missionary. In 1954, 23 churches reported 158 baptisms, 4,662 members, $134,647.06 total gifts, $26,105.73 mission gifts, $792,100.00 property value, and $43,315.00 church debt.

HIAWASSEE. Organized in 1849 by 24 churches of the Notla River and Valley River associations, located principally in Union and Towns counties. The Georgia Baptists operated a Baptist school, Hiawassee Institute, at the town of Hiawassee from 1886 to 1926. This association co-operates with Rabun County and White County associations in an associational missionary program. In 1954, 14 churches reported 37 baptisms, 2,926 members, $23,139.88 total gifts, $1,343.88 mission gifts, and $82,890.00 property value.

HIGHTOWER. Organized by 10 churches on Nov. 20, 1835, at Silver Springs, Forsyth County. Most of the churches came from the Chattahoochee Association and were located in Forsyth and Cherokee counties. In 1954, 59 churches reported 556 baptisms, 16,885 members, $94,577.13 total gifts, $2,534.13 mission gifts, $471,800.00 property value, and $15,500.00 church debt.

HOUSTON. Organized in 1830 by a group of churches from the Ebenezer Association. It took its name from Houston County. In 1833 there were 14 churches located in Dooly, Stewart, Lee, Sumpter, Irwin, and Pulaski counties. In 1954 churches were located in Crisp and Dooly counties. In 1954, 34 churches reported 289 baptisms, 6,949 members, $158,527.40 total gifts, $17,832.40 mission gifts, $688,150.00 property value, and $9,284.00 church debt.

KILPATRICK. Organized on Oct. 28, 1914, at Thomson Baptist Church by 26 churches located mostly in Warren and McDuffie counties in east Georgia. The churches came from the Georgia and Hephzibah associations. In 1954, 28 churches reported 239 baptisms, 5,573 members, $173,645.08 total gifts, $17,949.61 mission gifts, $540,000.00 property value, and $31,558.00 church debt.

KIMBELL. Organized Oct. 29, 1897, at County Line Church, Butts County, by 13 churches which withdrew from the Flint River Association located in Butts, Henry, and Monroe counties. The association adopted articles of faith similar to the Philadelphia Confession. In 1954, 23 churches reported 190 baptisms, 3,581 members, $75,150.86 total gifts, $11,136.59 mission gifts, $304,500.00 property value, and $5,780.36 church debt.

LAURENS COUNTY. Organized Nov. 30, 1911, at Blue Water Church by churches mostly from the Ebenezer and New Ebenezer associations. In 1914 there were 35 churches. It adopted the New Hampshire Confession of Faith. In 1954, 36 churches reported 305 baptisms, 8,261 members, $178,972.37 total gifts, $25,755.90 mission gifts, $698,000.00 property value, and $14,308.23 church debt.

LAWRENCEVILLE. Organized in 1854 at Hog Mountain Church in Gwinnett County. The churches in 1954 were located in DeKalb and Gwinnett counties. The association employs an associational missionary. In 1954, 27 churches reported 454 baptisms, 8,770 members, $289,101.54 total gifts, $42,181.54 mission gifts, $1,239,500.00 property value, and $48,148.00 church debt.

LIBERTY. Organized in 1868. In 1876 it met at Pleasant Hill Church, Hall County, and reported 16 churches located in the area between Toccoa, Ga., and Cornelia, Ga. These churches most probably came from the Tugalo and Chattahoochee associations. In 1954, 15 churches reported 86 baptisms, 2,518 members, $31,518.05 total gifts, $1,607.84 mission gifts, $71,000.00 property value, and $300.00 church debt.

LITTLE RIVER. Organized in 1880. At its fourth annual session there were 17 churches, located principally in Wilcox County. In 1893 two churches, which were expelled from this association because of their doctrinal belief in sinless perfection, joined with some churches in Florida and formed the Holiness Baptist Association of Georgia and Florida. In 1954, 19 churches reported 98 baptisms, 3,462 members, $53,375.72 total gifts, $5,022.72 mission gifts, and $154,100.00 property value.

LOOKOUT VALLEY. Organized in 1902 at Bethlehem Church, Overlook, Jackson County, Ala., by 11 churches located principally in Dade County, Ga. In 1954, 14 churches reported 58 baptisms, 1,513 members, $21,821.57 total gifts, $1,244.57 mission gifts, $71,500.00 property value, and $1,841.00 church debt.

MACON. Organized Oct. 14, 1954, at Mable White Church, Macon, Ga., by 37 churches which had withdrawn from the Rehoboth Association. Most of these churches are located in Bibb County. Mercer University, a Baptist college, is located at Macon, Ga. The association co-operates with the Baptist Convention of the State of Georgia and with the Southern Baptist Home Mission Board in a city missions program. In 1954, 39 churches reported 1,256 baptisms, 23,845 members, $1,106,578.11 total gifts, $121,143.11 mission gifts, $3,541,050.00 property value, and $382,924.00 church debt.

MALLARY. Organized in 1883 at Albany by about 17 churches located in Dougherty, Baker, Worth, Mitchell, Colquitt, and Lee counties. This association employs an associational missionary. In 1954, 31 churches reported 485 baptisms, 9,452 members, $261,039.79 total gifts, $30,994.32 mission gifts, $1,046,100.00 property value, and $83,812.00 church debt.

MARBLE VALLEY. Organized Apr. 30, 1939, at Cool Springs Baptist Church, Tate, Pickens

County, Ga., by six churches. In 1954, six churches reported 47 baptisms, 1,392 members, $47,320.12 total gifts, $6,552.80 mission gifts, $128,000.00 property value, and $8,247.00 church debt.

MELL. Organized in 1886 by 13 churches located in Berrien, Irwin, Lowndes, and Worth counties. In 1954, 21 churches reported 275 baptisms, 5,797 members, $219,571.21 total gifts, $21,067.38 mission gifts, $760,522.00 property value, and $29,293.00 church debt.

MEMORIAL. Organized Oct. 29, 1949, by seven churches which had withdrawn from the Gordon County Association. The churches are located in Gordon County. In 1954, 8 churches reported 35 baptisms, 1,457 members, $8,904.34 total gifts, $371.34 mission gifts, and $24,500.00 property value.

MERCER. Organized Feb. 6, 1874, at Boston, Ga., by approximately 32 churches located in Brooks, Lowndes, Colquitt, and Thomas counties. In 1954, 18 churches reported 89 baptisms, 3,180 members, $116,320.71 total gifts, $10,266.71 mission gifts, and $270,679.00 property value.

MERRITT. Organized Oct. 26, 1954, at Valley Grove Baptist Church, Woodland, Ga., by 14 churches coming from the Pine Mountain and Columbus associations. In 1955, 16 churches reported 150 baptisms, and 3,285 members. Gifts to local causes were $71,876, and to denominational causes, $20,753.

MIDDLE. Organized at New Providence Church, Effingham County, Ga., Dec. 14, 1841, by five churches, located in Effingham and Screven counties. Articles of faith were adopted. It was admitted to the Baptist Convention of Georgia in 1850. The association employs an associational missionary. In 1954, 39 churches reported 176 baptisms, 7,738 members, $195,287.22 total gifts, $22,124.30 mission gifts, $720,325.00 property value, and $23,151 church debt.

MIDDLE CHEROKEE. Organized at Mt. Moriah, Cass County, Ga., 1846. In 1848 there were 22 churches located in Murray, Cass, and Floyd counties. In 1854 this association "projected" the Cherokee Baptist College. In 1954, 32 churches reported 199 baptisms, 7,711 members, $156,626.45 total gifts, $19,653.00 mission gifts, $736,200.00 property value, and $42,503 church debt.

MORGAN COUNTY. Organized Sept. 18, 1918, at First Baptist Church, Madison, Ga. There were 13 churches located in Morgan County. These churches seem to have come from the Appalachee, Central, and Georgia associations. In 1954, 13 churches reported 96 baptisms, 2,092 members, $69,448.37 total gifts, $11,375.17 mission gifts, $254,600.00 property value, and $12,626.00 church debt.

MORGANTON. Organized in Fannin County, Ga., 1893. In 1898 there were 11 churches located in Fannin County. An associational missionary is employed. In 1954, 26 churches reported 156 baptisms, 5,583 members, $113,309.30 total gifts, $15,935.70 mission gifts, $428,960.00 property value, and $28,309.00 church debt.

MOUNT VERNON. Organized Feb. 7, 1859, at Riddleville, Ga., by five churches located in Washington, Johnson, Laurens, and Montgomery counties. These churches came from Washington Association. In 1954, 25 churches reported 75 baptisms, 3,738 members, $60,388.60 total gifts, $5,699.23 mission gifts, $306,550.00 property value, and $2,400.00 church debt.

MOUNTAINTOWN. Organized in 1885 by churches located in Gilmer County in north Georgia. At the sixth annual session in 1891 there were 14 churches in the association. These churches seem to have come from the Jasper and Ellijay associations, and most of them are located in Gilmer County. In 1954, 15 churches reported 83 baptisms, 2,454 members, $27,111.47 total gifts, $3,801.47 mission gifts, and $116,000.00 property value.

MULBERRY. Organized in Oct., 1874, by nine churches in Gwinnett, Jackson, and Barrow counties. In 1954, 24 churches reported 188 baptisms, 5,638 members, $58,686.71 total gifts, $4,028.04 mission gifts, $135,500.00 property value, and $2,600.00 church debt.

NEW SUNBURY. Organized at Jones Creek Church, Liberty County, Nov. 24, 1866, by 11 churches from the Sunbury, Union, and Piedmont associations. These churches were located in the territory between the Savannah and Altamaha rivers. The old Sunbury had voted to dissolve and join with the other churches from the Union and Piedmont associations in the formation of a new association. The new association was named the New Sunbury and it adopted the bylaws of the Georgia Association. In 1949, due to the long distances between some of the churches, the New Sunbury voted to divide and form two associations. The churches in and around Savannah organized and took the name Savannah Association and those to the west in Bryan, Liberty, Long, and McIntosh kept the name New Sunbury. In 1954, 15 churches reported 104 baptisms, 2,880 members, $132,314.63 total gifts, $12,324.63 mission gifts, $367,000.00 property value, and $17,000.00 church debt.

NEW UNION. Organized Oct. 7, 1876, at Salem Baptist Church, Lumpkin County, by six churches mostly located in Lumpkin County. The association was first known as Lumpkin County Association. In 1954, 8 churches reported 19 baptisms, 1,175 members, $14,881.20 total gifts, $1,349.96 mission gifts, $143,000.00 property value, and $3,649.00 church debt.

NOONDAY. Organized in 1858. At the 13th annual session 23 churches located in Cobb, Cherokee, and Pickins counties reported 1,715 members. The association employs a missionary and owns a home for the missionary. In 1954, 52 churches reported 808 baptisms, 17,631 members, $625,870.51 total gifts, $78,425.17 mission gifts, $2,203,300.00 property value, and $200,553.00 church debt.

NORTH GEORGIA. Organized at Popular Springs Church, Whitfield County, in the summer of 1862 by three churches. Most of the churches in the area belonged to the Middle Cherokee

Georgia Associations

Association. The first minutes in existence are dated 1870, and show there were 26 churches with 1,641 members, 95 of which were Negroes. One church in 1870 (Walnut Grove) was a Negro church with a Negro pastor. In 1871 this church, together with Negro members from six other churches, withdrew from the association and "joined an association of their own color." In 1954, 60 churches reported 708 baptisms, 13,-521 members, $369,630.30 total gifts, $33,817.42 mission gifts, $1,045,300.00 property value, and $66,419.00 church debt.

NOTLA RIVER. Organized by a number of churches in Union County, Ga., in 1840. It combined with the Valley River Association (organized c. 1843) to form the Hiawassee Association in 1849. In 1862 it became the Notla River Association. In 1954, 25 churches reported 129 baptisms, 3,211 members, $17,687.40 total gifts, $2,086.20 mission gifts, and $119,500.00 property value.

OGEECHEE RIVER. Organized as Bulloch County Association in 1898 by churches located mostly in Bulloch County. The first annual session was held with the Statesboro church in 1899. At that time there were 15 churches with a total membership of 1,163. A few of the churches were located in Candler County. In 1923 the association met at Brooklet Church and during the session voted to change its name to Ogeechee River. Its territory was expanded to include Bulloch, Candler, and part of Emanuel counties. Several churches from Emanuel County applied for membership in the association provided it would change its name. In 1954, 26 churches reported 246 baptisms, 4,779 members, $194,-897.88 total gifts, $16,903.55 mission gifts, $564,-500.00 property value, and $32,735.00 church debt.

OKEFENOKEE. Organized at Blackshear Church, Dec. 3, 1936, by 13 churches located in Pierce and Ware counties in southeast Georgia. Its churches came from the Piedmont Association. Plans have been made for the Georgia Baptist Home for the Aged to be located at Waycross in the area of this association. In 1954, 25 churches reported 339 baptisms, 6,341 members, $214,549.63 total gifts, $26,525.35 mission gifts, $914,107.77 property value, and $83,-410.00 church debt.

PIEDMONT. Organized in 1817 by five churches located in Liberty, McIntosh, and Tattnall counties. It was formed by churches to avoid connection with the missionary cause. It did not join the Baptist Convention of Georgia until 1848 and still opposed mission and benevolent causes. Various churches withdrew from it and formed the Okefenokee Association in 1936, the Altamaha Association in 1945, and the Southeast Association in 1953. In 1954, 32 churches reported 347 baptisms, 6,795 members, $259,729.65 total gifts, $24,252.65 mission gifts, $973,453.00 property value, and $40,632.00 church debt.

PINE MOUNTAIN. Organized in 1889. The early records of the association seem not to have been preserved. In 1919 at the annual meeting held at Hamilton, Harris County, 21 churches were located mostly in Harris, Meriwether, and Talbot counties. In 1954 a number of churches withdrew from this association and formed the Merritt Association. These churches were located in Meriwether and Talbot counties. In 1954, 26 churches reported 148 baptisms, 4,600 members, $130,826.32 total gifts, $18,222.18 mission gifts, $451,000.00 property value, and $5,063.25 church debt.

POLK COUNTY. Organized Oct., 1892, at Lake Creek church by seven churches from the Cave Spring Association (now extinct). The churches were located in Polk County in the northwestern part of Georgia. The association employs an associational missionary. In 1954, 31 churches reported 335 baptisms, 9,308 members, $169,-009.96 total gifts, $19,440.96 mission gifts, $697,-750.00 property value, and $4,376.00 church debt.

PULASKI-BLECKLEY. Organized Nov. 7, 1906, at Corinth Church in Pulaski County, by 14 churches from New Ebenezer, Ebenezer, Little River, and the Houston associations. In 1954, 21 churches reported 248 baptisms, 4,822 members, $133,272.64 total gifts, $14,227.27 mission gifts, $567,250.00 property value, and $28,318.00 church debt.

RABUN COUNTY. Organized in 1905. There are no records preserved until 1910. The churches in the organization probably came from the Mountain Association (now extinct). In 1910, 16 churches reported. Camp Pinnacle, one of the Georgia Baptist W.M.U. camps, is located at Clayton in this association. The association co-operates with White County and Hiawassee associations in an associational mission program.

REHOBOTH. Organized July 28, 1838, at Benevolence Church, Crawford County, by 10 churches. These churches had withdrawn or had been expelled from the Echeconnah Association because of the antimission spirit in that association. The churches in the new Rehoboth Association were located in Upson, Crawford, Houston, and Monroe counties. The association was organized in full harmony with the state convention's principles and policies, and it joined the state convention in 1839; from the beginning it was positively missionary. The association divided in 1953 into two divisions. Those churches located in Houston, Crawford, Peach, and Macon counties kept the name Rehoboth. The churches located in and around Macon, Ga., took the name Macon Association. The new Rehoboth Association was composed of 20 churches and the Macon Association was composed of 37 churches. In 1954, 27 churches reported 481 baptisms, 7,550 members, $362,801.98 total gifts, $29,719.22 mission gifts, $869,000.00 property value, and $91,-743.00 church debt.

ROSWELL. Organized Sept. 24, 1887. In 1890 there were nine churches located in Cobb, Milton, Gwinnett, Fulton, and DeKalb counties. In 1954, 25 churches reported 440 baptisms, 6,771 members, $110,981.95 total gifts, $8,101.95

mission gifts, $479,100.00 property value, and $49,521.00 church debt.

SAREPTA. Organized in Oct., 1798, by eight churches which had been dismissed from the Georgia Association to form a new association. Five new churches joined in the organization. The first session was held at Van's Creek Church, Elbert County, and the decorum and constitution of the Georgia Association were adopted. In 1820 Adiel Sherwood offered a resolution in this association recommending to the associations of the state the formation of a General Baptist Association. Messengers from the association met at Powelton, Hancock County, June 27, 1822, and formed the General Baptist Association of Georgia, which name was changed in 1828 to Baptist Convention of the State of Georgia. This association is the third oldest in Georgia. Its churches are located in Clark, Madison, Jackson, and Oglethorpe counties. It employs an associational missionary and owns a home for the missionary. In 1954, 63 churches reported 642 baptisms, 17,814 members, $374,582.80 total gifts, $46,380.70 mission gifts, $1,717,040.00 property value, and $32,000.00 church debt.

SAVANNAH. Organized Oct. 22, 1948, at Jasper Springs Church, Savannah, with 23 churches which came from a division in the New Sunbury Association. These churches were located principally in and around Savannah. The association adopted articles of faith in conformity to those agreed upon by Southern Baptist Convention, 1925. The association co-operates with the Georgia Baptist state convention and the Home Mission Board of the Southern Baptist Convention in a program of city missions. A superintendent of city missions is employed. In 1954, 37 churches reported 1,105 baptisms, 20,590 members, $646,442.91 total gifts, $102,834.42 mission gifts, $2,798,502.00 property value, and $384,774.00 church debt.

SMYRNA. Organized in 1857 at Sand Hill Church by 32 churches located mostly in Coffee and Bacon counties. In 1954, 32 churches reported 201 baptisms, 6,131 members, $398,062.00 total gifts, $44,701.00 mission gifts, $963,450.00 property value, and $236,876.00 church debt.

SOUTH RIVER. Organized at Zion Baptist Church, Newton County, Oct. 27, 1893, by 15 churches located in Newton and DeKalb counties. Articles of faith were adopted according to the New Hampshire Confession of Faith. In 1954, 17 churches reported 189 baptisms, 2,705 members, $17,515.18 total gifts, $289.18 mission gifts, and $140,500.00 property value.

SOUTHEAST GEORGIA. Organized Mar. 16, 1953, at Woodbine Church by seven churches from the Piedmont Association dismissed for the purpose. It is located in the southeastern corner of the state. In 1954, 10 churches reported 222 baptisms, 2,143 members, $76,958.50 total gifts, $8,029.50 mission gifts, $257,870.000 property value, and $28,404.00 church debt.

STONE MOUNTAIN. Known at first as Rock Mountain Association, it was organized in Oct., 1839, at Macedonia Church, DeKalb County, by 12 churches which had withdrawn from the Yellow River Association because of the antimission spirit in that association. The churches of the new association were located in DeKalb County. A majority of the churches forming the Atlanta Association came from this association. The churches are located in DeKalb, Rockdale, and Newton counties. In 1954, 24 churches reported 517 baptisms, 8,277 members, $290,181.82 total gifts, $32,070.41 mission gifts, $1,184,633.00 property value, and $73,709.00 church debt.

SUMMERHILL. Organized at Summerhill, Stewart County, in 1889 by 13 churches located in Randolph, Stewart, and Webster counties. In 1954, 24 churches reported 128 baptisms, 3,849 members, $85,678.42 total gifts, $12,284.72 mission gifts, $364,900.00 property value, and $19,000.00 church debt.

TALLAPOOSA. Organized in 1835. Ten years later it reported 20 churches located in Paulding and Cobb counties. In 1954, 23 churches reported 127 baptisms, 3,851 members, $41,058.04 total gifts, $5,155.35 mission gifts, $190,000.00 property value, and $119.00 church debt.

TATTNALL-EVANS. Organized Dec. 9, 1904, as Tattnall Association by 14 churches located principally in Tattnall County. The name was changed in 1923 to Tattnall-Evans and included churches located in both Tattnall and Evans counties. In 1954, 20 churches reported 125 baptisms, 3,581 members, $148,147.84 total gifts, $10,834.84 mission gifts, $477,650.00 property value, and $29,730.00 church debt.

TELFAIR. Organized in 1899 at Helena Baptist Church by 21 churches located principally in Telfair County. The churches came from the New Ebenezer Association. In 1954, 20 churches reported 147 baptisms, 3,185 members, $66,509.48 total gifts, $7,686.48 mission gifts, and $386,000.00 property value.

THOMAS COUNTY. Organized by 19 churches at Salem Church in 1910 as the Campbell Association. The association adopted the New Hampshire Confession of Faith, and has employed an associational missionary for many years. In 1954, 23 churches reported 333 baptisms, 7,691 members, $307,234.41 total gifts, $103,479.41 mission gifts, $822,875.00 property value, and $75,950.00 church debt.

TROUP COUNTY. Organized in Nov., 1937, at the First Baptist Church, LaGrange, by 12 churches from the Western Association. This association employs an associational missionary. In 1954, 35 churches reported 534 baptisms, 9,876 members, $426,477.52 total gifts, $37,895.52 mission gifts, $1,300,236.71 property value, and $15,479.45 church debt.

TUCKER. Organized in 1894 at Pelham, Mitchell County, by 14 churches located mostly in Mitchell County. It adopted the New Hampshire Confession of Faith. This association employs an associational missionary. In 1954, 25 churches reported 152 baptisms, 5,112 members, $102,059.37 total gifts, $13,069.37 mission

Georgia Associations

gifts, $382,577.00 property value, and $27,993.00 church debt.

TUGALO. Organized in 1817 by 11 churches dismissed from the Sarepta Association and located on either side of the Tugalo River in northeast Georgia and western South Carolina. In 1821 it constituted 19 churches of which 13 were located in Georgia. The association employs an associational missionary. In 1954, 43 churches reported 406 baptisms, 12,764 members, $233,438.28 total gifts, $25,618.00 mission gifts, $1,017,300.00 property value, and $7,388.00 church debt.

TURNER. Organized at Inaha Church in 1912 by 16 churches most of which came from the Little River Association. The churches were located in Wilcox, Worth, Irving, Crisp, and Turner counties. Practically all of the churches were located in Turner County. In 1954, 19 churches reported 131 baptisms, 3,645 members, $58,190.29 total gifts, $3,794.49 mission gifts, $180,893.00 property value, and $4,140.00 church debt.

VALDOSTA. Organized in 1905 at Naylor, Ga., by 26 churches from the Mercer and Homerville associations in Georgia, and three churches from Florida. This association employs a missionary and provides his home. The churches in 1954 were located in Lowndes, Brooks, Clinch, Lanier, Echols, and Berrien counties. In 1954, 33 churches reported 555 baptisms, 8,916 members, $359,043.63 total gifts, $38,928.83 mission gifts, $1,001,879.00 property value, and $57,984.00 church debt.

WASHINGTON. Organized in Dec., 1828, at Sisters Meetinghouse, Washington County, by five churches from the Hephzibah Association. The association joined the Baptist Convention of the State of Georgia in 1838. The association employs an associational missionary. In 1954, 34 churches reported 325 baptisms, 8,061 members, $235,511.22 total gifts, $39,810.22 mission gifts, $1,102,300.00 property value, and $281,633.00 church debt.

WESTERN. Organized at LaGrange, Ga., Nov. 7, 1829, by 16 churches. The churches seem to have come from the Flint River Association. At its second annual session in 1830, 16 churches joined. In 1837 a number of churches withdrew from this association because they were opposed to all missionary and benevolent institutions and formed an antimissionary association which was known as Primitive Western Association. Western joined the Baptist Convention of the State of Georgia in 1842. Its churches are located in Coweta, Heard, and Meriwether counties. The association employs an associational missionary. In 1954, 43 churches reported 464 baptisms, 9,334 members, $251,715.15 total gifts, $49,953.37 mission gifts, $1,136,000.00 property value, and $16,600.00 church debt.

WHITE COUNTY. Organized in 1921 by churches some of which had withdrawn from the Clarksville, Chattahoochee, and Hiawassee associations. These churches are located principally in White County. Truett-McConnell College is located at Cleveland within this association. This association co-operates with Rabun County and Hiawassee associations in an associational mission program. In 1954, 12 churches reported 41 baptisms, 1,889 members, $30,257.32 total gifts, $2,270.46 mission gifts, $78,700.00 property value, and $600.00 church debt.   ARTHUR HINSON

II. Extinct Associations. BALLGROUND. Organized in 1900 at the Baptist Church, Jasper, Ga., by four churches located in Pickens County. The first regular session was held in Aug., 1901. After the association became extinct about 1908, most of the churches went to Mountaintown and Ellijay associations.

BETHLEHEM. Composed of churches located in Polk, Haralson, and Floyd counties in Georgia and Cleburn County in Alabama. In 1890, 15 churches reported a total membership of 918. The association adopted articles of faith and co-operated with the Baptist convention of Georgia. Upon its dissolution, churches joined Polk, Floyd, and Haralson County associations.

CAVE SPRING. Organized in 1869 by some 13 churches located in Floyd, Chattooga, and Polk counties. It adopted articles of faith following closely the New Hampshire Confession of Faith. The association joined the Baptist convention of Georgia. At its third annual session in Oct., 1872, it reported a total membership of 14 churches with 1,444 members. Upon its dissolution, the churches joined the associations in Polk, Chattooga, and Floyd counties.

CENTRAL WESTERN. Organized in 1884 by a group of churches in Heard and adjoining counties. It seems never to have co-operated fully with the Baptist convention of Georgia. Some of its churches did contribute small amounts of money to denominational benevolent agencies. In 1955 only a few weak churches remained in the association.

CHESTATEE. Organized in 1839 by a group of churches in north central Georgia. It has never been co-operative with the Baptist convention of Georgia. In 1948, 20 churches reported 769 members.

CLARKSVILLE. Organized at Bethlehem Church, Habersham County, Ga., Sept. 5, 1851, by 13 churches located in Habersham, Lumpkin, and Hall counties. The total membership was 543. It voted in the first session to become a member of the Baptist convention of Georgia. It adopted articles of faith similar to the New Hampshire Confession. The name of the association later changed to Habersham County and most of the churches remained in it.

COOSAWATTEE. Organized in 1880 by a few churches located in Gordon and Whitfield counties. In 1929, 11 churches reported 827 members.

ELLIJAY. Organized in 1840 by churches located in several counties in north central Georgia. In 1954, 13 churches reported 1,487 members. Some of the churches contribute small amounts to benevolent causes of the Baptist convention of Georgia.

HARMONY. Organized in 1864 by churches from Cleburn County in Alabama; Haralson, Cherokee, and Polk counties in Georgia. In 1876 it reported 16 churches with 1,082 members. Upon dissolution most of the churches joined Haralson County Association.

HOMERVILLE. Organized in 1891 by a few churches located in the vicintiy of Homerville, Ga. Though listed in the Georgia Baptist convention *Annual* in 1901, it seems to have been Primitive in doctrine and practice and never joined the Baptist convention of Georgia.

JASPER UNITED. Organized in 1873 at Pleasant Hill Church, Gordon County. In 1877, 32 churches reported 1,654 members. In 1955 its churches were located in several counties in the vicinity of Jasper, Ga. It is antimissionary.

MILLER. Organized by churches located in Bullock, Emanuel, Tattnall, and Candler counties, Ga. In 1890 at the sixth annual session 20 churches reported a combined membership of 1,004. Most of the churches joined Ogeechee River, Tattnall Evans, and Emanuel County associations.

MOUNTAIN. Organized Nov. 6, 1832, at Mud Creek meetinghouse, Habersham County, Ga., by 14 churches. The associations reported eight ministers and 434 members. It joined the Baptist convention of Georgia in 1836. Upon its dissolution the churches joined White County, Hiawassee, Rabun, and Clarksville associations.

NEW EBENEZER. Organized in 1872 by 11 churches located in Pulaski, Dodge, and Laurens counties. At its second session in 1874, 20 churches reported 947 members and 118 baptisms. Upon its dissolution the churches joined Dodge, Pulaski-Bleckley, Laurens, Telfair, and Daniell associations.

NEW HOPE. Constituted at one time of approximately 100 churches located in northwest Georgia and northeast Alabama. In 1929, 30 churches reported 2,928 members. The churches are almost completely antimissionary.

OCHLOCHNEE. Constituted at Strickland's meetinghouse, Lowndes County, Ga., in 1827 by six churches. In 1838, 27 churches reported 16 ministers and a total membership of 834. It was never friendly to missionary causes, and became a Primitive association.

OCMULGEE. Organized in Nov., 1810, at Rooty Creek meetinghouse near Eatonton, Ga., by 24 churches. Twenty of the churches came from the Georgia Association, and four came from the Hephzibah Association. Four other churches joined it during the first session. It was the fifth Baptist association formed in the state. In 1830 it withdrew from the Baptist convention of Georgia because of a widespread antimission spirit within the association.

OOSTANAULA. Organized in 1851 by five churches located in Floyd County. In 1854 at the third annual session 11 churches were reported with a membership of 432. The association adopted articles of faith similar to Philadelphia Confession. At the last session in 1893, 22 of its 25 churches formed Floyd County Association.

PLEASANT GROVE. Organized in Oct., 1910, at Pleasant Hill Church, Rockdale County, by eight churches. It is now composed of 30 churches located in Gwinnett, DeKalb, and Rockdale counties, though its churches contribute small amounts to benevolent causes of the Baptist convention of Georgia.

PLEASANT VALLEY. Organized in 1890 in Bartow County by churches located in Paulding, Cobb, and Bartow counties. In 1933, 22 churches reported 3,956 members.

ST. MARY'S RIVER. Little is known about this association, but in 1898 it was listed in the minutes of the Baptist convention of Georgia and included five churches located in Kingsland, Ga.

SAVANNAH. Organized Apr. 5, 1802, by four churches. The creed adopted was the English Confession of 1688 and the summary of church discipline of the Charleston Association. At the 1803 session held in Savannah seven churches were admitted. In 1806 the name of the association changed to Savannah River, because the churches were located on either side of the river. In 1817 it was decided that two associations be formed using the Savannah River as the dividing line. In Nov., 1818, the churches on the Georgia side joined the Sunbury Association.

SECOND GEORGIA. Composed of churches located in Rockdale, Walton, DeKalb, and Gwinnett counties. In 1879 nine churches were reported with a total of 561 members. Possibly, these churches merged with the Stone Mountain, South River, and Pleasant Grove associations.

SUNBURY. Organized in 1818 after the division of Savannah River Association the previous year, with 12 churches having 3,541 members, most of whom were Negroes. In 1823 it resolved to become a "constituent member" of the Georgia general association. At first it was able to give good co-operation, and employ missionaries for work in its own territory, mainly with the Negroes. Later there were years when its delegates failed to attend the state body, and on Nov. 24, 1866, reduced in strength by war, it was dissolved. Churches from the Sunbury, Piedmont, and Union associations combined to form New Sunbury.

SOUTHWESTERN. Organized in 1879 by churches located in the southwestern part of Georgia and a few along the state line in Florida. In 1890 at the 11th annual session 13 churches reported a total membership of 445. The last session was held in 1926 with only six churches because most of the churches had united with the Bowen and Grady County associations.

YELLOW RIVER. Organized Sept. 18, 1824, at Harris Springs, Newton County, Ga., by seven churches dismissed from the Ocmulgee Association and six newly constituted churches. At first the association seems to have corresponded with other missionary churches and associations, but from the first was opposed to all missions, Bible societies, etc. It never joined the Baptist convention of Georgia. It eventually ceased to correspond with missionary associations and became a Primitive association.

ARTHUR HINSON

GEORGIA BAPTIST. A newspaper published at Vidalia, Ga., which was announced in 1905 at the Mount Vernon (Ga.) Association. This paper, now extinct, had a name similar to a paper published by Negro Baptists in Augusta and Macon, Ga.

JOHN J. HURT, JR.

GEORGIA BAPTIST BUILDING. At 291 Peachtree Street, Atlanta, Ga., the location of all of the offices of the Georgia Baptist convention. It provides accommodations for *The Christian Index*, Georgia Woman's Missionary Union, Georgia Baptist Foundation and Endowment Committee, the Atlanta Association, all eight departments of state missions, and the Georgia executive committee's work of administration and promotion. In addition, the ground floor is leased to the Southern Baptist Sunday School Board for the Baptist Book Store, and other space is leased also to provide income.

The building was purchased in 1943 for $190,000, and was occupied beginning in December of that year. It has four floors and two basements, covers a lot 100 by 177 by 77.5 by 134 feet, and provides approximately 50,000 square feet of space. Between 1952 and 1954 the building was modernized and remodeled; air conditioning and a new elevator were installed, and other improvements effected.

JAMES W. MERRITT

GEORGIA BAPTIST CHILDREN'S HOME. An institution providing care for orphan and indigent children, founded in 1872, and under the control of the Baptist Convention of the State of Georgia since 1898. The home was founded in Atlanta as a private institution called the Georgia Baptist Orphan's Home and in 1873 cared for 16 children. It prospered for several years until a period of decreased financial support prompted the trustees to recommend in 1880 that the home be dissolved.

The work was then taken up by the Baptist women of the Atlanta area, who, in 1888, obtained a charter for the Georgia Baptist Orphan's Home Association. In 1898 a committee of the Georgia Baptist convention recommended that the "orphanage should be taken under the fostering care of this Convention (and that) a committee . . . be created to prepare plans for its management and enlargement . . . the same to be reported at the next session of this Convention." This was done, and in 1899 the home was moved to a 50-acre tract of land in Hapeville. The name of the home was officially changed in 1943 to Georgia Baptist Children's Home, Inc. In 1946 a branch of the home was established at Baxley on property acquired from the Southern Industrial Home, a privately operated institution. Both branches are under one management.

In 1955 the home served a total of 500 children, with a daily average of 450. The budget for that year was $590,000, and property consisted of 1,995 acres of land and 120 buildings, the land, buildings, and equipment valued at $1,700,000. The home is financed through voluntary gifts from individuals, organizations, and Baptist churches throughout the state.

The children live in 22 cottages, with 20 to 25 children and two or three cottage parents in each building. By Dec., 1955, a total of 3,492 children had gone out from the home.

The boys and girls attend public schools of Hapeville and Baxley until they finish high school. Those who qualify are sent to college; some are given specialized training for a particular vocation; and others receive assistance in finding employment. Christian training for the children includes participation in the program and activities of local Baptist churches.

The children are not placed for adoption. Some, however, are returned to relatives when circumstances permit. In 1955 the total cost of caring for the children amounted to $2.71 per child per day.

JOHN C. WARR

GEORGIA BAPTIST FEMALE SEMINARY. A school for both boys and girls on the elementary and high school levels, established at Gainesville, Ga., in 1878. William Clay Wilkes, pastor at Gainesville, secured the help of local citizens in the school's establishment and served as agent and president. The state convention approved but did not own the school. In 1886 A. W. Van Hoose purchased the property and in 1893 sold half interest to H. J. Pearce. The seminary became Brenau College in 1900 and has operated continuously since that time, during which it has provided education of high quality, especially in the fine arts, for young women.

ARTHUR JACKSON

GEORGIA BAPTIST FOUNDATION. A corporation proposed by resolution Nov. 17, 1937, authorized, after committee study, by the Georgia Baptist convention in 1939, and chartered May 14, 1941. The foundation's purpose is to provide a promotional program for securing endowment funds for the institutions of Georgia Baptists and to furnish a positive approach toward meeting the financial needs of schools and other institutions; to provide management of endowment funds; to protect endowment funds from use other than endowment; and to place greater responsibility for securing funds on the whole Baptist constituency rather than on individual institutions.

The 1940 session of the convention, meeting in Macon, authorized $5,000 to finance a statewide fund-raising campaign for endowment, the amount to be paid out of funds to be raised. The convention elected five trustees of the foundation as follows: Leonard E. Bowen, Tifton; Chelton W. Coleman, La Grange (president); John H. Cheatham, Griffin (treasurer); Arthur Jackson, Savannah; Wiley Moore, Atlanta. The

FIRST SOUTHERN BAPTIST CHURCH, Phoenix, Ariz. Auditorium of Georgian Colonial architecture erected 1931, valued at approximately $350,000. Educational unit houses 25 Sunday school departments.

TRUETT MEMORIAL BAPTIST CHURCH, Hayesville, N. C. Organized 1850, auditorium of crab orchard stone and Colonial architecture dedicated debt-free in 1950, seats 350. Property evaluation, $110,000.

FIRST SOUTHERN BAPTIST CHURCH, San Diego, Calif. Established 1942, membership 1956 over 1,000. Auditorium of contemporary design erected 1955 with capacity of 1,100. Educational unit houses 1,000. Total property worth $135,000.

FIRST SOUTHERN BAPTIST CHURCH, Sanger, Calif. Organized 1940. Present building seating 300 erected 1950. Property, including Sunday school facilities for 250, valued at $35,000.

FIRST BAPTIST CHURCH, Nashville, Tenn. Founded 1820, Gothic main building erected 1886. Auditorium seats 1,200, Sunday school 2,300, membership 1956 totaled 3,000. Property valued at $1,000,000.

WALNUT STREET BAPTIST CHURCH, Louisville, Ky. Gothic design of Bedford stone completed 1902 on property acquired in 1900. Auditorium and educational units accommodate 1,500 each. Property valued at $1,400,000.

trustees were granted a charter by the Fulton Superior Court on May 14, 1941.

On Apr. 19, at Marietta, the campaign for endowment was launched with an address by George Washington Truett (q.v.). Approximately $35,000 was pledged, most of which was paid directly to the (then) five Georgia Baptist schools and colleges. After deducting expenses for the campaign, $7,424.75 was placed with the foundation for investment and administrative expenses. The income was divided between the five schools on a percentage basis.

The convention in its 1942 session in Macon set up an endowment committee consisting of the trustees of the foundation, the heads of the schools and colleges, and five members elected by the convention. An appropriation of $10,000 was authorized to employ an executive secretary and pay the expenses of this program.

At the meeting of the endowment committee Aug. 26, 1943, Arthur Jackson accepted the position of executive secretary. He began his service on Sept. 15. On Jan. 1 of the following year, an office was opened in the Baptist Building in Atlanta.

By Oct. 1, 1943, Columbus Roberts (q.v.) had given the foundation $50,000 and directed the income to be used for the benefit of ministerial students at Mercer, Norman College, and Brewton-Parker Junior College in equal amounts. This was the first significant gift to the foundation. Roberts later gave $25,000 for Truett-McConnell Junior College for the same purpose. The income from his final gift of $200,000, after certain reservations, was to be divided between Georgia Baptist schools and colleges in proportion to the amount of endowment each had at the close of each calendar year.

In 1948 the number of the foundation's trustees was increased to seven; and on Jan. 1, 1956, it had an operating budget of $25,000 annually. The endowment assets increased from $7,424.75 on Sept. 15, 1943, to $2,147,515.20 on Dec. 31, 1955, at which time Arthur Jackson retired. At the meeting of the endowment committee and trustees in June, 1955, Harry V. Smith was elected to succeed Jackson as executive secretary. He assumed office on Dec. 15, 1955.   ARTHUR JACKSON

GEORGIA BAPTIST HISTORY, COMMITTEE ON THE PRESERVATION OF. A standing committee, created by Georgia Baptist convention in 1944 and charged with collecting Georgia Baptist historical materials and with promoting interest in their history. The earliest Baptist records in Georgia were preserved by Henry Holcombe (q.v.), editor and publisher of *The Analytical Repository* (Savannah, 1802–03), and Adiel Sherwood (q.v.), who "left an incomplete manuscript history of Georgia Baptists." In 1878 the first organization was formed, as a result of a resolution offered by Washington Lafayette Kilpatrick (q.v.) to the Georgia Baptist convention. This organization, called the Georgia Baptist Historical Society, was active until 1888. In 1899, at the instigation of Lansing Burrows (q.v.), the society was reorganized. A committee on Georgia Baptist history was appointed in 1910 by the conference of associational officers and operated for several years with Spencer Bidwell King, Sr. (q.v.), as chairman. In 1947 the Georgia Baptist convention approved a recommendation providing for the appointment of "a permanent Committee on Baptist history." J. C. Wilkinson was chairman.

Mercer University Library is the official depository of Georgia Baptist historical records. Manuscripts and microfilm copies of church minutes are preserved there; and a well-kept but as yet incomplete file of published associational minutes is available for research. The library also contains published and unpublished histories of associations and individual churches, memoirs and biographies, and *The Christian Index* (1822–) in bound volumes and on microfilm. Among several published histories of Georgia Baptists, the best known are *A History of the Baptist Denomination in Georgia* (1881); B. D. Ragsdale, *Story of Georgia Baptists*, 3 vols. (1932–38); J. H. Campbell, *Georgia Baptists: Historical and Biographical* (1874); S. G. Hillyer, *Reminiscences of Georgia Baptists* (1902); Memoirs of Elder Jesse Mercer, C. D. Mallary (1844); Memoir of Adiel Sherwood, by Julia W. Sherwood (1884). The first two named are more generally used.   H. LEWIS BATTS

GEORGIA BAPTIST HOME FOR THE AGED. An institution established as the result of a study authorized by the Georgia Baptist convention in Nov., 1953, and opened for operation early in 1957. The home is located on a tract of about 530 acres, one and a half miles southwest of Waycross, Ga. A charter was secured, and Harvey L. Mitchell, former pastor in Barnesville, Ga., was employed as the home's administrator. An ultimate capacity of 300 residents was planned.   DICK H. HALL, JR.

GEORGIA BAPTIST HOSPITAL. An institution founded in 1901 and owned and controlled by the Georgia Baptist convention since 1913. It was established in connection with the Tabernacle Baptist Church, Atlanta, under the leadership of the pastor, Len (Leonard Gaston) Broughton, who had had medical as well as theological training and strongly favored medical work under distinctly Christian auspices.

The hospital, then called the Tabernacle Infirmary, was opened in 1903 in a small rented house on Courtland Street in Atlanta. Broughton personally paid the first month's rent of $25, and a group of women from his church renovated and equipped the building with furniture from their homes. Two women who had been unable to secure aid from the community were the first patients.

Georgia Barnett of Roanoke, Va., was the first employee of the infirmary, and E. C. Davis was the first president of the staff. T. C. Davison and J. T. Floyd were the first interns. The infirmary grew, and soon was moved to Luckie Street near the present imposing meeting house of the Tabernacle Baptist Church. In 1912 Broughton accepted the call to Christ Church, London, England, and the next year the infirmary was sold to the Georgia Baptist convention for $85,000. The name was changed to Georgia Baptist Hospital. In 1921 it was moved from Luckie Street to its present location, 300 Boulevard, N. E., Atlanta.

Prominent among the early executives of the Georgia Baptist Hospital were: Mrs. Martha Harris, Elizabeth Coates, Ada Foster, Mrs. Margaret Welsh, Jean Harrell. J. M. Long served as superintendent, 1916–21; Mrs. Welsh, 1921–22; Miss Harrell, 1922–23; Eugene Elder, 1923–27; J. B. Franklin, 1927–31. Then followed the longest term of any superintendent, that of W. D. Barker, 1931–46, terminated by his death. The name of the chief executive was changed from superintendent to administrator with the coming of Edwin B. Pel in 1946.

The hospital is owned and operated by the Georgia Baptist convention through its executive committee. A five-man commission composed of two members of the executive committee of the convention, two members of the board of trustees, and the executive secretary-treasurer of the executive committee actually directs the work of the hospital and is accountable to the executive committee of the convention.

In 1955 the hospital property included 21 buildings and was valued at $7,546,765. The bed capacity is 475 beds, plus 75 bassinets. In 1955 there were 147,077 days of patient care. There were 3,327 babies born in the hospital in 1955. There were 23,959 bed patients in 1955, and 16,837 outpatients, from 143 counties in Georgia, 26 other states, and two foreign countries.

There are 365 doctors on the staff, 20 interns, and 19 resident physicians. There are 356 student nurses enrolled and 119 graduate nurses on the staff. There are 754 salaried employees. During 1955, 1,794 persons were given free or part free services, representing a cost to the hospital of $316,691.35. Georgia Baptists gave $128,928 in 1955 toward this charity service. The hospital is accredited by the Joint Commission on Accreditation of American Hospitals. The hospital conducts accredited schools of nursing, X-ray technology, and medical technology.

LOUIE D. NEWTON

GEORGIA FEMALE COLLEGE. Founded at Madison, Ga., in 1849, primarily local in sponsorship and patronage. It attracted some students, however, who otherwise would have probably gone to Penfield Female Seminary, and its establishment was, therefore, one probable reason for the closing of that school. George Y. Browne was the first principal. Stockholders, who owned stock at $25 a share, managed the school and elected seven to 21 trustees, the majority of whom were Baptists. The school did not last through the post-war reconstruction period.

ARTHUR JACKSON

GEORGIA TEMPERANCE LEAGUE. Organized Oct. 1, 1943, at the Atlanta Biltmore Hotel. Three hundred prominent citizens of Georgia answered the call of Bishop Arthur J. Moore of the Methodist church in Georgia, Louie DeVotie Newton of the Georgia Baptist Convention, and J. R. McCain, president of Agnes Scott College, representing the Presbyterians of Georgia, to meet for the purpose of coordinating the efforts of the evangelical forces of Georgia in resistance to the growth of the alcohol traffic in the state.

For a number of years the opponents of legal and illegal liquor in Georgia had been divided into small and ineffective organizations, and many concerned Christians felt little hope of accomplishing any lasting results. The Woman's Christian Temperance Union gave its hearty support to the idea of forming the Georgia Temperance League, and the WCTU has worked with the organization in complete harmony, though maintaining its separate organization, in co-operation with the National WCTU.

Leighton Shepard of Fort Valley was elected the first president of the Georgia Temperance League and served until his sudden death in 1944. He was succeeded by Columbus Roberts of Columbus, who served until his death in 1951. H. W. Pitman of Macon was named president in 1951, serving until 1954, when Walter Harrison was elected president. B. L. Bugg served as treasurer until his death, and was succeeded by Parks Warnock.

The Georgia Temperance League is supported by the Georgia Baptist Convention and the two Methodist Conferences in Georgia. In addition a number of local churches in both denominations put the league in their budgets for definite annual sums.

Norman Lovein served as executive secretary of the league from 1944 to 1954. He was succeeded by Bruce Wilson. Wilson directs the work of the league from the state headquarters office, 63 Auburn Avenue, N.E., Atlanta. The plan of organization reaches down to the county level, with county organizations, including representatives from the local churches.

Since its organization in 1943, the Georgia Temperance League has been active in numerous county and municipal elections, successfully resisting the beer, wine, and liquor forces in 66 elections. The league has concentrated its efforts on local option elections on the county and municipal levels. LOUIE D. NEWTON

GERMANY, BAPTISTS OF. The founder and pioneer of this group was Johann Gerhard Oncken (q.v.) who was converted in a Methodist chapel in London and returned to his native Hamburg several years later to do religious work. Convinced of believers' baptism, he sought for some time a way of being baptized. On Apr. 22, 1834, he, his wife, and five other people were baptized in the Elbe River by the American professor Barnas Sears. A Baptist church was organized with Oncken as pastor, and shortly thereafter he was employed as a missionary by American Baptists.

In spite of initial serious opposition, involving the imprisonment of Oncken and others, the Baptist movement grew rapidly in Hamburg and other Protestant areas of Germany and spread into many other countries. Oncken has been called "the father of German Baptists" and "the father of continental Baptists." Closely associated with him were Julius Köbner, son of a Danish rabbi, and Gottfried Wilhelm Lehmann, of Berlin. When Oncken died in 1884 there were 31,000 Baptists in Germany. The remarkable growth was probably due to the following factors: (1) the indigenous quality of the Baptist movement, (2) favorable conditions, (3) capable leaders, and (4) the spirit of missions which was inspired by Oncken's conviction that every Baptist should be a missionary.

In 1849 the Union of the Associated Churches of Baptized Christians in Germany and Denmark was established. Later limited to Germany, it had a centralizing effect upon Baptist work. During World War II, Baptists united with two other groups to form the Federation of Evangelical and Free-Church Congregations. The preachers' seminary dates from 1880, and even earlier Oncken had conducted short courses for missionary workers. Destroyed during World War II, the seminary was rebuilt, and a youth seminary for the training of workers with children, students, and other young people has been well developed. The publishing house in Kassel, which bears Oncken's name, was destroyed during the war but was rebuilt. *Die Gemeinde*, the official Baptist organ, is published weekly, and there are also papers for children, young people, women, and pastors. Long interested in missions to the heathen, German Baptists sent their first missionary to the Cameroons in 1891. War interrupted this activity, but German Baptists now co-operate with the European Baptist Missionary Society. There is an active women's organization, and several hundred deaconesses operate hospitals, orphanages, and homes for the aged; otherwise care for the sick; and serve as church assistants.

Many churches were destroyed during World War II, but these have been rebuilt, partly with American or other foreign aid. The loss to Germany of the territory in which many Baptists lived led to their resettlement elsewhere and incidentally to the strengthening of existing churches and the establishing of refugee congregations, several in Catholic sections where before the war Baptists were unknown. German Baptists, divided by the division of their country, in 1956 numbered 61,855 in Western Germany and 38,071 in Eastern Germany. Baptist headquarters, including the office of the general secretary, are in Bad Homburg.

BIBLIOGRAPHY: J. D. Franks, ed., *European Baptists Today* (1952). H. Luckey, *Free Churches in Germany* (1956); *Johann Gerhard Oncken und die Anfänge des deutschen Baptismus* (1934). J. A. Moore, "Beginning in Europe—Oncken in Hamburg, 1834," *The Quarterly Review* (Apr., May, June 1955). J. H. Rushbrooke, *The Baptist Movement in the Continent of Europe* (1923).

J. D. HUGHEY, JR.

GETHSEMANE. See JESUS CHRIST.

GHANA, A MISSION IN. See GOLD COAST, MISSION IN.

GIBSON BAPTIST ASSEMBLY, INC. Founded west of Boise City, Okla., in 1923, now located on a 20-acre plot 25 miles east of Guymon. The assembly is valued at $12,000. The 1944–51 sessions were held on the campus of Panhandle A. & M. College, Goodwell. In 1951 the assembly moved to its present location on grounds made available by the Harold Gibsons. It is operated by the board of trustees of Panhandle Association. In 1955 it reported an enrolment of 223, high attendance of 700, $1,848 income, and 23 professions of faith. The G.A. camp had 49 registered with three conversions and the R.A. camp had 43 enrolled with seven conversions.

M. JUDSON COOK

GIBSON-MERCER ACADEMY. Founded by Hebron Association in 1892, located at Bowman, Ga. A member of the Mercer system, it existed until 1925.

ARTHUR JACKSON

GIFTS OF THE SPIRIT. See HOLY SPIRIT.

GILL, EVERETT, JR. (b. Hannibal, Mo., July 31, 1901; d. Richmond, Va., Apr. 25, 1954). Foreign Mission Board secretary for Latin America. Son of Southern Baptist missionaries to Europe, Gill's early home was abroad. He was educated in schools of Europe, at William Jewell College, at the United States Naval Academy, at the Southern Baptist Theological Seminary, and at the University of Edinburgh. After serving as pastor of the First Baptist Church, Marshall, Mo., 1927–34, and of St. Charles Baptist Church, New Orleans, La., 1934–41, he became secretary for Latin America, under the Foreign Mission Board, and served from 1941 to 1954. He had married Rachel Truex on Apr. 21, 1928, and they had three children, Elizabeth, Everett III, and Jane. As secretary for Latin America, Gill supervised Southern Baptist foreign mission work in Brazil, Argentina, Uruguay, Chile, Paraguay, Ecuador, Peru, Colombia, Venezuela, Mexico, Costa Rica, Honduras, Guatemala, the Bahamas, and Jamaica. Almost every year he visited some or all of the mission areas in Latin America, and he and his family lived in strategic mission centers in South America, 1945–47. During his secretaryship, eight new Latin American fields were occupied; the third Brazilian mission was established (Equatorial); hospitals and seminaries were built; language schools were utilized; transportation and radio communication were improved; publishing houses were enlarged and well equipped; home mission agencies were strengthened; foreign mission efforts were projected by Brazilian Baptists; and inter-American relations were intensified. Gill saw all South American republics, except Bolivia, occupied by missionaries of the Southern Baptist Convention. He was author of *Pilgrimage to Spanish America* and *Pilgrimage to Brazil.*

In contacts with his associates in mission service, Gill was intensely human, yet devoutly Christian. He was master of the art of easing tensions with wholesome humor. His last words heard by friends and members of his family were, "Isn't God good?"

BIBLIOGRAPHY: *The Commission* (June, 1954). E. Gill, Jr., *Pilgrimage to Spanish America* (1951). E. Gill, Jr., *Pilgrimage to Brazil* (1954).

E. C. ROUTH

GILL, JOHN. (b. Kettering, Northamptonshire, England, Nov. 23, 1697; d. Camberwell, England, Oct. 14, 1771). Theologian and pastor. Ordained on Mar. 22, 1720, Gill served the Horselydown, Southwark, church in London, England, until his death 51 years later. His father was Edward Gill, who led in the organization of the first Particular Baptist church in Kettering, England; this church later ordained him as a deacon. While yet a youth, Gill early demonstrated his exceptional ability as a student. Since his father was a dissenter, he was forced to pursue his education largely at his own initiative. His studies included Latin, Greek, and Hebrew as well as logic, rhetoric, and natural and moral philosophy. He was converted and baptized in 1716, and became a member of the Particular Baptist church at Kettering. Soon after his baptism he began to preach. Four years later he accepted the pastorate at Horselydown, the first and only pastorate of his life. Almost immediately after going to London, Gill's ministry began to attract wide attention; and during the ensuing years his influence continued to grow until he became one of the best-known theologians of his generation. In 1748 Gill received the D.D. degree from Marischal College of Aberdeen. Upon that occasion it was said that he had "extraordinary proficiency in sacred literature, the Oriental tongues and Jewish antiquities."

A hyper-Calvinist, Gill never addressed the ungodly or offered an invitation for the lost to trust Christ as Saviour. He became the soul of orthodoxy and supreme source of human authority among the Particular Baptists. Among the General Baptists he was disliked to the same degree that he was esteemed by his Particular Baptist friends. John Ryland, a contemporary Particular Baptist pastor, wrote: "Dr. Gill leads into an ocean of divinity by a system of doctrinal and practical religion, and by a judicious and learned exposition of the Old and New Testaments." By way of contrast, upon hearing a Welshman express the desire that Gill's works might have been written in the Welsh language, Robert Hall replied, "I wish they had, sir; I wish they had, with all my heart, sir, for then I should never have read them! They are a continent of mud, sir!"

Gill's published works include: *A Dissertation Concerning the Antiquity of the Hebrew Language, Letters, Vowel Points, and Accents; A Body of Doctrinal Divinity* in three volumes; a volume entitled *Infant-Baptism;* and a commentary, *Annotations on the Bible.* A complete set of Gill's works are housed in the library of Brown University, Providence, R. I.

W. R. ESTEP, JR.

GILLSBURG COLLEGIATE INSTITUTE. A Mississippi Baptist school established about 1882 with W. K. Nettles principal. Enrolment increased from 125 in 1890 to 150 in 1897, but the date of the school's discontinuance is uncertain.

J. L. BOYD

GILMORE, WALTER MURCHISON (b. Moore County, N. C., Jan. 10, 1869; d. Nashville, Tenn., Dec. 19, 1946). Pioneer in the promotional work of the Executive Committee of the Southern Baptist Convention. The son of David Chandler and Margaret Frances (Murchison) Gilmore, he received his education in the Mount Vernon Springs Academy, Sanford High School, Wake Forest College (A.B.), Southwestern Baptist Theological Seminary (Th.B.). He was ordained to the Baptist ministry in Oct., 1892, and served as pastor of the First Baptist Church, Burnswick, Ga., 1895–1904; Marshallville, Ga., 1904–06; Eastman, Ga., 1906–09; Immanuel Baptist Church, Atlanta, Ga., 1910–11; Louisburg, N. C., 1911–18; First Baptist Church, Sanford, N. C., 1918–23. From 1923 to 1930, he was stewardship and mission secretary in North Carolina. From 1930 until his death, he served the Executive Committee of the Southern Baptist Convention except for a brief period when part of the work of the Executive Committee was done by the Promotion Committee of the Southern Baptist Convention. Other denominational responsibilities include long service as recording secretary of the North Carolina state convention, 1914–30. During his service with the Executive Committee he served as editor of the *Baptist Program* and the director of the Baptist Bulletin Service. It was under his direction that the first modern approach to newspapers in convention cities was made. He carried the title Press Representative of the Southern Baptist Convention and developed the system of preparing newspaper stories of reports and speeches in advance of the convention itself. On Nov. 4, 1904, Gilmore was married to Mary Estelle Taylor of Dunn, N. C., to which union was born one child, Walter Sledge Gilmore.

ALBERT MC CLELLAN

GIRLS' AUXILIARY. A missionary organization for girls aged 9–16, fostered by the Woman's Missionary Union. Membership in 1954 totaled 206,709 girls in 20,613 auxiliaries, making the Girls' Auxiliary the largest evangelical denominational organization for girls in the world. The movement was originally a spontaneous effort promoted by the girls themselves. Before the organization of Woman's Missionary Union in 1888, girls attended sewing circles and missionary meetings with their mothers, and caught some of the fervor which characterized the early missionary organizations. As early as 1818 Luther Rice (*q.v.*) tells of preaching a sermon to aid the collection of funds for missions by the Juvenile Female Cent Society in Richmond, Va. Rice was impressed by the fact that young girls 6–14 years old had formed a mission society.

Early missionary organizations for girls were known as Young Ladies' Societies, Girls' Bands, Young Women's Circles, and by similar names. After organization of Young Woman's Auxiliary in 1907, girls over 16 had a definite place in Woman's Missionary Union, and Sunbeam Bands had been the missionary organizations for children under 12 for several years. In 1908, referring to boys and girls between 12 and 16 as "the mission link," Woman's Missionary Union asked that programs and leaflets be provided for them, after which meeting plans for "Junior Y.W.A.'s" appeared in *Our Mission Fields* in Oct., 1909.

Minutes from the annual meeting of 1909 include a recommendation that girls 12 to 16 be organized into Junior Young Woman's auxiliaries. Girls' Auxiliary dates its actual organization to 1913 when Junior Young Woman's auxiliaries were first listed in the statistical tables of Woman's Missionary Union minutes as a separate organization. At that time 173 auxiliaries were reported, 59 of which had been organized that year. Girls' Auxiliary became the official name of the organization in 1914, and a Standard of Excellence was suggested. Definite work in personal service was assigned, and Girls' Auxiliaries were asked to help support hospitals in the foreign fields and frontier missions on the home field.

Mary Faison Dixon, elected young people's secretary in 1916, introduced a correspondence course for Girls' Auxiliary counselors the following year, but after her resignation in 1919 the work was carried on by volunteer help until the election of Juliette Mather as young people's secretary in 1921. Miss Mather served until 1948 when she was succeeded by Margaret Bruce.

The Girls' Auxiliary manual, similar to the Young Woman's Auxiliary manual until 1924, was changed when Junior Girls' Auxiliary for girls 9–13 and Intermediate Girls' Auxiliary for girls 13–16 were formed. A new manual was written at that time and used until 1937 when separate manuals for the two age groups and a *Guide for Counselors of Girls' Auxiliary* were published.

"We've a Story to Tell" was selected as the Girls' Auxiliary hymn in 1924; "Arise, Shine; For Thy Light Is Come" (Isa. 60:1) was chosen for the watchword; and an initiation service was written. Introduced in 1928, the first four Forward Steps gave individual recognition in coronation services for Scripture memory work and reading and study of missionary and denominational activities. The steps were named Maiden, Lady-in-Waiting, Princess, and Queen, and by 1933 the enthusiastic response given them led to the addition of two higher steps for Intermediate G.A.'s, Queen-with-a-Scepter and Queen Regent. A white star bearing the gold Girls' Auxiliary monogram, enclosed by a green octagon edged in gold, is the organization's emblem. The pin, a replica of the emblem, was first introduced in 1915. The star ideals—abiding in him through prayer, advancing in wisdom by Bible study, acknowledging my stewardship, adorning myself with good works, and accepting the challenge of the Great Commission—reflect Woman's Missionary Union fundamentals. The Girls' Auxiliary allegiance incorporates these ideals.

Although its primary purpose is missionary education, the organization also provides social outlets through parties, banquets, and teas. Girls' Auxiliary Focus Week has been an annual affair since 1935. The first state Girls' Auxiliary camp was held in Virginia in 1919, at Virginia Beach, and the state house party idea began in Arkansas at Central College in 1924. Materials for use in meetings are found in *Tell: A Missions Magazine for Girls*, first published in May, 1953, to celebrate the 40th anniversary of Girls' Auxiliary. The programs, presented in a variety of ways to give missionary information and challenge missionary interest, teach girls to think and speak at ease in public. Members serve on committees, make motions, and conduct business.

Community missions activities; mission study; participation in the weeks of prayer for foreign and home missions and the season of prayer for state missions; contributions to missions through the Cooperative Program, Lottie Moon, Annie Armstrong, and other mission offerings: these are all important emphases in Girls' Auxiliary. International in scope, the organization had two Girls' Auxiliaries in China in 1915 with 55 members, and one auxiliary in Nigeria in 1917. Now there are auxiliaries in most of the 37 countries where Southern Baptists have missionaries.

The need of a Girls' Auxiliary secretary was first expressed in 1915 when the executive committee of Woman's Missionary Union suggested "that when practical and advisable a special leader for G.A. be secured." Under direction of the young people's secretary for many years, the Girls' Auxiliary secured its first Convention-wide secretary in 1955.

BIBLIOGRAPHY: E. B. Cox, *Following in His Train* (1938). Mrs. G. E. Davis, "The Story of G.A. Beginnings," *World Comrades* (Jan., Feb., Mar., 1938). *Guide for Counselors of Girls' Auxiliary* (1938).

Manual of the Junior Girls' Auxiliary (n.d.). *Manual of the Intermediate Girls' Auxiliary* (n.d.). *W.M.U., Annual Report* (1922). *W.M.U. Year Book 1954.*

DOROTHY LOUISE WEEKS

GLEBES, VIRGINIA. Plantations acquired in each parish by taxation for the residences and support of the clergy of the Established Church. While their possession by the church was considered a secondary target, advocates of religious freedom, especially Baptists, were not satisfied that disestablishment of the church was complete until the glebes had reverted to the Commonwealth of Virginia.

Question concerning the glebes arose in the first general assembly in Virginia, 1776, but a resolution was adopted holding that "reservation ought to be made to the use of the said church, in all times coming, of the several tracts of glebe lands. . . ." Later, when the Episcopal church was removed from state control by an Act of Incorporation in 1784, the glebe lands were still confirmed to that church. Baptists opposed both the incorporation and the confirmation of the possession of glebe lands as violations of the Bill of Rights and as dangerous precedents. Repeated protests from the General Committee of the Baptist Associations in Virginia were submitted to the general assembly, and finally in Jan., 1794, the general assembly repealed every prior act that had anything to do with religion except the Act for Establishing Religious Freedom. This action returned the gleebs to the state, and in Jan., 1802, the assembly passed a law calling for the sale of the glebes and proper appropriation of the proceeds. With the sale of the glebes the last trace of religious establishment in Virginia was removed.

L. D. JOHNSON

GLEN DALE CHILDREN'S HOME. An institution owned by Kentucky Baptists, Kentucky's largest non-tax-supported home for dependent children. The home is located at Glendale, Hardin County, Ky., on the site formerly occupied by Lynnland College. It was established in 1914 by the General Association of Baptists in Kentucky in response to a memorial presented in the annual meeting of that body at Somerset, Ky., by the Ohio County Baptist Association. The home opened the following year, on June 23, at its present location. From its establishment to July 10, 1956, the legal name of the institution was The Kentucky Baptist Children's Home. On that date the name was changed officially to Glen Dale. The institution is incorporated under the laws of the Commonwealth of Kentucky and is governed by a board of 20 trustees who also constitute the Kentucky Baptist Board of Child Care. The members of this board are elected by the General Association of Baptists in Kentucky in its annual meetings.

During its more than 41 years of continuous operation, Glen Dale has cared for approximately 1,600 children, and has grown from an original investment of $3,500 in 16 acres of campus and one old college building to seven major buildings, 588 acres of land, and total assets amounting to more than $1,250,000. On Nov. 1, 1956, there were 225 children under care, and 260 had received care during the first 10 months of that year.

The superintendents who have served Glen Dale since its foundation, together with their years of service, are as follows: A. B. Gardner, 1915–16; J. W. Vallandingham, 1917–19; M. George Moore, 1919–29; W. M. Stallings, 1929–31; H. C. Compton, 1931–32; C. K. Hoagland, 1933–37; J. G. Barbe, 1937–40; T. E. Ennis, 1941; E. F. Glenn, 1942–48; C. Ford Deusner, 1948 to date.

C. FORD DEUSNER

GLOBE ACADEMY. A Baptist school at Globe, Caldwell County, N. C., founded in Caldwell Association in 1883 by R. L. Patton. In 1886 W. F. Marshall, clerk of the association, became its principal. In 1896 it was adopted by Caldwell Association, but it was closed shortly after the turn of the century.

D. L. SMILEY

GLORIETA BAPTIST ASSEMBLY. A Southern Baptist Convention assembly located at Glorieta, N. Mex., which began operations in 1952. The success of the Ridgecrest Baptist Assembly, Ridgecrest, N. C., and the growth of the Convention constituency in the western area of the nation led to agitation for another Convention-wide assembly. The Southern Baptist Convention in May, 1947, appointed a committee to study the matter. Careful investigation was made, not only by the committee, but by interested states and leaders. The result was the selection by the Convention in 1949 of Glorieta, N. Mex., as the site. The assembly was conceived as a Convention-wide rather than a strictly Western assembly.

The Convention in 1950 charged the Sunday School Board with the responsibility of raising funds, erecting buildings, developing and operating the new assembly. The New Mexico Baptist General Convention and its churches made the first gift of 880 acres of land with an estimated value of $50,000. For protective purposes the board purchased additional property, the toal acreage being increased to 1,238 acres. The location is 19 miles from Santa Fe, N. Mex., at an altitude of approximately 7,500 feet. The assembly is served by the Santa Fe Railroad and Central Pan American Highway.

The first step in building the assembly involved the development of long-range plans for landscaping and buildings. The first year (1950) was spent in an engineering study of the grounds, laying out roadways, laying water and sewer lines, drilling a ten-inch-diameter well 720 feet deep, erecting a 500,000-gallon reservoir tank with an auxiliary pump house for pumps and water controls, locating the first major buildings, and working out tentative building schedules. E. A. Herron, a native of New Mexico then serving as the state Sunday school secretary in Alabama, was elected the first manager; he assumed this responsibility in June, 1950.

The initial building plans provided for an administration building to be known as New Mexico Hall, an auditorium and conference room building later to be known as the Holcomb Auditorium, a dining hall and kitchen, and hotel and housing units. A building committee was appointed by the Sunday School Board to direct the building operations. Staff members in the Department of Church Architecture of the board assisted the building committee. Through the initiative of Thomas Luther Holcomb, executive secretary of the board, state conventions were encouraged to make gifts toward the erection of the initial buildings. Substantial contributions were made by New Mexico ($54,469.83) for New Mexico Hall; Texas ($100,000) for Texas Hall; and Oklahoma ($40,000) for Oklahoma Hall. Mississippi, Kentucky, Florida, Missouri, Arkansas, Virginia, Tennessee, California, and Illinois contributed $2,500 each, and Louisiana $1,500 for the Hall of States. These contributions, together with miscellaneous gifts, amounted (through June, 1956) to $329,955.83. The initial buildings—also cottages for staff workers and guests—were constructed in 1952 and the early months of 1953.

Three years after approval by the Convention, Glorieta Baptist Assembly launched its first week of program activities as Pioneer Week, Aug. 7-13, 1952. Housing accommodations were limited to about 200 guests, but more than 1,400 people registered during the week, many using tents or other camping facilities or neighboring motels and hotels in Santa Fe. Meals were served in a tent-covered area, while the first auditorium was a temporary wooden structure hastily constructed. Beginning with the summer of 1953, a complete assembly program was inaugurated for all the phases of a church educational program and for the various denominational emphases, a program comparable to the one at the Ridgecrest Assembly.

A continuous building program has been pursued, dependent on available funds, to provide the facilities needed by the assembly. An investment exceeding $2,000,000 had been made by the Sunday School Board through 1955. Strong churches have erected housing facilities to accommodate their members in attendance at the assembly. The attendance for the first full season was 5,958. For the 1955 season the total registration was more than 10,000.

ROBERT L. MIDDLETON

GOD. God may be defined as:

. . . the supreme personal Spirit; perfect in all his attributes; who is the source, support, and end of the universe; who guides it according to the wise, righteous, and loving purpose revealed in Jesus Christ; who indwells in all things by his Holy Spirit, seeking ever to transform them according to his own will and bring them to the goal of his kingdom.

This definition is probably typical of the idea of God among Baptists although it, like all definitions of God, is insufficient. At best, the living God can only be "characterized," and Baptists, for the most part, have been content to depend upon the many-faceted biblical characterization of God. However, divergent views of God have appeared in Christian thought as a result of nonbiblical influences such as Greek philosophy and other social and cultural thought patterns.

The writers of the Bible make no attempt to argue for the existence of God. They seem to regard as unnecessary an explanation of the existence of God, who speaks to them and moves them to action by his mighty power and glorious presence (cf. Amos 3:8). Rather, they declare his majestic presence and will (Isa. 6; Deut. 30:11-20; Rom. 10:8; Acts 4:20).

In the Old Testament appear various "names" of God, descriptive of his nature, character, and work. A person's name was so important to the Hebrews that a change in a person's character called for a change in name, e.g., Abram to Abraham (Gen. 17:5), Jacob to Israel (Gen. 32:27-28), Solomon to Jedidiah (II Sam. 12:25), etc. The names of God were likewise important; by them the Hebrews expressed God's attributes and his relationships to them. Two names, *Elohim* and *Yahweh,* are especially significant. *Elohim* was a general name for God which the Hebrews shared with their neighbors; it had no special meaning other than signifying power or strength (Gesenius, Dillman), possibly governor or leader (Nöldeke), or even goal or end (Lagarde). Other combinations involving the term *El*, such as *El-Shaddai* and *El-Elyon,* were descriptive titles for God, probably meaning God Almighty and God Most High, respectively. *Eloach,* a literary variation for *El* or *Elohim,* occurred primarily in poetry, sometimes in prose. Although *El-Shaddai* seems to have been the principal term of the patriarchal period (Gen. 17:1; Exod. 6:3), this does not mean that the name *Yahweh* was wholly unknown to the patriarchs; rather, it was not yet clearly known to them. *Elohim,* a plural name, was used regularly with a singular verb except in a very few cases. Its plural form denoted the fulness and, perhaps, majesty of the divine power.

The *personal* name for God, *Yahweh,* was peculiar to the people of Israel, although there are traces of its use in proper names among their neighbors. For the Israelites *Yahweh* had great meaning; it signified that God had chosen them to be his missionary people and had made a covenant with them to bless them and through them to bless all nations.

It was in connection with the Exodus from Egypt under the leadership of Moses that the meaning of *Yahweh* was revealed more specifically to the Israelites. Its significance lies in the verbal root *to be.* However, in the vivid setting of the Exodus, amid its practical and simple lessons (Exod. 3-6), such an abstract idea as the Eternal One is out of place. When God revealed to Moses, the refugee in Midian, the name by which he would be known to the Israelite slaves in Egypt (Exod. 3:13–14), God intended it to convey in its meaning his faithfulness, a reassurance to the Israelites that he would be with them all the way. The "I am" of Exodus 3:12, 14 is in the imperfect tense and must mean not merely "I am" but "I will be." In this way God assured Moses that what he had said he would be, he would be.

He is the Faithful One who keeps every promise. This attribute of faithfulness is identified with JHWH and is a very important step in the making of the Name to be a synonym for the moral attributes of God.

In the New Testament the significant name for God is *Father*, which will be discussed in more detail below.

Who God is and what he is doing is the essential question posed in the Scriptures. No question is raised concerning the fact of God's existence or the fact of his being known by men. The assertion of what God is doing answers the question of who God is. He is what he does; he does what he is. God's identity and action must be understood in relation to the response of men to him. The Bible is a record of God's work and man's response to that work. Essential to its message is its assertion that God works to save man from sin and tragedy, but the effectiveness of God's work depends upon man's response of faith, love, and obedience.

Men know who God is and what he is doing through revelation. The absolute personal Spirit is the living, acting, self-revealing God. Apart from his self-revelation man could not know him or commune with him. The Bible, however, does not lead the reader to construe revelation as taking place by the sudden or preternatural conveyance of mere information or bare doctrinal ideas. God did not reveal abstract truth or systems of thought for men to wrestle with philosophically. Rather, he revealed *himself* to them progressively in the living experience of his presence and in the events of history interpreted by them with the help of his Spirit. By their faith he was present with them personally to give historical events transcendent meaning and predictive significance of greater divine guidance in the future.

First, the Bible stresses God's revelation of himself as *personal*. "He that planted the ear, shall he not hear? he that formed the eye, shall he not see?" (Psalm 94:9). God "knows," "wills," "loves," and "hates." There is much anthropomorphism in the Scriptures, but it is all rooted in the idea of God as personal; because God is personal, men may have fellowship with him.

Second, the absolute personal Spirit is the *ground* and *source* of all things, the *creator* (Gen. 1:1). His ability to create expresses the attribute of *power*. He is the all-powerful one, as the name *Elohim* indicates. In him and by his power, all things live and move and have their being (Acts 17:24, 28). By his power expressed in his Word all things were made, and without the Word revealed in Christ "was not any thing made that was made" (John 1:1–3).

Third, God reveals himself as the *one*, the *only* God. "Hear, O Israel: the Lord [*Yahweh*] our God [*Elohim*] is one Lord [*Yahweh*]" (Deut. 6:4). This is a classic statement of monotheism in the Scriptures. Jews, especially since the time of Maimonides (A.D. 1135–1204), have interpreted the "one" of this passage as an indivisible monad in the philosophical sense. They have used the verse in opposition to the Christian teaching concerning the Trinity. But Christains have interpreted the "one" to mean a unity with distinctions like those of the persons of the Godhead, or like the unity, the oneness, of two people in marriage (Gen. 2:24). This is not to say that the Trinity is explicitly taught in the Old Testament, but there appears to be nothing in the Old Testament teaching about God that would clearly contradict the New Testament teaching of the Trinity.

Fourth, God reveals himself as the *moral ground* of the universe, the supreme *lawgiver*. It is by his natural, spiritual, and moral laws that he *supports* and *controls* the universe and men. By his *moral power*, his goodness and righteousness, he directs the universe toward the goal of his kingdom of love and righteousness. Because God is the ethical one, he is man's ultimate Judge and Saviour from sin and death. While God's moral nature constitutes the ground of all natural, personal, and social laws, the operation of these laws is neither arbitrary nor expressive of sheer power. God's power is a moral power, described in the Scriptures as the holiness of God. God is the Holy One who works in the midst of men by the Holy Spirit. Jesus promised to his followers the coming of the Holy Spirit, the Comforter, who would "reprove the world of sin, and of righteousness, and of judgment," and guide the believers into all truth. The holiness of God reacts in judgment of and punishment for the sin of disobedience. Because God is holy, absolute in moral purity, he cannot ignore wickedness but must act to punish or deliver. For God to act with indifference toward moral evil would result in moral chaos in the universe. God demands that men be holy and keep his statutes; he can demand no less. He is the absolute moral standard, the Holy One who rules on the throne of the universe.

The root idea of the word *holy* (*kadōsh*) appears to be to separate, to set apart, hence to devote or consecrate to deity. The holy God is *Yahweh*, "high and lifted up" (Isa. 6:1). "Holy" is also used frequently in the Old Testament with regard to things, persons, groups, and actions. When so used, the idea of being set apart or consecrated is normally intended, meaning set apart for *Yahweh*, for deity. Perhaps no other biblical passage combines the idea of "holy" with worship, confession of sin, and moral responsibility more fully than Isaiah 6. All the elements of the "holy" are present: the *numinous,* the *mysterium tremendum,* which strikes one with awe and wonder, and with fearful fascination both repels from and attracts to the deity. The holy God, although high and lifted up in his mighty power and awe-inspiring majesty and glory, *comes down* to purge the sin of the repentant Isaiah, who worships, surrenders to the divine call, and goes forth in obedience to speak for *Yahweh.* Isaiah experienced what Martin Luther called the holy *Deus absconditus* (God hidden), *Deus nudus* (God in his naked majesty), *Deus velatus* (God veiled in the smoke of the Temple), and *Deus revelatus* (God revealed in the voice, in the divine forgiveness, and in the divine commission).

Fifth, God reveals himself as the *rational ground* of the universe. Because he is absolute in *wisdom,* all things were made; they function in keeping with his all-wise plan (Psalms 104:24; 136:5; Prov. 3:19; Jer. 10:12–13). Nothing happens without his notice (Matt. 10:29). He grants wisdom and understanding to all—kings, shepherds, artisans, etc.—who will trustingly obey his word (Exod. 31:3; I Kings 3:28; 4:29–34; Psalms 51:6; 111:10; Prov. 2:6). While the wisdom of God is *personified* in Proverbs, the wisdom of God becomes *personal* in Christ. Jesus spoke of himself as the way, the *truth,* and the life (John 14:6).

Paul, the highly trained Jew of Tarsus, found in Jesus, the crucified and risen Lord, the true power and *wisdom* of God which renders foolish the wisdom of this world (I Cor. 1:17–30). In Jesus Paul saw hidden all the treasures of wisdom and knowledge (Col. 2:3). To Paul Christ was the mind of God, the rational ground and structure of the universe, revealed to men in a historical person, risen and glorified and living in the church, which is his body (cf. Eph. 1:7–23; Phil. 2:5–11; 4:7–13; Col. 1:12–20; 2:2 to 3:4). In and through this church, the body of Christ, "the pillar and ground of *truth,*" God in Christ works to save all men and bring them to "the knowledge of the truth" (I Tim. 2:4; 3:15).

Sixth, God reveals himself as *Saviour,* the deliverer from sin and its consequences. God, as holy, just, and morally perfect and as the supreme *lawgiver,* must demand that all things conform to his will and purpose. But all things do not conform, for God created human beings who bear his image, who think, feel, will, and act "like" him and are therefore moral creatures, free and accountable, who have rebelled against him and like sheep have *gone their own way* (Isa. 53:6).

Since men are moral creatures, weak and helpless like sheep, God is pictured as the good shepherd who goes out in search of the lost ones. God is not an all-powerful tyrant or an unbending judge who must defend his law at all costs, but rather a loving God, a Saviour, the Father of the Lord Jesus Christ. He is like the father in Jesus' immortal story of the prodigal son, who lovingly received his wayward son back into his bosom and rejoiced that the lost son had been found (Luke 15:11–24). He is the God who not only demands but gives. God is *light* and *love* (I John 1:5; 4:16). The Old Testament provided preparation for understanding God as the loving Heavenly Father. Hosea's God of redeeming love prefigured the coming of God in Christ to seek and to save the lost. Jeremiah, the weeping and suffering prophet, was a foreshadow of the humble Jesus of Nazareth, the man of sorrows who took upon himself the sins of the world. Isaiah, the prince of prophets, through the eye of faith foresaw the Suffering Servant who would offer himself for the sins of many. The meaning of the name *Yahweh* as proclaimed to Moses revealed God as merciful, gracious, long-suffering, abundant in goodness and truth, forgiving iniquity and transgression and sin, and yet one whose love was not soft and indulgent but as morally demanding as his holy law (Exod. 34:5–7). All these ideas found expression in Jesus' teachings about God as Father. The holy love of *Yahweh* was expressed in Jesus, who by Paul was described as *Yahweh* himself: "Jesus Christ is Lord" (Phil. 2:11). The word "Lord" is the translation of the Greek word *Kurios* used in the Septuagint for the name *Yahweh.*

Throughout the Bible the idea of the kingdom of God (heaven) expresses the unfolding of God's divine purpose. God is working to establish his kingdom of love and righteousness. In the Old Testament *Yahweh* of hosts is King, King over Israel and King over all the earth. The kings of Israel and the kings of all nations rule only under the permissive sovereign will of King *Yahweh.* God sets them upon their thrones and removes them when they rule unwisely, unjustly, and unrighteously (Deut. 17:14–15; I Sam. 12:12–25; Psalms 2; 10:16; 24:7; 29:10; 47:2; Isa. 43:15; Jer. 10:7, 10; Zech. 9:9–10; 14:9, 16–17; etc.). And the sovereign, glorious King *Yahweh* of the Old Testament comes to earth in Jesus of Nazareth (*Immanuel,* God with us), becomes meek and humble, riding on an ass (Zech. 9:9–10; Matt. 21:5). The sovereign *Yahweh* of the Old Testament revelation is thus identified with the Christ of the New Testament, who, also a King, comes to announce the coming universal reign (kingdom) of God. It is in this way that the idea of the sovereign kingship of *Yahweh* becomes linked with the idea of God as Father, as taught by Jesus to his followers. Taking the Old and New Testaments together, God is revealed as the sovereign Father, i.e., King over all the universe, yet a loving Heavenly Father. God's attributes— his absolute power, holiness, wisdom, and love— are blended in the highly significant names given to him. God is the supreme *personal* Spirit who unites in himself all perfections and powers and shares his life and blessing with all who will trust, love, and serve him in righteousness.

The personal, sovereign Spirit who reveals himself as the all-powerful *creator,* the holy *lawgiver,* and the *saving Father* uses various modes to make himself known to man. In the Scriptures God is described as using both natural and supernatural means (miracles) for his self-revelation. His most effective mode was by personal contact with men of faith who recognized him as God and honored him in obedient service: Abraham, Isaac, Jacob, David, Jeremiah, etc. As a result of the divine-human encounter, men of pre-Christian days wrote a record of God's working among them, the Old Testament. With the coming of Christ, all that had gone before was viewed as a preparation for the incarnation, the supreme revelation of God in a living person, truly man and truly God. Jesus' followers, those who shared in the life of God mediated in Christ, banded themselves together in a fellowship of faith, a spiritual fellowship (koinōnia), the household (family) of God, the church. The divine-human encounter goes on continually in this living fellowship; through the church, as the divine-human agency, God still extends his offer of salvation to all who will respond in repentance and faith. In this fellowship the Holy Spirit supplies the power and the guidance. As the church lives within the events of human history, God continues to speak through it to all men. The Holy Spirit is the voice of God, speaking to men through nature, in the Scriptures, and in the living church; the Holy Spirit makes Christ known to men (John 14:26; 15:26; 16:7-15; Rom. 8; Eph. 2:22; 3:20-21).

Early in the history of Christian theology, the influence of Greco-Roman and Greco-Oriental thought was felt. Such an apologist as Justin Martyr thought of God as incomprehensible and nameless, without desire and feeling. Under the influence of Greek ideas concerning the Logos, God, the sovereign Father, more and more was relegated to the realm of the transcendent, the realm of the unknown and the unseen. God became the impassive, unchanging One, a sheer abstraction, untouched by the imperfect, evil flux of the world of things. Great and influential theologians were affected by the trend. Augustine sometimes thought of God, in Platonic terms, as a finite, impersonal universal of the Good, the True, and the Beautiful. Thomas Aquinas was influenced by Aristotle's idea of God as the impersonal, Unmoved Mover, oblivious to both the physical and moral orders. The personal, evangelical God as revealed in Christ was consequently neglected.

Between the times of Thomas Aquinas and Martin Luther, a reaction against scholasticism and its logical sterility took place. Due to the "secularizing" tendencies of the Renaissance influence and also due to the rising scientific spirit, philosophy and theology began to separate. As a result, philosophy, cut off from its roots in the Christian tradition and feeling its newly found freedom in the Western world, soared to the heights of speculation and fathered ideas of God strangely inconsistent with the Hebrew-Christian (biblical) concept of God. Yet in a sense these ideas were not new but were often influenced by the Platonic and Aristotelian ideas which found expression in a variety of ways in post-Reformation thought. For example, Spinoza's (1632-77) monistic and pantheistic philosophy pictured God as the one fixed Substance, the All, impersonal and absolute, unknown and unknowable, lost in a universe which at the same time *is* God. Spinoza's monism shows many similarities to the Neo-Platonism (New-Idealism) of Plotinus (203-279), a man whose influence on the thought of the Middle Ages was great. Hegel (1770-1831) also illustrates the philosophical approach to God; like Spinoza, Hegel defined God as absolute and identified with the universe. But Hegel's absolute Spirit was dynamic process, becoming, while Spinoza's absolute Substance was fixed and unchanging, as were Plato's fixed universals. Both Spinoza and Hegel exerted a great influence upon modern philosophy and theology. The end result of their speculations was a view of God at some points akin to biblical revelation (due, no doubt, to the influence of Christianity upon them) but for the most part radically different from the Person of the biblical revelation, transcendent yet at the same time working in history to draw men into a living fellowship with himself. The pantheism of both Hegel and Spinoza renders God impersonal and abstract, found only in intellectual exercise; at the same time, by confusing God and the universe, their philosophy relegates human persons to the role of mere parts of the whole which is God.

Although inadequate, this analysis of the interplay between philosophy—especially Greek philosophy—and Christian theology should at least serve to illustrate the part philosophy has played, both in deepening man's concept of the divine Spirit and also in turning men's minds away from the living, personal, self-revealing, loving, sovereign Father, spoken of in the Scriptures and experienced through faith and repentance in a personal fellowship in the Spirit. In the present, as in the time of Martin Luther and John Calvin, a renewed interest in the biblical revelation of God is evident, in reaction against the idea of God in speculative philosophy.

See also ATTRIBUTES OF GOD, FOREKNOWLEDGE, JUSTICE OF GOD, IMMANENCE, MONOTHEISM, PANTHEISM, RIGHTEOUSNESS, TRANSCENDENCE, and TRINITY.

BIBLIOGRAPHY: J. Dillenberger, *God Hidden and Revealed* (1953). A. E. Garvie, *The Christian Doctrine of the Godhead* (1925). A. C. Knudson, *The Doctrine of God* (1930). J. Orr, *The Christian View of God and the World* (1897). P. Tillich, *Systematic Theology* (1951).

TED R. CLARK

GODBOLD, EDGAR (b. near Auburn, Miss., Dec. 2, 1879; d. Alexandria, La., Nov. 21, 1952). Educator and denominational leader. After receiving the Bachelor of Science degree from Mississippi College in 1905, he served a year as principal of Lawrence County High School.

The next year he returned to Mississippi College as professor of biology and meanwhile earned his M.A. degree in 1910. In 1912 he became educational secretary for Louisiana Baptists and the first professor of Biology of Louisiana College. Godbold served as chairman of the advertising committee of the Laymen's Movement in 1914. In 1916 he served on the Hospital Committee which founded the Baptist hospital for Louisiana in Alexandria. After one year of service overseas in the Y.M.C.A., he was elected in 1919 as Louisiana state publicity director in the 75 Million Campaign. He succeeded the retiring corresponding secretary of the state convention in 1920. In 1923 Godbold was elected president of Howard Payne College. He placed the college in the hearts of Texas Baptists and was active in the Texas Conquest Campaign of 1927–28 for liquidating debts. In 1929 he resigned to become secretary of the Baptist executive board in Missouri. In 1942 he accepted the presidency of Louisiana College, remaining there until his retirement in 1951. Under his leadership the value of the college property increased almost a million and a half dollars, and countless improvements were made on existing property. He continued his service in the capacity of financial agent for the college. In 1950 he was elected president of the Louisiana Baptist Convention, and he was re-elected in 1951. While en route to the 1952 meeting he had an automobile accident on Nov. 10 and died from his injuries on Nov. 21. He was among the best-known educators in the South, and he served in many civic and denominational posts.   W. S. TAYLOR

GOLD COAST, MISSION IN. The first congregation of Baptists in the Gold Coast, Yoruba-speaking traders from Nigeria, met in Tarkwa in 1918. Yoruba Baptists in other towns formed congregations, each using one of its own men as leader. Representatives from 20 congregations met at Kumasi, June 22, 1925, when they decided to hold annual meetings and asked the Nigerian mission to send missionaries.

When Homer Richerson and Ossie (Price) Littleton, Southern Baptist missionaries, went to the Gold Coast in 1947 with two Nigerian missionaries, there were 24 congregations (churches not yet organized by New Testament standards) with 1,050 members. By 1955, 53 congregations (including six organized churches) had 1,820 members, seven pastors, a fieldworker, and six Southern Baptist missionaries. Baptists have a large school in Kumasi.

Among the churches in 1955 were two churches and 11 preaching places with 78 members among the Ashanti, Fanti, and Dagomba tribes native to the Gold Coast, among whom mission work began in 1950.

HOMER R. LITTLETON

GOLDEN AGE. A publication edited by W. D. Upshaw which began on Feb. 22, 1906, in Atlanta, Ga., as a literary weekly. It probably superseded the *Religious Forum*, which had been published from Feb. 22, 1905, to Feb. 14, 1906. By 1910 circulation was 12,000. By 1914 it had become a literary and religious publication, and the circulation had dropped to 10,000. In 1919, as a monthly devoted to religion and temperance, it had a circulation of 16,000. The next year the circulation had dropped to 6,000 and the paper thereafter disappeared from record.   JUDSON BOYCE ALLEN

GOLDEN GATE BAPTIST THEOLOGICAL SEMINARY. A coeducational institution owned and operated by the Southern Baptist Convention, founded July 12, 1944, and located at 1908 Addison Street, Berkeley, Calif.

By the time California was admitted to the Union in 1850, Baptists from the South had located in California. The Board of Domestic Missions of the Southern Baptist Convention soon had missionaries organizing churches throughout the central area. Among these missionaries was Harvey Gilbert, who received a commission from the board in 1858. He then served for a few months as mission pastor of the Baptist church in Oakland. But Gilbert was primarily interested in Christian education, and he had a dream of establishing a Baptist theological seminary in the state where the need for ministers was so much greater than the supply. He gave up the Oakland church and moved to Marin County in 1859 to endeavor to make his dream a reality. In a letter to the board, he gave a glowing description of the beauties of Marin County, with its lovely hills and fertile valleys, and its desirability as a location for such a school. Within a few months he raised the funds necessary for the erection of a building and began operation of the San Rafael Baptist Institute. During this entire period he was still in the employment of the domestic board. John Lewis Shuck (*q.v.*), then serving as general missionary of the board to California, wrote concerning the school, "It is the beginning of a great Baptist theological school."

But the War Between the States, the impoverishment of reconstruction days, and changes in Southern Baptists' home mission emphasis caused this early institution to pass out of existence; nearly 100 years elapsed before another attempt was made to establish a Southern Baptist theological seminary in California.

In the period from 1936 to 1940, many Southern Baptists moved to California from the drought-ridden regions of the Midwest. Some of these soon founded churches similar in doctrine and practice to the ones with which they were familiar in their former homes. In 1940 messengers from these newly established churches organized the Southern Baptist General Convention of California.

With the coming of World War II, additional thousands of Southern Baptists moved to Cal-

Golden Gate Baptist Theological Seminary

ifornia to work in the shipyards and war plants. The dream of 1859 soon began to live again in the hearts of some of these Baptists.

Isam B. Hodges became the leader in the movement to found a seminary. Hodges, a graduate of Ouachita College, came to California in 1935, and in 1937 he became pastor of the Golden Gate Baptist Church of Oakland. He held the Th.M. degree from Southwestern Baptist Theological Seminary, and the M.A. degree from Berkeley Baptist Divinity School. In 1944 he was serving as president of the Southern Baptist General Convention of California.

Hodges enlisted the help of Dallas G. Faulkner, pastor of the First Southern Baptist Church of San Francisco. Faulkner was also a Ouachita graduate and held the Th.D. degree from Southern Baptist Theological Seminary.

Their two churches elected trustees, and the Golden Gate Southern Baptist Theological Seminary was incorporated under the laws of the state of California on July 12, 1944. With Hodges as president, the first term opened Sept. 2, 1944, in the building of the Golden Gate Baptist Church on Fifty-fourth and Gaskill streets in Oakland. On Sept. 22 the Golden Gate Baptist Association voted to give the institution its "prayerful and moral support." The association then elected six additional trustees to serve with the 12 elected by the two churches. There was no provision for financial support from any sponsoring body.

The records show that seven regular students attended classes throughout the first session. Twenty students were enrolled for the school term beginning Sept., 1945. Interest in the new institution was awakened sufficiently that the Southern Baptist General Convention of California in its annual meeting in Nov., 1945, acceded to the request of the seminary trustees and voted to assume ownership and control of the school. A new board of trustees was elected by the convention.

In May, 1946, Benjamin Oscar Herring accepted an offer of the trustees to become the seminary's second president. He had served for 21 years on the Bible faculty of Baylor University, from which institution he held the A.B. and A.M. degrees. He was also a graduate of Southern Baptist Theological Seminary with the Th.M. and Th.D. degrees.

Herring faced a difficult task as he began his work on Sept. 2, 1946. Thirty-one students were enrolled, coming from 11 colleges and universities. Among them was Helen Nixon, later to serve as a missionary in Argentina. The president and a part-time secretary were the only salaried employees.

On Apr. 2, 1947, the board of directors of the state convention authorized the seminary trustees to purchase from the Calvary Baptist Church its property located at Grove and Addison streets in Berkeley. The transaction was consummated in time for the fall term of 1947 to open in the new location. The enrolment reached 65 by the end of the spring semester.

During his first year of service, Herring carried a teaching load of 12 hours in addition to his administrative duties. He succeeded in securing the approval of the state board for an annual Christian Education Day offering for the seminary. This was in addition to 20 per cent of the distributable Cooperative Program funds given by California Southern Baptist churches. As more funds were made available, the faculty was increased and strengthened. Among the additions during the administration of Herring were R. Fletcher Royal, Mrs. Claudia Royal, A. J. Hyatt, L. A. Brown, Arthur Insko, Derward W. Deere, Jack W. Manning, Lysbeth Cox, and S. Madge Lewis, all of whom are still serving as members of the faculty or staff. S. G. Posey, now executive secretary of the California Southern Baptist General Convention, joined the faculty in 1947. The coming of Amos Lindsey Aulick (q.v.) in 1948 was of great importance to the seminary. Many of his former students from Eastern New Mexico University, where he had taught, were attracted to Golden Gate through his coming. His wise counsel was helpful to those who were responsible for decisions concerning the infant school.

In 1949 the 17 members of the first graduating class received their awards.

Two events of great importance took place during the administration of Herring. The first was the securing of a new charter in Nov., 1948, more clearly setting forth the purpose, powers, and government of the seminary in view of its connection with the state convention and granting the authority to confer degrees. In the new charter the word "Southern" was dropped from the title of the institution, in keeping with the common usage since the printing of the second catalogue. The second event was the acceptance of Golden Gate Seminary by the Southern Baptist Convention, meeting in Chicago in May, 1950. The charter was amended to meet the necessary requirements, and Jan. 1, 1951, the seminary began receiving support from the Convention.

Early in 1952 Herring resigned to become president of Grand Canyon College. The seminary trustees, meeting in Miami, Fla., May 13, 1952, elected as his successor, Harold Keaster Graves, pastor of the First Baptist Church, Bartlesville, Okla. He holds the Th.M. and Th.D. degrees from Southern Baptist Theological Seminary and was prominent as denominational leader before his election to this post. With his coming as president in July, 1952, Graves was charged by the trustees with the responsibility of continuing the strengthening and reorganization of the faculty and staff, the improvement of the physical plant, the working out of a program calling for complete accreditation, and the search for a more adequate and suitable location for the school.

The progress made in the next four years was gratifying. Two additional buildings were purchased for use as residences for single women and an apartment building was leased just across the street from the seminary property. Another building was leased and remodeled to house the cafeteria and the child care program and to provide additional faculty offices and classrooms. A home for the president was purchased, which is spacious enough for many of the seminary social functions.

The library was greatly enlarged, and in 1956 it listed more than 16,000 volumes. Ten thousand dollars is expended yearly in carefully selected works to build a theological library which will meet the requirements for the highest type of theological study. Golden Gate cooperates with the six other seminaries of the area in operation of a master catalogue and extends the privilege of its library to the other schools. In addition, students have access to the third largest university library in the United States, that of the University of California. The American Association of Theological Schools accepted Golden Gate as an associate member in Dec., 1954. It has been an associate member of the American Association of Schools of Religious Education since 1948.

Perhaps the most significant event in the first four years of Graves' presidency was the purchase of a campus site on beautiful Strawberry Point in Marin County. It consists of 126 acres jutting out into Richardson Bay, and the master plans for a complete seminary plant were approved by the trustees in 1956. The expenditure of $5,500,000 will be necessary before the school can move to its new site. The fall of 1959 will witness the official opening of the seminary in Marin County, just 100 years from the time that Gilbert began the San Rafael Baptist Institute, and only six miles from the site of the early educational venture.

The seminary accepts as a correct doctrinal statement the confession of faith presented by a committee of which Edgar Young Mullins (q.v.) was chairman and adopted by the Southern Baptist Convention in 1926. All faculty members are required to subscribe to the statement.

In addition to the catalogue and various phases of promotional literature, the seminary has since 1949 published the *Golden Gate*, the official organ of the institution. It began in Jan., 1949, as a quarterly publication, but now it appears monthly from October through July. The *Nugget* was published during 1951 by the student body but did not appear after that year.

The curriculum offered at Golden Gate is listed under three areas: Christian Sources and Origins, Christian Life and Thought, and Christian Work and Worship. The following degrees are offered: Bachelor of Theology, Bachelor of Divinity, Master of Theology, Bachelor of Religious Education, Master of Religious Education, Bachelor of Sacred Music, and Master of Sacred Music. The specifications of the American Association of Theological Schools are strictly adhered to, as well as a number of additional requirements. Under the provisions of the charter, the seminary has the right to offer courses leading to the doctorate in theology and in religious education. For the present no new students will be admitted to the candidacy for these degrees. Plans now call for full accreditation before the complete graduate program is resumed.

See also STUDENT ACTIVITIES, GOLDEN GATE BAPTIST THEOLOGICAL SEMINARY.

WILLIAM A. CARLETON

GOOD WILL CENTER WORK. A spiritual ministry developed by Woman's Missionary Union to meet the same needs growing out of the Industrial Revolution that prompted others in England and America about 1890 to begin the establishment of "social settlements" for underprivileged peoples. Beginning in 1912 with the "Baptist Training School Settlement" in Louisville, Ky., under the auspices of the W.M.U. Training School, and taking the name "Good Will Centers" in 1914, the movement has now grown to 65 centers. Each is supported and directed by one or more churches, Woman's Missionary Union (local, associational, district, or state), city mission boards or committees, associations, the Home Mission Board, the Foreign Mission Board, or, in some cases, a combination of two or more of these. The Home Mission Board participates in the support and direction of 18 centers, and the Foreign Mission Board has 11 abroad.

Originally designed to overcome social and economic barriers in bringing to underprivileged city people the full impact of the gospel, the Good Will Center program has extended also to overcome the barriers of race, nationality, language, religion, and geographic location. Under the leadership of one or more paid workers and as many volunteer helpers as can be enlisted from the churches, the Good Will Center wins souls and lifts lives through Bible-centered, Christ-centered activities built around the interests, abilities, and needs of the group served. These activities include: (1) day nursery, nursery school, or kindergarten; (2) graded clubs using recreation, music, dramatics, and handcrafts; (3) classes in Bible study, adult education, and homemaking; (4) medical clinics; (5) library; (6) visitation; (7) summer camps; and (8) Vacation Bible school. Good Will Center buildings range from one or two rooms to elaborate properties including living quarters for the paid workers, assembly rooms, club rooms, library, clinic room, storage and dispensary rooms, play rooms, work shops, and playgrounds.

Good Will Centers work in very close co-operation with other community agencies. The welfare agencies, public health services, juvenile courts, and schools welcome as a contribution to their own success the spiritual impetus that Good Will Centers provide. Good Will Centers, however, do not usurp the divinely appointed function of the church. The centers are the connecting link between their communities and the near-by churches, working together in winning souls and developing Christians that otherwise might be overlooked. The full and varied program of the Good Will Center offers opportunities for church members to engage in the practical missionary activity called for in the plans of work of the Woman's Missionary Union, Brotherhood, Training Union, and Sunday school. LOYD CORDER

GOOD WILL CENTERS IN MISSIONS. Social settlements with an evangelistic approach offered Southern Baptist women the opportunity to serve needy people, following the example of Toynbee Hall, pioneer settlement house begun in an industrial quarter of London in 1884, and Hull House established by Jane Addams and Ellen Gates Starr in Chicago in 1889. In 1914 at the suggestion of Mrs. H. M. Wharton (q.v.), personal service chairman of Woman's Missionary Union, the name "good will center" was given to these settlements, with the motto, "Peace on Earth, Good Will Among Men." The object was to provide for the enlistment of women in definite missionary activities within the community by promoting soul-winning in good will centers. In 1914 Woman's Missionary Union purchased an old residence in Louisville, Ky., remodeled it, and started the Baptist Training School Settlement.

The two Southern Baptist mission boards sponsor numerous good will centers, including 18 operated by the Home Mission Board with 41 missionaries, and 11 supported by the Foreign Mission Board in Argentina, Brazil, Chile, Mexico, Japan, and Malaya, with 10 missionaries directing and 59 nationals assisting. The purpose of each center is "to minister to all the needs of the people it serves, bettering home conditions and providing a wholesome environment for children, to win to Christ, and make the contact between the people and the church." The activities may include the graded system of clubs; kindergarten and nursery school; classes in sewing, cooking, handicraft, art, music, and frequently English; games, athletics, playground, library, dramatics, parties, family night entertainments; dental, medical, baby health, and prenatal clinics; and religious services such as Sunday school, Vacation Bible school, preaching, and prayer meeting. SARA TAYLOR

GOODNIGHT ACADEMY. A coeducational school, transferred to the Baptist General Convention of Texas in 1905. It was made a junior college in 1913 and closed in 1917. Annual enrolment never exceeded 100.

RUPERT N. RICHARDSON

GOODSPEED, CALVIN (b. Nashwaak, New Brunswick, May 5, 1842; d. Paradise, Nova Scotia, July 6, 1912). Minister, teacher, and editor. He was graduated from University of New Brunswick, and Regent's Park College, London, England, in 1868 and did additional study at Newton Theological Seminary and University of Leipzig. He was ordained at Andover, New Brunswick, in 1869, and he was pastor at Woodstock, Ontario, and Yarmouth, New Brunswick. He served as principal of the Baptist Seminary Fredericton, New Brunswick, and later as professor at Woodstock College, at the University of Ontario, and at McMaster University in Toronto. From 1905 to 1909, he was professor of Theoretical Theology of Southwestern Baptist Theological Seminary, then located at Waco, Tex. For a brief time he was editor of *Messenger and Visitor*, St. John, New Brunswick, and associate editor of the *Canadian Baptist*. CHARLES P. JOHNSON

GORDON, ADONIRAM JUDSON (b. New Hampton, Belknap County, N. H., Apr. 19, 1836; d. Boston, Mass., Feb. 2, 1895). A leader in the optimistic and aggressive program of the Church Militant (soon to be Triumphant) of the 19th century. Born in New Hampshire in a hyper-Calvinistic family, Gordon epitomizes the American transition from speculative to practical concerns, from doctrines to missions; his father was named for John Calvin, the theological systematician, but Gordon was named for the first American Baptist missionary to Burma. At the age of 15 he was converted. He was educated at New London, N. H. (1853–57), Brown University (1857–60), and Newton Theological Institute (1860–63). Immediately upon graduation he was ordained and became a pastor at Jamaica Plain, Mass., and soon thereafter he married Maria Hale. From 1867 he was sought for the pastorate of Clarendon Street Church, Boston, but he did not accept the position until late in 1869. Though Gordon was not a chronic controversialist, he defended Christianity against "a metaphysical jargon, a shallow Pelagianism, and a uniformed officialism." He attacked the growing agnosticism following in the wake of Darwinism, the negative propositions of Unitarianism, the "lavender-water theology" and "enlightened humanism" of Transcendentalism, the growing belief in baptismal regeneration, the doctrines of Christian Science, and the enervating influence of capitalism in evangelical churches (several "millionaire merchants," as he called them, were in his church). He was dominated by the conviction that nothing is practical except the spiritual and nothing is spiritual unless it is practical. He possessed a strong strain of mysticism which came both from his personal experience and from devotional classics; the new birth which effects a union of believer and Christ was primary. He was a persistent soul-winner and evangelistic preacher, and a participant in Moody's evangelistic efforts. Though Gordon emphasized individual salvation, he did not neglect the church's leavening responsibility in society; social transformation was designed both to facilitate and to preserve the conversion of individuals; in addition to participating in social campaigns, he either founded or supported institutions to aid drunkards, foreigners, laborers, paupers, etc. He insisted on spiritual worship by the entire congregation; his only stipulation in accepting the call to the Clarendon Street church was the replacement of the paid choir by congregational singing. He was a hymn writer, a composer of hymn tunes, and a compiler of hymnals. He assisted with the compilation of *The Service of Song for Baptist Churches* (Boston, 1871), and compiled *The Vestry Hymn and Tune Book* (Boston, 1872). Though he wrote several hymns, he is probably best known for his hymn tune "Gordon" sung to the hymn, "My Jesus, I love Thee." Gordon's influential work was related to missions; over one half of his travels and conferences were in behalf of world evangelism. He served more than 20 years as either member or executive chairman of the board of the American Baptist Missionary Union; though he favored sound financial support, he also emphasized the faith element in mission support. A precursor of fundamentalism, especially concerning inspiration, soul-winning, and premillennialism, he held the inerrancy and infallibility of the Bible, the constant presence of the Holy Spirit, and the imminence of the second coming. His premillennialism increased during his later years; his "new-departure theology" argued for Christ's early return on the basis of the universal promulgation of the gospel, the decline of the temporal power of the papacy, and the movement of Israel. His tombstone simply recorded his eschatological hope: "Pastor A. J. Gordon, 1836–1895, 'Until He Come.'"   HUGH WAMBLE

GOSPEL. The proclaimed good news of God's saving grace to be appropriated through faith in Christ. Isaiah's announcement of "good tidings" of deliverance to the suffering cities of Judah (40:9), the promise of One who would give good tidings to Jerusalem (41:27), the beautiful footsteps on the mountains of the messenger of salvation to Zion (52:7), and the messianic hope of the Spirit-anointed One to "preach good tidings unto the meek" (61:1)—all culminate in the dramatic story of salvation through the life, death, and resurrection of Christ, the "gospel of Jesus Christ, the Son of God" (Mark 1:1). Announced by the prophets, enacted in Christ, preached in the early church, the gospel is the whole message of Christian salvation.

The gospel is both the message of deliverance from sin and the effective power of God working through the Holy Spirit in those who believe unto salvation (Rom. 1:16). Never used in the New Testament to denote any book or books, the term came into general use by the second century in Ignatius, Justin Martyr, and others to designate any one or all of the first four New Testament books which record the life and teachings of Christ. In the New Testament Christ used the word to proclaim the "gospel of the kingdom" (Matt. 4:23; 11:5; Mark 1:14; Luke 4:18; 7:22); Paul spoke of the "gospel of Christ" (Rom. 1:16; 15:19; I Cor. 9:12, 18; Gal. 1:7) or simply the "gospel of God" (Rom. 1:1; I Thess. 2:2, 9; I Tim. 1:11). Peter and John preached the gospel in the villages of Samaria (Acts 8:25). Paul's response to the Macedonian vision was "to preach the gospel unto them" (Acts 16:10), and to the Ephesian elders he affirmed that his whole Christian calling was to witness to "the gospel of the grace of God" (Acts 20:24).

WAYNE E. WARD

GOSPEL EXPOSITOR. A newspaper published at Atlanta, Ga., and edited for a short time by E. R. Carswell, Jr., in the late 1880's. The paper is now extinct.   JOHN J. HURT, JR.

GOSPEL HERALD, THE. Published at Frankfort, Ky., and edited by Silas Mercer Noel (*q.v.*) in 1813. It was successor to *The Kentucky Missionary & Theological Magazine*, Frankfort, Ky., edited by Starke Dupuy in 1812. Under the heading, "Oldest Religious Paper West," Editor S. H. Ford wrote of this periodical on page 143 of *The Christian Repository*, and quoted four paragraphs from the 1813 publication. No file of this paper is extant.   GEORGE RALEIGH JEWELL

GOSPEL MESSENGER. A Primitive Baptist monthly newspaper published in Butler, Ga., 1878–96, then in Atlanta, Ga., where it remained for only a few months until it moved to Williamston, N. C. It continued publication in Williamston until its suspension in 1923. J. R. Repress and William M. Mitchell edited the paper.   JOHN J. HURT, JR.

GOSPEL MISSION MOVEMENT (NORTH AND CENTRAL CHINA). Fear that conventions and boards were, by centralizing authority in themselves, destroying the autonomy of churches on mission fields led to establishment of the Gospel Mission in China in 1894. Its founders claimed that the use of money in employing native workers and supporting schools on mission fields attracted people to the church with the false motive of pecuniary gain. Some of their distinctive views were: no financial remuneration to native Christians for any service rendered; no schools or other institutions supported by mission funds; boards to have no authority to appoint missionaries or direct their work on the field; a church or group of churches to choose the missionary, support him, and receive his reports directly. Some of the founders contended for the wearing of native dress, eating native food, and living in native houses.

Tarleton Perry Crawford (*q.v.*) and George P. Bostick withdrew from the North China Mission, Sept. 13, 1893. Delays in locating a new field detained them in Pingtu for the winter. During the winter William Dawson King and David Wells Herring joined them. Three new

Gospel Missionism

men came from the United States, F. M. Royall, William Elwyn Crocker, and T. L. Blalock. Other charter members were T. J. League, Florence Nightingale League, and Fannie Knight. By midsummer, 1894, the Gospel Mission was established with Taianfu as its center.

The Sino-Japanese War hindered progress, and the Boxer Rebellion forced complete evacuation. However, the organization has continued. The name was changed in 1920 to China Baptist Direct Mission and more recently to Independent Baptist Direct Mission, Inc., through which it has some legal connection with other independent Baptist bodies.

W. B. GLASS

GOSPEL MISSIONISM. A missionary policy, which developed into a movement, led by Tarleton Perry Crawford (*q.v.*), seeking direct support of missionaries by voluntary gifts from individuals, churches, and associations, rather than by the Foreign Mission Board. The policy also held that missionaries should conform to the social customs of the people with whom they worked. This movement appeared in Southern Baptist life in the 1880's and sought to revolutionize the foreign mission program of the Convention. Crawford, a long-time missionary of the Foreign Mission Board in China, was financially independent and was giving his service without remuneration when he presented his plan to the Convention in 1888. He was supported by D. W. Herring, C. W. Pruitt, and J. M. Joiner, all fellow missionaries to China.

This agitation continued for the next four years. In 1892 it was announced to the Southern Baptist Convention that Crawford's "name had been removed from the roll of missionaries." G. P. Bostick resigned, stating that he intended to ask his home association, King's Mountain of North Carolina, to withdraw support from the Foreign Mission Board and support him directly. Crawford, in his resignation, declared that "boards make pastors, editors, missionaries bow or perish."

The following year, 1893, it was reported to the Convention that T. J. League, D. W. Herring, their wives, and Mrs. Crawford had resigned from their appointments with the Foreign Mission Board because they could no longer work in harmony with the board. At this same Convention, a proposal from Herring was presented which recommended that local churches or groups of churches select, appoint, and support their own missionaries, that all money gathered for foreign missions be transmitted directly to the missionaries except for a small commission for gathering the funds, and that the board have no voice in the selection or approval of missionaries or the location or method of work.

In 1894 it was reported to the Convention that W. D. King and Fannie Knight, both missionaries to China, had resigned from the service of the Foreign Mission Board. The reason given was that they could no longer work in harmony with the board. These resignations weakened the mission work in China, but they eliminated the advocates of gospel missionism from a voice in the Southern Baptist Convention, and thus the threat to the Foreign Mission Board removed itself.

BIBLIOGRAPHY: T. P. Crawford, *Churches, To the Front!* (1892). *Foreign Missionary Journal* (May, 1892). *Religious Herald* (May 17, 1888).

JOHN F. GIBSON

GOSPEL SONG. A type of religious music characterized by melodious, rhythmic, easy-to-sing music and by lyrics which are emotional and subjective, including a chorus to be repeated after each verse. It has had a long and continuous use among Baptists and is the type of popular religious song most used in Southern Baptist churches today. Throughout most of their history, Southern Baptists have been a rural people strongly inclined toward folk traditions. The beginning of the gospel song goes deep into the history of American Baptists. There is evidence to support the theory that some of the early Baptist immigrants brought with them many folk hymns, largely songs of praise suited to group singing. Evidence also points to the possibility that Baptists spread this folk-hymn tradition first in the northeast and then in the southeast and the western territory, where it became the song tinder for the frontier revivals. It is probable, though unproven, that this folk-song tinder included the folk tunes which have been associated with the hymns.

Toward the end of the 18th century, the ballad tradition, as a survival from England or as an unconscious revival, welled up in the production of hymns with refrains. These were called "spiritual songs"; perhaps the earliest collection of the type was the *Divine Hymns* or *Spiritual Songs* (Norwich, 1784) of Joshua Smith, a New Hampshire layman. Spiritual songs became very popular and appeared in most Baptist hymnbooks. These books, suited to the popular liking, reflected in their lack of literary value the lack of culture of Baptist congregations and the lack of ministerial and cultural training among a ministry opposed to such training. In some of them, however, can be traced the rise of American folk hymnody.

Although many Baptists along the seaboard from New England to Georgia objected to the emotional excesses of the "camp meeting" type of evangelism which began to flourish at the beginning of the 19th century, the rural masses of the South and West were reached by its emotional appeal. From these meetings there developed a type of camp meeting hymn whose form was that of the popular ballad, whose speech was the plainest of everyday language, and whose poetic technique reflected carelessness or incapacity. The refrain or chorus was its most dominant feature. The verses were usually short, easily learned, and quite definite in their teachings. Both the traditional hymns and the folk hymns were literally sung to pieces and new music formed from those pieces, thereby achieving the folk level of song. Tunes used for these songs were usually very familiar or contagiously popular, traditional, or folk melodies and tunes which were developed in the meetings themselves.

The zeal for missions which developed during the first part of the 19th century created a demand by some for an educated ministry. These were sharply opposed by the "anti-effort" Baptists. Although Baptist hymnody was not thus divided, as a rule the less educated congregations, especially in the South, carried forward the use of spiritual songs. However, the desire for songs in the developing Sunday schools of the more progressive Baptist churches brought forth a new emphasis on church song of the more popular type. This emphasis was continued in the Y.M.C.A. songs and the songs used by soldiers in the armies during the Civil War.

By the time of the Civil War, Baptist revivals often came to be held in connection with regular church and associational meetings or in periods of several days or weeks, known as "protracted meetings." This was the era of the professional evangelist and singing evangelist. These singers led their congregations and choirs in the singing of what is now known as Moody and Sankey type of spiritual song or the modern gospel song. Neither the words nor the music of these gospel songs was of a type which was distinctively new or even clearly different from its predecessors. Although there were others before them, it was P. P. Bliss and Ira D. Sankey, from the 1870's, who became the heads of an evangelistic school of gospel song and tune writers whose works were used extensively by Baptists. The music and texts were fitted to the evangelistic sermons and were so overwhelmingly successful that they became the only music used in many Baptist churches.

As most rural people had learned the shape note method of musical notation, gospel song publishers published shape note editions of their books. Southern denominational houses, including the Southern Baptists', also put out shape note editions of their hymnals and gospel songbooks. This was an effort to supply the demands of their rural congregations, who preferred shape note books but not always the indigenous songs of the other publishers, and to keep them from buying nondenominational songbooks. This move extended the influence of the denominational songbooks into the rural sections, and the practice has been continued by Southern Baptists. As late as 1955, over 27 per cent of the total sales of the *Broadman Hymnal* was of the shape note edition. In spite of some opposition, the *Baptist Hymnal* (1955) was not published in a shape note edition.

Although the Sunday School Board published songbooks which contained gospel songs, the Robert H. Coleman Company of Dallas, Tex., was virtually the unofficial Southern Baptist songbook publisher. The company was eventually purchased by the Sunday School Board in 1945.

It may be seen that the gospel song is only the latest in the successive steps which the predominantly rural and musically uneducated masses have demanded in seeking a popular hymnody. These successive efforts have run more or less parallel to regular church hymnody and occasionally have influenced it. In each case, however, they were characteristic of the place and period in which they occurred.

Gospel songs are widely used in both rural and urban Baptist churches today. Many Baptist congregations are unaware that there is a difference between the hymns and the gospel songs which they sing. Many of the Baptists' favorite songs are gospel songs, and until recently, or perhaps until yet, gospel song writers have dominated Southern Baptist musical life. Until a few years ago the heads of the two oldest church music departments in the Southern Baptist seminaries and the head of the Church Music Department of the Sunday School Board were gospel song writers.

FLOYD PATTERSON

GRACE. God's attitude in Christ toward sinners, not a substance which God gives to men, as in Roman Catholic thought and as in some loose Protestant usage. It signifies God's love in action, redeeming men from their sin and sustaining them in the new life in Christ. To be in the "state of grace" means to be living within the operation of God's redeeming, forgiving, and sustaining love in Christ. The natural man is outside such gracious operation.

In the biblical revelation grace means God's free gift to men (Rom. 3:20–28; Gal. 2:16–21). As sinners having no claim upon God, they do not deserve love and mercy but wrath and judgment. Even their good works, which are contaminated by sinful pride, cannot save them. If such men are to be put right with God, justified, it will be by God's grace, an undeserved act of mercy which God performs in Christ (Rom. 5:18–21). Hence, grace receives concrete expression in the incarnation of Jesus Christ and becomes fully operative in his death and resurrection.

Further, God's grace, his free love in redemptive operation, is associated with the work of the Holy Spirit (Heb. 10:29), who makes God's redemption contemporaneous with us and effective in our lives. Grace, through the operation of the Spirit, convinces us of the truth of the gospel and sets us free to respond in the obedience of faith. Grace, further, continues to operate through the Spirit in the lives of redeemed men and women, sustaining them in the new life which Christ gives, strengthening their wills to fulfil God's purpose for their lives and obey his commands, warming their hearts and enabling them to grow in the love of God, enlightening their minds that they may understand more of the truth in Christ (Rom.

8). When II Peter 3:18 speaks of growing in grace, it means that the operation of the grace of God in our lives makes us more gracious, producing in us love of the same quality as that of Jesus. Grace, the free love of God in action, operates in our lives so that we, too, grow in a love that spends itself for others without reward, and so that we enter into a deepening knowledge of God as he reveals himself in Jesus Christ.

All is of grace, not of our works (Rom. 3:28; Eph. 2:5, 8). All that is left for sinful man is that commitment of faith which receives the gracious approach of God, a commitment which has to be renewed day by day so that his grace may continually operate within. Yet, paradoxically, even that faith which is *our* response is also *God's* gracious gift to our needy souls. We work out our own salvation, yet it is God who works in us.
E. C. RUST

GRACE McBRIDE YOUNG WOMAN'S AUXILIARY. Organized first in 1923 in Baptist hospitals in Alabama and Tennessee, by 1955 Grace McBride Young Woman's auxiliaries had been organized in Southern Baptist and other schools of nursing. The name Grace McBride was chosen in tribute to the first Southern Baptist nurse appointed by the Foreign Mission Board who died overseas. Miss McBride, appointed to Hwanghsien hospital in China, sailed in Mar., 1916, and two years later she joined the Red Cross to be sent with 471 other nurses to Siberia to serve the American Expeditionary Forces there. She died of typhus fever Dec. 23, 1918, at Tumen, Siberia, "a martyr to a holy cause," and she was awarded the American Red Cross Posthumous Medal and Citation in 1921.

See also YOUNG WOMAN'S AUXILIARY.
JULIETTE MATHER

GRADING IN THE CHURCH EDUCATIONAL PROGRAM. The principle of grading as practiced by Southern Baptists implies the grouping of pupils according to age and providing lesson materials, teaching methods, buildings, and equipment appropriate for the needs of each age group.

A brief look at the history of the modern Sunday school movement aids in understanding this principle.

Although there had been isolated instances where schools somewhat similar in character were initiated by individuals, it is generally agreed that the modern Sunday school movement, as we know it, had its beginnings with Robert Raikes's schools in 1780.

Those first schools, designed to take underprivileged boys and girls off the streets and to teach them the rudiments of education, were graded according to the knowledge of each pupil.

Hence, both in Britain and America, pupils were classified into four general divisions:

Infant—Alphabet and words of one syllable were taught.
Elementary—Words of two or more syllables were taught to pupils still unable to read.
Scripture—For pupils who could read but with difficulty.
Senior—For those who could read the New Testament without difficulty.

Such grading, with local adaptations, continued until the growth of public schools made it unnecessary to teach the rudiments of learning in Sunday schools. Sunday schools then had greater freedom in providing distinctive materials and methods. The purpose of Sunday school changed from teaching pupils to read and write to meeting the spiritual needs of members, and the age basis (for grading) evolved as the accepted method for grading the school.

About the turn of the century, Southern Baptists faced with more seriousness and determination the developing of distinctive methods in grading all educational organizations.

In *The Convention Normal Manual for Sunday School Work*, published in 1909, the following departmental grading plan was proposed: Cradle Roll, birth–3; Beginner, 4–5; Primary, 6–8; Junior, 9–12; Intermediate, 13–15; Senior, 16–20; Adult, 21–up.

In subsequent printings of this manual, the grading for Intermediates and above was changed to the groupings now being followed: Intermediates, 13–16; Young People, 17–24; Adults, 25–up.

In recent years, the provision for small children, birth–3, has been identified as the Nursery department. The term Cradle Roll is now applied to the church's ministry to the little child in the home before enrolment in the Sunday sessions. The present Extension Department ministry for those who are prevented from attendance by work or health reasons grew out of the Home Department of earlier years.

Other methods of grading tried by some churches include grading children and youth groups like the public school and grading adults on the functional basis of interest and need.

The acceptance of the relationship of age to the principle of "change" has been a decisive factor in adopting the age basis as a system for grading. Southern Baptist churches that grade on the age basis practice annual promotion and provide multiple units and departments wherever possible in all organizations. Southern Baptists, generally, feel that this is the most democratic, practical, and workable method that can be utilized in building better churches.
KEENER PHARR

GRAHAM, NORA AGNES (b. Yoakum, Tex., Feb. 22, 1888; d. Concepción, Chile, Jan. 15, 1947). Missionary to Chile. A mission volunteer after hearing Charles Edward Maddry, then pastor of University Baptist Church, Austin, Tex., preach on "The Upward Calling of God in Christ" (Phil. 3:13–14), Miss Graham was appointed to Chile on June 10, 1920. She led in building and directed *Colegio*

Bautista in Temuco, a Baptist school patronized by many Catholic families. Miss Graham, greatly loved by Chilean Baptists, was author of *Pioneering with Christ in Chile*.

BIBLIOGRAPHY: *The Commission* (1947). A. Graham, *Pioneering with Christ in Chile* (1942). *Charles E. Maddry: Autobiography* (1955). C. E. Maddry, *Christ's Expendables* (1949).   E. C. ROUTH

GRAND CANYON COLLEGE. An institution owned and operated by the Baptist General Convention of Arizona. It was approved by the Glendale session of the convention in 1946; trustees were selected by the convention's executive board in Mar., 1947; and the charter was received Aug. 1, 1949. The school opened in temporary quarters in an armory at Prescott, Ariz., in Sept., 1949. The first president was Willis J. Ray. There were 123 enrolled the first year. In the summer of 1951, the college was moved to a permanent 160-acre campus at 3300 West Camelback Road, Phoenix. Leroy Smith was then the president. Other presidents have been B. O. Herring and Loyed R. Simmons. The first graduating class (1951) had six members. At the end of the first seven years the graduates numbered 115. In 1955 the college had 10 semi-permanent and 10 temporary buildings, property valued at $536,164.41, a debt of $439,806.39, an operating budget of $285,076.50, and 396 students. Grand Canyon College is fully accredited by the state board of education for the certification of elementary teachers, for renewal of certificates, and for undergraduate training of high school teachers. The college is approved by the Veteran's Administration for the education of veterans and by the Immigration and Naturalization Service of the United States Government for alien students.   VERNON E. SHIPP

GRAND LAKE BAPTIST ASSEMBLY. Located seven miles northeast of Grove, Okla., founded in 1951 by Northeastern Baptist Association. The original property consisted of 60 acres of land adjacent to Grand Lake with 24 buildings, and it was purchased from the Tulsa YMCA for $20,000. It is owned by the Northeastern Association, whose executive committee sets the time of its meetings and in annual session elects its trustees. Governed by is own constitution, the assembly elects its officers annually, has separate committees in charge of various phases of its work, and makes reports to the association in annual session. Total enrolment at the assembly and auxiliary camps in 1955 was 459, and in 1956 property value was $100,000. It is financed by registration fees of those attending, designated gifts from churches, and a $500 annual supplement from the Baptist General Convention of Oklahoma.

J. M. GASKIN

GRAND VALLEY HOSPITAL (PRYOR, OKLA.). The county commissioners of Mayes County requested the Oklahoma convention to lease this new 40-bed hospital on a 25-year agreement at $25 per year. The lease was signed Oct. 29, 1954, and the hospital opened Dec. 9, 1954. Building and equipment are valued at $450,000.   TOM E. CARTER

GRANT, WILLIAM CALLAWAY (b. Habbersham County, Ga., Sept. 7, 1864; d. Portales, N. Mex., June 1, 1947). Pastor, teacher, newspaper publisher, associational missionary, children's home superintendent, fighter of "unionism." Son of John Cisero and Alie Lovenia (Deavours) Grant, the oldest of their 11 children, Grant moved to Brownwood, Tex., in Dec., 1885. Educated at Salt Creek High School and Howard Payne College, he was converted at 23 and baptized. He was elected deacon, licensed to preach in July, 1887, ordained in 1891, and called to the pastorate of Salt Creek Church. The father of six children, five girls and one boy, Grant arrived in Elida, N. Mex., in 1902, where he was co-owner and publisher of the newspaper *Elida News*. He served as an associational missionary for Portales Association from 1902 to 1909, assisting in organizing churches at Clovis, Texico, Fort Sumner, House, McAlister, Taft, and Dunlop; and for Central Association from 1909 to 1926, during which time he was mission pastor at Vaughn, Mountainair, and Venus, where he served 14 years. While missionary for the eastern area from 1926 to 1929, Grant had half-time pastorates at Belen and Forrest. He was superintendent of the children's home from 1929 to 1937, when he retired.   MRS. RICHARD THOMAS BAKER, SR.

GRAVES, HENRY LEE (b. Yanceyville, N. C., Feb. 22, 1813; d. Brenham, Tex., Dec. 4, 1881). Pastor, university president, educator. After graduating from the University of North Carolina in 1835, Graves tutored in mathematics at Wake Forest College from 1835 to 1837, and taught at Cave Springs, Ga., in 1838. Three years later he entered Hamilton Theological Seminary in New York, and returned to Georgia in 1843 to teach at Covington. While there he received notice Jan. 12, 1846, that he had been elected to the presidency of Baylor University at Independence, Tex., and called as pastor of the Independence Baptist Church. Graves served as president of the Baptist state convention in 1848, and was chairman of the convention which reorganized the Baptist Educational Society in 1872. During his administration of Baylor, enrolment increased, lectures in law were begun, and a substantial stone building was nearing completion when, because of trouble with his voice, he resigned on June 13, 1851, and retired to his plantation near Brenham. From 1859 to 1868, Graves served as principal of Fairfield Female Academy.

BIBLIOGRAPHY: G. J. Burleson, *Life and Writings of Rufus C. Burleson* (1901). J. M. Carroll, *A History of Texas Baptists* (1923). J. B. Link, *Texas Biographical and Historical Magazine* (c. 1891). L. M. Russell, "Life of Henry Lea Graves" (1955). Texas State Historical Association, *The Handbook of Texas* (1952).

GUY B. HARRISON, JR.

GRAVES, JAMES ROBINSON (b. Chester, Vt., Apr. 10, 1820; d. Memphis, Tenn., June 26, 1893). Preacher, publisher, author, and editor. He influenced Southern Baptist life of the 19th century in more ways, and probably to a greater degree, than any other person. As an agitator and controversialist of the first magnitude, he kept his denomination in almost continual and often bitter controversy for about 30 years. He also engaged in frequent and prolonged debates and controversies with outstanding representatives of other denominations. Being magnetic and dynamic, he won the enthusiastic and loyal support of thousands; but being acrimonious in his disputations and attacks, he made many determined enemies. For four decades he traveled from Maryland to Texas, enthralling great throngs who listened to him, often for hours, in amazement and rapt attention. Thomas Treadwell Eaton, in an editorial on his death, wrote: "We have seen him hold a congregation packed uncomfortably, for three hours and a half without any sign of weariness on their part. This was not done once or twice, but scores of times."

Although of Congregational heritage, he joined a Baptist church at the age of 15. At 19 he, with his mother and sister, moved to northern Ohio, and he became principal of a school which his elder brother Zuinglius Calvin Graves, who was teaching near by, had procured for him. He had had almost no schooling, because he had become fatherless when two weeks of age, and his father's business partner had defrauded his mother of the estate which his father had left. He, therefore, had to learn each night what he was to teach the next day.

Two years later (1841) he took charge of a school near Nicholasville, Ky. There, without a teacher, he learned a language each year for four years, completed the equivalent of a college education, and made a detailed study of the Bible. The neighboring Mount Freedom Baptist Church, which he joined, soon licensed him to preach and in 1844 ordained him.

He went to Nashville, Tenn., July, 1845, to teach, and joined the First Baptist Church. Soon afterward he became pastor of the Second Baptist Church (later, Central) and served it for about a year. When Robert Boyté Crawford Howell (*q.v.*) gave his newspaper *The Baptist* to the Baptist General Association of Tennessee and North Alabama, Nov., 1846, the association, through its education board, elected Graves assistant editor and made him and A. B. Shankland publishers and depository agents. They then established a bookstore. When Howell resigned as editor in June, 1848, Graves succeeded him. He edited the paper either as *The Baptist* or as the *Tennessee Baptist* until Aug., 1889, when it became *Baptist and Reflector*. Through it he reached thousands of people all over the South, the circulation at one time having been about 12,000. For some years after 1869 it also served as the official paper for Arkansas, Louisiana, and Mississippi, as well as for Tennessee.

Graves led in the Landmark movement from its beginning in 1851 and sought to make its ideology dominant in Southern Baptist life. During 1854–58, when Amos Cooper Dayton (*q.v.*) was corresponding secretary of the Southern Baptist Convention Bible Board (Nashville, 1851–62), Landmarkers were in control. Dayton resigned under pressure in Apr., 1858. Growing out of the conflict that developed, the Southern Baptist Convention in 1859 appointed no Landmarkers from Nashville to serve on the Bible Board.

Through his paper and through correspondence and travel, Graves, in 1858–59, led in a determined effort to take from the Foreign Mission Board its power to examine, choose, support, and direct its missionaries, on the ground that these were the rights of churches and associations, or groups of churches that might wish to work together. At Richmond, Va., in May, 1859, the Convention gave more than a day to the Graves proposals. Graves himself spoke for several hours. The atmosphere was tense, but the Convention at last voted unanimously not to make any change. It did provide that churches who sent out their own missionaries might send funds at their own expense through the Foreign Mission Board for the support of their missionaries. The gospel mission movement that developed among a few Southern Baptist missionaries in China (1886–93), and the Landmark Baptist conventions in Arkansas and Texas, organized about 1905, were logical developments of the views Graves sought to implement at Richmond in 1859.

In the 1850's Graves became a severe and sustained critic of the Southern Baptist Publication Society, Charleston, S. C. (1847–63), largely through the *Tennessee Baptist,* for what he considered its doctrinal deviations and its failure to meet the needs of the people. Through his paper, a tract society which he organized, and his publishing firm of Graves, Marks and Co., he became an active competitor of the publication society. He saw clearly the importance of the Sunday school and made Sunday school libraries available to the people. In 1857 he led in an effort to establish the Southern Baptist Sunday School Union. Strong opposition delayed complete organization until Nov., 1858, when, at Memphis, Tenn., several hundred made it a 100 per cent Landmark Union and located it at Nashville. It led a precarious existence until Feb., 1862, when the Union Army captured Nashville. Graves, Marks and Co. (the South Western Publishing House) and the *Tennessee Baptist* were heavy losers from Federal occupation, and were dormant until Feb., 1867. Then they began again in Memphis, the paper as *The Baptist*, and the publishing firm as Graves, Jones and Co. This private business, having insufficient funds, became in Dec., 1868, a stock company called the Southwestern Publishing Company. Several causes combined to bring about its collapse in Aug., 1871, with heavy losses to its stockholders.

The Sunday School Union was also moved to Memphis, 1867, where efforts failed to revitalize it. Graves and his associates then offered to give its very limited assets to the Sunday School Board of the Southern Baptist Convention, should it be moved to Memphis. The Convention considered this proposal at its 1867 session in Memphis but took no action. In 1868, at Baltimore, after full discussion, it voted by about three to one to accept the proposal. Discussions through the year had revealed a widespread desire among the people for a united Sunday school effort and the cessation of denominational strife.

However, moving the board from Greenville, S. C., to Memphis and its absorption of the union did not remove denominational tensions and weaknesses. Because of them, as well as problems inherent in the Reconstruction era and the panic of 1873, the Convention, at Mobile in 1873, consolidated the Sunday School Board with the Domestic and Indian Mission Board.

About 1869 Graves became convinced that the Sunday School Board would fail, and that, when it did so, the American Baptist Publication Society would provide Sunday school literature for the South. This led him, in 1870 at the Big Hatchie Association, to which the Memphis churches belonged, to propose the organization of another Southern Baptist Publication Society and to present a constitution and by-laws for it. (It had no relation whatever to the society by the same name which had its headquarters at Charleston, S. C., from its organization in 1847 until its end in late 1863 or soon thereafter.) The association gave hearty approval, and Graves went afield to raise funds. He procured pledges (bonds) and cash totaling $108,000, of which $50,000 was due Jan. 1, 1873. The society, relying on these pledges, bought a building, equipped it, and began printing in the fall of 1873. Nonpayment of most of the pledges, mismanagement, internal friction, and other causes led to its collapse in the spring of 1877 and its complete liquidation some months later. This failure ended Graves's efforts of more than 25 years to provide Southern Baptists with the kind of literature he thought they ought to have.

A succession of financial reverses in connection with his various publishing enterprises through the years, the deaths of his mother and wife from yellow fever in Memphis within a week of each other (1867), his paralytic stroke in Aug., 1884, a fall in his yard in early 1889 that crushed his side and put him in an invalid's chair for the rest of his life, and other sobering experiences during his years of almost unceasing conflict, produced in him a notable change in thought, attitude, manner, and disposition. A reading of his writings in *The Baptist* after 1877, the year his publication society failed, reveals that the man of thunder and conflict had subsided and a man of gentler and sweeter spirit was developing. He gave much less attention to controversial matters and dealt much more gently with those who did not agree with him. He magnified the doctrines of grace and preached with tenderness and love, becoming a revered and widely loved man. It is this Graves his friends and admirers, and their descendants, largely remember.

Graves held numerous denominational offices. He organized three tract societies (1847, 1869, and 1883). He organized the Nashville Indian and Missionary Association in 1846, and manifested a life-long interest in the Indians. He was one of the leaders in organizing Mary Sharp College (for women) at Winchester, Tenn., in 1850. He raised the money with which to endow the chair of theology of Union University. He established and was main editor of a quarterly, *The Christian Review* (1855-60), published for six years by his printing company, Graves, Marks and Co.

In addition to his editorials and articles, vast in number through the years, he was the author of the following books: *The Desire of All Nations, The Watchman's Reply, The Trilemma, The First Baptist Church in America, The Great Iron Wheel, The Little Iron Wheel, The Bible Doctrine of the Middle Life, Exposition of Modern Spiritism, The Little Seraph, Old Landmarkism, What Is It?* and *The Work of Christ in Seven Dispensations*.

With the assistance of James Madison Pendleton (*q.v.*), Graves published *The Southern Psalmist* (1858). He compiled and published *The New Baptist Psalmist for Churches and Sunday Schools* (1873), the preface of which states, "in this collection there will be found no hymns that teach the doctrine of baptismal remission or ritual efficacy, no praises to be sung to dead relatives or friends, nor are children taught to pray to the angels, or to desire to be angels."

Graves was an invalid for nearly 10 years after Aug. 17, 1884, when he had a stroke while preaching a sermon in the First Baptist Church, Memphis. He recovered sufficiently, after some months, to walk with a stick for several years. Then a fall in his yard put him in a wheel chair the rest of his life. He traveled over wide areas and made "chair talks," as he called them. His mind was clear and strong, though his body was enfeebled. He died June 26, 1893.

All the Baptist papers had editorials that gave an appraisal of Graves. Alfred Elijah Dickinson, in the *Religious Herald*, said:

As is well known by all who are acquainted with Baptist controversy in the South, the *Religious Herald* has constantly antagonized the Old Landmark theory, of which Brother Graves was the chief champion through all his public career, and we differed widely from him also on some other things. Pretty generally we were upon opposing sides, but through these two-score years of occasional earnest controversies we have never failed to give our deceased brother full credit for his candor, ability and enthusiastic devotion to what he believed to be the teaching of God's word.

Editors A. J. S. Thomas and W. W. Keys of *The Baptist Courier* wrote:

> He was a great power in some directions, and while he did his denomination great service in . . . particular lines, yet it is also true that in some other very important, even necessary denominational enterprises, his influence was not felt. In many respects he was a great and useful man. He stands out among his brethren a remarkable, exceptional and unique character.

BIBLIOGRAPHY: W. W. Barnes, *The Southern Baptist Convention, 1845–1953* (1954). J. H. Borum, *Biographical Sketches of Tennessee Baptist Ministers* (1880). J. J. Burnett, *Sketches of Tennessee's Pioneer Bapist Preachers* (1919). W. Cathcart, *The Baptist Encyclopedia* (1881). J. R. Graves, *Old Landmarkism: What It Is* (1928). J. H. Grime, *History of Middle Tennessee Baptists* (1902). O. L. Hailey, *J. R. Graves: Life, Times, and Teachings* (1929). H. C. Irby, *History of First Baptist Church, Jackson, Tennessee, 1837–1912* (n.d.). F. M. Masters, *A History of Baptists in Kentucky* (1933). D. B. Ray, *Baptist Succession* (1883). J. H. Spencer, *A History of Kentucky Baptists from 1769 to 1885* (1885). R. G. Torbet, *A History of the Baptists* (1950).

HOMER L. GRICE

GRAVES, ROSEWELL HOBART (b. Baltimore, Md., May 29, 1833; d. Canton, China, June 3, 1912). Pioneer missionary to China. After graduation from St. Mary's College, Graves studied medicine and was appointed a missionary by the Foreign Mission Board in 1856. A pioneer missionary in Kwangtung and Kwangsi provinces, he lived in the cities of Shiuhing and Canton, and worked in the West, Fu, and North River areas of South China. Graves never established a hospital but practiced medicine as he traveled. His greatest work, however, was preaching, teaching, and writing.

He founded Graves Theological Seminary because he realized that Christianity, to be permanent, needed a solid foundation of local churches led by Chinese pastors. He started this move by inviting a few prospective preachers to study the Bible in his home, combining three months of study with three months of preaching in the early program. The seminary with as many as 10 teachers, which grew out of the original class, trained hundreds of Chinese pastors during its 75-year history. Graves preferred to have prospective pastors prove their character, fitness, and ability before ordination. However, he encouraged the churches to pay their pastors.

Graves mastered the Chinese language. His books and tracts covered the whole realm of Christian doctrine and experience. Many people traced their conversion directly to reading his "Truth Manifested," a tract printed in successive editions for more than half a century. Among those converts was Chang Wen-kai, who edited *True Light Magazine* for many years. Graves was chosen as one of the best Chinese scholars to work with the committee on Bible translation.

J. T. WILLIAMS

GRAVES (JAMES ROBINSON) PUBLICATION ORGANIZATIONS. Graves (*q.v.*) as nearly self-educated as a man could have been, and without previous training for such work, became assistant editor of *The Baptist*, Nov., 1846, at age 27, a month after R. B. C. Howell (*q.v.*) gave the paper to the Baptist General Association of Tennessee. At the same time he and Alexander B. Shankland contracted to publish the paper and become agents for the Tennessee Baptist Depository. For about 40 years he gave much time to being an author, editor, publisher, and bookseller. He knew clearly from the beginning what he wanted to do as a publisher, and incorporated it in the constitution of the Tennessee Baptist Publication Society which he organized in the fall of 1847, and for which he procured a charter Feb. 2, 1848, namely: "to purchase and publish Bibles, Testaments, religious and Sabbath school books, tracts and other publications of theological, church, and a moral tendency, and the same to sell, and distribute gratuitously in the destitute portions of our country through colporters and otherwise." It was to be the organ of the Baptists of Tennessee and other states that wished to co-operate. Graves was its corresponding secretary.

The Baptist was transferred to the society in 1848. The society functioned poorly, did little, met rarely, and lent its funds of some $1,300 to Graves & Shankland, Agents. After some years, it became impossible to get a quorum at the directors' meetings, Graves took over the paper, and Graves & Shankland took over its funds. They dropped "Agents" after the firm name. When Graves and Shankland dissolved partnership in 1854, W. P. Marks, a brother-in-law of Graves, became Graves's partner. When J. B. Rutland bought an interest in the firm in Sept., 1855, it became Graves, Marks & Co., and adopted the trade name of South-Western Publishing House. In their first advertisement, Sept. 15, 1855, they said: "We design immediately to add the required presses and machinery until this house is complete in all the apartments and facilities for the prosecution of the publishing business upon a scale of magnitude commensurate with the wants of the great West and Southwest." All its advertisements carried South-Western Publishing House at the top, and Graves, Marks & Co. at the bottom.

Graves was critical of the Southern Baptist Publication Society, Charleston, S. C., from its beginning in 1847 until its end in 1863. (It was about six months older than the Tennessee Publication Society.) He was impatient with its minor accomplishments and critical of much it did and published. He established depositories for his publishing house in some states, and sought to make the *Tennessee Baptist* (the name of *The Baptist* after 1847) the dominant paper in many of them. His publishing house and his paper became the media for printing and distributing Landmark literature after he launched the Landmark movement in 1851. His aggressiveness brought him increasingly into conflict with many of the editors and other leaders in the Southern Baptist Convention. The "South" meant the states from Maryland to and including Alabama. The "Southwest" included Kentucky, Tennessee, Mississippi, and the states west of them. Graves's editorials and public efforts, and the name of his publishing house, made it clear that he purposed to make his company dominant in the Baptist life of the Southwest, and to gain as much influence as possible in the Southern states, especially Alabama and Georgia.

In an editorial, Nov. 17, 1855, Graves commented on the recently established Southern Methodist Publishing House, Nashville, and its vast output of literature. (It was on the opposite corner of the public square from his own house.) He asserted that his company could furnish the antidote for the Methodist "poison." He therefore appealed for Baptist support, not only because of what his house had already done, but also for what it was doing, and would do in even greater measure. He hoped, with God's blessings, that it would soon become a mighty force in the Southwest and the South, and be able to "snap its finger in the face of the Concern over the way, for its [his house] little finger may be thicker than even the thigh of that great concern."

Rutland, because of his health, sold his interest in the company Mar., 1857. Immediately thereafter A. C. Rogers of Chattanooga, and E. F. P. Poole of Virginia, each bought a fourth interest in the company. According to Graves, this put the company "upon a foundation broad and secure."

Graves tried unsuccessfully at the Southern Baptist Convention, Louisville, 1857, to move the *Home and Foreign Mission Journal* from Richmond to Nashville. When the Southern Baptist Sunday School Union began operations in Nashville in Jan., 1859, Graves, Marks & Co. underbid all other bidders by 40 per cent to do its printing. Thereafter it did the printing of the union until it ceased its work in Feb., 1862, following the capture of Nashville by the Union army. This capture also brought heavy loss to Graves, Marks & Co. and its South-Western Publishing House. They remained dormant until Feb., 1867, when, at Memphis, Graves, Marks & Co. became Graves, Jones & Co. P. S. Jones, a Baptist layman of Memphis, invested heavily in the company, but it was almost immediately in financial distress. Graves then, Oct., 1868, organized a stock company, the Southwestern Publishing Company, which absorbed Graves, Jones & Co. and the South-Western Publishing House. He went afield to sell stock. On the strength of what was sold, but mostly unpaid, the company bought a large building, invested heavily in equipment, and made large claims for itself, but it went into receivership in early 1871.

Graves anticipated this failure by 1870, for that fall at the Big Hatchie Association, of which the Memphis churches were members, he procured their enthusiastic endorsement of the Southern Baptist Publication Society, for which he presented a constitution. (It bore the same name as the Southern Baptist Publication Society, Charleston, but had no connection with or relationship to it in any way.) In reality it was not a society in the usual sense of the word, but a stock company of Baptists, whose purpose was to publish religious books and tracts, and promote "evangelical religion by means of the printing press and colportage."

Graves traveled far and wide, spoke often, and labored heroically to raise funds. He procured pledges totaling more than $100,000, of which about one fifth was paid. He was both president and general agent of the society but later withdrew from it because of criticism that arose. The society bought much equipment from the bankrupt Southwestern Publishing Company, and a building and much new equipment on the strength of the stock that had been sold. It began operations in the fall of 1873, made great claims, gave glowing accounts of its progress, and almost immediately paid the stockholders a 10 per cent dividend. However, the financial conditions prevailing, bad management, and the lack of funds led to its failure by May, 1877, and its complete liquidation in early 1878.

This collapse was, no doubt, a keen disappointment to Graves, for he had seen the approaching end of the first Baptist Sunday School Board after its removal to Memphis in 1868, when it absorbed the tiny remnants of the Southern Baptist Sunday School Union. It was abolished by the Southern Baptist Convention in May, 1873, and its assets, liabilities, and work assigned to the Domestic Mission Board. This left Southern Baptists without a publication house, and Graves was determined that his Southern Baptist Publication Society should fill the void. He disliked and actively opposed the American Baptist Publication Society, which, inactive in the South from 1847 until the close of the Civil War, was again aggressively entering a vast and needy field, and determined to supply Southern Baptists with religious literature of all kinds.

The failure of the Southern Baptist Publication Society after an effort of slightly more than three years brought to a close Graves's long, ambitious, arduous, and unsuccessful efforts to achieve the purpose he set forth in the charter of the Tennessee Baptist Publication Society, Feb. 2, 1848. He kept the ownership of the *Tennessee Baptist*, again called *The Baptist* after its removal to Memphis in 1867. He established the Southern Baptist Book House, Memphis, of which Graves & Son were at first the proprietors, and then Graves & Mehaffey.

If Graves had succeeded in his publishing efforts, Southern Baptists would have found it increasingly difficult to free themselves from the domination of his publishing house, over which the Southern Baptist Convention had no control. On the other hand, his series of failures, and the unfortunate experiences of both the first Sunday School Board and the Southern Baptist Sunday School Union made Southern Baptists skeptical about establishing another Sunday School Board or a publishing house. Instead, many were convinced that either private companies should print and sell religious literature to them, or that the American Baptist Publication Society should again serve them. This largely explains why the Southern Baptist Convention did not authorize its second Sunday School Board until May, 1891, and did not permit it to publish books until after May, 1910.

Graves's failure as a publisher resulted largely from too ambitious efforts, insufficient funds, bad management, and bitter controversies with many people and organizations that alienated them. He was a tireless worker and a superb promoter, but a poor businessman. He had a great vision and a deep insight into the book needs of preachers, families, churches, and Sunday schools. To make his vision real he gave his best, often sacrificially, for many years. He probably did more than anyone to make Southern Baptists conscious of their need for religious books and publications.   HOMER L. GRICE

GRAVES THEOLOGICAL SEMINARY, CANTON. See CHINA, MISSION IN.

GRAVES-HOWELL CONTROVERSY (1857–62). Between James Robinson Graves (*q.v.*) and Robert Boyté Crawford Howell (*q.v.*), it was personal, doctrinal, ecclesiastical, and denominational. It originated with two great men who were personally allergic to each other, but it soon became primarily a controversy between Graves and the First Baptist Church, Nashville, Tenn., the several state conventions, and the Southern Baptist Convention. Bitter, intense, devastating, it involved many people, dangerously threatened to split the denomination, and injured it seriously for many years.

Graves went to Nashville, July, 1845, to open a school. A stranger and almost without funds, he joined the First Baptist Church, of which Howell was pastor. Howell gave *The Baptist* (later the *Baptist and Reflector*) to the Baptist General Association of Tennessee and North Alabama in Oct., 1846. Through its board of education, the association contracted with Graves and Alex B. Shankland to publish the paper and made Graves assistant editor. When Howell resigned as editor, June, 1848, Graves (then 28) became editor.

Howell left Nashville, July, 1850, having been pastor there since Jan. 1, 1835, to become pastor of the Second Baptist Church, Richmond, Va.; but he returned to Nashville July 15, 1857, for his second pastorate. Meantime, Graves had become the acknowledged leader among Tennessee Baptists. The *Tennessee Baptist*, formerly *The Baptist*, had the largest and most widely distributed circulation of any Baptist paper in the South. Graves, Marks & Co., operating under the trade name of South-Western Publishing House (owned by four men who were members of the First Baptist Church), wished to be for Southern Baptists what the Methodist Book Concern was to the Methodists.

Critical of and hostile to the Southern Baptist Publication Society, Charleston, S. C. (organized 1847), Graves had a prolonged personal controversy in 1857–58 with J. P. Tustin, secretary of the society and also editor of the society's paper, the *Southern Baptist*. This wrangle led "Philander" to say in the *Southwestern Baptist*, Alabama, Aug. 6, 1857, that it deeply pained him that such wholly personal matters should be given to the public, especially in religious periodicals and about ministers, involving mutual friends in their acrimonious spirit, injuring the cause of Christ in general, and doing incalculable damage to the denomination.

Graves, an innate controversialist and formidable antagonist, also had heated controversies with the editors of the *New Orleans Weekly Baptist Chronicle* (1853–54), and the *Western Recorder*, Kentucky (1855). He was deeply involved (1854–56) with a fellow church member, William P. Jones, a physician. When the church failed to reconcile them, it invited an outside committee of five, with J. B. Taylor, secretary of the Foreign Mission Board, as chairman, to aid it, but its efforts were only partially successful.

The Big Hatchie Association, Tennessee, launched the Landmark movement in 1851 at Cotton Grove. Graves immediately became its leader and labored hard and long to make Landmarkism dominant in the Southern Baptist Convention. He enlisted two able associates, J. M. Pendleton (*q.v.*) and A. C. Dayton (*q.v.*), who soon became his associate editors. Pendleton became professor of theology at Union University in 1857 and pastor of the Baptist church at Murfreesboro, Tenn., and taught Landmarkism to the ministerial students. Dayton became secretary of the Southern Baptist Bible Board, Nashville, in Sept., 1854, succeeding William C. Buck, secretary from the board's beginning in 1851.

Graves knew the value of the Sunday school for teaching doctrines. His company had published many books for a Sunday school library. He and Dayton saw the need for Baptist Sunday school lesson materials for Southern Baptists. Their plans for providing it precipitated the famous controversy.

About two weeks after Howell's return to Nashville, the Concord Association held its annual session. By request Howell introduced a resolution, which was adopted, calling for a Southern Baptist Sunday school convention in Nashville, Oct. 23, 1857, just prior to the annual session of the Baptist General Association of Tennessee and North Alabama. When it met, 72 were present from Tennessee, and nine from outside the state. Two were from Virginia on personal or official business; one, from the

Southern Baptist Publication Society, Charleston, S. C.; and a missionary, from the Indian Territory. Of the other five, at least three were Landmarkers—two from Alabama, and one each from Georgia, Kentucky, and Mississippi.

Howell had supposed this would be a convention like others that had been previously held, but it was not. Dayton presented a constitution for a new organization, the Southern Baptist Sunday School Union, and led in the struggle for its establishment. One object was to provide and recommend suitable Sunday school books and periodicals. The corresponding secretary was to edit the books. The officers and seven managers were to contract with authors, publishers, and agents. After a heated discussion the organization was approved and the constitution adopted. The officers were: Dayton, president; Graves, recording secretary; and J. E. Sharpe, a Landmarker from Georgia, corresponding secretary. Of the seven managers elected, two were or had been part owners of Graves, Marks & Co., and some of the others were Landmarkers.

Howell, surprised, opposed the new union because (1) it would be another, and therefore unneeded, publication society; (2) too few were present to justify calling it Southern; and (3) it might be suspected by some to have been created to advance the interests of a private publishing firm. Besides, Howell was against Landmarkism and a supporter of the Southern Baptist Publication Society.

After its temporary organization the union adjourned to meet at Americus, Ga., Apr., 1858, just prior to the annual meeting of the Georgia Baptist Convention, where it was hoped a large number from over the South would effect a permanent organization. Graves, through his paper, urged Landmarkers to attend and control the meeting. The Americus church, because of the tense situation that developed, asked that the meeting not be held there. Graves and his associates then planned a meeting at Memphis, Tenn., Dec., 1858, where a 100 per cent Landmark Union was organized with enthusiasm.

The *Christian Index*, Georgia, Jan. 6, 1858, printed a letter from Howell explaining his opposition to the union and its board of managers, several of whom were his close personal friends. In February Graves, in his paper, assailed Howell for the article, and through the following months intensified his opposition to him, both personally, and because of his connection with the Bible Board, of which he (Howell) was an ex officio member as president of the Southern Baptist Convention. (He was in his fourth two-year term, having succeeded William B. Johnson, the first president, in 1851.) Strong opposition to Dayton developed in the board in the fall of 1857, primarily to some of his managerial procedures, and secondarily to his giving so much time to matters relating to the Sunday School Union. He resigned under pressure Apr. 5, 1858. Graves charged in his paper of May 15 that Dayton "was driven from his work he so dearly loved by an anti-Landmark combination that had its head [Howell] in this city, and a mouthpiece in Knoxville [Hillsman, ed., *Baptist Watchman*], Tuskegee [Samuel Henderson, ed., *Southwestern Baptist*], and Charleston [J. P. Tustin, sec., Southern Baptist Publication Society, and ed., *Southern Baptist*]." After Dayton's resignation Graves became an implacable enemy of the Bible Board. He attacked the character of the two men who, in a brief period, succeeded Dayton. He sought, but without success, to abolish the board at the Southern Baptist Convention in 1859 and then failed in his efforts to have it moved to Macon, Ga.

The First Baptist Church, through some of its members, tried to get Graves to cease his published and oral attacks on their pastor, but without success. Graves maintained that Howell was persecuting him and was determined to ruin him. July 17, 1858, he printed a long article which presented a hypothetical situation in which he presupposed that Dayton had been charged by anti-Landmark members of the Bible Board with deception and heinous wrongdoing; that board members had egregiously misrepresented him and treated him foully; that Dayton had published his defense, in which he had exposed their recent report, vindicated himself, and convicted them; that then, as a last resort, charges had been preferred against him in the church, and that a majority had pronounced him guilty and excluded him. Graves then predicted what would follow:

Another church would rehear Dayton's case and, assisted by a council, vote that he had been persecuted and greatly wronged and was innocent, and then receive him. The Concord Association would pronounce one of the churches in disorder. At this time, personal considerations would be brought in. The whole transaction would be charged upon Landmark Baptists or the editor of the *Tennessee Baptist* to divide and make a party. As a result, the association would divide, and churches throughout Tennessee and over the South would take sides. All this division would be charged to Landmarkers, but Dayton's innocence would be the real cause, should the denomination sustain him.

Graves then said that it was possible for churches sometimes to be used by an influential pastor to effect the ruin or lasting injury of an innocent member not altogether acceptable to him; and that he had lately heard of a pastor [Howell] who, when speaking about the exclusion of an influential member whom he opposed, said that his exclusion from the church would ruin him. Finally, assuming his suppositions were true, he wrote: "This is to confess a phase of designing craft and depravity unconceived of by us. What blasphemy! Using the church of God to gratify the feelings of personal revenge upon an innocent brother."

In this supposed case Graves was actually presenting his own case in advance and suggesting what would happen should the church exclude him. Sept. 8, 1858, the church preferred charges against him but gave him time to think over the matters involved. The trial began Oct. 12, and ended Oct. 18. The charge was "grossly immoral [nothing pertaining to sex] and unchristian conduct" with five specifications: (1) that he had sought to bring upon the pastor reproach and injury, and thus destroy his character and influence in the Southwest by forcing him into collision with Rev. A. C. Dayton, late corresponding secretary of the Bible Board, and now one of his associate editors, through the publication in his paper of various false and malicious misrepresentations; (2) that he had endeavored to distract and divide the church by means of a conflict between the pastor and four of the deacons, and several other influential members, which conflict he had labored to produce by various inflammatory articles published in his paper; (3) that he had uttered and published in his paper, against the pastor, sundry foul and atrocious libels; (4) that he had at various times in his paper attacked, slandered, and abused ministers and brethren of high character belonging to the denomination throughout the country; and (5) that he had uttered and published nine wilful and deliberate falsehoods.

Graves, accompanied by a number of supporters from in and around Nashville (not members of the church) attended the church conference. He spoke at length to a motion that the charges be dropped and insisted that the church proceed in harmony with Matthew 18:15-17, as the matters at issue were strictly personal. About midnight the church voted, 91 to 48, to proceed with the trial, whereupon Graves and about 23 other members withdrew and declared that they were the First Baptist Church, and the majority were no church but a faction. They elected Graves pastor and publicized themselves as the First Baptist Church. The church, which had obtained a charter Mar., 1858, at once warned them that legal action would be taken against them if they continued to call themselves the First Baptist Church. They then called themselves the Spring Street Baptist Church, saying: "We declare ourselves to be the regular and scriptural church of the Lord Jesus worshiping in this place; and in his name, claim for ourselves, as his true and proper church, all the rights, privileges, and authority which are by his word conferred upon his church."

The church tried Graves *in absentia*, found him guilty on all seven counts, with only one dissenting vote on one count, and excluded him Oct. 18. It then published its proceedings in a booklet, *The Trial of J. R. Graves*.

The Baptist General Association of Tennessee and North Alabama met at Lebanon five days later (Oct. 23) and, by an overwhelming vote, received those sent by the minority as the messengers of the First Baptist Church. The association refused to recognize those sent by the church, to permit them to be heard, or to receive their written protest, thereby declaring that the church, because it tried and excluded Graves, ceased to be a church.

The church immediately preferred charges against eight men, including Dayton and three deacons, for schism and specified seven counts. It postponed their trial because of Dayton's illness, but on Feb. 15, 1859, tried them *in absentia* and excluded them. Ten days later, it excluded 15 others of the minority, most of whom were employees or part owners of the South-Western Publishing House, employees of the *Tennessee Baptist*, or members of the families of the men involved. Nov. 9, 1859, the church excluded 21 others who had gone with the minority, and, Apr. 4, 1860, two more. This made a total of 47 excluded from several hundred members.

At the request of Spring Street Church, 40 men from 20 churches of the Concord Association, sitting as a council, heard Graves's side of the matter Mar. 1-3, 1859, with no one present from First Church. Each charge made by the church was presented in order, with Graves speaking to it (16 hours in all). The council voted on each count that he was innocent; that, from the evidence presented, it believed Howell and others had determined to ruin Graves and had tried him for that purpose; that Graves was justified in refusing to stand trial because of his unscriptural arraignment; that the actions of the church were null and void; that the minority did right in withdrawing from the disorderly dominant part (not the majority because a majority of the members were not present); and that by violating Christ's law (Matt. 18:15-17) it forfeited its right to be a church and became a faction. The Spring Street Church approved the findings and had them printed in a book, *Both Sides* (1859).

The Concord Association approved the council's findings at its July, 1859, session and, upon the recommendations of a special committee of which J. M. Pendleton was chairman, seated the messengers from Spring Street Church and refused to seat those from First Church.

The general association, at its annual meeting at Shelbyville in Oct., 1859, elected as officers three men who had been excluded by First Church: A. C. Dayton, moderator; J. B. Rutland, corresponding secretary; and A. B. Shankland, treasurer.

Because First Church had no way by which to present its case to the public at large, some members began a paper, the *Baptist Standard*, Nov. 10, 1858, and continued it until Dec., 1860. L. B. Woolfolk, a member of the church, proved to be an able editor who wrote simply, cogently, and objectively. He made clear the ecclesiastical and other issues that had been raised. Other Baptist papers gave more or less space to the broadening controversy, with some supporting Spring Street Church and others, First Church. The *Southwestern Baptist*, Alabama, attacked Graves as vehemently as Graves, through the years, had attacked many, including Howell.

Graves's next step was to defeat Howell for re-election as president of the Southern Baptist Convention at its Richmond session, May, 1859 (Howell had been president eight years), and get the Convention to approve the actions of the Concord Association and the general association concerning First Church, Nashville. He urged his followers to aid him in defeating Howell. Moreover, he was attacking both the Convention and its boards as unscriptural, and at the same time trying to get the conventions in other states to intervene in his behalf. Men like J. B. Taylor (*q.v.*), Foreign Mission Board, and John Albert Broadus (*q.v.*) were gravely concerned about the Southern Baptist Convention's existence, should this controversy get into its deliberations. Howell won on the first ballot against Jeremiah Bell Jeter (*q.v.*), Richard Fuller (*q.v.*), and some scattering votes. He accepted the office but immediately resigned, saying that he did not want personal matters to be injected into the proceedings of the Convention. It accepted his resignation and elected Fuller to succeed him.

Reference has been made to Graves's efforts at the Convention, first to abolish the Bible Board and then to move it from Nashville. He expressed himself as being satisfied with the decision of the Convention concerning its foreign mission work but deeply resented its not appointing any Nashville Landmarkers to the Bible Board. There were only two regularly organized Baptist churches in Nashville, First and Second, the latter very weak. The nominating committee, knowing that the Convention's board members and officers must be members of churches in union with the churches connected with the Convention, nominated as Nashville members of the Bible Board those who were First Church, none of whom were Landmarkers, for all of them had been excluded, having gone with the minority that left the church.

The following September, Graves said in his paper that those who did not fellowship Spring Street Church were the disturbers of the churches and driving in the wedge of schism, and that, unless they changed their course, the denomination would divide. That fall and winter, he toured Alabama, Arkansas, Georgia, Louisiana, Mississippi, Texas, Virginia, and possibly other states, agitating the several controversial matters which he had sponsored. What B. F. Riley wrote about Graves's tour of Alabama in his *History of Alabama Baptists* (1895) makes clear the situation that prevailed in other states:

Another cause of distraction arose from the repeated utterances of Rev. J. R. Graves, through the columns of the *Tennessee Baptist*, of the great injury which had been done him by his exclusion from the First Baptist Church, Nashville. He was not without many ardent friends and sympathizers in the state who were ready to resist any opposition to his expressed views. A tour of Mr. Graves through Alabama added greatly to the intensity of feeling on the part of his friends and opponents.

The Baptist General Association of East Tennessee met at Knoxville in the fall of 1859, and Howell, a visiting minister, was invited to a seat in the body. The Graves followers violently opposed this and, losing, tried to dissolve the body. Losing again, they withdrew from the convention for themselves, their churches, and their associations.

At the Georgia Baptist Convention, May, 1860, the Graves faction tried to deny the visiting corresponding secretary of the Bible Board a seat in the body but lost by a vote of 50 to 94. When a motion was introduced declaring that the reception of the secretary in his official capacity was not an endorsement of the Howell party, it also lost. A Georgia historian refers to this period as one of great commotion, when exciting questions, including the rights of minorities, board and antiboard, Landmark and anti-Landmark, and other discussions produced imminent threats of a split or a divided denomination.

Editor John E. Dawson discussed the question of direct or board missions in the *Southwestern Baptist*, Alabama, Mar., 1860, and declared that it was unnecessarily connected with the Graves-Howell controversy. He said:

Opposition to the Convention and the advocacy of the Nashville minority is so identic that they seem but parts of the same question. . . . We cannot call to mind a single individual who has taken a position against the Convention who is not decidedly in favor of the Spring Street party, and there is good reason to believe that no measure would be acceptable to that party, and its leader, or their friends, which did not recognize it as a regular Baptist church.

Further on in the editorial he added:

Whenever one, or one dozen men, can distract the whole Baptist denomination South, upturn established principles and usages, interrupt the harmonious operation of our whole system of benevolence—carry off hundreds of unsuspecting men with a shout of triumph, it is time for considerate men to pause and ask, Who is to be trusted? . . . Could the evils fall on the heads of the guilty only, it would be well, but while those often profit by the discord, the cause of Christ is wounded in the house of its friends.

The Mississippi State Baptist Convention adopted resolutions concerning the Graves-Howell controversy in May, 1860, and appointed a committee of 13 to go to Nashville and make an effort to adjust the controversy, but avowed that it had no ecclesiastical authority in the case. The First Baptist Church acknowledged a letter from the secretary of the committee, T. C. Teasdale, and said it would receive the committee, but within clearly specified limits. (During a debate in the Mississippi convention on this issue, Teasdale "prayed for the peace of Zion with a bias to one side of the mooted question manifested in his prayer; and when he had completed his prayer, some one moved that one be appointed by the chair to answer Dr. Teasdale's prayer.") Only five of the committee went to Nashville. According to Howell's account of the visit, it showed a bias in favor of Graves. After several days, in which it made no progress, it returned home.

A Mississippian wrote to his state paper about the convention's action. In a long letter he said: "We want peace; we are tired of war. Already the evil consequences of the strife are seen and felt in every quarter. . . . Is it not time that we sheathe the sword of internecine strife? . . . All our benevolent operations also are injuriously affected by these alienations and strifes."

In response to the situation that rapidly developed throughout the South, the First Baptist Church declared:

This church is in no sense responsible for the strifes, agitations, and tumults which have filled the country with respect to these excluded members, since they have been originated and kept up, not by the church, but by appeals of the recusants themselves through the public press, and by unauthorized action and inflammatory publications of churches, associations, and *ex parte* councils.

The meager recordings here of what happened in a few states indicate what occurred in other states. Graves and his associates urged their followers to split churches, associations, and conventions if their demands were not met. Graves issued an ultimatum in his paper, Dec. 15, 1860, demanding that half the board members and secretaries of the Southern Baptist Convention must be Landmarkers, and then added: "Let one or two other changes be made, and the denomination would again be united in missionary work—otherwise never."

Graves, May 28, 1859, named in his paper 37 men who, he said, were "distinguished for their bitter hostility to the Southern Baptist Sunday School Union." Among them were William Theophilus Brantly, Jr. (*q.v.*), Richard Fuller (*q.v.*), John Barnett Taylor (*q.v.*), John Lansing Burrows (*q.v.*), Jeremiah Bell Jeter (*q.v.*), Alfred Elijah Dickinson (*q.v.*), John Albert Broadus (*q.v.*), James Petigru Boyce (*q.v.*), Richard Furman (*q.v.*), Patrick Hues Mell (*q.v.*), and Robert Boyté Crawford Howell (*q.v.*).

The Christian Index, Georgia (1859), published a series of articles by P. H. Mell, then president of the Georgia Baptist Convention and later president of the Southern Baptist Convention, on *Corrective Church Discipline* (printed as a book in the spring of 1860 by the Southern Baptist Publication Society). Mell's positions were substantially those of the First Baptist Church. Graves and some of his friends accused Mell of writing these articles to injure him. Mell denied this.

By 1860 the tide began to turn against Graves. A knowledge of what was involved became well known and its significance understood. Many of Graves's followers were not willing to help split associations, state conventions, and the Southern Baptist Convention on the personal and denominational issues he had stressed, for they knew what the Campbellite and antimission splits had done to Southern Baptist life. Increasingly, they tired of warfare and yearned for peace. Even Teasdale, president of the Sunday School Union and a member of the Mississippi committee that visited Nashville, expressed himself in a letter, June 27, 1860, to the *Southern Baptist,* Charleston, S. C., in which he said:

In my humble opinion, an object of paramount importance to the denomination at large [is] that this internecine warfare should be brought to a close. It has been productive of incalculable evil already, and threatens much more unless it can be checked at once. Even now the tocsin of division in our ranks is being sounded in certain quarters. . . . For myself, I see only evil, as a deep, broad river, to flow from division. Our missions, our Publication Society, and last, though not least, our Southern Theological Institute, must all suffer incalculably, if division takes place.

The support of the Sunday School Union declined to such an extent that, by the close of 1861, it was in dire financial condition. Graves, Marks & Co. were also having financial troubles. The Baptist General Association of Tennessee and North Alabama became so involved in difficulties that after its 1859 session it seemingly did not meet again until after the close of the war. Nashville fell to the Union army in Feb., 1862, and Graves, Marks & Co. suffered heavy damage to their printing plant. The *Tennessee Baptist* was not published from Feb., 1862, until Nov., 1867, when its publication began again in Memphis, where Graves joined the First Baptist Church. The First Baptist Church building, Nashville, was used by the Union army for about two years, and Howell was imprisoned by the military governor, Andrew Johnson, for two months in 1862 because he would not take the oath of allegiance to the federal government. Howell retired as pastor in July, 1867, because of failing health and died Apr. 5, 1868. The Spring Street Church became the Central Church, and, in 1870, took over the building and most of the members of the disbanded Cherry (Second) Street Church.

At its July, 1868, annual session, the Concord Association rescinded the "offensive and injurious" actions which it had taken against the First Baptist Church 10 years earlier (July, 1857) and invited it to resume its connections with the association. The church unanimously accepted the invitation.

After 1867 Graves's policy was not to make personal attacks on prominent men. He limited his references to previous discords to a standing column in his paper, where he set forth his doctrinal and ecclesiastical beliefs, and gave his attention to contemporary affairs.

The people, the churches, the associations, the state conventions, and the Southern Baptist Convention, suffering sorely from the ravages of the Civil War and grappling with the many difficult problems of the Reconstruction era, had other things to think about than the Graves-Howell controversy, even though they still suffered from its wounds. The war brought at least one great blessing to Southern Baptists: It ended the greatest controversy that ever afflicted them.

BIBLIOGRAPHY: *Both Sides:* A Full Investigation of the Charges Presented Against Elder J. R. Graves by R. B. C. Howell and Others, by a Council Composed of Delegates from Twenty Churches of Concord Association, March 1-3, 1859 (1859). O. L. Hailey, *J. R. Graves—Life, Times, and Teachings* (1929). R. B. C. Howell, "A Memorial of the First Baptist Church, Nashville, Tenn., from 1820 to 1863" [1862]. *The Baptist Standard*, I–II (1858–60). *The Southwestern Baptist* (1857 ff.). *Tennessee Baptist* (1857–62). First Baptist Church, Nashville, Tenn., *The Trial of J. R. Graves* (1859).

HOMER L. GRICE and R. PAUL CAUDILL

GRAY, BARON DeKALB (b. near Waynesboro, Miss., June 18, 1855; d. Atlanta, Ga., Nov. 25, 1946). Pastor, college president, denominational leader. Until his 19th year he lived in the plantation home of his father, John L. Gray, working on the farm and attending neighborhood schools and Waynesboro Academy. He was converted at about the age of 16 and joined Salem Baptist Church at Waynesboro. Soon after that he felt the call to the ministry and was ordained and licensed to preach by his own church.

In Jan., 1874, he entered Mississippi College, the Baptist college of the state. He graduated in the summer of 1878 with an A.B. degree. The year after his graduation was spent as pastor of two country churches, Mound Bluff and New Hope, in Madison County, Miss.

In 1879 he entered the Southern Baptist Theological Seminary at Louisville; he graduated in the full course, and took postgraduate studies. During his seminary course he was copastor with W. M. Pratt of Midway Church, Kentucky; pastor of Buffalo Lick in Shelby County and East Baptist Church in Louisville. He remained with East Church one year after his graduation in 1883.

After graduating from the seminary he became pastor of the church at Clinton, Miss., and shortly thereafter he married Alma Ratliff, daughter of W. T. Ratliff, Dec. 9, 1884. In Jan., 1888, he accepted the call of the church at Hazlehurst, Miss., where he remained for more than five years. During this time he did gratuitous denominational work in the interest of missions and education. He was chairman for Mississippi of the Baptist Centennial of Missions and was state vice-president of the Foreign Mission Board. In the spring of 1893, he became pastor of the First Baptist Church in Birmingham, Ala.

Mississippi College, in 1904, conferred on him the D.D. degree, and Baylor University in 1911 conferred the LL.D. degree. He was in great demand for commencement addresses and addresses on special occasions.

In 1901 Gray accepted the presidency of Georgetown College, the Baptist college of Kentucky. His interest and influence with young people was felt by the whole student body and particularly by the young ministerial students. While there, he was chairman of the Cecil Rhodes Scholarship Committee for Kentucky.

In 1903, upon the resignation of Fernando Coello McConnell (*q.v.*), Gray accepted his nomination to become corresponding secretary of the Home Mission Board. The following is an excerpt from the report of the committee appointed by the board to recommend a man for the place:

The brother about to be nominated is widely known and as generally trusted and loved as any minister whom we are likely to secure. He is in the vigor of mature manhood. His personal appearance is impressive and commanding. His character is spotless. His disposition is most amiable but without the slightest suggestion of weakness. He is a recognized leader in all assemblies of Southern Baptists, wise in council, conservative in method, powerful in debate, eloquent in the advocacy of any cause which enlists his moral convictions, and untiring in his labors. As a man of business he is exact and painstaking.

Gray served in that capacity for 25 years and was retired in Nov., 1928, as executive secretary emeritus. After that he served at the call of the executive secretary, J. B. Lawrence, in prosecuting the work of the Home Mission Board in associations, churches, state conventions, and the Southern Baptist Convention. He was also frequently engaged as pulpit supply for churches in Atlanta and other parts of Georgia. He was always vitally interested in denominational work and represented Southern Baptists on many occasions.

The work of the Home Mission Board was greatly enlarged during his secretaryship, with many departments added, notably, church building and loan and evangelism. Great development in Cuban work was undertaken and extended to the Panama Canal Zone. During his term of office, the board assisted in the founding of the Baptist Hospital in New Orleans and the Baptist Bible Institute, also of that city, which Gray visited regularly as one of the trustees. Also the board assisted in the building of the Roger Williams Memorial Church in Washington, D. C.

J. B. LAWRENCE

GRAY, CLAUDE (b. near Jackson, Butts County, Ga., May, 1872; d. Tifton, Ga., Mar. 12, 1947). He was educated at Jackson High School, Monticello High School, and Mercer University (A.B., 1894). He taught at Hearn Academy, Cave Spring, Ga., 1894–95; was president of Locust Grove Institute, Locust Grove, Ga., 1897–1928; and taught at agricultural and mechanical schools in Dallas and Tifton, Ga., 1928–47. He declined invitations to professorships in colleges and chose to do his work in high schools and academies. His most significant work was the building of Locust Grove Institute, where he was president for 31 years. He married Daisey Smith, of Indian Springs, Ga., Dec. 31, 1902. They had two children: Martha Caroline and Claude Nelson.

SOLON B. COUSINS

GRAY, RUFUS FRANKLIN (b. Titusville, Fla., June 3, 1915; d. Philippines, Feb., 1942). Missionary appointee to China. A mission volunteer before entering college, Gray received the B.A. degree from Furman University and the Th.M. degree from the Southern Baptist Theological Seminary. He was appointed a Southern Baptist missionary to China in 1940, but was interned by the Japanese in 1941 while attending language school in Baguio, Philippines. Little is known concerning Gray's death. He was the only Southern Baptist missionary to lose his life in prison during World War II. Gray married Marian Peeler in 1939, by whom he had one son, William Gilman. IONE GRAY

GREAT BRITAIN AND IRELAND, BAPTIST UNION OF. Organized June 24, 1813, at a meeting held in the vestry of Carter Lane Baptist Church, Southwark, London, during the ministry of John Rippon (1751–1836). Before that event there had been two centuries of Baptist witness and growth in England. The pioneer English Baptist was John Smyth (d. 1612), a Cambridge scholar who led a group to Amsterdam in search of religious freedom. There he adopted Baptist views, baptized himself, his friend Thomas Helwys (1572–1616), and about 40 others. In 1611 Helwys and a few followers returned to London and founded in Spitalfields the first Baptist church in England, Arminian in theology. From this heroic beginning came the General Baptist movement in England. In the 1630's another Baptist group emerged in Southwark, Calvinistic in theology, under the leadership of Samuel Eaton and John Spilsbury.

These two streams of Baptist life and witness, the General Baptists and the Particular Baptists, gained in strength during the 17th century. Baptists took part in the Puritan struggle for political and religious freedom, with Cromwell's army containing numerous Baptists among both the officers and lower ranks. It was through the witness of Cromwellian soldiers that Baptist witness began in Ireland and Scotland. Baptists appeared in Wales during the early part of the 17th century; one of the Welsh Baptist leaders, John Myles of Ilston, moved to the New World.

During the 17th century both groups of Baptists in England were preoccupied with the struggle for religious liberty; thus it was not until the 18th century that the movement began for closer co-operation of the scattered church groups. This movement brought associations into being although there was still no attempt at national organization. The formation of the Baptist Missionary Society in 1792, however, turned Baptist minds toward co-operation on a national scale. Its leaders were Particular Baptists who, under the influence of men like Andrew Fuller (1754–1815) (*q.v.*), modified their narrower Calvinism and responded to William Carey's (*q.v.*) call to "Expect great things from God: attempt great things for God." (Not until the early part of the 19th century did the General Baptists form their missionary society.)

In 1812, 61 ministers from the Midlands and the South of England met together to approve a scheme of closer co-operation. A year later, at the meeting in Carter Lane, 45 ministers were present. They included John Rippon, Joseph Ivimey (1773–1834), William Newman (1773–1835), Francis Franklin, and John Sutcliffe (1752–1814). The main aims of the General Union of Baptist Ministers and Churches, as it was called, were to provide opportunities for fellowship and to support three enterprises: the Baptist Missionary Society; colleges for training ministers, of which three were by that time in existence: Bristol, Horton (now Rawdon College), and Stepney (now Regent's Park, Oxford); and village and itinerant preaching (for which a Home Missionary Society had been established in 1797). It was also decided to support the Particular Baptist Fund (founded in 1717 by the Particular Baptists of London to assist needy ministers and educate ministerial candidates) and to support the *Baptist Magazine* (started in 1809).

During the 20 years after its founding the union's activities were little more than the holding of an annual meeting in June at which special sermons were preached. The desire for a loan fund to help in the building and repair of meetinghouses led in 1824 to the establishment of the Baptist Building Fund. New impetus to the work of the union came from members of the Baptist Board (a ministers' society founded in 1724 and meeting in one of the London coffeehouses) and from reports on the state of the denomination. Two ministers were appointed joint secretaries of the union, and annual reports began to appear, especially during the secretaryship of John Howard Hinton (1791–1873), when an annual *Account of the Proceedings* of the union was published. This publication became the *Manual* and eventually the present *Handbook* of the union.

The latter part of the 19th century was an important period of development both for the union and its constituent bodies. Baptists of Wales formed the Welsh Baptist Union in 1866; Scotch Baptists formed a union in 1869. The growth of the parent body made it necessary to appoint a full-time secretary, and Samuel Harris Booth (1824–1902), was elected to this office. The union had its own premises for the first time, a modest room in the Baptist Mission House in Furnival Street, London. In 1891 the two main groups of Baptists in Britain, Particular Baptists and General Baptists, merged when the New Connexion of General Baptists (formed in the 18th century under the influence of the Evangelical Revival) joined the union.

Booth was succeeded as secretary of the union in 1898 by John Howard Shakespeare (1857–1928) who directed the affairs of the union until his resignation because of ill health in 1924. In 1903 new union headquarters were opened in Southampton Row, London, on the site of a Baptist church established in 1737, with Andrew Gifford and Joseph Ivimey among its pastors. The cost of the new building, £50,000, was largely provided from the Twentieth Century Fund, the first great fund raised by J. H. Shakespeare, who may be described as the architect of the Baptist union as it is today. In his devotion to the world range of Baptist life and thought (he took a leading part in the founding of the Baptist World Alliance and served as one of its first secretaries) and in his fraternal relations with the other free churches, Shakespeare set a policy which his successors in office have developed. His genius brought into being the Baptist Women's League which now has affiliated women's meetings in about 1,250 churches. In recent years the work of the Baptist Union Women's Department has included a hostel for business girls, a home for unmarried mothers and their children, and an adoption society. For many years deaconesses were trained in the Women's Training College, but they are now trained at Carey Hall, Birmingham. Baptist union youth work includes a Sunday school department and a department of moral and social questions. Biblical and theological studies are encouraged in a plan which trains students for the diploma of religious knowledge. The work of lay preachers is organized in the Lay Preachers' Federation. Schemes of ministerial settlement and superannuation are important in union activities. There are Baptist theological colleges at Bristol, Rawdon (near Leeds), Regent's Park (Oxford), Spurgeon's (London), Manchester, Cardiff, Bangor, Glasgow, and Dublin. The union has a weekly denominational organ, *The Baptist Times;* the Baptist Historical Society publishes a *Quarterly;* and the Baptist Ministers' Fellowship, a periodical *Fraternal.*

In 1953 Ernest A. Payne described the financial resources of the union as related to invested funds and individual stewardship:

> The churches and individual members of them have entrusted to the Union considerable financial resources. The Superannuation Fund, which is actuarially based and operated, has an invested capital of over £1,000,000. By careful management it has been possible to raise the annual payments to retired ministers and their widows well above the figure contemplated when the fund was first launched. The capital investments of the Sustentation Fund and the Original Home Work Fund amount to nearly £400,000. The interest on these investments amounts to some £15,000 a year. But grants to ministers and associations total some £48,000. To meet the difference between these last two figures, and to cover general administrative expenditure and the cost of all the services undertaken, the union depends upon annual contributions received by way of subscriptions from churches and personal members, contributions to the Home Work Fund, and grants from associated organisations like the Baptist Insurance Company and the Psalms and Hymns Trust. By far the largest and most important source of income is and must be the contributions to the Home Work Fund.

According to the union's constitution, its objects are primarily aimed toward "the advancement of the Christian religion" in accord with Baptist principles. The primary purposes include:

(1) the cultivation of Christian respect and love;

(2) the spread of the gospel through ministers and church directed mediums;

(3) the opportunity for conferences and for united action on questions affecting church welfare, ministerial support, and denominational growth;

(4) the promotion of international relations among Baptists;

(5) the gathering and distribution of accurate information concerning Baptists throughout the world; and

(6) the promotion of co-operation with other Christian groups.

Baptist polity assures complete autonomy for the local church. Churches in any locality are normally grouped in district unions, and there are in England some 25 county or larger associations. The union has 10 general superintendents who exercise advisory and organizational ministry in their areas. Normally an assembly of the union is held in the spring of each year; but union business, both spiritual and organizational, is dealt with by the Baptist Union Council, which meets twice for full session each year, and its various committees. The council, in addition to officers of the union, ex-presidents, principals of the theological colleges and the general superintendents, is composed of representatives from each affiliated association, 50 members of the assembly (25 ministers and 25 laymen) elected by ballot, and 20 other members elected by the council at its first meeting following the assembly.

The Baptist Missionary Society, founded in Kettering in 1792, and thus older than the union, has its own headquarters and organization. Its early fields were India, West Indies, Congo, and China. In the course of its history the society has also sent missionaries to East Indies, Brittany, Norway, Italy, Palestine, and Japan. In 1955 the society had 343 missionaries with 3,500 native colleagues in India, Pakistan, Ceylon, Belgian Congo, Angola, and West Indies. Since the withdrawal of missionaries from China in 1952, missionary projects have been undertaken in Hong Kong, Malaya, and Brazil. In 1954 the society's income from the churches reached the record total of £206,014.

The 19th century was a period of Baptist expansion in Britain. From 1801 to 1851 Baptist buildings increased from 652 to 2,789. By 1901 there were 4,012 church buildings, 2,747 churches, and 372,998 church members. The present century has evidenced the effects of the growth of secularism and two devastating world wars on religious life in Britain as a whole. Thus in the Baptist Union in 1954 there were: 3,831 church buildings, 3,273 churches, 325,896 church members, 2,018 pastors in charge, 4,582 lay preachers, 327,597 Sunday school scholars, and 7,895 baptisms. The period following the close of World War II has seen much rebuilding, the erection of churches or halls in new areas of population, and a marked attention to evangelism. There are many indications, especially in the vigor of work among young people, that the decline which marked the earlier decades of this century has been arrested and that the denomination has entered on a new period of expansion. The response of the churches to the Home Work Fund for the year 1955 reached the record total of £55,800.

When the union was formed in 1813 the Baptists of Britain could look back with pride to great personalities who had enriched the religious life of the nation: to men like Thomas Helwys in the struggle for religious liberty; to John Bunyan (1628–88) (q.v.) who holds a unique position in literature; to theologians and preachers like Andrew Fuller, Robert Hall (1764–1831), and John Ryland (1753–1825); to the genius of William Carey in the modern missionary movement; and to Benjamin Keach (1640–1704), who introduced hymn singing to British churches in the 17th century. In the Victorian era Baptists in Britain produced three outstanding pulpit figures, Charles Haddon Spurgeon (1834–92) (q.v.), Alexander Maclaren (1826–1910) (q.v.), and John Clifford (1826–1937). In many realms Baptists have left their impress through outstanding figures such as Joseph Livesey (1794–1884), pioneer of the total abstinence movement; Joseph Hughes (1769–1833), first secretary of the British and Foreign Bible Society; Thomas Cook (1808–92), pioneer of world travel; Thomas Sheraton (1751–1806), designer of beautiful furniture; David Lloyd George, orator and statesman. British Baptists have contributed to biblical scholarship. Henry Wheeler Robinson and Theodore H. Robinson attained international fame in Old Testament scholarship, and Terrot Reaveley Glover (1869–1943) was public orator in the University of Cambridge. At the present time three Baptists hold university chairs in Semitic studies. Notable in Baptist work throughout the world, James Henry Rushbrooke (1870–1947), served as a leader and for a time as president of the Baptist World Alliance. British Baptists have contributed three presidents to the alliance: John Clifford, elected in London in 1905; Rushbrooke, elected in Atlanta in 1939; and F. Townley Lord, elected in Cleveland in 1950.   F. TOWNLEY LORD

GREAT COMMISSION, THE. This term usually refers to Matthew 28:18–20, Christ's most definite and complete missionary command. It summarizes the continual emphasis of his ministry. The late William Owen Carver (q.v.) explained it: "Make all the nations learners from Me—enter them in My school;—baptizing them into the new relation and possibilities implied by the names Father, Son, Holy Spirit; then leading them on to guard the whole teaching of Him who taught you."

Note the continual mission emphasis of Jesus: The universal, searching love of God (Luke 15 is a strong illustration); the world (usually used by John to denote sphere of evil) as the object of that love (John 3:16); severe penalties for failure to fulfil God's purpose of sharing redemption through his Son (Matt. 21:33–44); and the appeal of the person of Jesus to every man in need (Matt. 11:28–30).

In sending the twelve (Luke 9) and the seventy (Luke 10), Jesus made specific application during his earthly ministry of the principle in the Great Commission. In John 20:21 he urged world coverage, a topic that dominated his resurrection conversations. In this case he based his sending the disciples on the fact that his Father had sent him. Each Gospel writer reported a specific command (Luke 24:47–49; Mark 16:15). Immediately before his ascension he commanded his followers to be witnesses "unto the uttermost part of the earth" (Acts 1:8), evidently desiring to leave that command ringing in their memories and seeming to leave the question, "Will you do it?"

The application today is clear: Since the missionary movement created the New Testament, the churches of Christ must move unitedly toward a world witness in order to resemble the New Testament church. In command, in example, and in spirit Jesus leads to ever stronger mission participation. To fail to render the fruits of obedience and love is to forfeit God's choicest blessings. To measure up is to open the door to his power, granted only to those who use it for his purposes.   CAL GUY

GREAT CONFESSION. See JESUS CHRIST.

GREEK ORTHODOX CHURCH. Sometimes called Eastern Orthodox. The adherents to the Orthodox faith claim theirs as the most ancient Christian church. When an Orthodox member speaks of the Orthodox Church, he means, first, the churches founded by the apostles or the disciples of the apostles, which have remained in communion with one another; and second, the churches which have come from missionary activity of the former or which were founded by separation without loss of communion. Orthodoxy today numbers 22 independent bodies with an estimated membership of 250,000,000. The word "Greek" is used because Greek was the first language of Christendom, the New Testament was written in Greek, and Christianity grew fastest among the Greeks and Hellenized Jews. The word "orthodox" is derived from two Greek words meaning to believe correctly or to worship correctly.

As defined by its creed, the Greek Orthodox Church is the one, holy, catholic, and apostolic church: *one*, because Jesus founded only one church; *holy*, because it seeks to save and sanctify its members through the sacraments; *catholic*, because it is universal in its mission; *apostolic*, because it was built on the "foundation of the apostles and prophets, Jesus Christ

FIRST BAPTIST CHURCH, Winston-Salem, N. C. Organized 1871, auditorium of English Renaissance architecture completed 1925, total property worth over $1,000,000. Membership 1956 over 3,200, Sunday school enrolment 2,500.

FIRST BAPTIST CHURCH, West Palm Beach, Fla. Founded 1901, membership 1956 approximately 2,700. Auditorium of Mediterranean Romanesque built 1934, seats 800, educational unit serves 1,500, property evaluation, $600,000.

himself being the chief corner stone" (Eph. 2:20).

The sources of the teachings of Greek Orthodoxy are divided under two headings: Holy Scripture and Sacred Tradition. Holy Scripture comprises the Septuagint version of the Old Testament and the Greek New Testament. Sacred Tradition, regarded as an essential complement of Scripture, includes (a) the oral teachings of Christ to the apostles and their oral teachings before the New Testament was written; (b) the decrees of the first seven ecumenical councils; (c) the creed, as fixed by the first two councils; (d) the sacraments (seven in number: baptism, thrice by immersion in water; chrismation, performed immediately after baptism; penance; holy eucharist, with laity taking both bread and wine; holy orders; holy matrimony; holy unction, administered to an ill person as an act of healing; the first four are obligatory, the others optional); (e) the doctrines and ecclesiastical services as handed down from generation to generation; (f) the writings of the Great Fathers of the undivided church to about A.D. 800.

The Catholic Church was undivided until 1054 A.D., when papal legates laid on the altar of St. Sophia in Constantinople a sentence of excommunication of the Patriarch of Constantinople and his followers. Four reasons for the separation were racial differences, the separation of the Eastern and Western empires, rivalry between the patriarchates of Rome and Constantinople, and controversy over the *filioque* clause of the Nicene Creed (the Greek Orthodox Church maintains that the Holy Spirit proceeds from the Father alone *through* the Son; the Western Church, that he proceeds from the Father *and* the Son as a joint source).

The modern Greek Orthodox Church disagrees with the Roman Church on the procession of the Holy Spirit and denies the doctrines of the immaculate conception, the infallibility of the pope, and purgatory. Though the Greek Orthodox Church denies the immaculate conception of Mary, the Orthodox faithful venerate and honor her exceedingly. They also venerate and honor the saints and sacred images and relics.

BIBLIOGRAPHY: W. F. Adeney, *The Greek and Eastern Churches* (1923). D. T. Andrews, *The Eastern Othodox Church, A Bibliography* (1953). M. Constantinides, *The Greek Orthodox Faith* (n.d.); *The Orthodox Church*, second ed. (1952). Demetrius (Bishop of Olympus), *The Sacrament of Chrismation* (n.d.). R. M. French, *The Eastern Orthodox Church* (1951). A. Kokkinakis, *Christian Orthodoxy and Roman Catholicism* (1952). S. P. Pendias, *An Outline of Greek Orthodoxy* (1953). GRAY ALLISON

GREEN, ANANIAS (b. Salem, Perry County, Ala., Oct. 12, 1824; d. Carlsbad, N. Mex., June 4, 1906). Probate judge, associational leader, Baptist historian. Son of Jesse and Jemina Green, he married Sarah Griffis of Choctaw County, Miss., in 1845, and had six sons and three daughters. Green came to Seven Rivers, Lincoln County, N. Mex., in July, 1886, from Lean County, Tex., and was instrumental in securing the first pastor for this south central area. Finding locations for churches, he brought in pastors and thus became an agent in the founding of many churches. Green, elected moderator of Lincoln Association at its organizational meeting in 1888, serving in that capacity for 18 years, wrote an early history of Baptist work in the area upon authorization of the association. He served his church as deacon. Following the organization of the territorial convention at Las Cruces in 1900, Green was elected second vice-president, and the following year, first vice-president. He was known as Judge Green, and served as justice of the peace, 1886–87; Lincoln County commissioner, 1888–99; and probate judge, Eddy County, 1900–06. MRS. RICHARD THOMAS BAKER, SR.

GREEN, JESSE MERCER (b. Sharp Mountain Creek, Cherokee County, Ga., Apr. 7, 1836; d. Jan. 3, 1926). Baptist preacher and editor. Green started west by horse and ox teams in 1854 but was delayed a year en route by necessity of temporary employment. He arrived in west Texas in 1855. In Jan., 1858, he joined the Texas Rangers. In June, 1862, he enlisted in the Texas Cavalry as a Confederate soldier; he received a medical discharge in 1863. Green moved to Polk County, Ark., in Sept., 1868, and then to Mansville, Chickasaw Nation, Indian Territory, in 1890. He served as pastor of many churches in western Arkansas and eastern Oklahoma. He was a leader for many years in the Baptist General Association of Western Arkansas and Indian Territory; he served as moderator of that body, 1897–1900, and as editor of the *Baptist Signal* for three years. He is buried at Fillmore, Okla. J. M. GASKIN

GREEN RIVER BAPTIST. A weekly paper published in Hartford, Ky., Jan. 1–Aug. 12, 1864, Volume 1, Numbers 1–32, edited by James Smith Coleman (*q.v.*). This paper was dedicated to the "advocacy and defense of Baptist principles and practices, and to the diffusion of scriptural knowledge and holiness." It was directed against the teachings of Alexander Campbell. It was discontinued because of lack of funds. J. M. GREEN

GREEN RIVER BAPTIST EDUCATION SOCIETY. See BETHEL COLLEGE, RUSSELLVILLE, KY.

GREENE, JOHN PRIEST (b. Scotland County, Mo., Aug. 20, 1849; d. Santa Ana, Calif., March 10, 1933). Pastor and educator. For over three decades he was president of William Jewell College, Liberty, Mo. Educated at LaGrange College and Southern Baptist Theological Seminary, he taught mathematics at LaGrange from 1872 to 1875 and at the same time served as pastor of various churches in that area. He was pastor of the East Baptist Church, Louisville, Ky., 1877–82, and the Third Baptist Church,

St. Louis, Mo., 1882-92. During the latter pastorate he accomplished much in the work of city missions. Greene became president of William Jewell College in June, 1892. Through his effective administration of 31 years the institution made remarkable progress. The administration building constructed on the campus in 1948 bears his name and is a memorial to him. Upon his retirement from the presidency of the institution in June, 1923, he moved to Santa Ana, Calif., where he resided until his death.

MRS. R. W. PRATHER, JR.

GREENE, SAMUEL HARRISON (b. Enosburg, Vt., Dec. 25, 1845; d. Washington, D. C., Sept. 7, 1920). District of Columbia denominational leader. He was born in a Baptist parsonage and educated in the public schools of Fairfax and Brandon, and at Norwich University and Colgate University. At 17 he became secretary to a Union army officer, but he became ill and was discharged. He returned to Vermont to enter the legal profession and started clerking in his father's store.

Greene made his profession of faith at the age of 18. Two years later he married the pastor's daughter, Laura A. Buzzell. At 23 he entered Madison (Colgate) University, and he earned the A.B. degree in 1873. He took a two-year theological course at Madison (Colgate-Rochester) Theological Seminary. He earned the M.A. degree from Colgate in 1876. In 1875 he was ordained by, and became pastor of, Cazenovia Baptist Church, New York, and he served this church until he was called to Calvary Church, Washington, D. C., in 1879.

Five honorary degrees were conferred upon him—D.D. by Norwich in 1883, D.D. by Colgate and University of Rochester in 1891, and LL.D. by Columbian and Howard universities in 1895.

He served as pastor of Calvary Church 41 years, during which time he was a pioneer and outstanding leader in Sunday school development and in the ministry to the deaf, to the Chinese, and to a growing capital city. He was four times moderator of Columbia Association of Baptist Churches (now District of Columbia Baptist Convention). He served as a trustee and acting president of Columbian College (George Washington University). In 1907 when the Northern (now American) Baptist Convention was organized, he was pastor of the host church and was elected one of the vice-presidents of the Convention.

M. CHANDLER STITH

GREENSBORO FEMALE SEMINARY. An elementary and high school for girls located at Greensboro, Hale County, Ala., founded by the Cahaba Association c. 1849, with C. F. Sturgis as first principal. It is now extinct.

JAMES E. DAVIDSON

GREENUP BAPTIST ASSOCIATION CAMP. Begun in 1953, supported by the associational Woman's Missionary Union, Kentucky. Facilities were rented from Carter Caves in 1953-54. The "Mad Anthony Wayne" camp of Huntington, W. Va., was rented in 1955. Camps are for Royal Ambassadors, Girls' Auxiliary, and Young Woman's Auxiliary, and are operated two or more weeks annually.

ELDRED M. TAYLOR

GREENVILLE WOMAN'S COLLEGE. The woman's college of Furman University, Greenville, S. C. It was founded by the state Baptist convention in 1854. The Baptists were influenced in their selection of a site for the college by a generous offer made by the trustees of two academies, established by the citizens of Greenville in 1819, to transfer to the state Baptist convention all property rights to the buildings and 30 acres of land as an inducement to bring the college to Greenville. This offer was accepted, and the legal transfer was made Dec. 26, 1854. The Greenville Baptist Female College opened Feb. 7, 1855, under control of the trustees of Furman University, Baptist college for men in Greenville. Not until 1909, however, was the Woman's College granted a separate charter authorizing a separate board of trustees. The first building, now the Administration Building, was erected in 1855; the second, Townes Building, in 1870, honoring Professor A. S. Townes; and the third, Gardner Hall, in 1900, named in honor of Charles Spurgeon Gardner. These three buildings constituted the physical plant when David M. Ramsay became president in 1911. At this time the much-needed expansion was provided for by the issuance of bonds on college property, whereby money was secured for financing the construction of West and North buildings and the remodeling and refurnishing of the old buildings. The college acquired the Orr property, adjoining the campus, in 1912 through the activities of the Alumnae Association. Some years later a $20,000 gift from the alumnae made possible the conversion of the building into an adequate library. The David M. Ramsay Fine Arts Building, financed by a $200,000 donation from the 75 Million Campaign and dedicated in 1922, completed the college plant as it stands today.

During these years of development, the curriculum was strengthened, laboratories were enlarged and equipped, and library facilities were increased. The preparatory department was discontinued, and all diplomas were eliminated except those for the degrees of Bachelor of Arts, Bachelor of Science, and Bachelor of Music. Throughout this period graduates of the college were accepted for graduate standing in leading universities. The college reached the point where the only requirement needed for recognition by all accrediting agencies was the stipulated $500,000 endowment. When this sum could not be realized, arrangements were worked out for the co-ordination of the Woman's College with Furman University. The Furman board voted approval Apr. 6, 1933. The college, the name of which had been changed to the Greenville Woman's College in 1914, then became the Woman's College of Furman University.

The character and scholastic excellence of the men and women connected with the college as administrators and faculty have been its richest asset. These educators, embodying the ideals of the founders in establishing the college, have provided the best in Christian education and cultural development. They have also, through the quality of their instruction and high regard for academic achievement, enabled the college through the years to attract and graduate young women of superior ability, in whom has been realized the fulfilment of the vision of the founding fathers.

Soon after the college was chartered in 1854, H. A. Duncan was chosen president. He served until 1860. Following him were C. J. Radford, 1860–61; C. R. Twitty, 1861–63; Charles Hallette Judson, 1863–78; Alexander Sloan Townes, 1878–94; M. M. Riley, 1894–1900; Edgar Hunter Murfee, 1900–01; Edward Carroll James, 1901–11; David Marshall Ramsay, 1911–30; Miss Rosa Catherine Paschal, acting president, 1930–31; and Herbert Winston Provence, 1931–33, president at the time of the co-ordination.

BIBLIOGRAPHY: Mrs. E. R. Alford, "The Story of 'Our Mother,'" (*Bulletin*, Greenville Woman's College, Vol. XXIII, No. 2, 1925). H. T. Cook, "The Greenville Female College, 1853–1863," *Baptist Courier* (Dec. 9, 1909). S. S. Crittenden, *The Greenville Century Book* (1903). R. N. Daniel, *Furman University, A History* (1951).   AILEEN COGGINS

GREGORY, OLIVER FULLER (b. Charleston, S. C., Mar. 1844; d. Baltimore, Md., Jan. 12, 1919). Preacher and denominational leader. His education was received in the schools and in the college at Charleston. While serving in the Confederate army, he suffered several wounds. He was taken prisoner in 1863 and was held until 1865. He was baptized in the First Baptist Church, Charleston, and after suitable preparation he was ordained in that church in 1871.

Gregory served as pastor at Mount Pleasant Church, South Carolina, for five years; at the Baptist church of Kingston, S. C., for one year; at churches at Eufaula and Tuscaloosa, Ala., 1877–80; at churches at Cheraw and Florence, S. C., for five years; at Valence Street Church, New Orleans, La.; at Fourth Church, Baltimore, Md., for 17 years; at Adams Street Church, Montgomery, Ala., for three years; and at First Church, Staunton, Va., for nine years. In 1912 he moved back to Baltimore to become pastor of a suburban church in Govans, where he remained until his death in 1919. As a tribute to his faithful and successful work there, the name of the church was changed on Oct. 24, 1917, to the Gregory Memorial Baptist Church.

For more than 16 years Gregory served as secretary of the state mission board of Maryland in connection with his pastorate at Fourth Church from 1888 until 1902.

He served as a secretary of the Southern Baptist Convention from 1880 until 1918. He was an able, efficient secretary, eloquent preacher, and successful denominational leader. He is buried in Baltimore city cemetery.   W. H. BRANNOCK

GRIME, JOHN HARVEY (b. Putnam County, Tenn., near Cookeville, July 29, 1851; d. Lebanon, Tenn., Aug. 8, 1941). Preacher, editor, author, historiographer. Grime's early education consisted of a study of Webster's "old blue-backed speller" and simple arithmetic. For the most part, his young manhood was spent carving out a livable homestead from an unbroken wilderness. In 1883 at the age of 31 he entered school again. At this time, accompanied by his eight-year-old daughter, he enrolled at Round Lick Male and Female Academy at Watertown, Tenn. His studies consisted "of . . . Latin, Greek, Higher Arithmetic, Algebra, Geometry and Rhetoric."

In Dec., 1868, Grime was converted at the Boiling Springs Baptist Church of Putnam County, Tenn. He was baptized in Jan., 1869, in the midst of winter. Ice froze on his garments as he came from the baptismal waters of Cane Creek in Putnam County. He was licensed to preach by the Pistole Baptist Church in White County, July 17, 1875. This same church ordained him to the gospel ministry Mar. 27, 1876.

From 1891 until 1897 Grime was either editor, field editor, associate editor, or contributing editor to no less than nine different religious papers. One of these papers was the *Baptist and Reflector* of Tennessee, for which he worked as field editor.

His pastoral ministry extended beyond the borders of Tennessee into Kentucky and Texas. Most of his ministry, however, was spent with the churches of Wilson County, Tenn. During his pastoral ministry he served at least 50 different churches and preached at least 4,000 sermons. According to Grime's personal account, under his ministry 20 men decided to preach. He helped to organize two associations, viz., New Salem Association in 1888 and the Wilson County Association in 1921. Under his leadership the Boiling Springs Baptist Church was reorganized and in 1888 was brought back into the fellowship of regularly associated Baptists. In 1891 he wrote the constitution for the Wiseman Association. Six houses of worship were erected under his leadership. He was the author of 30 publications consisting of both books and tracts. His largest publication was his *History of Middle Tennessee Baptists*, which consisted of nearly 600 pages. He also served at one time on the Historical Committee of the Tennessee Baptist Convention. To use his own language, Grime was "a strong uncompromising Land-Mark Baptist."   DEWEY ROACH

GRONER, FRANK SHELBY (b. Collin County, Tex., Jan. 3, 1877; d. Marshall, Tex., Nov. 8, 1943). Denominational leader, college

Groner, Orville

president, pastor. Educated in law, Groner taught school and served as county attorney before entering the ministry in 1905. Following two Texas pastorates at First Baptist Church, Stamford, 1905-11, and Columbus Avenue Baptist Church, Waco, 1911-18, he became corresponding secretary of the executive board of the Baptist General Convention of Texas, 1918-28, and in this position led Texas Baptists to subscribe $15,400,000 in the 75 Million Campaign. From 1928 to 1942 Groner was president of the College of Marshall (now East Texas Baptist College), after which he was president emeritus until his death. He became the first chairman of the Southern Baptist Hospital Commission in 1916.

BIBLIOGRAPHY: J. H. Boyd, "History of the College of Marshall" (1944). J. M. Carroll, *A History of Texas Baptists* (1923). J. M. Dawson, *A Century with Texas Baptists* (1947). L. R. Elliott, ed., *Centennial Story of Texas Baptists* (1936). *Who's Who in America*, XXIII (1945). A. B. RUTLEDGE

GRONER, ORVILLE (b. Jacksboro, Tex., Mar. 21, 1896; d. Dallas, Tex., Jan. 4, 1954). Treasurer of the Relief and Annuity Board for 30 years. Groner was educated in the public schools of Jacksboro, Stamford, and Waco, Tex., and was graduated from Tobeys Business College in Waco in 1915. He came to Dallas, Tex., in 1918 and for three months was active in promoting the 75 Million Campaign which was being conducted by his brother, the late Frank S. Groner (q.v.), then executive secretary of the Baptist General Convention of Texas. Groner joined the Relief and Annuity Board in Apr., 1923, as general accountant. He was made treasurer of the relief fund in 1924 and general treasurer in 1933, a position he held until his death in 1954. He scored success in the field of investments for the Relief and Annuity Board. When he joined the board, assets stood at $2,242,325; they increased during the 30 years he served as treasurer to $30,000,000, of which over $19,000,000 was in investment earnings. He married Billie Jones of Texas; they had one son, Orville, Jr., and two daughters, Aline and Gwen. RETTA O'BANNON

GROWTH OF SOUTHERN BAPTISTS. In 1845 Southern Baptists reported a membership of 351,951, of whom probably 150,000 were Negroes, in 4,126 churches. By 1900 the number of churches had increased to 19,558, and these churches reported a total white membership of 1,657,996. Twenty-two years later, in 1922, Southern Baptists had more than doubled their membership over 1900, and reported 3,366,211 members in 27,919 churches. However, the greatest growth was during the period of 1945-55, during which time church membership increased from 5,865,554 to 8,474,741, a net gain of 2,609,187. Total churches increased from 26,191 to 30,377 during this 10-year period. In 1955 Southern Baptists were the second largest Protestant group in the United States, second only to Methodists, who reported a membership of 9,292,046.

Southern Baptist Sunday school growth has been almost phenomenal. It took 63 years to reach the first million in Sunday school enrolment, but it took only 13 additional years to reach a two million enrolment, and 11 years to reach three million. The greatest growth was recorded in 1954, when a net gain of 597,361 was reported, which was almost 92,000 greater than the gains of 1952 and 1953 combined. The *Yearbook of American Churches*, in 1956, reported a total Sunday school enrolment of 37,623,530 in 242 religious bodies. Southern Baptist Sunday school enrolment represented 16.9 per cent of this total.

The Baptist Young People's Union, auxiliary to the Southern Baptist Convention, was organized on Nov. 21, 1895, in Atlanta, Ga. The Southern Baptist Convention, in its Chattanooga meeting in 1896, put its stamp of approval upon the new organization and in 1918 entrusted to the Sunday School Board the responsibility for Baptist Young People's Union work. At that time there was a Baptist Young People's Union membership of 230,540 in Southern Baptist churches. In 1934 the name Baptist Training Union was adopted, and a fully graded Training Union program was promoted. Fourteen years later, in 1948, the Training Union enrolment had reached the one million mark, and it reached the second million enrolment in 1954. In 1955 there was a total membership of 2,223,502 in 21,217 churches.

In 1923 Woman's Missionary Union enrolment had reached 148,108. In 1955 membership had climbed to 1,245,358. In 1942 the Brotherhood enrolment in Southern Baptist churches had reached 54,868. In 1955 they reported a membership of 404,281. In 1955 the responsibility for promoting Royal Ambassador work in the churches was transferred by the Convention from the Woman's Missionary Union to the Brotherhood. Prior to 1955 the Royal Ambassador enrolment was reported in the Woman's Missionary Union enrolment; after 1955 it was included in the Brotherhood enrolment.

The growth of Southern Baptists is also reflected in the total and mission gifts through the churches. In 1885 a total of $1,513,640 was given through 14,488 churches. Of this amount $202,170 was reported as mission gifts. By 1900 total gifts had climbed to $3,456,014; by 1946, $115,226,949; and in 1955 a total of $334,836,283 was reported from 30,377 churches. In the meantime, mission gifts climbed to $58,360,247 in 1955, which was greater than total gifts in 1942. Total per capita gifts in 1955 was $39.51, compared with $6.12 in 1935.

Cooperative Program receipts in 1955 were $35,717,008, of which $13,588,160 was distributed to Convention-wide causes. By comparison, Cooperative Program receipts in 1935 were $2,264,420.47.

Southern Baptists have grown in their foreign mission program. Missionary personnel has increased from 446 in 1940 to 1,020 in 1955. The Lottie Moon offering increased from $360,000 in 1940 to $3,951,000 in 1955. Total foreign mission income increased from $1,345,918 in 1940 to $11,287,775 in 1955.

The following additional facts have been gleaned from the 1955 reports of the Convention's agencies, commissions, and institutions:

The Home Mission Board employed 1,105 missionaries, who reported 37,475 baptisms in 1955; the organization of 725 new missions; and a total income from denominational sources of $3,134,363.86.

The Sunday School Board published and circulated in 1955 more than 65 million periodicals; printed 1,377,497 copies of new books and 2,296,356 reprints; distributed 9,631,460 general tracts; issued 1,391,173 Sunday school, Training Union, and music training awards; assisted 8,804 churches with their building program; and reported $1,782,027 in denominational appropriations.

Southern Baptist seminaries reported a total enrolment in 1955 of 5,885, property valued at $21,353,809, and a total endowment of $26,659,309.

Thirty Southern Baptist senior colleges and universities reported a total enrolment of 43,945, property valued at $96,968,766, and a total endowment of $142,157,857.

Thirty-three Baptist junior colleges, academies, and Bible schools reported a total enrolment of 11,574, property valued at $25,370,000, and a total endowment of $29,982,000.

Thirty-seven Southern Baptist hospitals reported a total bed capacity of 8,836, property valued at $97,817,000, and a total of 374,086 patients treated.

See also WESTWARD EXPANSION, SOUTHERN BAPTIST.   J. P. EDMUNDS

GUARDIAN, THE. A Baptist newspaper of Georgia published from 1881 to 1906 when it was succeeded by *The Bible Studio*.

JOHN J. HURT, JR.

GUATEMALA-HONDURAS, MISSION IN. The beginning of Baptist work in Guatemala and Honduras was precipitated by the visit of Paul C. Bell, Sr., in 1946. At that time Bell was superintendent of Baptist Home Mission Board work in Panama. He organized several congregations into churches, and the work remained under his supervision until January of 1947 when it came under the supervision of the Foreign Mission Board. William Jackson Webb of the Mexican mission made periodic visits to oversee the work during 1947, and in 1948 he moved to Guatemala City with his family. Six additional missionaries were named in 1952 for service in Guatemala and Honduras. Following language study in Costa Rica, Harold Edward and Alice (Leavitt) Hurst went to Honduras in Jan., 1954; Chester Samuel Cadwallader, Jr., and Dorothy (Bell) Cadwallader to Guatemala in Feb., 1954; and John Durwood and Wyona (Haragan) Ratliff to Honduras in Apr., 1954.

In 1953 the board named six more missionaries for the two countries. Paul C. Bell, Jr., and Carolyn (Crunk) Bell, appointed for Honduras, were reassigned to Guatemala and served an interim period of six months before entering language school. William M. Dyal, Jr., and Edith (Colvin) Dyal reached Guatemala in Dec., 1954, and Alton Clark and Sarah (Martin) Scanlon, in Feb., 1955.

The missionaries are stationed in Guatemala City and in Tegucigalpa, Honduras.

JOHN DURWOOD RATLIFF

GUATEMALA-HONDURAS BAPTIST CONVENTION. Baptist work in Guatemala and Honduras dates from a visit made to the sister republics in 1946 by Paul C. Bell, Sr., then superintendent of Southern Baptist Home Mission Board work in Panama. Bell's visit was precipitated by correspondence with representatives of the Convention of Evangelical Independent Churches in Guatemala, and with an independent pastor in Honduras whose congregation considered itself Baptist in doctrine.

Following Bell's visit members of the small congregation in Honduras were baptized, and organized the first Baptist church in Honduras in Jan., 1946. Since 1946 four churches have been established, and they maintain 22 mission congregations.

In Guatemala the original Convention of Independent Evangelical Churches was composed of nine self-supporting churches with approximately 700 members and six pastors. As far back as 1931 they had begun to use Baptist literature, and in 1939 had adopted the *Manual for Baptist Churches* by Hiscox as their guide. Bell found them to be Baptist in practice and belief and effected their organization into a convention of Baptist churches.

The Home Mission Board maintained the work for one year, but on Jan. 1, 1947, the Foreign Mission Board took it over and placed it temporarily under the supervision of the Mexican Baptist Mission. William Jackson Webb made periodic visits from Torreon, Mexico, during succeeding months. In 1948 he moved to Guatemala City with his family.

At present the Guatemala-Honduras Convention consists of 18 churches with 1,700 members. Four missionary families live in Guatemala and two in Honduras.   JOHN D. RATLIFF

GUILT. The condition following the deliberate violation of the moral law. Guilt is represented in the Bible as universal, "for all have sinned" (Rom. 3:22-23). It involves responsibility. Man is guilty, not because of what Adam did, but because of what he has done with the sinful disposition received from Adam. The fall of Adam was individual, but it had collective consequences, which, however, do not necessarily imply that those suffering them share the guilt which preceded them. Psalm 51 is a moving confession of individual guilt. Man's guilt means that he deserves the condemnation of God.

BIBLIOGRAPHY: H. W. Robinson, *The Christian Doctrine of Man* (1947). H. R. Mackintosh, *The Christian Experience of Forgiveness* (1921).

CHARLES A. TRENTHAM

GWALTNEY, LESLIE LEE, SR. (b. Elberon, Surry County, Va., Mar. 5, 1876; d. Birmingham, Ala., Nov. 10, 1955). Preacher, denominational leader, editor, and statesman. His parents were John Avington Merritt and Sarah Rebecca (Deering) Gwaltney. He married Richie Thornton Peters, and they had three children—Leslie Lee, Jr., Richard Merritt, and Raecile (Mrs. Fred Alvis Davis). Gwaltney was baptized in 1888 and ordained to the ministry in 1902. He was a graduate student of University of Richmond, 1899-1904; Union Theological Seminary, Richmond, 1904-05; received the Th.M. degree, Southern Baptist Theological Seminary, Louisville, Ky., 1908; S.T.D. degree, Potomac University, 1909; Litt.D. degree, Howard College, Birmingham, Ala., 1927. He went to Alabama in 1908 and served the following churches consecutively: Prattville, Greenville, and Florence, First. In 1919 he was elected editor of the *Alabama Baptist* and served in this capacity until July 1, 1950. He was editor emeritus of the same paper until his death, president of the Alabama Baptist State Convention 1935-37, president of the Alabama Temperance Alliance, and trustee of the Southern Baptist Theological Seminary. He was the author of the following books: *Man's Fairest Hope, A Rosary of Facts, Christ and Our Liberties, Heralds of Freedom, Forty of the Twentieth, A Message for Today,* and *World's Greatest Decade.* He was a leader in the organization of the Alabama Temperance Alliance and the Baptist Foundation of Alabama; and his influence as an editor, preacher, and statesman was felt throughout the Southern Baptist Convention. He was a strong advocate of the separation of church and state.

LEON MACON

GWATKIN, JAMES EDWARD (b. Bedford County, Va., Mar. 19, 1866; d. New Orleans, La., Oct. 27, 1941). Son of Charles Henry and Fredonia (Chewning) Gwatkin, he attended public schools in Bedford County, the preparatory school of the University of Virginia, University of Virginia, and Southern Baptist Theological Seminary, where he received the Th.M. and Th.D. degrees. The influence of dedication in infancy by his godly mother and inspiration received from a country schoolteacher remained with Gwatkin through life. He was converted as a youth and ordained at First Baptist Church, Charlottesville, Va. Gwatkin served pastorates at several places in Virginia, Kentucky, Oklahoma, and Colorado, and served as associate editor of the *Baptist Argus* while in Louisville, Ky. He wrote Sunday school lessons for Southern Baptist publications, articles for *The Teacher,* and many poems published in religious papers. A member and supporter of the Anti-Saloon League of America, he became a member of the first faculty of the Baptist Bible Institute, New Orleans, La., in 1918, and was also business manager; he served as professor of biblical introduction, 1918-41. Associate professor of New Testament interpretation for a time, Gwatkin was one of three professors who continued to serve the institute without salary when a default in bonded indebtedness required drastic budget reductions in 1932. His support of the institute's press led to its being named the James E. Gwatkin Memorial Press.

J. WASH WATTS

H

HAGARVILLE ACADEMY. A mission school established in 1919, operated by the Home Mission Board and the Arkansas Baptist state mission board. With two buildings financed locally, the academy had an average enrolment of 123 from 1919 to 1922; it closed in 1927.

H. D. MORTON

HAILEY, ORREN LUICO (b. Fayette County, Tenn., June 21, 1852; d. Nashville, Tenn., Feb. 10, 1934). Son of Luico Sanders and Elizabeth (Griffin) Hailey. He attended McKenzie College, Henderson Masonic Institute, Southwestern Baptist University, and Southern Baptist Theological Seminary, where he graduated in 1884. He married Nora Snider Graves, daughter of James Robinson Graves (*q.v.*). He was ordained to the ministry in 1879, and was pastor of churches at Aberdeen, Miss.; Knoxville and Nashville, Tenn.; Oxford, Miss.; Ft. Smith, Ark.; and Texarkana, Comanche, Corsicana, Plainview, and Dallas, Tex. He was also president of Wayland Baptist College, 1915-17.

Hailey was active in denominational affairs

and particularly in support of Negro theological education. He was chairman of the committee on order of business for Southern Baptist Convention, 1913-24; member of the joint commission from Northern (now American) Baptist Convention and Southern Baptist Convention, 1917-19; secretary of the commission from the Southern Baptist Convention to assist in establishing the American Baptist Theological Seminary, Nashville, Tenn., 1919-34.

Of Hailey's work it was said, "Dr. O. L. Hailey, while a member of the faculty, has devoted himself to the promotion of the Seminary and its maintenance. He has intimate association with the teachers and the business affairs of the Seminary and is in close co-operation with all the Seminary activities. It is the desire of the members of both conventions, that he should be closely identified with all the features of the Seminary. He has been elected as general secretary of the Board of Directors, as well as a member of the faculty."

His published works consist of *Why They Did Not Join the Methodists; Life, Time and Teachings of Dr. J. R. Graves; Sermons of Dr. J. R. Graves;* and *Three Prophetic Days.*

L. S. SEDBERRY

HAITI, BAPTIST UNION OF. A new and growing organization and a direct outgrowth of the missionary work conducted by the American Baptist Home Mission Society of the American Baptist Convention.

Missionaries are helping local churches achieve self-sufficiency in church government, administration, and support. Constituting the Haiti Baptist Union are 64 churches and 500 missions and outstations with 22,761 church members, through which 193 Sunday schools and 43 day schools are conducted with average attendance of 9,477 and 2,663 respectively.

Visitation evangelism has resulted in hundreds of converts who are made ready for baptism in instruction classes. Six pastors recently conducted a mass baptismal service for 250 converts.

Better-trained men and policy decisions are results of annual pastors' conferences. These conferences have encouraged churches to give toward the work in Haiti by accepting quotas on a per capita basis. This is a marked step toward self-support.

The seminary trains new pastors but never in sufficient numbers to supply the pastorless churches. The seminary staff, with the assistance of some local pastors, provides an extension program of local Bible institutions and leadership training conferences. Steady progress in Christian education is being made through a newly organized National Youth Association, well-attended summer conferences, and conferences for Sunday school teachers and lay preachers in local churches.

The number of primary schools increases annually. Although it is difficult to pay adequate salaries and hold good teachers, the standard of education is improving. The Good Samaritan Hospital has treated hundreds of patients in its dispensary.

MRS. MILO E. WENGER

HALE, SARAH ALICE (b. Monroe County, Tenn., Nov. 25, 1856; d. Fort Smith, Ark., Feb. 10, 1952). Writer, translator, missionary to Mexico. Educated at Carson-Newman College, Miss Hale went to Saltillo, Mexico, as a self-supported missionary in Nov., 1883, then was appointed by the Southern Baptist Foreign Mission Board in 1891. Ill health forced her resignation in Jan., 1900. After touring Europe and Palestine, she lived in Monterrey, Mexico, from 1908 until Apr., 1951. She translated 70 books into Spanish and published them at her own expense, wrote two books in Spanish, and wrote an English novel, *Mercedes.* Through her initiative the Baptist Woman's Missionary Union of Mexico was organized in 1919.

FRANK W. PATTERSON

HALL, JOHN NEWTON (b. Clinton County, Ky., Feb. 5, 1849; d. Fulton, Ky., Dec. 4, 1905). Preacher, editor, controversialist. He was converted at the age of 14 at Cane Run Baptist Church near Arlington, Ky. His formal education consisted of three years' attendance at Milburn Academy, Milburn, Ky. He was licensed to preach in 1871 and in 1872 was ordained by Hopewell Baptist Church in West Kentucky Association. Hall was married July 6, 1871, to Millie Earl, who died Dec. 12, 1899; and on Aug. 8, 1900, to Lillian J. Smith, who survived him. His pastorates were Martin, Dyersburg, and Newburn, Tenn.; Fulton, Ky. (1893-99); Trezevant, Tenn. (1900); again at Fulton, Ky. (1901-03); Arlington, Ky.; and Bolivar, Tenn.

His career as an editor extended from 1879 until his death. During this time he was connected with the following papers: the *Baptist Gleaner,* Fulton, Ky., the *Banner and Gleaner,* with W. P. Throgmorton; then the *Baptist Gleaner,* with J. B. Moody; then he bought the *Baptist Reaper* and changed the name to *Baptist Gleaner,* which was finally sold to the *Western Recorder,* with Hall as editor of the Gleaner department. When the *American Baptist Flag,* of St. Louis, Mo., was sold at auction in 1898, Hall bought the paper and removed it to Fulton, Ky. It later became the *Baptist Flag.*

Hall's career as an editor and controversialist was chiefly concerned with issues involving Landmark doctrines and missionary methods. Landmarkist in his belief in the supremacy and autonomy of the individual congregation in all religious matters, he consistently opposed all boards or other co-operative religious institutions which possessed administrative powers independent of specific mandates from individual churches. He was not opposed to committees which were the servants of individual or co-operating churches in such matters as the transmittal of funds to missionaries, but did oppose all boards which chose, appointed, or in any way directed the work of missionaries. These responsibilities, he thought, belonged to individual churches. He also opposed the financial basis of representation then in force in the Southern Baptist Convention, believing that it made richer churches and individuals improperly influential.

His pungent editorials, sprinkled with wit and sarcasm, proved him an able polemicist, and his paper, the *Baptist Flag*, was read in many parts of the South. Toward the end of his life he "greatly modified his mission views" and, it is said, grew quite wealthy.

LEO T. CRISMON

HALL, ROBERT, JR. (b. Arnsby, Leicestershire, England, May 2, 1764; d. Bristol, England, Feb. 21, 1831). English Baptist divine. The 14th child of Robert Hall, Sr., a respected Baptist minister, Hall taught himself the alphabet with the help of gravestones. He was educated in village schools and sent at his mother's death in 1776 to the boarding school of John Ryland, Sr., at Northampton, after which he attended Bristol Baptist Academy and King's College, Aberdeen, receiving the M.A. degree in 1784. He began his ministry as assistant pastor at Broadmead Church, Bristol (1785–91), and held successive pastorates at Cambridge (1791–1806), Harvey Lane in Leicester (1806–25), and Broadmead in Bristol (1825–31).

Hall had a keen mind which he developed from his childhood. By the age of nine he had written hymns and was well acquainted with Jonathan Edwards, the creative American theologian, and other metaphysical thinkers. He delivered his first sermon at an ordination in July, 1779, and was ordained the following year in his father's church at Arnesby. He became a liberal political theorist and spoke effectively for separation of church and state, freedom of the press, and the rights of the working man. In church polity he was also liberal and progressive, a hardy proponent of open communion, participating in the last great controversy on the subject among English Baptists with Joseph Kinghorn. Hall excelled in private conversation and could speak on almost any subject with genuine understanding, while salting his remarks with sharp wit.

As assistant pastor at Broadmead, Hall served under Caleb Evans, under whom he had studied at Bristol Academy, where Hall himself became a tutor. Hall moved in his theological thinking from Calvinism to Arminianism during this period; he was a firm believer in the divinity and atonement of Christ. Differences with Evans prompted Hall to resign his position in 1791, after which he moved to his pastorate in Cambridge. While there, in 1800, his delivery and subsequent publication of his discourse entitled "Modern Infidelity" made a great sensation.

Poor health bothered Hall from his frail childhood. He was chronically afflicted with kidney stone attacks and suffered pain almost constantly. Hall had hypochondria attacks and two short seizures of mental illness between 1804 and 1806. Recovery was complete, however, and marked an important turning point in his religious life, the point from which he dated his real conversion experience. He resigned his Cambridge pastorate and went to Harvey Lane, Leicester, Oct. 7, 1807, where he did his best work; he also married. At Harvey Lane, Hall had two congregations, the morning one an open communion group. Although his previous religious life had always been spiritually strong, he solemnly rededicated his life, and each year renewed this dedication. As he advanced in years, he increased both in piety and in wholehearted devotion to evangelical doctrines. Hall returned to Bristol in Mar., 1826, succeeding John Ryland as pastor at Broadmead. Still an avid reader, he was learning Italian in order to read Dante. His health became worse, however, aggravated by heart disease in 1830, and Hall preached his last sermon in Jan., 1831.

The excellent reputation which Hall enjoyed during his lifetime was due to his few published sermons dealing with national concerns, which were so well done and so widely acclaimed that Hall won the reputation of being an orator equaling those of Greece and Rome. These sermons, however, are now seldom read and are by modern standards far too verbose. Hall's biographer, Olinthus Gregory, considered his published work inferior to his pulpit address because in the former he strained for perfection, while when preaching to a congregation, he poured forth a torrent of lofty ideas clothed in superb language and undergirded by complete sincerity. It was not unusual for a majority of his auditors to rise from their seats during his preaching. Certainly Hall is properly numbered with Spurgeon and Maclaren as one of the three giants of the English Baptist pulpit during the 19th century.

Hall's chief published works include *Apology for the Freedom of the Press* (1793); *Reflections on War* (1802); *The Advantage of Knowledge to the Lower Classes* (1810); *On Terms of Communion* (1815); and *A Sermon Occasioned by the Death of . . . Princess Charlotte* (1817). His *Works* were collected in 1832 in six volumes, with a memoir by Olinthus Gregory.

BIBLIOGRAPHY: *Dictionary of National Biography*, Vol. XXIX.

W. C. SMITH, JR.

HALL-MOODY JUNIOR COLLEGE. A West Tennessee school founded as an institute in 1900 by the Martin and Beulah Baptist associations, and under the control of the Tennessee Baptist Convention from 1917 to 1927. The school, first called Hall-Moody Institute, enjoyed an early success under its associational direction. There was, however, a feeling among Tennessee Baptists that their educational work was in need of correlation, and in 1910 the convention adopted a resolution instructing its education commission to effect this correlation. Hall-Moody Institute, which had a program duplicating, to a large extent, the one offered at Union University, came under the control of the state convention in 1917. It was agreed that Hall-Moody would maintain a standard high school and two years of college work and that after June 1, 1918, Union University would discontinue its preparatory department.

Hall-Moody received support from the Tennessee Baptist Convention for current expenses until the year 1918, after which date it received no support for current expenses but shared proportionately with Union University in funds raised for indebtedness. In Dec., 1926, as a result of a growing sentiment that Tennessee Baptists had more schools than they were able to support, the convention's executive board voted to consolidate Hall-Moody Junior College with Union University at the close of that school year. Hall-Moody's property was to be sold for its debts, and its records and alumni were to become a part of Union University. This action was later approved by both boards of trustees.   HARLEY FITE

HAMBURG SCHOOL. A school under Baptist control in Jackson County, N. C. In 1889, as Hamburg Normal High School, with A. E. Pinckard as its principal, it had a theological department for ministerial students. In 1891, A. T. Hord, of Glenville, N. C., became the principal, and two years later the school was adopted by Haywood Association.   D. L. SMILEY

HAMILTON, ROBERT (b. Thornton, Ind., Jan. 7, 1861; d. Okmulgee, Okla., Mar. 23, 1948). Indian missionary and Oklahoma denominational leader. He received common school education, was ordained at Wellington, Kans., 1892, and served as pastor at Omega, Okla. In 1895 he was appointed by the Home Mission Society as missionary to Cheyennes; in 1913, as missionary to the Osages. From 1915 to 1930 he ministered to Indians in Government schools. He is buried at Okmulgee, Okla.   O. O. MORGAN

HANNIBAL–LAGRANGE COLLEGE. A liberal arts junior college located at Hannibal, Mo. Established in 1858 at LaGrange, Mo., as LaGrange College, the school became known as Hannibal-LaGrange College after being moved to Hannibal in 1928. In 1856 the Wyaconda Baptist Association laid plans to "establish a male and female seminary of the highest order." Principal among its founders were Trustees J. A. Hay, Thomas Richardson, Ralph Smith, James M. Lillard, George K. Biggs, and Ezra Kerfoot. Abandonment to Federal troops in 1860 and financial difficulties marked critical periods in the early history of the college.

The Wyaconda Baptist Association was the chief support of the college until 1919 when additional associations and churches of Northeast Missouri began to provide funds. In 1928, when the college was moved to Hannibal, citizens of that town pledged $232,000 for its support. That same year the charter was amended to provide for a board of trustees approved by the Missouri Baptist General Association, which now regularly supports the college.

Situated on a former Indian site, the college now occupies a campus of 120 acres overlooking the Mississippi River. The buildings, arranged in horseshoe style, include the Administration Building, Pulliam Hall for women, Nunn-Cook Hall for men, faculty housing units, student apartments, a student center, Muir Science Hall, modest farm units, and the president's home. A golf course, badminton and tennis courts, a softball diamond, and picnic park complete the campus. A program for future expansion will include a new boys' dormitory, library, science, and office buildings, and additional housing units.

Hannibal-LaGrange College is fully accredited by the University of Missouri and has applied for membership in the North Central Association of Colleges and Secondary Schools. The teaching staff consists of 15 full-time teachers and five part-time teachers. The annual operating budget is approximately $250,000. Endowments total $9,774.14. The college has served 7,450 students, the annual enrolment for the early years being approximately 150, and in recent years approximately 325.

BIBLIOGRAPHY: R. A. Duncan, *A History of Baptists in Missouri* (1882). *Hannibal-Courier Post* (Nov. 25, 1929; June 15, 1955). *Hannibal-LaGrange College Catalogue* (Apr., 1931). *1955 Book of Reports to the Missouri Baptist General Association. Leaders in Education*, Third Edition (1948). *Pro Forma Decree*, Marion County Court Record, Palmyra, Mo. *Self Survey Report of Hannibal-LaGrange College* (July 1, 1955). J. H. Terrill, *A Historical Chart, LaGrange College*, LaGrange, Mo. [n.d.]. *Who Was Who in America, 1897–1942. Who's Who in America*, Vol. 28, 1954–55.   FLORENCE GROVES

HARALSON, JONATHAN (b. Lowndes County, Ala., Oct. 18, 1830; d. Montgomery, Ala., July 11, 1912). Eminent jurist, leading Baptist layman in Alabama for over a half century. The son of wealthy planter William Browning and Temperance Martin (Dunklin) Haralson, he received his education in country schools, University of Alabama (A.B., 1851, and A.M., 1854), and University of Louisiana (LL.B., 1853). Mercer University conferred honorary LL.D. degree on him in 1892. He entered law practice in Selma, Ala., in 1853. He was appointed to city court at Selma by Governor Houston in 1876 and held that position until 1892 when he was made associate justice of Alabama Supreme Court. He was re-elected to that position repeatedly until 1910.

Haralson married his first wife, Mattie Ellen Thompson, Apr. 9, 1859, and his second, Lida J. McFaden, May 20, 1869. He had three daughters: Mary, Caroline, and Willie Browning.

Converted and baptized at age 14, he became active in religious work early. He was made deacon at age 25. He was elected president of Alabama Baptist State Convention in 1874 and held that position until 1892 when "impervious necessity" kept him away for the first time in 18 years. He was also elected president of the Southern Baptist Convention in 1888 and served continuously for 10 years. He was a trustee of Howard College, a member of the American Baptist Education Society, and a trustee of Dallas Academy. From 1876 until his death Haralson served as trustee of the Alabama Agricultural and Mechanical College (now the Alabama Polytechnic Institute).

Riley said of him: "Judge Jonathan Haralson was an eminent type of that generation of southern gentlemen who were a connecting link between the old and the new South." He was free of self-seeking, never ostentatious, exact, firm, but gentle. His Christian traits made him much sought after, and he was a master parliamentarian. He was the most distinguished layman in the denomination of the state during that time. He died at the age of 82 and was buried in Selma, Ala.

BIBLIOGRAPHY: W. Cathcart, ed., *The Baptist Encyclopedia* (1883). W. B. Crumpton, *A Book of Memories 1842–1920*, (1921). A. H. Newman, *A History of the Baptist Churches in the United States* (1894). T. M. Owen, *History of Alabama and Dictionary of Alabama Biography* (1921). B. F. Riley, *Makers and Romance of Alabama Baptists* (n.d.); *A Memorial History of the Baptists of Alabama* (1923). C. A. Stakely, *The History of the First Baptist Church of Montgomery* (1930).   GARNETT E. PUCKETT

HARDIN-SIMMONS UNIVERSITY. A coeducational, liberal arts school, located at Abilene, Tex., founded as Abilene Baptist College by Sweetwater Association in 1891. At that time the association included all the territory along the Texas and Pacific Railroad from Callahan County to El Paso. At the 14th annual meeting of Sweetwater Association, Aug. 10, 1890, the moderator appointed a committee of seven men with plenary powers to accept bids for the location of the school and who "shall jointly with the church where the school shall be located have plenary powers to appoint a Board of Trustees and do all other things necessary to the establishment of said school."

The cornerstone for the first building was laid July 4, 1891, and at the meeting of the association, Aug. 1, 1891, the committee reported that the school had been located in Abilene and chartered; that a board of trustees had been appointed, and a brick building was being erected; that James B. Simmons, a Baptist minister in New York City, had donated $5,000 to the school making possible the completion of the first building, after which the name was changed to Simmons College; and that a president had been appointed.

In allowing the college to use his name, Simmons entered into the Foundation Agreement, much of which he wrote, which specified in part:

AND WHEREAS no Barbarous tribe or heathen nation or infidel conclave ever becomes Christian of itself, but all true Christian enlightenment and progress, whether in tribe or nation or conclave, the same as in individual men, must come from a source outside of themselves, namely from the Spirit of God, through the teachings of the Son of God, as revealed in the Word of God;

AND WHEREAS the conquest of this world unto Jehovah is not likely to be accomplished except through the instrumentality of Christian Schools and colleges, in which Christianity shall be the confessed and formative principle of their whole organization, method and life, and in which it shall be the constant aim of the teachers by a truly liberal and Christian culture:

(1) To bring young men and women to Christ;
(2) To teach them of Christ; and
(3) To train them for the service of Christ;

AND WHEREAS such truly Christian College must give actual Christian instruction, not only in other departments of Liberal Culture, but especially
(1) In the Word of God, the greatest classic;
(2) In the Story of the Church, the greatest history;
(3) In the Doctrine of the Bible, the greatest science;
(4) In Christian Ethics, the noblest morality . . .

AND WHEREAS, in order to this end, it is indispensable that the President, Professors, Tutors, and Teachers (but especially the President) should be chosen, other things being equal, first of all because of a hearty sympathy with the above named views and principles.

That the Roger Williams doctrine of entire liberty in religious concernments is a great and distinguishing doctrine of the Baptists, no religious test shall ever hinder any person . . . from entering and receiving instruction in said Simmons College.

Later because of his interest in the college as a new outpost of Christian culture and education, Simmons left a provision which enabled Simmons College to receive at his death a portion of his estate valued at $40,000.

The college began its first session in Sept., 1892, and because of its growth and expansion became Simmons University in 1925, the same year in which provisions for graduate study were authorized and work leading to the Master of Arts degree was instituted. In 1927, the university was admitted to the Southern Association of Secondary Schools and Colleges, American Association of Colleges, and in 1930 became a member of the National Association of Schools of Music.

In 1934 John G. Hardin and his wife, of Burkburnett, Tex., made the institution a gift totaling $900,000. Sometime later the board of trustees voted to change the name, and an amendment to the charter was filed with the Secretary of State, changing the name to Hardin-Simmons University. Since 1941 the university has been controlled by the Baptist General Convention of Texas with the trustees recommended by Sweetwater Association and elected by the convention.

The liberal arts curriculum offers B.A., B.S., B.B.A., B.M., M.A., M.Ed., and M.M. degrees. In 1952, at the invitation of the board of trustees, the Department of the Army established a unit of the Reserve Officer Training Corps, Branch General.

Capital outlay consists of a main campus of 40 acres with 21 buildings, the president's home, and football stadium; a secondary campus (two blocks west of main campus) on which are located inexpensive housing for 108 married students, the riding school, and rodeo grounds. Other supplementary housing near the university consists of two dwellings, one duplex, and two three-room apartment buildings. The aggregate outlay is $4,336,674.45. Total annual enrolment in 1954-55 was 2,274 and endowment, $1,814,980.63. Hardin-Simmons has been served by nine presidents, including Owen Clinton Pope (q.v.), 1898-1901; Oscar Henry Cooper (q.v.), 1902-09; and Jefferson Davis Sandefer (q.v.), 1909-40.   W. T. WALTON

HARDY, JOHN CRUMPTON (b. Newton County, Miss., 1864; d. Belton, Tex., 1938). Educator. Graduating from Mississippi College where he received both A.B. and A.M. degrees, Hardy served as superintendent of public schools in Jackson, Miss., from 1890 to 1900, and as president of Mississippi Agricultural and Mechanical College, 1900-12. Hardy became president of Mary Hardin-Baylor College, Belton, Tex., 1912-37, and under his administration Mary Hardin-Baylor's campus was expanded from 20 to 75 acres, including its farm; the number of buildings increased from two to seven; and an endowment of $609,490 was raised, in addition to equity in the Hardin Trust, amounting to $1,000,000. Hardy was also president of the Baptist General Convention of Texas, 1932-35.   FRANK BURKHALTER

HARDY, WILLIAM HARRIS (b. near Montgomery, Ala., Feb. 12, 1837; d. Gulfport, Miss., Feb. 17, 1917). Attorney, orator, Mississippi Baptist leader. After attending Cumberland University at Lebanon, Tenn., Hardy taught school at Montrose, Miss., and founded an academy at Sylviarena in Smith County. In 1858 Hardy began the practice of law at Raleigh, and on Apr. 27, 1861, he was elected captain of a company of volunteers, Defenders of Smith County. He moved to Paulding as a lawyer in 1865, but eight years later moved to Meridian to promote the New Orleans and Northeastern Railroad from Meridian to New Orleans, which he had advocated since 1868. Hattiesburg, Miss., laid out by Hardy in 1883, was named for his second wife. He reorganized the Gulf and Ship Island Railroad in 1886 and founded the city of Gulfport on its southern terminus. Governor Vardman appointed Hardy circuit judge of the second district, Jan. 1, 1906. A talented orator, Hardy eulogized Jefferson Davis in New York City in 1889 and made his greatest contribution to the Baptist cause in Mississippi through his strong appeals, while president of the state convention from 1880 to 1885, for unification of the work and co-operation of all Baptist agencies. He served as vice-president of the Southern Baptist Convention, trustee of Mississippi College, and member of the old state mission board.

BIBLIOGRAPHY: J. L. Boyd, *A Popular History of the Baptists in Mississippi* (1930). *Goodspeed's Biographical and Historical Memoirs of Mississippi*, Vol. I (1891). T. A. Hardy, *No Compromise with Principle, Autobiography and Biography of William Harris Hardy* (1946). D. Malone, ed., *Dictionary of American Biography* (1933).   C. B. HAMLET III

HARGRAVE MILITARY ACADEMY. T. Ryland Sanford, pastor of the Baptist church in Chatham, Va., became greatly concerned about the need for facilities for secondary education in the county. With the able assistance and financial backing of one of his deacons, J. Hunt Hargrave, Chatham Training School was opened in Sept., 1909, with 18 students. Sanford was president until 1917, when he was succeeded by A. H. Camden, who was president until his retirement in 1951. He was succeeded by Joseph H. Cosby, the present president.

From the beginning, emphasis was placed on preparation for college, particularly Richmond College. Military training was introduced in 1919. In 1925 the name of the school was changed to Hargrave Military Academy to honor Hargrave, who was a founder, the principal benefactor, and chairman of the board of trustees.

A disastrous fire in 1950 destroyed a large part of the main building. Through contributions from alumni and friends, insurance receipts, and by anticipation of Cooperative Program funds, the academy was able to replace its losses with a more modern and commodious building.

The school is fully accredited by the state and the Southern Association of Colleges and Secondary Schools. The enrolment has been at capacity—361 in 1955-56. Through the efforts of Sanford and others, the school received help from the denomination from the first year. For 1955-56 denominational support amounted to $74,547. There is an endowment of only $3,-282, but total assets are $1,018,815. The control of the school is vested in a self-perpetuating board of trustees nominated by the Baptist General Association of Virginia.

RALPH MCDANEL

HARRIS, HENRY HERBERT (b. Louisa County, Va., Dec. 17, 1837; d. Lynchburg, Va., Feb. 4, 1897). College and seminary professor, minister, editor. After studying at home and in a community school, Harris entered Richmond College in 1854 and graduated in 1856. He taught high school for a year and then entered the University of Virginia where he received an M.A. degree in 1860. When his company in the Confederate Army disbanded in 1862, Harris entered Southern Baptist Theological Seminary for one month but then reenlisted for the remainder of the Civil War. After teaching at Albemarle Female Institute and at Richmond College as professor of Greek, from 1866 to 1895, Harris became professor of polemics and biblical introduction in Southern Seminary and served until his death.

Ordained in 1858, Harris served as a pastor and as clerk of Dover Association in Virginia. He was editor of *Foreign Mission Journal* and *Religious Herald* and lesson writer in the *Baptist Teacher* and *Advanced Quarterly* of the American Baptist Publication Society. Harris traveled in Europe, Egypt, and Palestine in 1878 and later visited mission fields in Mexico. Member of the Foreign Mission Board from 1876 to 1895 and president of the board the last nine of those years, he published *Three Lectures on Missions* through the American Baptist Publication Society, which were delivered as Gay Lectures at Southern Seminary in 1895.

LEO T. CRISMON

HARRIS, SAMUEL (b. Hanover County, Va., Jan. 12, 1724; d. between Jan. 13 and Oct. 17, 1799; buried at his homestead, Pittsylvania Co., Va.). In early life Samuel Harris settled in Pittsylvania where he became justice of the peace, burgess, colonel, captain of Fort Mayo, commissary, judge, church warden, sheriff. At the age of 34 Harris was joyously converted and baptized, 1758. Relinquishing his "worldly honors," Harris began his ministry the following year, though he was not ordained until 1769. Starting in Pittsylvania, his work extended throughout Virginia to North Carolina. Bearing for a few months the title "Apostle of Virginia," Samuel Harris founded, or helped to found, at least 26 Baptist churches and is credited with being the major influence in the growth of Baptist work in Virginia. Asked to preside at most of the associations and business meetings he attended, Harris was moderator of the General Association of Virginia at least six times. As chairman of the General Committee of the Baptists of Virginia, he signed the letter to President Washington, Aug. 8, 1789, "fearing that the liberty of conscience . . . was not sufficiently secured" in the Constitution.

Samuel Harris married Lucy Camp. Their children were Samuel, John, Mary, Nathaniel, Benjamin, and Elizabeth.

James Ireland (*q.v.*), the first candidate Harris baptized, says of him, "He was like another Paul among the churches."

BIBLIOGRAPHY: M. Edwards, *Materials Towards a History of the Baptists of Virginia* (1772). W. B. Hackley, "The Life and Times of Samuel Harris," *Religious Herald* (Jan. 13, 1955). J. Ireland, *The Life of the Reverend James Ireland* . . . (1819). G. Ryland, *The Baptists of Virginia 1699–1926* (1955). J. B. Taylor, *Lives of Virginia Baptist Ministers* (1838).

J. LEVERING EVANS

HARRISON, JAMES BUCHANAN, CHAIR OF NEW TESTAMENT INTERPRETATION. A businessman in Greensboro, N. C., James Buchanan Harrison became interested in the progress of Southern Baptist Theological Seminary at least as early as 1924, when he made gifts and pledges to the seminary totaling $10,000. In 1925, after conferring with his pastor, John Clyde Turner (1878–), an alumnus of the seminary, Harrison decided to increase his initial gift to $75,000 in order to endow a Chair of New Testament Interpretation. At his death on Mar. 27, 1930, Harrison had paid $40,000 of his pledge, and in his will he directed his son, J. Frank Harrison, as executor of the estate, to pay the balance due. This provision of the will was fully carried out during the next three years, and on Oct. 21, 1933, the executive committee of the seminary's board of trustees voted unanimously to name the chair after its donor. Archibald Thomas Robertson (*q.v.*) occupied the chair during the closing months of his life, and since that time the chair has been held by William Hersey Davis (*q.v.*), 1934–50, and William Walter Adams, since 1954.

H. E. TURLINGTON

HARRISON, JOHN GREEN (b. Washington County, Ga., Apr. 27, 1869; d. Harrison, Ga., Jan. 28, 1934). Educator. Harrison was graduated from Mercer University in 1889 and received the Th.M. degree from the Southern Baptist Theological Seminary in 1899. He studied education under Francis W. Parker at Chautauqua Lake and did graduate work at the University of Chicago and the University of Berlin (1905–06). He received the honorary degrees of Doctor of Divinity from Mercer University (1901) and Doctor of Laws from Louisiana College (1932).

Converted and baptized in 1886, he determined to enter the ministry in 1889 and was ordained in 1896. He taught and preached in several communities and served as president of Hiawassee Institute, Hiawassee, Ga. (1891). After several pastorates he became pastor of Tattnall Square Baptist Church, Macon, Ga. (1899–1905).

He served the cause of Christian education in Georgia as a trustee of Mercer University (1903–05), then as professor (1907–34), dean of the School of Christianity (1929–34), and secretary of the Georgia Baptist Education Board (1915–19). He was a member and chairman of the Georgia State Board of Welfare (1920–29) and a member of the Georgia State Board of Education (1929–34). His contribution to Georgia Baptist bibliography is *Life and Service of David Denton* (1926).

He married Bessie Winn Gilmore, Dec. 28, 1893 (d. 1902). He married Ruth Barrett, June 22, 1911, by whom he had three children.

BIBLIOGRAPHY: *Who's Who in America*, Vol. 17. *Who's Who in S.A.E.* (1912).

PARK HARRIS ANDERSON, JR.

HARRISON-CHILHOWEE BAPTIST ACADEMY. A four-year high school and preparatory school, located in East Tennessee, founded about 1840, and operated by various Tennessee Baptist organizations since 1887. The institution grew out of McCroskey School, known locally as Owl

College, and under the direction of John and Sam McCallie. The school passed from their control in 1880 or 1881, and became Boyd's Creek Academy. From 1884 to 1889 the school was called Harrison Seminary, and then Harrison-Chilhowee Normal Academy. In 1887 the Chilhowee Baptist Association assumed control, and the next year joined with the Sevier County Baptist Association in sponsorship. For many years the school gave teacher training courses for those who were not able to go to college and were to teach in the public schools of the area. In 1894 the word "Normal" was dropped from the school's name. After other name changes (Chilhowee Institute, 1900; Harrison-Chilhowee Institute, 1911) the school came under the control of the Tennessee Baptist Convention and was rechartered in 1932 as Harrison-Chilhowee Baptist Academy.

The school was founded in an era when academies were numerous, and short-lived. That it survived is due in no small measure to the abilities of its founders and to the guidance of its sponsors. From the first the school had a high local reputation, and soon made its place in the Baptist life as well. Even before it came formally under Baptist control, some of its earlier leaders were Baptists. It is now the only Baptist school of its kind in the state. Its purpose is to furnish a complete high school education under distinctly Christian and Baptist influence. Particular emphasis has been placed on the training of preachers and denominational workers.

Since the days of the McCallies, Chilhowee has had some 14 executives in 114 years. The earlier leaders were designated principal. In 1945 Roy Anderson was elected the school's first president. Walter Stuart Rule succeeded Anderson in 1952. In 1954-55 the enrolment was 239, operating income was $70,761, and property value was $658,547. From its founding to 1956 a total of 13,896 students attended the school, and 1,194 graduated. WALTER STUART RULE

HART, OLIVER (b. Warminster, Pa., July 5, 1723; d. Hopewell, N. J., Dec. 31, 1795). American Revolutionary patriot and founder of the Charleston Association. He was converted at 17 and baptized by Jenkins Jones on April 3, 1741, at Southampton, Bucks County, Pa. Upon the insistence of his church, he surrendered to preach on Dec. 20, 1746. At the annual meeting of the Philadelphia Association on Sept. 19, 1749, a letter was read appealing for ministers for the colony of South Carolina. Hart determined to offer his services there. He was ordained at Southampton on Oct. 18, 1749, and on Nov. 13 he embarked at Philadelphia. He arrived in Charleston (spelled Charles Town before the Revolution) on Dec. 2, the day the Charleston Baptists were burying the next to the last Baptist minister in the colony. Hart accepted the pastorate of the Baptist church at Charleston on Feb. 16, 1750, and remained with it for 30 years.

The benefits of the Philadelphia Association were long familiar to Hart, and he soon began planning a similar organization in South Carolina. The first meeting of the Charleston Association, with four participating churches, was held in Charleston on Oct. 21, 1751. Early in 1754 the Religious Society, sponsored by the association to gather funds for training ministerial students, was formed by Hart. For the first quarter century of its life, Hart furnished the guiding hand in all the association's undertakings.

Rhode Island College, at its first commencement on Sept. 7, 1769, bestowed the honorary A.M. degree upon Hart. In July, 1775, Hart, William Henry Drayton, and William Tennant were appointed by the Revolutionary Council of Safety to travel over South Carolina to win support, especially among Tories of the backcountry, for the American Revolutionary cause. Hart fled twice before the British; and on Feb. 2, 1780, he left Charleston never to return. The following October he was invited to accept the pastorate of the Baptist church at Hopewell, N. J., and he remained in this pastorate until his death.

Hart was twice married: to Sarah Brees on Feb. 25, 1747/48, and to Mrs. Anne Sealey Grimball on Apr. 5, 1774. Four children, all by his first wife, survived infancy.

BIBLIOGRAPHY: W. Cathcart, *The Baptist Encyclopedia* (1883). O. Hart, "A memorandum containing some of the most remarkable concurrencies on providence relative to or noticed by an unworthy traveler towards the New Jerusalem, who desires ever to esteem himself a stranger and sojourner in this dreary wilderness." Parts of a diary in the Furman University Library. L. Townsend, *South Carolina Baptists, 1670-1805* (1935). H. A. Tupper, *Two Centuries of the First Baptist Church of South Carolina, 1683-1883* (1889). LOULIE LATIMER OWENS

HARVEY, WILLIAM PATRICK (b. County Galway, Ireland, Mar. 15, 1841; d. Louisville, Ky., Sept. 29, 1929). Educator, denominational leader. As a boy of seven, Harvey came with his mother to America with the purpose of joining the father in Mason County, Ky., near Maysville. Harvey was educated in schools at Maysville, and later at Georgetown College and Kentucky (now Transylvania) University. He was ordained a minister in 1872 and became pastor at Harrodsburg and other churches.

Harvey was the Sunday school and mission secretary for Baptists in eastern Kentucky. For four years he was vice-president of Georgetown College and later served 20 years as a trustee of that institution. For 20 years he was president of the Baptist Book Concern and manager of the *Western Recorder*, holding this position until 1908, after which time he became manager of the Baptist World Publishing Company. He was auditor of the Southern Baptist Convention for 32 years.

He was married to Katherine Payne, to whom were born two sons. LEO T. CRISMON

HATCHER, WILLIAM ELDRIDGE (b. Bedford County, Va., July 25, 1834; d. Fork Union, Va., Aug. 24, 1912). Pastor, editor, writer. Son of Henry Hatcher, a hardy farmer, and of a mother who died when he was four years old, Hatcher graduated from Richmond College in June, 1858. He held pastorates at Bainbridge Street Baptist Church, Manchester, Va.; Franklin Square Church, Baltimore, Md.; First Baptist Church, Petersburg, Va.; and Grace Street Church, Richmond. During his 26 years at Grace, beginning in May, 1875, he and his members helped to form Clay Street, West View, Immanuel, and Barton Heights churches. Hatcher's leadership in the Southern Baptist Convention was recognized; he delivered the annual sermon in 1893. In 1888 he was elected president of the Baptist General Association of Virginia, and in 1901, after resigning the pastorate of Grace Baptist Church, he founded Fork Union Academy, Fluvanna County, Va. Hatcher was at different times editor of the *Religious Herald*, the *Baltimore Baptist*, and associate editor of the *Baptist World*, Louisville, Ky. His published works include *Life of J. B. Jeter*, *The Pastor and the Sunday School*, *John Jasper*, and *Along the Trail of the Friendly Years*, his autobiography. On Dec. 22, 1864, Hatcher married Virginia Snead. J. L. ROSSER

HAWAII, MISSION IN. Organized Dec. 12, 1940, with 11 members, all of whom were transferred from war-closed mission fields in the Orient. Lonnie Elwood and Gladys (Yates) Blackman were transferred from China to Hawaii in 1938; James Dalby and Martha (Bigham) Belote, and Hannah Plowden from China, H. B., Jr., and Vera Mabel (Howard) Ramsour from Japan, and Charles Alexander and Evelyn (Corbitt) Leonard, Victor and Aurora Lee (Hargrove) Koon from Manchuria in 1940.

The Foreign Mission Board voted Dec. 9, 1937, to "lend" missionaries to Hawaii after China missionary Park Harris Anderson surveyed the field and recommended that the board send missionaries. He spent seven months in the islands and helped organize a trusteeship called the Hawaiian Baptist Mission, to hold deeds to church property. One of the trustees was Charles J. McDonald, who started Baptist work in Hawaii. Others were Anderson, C. K. Tom, Ayako Saito, and Mrs. Rebecca C. McDonald.

McDonald, a Baptist businessman and lay preacher in Hawaii, had started a Sunday school in the park pavilion at the town of Wahiawa. A Baptist church was organized in 1934.

At its Sept. 1, 1941, meeting the Hawaiian Mission of the Southern Baptist Convention voted to "accept with gratitude the offer of the Hawaiian Baptist Mission in assuming joint responsibility in administration" of work and property. A board of directors was elected: four missionaries and three local church members. Under joint control a charter of incorporation was granted by the Territory of Hawaii Dec. 18, 1941. This corporation, Hawaiian Baptist Mission, became the property-holding body for local churches and the Foreign Mission Board; was approved by Charles Edward Maddry, then executive secretary of the Foreign Mission Board, who was visiting Hawaii in Dec., 1941.

Both Chinese-speaking and Japanese-speaking missionaries worked temporarily in Hawaii. When some of them returned to their fields after the war, several new appointees were sent to the Hawaiian Mission. Following is the list of Baptist churches with the dates of organization: Wahiawa, Oahu (1934); Olivet, Honolulu (1941), which grew out of a mission church established earlier by a Baptist lay preacher, Joseph Tyssowski; Nuuanu, Honolulu (1943); Waimea, Kauai (1943), which grew out of a mission established by a family named Tamashiro; Kahului, Maui (1945); University Avenue, Honolulu (1946); Kinoole, Hilo (1946); Waialae, Honolulu (1949); Kaunakakai, Molokai (1950); Kaumana Drive, Hilo (1951); Kalihi, Honolulu (1952); Pali View, Oahu (1952); Waikiki, Honolulu (1952); Wailuku, Maui (1952); Waianae, Oahu (1953); Aina Haina, Honolulu (1955).

The Baptist Bible School, founded Oct., 1941, to train local leaders, was located near the University of Hawaii. Its first principal was Hannah Plowden. Changed to a Baptist student center in 1954, it has dormitory space for 24 students who attend the university or other schools.

The Baptist Student Union, begun in 1946 by Josephine Harris, reaches about 100 students in the University of Hawaii and other schools. It has a building adjacent to the university campus.

The Hawaiian Baptist Academy was founded in Sept., 1949, under the leadership of Hugh Pendleton and Mary (Reeks) McCormick, formerly missionaries to Nigeria. It began with the seventh and eighth grades. In 1955 it was a complete primary and high school with an enrolment of 250. VICTOR KOON

HAWAIIAN BAPTIST ACADEMY. See HAWAII, MISSION IN.

HAWAIIAN BAPTIST CONVENTION. Formally organized Dec. 12, 1940, although the Southern Baptist Foreign Mission Board sent missionaries to Hawaii as early as 1938. By 1943 there were five Baptist churches in the islands: Calvary, Nuuanu, and Olivet Baptist churches in Honolulu; Wahiawa Baptist Church, Oahu; and Waimea Baptist Church, Kauai. Messengers from these churches met July 16, 1943, at the Baptist Bible School of Hawaii in Honolulu to organize a Baptist association for the islands. Edwin B. Dozier was elected moderator; Edward Shipman, secretary; and Victor Koon, treasurer.

The messengers voted that the new body would be known as the Association of Baptist Churches in Hawaii and elected committees for evangelism and missions, literature and publicity, Woman's Missionary Union, Baptist Training Union, Sunday school, and Brotherhood.

The Baptist book store originally located at the Olivet Church in 1944, moved later to a downtown location. The convention began work on the island of Maui in 1944 with Hannah Plowden, first resident missionary, and on the island of Molokai the next year. The name of the association was changed in 1945 to Hawaii Baptist Convention, and an annual budget of $3,000 was adopted for territorial missions.

In 1946 the convention added to its organization a Board of Christian Education and Student Work, and a Commission on Social Service. The Baptist Student Union was organized in 1946 with Josephine Harris as director, and a student center was established adjacent to the University of Hawaii. *The Hawaii Baptist*, convention periodical, began publication in 1947. David Petherbridge is editor of the magazine, which has a circulation (1955) of 1,000 per month.

In 1949 the convention began work on the island of Lanai and purchased summer assembly grounds located near a beach in November of that year at Puu Kahea. The Hawaiian Baptist Academy enrolled 36 pupils in the seventh and eighth grades at its first session, Sept. 2, 1949. Since then, with Hugh Pendleton McCormick as principal, it has increased to 250 students in the first twelve grades.

The Hawaii Baptist Convention co-operates with the Southern Baptist Convention and contributes to the Southwide Cooperative Program. It supports entirely mission work on the islands of Molokai and Lanai, owns and operates the Baptist book store in Honolulu, the assembly camp at Puu Kahea, and *The Hawaii Baptist*. It co-operates with the Hawaiian Mission of the Southern Baptist Convention in operating the Baptist Student Center, the Hawaiian Baptist Academy, and the Baptist Hour broadcast. The Woman's Missionary Union of the convention promotes all departments of the organization; Sue Saito is full-time secretary. In 1955, 18 churches reported 3,539 members.   VICTOR KOON

HAWTHORNE, JAMES BOARDMAN (b. Wilcox County, Ala., May 16, 1837; d. Richmond, Va., Feb. 23, 1910). Confederate soldier, minister, evangelist, lecturer, and denominational leader. The son of Kedar and Martha (Baggett) Hawthorne, he married Emma Matilda Hutchison, Mobile, Ala. Their children were Hartwell and Charles. Hawthorne completed literary studies at Howard College. He practiced law in Mobile three years, then re-entered Howard as ministerial student where he gained acclaim as evangelist. He was ordained at Friendship Church, Wilcox County, 1859. He served as captain of 24th Alabama Infantry Regiment in the Confederate army until 1863, when he resigned to become chaplain.

Hawthorne was pastor of many large churches in both South and North, including these: Franklin Square, Baltimore, Md.; First, Albany, N. Y.; Broadway, Louisville, Ky.; Tabernacle, New York, N. Y.; First, Montgomery, Ala., 1876; First, Richmond, Va., 1879; First, Atlanta, Ga., 1884; First, Nashville, Tenn., 1896; and Grove Avenue, Richmond, Va., 1899. He was elected president of the Board of Education of the Alabama Baptist State Convention, 1876, and a corresponding editor of *The Alabama Baptist*, 1877. He was for many years the acknowledged orator of the Southern Baptist Convention. It was said of him that his words "convicted the judgment, kindled the imagination, moved the feelings, and gave a powerful impulse to the will." A great foe of the liquor traffic, he was instrumental in abolishing saloons in Atlanta in 1887. Hawthorne was a member of the Home Mission Board while serving as pastor in Atlanta, and he was one of the first to advocate establishing a Sunday school board to publish Baptist literature. He was distinguished for his wisdom and judgment in the counsels of his denomination.

BIBLIOGRAPHY: Alabama State Convention, *Annuals* (1876–77). M. P. Blue, *Churches of the City of Montgomery* (1878). W. Cathcart, *The Baptist Encyclopedia* (1883). J. S. Dill, *Lest We Forget* (1938); *The Golden Age* (May 16, 1907); *The Montgomery Advertiser* (Feb. 25, 1910). T. M. Owen, *History of Alabama and Dictionary of Alabama Biography* (1921). B. F. Riley, *A Memorial History of the Baptists of Alabama* (1923); *History of the Baptists of Alabama, 1808–1894* (1895). C. A. Stakely, *History of the First Baptist Church of Montgomery, Alabama* (1930).
LESLIE S. WRIGHT

HAYS, JOHN BRADFORD (b. Henderson County, Tenn., Jan. 29, 1856; d. Mar. 6, 1922). Pioneer missionary preacher. He was educated in Tennessee and Texas schools. He married Mary Ann Wells in 1878. Beginning in 1887, he was active in mission work for 31 years in central southern Oklahoma. He organized a number of churches, including Duncan, 1889, and Marlow, 1891. An example of his work is reflected in a report to the Enon Association for 1892, which indicated 2,411 miles of travel by horseback or in a buggy, 150 sermons, 450 homes visited, and three churches organized.
R. L. MCCLUNG

HAYWOOD INSTITUTE. A Baptist school at Clyde, Haywood County, N. C. In 1886, citizens of Clyde organized a joint stock company, known as Pigeon Valley Education Association, secured a site and erected a school building. In the fall of 1886 the school was opened as Pigeon Valley Academy, with P. L. Frazier as principal. Due to the turnover of teachers and stock owners, the school was in a difficult situation in 1888, and in 1893 was sold at auction. It was purchased by a company of seven men who presented it as a gift to Haywood Association to be held in trust as an associational school. The association elected a board of trustees, and the school was opened under Baptist control. In 1905 the school was chartered by the state legislature, under the name Haywood Institute. A year earlier the school had begun to receive financial assistance from the Home Mission Board's program of aid to mountain schools. By 1927 the school had received over $42,000, including nearly $22,000 for capital improvements.

D. L. SMILEY

HAZARD BAPTIST INSTITUTE. Operated at Hazard, Ky., from 1903 to 1938. It was established under the leadership of A. S. Petrie, the local Baptist pastor. Four years later it became a part of the mountain school system of the Southern Baptist Home Mission Board, offering grade and high school work. After Home Mission Board support was discontinued, and after the establishment of tax supported public schools, local supporters tried to change the institute into a junior college but could get no support from the depression-pinched Baptist Education Society of Kentucky. Ultimately, debt forced the school into receivership, and the property was secured by the Hazard City School.

GEORGE RALEIGH JEWELL

HEALING SPRINGS INDUSTRIAL ACADEMY. A coeducational school on the elementary and high school level, located in Washington County. It was founded by the Antioch Baptist Association, under the leadership of J. B. Hamberline, with J. F. Brock as president, a few years before 1900. The Alabama Baptist State Convention assumed ownership and control of the school in 1905, at which time the enrolment was 63. The school was closed in 1915 due to lack of support.

JAMES E. DAVIDSON

HEARN MANUAL LABOR SCHOOL, THE. Opened in Jan., 1839, with its charter approved in December, in Floyd County, Ga., promoted by citizens from Vann's Valley and neighboring areas. The 15 trustees, one of whom was Humphrey Posey (*q.v.*), sought friendly relations with the Baptist Convention of the State of Georgia, resulting in the convention's appointment of a committee to work with them, requiring that the trustees be "orderly members of Baptist churches." In 1842 a bequest of $25,000 to the school was included in the will of Lott Hearn of Putnam County. The school's existence, one of struggle and local discord, continued through more than two decades of the 20th century. In 1920 it became a member of the Mercer system, which placed all Georgia Baptist schools under the Mercer University Board of Trustees, with Rufus W. Weaver, Mercer president, chancellor of the system from 1920–25. It is now extinct.

ARTHUR JACKSON

HEAVEN. The eternal abode of the righteous or the redeemed (Matt. 25:34–40, 46; I Peter 1:3–5; Rev. 21:1 to 22:5). The terms "paradise" (Luke 23:43; II Cor. 12:4; Rev. 2:7) and "Abraham's bosom" (Luke 16:22) are used synonymously for heaven. The New Testament presents heaven as both state and place, as both internal realization and environmental condition. Among its characteristics are full deliverance from sin (I John 3:2; Rev. 21:8, 27; 22:15), removal of want, sorrow, pain, and death (Rev. 7:16–17; 21:4; 22:3), blessedness of unhindered fellowship with God (Matt. 5:8; Phil. 1:23; Rev. 21:3, 22; 22:5), rest from earthly labors and continual service to God (Rev. 7:15; 14:13; 22:3). The eternal state is described as "a place" of "many mansions" (John 14:2–3), "new heaven and a new earth" (II Peter 3:13; Rev. 21:1), and "new Jerusalem" (Rev. 21:2).

BIBLIOGRAPHY: J. S. Bonnell, *Heaven and Hell* (1956). E. Brunner, *Eternal Hope* (1954). W. T. Conner, *The Gospel of Redemption* (1945).

JAMES LEO GARRETT

HECK, FANNIE EXILE SCUDDER (b. Buffalo Lithia Springs, Mecklenburg County, Va., June 16, 1862; d. Raleigh, N. C., Aug. 25, 1915). North Carolina and Convention-wide Woman's Missionary Union leader. Her father, McGee Heck, whose paternal ancestors came to America from the Palatinate before the Revolutionary War in search of religious liberty, was a lawyer, a lieutenant colonel in the Confederate army, a successful businessman, and a prominent Baptist. Fannie Heck was given the name "Exile" in memory of her birthplace to which her mother, Anna Callendine Heck, had gone for refuge from Morgantown, Va. (now W. Va.) because of the Civil War. In later years Miss Heck herself added Scudder, the maiden name of her mother's grandmother, Jane Scudder Chadwick. She was proud to be a descendant of the Scudder family, famous for its American ministers and foreign missionaries, and she wanted particularly to pay tribute to the ancestor who, because of her convictions, united with the Baptists and for years was the only Baptist in her community.

After the Civil War, Fannie Heck's parents settled in Raleigh, N. C., where she attended Hobgood Seminary, an elementary school for girls. Later she went to Hollins Institute (now College) near Roanoke, Va., and at 18 joined the First Baptist Church, Raleigh, N. C., where her parents were members. She also began teaching a Sunday school class of young boys. Active in a mission church in the slum section of Raleigh, she led in cultural and civic improvements in her home city and beyond. Miss Heck was a member and vice-president of the Southern Sociological Congress and member of the North Carolina Society of Social Work.

President of the Woman's Missionary Union of North Carolina from its beginning in Jan., 1886, until her death in 1915, she was also president of the Convention-wide Woman's Missionary Union, 1892–94, 1895–99, 1906–15. She was one of the founders of the Woman's Missionary Union Training School (now Carver School of Missions and Social Work) in Louisville, Ky. Under her guidance Woman's Missionary Union adopted definite courses of mission study for women and young people, inaugurated *Royal Service*, its official monthly publication (originally *Our Mission Fields*), began a department of personal service (now known as community missions), published the Woman's Missionary Union *Year Book,* an annual book of plans and methods for use by local missionary societies, and established Standards of Excellence for societies and auxiliaries to insure more efficient service in all phases of missionary education.

Memorials commemorating her service include the Fannie E. S. Heck Memorial Chapel in the main building of the Carver School of Missions and Social Work and the Memorial Fountain on the campus of Meredith College. The Fannie E. S. Heck offering, contributed each summer by the North Carolina Woman's Missionary Union for selected mission projects, and the part of the Lottie Moon Christmas Offering which supports training schools overseas are in her memory.

Books written by Miss Heck, author of the Woman's Missionary Union hymn, "Come, Women, Wide Proclaim," and numerous tracts and articles, include *In Royal Service* (1913); *Everyday Gladness* (1915); *Sunrise and Other Poems* (1916); and *The Pageant of the Golden Rule* (1916).

On Jan. 9, 1912, the eight living members of the original 12 young boys whom Miss Heck taught in her first Sunday school class 39 years before presented a tablet, which reads in part: "Our teacher, who illustrated precept by example: vitalized letter by spirit: and illuminated truth with life. This tablet is a memorial of the grateful love of a class of boys, who now in mature years count their association with her among their greatest blessings."

MRS. W. C. JAMES

HELL. The eternal abode of the unrepentant or unredeemed, characterized by eternal punishment and separation from God. In the teaching of Jesus, hell is described as "Gehenna," the term used for Jerusalem's valley of refuse (Matt. 5:22, 29-30; 10:28; 18:9; 23:15), "the outer darkness" (Matt. 8:12; 22:13; 25:30), "everlasting punishment" (Matt. 25:46), and "everlasting fire" (Matt. 25:41). The term "Hades" in some uses (Matt. 11:23; Luke 16:23) is virtually a synonym for Gehenna. In Revelation (20:10, 14-15; 21:8) the term is "the lake of fire [and brimstone]."

The biblical doctrine of eternal punishment is denied both by annihilationism or conditional immortality and by universalism or restorationism. Contemporary defenders of universalism, which originated with Origen, contend for it on such bases as that the suffering of hell is remedial, that God's love prevents hell's eternity, and that God's complete victory over evil demands the salvation of all men.

BIBLIOGRAPHY: J. S. Bonnell, *Heaven and Hell* (1956). C. S. Lewis, *The Great Divorce* (1946).

JAMES LEO GARRETT

HELM, SQUIRE LARUE (b. Hardin County, Ky., May 16, 1816; d. Fayette County, Ky., Oct. 26, 1885). Pastor and evangelist. The son of George and Rebecca (LaRue) Helm and brother of John LaRue Helm, he was governor of Kentucky in 1807. He had few educational advantages. He lived on a farm until he was 17, then was apprenticed to a tanner for three and a half years and later went into business for himself. In 1834 he was converted and was baptized by Jacob Rogers into the fellowship of Severns Valley Church. He was licensed to preach on Dec. 31, 1836. On Apr. 7, 1838, he became one of the founders of the General Association of Baptists in Kentucky.

He preached to many prominent city and country churches and filled many important positions for a period of 47 years. He died of cancer in Fayette County, Ky., Oct. 26, 1885, at the age of 70.

LEO T. CRISMON

HENDERSON, JOHN THOMPSON (b. Belltown, Tenn., July 27, 1858; d. Knoxville, Tenn., Jan. 7, 1946). College president, denominational leader, author, a leader of the Laymen's Missionary Movement and the Baptist Brotherhood for 30 years. His parents were Benjamin Peck and Margaret A. (Hammontree) Henderson.

When young Henderson reached college age he entered Carson College (now Carson-Newman College) at Jefferson City, Tenn., where he received his A.B., A.M. and LL.D. degrees. From 1883 to 1892, he was professor of mathematics at Carson-Newman, and for 11 years he was president of the school. Later, Henderson moved to Virginia to become president of Virginia Intermont College at Bristol, which office he held from 1903 to 1914. He served also as trustee of both schools.

For 11 years he was president of the Tennessee Baptist Convention. He also served as moderator of the Baptist General Association of Virginia. In 1898 and again in 1917 he was vice-president of the Southern Baptist Convention.

In 1908 Henderson became the first general secretary of the newly organized Laymen's Missionary Movement, and in 1926 he was elected general secretary of its successor, Baptist Brotherhood of the South, which office he held until his voluntary retirement in 1938. Thus 30 years of his life were actively dedicated to arousing in Baptist men everywhere a keener conciousness of their Christian responsibilities and a more active enlistment in the whole program of their church and denomination.

Henderson wrote three books—*Financing a Church, The Preacher from the Layman's View Point, The Office of Deacon.*

On May 14, 1883, Henderson married Martha C. Williams of Rural Vale, Tenn., and there were two children born of this union: Maude Lee (Mrs. J. V. Henderson) and Margaret Mata.

LAWSON H. COOKE

HENDON, JOHN HENRY (b. Alabama, Nov. 12, 1848; d. near Kyle, Tex., July 15, 1886). Baptist minister. Though he made a profession of faith at the age of nine, he did not join a Baptist church until he was 18. His father, a Baptist minister, baptized him. After graduating from Howard College, he went to Mobile to work but was not satisfied. He entered the ministry at 21. For years he taught school and preached; in 1875 he became pastor at Union Springs. He married Elizabeth Mabson, Dec. 20, 1876, and they had four children. In Dec., 1877, he received a call to the First Baptist Church of Birmingham, which prior to his acceptance had had preaching only once a month. There were 40 members when he went to the church; when he left the church in 1883, the church had about 240 members. His health forced his retirement, and he moved with his family to San Antonio, Tex., where they lived in a tent. When his health improved, he accepted the call to the San Marcos Baptist Church, but again his health failed after a few months. He died on a train en route to Battle Creek, Mich., to seek a cure, and his body was returned to Kyle, Tex., and buried there. G. NELSON DUKE

HENDRICK, THOMAS GOULD (b. Paradise, Ky., Oct. 23, 1862; d. Abilene, Tex., July 8, 1946). Benefactor of Baptist institutions. Son of Bernard C. and Mary (Coleman) Hendrick, he moved to Texas with his parents in 1871 and grew up in Frio County. At 16 he left home and sought his fortune. Hendrick became county judge of Ector County in 1927 and divided his time between ranching and banking interests. One ranch of 36,000 acres became Hendrick Oil Field and brought Hendrick a fortune in excess of $5,000,000. Major benefactions at Hendrick's death included $100,000 to Hardin-Simmons University; $200,000 to Scottish Rite Hospital, Dallas; $1,000,000 to Hendrick Memorial Hospital, Abilene; and $1,000,000 to several Baptist denominational causes. Hendrick Home for Children, at Abilene, was built for approximately 100 children and was endowed by the Hendrick fortune. R. N. RICHARDSON

HENDRICK MEMORIAL HOSPITAL. Located at Abilene, Tex., and originally called the West Texas Baptist Sanitarium, it opened to receive patients Sept. 16, 1924, as a 75-bed hospital. The original trustees were elected by trustees of Hardin-Simmons University and approved by Sweetwater Association. In 1936 the name of the hospital became Hendrick Memorial Hospital, and the property was transferred to the Baptist General Convention of Texas. The hospital is a memorial to Thomas Gould and Ida Hendrick, who paid off indebtedness and provided an addition to the hospital. Hendrick Memorial received an endowment from the Hendrick estate of $600,000. A nonprofit, general hospital serving patients without regard to race, creed, or color, it is fully approved by the Joint Commission on Accreditation of Hospitals.

In 1954–55 the hospital reported 225 beds, 11,221 patients, $30,481 charity service, $1,267,-384 income from patients, $1,233,826 total operating expense, $46,214 Baptist general convention gifts. Land, buildings, and equipment are valued at $2,500,000. E. M. COLLIER

HENRICIANS. A sect which originated c. 1101 in southern France through the preaching of Henry of Lausanne, once a Benedictine monk. As a preacher of ascetic righteousness, he denied the validity of sacraments administered by unworthy priests, condemned the wealthy and power-seeking clergy, and rejected infant baptism. Whole congregations, including many priests, left their churches to join the movement. The Roman Church condemned Henry in 1148, but his followers continued to propagate his doctrine until they were absorbed by the Waldenses. LYNN E. MAY, JR.

HENRY MALE AND FEMALE INSTITUTE. A secondary school, operated 1873–75 at New Castle, Ky., by Robert Ryland, pastor of the New Castle Baptist Church and former president of Lexington Baptist Female College. The school was patronized by the Sulphur Forks Baptist Association. GLYNN R. FORD

HEPZIBAH HIGH SCHOOL. Opened at Hepzibah, Ga., in Feb., 1861, projected by Hepzibah Association. Vincent Thornton was the first principal of this school, which passed to local control at the end of the century.
ARTHUR JACKSON

HIAWASSEE HIGH SCHOOL. Established in 1886 by George Washington Truett (q.v.), following a speech which he made at the courthouse in Hiawassee, Ga., urging its establishment. Truett himself had been walking nearly 12 miles to the nearest school, and after founding Hiawassee he taught there for three years. In 1905 Hiawassee Association assumed control of the school, and in 1925 the Home Mission Board, which had contributed to it for several years, began management. Chief inspiration and guiding power of the school came from Fernando Coello McConnell (q.v.).
ARTHUR JACKSON

HICKMAN, WILLIAM (b. King and Queen County, Va., Feb. 4, 1747; d. Frankfort, Ky., 1830). Kentucky pioneer preacher. Orphaned at an early age, he had little formal schooling. At 14 he was apprenticed to John Shackleford (q.v.). At 23 he married his master's daughter. In that year, 1770, he first saw and heard Baptist preachers. In Apr., 1773, he was baptized by Reuben Ford.

On a visit to Kentucky in Apr., 1776, he preached his first sermon, at Harrodsburg, before he was licensed or ordained. He ministered in Virginia until Aug., 1784. Pastor of several churches in Kentucky, he organized Forks of Elkhorn Church "the second Saturday in June, 1788" and was pastor of the church until his death in 1830, with an interim of about two years. During this period he was out of fellowship with the church because of his opposition to slavery "as being tolerated by the members of a Baptist Society."

His memoirs under title *The Life and Travels of William Hickman* were published in 1828 and republished in 1873. After the death of his first wife, June 9, 1812, he married Mrs. Elizabeth Abbott, Dec. 25, 1814.　　LEO T. CRISMON

HIGHLAND LAKES BAPTIST ENCAMPMENT. A Texas encampment located on Lake Travis, 35 miles from Austin.　　J. E. ROTH

HIGHTOWER BAPTIST COLLEGE. Established at Cumming, Ga., in 1893, sponsored by Hightower Association and housed in buildings of the old Piedmont College. The school existed until 1908.　　ARTHUR JACKSON

HILL, ALLEN (b. Pittsylvania County, Va., on the Dan River, Dec. 27, 1769; d. Madison County, Tenn., 1840). Pioneer Baptist preacher. He migrated to east Tennessee where he was married to Sarah Garrett, Aug. 28, 1795. The couple moved to Davidson County where their first son, Jacob, was born Aug. 28, 1796. Both father and son served under General Andrew Jackson during the War of 1812 and fought in the Battle of Pensacola. Allen Hill was promoted to captain. When the land west of the Tennessee River was opened for settlement, the family moved to Madison County where Allen received a tract of land five miles south of Jackson, for his military services. He led in the organization of the first Baptist church in Madison County—Cane Creek Baptist Church. The organization took place in the home of Jacob Hill, who served as a deacon. Allen Hill served as pastor from the date of organization until 1840, when he was succeeded by Obadiah Dodson (q.v.). The congregation worshiped in homes until 1822, when a frame building was constructed and became known as the Old Cane Creek Baptist Church. The First Baptist Church of Jackson, Madison Hall Baptist Church, and Malesus Baptist Church are outgrowths of Cane Creek Baptist Church. When the dispute over missions arose during the 1830's, Cane Creek Church remained loyally missionary. Cane Creek Church disbanded in 1925 and the members transferred to Jackson, Madison Hall, and Malesus.　　R. H. WARD

HILLCREST MEMORIAL HOSPITAL. A Texas Baptist hospital located at Waco, Tex., projected by the Waco Baptist Association in 1915, opened in 1920, and the property of the Baptist General Convention of Texas since 1945. The first suggestion of a hospital in the region was made in 1909 by Arthur James Barton (q.v.), pastor of the Waco First Baptist Church. In 1915 the Waco Baptist Association appointed a board of directors for the project. Construction began in 1917 and progressed in spite of material shortages during World War I, so that the hospital was officially opened on May 25, 1920, as the Central Texas Baptist Sanitarium. On Mar. 14, 1938, the name was changed to Hillcrest Memorial Hospital, and on Jan. 16, 1945, the hospital became the property of the Baptist General Convention of Texas.

Originally the hospital was a single unit which accommodated 65 patients. In 1955 the hospital had 190 beds and four buildings; its land, equipment, and other assets were valued at $2,026,190. The hospital's indebtedness in 1955 was $345,205.

Serving all races, Hillcrest, from its beginning to 1955, admitted 141,000 patients, of whom 13,603 were served during 1954. Charity work done by the hospital in 1954 amounted to $16,061; total income from patients was $1,002,406. To aid the hospital in carrying out its program of healing, teaching, benevolence, and evangelism, the Baptist General Convention of Texas provided $82,767 through the Cooperative Program, and friends of the hospital designated $16,810 in gifts.

In a Christ-centered educational program young men and women pursue courses of study as laboratory technicians, X-ray technicians, and registered nurses. In 1954 the school of nursing student body numbered 24. Hillcrest is an accredited hospital, but is not approved for internships. In 1955 Julian H. Price was administrator of the hospital and had served as such since 1943.

BIBLIOGRAPHY: *Annual Report of Examination, Hillcrest Memorial Hospital for the Year Sept. 1, 1954—Oct. 31, 1955.* F. E. Burkhalter, *A World-Visioned Church* (1946). Hillcrest Memorial Hospital (Waco, Texas), Board of Directors, *Minutes.* Waco Baptist Association (Texas), *Minutes.*　　ALTON PEARSON

HILLMAN COLLEGE. A girls' school in Clinton, Miss., initiated by Central Baptist Association when the board of trustees of Mississippi College decided in 1851 to operate Mississippi College as a boys' school only. Established "side by side the Mississippi College, just as it should be," the girls' school, founded as Central Baptist Female Institute in 1853, was chartered in 1854. Walter Hillman, of Massachusetts, became principal in 1856, and by 1860 enrolment had reached 162, with about 30 turned away for lack of room. Average attendance during the war period was 102, but after the war, the title of the property passed to Hillman to satisfy debts due him. He jointly served both Hillman and Mississippi Colleges as president during the period of stress from 1867 to 1873.

In 1891 the name of Central Female Institute was changed to Hillman College, and in 1908 the institution was sold to the Lowrey and Berry families of Blue Mountain. Seven years later it became a junior college. M. P. L. Berry, who had served the school as business manager since 1911, became vice-president in 1919 and bought Lowrey and Berry interests in 1921, thus becoming president and sole owner. In 1921 the school became a full member of the American Association of Junior Colleges and the Southern Association of Colleges for Women. An enlargement campaign launched in 1929 resulted in the building of two brick cottages, each accommodating 12 girls, with a teacher as counselor.

Although Hillman College survived the depression, it could not cope with the adverse circumstances which followed. As a result, the owner leased the property to Mississippi College in 1942 and deeded it in 1946. Mississippi College then reverted to its original status as a coeducational institution.   JOE ABRAMS

HILLSMAN, MATTHEW (b. Knox County, near Knoxville, Tenn., Aug. 7, 1814; d. Trenton, Tenn., Oct. 2, 1892). With the exception of two years spent in Talladega, Ala., all his life was lived in Tennessee. Converted at the age of 19 and ordained as a Baptist preacher at the age of 21 (1835), he began supplying a number of churches. In 1839 while residing at Chattanooga, he was instrumental in organizing the first Baptist church in that settlement. He was pastor of First Baptist Church in Murfreesboro, 1849–52. During his pastorate the church sent out George Washington Burton (1851), Tarlton Perry Crawford (1851), and Charles Washington Gaillard (1853) as missionaries. He served as pastor of Trenton Baptist Church. Other services included the presidency of Mossy Creek Baptist College (1858–59), which later became Carson-Newman College, and corresponding secretary of the Bible Board of the Southern Baptist Convention, 1859–60. He served as president of the West Tennessee Baptist Convention, and of its board of missions. When a trustee of the Southern Baptist Theological Seminary he was one of the committee that selected Louisville as its new site. He was one of a committee which presented a plan to organize Southwestern Baptist University (now Union) in Jackson. He is reported to have served as one of the editors of the *Nashville Reflector*. In recognition of his scholarship and ability, Union University in 1870 conferred upon him the D.D. degree. For more than 40 years he was intimately connected with the educational, missionary, and benevolent work of Tennessee.   G. ALLEN WEST

HILLYER, SHALER GRANBY (b. Wilkes County, Ga., June 20, 1809; d. 1900). He was graduated from the University of Georgia in 1829 and received the D.D. degree from Mercer University in 1850. In 1831 he was admitted to the bar in Clarke County, Ga., and in 1834 was elected tutor of languages in the state university. The following year he became principal of the Male Academy. His three marriages were to Elizabeth J. Thompson in 1836, to Elizabeth T. Dagg in 1846, and to Mrs. William Lawton in 1870. In 1835 he was ordained to the ministry by the Cabin Creek Baptist Church in Jackson County. He served as pastor of Baptist churches at Athens, Milledgeville, Rome, Forsyth, and Macon. Other positions held include principal of Scottsboro Female College and of Penfield Female Academy; professor of belles-lettres at Mercer University, 1845–56; chaplain of Mercer, 1859; trustee of Mercer, 1838–47; professor of theology at Penfield, 1859; president of Monroe College, Forsyth, 1867–76. In 1876 he resigned to devote full time to the Forsyth church. In 1873 at the Georgia Baptist Convention in Rome, he introduced resolutions pointing out needs for a "well-endowed institution of learning for the higher education of our daughters, under control of the Convention." His contributions to Baptist life and institutions were many and lasting.   LESLIE S. WILLIAMS

HISTORIC CHURCHES. With the exception of District of Columbia and Texas, churches defined as "historic" are those constituted prior to the organization of their state conventions. All of the churches listed here are still active; no extinct churches are given. The lists are arranged by states, chronologically by dates of organization, together with names, post offices (or counties or associations), and membership statistics. See introductions following names of states for further explanation.

ALABAMA. The Alabama Baptist State Convention was organized in 1823. There were 57 churches organized prior to 1823 that are inactive today. Most of these extinct churches were located in the northern and southern parts of the state. Baptist beginnings in Alabama occurred almost simultaneously in these two sections.

Year	Name	Post Office	Members 1955
1808	First *	Huntsville	1,732
1810	Mt. Tabor	Blountsville, Rt. 2	180
1812	Bethel	Columbiana, Rt. 1	176
1816	First	Monroeville	835
1817	Cahaba Valley	Brierfield, Rt. 1	200
1817	Old Salem	Frisco City, Rt. 1	67
1817	Round Island	Athens, Rt. 7	232
1817	Springville	Springville	273
1818	Canaan	Bessemer	707
1818	Catawba Springs	Flomaton, Rt. 1	290
1818	Chestnut Creek	Cooper	499
1818	Conecuh River	Andalusia, Rt. 1	109
1818	First	Tuscaloosa	2,140
1818	Friendship	Danville, Rt. 1	214
1818	Greensboro	Greensboro	479
1818	Poplar Creek	Athens, Rt. 5	238
1818	Town Creek	Moulton, Rt. 1	111
1819	Ebenezer	Stanton, Rt. 1	214
1819	Enon	Centerville, Rt. 2	40
1819	Enon	Moulton, Rt. 2	272
1819	Rehobeth	Lawley	241
1819	Ruhama	Birmingham	3,068
1819	Shiloh	Sardis	171
1820	Big Creek	Coker	131
1820	First	Athens	956
1820	Linden	Linden	645
1820	Ocmulgee	Suttle, Rt. 1	150
1821	Belleville	Belleville	85
1821	Brooklyn	Brooklyn	180
1821	Fairmount	Red Level, Rt. 1	389
1821	First	Wetumpka	954

Year	Name	Post Office	Members 1955
1821	Trussville	Trussville	621
1822	Friendship	Pine Hill	129
1822	Hopewell	Marion, Rt. 1	89
1822	New Salem	Baileytown, Rt. 1	117
1822	Siloam	Marion	918
1823	Sister Springs	Selma	165

Flint River was the first church organized in Alabama. The church divided and the West Fork of Flint River became known as Enon Church and later First Baptist Church of Huntsville.

BLOUNT DAVIDSON and LEON MACON

ARIZONA. The Baptist General Convention of Arizona was founded in 1928. Some of the churches organized before that time have left the Southern Baptist Convention and no records are available concerning 1955 membership. Such churches are indicated by an asterisk (*) following their names.

Year	Name	Post Office	Members 1955
1911	First	Chandler	657
1917	Willcox *	Willcox	
1919	Young	Young	84
1921	First Southern	Phoenix	1,468
1923	Pima	Sacaton	86
1925	First Southern	Buckeye	382
1925	Grace *	Phoenix	
1926	First Southern	Glendale	679
1926	First Southern	Globe	
?	Prescott *	Prescott	

BERNEICE ROBINSON

ARKANSAS.

Year	Name	Post Office	Members 1955
1829	Rehoboth	Morefield	111
1830	Old Union	Benton, Rt. 2	87
1832	Liberty	El Dorado, Rt. 5	108
1836	First	Benton	1,597
1836	First	Hot Springs	918
1836	First	Nashville	809
1836	Mt. Bethel	Arkadelphia, Rt. 3	78
1836	Washington	Washington	133
1838	Mt. Gilead	Norman	104
1840	Dardanelle	Dardanelle	309
1840	Mt. Zion	Paragould, Rt. 3	288
1842	First	Camden	1,673
1842	Twelve Corners	Garfield	99
1843	New Hope	Sparkman	109
1844	New Hope #1	Smithville	150
1845	Bingen	Nashville, Rt. 1	84
1845	First	Batesville	883
1845	First	El Dorado	2,506
1845	Fountain Hill	Fountain Hill	277
1846	New Hope	Pollard	261
1846	Union	El Dorado, Rt. 3	351
1847	First	Springdale	1,238
1848	Antioch	Hermitage, Rt. 1	98
1848	Harmony Hill	Arkadelphia, Rt. 4	134
1848	Holly Springs	Hermitage	237
1848	Salem	Stephens, Rt. 1	131
1848	Spring Valley	Spring Valley	100

L. C. TEDFORD

DISTRICT OF COLUMBIA. The situation in this area is rather unique. Three early churches of special importance are presented below.

First Baptist.—This church was begun in the Treasury Building in Washington, and was organized on Mar. 7, 1802, in a private home with six charter members. Four clergymen, Lewis Richards, Adam Freeman, Jeremiah Moore, and William Parkinson, were present. Richards was pastor of the First Baptist Church of Baltimore, Moore was a famous Virginia clergyman, retired, and Parkinson was chaplain of the House of Representatives.

The church constructed a house of worship at 19th and I streets. The first pastor, Obadiah B. Brown, was called in May, 1807. He served for 43 years, and was active in local civic and educational affairs as well, serving as trustee of Columbian College and Washington Public Orphanage, and president of the Baptist General Tract Association.

Luther Rice worshiped at First Church from 1813 until 1836. He was responsible for establishing in First Church the first Sunday school in the city and helped to foster general interest in Baptist missions and education. The Triennial Convention met in First Church in 1823.

Originally a member of the Baltimore Association, the church was a charter member of the Potomac Association in Virginia when it was formed in 1820, and entered the Washington city association, now the District of Columbia Convention, in 1882. Through the latter it contributes equally to both the American and Southern conventions.

The second building at Tenth and E streets was sold to John Ford who in 1863 built at the site the theatre in which Lincoln was shot. The church has recently completed a new million-dollar structure dedicated Christmas, 1955, at its old 16th and O Street site. President Harry S Truman was a member of the First Church. In 1955 membership was 1,676; budget, $923,684.55; gifts to missions, $32,126.00; total property value, $1,900,000.00. The pastor was Edward H. Pruden.

Second Baptist.—This church was formed as the Navy Yard Baptist Church in 1810 with five members. It was first led by Jeremiah Moore, famous Virginia preacher, and by Stephen Cone, converted actor and long-time pastor in New York City. Organized in McLeod's schoolhouse near the Navy Yard, the church constructed its first building at Fourth and G streets, S.E., moving to a new brick building at Virginia Avenue and Fourth Street in 1823. With four other churches Second Church led in the forming of the Maryland Baptist Union Association in 1836 and was one of the charter members of the Columbia Association of Baptist Churches, forerunner of the District of Columbia Baptist Convention. Co-operating through the latter, it is a member of both the Southern and American conventions. Second Church is credited with the establishment of the third permanent Washington Baptist

Church, now Temple, carefully fostering and shepherding the new colony as a downtown mission in 1842. Second Baptist, Negro, grew out of the church, and was separately constituted in 1848. Second Church aided in the establishment of Metropolitan Church in 1878 and Centennial Church, founded in 1884. The church prospered significantly under the ministry of Isaac Cole. Another eminent pastor was Hez Swem who served from 1884 to 1910. In 1955 membership was 1,389; budget, $52,189.16; total property value, $355,000.00. The pastor was J. Ray Garrett.

Temple Baptist.—This church was constituted as the Third Regular Baptist Church of Washington, D. C. (later known as E Street Church), on Oct. 6, 1842, with 21 members, 13 being from Second Church. After a three-month revival meeting held in a dance hall, some 200 members were gathered into the church, which then called as its first pastor George Whitefield Samson, a student at Newton Theological Seminary. After his ordination by the church, he served, with the exception of three years, until 1859 when he became simultaneously president of Columbian College and pastor of First Baptist Church. General Sam Houston, while serving as senator from Texas, was converted under his ministry in E Street Church.

During the Civil War the Temple Church building was taken over to be used as a government hospital, and the church split over Northern and Southern sentiments. The pastor, Joseph Spencer Kennard, resigned when the majority refused to receive Northerners as members. Taking about one-third of the members, he constituted the element that eventually became Calvary Baptist Church. The original group returned to their building after the war, having been led by Samuel Shute, professor at Columbian College, and Zalmon Richards, the first president of the National Education Association.

A mother of churches, Temple was responsible for the formation of five churches between 1853 and 1881, colonies from the church forming Fourth Baptist in 1853, Fifth Baptist in 1857, Calvary Baptist in 1862, Metropolitan Baptist in 1878, and Brookland Baptist in 1881. J. J. Muir served as pastor from 1889 to 1924.

In 1955 membership was 737; budget, $16,-415.04; total property value, $225,000.00. The pastor was Melvine Crump.   R. BAINE HARRIS

FLORIDA. The Florida Baptist State Convention was founded in 1854. These historic churches, still in existence, were constituted before that time.

Year	Name	Post Office	Members 1955
1825	First	Campbellton	157
1828	Ebenezer (Jefferson)	Monticello *	153
1829	Indian Springs	Monticello *	100
1832	Old Providence	Lake City *	178
1832	New River	Brooker *	34
1834	Hickory Hill	Ponce de Leon *	60
1834	Elizabeth	Aucilla *	228
1838	First	Jacksonville	2,700
1841	Callahan	Callahan	445
1841	First	Monticello	412
1842	Olive	Monticello *	148
1842	Providence	Greensboro *	282
1843	Aenon	Tallahassee *	50
1843	Arran	Crawfordville *	64
1843	Limestone	Darlington *	126
1844	Fellowship	Ocala *	223
1844	First	Key West	575
1845	Cluster Springs	DeFuniak Springs *	75
1845	Eden	Brooksville *	266
1845	Ephesus	Hilliard *	153
1845	Greenwood	Greenwood	142
1846	Ebenezer	Vernon *	13
1846	New Hope	Pittman *	97
1847	Bethlehem	Marianna *	140
1847	First	Milton	866
1847	First	Pensacola	2,533
1849	Ft. McCoy	Ft. McCoy	111
1849	First	Tallahassee	3,697
1850	Alafia	Plant City *	244
1850	Apalachicola	Apalachicola	225
1850	Bethel	Branford *	20
1850	Beulah	Starke *	60
1850	First	Madison	621
1850	Micanopy	Micanopy	223
1850	Mt. Gilead	Lamont *	34
1850	First	Ocala	1,966
1851	Antioch	Live Oak *	136
1851	Bethlehem	Lake City *	82
1852	First	Brooksville	657
1852	Peniel	Palatka *	277
1852	Pine Barren	Bratt *	127
1853	DeCoy	Green Cove Springs *	99
1853	Hawthorne	Hawthorne	250
1853	Sopchoppy	Sopchoppy	234
1854	East Thonotosassa	Plant City *	254
1854	Mt. Elon	Sopchoppy *	148
1854	Peace Creek	Bartow *	104

* Town nearest this rural or village church.

W. G. STRACENER

GEORGIA. Of the Baptist churches in Georgia at the time of the organization of the state convention (1822), 120 have continued until now. Nearly all are in the eastern half of the state, with the bulk in two contiguous clusters. Forty-nine are within a radius of 40 miles of Warrenton, and 39 are within the same distance of Homer.

In an undetermined number, certain churches in Georgia might trace their origin to old churches of the 18th and early 19th centuries, but somewhere the connecting link in the chain was broken. A good example of such a case is the Davisboro church, which, when founded in 1877, took in some members from the old Williamson's Swamp church, which was constituted

Historic Churches

in 1792 or perhaps a year or so earlier. However, the church had not existed between 1865 and 1877, and when Davisboro was constituted in 1877, it did not fall "heir to its name, its location, or any of its property." These churches are not included in this list.

Year	Name	Post Office	Members 1955
1772	Kiokee	Appling	204
1773	Botsford	Waynesboro	114
1774	Abilene	Martinez	241
1777	Little Briar Creek	Warrenton	61
1779	Mt. Moriah	Buford	208
1783	Fishing Creek	Washington	141
1784	Greenwood	Amity	133
1785	Bethesda	Union Point	185
1785	Phillip's Mill	Washington	336
1785	Providence	Avera	70
1785	Vans Creek	Elberton	82
1786	Long Creek	Warrenton	160
1786	Powelton	Mayfield	85
1787	Bethlehem	Girard	65
1787	Ebenezer	Washington	52
1787	Goshen	Lincolnton	102
1788	Bark Camp	Midville	72
1788	Bethany	Lexington	87
1788	Cloud's Creek	Comer	252
1788	Doves Creek	Elberton	273
1788	Oconee	Jefferson	270
1788	Sardis	Rayle	208
1789	Brushy Creek	Keysville	73
1789	Clark's Station	Tignall	105
1789	Salem	Lexington	191
1790	Bethlehem	Warthen	186
1790	Little Ogeechee	Oliver	142
1791	Beulah	Devereux	115
1791	Darien	Linton	171
1791	Falling Creek	Elberton	193
1792	Horeb	Mayfield	114
1792	Ohoopee	Tennille	104
1792	Sparta	Sparta	377
1793	North Newington	Newington	186
1794	Island Creek	Devereux	79
1795	Bethel	Bartow	147
1795	Danburg	Danburg	130
1795	Holly Springs	Canon	382
1795	Shiloh	Woodville	222
1796	Cabin Creek	Commerce	221
1797	County Line	Rayle	181
1797	Nails Creek	Homer	619
1799	Mars Hill	Bogart	195
1799	Sharon	Appling	114
1800	Carlton	Carlton	286
1800	Danville	Danville	110
1800	Fellowship	Gibson	177
1800	First	Savannah	1,879
1800	Mt. Zion	Turnerville	229
1800	New Hope	Madison	76
1800	Old Canon	Canon	165
1800	Pleasant Grove	Blairsville	155
1800	Sardis	Gainesville	450
1800	Silver Run	Dearing	243
1801	Double Branches	Carnesville	205
1801	Middle River	Carnesville	378
1801	Shiloh	Danielsville	124
1801	Shoal Creek	Lavonia	317
1802	Bairds	Bairdstown	107
1802	Bethel	Culverton	120
1802	Crawfordville	Crawfordville	426
1802	Sweetwater	Thomson	342
1802	The Line	Homer	60
1802	Walnut Fork	Hoschton	335
1803	Blacks Creek	Commerce	161
1803	Crooked Creek	Jefferson	128
1803	Double Branches	Lincolnton	78
1803	Sardis	Sardis	381
1804	Bethany	Tennille	171
1805	Poplar Springs	Lavonia	315
1806	Harmony	Eatonton	107
1806	Rehoboth	Washington	198
1806	White Plains	White Plains	181
1807	Poplar Springs	Dublin	282
1808	First	Monticello	348
1808	Grove	Grovetown	228
1808	Hopewell	Gainesville	186
1808	Sandy Creek	Madison	71
1808	Shiloh	Shady Dale	210
1808	Stone Creek	Dry Branch	393
1809	Antioch	Godfrey	130
1809	Big Sandy	Irwinton	127
1809	Evergreen	Cochran	127
1809	Union	Thomson	60
1810	Academy	Jefferson	116
1810	Eastanollee	Eastanollee	426
1810	Jones Creek	Ludowici	175
1810	Providence	Shady Dale	127
1811	Antioch	Dry Branch	262
1811	New Providence	Irwinton	129
1811	Sardis	Hartwell	539
1812	Corinth	Egypt	251
1812	Elam	Gray	127
1812	Hunter's Creek	Carnesville	254
1812	Pleasant Grove	Oglethorpe	113
1812	Ten-Mile Creek	Baxley	403
1813	Antioch	Stephens	75
1813	Bethabara	Auburn	449
1814	Powers	Eden	60
1815	First	Milledgeville	1,306
1815	Hopeful	Blythe	88
1816	Reedy Creek	Stapleton	331
1817	First	Augusta	3,044
1817	Ways	Stellaville	208
1818	Bethlehem	Clarksville	646
1818	Clark's Creek	Martin	117
1818	First	Eatonton	435
1818	Flat Creek	Oakwood	275
1818	Mt. Salem	Buford	277
1818	Tugalo	Toccoa	119
1818	Walthourville	Walthourville	58
1819	First	Clayton	558
1820	Damascus	Appling	167
1820	Lakeland	Lakeland	312
1820	Mt. Pleasant	Denton	104
1820	Providence	Danielsville	217

Historic Churches

Year	Name	Post Office	Members 1955
1820	Salem	Conyers	90
1821	Bethlehem	Dublin	182
1821	Greensboro	Greensboro	784
1821	Mud Creek	Alto	175

W. J. CARSWELL

ILLINOIS. The Illinois Baptist State Association organized in 1907 was preceded by the Illinois Baptist Convention which dated from 1834. The historic churches listed are those whose origin antedates the first Baptist general body in the state.

Year	Name	Post Office	Members 1955
1817	Saline Ridge	Carrier Mills	98
1817	Shiloh	Mounds	126
1818	First	Jonesboro	534
1820	Providence	Carrollton, Rt. 2	176
1820	Ten Mile	McLeansboro, Rt. 2	223
1828	Mt. Pleasant	Benton, Rt. 3	71
1829	Modesto	Girard	173
1829	Nine Mile	Tamaroa	78
1830	Hickory Grove	Wrights	292
1832	Bethel	Odin, Rt. 1	142
1832	Liberty	Harrisburg, Rt. 1	140
1832	Mt. Pleasant	Medora	214
1832	Westfield	Charleston	70

W. J. PURDUE

KENTUCKY. Two hundred and eighty Baptist churches, still in existence in 1955, were organized in Kentucky between 1781 and 1837, when the General Association of Baptists in Kentucky was organized. This represents slightly over 12 per cent of the 2,278 churches affiliated with the general association in 1955. In 1955 these historic churches claimed a membership slightly in excess of 105,000, which represents more than 18 per cent of the total Kentucky Baptist membership in 1955. (In only one year, 1784, was there no church formed; and in all but five years, 1782, 1787, 1793, 1795, and 1807, at least two churches were organized.)

Year	Name	Association	Members 1955
1781	Cedar Creek	Nelson	325
1781	Severns Valley	Severns Valley	1,955
1782	Forks of Dix River	South District	175
1783	Providence	Boone's Creek	110
1783	South Elkhorn	Elkhorn	501
1785	Boone's Creek	Boone's Creek	505
1785	Clear Creek	Elkhorn	402
1785	Cox's Creek	Nelson	303
1785	Great Crossing	Elkhorn	628
1785	Tate's Creek	Tate's Creek	378
1786	First, Lexington	Elkhorn	1,005
1786	Long Run	Long Run	258
1787	East Hickman	Elkhorn	496
1788	Forks of Elkhorn	Franklin County	378
1788	Shawnee Run	South District	390
1789	Mays Lick	Bracken	233
1789	Pisgah	Blackford	82
1789	Salt River	South District	229
1790	Indian Creek	Union	34
1790	Salem	Boone's Creek	23
1791	Bloomfield	Nelson	692
1791	Campbellsville	Russell Creek	1,304
1791	Crab Orchard	Lincoln	369
1792	Brush Creek	Russell Creek	273
1792	Cedar Creek	Long Run	606
1792	Falmouth	Union	490
1793	Mill Creek	Nelson	176
1794	Bullitsburg	North Bend	197
1794	Cold Spring	Campbell County	361
1794	Elk Creek	Long Run	334
1794	Eminence	Henry County	610
1795	Stamping Ground	Elkhorn	399
1796	Deep Creek	South District	391
1796	Good Hope	East Lynn	224
1796	McKinney	Lincoln County	346
1797	Harrods Creek	Sulphur Fork	241
1797	Hazel Creek	Muhlenberg County	239
1797	Viney Fork	Tates Creek	138
1798	Beaver Dam	Ohio County	999
1798	Mill Creek	Monroe (Barren)	149
1798	Muddy River	Bethel	174
1799	Christiansburg	Shelby County	247
1799	Finchville	Shelby County	363
1799	Flat Lick	Pulaski County	319
1799	New Castle	Henry County	266
1800	Aetna Grove	Lynn	385
1800	Corn Creek	Sulphur Fork	140
1800	Eighteen-Mile	Sulphur Fork	69
1800	Freedom	Tates Creek	233
1800	Ghent	Whites Run	312
1801	Bethlehem	Allen County	199
1801	Burks Branch	Shelby County	440
1801	Campbellsburg	Henry County	346
1801	Clover Bottom	Elkhorn	372
1801	Davids Fork	Elkhorn	390
1801	Doctor's Fork	South District	132
1801	Drennons Ridge	Henry County	243
1801	Glens Creek	Elkhorn	370
1801	Liberty	East Lynn	261
1801	Little Mount	Shelby County	415
1801	Mt. Gilead	Russell Creek	101
1801	Mt. Pleasant	Elkhorn	328
1801	New Liberty	Owen County	266
1801	New Salem	Nelson	459
1801	North Fork	Franklin County	414
1801	Rolling Fork	East Lynn	123
1801	Salem	Liberty	374
1801	Silas	Elkhorn	203
1802	Bethel	Franklin County	392
1802	Hillsboro	Elkhorn	339
1802	Mt. Moriah	Nelson	325
1802	Persimmon Grove	Campbell County	69
1802	Smithfield	Henry County	209
1802	South Fork	Lynn	294

Historic Churches

Year	Name	Association	Members 1955
1802	Union	Union	199
1802	Zion	Russell Creek	38
1803	Dry Run	Elkhorn	471
1803	Fishing Creek	Pulaski County	40
1803	Lonoke	Liberty	168
1803	Nelson Creek	Muhlenberg County	331
1803	Nolynn	Severns Valley	213
1804	Barbourville	North Concord	1,632
1804	Big Sinking	Wayne	218
1804	Double Springs	Lincoln County	468
1804	Knoxes Creek	Lynn	280
1804	Liberty	Tates Creek	299
1804	Little River	Christian County	140
1804	Providence Knob	Warren	155
1804	Ten Mile	Ten Mile	279
1804	Wilmington	Campbell County	390
1805	Bethlehem	Central	393
1805	Buffalo Lick	Shelby County	284
1805	First, Morgantown	Gasper River	498
1805	Long Lick	Elkhorn	231
1805	Lynn Camp	Lynn Camp	278
1805	Monticello	Gasper River	215
1805	Old Salem	Ohio River	136
1805	Pleasant Grove	Long Run	567
1805	Sandy Creek	Gasper River	277
1806	Indian Fork	Shelby County	180
1806	Mill Creek	Severns Valley	320
1807	Friendship	Russell Creek	104
1808	Gap Creek	Wayne	346
1808	Goshen	Breckenridge	119
1808	Salem	Freedom	27
1809	Beaver	Union	260
1809	Jellico Creek	South Union	252
1810	Bethel	South Concord	394
1810	Center	Logan County	165
1810	Cumberland Union	South Union	244
1810	Georgetown	Elkhorn	1,473
1810	Little Flock	Long Run	416
1810	Plum Creek	Long Run	381
1810	Red Bird	South Union	120
1810	Union	Ohio River	282
1810	Whites Run	Whites Run	300
1811	Fairview	Ohio County	104
1811	Salem	Shelby County	638
1812	Buck Creek	Daviess-McLean	227
1812	Dover	Shelby County	229
1812	First, Newport	Campbell County	1,769
1812	Goshen	Baptist	266
1812	Lancaster	South District	825
1812	New Bethel	Caldwell	139
1812	Smiths Grove	Warren	244
1812	Three-Forks Bacon Creek	Lynn	285
1812	Union City	Boones Creek	287
1812	Unity	Muhlenberg County	50
1813	Concord	North Concord	200
1813	Hays Fork	Tates Creek	148
1813	Mount Vernon	Gasper River	208
1813	Port Royal	Henry County	324
1813	Yelvington	Daviess-McLean	156
1814	Bethel	Allen County	198
1814	Clearfork	East Union	270
1814	Donaldson Creek	Little River	148
1814	Fordsville	Ohio County	216
1814	Green Grove	Little Bethel	104
1814	Walton's Creek	Ohio County	148
1815	Bardstown	Nelson	909
1815	Mt. Gilead	Bethel	143
1815	Panther Creek	Blackford	122
1815	Providence	Laurel River	187
1815	Steubenville	Wayne	385
1815	Walnut Street	Long Run	5,661
1816	Bethel	Baptist	499
1816	Bethel	Christian County	335
1816	First, Frankfort	Franklin County	2,711
1816	First, Russellville	Bethel	996
1816	Walnut Grove	Breckenridge	260
1817	Dry Ridge	Crittenden	508
1817	First, Leitchfield	Goshen	618
1817	Mt. Carmel	East Lynn	217
1817	Mussel Shoals	Owen County	110
1817	Panola	Boone's Creek	120
1817	Unity	Crittenden	508
1818	Antioch	Logan County	280
1818	Augusta	Bracken	132
1818	Buck Run	Franklin County	200
1818	First, Bowling Green	Warren	3,010
1818	First, Hopkinsville	Christian County	1,817
1818	First, Paris	Elkhorn	1,080
1818	First, Twelve-Mile	Campbell County	193
1818	Glasgow	Liberty	1,773
1818	Holly Springs	Edmonson	184
1818	Perryville	South District	371
1818	Willow	Union	157
1819	Buck Fork	South District	168
1819	Carlisle	Bracken	424
1819	Cecilia	Severns Valley	232
1819	First, Shelbyville	Shelby County	1,383
1819	Hopewell	Henry County	119
1819	Mt. Moriah	Shelby County	400
1819	Mt. Vernon	Russell County	58
1819	Sand Run	North Bend	391
1820	Bell's Run	Ohio County	242
1820	Concord	South Concord	262
1820	Green Brier	Daviess-McLean	262
1820	Liberty	Wayne	340
1820	Long Ridge	Owen County	405
1820	Mt. Zion	Bethel	167
1820	Pleasant Run	Laurel River	68
1820	Pond Run	Ohio County	190
1820	Spring Valley	Bethel	142
1820	Union	Henry County	201
1821	Chaplin Fork	Nelson	216
1821	Wolf Creek	Salem	148
1822	Greenup Fork	Owen County	142
1822	Hill Grove	Salem	161
1822	Mt. Pleasant, Lewisburg	Logan County	339
1822	Mt. Vernon	Elkhorn	502

Historic Churches

Year	Name	Association	Members 1955
1823	Black Grove	Ohio Valley	138
1823	Deer Creek	Ohio River	110
1823	Donaldson	Caldwell	318
1823	First, Danville	South District	2,028
1823	Greensburg	Russell Creek	582
1823	Rocky Spring	Warren	125
1824	Elkhorn	Russell Creek	123
1824	Gilead	Severns Valley	532
1824	Little Obion	Graves County	175
1824	Mayfield Creek	West Kentucky	140
1824	New Salem	Wayne	223
1824	Trace Creek	Graves County	322
1824	Woodland	Ohio Valley	174
1825	Bethabara	Daviess-McLean	189
1825	Blackford	Blackford	409
1825	Boiling Springs	Lynn	466
1825	Elkston	Bethel	394
1825	Lebanon	Franklin County	415
1825	New Hope	South Concord	196
1825	North Benson	Franklin County	363
1825	Pigeon Fork	Shelby County	317
1825	Salem	Salem	228
1826	Cane Run	Elkhorn	269
1827	Ballardsville	Sulphur Fork	356
1827	Keysburg	Bethel	143
1827	Macedonia	Christian County	199
1827	Mt. Zion	Ten Mile	402
1827	Olivet	Christian County	212
1827	Poplar Grove	Ten Mile	141
1827	Providence	Sulphur Fork	97
1827	Salem	Christian County	173
1827	Wolf Creek	South Union	228
1828	Columbia	Russell Creek	720
1828	First, Taylorsville	Long Run	714
1828	Liberty	Logan County	211
1828	Mt. Carmel	Franklin County	75
1828	Mt. Pleasant	Rockcastle	150
1828	Patterson Creek	South Union	150
1828	Poplar Grove	West Kentucky	139
1829	First, Fountain Run	Monroe	254
1829	First, Richmond	Tates Creek	1,294
1829	Mt. Gilead	Allen County	97
1829	New Hope	Central	339
1829	Phillips Memorial	Salem	355
1829	Pleasant Hill	Monroe	218
1829	Stone Lick	Bracken	61
1829	Younger's Creek	Severns Valley	214
1830	Bedford	Sulphur Fork	431
1830	Gracey	Christian County	238
1830	Guthrie	Bethel	437
1830	Liberty	West Kentucky	231
1830	Richland	Union	156
1830	Rolling Fork	Nelson	193
1830	Simpsonville	Shelby County	326
1831	Liberty Hill	Edmonson	42
1831	Spring Creek	Blood River	109
1831	Welfare	Russell County	88
1832	Cloverport	Breckenridge	585
1832	Emmaus	West Kentucky	106
1832	Middle Creek	Severns Valley	173
1832	Mt. Freedom	Elkhorn	300
1832	Short Creek	Crittenden	151
1832	Slate Hill	Laurel River	148
1833	First, Clinton	West Kentucky	347
1833	First, Franklin	Simpson	919
1833	Flagg Spring	Campbell County	87
1833	New Hope	West Kentucky	54
1834	Canada's Creek	South Concord	351
1834	Greasy Creek	North Concord	200
1834	Lawrenceburg	Baptist	791
1834	New Friendship	Logan County	274
1834	Rock Springs	Gasper River	126
1834	Rocky Ford	Casey County	271
1834	Sulphur Spring	Simpson	434
1834	Whipporwill	Simpson	232
1835	Big Creek	Russell Creek	70
1835	Crooked Creek	Ohio River	96
1835	First, Owensboro	Daviess-McLean	2,459
1835	Indian Creek	Monroe	279
1835	Pleasant Grove	Daviess-McLean	421
1835	Union	Blackford	86
1836	Blood River	Blood River	58
1836	Clear Fork	Warren	200
1836	Green River	Ohio County	228
1836	Mt. Olivet	Graves County	126
1836	New Hope	Logan County	110
1836	Pleasant Ridge	Owen County	263
1836	White Mills	Severns Valley	95

HUGH WAMBLE

LOUISIANA. Due to Catholic domination, no Baptist churches were constituted in Louisiana prior to 1812, the year the territory achieved statehood. Before that time, missionary efforts had been frustrated by legal and social persecution. Between 1812 and 1848, the year of the organization of the Louisiana state convention, the following churches, still in existence, were organized:

Name	Year	Post Office
Calvary	1812	Ville Platte
First	1812	Vienna
Mt. Nebo	1813	Roseland
Hays Creek	1817	Franklinton
Antioch	1826	DeQuincy
Zion Hill	1826	Negreet
Amiable	1828	Forest Hill
Hebron	1831	Bush
Occupy No. 1	1832	Pitkin
First	1833	Franklinton
Old Union	1834	Grayson
First	1835	Jackson
First	1836	Clinton
Mount Lebanon	1837	Gibsland
Hebron	1837	Denham Springs
Toro	1837	Florien
Mt. Vernon	1837	West Monroe
Enon	1838	Franklinton
Line Creek	1839	Osyka, Miss.
Palestine	1840	Columbia
Bethel	1840	Lillie
Sandy Creek	1840	Pride

Name	Year	Post Office
Bayou Rouge	1841	Evergreen
Amite	1841	Denham Springs
Bluff Creek	1841	Clinton
Carolina	1842	Saline
Old Bethel	1842	Grayson
Gilgal	1842	Minden
Zion Hill	1842	Farmerville
First	1843	Jena
First	1843	New Orleans
Old Saline	1844	Saline
Salem	1844	Plain Dealing
Mt. Pleasant	1844	Columbia
First	1844	Minden
Friendship	1845	Bienville
First	1845	Shreveport
First	1845	Homer
Bayou des Galizes	1845	Hamburg
Rocky Springs	1845	Lisborn
Big Cane	1846	Morrow
Liberty	1846	Calhoun
Walnut Creek	1846	Arcadia
First	1847	Arcadia
Summer Grove	1847	Shreveport
First	1847	Farmerville
New Friendship	1847	Grand Cane
Old Bethel	1847	Natchitoches
Pleasant Hill	1847	Pleasant Hill
Little Flock	1848	Negreet
Ringgold	1848	Ringgold
Fellowship	1848	Dubach
Hebron	1848	Bernice
Spearsville	1848	Lillie

T. W. GAYER

MARYLAND. The Maryland Baptist Union Association was founded in 1835. Nine of its present churches were organized prior to that date.

Year	Name	Post Office	Members 1955
1742	Saters	Lutherville	119
1785	First	Baltimore	512
1793	Nanjemoy	Nanjemoy	351
1797	Second*	Baltimore	325
1805	Upper Seneca	Upper Seneca	210
1806	Gunpowder	Gunpowder	187
1817	Pitts Creek	Pitts Creek	117
1821	First	Rockville	393
1834	Huntingdon	Baltimore	466

* *In 1916 merged with Fourth Church to become known as East Baltimore Baptist Church.*

LAURENCE A. FREE

MISSISSIPPI. On Dec. 24, 1836, the Mississippi Baptist Convention was founded. Already there were many Baptist churches in that state, many of which still exist.

Year	Name	Post Office	Members 1955
1800	Woodville	Woodville	400
1806	Ebenezer	Centerville	110
1810	East Fork	Liberty	346
1810	Sarepta	Meadville	103
1811	Zion Hill	Liberty	204
1812	Bogue Chitto	Tylertown	236
1813	Hopewell	Bude	69
1814	Antioch	Columbia	133
1814	Silver Creek	McComb	367
1815	Fair River	Brookhaven	220
1815	Fellowship	Hermanville	102
1815	Mars Hill	Summit	334
1817	Friendship	McComb	474
1817	Hepzibah	Silver Creek	249
1818	Little Bahala	Wesson	170
1818	Mt. Zion	Meadville	167
1818	New Hope	Meadville	151
1818	Providence	Hattiesburg	349
1818	Silver Creek	Silver Creek	134
1819	Antioch	Vicksburg	51
1819	Bethany	Prentiss	153
1820	Ebenezer	Bassfield	300
1820	Ramah	McCall	197
1821	Old Hebron	New Hebron	268
1822	First	Waynesboro	531
1823	Mt. Zion	Brookhaven	397
1823	New Zion	Tylertown	412
1824	Antioch	Hazlehurst	102
1824	Galilee	Gloster	353
1824	Mt. Zion	Mt. Olive	399
1824	Society Hill	Oakvale	280
1825	Damascus	Hazlehurst	195
1826	First	Magnolia	773
1827	Palestine	Raymond	86
1827	Strong River	Pinola	95
1828	County Line	Crystal Springs	284
1828	Galilee	Hazlehurst	175
1828	Hopewell	Hopewell	163
1828	New Providence	Hazlehurst	55
1829	Leaf River	Mt. Olive	137
1830	Friendship	Brookhaven	266
1830	Providence	Grenada	164
1831	Beulah Memorial	Bolton	240
1831	Mt. Pisgah	Sand Hill	194
1831	Steen's Creek	Florence	434
1831	Zion	Pontotoc	386
1832	First	Columbus	2,959
1833	Carrollton	Carrollton	115
1833	New Hope	Sumrall	374
1834	Harmony	Mize	151
1834	Utica	Utica	432
1835	Bethlehem	Ackerman	93
1835	Double Springs	Maben	718
1835	Elim	Mashulaville	174
1835	Fellowship	Bellfontaine	272
1835	Fellowship	Meridian	310
1835	First	Louisville	1,082
1835	First	Macon	337
1835	Union	Sardis	166
1836	Bay Springs	Oxford	186
1836	Bethany	Slate Springs	314
1836	Bethlehem	Tishomingo	99
1836	Burnsville	Burnsville	348
1836	Clarke-Venable Memorial	Decatur	745
1836	Clear Creek	Oxford	194
1836	DeKalb	DeKalb	146

J. L. BOYD

Historic Churches

MISSOURI. The organization of the Missouri Baptist General Association was on Aug. 29, 1834. Fifty-one churches organized prior to that time have existed continuously until the present.

the state convention of 1912. In instances where records vary as to dates of organization, the earliest dates have been followed, unless the churches have already chosen other dates to observe.

Year	Name	Post Office	Members 1955
1807	Fee Fee	Pattonsville	897
1808	Lathrop	Lathrop	220
1809	Salem	Florissant, R.F.D.	127
1812	New Franklin	New Franklin	110
1815	First	Troy	373
1816	Liberty	Belgrade	53
1816	Ramsey Creek	Clarksville, R.F.D.	88
1817	Mt. Zion	Fayette, R.F.D.	26
1818	Black River	Williamsville	46
1818	Little Bonne Femme	Columbia, R.F.D.	210
1819	Peno	Bowling Green	52
1819	Pisgah	Bunceton	162
1820	Chariton	Glasgow, R.F.D.	54
1820	Mt. Gilead	Fayette, R.F.D.	60
1820	Mt. Nebo	Pilot Grove	87
1821	New Hope	Elsberry, R.F.D.	112
1821	Union	Jamestown	78
1822	New London	New London	153
1823	Bethel	Palmyra	122
1823	First	Columbia	1,276
1823	Mt. Pleasant	Clarksburg	142
1824	First	Jackson	669
1824	Sandy	Crystal City, R.F.D.	181
1825	Lexington	Lexington	522
1825	Six Mile	Buckner, R.F.D.	215
1826	Providence	New Bloomfield	305
1827	Zoar	Napton	129
1828	New Salem	Ashland, R.F.D.	192
1829	Bethlehem	Grubville, R.F.D.	46
1829	Calvey	Catawissa, R.F.D.	26
1829	Cedar Hill	Cedar Hill	107
1829	Courtois	Barryman, R.F.D.	41
1829	Friendship	Armstrong, R.F.D.	73
1829	Liberty	Owensville, R.F.D.	183
1829	New Salem	Owensville, R.F.D.	18
1830	Pleasant Grove	Crosstown, R.F.D.	8
1830	Roanoke	Armstrong	48
1831	Paris	Paris	408
1831	Providence	Bonne Terre, R.F.D.	146
1831	Wyaconda	Canton, Rt. 2	39
1832	Blue Springs	Blue Springs	480
1832	High Point	Windsor	133
1832	Mt. Horeb	Mineola	57
1832	Salem	Center, R.F.D.	90
1832	Sulphur Lick	Davis, R.F.D.	36
1832	Three Rivers	Farmington, Rt. 2	218
1833	First	California	832
1833	First	Palmyra	521
1833	Grand River	Jameson, R.F.D.	69
1833	Lebanon	Bloomsdale	173
1833	Mt. Zion	California, R.F.D.	96

CURTIS A. HUTCHERSON

NEW MEXICO. Churches listed here, 51 in number, have had continuous existence during the 63-year period antedating the formation of

Year	Name	Post Office	Members 1955
1880	First	Las Vegas	271
1881	First	Raton	504
1887	First	Albuquerque	2,181
1890	First, Eddy (Carlsbad)	Carlsbad	2,032
1891	Aztec	Aztec	393
1891	Cloudcroft	Cloudcroft	62
1892	Weed	Weed	41
1892	Hope	Hope	22
1894	First	Roswell	2,977
1896	Hagerman	Hagerman	345
1898	First	Alamogordo	978
1899	First	Las Cruces	1,285
1899	First	Deming	632
1899	First	Silver City	461
1900	First	Portales	1,125
1900	Capitan	Capitan	79
1901	First	Clayton	516
1903	Mayhill	Mayhill	62
1903	Elida	Elida	319
1903	Floyd	Floyd	185
1903	Pinon	Pinon	59
1904	First	Tucumcari	1,385
1904	Estancia	Estancia	179
1904	First	Artesia	1,516
1905	Lake Arthur	Lake Arthur	50
1905	Logan	Logan	78
1905	Texico	Texico	287
1905	Dexter	Dexter	247
1905	Corona	Corona	246
1906	Melrose	Melrose	496
1906	Tularosa	Tularosa	232
1907	Kenna	Kenna	67
1907	Carrizozo	Carrizozo	139
1907	Lordsburg	Lordsburg	210
1907	Mountainair	Mountainair	314
1907	House	House	225
1907	First	Clovis	1,671
1907	Grady	Grady	158
1907	Ruidoso	Ruidoso	264
1908	Monument	Monument	256
1908	Dora	Dora	174
1908	Bellville (Rosedale)	Bellview	233
1908	San Jon	San Jon	168
1908	Vaughn	Vaughn	69
1908	Causey	Causey	107
1908	Des Moines	Des Moines	104
1909	Hudson	Tucumcari	37
1909	First	Lovington	1,205
1911	Roy	Roy	122
1911	Salem	Salem	115
1911	First	Farmington	589

LEWIS A. MYERS

NORTH CAROLINA. The Baptist State Convention of North Carolina was founded in 1830. Of the churches existing in that state in 1955, 167 were organized before or during 1830.

Historic Churches

Year	Name	Post Office	Members 1955	Year	Name	Post Office	Members 1955
1727	Shiloh	Shiloh	596	1802	Seven Creeks	Whiteville, Rt. 4	142
1729	Meherrin	Murfreesboro	472	1803	First	Canton	1,001
1749	Rowan	Clinton, Rt. 2	502	1803	Mt. Carmel	Chapel Hill, Rt. 3	338
1750	Sandy Run	Roxobel	373	1803	Republican	Ahoskie	174
1754	Grassy Creek	Oxford	449	1803	Salem	Elizabeth City	225
1755	Fishing Creek	Whitakers, Rt. 2	138	1804	Ahoskie	Ahoskie	1,252
1755	Jersey	Lexington, Rt. 7	236	1804	Concord	Bostic, Rt. 1	300
1756	Well's Chapel	Wallace	318	1804	Holly Grove	Harrellsville	72
1758	Rock Springs	Pittsboro	148	1804	Mud Creek	Hendersonville	543
1760	Forks of Little River	Star	80	1804	Ross	Windsor	330
				1805	Cool Springs	East Bend	263
1762	Mount Pisgah	Supply	229	1805	Middle Fork	Mars Hill, Rt. 2	192
1765	White Marsh	Whiteville	248	1806	Antioch	Chapel Hill, Rt. 1	288
1771	Bethel Hill	Woodsdale	239	1806	Fairview	Fairview	201
1771	New Light	Durham, R.F.D.	132	1806	Middleswamp	Gatesville	153
1772	Long Creek Memorial	Dallas	429	1807	Center Grove	Powellsville	250
				1807	First	Washington	680
1772	Sandy Run	Mooresboro	438	1808	Potecasi	Jackson	338
1773	Philadelphia	Marshville, Rt. 1	402	1808	Ramoth Gilead	Elizabeth City	233
1775	Yeopin	Edenton	117	1808	Roanoke Island	Nags Head	74
1776	Hoopers Creek	Balfour	255	1809	First	New Bern	942
1776	Mill Creek	Winnabow	306	1809	Hephzibah	Wendell, Rt. 2	542
1776	Rocky River	Polkton, Rt. 2	33	1809	Peachtree	Spring Hope	412
1776	Sandy Creek	Louisburg, Rt. 2	384	1810	Cherry Grove	Fair Bluff	382
1777	Cashie	Windsor	624	1810	Wingate	Wingate	603
1777	Lilesville	Lilesville	219	1811	First	Clayton	673
1779	Beaver Creek	Boomer	144	1811	Flat Creek	Stocksville	321
1781	Ballard's Bridge	Tyner	440	1812	First	Raleigh	1,809
1782	Concord	Creedmoor	125	1812	Hominy	Candler	414
1783	Brier Creek	Ronda	87	1812	Juniper Springs	Goldston	229
1783	Flat Rock	Hamptonville	420	1812	New Britton	Loris, S. C.	215
1785	Bear Swamp	Lake View, S. C.	318	1812	Shady Grove	Wake County	105
1785	Bill's Creek	Lake Lure, Rt. 1	270	1813	Cathey's Creek	Candler, Rt. 3	196
1785	Spring Branch	Dunn, Rt. 1	366	1813	Concord	Magnolia	111
1785	Warren Plains	Warrenton, Rt. 1	303	1813	Spring Hill	Wagram	165
1786	First	Elizabeth City	969	1814	Mount Holly	Burgaw	145
1786	Wake Union	Wake Forest, Rt. 1	180	1814	Mount Pisgah	Apex, Rt. 3	268
1787	Bear Creek	Goldston	149	1814	Riley's Creek	Rocky Point	316
1787	Lick Creek	Lexington, Rt. 9	76	1814	Union	Lenoir, Rt. 2	417
1788	Saddle Tree	Proctorville	64	1814	Zion Hill	Taylorsville	249
1789	Antioch	Lumberton, Rt. 5	509	1815	Bells	Durham	325
1789	Colerain	Colerain	566	1816	Brown's	Fayetteville	179
1789	Connaritsa	Roxobel	374	1816	Mt. Ruhama	Alexis	462
1789	Mountain Creek	Gilkey	250	1816	Zion	Shelby, Rt. 5	437
				1817	Ebenezer	Hendersonville, Rt. 1	596
1789	Mountain Page	Tryon	267				
1789	Wake Cross Roads	Wake County	469	1818	Big Springs	Ellenboro, Rt. 1	272
				1818	Bull Creek	Marshall, Rt. 2	216
1790	Coldwater	Concord, Rt. 13	252	1818	Old Bull Creek	Black Mountain	240
1790	Sawyer's Creek	Belcross	288	1819	First Broad	Bostic, Rt. 2	231
1792	Bear Creek	Troutman	194	1819	First	Tarboro	678
1792	French Broad	Hendersonville	75	1819	Neill's Creek	Buie's Creek	331
1792	Lewis Fork	Purlear	290	1820	Beulah	Hendersonville	274
1794	First	Fairmont	976	1820	Cartledge Creek	Rockingham, Rt. 4	159
1795	Little Ivy	Mars Hill	201				
1796	Cheerful Hope	Delco	70	1820	Cumberland Union	Fuquay Springs, Rt. 1	105
1799	Fall Creek	Star	264				
1800	Cedar Creek	Fayetteville, Rt. 5	356	1820	Piney Grove	Fuquay Springs, Rt. 1	459
1800	Lennon's Cross Roads	Lumberton	244				
				1820	Union	Ronda	246
1800	Orrum	Orrum	162	1821	Big Ivy	Barnardsville	208
1800	Union	Kinston	125	1821	Cullowhee	Cullowhee	381
1802	Island Creek	Rose Hill	320	1821	Mt. Carmel	Enfield	166
1802	Mays Chapel	Chapel Hill	60	1822	Camp Creek	Gaffney, S. C., Rt. 2	457
1802	New Found	Leicester	356				

Historic Churches

Year	Name	Post Office	Members 1955
1822	First	Franklin	874
1822	Fishing Creek	Elkin	426
1822	Holly Springs	Holly Springs	183
1822	Island Creek	Henderson	564
1823	Brassfield	Creedmoor	115
1823	First	Waynesville	885
1823	Hester	Oxford	510
1823	Lewis	North Wilkesboro, Rt. 3	129
1823	Mt. Moriah	Durham	222
1823	Red Bud	Castalia, Rt. 1	258
1823	Samaria	Middlesex, Rt. 2	212
1824	Brush Creek	Siler City	199
1824	Capeharts	Merry Hill	311
1824	Flat Rock	Youngsville	637
1824	Mt. Gilead	Pittsboro, Rt. 1	193
1825	First	High Point	1,659
1825	Harrellsville	Harrellsville	305
1825	Loves Creek	Siler City	359
1825	North Catawba	Lenoir, Rt. 3	139
1825	Swan Creek	Jonesville	526
1826	Antioch	Taylorsville, Rt. 2	384
1826	Lower Creek	Lenoir, Rt. 2	625
1826	Mt. Zion	Liberty, Rt. 3	271
1826	Olive Branch	Roxboro	365
1826	Providence	Elizabeth City	268
1826	Sharon	Rockingham	86
1827	Powell's Point	Point Harbor	122
1828	Brown Creek	Polkton	160
1828	Cowee	Franklin, Rt. 3	389
1828	Iron Hill	Tabor City	170
1828	Liberty	Thomasville, Rt. 2	229
1828	Mountain View	Black Mountain	188
1828	Mt. Moriah	Pageland, S. C., Rt. 1	215
1828	Reynoldson	Gates	326
1828	Smyrna	Morganton, Rt. 5	64
1829	First	Asheville	2,779
1829	Gum Springs	Moncure, Rt. 1	115
1829	Roan Mountain	Bakersville	273
1829	Smyrna	Smyrna	81
1830	Bear Creek	Bakersville, Rt. 3	500
1830	Brown's	Warrenton, Rt. 2	129
1830	Clement	Hurdle Mills, Rt. 2	224
1830	Kendall's	New London, Rt. 1	155
1830	Marshall	Marshall	237
1830	New Hope	Wilbar	231
1830	Scots Creek	Sylva	717
1830	Silver Creek	Morganton, Rt. 6	67

HENRY SMITH STROUPE

OKLAHOMA. This list includes churches organized 1832–83, up to formation of the Baptist Missionary and Educational Convention of Indian Territory, the first general convention in what is now Oklahoma. Documentation is insufficient to prove survival of churches organized prior to the Civil War, except that in similar localities and names they reappear after 1865. Ottawa was organized in Kansas and migrated intact to Indian Territory. Fountain is Negro, and Old Baptist Mission, Ottawa, Philadelphia, Indian Spring, Rock Creek, Boiling Springs, Ephesus, Cedar, Rock Springs, and Belle Fonte are Indian. The others are white.

Year	Name	Post Office	Members 1955
1832	Fountain	Porter, Rt. 1	50
1839	Old Baptist Mission	Westville	30
1840	Ottawa	Miami, Rt. 1	72
1846	Philadelphia	Durant, Rt. 1	5
1850	Indian Spring	Sasakwa	247
1851	Rock Creek	Red Oak	30
1852	Boiling Springs	Wilburton	30
1854	Ephesus	Wilburton	20
1861	Cedar	Wilburton	25
1869	First	Atoka	1,062
1870	Double Branch	Poteau, Rt. 2	135
1874	Rock Springs	Anadarko	34
1875	Choate Prairie	Indianola	215
1875	Second	North McAlester	504
1877	First	Tahlequah	823
1878	Belle Fonte	Sallisaw	37
1879	Liberty Hill	Cameron	111
1880	First	Webbers Falls	267
1880	Leon	Leon	172
1881	Catoosa	Catoosa	333
1881	Macedonia	Ft. Smith, Ark., Rt. 3	109
1883	Burneyville	Burneyville	131

J. M. GASKIN

SOUTH CAROLINA. These existing Baptist churches were constituted by 1821, the year of the first meeting of the South Carolina Baptist Convention. This list has no reference to size or influence.

Year	Name	Post Office	Members 1954
1682	First	Charleston	1,323
1734	Glassy Mountain	Landrum	57
1737	Langston	Clinton	62
1738	Welsh Neck	Society Hill	239
1740	Pawley Swamp	Conway	155
1745	Euhaw	Ridgeland	93
1752	Brushy Creek	Greer	362
1754	Mechanicsville	Darlington	266
1755	Congaree	Gadsden	59
1756	Matlock	Jackson	217
1759	Beech Branch	Fairfax	86
1760	Upper Fair Forest	Union	337
1762	Lower Fair Forest	Union	121
1763	Horn's Creek	Edgefield	24
1765	Sandy Level	Blythewood	322
1765	Friendship	Pauline	364
1768	Little River	Jenkinsville	62
1768	Calvary	Pinewood	25
1768	Enoree	Newberry	84
1770	Goucher	Gaffney	329
1770	High Hills	Dalzell	19
1771	Bush River	Kinards	181
1772	First	McCall	368
1772	Healing Springs	Blackville	170
1773	Big Stevens Creek	Augusta	56
1773	Durbin Creek	Fountain Inn	130
1775	Gapway	Mullins	436

Historic Churches

Year	Name	Post Office	Members 1954	Year	Name	Post Office	Members 1954
1775	Lawtonville	Estill	335	1802	Providence	Gaffney	291
1775	Turkey Creek	Donalds	146	1803	Beaverdam	Fairplay	394
1776	Buffalo	McCormick	120	1803	Dean Swamp	Springfield	38
1776	Ebenezer	Timmonsville	283	1803	Double Springs	Taylors	331
1776	Flat Creek	Kershaw	240	1803	El Bethel	Gaffney, Rt. 6	105
1776	Skull Shoals	Gaffney	92	1803	First	Landrum	636
1778	Centenary	Centenary	87	1803	Hopewell	Anderson	180
1778	Reedy River	Travelers Rest	595	1803	Middle River	Cleveland	315
1780	Bethel	Sumter	409	1803	Old Hepsibah	Seneca	50
1780	Fork Shoals	Pelzer	555	1803	Philadelphia	Pauline	389
1780	Liberty	Liberty	314	1803	Springtown	Bamberg	172
1781	Little River	Honea Path	295	1804	Antioch	Modoc	152
1781	Robertsville	Pineland	31	1804	Bethel	Monetta	282
1782	Cheraw	Cheraw	639	1804	Cedar Shoals	Enoree	272
1782	Spears Creek	Blaney	385	1804	Dry Creek	Saluda	63
1783	Salem	Bennettsville	153	1804	Gilead	Jonesville	340
1783	Swift Creek	Darlington	488	1804	Good Hope	Saluda	364
1784	Padgetts Creek	Union	276	1804	Green Pond	Woodruff	223
1784	Red Bank	Saluda	507	1804	Holly Springs	Inman	743
1784	Wassamassaw	Moncks Corner	89	1804	New Hope	Cross Anchor	312
1785	Keowee	Six Mile	115	1804	Rosemary	Williston	137
1785	Plum Branch	Plum Branch	310	1804	Sardis	Saluda	423
1785	Secona	Pickens	321	1805	Republican	Modoc	95
1786	Elim	Effingham	240	1805	Willow Swamp	Norway	293
1787	Cedar Spring	Spartanburg	388	1806	Beulah	Lykesland	218
1787	First	Whitmire	576	1806	Hebron	Union	163
1787	First	Woodruff	740	1807	Black Creek	White Hall	228
1788	Big Creek	Belton	293	1807	Carter's Ford	Lodge	416
1788	Cross Roads	Easley	404	1807	Green Sea	Green Sea	452
1789	Brownsville	Blenheim	186	1807	New Home #1	Loris	158
1789	Little Stevens Creek	Edgefield	216	1808	Beaverdam	Mountville	76
				1808	Bethany	McCormick	85
1789	Mountain Creek	Anderson	313	1809	Chestnut Hill	Saluda	83
				1809	First	Columbia	3,654
1789	Woodward	Chester	123	1810	Bethlehem	Round O	91
1790	Great Saltkehatchie	Ulmers	153	1810	First	Camden	1,311
				1810	Gilgal	Landrum	201
1790	West Creek	Batesburg	255	1810	Mt. Moriah	Greenwood	180
1791	Lebanon	Pendleton	443	1810	Mt. Olivet	Pinopolis	138
1792	Catawba	Rock Hill	374	1810	Warrior Creek	Gray Court	351
1792	Flint Hill	Fort Mill	372	1812	Coneross	Westminster	134
1792	Killian	Columbia	244	1812	New Providence	Hartsville	372
1792	State Line	Gaffney	485	1812	Red Oak Grove	Modoc	174
1793	Bethabara	Wagener	62	1812	Rocky Grove	Salley	177
1793	Mount Tabor	Anderson	285	1812	Rocky Springs	Wagener	129
1794	Boiling Springs	Inman	1,087	1812	Salem	North	144
1794	First	Georgetown	973	1813	Antioch	Grover, N. C.	311
1794	Poplar Springs	Ware Shoals	337	1813	First	Sumter	1,589
1795	Oolenoy	Pickens	230	1813	Fork Hill	Heath Springs	242
1795	Rocky River	Iva	250	1813	Four Holes	Orangeburg	386
1796	Gum Branch	McBee	405	1813	Old Lexington	Leesville	115
1797	Beaver Creek	Chester	44	1814	Beaver Creek	Heath Springs	106
1797	Providence	Hodges	265	1814	Cross Roads	Chappells	55
1798	Mountain Creek	Callison	145	1814	Cypress Creek	Varnville	86
				1814	Phillippi	Johnston	435
1798	Salem	Anderson	148	1814	Steep Bottom	Furman	153
1798	Siloam	Greenwood	110	1816	Bull Swamp	North	223
1800	Beaufort	Beaufort	1,156	1817	Darien	Windsor	95
1800	Bethel	Walterboro	92	1818	Standing Springs	Simpsonville	222
1800	Bethlehem	Roebuck	449				
1800	Gloverville	Gloverville	319	1819	Clear Springs	Simpsonville	620
1800	Salem	Saluda	127	1819	Lake Swamp	Timmonsville	395
1800	Tyger	Taylors	193	1819	Washington	Greer	567
1802	Catfish Creek	Latta	240	1820	Gowensville	Gowensville	297
1802	Neal's Creek	Belton	176	1820	Macedonia	Gaffney	395

Historic Churches

Year	Name	Post Office	Members 1954
1820	New Prospect	Inman	464
1820	Thomas Memorial	Bennettsville	788
1821	Buck Creek	Loris	253
1821	Chestnut Ridge	Laurens	205
1821	Lake City	Lake City	932
1821	Washington	Pelzer	402

H. JACK FLANDERS, JR.

TENNESSEE. The first Tennessee Baptist Convention was organized in 1833. Additional information about these historic churches may be obtained by writing directly to the post office addresses given.

Year	Name	Post Office	Members 1955
1779	Buffalo Ridge	Fordtown	212
1780	Cherokee	Jonesboro	214
1780	Stock Creek	Knoxville	368
1783	Sinking Creek	Johnson City	261
1785	Whitesburg	Whitesburg	223
1786	Dandridge	Dandridge	312
1789	First	Sevierville	1,011
1789	Providence	Sevierville	149
1791	Red River	Adams	350
1792	Buffalo	Rutledge	263
1792	Mouth of Richland	Blaine	313
1792	New Bethel	Goodlettsville	334
1793	Warrensburg	Mohawk	218
1794	Mountain City	Mountain City	192
1795	Mill Creek	Nashville	246
1795	Pleasant Hill	Fountain Head	200
1797	Dumplin	New Market	125
1797	Little Flat Creek	Coryton	223
1800	Beaver Dam	Fountain City	313
1800	Dixon Creek	Dixon Springs	145
1800	Enon	McKenzie	210
1800	Gum Springs	Cleveland	148
1800	Mt. Pelia	Martin	237
1800	Mt. Pleasant	Rockvale	180
1800	Republican Grove	Murfreesboro	132
1801	Brush Creek	Brush Creek	232
1801	Kyles Ford	Kyles Ford	185
1802	Ball Camp	Knoxville	340
1802	Millers Cove	Walland	244
1802	Paw Paw Hollow	Kodak	482
1802	Shiloh	Woodbury	174
1803	First	Morristown	1,623
1803	McPheeters Bend	Church Hill	357
1803	Round Lick	Watertown	427
1804	Bethel	Sevierville	185
1805	Crockett's Creek	Model	137
1806	Hickman	Hickman	123
1806	Hopewell	Bethpage	55
1806	Smith Fork	Statesville	240
1807	Blooming Grove	Woodlawn	299
1807	Caney Fork	Cookeville	174
1807	Slick Rock	Robbins	134
1808	Burt	Woodbury	142
1808	Mulberry	Mulberry	85
1808	Spring Creek	Clarksville	318
1809	Salem	Liberty	256
1810	Boyd's Creek	Sevierville	275
1810	Friendship	Culleoka	201
1810	Hogan's Creek	Carthage	74
1810	Shellsford	McMinnville	515
1811	Richardson Creek	Lee Valley	119
1812	Hiwassee	Calhoun	95
1812	Peyton's Creek	Monoville	268
1812	Six Mile	Maryville	295
1812	Zion	Powell's Station	286
1813	Antioch	Dandridge	59
1813	Cedar Grove	Lebanon	338
1813	New Friendship	Cleveland	194
1813	New Hope	Wartrace	78
1813	Robertson Creek	Bulls Gap	114
1814	Antioch	Antioch	214
1814	Knob Spring	Lebanon	64
1814	Oak Hill	Leoma	153
1815	Hurricane	Norene	233
1816	Lebanon	Gatlinburg	221
1817	Hillsdale	Dixon Springs	177
1818	Egypt	Raleigh	299
1818	Head of Richland	Rutledge	145
1818	Little West Fork	Clarksville	176
1818	Pisgah	Ten Mile	189
1819	Bradley's Creek	Milton	242
1819	Eagleville	Eagleville	254
1819	Estanlee	Riceville	202
1819	New Hope	Alexandria	133
1820	Elim	Ripley	168
1820	First	Nashville	3,711
1820	First	Sweetwater	986
1820	Hickory Cove	Rogersville	289
1820	Old Sweetwater	Sweetwater	192
1820	Smyrna	Burlison	217
1821	Concord	Nolensville	303
1821	First	Lebanon	1,206
1821	Little Cedar Lick	Watertown	83
1821	New Blackwell	Rutledge	225
1821	Puncheon Camp	Luttrell	143
1821	Puncheon Camp	Washburn	136
1821	Rutland	Mt. Juliet	67
1822	Auburn	Auburntown	342
1822	Fall Creek	Norene	248
1822	First	Erwin	1,169
1822	Liberty	Lafayette	99
1822	Stony Creek	Elizabethton	440
1822	Union Hill	Ardmore	160
1822	Zion Hill	Englewood	130
1823	Bird's Creek	Paris	222
1823	Concord	Mohawk	133
1823	Decatur	Decatur	257
1823	Ellejoy	Walland	195
1823	North Fork	Puryear	360
1823	Shiloh	Ten Mile	214
1823	Spring Creek	Mansfield	65

FIRST BAPTIST CHURCH, El Dorado, Ark. Organized 1845, auditorium of classical style built 1923 to accommodate 800, educational facilities for 1,000. Membership 1956 estimated 2,600, property valued at $750,000.

FIRST BAPTIST CHURCH, Jennings, La. Begun 1894, present auditorium of Colonial design seating 500 erected 1952. Membership 1956 about 850; property worth $360,000, including Sunday school facilities for 550.

Year	Name	Post Office	Members 1955
1824	Chestua	Madisonville	174
1824	Concord	Ten Mile	78
1824	First	Athens	1,209
1824	First	Madisonville	639
1824	Good Hope	Big Springs	111
1824	Shady Grove	Buchanan	144
1825	First	Brownsville	896
1825	Muddy Creek	Bluff City	130
1825	Palestine	Hornsby	80
1826	Clover Creek	Medon	354
1826	Friendship	Benton	199
1826	Hopewell	Springfield	421
1826	Knob Creek	Columbia	196
1826	Lawrence Grove	Thompson Station	36
1826	Prospect	Loudon	261
1826	Rock Springs	Pulaski	194
1827	Fall Branch	Fall Branch	365
1827	Hannah's Gap	Petersburg	177
1827	Higgins Chapel	Erwin	157
1827	Holston	Bristol	255
1827	Woodville	Ripley	91
1828	Bethlehem	Whiteville	70
1828	Christianburg	Sweetwater	192
1828	Clay Creek	Newport	207
1828	Clear Creek	Selmer	240
1828	Eldad	Trenton	67
1828	Falling Springs	Allred	169
1828	Fellowship	Ten Mile	58
1828	Goodfield	Decatur	205
1828	New Providence	Tellico Plains	220
1828	Pleasant Grove	Saulsbury	88
1829	Chilhowee	Tallessee	60
1829	Fellowship	Mt. Juliet	295
1829	Hopewell Springs	Madisonville	525
1829	Mulberry Gap	Sneedville	212
1830	Alder Branch	Sevierville	305
1830	Antioch	Humboldt	111
1830	Big Creek	Lucy	217
1830	Big Rock	Big Rock	172
1830	First, Hunter	Elizabethton	275
1830	Paint Rock	Paint Rock	350
1831	First	Clarksville	1,853
1831	Mt. Harmony	Ducktown	166
1831	Zion	Brownsville	218
1832	Macedonia	Kenton	242
1832	Orlinda	Orlinda	500
1832	Pleasant Hill	Lenoir City	515
1832	Pleasant Plains	Jackson	162
1833	Bethel	Fountain City	549
1833	Bethlehem	Rutherford	106
1833	Blountville	Blountville	208
1833	Del Rio	Del Rio	115
1833	First	Paris	1,040
1833	Indian Creek	Jacksboro	238
1833	Rocky Valley	New Market	181

L. G. FREY

TEXAS. The number of churches constituted in Texas prior to the organization of the first general body is uncertain, due to incomplete early records and also to some doubt about the accuracy of such records. The first general body was the Baptist State Convention of Texas organized at Anderson, Grimes County, 1848. Prior to this date there were 11 churches, four whose continuation to the present time is seriously doubted. They are LaGrange in Fayette County, 1839, 9 members; Plum Grove, Fayette County, 1839, 13 members; Antioch, Grimes County, 1844, 7 members; Matagorda, Matagorda County, 1846.

It seems that Independence Baptist Church, Washington County, organized in 1839, holds the honor of having the longest continued existence. Thomas Spraggins led in the organization. The charter members were John, Ivey, Mary, and Jeannette McNeese, J. J. and Biddy Davis, Thomas and Martha Tremmier. A little later these three were added: O. H. P. Garrett, J. L. Davis, and Diadema Matson. T. W. Cox was called as the first pastor. This church is also distinguished as being the church where worshiped the teachers and students of Baylor University at Independence. In 1955 the membership was 56; value of church property, $6,000; total gifts, $1,367. Its post office address is Independence, Tex.

The First Baptist Church of Galveston, Tex., was organized June 13, 1840, with nine members, and James Huckins was moderator. Three other members were received at the time who did not have church letters in hand. The membership in 1955 was 3,898; value of church property, $500,000; total contributions, $142,164.33. The post office address is First Baptist Church, Galveston, Tex.

The First Baptist Church, Houston, Tex., was organized Apr. 10, 1841, with nine members, James Huckins assisting in the organization. In 1955 there were 5,577 members holding church property valued at $1,399,453, making total gifts of $289,505. The post office address is First Baptist Church, Houston, Tex.

Providence Church was organized in Washington County May 13, 1841, with nine members. This church had a distinguished group to lead in the organization—W. M. Tryon (q.v.), R. E. B. Baylor (q.v.), Hosea Garrett, and Elias Rogers. Tryon served as the first pastor for nearly four years and was succeeded by Hosea Garrett. In 1955 there were 75 members holding church property valued at $12,000, making total gifts of $5,323. The post office address is Providence Baptist Church, R.F.D., Brenham, Tex.

There were two churches organized at Gonzales, Gonzales County, before 1848. The first was constituted near the end of 1841 with 10 members. Z. N. Morrell (q.v.) was the leading spirit in this movement. The last reference to the church in the minutes of Union Association appears in 1845. After that the church dropped out of any recorded existence. The present church at Gonzales was organized on July 31, 1847, with nine members. The organizing council consisted of Richard B. Ellis and P. B. Chandler. Ellis became pastor and Thomas J. Pilgrim (q.v.) was elected clerk. In 1955 the membership stood at 993, the value of the church property was $290,000, and total gifts were $40,-

Historic Churches

718. The post office address is Gonzales, Tex.

The First Baptist Church at Austin, Travis County, was organized July, 1847, by R. H. Taliaferro with eight members. In 1955 the membership was 3,262; total expenditures, $263,182; value of church property, $985,859. The post office address is First Baptist Church, Austin, Tex.

The First Baptist Church at Wharton, in Wharton County, was organized May 22, 1846. Noah Hill became pastor in the fall of 1846. In 1851 Wharton Church had a membership of 94 Negroes and only 24 white people. In 1955 the membership was 893; the value of church property was $143,500; and gifts to all causes totaled $36,274. Its post office address is Wharton, Tex.

BIBLIOGRAPHY: J. M. Carroll, *A History of Texas Baptists* (1923). B. F. Fuller, *History of Texas Baptists* (1900). J. B. Link, *Texas Historical and Biographical Magazine* (1891). Z. N. Morrell, *Flowers and Fruits from the Wilderness* (1872).

L. R. ELLIOTT

VIRGINIA. The Baptist General Association of Virginia was founded in 1823. The following extant churches were constituted before that date.

Year	Name	County	Members 1955
1762	Broad Run	Fauquier	201
1762	Oak Grove	Princess Anne	293
1765	Zion	Greenville	220
1767	Craigs	Spotsylvania	440
1769	Blue Run	Culpeper	148
1769	Little River	Loudoun	210
1769	Wallers	Spotsylvania	360
1770	Gold Mine	Louisa	119
1771	County Line	Pittsylvania	201
1771	Ebenezer	Amherst	51
1771	Goochland	Goochland	345
1771	Meherrin	Lunenburg	173
1771	Morgan's	Bedford	319
1771	Old Powhatan	Powhatan	146
1772	Antioch	Sussex	177
1772	Berryville	Clarke	446
1772	Bethany	Spotsylvania	492
1772	Bethel	Mecklenburg	321
1772	Crooked Run	Culpeper	136
1772	Glebe Landing	Middlesex	211
1772	Lower King and Queen	King and Queen	187
1772	Rocks	Appomattox	123
1772	Sappony	Sussex	94
1772	Upper Essex	Essex	397
1773	Carmel	Caroline	366
1773	Chestnut Grove	Albemarle	211
1773	Dover	Goochland	182
1773	Jeffersonton	Culpeper	127
1773	Winns Creek	Halifax	210
1774	Blackwater	Princess Anne	124
1774	Culpeper	Culpeper	1,088
1774	Fork Union	Fluvanna	492
1774	Lyles	Fluvanna	168
1774	Mill Swamp *	Isle of Wight	292
1774	Mount Zion	Essex	209
1774	Muddy Creek	Powhatan	102
1774	North Pamunkey	Orange	247
1774	Upper King and Queen	King and Queen	402
1775	Black Creek	Hanover	101
1775	Hunting Creek	Halifax	314
1775	Quaker	Bedford	305
1775	Sharon	King William	172
1775	South Quay	Southampton	161
1776	Antioch	Henrico	162
1776	Buckingham	Buckingham	205
1776	Catawba	Halifax	336
1776	Emmaus	New Kent	95
1776	Liberty Chapel	Appomattox	109
1776	Mathews	Mathews	350
1776	Mt. Pleasant	Charles City	140
1776	Red Oak	Appomattox	223
1776	Reedy Creek	Brunswick	135
1776	Smyrna	Goochland	180
1776	Tomahawk	Chesterfield	157
1776	Winns	Hanover	343
1777	Lower Northampton	Northampton	36
1777	Tussekiah	Lunenburg	184
1778	Buffalo	Mecklenburg	342
1778	F. T.	Rappahannock	80
1778	Kentuck	Pittsylvania	373
1778	Morattico	Lancaster	139
1778	North Fork	Washington	117
1778	Skinquarter	Chesterfield	203
1779	Sandy Creek	Amelia	166
1779	Scottsburg	Halifax	304
1779	Western Branch	Nansemond	330
1780	First	Richmond	3,766
1781	Four Mile Creek	Henrico	520
1781	New Prospect	Amherst	145
1781	Preddy's Creek	Albemarle	91
1783	Red Bank	Northampton	277
1784	County Line	Caroline	442
1784	Hebron	Southampton	87
1784	London Bridge	Princess Anne	609
1785	Arbor	Halifax	162
1785	Childrey	Halifax	660
1785	Churchland	Norfolk	426
1786	Black Creek	Southampton	445
1786	Chincoteague	Accomack	31
1786	Ebenezer	Campbell	387
1786	Long Branch	Fauquier	204
1786	Mulberry Grove	Buckingham	102
1786	Nomini	Richmond	233
1787	Cut Bank	Dinwiddie	104
1787	Elam	Sussex	48
1787	Fountain Creek	Greenville	235
1787	High Hills	Sussex	319
1787	Mt. Hermon	Bedford	130
1787	Rapidan	Madison	178
1787	Reynolds Memorial	Sperryville	104
1788	Massaponax	Spotsylvania	277
1788	Wilderness	Spotsylvania	186
1789	Court Street	Portsmouth	975
1789	Hanover	King George	149
1789	Hermitage	Middlesex	262
1789	Millstone	Halifax	353

Year	Name	County	Members 1955
1790	Bethlehem	Chesterfield	269
1790	Bruington	King and Queen	282
1790	Deep Run	Henrico	251
1790	Farnham	Richmond	189
1790	Hollies	Northampton	129
1790	Staunton	Bedford	96
1791	Colosse	King William	163
1791	Gourdvine	Culpeper	212
1791	Hampton	Hampton	1,076
1791	Little River	Louisa	171
1791	Mine Road	Louisa	262
1792	Charles Town	Jefferson, W. Va.	434
1792	Falling River	Campbell	426
1795	Berea	Louisa	287
1797	Salem	Chesterfield	182
1798	Riceville	Pittsylvania	287
1800	Bethel	Caroline	185
1800	Greenfield	Pittsylvania	375
1800	Northwest	Norfolk	218
1800	Thompson's Settlement	Lee	130
1801	Bedford	Bedford	739
1801	Union	Gloucester	919
1802	Ash Camp	Charlotte	394
1802	Dan River	Halifax	335
1802	Hardware	Albemarle	72
1802	Republican Grove	Halifax	356
1802	Salem	Caroline	350
1803	Beaverdam	Bedford	278
1803	Bethel	Culpeper	295
1803	First	Alexandria	2,290
1803	Providence	Charlotte	155
1803	Shockoe	Pittsylvania	197
1804	Coan	Northumberland	297
1805	Suck Spring	Bedford	235
1805	Timber Ridge	Bedford	248
1805	Zoar	Spotsylvania	222
1805	First	Norfolk	1,362
1807	Hopeful	Hanover	359
1807	New Chapel	Campbell	363
1807	Poroporone	King and Queen	231
1807	Tucker Swamp	Southampton	210
1809	Zoar	Middlesex	245
1810	Second Branch	Chesterfield	166
1811	Grove	Fauquier	148
1812	Antioch	Charlotte	215
1812	Beulah	King William	225
1812	Clover	Halifax	349
1812	Ellis Creek	Halifax	206
1812	Mt. Hermon	Spotsylvania	123
1812	Pope's Creek	Westmoreland	136
1812	Rock Hill	Stafford	97
1813	Elk Creek	Louisa	94
1813	Kempsville	Princess Anne	620
1813	Zion	Orange	282
1814	Branch's	Chesterfield	1,331
1814	Cross Roads	Halifax	164
1815	First	Lynchburg	1,241
1815	First	Petersburg	1,018
1816	Clarksville	Mecklenburg	525
1816	Neriah	Rockbridge	116
1817	Bethel	Chesterfield	169
1818	Moore's Swamp	Surry	232
1819	South Anna	Louisa	245
1820	Enon	Essex	174
1820	Goshen	Rockbridge	95
1820	Round Hill	King George	240
1820	Second	Richmond	849
1820	Straitstone	Pittsylvania	422
1822	Winchester	Frederick	867
1823	Beth Car	Madison	128
1823	Chestnut Grove	Buckingham	77

* In his pamphlet "The First Baptist Church in Virginia," Parke Poindexter Deans claims that the Mill Swamp Church was established in 1714. But see "Mill Swamp Creek" in the index of Garnett Ryland's The Baptists of Virginia, 1899–1926 (1955).

RAYMOND BRYAN BROWN

HISTORICAL COMMISSION OF THE SOUTHERN BAPTIST CONVENTION. The Historical Commission of the Southern Baptist Convention began its official existence in 1947 with the adoption of the Southern Baptist Historical Society as the "duly recognized agency of the . . . Convention for the collection and preservation of Baptist History." It was given the status of a commission. Prior to this time the historical interest of most Southern Baptists had been sporadic and small.

After 1869 the Convention passed several resolutions of encouragement to the American Baptist Historical Society, which was chartered in 1853, and which included in its membership some Southerners. In 1887 a resolution was adopted commending the *History of the Baptists* written by Thomas Armitage, and in 1895 another requested more historical material in the Sunday school curriculum; but it was not until 1916 that Southern Baptists began to work for a history of their own. In that year the Sunday School Board was made responsible for preparing a "history of the Baptists of the South." A writer was secured and a manuscript delivered in 1919. It was found unsuitable and was never published.

In 1921 the Southern Baptist Convention appointed a committee on the preservation of Baptist history. This committee's activities were largely promotional. It encouraged interest in history generally, worked for the establishment of state historical societies and archives, and promoted the writing of histories. During the time of this committee's existence, the Southern Baptist Convention adopted recommendations proposing the compilation of a Baptist encyclopedia, a literary history of American Baptists, and a hymnology; the preparation of a bibliography of Southern Baptist historical materials; and the co-ordination of all American Baptist historical collections; in addition it requested that all possible Baptist minutes, journals, and papers be deposited with the Sunday School Board. Not a great deal of this ambitious program was ever accomplished; and after the death of its chairman, A. J. Holt (q.v.), in 1933, the committee was discontinued, and its work transferred to the Sunday School Board.

ORGANIZATION DATA OF SOUTHERN BAPTIST CHURCHES
as Reported on 1953 Church Letters

State	Churches	Before 1870	1870–1879	1880–1889	1890–1899	1900–1909	1910–1919	1920–1929	1930–1939	1940–1949	1950–1954	Date Not Given
Alabama	2,693	527	129	290	201	261	198	171	191	304	157	264
Arizona	175	—	—	—	—	—	2	7	8	54	93	11
Arkansas	1,136	101	52	84	79	101	92	77	97	145	109	199
California	456	1	—	—	1	1	—	—	16	172	192	73
Dist. of Col.	48	6	1	4	3	5	5	3	3	4	14	—
Florida	1,038	85	46	90	73	108	94	106	92	154	126	64
Georgia	2,744	701	174	255	252	273	189	97	137	221	146	299
Illinois	694	176	35	59	56	50	53	30	36	63	87	49
Kansas	99	1	3	3	—	3	4	1	3	27	49	5
Kentucky	2,253	684	138	216	181	174	139	146	122	184	113	156
Louisiana	1,146	136	60	78	74	105	96	120	123	184	121	49
Maryland	126	4	3	5	3	2	5	2	2	7	4	89
Mississippi	1,715	381	105	185	117	210	133	100	97	158	92	137
Missouri	1,699	431	170	250	184	146	79	70	63	113	77	116
New Mexico	216	—	—	3	6	30	20	14	30	56	38	19
North Carolina	3,149	605	179	321	251	271	292	178	229	352	211	260
Ohio	50	2	—	—	—	—	—	1	8	9	30	—
Oklahoma	1,246	2	5	29	135	252	130	112	114	159	123	185
Oregon-Wash.	93	—	—	1	—	1	1	1	2	15	67	2
South Carolina	1,386	407	107	158	89	115	127	81	44	91	89	78
Tennessee	2,570	456	145	207	170	177	167	164	219	324	178	363
Texas	3,583	252	246	331	300	453	309	306	295	430	369	292
Mexican	266	—	—	—	—	—	—	—	—	—	—	266
Virginia	1,282	445	99	123	109	128	75	71	33	117	51	31
Alaska	20	—	—	—	—	—	—	—	—	5	12	3
Hawaii	16	—	—	—	—	—	—	—	1	7	8	—
Total	29,899	5,403	1,697	2,692	2,284	2,866	2,210	1,858	1,965	3,358	2,556	3,010

Department of Survey, Statistics, and Information
Sunday School Board of the Southern Baptist Convention

Three years later, another committee on the preservation of Baptist history was authorized. It eventually led to the establishment of the Historical Commission. This committee, led by W. O. Carver (q.v.), chairman, who continued until his death in 1954, Rufus W. Weaver (q.v.), E. C. Routh, W. W. Barnes, H. I. Hester, J. H. Chapman, J. L. Boyd, and others, developed interest and prepared the way for expansion. Work was begun on a master catalogue of state historical materials. A Southern Baptist historical Society was organized on May 13, 1938. Interest in the writing of Baptist history was stimulated, and an organization was finally effected (Aug. 3, 1938) which would superintend the preparation of volumes of Baptist history for the centennial of the Southern Baptist Convention in 1945. Activity in the states grew. The Historical Society began a permanent collection and appointed a curator. On Dec. 12, 1945, the executive committee of the convention was requested to transfer the committee's work to the Historical Society. After the Convention had given its approval (May 8, 1947), the Southern Baptist Historical Society served as the Convention's history agency until Aug. 24, 1951, when a historical commission, already elected by the Convention, was chartered under the laws of the state of Tennessee "to encourage and motivate, conserve and utilize the history interests of the Southern Baptist Convention . . . to establish a library . . . of basic Baptist historical materials and books of a general nature; to publish whatever is related to its work or general interest; and to serve the general Baptist library [sic, historical] interest in whatever way seems desirable." The Southern Baptist Historical Society was then reconstituted as an auxiliary to the new Historical Commission.

After the history interests of Southern Baptists were thus committed to a permanent institution, progress was rapid. From an appropriation of $5,000 per year in 1949, its annual support has grown to $30,000, plus quarters and library personnel furnished by the Sunday School Board. By Aug., 1949, the collection of the society amounted to 1,235 catalogued volumes and a large amount of unprocessed material, including associational minutes. That same year, the Sunday School Board offered to furnish quarters for the offices and library of the Historical Society. On Aug. 19, 1950, the commission elected Norman Wade Cox to be its executive secretary, and he began his work Feb. 15, 1951. The permanent ministry of the commission was founded on a basis of broad cooperation with all the agencies of the Convention. The collection of the Historical Society was integrated with the Dargan Library of the Sunday School Board under an agreement adopted Mar. 8, 1951, between representatives of the society and the Board. The commission moved into its new quarters in Dec., 1952, and the new joint library, renamed the Dargan-Carver Library, was formally dedicated on June 16, 1953. At the end of 1954, approximately 35,000 books had been accessioned, and some 50,000 items of archival material processed. Between 1953 and 1955 these resources and the library's microfilm collection were used by more than 250 editors, writers, and graduate students for extended periods.

As expanding financial resources made it possible, the Historical Commission began other projects. It increased the collection and use of the historical materials of Southern Baptists and at the same time promoted interest in history among the constituency generally.

In 1952 the Historical Commission began a microfilm department; by July, 1955, over 2,000,000 pages of basic Baptist historical material, some of it dating back to the 15th century, had been filmed. Most of this material previously had been scattered throughout this country and Europe. Copies of all this material are available to college, university, and seminary libraries.

In Aug., 1952, the commission, upon the recommendation of Norman W. Cox, initiated and from that time sponsored the work of creating this encyclopedia.   JUDSON BOYCE ALLEN

HISTORIOGRAPHY, BAPTIST. The study of the writing of Baptist history begins with Thomas Crosby (q.v.) (fl. 1740), the first Baptist historiographer. He wrote *The History of the English Baptists* (four vols., 1738–40), which, although preserving many valuable writings, possesses some defects, e.g., poor organization of narratives, failure to distinguish General from Particular Baptists, and the tendency to insert material uncritically and without verification.

Joseph Ivimey (1773–1834) sought to bring Crosby's work up to date in *A History of the English Baptists* (four vols., 1811–30). Ivimey followed Crosby's volumes rather closely, with similar weaknesses resulting.

In America, John Comer (1704–34) and John Callender (1706–48) contributed extensively to Baptist historiography by investigating, copying, and arranging material on early American Baptists. Subsequent historians have drawn heavily from their labors.

The historical luminaries of the century, however, were Morgan Edwards (1722–95) and Isaac Backus (q.v.) (1724–1806). Edwards planned to write a history of Baptists in 12 volumes. Actually published were histories for Pennsylvania (1770), New Jersey (1792), Rhode Island (1867), and Delaware (1885), the latter two posthumously. Backus wrote *A History of New England with Particular Reference to . . . Baptists* (three vols., 1777, 1784, 1796).

In the 19th century historians expanded their interests, treating Baptists in general. For example, David Benedict (1779–1874) wrote *A General History of the Baptist Denomination in America, and Other Parts of the World* (two vols., 1813; rev. 1848). Thomas Armitage (1819–96) compiled *A History of the Baptists* (1886). *The Baptist Encyclopaedia* (two vols., 1881) was published by William Cathcart (*q.v.*) (1826-1908).

With the growing interest in Baptist history there was unfortunately not a commensurate improvement in objective research and accuracy. Some histories were characterized by excessive use of and dependence on secondary sources, inclusion of irrelevant and unverified material, and gross carelessness in the use of quoted material. An unscientific disposition was further displayed by the attempt to project partiality rather than letting the primary source material dictate the conclusions. Typical of these histories are: *A Concise History of Foreign Baptists* (1838) by G. H. Orchard (d. 1864); *The Origin of the Baptists* (*c.* 1860) by S. H. Ford (1823-1905); *Baptist Church Perpetuity* (1894) by W. A. Jarrel. Numbers of pamphlets and booklets also compose this historiographical body of Baptist literature.

It was not until the last quarter of the 19th century that modern techniques of historical research were scrupulously applied to the study of Baptist history. Baptist historians had been more apologetic than critical, resulting in volumes of questionable worth. But with the investigations of George Gould, H. C. Vedder, and William Heth Whitsitt (*q.v.*) a new era in historical competence began. Rigidly applying scientific methodology to the study of Baptist history were Vedder (1853-1935) in *A Short History of the Baptists* (1891; rev. 1907); Whitsitt (1841-1911) in *A Question in Baptist History* (1896); A. H. Newman (1852-1933) in *A History of the Baptist Churches in the United States* (1894); and George Augustus Lofton (*q.v.*) (1839-1914) in *Defense of the Jessey Records and Kiffin Manuscript* (1899) and *English Baptist Reformation* (1899). Throughout the transitional period the older positions were maintained by many, of whom two were John Tyler Christian (*q.v.*) (1854-1925) in *A History of the Baptists* (two vols., 1922-26) and D. B. Ray (1830-1922) in *Baptist Succession* (rev. 1912).

In 1860 George Gould (1818-82) published *Open Communion and the Baptists of Norwich,* which marked the beginning of the historical method among English historians. Shortly afterward, Benjamin Evans (1803-71) wrote *The Early English Baptists* (two vols., 1862-64). Two later historiographers have been W. T. Whitley (1861-1942), who wrote *A History of British Baptists* (1923) and compiled *A Baptist Bibliography* (two vols., 1916-22), and A. C. Underwood (1885-1948), who wrote *A History of the English Baptists* (1947).

Two recent American works are *A History of the Baptists* (1950) by Robert G. Torbet (1912-   ) and *The Southern Baptist Convention 1845-1953* (1954) by W. W. Barnes (1883-   ).

In Wales, Joshua Thomas (1718-97), the earliest Welsh historian, published *Hanes y Bedyddwyr* (1778; rev. 1885 by B. Davies) and *A History of the Baptist Association in Wales* (1795).

An exhaustive treatment of Welsh Baptists is contained in *Hanes y Bedyddwyr yng Nghymru* (four vols., 1893-1907) by J. Spinther James (1837-1914). A recent work, *Penodau yn Hanes y Bedyddwyr Cymraeg* (1949), was written by W. J. Rhys.

Considerable credit is due to church clerks, compilers, diarists, and "historiophiles," who, although not historians, wrote and preserved the materials indispensable to historiography. Many other works on Baptist history may be found dealing with individual churches, associations, states, sections, and countries.

See also HISTORY, BAPTIST RESOURCES FOR THEIR.

BIBLIOGRAPHY: W. M. Patterson, "Baptist History in America in the Eighteenth Century," *Review and Expositor* (Oct., 1955); "A Critique of the Successionist Concept in Baptist History" (1956).

W. MORGAN PATTERSON

HISTORY, BAPTIST RESOURCES FOR THEIR. *Resources on various subjects.*—
1. Churches—The primary historical materials of a Baptist church are its minutes, the title to its property, which is on file in court records, the minutes of its auxiliaries, and photographs. Secondary historical materials of a Baptist church are its own printed bulletins, associational minutes, items that have been published in papers, histories it has published, memoirs of members, letters, and relevant records of outside sources. Not one half of the churches that are 20 years old and older have complete records. In too many instances they have total gaps of one to 20 years.

2. Associations—Their primary records are their minutes and the primary records of their affiliated churches. Their secondary records are minutes of their state convention, newspaper files, histories (published or unpublished), letters, memorabilia of members and friends, and relevant records of other outside sources.

3. Conventions—Their primary records consist of minutes of their own body, executive board, or committee, files of their offices and auxiliary offices, and reports of standing committees or special committees. Secondary materials are minutes of related associations and churches, plus Baptist paper files, newspaper files, special or promotional publications, histories, memorabilia, letters, and relevant records of outside sources.

4. Institutions—Their primary records are minutes of the trustees or governing board, official records of transactions, court records, files of officers and others, pictures, minutes of committees, and official reports. Secondary records are files of the minutes of related Baptist organizations and periodicals, newspapers, histories, pictures, memorabilia, letters, and relevant outside sources.

5. Miscellaneous—In addition to the Baptist historical materials described above there are certain miscellaneous materials that deserve consideration, such as letters written by those

present to those who are interested who were not present and addresses that were supposed to communicate information based on accurate knowledge. In recent years the full programs or portions of many Baptist meetings have been recorded. Since 1953 the entire proceedings and program of the sessions of the Southern Baptist Convention have been recorded and are kept in the custody of the Convention's Historical Commission.

Collections.—Each Baptist church, association, convention, and institution is supposed to be the repository of its own basic historical materials. However, in too many instances this is not true. Many educational institutions have collected some or a considerable amount of Baptist historical material. Beginning in 1876, some Virginia Baptists created their Virginia Baptist Historical Society. From then until now, each of the state conventions, or the Baptists in that state, and the Southern Baptist Convention have developed either a society or a historical commission. This has resulted in substantial Baptist historical collections in the several states. Their chief interest is the historical materials that are relevant to their churches, associations, conventions, and institutions.

The following states have definite historical collections that are kept, processed, and serviced by the custodian indicated:

Alabama, library, Howard College, Birmingham.

Arizona, executive board, Arizona Baptist Convention, Phoenix.

Arkansas, library, Ouachita College, Arkadelphia.

California, executive board, the Southern Baptist General Convention of California, Fresno.

District of Columbia, office, District of Columbia Baptist Convention, Washington.

Florida, library, Stetson University, DeLand.

Georgia, library, Mercer University, Macon.

Illinois, executive board, Illinois Baptist State Association, Carbondale.

Kansas, office, Kansas Convention of Southern Baptists, Wichita.

Kentucky, library, Southern Baptist Theological Seminary, Louisville.

Louisiana, library, New Orleans Baptist Theological Seminary, New Orleans.

Maryland, office, Maryland Baptist Union Association, Baltimore.

Mississippi, library, Mississippi College, Clinton.

Missouri, library, William Jewell College, Liberty.

New Mexico, office, *Baptist New Mexican,* Albuquerque.

South Carolina, library, Furman University, Greenville.

Tennessee, executive board, Tennessee Baptist Convention, Nashville.

Texas, library, Southwestern Baptist Theological Seminary, Fort Worth.

Virginia, Boatwright Library, University of Richmond, Richmond, in a substantial wing, the cost of which was provided by the Woman's Missionary Union of Virginia.

Special Baptist collections are as follows:

American Baptist Historical Society collection, integrated with the Colgate collection, housed at Colgate-Rochester Theological Seminary, Rochester, N. Y.

Isaac Backus Library, Andover-Newton Theological Seminary, Newton Centre, Mass.

Dargan-Carver Library, Historical Commission, Southern Baptist Convention, Nashville, Tenn.

Much important Baptist historical material is in the libraries and archives of the departments of archives and history of the various states. Such libraries as the Library of Congress, the New York Public Library, Yale, Harvard, University of Chicago, Duke, and many state university libraries have much Baptist historical material.

Great Britain has quantities of Baptist historical material, particularly in its British Museum and in the Bodleian and Cambridge libraries. In addition there is a rich treasury of such material in the library of Dr. Williams, Gordon Square, London, and in the following places:

Regent's Park College, Oxford.
Bristol Baptist College, Bristol.
Spurgeon's College, London.
Rawdon College, Leeds, Yorkshire.
Manchester College, Manchester.
Cardiff College, Cardiff, South Wales.
Bangor College, Bangor, North Wales.
Library of G. M. Hardie, Glasgow, Scotland.
Baptist College, Dublin, North Ireland.
Baptist Historical Society Library, Baptist College, Bristol.
Baptist Union Library, Baptist Church House, London.

See also HISTORIOGRAPHY.   NORMAN W. COX

HOBBS, JAMES RANDOLPH (b. Hinds County, Miss., Sept. 16, 1874; d. Apr. 23, 1942). Pastor of First Baptist Church, Birmingham, Ala., from 1919 until 1938. He was educated in rural schools in Mississippi and at Mississippi College, Clinton, where he graduated with the Ph.D. degree in May, 1903. He was ordained to the Baptist ministry by the Crystal Springs, Miss., church on Jan. 1, 1901. He studied at the Southern Baptist Theological Seminary in Louisville in the fall of 1903. He married Elizabeth Brown Drake in 1905. His pastorates included Mt. Sterling, Ky.; Walnut Street in Owensboro, Ky.; Shelbyville, Tenn.; Jonesboro, Ark.; and First Baptist, Birmingham, Ala. He served on the Executive Committee, Southern Baptist Convention, and was vice-president of the Convention, 1921–22 and 1935–36. He preached the annual sermon for the Convention in Chattanooga in 1928. He also served as president of the Alabama Baptist State Convention, moderator of the Birmingham Association, president of the Anti-Saloon League of America, and member of the Foreign Mission Board of the Southern Baptist Convention. In 1924 he published *The Pastor's Manual*. He was the father of the hospital program for the Birmingham Baptist Association.   JOHN BOB RIDDLE

HOGUE, ROBERT JASPER (b. Greene County, Ga., Mar. 8, 1820; d. Atoka, Okla., Oct. 10, 1906). Pioneer Baptist preacher and missionary. He was converted and united with the Baptist church at LaGrange, Ga., 1838; he married Clarissa Jenkins on Oct. 12, 1843; he was licensed to preach, 1847, and ordained, 1850. In 1857 he was appointed by the Board of Domestic and Indian Missions, Southern Baptist Convention, to mission work among the Choctaw Indians, Indian Territory. In November of that year the Bethel Association meeting at the Friendship Church, Sumpter County, Ga., adopted him as their missionary at a salary of $600 per year. On Feb. 22, 1858, he started west with his family. Upon arrival in the Choctaw Nation in Mar., 1858, he served as pastor of Philadelphia and Ephesus churches. The same year he organized the first church in the Chickasaw Nation in Panola County. In 1860 he assisted in the organization of Ramsey Association. In 1899 the failure of his health forced him into retirement, and he died seven years later.   LOREN J. BELT

HOLCOMBE, HENRY (b. Prince Edward County, Va., Sept. 22, 1762; d. Philadelphia, Pa., May 22, 1824). Pastor in Savannah, Ga., and Philadelphia, Pa.

At an early age Holcombe moved with his family from Virginia to South Carolina. At the age of 22 he was converted while serving as a Revolutionary army captain. During his military service he preached his first sermon from horseback to the men of his command. Ordained to the ministry a year later, he became one of the outstanding preachers of the Southeast. In Apr., 1786, he married Frances Tanner of North Carolina and baptized her, along with her mother and brother, the following June. In 1799, while serving a pastorate in Beaufort, S. C., he was called to supply the pulpit of a congregation of Presbyterians and Baptists in Savannah.

On Nov. 26, 1800, Henry Holcombe, his wife, and 14 others constituted the Baptist Church in Savannah, now known as the First Baptist Church. On Mar. 24, 1802, he accepted the pastorate of the church at a salary of $2,100 per year, the largest ministerial salary in the United States at that time. In August of that year the Presbyterians withdrew to their new house of worship. Holcombe served with distinction in the Savannah pastorate until Dec., 1810, when he resigned and moved to Mount Enon because of his impaired health. He kept up an interesting exchange of letters with the church until the end of 1811. In Aug., 1811, he accepted a call to the pastorate of the First Baptist Church in Philadelphia.

In 1800 Holcombe received the honorary degree of Master of Arts from Rhode Island College (Brown University), Providence, R. I. He was awarded in 1812 the D.D. degree by South Carolina College. During his Savannah pastorate he led a movement to improve the Georgia penitentiary system. He was one of the founders of the Savannah Female Orphan Asylum. He led the Baptists of Georgia in organizing a general committee which later developed into the Georgia Baptist convention. In spite of the general hostility to education then characteristic of many Baptists, he established Mount Enon Academy, a forerunner of Mercer University, near Augusta. In May, 1802, Holcombe began publishing the *Georgia Analytical Repository* (1802–03). This was the first religious periodical published in the Southeastern states. Upon the death of George Washington he was invited by the city council to preach a memorial sermon.

While in Savannah, Holcombe declined a call to the First Baptist Church in Boston, Mass. Later he accepted a call to First Church, Philadelphia. His death closed a very influential pastorate there of more than 12 years. The report of his funeral in Philadelphia stated, "The whole city did honor to his memory; it is said that the concourse of people in attendance was, for numbers, such as was never before seen in Philadelphia."

Holcombe was a large man, six feet two inches tall and weighing three hundred pounds. Though his formal education ended when he was 11 years of age, his wide interests and thorough study made him a person of unusual culture; the honorary degrees which he received were in his day a recognition of real attainment. His major published works include *First Fruits, in a Series of Letters* (1812) and *Primitive Theology, in a Series of Lectures* (1823).

LEROY G. CLEVERDON

HOLCOMBE, HOSEA (b. Union District, S. C., July 20, 1780; d. Jonesboro, Ala., July 31, 1840). Pioneer Alabama Baptist leader and historian. He was married to Cassie Jackson, June 7, 1802, and was ordained Aug. 17, 1805. After several years of pastoral ministry in upper South Carolina, he moved to Jones Valley, Ala., in 1818. While there he was instrumental in effecting the organization of a number of churches in that area, including Ruhama in 1819. He was moderator of the Cahawba Baptist Association and gave approval to the plans for organizing a convention for the state of Alabama in 1822. As a representative of the Jonesboro Ladies Society for foreign missions, he participated in the constitution of the Baptist state convention in Alabama in 1823 at Salem Church near Greensboro and served on the committee to prepare a constitution for the convention. He was elected one of 15 domestic missionaries of the convention and assigned to work in the middle district of the state. Later he was elected president of the convention and served in this office for six years. Previously he had served on the board of managers for the convention. And in 1833 he was elected to a committee to establish a school. The next year he was chosen an agent to locate the proposed Manual Labor Institute.

In 1835 the convention designated him to prepare a history of the Baptists of the state. In 1840 his book was finished and in 1841 was presented to the convention. Pickett, the historian, speaks of Holcombe's *History of the Baptists in Alabama* as being "the first distinctively historical volume published in the state." In addition to this history, he compiled a collection of hymns which was published in 1815.

In his missionary activity when Holcombe could not work with the antimission forces he separated from them and followed his convictions. Such was the case in the organization on Sept. 16, 1833, of the Canaan Baptist Association of which he was the first moderator. The churches came from the Mount Zion Association for "the purpose of giving full expression to their views upon certain matters and for fullest enjoyment of liberty in the exercise of conviction."

Holcombe died July 31, 1841, at his home near Jonesboro, after laboring for 25 years to build up the Baptist denomination in Alabama. His body was buried in the Sadler Cemetery, now located in Bessemer. In 1912 the Baptists of Alabama erected a monument over his grave which replaced the roughhewn rock marker erected by his son.   DAVIS WOOLLEY

HOLDING COMMISSION, GEORGIA. A corporation created to hold legal title to all property of all convention interests, authorized by the Georgia Baptist convention in 1916, and its scope of work, regulations governing its operations, and authority to secure charter were outlined. The charter secured in Bibb County, Ga., was given convention approval and printed in convention minutes in 1917. In 1938 the Holding Commission was ordered dissolved. Its final statement to the convention, which reported return of all assets to the various institutions and expiration of its charter, was given in 1940.   JAMES W. MERRITT

HOLINESS. See SANCTIFICATION.

HOLLAND FOUNDATION LECTURES. The first endowed lectureship of Southwestern Baptist Theological Seminary, provided by Lewis Holland of San Antonio, Tex. He donated $2,500 in 1914 in order to "assist young preachers in qualifying themselves to preach the gospel." The agreement with the seminary provided that the principal should constitute a permanent endowment and the interest only should be used to secure a lecturer, if possible, each year. It was required that the speaker be a Baptist whose doctrinal position was generally that of the New Hampshire Confession of Faith. The first lecture under this foundation was delivered by George Washington Truett (*q.v.*), First Baptist Church, Dallas, Tex., in the spring of 1914. Distinguished Baptists from both the North and the South have been heard under this lectureship.   ROBERT A. BAKER

HOLLINGSWORTH HIGH SCHOOL. Established in 1890 in Banks County, Ga., transferred from the North Georgia Convention to Liberty Association in 1898. The school existed until about 1901.   ARTHUR JACKSON

HOLLUMS, JAMES WALTER (b. Milton County, Ga., Mar. 3, 1878; d. Oklahoma City, Okla., Feb. 22, 1953). Baptist minister and financier. He moved by covered wagon to Westminister, Collin County, Tex., in 1892. He was converted in 1899 and attended Baylor University Preparatory School in 1901 by selling his horse and buggy to pay tuition. He was ordained in 1903; he graduated from North Texas Baptist Academy, Westminister, in 1906 and married Elizabeth Gaddy in 1907. He served as pastor of several churches in Oklahoma and Texas. A charter member of the Baptist Foundation of Oklahoma, he gave it $65,000 equity in the Hollums Building, Oklahoma City, Okla. In early married life the Hollumses denied themselves the ordinary comforts of life and used corncobs for kitchen fuel, but later because of this frugality with wise investments of money they were able to give $100,000 to Baptist causes. He died of a heart attack while visiting a sick friend. He is buried in Rose Hill Cemetery, Oklahoma City.   HERBERT M. PIERCE

HOLLY SPRINGS SCHOOL. A Baptist school at Holly Springs, Macon County, N. C., founded and opened in 1896 by Tuckaseige Association. Two years later the building was destroyed by fire, but by Oct. 1, 1898, a new building had been erected. A year later Tuckaseige Association closed the school and subsequently joined with other associations to support Sylva Collegiate Institute. In 1906 Holly Springs School property was given to Macon County Association.   D. L. SMILEY

HOLMES, JAMES LANDRUM (b. Preston County, W. Va., May 16, 1836; d. North China, Oct. 1, 1861). Missionary to China. Reared in the Methodist faith, Holmes joined the Baptists after reading a copy of Richard Fuller's *Baptism and Communion*. Following graduation from Columbian College in June, 1858, and marriage to Sallie J. Little in July, Holmes and his wife sailed to China, Aug. 21, 1858, under appointment of the Southern Baptist Foreign Mission Board. Their station was Chefoo, North China. Holmes and a missionary of the Episcopal mission were murdered by rebels of the Taipeng Rebellion.

BIBLIOGRAPHY: C. E. Maddry, *Christ's Expendables* (1949). H. A. Tupper, *Foreign Missions of the Southern Baptist Convention* (1880).   E. C. ROUTH

HOLMES, OBADIAH (b. Preston, Lancashire, England, 1606; d. Newport, R. I., Oct. 15, 1682).

Son of religious parents, who sent at least three sons to Oxford. Holmes might not have been one of these, for he claims to have been a rebellious and wicked youth. His eventual reformation and conversion came after a lengthy period of spiritual disturbance, which lasted until a short while after he emigrated to Salem, Mass., in 1639. Here he established a glass works on money lent by the town, taking as his partner one Lawrence Southwick, a Quaker whose children were once almost sold into slavery to pay the fines his beliefs had incurred. Moving to Rehoboth (Plymouth Colony) in 1646, he united with the church there but after four years a disagreement with his pastor on the question of authority for church government caused him to withdraw, with several others, and to form his own church, receiving baptism from John Clarke (q.v.). Excommunication by the Rehoboth church and indictment by the Plymouth court followed (Oct. 2, 1650), and Holmes moved to Newport and to John Clarke's own church.

In July, 1651, Holmes went with John Clarke and John Crandall to Lynn, Mass., to conduct services in the home of an aged, blind member of the church at Newport. They were arrested and tried in a most insulting and illegal manner by the authorities at Boston, and were sentenced to pay heavy fines or be "well whipt." Friends paid the fines of Clarke and Crandall, but Holmes, by his own choice, suffered a brutal beating the following September.

Back at Newport, Holmes served as pastor of the church during the 12 years of Clarke's absence in England (1651–63), and again after Clarke's death (Apr. 20, 1676). He was buried on his farm in Middletown, near Newport.

BIBLIOGRAPHY: I. Backus, *History of New England*, 2 vols. (1871). J. Clarke, *Ill Newes From New England* (1651). W. Nelson, *The Hero of Aquidneck* (1938).

JUDSON BOYCE ALLEN

HOLSTON BAPTIST FEMALE INSTITUTE. Founded by the Holston Baptist Association in 1853 at Jonesboro, Tenn. R. H. Keeling, the first principal of this elementary and secondary school, reported an enrolment of 85 in 1854. The property was sold in 1861 for payment of a debt but was redeemed and the school reopened as a male institute in 1867. It had passed from under Baptist control by 1871.

LYNN EDWARD MAY, JR.

HOLT, ADONIRAM JUDSON (b. Somerset, Ky., Dec. 1, 1847; d. Arcadia, Fla., Apr. 15, 1933). Pastor, mission secretary, Baptist historian. Holt, who felt the impact of the slavery struggle in the separation of his abolitionist father and his pro-Southern mother before he was six years of age, immigrated to Texas with his mother in 1858, where he came under the influence of his uncle, Robert Cooke Buckner (q.v.). Encouraged by Buckner to secure an education, Holt attended McKenzie College in Paris, Tex., and later was a student on two different occasions at Southern Baptist Theological Seminary in Greenville. Another uncle, Henry Frieland Buckner, was responsible for Holt's appointment as missionary to the Seminole and Plains Indians in Oklahoma, where he worked from 1876 to 1879. Holt spent the following nine years in Texas as state missionary and as secretary of missions for the General Association and the Baptist General Convention of Texas. He later served the Tennessee Baptist Convention as secretary of missions. Holt used his organizational and pulpit abilities in pastorates in Texas, Oklahoma, Arkansas, Tennessee, and Florida. At intervals between 1886 and 1912 he owned or edited five Baptist newspapers, and was chairman of Southern Baptists' first committee on the Preservation of Baptist History, established in 1921.

BIBLIOGRAPHY: *Baptist Standard* (1933). J. B. Cranfill, *Dr. J. B. Cranfill's Chronicle* (1916). A. J. Holt, *Pioneering in the Southwest* (1923).

T. R. HAVINS

HOLY SPIRIT. The doctrine of the Holy Spirit as the third person of the Trinity, assumed in the teaching of the New Testament (Matt. 28:19 ff.; II Cor. 13:14) but not fully formulated until the Council of Constantinople, A.D. 381, was nevertheless rooted in the Old Testament concept of "Spirit." This is not to say, however, that there is a full-blown doctrine of the Holy Spirit, in the formal sense, in the Old Testament, or even in the New Testament. There is, rather, a development of the doctrine as the people of God progressed in their understanding of God's self-disclosure. Hence, the subject is traced through the Old and New Testaments and the historic creeds.

IN THE OLD TESTAMENT. The basic term for "spirit" in the Old Testament is *ruach*. *Ruach* in its original meaning implies the idea of violent power, coming as it does, from a root meaning "to breathe out through the nose with violence," thus indicating strong, hard breathing. The counterpart of this word is *neshamah*, "breath," which usually indicates soft breathing.

The basic meaning of *ruach*, then, is power. So in Isaiah 31:3 the prophet is contrasting the weakness of flesh (*basar*, men and animals) and the power of *ruach*, which is God's nature. Primarily, *ruach* is used to indicate God's operation in the world. In the Old Testament its usage may be classified in four different relations:

The ruach *in relation to God.*—The term "Holy Spirit" occurs only three times in the Old Testament (Psalm 51:11; Isa. 63:10–11); in these places it should be more properly translated "spirit of holiness," that is, the energizing principle of God's holiness. However, *ruach* is properly the possession of God, not men, so "Holy Spirit" is proper. The idea of *ruach* develops from its use as an agent of God (Isa. 40:7), through its use as a hypostatization of God (Isa. 59:21), to its use as an actual equivalent for his presence (Hag. 2:5; Zech. 4:6; 6:8; Psalms 104:33; 139:7; Isa. 30:1; 34:16).

The work of the spirit is, in fact, the work of God himself, hence the common names of *Ruach Yahweh* and *Ruach-Elohim*. *Ruach* and *Yahweh* are never connected by a makkeph, while *Ruach-Elohim* are so joined, and thus become one word in Hebrew. This latter conviction is possible because the name *Elohim* itself implies power, while *Yahweh* is the special covenant name for God.

The ruach *in relation to the world.*—Genesis 1 indicates the relation of the *ruach* of God to the act of original creation, picturing it as hovering, or brooding, like a bird over her nest. This chapter also indicates the close relation of *ruach* with the Word of God, like the relation of breath to the spoken word (cf. Job 34:14–15). This same idea is reiterated in Psalm 33:6.

Every living thing derives its life from the *ruach* of God (Gen. 2:7; Eccl. 11:5; Job 33:4; Psalm 104:29–30), which is also the principle of vitality in animate life (Gen. 7:22) and is frequently used as a psychological term to denote "dominant disposition." Examples of this latter use are "bitterness of *ruach*" (Gen. 26:35), the "*ruach* of jealousy" (Num. 5:14, 30), impatience (Exod. 6:9), hardness (I Sam. 1:15), etc. Later usage of *ruach* as the spirit of a living being makes it practically synonymous with *nephesh*, the soul (Isa. 26:9; Job 7:11), although in such instances *ruach* is not considered as the natural possession of man, but rather as coming forth from God (Zech. 12:1) and returning to him (Eccl. 12:7). In accord with this emphasis, *ruach* is thought of as bestowing both intellectual and physical gifts upon man. Bezalel and the other workmen were said to be specially equipped by the spirit (Exod. 31:3; 35:31–32), as were those who made Aaron's garments (Exod. 28:3). The "spirit of wisdom" was imparted to Joshua by Moses, who laid his hands upon him (Deut. 34:9; cf. Acts 13:3; 19:6; I Tim. 4:14).

To designate God's controlling and energizing activity in the world, both physical and animate, *ruach* is the "wind" of God. The violent wind is associated with the *geshem*, the heavy downpour of monsoon rains when black clouds make the sky heavy (I Kings 18:45; II Kings 3:17; Ezek. 13:11; Prov. 25:14, 23). So, the instrument of God's judgment on Egypt was the wind (Exod. 10:13, 19); it was also his instrument for the deliverance of Israel (Exod. 14:21 ff.) and his provision for them (Num. 11:31–32).

The ruach *in relation to prophecy.*—Primitive prophecy was attributed to the *ruach* of Yahweh (Num. 11:29); the bands of prophets described in I Samuel 10–11 who met Saul and with whom Samuel associated (I Sam. 19:18 ff.) were moved by the spirit to contagious abnormal behavior. They were noticeably ecstatic and later were looked upon as mad (Hos. 9:7). In their case, the action of the spirit did not impart the word of God but inspired abnormal conduct. The unusual feats of the judges ("former prophets") were attributed to the work of the spirit (Judg. 3:10; 6:34; 11:29; 13:27), as were those of Saul (I Sam. 11:6–7), Elijah, and Elisha (II Kings 2:13–15). The *ruach*, demonstrating itself in power and prophecy, during this early period was completely nonmoral. The earliest definite moral distinction in the operation of *ruach* is in the case of Saul, when the *Ruach Yahweh* ("spirit of the Lord") departed from him and an "evil *ruach*" from God afflicted him (I Sam. 16:14). A similar distinction is evident in the case of Micaiah ben Imlah (I Kings 22:23), where the *ruach* was a "lying spirit" in the mouths of the court prophets of Ahab. From this instance on, there is a change of emphasis in prophetic claims. The later prophets evidence an amazing reticence to use the term *ruach* in speaking of their call or authority from God, and Deuteronomy has no use of the word at all, possibly because of its undesirable association with primitive prophecy. More dominant in the prophets, from Amos on, is the prophetic consciousness of being in the "council" of God, of having received his word (Jer. 1:4). This "prophetic consciousness" had its definite beginning with Elijah on Mt. Horeb (I Kings 19:12), where God spoke to the fleeing prophet by a "sound of gentle stillness." Gradually, however, *ruach* was restored to favor, with Isaiah using *ruach* to speak of Messiah and Ezekiel restoring its usage for prophetic inspiration (Ezek. 2:2; 3:24; 11:5).

The ruach *in relation to the Messiah.*—Two passages definitely associate the spirit with the Messiah, Isaiah 11:1–4 and 61:1–3. In the first the emphasis is upon special endowments which the messianic King will have which will equip him to rule. N. H. Snaith points out the association of *ruach* and "wisdom" as being comparable to that in Proverbs 8:16. Isaiah 61:1–3 affirms that the spirit is to empower the special mission of the Messiah. Another passage (Isa. 42:1–4) speaks of the Servant of Yahweh as being endowed with the spirit, but the Jews did not identify this Servant with the Messiah (although Jesus did).

The messianic concept also embraced a special people who would be possessed by the spirit. Jeremiah's idea of the "new covenant" (31:31 ff.) was elaborated by Ezekiel to include a "new *ruach*" (Ezek. 36:26–27; cf. Ezek. 11:19; 18:31). The spirit's inspiration of the people, graphically presented in the vision of the valley of dry bones (37:1–14), is stated as an accomplished fact in Ezekiel 39:29, a passage which may be considered as a response to the pleas of Isaiah of the Exile for God to let his spirit once more cause his people to rest (Isa. 63:14), and for God to put his holy spirit again on his holy people (Isa. 63:11, 18; 64:9). This would, of course, take place in the new age spoken of by Joel (2:28), Zechariah (12:10), and Isaiah (44:3).

IN THE NEW TESTAMENT. The New Testament preserves the basic concept of spirit as power, maintaining the same identity of terminology with "wind" (Greek *pneuma* in John 3:8), but unusual prominence is given to the "Holy Spirit"

Holy Spirit

(*to pneuma to hagion* and variants), which is used 88 times. The usual Septuagint term for the "Spirit of God" (*to pneuma tou theou . . . kuriou*), however, is comparatively rare in the New Testament, replaced, to some extent, by the more personal "Spirit of the Father" (Matt. 10:20). Further, the New Testament uses some phrases unknown in the Old Testament or Septuagint, such as "the Spirit of his Son" (Gal. 4:6), "the Spirit of Christ" (Rom. 8:9; I Peter 1:11), and, of course, "the Spirit of Jesus" (Acts 16:9), all of which are identified with "the Spirit of God." The distinct personality of the Spirit is evidenced by the special name, the Paraclete, assigned to him in John (John 14:16, etc.), and by attributing personal characteristics to the Spirit in Acts (13:2). Of course, *pneuma* may designate a vital part of human personality, also (I Thess. 5:23), and the prominence of "spirit" in general is witnessed by its appearance in every New Testament book except three short, personal ones, Philemon and II and III John.

The Spirit and the Christ.—The Synoptic Gospels, Luke especially, make clear the special and full residence of the Spirit in the person of Christ. Before the birth of Christ, John the Baptist, the prophetic forerunner, was said to be "filled with the Holy Spirit" (Luke 1:15 ASV). This phrase, characteristic of Luke (cf. Exod. 28:3; 35:31) is also applied to John's father, Zacharias (Luke 1:67), and his mother, Elisabeth (Luke 1:39). The mention of Simeon ("the Holy Spirit was upon him," Luke 2:25 ASV) and Anna, the prophetess (Luke 2:36), has led Swete to assert that a resurgence of prophetic gifts had occurred which had not taken place since the time of the post-Exilic prophets. Certainly, John was in the line of Old Testament prophets, as one "in the spirit and power of Elijah" (Luke 1:17 ASV).

Christ, however, was conceived by the Holy Spirit. The miraculous conception of the Son of God by the Holy Spirit is the major emphasis in the birth accounts of both Matthew (1:18, 20) and Luke (1:35). Luke 1:38 indicates that Mary, like Sarah before her, "by faith" received power to conceive, and since the child was begotten by the Holy Spirit, he "grew, and waxed strong in spirit, filled with wisdom: and the grace of God was upon him" (Luke 2:40). Isaiah 11:2 and other messianic prophecies are thus fulfilled.

Christ was commissioned to begin his ministry by a special endowment of the Holy Spirit. The basic contrast between John the Baptist and Jesus is clarified by the fact that John, who was only filled with the Spirit, could not impart it to others but could only preach in the Spirit; while Christ, conceived by the Spirit, baptized with the Spirit and power (Luke 3:16-17). In fulfilment of Ezekiel 36:25 ff. and Joel 2:28 ff., spiritual baptism inaugurated and characterized the messianic age; it was the prerogative of the Messiah to bestow it. The appearance of the dove indicates the manner of descent and not the nature of the Spirit (although Luke 3:22 says "bodily form"). The temptation following Christ's baptism was the first step in the events of Christ's life which were the direct work of the Spirit (Luke 4:1 ff. and parallels). It is possible that Luke meant to imply that the Spirit not only urged the Lord into the conflict with Satan, as Mark 1:12 states, but also equipped him for it and carried him through it. Following this trial of Christ as Messiah, he began his public ministry at Nazareth, where he applied Isaiah 61:1 to himself and his ministry, with the Holy Spirit as the agent, who ushered in the jubilee year of the messianic people (Luke 4:16 ff.).

Christ's miraculous works were accomplished by the power of the Spirit; hence, attributing them to the power of Beelzebub was a sin of blasphemy against the Spirit (Matt. 12:32 and parallels). Christ's teaching authority (Matt. 7:29) and preaching power (Mark 1:27) stemmed from the Holy Spirit. When the 70 apostles returned from their preaching tour, Christ "rejoiced in the Holy Spirit" (Luke 10:21 ASV), and then, according to the Synoptic Gospels, revealed himself (Matt. 11:25-30). On the basis of these passages and other evidence, Otto suggests that Christ was of the "charismatic type," having a "charismatic character and endowment." Paul considered the resurrection of Christ as a work of the Holy Spirit (Rom. 1:4) and the writer of Hebrews viewed the entire passion as being endured by the power of the Spirit (Heb. 9:14; 12:2).

John's writings attribute to the Holy Spirit definite personal characteristics as the Paraclete, which means "one called alongside" (Latin *advocare*=English advocate). Christ called "advocate" in I John 2:1, promised his disciples that he would pray the Father to send "another of the same kind" which the world could not take away from them (John 14:15-17), a Paraclete who would reveal Christ to the disciples and cause them to recall his teachings (John 14:25-26). This function of the Paraclete is repeated in John 15:26, which also affirms that the Paraclete is the Spirit of truth, sent by Christ (though earlier, 14:26, he says the Father sends the Paraclete) and proceeding from the Father. A fourth reference to the Paraclete indicates that the Spirit could not dwell within the disciples until the mission of Christ among them was ended (16:7), and that the work of the Paraclete in the world would be to convict with reference to Christ as to sin, righteousness, and judgment. A fifth reference indicates that the Paraclete would build upon the work of Christ and impart the teachings which the disciples would not have been able to bear from him (16:12-15). Whereas the Synoptics and John agree that the disciples did not receive the Spirit until after the resurrection (John 7:39), John supplements the Synoptic tradition concerning the "promise of my Father" (Luke 24:49) by his teachings regarding the Paraclete. In addition John teaches that the Spirit is the power of the new birth (3:5-8), the new worship (4:24), the new gospel (6:63), and the new age (7:37–39).

The Spirit and the early church.—Just as Luke's "former treatise" was concerned with the Spirit in Christ, Acts is concerned with the Spirit of Christ in the church. The continuing work of Christ by the Spirit is stated in Acts 1:1–5; the apostolic witness is empowered by the Spirit in Acts 1:8. Apostolic preaching declared that the presence of the Holy Spirit in the church was the sign of Christ's present power and glory (Acts 2:33; 5:32). As the apostles anticipated the Spirit's coming, they realized that their number was deficient by one, Judas, and Peter attributed the scriptural teaching on his replacement to the Holy Spirit in Acts 1:16, a passage which has become a standard designation for the inspiration of the Holy Scripture (cf. I Peter 1:11; Heb. 3:7). The manner of choice by casting lots (Acts 1:26), however, is not repeated again in the history of the church; after Pentecost the "mind of the Spirit" was imparted to it.

The Pentecostal outpouring of the Spirit, the necessary consequence of the ascension of Christ (Acts 1:8–11; 2:33), was interpreted by Peter as the fulfilment of Joel's prophecy (2:14–21). It was the inauguration of the new age and was attended by supernatural phenomena. The gift of tongues, the most evident phenomenon, became a mark of Spirit-possession. Pentecost imparted the gift of prophecy to the church, and thus, that which had been reserved for a select group in ancient Israel was given to all believers, though selectivity was later evidenced. The association of wind and spirit is in accord with primitive concept; fire had been a common expression of divine presence (Exod. 3:2; I Kings 18:38; 19:12). Swete indicates the importance of the fact that Pentecost fell on the first day of the week, like the resurrection of Christ, giving double significance to the Lord's Day. So closely identified did the Spirit become with the church that any offense against the fellowship of believers was considered an offense against the Spirit (Acts 5:3, 9). At times the gift of the Spirit is associated with baptism (Acts 2:38; cf. I Cor. 12:13) and at other times with the laying on of hands (Acts 13:3–4; 19:6; cf. I Tim. 4:14). Twice in Acts occurrences of receiving the Spirit similar to Pentecost are found (4:31; 10:44 ff.). There was a strict judgment on Simon, the sorcerer, for attempting to purchase or otherwise manipulate the reception of the Spirit (Acts 8:9–24).

The Spirit in Paul's teaching.—The most elaborate biblical teaching on the Holy Spirit is that by the apostle Paul, who in his epistles mentioned the Holy Spirit nearly 120 times. Although Paul was not a systematic theologian, his treatment of the Holy Spirit lends itself to the following arrangement:

1. In relation to God, the Spirit is personalized, and there is no longer the strict identification of the Spirit and God. Thus the Spirit of God bears witness with the spirits of men (Rom. 8:26), helps their infirmity, and makes entreaty for them before God. At the same time he abides within the life of God and knows the depths of his thoughts, just as the spirits of men know their thoughts (I Cor. 2:11). Paul makes a fourfold distinction of *pneuma* (I Cor. 2:8–12): *to pneuma tou anthropou*, the spirit of man in man, or simply the man's "self"; *to pneuma tou theou*, the Spirit of God in God; *to pneuma tou kosmou (toutou)*, the spirit of the world, not like Stoic reality permeating the entire natural universe, but rather a personification of the sum total of the "rulers" (v. 8) or the "angels and principalities" (Rom. 8:38) arrayed against the kingdom of God; *to pneuma to ek tou theou*, the Spirit of God in man and the world. Paul's differentiation of *pneuma* is basic to his thought throughout his letters. The Spirit of God is eternal and uncreated, since the Spirit is internal to the essence of God; where the Spirit dwells and works, there God dwells and works (I Cor. 3:16; 6:19). This identity of God and Spirit, however, is not so as to eliminate distinctions of Persons in the Godhead (I Cor. 13:14).

2. The Spirit is also the Spirit of Christ (Rom. 8:7), both because Christ was anointed by the Spirit and because of a unique relationship to the Son (Gal. 4:6) reminiscent of the Paraclete sayings. The closest identification of Christ with the Spirit is II Corinthians 3:17–18. According to James Stewart,

> Paul's thought of the living Christ is so closely bound up with his thought of the Holy Spirit that he seems on occasion to use the two names almost interchangeably.... It is the Spirit who makes Christ real to us and mediates Christ's gifts to us; this is not "identity." Still, so close are the ideas of Christ and the Spirit in Paul's mind that he can pass almost without any sense of distinction from the one to the other.

In one place Paul uses "the spirit of holiness" to mean, possibly, our Lord's human spirit (Rom. 1:4), but the Spirit operative in believers is also the Spirit of Christ (Rom. 8:9–10). Hence, there is a fluidity of usage which both distinguishes the Spirit from Christ and relates them intimately.

3. In relation to man, the Spirit is the source of his sanctification (I Thess. 4:8), sonship (Rom. 8:14–16; Gal. 4:4–6), and spiritual life (Rom. 8). Beyond the normal character of the Christian, which is itself the "fruit [singular] of the Spirit" (Gal. 5:22–23, nine qualities), Paul associates the unusual, special "gracious gifts" from God with the Spirit. Paul distinguishes eight special spiritual gifts (I Cor. 12:4–11), with the unifying principle being the one Spirit from which they all proceed; he mentions nine types of "gifted persons" (12:28–30), the unifying principle here being the one Body of which they have all been made a part by the Spirit. The "more excellent way" of love is to be preferred to the spiritual gifts which are externally manifested and transitory, because the way of love is eternal (I Cor. 13:1–3, 9–13). Prophecy is distinguished from and preferred to

tongue-speech because it is more profitable in evangelizing the heathen (I Cor. 14). While prophecy had earlier been identified with ecstasy (I Thess. 5:19-20), it is now defined as intelligible discourse, and tongue-speech is identified with ecstasy. The later list of "gifts" neglects tongue-speech entirely (Eph. 4:8-16). Man's knowledge of God's "mysteries" is by revelation of the Spirit (I Cor. 2:1-12).

The gift of the Spirit is but a foretaste of future inheritance; the Spirit is related to man's eschatological hope. Present participation in the Spirit is but the "first-fruits" (Rom. 8:23); the Spirit in man is the "down payment" of his inheritance (Eph. 1:14), assuring him of the trustworthiness of God's promises (II Cor. 1:22). In the believer's hope for resurrection from the dead and a "spiritual body" (I Cor. 15:45 ff.), the threefold relation of the Spirit, his operation in man, and Christ, the second Adam (cf. Rom. 8:11), becomes more evident.

The entirety of the Spirit's relation to men may be summed up in the concept of a congregation of believers as the "temple of God" wherein the Spirit dwells (I Cor. 3:16 f.; cf. Eph. 2:22), and of an individual believer as a "temple of the Holy Spirit" (I Cor. 6:19-20). Paul's prison epistles elaborate this idea of the church. The Spirit is the unity of the church in general (Eph. 4:3-4; Phil. 2:1-2); the holiness of the local congregation. The pastoral epistles of Paul make the Spirit the source of ministerial gifts (II Tim. 1:6-7, 14; I Tim. 4:14), and the Scriptures are "God-breathed" (II Tim. 3:16). The Spirit himself has a complete personality (I Tim. 4:1).

The Spirit in the remainder of the New Testament.—John contributes the idea of the "spirit of antichrist" (I John 3:3) and makes what may be a reference to the Trinity (I John 5:7-8). First Peter 1:11 identifies the Spirit of Christ with the spirit of prophecy in the Old Testament, an identification apparent also in the Revelation (1:10; 2:7, etc.; 4:2; 19:10), where the Spirit is the voice of God to the man of God (14:13) and joins in the great invitation to men (22:17). Scriptural inspiration and the spirit of prophecy are related in II Peter 1:19-21.

IN THE HISTORIC CREEDS. The task of Christian thinkers from post-apostolic times to the present has been to elaborate and clarify what is stated or emphasized in the Scriptures about the Spirit. H. B. Swete in *The Holy Spirit in the Ancient Church* has given an extensive treatment of the teachings of the ancient church down to John of Damascus in the East and Gregory the Great in the West. Major turning points in the historical formulation of the doctrine of the Spirit may be stated only simply here.

The person of the Spirit.—The ordinance of baptism incorporated the trinitarian form into the confession of the church as early as the *Didache* in the first half of the second century. No serious formulation of the doctrine of the Spirit is found in the pre-Nicene age, although Irenaeus came closer to it than anyone. Only when it was evident that the Arian heresy was endangering the dignity not only of the Son, but of the Holy Spirit as well, did the post-Nicene fathers treat seriously the Spirit's relation to the Godhead. Basil of Caesarea was first with his *De Spiritu Sancto*, and the doctrine was definitely stated in the "Niceno-Constinopolitan" Creed of A.D. 381 reading, "And [I believe] in the Holy Ghost, the Lord and Giver of life; who proceedeth from the Father [and the Son]; who with the Father and the Son together is worshipped and glorified; who spake by the Prophets." This statement sufficiently established the eternal divine nature of the Spirit alongside the Son and the Father. Augustine's teaching on the Spirit in his *De Trinitate* became the standard Western formulation.

The Eastern church, emphasizing the Father as fountain of the Godhead, spoke of the Spirit as proceeding from the Father only. However, the West was concerned with retaining the essential unity of the Father and the Son and therefore conceived of the Spirit as proceeding from the Son as well. These opposing concepts gave rise to the famous "filioque" controversy (the Latin for "and the son" which the West wanted inserted in the creed).

The work of the Spirit.—The primary contribution of the Reformation doctrine of the Holy Spirit was its emphasis on the work of the Spirit in salvation. The ecclesiasticism and sacerdotalism of the medieval church had all but eliminated any understanding of the Spirit's work in the human heart, but the Reformers, with their emphasis on the "inner witness of the Holy Spirit," recovered the personal interpretation of the Spirit for succeeding generations. The outgrowth of their viewpoint was German pietism and the revival movement of the Wesleys, George Whitfield (*q.v.*), Newton, and Edwards, and later Dwight L. Moody.

See also PARACLETE and SPIRIT.

BIBLIOGRAPHY: F. W. Dillistone, *The Holy Spirit in the Life of Today* (1947). N. H. Snaith, *Distinctive Ideas of the Old Testament* (1950). H. B. Swete, *The Holy Spirit in the New Testament* (1909); *The Holy Spirit in the Ancient Church* (1912). W. H. G. Thomas, *The Holy Spirit of God* (1955).

JOSEPH R. ESTES

HOME AND FOREIGN FIELDS. See MISSIONARY JOURNALS, EXTINCT.

HOME AND FOREIGN JOURNAL. See MISSIONARY JOURNALS, EXTINCT.

HOME DAILY BIBLE READINGS. A list of Bible references accompanying the International Sunday School Lessons prepared for day-by-day study and meditation. The complete outline for a year includes each Sunday's lesson title, the basic Bible material for each lesson, and, within each week, a topic and Scripture passage such as will provide an adequate basis for a full study of the lesson.

Southern Baptists, through representation on the Committee on the Uniform Series, co-operate in the preparation of the Home Daily Bible Readings. The readings (topics and Scripture references) are printed with each week's lesson in Sunday school lesson quarterlies for teachers and pupils, chiefly from the older age groups. The principal and distinctive use by Southern Baptists of the Home Daily Bible Readings is in their adaptation for family worship in the "Altar Fires" section of *Home Life*. Although the readings are selected primarily for study purposes, they are chosen also to serve the values of religious education and worship in the home. Thus, they make it possible for families to have a daily worship experience centered around the Sunday school lesson. No effort has been made to discover how widely this family worship material in *Home Life* is used, but some indication is gained through the fact that *Home Life*'s circulation is more than 750,000 each month.

JOE W. BURTON

HOME LIFE, A CHRISTIAN FAMILY MAGAZINE. Published by the Sunday School Board of the Southern Baptist Convention. The first issue appeared Jan., 1947. The content is popular in style, fiction, feature material, and poetry being selected for their human interest representation of the many facets of Christian family living. A major purpose is to interpret the values of Christian family life and give motivation and help to parents for Christian home building. Each issue includes some 15 pages of guidance materials for family worship. The over-all distribution plan is to reach every family through all departments of the Sunday school. The circulation in 1956 was 775,158.

JOE W. BURTON

HOME MISSION BOARD OF THE SOUTHERN BAPTIST CONVENTION. American Baptists have been missionary in spirit and in practice from their beginnings on the continent. First churches and then associations, as they were being formed, endeavored to give the gospel to the Indians, to the increasing number of European immigrants and their descendants, and to Negro slaves. The method varied with the necessity and the opportunity. To the end of the 18th century, churches and associations continued to serve as mission agencies. With the opening of the 19th century, immigration into the Mississippi Valley greatly increased (Louisiana Purchase, 1803).

In 1814 the General Missionary Convention of the Baptist Denomination in the United States of America for Foreign Missions (popularly called the Triennial Convention) was formed to seize the opportunity presented by the conversion of Luther Rice and Adoniram Judson to Baptist views. Several leaders at the time, mainly from the South, desired an all-comprehensive body to carry on home missions and other objectives, also. The increasing population west of the Alleghenies and in the then Southwest was calling for home mission activity. In 1817 the Triennial Convention enlarged its scope to include home missions and other activities. But reaction set in. These activities were dropped at the next triennial meeting of the convention (1820). The final decision (1826) was to confine the Triennial Convention to foreign missions.

The Massachusetts Baptist Missionary Society (1802) carried on in the upper Mississippi Valley until its work led to the formation of the American Baptist Home Mission Society (1832). Almost from the beginning of this society's work, Baptists in the South complained that the society was neglecting the lower valley. State conventions and missionary societies were being formed in the South, but they did not meet the wider need. In 1839 Robert T. Daniel led in forming the Southwestern Baptist Home Mission Society (Columbus, Miss.). This society lapsed with the death of Daniel (1842).

The increasing need of home missions in the South and Southwest and the seeming neglect of the need and the opportunity by the American Baptist Home Mission Society constituted one of the divisive factors entering into the relations between Northern and Southern Baptists in the 1840's. When the Southern Baptist Convention was formed, the constitution (Article V) authorized the Convention to "elect at each triennial meeting as many Boards of Managers as in its judgment will be necessary." Two boards were set up—the Foreign Mission Board at Richmond, Va., and the Board of Domestic Missions at Marion, Ala.

The domestic board faced difficulty in the very beginning. Complaints had been made that the South was being neglected by the Home Mission Society. Now with a Southern organization and a domestic board thereof, "our brethren prefer carrying on their domestic missionary operations through their Associations and State Conventions." This board has been forced to prove its place in the life and work of Southern Baptists about once in every generation. Economic pressure has been the occasion; but the theory has been advanced that if each state convention and the associations affiliated therewith do the mission work within their own borders, there will be no need for a convention-wide domestic mission board.

An incident occurred in the beginning of the board's activity that portended a possible source of difficulty in the years ahead—a struggle to possess its very home base. The American Baptist Home Mission Society sent James Huckins to the Republic of Texas in Jan., 1840. After a few years he ceased to be a missionary of the society in Texas. Soon after the formation of the Southern Baptist Convention, the society reopened its mission in Texas. Secretary Russell Holman of the Board of Domestic Missions wrote to J. S. Baker of the *Christian Index* (Apr. 8, 1846):

The first thing we notice is the appointment of Mr. Taliaferro, missionary to Texas, by the American Baptist Home Mission Society. We have seen some notice of this before, but did not consider it worthy of attention. We should pass it by now were it not for the statement that Brother T. had made application to the Southern Board, but for the want of funds he could not be appointed. This was the first notice we had of any such application. Had it been made during the last six months the appointment would have been made.

Some fears have been expressed that such an appointment will create difficulty in that field, and the motives were not such as should characterize Christian actions. Whatever may have been the motive, we think there was an impropriety in the appointment. Texas is a wide and destitute field, and if the Gospel be preached there, whether through envy, or good will, let us rejoice. Providence seems to have marked out the appropriate fields for the Northern and Southern boards to occupy, in which each may labor without disturbing those jealousies and unpleasant feelings which have so long annoyed our churches; and it appears to us there is great propriety, to say the least, in each Board occupying its appropriate field. We know the Southern field is sufficient to engage all our resources and energies; and we are quite certain the Northern field is equal to the abilities of the Northern Board.

Texas was abandoned by them previous to the division; after the Southern organization, it was occupied by this Board. This, together with its geographical position, will furnish an apology for calling it "our field." Yet, if the Northern Board have sufficient funds to "preach the gospel to every creature" in the Northern and Western states and territories, and can occasionally send a missionary to Texas, we will find no fault.

Field of work.—The preamble to the first constitution of the Southern Baptist Convention begins: "We, the delegates from Missionary Societies, churches, and other religious bodies of the Baptist denomination, in various parts of the United States . . ." Article II of the constitution declares the purpose of the Convention is "to combine . . . such portions of the Baptist Denomination in the United States . . . for Christian benevolence."

In the first three annual reports (1846-48), the domestic board limited its activities to the Southern (slaveholding) states, with the exception of Delaware. This was done because of the circumstances leading to the formation of the Convention, the vast extent of territory in even those states, the overwhelming need, and the limited resources of the board.

It embraces fourteen states, with an aggregate area of 955,664 square miles, and a population of about eight million. . . . It is painfully true, that there are many of our white population of mature age, in each state, embraced in our field of labor who have never heard the Gospel. . . . Add to this matter the wants of our colored population. Although vast numbers of them enjoy religious advantages far superior to multitudes of our poor white citizens, yet greater numbers are in a condition to require special attention of this body.

In the fourth annual report (1849) the domestic board began to recognize its nationwide field of activity indicated in the constitution of the Southern Baptist Convention and to justify its self-imposed limitation in area.

The Board have deemed it expedient to confine their labors within the Southern or slave-holding states, although applications have been made for appointments in the free states.

There are sufficient reasons why each Board, Southern and Northern, should occupy its own field. Each has more than ample field to require all its energies and resources. . . . [We] have an ample field. More than we can at present cultivate. Yet we must cultivate it or it will remain without culture. Very little was done in the Southern field by any domestic missionary organization, even previous to the unhappy discussion touching our civil institutions. Much less can be expected now. Aside from the hindrance alluded to, there is good reason why other organizations should bestow most of their efforts upon the free States. From the best information furnished by various published reports, the destitution North is nearly or quite equal to the destitution South. . . . We must cultivate our own field. Our political ties, social relations, and religious sympathies, are so identified as to impose a peculiar and strong obligation upon all parts of the field to engage in this work. . . . Since the last meeting of this body, much territory has been added to this government. . . . Much interest has been excited in California. . . . Several applicants have requested appointments by the Southern Board, all of which have been duly considered. But from the time the first application was made to the present, the finances of the Board would not justify any such undertaking; . . . they wait any recommendation or instruction of the Convention.

The steadily increasing interest in the far West is seen in the successive reports of the domestic board. In 1852 special attention was paid to California.

There is hardly one of our larger churches that has not one or more of its members, and several of its congregation, scattered in those regions. Several communications have been received imploring us to send them aid. Judge Willis, late of Virginia, sent an appeal in behalf of Sacramento City Church. No doubt is expressed in any of our communications that ministers of the right character would speedily be supported. Little more is necessary than that their journeying expenses should be paid, and their support secured until they become known and established. . . . If it is the desire of the churches that we should assist in this work we entreat them to express it. . . . An effort should be speedily made for the Chinese providentially brought to our shores. Many of these might, by the blessings of God, soon become Christian missionaries themselves, and go back to declare to their own people the wonderful words of God.

Within the following year John Lewis Shuck (*q.v.*), who had been for 16 years missionary in China, was sent by the Board of Domestic Missions to work among the Chinese in California. Shuck preached for the Baptist church in Sacramento, also. A church was established in Oakland and supported by the domestic board. A special committee on California missions made a ringing report to the Convention, stressing the importance of work under the domestic board among both English-speaking and Chinese elements in the population.

At this session of the Convention (1855), the offer of the American Indian Mission Association to transfer its assets and work to the Convention was accepted. The association, a special missionary society, had been formed in 1842 by Isaac McCoy, headquarters at Louisville, Ky. McCoy died in 1846. The work was placed under the direction of the domestic board, the name of which was changed to the Domestic and Indian Mission Board.

The board continued to expand its work westward as funds were available. It entered Kansas, following instructions of the Convention, 1855. The work continued to expand in California under Shuck, general missionary of the board, until the Civil War.

By the end of the first 15-year period, the domestic board was just beginning to function well. In the earliest years it had had to prove its place in the life of the new Convention. By 1860 the work of the board among the native-born whites, the Negro slaves, the Indians in the Indian Territory, the Chinese in California, and the Germans in Louisiana, Missouri, Kentucky, and Maryland was giving evidence of increasing success. The acrimonious discussions in the late fifties were not having any great effect upon the progress of the work. In 1861 the board reported:

Though there have been many conflicting views among our brethren in regard to the mode of conducting missionary operations [Landmarkism], there has been a flattering partiality shown to the agencies of the Convention; and we cannot fail to discover that the wisdom of our fathers is daily becoming more apparent in the adoption of our constitutional usages [the convention method as contrasted with the society method].

The progress of our work is the best evidence of the hold upon the confidence and regards of the friends of missions. And though this advance has been temporarily interrupted in consequence of the short crops of the past season throughout the Southern country; and the unhappy national agitations that have so entirely engrossed the minds of our people, yet this is not to be regarded as arising from a want of interest and lack of confidence in the plan of operations. On the contrary, scores of evidences may be found on our files encouraging the Board to keep to its one object and prosecute it as faithfully as the circumstances of the times may justify. Had not the above causes existed, the receipts of the year would probably have exceeded those of the past by not less than ten thousand dollars. Up to the 1st of September the receipts into the treasury were considerably ahead of those of the same period of the preceding year.

With a judicious regard for the interests of the Convention, and under a lively sense of their obligations, the Board determined as soon as they discovered the difficulties that threatened them, to enter, without hesitation, upon a system of retrenchment that would guard against the possibility of a debt, so much to be deprecated. Consequently, the number of missionary appointments for the year has been greatly diminished, and the aggregate of work done much less than the preceding year. But we feel confident that this course will receive the approval of the Convention, and not fail to result in the ultimate welfare of the trust committed to our charge. . . . Should the resources of the Board be replenished, no delay need to exist in giving expansion to our work.

In this report the board was particularly encouraged concerning the work among the Negro slaves:

In the providence of God, a large number of the descendants of Africa are found in our midst; and such is their relation to us, that they are almost entirely dependent upon the white man for the bread they eat, and specially for that instruction that shall make them wise unto eternal life. Our obligations, then, in this regard, are weighty, and address themselves to our most serious consideration. Have we been as solicitous for their spiritual welfare as duty requires? Many of them are located at a distance from the sanctuaries frequented by the families to which they are attached; and unless special provision is made for them, they must remain deprived of all wholesome religious Sabbath instruction. It has been the design of the Board to supply this want as far as possible. Several of our missionaries devote all their time to their benefit; and many, if not all, give a portion directly to their religious training. They are encouraged in this work by the masters of the slaves, and now that we are (as it is to be hoped) removed from those political exciting causes that have had, for years, a tendency to embarrass our evangelical efforts for the good of the black man, we look forward to a brighter day, when no suspicions can be thrown upon devoted, honest labor for the religious instruction of members of our families.

There is no class of people among us that more sincerely appreciate the efforts of our missionaries than the slaves that work our soil. Let us, then, give them the pure Word of Life that has elevated them so far above the condition of their race in the mother land.

This report was optimistic about the work in California among the whites and Chinese and also among German-speaking people in different states of the Southland.

All of this promising work was disrupted by the outbreak of war; the disruption was especially severe among the Indians in the West. The board had been working among Indians in Kansas and in the Indian Territory. Some of the Indians, through the influence of missionaries from Northern states, took the Northern side; others, through contacts with missionaries from Southern states, took the Southern side. By the opening of the year 1862, the domestic board decided to give its major effort to religious work among the soldiers in the Confederate armies. In some of the states in which armies of the Confederacy were stationed, the boards of the state conventions carried on religious work. This was especially true in Virginia, where soldiers were gathered from most of the Southern states and where so much of the fighting for the next four years took place.

The story of religious work in the armies in Virginia is told in detail by John William Jones, *Christ in the Camp*. Jones was closely associated with Robert E. Lee, Thomas J. Jackson, J. B. Gordon, and others high in the military of the Confederacy—leaders well known for their deep personal religion and for their interest in the religious welfare of the soldiers.

Home Mission Board

The domestic board in some instances carried on direct missionary and evangelistic work in the armies or worked with and through the boards of the state conventions that were conducting such work. This was especially true in Virginia. In the report to the Convention, 1863, the board indicated the general plan of the work as follows:

Missionary operations in the army are diversified, but on this account are not less valuable. Sometimes the missionary is accompanying the regiment or brigade upon their long marches, and preaches as he finds it convenient. Sometimes he moves from camp to camp, conversing with the men, distributing tracts, Testaments, religious newspapers, and holding meetings for prayer, and exhortation; and sometimes he is found located for a time within the massive walls of the strong and defiant fort, where he has access to its defenders, always anxious to wait upon his ministry.

Much of the work of the army missionaries was based on the distribution of religious literature.

Notwithstanding such large numbers of tracts, books, and religious newspapers have been put into circulation, there still is found to exist a demand that is difficult to meet. Says one of our missionaries, "There is great thirst for reading among soldiers—even among those who had little taste for it when at home. The reason is simply this, they are now cut off from almost every other source of information. . . . Hence they will read—read anything. *Testaments*, too, are greatly needed. The absence of God's word from our army is distressing. The soldiers feel this want. They appreciate the Bible as they never did before. The appeals to the missionaries for it are truly affecting. During one of the visits of a missionary to one of the Hospitals in Mobile, as he entered one of the wards he announced in the hearing of all, that he had procured for them a few Testaments. The patients immediately and almost simultaneously, scrambled from the couches, and with eager haste made their way toward him to receive the prize, forgetful of sickness and pain."

Through the assistance of the Colportage Board of Virginia (A. E. Dickinson, superintendent), the domestic board distributed a large amount of religious literature. "Bro. D. thinks that not less than 5,000,000 pages of tracts have been given them [the missionaries of the board] for this object. Add to this the amount purchased of other publishing houses by the Board, and you have some idea of the volume of the truth scattered among our soldiers for their spiritual instruction."

As the war progressed and the Federal armies gained control of the Mississippi River, it became impossible for the domestic board to carry on directly its mission activities west of the river. To meet the situation, the board established the Trans-Mississippi Department. In the report closing Apr. 1, 1865 (submitted to the Convention, 1866, p. 40), the board stated:

Owing to the difficulties of communication with this department, and the demands of the field, it was thought desirable to establish an agency of the Board in Texas. Rev. J. B. Link, for some time the efficient agent of the Board in Mississippi, was sent out to occupy this position. He was expected to make an acquaintance with the brethren in Texas, secure their cooperation, if possible, collect funds, and pay them out to the brethren who might be employed as Missionaries in the army, or as pastors of destitute churches. Up to the close of the year, we had heard nothing from Bro. Link, as he had not had time to communicate his plans of operation. We anticipate good results from this arrangement. Bro. Link is expected to render a quarterly report of his services and the business of his department to the Board.

The Executive Committee, too, of the Louisiana Baptist State Convention, had voted to co-operate with the Board, and act as its agent in the appointment of Missionaries to the number of ten, for whose salaries the Board would be responsible, provided there should be any deficit. It will be seen, then, that the Board has not been indifferent to the necessities and demands of the most distant portions of the field entrusted to their supervision. We need only money to inaugurate a most extensive and promising scale of operations. The field is large—the laborers needing assistance are many.

The coming of peace left the South "in the midst of confusion and disorganization. The country presented one continuous scene of desolation and ruin—the hopes of the people disappointed—their finances exhausted. The prospect was truly dark and disappointing." Maryland, Kentucky, and Missouri came to the rescue of the mission boards. The domestic board placed 55 men in the field, distributed from Virginia to Texas.

In 1867 the board reported its current field of operations to be the original 14 states occupied by the board (1846) with West Virginia (a part of Virginia in 1846) and the Indian Territory added. One hundred and twenty-four missionaries and evangelists worked under the board in co-operation with the associations in the several states. In the early 1870's the financial condition of the country necessitated retrenchment on the part of the Board of Domestic Mission and other boards of the Convention. In 1873 the work of the Sunday School Board (1863) was consolidated with that of the domestic board. The name of the consolidated board became The Domestic and Indian Mission and Sunday School Board of the Southern Baptist Convention. The next year (1874), the name was changed to The Home Mission Board of the Southern Baptist Convention. The Sunday school work was continued under the new name.

The general economic conditions in the country and the special situation in the South during the reconstruction curtailed the activities of the Home Mission Board. In 1881 the board reported domestic mission work in eight of the states connected with the Convention. The Chinese work in California and the mission work in the Indian Territory were prospering under limitations. (The work among the Chinese had been reopened in 1879.) But the income of the board continued to decline.

In 1882 the Convention, in session at Greenville, S. C., faced the question of discontinuing the board or removing it from Marion, Ala. The board was moved to Atlanta, Ga., and Isaac Taylor Tichenor (*q.v.*) became corresponding secretary (July 1, 1882). The new board published the following statement of facts:

1. The Board is convinced that, in order to meet the wishes of the denomination and to supply the necessities of the field, its operations must be greatly enlarged.

In *California,* our missionaries to the Chinese need to be reinforced—Bro. J. B. Hartwell being our sole male missionary to the thousands of that race who have come to our shores. A year ago the Southern Baptist Convention recommended the appointment of two additional men to this field. The existence of that mission as now organized is dependent upon Bro. Hartwell, whose success only makes us the more anxious to comply with the instruction of the Convention.

2. The *Indian* mission, which has for so many years awakened the interest and solicitude of our brethren, merits and will receive at our hands great consideration, and calls for increased expenditure.

3. The rapidly increasing population of the States and Territories of *the South West,* Arkansas, Texas, New Mexico, and Arizona, and the building up of towns and cities on the lines of railroads now being so rapidly constructed in that section of the country, open a large and inviting field for our Convention. The duty of adequately supplying the wants of this field with men and means and thus laying the foundation of permanent denominational prosperity must be apparent to every thinking mind.

4. In *Florida,* the increasing tide of population, attracted by the development of the wonderful resources of that semi-tropical State, is creating new centres of life and activity, in which we should establish churches of our faith.

5. From the *older States,* east of the Mississippi river, the Board is already receiving pressing applications for aid from important centres. The growing commercial, mining and manufacturing interests are bringing into existence new communities which ought to receive from us the Bread of Life.

6. Our relations and obligations to the *Negroes* of the South have already claimed attention from the Board; a judicious committee has been appointed to take this whole subject into consideration, and to report at an early day the best plans for reaching, with the Gospel influences, this large part of our population. We are profoundly impressed with the importance and magnitude of this work.

7. *New Orleans,* the great and growing commercial emporium of the lower Mississippi valley, must in time become not only the social, but the great trade center of the Western hemisphere. No language can exaggerate its future influence upon our country. In this great city we have but two Baptist churches, both of which require aid from a board. The occupying of this field is imperatively demanded. Brethren from every section are pressing upon us its claims. The Mississippi Baptist Convention, which is thoroughly informed with reference to this field, at its late session resolved that the Baptists of the South ought to raise for it this year, at least $25,000. Rev. Dr. Landrum, Pastor of the Coliseum Place Baptist Church, New Orleans, has already pointed out a half dozen important points in that city which should be immediately occupied by missionaries. Will the funds be supplied that vigorous efforts may be made to meet these demands?

Properly to occupy these fields, and to meet their demands, the Board should have at its disposal during the current year not less than $100,000, and we cannot even do *effective* work in all of them with less than $50,000. So large an increase of funds will demand a corresponding increase of the liberality of our brethren. We confidently expect that the denomination, which, without solicitation on our part, has transferred this work to our hands, will cheerfully and liberally supply us with the funds needed for its prosecution. We request every pastor to raise during the year at least one collection for our treasury. The Home Mission Board earnestly desires the hearty co-operation of the several State Boards, and asks that they give encouragement to State Vice-Presidents and other representatives of our interests.

Our corresponding Secretary has been instructed to visit, if possible, each State, with the view of conferring with the State Boards and other brethren, and of thoroughly organizing this work which the Master has intrusted, not merely to the Board, but to all our brethren throughout the South. We heartily commend him to the churches, praying upon his labors the favor of God, whose he is and whom he serves.

The new Home Mission Board began its life in Atlanta, July 1, 1882. Two days later, the board ordered this statement of facts, this survey of the field, to be published. Tichenor, the new secretary, spent the last six months of the year studying the field and its problems and opportunities. He attended the annual meetings of state conventions and associational meetings. There is evidence to lead to the conclusion that he encouraged consolidation of two or more conventions in a state, the consolidated body becoming allied with the Home Mission Board. The women of the South were in process of forming a Southwide organization—auxiliary to the Southern Baptist Convention. Again Tichenor's hand may be seen. These two objectives—consolidated state bodies and a Southwide organization of women, all allied with the Convention—and the Sunday school work of the Home Mission Board constituted his strategy in the program of saving the home front of the Convention. In 1884 the board announced the closing of mission work among the Chinese in California, due to financial conditions.

Early in the 1880's the fortunes of the Home Mission Board reached the lowest ebb. The economic situation in the South curtailed the board's income. Associations and state conventions turned to the American Baptist Home Mission Society for financial alignment in domestic missions. This, in turn, further depleted the income of the board. The society had abandoned its Texas mission in the late 1840's. It did no further work in the South through the next decade. During the Civil War work was begun among the Negroes who had sought refuge near the Federal armies, particularly in areas adjacent to Washington, D. C., and Norfolk, Va. Furthermore,

. . . as the war advanced and the military resources of the South deminished, the extending military control of the North over the territory of the Southern Baptist Convention vitally affected the life and work of the churches. After the fall of Vicksburg and the Battle of Gettysburg the fortunes of the South began to wane. The Federal armies controlled more and more of Southern territory. The American Baptist Home Mission Society, through its president, U. S. Senator Harris of New York, made application for the authority to take charge of abandoned Baptist meeting-houses in the controlled territory. The Secretary of War granted more than was asked, but the Society did not decline the added privileges.

Addressing the military authorities in the field, the secretary wrote: "You are hereby directed to place at the disposal of the American Baptist Home Mission Society all houses of worship belonging to the Baptist Churches, South, in which a loyal minister of said church does not now officiate."

Many of the churches whose pastors were displaced under this military order were members of associations in working agreement with the Home Mission Board. The Coliseum Place Church, New Orleans, La., was owned by the Home Mission Board. Thus, during the war the Home Mission Society was established among both white and Negro Baptists in the South. Following the war the economic conditions invited the society to expand its work in the South. The society's name—American—gave further justification for the move. Work among the Negroes—evangelistic and educational—was enlarged, and white churches and associations were assisted when they desired it and the society's funds were adequate. When the funds of the Home Mission Board began to decline toward their lowest point, associations and state conventions began to turn to the Home Mission Society for assistance.

Secretary Tichenor and the new board prepared for aggressive action. During the last half of the year 1882, he surveyed the field, visiting the state conventions and associations, while the retiring secretary, William Hilary McIntosh, cared for the office work in Atlanta. The tide began to turn, and the aggressive program began to pay off. The board was cultivating its territory more deeply, regaining territory lost during the preceding two decades, and moving toward the tremendous increase of territory in the first half of the 20th century. In 1892 Tichenor could report:

Ten years ago the Convention then in session at Greenville, S. C., resolved to move the Board from Marion, Ala., to Atlanta [Ga.]. The condition of the Board at that time excited the gravest apprehensions. Its total receipts for the year were about $28,000. It had but forty missionaries. Except those in the Indian Territory, it had few west of the Mississippi river. The Baptist Convention in Arkansas was in co-operation with the Home Mission Society of New York. Nothing had been attempted in Missouri for years, and that state seemed lost to the Board forever. Texas was divided into five missionary organizations, four of which were receiving aid from the Home Mission Society, and the fifth was paralyzed by its own dissensions. Thus the territory west of the Mississippi river had passed out of the hands of the Board.

East of the river, Mississippi was in alliance with the Publication Society, Georgia was co-operating with the Society in New York in work among the negroes, while Florida was hesitating between remaining with the Board or forming alliance with the same Society. The State Boards had grown vigorously, and from several of the States the Home Mission Board was excluded by action of their State Conventions. It is not to be wondered that the Convention at Greenville pondered the question whether removal or abandonment was the wiser policy. When it was decided to remove it to Atlanta, and the present Board was put in charge of its affairs, the outlook was by no means assuring. A survey of the field indicated a great defeat and a lost cause.

Impressed with the conviction that the existence of this Convention depended upon the resucitation of its fortunes, the new Board threw itself into the arduous work before it with the determination to use every proper effort to reclaim its lost territory, and make itself a support of the Convention. This could not be done without money, and our impoverished and disheartened people could not be expected to give a speedy or liberal response to its demands. But such were the earnestness of its efforts and the happy results of its policy, that in five years there was not a missionary to the white people of the South who did not bear a commission from either the Home Mission Board of the Southern Baptist Convention, or one of our State Boards in alliance with it. Its territories had been reclaimed. Texas had been united in one great Convention in hearty sympathy and co-operation with the Board. So was Arkansas, so was Louisiana. A new spirit had possessed Missouri, and our cause has risen there until that State is among the strongest supporters of the Board, and of the Convention. The Board had demonstrated its right to live, and had won the confidence of the denomination.

In 1894, after several efforts on the part of secretary Tichenor, the board of the Home Mission Society agreed to confer with the Home Mission Board of the Southern Baptist Convention on a *modus operandi* among and with the Negro Baptists of the South. The conference was held at Fortress Monroe, Va., Sept., 1894, and reached the following agreement:

I. *As to Schools among Colored People.* 1. That the Home Board of the Southern Baptist Convention appoint an advisory local committee at each point where a school controlled by the American Baptist Home Mission Society is, or shall be located, and that this committee shall exercise such authority as shall be conferred upon it from time to time by the American Baptist Home Mission Society. 2. That the control of the school shall remain in the hands of the American Baptist Home Mission Society; but these local advisory committees shall recommend to the American Baptist Home Mission Society any changes in the conduct or in the teaching forces of these schools, including the filling of vacancies, with the reasons for their recommendations. 3. That the Southern Baptist Convention, through its Home Mission Board, shall appeal to the Baptists of the South for the moral and financial support of these schools, and that these local committees shall encourage promising young colored people to attend these institutions. 4. That the joint committee recommend to the respective bodies appointing them the adoption of the foregoing section as unanimously expressing their views as to the work in the schools among the colored people.

II. *As to Mission Work among the Colored People.* It is unanimously voted by the joint committee to recommend to our respective bodies that the American Baptist Home Mission Society and the Home Mission Board of the Southern Baptist Convention coöperate in the mission work among the colored people of the South, in connection with the Baptist state bodies, white and colored, in the joint appointment of general missionaries, in holding ministers' and deacons' institutes, and in the better organization of the missionary work of the colored Baptists. The details of the plan are to be left to be agreed upon by the bodies above named.

III. *As to Territorial Limits.* The committee of the American Baptist Home Mission Society, not being instructed to consider any subject except coöperation in labor for the colored race, respectfully refers to the Board of the American Baptist Home Mission Society the proposition of the committee of the Southern Baptist Convention on the subject of territorial limits, and asks for its favorable consideration.

The following is the text of the proposition referred to: "We believe that, for the promotion of fraternal feeling and of the best interests of the Redeemer's kingdom, it is inexpedient for two different organizations of Baptists to solicit contributions or to establish missions in the same locality, and for this reason we recommend to the Home Mission Board of the Southern Baptist Convention and to the American Baptist Home Mission Society that, in the prosecution of their work already begun on contiguous fields or on the same field, all antagonisms be avoided, and that their officers and employees be instructed to co-operate in all practicable ways in the spirit of Christ. That we further recommend to these bodies and their agents, in opening new work, to direct their efforts to localities not already occupied by the other."

By direction of the joint committee their action was furnished to the denominational press, and has been widely published. Everywhere there has been hearty approval, and earnest hopes are generally cherished that a brighter day has dawned upon our denominational work among the colored people, and in regard to friction arising and liable to arise in reference to territorial limits. It gives us pleasure to say that the proposition agreed to at the joint meeting of the committees in regard to territorial limits was approved unanimously both by the Board of the Home Mission Society and our Home Mission Board. We therefore recommend that the Convention approve of the conclusions reached at Fortress Monroe and direct our Home Mission Board to carry them into effect. We also recommend that the Home Mission Society, soon to meet in Saratoga, N. Y., be notified of this action of the Convention.

This report was adopted by the Convention the following year without discussion. There was no further friction between the Home Mission Board and the Home Mission Society over territorial limits until the early years of the 20th century.

Work in Cuba and Panama—In these two areas the Home Mission Board has had work for more than 50 years and both are treated separately under their own names. Cuba, normally a foreign mission field, came under direction of the Home Mission Board by Convention action in 1886, after that board had reported on work done for Cuba by the Florida Baptist State Convention in the name of the Home Mission Board. The first Baptists in Cuba were persons who had been attracted to Baptist principles while living in the United States; the earliest accomplishments were largely caused by various contacts between native Cubans and Baptists on the southern coasts of the United States. Under Home Mission Board leadership the work was promoted through a strategically located church, a seminary, and a strong emphasis upon the importance of native leadership.

Baptist work in Panama was begun in 1900 by Jamaican Baptists, whose evangelization had been begun a hundred years before by a freed slave from Georgia, George Leile. In 1905 the Home Mission Board appointed a missionary to the area. Since that time, in spite of the handicaps of a transient population and the church union ideas of the government chaplains and Y.M.C.A. workers who also ministered to those working on the construction of the Canal, progress was made. Successes in neighboring countries led to Foreign Mission Board work in those countries, while the Home Mission Board continued in Panama, working with Indians, Spanish-speaking Panamanians, and North Americans.

Sunday school work of the board.—By the early 1870's the economic situation in the South was such that the Sunday School Board, created in 1863, was consolidated with the Domestic and Indian Mission Board in 1873. The following year, the name of the consolidated board was changed to Home Mission Board. A debt on the Sunday School Board was assumed by the Home Mission Board, which continued the publication of the Sunday school paper *Kind Words*. The old debt was gradually reduced through the profits made on this publication. The Home Mission Board ceased publishing the Sunday school periodicals but printed in *Kind Words* the Sunday school lesson of the week. By 1878 the board reported that "its lessons were now guiding the study of God's word of one hundred and fifty thousand persons every week . . . the number of papers issued Monthly (Weekly, Semi-Monthly, Monthly, and Lesson Papers) is 176,000."

The success of the Sunday school publications of the Home Mission Board gradually paid off the debt of the old Sunday School Board. By Jan., 1884, the debt was liquidated, and from then on, profits made on the Sunday school publications went into the treasury of the board. In 1885 the board reported that the treasury was receiving $1,000 a year royalty on the Sunday school publications. Inasmuch as the contract with the publishers would expire in June, 1886, the board suggested that a forward step should be planned in facing the new situation.

A committee of wise and prudent brethren ought to give earnest consideration to the question how far it is proper for the Board to attempt to furnish Sunday-school literature to the Baptist churches of the South. Here is a wide field of usefulness and

Home Mission Board

future influence. Shall we attempt it, or shall we surrender it to others?

The Convention in session at Augusta, Ga., 1885, approved the following report of a committee:

In view of the early expiration of the contract for the publication of *Kind Words*, we suggest to the Home Board to mature some plan by which these growing demands may be met. With Rev. Samuel Boykin as chief, supported by such talent as can be found in our midst, this paper would meet all of the demands of the case, and none of our people would look either North or West for any Sabbath-school literature.

The following year, in the Home Mission Board report Secretary Tichenor announced to the Convention that the board, in obedience to the suggestion of the previous year, had made provision for the continued publication of *Kind Words*

... and also to bring out by or before October next a full grade of *Quarterlies,* three in number, and a *Magazine for Teachers.* ... The Board bespeaks for the new publisher that will assume the publication of our Sunday-school periodicals, on the first of June next, the general and hearty support of the Baptist Sunday-schools in the South.

The new venture of the Home Mission Board in the field of Sunday school literature aroused opposition on two grounds. Many Baptist pastors thought that a mission board ought not to go into the publication of Sunday school literature. Others opposed the venture on the grounds that it was not necessary, since the American Baptist Publication Society, after a history of more than 65 years, was furnishing satisfactory literature to the Baptist Sunday schools in the South. But nothing succeeds like success:

... some of our pastors have expressed the opinion that the International series does not fully meet the needs of our Sunday-schools; that we should have something which shall bring our denominational principles and practices more frequently and more strongly in contact with the minds of our children. The Board sympathizes with this view, and respectfully suggest to the Convention the desirableness of adopting some measures, either by modification of the International Lessons, or something in addition to them, to meet a want so vital to the best interest of our churches.

The increasing success of the Sunday school program of the Home Mission Board brought increasing complications. By 1890 the success of the venture and the consequent opposition to such work's being carried on by a mission board were so great that many ardent supporters of the Home Mission Board began to think that the Sunday school work should be undertaken by a separate board. In 1890 Tichenor, in the Home Mission Board report to the Convention, gave a survey of the situation and comments on new suggestions now being made.

Nearly thirty years ago the Convention entered upon the work of Sunday-school publication, which has been continued by its order and under its direction to the present time.

When the Board was removed to Atlanta it found a number of these publications placed in its charge. A contract with Burke & Co., of Macon, Ga., having five years to run, was then in process of execution. They were yielding the Convention a net income of one thousand dollars per annum. The then recent introduction of the *International Lessons* had caused rapid improvement in the character of the literature furnished the Sunday-schools of the land. The Board saw that during the existence of this contract with Burke & Co., it would be difficult, if not impossible, to improve the publications of the Convention so as fully to adapt them to the wants of our schools, and that unless this was done it was only a question of time when they would be superseded by others, and a valuable property of the Convention perish in its hands.

To avoid such a disaster and to carry out the purpose of the Convention in calling them into existence, the Board submitted to the Convention the question of improving them and under its direction subsequently submitted a contract for that purpose. Both the suggestion for the improvement and the contract for that purpose received the approval of the Convention without a word of opposition or a dissenting vote.

The present *Kind Words* series, after its appearance, received the heartiest indorsement of the Convention, and its unanimous resolve "to do all in its power to foster, sustain and advance this great interest of the denomination." Under the existing arrangement these publications have attained a success most gratifying to the Board. They are conducted with an ability that from their first issue has placed them among the best Sunday-school periodicals in the land. Their teachings have commanded the confidence and the admiration of many of our best Sunday-school workers. They have escaped criticism at a time when there was every incentive to attack. They have, year by year, steadily increased, and are now rapidly enlarging the circulation. Their success is no longer problematical. The property of the Convention in them has, in little more than three years, so augmented in value that what could not then have been sold for exceeding five thousand dollars is now worth thirty thousand, and at the expiration of the present contract can be made to yield to the Convention ten per cent annually upon this amount.

An honored brother of this body, having given notice that he would advocate at this session of the Convention the appointment of a Board of Sunday-school publications to which they shall hereafter be committed, the board deems it proper to say:

1. That, in all its acts as they relate to these publications, it has, at every step, carefully sought and implicitly obeyed the instructions of this body.

2. That, in the difficult and delicate task of managing these publications, it has, according to the wisdom given it, sought the best interest of the Convention and of the churches it represents.

3. It has sometimes been silent when its failure to speak might be construed into confession of wrong or mistaken action, because it desired peace in our brotherhood more than it wanted justice for itself. Standing to-day in the presence of this body, which has so long honored it with its confidence, it can say, in all good conscience before God and men, that the review of its connection with these publications fails to bring to light one action taken by it that it would

wish to change, or one word it has spoken which it would wish to blot from its record.

Holding the highest estimate of the importance of this work, of its present and future value to the Convention and to the denomination, and yielding to none in our desire to promote through them the religious welfare of our people the Board, cheerfully submits this question to the Convention. If it [sic] shall be your pleasure to commit this great and growing interest to a separate Board, we will rejoice that the success it has attained in our hands has made such a separation an act of wisdom, and we will heartily co-operate with the new Board in the work of the Convention. Should the Convention continue these publications in our hands we will, as heretofore, comply with its instructions and use our best endeavors to increase their circulation and their usefulness.

Out of this complicated situation the Convention created the second Sunday School Board and ordered the Home Mission Board to transfer to the new board all of its publications and Sunday school activities. Tichenor, in his program to save the home front of the Southern Baptist Convention, using the teaching in the Sunday schools of the Baptist churches of the South as one of his major lines of defense and attack, had succeeded so well that a great field of activity and progress was opened to Southern Baptists in the new Sunday school program.

The administration of Baron DeKalb Gray (*q.v.*).—The work which had been so successfully developed was continued under the direction of B. D. Gray, who succeeded Fernando Coello McConnell (*q.v.*), and who served from 1903 to 1928. During this period the board's interest in New Orleans was pursued with renewed strength. As a result of various programs over many years, the board built a notable hospital ministry and a Bible institute which became the center of increasingly successful mission work. The two permanent institutions which resulted—Southern Baptist Hospital and the New Orleans Baptist Theological Seminary—have become vital assets to the Southern Baptist Convention.

In addition during the period of Gray's administration the board built its system of mountain mission schools, which were allowed to perish in the depression after local public school systems had in some measure replaced them, but which for many years filled major educational and religious needs in what was then one of the most backward sections of the South. The various church building loan funds through which the board reinforces and encourages new and expanding churches throughout the territory of the Convention were also created. For many years the board had extended aid to a few churches but only in a token way. Not until this period were funds accumulated which could make the church loan ministry helpful to the denomination as a whole. The program of organized evangelism which became, after interruption during the 1930's, such a significant force in Southern Baptist growth, was established during this period, and its basic policies and patterns created.

Home Missions Council.—In the opening years of the 20th century, there was developing a vigorous interdenominational and unionist movement. In 1909 the Home Mission Board, in its report to the Convention, presented the following statement:

There has been formed in New York City since our last Convention an organization, known as the "Home Missions Council." It is composed of representatives from the various Home Mission organizations in the United States, and has for its aim the furtherance of Home Missions throughout the country. Your Board has been asked to join this Council, but we have felt constrained, in view of its importance, to refer the matter to the Convention for advice or instruction. We are authorizing our Corresponding Secretary to have copies of the by-laws of the Council convenient for use at the Convention and we ask the Convention to advise us as to whether we should join this inter-denominational Council.

The Convention appointed a committee of nine, of which William E. Hatcher of Virginia was chairman. He presented the following report. It was adopted by a rising vote.

Our Home Mission Board having appealed to this Convention to define the relation which it shall bear to the Home Missions Council located in New York City, and representing many Christian denominations of this country, respectfully recommend that this Convention shall make the following deliverance for the guidance of the Board:

1. That we rejoice heartily in the courtesy and fraternity which has always marked the relations between our Board with kindred organizations in the past, and most sincerely desire that this spirit of neighborship and kindliness shall always continue.

2. We desire also that our Board shall have ample liberty for conference and for such concert of action with other Home Mission Boards, so far as it may deem proper for the maintenance of kindly relations and good understanding as to the vast and unspeakably important work of Home evangelization.

3. We feel it to be of the utmost importance, however, to remind our Board that the people who make the Convention, hold doctrines set forth in the Scriptures, which are held only in part or not at all by many of our brethren of other denominations, who are engaged in Home Mission work. These doctrines we hold only as we find them in the Scriptures, and they constitute, very largely, the reason for our denominational existence, and we can not look with approval upon any alliances on the part of our Board that could possibly imperil these doctrines.

4. We deem it necessary to say further to our Board, that we cannot justify its entrance into any relations with other Boards which can possibly circumscribe our independence or liberty as to the fields which we are to occupy, or the methods which we are to adopt in carrying forward the work which we feel that the Lord has committed to us. Our churches, which make up this body, are independent of each other so far as their internal government is concerned, and therefore, cannot be lined up in any sort of federation that can subject them to any external authority, or commit them to any special line of policy.

5. It is to us a matter of honest regret that our

honored brethren of other denominations seem unable to get our own point of view as to our attitude and spirit as a denomination. We do not mention this in any mood of critical or censorious complaint against any, for we love all, but we deem it essential to say to our Board that we can do none other than to maintain our position in such a manner as will leave to us the broadest freedom in proclaiming our distinctive doctrines and establishing churches of our faith wherever we can. We feel that it is our duty to lead the people, so far as possible, in accepting Christ, to adopt those doctrines which we believe to be of the gravest importance, though often overlooked by many brethren whom we love and honor. We believe in charity, but we believe the highest type of charity is that which sweetly, graciously and courageously seeks to present to the people the counsel of God.

6. We do, therefore, with the utmost earnestness and yet with the most cordial goodwill and brotherly kindness to all, say to our Home Mission Board that we deem it inadvisable to form any relations with the Home Missions Council which can in any [way] abridge its freedom, warp its policy or embarrass its action in the future.

Carnes affair.—The defalcation of the treasurer of the Home Mission Board was the greatest financial calamity ever to strike the work of the Southern Baptist Convention. The stealing of the funds of the board, which was carried out through a period of years, came to light in Aug., 1928.

Clinton S. Carnes became treasurer of the Home Mission Board during the Convention year 1919–20 and was given authority to handle the papers and the funds of the board over his own signature. He had had a penitentiary record in the city of Atlanta, but it did not come to light until after the defalcation. He was an expert bookkeeper and accountant and seemingly had no difficulty in securing a position in a firm of accountants during the period of World War I, when men who had ability were difficult to secure. With the best recommendations from business and church sources, the board engaged his services. By authority from the board, he was empowered to borrow money from banks in different states to carry on the work of the board. He so manipulated his financial dealings that his criminal acts were committed legally in different states. When his conduct came to light, it seemed to the lawyers employed by the board that it would be next to impossible to assemble all of the various threads of evidence necessary to convict him on his different acts of thievery. Since his crimes were committed legally in different states, he could not be tried in Georgia upon the indictments for every individual act.

Carnes returned to Atlanta and confessed his defalcation. He pleaded guilty to one of the indictments committed in Georgia and was sentenced to the limit the law allowed upon that conviction. He had taken $226,126.86 from the church building fund and $683,334.14 from the general fund of the board, making a total of $909,461.00. He assigned all his known assets, estimated at a minimum value of $225,000. Upon conviction his bond of $50,000 was paid to the board. On his person when he was arrested were found $3,000 in traveler's checks. The sum of these amounts repaid nearly one third of the amount of the defalcation.

The fact of defalcation and the amount of money involved, coming on the very eve of the depression that hit in the fall of 1929, left the board and its work in a fearful situation. To relieve the immediate situation, the churches of the South came forward with special offerings on Baptist Honor Day, in the amount of $397,444.23. This immediate relief and wise, efficient management of the affairs of the board carried its greatly limited work through to success in clearing all debts by 1943. Much credit is due to J. B. Lawrence and his faithful co-workers and the members of the board in meeting the situation so successfully.

The administration of John Benjamin Lawrence.—Lawrence began his work in 1929, when the financial position of the board, because of debt and loss, was exceedingly dangerous. The first years of his administration were therefore largely devoted to preservation and rebuilding. After this time several distinct advancements were made. The work of the board in evangelism was renewed and developed in a way which made possible increasingly comprehensive efforts. The former emphasis during the administration of Tichenor on a distinct and exclusively Southern territory was definitely reversed as the board supported increasingly active mission work in Western and Northern states. From 1940 until the end of Lawrence's term, the board expanded existing programs and created new ones in many areas: direct missions, Negro work, co-operative missions, church loans, and publications. Various new services in the field of promotion and general ministries were begun. In 1953, when Lawrence retired, Courts Redford, who had been Lawrence's associate, was elected executive secretary of the board.

Modern progress.—The first half of the 20th century saw tremendous changes in the life of the American people, especially in population shifts. Several causes of these changes may be seen: (1) the normal urge in human experience to move; (2) the facilities of travel and transportation available; (3) improvement in areas in the West due to irrigation; (4) mechanization of agriculture, thus releasing many laborers from farms; (5) development of industry in new areas; (6) shifting of population due to two world wars, especially the second.

The westward trek in this period is comparable to the expansion westward from the Atlantic seaboard states into the Mississippi Valley in the first half of the 19th century. It was this movement of population westward that called for home mission effort, resulting in various methods and different types of organization. The Southern Baptist Convention was formed, among other reasons, to meet the domestic need in what was then the West, as Baptists in the South saw that need. The

20th-century movement has not produced new methods and agencies so much as it has resulted in the expansion of fields of activity of already existing domestic missionary organizations. The Home Mission Board of the Southern Baptist Convention has seized the new opportunities, enlarging its working force and expanding its internal organization to meet the new challenge.

The migration of Southern Baptists westward into New Mexico (especially from Texas) began to raise questions of territorial limits and alignment. Baptists of Southern origin in New Mexico began to plead with the Home Mission Board to come over and help them. During the first years of the appeal, the finances of the board did not justify the expansion of its field of work. When its financial situation began to improve, the board began to heed the New Mexico call. Henry L. Morehouse, secretary of the American Baptist Home Mission Society, protested on the ground that the Fortress Monroe agreement (1894) precluded the Home Mission Board's entrance into New Mexico. Out of the discussion of the issue, a conference composed of five representatives each from the board and the society met in Washington, D. C., Apr. 15, 1909. "Prior to the formulation of the agreement there reached, all parties to the conference agreed that the Fortress Monroe agreement had expired and that its stipulations were not now in force of binding." The agreement reached at Washington was as follows:

Resolved. That we recommend that the Home Mission Board upon the consent of the New Mexico Convention relieve entirely the American Baptist Home Mission Society of further responsibility for mission work, in that territory, on the understanding that the Home Board give assurance that they will put into the work in New Mexico next year an amount equal to that expended by the Home Mission Society this year and will take over the Navahoe mission property at its cost to the Home Mission Society.

Resolved. Further, that we recommend that the question of territorial adjustment on the part of both Boards be considered settled for a period of at least five years.

Resolved. Further, that in case of the approval of this arrangement by the Southern Baptist Convention and the American Baptist Home Mission Society, a joint communication be addressed to the New Mexico Baptist churches to this effect, expressing the hope that they will regard this arrangement with favor.

The Southern Baptist Convention approved the action of the Washington conference, with the proviso "that nothing in the agreement shall be so construed as to limit any church, association, or other Baptist body in the free exercise of the inalienable right to make such alignments for co-operation as will, in its judgment, be for its own good and for the furtherance of the work it is in."

The Home Mission Society, at its session held in Portland, Oregon, in 1909, adopted a resolution, which says that the statement of this doctrine "gave such qualified approval to the agreement as practically to nullify the five-years' clause thereof," and, on this ground withheld its approval of the agreement, referring "the whole matter back to the Executive Board for such further action as it may deem advisable to take." So far the Home Board has received no advices concerning any further action, and your Committee learns from the published report of the Society submitted at its recent session in Chicago that the Society and its officers consider the incident closed, as far as they are concerned.

But the decisions of committees, societies, boards, and conventions could not check the westward urge of Southern Baptist life. The New Mexico situation came to the front again. A joint committee of nine from each of the conventions, Northern and Southern, met at Old Point Comfort, Va., Sept. 27-28, 1911, to consider this and related questions. It was recommended, on the approval of the two national and the two New Mexico state conventions, that New Mexico be considered, after three years, as within the field of activity of the Home Mission Board of the Southern Baptist Convention.

As the board's finances justified, mission work among Indians and whites in the West was continued and enlarged. During the period of World War I and in the midst of the financial conditions in the third and fourth decades of the century, no advance westward was made. In the 1940's, with debts paid and rapidly increasing migration toward the Pacific coast, mission work was expanded. In 1947 the board had a program of missions in the West that included "all the co-operative mission work done through the state mission boards in Arizona, California, and New Mexico." In 1949 Alaska was added to the field of direct missions. To its field of co-operative missions, two more state conventions—Kansas and Oregon—were added to the Western mission program in 1950. The following year, churches in Washington were affiliated with the Oregon convention. It became necessary for the board to set forth its policy in the program of entering new areas. In the annual report for 1953, it is declared that "the policy followed by the Home Mission Board is not to enter any field of service until some church or churches in the area are affiliated with one of the state conventions through which the Home Board may aid on the recommendation and request of the state convention."

Due to the accelerated emigration of Baptists from the South into all areas of the nation and to the fact that conservative-minded Baptists in hitherto non-Southern Baptist areas were appealing to the Home Mission Board for assistance, the board further clarified its program and method in its report to the Convention, 1954:

The western and pioneer work has been put under one heading because pioneer work of the eastern areas of our Convention is the same type as that of the western work and is carried on in the same way. The Western Mission Program consists of that work which the Home Mission Board does in co-operation with the state conventions of New Mexico, Arizona, Kansas, Oregon-Washington, and California. Through these state conventions work is being done also in Utah, Nevada, Idaho, Colorado, Wyoming, Montana, North Dakota, and South Dakota, in each of which there are now co-operating Southern Baptist churches.

The Home Mission Board co-operates in the eastern area in this pioneer work with Illinois, Maryland, Arkansas, and Kentucky. Through these states work is done in Wisconsin, Indiana, Michigan, and Ohio. The work in Ohio has been under the Kentucky General Association, and was constituted into its own convention on January 8, 1954.

In the report for 1955 Delaware and Pennsylvania were added as areas in which churches, affiliated with adjacent state conventions, were co-operating with the board. "There are many requests that came from other areas for our co-operation, but the Home Mission Board can only reach them through the state conventions with which they may become affiliated."

Thus the Southern Baptist Convention, through its Home Mission Board, is realizing, after more than a century, the objective of 1845: "to combine ... such portions of the Baptist denomination in the United States, as may desire a general organization for Christian benevolence."

BIBLIOGRAPHY: W. W. Barnes, *The Southern Baptist Convention, 1845–1953* (1954). *Christian Index* (July 13, 1882; Feb. 14, Nov. 14, 1929). *Home and Foreign Journal* (Apr. 10, 1852). M. N. McCall, *A Baptist Generation in Cuba* (1942).

JOHN CAYLOR

HOME MISSION BOARD STATISTICAL SUMMARY

Year	Number of Missionaries	Number of Conversions	Number of Churches Constituted	Income	Net Worth	Corpus Loan Funds
1855	100	3,320	...	$ 37,729.91	....	....
1860	100	1,941	30	35,274.50	....	....
1880	35	435	...	20,942.41	....	....
1902	671	8,969	127	109,483.29	....	....
1915	1,409 *	43,792	167	382,051.96	....	$ 116,796.64
1920	1,656 *	45,092	258	1,462,327.53	$1,542,418.72	....
1925	833	19,774	100	624,682.25	1,561,061.23	1,072,105.20
1935	174	3,822	16	409,650.62	641,650.62	1,151,585.49
1945	645 **	16,833	123	1,613,979.59	3,504,789.16	1,558,527.55
1955	1,105 **	37,475	410	3,328,662.73	9,665,798.63	3,410,957.81

* Including associational missionaries.
** Excluding student summer workers.

SAMUEL COURTS REDFORD

HOME MISSION BOARD OF THE SOUTHERN BAPTIST CONVENTION
Organization and Ministry

EXECUTIVE COMMITTEE
ADMINISTRATIVE COMMITTEE

ADMINISTRATIVE OFFICERS: Executive Secretary-Treasurer, Assistant Executive Secretary-Treasurer, Executive Assistant, Financial Secretary, Business Manager, Director of Promotion, Attorney.

PROMOTIONAL SERVICES: Visual Aids—Newspaper Publicity—Denominational Press—Baptist News—Displays, Exhibits.

GENERAL MINISTRIES: Migrant Missions—Summer Mission Program—Tentmakers Program—Pioneer Ranch Ministry—Conferences: Ridgecrest, Glorieta—W.M.U. Work in Undeveloped Areas.

FIELD WORKERS: General—Colleges and Seminaries—Catholicism and Mixed Marriages—Mission Buildings.

COMMITTEE ON MISSIONARY EDUCATION

Schools of Missions—Camps and Institutes—Speakers Bureau—Biographical Materials—Mission Conferences.

COMMITTEE ON EDITORIAL SERVICE

Monthly Publication, *Home Missions*—Home Mission Books—Edit All Printed Materials—Mission Information to Other Denominational Publications—Mission Stories and Articles—Library Services—Research.

COMMITTEE ON NEGRO WORK

Teacher-Missionaries—Negro Centers—Extension Centers—Negro Institutes—Negro Evangelism—Negro B.S.U. Work—Negro Scholarships—Summer Mission Program for Negro Students—Negro Good Will Centers—Literature—Conferences—Co-operate with States in Negro Work.

Home Mission Board Sunday School Work

COMMITTEE ON EVANGELISM	Convention-wide Promotion—Transfer Church Membership Crusade—Conservation of Results in Evangelism—Co-operation with States in Promotion of Evangelism—Promotion of Simultaneous Revivals—Evangelistic Conferences—Evangelism Among Special Groups—Promotion of Evangelistic Church Councils—Production and Distribution of Literature.
COMMITTEE ON DIRECT MISSIONS	Direct Mission Work Among: Indians, Spanish, Mexicans, Cubans, French, Italians, Chinese, Japanese, Russians, Students in International Center, Deaf—Work in Good Will Centers, Rescue Homes, Outposts: Cuba, Panama, Canal Zone—Conferences and Institutes for Language Groups and Good Will Centers—Scholarship Funds—Mission Buildings—Co-operate with State and Local Workers in These Fields.
COMMITTEE ON CO-OPERATIVE MISSIONS	City Missions—Rural Missions—Mountain Missions—Alaska, Western, and Pioneer Missions—Work in Behalf of Juvenile Delinquents—Ministry to Military Personnel—Ministry in Industrial Areas—Conferences on Co-operative Mission Work—Correspondence Bible Course.
CHAPLAINS COMMISSION	Endorse Chaplains for Military Services—Encourage Training for the Chaplaincy—Obtain and Classify Information on Prospective Chaplains—Maintain Contacts with Chaplains—Plan Conferences for Chaplains and Their Wives—Produce and Distribute Helpful Literature—Certify to Draft Boards Information on Ministerial Status of Ordained and Licensed Personnel—Inform Denominational Agencies as to Availability for Civilian Ministry.
COMMITTEE ON CHURCH LOANS	Recommend Loan Policies—publicize Three Loan Plans: Church Building Loan, Church Extension Loan, Bond Purchase—Receive Loan Applications—Make Necessary Surveys—Approve Loans When Requirements Are Met—Administer Loans—Help Churches to Secure Commercial Loans—Seek Ways and Means to Increase Loan Funds.
COMMITTEE ON JEWISH EVANGELISM	Co-operate with State and Local Forces in Jewish Evangelism—Promote Jewish Fellowship Week—Promote "Jewish Night" in Revivals—Appoint and Direct Specialized Workers Among the Jews—Produce and Distribute Literature—Plan Conferences and General Promotion.
COMMITTEE ON INVESTMENT-PROPERTY-INSURANCE	Recommendations Concerning Properties of the Board—Consider Matters Pertaining to Insurance—Investment of Available Funds.

HOME MISSION BOARD SUNDAY SCHOOL WORK. By the early 1870's the economic situation in the South was such that the Southern Baptist Sunday School Board, created in 1863, was consolidated with the Domestic and Indian Mission Board in 1873. The following year, the name of the consolidated board was changed to Home Mission Board. A debt on the Sunday School Board was assumed by the consolidated Home Mission Board, which continued the publication of the Sunday school paper *Kind Words*. The old debt was gradually reduced through the profits made on this publication. The Home Mission Board ceased the publication of the Sunday school periodicals but published in *Kind Words* the Sunday school lesson of the week. By 1878 the board reported that "its lessons are now guiding the study of God's word of one hundred and fifty thousand persons every week. . . . The number of papers issued Monthly (Weekly, Semi-Monthly, Monthly, and Lesson Papers) is 176,000."

By Jan., 1884, the debt on the old Sunday School Board was liquidated. From then on, profits made on the Sunday school publications went into the board's treasury. The board reported in 1885 that the treasury was receiving $1,000 a year royalty on its Sunday school publications. Inasmuch as the contract with the publishers would expire in June, 1886, the board suggested that a forward step should be planned in facing the new situation.

> A committee of wise and prudent brethren ought to give earnest consideration to the question how far it is proper for the Board to attempt to furnish Sunday-school literature to the Baptist churches of the South. Here is a wide field of usefulness and future influence. Shall we attempt it, or shall we surrender it to others?

The Convention in session at Augusta, Ga., 1885, approved the following report of a committee:

> In view of the early expiration of the contract for the publication of *Kind Words*, we suggest to the Home Board to mature some plan by which these growing demands may be met. With Rev. Samuel Boykin [q.v.] as chief, supported by such talent as can be found in our midst, this paper would meet all of the demands of the case, and none of our people would look either North or West for any Sabbath-school literature.

The following year, Secretary Isaac Taylor Tichenor (q.v.) in the Home Mission Board report announced to the Convention that the board, in obedience to the suggestion of the previous year, had made arrangements to continue the publication of *Kind Words* "and also to bring out by or before October next a full grade of *Quarterlies* three in number, and a *Magazine for Teachers*. . . . The Board bespeaks for the new publisher that will assume the publication of our Sunday-school periodicals, on the first of June next, the general and hearty support of the Baptist Sunday-schools in the South."

The new venture of the Home Mission Board in the field of Sunday school literature aroused opposition on two grounds. Many Baptist pastors thought that a mission board ought not to go into the publication of Sunday school literature. Others opposed the venture because they believed that the American Baptist Publication Society, after a history of more than 65 years, was furnishing satisfactory literature to the Baptist Sunday schools of the South. But there were reasons for the new venture. The Home Mission Board reported:

Some of our pastors have expressed the opinion that the International series does not fully meet the needs of our Sunday-schools; that we should have something which shall bring our denominational principles and practices more frequently and more strongly in contact with the minds of our children. The Board sympathizes with this view, and respectfully suggests to the Convention the desirableness of adopting some measures, either by modification of the International Lessons, or something in addition to them, to meet a want so vital to the best interest of our churches.

The increasing success of the Sunday school program of the Home Mission Board brought increasing complications. By 1890 the success of the venture and the opposition to its being carried on by a mission board were such that many ardent supporters of the Home Mission Board began to think that the Sunday school work should be undertaken by a separate board. In 1890 Secretary Tichenor in the home mission report to the Convention gave a survey of the situation.

Nearly thirty years ago the Convention entered upon the work of Sunday-school publication, which has been continued by its order and under its direction to the present time.

When the Board was removed to Atlanta it found a number of these publications placed in its charge. A contract with Burke & Co., of Macon, Ga., having five years to run, was then in process of execution. They were yielding the Convention a net income of one thousand dollars per annum. The then recent introduction of the *International Lessons* had caused rapid improvement in the character of the literature furnished the Sunday-schools of the land. The Board saw that during the existence of this contract with Burke & Co., it would be difficult, if not impossible, to improve the publications of the Convention so as to adapt them to the wants of our schools, and that unless this was done it was only a question of time when they would be superseded by others, and a valuable property of the Convention perish in its hands.

To avoid such a disaster and to carry out the purpose of the Convention in calling them into existence, the Board submitted to the Convention the question of improving them and under its direction subsequently submitted a contract for that purpose. Both the suggestion for the improvement and the contract for that purpose received the approval of the Convention without a word of opposition or a dissenting vote.

The present *Kind Words* series, after its appearance received the heartiest indorsement of the Convention, and its unanimous resolve "to do all in its power to foster, sustain and advance this great interest of the denomination." Under the existing arrangement these publications have attained a success most gratifying to the Board. They are conducted with an ability that from their first issue has placed them among the best Sunday-school periodicals in the land. Their teachings have commanded the confidence and the admiration of many of our best Sunday-school workers. They have escaped criticism at a time when there was every incentive to attack. They have, year by year, steadily increased, and are now rapidly enlarging their circulation. Their success is no longer problematical. The property of the Convention in them has, in little more than three years, so augmented in value that what could not then have been sold for exceeding five thousand dollars is now worth thirty thousand, and at the expiration of the present contract can be made to yield to the Convention ten per cent annually upon that amount.

An honored brother of this body, having given notice that he would advocate at this session of the Convention the appointment of a Board of Sunday-school publications to which they shall hereafter be committed, the Board deems it proper to say:

1. That, in all its acts as they relate to these publications, it has, at every step, carefully sought and implicitly obeyed the instructions of this body.

2. That, in the difficult and delicate task of managing these publications, it has, according to the wisdom given it, sought the best interest of the Convention and of the churches it represents.

3. It has sometimes been silent when its failure to speak might be construed into confession of wrong or mistaken action, because it desired peace in our brotherhood more than it wanted justice for itself. Standing to-day in the presence of this body, which has so long honored it with its confidence, it can say, in all good conscience before God and man, that the review of its connection with these publications fails to bring to light one action taken by it that it would wish to change, or one word it has spoken which it would wish to blot from its record.

Holding the highest estimate of the importance of this work, of its present and future value to the Convention and to the denomination, and yielding to none in our desire to promote through them the religious welfare of our people the Board, cheerfully submits this question to the Convention. If it shall be your pleasure to commit this great and growing interest to a separate Board, we will rejoice that the success it has attained in our hands has made such a separation an act of wisdom, and we will heartily cooperate with the new Board in the work of the Convention. Should the Convention continue these publications in our hands we will, as heretofore, comply with its instructions and use our best endeavors to increase their circulation and their usefulness.

Out of this complicated situation the Convention created the second Sunday School Board and ordered the Home Mission Board to transfer to the new Sunday School Board all of its publications and Sunday school activities. Tichenor, in his program to save the home front of the Southern Baptist Convention, using the teaching in the Sunday schools of the Baptist churches of the South as one of his major lines of defense and attack, succeeded so well that a great field of activity and progress was opened to Southern Baptists in the new Sunday school program.

BIBLIOGRAPHY: Southern Baptist Convention, *Annuals* (1873–90).

W. W. BARNES

HOME MISSION STUDY BOOKS AND BOOKS PUBLISHED. The Home Mission Board, through its Department of Editorial Service, edits and produces annually five mission study books, graded according to age groups: Adults, Young People, Intermediates, Juniors, and Primaries or Sunbeams. For each textbook a pamphlet of background material and teaching helps is produced. The board handles its own printing contracts in Atlanta and the books are distributed through state Baptist Book Stores, owned and operated by the Sunday School Board. The theme for annual mission study is chosen by the committee on editorial service. Usually, the theme is the same as the interdenominational theme of about 35 Protestant denominations. The Protestant groups are combined in the Joint Commission on Missionary Education of the National Council of Churches. Before the affiliation of the Missionary Education Movement with the National Council of Churches, the Home Mission Board editor visited and co-operated with the movement in the choice of themes and in the selection of books which might be usable for background material in mission study among Southern Baptists. While the theme, if it suits the purposes of the administration, is followed as a matter of convenience, there is no affiliation with the Joint Commission. The Missionary Education Council of Southern Baptist Agencies, made up of editorial representatives of Southern Baptist agencies, renders invaluable assistance in the selection of themes, titles, and in setting up specifications for mission study courses and books.

In 1955, Baptist Book Stores handled 222,767 home mission books. In addition to the present editor, John Caylor, other editors, including Joe W. Burton, Una Roberts Lawrence, and Victor Irvine Masters (*q.v.*) have served. Department heads and missionaries of the board have contributed largely to the writing of mission study books.

Woman's Missionary Union, in its promotion of missionary education, the schools of missions program, and all-church study courses, promotes the study of home mission books.

JOHN CAYLOR

HOME MISSIONS. The official organ of publicity for the Home Mission Board, a 32-page monthly publication, lithographed and circulated by subscription plan. Circulation is promoted through joint subscriptions with *The Commission*, Foreign Mission Board journal; individual subscription rates; and a club rate for 10 or more. The magazine is edited by John Caylor; Mrs. Mildred Dunn is associate editor. Courts Redford, executive secretary-treasurer, writes an editorial page for each issue, setting forth the administrative angle. Material for the magazine is submitted largely by missionaries, no paid writers being used. Advertising, furnished by a national advertising agency, is used with limitation and restrictions. A circulation department provides stencils and keeps up circulation files. Department heads consider the magazine their own publication and promote both subscriptions and the solicitation and production of articles for use in the magazine.

The 1955 circulation of *Home Missions* averaged almost 150,000, with peak printing 155,000 in December. In its present form *Home Missions* has been in continuous production since 1930, when Secretary J. B. Lawrence enlarged his periodic tract into a monthly publication. He served as editor of the magazine until his retirement from the board in 1953, when the present editor was named. In September, 1954, the name *Southern Baptist Home Missions* was changed to *Home Missions*.

Predecessors of *Home Missions* are *Southern Baptist Home Missions*, *Home and Foreign Fields*, and *Our Home Field*.

JOHN CAYLOR

HOMER MEMORIAL HOSPITAL. Built by the city of Homer, La., in 1949 and leased to the Louisiana Baptist Convention for 20 years at $1 per year. The trustees are elected by the convention. The hospital was opened for service in July, 1949. In 1954 it treated 7,128 patients for which it received $618,457.03. Its capacity was 29 beds, and a 15-bed extension was under construction. Its total value was $304,016.42. It treats all races, is conditionally accredited, is not approved for internship, and has no debt. Its charity work in 1954 totaled $2,000.

R. HOUSTON SMITH

HOMILETICS. See SERMON PREPARATION.

HONDURAS. See GUATEMALA-HONDURAS, MISSION IN.

HONESTY. A disposition to truthfulness in thought, speech, and conduct. In general the term means freedom from deception. Complete honesty includes both inward integrity and outward truthfulness.

In Christian morality honesty has its sanction in the experience of redemption whereby the righteousness and truth of God come to expression in the life of the believer by the power of the Holy Spirit. It is the nature of the child of God that he is honest, truthful, and trustworthy. Having received the word of the kingdom, the "honest and good heart" keeps this word and brings "forth fruit with patience" (Luke 8:15). The Christian life is characterized by inward integrity, love of the truth, pursuit of the truth, and a sincere effort to bring life into conformity with the truth.

It follows that there is no place in the Christian's life for deception either of self or of others. The Christian rejects all forms of hypocrisy. He faces realities without self-deceiving rationalizations, and accepts responsibility for his deeds without blaming others. Regarding his own life, he permits neither vain pretensions nor utter self-contempt. Truthfulness is the law of his thinking.

This inward integrity is validated in words and deeds. The speech of the Christian is marked by sincerity. At no time is there a conscious effort to deceive others. Such complete truthfulness in speech excludes the use of "mental reservations." Likewise, falsehoods for purpose of suggestion and altruistic lying for the benefit of the deceived have no justification. An earnest effort is made to guard against practicing social deceptions. Expressions of courtesy are spoken with sincerity, and all verbal agreements and promises are kept inviolate.

In his vocation and in all financial transactions a genuine Christian is conscientious and dependable. There is no stealing of another's possessions or ideas, no cheating in weights and measures or in hours and wages. Just debts are honored and taxes are paid without evasions. In the interest of stable government he has respect for existing laws, and he seeks equity and justice in making and enforcing laws. Recognizing the infinite worth of the individual, he has regard for the rights and possessions of each person. In all the varying circumstances of economic, political, and social life, it is the Christian's sincere intention to act, think, and speak truthfully.

BIBLIOGRAPHY: R. C. Cabot, *Honesty* (1938). *Encyclopedia of Religion and Ethics* (1951). L. H. Marshall, *The Challenge of New Testament Ethics* (1950).

C. A. INSKO

HONG KONG BAPTIST ASSOCIATION. Organized in 1937 with 44 representatives from three churches and three mission chapels, with approximately 1,000 members. In 1955 the association reported 14 churches, 20 mission chapels, 8,500 members, 14 ordained Chinese pastors, and 34 unordained Chinese preachers, Bible women, and pastor's assistants. The work of the association is divided into 10 boards: evangelism, education, Sunday school, Young People, publication, benevolence, seminary, college, Woman's Missionary Union, and medical. The Hong Kong Baptist Theological Seminary, organized in 1951, now has an enrolment of 54 men and women who are preparing for work in the Baptist churches of Hong Kong and among the Chinese in other parts of the Orient. A clinic was established in Hong Kong in Jan., 1956. Three high schools—Pooi Ching, Pooi To, and Henrietta Hall Shuck—and one primary school are affiliated with the Hong Kong association.

Baptists form one fourth of the entire non-Catholic Christian community on Hong Kong Island and the leased territories of mainland China, generally known as Kowloon and the New Territories. (The total population of Hong Kong Island and the leased territories is estimated at 2,500,000.)

MARY C. ALEXANDER

HONG KONG BAPTIST THEOLOGICAL SEMINARY. See HONG KONG–MACAO, MISSION IN.

HONG KONG–MACAO, MISSION IN. Organized May, 1952, with seven missionaries, three relocated in the British colony of Hong Kong from the mainland of China, and four stationed in the Portuguese colony of Macao. John Lewis Shuck (*q.v.*) and Henrietta Hall Shuck (*q.v.*) arrived in Macao in 1836, and they with Issachar Jacox Roberts began the first Baptist mission work in Hong Kong in 1842. Although they have been in Macao since 1910, no Southern Baptists were stationed in Hong Kong until 1949. Co-operating with national leaders, 19 missionaries in Hong Kong and two in Macao carried on evangelistic work in 1955 through 18 chapels and 14 organized Baptist churches, the largest of which is the Kowloon City Baptist Church with 2,000 members; total Baptist membership is 8,399. Hong Kong Baptist Association was organized in 1937. Six Baptist day schools enrol 6,000 pupils through senior high school level. The Baptist press, formally organized in 1952, publishes and circulates throughout Southeast Asia Bibles, books, tracts, and periodicals for Sunday schools and other church organizations. The Hong Kong Baptist Theological Seminary, founded in 1951, has 50 young people in training for future Baptist leadership. Medical work was formally begun with the establishment of the Hong Kong Baptist Clinic in Jan., 1956.

JAMES D. BELOTE

HOPKINS, GRANVILLE SHELBY (b. Neosho, Mo., Oct. 10, 1878; d. Dallas, Tex., Aug. 2, 1953). A schoolteacher and acting postmaster at Amarillo, Tex., Hopkins was a zealous promoter of Sunday school training and enlargement. He served as education director of Cliff Temple Baptist Church, Dallas, Tex., 1919–26; and as the third Sunday school secretary of the Baptist General Convention of Texas, 1926–48, during which time Texas Sunday school enrolment increased from 387,515 to 712,780. Hopkins inspired church leaders to make wider use of the Sunday school in evangelism, stewardship, and enlistment. Author of *Tomorrow You Lead*, a training course book designed to encourage young people to prepare for service, he was a vigorous promoter of higher standards in Sunday school administration and the improvement of buildings for educational purposes. Hopkins planned and supervised annual Sunday school conventions which in 1948 reached a registration of 5,378.

ANDREW ALLEN

HOSPITAL COMMISSION OF KENTUCKY BAPTISTS. Established in 1951 to promote and enlarge the Baptist hospital program in Kentucky by putting all activities of the Baptist

hospitals under one control. It was authorized by the General Association of Baptists in Kentucky. The commission is composed of 12 members elected by and from the boards of trustees of the three Baptist hospitals located at Lexington, Louisville, and Paducah. The general purpose of the hospital commission was to complete and equip the Western Baptist Hospital, Paducah, and the Central Baptist Hospital, Lexington; to build an addition to Kentucky Baptist Hospital, Louisville; and to have general supervision over all operations and affairs of the three hospitals. H. L. Dobbs, of Kentucky Baptist Hospital, is executive secretary of the hospital commission. In this capacity he is general administrator of the three hospitals and liaison officer between the three boards of trustees and the hospital commission. Under the direction of their hospital commission, Kentucky Baptists now own and operate three hospitals with a total of 725 beds. The three hospitals are valued at almost $10,000,000.
H. L. DOBBS

HOSPITALS, BAPTIST. A hospital is an institution in which medical treatment is given to the sick and injured. Originally hospitals were little more than houses of refuge where the homeless, sick, poor, and infirm were received and cared for at no cost. Frequently the term "pesthouse" was applied to these early institutions. The first hospitals were established and operated by churches and benevolent societies, and in many instances the religious emphasis was given greater consideration than nursing skill and medical science. However, these services have improved through the years, and the modern hospital is headquarters for health, engaged in four distinct functions: the care of the sick, preventive medicine, research, and professional education for doctors and nurses.

Hospitals operated by Southern Baptist groups have sought to pattern their ministry of healing after the teachings and example of Jesus Christ. To the functions of many other first-class and accredited hospitals, Baptists have added the teaching of the Bible in courses required for graduation from their schools of nursing, the preaching of the gospel by specially trained chaplains, and personal witnessing for Christ by dedicated Christian nurses and other hospital personnel. Many Scripture references have been cited fully justifying such a program, but the one most frequently used is, "Jesus went about all the cities and villages, teaching in their synagogues, and preaching the gospel of the kingdom, and healing every sickness and every disease among the people" (Matt. 9:35).

It has been found that the patient and his family respond most favorably to such a program; hence the Baptist hospital has become an effective ministry and evangelistic agency of the denomination. Many Baptist hospitals have provided facilities for carrying on the threefold program in the design of the building. Radio and public address systems have been installed with speakers at the patient's bedside, enabling the chaplain to deliver gospel messages at regularly scheduled times. In many of the hospitals the day is begun with an encouraging scriptural devotion which can be heard by the patients and hospital personnel. Chapel services are provided for employees, ambulatory patients, and visitors. The chaplains make daily visits to the patients' rooms and wards and hold conferences in their offices. The team concept in providing for the patient's total needs is receiving enthusiastic approval by the doctor, nurse, and chaplain.

There is a growing conviction on the part of many Southern Baptists that the obligation to provide their own hospitals where young women can train for the nursing profession and young doctors can serve their internship and residences in a Christian atmosphere is no less than the obligation to maintain Christian colleges and seminaries. It is pointed out that Christian physicians and nurses are greatly needed on the mission fields and that Baptists cannot expect other groups to train them. The doctor and nurse minister to the families in times of greatest need; if they have a high quality of professional training plus Christian compassion and love, they can be very effective in witnessing for Christ and making friends for the Baptist cause.

Hospital boards, executives, and administrators are definitely committed to a program which has as its principal objective the creation of an atmosphere or climate in the hospital which will be friendly to the patient's needs, both physical and spiritual. That such efforts are being successful is evidenced by the increasing demand for the services of the hospitals and by requests for the establishment of additional Baptist hospitals in towns and cities throughout the Convention territory.

The Missouri Baptist Sanitarium, now Missouri Baptist Hospital, located in St. Louis, is credited with being the first Baptist hospital to be established within the territory of the Convention. In 1890 W. G. Mayfield, a practicing physician and Baptist layman, on his own initiative opened the hospital in an old residence with less than a dozen beds. After a great struggle the Missouri Baptist General Association assumed responsibility for ownership and management and established it as an agency of the association.

In 1903 Len G. Broughton, pastor of the Tabernacle Baptist Church of Atlanta, Ga., and former practicing physician, convinced that the ministry of healing was a Christian obligation, led his church in establishing what is now the Georgia Baptist Hospital. In 1913 the Baptist Convention of Georgia took it over and expanded its facilities until today it is one of the largest church-owned hospitals in the South.

At the meeting of the Southern Baptist Convention in Houston in 1915 an organization was formed of representatives from the various

STATISTICAL INFORMATION—BAPTIST HOSPITALS—1954

State	Name and Location	Bed Capacity	Bassinets	Admissions	Births	Receipts from Operations	Receipts from Denomination	No. of Bldgs.	Value of Bldgs.	Expended on Charity	Nurses in Training
Alabama	Baptist, Birmingham	300	27	14,365	1,582	$2,173,350	$ 51,400	4	$ 1,525,250	$ 24,835	119
Alabama	Baptist, Gadsden	92	22	5,176	1,073				301,000		0
Arkansas	Arkansas Baptist, Little Rock	305	41	21,121	1,803	1,694,630	45,000	3	1,303,411	103,011	219
Florida	Baptist, Pensacola	150	30	16,188	892	907,230		1	2,000,000	20,098	0
Florida	Baptist Memorial, Jacksonville	310	not open in 1954								
Florida	South Florida Baptist, Plant City	100	30	4,038	768	320,509		4	1,275,687	15,961	0
Georgia	Georgia Baptist, Atlanta	475	65	21,978	3,036	2,918,741	100,000	21	4,841,007	270,844	352
Kentucky	Southeastern Kentucky Baptist, Corbin	55	20	2,264	414	345,662	76,614		70,000		0
Kentucky	Central Baptist, Lexington	173	25	2,663	534	2,434,416	7,274	2	2,160,141	106,185	0
Kentucky	Kentucky Baptist, Louisville	345	50	31,672	2,984	432,036	2,543	5	2,920,770	9,807	165
Kentucky	Western Kentucky Baptist, Paducah	117	16	7,512	592	1,378,721		3	1,420,180	31,607	0
Louisiana	Baptist, Alexandria	214	28	22,125	814	1,807,888		3	1,876,262	19,942	47
Louisiana	Baton Rouge General, Baton Rouge	250	40	16,107	2,448	130,163	102	8	2,425,855	1,000	44
Louisiana	Beauregard Memorial, DeRidder	31	11	1,586	371	144,980	334	1	241,000		0
Louisiana	Homer Memorial, Homer	28	6	1,437	192	3,164,142	160,000	1	309,410	106,957	0
Louisiana	Southern Baptist, New Orleans	500	85	51,210	3,978	2,158,274	33,889	7	5,011,832	83,385	190
Mississippi	Mississippi Baptist, Jackson	308	40	24,971	1,587	2,458,063	33,137	6	1,637,879	120,000	221
Missouri	Missouri Baptist, St. Louis	486	39	19,399	1,162			14	3,088,251		144
North Carolina	North Carolina Baptist, Winston-Salem	338	62	67,753	1,724	1,516,964	69,237	2	4,900,000	500,247	175
Oklahoma	Southwest Baptist, Mangum	50	10	1,369	148	116,652	578	1	209,014	528	0
Oklahoma	Miami Baptist, Miami	60	12	5,317	491	235,725		3	220,200	3,112	0
Oklahoma	Oklahoma Baptist, Muskogee	88	16	2,282	352	279,923		4	475,000	11,066	45
Oklahoma	Grand Valley, Pryor	35	11	115	18	3,223		1	500,000		0
Oklahoma	Bristow Memorial, Bristow	28	7	152	10 (Dec.)	3,030			264,000		0
Oklahoma	Enid General, Enid	110	20	2,963	244	439,969	5,000	1	402,092	13,243	28
Oklahoma	Memorial, Perry	28	7	924	120	100,084		1	350,000	5,251	0
Oklahoma	Municipal Hospital, Stillwater	85	24	5,510	650	314,416		1	491,500	6,123	0
South Carolina	South Carolina Baptist, Columbia	212	33	9,495	1,120	1,205,272	108,271	3	2,054,914	162,710	200
Tennessee	East Tennessee Baptist, Knoxville	254	36	13,125	1,935	1,583,087	91,277	3	4,000,000	34,832	128
Tennessee	Mid-state Baptist, Nashville	245	55	14,974	2,753	1,898,162	68,458	12	5,000,000	141,233	98
Tennessee	Baptist Memorial, Memphis	550	50	66,038	3,087	5,412,758	42,236	3	14,500,000	430,411	296
Texas	Hendrick Memorial, Abilene	205	20	11,624	1,118	1,207,242		2	928,778	94,525	60
Texas	Baptist of Southeast Texas	125	20	6,693	976	896,626	27,876	2	1,016,627	20,016	30
Texas	Baylor University, Dallas	600	109	34,196	1,935	4,696,981	178,038	5	10,000,000	520,857	135
Texas	Valley Baptist, Harlingen	153	28	7,019	766	728,433	40,000	3	2,176,000	70,120	0
Texas	Memorial Baptist, Houston	402	60	26,195	2,466	2,858,523	106,716	3	8,105,887	37,103	138
Texas	Baptist Memorial, San Antonio	278	75	14,777	4,042	2,134,674	53,164	8	3,000,000	103,077	108
Texas	Hillcrest Memorial, Waco	165	27	12,187	1,454	966,451	71,460	4	1,353,231	66,487	25
Virginia	Virginia Baptist, Lynchburg	100	24	4,080	1,054	426,471	63,769	5	1,169,935	20,827	60

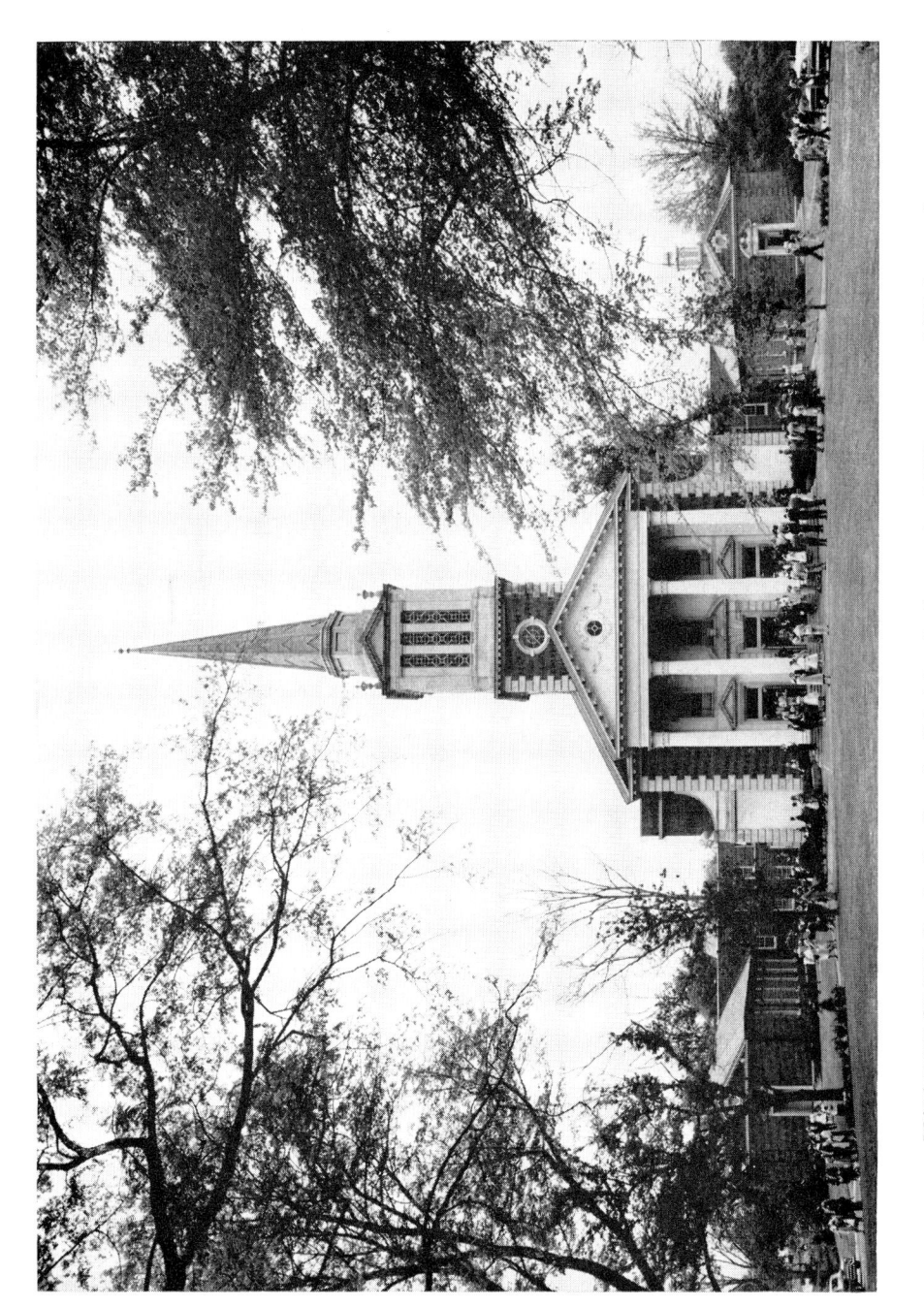

FIRST BAPTIST CHURCH, Decatur, Ga. Georgian Colonial auditorium completed 1951, seats over 1,600. Property including 38-department educational unit worth $1,900,000.

FIRST BAPTIST CHURCH, Jackson, Miss. Formed 1830, auditorium of English Gothic architecture seating 1,900 erected 1925. Membership 1956 almost 5,000. It has Sunday school accommodations for 3,000. Right wing was built in 1954. Property worth $3,000,000.

Baptist hospitals in the South. This organization took the name of "Southern Baptist Hospital Conference." The American Hospital Association, at its meeting in Sept., 1916, had amended its constitution "to provide for sectional meetings," and plans were under way for two sections to be established in the South, one west of the Mississippi and one east. The hospital committee recommended that the hospital workers participate in these meetings to the end "that our Baptist institutions be kept abreast with the latest hospital methods and management, and that the consideration of our hospital work become a part of the regular program of this Convention."

Gradually Southern Baptists felt the need for more hospitals and established institutions in nearly all of the Southern states. By 1918 there were 11 hospitals with a value of $2,000,000 and a bed capacity of 1,250. At the end of 1954 there were 39 Baptist hospitals already established, one under construction, and two proposed. Two of these are owned by the Convention and operated by its Hospital Board; and a few are owned and operated by district associations, but the majority are owned and operated by state conventions. These hospitals treat approximately 400,000 patients per year. Their property is valued at $99,954,372.33, with a bed capacity of 7,534 and 1,248 bassinets for newborn babies.

FRANK TRIPP

HOUSTON, SAMUEL (b. Rockbridge County, Va., Mar. 2, 1793; d. Huntsville, Tex., July 26, 1863). Baptist layman, president of the Republic of Texas, member of the United States Senate, governor of Texas. Houston, said to have been irreligious during his youth, was baptized Nov. 19, 1854, by Rufus C. Burleson (q.v.) and was an active and liberal member of the Independence Baptist Church during the latter part of his life. His conversion was doubtless due primarily to the influence of his devout wife, who was Margaret Lea before their marriage in 1840. Houston then attended preaching and prayer meeting services regularly, attended district associations and state conventions, both of which he addressed on such topics as temperance, education, and work among the Indians. He made a special contribution of $350 to Baylor University and served on the advisory board of the school. Houston was also at one time a member of the board of directors for the Baptist state convention and a life member of the convention.

Receiving only a few terms of formal schooling, Houston worked for a short time as a village store clerk, spent nearly three years with the Cherokee Indians, enlisted in the United States Army, and in succeeding years became a lieutenant, lawyer, district attorney, adjutant general, Congressman, and Tennessee governor. When his first marriage to Eliza H. Allen ended in failure after four months, Houston resigned his governorship, left for Arkansas, and spent the next six years in diplomatic and business work among the Cherokees, who granted him citizenship and an Indian wife, Tiana Rogers, whom he married in 1830.

After applying for a grant of land, Houston arrived in Texas in Dec., 1832, and made his way to Nacogdoches. Soon caught up in the rising storm of opposition to Mexico in 1835, Houston, with his commanding presence and capacity to arouse confidence and enthusiasm, rose quickly to prominence. Elected major general of the Texas army Nov. 12, 1835, he later became a delegate to the 1836 Convention in Texas, signed the March declaration of independence, and two days later was elected commander-in-chief of the army. His decisive victory at the Battle of San Jacinto came on Apr. 21, 1836. Houston was elected president of the republic on Sept. 5, 1836, and later secured recognition of the republic by the United States, served as a representative to the Texas congress, was again elected president, served in the United States Senate for 14 years, and was inaugurated governor of Texas Dec. 21, 1859. On Feb. 23, 1861, the people of Texas voted to secede from the United States, and when Houston opposed that action, the governor's office was declared vacant. Lieutenant Governor Edward Clark was made governor, and Houston, deposed, relinquished his office and retired to his farm at Huntsville, Tex.

JACK D. HARWELL

HOUSTON FEMALE COLLEGE. Began in 1853 as Perry Baptist Female Seminary, located at Perry, Ga., in Houston County. It was chartered Feb. 18, 1854, as Houston Female College. The chief figure in its establishment was Henry M. Holtzclaw, and its self-perpetuating board of directors, called incorporators, was composed of citizens of Houston County. In the late 1880's the school merged with a school for boys and was sold soon after to the town of Perry.

ARTHUR JACKSON

HOUSTON HIGH SCHOOL. Established at Arabi, Ga., in Houston Association, from which it received its name, in 1897. The school existed until about 1902.

ARTHUR JACKSON

HOWARD, ROBERT CLINTON (b. Devine County, Tex., June 26, 1887; d. Oklahoma City, Okla., May 6, 1947). Baptist pastor, businessman, denominational leader. From the age of 19 until his death, he sold insurance for Heralds of Liberty, now Liberty National Life Insurance Company. In May, 1924, he became pastor of Kelham Avenue Baptist Church, Oklahoma City; and for 23 years he served without salary, received more than 6,500 additions, more than one half coming for baptism, and led his church to organize 23 missions. He was a charter director of the Baptist Foundation of Oklahoma and president of the Baptist General Convention of Oklahoma at the time of his death.

DAVID C. HALL

HOWARD COLLEGE. As early as 1830, Baptist leaders in Alabama, under the impulse of the foreign mission movement, were discussing the need to educate their preachers. The state conventions of 1832, 1833, and 1834 moved toward a plan for a manual labor institute of a type being tried in several states. Such a school was opened in Jan., 1836, on a farm near Greensboro. Faults soon apparent in that type of education led to the abandonment of the school in less than two years.

The experiment had, however, emphasized a need. The convention in 1841 procured a charter for a school with both literary and theological departments, which opened as Howard College in Marion, Jan. 3, 1842, with nine boys. Connected with the school's beginnings were E. D. King, a wealthy planter who had moved to Alabama from South Carolina, and Milo P. Jewett, James Harvey DeVotie (q.v.), and Daniel Perrin Bestor, Sr. (q.v.), all preachers who had come to Alabama from New England by way of South Carolina. Basil Manly, Sr. (q.v.), president of the University of Alabama and valued adviser to the founders of Howard College, had been pastor in Charleston, S. C. Under the first president, Samuel Sterling Sherman, a graduate of Middlebury College in Vermont, the college grew rapidly. In 1848 it had 145 students and graduated its first class, four members having B.A. degrees and three having B.S. degrees. Henry Talbird, coming from the First Baptist Church of Montgomery to succeed Sherman in 1852, built a larger college with greater facilities when the first was destroyed by fire in 1854. He brought the endowment of the college to more than $200,000.

When war broke out in 1861, Talbird and most of the faculty and students entered the Confederate army, where Talbird served with distinction as colonel. One or two older professors and a few young boys carried on classes through most of the war. In 1863 the trustees authorized the use of two dormitories as a Confederate hospital. In 1865 Federal troops housed Negro freedmen in one of the dormitories. When Talbird declined to resume the presidency after the war, Jabez Lamar Monroe Curry (q.v.) was elected. Though Curry later became one of the greatest builders of the new South, he wrote ruefully to J. H. DeVotie that everywhere he found spirits willing but pocketbooks weak. After two years he resigned. E. Q. Thornton, who acted as president one year (1868–69), and S. R. Freeman, who was president two years (1869–71), also served during periods of financial stress. In 1867–68 only 50 students were enrolled. In the next session there were 184. The struggle of the college was the same as that of the entire South during reconstruction. The college did not close, though between 1866 and 1878 it sometimes graduated only one man.

J. T. Murfee, president from 1871 to 1887, was an excellent organizer, disciplinarian, and teacher. Associated longest with him and with the college were Thomas J. Dill, professor of Greek and Latin for 30 years (1869–99), and A. D. Smith, who began in 1881 a continuous service of 62 years as professor of mathematics, acting president, and trustee. From the classrooms of these men and their colleagues went students who distinguished themselves in many fields. David Gordon Lyon, '75, became Harvard University's authority in Semitic languages. John R. Tyson, '77, was chief justice of the supreme court of Alabama. Samuel W. Welsh, '80, established in Alabama a public health service that was copied in most of the nation. John Richard Sampey (q.v.), '82, was for a generation professor of Hebrew in Southern Baptist Theological Seminary and for many years its president. William Garrott Brown, '86, wrote a history of the South and was a contributing editor to Harper's *Weekly*. John William McCollum (q.v.), '86, was the first Southern Baptist missionary to Japan.

Offers of a site and of large support led the convention and most of the faculty to favor moving the college to the rapidly growing industrial city of Birmingham. The college opened the fall session of 1887 in Birmingham with 85 students. B. F Riley, president 1888–93, erected permanent buildings and brought the enrolment to 206. The panic of 1893 threw most of Birmingham into bankruptcy and halted the promise of swift growth in the college. The administrations of A. W. McGaha (1893–96), A. D. Smith (1896–97), and Frank M. Roof (1897–1902) were holding actions during which the faculty saved the college as they had saved it in Marion. In 1902 A. P. Montague came from the presidency of Furman University to begin 10 years of notable service at Howard. He built Renfroe Hall, the principal dormitory, and Montague Hall, the present library, and raised nearly $100,000 of endowment.

James M. Shelburne (1912–17) abolished the military system which had governed Howard students since the War Between the States. He opened the college to women in 1913, established the summer school in 1915, and the next year dropped the preparatory courses which had been carried in the Howard Academy. From the 75 Million Campaign, Howard received $300,000 for endowment.

John C. Dawson, professor of modern languages since 1903 and president, 1921–31, expanded and strengthened the faculty and earned new academic recognition. He was principally responsible for Howard's being admitted into the Southern Association of Colleges and Secondary Schools in 1920—the second college in Alabama to be admitted, the University of Alabama having been the first. In 1926 the Association of American Universities put Howard on its list of approved colleges, and the American Association of University Women reaffirmed the approval it had given in 1918. Extension classes first offered to public schoolteachers in 1920 were enrolling 272 in 1925, and the attendance in day classes in regular session rose to 600 in the same year. A. D. Smith Science Hall was built in 1922, Mamie Mell Smith Hall for women in 1928, and the gymnasium in 1930. A civic campaign in Birmingham in 1926 added $350,000 to the endowment and made possible the procuring of $150,000 from the General Education Board. In the spring of 1927 the college opened a Division of Pharmacy.

The administration of T. V. Neal (1932–39) fell during the hard years of the depression. Enrolments, however, held up, and there was never a question of suspending any major activity.

In 1939 Harwell G. Davis was called from his law practice to the presidency of Howard. With the support of a determined board of trustees, he wiped out a debt of $400,000, restored the credit of the college, and gave security to the faculty. He repaired and enlarged college buildings and bought adjacent property. A Navy V-12 training program gave the college a stable enrolment and income in World War II. A centennial campaign for 1942 brought approximately $400,000 before it was interrupted by the war.

In 1947 the college set up an Extension Division for Christian Training for adults, particularly preachers and Sunday school teachers, in communities throughout the state. The division has grown from 15 centers and 500 students to 54 centers with more than 120 instructors and 2,300 students (in 1956). This project, generally known as the Howard Plan, has been adopted by several Baptist colleges in other states.

An Evening Division, inaugurated in 1951, on the campus had grown to an enrolment of 252 students in the spring of 1956. Between 1925 and World War II, attendance in regular session averaged 600. Returning veterans brought a peak enrolment of 1,335 in the fall of 1947. The receding tide of veterans dropped attendance to 897 in 1951. Since 1951 attendance has climbed to 1,697 in day and evening classes on the campus. The total enrolment in campus and off-campus classes was more than 4,600 in 1955. Since the college opened in 1842, it has enrolled, to June 15, 1956, more than 28,100 students and has graduated 6,421.

In 1956 the total income of the institution from tuition and fees, endowment, auxiliary enterprises, activities, Extension Division, Cooperative Program, and other sources was $908,-000. Total expenses for the same year were $906,000. In 1952 Howard College was admitted to the American Association of Colleges for Teacher Education and to the American Association of Colleges of Pharmacy. It is rated as an "A" institution by the American Council of Pharmaceutical Education. In 1954 the college became a member of the National Association of Schools of Music. The college is approved by the Alabama State Department of Education for the training of elementary and high school teachers.

The first library was collected by President Sherman, who trundled in a wheelbarrow 1,200 books given by the citizens of Marion. The present library has 80,000 volumes and 620 current periodicals. A new library under construction can house 500,000 books.

Howard has always been a college of liberal arts and sciences. For nearly 70 years Greek and Latin were required for the A.B. degree. As late as 1930, two modern foreign languages were required. Across the decades the prescribed curriculum has, course for course, paralleled that of other standard colleges. Howard has, however, made innovations. Its ideal is "the development of the many-sided, full-orbed man and woman." In 1945 it adopted a program of general education which it named the Nuclear Curriculum, to indicate the central core or nucleus of subjects about which educated persons should have competent knowledge. It has since modified that too-rigid list of fixed courses. All students take at least 42 semester hours of work in the areas of science, history, English, literature, social studies, Bible, and fine arts.

Howard has always been owned, controlled, and supported by the Alabama Baptist State Convention. The college actively promotes religion. Chapel exercises, vigorous religious organizations, and religious focus week indicate the purpose of the college to maintain the spirit of the founders. The motto on the college seal, *Deo et Doctrinae,* has always been translated "For God and Learning."

The trustees in 1946 bought 400 acres in the Shades Valley section of Birmingham for a new campus. The college added to its building fund about $1,250,000 in 1948. In 1951 the convention projected a plan to raise in five years $2,500,000 for buildings on the new campus and in 1955 authorized a second five-year plan to raise $500,000 a year for building. The master plan calls for 18 or 20 buildings of Southern Colonial (Williamsburg) exterior design but completely modern and functional inside. The library has been completed, and enough buildings have been constructed for the college to open all classes on the new campus in September, 1957.

BIBLIOGRAPHY: H. Holcombe, *History of the Rise and Progress of the Baptists in Alabama* (1840). C. D. Johnson, *Higher Education of Southern Baptists* (1955). B. F. Riley, *Memorial History of the Baptists of Alabama* (1923). H. A. Tupper, *A Decade of Foreign Missions, 1880–1890* (1891). P. P. BURNS

HOWARD PAYNE COLLEGE. Located at Brownwood, Tex., a coeducational institution of Texas Baptists offering B.A., B.S., and M.Ed. degrees; was founded by Pecan Valley Association on June 29, 1889. The founder was J. D. Robnett, pastor of the First Baptist Church of Brownwood, who stimulated interest in establishing the school and, as president of the board of trustees and financial agent, led in securing the first funds, faculty, equipment, and students. In Aug., 1889, he obtained a substantial gift from his brother-in-law, Edward Howard Payne, of Fulton, Mo., and the college was named for this donor.

Howard Payne opened Sept. 16, 1890, with A. J. Emerson as president and a faculty of nine. While the Main Administration Building was being constructed in 1890 and 1891, the school was conducted in Robnett Hall, a temporary three-story structure with 21 rooms, situated where the First Baptist Church now stands. When the Main Building became available in the fall of 1891, Robnett Hall was converted into a girls' dormitory until destroyed by fire in 1902.

An accumulated debt of $30,000, a drought, and the financial panic of 1893 precipitated a serious crisis. The president resigned, and Robnett was elected. He sacrificed both health and his own modest wealth to keep the college open. While he sought funds and students, J. H. Grove as dean directed academic affairs. Broken in health, Robnett accepted a Dallas pastorate in 1896, and Grove became president under contract to operate the school without cost to the trustees and association. By wise management this was accomplished, and when he resigned in 1908 the enrolment had increased from 164 to 353.

Howard Payne entered the correlation system, started by the Texas Baptist Education Commission in 1897, and ownership was transferred from Pecan Valley Association to the Baptist General Convention of Texas. This resulted in the liquidation of all indebtedness by 1901. Howard Payne, according to the correlation agreement, operated as a junior college and no degrees were conferred after 1901 until 1915. In 1907 a wing was added to the Main Administration Building.

John S. Humphreys served as acting president from 1908 until R. H. Hamilton became president in 1910. In 1911 Humphreys became president and in 1912 a girls' dormitory, Howard Payne Hall, was erected. James Milton Carroll (q.v.) was president in 1913 and 1914, and the college resumed offering four years of work. A deficit in operational expenses, aggravated by the financial reaction of World War I, produced a second serious crisis. Anderson Edith Baten (q.v.) was acting president until J. A. Tolman became president in 1917. A unit of the Students' Army Training Corps was set up in 1918 and two barracks erected. During the presidency of L. J. Mims, 1919–22, the Mims Auditorium was erected and an old high school building was purchased for an academy (now called Science Hall).

W. R. Hornburg acted as president until the election of Edgar Godbold in 1923, who served until 1929, when Thomas H. Taylor was chosen. The beginning of the depression in the fall of 1929 caught Howard Payne with a deficit that had accumulated from almost continuous operation through the twenties with an unbalanced budget. This precipitated the third serious financial crisis for the college.

Taylor inaugurated a policy of strict economy, "more and more on less and less." Operational expenses were stabilized, confidence restored, and, stimulated by the offer of a bequest from John G. Hardin, friends liquidated the indebtedness in 1934. The Hardin bequest of $305,000 became available at his death in 1939. J. A. Walker, long-time friend of the college, left a million dollars of endowment, which became available at his death in 1943.

John D. Robnett, Jr., was the first graduate of Howard Payne in 1895. Over 15,000 students have enrolled and 3,364 have received degrees (181 received diplomas during the junior college period). Among the distinguished graduates are William Richardson White, president of Baylor University; James Winfred Edgar, Texas State Commissioner of Education; Judge Few Brewster of the Supreme Court of Texas; and Anderson Monroe Baten, author and anthologist. The total enrolment for 1953–54 was 1,129; faculty totaled 50. Total income for the same year was $598,426.06. Gifts and grants from Texas Baptists provided $90,879.82 of this amount; endowment provided $64,932.41; and tuition and other sources provided the remainder.

In 1955 the main campus contained 11 acres with 10 permanent buildings, including a $903,-000 girls' dormitory completed that year. The college plant was valued at more than two and a half million dollars and the endowment was $1,895,804.70 at the close of 1954. Daniel Baker College, founded by Presbyterians in 1888 and in continuous operation since 1890, merged with Howard Payne in 1953, adding a campus with four permanent buildings with an endowment of $309,707.98.

BIBLIOGRAPHY: B. M. David, "A History of Howard Payne College." B. M. Hitt, "History of Howard Payne College" (1951). W. F. Ledlow, "The Development of Protestant Education in Texas" (1924). M. P. Moore, "The History of Howard Payne College from 1890 to 1898" (1940). W. A. Todd, "History of Pecan Valley and Brown County Associations" (1940).

D. D. TIDWELL

HOWELL, ROBERT BOYTÉ CRAWFORD (b. Wayne County, N. C., Mar. 10, 1801; d. Nashville, Tenn., Apr. 5, 1868). As a speaker, writer, and leader, he helped to lay the foundations of the Southern Baptist Convention. Of Episcopal heritage, he joined a rural Baptist church 14 miles from his home in 1821. He attended Columbian College, Washington, D. C. After the 1825–26 session he left for home to become a lawyer. However, at Portsmouth, Va., he was induced to become a missionary. Ordained in Jan., 1827, he became pastor of the Cumberland Street Baptist Church, Norfolk.

In July, 1834, he visited Nashville, Tenn., a town of 6,000 people. He accepted an appointment as a missionary to the West from the American Baptist Home Mission Society and the pastorate of the Nashville church, effective Jan. 1, 1835. The church, established in 1820, lost its pastor, nearly all of its members, and its building to Campbellism May 24, 1828, and was nonexistent until reconstituted Oct. 10, 1830. Howell led in the erection of a commodious and beautiful building which the church dedicated late in 1837 or early 1838. He restored respect and honor for the Baptist name in the community. June 18, 1838, the church excluded a minority of about 100 antimissionary members, who claimed they were the true church and the majority no church at all.

Howell began *The Baptist*, a monthly paper, Jan., 1835, and edited it most of the time until he gave it to the Tennessee Baptists in Oct., 1846, then continued as editor until June, 1848. In Apr., 1835, he revived a Sunday school which had existed for a short while in 1834. It was then the only Baptist Sunday school in a vast area. During 1836–41 Howell organized or led in organizing societies for education and ministerial improvement, Bible distribution and publication, colportage, and Sunday school work. He also resuscitated a missionary society Luther Rice had organized Dec., 1816, in Tennessee. He led in establishing an early school called Union University, and in the organization (May, 1842) of the Baptist General Association of Tennessee and North Alabama to replace a convention (organized 1833) destroyed by antimissionary Baptists. The several societies were consolidated and merged into the general association (1842). In 1847 he advocated the establishment of a theological seminary at some central point and championed it at the 1849 session of the Southern Baptist Convention in Nashville. What he wanted materialized 10 years later with the establishment of the Southern Baptist Theological Seminary at Greenville, S. C., later moved to Louisville.

July, 1850, Howell became pastor of the Second Baptist Church, Richmond, Va., which he served until his return to Nashville, July, 1857, for his second pastorate. During his absence from Tennessee, Landmarkism became powerful in Tennessee under the leadership of James Robinson Graves (*q.v.*). Howell opposed Landmarkism and was active in freeing the Bible Board, Nashville, from Landmark domination. He opposed the creation (1857–58) of the Southern Baptist Sunday School Union at Nashville by Graves and his associates, and its close tie-in with Graves, Marks & Co., the proprietors of the South-Western Publishing House. He was loyal to the Southern Baptist Publication Society, Charleston, S. C., and saw no Baptist need for the union. Out of the situation developed the Graves-Howell controversy and conditions in the First Baptist Church which threatened its very existence—the third time for such an experience in its 30 years.

The Union army captured Nashville in Feb., 1862. Shortly thereafter the military governor, Andrew Johnson, had Howell, with three or four other ministers, imprisoned because they refused to take the oath of allegiance to the Federal Government. His two months' imprisonment affected his health. The army soon took possession of the church building for military purposes and left Howell and the church to get on with their work as best they could. He resigned in July, 1867, because of failing health and died some 10 months later. He was buried at Mount Olivet Cemetery, Nashville.

Howell was the second president of the Southern Baptist Convention. He served four two-year terms (1851–58), and was elected again at the Richmond Convention in 1859 over the prolonged and bitter opposition of Graves. He immediately resigned, saying that he did not want the Graves-Howell controversy to get into the Convention.

Howell was the author of several books, as follows: *Terms of Sacramental Communion* (1841)—in later editions, *Terms of Communion at the Lord's Table* (1846) and *Terms of Christian Communion* (1854); *The Deaconship* (1846 —several editions); *The Way of Salvation* (1849); *The Evils of Infant Baptism* (1851); *The Cross* (1854); *The Covenants* (1856)— later revised in manuscript only as "The Christology of the Pentateuch"; *The Early Baptists of Virginia*, an address delivered in 1856 before the American Baptist Historical Society and published as a tract, enlarged and published as a book in 1856, then enlarged again in 1864 and published posthumously by the American Baptist Publication Society; "A Memorial of the First Baptist Church, Nashville, Tennessee, from 1820 to 1863"—a two-volume manuscript edition of the church's history, with the author always referred to in the third person; and the author's sermons in 80 bound manuscript volumes.

Howell filled many important positions through the years. He married Mary Ann Morton Toy in Apr., 1829. Of their 10 children, two died in infancy. He was greatly beloved by his churches. Though urbane, genial, and kind, he was also possessed of great courage and determination. He ranked high as a preacher and author. Georgetown College, Kentucky, conferred on him the D.D. degree about 1844.

BIBLIOGRAPHY: P. E. Burroughs, *The Spiritual Conquest of the Second Frontier* (1942). R. B. C. Howell, "A Memorial of the First Baptist Church, Nashville, Tennessee, from 1820 to 1863," 2 vols. MS. (Dargan-Carver Library, Nashville, Tenn.). HOMER L. GRICE

HOYT, JAMES ALFRED (b. Waynesboro, Va., Oct. 11, 1837; d. Greenville, S. C., May 27, 1904). Editor, businessman, South Carolina Baptist leader. Son of Jonathan Perkins and Jane (Johnson) Hoyt, he moved with his family to Laurens, S. C., where he attended school, but was forced to go to work when only 14 and thus learned the printer's trade. After moving to Anderson as foreman of the Anderson *Gazette*, Hoyt soon became editor and later established the Anderson *Intelligencer*. Publication was suspended when Hoyt entered the

Hübmaier, Balthasar

Confederate army but was resumed after the surrender.

Hoyt went to the state capital in 1877 as editor of the Columbia *Register*. In 1879 he purchased the *Baptist Courier*, moved it to Greenville, and remained in charge of the paper as editor and part owner until 1892, when he became editor and proprietor of the Greenville *Mountaineer*. Shortly after Hoyt assumed control of the *Baptist Courier*, his wife became editor of "Hearth and Home" and "Our Little Ones" departments, and for 30 years or more her initials, R. C. H., were familiar to readers of the *Courier*. Although he lacked a formal education, Hoyt wrote forceful, clear English, and his editorial work showed the influence of the English classics, in which he was well read. "As an editor he was fair, honest, courageous, courteous, and considerate. He expressed his views in a remarkably clear and discriminating style."

President of the South Carolina state convention from 1885 to 1893, and trustee of Furman University, 1880-97, Hoyt was vice-president of the Southern Baptist Convention, the American Baptist Education Society, and the American Baptist Publication Society.

In 1900 Hoyt was nominated by the Prohibition Convention for governor in the Democratic primary and made an active canvass of the state, advocating abolition of the state liquor dispensary system. Through the active opposition of Senator B. R. Tillman, he was defeated in the second primary. One of the organizers of the South Carolina State Press Association in 1875 and its first president, Hoyt also helped organize the Peoples National Bank of Greenville in 1887 and was director and inactive vice-president until his death.

BIBLIOGRAPHY: Files of the *Baptist Courier*. D. W. Hoyt, *Genealogical History of Hoyt, Haight, and Hight Families* (1871). J. A. Hoyt, "The Palmetto Riflemen" (1886). J. A. Hoyt, Jr., "Sketch of Col. James A. Hoyt," in Greenville *News* (June 4, 1925). South Carolina Baptist State Convention, *Annual* (1904). The Yorkville *Inquirer* (July 25, 1900).

JAMES A. HOYT, JR.

HÜBMAIER, BALTHASAR (b. Friedberg, Germany, c. 1481; d. Vienna, Austria, Mar. 10, 1528). Evangelical reformer and early Anabaptist leader, received an M.A. degree from Freiburg University in 1511, and in 1512 a Th.D. degree from Ingolstadt University, where he taught and served as the university preacher several years. Once a pupil of John Eck, then colleague and friend of this opponent of Luther, Hübmaier remained a zealous Catholic until 1522, when, after much Bible study and reading of Luther's writings, he embraced Protestant views. He then succeeded in effecting reform in Waldshut, where he served as pastor. As early as May, 1523, he doubted the validity of infant baptism, since he found no scriptural warrant for it. Neither Hübmaier nor those who accepted his view translated theory into practice until 1525. Hübmaier published treatises against the mass, image-worship, purgatory, celibacy, etc., in 1524. Because of his reaction against the Catholic Church and the half-way measures of other reformers, and his emphasis on the authority of the Scriptures in determining faith and practice, Hübmaier became a leading Anabaptist and a champion of believer's baptism. The Anabaptist, Wilhelm Röubli, baptized (sprinkled) Hübmaier in Apr., 1525. On Easter Day Hübmaier baptized in his church at Waldshut 300 men out of a milk pail filled with water. In his treatise *On the Christian Baptism of Believers* he stated that "to baptise in water is to pour outward water over the confessor of sins." There is "no good reason to suppose that Hübmaier ever changed his practice [affusion]." He taught that baptism was not essential to salvation but was necessary for obedience and was the doorway into the church. Hübmaier held that the local church was "a particular, external congregation" of the universal church—the totality of the redeemed. He viewed the Lord's Supper as the "pledge of brotherly love" and the "memorial of Christ's sufferings." He was a literalist and a legalist in his interpretation of the Scriptures.

In Dec., 1525, Catholic forces occupied Waldshut. Hübmaier sought refuge in Zurich but was imprisoned and tortured there. He fled in 1526 to Moravia, where he propagated the Anabaptist movement with much success until Catholic authorities burned him at the stake on Mar. 13, 1528, and his wife was drowned.

LYNN E. MAY, JR.

HUCKINS, JAMES (b. New Hampshire, 1808; d. Charleston, S. C., 1863). Church organizer, pastor, educator. The first missionary sent to Texas by the American Baptist Home Mission Society, Huckins reached Galveston on Jan. 24, 1840, conducted a week's revival, and organized the First Baptist Church with nine charter members Feb. 3, 1840. Huckins toured several South Texas counties, preaching and paving the way for churches, and in 1841 organized the First Baptist Church of Houston. He helped organize Union Association in 1840; Texas Baptist Home Mission Society and Texas Baptist Educational Society, 1841; Baylor University, 1845; and the Texas Baptist convention, 1848. First to conceive the need of a Baptist university in Texas, Huckins was a charter trustee of Baylor University and president for three terms of the Texas Baptist convention. In 1847 Huckins became Baylor's financial agent and rode horseback over several states, South and North, raising $40,000 for equipment and endowment, thus making it possible for the school to continue operation. After 19 years in Texas, Huckins accepted a pastorate in Charleston, S. C., in 1859, where he died in 1863.

FRANK BURKHALTER

HUDGINS, WILLIAM DOUGLAS (b. near Estill Springs, Tenn., Apr. 6, 1872; d. Tullahoma, Tenn., Oct. 17, 1934). First state Sunday school and Baptist Young People's Union secretary of the Tennessee Baptist Convention and consecrated layman, who for 27 years (1908–34) set forward the education program of Tennessee Baptists, establishing work with laymen and students and popularizing the Six Point Record System. Son of Henry S. and Rebecca (Muse) Hudgins, he finished public school and graduated from Terrell College at Decherd, taught school several years, and was principal of the Lewisburg public school. He married Eula Hardison, who lived less than a year afterward. In 1902 he married Lelia Barrow of Hopkinsville, Ky. Two sons were born: William Douglas, Jr., and Richard Brooks. He entered mercantile business at Estill Springs in 1903. In 1905 he attended the first Tennessee Baptist encampment, where he was influenced by denominational leaders Bernard Washington Spilman (q.v.), Arthur Flake (q.v.), Landrum Pinson Leavell (q.v.), John Richard Sampey (q.v.), and Hight C Moore. His deep interest in state Baptist activities led W. C. Golden, state mission secretary, to invite him to become Sunday school secretary. Hudgins wrote *The Deaconship*, contributed original ideas now incorporated in study course books, developed leaders at Ovoca, and advocated preachers' schools. His death resulted from an automobile accident which occurred on the way from an associational meeting.   ROBERT PALMER

HUFHAM, JAMES DUNN (b. Duplin County, N. C., May 26, 1834; d. Raleigh, N. C., Mar. 27, 1921). Minister, editor. The son of a minister, George Washington Hufham, and Frances Dunn, James Hufham received the B.A. degree from Wake Forest College in 1856, the M.A. degree in 1860, and the D.D. degree in 1877. He was ordained in 1857. In 1861 he purchased the *Biblical Recorder* and was its editor until 1867. During the war years the youthful editor claimed "perfect liberty to say what I believe." He was able to keep the *Biblical Recorder* alive during the war and held the interest of North Carolina Baptists in their journal when many other papers failed to survive. Hufham was a member of the Board of Education of the Baptist State Convention of North Carolina from its beginning in 1862, served as corresponding secretary of the convention from 1864 to 1868, and was corresponding secretary of its mission board from 1870 to 1874. He held a number of pastorates, including Lanyine, Bear Marsh, Sawyers Creek, Tabernacle in Raleigh, First Baptist in Scotland Neck, Tarboro, First Baptist in Shelby, and First Baptist in Henderson. After he left the *Biblical Recorder* he still continued to write for it. He became famous in the North Carolina Baptist State Convention as "the walking delegate," because he would walk up and down the aisles and speak to his friends during the sessions while at the same time being on the alert and ready to reply to any speaker from the floor.

He was married to Mariana Faison, July 23, 1863, and their children were: George, James, Annie Hinton, Thomas McDowell, James Dunn, Jr., and Mary Faison.   GARLAND A. HENDRICKS

HUMANISM. "Man is the measure of all things" is the fundamental tenet of the philosophy of humanism. The humanist puts his trust in man's natural powers and rejects a miracle-working God as a factor in man's existence. A literary movement at first (Renaissance), humanism soon entered religious thought (e.g. Petrarch, 1304–74) and in time greatly altered Christian theology in the direction of rationalism and moralism (e.g. theological liberalism). Humanism in America has been represented by J. H. Dietrich, John Dewey, Corliss Lamont, *et al*. Baptists have steadily resisted humanism in its theological implications, but are themselves "humanistic" in their insistence on human dignity, freedom, and rights.

BIBLIOGRAPHY: A. J. Balfour, *Theism and Humanism* (1915). W. M. Horton, *Theism and the Modern Mood* (1930). C. Lamont, *Humanism as a Philosophy* (1949).   TED R. CLARK

HUNDRED THOUSAND CLUB. A plan used in the years 1933–43 to pay the debts of Southern Baptists, which for years had threatened to strangle the Convention's institutions and mission program. Because of a financial depression which began in 1921, only $58,000,000 of the $92,000,000 pledged to the 75 Million Campaign was finally collected, $17,000,000 short of the original five-year goal. Each year thereafter Convention causes as well as state causes showed deficits. By Dec. 31, 1926, Convention causes had accumulated a debt of approximately $6,500,000. Money was borrowed at high interest rates. Agencies were not able to meet payments on bonds and loans. Loans had to be renewed without payment on principal. Creditors clamored for payment, some threatening legal proceedings. Baptists were despondent and discouraged, and the morale was at the breaking point.

The Executive Committee met Apr. 12–13, 1933, to give consideration to the debt situation. After consideration of all plans proposed, it adopted those suggested by Frank Tripp for a Baptist Hundred Thousand Club. After long discussion this plan was adopted by the Convention in Washington, D. C., on May 20, 1933. The plan of the club called for equal treatment of all creditors and application of all funds received through it on the principal of the debts. Its object was "the liquidation of the present debt of all the agencies of the . . . Convention," the membership to "consist of persons paying one dollar ($1) per month over and above their regular subscription to the church budget." Luther Rice Memorial Memberships at $10 per member were also promoted. The plan of the club called for a general leader, a state leader in each state, an associational leader in each association, and a leader in each church. Tripp was elected general leader; his church in St. Joseph, Mo., gave him leave of absence to direct the club, continuing his salary. The Sunday School Board paid all operating expenses of the club, so that every dollar of receipts was applied on the principal of the debts.

The initial membership drive was hurriedly made in 1933. The first annual report to the Convention in 1934 indicated membership pledges totaling $360,000, indicating approximately 30,000 members. Annual membership campaigns were conducted in January and February of the years 1934–43 inclusive. All funds received through the club were transmitted promptly to the several agencies of the Convention "according to percentages determined by the Executive Committee in ratio to the debt needs of the several agencies."

At the 1935 Convention meeting in Memphis, Tenn., a memorial from the state secretaries to the Executive Committee was presented to the Convention, requesting that the plan be enlarged to include the payment of state debts. The Convention recommended further conference. A memorial from South Carolina requested the Convention "not to try to set up" the club for the payment of Convention debts in South Carolina. Tripp's first report to the Convention reported:

Virginia, North and South Carolina have not yet officially approved the plan; however, there are quite a number of members in each of these states. . . . Your general leader has tried to respect the wishes of the state secretaries and their boards in these states by not attempting to set up state and associational organizations for the promotion of the movement.

In the 1937 Convention the club was enlarged so that states desiring to do so might participate in its receipts.

After three years of leadership, Tripp declined to serve longer. Upon recommendation of the Executive Committee, the Convention authorized the "election of a Director of Promotion under the Executive Committee who shall promote the Cooperative Program and the Baptist Hundred Thousand Club." Tripp was elected director of promotion by the Executive Committee, but he declined. James Edgar Dillard (q.v.), president of the Executive Committee and pastor of Southside Baptist Church, Birmingham, Ala., was elected director of promotion and began work on Aug. 1, 1936.

In the 1941 Convention, plans were inaugurated for a Victory Campaign for cash to be promoted in 1943 in order to achieve the recommended goal of "a debtless denomination by 1945." During 1942 it appeared feasible and Dillard proposed that Southern Baptists be debt-free in 1943 and popularized the slogan, "Debt Free in '43—Count on Me." In 1943 the Executive Committee reported "our Foreign Mission Board for the first time in forty years is entirely out of debt." By the close of the year every Convention agency and institution was entirely out of debt with $38,846.49 balance in the debt-paying fund.

While the objective of 100,000 members of the club was not reached, it was one of the significantly successful movements among Southern Baptists. This plan aroused Southern Baptists to recognize the burdensome nature of debts and the urgency of paying them, encouraged the agencies themselves to put every possible dollar from their own funds into debt retirement, stimulated other large gifts for the purpose, and saved hundreds of thousands of dollars in interest. It led the way out of debt. Receipts of the club for Convention causes by years were as follows: 1933, $37,588.28; 1934, $160,565.96; 1935, $198,372.31; 1936, $191,296.88; 1937, $191,500.00; 1938, $161,726.07; 1939, $159,447.96; 1940, $158,279.43; 1941, $261,143.63; 1942, $377,277.82; 1943, $730,624.02; total, $2,627,822.36. By agreement six states during the last seven years, 1937–43 inclusive, retained one half their club receipts and applied them on their state debts. These amounts are not included in the above.

The Executive Committee in 1936 expressed "undying gratitude" to Tripp and the First Baptist Church, St. Joseph, Mo., for their contributions to the club movement "which to a large extent saved our mission causes." In 1943 the committee gave high praise to Dillard "for his untiring and efficient work in bringing to pass his aim, 'Debt Free in '43.'"

MERRILL D. MOORE

HUNGARIAN BAPTIST UNION OF AMERICA. Organized in Homestead, Pa., Apr. 11, 1908, under the leadership of Frank Balogh, John Leber, and Michael Veg. In the beginning there were only three ordained Hungarian Baptist ministers in America and about 100 members. By 1934 the membership had increased to 2,500 with 26 ordained ministers and missionaries. Soon after its organization, the union began to publish a monthly paper in Hungarian, called *Gospel Messenger*, now published every two weeks. Ten years after originating the *Messenger*, the union published in Hungarian the *Bible Expositor* of the international Sunday school lessons, a book still in use. For about 15 years the union had a large group of students in the International Baptist Theological Seminary in East Orange, N. J., with a talented Hungarian professor. At present Hungarian Baptist students are scattered all over the country. The Ladies' Aid, Sunday school, and the Young People's and Deacons' Conference, three branches of the union, meet annually at the convention of the union. A convenient old people's home in Watervliet, Mich., and a mission field in South America with two missionaries are sponsored by the union. The financial income for all mission purposes totals about $125,000 annually.   ALBERT M. PETRE

HUNGARY, MISSION IN. Southern Baptists came to the assistance of Hungarian Baptists following World War I and the London Conference of 1920. They found a well-organized Baptist Union (formed in 1907), with seminary, orphanage, publishing house, two homes for old people, and three denominational papers.

Territorial losses after the war decreased Hungarian Baptists from 24,000 to 7,000. Through the help of the Foreign Mission Board, seminary property was provided in 1925. A girls' school opened in 1937, following arrival in 1935 of missionary teachers, Mrs. Emil Bretz (nee Jane Maude Cobb), Mrs. James Stuart (nee Doris Ruth Mahan), and Mrs. Bela Udvarnoki (nee Ruby Inez Daniel). In 1938 Everett Gill, Sr., directing European missions, moved to Budapest, and Mrs. Gill assisted with the school.

Buildings of the schools were destroyed by bombs during World War II. Missionaries were unable to re-enter the country, but new seminary property was purchased with mission reconstruction funds, and the Foreign Mission Board sent financial assistance from time to time. Baptists numbering about 17,000 are maintaining their work with difficulties under Communist domination.

MRS. RUBY DANIEL UDVARNOKI

HUNT, MARION PALMER (b. Auxvasse, Calloway County, Mo., July 1, 1860; d. Louisville, Ky., Aug. 5, 1944). Minister, organizer, hospital founder. Son of William Bearl and Jane Nicholson (Palmer) Hunt, he attended William Jewell College, Liberty, Mo., and Southern Baptist Theological Seminary, Louisville, Ky. After ordination at Holt Baptist Church, Clay County, Mo., May 17, 1884, Hunt's early pastorates were at Gallatin, Mo., and Ellsworth, Kans.

On three different occasions Hunt was pastor of Twenty-second and Walnut Street Baptist Church, Louisville; he held pastorates at Patee Park, St. Joseph, Mo.; Fort Collins, Colo., 1911–13; Fayetteville, Ark., 1914–16; West Broadway Baptist Church, Louisville, Ky., 1916–22; and Eighteenth Street Baptist Church, Louisville, 1924–42.

In 1897 Hunt and John Newton Prestridge founded and promoted a newspaper, *The Baptist Argus,* which later became *The Baptist World,* Louisville, Ky. In 1904–05 he was western secretary for the Foreign Mission, Home Mission, and Sunday School boards, with headquarters in Kansas City, Mo. Hunt served as executive secretary of the Churchmen's Federation, Louisville, 1918–19; and of the Anti Race Track Gambling Commission of Kentucky, 1920–21.

During the early and middle 1920's Hunt campaigned for the first Baptist hospital in Kentucky. Kentucky Baptist Hospital was founded largely as a result of his efforts, and Hunt was a trustee of the hospital from its organization until his death, which occurred while he was a patient in the hospital. For many years Hunt was Kentucky's trustee on the board of the Southern Baptist Hospital, New Orleans.

Hunt's published works include *Paul's Superlatives and Sermons; The Exposure of Millennial Dawnism, the Preacher's Imperial Duty; Christian Science* vs. *The Bible;* and *The Story of My Life,* his autobiography. He also wrote tracts and articles for the denominational press.

GEORGE RALEIGH JEWELL

HYMN WRITERS, BAPTIST. Christian hymnody has been enriched by the contributions of many hymn writers. The last 250 years have produced far greater activity in this area than any previous period. Baptist hymn writers have made a significant contribution to that long procession of stalwart Christians who have written the great heritage of hymnic literature. Aside from the very few hymns dealing with believers' baptism, there is little or nothing to distinguish the hymns written by Baptists from those written by members of other denominational groups during related periods in our history. As is true with other denominational groups, the vast majority of these hymn writers were ordained ministers; few laymen were represented. The trend of the last century indicates a great increase in hymn writing activity on the part of the laity, and a great decrease on the part of the clergy, which has resulted in shallowness of thought and triteness of expression.

The following is a list of important Baptist hymn and hymn tune writers. In each case the author's name is given first, followed by his dates, followed by his best-known work. Hymns are listed by first lines; hymn tunes by their names. Whenever a hymn or hymn tune appears in the *Baptist Hymnal* (1956), its number is given in parentheses following its name. Asterisks indicate persons who were preachers.

In England.—John Bunyan,* 1628–88, "He who would valiant be"; Benjamin Keach,* 1640–1704, "The Lord, He is our sun and shield"; John Needham,* d. c. 1786, "Awake, my tongue, thy tribute bring" (24); Anne Steele, 1716–78, "Father, whate'er of earthly bliss"; Benjamin Beddome,* 1717–95, "Did Christ o'er sinners weep"; Edmond Jones,* 1722–65, "Come, humble sinner, in whose breast"; Samuel Stennett,* 1727–95, "On Jordan's stormy banks I stand" (479); Robert Robinson,* 1735–90, "Come, thou Fount of every blessing" (313); Samuel Medley,* 1738–99, "Awake, my soul, in joyful lays" (26); John Fawcett,* 1739–1817, "Blest be the tie that binds" (366); Robert Keene (?), "How firm a foundation" (263); Richard Burnham,* 1749–1810, "Jesus, Thou art the sinner's friend"; John Rippon,* 1751–1836, "Here, Lord, my soul convicted stands"; John Burton, Sr., 1773–1822, "Holy Bible, Book divine" (179); Bourne Hall Draper,* 1775–1843, "Ye Christian heralds! go proclaim" (459); Edward Mote,* 1797–1874, "My hope is built on nothing less" (283); John Eustace Giles,* 1815–75, "Thou hast said, exalted Jesus" (390); Charles Haddon Spurgeon* (*q.v.*),

1834-92, "The Holy Ghost is here" (168); Marianne Hearn, 1834-1909, "Just as I am, Thine own to be" (249); John Murch Wigner, 1844-1911, "Come to the Saviour now" (226); William H. Parker, 1845-1929, "Tell me the stories of Jesus" (505); Frederick William Goadby,* 1845-79, "O Thou whose hand hath brought us" (379).

In America.—Benjamin Cleaveland, 1733-1811, "O could I find from day to day"; Henry Alline,* 1748-84, "Amazing sight, the Saviour stands"; John Leland* (q.v.), 1754-1841, "The day is passed and gone"; Richard Furman* (q.v.), 1755-1825, "Sovereign of all the world's above"; Jesse Mercer* (q.v.), 1769-1841, "In sin's howling waste my poor soul was forlorn"; William Staughton* (q.v.), 1770-1829, "Ye sons of God awake to glory"; Andrew Broaddus* (q.v.), 1770-1848, "Help Thy servant, gracious Lord"; Robert T. Daniel,* 1773-1840, "Lord, in humble, sweet submission"; Joseph B. Cook,* 1775-1833, "Bought with the Saviour's precious blood"; William Dossey,* 1780-1853, "O sinners, to the Saviour go"; Adoniram Judson* (q.v.), 1788-1850, "Come, Holy Spirit, Dove divine" (385); William Calmes Buck* (q.v.), 1790-1872, "Behold, O Lord, at Thy command"; Stephen P. Hill,* 1806-84, "My soul, the Lord adore"; Samuel Francis Smith,* 1808-95, "My country, 'tis of thee" (487); Lydia Baxter, 1809-74, "Take the name of Jesus with you" (305); Abram Maer Poindexter* (q.v.), 1809-72, "O our Redeemer God"; Sewall S. Cutting,* 1813-82, "God of the world, near and afar"; Sidney Dyer,* 1814-98, "Go, proclaim the wondrous story"; J. M. D. Cates,* 1815-87, "The sacred day of rest"; Sylvanus Dryden Phelps,* 1816-95, "Saviour, Thy dying love" (400); James Tupper (q.v.), 1819-68, "Dark was the hour, when Jesus bore"; Basil Manly, Jr.* (q.v.), 1825-92, "Soldiers of Christ in truth arrayed"; Robert Lowry,* 1826-99, "Shall we gather at the river" (481); Joseph Henry Gilmore,* 1834-1918, "He leadeth me, O blessed thought"; Annie Sherwood Hawks, 1835-1918, "I need Thee every hour" (334); Adoniram Judson Gordon* (q.v.), 1836-95, "O Spirit's anointing"; John Henry Yates,* 1837-1900, "Faith is the victory" (256); Philip Paul Bliss,* 1838-76, "I will sing of my Redeemer" (143); Charles Clinton Luther,* 1847-1924, "Must I go and empty-handed" (430); E. Taylor Cassell,* 1849-1930, "From over hill and plain" (407); Howard B. Grose,* 1851-1939, "Give of your best to the Master" (353); Edward Smith Ufford,* 1851-1910, "Throw out the lifeline" (217); Francis H. Rowley,* 1854-1952, "I will sing the wondrous story" (144); Peter P. Bilhorn,* 1861-1936, "Sweet peace, the gift of God's love" (299); Civilla Durfee Martin, 1869-1948, "God will take care of you" (274); Ernest Orlando Sellers (q.v.), 1869-1952, "Thy word is a lamp to my feet" (180); Harper G. Smyth, 1873-1945, "Make me a channel of blessing" (438); John L. Rosser,* 1875-   , "To Him who hallows all our days" (499); Harry Emerson Fosdick,* 1878-   , "God of grace and God of glory" (465); Charles Butler,* 1879-1929, "There's none other name"; Albert Simpson Reitz,* 1879-   , "Teach me to pray" (330); Isham Emanuel Reynolds (q.v.), 1879-1949, "Jesus is the friend you need" (214); Jack P. Scholfield, 1882-   , "Saved, Saved" (197); Baylus Benjamin McKinney (q.v.), 1886-1952, "Have faith in God" (253); Eugene M. Bartlett, 1885-1941, "Victory in Jesus"; James C. Moore,* 1888-   , "Thou, O Christ of Calvary" (189); Edwin McNeely, 1891-   , "Jehovah the Lord, our Saviour and King" (494); John Roy Harris, 1891-   , "Great Redeemer, we adore Thee" (154); James Edwin McConnell, 1892-1954, "'Whosoever' meaneth me" (209); Edward Hughes Pruden,* 1903-   , "O God of our fathers" (500).

Baptist Hymn Tune Writers.—Oliver Holden, 1765-1844, "Coronation" (132); Benjamin Franklin White (q.v.), 1800-79, "The Morning Trumpet" (in *Sacred Harp*); William Walker, 1809-75, "Jerusalem" (in *Southern Harmony*); William Batchelder Bradbury, 1816-68, "He Leadeth Me" (58); John Gordon McCurry, 1821-86, "Teasley" (*Social Harp*); Robert Lowry, 1826-99, "Hanson Place" (481); William Fiske Sherwin, 1826-88, "Chautauqua" (29); William Howard Doane, 1832-1915, "Near the Cross" (97); Adoniram Judson Gordon, 1836-95, "Gordon" (289); Philip Paul Bliss, 1838-76, "Ville de Havre" (265); George Coles Stebbins, 1846-1945, "Jesus, I Come" (233); Edward Smith Ufford, 1851-1929, "Lifeline" (217); Flora Hamilton Cassel, 1852-1911, "Lambdin" (407); Peter P. Bilhorn, 1861-1936, "Wondrous Story" (144); William Stillman Martin, 1862-1935, "God Cares" (274); Ernest O. Sellers, 1869-1952, "New Orleans" (142); John Hughes, 1873-1932, "Cwm Rhondda" (55); Harper G. Smyth, 1873-1945, "Euclid" (438); Charlie Butler, 1879-1929, "No Other Name"; Albert Simpson Reitz, 1879-   , "Reitz" (330); Isham Emanuel Reynolds, 1879-1949, "Venting" (285); Jack P. Scholfield, 1882-   , "Rapture" (197); Luther B. Bridgers, 1884-1948, "Sweetest Name" (307); Baylus Benjamin McKinney, 1886-1952, "Falls Creek" (347); James C. Moore, 1888-   , "Moore" (189); Paolo Conte, 1891-   , "Redentore" (154); Harry Dixon Loes, 1892-   , "Redeemer" (106); James Edwin McConnell, 1892-1954, "McConnell" (209); Walter Hines Sims, 1907-   , "McComb" (384).

WILLIAM J. REYNOLDS

HYMNALS, BAPTIST. The first Baptist hymnbook published in America was *Hymns and Spiritual Songs, Collected from the Works of Several Authors.* It was printed by Samuel Hall in Newport, R. I., in 1766. Prior to this, Baptists had probably been using, according to Louis F. Benson, English publications, namely Ainsworth's version of the *Book of Psalms* and *The Bay Psalm Book* (1640).

As hymn singing in America developed, some

Baptist groups wanted only metrical versions of psalms, while others desired the addition of "hymns of human composure" such as those Isaac Watts was producing in England. This state of affairs resulted in the publication of hymnals by various individuals, churches, and associations to satisfy their convictions and needs. Since no denominational publication agencies existed, no official hymn compilation could be commissioned.

Hymnals which may be termed Baptist and which contributed to strengthening Baptist hymnody, particularly Southern Baptist, follow in chronological order with the compiler or author first given, then the title, publication date, and place of publication: William Reid, *Hymns and Spiritual Songs,* 1773, Williamsburg, Va.; Joshua Smith (later editions use Samuel Sleeper), *Divine Hymns, or Spiritual Songs for the Use of Religious Assemblies and Private Christians,* 1784, Philadelphia, Pa. (11 editions); Andrew Broaddus (q.v.) and Richard Broaddus, *Collection of Sacred Ballads,* 1790, Caroline County, Va.; Samuel Jones and Burgis Allison, *A Selection of Psalms and Hymns, Done Under the Appointment of the Philadelphia Association,* 1790, Philadelphia, Pa. (several editions).

In 1787 John Rippon published, in London, his *Selection of Hymns from the Best Authors* and in 1792 published, in Elizabethtown, N. J., *An American Edition of "Rippon's Selections"* which linked English and American hymnody. Following were Eleazer Clay, *Hymns and Spiritual Songs, Selected from Several Approved Authors and Recommended by the Baptist General Committee of Virginia,* etc., 1793, Richmond, Va.; John Courtney, *The Christian's Pocket Companion,* 1805, Richmond (revised, with appendix, 1831); Daniel Dodge, *A Selection of Hymns and Psalms* (an effort to combine the best from Watts and Rippon), 1808, Wilmington, Del.; William Parkinson, *A Selection of Hymns and Spiritual Songs,* 1809, New York; Jesse Mercer (q.v.), *The Cluster of Spiritual Songs, Divine Hymns and Social Poems,* three editions before 1817 in Augusta, Ga., 5th edition, 1835, in Philadelphia, Pa.; George C. Sedgwick, *A Selection of Hymns and Spiritual Songs,* 1815, Fredericksburg, Va.; Starke Dupuy, *Hymns and Spiritual Songs,* 1818, Louisville, Ky. (22 editions; revised in 1843 by J. M. Peck [q.v.]); William Dossey, *Dossey's Choice,* 1820, Philadelphia, Pa.; Lewis Skidmore, *The Choice Collection of the Latest Social and Camp Meeting Hymns and Spiritual Songs,* 1825, Baltimore, Md.; Andrew Broaddus (q.v.), *Dover Selection of Spiritual Songs,* 1828, Virginia (2nd edition, 1829); Andrew Broaddus, *Virginia Selection of Psalms, Hymns, and Spiritual Songs,* 1836; John Purify, *A Selection of Hymns and Spiritual Songs,* 1831, Wake Forest, N. C.; Staunton S. Burdette, *The Baptist Harmony,* 1834, South Carolina; William Walker, *Southern Harmony,* 1835, New Haven, Conn. (a singing school book of hymns and folk songs); and Sewall S. Cutting, *Hymns for the Vestry and the Fireside,* 1841, Boston, Mass.

William Calmes Buck (q.v.) published *The Baptist Hymnbook* in 1842 in Boston, Mass. It failed to gain popularity. Baron Stowe and Samuel F. Smith published *The Psalmist* in 1843 in Boston, which was popular in the North, then gained favor in the South when a supplement by Richard Fuller (q.v.) and Jeremiah Bell Jeter (q.v.) was published in 1847. Basil Manly, Sr. (q.v.), and his son, Basil, Jr. (q.v.), published *Baptist Psalmody* in 1850 in Charleston, S. C., which joined *The Psalmist* in becoming extensively used. In 1851 the Southern Baptist Publication Society asked its corresponding secretary, Edwin T. Winkler, to compile *The Sacred Lute,* which was published in 1855 in Charleston, S. C. Others of the period were William Carey Crane (q.v.), *The Prayer Meeting Hymnbook,* 1857, Baltimore, Md.; James Robinson Graves (q.v.) and James Madison Pendleton (q.v.), *The Southern Psalmist,* 1858, Nashville, Tenn.; Basil Manly, *Baptist Chorals,* 1859, Richmond, Va.; J. M. D. Cates, *The Sacred Harp,* 1867, Nashville, Tenn.; S. L. Caldwell and Adoniram Judson Gordon (q.v.), *Service of Song for Baptist Churches,* 1871, Boston, Mass.; American Baptist Publication Society with Louis Albert Banks, *The Baptist Hymn and Tune Book for Public Worship,* 1871, Philadelphia, Pa.; James Robinson Graves, *The New Baptist Psalmist,* 1873, Memphis, Tenn.; Robert Lowry and Will H. Doane, *Gospel Hymn and Tune Book,* 1879, Philadelphia, Pa.; A. B. Cates, *Baptist Songs with Music,* 1879, Louisville, Ky.; Rowland, Henson, Hornberger, and Doane, *Baptist Hymnal,* 1883, Philadelphia, Pa.; and Basil Manly, Jr., *Manly's Choice* (for Sunday school), 1892, Richmond, Va.

Lansing Burrows (q.v.) edited, and the Sunday School Board published, *The Baptist Hymn and Praise Book,* 1904, Nashville, Tenn., and the same year William H. Doane and William Kirkpatrick released *Glorious Praise* in Louisville, Ky. From this point the churches of the Southern Baptist Convention used almost exclusively the hymnals and songbooks published by Robert Henry Coleman (q.v.), of Dallas, Tex., and the Sunday School Board of Nashville. Coleman's principal books were: *Popular Hymnal,* 1918; *Harvest Hymns,* 1924; *The Modern Hymnal,* 1826; *Gospel Melodies,* 1928; *Majestic Hymns,* 1930; *Service Songs,* 1931; *The American Hymnal,* 1933; *Pilot Hymns,* 1934; *Leading Hymns,* 1936; *Precious Hymns,* 1938. Coleman sold his publishing business, hymnals, copyrights, and good will to the Sunday School Board in 1945.

The principal hymnals and songbooks published by the Sunday School Board, which is also known as Broadman Press and Convention Press, are as follows: John L. Hill, *The Chapel Book,* 1923; *The New Baptist Hymnal,* 1926 (a revision of the 1883 hymnal by a joint committee of American Baptist Publication Society and the Sunday School Board); *Songs of*

Faith, 1933; *Abiding Songs,* 1936; Baylus Benjamin McKinney (q.v.), *Songs of Victory,* 1937; McKinney, *The Broadman Hymnal,* 1940; McKinney, *Voice of Praise,* 1947; and Walter Hines Sims, *Baptist Hymnal,* 1956 (compiled by a select committee of 37 editors, musicians, and religious leaders from Southern Baptist Convention).   WALTER HINES SIMS

HYMNS, THEOLOGICAL IMPLICATIONS OF. The poetic material of hymns has always offered a fertile field for the theological thoughts of both the writer and the singer. Probably the main emphasis in hymns, at least the earliest, was *adoration,* as expressed in the psalms. But this adoration was based largely on the theological implications concerning God, man, and salvation as presented in the psalms. The second emphasis in hymnody was certainly *doctrinal* in that definite efforts were made by the hymnodists to express their views concerning God, man, and salvation. The third emphasis was the *evangelistic* or *missionary* concept—this being based upon the character and purpose of God, the value of man as related to his salvation, and his resulting responsibility to both God and his fellow man.

In earliest Christian history emphasis was always on the message, not on the music. The music was the vehicle of the message. This message emphasis made for definite "thought" or "doctrine" in each hymn. In the institution of the Lord's Supper, Christ and his disciples probably joined in chanting the Hallel psalms, which were definite doctrinal expressions. The early use of hymns, doctrinally, was most forceful in the Arian controversy when hymns were of definite doctrinal content for the purpose of winning converts. From that time on, in the full sweep of church history, the hymn has been a common and successful doctrinal carrier for Christian faith. The remark of the Roman Catholic prelate to the effect that Martin Luther did more evil by his singing than he did by his sermons expresses the value and power of the hymn in its doctrinal emphasis. Through the 18th and 19th centuries, a variety of doctrinally divergent views was held, but Watts in his Calvinism, Wesley in his Arminianism, great theologians and flaming evangelists all admitted the place and power of hymnody, and all used the hymn with its most valued doctrinal emphasis.

Unfortunately the 20th century lays too much stress upon the rhythmic and melodic, a practice which weakens the effectiveness of the doctrinal message. Thus there exists the danger of an emotional, superficial, and rather irrational hymnology in this day, without much doctrinal emphasis.

It is further to be noted that there is little heresy in standard hymnody. There may be heresy in the sermon; but the people sing with the orthodox. All denominations sing the same great, time-tested hymns, all of which are definite in their theological messages. In practically all the larger hymnbooks used by most denominations the hymns are evangelical in their doctrinal connotations. This is true although the hymns may have been written by Arminians, Calvinists, Roman Catholics, Unitarians, or others.

It is surely plain that the hymnody of each period of history exemplifies the theological emphasis of that period. This is particularly true when the period is one of theological controversy as well as when the personal element of Christian experience is paramount. The major doctrines of the Christian faith, such as concepts of God, man, and salvation, as well as the various phases of practical religious experience, are doctrinally and comprehensively covered in hymnology. In these hymns all people unite in both praise and practice through an evangelical and, in the main, an evangelistic worship. Corporate worship is usually theologically orthodox so far as its hymnody is concerned.   ALBERT VENTING

I

ILLINOIS ASSOCIATIONS. ANTIOCH UNITED MISSIONARY BAPTIST. Organized in Sept. 1908, at Brownfield, by 6 churches in Hardin and Pope counties, 2 churches from Union, and 2 from Big Saline associations. Its total membership was 439. The New Hampshire Confession of Faith was adopted. It is served by an associational missionary. In 1954, 13 churches reported 122 baptisms, 1,103 members, $49,536 total gifts, $7,513 mission gifts, $101,800 property value, and $2,325 church debt.   L. L. LEININGER

BAY CREEK. Organized Aug., 1864, as the Pleasant Hill Baptist Association by six churches in Pike County. Several years later the name was changed to Bay Creek. In 1954, 10 churches reported 105 baptisms, 1,008 members, $36,666 total gifts, $3,834 mission gifts, $93,000 property value, and $3,500 church debt.   GILBERT WAUD

BIG SALINE. Organized by 5 churches in Oct., 1854, as Big Saline Association of United Baptists, now Big Saline Missionary Baptist Association. Little of its early history is available. The 1904 annual report gives 24 churches; the 1924, 21 churches; and the 1939, 16 churches. The New Hampshire Declaration of Faith is used; it is served by a missionary, and is located in Hardin, Saline, and Pope counties. In 1954, 15 churches reported 48 baptisms, 1,224 members, $27,098 total gifts, $2,956 mission gifts, $43,900 property value, and $887 church debt.

CLEAR CREEK. Organized at Old Clear Creek Baptist Church near Jonesboro in 1831 by six churches in Pulaski, Alexander, Union, and Jackson counties. The Clear Creek and Shiloh churches were from the Cape Girardeau Association of Missouri in 1824. It is served by an associational missionary.

In 1868, 38 churches reported 232 baptisms and 2,102 members. In 1878, 37 churches reported 257 baptisms and 2,164 members. In 1954, 42 of its 44 churches reported 339 baptisms, 9,140 members, $260,338 total gifts, $50,019 mission gifts, $696,475 property value, and $68,030 church debt.

EAST ST. LOUIS. Organized Oct. 16, 1917, by 6 churches in St. Clair and Madison counties, west central part of Illinois, with membership of 1,069. The New Hampshire Declaration of Faith was adopted. The Southern Baptist Convention articles of faith were adopted in 1928. In 1945, 13 of its 32 churches formed the Madison County Association, and the original body remained the same. It conducts the Home Mission Board city missions program, has a city missionary, owns a missionary's home, has a Good Will Center and a rescue mission. In 1954, 22 churches reported 695 baptisms, 9,873 members, $505,785 total gifts, $89,127 mission gifts, $1,498,073 property value, and $262,400 church debt.   L. L. LEININGER

EASTERN INDIANA. Organized Oct., 1951, as the Indiana Association of Missionary Baptists by seven churches in east central Indiana, adopting articles of faith. In 1954 the name was changed to Eastern Indiana Association and affiliation with the Illinois Baptist State Association was consummated. It has been served by an associational missions superintendent since 1951. In 1954, 14 churches reported 167 baptisms, 1,313 members, $72,903 total gifts, $3,997 mission gifts, $250,000 property value, and $50,000 church debt.   GILBERT WAUD

FAIRFIELD. Organized in 1856. The earliest report on file, 1880, gives 38 churches and 2,508 members. It employs a missionary and is located in Hamilton and White counties. In 1954, 28 churches reported 133 baptisms, 3,813 members, $68,884 total gifts, $11,496 mission gifts, $278,050 property value, and $41,500 church debt.

FRANKLIN. Organized as Union United Baptist Association Oct. 16, 1841, at East York Meetinghouse, Franklin County, by seven churches located in Franklin and Williamson counties. The churches came out of Bethel Association of United Baptists because of "Hardshell antimissionism." In 1843 its name was changed to Franklin United Baptist Association, and by 1851 there were 50 churches, 2,319 members, and $5,895 total gifts. In 1954 at its 114th annual session 49 churches reported 355 baptisms, 10,695 members, $166,264 total gifts, $52,424 mission gifts, and $906,050 property value.

L. L. LEININGER

GREAT LAKES. Organized Dec., 1943, by six churches in the South Chicago area, four formerly affiliated with Salem South Association. Since 1946 it has been served by an associational missions superintendent, and owns a home for him. In 1954, 34 churches (located in Illinois, Indiana, Michigan, and Wisconsin) reported 620 baptisms, 4,060 members, $242,447 total gifts, $29,570 mission gifts, $525,750 property value, and $164,228 church debt.

ILLINI. Organized July, 1954, by seven churches located in six east central Illinois counties formerly in Sangamon Valley Association. It adopted articles of faith at that time. In 1954, 8 churches reported 146 baptisms, 1,084 members, $56,325 total gifts, $7,996 mission gifts, $135,000 property value, and $65,000 church debt.

ILLINOIS VALLEY. Organized June, 1950, by 11 churches in seven central Illinois counties between Springfield and Peoria. It adopted articles of faith in 1950 and has been served by an associational missions superintendent since 1951. In 1954, 21 churches reported 268 baptisms, 3,028 members, $140,190 total contributions, $16,981 mission gifts, $615,000 property value, and $178,809 church debt.

KASKASKIA. Organized in 1840 as the Centralia Baptist Association by 14 churches located primarily in the old Illinois and Sangamon communities. Articles of faith were adopted in 1840. In 1912 the name was changed to Kaskaskia Baptist Association. Since 1944 it has been served by an associational missions superintendent, and owns a home for him. In 1954, 29 churches reported 338 baptisms, 5,333 members, $274,425 total gifts, $41,723 mission gifts, $1,197,550 property value, and $246,131 church debt.

LOUISVILLE. Organized Oct., 1850, with the number of constituting churches not known. In 1893 there were 14 churches in Effingham, Fayette, and Clay counties, with 1,032 members. The association adopted articles of faith in 1953. In 1954, 16 churches reported 147 baptisms, 2,212 members, $90,252 total gifts, $12,044 mission gifts, $378,028 property value, and $68,518 church debt.

MACOUPIN. Organized in 1859 by 10 churches in Macoupin County as Macoupin Association of the United Baptists. Articles of faith were adopted at that time. About 1875 the name was changed to Macoupin County Baptist Association. In 1863 a resolution was adopted to observe footwashing as a church ordinance. Ten years later when one church had ceased doing so, the association attempted to force it to resume the practice but failed. Two other associations organized in part from Macoupin are Sangamon Valley and Illinois Valley in 1950. Since 1945 it has been served by an associational missions superintendent. In 1954, 31 churches reported 328 baptisms, 4,442 members, $183,725 total gifts, $27,260 mission gifts, $411,500 property value, and $13,222 church debt. GILBERT WAUD

MADISON. Organized as Madison County Baptist Association Oct. 5, 1945, by 13 churches from East St. Louis Association. The Southern Baptist Convention articles of faith (May 14, 1925) were adopted. It employs a missionary and is located in Madison County. In 1945, 13 churches reported 202 baptisms and 4,515 members. In 1954, 23 churches reported 765 baptisms, 6,430 members, $391,168 total gifts, $65,594 mission gifts, $1,134,200 property value, and $177,613 church debt. L. L. LEININGER

MOUNT ERIE. Organized Oct., 1882, by nine churches in Wayne County formerly in Fairfield Association. In 1954, 23 churches reported 114 baptisms, 3,074 members, $113,636 total gifts, $17,129 mission gifts, $257,500 property value, and $24,800 church debt. GILBERT WAUD

NINE MILE. Organized at the Nine Mile Baptist Church, Perry County, Oct. 4, 1845, by 7 churches from Clear Creek and Saline associations with membership of 280. A summary of faith was adopted. It employs a missionary and is located in Jackson, Perry, Randolph, and Washington counties.

In 1954, 42 churches reported 409 baptisms, 10,062 members, $501,252 total gifts, $67,816 mission gifts, $1,587,400 property value, and $233,072 church debt. L. L. LEININGER

OLNEY. Organized Sept., 1861, by 13 churches in Richland, Jasper, Lawrence, Wabash, and Edwards counties. It adopted articles of faith at that time. In 1954, 11 churches reported 58 baptisms, 1,067 members, $30,085 total gifts, $5,244 mission gifts, $71,000 property value, and $6,410 church debt. GILBERT WAUD

PALESTINE. Organized in 1840 at the Old Lamotte Church (oldest Baptist church in eastern Illinois, organized at Fort Lamotte, Palestine, Ill., in 1812).

Six churches were represented with 200 members. Its original location was in Clark, Crawford, and Lawrence counties in Illinois, and Vigo County, Ind. Some of the original churches were from the Union Association of Indiana. In 1851, 13 churches reported 20 baptisms and 271 members.

From it the Westfield, Olney, and Mattoon associations were formed. It is served by a missionary and is located in Lawrence, Crawford, and Jasper counties. In 1954, 19 of the 21 churches reported 70 baptisms, 1,816 members, $46,198 total gifts, $15,078 mission gifts, $168,050 property value, and $10,200 church debt.

REHOBOTH. Organized in 1860. It is served by a missionary and is located in Fayette, Bond, Montgomery, Shelby, Christian, and Macon counties. Its first annual session, Oct. 4, 1861, reported 7 churches.

In 1861, 6 churches reported 20 baptisms and 295 members. In 1910, 32 churches reported 203 baptisms and 2,460 members. In 1954, 43 churches reported 289 baptisms, 4,148 members, $87,527 total gifts, $9,358 mission gifts, $340,400 property value, and $27,457 church debt. L. L. LEININGER

SALEM SOUTH. Organized May, 1854, as Salem Association of United Baptists with no record of the number of constituting churches. In 1890 United was dropped from the name, and in 1897 South was added to distinguish it from another association named Salem. Since 1940 it has been served by an associational missions superintendent. In 1954, 35 churches reported 395 baptisms, 6,025 members, $210,249 total gifts, $26,156 mission gifts, $595,350 property value, and $71,417 church debt. GILBERT WAUD

SALINE. Organized Oct. 10, 1890, at First Baptist Church, Harrisburg, Ill., by 10 churches with 969 members. The New Hampshire Declaration of Faith is used. It employs a missionary and is located in Saline and Gallatin counties. In 1954, 32 churches reported 269 baptisms, 8,333 members, $301,039 total gifts, $53,930 mission gifts, $1,172,250 property value, and $54,565 church debt. L. L. LEININGER

SANDY CREEK. Organized June, 1858, by three churches in west central Illinois, adopting articles of faith. Present churches are in Cass, Morgan, Scott, and Green counties. Owning a camp site where the association was organized, it has been served by an associational missions superintendent since 1930. In 1954, 41 churches reported 187 baptisms, 4,534 members, $100,373 total gifts, $13,047 mission gifts, $275,800 property value, and $21,218 church debt.

SANGAMON VALLEY. Organized Aug., 1950, by seven churches in Macon, Dewitt, and Champaign counties, six of which were affiliated with Macoupin, Great Lakes, and Louisville associations. It adopted articles of faith in 1950 and has been served by an associational missions superintendent since 1951. In 1954, 19 churches reported 361 baptisms, 2,556 members, $169,982 total gifts, $18,322 mission gifts, $462,850 property value, and $100,020 church debt. GILBERT WAUD

UNION. Organized at Vienna, Ill., in Oct., 1867, by 14 churches with 708 members. Articles of faith have been adopted. It employs a missionary and is located in Massac and Johnson counties. In 1910, 35 churches reported 89 baptisms and 1,728 members. In 1925, 21 churches reported 133 baptisms and 2,225 total members. In 1954, 25 churches reported 393 baptisms, 4,664 members, $232,868 total gifts, $28,211 mission gifts, $589,581 property value, and $103,152 church debt.

WABASH VALLEY SOUTHERN BAPTIST. Organized Mar. 15, 1948, at Grayville by five churches in White, Edwards, and Wabash counties.

Minutes of the first annual session reported 186 baptisms, 1,851 members, $90,131.76 total gifts, and $8,810.55 mission gifts. In 1954, 9 churches reported 151 baptisms, 2,322 members, $105,592 total gifts, $23,263 mission gifts, $471,000 property value, and $85,104 church debt.

L. L. LEININGER

WESTFIELD. Organized in 1862 by eight churches in Clark, Cumberland, and Cole counties formerly affiliated with Palestine Association. It adopted articles of faith in 1862. In 1954, 20 churches reported 92 baptisms, 2,032 members, $78,248 total gifts, $10,920 mission gifts, $254,880 property value, and $38,395 church debt.

GILBERT WAUD

WILLIAMSON COUNTY. Organized Feb. 20, 1880, at Shiloh Baptist Church by five churches with 12 members present. The New Hampshire Declaration of Faith has been adopted. It is served by an associational missionary and is located in Williamson and Johnson counties. In 1900, 31 churches reported 139 baptisms, and 2,346 members. In 1920, 24 churches reported 199 baptisms and 4,241 members. In 1954, 33 churches reported 504 baptisms, 9,522 members, $339,610 total gifts, $35,372 mission gifts, $1,117,050 property value, and $27,373 church debt.

L. L. LEININGER

ILLINOIS BAPTIST. A newspaper, now extinct, started by S. H. Bundy at Benton, Ill., in 1856, the year after the committee on periodicals of Franklin Association had pointed out the need of a paper in southern Illinois. Because of financial difficulty, in 1857 he transferred the paper to "brethern [sic] Wither and Grover," who established the paper at Bloomington, Ill., where H. J. Eddy and E. H. Roe joined the editorial staff. M. P. Heartly edited the paper in 1863. After continuing publication for several years, the paper was merged with *The Standard* of Chicago.

LYNN E. MAY, JR.

ILLINOIS BAPTIST, THE. A weekly newspaper which is the official publication of the Illinois Baptist State Association. The Illinois Baptist Founding Fund Association established the paper at Marion, Ill., maintained it, and guaranteed the editor's salary for five years. William Pinckney Throgmorton (*q.v.*), editor, and James H. Felts (1866–1932), publisher, produced the Thanksgiving number of 1905 as the first issue. The paper was in charge of a board of managers consisting of D. H. Prior, president; Clarence Hodge, secretary; C. E. Hitt, treasurer; G. W. Danbury, J. K. Trovillion, L. L. Stierwalt, J. H. Nyberg, H. A. Todd, and B. F. Baker. The executive committee consisted of Trovillion, Hitt, and Danbury. The *Primitive Missionary* (*q.v.*) was merged with the paper and Joseph O. Raines (*q.v.*) became associate editor along with George W. Stoddard, Tuscola, Ill.

The paper was the effective instrument used by Throgmorton in publicizing his famous resolution which resulted in the division of the Illinois Baptist State Convention (Northern, now American Baptist) and the call for and organization of the Illinois Baptist State Association Jan. 31, 1907. After the latter body had united with the Southern Baptist Convention, the paper became the official publication of the association in 1910, its circulation reaching 5,200. After Throgmorton's retirement on Dec. 1, 1927, Felts, the publisher, served as editor until his death on Jan. 12, 1932. Under the editorship of his successor, Elbert Waller (1870–1956), the state association moved the paper to Pinckneyville and published it there until Mar. 15, 1935, when the body transferred it to Cobden and elected W. W. Hunsaker (1895–   ) editor. The association, on Dec. 1, 1936, combined its Sunday school and Training Union departments with the paper and appointed I. E. Lee (1887–   ) secretary and editor. It also transferred the paper at that time to Carbondale where the editing has been done to date. Lee resigned as editor to become pastor in Nov., 1939.

At the end of 1955, the paper, owned by the Illinois Baptist State Association, retained its original name *The Illinois Baptist*. Editor B. J. Murrie (1900–   ) began his service with the Thanksgiving issue of 1939, when the paper had a circulation of 1,500 and a total printing of 1,700. Circulation in 1955 was 12,852 with 315 churches using the budget plan to send a copy into each home. The paper is the official publication of the state association and is under the general control of the 63-member board of directors and under specific direction of the nine-member Literature Committee of the board, which is a subsidiary chartered corporation under the laws of Illinois under the corporate name of *The Illinois Baptist*. The editor is elected by the board on the recommendation of the Literature Committee.

The 1956 budget of the association allowed $25,200 for the entire cost of operating the paper. All receipts of the paper from subscriptions and advertising are paid to the association, and all bills are paid by its treasurer on approval of the editor. Any difference between receipts and expense is the amount contributed by the association. Inventory value of furniture, office equipment, supplies, and mailing machine (less depreciation) is $4,042.18. Subscriptions value is $64,260.00, and total inventory value, $68,302.18. With the exception of Volume I, and an occasional missing issue, the files are complete and have been microfilmed.

B. J. MURRIE

ILLINOIS BAPTIST BUILDING. On Nov. 16, 1950, a site for a building for Illinois Baptists was purchased at 306 W. Main, Carbondale. Construction was begun on June 9, 1952, and 25 rooms were occupied on Aug. 28, 1953, by the state offices. The building was completed in July, 1954, at a cost of $525,975, including the cost of the site. The exterior walls are of brick and stone; the interior walls are of lightweight, acoustical, masonry blocks. The floors are concrete covered with asphalt tile and terrazzo. The building is a three-story structure,

140 by 69 feet. It is equipped with an elevator and air conditioning. There are approximately 30,000 square feet of floor space. The Baptist Book Store occupies about 5,560 square feet in the basement and on the ground floor. The remainder of the ground floor and basement is leased to tenants. In addition to the Baptist offices on the top floor of the building, there is a chapel seating 75. Before the erection of this building, the Baptist state association used rented rooms for office space. NOEL TAYLOR

ILLINOIS BAPTIST CHILDREN'S HOME. Its establishment followed a controversy in *The Illinois Baptist* in 1913–14 over the management, control, and a will connected with the Huddleston (Baptist) Orphanage, Irvington, now Centralia, which was supported by both state bodies, Illinois Baptist State Convention (American) and Illinois Baptist State Association (Southern). An efficiency committee of the state association recommended appointment of a seven-member orphanage committee on Oct. 22, 1914, to consider the "advisability and possibility of establishing a Baptist Orphanage which shall be under the direction and control of the Ill. Baptist State Ass'n." After the committee expressed an affirmative opinion in 1915, the association accepted a gift of 40 acres of land near Carmi from citizens of White County on July 19, 1916, and adopted methods of management, control, and operation Oct. 24, 1917.

Originally only full orphans were received and children from the same family were kept together until self-supporting. Until 1948 elementary school grades were taught in the home, but children are now sent to elementary and high school in Carmi. The total number of children cared for to July, 1956, was 508. With a licensed capacity for 64, the home cared for 64 children in 1956. Its name was changed from orphanage to *Baptist Children's Home, Inc., Carmi, Illinois,* Aug. 31, 1948. Grounds consist of 450 acres on which are seven buildings, including four cottages for children, and administration building, shop-laundry-apartment, two farmsteads, and auxiliary buildings. Total property value is $350,303.12. The home is incorporated with nine directors, who compose the benevolence committee of the association's state board of directors. Supported by gifts, offerings, and budget designations from individuals and churches, the home does not share in the Cooperative Program. Receipts for 1955 totaled $141,797.17 and the budget for 1957, $147,940.00. B. J. MURRIE

ILLINOIS BAPTIST STATE ASSOCIATION.
I. Baptist Beginnings. Prior to the organization of the Baptist General Association of Illinois in 1845, the history of Illinois Baptists can be divided into three periods: the pioneer period, the period of controversy, and the period of unification. In point of time, these periods overlap. During the first period (1796–1833) the Illinois Territory was settled and attained statehood and the first Baptist churches in Illinois were organized. Illinois Territory was part of the Northwest Territory and was Indian country, peopled by the Algonquin and the Iroquois Indians, among whom the Kaskaskias, Cahokias, Illini, Peorias, and Kickapoos were most numerous. Except for French and English traders, no white immigration was begun until the American Revolution. Following the French and Indian War, after which the territory was ceded to England, the king of England gave the Illinois Territory by charter to Virginia. The first settlers were Virginians, and the first churches were organized by these Virginia settlers. The second period (1809–45) was a period of growth and controversy. Many churches were organized and local associations were formed, but controversies marred the fellowship of these youthful bodies. Contention over slavery and over the attempt to make Illinois a slave state entered the churches, despite the Northwest Ordinance of 1787. The contention of the East, between Regular and Separate Baptists, and questions concerning mission work also divided these churches. To some degree the alignments found the proslavery and the antimission groups arrayed against the antislavery and promission people. The third period, which overlapped the preceding era (1818–45), was the period of unification, which resulted finally in a state body of Baptists with some degree of unity in its program.

Pioneer period.—The first American settlers in Illinois Territory were the soldiers of George Rogers Clark, who, after their period of enlistment, returned to the new territory. Clark had been commissioned by the Virginia legislature to march against the forts in Illinois Territory held by the British. In 1778 Clark with his Virginia and Kentucky soldiers captured Fort Massac, Fort Kaskaskia, and Vincennes. In 1781 a group of the American soldiers returned with their families to the new territory and established New Design in what is now Monroe and St. Clair counties in west central Illinois. By 1787 several scores of people lived in New Design and were visited by James Smith, a Baptist preacher from Kentucky. In the meetings conducted by Smith several were converted, including James Lemen (*q.v.*) and his wife. Lemen became the first Baptist in Illinois. A subsequent revival was interrupted by an Indian raid; but in Feb., 1794, Josiah Dodge, also of Kentucky, visited the settlement and baptized James Lemen, Catherine Lemen, John Gibons, and Isaac Enoch. In 1796 following a series of meetings conducted by David Badgely, the Baptist church of New Design was constituted on May 28 with 28 members. On Apr. 28, 1798, near the present city of Chester, the Bottoms Baptist Church was organized with 25 members. In 1804 a community of Kentuckians settled in what is now St. Clair County. Before leaving Kentucky they had organized a Baptist church and called a pastor. In Illinois they named their church Richland Baptist Church. In 1806 William Jones of North Carolina settled in what is now Madison County and the next year organized the Wood River Baptist Church. On Sept. 12, 1807, an arm of the New Design Church was constituted the Richland Creek Baptist Church. James Lemen and his family became charter members.

In 1809 settlements were made in eastern Illinois Territory by immigrants from Ohio and Pennsylvania. These settlements on the Wabash River at Palestine, Salt Springs (near Shawneetown), and old Fort Massac were visited by Isaac McCoy (q.v.), pastor of Maria Creek Church across the river in Indiana. In 1812 McCoy organized the Lamotte Baptist Church near Palestine. This was the first Baptist church in eastern Illinois. By 1820 Little Village, Grand Prairie, Little Wabash, and Little Prairie churches existed along the western banks of the Wabash River.

In the extreme southern tip of Illinois, between the Ohio and Mississippi rivers, Baptists in Illinois had a third beginning. Settlers from Tennessee, Kentucky, and the Carolinas made their homes here. In 1806 William Jones, enroute to New Design, visited these settlements and met Stephen Stilley; together they searched out the Baptist families. On July 19, 1806, they organized the Big Creek Baptist Church in what is now Pope County. This was the third church to be constituted in Illinois Territory, since the Richland Church was actually constituted in Kentucky. In the next 12 years several churches were organized. Lusk's Creek, Bankston Forks, Island Ripple, East Fork, Middle Fork and Muddy River, Hopewell, Bethel Creek, and Ten Mile churches were organized between 1806 and 1820. Ten Mile, Bankston Forks, and Raleigh (old Bethel Creek) are still active.

Another settlement of Baptists, undocumented except by land deeds, took place in what is now Williamson County. These Baptists were from North Carolina, members of Grassy Creek Church there. When they arrived in Illinois in 1800, they soon organized a Grassy Creek Church southeast of the present city of Carbondale. Although this church is extinct, it mothered many churches in this area.

The fifth beginning of Baptist churches in Illinois was in the area of what is now Chicago. In 1825 Isaac McCoy preached the first Baptist sermon in Fort Dearborn. For some years services were held irregularly by missionaries. In 1833 Allen B. Freeman arrived in Chicago. He found several Baptist laymen from the East, among them John Temple. The same year the First Church of Chicago was organized by Freeman. Within a few years Baptist churches were organized in Dupage, Plainfield, and Long Grove. The young missionary died in Dec., 1834, as a result of exposure suffered in a storm.

From these five general areas of settlement, Baptist work in Illinois began. Three separate attitudes were developed that influence Baptist life in Illinois to the present time.

Growth and controversy.—The new churches in Illinois were revival-born and were intensely missionary. New Design extended an arm to the Bottoms community and to the Richland community. Churches resulted in both places. John Clark, who reached New Design in 1797 and was baptized in 1803, preached extensively in southern Illinois. After uniting with the Bethel Baptist Church, he and Stephen Stilley helped to form a dozen churches over a period of 20 years in what is now the area of Union, Massac, Alexander, Johnson, and Pope counties. Two of the churches of this area—Shiloh Baptist Church, organized in 1817, and Jonesboro Baptist Church, organized in 1818—are the oldest churches in Illinois with a continuous history. In eastern Illinois the Lamotte Church and her preachers had led in the formation of four other churches by 1820.

In 1807 the four churches in the New Design area sent messengers to a meeting at Anthony Badgely's home in the Bottoms community. Out of this meeting on June 24, 1807, the Illinois Baptist Association was formed, the first association of Baptists in Illinois.

While the churches were revival-born and knew nothing of controversies in the Baptist world, older brethren from outside brought controversies with them. The division between Regular and Separate Baptists decades before had been healed in a union that gave to Baptists the name United Baptists. In the first meeting of this new association, it was suggested that correspondence be made with the nearest association of United Baptists in Kentucky. The abolitionists from Virginia in New Design wanted no fellowship with slave-holding Baptists. Tacitly they agreed to doctrinal fellowship with United Baptists but not to any correspondence with slave-holding Baptists. In 1808 another disagreement arose. In the June meeting the association voted to send out preachers into destitute areas, two by two in the pattern of the New Testament. In the fall meeting the Wood River Church raised an objection, and the June action was rescinded. Thus the method of doing mission work was brought into sharp focus. These two questions, slavery and missions, were to plague Illinois Baptists for years.

In 1809 the association met at the Bottoms Church in its last session. The question before it was, "Shall we retain the name of United Baptists and fellowship slave-holding churches?" Two papers were drawn up for signatures. One was headed United Baptists, and the other bore the title Baptists, Friends to Humanity. This name was suggested by James Lemen. The association divided; the slavery brethren took the name United Baptists, the New Design and Richland churches took the name Illinois Union, and the antislavery brethren called themselves Baptists, Friends to Humanity. Following this meeting James Lemen, his wife, their three sons and their wives, and Benjamin Ogle, on Dec. 10, 1809, were organized into the Cantine Baptized Church of Christ, Friends to Humanity. After the storm the brethren of the old association gathered to consider the situation. A committee was appointed to visit all the churches involved, with the result that the name of the association became the Illinois Union Baptist Association.

The Lemen family and the Cantine Church stood alone as the Baptists, Friends to Humanity. This was a vigorous family. The father and two sons were preachers. Within a few years they numbered six churches and some 130 members and were a moral force worthy of a place in history. They did not bolt the denomination. They considered themselves Baptists but were opposed to slavery.

In 1818 the Illinois Union Baptist Association adopted a plan of co-operation with the Board of Foreign and Home Missions. Soon they numbered 10 churches and 190 members.

While these two groups gained followers in western Illinois, another controversy gathered momentum in eastern Illinois in the Wabash Association, which had been formed of Indiana and Illinois churches in 1809. Daniel Parker (q.v.) of Tennessee moved into what is now Crawford County, Ill., in 1818. Parker was uneducated and uncouth but was possessed of fanatical zeal and rare eloquence. He first circulated a paper attacking the work of the American Baptist Home Mission Society on the basis of material in the only two board reports which he had read. In 1826 he developed his "two-seed" doctrine in which he contended that some were born of the devil and therefore were irrevocably lost. Those who followed Parker took the name Regular, No Effort, or Primitive Baptist. Controversy raged until well in the 1840's. Churches divided, new associations were formed, churches were excluded or withdrew from existing associations. Notable among these new associations of No Effort Baptists were the Okaw and Vermillion associations. In 1833 Parker left Illinois and migrated to Texas.

In the slavery controversy, for a few years the Cantine Creek Church, Friends to Humanity, stood alone. In 1811 a portion of the Silver Creek Church withdrew and was constituted a separate church. By 1824 the old Illinois Union Baptist Association began to be antimission. By 1827 the Friends to Humanity had 13 churches and were the largest single association of Baptists in Illinois. In 1830 a revival was experienced among these churches, and three associations were formed. None of these three groups, the United Baptists, Friends to Humanity, nor the antimission Baptists, was finally to dominate Baptist life in Illinois.

Into this pioneer Baptist life in 1817 came John Mason Peck (q.v.), an Eastern preacher sent by the Philadelphia missionary board of managers to evangelize the West. Peck spent four years in Missouri, during which time he visited the Illinois churches. He was on hand at the meeting of the Illinois Union Baptist Association to write the provision for the association which pledged them to co-operate with the new United Society for the Spread of the Gospel.

In 1822 following disagreement with the Philadelphia board, Peck moved to Rock Springs, Ill., to begin work under the Massachusetts Baptist Missionary Society. There he organized the Rock Springs Church and founded the Rock Springs Theological Seminary. His home and the seminary were well known. He soon organized a society known as Friends of Freedom, an antislavery movement which became a close ally with the Friends to Humanity. He led in the fight in 1824 against the proslavery advocates who were trying to make the new state a slave state. Following this victory he was a figure to be reckoned with in Illinois. He met Daniel Parker in debate before associations and became the leader of missionary forces. From the church at Rock Springs, he organized several other churches in the Alton and Edwardsville areas. Soon the issue began to narrow, and Baptists aligned themselves either with Peck and missions, his Gospel Tract Society and his Sunday School Society, or with the Parker antimission group. In his fight for Baptist democracy and missions as against the ecclesiasticism of the antimission group, Peck published in 1829 the first Baptist periodical in Illinois under the name *The Pioneer*. In 1836 the paper was published from Alton and called the *Western Pioneer and Baptist Standard Bearer*. Parker's publication began about the time *The Pioneer* appeared and bore the title *Advocate*. When Parker moved to Texas, his paper disappeared.

As the result of Peck's labors, the Edwardsville Association was organized in 1830. The Illinois Baptist Association had been formed in 1807. In 1810 the name was changed to Illinois Union Baptist Association. Wabash Baptist Association had been formed in 1809, and the Baptists, Friends to Humanity, in 1811. In 1820, 11 churches in extreme southern Illinois, organized by Stilley, Jones, Clark, and others, formed the Muddy River Association. In 1825 this association divided, and the missionary churches joined with the missionary churches of old Wabash Association to form the Little Wabash Association. In 1829 Muddy River Association divided again to form Bethel Association. In 1823 the old Illinois Union Association divided, forming Sangamon Valley Association. The body was shortlived and in 1826 changed its name from United to Regular Baptists. Other associations forming shortly after the Edwardsville Association were Clear Creek, Apple Creek, Okaw, and Vermillion in 1831, Blue River Association in 1833, Salem Association of United Baptists in 1834, and Saline Association in 1834. In 1841 Palestine Association was formed, with messengers of the missionary churches of the old Wabash and Little Wabash associations as the forming members. In this same year the Union Association was organized on Oct. 16. In 1843 the name Union Association was changed to Franklin Association. Vandalia Association was also formed in 1841.

Edwardsville Association was Peck's answer to antimissions and to the eccentric elements in Baptist life. It was not based on the old Union Association idea nor on the Friends to Humanity ideal. Using this association as a fulcrum, Peck began his crusade for unity among Baptists in Illinois.

The period of unification.—In 1830 Edwardsville Association called for a general meeting of Illinois Baptists on July 22, 1831, at Edwardsville. A committee of correspondence was appointed to contact all Baptists of the state. The chairman was James Lemen. Members were Paris Mason, B. F. Edwards, James Pulliam, Hubbel Loomis, and John Mason Peck. This committee employed a traveling missionary, Peck, a part of whose work was to publish the semimonthly paper *Pioneer and Western Baptist*. Each year the brethren in sympathy met in a union fellowship meeting. One of these meetings, Oct. 9–12, 1834, sought to form a state body. Thirty-one brethren came, but being denied the use of Whitehall Baptist Church by the antimission faction, they met in a barn belonging to Aaron Hicks, a brother of the missionary persuasion. The new body took the name Baptist Convention of Illinois. This body commended Sunday schools, regular preaching, missions, the Baptist Tract Society, and the *Pioneer and Western Baptist*. The new body continued to meet annually, with a program that covered the state. In 1837 they had 20 missionaries. By 1840 the new body had considerable strength, particularly in central Illinois.

However, there were other groups of Baptists, located to the north and to the south of the state, which were so far removed as to make close co-operation difficult. One of these groups was located around Chicago, which had grown as a city and as a power in Baptist life. In 1840 Baptist laymen and pastors in Chicago issued a call for a meeting of Baptists of northern Illinois, northern Indiana, and Wisconsin. On Jan. 6, 1841, the Northwestern Convention of Baptists was organized. Minutes of the 1842 convention meeting at Payson deprecated the action of these northern brethren. In the following years economic pressures, as well as the fact that both bodies in 1842 placed the same man on their respective executive boards, brought discussion of the desirability of a union of the two. The result of this conference was the adoption of a constitution for the General Baptist Association of Illinois to be submitted at a joint meeting in Fremont on Oct. 18, 1845. In this meeting the old conventions dissolved and the General Baptist Association of Illinois was constituted. The chief difference between the new and the old was a money basis of representation. The membership of the old convention was composed of delegates from the churches. The membership of the new association was composed of delegates from contributing churches. The new body had a modest beginning, with only 60 messengers present. Over the next years other churches and associations affiliated with this body. In 1852 Peck read to the association a corresponding letter from the Baptist Convention of Southern Illinois, naming messengers and expressing felicitations. Peck made the motion for acceptance. This group of southern Baptists was the other group of Baptists that had never affiliated with the Illinois convention of 1834 or with the general association of 1845. Most of these associations had preferred to maintain correspondence with associations in Kentucky and Tennessee. By 1855 the new state body numbered 350 churches with 24,643 members. This body remained intact until 1906.

II. History of State Association. *Organization of the state association.*—For most of their history Baptists in Illinois have been divided. Baptists in southern Illinois were descendants of pioneers from Kentucky, Tennessee, and the Carolinas. Not until 1855 did any of the southern associations affiliate with the Baptist General Association. Until then fraternal greetings were exchanged, but no co-operative work was undertaken. Following the Civil War Baptists in southern Illinois had their own privately owned publications, the *Baptist News* and the *Illinois Baptist*.

The break among Baptists in Illinois came in 1906 and centered about the authority of the state body to disfellowship Unitarian and open-communion churches. George Burman Foster of the University of Chicago, a member of a Baptist church in Chicago, was the author of a widely criticized book, *The Finality of the Christian Religion*, in which he allegedly questioned the deity of Christ. He was defended by a member of the state executive board, among others. Another member of the board and pastor of the Galesburg church espoused open communion in a booklet, *What Saith the Scriptures*. The *Illinois Baptist* editorially attacked both these books. In 1906 at the meeting of the general association in Carbondale, William Pinckney Throgmorton (*q.v.*), editor of the *Illinois Baptist* and pastor of the First Baptist Church, Marion, Ill., introduced a motion to amend the constitution by adding an article which declared that the association should be composed of members of Baptist churches in the state of Illinois. The amendment went on to define a Baptist church as a group which

avowedly believes and distinctly teaches, among other Bible tenets the following: (1) The essential Deity of Jesus Christ; (2) the full inspiration and authority of the Bible as the written word of God; (3) the absolute necessity of spiritual regeneration; (4) Salvation by Grace through Faith in Christ's atoning blood; (5) Scriptural baptism and membership in a Baptist church as orderly and essential prerequisites to communion at the Lord's Supper as observed among our people.

This amendment was defeated by a vote of three to one. A resolution which affirmed the essential deity of Christ and the authority of the Scriptures was then offered and passed. Strangely, the minutes of the state body contained no reference to the proposed amendment, but the

Baptist Standard of Chicago and the *Illinois Baptist* both gave running accounts of the procedure. Those who favored the proposed amendment assumed because of its defeat that the state association thus explicitly refused to disfellowship any Unitarian or open-communion churches. Hundreds of questionnaires were sent out by the editor of the *Illinois Baptist* asking three questions:

> Shall we continue to work with the Illinois Baptist State Convention [the general association in its 1906 meeting incorporated as the Illinois Baptist State Convention] and try to bring it to our way of thinking?
> Shall we agree on the old Baptist faith held by our fathers and form another convention based on strict Baptist principles?
> Will we stand by what the majority vote thus taken decides?

Response to this inquiry led to a meeting at the First Baptist Church of Pinckneyville, Ill., to formulate a constitution and articles of organization. It was decided that if 200 churches adopted the proposed constitution, a new state body would be organized. On Jan. 31, 1907, at the First Baptist Church, Pinckneyville, Ill., 226 churches reported favorably on the new constitution, and it was moved to complete the organization of a new body. Messengers were enrolled. Judge R. H. Flannigan of East St. Louis was elected moderator, and Elder C. E. Hitt of Carterville, secretary. The new body incorporated under the name The Illinois Baptist State Association.

Constitutional structure.—The constitution of the new body provided that membership should be composed of members of Baptist churches, and a Baptist church was defined in the words of the amendment defeated by the old convention in 1906. The object of the new body as stated in the constitution was to plant and support Baptist churches in Illinois and to foster all Baptist interests, such as, education, literature, home and foreign missions, and general benevolence. A mission board of 30 members was authorized to conduct all business of the body. An executive board, composed of five members elected by the mission board, was empowered to act ad interim for both the mission board and the association. Standing committees on the state of religion, Christian stewardship, Sunday school work, young people's work, Christian education, religious literature, and auditing were to be elected annually by the state association. The board was to elect a financial secretary who would solicit money. The New Hampshire Confession of Faith was adopted as the doctrinal statement of the association. In 1909 the constitution was amended by Article XI, which provided for acceptance of institutions of learning for support, and in 1910 by Article XII, which provided for publication and control of the *Illinois Baptist*. This constitution was amended in 1918 to increase the mission board from 30 to 45 members and to change the name financial secretary to secretary of missions. Again in 1920 the constitution was amended, changing the board of missions to a board of 60 members and calling this group the Board of Directors, with an executive committee composed of the chairman and secretary and the chairman of each committee in the board. The board was to organize into committees, and these committees were to direct the work assigned them. The state association was composed of members of Baptist churches sent on a numerical basis. Each association was entitled to one messenger and to one additional member for each 1,000 members. The purpose of the association was enlarged to make room for all benevolent projects and for Christian education and publications. This constitution remained in use until 1939, when a new constitution was adopted and substituted for the constitution of 1920. The new constitution provided that membership be composed of messengers elected by regular Missionary Baptist Churches "of like faith" which co-operate in district associations in Illinois. Board membership was restricted to 60 members, not to exceed one from each church and not more than five from an association. Provisions were made in the constitution for the incorporation of various agencies of the state association and the addition of an endowment committee. In 1951 the constitution was revised, changing the name of the presiding officer from moderator to president, removing any limitation on the number of laymen who might serve on the board of directors, and limiting the period of board membership to two consecutive terms.

Denominational affiliation.—The new state body in 1909 voted to co-operate with the Southern Baptist Convention in home and foreign missions and to employ a field secretary to promote this new project. By 1910 money sent to Southern agencies permitted the sending of messengers to the Southern Baptist Convention. Accordingly, in the 1910 convention held in Baltimore three state messengers and five associational messengers, in keeping with the plan of membership of the Southern Baptist Convention, were present to represent Illinois. The enrolment committee accepted their credentials, and the messengers were seated. The report of this action as found in the *Baptist and Reflector* and in the *Illinois Baptist* is as follows: "The anticipated trouble over reception of the Illinois delegates did not appear in the organization. The three state representatives; W. P. Throgmorton, W. H. Carver, and Marion Teague were formally seated. The following associational delegates were also seated: C. E. Perryman, A. L. Smith, D. W. Holtslaw, James Biggs, and W. R. Mizell." From that time the closest fellowship and co-operation existed between the two bodies. Illinois received full representation on all boards and agencies, and the Convention through its Sunday School Board and Home Mission Board reinforced the program of Baptists in Illinois.

Institutions.—Until Article XI was added to the constitution, the new association had no institutions. By this amendment Creal Springs Academy and Ewing College became affiliated with the state body.

In 1938 the state association authorized the establishment of a school in Carbondale, Ill., and that year the school was begun under the name Illinois Baptist Foundation. George L. Johnson was elected dean and later president, when the name was changed to the Southern Illinois Baptist College of the Bible. In 1954 property was bought in Champaign, Ill., near the University of Illinois and the same type of work begun.

Illinois' oldest institution is the Baptist Children's Home at Carmi. In 1917 the First Baptist Church of Carmi gave the state association a tract of land. Other land was purchased, and the Carmi Baptist Children's Home was begun. George Washington Danbury was the first superintendent and supervised the building of the two early units. Joseph Dodge Mathias (*q.v.*) later became superintendent and for many years guided the home's policies.

Administration.—The state association has had but four executive secretaries. B. F. Rodman (*q.v.*) served in this capacity for the first 17 years. In 1911 a field secretary for home and foreign missions was employed when Miss Dora Cain became the first Woman's Missionary Union secretary. From this meager staff the administration and promotion of the work have grown to include 11 separate departments. In 1915 J. L. Corzine of Anna was elected secretary of the Sunday School and Training Union Department. In 1925 J. M. Pepper was elected general secretary. These were years of advancing and expanding programs of work but of burdensome debts. In 1925 the debt of Illinois Baptists was $135,465.11. During Pepper's administration the debt was reduced to $57,988.11. E. W. Reeder (*q.v.*) was elected secretary in 1929 and served for 17 years. During these years the indebtedness was paid, the membership of the churches greatly increased, and a large measure of stability added to the work. In 1946 there were 577 churches with a membership of 92,023. Total gifts to all causes were $1,647,042.42 in contrast to $158,005.00 in 1929. In 1946 Noel M. Taylor was elected executive secretary. The number of churches increased to 694 in 1954, and over-all gifts amounted to approximately $5,000,000 in 1953. In 1954 the chair of Bible at the University of Illinois was founded, the state office building erected, and more than 100 new churches organized.

III. Program of Work of Illinois Baptists.

Board of directors.—The administrative board of the Illinois Baptist State Association is called the board of directors. It is composed of 63 members, one third of whom are elected annually by the state association. Each association must be represented by at least one and not more than five members. Twelve members must be women and nine must be laymen. Persons receiving remuneration from any institution or office of the denomination are ineligible. Churches are limited to one member, who must have had membership in a church affiliated with the convention for at least one year prior to his election. Board membership is limited to two consecutive terms of three years each. Persons become eligible for re-election after one year. The state body grants to this board authority to supervise and control all business and work, including missions and stewardship, education, literature, Sunday school, Training Union, W.M.U., Brotherhood, evangelism, music, beneficences, and camp activities, in the interim of the annual sessions. Four meetings of the board are held annually. Twelve members constitute a quorum.

The board elects its own chairman and secretary and organizes into committees. The chairmen of these committees become, with the chairman and secretary of the board, the executive committee. This committee has the authority to act for the board of directors in all matters between board meetings except to sell or exchange property, unless specifically authorized by the board. The executive committee is named the budget committee and instructed to prepare a suggested budget yearly for the consideration of the board. The committees and the membership of each committee are specified as follows: missions and stewardship, five members; education, nine members; literature, nine members; Sunday school, five members; Training Union, five members; Brotherhood, five members; evangelism, five members; music, five members; benevolence, nine members; and W.M.U., five members. Each committee manages the interest committed to it subject to the direction of the board. Three committees (benevolence, literature, and education) are incorporated as boards of trustees: the benevolence committee for the Baptist Children's Home, the literature committee for the *Illinois Baptist,* and the education committee for the Southern Illinois College of Bible, usually known as the Illinois Baptist Foundation.

The board of directors elects the executive secretary, whose duties are set forth in the constitution. He is to promote missions, Christian education, benevolence, and such interests as the board may authorize. He also receives all money coming to the association and makes a report of all funds as per the auditor's report to the quarterly meetings of the board and the annual meeting of the state association. He holds in safekeeping all evidences of property and documents belonging to the state association and gives inventory of same to the board of directors annually. The interpretation of these directives to the executive secretary is that he give guidance and direction to all the administrative and promotional phases of Baptist life within the province of the association as specified by it in its constitution. Noel Myron Taylor, the present (1956) executive secretary, came to this office in 1946.

Missions.—The state mission program includes a city mission program and a pioneer mission program with subsidies for ministers in mission areas and a church revolving loan fund. In 1954, 23 churches received pastoral subsidy. Six associations received aid from state mission funds in the support of their associational missionaries. On July 1, 1953, Walter W. Mihlfeld became the state rural missionary to give co-ordination to the program of local associations. In 1954 there were 18 superintendents of associational missions on the field. Illinois has one city mission program, located at East St. Louis. Fred Propst is the city missions superintendent.

In co-operation with the Home Mission Board of the Southern Baptist Convention, two pioneer missionaries are located in northern Illinois. These men are charged with the responsibility of beginning new work. In 1954, 21 of these missions and mission churches were aided with pastoral subsidy through the co-operative missions department of the Home Mission Board. A limited fund known as the Church Revolving Loan Fund is provided by the missions department for state mission funds and in 1954, 32 such loans were in force.

The department of missions and evangelism was set up in 1949 with S. Otho Williams as secretary. In 1952 a new department of stewardship and missions was created. E. H. Moore became secretary of the department and at present heads this phase of the work. The evangelism department was established in July, 1953, with L. H. Moore as secretary. Formerly the work of evangelism had been directed in connection with other departments. Since 1951 the state has co-operated with the Home Mission Board and the Convention-wide department of evangelism in the promotion of evangelism.

Educational ministry.—Sunday school, Training Union, Woman's Missionary Union, Baptist Student Union, Brotherhood, and music, each has departmental status with a secretary directing its promotion. In 1954 the Sunday school department, Wheeler L. Thompson, secretary, reported enrolment gains of approximately 17,000 in net enrolment with a total enrolment of 106,000 and 10,281 training awards. Three hundred and eighty Vacation Bible schools were reported. The Training Union department, Bluford M. Sloan, secretary, reported a Training Union enrolment of 28,707 with 50 additional churches having new units of Training Union work. "M" Night attendance had been 6,694 in Dec., 1953. In 1954 the Woman's Missionary Union reported 1,339 organizations in 382 of the 694 churches in the state. Helen Sinclair was elected secretary of this department in Jan., 1955. Baptist Student Union work, M. V. Entrekin, secretary, reported three B.S.U. organizations in the state: one at Southern Illinois University, Carbondale, Lucille Steele, director; one at the University of Illinois, Champaign; and one at Wheaton College, Wheaton. The present Brotherhood secretary, George E. Wheeler, came to the department in June, 1954; he reported 225 churches having Brotherhood organizations that year. The music department, Eugene F. Quinn, secretary, reported organizations in all associations. More than 1,000 awards were granted by this department. The Radio and Television Committee and the Baptist Historical Society are elected by the state association in its annual meeting; neither has a paid director. Both committees have budget allocations. The Historical Society has gathered considerable historical data. Much material has been microfilmed. The Radio and Television Committee arranged for statewide broadcasts in 1954 during the simultaneous revivals in April. The budget of the committee is used principally in subsidizing local Baptist broadcasts.

Institutions and properties.—Southern Baptists in Illinois have three institutions: the Baptist Children's Home, the Southern Illinois College of Bible, and the chair of Bible, Champaign. The Children's Home is located on a 160-acre farm near Carmi. The home is fully accredited with the state of Illinois. Modern cottages can accommodate 70 children. The home does not share in co-operative receipts but is supported by direct offerings from the churches. Wade B. East is superintendent.

The Southern Illinois College of Bible at Carbondale has a staff of three teachers besides the housemothers and dormitory workers. The administration building has three units: the classrooms, the Wasson Memorial Chapel, and a modern cafeteria. Doyle Dormitory houses the men students and Johnson Hall, the women students. George L. Johnson is president of this institution, and Harral A. Hall is the dean. All courses taught are accredited at Southern Illinois University. Four hundred and sixty-one students were enrolled in the college in 1953–54.

The chair of Bible at Champaign is of recent origin. At present the state B.S.U. secretary teaches classes which meet in the property purchased in 1953. Work here is accepted by the University of Illinois toward degrees. Twenty students were enrolled in these classes.

Illinois Baptists also own an encampment ground known as Lake Sallateeska near Pinckneyville. Forty acres of land with 25 cabins, an auditorium, a dining room, and a superintendent's home comprise this property. The W.M.U. and Brotherhood departments conduct auxiliary encampments here.

In 1954 the Baptist Building was completed in Carbondale at a cost of $525,000. This two-story building houses the Baptist Book Store on the first floor and Baptist offices on the second floor. The other area is rental space occupied by business interests.

Promotional work.—The *Illinois Baptist* has been the organ of publicity of the state association since 1909. B. J. Murrie, editor, reports a circulation of 12,196. All the departments have access to the paper's columns. The paper is supported by Cooperative Program receipts and subscriptions. There is no department of promotion in the state. Most general promotion has been delegated to the department of missions and stewardship.

IV. ILLINOIS STATISTICAL SUMMARY

Year	Associations	Churches	Church Membership	Baptisms	S. S. Enrolment	V.B.S. Enrolment	T. U. Enrolment	W.M.U. Enrolment	Brotherhood Enrolment	Mission Gifts	Total Gifts	Value Church Property	State Capital Worth
1830													(Explanation: This column includes total value of Schools, Children's Homes, Hospitals, Foundation, Buildings, etc.)
1840													
1850													
1860													
1870													
1880													
1890													
1900													
1905													
1910													
1915	25	605	62,981	3,943	43,194	....	....	....	....	$ 33,021	$ 260,100	$ 1,284,590	....
1920	25	586	57,672	2,932	42,338	....	3,500	....	....	146,818	510,161	1,794,568	....
1925	25	594	62,319	3,119	48,446	963	6,093	....	....	80,888	539,502	2,794,623	....
1930	23	581	63,267	2,793	49,200	1,065	5,760	....	....	70,153	450,572	2,904,046	....
1931	23	567	64,177	3,574	50,347	1,087	6,355	....	....	58,523	405,337	2,731,978	....
1932	23	568	66,220	4,096	53,272	821	6,654	4,963	....	48,930	367,730	2,638,112	....
1933	23	568	67,151	3,435	53,463	496	6,872	4,656	....	35,018	308,514	2,586,369	....
1934	23	584	69,770	3,021	53,351	1,889	8,046	5,208	....	37,583	312,196	2,517,645	....
1935	23	584	70,854	3,101	55,653	3,432	7,973	6,814	....	43,173	346,035	2,566,741	$ 185,000
1936	23	587	73,205	3,177	56,494	4,982	9,749	6,621	....	53,469	422,972	2,594,917	....
1937	23	588	74,213	2,763	55,355	5,141	12,278	6,308	....	58,384	412,651	2,623,795	....
1938	23	578	77,026	3,719	59,219	7,644	11,136	7,504	....	64,862	470,407	2,728,054	....
1939	21	549	78,282	4,621	60,310	13,723	12,907	7,896	....	81,024	511,040	2,805,699	....
1940	21	564	81,382	3,659	62,334	14,601	9,677	8,332	1,070	93,770	641,311	2,914,888	....
1941	21	565	83,516	3,605	62,794	17,471	10,416	8,484	1,322	115,704	683,795	2,951,739	....
1942	21	568	83,239	2,857	59,192	14,645	9,968	8,559	806	152,150	862,569	3,187,393	....
1943	21	577	86,514	2,818	58,274	13,197	9,555	8,508	1,035	193,232	939,825	3,228,556	....
1944	22	573	89,240	3,114	59,600	16,268	9,455	8,929	894	238,460	1,161,096	3,373,301	309,967
1945	23	580	92,270	3,375	63,539	17,506	10,714	8,814	897	301,709	1,464,961	3,464,099	....
1946	23	590	94,793	3,424	63,705	21,399	13,241	9,701	1,104	386,465	1,608,326	4,172,112	....
1947	23	589	94,729	3,920	65,196	23,096	13,512	10,792	1,690	367,832	1,875,609	4,862,724	....
1948	24	586	97,624	4,827	69,782	23,724	15,194	11,905	1,860	389,460	2,237,003	5,889,861	....
1949	24	587	100,224	4,838	72,927	26,242	17,521	11,887	2,465	425,161	2,485,882	7,002,267	....
1950	26	602	103,821	5,991	79,207	29,138	18,500	13,087	3,093	430,556	2,724,716	7,999,343	....
1951	26	619	108,848	6,662	83,459	28,008	20,156	14,710	3,098	494,196	3,129,774	9,620,071	....
1952	26	638	114,451	6,040	88,791	30,906	22,368	15,784	3,517	658,662	3,684,942	11,879,356	....
1953	26	650	118,646	6,260	92,339	29,351	24,865	15,876	3,810	691,330	4,144,532	13,501,642	....
1954	28	694	125,797	7,769	106,871	40,256	28,705	18,163	4,196	751,634	4,932,450	16,058,757	1,320,138

NOEL M. TAYLOR

BIBLIOGRAPHY: Baptist General Association of Illinois *Minutes*, 1945-51. *Baptist News* (1901, 1910). D. Benedict, *A General History of Baptist Denomination of America* (1850). E. P. Brand, *A History of Illinois Baptists* (1930). Clear Creek Association *Minutes* (1886). *Illinois Baptist*. Illinois Baptist State Convention *Minutes*. Illinois Baptist State Association *Minutes* (1909-54). M. Lawrence, *John Mason Peck* (1940). T. J. Wheeler and H. Etter, *History of Illinois Baptist State Association* (1940).   L. H. MOORE

IMAGE OF GOD. This term is the scriptural designation for the likeness of God in Christ and in man. The image of God in Christ, who is the only true and perfect likeness, is related both to the orders of creation and redemption. As "the image of the invisible God" Christ is the agent through whom all things were originally created and in whom they hold together (Col. 1:15-17). As the image of God, he is also agent of the new creation in whom all things pass away and become new again (II Cor. 4:3-6; 5:17). Perfect lordship over the original creation and perfect love in the new creation sum up the meaning of the image of God in Christ.

The image of God in the original creation of man is the dominion of man over the whole created order. The Creator is the Lord of man, and man is the lord of creation. His dominion (Gen. 1:26-27) over all created things is his likeness to God, a likeness which applies to the dual nature of man as both male and female (Gen. 5:1-2). The dignity of man, thus attained, forbids murder (Gen. 9:6) and makes the cursing of man a contradiction (Jas. 3:9).

The image of God in the Christian includes the dominion of man over creation, but the essential point is his dynamic existence in the love of God. God's image in man, in both the senses, is the revelation that man was created to be lord over creation and to love the Creator. Dynamic existence in the love of God is the renewal of man "in knowledge after the image of him that created him" (Col. 3:10). This image is seen in the present transformation of man by the Holy Spirit from one degree of glory to another (II Cor. 3:17) and the future conformity of man to the image of the Son of God (Rom. 8:29; I Cor. 15:49).

See also GOD and MAN.

BIBLIOGRAPHY: D. S. Cairns, *The Image of God in Man* (1953).   DALE MOODY

IMMACULATE CONCEPTION. Pope Pius IX (1792-1878) promulgated the dogma of the immaculate conception of the virgin Mary before an assembly of cardinals and bishops in St. Peter's in Rome on Dec. 8, 1854. This was one result of the ultramontanism, led by the restored Jesuits, which also produced the syllabus of errors and the decree of infallibility. Thus debate on the question was ended in the Roman Catholic Church.

The issue was not Mary's perpetual virginity, held widely since Jerome's *De perpetua Virginitate B. Mariae*, but whether or not she was free from sin when she was conceived. Anselm of Canterbury (1033-1109) believed Mary was both conceived and born in sin. Thomas Aquinas (1225?-74) taught that she was conceived in sin but sanctified before birth, a view in which he was followed by the Dominicans. John Duns Scotus (1265?-1308) and the Franciscans argued for the immaculate conception. In 1483, Pope Sixtus IV (1414-84) reminded Roman Catholics that the question of the character of Mary's conception was undecided.

The dogma, allegedly "revealed by God," declares that "the blessed Virgin Mary was, in the first instance of her conception, preserved untouched by any taint of original guilt, by a singular grace and privilege of Almighty God, in view of the merits of Christ Jesus the Saviour of mankind."

BIBLIOGRAPHY: H. Bettenson, *Documents of the Christian Church* (1947). *Decretum PII IX De Immaculata Conceptione Beatae Virginis Mariae*, in *The Creeds of Christendom*, Vol. II, ed. P. Schaff (1919). F. G. Holweck, "Immaculate Conception," *The Catholic Encyclopedia*, ed. C. G. Herbermann (1910), Vol. VII. P. Schaff, "The Papal Definition of the Immaculate Conception of the Virgin Mary, 1854," *The Creeds of Christendom* (1919). F. J. Paul, *Romanism and Evangelical Christianity, A Study of Origins and Development* (1940).   PENROSE ST. AMANT

IMMANENCE. The indwelling of God in the universe, including man. In biblical teaching, God not only transcends the universe but is also actively present within it (Gen. 1:1; 3:8; Rom. 1:20; Eph. 4:6). While deism stresses the absolute independence (transcendence) of God from the universe, and pantheism, the absolute identification (immanence) of God with the universe, Hebrew-Christian theism holds that God is immanent in the universe but not exhausted in it, i.e., that God is everywhere (omnipresent) in the universe but infinitely more than the universe at the same time. The doctrines of revelation, incarnation, salvation, Holy Spirit, the church, etc., are all rooted in the doctrine of divine immanence.

See also DEISM, GOD, PANTHEISM, THEISM.

BIBLIOGRAPHY: B. P. Bowne, *The I. of God* (1905). A. H. Strong, *Systematic Theology* (1907). J. Dillenberger, *God Hidden and Revealed* (1953).
       TED R. CLARK

IMMERSION. See BAPTISM.

IMMORTALITY. Classical and Christian views of immortality have been so confused in the history of Christian thought that it has become necessary to distinguish clearly between them. The classical idea, as expressed in the writings of Plato and Aristotle, bases belief in immortality on the nature of man. The first of Plato's five idealistic arguments holds that life must exist over against death to avoid the destruction of all things by death (*Phaedo*, 61e). In a second argument Plato, insisting on the existence of the soul before it dwelt in the body, holds that it is possible for the soul to exist after the death of the body (*Phaedo*,

70c–72e). A third view assumes the soul to be a simple substance which cannot be divided and refuses the idea that the disintegration of physical death can divide and destroy the soul (*Phaedo*, 80b). In his fourth argument Plato holds that the soul participates in life-in-itself and cannot die (*Phaedo*, 103b–107b). The final statement of the theory argues for the principle of eternal motion—in the self-existence of the soul (*Phaedrus*, 245c–246a; *Laws*, 893–896). Plato's views have often been confused with biblical teachings, but Aristotle's naturalistic idea that only the race of man is imperishable and that only what is part of God survives death is not so easy to confuse with truth (*De Anima*, 408–430). The tendency to identify God and man makes it difficult to find a relation between these classical theories and biblical thought.

Christian thought bases belief in immortality on the nature of God. The tree of knowledge (Gen. 3:1–7) proclaims the fact that man is very wise, and the tree of life (Gen. 3:22–24) is guarded by a flaming sword to remind sinful man that immortality is the gift of God. In the New Testament immortality is a quality of deity (I Tim. 1:17) and is possessed by God alone (I Tim. 6:14–16). Immortality becomes possible for man with the "appearing of our Saviour Jesus Christ, who hath abolished death, and hath brought life and immortality to light through the gospel" (II Tim. 1:10). This statement does not mean that some men do not survive death; it rather means that immortality is far more than mere survival after death. Immortality means sharing the very life of God, who gives immortality to the redeemed in two stages. The first stage is the clothing of the human spirit with immortality when it leaves the body. Death appears as a dissolution (*katalysis*) as far as the body is concerned (II Cor. 4:16 to 5:10), but from the perspective of faith, death is a departure (*analysis*) to be with the Lord (Phil. 1:23; II Tim. 4:6–8). The second stage is the immortality of the body, which, according to biblical thought, is clothed with immortality at the resurrection of the dead (I Cor. 15). Other biblical writings, especially Hebrews and Revelation, sustain this view of life after death.

See also DEATH and INTERMEDIATE STATE.

BIBLIOGRAPHY: J. Baillie, *And the Life Everlasting* (1934). F. T. Lord, *The Conquest of Death* (1942). A. E. Taylor, *The Christian Hope of Immortality* (1946).

DALE MOODY

INCARNATION. Denotes the career and person of Christ, conceived of as the life and acts of God in and through the life of a man. Christian theology, based on the scriptural presentations of Christ, maintains that the eternally pre-existent Son of God, the eternal Word, Very God, became incarnate in the man Jesus. In him perfect God was conjoined with perfect man in an organic and total unity of personality, without any loss of identity or change and confusion of nature. Christ was and continues to be forever God and Man in one unique personality.

See also JESUS CHRIST.

BIBLIOGRAPHY: D. M. Baille, *God Was in Christ, An Essay on Incarnation and Atonement* (1948). J. E. Davidson, "The Principle of Incarnation in Pauline Theology" (1951).

JAMES E. DAVIDSON

INDEPENDENCY AND CO-OPERATION, BAPTIST. The history of the Baptist denomination shows that its polity is not a static thing. Traditional ways of doing and thinking are sometimes challenged and are occasionally modified or even reversed. Although there is no special authority for some traditions, mainly the features of Baptist polity are based on principles derived from the Scriptures, usage through the years, and the consensus of Baptist writers.

The independency and co-operation of Baptist churches and general bodies are a paradox to many people. Baptists themselves, trusting to the leadership and guidance of the Holy Spirit, believe it to be the strength of their organization. The following is a statement of the traditional Southern Baptist polity of independency and co-operation as it generally prevailed in the middle of the 20th century.

Baptists stand strongly for the independence of the individual and hold that the individual conscience must stand against any religious body. The power of the church is entirely moral and spiritual. This power extends over its own members only and, even there, is limited by the rights of private judgment and individual conscience.

The Baptist view of the constitution and polity of the church holds that each church is a free, independent, and self-governing body. The local church's independency is a cardinal and directive tenet. In fact, it may be said that this is the fundamental principle of Baptist church polity upon which all else rests. Baptist churches are not interdependent; in themselves they are autonomous entities which are separate from every other church.

Although the government of the church is administered by its members, Baptist churches are practical democracies, not pure democracies. The existence of the pastoral office and the office of deacon imply practical self-imposed limitations on congregational action. Various committees and organizations carry this limitation even further. Although, when the church is in conference, no one possesses a pre-eminence of authority, and each enjoys an equality of rights, the responsibility for leadership to a significant extent has already been distributed to various functionaries and organizations.

The democratic theory of majority rule holds except when a minority refuses to abide by the decision of the majority. In differences of opinion in Baptist churches, a simple majority or other previously agreed-upon majority decides. It is the duty of the minority to concur in this decision up to the point of the violation of individual conscience.

Church action is final, and the power of the church is not to be transferred or alienated, nor is the church to empower any man or body of men to do anything which impairs its independency.

General bodies among Southern Baptists (district associations, state conventions, the Southern Baptist Convention) are composed of individual Baptists who have voluntarily associated themselves together. These usually are chosen by co-operating churches; but sometimes, notably in the cases of state conventions, several of which include individuals chosen by district associations, other means of selection are used.

The basic principles of general bodies are derived from the nature and the basic principles of the local churches. Therefore, the general bodies function under the following principles: The members of general bodies must be equal in rank and privilege. The organizing and operating principle is voluntary co-operation. General bodies are autonomous and independent. Like local churches, they are purely advisory and exemplary in their relations to other general bodies and to churches. While separate from the churches and sovereign in their own spheres, general bodies exist chiefly to enable the churches co-operating through this to carry out their divinely ordained tasks more effectually and expeditiously. To this end they are authorized to create agencies, devise plans, foster institutions, and employ means in keeping with the teachings and examples of New Testament churches. General bodies, as well as Baptist churches, are created by free and voluntary action of their members and may be dissolved or disbanded by the same action.

From these principles are derived inherent powers which are not to be abrogated or delegated to other Baptist bodies. These include the power to carry out the objectives of fellowship, conference, and promotion; the power to employ agents; and the power to call on individuals, churches, and other general bodies to co-operate, and likewise the power to co-operate with other general bodies and with churches.

General bodies, by their nature, have limitations. They are not to take into their membership any other Baptist body; they may be composed only of individuals. There is to be no rank or special privilege in the body of the membership nor any attempt to compel the co-operation of any Baptist individual, church, or other general body. They are not to exercise the functions of any other Baptist body. They cannot pass rules or regulations for other Baptist bodies, nor may they arrange themselves into a graded system of synods and exercise any presbyterial, episcopal, or hierarchical jurisdiction over any individual or any Baptist body. The general bodies are not to be regarded as church bodies or exercise any distinct church function. Neither are they to set absolute territorial limitations.

The autonomous general bodies among themselves are of equal rank. Their voluntary co-operation with one another is the co-operation of equals. In other words, one does not proceed from the state convention "up" to the Southern Baptist Convention or "down" to the district association. Rather, one goes "across" from equal to equal. Also, one general body is as near to its affiliated churches as another, as the relationship is spiritual rather than physical.

Although messengers come from churches into meetings of general bodies, there is no conflict of jurisdiction between the church and the general body. As members of the general body, they vote and act as individuals. If they act under the influence of the known wishes of their churches in measures which are considered in the general body, they are acting under spiritual influence, not ecclesiastical compulsion.

The foregoing descriptions of churches, general bodies, and their relationships to each other, represent the traditional Southern Baptist stand ideologically and theoretically. It emphasizes the independence of the local church. Nevertheless, these independent local churches believe they should co-operate, and their media for co-operation are the district associations, the state conventions, and the Southern Baptist Convention.

The associational principle involved in this co-operation is not considered an abridgment of local independency or local autonomy but rather, an enlargement of it. Whereas independency and autonomy might easily become isolation and strangulation, association gives outlet for the strength and wisdom generated in the local group. Thus considered, the associational principle becomes, next to independency, the most potent single development in Baptist polity.

It may be said that independency is the ideal, and co-operation is the practical. Therefore, Baptist churches and general bodies are constantly seeking the formula which most safely guards the essential life of the independent unit, while at the same time it allows association with other independent denominational units in co-operative enterprise.

See also POLITY, BAPTIST CHURCH.

FLOYD PATTERSON

INDEPENDENT BAPTIST CHURCH OF AMERICA. A body of Swedish Free Baptists that dates back to 1893. Their doctrinal position includes laying on of hands at time of conversion. They are generally pacifist. In 1927 they reported 13 churches, seven of them in Minnesota, with a membership of 222. In 1952 they reported two churches with 50 members and two pastors.   ALBERT MCCLELLAN

INDEPENDENTS. A name applied to those

who, from the middle of the 16th century, believed that each particular and individual congregation should be free from all external ecclesiastical control. They held no ecclesiastical authority to be higher than the local church, whether that body exercised "its powers in a purely democratic fashion in congregational meeting or through a committee of officials similar to that on the first level in the Presbyterian system." These reformers did not wait for internal church reform but at once "set up some completely independent congregation or other," says William Haller. "These were the Brownists, Barrowists and separatists of all sorts." Robert Browne (1550?–1633) described the church as

...a companie or number of Christians or beleeuers, which by a willing couenant made with their God, are vnder the gouernment of god [sic] and Christ, and kepe his lawes in one holie communion: because Christ hath redeemed them vnto holines & happines for euer, from which they were fallen by the sinne of Adam.

The earliest churches of the Separation were isolated from one another, whether deliberately or not, and the term applies to them. From the beginning of the 18th century, Independent churches have preserved a congregational polity, but did not do so under the Commonwealth and Protectorate.

Henry Jacob (1563–1624), who established the first Independent church at Southwark in 1616, declared that "a true Visible or Ministeriall Church of Christ is a particular Congregation being a spirituall perfect Corporation of Believers, & having power in it selfe immediatly from Christ to administer all Religious meanes of faith to the members thereof." Puritans like Jacob, who did not separate from the Church of England, were also regarded as Independents. These nonseparating Puritans took a position of church polity between the Brownists and the Presbyterians. From the Civil War period in England, the terms "Congregational" and "Congregationalist" came into use to avoid the odiousness of Independent separatism. The terms Independent, Congregational, and Congregationalist henceforth were used interchangeably; "the duplication," M. M. Knappen believed, was "due solely to party passions."

BIBLIOGRAPHY: C. Burrage, *The Early English Dissenters in the Light of Recent Research (1550–1641)* (1912). I. B. Calder, ed., *Letters of John Davenport* (1937). J. Canne, *A Necessity of Separation* (1849). R. W. Dale, *History of English Congregationalism* (1907). W. Haller, *The Rise of Puritanism* (1938). B. Hanbury, *Historical Memorials* (1839). M. M. Knappen, *Tudor Puritanism* (1939). M. MarPrelate, *An Epistle to the Terrible Priests* (1843). J. B. Marsden, *The History of the Early Puritans* (1850); *The History of the Later Puritans* (1852). H. Martin, *Puritanism and Richard Baxter* (1954). P. Miller, *Orthodoxy in Massachusetts* (1933). D. Neal, *The History of the Puritans*, ed., J. C. Choules (1843). A. Peel and L. H. Carlson, eds., *The Writings of Robert Harrison and Robert Browne* (1953). J. W. Platner, et al., *Religious History of New England* (1917). J. Waddington, *Congregational History, 1567–1700* (1874). W. Walker, *A History of the Christian Church* (1952). C. E. Whiting, *Studies in English Puritanism from the Restoration to the Revolution, 1660–1688* (1931). W. T. Whitley, *A History of British Baptists* (1923). A. S. P. Woodhouse, *Puritanism and Liberty* (1951).

ROBERT B. BARNES

INDIAN MISSION SCHOOLS, OKLAHOMA. Baptist mission schools began with the establishment of churches in what is now Oklahoma. Pioneer missionaries often served in a dual role as missionary for some mission board or society and Indian agent for the United States Government. The organization of a church frequently meant a school would soon be established.

One of the first mission schools in Indian Territory was founded among the Choctaws in 1832, by Charles E. Wilson at the Choctaw Agency on the Arkansas River a short distance west of the present city of Fort Smith, Ark. This school soon closed because of a smallpox epidemic. Duncan O'Bryant, a missionary pastor among the Western Cherokees, started a mission about 70 miles northwest of Fort Smith on the Illinois River May 6, 1832, where 20 pupils were enrolled in a school shortly thereafter. Ramsey Potts began a school at Providence, Choctaw Nation, about 10 miles west of Fort Towson, in 1835, and nine years later this school reported 10 pupils. In 1842 Jesse Bushyhead (q.v.) founded the Cherokee Female Seminary for high school girls, at Cherokee, near the Arkansas line in the Cherokee Nation. About the same time there was a school at Delaware Town, 40 miles northwest of Cherokee. By 1844 there were four mission schools among the Cherokees. Ramsey Potts founded Armstrong Academy under the auspices of the American Indian Mission Association near the present town of Bokchito, Okla., in 1844. It was transferred to the Cumberland Presbyterians in 1855, and taken over by the United States Government during the Civil War. The school was named for William Armstrong, a Baptist layman and Government agent to the Choctaws.

Joseph Samuel Murrow (q.v.) founded Rehoboth Mission School at Muddy Boggy, now Atoka, Okla., just prior to May 6, 1869. He later founded the Atoka Baptist Academy, and the Choctaw Academy, in 1887, with an enrolment of 100. In 1902, this school merged with the Murrow Indian Orphanage and moved to Unchuka, and in 1910 it moved to its present location adjacent to the campus of Bacone College.

The Levering Mission School for the Creeks was opened Sept. 5, 1832, with a 160-acre tract of land, $6,000 annual appropriation from the Creek Council, and funds made available for building purposes by the Home Mission Board out of a $2,500 legacy from the estate of Mr. and Mrs. Joshua Levering (q.v.), Baltimore, Md. The school opened with 100 pupils, and operated successfully until 1891, when the Creek Nation decided to terminate all educational contracts with mission boards and purchased the Levering school buildings from the Home Mission Board for $3,000. The name Levering was later attached to the Nuyaka-Levering Indian School and Orphanage. Nuyaka Academy, an Indian Government school, was sold at auction in 1921, and bought by J. M. Wiley, general missionary of the Baptist General Convention of Oklahoma. In 1923 it was taken over by the Education Board of the Southern Baptist Convention. At that time there were 50 enrolled in the school. In 1929 it was taken over by the Home Mission Board and had, by 1930, six workers and 85 students, with eight tribes represented. It was closed in 1936.

In 1878 Almon C. Bacone (q.v.) came to the Cherokee Nation as a teacher, and in 1879 addressed the Cherokee Baptist Association in its annual meeting in an appeal for the establishment of a literary and theological school for Indians. A committee was appointed to study the matter, and a year later Bacone began a school with three Indian pupils in one room of the old Cherokee Mission building at Tahlequah. Sept. 1, 1880, Bacone officially began his work as principal of the Indian Normal and Theological School at Tahlequah under appointment by the American Baptist Home Mission Society. In 1885 the school was moved to its present location near Muskogee and named Indian University; after Bacone's death in 1896, the name of the school was changed to Bacone College, in his honor. This is the only college in the United States operated exclusively for Indians.

The Wetumka Boarding School was founded in 1881, jointly by the Creek Council and the Southern Baptist Convention. The Convention provided the staff and other needs, with financial assistance from the Creek Council until 1891, when the Council took charge of the school as one of its six national boarding schools. Other early mission schools in Indian Territory about which little or nothing is known include Tullehasee Manual Labor School, Seminole Female Academy at Sasakwa, Lone Wolf Mission among the Kiowas and Comanches, Dawes' Academy established at Anadarko in 1890, and Kulli Inla Mission School.

BIBLIOGRAPHY: R. Hamilton, *The Gospel Among the Red Men* (1930). S. Peck, *History of the Missions of the Baptist General Convention* (1840). L. W. Marks, "The Story of Oklahoma Baptists" (MS, Oklahoma Baptist University Library). W. A. Carleton, *Not Yours but You* (1954). V. Lackey, "Early Institutions of Indian Territory" (n.d.).

LOREN J. BELT

INDIAN MISSIONARY, THE. A Baptist monthly newspaper for Indian Territory, founded in Sept., 1884, by editors William P. Blake and Aaron Frank Ross (q.v.) at Eufaula and McAlester, Indian Territory, respectively. The paper was published in duplicate but not identical issues at these places until Sept., 1885, when Daniel Rogers (q.v.) succeeded Blake as co-editor and publication of the Eufaula edition changed to Tahlequah. In Nov., 1885, Rogers assumed the role of editor and Ross, business manager and publisher, with a single edition issued at McAlester. In May, 1886, the paper was moved to South Canadian, Indian Territory, and in Dec., 1886, to Atoka with Joseph Samuel Murrow (q.v.) as editor and proprietor. The paper was then an 8-page monthly, 22 × 30 inches, issued for 50 cents the year. During his first year as editor Murrow reported a circulation of 610 which by 1890 had increased to 1,000, the same year in which the paper's size was reduced to 11 × 15 inches. Murrow resigned his position with the paper Oct. 1, 1891, at which time it was purchased by a stock company of 14 men who deposited $100 each to make up a fund supplemented by the Baptist Missionary and Educational Convention of Oklahoma and Indian territories to continue publication. The paper had been endorsed by this convention in 1885 and adopted as a convention publication in 1886, a relationship which terminated after 10 months but was restored in 1892. In 1891 W. H. Nichols became editor. The paper consisted of news items, articles, letters, Scripture passages, sermons, exhortations, and hymns, mostly in English with occasional contributions in Indian languages. It merged with the *Baptist Watchman* in 1893.

J. M. GASKIN

INDIAN MISSIONS, FLORIDA. A work among the Seminoles in Florida, initiated in 1932 by the Baptist Mission Association of Oklahoma. The work is supported by the churches of the Miami Association and, since 1951, by the Home Mission Board. The first missionary was Willie King, an English-speaking Creek Indian sent by the Baptist Indian Association of Oklahoma. Churches of Miami Association provided him a home on a five-acre tract adjoining headquarters of the Federal Seminole Indian agency for Florida and helped to plan a mission building anchored on piles, thatched with palmetto fronds or leaves as the Seminole Indians roof their own huts. It was dedicated June 7, 1936, with 14 Oklahoma Indian Baptist preachers attending. Then the next day the first Florida Seminole Indian Baptist church was organized at Dania with 14 Indian charter members. By Dec., 1954, there were 86 local members.

In 1937 King retired to limited work at Brighton reservation near Lake Okeechobee. Here Billy Osceola joined him, helped build an "arbour," held full-time services, and received 64 prospective charter members for a new church. King was succeeded by Amos Marks, another Oklahoma Creek, who was supported for four years by the Woman's Missionary Union of Miami and Indian River associations.

In 1951 the Home Mission Board appointed Genus Edward Crenshaw to supervise the work among the Seminoles. He led in organizing a church with 88 members on Big Cypress reservation in July, 1952. All Florida native Indian pastors have been trained at the Baptist Bible Institute at Lakeland, Fla. In 1954 the Woman's Missionary Society in Central Church, Miami, completed a $10,000 concrete block infirmary-clinic on grounds adjoining the Seminole reservation near Dania, saw it equipped, dedicated, and turned over to the Home Mission Board, debt-free, made possible by gifts from eight states, not one cent solicited.

FRANK A. KEENE

INDIAN MISSIONS, NEW MEXICO. The American Baptist Home Mission Society opened work among the Indians of New Mexico, the oldest of the area's inhabitants, in 1852 with the appointment of Samuel Gorman. He located at Laguna and in six years' residence established the first all-Indian school and won the first convert, Jose Senon, whom he baptized and later led the Albuquerque church to license to the ministry. Senon, the first interpreter appointed in the work upon Gorman's departure for Santa Fe to continue the effort, remained until 1861. Other missionaries visited Taos, Pecos, and the strictly Indian regions of the upper Rio Grande Valley, continuing their missionary effort until suspension of the work by the society in 1866. In 1901 the society reopened work among the Indians with the appointment of R. B. Wright and his wife to take over the work of Two Gray Hills near Gallup. The second Indian school operated by Baptists was located here and the Wrights remained until 1906. This mission, along with other Indian property, was later taken over by other evangelicals.

The first effort of Southern Baptists, after the society turned over work in New Mexico to them in 1911, was among the Navajos of the Farmington area where F. E. Graham and his wife served, 1922–24. First Baptist Church, Albuquerque, launched a program for Indian students in 1925, work taken over by the Home Mission Board with the appointment of Thomas D. New and his wife in 1928. Later, under regional direction, this area of service was widened and missionary personnel increased. Converts were baptized into near-by white churches in all cases except Albuquerque, Alamo, and Isleta, where Indian churches had been organized.

There is regional supervision but no district or state convention for the Indians. Twenty-nine missionaries serve 15 missions; three churches have pastors. Mission buildings are valued at $250,000, and 500 Indians are Baptists. Directed by a co-ordinator, Milton S. Leach, the program is integrated with state work. A newspaper, the *All-Indian Baptist,* is published monthly, and an all-Indian camp is held each year.

CALOWA W. STUMPH

INDIAN MISSIONS, OKLAHOMA. Baptist missions among the Indians of Oklahoma began with the removal of the Five Civilized Tribes (Creek, Choctaw, Chickasaw, Cherokee, and Seminole) from east of the Mississippi River (1820–44). At first mission work was done by native leaders such as Jesse Bushyhead (*q.v.*), who migrated westward with the tribes and moved nuclei of their schools and churches intact. Henry Frieland Buckner (*q.v.*), who served under appointment of the American Indian Mission Association, and Joseph Samuel Murrow (*q.v.*), who was supported by the Rehoboth Association in Georgia, were white missionaries who worked among the Indians. Teachers frequently served under joint support of mission boards and tribal governments. Majors William Armstrong and I. G. Vore, Baptist laymen who served as Indian agents in the military, were influential in advancing missions causes. John McIntosh (*q.v.*) pioneered in Baptist missions among the Plains Indians of western Oklahoma in 1876. Prior to the organization of the Baptist General Convention of Oklahoma in 1906, emphasis was given to Indian missions in the constituent conventions of Oklahoma and Indian Territories, particularly in the Baptist General Convention of Indian Territory.

James Burley Rounds (b. Drumbo, Ontario, Canada, Mar. 9, 1876) was a leader in Oklahoma Baptist Indian missions from his appointment as missionary to the Choctaws and Chickasaws in 1901 until his retirement Apr. 1, 1951. He was secretary of Indian work for the Southern Baptist Home Mission Board, 1943–51.

Albert G. Washburn (*q.v.*) became superintendent of Indian Missions Feb. 1, 1907, succeeding William P. Blake, who had served as general missionary to the Five Civilized Tribes. Washburn resigned in June, 1917, at which time his office was abolished and the Indian work placed under the supervision of the corresponding secretary of the convention. At Washburn's recommendation General Lee Phelps (*q.v.*) was elected general missionary to the five tribes. On June 1, 1934, by mutual agreement of the boards involved all Indian mission work in Oklahoma was turned over to the Southern Baptist Home Mission Board. Bailey Otis Sewell became superintendent of Indian Missions in Oklahoma May 1, 1954, under a joint arrangement of the Home Board and the Baptist General Convention of Oklahoma.

In 1954 the Indian population of Oklahoma was c. 120,000. Five associations co-operating with the Southern Baptist Convention reported 125 churches, 7,815 members, 411 baptisms, 4,817 enrolled in Sunday school, 1,608 in Training Union, 984 in Woman's Missionary Union, and $5,521 total gifts.

BIBLIOGRAPHY: J. Belt, "Baptist Missions to the Indians of the Five Civilized Tribes of Oklahoma" (1955). J. P. Dane, "A History of Baptist Missions Among the Plains Indians of Oklahoma" (1955).

J. M. GASKIN and BAILEY SEWELL

INDIAN TERRITORY, BAPTIST GENERAL CONVENTION OF. Formed Dec. 1, 1898, at Oklahoma City, Okla. Territory, as a continuation of the Baptist Missionary and Educational Convention of Oklahoma and Indian Territories. It continued until Sept. 10, 1900, when it met at Durant, Indian Territory, and merged with the Baptist General Association of Indian Territory. The merger was formed by adopting recommendations framed at South McAlester Mar. 6, 1900, by a joint committee representing the General Association and the General Convention of Indian Territory. The recommendations provided for union on a "dual alignment" basis, and the new body continued until final unification of Oklahoma Baptists forces in the formation of the Baptist General Convention of Oklahoma in 1906.

J. M. GASKIN

INDIAN TERRITORY BAPTIST. Published at South McAlester, Okla., each Thursday in 1902–03. It was owned and edited by J. M. B. Gresham. The paper no longer exists.

J. M. GASKIN

INDIAN WARS AND RELIGION, TENNESSEE. During the first years of settlement in East Tennessee and until about 1784, the peril of Indian attacks greatly hindered the work of the churches. The first Baptist churches in Tennessee are said to have been organized sometime after 1765, but these were destroyed in the Indian War of 1774. During this time worship was difficult and dangerous, and travel was practically impossible. Men went to church armed; even preachers carried their guns into the pulpit in expectation of Indian attack. Emigrants had to travel in parties as large as 300 persons in order to provide necessary protection. In some cases entire churches were organized before leaving older settlements, and they moved together as a unit into new areas. Congregations were widely scattered, and the few ministers on the frontier found it almost impossible to travel enough to minister to their constituencies. No churches were developed in the Cumberland Valley until after 1784. One church which possibly decended from the destroyed earlier organizations was Glade Hollows, reconstituted by members returning after the war.

BIBLIOGRAPHY: D. Benedict, *A General History of the Baptist Denomination in America* (1813). J. G. M. Ramsey, *The Annals of Tennessee* (1853). P. M. Hamer, *Tennessee—A History 1673–1932* (1933). G. D. Free, *History of Tennessee* (1895–96).

W. FRED KENDALL

INDIANS, HOME MISSIONS TO. European Christian immigrants to America began early to take an evangelistic interest in the natives. Roger Williams in New England is a famous example. Others in the middle colonies and in the South carried on what might be called unofficial action, no record of which was kept. Native preachers appear now and then, with no record of when or how they came to a knowledge of Christ.

The evangelistic fervor of the Separate Baptists south of the Potomac had some influence in the South in efforts to reach the Indians. The first definite official plan among Baptists in the South appears in the record of the Charleston (S. C.) Association. Richard Furman, pastor of the First Baptist Church, Charleston, and the great leader of the association, was himself a convert of the Separate Baptist movement. In 1802

a mission . . . to the Catawba Indians, which had for some time been contemplated, was now commenced. Rev. John Rooker was engaged for a year to preach to them, at least once a month, and to consult with the chiefs and other persons of influence, on their disposition to have a school founded among them. Mr. Rooker the next meeting reported, that "the Indians had given him a very favorable reception; from the first expressed an earnest desire that a school might be established among them for the instruction of their youth. . . ." It was in consequence determined to continue the mission, and Mr. Rooker was authorized to employ a teacher to instruct the youth in the common branches of education, and the principles of Christianity. A school was accordingly established and has been continued. [This was published in 1811.] At the meeting in 1806, Robert Mursh, an Indian of the Pomunkey tribe, living with the Catawbas, and a licensed preacher, was present, and preached with acceptance to a large and affected audience.

On Dec. 17, 1819, the mission board of the Georgia Association announced plans for opening a mission. Two other associations in Georgia, the Ocmulgee and the Ebenezer, joined with the Georgia Association in conducting the school and the mission among the Creeks. Jesse Mercer, secretary of the board of trustees appointed by the three associations, addressed the churches of the associations on Feb. 26, 1822, announcing the appointment of Lee Compere, of Charleston, S. C., as missionary-teacher to the Creek Indians.

Sept. 26, 1821, the board of managers of the Triennial Convention issued instructions to Thomas Roberts, Isaac Cleaver, Evan Jones, and John Farrier, who were preparing to go to the Baptist mission stations in the Valley Towns, Cherokee Nation, Tenn. Humphrey Posey had already been sent (1817) to do mission work in the Valley Towns.

Isaac McCoy was appointed by the board of the Triennial Convention (1817) to labor among the Indians in the valley of the Wabash in Indiana. He became greatly interested in Indian mission work and endeavored to increase the work of the Triennial Convention. In order to enlarge a program of mission work, he led in forming the American Indian Mission Association, organized in Cincinnati, Ohio, Oct. 27, 1842, with headquarters at Louisville, Ky. McCoy's plan was to make the association auxiliary to the general convention and thereby put greater emphasis upon the convention's work among the Indians. However, due to clashes between personalities and other causes that seemed to be in the atmosphere of the time, there developed opposition even among some of the missionaries to the plan of making the Indian Mission Association auxiliary to the general convention. In the main the opposition was centered north of the Ohio. Perhaps some of the same influences tending toward division in the whole country entered into the situation. At any rate McCoy had more support south of the Ohio. He found that he could get more publicity in the Baptist papers of the South.

McCoy died in 1846. The success he had attained continued for some years, but the recently organized Southern Baptist Convention and the activities of its Domestic Mission Board seemed to absorb some of the support hitherto given to the Indian Mission Association. The funds of the association began to decrease and debt increased. In 1854 the work of the American Indian Mission Association was offered to the Domestic Mission Board of the Southern Baptist Convention. The Convention in session in 1855 accepted the offer. In the report of the Domestic and Indian Mission Board for 1856, the transfer of both the work and the assets of the association was given in detail. There was a debt of $8,000. From the Bureau of Indian Affairs (Washington), $3,000 were received, due for the work of the schools among the Indians. Contributions from churches up to Apr. 1, 1856, had reduced the debt to $1,000, and it was wiped out within a few months. The board announced mission work as follows:

Creek Nation.—Henry Frieland Buckner (*q.v.*), who had begun to work among the Creeks (1847) under the American Indian Mission Association, made a trip through the South gathering funds to wipe out the debt. He and 10 native preachers were appointed by the Domestic and Indian Mission Board. The support of native preachers was assured by churches in Alabama, Georgia, and Kentucky.

Choctaw Nation.—Joseph Smedley, in government service (schools) from 1836 and in the service of the Indian Mission Association from then until 1854, was appointed missionary by the Domestic Mission Board, together with 10 native preachers. Most of the support of the native preachers was assured by associations in Alabama.

Cherokee Nation.—David Foreman, a native preacher, was appointed by the Domestic Mission Board, his support being assured by the Coosa Association (Georgia). Several native preachers were to be appointed, the funds therefor coming from many friends in the churches.

The American Indian Mission Association began its work among the Indians in the Indian Territory about the time that the Five Civilized Tribes became settled after their removal from the East. For years, perhaps since the beginning of national life, there had been friction between state governments, Georgia in particular, and the Indians on one side, and between state governments and the federal government on the other. The federal government had made treaties with the Indian tribes, virtually recognizing them as independent nations. The government of Georgia refused to recognize an independent nation which occupied a portion of the area of the state. When Andrew Jackson became President, he informed the Indians they must go.

When time came for their removal, an army was sent under command of Gen. Winfield Scott to gather them into detention camps and transport them to their new land. . . . Four thousand perished on the way, and their graves mark the 'Trail of Tears' across the states of Tennessee and Arkansas. This was in the winter of 1839-40. . . . By July all were brought in, except a remnant who escaped to the mountains, determined to die there rather than to leave the only home they had ever known. . . . Everything was done that could be done to prevent suffering. But the Indians' hearts were broken, and many died of grief and homesickness, not caring to live. The Christians were said to have borne up better than the others. The missionaries with their families accompanied them. The native preachers were also distributed as best could be among the companies. . . . In the two companies attended by Mr. [Evan] Jones and [Jesse] Bushyhead, there were more than five hundred Baptists. At a place near Columbia, Tennessee, fifty-five were baptized in one day, and the Lord's Supper observed by the churches that night. When they reached Nashville, they remained over Sunday near the city. A party of Christian Indians with the missionaries attended service[s] at one of the Baptist churches. They were treated with great kindness and sympathy. . . . The company with which Mr. Bushyhead traveled was five months on the way. Eighty-two died while on the journey, sixty-six of whom were Baptists; two were licensed preachers. . . . Jesse Bushyhead did not live long after reaching the new country. Six years after their arrival he died, at the age of fifty years.

These five tribes had occupied much of the territory east of the Mississippi River and south of Kentucky. Among the great Southern Baptist missionaries who worked among them, two may be mentioned by way of illustration.

Henry Frieland Buckner (*q.v.*) was appointed missionary to the Creeks (1847) by the American Indian Mission Association. He labored among them devotedly and continued his work under the Domestic Mission Board after the transfer in 1855. During the Civil War he served as a pastor in Texas until 1871, when he returned to his beloved Creek Nation to repair the broken work. For 36 years he devoted himself to the Indian service.

Mr. Buckner was in some respects one of the most remarkable missionaries of any denomination who came into the Indian Territory, during the period of its greatest missionary activities. He was a powerful and persuasive preacher and he had a very marked personality. He came into the Creek Nation while yet there was much hostility toward preaching and preachers. The Creek Council did not consent to his presence, though they suffered him to remain. Slowly and patiently at first and then in his own more natural and impulsive way, he won the confidence and esteem of the Creek people, until his influence among them became powerful and widely felt.

Buckner died Dec. 3, 1883.

Another great missionary to the Indians was Joseph Samuel Murrow (*q.v.*). Writing to President N. M. Crawford of Mercer University, Buckner made an appeal for missionaries to the Indians. Crawford placed the matter before student Murrow, who finally accepted the call of duty. For 72 years he literally spent himself in behalf of the Indians, not only the Creek Nation, but also the whole Indian population of the territory. The Domestic Mission Board was not in financial position to support him. The Rehoboth Association (Ga.) was supporting a missionary in Africa. They agreed to support Murrow among the Indians, and the appointment was made by the Domestic Mission Board in 1857. In 1858 the association (under Landmark influence) decided to carry on the mission work (foreign and domestic) directly rather than through a mission board. From 1858 to 1885, Murrow served under the sponsorship of the Rehoboth Association. He was left free to direct his own time and labors, reporting to the association from time to time concerning the progress of his work. From 1885 to 1891, he was again under the Home Mission Board, but he could not adjust himself to the plans of Secretary Tichenor in his effort to unify the work in each state and territory into one organization allied with the board. Since Murrow could not, for the sake of the Indians, conscientiously join in Tichenor's plans, he resigned from the service of the board and later worked with the American Baptist Home Mission Society (New York). The main reasons for the change in alignment were not so much disagreement with the secretary in matters of organization as his deep devotion to the Indians and their evangelization and his fear that the Indian churches would be disrupted by efforts to implement the new program. Devotedly, he carried on in evangelization, education, and caring for Indian orphans. He died at the age of 94, beloved by the Indians to whom he had given nearly three quarters of a century of devotion.

The ultimate goal has been the establishing of self-supporting Indian churches, which would become centers of Christian activity at home and beyond. These Indian churches have fast been becoming self-supporting and allied with other churches in carrying on Christian work.

Our missions among the Indians are becoming year after year more assimilated to the missions among our own people. In consequence of English being the language of all the schools, and the rapid influx of white population, the necessity of preaching in the native language of these people is diminishing. Before many years among the Civilized Tribes this necessity will have been passed away forever.

In the expanding work of the Home Mission Board in the West, these Indian churches have joined in sending missionaries to the Blanket or Wild Tribes. The Association of the Creek Churches has sent missionaries to their close relatives, the Seminoles in Florida.

The missionary work among the Indians carried on by the Home Mission Board from 1855 onward was confined to the Indians west of the Mississippi River, through the rest of the 19th century and for some years of the 20th. In 1918 the board opened a mission among the remnant of the Cherokees located in the mountains of North Carolina and among the remnant of the Choctaws in Mississippi. Work had been conducted among the Eastern Cherokees before the Civil War. After the war the board was financially unable to carry on the work. When work was reopened, the missionary found 14 small Baptist churches among the Cherokees. Year by year, the board opened work among other groups of Indians in the East. In 1921 work was begun among the Croatans in Robeson County, N. C. These Indians claim to be descended from Sir Walter Raleigh's lost colony on Roanoke Island (1585) and the Indians with whom they amalgamated. There is only tradition to sustain the claim, but students of history have found reasons to believe the tradition is correct. There has been little religious work among them except by Baptists. In 1930 the board transferred this work to the North Carolina Convention, with which the Burnt Swamp Baptist Association is now affiliated.

The Home Mission Board (together with the Creek Indian Association in Oklahoma) has continued work among the Seminoles in Florida; among the Alabama Indians, 5,000 or more, north of Mobile; among fragments of Indian tribes near Richmond, Va., and others on the borderline of Virginia and North Carolina between Roxboro and South Boston. In the 1955 report the board was continuing work among Indians in Alabama, Arizona, Florida, Kansas, Mississippi, New Mexico, North Carolina, Oklahoma, and Utah.

BIBLIOGRAPHY: *American Baptist Magazine*, II (1819), III (1821). W. W. Barnes, *History of the Southern Baptist Convention, 1845–1953* (1954). *The Commission* (1956). W. Furman, *History of the Charleston Association* (1811). R. Hamilton, *Gospel Among the Red Men* (1930). C. C. Lister, *Baptist Missions Among the American Indians* (1944). J. Mercer, *History of the Georgia Association* (1838). Mrs. N. B. Moon, *Indian Source Book and Teaching Helps* (1956).
JOHN CAYLOR

INDONESIA, MISSION IN. On Christmas Day, 1951, three Southern Baptist missionaries—Charles Phillip Cowherd, William Buren Johnson, and Stockwell Bettes Sears—landed in Djakarta, Indonesia. They were sent by the Foreign Mission Board of the Southern Baptist Convention to begin Baptist mission work in the newly formed republic. On Feb. 25, 1952, after extensive negotiations, the Indonesian Ministry of Religions granted them permission to establish a mission in the country.

Bandung was the first mission center. The first Sunday school and preaching service were held the second Sunday in May, 1952, in a rented auditorium in the Masonic Temple. In November of that year the First Baptist Church of Bandung was organized with 20 charter members. In Jan., 1953, work began in the cities of Surabaya and Djakarta. A Baptist theological

FAMILY NIGHT (q.v.), First Baptist Church, Meridian, Miss. Showing a part of that weekly meeting group of approximately 400. Church was organized 1839. Present structure of Georgian Colonial architecture erected 1948–52, seats 1,000; Sunday school accommodates 1,500. Property worth $900,000.

FIRST BAPTIST CHURCH, Greensboro, N. C. Founded 1859, present auditorium of Colonial architecture erected 1952 with capacity of 1,800. Membership 1956 over 3,700, Sunday school facilities for 2,200. Property valued at $2,000,-000.

seminary was opened in Oct., 1954, in Semarang where mission work began the preceding July. Medical work was started in Kediri in Feb., 1955.

Four years after the arrival of the first three missionaries, there were Baptist mission stations in five principal cities on the island of Java, 33 missionaries under appointment to Indonesia, four organized Baptist churches with a membership of 300, one national pastor, a theological seminary, two medical clinics in operation, and a start toward the establishment of a general hospital and medical center. An organization for the production of Sunday school lessons, Training Union and W.M.U. programs, books, tracts, and other Christian literature has been established. W. B. JOHNSON

INDONESIAN SEMINARY, SEMARANG. See INDONESIA, MISSION IN.

INFANT BAPTISM. A term denoting the act of administering the rite of baptism to a child by means of immersion, sprinkling, or pouring water on the head. The rite is perpetuated under the belief that all human beings are born under the guilt of original sin and that baptism removes the guilt even apart from repentance. Some persons, however, view the act as a dedication of the child to God in the expectation that the individual will eventually decide for himself to accept Christ. Baptists insist that in characteristic New Testament practice baptism is administered to the believer who submits to the rite on conscious profession of faith, and that the rite itself consists of the immersion of the believer in water.

It is difficult to set a definite date for the beginning of the practice of infant baptism. Ireneus (died c. 200) is often cited for a definite reference to the practice, but his language is not at all convincing, and by no means is the doctrine explicitly taught by him. It is probably sufficient to say that the practice was clearly established by the time of the theologian Augustine (354–430) and, for practical purposes, was universal by the sixth or seventh century. After the conversion of the Emperor Constantine (274–337), there evolved a concept of a state church of which infant baptism was the symbol, and which crystallized in an authoritarian Western Catholic Church. The practice continued through the Middle Ages; it was embraced by the major Protestant Reformers but was under constant criticism by both medieval antichurchly groups and the sectarian reformers. The Protestants retained it usually on the pretext of the relationship between the old and new covenants and the relation of circumcision to baptism, although it is possible that their hopes for a state church probably moved them more deeply.

BIBLIOGRAPHY: K. Barth, *The Teaching of the Church Regarding Baptism* (1948). J. Calvin, *The Institutes of the Christian Religion* (1559). O. Cullman, *Baptism in the New Testament* (1950). J. W. F. Höfling, *Das Sacrament der Taufe* (1859). R. Ingham, *Christian Baptism: Its Subjects* (1871). M. Luther, *The Larger Catechism* (1529). J. Smyth, *The Character of the Beast* (1609). *The Ante-Nicene Fathers* (various editions). *The Nicene and Post-Nicene Fathers* (various editions). W. Wall, *The History of Infant Baptism* (1st ed., 1705).

ROBERT S. SOILEAU and EUGENE STOCKSTILL

INFANTS, SALVATION OF. The doctrine that all persons dying in infancy are eternally saved. The doctrine is based, ultimately, not upon specific scriptural teaching, but upon an understanding of the character of God as revealed in Christ. Infants have within them the seeds of evil and are involved in the Adamic transgression. Since the infant lacks the powers of self-consciousness and self-determination, however, he does not have personal guilt. Christ's atoning work for the world must be ratified by the personal faith of the individual. Up to the point of accountability, however, Christ's atonement covers the race, and all who die before reaching this stage of development are saved.

See also ADAM and INNOCENCE. J. E. TULL

INLOW YOUTH CAMP. Purchased by the Baptist Convention of New Mexico in 1940. Located 55 miles southeast of Albuquerque in the Manzano Mountains, Inlow Youth Camp's grounds and encampment, now greatly improved, include 30 buildings and land valued at $125,000. The terrain rises from a ranch house and farm in the valley to the lofty summit of rugged mountains. Owned by the Baptist convention and the Woman's Missionary Union of New Mexico, the camp is managed by the woman's organization and is named for Eva R. Inlow, state executive secretary of woman's work. Bernice Elliott, state youth director, lives on the grounds during the summer and supervises the camp program with local management under chaperons, recreational directors, group sponsors, and health nurses. Largely financed by summer fees, the camp is designed for Juniors, Intermediates, Young People, and Adults. In addition, international, all-Indian, Spanish, Negro, and scout camps are accommodated each season.

HERBERT E. BERGSTROM

INNOCENCE. The quality of stainless purity or freedom from sin which renders one guiltless. *Nikkāyōn* and the adjective *nākī*, meaning innocent in the sense of freedom from guilt, often occur in the Old Testament. This guiltlessness may be the result of knowledge (Gen. 20:5), divine forgiveness or acquittal (Job 9:28), or restraint from sin. *Akakos*, "without guile, free from guilt," is used in reference to Jesus (Heb. 7:26). In the absolute sense, innocence can be applied only to Jesus. The term, however, is applied to Adam and Eve before the Fall and to children before they reach the age of moral accountability.

See also FALL OF MAN; INFANTS, SALVATION OF; and MAN. R. E. GLAZE, JR.

INSPIRATION. The term applies to the action of the Holy Spirit upon the writers of Scripture to make them reliable witnesses to the divine revelation. From the original idea of God's breathing into the nostrils of man in the act of creation (Gen. 2:7) comes the developed idea of "God-breathed" Scriptures (*Theopnuestos*, God-breathed, II Tim. 3:16). In each case the fundamental fact is not the psychological or physiological manner in which God acted, but rather the dramatic assertion that God is the source of the life of man and of the Scriptures as well. In the King James Version the word "inspiration" is used only twice (Job 32:8; II Tim. 3:16), and in most modern versions the word has disappeared from the Job passage, in favor of the more literal translation "breath of the Almighty," emphasizing that man's life is grounded in God, with both his intellectual and his physical life dependent upon the spirit (breath) of God.

Inspiration has assumed importance in theology far beyond its scant occurrence in Scripture. It has become the technical term for the distinguishing characteristic of the Scriptures, by which they are divinely authoritative in matters of Christian faith and practice. There has been a tendency among many theologians to spin theories of Spirit-possession or passive instrumentality of the writer while the Spirit of God swept over him like a lute-player plucking the strings (Philo). Second Peter 1:21 does emphasize the manner of inspiration as "being carried along by the Holy Spirit," like a ship before the wind (cf. Acts 27:15, 17 where the same word occurs). However, hundreds of passages quote other Scriptures and simply assume divine authorship, bluntly asserting that "which was spoken of the Lord" (Matt. 1:22, 2:15), or that "which the Holy Ghost by the mouth of David spake" (Acts 1:16; see also Acts 28:25; Heb. 3:7; 10:15). Most citations to Scripture are introduced by the standard authoritative formula, "It is written . . ." This introduction places the emphasis in the doctrine of scriptural inspiration clearly upon the fundamental fact of God's responsible authorship, rather than upon psychological theories of the manner of his inspiration.   WAYNE E. WARD

INSPIRATION OF THE SCRIPTURES. God's influence on the content of the Christian revelation, which is the Bible. "Inspiration is that divine influence that secures the accurate transference of truth into human language by a speaker or writer, so as to be communicated to other men." It "is a general term including all those kinds and degrees of the Holy Spirit's influence which are brought to bear upon the minds of the Scripture writers, in order to secure the putting into permanent and written form of the truth best adapted to man's moral and religious needs."

Because of its basic importance, the doctrine of the inspiration of the Scriptures has been proclaimed and defended by Christian bodies since the first Christian century. The Bible, of course, must be the Word of God, or it becomes the mere product of man's thought and effort. If the Scriptures are the work of men only, unaided by the Holy Spirit, certain disastrous consequences must follow. As Basil Manly, Jr. (*q.v.*), points out, the Bible would then be deficient in three areas: (1) "It would furnish no infallible standard of truth." (2) "It would present no authoritative rule for obedience, and no ground for confident and everlasting hope." (3) "It would offer no suitable means for testing and cultivating the docile spirit, for drawing man's soul trustfully and lovingly upward to its Heavenly Father."

It is significant that the Scriptures themselves claim to be divinely inspired: "For no prophecy ever came by the will of man: but men spake from God, being moved by the Holy Spirit" (II Peter 1:21 ASV). "Every scripture inspired of God is also profitable for teaching, for reproof, for correction, for instruction which is in righteousness: that the man of God may be complete, furnished completely unto every good work" (II Tim. 3:16–17 ASV). In I Corinthians 2:10–13, Paul vigorously claims to teach by divine revelation through the Spirit and thus asserts that his writings have the authority of God. The key word *theopneustos* means divinely breathed upon or inspired. Holy men divinely breathed upon, or directed, wrote the books which constitute our Bible. As such they have an authority not true of any other writings.

There are various theories as to the extent and nature of inspiration. A. H. Strong (*q.v.*) lists four of these views: (1) the intuition theory, which holds that inspiration is simply a higher development of man's natural insight into truth; (2) the illumination theory, which views inspiration as simply an intensifying and elevating of the religious perceptions of men; (3) the dictation theory, affirming that the writers were so possessed by the Holy Spirit that they became passive instruments in the hands of God; (4) the dynamical theory, which holds that inspiration is neither natural, partial, nor mechanical, but supernatural, full, and dynamic. This view, held by the great majority of scholars, insists that the Scriptures are the production of God and of man and are not to be regarded merely as human or merely divine. Thus, the Bible has a double authorship—human and divine—both of which must be recognized. The Bible is God's word to man throughout, yet at the same time it is really and thoroughly man's composition. The Word is not *of* man as to its source; but it is by and through man, and he is voluntarily active and intelligent in its communication. "The Scriptures are thoroughly human (though without . . . error) in contents and form, in the mode of their rise, their compilation, their preservation, and transmission; yet at the same time they are thoroughly divine, both in thoughts and words, in origin, vitality, energy, and effect." H. I. HESTER

Southern Baptist affirmations.—Southern Baptists throughout their history have been characterized by a firm belief in the divine inspiration of the Bible. This fact is reflected in the articles of faith which are in common use among them, as well as by statements on the subject in books by some of their prominent theologians.

The opening article of a widely used Baptist doctrinal summary, the New Hampshire Confession of Faith (1833), begins as follows: "We believe that the Holy Bible was written by men divinely inspired, and is a perfect treasure of heavenly instruction; that it has God for its author, salvation for its end, and truth, without any mixture of error, for its matter. . . ." This confession also constitutes the Articles of Faith of Southwestern Baptist Theological Seminary, and in 1925 it was adopted by the Southern Baptist Convention in session at Memphis, Tenn., as a part of the report of its special Committee on Baptist Faith and Message. Of course, in the case of the churches and the Convention, the statement is not binding on members, but it does express the general doctrinal position held.

Another typical statement is the opening sentence of the Abstract of Principles of the Southern Baptist Theological Seminary, written by James Petigru Boyce (q.v.), first chairman of the faculty, and adopted previous to the opening of that institution in 1859. It reads: "The Scriptures of the Old and New Testaments were given by inspiration of God, and are the only sufficient, certain and authoritative rule of all saving knowledge, faith and obedience." Throughout the history of this institution, each new faculty member has been required to subscribe to this statement. These articles are also the Articles of Faith of Southeastern Baptist Theological Seminary. Golden Gate Baptist Theological Seminary, likewise Southwestern, has adopted the New Hampshire Confession. New Orleans Baptist Theological Seminary has articles of faith written by Byron Hoover DeMent (q.v.), which also contain a statement affirming the inspiration of the Scriptures.

Books by Southern Baptist theological professors on the subject include *The Bible Doctrine of Inspiration* (1888) by Basil Manly, Jr. (q.v.); and *Inspiration of the Bible* (1930) by Benajah Harvey Carroll (q.v.), published posthumously. Though quite different in tone and treatment, both authors hold to the full inspiration of the Scriptures, at the same time denying that this was something mechanical.

Perhaps an increasing number of Southern Baptists would agree with James McKee Adams (q.v.) in accepting the fact of inspiration without the need for "formal theory to make it real. The fruits or results of inspiration are the final and convincing arguments as to its reality."

See also REVELATION. HOWARD P. COLSON

INSURANCE. According to the minutes of the Southern Baptist Convention, only one real proposal has been made to the Convention concerning a plan of insurance. J. Calvin Moss of Virginia "moved that the Executive Committee be instructed to study the possible facilities for better fire insurance rates and the methods that may induce our churches to carry more adequate lines of insurance on all our church property; and the motion was adopted."

The committee made a study of the amount of fire insurance carried on property owned by churches and the denomination, and reported to the Convention in 1928 that at that time there were 24,326 churches owning property valued at $195,005,222. Of these churches, a total of 14,741 had no insurance whatever. In the matter of property value, 67.6 per cent was not covered by insurance.

Among other recommendations the Executive Committee recommended ". . . that if a majority of the state conventions recommend the organizing of a Southern Baptist Mutual Church Fire Insurance Company, the Executive Committee of the Southern Baptist Convention be instructed to present to the Convention next year the plans for perfecting such an organization."

In 1929 the following report was presented by the committee to the Convention

Concerning the matter of securing better fire insurance rates for churches, your Committee was instructed to confer with the states, and "that if a majority of the state conventions recommend the organizing of a Southern Baptist Mutual Church Fire Insurance Company, the Executive Committee of the Southern Baptist Convention be instructed to present to the Convention next year the plans of perfecting such an organization." Very few of the state conventions expressed any interest in the establishing of such a fire insurance company. Therefore your Committee has no recommendations to make on this point.

No further action was taken concerning the creation of a Southern Baptist Mutual Church Fire Insurance Company. AUSTIN CROUCH

INTER-AGENCY COUNCIL. A consultative group composed of members appointed by the Sunday School Board, the Foreign Mission Board, the Home Mission Board, the Woman's Missionary Union, and the Baptist Brotherhood. It works particularly to correlate, as far as possible, the educational materials prepared by these agencies for use in the churches, and also seeks to give assistance in the planning of their educational programs. It has no legislative power, but is supported by the influence of the bodies it represents. The council grew out of an earlier committee named by the Southern Baptist Convention in response to resolutions that came simultaneously from two sources. This committee, of which Gaines S. Dobbins was chairman, was instructed "carefully [to] study the organizational needs of our churches with respect to their auxiliaries; to define the functions and spheres of each; to propose in the light of our experience and need what changes or additions should be made." Earlier minor efforts at consultation on the part of the various agencies gave place to this committee, which then led in studies and conferences out of which in 1948 came the present Inter-Agency Council.

The council meets annually, or more often if necessary, to consider any problems which affect the denomination's ministry through educational materials. Reports of past activities are made, plans concerning new ventures by various agencies are shared and discussed, problems of schedule and calendar are worked out, efforts are made to avoid unnecessary overlappings and duplications, co-operation is encouraged on the basis of mutuality of interests and responsibility, and plans are made to prevent undue tensions and conflicts. Recommendations made to member agencies are not binding, but do provide a basis for constructive and co-operative planning and work at all levels of denominational activity. Among the accomplishments of the council has been the effecting of a plan called the Correlated Church Study Course, which provides for an "interchange of credits on comparable subjects" by the various agencies awarding such credit. GAINES S. DOBBINS

INTER-BOARD COMMISSION ON STUDENT RELIGIOUS ACTIVITIES. An agency created by the Southern Baptist Convention in 1921 and directed to begin and promote a Convention-wide program of Baptist student religious activity. The members of the commission were the secretary of the Woman's Missionary Union and the secretaries of the four general boards of the Convention. Frank Hartwell Leavell (q.v.), then state B.Y.P.U. secretary of Georgia, became the first executive secretary of the commission, Jan. 1, 1922. The offices were located in Memphis, Tenn. By September the work had grown. An associate secretary was employed, and the first issue of *The Baptist Student* appeared. The work continued under the direction of this independent agency until 1928. In that year, as a result of a study of Convention agencies and work made by a special efficiency committee, the work was transferred by the Convention to the Sunday School Board in Nashville, Tenn.; and the Inter-Board Commission was discontinued. G. KEARNIE KEEGAN

INTERCESSION OF CHRIST. Especially in the book of Hebrews, Christ is presented as man's great High Priest. Part of the work of a priest is to intercede for his people. "Wherefore he is able also to save them to the uttermost that come unto God by him, seeing he ever liveth to make intercession for them" (Heb. 7:25). The work of Christ as priest did not cease when he offered himself as an atonement for sin, for he stands in the presence of God ever interceding for his own. A part of the basis of Christian confidence and assurance is the realization that our Redeemer prayed while on earth for every man who would ever enter his kingdom (John 17:20). Even now he holds up hands of everlasting intercession so that "if any man sin, we have an advocate with the Father, Jesus Christ the righteous" (I John 2:1). Christ assured Peter that the steadfastness of human faith was grounded in the Redeemer's prayers (Luke 22:31–32). Isaiah declared that he would make intercession for the transgressors (Isa. 53:12; Luke 23:34). According to the biblical presentation Christ is with every praying heart, lifting every prayer to the Father (Matt. 18:19–20). He walks among his churches praying for them (Rev. 1:13).

See also CHRISTOLOGY.

BIBLIOGRAPHY: A. H. Strong, *Systematic Theology* (1943). E. Brunner, *The Mediator* (1934).

CHARLES A. TRENTHAM

INTERDENOMINATIONAL RELIGIOUS WORK FOUNDATION, INC. Started in Richmond in 1920 by a group of ministers and laymen representing various Protestant denominations in Virginia. They first presented to the state legislature a bill to provide for chaplains and other workers to conduct a program of worship and religious instruction in state institutions, and then, deciding that it was a missionary opportunity of churches rather than a responsibility of the state, withdrew the bill, constituted themselves The Committee for Religious Work in State Institutions, and secured support of the mission boards of their respective denominations to provide funds for the program.

After a few years the name of the organization was changed to The Interdenominational Board for Religious Work in State Institutions, and in 1942 the work was reorganized and incorporated under the present name. The 17 trustees are elected annually upon nomination of the 13 Protestant groups which support the foundation. These in turn elect officers and staff members, including an executive secretary who directs the program. Organization and maintenance of regular religious services, counseling on personal and religious problems, emergency aid to prisoners, and enlisting churches and church leaders in ministering to patients and prisoners in the institutions are all part of the program, and libraries are operated in a number of institutions.

The foundation co-operates with local ministers in serving the mental hospitals of the state. Chaplains are employed for full-time service at the Medical College of Virginia Hospital, The University of Virginia Hospital, and the State Penitentiary. Weekly worship services are maintained at the three tubercular sanatoria, Blue Ridge, Catawba, and Piedmont. Sunday schools are conducted in the juvenile institutions; regular worship services are held each Sunday at the four state farms, the three miscellaneous institutions, and the 30 prison road camps. Many of the services are made possible through the co-operation of pastors and lay workers in the areas in which the institutions are located.

W. RUSH LOVING

INTERMEDIATE STATE. The condition of the soul between death and final judgment. The term also represents the belief that the final spiritual body is not received at death (I Thess. 4:16-17; I Cor. 15:52). The soul of the believer at death enters the presence of Christ (II Cor. 5:1-8; Heb. 12:23; Eccl. 12:7). Departed saints are truly conscious (Matt. 22:32; Luke 23:43; John 11:26; Rev. 6:9-11; 14:13). Wicked souls are described as being in prison (I Pet. 3:19) and in conscious suffering (Luke 16:23; II Pet. 2:9). At the resurrection the saints shall come forth with glorified bodies to face judgment and enter into everlasting happiness (Rev. 20:12 ff.). The intermediate state is often portrayed as paradise for the righteous (Luke 23:42-43), and as a prison for the wicked (I Pet. 3:19). Nothing in the Bible indicates that the intermediate state has any gradations of experience or is different in quality or hope from the ultimate destiny of the soul.

See also DEATH and IMMORTALITY.

BIBLIOGRAPHY: J. Baillie, *And the Life Everlasting* (1951). A. H. Strong, *Systematic Theology* (1943).

CHARLES A. TRENTHAM

INTERPRETATION OF SCRIPTURES. HISTORY OF INTERPRETATION. The history of interpretation of the Scriptures may be divided into two general periods, the classical period and the Christian era. These may be subdivided into four periods each.

The classical period of interpretation of the Scriptures began with Ezra in the fifth century B.C. and ended with the Babylonian Talmud A.D. 500. During these approximately 10 centuries, there were four periods in the development of the Law.

The period of the Sopherim (c. 500-200 B.C.).—The Sopherim were scribes, the learned men who succeeded Ezra and his associates to carry on their authority in the explanation of the Law and its meaning to the people. During this period the professional interpreter occupied a position of authority, and the voice of a prophet was not heard.

The period of the zugoth (200 B.C.-A.D. 10). —"Zugoth" means the pairs. It was a name given by all the rabbis to the leading teachers, from Joses Ben Joase to Shammai and Hillel. During the period of the zugoth, the Haggadah (from *negad,* to tell), commentary material, and the Halakhah (from *halakh,* to go), oral law, were more fully developed. The Halakhah, when fixed, had even greater authority than the Scriptures of the Old Testament.

The period of the tannaim (A.D. 10-220).— The tannaim were teachers called by the title "rabbi." During this period there was produced a number of very important works, including the Targums and the Mishnah. The Targums were Aramaic translations and paraphrases of the Pentateuch and other parts of the Bible. The Mishnah was the codification of the oral law.

The period of the amoraim (A.D. 219-500). —Multitudes of possibilities were treated in the Mishnah, but these left open doubts for every single sentence. Therefore, the text of the Mishnah again became the point of learned discussion, carried on partly by logic and partly by the help of traditional matter which had not been included in the Mishnah. The Palestinian and Babylonian talmuds were completed during the period of the amoraim.

The Christian period.—The Bible of the early Christians was the Greek version of the Old Testament, known as the Septuagint. These early Christians also had the mass of legends and legal decisions which had gathered about the Old Testament since the time of Ezra. Various methods of Christian interpretation of the Scriptures have resulted from the influence of four distinct periods.

During the *formative period* of the Christian movement, the allegorical method of interpretation was widely used both by Jews and Christians. According to this method, interpreters claimed that there were hidden truths behind literal meanings. Also, during the period of apostolic Christianity, the typological, historical, and dogmatic methods of interpretation found root.

During the *medieval period,* from Augustine to the Reformation, interpretation became more and more arbitrary and artificial. This period produced the traditional, the scholastic, and the mystical types of interpretation.

During the Reformation period, the reformers interpreted the Scriptures with emphases upon doctrinal and devotional exegesis. There was a disposition to prove doctrine by the Bible, rather than to derive doctrine from the Bible. These methods often fell prey to extreme spiritualizing, detached proof texts, and theological bias.

The modern critical period has emphasized scientific principles in Biblical interpretation. This method stresses the grammatical, historical, logical, and spiritual factors in exegesis. Using this method, interpreters approach the Scriptures to find out what the writers said and to determine what was meant by what they said.

RAY ROBBINS

PRINCIPLES OF INTERPRETATION.—Interpretation is the art of correctly understanding the thought of an author or speaker and of communicating that thought to others. Because of various factors, there is difficulty in finding the true meaning of the Scriptures. God has spoken through various authors, in different languages, over a long period of time. In order to know what God has said, and is saying, it is necessary first to understand the thoughts of the men through whom he wrote. The writers of Scripture were Orientals, with social, religious, and cultural backgrounds vastly different from our own. Because of these and other difficulties, different theological groups through the centuries have given myriad interpretations to certain passages. Although interpretation is difficult, some basic principles will guide in interpreting the Scriptures correctly. The first principle of interpretation is to start with the right text, that which is as near to the original manuscript as possible. The recovery of the original text is the task of the textual critic, who has been trained to read various manuscripts and versions and to decide which of the extant readings are nearest to the autographs. The importance of having a reliable text is obvious, for we cannot interpret an author's thought if we do not have what he wrote. Many interpreters will not be textual critics, however, and will have to start with the work of others in the form of standard texts or translations.

After securing the most reliable text or translation, the interpreter should try to reconstruct the historical background of the particular passage or book under consideration.

The second principle of interpretation is usually called the historical principle. In considering a particular passage or book, the interpreter should try to reconstruct its historical background, including the identity of its author, the time of its writing, and the social, political, geographical, economic, and religious conditions of the period. H. H. Rowley says,

> The religion of both the Old Testament and the New has one characteristic that it shares with no other religion. It is religion that was born of history. . . . A religion which is rooted and grounded in history cannot ignore history. Hence a historical understanding of the Bible is not a superfluity. . . . The interpreter of the Bible must therefore seek to apprehend the fact as a historical fact, and must have a historical sense, relating the Bible first of all to its context of history and grasping the whole process through which the ideas were revealed.

Application of the third principle of interpretation, the grammatical principle, begins with the study of the etymology and use of each word. After the meaning of the words has been determined, the interpreter will study the relationship of the words within the sentence, noting the grammatical construction and the syntactical relations. The word order in the original text is often very important because it indicates where the emphasis lies.

A fourth principle of interpretation is the logical or contextual principle. In considering the meaning of an immediate passage, the larger contexts of the passage should be studied: the paragraph, the chapter, the book, the entire Bible. Closely related to the matter of context is the type of literature. The interpreter should note carefully whether a passage is prose or poetry, prophecy or apocalyptic, parable or history. C. T. Francisco says, "There is no result so tragic as an interpretation of a poetical passage by a prosaic theologian."

A fifth principle of interpretation is related to the work of the Holy Spirit. "The interpretation of Scriptures is a work of grace. We cannot of ourselves hear the Word of God or receive its meaning." When one has secured the right text, reconstructed the historical background, examined the words and phrases in their various contexts and relationships, he may not yet fully understand the thought of the writer. Because the Bible is a divine Book as well as a human Book, its spiritual truths must be spiritually discerned. One must be a member of the redeemed community before he can correctly interpret the Word of God.

Bernard Ramm says, "The leading of the Holy Spirit will never be as definite as that of the inspiration of the Bible, therefore, we can never claim infallible guidance. Nor does the Holy Spirit convey information as much as he influences attitudes." J. Angus and S. G. Green have pointed out that "the Spirit of God does not communicate to the mind of even a teachable, obedient, and devout Christian, any doctrine or meaning of Scripture which is not contained already in Scripture itself."

A final principle of interpretation is the application of the Scriptures to the conditions in our own day. A definition of interpretation includes the understanding of the thought of the authors and the communication of that thought to others. Rowley says:

> There is yet another principle . . . without which no interpretation can be adequately relevant. It is found in the application of the fundamental message of the Bible to conditions of our own day. In an unpublished lecture the late Principal H. Wheeler Robinson observed: "Wise application is the best form of exegesis, for it brings the past into which we can never wholly penetrate into relation with that present in which we actually live." This means that the theological interpretation of the Bible which is often called for, and which indeed is to be desired, is not sufficient. For the Bible is more than a theological book. It is a religious book; and religion is more than theology. Its study should do more than develop right views about God, man, and duty; it should nurture right relations to God.

BIBLIOGRAPHY: J. Angus and S. G. Green, *The Cyclopedic Handbook to the Bible* (1908). L. Berkhof, *Principles of Biblical Interpretation* (1950). C. A. Briggs, *The Study of the Holy Scripture* (1899). F. C. Conybeare, *History of New Testament Criticism* (1910). H. E. Dana, *Searching the Scriptures* (1946). A. Edersheim, *The Life and Times of Jesus the Messiah*, Vol. I (1904). F. W. Farrar, *History of Interpretation* (1886). C. T. Francisco, *Introducing the Old Testament* (1950). G. H. Gilbert, *Interpretation of the Bible: A Short History* (n.d.). C. Lockhart, *Principles of Interpretation* (1915). H. S. Nash, *History of Higher Criticism of the New Testament* (n.d.). B. Ramm, *Protestant Biblical Interpretation* (1950). A. Richardson and W. Schweitzer, *Biblical Authority for Today* (1951). M. S. Terry, *Biblical Hermenenties* (1911).

RALPH SMITH

IRELAND, JAMES (b. Edinburgh, Scotland, 1748; d. Berryville, Va., May 5, 1806). Minister, church organizer. Born in a Presbyterian family "denominated gentry," Ireland was well educated, but a turbulent spirit sent him to sea, and at 18 he was teaching school in Shenandoah

County, Va. Along with friends, Ireland, whose conversion began with the writing of a religious poem at the request of a Baptist acquaintance, decided to align himself with the Separate rather than the Regular Baptists, "as they had the warmest preachers and the most fire among them," but Ireland later became a Regular Baptist. In 1769, after returning from an associational meeting in Sandy Creek, N. C., Ireland was baptized by Samuel Harris (q.v.) in Pittsylvania County, Va., and received signed credentials for preaching from 11 ministers. That November, Harris and Ireland formed Carter's Run, the first church of the Separates in northern Virginia, which in three years grew to 240 members. So effective was Ireland as a preacher at only 21 that authorities put him in prison almost immediately. In the Culpeper jail, from Nov., 1769, to Apr., 1770, attempts were made to destroy him by explosives, suffocation, and poison—permanently injuring his health—but Ireland converted fellow prisoners and wrote letters "from my palace in Culpeper." Released on bail, he procured from Governor Botetourt and his council a license to preach and build a meetinghouse, which, with the application of the Toleration Act of William and Mary, forced the magistrates to free him. Extensive missionary journeys carried him from Chesapeake Bay to Ohio, during which he often faced physical violence. Teachers who attempted to create controversies with him found their congregations convinced by Ireland's replies. Ireland helped form churches in the Ketocton Association and for many years was pastor of the Buck Marsh (now Berryville), Waterlick, and Happy Creek churches in Frederick and Shenandoah counties, Va. In 1802 he baptized 93 persons, 52 of whom were received in one day. Although he suffered excruciating pain during his final illness, Ireland never neglected family worship, and he dictated his autobiography. In 1771 he married Jane Burgess, who died in 1790, and he married Ann Pollard the following year. The *Winchester Gazette* said of Ireland, "He was always distinguished as an able minister of the New Testament, rightly dividing the Word of Truth, giving to saint and sinner their portion in due season."

BIBLIOGRAPHY: J. Foster, comp., *The Life of the Rev. James Ireland* (1819). T. D. Gold, *History of Clarke County, Virginia* (1914). L. M. Ritter, "James Ireland, Martyr," *The Religious Herald* (Jan. 30, 1930). G. Ryland, *The Baptists of Virginia, 1699–1926* (1955); "James Ireland," (an address, May 20, 1931). R. B. Semple, *A History of the Rise and Progress of Baptists in Virginia* (1810); Revised and extended by G. W. Beale (1894). J. B. Taylor, *Virginia Baptist Ministers* (1859). E. W. Winfrey, "James Ireland," *The Religious Herald* (Feb. 13, 1930).

LEVERING EVANS

ISLANDS, JOSEPH (b. Georgia; d. North Fork Town, Creek Nation, Mar. 8, 1848). Baptist preacher, "Apostle to the Creeks," who was dramatically converted in 1842 after removal to the West with the Creeks. He preached from house to house among the Creeks as a local exhorter until his ordination in 1845 by Ramsey Potts and Joseph Smedley (q.v.), missionaries to the Choctaws. Islands was the first pastor of the North Fork Church (three years); and through his firm endurance of Creek persecution, he was instrumental in its abolition. He gave his own new residence to be the "first house of worship in the Creek Nation" for North Fork Church.

BIBLIOGRAPHY: J. M. Gaskin, *Trail Blazers of Sooner Baptists* (1953). E. C. Routh, *The Story of Oklahoma Baptists* (1932). M. E. Wright, *Missionary Work of the Southern Baptist Convention* (1902).

ROGER D. HEBARD

ISRAEL. Biblically "Israel" has at least four distinct usages: the new name given to Jacob (Gen. 32:28; 35:10), the Hebrew people or nation, the Northern Kingdom as distinguished from Judah, and Christians as the people of God. The term is also used today to describe the political state of Israel created in 1948. Rooted in the call of Abraham (Gen. 12:1–3), God's gracious election of Israel (Deut. 7:7 f.) was issued in the covenant (Exod. 19:3–8), according to which Israel was to mediate God's revelation to all mankind. Israel's disobedient failure to fulfil this mission led to the remnant doctrine and reached its climax in Israel's rejecting Jesus as the Christ. Paul stressed the "inward" Jew, Israel within Israel, and the remnant (Rom. 2:28 f.; 9:6; 11:5). The New Testament declares that Christians, whether Jew or Gentile, are "a chosen generation" (I Pet. 2:9), "heirs according to the promise" (Gal. 3:29), and veritably "the Israel of God" (Gal. 6:16). Modern dispensationalism denies this declaration.

BIBLIOGRAPHY: J. Bright, *The Kingdom of God* (1953). H. H. Rowley, *The Biblical Doctrine of Election* (1950).

JAMES LEO GARRETT

ISRAEL, MISSION IN. Baptist work in what is now the State of Israel was begun in 1911 by Shukri Mosa, a Syrian. Supported by Illinois Baptists, he opened work at Safed but moved to Nazareth the same year and established a church.

Southern Baptists took over this work following the London Conference of 1920 and sent W. A. Hamlett to Palestine in 1921. Although he reported that conditions were unsafe, four new missionaries reached Jerusalem early in 1923. Ill health forced Fred Bunyan and Ruth (Casey) Pearson home the following year. Thomas Washington and Mattie (Reid) Watts remained until 1928. Seven missionaries were under appointment to Palestine when World War II closed the mission. During the 20 years before the war, churches were organized at Jerusalem (1925) and Haifa (1936); a church building was erected at Nazareth; missionaries were stationed briefly at Tel Aviv; and a day school was opened in Nazareth in 1937.

Since the war two of the churches have been reorganized, Jerusalem in 1946 with 9 members and Nazareth in 1953 with 29 members. The school reopened in 1948 and has added a high school. The 19 children of the George W. Truett Orphanage, opened in Nazareth in 1946, were moved in 1955 to new buildings on a farm near Petach Tikva, which will serve also as a camp center. Fifteen missionaries were under appointment to Israel, Jan. 1, 1956.

GENEVIEVE GREER

ITALIAN BAPTIST CONVENTION. The first meeting of the convention was held in New York City from Apr. 30 to May 3, 1899. Its organization resulted from early attempts to evangelize Italians in this country dating back to 1887 when women of the Mt. Pleasant Baptist Church of Newark, N. J., at the inspiration of their pastor, F. C. A. Jones, went from house to house in the Italian quarters, distributing Italian tracts. The women soon started sewing classes for girls and weekly meetings in private houses. The children were gathered and taken to Mt. Pleasant for Sunday school although the church was rather far from the Italian section of the city. Those interested in the work saw the necessity of procuring near-by temporary quarters for the new enterprise. Similar evangelical attempts among Italians were made by local churches in other cities.

The American Baptist Home Mission Society entered the field of Italian work in 1894 in Buffalo, N. Y., through the young people's organization. In co-operation with the Baptist union of Buffalo and of the American Baptist Home Mission Society, the youth group procured the service of Ariel B. Bellondi, who had come to this country for a theological education. After a few months of work, 26 Italians were baptized in the Prospect Avenue Baptist Church, and in the next four years 15 mission stations were established in New York, New Jersey, Pennsylvania, Connecticut, Rhode Island, Massachusetts, and Vermont.

Missionaries of the various fields recognized the need for an Italian Baptist Association in America. A few of them met in the home of Joseph Boccaccio of Mount Vernon, N. Y., on May 2, 1898, and organized such an association. Pasquale De Carlo was elected president; Boccaccio, secretary and treasurer. The convention was organized, having no funds at that time with which to begin work. However, the body has met yearly since its organization with the exception of one year during World War II.

ANGELO DI DOMENICA

ITALIANS, HOME MISSIONS TO. It is estimated that there are 600,000 Italians living within the territory of the Southern Baptist Convention. The first work done with them by the Home Mission Board was in Tampa, Fla. L. Zarrilli was appointed to work with the Italians of Ybor City, Tampa, June 23, 1908. This work has been continued; at present the Cuscaden Park Baptist Church and the Armenia Avenue Baptist Church are assisted by the Home Mission Board and minister principally to the Italians of Tampa.

In Birmingham, Ala., work with the Italians was begun in 1922. This work still continues in the Immanuel Baptist Church and the Good Will Center, which are supported by the Home Mission Board. Abraham Wright and Mrs. Wright began work with the Italians and other foreign elements in Benld, Ill., and surrounding area on Nov. 10, 1945. Out of this work have come two self-sustaining churches in addition to the work at Benld, which continues under Wright's leadership. The Home Mission Board supported Frank DiMaggio and Mrs. DiMaggio in the Italian work of DuQuoin, Ill., from Jan., 1946, to Mar., 1949.

Brief but unsuccessful attempts were made to establish Italian work in Los Angeles, Calif., from June, 1948, to 1950, and in San Francisco, Calif., Dec., 1948, to Nov., 1949. The present work among the Italians of the San Francisco Bay area was begun in 1953 under the leadership of Amelio Giannetta and his wife. Their principal function is to enlist and assist the churches of that area in winning and enlisting the Italians of their communities. Giannetta also carries on a very effective radio ministry in Italian. A similar radio ministry is being carried on by S. A. Candal, of Birmingham, Ala.

The Home Mission Board has 10 missionaries to the Italians. It owns properties for Italian work in Tampa, Fla., Birmingham, Ala., and Benld, Ill.

The state conventions of both Louisiana and Illinois have for periods of time since 1926 engaged in mission work with the Italians within their states.

LOYD CORDER

ITALY, BAPTIST EVANGELICAL UNION OF. The *Unione Evangelica Battista d'Italia* had its origin in two Baptist beginnings. One was initiated in 1863 by James Wall, an Englishman, who was supported after 1871 by the Baptist Missionary Society of London. Alongside English Baptist work in Italy was that initiated by Southern Baptists. Although separate in financial and disciplinary administration, the two groups were united in evangelization, missionary propaganda, and educational and social work. Their united effort led to the formation of the Christian Apostolic Baptist Union of Italy in May, 1884.

As a result of this union the work carried on by the two Baptist groups merged, with the fusion officially effective Jan. 1, 1923, under the title *Opera* (later *Unione*) *Evangelica Battista d'Italia*, following the London Conference of 1920, when Southern Baptists accepted entire responsibility in the Italian Baptist missionary field. In 1920 the union consisted of about 50 churches and stations with about 2,700 members, a seminary, a publication house, two periodicals, and one journal. The G. B. Taylor Orphanage was founded in 1923.

In 1944–48, the Evangelical Baptist Union was reorganized on a basis of national self-administration with missionary collaboration. Through rehabilitation and material expansion, Baptist work in Italy took a new turn in 1950. The seminary (Philadelphia Institute at Rivoli) was reopened and enlarged, and a training school for young women (the Armstrong Memorial Training School in Rome) was founded; publication, auxiliary (Sunday school, Woman's Missionary Union, Training Union), and Christian social work (G. B. Taylor Orphanage, Old Folks Home, and Good Samaritan Dispensary after 1953) were strengthened; and churches were provided with more adequate quarters.

W. DEWEY MOORE

ITALY, MISSION IN. William Nelson Cote (q.v.), appointed by the Foreign Mission Board in 1870, initiated Baptist work in Italy. Serving for three years, he led in founding the first Baptist church in Rome, Jan. 29, 1871. George Boardman Taylor (q.v.) went to Italy in 1873 to direct the mission and after 34 years, left the first trained Italian pastors, a church periodical, several books, and 32 churches. In 1872 Americans pledged $20,000 for a chapel in Rome. Dedicated in 1878, it was the first of several built under Taylor's ministry and is still the home of Rome's first Baptist church (Teatro Valle). It served until 1923 as Baptist mission headquarters in Italy.

Susan Spottswood Taylor ministered among women and children in a work that grew into what is now the Woman's Missionary Union of Italy. John Howard and Olive M. (Board) Eager served with the Taylors for 16 years; Charles James Fox and Mary (Jordan) Anderson served three and a half years.

In Dec., 1900, the board appointed Dexter Gooch Whittinghill for seminary work, and as a result a school opened Nov. 26, 1901, in the Rome chapel. Whittinghill served as seminary president until 1938 and assumed direction of Italian mission work when Taylor retired. In 1905, he married Taylor's youngest daughter, Susan.

In 1911, Everett Gill, Sr., and James Percy Stuart became superintendents of the work in northern and southern Italy, respectively, while Whittinghill dedicated himself to the seminary and publication work. At the end of World War I, after Stuart's death and Gill's return to the States, Whittinghill again assumed administration of the mission. An Italian committee was formed in 1920 to co-operate in the administration.

Following the 1920 London Missionary Conference of the Baptist World Alliance, the Italian Mission of the Baptist Missionary Society of Great Britain, consisting of 3 missionaries, 12 Italian pastors, 16 churches, 8 church buildings, a publication house, and a headquarters building, was ceded (1923) to the Southern Baptist Mission. The G. B. Taylor Orphanage was opened in Rome in 1923 and expanded in 1952 to include a home for old folks.

The Whittinghills retired Jan. 1, 1939, leaving William Dewey and Alice (Speiden) Moore, in Italy since 1937, to direct Baptist work in co-operation with the first Italian Baptist executive secretary, Lodovico Paschetto. Mrs. Moore became director of the Taylor Home.

During World War II American missionaries in Italy were forced home temporarily. Four months before the war ended in 1945 a special relief team including Moore was sent to Italy to organize a Central European relief committee. Following the reopening of the mission in 1947 relief and rehabilitation work was added to regular mission work for the next four years.

Late in 1947 Benjamin Ray and Mary (Patterson) Lawton were sent to help reopen the Baptist seminary, closed since 1932. Relocated in Rivoli, near Turin, in newly purchased and adapted quarters the school was officially opened in 1949. Roy Franklin and Lillie Mae (Hylton) Starmer joined the mission staff in 1949, serving on the seminary faculty a year before going to Rome to head the publications department of the mission. Virginia Wingo became director of the Armstrong (Mrs. Frank W.) Memorial Training School which opened in 1950; Grace Tyler joined the teaching staff in 1952. The Good Samaritan Dispensary was opened in Rome in Dec., 1953, under the direction of Marco Fasulo, with quarters in the Armstrong Memorial Training School building; it began operation in separate quarters in 1955.

Further reorganization of Italian mission work in 1955 was designed to lead toward the goal of a full convention of Baptist churches working together autonomously.

BIBLIOGRAPHY: P. Chiminelli, *The Baptists in Italy* (1923). J. H. Eager, *Romanism in Its Home* (1899). E. P. Maddry, *Believers and Builders in Europe* (1939). L. and E. Paschetto, *They of Italy* (1939). G. B. Taylor, *Life and Letters of Rev. George Boardman Taylor, D.D.* (1910); *Southern Baptists in Sunny Italy* (1929). E. H. Trutza, *Modern Macedonia* (1940).

W. DEWEY MOORE

ITINERANCY, SOUTHERN BAPTIST MINISTERS'. The practice of itinerating began with the earliest settlers and gradually increased from the beginning of the 18th century to the American Revolution. The years between 1775 and 1830 could well be called "the itinerant era," being the period when almost every preacher spent at least some of his time traveling long distances and visiting from house to house to build up churches. He journeyed to the homes of the wealthy planters on the James River as well as to the cabin in the frontier clearing. Again and again in pioneer biography appear such statements as "He not only preached in his native county, but traveled much. . . ." "In 1801, according to the custom of ministers in that day, he made a preaching tour. . . ."

The well-known and the little-known preacher itinerated. Lewis Craig (q.v.), one of those who suffered persecution in Virginia, became an itinerant in Kentucky; William Bullein

Johnson (*q.v.*), first president of the Southern Baptist Convention, was told by doctors to make a journey for his health. He set out for New Orleans, his bags filled with tracts, to itinerate. Richard Furman (*q.v.*), first president of the Triennial Convention, itinerated on the islands around Charleston; Adiel Sherwood (*q.v.*) preached in almost every Atlantic state; Shubal Stearns (*q.v.*) "traveled extensively in his own region, preaching Jesus, organizing churches, and giving counsel to the new communities which were formed." Jesse Mercer (*q.v.*) attended the Triennial Convention in 1817, traveling from Georgia to Philadelphia "in his own carriage, and preaching very frequently." Oliver Hart (*q.v.*) also intinerated.

Nothing but a driving sense of mission sent the preacher itinerating. He received no honorarium, even in the form of salt, corn, wheat, flour, tallow, or whisky, which he might have expected now and then, had he remained at his home church. The homes he visited only furnished him food and lodging, stable and forage for his horse. When his clothes were soiled or worn thin, the women usually laundered and mended them. The clothes of the habitual itinerant were often furnished by these good women. Beside such individual assistance the churches sometimes encouraged itinerants. A church in South Carolina in 1804 furnished the pastor with a "letter of Recommendation to travel." The Charleston Association in 1779 appointed a standing committee to transact emergency business between sessions. One of its duties was to "recommend traveling Ministers of good character." The philosophy of the itinerant himself was simple. "He reasoned that the Lord would take care of them [his family] if he were dead so he might as well care for them in his absence."

Economic depression followed the American Revolution. There was no way to export excess commodities, so the people started West. The pre-Revolution settlers across the Alleghenies were largely hunters, wood-choppers, and Indian-fighters who established no cultural institutions and had little permanent influence. But the post-Revolution settlers were small farmers, lawyers, and artisans. Schools and churches followed them into the wilderness. Having fought for religious liberty (and won it in Virginia in 1785), they determined to enjoy it in the West. The Baptist preacher, with his democratic form of church government, his ideas about secular government, his economic status, was well qualified to attract the Western immigrants. The Methodists, Presbyterians, and other groups also followed the frontier. But "the Baptists . . . were the first to take an active interest in the frontier situation as migration moved westward."

In the new country the preacher lived and worked like the rest of his flock. He lived in a cabin with a dirt floor and slept on a skin-covered bunk instead of a bed. He cleared the ground, split rails, planted corn, and raised hogs. He was a farmer five to six days a week. But no sooner had the pioneer preacher set up his cabin, cleared land, and cultivated his first crop than he began to think of settlers who had not been reached by the gospel. Like Luke Williams who went to Missouri, he "left home and rode through all the settlements of the extreme western frontier preaching to destitute churches."

The itinerant Baptist preacher has been described as "home missionary, revivalist, Bible agent, Sunday school missionary, all in one, with miscellaneous service in speeches, addresses, and lectures." He did many duties of the pastor, such as house-to-house visitation, leadership in discipline of the churches, formation of churches, and baptisms in "the streams of the wilderness." The description of one preacher claimed that "he was an itinerant, always floating from place to place. . . . He would visit all parts of Southern Missouri and southwest Illinois with a little bundle tied up in a handkerchief swung on his shoulders, a walking stick in his hand."

Sometimes warm hospitality opened the pioneer door to the itinerant, but frequently he was not kindly received. John Gano (*q.v.*) once stopped at a farm house where he had heard that the master welcomed traders but shunned preachers. As he brought his things to the door, the owner asked, "Are you a trader?" "Yes," was the reply. He explained that he was a gospel trader, and the man reluctantly let him in. Again, as he journeyed, he rushed to a house to avoid a storm. It was in the time of the French and Indian War, and the master of the house mistook him for a recruiting officer. "Sir, are you a press-master?" he asked. "Yes," replied the preacher. "But you do not take married men?" The preacher assured him that he did, that the Master he wished him to serve was good, the wages great, and it would benefit his wife and children if he enlisted. The man made many excuses, but the preacher begged him to volunteer in the service of Chirst.

The stories of hardship and even persecution of the itinerant preacher would fill volumes. When Daniel Marshall (*q.v.*) itinerated into Georgia just before the Revolution, he was summoned to court while in his pulpit. He had violated the law which forbade all religious worship except the Anglican. But Marshall continued to preach in Georgia, and the constable who summoned him became a preacher.

James Freeman was sent, on request, by the American Home Mission Society to form a church in Chicago in 1833. He had no sooner built up a church of 15 members and erected a meetinghouse than he began to itinerate to adjoining settlements, where he organized several churches. Returning homeward during a storm over a distance of 50 miles, his horse gave out. Freeman had to walk the rest of the way through the storm and soon afterward died from the exposure.

Edmund Botsford, who was called "The Flying Preacher," began itinerating in South Carolina and Georgia in 1771. Invited to preach to some Baptists in a German settlement, he requested the keys of the Lutheran meetinghouse from the caretaker. The caretaker replied, "No, no! Tese Paptists are a very pad people. Day begin slow vurst; py and py all men follow dem." This was the prediction of an honest German when there was not a Baptist church in the colony.

In Burke County, Ga., as Botsford preached, a large proportion of his congregation suddenly jumped up, yelling, "The rum is come!" Soon they were all drunk and disorderly. When the service ended and Botsford emerged from the church, one rough old man grabbed the horse's reins and poked fun at the preacher. The man jokingly invited Botsford to preach near his home, and Botsford accepted. At this service the man's wife and several of his family were converted, and the man himself sobered up permanently.

In many places the Catholics harassed the itinerant preacher even after the Bill of Rights guaranteed religious liberty. One itinerant made an appointment to preach in a courthouse. A Roman Catholic loaded two guns and swore he would shoot the first preacher who darkened the door. The preacher was informed of this, and, gathering the people about him, he retired to the edge of town. There, he testified, "Under the shade of a beautiful elm tree, I blew the silver trumpet of the gospel to a crowd of attentive hearers." An itinerant to Missouri in 1801 "was threatened with arrest and imprisonment by the minions of the Pope," but he continued his labors undaunted.

The only accusation of actual persecution brought by the Baptists against South Carolina provincial authorities concerned the whipping of Joseph Cates, an itinerant, at Cheraw Hill in 1772.

The toils and privations of the itinerant were far from appreciated by many. In 1766 Lt.-Gov. Bull of South Carolina recommended an appropriation for an Anglican minister, "hoping . . . it will even put a stop to the progress of those Baptist vagrants . . ."

Luther Rice (q.v.), in his journeys, is reputed to have reached a stream too deep for his little sulky to cross. He dismounted, took the light vehicle apart, and swam it piece by piece to the opposite side. After swimming his horse across, he reassembled the sulky and proceeded on his journey.

Diaries of itinerants often reveal an urgent drive that rushed them from sermon to sermon, each in a different place. Adiel Sherwood kept a diary on a journey in 1820. It read, in part, as follows:

Nov. 1st—Preached from Jonah
Nov. 4th—Preached at Bethlehem
Nov. 11th—Preached for Brother Lumpkin
Sabbath—Preached from Matt. 5:4
Nov. 13th—Preached in Court House in Greenesboro
Nov. 19th—Preached at Lexington
Nov. 24th—Preached a funeral sermon
Nov. 26th—Preached on the "Priesthood of Christ"
Nov. 29—Preached at Mr. Norton's
Sabbath—Preached at County Line

Nobody has done better in describing the toils of the itinerant than Luther Rice. In his report for 1817, he wrote, "Since the date of my letter of the 19th of June, 1816, I have travelled 6,600 miles—in populous and in dreary portions of country—through wilderness and over rivers—across mountains and valleys—in heat and cold—by day and by night—in weariness, in painfulness, and fastings, and loneliness. . . ."

Rice furnished other statistics, "By my journal, it appears that I have travelled, since entering upon my 33rd year, which loses (sic) this day, 7,800 miles. . . ."

John Mason Peck (q.v.) wrote in 1822, "I have been absent from home 53 days, having traveled through 18 counties in Illinois and 9 in Indiana, rode 926 miles, preached regular sermons 31 times, besides delivering several speeches, addresses, lectures. I have been enabled to revive 3 Bible societies which would never have been reorganized but for my visit, to establish 7 new societies. . . . I have aided in forming 3 sabbath-schools."

Jacob Bower itinerated in the west between 1832 and 1848. He traveled 40,925 miles, preached 2,931 sermons, aided in organizing 14 churches, and ordained 12 preachers.

The results of all these sermons, visits, and miles traveled are shown through these figures, which indicate the trend they helped set in motion: In 1771, when Daniel Marshall and Edmund Botsford came to Georgia, there was not a single church in the colony and only 100 or 200 scattered Baptists. In 1794 there were 53 churches with 3,350 members. In 1772 there were 24 churches and 49 meetinghouses in South Carolina, with 1,100 members and 49 preachers. By 1790 there were 67 churches, 3,878 members, and 91 preachers. In Kentucky in 1790, there were 42 churches, 3,105 members, and 40 preachers. In 1820 there were 491 churches, 31,689 members, and 25 district associations.

The story is simply summarized. When the preacher itinerated, lost people were won, and churches were born. Churches produced other churches, associations, mission societies, sabbath schools; in short, the foundations of the Baptist denomination of today. A history of Brush Creek Church, S. C., states the record of hundreds like it. It says, "The church was organized in 1791 when Carter Tarrants itinerated there."   LOULIE LATIMER OWENS

IWO BAPTIST COLLEGE, IWO. See NIGERIA, MISSION IN.

J

JACKSON, DIXIE FARRIOR (b. Carroll Parish, La., May 6, 1860; d. Little Rock, Ark., June 7, 1929). W.M.U. executive. In 1872 her parents moved to Dardanelle, Ark. She was educated in Carroll Parish, La., and Dardanelle, Ark. She married J. G. Jackson in 1878 and had eight children. The family moved to Little Rock, Ark., in 1904. In 1912 Jackson died, and two years later his widow was elected executive secretary-treasurer of the Arkansas W.M.U., which office she held until her death. She closed her first year's report with these words, "And let the beauty of the Lord, our God, be upon us; and establish thou the work of our hands." She was an alert, persistent leader of Baptist women. MRS. W. I. STOUT

JACKSON FEMALE COLLEGE. Established in Jackson, Miss., in 1853, with Harvey Ball principal. The school was favorably commended by the state convention; however, it is now extinct. J. L. BOYD

JAMAICA, MISSION IN. The Foreign Mission Board aided Jamaican Baptists in reconstruction of churches following hurricanes between 1944 and 1951. In 1953 they asked that an official representative of the board be stationed in Jamaica to share in developing the "policies and program of the Jamaica Baptist Union."

Southern Baptist representatives Charles Wilson and Avis (Chaffin) McCullough, formerly stationed in Colombia's San Andres Island, were located at Kingston, Jamaica, from 1954 to 1956 in an advisory capacity. They introduced Sunday school and Training Union literature, held stewardship conferences, and arranged Vacation Bible schools and evangelistic campaigns. Groups of Southern Baptist students and ministers held special services occasionally.

An emancipated slave from Virginia started Baptist work in Jamaica in 1783. The Baptist Missionary Society of England sent missionaries to the colony between 1814 and 1842; the society continues to aid in times of crisis and helps maintain Calabar College for training ministers.

GENEVIEVE GREER

JAMES MEMORIAL TRAINING SCHOOL FOR GIRLS, BUCHAREST. See ROMANIA, MISSION IN.

JAMESON, SAMUEL YOUNG (b. Towns County, Ga., Oct. 1, 1859; d. Atlanta, Ga., Mar. 15, 1921). Minister, educator, denominational officer. He was of Scotch and French Huguenot descent. His father died in 1862, and his mother remarried and moved to Walhalla, S. C. He attended private schools and Newberry College there, then Hicks Academy in Hayesville, N. C. At 16 he opened a store in Westminster, S. C. In 1880 he entered the Baptist ministry, then attended Furman University and Southern Baptist Theological Seminary. He returned to Westminster as pastor of the church he organized, and in 1884 married Etta Bibb of Westminster. He was the first pastor of West End Baptist Church, Atlanta, 1888–99, where he served with great success until elected corresponding secretary of the Mission Board of the Georgia Baptist Convention. During his tenure, state contributions for missions increased from $44,848 in 1900 to $110,065 in 1905. He was president of Mercer University, 1906–13, during which time a new record of enrolment was set, a men's dormitory and a library were erected, and endowment was increased by $230,000. From 1913 to 1916 he was president of Ouachita College in Arkansas, and from 1916 to 1918 pastor of the First Baptist Church, Marietta, Ga. Jameson was a trustee of Mercer, 1893–1906, from which school he received the D.D. degree in 1898. He served as president of the Georgia Baptist Convention, 1909–11. In 1918 he became superintendent of enlistment of the Home Mission Board of the Southern Baptist Convention, where he served until his death. H. LEWIS BATTS

JAMISON, ATHA THOMAS (b. Murfreesboro, Tenn., Mar. 5, 1866; d. Greenwood, S. C., Aug. 9, 1947). Pioneer in social work. After receiving his early education from his schoolteacher father, Jamison attended Southern Baptist Theological Seminary for one term (1894–95). Four years later, while pastor at Camden, S. C., he was elected superintendent of Connie Maxwell Orphanage, where he served for 46 years until his retirement July 1, 1946. His work attracted national attention, and he led in the formation of the Tri-State Conference of Orphanage Workers in 1906 and the South Carolina Conference of Social Work in 1909. Vice-president of the Child Welfare League of America (1927, 1941–47) and of the National Conference of Social Work (1944), member of three White House Conferences on Child Care (1909, 1930, 1940), and delegate to the International Conference of Social Work (1936), Jamison helped develop programs for the protection of children at home and abroad. Author of five books, his *The Institution for Children* has been used widely. Jamison served as president of the South Carolina Baptist Convention three terms (1924–26). He married Emma Caldwell in 1889 (d. 1900), Mrs. Margaret Wallace Caldwell in 1904 (d. 1934), and Nancy K. Hudgens in 1946.   JOHN C. MURDOCH

JAPAN, MISSION IN. In the 1857 and 1859 biennial conventions Southern Baptists made possible the appointment in 1860 of missionaries for Japan, John Quincy Adams and Sarah (Robinson) Rohrer, who sailed Aug. 3 and were lost at sea. The Civil War and reconstruction delayed further action until 1882 and 1888, when the Foreign Mission Board was authorized by the convention to establish a Japan Mission, a "favorite project" of missionary-statesman Matthew Tyson Yates (q.v.) of China. John William McCollum (q.v.) and Dru (Collins) McCollum were appointed to Japan May 3, 1889, and John Alexander and Sophia (Boatwright) Brunson were transferred from appointments to China. The new missionaries arrived in Yokohama Nov. 5, 1889, and went immediately to Kobe for language study.

After conferring with Northern (American) Baptist missionary personnel, first Osaka and then the island of Kyushu, after a jinriksha survey trip in 1890, became fields of Southern Baptists. McCollum helped organize the Osaka church Mar. 5, 1891, also a day school, before joining Brunson who had moved to Kyushu. Work at Kokura, Wakamatsu, and Chofu was begun in 1888 by the American Baptist Missionary Union. After two years the Brunsons resigned, and at the end of the 1890's there were eight missionaries, six evangelists, one ordained pastor, 75 members (scattered over a 50-mile radius) in one organized church at Moji, and 11 preaching stations in major cities. Rented chapels caused frequent moves.

The Japan Mission was formally organized in Fukuoka Jan. 23, 1900, and Fukuoka's second church was organized in October of that year. Unprecedented evangelism developed in Nagasaki in 1901, and churches were organized in 1902 at Nagasaki, Sasebo, and Kumamoto. In 1903 churches were organized at Kokura and Kagoshima, and Southwestern Association was formed at Fukuoka. Joshua Levering initiated a Sunday School Board gift of $500 for literature, with the first paper published in 1905. The mission was legally recognized as a property-holding body Dec. 23, 1903. Missionary staff increased as three couples arrived together Sept. 27, 1906, at Nagasaki. Then in 1907 when Foreign Mission Board Secretary Robert Josiah Willingham (q.v.) visited Japan, negotiations with the American Baptist Missionary Union resulted in expanding territory on Honshu to Hiroshima and inclusion of Shikoku as a field. The theological seminary in Fukuoka was opened Oct. 17, 1907, with Y. Chiba as president, and missionaries began occupying Shimonoseki as a new field in 1908. In 1910 seminaries in Fukuoka (southern) and Yokohama (northern) merged at Tokyo, and a large English night school was developed in Fukuoka seminary buildings. The Foreign Mission Board approved literature work on an interdenominational basis in 1911. Appropriations of $30,000 and $10,000 were made for a boys' school and for literature respectively; Moji became the first self-supporting church in Japan in 1912. The publishing of the *Life of Adoniram Judson* and the founding of Maizuru kindergarten in 1913 and the beginning of railroad evangelism in 1914 increased the mission's scope. Seinan Gakuin (boys' school), founded Apr. 11, 1916, with 105 students, faced its first crisis with authorities because of insufficient funds for promised expansion. In 1918 Southwestern Association reorganized into a convention; in 1919 student hostel work was inaugurated in Tokyo; and in 1920 the Japan Woman's Missionary Union was organized at Fukuoka. Twelve missionaries arrived in 1921, and the Hiroshima-Kure field was occupied. Seinan Jo Gakuin (girls' school) was founded in Kokura Apr. 22, 1922, with 96 pupils; Training Union work was launched; and the seminary was reborn in 1923 as a department of Seinan Gakuin College. Following in succession, the Young Woman's Auxiliary, the Rinkosha Good Will Center at Tobata, and rural evangelism were established between 1926 and 1930.

Between 1931 and 1941 missionary ranks thinned and replacements became difficult. The first Christmas offering in 1931 was 89.39 yen, and Tobata church was organized. But also in 1931 the Asa-Kai, a reaction against spiritual formality and some convention leaders, swept away a number of younger pastors and caused church losses. A home mission movement was launched among North Kyushu churches, and the convention, of which the women's organization had become a department, dispatched its first missionary to Manchukuo in 1936. After the government approved inclusion of Japanese on the mission's legal holding body, which completed partnership responsibilities, the two Japanese conventions merged to form Japan Baptist Convention at Himeji in Jan., 1940, but the organization was denied entity under the New Religions Law, and Baptists were forced into Kirisuto Kyodan (union church) by Nov., 1941. Finally, W. Maxfield Garrott remained as the only missionary in Japan to be interned at the outbreak of the Pacific war.

World War II left only a remnant of Baptist work. The last graduate of Tokyo seminary was sent as a missionary to Palau, Caroline Islands, in 1942. Pressure to close or merge schools at Kokura and Fukuoka developed; Christian faith was tried by national Shinto; pastors were conscripted into war service; the membership of Koishikawa church formed a new Mejiro-gaoka church Apr. 9, 1944, outside the Kyodan framework; nine churches died, and membership dwindled from 2,700 to less than 500 by 1945.

Reconstruction and expansion followed at the end of the war by 1946. On Nov. 23 of that year a Southern Baptist representative conferred with former Japanese co-workers at Fukuoka, resulting in the formation of the new Japan Baptist Convention Apr. 3, 1947, composed of 16 churches. Seinan Jo Gakuin launched a junior college in 1946 and the seminary enrolled 18 students. Jordan Press was started in 1947; Hiroshima First Church was rebuilt in 1948; Oi-machi church (Tokyo) joined the convention; and Southern Baptist Military Fellowship was organized in Tokyo. In 1949 there were 22 churches and 18 missions; Mallory Memorial Auditorium (Kokura) was dedicated; Seinan Gakuin received senior college recognition. Work expanded still more in 1950 when 24 missionaries arrived together, and a pastors-missionaries conference stirred comradeship. Preaching missions in 1950 and 1951 lent encouragement. A mission and convention office building and a seminary dormitory were provided. By 1952, 20 self-supporting churches indicated solid growth; a university building at Fukuoka was dedicated. The Military Fellowship gave 10 acres of land for Amagi Assembly in 1953; medical work began in Kyoto. Missionaries were in 27 of the 49 prefectural states by 1954 when Rankin Memorial Chapel and Seinan Gakuin Library were dedicated. A hospital began operation July 12, 1955; a seminary building in Fukuoka and Hara Memorial building at the Kokura school were dedicated in October. With more than 50 church locations and buildings acquired by 1955, the mission reported 62 churches, 102 missionaries, 65 national pastors, and 9,119 members.

EDWIN B. DOZIER.

JAPAN CONVENTION OF BAPTIST CHURCHES. Japan was opened as a mission field by the American Baptist Free Mission Society, which transferred the work to the American Baptist Missionary Union May 21, 1872. Nathan Brown (1807–86) served as the union's first missionary. In 1875 two single women missionaries initiated the work among women and children. Brown, who had served previously in Burma and Assam, was 66 years old when he reached Yokohama. In spite of impaired health he learned the Japanese language and translated the New Testament from the Greek while ministering to his church. Brown's first convert became his assistant and the forerunner of many Japanese church and educational leaders, a number of whom have pursued graduate study in the United States. Major success has been with the intellectuals in the cities.

The first Baptist church in Tokyo opened June 14, 1876, followed by Misaki Tabernacle, an institutional church rendering varied services in a needy area, in 1908, opened due to the efforts of William Axling (1873–   ). In 1898 Captain Luke W. Bickel (1866–1917) began work among the islands of the Inland Sea in a "Gospel Ship."

During World War II churches in Japan were obliged to operate independently of both foreign funds and missionaries through the Kyodan, or Church of Christ in Japan, organized in 1941.

After the war Baptist churches affiliated with the American Baptist Foreign Mission Societies also formed the Shinseikai, or Baptist New Life Fellowship, which operates as a convention with Jin Sugaya as executive secretary. Union, or interdenominational, work is congenial to Japanese, whose first effort to establish a National Christian church in Japan was in 1877. Union institutions include the National Christian Council, Tokyo Woman's Christian College, the Japan Union Theological Seminary, Tokyo, and the Japan International Christian University, opened in 1953; in all these, churches related to American Baptist Foreign Mission Societies cooperate.

High schools for girls are located in Yokohama, Sendai, and Himeji. A kindergarten training school and many church-related kindergartens provide contact with family life; general youth work includes summer conferences and work camps. An Institute of Christian Studies is included at coeducational Kanto Gakuin University in Yokohama, and a Baptist student center at Waseda University, a private institution in Tokyo. In the industrial city of Osaka, a Christian Center program is carried on, and projects for neglected rural areas, both Baptist and union, are being developed.

DATA

	1934	1954 (Figures incomplete)
Churches	35	61
Baptisms	178	233
Church members	4,575	5,052
Missionaries	36	32
Japanese workers	300	554
Students	4,322	10,238
Schools	59	52
Patients	3,550	—
Dispensaries	2	2
Field contributions	$27,115	$52,497

ADA STEARNS.

JAPAN HOSPITAL, KYOTO. See JAPAN, MISSION IN.

JAPAN SEMINARY, FUKUOKA. See JAPAN, MISSION IN.

JAPANESE, HOME MISSIONS TO. Southern Baptist mission work with the Japanese began when the 125,000 Japanese of the West Coast were interned in relocation centers during World War II. On June 4, 1942, Elizabeth Watkins, former missionary to Japan, was appointed by the Home Mission Board to serve in the internment camp near Phoenix, Ariz. Bette Ishibashi Kira served in the relocation center at McGehee, Ark., from May 15, 1943, to Sept. 30, 1945. Maxfield Garrott and his wife were assigned by the Foreign Mission Board to the Home Mission Board to work in all the relocation centers in Southern Baptist Convention territory from Nov. 4, 1943, to Feb. 28, 1945.

Since the war, work has been begun with the Japanese of Los Angeles, Richmond, and Sacramento, Calif. George Fujita and Mrs. Fujita served in Los Angeles from June 1, 1948, until their return to Japan on July 1, 1951. They were succeeded by Toshio Sakamoto and Mrs. Sakamoto who have served there since July 1, 1951. Helen Ige began working with the Fujitas in Los Angeles on June 1, 1948, and was transferred to begin the work in Richmond on Feb. 1, 1949, where she continued to serve until Jan. 31, 1956. A. K. Bonham and his wife also served in Richmond from Sept. 1, 1951, to Jan., 1952. Richard Uejo and Mrs. Uejo served at Richmond from May 15, 1952, until their return to Hawaii June 30, 1955. Raymond Spence and Mrs. Spence, former missionaries to Japan, served in Richmond from Sept. 24, 1955, to June 10, 1956. The work at Sacramento was begun by the transfer of A. K. Bonham and Mrs. Bonham, who have continued to serve there since Jan., 1952. Their efforts have been directed toward the winning and enlistment of the Japanese into the Anglo-American Southern Baptist churches rather than the beginning of a separate Japanese Baptist congregation.

The properties used for Japanese missions in Los Angeles and Richmond, Calif., are worth $75,000.

Besides the 125,000 Japanese of the West Coast, there are small groups in several other parts of the country. The best approach to winning them outside their larger sections is to enlist them in the existing churches of the communities in which they live.   LOYD CORDER

JASPER, JOHN (b. Fluvanna County, Va., July 4, 1812; d. Mar. 30, 1901). Negro slave, preacher. Born a slave on a plantation owned by the Peachy family, Jasper was transferred to Charles City County, at the age of 22, where he became the property of John Blair Peachy, who lived near Williamsburg, Va. Later, he was sent to Richmond and became the property of Samuel Hargrove, who was engaged in the manufacture of tobacco. Hargrove gave Jasper, a stemmer in his factory, a holiday when he was converted and told him to go to tell his relatives and friends what the Lord had done for him. Jasper said his friend, "Rev." Johnson, taught him to read from an old New York spelling book. He had a passionate desire to know the Bible and spent hours reading it.

A close observer and imitator, Jasper picked up certain words and attitudes from white people in whose homes he worked, and he spoke of them in terms of affection after he was freed. Divorced by his first wife when he was sent to Richmond as the property of another owner, Jasper, with the sanction of the First African Baptist Church, then married Candus Jordan, who bore him several children. When she proved unfaithful, Jasper divorced her and married a third wife, who died in 1874. His fourth wife survived him.

Jasper began his preaching ministry in an abandoned house near the James River. Later, his congregation bought the church building at the corner of Duval and St. John streets, Richmond, owned by the Presbyterians, for $2,025. Soon this was not large enough, however, and the building was enlarged at a cost of $6,000. As membership increased to about 2,000, a new building became a necessity, and Jasper led in the movement for its erection. Many white people gave him money for "Sixth Mount Zion's" new building, and Jasper himself is reported to have given $3,000 to the building fund.

He became a national figure. For 25 years, as a slave, Jasper preached in Richmond and Petersburg, and for 30 more years, after he was freed, he continued to preach in Richmond, in many parts of Virginia, and out of the state. He is said to have repeated his famous "The Sun Do Move" sermon at least 250 times. On one of these occasions, the church was packed, probably a third of the congregation white people. Jasper held his congregation spellbound for more than an hour. His grammar was horrid, but his eloquence "carried everybody with him" as he proved "the sun do move" by quoting verse after verse, following the literal meaning. He stood erect, his eyes flashed, his long arms waved, as he shouted: "How in de name of Goad can the earth be round when de Bible speak of its four corners?" "Whar you going to put a corner on a round thing? Read your Bible and if it don't speak of dem four corners, next time you see me, Spit in my face!"

Jasper's funeral was conducted at his own Sixth Mount Zion Church, Apr. 4, 1901, at 11:30 A.M. Among the addresses delivered was one by Jasper's great friend and biographer, William Eldridge Hatcher (q.v.), on "Jasper as a Citizen." Hatcher died nearly 11 years later, Aug. 12, 1912, at his home in Fork Union, and as he lay dying, a friend heard him whisper, "John Jasper, we are brothers now and will live forever around the throne of God."

BIBLIOGRAPHY: R. E. Day, *Rhapsody in Black* (1953). W. E. Hatcher, *John Jasper* (1908). I. James, *The Sun Do Move* (1954). E. Randolph, *Life of Rev. John Jasper* (1884).   L. M. RITTER

JAYNE, MARY PROSSER (b. Iowa, Dec. 16, 1867; d. Muskogee, Okla., Jan. 5, 1937). Pioneer missionary; educator of Indians. After graduation from Women's Baptist Missionary Training School, Chicago, Ill., 1896, she was appointed by the Woman's Baptist Home Mission Society to work with the Cheyenne Indians in Oklahoma and assumed duties in that work at Watonga, Okla., the same year. In 1914 she moved to Pawnee, Okla., to work with that Indian tribe, and in 1924 she went to Bacone College as a housemother. In 1933 she retired to California, returned to Bacone in 1934, and remained until her death. First president of Woman's Home and Foreign Mission Society, Auxiliary to the Oklahoma Baptist State Convention, she served until 1905. Last corresponding secretary of that body (1905–06), she was also temporary secretary at the organization of

Woman's Missionary Union of Oklahoma, Nov. 8, 1906, and field secretary in western Oklahoma, 1906–07. She was superintendent of the W.M.U.'s traveling library service, 1908–12.

BIBLIOGRAPHY: Mrs. A. F. Wasson, *One Who Was Strong* (n.d.). J. M. GASKIN and L. E. MAPLES

JENKINS, WARWICK HOXIE (b. Washington, Tex., Nov. 14, 1847; d. Waco, Tex., Jan. 20, 1933). Attorney, active Texas layman. Son of James R. Jenkins, who in 1837 wrote the letter which induced the American Baptist Home Mission Society to send several missionaries to Texas, Jenkins attended Baylor and Waco universities at Independence and Waco, after which he served as a Baylor trustee for 55 years, vice-president 18 years, and board secretary 37 years. A member at First Baptist Church, Waco, Jenkins served 33 years as deacon, 28 as chairman; 31 years as clerk; 29 years as Sunday school superintendent; and as choir director, librarian, and teacher. While Texas Baptist headquarters were in Waco, Jenkins served several years as chairman of the state executive board. At the state convention in 1897, he challenged S. A. Hayden's right to a seat in that body, and his challenge was sustained five to one.

FRANK BURKHALTER

JENT, JOHN WILLIAM (b. Franklin, Simpson County, Ky., Mar. 17, 1877; d. Shawnee, Okla., May 29, 1941). Minister, college professor, author; educated at Pierce City Baptist Academy, Southern and Southwestern Baptist seminaries, Baylor, Yale, and Columbia universities. He was converted at Erie, Mo., July, 1886, and was baptized by his father at Pool's Prairie Baptist Church, Newton County, Mo., Aug., 1887; he was licensed to preach at Cedar Vale, Kans., Nov. 17, 1897; he was ordained at Oregon Baptist Church, Jasper County, Mo., July 6, 1899. Jent married Jessie Pollard at Moody, Tex., Aug. 4, 1905. As private secretary to Benajah Harvey Carroll (*q.v.*) for four years, he helped organize Southwestern Baptist Seminary and later helped map the course for Oklahoma Baptist University—beginning as registrar and professor of social sciences, 1915, he served as dean, 1922–26. He was professor of the rural church department and dean of Theological Seminary, Mercer University, 1926–28; president of Southwest Baptist College, Bolivar, Mo., 1928–30; and professor of education and sociology, Union University, Jackson, Tenn., 1930–32. He returned to Oklahoma Baptist University in 1932 as professor of psychology and philosophy, and served as dean of faculties in 1933, and vice-president from 1938 until his death. He was the author of: *The Primacy of Personality in Pedagogy, The Challenge of the Country Church, Rural Church Problems, After Fifty Eight Years, Sermons and Addresses, Rural Church Development,* and *The Philosophy of a Christian Philosopher.* He is listed in *Who's Who in America* (1926–43); *Who's Who in the Central States* (1929); *Who's Who Among American Authors* (1931); and *Leaders in Education* (1932). He was a member of the education board of the Southern Baptist Convention, 1925–26, and of the Southwestern Political Science Association. He was a democrat and a Mason.

HARRY M. ROARK

JERSEY SETTLEMENT CHURCH. In 1753 and soon after, a group of immigrants from New Jersey came to a section along the Yadkin River, east and southeast of Salisbury, N. C., which became known as the Jersey Settlement. Among these immigrants was Benjamin Miller, pastor of the Scotch Plains Baptist Church of New Jersey. He worked so effectively among the settlers that Hugh McAden, a Presbyterian minister on tour in 1755, found that many Presbyterians in the settlement had become Baptists. After Miller left, the Charleston Association sent John Gano on a missionary tour to the region in 1756, and at the insistence of the Jersey church he soon returned as pastor. The church, reconstituted, built a meetinghouse, which it used with other denominations. Particular Baptist in faith, the church was a member of the Charleston Association in 1759. Gano left the Jersey Settlement in 1760 because of Cherokee Indian raids, and the church ceased to function. The present Jersey church was organized in 1784 with the help of William Hill and Pastor Drury Sims. An early member of the Yadkin Association, it later joined the Pee Dee and Abbott's Creek Union; and when the latter body "split" in 1832, Jersey became a constituent member of Liberty Association, in which it has remained. G. W. PASCHAL

JESUS CHRIST. VIRGIN BIRTH. According to the Gospels of Matthew and Luke, Jesus of Nazareth was born of the virgin Mary through the operation of the power of the Holy Spirit and without the agency of a human father. This view appeared in the early confessions of the Christian faith. In the Apostles' Creed the confession reads, "I believe . . . in Jesus Christ . . . who was conceived by the Holy Ghost, born of the Virgin Mary," and in the Nicene Creed, "incarnate by the Holy Ghost of the Virgin Mary."

Until the latter part of the eighteenth century, the virgin birth remained a virtually undisputed part of the Christian faith. Beginning at that time and extending on to the present, many attacks have been made on the truth of the doctrine. These attacks have come from persons who have sought to find a natural explanation for the birth of Jesus rather than the supernatural one affirmed in the New Testament. While some have opposed the doctrine because of their skepticism regarding the supernatural, others have objected because they regarded the mode of Jesus' birth as having little doctrinal importance, or because the virgin birth was not a subject emphasized in the teaching of Jesus and the apostles, or because it is not affirmed in the New Testament outside of

Matthew and Luke. These objections are not valid. An appraisal of the doctrine must be made on the basis of the authenticity of the passages of Scripture where it appears, not on the basis of the silence of those who do not mention it.

It has been demonstrated with certainty that the virgin birth stories are an integral and original part of Matthew (1:18-25) and Luke (1:26-56; 2:1-20). All the early Greek manuscripts contain the accounts (Sinaiticus, Vaticanus, Ephraemi, Bezae; Alexandrinus is mutilated at this part of Matthew, but the Gospel of Luke is intact and contains chapters 1-2). The early Latin manuscripts, as well as the Syriac and Coptic, contain these accounts. There is only one exception, the Sinaitico-Syriac version, and its original form is a subject of great conjecture. This version's reading of Matthew 1:16 states that Joseph begat Jesus. In the light of such preponderance of evidence, however, the virgin birth stories must be regarded as a genuine part of Matthew and Luke, and it must be granted that the writers intended for readers to believe that Jesus was born of the virgin Mary by the power of the Holy Spirit, apart from the natural processes of human paternity.

While the remainder of the New Testament is silent on the subject of the virgin birth, there is nothing in the language of the other writers which would either preclude the doctrine or be inconsistent with it. The Gospel of Mark begins with the public ministry of the wonderworking Jesus, recording no part of his life up to that point. The Gospel of John begins with the pre-existent *Logos* and affirms the incarnation (John 1:14) but says nothing of the mode of the incarnation. Paul speaks of the pre-existence and incarnation (Phil. 2:5-11; II Cor. 8:9; I Cor. 8:6; 15:45, 47; Rom. 1:3-4; Rom. 8:3) but says nothing of the mode of the incarnation. Acts, Hebrews, James, Peter, the Johannine epistles, and Revelation do not deal with the virgin birth.

An argument from silence is never conclusive. Also, positive affirmations of the virgin birth of Jesus are unquestionably authentic in Luke and Matthew, with Matthew (1:23) finding a parallel (Isa. 7:14) in prophetic word.

BIBLIOGRAPHY: C. A. Briggs, *The Incarnation of the Lord* (1902). J. G. Machen, *The Virgin Birth of Christ* (1930). J. Orr, *The Virgin Birth of Christ* (1907). F. Palmer, *The Virgin Birth* (1924). P. Schaff, *The Creeds of Christendom* (1919). RAY SUMMERS

BAPTISM. The baptism of Jesus in the river Jordan at the hands of John the Baptist marks the beginning of his public life and points to his public ministry. The Gospels do not record the details of Jesus' life from his appearance in the Temple at the age of 12 (Luke 2:41-52) to his baptism at the age of 30 (Luke 3:23). John the Baptist, coming from a priestly family, began his ministry when he was 30; and Jesus, approximately six months younger than John, began his public life and ministry at the same age.

The details of Jesus' baptism are given in Mark 1:9-11; Matthew 3:13-17; Luke 3:21-23; and John 1:32-34. The baptism took place in the Jordan River, in the territory of Judea east of Jerusalem (Luke 3:2-3), the section where John was preaching and baptizing. The fact that Jesus journeyed from Nazareth in Galilee to be baptized by John in Judea (Mark 1:9; Matt. 3:13) indicates the importance of the act to him. Matthew's account describes John's reluctance to baptize Jesus, John thinking that it would be more appropriate for Jesus to baptize him. Jesus, however, requested that John proceed with the baptism in order that he might fulfil in that act all righteousness in the Father's purpose for him.

Jesus' coming to John, insisting on being baptized, has always been a perplexing matter. The baptism which John was administering was related to confession of sin (Matt. 3:6), repentance (Luke 3:3), and a new kind of life, demonstrating the sincerity of one's confession and repentance (Luke 3:8-14). All the New Testament records indicate that Jesus was without sin and that he was free of any consciousness of sin. There was no need for him to turn from an old life to a new one. Thus, the significance of his baptism must be explained in other ways.

Jesus had come into the world to align himself with mankind, whom he had come to redeem. In the act of baptism, he was doing this completely. He definitely aligned himself with the cause of his forerunner, John the Baptist, who was proclaiming a message of confession and repentance. Jesus felt that he must identify himself with that cause as well as with man, the object of his redemptive work.

The details of his baptism are few but clear. When Jesus was immersed in the Jordan river, he was in the spirit of prayer (Luke 3:21). Jesus saw the heavens open (the Greek of Mark's customarily graphic description says "rent asunder"—1:10); he saw the Spirit of God descending "in a bodily shape like a dove" (Luke 3:22) upon him. The dove was John's means of identifying Jesus as the one who was to come after him (John 1:32-34). Jesus heard a voice out of heaven, with the words spoken combining parts of Psalm 2:7 and Isaiah 42:1. Psalm 2:7, "Thou art my Son," identified Jesus as the Messiah. Isaiah 42:1, "Behold my servant, whom I uphold," identified him as the Suffering Servant Messiah of prophecy. These words were of particular importance to Jesus as he turned from his baptism to the temptation in the wilderness. In the initial experience of his public life, he was identified as the Suffering Servant Messiah, the anointed Son of God, who would suffer as the just for the unjust in his redemptive mission. RAY SUMMERS

TEMPTATION. The temptation of Jesus in the wilderness was representative of the temptation which he faced all through his earthly life.

This period of temptation (Mark 1:12-13; Matt. 4:1-11; Luke 4:1-13) followed immediately upon his baptism. When he was baptized, a voice from heaven identified him as the Son of God (Psalm 2:7, "Thou art my Son") and as the Suffering Servant Messiah of Isaiah's prophecy (Isa. 42:1, "Behold my servant, whom I uphold"). To Jesus this latter identification meant that the way to his messiahship was the long, hard way of suffering pictured by the prophet (Isa. 40-66). The temptation in the wilderness was related directly to his suffering role. Underlying all three temptation experiences was the basic temptation to take the easy way and thus avoid the suffering pictured by Isaiah. Jesus recognized the true nature of the temptation.

After 40 days of fasting, Jesus, with keen awareness of hunger, was tempted at the physical level to turn stones to bread (Luke 4:3-4; Matt. 4:3-4). The temptation was presented somewhat like this: "As the Son of God, you should not be hungry like ordinary men. Use your divine power and satisfy your human hunger." This temptation, like the two which followed, appealed to what was natural and normal. It involved, however, the application of a method not embraced in God's will for his Son as Suffering Messiah. In his answer (Luke 4:4) Jesus made it clear that while bread was important to him, his obedience to the Father's will was primary.

Resisting the first temptation, Jesus indicated his trust in the Father to care for his needs. The second temptation (Luke 4:9-12; Matt. 4:5-7) was at the level of the spectacular. Then Satan tempted Jesus to presume on the Father's favor by leaping from the top of the Temple, trusting God's angels to bear him up (Psalm 91:11-12). The worshipers, seeing him arrive unharmed on the ground, would immediately proclaim him as the Messiah. Jesus refused the temptation, knowing that spiritual ends cannot be achieved by unspiritual means and realizing the vast difference between faith and presumption.

The third temptation was at the level of power (Luke 4:5-8; Matt. 4:8-10). Satan tempted Jesus to take the way of popular demand, the way of the political revolutionist, as a means of winning a following. But as Jesus had refused to co-operate with Satan in the first two temptations, he refused again in this one.

Out of his temptation experience Jesus determined: (1) He would not use supernatural power to provide for his natural needs. (2) He would not use supernatural power as a means of display among men. (3) He would not stoop to the world's demand for an earthly kingdom brought about by worldly means and for like ends. (4) He would accept the long, hard road which would lead him to the cross.

BIBLIOGRAPHY: H. M. Battenhouse, *Christ in the Gospels* (1952). J. W. Bowman, *The Intention of Jesus* (1943). E. A. McDowell, *Son of Man and Suffering Servant* (1944). G. C. Morgan, *The Crises of the Christ* (n.d.). J. Stalker, *The Life of Christ* (1891). V. Taylor, *The Life and Ministry of Jesus* (1955).

RAY SUMMERS

THE SERMON ON THE MOUNT. This title designates the discourse of Jesus recorded in Matthew 5-7. In spite of the fact that Luke gives a similar outline of such teachings in Luke 6:20-49 and includes many other principles common to those recorded in Matthew, most scholars consider the basic Matthew record to be that of a continuous discourse given by Jesus at one time. Although the teachings of Jesus on that occasion were perhaps more lengthy than our record of them in Matthew, this account presents the main body of the principles he enunciated.

Both Matthew and Luke place the discourse early in the ministry of Jesus, about the time of his selection of the disciples. The sermon was apparently addressed primarily to these disciples. However, there is evidence that others were present. Jesus delivered the sermon on one of the hills overlooking the Galilean plain and the lake, probably near Capernaum. His references to "lilies," "grass," "fowls," "cities on a hill," and "salt" indicate their proximity and the familiarity of the people with them.

Dealing with the kingdom of heaven and its subjects, the sermon represents Jesus' highest teaching concerning the character, conduct, and destiny of God's children. The message of the sermon is centered in the character and conduct of the "kingdom man." The sermon is not to be considered the sum total of all Jesus' teachings, however, for many themes are omitted. In a sense it is like an inaugural address. Jesus sets forth his aims and purposes for man and describes the person he proposes man should become. Such a person is illustrated in Jesus' life, and he proposes to make such a life possible in his followers. Man's eternal destiny is determined by what he does with the principles set forth in this sermon. The doing of these things seems to be not the way to eternal life, but rather the evidence that one is a "kingdom man." Righteousness in character and conduct is the central theme.

Many good outlines have been made of the sermon. The following outline is based upon one given by the late William Hersey Davis, long-time professor of New Testament at Southern Baptist Theological Seminary, Louisville, Ky.:

Introduction. Matt. 5:1 f.
I. The Character of the Kingdom Man. Matt. 5:3-9
II. The Influence of the Kingdom Man. Matt. 5:10-19
   1. Negatively. 10-12
   2. Positively. 13-16
   3. On the law and prophets. 17-19
III. The Conduct of the Kingdom Man. Matt. 5:20 to 7:12
   1. Christ's ethical standard superior to the scribes. 5:20-48

2. Real righteousness unlike the empty righteousness of the Pharisees. 6:1–18
   3. Central devotion to God in contrast to worldly aims and anxieties. 6:19–34
   4. Christ's standard of judgment. 7:1–6
   5. Prayer and the Golden Rule. 7:7–12
IV. The Destiny of Man. Matt. 7:13–27
   1. Parable of the gates and ways. 7:13 f.
   2. Parable of the trees and fruit. 7:15–23
   3. Parable of the houses. 7:24–28

BIBLIOGRAPHY: G. G. Atkins, *From the Hillside* (1948). H. L. Eddleman, *The Teachings of Jesus* (1955). E. M. Ligon, *The Psychology of Christian Personality* (1949). A. W. Pink, *The Sermon on the Mount* (1951). E. T. Thompson, *The Sermon on the Mount* (1946). H. Windisch, *The Meaning of the Sermon on the Mount* (1937). On the Beatitudes: H. Martin, *The Beatitudes* (1953). H. B. Walker, *Ladder of Light* (1951).   HAROLD K. GRAVES

THE GREAT CONFESSION (Mark 8:27–30; Matt. 16:13–20; Luke 9:18–21). Near Caesarea Philippi Jesus tested his disciples' faith in his messiahship. They were there because the people in Galilee, who six months before had responded to Jesus as a popular hero, had turned away as the true nature of his messiahship became apparent. Although the people rejected him because he refused to be a national king and relieve them of Roman rule, those who had followed him for more than two years remained loyal. The disciples' early faith had been tinged by popular conceptions of the Messiah, but their growing appreciation of Jesus had produced a settled conviction that was revealed by his questions.

The first question, "Who do men say that I the Son of man am?" began the discussion and received a variety of answers which were suggestive of the characteristics of Jesus that impressed the people. John the Baptist, Elijah, Jeremiah, one of the prophets were identities recounted by the disciples. None of these satisfied; none was an acceptable basis for real discipleship; hence, Jesus pressed another question: "But whom say ye that I am?" Simon Peter answered for the group: "Thou art the Christ, the Son of the living God." Peter's response, which recognized not only the messianic office but the divine nature belonging to Jesus, was warmly received. Jesus openly accepted the title of Messiah.

Almost endless controversy has attended the words following the confession which were spoken to Peter by Jesus: "Thou art Peter, and upon this rock I will build my church." Unquestionably there is a play on the words "Peter" (*petros*) and "rock" (*petra*), but the significance has been much disputed. Three interpretations are most commonly given: (1) Peter himself is the rock upon which the church is to be built. (2) Peter is playing the part of a rock in his confession, the confession being the significant matter. (3) The rock refers to the divine nature and messiahship of Jesus confessed by Peter. The word "church" has caused much discussion. Many scholars understand the word in an institutional sense, though some do not. The emphasis seems to be upon Christ's activity, and the contrast is with the "church" of the Old Testament. Psalm 89, which is messianic, employs the significant terminology of this passage. The phrase "the gates of hell" refers to the region of death. The church is on the offensive with victory assured. "The keys of the kingdom" and the idea of binding and loosing have been related to the meaning of "rock." Some understand the reference to mean that ecclesiastical authority was vested in Peter (not all who understand "rock" to refer to Peter follow Roman Catholicism, but find the sense of Eph. 2:20); others suggest that both relate to the proclaiming of the truth of the confession. "Binding" and "loosing" were common terms among the Pharisees for what was forbidden and what was permitted, suggesting that not the souls of men but matters of Christian conduct are involved. Some notice that in the Talmud "the key" was used to represent control through teaching. One who was effective in teaching was referred to as binding; one who was ineffective, as loosing. The reference would then be to the preaching of the disciples and the content of their message. The verb tenses (future perfect, "shall have been bound") indicate that the disciples' success is conditioned by what has already taken place in heaven.

HUBER DRUMWRIGHT

TRANSFIGURATION. This event was directly related to Christ's messianic mission, which culminated in the cross and the resurrection. In the company of Peter, John, and James, Christ was praying on a mountain in Galilee when his appearance changed so that his clothes were brilliantly white, and his face was like the brightness of the sun (Mark 9:2–8; Matt. 17:1–8; Luke 9:28–36). Moses and Elijah appeared, discussing with Christ the death which would soon come to him in Jerusalem. Evidently the disciples were asleep and missed the conversation (Luke 9:32); but when they awoke and saw Moses and Elijah, Peter boldly suggested that he be permitted to build three booths, with all the company remaining on the mountain. Perhaps he was thinking that the Feast of Tabernacles, which was soon to be observed, could hold nothing greater than the joy of the present experience.

While Peter was speaking, a bright cloud came over the group, and a voice spoke out of the cloud saying, "This is my beloved Son: hear ye him." The disciples fell upon their faces in fear. When they looked up in response to Christ's command, they saw that Moses and Elijah had disappeared; Christ alone remained. How the disciples recognized Moses and Elijah is idle speculation. It could have been by spiritual perception or by Christ's explanation. The phenomena of the experience have fascinated interpreters throughout the Christian era—the deity of Christ, shining through a humanity that could not contain it. This phenomenon, however, is not the most significant point to be observed. The importance of the event lies in the fact that this experience, occurring one week after the great confession at Caesarea Philippi (Mark 8:27-30; Matt. 16:13-20; Luke 9:18-21), was directly related to Christ's redemptive work. Moses was the representative of the law; Elijah was the representative of the prophets. The law had spoken of sin; the prophets had spoken of a sin-bearer. In the transfiguration the two representatives who embodied the idea of authority in the Hebrew religion appeared talking with the Son of God, who had become man to carry out the redemptive work of God, the necessity of which is seen in the law and the reality of which is seen in the prophets.

When Moses and Elijah disappeared, Christ only "remained," and the voice from heaven said, "Hear ye him." Christ fulfils both the law and the prophets; he alone can speak with authority in the realm of religion.

BIBLIOGRAPHY: H. M. Battenhouse, *Christ in the Gospels* (1952). E. A. McDowell, *Son of Man and Suffering Servant* (1944). G. C. Morgan, *The Crises of the Christ* (n.d.). J. Stalker, *The Life of Christ* (1891). V. Taylor, *The Life and Ministry of Jesus* (1955).

RAY SUMMERS

GETHSEMANE. This scene of Jesus' agony on the night of his arrest has been from earliest times a stumbling block to many, because it appears to betray in Jesus conduct unworthy of the Son of God. Mark says Jesus "began to be greatly amazed, and sore troubled" (14:33 ASV), and quotes him as saying, "My soul is exceeding sorrowful even unto death" (14:34 ASV). Matthew writes that Jesus "began to be sorrowful and sore troubled" (26:37 ASV). Luke speaks of Jesus as "being in an agony" and records that as he prayed, "his sweat became as it were great drops of blood falling down upon the ground" (22:44 ASV). The author of Hebrews adds that Jesus' prayer was offered up "with strong crying and tears" (5:7). Obviously, if Gethsemane is to be explained at all, it must be explained in relation to Christ's death (Heb. 5:7-8). Opinions, however, differ widely when a more specific explanation is sought.

Sometimes the Lord's distress in the garden is attributed to a *dread of the physical suffering* involved in his death. If that were so, then it must be admitted that the Lord showed less courage and endurance than many of his followers. Martyrs in many ages have looked calmly upon death in its most terrifying forms, and some of them have endured its tortures with a song on their lips. Even the coarsest of criminals have climbed the scaffold without a tremor, and many a brutal murderer has met death with an unflinching countenance. Something more than physical sufferings, terrible as they were, must have been in the mind of Jesus in Gethsemane.

A more plausible explanation is that which finds the cause of Jesus' agony in the *mode* and *accompaniments* of his death. The thought of his death had long been in his mind, but, as he came face to face with it, he found that its form and conditions involved its perpetrators in what appeared inexpiable guilt. His act of redemption was to become the occasion of their crime. It seemed "as if into His very cup their crimes had been pressed, as if the very wine He had to drink were dark with their blood. . . . His soul stood, as it were, clothed in horror before a sacrifice so conditioned, a death so prepared and attended" (Fairbairn).

The most satisfactory view of Jesus' agony in the garden is that which relates it to the *expiatory* and *vicarious character* of his death. According to this view, Christ was seized with anguish in the garden because he began to feel in a terrifying way the crushing pressure of the world's sin, for which his death was to make atonement. He was to be "wounded for our transgressions, . . . bruised for our iniquities" (Isa. 53:5), and was to bear "our sins in his own body on the tree" (I Peter 2:24). He had no horror at death considered simply as physical dissolution. He had no dread of the physical torture of the cross; this he could face without a murmur (Mark 10:33-34). The secret ingredient which gave his death its poignant bitterness was consciousness of the fact that he was dying for sinners and must endure for them an interruption of his filial communion with God. He who knew no sin was to be made sin for man (II Cor. 5:21). It was not at all improper that the Son of God should recoil with horror from the anticipation of such an experience.

Although the dreadful cup did not pass away, the prayer was not unanswered, for the author of Hebrews says Christ was "heard for his godly fear" and became through his sufferings perfectly fitted to be "the author of eternal salvation" (5:7-9 ASV).

BIBLIOGRAPHY: A. B. Bruce, *With Open Face* (1896). A. Edersheim, *The Life and Times of Jesus the Messiah* (1953). A. M. Fairbairn, *Studies in the Life of Christ* (1899); *The Philosophy of the Christian Religion* (1947). F. W. Farrar, *The Life of Christ* (1906). A. E. Garvie, "Agony," *A Dictionary of Christ and the Gospels* (J. Hastings, ed.) (1911); *Studies in the Inner Life of Jesus* (n.d.). J. P. Lange, *The Life of the Lord Jesus Christ* (1864). D. M. Pratt, "Agony," *The International Standard Bible Encyclopaedia* (James Orr, ed.) (1949).

CURTIS VAUGHAN

CRUCIFIXION. Death by impalement on a stake was common in the ancient world. It was practiced at some time by the Persians, Babylonians, Phenicians, Carthaginians, and Romans. From impalement developed the agonizing death by crucifixion, which the Romans reserved for depraved criminals, slaves, and provincials. Treason, desertion, robbery, piracy, assassination, and sedition were crimes punishable by execution in this way. It was such a horrible and disgraceful death that it was contrary to Roman law to crucify a Roman citizen.

The precise form of the cross upon which Christ hung is not known with certainty. Sometimes the Romans used a single stake, the victim being tied to the stake or impaled upon it.

Crosses composed of two pieces were in the form of a T, X, or crossed-T. Earliest church traditions, in conjunction with references to the cross in the Gospels, favor the crossed-T as the form of the cross upon which Christ was hung.

Execution rapidly followed judgment; when the judge had given his verdict, there was no appeal. The victim was weakened through scourging, after which the procession formed. In front of the victim went a herald carrying the sign with the charge written upon it. Then the victim, carrying the crosspiece (not the entire cross, for the centerpiece was usually a permanent fixture), was driven, scourged, and beaten to the place of execution.

Arriving at the place, he was stripped of his garments and stretched out on the ground; then his hands were nailed to the crosspiece. Next he was lifted upon the erect central stake, and his feet were tied or secured to it with nails. Usually a support for the victim's body prevented its full weight from pulling on his hands, although some crosses were set at an angle to increase the pull of the body on the nails.

According to law the garments of the victim belonged to the executioners. The outer garment could be readily divided among the four soldiers but they gambled for Christ's seamless inner garment, which would be worthless if torn apart.

The typical cross was just high enough for the victim's feet to clear the ground, although unusually high crosses were used in special cases. Before the ordeal the victim was given a stupefying drink of wine; this is the drink which Christ refused. The shrieking, entreating, cursing, and pitiful wailing of the victims at times affected even those hardened through warfare. General shock, exposure, and pain created an intolerable thirst; tetanous convulsions made the victim tear his flesh. The suffering, the unnatural position, and the pain forced the blood to the head so that the victim probably felt as if his head would split open from the pressure.

Death seldom came before thirty-six hours, and life could be prolonged for days by feeding the victim. If his death was required in shorter time, cruel blows of a mallet broke the bones and hastened death.

The Gospels' account of the crucifixion coincides in great detail with historic knowledge of the Roman method.

The Jews detested crucifixion; the Romans abhorred it; thus the preaching of the cross was offensive to Jew and Gentile alike. However, the crucifixion of Jesus became the symbol of the power and wisdom of God to the Christian.

BERNARD RAMM

RESURRECTION. The resurrection of Christ was the climactic event of his redemptive mission on earth. Many times Christ predicted his own resurrection (Matt. 16:4, 21; 17:23; 20:19; Mark 9:31; 10:34; Luke 11:29; 18:33; John 2:19). Following the great confession at Caesarea Philippi, he often discussed his death and without exception also discussed his resurrection. The resurrection occupied a major place in Christ's thinking, it had great importance in his role as God's Suffering Servant Messiah.

The New Testament writers affirm the fact that the physical body of Jesus did not decay in the tomb, but was made alive again, not to resume the old physical functions, but gloriously transformed so that it was no longer limited by time and space. It is doubtful that any other event in the recorded life of Christ is supported by better evidence than his resurrection. Such an event could otherwise not be accepted. Evidence is found in Mark 16:1-19; Matthew 28:1-20; Luke 24:1-53; John 20:1 to 21:25; Acts 1:3-8; I Corinthians 15:3-7.

These passages indicate beyond question that the early Christians believed that Christ was raised from death, and that he appeared to his disciples. While many "theories" have been presented to explain the presence of these stories in the New Testament in such a way as to deny their historical veracity, able and reverent scholars have accepted the record at face value and have held that Christ was raised just as New Testament writers recorded.

On the main points of the resurrection, the records agree: The time of the resurrection was early morning; women came first to the tomb and found it open and empty; the tomb was guarded by angels, who announced the resurrection and sent messages to the disciples; Jesus appeared to his disciples several times (10 or 11 according to one's interpretation of Acts 1:3-8 and I Cor. 15:7, "all the apostles"). Slight differences in the accounts appear in regard to the exact hour of the visit of the women, the names and number of the women, the number of angels, and the exact wording of the message to the disciples.

The points of difference are not contradictory; they are complementary and reflect the particular purpose of each writer. Matthew reports those things which afford a touch with Jewish life; Mark reports those which arouse wonder; Luke reports those which indicate human interest and sympathy; John reports the effect of the resurrection on particular individuals, i.e., Mary Magdalene, Peter, "that disciple whom Jesus loved," Thomas. Thus the Gospel quartet sings in "harmony" but not in "unison"— each presents his own theme, with the combined result of striking beauty.

The appearances of Jesus following the resurrection are instructive. He appeared sometimes to one disciple (Mary, Peter), sometimes to two (Emmaus road appearance), sometimes to the apostolic group, one time to as many as 500, to his half brother James, to Saul of Tarsus, etc. The result was always the same. The person or persons to whom he appeared were convinced of the reality of the resurrection. While the demonstrations left no question as to the reality of the experience, they revealed the mystery of Jesus' body. The body was tangible enough to be touched, seen, heard; it could even partake of food, but it transcended the limitations of time, space, and the material. The fact that this body could never again be subject to death became the central idea in apostolic preaching of the doctrine of man's redemption and resurrection.

BIBLIOGRAPHY: W. T. Conner, *The Resurrection of Jesus* (1926). H. Grierson, *And the Third Day* (1948). S. M. Gwener, *The Glory of the Empty Tomb* (1947). D. A. Hayes, *The Resurrection Fact* (1932). J. McNaugher, *Jesus Christ, the Same Yesterday, Today, and Forever* (1947). W. Milligan, *The Resurrection of Our Lord* (1927). H. P. Sloan, *He Is Risen* (1942). J. H. Snowden, *A Wonderful Morning* (1921).

RAY SUMMERS

ASCENSION. The only Gospel writer who gives an account of the ascension is Luke, the sole Gentile contributor to the New Testament record. Mark refers to the ascension only briefly in 16:19. Although Luke is the only evangelist who actually notes the ascension, the other Gospel writers allude to it. Both Matthew and Mark quote the words of Jesus to the high priest: "Hereafter shall ye see the Son of man sitting on the right hand of power, and coming in the clouds of heaven" (Matt. 26:64; cf. Mark 14:62). The Fourth Gospel (John 6:62) records these words of Jesus: "What and if ye shall see the Son of man ascend up where he was before?" John 14:28; 16:10, 28 provide additional statements which indicate that Jesus was ascending to the Father.

In addition to the Gospel accounts and acknowledgments, the general tenor of the New Testament lends its support to the doctrine of the ascension. Paul, in Philippians 2:9, indicates that God has exalted Jesus, an action in direct contrast to Jesus' emptying himself. In I Timothy 3:16 the apostle also reveals that Jesus was "received up into glory." In Ephesians it is declared that Christ "that descended is the same also that ascended up far above all heavens" (Eph. 4:10). Ephesians 1:20 emphasizes the fact that Jesus is seated at the right hand of God in the heavenlies. Peter, furthermore, adds his testimony by speaking of Christ as one "who is gone into heaven, and is on the right hand of God" (I Peter 3:22). The author of the Epistle to the Hebrews states that Jesus is a high priest who has passed through the heavens and who has been exalted above them (Heb. 4:14; 7:26). In addition to the concept recorded in John's Gospel, the Revelation pictures the ascended Jesus as a powerful and glorified Saviour (Rev. 1:12-18).

Added to the biblical evidence is the patristic evidence as revealed in Henry Barclay Swete's *The Ascended Christ:* "Belief in the Ascension and Session was universal in the early church, both East and West." William Milligan supports Swete's view by stating that his belief "is not that of one or two witnesses who might be credulous or mistaken. It is that of communities, of widespread bodies of men, whose life had been changed by what they had felt compelled to receive as facts. . . ." Harvey Eugene Dana summarizes the patristic evidence when he states that "the Christ common to all Christian experience in the early days of Christianity was a risen and *Ascended* Christ."

The resurrected Christ remained upon earth for a period of 40 days (Acts 1:3), during which time he appeared on various occasions to the disciples. He ascended from Mount Olivet, a sabbath day's journey from Jerusalem (Acts 1:12, Luke 24:50). Christ ascended to heaven, a place with life separate and distinct from this world (Acts 1:9; John 14:1-6; Rev. 4:1 ff.; 21-22). The ascension completed the redemptive purposes begun in the incarnation. In the ascension Christ gained the reward which God had prepared for him; thus his enthronement initiated his exaltation (Phil. 2:8-11). The ascended Christ is active, reigning over his kingdom (Acts 2:30-31; 5:31; Matt. 28:18), crowned with his lordship (Matt. 28:18; Acts 2:33). To intercede eternally as a high priest from his seat at the right hand of God (Acts 7:56) is his aim (Heb. 7:25). No longer is Jesus' ministry local. He is spiritually omnipresent through his Spirit (John 16:7). The crowning fact of the ascension is that in this experience humanity was glorified, for Jesus carried the human nature which he had assumed on earth into heaven (cf. Phil. 3:21).

See also INCARNATION, MESSIAH, and PRE-EXISTENCE.

BIBLIOGRAPHY: W. T. Conner, *Revelation and God* (1949); *The Resurrection of Jesus* (1926). H. E. Dana, "The Ascension of Jesus" (MS). C. C. Dodson, *The Empty Tomb and the Risen Lord* (n.d., 2nd ed.). A. A. Lipscomb, *Studies in the Forty Days* (1884). W. Milligan, *The Ascension and Heavenly Priesthood of our Lord* (1901). H. B. Swete, *The Ascended Christ* (1910).

V. E. GIDEON

JETER, JEREMIAH BELL (b. Bedford County, Va., July 18, 1802; d. Richmond, Va., Feb. 18, 1880). Minister, Southern Baptist leader, first president of Foreign Mission Board. Baptized in Dec., 1821, Jeter began preaching shortly afterward. After spending some time in an itinerant ministry, he served nine years as pastor in northeastern Virginia, during which time he baptized about 1,000 persons. In Jan., 1836, Jeter became pastor of First Baptist Church, Richmond, Va., where he served more than 13 years. The church had 1,717 members at that time, 1,384 Negro and 333 white. Jeter encouraged organization of the African church in 1842, and the congregation occupied the old building where the First Baptist Church had worshiped.

From 1849 to 1852 Jeter was pastor of Second Baptist Church, St. Louis, Mo., after which he returned to Richmond as pastor of Grace Street Baptist Church. He was the first president of the Foreign Mission Board, 1845-49. Because of complicated conditions with Southern Baptist work in Italy, the Foreign Mission Board sent him to supervise their mission in 1872. Eventually, George Boardman Taylor (q.v.) was commissioned as missionary to Italy.

In 1865, Jeter and Alfred Elijah Dickinson (*q.v.*) purchased the *Religious Herald*, for which Jeter usually wrote from two to four columns a week, promoting Baptist faith and fellowship. With the assistance of Richard Fuller, Jeter had published an edition of *The Psalmist*, Boston, in 1843, adding a supplement to make it more acceptable to Baptist churches in the South.

Jeter never received a high degree of academic training, but made a distinctive contribution to the work of Southern Baptists. He attended more than one session of the Triennial Convention, had part in the organization of the Southern Baptist Convention, served as president of the trustees of Southern Baptist Theological Seminary and as trustee of Richmond College.

BIBLIOGRAPHY: W. E. Hatcher, *Life of J. B. Jeter* (1887). J. B. Jeter, *Recollections of a Long Life* (1891). G. B. Taylor, *Virginia Baptist Preachers* (1912).
E. C. ROUTH

JEWELL, WILLIAM (b. Loudon County, Va., Jan. 1, 1789; d. Liberty, Mo., Aug 7, 1852). Physician. After receiving the M.D. degree from Transylvania University in Kentucky, Jewell in 1822 moved to Columbia, Mo., where he established himself in the medical practice. Dr. Jewell gave $1,800 to help secure a location for the University of Missouri, and for several sessions he served as a member of the General Assembly of Missouri. In 1843 Jewell gave $10,000 for the establishment of a Missouri Baptist college. A committee of trustees selected Liberty as the location, and the school was named William Jewell College. Including later gifts, Jewell's contributions to the college totaled about $16,000.

The college was opened in 1849, with classes being held in the Second Baptist Church of Liberty. Because of the urgent need of buildings, Jewell personally supervised the construction of the first building of the college, Jewell Hall, even to the extent of making changes during construction. Jewell Hall stands today, more than 100 years later, as a memorial to Jewell. His death resulted from an illness caused by excessive summer heat, to which he was exposed while supervising the erection of this building.

BIBLIOGRAPHY: W. Cathcart, *Baptist Encyclopedia* (1883). R. S. Douglass, *History of Missouri Baptists* (1934). R. S. Duncan, *History of the Baptists in Missouri* (1882). J. C. Maple, *Missouri Baptist Centennial 1906* (1907). J. C. Maple and R. P. Rider, *Missouri Baptist Biography*, Vol. I (1914). W. P. Yeaman, *A History of Missouri Baptist General Association* (1899).
W. C. LINK, JR.

JEWS, HOME MISSIONS TO. Southern Baptists expressed their interest in Jewish work as early as May 11, 1867, when a resolution was unanimously adopted in the Memphis, Tenn., meeting, stating that it was the duty of Christians "to labor and pray for the conversion of Jews." Again, on May 10, 1873, when the Convention met in Mobile, Ala., the matter was brought before the body by Abraham Jaeger, a Jewish rabbi who had become a Baptist minister, when he was invited to address the Convention on the subject, "The Conversion of Jews to Christianity." After his address a resolution was offered on the floor of the Convention that he be recommended for appointment "through the Board of Domestic Missions as missionary to the Jews in this country." However, a substitute motion was offered, suggesting that the original motion and resolution be referred to a special committee of five: H. Clark, T. P. Miller, John Albert Broadus (*q.v.*), Mark Perrin Lowry (*q.v.*), and W. H. McIntosh.

The special committee reported:

Your committee, to whom was referred the duty of giving expression to the sense of this Convention in reference to the address of Bro. A. Jaeger, and to the narration of his experience in passing from Judaism to Christianity, recommend the adoption of the following resolutions:

Resolved, That we have heard with profound interest and sympathy the narration of the experience of Bro. Jaeger, and his address upon the subject of missions to the Jews.

Resolved, That this Convention recognizes the comprehensiveness of the Great Commission, and the obligation to provide for the preaching of Christ to the Jews as well as to the Gentiles.

Resolved, That should Bro. Jaeger now, or at a future time, be impressed with a sense of duty to preach Christ to his Jewish brethren, that this Convention pledges its sympathy, its prayers, and its active co-operation.

Resolved, That we commend Bro. Jaeger to the fraternal regard of the brethren everywhere, and ask for him such Christian courtesies as may facilitate his labors in the cause of our Divine Master.

In the Convention meeting in Charleston, S. C., on May 10, 1875, another resolution was adopted:

WHEREAS, In the providence of God there seems now to be a special call on Southern Baptists to make effort for the conversion of the Jews; therefore,

Resolved, That the Home Mission Board be instructed to inquire into the expediency of appointing, and if found practicable, to send out a missionary to the Jews, as soon as a suitable man can be found.

On Apr. 7, 1921, Baron DeKalb Gray (*q.v.*) stated that the Home Mission Board had for consideration at various times the question of work among the Jews and recommended the election of Jacob Gartenhaus for such work. There were at that time approximately 400,000 Jewish people in the territory of the South, and Baptist people felt an unusual responsibility toward their enlistment and evangelization. There were those in the Convention who felt that Southern Baptists could not ignore the work without being guilty before God.

By 1924 the number of Jews moving to the South had increased, and it was felt that Southern Baptists were doing very little for them. It was proposed that, as soon as possible, more workers be employed to help reach Jewish people.

Jacob Gartenhaus served from 1922 until the spring of 1949. He was the author of many tracts and books during his lengthy service with the Home Mission Board. Frank Halbeck became fieldworker in the Jewish Department on May 1, 1949. Substantially the same program of work was followed as formerly, placing the responsibility of the evangelizing of the Jewish people at the doors of every local Baptist church with Jewish people in its community.

In Sept., 1953, a precedent was set for the Jewish work by the appointment of three student workers, who were located in cities adjacent to Baptist theological seminaries. William B. Mitchell was the first missionary appointed to full-time service in a local field. He began his work in Houston, Tex., with the Home Mission Board, the Baptist General Convention of Texas, and the local association supporting the effort. Many reports of conversions have come from the efforts of the workers on the field.

Our Jewish Neighbors by Frank Halbeck, a book setting forth the enlarged program of work as well as presenting a study of Judaism as relating to Christianity, was published by the Home Mission Board in 1955.   FRANK HALBECK

JOHNSON, ARCHIBALD (b. Richmond, now Scotland, County, N. C., Aug. 29, 1859; d. Thomasville, N. C., Dec. 26, 1934). Editor. The son of Duncan and Catharine (Livingston) Johnson, he grew up in the Scottish settlement of Riverton. Johnson attended schools at Wagram and Red Springs, N. C. In 1883 he became a merchant in Laurinburg but after seven years returned to his old home to take up farming. He became editor of the *Laurinburg Exchange*, 1892-94, and established the *Red Springs Citizen* early in 1895. Johnson became editor of *Charity and Children*, organ of the Baptist Orphanage, Thomasville, N. C., in Sept., 1895, and for 30 years produced a wide-awake, interesting editorial page on which he discussed matters of moral and religious interest that concerned the country, as well as those that promoted the interests of the needy children. The circulation of the paper rose rapidly, and Johnson's terse, forceful editorials were quoted in papers throughout the South. Johnson was a deacon of the First Baptist Church, Thomasville, and a leader in denominational work in the state. He married Flora C. McNeill, Jan. 28, 1885; and to them were born five children.   I. G. GREER

JOHNSON, JULIA ANNA (TOY) (b. Norfolk, Va., Dec. 30, 1841; d. Clinton, Miss., Jan. 16, 1930). Julia Anna Toy, sister of Crawford Howell Toy of Harvard and Walter Dallam Toy of the University of North Carolina, married John Lipscomb Johnson, July 12, 1860. They were appointed as missionaries to Japan, but the illness of her husband prevented their sailing. While Johnson was head of the English department at the University of Mississippi, she was appointed in 1878 by the Foreign Mission Board to serve in Mississippi as president of the first Central Committee, "whose special work should be interesting Baptist women in the work of giving the gospel to the heathen." She served as president of the Central Committee for 10 years, as editor of the "Woman's Page" in *The Baptist Record*, and as president of the Woman's Missionary Society of Clinton. In addition to being the wife of a college professor, pastor, and editor, she taught a Bible class in her home.

BIBLIOGRAPHY: Mrs. A. J. Aven, "To the Memory of Our First President," *The Baptist Record* (Jan. 30, 1930). J. L. Boyd, *A Popular History of the Baptists in Mississippi* (1930). Miss. W.M.U., *Hearts the Lord Opened* (1954).   C. B. HAMLET III

JOHNSON, LIVINGSTON (b. Spring Hill community, Richmond, now Scotland, County, N. C., Nov. 7, 1857; d. Raleigh, N. C., Feb. 8, 1931). Minister, editor. He was the son of Duncan and Catharine (Livingston) Johnson. After attending Spring Hill Academy, Johnson studied at Wake Forest College during the 1877-78 session. For the next 10 years he worked in his home community as a farmer and as a teacher. Licensed to preach by Spring Hill Church, 1888, he spent the next session (1888-89) at Southern Baptist Theological Seminary. He was called to serve as pastor of the following churches in the Pee Dee Association: Rockingham, Lilesville, Pleasant Grove, Cartledge Creek, Roberdell, and Saron; Lumberton First, 1895; Greensboro First, 1895-1900. Johnson was corresponding secretary of the North Carolina Baptist State Convention, 1900-15. He served as pastor of First Church, Rocky Mount, 1915-17, and was editor of the *Biblical Recorder*, 1917-31. As trustee of Wake Forest College, Meredith College, and Southern Baptist Theological Seminary, a member of the Executive Committee of the Southern Baptist Convention, and a member of the executive committee of the Baptist World Alliance, he proved a wise counselor and leader. Author of *History of the Baptist State Convention of North Carolina* (1908) and *Christian Statesmanship* (1913), he led the way in shaping policies for Baptist affairs within the state.

BIBLIOGRAPHY: *Biblical Recorder* (1931). L. Johnson, "Led By an Unseen Hand" (pamphlet). *News and Observer* (1931). *Who Was Who in America*, Vol. I, 1897-1942 (1942).   E. NORFLEET GARDNER

JOHNSON, WALTER NATHAN (b. Sampson County, N. C., Mar. 24, 1875; d. Raleigh, N. C., June 24, 1952). Minister, denominational leader. Son of Calhoun Cornelius and Laura Ann (Alderman) Johnson, he was graduated in 1899 from Wake Forest College and received from the college in 1919 an honorary D.D. degree. In 1905 he did graduate work at the Southern Baptist Theological Seminary, and in 1911 at the University of Chicago. Following his ordination to the ministry in 1894, he held pastorates in North Carolina in Weldon (1899–1900); First Church, Rocky Mount (1900–02); Johnson's Church at Warsaw (1902–04); Wake Forest (1909–15); Badin (1920–23); and Kings Mountain (1923–25). In Louisiana he served as pastor in Natchitoches (1905–06) and Alexandria (1906–07). He served as secretary of missions in both Louisiana (1907–09) and North Carolina (1915–20). Later he became secretary of the Steward League of Baptist Ministers and editor of *The Next Step in the Churches,* the league's bulletin. His published works include *The Southern Baptist Crisis* (1905), *Stewardship Vitalized* (1926), *Which? Dominate or Permeate* (1929), *Spinal Adjustment in Southern Baptist Life* (1931), and *The Release of Power in Churches Vitalized to Save Our Modern World* (1946). On Aug. 15, 1900, he married Eva Alice Coppedge. To them were born six children.

W. R. CULLOM

JOHNSON, WILLIAM BULLEIN (b. John's Island, S. C., June 13, 1782; d. Greenville, S. C., Oct. 2, 1862). South Carolina Baptist leader and first president of the Southern Baptist Convention. Son of Joseph and Mary (Bullein) Johnson, he was taught at his boyhood home in Georgetown, S. C., by his mother and by private tutors. He came under the influence of William Staughton (1770–1829), John Waldo (1762–1826), Edmund Botsford (c. 1744–1819), Oliver Hart (q.v.) (1723–95), and Richard Furman (q.v.) (1755–1825). Johnson received the A.M. degree from Brown University in 1814. He studied law, expecting to make it his profession, but was converted during a revival at Beaufort, S. C., in 1804, and thereafter devoted his life to Christian service. He was pastor of churches at Edgefield, S. C., and at Euhaw near Beaufort; and founded churches at Greenville, S. C., and Columbia, where he was chaplain of South Carolina College. At Anderson, S. C., as chancellor of Johnson Female University (1853–58), he pioneered in higher education for women. He also had charge of schools at Savannah, Greenville, and Edgefield.

Johnson was in Savannah when Luther Rice (1783–1836) enlisted his interest in foreign missions, and Rice accepted Johnson's proposal to hold the first meeting of American Baptists in Philadelphia to form a general convention. Johnson, the only man who attended initial meetings of both the General Baptist Missionary Convention (1814) and the Southern Baptist Convention (1845), was also the only man who served as president of each; he had a large part in the framing of constitutions for the two bodies. Johnson was the last southern president of the general convention (1841–44), and justified the confidence placed in him by his able leadership in reconciling opposing forces and thus delaying disruption of the convention. When separation became inevitable in 1845, Baptists of the South and Southwest turned to Johnson for counsel, and as first president of the Southern Baptist Convention (1845–51), he led in shaping its far-reaching program.

From 1817 until his death, Johnson remained in South Carolina and was one of nine men who formed the South Carolina State Baptist Convention in 1821. Succeeding Richard Furman as president of the convention and serving for 27 years (1825–52), Johnson realized one of Furman's fondest dreams in helping found the school which became Furman University, out of which grew Southern Baptist Theological Seminary.

Johnson, author of *The Gospel Developed,* contributed to religious and secular publications. He married Henrietta Hornby in 1803, and among their eight children who reached maturity, a son, Francis C. Johnson, became a Southern Baptist missionary to China in 1846.

BIBLIOGRAPHY: W. W. Barnes, *The Southern Baptist Convention* (1954). R. N. Daniel, *Furman University* (1951). W. B. Johnson, "Reminiscences," (mss., University Caroliniana Library, Columbia, S. C.). Mrs. J. L. Mims, "History of the Edgefield Baptist Church," *The Edgefield Advertiser* (1923). H. Woodson, *Giant in the Land* (1950).

HORTENSE WOODSON

JOLLY, ROBERT GARLAND (b. Cave City, Ky., Mar. 27, 1885; d. Houston, Tex., May 14, 1952). Hospital administrator; Texas Baptist leader. Believed to have been the only man ever president of both the Protestant Hospital Association of America and the American Hospital Association, Jolly was administrator of Memorial Hospital in Houston 27 years, and helped raise $12,000 for the hospital's first X-ray department by singing in a revival meeting. Jolly's wife, the former Mrs. J. P. Burnett, was for 38 years head of the Memorial school of nursing, the first school of its kind in the United States to require a course of Bible study in its curriculum.

Jolly first worked three years as an auditor, then eight years as an evangelistic singer, and five years as an assistant pastor in Dallas and Houston churches. He was president of the Palacios Baptist Encampment 16 years; song leader for the South Main Baptist Church, Houston, 19 years; state president of the B.Y.P.U. Convention of Texas three years; president of the Texas Baptist Sunday School Convention three years; and a member, song leader, and director of several civic and community organizations, including the Houston Rotary Club, Chamber of Commerce, Symphony Society, and Better Business Bureau.

Jolly became a member of the American Hospital Association in 1923 and, before his death in 1952, was the organization's vice-president, president, and House of Delegates member. In 1929 he called a meeting of Texas hospital administrators to organize the Texas Hospital Association and was a trustee in 1932. After serving as president of the Protestant Hospital Association of America in 1931 and 1932, he became a charter fellow in the organization of the American College of Hospital Administra-

tors in 1933 and was a regent in 1936 and 1937. The South Texas Hospital Council elected Jolly its president in 1938.
JACK D. HARWELL

JONES, CARTER HELM (b. Oakley, Nelson County, Va., Nov. 30, 1861; d. Lynchburg, Va., May 6, 1946). Baptist minister. Son of John William and Judith Page (Helm) Jones, he was descended from distinguished Colonial and Revolutionary Virginia families. His father was a Baptist minister. Jones graduated from Richmond College in 1882, Southern Baptist Theological Seminary in 1885, and took a special course at the University of Virginia during the next session. Ordained by the First Baptist Church, Richmond, in 1884, Jones married Anne McCown of Gordonsville, Va., in 1886. After four years in his first pastorate at First Baptist Church, Elizabeth, N. J., Jones, at 29, became pastor of the First Baptist Church, Knoxville, Tenn. While there he preached the annual sermon to the Southern Baptist Convention, the youngest man ever so honored up to that time. Jones accepted the pastorate of McFerran Memorial Church, Louisville, Ky., in 1894, and of the Broadway Church, Louisville, in 1897. Other pastorates were at First Baptist churches in Lynchburg, Va.; Oklahoma City, Okla.; Seattle, Wash.; Philadelphia, Pa.; and Murfreesboro, Tenn.; Second Church, Atlanta, Ga.; St. Charles Avenue Church, New Orleans, La.; and Williamsburg Baptist Church, Williamsburg, Va. On Jan. 1, 1942, Jones retired to Lynchburg, Va., where he resided until his death. Jones' only book, *Prophetic Patriotism*, was published in 1941.
J. L. ROSSER

JONES, CHARLES ALFRED (b. London, England, Apr. 14, 1869; d. Columbia, S. C., June 4, 1942). Minister, South Carolina Baptist leader. Son of John Wells and Mary Ann (Cracknell) Jones, he was brought to the United States at an early age, living first in Batesburg and later in Columbia, S. C. Jones attended schools in Batesburg and received the B.A. degree from Furman University in 1895 and the Th.M. degree from Southern Baptist Theological Seminary in 1904. On Dec. 31, 1896, he married Jessie Berry of Pickens County, S. C., and they had three sons, Charles Wells (d. in infancy), Alfred Broadus, and Edwin Holmes. Ordained to the ministry in 1891, Jones served as pastor in Mullens, S. C.; Belleville, Ill.; and Bennettsville, S. C. He was elected secretary of the Baptist Education Board of South Carolina in 1914, and served until 1925. The state convention made him general secretary-treasurer in 1925 and retained him in that position until his death, at which time he was also serving as vice-president of the Southern Baptist Convention. Under his inspiration and leadership, the Minister's Retirement Plan was originated and adopted by all states of the Southern Baptist Convention.

BIBLIOGRAPHY: R. N. Daniel, *Furman University, A History* (1951). Fairfield Baptist Association, *Minutes* (1942). South Carolina Baptist State Convention, *Minutes* (1942). *Who's Who in America*, Vol. 15, 1928–29. *Who Was Who in America*, Vol. 2.
EDWIN HOLMES JONES

JONES, JOHN BUTTRICK (b. Valley Town, N. C., Dec. 24, 1824; d. Denver, Colo., June 13, 1876). Baptist preacher, scholar, translator, and missionary to Cherokee Indians. Son of Evan Jones, co-laborer of Jesse Bushyhead (q.v.) in establishing the first Cherokee Baptist church and the first newspaper in Indian Territory, the younger Jones graduated from Rochester University in 1855, was ordained to the ministry July 14, 1855, and joined his father in the mission work near the present Westville, Okla. He served as chaplain of Third Regiment, Indian Home Guards, a Cherokee regiment of the Union army in the Civil War, and as a Cherokee delegate signed the Treaty of Washington, July 9, 1866. A leader in the political, educational, and religious life of the Cherokees, he secured permission from the Cherokee Council to remove the Baptist Mission from Westville to Tahlequah, the Cherokee capital, in 1866 and the next year completed the transfer. Failing health sent him west, where he died in Denver, Colo. He is buried at Tahlequah, Okla.
J. M. GASKIN

JONES, JOHN WILLIAM (b. Louisa Courthouse, Va., Sept. 25, 1836; d. Columbus, Ga., Mar. 17, 1909). Chaplain, minister, writer. Son of Francis William and Ann Pendleton (Ashby) Jones, he was converted in 1855, and entered the University of Virginia that fall. In 1859 Jones matriculated as the first student of the first session of Southern Baptist Theological Seminary, Greenville, S. C. Ordained at Charlottesville, Va., in 1860 and appointed to missionary work in China less than a month later, Jones never sailed because of the impending civil strife. He enlisted in the Confederate Army as a private and soon became chaplain, then army evangelist, and zealously devoted himself to the religious welfare of the soldiers. At the close of the war, he became pastor of Goshen Bridge and Lexington Baptist churches, Virginia. Agent of Southern Seminary in 1871 and general superintendent of the Sunday School and Bible Board of the Baptist General Association of Virginia in 1874, Jones accepted a pastorate at Ashland, Va., in 1875, and at the same time was secretary of the Southern Historical Society. Later he became assistant secretary of the Southern Baptist Home Mission Board. For two years Jones was chaplain of the University of Virginia, Miller School, Albemarle County; chaplain-general of the United Confederate Veterans; and finally Superintendent of the Confederate Memorial Association. Published works include *Personal Reminiscences, Anecdotes, and Letters of R. E. Lee; Army of Northern Virginia, Memorial Volume; Jefferson Davis, Memorial Volume; School History of the United States; Life and Letters of R. E. Lee;* and *The Soldier and the Man.* On Dec. 20,

1860, Jones married Judith Page Helm, by whom he had five sons, four of them ministers, one of whom was Carter Helm Jones (*q.v.*).

J. L. ROSSER

JONES, SALLIE BAILEY (b. Greenville County, Va., Jan. 29, 1868; d. Raleigh, N. C., Nov. 25, 1943). Denominational leader. Daughter of C. T. Bailey, she was educated in Peace Institute, Raleigh, and Richmond Female Institute, Richmond, Va. She married Wesley Norwood Jones when she was 19. She joined the First Baptist Church of Raleigh when only a child and remained a member all her life. At the age of 17 she participated in the organization of the North Carolina Woman's Missionary Union; Fannie E. S. Heck was elected president and Sallie Bailey was elected secretary. From 1900 to 1916, Mrs. Jones was treasurer for her state W.M.U., and president from 1916 to 1936. She was also vice-president of the Convention-wide Woman's Missionary Union from 1916 to 1938.

S. L. MORGAN

JONESBORO COLLEGE. A school located at Jonesboro, Ark., managed by the Southern Baptist Home Mission Board, 1924–30, and then by Baptist associations in northeastern Arkansas until 1935. Mt. Zion Baptist Association began in 1920 a movement for the establishment of the school. Money was collected from the churches, and help came from the Home Mission Board. An administration building was begun at once on the campus of 90 acres. The old Woodland College dormitory was used.

Jonesboro Junior College formally opened Sept. 9, 1924, with J. N. Mallory president and 224 students enrolled. The college departments included academy, college, business, theology, music, expression, and extension. Lack of finances handicapped the building program. The Home Mission Board severed its connection with the college May 26, 1930, returning the property debt free to the Baptists of the region. A board representing these Baptists reopened Jonesboro Baptist College Sept. 8, 1930. Mallory continued as president until 1933. H. E. Watters, president in 1935, attempted to rebuild the college, but lack of funds forced it to close that year. Jonesboro College served 1,643 students. Jonesboro Special School District bought the property Nov. 22, 1939.

DOLLIE HIETT

JORDAN, MISSION IN. Except for brief residence in Taibe of a missionary family in 1948, Southern Baptist mission work in Jordan began in 1950 in Ajloun. Charles MacLean, a doctor whose work had been supported by British contributions, offered his hospital to Southern Baptists. The gift was accepted in Oct., 1950. A missionary moved to Ajloun in Feb., 1951, and the property was transferred June 1, 1952.

Under the missionary's supervision construction was completed in 1954 on three new buildings. By 1956 the 40-bed capacity had been increased to 50; the 5 buildings to 10. The mission includes two schools, one in Ajloun, the other in Debbin. A missionary directs the schools with national teachers assisting.

There was no Baptist church in Ajloun when Baptists began operating the hospital, but a congregation met regularly. A church was organized in Sept., 1953, with 22 members. Jerius Delleh, accountant for the hospital, was called as pastor.

GENEVIEVE GREER

JORDAN PRESS, TOKYO. See JAPAN, MISSION IN.

JOSEPH E. BROWN INSTITUTE. Began under this name in 1883 because of a gift of $5,000 from Joseph E. Brown, governor of Georgia, formerly operated under the name Crawford High School, located at Dalton, Ga. The school ceased to exist before 1890.

ARTHUR JACKSON

JOURNALISM, CHRISTIAN. Journalism is defined as "the occupation of writing for, editing, and conducting newspapers and other periodicals." Religious journalism, however, far antedates the appearance of daily and weekly papers. It goes back to the New Testament, particularly to the letters to the churches by the apostle Paul written to groups of individuals for circulation. This is especially true with the letter to the Ephesians. In the early years of Christianity, men depended upon letters and more formal types of writing, many times wound on scrolls to perpetuate the cause in which they believed. Kenneth Scott Latourette refers to what he calls the "Wedding of Christianity and Learning" in providing "the impulse which helped both perpetuate local tongues and create a literature in them." In modern times the use of the printed page for Christian and missionary purposes received its greatest forward thrust when Gutenberg printed his famous Protestant Bible in Germany between the years 1450 and 1456. The modern missionary movement was born with an emphasis on journalism. "If the Lord blesses," said the newly appointed missionary, William Carey (*q.v.*), to printer William Ward, in 1793, "we shall want a person of your business to enable us to print the scriptures." Baptists in the South can attribute part of their growth to Christian journalism. Through tracts and state papers people found out what their neighbors were doing and were inspired by their work. The westward sweep of the Baptist cause into Texas and Oklahoma and the Far West can be credited to the missionary letters that were written back by missionaries to state papers published in the East. Altogether in Southern Baptist life there have been more than 300 Baptist newspapers of a regional or provincial nature. Of these, nearly 30 exist today. Many were short-lived and were dropped when their purposes had been realized. Christian journalism lays claim to three areas: (1) direct writing or editing in the employment of a religious paper or publishing house; (2) religious or church reporting as either reporter or editor in the religion department of a secular magazine; (3) free-lance writing for newspapers and magazines offering material of the religious nature. The recognized requisites for entering these fields in Christian journalism are: (a) a well-rounded high school or college education, majoring either in English composition or writing for publication, depending upon the type of career expected; (b) a period of service in the seminary, becoming familiar with Baptist thought concepts and Baptist ideas; (c) considerable experience in the organizational life of a local church; (D) a life dedication to the cause of Christ as expressed in our Baptist point of view; (e) some experience on secular newspapers and magazines. The categories of religious journalism are editors, staff writers, copyreaders, artists, layout experts, press representatives, and public relations representatives. ALBERT MCCLELLAN

JOURNEYCAKE, CHARLES (Ne-She-Pa-Na-Cumin; b. Upper Sandusky, Ohio, Dec. 16, 1817; d. Alluwe, Indian Territory, Jan. 3, 1894). Last chief of the Delaware Indians, serving from 1861 until his death. He was the second Delaware converted to Christianity after the inhuman massacre of all but two Christian Delawares in 1782, at Gnadenhutten, Ohio, when American Rangers on pretense of friendship borrowed all the tools and weapons of the Christian Delawares and then, while the Indians were praying in their chapel, killed 99 of them. On Aug. 11, 1833, Journeycake was baptized west of the Mississippi River, the first Protestant baptized in what is now the state of Kansas.

Without formal education, but through the help of his mother and John Gill Pratt, Indian agent and missionary, he developed into an outstanding Indian statesman and Christian leader. He made 24 trips to Washington, D. C., in the interest of his tribe, and organized and built the first Delaware Baptist church in Indian Territory, at Alluwe, Nov. 8, 1871. He traveled widely, preaching the gospel to the Delawares and other Indian tribes.

BIBLIOGRAPHY: H. M. Roark, *C. J.: Indian Statesman and Christian Leader* (1948). HARRY M. ROARK

JOYNER, JAMES YADKIN (b. Davidson County, N. C., Aug. 7, 1862; d. La Grange, N. C., Jan. 24, 1954). Educator. Son of John and Sallie A. (Wooten) Joyner, he was orphaned at the age of one and a half years and lived with his maternal grandfather, and later an uncle. Joyner prepared for college at La Grange Academy. After graduating from the University of North Carolina in 1881, he served as principal of La Grange Academy for two years and as Lenoir County superintendent of schools. Joyner read law, was admitted to the bar, and practiced law in Goldsboro, 1886–89; served as superintendent of Goldsboro schools, 1889–93; taught in Greensboro (State Normal and Industrial School) four years; and was state superintendent of public instruction, 1902–19. He was elected president, National Education Association, 1910. Joyner retired in 1919 to his farm at La Grange but returned to Raleigh in 1922 to become active in co-operative marketing of tobacco and cotton. For 21 years Joyner emphasized progressive farming. He was a deacon in his local church and for many years was a trustee of Meredith College. He married Effie E. Rouse, of Lenoir County, Dec. 18, 1897, and to them were born two sons.

BIBLIOGRAPHY: S. A. Ashe, *Biographical History of North Carolina* (n.d.). R. D. W. Connor, *North Carolina, Rebuilding an Ancient Commonwealth* (1929). Lefler and Newsome, *North Carolina, the History of a Southern State* (n.d.).

C. SYLVESTER GREEN

JUDAISM. Judaism in its broader meaning is the religion, history, language, literature, culture, and civilization of the Jews from the time of Abraham until the present day. In a more restricted sense, Judaism connotes the religion of the Jews from post-Exilic days until the present with the emphasis upon the Torah (Law). The word "Judaism" occurs first in the apocryphal work II Maccabees, and there it means the religion of the Jews. The three basic doctrines of Judaism are (1) monotheistic belief in the one and only God, (2) the covenant election of Israel to be the bearer of this belief, and (3) belief in the Torah, the teaching which claimed obedience for the individual and corporate life of the Jews in order that they may be brought into subjection to the righteous and holy will of God. There are three groups within the Jewish faith: the orthodox, who adhere strictly to the traditional ceremonial regulations found in the Old Testament, the Talmud, and the teachings of the later rabbis; the conservative, who uphold the authority of the Jewish ritual law with a large number of important modifications; and the reform, who are less concerned about ceremonial and ritual practices and concentrate upon social, moral, and ethical teachings which the prophets advocated. Reform and many conservative Jews expect the messianic age to come about through the gradual enlightenment of men, while the orthodox Jews still look for a Messiah who will restore the national status of the Jews.

BIBLIOGRAPHY: S. W. Baron and J. L. Blau, *Judaism* (1954). I. Epstein, *Judaism* (1945).

TAYLOR C. SMITH

JUDGMENT. The judgment of God is first a process in history, the testing and dividing of men according to their character and relation to Christ. It is God's affirmation of righteousness and condemnation of sin in the events of history.

The New Testament foresees, also, a final judgment at the end of history in which God will judge the race, as well as the individuals of the race. God will be the Judge, because only he has the right and the power to decide human destiny. Christ, also, will be Judge with God the Father. This fact means not only that Christ will preside at the judgment, but also that God's judgment will be one of holy love, in which Christ is the standard by which character is tested and the Saviour through whom reconciliation with God is effected.

Christ will come to judge the living and the dead, and all men will stand before his judgment seat. He will demonstrate his eternal victory in the salvation of those who have faith in him and in the destruction of those who have persisted in rebellion against him. J. E. TULL

JUDSON, ADONIRAM (b. Malden, Mass., Aug. 9, 1788; d. at sea, Apr. 12, 1850). The first Baptist foreign missionary from the United States. Son of a Congregational minister and a graduate of Rhode Island College (Brown University), Judson entered Andover Seminary in 1808. His thoughts soon turned to missions, and with other Andover students, he petitioned the General Association of Massachusetts for advice as to how they might realize the desire to take the gospel to "the heathen." In 1810 this Congregational group responded by organizing the American Board of Commissioners for Foreign Missions, the first agency to send foreign missionaries from the United States.

On Feb. 5, 1812, Judson married Ann Hasseltine, and two weeks later the couple sailed for India as missionaries of the Congregational board. On the long sea voyage Judson studied the New Testament mode of baptism. Shortly after landing in India, he became convinced of the Baptist position and in turn convinced his wife. The two were baptized in Calcutta on Sept. 6, 1812, by William Ward, an English Baptist missionary. Luther Rice (*q.v.*), another American missionary who had sailed on a different ship, had a similar experience and was baptized on Nov. 1, 1812. Resigning from the Congregational mission, the Judsons wrote letters to Baptists in America, offering themselves as their missionary representatives, should Baptists see fit to organize for their support.

As a result of this challenge and in response to the vigorous efforts of Luther Rice, who returned to the United States to advocate the world missionary cause, the General Convention of the Baptist Denomination in the United States for Foreign Missions was formed in 1814. This organization, popularly known as "the Triennial Convention," served as the agency for the support of foreign missionaries of American Baptists, both of the North and of the South, until the organization of the Southern Baptist Convention in 1845.

Forced out of India by the British East India Company, the Judsons settled in Burma in 1813. Judson, with "marked linguistic and scholarly gifts," early began translating the Bible into Burmese, completing the task in 1834. He also wrote several hymns, the most familiar of which is "Come, Holy Spirit, Dove Divine." After many trials the Baptist cause was firmly established in Burma. For many years this remained the major mission field of American (Northern) Baptists. Ann (Hasseltine) Judson died in 1826, and in 1834 Judson married Sarah Boardman, widow of missionary George Dana Boardman. Shortly after her death in 1845, Judson returned to America for his only furlough. Receiving a hero's welcome, he stimulated interest in foreign missions wherever he went. In 1846 he married Emily Chubbuck, a well-known writer, and later that year they sailed for Burma. Judson's latter years were spent largely in work on a Burman-English dictionary. Chronic illness became more severe, and in 1850 his death occurred on an ocean voyage which had been prescribed as his only hope for improvement. He was buried at sea in the Bay of Bengal, Apr. 12, 1850.

Judson's achievements are summarized by one of his biographers as follows: "He was leader in the movement that made the dream of American foreign missions a reality; he was chief in the little group of stalwarts who first set forth as missionaries from America to the East; he inspired a great fellowship of churches to organize for the spreading of the gospel to earth's remotest bound." CAL GUY

JUDSON, ANN HASSELTINE (b. Bradford, Mass., Dec. 22, 1789; d. Amherst, Burma, Oct. 24, 1826). American missionary to India; wife of Adoniram Judson (*q.v.*). Ann ("Nancy") became a Christian when she was 16. In June, 1810, she attended a missionary meeting at the Bradford Congregational Church when four young students from Andover Theological Seminary petitioned to be sent as foreign missionaries. One of these young men was Adoniram Judson, who was invited to dine in the Hasseltine home. On Feb. 5, 1812, Judson and Ann Hasseltine were married, and they sailed for India Feb. 19. During the voyage they studied the question of baptism and were convinced that the Baptist position was scriptural. Arriving at Calcutta, they were baptized by one of the associates of William Carey (*q.v.*). Being ordered by the East India Company to leave India, they were permitted to go to the Isle of France, thence to Madras. When forced to leave Madras, they boarded the only ship in harbor ready to sail, which was bound for Rangoon, Burma; they arrived at that port July 13, 1813. They were in Burma six years before the first convert was baptized. In the bitter conflict between the British and Burmese armies, Judson was imprisoned many months and would have died had not Mrs. Judson, despite her own illness, managed to get food to him. After his release and their removal to Amherst, Mrs. Judson was stricken while her husband was absent on a mission to Ava, and she died Oct. 24, 1826.

BIBLIOGRAPHY: E. D. Hubbard, *Ann of Ava* (1913). J. D. Knowles, *Memoirs of Mrs. Judson* (1831).

E. C. ROUTH

JUDSON, CHARLES HALLETTE (b. Monroe, Conn., Apr. 20, 1820; d. Greenville, S. C., Jan. 12, 1907). College professor, educator. Educated at Hamilton Literary and Theological Institute (now Colgate University), Hamilton, N. Y., and the University of Virginia, Judson married Emily F. Bosher of Richmond, Va., in 1847. From 1851 on, he spent most of his life serving Furman University; he was the first member of its faculty, and he contributed to its support about $50,000, which he had accumulated by frugality and financial sagacity. He was "one of the ablest men ever to serve the University." At Furman, Judson was professor and professor emeritus of mathematics, 1851–1907, treasurer, 1855–94, member of the executive committee of the board of trustees, 1857–97; and acting president of the university, 1902–03. He was also a trustee of Southern Baptist Theological Seminary, 1880–1907; treasurer, 1860–97, and clerk, 1853–70, of the Baptist state convention; and deacon of the Greenville Baptist Church (now First Baptist), 1854–1907.

BIBLIOGRAPHY: *The Baptist Courier* (Apr. 22, 1897, and Jan. 17, 1907). R. N. Daniel, *Furman University, a History* (1951). Furman University, *Catalogue* (1852–1907). J. C. Garlington, *Men of the Time* (1902). J. C. Hemphill, ed., *Men of Mark in South Carolina* (1908). State Convention of the Baptist Denomination in South Carolina, *Minutes* (1855–1907).

ROBERT C. TUCKER

JUDSON BAPTIST. A short-lived newspaper of Tupelo, Miss., started in 1868. Known editors were John S. Carothers and L. A. Stovall.

A. L. GOODRICH

JUDSON BAPTIST INSTITUTE. Established in 1835 by the Mississippi Baptist Education Society and chartered in 1836 with L. B. Holloway president. In 1840 the school merged with Middleton Literary and Theological Institute, a four-year college, and averaged about 60 students in enrolment; but it collapsed in 1845.

J. L. BOYD

JUDSON COLLEGE. Plans for the founding of Judson Female Institute, Marion, Ala., were made in the fall of 1838, and the school was opened formally Jan. 7, 1839. The college was named for Ann Hasseltine Judson (*q.v.*), wife of Adoniram Judson (*q.v.*), "whose heroic energy and overwhelming sufferings, on an errand of mercy to the perishing heathen, have embalmed her memory in the hearts of millions."

While traveling through the South, looking for a place to establish a school, Milo P. Jewett of Vermont met Edwin D. King (1792–1862) in Tuscaloosa, Ala. King, a member of the board of trustees of the University of Alabama, invited Jewett to Marion, and together they discussed establishment of a school with Mrs. Julia Barron, a wealthy widow. As a result, plans were made for opening a school for young women under Baptist influence with Jewett as president. King, who became one of the wealthiest men in Alabama, was the chief founder of Judson College and president of its board of trustees from its founding until his death in 1862. "Devoted to the causes of religion and education, he was ever the steadfast friend of the Judson; and it is chiefly due to him that the school was firmly and successfully founded." Mrs. Barron, also credited as being one of the founders, provided the large wooden residence in which the school opened and paid rent on it for the first year and a half. She also took Jewett and his wife into her home as guests for six months and the two assistant teachers for over a year.

A year after the college was chartered on Jan. 8, 1841, the owners offered it to the Alabama Baptist State Convention, and at the next meeting of the convention, in 1843, the transfer was completed. The property was valued at between $25,000 and $30,000. One of the trustees, who was also an architect, drew plans for and supervised construction of the first permanent building, erected in 1839, for which Baptists of Marion raised $22,000.

Jewett, the first president, resigned in 1855 because the "cares and responsibilities connected with the management of so large an institution" had become "too heavy a burden for him. The school this year numbered 239." The college had opened in 1839 with nine students, three of whom were boys. At the end of the first five months enrolment numbered 47; at the end of the first ten-month term, 94. Enrolment increased steadily in succeeding years. A year or two after the founding of Judson, the Ann Hasseltine Missionary Society, named for Mrs. Judson, was founded. This society is credited with being the first of the present Ann Hasseltine auxiliaries in Baptist colleges.

Samuel Sterling Sherman (1815–1915), the school's second president, had served as president of Howard College and had resigned to purchase his own school in Georgia. He was called back to Marion in 1855 to succeed Jewett and served until 1859. Following Sherman, Noah K. Davis (1830–1910) was president from 1859 to 1865, when the school faced many problems incident to the war, but remained open the entire time. Of the school's contribution during this period, Davis said:

> I think it not too much to claim that the Judson has never been more useful than during this part of its noble career. For while its high standard of education was maintained . . . it served also as a . . . house of refuge for many hundreds of daughters and sisters whose homes were desolate while their fathers and brothers engaged in the stern business of battling for liberty and right.

After the Society of the Alumnae of Judson Female Institute was organized in 1868, the alumnae began sending students to Judson and began raising funds for a music hall, completed in 1885. "The Judson can be congratulated on the financial showing of this period: $12,000 of debt has been paid, $15,000 spent in buildings and repairs, $8,000 in pianos, and $3,000 in furniture."

Just as the college became free of debt, President Samuel W. Averett (1887-96) faced a still larger problem when the college building was completely destroyed by fire, Nov. 24, 1888. The school rented the King House (hotel) and used it for school purposes the rest of the session. Plans were immediately started for erection of another building, which was ready for the fall session of 1889. Constructed at a cost of $65,000, it raised the college debt to $34,500.

In the fall of 1889, when the state convention met in Selma, the Judson trustees made their first appeal for help. The second day the convention came to Marion and met in the Judson chapel. It raised $10,000 for furnishings and authorized a loan of $25,000 for the balance of indebtedness.

During the administration of Robert G. Patrick (1897-1913), the debt resulting from the fire was completely paid. The purchase of land for the present library in 1900, construction of an annex to the main building in 1901 and of the Alumnae Auditorium in 1902-04, purchase of McAllister Cottage (for teachers) in 1904, construction of Carnegie Library in 1908 and of the president's home in 1910, and acquisition of the John Trotwood Moore property all took place during Patrick's presidency. Although the school had given certificates of graduation, it was not authorized to grant degrees until 1903; its name was changed to Judson College, April 28, 1904.

During the administration of Paul V. Bomar (1913-23), efforts were continued to raise funds for endowment. The General Education Board of New York agreed to give $100,000 if Judson raised $200,000, part of which came through the 75 Million Campaign. The college secured the endowment necessary for admission to the Southern Association of Colleges in 1925.

President E. V. Baldy (1923-30) led in modernizing the main building and adding the Woman's Missionary Union dormitory, a gift from the Alabama union in 1925. His successor, L. G. Cleverdon (1931-41), faced the problems of mounting debts in depression years when support from the convention was directed toward debt retirement. Indebtedness was refunded in 1942 during the administration of Leroy Priest (1941-43) through debenture bonds of $250,000 with college income pledged for their retirement. In 1943 a statewide move for the payment of indebtedness on all Baptist institutions was inaugurated, and as a result the last of the Judson College bonds were burned during the commencement ceremony in May, 1945. Since that date the college has received regular support from the convention through a percentage of the Cooperative Program. In a special session, Apr. 27, 1947, the state convention voted to coordinate Judson and Howard colleges in Birmingham. However, there was such strong opposition to this move that the convention rescinded the action at its regular session the following November.

When Jewett Hall was destroyed by fire caused by lightning on July 15, 1947, friends rallied to the support of the college. With temporary buildings erected, the fall session opened on time, and plans were made for the erection of a modern, fireproof building to house offices, classrooms, parlors, and dormitory space, which was ready for use by 1951. Two years later, the addition of a wing housing the dining hall and Erskine Ramsay Memorial Chapel completed this unit at a cost of approximately $750,000. The largest single gift ever made to the college was received from Ramsay, Birmingham philanthropist, who contributed $100,000 toward the erection of Jewett Hall and in whose memory the chapel was named.

The present purpose of the college is essentially the same as it was in 1838, with its educational program remaining in harmony with modern educational trends. "Fundamentally a liberal and fine arts college, Judson aims to prepare young women for intelligent, cultured, and competent living by providing, under positive Christian influences, an integrated educational program." During its 118 years of history, approximately 12,000 young women have attended the college and 2,540 have graduated. The college has assets of over $2,225,000, including an endowment of $643,260.25 and a plant valued at $1,438,845.38.

BIBLIOGRAPHY: L. Manly, *History of Judson College* (1913). *Memorial of Milo Parker Jewett, LL.D.* (1882). T. M. Owen, *History of Alabama and Dictionary of Alabama Biography* (1921). S. S. Sherman, *Autobiography 1815-1910* (1910). S. A. Townes, *The History of Marion, Sketches of Life, etc., in Perry County, Alabama* (1844). MARY McMILLAN

JUDSON COLLEGE. College of the Western Baptist Convention of North Carolina, located at Hendersonville, N. C. About 1857 N. Bowen planned a girls' school at Hendersonville and began construction of a large stone building. The Civil War forced suspension of the construction, and not until 1879 was the building completed.

W. A. G. Brown, first president of Mars Hill College, was also the first president of Judson College. The girls' school idea was abandoned, and the college opened as a coeducational school —the first such college in the state.

In 1889 the college stock was donated to the Western Baptist Convention, but the school was never able to pay its debts. When, in 1898, the Western convention merged with the state convention, the college was sold to the town of Hendersonville and used for a public graded school. D. L. SMILEY

JUDSON FUND. Henry Alford Porter introduced a resolution at the 1911 session of the Southern Baptist Convention asking for a suitable observance of the 100th anniversary of the sailing of Adoniram Judson, first American foreign missionary. The Convention voted in 1912 to launch the Judson Centennial Movement, chief feature of which would be to raise a Judson Fund of $1,250,000 to be used by the Foreign Mission Board for educational missions. Advocates of the fund pointed out that on the foreign field "evangelism had outrun teaching, numbers had outstripped equipment." Thomas Bronson Ray (*q.v.*), educational secretary of the board, was named campaign head, assisted by a committee of one from each state. Fifteen field representatives were employed. Subscriptions were to be secured for a period of not over three years, ending not later than the 1915 Convention. Two years later at the 1914 Convention, the committee reported cash and pledges of $602,874.91. By 1915, $959,000 was reported in cash and pledges. World War I crippled efforts to raise the total goal. The last report on the fund was at the 1917 Convention, which showed actual cash receipts of $483,399.05.

ROBERT J. HASTINGS

JUMPER, JOHN (b. Florida, *c.* 1810; d. near Sasakwa, Okla., *c.* 1894). Seminole chief and Baptist preacher. He was the son of Chief Jumper who was associated with Osceola in the Seminole wars. Married early in life, he was the father of six boys and two girls. He migrated from Florida to Indian Territory in 1840. He was a man of physical, moral, and intellectual strength. At first a Presbyterian, he later became a Baptist through the influence of Joseph Samuel Murrow (*q.v.*). An intense hatred for all white men vanished after his conversion experience. He served as a lieutenant-colonel over a regiment of Seminoles in the Civil War. After the war he was ordained with James Factor (*q.v.*) to the gospel ministry in 1865. He was pastor of the Ash Creek Church near Sasakwa, Okla., part or all of the time 1860–94. He is buried in an unmarked grave about three miles southwest of Sasakwa.

JESS KIRKLEY

JUSTICE, AMOS ISAAC (b. Henderson County, N. C., Dec. 8, 1851; d. Dec. 21, 1945). Minister. Justice was educated in rural schools, and attended Judson and Weaver colleges. Converted at an early age, he began preaching at 16. Justice served as minister in Buncombe, Madison, and Polk counties. A strong advocate of Christian education, he was one of the founders of Fruitland Institute in a day when there were no high schools in adjacent counties. He became a leader in Carolina Association and the early Western North Carolina Baptist Association and was a leading figure in effecting a union of the Western convention with the rest of the state to form the North Carolina Baptist State Convention in 1898. Justice married Minerva Fisher, and they had six children.

BIBLIOGRAPHY: G. W. Paschal, *History of North Carolina Baptists*, Vol. II (1930).

C. SYLVESTER GREEN

JUSTICE OF GOD. Term referring to God's administration of law designed to maintain harmony in his universe. Being perfect in every respect, God demands perfection in all his creatures. Nonconformity to that perfection on the part of man results in disharmony, which in turn brings forth retribution. Not a matter of arbitrary will, retribution is the inevitable consequence of failure to conform to the holy will and purpose of the Creator. By his nature God is infinitely pure and cannot change. Therefore, in order for harmony to exist, man must be like God. Justice is the recognition and enforcement of this necessity.

See also GOD.

BIBLIOGRAPHY: W. N. Clarke, *An Outline of Christian Theology* (1908). A. H. Strong, *Systematic Theology* (1907).

N. W. CARPENTER, JR.

JUSTIFICATION. The redemptive act of God in Jesus Christ whereby the sinner, on the response of faith, becomes the saint whose life is now being fashioned and directed by God's love. The term "justification" in its Greek form means "to reckon as being in the right"; hence, "justification" and "righteousness" are identical in meaning. Man is the sinner, in the sense that he has rebelled against the person and authority of the Creator and, because of that action, constantly breaks God's law. To be justified cannot be accomplished by the sinner, for even should he begin to keep the law, he could not obliterate his earlier disobedience. The sinner is, therefore, subject to the law of sin and death (Rom. 8:2). Human justification depends not on man but on God, and God has acted on man's behalf in Jesus Christ. Jesus Christ is the gift (grace) of God's love to man, and the sinner who responds to Jesus Christ by surrendering his life and laying down his arms of rebellion is made right with God. Justification, then, is God's gracious and full acquittal, solely through the obedient and loving action of Jesus Christ, of sinners who believe in Christ.

W. C. STRICKLAND

JUVENILE DELINQUENCY. Conduct on the part of young persons which violates accepted standards of behavior or conflicts with the law. Such a broad definition is necessary since delinquency is both a sociological and legal concept. Legal delinquents are those committing acts which violate the law.

No reliable statistics are available as to the total volume of delinquency. It is estimated that more than one million youngsters in the United States between the ages of 10 and 18 are in trouble with the police each year. In 1954 arrests of juveniles under 18 increased 2.3 per cent, while arrests of adults decreased 1.9 per cent. The arrests of juvenile delinquents have increased each year since 1948.

Typical delinquent acts by boys are stealing, acts of carelessness, and malicious mischief. Most girl delinquents are referred to courts for being ungovernable, running away, and committing sex offenses. In 1954 juveniles under the age of 18 represented 18.7 per cent of all

FIRST BAPTIST CHURCH, Jackson, Mo. Organized Apr. 30, 1824, by a missionary-minded minority from Bethel, Missouri's oldest Baptist church organized in 1806, whose majority had become Hardshell. It is, therefore, properly a continuation of that first Missouri church. The present Colonial auditorium was erected in 1924 and educational unit in 1956. Value estimated at $200,000.

FIRST BAPTIST CHURCH, Clinton, Mo. Organized 1866, Colonial style auditorium seating 500 built 1927. Membership 1956 numbered over 1,400, Sunday school enrolment 862. Educational unit serves 850.

FIRST BAPTIST CHURCH, Clovis, N. M. Formed 1907, membership 1956 was 1,673. Auditorium of contemporary architecture seats 1,200, Sunday school accommodates 800. Property worth $427,000.

persons arrested for robbery, 49 per cent for burglary, 43.6 per cent for larceny, 57.6 per cent for auto theft, 2.2 per cent for embezzlement and fraud, 26 per cent for receiving stolen property, and 5.6 per cent for forgery and counterfeiting in 1,389 cities (total population 38,642,183). Approximately 35 per cent of all delinquents are repeaters who come before the courts on more than one occasion.

Causative factors in delinquency are complex and numerous. Traditional views that delinquent children are demon possessed, have certain physical configurations, and are natural-born thieves have been discarded by modern students of the problem. One of the basic causes of problem children is the defective family. Generally they come from homes broken by divorce, desertion, demoralization, and death and from homes where there is a lack of proper training, love, recognition, security, happiness, and care.

Communities characterized by slums, gangs, and a lack of wholesome recreational facilities are sources of problem children. The impact of war greatly increases the volume of delinquency. Economic prosperity, mass migration, anxiety, and the lessening of the bonds of moral restraint are products of war and adversely affect juvenile behavior. Radio, television, and the press are powerful forces for good or evil. Often they do not wield a wholesome influence upon children. Crime and comic books which glorify and glamorize the criminal tend to provide the mental food which motivates young people to wrongdoing.

Delinquency control has largely been confined to the usual single line of attack through the police, the court, and the various correctional institutions. But control of the problem is also a community responsibility. Youth organizations, welfare agencies, character-building groups such as scouts, boys' clubs, and Big Brothers are also means of preventing delinquency. Local newspapers, radio, and television can be vital forces in disseminating facts about delinquency and mobilizing the community to combat it.

Public schools can function to help prevent delinquency. Special attention should be given to children manifesting behavior problems. Educational facilities for exceptional children, vocational education and placement, and character and health education are important ways the school can help to meet the basic needs of children. Through the Parent-Teacher Association and teacher visitation, parents can be enlisted to work with the school as it seeks to help the child.

Churches generally have been slow to attack the problem of delinquency other than through the regular types of religious services. Southern Baptists are awakening to the need for special emphasis and action to aid young people in the solution of their problems. Churches are establishing playgrounds; furnishing indoor recreation; sponsoring summer camps, Scouting troops, and athletic activities.

At the associational level some Baptist churches co-operate with local courts in the assignment of boys and girls through the probation department to carefully selected homes in an effort to reclaim them for society. The Home Mission Board also provides what is called the Christian Sponsorship Program which works with the courts. Literature on delinquency is published by the Christian Life Commission and other agencies of the Southern Baptist Convention.   HENLEE BARNETTE

JUVENILE DELINQUENCY, HOME MISSION BOARD PROGRAM ON. The Home Mission Board, in its program on the broken home and juvenile delinquency, recognizing the tremendous need, attacked the problem through its city mission program. The Brotherhood Commission initiated the Man and Boy Movement, which made a man responsible for a boy not in Sunday school and church. In Louisville, Ky., the Boys Estate was developed as an effort to solve the problem of juvenile delinquency. J. Perry Carter, in 1946, led in constituting a home to care for boys in need of direction. Edward J. Lee, a student in Southern Baptist Theological Seminary, was active in leadership in Boys Estate. The next significant effort in reclamation of juvenile delinquents was promoted jointly by the city mission program of Knoxville, Tenn., and the Knox County Association Brotherhood. Later, Woman's Missionary Union co-operated in a similar program for girls. Co-operation of the courts led to the program of sponsorship in which boys were released from juvenile courts to designated men to look after them and girls were released to women sponsors. This program has spread to other cities, and many boys and girls have been reclaimed. In Feb., 1953, Leland Waters, of Richmond, Va., was elected by the Home Mission Board to promote and direct the program for juvenile delinquents and broken homes. Waters prepared several pamphlets on the subject: "Southern Baptist Ministry to Juvenile Delinquents and Broken Homes," "I Helped a Delinquent," "The Christian's Attitude Toward Delinquency," and "A Christian's Guiding Hand."   S. F. DOWIS

K

KANSAS ASSOCIATIONS.
I. Extant. BLUE STEM. Organized Apr. 15, 1954, with five churches previously affiliated with Kaw Valley and Twin Valley Baptist associations. In 1954 five churches reported 38 baptisms, 314 members, $13,946 total gifts, $1,235 mission gifts, $36,000 property value, and no church debt.

CHEYENNE. Organized Oct. 19, 1954, with four churches which came out of High Plains Baptist Association upon its dissolution Sept. 28, 1954. It includes an area of nine counties with the four charter churches in Barton County. In 1954 four churches reported 60 baptisms, 504 members, $34,762.13 total gifts, $5,305.23 mission gifts, $100,945.00 property value, and $31,948.00 church debt.

HIGH PLAINS. Organized Oct. 12, 1954, with six churches and two missions in northwestern Kansas which came out of High Plains Baptist Association at its dissolution, Sept. 28, 1954. In 1954 six churches and two missions reported 83 baptisms, 380 members, $22,722.82 total gifts, $2,914.84 mission gifts, $25,000.00 property value, and $10,188.00 church debt.

KANSAS CITY. Organized Oct. 4, 1953, with 10 churches in northeastern Kansas which came out of George W. Truett Memorial Association at its dissolution Sept., 1953. In 1954 eight churches and two missions reported 240 baptisms, 1,670 members, $138,606 total gifts, $11,868 mission gifts, and $359,000 property value.

KAW VALLEY. Organized in 1953 with 10 churches which came out of George W. Truett Memorial Association upon its dissolution Sept., 1953. In 1954 nine churches reported 122 baptisms, 537 members, $20,107 total gifts, $1,896 mission gifts, and $57,000 property value.

SEDGWICK COUNTY. Organized Dec. 6, 1951, with 10 churches in the Wichita area formerly affiliated with South Central Baptist Association. In 1954, 18 churches and one mission reported 487 baptisms, 5,113 members, $330,656 total gifts, $60,109 mission gifts, and $806,783 property value.

SOUTH-CENTRAL. Organized Oct., 1947, with six churches in south central Kansas which came out of the dissolution of Western Baptist Association. In 1954, 13 churches reported 201 baptisms, 1,469 members, $75,463 total gifts, $8,686 mission gifts, and $189,200 property value.

SOUTHERN PLAINS. Organized Oct. 14, 1954, in southwestern Kansas with five churches, four of which came out of High Plains Baptist Association upon its dissolution Sept. 28, 1954. In 1954 five churches reported 46 baptisms, 323 members, $28,793.61 total gifts, $3,542.75 mission gifts, $97,500.00 property value, and $29,904.00 church debt.

TRI-COUNTY. Organized June 2, 1949, with six churches in southeastern Kansas which came out of the dissolution of Southeastern Baptist Association May 26, 1949. Tri-County adopted articles of faith. In 1954, 14 churches reported 146 baptisms, 1,949 members, $72,309.51 total gifts, $8,918.50 mission gifts, and $140,500.00 property value.

TWIN VALLEY. Organized June, 1949, with five churches in southeastern Kansas which came out of the dissolution of Southeastern Baptist Association May 26, 1949. The association adopted articles of faith. In 1954, 10 churches and four missions reported 142 baptisms, 1,193 members, $78,954.30 total gifts, $8,186.52 mission gifts, $211,796.00 property value, and $43,377.00 church debt.

WHEATLAND. Organized Oct., 1947, in north central Kansas with eight churches which came from Western Baptist Association at its dissolution. Wheatland adopted articles of faith. In 1954, 12 churches reported 81 baptisms, 975 members, $49,226 total gifts, $5,619 mission gifts, $119,000 property value, and $29,512 church debt.

II. Extinct. GEORGE W. TRUETT MEMORIAL. Organized Feb. 10, 1948, with four co-operating churches. It dissolved Sept., 1953, the 20 churches forming Kaw Valley and Kansas City associations.

SOUTHEASTERN. Organized Oct., 1946, at First Baptist Church, Burden, with four co-operating churches, during the first annual session of the Kansas Convention of Southern Baptists. Southeastern dissolved May 26, 1949, the 11 churches forming Twin Valley and Tri-County Baptist associations.

WESTERN. Organized Oct., 1946, at First Baptist Church, Burden, with seven co-operating churches, during the first annual session of the Kansas Convention of Southern Baptists. Western dissolved Oct., 1947, the 14 churches forming Wheatland and South-Central associations.

HOYT S. GIBSON

KANSAS CONVENTION OF SOUTHERN BAPTISTS.
I. Baptist Beginnings. On May 15, 1855, the Southern Baptist Convention voted for its Board of Domestic Missions to take over the work of the destitute American Indian Mission Association. The transfer occurred on June 20,

1855. Shortly afterward, the board's secretary, Joseph Walker, visited Kansas. Involved were the Wea Mission School, Paoli, David Lykins, superintendent; and the Pottawatomie School, Topeka (enrolling 105 in 1860), John Jackson, director.

In 1857 John Hill Luther was sent to Kansas, but pre-Civil War fighting prevented his entry. During the same year Woodlief (also known as "W." and William) Thomas (q.v.) was given $200 per year salary supplement to serve as pastor of the Delaware City Baptist Church. On Oct. 1, 1858, he led in organizing the East Kansas Association of Baptists (Kansas' first) and became its moderator. Soon afterward, he moved to Austin, Tex. Work among the Wea Indians was discontinued prior to 1860, and among the Pottawatomies on Nov. 15, 1861, when most of that tribe became United States citizens.

The second period of Southern Baptist life in Kansas centered around 1910. A Missouri Baptist association reported in its constituency six Kansas churches, claiming 273 members, with church property valued at $2,100, including four buildings seating 700. Their location is not known.

The third period began in 1911 when the Wirtonia Baptist Church near Crestline joined Missouri's Spring River Association. By 1945 churches at Baxter Springs, Lawton, Arma, and Macedonia had followed. By 1943 Oklahoma Baptists listed 10 Kansas churches on their rolls (the 11th, First Baptist, Russell, joined Northern Baptists in 1942). These churches were located at Treece, Chetopa, Chanute, Coffeyville, Chautauqua, rural Chautauqua, Burden, Liberal, Ness City, and Ellinwood. Others once existing in Topeka and Arkansas City had disbanded. The Trinity Baptist Church, Chanute, had joined Northern Baptists by 1944. The churches working with one Missouri association developed a group consciousness. Those affiliating with six Oklahoma associations were isolated, having little knowledge of each other. Frank Calvin Medearis contributed 31 years of leadership to Kansas churches as pastor of the First Baptist Church, Burden (1915–22, 1933–41), and as missionary of Spring River Association during alternating periods, 1922–33 and 1941–46. He had ministered to six of the twelve Southern Baptist churches existing in 1946.

Steps were taken at the Baptist General Convention of Oklahoma, which met in Tulsa, Nov. 12–16, 1944, to bring the churches working with Oklahoma into closer fellowship.

N. J. WESTMORELAND

II. History of Convention. Kansas Southern Baptist Fellowship was organized Nov. 26–27, 1945, at Burden with representatives from First Baptist, Chautauqua; First Baptist, Burden; Calvary Baptist, Ellinwood; and Emmanuel Baptist, Coffeyville. Mar. 19, 1946, seven churches (First Baptist, Chautauqua; First Baptist, Burden; First Baptist, Chetopa; First Baptist, Treece; First Southern Baptist, Wichita; Trinity Baptist, Ness City; Emmanuel Baptist, Coffeyville) organized Kansas Convention of Southern Baptist Churches in a meeting at First Baptist, Chetopa. The name was changed to Kansas Convention of Southern Baptists during a meeting in Wichita in Oct., 1947. Recognition as a co-operating constituency of the Southern Baptist Convention was received in May, 1948.

The first annual meeting of the convention, held Oct. 14–16, 1946, at First Baptist Church, Burden, elected Ray Walker, president; Orbie Russell Clem, vice-president; Mrs. George Robert (Zola Gertrude Hunter) Mitchell, recording secretary; and N. J. Westmoreland, executive secretary-treasurer.

Southern Baptist Beams was the publication of the Kansas Southern Baptist Fellowship, and it was adopted by the convention as its official publication during the Mar., 1946, organization. Clem was editor of the paper, which became known as *Kansas Southern Baptist Beams* during 1946. The publication was named *Baptist Digest* in Apr., 1954.

The 100 Club was authorized Sept. 3, 1946, as part of the "Five Year Plan" to organize 100 new churches. Membership to the 100 Club was by monthly contribution of $1 or more as authorized by the executive board. The Revolving Building Loan Fund was established Oct. 12, 1948, to provide building loans for needy churches.

The Ministers Retirement Plan was made available to Kansas pastors Jan. 1, 1949.

The Kansas Southern Baptist Foundation was established Nov. 4, 1949. Howard Hiram Whatley was elected executive secretary of the first board of directors in 1952.

In June, 1949, a five-room suite was rented at 244½ North Main, Wichita, for state offices. A front room was used for the Baptist Book Store. The Baptist Building, 231 North Main, Wichita, was purchased June 26, 1952. The 25 × 130-foot building has two floors and a 60-foot basement. The first floor and basement were leased to the Sunday School Board for the Baptist Book Store. The second floor houses the state convention offices. One hundred and thirty acres south of Maria Des Cygnes River near Quenemo were purchased in late 1952 for the state assembly grounds.

A nonprofit corporation, Baptist Liberties, Inc., was chartered in Aug., 1950, to receive and disburse funds contributed toward the appeal of the Wyandotte County District Court decision in the Argentine Baptist Church case, which granted property to a minority group prior to organization of the Berean Baptist Church, Kansas City, Aug. 13, 1950. In the 1950 annual session the Kansas convention endorsed the program of Baptist Liberties, Inc., to restore the autonomy of the local Baptist church by seeking to have reversed the existing decision or any future decisions of the Kansas supreme court contrary to majority rule. The decision was sustained by the higher courts to favor minority vote.

The program for Kansas State Teachers College, Pittsburg, Baptist students was authorized by the executive board Mar. 11, 1947. The Pittsburg Baptist Student Union had its first formal program Feb. 18, 1949, at Trinity Baptist Church in Pittsburg. Stanley Alvin Gasswint was first part-time Baptist Student Union secretary. Zeb Linston Brister, professor of the Baptist Chair of Bible, Pittsburg, became secretary Aug. 1, 1952.

The Training Union Department was authorized Oct. 16, 1946, with Floyd Presley McDaniel serving as secretary without pay. The Sunday School Department began Oct. 16, 1946, with Lonnie Wells serving as secretary without pay. The two departments were combined under the Department of Religious Education with William Edwin Russell serving as secretary, Feb. 1, 1949, as authorized by the Oct., 1948, annual convention at Coffeyville. One hundred and eighty registered for the first annual Sunday school convention Mar. 22–23, 1949, at Salvation Army Citadel, Wichita.

William Andrew Burkey was elected secretary of the Department of Co-operative Missions and assumed the new work Aug. 20, 1951. Gordon Burke (Jack) Stanton, first superintendent of evangelism, began serving full time Jan. 1, 1952.

The Kansas Woman's Missionary Union began in auxiliary relation to the convention Mar. 20, 1946, with 113 enrolled in all auxiliary units. Mrs. James Douglas (Nellie Emeline Gentz) Williamson was elected Woman's Missionary Union president at the first annual meeting in Oct., 1946, in Burden. Jan. 1, 1950, Mrs. Orbie Russell (Lois Maurine Bondurant) Clem began full-time work as Woman's Missionary Union executive secretary-treasurer.

The Brotherhood Department was organized Oct. 14, 1948, with Robert Henry Hill serving as secretary without pay. The work continued on part-time status at the close of 1954.

In 1954, 104 churches reported 1,646 baptisms, 14,427 members, $865,546.37 total contributions, $118,280.84 mission gifts, $2,142,624.00 property value.

III. **Program of Work of Kansas Baptists.** *Executive board.*—The administrative board of the Kansas Convention of Southern Baptists is called the executive board. It is composed of 32 members. Ten members retire annually, and 10 members are elected by the annual convention for a three-year term. Six of the 10 members elected annually must be pastors of churches co-operating with the Kansas convention; all must be members of co-operating churches. The president and recording secretary of the convention are respectively chairman and secretary of the board. Board membership is limited to a three-year term. Persons become eligible for re-election after one year. No salaried employee of the convention or of any agency sponsored by the convention is eligible for membership. The state convention grants this board authority to act for the convention during the interim of the annual sessions, provided no action of the general convention be reversed or any action taken contrary to the constitution or principles of the convention. Four regular meetings of the board are held annually. Seventeen members constitute a quorum.

Since the board is organized into six committees, the chairman of these committees become with the chairman and secretary of the board the executive committee. The convention president, recording secretary, and executive secretary-treasurer present the names of the executive committee to the annual convention for approval. This committee conducts the business of the board between the quarterly meetings. Lay members of the board form the committee for laymen's and Brotherhood work. The committees are promotion, missions, religious education, evangelism, Brotherhood, and Woman's Missionary Union. Each committee is responsible for the direction of the interest committed to it, subject to the direction of the board.

Thirty trustees direct the Kansas Southern Baptist Foundation. Elected to a three-year term, 10 retire annually. There are seven members on both the board of managers for the Baptist Chair of Bible at Pittsburg and the board of directors for the *Baptist Digest*. Elected for a three-year term, two retire annually except every third year, when three retire.

The editor of the *Baptist Digest* is elected by the paper's board of directors subject to annual call. Other convention employees are extended an annual call by the convention, except the executive secretary-treasurer, who receives an indefinite call upon his election. The executive secretary-treasurer superintends the entire work of the board and has general charge of the educational, missionary, and benevolent interests of the state. He receives all monies coming to the convention and makes a report of all funds to the quarterly meetings of the board and the annual meeting of the state convention. N. J. Westmoreland, the present executive secretary, was elected in 1946.

Missions.—The state mission program includes associational and pastoral subsidy, an area mission program, and sharing the administration of a church revolving loan fund. In 1954, 28 churches received pastoral subsidy. Through the 100 Club and the pastoral aid fund of the Home Mission Board, $10,542.24 was provided. The state is divided into six mission areas with a missions committee for each area and a representative from each association. Six area missionaries are responsible for the promotion of the over-all program, assisting churches desiring help in establishing new missions and churches. The mission program is on a church-centered basis, a co-operative work between the churches, the associations, the state convention, and the Home Mission Board. The work is directed by the secretary of the Department of Missions. Since 1952 a full-time secretary of evangelism has directed the Department of Evangelism in cooperation with the Home Mission Board and the Convention-wide Department of Evangelism in the promotion of evangelism.

Educational ministry.—The Department of Religious Education has a secretary with departmental status to direct the promotion of Sunday school, Training Union, and Baptist Student Union. In 1954 the department secretary, Milton Ray Gilliland, reported 124 Sunday schools with an enrolment of 15,526; 107 Training Unions with an enrolment of 6,625. There were 7,792 enrolled in 88 Vacation Bible schools during the summer. M Night attendance was 1,703 in Dec., 1953. Three Baptist Student Union organizations were reported. The Woman's Missionary Union, convention auxiliary, reported a membership of 1,538 in 93 organizations in 1954. Ida Odell Polk, executive secretary-treasurer, reported 242 auxiliaries with a membership of 1,950. Elizabeth Carolyn Freeman became secretary for the promotion of young people's work in the auxiliaries in Nov., 1954. Forty-seven Brotherhood organizations in the state reported a total enrolment of 864 laymen in 1954.

Institutions.—The Baptist Chair of Bible at Kansas State Teacher's College, Pittsburg, offers courses accredited by Oklahoma Baptist University.

Promotional work.—The *Baptist Digest* has been the official organ of publicity of the state convention since 1954. Formerly named *Kansas Southern Baptist Beams*, the paper is supported by Cooperative Program receipts, subscriptions, and advertising. There is no Department of Promotion in the state. Most general promotion has been delegated to the executive secretary-treasurer and his budget and promotion committee.   HOYT S. GIBSON

KANSAS SOUTHERN BAPTIST BEAMS. See BAPTIST DIGEST.

KANSAS SOUTHERN BAPTIST FOUNDATION. Established by the Kansas Convention of Southern Baptists, Nov. 4, 1949, to promote, support, maintain, and foster the various causes, objects, and agencies of the convention. The Kansas Foundation applied for a charter on Jan. 2, 1952, and Howard Hiram Whatley was elected executive secretary of the first board of directors, whose members included Guy Eugene Caskey, president; Neal Erwin Huff; Harold LeRoy Roberts; and Clyde Hoffman. Income in 1954 from investments was $375; from capital assets, $2,363.13; from convention budget, $300. Assets Dec. 31, 1954, totaled $7,488.78.   HOYT S. GIBSON

KANSAS STATE TEACHERS COLLEGE, CHAIR OF BIBLE. Located at Kansas State Teachers College, Pittsburg, opened Sept. 11, 1952, with Zeb Linston Brister as director-professor. Eight pastors and laymen enrolled for three night classes meeting at Trinity Baptist Church. It is directed by a convention-elected board of managers consisting of seven members. The chair of Bible in 1953 secured a building adjoining the campus for the Baptist Student Center and Bible classes then available to college students. Work is accredited by Oklahoma Baptist University. In Dec., 1954, two courses were offered with a total enrolment of four.   HOYT S. GIBSON

KATHLEEN MALLORY-MAYFIELD TYZZER HOSPITAL, LAICHOWFU. See CHINA, MISSION IN.

KEACH, BENJAMIN (b. Stoke Hammond, North Buckinghamshire, England, Feb. 29, 1640; d. London, England, July 18, 1704). Particular Baptist preacher, author, printer, and bookseller; controversialist. Keach was a second-generation Baptist who became a General Baptist at the age of 15, began to preach and teach at 18, and became a minister (elder) to the small General Baptist church at Winslow in 1660. He was twice married, first to Jane Grove in 1660, who bore him five children, and, after her death (1670), to Widow Susanna Partridge (1672), who also bore him five children and who was, apparently, a Particular Baptist.

In 1664 Keach, a tailor as well as a General Baptist preacher, wrote and published a little dissenting book called *The Child's Instructor, or a New and Easy Primer*, containing the rudiments of learning. For writing, printing, and publishing this heretical (believer's baptism), schismatic (non-episcopally ordained preachers), and seditious (Christ is King, not Charles II) book, Keach was fined, imprisoned, and made to stand upon a pillory and watch his book burned. Keach rewrote the primer from memory, and its sales ran into many editions. It was published in Boston in 1685 and became the foundation of the New England Primer, which ran to scores of editions.

Soon after his imprisonment because of *The Child's Instructor*, Keach was encouraged to move to London where, in 1668, he received the first recorded dissenting ordination in London and became pastor of the General Baptist church meeting on Tooley Street, Southwark. Upon coming in contact with the prominent Particular Baptists, William Kiffin and Hanserd Knollys, and also perhaps influenced by his wife, Keach considered the points of difference between the General and Particular Baptists and declared himself a Calvinist. Taking a few converts with him from his church, he founded a Particular Baptist church in 1672 or 1673. After the Declaration of Indulgence was passed in 1672, the church built its first meetinghouse on Goat Street, Horsley-down, Southwark. Keach's services attracted large congregations, and it was necessary successively to enlarge the church building until it could hold nearly a thousand people. Some years after Keach's death, a group split from this church later became Carter's Lane Church and then (Spurgeon's) Metropolitan Tabernacle.

Keach led an active life as a preacher, writer, rhymester, apologist, and Baptist leader. He was a successful proselyter among the General Baptists. As a churchman, he was concerned with the elevation of the ministry. He continued in his belief in the General Baptist principle of laying hands on baptized believers and propagandized for the practice. He also insisted that the hands of ministers should be laid on ministerial candidates when they were ordained, and declared for the financial support of ministers beyond bare necessities, when the churches were able. He was also active in the development of ministerial fraternities.

Keach helped revive and extend the practice of the use of church covenants. In 1697 he and his son, Elias, who had been a minister in Pennsylvania, published a covenant which was used by their two (London) churches and was extensively copied by others. This confession was the first Baptist confession recorded in America. It was used as a basis for the restoration of harmony at the Middletown, N. J., church in 1712. The confession of the Philadelphia Baptist Association included articles from the confession of Keach and his son on the singing of psalms and the laying on of hands. When this confession was adopted by the second American association, the one at Charleston, S. C., in 1767, the article on singing was included, but the one on the laying on of hands was dropped.

Keach is best known today because under his leadership his church at Horsley-down seems to have been the first church in all England, established or dissenting, to introduce the congregational singing of hymns as distinct from paraphrases or psalms and to establish them as a regular part of the worship services. A hymn was always used at the end of the Lord's Supper from about 1673. Then the practice of hymn-singing was extended to "Days of Thanksgiving" and later to baptisms and other special occasions. Keach met with vigorous opposition, but he was determined to have congregational singing in his church and, although it brought upon him much trouble and ill will, he slowly brought it about. Keach began to write hymns to emphasize the points of his sermons, but it was not until about 1690 that the church was persuaded to the point of agreeing by church action to sing hymns every Lord's Day. Then they agreed to sing only after the sermon and when the prayers were ended so that any who disapproved of singing could leave without anyone's being offended by their action. Even this consideration of the feelings of others did not prevent splits in the church over the issue, one group joining another church and another group organizing a new church.

The regular Lord's Day use of hymns in the worship service of Keach's church precipitated a bitter controversy over singing among Particular Baptist churches. Keach and Isaac Marlow were the chief figures in the ensuing "Controversie of Singing," which grew so hot and abusive in its battle of pamphlets that the pamphleteers were censured by the General Assembly of Particular Baptists in 1692.

In 1691 Keach published *Spiritual Melody*, a pocket hymnbook of 222 hymns, many of which were intended to be used for congregational singing. While not the first book of its kind, it was the first actually used for this purpose by English congregations. Although Keach was one of the important pioneers, his hymns are not used today because of their lack of literary quality.

Keach's chief disciple, so far as hymn-writing was concerned, was Joseph Stennett, Sr. (1633–1713), a Seventh Day Baptist, who preached the funeral service of Benjamin Keach. Keach was buried in the Baptist burial ground in the former Park of the bishop of Winchester, Southwark.

BIBLIOGRAPHY: T. Crosby, *The History of the English Baptists* (1740). J. J. Goadby, *Bye-Paths in Baptist History* (1871). G. W. Hughes, "He Taught Us to Sing," Part II of "The Tercentenary of Benjamin Keach, Baptist Preacher, London, England," *The Chronicle*, III, No. 4 (1940). A. A. Reid, "Benjamin Keach, 1640," Part I of "The Tercentenary of Benjamin Keach, Baptist Preacher, London, England," *The Chronicle*, III, No. 4 (1940). H. Wamble, "Benjamin Keach, Churchman," *The Quarterly Review*, Vol. XVI, No. 2 (1956). W. T. Whitley, *A History of British Baptists* (1923); *The Baptists of London, 1612–1928* (n.d.); *Congregational Hymn-Singing* (1933).

FLOYD PATTERSON

KEATCHIE FEMALE COLLEGE. Located at Keatchie, DeSoto Parish, La., founded in 1857 by the Grand Cane Association, governed by a board of trustees selected from that body. It was a liberal arts college noted for a well-trained faculty and emphasis on fine arts. In 1879 it became coeducational under the name of Keatchie Male and Female College. The college, lacking endowment and depending upon tuition and gifts, reached its most productive year in 1890. Thereafter, it declined rapidly until it was transferred to the control of the Louisiana Baptist Convention in 1899. It was then renamed Louisiana Female College and administered by an educational commission of the convention. The school closed in 1911, and many of its students transferred to the newly organized Louisiana College in Pineville. (MRS.) LELA B. COSTELLO

KEHUKEE CHURCH. Established in 1742 near Scotland Neck, N. C., by William Sojourner and a group of General Baptists from the Virginia county, Isle of Wight, it was regarded as a mother of other churches in eastern North Carolina. Edward Brown and Thomas pope, Calvinists, succeeded Sojourner, preparing fertile ground for missionaries sent by the Philadelphia Baptist Association to win churches to the Particular faith. With Pope as pastor, the reconstituted Kehukee became the first Particular church in North Carolina on Dec. 11, 1755. After withdrawing from Charleston Association in 1762, the Kehukee Church was a constituent member of the old Kehukee Association in 1769, but did not join in its 1777 reorganization or in the organization of the North Carolina Baptist state convention in 1830. Because in 1827 it had identified itself with the antimission movement, the church now has only historical interest.

G. W. PASCHAL

KENDALL, AMOS (b. Dunstable, Mass., Aug. 16, 1789; d. Washington, D. C., Nov. 12, 1869). Educated in the public schools of Massachusetts, he taught in country schools and put himself through Dartmouth, graduating in 1811. He studied law at Groton, Mass.; migrated to Kentucky, 1814; served as a tutor in the family of Henry Clay. Later he practiced law and edited newspapers. He helped Andrew Jackson carry Kentucky in the 1828 presidential election, and he carried the state's electoral vote to Washington. Jackson appointed him auditor of the Treasury. He held this office for six years and was then appointed Postmaster General. Martin Van Buren reappointed him to the same post in 1837. He served in the Cabinet until 1840. In 1845 he became business agent for Samuel F. B. Morse, the inventor of the telegraph, and grew quite wealthy. He became associated with Calvary Church, Washington, D. C., in 1862, when his wife (Jane Kyle) moved her membership to Calvary from New Jersey. His profession of faith, baptism, and reception into Calvary Church took place in 1865. During the last seven years of his life he contributed money to build the first Calvary Church building and funds to replace the burned first building with a second. He also contributed large sums to build missions. He was a leader and contributor toward the establishment of Columbia Institution for the Deaf and Dumb (now Gallandet College). He served as deacon or trustee of Calvary Church during his entire association.

M. CHANDLER STITH

KENNEDY MEMORIAL HOME. Located at Falling Creek, N. C., midway between La Grange and Kinston in Lenoir County on a 1,200-acre tract of land which was deeded to the Baptist Orphanage of North Carolina, Inc., on May 12, 1912, by William Lafayette Kennedy and wife. Bernard Washington Spilman (q.v.), who married Mozelle Pollock, niece of Mrs. Kennedy, played an important part in interesting Captain and Mrs. Kennedy in leaving their farm to the Baptist Orphanage, and Spilman closely identified himself with Kennedy Home from its founding until his death. One of the cottages on the campus is named for him.

Consisting of 16 major buildings and several smaller ones, the plant includes nine cottages for children, a church, freezer locker, administration building, combined laundry-sewing room, gymnasium, pastorium, superintendent's home, and four residences for staff members. A large farm, with 500 acres under cultivation, provides much of the food. On Dec. 31, 1954, the home was caring for 185 children. A full-time pastor serves in the new campus church, built in 1955, and children attend school at La Grange, seven miles away. Adequate medical care and recreational opportunities are provided at the home, which receives financial support through the main offices of the Baptist Orphanage of North Carolina, Inc., at Thomasville. Kennedy Home's superintendent lives on the campus and directs work under supervision of the general superintendent of the incorporated organization.

J. MARSE GRANT

KENTUCKY, GENERAL ASSOCIATION OF BAPTISTS IN.

I. Baptist Beginnings. *Exploration and settlement.*—No other denomination profited more immediately from the development of Kentucky than did Baptists. As the pioneers of religion in the wilderness, Baptists were strongly represented among the original permanent settlers.

Squire Boone, brother of Daniel, was a Baptist preacher. Daniel Boone himself attended Baptist meetings, but never formally affiliated with any church, although several female members of his family joined Baptist churches. Though Squire was the first preacher on Kentucky soil, the Episcopalian John Lythe preached the first-mentioned sermon at Boonesboro on May 28, 1775. Thomas Tinsley and William Hickman preached the earliest known Baptist sermons at Harrodstown in Apr., 1776. It is altogether likely that Squire Boone conducted services before this date, but substantiating evidence is missing. At any rate, on Aug. 7, 1776, Squire performed the first marriage ceremony in Kentucky, that of Samuel Henderson (q.v.) and Elizabeth Callaway. He preached the first sermon in Louisville and appeared as the first Baptist preacher in Meade County.

Early Baptist churches.—The mass migration after 1779 included large numbers of Baptists, most of whom came from Virginia. Baptist preachers were liberally represented among the immigrants. During 1781 two churches were organized in Kentucky, and a third migrated as a body. Organized on June 18, 1781, Severn's Valley Church, now located in Elizabethtown, was the first Baptist church in Kentucky. It was begun by 18 persons, three of whom were Negro. The second church, Cedar Creek, located in Nelson County about five miles southwest of Bardstown, was organized on July 4, 1781. Severn's Valley Church was influential in forming Cedar Creek. The third church, Gilbert's Creek, was the famous "traveling church." Its history may be traced to Upper Spotsylvania, Va., where on Nov. 20, 1767, 25 persons constituted themselves as a church. In the fall of 1781, this church, with Lewis Craig (q.v.) as pastor, set out for Kentucky; the trip of around 600 miles took about five months. On Sept. 28, 1781, the church stopped at Abingdon, Va., and constituted another "traveling church." The Upper Spotsylvania Church continued on the Wilderness Road, and in December the party settled in Garrard County on the south side of the Kentucky River. On the second Sunday of December, the newly arrived church, containing around 200 members and four preachers, established itself on Gilbert's Creek, about a mile and a half from Lancaster. Craig served as pastor of the church until 1783, when he and a majority of the members moved north of the river and formed South Elkhorn Church. The original church, weakened by the removal of so many members, was dissolved around 1786.

In 1782 two churches were organized. NoLynn Church, now called South Fork Church, in LaRue County, was constituted in the summer. Soon after the church's constitution seven persons were baptized in Nolin River, while armed guards were posted to defend against Indians; this was probably the first baptismal service in Kentucky. The Forks of Dix River Church, in Garrard County, was organized by Lewis Craig in 1782. Three churches appeared in 1783. A Separate church was constituted in the vicinity of Gilbert's Creek "traveling church." The origin of the new church, also called Gilbert's Creek, is attributed to two removals of Regular Baptists and to the strong Separate leadership of Joseph Bledsoe. In the summer of 1783, Lewis Craig led a majority of the "traveling church" north of the Kentucky River, and in the fall these members constituted themselves as South Elkhorn Church. The third Baptist church which appeared in Kentucky in 1783 was Providence, a church which had been organized by the Gilbert's Creek "traveling church" at Abingdon, Va., on Sept. 28, 1781, while en route to Kentucky. Providence, also a "traveling church," arrived in Kentucky in Sept., 1783, after spending several months in East Tennessee. Settling for a year near the location of the original "traveling church," Providence in Nov., 1784, moved to the north side of Kentucky River, in Clark County. The only church organized in 1784 was Bear Grass Creek near Louisville; this church was lost to Campbellism around 1830.

The year 1785 witnessed a church-constituting boom for Baptists, seemingly influenced by the influx of Virginia immigrants who had profited from the Virginia revival of 1785. Nine churches are known to have been organized that year.

1. In April 30 members of South Elkhorn formed Clear Creek Church, in Woodford County, under the leadership of John Taylor, who, in the winter of 1784-85, initiated the first-known revival in Kentucky.

2. Limestone Church was constituted in Mason County, but in 1788 the church moved to the town of Washington, and in 1792 the name was changed to Washington.

3. Pottenger's Creek Church was constituted in the southern part of Nelson County, but after a good start it was dissolved in 1804.

4. On Apr. 17, 1785, Cox's Creek Church, in Nelson County, was constituted with 16 charter members.

5. Eight persons in Owen's Fort, near Shelbyville, constituted themselves as Brashear's Creek Church, the mother church in Shelby County, but Indians prevented their holding services in 1786-87. Late in 1788, however, the church was revived and in 1842 its name was changed to Clear Creek. Around 1858, however, it seemingly dissolved, with members being absorbed by the Shelbyville Church.

6. The Rush Branch Church, first to be organized in Lincoln County, was gathered, but in 1803 it withdrew from South Kentucky Association over a doctrinal matter and later disappeared.

7. Head of Boone's Creek Church, in Fayette County, was organized by Joseph Craig (q.v.).

8. On May 28, 1785, Lewis Craig and John Taylor gathered 16 persons into Great Crossings Church, near Georgetown. Early in the 1790's it suffered in a difficulty between pastor Elijah Craig (q.v.) and Joseph Redding, a popular preacher. It later experienced two remarkable revivals: 361 persons were baptized in 1801, and 359 were baptized in 1828.

9. The Tate's Creek (Regular) Church was organized in Madison County, between Boonesboro and Richmond; in 1810 the church split, with one faction remaining in the Elkhorn Association and the other becoming a charter member of the Licking Association.

Early associations.—From their beginnings there had been a kind of practical interrelationship of Kentucky churches. Many new churches owed their gathering to already existing churches, and the spirit of fellowship existed among them. Of course, distance, wilderness conditions, danger from Indians, and some doctrinal variants prevented the closest of fellowship. It was not until 1785, therefore, that formal associations were first organized.

On June 25 of that year, at South Elkhorn Church, Baptists (Regular) north of the Kentucky River met with Baptists (Separate) south of the river in an effort to resolve their differences and to establish a union. However, these messengers were unable to achieve these objectives; rather, the breach was widened, and local congregations began to divide along Regular-Separate lines. On Sept. 30, 1785, 16 messengers from six churches met in the community of Clear Creek and organized the Elkhorn Association, the first Baptist association in Kentucky. These messengers adopted the term "Regular Baptist" to distinguish themselves from other Baptists who held different views. On Oct. 29, 1785, messengers from four churches, in what was then the western area, met at Cox's Creek and organized Salem Association. Salem also adopted the term "Regular Baptist."

In Oct., 1787, at Tate's Creek Church, Separate Baptists, who had originally refused to join in any kind of association which would undermine local independence by setting up external authorities, formed the "South Kentucky Association of Separate Baptists." Eleven churches composed the new association which, because of Separate suspicion of external authority, was formed on an uncertain basis, requiring no doctrinal agreement. This condition permitted "Hell Redemptionism" or Universalism to create strife in the association between 1791 and 1801, resulting in the withdrawal of five churches in 1793 and the split of the original association in 1801 into two associations (South District and North District). In 1803 an unhealthy split occurred in South District, and a faction formed another association, calling itself "South Kentucky Association of Separate Baptists II." The five churches which withdrew in 1793 met at Jessamine Church in November of that year and organized Tate's Creek Association, which designated itself as "United Baptists," the first Kentucky use of this term. The fifth association, Bracken, was constituted at Bracken Church, in Mason County on May 28, 1799. Eight churches formed this association, five of which had peaceably separated from the Elkhorn Association. The sixth and last association formed before the Great Revival was Green River Association, constituted in June, 1800, at Mt. Tabor Church in Barren County. The association was composed of eight widely scattered churches. Holding a strong Regular Baptist position, Green River became hyper-Calvinistic during the antimissions controversy and since 1840 has been non-co-operating with Kentucky Baptists.

The Great Revival, 1800–03.—Between 1790 and 1800 the strength of Kentucky Baptists grew comparatively weaker. Several factors which contributed were (1) rapidly increased migration between 1790 and 1800; (2) preoccupation of Kentuckians with economic and political projects; (3) diversion of evangelism by doctrinal controversy; and (4) increasing immorality of society. This decline of religious vitality, in other denominations as well as among Baptists, was arrested, and a new era of spiritual and moral vigor was inaugurated in 1800 by the Great Revival, which broke out among Presbyterians in Logan County, under the preaching of James McGready, who emphasized repentance, faith, and regeneration. Camp meetings, drawing people from great distances, were begun. Accompanying the revival, especially in camp meetings, were ecstatic and frantic exercises, weird in nature but certainly fostered by conviction of sin and mass psychology; these exercises included groaning, crying, singing, shouting, falling, jerking, laughing, and dancing. Baptists were inclined to be wary of revivals, fearing that nondenominational meetings would undermine their doctrines of (1) believer's baptism and (2) a gathered or disciplined church. However, there was no permanent immunization to the contagion. As early as 1797, the Gasper River, Muddy River, and Red River congregations experienced revivals. In the spring of 1800, Baptists participated in a union revival meeting with Methodists at Carrollton.

During the years 1800–03 the number of Baptist churches doubled, and the membership tripled. Another consequence of the revivals was the union of Regulars and Separates.

Regular and Separate Baptists.—Kentucky Baptists were originally divided into two groups—Regular and Separates. Actually the division was not as fixed as it is sometimes described, and early Kentucky churches frequently contained both. However, when measures were taken to set up a standard of faith and an associational organization, differences became conspicuous, and a breach developed. The terms "Regular" and "Separate" refer to Baptists in the mid-18th century, as related to the Great Awakening. Regular Baptists constituted the older group, having direct kinship with English Particular Baptists. They perpetuated the confession of 1677 in the modified Philadelphia and Charleston confessions, and they promoted, as did early English Baptists, a system of associationalism based on the concept of the "Body of Christ" and the interdependence of local churches. Inasmuch as they were already in existence when the more zealous Separates appeared, they were identified as "Regulars."

Separate Baptists, on the other hand, were strictly a New England development. In view of the increasing unholy and mixed membership in Congregational churches and the adoption of the Saybrook Platform in 1708 (which undermined strict congregational government by making presbyterial concessions), hundreds of Congregationalists withdrew and formed "Separate" congregations. Initially these congregations were primarily interested in regenerate conversion, pure membership, and strict local independence. Within a half generation, however, members of these "Separate" or "New Light" congregations began to apply the Bible to church order and to arrive at Baptist positions, notably concerning the baptism of believers by immersion only. Because of several factors, during the 1750's many Separates migrated southward and inaugurated enthusiastic and successful evangelism in the Piedmont from Virginia to Georgia. It was from this territory that emigrants left for Kentucky and Tennessee in the late 1770's and early 1780's, bringing with them aversion to confessions, zeal for independence, and lax theology.

The union of Regular and Separate Baptists was a process. In 1786 in North Carolina and in 1787 in Virginia, it was completed when the term "United Baptists" was adopted. In Kentucky union was effected in 1801, although the process was going on during the 1780's. Most

Baptists who came to Kentucky were Separates, but they tended to become Regulars. Generally speaking, Regulars were located north of the Kentucky River and Separates, south of it. After the attempts at union in 1785 and 1789, Separate and Regular churches were often to be found in the same community.

One of the foremost results of the Great Revival was the union of Regulars and Separates. In 1800 Elkhorn Association (Regular) sent a committee to South Kentucky Association (Separate) to promote a union. Upon the favorable response of the latter, committees from both associations met in Oct., 1801, at Old Providence Church on Howard's Creek, in Clark County, and agreed on "Terms of General Union." The term "United Baptists" was adopted, and it soon became characteristic of most Kentucky Baptists. In time the name became simply "Baptists," but around 1840 new names, e.g., "Missionary," "Hardshell," or "Primitive," were applied, indicating the attitude toward missions.

Continued growth and foreign mission interest.—After the peak of the Great Revival in 1801, the revival rapidly waned, and by 1803 it had died. Baptists became absorbed with other things. In 1803 South District Association split, and a Separate Baptist body was organized which took a strong anticonfessional stand, claiming to recognize no authority in faith and practice except the Bible. In 1805 Long Run Association condemned Free Masonry, and a controversy continued for over a generation. Slavery was questioned by Salem Association as early as 1789, and around 1804 to 1807, this issue greatly agitated Elkhorn and North District associations. Being called to silence on emancipation, David Barrow and others organized a "Friends of Humanity" association. Over a period of five years, the discipline of a preacher, Jacob Creath of the Town Fork Church, who refused to pay for a slave girl who died soon after he bought her, troubled Elkhorn Association; finally in 1810 Elkhorn Association was dissolved and immediately reconstituted so as to exclude Creath; 11 protesting churches, therefore, withdrew and constituted Licking Association. Preoccupation with such concerns hindered evangelism and growth. Between 1810 and 1813, however, there was another period of growth. Revivalism was neither as spectacular nor as productive as the Great Revival, but there were hundreds of conversions. In 1810 Long Run Association reported 956 baptisms; in 1811 Elkhorn added 605; between 1811 and 1813 North District added 1,078, and Russell's Creek added 622. Before 1812 American Baptists had no united interest in foreign missions, but following the conversion of Luther Rice (q.v.) and the Adoniram Judsons (q.v.) to Baptist views, they quickly united. In 1814 American Baptists organized the Triennial Convention. Kentucky Baptists had no representative in its organization, but in 1815–16 Rice, the convention's traveling agent, received a hearty welcome from Kentucky churches and associations. Six mission societies were formed by the end of 1816, and gifts were as liberal as any that Rice had received elsewhere. Unfortunately, however, missionary enthusiasm was soon dampened.

Anti-effort controversy and Campbellite schism.—Prior to 1816 there was no Kentucky opposition to missions, but there soon developed throughout the frontier a bitter hostility to such efforts. This hostility was not limited to foreign missions, for it soon centered on all "efforts," such as Sunday schools, mission societies, theological education, tract societies, Bible societies, etc. The following factors were involved in this development: frontier suspicion of the East, the preachers' fear that an educated ministry would either dominate or displace them, dread of money power held by boards, and antagonism toward centralization which might weaken local independence. In 1817 the Triennial Convention undertook home missions, and this seemingly touched off frontier opposition.

Three persons, John Taylor, Daniel Parker (q.v.), and Alexander Campbell, were primarily responsible for spreading anti-effort sentiment. It is odd that Taylor attacked "means" or "efforts" which support missions, for it was he who had begun the first revival in Kentucky in 1784–85, and who was the most vigorous leader in spreading Baptist views and in organizing Baptist churches in the bluegrass region between 1785 and 1820. In 1820 Taylor published his pamphlet, *Thoughts on Missions*, in which he likened Rice to Tetzel, the priest who sold indulgences in Luther's day. Taylor feared money power which boards and societies held and attacked as unscriptural societies, conventions, theological education, and Sunday schools. Parker lived in Tennessee, but his views were circulated in Kentucky through pamphlets and his paper, *Church Advocate*, begun in 1829. In 1820 he published a pamphlet attacking the Triennial Convention's mission program, and in 1824 it was reprinted in Lexington, where antimissionism was radically vocal. He developed the peculiar doctrine of "Two-Seed-in-the-Spirit"; strictly deterministic (in this respect showing affinity to the hyper-Calvinist doctrine of double-edged predestination), this doctrine asserts that each person gets a seed from either God through Adam or from Satan, and that this seed determines whether one can be saved; those with God's seed must be saved, and those begotten of Satan cannot be saved; it is useless, therefore, to attempt the salvation of persons. Such a doctrine effectively paralyzes mission effort. Despite formidable opposition from men like Taylor and Parker, Baptist churches experienced a revival between 1817 and 1820. The mission societies founded by 1816 continued to promote missions. Choctaw Academy was founded at Georgetown by the Kentucky Missionary Society in 1819. Soon, however, opposition stifled energetic mission efforts.

Campbellism, the most disruptive force among

Baptists between 1820 and 1840, thrived on anti-effort sentiment. Thomas Campbell and his son Alexander were Scotch-Irish, and both were ministers in the Scottish Seceder Presbyterian Church. In 1807 Thomas Campbell came to America, settling in southwest Pennsylvania. After a year's study in Glasgow, Alexander, accompanied by the remainder of the family, arrived in 1809. Both men were formerly Presbyterians; in 1813 they were baptized as Baptists and organized Brush Run Church, which affiliated with Redstone Association. Although suspicion soon gathered around Alexander, he was able to evade discipline. In 1823 in what is now Bethany, W. Va., he began to publish *The Christian Baptist,* succeeded in 1830 by the *Millennial Harbinger.* Also in 1823 he made contact with Kentucky Baptists. His disputation with W. C. MacCalla, a Presbyterian debater, at Washington, Ky., gave him the reputation of a "Baptist champion," and he was hospitably received in several places as far west as Louisville. His paper was perhaps unexcelled in circulation in Kentucky, and his views were unsuspectingly swallowed by many Kentucky Baptists. Rejecting all creeds and claiming "the Bible alone," Campbell attacked everything for which he could find no biblical command. He repudiated missions, paid ministry, theological education, Sunday schools, etc.; by 1830 he had come to attach prime importance to baptism for the remission of sins. In 1824 and 1826 Campbell made tours in Kentucky, during which some Baptist leaders began to suspect both his doctrines and objectives. Soon churches and associations became troubled over Campbellism. Some outstanding Baptist leaders became ardent Campbell supporters; others opposed Campbellism. By 1827 the new movement was splitting associations. In July, 1830, Franklin Association, attended by ministers from five other associations, repudiated Campbellism; in a circular letter Franklin Association urged other associations to close pulpits to Campbellites and to deny communion to them; Baptists found it defensively necessary to sever contact with Campbell's followers. Between 1830 and 1832 almost 10,000 Baptists became Campbellites. At the same time Campbell's followers (known as "Reformers" or "Disciples") were united with the followers of Barton W. Stone (known as "Christians").

Even many Baptists who refused to follow Campbell held strictly antimissionary doctrines and practices. During the mid-1830's their churches and associations were refusing to cooperate with missionary-minded Baptists, and by 1842 some 7,000 had dissociated themselves. The Baptist membership of 1829 was 45,442, but in 1832 it was only 35,862. Despite the revival between 1837 and 1840, the membership of 1839 was only 39,806. By this time, however, missionary-minded Baptists had achieved a Baptist unity which insured their victory.

Consolidation of Kentucky Baptists.—Despite the efforts of men like Taylor, Parker, and Campbell, Kentucky Baptists were able to achieve a basic unity by 1837. Prior to that time associations maintained contact with each other through "circular letters" and "fraternal greetings." However, this was a haphazard program and did not constitute denominational unity. Moreover, poor transportation and communication prevented close contact. Journalism contributed to the building up of Baptist unity. The first Baptist paper in Kentucky, *Kentucky Missionary and Theological Magazine,* lived for only one year, 1812–13. *Gospel Herald,* started in 1813, was also short-lived. In 1826 *Baptist Register* (changed to *Baptist Recorder*) of Bloomfield was started, with the purpose of exposing the errors of Campbellism. It was able to survive for four or five years. In 1830 Uriel B. Chambers began to publish *Baptist Herald* (afterward *Baptist Chronicle*). This, too, was an unsuccessful venture. In 1832 Chambers began to edit *Cross and Baptist Banner,* the first weekly Baptist paper in Kentucky, which was soon adopted as the official organ of the Kentucky Baptist Convention. In 1834 James Wilson, M.D., of Shelbyville, started *Baptist Banner* as a rival of *Cross and Baptist Banner.* In 1835 John Lightfoot Waller (*q.v.*) became editor of the *Baptist Banner,* which under his leadership and that of W. C. Buck, his successor, became the leading Baptist journal in the West. It became the official paper of the general association after 1837. Due to various mergers with *The Baptist* of Nashville, Tenn., and *Western Pioneer* of Alton, Ill., its name has undergone several changes; since 1851 it has been called *Western Recorder.*

Compared to Baptists of other states, Kentucky Baptists were early in founding a college, Georgetown, in 1829. This was the first Baptist college west of the Allegheny Mountains. As early as 1788, Elijah Craig (*q.v.*) opened a classical school at Lebanon (now Georgetown). In 1798 the Kentucky legislature established Rittenhouse Academy at Georgetown; the school ceased to exist, but the property was given by the city to Georgetown College in 1829. During its first few years Georgetown suffered from Campbellism. A rival college (Bacon) was established in Georgetown by some of Campbell's followers.

The establishment of a permanent statewide organization of Baptists was only slowly realized. Silas Noel first proposed, in *Gospel Herald* in 1813, the forming of a "General Meeting of Correspondence," in which ministers and members would gather at least annually from throughout the state and consult together on mutual interests. In 1814 this suggestion met with disfavor, but in 1827, in *Baptist Record,* Spencer Clack and George Waller made a similar proposal. Although it was not immediately accepted, concerted effort became more necessary because of the growing threat of Campbellism during the late 1820's. Following the separation between Baptists and Campbellites in 1830, the subject of a general meeting was revived in 1831. On Dec. 11, 1831, "Frankfort Association, Auxiliary to the Kentucky Baptist Convention" (whose early organization was expected) was formed with 153 members. The association sent out an appeal defining the purpose of a convention and urging the immediate organization of other auxiliaries. On Mar. 29, 1832, 34 delegates, representing three auxiliary associations and nine churches, met at Bardstown and organized the Kentucky Baptist Convention. The constitution was adopted, and a sum of $190 was raised for convention expenses. The adjourned delegates met at New Castle in Oct., 1832; the convention adopted "rules of decorum" and named *Cross and Baptist Banner* as its organ. Six convention meetings were held between 1832 and 1836. At the seventh meeting, at Georgetown on June 3, 1837, it was recommended that a more general body than the convention be formed, for the convention's power was inadequate to achieve the objectives of supplying destitute places with preachers, sending out missionaries, and raising and disbursing needed funds. Doctrinal differences (such as Calvinism and Arminianism), antimissionism, and fears of centralized authority defeated the convention, so the "general association" plan was recommended. The General Association of Baptists in Kentucky was organized on Oct. 20, 1837, in Louisville; on Oct. 21-23 the convention held its final meeting and transferred its funds to the association. Though the convention failed, its underlying objectives were largely responsible for the successful launching of the general association.

WENDELL H. RONE

II. History of the General Association. *Beginning.*—Kentucky Baptists for a long period of time were unable to achieve any degree of unanimity on an organizational basis, but the general association was able eventually to establish itself as the focal center of a majority of Kentucky Baptists, although perennially plagued by dissident elements. The old Kentucky Baptist Convention was never able to achieve its objective of uniting Kentucky Baptists. Perhaps the greatest criticism concerned the convention's threat to local churches in raising monies and appointing evangelists. In 1835 the convention disclaimed any pre-eminence and affirmed that the local church is the only ecclesiastical authority, but this did not fully allay suspicion. Sponsors of the convention began to advocate a general association, realizing that Baptists were familiar with the associational concept (though some disfavored associations). Upon the recommendation of the Kentucky Baptist Convention, and the urging of the *Baptist Banner*, 57 Kentucky Baptists met in Louisville on Oct. 20, 1837, to organize a general association. Present were the certified delegates—20 ordained ministers, one licensed preacher, and 36 laymen—and Baptist leaders from some other states. Only 9 of the 43 associations were represented, but each major district of the state was represented. Areas where Campbellism and antimissionism had been most disruptive were weakly represented; most strongly represented were Long Run and Russell's Creek associations. At the organizational meeting the constitution, of 12 articles (later 10), was adopted, and the official title became "General Association of Baptists in Kentucky." Composed of representatives from Baptist churches and associations which contribute annually to the causes or co-operate through auxiliary associations, the general association has as its special aim to promote God's cause in the state. No ecclesiastical authority over churches is intended. Officers and duties, election procedure, recognition of visiting brethren, time of annual meeting, and procedure for constitutional changes are defined in the constitution. In anticipating inquiries or criticisms concerning its doctrinal viewpoint, the General Association stated that its avowed "sentiments" were those held by United Baptists (the terms of General Union of 1801).

Definition of objectives and process of consolidation.—Though it endorsed foreign missions, the general association construed state or home missions as its prime task. The destitute condition of Kentucky churches alarmed the general association. Only about 200 of the 500 churches had any preaching; only about one third of the 200 preachers were regularly employed in weekly preaching; only the Louisville church had a pastor on regular and adequate salary. This condition had been created by opposition to a paid and trained ministry, by preoccupation with theological speculation and ecclesiological controversy, and by the failure of churches to pursue evangelism. The general association urged churches to give financial support to their pastors, thereby providing them more time to do religious work and preventing the migration of qualified men to other states where they could secure a livelihood. To provide a competent preaching ministry, the general association promised to offer educational opportunities to God-called preachers. It did not seek to appoint missionaries to destitute areas; rather, it recommended that district associations undertake such work, calling upon others only if necessary.

Antimission Baptists, whose opposition had been largely responsible for the dissolution of the Kentucky Baptist Convention, attacked the general association from its beginning. They argued that it was unscriptural to raise monies for religious purposes, that the theological education was a detriment to preachers, and that it was both unscriptural and unnecessary to preach the gospel to sinners who could not repent and believe without divine grace. While creating a condition which prevented the immediate acceptance of the general association, these arguments were not successful in forcing the dissolution of the general body. Antimissioners, along with the money panic of 1841, influenced a decline in mission contributions between 1838 and 1842. Failing to frustrate the cause of missions, antimissioners gradually separated. By 1842 the two groups were effectively disunited, and thereafter missionary Baptists far outstripped antimissioners. Largely responsible for missionary strength was perennial evangelism. "Protracted meetings" were inaugurated soon after the organization of the general association. In 1843 missionary Baptists reported 7,271 baptisms, whereas antimissioners reported only 476; in 1845 the baptisms of the two groups were 2,885 and 273, respectively. Revivalism was found almost exclusively among those churches which co-operated with the general association. Moreover, missionary Baptists supported many projects—missions, education, evangelism, Sunday schools, Bible distribution, etc. For almost a century the following process was repeated over and over: A few interested individuals formed a society through which to promote a worthy cause, and later the society turned over its work to the general association and dissolved itself. In this way the general association's objectives became more numerous, diverse, and comprehensive, while independent agencies decreased.

State missions was the primary concern of the general association, but it took several decades for the details of this to become clear. In 1850 the general association stated its aim: to secure representation from each district association in the state, to establish a Baptist church in each county seat, to sustain missionary labor in destitute areas, and to encourage the circulation of Baptist literature. To implement these, the general agent was authorized to visit each district association in order to secure co-operation, to survey needs over the state, to recommend competent men to serve as missionaries, to supervise colportage service, and to represent the general association as occasion demanded. In 1860 the constitution was altered to define the areas of service as state, domestic, Indian, and foreign missions and Bible circulation. In 1861 book colportage, supervision of Sunday schools, and the hearing of reports on colleges and theological seminaries were included within the general association's scope. In 1866 it undertook the support of literary and theological education and the collection and preservation of Kentucky Baptist history. The latter work resulted in J. H. Spencer's *A History of Kentucky Baptists* (1885), F. M. Masters' *A History of Baptists in Kentucky* (1953), and other publications of the Kentucky Baptist Historical Society. In 1886 the primary responsibilities were defined as state missions, Sunday schools, and colportage; indirect responsibility was the supervision of the Southern Baptist Convention's home and foreign mission interests.

The general association encountered difficulty in carrying out its aims. The fear of centralization was a persistent consequence of antimissionism; although less conspicuous at times, this fear has always been alive in Kentucky Baptist history. As the general association undertook direct action consistent with its aims, both churches and district associations became zealous of their independence and security. District associations seemingly held stronger fears, because they viewed the general association as a competitor. In 1850 the situation was improved when the general association adopted a policy requiring a missionary to be approved by a majority of churches in a district association before he was sent there to labor.

The progress made in the 1850's was arrested and retarded by the Civil War and some controversies. The former weakened Kentucky Baptists, even though they sustained less loss than most Southern Baptists; the latter, although favoring missions and benevolent efforts, opposed the associational or conventional expression of interdependence, preferring instead a strong emphasis on local church independence and societal interrelations. By the exercise of wise patience, the general association gradually overcame obstacles and unified Kentucky Baptists. In 1869 its aims were stated: (1) to encourage closer relations between the general association and district associations; (2) to secure co-operation between churches and the general association; (3) to use experienced men as evangelists throughout the state; (4) to support the feeble churches; and (5) to establish Baptist work in neglected areas, especially in the 22 counties in the mountainous area of eastern Kentucky. The first two aims indicate that the general association was still encountering opposition or indifference from churches and associations. In 1881 fewer than one third of over 1,000 churches contributed to the general association's work. To improve this situation, it was proposed that a common fund be set up: A statewide survey would determine needs, missionary boards in each district association would conduct work in its area, and 50 per cent of funds collected by the general association would go to the district association out of which they came. In 1882 it was reported that 30 district associations, representing two thirds of the Baptist population in the state, had approved the plan, which had helped to establish "hearty fellowship throughout the denomination." In 1883 foreign, home, state, and district missions were called four aspects of the same mission task. Before the century was over, however, district missions were virtually nonexistent; their projects had been taken over by the general association. In the second quarter of the 20th century, the general association and district associations undertook co-operative enterprises, but the general association was the senior partner.

The general association also found it difficult to assume the projects of various societies. In the early years, when general association leaders were also leaders in various societies, the problem was less difficult. Generally, societies were eager to transfer their causes to the general association, thereby strengthening them. General Agent W. W. Gardner reported in 1851 that so many agents were soliciting funds from only a few liberal churches that all causes were suffering; some churches were adopting measures to exclude all agents. To solve this problem, it was proposed by the general association that all fund-raising societies be dissolved and their interests be taken over by the general association; Kentucky and Foreign Bible Society and Kentucky Foreign Mission Society immediately complied. However, it was easier for the general association to take over new work than to start it. Seemingly, the society method was more effective in inaugurating new efforts, for only a few people normally possessed enough conviction and enthusiasm to introduce them. As the general association grew in size, it became less venturesome and more conservative; therefore, new works had to be launched through organizations, e.g., women's missionary, Sunday school, minister's aid, education, children's home, etc. These acted as auxiliaries to the general association, holding their meetings in connection with the annual meeting of the general association and making reports to the state organization. Nevertheless, they had an independent existence, electing their own officers, conducting their own solicitation, and disbursing their monies independently of church or association action.

Method of financial support.—Throughout its history the general association has been compelled to review its method of support. In 1852 the general association was constrained to encourage churches to adopt a systematic method of placing benevolent causes before the people. It recommended that a single cause be presented at least quarterly, with all causes receiving some attention during the year, and that collections should be taken periodically and sent annually to the general association. To prevent the neglect of any cause, in 1854 the general association began to appoint committees to report on each cause at the annual meeting. This policy worked well for the general association's projects, but independent interests were less easily controlled.

As the South was coming out of the depression of the Reconstruction era, Kentucky Baptists were forced to develop systematic support. This was made increasingly urgent by the multiplication of financial responsibilities, especially in regard to educational institutions. For example Kentucky Baptists were asked by the Southern Baptist Convention to raise $300,000 in the 1870's in order to effect the removal of the Southern Baptist Theological Seminary from South Carolina to Louisville. Solicitation for such projects affected contributions to missions. In 1877 the general association proposed that a unified collection system be started. Direct contact with churches and individuals had to be continued, however, for it was reported in 1878 that they would not voluntarily support benevolent causes without on-the-spot solicitation. In 1879 the general association asked each church and district association to cultivate stewardship in its bounds and to make annual contributions to state causes. At this time each cause solicited the churches in its own behalf; therefore, in 1884 the constitution was altered to place all collections under the executive board.

Kentucky Baptists inaugurated work on such an ambitious scale that it became necessary in the 1880's to establish a dependable means of support. Prior to this time churches supported local needs by an annual or periodic collection, subscription, or apportionment; they contributed to nonlocal causes by taking up special collections when solicitors came before them. In 1887 Secretary J. W. Warder recommended that churches support the general association with an annual subscription, collectible in envelopes and payable in weekly instalments; he stated his hope that weekly offerings would become the "universal habit of church life."

Solicitation and special offerings continued to plague the general association, however. In 1896 Warder discouraged special offerings and urged the different causes to depend on regular offerings through the general association. To increase donors and total revenue, a system of apportionment was proposed in 1905, with each district association being asked to undertake to raise annually an amount determined in counsel with other associations in the general association and adequate to meet the needs of all causes. In 1914 a "committee on unification" was appointed and instructed to recommend a plan to prevent the representation of all causes at district associations, which had encouraged competition on a popularity basis. In 1915 the "Budget Plan" was adopted; independent societies and agencies (such as Kentucky Baptist Education Society, Ministers' Aid Society, Louisville Orphanage, and Kentucky Baptist Children's Home) were requested to co-operate with the general association in this plan; there was to be a united solicitation, and funds were to be divided among 12 causes.

Between 1919 and 1924 Kentucky Baptists participated in the 75 Million Campaign of Southern Baptists, the Kentucky quota being $1,300,000 annually. Kentucky Baptists exceeded their goal the first year, but in the succeeding years revenue declined. Agencies and institutions had projected their programs on an enormous scale, anticipating funds from the campaign. They soon found themselves in debt, a condition aggravated by the economic depression in the mid-1920's and the great depression between 1929 and 1934. This condition weakened the "unified" plan, which had been in the process of development since 1851 and which reached its theoretical definition in 1915 in the Budget Plan. Educational institutions had rejected the unified system as early as the 1890's when, primarily due to legal technicalities, all schools except Bardstown Institute opposed denominational control. During the 1920's their economic status became extremely insecure, so they revived solicitation for themselves. In 1923 the increase of designated gifts threatened to frustrate the objectives of the unified system. Advocates of general association control attacked the independence of the schools; some went so far as to urge the suspension of funds to all schools which refused to transfer property title to the general association (1926), which taught evolution (1926), and which permitted Greek letter societies (1930). These positions were symptomatic, not real; when needs far outnumbered resources, it became necessary to differentiate between causes. In 1930, realizing that it was unable to support all schools but yet being reluctant to kill some by withholding funds and aiding others by subsidy, the general association gave permission to all schools to solicit for existence. Similar permission had been granted to the Kentucky Baptist Children's Home in 1928, when the fourth Sunday in May (later changed to the Thanksgiving season) was set aside for special offering for children's work.

These policies, while reversing the trend of unified support, were perhaps necessary in view of economic insecurity. Many phases of work were either drastically reduced or killed because of nonsupport. Efforts were made to retain in the state funds earmarked, through the Cooperative Program, for Southern Baptist Convention causes. For example in 1931, $12,000 was withdrawn from the 50–50 per cent division of funds between state and Southwide causes, in order to meet the pressing debt of the *Western Recorder*. The campaign of the Hundred Thousand Club, inaugurated in 1934, enabled Kentucky Baptists to meet the most urgent needs. Improved administrative control (through budgeting and bookkeeping) and economic health combined to place Kentucky Baptists in a solvent condition around 1940. The Kentucky Baptist Foundation was established in 1944 to hold in trust the funds belonging to various institutions, thereby removing the future temptation for institutions to convert endowments to the liquidation of debts. Since the late 1930's the unified system has been established as the means of support to various causes undertaken by the general association.

Organization.—The organizational character of the general association has undergone change just as the method of support has. Originally, it was weak organizationally, but a stronger central organization would probably have stimulated more bitter reaction. The functioning agency of the general association was originally called the Board of Managers (or Directors), renamed the General Executive Board in 1853 and later State Board of Missions. It was empowered to promote domestic and foreign missions, ministerial education, and pastoral maintenance and to serve as the general association's disbursing agency. Through the years new responsibilities have fallen upon the board; these have in turn been delegated to directors, secretaries, or superintendents. With numerical growth and changes in religious education, stewardship, and promotion, the board has entered areas of work such as Sunday school, B.Y.P.U. (1894), Laymen's Movement or Brotherhood (1907), hospital (1918–24), children's home (1915), city missions (at various times), student work (1938), etc.

The membership of the board has fluctuated according to the needs. Since 1866 membership has been increased as additional associations have been created and new work undertaken; however, the policy-making power, while still belonging to the board, has been exercised by an executive committee. The board's office has been variously located so as to be convenient to the general agent: in Louisville in 1839, in Georgetown in 1844, in Louisville in 1853, in Lexington in 1861, and in Louisville in 1866. The office of general agent has also undergone change. His functions from the beginning have included promotion, solicitation of funds, and supervision of work. Through the years the duties have been specified in greater detail, but he has been able to administer them through junior officers. Originally the general agent conducted other work, such as the pastoral ministry, along with his work for the general association, but he came under full-time salary as his responsibilities increased. The weakness of the office is evidenced by the fact that between 1837 and 1854, 10 different men served as general agent, and in two years there was none. In 1856 the general association appointed a general agent for each of the four major districts of the state (six districts were named in 1858). This system proved unsuccessful, however, so the plan was dropped in 1859. The corresponding secretary of the board exercised some of the duties of the general agent between 1859 and 1866; in 1866 the title became corresponding secretary, and later it was changed to general secretary and treasurer. The office was filled by annual election (re-election was common, however) until 1946, when an indefinite call was extended to William Cook Boone.

Each church is permitted one messenger to the general association, with additional messengers being permitted for each 200 members in excess of 100. In 1909 the constitution was interpreted to mean that only men might be messengers; however, the constitution was never altered to this effect. In 1956 the general association specifically granted to women the right to serve as messengers and to speak on the floor. The annual meeting of the general association was held in May or June until 1907, when the time was changed to November in order to separate the state meeting from the Southern Baptist Convention and thereby encourage more successful promotion of both causes.

Areas of service.—The central area of service has always been state missions, even though the greatest percentage of monies has not always been given to this. Missionaries have been sent to destitute and neglected areas. One of the early objectives was the establishment of a Baptist church in each county-seat town. After the Civil War cities became the object of mission work. After 1900 city mission work increased, and in time rural missions suffered. During World War I the general association took concerted action to serve the religious needs of soldiers in Camp Taylor, Louisville. In 1944 the general association underscored its dual responsibility by providing rural church and city mission programs.

The general association gradually entered Sunday school work. In 1843 it recommended schools to the churches. In 1857 it reported that schools were weak; not over one fourth of the churches had schools, and they were sparsely attended by children only. After the Civil War Sunday school work increased, being promoted by a Sunday school board. In 1876 greater co-operation between the general association and Sunday schools was urged. F. H. Kerfoot (q.v.) promoted the motto, "a Baptist church in every community and a well-organized Sunday school in every church." The Sunday school board, and a convention which was later organized, proved ineffectual, however. During the 1880's the general association assumed greater control, considering schools the best agency through which to teach Baptist views. In 1882 they were termed a "church act" which deserved support from all members, not only from children. The effect of Sunday schools upon growth and missions is indicated by the statistics of 1883: Churches with schools showed an increase of $8\frac{1}{4}$ per cent, whereas churches without schools increased only 6 per cent; the support of missions was 33 and $2\frac{1}{2}$ cents, respectively. During the 1890's Kentucky Baptists profited from the labors of the new Sunday School Board of the Southern Baptist Convention. Early in the 1910's, however, there was a setback in Sunday school work due to lack of leadership, but this was soon overcome. Since then Sunday schools have been the most effective agency of Kentucky Baptists in enlistment and stewardship.

In the 1910's summer assemblies appeared in various places, and the trend continued during the 1920's. Following the example of Southern Baptists, the general association established an assembly in 1950 at Cedarmore, a picturesque estate near Bagdad. Work among young people was begun in 1894, simultaneously with the inauguration of the program among Southern Baptists. Local churches organized local young people's societies; in 1894 the general association appointed a committee to promote the cause. In 1934 this movement became the Baptist Training Union. In 1938 the general association created the Baptist Student Union Department to conserve, train, and enlist Baptist students on college campuses.

Throughout most of its history the general association has had a helpful auxiliary in the women's missionary work. In 1857 it urged churches to form female missionary societies "for the purpose of raising funds by monthly contributions in aid of the General Association." Again in 1876 it recommended the formation of female societies, or at least the enlistment of "the sisters," to further state missions. In 1903 representatives of women's societies organized "The Woman's Missionary Association of Kentucky, auxiliary to the General Association of Baptists of Kentucky." Since that time the W.M.U. has sponsored work with boys, girls, and young women; while giving major support to foreign missions, it has also carried on community missions in needy areas. Work among men began in 1907 when interested laymen organized "The Executive Committee of the Laymen's Missionary Movement of Kentucky"; this later became the Brotherhood Department.

Negroes were originally members of churches affiliated with the general association. A few Negro churches were formed, by friendly separation, before the Civil War, but the great split occurred after the war. The general association took steps to aid the Negroes in evangelism and ministerial education, but after 1870 relations between Negro and white Baptists became strained. Consequently, the general association decided in 1875 to provide help when it was requested, but not to attempt the conversion of Negroes without specific invitation. Shortly after 1900 several training institutes were held among Negroes, sponsored by the general association. There has been little formal connection between Negro Baptists and the general association since the 1870's.

The efforts of the general association in the field of education have been extensive. Georgetown College, begun in 1829, became a concern of the new organization in 1837 and has remained so ever since. In 1855 Bethel College grew out of the high school of Russellville. Female schools sprang up under local auspices in the 1850's, but the general association heartily endorsed them. In 1855 there were nine female schools, but in 1868, because of the Civil War, the number had declined to seven. During the 1870's Kentucky Baptists enlarged their efforts in education, a trend which continued for 30 years or more. In 1895 the general association requested schools and colleges to permit the state body to appoint trustees, using the relationship of the Southern Baptist Convention to the Southern Baptist Theological Seminary as a model. This precipitated a controversy, which lasted for half a century, in which the growing desire for denominational control met with increasing zealousness for autonomy by the schools. In 1898 the Baptist Educational Committee was created to make annual reports, and in 1906 the Baptist Education Society was organized to foster closer relations between educational institutions and the churches. In 1901 the Department of State Institute Work was established to provide training in doctrines, missions, education, promotion, and co-operation. In the 1920's other institutes were founded; in 1946 one of these, Clear Creek Mountain Preacher's School, became the property of the general association. During the 1920's Baptist schools enlarged rapidly and unwisely. When revenue did not come from the 75 Million Campaign, they found themselves in debt. For the next 20 years schools struggled for existence, and many succumbed. After World War II Kentucky Baptists supported only a few schools: Georgetown, Bethel, Campbellsville, Cumberland, and Clear Creek.

The general association's benevolent work has been restricted to children's homes and hospitals. In 1869 women of Walnut Street Church, Louisville, established an orphanage, later known as Louisville Baptist Orphans' Home and still later as Spring Meadows. In 1872 the general association began to hear reports on its work, and in 1891–92 Kentucky Baptists matched a large donation by the Norton family of Louisville. In 1915 the Kentucky Baptist Children's Home was established at Glendale, in property formerly belonging to the defunct Lynnland College. In 1955 Pine Crest was established near Morehead.

Although the general association did not own a paper until 1919, from its beginning it endorsed numerous papers and received from them support for mission causes. Early endorsements included *Baptist Banner* (later *Western Recorder*) (1838), *Western Baptist Review, Southern Journal* (1846), the mission journal of Southern Baptist Convention (1847), Ford's *Christian Repository* (1853), and *Baptist Sentinel* and *Prophetic Key* (1871). From the 1850's onward, the *Western Recorder* received most support from the general association. However, the state body strongly supported the *Baptist Argus*, begun in 1897 to defend W. H. Whitsitt (q.v.) and to serve as an organ of all departments of state work and enterprises of the Southern Baptist Convention. In 1908, following the organization of the Baptist World Alliance in 1905, the paper's name was changed to *Baptist World*. Realizing the need of an organ through which to promote the 75 Million Campaign, the general association purchased the *Western Recorder* in 1919, even though it was also offered the facilities of the *Baptist World*. Mismanagement and depression placed the *Western Recorder* in debt around 1930, but the debt was paid off by the general association. The *Western Recorder* presently serves as the official organ of Kentucky Baptists.

Special interests.—During its history the general association has been involved in various controversies. In 1847 the ministers' meeting, convening in connection with the general association, dissociated a minister, Gilbert Mason, for conduct unbecoming a minister. Gospel Missionism, with its plan for local church support of missions, plagued western Kentucky from the late 1880's until the early 1920's. In 1897–98 the Whitsitt controversy received special attention; Kentucky Baptists expressed a desire to support a new seminary if Whitsitt remained at the Louisville seminary. In 1907 alien immersion was opposed, but the mid-20th century has not witnessed a public controversy on the issue. During the 1920's the general association sympathetically heard frequent messages, reports, and resolutions condemning "modernism" and Darwinism. Between 1934 and 1941 nothing agitated the general association more than the refusal of Georgetown College trustees to fire President Henry Noble Sherwood, whose baptism was reportedly Campbellite. Harmony was not restored until he resigned. The general association has frequently approved resolutions dealing with social and legal problems, especially alcoholic beverages and gambling. The first petition against spirituous liquors was made in 1839, and the subject has since been a perennial problem. In 1940 the general association opposed the public subsidy of transportation for students attending religious and private schools; it also opposed President Roosevelt's appointment of a personal representative to the Vatican; these actions were made in defense of the principle of separation of church and state. Kentucky Baptists have since been alert to this problem, adopting several resolutions in support of separation.

Denominational affiliation.—The general association affiliated with the Southern Baptist Convention in 1845 and has maintained this relationship ever since. Prior to 1845 missionary Baptists in Kentucky were affiliated with the Triennial Convention (foreign missions) and the American Baptist Home Mission Society. In 1845 they united with the Southern Baptist Convention on the same terms which bound them to the Home Mission Society. The China Mission Society transferred to the Southern Baptist Convention the Roberts Fund, which had been established in 1836 to support the independent work of I. J. Roberts in China; when Roberts became an early appointee of the Convention, the fund was transferred. In 1848 the Kentucky Foreign Mission Society amended its constitution, making it an auxiliary to the Southern Baptist Convention. During the Civil War Kentucky Baptists helped to sustain the Convention's foreign missionaries whose means of communication was broken; inasmuch as Kentucky, Maryland, and Missouri Baptists possessed both resources and an avenue of communication with the North, they provided most of the support of the South's missionaries. In the 1850's Kentucky Baptists were enthusiastic supporters of a theological seminary, due in large measure to the defection of the Western Baptist Theological Institute to abolition views. The Southern Baptist Theological Seminary found a friend in the general association, a friendship which was vindicated after the Civil War when economic conditions forced the seminary to find a new home (in Louisville in 1877). The general association has spontaneously co-operated with the programs of the Southern Baptist Convention: Sunday School Board (established in 1891), 75 Million Campaign (1919), Cooperative Program (begun in 1925), Hundred Thousand Club (1934), etc. The areas of its work in most cases are the same as those of the Convention, although the Convention provides some services which the states cannot duplicate.

WENDELL H. RONE and HUGH WAMBLE

III. Program of Work of Kentucky Baptists.
The executive board.—The executive board of the General Association of Baptists in Kentucky is elected by, and subject to the control of, the general association. It is incorporated under the laws of the state of Kentucky, whereby it can buy, sell, and mortgage its property, sue and be sued, borrow funds, etc., in keeping with the actions of the general association. Members of the executive board are selected in the following way: Each co-operating district association annually makes two nominations for each place to be filled on the executive board, and the nominating committee of the general association selects one to serve for three years. Each association is allowed one member for the first 5,000 church members and one additional member for each additional 5,000. In case of death or removal, the general association by the same method elects members to fill out the unexpired term. No board member is eligible for re-election until one year has passed since the end of his term, except one elected to serve the unexpired term of another member.

The executive board meets annually on Tuesday after the first Sunday of December. Committees, which are divided according to the departments of work, meet to study the program of work for the ensuing year and then make specific recommendations for adoption by the entire group. The board is subject to call at any other time, upon approval of such a call by the executive committee, or its chairman, and the general secretary, for action on matters of major importance. Thirty members of the entire board constitute a quorum. The executive board has charge of the work of the general association during the intervals between annual sessions. It is granted the authority to appoint all officers and agencies that may be required to prosecute the work, limited only by the funds available and the exercise of sound discretion. The board makes a detailed annual report and recommends proposals of future work and policies to be followed. These recommendations are published in the *Western Recorder* at least 30 days before the annual meeting of the general association, according to the requirement of the constitution. This report includes the preparation of an annual budget by a subcommittee, its approval by the executive committee, and final approval by the general association.

The executive board elects its own chairman, vice-chairman, and secretary at each annual session. The chairman, with the help of the general secretary, appoints the various committees on departments of work, with their chairmen, and presides over the meetings. The moderator of the general association is an ex officio member of the executive board and also of its executive committee. The committees of the board in 1956 were appropriations, audit, Cedarmore Assembly, music conference, missions, department work, benevolence, promotion, and evangelism. The executive board, through appointment by the chairman, has an executive committee composed of 15 members. This committee meets several times each year through the call of the chairman, who is also chairman of the executive board. It has full authority to act for the executive board in the interim between meetings; it makes appropriations, fills vacancies, and carries on the work of the denomination in the state. In important matters, such as electing a department head, buying and selling property, etc., it is customary to poll the entire executive board by mail or call for a special meeting. Expenses for travel and lodging are provided in the state mission budget for the executive board, its executive committee, and any special committees working in its interest.

Since 1946, when William Cook Boone became the general secretary-treasurer, that officer has been elected for an indefinite period, dependent upon mutual satisfaction to both parties. This policy also applies to all department heads. The general secretary-treasurer is responsible for the administration and promotion of the work of the general association. At the annual meeting of the general association, he makes the report of the executive board, including the proposed new budget and other items of policy and promotion. The executive board has several departments under its supervision, with a secretary directing the promotion of each one. These departments are charged with the duties of promotion, teaching, training, enlargement, and direct missionary work; they are directly responsible to the executive board, making reports through the board to the general association. Departments are direct state missions, Cedarmore Assembly, Sunday school, Training Union, Brotherhood, church music, Baptist Student Union, and missionary and stewardship training. In addition to these departments, there are three groups of institutions which have their own executive secretary, but which are considered a part of, and are responsible to, the executive board. These are the Department of Christian Education, the Kentucky Baptist Board of Child Care, and the Kentucky Baptist Hospital Commission.

The Woman's Missionary Union of Kentucky is an auxiliary of the general association. It works harmoniously with the state organization, and makes annual reports to the general association, but it elects its own officers and employs its own personnel. The state missionary body follows the pattern of organization and work advocated by the Convention-wide auxiliary. In 1955 there were 1,205 women's societies with 40,123 members and 3,346 youth organizations. Regional and associational organizations are also maintained, together with several weeks of camps and conferences at Cedarmore Assembly each year. Mrs. George R.

Ferguson has been executive secretary of this department since 1949.

Missions.—The state mission program among Kentucky Baptists includes the subsidizing of, or outright provision for, associational and local missionaries; a rural church program; mountain missions; a city mission program; administering aid in a church building fund; schools of missions and stewardship; promotion of the state assembly at Cedarmore; regional meetings on stewardship and evangelism; the provision of student centers adjacent to college campuses in Kentucky; and the maintenance of good press relations and audio-visual aids for promotion. The state mission program has as its aim the placing of a state missionary in every association to evangelize, enlist, and train people and to seek the active and organizational support of all associations behind the work of the denomination. Out of 81 associations 69 had such missionaries in 1955. According to area and arrangement with the local association, the state mission program pays all or part of the salary and expenses of these missionaries. Eldred M. Taylor, associate to the general secretary, directs this work and also serves as the state secretary of evangelism. His office promotes the annual evangelistic conference, held in January each year in Louisville, at the Walnut Street Baptist Church, with all state missionaries participating in this and other conferences to promote the evangelistic program of the state. The state program has been aligned with the evangelistic program of the Southern Baptist Convention, through its Home Mission Board, since its beginning. In needy and pioneer areas the state board provides in whole or in part for the expenses and salaries of local church missionaries. Such assistance is maintained until the work becomes self-sustaining. Three regional missionaries, located in the western, central, and eastern areas of the state, promote the over-all work of the denomination in co-operation with the state and associational missionaries and the churches in the respective regions. In co-operation with the Home Mission Board of the Southern Baptist Convention, city mission programs are maintained in Louisville, the Covington-Newport area, and the Henderson, Ky.-Evansville, Ind., area. Probably most of the work in state missions in Kentucky is concentrated under the mountain mission program in the vast region of the mountains of eastern Kentucky. The eastern regional state missionary supervises this program. One of the most fruitful mission endeavors is the encouragement of churches in establishing outlying mission and preaching stations, many of which are growing rapidly and becoming churches.

The entire state mission force promotes the program of the Southern Baptist Convention and urges the churches to promote, financially support, and educate their memberships concerning all denominational enterprises. Kentucky has increased her gifts to the Cooperative Program from $775,529 in 1945 to $1,825,487 in 1955. Cedarmore Baptist Assembly, Bagdad, is a rapidly developing project of Kentucky Baptists. This assembly provides opportunities for young people and others in inspiration, recreation, and dedication to Christian service. The state W.M.U. and its auxiliaries use the grounds during the major part of the summer; however, all departments of state work are represented, with nearly 6,000 persons using the assembly's facilities in 1955. Enlarging, developing, and repaying the loan on the property engage the attention of Kentucky Baptists. Marvin M. Byrdwell is the superintendent.

Educational ministry.—The Sunday School Department has four regular workers engaged in associational promotion work, secretarial work, Vacation Bible schools, clinics, training schools, enlargement campaigns, conferences, conventions, and other types of work. In 1955 a total of 413,820 were enrolled in Kentucky Baptist Sunday schools, and a total of 40,935 awards were given in training schools. Standard Sunday schools numbered 137. That same year 1,701 Vacation Bible schools were conducted, with 2,405 professions of faith being made. Regional conferences are held annually in the eight regions of the state, and one week is given to the promotion of Sunday school work at Cedarmore Assembly each year. Roy E. Boatwright has been secretary since 1953.

The Training Union Department has six workers who do promotional work, conduct training schools and enlargement campaigns, hold regional conferences in the eight regions each March, promote "M" Night in associations in December, hold a state convention each April, and sponsor Junior, Young People's, and Intermediate drills and events. They also promote Youth Week, Youth Night, elementary workshops, associational work, and fall planning meetings in the associations, and conduct two weeks of Training Union emphasis at Cedarmore annually. In 1955, 96,139 were enrolled in Kentucky Baptist Training Unions, and 25,302 study course awards were given to 631 churches in 81 associations. James Whaley has been secretary since 1953.

The Brotherhood Department is one of the newest full-time departments in Kentucky Baptist life. The department majors on the enlistment of men in evangelism and missions. He supervises the work of the Royal Ambassadors and annually sponsors a tour of all Kentucky Baptist colleges, children's homes, and hospitals and a rally at Cedarmore Assembly. In 1955 there were reported 423 local Baptist Brotherhoods, with approximately 13,500 members. Lucien E. Coleman, Sr., has been secretary since Dec. 1, 1953.

A Department of Church Music, with Eugene F. Quinn as secretary, was set up by the executive committee, on instruction from the executive board in Aug., 1956.

Institutions.—The Department of Christian Education is responsible for all educational institutions operated by Kentucky Baptists. It has a separate board of trustees consisting of the presidents of all Baptist schools in the state, chairmen of the boards of trustees of the four colleges, and 12 additional members elected by the general association. Kentucky Baptists have one senior college, Georgetown, with H. Leo Eddleman as president. It has an investment in buildings and endowment of $2,600,000, an enrolment of 1,236, with 150 ministerial students, and 56 on its faculty and administrative staff. There are 35,000 volumes in the library. Cumberland College, Williamsburg, with J. M. Boswell as president, has an endowment and buildings investment of $2,085,694, an enrolment of 652, with 19 ministerial students, 28 on its faculty and administrative staff, and 12,000 volumes in the library. Campbellsville College, with John M. Carter as president, has an endowment and buildings investment of $1,074,076, an enrolment of 373, with 28 ministerial students, 25 on its faculty and administrative staff, and 9,000 volumes in the library. Bethel College, Hopkinsville, with W. E. Richardson as president, has an endowment and buildings investment of $446,742, an enrolment of 218, with 37 ministerial students, 18 on its faculty and administrative staff, and 10,276 volumes in the library. Clear Creek Mountain Preachers' Bible School, Pineville, with D. M. Aldridge as president, is primarily a school for underprivileged mountain preachers. It has an endowment and property valued at $455,527, an enrolment of 102, with 8 on its faculty and administrative staff, 70 ministerial students, and 5,100 volumes in the library. Magoffin Institute, Mountain Valley, Ky., and Oneida Institute are boarding schools for underprivileged mountain children in eastern Kentucky. These offer both elementary and high school courses. All Kentucky Baptist educational institutions have their own boards of trustees, elected by the general association. In 1955 Kentucky Baptist schools and colleges reported a total enrolment of 2,189 students, exclusive of part-time students.

The Baptist Student Union Department, with Chester Durham serving as the secretary since 1943, promotes annually a state convention in November, a spring retreat at Cedarmore, a fall training meeting, focus weeks, and the regular campus programs of work. Baptist student centers on, or adjacent to, the campuses of the larger colleges in Kentucky, are being built by the general association, in co-operation with local churches in these communities. Centers have been completed at Murray State College, the University of Kentucky at Lexington, the University of Louisville, Berea College, and Western Kentucky State College at Bowling Green. Centers are contemplated at Eastern Kentucky State College at Richmond and at Morehead State College. At present full-time B.S.U. directors are employed on eight college campuses and a part-time director on one other campus.

Kentucky Baptists support three children's homes: Spring Meadows, Middletown, with Sam Ed Bradley as superintendent; Glendale, with C. Ford Duesner as superintendent; and Pine Crest, Morehead, with Sam Ed Bradley as superintendent. In 1955 a total of 255 children were cared for by Glendale and 256 at Spring Meadows. Pine Crest, which has just been completed, will care for 50 children when filled. For several years a special offering has been taken to go toward the support and enlargement of these homes. The Kentucky Baptist Board of Child Care, composed of 24 members elected by the general association, operates all homes for the Baptists of Kentucky. The homes have an endowment of $669,765.

The hospital ministry of Kentucky Baptists includes Western Baptist Hospital at Paducah, Central Baptist Hospital at Lexington, and Kentucky Baptist Hospital at Louisville. They had 117, 173, and 285 beds respectively, a total property evaluation of $6,992,734, and an indebtedness of $2,837,477 in 1955. Each hospital has its own board of trustees, elected by the general association. There is also a Kentucky Baptist Hospital Commission composed of eight trustees of Kentucky Hospital, two trustees of Central Hospital, and two trustees of Western Hospital. H. L. Dobbs is executive secretary of the commission, general administrator of the three hospitals, and also administrator of the Kentucky Baptist Hospital. Homer D. Coggins is administrator of Central Hospital, and Emmett R. Johnson serves in the same capacity at Western Hospital. The hospitals served over 28,500 patients in 1955, and a total of 4,943 babies were born in them during that year. Almost $150,000 was expended on charity patients, and 143 nurses were in training in 1955.

The general association co-operates in all the plans of the Relief and Annuity Board of the Southern Baptist Convention, and about 630 ministers and 1,100 churches participate in the plans.

Promotional work.—The *Western Recorder*, the Kentucky Baptist official organ of promotion, is owned by the general association and operated through a board of managers consisting of nine persons elected by the general association. R. T. Skinner was editor in 1956, and Robert L. Pogue, business manager. Its weekly circulation in 1956 was approximately 58,000. All departments of state and Convention-wide work are regularly promoted by the paper. For this service the general association appropriates about $10,000 annually as a preferred item from the Cooperative Program. The director of press relations and audio-visual aids is Gainer E. Bryan, Jr., and through this new department the work of promotion is carried on. Excellent press relations are constantly maintained with secular papers in the commonwealth. W. H. Curl is the director of missionary and stewardship training and is responsible for the promotion of schools of missions, stewardship revivals, and church and denominational night programs. All departments constantly promote by mail their respective phases of denomina-

IV. KENTUCKY STATISTICAL SUMMARY

Year	Associations	Churches	Church Membership	Baptisms	S. S. Enrolment	V.B.S. Enrolment	T. U. Enrolment	W.M.U. Enrolment	Brotherhood Enrolment	Mission Gifts	Total Gifts	Value Church Property	State Capital Worth
182–	25	491	31,639	....	....	....	....	....	....	....	....	....	$ 6,000. (Explanation:
1830	35	574	39,957	831	....	....	....	....	....	....	....	....	26,000. tion:
1840	50	711	49,308	6,251	....	....	....	....	....	....	....	....	133,000. This column
1850	43	757	65,489	3,835	....	....	....	....	....	....	....	....	285,000. includes
1860	44	880	84,403	5,136	....	....	....	....	....	....	....	....	383,000. total value
1870	46	1,023	87,127	....	....	....	....	....	....	$ 6,426.82	....	....	512,000. of Schools,
1880	57	1,246	108,860	4,496	20,536	....	....	....	....	18,084.46	....	....	625,000. Children's
1890	61	1,441	143,288	9,267	41,113	....	....	....	....	14,092.84	....	....	624,000. Homes, Hos-
1900	67	1,615	183,181	9,096	53,589	....	....	....	....	26,585.77	309,900.02	$ 996,248.00	965,000. pitals,
1905	75	1,635	202,801	9,769	64,101	....	....	....	....	47,846.72	385,261.42	2,112,150.00	990,000. Foundation,
1910	75	1,774	224,239	13,511	93,058	....	....	....	....	106,558.78	491,528.77	....	1,604,000. Buildings,
1915	76	1,851	252,562	14,414	126,837	....	....	....	....	114,586.76	693,986.30	3,293,017.00	1,447,000. etc.)
1920	76	1,877	258,663	12,981	141,879	1,328	23,995	....	....	142,118.21	1,127,015.16	5,011,483.00	2,332,216.
1925	80	2,020	298,040	16,202	217,316	4,811	18,536	....	....	1,175,142.22	2,676,509.06	7,253,169.00	3,702,400.
1930	81	1,939	354,077	12,757	174,393	....	20,119	36,180	....	534,465.22	2,339,332.38	10,784,480.00	4,332,278.
1931	81	1,935	314,941	13,268	188,561	9,291	20,679	37,030	....	531,081.94	2,753,033.68	17,014,326.00	3,567,698.
1932	79	1,942	319,866	14,959	191,890	9,567	24,924	39,886	....	404,256.40	2,241,508.34	15,178,313.00	3,904,776.
1933	79	1,963	327,746	15,963	208,794	10,093	23,941	49,886	....	347,416.28	1,936,513.81	15,380,529.00	3,455,341.
1934	79	1,971	339,890	14,151	204,959	15,162	23,807	40,954	....	279,266.29	1,629,947.72	17,225,629.00	3,577,093.
1935	80	1,901	344,474	15,171	219,925	19,782	22,011	43,243	....	309,415.64	1,686,170.08	15,167,995.00	3,629,731.
1936	80	2,043	351,555	12,714	188,863	24,804	23,281	44,539	....	332,306.22	1,968,895.37	15,927,636.00	3,843,181.
1937	79	1,983	358,067	13,712	207,254	43,383	26,285	47,020	....	343,392.31	1,910,565.83	14,923,023.00	3,501,569.
1938	79	2,018	369,232	16,807	218,392	49,318	28,615	41,738	....	375,235.44	1,282,562.92	15,608,348.00	3,578,748.
1939	80	2,013	383,629	17,838	223,226	60,456	30,684	48,292	....	402,129.73	2,396,525.73	15,472,822.38	3,789,103.
1940	79	2,062	402,383	17,672	252,562	62,068	32,185	48,793	....	405,858.33	2,360,418.04	15,975,061.73	3,845,290.
1941	79	2,002	388,377	16,327	253,266	58,462	30,138	54,289	4,000	450,136.08	2,464,654.28	15,074,321.00	3,848,438.
1942	79	2,023	417,761	14,817	230,620	19,077	27,845	48,843	839	586,739.15	2,943,958.92	16,424,273.28	3,853,438.
1943	79	2,068	420,806	13,778	232,752	30,060	29,945	49,016	1,207	820,103.54	3,671,373.28	17,134,358.26	3,171,901.
1944	79	2,130	426,194	15,424	234,559	53,189	35,309	41,711	1,429	944,085.43	4,060,591.96	16,991,539.56	4,856,956.
1945	79	2,149	437,160	17,463	240,238	72,866	39,902	43,236	3,142	1,298,509.04	5,132,084.29	18,252,112.90	4,998,008.
1946	80	2,168	458,572	17,428	256,003	86,696	44,770	42,500	4,451	1,753,823.42	7,536,320.15	17,691,425.08	4,997,392.
1947	80	2,165	473,701	19,715	279,186	102,509	52,281	45,173	5,222	2,284,322.16	7,648,514.95	27,042,574.52	5,705,490.
1948	79	2,254	496,580	22,907	307,886	76,212	43,163	51,898	6,361	2,128,895.24	8,618,887.88	23,360,707.52	6,802,022.
1949	78	2,228	507,990	24,874	226,760	121,758	71,660	55,977	7,032	2,222,899.00	10,196,245.00	29,975,974.00	7,620,944.
1950	79	2,243	527,362	28,183	353,235	126,411	78,447	58,834	8,016	2,142,767.00	11,630,236.00	34,500,107.00	8,498,539.
1951	80	2,277	550,403	26,663	368,523	131,305	80,913	61,775	7,213	2,254,233.00	11,776,250.00	39,021,147.00	9,917,963.
1952	80	2,295	559,653	23,214	396,660	144,418	87,178	63,681	8,780	2,438,768.00	3,291,385.00	44,963,179.00	10,054,224.
1953	80	2,332	571,472	23,296	387,219	175,717	102,139	62,506	10,689	3,024,495.00	15,044,717.00	52,678,991.00	11,262,224.
1954	80	2,253	579,683	24,668	422,680	175,717	102,139	67,859	10,689	3,043,450.00	16,928,395.00	64,854,238.00	11,510,680.

tional work. Through its tract ministry the state executive board reaches an ever-enlarging number of churches and individuals.

A major project to be completed in 1957 by Kentucky Baptists is their new state Baptist Building, being erected on a five-acre plot adjacent to the Spring Meadows Children's Home, at Middletown, about 10 miles from Louisville. The new two-story brick building, fully air-conditioned, will provide for all departments of state work and for the *Western Recorder*. Estimated cost is slightly in excess of $400,000, to be provided through sale of the present headquarters building and a loan to be repaid in 20 years. Adequate parking space will allow large groups, such as the executive board, to meet there. The plan also allows for future expansion to meet the needs of the Baptists of the state.

The Kentucky Baptist Foundation, with a board of directors composed of nine members elected by, and responsible to the general association, cares for and invests the funds received by the various participating agencies. The foundation passed the million dollar mark in assets in 1955. A. M. Vollmer has been the executive secretary-treasurer of the foundation since its incorporation in 1945; he also promotes the Cooperative Program in the state. Kentucky Baptists do not have a department on radio and television, but annual reports are made on the Southern Baptist Convention agency, and many Kentucky radio stations carry the "Baptist Hour" regularly. A number of associations and churches have individual radio programs, and an effective ministry is maintained through this medium. The Kentucky Baptist Historical Society, with Leo T. Crismon as president, and George R. Jewell as secretary-treasurer, reports regularly to the general association. Recently this society promoted the printing and sale of F. M. Masters' *History of Baptists in Kentucky*, with the financial help of the general association. Only a few Baptists keep up their annual dues and hold membership in this organization. Its archives are in the library of the Southern Baptist Theological Seminary in Louisville.

Co-operative work.—Annual reports are made to the general association, and to most of the district associations, concerning the work of the American Bible Society. By arrangement with the Temperance League of Kentucky, the general association elects a total of 15 Baptists to serve on its board of trustees for terms of three years each, with the terms of five expiring each each year.

BIBLIOGRAPHY: L. T. Crismon, *The Boone Family and Kentucky Baptists* (1946). F. M. Masters, *A History of Baptists in Kentucky* (1937). W. D. Nowlin, *Kentucky Baptist History, 1770–1922* (1922). W. W. Sweet, *Religion on the Frontier* (1931). J. Taylor, *The History of Ten Baptist Churches* (1823).

WENDELL H. RONE

KENTUCKY AND FOREIGN BIBLE SOCIETY. Organized in Lexington, Ky., May 3, 1839. In spite of antisociety sentiments, fostered by antimissioners and Alexander Campbell, several Bible societies, auxiliary to the American Bible Society, had been formed in Kentucky prior to 1836 when Baptists formed the American and Foreign Bible Society in protest against the American society's refusal to publish Judson's Burmese version in which "baptize" was translated by a word meaning immerse. When the break came, these Kentucky Baptist societies affiliated with the American and Foreign Bible Society. In 1838 they urged the formation of a Kentucky society, and in Oct., 1839, delegates from seven associational or local societies (Shelby County, Goshen, Green River, Gasper River, Bowling Green, Georgetown, and Second Baptist Church of Louisville) elected John Lightfoot Waller (*q.v.*) as president and A. D. Sears as corresponding secretary; the society was located in Louisville, but in 1849 it was removed to Lexington. During the 1840's the Bible cause became the most strongly supported benevolent project among Kentucky Baptists, sometimes receiving five times as much money as foreign missions. Records are not uniform, but it appears that almost $14,000 was sent to the American and Foreign Bible Society between 1839 and 1851. The Bible interest was so intense that the Kentucky society continued as an auxiliary to the national society, in spite of agitation for a division on a "North-South" basis. In response to a request for a pure English version, the American and Foreign Bible Society affirmed in 1850 that it would distribute only "the commonly received version (King James), without note or comment." Revisionists immediately withdrew and formed the American Bible Union, which received increasing support from Kentucky Baptists. In 1851, upon a request from the general association to all co-operating but independent societies, the Kentucky and Foreign Bible Society was disbanded and its funds were transferred to the general association.

HUGH WAMBLE

KENTUCKY ASSOCIATIONS.

I. Extant Associations. ALLEN. Constituted in 1841 of Bethel and Trammels Fork churches of Allen County and Rocky Spring Church in Warren County, first called Drake's Creek Association of United Baptists. In 1845 the name was changed to Bays Fork and in 1913 to Allen Baptist Association. In 1954, 28 churches reported 78 baptisms, 4,482 members, $40,140 total gifts, $5,872 mission gifts, and $130,150 property value.

BAPTIST. Constituted of messengers from four churches which broke off from Elkhorn Association, organized at Glen's Creek meetinghouse, Woodford County, in Oct., 1826. Adopting the Philadelphia Confession of Faith, the messengers considered the preamble unbaptistic since they regarded themselves as the Authorized Delegates of the Baptist Churches of Jesus Christ. The association was soon established firmly on Baptist grounds, however, and in

1852 became an auxiliary to the Kentucky general association. In 1954, 17 churches reported 200 baptisms, 4,871 members, $126,812 total gifts, $16,116 mission gifts, and $566,000 property value.

BELL COUNTY. Constituted at Walnut Grove Baptist Church in Bell County in Sept., 1896, with 11 churches from North Concord Association. Designated by the name East Concord until the 1907 session, its name was then changed to the Bell County Association of Baptists. In 1954, 81 churches reported 511 baptisms, 13,635 members, $254,287 total gifts, $25,847 mission gifts, and $956,650 property value.

BETHEL. Constituted Oct. 29, 1825, at Mt. Gilead Church, Allensville, Todd County, as a result of a division in Red River Association. The constitution, abstracts of faith, and rules of order of Red River Association were adopted. Missionary work was established in 1839; and in less than 30 years after its origin, the association founded two colleges, Bethel at Russellville and Bethel Female College at Hopkinsville. Progress numerically during the first 35 years of its existence was greater than that of any other association in the state. In 1954, 21 churches reported 225 baptisms, 5,644 members, $171,789 total gifts, $42,446 mission gifts, and $643,650 property value.

BLACKFORD. Located principally in Hancock County, organized in Bethlehem Church Nov. 30, 1877, with 14 churches dismissed from Goshen Association for that purpose. In 1954, 20 churches reported 140 baptisms, 3,196 members, $75,516 total gifts, $16,418 mission gifts, $163,500 property value, and (1953) $4,950 church debt.

BLOOD RIVER. Formed Oct. 28, 1870, at Johnathan's Creek Church, later known as Elm Grove, with 11 churches dismissed from West Union, Little River, and Western District associations. In 1954, 43 churches reported 508 baptisms, 10,090 members, $386,709 total gifts, $76,306 mission gifts, $1,160,037 property value, and (1952) $963,500 church debt.

BOONE'S CREEK. Constituted at the Mt. Gilead meetinghouse in Fayette County, May 28, 1823, with messengers from four churches dismissed from Elkhorn and Tate's Creek associations. At their meeting in 1828, messengers reported 13 churches with 1,835 members, 869 of which had been received by baptism that year as a result of the teaching of Alexander Campbell. Separation between Baptists and Campbellites began in 1830, and by 1836 the body was reduced to seven churches with only 412 members. The association then became a missionary organization and began to grow; in 1840 division developed concerning missions, causing a temporary setback, but the association began to increase again within three years. In 1954, 31 churches reported 199 baptisms, 6,831 members, $173,467 total gifts, $21,710 mission gifts, and $600,235 property value.

BOONEVILLE. Located in the mountains of eastern Kentucky, constituted by 16 churches from Irvine Association of United Regular Baptists in Sept., 1871, at Beattyville, county seat of Lee County. Crisis developed in 1904–07 over the heresy of "hardshellism," but through the leadership of Hughes Bowling, moderator of the association for 17 years, the churches remained missionary. The association's territory has extended into Clay, Owsley, Lee, Jackson, Knott, Perry, and Wolf counties. In 1954, 21 churches reported 184 baptisms, 4,088 members, $41,616 total gifts, $6,097 mission gifts, $374,800 property value, and (1951) $2,500 church debt.

BRACKEN. The fifth constituted in Kentucky, organized by messengers from eight churches with 539 members at the Bracken meetinghouse in Mason County, May 28, 1799. Five of the eight churches had been dismissed from Elkhorn to form a new association. Beginning about 1805 there was continued agitation over slavery, resulting in the loss of several churches to the emancipation movement, and by 1812 the situation was so discouraging that the propriety of dissolving the association was discussed. Walter Warder became pastor of some of the churches, and by 1821 the number of churches had increased to 17 with 1,522 members. Following this growth Alexander Campbell's appearance, resulting in the separation of his disciples, left 16 churches with only 890 members. The association grew rapidly after this until the Civil War. In 1954, 26 churches reported 152 baptisms, 3,536 members, $112,858 total gifts, $14,260 mission gifts, $574,600 property value, and $10,504 church debt.

BRECKENRIDGE. Constituted at Clover Creek Church Nov. 27, 1903, by 11 churches from Goshen and Salem associations. In 1954, 17 churches reported 106 baptisms, 3,140 members, $82,437 total gifts, $12,103 mission gifts, $230,200 property value.

CALDWELL COUNTY. Organized Sept. 24, 1924, by 17 churches formerly in Little River Association. In 1954, 30 churches reported 414 baptisms, 7,212 members, $217,535 total gifts, $44,500 mission gifts, $757,100 property value, and $56,728 church debt.

CAMPBELL COUNTY. Constituted at Brush Creek Church Sept. 21, 1827, with eight churches from North Bend Association. Discord and dissension which prevailed in the body from its beginning were caused by the Alexander Campbell division, and soon after this, by the antimission minority in the churches. After these forces split off, conditions improved. In 1848 the association recommended Georgetown College and Western Baptist Theological Institute at Covington. In 1954, 20 churches reported 311 baptisms, 6,969 members, $279,745 total gifts, $48,138 mission gifts, $1,126,500 property value, and $210,225 church debt.

LEO T. CRISMON

CASEY COUNTY. Organized in 1845 under the leadership of a preacher named Jesse C. Portman. The organization was called the South Kentucky Association for the first 110 years of its existence—from 1845 to 1955. It was made up of churches which came from Garrard, Lincoln, and Casey counties. Portman started preaching when Campbellism was experiencing rapid growth in that section. He fought this movement and discouraged many Baptist churches from joining with Campbell. From this association came the missionary to the Indians, H. F. Buckner (q.v.), whose descendants have become famous for their labors in orphanage work in Texas. In 1954, 11 churches reported 71 baptisms, 1,966 members, $30,127 total gifts, $2,840 mission gifts, $111,100 property value, and $1,900 church debt.

GEORGE RALEIGH JEWELL

CENTRAL. Constituted at the Bethlehem Church in Washington County Oct. 22, 1889, of churches which had been lettered out of South District Association. In 1954, 12 churches reported 223 baptisms, 5,659 members, $128,483 total gifts, $24,602 mission gifts, $624,200 property value, and (1951) $13,685 church debt.

CHRISTIAN COUNTY. Organized Oct. 9, 1923, by 24 churches in that county which had 3,777 members. In 1954, 29 churches reported 325 baptisms, 8,121 members, $260,003 total gifts, $54,176 mission gifts, and $976,200 property value.

CRITTENDEN. Constituted Oct. 12, 1860, at the Crittenden meetinghouse in Grant County of seven churches with 403 members. It was missionary in sentiment and endorsed the work of the general association, but was deficient in liberality. The association resolved that only men were to be appointed by churches as messengers. In 1954, 24 churches reported 114 baptisms, 4,313 members, $98,647 total gifts, $17,398 mission gifts, $376,600 property value, and (1953) $13,102 church debt.

DAVIESS-MCCLEAN. Constituted as the Daviess County Association of United Baptists by 9 churches dismissed from the Goshen Association of United Baptists Nov. 1, 1844, in the meetinghouse of Bethabara Baptist Church in Daviess County. A missionary body from the beginning, it favored various benevolent objects of the general association, approving and organizing a Bible Society, and approving the Indian Mission Association. Several times the association advised its churches against receiving alien immersion. Its name was changed to Daviess-McClean in 1926.

The association's growth has been even and rapid, with membership almost doubled during the first 10 years of its existence. In 1954, 51 churches reported 675 baptisms, 14,813 members, $741,196 total gifts, $149,715 mission gifts, $2,531,500 property value, and $190,279 church debt.

EAST LYNN. Constituted in the fall, 1893, of rural churches, located principally in La Rue County. At its fourth session in 1896, it had 13 churches. In 1954, 13 churches reported 35 baptisms, 2,292 members, $39,760 total gifts, $3,981 mission gifts, and $102,100 property value.

EAST UNION. Organized Nov. 27, 1891, at the Boston Church. At the second session it was composed of messengers from eight churches. In 1954, 26 churches reported 112 baptisms, 3,862 members, $24,865 total gifts, $1,652 mission gifts, and $107,600 property value.

EDMONSON. Organized by five churches at Brownsville, Edmonson County, June 25, 1894. In 1954, 14 churches reported 117 baptisms, 2,300 members, $20,589 total gifts, $2,783 mission gifts, and $77,500 property value.

ELKHORN. Organized as a result of a convention which met June 25, 1785, with South Elkhorn Church, Fayette County, near Lexington, with five Regular Baptist churches sending messengers, including well-known preachers Lewis Craig, Benjamin Craig, William Hickman (q.v.), John Taylor (q.v.), and Elijah Craig (q.v.).

Two big questions were raised and settled in this meeting. The first was whether the Philadelphia Confession of Faith, adopted by the Baptists, should be adhered to as the rule of the union; or whether a suspension thereof, for the sake of society, would be best. Since the Separates had refused to adopt any confession of faith, the grave question involved the hope of effecting a union between the Regular and Separate Baptists. When the convention adopted the Philadelphia Confession of Faith "to be strictly adhered to," the Separates rejected union, and the breach widened between the two groups. The second question concerned the propriety of forming an association. Deciding in the affirmative, six churches sent messengers to meet Sept. 30, 1785, at Clear Creek Church. They adopted articles of faith and identified themselves as Regular Baptists.

On the following day, Oct. 1, 1785, Elkhorn, the first Baptist association west of the Allegheny Mountains, was constituted, declaring that all matters of business should be determined by majority vote. Questions confronting the association at various sessions included advisability of Christians holding public office, question of scriptural basis for ministers' self-support, and foot washing. It was agreed that the association had no right to interfere with internal affairs of an orderly church.

From 1926 to 1947 the association was divided into two groups with separate sets of officers, with the annual meetings being held at different places, often on the same days. The separation resulted from personal grievances growing out of disagreements over the choice of place of meeting for 1926. In 1954, 55 churches reported 1,312 baptisms, 38,059 members, $1,074,747 total gifts, $190,356 mission gifts, $5,144,012 property value, and $573,700 church debt.

ENTERPRISE. Constituted at Providence Church in Carter County Nov. 10, 1876, of eight churches dismissed from Greenup Association, in Johnson, Lawrence, and Carter counties. Although located in antimissionary territory, the association has grown steadily from the beginning. In 1954, 33 churches reported 364 baptisms, 5,564 members, $232,992 total gifts, $26,-166 mission gifts, $712,735 property value, and (1951) $33,581 church debt.

FRANKLIN. Constituted in 1815 and named for the county in which most of the churches were located. At the 1816 session with 12 churches represented, a great revival began which continued through the ensuing year and resulted in 351 converts. In 1821 the association lost a number of churches and preachers when Concord Association was constituted on its northern borders, but by 1824 it had regained the loss as a result of "gracious revivals" which prevailed in the churches. Among eminent pastors in the association were William Hickman, son of a pioneer preacher by that name (William Hickman [q.v.]); Silas M. Noel; J. M. Frost, Jr.; Porter Clay, son of John Clay of Virginia, and brother of statesman Henry Clay; and Joseph M. Taylor. In 1954, 18 churches reported 285 baptisms, 8,207 members, $231,530 total gifts, $49,194 mission gifts, and $762,000 property value.

FREEDOM. Constituted by six churches from Cumberland and Clinton counties at Beech Grove meetinghouse in Nov., 1843. The churches had been dismissed from Stockton's Valley Association because they refused to submit to its antimission policies. In the 1845 session a resolution concerning alien baptism advised churches "that they had better not receive members from other denominations without first administering baptism." In 1954, 12 churches reported 29 baptisms, 1,482 members, $31,109 total gifts, $2,788 mission gifts, and $196,500 property value.

GASPER RIVER. Constituted at Providence Church in Warren County, Sept. 26, 1812, and named for a small stream which flowed through its territory. Organization resulted from a division of the territory of the Green River Association at its annual session in 1812. The original territory of Gasper River extended into several counties, but in 1818 Smiths Grove Church was dismissed to join Green River, and Tanners and Panther Creek were lettered out to Goshen Association, and by 1820, when its territory was divided, with 13 churches constituting Drake's Creek Association, Gasper River was reduced to 11 churches with 693 members. In 1954, 23 churches reported 172 baptisms, 4,596 members, $47,689 total gifts, $6,974 mission gifts, and $128,500 property value.

GOOSE CREEK. Organized by 11 churches in New Home Baptist Church in Clay County, Sept. 24–25, 1897. Evidently constituted in 1896, since the 1897 session was called to order by J. W. Jones, "the Moderator of last year," but the association has no records to verify the earlier date. Messengers in the session of 1898 resolved: "We do believe this Association should appoint a committee of three members, to get up a history of the United Baptists of Kentucky, so we Baptists of the mountains can show our successors back to England and Holland." In 1954, 16 churches reported 22 baptisms, 1,226 members, $3,023 total gifts, $30 mission gifts, and $35,000 property value.

GOSHEN. Constituted in the fall of 1817 by 11 churches dismissed from the Old Salem fraternity for that purpose. Daniel Parker's two-seeds doctrine became evident in some of the churches about 1832 and resulted in strong opposition to missions. In 1839 the association opened correspondence and became an auxiliary to the General Association of Baptists in Kentucky. Goshen was then committed to the mission system, and by 1842 the antimission system had withdrawn. In 1954, 17 churches reported 97 baptisms, 2,415 members, $40,658 total gifts, $12,594 mission gifts, and $171,000 property value.

GRAVES COUNTY. Constituted Nov. 22, 1893, in the Mayfield Baptist Church by 29 churches located in Graves County. The association was formed as the result of action taken by the Mt. Olivet Association in 1892 to divide the territory occupied by Mt. Olivet and West Union into three associations: the churches in Graves County to compose one association, those in McCracken and Ballard counties to compose the second, and those in Carlisle, Hickman, and Fulton counties to compose the third. In 1954, 41 churches reported 533 baptisms, 10,799 members, $374,538 total gifts, and $75,411 mission gifts.

GREEN RIVER. Organized in 1800. Because the antimission party was in majority in the 1839 session, it brought charges against Bowling Green, Glasgow, and Mt. Olive churches "for having joined, or represented themselves, as churches, in the General Association." The missionary party's proposition that "the Association come to a friendly division" was deferred until the next annual meeting. A convention for consultation composed of eight churches, including Glasgow and Bowling Green, convened at Glasgow June 12, 1840. They resolved to "withdraw from said (Green River) Association . . . and labor for the extension of the Kingdom of Christ." The newly organized missionary association was called Liberty. In 1954, 39 churches reported 242 baptisms and 5,229 members.

GREENUP. Constituted by three churches from Ohio Association in the latter part of 1841 in the meetinghouse of Palmyra Baptist Church. Division in the association resulted from intemperate use of intoxicating drinks among the churches, and a new temperance association, composed of four churches, was constituted Dec. 29, 1850, named Friendship. In 1854 the body dissolved, and churches returned to Greenup Association. Greenup grew slowly until 1868 when a revival began and continued several years; it dismissed eight churches to form Enterprise Association in Nov., 1876. In 1954, 54 churches reported 725 baptisms, 10,-447 members, $480,651 total gifts, $75,356 mission gifts, and $1,964,000 property value.

GREENVILLE. Constituted at Greenville Church Nov. 7, 1879, by six churches located principally in Wolf County. Organization resulted from division of the territory of Booneville Association, with the new association originally named Greenville Association of United Regular Baptists. In 1954, 15 churches reported 107 baptisms, 1,318 members, $15,994 total gifts, $2,306 mission gifts, and $161,000 property value.

HENRY COUNTY. Constituted by 11 churches Oct. 13, 1915, at Drennon's Ridge Church, Franklinton. In 1954, 14 churches reported 145 baptisms, 3,424 members, $104,856 total gifts, $17,764 mission gifts, $405,000 property value, and $329 church debt.

IRVINE. Constituted by seven churches in Oct., 1859, at the Drowning Creek meetinghouse in Madison County. The association had increased to 33 churches in 1870, when 17 were dismissed to form Booneville Association. In 1954, 7 churches reported 19 baptisms, 825 members, $4,827 total gifts, $570 mission gifts, and $25,155 property value.

JACKSON COUNTY. Formed by 13 churches at Grayhawk Sept. 18, 1925, under the name of Jackson County Association of Missionary Baptists. It adopted the New Hampshire Confession of Faith. In 1954, 29 churches reported 85 baptisms, 3,489 members, $14,652 total gifts, $4,165 mission gifts, and $96,600 property value.

LAUREL RIVER. Constituted Sept. 30, 1831, by five churches dismissed from South Union Association. Disturbed during the War Between the States by the political conditions of the times, the London and Robinson Creek churches introduced into the association in 1863 the query: "Do we fellowship the principles of secession and rebellion against the Government?" The association answered, "Nay." This question became a test of fellowship until 1867, when a statement was adopted saying, "This Association believes it committed an error in making politics a test of fellowship; therefore, we rescind said act." In 1868 the 10 churches south of Laurel River constituted Lynn Camp Association. In 1954, 35 churches reported 163 baptisms, 6,271 members, $122,626 total gifts, $14,472 mission gifts, and $658,101 property value.

LIBERTY. Constituted at Mt. Tabor Church, near Glasgow, July 31, 1840, by nine churches which had withdrawn from Green River Association. Liberty, a missionary Baptist association, prospered from the beginning, with 7,401 converts in the churches from 1840 until 1882. In 1954, 40 churches reported 197 baptisms, 8,760 members, $153,556 total gifts, $30,722 mission gifts, and $713,375 property value.

LINCOLN COUNTY. Constituted by 11 churches in Sept., 1924, in Pleasant Point Baptist Church. In 1954, 23 churches reported 249 baptisms, 5,443 members, $118,595 total gifts, $12,684 mission gifts, and $421,500 property value.

LITTLE BETHEL. Constituted in Sept., 1836, at Flat Creek meetinghouse in Hopkins County by four churches which had split off from the antimission Highland Association. The reason for withdrawal from Highland was recorded as "the violent opposition of a majority of that body to the benevolent institutions of the day" and "its repeated violation of the spirit and letter of its constitution." In 1954, 43 churches reported 556 baptisms, 9,621 members, $326,965 total gifts, $44,157 mission gifts, and $1,334,250 property value.

LITTLE RIVER. Constituted in Nov., 1813, at the Eddy Grove Church in Caldwell County, formed as a result of the division of the Red River Association territory, which contained 40 churches extending from Clarksville, Tenn., to near Henderson, Ky. Only two churches which went into the formation of Little River Association in 1813 are still in existence, Mt. Pleasant in Trigg County and New Bethel in Lyon County. In 1954, 31 churches reported 251 baptisms, 5,048 members, $148,240 total gifts, $25,259 mission gifts, and $371,000 total property value.

LOGAN COUNTY. Constituted at the 44th annual session of Clear Fork Association held at Green Ridge Baptist Church, Logan County, Aug. 11-12, 1903, when the association "Resolved that Article I of our constitution be amended by striking out 'Clear Fork' and submitting, 'Logan County' in the room thereof." In 1954, 22 churches reported 105 baptisms, 3,861 members, $66,812 total gifts, $12,970 mission gifts, and $153,500 property value.

LONG RUN. Constituted Sept. 16, 1803, at Long Run meetinghouse in Jefferson County by 24 churches which had been dismissed from Salem Association. Long Run adopted the Philadelphia Confession of Faith, "excepting some things contained in the 3rd and 5th articles, if construed so as to make God the author of sin. Also, in the 31st article, respecting laying hands on newly baptized persons, that the using or not using that ceremony, be no bar to fellowship."

Churches were dismissed from Long Run Association to assist in forming Silver Creek (Ind.), Franklin, Sulphur Fork, Middle District, and Shelby County associations. By 1825 agitation had increased among the churches because of the teaching of Alexander Campbell, and from 1825 to 1830 Campbell's forces were zealously engaged in propagating their beliefs among the churches. In 1830 the association issued the statement: ". . . as the writings of Alexander Campbell are in direct opposition to the existence and general dictates of our constitution, we, therefore, advise our brethren, that they discountenance those writings, and all those who support that course of rebellion against the principles of our Associational existence." The loss to the association, due to Campbell's influence, totaled 1,112 members.

In 1877 the Southern Baptist Theological Seminary was moved within the association's boundaries. The presence of seminary professors and ministerial students stimulated the churches, and the number of baptisms began to increase each year. In 1954, 92 churches reported 3,501 baptisms, 69,951 members, $3,172,001 total gifts, $702,121 mission gifts, and $11,877,273 property value.

LYNN. Constituted Nov. 8, 1856, in the meetinghouse of the South Fork Church, Nolin, by 12 churches located in La Rue, Hart, and Taylor counties. In 1860 a resolution was adopted, recommending to the churches the importance of "a more fervent, united prayer to God to send forth more laborers into the harvest. . . ." The association, composed entirely of small town and country churches, has been one of the most prosperous in the state. In 1954, 38 churches reported 243 baptisms, 8,054 members, $85,346 total gifts, $10,498 mission gifts, and $357,400 property value.

LYNN CAMP. Constituted at Lynn Camp Church, Knox County, Nov. 6, 1868, by 10 churches coming from the division of Laurel River Association the previous year. A constitution was adopted, and the organization designated Lynn Camp Association of United Baptists. In 1954, 24 churches reported 131 baptisms, 3,973 members, $40,336 total gifts, $2,113 mission gifts, $118,750 property value.

LEO T. CRISMON

McCREARY COUNTY. Organized by six churches in 1913. Within three years the word "United" was dropped from its name, and five years later the word "missionary" was added. It is located on the Tennessee line in south central Kentucky. In 1954, 17 churches reported 165 baptisms, 2,806 members, $42,045 total gifts, $4,411 mission gifts, $134,700 property value, and $4,242 church debt.

MERCER. Organized in 1955 in the northern part of South District Association by churches in Mercer County.

MIDDLE FORK. Organized in 1952 by three churches in the mountains of southeastern Kentucky. In 1954, 5 churches reported 5 baptisms, 538 members, $156 total gifts, $60 mission gifts, $4,500 property value.

MONROE. Organized in 1954 by nine churches from Barren River Association. Tompkinsville is its largest church. In its first year of organization it reported 91 baptisms, 2,217 members, $21,239 total gifts, $4,011 mission gifts, and $83,000 property value.

MOUNT ZION. Organized Oct. 30, 1885, with 11 churches in the southeastern Kentucky mountains, near the Tennessee state boundary. Three of its churches today have more than 1,000 members. This association is situated in a rich coal producing section. Williamsburg is the seat of Cumberland College. In 1954, 39 churches reported 352 baptisms, 9,207 members, $186,987 total gifts, $37,443 mission gifts, and $1,014,300 property value.

MUHLENBERG COUNTY. Organized in 1907 by churches from several adjoining associations with Greenville and Central City as its focal center. This association is situated in the heart of the coal mining operations in western Kentucky. In 1954, 45 churches reported 378 baptisms, 10,078 members, $285,523 total gifts, $57,406 mission gifts, $788,025 property value, and $35,772 church debt.

NELSON. Organized in 1849 by 11 churches from Salem Association. These were Cox's Creek, Bloomfield, Bardstown, Mill Creek, Little Union, New Salem, Mt. Washington, Shepherdsville, Hardin's Creek, New Hope, and Rolling Fork. Some of these churches were among the strongest in the state. Mostly rural in territory and with a predominantly prosperous farm constituency, its growth has been steady throughout the years. In 1954, 25 churches reported 318 baptisms, 8,069 members, $211,862 total gifts, $39,746 mission gifts, $764,774 property value, and $64,299 church debt.

NORTH BEND. Organized in 1803, covering Boone and Kenton counties in the Big Bend of the Ohio River opposite Cincinnati, Ohio. Covington, the largest Kentucky city in that area, is the second largest city in Kentucky. In 1954, 36 churches reported 842 baptisms, 15,892 members, $731,487 total gifts, $139,859 mission gifts, $3,403,898 property value, and $509,164 church debt.

NORTH CONCORD. Constituted in 1843 by eight churches from the South Union Association in three large mountain counties in southeastern Kentucky, viz., Knox, Whitley, and Bell. This association established Sunday schools and supported missions and educational work, but in the last quarter of the 19th century, probably due to the utter isolation of the region from the outside world at the time, they languished. An attempt to establish a Baptist high school also failed. However, Barbourville Baptist Institute (also called Southeastern Kentucky Baptist Institute), instituted in 1899, was operated for about 30 years. In 1954, 39 churches reported 195 baptisms, 7,220 members, $79,029 total gifts, $6,785 mission gifts, and $284,800 property value.

OHIO COUNTY. Constituted in 1901 by 22 churches from the Daviess County Association. Some of its churches had at one time held membership in the Panther Creek Association of United Baptists (antimissionary), which was organized in 1843. J. S. Coleman (q.v.), who had long been moderator of the Daviess County Association and the General Association of Baptists in Kentucky, was its first moderator. In 1954, 40 churches reported 230 baptisms, 7,076 members, $176,457 total gifts, $26,145 mission gifts, $535,074 property value, and $68,200 church debt.

OHIO RIVER. Organized Oct. 13, 1883, at Crooked Creek Church in Crittenden County. This body was formed by 15 churches from the Little River Association, with an aggregate membership of 1,425. In 1954, 34 churches reported 240 baptisms, 4,858 members, $182,768 total gifts, $21,100 mission gifts, and $519,000 property value.

OHIO VALLEY. Organized in 1888, as a result of the union of Union County (1878) and Henderson County (1868) associations. Includes churches in Henderson, Union, and Webster counties. In the first half of the 20th century the co-operating churches spread their territory over into Evansville, Ind. In 1948, 25 churches in Henderson, Ky., and Evansville, Ind., withdrew from this association and organized the West Kentuckiana Association. Twenty-two churches remained in the Ohio Valley. In 1954, these 22 churches reported 207 baptisms, 5,473 members, $183,562 total gifts, $35,386 mission gifts, $587,800 property value, and $9,737 church debt.

OWEN COUNTY. Organized in 1925 to replace the Concord Association which was disbanded in 1924. Twenty-eight churches reported to the initial meeting of this new organization. In 1954, 26 churches reported 117 baptisms, 5,531 members, $115,344 total gifts, $24,397 mission gifts, $428,200 property value, and $3,500 church debt.

PINE MOUNTAIN. Organized in 1954 in the coal mining regions of Letcher County, in southeastern Kentucky. Whitesburg and Lynch churches are the largest in this association. In its initial year 16 churches reported 169 baptisms, 4,188 members, $99,784 total gifts, $16,921 mission gifts, $449,000 property value, and $52,806 church debt.

PULASKI COUNTY. The South Kentucky Association was so large in 1904 that the churches in Pulaski County formed the Pulaski County Association, with Somerset as its center. In 1954, 45 churches reported 442 baptisms, 10,892 members, $235,525 total gifts, $38,857 mission gifts, $1,013,800 property value, and $70,177 church debt.

RED RIVER. Organized in 1955 by five churches in five county seats of five counties. The five churches initiating this association were: Campton, Wolfe County; Frenchburg, Menifee County; Jackson, Breathitt County; Stanton, Powell County; and West Liberty, Morgan County. This new Red River Association is not to be confused with the Red River Association in Robertson County, Tenn., which in the early history of Kentucky, lapped over into Logan, Christian, and Trigg counties in southern and western Kentucky.

ROCKCASTLE. Formed in 1871 by 14 churches with a total membership of 764, which came from the old Cumberland River Association. Its territory lies in parts of Pulaski and Rockcastle counties. In 1954, 27 churches reported 185 baptisms, 4,665 members, $67,688 total gifts, $4,096 mission gifts, and $230,050 property value.

RUSSELL COUNTY. Formed in 1916 by the merging of the South Cumberland River Association (organized in 1841) and the Second North Concord Association (organized in 1876). In 1954, 20 churches reported 86 baptisms, 2,154 members, $37,057 total gifts, $7,805 mission gifts, and $138,000 property value.

RUSSELL CREEK. Organized in 1804 by 11 churches from Green River Association. One of the largest associations in Kentucky, Russell Creek is situated in the geographical center of the state. It established Campbellsville Junior College, formerly Russell Creek Academy, at Campbellsville. In 1954, 48 churches reported 346 baptisms, 9,431 members, $243,836 total gifts, $41,061 mission gifts, $1,147,878 property value, and $49,979 church debt.

SALEM. Organized at Cox's Creek Church in 1785, Salem was the second association to be organized in the commonwealth. From it has come all the Kentucky district associations west of the Kentucky River. Though, theoretically, it included everything west of the Kentucky River, it never actually covered that much territory, for, as the churches were organized and developed, they tended to break off and form associations near their home bases. The four original churches of Salem Association were: Severns Valley, Elizabethtown (now in Severns Valley Association); Cedar Creek and Cox's Creek (both now in Nelson Association); and Bear Grass, in Jefferson County (now extinct, though earlier it was in the Long Run Association). In the days of heavy river traffic in the vicinity of Brandenburg, this was a thriving, prosperous association, but in recent years its growth has declined. In 1954, 20 churches reported 186 baptisms, 3,918 members, $92,782 total gifts, $19,428 mission gifts, $260,600 property value, and $4,800 church debt.

SEVERNS VALLEY. Organized in 1899 with 19 churches and 2,381 members from the Salem Association. The historic cities of Elizabethtown and Hodgenville were its centers of population. Today this association serves a more or less floating and fluctuating population, due to the United States Government's expansion of Fort Knox into Severns Valley territory. Lynnland College was located at Glendale. Its buildings are now occupied by Glen Dale, the Kentucky Baptist Children's Home. In 1954, 39 churches reported 403 baptisms, 9,090 members, $347,764 total gifts, $65,142 mission gifts, $1,045,615 property value, and $14,582 church debt.

SHELBY COUNTY. Organized Aug. 16, 1872, at Clayvillage Church, Clayvillage, Ky., with 14 churches participating, having a combined membership of 1,797. It is situated in a rich farming county between the Blue Grass region and Louisville. In 1954, 24 churches reported 171 baptisms, 8,837 members, $216,076 total gifts, $40,685 mission gifts, $632,000 property value, and $17,988 church debt.

SIMPSON. Organized in 1900 by seven churches from the Bethel Association in Simpson County, in southern Kentucky, with Franklin as its center. In 1954, 12 churches reported 79 baptisms, 3,176 members, $75,992 total gifts, $13,877 mission gifts, $191,000 property value, and $5,650 church debt.

SOUTH CONCORD. Organized in 1825 with 11 churches from the Cumberland Association in southern Kentucky. In 1954, 22 churches reported 112 baptisms, 3,926 members, $7,387 total gifts, $35 mission gifts, and $63,600 property value.

SOUTH DISTRICT. Beginning in 1802, this body

soon became involved in a dispute which divided the group into two associations—South District, the minority group; and South Kentucky Association, the majority group. South District lies largely in Mercer and Boyle counties—the center of much of Kentucky's earliest settlements at Harrodsburg, and its early constitutional government formed at Danville. In 1954, 31 churches reported 496 baptisms, 13,206 members, $352,130 total gifts, $58,068 mission gifts, $1,434,390 property value, and $39,797 church debt. In 1955 churches in Mercer County formed a separate organization.

SOUTH UNION. Organized in 1815 of churches in Whitley and Knox counties. In 1830 it had 18 churches with 489 members. In 1954, 34 churches reported 133 baptisms, 4,167 members, $31,850 total gifts, $1,964 mission gifts, and $105,050 property value.

SULPHUR FORK. Organized in 1826 of nine churches coming from Long Run Association, this body lies on the Kentucky side of the Ohio River, just northeast of Louisville, Ky., in a rich farming area in Oldham and Trimble counties. In 1954, 16 churches reported 236 baptisms, 3,390 members, $86,327 total gifts, $14,399 mission gifts, $350,661 property value, and $7,273 church debt.

TATES CREEK. Organized in 1793, the fourth district association constituted in Kentucky, and composed of five churches from the old South Kentucky Association. It is situated in Madison and Garrard counties. It was to this area that Lewis Craig (q.v.) brought his "Travelling Church" from Upper Spotsylvania, Va., in 1781, and settled at Gilbert's Creek, near Lancaster. In 1954, 26 churches reported 215 baptisms, 8,332 members, $145,421 total gifts, $21,806 mission gifts, $740,000 property value, and $52,610 church debt.

TEN MILE. Organized in 1831 with nine churches and 383 members. It is a small association made up entirely of small rural churches, situated among the hills of northern Kentucky, along the Ohio River just a few miles southwest of Cincinnati, but it has an extremely active constituency. For years Ten Mile's Sunday school organization has been standard. In 1954, 14 churches reported 76 baptisms, 3,263 members, $59,169 total gifts, $6,929 mission gifts, $237,169 property value, and $9,095 church debt.

THREE FORKS. Organized with seven churches in 1901, in the rugged mountain regions of Perry, Leslie, and Knott counties. Among the stalwarts who labored there, was A. S. Petrey, "The Prophet of Little Cane Creek," who founded Hazard Baptist Institute. In 1954, 22 churches reported 208 baptisms, 3,919 members, $90,971 total gifts, $9,186 mission gifts, $415,500 property value, and $17,775 church debt.

UNION. Constituted in 1813 by five churches with 216 members from the Elkhorn Association. Its territory reaches from the Blue Grass region to the Ohio River, including Pendleton, Harrison, and Bracken counties. In 1954, 17 churches reported 131 baptisms, 3,181 members, $106,108 total gifts, $18,403 mission gifts, $435,000 property value, and $11,150 church debt.

UPPER CUMBERLAND. Organized in 1890 of seven churches, located along the Kentucky-Virginia boundary line (Harlan County) amid the mountains and valleys in southeastern Kentucky. In 1954, 46 churches reported 562 baptisms, 9,876 members, $207,770 total gifts, $19,627 mission gifts, $974,300 property value, and $18,892 church debt.

WARREN. Formed in 1890 at Bowling Green, Ky., by seven churches in Warren County. It is situated in a rich agricultural section, in which have been located a number of schools and colleges, including Western State Teachers College and Bowling Green Business University at the county seat. In 1954, 30 churches reported 313 baptisms, 8,078 members, $254,492 total gifts, $39,135 mission gifts, $1,460,700 property value, and $43,532 church debt.

WAYNE COUNTY. Organized in 1905 by 15 churches and located in the south central portion of Kentucky, near the Tennessee line. In 1954, 20 churches reported 165 baptisms, 4,407 members, $43,631 total gifts, $6,310 mission gifts, and $208,900 property value.

WEST KENTUCKIANA. Organized in 1948 by 25 churches in the Ohio Valley Association. These churches were located in Henderson, Ky., and Evansville, Ind., for the most part. With strong city churches in the two major populated areas of that sector, the association avoided many of the early struggles for existence through which many of the associations passed. The churches are progressive, alert, missionary, and evangelistic. In 1954, 42 churches reported 1,010 baptisms, 13,054 members, $554,901 total gifts, $81,014 mission gifts, $2,078,500 property value, and $115,430 church debt.

WEST KENTUCKY. Organized in 1893 by messengers from 26 churches in Carlisle, Hickman, and Fulton counties—the most southwestern of all Kentucky counties, situated on the Mississippi River. For years the *American Baptist Flag* was published at Fulton, Ky., in this territory. Many doctrinal and ecclesiastical debates were held there, too. In 1954, 41 churches reported 444 baptisms, 8,423 members, $281,845 total gifts, $49,721 mission gifts, $831,331 property value, and $66,404 church debt.

WEST UNION. Organized in 1834 by 10 churches in McCracken County, this association is located between the Tennessee and Cumberland rivers where they pour into the Ohio, following the curve of the Ohio into the Mississippi on the west. Paducah is its largest city, prominent throughout its history as a river town. In 1954, 42 churches reported 995 baptisms, 16,365 members, $801,048 total gifts, $155,210 mission gifts, $2,165,950 property value, and $101,230 church debt.

WHITES RUN. Established by 10 churches from the Concord Association in 1900. It is located in a small region around Carrollton, where the Kentucky River flows into the Ohio, about halfway between Louisville and Cincinnati. In 1954, 11 churches reported 70 baptisms, 3,033 members, $56,125 total gifts, $9,780 mission gifts, $178,000 property value, and $577 church debt.

GEORGE RALEIGH JEWELL

II. Extinct Associations. BARREN RIVER. Constituted Sept. 15, 1830, at the Mt. Pleasant meeting house with 15 churches in Barren, Allen, and Monroe counties and in present Tennessee counties, Metcalf and Smith. In 1835, composed of churches from the Old Green River Association, influenced by Andrew Nuckols, the association declared nonfellowship with the Baptist state convention and all institutions of the day; however, this resolution was rescinded the following year. Antimission forces, the minority group, withdrew from the association, and the remaining churches began strong missionary movements. In 1953, 46 churches reported 8,149 members. The association withdrew from the general association in 1954.

BAY'S FORK. See Allen Baptist Association, Kentucky.

CLEAR FORK. Constituted in 1860 by five churches located in Logan, Warren, and Simpson counties. In 1861 a missionary board was appointed, Sunday schools were endorsed, and the organization of a pastors' and deacons' meeting was advised. The association took no interest in missions outside of its own territory. In 1903 it dissolved, and in 1904 churches went into the organization of Logan County Association, embracing the northern part of the county.

CLOVER BOTTOM. Organized in 1898 by five churches with 207 members. In 1908 there were 4 churches with 345 members. Its territory was largely included in Jackson County Association when it was organized in 1925.

CONCORD. Constituted at White's Run Church, Carroll County, Sept. 28, 1821, by eight churches, six of which were dismissed from Long Run Association. The association, requested to advise churches concerning the teaching of followers of Alexander Campbell, urged churches not to invite them into their meeting houses or into their homes, or encourage them in any way. As a result Campbell's followers never gained a foothold in this association. In 1831 Ten Mile Association, formed near Concord, reduced it to 11 churches, but there was a constant growth during 10 years. In 1838 a plan to pay pastors met stern opposition. Several churches divided into two violent parties and set up mission and antimission churches. In 1900 nine churches were dismissed to go into the constitution of White's Run Association, and in 1924 when Owen County Association was formed Concord dissolved.

CUMBERLAND RIVER. Constituted in Oct., 1809, by six churches dismissed from Tate's Creek Association. In 1811, 13 member churches had 447 members, and as a result of the 1811–12 revival, churches reported 368 baptisms. Only nominally missionary, the association contained an antimissionary element which kept growing and began to defeat every effort to promote any form of benevolent work. In 1861 Cumberland River divided, and 11 churches with 683 members formed an antimissionary association. The remaining group did little to promote the spread of the gospel beyond its own bounds and in 1903 went out of existence.

DAVIESS COUNTY ASSOCIATION OF UNITED BAPTISTS. See Daviess-McClean Association, Kentucky.

DRAKE'S CREEK. Continued Oct. 6, 1820, by 13 churches, as a result of the division of territory of Gasper River Association. In spite of an auspicious beginning, the association made little progress for more than 10 years. Three of the pastors had to be dismissed for immorality, drunkenness, and falsehood; and a two-year epidemic of cholera hampered the work. But by 1833 this had passed, and the association expressed its thankfulness for the 329 baptisms reported for the previous year. The year before, however, the churches and members were advised to abstain from joining temperance, Bible, tract, and missionary societies, and the Sunday school union. In 1835, as a further expression of antimission sentiment, the churches were urged to have no correspondence with the general association, and in 1841 the association assumed the name Drake's Creek Baptist Association United Upon the Doctrine of Predestination and Election, which name it retained for 30 years. The report of 1879, from 13 churches with 273 members, is the last evidence of this antimissionary organization, which soon thereafter ceased to exist.

DRAKE'S CREEK ASSOCIATION OF UNITED BAPTISTS. See Allen Baptist Association, Kentucky.

EAST CONCORD ASSOCIATION. See Bell County Association of Baptists, Kentucky.

FRIENDSHIP. Formed Oct. 29, 1927, by four churches which withdrew from Boone's Creek Association. It existed only until 1939 when two of its churches went into Elkhorn, and others returned to Boone's Creek Association.

HENDERSON COUNTY. Formed in the latter part of Oct., 1868, by eight churches dismissed from Little Bethel Association. In Nov., 1888, Union County and Henderson County associations met at Corydon for the purpose of uniting, which they did under the name The Ohio Valley Association of Baptists.

MIDDLE DISTRICT. Organized on Apr. 9, 1837, by four churches with 704 members. In 1844 there were nine churches with 1,436 members. An antimissionary spirit prevailed, and the association declined so that it was formally dissolved in 1872 when the Shelby County Association was organized.

MOUNT OLIVET. Organized "on Saturday before the first Sunday in July, 1848," by four churches with 199 members, as a result of a personality dispute. In 1893 there were 17 churches with 1,608 members. In that same year the association dissolved and its churches went into the organization of Graves County Association.

Mountain. Organized in 1913. In 1923 there were 27 churches with 1,244 members. In 1942 there were eight churches with 1,021 members.

Second North Concord. See Russell County Association.

South Cumberland River. See Russell County Association.

South Kentucky. See Casey County Association.

South Kentucky Association of Separate Baptists, No. 1. After a preliminary meeting in Oct., 1787, at Tates Creek Church in Madison County, it was organized in May, 1788. No early minutes are available, but 11 Separate Baptist churches were known to be extant in that area at that time according to J. H. Spencer. This association grew to include 31 churches with 2,383 members in 1801, at which time after the General Union its territory was divided up by South District and North District associations, and it disbanded.

South Kentucky Association of Separate Baptists, No. 2. Had its origin in the division of South Kentucky Association of Separate Baptists, No. 1, in 1802 into North District and South District associations of United Baptists and a further division (1803) of South District between the United Baptists and those who held heretical views who again designated themselves Separate Baptists (1806), which was the only Separate Baptist association in Kentucky at that time. It declared against missions in 1816. In 1819 it had grown to 50 churches with a membership of 2,000. By 1824 it had been reduced to 26 churches with 1,230 members. Weakened further by divisions, it had only 16 churches with 860 members in 1879. When it died is not known.

Union County. See Ohio Valley Association.

LEO T. CRISMON

KENTUCKY BAPTIST, THE. A four-page weekly paper published at Franklin, Ky., May 17, 1866, to June 22, 1867 (Vol. 1, No. 1, to Vol. 2, No. 5), for "the diffusion of religious, literary and general intelligence."

LEO T. CRISMON

KENTUCKY BAPTIST, THE. A four-page weekly paper, published at Louisville, Ky., from 1888 until 1895, edited by Charles E. Nash. It was devoted primarily to reporting the news of Kentucky Baptist churches, and devotional materials. The earliest extant issue is Sept. 28, 1893, Volume 6, Number 11. With the issue of July 4, 1895, the paper was sold to James Britton Cranfill (q.v.) of Waco, Tex., and similar editions were published at Waco as the *Kentucky Baptist Standard* and the *Texas Baptist Standard*, both editions taking the volume and issue numbers of the *Texas Baptist Standard*. The last issue of the Kentucky edition presently located is for Aug. 29, 1895.

J. M. GREEN

KENTUCKY BAPTIST FOUNDATION. Created by an act of the General Association of Baptists in Kentucky at its annual meeting in Lexington, Ky., Nov. 14–16, 1945, at which time its charter was approved. Its purpose and work is to solicit, receive, and administer gifts and bequests in the form of trusts for the benefit of those Baptist institutions and agencies, both state and Convention-wide, designated by the donor.

Nine directors, three of which are elected each year by the General Association of Baptists in Kentucky to serve for a term of three years, direct the affairs of this agency. The first directors were George D. Caldwell, W. T. Chapin, T. C. Ecton, C. W. Elsey, John D. Freeman, J. C. Iler, Sr., F. H. Mason, N. B. Perkins, and George S. Wilson, Sr. The directors elect the executive secretary-treasurer. A. M. Vollmer has served in this capacity from the time the foundation began operation until the present (1955).

The foundation began operations with assets totaling $183,000, which were trust funds held by the Kentucky Baptist State Mission Board. On Oct. 31, 1955, its assets totaled $1,056,964.58. Of this amount $350,000 were funds not in the hands of any institution when the foundation began operations. The balance was endowment on hand and placed with the foundation by various institutions for administration.

The annual income from present investments is approximately $40,000. The operating budget of the foundation is received from the Cooperative Program.

A. M. VOLLMER

KENTUCKY BAPTIST HISTORICAL SOCIETY. In 1866 the constitution of the General Association of Baptists in Kentucky was amended to contain the following expression of its purpose: ". . . and to collect and preserve our Denominational History of Kentucky." A committee of six, with headquarters at Covington, was appointed to carry on this work. In 1876 the matter of collecting materials and writing a history was transferred to John Henderson Spencer (q.v.) (1826–97), who published *A History of Kentucky Baptists* in two volumes in 1885.

The Kentucky Baptist Historical Society was first established with headquarters to be located at Frankfort, and it was chartered on Mar. 21, 1871. On May 12, 1890, the charter was revised to provide for headquarters at Louisville with the depository of materials at the library of the Southern Baptist Theological Seminary. In 1903, seemingly without knowledge of the previous acts, the matter of obtaining a charter was taken up again, and the society was chartered on June 20, 1905.

The society ceased to function from 1919 until 1939. It was then revived through interest stimulated by the organization of the Southern Baptist Historical Society, with which it became affiliated.

The society does not receive regularly allocated funds from the general association. It is financed through membership subscriptions and through the sale of its publications. The general association financed the writing and publication of *A History of Baptists in Kentucky*, by Frank Mariro Masters (1870-   ), which was published by the society in 1953.

The collection of materials belonging to the society is located in the fireproof stack room of the Southern Baptist Theological Seminary. It consists of about 400 volumes of books and about 2,000 issues of minutes of associations within the state.   LEO T. CRISMON

KENTUCKY BAPTIST HOSPITAL. A corporation chartered Sept. 12, 1918, by the state of Kentucky, established by the General Association of Baptists in Kentucky, and located in Louisville.

The first mention of a Baptist hospital for Kentucky was made by a lady in the *Western Recorder* in 1892. Next mention was by Marion Palmer Hunt (*q.v.*), former pastor of Twenty-third and Broadway and Eighteenth Street Baptist churches, when he spoke before a Baptist pastors' conference in Oct., 1897.

Kentucky Baptist Hospital was formally opened on Nov. 17, 1924. The building and equipment represented a total investment of $624,879. The total capacity at the time of opening was 130 beds and 20 bassinets. In 1954 the hospital had a total capacity of 345 beds and 50 bassinets.

Kentucky Baptist Hospital is fully accredited by the Joint Commission on Accreditation. It is approved for one-year internship training and for the teaching of X-ray and laboratory technicians. It is a member of the American Hospital Association, the Kentucky Hospital Association, the American Protestant Hospital Association, and the Southwide Baptist Hospital Association.

Annually more than 18,000 patients are admitted, approximately 7,500 operations are performed, and over 3,400 babies are delivered. The physical plant is now valued at more than $5,900,000. H. L. Dobbs is administrator.

The School of Nursing was chartered in 1918 and organized in 1924. A diploma school, it is affiliated with the University of Louisville. The first five students accepted were sent to the Baptist Hospital in Missouri until Kentucky Baptist Hospital was opened in Nov., 1924. Average enrolment is about 160 students.
          H. L. DOBBS

KENTUCKY BAPTIST SUMMER ASSEMBLY. Founded in 1908 at Georgetown, Ky., using the facilities of Georgetown College. Purposes of the assembly were inspiration and instruction, with study classes covering many phases of church and denominational life. Later the name was changed to Kentucky Baptist Assembly at Georgetown because of the West Kentucky Baptist Assembly at Dawson Springs. The assembly was held for 24 consecutive years, for the last time in July, 1931. Extreme financial hardship caused the canceling of plans for the assembly in 1932.   ELDRED M. TAYLOR

KENTUCKY COLLEGE. Organized at Pewee Valley, Ky., as an nondenominational secondary school for girls in 1863, but became Baptist in 1897 when it passed into the hands of T. Simpson McCall, former president of Bethel Female College. It was under the patronage of the Long Run Baptist Association until it was discontinued in 1900.   GLYNN R. FORD

KENTUCKY MISSION MONTHLY. Published at Louisville, Ky., from May, 1902, to 1919, it was started as a small monthly bulletin by Jonathan Goforth Bow while he was corresponding secretary of the executive board of the General Association of Baptists in Kentucky. The leaflet was intended to stimulate interest in state missions and all the interests fostered by the state mission board. Within six months its size was increased to 11 x 15 inches. It remained that size until Jan., 1905, when it became 6 x 9 inches and included 16 pages. William David Powell (*q.v.*) became its editor Jan., 1909, when he succeeded Bow as corresponding secretary, and Oscar Eugene Bryan (*q.v.*) became editor when he was elected to succeed Powell in 1919. With the launching of the 75 Million Campaign, the executive board of the General Association of Baptists in Kentucky purchased *The Baptist World* and *The Western Recorder*, merged them with the *Kentucky Mission Monthly* and continued them as one publication under the name of *The Western Recorder*.
          GEORGE RALEIGH JEWELL

KENTUCKY MISSIONARY & THEOLOGICAL MAGAZINE, THE. Frankfort, Ky., edited by Starke Dupuy after May 1, 1812. It was the first Baptist periodical published west of the Alleghenies. No known copies of this publication have survived. In the first issue, Editor Dupuy wrote:

I shall do everything in my power to make it [the magazine] pleasing and profitable. I find, however, that the number of subscribers is very inconsiderable. So much so, that I can barely venture to publish.

Brethren and friends will be so good as to obtain what subscribers they can, and inform me (Starke Dupuy) in Shelby County or Mr. William Gerard, the public printer, Frankfort.

It is said that the conditions incident to the War of 1812 made it difficult to continue this paper. It was sold to Silas Mercer Noel (*q.v.*), Frankfort, Ky., and was continued under the name of *The Gospel Herald* (1813).

Starke Dupuy compiled *Dupuy's Hymns*, a book widely used in Baptist churches throughout the Southern and Western states. He revised it twice, until it had a circulation of 100,000 and reached 22 large editions. After he died, John Mason Peck revised it.

BIBLIOGRAPHY: B. H. Dupuy, *The Huguenot Bartholomew Dupuy and His Descendants* (1908). J. H. Spencer, *History of Kentucky Baptists* (1886). W. B. Warder, Personal correspondence with George R. Jewell (1938).   GEORGE RALEIGH JEWELL